Hoover's MasterList of U.S. Companies

2024

Hoover's MasterList of U.S. Companies is intended to provide readers with accurate and authoritative information about the enterprises covered in it. The information contained herein is as accurate as we could reasonably make it. We do not warrant that the book is absolutely accurate or without error. Readers should not rely on any information contained herein in instances where such reliance might cause financial loss.

The publisher, the editors, and their data suppliers specifically disclaim all warranties, including the implied warranties of merchantability and fitness for a specific purpose. This book is sold with the understanding that neither the publisher, the editors, nor any content contributors are engaged in providing investment, financial, accounting, legal, or other professional advice.

Mergent Inc., provided financial data for most public companies in this book. For private companies and historical information on public companies prior to their becoming public, we obtained information directly from the companies or from third-party material that we believe to be trustworthy. Hoover's, Inc., is solely responsible for the presentation of all data.

Many of the names of products and services mentioned in this book are the trademarks or service marks of the companies manufacturing or selling them and are subject to protection under US law. Space has not permitted us to indicate which names are subject to such protection, and readers are advised to consult with the owners of such marks regarding their use. Hoover's is a trademark of Hoover's, Inc.

Copyright © 2024 by Hoover's, Inc. All rights reserved. No part of this book may be reproduced or transmitted in any form or by any means, electronic or mechanical, including by photocopying, facsimile transmission, recording, rekeying, or using any information storage and retrieval system, without permission in writing from Hoover's, except that brief passages may be quoted by a reviewer in a magazine, in a newspaper, online, or in a broadcast review.

10 9 8 7 6 5 4 3 2 1

Publishers Cataloging-in-Publication Data

Hoover's MasterList of U.S. Companies 2024,

   Includes indexes.

   ISBN: 979-8-89251-053-0

   ISSN 1549-6457

   1. Business enterprises — Directories. 2. Corporations — Directories.

HF3010 338.7

U.S. AND WORLD BOOK SALES

Mergent Inc.
28 Liberty ST
58th Floor
New York, NY 10005
Phone: 704-559-6961

e-mail: skardon@ftserussell.com
Web: www.mergentbusinesspress.com

Mergent Inc.

Executive Managing Director: John Pedernales

Publisher and Managing Director of Print Products: Thomas Wecera

Director of Print Products: Charlot Volny

Quality Assurance Editor: Wayne Arnold

Production Research Assistant: Davie Christna

Data Manager: Allison Shank

MERGENT CUSTOMER SERVICE-PRINT PRODUCTS

Support and Fulfillment: Stephanie Kardon

Phone: 704-559-6961
email: skardon@ftserussell.com
Web: www.mergentbusinesspress.com

ABOUT MERGENT INC.

For over 100 years, Mergent, Inc. has been a leading provider of business and financial information on public and private companies globally. Mergent is known to be a trusted partner to corporate and financial institutions, as well as to academic and public libraries. Today we continue to build on a century of experience by transforming data into knowledge and combining our expertise with the latest technology to create new global data and analytical solutions for our clients. With advanced data collection services, cloud-based applications, desktop analytics and print products, Mergent and its subsidiaries provide solutions from top down economic and demographic information, to detailed equity and debt fundamental analysis. We incorporate value added tools such as quantitative Smart Beta equity research and tools for portfolio building and measurement. Based in the U.S., Mergent maintains a strong global presence, with offices in New York, Charlotte, San Diego, London, Tokyo, Kuching and Melbourne. Mergent, Inc. is a member of the London Stock Exchange plc group of companies. The Mergent business forms part of LSEG's Information Services Division, which includes FTSE Russell, a global leader in indexes.

Abbreviations

AFL-CIO – American Federation of Labor and Congress of Industrial Organizations
AMA – American Medical Association
AMEX – American Stock Exchange
ARM – adjustable-rate mortgage
ASP – application services provider
ATM – asynchronous transfer mode
ATM – automated teller machine
CAD/CAM – computer-aided design/computer-aided manufacturing
CD-ROM – compact disc – read-only memory
CD-R – CD-recordable
CEO – chief executive officer
CFO – chief financial officer
CMOS – complementary metal oxide silicon
COO – chief operating officer
DAT – digital audiotape
DOD – Department of Defense
DOE – Department of Energy
DOS – disk operating system
DOT – Department of Transportation
DRAM – dynamic random-access memory
DSL – digital subscriber line
DVD – digital versatile disc/digital video disc
DVD-R – DVD-recordable
EPA – Environmental Protection Agency
EPROM – erasable programmable read-only memory
EPS – earnings per share
ESOP – employee stock ownership plan
EU – European Union
EVP – executive vice president
FCC – Federal Communications Commission
FDA – Food and Drug Administration
FDIC – Federal Deposit Insurance Corporation
FTC – Federal Trade Commission
FTP – file transfer protocol
GATT – General Agreement on Tariffs and Trade
GDP – gross domestic product
HMO – health maintenance organization
HR – human resources
HTML – hypertext markup language
ICC – Interstate Commerce Commission
IPO – initial public offering
IRS – Internal Revenue Service
ISP – Internet service provider
kWh – kilowatt-hour
LAN – local-area network
LBO – leveraged buyout
LCD – liquid crystal display
LNG – liquefied natural gas
LP – limited partnership
Ltd. – limited
mips – millions of instructions per second
MW – megawatt
NAFTA – North American Free Trade Agreement
NASA – National Aeronautics and Space Administration
NASDAQ – National Association of Securities Dealers Automated Quotations
NATO – North Atlantic Treaty Organization
NYSE – New York Stock Exchange
OCR – optical character recognition
OECD – Organization for Economic Cooperation and Development
OEM – original equipment manufacturer
OPEC – Organization of Petroleum Exporting Countries
OS – operating system
OSHA – Occupational Safety and Health Administration
OTC – over-the-counter
PBX – private branch exchange
PCMCIA – Personal Computer Memory Card International Association
P/E – price to earnings ratio
RAID – redundant array of independent disks
RAM – random-access memory
R&D – research and development
RBOC – regional Bell operating company
RISC – reduced instruction set computer
REIT – real estate investment trust
ROA – return on assets
ROE – return on equity
ROI – return on investment
ROM – read-only memory
S&L – savings and loan
SCSI – Small Computer System Interface
SEC – Securities and Exchange Commission
SEVP – senior executive vice president
SIC – Standard Industrial Classification
SVP – senior vice president
USB – universal serial bus
VAR – value-added reseller
VAT – value-added tax
VC – venture capitalist
VP – vice president
VoIP – Voice over Internet Protocol
WAN – wide-area network
WWW – World Wide Web

CONTENTS

Volume 1

Company Lists 2a-14a
   Top 500 Companies By Sales 2a
   Top 500 Companies By Employees 7a
   Top 500 Companies by Net Profit 12a

Company Listings A – L 2

Volume 2

Company Listings M – Z 819

Indexes 1555
   By Company 1557
   By Headquarters Location 1599

Hoover's MasterList of U.S. Companies

Company Rankings

Top 500 Companies by Sales in Hoover's MasterList of U.S. Companies 2024

Rank	Company	Headquarters	Sales ($ Mil)
1	Walmart Inc	AR	$648,125
2	Amazon.com Inc	WA	$574,785
3	Apple Inc	CA	$383,285
4	UnitedHealth Group Inc	MN	$371,622
5	Berkshire Hathaway Inc	NE	$364,482
6	CVS Health Corp	RI	$357,776
7	Exxon Mobil Corp	TX	$344,582
8	Alphabet Inc	CA	$307,394
9	McKesson Corp	TX	$276,711
10	Cencora Inc	PA	$262,173
11	Costco Wholesale Corp	WA	$242,290
12	JPMorgan Chase & Co	NY	$239,425
13	Microsoft Corporation	WA	$211,915
14	Cardinal Health, Inc.	OH	$205,012
15	Chevron Corporation	CA	$200,949
16	The Cigna Group	CT	$195,265
17	Ford Motor Co. (DE)	MI	$176,191
18	Bank of America Corp	NC	$171,912
19	General Motors Co	MI	$171,842
20	Elevance Health Inc	IN	$171,340
21	Citigroup Inc	NY	$156,820
22	Centene Corp	MO	$153,999
23	Home Depot Inc	GA	$152,669
24	Marathon Petroleum Corp.	OH	$150,307
25	Phillips 66	TX	$149,890
26	Kroger Co (The)	OH	$148,258
27	Valero Energy Corp	TX	$144,766
28	Fannie Mae	DC	$141,240
29	Walgreens Boots Alliance Inc	IL	$139,081
30	Meta Platforms Inc	CA	$134,902
31	Verizon Communications Inc	NY	$133,974
32	AT&T Inc	TX	$122,428
33	Federal Reserve System	DC	$122,368
34	Comcast Corp	PA	$121,572
35	Goldman Sachs Group Inc	NY	$108,418
36	Freddie Mac	VA	$108,050
37	Target Corp	MN	$107,412
38	Humana, Inc.	KY	$106,374
39	Tesla Inc	TX	$96,773
40	Morgan Stanley	NY	$96,194
41	Archer Daniels Midland Co.	IL	$93,935
42	PepsiCo Inc	NY	$91,471
43	United Parcel Service Inc	GA	$90,958
44	FedEx Corp	TN	$90,155
45	Disney (Walt) Co. (The)	CA	$88,898
46	Dell Technologies Inc	TX	$88,425
47	Lowe's Companies Inc	NC	$86,377
48	Johnson & Johnson	NJ	$85,159
49	Procter & Gamble Co (The)	OH	$82,006
50	Energy Transfer LP	TX	$78,586
51	T-Mobile US Inc	WA	$78,558
52	Boeing Co.	VA	$77,794
53	Albertsons Companies Inc	ID	$77,650
54	Sysco Corp	TX	$76,325
55	RTX Corp	VA	$68,920
56	General Electric Co	MA	$67,954
57	Federal Reserve Bank Of New Y	NY	$67,807
58	American Express Co.	NY	$67,364
59	Bunge Global SA	MO	$67,232
60	Caterpillar Inc.	TX	$67,060
61	MetLife Inc	NY	$66,905
62	HCA Healthcare Inc	TN	$64,968
63	Progressive Corp. (OH)	OH	$62,109
64	International Business Machines Corp.	NY	$61,860
65	Deere & Co.	IL	$61,251
66	NVIDIA Corp	CA	$60,922
67	Merck & Co Inc	NJ	$60,115
68	StoneX Group Inc	NY	$59,996
69	Pfizer Inc	NY	$58,496
70	Delta Air Lines Inc (DE)	GA	$58,048
71	TD SYNNEX Corp	CA	$57,555
72	Publix Super Markets, Inc.	FL	$57,534
73	Performance Food Group Co	VA	$57,255
74	Allstate Corp	IL	$57,094
75	Cisco Systems Inc	CA	$56,998
76	Charter Communications Inc (New)	CT	$54,607
77	AbbVie Inc	IL	$54,318
78	Intel Corp	CA	$54,228
79	Prudential Financial Inc	NJ	$53,979
80	HP Inc	CA	$53,718
81	United Airlines Holdings Inc	IL	$53,717
82	Tyson Foods Inc	AR	$52,881
83	American Airlines Group Inc	TX	$52,788
84	NIKE Inc	OR	$51,217
85	Oracle Corp	TX	$49,954
86	TJX Companies, Inc.	MA	$49,936
87	Enterprise Products Partners L.P.	TX	$49,715
88	Capital One Financial Corp	VA	$49,484
89	Plains All American Pipeline LP	TX	$48,712
90	World Kinect Corp	FL	$47,711
91	American International Group Inc	NY	$46,802
92	Coca-Cola Co (The)	GA	$45,754
93	CHS Inc	MN	$45,590
94	Bristol Myers Squibb Co.	NJ	$45,006
95	Dow Inc	MI	$44,622
96	Best Buy Inc	MN	$43,452
97	Thermo Fisher Scientific Inc	MA	$42,857
98	General Dynamics Corp	VA	$42,272
99	Travelers Companies Inc (The)	NY	$41,364
100	Warner Bros Discovery Inc	NY	$41,321
101	U.S. Bancorp (DE)	MN	$40,624
102	Abbott Laboratories	IL	$40,109
103	Northrop Grumman Corp	VA	$39,290
104	Dollar General Corp	TN	$38,692
105	PBF Energy Inc	NJ	$38,325
106	Uber Technologies Inc	CA	$37,281
107	Liberty Mutual Holding Company Inc.	MA	$36,944
108	Honeywell International Inc	NC	$36,662
109	Mondelez International Inc	IL	$36,016
110	Starbucks Corp.	WA	$35,976
111	Qualcomm Inc	CA	$35,820
112	Broadcom Inc (DE)	CA	$35,819
113	US Foods Holding Corp	IL	$35,597
114	DR Horton Inc	TX	$35,460
115	Philip Morris International Inc	CT	$35,174
116	Paccar Inc.	WA	$35,127
117	Salesforce Inc	CA	$34,857
118	Nucor Corp.	NC	$34,714
119	Jabil Inc	FL	$34,702
120	Lennar Corp	FL	$34,233

Top 500 Companies by Sales in Hoover's MasterList of U.S. Companies 2024 (continued)

Rank	Company	Headquarters	Sales ($ Mil)
121	Eli Lilly & Co	IN	$34,124
122	Molina Healthcare Inc	CA	$34,072
123	Cummins, Inc.	IN	$34,065
124	Bank of New York Mellon Corp	NY	$33,805
125	Netflix Inc	CA	$33,723
126	Truist Financial Corp	NC	$33,246
127	Arrow Electronics, Inc.	CO	$33,107
128	Linde PLC (New)	CT	$32,854
129	3M Co	MN	$32,681
130	Visa Inc	CA	$32,653
131	Apollo Global Management Inc (New)	NY	$32,644
132	Citgo Petroleum Corp.	TX	$32,277
133	HF Sinclair Corp	TX	$31,964
134	CBRE Group Inc	TX	$31,949
135	PNC Financial Services Group (The)	PA	$31,882
136	Lithia Motors Inc	OR	$31,042
137	Dollar Tree Inc	VA	$30,604
138	United Natural Foods Inc.	RI	$30,272
139	PayPal Holdings Inc	CA	$29,771
140	Carmax Inc.	VA	$29,685
141	Paramount Global	NY	$29,652
142	Penske Automotive Group Inc	MI	$29,527
143	Hewlett Packard Enterprise Co	TX	$29,135
144	Duke Energy Corp	NC	$29,060
145	Occidental Petroleum Corp	TX	$28,918
146	NRG Energy Inc	TX	$28,823
147	Amgen Inc	CA	$28,190
148	NextEra Energy Inc	FL	$28,114
149	Gilead Sciences Inc	CA	$27,116
150	AutoNation, Inc.	FL	$26,949
151	Kraft Heinz Co (The)	PA	$26,640
152	Avnet Inc	AZ	$26,537
153	Applied Materials, Inc.	CA	$26,517
154	Southwest Airlines Co	TX	$26,091
155	Charles Schwab Corp	TX	$25,521
156	Baker Hughes Company	TX	$25,506
157	McDonald's Corp	IL	$25,494
158	Southern Co.	GA	$25,253
159	Mastercard Inc	NY	$25,098
160	Hartford Financial Services Group Inc.	CT	$24,527
161	Altria Group Inc	VA	$24,483
162	Exelon Generation Co LLC	PA	$24,440
163	PG&E Corp (Holding Co)	CA	$24,428
164	United Services Automobile A	TX	$24,361
165	EOG Resources, Inc.	TX	$24,186
166	New York Life Insurance Co.	NY	$24,148
167	Union Pacific Corp	NE	$24,119
168	Rite Aid Corp.	PA	$24,092
169	Danaher Corp	DC	$23,890
170	Marriott International, Inc.	MD	$23,713
171	Northwestern Mutual Life Ins.	WI	$23,595
172	Lear Corp.	MI	$23,467
173	Genuine Parts Co.	GA	$23,091
174	Sunoco LP	TX	$23,068
175	Citigroup Global Markets Hol	NY	$23,065
176	Sherwin-Williams Co (The)	OH	$23,052
177	Halliburton Company	TX	$23,018
178	Freeport-McMoRan Inc	AZ	$22,855
179	Live Nation Entertainment Inc	CA	$22,749
180	Marsh & McLennan Companies Inc.	NY	$22,736
181	Advanced Micro Devices Inc	CA	$22,680
182	First Citizens BancShares Inc (DE)	NC	$22,466
183	Wesco International, Inc.	PA	$22,385
184	Carrier Global Corp	FL	$22,098
185	Cleveland-Cliffs Inc (New)	OH	$21,996
186	Block Inc	CA	$21,916
187	Exelon Corp	IL	$21,727
188	Carnival Corp	FL	$21,593
189	Murphy USA Inc	AR	$21,529
190	CDW Corp	IL	$21,376
191	Booking Holdings Inc	CT	$21,365
192	Baker Hughes Holdings LLC	TX	$21,156
193	Quanta Services, Inc.	TX	$20,882
194	Jones Lang LaSalle Inc	IL	$20,761
195	Burlington Northern & Santa F	TX	$20,747
196	Discover Financial Services	IL	$20,606
197	Tenet Healthcare Corp.	TX	$20,548
198	Stryker Corp	MI	$20,498
199	Kimberly-Clark Corp.	TX	$20,431
200	Waste Management, Inc. (DE)	TX	$20,426
201	Cheniere Energy Inc.	TX	$20,394
202	WestRock Co	GA	$20,310
203	General Mills Inc	MN	$20,094
204	Goodyear Tire & Rubber Co.	OH	$20,066
205	BJs Wholesale Club Holdings Inc	MA	$19,969
206	Massachusetts Mutual Life Insurance Co. (Springfield, MA)	MA	$19,687
207	Colgate-Palmolive Co.	NY	$19,457
208	Whirlpool Corp	MI	$19,455
209	L3Harris Technologies Inc	FL	$19,419
210	Adobe Inc	CA	$19,409
211	Becton Dickinson And Co	NJ	$19,372
212	Pioneer Natural Resources Co	TX	$19,362
213	Cognizant Technology Solutions Corp.	NJ	$19,353
214	Fiserv Inc	WI	$19,093
215	Parker-Hannifin Corp	OH	$19,065
216	American Electric Power Co Inc	OH	$18,982
217	International Paper Co	TN	$18,916
218	ManpowerGroup	WI	$18,915
219	Aramark	PA	$18,854
220	Steel Dynamics Inc.	IN	$18,795
221	AFLAC Inc.	GA	$18,701
222	Ross Stores Inc	CA	$18,696
223	Reinsurance Group of America, Inc.	MO	$18,567
224	State Street Corp.	MA	$18,366
225	Florida Power & Light Co.	FL	$18,365
226	PPG Industries Inc	PA	$18,246
227	United States Steel Corp.	PA	$18,053
228	Automatic Data Processing Inc.	NJ	$18,012
229	Group 1 Automotive, Inc.	TX	$17,874
230	BlackRock Inc	NY	$17,859
231	ONEOK Inc	OK	$17,677
232	Robinson (C.H.) Worldwide, Inc.	MN	$17,596
233	Texas Instruments, Inc.	TX	$17,519
234	Kohl's Corp.	WI	$17,476
235	AutoZone, Inc.	TN	$17,457
236	Lam Research Corp	CA	$17,429
237	Pilgrims Pride Corp.	CO	$17,362
238	Builders FirstSource Inc.	TX	$17,097
239	EchoStar Corp	CO	$17,016

Top 500 Companies by Sales in Hoover's MasterList of U.S. Companies 2024 (continued)

Rank	Company	Headquarters	Sales ($ Mil)
240	Delek US Holdings Inc (New)	TN	$16,917
241	Sempra	CA	$16,720
242	Sears Holdings Corp	IL	$16,702
243	DISH Network Corp	CO	$16,679
244	Global Partners LP	MA	$16,492
245	Grainger (W.W.), Inc.	IL	$16,478
246	Time Warner Entertainment Co	NY	$16,425
247	Jacobs Solutions Inc	TX	$16,352
248	Edison International	CA	$16,338
249	Southern California Edison C	CA	$16,275
250	MGM Resorts International	NV	$16,164
251	Illinois Tool Works, Inc.	IL	$16,107
252	PulteGroup Inc	GA	$16,062
253	Targa Resources Corp	TX	$16,060
254	Ally Financial Inc	MI	$15,971
255	Loews Corp.	NY	$15,901
256	Santander Holdings USA Inc.	MA	$15,820
257	O'Reilly Automotive, Inc.	MO	$15,812
258	Markel Group Inc	VA	$15,804
259	Stanley Black & Decker Inc	CT	$15,781
260	Union Pacific Railroad Co	NE	$15,546
261	Micron Technology Inc.	ID	$15,540
262	Ameriprise Financial Inc	MN	$15,535
263	Fluor Corp.	TX	$15,474
264	Leidos Holdings Inc	VA	$15,438
265	Kinder Morgan Inc.	TX	$15,334
266	Ecolab Inc	MN	$15,320
267	Devon Energy Corp.	OK	$15,258
268	Emerson Electric Co.	MO	$15,165
269	Casey's General Stores, Inc.	IA	$15,094
270	DCP Midstream LP	CO	$14,993
271	IQVIA Holdings Inc	NC	$14,984
272	Republic Services Inc	AZ	$14,965
273	Fox Corp	NY	$14,913
274	Gap Inc	CA	$14,889
275	Keurig Dr Pepper Inc	MA	$14,814
276	Baxter International Inc	IL	$14,813
277	Reliance Inc	AZ	$14,806
278	Asbury Automotive Group Inc	GA	$14,803
279	Vistra Corp	TX	$14,779
280	Andersons Inc	OH	$14,750
281	Nordstrom, Inc.	WA	$14,693
282	Omnicom Group, Inc.	NY	$14,692
283	Consolidated Edison Inc	NY	$14,663
284	CSX Corp	FL	$14,657
285	Lumen Technologies Inc	LA	$14,557
286	Tractor Supply Co.	TN	$14,556
287	KKR & Co Inc	NY	$14,499
288	DXC Technology Co	VA	$14,430
289	AGCO Corp.	GA	$14,412
290	Dominion Energy Inc (New)	VA	$14,393
291	AECOM	TX	$14,378
292	Sonic Automotive, Inc.	NC	$14,372
293	Intuit Inc	CA	$14,368
294	United Rentals Inc	CT	$14,332
295	Universal Health Services, Inc.	PA	$14,282
296	Boston Scientific Corp.	MA	$14,240
297	Otis Worldwide Corp	CT	$14,209
298	Xcel Energy Inc	MN	$14,206
299	BorgWarner Inc	MI	$14,198
300	Qurate Retail Inc - Com Ser B	CO	$14,177
301	Ball Corp	CO	$14,029
302	Royal Caribbean Group	FL	$13,900
303	LKQ Corp	IL	$13,866
304	Mosaic Co. (The)	FL	$13,696
305	Textron Inc	RI	$13,683
306	Principal Financial Group Inc	IA	$13,666
307	Federal Deposit Insurance Cor	DC	$13,380
308	CNA Financial Corp	IL	$13,299
309	Consolidated Edison Co. of N	NY	$13,268
310	Kellanova	IL	$13,122
311	Regeneron Pharmaceuticals, Inc.	NY	$13,117
312	Land O' Lakes Inc	MN	$13,008
313	Raymond James Financial, Inc.	FL	$12,992
314	Dick's Sporting Goods, Inc	PA	$12,984
315	Federal Reserve Bank of San F	CA	$12,941
316	Toyota Motor Credit Corp.	TX	$12,909
317	FirstEnergy Corp	OH	$12,870
318	Expedia Group Inc	WA	$12,839
319	Hunt (J.B.) Transport Services, Inc.	AR	$12,830
320	M & T Bank Corp	NY	$12,752
321	DTE Energy Co	MI	$12,745
322	AES Corp	VA	$12,668
323	Berry Global Group Inc	IN	$12,664
324	Fifth Third Bancorp (Cincinnati, OH)	OH	$12,641
325	Air Products & Chemicals Inc	PA	$12,600
326	Corning Inc	NY	$12,588
327	EMCOR Group, Inc.	CT	$12,583
328	Amphenol Corp.	CT	$12,555
329	Westlake Corp	TX	$12,548
330	S&P Global Inc	NY	$12,497
331	Community Health Systems, Inc.	TN	$12,490
332	Unum Group	TN	$12,386
333	Henry Schein Inc	NY	$12,339
334	Western Digital Corp	CA	$12,318
335	Analog Devices Inc	MA	$12,306
336	Conagra Brands Inc	IL	$12,277
337	Jones Financial Companies LL	MO	$12,269
338	Citizens Financial Group Inc (New)	RI	$12,187
339	Liberty Media Corp (DE)	CO	$12,164
340	LabCorp	NC	$12,162
341	Norfolk Southern Corp	GA	$12,156
342	Entergy Corp. (New)	LA	$12,147
343	WR Berkley Corp	CT	$12,143
344	DaVita Inc	CO	$12,140
345	Northern Trust Corp	IL	$12,117
346	Hormel Foods Corp.	MN	$12,110
347	DuPont de Nemours Inc	DE	$12,068
348	Tennessee Valley Authority	TN	$12,054
349	Crown Holdings Inc	FL	$12,010
350	Avis Budget Group Inc	NJ	$12,008
351	Wayfair Inc	MA	$12,003
352	MasTec Inc. (FL)	FL	$11,996
353	Eversource Energy	MA	$11,911
354	Newmont Corp	CO	$11,812
355	Ryder System, Inc.	FL	$11,783
356	Fidelity National Financial Inc	FL	$11,752
357	Lincoln National Corp.	PA	$11,645
358	VF Corp.	CO	$11,612
359	Caesars Entertainment Inc (New)	NV	$11,528

Top 500 Companies by Sales in Hoover's MasterList of U.S. Companies 2024 (continued)

Rank	Company	Headquarters	Sales ($ Mil)
360	International Flavors & Fragrances	NY	$11,479
361	Huntington Ingalls Industries, Inc.	VA	$11,454
362	Advance Auto Parts Inc	NC	$11,288
363	MPLX LP	OH	$11,281
364	Public Service Enterprise Group Inc	NJ	$11,237
365	Ulta Beauty Inc	IL	$11,207
366	Hershey Company (The)	PA	$11,165
367	Chewy Inc	FL	$11,148
368	American Tower Corp (New)	MA	$11,144
369	Mohawk Industries, Inc.	GA	$11,135
370	Assurant Inc	GA	$11,132
371	Thor Industries, Inc.	IN	$11,122
372	Citigroup Global Markets Holdings Inc	NY	$11,049
373	Yum China Holdings Inc	TX	$10,978
374	Celanese Corp (DE)	TX	$10,940
375	Qurate Retail Inc	CO	$10,915
376	Interpublic Group of Companies Inc.	NY	$10,889
377	Ovintiv Inc	CO	$10,883
378	Icahn Enterprises LP	FL	$10,847
379	Huntington Bancshares Inc	OH	$10,837
380	Carvana Co	AZ	$10,771
381	Hess Corp	NY	$10,645
382	Dana Inc	OH	$10,555
383	Alcoa Corporation	PA	$10,551
384	Graybar Electric Co., Inc.	MO	$10,534
385	Equitable Holdings Inc	NY	$10,528
386	KLA Corp	CA	$10,496
387	Darden Restaurants, Inc. (United States)	FL	$10,488
388	Alaska Air Group, Inc.	WA	$10,426
389	KeyCorp	OH	$10,397
390	Qurate Retail Inc - Com Ser A	CO	$10,381
391	Las Vegas Sands Corp	NV	$10,372
392	Owens & Minor, Inc. (New)	VA	$10,334
393	Hilton Worldwide Holdings Inc	VA	$10,235
394	Credit Suisse (USA) Inc	NY	$10,232
395	Georgia Power Co	GA	$10,118
396	eBay Inc.	CA	$10,112
397	Gallagher (Arthur J.) & Co.	IL	$10,072
398	LPL Financial Holdings Inc.	CA	$10,053
399	Cincinnati Financial Corp.	OH	$10,013
400	Toll Brothers Inc.	PA	$9,995
401	Motorola Solutions Inc	IL	$9,978
402	Airbnb Inc	CA	$9,917
403	Intercontinental Exchange Inc	GA	$9,903
404	News Corp (New)	NY	$9,879
405	Chipotle Mexican Grill Inc	CA	$9,872
406	Vertex Pharmaceuticals, Inc.	MA	$9,869
407	Biogen Inc	MA	$9,836
408	Fidelity National Information Services Inc	FL	$9,821
409	GXO Logistics Inc	CT	$9,778
410	SpartanNash Co	MI	$9,729
411	Burlington Stores Inc	NJ	$9,727
412	NVR Inc.	VA	$9,687
413	Owens Corning	OH	$9,677
414	Cheniere Energy Partners L P	TX	$9,664
415	Oshkosh Corp (New)	WI	$9,658
416	Global Payments Inc	GA	$9,654
417	Albemarle Corp.	NC	$9,617
418	JetBlue Airways Corp	NY	$9,615
419	Virginia Electric & Power Co	VA	$9,573
420	Seaboard Corp.	KS	$9,562
421	Constellation Brands Inc	NY	$9,453
422	Graphic Packaging Holding Co	GA	$9,428
423	ARKO Corp	VA	$9,413
424	CoBank, ACB	CO	$9,392
425	Hertz Global Holdings Inc (New)	FL	$9,371
426	Campbell Soup Co	NJ	$9,357
427	Expeditors International of Washington, Inc.	WA	$9,300
428	A-Mark Precious Metals, Inc	CA	$9,287
429	Booz Allen Hamilton Holding Corp.	VA	$9,259
430	Quest Diagnostics, Inc.	NJ	$9,252
431	CVR Energy Inc	TX	$9,247
432	Altice USA Inc	NY	$9,237
433	Eastman Chemical Co	TN	$9,210
434	Insight Enterprises Inc.	AZ	$9,176
435	Regions Financial Corp	AL	$9,153
436	Beacon Roofing Supply Inc	VA	$9,120
437	Rockwell Automation, Inc.	WI	$9,058
438	PVH Corp	NY	$9,024
439	ServiceNow Inc	CA	$8,971
440	Sirius XM Holdings Inc	NY	$8,953
441	Prudential Annuities Life As	NJ	$8,948
442	Sanmina Corp	CA	$8,935
443	Polaris Inc	MN	$8,934
444	UGI Corp.	PA	$8,928
445	WEC Energy Group Inc	WI	$8,893
446	HSBC USA, Inc.	NY	$8,842
447	Cintas Corp	OH	$8,816
448	Commercial Metals Co.	TX	$8,800
449	Foot Locker, Inc.	NY	$8,759
450	Chesapeake Energy Corp.	OK	$8,721
451	CenterPoint Energy, Inc	TX	$8,696
452	NGL Energy Partners LP	OK	$8,695
453	Pacific Mutual Holding Compa	CA	$8,642
454	DoorDash Inc	CA	$8,635
455	NOV Inc	TX	$8,583
456	Norwegian Cruise Line Holdings Ltd	FL	$8,550
457	Zoetis Inc	NJ	$8,544
458	Smucker (J.M.) Co.	OH	$8,529
459	Microchip Technology Inc	AZ	$8,439
460	Dover Corp	IL	$8,438
461	Diamondback Energy, Inc.	TX	$8,412
462	Avery Dennison Corp	OH	$8,364
463	PPL Corp	PA	$8,312
464	Avangrid Inc	CT	$8,309
465	Southern California Gas Co.	CA	$8,289
466	ON Semiconductor Corp	AZ	$8,253
467	Par Pacific Holdings Inc	TX	$8,232
468	APA Corp	TX	$8,192
469	Equinix Inc	CA	$8,188
470	New York Community Bancorp Inc.	NY	$8,178
471	Ingredion Inc	IL	$8,160
472	Newell Brands Inc	GA	$8,133
473	ABM Industries, Inc.	NY	$8,096
474	Blackstone Inc	NY	$8,023
475	Prologis Inc	CA	$8,023
476	Skechers USA Inc	CA	$8,000
477	Guardian Life Insurance Co.	NY	$7,967
478	Masco Corp.	MI	$7,967
479	Rush Enterprises Inc.	TX	$7,925

Top 500 Companies by Sales in Hoover's MasterList of U.S. Companies 2024 (continued)

Rank	Company	Headquarters	Sales ($ Mil)
480	Duke Energy Carolinas LLC	NC	$7,857
481	Franklin Resources Inc	CA	$7,849
482	ODP Corp (The)	FL	$7,831
483	American Financial Group Inc	OH	$7,827
484	TechnipFMC plc	TX	$7,824
485	Federal Reserve Bank Of Atlan	GA	$7,805
486	Packaging Corp of America	IL	$7,802
487	Vulcan Materials Co (Holding Company)	AL	$7,782
488	Williams Sonoma Inc	CA	$7,751
489	XPO Inc	CT	$7,744
490	Weyerhaeuser Co	WA	$7,674
491	Ameren Corp	MO	$7,500
492	Genworth Financial, Inc. (Holding Co)	VA	$7,488
493	CMS Energy Corp	MI	$7,462
494	Science Applications International Corp (New)	VA	$7,444
495	Bath & Body Works Inc	OH	$7,429
496	Electronic Arts	CA	$7,426
497	Taylor Morrison Home Corp (Holding Co)	AZ	$7,418
498	Spectrum Group International Inc	CA	$7,406
499	SVB Financial Group	CA	$7,401
500	Zimmer Biomet Holdings Inc	IN	$7,394

Top 500 Companies by Employees in Hoover's MasterList of U.S. Companies 2024

Rank	Company	Headquarters	Employees
1	Walmart Inc	AR	2,100,000
2	Amazon.com Inc	WA	1,525,000
3	Home Depot Inc	GA	463,100
4	United Parcel Service Inc	GA	462,000
5	UnitedHealth Group Inc	MN	440,000
6	Yum China Holdings Inc	TX	432,000
7	Kroger Co (The)	OH	430,000
8	Target Corp	MN	415,000
9	Berkshire Hathaway Inc	NE	396,500
10	Starbucks Corp.	WA	381,000
11	Cognizant Technology Solutions Corp.	NJ	347,700
12	Walgreens Boots Alliance Inc	IL	331,000
13	TJX Companies, Inc.	MA	329,000
14	PepsiCo Inc	NY	318,000
15	Costco Wholesale Corp	WA	316,000
16	HCA Healthcare Inc	TN	310,000
17	JPMorgan Chase & Co	NY	309,926
18	International Business Machines Corp.	NY	305,300
19	CVS Health Corp	RI	300,000
20	Albertsons Companies Inc	ID	290,000
21	Lowe's Companies Inc	NC	284,000
22	Aramark	PA	262,550
23	Publix Super Markets, Inc.	FL	253,000
24	FedEx Corp	TN	244,000
25	Citigroup Inc	NY	239,000
26	Jabil Inc	FL	236,000
27	Disney (Walt) Co. (The)	CA	225,000
28	Microsoft Corporation	WA	221,000
29	Bank of America Corp	NC	213,000
30	Dollar Tree Inc	VA	211,826
31	Darden Restaurants, Inc. (United States)	FL	187,384
32	Lear Corp.	MI	186,600
33	Comcast Corp	PA	186,000
34	RTX Corp	VA	185,000
35	Alphabet Inc	CA	182,502
36	Hilton Worldwide Holdings Inc	VA	178,000
37	Ford Motor Co. (DE)	MI	177,000
38	Boeing Co.	VA	171,000
39	Oracle Corp	TX	164,000
40	General Motors Co	MI	163,000
41	Apple Inc	CA	161,000
42	McDonald's Corp	IL	150,000
43	Marriott International, Inc.	MD	148,000
44	Tesla Inc	TX	140,473
45	Tyson Foods Inc	AR	139,000
46	American Airlines Group Inc	TX	132,100
47	Johnson & Johnson	NJ	131,900
48	Barrett Business Services, Inc.	WA	130,513
49	CBRE Group Inc	TX	130,000
50	DXC Technology Co	VA	130,000
51	General Electric Co	MA	125,000
52	Intel Corp	CA	124,800
53	ABM Industries, Inc.	NY	123,000
54	Thermo Fisher Scientific Inc	MA	122,000
55	Dell Technologies Inc	TX	120,000
56	AutoZone, Inc.	TN	119,000
57	Chipotle Mexican Grill Inc	CA	116,068
58	Abbott Laboratories	IL	114,000
59	Caterpillar Inc.	TX	113,200
60	General Dynamics Corp	VA	111,600
61	Procter & Gamble Co (The)	OH	107,000
62	Carnival Corp	FL	106,000
63	Jones Lang LaSalle Inc	IL	106,000
64	Tenet Healthcare Corp.	TX	105,600
65	Verizon Communications Inc	NY	105,400
66	Elevance Health Inc	IN	104,900
67	United Airlines Holdings Inc	IL	103,300
68	Delta Air Lines Inc (DE)	GA	103,000
69	Charter Communications Inc (New)	CT	101,100
70	Northrop Grumman Corp	VA	101,000
71	Ross Stores Inc	CA	101,000
72	Royal Caribbean Group	FL	98,200
73	Kohl's Corp.	WI	96,000
74	Amphenol Corp.	CT	95,000
75	Honeywell International Inc	NC	95,000
76	Mondelez International Inc	IL	91,000
77	Texas Roadhouse Inc	KY	91,000
78	O'Reilly Automotive, Inc.	MO	90,302
79	Sears Holdings Corp	IL	89,000
80	Pfizer Inc	NY	88,000
81	Bloomin' Brands Inc	FL	87,000
82	GXO Logistics Inc	CT	87,000
83	IQVIA Holdings Inc	NC	87,000
84	3M Co	MN	85,000
85	Best Buy Inc	MN	85,000
86	Gap Inc	CA	85,000
87	Marsh & McLennan Companies Inc.	NY	85,000
88	Cisco Systems Inc	CA	84,900
89	NIKE Inc	OR	83,700
90	Deere & Co.	IL	83,000
91	Philip Morris International Inc	CT	82,700
92	HireQuest Inc	SC	82,223
93	Morgan Stanley	NY	80,000
94	Coca-Cola Co (The)	GA	79,100
95	Cracker Barrel Old Country Store Inc	TN	77,000
96	Omnicom Group, Inc.	NY	75,900
97	Cummins, Inc.	IN	75,500
98	U.S. Bancorp (DE)	MN	75,465
99	Southwest Airlines Co	TX	74,806
100	American Express Co.	NY	74,600
101	Community Health Systems, Inc.	TN	74,000
102	Universal Health Services, Inc.	PA	73,350
103	Becton Dickinson And Co	NJ	73,000
104	Salesforce Inc	CA	72,682
105	The Cigna Group	CT	72,500
106	Merck & Co Inc	NJ	72,000
107	Sysco Corp	TX	72,000
108	Burlington Stores Inc	NJ	71,049
109	Goodyear Tire & Rubber Co.	OH	71,000
110	Otis Worldwide Corp	CT	71,000
111	Advantage Solutions Inc	CA	70,000
112	DaVita Inc	CO	70,000
113	Advance Auto Parts Inc	NC	69,000
114	Brinks Co (The)	VA	68,200
115	Centene Corp	MO	67,700
116	Humana, Inc.	KY	67,600
117	Meta Platforms Inc	CA	67,317
118	Emerson Electric Co.	MO	67,000
119	LabCorp	NC	67,000
120	T-Mobile US Inc	WA	67,000

Top 500 Companies by Employees in Hoover's MasterList of U.S. Companies 2024 (continued)

Rank	Company	Headquarters	Employees
121	Linde PLC (New)	CT	66,323
122	Brinker International, Inc.	TX	64,323
123	Sherwin-Williams Co (The)	OH	64,088
124	Automatic Data Processing Inc.	NJ	63,000
125	Danaher Corp	DC	63,000
126	MGM Resorts International	NV	63,000
127	Parker-Hannifin Corp	OH	62,730
128	Exxon Mobil Corp	TX	62,000
129	Hewlett Packard Enterprise Co	TX	62,000
130	Progressive Corp. (OH)	OH	61,400
131	Pilgrims Pride Corp.	CO	61,200
132	TTEC Holdings Inc	CO	60,055
133	Baxter International Inc	IL	60,000
134	Fidelity National Information Services Inc	FL	60,000
135	Genuine Parts Co.	GA	60,000
136	Jacobs Solutions Inc	TX	60,000
137	Conduent Inc	NJ	59,000
138	Whirlpool Corp	MI	59,000
139	Baker Hughes Company	TX	58,000
140	HP Inc	CA	58,000
141	Interpublic Group of Companies Inc.	NY	57,400
142	Bath & Body Works Inc	OH	57,157
143	PNC Financial Services Group (The)	PA	56,411
144	Vail Resorts Inc	CO	56,400
145	WestRock Co	GA	56,100
146	Ulta Beauty Inc	IL	56,000
147	Dick's Sporting Goods, Inc	PA	55,500
148	Baker Hughes Holdings LLC	TX	55,000
149	Select Medical Holdings Corp	PA	54,600
150	ExlService Holdings Inc	NY	54,000
151	Nordstrom, Inc.	WA	54,000
152	Allstate Corp	IL	53,400
153	Bank of New York Mellon Corp	NY	53,400
154	Epam Systems, Inc.	PA	53,150
155	Cedar Fair LP	OH	53,050
156	Carrier Global Corp	FL	53,000
157	Western Digital Corp	CA	53,000
158	Quanta Services, Inc.	TX	52,500
159	AECOM	TX	52,000
160	Gallagher (Arthur J.) & Co.	IL	52,000
161	Stryker Corp	MI	52,000
162	Capital One Financial Corp	VA	51,987
163	Caesars Entertainment Inc (New)	NV	51,000
164	Hyatt Hotels Corp	IL	51,000
165	Jones Financial Companies LL	MO	51,000
166	McKesson Corp	TX	51,000
167	Truist Financial Corp	NC	50,832
168	Stanley Black & Decker Inc	CT	50,500
169	Union Pacific Railroad Co	NE	50,379
170	AbbVie Inc	IL	50,000
171	L3Harris Technologies Inc	FL	50,000
172	Qualcomm Inc	CA	50,000
173	Tractor Supply Co.	TN	50,000
174	Corning Inc	NY	49,800
175	LKQ Corp	IL	49,000
176	Boston Scientific Corp.	MA	48,000
177	Cardinal Health, Inc.	OH	48,000
178	Ecolab Inc	MN	48,000
179	Halliburton Company	TX	48,000
180	HanesBrands Inc	NC	48,000
181	Quest Diagnostics, Inc.	NJ	48,000
182	Waste Management, Inc. (DE)	TX	48,000
183	Cheesecake Factory Inc. (The)	CA	47,900
184	Ryder System, Inc.	FL	47,500
185	Leidos Holdings Inc	VA	47,000
186	Rite Aid Corp.	PA	47,000
187	Foot Locker, Inc.	NY	46,880
188	State Street Corp.	MA	46,451
189	Chevron Corporation	CA	45,600
190	Goldman Sachs Group Inc	NY	45,300
191	Illinois Tool Works, Inc.	IL	45,000
192	MetLife Inc	NY	45,000
193	Cintas Corp	OH	44,500
194	Berry Global Group Inc	IN	44,000
195	Genesis Healthcare Inc	PA	44,000
196	Huntington Ingalls Industries, Inc.	VA	44,000
197	Mohawk Industries, Inc.	GA	43,300
198	American Eagle Outfitters, Inc.	PA	43,100
199	Eli Lilly & Co	IN	43,000
200	Micron Technology Inc.	ID	43,000
201	Casey's General Stores, Inc.	IA	42,982
202	Cencora Inc	PA	42,000
203	Fiserv Inc	WI	42,000
204	Archer Daniels Midland Co.	IL	41,802
205	Dana Inc	OH	41,800
206	Burlington Northern & Santa F	TX	41,000
207	Kimberly-Clark Corp.	TX	41,000
208	Norwegian Cruise Line Holdings Ltd	FL	41,000
209	Republic Services Inc	AZ	41,000
210	Prudential Financial Inc	NJ	40,658
211	S&P Global Inc	NY	40,450
212	Citigroup Global Markets Hol	NY	40,000
213	BorgWarner Inc	MI	39,900
214	MAXIMUS Inc.	VA	39,600
215	International Paper Co	TN	39,000
216	Las Vegas Sands Corp	NV	38,400
217	EMCOR Group, Inc.	CT	38,300
218	XPO Inc	CT	38,000
219	Brookdale Senior Living Inc	TN	36,000
220	Kraft Heinz Co (The)	PA	36,000
221	Dow Inc	MI	35,900
222	Ensign Group Inc	CA	35,300
223	Warner Bros Discovery Inc	NY	35,300
224	U-Haul Holding Co	NV	35,100
225	Avery Dennison Corp	OH	35,000
226	Performance Food Group Co	VA	35,000
227	Textron Inc	RI	35,000
228	Addus HomeCare Corp	TX	34,846
229	Hunt (J.B.) Transport Services, Inc.	AR	34,718
230	Knight-Swift Transportation Holdings Inc	AZ	34,300
231	Bristol Myers Squibb Co.	NJ	34,100
232	Applied Materials, Inc.	CA	34,000
233	BJs Wholesale Club Holdings Inc	MA	34,000
234	Colgate-Palmolive Co.	NY	34,000
235	General Mills Inc	MN	34,000
236	KBR Inc	TX	34,000
237	Sanmina Corp	CA	34,000
238	Texas Instruments, Inc.	TX	34,000
239	AMC Entertainment Holdings Inc.	KS	33,812
240	NOV Inc	TX	33,676

Top 500 Companies by Employees in Hoover's MasterList of U.S. Companies 2024 (continued)

Rank	Company	Headquarters	Employees
241	Healthcare Services Group Inc.	PA	33,400
242	Mastercard Inc	NY	33,400
243	Travelers Companies Inc (The)	NY	33,300
244	Charles Schwab Corp	TX	33,000
245	Mattel Inc	CA	33,000
246	VF Corp.	CO	33,000
247	Union Pacific Corp	NE	32,973
248	Paccar Inc.	WA	32,400
249	Big Lots, Inc.	OH	32,200
250	Regal Rexnord Corp	WI	32,100
251	Nucor Corp.	NC	32,000
252	Sprouts Farmers Market Inc	AZ	32,000
253	Topgolf Callaway Brands Corp	CA	32,000
254	Booz Allen Hamilton Holding Corp.	VA	31,900
255	Time Warner Entertainment Co	NY	31,200
256	PVH Corp	NY	31,000
257	Amdocs Ltd.	MO	30,695
258	Carmax Inc.	VA	30,621
259	Uber Technologies Inc	CA	30,400
260	Fluor Corp.	TX	30,187
261	ON Semiconductor Corp	AZ	30,100
262	US Foods Holding Corp	IL	30,000
263	Yellow Corp (New)	TN	30,000
264	Adobe Inc	CA	29,945
265	Dillard's Inc.	AR	29,900
266	R1 RCM INC New	UT	29,900
267	Abercrombie & Fitch Co	OH	29,600
268	NVIDIA Corp	CA	29,600
269	United Natural Foods Inc.	RI	29,455
270	Builders FirstSource Inc.	TX	29,000
271	Petco Health & Wellness Co Inc	CA	29,000
272	Rockwell Automation, Inc.	WI	29,000
273	Laureate Education Inc	FL	28,900
274	Visa Inc	CA	28,800
275	Amkor Technology Inc.	AZ	28,700
276	Qurate Retail Inc - Com Ser A	CO	28,255
277	Keurig Dr Pepper Inc	MA	28,100
278	Southern Co.	GA	28,100
279	Cleveland-Cliffs Inc (New)	OH	28,000
280	Lumen Technologies Inc	LA	28,000
281	Penske Automotive Group Inc	MI	28,000
282	United Services Automobile A	TX	28,000
283	Universal Corp	VA	28,000
284	AGCO Corp.	GA	27,900
285	ManpowerGroup	WI	27,900
286	Wynn Resorts Ltd	NV	27,800
287	Lithia Motors Inc	OR	27,446
288	Freeport-McMoRan Inc	AZ	27,200
289	PayPal Holdings Inc	CA	27,200
290	Duke Energy Corp	NC	27,037
291	Global Payments Inc	GA	27,000
292	Hertz Global Holdings Inc (New)	FL	27,000
293	Iron Mountain Inc (New)	NH	27,000
294	Sally Beauty Holdings Inc	TX	27,000
295	Tetra Tech Inc	CA	27,000
296	Vertiv Holdings Co	OH	27,000
297	Cinemark Holdings Inc	TX	26,800
298	Amgen Inc	CA	26,700
299	Coherent Corp	PA	26,622
300	SS&C Technologies Holdings Inc	CT	26,600
301	Qurate Retail Inc - Com Ser B	CO	26,508
302	Ingles Markets Inc	NC	26,420
303	United Rentals Inc	CT	26,300
304	Grainger (W.W.), Inc.	IL	26,100
305	Alaska Air Group, Inc.	WA	26,043
306	Advanced Micro Devices Inc	CA	26,000
307	Analog Devices Inc	MA	26,000
308	Urban Outfitters, Inc.	PA	26,000
309	Encompass Health Corp	AL	25,308
310	AutoNation, Inc.	FL	25,300
311	American International Group Inc	NY	25,200
312	Crown Holdings Inc	FL	25,000
313	Dover Corp	IL	25,000
314	Henry Schein Inc	NY	25,000
315	News Corp (New)	NY	25,000
316	Plexus Corp.	WI	25,000
317	SPAR Group, Inc.	MI	25,000
318	Yum! Brands Inc	KY	25,000
319	Service Corp. International	TX	24,922
320	Thor Industries, Inc.	IN	24,900
321	Newell Brands Inc	GA	24,600
322	Avis Budget Group Inc	NJ	24,500
323	Carrols Restaurant Group Inc	NY	24,300
324	DuPont de Nemours Inc	DE	24,000
325	O-I Glass Inc	OH	24,000
326	Science Applications International Corp (New)	VA	24,000
327	Booking Holdings Inc	CT	23,600
328	Graphic Packaging Holding Co	GA	23,500
329	Vishay Intertechnology, Inc.	PA	23,500
330	JetBlue Airways Corp	NY	23,388
331	PENN Entertainment Inc	PA	23,333
332	Bon-Ton Stores Inc	PA	23,300
333	Ralph Lauren Corp	NY	23,300
334	Fastenal Co.	MN	23,201
335	Howmet Aerospace Inc	PA	23,200
336	Northern Trust Corp	IL	23,100
337	Air Products & Chemicals Inc	PA	23,000
338	Bunge Global SA	MO	23,000
339	CACI International Inc	VA	23,000
340	Cooper-Standard Holdings Inc	MI	23,000
341	CSX Corp	FL	23,000
342	Kellanova	IL	23,000
343	Sonoco Products Co.	SC	23,000
344	TD SYNNEX Corp	CA	23,000
345	Weis Markets, Inc.	PA	23,000
346	Xylem Inc	DC	23,000
347	Old Dominion Freight Line, Inc.	NC	22,902
348	TechnipFMC plc	TX	22,762
349	Dave & Busters Entertainment Inc	TX	22,748
350	ServiceNow Inc	CA	22,668
351	Microchip Technology Inc	AZ	22,600
352	Red Robin Gourmet Burgers Inc	CO	22,516
353	Fidelity National Financial Inc	FL	22,293
354	M & T Bank Corp	NY	22,223
355	Arrow Electronics, Inc.	CO	22,100
356	Academy Sports & Outdoors Inc	TX	22,010
357	Five Below Inc	PA	22,000
358	Marriott Vacations Worldwide Corp.	FL	22,000
359	Paramount Global	NY	21,900
360	United States Steel Corp.	PA	21,803

Top 500 Companies by Employees in Hoover's MasterList of U.S. Companies 2024 (continued)

Rank	Company	Headquarters	Employees
361	Newmont Corp	CO	21,700
362	Align Technology Inc	AZ	21,610
363	BrightView Holdings Inc	PA	21,600
364	Markel Group Inc	VA	21,600
365	AMETEK Inc	PA	21,500
366	International Flavors & Fragrances	NY	21,500
367	Charles River Laboratories International Inc.	MA	21,400
368	ModivCare Inc	CO	21,200
369	Discover Financial Services	IL	21,100
370	Clean Harbors Inc	MA	21,021
371	Ball Corp	CO	21,000
372	BJ's Restaurants Inc	CA	21,000
373	Diebold Nixdorf AG	OH	21,000
374	Motorola Solutions Inc	IL	21,000
375	Education Management Corp	PA	20,800
376	Norfolk Southern Corp	GA	20,700
377	Spirit AeroSystems Holdings Inc	KS	20,655
378	Hershey Company (The)	PA	20,505
379	Qurate Retail Inc	CO	20,300
380	Synopsys Inc	CA	20,300
381	Gartner Inc	CT	20,237
382	Regions Financial Corp	AL	20,101
383	Xerox Holdings Corp	CT	20,100
384	Bed, Bath & Beyond, Inc.	NJ	20,000
385	Broadcom Inc (DE)	CA	20,000
386	CH2M Hill Companies Ltd	CO	20,000
387	CommScope Holding Co Inc	NC	20,000
388	Hormel Foods Corp.	MN	20,000
389	JOANN Inc	OH	20,000
390	Synchrony Financial	CT	20,000
391	Wesco International, Inc.	PA	20,000
392	Exelon Corp	IL	19,962
393	Huntington Bancshares Inc	OH	19,955
394	Graham Holdings Co.	VA	19,900
395	SP Plus Corp	IL	19,900
396	BlackRock Inc	NY	19,800
397	Edwards Lifesciences Corp	CA	19,800
398	Principal Financial Group Inc	IA	19,800
399	Timken Co. (The)	OH	19,602
400	DoorDash Inc	CA	19,300
401	Leggett & Platt, Inc.	MO	19,300
402	First American Financial Corp	CA	19,210
403	Levi Strauss & Co.	CA	19,100
404	Rollins, Inc.	GA	19,031
405	American Axle & Manufacturing Holdings Inc	MI	19,000
406	FirstCash Holdings Inc	TX	19,000
407	Travel + Leisure Co	FL	19,000
408	Workday Inc	CA	18,800
409	Fifth Third Bancorp (Cincinnati, OH)	OH	18,724
410	Hartford Financial Services Group Inc.	CT	18,700
411	Conagra Brands Inc	IL	18,600
412	Parsons Corp (DE)	VA	18,500
413	Polaris Inc	MN	18,500
414	Tapestry Inc	NY	18,500
415	Weatherford International Plc	TX	18,500
416	Hubbell Inc.	CT	18,317
417	Intuit Inc	CA	18,200
418	Marathon Petroleum Corp.	OH	18,200
419	NRG Energy Inc	TX	18,131
420	Agilent Technologies, Inc.	CA	18,100
421	Chewy Inc	FL	18,100
422	Expeditors International of Washington, Inc.	WA	18,100
423	Fortive Corp	WA	18,000
424	Genesco Inc.	TN	18,000
425	Gilead Sciences Inc	CA	18,000
426	Ingersoll Rand Inc	NC	18,000
427	Masco Corp.	MI	18,000
428	Molina Healthcare Inc	CA	18,000
429	Owens Corning	OH	18,000
430	Zimmer Biomet Holdings Inc	IN	18,000
431	Catalent Inc	NJ	17,800
432	Dominion Energy Inc (New)	VA	17,700
433	JELD-WEN Holding Inc	NC	17,700
434	Citizens Financial Group Inc (New)	RI	17,570
435	KeyCorp	OH	17,333
436	Mettler-Toledo International, Inc.	OH	17,300
437	Oshkosh Corp (New)	WI	17,300
438	Schneider National Inc (WI)	WI	17,300
439	RPM International Inc (DE)	OH	17,274
440	American Electric Power Co Inc	OH	17,250
441	Lam Research Corp	CA	17,200
442	Expedia Group Inc	WA	17,100
443	Acadia Healthcare Company Inc.	TN	17,000
444	Coca-Cola Consolidated Inc	NC	17,000
445	Littelfuse Inc	IL	17,000
446	Sealed Air Corp.	NC	17,000
447	SpartanNash Co	MI	17,000
448	Sempra	CA	16,835
449	NextEra Energy Inc	FL	16,800
450	Roper Technologies Inc	FL	16,800
451	Brunswick Corp.	IL	16,608
452	Paychex Inc	NY	16,600
453	Unisys Corp	PA	16,500
454	United Parks & Resorts Inc	FL	16,500
455	GEO Group Inc (The) (New)	FL	16,400
456	Brown & Brown Inc	FL	16,152
457	Boyd Gaming Corp.	NV	16,129
458	Stater Bros. Holdings Inc.	CA	16,100
459	First Citizens BancShares Inc (DE)	NC	16,021
460	Group 1 Automotive, Inc.	TX	16,011
461	Flowserve Corp	TX	16,000
462	Unifirst Corp	MA	16,000
463	Avnet Inc	AZ	15,800
464	Comfort Systems USA Inc	TX	15,800
465	Darling Ingredients Inc	TX	15,800
466	TTM Technologies Inc	CA	15,800
467	UFP Industries Inc	MI	15,800
468	Dycom Industries, Inc.	FL	15,611
469	Murphy USA Inc	AR	15,600
470	Westlake Corp	TX	15,520
471	NCR Voyix Corp	GA	15,500
472	TransDigm Group Inc	OH	15,500
473	Americold Realty Trust Inc	GA	15,484
474	EchoStar Corp	CO	15,300
475	Wendy's Co (The)	OH	15,300
476	Robinson (C.H.) Worldwide, Inc.	MN	15,246
477	Carter's Inc	GA	15,230
478	KLA Corp	CA	15,210
479	Party City Holdco Inc	NJ	15,200
480	Moody's Corp.	NY	15,151

Top 500 Companies by Employees in Hoover's MasterList of U.S. Companies 2024 (continued)

Rank	Company	Headquarters	Employees
481	CDW Corp	IL	15,100
482	Chemed Corp	OH	15,087
483	Icahn Enterprises LP	FL	15,038
484	ArcBest Corp	AR	15,000
485	Asbury Automotive Group Inc	GA	15,000
486	Cooper Companies, Inc.	CA	15,000
487	DENTSPLY SIRONA Inc	NC	15,000
488	Hilton Grand Vacations Inc	FL	15,000
489	Reliance Inc	AZ	15,000
490	Robert Half Inc	CA	15,000
491	Under Armour Inc	MD	15,000
492	MDU Resources Group Inc	ND	14,929
493	Equifax Inc	GA	14,900
494	Keysight Technologies Inc	CA	14,900
495	Packaging Corp of America	IL	14,900
496	Teledyne Technologies Inc	CA	14,900
497	Broadridge Financial Solutions Inc	NY	14,700
498	Gates Industrial Corp PLC	CO	14,700
499	Live Nation Entertainment Inc	CA	14,700
500	Consolidated Edison Inc	NY	14,592

Top 500 Companies by Net Profit in Hoover's MasterList of U.S. Companies 2024

Rank	Company	Headquarters	Net Income ($ Mil)
1	Apple Inc	CA	$96,995
2	Berkshire Hathaway Inc	NE	$96,223
3	Alphabet Inc	CA	$73,795
4	Microsoft Corporation	WA	$72,361
5	JPMorgan Chase & Co	NY	$49,552
6	Meta Platforms Inc	CA	$39,098
7	Exxon Mobil Corp	TX	$36,010
8	Johnson & Johnson	NJ	$35,153
9	Amazon.com Inc	WA	$30,425
10	NVIDIA Corp	CA	$29,760
11	Bank of America Corp	NC	$26,515
12	UnitedHealth Group Inc	MN	$22,381
13	Chevron Corporation	CA	$21,369
14	Fannie Mae	DC	$17,408
15	Visa Inc	CA	$17,273
16	Walmart Inc	AR	$15,511
17	Comcast Corp	PA	$15,388
18	Home Depot Inc	GA	$15,143
19	Tesla Inc	TX	$14,999
20	Procter & Gamble Co (The)	OH	$14,653
21	AT&T Inc	TX	$14,400
22	Broadcom Inc (DE)	CA	$14,082
23	Federal Deposit Insurance Cor	DC	$13,305
24	Emerson Electric Co.	MO	$13,219
25	Cisco Systems Inc	CA	$12,613
26	Burlington Northern & Santa F	TX	$12,119
27	Verizon Communications Inc	NY	$11,614
28	First Citizens BancShares Inc (DE)	NC	$11,466
29	Mastercard Inc	NY	$11,195
30	Coca-Cola Co (The)	GA	$10,714
31	Freddie Mac	VA	$10,538
32	Caterpillar Inc.	TX	$10,335
33	Deere & Co.	IL	$10,166
34	General Motors Co	MI	$10,127
35	Cheniere Energy Inc.	TX	$9,881
36	Marathon Petroleum Corp.	OH	$9,681
37	General Electric Co	MA	$9,481
38	Citigroup Inc	NY	$9,228
39	Morgan Stanley	NY	$9,087
40	PepsiCo Inc	NY	$9,074
41	Valero Energy Corp	TX	$8,835
42	Goldman Sachs Group Inc	NY	$8,516
43	Oracle Corp	TX	$8,503
44	McDonald's Corp	IL	$8,469
45	American Express Co.	NY	$8,374
46	CVS Health Corp	RI	$8,344
47	T-Mobile US Inc	WA	$8,317
48	Altria Group Inc	VA	$8,130
49	Bristol Myers Squibb Co.	NJ	$8,025
50	Philip Morris International Inc	CT	$7,813
51	Lowe's Companies Inc	NC	$7,726
52	EOG Resources, Inc.	TX	$7,594
53	International Business Machines Corp.	NY	$7,502
54	NextEra Energy Inc	FL	$7,310
55	Qualcomm Inc	CA	$7,232
56	Phillips 66	TX	$7,015
57	Applied Materials, Inc.	CA	$6,856
58	Amgen Inc	CA	$6,717
59	United Parcel Service Inc	GA	$6,708
60	Texas Instruments, Inc.	TX	$6,510
61	Union Pacific Corp	NE	$6,379
62	Costco Wholesale Corp	WA	$6,292
63	Linde PLC (New)	CT	$6,199
64	Thermo Fisher Scientific Inc	MA	$5,995
65	Elevance Health Inc	IN	$5,987
66	Abbott Laboratories	IL	$5,723
67	Gilead Sciences Inc	CA	$5,665
68	Honeywell International Inc	NC	$5,658
69	PNC Financial Services Group (The)	PA	$5,578
70	Enterprise Products Partners L.P.	TX	$5,532
71	BlackRock Inc	NY	$5,502
72	U.S. Bancorp (DE)	MN	$5,429
73	Adobe Inc	CA	$5,428
74	Netflix Inc	CA	$5,408
75	HCA Healthcare Inc	TN	$5,242
76	Eli Lilly & Co	IN	$5,240
77	The Cigna Group	CT	$5,164
78	NIKE Inc	OR	$5,070
79	Charles Schwab Corp	TX	$5,067
80	Apollo Global Management Inc (New)	NY	$5,047
81	Prudential Annuities Life As	NJ	$4,965
82	Mondelez International Inc	IL	$4,959
83	Pioneer Natural Resources Co	TX	$4,894
84	Capital One Financial Corp	VA	$4,887
85	AbbVie Inc	IL	$4,863
86	Airbnb Inc	CA	$4,792
87	Danaher Corp	DC	$4,764
88	DR Horton Inc	TX	$4,746
89	Occidental Petroleum Corp	TX	$4,696
90	AFLAC Inc.	GA	$4,659
91	Delta Air Lines Inc (DE)	GA	$4,609
92	Paccar Inc.	WA	$4,601
93	Charter Communications Inc (New)	CT	$4,557
94	Florida Power & Light Co.	FL	$4,552
95	Nucor Corp.	NC	$4,525
96	Lam Research Corp	CA	$4,511
97	Publix Super Markets, Inc.	FL	$4,349
98	Ford Motor Co. (DE)	MI	$4,347
99	Booking Holdings Inc	CT	$4,289
100	Cheniere Energy Partners L P	TX	$4,254
101	PayPal Holdings Inc	CA	$4,246
102	Target Corp	MN	$4,138
103	Salesforce Inc	CA	$4,136
104	Starbucks Corp.	WA	$4,125
105	Southern Co.	GA	$3,976
106	FedEx Corp	TN	$3,972
107	Regeneron Pharmaceuticals, Inc.	NY	$3,954
108	Lennar Corp	FL	$3,939
109	Energy Transfer LP	TX	$3,935
110	MPLX LP	OH	$3,928
111	Progressive Corp. (OH)	OH	$3,902
112	Marsh & McLennan Companies Inc.	NY	$3,756
113	Devon Energy Corp.	OK	$3,747
114	KKR & Co Inc	NY	$3,732
115	CSX Corp	FL	$3,715
116	American International Group Inc	NY	$3,643
117	Vertex Pharmaceuticals, Inc.	MA	$3,620
118	McKesson Corp	TX	$3,560
119	TJX Companies, Inc.	MA	$3,498
120	Archer Daniels Midland Co.	IL	$3,483

Top 500 Companies by Net Profit in Hoover's MasterList of U.S. Companies 2024 (continued)

Rank	Company	Headquarters	Net Income ($ Mil)
121	Automatic Data Processing Inc.	NJ	$3,412
122	KLA Corp	CA	$3,387
123	Analog Devices Inc	MA	$3,315
124	General Dynamics Corp	VA	$3,315
125	Bank of New York Mellon Corp	NY	$3,286
126	HP Inc	CA	$3,263
127	CME Group Inc	IL	$3,226
128	Dell Technologies Inc	TX	$3,211
129	RTX Corp	VA	$3,195
130	Stryker Corp	MI	$3,165
131	Diamondback Energy, Inc.	TX	$3,143
132	General Motors Financial Co	TX	$3,084
133	Marriott International, Inc.	MD	$3,083
134	Sempra	CA	$3,075
135	Fiserv Inc	WI	$3,068
136	Prologis Inc	CA	$3,059
137	Travelers Companies Inc (The)	NY	$2,991
138	Illinois Tool Works, Inc.	IL	$2,957
139	Discover Financial Services	IL	$2,940
140	APA Corp	TX	$2,855
141	Kraft Heinz Co (The)	PA	$2,855
142	Duke Energy Corp	NC	$2,841
143	eBay Inc.	CA	$2,767
144	M & T Bank Corp	NY	$2,741
145	Centene Corp	MO	$2,702
146	ONEOK Inc	OK	$2,659
147	Baxter International Inc	IL	$2,656
148	Halliburton Company	TX	$2,638
149	S&P Global Inc	NY	$2,626
150	United Airlines Holdings Inc	IL	$2,618
151	PulteGroup Inc	GA	$2,602
152	General Mills Inc	MN	$2,594
153	Public Service Enterprise Group Inc	NJ	$2,563
154	Ameriprise Financial Inc	MN	$2,556
155	Toyota Motor Credit Corp.	TX	$2,535
156	AutoZone, Inc.	TN	$2,528
157	Consolidated Edison Inc	NY	$2,519
158	Hartford Financial Services Group Inc.	CT	$2,504
159	Humana, Inc.	KY	$2,489
160	Prudential Financial Inc	NJ	$2,488
161	Steel Dynamics Inc.	IN	$2,451
162	United Rentals Inc	CT	$2,424
163	Chesapeake Energy Corp.	OK	$2,419
164	Kinder Morgan Inc.	TX	$2,391
165	Sherwin-Williams Co (The)	OH	$2,389
166	Intuit Inc	CA	$2,384
167	Intercontinental Exchange Inc	GA	$2,368
168	Entergy Corp. (New)	LA	$2,362
169	Disney (Walt) Co. (The)	CA	$2,354
170	Fifth Third Bancorp (Cincinnati, OH)	OH	$2,349
171	O'Reilly Automotive, Inc.	MO	$2,347
172	Zoetis Inc	NJ	$2,344
173	Exelon Corp	IL	$2,328
174	Waste Management, Inc. (DE)	TX	$2,304
175	DISH Network Corp	CO	$2,303
176	Air Products & Chemicals Inc	PA	$2,300
177	Colgate-Palmolive Co.	NY	$2,300
178	Simon Property Group, Inc.	IN	$2,283
179	United Services Automobile A	TX	$2,272
180	PG&E Corp (Holding Co)	CA	$2,256
181	Kroger Co (The)	OH	$2,244
182	Microchip Technology Inc	AZ	$2,238
183	Synchrony Financial	CT	$2,238
184	American Electric Power Co Inc	OH	$2,208
185	ON Semiconductor Corp	AZ	$2,184
186	Keurig Dr Pepper Inc	MA	$2,181
187	Public Storage	CA	$2,148
188	PBF Energy Inc	NJ	$2,141
189	Cognizant Technology Solutions Corp.	NJ	$2,126
190	Pfizer Inc	NY	$2,119
191	Arista Networks Inc	CA	$2,087
192	Ovintiv Inc	CO	$2,085
193	Parker-Hannifin Corp	OH	$2,083
194	Georgia Power Co	GA	$2,080
195	Regions Financial Corp	AL	$2,074
196	Credit Suisse (USA) Inc	NY	$2,063
197	Northrop Grumman Corp	VA	$2,056
198	Hewlett Packard Enterprise Co	TX	$2,025
199	Citigroup Global Markets Holdings Inc	NY	$2,022
200	Markel Group Inc	VA	$1,996
201	Dominion Energy Inc (New)	VA	$1,994
202	Ford Motor Credit Company LLC	MI	$1,989
203	Celanese Corp (DE)	TX	$1,960
204	Huntington Bancshares Inc	OH	$1,951
205	State Street Corp.	MA	$1,944
206	Baker Hughes Company	TX	$1,943
207	Amphenol Corp.	CT	$1,928
208	CHS Inc	MN	$1,900
209	Uber Technologies Inc	CA	$1,887
210	Hershey Company (The)	PA	$1,862
211	Freeport-McMoRan Inc	AZ	$1,848
212	Cincinnati Financial Corp.	OH	$1,843
213	Grainger (W.W.), Inc.	IL	$1,829
214	Norfolk Southern Corp	GA	$1,827
215	Liberty Media Corp (DE)	CO	$1,815
216	Spectrum Brands Holdings Inc (New)	WI	$1,802
217	Intuitive Surgical Inc	CA	$1,798
218	T Rowe Price Group, Inc.	MD	$1,789
219	Xcel Energy Inc	MN	$1,771
220	Sysco Corp	TX	$1,770
221	Kimberly-Clark Corp.	TX	$1,764
222	Cencora Inc	PA	$1,745
223	Raymond James Financial, Inc.	FL	$1,739
224	EQT Corp	PA	$1,735
225	Republic Services Inc	AZ	$1,731
226	ServiceNow Inc	CA	$1,731
227	CNX Resources Corp	PA	$1,721
228	Motorola Solutions Inc	IL	$1,709
229	Royal Caribbean Group	FL	$1,697
230	Intel Corp	CA	$1,689
231	SVB Financial Group	CA	$1,672
232	First Republic Bank (San Francisco, CA)	CA	$1,665
233	Dollar General Corp	TN	$1,661
234	New York Life Insurance Co.	NY	$1,655
235	Avis Budget Group Inc	NJ	$1,632
236	Monster Beverage Corp (New)	CA	$1,631
237	Coterra Energy Inc	TX	$1,625
238	Bunge Global SA	MO	$1,610
239	Citizens Financial Group Inc (New)	RI	$1,608
240	Moody's Corp.	NY	$1,607

Top 500 Companies by Net Profit in Hoover's MasterList of U.S. Companies 2024 (continued)

Rank	Company	Headquarters	Net Income ($ Mil)
241	Duke Energy Carolinas LLC	NC	$1,600
242	Southern California Edison C	CA	$1,597
243	Yum! Brands Inc	KY	$1,597
244	Boston Scientific Corp.	MA	$1,593
245	NVR Inc.	VA	$1,592
246	HF Sinclair Corp	TX	$1,590
247	MetLife Inc	NY	$1,578
248	Albemarle Corp.	NC	$1,573
249	Union Pacific Railroad Co	NE	$1,570
250	Paychex Inc	NY	$1,557
251	Southwestern Energy Co	TX	$1,557
252	Marathon Oil Corp.	TX	$1,554
253	Builders FirstSource Inc.	TX	$1,541
254	CF Industries Holdings Inc	IL	$1,525
255	Albertsons Companies Inc	ID	$1,514
256	Ross Stores Inc	CA	$1,512
257	CoBank, ACB	CO	$1,507
258	Crown Castle Inc	TX	$1,502
259	Vistra Corp	TX	$1,493
260	Becton Dickinson And Co	NJ	$1,484
261	American Tower Corp (New)	MA	$1,483
262	International Finance Corp.	DC	$1,483
263	Virginia Electric & Power Co	VA	$1,452
264	Loews Corp.	NY	$1,434
265	Valvoline Inc	KY	$1,420
266	Edison International	CA	$1,407
267	Otis Worldwide Corp	CT	$1,406
268	Jones Financial Companies LL	MO	$1,404
269	Edwards Lifesciences Corp	CA	$1,402
270	DTE Energy Co	MI	$1,397
271	Blackstone Inc	NY	$1,391
272	Omnicom Group, Inc.	NY	$1,391
273	Consolidated Edison Co. of N	NY	$1,390
274	Rockwell Automation, Inc.	WI	$1,387
275	Roper Technologies Inc	FL	$1,384
276	Hess Corp	NY	$1,382
277	Workday Inc	CA	$1,381
278	WR Berkley Corp	CT	$1,381
279	GoDaddy Inc	AZ	$1,375
280	Ecolab Inc	MN	$1,372
281	Toll Brothers Inc.	PA	$1,372
282	Alabama Power Co	AL	$1,370
283	IQVIA Holdings Inc	NC	$1,358
284	Carrier Global Corp	FL	$1,349
285	Gen Digital Inc	AZ	$1,349
286	Cintas Corp	OH	$1,348
287	Targa Resources Corp	TX	$1,346
288	Signature Bank (New York, NY)	NY	$1,337
289	Reliance Inc	AZ	$1,336
290	WEC Energy Group Inc	WI	$1,333
291	FMC Corp.	PA	$1,322
292	Genuine Parts Co.	GA	$1,317
293	AMETEK Inc	PA	$1,313
294	Equitable Holdings Inc	NY	$1,302
295	TransDigm Group Inc	OH	$1,298
296	Ulta Beauty Inc	IL	$1,291
297	Unum Group	TN	$1,284
298	Netapp Inc	CA	$1,274
299	Cogent Communications Holdings, Inc.	DC	$1,273
300	PPG Industries Inc	PA	$1,270
301	Sirius XM Holdings Inc	NY	$1,258
302	Best Buy Inc	MN	$1,241
303	Agilent Technologies, Inc.	CA	$1,240
304	Old Dominion Freight Line, Inc.	NC	$1,240
305	Fox Corp	NY	$1,239
306	Copart Inc	TX	$1,238
307	Plains All American Pipeline LP	TX	$1,230
308	Synopsys Inc	CA	$1,230
309	Chipotle Mexican Grill Inc	CA	$1,229
310	L3Harris Technologies Inc	FL	$1,227
311	Las Vegas Sands Corp	NV	$1,221
312	Qurate Retail Inc - Com Ser A	CO	$1,208
313	CNA Financial Corp	IL	$1,205
314	Qurate Retail Inc - Com Ser B	CO	$1,204
315	Owens Corning	OH	$1,196
316	AGCO Corp.	GA	$1,171
317	Martin Marietta Materials, Inc.	NC	$1,169
318	Mosaic Co. (The)	FL	$1,165
319	Biogen Inc	MA	$1,161
320	East West Bancorp, Inc	CA	$1,161
321	Fastenal Co.	MN	$1,155
322	Ameren Corp	MO	$1,152
323	MSCI Inc	NY	$1,149
324	Fortinet Inc	CA	$1,148
325	MGM Resorts International	NV	$1,142
326	Hilton Worldwide Holdings Inc	VA	$1,141
327	Northern Trust Corp	IL	$1,107
328	Tractor Supply Co.	TN	$1,107
329	CDW Corp	IL	$1,104
330	FirstEnergy Corp	OH	$1,102
331	Interpublic Group of Companies Inc.	NY	$1,098
332	Molina Healthcare Inc	CA	$1,091
333	Viasat Inc	CA	$1,085
334	LPL Financial Holdings Inc.	CA	$1,066
335	Nasdaq Inc	NY	$1,059
336	Dover Corp	IL	$1,057
337	Keysight Technologies Inc	CA	$1,057
338	Penske Automotive Group Inc	MI	$1,053
339	DCP Midstream LP	CO	$1,052
340	Dick's Sporting Goods, Inc	PA	$1,047
341	Cadence Design Systems Inc	CA	$1,041
342	Chord Energy Corp	TX	$1,024
343	Zimmer Biomet Holdings Inc	IN	$1,024
344	Western Midstream Partners LP	TX	$1,022
345	AutoNation, Inc.	FL	$1,021
346	Ally Financial Inc	MI	$1,020
347	Snap-On, Inc.	WI	$1,011
348	Lamb Weston Holdings Inc	ID	$1,009
349	Lithia Motors Inc	OR	$1,001
350	NOV Inc	TX	$993
351	CBRE Group Inc	TX	$986
352	Global Payments Inc	GA	$986
353	United Therapeutics Corp	MD	$985
354	Skyworks Solutions Inc	CA	$983
355	Corplay Inc	GA	$982
356	Darden Restaurants, Inc. (United States)	FL	$982
357	Globe Life Inc	TX	$971
358	Gallagher (Arthur J.) & Co.	IL	$970
359	Equinix Inc	CA	$969
360	KeyCorp	OH	$967

Top 500 Companies by Net Profit in Hoover's MasterList of U.S. Companies 2024 (continued)

Rank	Company	Headquarters	Net Income ($ Mil)
361	Kellanova	IL	$951
362	Williams Sonoma Inc	CA	$950
363	Digital Realty Trust Inc	TX	$949
364	American Water Works Co, Inc.	NJ	$944
365	LKQ Corp	IL	$936
366	Tapestry Inc	NY	$936
367	Santander Holdings USA Inc.	MA	$933
368	Vulcan Materials Co (Holding Company)	AL	$933
369	AvalonBay Communities, Inc.	VA	$929
370	Northern Oil & Gas Inc (MN)	MN	$923
371	U-Haul Holding Co	NV	$923
372	Textron Inc	RI	$921
373	CenterPoint Energy, Inc	TX	$917
374	Duke Energy Florida LLC	FL	$909
375	Masco Corp.	MI	$908
376	Oncor Electric Delivery Co	TX	$905
377	Arrow Electronics, Inc.	CO	$904
378	Reinsurance Group of America, Inc.	MO	$902
379	ResMed Inc.	CA	$898
380	First Horizon Corp	TN	$897
381	United States Steel Corp.	PA	$895
382	Eastman Chemical Co	TN	$894
383	Dillard's Inc.	AR	$892
384	CMS Energy Corp	MI	$887
385	Atmos Energy Corp.	TX	$886
386	Teledyne Technologies Inc	CA	$886
387	Franklin Resources Inc	CA	$883
388	Gartner Inc	CT	$882
389	Comerica, Inc.	TX	$881
390	Bath & Body Works Inc	OH	$878
391	Realty Income Corp	CA	$872
392	Brown & Brown Inc	FL	$871
393	Range Resources Corp	TX	$871
394	Webster Financial Corp (Waterbury, Conn)	CT	$868
395	Consumers Energy Co.	MI	$867
396	Fortive Corp	WA	$866
397	Duke Realty L.P.	IN	$861
398	Commercial Metals Co.	TX	$860
399	Campbell Soup Co	NJ	$858
400	Entergy Louisiana LLC (New)	LA	$855
401	Advanced Micro Devices Inc	CA	$854
402	Quest Diagnostics, Inc.	NJ	$854
403	American Financial Group Inc	OH	$852
404	Idexx Laboratories, Inc.	ME	$845
405	Weyerhaeuser Co	WA	$839
406	Equity Residential	IL	$835
407	First Solar Inc	AZ	$831
408	Liberty Mutual Holding Company Inc.	MA	$829
409	Yum China Holdings Inc	TX	$827
410	Autodesk Inc	CA	$823
411	American Airlines Group Inc	TX	$822
412	Jabil Inc	FL	$818
413	SM Energy Co.	CO	$818
414	Verisign Inc	VA	$818
415	Southern California Gas Co.	CA	$812
416	Extra Space Storage Inc	UT	$803
417	Electronic Arts	CA	$802
418	Expedia Group Inc	WA	$797
419	National Rural Utilities Coo	VA	$796
420	Hormel Foods Corp.	MN	$794
421	Crocs Inc	CO	$793
422	Mettler-Toledo International, Inc.	OH	$789
423	Avangrid Inc	CT	$786
424	Caesars Entertainment Inc (New)	NV	$786
425	Civitas Resources Inc	CO	$784
426	Brown-Forman Corp.	KY	$783
427	Ingersoll Rand Inc	NC	$779
428	DTE Electric Company	MI	$772
429	Avnet Inc	AZ	$771
430	CVR Energy Inc	TX	$769
431	Taylor Morrison Home Corp (Holding Co)	AZ	$769
432	Carlisle Cos., Inc.	AZ	$767
433	Wesco International, Inc.	PA	$766
434	Howmet Aerospace Inc	PA	$765
435	Packaging Corp of America	IL	$765
436	Cboe Global Markets Inc	IL	$761
437	Hubbell Inc.	CT	$760
438	Peabody Energy Corp (New)	MO	$760
439	Cal-Maine Foods Inc	MS	$758
440	Church & Dwight Co Inc	NJ	$756
441	Expeditors International of Washington, Inc.	WA	$753
442	Quanta Services, Inc.	TX	$745
443	Host Hotels & Resorts Inc	MD	$740
444	PPL Corp	PA	$740
445	Meritage Homes Corp	AZ	$739
446	Government National Mortgage	DC	$738
447	Cummins, Inc.	IN	$735
448	Evergy Inc	MO	$731
449	Wynn Resorts Ltd	NV	$730
450	Par Pacific Holdings Inc	TX	$729
451	Hunt (J.B.) Transport Services, Inc.	AR	$728
452	Graphic Packaging Holding Co	GA	$723
453	Western Alliance Bancorp	AZ	$722
454	Bread Financial Holdings Inc	OH	$718
455	Universal Health Services, Inc.	PA	$718
456	NiSource Inc. (Holding Co.)	IN	$714
457	MGIC Investment Corp. (WI)	WI	$713
458	W.P. Carey Inc	NY	$708
459	Ball Corp	CO	$707
460	Harley-Davidson Inc	WI	$707
461	National CineMedia Inc	CO	$705
462	Alliant Energy Corp	WI	$703
463	Revvity Inc	MA	$693
464	DaVita Inc	CO	$692
465	Bank OZK	AR	$691
466	Atkore Inc	IL	$690
467	Conagra Brands Inc	IL	$684
468	Huntington Ingalls Industries, Inc.	VA	$681
469	McCormick & Co Inc	MD	$681
470	Zions Bancorporation, N.A.	UT	$680
471	Aramark	PA	$674
472	Affiliated Managers Group Inc.	FL	$673
473	Allison Transmission Holdings Inc	IN	$673
474	Jacobs Solutions Inc	TX	$666
475	Murphy Oil Corp	TX	$662
476	Pacific Mutual Holding Compa	CA	$661
477	Kimco Realty Corp	NY	$654
478	Darling Ingredients Inc	TX	$648
479	Northwestern Mutual Life Ins.	WI	$645
480	Assurant Inc	GA	$643

Top 500 Companies by Net Profit in Hoover's MasterList of U.S. Companies 2024 (continued)

Rank	Company	Headquarters	Net Income ($ Mil)
481	Ingredion Inc	IL	$643
482	Waters Corp.	MA	$642
483	OneMain Holdings Inc	IN	$641
484	Super Micro Computer Inc	CA	$640
485	Zoom Video Communications Inc	CA	$637
486	EMCOR Group, Inc.	CT	$633
487	Broadridge Financial Solutions Inc	NY	$631
488	Alliance Resource Partners L	OK	$630
489	TD SYNNEX Corp	CA	$627
490	Western Union Co	CO	$626
491	BorgWarner Inc	MI	$625
492	Citgo Petroleum Corp.	TX	$625
493	Principal Financial Group Inc	IA	$623
494	Wintrust Financial Corp (IL)	IL	$623
495	Rithm Capital Corp	NY	$622
496	Boyd Gaming Corp.	NV	$620
497	Hertz Global Holdings Inc (New)	FL	$616
498	Air Lease Corp	CA	$615
499	Verisk Analytics Inc	NJ	$615
500	TopBuild Corp	FL	$614

Hoover's MasterList
of U.S. Companies

Company Listings
---

1 SOURCE CONSULTING, INC.

9500 MEDICAL CENTER DR STE 450
LARGO, MD 20774
Phone: 202 850-0073
Fax: –
Web: www.1-sc.com

CEO: William Teel Jr
CFO: Kimberly Logan
HR: Brandon Teele
FYE: December 31
Type: Private

1 Source Consulting isn't the only company to provide information technology and strategic consulting services to the US government, but it would like to be at the top of the list. The company offers IT systems design, development, and integration services, as well as security management, program management, infrastructure and operations consulting, and systems development. 1 Source has served federal agencies such as the departments of Homeland Security, Energy, Transportation, as well as the ATF and SEC. The company operates from offices in Germantown, Maryland and Washington, D.C. 1 Source was founded in 1999 by CEO William R. Teel, Jr.

	Annual Growth	12/05	12/06	12/07	12/08	12/09
Sales ($mil.)	51.8%	–	–	6.5	12.5	14.9
Net income ($ mil.)	39.6%	–	–	5.1	10.0	10.0
Market value ($ mil.)	–	–	–	–	–	–
Employees	–	–	–	–	–	70

1-800 FLOWERS.COM, INC.

NMS: FLWS

Two Jericho Plaza, Suite 200
Jericho, NY 11753
Phone: 516 237-6000
Fax: –
Web: www.1800flowers.com

CEO: James F McCann
CFO: William E Shea
HR: –
FYE: July 2
Type: Public

1-800-FLOWERS.COM is a leading provider of gifts designed to help customers express, connect and celebrate. sells fresh-cut flowers, floral arrangements, and plants through its toll-free number and websites; it also markets gifts via catalogs, TV and radio ads, and online affiliates. Through subsidiaries, the company offers gourmet foods (Harry & David), popcorn (The Popcorn Factory), baked goods (Cheryl's), fruit arrangements (FruitBouquets.com), and a host of other products. Its BloomNet service provides products and services to florists. Founder and chairman James McCann launched the company in 1976. In 2020, the company has completed its acquisition of PersonalizationMall.com.

	Annual Growth	06/19	06/20	06/21*	07/22	07/23
Sales ($mil.)	12.7%	1,248.6	1,489.6	2,122.2	2,207.9	2,017.9
Net income ($ mil.)	–	34.8	59.0	118.7	29.6	(44.7)
Market value ($ mil.)	(19.8%)	1,223.0	1,287.1	2,181.7	621.2	505.3
Employees	0.6%	4,095	4,300	4,800	4,700	4,200

*Fiscal year change

123GREETINGS.COM, INC.

255 EXECUTIVE DR STE 400
PLAINVIEW, NY 118031707
Phone: 347 759-6138
Fax: –
Web: www.123greetings.com

CEO: –
CFO: –
HR: –
FYE: March 31
Type: Private

Sending an electronic greeting is easier than counting to three. 123Greetings.com seems to think so, anyway. With an offering of more than 150,000 products (including free e-mail cards) the company's greetings run the gamut, offering a variety of cards celebrating secular occasions (birthdays, anniversaries, and others plus lots of other events throughout the year). 123Greetings.com also provides a wireless service that allows subscribers to access, personalize, and send greeting cards through their mobile phones.

1399 INTERNET TECHNOLOGY APPLICATION GROUP INC

NBB: YSGG

7702 E Doubletree Ranch, Suite 300
Scottsdale, AZ 85258
Phone: 480 905-5550
Fax: –
Web: –

CEO: Medhat Mohamed
CFO: –
HR: –
FYE: December 31
Type: Public

LaSalle Brands (formerly Diners Acquisition Corp.) owns LaSalle Ice Cream, a premium frozen dairy brand that is distributed primarily in pints throughout the New York City area. LaSalle is popular for its variety of ice cream flavors, as well as gelato and fruit sorbet. The company also sells branded coffee and imported cookies. LaSalle Brands was founded in 1972. The company opened its first retail location in New York in 2005; it has since announced a franchising plan that calls for more than 30 dessert cafes to be operating throughout the US by the end of 2009.

	Annual Growth	12/02	12/03	12/04	12/05	12/06
Sales ($mil.)	–	–	–	–	0.0	0.0
Net income ($ mil.)	–	–	–	(0.0)	(5.6)	(2.9)
Market value ($ mil.)	9.5%	–	–	0.0	0.0	0.0
Employees	–	–	–	–	7	–

180 DEGREE CAPITAL CORP

NMS: TURN

7 N. Willow Street, Suite 4B
Montclair, NJ 07042
Phone: 973 746-4500
Fax: 973 746-4508
Web: www.180degreecapital.com

CEO: Kevin Rendino
CFO: Daniel B Wolfe
HR: –
FYE: December 31
Type: Public

Harris & Harris Group likes to think small. The business development company invests mostly in startup firms developing so-called "tiny technology" -- microsystems, microelectromechanical systems, and nanotechnology used in applications in such sectors as electronics, medical devices, pharmaceuticals, semiconductors, telecommunications, and clean technology. The company seeks out small, thinly capitalized firms lacking operating history or experienced management. Harris & Harris has made more than 80 venture capital investments since 1983; its current portfolio consists of interests in some 30 firms, including Nanosys and NeoPhotonics.

	Annual Growth	12/19	12/20	12/21	12/22	12/23
Sales ($mil.)	(50.3%)	0.9	3.5	2.8	0.3	0.0
Net income ($ mil.)	–	(4.8)	(0.5)	(3.5)	(2.6)	(3.7)
Market value ($ mil.)	17.5%	21.5	22.2	73.5	52.8	41.0
Employees	–	–	–	–	–	–

1ST COLONIAL BANCORP INC

NBB: FCOB

210 Lake Drive East, Suite 300, Woodland Falls Corporate Park
Cherry Hill, NJ 08002
Phone: 877 785-8550
Fax: 856 321-8272
Web: www.1stcolonial.com/

CEO: Robert B White
CFO: Frank J Monaghan
HR: –
FYE: December 31
Type: Public

1st Colonial Bancorp is the holding company for 1st Colonial National Bank. Founded in 2000, the bank serves Camden County in southern New Jersey through branches in the communities of Cinnaminson, Collingswood, and Westville. With an emphasis on personalized service, it caters to small and midsized businesses, professional practices, and local government entities, as well as consumers. The bank provides traditional deposit products such as checking, savings, and money market accounts and certificates of deposit. Additional services include check cards, online banking, and safe deposit boxes.

	Annual Growth	12/17	12/18	12/19	12/20	12/21
Assets ($mil.)	6.0%	540.1	543.9	575.2	636.1	682.8
Net income ($ mil.)	15.8%	4.0	5.2	3.2	4.8	7.3
Market value ($ mil.)	(4.6%)	54.4	58.1	49.4	36.7	45.1
Employees	–	–	–	–	–	–

1ST FRANKLIN FINANCIAL CORP.

135 East Tugalo Street, Post Office Box 880
Toccoa, GA 30577
Phone: 706 886-7571
Fax: –
Web: www.1ffc.com

CEO: Virginia C Herring
CFO: A R Guimond
HR: –
FYE: December 31
Type: Public

Benjamin Franklin was known for doling out sage financial advice to "common folk." Today, 1st Franklin Financial is known for doling out direct cash loans and first and second home mortgages to a similar demographic. Secured direct cash loans make up the lion's share of the company's lending activity; finance charges on loans account for the majority of its revenues. 1st Franklin also offers credit insurance to borrowers and supplements its business by purchasing and servicing sales finance contracts from retailers. The firm operates through about 250 branch offices in the Southeast. Chairman and CEO Ben Cheek III and his family own 1st Franklin, which was founded by his father in 1941.

	Annual Growth	12/18	12/19	12/20	12/21	12/22
Assets ($mil.)	9.9%	796.4	939.2	1,013.7	1,118.2	1,162.9
Net income ($ mil.)	(1.7%)	17.3	13.3	15.9	41.9	16.2
Market value ($ mil.)	–	–	–	–	–	–
Employees	1.4%	1,488	1,513	1,476	1,442	1,575

1ST SOURCE CORP

100 North Michigan Street
South Bend, IN 46601
Phone: 574 235-2000
Fax: –
Web: www.1stsource.com

NMS: SRCE
CEO: Christopher J Murphy III
CFO: Brett A Bauer
HR: –
FYE: December 31
Type: Public

1st Source Corporation, parent of 1st Source Bank, provides commercial and consumer banking services trust and wealth advisory services, and insurance to individual and business clients through its about 80 banking centers locations in nearly 20 counties in Indiana and Michigan and Sarasota County in Florida. The bank provides commercial, small business, agricultural, and real estate loans to private owned business clients and traditional banking services include checking and savings accounts certificate of deposits and individual retirement accounts. Its specialty finance group provides financing for aircraft, automobile fleets, trucks, and construction and environmental equipment, new construction equipment, new and used aircraft, auto and light trucks, and medium and heavy-duty trucks. It was founded in 1863.

	Annual Growth	12/19	12/20	12/21	12/22	12/23
Assets ($mil.)	7.1%	6,622.8	7,316.4	8,096.3	8,339.4	8,728.0
Net income ($ mil.)	8.0%	92.0	81.4	118.5	120.5	124.9
Market value ($ mil.)	1.4%	1,267.7	984.7	1,212.0	1,297.2	1,342.7
Employees	(0.1%)	1,175	1,175	1,130	1,150	1,170

2U INC

7900 Harkins Road
Lanham, MD 20706
Phone: 301 892-4350
Fax: –
Web: www.2u.com

NMS: TWOU
CEO: Paul Lalljie
CFO: Matt Norden
HR: –
FYE: December 31
Type: Public

2U, Inc. is a leading digital transformation partner for nonprofit colleges and universities delivering high-quality online education at scale. It serves more than 230 top-ranked global universities and other leading organizations and offers over 4,000 high-quality online learning opportunities, including open courses, executive education offerings, boot camps, micro-credentials, professional certificates as well as undergraduate and graduate degree programs. Its platform consists of a seamlessly integrated ecosystem of technology, people, and data. Through its platform, the company provides the tools and services clients need to bring their education offerings online. Its edX.org provides access to the full catalog of online offerings that the company enables, ranging from free offerings to graduate degrees. It provides technology and services to enable its clients to provide a range of non-degree credentials and other courses to learners.

	Annual Growth	12/19	12/20	12/21	12/22	12/23
Sales ($mil.)	13.3%	574.7	774.5	945.7	963.1	946.0
Net income ($ mil.)	–	(235.2)	(216.5)	(194.8)	(322.2)	(317.6)
Market value ($ mil.)	(52.4%)	1,973.4	3,291.2	1,651.0	515.8	101.2
Employees	(1.2%)	5,848	6,606	7,188	7,144	5,568

374WATER INC

701 W Main Street, Suite 410
Durham, NC 27701
Phone: 919 888-8194
Fax: –
Web: www.powerverdeenergy.com

NAS: SCWO
CEO: Yaacov Nagar
CFO: John Hofmann
HR: –
FYE: December 31
Type: Public

PowerVerde (formerly known as Vyrex) has abandoned its quest for a molecular fountain of youth. These days, it's only interested in power. The development-stage biotech company had been researching antioxidants to develop cures for respiratory, cardiovascular, and neurodegenerative diseases, and other conditions related to aging. Unable to continue funding its activities, however, Vyrex executed a reverse merger with PowerVerde, which has designed a power system that generates electricity with zero emissions. The system, created by the company's founders George Konrad and Fred Barker, uses solar-heated water to power an environmentally friendly motor.

	Annual Growth	12/18	12/19	12/20	12/21	12/22
Sales ($mil.)	99.6%	0.2	0.0	0.0	0.0	3.0
Net income ($ mil.)	–	(0.7)	(0.5)	(0.5)	(3.2)	(4.7)
Market value ($ mil.)	172.3%	6.6	11.4	106.4	361.1	362.4
Employees	134.0%	1	1	1	17	30

3D SYSTEMS CORP. (DE)

333 Three D Systems Circle
Rock Hill, SC 29730
Phone: 803 326-3900
Fax: –
Web: www.3dsystems.com

NYS: DDD
CEO: Jeffrey A Graves
CFO: Jeffrey Creech
HR: –
FYE: December 31
Type: Public

3D Systems provides comprehensive 3D printing and digital manufacturing solutions, including 3D printers for plastics and metals, materials, software, on demand manufacturing services and digital design tools. The company's solutions support advanced applications in a wide range of industries and verticals, including healthcare, dental, aerospace, automotive and durable goods. The company also offers several 3D printing technologies, such as selective laser sintering, direct metal printing, Multi Jet printing, and ColorJet printing. The company generates approximately half of its sales domestically.

	Annual Growth	12/18	12/19	12/20	12/21	12/22
Sales ($mil.)	(6.0%)	687.7	629.1	557.2	615.6	538.0
Net income ($ mil.)	–	(45.5)	(69.9)	(149.6)	322.1	(122.7)
Market value ($ mil.)	(7.6%)	1,334.4	1,148.1	1,375.0	2,826.2	970.9
Employees	(6.2%)	2,620	2,472	1,995	1,721	2,032

3M CO

3M Center
St. Paul, MN 55144
Phone: 651 733-1110
Fax: 651 733-9973
Web: www.3m.com

NYS: MMM
CEO: Michael F Roman
CFO: –
HR: –
FYE: December 31
Type: Public

3M Company is a diversified technology company with a global presence in the following businesses: Safety and Industrial; Transportation and Electronics; Health Care; and Consumer. 3M is among the leading manufacturers of products for many of the markets it serves. Most 3M products involve expertise in product development, manufacturing and marketing, and are subject to competition from products manufactured and sold by other technologically oriented companies. Some of its brands and offerings include 3M Cubitron II abrasives and Scotch-Brite Abrasives. It generates majority of its revenue from the Americas region. The company began its operations in 1902.

	Annual Growth	12/19	12/20	12/21	12/22	12/23
Sales ($mil.)	0.4%	32,136	32,184	35,355	34,229	32,681
Net income ($ mil.)	–	4,570.0	5,384.0	5,921.0	5,777.0	(6,995.0)
Market value ($ mil.)	(11.3%)	97,486	96,586	98,155	66,266	60,408
Employees	(3.0%)	96,163	95,000	95,000	92,000	85,000

5LINX HOLDINGS INC.

400 ANDREWS ST STE 400
ROCHESTER, NY 146041429
Phone: 585 359-2922
Fax: –
Web: www.myepiccompany.com

CEO: –
CFO: –
HR: –
FYE: December 31
Type: Private

You won't see 5LINX stores popping up anytime soon, but the telecommunications company is still a fast growing enterprise. Relying on a network of independent marketing representatives to sell its products (similar to the model employed by Mary Kay), 5LINX provides an array of telecommunications products and services. Among these are cellular phones and plans from major US carriers; satellite TV service from DISH Network and DIRECTV; and broadband Internet and home security services. Representatives also sell GLOBALINX VoIP services for residential and business customers; a subsidiary of 5LINX, GLOBALINX products include Wi-Fi phones and digital phone services.

	Annual Growth	12/08	12/09	12/10	12/11	12/12
Sales ($mil.)	43.9%	–	–	50.0	81.4	103.6
Net income ($ mil.)	76.3%	–	–	1.2	1.5	3.8
Market value ($ mil.)	–	–	–	–	–	–
Employees	–	–	–	–	–	35

8POINT3 ENERGY PARTNERS LP

77 RIO ROBLES
SAN JOSE, CA 951341859
Phone: 408 240-5500
Fax: –
Web: –

CEO: Charles D Boynton
CFO: Mark R Widmar
HR: –
FYE: November 30
Type: Private

8point3 Energy Partners was formed by First Solar and SunPower to own, operate, and buy solar energy generation projects. Its primary objective is to generate cash distributions that grow at a sustainable rate by acquiring premium solar assets primarily developed by First Solar and SunPower that serve utility, commercial, industrial, and residential customers in the US and in other markets within the Organization for Economic Cooperation and Development (OECD). 8point3 Energy Partners' initial portfolio includes stakes in 432 MW of solar energy projects. The partnership went public in 2015.

8X8 INC

675 Creekside Way
Campbell, CA 95008
Phone: 408 727-1885
Fax: 408 980-0432
Web: www.8x8.com

NMS: EGHT
CEO: Samuel Wilson
CFO: Kevin Kraus
HR: –
FYE: March 31
Type: Public

8x8 is transforming the future business communications as a leading Software-as-a-Service (SaaS) provider of contact center, voice, video, chat, contact center, and enterprise-class API solutions powered by one global cloud communications platform. The company empowers workforces worldwide by connecting individuals and teams so they can collaborate faster and work smarter from anywhere. 8x8 provides real-time business analytics and intelligence giving its customers unique insights across all interactions and channels on its platform, so the company can support a distributed and hybrid working model while delighting its end-customers and accelerate its business. 8x8 has more than 2.5 million paid business licenses with users in more than 180 countries. More than 70% of its total revenue comes from its US customers.

	Annual Growth	03/19	03/20	03/21	03/22	03/23
Sales ($mil.)	20.5%	352.6	446.2	532.3	638.1	743.9
Net income ($ mil.)	–	(88.7)	(172.4)	(165.6)	(175.4)	(73.1)
Market value ($ mil.)	(32.6%)	2,316.1	1,589.2	3,719.5	1,443.6	478.1
Employees	6.4%	1,497	1,675	1,696	2,216	1,921

99 CENTS ONLY STORES LLC

4000 UNION PACIFIC AVE
COMMERCE, CA 900233202
Phone: 323 980-8145
Fax: –
Web: www.99only.com

CEO: –
CFO: –
HR: –
FYE: January 30
Type: Private

99 Cents Only Stores is the leading operator of extreme value stores in California and the Southwestern US. It sells name-brand closeout and regular general merchandise for 99 cents (or less) through about 385 stores in four states. The company sells name-brand and private-label food and grocery products, along with health and beauty aids, household and seasonal goods, hardware, stationary, party products, and more. Its Bargain Wholesale unit distributes discounted merchandise to retailers, distributors, wholesalers, online sellers, and exporters. 99 Cents Only Stores was founded in 1982.

A & E STORES, INC.

1000 HUYLER ST STE 1
TETERBORO, NJ 076081125
Phone: 201 393-0600
Fax: –
Web: www.aestores.com

CEO: –
CFO: –
HR: –
FYE: December 31
Type: Private

Working women who have never heard of A & E Stores are more likely to be familiar with its Strawberry and Bolton's chains. The company operates more than 15 Strawberry and Bolton's stores that sell junior's and women's career and casual apparel, shoes, and accessories. The stores are concentrated in prime office districts in New York City. A & E's third retail chain, Pay/Half, operates more than 45 discount family clothing stores in half a dozen northeastern states, the Chicago area, and Wisconsin. A & E Stores was formed in 1973 by Alan Ades and Albert and Dennis Erani.

A & K RAILROAD MATERIALS, INC.

1505 S REDWOOD RD
SALT LAKE CITY, UT 841045106
Phone: 801 974-5484
Fax: –
Web: ak-railway-materials.mybigcommerce.com

CEO: Kern Shumacher
CFO: Vic Davis
HR: Cheryl Norton
FYE: December 31
Type: Private

You won't find A & K Railroad next to B&O Railroad on a Monopoly board, but you will find the company's pieces all over the railroad. A & K Railroad Materials sells a multitude of new and used railroad supplies, including steel and wood railroad ties and tie plugs, landscaping railroad ties (reclaimed), frogs (plates used to guide rail wheels at crossings), guard rails, switches and components (braces, clips, and plates), rails, and rail tools. Services offered by A & K Railroad Materials include track removal/salvage and custom rail welding. Its lineup is used for railroads, as well as mines and cranes, in North and South America. About 90% of the company is owned by its founder and chairman, Kern Schumacher.

	Annual Growth	01/01	01/02	01/03	01/04*	12/14
Sales ($mil.)	7.8%	–	60.9	67.8	59.7	150.2
Net income ($ mil.)	–	–	(3.2)	0.3	0.4	16.9
Market value ($ mil.)	–	–	–	–	–	–
Employees	–	–	–	–	–	250

*Fiscal year change

A & T SYSTEMS, INC.

12200 TECH RD STE 200
SILVER SPRING, MD 209041971
Phone: 301 384-1425
Fax: –
Web: www.ats.com

CEO: Jeffrey Williams
CFO: –
HR: Melissa Rawls
FYE: June 30
Type: Private

A&T Systems serves up technology for government and business clients. The company provides its customers with a variety of information technology products and services including systems design, management, and maintenance, as well as software development and e-commerce services. A&T Systems also specializes in systems for telecommunications and health care applications. Additionally, it provides a range of more general professional services such as business consulting and technical staffing. The company deals in hardware, software, peripherals, and networking equipment made by such vendors as Dell, Ricoh, and BlackBerry. A&T Systems was founded in 1984 by CEO Dr. Ashok Thareja.

	Annual Growth	06/18	06/19	06/20	06/21	06/22
Sales ($mil.)	4.1%	–	–	23.9	23.9	25.9
Net income ($ mil.)	(65.0%)	–	–	1.2	1.2	0.1
Market value ($ mil.)	–	–	–	–	–	–
Employees	–	–	–	–	–	119

A-1 EXPRESS DELIVERY SERVICE, INC.

1450 W PEACHTREE ST NW # 200
ATLANTA, GA 303092955
Phone: 877 219-7737
Fax: –
Web: www.a1express.com

CEO: –
CFO: –
HR: –
FYE: December 31
Type: Private

From the CNN Center to the High Museum of Art, from the Georgia Dome to the Margaret Mitchell House, A-1 Express Delivery Service provides same-day courier services. The company makes its own deliveries in the Atlanta area and partners with other couriers and third-party carriers to serve cities throughout the US. It has about 1,500 clients, including some FORTUNE 500 companies. Working with its partners, A-1 Express Delivery Service can arrange the delivery of freight by a variety of methods, ranging from bicycles to tractor-trailers. The company was founded in 1997.

	Annual Growth	12/05	12/06	12/07	12/08	12/09
Sales ($mil.)	(3.7%)	–	4.4	5.2	4.7	4.0
Net income ($ mil.)	(43.4%)	–	0.1	0.0	(0.0)	0.0
Market value ($ mil.)	–	–	–	–	–	–
Employees	–	–	–	–	–	300

A-1 FREEMAN MOVING & STORAGE, L.L.C.

11517 BROADWAY EXT
OKLAHOMA CITY, OK 731146607
Phone: 405 751-7561
Fax: –
Web: www.northamerican.com

CEO: –
CFO: –
HR: –
FYE: December 30
Type: Private

A-1 Freeman Moving & Storage provides household and corporate relocation services, primarily in the southern US. It offers tracking systems, international relocation services, and specialized transportation services for items such as medical equipment, exhibits, artifacts, and other highly valued products. The company operates from offices in Georgia, Oklahoma, and Texas. A-1 Freeman is an agent of North American Van Lines, which is a unit of SIRVA. (As an agent, A-1 Freeman handles moves within its assigned territories and cooperates with other North American Van Lines agents on interstate moves.) CEO James Freeman founded the company in 1974.

	Annual Growth	12/04	12/05	12/06	12/07	12/09
Sales ($mil.)	(12.0%)	–	–	57.4	51.6	39.2
Net income ($ mil.)	(14.9%)	–	–	1.4	1.7	0.9
Market value ($ mil.)	–	–	–	–	–	–
Employees	–	–	–	–	–	400

A-MARK PRECIOUS METALS, INC

NMS: AMRK

2121 Rosecrans Ave. Suite 6300
El Segundo, CA 90245
Phone: 310 587-1477
Fax: –
Web: www.amark.com

CEO: Gregory N Roberts
CFO: Kathleen S Taylor
HR: –
FYE: June 30
Type: Public

A-Mark Precious Metals is a fully integrated precious metals platform that offers an array of gold, silver, platinum, palladium, and copper bullion, numismatic coins, bars, wafers, and grain for central banks, manufacturers, and individuals around the world. It also distributes coins for government mints, including those of Australia, Austria, Canada, China, Mexico, South Africa, the UK, and the US. A-Mark, which generates most of its revenue in the US, offers related services such as financing and logistics and secure storage. It also sells and purchases directly to the retail market. The company was founded in 1965.

	Annual Growth	06/19	06/20	06/21	06/22	06/23
Sales ($mil.)	18.0%	4,783.2	5,461.1	7,613.0	8,159.3	9,286.6
Net income ($ mil.)	189.5%	2.2	30.5	159.6	132.5	156.4
Market value ($ mil.)	30.1%	304.5	444.6	1,085.1	752.6	873.6
Employees	23.2%	186	220	351	384	429

A-MRAZEK MOVING SYSTEMS, INC.

545 LEFFINGWELL AVE
SAINT LOUIS, MO 631226454
Phone: 314 822-4200
Fax: –
Web: www.a-mrazek.com

CEO: –
CFO: Celeste Roloff
HR: –
FYE: March 31
Type: Private

A-Mrazek Moving Systems, an agent of United Van Lines, is a full-service moving company. The company's offerings include local, long distance, and international relocations, office relocations, trade show moves, and storage. A-Mrazek Moving Systems is able to offer services outside its St. Louis home region by working with other agents of United Van Lines and with other affiliates of UniGroup, which owns United Van Lines. The company is the official mover of the city's sports teams, the Saint Louis Cardinals (MLB) and the Saint Louis Rams (NFL).

A. DUDA & SONS, INC.

1200 DUDA TRL
OVIEDO, FL 327654505
Phone: 407 365-2111
Fax: –
Web: www.duda.com

CEO: Joseph A Duda
CFO: Palmer B Weeks
HR: Donna Taylor
FYE: August 27
Type: Private

A. Duda & Sons (known as DUDA) is a diversified land company with some DANDY operations in agriculture and real estate spanning nearly 90,000 acres nationwide. Through its Duda Farm Fresh Foods unit, it grows and markets fresh fruits and vegetables as well as value-added products under the DANDY label. DUDA sells them to retail and foodservice customers in North America, Europe, and Asia. Its products portfolio consists of celery, lettuce, onions, sweet corn, and citrus fruits. The Duda Products division operates citrus groves and processing operations. Duda Ranches oversees cattle, sugarcane, and sod operations. DUDA's Viera division develops and manages commercial and residential properties in Florida.

A. DUIE PYLE INC.

650 WESTTOWN RD
WEST CHESTER, PA 193824900
Phone: 610 696-5800
Fax: –
Web: www.aduiepyle.com

CEO: –
CFO: –
HR: –
FYE: December 31
Type: Private

A. Duie Pyle has piled up a collection of transportation-related businesses. The company's services include less-than-truckload (LTL) and truckload freight hauling, warehousing, third-party logistics, and equipment leasing. (LTL carriers consolidate freight from multiple shippers into a single trailer.) A. Duie Pyle's LTL business operates primarily in the Northeast US and in Canada from a network of more than 15 service depots. The LTL unit maintains a fleet of about 800 tractors and 1,900 trailers; another 325 tractors for heated truckload hauling. The company offers service outside its core region through alliances with other carriers. A. Duie Pyle maintains more than 2 million sq. ft. of warehouse space.

A. STUCKI COMPANY

360 WRIGHT BROTHERS DR
CORAOPOLIS, PA 151086807
Phone: 412 424-0560
Fax: –
Web: www.stucki.com

CEO: John O'Bryan
CFO: David Brown
HR: Rick Clary
FYE: December 31
Type: Private

A. Stucki Company has been working on the railroad, all the live long day. The company designs and manufactures ball bearings, including roller side bearings, long travel side bearings, body side bearings, and resilient friction elements, for railroad freight cars worldwide. It also offers repair and reconditioning services, as well as rail car parts through its subsidiary operations. A. Stucki invests much of its revenue in R&D and designs turnkey systems. Besides the US, the company has operations in Australia, Brazil, Mexico, and the Ukraine. Arnold Stucki, a Swiss mechanical engineer and the author of Steel Car Design, founded the company in 1911. Gladstone Investment is a leading investor in A. Stucki.

A. EPSTEIN AND SONS INTERNATIONAL, INC.

600 W FULTON ST FL 9
CHICAGO, IL 606611253
Phone: 312 454-9100
Fax: –
Web: www.epsteinglobal.com

CEO: –
CFO: –
HR: Christine Paccione-Anders
FYE: March 31
Type: Private

From the jazz age to the tech age, Epstein has made its mark. The company provides architectural, engineering, and construction management services in the US and Europe. Epstein serves the commercial, industrial, and public sector markets, building and designing projects such as office buildings, corporate headquarters, manufacturing plants, convention centers, hospitals, and schools. It has worked on O'Hare International Airport and Whirlpool's headquarters, as well as projects for Apple, Serta, and Hyatt. The employee-owned firm was founded in 1921 by Abraham Epstein. The company has offices in the US, Poland, and Romania.

A.B.C. HOME FURNISHINGS, INC.

11111 SANTA MONICA BLVD
LOS ANGELES, CA 900250437
Phone: 212 473-3000
Fax: –
Web: www.abchome.com

CEO: Aaron Rose
CFO: –
HR: Patricia Baroncini
FYE: December 31
Type: Private

ABC Home Furnishings (aka ABC Carpet & Home) is one of the largest and most diverse rug and home collections in the world. The specialty home furnishings retailer operates a handful of US stores. ABC offers high-quality furniture, rugs, and related accessories. In addition, its ABC Kitchen is an upscale restaurant in New York City. In late 2021, ABC Carpet & Home filed for chapter 11 bankruptcy protection. It enters bankruptcy with a roughly $15.3 million offer to take over its business. In the same year, the lifestyle brand with a rich legacy in home and hospitality was acquired by investment vehicle 888 Capital Partners, the company's lead bidder.

A. P. HUBBARD WHOLESALE LUMBER CORPORATION

138 E MURPHY ST STE 1
MADISON, NC 270251967
Phone: 336 275-1343
Fax: –
Web: www.hubbardlumber.com

CEO: –
CFO: –
HR: –
FYE: March 31
Type: Private

A.P. Hubbard Lumber manufactures lumber and lumber products for the construction industry. Its offerings include air- and kiln-dried lumber made from cypress, hardwoods, softwoods, and eastern white pine, as well as engineered wood products such as glue-laminated timber, rim board, wood decking, sheathing, and framing lumber. The company distributes its products in the Carolinas, Virginia, and Maryland. A.P. Hubbard Lumber was founded in Greensboro, North Carolina in 1952.

A.L.L. MASONRY CONSTRUCTION CO., INC.

1425 S 55TH CT
CICERO, IL 608041841
Phone: 773 489-1280
Fax: –
Web: www.allconstructiongroup.com

CEO: –
CFO: –
HR: –
FYE: July 31
Type: Private

A.L.L. Masonry Construction offers a variety of masonry construction services, including installations, pavers, and walls. The company primarily serves commercial, industrial, and institutional customers in and around Chicago. Its list of clients reads like a who's who of area institutions, including Northwestern University, The University of Chicago, Soldiers Field, the Lincoln Park Zoo, and the Chicago Public Library, as well as churches, schools, and apartment communities. Minority-owned A.L.L. Masonry Construction was founded in 1959. It is controlled by CEO Luis Puig.

	Annual Growth	03/08	03/09	03/10	03/11	03/12
Sales ($mil.)	20.2%	–	8.8	8.8	11.7	15.3
Net income ($ mil.)	46.5%	–	0.0	0.0	0.0	0.0
Market value ($ mil.)	–	–	–	–	–	–
Employees		–	–	–	–	5

A.V. THOMAS PRODUCE, INC.

3900 SULTANA AVE
ATWATER, CA 953019605
Phone: 209 394-7514
Fax: –
Web: www.avthomasproduce.com

CEO: –
CFO: –
HR: –
FYE: December 31
Type: Private

A.V. Thomas Produce knows a sweet potato is not just a yam by another name. The California grower produces, packages, and sells several varieties of yams and the yam's sweeter cousin, the sweet potato. (Though the names are used interchangeably in this country, most US-grown "yams" are actually sweet potatoes.) With 1,700 acres in production, its brands include Best West, Court House, Nature's Pride, Oriental Beauty, Royal Flush, Sweetie Pie, Thomas, and Winner; it is also a major US producer of organic sweet potatoes, which it sells under the Natural Beauty label. Founded in 1960 by Antonio Vieira Tomas, an immigrant from the Azores Islands, A.V. Thomas is owned and run by Tomas's nephew, CEO Manuel Vieira.

	Annual Growth	12/09	12/10	12/11	12/12	12/13
Sales ($mil.)	7.1%	–	–	60.8	65.5	69.7
Net income ($ mil.)	16.6%	–	–	10.6	9.0	14.5
Market value ($ mil.)	–	–	–	–	–	–
Employees	–	–	–	–	–	166

A10 NETWORKS INC

2300 Orchard Parkway
San Jose, CA 95131
Phone: 408 325-8668
Fax: –
Web: www.a10networks.com

NYS: ATEN
CEO: Dhrupad Trivedi
CFO: Brian Becker
HR: –
FYE: December 31
Type: Public

A10 Networks is a leading provider of networking solutions that enable next-generation networks focused on reliability, availability, scalability and cybersecurity. Its portfolio supports customers operating in the cloud, on-premise or in hybrid environments providing rapid return on their investment as well as investment protection with best-in-class technical performance. A10's products center on its Advanced Core Operating System (ACOS) platform. Application Delivery Controllers (ADCs) optimize a data center's performance, while its Carrier Grade Network Address Translation (CGN) products provide address and protocol translation services for service provider networks. The company's Distributed Denial of Service Threat Protection System (TPS) offers network-wide security protection. About 45% of the company's sales were generated in the US.

	Annual Growth	12/19	12/20	12/21	12/22	12/23
Sales ($mil.)	4.3%	212.6	225.5	250.0	280.3	251.7
Net income ($ mil.)	–	(17.8)	17.8	94.9	46.9	40.0
Market value ($ mil.)	17.7%	510.8	733.2	1,232.9	1,236.6	979.3
Employees	(10.3%)	810	749	590	575	525

AAA COOPER TRANSPORTATION

1751 KINSEY RD
DOTHAN, AL 363035877
Phone: 334 793-2284
Fax: –
Web: www.aaacooper.com

CEO: Reid Dove
CFO: J S Roy
HR: Renee Lingo
FYE: January 01
Type: Private

AAA Cooper Transportation (AACT), an independent subsidiary of Knight-Swift Transportation Holdings, is an asset-based multi-regional transportation solutions provider offering less-than-truckload, truckload, dedicated contract carriage, brokerage, fleet maintenance, and international services. Its cross-brand integrations with other KNX subsidiaries provide extended direct coverage and resources across a substantial area of the US. In addition, robust Affiliate Carrier Program extends AACT's coverage area into Canada, Mexico, and across the globe. The company's fleet includes 3,000 tractors and 7,500 trailers.

	Annual Growth	12/12	12/13	12/14*	01/16	01/17
Sales ($mil.)	0.9%	–	–	576.9	595.4	592.0
Net income ($ mil.)	(4.3%)	–	–	20.1	14.1	17.7
Market value ($ mil.)	–	–	–	–	–	–
Employees	–	–	–	–	–	4,933

*Fiscal year change

AAC GROUP HOLDING CORP.

7211 CIRCLE S RD
AUSTIN, TX 787456603
Phone: 512 444-0571
Fax: –
Web: –

CEO: –
CFO: Kris G Radhakrishnan
HR: –
FYE: August 29
Type: Private

School spirit tops the shopping list of customers of AAC Group. Doing business as American Achievement, the company manufactures and supplies class rings, yearbooks, and letter athletic jackets, as well as graduation items, such as caps and gowns, diplomas, and announcements for the US elementary through high school and college markets. Its ring and accessory brands include ArtCarved, Balfour, and Keepsake. Although scholastic products account for most of its sales, AAC Group also makes commemorative jewelry for families, bridal jewelry, personalized rings for the military, bowling tournaments, and pro sports such as World Series, Super Bowl, and Stanley Cup. The memorabilia maker is owned by Fenway Partners.

AALFS MANUFACTURING, INC.

1005 4TH ST
SIOUX CITY, IA 511011806
Phone: 712 252-1877
Fax: –
Web: www.aalfs.com

CEO: –
CFO: –
HR: –
FYE: December 31
Type: Private

Aalfs Manufacturing Company, owned and run by the founding Aalfs family, just might have a gene for the jeans business. The company designs, makes, and markets clothing (primarily jeans and denimwear) to big-name retailers nationwide. Clients include J.C. Penney (since 1943), American Eagle, Tommy Hilfiger, Gap, Old Navy, and even Harley Davidson. Aalfs also makes and sells its own 4 Stroke brand of denim apparel. Founded in Iowa in 1892 by H.A. Baker and renamed the Aalfs-Baker Manufacturing Company in 1929, when Wilbur Aalfs held the presidential title, the apparel manufacturer officially became Aalfs Manufacturing Company in 1959.

AAON, INC.

2425 South Yukon Ave.
Tulsa, OK 74107
Phone: 918 583-2266
Fax: –
Web: www.aaon.com

NMS: AAON
CEO: Gary D Fields
CFO: Rebecca A Thompson
HR: –
FYE: December 31
Type: Public

AAON is the world's leading manufacturer of premium HVAC equipment, creating comfortable and healthy indoor environments. Operating through subsidiaries, the company makes and markets air conditioning and heating equipment for commercial and industrial buildings, primarily in the US. AAON's products include rooftop units, air-handling and make-up air units, chillers, and energy recovery units, as well as condensing units and geothermal/water-source heat pumps and coils. The company sells to property owners and contractors in both the new construction and replacement markets looking for a higher quality and more options than offered by standardized manufacturers.

	Annual Growth	12/19	12/20	12/21	12/22	12/23
Sales ($mil.)	25.6%	469.3	514.6	534.5	888.8	1,168.5
Net income ($ mil.)	34.9%	53.7	79.0	58.8	100.4	177.6
Market value ($ mil.)	10.6%	4,027.3	5,430.9	6,474.2	6,139.2	6,021.0
Employees	13.9%	2,290	2,268	2,881	3,666	3,856

AAR CORP
NYS: AIR

One AAR Place, 1100 N. Wood Dale Road
Wood Dale, IL 60191
Phone: 630 227-2000
Fax: 630 227-2019
Web: www.aarcorp.com

CEO: John M Holmes
CFO: Sean M Gillen
HR: –
FYE: May 31
Type: Public

AAR Corp. is a diversified provider of services and products to the worldwide commercial aviation and government and defense markets. The company sells and leases new and overhauled and repaired aircraft engines and airframe parts to commercial aviation, military, and government/defense customers. AAR provides supply chain management services, parts, and MRO (aircraft maintenance, repair, and overhaul) services. The company also supplies government agencies and non-governmental organizations (NGOs) with transportation pallets, containers, shelters, mobility systems, and control systems used in support of military deployments and humanitarian activities. More than 75% of AAR's revenue comes from North America. The company traces its historical roots to 1951.

	Annual Growth	05/19	05/20	05/21	05/22	05/23
Sales ($mil.)	(0.8%)	2,051.8	2,072.0	1,652.3	1,820.0	1,990.5
Net income ($ mil.)	86.2%	7.5	4.4	35.8	78.7	90.2
Market value ($ mil.)	13.6%	1,050.6	704.2	1,457.7	1,683.6	1,749.6
Employees	(6.5%)	6,550	5,400	4,920	4,850	5,000

AARON AND COMPANY, INC.

30 TURNER PL
PISCATAWAY, NJ 088543839
Phone: 732 752-8200
Fax: –
Web: www.ferguson.com

CEO: Barry Portnoy
CFO: Victor D Rosa
HR: –
FYE: December 31
Type: Private

Aaron & Company knows a thing or two about staying cool. Catering primarily to contractors in New Jersey and eastern Pennsylvania, the wholesaler offers plumbing and HVAC supplies through more than five locations in the Garden State. Three of these outlets house Aaron Kitchen & Bath Design Galleries, which feature complete kitchen and bathroom set-ups to help customers with building and remodeling plans. Aaron & Company is served by a single 120,000-sq.-ft. distribution center that is stocked with more than 15,000 items.

	Annual Growth	12/15	12/16	12/17	12/18	12/19
Sales ($mil.)	5.3%	–	86.6	89.0	99.6	101.1
Net income ($ mil.)	–	–	(0.4)	1.9	1.7	1.9
Market value ($ mil.)	–	–	–	–	–	–
Employees	–	–	–	–	–	188

AARP

601 E ST NW
WASHINGTON, DC 200490003
Phone: 202 434-2277
Fax: –
Web: www.aarp.org

CEO: Jo A Jenkins
CFO: Robert R H Jr
HR: –
FYE: December 31
Type: Private

AARP is a nonprofit, nonpartisan organization, with a membership of nearly 38 million current members. With staffed offices in all 50 states, the District of Columbia, Puerto Rico, and the US Virgin Islands, AARP works to strengthen communities and advocate for what matters most to families?with a focus on health security, financial stability, and personal fulfillment. AARP also advocates for individuals in the marketplace by selecting products and services of high quality and value to carry the AARP name. It also produces the world's largest circulation magazine, AARP The Magazine and AARP Bulletin. The American Association of Retired Persons, now known as AARP, was founded in 1958 by Ethel Percy Andrus, a retired high school principal.

	Annual Growth	12/11	12/12	12/13	12/14	12/16
Sales ($mil.)	3.7%	–	–	1,439.0	1,399.0	1,605.0
Net income ($ mil.)	(29.8%)	–	–	408.8	84.5	141.2
Market value ($ mil.)	–	–	–	–	–	–
Employees	–	–	–	–	–	1,800

AATRIX SOFTWARE, INC.

2617 S COLUMBIA RD STE 1
GRAND FORKS, ND 582016003
Phone: 701 746-6801
Fax: –
Web: www.aatrix.com

CEO: Steve Lunseth
CFO: –
HR: –
FYE: December 31
Type: Private

Founded in 1987, Aatrix Software provides payroll processing, time and attendance, accounting, and financial software for small businesses. Its Aatrix 1099 Utility collects data from QuickBooks and prints it out in a form. Aatrix Top Pay allows users to track deductions, employer-paid contributions, and vacation, sick, and holiday time and automatically posts the payroll information into QuickBooks. The company also offers eFiling services for government payroll reports for all 50 states and the federal government, and it offers more than 300 electronic business forms that are compatible with its software, which come in versions for both Windows and Mac operating systems.

	Annual Growth	12/04	12/05	12/06	12/07	12/08
Sales ($mil.)	10.8%	–	–	2.1	2.2	2.6
Net income ($ mil.)	(28.2%)	–	–	0.0	0.0	0.0
Market value ($ mil.)	–	–	–	–	–	–
Employees	–	–	–	–	–	40

ABATIX CORP.

2400 SKYLINE DR STE 400
MESQUITE, TX 751491990
Phone: 214 381-0322
Fax: –
Web: www.abatix.com

CEO: Terry W Shaver
CFO: Frank J Cinatl IV
HR: Elisabeth Parker
FYE: December 31
Type: Private

Following a huff and a puff, Abatix cleans up. The company distributes more than 30,000 personal protection and safety equipment products to environmental contractors as well as construction and industrial safety companies. Abatix's lineup is used by workers involved in cleanup projects, such as asbestos and lead abatement, and natural disasters. Products include sheeting and bags, dehumidifiers, air scrubbers and filters, and germicidals, and fire retardant and disposable protective clothing. Abatix serves some 6,000 customers located throughout the US. It operates a dozen sales and distribution centers in Texas, Arizona, Georgia, Louisiana, Nevada, California, Washington, and Florida.

	Annual Growth	12/17	12/18	12/19	12/20	12/21
Sales ($mil.)	1.3%	–	–	–	129.6	131.2
Net income ($ mil.)	(6.7%)	–	–	–	9.8	9.1
Market value ($ mil.)	–	–	–	–	–	–
Employees	–	–	–	–	–	180

ABAXIS, INC.

3240 WHIPPLE RD
UNION CITY, CA 945871217
Phone: 510 675-6500
Fax: –
Web: www.abaxis.com

CEO: Clinton H Severson
CFO: Ross Taylor
HR: –
FYE: March 31
Type: Private

The genesis of the Abaxis technology took place at the Oak Ridge National Laboratory, where under contract to the National Aeronautics and Space Administration, scientists sought to develop and manufacture a small biochemical analyzer for use in space laboratories. Founded in 1989, Abaxis licenses and manufactures reagents utilizing the Orbos technology to other companies. It introduces Piccolo and VETSCAN analyzer in the market. The company covers more than 90% of the general chemistry tests normally used in medical and veterinary diagnostics. Abaxis sells to primary care physicians, pediatric caregivers, hospitals, managed care organizations, and the military.

	Annual Growth	03/14	03/15	03/16	03/17	03/18
Sales ($mil.)	6.5%	–	202.6	218.9	227.2	244.7
Net income ($ mil.)	(0.2%)	–	27.3	31.6	32.7	27.2
Market value ($ mil.)	–	–	–	–	–	–
Employees	–	–	–	–	–	656

ABBOTT LABORATORIES   NYS: ABT

100 Abbott Park Road   CEO: Robert B Ford
Abbott Park, IL 60064-6400   CFO: Philip P Boudreau
Phone: 224 667-6100   HR: –
Fax: –   FYE: December 31
Web: www.abbottinvestor.com   Type: Public

Abbott Laboratories is a global healthcare leader that helps people live more fully at all stages of life. It develops, manufactures, and sells a broad and diversified line of health care products. Abbott has product lines of branded generic pharmaceuticals, diagnostic systems and tests, pediatric and adult nutritional products (including well-known brands such as Similac and PediaSure), and medical devices for the treatment of cardiovascular diseases, including diabetes care products for people with diabetes, neuromodulation devices for chronic pain and movement disorder management. The US accounts for more than 40% of company's total sales. Abbott was founded in 1888 by physician and drug store proprietor Dr. Wallace C. Abbott.

	Annual Growth	12/19	12/20	12/21	12/22	12/23
Sales ($mil.)	5.9%	31,904	34,608	43,075	43,653	40,109
Net income ($ mil.)	11.6%	3,687.0	4,495.0	7,071.0	6,933.0	5,723.0
Market value ($ mil.)	6.1%	150,622	189,864	244,054	190,384	190,870
Employees	1.6%	107,000	109,000	113,000	115,000	114,000

ABBOTT NORTHWESTERN HOSPITAL

800 E 28TH ST   CEO: Gordon M Sprenger
MINNEAPOLIS, MN 554073799   CFO: –
Phone: 612 863-4000   HR: Jeffrey Peterson
Fax: –   FYE: December 31
Web: www.allinahealth.org   Type: Private

Abbott Northwestern Hospital helps bring twins into the Twin Cities -- along with triplets, quadruplets, and even quintuplets. The not-for-profit hospital boasts some 650 beds and provides general medical and surgical health, specialty care, and diagnostic services to the Minneapolis-St. Paul metro area. Abbott Northwestern Hospital includes a cardiovascular, neuroscience, mental health, and orthopedic centers and the Virginia Piper Cancer Institute, as well as home health and hospice agencies. It is one of four hospital-based locations of the Sister Kenny Rehabilitation Institute. Its medical staff includes more than 1,400 physicians. Abbott Northwestern Hospital is a member of Allina Hospitals and Clinics.

ABBVIE INC   NYS: ABBV

1 North Waukegan Road   CEO: Richard A Gonzalez
North Chicago, IL 60064-6400   CFO: Scott Reents
Phone: 847 932-7900   HR: –
Fax: –   FYE: December 31
Web: www.abbvie.com   Type: Public

AbbVie is a global, research-based biopharmaceutical company. The company has a portfolio of products across immunology, hematologic oncology, neuroscience, aesthetics and eye care. AbbVie uses its expertise, dedicated people and unique approach to innovation to develop and market advanced therapies that address some of the world's most complex and severe diseases. AbbVie's products are sold globally directly to wholesalers, distributors, government agencies, health care facilities, specialty pharmacies and independent retailers from AbbVie-owned distribution centers and public warehouses. The US is AbbVie's largest market, accounting for about 65% of total revenue.

	Annual Growth	12/19	12/20	12/21	12/22	12/23
Sales ($mil.)	13.0%	33,266	45,804	56,197	58,054	54,318
Net income ($ mil.)	(11.4%)	7,882.0	4,616.0	11,542	11,836	4,863.0
Market value ($ mil.)	15.0%	156,356	189,221	239,108	285,394	273,668
Employees	13.6%	30,000	47,000	50,000	50,000	50,000

ABDON CALLAIS OFFSHORE, LLC

1300 N ALEX PLAISANCE BLVD   CEO: –
GOLDEN MEADOW, LA 703572612   CFO: –
Phone: 985 475-7111   HR: –
Fax: –   FYE: December 31
Web: –   Type: Private

Abdon Callais Offshore provides freight and passenger transportation services to the offshore oil and gas industry. The company operates its fleet of about 75 supply vessels, utility vessels, and crew boats in the Gulf of Mexico, serving coastal, shelf, and deepwater projects. It counts both production companies and service companies among its customers. The company was founded in 1945 by Abdon Callais, grandfather of president and CEO Peter Callais. The Callais family controls the company; other backers have included private equity firm Stonehenge Capital.

	Annual Growth	12/07	12/08	12/09	12/10	12/12
Sales ($mil.)	15.8%	–	–	–	75.5	101.2
Net income ($ mil.)	65.1%	–	–	–	14.4	39.3
Market value ($ mil.)	–	–	–	–	–	–
Employees	–	–	–	–	–	430

ABEONA THERAPEUTICS INC   NAS: ABEO

6555 Carnegie Avenue, 4th Floor   CEO: Vishwas Seshadri
Cleveland, OH 44103   CFO: Joseph Vazzano
Phone: 646 813-4701   HR: –
Fax: –   FYE: December 31
Web: www.abeonatherapeutics.com   Type: Public

Abeona Therapeutics (formerly PlasmaTech Pharmaceuticals) is developing treatments to tap into the cancer therapy market. The company makes pharmaceutical products based on nanopolymer chemistry and other drug delivery technologies. Its FDA-approved MuGard is a prescription oral rinse for the treatment of mucositis, or mouth ulceration, a common side effect of chemotherapy or radiation. MuGard has marketing approval in the US, and it is available in Europe through partner SpePharm. Other Abeona products, include ovarian cancer treatments and drug delivery technologies for solid tumors and diabetes.

	Annual Growth	12/19	12/20	12/21	12/22	12/23
Sales ($mil.)	–	–	10.0	3.0	1.4	3.5
Net income ($ mil.)	–	(76.3)	(84.2)	(84.9)	(39.7)	(54.2)
Market value ($ mil.)	11.3%	86.7	41.6	8.9	81.7	132.9
Employees	(1.2%)	88	76	90	57	84

ABERCROMBIE & FITCH CO   NYS: ANF

6301 Fitch Path   CEO: Fran Horowitz
New Albany, OH 43054   CFO: Scott D Lipesky
Phone: 614 283-6500   HR: –
Fax: –   FYE: January 28
Web: www.abercrombie.com   Type: Public

Abercrombie & Fitch (A&F) is a global multi-brand omnichannel specialty retailer that offers a broad assortment of apparel, personal care products and accessories for men, women and kids, which are sold primarily through its digital channels and company-owned stores, as well as through various third-party arrangements. The company's two brand-based operating segments are Hollister, which includes the company's Hollister, Gilly Hicks and Social Tourist brands, and Abercrombie, which includes the company's Abercrombie & Fitch and abercrombie kids brands. The company's approximately 760 stores are found mainly in the US but also in Europe, the Asia Pacific region, and the Middle East, while A&F ships globally online. The US is its largest market accounting for about 75% of total revenue.

	Annual Growth	02/19	02/20*	01/21	01/22	01/23
Sales ($mil.)	0.7%	3,590.1	3,623.1	3,125.4	3,712.8	3,697.8
Net income ($ mil.)	(55.9%)	74.5	39.4	(114.0)	263.0	2.8
Market value ($ mil.)	6.3%	1,047.2	801.7	1,130.5	1,788.1	1,338.2
Employees	(8.4%)	42,000	44,000	34,000	31,500	29,600

*Fiscal year change

ABF FREIGHT SYSTEM, INC.

3801 OLD GREENWOOD RD
FORT SMITH, AR 729035937
Phone: 479 785-8700
Fax: -
Web: www.arcb.com

CEO: Robert A Young III
CFO: -
HR: Dave Ayers
FYE: March 31
Type: Private

ABF Freight System knows the ABCs of freight transportation. The largest subsidiary of ArcBest Corporation, ABF Freight System is one of the nation's largest and most trusted less-than-truckload carriers. With 100 years of experience, a detailed quality improvement process, and an innovative transportation network of over 240 service centers across all 50 states, Canada and Puerto Rico, ABF delivers LTL freight with precision and skill. ABF Freight also provides motor carrier freight transportation services to customers in Mexico through arrangements with trucking companies in that country.

	Annual Growth	12/06	12/07	12/08*	03/12	03/13
Sales ($mil.)	(25.7%)	-	-	1,758.8	-	398.3
Net income ($ mil.)	-	-	-	28.1	-	(12.8)
Market value ($ mil.)	-	-	-	-	-	-
Employees	-	-	-	-	-	1,000

*Fiscal year change

ABILENE CHRISTIAN UNIVERSITY INC

1600 CAMPUS CT
ABILENE, TX 796013761
Phone: 325 674-2000
Fax: -
Web: www.acu.edu

CEO: -
CFO: Lori Herrick
HR: -
FYE: May 31
Type: Private

Abilene was once the home where the buffalo roamed, but now it's where the Abilene Christian University Wildcats play. The private Church of Christ-affiliated university, which requires Bible study courses and daily chapel attendance, has an enrollment of about 4,600 students. By 2020 the school intends to be the world's premier Christ-centered university. It offers some 70 baccalaureate majors that include more than 125 areas of study, in addition to about 25 graduate academic programs, one doctoral program, and study abroad programs in Oxford, England; Montevideo, Uruguay; and Leipzig, Germany. The student-teacher ratio is 15:1. Abilene Christian was founded in 1906.

	Annual Growth	05/16	05/17	05/18	05/20	05/21
Sales ($mil.)	2.2%	-	131.6	135.6	139.3	143.8
Net income ($ mil.)	65.7%	-	33.8	44.6	11.2	254.9
Market value ($ mil.)	-	-	-	-	-	-
Employees	-	-	-	-	-	675

ABILITYPATH

350 TWIN DOLPHIN DR STE 123
REDWOOD CITY, CA 940651458
Phone: 650 259-8500
Fax: -
Web: www.abilitypath.org

CEO: Sheryl Young
CFO: -
HR: -
FYE: June 30
Type: Private

It's not exactly the yellow brick road but Community Gatepath leads disabled people in San Mateo County, California to a place even better than Oz. The not-for-profit organization serves more than 1,100 individuals and their families by promoting independence and integration into the community. It offers adults and children rehabilitative therapy, support groups, educational and vocational classes, and socialization training. Community Gatepath also provides services to local businesses and individuals that include production work (hand assembly, mail sorting, collating, shrink-wrapping, and delivery), staffing, and landscape work. It was formed when community centers Poplar Center and Peninsula ReCare merged.

ABINGTON MEMORIAL HOSPITAL

1200 OLD YORK RD
ABINGTON, PA 190013788
Phone: 215 481-2000
Fax: -
Web: www.abingtonradiology.com

CEO: Laurence M Merlis
CFO: -
HR: Christine Rue
FYE: June 30
Type: Private

Jefferson Health-Abington (formerly Abington Memorial Hospital) brings is reimagining health care through its service-minded and diverse community of providers and specialists. The not-for-profit community hospital has some 800 beds. In addition to general medical and surgical care, the hospital offers specialized care centers for cancer and cardiovascular conditions, operates high-tech orthopedic and neurological surgery units, and serves as a regional trauma care facility. With approximately 126,000 inpatient admissions, 499,000 Emergency Department visits, and four million outpatient visits annually, it also runs an inpatient pediatric unit in affiliation with Nemours Children's Health. Jefferson Health-Abington?operates the neighboring 140-bed Lansdale Hospital? Jefferson Health and range of inpatient and outpatient facilities.

	Annual Growth	06/12	06/13	06/14	06/15	06/16
Sales ($mil.)	1.5%	-	708.5	697.3	697.7	740.9
Net income ($ mil.)	19.2%	-	20.9	0.7	28.5	35.3
Market value ($ mil.)	-	-	-	-	-	-
Employees	-	-	-	-	-	4,018

ABL MANAGEMENT, INC.

300 S TRYON ST STE 400
CHARLOTTE, NC 282020136
Phone: 704 424-1071
Fax: -
Web: -

CEO: Olivier Poirot
CFO: -
HR: -
FYE: December 25
Type: Private

A leading provider of contract food services, ABL Management makes lunchtime possible for students and inmates alike. Through ABL Educational Enterprise, the company provides food services at colleges and universities, including residential cafeterias and retail dining areas. For prison operators, it provides meals, runs commissaries, and offers laundry services. In addition, ABL provides on-site food services for other customers in both the public and private sectors, including government agencies, health care facilities, and commercial employee cafeterias. It also offers corporate dining services and special events catering.

	Annual Growth	09/06	09/07	09/08*	12/08	12/09
Sales ($mil.)	29.3%	-	-	34.5	45.6	44.7
Net income ($ mil.)	586.3%	-	-	0.3	0.5	2.1
Market value ($ mil.)	-	-	-	-	-	-
Employees	-	-	-	-	-	950

*Fiscal year change

ABM INDUSTRIES, INC.

One Liberty Plaza, 7th Floor
New York, NY 10006
Phone: 212 297-0200
Fax: -
Web: www.abm.com

NYS: ABM

CEO: Scott Salmirs
CFO: Earl R Ellis
HR: -
FYE: October 31
Type: Public

ABM Industries is a leading provider of integrated facility solutions. The company primarily offers janitorial services to owners and operators of office buildings, hospitals, manufacturing plants, schools, shopping centers, catering logistics, parking and transportation facilities. ABM also provides maintenance of mechanical, air cabin, facilities engineering, electrical and plumbing systems and it operates parking services and garages, mainly at airports across all 50 states. ABM makes most of its revenue in the US. The company's history dates back to 1909.

	Annual Growth	10/19	10/20	10/21	10/22	10/23
Sales ($mil.)	5.6%	6,498.6	5,987.6	6,228.6	7,806.6	8,096.4
Net income ($ mil.)	18.5%	127.4	0.3	126.3	230.4	251.3
Market value ($ mil.)	1.9%	2,291.4	2,182.1	2,765.9	2,797.3	2,472.4
Employees	(3.2%)	140,000	114,000	124,000	127,000	123,000

ABS CAPITAL PARTNERS III, L.P.

201 INTERNATIONAL CIR STE 150
COCKEYSVILLE, MD 210301929
Phone: 410 246-5600
Fax: –
Web: www.abscapital.com

CEO: –
CFO: –
HR: –
FYE: December 31
Type: Private

ABS Capital Partners seeks out companies that have learned their business ABCs. The firm typically invests $10 million to $30 million per transaction in late-stage (but growing) US companies in the business services, health care, media and communications, and technology sectors. It provides capital for expansions, acquisitions, management buyouts, and recapitalizations. In addition to taking a seat on the boards of its portfolio companies, the firm also provides strategic and financial advice to them, but usually does not get involved with their day-to-day operations. ABS Capital Partners has interests in more than two dozen companies, including Liquidity Services, Rosetta Stone, and Vibrant Media.

ACACIA RESEARCH CORP   NMS: ACTG

767 Third Avenue, 6th Floor
New York, NY 10017
Phone: 332 236-8500
Fax: 949 480-8301
Web: www.acaciaresearch.com

CEO: Clifford Press
CFO: Richard Rosenstein
HR: –
FYE: December 31
Type: Public

Acacia Research is an opportunistic capital platform that purchases businesses based on the differentials between public and private market valuations. The company invests in intellectual property, and related absolute return assets, and engages in the licensing and enforcement of patented technologies. The company established a proven track record of licensing and enforcement success with over 1,600 license agreements across nearly 200 patent portfolio licensing and enforcement programs. Acacia Research partners with inventors, universities, research institutions, technology companies, and others. The US generates roughly 60% of the company's total sales.

	Annual Growth	12/19	12/20	12/21	12/22	12/23
Sales ($mil.)	82.6%	11.2	29.8	88.0	59.2	125.1
Net income ($ mil.)	–	(17.1)	113.4	149.2	(125.1)	67.1
Market value ($ mil.)	10.2%	265.7	393.6	512.5	420.6	391.6
Employees	77.8%	17	20	293	269	170

ACADEMY OF MOTION PICTURE ARTS & SCIENCES

8949 WILSHIRE BLVD
BEVERLY HILLS, CA 902111907
Phone: 310 247-3000
Fax: –
Web: www.oscars.org

CEO: Dawn Hudson
CFO: Andy Horn
HR: –
FYE: June 30
Type: Private

And the Oscar goes to ... the Academy of Motion Picture Arts and Sciences (AMPAS). The not-for-profit organization promotes the movie industry by recognizing excellence, fostering cultural progress, providing a forum for various crafts, and cooperating in technical research. It is best known for the annual Academy Awards in which Britannia metal trophies (known as the Oscars) are awarded for outstanding achievements in the motion picture industry. The more than 6,000 AMPAS members (who pick the Oscar winners) represent 15 branches of the industry, including actors, directors, producers, and executives. The organization was founded in 1927 and is governed by seven officers and a board of governors.

	Annual Growth	06/18	06/19	06/20	06/21	06/22
Sales ($mil.)	24.9%	–	147.9	158.4	210.7	288.0
Net income ($ mil.)	–	–	44.1	32.7	104.6	(49.4)
Market value ($ mil.)	–	–	–	–	–	–
Employees	–	–	–	–	–	174

ACADEMY OF TELEVISION ARTS AND SCIENCES

5220 LANKERSHIM BLVD
NORTH HOLLYWOOD, CA 916013109
Phone: 818 754-2800
Fax: –
Web: www.emmys.com

CEO: Dick Askin
CFO: –
HR: Kisha Hollins
FYE: December 31
Type: Private

And the award for best organization that honors the television industry goes to: the Academy of Television Arts & Sciences (ATAS). ATAS, which has more than 13,000 members, presents the annual Emmy Awards and sponsors various television-related conferences and activities. The organization also oversees the Daytime and L.A. Area Emmy Awards, publishes emmy magazine, manages archival and educational programs through its ATAS Foundation, and operates Web sites such as emmys.tv and emmys.com. The Emmy statuette features a winged woman holding an atom aloft to symbolize the melding of art and science. The award's name is a deviation of "Immy," an early television camera. ATAS was founded in 1946.

	Annual Growth	12/13	12/14	12/16	12/21	12/22
Sales ($mil.)	5.1%	–	29.0	33.1	33.0	43.3
Net income ($ mil.)	–	–	(7.6)	1.7	2.7	5.1
Market value ($ mil.)	–	–	–	–	–	–
Employees	–	–	–	–	–	65

ACADEMY SPORTS & OUTDOORS INC   NMS: ASO

1800 North Mason Road
Katy, TX 77449
Phone: 281 646-5200
Fax: –
Web: www.academy.com

CEO: Steven P Lawrence
CFO: Carl Ford
HR: –
FYE: February 3
Type: Public

Academy Sports and Outdoors is one of the leading full-line sporting goods and outdoor recreation retailers in the US. Operates nearly 270 stores across nearly 20 contiguous states, its product assortment focuses on key categories of outdoor, apparel, sports and recreation, and footwear through both leading national brands and a portfolio of approximately 20 owned brands, which go well beyond traditional sporting goods and apparel offerings. It has premium access to hundreds of well-recognized national brands, such as Nike, Under Armour, Adidas, Winchester, Brooks, Crocs, Wilson, Spaulding, Yeti, the North Face, and Columbia Sportswear. Academy Sports and Outdoors regularly analyzes consumer trends on media consumption and relies on various media channels to communicate with its customers. The company was originally founded in 1938 as a family business in Texas.

	Annual Growth	02/20*	01/21	01/22	01/23*	02/24
Sales ($mil.)	6.3%	4,829.9	5,689.2	6,773.1	6,395.1	6,159.3
Net income ($ mil.)	44.2%	120.0	308.8	671.4	628.0	519.2
Market value ($ mil.)	–	–	1,598.5	2,800.0	4,137.6	4,794.1
Employees	1.2%	21,000	22,000	22,000	22,000	22,010

*Fiscal year change

ACADIA HEALTHCARE COMPANY INC.   NMS: ACHC

6100 Tower Circle, Suite 1000
Franklin, TN 37067
Phone: 615 861-6000
Fax: –
Web: www.acadiahealthcare.com

CEO: –
CFO: –
HR: –
FYE: December 31
Type: Public

Acadia Healthcare is a leading pure-play provider of behavioral health services. Acadia operates about 250 behavioral health facilities with approximately 11,000 licensed beds in some 40 US states and Puerto Rico. Its specialty treatment facilities include residential recovery facilities, eating disorder facilities and CTCs which include detoxification, partial hospitalization, and outpatient programs. The majority of its specialty treatment services are provided to patients who abuse addictive substances such as alcohol, illicit drugs or opiates, including prescription drugs. Some of its facilities also treat other addictions and behavioral disorders such as chronic pain, sexual compulsivity, compulsive gambling, mood disorders, emotional trauma and abuse.

	Annual Growth	12/19	12/20	12/21	12/22	12/23
Sales ($mil.)	(1.5%)	3,107.5	2,089.9	2,314.4	2,610.4	2,928.7
Net income ($ mil.)	–	108.9	(672.1)	190.6	273.1	(21.7)
Market value ($ mil.)	23.7%	3,031.8	4,586.9	5,539.7	7,512.9	7,096.7
Employees	(20.6%)	42,800	42,200	22,500	23,000	17,000

ACADIA PHARMACEUTICALS INC   NMS: ACAD

12830 El Camino Real, Suite 400 — CEO: -
San Diego, CA 92130 — CFO: -
Phone: 858 558-2871 — HR: -
Fax: - — FYE: December 31
Web: www.acadia.com — Type: Public

ACADIA Pharmaceuticals develops small molecule drugs for the treatment of central nervous system disorders. The biopharmaceutical company's pimavanserin (Nuplazid) was approved by the FDA in 2016 as a treatment for Parkinson's disease psychosis, a common development with the disease. Two other clinical-stage candidates are being developed in collaboration with Allergan to treat patients with chronic pain. The company's pipeline also includes pre-clinical candidates in development for chronic pain and Parkinson's disease. All candidates are birthed from ACADIA's own R-SAT drug discovery platform.

	Annual Growth	12/19	12/20	12/21	12/22	12/23
Sales ($mil.)	21.0%	339.1	441.8	484.1	517.2	726.4
Net income ($ mil.)	-	(235.3)	(281.6)	(167.9)	(216.0)	(61.3)
Market value ($ mil.)	(7.5%)	7,043.7	8,802.2	3,842.9	2,621.2	5,155.2
Employees	4.4%	503	601	514	513	597

ACADIA REALTY TRUST   NYS: AKR

411 Theodore Fremd Avenue, Suite 300 — CEO: Kenneth F Bernstein
Rye, NY 10580 — CFO: John Gottfried
Phone: 914 288-8100 — HR: -
Fax: - — FYE: December 31
Web: www.acadiarealty.com — Type: Public

Acadia Realty acquires, redevelops, and manages retail properties located primarily in high-barrier-to-entry, supply-constrained, densely populated metropolitan areas in the US. The self-managed real estate investment trust (REIT) specializes in community shopping centers and mixed-use properties in suburban areas. It owns more than 190 properties with about 13.2 million sq. ft. of leasable space -- mostly shopping centers anchored by a grocery store, drug store, big box store, and sporting goods stores. The REIT's largest tenants include Target, H&M, Walgreens, TJX Companies, Royal Ahold, and Fast Retailing, among others. Acadia Realty has operations in New York, Chicago, Los Angeles, San Francisco, Washington DC, and Boston.

	Annual Growth	12/19	12/20	12/21	12/22	12/23
Sales ($mil.)	3.5%	295.3	255.5	292.5	326.3	338.7
Net income ($ mil.)	(21.8%)	53.0	(8.8)	23.5	(35.4)	19.9
Market value ($ mil.)	(10.0%)	2,472.7	1,353.2	2,081.7	1,368.4	1,620.2
Employees	(0.2%)	118	120	123	115	117

ACADIAN AMBULANCE SERVICE, INC.

130 E KALISTE SALOOM RD — CEO: Richard E Zuschlag
LAFAYETTE, LA 705088308 — CFO: David L Kelly
Phone: 337 291-3333 — HR: Chari Foster
Fax: - — FYE: December 31
Web: www.acadianambulance.com — Type: Private

Acadian Ambulance Service is one of the nation's largest privately-held medical transportation companies. The company covers over 70 parishes and counties that are home to more than 24 million residents in Louisiana, Mississippi, Tennessee, and Texas. Along with its ground ambulances, the company also operates a handful of helicopter ambulances and fixed-wing airplanes. Its services include emergency transportation, air services, non-emergency transportation, special services, mobile healthcare, medical education, offshore & industrial health and medical alert systems. Established in 1971, Acadian Ambulance Service is owned by its employees through a private stock option plan.

	Annual Growth	12/07	12/08	12/09	12/10	12/11
Sales ($mil.)	14.4%	-	-	290.8	358.3	380.6
Net income ($ mil.)	39.5%	-	-	4.8	7.2	9.3
Market value ($ mil.)	-	-	-	-	-	-
Employees	-	-	-	-	-	4,000

ACAS, LLC

2 BETHESDA METRO CTR FL 14 — CEO: R K Deveer
BETHESDA, MD 208146320 — CFO: -
Phone: 301 951-6122 — HR: Kasey Reisman
Fax: - — FYE: December 31
Web: - — Type: Private

Whether you make musical instruments or mints, salon appliances or safes, this company has a strategy for you. Founded in 1986, American Capital invests in a diverse selection of middle-market companies both directly and through its global asset management business. It typically provides up to $300 million per transaction to companies for management and employee buyouts and private equity buyouts. The firm also directly provides capital to companies. Other investments include financial products such as commercial mortgage-backed securities and collateralized loan obligations. American Capital's portfolio consists of stakes in more than 150 companies and has a focus on manufacturing, services, and distribution. Ares Capital Corp agreed to buy American Capital for $3.4 billion in May 2016.

ACCELERATE DIAGNOSTICS INC   NAS: AXDX

3950 South Country Club Road, Suite 470 — CEO: Jack Phillips
Tucson, AZ 85714 — CFO: David Patience
Phone: 520 365-3100 — HR: -
Fax: - — FYE: December 31
Web: www.acceleratediagnostics.com — Type: Public

Accelerate Diagnostics is an in vitro diagnostics company dedicated to providing solutions that improve patient outcomes and lower healthcare costs through the rapid diagnosis of serious infections. The Accelerate PhenoTest BC Kit is indicated as an aid, in conjunction with other clinical and laboratory findings, in the diagnosis of bacteremia and fungemia. The device provides identification (ID) results followed by antibiotic susceptibility testing (AST) for certain pathogenic bacteria commonly associated with or causing bacteremia. This test kit utilizes genotypic technology to identify infectious pathogens and phenotypic technology to conduct AST, which determines whether live bacterial cells are resistant or susceptible to a particular antimicrobial. Multiple external studies have proven that Accelerate technology platform is intended to address these challenges by delivering significantly faster testing of infectious pathogens in various patient sample types. About 85% of total revenue accounts from its domestic operations.

	Annual Growth	12/18	12/19	12/20	12/21	12/22
Sales ($mil.)	22.5%	5.7	9.3	11.2	11.8	12.8
Net income ($ mil.)	-	(88.3)	(84.3)	(78.2)	(77.7)	(62.5)
Market value ($ mil.)	(50.2%)	112.1	164.7	73.9	50.9	6.9
Employees	(11.1%)	287	275	224	220	179

ACCELPATH INC

137 National Plaza, Suite 300 — CEO: -
National Harbor, MD 20745 — CFO: -
Phone: 240 273-3295 — HR: -
Fax: - — FYE: June 30
Web: - — Type: Public

Technest Holdings can help you get a better picture of your security efforts or better diagnose your patients. The company makes 3-D modeling and imaging software and equipment, primarily for the security and health care industries. Technest's products include intelligent surveillance, 3-D facial recognition, and 3-D imaging devices and systems. The company's customers have included the Department of Defense and the National Institute of Health.

	Annual Growth	06/10	06/11	06/12	06/13	06/14
Sales ($mil.)	-	-	0.4	0.6	0.3	0.2
Net income ($ mil.)	-	(0.3)	(2.9)	(2.1)	(2.0)	(2.5)
Market value ($ mil.)	(78.9%)	0.8	1.3	0.2	0.0	0.0
Employees	-	-	11	5	1	1

ACCESS BUSINESS GROUP LLC

7575 FULTON ST E
ADA, MI 493550001
Phone: 616 787-3000
Fax: -
Web: www.amwayglobal.com

CEO: -
CFO: -
HR: -
FYE: December 31
Type: Private

Somehow all those Amway products have to get from factories to the sales floor, and that's where Access Business Group (ABG) comes in. The company manufactures and distributes cosmetics, nutritional supplements, home care, and personal care products for its sister company, Amway. (Both companies are units of Alticor.) It also offers contract manufacturing services for third-party consumer goods companies, but to a lesser extent. Other offerings include product packaging services, as well as catalog and direct mail printing services. In addition, the company operates R&D labs that develop and test products for Amway. Alticor is the parent company of Access Business Group, as well as Amway, and is a holding company for Amway's non-direct selling companies.

	Annual Growth	12/11	12/12	12/13	12/14	12/15
Sales ($mil.)	(5.7%)	-	-	1,135.5	1,068.1	1,009.9
Net income ($ mil.)	-	-	-	-	-	-
Market value ($ mil.)	-	-	-	-	-	-
Employees	-	-	-	-	-	3,000

ACCESS CAPITAL, INC.

405 PARK AVE FL 16
NEW YORK, NY 100224405
Phone: 212 644-9300
Fax: -
Web: www.accesscapital.com

CEO: Terry M Keating
CFO: -
HR: Ethan Aronoff
FYE: June 30
Type: Private

Access Capital gives business owners access to much needed capital. The business lender offers payroll funding, asset-based lending, and acquisition financing/senior term loans to over a thousand companies in a broad range of industries, ranging from small start-ups to large corporations. The New York-based firm's typical clients include growing business services companies from IT staffing and engineering, legal, light industrial, media companies, distributors and manufacturers.

	Annual Growth	06/08	06/09	06/10	06/17	06/21
Assets ($mil.)	15.3%	-	0.3	0.3	1.3	1.8
Net income ($ mil.)	-	-	-	(0.0)	0.8	1.2
Market value ($ mil.)	-	-	-	-	-	-
Employees	-	-	-	-	-	34

ACCESS WORLDWIDE COMMUNICATIONS, INC.

1820 North Fort Myer Drive
Arlington, VA 22209
Phone: 703 292-5210
Fax: -
Web: www.accessww.com

CEO: -
CFO: -
HR: -
FYE: December 31
Type: Public

This firm doesn't want place any geographic limits on its business services. Operating from locations in the US, Latin America, Europe, Africa, and the Asia/Pacific region, Access Worldwide offers business process outsourcing (BPO) capabilities to a variety of clients. Services include inbound and outbound sales, lead generation, order entry, appointment setting, billing management, and support services for hardware and software. The company caters to the banking, retail, telecommunications, and media industries. It provides BPO support in more than 15 languages across all forms of media. Major clients have included AT&T and E*TRADE. Access Worldwide was established in 1983. Examples of services Access Worldwide has provided include helping clients find an effective way to generate leads and creating outbound campaigns to educate and up-sell clients on products. The company also conducts market research services such as survey administration and other methods of data collection. All total, its staff has executed more than 400 marketing campaigns, customer activations, and customer service programs for its clients.

	Annual Growth	12/03	12/04	12/05	12/06	12/07
Sales ($mil.)	(10.5%)	51.1	47.5	38.9	27.7	32.8
Net income ($ mil.)	-	(11.6)	(1.4)	(4.7)	2.9	(5.0)
Market value ($ mil.)	(12.9%)	28.5	27.9	15.8	20.5	16.4
Employees	(6.3%)	1,300	700	1,000	1,000	1,000

ACCESSLEX INSTITUTE

10 N HIGH ST STE 400
WEST CHESTER, PA 193803014
Phone: 484 653-3300
Fax: -
Web: www.accesslex.org

CEO: Christopher P Chapman
CFO: -
HR: -
FYE: March 31
Type: Private

As if paying for Albert's undergraduate degree didn't set you back enough, now your little Einstein wants to attend graduate school. It may be time to contact Access Group, a not-for-profit organization that offers graduate and professional student lending. The company issues and services private student loans for continuing education, part-time, and international students, and their parents. It specializes in financing educations in business, dental, law, medical, engineering, and other professional courses of study. The company also issues specialized loans for bar and dental board exams and medical and dental residencies. Access Group was founded in 1983 to provide funding to law students.

	Annual Growth	03/15	03/16	03/17	03/20	03/22
Assets ($mil.)	(13.1%)	-	5,057.0	4,584.2	3,251.7	2,183.4
Net income ($ mil.)	(19.7%)	-	16.8	91.5	21.1	4.5
Market value ($ mil.)	-	-	-	-	-	-
Employees	-	-	-	-	-	60

ACCION INTERNATIONAL

1101 15TH ST NW STE 400
WASHINGTON, DC 200055002
Phone: 202 393-5113
Fax: -
Web: www.accion.org

CEO: Michael Schlein
CFO: Livingston Parsons
HR: -
FYE: December 31
Type: Private

This group helps people take action to help themselves. ACCION International, Spanish for "action," gives the poor the means to achieve economic independence by providing micro loans for starting small businesses. Enterprises are typically making and selling food, sewing clothing, or growing and selling produce. The organization works with lenders to support programs in about 20 countries in Africa, Asia/Pacific, the Caribbean, and Latin America. It loans about $5 billion each year to nearly 3 million people. First-time loans average about $600 each. The program's repayment rate is more than 97%. ACCION was formed in 1961 to fight poverty in Latin American cities.

ACCO BRANDS CORP

Four Corporate Drive
Lake Zurich, IL 60047
Phone: 847 541-9500
Fax: -
Web: www.accobrands.com

NYS: ACCO
CEO: Boris Elisman
CFO: Deborah A O'Connor
HR: -
FYE: December 31
Type: Public

ACCO Brands is one of the world's largest designers, marketers, and manufacturers of branded academic, consumer, and business products. The company makes office, school, and consumer products under a host of brand names recognizable to anyone who has shopped for school or office supplies, including Artline, Mead, Five-Star, AT-A-GLANCE, and Rexel. It offers items for storage and organization, laminating and binding, and shredding, as well as writing instruments, whiteboards, notebooks, calendars, and computer accessories. ACCO sells mostly through retail superstores, mass merchandisers, commercial stationers, wholesalers, e-tailers, and warehouse clubs. It operates worldwide, with about 45% of sales coming from the US.

	Annual Growth	12/19	12/20	12/21	12/22	12/23
Sales ($mil.)	(1.6%)	1,955.7	1,655.2	2,025.3	1,947.6	1,832.8
Net income ($ mil.)	-	106.8	62.0	101.9	(13.2)	(21.8)
Market value ($ mil.)	(10.2%)	888.5	802.1	784.1	530.6	577.1
Employees	(5.4%)	7,000	6,100	6,000	6,000	5,600

ACCUCODE, INC.

65 INVERNESS DR E STE 300
ENGLEWOOD, CO 801125141
Phone: 303 639-6111
Fax: –
Web: www.accucode.com

CEO: –
CFO: –
HR: –
FYE: December 31
Type: Private

AccuCode designs and installs customized asset-tracking systems that combine mobile computing with automated data collection tools such as bar codes and radio-frequency identification (RFID). The company's offerings include hardware from manufacturers such as Datalogic Scanning, Intermec, Motorola Solutions, and Psion Teklogix, as well as proprietary software. Its customers -- which include airlines, delivery service providers, retail stores, manufacturers, and health care providers -- use AccuCode's systems to track warehouse inventory and corporate assets, monitor patients, and manage assembly-line efficiency. The company counts British Airways, Corporate Express, DHL, and Kroger among its clients.

ACCURAY INC (CA)

NMS: ARAY

1240 Deming Way
Madison, CA 53717
Phone: 608 824-2800
Fax: –
Web: www.accuray.com

CEO: Suzanne Winter
CFO: Ali Pervaiz
HR: –
FYE: June 30
Type: Public

Accuray Incorporated is a radiation therapy company that develops, manufactures, sells and supports market-changing solutions that are designed to deliver radiation treatments for even the most complex cases, while making commonly treatable cases even more straightforward, to meet the full spectrum of patient needs. Doctors can use CyberKnife to treat tumors anywhere in the body; the system tracks and adjusts for movement in real time, allowing for patient and tumor movement. Accuray also offers the TomoTherapy systems, which allow doctors to change the intensity of the radiation beam to adapt to the shape, location, and size of a tumor. Accuracy generates most of its sales internationally.

	Annual Growth	06/19	06/20	06/21	06/22	06/23
Sales ($mil.)	1.7%	418.8	382.9	396.3	429.9	447.6
Net income ($ mil.)	–	(16.4)	3.8	(6.3)	(5.3)	(9.3)
Market value ($ mil.)	–	373.6	196.0	436.3	189.2	373.6
Employees	2.0%	947	932	995	1,044	1,024

ACCURIDE CORPORATION

38777 6 MILE RD STE 410
LIVONIA, MI 481522642
Phone: 812 962-5000
Fax: –
Web: www.accuridecorp.com

CEO: Robin Kendrick
CFO: Michael A Hajost
HR: Isaac M Alcala Hr
FYE: December 31
Type: Private

Accuride is a leading manufacturer and supplier of wheel-end systems to the global commercial vehicle markets. Its products include steel and aluminum commercial vehicle wheels and wheel-end components and assemblies; and steel wheels for the European automotive and global agricultural, construction and industrial equipment markets. The company's brands include Accuride, KIC, Gunite, and Accuride Wheel End Solutions. The company supports its product portfolio with strong sales, marketing, and design engineering capabilities. Its products are manufactured in facilities throughout North America, Europe and Asia.

ACE HARDWARE CORP.

2200 Kensington Court
Oak Brook, IL 60523-2100
Phone: 630 990-6600
Fax: –
Web: www.acehardware.com

CEO: John Venhuizen
CFO: William Guzik
HR: Patrick J Jones
FYE: December 31
Type: Public

Ace Hardware is the largest retailer-owned hardware cooperative in the world with more than 5,800 locally owned and operated hardware stores in approximately 60 countries. The overall home improvement industry is consists of a broad range of products and services, including lawn and garden products, paint and sundries, certain building supplies and general merchandise. Ace also provides value-added services such as advertising, market research, merchandising assistance, and store location and design services. Ace owns Ace Hardware Home Services, a collection of local service companies with experienced professionals dedicated to helping homeowners complete home maintenance tasks. Ace was founded in 1924 by a group of Chicago hardware store owners.

	Annual Growth	12/01	12/02*	01/04	01/05*	12/05
Sales ($mil.)	4.6%	2,894.4	3,029.1	3,159.3	3,288.7	3,466.0
Net income ($ mil.)	8.3%	73.1	82.1	100.7	101.9	100.4
Market value ($ mil.)	–	–	–	–	–	–
Employees	–	5,229	5,368	–	–	–

*Fiscal year change

ACE RELOCATION SYSTEMS, INC.

5608 EASTGATE DR
SAN DIEGO, CA 921212816
Phone: 858 677-5500
Fax: –
Web: www.acerelocation.com

CEO: Lawrence R Lammers
CFO: –
HR: –
FYE: December 31
Type: Private

Hoping to trump the kings and queens of the moving industry, Ace Relocation Systems provides corporate and household relocation services. The family owned company operates from more than half a dozen offices spread throughout the US. Ace Relocation Systems is an agent of Atlas Van Lines; as an agent, Ace Relocation Systems operates within its assigned geographic territories and cooperates with other Atlas agents on interstate moves. In addition, the company can arrange international moves and provide transportation of items such as trade show exhibits through the Atlas network. Ace Relocation Systems was founded in 1968.

	Annual Growth	12/14	12/15	12/16	12/19	12/20
Sales ($mil.)	5.0%	–	65.1	67.3	–	83.2
Net income ($ mil.)	17.9%	–	1.3	0.9	–	2.9
Market value ($ mil.)	–	–	–	–	–	–
Employees	–	–	–	–	–	255

ACENTRA HEALTH, LLC

1600 TYSONS BLVD STE 1000
MC LEAN, VA 221024859
Phone: 703 214-3370
Fax: –
Web: www.cns-inc.com

CEO: Kristin Robinson
CFO: Lawrence Sinnott
HR: Patricia Scott
FYE: December 31
Type: Private

Client Network Services, Inc. (CNSI) provides IT and business process outsourcing services to corporate and government clients in the US. Its offerings include consulting, systems integration, project management, application development, legacy migration, and software architecture. The company is particularly active in the health care industry, and worked as a subcontractor to support the Federal Health Exchange. It also supports the defense, transportation, energy, and financial industries. CNSI takes an agnostic approach to technology and partners with a range of vendors, including IBM, Microsoft, and Oracle. The company counts Best Buy, Health and Human Services, and the National Institutes of Health among its clients.

	Annual Growth	12/11	12/12	12/13	12/14	12/15
Sales ($mil.)	13.7%	–	109.1	148.6	143.0	160.2
Net income ($ mil.)	29.0%	–	8.9	12.1	15.6	19.0
Market value ($ mil.)	–	–	–	–	–	–
Employees	–	–	–	–	–	1,000

ACH FOOD COMPANIES, INC.

1 PARKVIEW PLZ STE 500
OAKBROOK TERRACE, IL 601814495
Phone: 866 386-8282
Fax: –
Web: www.achfood.com

CEO: Imad Bazzi
CFO: Stephen Zaruba
HR: –
FYE: August 27
Type: Private

ACH Food Companies is a leading marketer of core ingredients long-valued by those who cook with care. The company manufactures and sells a variety of cooking oils and other food ingredients, such as cornstarch, corn syrup, and yeast. From marinating and saut ing to deep-frying and baking, our oils help consumers cook with care. Its lineup is led by well-known brands, including Mazola (the #1 corn oil brand in North America), Argo cornstarch, Fleischmann's Yeast, and Karo corn syrup. The company has been a dedicated partner to the food service industry, and its portfolio of well-known ingredient brands are trusted staples for chefs throughout the country. ACH is a subsidiary of UK food giant Associated British Foods.

ACHIEVE LIFE SCIENCE INC

22722 29th Drive S.E., Suite 100
Bothell, WA 98021
Phone: 604 210-2217
Fax: –
Web: www.achievelifesciences.com

NAS: ACHV
CEO: –
CFO: –
HR: –
FYE: December 31
Type: Public

Achieve Life Sciences (formerly OncoGenex Pharmaceuticals) is dedicated to getting the world to quit nicotine once and for all. The company promotes the use of cytisine, a plant-based alkaloid, to help fight nicotine addiction. Cytisine is approved and marketed in Central and Eastern Europe; Achieve Life Sciences intends to begin a late-stage trial of the treatment in the US in 2018. In mid-2017, cancer therapy development firm OncoGenex Pharmaceuticals (which had suffered setbacks in drug trials in 2016) merged with smoking cessation firm Achieve Life Sciences, the surviving entity.

	Annual Growth	12/18	12/19	12/20	12/21	12/22
Sales ($mil.)	–	–	–	–	–	–
Net income ($ mil.)	–	(12.7)	(16.4)	(14.7)	(33.2)	(42.4)
Market value ($ mil.)	19.3%	21.7	9.5	145.0	139.2	43.8
Employees	13.6%	12	14	13	16	20

ACHILLION PHARMACEUTICALS INC

1777 SENTRY PKWY W STE 200
BLUE BELL, PA 194222207
Phone: 215 709-3040
Fax: –
Web: –

CEO: –
CFO: –
HR: –
FYE: December 31
Type: Private

Achillion Pharmaceuticals is looking for the Achilles heel of infectious disease. The firm is developing novel small molecule therapeutics to treat patients with certain diseases of the immune system. Its complement inhibitor platform targets a specific protein that plays a critical role in a number of disease conditions. Its lead candidate, ACH-4471, is in studies for a rare kidney disease and a rare blood disorder. In 2018, after Johnson & Johnson dumped its hepatitis C program with Achillion, the company announced plans to cut 20% of its workforce to save cash. The firm agreed to be acquired by Alexion Pharmaceuticals in 2019.

ACI WORLDWIDE INC

2811 Ponce de Leon Blvd, PH 1
Coral Gables, FL 33134
Phone: 305 894-2200
Fax: –
Web: www.aciworldwide.com

NMS: ACIW
CEO: Thomas W Warsop III
CFO: Scott W Behrens
HR: –
FYE: December 31
Type: Public

ACI Worldwide develops markets, installs, and supports a broad line of software products and solutions primarily focused on facilitating real-time digital payments. The company provides enterprise payments capabilities that target any channel, any network, and any payment type and its solutions empower customers to regain control, choice, and flexibility in today's complex payments environment, get to market more quickly, and reduce operational costs. In addition, the company products and services are used globally by banks, intermediaries, merchants and billers, such as third-party digital payment processors, payment associations, and a wide range of transaction-generating endpoints, including automated teller machines (ATM), merchant point-of-sale (POS) terminals, bank branches, corporations and more. The US accounts for about 60% of the company's revenue. The company was founded in 1975.

	Annual Growth	12/19	12/20	12/21	12/22	12/23
Sales ($mil.)	3.7%	1,258.3	1,294.3	1,370.6	1,421.9	1,452.6
Net income ($ mil.)	16.0%	67.1	72.7	127.8	142.2	121.5
Market value ($ mil.)	(5.2%)	4,094.5	4,153.4	3,750.3	2,485.8	3,307.2
Employees	(5.4%)	4,018	3,768	3,610	3,349	3,212

ACKERMANN PR, INC.

1111 N NORTHSHORE DR N425
KNOXVILLE, TN 379194088
Phone: 865 584-0550
Fax: –
Web: www.thinkackermann.com

CEO: Cathy G Ackermann
CFO: –
HR: –
FYE: December 31
Type: Private

Ackermann PR thinks its only fair that every company have good public relations. The company, which has its roots in founder Cindy Ackerman's work with the 1982 World's Fair in Knoxville, Tennessee, offers media relations, branding, investor relations, and crisis communications among other PR services. It also offers market research and public opinion polling. Ackerman has three offices in Tennessee (Oak Ridge, Knoxville, and Nashville) and one in Dallas. The agency focuses on work in the technology, health care, consumer products, economic and tourist development, and real estate development industries. Clients have included Siemens, Vista Radiology, Ruby Tuesday, DFW International Airport, and Saddlebrook.

	Annual Growth	12/11	12/12	12/13	12/14	12/16
Sales ($mil.)	(5.0%)	–	–	1.7	1.5	1.5
Net income ($ mil.)	–	–	–	(0.1)	(0.0)	0.0
Market value ($ mil.)	–	–	–	–	–	–
Employees	–	–	–	–	–	31

ACMAT CORP.

30 South Road
Farmington, CT 06032-2418
Phone: 860 415-8400
Fax: –
Web: www.acmatcorp.com

NBB: ACMT A
CEO: Henry W Nozko Jr
CFO: –
HR: –
FYE: December 31
Type: Public

ACMAT does its part to wipe out asbestos. Originally a contracting firm focused on asbestos abatement, the company moved into the insurance industry when it was dropped by its own insurer. Through its ACSTAR Insurance subsidiary the company handles liability insurance and supply bonds to customers such as general, specialty trade, environmental, and asbestos and lead abatement contractors. ACMAT's insurance products are sold nationwide. AMCAT still provides design and construction contracting services for commercial and government customers through its ACMAT Contracting division.

	Annual Growth	12/16	12/17	12/18	12/19	12/20
Sales ($mil.)	(8.1%)	4.2	3.7	2.8	4.0	3.0
Net income ($ mil.)	(2.4%)	0.8	0.3	0.7	1.5	0.7
Market value ($ mil.)	12.3%	16.8	15.5	22.4	25.0	26.6
Employees	–	–	–	–	–	–

ACME COMMUNICATIONS, INC.

4790 IRVINE BLVD STE 105　　　　　　　　　　　　　　　　CEO: –
IRVINE, CA 926201998　　　　　　　　　　　　　　　　　　CFO: –
Phone: 714 245-9499　　　　　　　　　　　　　　　　　　　HR: –
Fax: –　　　　　　　　　　　　　　　　　　　　　FYE: December 31
Web: www.acmecommunications.com　　　　　　　　　Type: Private

ACME Communications' relationship with Warner Bros. has nothing to do with a wily coyote, rockets, or any other explosives. The company owns and operates three television stations in midsized markets (KWBQ and KASY in Albuquerque/Santa Fe, New Mexico and WBUW in Madison, Wisconsin), most of which are affiliated with The CW Network, a joint venture between Time Warner's Warner Bros. Entertainment and CBS Corporation. In addition to its stations, ACME Communications produces a syndicated morning program called The Daily Buzz that airs on about 150 TV stations throughout the country.

ACME UNITED CORP.　　　　　　　　　　　　　　　　　　ASE: ACU

1 Waterview Drive　　　　　　　　　　　　　　　　CEO: Walter C Johnsen
Shelton, CT 06484　　　　　　　　　　　　　　　　　CFO: Paul G Driscoll
Phone: 203 254-6060　　　　　　　　　　　　　　　　　　HR: Lisa Tesoro
Fax: –　　　　　　　　　　　　　　　　　　　　　FYE: December 31
Web: www.acmeunited.com　　　　　　　　　　　　　　　Type: Public

Acme United has the goods for measuring twice and cutting once ... even if you cut yourself in the process. The company supplies measuring instruments (including rulers, protractors, tape measures), cutting devices (scissors, paper trimmers), and safety items (first-aid kits, personal protection products) under the Westcott, Camillus, Clauss, PhysiciansCare, and Pac-Kit brands, as well as under private labels. Acme's products are sold to stationery and industrial supply distributors, office supply stores, drugstores, hardware chains, mass merchants, and florists. Its operations span Canada, Germany, Hong Kong, China, and the US (its biggest market). Chairman and CEO Walter Johnsen owns about 15% of the company.

	Annual Growth	12/19	12/20	12/21	12/22	12/23
Sales ($mil.)	7.7%	142.5	164.0	182.1	194.0	191.5
Net income ($ mil.)	34.0%	5.5	8.1	13.7	3.0	17.8
Market value ($ mil.)	15.9%	86.7	109.8	122.3	79.8	156.2
Employees	10.0%	441	552	654	619	645

ACNB CORP　　　　　　　　　　　　　　　　　　　　　　NAS: ACNB

16 Lincoln Square　　　　　　　　　　　　　　　　　CEO: James P Helt
Gettysburg, PA 17325　　　　　　　　　　　　　　　CFO: David W Cathell
Phone: 717 334-3161　　　　　　　　　　　　　　　　　HR: Carolyn Dull
Fax: –　　　　　　　　　　　　　　　　　　　　　FYE: December 31
Web: www.acnb.com　　　　　　　　　　　　　　　　　　Type: Public

Seven score and a few years ago, ACNB Corporation's fathers brought forth a small-town bank. Now ACNB is dedicated to the proposition of being the holding company for Adams County National Bank, operating more than 20 branches in the Gettysburg and Newville areas of Pennsylvania. It is altogether fitting and proper that the bank offers traditional retail banking services. The world may long note and remember that the bank also provides residential mortgage (about 60% of the portfolio), commercial real estate, consumer, and business loans. In addition, ACNB gives a full measure of devotion to insurance products; provides trust services; and hopes that community banking shall not perish from the earth.

	Annual Growth	12/19	12/20	12/21	12/22	12/23
Assets ($mil.)	8.9%	1,720.3	2,555.4	2,787.0	2,525.5	2,418.8
Net income ($ mil.)	7.5%	23.7	18.4	27.8	35.8	31.7
Market value ($ mil.)	4.3%	321.9	212.8	266.2	338.8	381.0
Employees	2.5%	374	396	397	397	413

ACOLAD INC

2365 WILLIS MILLER DR　　　　　　　　　　　　CEO: Shannon Zimmerman
HUDSON, WI 540167999　　　　　　　　　　　　　CFO: Thomas P Skiba
Phone: 715 426-9505　　　　　　　　　　　　　　　　　　HR: –
Fax: –　　　　　　　　　　　　　　　　　　　　　FYE: December 31
Web: www.acolad.com　　　　　　　　　　　　　　　　Type: Private

Sajan wants to make sure nothing is lost in translation. Formerly known as MathStar, Sajan offers global language services and software for document and translation management, Web site localization, and multilingual desktop publishing. The company's offerings, which are supported by its Global Communication Management Systems (GCMS) Web-based platform, allow companies to expand into untapped international markets by making their Web sites accessible and culturally suitable for target audiences. Sajan also adapts Web pages for images, e-learning, and search engine optimization. The company's Ireland-based subsidiary Sajan Software covers markets in Europe, Africa, and the Middle East.

ACORDA THERAPEUTICS INC　　　　　　　　　　　　　　NMS: ACOR

2 Blue Hill Plaza, 3rd Floor　　　　　　　　　　　　　　　　CEO: –
Pearl River, NY 10965　　　　　　　　　　　　　　　　　　CFO: –
Phone: 914 347-4300　　　　　　　　　　　　　　　　　　HR: –
Fax: 914 347-4560　　　　　　　　　　　　　　　　FYE: December 31
Web: www.acorda.com　　　　　　　　　　　　　　　　Type: Public

Acorda Therapeutics is a biopharmaceutical company focused on developing prescription drugs that aim to restore neurological function for patients with central nervous system disorders. The company's marketed drugs include Ampyra, which enhances conduction in nerves damaged from multiple sclerosis (MS); and Inbrija treatment for OFF periods in people with Parkinson's disease. Acorda's other drug candidates include therapies for MS and other central nervous system disorders, as well as cardiac conditions. Acorda markets its product in the US through its own specialty sales force and being distributed primarily through a network of specialty pharmacies.

	Annual Growth	12/18	12/19	12/20	12/21	12/22
Sales ($mil.)	(29.2%)	471.4	192.4	153.0	129.1	118.6
Net income ($ mil.)	–	33.7	(273.0)	(99.6)	(104.0)	(65.9)
Market value ($ mil.)	(52.9%)	19.0	2.5	0.8	2.9	0.9
Employees	(29.1%)	484	344	168	130	122

ACORN ENERGY INC　　　　　　　　　　　　　　　　　　NBB: ACFN

1000 N West Street, Suite 1200　　　　　　　　　　CEO: Jan H Loeb
Wilmington, DE 19801　　　　　　　　　　　　　　CFO: Tracy Clifford
Phone: 410 654-3315　　　　　　　　　　　　　　　　　　HR: –
Fax: –　　　　　　　　　　　　　　　　　　　　　FYE: December 31
Web: www.acornenergy.com　　　　　　　　　　　　　Type: Public

Acorn Energy is hopeful that its seedling energy technology companies might one day grow into big trees. The company has controlling or equity positions in four energy infrastructure firms -- Energy & Security Sonar Solutions, GridSense Systems, OmniMetrix, US Sensor Systems (USSI). Its largest company, Israel-based Energy & Security Sonar Solutions, offers underwater acoustic and sonar security systems for the military and offshore oil rigs through 84%-owned DSIT Solutions. GridSense makes electronic monitoring systems for utility companies, and USSI designs fiber optic sensing systems for energy companies. OmniMetrix is engaged in remote monitoring of emergency back-up power generation systems.

	Annual Growth	12/19	12/20	12/21	12/22	12/23
Sales ($mil.)	10.1%	5.5	5.9	6.8	7.0	8.1
Net income ($ mil.)	–	(0.6)	0.0	(0.0)	(0.6)	0.1
Market value ($ mil.)	101.4%	0.9	0.9	1.5	0.9	14.8
Employees	2.1%	23	23	25	28	25

ACRE REALTY INVESTORS INC
ASE: AIII

c/o Avenue Capital Group, 399 Park Avenue, 6th Floor
New York, NY 10022
Phone: 212 878-3504
Fax: -
Web: www.acrerealtyinvestors.com

CEO: -
CFO: -
HR: -
FYE: December 31
Type: Public

Roberts Realty Investors really wants to get it REIT. A self-administered real estate investment trust (REIT), Roberts Realty owns and operates commercial real estate and land, primarily in metropolitan Atlanta. The company sold a 400-unit apartment community in 2008; it followed that sale with a handful of other property divestitures. The REIT now owns about five retail and office assets and approximately 150 acres of land, which it plans to develop into residential and mixed-use properties. Roberts Realty Investors operates through its majority-owned Roberts Properties Residential partnership.

	Annual Growth	12/12	12/13	12/14	12/15	12/16
Sales ($mil.)	-	1.4	0.0	0.0	0.0	-
Net income ($ mil.)	-	(6.9)	(0.5)	(2.4)	(1.5)	(3.3)
Market value ($ mil.)	(1.3%)	24.0	18.4	21.7	25.8	22.7
Employees	-	-	1	1	1	-

ACRES COMMERCIAL REALTY CORP
NYS: ACR PRC

390 RXR Plaza
Uniondale, NY 11556
Phone: 516 535-0015
Fax: -
Web: www.acresreit.com

CEO: Mark S Fogel
CFO: David J Bryant
HR: -
FYE: December 31
Type: Public

Exantas (formerly Resource Capital) is looking to pump some capital into real estate resources. The real estate investment trust (REIT) was launched in 2005 and invests in originating, holding and managing commercial real estate, or CRE, mortgage loans and other commercial real estate-related debt investments. To a lesser extent, the REIT invests in commercial finance assets, such as syndicated corporate loans and direct financing leases. CRE loans account for more than 80% of the REIT's portfolio. The firm's investments are managed by Resource Capital Manager, a subsidiary of Resource America.

	Annual Growth	12/19	12/20	12/21	12/22	12/23
Sales ($mil.)	(11.0%)	145.0	108.3	111.7	157.5	91.1
Net income ($ mil.)	(11.2%)	36.0	(197.7)	33.9	10.6	22.4
Market value ($ mil.)	(5.0%)	93.0	31.4	98.2	65.1	75.8
Employees	-	-	-	-	-	-

ACT, INC.

500 ACT DR
IOWA CITY, IA 522439003
Phone: 319 337-1000
Fax: -
Web: www.act.org

CEO: Marten Roorda
CFO: Thomas J Goedken
HR: -
FYE: August 31
Type: Private

ACT is a mission-driven, nonprofit organization dedicated to helping people achieve education and workplace success. It serves millions of students, job seekers, schools, government agencies, and employers in the US and around the world with learning resources, assessments, research, and credentials designed to help them succeed from elementary school through their careers. It offers Assessment Solutions for Schools and Districts and services for Schools and Districts. The non-for-profit organization was founded in 1959 by E. F. Lindquist and Ted McCarrel, who sought to create an exam to measure potential college students' capacity for critical thinking.

	Annual Growth	08/13	08/14	08/16	08/21	08/22
Sales ($mil.)	(3.6%)	-	328.8	350.1	243.6	244.4
Net income ($ mil.)	-	-	9.9	18.0	(6.1)	(12.0)
Market value ($ mil.)	-	-	-	-	-	-
Employees	-	-	-	-	-	1,202

ACTELIS NETWORKS INC
NAS: ASNS

4039 Clipper Court
Fremont, CA 94538
Phone: 510 545-1045
Fax: -
Web: -

CEO: -
CFO: -
HR: -
FYE: December 31
Type: Public

Actelis Networks prefers copper over glass. The company's transmission equipment enables carriers and telecom providers to deliver Ethernet services over copper wires. Its products are intended to increase the data-carrying capacity of the copper lines and eliminate the need for installing fiber optics in the "last mile" between service providers' networks and their subscribers. Actelis targets regional telephone companies, independent and competitive local exchange carriers, and alternative carriers worldwide. Customers include more than 200 service providers around the world, such as Easynet and Frontier. Founded in 1998 by Tuvia Barlev, Actelis operates from its headquarters in California and a R&D center in Israel.

	Annual Growth	12/19	12/20	12/21	12/22	12/23
Sales ($mil.)	(13.1%)	-	8.5	8.5	8.8	5.6
Net income ($ mil.)	-	-	(1.5)	(5.3)	(11.0)	(6.3)
Market value ($ mil.)	-	-	-	-	1.4	3.4
Employees	-	-	-	45	48	43

ACTION FOR BOSTON COMMUNITY DEVELOPMENT, INC.

178 TREMONT ST
BOSTON, MA 021111006
Phone: 617 357-6000
Fax: -
Web: www.bostonabcd.org

CEO: John McGahan
CFO: Marjorie Lombard
HR: -
FYE: August 31
Type: Private

Action For Boston Community Development (ABCD) strives to make helping others as easy as 1-2-3. The not-for-profit serves more than 100,000 low-income people in New England in areas such as advocacy, child care, consumer services, education, health, and housing. The group operates through a decentralized model that utilizes a citywide network of Area Planning Action Councils, Neighborhood Service Centers, and Family Service Centers. It partners with more than a dozen programs like SUMMERWORKS (work experience for low-income teens), Foster Grandparents, Urban College of Boston, and another 10 or so government agencies. ABCD was established in 1962 as one of several national programs to combat poverty.

	Annual Growth	08/14	08/15	08/16	08/21	08/22
Sales ($mil.)	3.8%	-	176.0	168.9	203.3	227.9
Net income ($ mil.)	20.3%	-	0.2	(0.1)	1.2	0.8
Market value ($ mil.)	-	-	-	-	-	-
Employees	-	-	-	-	-	1,000

ACTIONET, INC.

2600 PARK TOWER DR STE 1000
VIENNA, VA 22180
Phone: 703 204-0090
Fax: -
Web: www.actionet.com

CEO: Ashley W Chen
CFO: -
HR: Nancy Graves
FYE: December 31
Type: Private

ActioNet is an IT engineering service firm with strong qualifications and expertise in cloud-based solutions, cyber security and Agile software engineering. It provides cybersecurity, cloud solutions, as well as managed services. Customers have included US Agencies such as Army, Navy, Air Force, Department of Transportation, and more. ActioNet was founded in 1998 by president and CEO Ashley Chen.

	Annual Growth	12/12	12/13	12/14	12/15	12/16
Sales ($mil.)	12.5%	-	298.5	352.6	411.5	425.5
Net income ($ mil.)	11.3%	-	23.8	25.3	32.0	32.8
Market value ($ mil.)	-	-	-	-	-	-
Employees	-	-	-	-	-	1,400

ACTIONTEC ELECTRONICS, INC.

2445 AUGUSTINE DR STE 501
SANTA CLARA, CA 950543033
Phone: 408 752-7700
Fax: –
Web: www.actiontec.com

CEO: Dean Chang
CFO: Brian Paul
HR: –
FYE: December 31
Type: Private

Actiontec Electronics aims to broaden your approach to networking. The company makes gateways, routers, modems, and other broadband connection equipment used to create wireless home networks. Its fiber optic routers allow broadband television and other content to be distributed to multiple devices throughout the home over coaxial cables. Actiontec sells its equipment through partnerships with broadband service providers and equipment makers such as Qwest, Verizon,& Cisco, and Entropic. It also sells directly through retailers including Amazon.com, Best Buy, and Wal-Mart.

	Annual Growth	12/04	12/05	12/06	12/07	12/10
Sales ($mil.)	2.8%	–	–	145.6	183.1	162.3
Net income ($ mil.)	–	–	–	–	–	1.8
Market value ($ mil.)	–	–	–	–	–	–
Employees	–	–	–	–	–	350

ACTIVE MEDIA SERVICES, INC.

1 BLUE HILL PLZ STE 1705
PEARL RIVER, NY 109656170
Phone: 845 735-1700
Fax: –
Web: www.activeinternational.com

CEO: –
CFO: –
HR: –
FYE: December 31
Type: Private

Doing business as Active International, the corporate trading firm acquires underperforming assets including surplus inventory, capital equipment, real estate, and receivables. It exchanges these for cash and/or trade credit, which is used to offset expenses or purchase such services as advertising, freight, printing, shipping, event planning, and travel. Clients may barter future manufacturing capacity for services, including advertising across all mediums. Active International also provides traditional marketing services. Alan Elkin and Art Wagner founded the employee-owned company in 1984.

ACTIVIDENTITY CORPORATION

6623 DUMBARTON CIR
FREMONT, CA 945553603
Phone: 510 574-0100
Fax: –
Web: www.iamsportal.hidglobal.com

CEO: –
CFO: –
HR: –
FYE: September 30
Type: Private

ActivIdentity isn't passive about data security. The company provides a variety of authentication and user management products, including smart cards, biometric readers, tokens, and USB keys. Its products are used to control and monitor access to intranets, extranets, and the Internet, enabling businesses to digitally authenticate and manage the identities of employees, customers, and trading partners. The company's commercial customers have included Citibank, Novell, and Oracle; the US Department of Defense is also a client. About half of ActivIdentity's business is done outside of North America. It also offers services such as consulting, support, and training. The company is a subsidiary of ASSA ABLOY.

	Annual Growth	09/05	09/06	09/07	09/08	09/09
Sales ($mil.)	(82.5%)	–	–	2,034.2	59.0	62.3
Net income ($ mil.)	–	–	–	0.0	(76.5)	(5.5)
Market value ($ mil.)	–	–	–	–	–	–
Employees	–	–	–	–	–	218

ACTS RETIREMENT-LIFE COMMUNITIES, INC.

420 DELAWARE DR
FORT WASHINGTON, PA 190342711
Phone: 215 661-8330
Fax: –
Web: www.actsretirement.org

CEO: Gerald T Grant
CFO: –
HR: –
FYE: March 31
Type: Private

No acting here! ACTS is serious about providing seniors with the opportunity to live independently, but with a helping hand when needed. ACTS develops, owns, and operates continuing-care retirement communities (CCRSs) in nine US states along the Eastern Seaboard. The company's properties feature resort-style amenities in Christian environments (ACTS comes from a Biblical reference). One of the largest not-for-profit operators of CCRCs in the US, ACTS serves about 8,500 older adults at about 25 communities from Pennsylvania to Florida. The not-for-profit organization was founded as Open Door Estates by a group of Pennsylvania church members in 1971.

ACTUA CORP

555 East Lancaster Ave., Suite 640
Radnor, PA 19087
Phone: 610 727-6900
Fax: –
Web: www.actua.com

CEO: –
CFO: –
HR: –
FYE: December 31
Type: Public

Actua Corporation (formerly ICG Group) actually invests in companies in the business-to-business (B2B) market, working with its holdings to develop strategy. It owns stakes in roughly a handful of cloud-based companies involved in technology-enabled business process outsourcing, cloud-based software, and software as a service (SaaS), including government-focused communications provider GovDelivery, wealth management platform FolioDynamix, EHS compliance software provider MSDSonline, and property/casualty insurance distribution platform Bolt Solutions. Actua works closely with its companies, often helping in day-to-day management.

	Annual Growth	12/13	12/14	12/15	12/16	12/17
Sales ($mil.)	–	59.2	84.8	133.4	109.3	–
Net income ($ mil.)	(4.5%)	209.1	(23.6)	(96.1)	70.1	174.0
Market value ($ mil.)	(4.3%)	593.9	588.8	365.0	446.3	497.3
Employees	(60.1%)	551	761	867	186	14

ACTURUS, INC.

270 FARMINGTON AVE STE 200
FARMINGTON, CT 060321909
Phone: 860 242-2005
Fax: –
Web: www.metrixlab.com

CEO: –
CFO: –
HR: –
FYE: December 31
Type: Private

The Pert Group (formerly PERT Survey Research) can provide quantitative and qualitative research but most importantly, it helps clients understand their customers. The firm's custom market research services tackle such topics as customer satisfaction, market segmentation, ad tracking, and positioning (brands, products, or corporate). In addition to their consumer research services, Pert Group helps clients to assess their training needs and develop job satisfaction surveys. It has offices in Connecticut, Missouri, and Pennsylvania. The Pert Group was formed in 2009 when the former PERT Survey Research merged with two other research firms: Pulsar Research & Consulting; and Market Directions.

	Annual Growth	12/06	12/07	12/08	12/09	12/10
Sales ($mil.)	–	–	–	(1,569.7)	16.3	21.7
Net income ($ mil.)	914.1%	–	–	0.0	0.0	1.7
Market value ($ mil.)	–	–	–	–	–	–
Employees	–	–	–	–	–	99

ACUATIVE CORPORATION

695 US HIGHWAY 46 STE 305
FAIRFIELD, NJ 070041561
Phone: 862 926-5600
Fax: –
Web: www.acuative.com

CEO: Vincent Sciarra
CFO: Patrick J Danna
HR: –
FYE: December 31
Type: Private

Acuative Corporation is a leading provider of managed network lifecycle solutions. It provides the world's leading companies with a complete range of advanced technology and managed services, enabling customers to utilize a single source provider for all of their network requirements. Acuative has a specific focus and expertise in implementing and managing voice and data networks in a highly secure environment. The company was founded in 1984 by Vince Sciarra and Rich Ackerman as Telesource Corp ? a field services company.

	Annual Growth	12/14	12/15	12/16	12/17	12/18
Sales ($mil.)	(6.5%)	–	120.2	112.4	95.8	98.2
Net income ($ mil.)	–	–	0.3	0.8	(1.2)	(2.0)
Market value ($ mil.)	–	–	–	–	–	–
Employees	–	–	–	–	–	325

ACUITY BRANDS INC (HOLDING COMPANY)   NYS: AYI

1170 Peachtree Street, N.E., Suite 1200
Atlanta, GA 30309
Phone: 404 853-1400
Fax: –
Web: www.acuitybrands.com

CEO: –
CFO: –
HR: –
FYE: August 31
Type: Public

Acuity Brands is a market-leading industrial technology company. It uses technology to solve problems in spaces and light, and designs, manufactures, and brings to market products and services that makes a valuable difference in people's lives. Its products ? marketed under brands like Lithonia, Holophane, Peerless, Mark Architectural, and Gotham include luminaires, lighting controls, controls for building systems, as well as an integrated lighting systems for indoor and outdoor applications. The company serves customers such as electrical distributors, retail home improvement centers, electric utilities, national accounts, system integrators, digital retailers, lighting showrooms, and energy service companies. Majority of the company's sales are generated domestically.

	Annual Growth	08/19	08/20	08/21	08/22	08/23
Sales ($mil.)	1.9%	3,672.7	3,326.3	3,461.0	4,006.1	3,952.2
Net income ($ mil.)	1.2%	330.4	248.3	306.3	384.0	346.0
Market value ($ mil.)	6.5%	3,893.9	3,393.3	5,729.5	5,089.9	5,007.6
Employees	0.4%	12,000	11,500	13,000	13,200	12,200

ACURA PHARMACEUTICALS INC   NBB: ACUR

616 N. North Court, Suite 120
Palatine, IL 60067
Phone: 847 705-7709
Fax: –
Web: www.acurapharm.com

CEO: Robert B Jones
CFO: Peter A Clemens
HR: –
FYE: December 31
Type: Public

Acura Pharmaceuticals is working to provide accurate dosages of powerful drugs while preventing drug abuse. The company has developed a technology to add abuse-deterring agents to commonly abused pharmaceuticals. If a drug with these agents (what Acura calls Aversion Technology) is crushed and inhaled, certain ingredients will cause nasal irritation, and if an abuser attempts to dissolve the powder, it will form a non-injectable gel. Its Impede Technology works with pseudoephedrine to disrupt the process used to turn the decongestant into meth. Acura's approved products include prescription Aversion oxycodone and over-the-counter Nexafed (pseudoephedrine with Impede ingredients).

	Annual Growth	12/17	12/18	12/19	12/20	12/21
Sales ($mil.)	(14.8%)	3.0	0.4	2.7	3.6	1.6
Net income ($ mil.)	–	(5.7)	(3.8)	(3.8)	(1.2)	(0.9)
Market value ($ mil.)	5.5%	26.3	7.5	15.0	13.7	32.5
Employees	–	14	13	13	13	–

ACUSHNET HOLDINGS CORP   NYS: GOLF

333 Bridge Street
Fairhaven, MA 02719
Phone: 800 225-8500
Fax: –
Web: www.acushnetholdingscorp.com

CEO: David Maher
CFO: Sean Sullivan
HR: –
FYE: December 31
Type: Public

Acushnet is the global leader in the design, development, manufacture, and distribution of performance driven golf products such as golf balls, clubs, shoes, gloves, and other equipment and accessories. Its famous Titleist golf balls and FootJoy golf shoes and gloves are the #1 sellers in US professional golf. Other products include value-priced Pinnacle golf balls, Titleist golf clubs, Scotty Cameron putters, and Vokey Design wedges, as well as golf bags and outerwear. Products are sold worldwide through on-course golf pro shops, and select off-course golf specialty stores, sporting goods stores, and other qualified retailers; the US accounts for about 55% of revenue. Acushnet was originally founded as Acushnet Process Company in Acushnet, Massachusetts by Phil "Skipper" Young in 1910.

	Annual Growth	12/19	12/20	12/21	12/22	12/23
Sales ($mil.)	9.1%	1,681.4	1,612.2	2,147.9	2,270.3	2,382.0
Net income ($ mil.)	13.1%	121.1	96.0	178.9	199.3	198.4
Market value ($ mil.)	18.1%	2,061.5	2,571.4	3,366.8	2,693.2	4,006.8
Employees	8.8%	5,213	5,365	6,500	7,300	7,300

ADAC PLASTICS, INC.

5690 EAGLE DR SE
GRAND RAPIDS, MI 495122057
Phone: 616 957-0311
Fax: –
Web: www.adacautomotive.com

CEO: Jon Husby
CFO: –
HR: Katherine Exton
FYE: December 31
Type: Private

ADAC Plastics, which does business as ADAC Automotive, has a handle on what automakers need. The company (privately owned by the Teets and Hungerford families) supplies automakers and tier 1 suppliers worldwide with door handles and components, exterior trim, and marker lighting. Other products include cowl vent grilles and fuel filler doors. Services provided by ADAC Automotive include design, molding, painting, and assembly. Its ADAC Technologies subsidiary is a leading supplier of plastic moldings, subassemblies, and decorative finishes. It is part of the VAST (Vehicle Access Systems Technology) Alliance, along with fellow automotive suppliers STRATTEC SECURITY and WITTE Automotive of Velbert, Germany.

	Annual Growth	12/03	12/04	12/05	12/06	12/07
Sales ($mil.)	–	–	–	(1,820.3)	177.2	177.2
Net income ($ mil.)	32691.6%	–	–	0.0	3.8	25.8
Market value ($ mil.)	–	–	–	–	–	–
Employees	–	–	–	–	–	800

ADAMS FAIRACRE FARMS, INC.

765 DUTCHESS TPKE
POUGHKEEPSIE, NY 126032000
Phone: 845 454-4330
Fax: –
Web: www.adamsfarms.com

CEO: Patrick Adams
CFO: –
HR: Jennifer Giammatteo
FYE: January 31
Type: Private

From seeds to seafood and fertilizer to fencing, Adams Fairacre Farms has a few things covered. The company's four locations in New York's Hudson River Valley offer groceries, including fresh produce, power equipment (John Deere tractors and mowers, chippers, chain saws), fencing supplies, landscaping materials, and gifts and gardening supplies (plants, seeds, soil, pest control). Adams Fairacre Farms was founded in 1919 by Ralph Adams Sr. as a roadside produce stand where the Adams family sold the excess from its 50-acre farm. The company added other items as customers requested them. Descendants of Adams, including some third-generation members, own and run the family business.

	Annual Growth	01/07	01/08	01/09	01/11	01/12
Sales ($mil.)	2.4%	–	–	113.7	115.6	122.1
Net income ($ mil.)	(23.5%)	–	–	1.8	1.6	0.8
Market value ($ mil.)	–	–	–	–	–	–
Employees	–	–	–	–	–	550

ADAMS RESOURCES & ENERGY, INC.   ASE: AE

17 South Briar Hollow Lane, Suite 100
Houston, TX 77027
Phone: 713 881-3600
Fax: –
Web: www.adamsresources.com

CEO: Kevin J Roycraft
CFO: Tracy E Ohmart
HR: –
FYE: December 31
Type: Public

Adams Resources & Energy (AE) markets, transports and stores crude oil across the US, Mexico and Canada. The company had various crude oil and natural gas basins in the lower 48 states of the US. Based in Houston, the company owns terminals in the Gulf Coast region of the US, and provides liquid chemicals, dry bulk, and tank truck transportation services through its two wholly-owned subsidiaries GulfMark and Service Transport. AE reports approximately 889,000 barrels of crude oil storage capacity. The company was established in 1973.

	Annual Growth	12/19	12/20	12/21	12/22	12/23
Sales ($mil.)	11.0%	1,811.2	1,022.4	2,025.2	3,366.9	2,745.3
Net income ($ mil.)	(59.9%)	8.2	1.0	11.9	3.5	0.2
Market value ($ mil.)	(8.9%)	97.0	61.4	70.8	99.1	66.7
Employees	2.8%	664	726	710	882	741

ADAMS STATE UNIVERSITY

208 EDGEMONT BLVD
ALAMOSA, CO 811012320
Phone: 719 587-7011
Fax: –
Web: www.adams.edu

CEO: –
CFO: –
HR: Shannon Heersink
FYE: June 30
Type: Private

Adams State University (ASU) hasn't quite been around since the beginning of time, but it has seen the eve of a few decades. The school confers bachelor's degrees in 16 majors, with 28 minors and emphases. It also offers six master's degree programs, as well as associate degree and pre-professional programs. The college provides online learning programs for non-traditional students as well. It draws some 3,700 students annually to its San Luis Valley, Colorado, campus, in addition to more than 10,000 extended study students. Founded in 1921 as a teachers' college by Billy Adams, a Colorado legislator who would later become the state's governor, Adams converted from a college to a university in 2012.

	Annual Growth	06/17	06/18	06/19	06/20	06/21
Sales ($mil.)	(5.0%)	–	42.3	46.3	46.3	36.2
Net income ($ mil.)	–	–	(18.6)	9.1	19.1	17.7
Market value ($ mil.)	–	–	–	–	–	–
Employees	–	–	–	–	–	254

ADAMS WOOD PRODUCTS, INC.

5436 JEFFREY LN
MORRISTOWN, TN 378131110
Phone: 423 587-2942
Fax: –
Web: www.adamswoodproducts.com

CEO: –
CFO: –
HR: –
FYE: December 31
Type: Private

Adams Wood Products knows it has a leg to stand on. The company manufactures wooden furniture components, including bed posts, bun feet, cabinet onlays, corbels, finials, and legs for chairs, sofas, and tables. It also sells hardware and unfinished ready-to-assemble furniture kits (for building chairs, desks, and tables). Adams Wood Products serves furniture manufacturers as well as customers in the health care, hospitality, institutional, and retail industries. The company was founded in 1975.

ADAMS-COLUMBIA ELECTRIC COOPERATIVE

401 E LAKE ST
FRIENDSHIP, WI 539348050
Phone: 800 831-8629
Fax: –
Web: www.acecwi.com

CEO: Martin Hillard Jr
CFO: John West
HR: Bill Gneiser
FYE: December 31
Type: Private

With a name that harkens back to Christopher Columbus and the Founding Fathers, Adams-Columbia Electric Cooperative provides power to more than 36,000 member-owners in 12 counties in central Wisconsin. The rural distribution cooperative operates nearly 5,300 miles of transmission and distribution lines. Adams-Columbia Electric was formed through the merger of Adams-Marquette Electric Cooperative and Columbus Rural Electric Cooperative in 1987. The utility expanded further through its 1992 acquisition of Waushara Electric Cooperative. The cooperative covers a 2,500 sq. ml. geographic service area.

	Annual Growth	12/17	12/18	12/19	12/21	12/22
Sales ($mil.)	5.9%	–	72.9	72.1	77.4	91.8
Net income ($ mil.)	–	–	–	1.2	3.0	0.2
Market value ($ mil.)	–	–	–	–	–	–
Employees	–	–	–	–	–	115

ADAPTHEALTH CORP   NAS: AHCO

220 West Germantown Pike, Suite 250
Plymouth Meeting, PA 19462
Phone: 610 424-4515
Fax: –
Web: www.adapthealth.com

CEO: Stephen Griggs
CFO: Jason A Clemens
HR: –
FYE: December 31
Type: Public

AdaptHealth Corp. is a national leader in providing patient-centered, healthcare-at-home solutions including home medical equipment (HME), medical supplies, and related services. It focuses primarily on providing sleep therapy equipment, supplies, and related services (including CPAP and bi-PAP services); medical devices and supplies; home medical equipment; oxygen and related chronic therapy services in the home; and other HME devices and supplies on behalf of chronically ill patients with wound care, urological, incontinence, ostomy, and nutritional supply needs. The company services beneficiaries of Medicare, Medicaid, and commercial insurance payors. It serviced approximately 3.9 million patients annually in all 50 states through the company's network of approximately 725 locations in more than 45 states.

	Annual Growth	12/19	12/20	12/21	12/22	12/23
Sales ($mil.)	56.8%	529.6	1,070.7	2,465.1	2,970.6	3,200.2
Net income ($ mil.)	–	(15.0)	(64.5)	156.2	69.3	(678.9)
Market value ($ mil.)	(9.7%)	1,456.3	4,981.8	3,244.2	2,549.2	966.9
Employees	42.6%	2,590	4,700	10,700	10,900	10,700

ADCO ELECTRICAL CORP.

201 EDWARD CURRY AVE
STATEN ISLAND, NY 103147105
Phone: 718 494-4400
Fax: –
Web: www.adcoonline.com

CEO: –
CFO: –
HR: –
FYE: December 31
Type: Private

Customers rely on ADCO Electrical to keep their currents live and running. The company is an electrical and telecommunications contractor that specializes in installing electrical components and wiring, cabling infrastructure, computer networking, and security systems. Other services include conducting electrical equipment testing to ensure operational safety, procuring hardware and software, and providing project management and technical consulting. ADCO Electrical, with its fleet of 20 trucks, serves commercial, institutional, and public sector clients primarily around the New York metropolitan area. It has completed projects for American Express, Citigroup, Grubb & Ellis, Time Warner, and Bloomingdale's.

ADDUS HOMECARE CORP
NMS: ADUS

6303 Cowboys Way, Suite 600
Frisco, TX 75034
Phone: 469 535-8200
Fax: –
Web: www.addus.com

CEO: R D Allison
CFO: Brian Poff
HR: –
FYE: December 31
Type: Public

Addus HomeCare is a provider of home care services that primarily include personal care services that assist with activities of daily living, as well as hospice and home health services. Addus HomeCare's consumers are primarily persons who, without these services, are at risk of hospitalization or institutionalization, such as the elderly, chronically ill and disabled. Addus HomeCare's payor clients include federal, state and local governmental agencies, managed care organizations, commercial insurers and private individuals. Addus HomeCare currently provides home care services to approximately 44,500 consumers through more than 205 locations across some 20 US states.

	Annual Growth	12/19	12/20	12/21	12/22	12/23
Sales ($mil.)	13.0%	648.8	764.8	864.5	951.1	1,058.7
Net income ($ mil.)	25.5%	25.2	33.1	45.1	46.0	62.5
Market value ($ mil.)	(1.1%)	1,577.6	1,900.0	1,517.4	1,614.4	1,506.7
Employees	1.2%	33,238	35,139	31,915	33,182	34,846

ADDVANTAGE TECHNOLOGIES GROUP, INC.
NBB: AEYG Q

1430 Bradley Lane, Suite 196
Carrollton, TX 75007
Phone: 918 251-9121
Fax: –
Web: www.addvantagetechnologies.com

CEO: –
CFO: –
HR: –
FYE: December 31
Type: Public

ADDvantage Technologies provides turn-key wireless infrastructure services for wireless carriers, tower companies and equipment manufacturers, and distributes and services a comprehensive line of electronics and hardware for the telecommunications industry. For its telecommunications subsidiaries, it sells new, surplus-new, and refurbished equipment that it purchases in the market as a result of telecommunications system upgrades or overstock supplies. It maintains one of the industry's largest inventories of new and used equipment, which allows it to expedite the delivery of system-critical products to its customers. ADDvantage gets most of its sales in the US.

	Annual Growth	09/19	09/20	09/21*	12/21	12/22
Sales ($mil.)	20.7%	55.1	50.2	62.2	18.7	97.0
Net income ($ mil.)	–	(5.3)	(17.3)	(6.5)	(2.0)	0.5
Market value ($ mil.)	(10.2%)	2.8	2.7	3.3	2.4	2.0
Employees	(7.9%)	188	124	170	–	147

*Fiscal year change

ADDX CORPORATION

4825 MARK CENTER DR STE 300
ALEXANDRIA, VA 223111846
Phone: 703 933-7637
Fax: –
Web: www.addxcorp.com

CEO: Bill Millward
CFO: –
HR: Janet Pace
FYE: December 31
Type: Private

Information technology services, management consulting, and program management services -- put them all together and it adds up to Addx Corporation. The consulting firm specializes in providing government clients with management of large technical projects that involve many different methods of project, personnel, and cost management. At the core lies technology planning, design, and testing. The company boasts a virtual, computer-based testing environment known as CONOP Studio. Clients have included the Department of Defense, the Department of Homeland Security, and the Department of Energy.

	Annual Growth	12/05	12/06	12/07	12/08	12/09
Sales ($mil.)	21.1%	–	–	10.2	12.3	15.0
Net income ($ mil.)	53.1%	–	–	0.5	0.1	1.1
Market value ($ mil.)	–	–	–	–	–	–
Employees	–	–	–	–	–	50

ADEIA INC
NMS: ADEA

3025 Orchard Parkway
San Jose, CA 95134
Phone: 408 473-2500
Fax: –
Web: www.adeia.com

CEO: Paul Davis
CFO: Keith Jones
HR: –
FYE: December 31
Type: Public

Xperi Corp. (formerly Tessera Technologies) licenses its portfolio of patented technologies for semiconductor packaging, interconnects, and imaging in exchange for royalty payments. More than 100 companies, such as Intel, Sony, LG Electronics, and Samsung, use its designs to produce high-performance packages for mobile computing and communications, memory and data storage, and 3D integrated circuit technologies. Xperi has more than 4,000 US and foreign patents and patents applications. The US is the company's biggest geographic market. The company changed its named to Xperi in 2017 to better reflects a broader range of technologies it offers.

	Annual Growth	12/19	12/20	12/21	12/22	12/23
Sales ($mil.)	8.5%	280.1	892.0	877.7	438.9	388.8
Net income ($ mil.)	–	(62.5)	146.8	(55.5)	(295.9)	67.4
Market value ($ mil.)	(9.5%)	1,986.6	2,244.3	2,030.6	1,018.0	1,330.5
Employees	(34.4%)	700	1,850	1,900	120	130

ADELBERG, RUDOW, DORF, HENDLER, LLC

10400 LITTLE PATUXENT PKWY
COLUMBIA, MD 210443518
Phone: 410 539-5195
Fax: –
Web: www.adelberg.com

CEO: –
CFO: –
HR: –
FYE: December 31
Type: Private

Adelberg, Rudow, Dorf & Hendler offers a broad range of legal services through offices in Baltimore and Towson, Maryland. The firm has 11 practice areas covering the legal intricacies of litigation, business, real estate, banking, family law, intellectual property, and white-collar defense and also offers alternate dispute-resolution services. Founded in 1927, the firm has almost 30 attorneys serving individuals, businesses, and institutions.

ADELPHI UNIVERSITY

1 SOUTH AVE
GARDEN CITY, NY 115304299
Phone: 516 877-3000
Fax: –
Web: www.adelphi.edu

CEO: –
CFO: –
HR: –
FYE: August 31
Type: Private

It may not house an oracle, but Adelphi University hopes to provide answers to students' questions about their future. Founded in 1896, the university has about 7,700 students enrolled at its four campuses located in New York (Garden City, Hauppage, Manhattan, and the Hudson Valley). Adelphi University, a private institution, offers graduate, undergraduate, and continuing education programs in areas including business management, education, nursing, and social work. Its Swirbul Library contains about 600,000 books and documents and 33,000 audiovisual materials. The school counts Nextel co-founder Brian McAuley, US Chamber of Commerce CEO Thomas Donahue, and author Alice Hoffman among its alumni.

	Annual Growth	08/18	08/19	08/20	08/21	08/22
Sales ($mil.)	12.2%	–	233.6	247.5	264.5	329.9
Net income ($ mil.)	(5.3%)	–	8.8	15.4	38.4	7.5
Market value ($ mil.)	–	–	–	–	–	–
Employees	–	–	–	–	–	1,400

ADENA HEALTH SYSTEM

272 HOSPITAL RD
CHILLICOTHE, OH 456019031
Phone: 740 779-7500
Fax: –
Web: www.adena.org

CEO: Jeffrey J Graham
CFO: Lisa Carlson
HR: Mark H Shuter
FYE: December 31
Type: Private

Adena Health System serves the residents of about a dozen counties in south and south-central Ohio, centered on the city of Chillicothe. Its main facility is the 266-bed Adena Regional Medical Center, which provides general medical and surgical care, as well as specialty care in a number of areas, including cardiology, women's health, oncology, and rehabilitation. Its Adena Home Care provides highly personalized, quality care to patients of four service lines -- home health, hospice, home respiratory and home infusion. The not-for-profit health system also features four hospitals, six regional clinics, surgery centers, and a counseling center, among other facilities. Adena Health System traces its roots back to 1895.

	Annual Growth	12/16	12/17	12/19	12/21	12/22
Sales ($mil.)	7.6%	–	470.6	–	472.3	678.6
Net income ($ mil.)	(22.7%)	–	29.5	–	102.6	8.1
Market value ($ mil.)	–	–	–	–	–	–
Employees	–	–	–	–	–	3,000

ADEPTUS HEALTH INC.

2200 ROSS AVE STE 3600
DALLAS, TX 752017921
Phone: 972 899-6666
Fax: –
Web: www.adhc.com

CEO: Frank R Williams
CFO: James Hopwood
HR: Lyn Kruger
FYE: December 31
Type: Private

Adeptus wants to be your first choice for emergency medicine. The company owns and operates First Choice freestanding emergency rooms in Texas. Its approximately 100 locations offer emergency care for things like head injuries, heart attacks, and other life-threatening conditions. First Choice locations are open 24 hours a day, focus on getting patients in front of a doctor quickly, include full radiology and lab facilities, and most include special rooms for pediatrics and ob/gyn patients. The company maintains partnerships with local hospitals for direct admissions when needed. The company was formed as First Choice ER in 2002. Adeptus exited Chapter 11 bankruptcy in October 2017; it is now owned by hedge fund Deerfield Management Company.

ADHERA THERAPEUTICS INC

NBB: ATRX

8000 Innovation Parkway
Baton Rouge, LA 70820
Phone: 919 518-3748
Fax: –
Web: www.adherathera.com

CEO: Andrew Kucharchuk
CFO: –
HR: –
FYE: December 31
Type: Public

Marina Biotech is a biopharmaceutical with a focus on arthritis, pain, oncology, and hypertension therapies. In addition to developing and commercializing non-addictive pain medicines, the company also studies combination therapies of approved drugs. Its pipeline includes next-generation versions of non-steroidal anti-inflammatory drug (NSAID) celecosib, which, due to dangerous side effect of swelling, is currently limited in its usage. The company's Prestalia drug is commercially available for the treatment of hypertension. Formerly dedicated to gene-silencing treatments, the struggling Marina Biotech altered its course with the late 2016 merger with IthenaPharma.

	Annual Growth	12/18	12/19	12/20	12/21	12/22
Sales ($mil.)	–	0.0	0.3	–	–	–
Net income ($ mil.)	–	(16.8)	(12.0)	(3.8)	(6.4)	(2.1)
Market value ($ mil.)	30.8%	0.9	0.2	0.1	0.2	2.6
Employees	–	24	2	–	–	–

ADHESIVES RESEARCH, INC.

400 SEAKS RUN RD
GLEN ROCK, PA 173279500
Phone: 717 235-7979
Fax: –
Web: www.adhesivesresearch.com

CEO: –
CFO: –
HR: –
FYE: June 30
Type: Private

In times of stress, please watch your step around Adhesives Research's products -- they're pressure-sensitive. The company manufactures pressure-sensitive adhesives for the medical (for wound care and intravenous attachments), electronics (used in the assembly stages for mobile devices, hard drives, etc.), industrial (automotive, glass treatment), and splicing (pulp and paper industry) markets. Adhesives Research manufactures its products on a custom basis, working with customers worldwide. It operates technical design and manufacturing facilities in Colombia, Ireland, and the US.

ADIRONDACK COMMUNITY COLLEGE (INC)

640 BAY RD
QUEENSBURY, NY 128041445
Phone: 518 743-2200
Fax: –
Web: www.sunyacc.edu

CEO: –
CFO: –
HR: Marjorie Kelly
FYE: June 30
Type: Private

Adirondack Community College (ACC) is a public, two-year institution with an enrollment of approximately 3,400 students (about 2,000 full time and 1,400 full time); about half go on to a four-year college or university. ACC offers associate degree and certificate programs in more than 30 fields of study in the humanities, liberal arts, social science, and mathematics and science, as well as specialized fields such as adventure sports leadership and management, allied health, computer science, criminal justice, and food service. Founded in 1961, Adirondack Community College is part of the State University of New York, or SUNY, system.

	Annual Growth	06/07	06/08	06/09	06/21	06/22
Sales ($mil.)	(1.0%)	–	0.8	0.7	0.7	0.7
Net income ($ mil.)	–	–	(1.1)	(0.3)	(0.2)	0.0
Market value ($ mil.)	–	–	–	–	–	–
Employees	–	–	–	–	–	501

ADM TRONICS UNLIMITED, INC.

NBB: ADMT

224-S Pegasus Avenue
Northvale, NJ 07647
Phone: 201 767-6040
Fax: 201 784-0620
Web: www.admtronics.com

CEO: Andre Dimino
CFO: Andre Dimino
HR: –
FYE: March 31
Type: Public

ADM Tronics has had its own Industrial Revolution. While the company previously focused on the making of medical devices, ADM has shifted its main focus to water-based chemical products for industrial use. These products include coatings, resins, primers, and additives, primarily for the printing and packaging industries. The firm licenses many of its medical products, which include the Sonotron line of devices (used to treat osteoarthritis and inflammatory joint ailments with radio waves). Its Pros-Aide unit makes adhesives used in professional makeup products. ADM spun off Ivivi Technologies in 2006 but still owns about a third of the company. The founding DiMino family owns nearly half of ADM Tronics.

	Annual Growth	03/19	03/20	03/21	03/22	03/23
Sales ($mil.)	5.1%	3.0	3.5	3.1	3.2	3.7
Net income ($ mil.)	–	(0.3)	(0.1)	(0.6)	(1.4)	(0.1)
Market value ($ mil.)	(6.8%)	10.7	10.8	8.1	6.6	8.1
Employees	–	30	–	–	–	–

ADOBE INC NMS: ADBE

345 Park Avenue
San Jose, CA 95110-2704
Phone: 408 536-6000
Fax: -
Web: www.adobe.com

CEO: Shantanu Narayen
CFO: Daniel Durn
HR: -
FYE: December 1
Type: Public

Adobe is one of the largest and most diversified software companies in the world. It has been known for brands such as Acrobat, Photoshop, and Adobe Document Cloud. Adobe serves customers such as content creators and web application developers with its digital media products, and marketers, advertisers, publishers, and others with its digital marketing business. Its creative cloud offering is a cloud-based subscription offering that enables creative professionals and enthusiasts alike to express themselves with apps and services for video, design, photography and the web that connect across devices, platforms and geographies. The Americas account for about 60% of revenue. The company was founded in 1982.

	Annual Growth	11/19	11/20*	12/21	12/22	12/23
Sales ($mil.)	14.8%	11,171	12,868	15,785	17,606	19,409
Net income ($ mil.)	16.5%	2,951.5	5,260.0	4,822.0	4,756.0	5,428.0
Market value ($ mil.)	18.6%	140,836	217,049	280,521	155,396	278,674
Employees	7.2%	22,634	22,516	25,988	29,239	29,945

*Fiscal year change

ADOLFSON & PETERSON INC

5500 WAYZATA BLVD STE 600
MINNEAPOLIS, MN 554163576
Phone: 952 544-1561
Fax: -
Web: www.a-p.com

CEO: Jeffrey Hansen
CFO: -
HR: Anthony Govind
FYE: February 29
Type: Private

This A&P serves clients in the market for construction services. Adolfson & Peterson (A&P) provides general construction, construction management, design/build, and facilities maintenance services. With eight US offices, the company provides services for health care, multifamily, education, and institutional projects. A&P also works on retail, office, hospitality, and manufacturing and distribution projects and offers historic renovation services. George Adolfson and Gordon Peterson established the company as a homebuilder in 1946. The Adolfson family has a majority stake in the firm.

ADS MEDIA GROUP, INC.

12758 CIMARRON PATH
SAN ANTONIO, TX 782493426
Phone: 210 655-6613
Fax: -
Web: -

CEO: -
CFO: -
HR: -
FYE: December 31
Type: Private

ADS Media Group brings business right to your door. Through its Alternative Delivery Solutions subsidiary, the company specializes in direct marketing for companies in Canada, Mexico, Puerto Rico, and the US. It delivers promotional products directly to the doors of homes, apartments, and businesses across North America. ADS can target its marketing efforts down to the neighborhood level, delivering materials to households based on specific demographic information. One key branded product is its La Canasta de Valores (basket of values) campaign, a package containing advertising inserts and a promotional magazine geared toward the Hispanic consumer. The company was founded in 2001.

ADSTAR, INC. NBB: ADST

4553 Glencoe Avenue, Suite 300
Marina Del Rey, CA 90292
Phone: 310 577-8255
Fax: 310 577-8266
Web: www.adstar.com

CEO: -
CFO: -
HR: -
FYE: December 31
Type: Public

Adstar deals with matters that are strictly classified. More than 70 publishers use Adstar's technology, which enables advertisers to compose, format, schedule, and submit newspaper classified ads electronically. Adstar also provides mobile advertising solutions through a partnership with Relevantis, a provider of software used to measure advertising effectiveness in the mobile advertising and mobile video games sectors. Through subsidiary Edgil Associates, Adstar markets and sells credit card payment processing software. Leslie Bernhard (president and CEO) and Eli Rousso (EVP and CTO) co-founded the company in 1986.

	Annual Growth	12/03	12/04	12/05	12/06	12/07
Sales ($mil.)	13.8%	2.8	4.9	5.2	5.1	4.8
Net income ($ mil.)	-	(2.8)	(3.6)	(1.1)	(1.4)	(3.3)
Market value ($ mil.)	(34.0%)	40.3	22.0	44.9	46.3	7.7
Employees	(8.7%)	36	28	32	32	25

ADT INC (DE) NYS: ADT

1501 Yamato Road
Boca Raton, FL 33431
Phone: 561 988-3600
Fax: -
Web: www.adt.com

CEO: James D Devries
CFO: Kenneth J Porpora
HR: Audrey Courseault
FYE: December 31
Type: Public

ADT is a leading provider of security, automation, and smart home solutions serving consumer and business customers in the US. The company primarily offer its portfolio of products and services under its ADT brand, which includes burglar alarm, security automation, and other smart home solutions and fire detection, suppression, and access control systems as well as solar systems and energy storage solutions. It offers its services to residential, small business, and large commercial customers. All of the company's revenue were generated in the US from about 6.7 million customers.

	Annual Growth	12/19	12/20	12/21	12/22	12/23
Sales ($mil.)	(0.7%)	5,125.7	5,314.8	5,307.1	6,395.3	4,982.7
Net income ($ mil.)	-	(424.2)	(632.2)	(340.8)	172.6	463.0
Market value ($ mil.)	(3.7%)	7,312.9	7,239.1	7,755.5	8,364.1	6,289.2
Employees	(4.9%)	17,500	20,500	25,000	22,000	14,300

ADTALEM GLOBAL EDUCATION INC NYS: ATGE

500 West Monroe Street
Chicago, IL 60661
Phone: 312 651-1400
Fax: -
Web: www.adtalem.com

CEO: Stephen W Beard
CFO: Robert J Phelan
HR: Doug Offutt
FYE: June 30
Type: Public

Adtalem Global Education is a national leader in post-secondary education and a leading provider of professional talent to the healthcare industry. Adtalem's institutions offer a wide array of programs, with a primary focus on healthcare programs. Its Chamberlain segment, through Chamberlain University, offers its programs through its College of Nursing and College of Health Professions. Walden provides an engaging learning experience for working professionals. It supports more than 100 degree and certificate programs including programs at the bachelor's, master's, education specialist, and doctoral levels with over 350 specializations and concentrations. Walden has some 37,580 students enrolled. Medical and Veterinary, which caters to some 4,870 students, offers degree and non-degree programs in the medical and veterinary postsecondary education industry. The US accounts for about 75% of total revenue.

	Annual Growth	06/19	06/20	06/21	06/22	06/23
Sales ($mil.)	4.0%	1,239.7	1,052.0	1,112.4	1,387.1	1,450.8
Net income ($ mil.)	(0.5%)	95.2	(85.3)	76.9	317.7	93.4
Market value ($ mil.)	(6.6%)	1,906.1	1,318.0	1,507.9	1,521.9	1,452.9
Employees	(4.0%)	11,356	4,299	4,426	4,682	9,655

ADTRAN HOLDINGS INC   NMS: ADTN

901 Explorer Boulevard
Huntsville, AL 35806-2807
Phone: 256 963-8000
Fax: –
Web: www.adtran.com

CEO: Thomas R Stanton
CFO: Michael K Foliano
HR: –
FYE: December 31
Type: Public

ADTRAN is a leading global provider of open networking and communications platforms, software, and services focused on the broadband access market. Its innovative solutions and services enable voice, data, video, and internet communications across network infrastructures and are currently in use by millions of people worldwide. It offers a broad portfolio of flexible software and hardware network solutions and services that enable service providers to meet today's service demands, while also enabling them to transition to the fully converged, scalable, highly-automated, cloud-controlled voice, data, internet, and video network. ADTRAN has a diverse global customer base that includes Tier-1, -2, and -3 service providers, alternative service providers, such as utilities, municipalities and fiber overbuilders, cable/MSOs, SMBs, and distributed enterprises. The US accounts for about 50% of the company's revenue.

	Annual Growth	12/18	12/19	12/20	12/21	12/22
Sales ($mil.)	18.0%	529.3	530.1	506.5	563.0	1,025.5
Net income ($ mil.)	–	(19.3)	(53.0)	2.4	(8.6)	(2.0)
Market value ($ mil.)	15.0%	836.5	770.3	1,150.4	1,778.2	1,463.5
Employees	14.9%	1,900	1,790	1,405	1,335	3,307

ADVANCE AUTO PARTS INC   NYS: AAP

4200 Six Forks Road
Raleigh, NC 27609
Phone: 540 362-4911
Fax: –
Web: www.advanceautoparts.com

CEO: Shane M O'Kelly
CFO: Anthony A Iskander
HR: –
FYE: December 30
Type: Public

Advance Auto Parts a leading automotive aftermarket parts provider in North America, serving both professional installers (professional) and do-it-yourself (DIY) customers, as well as independently owned operators. The company operates approximately 4,770 stores and about 315 branches under the Advance Auto Parts, Carquest, and Worldpac banners in the US and Canada. Its stores carry brand-name and private-label replacement parts, batteries, maintenance items, and automotive chemicals for individual car and truck owners. The company's Carquest and Worldpac stores cater to commercial customers, including garages, service stations, and auto dealers. The company also serves about 1,310 independently owned Carquest stores with shipments directly from its distribution centers.

	Annual Growth	12/19*	01/21	01/22*	12/22	12/23
Sales ($mil.)	3.8%	9,709.0	10,106	10,998	11,155	11,288
Net income ($ mil.)	(50.3%)	486.9	493.0	616.1	501.9	29.7
Market value ($ mil.)	(21.2%)	9,423.7	9,373.7	14,276	8,750.0	3,632.0
Employees	0.7%	67,000	68,000	68,000	67,000	69,000

*Fiscal year change

ADVANCED COMPOSITE STRUCTURES, LLC

1026 LEGRAND BLVD
CHARLESTON, SC 294927672
Phone: 843 588-5590
Fax: –
Web: www.aerotuf.com

CEO: Thomas Pherson
CFO: –
HR: –
FYE: December 31
Type: Private

Sometimes it's OK to think inside the box; Advanced Composites Structures (formerly AeroBox) has been doing just that and hopes to turn its kind of thinking into cash. The company manufactures shipping containers used on cargo flights; it has several products either in use or in trials by airlines. ACS touts its composite-material containers as more durable and less expensive to repair than aluminum containers. The company filed for Chapter 11 bankruptcy protection in 2007 under the AeroBox name and emerged the following year as Advanced Composites Structures. That name had been the name of its subsidiary, which maintains manufacturing operations in New Mexico.

ADVANCED DISPOSAL SERVICES, INC.

90 FORT WADE RD STE 200
PONTE VEDRA, FL 320815112
Phone: 904 737-7900
Fax: –
Web: www.dwloftonconsulting.com

CEO: –
CFO: Leslie K Nagy
HR: Misty Peffer
FYE: December 31
Type: Private

Advanced Disposal Services offers waste disposal, collection and recycling services for residential, commercial, industrial and construction customers. For businesses, it offers collection services, and disposal and recycling services. It also offers industry-specific solutions used for industrial/manufacturing, colleges and universities, and healthcare industries, to name a few. Acquired in 2020, it becomes a wholly-owned subsidiary of Waste Management, a leading provider of comprehensive waste management environmental services in North America which provides collection, transfer, disposal services, and recycling and resource recovery. It is also a leading developer, operator and owner of landfill gas-to-energy facilities in the United States.

ADVANCED DRAINAGE SYSTEMS INC   NYS: WMS

4640 Trueman Boulevard
Hilliard, OH 43026
Phone: 614 658-0050
Fax: –
Web: www.adspipe.com

CEO: D S Barbour
CFO: Scott A Cottrill
HR: –
FYE: March 31
Type: Public

Advanced Drainage Systems (ADS) is the leading manufacturer of innovative water management solutions in the stormwater and onsite septic wastewater industries, providing superior drainage solutions for use in construction and agriculture marketplaces. In addition, ADS makes high-density polyethylene (HDPE) pipes for storm and sanitary sewers, agricultural drainage, highway edge drains, septic systems, and other construction applications. ADS is one of the largest plastic recycling companies in North America, ensuring over half a billion pounds of plastic is kept out of landfills every year. Its IM-Series line of septic tanks are injection-molded polypropylene plastic tanks manufactured from recycled materials. Major customers include Ferguson Enterprises and Core and Main. Majority of the company's revenue comes from the US market.

	Annual Growth	03/19	03/20	03/21	03/22	03/23
Sales ($mil.)	22.0%	1,384.7	1,673.8	1,982.8	2,769.3	3,071.1
Net income ($ mil.)	59.8%	77.8	(193.2)	224.2	271.3	507.1
Market value ($ mil.)	34.5%	1,791.5	2,046.6	7,187.5	8,259.4	5,854.1
Employees	7.5%	4,400	4,950	5,000	5,635	5,870

ADVANCED ENERGY INDUSTRIES INC   NMS: AEIS

1595 Wynkoop Street, Suite 800
Denver, CO 80202
Phone: 970 407-6626
Fax: –
Web: www.advancedenergy.com

CEO: Stephen D Kelley
CFO: Paul R Oldham
HR: –
FYE: December 31
Type: Public

Advanced Energy Industries designs, manufactures, sells, and supports precision power products that transform, refine, and modify the raw electrical power coming from either the utility or the building facility and convert it into various types of highly controllable, usable power that is predictable, repeatable, and customizable to meet the requirements for powering a wide range of complex equipment. Its broad portfolio of high and low voltage power products are used in a wide range of applications, such as semiconductor equipment, industrial production, medical and life science equipment, data centers computing, networking, and telecommunications. It also supply related sensing, controls, and instrumentation products primarily for advanced measurement and calibration of power and temperature for multiple industrial markets. The company gets some 40% of its revenue from the US.

	Annual Growth	12/19	12/20	12/21	12/22	12/23
Sales ($mil.)	20.4%	788.9	1,415.8	1,456.0	1,845.4	1,655.8
Net income ($ mil.)	18.6%	64.9	134.7	134.7	199.7	128.3
Market value ($ mil.)	11.2%	2,657.0	3,618.7	3,398.2	3,201.1	4,064.7
Employees	(2.2%)	10,917	10,000	10,000	12,000	10,000

ADVANCED LIGHTING TECHNOLOGIES, LLC

6675 PARKLAND BLVD
SOLON, OH 441394345
Phone: 888 440-2358
Fax: -
Web: www.adlt.com

CEO: -
CFO: -
HR: -
FYE: June 30
Type: Private

And then there was light, the metal halide kind. Made by Advanced Lighting Technologies (ADLT), metal halide simulates sunlight more closely and efficiently than other technologies. ADLT subsidiary Venture Lighting produces metal halide lamps and ballast systems. Its lineup includes lamp components, power supplies, and lamp-making equipment for commercial and industrial markets. ADLT's Materials segment makes the metal halide salts used in its products as well as sells the salts to other manufacturers. Via its Deposition Sciences subsidiary ADLT also produces durable thin-film optical coatings for industrial, medical, and biological sciences instrumentation.

ADVANCED MICRO DEVICES INC
NMS: AMD

2485 Augustine Drive
Santa Clara, CA 95054
Phone: 408 749-4000
Fax: -
Web: www.amd.com

CEO: Lisa T Su
CFO: Jean Hu
HR: -
FYE: December 30
Type: Public

Incorporated in 1969, Advanced Micro Devices (AMD) produces microprocessors as standalone devices or as incorporated into an accelerated processing unit (APU), chipsets, discrete and integrated graphics processing units (GPUs), data center and professional GPUs, and development services and servers and embedded processors, semi-custom System-on-Chip (SoC) products, development services and technology for game consoles. In recent years, the company has armed itself with new product families: Radeon for graphics and Ryzen for computing to strengthen its position against longtime rival and market leader, Intel. Majority of AMD's sales come from international customers.

	Annual Growth	12/19	12/20	12/21	12/22	12/23
Sales ($mil.)	35.5%	6,731.0	9,763.0	16,434	23,601	22,680
Net income ($ mil.)	25.8%	341.0	2,490.0	3,162.0	1,320.0	854.0
Market value ($ mil.)	33.7%	74,627	148,365	236,162	104,668	238,215
Employees	22.9%	11,400	12,600	15,500	25,000	26,000

ADVANCEPIERRE FOODS, INC.

9990 PRINCETON GLENDALE RD
WEST CHESTER, OH 452461116
Phone: 513 874-8741
Fax: -
Web: www.tysonfoodservice.com

CEO: Tom Hayes
CFO: Dennis Leatherby
HR: Terry Walker
FYE: January 02
Type: Private

Advancepierre Foods Holdings, Inc. is a nationally recognized supplier of value-added proteins and sandwich products to foodservice, retail, schools and convenience channels across the United States. It collaborates and innovates with its customers to make great-tasting foods, and takes pride in driving profitable growth for every retailer, every kitchen, every menu and every plate. It is also an industry leader in supplying quality beef, chicken and pork products, and is America's #1 provider of sandwiches, fully cooked burgers, Philly steak, stuffed chicken breasts and country fried steaks. The Ohio-based company's products are sold under brand names Barber Foods, Fast Fixin, and Hot n Ready, to name a few.

ADVANCIA CORPORATION

755 RESEARCH PKWY STE 150
OKLAHOMA CITY, OK 731043621
Phone: 405 996-3000
Fax: -
Web: www.advancia.com

CEO: -
CFO: David Sperle
HR: -
FYE: September 30
Type: Private

Advancia can help your hardware and software get ahead. The company provides systems integration and other information technology services primarily for state and federal government agencies involved in homeland security, aviation, and defense. Advancia also offers engineering, consulting, training, logistics, and environmental mitigation services. Clients have included the US Air Force, the Federal Aviation Administration, and the Air National Guard. Founded in 1982, Advancia operates from fifteen US offices located from the District of Columbia to Alaska. The company was acquired in 2007 by a division of Native American investment firm Potawatomi Business Development Corporation.

	Annual Growth	09/08	09/09	09/10	09/11	09/12
Sales ($mil.)	(26.5%)	-	-	28.5	27.5	15.4
Net income ($ mil.)	(24.5%)	-	-	2.1	2.9	1.2
Market value ($ mil.)	-	-	-	-	-	-
Employees	-	-	-	-	-	252

ADVANSIX INC
NYS: ASIX

300 Kimball Drive, Suite 101
Parsippany, NJ 07054
Phone: 973 526-1800
Fax: -
Web: www.advansix.com

CEO: Erin N Kane
CFO: Michael Preston
HR: Lavonnia Downey
FYE: December 31
Type: Public

Emerging from its long incubation as part of Honeywell International, the company was spun off as AdvanSix, a major producer and global supplier of Nylon 6 materials. AdvanSix makes Nylon 6 (a polymer resin sold under the Aegis brand) to produce engineered plastics, fibers, filaments, and films. These in turn are used in end products such as automotive, electronic components, food, and industrial packaging. AdvanSix also produces caprolactam, the main feedstock for producing nylon; Capran nylon film; Sulf-N ammonium sulfate fertilizers; and chemical intermediates, including phenol, acetone, and Nadone cyclohexanone. The US is the company's largest market, accounting for about 85% of total sales.

	Annual Growth	12/19	12/20	12/21	12/22	12/23
Sales ($mil.)	4.3%	1,297.4	1,157.9	1,684.6	1,945.6	1,533.6
Net income ($ mil.)	7.2%	41.3	46.1	139.8	171.9	54.6
Market value ($ mil.)	10.7%	533.9	534.7	1,264.0	1,017.1	801.4
Employees	(1.2%)	1,520	1,400	1,375	1,458	1,450

ADVANT-E CORPORATION

2434 Esquire Dr.
Beavercreek, OH 45431
Phone: 937 429-4288
Fax: -
Web: www.advant-e.com

CEO: Jason K Wadzinski
CFO: James E Lesch
HR: -
FYE: December 31
Type: Public

Advant-e makes B2B e-commerce EZ. Through subsidiaries Edict Systems and Merkur Group, the holding company offers Electronic Data Interchange (EDI) and electronic document management software for small and midsized businesses. Edict Systems' GroceryEC.com helps suppliers such as Associated Grocers do business with retailers by automating invoices and purchase orders. Merkur Group sells document management software that works within a company's Oracle, SAP, or Microsoft application. President and CEO Jason Wadzinski founded Edict System when he was 25.

	Annual Growth	12/08	12/09	12/10	12/11	12/12
Sales ($mil.)	3.3%	8.9	8.6	9.3	9.6	10.1
Net income ($ mil.)	17.1%	1.1	1.2	1.6	1.7	2.0
Market value ($ mil.)	-	-	-	-	-	-
Employees	4.4%	59	66	65	68	70

ADVANTAGE SOLUTIONS INC
NMS: ADV

15310 Barranca Parkway, Suite 100
Irvine, CA 92618
Phone: 949 797-2900
Fax: –
Web: www.advantagesolutions.net

CEO: David A Peacock
CFO: Christopher Growe
HR: –
FYE: December 31
Type: Public

Advantage Solutions Inc. is a leading provider of outsourced solutions to consumer goods companies and retailers. It has a strong platform of competitively advantaged sales and marketing services built over multiple decades ? essential, business critical services like headquarter sales, retail merchandising, in-store sampling, digital commerce, and shopper marketing. It provides a full suite of outsourced solutions to enhance sales in the traditional retail, foodservice, and e-commerce channels and has been predominately centered around providing solutions to branded consumer goods manufacturers such as non-private label manufacturers. It also serve select retailers as their exclusive provider, and other retailers as an authorized provider, of in-store merchandising or reset services. Majority of its sales were generated in the North American markets.

	Annual Growth	12/19	12/20	12/21	12/22	12/23
Sales ($mil.)	–	–	3,155.7	3,602.3	4,049.7	4,224.8
Net income ($ mil.)	–	–	2.5	(162.4)	54.5	(1,380.5)	(63.3)
Market value ($ mil.)	(23.2%)	3,313.8	4,196.4	2,555.5	662.8	1,153.5
Employees	1267.8%	2	62,000	70,000	75,000	70,000

ADVANTEGO CORP
NBB: ADGO

3801 East Florida Ave., Ste. 400
Denver, CO 80210
Phone: 949 627-8977
Fax: –
Web: –

CEO: –
CFO: –
HR: –
FYE: December 31
Type: Public

In search of gold and copper, Golden Eagle International has spread its wings in Bolivia. The company is exploring prospects in the Tipuani-Cangalli area north of La Paz and in eastern Bolivia's Precambrian Shield area. Gold production on the company's Cangalli claims was halted in 2004 because of a farmers' strike and has not yet restarted; the company has yet to produce minerals on its other properties. Golden Eagle has generated no revenue since late 2004.

	Annual Growth	12/15	12/16	12/17	12/18	12/19
Sales ($mil.)	–	–	–	0.0	0.2	0.1
Net income ($ mil.)	–	(0.1)	(0.2)	(0.6)	(1.3)	(2.5)
Market value ($ mil.)	(57.3%)	1.5	12.2	41.4	83.6	0.0
Employees	18.9%	2	3	4	13	4

ADVANZEON SOLUTIONS INC
NBB: CHCR

2901 W. Busch Blvd., Suite 701
Tampa, FL 33618
Phone: 813 517-8484
Fax: –
Web: www.advanzeonshareholders.com

CEO: Clark Marcus
CFO: Arnold B Finestone
HR: –
FYE: December 31
Type: Public

It's not comprehensive health care if doesn't cover body and mind. That's why Comprehensive Care helps commercial and government-run health plans nationwide offer behavioral health care services. Through its Comprehensive Behavioral Care subsidiary (CompCare, for short), the company manages behavioral health care, including psychiatric and substance abuse services, through a network of about 21,000 health care providers in 39 states and Puerto Rico. For the most part it operates under capitation agreements, in which the plans pay CompCare a fixed monthly fee for each member.

	Annual Growth	12/15	12/16	12/17	12/18	12/19
Sales ($mil.)	(9.0%)	0.4	0.2	0.6	0.5	0.3
Net income ($ mil.)	–	(3.6)	(4.5)	(5.9)	4.8	(3.3)
Market value ($ mil.)	35.4%	8.5	4.7	9.1	6.9	28.7
Employees	7.5%	9	12	12	9	12

ADVENTIST HEALTH SYSTEM/SUNBELT, INC.

900 HOPE WAY
ALTAMONTE SPRINGS, FL 327141502
Phone: 407 357-1000
Fax: –
Web: www.adventhealth.com

CEO: –
CFO: –
HR: –
FYE: December 31
Type: Private

Florida Hospital Heartland Medical Center provides care to residents of central Florida. The not-for-profit, 160-bed medical center is the flagship facility of the Florida Hospital Heartland division of Adventist Health System. Other facilities in the Heartland system include Florida Hospital Lake Placid (a 50-bed community hospital), Florida Hospital Wauchula (25 beds), various fitness centers, medical clinics, and counseling agencies. Together the facilities provide primary and acute care, as well as specialty medical services including diagnostics, obstetrics, cardiac care, and cancer treatment. The Florida Hospital Heartland Medical Center opened in 1997.

	Annual Growth	12/07	12/08	12/14	12/15	12/16
Sales ($mil.)	6.7%	–	126.5	167.2	193.7	212.8
Net income ($ mil.)	189.3%	–	0.0	(14.1)	(6.1)	7.3
Market value ($ mil.)	–	–	–	–	–	–
Employees	–	–	–	–	–	1,200

ADVENTIST HEALTH SYSTEM/SUNBELT, INC.

6838 HOFFNER AVE STE 1200
ORLANDO, FL 328223580
Phone: 407 664-0167
Fax: –
Web: www.adventhealth.com

CEO: Terry D Shaw
CFO: –
HR: –
FYE: December 31
Type: Private

Adventist Health System Sunbelt (AdventHealth) provides full system care from everyday wellness and preventive health care to life-saving diagnostic services and innovative medical treatments in cancer, heart failure and more. Its integrated network of health care serves neighbors across more than 130 facilities nationwide, including hospital campuses, urgent-care centers, home-health and hospice agencies, and nursing homes across nine states. AdventHealth was formally founded in 1973 but traces its roots back to 1866 with a team of Seventh-day Adventist medical pioneers in Battle Creek, Michigan.

	Annual Growth	12/08	12/09	12/19	12/20	12/21
Sales ($mil.)	201.9%	–	0.0	11,892	12,623	14,883
Net income ($ mil.)	–	–	–	1,607.3	951.4	1,512.3
Market value ($ mil.)	–	–	–	–	–	–
Employees	–	–	–	–	–	46,960

ADVENTIST HEALTH SYSTEM/WEST, CORPORATION

1 ADVENTIST HEALTH WAY
ROSEVILLE, CA 956613266
Phone: 844 574-5686
Fax: –
Web: www.adventisthealth.org

CEO: Kerry Heinrich
CFO: John Beaman
HR: Roger Ashley
FYE: December 31
Type: Private

Adventist Health System/West, doing business as Adventist Health, is a faith-based, nonprofit integrated health system serving more than 80 communities on the West Coast and Hawaii. Annually, Adventist Health has more than 127,700 admissions, 682,300 emergency department visits, 246,570 home health visits, 2.4 million clinic visits, and 1.6 million outpatient visits. Adventist Health maintains strong ties to the Seventh-day Adventist Church but is independently owned. A sister organization, Adventist Health System, operates in the central and southern parts of the country.

	Annual Growth	12/18	12/19	12/20	12/21	12/22
Sales ($mil.)	2.0%	–	–	–	789.4	805.1
Net income ($ mil.)	–	–	–	–	(119.1)	(185.7)
Market value ($ mil.)	–	–	–	–	–	–
Employees	–	–	–	–	–	19,512

ADVENTIST HEALTHCARE, INC.

820 W DIAMOND AVE STE 600　　　　　　　　　　　CEO: –
GAITHERSBURG, MD 208781469　　　　　　　　　　CFO: –
Phone: 301 315-3030　　　　　　　　　　　　　　　HR: –
Fax: –　　　　　　　　　　　　　　　　　　　　FYE: December 31
Web: www.adventisthealthcare.com　　　　　　　　Type: Private

Adventist HealthCare is the first and largest provider of healthcare in Montgomery County, Maryland. The not-for-profit system, with more than 2,205 physicians and medical providers, is home to five acute care hospitals, and more than 445,355 outpatient visits. Its hospitals are Adventist HealthCare Shady Grove Medical Center (Rockville), White Oak Medical Center (Silver Spring), Fort Washington Medical Center (Fort Washington), Germantown Emergency Center, and Adventist HealthCare Rehabilitation (Rockville). Among its specialized medical services include heart and vascular care, mental health care, pregnancy care and birth and radiology and diagnostic imaging. Adventist HealthCare, which is affiliated with the Seventh-day Adventist Church, has been in operation since 1907.

	Annual Growth	12/18	12/19	12/20	12/21	12/22
Sales ($mil.)	10.1%	–	862.5	974.9	1,154.3	1,151.6
Net income ($ mil.)	–	–	32.8	42.1	30.0	(32.9)
Market value ($ mil.)	–	–	–	–	–	–
Employees	–	–	–	–	–	5,236

ADVERUM BIOTECHNOLOGIES INC　　　　　　NAS: ADVM

100 Cardinal Way　　　　　　　　　　　　　CEO: Laurent Fischer
Redwood City, CA 94063　　　　　　　　　　CFO: Leone Patterson
Phone: 650 656-9323　　　　　　　　　　　　HR: Dena House
Fax: –　　　　　　　　　　　　　　　　　　FYE: December 31
Web: www.adverum.com　　　　　　　　　　Type: Public

Adverum is a clinical-stage company that aims to establish gene therapy as a new standard of care for highly prevalent ocular diseases. It develops gene therapy product candidates intended to provide durable efficacy by inducing sustained expression of a therapeutic protein. Its core capabilities include novel vector discovery, non-clinical and clinical development, and pre-commercial planning. In addition, it has in-house manufacturing expertise, specifically in scalable process development, assay development, and current Good Manufacturing Practices (GMP) quality control. Its next-generation discovery platform is based on vectors derived from AAV, which is a small, non-pathogenic virus, which carry a therapeutic DNA instead of the viral genes.

	Annual Growth	12/19	12/20	12/21	12/22	12/23
Sales ($mil.)	94.8%	0.3	–	7.5	–	3.6
Net income ($ mil.)	–	(64.5)	(117.5)	(145.5)	(154.5)	(117.2)
Market value ($ mil.)	(49.4%)	116.9	110.0	17.9	5.9	7.6
Employees	1.5%	114	167	188	123	121

ADVOCATE AURORA HEALTH INC.

3075 HIGHLAND PKWY STE 600　　　　　　　CEO: Eugene A Woods
DOWNERS GROVE, IL 605155563　　　　　　　CFO: Anthony C Defurio
Phone: 630 572-9393　　　　　　　　　　　　HR: Agnes Pociecha
Fax: –　　　　　　　　　　　　　　　　　　FYE: December 31
Web: www.advocatehealth.com　　　　　　　　Type: Private

Advocate Aurora Health is a not-for-profit, integrated health care network with some 500 care sites serving Illinois and Wisconsin. The organization includes about 30 acute and specialty care hospitals (including Advocate Christ Medical Center, Aurora St. Luke's Medical Center, Aurora Lakeland Medical Center, and Lutheran General Hospital) with more than 7,000 beds, as well as community health clinics, walk-in clinics (with Walgreen's), physician offices, and home health care and hospice agencies. The company was formed when Illinois-based Advocate Health merged with Wisconsin-based Aurora Health Care in 2018, creating one of the nation's largest not-for-profit health systems.

ADVOCATE CHARITABLE FOUNDATION INC

3075 HIGHLAND PKWY FL 6　　　　　　　　　CEO: –
DOWNERS GROVE, IL 605155563　　　　　　　CFO: –
Phone: 630 929-6900　　　　　　　　　　　　HR: –
Fax: –　　　　　　　　　　　　　　　　　　FYE: December 31
Web: www.advocateaurorahealth.org　　　　　　Type: Private

They may not want you to give until it hurts, but they do want you to give. Advocate Charitable Foundation is the faith-based philanthropic arm of Advocate Health Care. Its mission is to build relationships and partnerships across Chicago and to inspire charitable giving by individuals, foundations, corporations, and organizations. The not-for-profit group funds programs that offer patient care, research, education, and community-based health services. These include caregiver education classes, family-focused support groups, cancer research facilities, and specialized clinics throughout the city. Advocate Charitable Foundation began as Evangelical Health Foundation in 1984 and took its current name in 1995.

	Annual Growth	12/13	12/14	12/17	12/18	12/22
Sales ($mil.)	(16.9%)	–	42.8	34.0	22.9	9.8
Net income ($ mil.)	–	–	11.9	(5.5)	(3.4)	(7.9)
Market value ($ mil.)	–	–	–	–	–	–
Employees	–	–	–	–	–	16

ADVOCATE HEALTH AND HOSPITALS CORPORATION

1775 DEMPSTER ST　　　　　　　　　　　　CEO: –
PARK RIDGE, IL 600681143　　　　　　　　　CFO: –
Phone: 847 723-6610　　　　　　　　　　　　HR: –
Fax: –　　　　　　　　　　　　　　　　　　FYE: December 31
Web: www.advocatehealth.com　　　　　　　　Type: Private

Advocate Lutheran General Hospital, also known simply as Lutheran General, provides acute and long-term medical and surgical care to the residents of Park Ridge, Illinois and the surrounding northern suburban Chicago area. As one of the largest hospitals in the region, Lutheran General boasts nearly 640 beds and a Level I trauma center. Its operations also include a complete children's hospital and pediatric critical care center. Lutheran General serves as a teaching hospital and its specialized programs include oncology, cardiology, women's health, emergency medicine, and hospice care. Lutheran General is part of the Advocate Health Care network.

	Annual Growth	12/14	12/15	12/16	12/17	12/21
Sales ($mil.)	5.3%	–	752.1	785.3	790.5	1,025.2
Net income ($ mil.)	11.5%	–	104.8	118.4	79.3	200.9
Market value ($ mil.)	–	–	–	–	–	–
Employees	–	–	–	–	–	4,818

ADVOCATE HEALTH CARE NETWORK

2025 WINDSOR DR　　　　　　　　　　　　CEO: –
OAK BROOK, IL 605231585　　　　　　　　　CFO: –
Phone: 630 572-9393　　　　　　　　　　　　HR: –
Fax: –　　　　　　　　　　　　　　　　　　FYE: December 31
Web: www.advocatehealth.com　　　　　　　　Type: Private

Advocate Health Care (Advocate) is part of Advocate Health, the fifth-largest nonprofit integrated health system in the US. Advocate offers more than 250 sites of care, with a dozen of acute-care hospitals, including a children's hospital with two campuses and the state's largest integrated children's network. It has the largest emergency and Level I Trauma network in Illinois. Advocate treats more pediatric patients than any other hospital or system in the state, and more people trust their hearts to Advocate than to any other hospital or system in the state. Additionally, Advocate diagnoses and treats more cancer than any other hospital or system in Illinois.

	Annual Growth	12/03	12/04	12/05	12/06	12/19
Sales ($mil.)	(22.4%)	–	–	2,973.9	3,268.3	85.5
Net income ($ mil.)	(14.8%)	–	–	140.6	286.8	15.0
Market value ($ mil.)	–	–	–	–	–	–
Employees	–	–	–	–	–	25,000

AECOM
NYS: ACM

13355 Noel Road
Dallas, TX 75240
Phone: 972 788-1000
Fax: –
Web: www.aecom.com

CEO: W T Rudd
CFO: Gaurav Kapoor
HR: –
FYE: September 30
Type: Public

AECOM is one of the world's top engineering and design groups. The company provides planning, consulting, architectural, and engineering design services for civil and infrastructure construction to public and private clients. The company also offers other services including logistics and consulting in a range of end markets that include transportation, facilities, environmental, energy, water, and government. Some of AECOM's major projects include World Trade Center, Port of Los Angeles Waterfront, Mercedes Benz Stadium, Golden 1 Center and Warner Bros. World Abu Dhabi. AECOM generates around 70% of sales in the Americas region.

	Annual Growth	09/19	09/20	09/21	09/22	09/23
Sales ($mil.)	(8.1%)	20,173	13,240	13,341	13,148	14,378
Net income ($ mil.)	–	(261.1)	(186.4)	173.2	310.6	55.3
Market value ($ mil.)	21.9%	5,116.1	5,699.1	8,601.7	9,312.7	11,311
Employees	(11.8%)	86,000	54,000	51,000	50,000	52,000

AEGION CORPORATION

580 GODDARD AVE
CHESTERFIELD, MO 630051120
Phone: 636 530-8000
Fax: –
Web: www.aegion.com

CEO: –
CFO: –
HR: –
FYE: December 31
Type: Private

Aegion is a global leader in infrastructure protection that combines innovative technologies with market leading expertise to maintain, rehabilitate and strengthen pipelines and other infrastructure around the world. Aegion is the parent company for Aegion Coating Services, Corrpro, EN-TECH Infrastructure, Fibrwrap, Insituform, MTC, Underground Solutions, and Infraspec Services. Aegion provides proprietary technologies and services for the corrosion protection of industrial pipelines and the rehabilitation and strengthening of wastewater, water, energy and mining piping systems, buildings, bridges and tunnels and waterfront structures.

AEGIS AEROSPACE, INC.

18050 SATURN LN STE 300
HOUSTON, TX 770584502
Phone: 281 283-6200
Fax: –
Web: www.aegisaero.com

CEO: Mark Gittleman
CFO: –
HR: Pedro Flores
FYE: December 31
Type: Private

Aegis Aerospace Inc. (formerly MEI Technologies) which changed name in 2021 after it merged with Alpha Space Test & Research Alliance) provides commercial, turn-key space services, spaceflight product development, and engineering services for the civil and commercial space and defense industries. It develops, integrates, and operates lunar surface systems, 100kg-class satellites, attached ISS payloads and commercial vehicle payloads, and provides Advanced Engineering and Technical Services for NASA, the US Space Force, US Air Force, and commercial customers. It also offers a unique range of commercial space services, technology and engineering services, and products to the space and defense industries, all under a single, woman-owned roof.

	Annual Growth	12/05	12/06	12/07	12/08	12/12
Sales ($mil.)	3.4%	–	–	116.1	118.9	137.2
Net income ($ mil.)	15.4%	–	–	2.3	(0.9)	4.8
Market value ($ mil.)	–	–	–	–	–	–
Employees	–	–	–	–	–	721

AEHR TEST SYSTEMS
NAS: AEHR

400 Kato Terrace
Fremont, CA 94539
Phone: 510 623-9400
Fax: 510 623-9450
Web: www.aehr.com

CEO: –
CFO: –
HR: –
FYE: May 31
Type: Public

Aehr Test Systems' products don't test air, but rather silicon. Aehr (pronounced "air") makes gear that tests logic and memory semiconductors to weed out defective devices. Its burn-in systems test chips' reliability under stress by exposing them to high temperatures and voltages. Aehr also makes massively parallel test systems for handling thousands of chips simultaneously, die carriers for testing unpackaged chips, custom-designed fixtures for test equipment, and other memory test products. Top customers include Spansion (about 80% of sales) and Texas Instruments. Aehr gets more than one-third of its business outside the US.

	Annual Growth	05/19	05/20	05/21	05/22	05/23
Sales ($mil.)	32.5%	21.1	22.3	16.6	50.8	65.0
Net income ($ mil.)	–	(5.2)	(2.8)	(2.0)	9.5	14.6
Market value ($ mil.)	108.4%	49.9	47.1	64.2	239.2	942.4
Employees	7.1%	79	71	79	91	104

AEOLUS PHARMACEUTICALS INC
NBB: AOLS

26361 Crown Valley Parkway, Suite 150
Mission Viejo, CA 92691
Phone: 949 481-9825
Fax: –
Web: www.aolsrx.com

CEO: –
CFO: –
HR: –
FYE: September 30
Type: Public

Aeolus Pharmaceuticals wants to put an end to free radicals' free-wheeling, cell-damaging fun. The development-stage company is focusing its attention on developing catalytic antioxidant drugs, which can neutralize free radicals. Aeolus' drug candidates could battle amyotrophic lateral sclerosis (ALS, better known as Lou Gehrig's disease), stroke, Parkinson's disease, and other neurodegenerative conditions. The company is also developing antioxidant drugs to treat respiratory conditions and protect healthy tissue from cancer-fighting radiation. Chairman David Cavalier controls about half of the company through investment company XMark Asset Management.

	Annual Growth	09/12	09/13	09/14	09/15	09/16
Sales ($mil.)	(27.0%)	7.3	3.9	9.6	3.1	2.1
Net income ($ mil.)	–	1.7	(3.2)	(0.1)	(2.6)	(3.6)
Market value ($ mil.)	(15.3%)	56.3	42.6	38.0	36.6	28.9
Employees	(5.4%)	5	4	4	4	4

AEON GLOBAL HEALTH CORP

2225 Centennial Drive
Gainesville, GA 30504
Phone: 888 661-0225
Fax: –
Web: www.authentidate.com

CEO: Hanif A Roshan
CFO: –
HR: –
FYE: June 30
Type: Public

AuthentiDate Holding wants to leave its technological stamp of approval on the US health care industry. Through its subsidiaries, the company provides secure workflow management software and remote patient monitoring technology to health care companies and government entities. Its hosted Inscrybe platform facilitates administrative functions like electronic signing, identity management, and content authentication, while its ExpressMD Solutions subsidiary makes in-home patient vital signs monitoring systems. Other offerings include Inscrybe Office, which extends its Web-based workflow management software to personal and business customers. Major customers include the US Department of Veterans Affairs.

	Annual Growth	06/15	06/16	06/17	06/18	06/19
Sales ($mil.)	36.8%	3.7	34.6	20.2	16.3	12.9
Net income ($ mil.)	–	(9.7)	5.3	(32.1)	(8.0)	(8.0)
Market value ($ mil.)	11.5%	1.9	30.2	15.9	9.4	2.9
Employees	20.1%	25	76	137	108	52

AEP TEXAS CENTRAL CO

1 Riverside Plaza
Columbus, OH 43215-2373
Phone: 614 716-1000
Fax: -
Web: www.aeptexas.com

CEO: -
CFO: -
HR: -
FYE: December 31
Type: Public

The lights are big and bright deep in the heart of the Lone Star State, thanks to AEP Texas Central (TCC). The utility, formerly named Central Power and Light, provides regulated electric utility services to 766.000 customers in its 100,000 sq. ml. service territory in south and west Texas. TCC operates more than 29,600 miles of transmission and distribution lines in Texas; its transmission assets are managed by ERCOT. In addition to distributing power, AEP Texas also reads electric meters, maintains and repairs power lines, and takes care of connections and disconnections.

	Annual Growth	12/02	12/03	12/04	12/05	12/06
Sales ($mil.)	(20.8%)	1,690.5	1,747.5	1,175.3	793.2	664.7
Net income ($ mil.)	(37.7%)	275.9	217.7	174.1	(173.8)	41.6
Market value ($ mil.)	-	-	-	165.9	144.9	149.3	162.6
Employees	(0.5%)	1,248	1,203	933	1,160	1,224

AEROKOOL AVIATION CORPORATION

1495 SE 10TH AVE
HIALEAH, FL 330105916
Phone: 305 887-6912
Fax: -
Web: www.aerokool.com

CEO: Jeffrey Kelly
CFO: -
HR: -
FYE: December 31
Type: Private

AeroKool Aviation makes sure aircraft pilots are not left out in the cold. The aircraft maintenance company, which has its own engineering and manufacturing departments, provides airframe and engine accessory repair and overhaul services. AeroKool works on a wide range of equipment, including air cycle machines, air starters, fuel heaters, heat exchangers, oil tanks and coolers, refrigeration packs, valves (both electro-mechanical and electro-pneumatic), and water separators. The company also sells airframe and engine accessories and designs and manufactures replacement parts. AeroKool was founded in 1959.

	Annual Growth	12/04	12/05	12/06	12/08	12/09
Sales ($mil.)	3.6%	-	-	8.3	9.5	9.2
Net income ($ mil.)	(30.2%)	-	-	1.0	0.4	0.3
Market value ($ mil.)	-	-	-	-	-	-
Employees	-	-	-	-	-	42

AERONET WORLDWIDE, INC.

42 CORPORATE PARK STE 100
IRVINE, CA 926063101
Phone: 949 474-3000
Fax: -
Web: www.aeronet.com

CEO: -
CFO: -
HR: -
FYE: December 31
Type: Private

Aeronet is casting a wide net for its logistics business. The company provides a full range of logistics services both in the US and overseas. Offerings include time-guaranteed domestic freight delivery (ranging from same-day to five-day), air and ocean freight forwarding, customs brokerage, shipment tracking, supply chain management, and warehousing and distribution. As a freight forwarder, the company purchases transportation capacity from carriers and resells it to customers. Aeronet maintains 10 offices near major trade gateways throughout the US and operates through agents in other regions.

	Annual Growth	12/18	12/19	12/20	12/21	12/22
Sales ($mil.)	35.0%	-	-	-	175.3	236.7
Net income ($ mil.)	(14.3%)	-	-	-	5.3	4.5
Market value ($ mil.)	-	-	-	-	-	-
Employees	-	-	-	-	-	175

AEROTEK AFFILIATED SERVICES, INC.

7301 PARKWAY DR
HANOVER, MD 210761159
Phone: 410 694-5100
Fax: -
Web: www.aerotek.com

CEO: -
CFO: Thomas B Kelly
HR: Laura Stovie
FYE: December 31
Type: Private

For more than 35 years, Aerotek has been linking qualified professionals to businesses in need of temporary, temp-to-perm, or permanent labor. With access to a wide range of skill sets, the company has grown to become one of the biggest industrial staffing firms in North America. Its team collaborates with dependable experts in light industry, manufacturing trades, construction trades, facilities and maintenance, and aviation. Along with aerospace, auto, and engineering companies, Aerotek's clients include companies from the construction, energy, manufacturing, health care, and finance industries. Operates through more than 250 offices, the company supports over 13,000 clients across North America's leading industries. Aerotek is an operating company within Allegis Group, a global leader in talent solutions.

	Annual Growth	12/16	12/17	12/18	12/19	12/20
Sales ($mil.)	(1.2%)	-	6,070.1	6,586.3	6,662.1	5,859.1
Net income ($ mil.)	-	-	-	-	-	-
Market value ($ mil.)	-	-	-	-	-	-
Employees	-	-	-	-	-	9,300

AEROVIRONMENT, INC.

NMS: AVAV

241 18th Street, Suite 415
Arlington, VA 22202
Phone: 805 520-8350
Fax: -
Web: www.avinc.com

CEO: Wahid Nawabi
CFO: Kevin McDonnell
HR: -
FYE: April 30
Type: Public

AeroVironment (AV) designs, develops, produces, delivers and supports a technologically-advanced portfolio of intelligent, multi-domain robotic systems, and related services for government agencies and businesses. The company designs and manufactures a line of small unmanned aircraft systems (UAS), tactical missile systems (TMS), unmanned ground vehicles (UGV) and related services primarily for the Department of Defense (DoD). The business addresses the increasing value of intelligent, network-centric intelligence, surveillance and reconnaissance (ISR), communications, remote sensing, effects delivery and remote materials handling with innovative UAS, TMS, and UGV solutions. The company generates almost 60% of total revenue domestically.

	Annual Growth	04/19	04/20	04/21	04/22	04/23
Sales ($mil.)	14.5%	314.3	367.3	394.9	445.7	540.5
Net income ($ mil.)	-	47.4	41.1	23.3	(4.2)	(176.2)
Market value ($ mil.)	10.1%	1,797.4	1,579.8	2,893.6	2,105.7	2,639.8
Employees	16.3%	699	828	1,177	1,223	1,279

AES CORP

NYS: AES

4300 Wilson Boulevard
Arlington, VA 22203
Phone: 703 522-1315
Fax: 703 528-4510
Web: www.aes.com

CEO: Andres R Gluski
CFO: Stephen Coughlin
HR: -
FYE: December 31
Type: Public

The AES Corporation is a global energy company accelerating the future of energy. The company operates across four continents and serves 2.6 million customers in about 15 countries. AES has a generation portfolio of about 32,325 MW. Its main products include renewables (about 45%), natural gas (more than 30%), coal (about 20 %) and oil, diesel and pet coke (less than 5%). AES sells electricity to utilities, industrial users, and intermediaries. The company also sells power directly to end-users, such as homes and businesses. The non-regulated generates the biggest share of electricity, while regulated generates about 30%. The US supplies about 35% of AES' revenue.

	Annual Growth	12/19	12/20	12/21	12/22	12/23
Sales ($mil.)	5.6%	10,189	9,660.0	11,141	12,617	12,668
Net income ($ mil.)	(4.8%)	303.0	46.0	(409.0)	(546.0)	249.0
Market value ($ mil.)	(0.8%)	13,327	15,738	16,274	19,260	12,892
Employees	-	-	8,200	8,450	9,100	9,600

AETEA INFORMATION TECHNOLOGY, INC.

1445 RESEARCH BLVD STE 210
ROCKVILLE, MD 20850
Phone: 301 721-4200
Fax: –
Web: www.aetea.com

CEO: –
CFO: Charles V Brown III
HR: Toni Ricca
FYE: December 31
Type: Private

AETEA knows information technology backward and forward. The company provides systems integration, enterprise resource management software consulting, and other IT services. It also offers IT staffing services to a variety of customers, ranging from large global enterprises to small and midsized companies. Industries served include financial services, pharmaceuticals, and health care. AETEA also has a unit devoted to public sector clients, which targets the US Department of Defense, as well as civilian agencies. Clients have included ADP, BNP Paribas, and Bristol-Myers Squibb. The company operates from offices in Maryland, New Jersey, New York, Pennsylvania, and Washington. AETEA was established in 1979.

	Annual Growth	12/02	12/03	12/04	12/06	12/07
Sales ($mil.)	(2.6%)	–	–	74.2	73.8	68.5
Net income ($ mil.)	(20.2%)	–	–	7.7	0.6	3.9
Market value ($ mil.)	–	–	–	–	–	–
Employees		–	–	–	–	350

AETERNA ZENTARIS INC
NAS: AEZS

315 Sigma Drive, Suite 302D
Summerville, SC 29486
Phone: 843 900-3223
Fax: –
Web: www.zentaris.com

CEO: –
CFO: –
HR: –
FYE: December 31
Type: Public

terna Zentaris, formerly terna Laboratories, knows seriously ill patients can't wait an eternity for new drugs, so the firm is working to take lead drug candidates through trials and to approvals as quickly as possible. The company's pipeline got a boost from the purchase of Zentaris, which has drugs on the market and a dozen others in development for the treatment of cancer and endocrinology disorders. The firm's flagship drug, Centrotide, is an endocrine therapy used for in vitro fertilization. It is approved in 80 countries and is marketed worldwide (except for Japan) by Merck Serono; Shionogi and Nippon Kayaku market the drug in Japan.

	Annual Growth	12/18	12/19	12/20	12/21	12/22
Sales ($mil.)	(32.3%)	26.9	0.5	3.7	5.3	5.6
Net income ($ mil.)	–	4.2	(6.0)	(5.1)	(8.4)	(22.7)
Market value ($ mil.)	2.0%	14.3	4.4	2.1	1.7	15.4
Employees	17.5%	22	11	11	17	42

AFFILIATED FOODS MIDWEST COOPERATIVE, INC.

1301 W OMAHA AVE
NORFOLK, NE 687015872
Phone: 402 371-0555
Fax: –
Web: www.afmidwest.com

CEO: –
CFO: –
HR: –
FYE: June 26
Type: Private

Affiliated Foods Midwest Cooperative is a wholesale food distribution cooperative that supplies more than 800 independent grocers in some 15 states in the Midwest. From its handful of distribution centers in Kansas, Nebraska, and Wisconsin, the co-op distributes fresh produce, meats, deli items, baked goods, dairy products, and frozen foods, as well as general merchandise and equipment. It distributes goods under the Shurfine brand (from Topco Associates) and IGA labels. Additionally, Affiliated Foods Midwest provides marketing, merchandising, and warehousing support services for its members. The cooperative was formed in 1931 to make wholesale purchases for a group of retailers in Nebraska.

	Annual Growth	06/11	06/12	06/13	06/14	06/15
Sales ($mil.)	0.9%	–	1,486.3	1,391.7	1,477.5	1,527.3
Net income ($ mil.)	(19.5%)	–	2.8	2.7	2.8	1.5
Market value ($ mil.)	–	–	–	–	–	–
Employees		–	–	–	–	850

AFFILIATED FOODS, INC.

1401 W FARMERS AVE
AMARILLO, TX 791186134
Phone: 806 372-3851
Fax: –
Web: www.afiama.com

CEO: Randy Arceneaux
CFO: Noman Burr
HR: Sally Noriega
FYE: October 01
Type: Private

This company helps keep pantries stocked in the Texas Panhandle and elsewhere. Affiliated Foods is a leading wholesale distribution cooperative that supplies grocery stores and restaurants in about a half a dozen states, including Texas, New Mexico, and Oklahoma. It distributes fresh produce, meat, and non-food products, as well as dairy products and beverages through its Plains Dairy unit. Its Tri State Baking Company supplies bread and other baked goods. In addition, Affiliated Foods owns a stake in private-label products supplier Western Family Foods. The company was founded in 1946 as Panhandle Associated Grocers, which merged with South Plains Associated Grocers to form Affiliated Foods in 1968.

	Annual Growth	09/18	09/19*	10/20	10/21	10/22
Sales ($mil.)	4.4%	–	1,450.9	1,556.9	1,532.4	1,652.3
Net income ($ mil.)	(32.5%)	–	2.0	1.6	1.7	0.6
Market value ($ mil.)	–	–	–	–	–	–
Employees		–	–	–	–	1,200

*Fiscal year change

AFFILIATED MANAGERS GROUP INC.
NYS: AMG

777 South Flagler Drive
West Palm Beach, FL 33401
Phone: 800 345-1100
Fax: –
Web: www.amg.com

CEO: Jay C Horgen
CFO: Thomas M Wojcik
HR: –
FYE: December 31
Type: Public

Affiliated Managers Group, Inc. (AMG) is a leading partner to independent active investment management firms globally. AMG's Affiliates manage about $651 billion in assets across a broad range of return-oriented strategies. Through its affiliates, the company provides a comprehensive and diverse range of return-oriented strategies designed to assist institutional and retail investors as well as high net worth clients. AMG offers centralized capabilities including strategy, marketing and distribution, and product development. Affiliates currently manage assets for investors in more than 50 countries, including all major developed markets. Majority of the company's sales comes from the US.

	Annual Growth	12/19	12/20	12/21	12/22	12/23
Sales ($mil.)	(2.1%)	2,239.6	2,027.5	2,412.4	2,329.6	2,057.8
Net income ($ mil.)	155.9%	15.7	202.2	565.7	1,145.9	672.9
Market value ($ mil.)	15.6%	2,813.4	3,376.4	5,461.7	5,259.9	5,027.1
Employees	–	4,000	3,900	4,050	3,950	4,000

AFFINITY INTERACTIVE

3755 BREAKTHROUGH WAY STE 300
LAS VEGAS, NV 891353051
Phone: 702 341-2400
Fax: –
Web: www.affinitygaming.com

CEO: Andrei Scrivens
CFO: Mary E Higgins
HR: Ana Flores
FYE: December 31
Type: Private

Affinity Gaming operates nine casinos, hotels, RV parks, and slot routes in Nevada and the Midwest. The Primm Valley Resort & Casino in Primm, Nevada has about 625 hotel rooms and some 600 slot machines, as well as more than 20 table games and a William Hill race and sports book. It also houses restaurants, lounges, a gift shop, and a video arcade. Other Affinity properties are located in smaller towns throughout Nevada, including Whiskey Pete's, Buffalo Bill's, and Rail City. In addition, the firm has a handful of locations in Iowa and Missouri.

AFFINITY SOLUTIONS, INC.

112 W 34TH ST FL 18
NEW YORK, NY 101200001
Phone: 212 822-9600
Fax: -
Web: www.affinity.solutions

CEO: Jonathan Silver
CFO: Gary Starr
HR: -
FYE: December 31
Type: Private

Affinity Solutions is a relationship marketing agency that specializes in loyalty programs for such companies as financial services providers, insurance agencies, and publishers. The firm designs and implements marketing campaigns that integrate rewards, benefits, advice, and interactive services with goal of creating customer loyalty towards its clients. In addition, Affinity Solutions offers such services as database marketing, data analytics, and creative marketing services. The company, which is headquartered in New York City, was founded in 1998.

	Annual Growth	12/02	12/03	12/04	12/06	12/07
Sales ($mil.)	77.1%	-	-	3.0	4.3	16.6
Net income ($ mil.)	(48.8%)	-	-	2.5	2.9	0.3
Market value ($ mil.)	-	-	-	-	-	-
Employees	-	-	-	-	-	140

AFFIRMATIVE INSURANCE HOLDINGS INC

4450 Sojourn Drive, Suite 500
Addison, TX 75001
Phone: 972 728-6300
Fax: -
Web: -

CEO: Michael J McClure
CFO: Earl R Fonville
HR: Jacqueline Debowski
FYE: December 31
Type: Public

If you've got an iffy driving record or let your insurance lapse, can you still get auto coverage? This company answers in the Affirmative. Affirmative Insurance Holdings, through its subsidiaries, writes nonstandard auto insurance policies -- that is, coverage for drivers in high-risk categories due to their age, driving records, and other factors. It sells its policies through about 5,300 independent agents in seven southern and mid-western states. Affirmative sold its nearly 200 company-owned retail locations (including A-Affordable, Driver's Choice, InsureOne, and USAgencies stores) in late 2013. Investment firm J.C. Flowers controls more than half of the company.

	Annual Growth	12/10	12/11	12/12	12/13	12/14
Assets ($mil.)	(18.0%)	745.7	444.8	338.4	386.8	337.7
Net income ($ mil.)	-	(88.9)	(164.2)	(51.9)	30.7	(32.2)
Market value ($ mil.)	(17.4%)	43.1	8.6	2.3	41.2	20.0
Employees	(21.2%)	1,268	1,078	949	522	489

AFFYMAX INC
NBB: AFFY

19200 Stevens Creek Blvd. Suite 240
Cupertino, CA 95014
Phone: 650 812-8700
Fax: -
Web: www.affymax.com

CEO: Jonathan M Couchman
CFO: Mark G Thompson
HR: -
FYE: December 31
Type: Public

Affymax is training peptides to give red blood cells a pep talk. The biotechnology firm is researching and developing drugs based upon peptides, which can help regulate biological processes. Its leading drug candidate, Omontys (peginesatide), was approved by the FDA in 2012 as a treatment for anemia due to chronic kidney disease. Affymax believes Omontys, which was developed and commercialized through a partnership with Japan's Takeda Pharmaceutical, will prove to be cheaper and longer lasting than the EPO stimulants currently used on dialysis patients. However, the product was recalled in 2013 due to adverse reactions to the drug.

	Annual Growth	12/09	12/10	12/11	12/12	12/13
Sales ($mil.)	(67.0%)	114.9	112.5	47.7	94.4	1.4
Net income ($ mil.)	-	(76.5)	(14.1)	(61.4)	(93.4)	(14.4)
Market value ($ mil.)	(57.9%)	927.5	249.3	247.8	711.9	29.2
Employees	(59.1%)	143	140	130	304	4

AFFYMETRIX, INC.

3380 CENTRAL EXPY
SANTA CLARA, CA 950510704
Phone: 408 731-5000
Fax: -
Web: www.thermofisher.com

CEO: -
CFO: -
HR: Anna Gregorio
FYE: December 31
Type: Private

Affymetrix microarray solutions are now branded Applied Biosystems and include all necessary components for a microarray experiment, from arrays and reagents to instruments and software. Its solutions enable scientists and clinicians to understand underlying disease mechanisms, identify biomarkers for personalized medicine, create novel molecular diagnostic tests, and improve genetic marker-assisted breeding programs in agriculture, thereby translating research results into biology for a better world. Its popular products have included Clariom D Assay, Axiom Precision Medicine Research Array, and CarrierScan Assay. Its key applications have also included Transcriptome Analysis, Human Genotyping for Precision Medicine Research, Cytogenetics Analysis, miRNA Profiling, Large-scale Biobank Genotyping, and Plant and Animal Genotyping.

	Annual Growth	12/10	12/11	12/12	12/13	12/14
Sales ($mil.)	8.7%	-	-	295.6	330.4	349.0
Net income ($ mil.)	-	-	-	(10.7)	(16.3)	(3.8)
Market value ($ mil.)	-	-	-	-	-	-
Employees	-	-	-	-	-	1,100

AFLAC INC
NYS: AFL

1932 Wynnton Road
Columbus, GA 31999
Phone: 706 323-3431
Fax: 706 596-3488
Web: www.aflac.com

CEO: Daniel P Amos
CFO: J T Daniels
HR: -
FYE: December 31
Type: Public

Aflac sells supplemental health and life insurance products, including first sector insurance coverage and third sector insurance coverage for cancer, hospitalization, and income support in Japan; and cancer, accident, critical illness and short-term disability insurance in the US. Aflac Japan is the largest insurer in Japan in terms of cancer and medical (third sector insurance products) policies in force, while Aflac US is expanding its product offerings to network dental and vision and employer paid group life and disability. Aflac sells policies that pay cash benefits to more than 50 million people worldwide. The company generates some 65% of its revenue outside of the US.

	Annual Growth	12/19	12/20	12/21	12/22	12/23
Assets ($mil.)	(4.6%)	152,768	165,086	157,542	131,017	126,724
Net income ($ mil.)	9.0%	3,304.0	4,778.0	4,325.0	4,201.0	4,659.0
Market value ($ mil.)	11.8%	30,602	25,725	33,777	41,616	47,725
Employees	2.2%	11,729	6,239	6,492	12,882	12,785

AFP IMAGING CORP.

250 Clearbrook Road
Elmsford, NY 10523
Phone: 914 592-6100
Fax: 914 592-6148
Web: www.afpimaging.com

CEO: -
CFO: -
HR: -
FYE: June 30
Type: Public

Getting ready for a dental implant, or just wanting to look that gift horse in the mouth? AFP Imaging (dba ImageWorks) can assist you. The company makes imaging systems, for medical, dental, veterinary, and industrial markets. Products range from good old-fashioned film-based X-ray machines and film processors to digital computed tomography scanners and three-dimensional digital radiography systems (including both the sensors and display software). Its digital radiography systems are designed for use in both human and animal dental diagnostics. Its brands include Dent-X, EVA-Vet, and Mini-Medical. ImageWorks also distributes the NewTom line of cone beam 3-D imaging units for Italy's Quantitative Radiology.

	Annual Growth	06/04	06/05	06/06	06/07	06/08
Sales ($mil.)	14.7%	19.8	23.1	25.0	28.7	34.3
Net income ($ mil.)	-	1.3	1.9	1.0	(4.7)	(11.0)
Market value ($ mil.)	(34.3%)	0.0	0.0	0.0	0.0	0.0
Employees	10.1%	83	84	83	115	122

AFRICARE

1100 CONNECTICUT AVE NW STE 330
WASHINGTON, DC 200364154
Phone: 202 328-5320
Fax: –
Web: www.africare.org

CEO: –
CFO: –
HR: –
FYE: June 30
Type: Private

Africare helps Africans help themselves. The not-for-profit organization provides support to communities in Africa in areas such as health care and HIV/AIDS prevention, food security, agriculture, education, environmental management, and water resource development. It also works to help people create small businesses, such as growing sunflowers and pressing the seeds into cooking oil, and to provide emergency humanitarian aid when needed. Africare has given more than $800 million in aid to some 35 countries in Africa, funding more than 2,500 projects. William and Barbara Kirker founded the organization in 1970.

	Annual Growth	06/09	06/10	06/11	06/15	06/18
Sales ($mil.)	(13.2%)	–	54.8	76.9	49.2	17.6
Net income ($ mil.)	–	–	(1.1)	0.8	(2.2)	(2.7)
Market value ($ mil.)	–	–	–	–	–	–
Employees	–	–	–	–	–	1,000

AFTER, INC.

1 SELLECK ST STE 5
NORWALK, CT 068551117
Phone: 203 254-5330
Fax: –
Web: www.afterinc.com

CEO: –
CFO: –
HR: –
FYE: December 31
Type: Private

After, Inc. is a pioneer in the warranty business ? providing product registration, marketing, analytics, and program administration to warranty organizations across a wide range of industries. After, Inc. partners with some of the world's top brands to help transform their warranty businesses, driving customer satisfaction post-purchase, higher product reliability, deeper brand equity and additional revenue/profit opportunities. Headquartered in Norwalk, Connecticut and with offices in New York City, After, Inc. is part of Galway Holdings Group, a financial services distribution company. The company was founded in 2005.

	Annual Growth	12/03	12/04	12/05	12/06	12/07
Sales ($mil.)	6.3%	–	–	9.9	9.1	11.2
Net income ($ mil.)	–	–	–	0.2	0.0	(0.1)
Market value ($ mil.)	–	–	–	–	–	–
Employees	–	–	–	–	–	105

AG MORTGAGE INVESTMENT TRUST INC

NYS: MITT

245 Park Avenue, 26th Floor
New York, NY 10167
Phone: 212 692-2000
Fax: –
Web: www.agmit.com

CEO: –
CFO: –
HR: –
FYE: December 31
Type: Public

AG Mortgage Investment Trust invests in, acquires, and manages a diverse portfolio of residential mortgage assets, as well as other real estate-related securities and financial assets. Residential mortgage-backed securities backed by US government agencies, including Fannie Mae, Freddie Mac, and Ginnie Mae, known as "Agency RMBS," make up more than 50% of the mortgage real estate investment trust's (REIT) portfolio. Credit assets, including RMBS not issued or backed by the government, account for most of the rest. Formed in 2011 by executives of investment adviser Angelo Gordon looking to profit from a recovery in the US mortgage bond market, the mortgage REIT is managed by a subsidiary of Angelo Gordon.

	Annual Growth	12/19	12/20	12/21	12/22	12/23
Assets ($mil.)	9.0%	4,347.8	1,400.0	3,362.7	4,369.8	6,126.4
Net income ($ mil.)	(12.8%)	92.9	(420.9)	104.2	(53.1)	53.8
Market value ($ mil.)	(19.9%)	453.9	86.8	301.7	156.3	186.9
Employees	–	–	–	–	–	–

AG PROCESSING INC A COOPERATIVE

12700 W DODGE RD
OMAHA, NE 681542154
Phone: 402 496-7809
Fax: –
Web: www.agp.com

CEO: Chris Schaffer
CFO: Kyle Droescher
HR: Chris Tibbs
FYE: August 31
Type: Private

Soy far, soy good for Ag Processing (AGP), the largest farmer-owned soybean processor in the world, and roughly the fourth-largest soybean processor in the US based on capacity. It purchases and processes more than 5.5 million acres of members' soybeans per year. The farmer-owned cooperative is also a leading supplier of refined vegetable oil in the US. It procures, processes, markets, and transports grains and grain products, ranging from human food ingredients to livestock feed to renewable fuels. AGP is owned by about 180 local and regional cooperatives and represents more than 250,000 farmers in 15 states throughout the US.

	Annual Growth	08/17	08/18	08/19	08/20	08/21
Sales ($mil.)	44.3%	–	–	–	4,043.9	5,836.0
Net income ($ mil.)	(35.4%)	–	–	–	294.6	190.4
Market value ($ mil.)	–	–	–	–	–	–
Employees	–	–	–	–	–	1,456

AG&E HOLDINGS INC.

223 PRATT ST
HAMMONTON, NJ 080371719
Phone: 609 704-3000
Fax: –
Web: agegamingcom.wordpress.com

CEO: Anthony Tomasello
CFO: Francis McCarthy
HR: –
FYE: December 31
Type: Private

After selling assets and losing a key contract, AG&E Holdings, formerly known as Wells-Gardner Electronics, is resetting its business as a distributor of electronic parts to the casino and gaming markets. The company sells parts for video gaming machines to some 700 casinos in the US. In 2014 the company sold its LCD business and in 2015 it lost a contract with GTech to supply video lottery terminals for the Illinois Lottery. In 2016 AG&E bought Advanced Gaming Associates (AGA), which services slot machines in the US. AG&E changed its name from Wells-Gardner in 2014.

AGCO CORP.

NYS: AGCO

4205 River Green Parkway
Duluth, GA 30096
Phone: 770 813-9200
Fax: –
Web: www.agcocorp.com

CEO: Eric P Hansotia
CFO: Damon J Audia
HR: Dennis Branch
FYE: December 31
Type: Public

AGCO makes tractors, combines, hay and forage tools, sprayers, grain storage and protein production systems, seeding and tillage implements, and replacement parts for agricultural end uses. It sells through a global network of almost 3,200 dealers and distributors spanning about 140 countries. It also builds diesel engines, gears, and generators through its power engines unit. Core brands include Challenger, Fendt, GSI, Massey Ferguson, Precision Planting and Valtra. AGCO Finance offers financing services to retail customers and dealers via a venture with Rabobank, a Dutch bank specializing in agricultural loans. Europe accounts for nearly 60% of AGCO's sales.

	Annual Growth	12/19	12/20	12/21	12/22	12/23
Sales ($mil.)	12.4%	9,041.4	9,149.7	11,138	12,651	14,412
Net income ($ mil.)	74.9%	125.2	427.1	897.0	889.6	1,171.4
Market value ($ mil.)	12.0%	5,756.5	7,682.1	8,645.6	10,335	9,047.2
Employees	7.4%	21,000	21,400	23,300	25,600	27,900

HOOVER'S MASTERLIST OF U.S. COMPANIES 2024

AGE GROUP LTD.

2 PARK AVE FL 18
NEW YORK, NY 100165675
Phone: 212 213-9500
Fax: –
Web: www.agegroup.com

CEO: Harold Ebani
CFO: –
HR: –
FYE: December 31
Type: Private

People like to be comfy under there, no matter what their age group. Age Group makes and markets sleepwear, lingerie, and underwear under the brand name Of the Moment, as well as apparel and accessories under licensed names including Hello Kitty, Disney, Roca Wear, and American Tourister, and others. A leading wholesaler, Age Group also manufactures and designs pet accessories, including an exclusive line of pet apparel, bedding, and grooming supplies under the Martha Stewart brand, for sale in PetSmart stores. The company's products are distributed through large-scale department stores nationwide. Age Group's age? The company has been in the design and manufacturing business for more than 25 years.

AGENUS INC   NAS: AGEN

3 Forbes Road
Lexington, MA 02421
Phone: 781 674-4400
Fax: –
Web: www.agenusbio.com

CEO: Garo H Armen
CFO: –
HR: Hannah Soulard
FYE: December 31
Type: Public

Agenus is a clinical-stage company advancing an extensive pipeline of immune checkpoint antibodies, adoptive cell therapies (through its subsidiary MiNK Therapeutics, Inc. (MiNK)) and adjuvants and vaccines (through its subsidiary SaponiQx, Inc. (SaponiQx)) to fight cancer and other immune related diseases. This robust product pipeline is supported by its in-house capabilities, including current good manufacturing practice (cGMP) manufacturing and a clinical operations platform. The company's lead drug candidate in the series, its most advanced antibody candidates are balstilimab (an anti-PD-1 antibody) and zalifrelimab (an anti-CTLA-4 antibody), which are in Phase 2 trials of balstilimab monotherapy and balstilimab/zalifrelimab combination for patients with second-line cervical cancer. Agenus is also developing viral vaccines and QS-21 Stimulon, an improved vaccine adjuvant to make vaccines more effective. The vast majority of its revenue comes from its domestic operations.

	Annual Growth	12/19	12/20	12/21	12/22	12/23
Sales ($mil.)	1.0%	150.0	88.2	295.7	98.0	156.3
Net income ($ mil.)	–	(107.7)	(180.9)	(23.9)	(220.1)	(245.8)
Market value ($ mil.)	(32.8%)	1,605.1	1,254.1	1,269.9	946.5	326.5
Employees	–	328	359	441	533	–

AGEAGLE AERIAL SYSTEMS INC (NEW)   ASE: UAVS

8863 E. 34th Street North
Wichita, KS 67226
Phone: 620 325-6363
Fax: –
Web: www.ageagle.com

CEO: –
CFO: –
HR: –
FYE: December 31
Type: Public

When other oil companies have given up, EnerJex Resources steps in and injects some capital. The oil and gas exploration and production company works primarily in Eastern Kansas, buying producing properties that it feels are undervalued or that were abandoned by other oil companies when oil prices were below $10 a barrel. The company, which has proved reserves of 1.2 million barrels of oil equivalent, holds full or partial interest in half a dozen oil, gas, and oil and gas projects across Kansas. It uses enhanced drilling techniques to recover additional oil and gas from already explored fields.

AGFIRST FARM CREDIT BANK

1901 MAIN ST
COLUMBIA, SC 292012443
Phone: 803 799-5000
Fax: –
Web: www.agfirst.com

CEO: –
CFO: –
HR: –
FYE: December 31
Type: Private

AgFirst Farm Credit Bank is a member of the Farm Credit System, the largest agricultural lending organization in the US and one of the four banks in the Farm Credit Systems. Boasting $40 billion in assets, Agfirst provides financing to about 20 farmer-owned financial cooperatives in about 15 Eastern states and Puerto Rico. These Associations provide real estate and production financing to more than 80,000 farmers, agribusinesses and rural homeowners. It also offer direct continuing education to agricultural producers and the lenders who support them through its Farm Credit University. AgFirst Farm Credit Bank was founded in 1916.

	Annual Growth	12/12	12/13	12/14	12/15	12/17
Assets ($mil.)	3.0%	–	–	–	30,621	32,487
Net income ($ mil.)	1.2%	–	–	–	336.8	344.7
Market value ($ mil.)	–	–	–	–	–	–
Employees	–	–	–	–	–	530

AGENT INFORMATION SOFTWARE INC   NBB: AIFS

10535 Foothill Blvd., Suite 200
Rancho Cucamonga, CA 91730
Phone: 800 776-6939
Fax: –
Web: www.auto-graphics.com

CEO: –
CFO: –
HR: –
FYE: December 31
Type: Public

Agent Information Software (AIS) seeks to organize information on your behalf. A holding company, AIS owns two niche information management software subsidiaries: Auto-Graphics and AgentLegal. Auto-Graphics, which primarily serves public libraries, offers hosted software used to manage, share (e.g. interlibrary loans), and search library resources. On the other hand, AgentLegal's software caters to law firm professionals, including firm CFOs looking to manage the cost of search resources; law librarians and IT departments who manage and protect information; and researchers who gather information. AIS was formed in 2009 to take over Auto-Graphics' stock.

AGILE THERAPEUTICS INC   NAS: AGRX

500 College Road East, Suite 300
Princeton, NJ 08540
Phone: 609 683-1880
Fax: –
Web: www.agiletherapeutics.com

CEO: Al Altomari
CFO: Scott M Coiante
HR: –
FYE: December 31
Type: Public

If you'd rather have a patch than The Pill, Agile Therapeutics is positioned to provide. The development-stage pharmaceutical company uses its proprietary SkinFusion patch technology to create hormone-based contraceptive products for women. Its FDA approved product Twirla, a once-weekly patch that uses the same hormone combination as oral contraceptives but delivers it at a sustained level. It's the first patch to deliver levonorgestrel, a synthetic hormone. Other products in Agile's pipeline are also contraceptives but with different hormone configurations. Founded in 1997, Agile Therapeutics has operation in Princeton, New Jersey.

	Annual Growth	12/18	12/19	12/20	12/21	12/22
Sales ($mil.)	264.8%	0.1	0.3	1.3	9.8	19.1
Net income ($ mil.)	–	(2.1)	(2.5)	(4.9)	(30.1)	(58.3)
Market value ($ mil.)	(11.3%)	2.5	2.0	26.5	6.9	1.5
Employees	98.4%	6	10	11	124	93

	Annual Growth	12/18	12/19	12/20	12/21	12/22
Sales ($mil.)	0.5%	5.2	5.6	5.4	5.2	5.3
Net income ($ mil.)	(7.5%)	0.5	0.5	0.4	0.0	0.4
Market value ($ mil.)	18.6%	3.8	10.5	11.8	8.9	7.5
Employees	–	–	–	–	–	–

	Annual Growth	12/19	12/20	12/21	12/22	12/23
Sales ($mil.)	–	–	0.7	4.1	10.9	19.6
Net income ($ mil.)	–	(18.6)	(51.9)	(74.9)	(25.4)	(14.5)
Market value ($ mil.)	(6.0%)	7.4	8.5	1.4	0.7	5.8
Employees	6.1%	15	28	30	22	19

AGILENT TECHNOLOGIES, INC.　　　　　　　　　　　NYS: A

5301 Stevens Creek Blvd.　　　　　　　　　　　　　CEO: –
Santa Clara, CA 95051　　　　　　　　　　　　　　CFO: –
Phone: 800 227-9770　　　　　　　　　　　　　　　HR: –
Fax: 408 345-8474　　　　　　　　　　　　FYE: October 31
Web: www.agilent.com　　　　　　　　　　　　Type: Public

Agilent Technologies is a leading maker of scientific testing equipment. Agilent supplies a slew of analytical and measurement instruments, including gas and liquid chromatographs, mass spectrometers, spectroscopy, software and informatics, lab automation and robotics, vacuum technology and cell analysis. Its operations include products used in the pharmaceutical, biotechnology, academic and government, chemical and energy, food, and environment and forensics markets. The company's domestic sales accounts for about a third of total revenue.

	Annual Growth	10/19	10/20	10/21	10/22	10/23
Sales ($mil.)	7.3%	5,163.0	5,339.0	6,319.0	6,848.0	6,833.0
Net income ($ mil.)	3.7%	1,071.0	719.0	1,210.0	1,254.0	1,240.0
Market value ($ mil.)	8.1%	22,128	29,823	46,006	40,415	30,197
Employees	2.7%	16,300	16,400	17,000	18,100	18,100

AGILITI HEALTH, INC.

6625 W 78TH ST STE 300　　　　　　　　　CEO: Thomas Leonard
MINNEAPOLIS, MN 554392650　　　　　　　CFO: James Pekarek
Phone: 952 893-3200　　　　　　　　　　　　　　　HR: –
Fax: –　　　　　　　　　　　　　　　　　　FYE: December 31
Web: www.uhs.com　　　　　　　　　　　　　Type: Private

When it comes to medical equipment, Universal Hospital Services (UHS) has a whole galaxy of offerings. Founded in 1939, the company leases movable medical equipment to hospitals and care providers throughout the US. UHS has a pool of more than 700,000 pieces of equipment in specialty areas such as critical care, respiratory therapy, and newborn care, which it leases to more than 7,000 hospitals and alternate site care providers throughout all 50 states. The company also sells new and used equipment and disposable supplies, and it provides equipment maintenance services. UHS, which is owned by investment firm Irving Place Capital Management, plans to go public as Agiliti.

AGILYSYS INC (DE)　　　　　　　　　　　　　　NMS: AGYS

3655 Brookside Parkway, Suite 300　　　　　　CEO: Ramesh Srinivasan
Alpharetta, GA 30022　　　　　　　　　　　CFO: William D Wood III
Phone: 770 810-7800　　　　　　　　　　　　HR: Theresa Putnal
Fax: –　　　　　　　　　　　　　　　　　　　FYE: March 31
Web: www.agilysys.com　　　　　　　　　　　Type: Public

Agilysys is a leading provider of IT services and software to customers across the hospitality industry. Its areas of expertise include point-of-sale (POS) systems, payment, reservation and table management, property management, inventory and procurement, business analytics, and guest loyalty programs. The company delivers cloud-native SaaS and on-premise-ready guest-centric technology solutions for hotels, resorts and cruise lines, casinos, corporate food service management, restaurants, universities, stadiums, and healthcare sectors. The Agilysys Hospitality Experience Cloud offers solution ecosystems that combine core operational systems for property management (PMS), point-of-sale (POS), and Inventory and Procurement (I&P) with Experience Enhancers that meaningfully improve interactions for guests and employees. Its Core solutions and Experience Enhancers are selectively combined in Hospitality Solution Studios tailored to specific hospitality settings and business needs. Organized in 1963 as Pioneer-Standard Electronics.

	Annual Growth	03/19	03/20	03/21	03/22	03/23
Sales ($mil.)	8.9%	140.8	160.8	137.2	162.6	198.1
Net income ($ mil.)	–	(13.2)	(34.1)	(21.0)	6.5	14.6
Market value ($ mil.)	40.5%	536.2	423.0	1,214.7	1,010.0	2,089.7
Employees	14.3%	936	1,275	1,350	1,400	1,600

AGIOS PHARMACEUTICALS INC　　　　　　　　NMS: AGIO

88 Sidney Street　　　　　　　　　　　　　　CEO: Brian Goff
Cambridge, MA 02139　　　　　　　　　　　CFO: Cecilia Jones
Phone: 617 649-8600　　　　　　　　　　　　　　　HR: –
Fax: –　　　　　　　　　　　　　　　　　　FYE: December 31
Web: www.agios.com　　　　　　　　　　　　Type: Public

Agios Pharmaceuticals wants to say " adios " to cancer. The biopharmaceutical company is developing metabolic treatments for certain types of cancer and rare genetic diseases. Its lead drug candidates, AG-221 and AG-120, are oral tablets that apply cellular metabolism to treat patients with cancers that harbor certain mutations. Agios has a development collaboration agreement with Celgene for its cancer metabolism program. Another drug candidate, AG-348, would treat a form of hemolytic anemia known as pyruvate kinase deficiency, or PK deficiency. Agios went public in 2013, raising about $106 million in its IPO, which it plans to use to further fund clinical development for its drug candidates.

	Annual Growth	12/19	12/20	12/21	12/22	12/23
Sales ($mil.)	(30.9%)	117.9	203.2	–	14.2	26.8
Net income ($ mil.)	–	(411.5)	(327.4)	1,604.7	(231.8)	(352.1)
Market value ($ mil.)	(17.4%)	2,671.4	2,424.1	1,838.9	1,570.9	1,245.9
Employees	(7.9%)	536	562	392	393	386

AGNC INVESTMENT CORP　　　　　　　　　　NMS: AGNC

2 Bethesda Metro Center, 12th Floor　　　　　　CEO: Gary D Kain
Bethesda, MD 20814　　　　　　　　　　　　CFO: Bernice E Bell
Phone: 301 968-9315　　　　　　　　　　　　　　　HR: –
Fax: 301 968-9301　　　　　　　　　　　　　FYE: December 31
Web: www.agnc.com　　　　　　　　　　　　Type: Public

AGNC Investment (formerly known as American Capital Agency) is a leading provider of private capital to the US housing market, enhancing liquidity in the residential real estate mortgage markets and, in turn, facilitating home ownership in the US. The internally-managed mortgage real estate investment trust (REIT) invests primarily in Agency residential mortgage-backed securities (Agency RMBS) on a leveraged basis. These investments consist of residential mortgage pass-through securities and collateralized mortgage obligations for which the principal and interest payments are guaranteed by Fannie Mae, Freddie Mac and Ginnie Mae. The company may also invest in other assets related to the housing, mortgage or real estate markets that are not guaranteed by a GSE or US Government agency. Founded in 2008, AGNC is headquartered in Bethesda, Maryland.

	Annual Growth	12/19	12/20	12/21	12/22	12/23
Assets ($mil.)	(10.8%)	113,082	81,817	68,149	51,748	71,596
Net income ($ mil.)	(31.1%)	688.0	(266.0)	749.0	(1,190.0)	155.0
Market value ($ mil.)	(13.7%)	12,275	10,831	10,442	7,186.0	6,811.1
Employees	1.0%	51	50	50	51	53

AGNES SCOTT COLLEGE, INC.

141 E COLLEGE AVE　　　　　　　　　　　　CEO: Elizabeth Kiss
DECATUR, GA 300303797　　　　　　　　　　CFO: John Hegman
Phone: 404 471-6000　　　　　　　　　　　　HR: Amanda Garlin
Fax: –　　　　　　　　　　　　　　　　　　FYE: June 30
Web: www.agnesscott.edu　　　　　　　　　　Type: Private

Great Scott, Agnes, it's a liberal arts college for women! Agnes Scott College (ASC) offers bachelor of arts degrees in 33 majors and 27 minors, with pre-law and pre-medicine programs and dual degree programs in architecture, engineering, and nursing, as well as post-baccalaureate programs. The school also grants master of arts in teaching degrees in English, biology, chemistry, physics, and mathematics. Enrollment in 2008 was about 850 students. Founded in 1889, ASC is affiliated with the Presbyterian Church and has an endowment of about $300 million. Tuition, fees, room and board cost $39,000 per year. The 100-acre campus, rated one of the most beautiful in the country, is in Decatur, Georgia.

	Annual Growth	06/15	06/16	06/20	06/21	06/22
Sales ($mil.)	8.0%	–	58.8	81.4	76.7	93.2
Net income ($ mil.)	–	–	(16.5)	(4.8)	(3.0)	3.8
Market value ($ mil.)	–	–	–	–	–	–
Employees	–	–	–	–	–	350

AGREE REALTY CORP.
NYS: ADC

70 E. Long Lake Road
Bloomfield Hills, MI 48304
Phone: 248 737-4190
Fax: 248 737-9110
Web: www.agreerealty.com

CEO: Joel Agree
CFO: Peter Coughenour
HR: –
FYE: December 31
Type: Public

Shopping sprees really agree with Agree Realty. The self-managed real estate investment trust (REIT) owns, develops, and manages retail real estate. It owns around 820 retail properties spanning approximately 14.6 million square feet of leasable space across 45-plus states. Most of its tenants are national retailers, with its largest tenants being Sherwin-Williams, Wal-Mart, and TJX Companies. The REIT typically acquires either property portfolios or single-asset, net lease retail properties worth approximately $702.9 million with creditworthy tenants. It was founded in 1971 by CEO Richard Agree.

	Annual Growth	12/19	12/20	12/21	12/22	12/23
Sales ($mil.)	30.1%	187.5	248.6	339.3	429.8	537.5
Net income ($ mil.)	20.7%	80.1	91.4	122.3	152.4	170.0
Market value ($ mil.)	(2.7%)	7,053.4	6,692.6	7,173.1	7,129.8	6,327.7
Employees	15.1%	41	49	57	76	72

AGRIBANK, FCB

30 7TH ST E STE 1600
SAINT PAUL, MN 551011850
Phone: 651 282-8800
Fax: –
Web: www.agribank.com

CEO: William J Thone
CFO: –
HR: Laura Kemmerer
FYE: December 31
Type: Private

AgriBank puts the "green" in green acres. The borrower-owned bank provides wholesale lending and business services to Farm Credit System (FCS) associations in America's heartland. Established by Congress in 1916, the FCS is a nationwide network of cooperatives that provide loans and financial services for farmers, ranchers, agribusiness, timber producers, and rural homeowners. The co-ops write loans for homes, land, equipment, and other farm operating costs. AgriBank also provides credit to rural electric, water, and telephone systems. The largest bank in the FCS, its footprint includes more than half of the cropland in the US, covering 15 states from Ohio to Wyoming and Minnesota to Arkansas.

	Annual Growth	12/05	12/06	12/07	12/08	12/09
Assets ($mil.)	(99.9%)	–	–	–	63,286	73.8
Net income ($ mil.)	(99.7%)	–	–	–	329.2	0.9
Market value ($ mil.)	–	–	–	–	–	–
Employees	–	–	–	–	–	283

AGRITECH WORLDWIDE INC

1120 Avenue of the Americas, Suite 1514
New York, NY 10036
Phone: 847 549-6002
Fax: –
Web: www.ztrim.com

CEO: –
CFO: –
HR: –
FYE: December 31
Type: Public

Z Trim Holdings is trying to cut the fat while at the same time allowing users to chew the fat. Its core product Z Trim, developed and licensed by the USDA, is a zero-calorie fiber ingredient typically made from corn or oats that is manufactured into gel and powdered form to replace fat, gums, starches, and carbohydrates in foods. Z Trim sells its fat-replacement products as ingredients to food manufacturers, and foodservice companies. Founder and former CEO Gregory Halpern owns about 13% of Z Trim Holdings; individual investor Nurieel Akhamzadeh owns 5%.

	Annual Growth	12/12	12/13	12/14	12/15	12/16
Sales ($mil.)	(2.0%)	1.3	1.4	1.1	1.2	1.2
Net income ($ mil.)	–	(9.6)	(13.4)	(5.6)	(24.0)	(3.2)
Market value ($ mil.)	(72.4%)	269.7	86.8	58.1	6.5	1.6
Employees	(7.4%)	19	21	13	14	14

AGTEGRA COOPERATIVE

908 LAMONT ST S
ABERDEEN, SD 574015515
Phone: 605 225-5500
Fax: –
Web: www.agtegra.com

CEO: Jason Klootwyk
CFO: Robert Porter
HR: Patrick King
FYE: July 31
Type: Private

Who loves you a bushel and a peck? South Dakota Wheat Growers may; it is an agricultural co-op comprising some 6,800 member-farmers. It provides a grain warehouse along with grain marketing services intended to compete with big food and ag companies. In addition to storage and drying, Wheat Growers offers agronomy spreading and spraying, and transportation. It supplies feed, fertilizer, chemicals, and other farm-related provisions for members in and around counties in North and South Dakota. Wheat Growers generates more than half of its revenues through marketing some 160 million bushels of grain (corn, wheat, and soybeans) each year. Remaining revenues are made through agronomy and retail sales and services.

	Annual Growth	07/15	07/16	07/17	07/18	07/19
Sales ($mil.)	7.7%	–	1,209.2	1,275.6	1,544.3	1,509.7
Net income ($ mil.)	–	–	6.7	22.8	32.5	(6.0)
Market value ($ mil.)	–	–	–	–	–	–
Employees	–	–	–	–	–	638

AGWEST FARM CREDIT, FLCA

2001 S FLINT RD
SPOKANE, WA 992249198
Phone: 509 838-2429
Fax: –
Web: www.agwestfc.com

CEO: Phil Dipofi
CFO: –
HR: Kathy Payne
FYE: December 31
Type: Private

Northwest Farm Credit Services is a financial cooperative providing financing and related services to farmers, ranchers, agribusinesses, commercial fishermen, timber producers, rural homeowners and crop insurance customers in Montana, Idaho, Oregon, Washington and Alaska. The company has a network of around 45 branches and offers a broad range of flexible loan programs to meet the needs of people in the agriculture business. Northwest Farm Credit also provides equipment financing, appraisal services and crop and livestock insurance programs. It is part of the Farm Credit System, a network of lenders serving the US agriculture industry.

	Annual Growth	12/09	12/10	12/11	12/12	12/13
Assets ($mil.)	5.1%	–	–	8,696.7	9,471.2	9,604.7
Net income ($ mil.)	22.0%	–	–	159.2	187.3	236.9
Market value ($ mil.)	–	–	–	–	–	–
Employees	–	–	–	–	–	500

AGY HOLDING CORP.

2556 WAGENER RD
AIKEN, SC 298019572
Phone: 888 434-0945
Fax: –
Web: www.agy.com

CEO: Patrick J Burns
CFO: Jay W Ferguson
HR: Mary Flanigan
FYE: December 31
Type: Private

You may think of yarn as a soft textile but AGY Holding will make you think again. The company produces glass yarns (thin filaments of glass twisted together to form advanced fiber), which are used in myriad aerospace, automotive, construction, defense, electronics, industrial, and recreational applications. The US military, for example, reinforces Humvees and other armored vehicles with AGY's proprietary glass fiber. AGY products are differentiated by glass chemistry, coating technology, and form; brands include L Glass, S-2 Glass, and S-1 HM Glass. It makes glass fibers at two plants in the US and one in Hong Kong. Private equity firm Kohlberg & Co. owns AGY.

AHMC ANAHEIM REGIONAL MEDICAL CENTER LP

1111 W LA PALMA AVE
ANAHEIM, CA 928012804
Phone: 714 774-1450
Fax: –
Web: www.ahmchealth.com

CEO: –
CFO: –
HR: –
FYE: June 30
Type: Private

If you're feeling light-headed in the land of Angels, you might want to check yourself into AHMC Anaheim Regional Medical Center. The acute care Anaheim facility has some 220 beds and serves northern Orange County in California. Anaheim Regional also offers centers specifically devoted to diagnostic testing, heart care, orthopedics, pain management, and women's health and wellness. Its Advanced Endovascular Institute provides patients with specific programs and treatment options for circulatory problems. Anaheim Regional is owned by private hospital operator AHMC Healthcare.

	Annual Growth	09/92	09/93	09/94	09/95*	06/14
Sales ($mil.)	(1.7%)	–	–	–	0.0	0.0
Net income ($ mil.)	–	–	–	–	(0.0)	(0.0)
Market value ($ mil.)	–	–	–	–	–	–
Employees	–	–	–	–	–	4,230

*Fiscal year change

AHS HILLCREST MEDICAL CENTER, LLC

1120 S UTICA AVE
TULSA, OK 741044012
Phone: 918 579-1000
Fax: –
Web: www.hillcrestmedicalcenter.com

CEO: Kevin Gross
CFO: Joseph Mendoza
HR: Becky Billingslea
FYE: June 30
Type: Private

Hillcrest Medical Center, as part of the Hillcrest HealthCare System, provides a helping hand to health care patients in northeastern Oklahoma. The medical center operates health care facilities in Tulsa and surrounding areas. The main hospital facility has about 730 beds and offers emergency, cancer, cardiology, neurology, rehabilitation, and other acute and specialty care services. Hillcrest Medical Center also operates outpatient and extended care facilities, including general health and specialty clinics, and provides home health, foster care, and hospice services. The health care organization is part of Ardent Health Services.

	Annual Growth	06/12	06/13	06/14	06/15	06/16
Sales ($mil.)	7.5%	–	–	–	472.5	508.0
Net income ($ mil.)	89.4%	–	–	–	7.7	14.7
Market value ($ mil.)	–	–	–	–	–	–
Employees	–	–	–	–	–	2,126

AIADVERTISING INC

321 Sixth Street
San Antonio, TX 78215
Phone: 805 964-3313
Fax: –
Web: www.aiadvertising.com

NBB: AIAD
CEO: –
CFO: –
HR: –
FYE: December 31
Type: Public

Warp 9 (formerly Roaming Messenger) hopes to get all sorts of messages across. The company provides software used for e-commerce applications such as product presentation, online catalogs, and store management. Warp 9 also offers a Web-based e-mail and list management system that can be used for marketing and customer loyalty campaigns. Former chairman, president, and CFO Jonathan Lei owns about 48% of the company.

	Annual Growth	12/18	12/19	12/20	12/21	12/22
Sales ($mil.)	(13.0%)	11.8	9.2	9.7	6.9	6.7
Net income ($ mil.)	–	(2.9)	(10.1)	(1.3)	(8.5)	(8.5)
Market value ($ mil.)	(30.7%)	16.3	2.2	7.5	14.9	3.8
Employees	(17.6%)	65	49	31	50	30

AIM IMMUNOTECH INC

2117 SW Highway 484
Ocala, FL 34473
Phone: 352 448-7797
Fax: –
Web: www.aimimmuno.com

ASE: AIM
CEO: William M Mitchell
CFO: Robert Dickey IV
HR: –
FYE: December 31
Type: Public

Targeting chronic viral diseases and immune disorders, Hemispherx Biopharma hopes to do a world of good with its RNA (ribonucleic acid) and other drugs. The company has acquired the rights to Alferon N, an FDA-approved drug for genital warts that the company is developing to fight other viral diseases, such as West Nile virus. Hemispherx also is developing Ampligen, an intravenously administered RNA drug that is in clinical trials to treat HIV and chronic fatigue syndrome (CFS). Ampligen is also being tested as an adjuvant for vaccines conditions including seasonal flu and bird flu. The compound has received orphan status from the FDA for kidney cancer, melanoma, CFS, and HIV.

	Annual Growth	12/18	12/19	12/20	12/21	12/22
Sales ($mil.)	(21.3%)	0.4	0.1	0.2	0.1	0.1
Net income ($ mil.)	–	(9.8)	(9.5)	(14.4)	(19.1)	(19.4)
Market value ($ mil.)	14.6%	8.7	26.2	86.1	44.2	15.0
Employees	(7.7%)	33	26	23	23	24

AINOS INC

8880 Rio San Diego Drive, Suite 800
San Diego, CA 92108
Phone: 858 869-2986
Fax: –
Web: www.amarbio.com

NAS: AIMD
CEO: Chun-Hsien Tsai
CFO: –
HR: –
FYE: December 31
Type: Public

Amarillo -- home to cattlemen, prairies, and...interferon? Amarillo Biosciences hopes its low-dose interferon alpha (IFNa), which modulates the immune system, will help those suffering from a range of maladies, including viral and autoimmune diseases. The company's interferon technology, which uses a low-dose dissolving tablet, potentially offers effective treatment with fewer side effects than injectable forms of the drug. Amarillo Biosciences is developing its interferon technology as a treatment for flu, oral warts in HIV patients, and chronic cough. Through research partners, it is also investigating the drug in relation to Behcet's disease (a severe inflammatory disorder) and hepatitis C.

	Annual Growth	12/19	12/20	12/21	12/22	12/23
Sales ($mil.)	79.6%	0.0	0.0	0.6	3.5	0.1
Net income ($ mil.)	–	(1.6)	(1.5)	(3.9)	(14.0)	(13.8)
Market value ($ mil.)	–	–	–	–	2.9	9.6
Employees	84.2%	4	4	35	43	46

AIR LEASE CORP

2000 Avenue of the Stars, Suite 1000N
Los Angeles, CA 90067
Phone: 310 553-0555
Fax: –
Web: www.airleasecorp.com

NYS: AL
CEO: –
CFO: –
HR: –
FYE: December 31
Type: Public

Air Lease doesn't really lease air, unless of course you include the air inside the cabins of its fleet of airplanes. An aircraft leasing company, Air Lease buys new and used commercial aircraft from manufacturers and airlines and then leases to airline carriers in Europe, the Asia-Pacific region, and the Americas. It owns a fleet of almost 240 aircraft comprised of 181 single-aisle narrowbody jet aircraft, 40 twin-aisle widebody jet aircraft, and 19 turboprop aircraft. In addition to leasing, Air Lease also offers fleet management services such as lease management and sales.

	Annual Growth	12/19	12/20	12/21	12/22	12/23
Sales ($mil.)	7.4%	2,016.9	2,015.4	2,088.4	2,317.3	2,685.0
Net income ($ mil.)	1.2%	587.1	516.3	436.6	(97.0)	614.6
Market value ($ mil.)	(3.1%)	5,276.0	4,931.8	4,910.7	4,265.7	4,656.5
Employees	8.6%	117	120	129	151	163

AIR METHODS LLC

5500 S QUEBEC ST STE 300
GREENWOOD VILLAGE, CO 801111926
Phone: 855 896-9067
Fax: -
Web: www.airmethods.com

CEO: Jaelynn Williams
CFO: Peter Csapo
HR: -
FYE: December 31
Type: Private

Air Methods is the leading air medical service, delivering lifesaving care to more than 100,000 people every year. Air Methods is the preferred partner for hospitals and one of the largest community-based providers of air medical services. United Rotorcraft is the company's products division specializing in the design and manufacture of aeromedical and aerospace technology. Air Methods' fleet of owned, leased, or maintained aircraft features more than 450 helicopters and fixed wing aircraft. Annually, the company conducts over 100,000 transports amassing over 150,000 flight hours. Air Methods was founded in 1980 by Roy Morgan.

	Annual Growth	12/11	12/12	12/13	12/14	12/15
Sales ($mil.)	11.0%	-	-	881.6	1,004.8	1,085.7
Net income ($ mil.)	32.7%	-	-	62.1	95.5	109.3
Market value ($ mil.)	-	-	-	-	-	-
Employees	-	-	-	-	-	5,133

AIR PRODUCTS & CHEMICALS INC

NYS: APD

1940 Air Products Boulevard
Allentown, PA 18106-5500
Phone: 610 481-4911
Fax: 610 481-5900
Web: www.airproducts.com

CEO: Seifollah Ghasemi
CFO: Melissa N Schaeffer
HR: -
FYE: September 30
Type: Public

Air Products and Chemicals produces and distributes atmospheric, process, and specialty gases in the US and across the world. It is a leading hydrogen supplier as well as helium and liquefied natural gas (LNG) process technology and equipment. Air Products and Chemicals, which generates more than 40% revenue outside the US, also provides related equipment and services (air separation, hydrocarbon recovery, natural gas liquefaction, etc.) to customers in the refining, gasification, electronics, chemicals, metals, manufacturing, and food and beverage industries. The company was founded in 1940.

	Annual Growth	09/19	09/20	09/21	09/22	09/23
Sales ($mil.)	9.0%	8,918.9	8,856.3	10,323	12,699	12,600
Net income ($ mil.)	6.9%	1,760.0	1,886.7	2,099.1	2,256.1	2,300.2
Market value ($ mil.)	6.3%	49,297	66,184	56,908	51,713	62,971
Employees	6.8%	17,700	19,275	20,875	21,900	23,000

AIR SERV INTERNATIONAL, INC.

410 ROSEDALE CT STE 190
WARRENTON, VA 201864329
Phone: 540 428-2323
Fax: -
Web: www.airserv.org

CEO: Dave Carlstrom
CFO: -
HR: -
FYE: December 31
Type: Private

Not your typical cargo carrier, Air Serv International transports relief supplies for humanitarian organizations. The nonprofit organization flies food, medicine, and other needed items to destinations all over the world that have been affected by wars or natural disasters, including Iraq, Afghanistan, and several countries in Africa. Its fleet, based in various locations overseas, consists of several models of single- and twin-engine planes and helicopters, and it leases additional aircraft as needed. Support for the organization's efforts comes mainly from government grants and contracts. Air Serv International was founded in 1984.

	Annual Growth	12/16	12/17	12/18	12/21	12/22
Sales ($mil.)	(4.7%)	-	2.1	2.1	2.3	1.7
Net income ($ mil.)	-	-	0.4	0.6	0.5	(0.3)
Market value ($ mil.)	-	-	-	-	-	-
Employees	-	-	-	-	-	20

AIR T INC

NMS: AIRT

11020 David Taylor Drive, Suite 305
Charlotte, NC 28262
Phone: 980 595-2840
Fax: -
Web: www.airt.net

CEO: -
CFO: -
HR: -
FYE: March 31
Type: Public

Air T helps FedEx deliver the goods. The company owns two overnight air cargo subsidiaries -- Mountain Air Cargo (MAC) and CSA Air -- which operate under contracts with FedEx. MAC and CSA Air fly mainly in the Eastern and Midwest regions of the US, as well as the Caribbean and South America. Its combined fleet consists of about 80 turboprop Cessna aircraft, most of which are leased from FedEx. Air Cargo Services accounts for about half of its sales. Air T's Aircraft Ground Service Equipment and Service business comprises Global Ground Support (GGS; de-icing and scissor-lift equipment used at airports) and Global Aviation Services (GAS; provides related maintenance services).

	Annual Growth	03/19	03/20	03/21	03/22	03/23
Sales ($mil.)	(0.3%)	249.8	236.8	175.1	177.1	247.3
Net income ($ mil.)	-	1.3	7.7	(7.3)	10.9	(12.3)
Market value ($ mil.)	(4.6%)	85.1	35.3	67.0	64.1	70.6
Employees	(6.6%)	769	478	452	500	584

AIR TRANSPORT SERVICES GROUP, INC.

NMS: ATSG

145 Hunter Drive
Wilmington, OH 45177
Phone: 937 382-5591
Fax: -
Web: www.atsginc.com

CEO: Joe Hete
CFO: Quint O Turner
HR: Shawnna Wharton
FYE: December 31
Type: Public

Air Transport Services Group (ATSG) leases aircraft and provide airline operations, aircraft modification and maintenance services, ground services, and other support services to the air transportation and logistics industries. It offers a range of complementary services to delivery companies, freight forwarders, e-commerce operators, airlines, and government customers. In addition, it is a provider of passenger charter service to the US Department of Defense (DoD). ATSG's Cargo Aircraft Management (CAM) subsidiary leases Boeing 777, 767, and 757 aircraft and aircraft engines, and ACMI Services includes the cargo and passenger transportation operations of its three airlines. The company was founded in 1980.

	Annual Growth	12/19	12/20	12/21	12/22	12/23
Sales ($mil.)	9.3%	1,452.2	1,570.6	1,734.3	2,045.5	2,070.6
Net income ($ mil.)	(0.4%)	61.2	32.1	231.4	198.6	60.3
Market value ($ mil.)	(6.9%)	1,530.6	2,044.7	1,916.8	1,695.0	1,148.9
Employees	3.9%	4,380	5,305	5,280	5,320	5,095

AIRBNB INC

NMS: ABNB

888 Brannan Street
San Francisco, CA 94103
Phone: 415 510-4027
Fax: -
Web: www.airbnb.com

CEO: -
CFO: -
HR: -
FYE: December 31
Type: Public

Airbnb is one of the world's largest marketplaces for unique, authentic places to stay and things to do, has grown to over 4 million Hosts who have welcomed over 1 billion guest arrivals to over 100,000 cities and towns in almost every country and region. Airbnb hosts are everyday people that share their worlds to provide guests with the feeling of connection and being at home. The company was established in 2007. The US accounts for about 50% of the company's total revenue.

	Annual Growth	12/19	12/20	12/21	12/22	12/23
Sales ($mil.)	19.9%	4,805.2	3,378.2	5,991.8	8,399.0	9,917.0
Net income ($ mil.)	-	(674.3)	(4,584.7)	(352.0)	1,893.0	4,792.0
Market value ($ mil.)	-	-	93,658	106,221	54,549	86,857
Employees	6.0%	5,465	5,597	6,132	6,811	6,907

AIRCASTLE LIMITED

201 TRESSER BLVD STE 400　　　　　　　　　CEO: Michael Inglese
STAMFORD, CT 069013435　　　　　　　　　　CFO: Aaron Dahlke
Phone: 203 504-1020　　　　　　　　　　　　HR: Brooke Call
Fax: –　　　　　　　　　　　　　　　　　　　FYE: February 28
Web: www.aircastle.com　　　　　　　　　　Type: Private

Aircastle acquires, leases, and sells commercial jet aircraft to airlines throughout the world. The company owns a lineup of utility jet aircraft that it adds to, leases, and sells to passenger and cargo markets. Aircastle touts a portfolio of nearly 250 aircraft, which are leased to about 75 customers located in some 45 countries. Lessees of Aircastle's aircraft maintain the planes, as well as pay operating and insurance expenses. Some of its customers include IndiGo, LATAM, KLM, Viva Aerobus, and Lion Air, among others. Aircastle Limited is owned by Japan's Marubeni Corp. and Mizuho Leasing Co.

AIRNET SYSTEMS, INC.

7250 STAR CHECK DR　　　　　　　　　　　　CEO: Joan C Makley
COLUMBUS, OH 432171025　　　　　　　　　　CFO: Fred Deleeuw
Phone: 614 409-4900　　　　　　　　　　　　HR: –
Fax: –　　　　　　　　　　　　　　　　　　　FYE: December 31
Web: www.airnet.com　　　　　　　　　　　　Type: Private

Air cargo carrier AirNet Systems helps banks keep their records straight. Transporting canceled checks and other bank documents accounts for the majority of the company's sales. AirNet also offers express delivery of such cargo as human organs and time-sensitive medications, as well as general freight. Founded in 1974, it provides both scheduled and charter cargo services. Overall, AirNet operates a fleet of aircraft, including jets and turboprops. It serves more than 80 markets in the US. In 2008, AirNet was acquired by an affiliate of investment firm Bayside Capital.

AIRE-MASTER OF AMERICA, INC.

1821 N STATE HIGHWAY CC　　　　　　　　　CEO: Douglas McCauley
NIXA, MO 657148015　　　　　　　　　　　　CFO: David Knewtson
Phone: 417 725-2691　　　　　　　　　　　　HR: Phyllis O 'neal
Fax: –　　　　　　　　　　　　　　　　　　　FYE: March 31
Web: www.airemaster.com　　　　　　　　　Type: Private

Rather than mask unpleasant bathroom odors with perfumed sprays, Aire-Master of America wants to wipe them out altogether. The company manufactures restroom hygiene and commercial odor control products, including air sanitizers, hand soap, cleaning products, disinfecting soaps, and paper towels. It also makes private-label products for janitorial suppliers and companies with similar product offerings. Aire-Master operates through more than 80 independent franchises and four company-owned stores in the US and Canada. Clients have included corporate offices, hotels, medical facilities, and restaurants such as Wendy's and Pizza Hut. Founded in 1958, Aire-Master launched its first franchise in 1976.

	Annual Growth	03/13	03/14	03/15	03/16	03/17
Sales ($mil.)	6.3%	–	9.4	9.7	10.7	11.2
Net income ($ mil.)	20.9%	–	0.2	0.2	0.3	0.3
Market value ($ mil.)	–	–	–	–	–	–
Employees	–	–	–	–	–	63

AJAX METAL PROCESSING, INC.

4651 BELLEVUE ST　　　　　　　　　　　　　CEO: Derek J Stevens
DETROIT, MI 482071713　　　　　　　　　　CFO: Daniel L Morrell
Phone: 313 267-2100　　　　　　　　　　　　HR: –
Fax: –　　　　　　　　　　　　　　　　　　　FYE: December 31
Web: www.ajaxmetal.com　　　　　　　　　　Type: Private

Ajax Metal Processing is cleaning up the market when it comes to hardening and protecting small metal parts, such as nuts and bolts, primarily for customers in the automobile manufacturing industry. Services include heat treating, plating, adhesive and sealant application, annealing, cleaning, and coating. The company's wire rod annealing and pickling equipment includes four surface combustion batch-type furnaces with a total annealing capacity of 230 tons per day. Ajax Metal Processing operates two plants in Michigan and one in Indiana. The company opened for business in 1967.

AIRGAS, INC.

259 N RADNOR CHESTER RD STE 100　　　　　CEO: –
RADNOR, PA 190875240　　　　　　　　　　　CFO: –
Phone: 610 687-5253　　　　　　　　　　　　HR: –
Fax: –　　　　　　　　　　　　　　　　　　　FYE: March 31
Web: www.airgas.com　　　　　　　　　　　　Type: Private

Airgas is a subsidiary of Air Liquide, a leading supplier of industrial, medical, and specialty gases in the US. The company also offers a diverse range of hard goods and related products, as well as safety products, making it a reliable one-stop-shop for customers' needs. Airgas prides itself on its ability to support over 1 million customers by providing dependable products, services, and expertise to help them grow and improve their business performance. Its robust eBusiness platform, Airgas Total Access telesales channel, and 1,400 locations, all staffed by nearly 18,000 associates, ensure that customers can access its products and services with ease. As an Air Liquide company, Airgas benefits from unparalleled global reach, innovation, and technology, which enables it to provide customers with world-class solutions. Airgas was founded in 1982 with the acquisition of a local distributor, Connecticut Oxygen.

	Annual Growth	03/10	03/11	03/12	03/13	03/15
Sales ($mil.)	3.4%	–	–	–	4,957.5	5,304.9
Net income ($ mil.)	3.9%	–	–	–	340.9	368.1
Market value ($ mil.)	–	–	–	–	–	–
Employees	–	–	–	–	–	17,004

AKAL SECURITY, INC.

3 RAM DAS GURU PL　　　　　　　　　　　　CEO: –
ESPANOLA, NM 875328213　　　　　　　　　CFO: –
Phone: 505 692-6600　　　　　　　　　　　　HR: –
Fax: –　　　　　　　　　　　　　　　　　　　FYE: December 31
Web: www.akalglobal.com　　　　　　　　　　Type: Private

Unarmed? Akal Security provides contract security guard services for customers in the US and abroad. Akal's Judicial Security division specializes in security services for protecting federal courthouses in approximately 40 states. It also transports prisoners and illegal aliens for homeland security efforts. In addition, Akal supplies security officers for detention facilities and military installations, and offers electronic security, surveillance, and access control system design, installation, and integration. The company serves federal agencies as well as commercial clients and state and local government facilities.

	Annual Growth	12/07	12/08	12/09	12/10	12/11
Sales ($mil.)	(1.9%)	–	–	479.6	466.2	461.5
Net income ($ mil.)	11.2%	–	–	2.9	2.5	3.6
Market value ($ mil.)	–	–	–	–	–	–
Employees	–	–	–	–	–	15,000

AKAMAI TECHNOLOGIES INC
NMS: AKAM

145 Broadway
Cambridge, MA 02142
Phone: 617 444-3000
Fax: 617 444-3001
Web: www.akamai.com

CEO: F T Leighton
CFO: Edward McGowan
HR: -
FYE: December 31
Type: Public

Akamai Technologies provides solutions for securing and delivering content and business applications over the internet. The company's cloud services help its customers ? corporations and government agencies ? deliver digital content over the internet at optimal speeds and security. Specifically, the company offers services that keep infrastructure, websites, applications, application programming interfaces ("APIs") safe from cyberattacks. Its software works from a network of more than 350,000 servers in over 130 countries. Customers include IKEA, Sony Interactive Entertainment, Toshiba, WarnerMedia, the Coca-Cola Company, and PayPal. More than 50% of the company's total revenue comes from the US.

	Annual Growth	12/19	12/20	12/21	12/22	12/23
Sales ($mil.)	7.1%	2,893.6	3,198.1	3,461.2	3,616.7	3,811.9
Net income ($ mil.)	3.5%	478.0	557.1	651.6	523.7	547.6
Market value ($ mil.)	8.2%	13,063	15,878	17,700	12,749	17,898
Employees	7.3%	7,724	8,368	8,700	9,800	10,250

AKELA PHARMA INC

Suite 130, 11501 Domain Drive
Austin, TX 78758
Phone: 512 531-6676
Fax: 512 339-3050
Web: www.akelapharma.com

CEO: Rudy Emmelot
CFO: -
HR: -
FYE: December 31
Type: Public

Drug developer Akela Pharma is hoping to be there before the last dose of pain meds wears off and the next dose kicks in. The company's lead product candidate is Fentanyl Taifun, an inhaled formulation of cancer pain fighter fentanyl, to be used in conjunction with other drugs to manage severe pain. Akela Pharma is also working on research in areas not related to pain relief; it is developing a growth hormone stimulator to help treat frailty and malnutrition in patients with kidney failure. Akela Pharma's subsidiary PharmaForm provides contract drug development services and specializes in controlled-release drug delivery technology.

	Annual Growth	12/07	12/08	12/09	12/10	12/11
Sales ($mil.)	20.0%	12.6	14.8	13.9	13.3	26.2
Net income ($ mil.)	-	(32.7)	(26.0)	(21.0)	1.4	13.9
Market value ($ mil.)	(53.4%)	106.9	3.2	5.5	5.5	5.0
Employees	-	-	-	65	57	57

AKRON GENERAL HEALTH SYSTEM

1 AKRON GENERAL AVE
AKRON, OH 443072432
Phone: 330 344-6000
Fax: -
Web: www.akrongeneral.org

CEO: Thomas L Stover
CFO: Pat McMahon
HR: -
FYE: December 31
Type: Private

Akron General Health System serves the residents of Akron and northeastern Ohio through the not-for-profit organization's primary Akron General Medical Center, a tertiary care teaching hospital with more than 500 beds. Other facilities that are part of the health care network include the Lodi Community Hospital, a rural hospital with 25 beds that has been designated a critical access facility, and the Rose Lane Health Center, a long-term care facility with about 170 beds. The system also runs several Edwin Shaw Rehabilitation Institute locations. Akron General Health System boasts a satellite general practice, radiology, and specialty care clinics, as well as home health and hospice facilities.

	Annual Growth	12/01	12/02	12/04	12/05	12/13
Sales ($mil.)	(41.1%)	-	452.9	0.3	0.3	1.3
Net income ($ mil.)	-	-	7.8	(5.1)	(4.5)	(0.2)
Market value ($ mil.)	-	-	-	-	-	-
Employees	-	-	-	-	-	5,200

AKRON GENERAL MEDICAL CENTER INC

1 AKRON GENERAL AVE
AKRON, OH 443072432
Phone: 330 344-6000
Fax: -
Web: www.akrongeneral.org

CEO: F W Steere
CFO: -
HR: Rick Slater
FYE: December 31
Type: Private

Akron General Medical Center, the flagship hospital of Akron General Health System, is a not-for-profit teaching hospital that boasts more than 530 acute care beds. The hospital serves the residents of Northeast Ohio as a regional referral center in a number of medical specialties, including cardiovascular disease, heart surgery, cancer care, women's health, orthopedics, sports medicine, and trauma care. Akron General Medical also operates Edwin Shaw Rehab, the area's only rehabilitation hospital. Edwin Shaw has 35 beds and treats patients who have experienced stroke, head trauma, and other critical injuries. Akron General Medical was founded in 1914 as Peoples Hospital.

ALABAMA FARMERS COOPERATIVE, INC.

121 SOMERVILLE RD NE
DECATUR, AL 356012659
Phone: 256 353-6843
Fax: -
Web: www.alafarm.com

CEO: Mary Grier
CFO: Thomas Hallin
HR: Susana Salcido
FYE: September 30
Type: Private

Alabama Farmers Cooperative (AFC) provides farmers in the Yellowhammer state with a range of agricultural supplies and services. The co-op offers animal feed, crop fertilizer, and home-gardening items, such as seed and hand tools, as well as grain storage and hardware. AFC comprises 37 member associations, including about 90 retail locations. Expanding through joint ventures, it boasts one of the largest farmer-owned agriculture businesses in the southeastern US. Its Bonnie Plants is one of the biggest suppliers of vegetable and herb plants for home gardeners. BioLogic makes forage products for wild game. AFC supplies the foodservice industry with fresh fish through its SouthFresh Farms catfish farm.

	Annual Growth	07/08	07/09	07/10	07/11*	09/15
Sales ($mil.)	(57.3%)	-	2,088.8	401.0	450.8	12.7
Net income ($ mil.)	277.6%	-	0.0	8.1	9.2	0.5
Market value ($ mil.)	-	-	-	-	-	-
Employees	-	-	-	-	-	3,000

*Fiscal year change

ALABAMA POWER CO
NBB: APRD M

600 North 18th Street
Birmingham, AL 35203
Phone: 205 257-1000
Fax: -
Web: www.alabamapower.com

CEO: Jeff Peoples
CFO: Philip C Raymond
HR: Brad Hilsmier
FYE: December 31
Type: Public

Founded in 1906, Alabama Power, a wholly-owned subsidiary of the Southern Company, is a vertically integrated utility that provides electric service to retail customers in three Southeastern states and to wholesale customers in the Southeast region. It owns or operates more than 75 electric generating units with total nameplate capacity of more than 12 million kilowatts. These generating units are located at 25 facilities. Alabama Power owns coal reserves near its Plant Gorgas site and uses their output in its generating plants. In addition, Alabama Power sells, and cooperates with dealers in promoting the sale of, electric appliances and products and also markets and sells outdoor lighting services.

	Annual Growth	12/19	12/20	12/21	12/22	12/23
Sales ($mil.)	3.6%	6,125.0	5,830.0	6,413.0	7,817.0	7,050.0
Net income ($ mil.)	6.0%	1,085.0	1,165.0	1,253.0	1,351.0	1,370.0
Market value ($ mil.)	-	3,256.9	3,301.5	3,441.0	-	-
Employees	(0.5%)	6,324	6,200	6,100	61,000	6,200

ALABAMA STATE PORT AUTHORITY

250 N WATER ST
MOBILE, AL 366024000
Phone: 251 441-7200
Fax: –
Web: www.alports.com

CEO: James Lyons
CFO: Larry R Downs
HR: –
FYE: September 30
Type: Private

Offering a gateway to the Gulf of Mexico, the Alabama State Port Authority (ASPA), a government agency, operates the deepwater port facilities in Mobile. The port complex includes facilities for handling general cargo, such as containers, forest products, and metals, as well as liquid bulk and dry bulk cargo, such as chemicals, coal, iron ore, and steel. The port complex features more than 4 million sq. ft. of warehouse space and open yards and almost 40 berths. A 75-mile rail line links Port of Mobile facilities and provides connections to major freight railroads. The ASPA began operations in 1928.

	Annual Growth	09/16	09/17	09/18	09/19	09/22
Sales ($mil.)	5.5%	–	125.9	134.9	158.4	164.5
Net income ($ mil.)	66.1%	–	1.2	4.7	8.5	14.6
Market value ($ mil.)	–	–	–	–	–	–
Employees	–	–	–	–	–	495

ALAMANCE REGIONAL MEDICAL CENTER, INC.

1240 HUFFMAN MILL RD
BURLINGTON, NC 272158700
Phone: 336 538-7000
Fax: –
Web: –

CEO: –
CFO: Rex A Street
HR: Mandy Parham
FYE: September 30
Type: Private

Alamance Regional Medical Center is a not-for-profit hospital serving the residents of North Carolina. the medical center has some 240 beds. Services include cancer care, behavioral health, cardiology, radiology, women's services, and home health care. It also provides a sleep lab, pain center, and birthing center. Its satellite Mebane Medical Park includes general practice, surgery, and cancer centers, and the West End Medical Park provides primary care. Other facilities include a pediatric rehabilitation clinic, sports rehabilitation center, a nursing home, and a retirement community. Alamance Regional Medical Center is a part of not-for-profit Cone Health's regional network of healthcare providers.

	Annual Growth	09/13	09/14	09/15	09/20	09/21
Sales ($mil.)	2.5%	–	–	240.4	303.7	279.3
Net income ($ mil.)	2.0%	–	–	48.6	101.3	54.7
Market value ($ mil.)	–	–	–	–	–	–
Employees	–	–	–	–	–	1,500

ALAMBIC, INC.

3001 S STATE ST STE 35
UKIAH, CA 954826969
Phone: 707 462-0314
Fax: –
Web: www.caddellwilliams.com

CEO: –
CFO: Denise Niderost
HR: –
FYE: December 31
Type: Private

Germain-Robin Alambic produces hand-distilled brandies and bourbons under the Anno Domini, Select Barrel XO, Shareholders Reserve, and Grappa labels. Germain-Robin products, said to rival the great French brandies (called cognac), are distilled from premium wine grapes such as Pinot Noir, Merlot, and Viognier (grappa is made from apples). Germain-Robin was founded by Ansley Coale and Hubert Germain-Robin who, according to company legend, set out to make brandy using an antique still found in an abandoned cognac distillery.

	Annual Growth	12/00	12/01	12/06	12/07	12/08
Sales ($mil.)	34.0%	–	1.2	8.6	8.8	9.6
Net income ($ mil.)	–	–	(0.6)	0.1	0.3	0.0
Market value ($ mil.)	–	–	–	–	–	–
Employees	–	–	–	–	–	15

ALAMEDA CORRIDOR TRANSPORTATION AUTHORITY

3760 KILROY AIRPORT WAY STE 200
LONG BEACH, CA 908062443
Phone: 310 233-7480
Fax: –
Web: www.acta.org

CEO: –
CFO: –
HR: –
FYE: June 30
Type: Private

There's nothing illicit about the underground activities of the Alameda Corridor Transportation Authority; in fact, the agency's mission -- to facilitate efficient rail transportation of containerized cargo in Southern California -- is strictly aboveboard. The Alameda Corridor Transportation Authority maintains 20 miles of freight rail lines between the ports of Long Beach and Los Angeles and the main rail terminals near downtown Los Angeles. The agency's system, known as the Alameda Corridor, includes the Mid-Corridor Trench, a 10-mile section of railroad constructed 30 feet underground.

	Annual Growth	06/15	06/16	06/17	06/18	06/19
Sales ($mil.)	4.7%	–	–	107.7	117.9	118.1
Net income ($ mil.)	–	–	–	(28.5)	(18.6)	(16.2)
Market value ($ mil.)	–	–	–	–	–	–
Employees	–	–	–	–	–	15

ALAMO COMMUNITY COLLEGE DISTRICT

2222 N ALAMO ST
SAN ANTONIO, TX 782151195
Phone: 210 485-0000
Fax: –
Web: www.alamo.edu

CEO: –
CFO: –
HR: Donn Kraft
FYE: August 31
Type: Private

San Antonio, Texas, high school students are encouraged to remember the Alamo ... the Alamo Community College District, that is. The district oversees five schools -- Northeast Lakeview College, Northwest Vista College, Palo Alto College, St. Philip's College, and San Antonio College -- all of which serve the post-secondary education needs of the greater San Antonio area. The colleges offer 325 degree and certificate programs. Classes are available during the day, in the evening, and on weekends through six campuses, the Internet, and at various off-campus sites. The Alamo Community College District serves more than 52,000 students, about half of whom are Hispanic.

	Annual Growth	08/18	08/19	08/20	08/21	08/22
Sales ($mil.)	1.1%	–	89.9	86.5	93.3	92.8
Net income ($ mil.)	22.1%	–	46.2	31.1	78.9	84.1
Market value ($ mil.)	–	–	–	–	–	–
Employees	–	–	–	–	–	2,134

ALAMO GROUP, INC.

1627 East Walnut
Seguin, TX 78155
Phone: 830 379-1480
Fax: 830 372-9683
Web: www.alamo-group.com

NYS: ALG
CEO: Jeffery A Leonard
CFO: Richard J Wehrle
HR: Allison Boechlerlyautey
FYE: December 31
Type: Public

Alamo Group is a leader in the design and manufacture of hig-quality agricultural equipment and infrastructure maintenance equipment for governmental and industrial use. Its branded lines, Alamo Industrial and Tiger hydraulically powered tractor-mounted mowers, serve US government agencies. Rhino Products and M&W Gear subsidiaries sell rotary cutters and other equipment to farmers for pasture upkeep. UK McConnel and Bomford, and France's S.M.A. subsidiaries market vegetation maintenance equipment, such as hydraulic boom-mounted hedge and grass mowers. The company generates the majority of its revenue domestically.

	Annual Growth	12/19	12/20	12/21	12/22	12/23
Sales ($mil.)	10.8%	1,119.1	1,163.5	1,334.2	1,513.6	1,689.7
Net income ($ mil.)	21.3%	62.9	56.6	80.2	101.9	136.2
Market value ($ mil.)	13.7%	1,502.1	1,650.5	1,760.9	1,694.1	2,514.8
Employees	0.5%	4,270	3,990	4,200	4,200	4,350

ALANCO TECHNOLOGIES INC

7950 E. Acoma Drive, Suite 111
Scottsdale, AZ 85260
Phone: 480 607-1010
Fax: –
Web: www.alanco.com

CEO: John A Carlson
CFO: Danielle L Haney
HR: –
FYE: June 30
Type: Public

Having failed to strike gold and feeling lost, Alanco Technologies is looking for a new business venture. The company once made pollution control systems, owned gold mines, and made unsuccessful forays into both the data storage and restaurant fryer businesses. It also made radio-frequency ID (RFID) tracking devices for correctional facilities through its TSI PRISM subsidiary until that line of business was sold in 2010 to Alabama-based Black Creek Integrated Systems for about $2 million in cash. Alanco then offered subscription-based GPS tracking data services for the refrigerated transport industry through StarTrak Systems (acquired for $15 million in 2006), but sold that business to ORBCOMM in 2011.

	Annual Growth	06/12	06/13	06/14	06/15	06/16
Sales ($mil.)	–	–	–	0.4	0.6	0.8	0.2
Net income ($ mil.)	–	–	(0.6)	(0.7)	(0.1)	(0.9)	(1.6)
Market value ($ mil.)	(38.0%)	7.4	2.2	2.4	1.4	1.1
Employees	–	–	–	2	1	5	3

ALASKA AIR GROUP, INC.

19300 International Boulevard
Seattle, WA 98188
Phone: 206 392-5040
Fax: –
Web: www.alaskaair.com

NYS: ALK

CEO: Benito Minicucci
CFO: Shane R Tackett
HR: Michaela Littman
FYE: December 31
Type: Public

The fifth-largest airline in the US, Alaska Air Group offers unparalleled guest service, connectivity and schedules from its hub markets along the West Coast. With its regional partners, Alaska Air flies to over 120 destinations through the US and North America. Alaska operates a fleet of narrowbody passenger jets on primarily longer stage-length routes, and contracts primarily with Horizon and SkyWest Airlines, Inc. (SkyWest) for shorter-haul capacity, such that Alaska receives all passenger revenue from those flights. Alaska Airlines' fleet is comprised of about 240 aircraft.

	Annual Growth	12/19	12/20	12/21	12/22	12/23
Sales ($mil.)	4.4%	8,781.0	3,566.0	6,176.0	9,646.0	10,426
Net income ($ mil.)	(25.6%)	769.0	(1,324.0)	478.0	58.0	235.0
Market value ($ mil.)	(12.9%)	8,542.6	6,556.7	6,569.3	5,414.3	4,926.4
Employees	1.9%	24,134	21,997	22,833	25,469	26,043

ALASKA COMMUNICATIONS SYSTEMS GROUP, INC.

600 TELEPHONE AVE
ANCHORAGE, AK 995036010
Phone: 907 297-3000
Fax: –
Web: www.alaskacommunications.com

CEO: –
CFO: –
HR: –
FYE: December 31
Type: Private

Alaska Communications Systems Group keeps customers in the largest US state connected. Through subsidiaries the telecom carrier operates the leading local-exchange network in the state, providing wired local and long-distance voice and data services mostly to enterprise customers. It also offers wireless phone service through a joint venture with GCI that offers mobile devices from Apple, HTC, and Samsung. The company has about 130,000 wired phone lines in service, about 110,000 wireless subscribers, and about 55,000 Internet customers. Alaska Communications sells to consumers in part through its network of retail stores.

ALASKA CONSERVATION FOUNDATION

1227 W 9TH AVE STE 300
ANCHORAGE, AK 995013279
Phone: 907 433-8208
Fax: –
Web: www.alaskaconservation.org

CEO: –
CFO: –
HR: –
FYE: June 30
Type: Private

Whales, and otters, and bears, oh my! The Alaska Conservation Foundation strives to protect the environment (and all its inhabitants) in Alaska, as well as help the state's native people retain their cultural connections to the land. The foundation has awarded more than $22 million in grants to about 200 organizations. Its projects include the Alaska Coalition (national parks, wildlife refuges, and other federal lands), Alaska Oceans Program (conservation and sustainable fishing), Alaska Conservation for the Majority (finding common ground between conservationists and state residents), and Climate Change Program (minimizing individual impact). The Alaska Conservation Foundation was formed in 1980.

	Annual Growth	06/17	06/18	06/19	06/20	06/22
Sales ($mil.)	8.8%	–	2.9	3.1	3.5	4.0
Net income ($ mil.)	34.8%	–	0.2	0.6	1.0	0.8
Market value ($ mil.)	–	–	–	–	–	–
Employees	–	–	–	–	–	33

ALASKA NATIVE TRIBAL HEALTH CONSORTIUM

4000 AMBASSADOR DR
ANCHORAGE, AK 995085909
Phone: 907 729-1900
Fax: –
Web: www.anthc.org

CEO: –
CFO: –
HR: Danielle Blanchard
FYE: September 30
Type: Private

The Alaska Native Tribal Health Consortium (ANTHC) brings good health to Alaska Natives. The company is a not-for-profit, statewide health care organization managed by regional tribal governments and their respective regional health organizations. The organization connects disparate medical providers by providing a range of health programs and services, including community health care, public health advocacy and education initiatives, health research (including water and sanitation), and medical supply distribution. The nearly 175-bed Alaska Native Medical Center (ANMC), a native-owned hospital, is jointly managed by ANTHC and Southcentral Foundation, a regional health corporation based in the Cook Inlet region.

	Annual Growth	09/13	09/14	09/15	09/16	09/20
Sales ($mil.)	–	–	(1,780.2)	511.9	587.0	687.2
Net income ($ mil.)	1063.2%	–	0.0	3.3	72.9	22.3
Market value ($ mil.)	–	–	–	–	–	–
Employees	–	–	–	–	–	1,850

ALASKA RAILROAD CORPORATION

327 W SHIP CREEK AVE
ANCHORAGE, AK 995011671
Phone: 907 265-2494
Fax: –
Web: www.alaskarailroad.com

CEO: William G O'Leary
CFO: Barbara Amy
HR: Keri Meszaros
FYE: December 31
Type: Private

Alaska Railroad operates freight and passenger trains that run between Anchorage, near the Gulf of Alaska, up through scenic Denali National Park, and north to Fairbanks. Known as the railbelt, the area between Anchorage and Fairbanks is home to 70% of Alaska's population. Cargo carried by the railroad includes chemicals, coal, consumer goods, gravel, oil field and mining supplies, and petroleum products. The company's rail network spans some 465 miles of main line track, 80 miles of branch line, and 110 miles of rail siding (auxiliary track used to store cars waiting to load or unload). The Alaska Railroad Corporation also owns more than 35,000 acres of land, about half of which is leased.

	Annual Growth	12/17	12/18	12/19	12/20	12/21
Sales ($mil.)	0.6%	–	163.4	177.6	129.9	166.2
Net income ($ mil.)	19.8%	–	18.0	21.6	(7.8)	30.9
Market value ($ mil.)	–	–	–	–	–	–
Employees	–	–	–	–	–	775

ALASKAN COPPER COMPANIES, INC.

27402 72ND AVE S
KENT, WA 980327366
Phone: 206 623-5800
Fax: –
Web: www.alaskancopper.com

CEO: William M Rosen
CFO: Brian Lucarelli
HR: Arthur Grunbaum
FYE: September 30
Type: Private

The companies in question are Alaskan Copper & Brass and Alaskan Copper Works. Alaskan Copper processes and distributes corrosion-resistant alloy products. Offerings include bar, fittings, flanges, plate, pipe, rod, and tubing, made from materials such as aluminum, brass, bronze, copper, copper-nickel, and stainless steel. Alaskan Copper also fabricates products such as heat exchangers and pressure vessels. Founded in 1913, Alaskan Copper has facilities in Oregon, Washington, and British Columbia.

ALAUNOS THERAPEUTICS INC   NAS: TCRT

8030 El Rio Street
Houston, TX 77054
Phone: 346 355-4099
Fax: –
Web: www.alaunos.com

CEO: Dale C Hogue Jr
CFO: Timothy Cunningham
HR: –
FYE: December 31
Type: Public

Alaunos Therapeutics (formerly known as Ziopharm Oncology) is a clinical-stage oncology-focused cell therapy company developing adoptive TCR engineered T-cell therapies, or TCR-T, designed to treat multiple solid tumor types in large cancer patient populations with unmet clinical needs. The company is leveraging its proprietary, non-viral Sleeping Beauty gene transfer platform to design and manufacture patient-specific cell therapies that target neoantigens arising from common tumor-related mutations in key oncogenic genes, including KRAS, TP53, and EGFR. In early 2022, the company changed its name from Ziophatm Oncology to Alaunos Therapeutics.

	Annual Growth	12/18	12/19	12/20	12/21	12/22
Sales ($mil.)	111.5%	0.1	–	–	0.4	2.9
Net income ($ mil.)	–	(53.1)	(117.8)	(80.0)	(78.8)	(37.7)
Market value ($ mil.)	(23.2%)	30.0	75.6	40.4	17.5	10.4
Employees	(8.3%)	48	73	106	41	34

ALBAN TRACTOR, LLC

8531 PULASKI HWY
BALTIMORE, MD 212373005
Phone: 410 686-7777
Fax: –
Web: www.caterpillar.com

CEO: –
CFO: Jim Sweeney
HR: Marianne Bishoff
FYE: December 31
Type: Private

Alban Tractor sells and rents new and used Caterpillar construction equipment and power systems, and a range of work tools and parts. In recent years the company has added Allianz Sweepers, Peterson Grinders, and Weiler Pavers to its list of equipment. Alban Tractor provides engines for large trucks and RVs, as well as industrial and marine machinery. The company also offers preventative maintenance, repair, and remanufacturing services for power generation equipment. It serves government agencies and industrial, energy, and healthcare customers in the mid-Atlantic region of the US.

ALBANY COLLEGE OF PHARMACY AND HEALTH SCIENCES

106 NEW SCOTLAND AVE
ALBANY, NY 122083425
Phone: 518 459-1975
Fax: –
Web: www.acphs.edu

CEO: –
CFO: –
HR: Kelly O'brien
FYE: June 30
Type: Private

Students with a prescription for medical and pharmaceutical training get their fill at Albany College of Pharmacy and Health Sciences (ACPHS). The college offers health care degree programs, including pharmacy, pre-med, clinical laboratory sciences, cytotechnology, and biomedical technology. The school also is home to the Pharmaceutical Research Institute and Center for NanoPhamaceuticals, which focuses on drug discovery and development. A satellite campus in Vermont offers doctor of pharmacy degrees. ACPHS enrolls more than 1,500 students and was founded in 1881. The school changed its name to include "Health Sciences" in 2008. The change was made to better reflect the school's range of offerings.

	Annual Growth	06/16	06/17	06/18	06/20	06/22
Sales ($mil.)	(3.2%)	–	58.7	61.9	69.2	49.8
Net income ($ mil.)	–	–	1.4	2.6	4.8	(1.6)
Market value ($ mil.)	–	–	–	–	–	–
Employees	–	–	–	–	–	310

ALBANY INTERNATIONAL CORP   NYS: AIN

216 Airport Drive
Rochester, NH 03867
Phone: 603 330-5850
Fax: –
Web: www.albint.com

CEO: A W Higgins
CFO: Stephen M Nolan
HR: Andrew Schoen
FYE: December 31
Type: Public

Albany International is a leading developer and manufacturer of engineered components, using advanced materials processing and automation capabilities. The company makes Machine Clothing (custom-designed, consumable fabrics and process belts essential for the manufacture of all grades of paper products. It markets these products to customer end-users worldwide, and it also provides nonwoven for building products, tannery, and textile industries. Its other business segment, Albany Engineered Composites (AEC), makes highly engineered advanced composite parts for the commercial and defense aerospace industries. Over 55% of the company's sale comes from the US. Albany International was started by three businessmen in 1895 as the Albany Felt Co. in New York's state capital.

	Annual Growth	12/19	12/20	12/21	12/22	12/23
Sales ($mil.)	2.2%	1,054.1	900.6	929.2	1,034.9	1,147.9
Net income ($ mil.)	(4.3%)	132.4	98.6	118.5	95.8	111.1
Market value ($ mil.)	6.7%	2,368.3	2,290.3	2,759.2	3,075.5	3,064.0
Employees	5.0%	4,600	4,000	4,100	4,100	5,600

ALBANY MED HEALTH SYSTEM

43 NEW SCOTLAND AVE
ALBANY, NY 122083412
Phone: 518 262-3125
Fax: –
Web: www.amc.edu

CEO: James J Barba
CFO: William C Hasselbarth
HR: Katie Vandenburgh
FYE: December 31
Type: Private

Albany Medical Center (AMC) is northeastern New York's only academic medical center and one of the largest private employers in the Capital Region. It incorporates a 766-bed hospital, which offers the widest range of medical and surgical services in the region, and Albany Medical College, which trains the next generation of doctors, scientists, and other health care professionals. The general medical-surgical facility also provides specialty care in such areas as oncology, rehabilitation, and organ transplantation. AMC also features a children's hospital, an outpatient surgery center, and a group medical practice. One of the nation's first private medical schools, AMC traces its roots to 1849.

	Annual Growth	12/12	12/13	12/15	12/16	12/17
Sales ($mil.)	(9.3%)	–	980.6	1,167.2	317.8	664.8
Net income ($ mil.)	23.4%	–	115.1	5.4	78.0	267.0
Market value ($ mil.)	–	–	–	–	–	–
Employees	–	–	–	–	–	8,760

ALBEMARLE CORP.

NYS: ALB PRA

4250 Congress Street, Suite 900
Charlotte, NC 28209
Phone: 980 299-5700
Fax: –
Web: www.albemarle.com

CEO: J K Masters Jr
CFO: Neal Sheorey
HR: Jeff Vitters
FYE: December 31
Type: Public

Albemarle develops, makes, and sells specialty chemicals for a wide range of markets, including automotive, construction, consumer electronics, crop protection, lubricants, pharmaceuticals, plastics, and refining. It is a major producer of lithium compounds used in batteries for consumer electronics; thermoplastic elastomers for car tires, rubber soles, and plastic bottles; and catalysts for chemical reactions. Its bromine and bromine-based business includes products used in fire safety solutions and other specialty chemical applications. About 90% of the company's revenue comes from outside the US.

	Annual Growth	12/19	12/20	12/21	12/22	12/23
Sales ($mil.)	27.9%	3,589.4	3,128.9	3,328.0	7,320.1	9,617.2
Net income ($ mil.)	31.1%	533.2	375.8	123.7	2,689.8	1,573.5
Market value ($ mil.)	18.6%	8,571.7	17,312	27,434	25,450	16,956
Employees	10.7%	6,000	5,900	6,000	7,400	9,000

ALBERICI CORPORATION

8800 PAGE AVE
SAINT LOUIS, MO 631146106
Phone: 314 733-2000
Fax: –
Web: www.alberici.com

CEO: John S Alberici
CFO: –
HR: Tony Destefano
FYE: December 31
Type: Private

Alberici helped shape the St. Louis skyline; it now sets its sights -- or its construction sites -- across North America. As the parent company of Alberici Constructors, the company encompasses a group of enterprises with a presence in North America, Central America, South America, and Europe. Operations include construction services, building materials, and steel fabrication and erection units. Alberici offers general contracting, design/build, construction management, demolition, and specialty contracting services, while also offering facilities management. Founded in 1918, the Alberici family still holds the largest share of the employee-owned firm.

	Annual Growth	12/14	12/15	12/20	12/21	12/22
Sales ($mil.)	3.9%	–	1,886.0	2,124.4	2,097.4	2,459.3
Net income ($ mil.)	–	–	–	–	–	–
Market value ($ mil.)	–	–	–	–	–	–
Employees	–	–	–	–	–	2,080

ALBERTSONS COMPANIES INC

NYS: ACI

250 Parkcenter Blvd.
Boise, ID 83706
Phone: 208 395-6200
Fax: –
Web: www.albertsonscompanies.com

CEO: Vivek Sankaran
CFO: Sharon McCollam
HR: –
FYE: February 25
Type: Public

Albertsons Companies is one of the biggest supermarket retailers in the US with nearly 2,270 stores in about 35 states and the District of Columbia. In addition to traditional grocery items, many of the stores offer pharmacies and coffee shops and around 400 include adjacent gas stations. The company operates under roughly 25 banners, including Albertsons, Vons, Pavilions, Randalls, Tom Thumb, Carrs, Jewel-Osco, Shaw's, Star Market, Safeway, Market Street, Haggen, and United Supermarkets. It also owns a meal kit company Plated. Albertsons, which traces its roots to 1939, is owned by Cerberus Capital Management, and went public in mid-2020.

	Annual Growth	02/19	02/20	02/21	02/22	02/23
Sales ($mil.)	6.4%	60,535	62,455	69,690	71,887	77,650
Net income ($ mil.)	84.3%	131.1	466.4	850.2	1,619.6	1,513.5
Market value ($ mil.)	–	–	–	9,211.5	16,931	11,701
Employees	2.1%	267,000	270,000	300,000	290,000	290,000

ALBION COLLEGE

611 E PORTER ST
ALBION, MI 492241887
Phone: 517 629-1000
Fax: –
Web: www.albion.edu

CEO: –
CFO: Gary Black
HR: Lisa Locke
FYE: June 30
Type: Private

Albion College is a private, co-educational, liberal arts college in Michigan associated with the Methodist church. The college offers Bachelor of Arts in about 30 subjects and Bachelor of Fine Arts degrees in art and art history. It employs some 130 full-time faculty members and has an enrollment of almost 2,000. Albion can trace its roots to 1835 when early Methodist settlers of the Michigan Territory worked to get the college a charter from the Michigan Territorial Legislature. Notable alumni include chairman and editor-in-chief of Newsweek magazine Richard Smith and Broadway producer Michael David, founder of Dodger Theatricals.

	Annual Growth	06/17	06/18	06/19	06/20	06/22
Sales ($mil.)	2.0%	–	56.3	71.2	106.4	60.9
Net income ($ mil.)	–	–	(1.9)	0.3	(7.4)	(24.1)
Market value ($ mil.)	–	–	–	–	–	–
Employees	–	–	–	–	–	600

ALBRIGHT COLLEGE

1621 N 13TH ST
READING, PA 196041708
Phone: 610 921-7520
Fax: –
Web: www.albright.edu

CEO: –
CFO: –
HR: –
FYE: May 31
Type: Private

Students' futures are bright at Albright College. The school is a private, liberal arts university that offers bachelor's of arts and science degrees, as well as masters in education degrees. More than 1,600 students study at Albright College, which offers programs in areas such as art, biology, English, psychology, mathematics, and communications. The college employs about 110 faculty members. Affiliated with the United Methodist Church, Albright College was established in 1856 and sits upon 118 acres in Reading, Pennsylvania. The College is named for Jacob Albright, a German evangelical preacher.

	Annual Growth	05/16	05/17	05/20	05/21	05/22
Sales ($mil.)	5.1%	–	57.1	42.3	46.4	73.1
Net income ($ mil.)	–	–	7.6	(9.2)	(4.1)	(4.6)
Market value ($ mil.)	–	–	–	–	–	–
Employees	–	–	–	–	–	394

ALC HOLDINGS, INC.

4005 ALL AMERICAN WAY
ZANESVILLE, OH 437017251
Phone: 740 452-2500
Fax: –
Web: www.axionintl.com

CEO: –
CFO: –
HR: –
FYE: December 31
Type: Private

Axion International Holdings surveyed the landscape and decided to shift into a new line of business. Formerly operating as Analytical Surveys, the company completed a reverse merger with Axion in 2008 and adopted that company's name and line of business. Axion is a licensee of technology regarding the manufacture of plastic composites used for structural applications such as railroad crossties, bridge infrastructure, marine pilings, and bulk headings. While the company is initially targeting the railroad industry, it has yet to generate any significant revenues.

ALCO STORES, INC.

751 FREEPORT PKWY
COPPELL, TX 750194411
Phone: 469 322-2900
Fax: –
Web: www.alcostores.com

CEO: –
CFO: –
HR: –
FYE: February 02
Type: Private

Some retailers prize locations where they can battle competitors toe-to-toe; ALCO Stores (formerly Duckwall-ALCO) covets locations big national discounters, such as Wal-Mart and Target, won't even consider. The retailer runs some 200 ALCO and ALCO Market Place discount stores in small towns in some two dozen states, primarily in the central US. Situated in towns with populations of 5,000 or fewer, ALCO stores offer a broad line of merchandise that includes automotive, apparel, consumables, crafts, electronics, fabrics, furniture, hardware, health and beauty aids, toys, and more. The company closed all of its smaller Duckwall stores to focus on growing its larger and more profitable ALCO chain.

ALCOA CORPORATION

NYS: AA

201 Isabella Street, Suite 500
Pittsburgh, PA 15212-5858
Phone: 412 315-2900
Fax: –
Web: www.alcoa.com

CEO: William Oplinger
CFO: Molly S Beerman
HR: –
FYE: December 31
Type: Public

Alcoa Corporation is a vertically integrated aluminum company comprised of bauxite mining, alumina refining, aluminum production (smelting and casting), and energy generation. With an extensive operational portfolio, the company conducts business across nine countries, where it operates more than 25 locations. It offers a comprehensive portfolio of products manufactured through low-carbon emitting processes in its Sustana family of products, including EcoDura aluminum, EcoLum aluminum, and EcoSource alumina. The company generates about 55% of its revenue from international customers. Formed in 2016, Alcoa consists of the upstream operations of its former parent company Alcoa Inc.

	Annual Growth	12/19	12/20	12/21	12/22	12/23
Sales ($mil.)	0.3%	10,433	9,286.0	12,152	12,451	10,551
Net income ($ mil.)	–	(1,125.0)	(170.0)	429.0	(123.0)	(651.0)
Market value ($ mil.)	12.1%	3,838.9	4,113.8	10,633	8,115.1	6,068.1
Employees	(0.4%)	13,800	12,900	12,200	13,100	13,600

ALCOR LIFE EXTENSION FOUNDATION

7895 E ACOMA DR STE 110
SCOTTSDALE, AZ 852606916
Phone: 480 905-1906
Fax: –
Web: www.alcor.org

CEO: –
CFO: –
HR: –
FYE: December 31
Type: Private

Alcor Life Extension Foundation is all about the future. The foundation, a provider of cryonics services, is the largest operation of its kind worldwide. Alcor has enlisted more than 840 members and has frozen some 80 people and animals in the first step to resuscitating them someday. Patients are frozen or "suspended" using liquid nitrogen -- which typically costs more than $150,000 for the process -- and stored in containers called "Dewars." Neurosuspensions (head-only) are $80,000 and whole-body suspensions are $150,000. Cryonic suspensions are usually funded through life insurance policies but some are paid for outright. Baseball great Ted Williams became the foundation's 50th suspension in July 2002.

	Annual Growth	12/13	12/14	12/15	12/17	12/19
Sales ($mil.)	10.4%	–	2.0	2.0	3.8	3.3
Net income ($ mil.)	–	–	0.3	0.1	2.1	(1.6)
Market value ($ mil.)	–	–	–	–	–	–
Employees	–	–	–	–	–	10

ALDEYRA THERAPEUTICS INC

NAS: ALDX

131 Hartwell Avenue, Suite 320
Lexington, MA 02421
Phone: 781 761-4904
Fax: –
Web: www.aldeyra.com

CEO: –
CFO: –
HR: –
FYE: December 31
Type: Public

Aldeyra Therapeutics focuses on the development of products to treat immune-mediated, inflammatory, orphan, and other rare diseases related to a naturally occurring toxic chemical species (free aldehydes). The company discovered and is developing NS2, a product candidate designed to trap and allow for the disposal of free aldehydes for the treatment of Sj gren-Larsson Syndrome (SLS, caused by mutations in an enzyme that metabolizes fatty aldehydes), and acute anterior uveitis, an inflammatory eye disease. Aldeyra is hoping to commercially develop NS2 and related products as an alternative to corticosteroids (which has toxic side effects). The company raised $12 million in 2014 IPO.

	Annual Growth	12/19	12/20	12/21	12/22	12/23
Sales ($mil.)	–	–	–	–	–	–
Net income ($ mil.)	–	(60.8)	(37.6)	(57.8)	(62.0)	(37.5)
Market value ($ mil.)	(11.8%)	343.9	406.1	236.8	412.0	207.8
Employees	(15.9%)	20	11	12	15	10

ALDRIDGE ELECTRIC, INC.

844 E ROCKLAND RD
LIBERTYVILLE, IL 600483358
Phone: 847 680-5200
Fax: –
Web: www.aldridgegroup.com

CEO: Alex Aldridge
CFO: Gene Huebner
HR: –
FYE: March 31
Type: Private

Aldridge Electric powers up the Windy City and other parts of the Midwest. The electrical contractor divides its business into six main areas: airport, industrial, power, drilling, highway, and transit. It works on projects ranging from Chicago's subway system to its airport runways. Additional activities include services for street lighting, traffic signals, high-voltage cabling and splicing, and foundation drilling. Aldridge Electric has worked for clients such as Commonwealth Edison Company and Exelon Corporation. It sister companies in the family-owned AldridgeGroup include Aldridge Construction, GFS Construction, and Woodward Brothering.

	Annual Growth	03/08	03/09	03/10	03/11	03/17
Sales ($mil.)	6.3%	–	–	272.2	208.9	417.2
Net income ($ mil.)	–	–	–	10.5	2.1	–
Market value ($ mil.)	–	–	–	–	–	–
Employees	–	–	–	–	–	850

ALEGENT CREIGHTON HEALTH

12809 W DODGE RD
OMAHA, NE 681542155
Phone: 402 343-4300
Fax: –
Web: www.chisaintjosephhealth.org

CEO: Jeanette Wojtalewicz
CFO: Nick O 'toole
HR: Donna Cloonan
FYE: June 30
Type: Private

CHI Health (formerly Alegent Creighton Health) pledges allegiance to medical well-being in its corner of the Midwest. The not-for-profit health care system operates 15 hospitals with about 3,000 beds in Omaha and surrounding communities in eastern Nebraska and southwestern Iowa, including Bergan Mercy Medical Center and Immanuel Medical Center. Alegent Creighton Health's hospitals provide specialty services including cardiovascular, orthopedic, and cancer care; it also operates psychiatric, long-term care, home health, and outpatient centers. The health system is sponsored by Catholic Health Initiatives and is affiliated with Creighton University.

	Annual Growth	06/18	06/19	06/20	06/21	06/22
Sales ($mil.)	(7.2%)	–	599.1	636.9	528.1	479.5
Net income ($ mil.)	(55.5%)	–	27.8	12.8	9.0	2.5
Market value ($ mil.)	–	–	–	–	–	–
Employees	–	–	–	–	–	10,000

ALERE INC.

51 SAWYER RD STE 200
WALTHAM, MA 024533448
Phone: 781 647-3900
Fax: -
Web: www.globalpointofcare.abbott

CEO: -
CFO: -
HR: -
FYE: December 31
Type: Private

Alere manufactures professional and consumer diagnostic health tests. Its professional diagnostic products include tests for cancers, cardiovascular disease, drugs of abuse, infectious diseases, and women's health, including pregnancy tests and fertility monitors. Alere also makes consumer diagnostics, including First Check drug tests, through a venture with Procter & Gamble . Branded products include Cholestech (lipid and cholesterol testing), Determine (HIV, tuberculosis, hepatitis B, and syphilis detection), Toxicology (drug and alcohol testing), and Nycocard (diabetes diagnosis and management). Abbott Laboratories acquired Alere for $5.3 billion in October 2017.

ALERISLIFE INC.

255 WASHINGTON ST STE 300
NEWTON, MA 024581634
Phone: 617 796-8387
Fax: -
Web: www.fivestarseniorliving.com

CEO: Jeff Leer
CFO: Heather Pereira
HR: Beronica Galindo
FYE: December 31
Type: Private

AlerisLife, is the provider of an evolving portfolio of residential and lifestyle services to older adults that are financially flexible and choice-based. With roots in senior living, the company is expanding its reach and vision, seeking to pioneer nontraditional ways to meet the needs of coming generations of aging adults. Its offerings span physical spaces, life enrichment programs and innovative conveniences, with curated choices to honor personal preferences, enable newfound freedoms and inspire daily discoveries. In 2023, AlerisLife was acquired by ABP Acquisition LLC, or ABP, for $43.8 million.

ALEX LEE, INC.

120 4TH ST SW
HICKORY, NC 286022947
Phone: 828 725-4424
Fax: -
Web: www.alexlee.com

CEO: Brian A George
CFO: Andrew Almquist
HR: Rafeal Lanier
FYE: October 01
Type: Private

The Alex Lee family of companies includes Lowes Foods and Merchants Distributors (MDI). Alex Lee grew out of Merchants Produce Company which was founded in 1931 by Alex and Lee George. MDI supplies food and general merchandise to more than 600 retailers with food and non-food items in over 10 Eastern states. The company's Consolidation Services supplies an array of warehousing and logistics services. As part of its business, Alex Lee also operates Lowes Food stores, a chain of approximately 75 grocery stores located in the Carolinas and Virginia. In addition to small grocery stores, the company serves customers across restaurants, schools, hospitals, and mill stores. The George family continues to control Alex Lee.

	Annual Growth	09/18	09/19*	10/20	10/21	10/22
Sales ($mil.)	19.3%	-	2,286.1	3,192.2	3,556.2	3,880.5
Net income ($ mil.)	12.3%	-	25.2	56.4	88.3	35.7
Market value ($ mil.)	-	-	-	-	-	-
Employees	-	-	-	-	-	9,550

*Fiscal year change

ALEXANDER & BALDWIN INC (REIT)

822 Bishop Street, P.O. Box 3440
Honolulu, HI 96801
Phone: 808 525-6611
Fax: -
Web: www.alexanderbaldwin.com

NYS: ALEX
CEO: -
CFO: James E Mead
HR: -
FYE: December 31
Type: Public

Alexander & Baldwin (A&B) is the only publicly-traded real estate investment trust to focus exclusively on Hawai'i commercial real estate and is the state's largest owner of grocery-anchored, neighborhood shopping centers. The company has been operating ever since 1870. The company operated through its segments; Commercial Real Estate and Land operation. A&B operates a commercial portfolio comprising of about 20 retail centers, around 10 industrial assets, and four office properties, includes about 3.9 million square feet of gross leasable area as well as about 140.7 acres of land.

	Annual Growth	12/19	12/20	12/21	12/22	12/23
Sales ($mil.)	(16.8%)	435.2	305.3	379.3	230.5	208.9
Net income ($ mil.)	-	(36.4)	5.6	35.4	(50.6)	29.8
Market value ($ mil.)	(2.4%)	1,517.5	1,243.8	1,816.5	1,356.1	1,377.0
Employees	(39.8%)	793	618	611	144	104

ALEXANDER'S INC

210 Route 4 East
Paramus, NJ 07652
Phone: 201 587-8541
Fax: -
Web: www.alx-inc.com

NYS: ALX
CEO: Steven Roth
CFO: Matthew Iocco
HR: -
FYE: December 31
Type: Public

Alexander's is a real estate investment trust (REIT) that owns, manages, and leases more than five properties in metropolitan New York City. Once a department store chain, Alexander's held on to its property interests, including the site of its erstwhile flagship store -- an entire block on Manhattan's Lexington Avenue. The REIT leases space at the mixed-use site to tenants such as Bloomberg, The Home Depot, and The Container Store. The Lexington site is also home to about 105 condominiums. In total, Alexander's has about 2.7 million sq. ft. of leasable space. Vornado Realty Trust manages the company and leases and develops its properties.

	Annual Growth	12/19	12/20	12/21	12/22	12/23
Sales ($mil.)	(0.2%)	226.4	199.1	206.1	205.8	225.0
Net income ($ mil.)	14.3%	60.1	41.9	132.9	57.6	102.4
Market value ($ mil.)	(10.3%)	1,687.2	1,416.5	1,329.4	1,123.9	1,090.8
Employees	7.5%	69	70	70	69	92

ALEXANDRIA EXTRUSION COMPANY

401 COUNTY ROAD 22 NW
ALEXANDRIA, MN 563084974
Phone: 320 763-6537
Fax: -
Web: www.alexandriaindustries.com

CEO: -
CFO: -
HR: Janelle Wunderlich
FYE: December 31
Type: Private

Alexandria Extrusion Company (doing business as Alexandria Industries) is a multifaceted, high quality, short lead-time producer of engineered products that meet customers' exact specifications. The company delivers customized aluminum extrusions, precision machining of ferrous and non-ferrous products, heatsinks, and plastic injection and foam molded components, as well as finishing, welding and assembly services. Its collective scope of processes and services simplifies supply chain management. Alexandria Industries markets its products to companies in a variety of industries, such as engineering and design, firearms, education, electronics, marine and recreation, medical, automotive, DOT sign manufacturing, and transportation. CEO Tom Schabel owns the company, which was founded in 1966.

	Annual Growth	12/08	12/09	12/10	12/11	12/12
Sales ($mil.)	16.8%	-	-	62.5	72.2	85.3
Net income ($ mil.)	-	-	-	-	-	-
Market value ($ mil.)	-	-	-	-	-	-
Employees	-	-	-	-	-	600

ALEXANDRIA INOVA HOSPITAL

4320 SEMINARY RD
ALEXANDRIA, VA 223041535
Phone: 703 504-3000
Fax: –
Web: www.inova.org

CEO: Jennifer McCarthy
CFO: Thomas Knight
HR: Marianne Castillo
FYE: December 31
Type: Private

Inova Alexandria Hospital provides medical, surgical, and therapeutic services in northeastern Virginia. The hospital was founded in 1872 and became part of the not-for-profit Inova Health System in 1997. Inova Alexandria Hospital has about 320 beds. The hospital offers specialty services such as heart and cancer treatment, women's and children's health care, emergency medicine, vascular procedures, interventional radiology, and sleep disorder and heartburn treatment services. The Inova Health System provides health care services in northern Virginia through a network of hospitals, clinics, assisted living centers, and other provider facilities.

	Annual Growth	12/14	12/15	12/17	12/18	12/21
Sales ($mil.)	3.2%	–	369.3	387.4	403.1	446.3
Net income ($ mil.)	0.3%	–	63.4	52.3	56.0	64.4
Market value ($ mil.)	–	–	–	–	–	–
Employees	–	–	–	–	–	1,750

ALEXANDRIA REAL ESTATE EQUITIES INC   NYS: ARE

26 North Euclid Avenue
Pasadena, CA 91101
Phone: 626 578-0777
Fax: –
Web: www.are.com

CEO: Peter M Moglia
CFO: Dean A Shigenaga
HR: –
FYE: December 31
Type: Public

Alexandria Real Estate Equities owns, develops, and operates offices and labs to life science tenants, including biotech and pharmaceutical companies, universities, research institutions, medical office developers, and government agencies. A real estate investment trust (REIT), Alexandria owns over 430 specialized properties with approximately 47.4 million sq. ft. of rentable space in the US and Canada. Its portfolio is largely located in high-tech hotbeds such as Greater Boston, New York City, the San Francisco Bay area, San Diego, Seattle, Maryland, and Research Triangle. The company was founded in 1994.

	Annual Growth	12/19	12/20	12/21	12/22	12/23
Sales ($mil.)	17.2%	1,531.3	1,885.6	2,114.2	2,589.0	2,885.7
Net income ($ mil.)	(26.9%)	363.2	771.0	571.2	521.7	103.6
Market value ($ mil.)	(5.9%)	27,777	30,638	38,329	25,042	21,793
Employees	6.7%	439	470	559	593	568

ALEXIAN BROTHERS HEALTH SYSTEM

200 S WACKER DR FL 12
CHICAGO, IL 606065801
Phone: 847 437-5500
Fax: –
Web: www.alexianbrothershealth.org

CEO: Mark A Frey
CFO: –
HR: –
FYE: June 30
Type: Private

O brother, can you spare some health care? Alexian Brothers Health System -- which follows the principles set forth by St. Alexius of Rome, the patron of beggars and pilgrims -- runs two acute care medical centers, a psychiatric hospital, and a rehabilitation hospital. It also operates numerous occupational health and community health clinics in the northwestern suburbs of Chicago, as well as home health and hospice agencies. With some 800 beds, Alexian Brothers Health System's hospitals emphasize such specialties as cardiology, obstetrics, orthopedics, and oncology. The health system was acquired by Catholic hospital operator Ascension Health in 2012.

	Annual Growth	06/17	06/18	06/19	06/20	06/21
Sales ($mil.)	(76.6%)	–	–	–	293.1	68.7
Net income ($ mil.)	–	–	–	–	(327.5)	(30.1)
Market value ($ mil.)	–	–	–	–	–	–
Employees	–	–	–	–	–	8,000

ALFA TECH CONSULTING ENGINEERS, INC.

1321 RIDDER PARK DR NO 50
SAN JOSE, CA 951312306
Phone: 408 487-1200
Fax: –
Web: www.atce.com

CEO: Jeff Fini
CFO:
HR: –
FYE: December 31
Type: Private

Alfa Tech Cambridge Group (ATCG) provides construction and project management, mechanical and electrical engineering, and IT planning for corporate facilities and high-tech buildings in both the public and private sectors, mainly in California. ATCG has done project work on banks, cultural institutions, hospitals, hotels, office buildings, residential complexes, and schools. Clients have included Apple, Kaiser Permanente, Lawrence Berkeley National Laboratory, and Stanford University. Formerly known as Alfa Tech Consulting Engineers, ATCG was formed from the 2006 merger between Alfa Tech and Cambridge Construction Management. The group is employee-owned.

	Annual Growth	06/97	06/98	06/99*	12/06	12/07
Sales ($mil.)	–	–	–	(1,075.3)	50.6	23.0
Net income ($ mil.)	219.0%	–	–	0.0	0.4	0.5
Market value ($ mil.)	–	–	–	–	–	–
Employees	–	–	–	–	–	86

*Fiscal year change

ALFRED NICKLES BAKERY, INC.

26 MAIN ST N
NAVARRE, OH 446621158
Phone: 330 879-5635
Fax: –
Web: www.nicklesbakery.com

CEO: –
CFO: –
HR: Gary Prato
FYE: December 25
Type: Private

Founded by Swiss immigrant Alfred Nickles in 1909, Alfred Nickles Bakery makes a broad range of fresh-baked goods. Thousands of customers have enjoyed the freshly baked bread, rolls, cakes, donuts and almost every baked food imaginable which has contributed to Nickles famous reputation as one of America's finest bakeries. Products include dinner rolls, deli-style, pastries, sweet rolls, and breakfast items. It has expanded its distribution area to meet the needs of customers in seven Midwestern states. Alfred Nickles operates about 20 distribution branches and three modern bakeries in West Virginia, Ohio and Pennsylvania.

ALFRED UNIVERSITY

1 SAXON DR
ALFRED, NY 148021232
Phone: 607 871-2111
Fax: –
Web: www.alfred.edu

CEO: –
CFO: –
HR: –
FYE: June 30
Type: Private

Alfred University was a progressive bastion of learning from the start. A private university in Western New York, the small non-sectarian school serves about 2,400 students. Its academic programs range from the liberal arts and sciences to engineering, business, and art and design, with degrees from a bachelor's to a Ph.D. The school also houses the New York State College of Ceramics. The student-faculty ratio is 12-to-1. The university was founded as the Select School in 1836, providing a coeducational environment from the school's beginnings. Alfred University (and the village it's in) is named for Alfred the Great, ninth-century ruler of southern England. Its mascot is, of course, the Saxons.

	Annual Growth	06/14	06/15	06/20	06/21	06/22
Sales ($mil.)	9.0%	–	67.3	–	114.9	123.0
Net income ($ mil.)	16.3%	–	4.0	–	10.1	11.5
Market value ($ mil.)	–	–	–	–	–	–
Employees	–	–	–	–	–	530

ALICO, INC.
NMS: ALCO

10070 Daniels Interstate Court, Suite 200
Fort Myers, FL 33913
Phone: 239 226-2000
Fax: -
Web: www.alicoinc.com

CEO: John E Kiernan
CFO: Bradley Heine
HR: -
FYE: September 30
Type: Public

Alico is an agribusiness with a legacy of achievement and innovation in citrus and conservation. One of the largest citrus producers in the US, its principal lines of business are citrus groves and land management. The company operates two divisions: Alico Citrus, a citrus producer on its own land and as a manager of citrus groves for third parties, and Land Management and Other Operations, which includes land conservation, encompassing environmental services, land leasing, and related support operations. All of its operating revenues are generated in the US.

	Annual Growth	09/19	09/20	09/21	09/22	09/23
Sales ($mil.)	(24.4%)	122.3	92.5	108.6	91.9	39.8
Net income ($ mil.)	(53.1%)	37.8	23.7	34.9	12.5	1.8
Market value ($ mil.)	(7.4%)	258.9	217.8	260.6	214.9	190.0
Employees	(4.7%)	235	251	222	206	194

ALIGHT

1325 QUINCY ST NE # 1A
MINNEAPOLIS, MN 554131540
Phone: 612 872-7060
Fax: -
Web: www.wearealight.org

CEO: -
CFO: -
HR: Anne Gabagaya
FYE: March 31
Type: Private

ARC has an overreaching mission to help people. The American Refugee Committee provides humanitarian aid for about two million refugees and displaced persons in the areas of health care and training, shelter repair and construction, water and sanitation, and psychosocial services and environmental rehabilitation. ARC works with people caught in the middle of war or civil conflicts in Africa, Asia, and Europe. It also worked to help Americans forced to flee the US Gulf Coast by hurricanes Katrina and Rita, by bringing a group of Minnesota medical personnel from Mayo Clinic, the University of Minnesota, the College of St. Catherine, and Nechama to Louisiana.

ALIGN COMMUNICATIONS INC.

608 RUSTIC RIDGE CT
SOUTHLAKE, TX 760928684
Phone: 212 207-2600
Fax: -
Web: www.align.com

CEO: -
CFO: -
HR: Amanda Pariaros
FYE: December 31
Type: Private

Align is a good match for businesses with a need to straighten out their information technology (IT) assets and services. The company specializes in data center design and build services, network and systems infrastructure, consolidating and relocating technology, and managed services such as help desk support and hosted computing for companies mainly in North America and the UK. Align, which has offices in six US states and the UK, serves clients in such industries as finance, health care, insurance, retail, and energy. Clients have included Blackrock, BP, and Dun & Bradstreet (the publisher of this profile). The company was founded in 1986.

ALIGN TECHNOLOGY INC
NMS: ALGN

410 North Scottsdale Road, Suite 1300
Tempe, AZ 85288
Phone: 602 742-2000
Fax: -
Web: www.aligntech.com

CEO: Joseph M Hogan
CFO: John F Morici
HR: -
FYE: December 31
Type: Public

Align Technology is a global medical device company engaged in the design, manufacture and marketing of Invisalign clear aligners and iTero intraoral scanners and services for dentistry, and exocad computer-aided design and computer-aided manufacturing (CAD/CAM) software for dental laboratories and dental practitioners. Its products are intended primarily for the treatment of malocclusion or the misalignment of teeth and are designed to help dental professionals achieve the clinical outcomes that they expect and the results patients' desire. To date, over 15 million people worldwide have been treated with Invisalign System. Most of the company's revenue comes from the US.

	Annual Growth	12/19	12/20	12/21	12/22	12/23
Sales ($mil.)	12.6%	2,406.8	2,471.9	3,952.6	3,734.6	3,862.3
Net income ($ mil.)	0.1%	442.8	1,775.9	772.0	361.6	445.1
Market value ($ mil.)	(0.5%)	20,949	40,119	49,338	15,833	20,571
Employees	10.4%	14,530	18,070	22,540	23,165	21,610

ALIMERA SCIENCES INC
NMS: ALIM

6310 Town Square, Suite 400
Alpharetta, GA 30005
Phone: 678 990-5740
Fax: -
Web: www.alimerasciences.com

CEO: Richard S Eiswirth Jr
CFO: Elliot Maltz
HR: -
FYE: December 31
Type: Public

Alimera Sciences wants to see clear into the future. The biopharmaceutical develops prescription ophthalmic medicines, particularly those aimed at treating ocular diseases affecting the retina. Alimera's first commercialized product, Iluvien, is an injectable insert -- smaller than a grain of rice -- that slowly releases a corticosteroid to the back of the eye to treat diabetic macular edema (DME). DME, a retinal disease affecting diabetics, can lead to severe vision loss and blindness. Iluvien is approved in the US (where it became commercially available in 2015) and in about 20 nations in Europe. Alimera is investigating another group of drugs as potential treatments for macular degeneration and diabetic retinopathy.

	Annual Growth	12/19	12/20	12/21	12/22	12/23
Sales ($mil.)	10.6%	53.9	50.8	59.0	54.1	80.8
Net income ($ mil.)	-	(10.4)	(5.3)	(4.4)	(18.1)	(20.1)
Market value ($ mil.)	(13.1%)	396.8	220.9	268.6	141.9	226.2
Employees	5.8%	127	140	154	158	159

ALINABAL HOLDINGS CORPORATION

28 WOODMONT RD
MILFORD, CT 064602872
Phone: 203 877-3241
Fax: -
Web: www.alinabal.com

CEO: -
CFO: -
HR: -
FYE: January 01
Type: Private

Alinabal Holdings operates through its individual business units that serve the automotive, aerospace, and printing industries. Alinabal Motion Transfer Devices manufactures spherical bearings, stamped molded bearing and linkage assemblies, and standard/custom rod ends. Alinabal Engineered Products produces complex mechanical assemblies and precision stampings. Its Alinabal Practical Automation unit provides printers (for use in ticket kiosks and ATMs), and the company also makes aircraft instrumentation (desiccators and dehumidifiers) and optical shutters (aka "beam blockers") through its DACO Instrument subsidiary. Alinabal was founded in 1913.

	Annual Growth	12/17	12/18	12/19*	01/21	01/22
Sales ($mil.)	-	-	57.0	56.0	49.7	56.9
Net income ($ mil.)	17.9%	-	4.6	4.0	1.1	8.9
Market value ($ mil.)	-	-	-	-	-	-
Employees	-	-	-	-	-	340

*Fiscal year change

ALITHYA USA, INC.

2500 NORTHWINDS PKWY STE 600
ALPHARETTA, GA 300092247
Phone: 781 246-3343
Fax: –
Web: –

CEO: –
CFO: –
HR: –
FYE: December 31
Type: Private

Edgewater Technology tries to stay on the cutting edge of technology management consulting. The company provides management consulting, designs customized software applications, implements third-party software, and helps enterprises optimize business processes. Its managed services division allows clients to outsource management and maintenance of IT facilities. Edgewater Technology has expertise in such markets as financial services, health care, insurance, and higher education and targets middle-market clients and divisions of large (Global 2000) firms located mostly in the US. Edgewater counts more than 400 customers, and its consultants work onsite at clients' facilities.

ALJ REGIONAL HOLDINGS INC

244 Madison Avenue, PMB #358
New York, NY 10016
Phone: 888 486-7775
Fax: –
Web: www.aljregionalholdings.com

NBB: ALJJ

CEO: –
CFO: –
HR: –
FYE: September 30
Type: Public

ALJ Regional Holdings owns a steel mini-mill in Kentucky, which it acquired in 2005. The mill is operated by Kentucky Electric Steel, which produces bar flat products that it sells to service centers as well as makers of truck trailers, steel springs, and cold drawn bars. Kentucky Electric Steel produces steel in both Merchant Bar Quality and Special Bar Quality. The company also recycles steel from scrap to produce steel. Kentucky Electric Steel operates mainly in the US, Canada, and Mexico.

	Annual Growth	09/18	09/19	09/20	09/21	09/22
Sales ($mil.)	(10.0%)	369.8	355.0	389.1	440.9	242.5
Net income ($ mil.)	–	(7.3)	(16.0)	(67.7)	(4.6)	144.1
Market value ($ mil.)	3.3%	63.6	51.7	27.0	39.4	72.5
Employees	–	2	6,322	8,407	6,963	–

ALL AMERICAN CONTAINERS, INC.

9330 NW 110TH AVE
MEDLEY, FL 331782519
Phone: 305 887-0797
Fax: –
Web: www.veritivcontainers.com

CEO: Salvatore Abbate
CFO: Stephen Smith
HR: –
FYE: December 31
Type: Private

It has become an All American pastime to put liquid consumer products (everything from beer, to honey, to cleaning products) in safe, sturdy, and attractive containers. All American Containers supports this tradition by making containers for the beverage, chemical, cosmetic, food, liquor, perfume, and pharmaceutical industries. The manufacturer's range of products includes glass, plastic, and metal tubes and dispensers, and plastic and metal closures. The company exports its products to more than 50 countries around the world. Major customers include Coca-Cola, McCormick, PepsiCo, and Seven-Up. All American Containers was founded by female Floridian and CEO Remedios Diaz-Oliver in 1991.

	Annual Growth	12/01	12/02	12/03	12/06	12/07
Sales ($mil.)	2.7%	–	96.0	104.0	102.1	109.7
Net income ($ mil.)	9.4%	–	2.6	2.3	5.9	4.0
Market value ($ mil.)	–	–	–	–	–	–
Employees	–	–	–	–	–	260

ALL POINTS COOPERATIVE

120 8TH ST
GOTHENBURG, NE 691381006
Phone: 308 537-7141
Fax: –
Web: www.allpoints.coop

CEO: –
CFO: –
HR: –
FYE: September 30
Type: Private

All Points Cooperative provides agricultural support services to farmers and ranchers in central Nebraska. The cooperative offers seed, energy, fuel, agronomy, storage and purchasing services, along with financial, credit marketing, and purchasing assistance for its member/farmers. Its agronomy services include fertilizer application, soil sampling, and crop planning and management. Its energy division offers bulk fuel, bulk oil, heating oil and propane delivery. It also operates retail outlets, including two Ampride Convenience Stores and the Trustworthy Feed and Hardware Store. In addition to its headquarters in Gothenburg, Nebraska, All Points has cooperative operations in 12 other communities.

ALL SENSORS CORPORATION

16035 VINEYARD BLVD
MORGAN HILL, CA 950375480
Phone: 408 776-9434
Fax: –
Web: www.allsensors.com

CEO: –
CFO: –
HR: –
FYE: December 31
Type: Private

All Sensors Corporation is not afraid to discuss sensitive subjects. The company specializes in pressure sensor product development and manufacturing primarily focused on low pressure sensors for medical and industrial applications. In the medical industry the company's products are used for breathing monitoring and sensing differential pressure to calculate flow measurments. The company produces high accuracy sensors that offer pressure ranges from 1/2" of water full scale to 100 psi. The company's sensors see use in such applications as oxygen tanks and HVAC systems. The company was founded in 1999 by company president Dennis Dauenhauer.

	Annual Growth	12/07	12/08	12/09	12/10	12/11
Sales ($mil.)	11.6%	–	–	7.4	9.4	9.2
Net income ($ mil.)	1.0%	–	–	0.4	0.5	0.4
Market value ($ mil.)	–	–	–	–	–	–
Employees	–	–	–	–	–	38

ALL STAR GLASS, INC.

1845 MORENA BLVD
SAN DIEGO, CA 921103699
Phone: 619 275-3343
Fax: –
Web: www.allstarglass.net

CEO: –
CFO: –
HR: –
FYE: December 31
Type: Private

All Star Glass can help you out if a star, or something more terrestrial like a rock, collides with your windshield. The company repairs windshields and car windows through about 40 locations in California. All Star also refers out-of-state clients to one of 1,500 affiliates nationwide. It works with insurance agents and adjusters in hopes of smoothing the process for all involved. The company also works with fleet managers and performs on-site repairs. All Star keeps a 90-day inventory of glass on hand, allowing it to guarantee the parts are in stock. The Scharaga family, including CEO Sam Scharaga, owns the company.

	Annual Growth	12/15	12/16	12/17	12/18	12/20
Sales ($mil.)	3.0%	–	23.8	25.0	24.1	26.8
Net income ($ mil.)	28.2%	–	1.1	0.9	0.3	3.0
Market value ($ mil.)	–	–	–	–	–	–
Employees	–	–	–	–	–	215

ALL STAR PREMIUM PRODUCTS, INC

660 MAIN ST
FISKDALE, MA 015181259
Phone: 508 347-7672
Fax: –
Web: www.allstarincentivemarketing.com

CEO: Edward Galonek Sr
CFO: Ann Galonek
HR: Geri Labonte
FYE: December 31
Type: Private

Want to improve your business performance? The answer may lie within your incentives packaging. All Star Premium Products -- which does business as All Star Incentive Marketing -- provides solutions for companies wishing to develop, implement, and manage incentive programs and to make the best use of promotional products. All Star's incentive programs target sales teams, employees, customers, and prospects to improve business performance. The company's services include program design, product sourcing, fulfillment, measurement and reporting. The incentives marketing firm traces its roots back to 1967.

	Annual Growth	12/14	12/15	12/16	12/19	12/20
Sales ($mil.)	14.6%	–	30.3	31.0	32.6	59.9
Net income ($ mil.)	52.4%	–	0.4	0.3	0.9	3.1
Market value ($ mil.)	–	–	–	–	–	–
Employees	–	–	–	–	–	46

ALLAN MYERS, INC.

1805 BERKS RD
WORCESTER, PA 19490
Phone: 610 222-8800
Fax: –
Web: www.allanmyers.com

CEO: –
CFO: –
HR: –
FYE: December 31
Type: Private

American Infrastructure provides heavy civil construction services for projects in the Mid-Atlantic. Operating as Allan A. Myers in Pennsylvania and Delaware and as American Infrastructure in Maryland and Virginia, the family-run business builds and reconstructs highways, water treatment plants, medical facilities, and shopping centers, and offers site development for homebuilders. Its quarries and asphalt plants operate under the Independence Construction Materials (ICM) subsidiary, which supplies aggregates, asphalt, and ready-mixed concrete to its construction companies. The company is ranked by Engineering News-Record as 25th on the country's Top 50 list of heavy civil contractors.

	Annual Growth	12/18	12/19	12/20	12/21	12/22
Sales ($mil.)	7.9%	–	989.3	1,025.7	1,157.9	1,243.7
Net income ($ mil.)	(12.2%)	–	49.0	33.6	37.7	33.1
Market value ($ mil.)	–	–	–	–	–	–
Employees	–	–	–	–	–	2,000

ALLEGHENY COLLEGE

520 N MAIN ST
MEADVILLE, PA 163353902
Phone: 814 332-3100
Fax: –
Web: www.allegheny.edu

CEO: –
CFO: David McInally
HR: –
FYE: June 30
Type: Private

Allegheny College ranks among the oldest colleges and universities in the US. The private, co-educational liberal arts school was founded in 1815 with a class of just four students. Today, approximately 2,100 enrolled students can pursue Bachelor of Arts and Bachelor of Science degrees in more than 50 academic programs, including art, biology, communications, computer science, English, history, math, music, philosophy, psychology, and religious studies. It also offers accelerated master's and doctorate programs in partnership with other universities. Though the college is non-sectarian, it maintains a historic affiliation with the United Methodist Church.

	Annual Growth	06/18	06/19	06/20	06/21	06/22
Sales ($mil.)	(1.5%)	–	86.3	80.4	73.8	82.6
Net income ($ mil.)	–	–	13.6	1.3	64.4	(30.8)
Market value ($ mil.)	–	–	–	–	–	–
Employees	–	–	–	–	–	479

ALLEGHENY ENERGY SUPPLY COMPANY, LLC

800 CABIN HILL DR
GREENSBURG, PA 156011650
Phone: 724 837-3000
Fax: –
Web: www.alleghenyenergysupply.com

CEO: –
CFO: –
HR: –
FYE: December 31
Type: Private

First things first. FirstEnergy Solutions (formerly Allegheny Energy Supply) serves more than one million residential, commercial and industrial customers in the Northeast, Midwest and Mid-Atlantic regions. It operates 35 plants with 23,000 MW of generating capacity and supplies electricity to customers in Illinois, Maryland, Michigan, New Jersey, Ohio and Pennsylvania. It also manages the energy and procurement needs for more than 120,000 business clients. Allegheny Energy Supply, the former power production subsidiary of utility holding company Allegheny Energy, which was acquired by FirstEnergy in 2011, was merged into FirstEnergy Solutions.

ALLEGHENY GENERAL HOSPITAL INC

320 E NORTH AVE
PITTSBURGH, PA 152124772
Phone: 412 359-3131
Fax: –
Web: www.ahn.org

CEO: –
CFO: –
HR: –
FYE: June 30
Type: Private

If there is a critical trauma anywhere near Pittsburgh, Allegheny General Hospital (AGH) is ready to take it on. The roughly 630-bed hospital is the Level I Shock Trauma Center for the five-state region surrounding Steel City. AGH offers traditional medical and surgical services as well as cardiology care and organ transplants. The hospital also is engaged in research in areas such as neuroscience, oncology, trauma, and genetics. AGH, which treats nearly 22,000 patients each year, has about 800 physicians on its staff. The hospital, which is affiliated with Philadelphia's Drexel University College of Medicine, is a subsidiary of Allegheny Health System, which itself is owned by Highmark, Inc.

	Annual Growth	06/12	06/13	06/14	06/15	06/16
Sales ($mil.)	2.8%	–	–	–	700.5	720.3
Net income ($ mil.)	(31.7%)	–	–	–	107.5	73.4
Market value ($ mil.)	–	–	–	–	–	–
Employees	–	–	–	–	–	5,064

ALLEGIANT TRAVEL COMPANY

NMS: ALGT

1201 North Town Center Drive
Las Vegas, NV 89144
Phone: 702 851-7300
Fax: –
Web: www.allegiant.com

CEO: Maurice J Gallagher Jr
CFO: Robert J Neal
HR: –
FYE: December 31
Type: Public

Allegiant Travel is a leisure travel company focused on providing travel and leisure services and products to residents of under-served cities in the US. The company provides scheduled air transportation on limited-frequency, nonstop flights predominantly between under-served cities and popular leisure destinations. Besides providing scheduled air transportation which sells travel on about 575 routes to some 125 cities, the company also supply unbundled air-related services and products, as well as offering third party travel products such as hotel rooms and ground transportation to its passengers.

	Annual Growth	12/19	12/20	12/21	12/22	12/23
Sales ($mil.)	8.1%	1,841.0	990.1	1,707.9	2,301.8	2,509.9
Net income ($ mil.)	(15.6%)	232.1	(184.1)	151.9	2.5	117.6
Market value ($ mil.)	(17.0%)	3,179.6	3,457.2	3,417.1	1,242.1	1,509.2
Employees	9.2%	4,697	4,068	4,733	5,315	6,686

ALLEGIS GROUP, INC.

7301 PARKWAY DR
HANOVER, MD 20761159
Phone: 410 579-3240
Fax: –
Web: www.allegisgroup.com

CEO: Jay Alvather
CFO: –
HR: Stacie Forrester
FYE: December 31
Type: Private

Allegis Group is a global leader in talent solutions. Its companies include Aerotek; TEKsystems; Aston Carter; Actalent; Allegis Global Solutions; Major, Lindsey & Africa; Allegis Partners; MarketSource; Getting Hired; CareerCircle; QuantumWork; and QuantumWork Advisory. Allegis Group operates through more than 500 locations worldwide. The company and its network of specialized companies provide a full suite of complementary talent solutions that solves nearly every workforce challenge to empower business success while consistently delivering an unsurpassed quality experience. It will continue to focus on creating significant opportunity for people to grow their careers and for businesses to solve their most pressing challenges.

	Annual Growth	12/18	12/19	12/20	12/21	12/22
Sales ($mil.)	13.8%	–	–	12,269	14,478	15,876
Net income ($ mil.)	–	–	–	–	–	–
Market value ($ mil.)	–	–	–	–	–	–
Employees	–	–	–	–	–	85,000

ALLEGRO CORPORATION

20048 NE SAN RAFAEL ST
PORTLAND, OR 972307459
Phone: 503 491-8480
Fax: –
Web: www.allegromediagroup.com

CEO: –
CFO: –
HR: –
FYE: December 31
Type: Private

Allegro Corporation is one of the largest independent distributors of music in North America. The company distributes releases by more than 200 alternative, blues, classical, jazz, new age, and pop independent record labels. Allegro works with labels that have no fewer than 12 artists and/or 25 titles, including Knit Media's Knitting Factory Records, E1 Music, and K-Tel International. The company sells wholesale to CD retailers. It also sells directly to consumers through its online catalog and monthly new release books. Allegro was founded in 1982.

ALLEGRO MICROSYSTEMS, LLC

955 PERIMETER RD
MANCHESTER, NH 031033353
Phone: 603 626-2300
Fax: –
Web: www.allegromicro.com

CEO: Vineet Nargolwala
CFO: Mark Feragne
HR: –
FYE: March 30
Type: Private

Allegro MicroSystems is a leading global designer, developer, fabless manufacturer, and marketer of sensor integrated circuits (ICs) and application-specific analog power ICs enabling critical technologies in the automotive and industrial markets. Allegro is a leading supplier of magnetic sensor IC solutions worldwide. Its sensor ICs enable its customers to precisely measure motion, speed, position and current, while its power ICs include high-temperature and high-voltage capable motor drivers, power management ICs, light emitting diode (LED) driver ICs, and isolated gate drivers. Its solutions are based on its monolithic Hall effect and xMR technology that allows customers to develop contactless sensor solutions that reduce mechanical wear and provide greater measurement accuracy and system control. Asian markets, particularly China, generated the majority of its revenue.

	Annual Growth	03/12	03/13	03/16	03/17	03/18
Sales ($mil.)	6.0%	–	489.9	526.3	600.1	654.9
Net income ($ mil.)	9.7%	–	45.8	43.7	65.5	72.6
Market value ($ mil.)	–	–	–	–	–	–
Employees	–	–	–	–	–	3,500

ALLEN & COMPANY INCORPORATED

711 5TH AVE FL 9
NEW YORK, NY 100223168
Phone: 212 832-8000
Fax: –
Web: –

CEO: Donald R Keough
CFO: –
HR: –
FYE: December 31
Type: Private

For Allen & Company, there's no business like financing show business. The investment bank serves variously as investor, underwriter, and broker to some of the biggest names in entertainment, technology, and information. Viewed as something of a secret society, the firm has had a quiet hand in such hookups as Seagram (now part of Vivendi) and Universal Studios, Hasbro and Galoob Toys, and Disney and Capital Cities/ABC. The notoriously secretive firm's famous annual retreat in Sun Valley, Idaho, attracts more moguls than a double-black diamond ski run (Warren Buffett, Bill Gates, Rupert Murdoch, and Oprah Winfrey have attended).

ALLEN COMMUNICATION LEARNING SERVICES, INC.

55 W 900 S
SALT LAKE CITY, UT 841012931
Phone: 801 537-7800
Fax: –
Web: www.allencomm.com

CEO: Ron Zamir
CFO: Paul Zackrison
HR: Ryan Shurtz
FYE: December 31
Type: Private

Allen Communication Learning Services helps improve organizations' performance and productivity by developing customized training offerings. Founded in 1981, the employee-owned company provides systems like e-learning courseware and multimedia instruction (i.e. combining electronic courseware with Web meetings, podcasts, and e-mail), as well as related consulting, presentation preparation, and technical support services. The company's training courses address issues such as compliance, ethics, safety, and management effectiveness. Catering to a variety of industries, Allen has served clients such as Deutsche Bank, Avon, American Express, Rockwell Collins, Northrop Grumman, and Pfizer.

	Annual Growth	12/14	12/15*	04/17*	12/17	12/18
Sales ($mil.)	(5.2%)	–	14.8	13.7	15.0	12.6
Net income ($ mil.)	–	–	1.7	(0.0)	0.9	(0.1)
Market value ($ mil.)	–	–	–	–	–	–
Employees	–	–	–	–	–	53

*Fiscal year change

ALLEN LUND COMPANY, LLC

4529 ANGELES CREST HWY
LA CANADA FLINTRIDGE, CA 910113247
Phone: 800 811-0083
Fax: –
Web: www.allenlund.com

CEO: –
CFO: –
HR: –
FYE: December 31
Type: Private

The Allen Lund Company (ALC) knows loads; it matches shippers' loads with a network of truckload and less-than-truckload (LTL) carriers. (LTL carriers collect, consolidate, and haul freight from multiple shippers.) The brokerage firm arranges the transport of dry, refrigerated (predominantly produce), and flatbed cargo. It operates from 30 offices throughout more than 20 US states. ALC Logistics, ALC Perishable Logistics, and ALC International (an international division) assist shippers in managing transportation costs, tracking and tracing shipments, managing appointments, and executing freight forward management services overseas. The company was founded in 1976 by Allen Lund and his wife, Kathie Lund.

	Annual Growth	12/14	12/15	12/16	12/17	12/18
Sales ($mil.)	13.1%	–	457.5	426.3	516.0	661.8
Net income ($ mil.)	15.1%	–	13.2	12.4	10.3	20.1
Market value ($ mil.)	–	–	–	–	–	–
Employees	–	–	–	–	–	310

ALLERGY RESEARCH GROUP LLC

2300 S MAIN ST
SOUTH SALT LAKE, UT 841152734
Phone: 510 263-2000
Fax: –
Web: www.allergyresearchgroup.com

CEO: Stephen Levine
CFO: Stephen Levine
HR: –
FYE: December 31
Type: Private

You might only think about allergies once a year, but Allergy Research Group thinks about them every day. Through its Nutricology subsidiary, the company develops and markets hypoallergenic vitamins and nutritional supplements including amino acids, fatty acids, glandular tissue products, minerals, and multivitamins. It markets products directly to doctors, nutritionists, and other health care professionals under the Allergy Research Group label, and it distributes products to health food stores and pharmacies through its NutriCology label. The company was acquired by KI NutriCare, a subsidiary of Kikkoman Corporation, in 2008.

ALLETE INC

30 West Superior Street
Duluth, MN 55802-2093
Phone: 218 279-5000
Fax: –
Web: www.allete.com

NYS: ALE
CEO: Bethany M Owen
CFO: Robert J Adams
HR: Dustin Puchalla
FYE: December 31
Type: Public

ALLETE is well-positioned as a reliable provider of competitively-priced energy in the Upper Midwest and invests in transmission infrastructure and other energy-centric businesses. Most of its business is classified within its regulated operations, which include electric, gas, and water utilities located in northeastern Minnesota and northwestern Wisconsin. Those operations are conducted through subsidiaries Minnesota Power (approximately 150,000 retail customers) and Superior Water Light and Power (some 15,000 electric, nearly 13,000 gas, and some 10,000 water customers). ALLETE's other segment includes coal mining operations, emerging technologies related to electric utilities, and a real estate business (large land tracts in Florida). Subsidiary BNI Energy operates a mine in North Dakota that supplies, primarily, two generating co-ops, Minnkota Power and Square Butte.

	Annual Growth	12/19	12/20	12/21	12/22	12/23
Sales ($mil.)	11.0%	1,240.5	1,169.1	1,419.2	1,570.7	1,879.8
Net income ($ mil.)	7.4%	185.6	174.2	169.2	189.3	247.1
Market value ($ mil.)	(6.8%)	4,675.4	3,567.7	3,821.8	3,715.6	3,522.8
Employees	3.9%	1,339	1,342	1,365	1,494	1,560

ALLEY-CASSETTY COMPANIES, INC.

2 OLDHAM ST
NASHVILLE, TN 372131107
Phone: 615 244-7077
Fax: –
Web: www.alley-cassetty.com

CEO: –
CFO: –
HR: –
FYE: April 30
Type: Private

Some build with blood, sweat, and tears; Alley-Cassetty Companies do it with trucks, bricks, and coal. The company's trucking division specializes in hauling liquid- and dry-bulk cargo, including hazardous materials, while the Alley-Cassetty Truck Center sells and services commercial trucks. The building supply division, which operates in Georgia, Kentucky, and Tennessee, produces and distributes bricks and other masonry products. Alley-Cassetty also provides coal to commercial and industrial users, arranging its transportation via barge, train, and truck. Originally a coal company, Alley-Cassetty was formed in 1964 through the merger of two Nashville residential coal delivery companies dating to the 1880s.

	Annual Growth	03/06	03/07	03/08	03/09*	04/10
Sales ($mil.)	(28.5%)	–	–	–	114.0	81.5
Net income ($ mil.)	–	–	–	–	1.0	(0.3)
Market value ($ mil.)	–	–	–	–	–	–
Employees	–	–	–	–	–	350

*Fiscal year change

ALLIANCE FIBER OPTIC PRODUCTS, INC.

840 N MCCARTHY BLVD
MILPITAS, CA 950355114
Phone: 408 736-6900
Fax: –
Web: –

CEO: –
CFO: –
HR: –
FYE: December 31
Type: Private

Alliance Fiber Optic Products (AFOP) is no lightweight in light waves. Communications equipment designers and manufacturers plug AFOP's fiber-optic components into products used to build networks that connect cities, regions within cities, and telecommunications service providers with their individual customers. Its optical path integration and optical fiber amplifier components, which include attenuators, couplers, depolarizers, multiplexers, and splitters, account for most of sales. The company sells directly to telecom equipment makers, primarily in North America, where it gets about half of sales. AFOP has more than 200 customers; in mid-2016 it was acquired by Corning.

ALLIANCE FOR AUDITED MEDIA

4513 LINCOLN AVE STE 105B
LISLE, IL 605321290
Phone: 224 366-6939
Fax: –
Web: www.auditedmedia.com

CEO: –
CFO: –
HR: –
FYE: August 31
Type: Private

The Alliance for Audited Media (AAM; formerly Audit Bureau of Circulations) audits circulation data for print media in the US and Canada, including newspapers, consumer magazines, and farm and business publications. Advertising agencies and advertisers use AAM's audit data to make media purchasing decisions. AAM, which was founded in 1914, is the world's largest independent auditing organization for publication circulation. The company also provides auditing services for nontraditional media and trade shows. AAM makes its money primarily from charging fees for its audits and selling the related reports.

	Annual Growth	08/10	08/11	08/14	08/15	08/16
Sales ($mil.)	1.4%	–	23.4	21.7	24.9	25.1
Net income ($ mil.)	32.3%	–	1.0	(0.8)	3.7	4.1
Market value ($ mil.)	–	–	–	–	–	–
Employees	–	–	–	–	–	250

ALLIANCE FOR COOPERATIVE ENERGY SERVICES POWER MARKETING LLC

4140 W 99TH ST
CARMEL, IN 460327731
Phone: 317 344-7000
Fax: –
Web: www.acespower.com

CEO: Michael T Steffes
CFO: –
HR: –
FYE: December 31
Type: Private

A power lobby in its own right, Alliance for Cooperative Energy Services Power Marketing (or ACES Power Marketing), provides wholesale electricity and natural gas trading services to its member/owners, which operate in the eastern, southern, and Midwestern US. Its risk management services include portfolio analysis, transaction administration, consulting, training, and policy development. The company is owned by 17 power supply cooperatives which collectively have 35,000 MW of generating capacity. It also provides marketing and risk management services to utilities, power producers, and other end-users (such as public water agencies, municipalities, and industrial companies).

	Annual Growth	12/04	12/05	12/06	12/07	12/08
Sales ($mil.)	7.7%	–	–	25.0	27.4	29.0
Net income ($ mil.)	(29.8%)	–	–	1.0	0.4	0.5
Market value ($ mil.)	–	–	–	–	–	–
Employees	–	–	–	–	–	200

ALLIANCE HEALTHCARE SERVICES, INC.

18201 VON KARMAN AVE STE 600
IRVINE, CA 926121000
Phone: 800 544-3215
Fax: –
Web: www.alliancehealthcareservices-us.com

CEO: Percy C Tomlinson
CFO: –
HR: Aljelyn A Mshrm
FYE: December 31
Type: Private

Alliance HealthCare Services is a leading national provider of outsourced advanced radiology and radiation therapy services across 45 states in the US. Alliance partners with more than 1,000 hospitals, health systems and physician practices to provide a full continuum of solutions, including onsite outpatient services and comprehensive service line management. Alliance's roots date back more than 35 years, when Radiology division was founded as a mobile CT provider and shortly thereafter purchased its first MRI unit. In late 2021, Alliance was acquired by Akumin, a premier provider of outpatient radiology services in the US, for $820 million.

ALLIANCE HOLDINGS GP, L.P.

1717 S BOULDER AVE STE 400
TULSA, OK 741194805
Phone: 918 295-1415
Fax: –
Web: www.arlp.com

CEO: Joseph W Craft III
CFO: Brian L Cantrell
HR: –
FYE: December 31
Type: Private

When it comes to coal mining, it takes more than one company to make this Alliance work. Alliance Holdings GP owns Alliance Resource Management GP, the managing general partner of major coal mining company Alliance Resource Partners, L.P. The company is currently the second largest coal producer in the eastern United States with about 10 underground mining complexes in Illinois, Indiana, Kentucky, Maryland and West Virginia as well as a coal-loading terminal in Indiana. The company manage and report coal operations primarily under two regions, Illinois Basin and Appalachia. Alliance Resource market coal production to major domestic and international utilities and industrial users. The company has coal reserves totaling 1.76 billion tons. Alliance Resource owns both mineral and royalty interests in approximately 1.4 million gross acres in premier oil & gas producing regions in the United States, primarily the Permian, Anadarko and Williston Basins.

ALLIANCE LAUNDRY HOLDINGS LLC

221 SHEPARD ST
RIPON, WI 549711390
Phone: 920 748-3121
Fax: –
Web: www.alliancelaundry.com

CEO: Michael D Schoeb
CFO: –
HR: –
FYE: December 31
Type: Private

Laundry day can't come often enough for Alliance Laundry Holdings (ALH). Through its wholly owned subsidiary, Alliance Laundry Systems, the company designs, makes, and markets commercial laundry equipment used in Laundromats, multi-housing laundry facilities (such as apartments, dormitories, and military bases), and on-premise laundries (hotels, hospitals, and prisons). Its washers and dryers are sold under the brands Speed Queen, UniMac, Huebsch, IPSO, and Cissell. They're sold primarily in the US and Canada, but also overseas. Investment firm BDT Capital Partners controls the company, which was founded in 1908.

	Annual Growth	12/07	12/08	12/09	12/12	12/14
Sales ($mil.)	13.1%	–	–	393.2	505.5	726.3
Net income ($ mil.)	12.3%	–	–	16.6	16.4	29.6
Market value ($ mil.)	–	–	–	–	–	–
Employees	–	–	–	–	–	2,787

ALLIANCE OF PROFESSIONALS & CONSULTANTS, INC.

8200 BROWNLEIGH DR
RALEIGH, NC 276177411
Phone: 919 510-9696
Fax: –
Web: www.apcinc.com

CEO: –
CFO: –
HR: Kimberly Rogov
FYE: December 31
Type: Private

Alliance of Professionals & Consultants (APC) provides information technology and other technical staffing services for clients in the telecommunications, financial, manufacturing, e-commerce, pharmaceutical, and health care industries. The company offers temp-to-hire and permanent placement -- as well as total outsourcing arrangements -- in such areas as application development, quality assurance and testing, network engineering and security, and project management. It also operates staffing and consulting practices in engineering and business services. APC, which was founded in 1993, uses subcontractors to supply its clients with personnel for some projects.

	Annual Growth	12/15	12/16	12/17	12/19	12/22
Sales ($mil.)	(1.2%)	–	63.1	70.7	65.1	58.9
Net income ($ mil.)	10.0%	–	1.1	1.5	1.2	2.0
Market value ($ mil.)	–	–	–	–	–	–
Employees	–	–	–	–	–	735

ALLIANCE RESOURCE PARTNERS LP

NMS: ARLP

1717 South Boulder Avenue, Suite 400
Tulsa, OK 74119
Phone: 918 295-7600
Fax: –
Web: www.arlp.com

CEO: Joseph W Craft III
CFO: Brian L Cantrell
HR: –
FYE: December 31
Type: Public

Coal is the main resource of Alliance Resource Partners, which operates in the Illinois Basin, Central Appalachia, and Northern Appalachia. The company has 11 underground coal mining complexes in Illinois, Indiana, Kentucky, Maryland, Pennsylvania, and West Virginia. Alliance controls about 650 million tons of reserves. Approximately 205 million tons of these reserves, located in Hamilton County, Illinois, are leased to independent coal company White Oak Resources. Alliance produces about 32 million tons of coal annually, nearly all of which is sold to electric utilities.

	Annual Growth	12/19	12/20	12/21	12/22	12/23
Sales ($mil.)	7.0%	1,961.7	1,328.1	1,570.0	2,406.5	2,566.7
Net income ($ mil.)	12.1%	399.4	(129.2)	178.2	577.2	630.1
Market value ($ mil.)	18.3%	1,375.5	569.5	1,606.9	2,583.2	2,692.5
Employees	–	3,602	2,902	2,990	2,067	3,595

ALLIANCE SHIPPERS INC.

15515 S 70TH CT
ORLAND PARK, IL 604625105
Phone: 708 802-7000
Fax: –
Web: www.alliance.com

CEO: –
CFO: –
HR: –
FYE: June 30
Type: Private

Alliance Shippers knows that it often takes more than one company to move freight from origin to destination. A logistics provider, Alliance Shippers arranges the transportation of freight by rail, road, air, and sea. The company specializes in arranging intermodal freight transportation, in which goods move by multiple methods, such as train and truck. Alliance Shippers operates through about a dozen divisions, including units devoted to government customers and to temperature-controlled transportation. The company traces its historical roots back to 1977.

ALLIANCEBERNSTEIN HOLDING L.P.

501 COMMERCE ST
NASHVILLE, TN 372036039
Phone: 212 969-1000
Fax: –
Web: www.alliancebernstein.com

CEO: Seth P Bernstein
CFO: William R Siemers
HR: –
FYE: December 31
Type: Private

Boasting some $779 billion in assets under management, AllianceBernstein offers domestic and international mutual funds, as well as managed accounts, hedge funds, and defined-contribution investments, on behalf of individual investors and institutional clients, including public retirement funds, employee benefit plans, foundations, endowments, government entities, and insurance firms. AB also provides distribution, shareholder servicing, transfer agency services and administrative services to the mutual funds it sponsors. The US accounts for about 55% of company's total revenue. AB was founded in 1967 by Sanford C. Bernstein as a private securities firm.

ALLIANCEBERNSTEIN HOLDING LP   NYS: AB

501 Commerce Street
Nashville, TN 37203
Phone: 615 622-0000
Fax: –
Web: www.alliancebernstein.com

CEO: –
CFO: –
HR: –
FYE: December 31
Type: Public

The raison d'etre of AllianceBernstein Holding is its more than 35% stake in investment manager AllianceBernstein. (French insurer AXA, through its AXA Financial unit, owns a majority of the subsidiary.) AllianceBernstein, which has more than $420 million of client assets under management, administers about 200 mutual funds invested in growth and value equities, fixed-income securities, and index and blended strategies. The subsidiary also offer separately managed accounts, closed-end funds, structured financial products, and alternative investments such as hedge funds. It mainly serves institutional clients such as pension funds, corporations, and not-for-profits, in addition to retail investors.

	Annual Growth	12/18	12/19	12/20	12/21	12/22
Sales ($mil.)	3.1%	270.6	266.3	308.4	416.3	305.5
Net income ($ mil.)	3.1%	242.4	238.6	279.4	385.8	274.2
Market value ($ mil.)	5.9%	3,109.0	3,443.6	3,843.1	5,558.0	3,911.3
Employees	5.1%	3,641	3,811	3,929	4,118	4,436

ALLIANT ENERGY CORP   NMS: LNT

4902 N. Biltmore Lane
Madison, WI 53718
Phone: 608 458-3311
Fax: 608 458-4824
Web: www.alliantenergy.com

CEO: John O Larsen
CFO: Robert J Durian
HR: Kevin Cline
FYE: December 31
Type: Public

Alliant Energy is a US energy company that engages in electric generation and the distribution of the electricity and natural gas. Alliant Energy is the parent of two regulated utility companies, Interstate Power and Light (IPL) and Wisconsin Power and Light (WPL), which together serve approximately 995,000 electricity customers and approximately 425,000 natural gas customers in Iowa and Wisconsin. In addition to providing retail energy, the utilities sell wholesale electricity in Iowa, Illinois, and Minnesota.

	Annual Growth	12/19	12/20	12/21	12/22	12/23
Sales ($mil.)	2.5%	3,647.7	3,416.0	3,669.0	4,205.0	4,027.0
Net income ($ mil.)	5.5%	567.4	624.0	674.0	686.0	703.0
Market value ($ mil.)	(1.6%)	14,014	13,197	15,742	14,139	13,138
Employees	(2.3%)	3,597	3,375	3,313	3,129	3,281

ALLIANT INTERNATIONAL UNIVERSITY, INC.

10455 POMERADO RD
SAN DIEGO, CA 921311799
Phone: 415 955-2000
Fax: –
Web: www.alliant.edu

CEO: Andy Vaughn
CFO: Tarun Bhatia
HR: –
FYE: June 30
Type: Private

Alliant International University churns out mental health professionals, lawyers, teachers, businessmen, and forensic specialists. The university prepares students (graduates and undergraduates who've completed at least two years of college) for careers in psychology and applied social sciences. Alliant International University consists of five graduate schools specializing in psychology, business management, forensics, law, and education. It also operates two undergraduate educational centers and has an affiliation with the Presidio Graduate School, which focuses on sustainable management. It serves more than 4,000 students from its seven campus locations in California, as well as three satellite locations overseas.

	Annual Growth	06/07	06/08	06/09	06/10	06/14
Sales ($mil.)	(0.3%)	–	73.1	78.3	76.3	71.7
Net income ($ mil.)	–	–	1.8	8.5	1.9	(5.2)
Market value ($ mil.)	–	–	–	–	–	–
Employees	–	–	–	–	–	471

ALLIED BEVERAGE GROUP L.L.C.

700 KAPKOWSKI RD
ELIZABETH, NJ 072012131
Phone: 201 842-6200
Fax: –
Web: home.alliedbeverage.com

CEO: –
CFO: –
HR: –
FYE: March 31
Type: Private

A business with the mostest: What do you buy from a company that claims to be New Jersey's largest and most extensive wine and spirits distributor? Size aside, Allied Beverage specializes in supplying fine wines and spirits. It distributes alcoholic beverages and related products to restaurants and other licensed establishments (package stores, hotels, and clubs). Allied owns more than a dozen general and specialized sales and marketing companies, including Flagstaff Distributors, Meritage Wine Group, and J&J Distributing. Its core subsidiary, Majestic Wine & Spirits is a Pennsylvania-based brokerage and direct wholesaler; its services provide merchandising and promotional representation for several suppliers.

	Annual Growth	01/05	01/06	01/07*	03/09	03/20
Sales ($mil.)	(40.5%)	–	521.5	553.8	0.2	0.4
Net income ($ mil.)	(44.8%)	–	13.3	13.1	–	0.0
Market value ($ mil.)	–	–	–	–	–	–
Employees	–	–	–	–	–	815

*Fiscal year change

ALLIED HEALTHCARE PRODUCTS INC   NBB: AHPI Q

1720 Sublette Avenue
St. Louis, MO 63110
Phone: 314 771-2400
Fax: –
Web: www.alliedhpi.com

CEO: –
CFO: –
HR: –
FYE: June 30
Type: Public

Allied Healthcare Products helps medical workers get oxygen flowing. The medical equipment maker produces respiratory equipment used in hospitals, surgery centers, ambulances, and other medical facilities, as well as in patient homes. Its products include anesthesia equipment, oxygen cylinders, and nebulizers used in home respiratory therapy, as well as emergency resuscitation products. It also makes medical gas system components installed in hospital walls during construction, as well as spine immobilization backboards and other items used in trauma situations. Allied Healthcare sells directly to hospitals and through equipment dealers in the US and abroad.

	Annual Growth	06/18	06/19	06/20	06/21	06/22
Sales ($mil.)	(5.4%)	33.8	31.4	31.9	36.3	27.0
Net income ($ mil.)	–	(2.2)	(2.1)	(3.0)	1.7	(5.4)
Market value ($ mil.)	(9.3%)	9.7	7.5	47.3	16.7	6.5
Employees	(7.8%)	202	181	218	189	146

ALLIED INTERNATIONAL CORPORATION OF VIRGINIA

101 DOVER RD NE
GLEN BURNIE, MD 210606561
Phone: 410 424-4003
Fax: –
Web: www.alliedint.com

CEO: –
CFO: –
HR: –
FYE: December 31
Type: Private

Allied International imports packed food products from more than 35 countries for distribution to grocery retailers throughout the US. Its product portfolio includes breakfast cereals, candy, condiments, cookies, and crackers, as well as pasta products, oils, and salad dressings. It distributes such brands as Forrelli, Smith & Johnson, and Sunrise Valley. In addition, Allied International imports and distributes kosher products and general merchandise including cleaning products and personal care items. The family-owned company was formed in 1980.

	Annual Growth	12/18	12/19	12/20	12/21	12/22
Sales ($mil.)	25.3%	–	–	15,575	20,165	24,437
Net income ($ mil.)	12.9%	–	–	749.9	902.9	956.2
Market value ($ mil.)	–	–	–	–	–	–
Employees	–	–	–	–	–	17

ALLIED RESOURCES INC

NBB: ALOD

1403 East 900 South
Salt Lake City, UT 84105
Phone: 801 232-7395
Fax: –
Web: www.alliedresourcesinc.com

CEO: Ruairidh Campbell
CFO: Ruairidh Campbell
HR: –
FYE: December 31
Type: Public

Allied Resources has allied with Allstate Energy to get the most out of its Appalachian energy resources. The company is an oil and natural gas exploration and production enterprise with primary operations in West Virginia (in Calhoun and Ritchie counties). Allied Resources produces oil and natural gas from 145 wells, which are maintained and operated by Allstate Energy. The depth at which the wells produce ranges from 1,730 feet to more than 5,470 feet. The company also owns 13 gross wells in Goliad, Edwards, and Jackson counties, Texas. In 2008 Allied Resources reported proved reserves of 18,950 barrels of oil, and 1.4 billion cu. ft. of natural gas. CEO Ruairidh Campbell owns 27% of the company

	Annual Growth	12/17	12/18	12/19	12/20	12/21
Sales ($mil.)	0.2%	0.3	1.1	0.9	0.1	0.3
Net income ($ mil.)	–	(0.2)	0.6	0.3	(0.2)	(0.1)
Market value ($ mil.)	8.9%	1.1	0.8	1.1	1.8	1.6
Employees	–	–	–	–	–	–

ALLIED SECURITY HOLDINGS LLC

161 WASHINGTON ST STE 600
CONSHOHOCKEN, PA 194282083
Phone: 484 351-1300
Fax: –
Web: www.aus.com

CEO: William C Whitmore Jr
CFO: –
HR: –
FYE: December 31
Type: Private

Better than a blanket, Allied Security Holdings gives customers a sense of security. One of the largest private contract security firms in the US, it does business as AlliedBarton Security Services. It recruits and employs trained security guards to serve thousands of customers (some of which are large FORTUNE 500 companies) and their facilities. They include government facilities, hospitals, offices, ports, residential communities, shopping centers, and universities. The firm also provides employment and background screening services through its HR Plus subsidiary. In mid-2016, AlliedBarton merged with Universal Services of America to create Allied Universal, North America's largest security services group.

	Annual Growth	12/10	12/11	12/12	12/13	12/14
Sales ($mil.)	5.7%	–	–	1,923.9	2,042.4	2,149.2
Net income ($ mil.)	(25.0%)	–	–	43.8	51.7	24.7
Market value ($ mil.)	–	–	–	–	–	–
Employees	–	–	–	–	–	53,760

ALLIED UNIVERSAL ELECTRONIC MONITORING US, INC.

1838 GUNN HWY
ODESSA, FL 335563524
Phone: 813 749-5454
Fax: –
Web: www.attentigroup.com

CEO: –
CFO: –
HR: –
FYE: December 31
Type: Private

Pro Tech Monitoring helps keep an eye on parolees. Using global positioning system (GPS) satellites, the company's equipment and related services track offenders 24 hours a day, seven days a week. Offenders wear tamper-resistant ankle bracelets that transmit signals, traceable by GPS. A radio frequency monitoring line by Pro Tech offers home curfew reporting, too. Pro Tech's SMART Ware branded systems supervises offenders through a data center in Florida, providing different levels of surveillance. The company's customers include federal, state, and local government agencies throughout the US. Pro Tech is a subsidiary of Israeli monitoring technology company Attenti (formerly Dmatek).

ALLIENT INC

NMS: ALNT

495 Commerce Drive
Amherst, NY 14228
Phone: 716 242-8634
Fax: –
Web: www.alliedmotion.com

CEO: Richard S Warzala
CFO: Michael R Leach
HR: –
FYE: December 31
Type: Public

Allied Motion Technologies is a global company that designs, manufactures and sells precision and specialty controlled motion products and solutions used in a broad range of industries. The company makes nano-precision positioning systems, servo control systems, motion controllers, digital servo amplifiers and drives, brushless servo, torque, and coreless motors, brush motors, and integrated motor-drives. Its products are incorporated into a number of end products, including high-definition printers, scanners, surgical tools and equipment, surgical robots, diagnostic equipment, test equipment, patient mobility and rehabilitation equipment, hospital beds, and mobile equipment carts. Allied Motion's target markets include vehicle, aerospace and defense, industrial, and medical. The North America was responsible for about 65% of the total sales.

	Annual Growth	12/19	12/20	12/21	12/22	12/23
Sales ($mil.)	11.7%	371.1	366.7	403.5	503.0	578.6
Net income ($ mil.)	9.1%	17.0	13.6	24.1	17.4	24.1
Market value ($ mil.)	(11.2%)	790.9	833.3	595.1	567.7	492.7
Employees	7.7%	1,700	1,770	1,950	2,254	2,287

ALLIN CORP

381 Mansfield Avenue, Suite 400
Pittsburgh, PA 15220-2751
Phone: 412 928-8800
Fax: 412 928-0887
Web: www.allin.com

CEO: –
CFO: –
HR: –
FYE: December 31
Type: Public

Allin wants to be an all-in-one information technology (IT) provider on the high seas and dry land. The company (pronounced "all in") offers interactive media development and integration for cruise lines, technology infrastructure services, and systems integration. The company uses video equipment and services provided by On Command for its interactive TV operations. Formerly a provider of Microsoft-focused services, the company sold that business to PC maker Dell in 2009. With warrants, Pittsburgh investor Henry Posner controls just over 50% of Allin.

	Annual Growth	12/03	12/04	12/05	12/06	12/07
Sales ($mil.)	18.1%	12.9	12.6	14.3	19.0	25.1
Net income ($ mil.)	43.9%	0.8	0.3	(1.0)	1.9	3.3
Market value ($ mil.)	26.7%	0.0	0.0	0.0	0.0	0.0
Employees	18.7%	84	101	128	139	167

ALLINA HEALTH SYSTEM

2925 CHICAGO AVE
MINNEAPOLIS, MN 554071321
Phone: 612 262-5000
Fax: –
Web: www.allinahealth.org

CEO: Tom Lindquist
CFO: Duncan Gallagher
HR: –
FYE: December 31
Type: Private

Allina Health System is a not-for-profit health care system that cares for patient from beginning to end of life. The health system owns and operates more than 10 hospitals, around 90 clinics, 15 retail pharmacies, specialty care centers and specialty medical services, home care, and emergency medical transportation services. Alina Health System provides prevention and treatment of illness to improve the health of individuals, families, and communities throughout Minnesota and western Wisconsin. Allina Health System traces its roots back to 1855.

	Annual Growth	12/13	12/14	12/15	12/16	12/22
Sales ($mil.)	(80.5%)	–	–	–	3,947.7	0.2
Net income ($ mil.)	–	–	–	–	74.9	(0.1)
Market value ($ mil.)	–	–	–	–	–	–
Employees	–	–	–	–	–	26,400

ALLISON TRANSMISSION HOLDINGS INC   NYS: ALSN

One Allison Way
Indianapolis, IN 46222
Phone: 317 242-5000
Fax: –
Web: www.allisontransmission.com

CEO: –
CFO: –
HR: –
FYE: December 31
Type: Public

Allison Transmission is the world's largest manufacturer of fully-automatic transmissions for medium- and heavy-duty commercial vehicles and medium- and heavy-tactical US defense vehicles and a leader in electrified propulsion systems. Its products are used in a wide variety of applications, including on-highway trucks (distribution, refuse, construction, fire, and emergency), buses (primarily school and transit), motorhomes, off-highway vehicles and equipment (primarily energy, mining, and construction applications) and defense vehicles (tactical wheeled and tracked). Allison's customers include original equipment manufacturers (OEMs) as well as the US Department of Defense. The company also makes electric drives for transit buses and shuttles and its ReTran remanufactured transmissions for aftermarket customers. The US accounts for most of the company's revenue, but Allison also serves customers in Europe, Africa, Asia, and South America. The company traces its historical roots back to 1915.

	Annual Growth	12/19	12/20	12/21	12/22	12/23
Sales ($mil.)	3.0%	2,698.0	2,081.0	2,402.0	2,769.0	3,035.0
Net income ($ mil.)	2.7%	604.0	299.0	442.0	531.0	673.0
Market value ($ mil.)	4.7%	4,235.2	3,780.3	3,186.0	3,646.2	5,096.7
Employees	–	3,700	3,300	3,400	3,500	3,700

ALLSTATE CORP   NYS: ALL

3100 Sanders Road
Northbrook, IL 60062
Phone: 847 402-5000
Fax: –
Web: www.allstate.com

CEO: Thomas J Wilson
CFO: Jesse E Merten
HR: –
FYE: December 31
Type: Public

Serving more than 190.9 million policies in force, Allstate is one of the top overall property/casualty insurers. Its Allstate Protection segment sells auto, homeowners, and other property/casualty insurance products in Canada and the US. Other divisions provide life insurance, voluntary benefits such as short-term disability and critical illness policies, and consumer protection plans. In early 2021, Allstate closed the sales Allstate Life Insurance Company and certain affiliates Wilton Reassurance Company for $400 million.

	Annual Growth	12/19	12/20	12/21	12/22	12/23
Assets ($mil.)	(3.7%)	119,950	125,987	99,440	97,957	103,362
Net income ($ mil.)	–	4,847.0	5,576.0	1,599.0	(1,311.0)	(188.0)
Market value ($ mil.)	5.6%	29,462	28,802	30,824	35,527	36,675
Employees	3.6%	46,290	42,160	54,700	54,500	53,400

ALLY BANK

6985 S UNION PARK CTR STE 435
MIDVALE, UT 840474177
Phone: 801 790-5005
Fax: –
Web: www.ally.com

CEO: Jeffrey J Brown
CFO: –
HR: Laura Tritle
FYE: December 31
Type: Private

Ally Bank is on your side when it comes to banking. Formerly known as GMAC Bank, Ally Bank (which is a subsidiary of government-backed Ally Financial) offers savings and money market accounts, as well as traditional and no-penalty CDs. The online bank also offers interest checking accounts. The bank offers its services online and over the phone; it operates no physical branch locations. Clients also can use any ATM in the US and Ally will reimburse any fees charged by other banks. Ally Bank was revamped and renamed in 2009 in the midst of GM's (very public) financial difficulties. Predecessor GMAC Bank had been in operation since 2001.

	Annual Growth	06/04	06/05	06/06*	12/07	12/16
Assets ($mil.)	42.5%	–	–	3,586.2	28,473	123,548
Net income ($ mil.)	131.3%	–	–	0.3	291.4	1,273.3
Market value ($ mil.)	–	–	–	–	–	–
Employees	–	–	–	–	–	10,363

*Fiscal year change

ALLY FINANCIAL INC   NYS: ALLY

Ally Detroit Center, 500 Woodward Avenue, Floor 10
Detroit, MI 48226
Phone: 866 710-4623
Fax: –
Web: www.ally.com

CEO: Jeffrey J Brown
CFO: Bradley J Brown
HR: –
FYE: December 31
Type: Public

Ally Financial is a financial-services company with the nation's largest all-digital bank and an industry-leading automotive financing and insurance business. The company serves customers through a full range of online banking services (including deposits, mortgage lending, point-of-sale personal lending and credit-card products) and securities brokerage and investment advisory services. It also includes a corporate finance business that offers capital for equity sponsors and middle-market companies, as well as auto financing and insurance offerings.

	Annual Growth	12/19	12/20	12/21	12/22	12/23
Assets ($mil.)	2.1%	180,644	182,165	182,114	191,826	196,392
Net income ($ mil.)	(12.2%)	1,715.0	1,085.0	3,060.0	1,714.0	1,020.0
Market value ($ mil.)	3.4%	9,243.2	10,786	14,400	7,395.1	10,562
Employees	6.3%	8,700	9,500	10,500	11,600	11,100

ALMA COLLEGE

614 W SUPERIOR ST
ALMA, MI 488011599
Phone: 989 463-7111
Fax: –
Web: www.alma.edu

CEO: –
CFO: –
HR: –
FYE: June 30
Type: Private

Alma College is glad to show off its Gaelic garb. The school is a undergraduate liberal arts college situated on 100 acres in central Michigan and has an enrollment of about 1,400 students. Founded in 1886 by Presbyterians, the college has several Scottish traditions including a marching band clad in Kilts, a Scottish dance troupe, and its own official registered tartan. Each year Alma College hosts the Alma Highland Festival and Games, which feature traditional Scottish games and revelry.

	Annual Growth	06/18	06/19	06/20	06/21	06/22
Sales ($mil.)	1.1%	–	50.3	54.8	54.8	51.9
Net income ($ mil.)	–	–	(1.1)	2.7	34.2	(23.7)
Market value ($ mil.)	–	–	–	–	–	–
Employees	–	–	–	–	–	300

ALMOST FAMILY, INC.

9510 ORMSBY STATION RD STE 300
LOUISVILLE, KY 402235016
Phone: 502 891-1000
Fax: –
Web: www.almostfamily.com

CEO: –
CFO: –
HR: –
FYE: December 29
Type: Private

Almost Family steps in when you're more than an arm's reach from family members with health needs. With its home health nursing services, Almost Family offers senior citizens in 26 states (including Florida) an alternative to institutional care. Its Visiting Nurse unit provides skilled nursing care and therapy services at home under a variety of names, including Apex, Caretenders, Community Home Health, and Mederi-Caretenders. Its Personal Care Services segment, operating under the Almost Family banner, offers custodial care, such as housekeeping, meal preparation, and medication management. Almost Family operates 175 Visiting Nurse agencies and about 65 Personal Care Services locations.The company is merging with LHC Group.

	Annual Growth	12/13	12/14*	01/16*	12/16	12/17
Sales ($mil.)	17.1%	–	495.8	532.2	623.5	797.0
Net income ($ mil.)	14.7%	–	13.5	19.5	18.2	20.4
Market value ($ mil.)	–	–	–	–	–	–
Employees	–	–	–	–	–	14,200

*Fiscal year change

ALNYLAM PHARMACEUTICALS INC

675 West Kendall Street, Henri A. Termeer Square
Cambridge, MA 02142
Phone: 617 551-8200
Fax: 617 551-8101
Web: www.alnylam.com

NMS: ALNY

CEO: Yvonne L Greenstreet
CFO: Jeffrey V Poulton V
HR: –
FYE: December 31
Type: Public

Like a genetic linebacker, Alnylam Pharmaceuticals runs interference with RNA to prevent the forward progress of disease. RNA interference (RNAi) technology developed by the biotech firm can selectively shut off harmful genes. The company is developing a pipeline of candidates both individually and through collaborations with other drugmakers. Its disease targets include neurological ailments, hypercholesterolemia, and hemophilia. In mid-2018, the FDA approved the firm's patisiran drug for the treatment of neuropathy (nerve damage); it was the first RNAi-based therapy to gain approval in the US. Alnylam has additional partner-based programs in clinical or development stages, including candidates targeting respiratory syncytial virus (RSV) infection and liver cancers.

	Annual Growth	12/19	12/20	12/21	12/22	12/23
Sales ($mil.)	69.8%	219.8	492.9	844.3	1,037.4	1,828.3
Net income ($ mil.)	–	(886.1)	(858.3)	(852.8)	(1,131.2)	(440.2)
Market value ($ mil.)	13.5%	14,488	16,349	21,332	29,895	24,078
Employees	12.2%	1,323	1,453	1,665	2,002	2,100

ALON USA PARTNERS, LP

12700 PARK CENTRAL DR STE 1600
DALLAS, TX 752511500
Phone: 972 367-3600
Fax: –
Web: www.delekus.com

CEO: Alan Moret
CFO: Shai Even
HR: Eric Nystrom
FYE: December 31
Type: Private

The crude oil refinery of Alon USA Partners doesn't exactly stand alone, seeing as how it's situated right in the middle of the West Texas oil patch. Located in Big Spring with a capacity of 70,000 barrels per day, it powers the company's petroleum products refining and marketing business. The refinery mainly produces gasoline and diesel and jet fuel along with asphalt and petrochemicals, and the company markets them in Arizona, New Mexico, Oklahoma, and Texas. In 2012 Alon USA Partners was spun off by Alon USA Energy, which in turn is majority-owned by Alon Israel Oil. The same year the company went public through an IPO that raised $184 million.

ALPHA NATURAL RESOURCES, INC.

636 SHELBY ST STE 1C
BRISTOL, TN 376202236
Phone: 423 574-5100
Fax: –
Web: www.alphametresources.com

CEO: David Stetston
CFO: Andy Eidson
HR: –
FYE: December 31
Type: Private

The alpha and omega of Alpha Natural Resources is coal mining. One of the top coal producers in the US, the company produces steam and metallurgical coal at 19 active mines and 7 coal preparation plants, primarily in West Virginia and Kentucky. Alpha's sales are split between low-sulfur steam coal, used mainly for electricity generation, and metallurgical coal, used primarily to make coke -- a key component in the steelmaking process. The company produces about 84 million tons of coal per year. In April 2018, Alpha agreed to merge with Contura Energy Inc to create the largest US producer of met coal, reuniting the two companies that were split by the 2015 bankruptcy.

ALPHA-EN CORP

28 Wells Avenue, 2nd Floor
Yonkers, NY 10701
Phone: 914 418-2000
Fax: –
Web: www.alpha-encorp.com

NBB: ALPE

CEO: Sam Pitroda
CFO: Nathan J Wasserman
HR: –
FYE: December 31
Type: Public

alpha-En Corporation (formerly Avenue Entertainment) once brought entertainment to the street where you live. The company produced films such as Closer and The Merchant of Venice , and made-for-TV and cable movies, including Angels in America and Path To Paradise: The Untold Story of the World Trade Center Bombing , both for HBO. Its Wombat Productions created one-hour profiles of Hollywood celebrities, shown on networks such as PBS, A&E, and Bravo. The company halted production activities and sold its assets in 2007. It is seeking another business to acquire.

	Annual Growth	12/14	12/15	12/16	12/17	12/18
Sales ($mil.)	–	–	–	–	–	–
Net income ($ mil.)	–	(0.0)	(1.8)	(3.6)	(6.5)	(5.3)
Market value ($ mil.)	34.8%	9.9	37.9	49.8	109.2	32.6
Employees	–	–	10	10	8	13

ALPHABET INC

1600 Amphitheatre Parkway
Mountain View, CA 94043
Phone: 650 253-0000
Fax: –
Web: www.abc.xyz

NMS: GOOG L

CEO: Sundar Pichai
CFO: Ruth M Porat
HR: –
FYE: December 31
Type: Public

Alphabet is the holding company of Google, the firm behind the world's largest search engine, the world's most used smartphone operating system (Android), and a multitude of other internet-based services, including the world's largest video-sharing site (YouTube). Alphabet's other holdings include Chrome, Gmail, Google Drive, Google Maps, Google Photos, Google Play, Search; and the Other Bets include emerging businesses at various stages of development, ranging from those in the research and development phase to those that are in the beginning stages of commercialization. It generates over 50% of its revenue outside the US.

	Annual Growth	12/19	12/20	12/21	12/22	12/23
Sales ($mil.)	17.4%	161,857	182,527	257,637	282,836	307,394
Net income ($ mil.)	21.1%	34,343	40,269	76,033	59,972	73,795
Market value ($ mil.)	(43.2%)	16,688,799	21,837,894	36,097,118	1,099,346	1,740,537
Employees	11.3%	118,899	135,301	156,500	190,234	182,502

ALPHATEC HOLDINGS INC

NMS: ATEC

1950 Camino Vida Roble
Carlsbad, CA 92008
Phone: 760 431-9286
Fax: –
Web: www.atecspine.com

CEO: Patrick S Miles
CFO: J T Koning
HR: –
FYE: December 31
Type: Public

Alphatec Holdings aims to help people stand up straight and keep moving. The company develops and manufactures products used to treat spinal disorders including stenosis, compression fractures, and degenerating discs. Through its Alphatec Spine subsidiary, the company makes a variety of FDA-approved products for the spinal fusion market in the US, the world's largest spinal fusion market. Its spinal implant products include screws, plates, fixation systems, grafting materials, and surgical instruments. Alphatec markets its products to surgeons through a network of independent but exclusive distributors, as well as a direct sales force. The company develops its products through its manufacturing facilities in California and France.

	Annual Growth	12/19	12/20	12/21	12/22	12/23
Sales ($mil.)	43.6%	113.4	144.9	243.2	350.9	482.3
Net income ($ mil.)	–	(57.0)	(79.0)	(144.3)	(152.1)	(186.6)
Market value ($ mil.)	20.8%	987.9	2,021.8	1,591.6	1,719.7	2,104.0
Employees	38.7%	227	296	561	705	839

ALPINE AIR EXPRESS, INC.

1177 ALPINE AIR WAY
PROVO, UT 846018270
Phone: 801 373-1508
Fax: –
Web: www.alpine-air.com

CEO: Michael Dancy
CFO: –
HR: Max Crandall
FYE: October 31
Type: Private

Alpine Air Express flies the western skies to cart cargo for its customers. The air cargo company provides scheduled transportation of mail, packages, and other time-sensitive freight to more than 25 cities in the western half of the US mainland and in Hawaii. Its primary customers, the United States Postal Service and United Parcel Service, together account for more than 85% of sales. Alpine Air operates a fleet of about 25 Beechcraft turboprop planes from bases in Hawaii, Montana, and Utah. Along with its cargo operations, the company provides pilot training and aircraft maintenance services. CEO Eugene Mallette owns a controlling stake in Alpine Air.

ALRO STEEL CORPORATION

3100 E HIGH ST
JACKSON, MI 492036413
Phone: 517 787-5500
Fax: –
Web: www.alro.com

CEO: Randy Glick
CFO: Steve Laten
HR: –
FYE: May 31
Type: Private

Alro Steel runs its service centers like a grocery store for metals, keeping what customers need in easy reach. The service center operator, which has a dozen facilities in the US Northeast, Midwest, and Southeast, provides processing services such as aluminum circle cutting, CNC flame cutting, forming, and machining. The company carries an extensive inventory of steel products, along with industrial tools and supplies. It also offers plastic sheet, rod, tube, and film through its Alro Plastics division and distributes industrial tools and materials through subsidiary Alro Industrial Supplies.

	Annual Growth	05/16	05/17	05/18	05/19	05/22
Sales ($mil.)	16.6%	–	–	1,989.0	2,213.2	3,682.3
Net income ($ mil.)	32.5%	–	–	165.8	198.5	510.6
Market value ($ mil.)	–	–	–	–	–	–
Employees	–	–	–	–	–	2,400

ALS THERAPY DEVELOPMENT FOUNDATION INC

480 ARSENAL ST
WATERTOWN, MA 024722805
Phone: 617 441-7200
Fax: –
Web: www.als.net

CEO: Steve Perrin
CFO: –
HR: –
FYE: December 31
Type: Private

The ALS Therapy Development is a not-for profit biotechnology company that conducts medical research on amyotrophic lateral sclerosis, also known as Lou Gehrig's disease. The degenerative disease progressively attacks neurons in the brain and spinal cord. When these neurons can no longer send impulses to the body's voluntary muscles (due to ALS), the muscles begin to waste away. The organization focuses on drug discovery and development for a cure for ALS, both independently and through collaborations with drug and research entities. Director James Heywood established the company in 1999.

	Annual Growth	12/17	12/18	12/19	12/21	12/22
Sales ($mil.)	(6.8%)	–	15.0	13.1	12.4	11.4
Net income ($ mil.)	(13.2%)	–	2.7	1.7	3.4	1.5
Market value ($ mil.)	–	–	–	–	–	–
Employees	–	–	–	–	–	30

ALSCO INC.

505 E 200 S STE 101
SALT LAKE CITY, UT 841022007
Phone: 801 328-8831
Fax: –
Web: www.alsco.com

CEO: –
CFO: –
HR: Bettie Wicks
FYE: December 31
Type: Private

Alsco provides uniform laundry services and other products that keep businesses clean and safe for all kinds of customers in the healthcare, automotive, industrial, and hospitality industries. Operating from more than 180 branches in about 15 countries worldwide, the company rents and sells uniforms, linens, towels, napkins, and soft blankets to more than 355,000 customers worldwide. It also manages janitorial services, provides washroom supplies, and soap and sanitizer services. In addition, Alsco provides professional textile rental services and offers first aid that is fresh and budget-friendly. Alsco has locations in Australia, Brazil, Canada, Germany, Italy, New Zealand, Singapore, Malaysia, Thailand, the UK, and the US. The company was founded in 1889 by George Steiner and is still owned and operated by the Steiner family.

	Annual Growth	12/13	12/14	12/15	12/16	12/17
Sales ($mil.)	14.3%	–	–	683.4	704.3	892.3
Net income ($ mil.)	45.2%	–	–	30.6	38.5	64.6
Market value ($ mil.)	–	–	–	–	–	–
Employees	–	–	–	–	–	16,000

ALSERES PHARMACEUTICALS INC

NBB: ALSE

275 Grove Street Suite 2-400
Auburndale, MA 02466
Phone: 508 497-2360
Fax: –
Web: –

CEO: –
CFO: –
HR: –
FYE: December 31
Type: Public

Unlike most people, the folks at Alseres Pharmaceuticals (formerly Boston Life Sciences) want to get on your nerves. The biotechnology company is developing therapies and diagnostics related to nervous system conditions, such as spinal cord injury, Parkinson's disease, and attention deficit hyperactivity disorder (ADHD). Its lead candidate is Altropane, a molecular imaging agent for diagnosing Parkinson's disease and ADHD. Another candidate, Cethrin, aims to repair nerve damage caused by spinal cord injury; Alseres licensed Cethrin from Canadian firm BioAxone Therapeutic in 2006.

	Annual Growth	12/09	12/10	12/11	12/12	12/13
Sales ($mil.)	–	–	–	–	0.5	0.5
Net income ($ mil.)	–	(10.8)	0.5	(2.9)	(1.6)	(0.9)
Market value ($ mil.)	(41.5%)	0.0	0.0	0.0	0.0	0.0
Employees	(12.0%)	5	4	3	3	3

ALSTON & BIRD LLP

1201 W PEACHTREE ST NE STE 4900
ATLANTA, GA 303093424
Phone: 404 881-7000
Fax: –
Web: www.alston.com

CEO: –
CFO: Richard G Levinson
HR: Jessica Ferko
FYE: December 31
Type: Private

One of the leading local, national, and international law firms, Alston & Bird groups its practices into six main areas: corporate and finance, intellectual property, international, litigation, regulatory and specialty, and tax. The firm's intellectual property practice group is one of the nation's largest. Alston & Bird has a diverse network of attorneys, policy advisers, and patent agents. The firm serves a wide range of domestic and international clients, which have included Rocky Research. Alston & Bird traces its roots to a law practice founded in 1893.

ALSTON CONSTRUCTION COMPANY, INC.

400 CAPITOL MALL
SACRAMENTO, CA 958144436
Phone: 916 340-2400
Fax: –
Web: www.alstonco.com

CEO: Paul D Little
CFO: Adam Nickerson
HR: Heather S Clark
FYE: December 31
Type: Private

Alston Construction (formerly Panattoni Construction) offers a broad platform of general contracting, construction management, design-build services and virtual design management construction. The company serves a diverse array of industries, including healthcare, food and beverage, industrial, office, athletic facilities, and retail, among others. Refurbishing and extending buildings from its network of offices throughout the US, Alston Construction provides construction management services for such clients as Amazon.com, Bridgestone, Caterpillar, Clorox, FedEx, Petco, Helen of Troy, Under Armour, and Whirlpool. Completed approximately 6,010 projects, Alston Construction started in 1986.

	Annual Growth	12/14	12/15	12/17	12/18	12/19
Sales ($mil.)	18.6%	–	642.5	865.5	909.9	1,271.4
Net income ($ mil.)	28.4%	–	6.9	13.7	14.2	18.7
Market value ($ mil.)	–	–	–	–	–	–
Employees	–	–	–	–	–	200

ALTA MESA RESOURCES, LP

15021 KATY FWY STE 400
HOUSTON, TX 770941900
Phone: 281 530-0991
Fax: –
Web: –

CEO: –
CFO: –
HR: –
FYE: December 31
Type: Private

If Alta Mesa Holdings were your dinner companion, it'd ask, "Are you going to finish that?" The company goes over established oil and natural gas fields looking for what's left behind. It exploits mature fields originally developed by the big boys -- Shell, Chevron, and Exxon-- using enhanced oil recovery techniques that boost the amount of extractable oil and gas. Its properties are located in South Louisiana, Oklahoma, the Deep Bossier resource play of East Texas, Eagle Ford Shale play and Indian Point field in South Texas, the Blackjack Creek field in Florida, and the Marcellus Shale in West Virginia. The company reports proved reserves of 325 billion cu. ft. of natural gas and about 250 producing wells. In 2019 the company filed for Chapter 11 bankruptcy protection.

ALTABA INC.

140 E 45TH ST FL 15
NEW YORK, NY 100173144
Phone: 646 679-2000
Fax: –
Web: www.altaba.com

CEO: –
CFO: –
HR: –
FYE: December 31
Type: Private

Altaba Inc. is stocked with stock ? and that's about all. The company (formerly Yahoo Inc.) is a publicly traded, closed-end management investment which tracks the shares of Alibaba Group Holding Co., an online retailer based in China, and Yahoo Japan Corp., an internet company based in Japan. Altaba is the spinoff of the Yahoo assets that were left after Verizon Communications bought Yahoo's operating business for $4.4 billion in 2017.

ALTAIR ENGINEERING INC

NMS: ALTR

1820 East Big Beaver Road
Troy, MI 48083
Phone: 248 614-2400
Fax: –
Web: www.altair.com

CEO: James R Scapa
CFO: Matthew Brown
HR: –
FYE: December 31
Type: Public

Altair is a global leader in computational science and artificial intelligence enabling organizations across broad industry segments to drive smarter decisions in an increasingly connected world. It delivers software and cloud solutions in the areas of simulation, high-performance computing (HPC), data analytics, and artificial intelligence (AI). Its simulation and AI-driven approach to innovation is powered by its broad portfolio of high-fidelity and high-performance physics solvers, its market-leading technology for optimization and HPC, and its end-to-end platform for developing AI and digital twin solutions. Altair's software products represent a comprehensive, open architecture solution for computational science and AI to empower decision-making for improved product design and development, manufacturing, energy management and exploration, financial services, health care, and retail operations. The US operations generate almost half of the company's revenue.

	Annual Growth	12/19	12/20	12/21	12/22	12/23
Sales ($mil.)	7.5%	458.9	469.9	532.2	572.2	612.7
Net income ($ mil.)	–	–	(7.5)	(10.5)	(8.8)	(43.4)	(8.9)
Market value ($ mil.)	23.7%	2,946.6	4,773.9	6,344.4	3,731.0	6,904.8
Employees	6.4%	2,500	2,700	2,800	3,200	3,200

ALTAIR NANOTECHNOLOGIES INC

204 Edison Way
Reno, NV 89502-2306
Phone: 775 856-2500
Fax: –
Web: www.altairnano.com

CEO: –
CFO: –
HR: –
FYE: December 31
Type: Public

When Altair Nanotechnologies paints the town, its pigment of choice is titanium dioxide (TiO_2). The company produces titanium dioxide particles used in paints, coatings, and sensors. Altair intends to create new applications and products with its nanocrystalline technology. Its major development thus far has been its nano lithium-titanate battery materials, which offer superior performance, the company says, to other rechargeable batteries. In 2011, Canon Investment Holdings, through a subsidiary, purchased a 49% share in Altair for $57.5 million. The deal includes the transfer of Altair's lithium-titanate manufacturing process for producing battery cells to Canon's Energy Storage Technology (China) Group.

	Annual Growth	12/12	12/13	12/14	12/15	12/16
Sales ($mil.)	143.8%	1.5	8.2	14.3	54.7	54.7
Net income ($ mil.)	–	(18.0)	(14.6)	(16.0)	(19.5)	(3.6)
Market value ($ mil.)	–	25.0	45.5	12.9	0.3	–
Employees	88.0%	90	–	–	631	1,125

ALTAR PRODUCE, LLC

205 GRANT ST
CALEXICO, CA 922312272
Phone: 760 357-6762
Fax: –
Web: www.altarproduce.com

CEO: –
CFO: –
HR: –
FYE: September 30
Type: Private

Altar Produce is a leading supplier of fresh vegetables and fruits, specializing in asparagus. The company also offers chili peppers, spinach, and table grapes. It sources and markets fresh produce from growers in Mexico. Areas of production include Caborca, Sonora; Mexicali, Baja California; and Ciudad Constitucion, Baja California Sur. The company also has a cooling facility close to the Mexican border in California. Altar Produce ships its fruits and vegetables to food retailers and wholesalers worldwide; however, the majority of its customers are located in Canada and the US.

ALTARUM INSTITUTE

3520 GREEN CT STE 300
ANN ARBOR, MI 481051566
Phone: 734 302-4600
Fax: –
Web: www.altarum.org

CEO: Michael Monson
CFO: Mark Kielb
HR: Kathy Lowell
FYE: December 31
Type: Private

The Altarum Institute is a not-for-profit organization that provides health care research and consulting services primarily to government agencies. Altarum's services include policy analysis, program development and management, business operations planning and finance, clinical research support, strategic communications, and event design and management. Key customers include the US Department of Health and Human Services, the US Department of Defense Military Health System, and the US Department of Veterans Affairs. Altarum operates in California, Georgia, Maine, Michigan, Texas, and the Washington, DC area.

	Annual Growth	12/12	12/13	12/14	12/17	12/19
Sales ($mil.)	(7.3%)	–	79.0	59.9	56.9	50.0
Net income ($ mil.)	–	–	(1.8)	0.4	(2.4)	(0.7)
Market value ($ mil.)	–	–	–	–	–	–
Employees	–	–	–	–	–	455

ALTENBURG HARDWOOD LUMBER CO INC

10220 MAIN ST
ALTENBURG, MO 637326176
Phone: 573 824-5265
Fax: –
Web: www.altenburghardwood.com

CEO: –
CFO: –
HR: –
FYE: December 31
Type: Private

Altenburg Hardwood Lumber sells hardwood dimension lumber, plywood, and other wood products. The company also buys logs and processes such native American hardwoods as hard and soft maple, oak, walnut, and other species. Altenburg Hardwood Lumber sells its products to flooring manufacturers and other building materials providers in the US and abroad.

	Annual Growth	12/04	12/05	12/07	12/09	12/13
Sales ($mil.)	–	–	(1,794.0)	9.4	7.1	10.6
Net income ($ mil.)	145.3%	–	0.0	(0.2)	(0.4)	0.2
Market value ($ mil.)	–	–	–	–	–	–
Employees	–	–	–	–	–	55

ALTERA CORPORATION

101 INNOVATION DR
SAN JOSE, CA 951341941
Phone: 408 544-7000
Fax: –
Web: www.intel.com

CEO: John P Daane
CFO: Ronald J Pasek
HR: –
FYE: December 31
Type: Private

Altera is a fabless semiconductor company that specializes in high-density programmable logic devices (PLDs) -- integrated circuits (ICs) that OEMs can program to perform logic functions in electronic systems. PLDs are an alternative to custom-designed ICs, and offer a quick, reduced-cost chip. The company's products are used by its more than 12,500 customers worldwide in communications network gear, consumer electronics, medical systems, and industrial equipment. Altera outsources fabrication of the devices to top silicon foundry Taiwan Semiconductor Manufacturing Company. Customers outside the US represent most of the company's sales. Altera became a part of Intel in a $16.7 billion deal in late 2015.

ALTERRA MOUNTAIN COMPANY

3501 WAZEE ST STE 400
DENVER, CO 802163787
Phone: 303 749-8200
Fax: –
Web: www.alterramtn.co

CEO: Jared Smith
CFO: –
HR: –
FYE: June 30
Type: Private

Alterra Mountain is a family of over 15 iconic year-round resorts, the world's largest heli-skiing operation, and Ikon Pass - the premier ski and snowboard season pass offering access to more than 6,500 trails and 50 iconic mountain destinations throughout the Americas, Europe, Australia, New Zealand, and Japan. Its mountain resorts offer activities combining outdoor adventure and fitness with services and amenities such as retail, equipment rental, dining, lodging, ski school, spa services, golf, mountain biking, and other winter and summer activities. The company was formed in 2018 after a ski resort group led by KSL Capital Partners acquired Mammoth Resorts and Intrawest.

ALTERYX, INC.

17200 LAGUNA CANYON RD
IRVINE, CA 926185403
Phone: 888 836-4274
Fax: –
Web: www.alteryx.com

CEO: Kevin Rubin
CFO: Kevin Rubin
HR: Brandon Carroll
FYE: December 31
Type: Private

Alteryx is a leader in Analytic Process Automation (APA). The company's software unifies analytics, data science and business process automation in one self-service platform to accelerate digital transformation, deliver high-impact business outcomes, accelerate the democratization of data and rapidly upskill modern workforces. It sells what it calls self-service data analytics software by subscription. Alteryx's platform includes the Designer, Server, Promote, Connect, Analytics Hub and Intelligence Suite products that are available on-premise or as a service. Started in 1997, the company now sells to enterprises such as Chevron Corporation, Anheuser Busch, Barclays Capital, Biogen Idec and General Mills. The US accounts for around 70% of the company's total sales.

ALTEVA, INC.

400 MARKET ST STE 1100
PHILADELPHIA, PA 191062502
Phone: 877 258-3722
Fax: –
Web: www.alteva.com

CEO: William J Fox III
CFO: Matthew G Conroy
HR: –
FYE: December 31
Type: Private

Alteva (formerly Warwick Valley Telephone) provides communications services from its quiet niche. The independent facilities-based telecom company was established in 1902 and has about 20,000 access lines in operation. It provides local and long-distance services to consumers and businesses in a mostly rural area in southeastern New York (Warwick, Wallkill, and Goshen) and northwestern New Jersey (Vernon and West Milford). The company's Warwick Online unit offers dial-up and DSL Internet access, digital video, and a VoIP computer telephony service that is sold under the VoiceNet brand. Alteva's services for business customers include hosted conferencing and wholesale voice access.

ALTEX INDUSTRIES, INC.   NBB: ALTX

700 Colorado Blvd. #273
Denver, CO 80206
Phone: 303 265-9312
Fax: –
Web: –

CEO: –
CFO: –
HR: –
FYE: September 30
Type: Public

More OilRockies than AllTex(as), Altex Industries buys and sells oil and gas properties, participates in drilling exploratory wells, and sells oil and gas production to refineries, pipeline operators, and processing plants. The oil and gas exploration and production independent owns interests in two gross productive oil wells and 200 gross developed acres in Utah and Wyoming. Over the last few years Altex Industries has been forced to sell most of its oil and gas assets in order to pay down debt. CEO Steven Cardin holds a majority stake in the company.

	Annual Growth	09/19	09/20	09/21	09/22	09/23
Sales ($mil.)	(13.1%)	0.0	0.0	0.0	0.0	0.0
Net income ($ mil.)	–	(0.0)	(0.1)	(0.1)	0.3	(0.1)
Market value ($ mil.)	19.7%	0.9	0.9	1.4	1.0	1.8
Employees	–	1	1	1	1	1

ALTICE USA INC   NYS: ATUS

1 Court Square West
Long Island City, NY 11101
Phone: 516 803-2300
Fax: –
Web: www.alticeusa.com

CEO: Dennis Mathew
CFO: Marc Sirota
HR: –
FYE: December 31
Type: Public

Altice USA, Inc., through its brands such as Optimum and Suddenlink, provides broadband communications and video services in the US. Most of its customers are mainly in the New York metropolitan area and south-central US. The company provides broadband, video, telephony, and mobile services to 4.9 million residential and business customers in more than 20 states through a fiber-rich hybrid-fiber coaxial (HFC) broadband network and a fiber-to-the-home (FITH) network. In addition, the company's connectivity enables 4K ultra-high-definition (UHD) and high-definition (HD) video on multiple devices, online multi-player video game streaming platforms, video chatting, streaming music, high-quality virtual-and augmented reality experiences, and downloading of large files, which are all data-intensive.

	Annual Growth	12/19	12/20	12/21	12/22	12/23
Sales ($mil.)	(1.4%)	9,760.9	9,894.6	10,091	9,647.7	9,237.1
Net income ($ mil.)	(21.3%)	138.9	436.2	990.3	194.6	53.2
Market value ($ mil.)	(41.3%)	12,467	17,269	7,378.0	2,097.6	1,482.0
Employees	(0.2%)	10,700	8,900	9,000	11,000	10,600

ALTICOR INC.

7575 FULTON ST E
ADA, MI 493550001
Phone: 616 787-1000
Fax: –
Web: www.amway.com

CEO: –
CFO: Michael Cazer
HR: Claire Groen
FYE: December 31
Type: Private

Where there's a will (and an army of independent sales representatives), there's Amway. Operated through holding company Alticor, Amway is the world's top direct-selling company with millions of individual ABOs (Amway Business Owners) pitching everything from air filters to vitamins. The company makes some 450 unique products across the categories of nutrition (which generates about half of sales), beauty and personal care, and home. It is active in more than 100 countries across the globe with Asia (led by China) its largest market. Alticor is controlled by the families of Rich DeVos and Jay Van Andel, who founded Amway in 1959.

	Annual Growth	12/11	12/12	12/13	12/14	12/15
Sales ($mil.)	(10.3%)	–	–	11,754	10,805	9,459.8
Net income ($ mil.)	–	–	–	–	–	–
Market value ($ mil.)	–	–	–	–	–	–
Employees	–	–	–	–	–	14,000

ALTIGEN COMMUNICATIONS INC   NBB: ATGN

670 N. McCarthy Blvd., Suite 200
Milpitas, CA 95035
Phone: 408 597-9000
Fax: 408 597-2020
Web: www.altigen.com

CEO: –
CFO: –
HR: –
FYE: September 30
Type: Public

AltiGen Communications helps businesses find their calling on the Internet. The company provides Microsoft brand voice-over-IP (VoIP) telephone systems and administration software to small and midsized businesses and call centers. Its phone systems utilize both the Internet and public telephone networks to transmit voice signals. Its MaxCommunications Server (MaxCS) systems include voicemail, auto attendant menus, and other features of traditional business PBX systems; its AltiContact Manager product adds advanced call center functionality. AltiGen deals primarily through resellers and distributors, counts thousands of customers, most of them in the US.

	Annual Growth	09/18	09/19	09/20	09/21	09/22
Sales ($mil.)	4.4%	10.0	10.6	11.8	11.0	11.9
Net income ($ mil.)	–	9.8	1.9	1.4	(0.5)	(0.7)
Market value ($ mil.)	18.3%	12.4	26.9	55.7	54.5	24.2
Employees	10.1%	51	53	64	61	75

ALTIMMUNE INC   NMS: ALT

910 Clopper Road, Suite 201S
Gaithersburg, MD 20878
Phone: 240 654-1450
Fax: –
Web: www.altimmune.com

CEO: –
CFO: –
HR: –
FYE: December 31
Type: Public

Anthrax beware, Altimmune is out to get you and your brethren. Formerly known as PharmAthene, the clinical-stage immunotherapeutics firm develops medical products that protect against biological and chemical threats. Treatments under development include SparVax, an antigen anthrax vaccine; NasoVAX, a single-dose influenza vaccine; and HepTcell, an immunotherapeutic for chronic hepatitis B. Altimmune has two proprietary platforms (RespirVec and Densigen) which activate the body's immune system differently than traditional vaccines. Pharmathene merged with private firm Altimmune in May 2017.

	Annual Growth	12/18	12/19	12/20	12/21	12/22
Sales ($mil.)	–	10.3	5.8	8.2	4.4	(0.1)
Net income ($ mil.)	–	(39.2)	(20.5)	(49.0)	(97.1)	(84.7)
Market value ($ mil.)	68.1%	101.4	93.0	555.0	450.7	809.3
Employees	17.8%	27	25	43	47	52

ALTO INGREDIENTS INC NAS: ALTO

1300 South Second Street
Pekin, IL 61554
Phone: 916 403-2123
Fax: 916 446-3937
Web: www.pacificethanol.com

CEO: Bryon T McGregor
CFO: –
HR: –
FYE: December 31
Type: Public

Alto Ingredients (formerly Pacific Ethanol) is the leading producer and marketer of specialty alcohols and essential ingredients, and the largest producer of specialty alcohols in the US. The company sells co-products such as wet distillers grain (WDG), a nutritional animal feed, dried distillers grains with solubles (DDGS), wet and dry corn gluten feed, condensed distillers solubles, corn gluten meal, corn germ, corn oil, dried yeast, and CO_2. Its wholly-owned subsidiary, Eagle Alcohol Company LLC, or Eagle Alcohol, specializes in break bulk distribution of specialty alcohols. Eagle Alcohol purchases bulk alcohol from suppliers and then stores, denatures, packages, and resells alcohol products in smaller sizes, including tank trucks, totes, and drums, that typically garner a premium price to bulk alcohols. On an annualized basis, the company markets about 420 million gallons combined of its own alcohols and over 1.6 million tons of essential ingredients.

	Annual Growth	12/19	12/20	12/21	12/22	12/23
Sales ($mil.)	(3.7%)	1,424.9	897.0	1,207.9	1,335.6	1,222.9
Net income ($ mil.)	–	(88.9)	(15.1)	46.1	(41.6)	(28.0)
Market value ($ mil.)	42.2%	49.2	411.1	364.1	218.0	201.4
Employees	–	500	370	417	439	–

ALTRIA GROUP INC NYS: MO

6601 West Broad Street
Richmond, VA 23230
Phone: 804 274-2200
Fax: –
Web: www.altria.com

CEO: William F Gifford Jr
CFO: Salvatore Mancuso
HR: Ananda Lopezcarter
FYE: December 31
Type: Public

Altria Group is one of the largest cigarette companies in the US. Altria operates through subsidiary Philip Morris USA, which sells Marlboro ? one of the world's leading cigarette brand. It manufactures cigarettes under the Parliament, Benson & Hedges and Nat's, Chesterfield, Virginia Slims, and Basic brands, among many others. Altria, however, has diversified from solely a cigarette maker to a purveyor of cigars and pipe tobacco through John Middleton Co.; and smokeless tobacco products through UST. The group's investments in equity securities consisted of Anheuser-Busch InBev, Cronos Group, and JUUL Labs.

	Annual Growth	12/19	12/20	12/21	12/22	12/23
Sales ($mil.)	(0.6%)	25,110	26,153	26,013	25,096	24,483
Net income ($ mil.)	–	(1,293.0)	4,467.0	2,475.0	5,764.0	8,130.0
Market value ($ mil.)	(5.2%)	88,014	72,302	83,570	80,608	71,138
Employees	(3.2%)	7,300	7,100	6,000	6,300	6,400

ALTRU HEALTH SYSTEM

1200 S COLUMBIA RD
GRAND FORKS, ND 582014044
Phone: 701 780-5000
Fax: –
Web: www.altru.org

CEO: Todd Forkel
CFO: Craig Faerber
HR: –
FYE: December 31
Type: Private

Altru Health System provides medical care to over 230,000 residents throughout northeastern North Dakota and northwestern Minnesota. The integrated health care network administers everything from primary care to inpatient medical and surgical care through its Altru Hospital (with more than 255 beds) and Altru Specialty Centers (with about 40 beds). It also operates a cancer center, a rehabilitation center, dialysis facilities, and home health providers. A community of approximately 3,500 health professionals and support staff, the not-for-profit center was formed in 1997 by the integration of Grand Forks Clinic and United Health Services.

	Annual Growth	12/18	12/19	12/20	12/21	12/22
Sales ($mil.)	2.3%	–	589.2	595.3	557.1	630.7
Net income ($ mil.)	21.4%	–	10.5	45.8	47.2	18.8
Market value ($ mil.)	–	–	–	–	–	–
Employees	–	–	–	–	–	3,500

ALTUM, INCORPORATED

11921 FREEDOM DR STE 550
RESTON, VA 201905635
Phone: 703 964-5858
Fax: –
Web: www.altum.com

CEO: Steve Pinchotti
CFO: Wendy Fyock
HR: –
FYE: December 31
Type: Private

Altum hopes to provide alternatives to old fashioned data management solutions such as filing cabinets, paper, and pen. The company provides software and services that clients use to access, analyze, and manage enterprise data. Altum's software products include applications for data collection, collaboration, reporting, and text searches, as well as tools that enable grant-making organizations to analyze and manage their grant programs. The company also offers services such as consulting, training, support, and maintenance. Altum was founded in 1997.

	Annual Growth	03/06	03/07	03/08*	12/12	12/14
Sales ($mil.)	35.3%	–	–	2.3	8.4	14.0
Net income ($ mil.)	(31.3%)	–	–	2.1	0.2	0.2
Market value ($ mil.)	–	–	–	–	–	–
Employees	–	–	–	–	–	50

*Fiscal year change

ALVERNIA UNIVERSITY

400 SAINT BERNARDINE ST
READING, PA 196071737
Phone: 610 796-8200
Fax: –
Web: www.alvernia.edu

CEO: –
CFO: Joshua E Hoffman
HR: –
FYE: June 30
Type: Private

Alvernia University (formerly Alvernia College) is a private, Catholic, Franciscan liberal arts college. It offers about 40 undergraduate majors and about 20 undergraduate minors, as well as associate of science degrees in business and computer information systems, six master's degrees programs, and a doctor of philosophy program. Its main campus is located in Reading, Pennsylvania, with additional courses taught in Pottsville and Philadelphia. The university has a total enrollment of some 3,000 students. Alvernia was founded in 1958 by the Bernardine Franciscan Sisters. The institution gained university status in 2008.

	Annual Growth	06/18	06/19	06/20	06/21	06/22
Sales ($mil.)	(6.5%)	–	87.5	90.0	74.2	71.6
Net income ($ mil.)	54.1%	–	2.6	0.5	16.1	9.5
Market value ($ mil.)	–	–	–	–	–	–
Employees	–	–	–	–	–	293

ALVERNO COLLEGE

3400 S 43RD ST
MILWAUKEE, WI 532194844
Phone: 414 382-6000
Fax: –
Web: www.alverno.edu

CEO: –
CFO: –
HR: Cindi Maier
FYE: June 30
Type: Private

Alverno College is an independent liberal arts institution with an enrollment of more than 2,100 undergraduates and about 500 graduate students. It confers associate's, bachelor's, and master's degrees in more than 60 areas of study at four schools: Arts and Sciences, Business, Education, and Nursing. Matriculating only women in its undergraduate programs, Alverno accepts men as graduate students. Alverno takes its name from a mountain in Italy (La Verna) that was given to St. Francis as a gift and used by his followers as a place of reflection. The school was founded by the School Sisters of St. Francis in 1887.

	Annual Growth	06/16	06/17	06/20	06/21	06/22
Sales ($mil.)	(2.7%)	–	57.5	48.4	57.2	50.2
Net income ($ mil.)	–	–	4.3	(2.3)	4.5	(3.7)
Market value ($ mil.)	–	–	–	–	–	–
Employees	–	–	–	–	–	1,000

ALY ENERGY SERVICES INC (DE)

3 Riverway, Suite 920
Houston, TX 77056
Phone: 713 333-4000
Fax: –
Web: www.alyenergy.com

CEO: –
CFO: –
HR: –
FYE: December 31
Type: Public

A Preferred Voice may be one that makes life easier. Preferred Voice answers that call with a host of integrated voice-driven products and services. The company's Global Application Platform (GAP) lets telecommunications providers offer enhanced services such as ringtones and games, reminders, voice-activated dialing, and conferencing. The company's My Phone Services Suite features a network-based address book with offerings such as its flagship Rockin' Ringback and Emma, the virtual receptionist. Preferred Voice offers its services through half-a-dozen carriers, but wireless service provider MetroPCS Communications is its biggest customer, accounting for 52% of sales.

	Annual Growth	12/14	12/15	12/16	12/17	12/18
Sales ($mil.)	(20.1%)	42.5	29.1	11.0	14.6	17.3
Net income ($ mil.)	(39.8%)	2.6	(15.9)	(22.1)	(0.4)	0.3
Market value ($ mil.)	77.5%	0.6	0.9	0.0	0.2	5.6
Employees	(27.5%)	210	110	50	65	58

ALY ENERGY SERVICES, INC.

3 RIVERWAY STE 920
HOUSTON, TX 770561982
Phone: 713 333-4000
Fax: –
Web: www.alyenergy.com

CEO: –
CFO: –
HR: –
FYE: December 31
Type: Private

A Preferred Voice may be one that makes life easier. Preferred Voice answers that call with a host of integrated voice-driven products and services. The company's Global Application Platform (GAP) lets telecommunications providers offer enhanced services such as ringtones and games, reminders, voice-activated dialing, and conferencing. The company's My Phone Services Suite features a network-based address book with offerings such as its flagship Rockin' Ringback and Emma, the virtual receptionist. Preferred Voice offers its services through half-a-dozen carriers, but wireless service provider MetroPCS Communications is its biggest customer, accounting for 52% of sales.

ALYESKA PIPELINE SERVICE COMPANY

3700 CENTERPOINT DR
ANCHORAGE, AK 995035827
Phone: 907 787-8842
Fax: –
Web: www.alyeska-pipe.com

CEO: –
CFO: –
HR: Eric McGhee
FYE: December 31
Type: Private

Named after the Aleut word for mainland, The Alyeska Pipeline Service Company operates the 800-mile-long, 48-inch-diameter pipeline that transports crude oil and natural gas liquids from Alaska's North Slope to the marine oil terminal of Valdez in Prince William Sound. Founded in 1970 to make the newly discovered finds in Prudhoe Bay commercially accessible, the company was assigned the task of designing, building, operating, and maintaining the Trans-Alaska Pipeline System (TAPS). TAPS is owned by a consortium of oil and gas firms, including BP (49%), ConocoPhillips (29%), Exxon Mobil (21%), and Chevron (Unocal Pipeline, 1%).

ALZHEIMER'S DISEASE AND RELATED DISORDERS ASSOCIATION, INC.

225 N MICHIGAN AVE FL 17
CHICAGO, IL 606017652
Phone: 312 335-8700
Fax: –
Web: www.alz.org

CEO: Harry Johns
CFO: –
HR: –
FYE: June 30
Type: Private

Alzheimer's Association wants you to "maintain your brain". The charitable organization is working to prevent, treat, and ultimately cure Alzheimer's, a progressive brain disorder that destroys memory and the ability to learn, reason, and do other daily activities. The group has more than 80 local chapters throughout the US and numerous service programs including a 24-hour helpline, support groups, information libraries, public advocacy, an online community, and a registration program so wandering Alzheimer patients can be returned home safely. Alzheimer's Association also funds research and hosts national and international conferences for scientists and caregivers. Its annual fund raiser is the Walk to End Alzheimer's.

	Annual Growth	06/15	06/16	06/19	06/20	06/22
Sales ($mil.)	156.5%	–	1.8	389.7	403.1	502.0
Net income ($ mil.)	214.3%	–	0.0	3.1	15.3	58.9
Market value ($ mil.)	–	–	–	–	–	–
Employees	–	–	–	–	–	200

AM OPTERNA INC

6176 E MOLLOY RD
EAST SYRACUSE, NY 130571020
Phone: 703 653-1130
Fax: –
Web: –

CEO: Javad K Hassan
CFO: Saju Thomas
HR: –
FYE: December 31
Type: Private

AM Networks wants your network equipment to rise and shine each morning with a sparkle in its eye. The company provides network monitoring products and services for cable TV and broadband system operators. AM Networks' products include hardware and software to monitor and manage multiple types and brands of network equipment. The company has installed more than 500,000 network transponders around the world. As AM Communications, the company filed for Chapter 11 in 2003 and certain of its assets were purchased by NeST Technologies that year. AM Communications converted its bankruptcy case to Chapter 7 liquidation in 2004.

AMACORE GROUP INC

NBB: ACGI

Maitland Promenade 1, 485 North Keller Road, Suite 450
Maitland, FL 32751
Phone: 407 805-8900
Fax: –
Web: amacoregroup.com

CEO: Jay Shafer
CFO: G S Smith
HR: –
FYE: December 31
Type: Public

The Amacore Group wants you to be able to see a smaller optometry bill. Amacore is a provider of non-insurance based discount plans for eyewear and eyecare services, including surgery. Amacore Group's products are marketed to individuals, families, and businesses, as well as through the company's affiliations with insurance companies and other membership groups. The company has expanded its discount program offerings to include dental, hearing, chiropractic, and other health services. It also offers traditional health plans through partnerships with insurance providers.

	Annual Growth	12/05	12/06	12/07	12/08	12/09
Sales ($mil.)	158.3%	–	–	4.3	29.5	28.8
Net income ($ mil.)	–	–	–	(21.2)	(33.9)	(10.7)
Market value ($ mil.)	(74.6%)	–	–	471.6	120.5	30.4
Employees	–	–	–	–	103	89

AMAG PHARMACEUTICALS, INC.

1150 1ST AVE STE 910
KING OF PRUSSIA, PA 194061335
Phone: 617 498-3300
Fax: –
Web: www.covispharma.com

CEO: Michael Porter
CFO: Ozgur Kilic
HR: Kate Gaston
FYE: December 31
Type: Private

AMAG Pharmaceuticals is a commercial-stage pharmaceutical company focused on bringing innovative products to patients with unmet medical needs. The company develops and delivers innovative medicines for complex yet under-treated health conditions across a range of therapeutic areas. The company develops products such as Makena which helps reduce the risk of preterm birth in the indicated patient population. Feraheme is indicated for treatment of iron deficiency anemia (IDA) in adult patients. AMAG Pharmaceuticals, Inc. is now a subsidiary of the Covis Pharma Group, a Swiss specialty pharmaceutical company.

AMALGAMATED FINANCIAL CORP
NMS: AMAL

275 Seventh Avenue
New York, NY 10001
Phone: 212 255-6200
Fax: –
Web: www.amalgamatedbank.com

CEO: Keith Mestrich
CFO: Andrew Labenne
HR: Ruben Vargas
FYE: December 31
Type: Public

Amalgamated Bank serves working-class consumers, trade unions, and businesses through 20 branches in and around New York City, as well as through locations in California, New Jersey, Nevada, and Washington, DC. Services include deposit accounts, fund administration, and asset-based lending. Through its investment management division, the bank is also one of the leading providers of investment and trust services to Taft-Hartley plans in the US. Amalgamated Bank is controlled by UNITE HERE, a trade union of textile and hospitality trade employees, and 40% owned by both The Yucaipa Companies and WL Ross & Co. The FDIC-insured commercial bank has $3.5 billion in assets.

	Annual Growth	12/18	12/19	12/20	12/21	12/22
Sales ($mil.)	10.1%	192.3	215.2	231.1	208.9	282.4
Net income ($ mil.)	16.2%	44.7	47.2	46.2	52.9	81.5
Market value ($ mil.)	4.3%	598.7	597.1	421.8	514.8	707.3
Employees	(0.7%)	421	398	370	375	409

AMALGATED SUGAR COMPANY

1951 S SATURN WAY STE 100
BOISE, ID 837092924
Phone: 208 383-6500
Fax: –
Web: www.amalgamatedsugar.com

CEO: –
CFO: –
HR: Aubrey Nash
FYE: December 31
Type: Private

The Amalgamated Sugar Company, with roots reaching back to 1915, turns beets into sweets. It's the second-largest US sugar producer, processing sugar beets grown on about 180,000 acres in Idaho, Oregon, and Washington. The company manufactures granulated, coarse, powdered, and brown consumer sugar products marketed under the brand White Satin. It also makes products for retail grocery chains under private labels. The sugar company produces beet pulp, molasses, and other beet by-products for use by food and animal-feed manufacturers. Since 1997 Amalgamated Sugar has been owned by the Snake River Sugar Company, a cooperative that comprises sugar beet growers in Idaho, Oregon, and Washington.

	Annual Growth	12/09	12/10	12/11	12/12	12/13
Sales ($mil.)	3.7%	–	–	886.1	907.9	953.1
Net income ($ mil.)	16.0%	–	–	46.7	14.7	62.8
Market value ($ mil.)	–	–	–	–	–	–
Employees	–	–	–	–	–	1,500

AMANASU ENVIRONMENT CORP
NBB: AMSU

244 Fifth Avenue, 2nd Floor
New York, NY 10001
Phone: 604 790-8799
Fax: –
Web: –

CEO: Atsushi Maki
CFO: Atsushi Maki
HR: –
FYE: December 31
Type: Public

Development stage environmental engineering company Amanasu Environment Corporation owns the licensing rights to produce and market high-temperature furnaces, hot-water boilers that extract heat energy from waste tires, a patented process for purifying seawater and removing hazardous pollutants from wastewater, and a range of solar panels. Amanasu Environment, however, has not developed any products for commercial sale, although it has developed prototypes. The firm was incorporated in 1999. Chairman and president Atsushi Maki owns about 73% of the company.

	Annual Growth	12/17	12/18	12/19	12/20	12/21
Sales ($mil.)	–	–	–	–	–	–
Net income ($ mil.)	–	(0.1)	(0.1)	(0.1)	(0.1)	(0.1)
Market value ($ mil.)	(12.7%)	4.0	2.2	2.6	4.4	2.3
Employees	–	–	–	–	–	–

AMAZON.COM INC
NMS: AMZN

410 Terry Avenue North
Seattle, WA 98109-5210
Phone: 206 266-1000
Fax: 206 266-1821
Web: www.amazon.com

CEO: –
CFO: –
HR: –
FYE: December 31
Type: Public

Amazon.com designs its stores to enable hundreds of millions of unique products to be sold by the company and by third parties across dozens of product categories. Customers access its offerings through its websites, mobile apps, Alexa, devices, streaming, and physically visiting its stores. In terms of electronics, Amazon manufactures and sells electronic devices, including Kindle, Fire tablet, Fire TV, Echo, Ring, and other devices, and develops and produces media content. Amazon serve consumers, sellers, developers, enterprises, content creators, advertisers, and employees. Amazon acquired 1Life Healthcare, Inc. (One Medical) for approximately $3.9 billion in 2022. Almost 70% of sales were generated in US.

	Annual Growth	12/19	12/20	12/21	12/22	12/23
Sales ($mil.)	19.6%	280,522	386,064	469,822	513,983	574,785
Net income ($ mil.)	27.3%	11,588	21,331	33,364	(2,722.0)	30,425
Market value ($ mil.)	(46.5%)	19,186,123	33,816,704	34,620,452	872,172	1,577,593
Employees	17.6%	798,000	1,298,000	1,608,000	1,541,000	1,525,000

AMB FINANCIAL CORP
NBB: AMFC

7880 Wicker Ave., Suite 101
St. John, IN 46373
Phone: 219 365-6700
Fax: 219 365-9106
Web: www..acbanker.com

CEO: Michael Mellon
CFO: Steven A Bohn
HR: –
FYE: December 31
Type: Public

AMB Financial is the holding company for American Savings, a thrift serving Lake County, Indiana, near the southern tip of Lake Michigan. It operates four offices in Dyer, Hammond, Munster, and Schererville. Catering to local families and businesses, the bank offers checking and savings accounts, money market accounts, certificates of deposit, and IRAs. It mainly uses these deposit funds to originate real estate, construction, consumer, commercial, land, and other loans. One- to four-family residential mortgages account for approximately three-quarters of its loan portfolio. American Savings offers financial planning services through its American Financial Services division.

	Annual Growth	12/19	12/20	12/21	12/22	12/23
Assets ($mil.)	11.4%	228.6	262.3	288.0	324.8	352.4
Net income ($ mil.)	12.9%	1.3	2.8	3.8	3.2	2.2
Market value ($ mil.)	1.9%	15.4	14.5	22.6	19.0	16.6
Employees	–	–	–	–	–	–

AMBAC FINANCIAL GROUP, INC.

NYS: AMBC

One World Trade Center
New York, NY 10007
Phone: 212 658-7470
Fax: 212 208 3414
Web: www.ambac.com

CEO: Claude Leblanc
CFO: David Trick
HR: –
FYE: December 31
Type: Public

Holding company Ambac Financial operates through subsidiaries including its flagship unit Ambac Assurance, Everspan Financial Guarantee, and Ambac Assurance UK. The businesses offered financial guarantees and related services to customers around the world. Ambac Assurance guaranteed public finance, structured finance and international finance obligations.

	Annual Growth	12/19	12/20	12/21	12/22	12/23
Assets ($mil.)	(10.8%)	13,320	13,220	12,303	7,973.0	8,428.0
Net income ($ mil.)	–	(216.0)	(437.0)	(17.0)	523.0	4.0
Market value ($ mil.)	(6.5%)	974.9	695.1	725.4	788.2	744.8
Employees	14.4%	104	125	122	145	178

AMBARELLA, INC.

NMS: AMBA

3101 Jay Street
Santa Clara, CA 95054
Phone: 408 734-8888
Fax: –
Web: www.ambarella.com

CEO: Feng-Ming Wang
CFO: Brian C White
HR: Darlene Forsythe
FYE: January 31
Type: Public

Ambarella is a leading developer of low-power system-on-a-chip, or SoC, semiconductors and software for edge artificial intelligence, or AI, applications. The company's system-on-a-chip, or SoC, designs fully integrate high-definition video processing, image processing, artificial intelligence (AI) computer vision algorithms, audio processing and system functions onto a single chip. These low power SoCs deliver exceptional video and image quality and can extract valuable data from high-resolution video and radar streams. The company is currently addressing a broad range of human and computer vision applications, including video security, advanced driver assistance systems (ADAS), electronic mirrors, drive recorders, driver/cabin monitoring systems, autonomous driving, and industrial and robotic applications. Ambarella generates about 95% of its revenue from outside the US.

	Annual Growth	01/19	01/20	01/21	01/22	01/23
Sales ($mil.)	10.3%	227.8	228.7	223.0	331.9	337.6
Net income ($ mil.)	–	(30.4)	(44.8)	(59.8)	(26.4)	(65.4)
Market value ($ mil.)	–	–	–	–	–	–
Employees	5.7%	750	761	786	899	937

AMBASSADOR PROGRAMS, INC.

157 S HOWARD ST
SPOKANE, WA 992014422
Phone: 509 568-7700
Fax: –
Web: www.peopletopeople.com

CEO: –
CFO: –
HR: –
FYE: December 31
Type: Private

Ambassador Programs people are people people. The group operates the People to People Student Ambassador Program, an invitation-only educational program for students from grade school to high school. The organization sends groups of students abroad to fulfill the Ambassador Programs mission set forth by President Dwight Eisenhower: "To promote peace through understanding." Ambassadors have traveled to countries in Asia, Europe, the South Pacific, and other regions around the world to promote cultural, political, and historical understanding between nations, potentially earning school credits.

AMBER ROAD, INC.

1 MEADOWLANDS PLZ STE 1500
EAST RUTHERFORD, NJ 070732151
Phone: 201 935-8588
Fax: –
Web: www.e2open.com

CEO: James W Preuninger
CFO: Thomas E Conway
HR: Roy Montfort
FYE: December 31
Type: Private

Amber Road is a top provider of cloud-based global trade management (GTM) technology, it automates import and export processes to allow goods to flow across borders efficiently, legally, and profitably. Amber Road combines enterprise-class software and trade content (sourced in more than 145 countries) with a global supply chain network connecting customers with trading partners, including suppliers, freight forwarders, customs brokers, and transportation carriers. It delivers its GTM via a Software-as-a-Service (SaaS) model. Most of Amber Road's revenue comes from customers in the US. The company agreed to a $425 million acquisition offer from E2open in 2019.

AMC ENTERTAINMENT HOLDINGS INC.

NYS: AMC

One AMC Way, 11500 Ash Street
Leawood, KS 66211
Phone: 913 213-2000
Fax: –
Web: www.amctheatres.com

CEO: Adam M Aron
CFO: Sean D Goodman
HR: –
FYE: December 31
Type: Public

AMC Entertainment is one of the largest theater operators around the world. The world's largest theatrical exhibition company and an industry leader in innovation and operational excellence owns, partially owns, or operates approximately 940 theaters with over 10,500 screens worldwide, most of which are in megaplexes (units with more than 10 screens and stadium seating). It also has a significant presence in Europe through London-based subsidiary Odeon & UCI Cinemas Group. The company's theatrical exhibition revenues are generated primarily from box office admissions and theatre food and beverage sales. Most of its revenue were generated from the US. The company was founded in 1920.

	Annual Growth	12/19	12/20	12/21	12/22	12/23
Sales ($mil.)	(3.2%)	5,471.0	1,242.4	2,527.9	3,911.4	4,812.6
Net income ($ mil.)	–	(149.1)	(4,589.1)	(1,269.1)	(973.6)	(396.6)
Market value ($ mil.)	(4.1%)	1,886.6	552.4	7,087.6	1,060.5	1,594.7
Employees	(3.4%)	38,862	25,019	31,198	33,694	33,812

AMC NETWORKS INC

NMS: AMCX

11 Penn Plaza
New York, NY 10001
Phone: 212 324-8500
Fax: –
Web: www.amcnetworks.com

CEO: –
CFO: –
HR: –
FYE: December 31
Type: Public

AMC Networks is a global entertainment company known for its popular and award-winning content. It distributes its content to audiences globally on an array of distribution platforms, including linear networks and subscription streaming services, as well as through licensing arrangements. Its library of television and film properties includes The Walking Dead Universe, Anne Rice catalog, and Agatha Christie library. It operates in the entertainment industry for more than 40 years, powered by distinguished brands, including AMC, AMC+, BBC AMERICA (which the company operates through a joint venture with BBC Studios), IFC, SundanceTV, ALLBLK, HIDIVE, and IFC Films. Internationally, AMC Networks delivers programming that reaches subscribers in approximately 110 countries and territories around the world. It generates the majority of its revenue from the US.

	Annual Growth	12/19	12/20	12/21	12/22	12/23
Sales ($mil.)	(3.0%)	3,060.3	2,815.0	3,077.6	3,096.5	2,711.9
Net income ($ mil.)	(13.3%)	380.5	240.0	250.6	7.6	215.5
Market value ($ mil.)	(17.0%)	1,720.7	1,558.2	1,500.2	682.6	818.5
Employees	(11.2%)	3,062	2,357	2,026	1,948	1,900

AMCON DISTRIBUTING COMPANY
ASE: DIT

7405 Irvington Road
Omaha, NE 68122
Phone: 402 331-3727
Fax: 402 331-4834
Web: www.amcon.com

CEO: Christopher H Atayan
CFO: Charles J Schmaderer
HR: –
FYE: September 30
Type: Public

AMCON Distributing enjoys a healthy meal, but the company is not without its vices. A leading consumer products wholesaler, AMCON distributes more than 16,000 different consumer products, including cigarettes and other tobacco products, as well as candy, beverages, groceries, paper products, and health and beauty aids. AMCON serves about 4,500 convenience stores, supermarkets, drugstores, tobacco shops, and institutional customers in the Great Plains and Rocky Mountain regions. Throughout the Midwest and Florida, the company also operates a growing chain of health food stores under the Chamberlin's Natural Foods and Akin's Natural Foods Market banners.

	Annual Growth	09/19	09/20	09/21	09/22	09/23
Sales ($mil.)	16.2%	1,392.4	1,521.3	1,672.4	2,010.8	2,540.0
Net income ($ mil.)	37.9%	3.2	5.5	15.5	16.7	11.6
Market value ($ mil.)	28.2%	46.4	39.3	90.7	127.8	125.4
Employees	12.8%	912	929	934	1,217	1,476

AMDOCS LTD.
NMS: DOX

Amdocs, Inc., 625 Maryville Centre Drive, Suite 200
Saint Louis, MO 63141
Phone: 314 212-7000
Fax: –
Web: www.amdocs.com

CEO: –
CFO: –
HR: –
FYE: September 30
Type: Public

Amdocs helps bring telecom companies and their customers together. The company is a leading supplier of customer experience software and services for business support systems (BSS) and operational support systems (OSS), used by telecommunications providers to manage delivery of voice, data, and wireless services. Its applications help automate customer relationship management (CRM), sales, and billing operations. Amdocs also develops publishing software for creating print and online directories. In addition, the company offers outsourced customer service and data center services. Amdocs gets more than 70% of sales from customers in North America.

	Annual Growth	09/19	09/20	09/21	09/22	09/23
Sales ($mil.)	4.6%	4,086.7	4,169.0	4,288.6	4,576.7	4,887.6
Net income ($ mil.)	3.1%	479.4	497.8	688.4	549.5	540.7
Market value ($ mil.)	–	–	–	–	–	–
Employees	5.8%	24,516	25,875	27,176	30,288	30,695

AMEDISYS, INC.
NMS: AMED

3854 American Way, Suite A
Baton Rouge, LA 70816
Phone: 225 292-2031
Fax: –
Web: www.amedisys.com

CEO: Paul Kusserow
CFO: Scott G Ginn
HR: –
FYE: December 31
Type: Public

Through over 530 home health care agencies located throughout the US, Amedisys is a leading healthcare services company committed to helping its patients age in place by providing clinically excellent care and support in the home. It provides skilled nursing and home health services, primarily to geriatric patients covered by Medicare. It is also a post-acute care partner to over 3,000 hospitals and some 102,000 physicians across the country. In addition to home health services, Amedisys owns or manages about 165 hospice centers that offer palliative care to terminally ill patients. Amedisys provides home health, hospice care, personal care, and high acuity care services to more than 465,000 patients annually.

	Annual Growth	12/19	12/20	12/21	12/22	12/23
Sales ($mil.)	3.4%	1,955.6	2,105.9	2,227.4	2,223.2	2,236.4
Net income ($ mil.)	–	126.8	183.6	209.1	118.6	(9.7)
Market value ($ mil.)	(13.1%)	5,452.9	9,582.4	5,288.2	2,729.1	3,105.4
Employees	–	21,300	21,000	21,000	20,000	–

AMEN PROPERTIES INC
NBB: AMEN

P.O. Box 835451
Richardson, TX 75080
Phone: 972 999-0494
Fax: –
Web: www.amenproperties.com

CEO: –
CFO: –
HR: –
FYE: December 31
Type: Public

AMEN Properties is hoping that the answer to its prayers are power and energy, and a little property thrown in for good measure. The company's Priority Power subsidiary provides energy management and consulting services. This unit has current or previous business activities in Texas and 21 other states, and serves more than 1,200 clients (including a large number of oil and gas companies.) These activities include electricity load aggregation, natural gas and electricity procurement, energy risk management, and energy consulting. AMEN Properties also invests in commercial real estate in secondary markets and in oil and gas royalties.

	Annual Growth	12/17	12/18	12/19	12/20	12/21
Sales ($mil.)	3.4%	2.7	4.6	2.7	1.1	3.1
Net income ($ mil.)	(7.6%)	2.4	5.1	0.0	(0.5)	1.8
Market value ($ mil.)	(2.7%)	25.8	36.7	39.9	21.1	23.1
Employees	–	–	–	–	–	–

AMERAMEX INTERNATIONAL INC
NBB: AMMX

3930 Esplanade
Chico, CA 95973
Phone: 530 895-8955
Fax: 530 895-8959
Web: www.ammx.net

CEO: Lee Hamre
CFO: Hope Stone
HR: –
FYE: December 31
Type: Public

Let AmeraMex take care of the heavy stuff. The company sells, leases, services, and maintains heavy equipment to businesses such as heavy construction, surface mining, infrastructure, logging, shipping, and transportation. AmeraMex has four business units: Hamre Equipment, Hamre Heavy Haul Industry, Hamre Parts and Service, and John's Radiator. Its inventory includes front-end loaders, excavators, container handlers, and trucks and trailers; manufacturers represented include Taylor Machine Works, Terex Heavy Equipment, and Barko Hydraulics. The firm is active in the Americas, Europe, the Middle East, and Asia. AmeraMex also provides heavy hauling services throughout the US.

	Annual Growth	12/17	12/18	12/19	12/20	12/21
Sales ($mil.)	29.3%	8.8	10.1	13.4	12.3	24.7
Net income ($ mil.)	(0.8%)	1.7	1.4	0.3	(0.6)	1.6
Market value ($ mil.)	172.7%	0.0	0.2	0.1	7.2	5.0
Employees	–	–	–	–	16	21

AMEREN CORP
NYS: AEE

1901 Chouteau Avenue
St. Louis, MO 63103
Phone: 314 621-3222
Fax: –
Web: www.ameren.com

CEO: –
CFO: Michael L Moehn
HR: –
FYE: December 31
Type: Public

Missouri-based Ameren is a public utility holding company whose primary assets are its equity interests in its subsidiaries. As the sole distributor in its service region, the holding company distributes electricity to 1.2 million customers and natural gas to 100,000 customers. Ameren has generating capacity of around 5 million net kilowatt of primarily coal-fired power, most of which is owned by Ameren Missouri. About 97% of Ameren Missouri's coal is purchased from the Powder River Basin in Wyoming, which has a limited number of suppliers. The remaining coal is typically purchased from the Illinois Basin.

	Annual Growth	12/19	12/20	12/21	12/22	12/23
Sales ($mil.)	6.1%	5,910.0	5,794.0	6,394.0	7,957.0	7,500.0
Net income ($ mil.)	8.6%	828.0	871.0	990.0	1,074.0	1,152.0
Market value ($ mil.)	(1.5%)	20,452	20,787	23,703	23,679	19,264
Employees	0.1%	9,323	9,183	9,116	9,244	9,372

AMEREN ILLINOIS CO
NBB: AILL I

10 Richard Mark Way
Collinsville, IL 62234
Phone: 618 343-8150
Fax: –
Web: www.amereninvestors.com

CEO: Richard J Mark
CFO: Michael L Moehn
HR: –
FYE: December 31
Type: Public

Ameren Illinois brings gas and electric services to customers across the Land of Lincoln. The Ameren subsidiary operates a rate-regulated electric and natural gas transmission and distribution business in Illinois, serving more than 1.2 million electricity and 806,000 natural gas customers in 85 of Illinois' 102 counties. The multi-utility has a service area of 43,700 square miles. Ameren Illinois operates 4,500 miles of transmission lines, 45,400 miles of power distribution lines, and 18,000 miles of gas transmission and distribution mains. It also has 12 underground natural gas storage fields.

	Annual Growth	12/19	12/20	12/21	12/22	12/23
Sales ($mil.)	8.3%	2,527.0	2,535.0	2,895.0	3,756.0	3,482.0
Net income ($ mil.)	15.2%	346.0	382.0	427.0	515.0	609.0
Market value ($ mil.)	(6.3%)	2,639.3	2,658.4	2,632.9	2,397.0	2,033.6
Employees	(1.4%)	3,476	3,304	3,239	3,243	3,280

AMERESCO INC
NYS: AMRC

111 Speen Street, Suite 410
Framingham, MA 01701
Phone: 508 661-2200
Fax: –
Web: www.ameresco.com

CEO: George P Sakellaris
CFO: Spencer D Hole
HR: –
FYE: December 31
Type: Public

Ameresco is a leading clean technology integrator and renewable energy asset developer, owner, and operator. Its comprehensive portfolio includes energy efficiency, infrastructure upgrades, asset sustainability, and renewable energy solutions. Its core offerings include the development, design, arrangement of financing, construction, and installation of solutions that deliver measurable cost and energy savings while enhancing the operations, energy security, infrastructure, and resiliency of a facility. These solutions range from upgrades to a facility's energy infrastructure to the development, construction, and operation of renewable energy plants. Ameresco has approximately 60 regional offices in North America and the UK. The US accounts for about 95% of company's revenue.

	Annual Growth	12/19	12/20	12/21	12/22	12/23
Sales ($mil.)	12.2%	866.9	1,032.3	1,215.7	1,824.4	1,374.6
Net income ($ mil.)	8.9%	44.4	54.1	70.5	94.9	62.5
Market value ($ mil.)	16.0%	914.9	2,731.0	4,257.5	2,987.1	1,655.6
Employees	7.5%	1,127	1,141	1,272	1,363	1,503

AMERICA CHUNG NAM (GROUP) HOLDINGS LLC

1163 FAIRWAY DR
CITY OF INDUSTRY, CA 917892846
Phone: 909 839-8383
Fax: –
Web: www.acni.net

CEO: Teresa Cheung
CFO: Kevin Zhao
HR: –
FYE: December 31
Type: Private

America Chung Nam (ACN) is one of the world's largest exporters of recovered paper in the US and a leading exporter in Europe and Asia. The company sells recovered fiber sources to Chinese paper mills where it can be converted into fiberboard, cardboard, and packaging. It also collects and exports a number of grades of post-consumer plastics. Engaged in the export of recovered paper in America, Europe, and Asia, the company sources its materials through exclusive relationships with recycling facilities, waste management companies, and distribution centers. ACN has access to virtually all global shipping, rail and trucking routes, as well as ports in major cities around the world. Yan Cheung and Ming Chung Liu founded the ACN in 1990.

	Annual Growth	12/07	12/08	12/09	12/18	12/21
Sales ($mil.)	(2.8%)	–	1,363.3	1,125.2	1,711.7	943.5
Net income ($ mil.)	14.5%	–	7.9	16.9	216.3	46.1
Market value ($ mil.)	–	–	–	–	–	–
Employees	–	–	–	–	–	200

AMERICA'S CAR-MART INC
NMS: CRMT

1805 North 2nd Street, Suite 401
Rogers, AR 72756
Phone: 479 464-9944
Fax: –
Web: www.car-mart.com

CEO: Douglas W Campbell
CFO: Vickie D Judy
HR: –
FYE: April 30
Type: Public

America's Car-Mart is one of the largest publicly held automotive retailers in the US focused exclusively on the integrated auto sales and finance segment of the used car market. The company's subsidiaries operate about 155 used car dealerships in more than 10 states, primarily in smaller urban and rural markets throughout the US South-Central region. Dealerships focus on selling basic and affordable transportation, with an average retail sales price of about $16,080 per unit in fiscal 2023. Bill Fleeman founded America's Car-Mart in 1981.

	Annual Growth	04/19	04/20	04/21	04/22	04/23
Sales ($mil.)	20.4%	669.1	744.6	918.6	1,212.4	1,405.5
Net income ($ mil.)	(19.1%)	47.6	51.3	104.1	93.3	20.4
Market value ($ mil.)	(5.1%)	631.3	420.3	961.3	515.3	512.4
Employees	9.0%	1,600	1,750	1,850	2,100	2,260

AMERICA'S CHARITIES

14200 PARK MEADOW DR
CHANTILLY, VA 201514210
Phone: 703 222-3861
Fax: –
Web: www.charities.org

CEO: James E Starr
CFO: –
HR: –
FYE: December 31
Type: Private

America's Charities makes it easier for corporate America to give 'til it hurts. The not-for-profit group is a federation of some 200 national and regional charities that participate in workplace giving campaigns. The organization helps employers conduct campaigns, which distribute employee gifts to designated charities. Members are screened for fiscal responsibility and effectiveness and include Make-A-Wish Foundation, the NAACP Legal Defense and Educational Fund, Junior Achievement, and Ronald McDonald House. It works with American Express, Hewlett Packard, Sears, Booz Allen Hamilton, and other companies. America's Charities also offers an online giving tool. It was founded in 1980.

	Annual Growth	12/16	12/17	12/18	12/21	12/22
Sales ($mil.)	10.9%	–	23.8	26.4	37.3	39.9
Net income ($ mil.)	125.0%	–	0.0	0.2	0.0	3.7
Market value ($ mil.)	–	–	–	–	–	–
Employees	–	–	–	–	–	40

AMERICA'S HOME PLACE, INC.

2144 HILTON DR
GAINESVILLE, GA 305016172
Phone: 770 532-1128
Fax: –
Web: www.americashomeplace.com

CEO: Barry G Conner
CFO: –
HR: –
FYE: December 31
Type: Private

America's Home Place builds custom homes on its customers' land. The company builds single-family, detached houses with more than 100 custom floor plans and designs. Its two- to five-bedroom cabin, chalet, ranch, two-story, and split-level houses range in price from about $80,000 to more than $300,000. Sizes start at about 900 sq. ft. and go up to to 4,000 sq. ft. America's Home Place operates nearly 40 home building and model centers in the southeastern US. Buyers typically already own their land, from a single lot to many acres. The company also assists buyers who are not landowners in locating available property. President Barry Conner owns the company he founded in 1972.

AMERICAN ACADEMY OF PEDIATRICS

345 PARK BLVD
ITASCA, IL 601432644
Phone: 847 228-5005
Fax: –
Web: www.aap.org

CEO: Mark D Monte
CFO: John Miller
HR: Rebecca D Cruz
FYE: June 30
Type: Private

The American Academy of Pediatrics (AAP) is a membership group of some 64,000 pediatricians, pediatric specialists, and pediatric surgeons dedicated to improving the health and well-being of infants, children, teenagers, and young adults. The not-for-profit organization executes research on a number of topics, including school health, common childhood illnesses, and immunizations and acts as an advocate on behalf of children's health needs. It also provides continuing education for its members through courses, scientific meetings, and publications such as Pediatrics and Pediatrics in Review . The organization is funded by membership dues, grants, gifts, and its own activities. AAP was founded in 1930.

	Annual Growth	06/14	06/15	06/17	06/20	06/22
Sales ($mil.)	3.1%	–	111.2	126.6	–	137.4
Net income ($ mil.)	–	–	(0.2)	6.0	–	12.0
Market value ($ mil.)	–	–	–	–	–	–
Employees	–	–	–	–	–	400

AMERICAN AIRLINES GROUP INC

NMS: AAL

1 Skyview Drive
Fort Worth, TX 76155
Phone: 682 278-9000
Fax: 817 967-9641
Web: www.aa.com

CEO: Robert D Isom Jr
CFO: Devon E May
HR: –
FYE: December 31
Type: Public

American Airlines Group (AAG) is one of the largest airline in the world. The company's primary business activity is the operation of a major network air carrier, providing scheduled air transportation along with its group of regional subsidiaries and third-party regional carriers operating as American Eagle. It also offers freight and mail services through its cargo division. In all, American operates an average of nearly 6,700 flights daily to some 350 destinations in about 50 countries. It operates some 925 mainline aircraft and around 535 regional aircraft. American Airlines Group is also a founding member of oneworld alliance, where member-carriers share airport lounge facilities and offer interconnected loyalty programs. About 75% of passenger sales of American Airlines Group is generated from the US.

	Annual Growth	12/19	12/20	12/21	12/22	12/23
Sales ($mil.)	3.6%	45,768	17,337	29,882	48,971	52,788
Net income ($ mil.)	(16.4%)	1,686.0	(8,885.0)	(1,993.0)	127.0	822.0
Market value ($ mil.)	(16.8%)	18,765	10,318	11,751	8,322.4	8,989.7
Employees	(0.3%)	133,700	102,700	123,400	129,700	132,100

AMERICAN ARBITRATION ASSOCIATION, INC.

120 BROADWAY FL 21
NEW YORK, NY 102712700
Phone: 212 716-5800
Fax: –
Web: www.adr.org

CEO: India Johnson
CFO: Francesco Rossi
HR: Eric Dill
FYE: December 31
Type: Private

The American Arbitration Association (AAA) wants to keep things civil. The organization provides arbitration, mediation, and other forms of alternative dispute resolution services -- alternatives, that is, to going to court. It maintains a panel of more than 7,000 arbitrators and mediators who can be engaged to hear cases and supports their work. Every year more than 185,000 cases are filed with AAA in a full range of matters including commercial, construction, labor, employment, insurance, international, and claims program disputes. The association's services include development of alternative dispute resolution (ADR) systems for corporations, unions, government agencies, law firms, and the courts.

	Annual Growth	12/04	12/05	12/06	12/08	12/09
Sales ($mil.)	(67.2%)	–	–	1,929.9	70.7	67.9
Net income ($ mil.)	716.4%	–	–	0.0	(23.0)	8.9
Market value ($ mil.)	–	–	–	–	–	–
Employees	–	–	–	–	–	750

AMERICAN ASSETS TRUST, INC.

3420 CARMEL MOUNTAIN RD STE 100
SAN DIEGO, CA 921211069
Phone: 858 350-2600
Fax: –
Web: www.americanassetstrust.com

CEO: –
CFO: –
HR: –
FYE: December 31
Type: Private

American Assets Trust is a self-administered real estate investment trust (REIT) that owns, develops, and operates upscale retail, office, and residential property mostly in Northern and Southern California, but also in Oregon, Washington, Texas, and Hawaii. Its approximately 3.1 million square foot portfolio includes more than 10 shopping centers, about 101 of office buildings, a 369-room hotel and retail complex, and more than five multi-family residential properties. Its tenants include SalesForce, Autodesk, the Veterans Benefits Administration, and well-known retailers such as Kmart, Lowe's, Sports Authority, Old Navy, and Vons. Formed in 1967 as American Assets, the firm went public in 2011.

	Annual Growth	12/13	12/14	12/15	12/16	12/17
Assets ($mil.)	5.2%	–	1,941.8	1,978.4	1,986.9	2,259.9
Net income ($ mil.)	8.8%	–	31.1	53.9	45.6	40.1
Market value ($ mil.)	–	–	–	–	–	–
Employees	–	–	–	–	–	113

AMERICAN ASSOCIATION FOR THE ADVANCEMENT OF SCIENCE

1200 NEW YORK AVE NW
WASHINGTON, DC 200053928
Phone: 202 326-6730
Fax: –
Web: www.aaas.org

CEO: Sudip Parikh
CFO: Colleen Strusss
HR: –
FYE: December 31
Type: Private

The American Association for the Advancement of Science (AAAS) is the world's largest multidisciplinary scientific society and a leading publisher of cutting-edge research through its Science family of journals. Membership is open to anyone who shares its goals and belief that science, technology, engineering, and mathematics can help solve many of the challenges the world faces today. AAAS fulfills its mission to advance science and serve society through initiatives in science policy, diplomacy, education, career support, public engagement with science, and more. Operates in about 90 countries worldwide, AAAS was founded in 1848.

	Annual Growth	12/08	12/09	12/13	12/21	12/22
Sales ($mil.)	2.1%	–	87.8	107.0	112.3	114.9
Net income ($ mil.)	(2.4%)	–	3.6	12.2	4.1	2.6
Market value ($ mil.)	–	–	–	–	–	–
Employees	–	–	–	–	–	475

AMERICAN ASSOCIATION OF ADVERTISING AGENCIES, INC.

25 W 45TH ST FL 16
NEW YORK, NY 100364902
Phone: 212 682-2500
Fax: –
Web: www.aaaa.org

CEO: Marla Kaplowitz
CFO: Laura J Bartlett
HR: Helen Siguenza
FYE: March 31
Type: Private

The American Association of Advertising Agencies (AAAA) is aaaall aaaabout aaaadvertising aaaalways. The not-for-profit national trade association represents nearly 1,200 advertising companies in the US. AAAA offers its members insurance and investment benefits, a searchable member database, conferences and an annual trade show (Advertising Week), and tools to communicate and do business with other ad agencies. The group also runs The Institute of Advanced Advertising Studies, offering evening courses for young professionals, and publishes marketing and ad industry research. AAAA was founded in 1917 and operates through about 25 local councils.

	Annual Growth	03/14	03/15	03/17	03/19	03/22
Sales ($mil.)	(1.0%)	–	17.5	16.8	16.4	16.3
Net income ($ mil.)	–	–	(0.7)	(0.4)	(1.7)	0.5
Market value ($ mil.)	–	–	–	–	–	–
Employees	–	–	–	–	–	84

AMERICAN AXLE & MANUFACTURING HOLDINGS INC   NYS: AXL

One Dauch Drive
Detroit, MI 48211-1198
Phone: 313 758-2000
Fax: –
Web: www.aam.com

CEO: David C Dauch
CFO: Christopher J May
HR: Susan Novak
FYE: December 31
Type: Public

American Axle & Manufacturing (AAM) is a global Tier 1 supplier to the automotive industry. AAM manufactures, engineers, and designs axles, driveshafts, and transmission shafts, mainly for light trucks and SUVs, but also for cars and crossover vehicles. The Tier 1 supplier gets about 40% of its business from GM. Other customers include Ford, Chrysler Pacifica, and Lincoln Nautilus. AAM operates nearly 80 manufacturing facilities in about 20 countries around the world and generates more than 75% of its revenue from North America.

	Annual Growth	12/19	12/20	12/21	12/22	12/23
Sales ($mil.)	(1.8%)	6,530.9	4,710.8	5,156.6	5,802.4	6,079.5
Net income ($ mil.)	–	(484.5)	(561.3)	5.9	64.3	(33.6)
Market value ($ mil.)	(4.9%)	1,260.0	976.6	1,092.5	915.7	1,031.7
Employees	(1.3%)	20,000	20,000	18,000	19,000	19,000

AMERICAN BANCORP, INC (LA)

321 East Landry Street
Opelousas, LA 70570
Phone: 337 948-3056
Fax: –
Web: www.americanbankandtrust.com

CEO: –
CFO: Elaine Ardoin
HR: –
FYE: December 31
Type: Public

American Bancorp provides banking on the bayou. Through subsidiary American Bank and Trust, the company operates six bank offices in southern Louisiana. It offers checking and savings accounts, CDs, and loans to area businesses and consumers. Residential and commercial mortgages dominate the company's lending portfolio. Interest from investments in mortgage-backed securities, US Treasuries, municipal bonds, and other securities are another major source of American Bancorp's revenue. Members of the Diesi family, including company chairman Salvador, his uncle J. C. (a director), and CEO Ronald Lashute (Salvador's cousin) are major shareholders of American Bancorp.

	Annual Growth	12/99	12/00	12/01	12/02	12/03
Assets ($mil.)	5.9%	80.2	82.8	91.6	99.7	100.9
Net income ($ mil.)	(2.6%)	1.1	1.2	1.1	1.3	1.0
Market value ($ mil.)	28.7%	6.2	6.2	6.2	6.2	16.9
Employees	0.6%	44	45	45	45	45

AMERICAN BANK INC (PA)   NBB: AMBK

615 Waterfront Drive, Suite 501
Allentown, PA 18102
Phone: 610 366-1800
Fax: 610 366-1900
Web: www.ambk.com

CEO: –
CFO: –
HR: –
FYE: December 31
Type: Public

American Bank Incorporated is the holding company for American Bank, which operates a single branch in Allentown, Pennsylvania. It serves customers throughout the US via its pcbanker.com Web site. The bank's products and services include checking and savings accounts, money market accounts, CDs, credit cards, and discount brokerage. It primarily originates real estate loans although it also offers commercial mortgages and residential mortgages. The Jaindl family, including company president and CEO Mark Jaindl, owns a majority of American Bank Incorporated.

	Annual Growth	12/18	12/19	12/20	12/21	12/22
Assets ($mil.)	10.5%	621.9	641.6	734.3	849.2	927.3
Net income ($ mil.)	10.3%	6.8	7.9	8.7	10.1	10.1
Market value ($ mil.)	9.4%	79.1	76.0	76.0	99.7	113.5
Employees	–	–	–	–	–	–

AMERICAN BANKERS ASSOCIATION INC

1333 NEW HAMPSHIRE AVE NW STE 700
WASHINGTON, DC 200361532
Phone: 202 663-7575
Fax: –
Web: www.aba.com

CEO: Rob Nichols
CFO: –
HR: Dee Castille
FYE: August 31
Type: Private

The American Bankers Association (ABA) brings together banks of various types and sizes. Its members include bank holding companies, savings associations, savings banks, trust companies, and community, regional, and money center banks. The ABA serves as an advocate for its members in legislative and regulatory arenas. It also engages in consumer education, research, and training efforts. The ABA's BankPac, the banking industry's largest political action committee, provides financial support to candidates for the US Senate and House of Representatives. The ABA was founded in 1875 and claims to represent more than 95% of banking assets. The group merged with the America's Community Bankers association in 2007.

	Annual Growth	08/06	08/07	08/08	08/09	08/10
Sales ($mil.)	(1.9%)	–	–	83.9	64.0	80.7
Net income ($ mil.)	–	–	–	(2.1)	(22.3)	0.8
Market value ($ mil.)	–	–	–	–	–	–
Employees	–	–	–	–	–	354

AMERICAN BANKNOTE CORPORATION

1055 WASHINGTON BLVD FL 6
STAMFORD, CT 069012216
Phone: 617 325-9600
Fax: –
Web: www.abcorp.com

CEO: William Brown
CFO: –
HR: –
FYE: December 31
Type: Private

American Banknote Corporation (ABCorp) designs, manufactures, and personalizes contactless credit cards, 3D print highly detailed prototypes and parts, and deliver omni-channel content to elevate the customer experience. Customer include federal, state, and local government agencies, and world-class companies spanning in more than 120 countries. The company serves aerospace and defense, automotive, robotics, consumer goods, government, healthcare, commercial, and financial industries. The company traces its roots to 1795 when it helped the First Bank of the United States produce counterfeit-resistant currency.

	Annual Growth	12/02	12/03	12/04	12/05	12/08
Sales ($mil.)	0.7%	–	222.6	162.3	–	230.8
Net income ($ mil.)	–	–	(46.6)	46.2	–	3.6
Market value ($ mil.)	–	–	–	–	–	–
Employees	–	–	–	–	–	703

AMERICAN BAR ASSOCIATION

321 N CLARK ST
CHICAGO, IL 606547598
Phone: 312 988-5000
Fax: –
Web: www.americanbar.org

CEO: Michael E Burke
CFO: –
HR: –
FYE: August 31
Type: Private

The world's largest voluntary professional organization, American Bar Association (ABA) promotes improvements in the American justice system and develops guidelines for the advancement of the legal profession and education. The association provides law school accreditation, continuing education, legal information, and other services to assist legal professionals. The ABA's roster of about 400,000 members includes lawyers, judges, court administrators, law librarians, and law school professors and students. The organization cannot discipline lawyers nor enforce its rules; it can only develop guidelines. The ABA was founded in 1878.

	Annual Growth	08/12	08/13	08/14	08/15	08/19
Sales ($mil.)	(17.2%)	–	206.0	204.4	151.7	66.5
Net income ($ mil.)	–	–	39.4	35.9	(7.4)	(10.3)
Market value ($ mil.)	–	–	–	–	–	–
Employees	–	–	–	–	–	900

AMERICAN BILTRITE INC.

NBB: ABLT

57 River Street, Suite 302
Wellesley Hills, MA 02481-2097
Phone: 781 237-6655
Fax: -
Web: www.ambilt.com

CEO: Roger S Marcus
CFO: Howard N Feist III
HR: Claire Frazier
FYE: December 31
Type: Public

American Biltrite (ABI), which makes and distributes commercial flooring and industrial rubber, has its hand in several different pots, some of which are sticky. Its Tape division makes adhesive-coated, pressure-sensitive tapes and films used to protect materials during handling and storage, as well as for applications in the heating, ventilation, and air conditioning, automotive, and electrical industries. ABI also designs and distributes wholesale jewelry and accessories to stores through its K&M subsidiary, while its AB Canada subsidiary makes floor tile and rubber products. The founding Marcus family controls ABI.

	Annual Growth	12/18	12/19	12/20	12/21	12/22
Sales ($mil.)	(1.9%)	202.6	204.8	162.5	190.7	187.7
Net income ($ mil.)	-	8.3	(4.6)	(14.1)	1.8	(5.8)
Market value ($ mil.)	(29.2%)	16.6	13.1	8.3	5.7	4.2
Employees	-	-	-	-	-	-

AMERICAN BIO MEDICA CORP.

NBB: ABMC

122 Smith Road
Kinderhook, NY 12106
Phone: 518 758-8158
Fax: -
Web: www.abmc.com

CEO: -
CFO: -
HR: -
FYE: December 31
Type: Public

There's a thin line between employment and unemployment, and that line might just be on one of American Bio Medica's drug-testing kits. The company's Rapid Drug Screen products indicate within minutes the presence in a urine sample of such illegal substances as marijuana, cocaine, amphetamines, and opiates. Used by employers, law enforcement agencies, hospitals, schools, and other institutions, the tests offer up to 10-panel options (each panel tests for different substances). The company's Rapid One is a line of single-drug specific tests; its Rapid Tec and Rapid TOX products detect multiple drug classes on one panel. American Bio Medica also offers saliva-based tests for law enforcement customers.

	Annual Growth	12/18	12/19	12/20	12/21	12/22
Sales ($mil.)	(30.3%)	3.9	3.7	4.1	2.2	0.9
Net income ($ mil.)	-	(1.0)	(0.7)	(0.8)	(0.5)	(1.4)
Market value ($ mil.)	(46.8%)	3.3	3.4	6.3	1.8	0.3
Employees	(13.6%)	43	48	42	37	24

AMERICAN BLUE RIBBON HOLDINGS, LLC

3038 SIDCO DR
NASHVILLE, TN 372044506
Phone: 615 256-8500
Fax: -
Web: www.villageinn.com

CEO: Hazem Ouf
CFO: -
HR: Dawn Ellspermann
FYE: March 17
Type: Private

American Blue Ribbon Holdings (ABRH) is a leading multi-concept restaurant operator that operates two distinct regional family dining restaurant brands ? Village Inn (with corporate and franchise restaurants totaling more than 100, primarily located in the Rocky Mountain region, the Midwest, Arizona, and Florida) and Bakers Square (with operations primarily in Illinois, Michigan, Minnesota, and Ohio), as well as an award-winning bakery operation, Legendary Baking (one of the largest pie producers in Canada). ABRH restaurant portfolio currently has a national footprint consisting of company-operated and franchised restaurants.

AMERICAN BOOKSELLERS ASSOCIATION, INC.

333 WESTCHESTER AVE S202
WHITE PLAINS, NY 106042911
Phone: 914 406-7500
Fax: -
Web: www.bookweb.org

CEO: Oren Teicher
CFO: Robyn Deshotel
HR: -
FYE: September 30
Type: Private

The American Booksellers Association (ABA) offers strength in numbers for independent booksellers in a bind over how to battle the superstores. The organization is dedicated to protecting book retailers' interests. For an annual fee, ABA provides its members with an annual trade conference, industry news and information, professional development services, and advertising and promotional opportunities. Its members include independent bookstores and chains, university stores, and specialty shops. To help members compete against large Internet booksellers, ABA has launched an online sales network, BookSense.com. The association was founded in 1900.

	Annual Growth	09/16	09/17	09/18	09/19	09/21
Sales ($mil.)	(33.0%)	-	-	6.5	-	2.0
Net income ($ mil.)	-	-	-	1.1	-	(2.1)
Market value ($ mil.)	-	-	-	-	-	-
Employees	-	-	-	-	-	34

AMERICAN BUREAU OF SHIPPING

1701 CITY PLAZA DR
SPRING, TX 773891878
Phone: 281 877-6000
Fax: -
Web: www.eagle.org

CEO: Robert D Somerville
CFO: -
HR: Reagan Nelson
FYE: December 31
Type: Private

One of the world's largest ship classification societies, American Bureau of Shipping (ABS) offers inspection and analysis services to verify that vessels are mechanically and structurally fit. The not-for-profit company's surveyors examine ships in major ports throughout the world, assessing whether the vessels comply with ABS rules for design, construction, and maintenance. Additionally, its engineers consult with shipbuilders on proposed designs and repairs. The not-for-profit company operates from more than 150 offices in about 70 countries. For-profit subsidiaries ABS Group offers risk management consulting services, while ABS Nautical Systems provides fleet management software. ABS was founded in 1862.

	Annual Growth	12/10	12/11	12/12	12/21	12/22
Sales ($mil.)	(3.6%)	-	726.7	1,134.3	455.2	487.8
Net income ($ mil.)	(7.6%)	-	143.6	155.3	46.1	60.3
Market value ($ mil.)	-	-	-	-	-	-
Employees	-	-	-	-	-	3,000

AMERICAN BUS ASSOCIATION INC.

111 K ST NE FL 9
WASHINGTON, DC 200028110
Phone: 202 842-1645
Fax: -
Web: www.buses.org

CEO: Peter J Pantuso
CFO: Eric Braendel
HR: -
FYE: December 31
Type: Private

The American Bus Association (ABA) doesn't want its members taken for a ride. The trade association looks out for the interests of bus company owners and operators. It promotes and lobbies for the interests of the intercity bus industry and facilitates relationships between the North American motor coach and tour companies. The ABA also publishes Destinations Magazine . The organization has more than 3,000 members, including about 1,000 motor coach and tour companies in the US and Canada. Other members include travel and tourism organizations and suppliers of bus products. The American Automobile Association started the organization in 1924 as a separate division of the AAA. It became a separate entity in 1926.

	Annual Growth	12/13	12/14	12/18	12/21	12/22
Sales ($mil.)	(3.1%)	-	5.5	5.5	2.7	4.3
Net income ($ mil.)	-	-	0.5	(0.3)	(1.3)	(0.6)
Market value ($ mil.)	-	-	-	-	-	-
Employees	-	-	-	-	-	14

AMERICAN BUSINESS BANK (LOS ANGELES, CA)   NBB: AMBZ

400 South Hope Street, Suite 300
Los Angeles, CA 90071
Phone: 213 430-4000
Fax: –
Web: www.americanbb.bank

CEO: Leon Blankstein
CFO: Karen Schoenbaum
HR: –
FYE: December 31
Type: Public

What's a middle-market, closely held, owner-managed business gotta do to get FORTUNE 500 treatment from a bank? American Business Bank (ABB) caters to private companies in Southern California with annual sales between $5 million and $200 million, with an emphasis on wholesalers, manufacturers, service businesses, not-for-profit organizations, and professionals. The bank's commercial lending services include commercial real estate loans (more than half of its portfolio), asset-based lending, equipment finance, construction loans, and revolving lines of credit. Its deposit products consist of checking, savings, and money market accounts, and CDs.

	Annual Growth	12/18	12/19	12/20	12/21	12/22
Assets ($mil.)	15.5%	2,157.4	2,401.9	3,454.3	3,912.3	3,840.8
Net income ($ mil.)	31.2%	16.4	22.1	28.8	39.2	48.6
Market value ($ mil.)	6.0%	282.8	319.5	285.3	354.0	356.7
Employees		–	–	–	–	–

AMERICAN CAMPUS COMMUNITIES LLC

12700 HILL COUNTRY BLVD STE T200
AUSTIN, TX 787386307
Phone: 512 732-1000
Fax: –
Web: www.americancampus.com

CEO: Rob Palleschi
CFO: –
HR: –
FYE: December 31
Type: Private

American Campus Communities (ACC) is a fully integrated, self-managed and self-administered real estate investment trust (REIT) with expertise in the acquisition, design, financing, development, construction management, leasing, and management of student housing properties. The company leases the ground for on-campus properties from the schools, which in turn receive about half of the net cash flow from these properties. ACC also works with schools to develop new properties and renovate existing housing, and provides third-party leasing and management services for other student housing owners. In all, the REIT manages more than 200 properties with some 140,900 beds at some 95 schools in the US and Canada. In 2022, ACC was acquired by Blackstone, a global leader in real estate investing, for $12.8 billion.

AMERICAN CANNABIS CO INC   NBB: AMMJ

200 Union Street, Ste. 200
Lakewood, CO 80228
Phone: 303 974-4770
Fax: –
Web: –

CEO: Terry Buffalo
CFO: David M Godfrey
HR: –
FYE: December 31
Type: Public

NatureWell hopes to offer relief out of the mist to migraine sufferers in a fog. The company has developed its MICROMIST technology to deliver homeopathic and natural remedies under the tongue. Currently, the company's only product is over-the-counter migraine treatment MigraSpray, which can be used both as a preventative measure and to relieve the acute pain of migraines. It is only available through healthcare professionals and by mail order. NatureWell outsources manufacturing, distribution, and customer service functions. It is exploring new product offerings for arthritis and general pain, including Arthrispray, PMS Spray, and Allerspray.

	Annual Growth	12/18	12/19	12/20	12/21	12/22
Sales ($mil.)	109.2%	1.0	2.1	1.6	2.4	18.8
Net income ($ mil.)	–	(1.0)	(0.3)	(0.5)	(1.4)	(0.6)
Market value ($ mil.)	(44.7%)	27.6	8.9	6.6	6.5	2.6
Employees	41.4%	6	9	5	21	24

AMERICAN CARESOURCE HOLDINGS INC   NBB: GNOW

55 Ivan Allen Jr. Blvd., Suite 510
Atlanta, GA 30308
Phone: 404 465-1000
Fax: –
Web: www.americancaresource.com

CEO: –
CFO: –
HR: –
FYE: December 31
Type: Public

American CareSource owns and operates a chain of about a dozen urgent and primary care centers (branded GoNow and Medac) in the Southeast US. However, the firm has found itself in high levels of debt. In early 2017, the company sold subsidiary Ancillary Care Services, which negotiates contracts with specialty health care providers with (i.e., outpatient surgery, rehabilitation, hospice, laboratory, and other services). It is also exploring the sale of its urgent care assets. American CareSource's clients have included preferred provider organizations (PPOs), health maintenance organizations (HMOs), third-party administrators, and self-insured employers. The firm's roots go back to the mid-1990s.

	Annual Growth	12/11	12/12	12/13	12/14	12/15
Sales ($mil.)	(32.7%)	48.9	34.9	26.8	27.1	10.0
Net income ($ mil.)	–	(7.2)	(3.1)	(3.8)	(6.8)	(13.3)
Market value ($ mil.)	(1.1%)	7.1	23.7	27.2	48.1	6.8
Employees	35.4%	56	56	52	141	188

AMERICAN CAST IRON PIPE COMPANY

1500 32ND AVE N
BIRMINGHAM, AL 352074110
Phone: 205 325-7701
Fax: –
Web: www.american-usa.com

CEO: J M Obrien
CFO: Cook J M
HR: Delilah Landrum
FYE: December 31
Type: Private

American Cast Iron Pipe Company (ACIPCO) operates one of the largest ductile iron pipe casting plants in the world. Its divisions ? including American Ductile Iron Pipe, American Flow Control, American SpiralWeld Pipe, and American Steel Pipe ? make ductile iron pipe and fittings, cast steel tubes, fire hydrants and fire truck pumps, and valves for water treatment and energy production. It also makes specialized products for the water utility industry and electric-resistance steel pipe for the oil and natural gas industries. ACIPCO has eight manufacturing plants in six states and inventory locations across the country. The company has been exporting pipes and related products since 1905.

AMERICAN CENTURY COMPANIES, INC.

430 W 7TH ST
KANSAS CITY, MO 641051407
Phone: 816 531-5575
Fax: –
Web: corporate.americancentury.com

CEO: Jonathan Thomas
CFO: –
HR: Kristin Overman
FYE: December 31
Type: Private

Founded in 1958, American Century Investments is a leading global asset manager focused on delivering investment results and building long-term client relationships while supporting breakthrough medical research. Delivering investment results to clients enables American Century Investments to distribute over 40% of its dividends to the Stowers Institute for Medical Research, a 500-person, non-profit basic biomedical research organization. The Institute owns more than 40% of American Century Investments and has received dividend payments of nearly $2 billion since 2000.

	Annual Growth	12/05	12/06	12/07	12/08	12/22
Assets ($mil.)	0.9%	–	–	–	4.8	5.4
Net income ($ mil.)		–	–	–	–	0.3
Market value ($ mil.)		–	–	–	–	–
Employees		–	–	–	–	1,837

AMERICAN CHEMICAL SOCIETY

1155 16TH ST NW
WASHINGTON, DC 200364892
Phone: 202 872-4600
Fax: -
Web: www.acs.org

CEO: Albert G Horvath
CFO: Brian Bernstein
HR: -
FYE: December 31
Type: Private

With more than 151,000 members, the American Chemical Society (ACS) is the world's largest scientific society. The not-for-profit organization provides information, career services, engagement programs, and educational resources to members and scientists. The company also publishes magazines, journals, and books. Its Chemical Abstract Service provides the most comprehensive repository of research in chemistry and related sciences. ACS also serves as an advocate for its members on public policy issues. The ACS Member Insurance Program provides insurance plans to its members. The company was founded in 1876.

	Annual Growth	12/18	12/19	12/20	12/21	12/22
Sales ($mil.)	(16.5%)	-	-	-	851.3	711.0
Net income ($ mil.)	(90.7%)	-	-	-	244.2	22.7
Market value ($ mil.)	-	-	-	-	-	-
Employees	-	-	-	-	-	2,000

AMERICAN CIVIL LIBERTIES UNION FOUNDATION, INC.

125 BROAD ST FL 18
NEW YORK, NY 100042454
Phone: 212 549-2500
Fax: -
Web: www.aclu.org

CEO: -
CFO: -
HR: Marcella Granick
FYE: March 31
Type: Private

The philosopher Socrates once said, "I am that gadfly which God has given the state." While the American Civil Liberties Union (ACLU) might have a quarrel with the "God" part, the group has at times proved a stinging critic in its efforts to defend individual rights. It acts as a legal and legislative advocate in matters related to civil liberties and the Bill of Rights. The ACLU has participated in such cases as the 1925 Scopes trial (challenged a ban on teaching evolution), Brown v. Board of Education (school desegregation), Roe v. Wade (abortion rights), and Romer v. Evans (gay and lesbian rights). The group, which has more than 500,000 members, has offices throughout the US. It was founded in 1920.

	Annual Growth	03/14	03/15	03/16	03/20	03/22
Sales ($mil.)	8.1%	-	94.0	95.9	185.5	162.2
Net income ($ mil.)	-	-	8.4	3.9	44.1	(0.7)
Market value ($ mil.)	-	-	-	-	-	-
Employees	-	-	-	-	-	350

AMERICAN COASTAL INSURANCE CORP

NAS: ACIC

800 2nd Avenue S.
St. Petersburg, FL 33701
Phone: 727 895-7737
Fax: -
Web: www.upcinsurance.com

CEO: R D Peed
CFO: Svetlana Castle
HR: -
FYE: December 31
Type: Public

United Insurance Holdings is a holding company engaged in the personal residential and commercial residential property and casualty insurance business in the US. Its largest insurance subsidiary is United Property & Casualty Insurance Company (UPC), and it also write business through American Coastal Insurance Company (ACIC), Family Security Insurance Company, Inc. (FSIC), Interboro Insurance Company (IIC), and Journey Insurance Company (JIC). Its insurance subsidiaries provide personal residential and commercial property and casualty insurance products that protect its policyholders against losses due to damages to structures and their contents. Some of its insurance subsidiaries sell policies that protect against liability for accidents as well as property damage. Its non-insurance subsidiaries support our insurance and investment operations. Approximately 45% of its policies in-force were written in Florida.

	Annual Growth	12/19	12/20	12/21	12/22	12/23
Assets ($mil.)	(19.0%)	2,467.2	2,848.9	2,698.6	2,837.5	1,060.4
Net income ($ mil.)	-	(29.9)	(96.5)	(57.9)	(469.9)	309.9
Market value ($ mil.)	(6.9%)	589.9	267.6	203.0	49.6	442.5
Employees	(33.5%)	363	478	472	269	71

AMERICAN COLLEGE OF HEALTHCARE EXECUTIVES

300 S RIVERSIDE PLZ STE 1900
CHICAGO, IL 606066613
Phone: 312 424-9190
Fax: -
Web: www.ache.org

CEO: -
CFO: Richard Hovland
HR: -
FYE: December 31
Type: Private

ACHE is made up of people who don't want you to have any aches at all. The American College of Healthcare Executives (ACHE) is a professional membership society of more than 30,000 health care executives, including leaders of hospitals, health care systems, and other health care organizations. The group credentials, establishes ethics guidelines, and hosts conventions and educational programs for members. ACHE boasts a network of more than 80 chapters nationwide. The organization's publishing division, Health Administration Press, publishes books and journals on the topics of health services management, as well as college textbooks. The group was founded in 1933.

	Annual Growth	12/15	12/16	12/17	12/21	12/22
Sales ($mil.)	0.2%	-	11.9	12.2	21.4	12.1
Net income ($ mil.)	-	-	0.1	(0.5)	9.2	(1.5)
Market value ($ mil.)	-	-	-	-	-	-
Employees	-	-	-	-	-	94

AMERICAN COMMERCE SOLUTIONS INC

NBB: AACS

1400 Chamber Drive
Bartow, FL 33830
Phone: 863 533-0326
Fax: -
Web: www.aacssymbol.com

CEO: Daniel L Hefner
CFO: Frank D Puissegur
HR: -
FYE: February 29
Type: Public

Holding company American Commerce Solutions (ACS), through its International Machine and Welding subsidiary, provides specialized machining and repair services for heavy equipment used in the agricultural, construction, forestry, mining, and scrap industries. Its Chariot Manufacturing Company subsidiary (which includes Chariot Trailers) manufactures open and enclosed trailers to carry motorcycles. ACS also sells aftermarket repair parts. The company also has a strategic relationship with American Fiber Green Products. The Mosaic Company generates about 36% of sales.

	Annual Growth	02/12	02/13	02/14	02/15	02/16
Sales ($mil.)	(4.3%)	2.4	2.4	2.7	2.2	2.1
Net income ($ mil.)	-	0.0	(0.0)	(0.2)	(0.1)	(0.2)
Market value ($ mil.)	23.1%	1.2	2.9	3.9	2.4	2.7
Employees	22.1%	18	19	21	20	40

AMERICAN COMMUNITY PROPERTIES TRUST INC

10400 ODONNELL PL STE 200
SAINT CHARLES, MD 206037291
Phone: 301 843-8600
Fax: -
Web: -

CEO: Alan Shearer
CFO: Matthew M Martin
HR: -
FYE: December 31
Type: Private

American Community Properties Trust (ACPT) develops, builds, owns, and manages primarily residential real estate in Washington, DC; Maryland; and Virginia. The self-managed real estate investment trust (REIT) has ownership in more than 20 multi-family apartment communities (about 3,200 units) and 4,000 acres of undeveloped land in a planned residential community in St. Charles, Maryland. More than half of its apartment units participate in low-income housing programs. Subsidiary American Rental Management Company manages apartments for ACPT and for third parties. ACPT was acquired by real estate investment company Federal Capital Partners for $43.6 million in 2009.

AMERICAN COUNCIL OF THE BLIND INC

1703 N BEAUREGARD ST # 420　　　　　　　　　　　CEO: –
ALEXANDRIA, VA 223111744　　　　　　　　　　　　CFO: –
Phone: 202 467-5081　　　　　　　　　　　　　　　HR: –
Fax: –　　　　　　　　　　　　　　　　　　FYE: December 31
Web: www.acb.org　　　　　　　　　　　　　　　Type: Private

ACB sees 20/20 when it comes to issues affecting blind and visually impaired Americans. The American Council of the Blind strives to improve the lives of it members by offering scholarship assistance, referral services, public education, leadership and legislative training, and helping businesses hire blind people. The group also hosts an annual national convention, publishes The Braille Forum magazine each month, and runs Washington Connection, a national legislative hotline. ACB has more than 70 affiliates nationwide, including special interest and professional groups. It was founded in 1961.

	Annual Growth	12/18	12/19	12/20	12/21	12/22
Sales ($mil.)	13.9%	–	1.8	1.8	2.2	2.6
Net income ($ mil.)	16.7%	–	0.0	0.0	0.2	0.1
Market value ($ mil.)	–	–	–	–	–	–
Employees	–	–	–	–	–	15

AMERICAN CRYSTAL SUGAR COMPANY

101 3RD ST N　　　　　　　　　　　　　　CEO: David A Berg
MOORHEAD, MN 565601990　　　　　　　　CFO: Thomas S Astrup
Phone: 218 236-4400　　　　　　　　　　　　HR: Wendy Maurstad
Fax: –　　　　　　　　　　　　　　　　　　FYE: August 31
Web: www.crystalsugar.com　　　　　　　　　　Type: Private

American Crystal Sugar is the largest beet sugar producer in the US. The cooperative is owned by some 2,800 growers in the Red River Valley of North Dakota and Minnesota who farms approximately 425,000 acres of cropland. The company has sugar packaging facilities located at East Grand Forks, Crookston, and Moorhead in Minnesota, and Drayton and Hillsboro in North Dakota. The cooperative's products are sold in the US and other markets to industrial users and retail and wholesale customers under the Crystal name, as well as under private labels through marketing co-ops United Sugars and Midwest Agri-Commodities. American Crystal Sugar was founded by Henry Oxnard in 1890.

	Annual Growth	08/15	08/16	08/17	08/18	08/19
Sales ($mil.)	5.8%	–	1,290.8	1,420.0	1,515.1	1,528.2
Net income ($ mil.)	3.6%	–	561.7	511.9	650.9	624.4
Market value ($ mil.)	–	–	–	–	–	–
Employees	–	–	–	–	–	1,365

AMERICAN DEFENSE SYSTEMS INC

420 McKinney Pkwy　　　　　　　　　　　　　NBB: ADFS
Lillington, NC 27546　　　　　　　　　　　　　CEO: –
Phone: 910 514-9701　　　　　　　　　　　　　CFO: –
Fax: –　　　　　　　　　　　　　　　　　　　HR: –
Web: www.adsiarmor.com　　　　　　　　　FYE: December 31
　　　　　　　　　　　　　　　　　　　　　　Type: Public

American Defense Systems, Inc. (ASDI) does a bang-up job of supporting our troops. The company makes custom bulletproof steel plates and glass panes that provide protection to US military vehicles in combat. It also manufactures bullet- and blast-resistant transparent armor, walls, and doors to protect buildings, as well as barriers, steel gates, and bollards to keep vehicles from crashing into them. ASDI earns all of its revenues from the Departments of Defense and Homeland Security and branches of the US military. In addition, the company runs the American Institute for Defense and Tactical Studies, which offers tactical training courses. CEO Tony Piscitelli owns almost three-quarters of the company's stock.

	Annual Growth	12/08	12/09	12/10	12/11	12/12
Sales ($mil.)	(35.6%)	35.6	45.9	39.5	8.7	6.1
Net income ($ mil.)	–	(1.6)	(16.3)	(9.4)	9.4	(1.1)
Market value ($ mil.)	(52.1%)	32.0	22.4	9.5	0.9	1.7
Employees	–	94	102	45	28	–

AMERICAN DENTAL ASSOCIATION

211 E CHICAGO AVE　　　　　　　　　　　　　CEO: –
CHICAGO, IL 606112637　　　　　　　　　　CFO: Paul Sholty
Phone: 312 440-2500　　　　　　　　　　　　　HR: –
Fax: –　　　　　　　　　　　　　　　　　　FYE: December 31
Web: www.ada.org　　　　　　　　　　　　　　Type: Private

Four out of five dentists recommend the ADA to their peers who join organizations. The American Dental Association is the world's oldest and largest dental association, representing some 158,000 dentists. The ADA provides information on oral health, promotes dental science, and conducts research, development, and testing on dental products and materials. If products are up to the organization's standards, they are allowed to carry the ADA Seal of Acceptance. The group's Professional Product Review (PPR) evaluates and reports on products used by dental professionals. The ADA was founded in 1859 by 26 representatives from dental societies around the country.

	Annual Growth	12/15	12/16	12/19	12/21	12/22
Sales ($mil.)	2.0%	–	123.5	134.8	138.6	138.8
Net income ($ mil.)	–	–	6.4	(0.5)	13.7	(3.5)
Market value ($ mil.)	–	–	–	–	–	–
Employees	–	–	–	–	–	475

AMERICAN DENTAL ASSOCIATION FOUNDATION

100 BUREAU DR STOP 8546　　　　　　　　CEO: Marcelo Araujo
GAITHERSBURG, MD 208998546　　　　　　　　CFO: –
Phone: 312 440-2549　　　　　　　　　　　　　HR: –
Fax: –　　　　　　　　　　　　　　　　　　FYE: December 31
Web: –　　　　　　　　　　　　　　　　　　Type: Private

The American Dental Association Foundation wants you to keep your pearly whites. It is the charitable arm of the American Dental Association (ADA) and supports grants in a number of areas, including dental research and development, education, scholarships, and access to dental care for low-income communities and underserved rural areas. The foundation also funds grants for dentists and their families who need support because of an injury or medical condition and those who have been victims of disasters. The ADA started the organization in 1964.

	Annual Growth	12/13	12/14	12/15	12/16	12/18
Sales ($mil.)	6.7%	–	5.8	8.9	6.2	7.5
Net income ($ mil.)	–	–	(0.4)	1.5	(1.9)	(1.4)
Market value ($ mil.)	–	–	–	–	–	–
Employees	–	–	–	–	–	10

AMERICAN DENTAL EDUCATION ASSOCIATION

655 K ST NW STE 800　　　　　　　　　　　CEO: Lily T Garcia
WASHINGTON, DC 200012399　　　　　　　　CFO: –
Phone: 202 289-7201　　　　　　　　　　　　HR: –
Fax: –　　　　　　　　　　　　　　　　　　FYE: June 30
Web: www.adea.org　　　　　　　　　　　　　Type: Private

The American Dental Education Association (ADEA) is the primary not-for-profit educational organization representing dental schools and the people associated with them throughout the US and Canada. The organization conducts research, organizes conferences, and issues a monthly newsletter and other publications, including the Journal of Dental Education (published monthly). Established in 1923, the American Dental Education Association has approximately 18,000 individual members. The organization has more than 800 allied and advanced dental education programs.

	Annual Growth	06/18	06/19	06/20	06/21	06/22
Sales ($mil.)	7.3%	–	25.8	24.2	28.8	31.9
Net income ($ mil.)	–	–	(0.9)	1.6	4.6	3.8
Market value ($ mil.)	–	–	–	–	–	–
Employees	–	–	–	–	–	75

AMERICAN DG ENERGY INC.

45 1ST AVE
WALTHAM, MA 024511105
Phone: 781 622-1120
Fax: -
Web: www.americandg.com

CEO: Benjamin M Locke
CFO: Bonnie Brown
HR: -
FYE: December 31
Type: Private

Doggone tired of high utility bills? American DG Energy wants to put an end to that. The company provides DG, or distributed generation, energy by installing electricity generating equipment on-site to save on energy loss during transmission. The equipment, which the company owns and maintains, uses clean natural gas to generate power and for heating and cooling; it captures waste heat for water chilling and heating. While the technology is in wide use by consumers of more than 10 MW of power, American DG Energy targets smaller users, one MW and less. The Hatsopoulos family, including chairman George Hatsopoulos and CEO John Hatsopoulos, control about 25% of the company.

AMERICAN DIABETES ASSOCIATION

2451 CRYSTAL DR STE 900
ARLINGTON, VA 222024804
Phone: 703 549-1500
Fax: -
Web: www.diabetes.org

CEO: Kevin Hagan
CFO: Charlotte Carter
HR: Tony Webster
FYE: December 31
Type: Private

The American Diabetes Association (ADA) lives for the day when it has no customers, but for now seeks to serve the some 30 million children and adults in the US who have the disease. It is a nonprofit research, information, and advocacy organization that works to prevent and cure diabetes while also focusing on improving the lives of people affected by diabetes. The ADA has a number of fundraising programs, Step Out: Walk to Fight Diabetes is the group's main fundraiser; others include the Tour de Cure (cycling); School Walk for Diabetes; and Kiss-A-Pig, which honors the pig for its role in discovering the effectiveness of insulin in controlling diabetes.

AMERICAN EAGLE OUTFITTERS, INC. NYS: AEO

77 Hot Metal Street
Pittsburgh, PA 15203-2329
Phone: 412 432-3300
Fax: -
Web: www.ae.com

CEO: Jay L Schottenstein
CFO: Michael A Mathias
HR: -
FYE: February 3
Type: Public

American Eagle Outfitters is a leading global specialty retailer. The company offers a broad assortment of high quality, on-trend apparel, accessories, and personal care products at affordable prices for men and women under the American Eagle brand, and intimates, apparel, active wear, and swim collections under the Aerie brand. It sells directly to consumers through its retail channel, which includes the company's stores and concession-based shop-within-shops. It also operates Todd Snyder New York (a premium menswear) and Unsubscribed (new brand with a focus on consciously-made, slow fashion). The company operates or licenses over 1,400 stores worldwide, of which approximately 1,175 were company-owned; it generates the majority of its sales in the US.

	Annual Growth	02/20*	01/21	01/22	01/23*	02/24
Sales ($mil.)	5.1%	4,308.2	3,759.1	5,010.8	4,989.8	5,261.8
Net income ($ mil.)	(2.9%)	191.3	(209.3)	419.6	125.1	170.0
Market value ($ mil.)	9.6%	2,835.9	4,468.5	4,411.4	3,084.0	4,090.4
Employees	(1.6%)	46,000	37,000	40,800	40,000	43,100

*Fiscal year change

AMERICAN ELECTRIC POWER CO INC NMS: AEP

1 Riverside Plaza
Columbus, OH 43215-2373
Phone: 614 716-1000
Fax: 614 223-1823
Web: www.aep.com

CEO: Nicholas K Akins
CFO: Charles Zebula
HR: Ashlee Gates
FYE: December 31
Type: Public

Serving markets in Ohio, Michigan, Indiana, and other midwestern states, American Electric Power (AEP) is one of the largest power generators and distributors in the US. The holding company owns the nation's largest electricity transmission system and distribution lines, comprising a network of approximately 131,000 miles. AEP's electric utilities boast 5 million customers in about 10 states. The public utility subsidiaries of AEP have traditionally provided electric service, consisting of generation, transmission and distribution, on an integrated basis to their retail customers.

	Annual Growth	12/19	12/20	12/21	12/22	12/23
Sales ($mil.)	5.1%	15,561	14,919	16,792	19,640	18,982
Net income ($ mil.)	3.5%	1,921.1	2,200.1	2,488.1	2,307.2	2,208.1
Market value ($ mil.)	(3.7%)	49,730	43,815	46,815	49,961	42,737
Employees	(0.2%)	17,408	16,787	16,688	16,974	17,250

AMERICAN EQUITY INVESTMENT LIFE HOLDING CO NYS: AEL PRB

6000 Westown Parkway
West Des Moines, IA 50266
Phone: 515 221-0002
Fax: -
Web: www.american-equity.com

CEO: -
CFO: -
HR: -
FYE: December 31
Type: Public

American Equity Investment Life Holding (American Equity Life) is a leader in the development and sale of fixed index and fixed rate annuity products. The company issues and administers fixed annuity products through subsidiaries American Equity Investment Life Insurance, Eagle Life Insurance Company, and American Equity Investment Life Insurance Company of New York. Its target market includes individuals, typically ages 40 or older, who are seeking to accumulate tax-deferred savings or create guaranteed lifetime income. Licensed in all 50 states and the District of Columbia, the company sells its products through various channels including nearly 28,640 independent agents and some 50 national marketing organizations.

	Annual Growth	12/19	12/20	12/21	12/22	12/23
Assets ($mil.)	3.5%	69,697	71,390	78,349	73,926	79,918
Net income ($ mil.)	(3.8%)	246.1	671.5	474.0	1,220.9	210.5
Market value ($ mil.)	16.9%	2,374.6	2,194.5	3,087.8	3,619.4	4,427.1
Employees	13.1%	608	657	800	940	995

AMERICAN EXPRESS CO. NYS: AXP

200 Vesey Street
New York, NY 10285
Phone: 212 640-2000
Fax: 212 640-0404
Web: www.americanexpress.com

CEO: Stephen J Squeri
CFO: Christophe L Caillec
HR: -
FYE: December 31
Type: Public

American Express is a globally integrated payments company that provides its customers with access to products, insights and experiences that enrich lives and build business success. The company is also a leader in providing credit and charge cards to consumers, small businesses, mid-sized companies, and large corporations worldwide. In addition, the company still issues travelers cheques. Further, the company's charge and credit cards are its bread and butter; American Express boasts approximately $1.3 trillion in worldwide proprietary billed business, and has some 71.4 million proprietary cards-in-force worldwide. Nearly 80% of company's total sales comes from the US.

	Annual Growth	12/19	12/20	12/21	12/22	12/23
Assets ($mil.)	7.1%	198,321	191,367	188,548	228,354	261,108
Net income ($ mil.)	5.5%	6,759.0	3,135.0	8,060.0	7,514.0	8,374.0
Market value ($ mil.)	10.8%	90,006	87,418	118,283	106,823	135,447
Employees	3.7%	64,500	63,700	64,000	77,300	74,600

AMERICAN FARMS, LLC

1484 KEANE AVE
NAPLES, FL 341172926
Phone: 239 455-0300
Fax: –
Web: www.american-farms.com

CEO: –
CFO: –
HR: –
FYE: December 31
Type: Private

American Farms certainly hopes that its corporate strategies lead to perennial success. Established in 1991 with 10 acres, the company, a wholesale grower of flowering pot crops, now comprises more than 100 acres in Florida. It produces more than 100 varieties of annuals and herbaceous perennials, as well as flowering tropicals, landscape ferns and grasses, seasonal crops, and more. The majority of American Farms' sales are in the state of Florida, where it's one of the top growers of flowering plants, and more than half are to mass merchandisers (Home Depot, Target, Wal-Mart) in the southeastern US. In addition, the company sells to independent garden centers and landscapers.

	Annual Growth	12/09	12/10	12/11	12/12	12/14
Sales ($mil.)	4.2%	–	–	–	22.0	23.9
Net income ($ mil.)	(0.5%)	–	–	–	3.6	3.5
Market value ($ mil.)	–	–	–	–	–	–
Employees	–	–	–	–	–	170

AMERICAN FEDERATION OF LABOR & CONGRESS OF INDUSTRIAL ORGANZATION

815 16TH ST NW
WASHINGTON, DC 200064101
Phone: 202 637-5000
Fax: –
Web: www.aflcio.org

CEO: –
CFO: –
HR: –
FYE: June 30
Type: Private

Talk about spending a long time in labor: The AFL-CIO (American Federation of Labor and Congress of Industrial Organizations) has been focused on the task for more than a century. The AFL-CIO is an umbrella organization for more than 55 autonomous national and international unions. Altogether, the AFL-CIO represents more than 12 million workers -- from actors and airline pilots to marine engineers and machinists. It fights to improve wages and working conditions. The organization charters 50-plus state federations and about 500 central labor councils. Union members generally receive about 30% higher pay and more benefits than non-members. The AFL-CIO was created in 1955 by the merger of the AFL and the CIO.

	Annual Growth	06/14	06/15	06/16	06/19	06/22
Sales ($mil.)	(4.4%)	–	152.1	154.8	126.3	111.4
Net income ($ mil.)	–	–	(3.9)	5.8	9.9	8.9
Market value ($ mil.)	–	–	–	–	–	–
Employees	–	–	–	–	–	380

AMERICAN FEDERATION OF STATE COUNTY & MUNICIPAL EMPLOYEES

1625 L ST NW
WASHINGTON, DC 200365665
Phone: 202 429-1000
Fax: –
Web: www.afscme.org

CEO: –
CFO: –
HR: –
FYE: December 31
Type: Private

American Federation of State, County and Municipal Employees, AFL-CIO (AFSCME) finds strength in its numbers. The 1.6 million member labor union represents public sector employees in industries such as health care, education, social services, transportation, and public works. The group advocates and seeks legislative change for issues relating to social and economic justice in the workplace. AFSCME has more than 3,400 local unions in some 45 states, the District of Columbia and Puerto Rico. The union is a member of The American Federation of Labor-Congress of Industrial Organizations (AFL-CIO). AFSCME began in 1932 as the Wisconsin State Administrative, Clerical, Fiscal and Technical Employees Association.

	Annual Growth	12/11	12/12	12/15	12/17	12/22
Sales ($mil.)	(1.3%)	–	160.2	168.3	177.7	140.2
Net income ($ mil.)	–	–	(15.8)	27.8	47.5	(2.8)
Market value ($ mil.)	–	–	–	–	–	–
Employees	–	–	–	–	–	450

AMERICAN FEDERATION OF TEACHERS AFL-CIO AFT COMMITTEE ON POLITICAL

555 NEW JERSEY AVE NW
WASHINGTON, DC 200012029
Phone: 202 879-4400
Fax: –
Web: www.aft.org

CEO: –
CFO: –
HR: Tammelleo Sarah
FYE: June 30
Type: Private

This union could really take you to school. American Federation of Teachers (AFT) represents the economic, social, and professional interests of pre-K through 12th-grade teachers, faculty, and staff in higher education, as well as school-related personnel, health care professionals, and public employees. Its more than 1.5 million members are organized into 43 state affiliates and 3,000 local affiliates. About 170,000 of its members are retired. The union provides its constituents with workshops, publications, an insurance and discount services benefits program, nationwide salary surveys, and representation before Congress. AFT is an affiliate of the AFL-CIO.

	Annual Growth	06/13	06/14	06/15	06/21	06/22
Sales ($mil.)	127.8%	–	–	0.6	207.2	206.0
Net income ($ mil.)	108.1%	–	–	0.0	11.1	15.6
Market value ($ mil.)	–	–	–	–	–	–
Employees	–	–	–	–	–	320

AMERICAN FIBER GREEN PRODUCTS INC

NBB: AFBG

4209 Raleigh Street
Tampa, FL 33619
Phone: 813 247-2770
Fax: –
Web: www.americanfibergreenproducts.com

CEO: –
CFO: –
HR: –
FYE: December 31
Type: Public

The recycled fiberglass molding to be made by American Fiber Green Products will come in more colors than green. American Fiber Green Products announced plans in 2008 to build the first fiberglass recycling plant in the US. Its subsidiaries, including American Leisure Products and Chariot Manufacturing, will incorporate the recycled resin products into their manufacturing process to build such products as picnic tables, park benches, trailers, boats, and vehicle bodies for replicas of vintage cars. American Fiber Green Products is working on other uses to circumvent fiberglass away from landfills. Company president and CEO Dan Hefner also holds those positions for American Commerce Solutions.

	Annual Growth	12/11	12/12	12/13	12/14	12/15
Sales ($mil.)	47.8%	0.1	0.3	0.3	0.4	0.5
Net income ($ mil.)	–	(0.1)	(0.2)	(0.1)	(0.3)	(0.2)
Market value ($ mil.)	(14.3%)	8.9	3.5	5.3	2.8	4.8
Employees	–	3	3	3	3	3

AMERICAN FINANCIAL GROUP INC

NYS: AFG

301 East Fourth Street
Cincinnati, OH 45202
Phone: 513 579-2121
Fax: –
Web: www.afginc.com

CEO: Carl H Lindner III
CFO: Brian S Hertzman
HR: –
FYE: December 31
Type: Public

American Financial Group (AFG) insures American businessmen in pursuit of the Great American Dream. Through the operations of Great American Insurance Company, AFG offers commercial property/casualty insurance, and in the sale of traditional fixed and indexed annuities in the retail, financial institutions, broker-dealer and registered investment advisor markets. AFG's property and casualty insurance operations provide a wide range of commercial coverages through approximately 35 insurance businesses that make up the Great American Insurance Group. The company also provides surety and fidelity coverage and risk management services. It was founded in 1959 but its insurance roots started in 1872

	Annual Growth	12/19	12/20	12/21	12/22	12/23
Assets ($mil.)	(19.3%)	70,130	73,566	28,931	28,831	29,787
Net income ($ mil.)	(1.3%)	897.0	732.0	1,995.0	898.0	852.0
Market value ($ mil.)	2.0%	9,170.7	7,328.2	11,485	11,482	9,943.5
Employees	2.5%	7,700	7,300	6,600	6,900	8,500

AMERICAN FORESTS

1220 L ST NW STE 750
WASHINGTON, DC 200054079
Phone: 202 737-1944
Fax: –
Web: www.americanforests.org

CEO: James Daley
CFO: –
HR: –
FYE: September 30
Type: Private

Talk about old growth -- founded in 1875, American Forests is the oldest nonprofit citizens' conservation agency in the US. The environmental restoration organization assists communities in planning and implementing tree planting and forest conservation activities. Its efforts include planting memorial trees, replanting trees in areas devastated by wildfires and war, and planting trees to help Siberian tigers in Russia. The group has planted trees for about 500 projects across more than 20 countries. It also encourages individuals to plant trees at homes and businesses in urban areas in the US. American Forests was founded by a group of citizens concerned about the waste of America's forests.

	Annual Growth	09/18	09/19	09/20	09/21	09/22
Sales ($mil.)	29.6%	–	10.1	11.2	16.0	21.9
Net income ($ mil.)	11.1%	–	2.5	(0.2)	3.1	3.4
Market value ($ mil.)	–	–	–	–	–	–
Employees		–	–	–	–	55

AMERICAN FRUIT & PRODUCE, CORP.

12805 NW 42ND AVE
OPA LOCKA, FL 330544401
Phone: 305 681-1880
Fax: –
Web: www.americanfruitandproduce.com

CEO: Hugo J Acosta
CFO: –
HR: –
FYE: December 31
Type: Private

American Fruit & Produce's (AFP) patriotic duty is to distribute fresh fruits and vegetables. The company supplies everything from apples to zucchini to US wholesale, foodservice, and retail customers. AFP also exports fresh fruits and vegetables from Florida ports to locations in the Americas and Europe. It is the largest US supplier of fresh produce to Caribbean countries. Hugo Acosta and his uncle, Delio Medina, opened their small produce outfit in Miami in 1983. The company has grown to include some 300,000 sq. ft. of floor space situated on 32 acres in South Florida. American Fruit & Produce is still owned and operated by the its founders and their families.

AMERICAN FURNITURE WAREHOUSE CO.

8820 AMERICAN WAY
ENGLEWOOD, CO 801127056
Phone: 303 799-9044
Fax: –
Web: www.afw.com

CEO: Jake Jabs
CFO: –
HR: Ashley Maestas
FYE: March 31
Type: Private

Tony the Tiger hawking home furnishings might give some marketers pause, but the combination seems to work for American Furniture Warehouse. American Furniture's television commercials often spotlight white-haired president and CEO Jake Jabs (who has become a well-known personality in the state, as well as in the home furnishings industry) accompanied by baby exotic animals, mostly tigers. The company sells furniture, electronics, and decor at discounted prices. It boasts about a dozen retail locations in Colorado and Arizona and sells through its website, which also features bridal and gift registries. The company has built a reputation as a home-spun, local furniture retailer. Jabs bought the company in 1975.

	Annual Growth	03/18	03/19	03/20	03/21	03/22
Sales ($mil.)	12.6%	–	694.5	740.8	845.0	992.8
Net income ($ mil.)	17.6%	–	29.8	21.2	50.4	48.5
Market value ($ mil.)	–	–	–	–	–	–
Employees		–	–	–	–	4,312

AMERICAN FUTURE SYSTEMS, INC.

660 AMERICAN AVE STE 203
KING OF PRUSSIA, PA 194064032
Phone: 610 695-8600
Fax: –
Web: www.pbp.com

CEO: –
CFO: Tom Schubert
HR: –
FYE: December 31
Type: Private

Progressive Business Publications (PBP) wants to help business executives take more than a few steps forward. The company's publishing division includes a line of about 25 subscription-based business-to-business newsletters on business, non-profit, and medical topics. Titles include The Selling Advantage and Nonprofit Board Report. PBP also publishes websites and e-newsletters, legal information, executive reports and summaries, and buyer's guides. In addition, the company has divisions devoted to education and training for professional development, as well as selling business products related to gifts and incentives, and other human resources-related items. PBP was founded by President Ed Satell in 1989.

	Annual Growth	12/18	12/19	12/20	12/21	12/22
Sales ($mil.)	31.6%	–	–	–	0.0	0.0
Net income ($ mil.)		–	–	–	0.0	(0.0)
Market value ($ mil.)		–	–	–	–	–
Employees		–	–	–	–	600

AMERICAN GAMING ASSOCIATION

799 9TH ST NW STE 700
WASHINGTON, DC 200015326
Phone: 202 552-2675
Fax: –
Web: www.americangaming.org

CEO: –
CFO: –
HR: –
FYE: December 31
Type: Private

The American Gaming Association (AGA) makes sure the house always wins. The AGA is the trade association and lobbying firm for the commercial casino and gaming industry. It works to address federal legislative and regulatory issues surrounding the casino entertainment industry, such as federal taxation, regulatory issues, and travel and tourism. The AGA also has a bipartisan political action committee, AGA PAC, that supports likeminded political candidates through campaign donations. The AGA is led by CEO Frank Fahrenkoph Jr., former chairman of the Republican National Committee.

	Annual Growth	12/16	12/17	12/18	12/21	12/22
Sales ($mil.)	(0.5%)	–	16.1	18.7	12.8	15.6
Net income ($ mil.)	24.9%	–	0.9	3.0	0.5	2.6
Market value ($ mil.)		–	–	–	–	–
Employees		–	–	–	–	15

AMERICAN GREETINGS CORPORATION

1 AMERICAN BLVD
CLEVELAND, OH 441458151
Phone: 216 252-7300
Fax: –
Web: www.americangreetings.com

CEO: Joe Arcuri
CFO: Gregory M Steinberg
HR: Jacquilyn Rybka
FYE: February 28
Type: Private

American Greetings is a global leader in the large and enduring Celebrations marketplace. It produces greeting cards, party goods, and gift wraps under iconic brand names such as American Greetings, Papyrus, Recycled Paper Greetings, and Carlton Cards. Its digital business unit, AG Interactive, is a leading provider of digital greetings and premium celebrations content through proprietary technology platforms and apps. Clayton, Dubilier & Rice owns 60% stake in family-owned American Greetings. The Weiss Family, descendants of Jacob Sapirstein, who founded the company, in 1906, retained a 40% stake in the business.

AMERICAN HEALTHCHOICE, INC.

7350 Hawk Road
Flower Mound, TX 75022
Phone: 972 538-0122
Fax: 972 538-0130
Web: www.americanhealthchoice.com

CEO: Joseph W Stucki
CFO: John Stuecheli
HR: –
FYE: September 30
Type: Public

American HealthChoice operates medical clinics, makes medical devices, and provides other health related services in the southeastern US. Its AHC Medical Clinics unit owns and operates eight medical clinics in Texas and Tennessee and provides support services to about 35 affiliated clinics. Through its TelmedCo unit, American HealthChoice offers telemedicine services, allowing doctors at its own and third-party clinics to get second opinions from remote specialists. A third unit, RehabCo, has developed the OmniBody Scan medical imaging system, which uses infrared technology to detect breast cancer and other conditions.

	Annual Growth	09/01	09/02	09/03	09/04	09/05
Sales ($mil.)	4.5%	5.5	4.8	4.5	5.3	6.6
Net income ($ mil.)	37.3%	0.2	(3.1)	(1.8)	(1.5)	0.5
Market value ($ mil.)	48.3%	1.7	0.6	0.6	2.2	8.0
Employees	1.2%	62	62	62	51	65

AMERICAN HOCKEY LEAGUE INC

1 MONARCH PL STE 2400
SPRINGFIELD, MA 011442400
Phone: 413 781-2030
Fax: –
Web: www.theahl.com

CEO: –
CFO: –
HR: –
FYE: June 30
Type: Private

The American Hockey League is a minor league sports organization that serves as a farm system for the National Hockey League. Each of its 29 teams is affiliated with at least one professional franchise, providing a training ground for young players and offering a reserve roster of players who can be called up to the NHL. Established in 1936, the league has teams located throughout the US and in Canada. It regulates franchise ownership and oversees such business operations as sponsorships and marketing. The AHL season runs from October through April, followed by a playoff for the Calder Cup championship trophy.

	Annual Growth	06/16	06/17	06/18	06/19	06/22
Sales ($mil.)	(0.3%)	–	12.1	11.6	12.4	12.0
Net income ($ mil.)	–	–	0.7	–	–	–
Market value ($ mil.)	–	–	–	–	–	–
Employees	–	–	–	–	–	10

AMERICAN HOMESTAR CORPORATION

2450 S SHORE BLVD STE 300
LEAGUE CITY, TX 775732997
Phone: 281 334-9700
Fax: –
Web: www.americanhomestar.com

CEO: Finis F Teeter
CFO: Craig A Reynolds
HR: Katherine Santos
FYE: June 30
Type: Private

American Homestar shines brightly in the manufactured housing industry. The company produces factory-built modular, multi-section and single-section manufactured homes, and commercial structures under the Oak Creek and Platinum brand names. Its homes, which typically range from about 1,200 to 2,600 sq. ft., have average prices comparable to site-built homes. Its multi-section homes have as many as six bedrooms. American Homestar sells its homes through company-owned home centers and franchised retail centers in the South and the Southeast. Other operations include insurance and mortgage financing services.

	Annual Growth	06/13	06/14*	07/15	07/16*	06/17
Sales ($mil.)	8.7%	–	108.8	120.4	125.5	139.9
Net income ($ mil.)	102.6%	–	0.4	0.2	1.5	3.4
Market value ($ mil.)	–	–	–	–	–	–
Employees	–	–	–	–	–	568

*Fiscal year change

AMERICAN HONDA FINANCE CORPORATION

1919 TORRANCE BLVD
TORRANCE, CA 905012722
Phone: 310 972-2239
Fax: –
Web: www.honda.com

CEO: Hideo Tamaka
CFO: John Weisickle
HR: Breanna Robinson
FYE: March 31
Type: Private

If you're fonda the idea of driving a Honda, you might want to call on American Honda Finance. Operating as Honda Financial Services, the company provides retail financing in the US for Honda and Acura automobiles, motorcycles, all-terrain vehicles, power equipment, and outboard motors. Its American Honda Service division administers service contracts, while Honda Lease Trust offers leases on new and used vehicles. Honda Financial Services also offers dealer financing and related dealer services. Ancillary services include servicing loans and securitizing and selling loans into the secondary market. A subsidiary of American Honda Motor, the company began as a wholesale motorcycle finance provider in 1980.

	Annual Growth	03/06	03/07	03/08	03/16	03/17
Assets ($mil.)	5.4%	–	41,431	50,527	66,653	69,854
Net income ($ mil.)	6.7%	–	394.9	(45.2)	910.0	753.0
Market value ($ mil.)	–	–	–	–	–	–
Employees	–	–	–	–	–	1,000

AMERICAN HOSPITAL ASSOCIATION

155 N WACKER DR STE 400
CHICAGO, IL 606061719
Phone: 312 422-3000
Fax: –
Web: www.aha.org

CEO: Richard J Pollack
CFO: Christina Fisher
HR: Jean Montgomery
FYE: December 31
Type: Private

The American Hospital Association (AHA) represents some 5,000 hospitals and other health care providers and some 43,000 individuals from various health care fields. The AHA acts as an advocate in national health care policy development and provides services to its members, such as helping hospitals and other health care providers form networks for patient care, conducting research and development projects on the structuring and delivery of health care services, and producing educational programs and publications. The AHA Resource Center maintains an extensive collection of books and documents relating to hospitals and health care. The AHA was founded in 1898.

	Annual Growth	12/12	12/13	12/19	12/21	12/22
Sales ($mil.)	1.2%	–	124.4	142.8	128.9	138.8
Net income ($ mil.)	(1.3%)	–	7.4	6.6	10.3	6.6
Market value ($ mil.)	–	–	–	–	–	–
Employees	–	–	–	–	–	508

AMERICAN INDIAN COLLEGE FUND, THE (INC)

8333 GREENWOOD BLVD STE 120
DENVER, CO 802214483
Phone: 303 426-8900
Fax: –
Web: www.collegefund.org

CEO: –
CFO: Tamela M Carlson
HR: –
FYE: June 30
Type: Private

The American Indian College Fund helps kids get a reservation education. The nonprofit provides more than 3,500 scholarships a year for American Indian students to attend one of more than 30 tribal colleges operating on reservations. The organization also provides funding for programs in areas such as teacher training, culture preservation, and construction. Events like Celebration of Native Peoples held in various US cities benefit the American Indian College Fund. The organization was formed in 1989.

	Annual Growth	06/17	06/18	06/19	06/20	06/22
Sales ($mil.)	22.5%	–	25.5	27.9	48.8	57.4
Net income ($ mil.)	110.7%	–	0.9	3.0	20.6	17.4
Market value ($ mil.)	–	–	–	–	–	–
Employees	–	–	–	–	–	40

AMERICAN INSTITUTE FOR FOREIGN STUDY, INC.

1 HIGH RIDGE PARK
STAMFORD, CT 069051323
Phone: 203 399-5000
Fax: –
Web: www.aifs.com
CEO: William L Gertz
CFO: –
HR: Charlotte Mitchener
FYE: December 31
Type: Private

Making fun of, or hitting on, the foreign exchange student has become a rite of passage, thanks to AIFS. With offices in 15 countries, the American Institute for Foreign Study (AIFS) organizes cultural exchange programs around the globe for more than 50,000 students each year. Founded in 1964, the for-profit organization works with 500 colleges and universities in the US. Its Au Pair in America program has placed more than 60,000 au pairs since it was founded in 1986. AIFS also operates an American-style liberal arts college in the UK -- Richmond, The American International University. AIFS, a for-profit organization, was co-founded by chairman Cyril Taylor in 1964. AIFS has annual revenues of $180 million.

AMERICAN INSTITUTE OF ARCHITECTS, INC

1735 NEW YORK AVE NW
WASHINGTON, DC 200065209
Phone: 202 626-7300
Fax: –
Web: store.aia.org
CEO: Robert Ivy Jr
CFO: Tracy Harris
HR: –
FYE: December 31
Type: Private

The American Institute of Architects (AIA) knows how to raise the roof. The group represents the interests of some 83,000 professional architects through more than 300 chapters in every state in the US and in Asia, Europe, and South America. Members adhere to a code of ethics and the AIA disciplines members who break the rules with censure, admonition, suspension of membership, or permanent termination of membership. The organization's member benefits include educational programs, referrals, discounted contract documents, and job search assistance. It also lobbies government bodies on behalf of its members and provides media relations support.

	Annual Growth	12/07	12/08	12/10	12/13	12/15
Sales ($mil.)	1.5%	–	59.5	57.3	60.5	66.1
Net income ($ mil.)	1.6%	–	2.3	2.6	0.9	2.6
Market value ($ mil.)	–	–	–	–	–	–
Employees	–	–	–	–	–	200

AMERICAN INSTITUTE OF BAKING

1213 BAKERS WAY
MANHATTAN, KS 665024576
Phone: 785 537-4750
Fax: –
Web: cookingcareer.shawguides.com
CEO: –
CFO: –
HR: –
FYE: December 31
Type: Private

AIB isn't so interested in the butcher and candlestick maker -- they can find their own institutes. The American Institute of Baking (AIB) is a nonprofit that focuses on education, and research for the baking and food industry. The organization performs food safety audits and certifications in the US and around the world. AIB also sets standards for food packaging, and conducts occupational safety training. Its School of Baking offers resident courses, seminars, and correspondence and online education programs. AIB has more than 900 members worldwide, including ARAMARK Uniform Division and Otis Spunkmeyer. Founded in 1919, The AIB has offices in US, as well as Latin America, Europe, and Asia.

	Annual Growth	12/17	12/18	12/19	12/21	12/22
Sales ($mil.)	0.6%	–	2.7	3.3	5.4	2.8
Net income ($ mil.)	–	–	(1.8)	(1.0)	2.8	0.1
Market value ($ mil.)	–	–	–	–	–	–
Employees	–	–	–	–	–	185

AMERICAN INSTITUTE OF CERTIFIED PUBLIC ACCOUNTANTS

220 LEIGH FARM RD
DURHAM, NC 277078110
Phone: 919 402-0682
Fax: –
Web: –
CEO: Barry C Melancon
CFO: Scott H Spiegel
HR: –
FYE: December 31
Type: Private

When you add it all up, the American Institute of Certified Public Accountants (AICPA) makes perfect sense. One of the nation's leading nonprofit professional associations, the AICPA has more than 431,000 members from some 130 countries who are involved in public accounting, business, education, law, and government. The group promotes awareness of the accounting profession; identifies financial trends; sets certification, licensing, and professional standards; and provides information and advice to CPAs. The AICPA distributes its information through websites, conferences and forums, and publications. The group was founded in 1887.

	Annual Growth	07/08	07/09	07/13	07/15*	12/17
Sales ($mil.)	3.7%	–	199.8	219.9	247.5	266.8
Net income ($ mil.)	–	–	(13.6)	15.2	(7.2)	13.5
Market value ($ mil.)	–	–	–	–	–	–
Employees	–	–	–	–	–	800

*Fiscal year change

AMERICAN INSTITUTE OF PHYSICS INCORPORATED

1 PHYSICS ELLIPSE
COLLEGE PARK, MD 207403841
Phone: 301 209-3100
Fax: –
Web: www.aip.org
CEO: Michael Moloney
CFO: Catherine Swartz
HR: –
FYE: December 31
Type: Private

Who says scientists don't know how to get physical? The American Institute of Physics (AIP) publishes magazines (Physics Today) , journals (Journal of Applied Physics), conference proceedings, online products, and other publications in the sciences of physics and astronomy. The company provides publishing services for its own publications, as well as for its member societies and other publishers. Scitation, AIP's online publishing platform, hosts 1.6 million articles from 190 sources. AIP was founded in New York in 1931 by a group of American physical science societies. It was chartered as a membership corporation to advance and diffuse knowledge of the science of physics and its applications to human welfare.

	Annual Growth	12/17	12/18	12/19	12/21	12/22
Sales ($mil.)	3.7%	–	70.4	83.1	82.3	81.4
Net income ($ mil.)	–	–	(13.1)	10.0	0.4	(5.5)
Market value ($ mil.)	–	–	–	–	–	–
Employees	–	–	–	–	–	110

AMERICAN INSTITUTES FOR RESEARCH IN THE BEHAVIORAL SCIENCES

1400 CRYSTAL DR FL 10
ARLINGTON, VA 222023289
Phone: 202 403-5000
Fax: –
Web: www.air.org
CEO: David Myers
CFO: Marijo Ahlgrimm
HR: –
FYE: December 31
Type: Private

The American Institutes for Research (AIR) lives and breathes to enhance human performance. The not-for-profit organization conducts behavioral and social science research on topics related to education and educational assessment, health, international development, and work and training. Clients, including several federal agencies, use AIR's research in developing policies. As a major ongoing initiative, the organization provides tools to improve education both in the US and internationally, particularly in disadvantaged areas. John C. Flanagan, who developed the Critical Incident Technique personnel-selection tool to identify human success indicators in the workplace, founded the organization in 1946.

	Annual Growth	12/14	12/15	12/16	12/17	12/19
Sales ($mil.)	14.2%	–	488.3	474.1	497.6	829.6
Net income ($ mil.)	72.5%	–	45.1	43.6	55.1	398.1
Market value ($ mil.)	–	–	–	–	–	–
Employees	–	–	–	–	–	1,500

AMERICAN INSURANCE ASSOCIATION INC.

555 12TH ST NW STE 5
WASHINGTON, DC 200041211
Phone: 202 828-7100
Fax: –
Web: www.aiadc.org

CEO: –
CFO: –
HR: –
FYE: December 31
Type: Private

The American Insurance Association (AIA) is betting that everything will be alright. The group represents the interests of some 350 major property and casualty insurers. In addition to its Washington, DC, headquarters, the organization has offices in New York, Georgia, Massachusetts, Texas, Illinois, and California. AIA lobbies state and federal law makers on issues including asbestos, auto insurance, regulatory and legal reform, workers' compensation, and tort reform and litigation management, among others. It also holds conferences and workshops and publishes newsletters and books for its members and contributes heavily to issue ads like those for asbestos litigation reform.

	Annual Growth	12/07	12/08	12/09	12/13	12/17
Sales ($mil.)	39.2%	–	1.0	24.8	–	18.9
Net income ($ mil.)	–	–	(0.1)	(2.4)	–	1.1
Market value ($ mil.)	–	–	–	–	–	–
Employees	–	–	–	–	–	70

AMERICAN INTERNATIONAL GROUP INC   NYS: AIG

1271 Avenue of the Americas
New York, NY 10020
Phone: 212 770-7000
Fax: –
Web: www.aig.com

CEO: Peter S Zaffino
CFO: Sabra Purtill
HR: –
FYE: December 31
Type: Public

American International Group (AIG) is one of the world's largest insurance company. The company provides general property/casualty insurance, life insurance, and retirement and financial services to commercial, institutional, and individual customers in about 70 countries around the world. North America accounts for more than 70% of its total revenue. The company traces its roots back to 1919, when Cornelius Vander Starr founded American Asiatic Underwriters in Shanghai.

	Annual Growth	12/19	12/20	12/21	12/22	12/23
Assets ($mil.)	0.7%	525,064	586,481	596,112	526,634	539,306
Net income ($ mil.)	2.1%	3,348.0	(5,944.0)	9,388.0	10,276	3,643.0
Market value ($ mil.)	7.2%	35,358	26,079	39,167	43,562	46,669
Employees	(14.0%)	46,000	45,000	36,600	26,200	25,200

AMERICAN INTERNATIONAL INDUSTRIES INC   NBB: AMIN

601 Cien Street, Suite 235
Kemah, TX 77565-3077
Phone: 281 334-9479
Fax: 281 334-9508
Web: www.americanii.com

CEO: –
CFO: –
HR: –
FYE: December 31
Type: Public

Nothing says Texas like oil and real estate. American International Industries (AII) covers those bases -- and more -- from its home in the Houston metro area. The company typically takes a controlling interest in undervalued companies; it holds investments in oil wells, real estate, and various industrial manufacturers. AII owns Delta Seaboard International (formerly Hammonds Industries), which operates technical services, fuel additives, and water treatment systems divisions. Its Northeastern Plastics subsidiary makes automotive after-market products. International Diversified Corporation (a firm connected with the brother of chairman and CEO Daniel Dror) owns 27% of the firm.

	Annual Growth	12/10	12/11	12/12	12/13	12/14
Sales ($mil.)	(80.8%)	24.3	21.7	8.0	7.2	0.0
Net income ($ mil.)	–	0.0	(3.3)	(2.1)	(1.8)	(2.4)
Market value ($ mil.)	6.0%	1.5	0.6	5.8	4.2	1.9
Employees	(22.9%)	51	60	18	18	18

AMERICAN JEWISH WORLD SERVICE, INC.

45 W 36TH ST FL 10
NEW YORK, NY 100187641
Phone: 212 792-2900
Fax: –
Web: www.ajws.org

CEO: –
CFO: –
HR: –
FYE: April 30
Type: Private

The American Jewish World Service (AJWS) helps poor people around the globe in areas such as health, nutrition, education, housing, and women's issues. It offers grants, technical assistance, advocacy, and emergency relief through hundreds of organizations in more than 35 developing nations worldwide. Projects include anti-sexual exploitation clinics, building orphanages, helping street children, entrepreneur programs for women, HIV/AIDS education and intervention, and sustainable agriculture programs. AJWS was founded in 1985 to help American Jews do tzedakah, or good deeds, which is part of a Jewish obligation to help the world.

	Annual Growth	04/17	04/18	04/19	04/20	04/22
Sales ($mil.)	(8.2%)	–	64.7	39.6	44.5	46.0
Net income ($ mil.)	–	–	12.3	(4.4)	1.9	(1.0)
Market value ($ mil.)	–	–	–	–	–	–
Employees	–	–	–	–	–	112

AMERICAN LEARNING CORPORATION

1 JERICHO PLZ
JERICHO, NY 117531680
Phone: 516 938-8000
Fax: –
Web: www.interactivetherapygroup.com

CEO: –
CFO: –
HR: –
FYE: March 31
Type: Private

American Learning (formerly American Claims Evaluation) has undergone a transition. The company historically provided vocational rehabilitation and disability management services through its RPM Rehabilitation & Associates subsidiary; but in 2008 it sold those operations and got into the business of helping kids with developmental delays and disabilities. It acquired private New York-based Interactive Therapy Group Consultants, which provides comprehensive therapy services, including early intervention programs, preschool programs, and school staffing services, to developmentally delayed and disabled children, primarily in New York. Chairman, president, and CEO Gary Gelman owns two-thirds of the company.

AMERICAN LIBRARY ASSOCIATION

225 N MICHIGAN AVE STE 1300
CHICAGO, IL 606017616
Phone: 800 545-2433
Fax: –
Web: www.ala.org

CEO: –
CFO: –
HR: –
FYE: August 31
Type: Private

Shhhh! The American Library Association (ALA) is a not-for-profit that works to develop, promote, and improve library and information services. Governed by an elected council, the ALA works with libraries of all types, from public to academic to prison. The 58,000-member organization consists of 11 divisions, as well as affiliated organizations and chapters in all 50 states, all working to advance ALA causes, such as Banned Books Week, an annual event promoting awareness about efforts to ban certain books from libraries. The ALA's Washington, DC branch office tries to influence federal legislative policy to ensure the public's right to free access to information. The group was founded in 1876.

	Annual Growth	08/16	08/17	08/19	08/21	08/22
Sales ($mil.)	4.6%	–	49.0	50.0	46.4	61.2
Net income ($ mil.)	4.2%	–	9.5	(4.1)	4.2	11.7
Market value ($ mil.)	–	–	–	–	–	–
Employees	–	–	–	–	–	275

AMERICAN LOCKER GROUP, INC.

2701 Regent Blvd., Suite 200   CEO: –
DFW Airport, TX 75261   CFO: –
Phone: 817 329-1600   HR: –
Fax: –   FYE: December 31
Web: www.americanlocker.com   Type: Public

Ever carried around one of those orange plastic-capped locker keys at the theme park? That's American Locker Group. The company sells and rents coin-, key-, and electronically controlled lockers used by health clubs, amusement parks, ski resorts, bus stations, and employee locker rooms. Customers include SeaWorld, Vail Resorts, Walt Disney World, The UPS Store, and the University of Colorado. Postal mailboxes, such as those used by apartment complexes, make up about a third of sales. Besides the US, American Locker Group serves customers in Canada, Chile, Greece, India, Mexico, and the UK (less than 20% of sales in 2009). The company was founded in 1958.

	Annual Growth	12/09	12/10	12/11	12/12	12/13
Sales ($mil.)	4.0%	12.5	12.1	13.4	13.7	14.6
Net income ($ mil.)	–	(0.4)	0.0	0.0	(0.6)	(2.8)
Market value ($ mil.)	5.1%	2.7	1.9	2.5	2.9	3.3
Employees	(3.3%)	137	103	110	108	120

AMERICAN LUNG ASSOCIATION

55 W WACKER DR STE 1150   CEO: Harold Wimmer
CHICAGO, IL 606011796   CFO: Laura Scott
Phone: 312 801-7600   HR: Mariel Guzman
Fax: –   FYE: June 30
Web: www.lung.org   Type: Private

Many Americans breathe easier because of the American Lung Association. Dedicated to the prevention and cure of lung disease, the group focuses on asthma management, air quality, and tobacco control. It funds research, develops public education materials, sponsors conferences, and lobbies for legislation. It operates through a network of about 200 local offices across the US as well as in Puerto Rico and the US Virgin Islands. About half of the American Lung Association's support comes in response to direct-mail solicitations, including the annual Christmas Seals drive. It also receives grants from companies, foundations, and government agencies. The group was founded in 1904 to fight tuberculosis.

	Annual Growth	06/05	06/06	06/07	06/20	06/22
Sales ($mil.)	6.1%	–	50.3	–	104.4	129.4
Net income ($ mil.)	–	–	–	–	(1.6)	27.5
Market value ($ mil.)	–	–	–	–	–	–
Employees	–	–	–	–	–	500

AMERICAN MANAGEMENT ASSOCIATION INTERNATIONAL, INC.

1601 BROADWAY   CEO: Manos Avramidis
NEW YORK, NY 100197420   CFO: Vivianna Guzman
Phone: 212 586-8100   HR: Barbara Zung
Fax: –   FYE: March 31
Web: www.amanet.org   Type: Private

American Management Association (AMA) is a not-for-profit membership association that provides a variety of educational and management development services to businesses, government agencies, and individuals. The associations is engaged in professional development, advancing the skills of individuals. AMA offers more than 140 training seminars in more than 25 subject areas of business management and workforce development. It also sponsors conferences and workshops and provides webcasts, podcasts, and books in such areas as communication, leadership, project management, sales and marketing, human resources, and finance and accounting.

	Annual Growth	03/13	03/14	03/20	03/21	03/22
Sales ($mil.)	(9.7%)	–	84.5	58.0	30.6	37.4
Net income ($ mil.)	–	–	(2.1)	0.7	(4.2)	(0.7)
Market value ($ mil.)	–	–	–	–	–	–
Employees	–	–	–	–	–	500

AMERICAN MARKETING ASSOCIATION INC

130 E RANDOLPH ST FL 22   CEO: Dennis Dunlap
CHICAGO, IL 606016320   CFO: –
Phone: 312 542-9000   HR: Jennifer Howell
Fax: –   FYE: June 30
Web: www.ama.org   Type: Private

The largest marketing association in North America, the American Marketing Association (AMA) offers services to marketing professionals including best practices and research studies, job resources, and publications and directories. AMA publications include the flagship semi-monthly magazine Marketing News, as well as the Journal of Marketing, Journal of Public Policy & Marketing, and a variety of newsletters. The AMA Web site, MarketingPower.com, updates industry news and articles daily. The AMA has some 400 local chapters throughout the US and Canada about 40,000 members worldwide.

	Annual Growth	06/12	06/13	06/14	06/15	06/20
Sales ($mil.)	(42.6%)	–	16.7	17.3	17.3	0.3
Net income ($ mil.)	(60.2%)	–	3.5	1.0	(2.0)	0.0
Market value ($ mil.)	–	–	–	–	–	–
Employees	–	–	–	–	–	65

AMERICAN MEDICAL ASSOCIATION INC

330 N WABASH AVE STE 39300   CEO: James Madera
CHICAGO, IL 606115885   CFO: –
Phone: 312 464-5000   HR: Kevin Collins
Fax: –   FYE: December 31
Web: www.ama-assn.org   Type: Private

The AMA knows whether there's a doctor in the house. The American Medical Association (AMA) prescribes the standards for the medical profession. The membership group's activities include advocacy for physicians, promoting ethics standards in the medical community, and improving health care education. Policies are set by the AMA's House of Delegates, comprised of elected representatives. The AMA is also a publisher of books for physicians, and provides an online physician network through a partnership with Medfusion, sells medical malpractice insurance, and helps doctors fight legal claims. Founded in 1847 by a physician to establish a code of medical ethics, AMA has nearly 225,000 members.

	Annual Growth	12/12	12/13	12/14	12/15	12/22
Sales ($mil.)	6.3%	–	258.5	261.4	284.3	446.7
Net income ($ mil.)	–	–	(7.0)	29.1	30.0	76.8
Market value ($ mil.)	–	–	–	–	–	–
Employees	–	–	–	–	–	1,150

AMERICAN MEDICAL TECHNOLOGIES INC   NBB: ADLI

5555 Bear Lane   CEO: Judd D Hoffman
Corpus Christi, TX 78405   CFO: –
Phone: 361 289-1145   HR: –
Fax: –   FYE: December 31
Web: www.americandentaltech.com   Type: Public

American Medical Technologies (AMT) can get you a good deal on dental products. The company makes the Hydro Jet system, which removes tooth decay with a stream of tiny particles and water propelled by compressed air. However, as the market for the system has softened, AMT is increasingly focused on its role as a distributor or broker for products made by others. It uses its worldwide network of dealers and sales representatives to distribute the tooth-whitening products of Spectrum Dental, for instance, as well as crowns, bridges, dental head light systems, and other oral care products made by third parties.

	Annual Growth	12/03	12/04	12/05	12/06	12/07
Sales ($mil.)	1.6%	3.0	2.3	2.2	2.8	3.2
Net income ($ mil.)	–	0.0	0.0	(1.5)	(1.4)	(0.9)
Market value ($ mil.)	(23.3%)	5.3	4.5	1.7	1.6	1.8
Employees	(4.7%)	17	24	20	17	14

AMERICAN MILLENNIUM INC

110 North Rubey Drive, Suite 100A
Golden, CO 80403
Phone: 303 279-2002
Fax: –
Web: –

NBB: AMCI E
CEO: Bruce R Bacon
CFO: David E Welch
HR: –
FYE: July 31
Type: Public

American Millennium Corporation, Inc. (AMCi) can help you keep track of all your assets. The company offers hardware and software that tracks and monitors remote commercial or industrial assets, such as vehicles, oil-field equipment, and large tanks for fluids or gases. The company is a value-added reseller for the Transcore/Vistar GlobalWave and for the Globalstar Telecommunications SENS satellite communications systems. AMCi's product line includes the SatAlarm-Sentry, SatAlarm-Server, and SatAlarm-Watchdog. The company was established in 1979.

	Annual Growth	07/98	07/99	07/00	07/01	07/02
Sales ($mil.)	22.0%	0.3	0.1	0.3	0.3	0.7
Net income ($ mil.)	–	(6.1)	(1.5)	(2.7)	(2.9)	(1.7)
Market value ($ mil.)	(49.3%)	57.8	14.0	34.5	16.6	3.8
Employees	12.0%	7	6	13	10	11

AMERICAN MOTORCYCLE ASSOCIATION

13515 YARMOUTH DR
PICKERINGTON, OH 431478273
Phone: 614 856-1900
Fax: –
Web: www.americanmotorcyclist.com

CEO: –
CFO: Jeff Wolens
HR: Carolyn Stewart
FYE: September 30
Type: Private

For those who feel the need for two-wheeled speed, there's the American Motorcyclist Association (AMA). The group promotes the interests of its about 300,000 biking enthusiast members by offering a roadside assistance program, lobbying government at all levels, and publishing American Motorcyclist magazine. As a member of the F d ration Internationale de Motocyclisme, it organizes some 100 annual professional, amateur, and pro-am racing events through its AMA Pro Racing unit. The AMA also runs the Motorcycle Hall of Fame Museum and an online database of riding trips, gear and bikes for sale, and stories of motorcycle glory. The AMA was founded in 1924 but traces its roots to the 1903 New York Motorcycle Club.

	Annual Growth	09/18	09/19	09/20	09/21	09/22
Sales ($mil.)	4.3%	–	11.8	11.6	12.0	13.4
Net income ($ mil.)	–	–	(0.2)	1.7	1.2	1.6
Market value ($ mil.)	–	–	–	–	–	–
Employees	–	–	–	–	–	55

AMERICAN MUNICIPAL POWER, INC.

1111 SCHROCK RD STE 100
COLUMBUS, OH 432291155
Phone: 614 540-1111
Fax: –
Web: www.amppartners.org

CEO: Jon Bisher
CFO: Robert W Trippe
HR: –
FYE: December 31
Type: Private

Power to the Public is the motto of American Municipal Power (AMP). The non-profit membership organization supplies wholesale power to more than 80 community-owned distribution utilities in Ohio, 30 in Pennsylvania, 6 in Michigan, 5 in Virginia, 3 in Kentucky, 2 in West Virginia, 1 in Indiana, and 1 in Delaware (a joint action agency). AMP and its members own and operate plants that generate more than 1500 MW of power. The company also handles projects on behalf of the Ohio Municipal Electric Generating Agency (OMEGA) Joint Ventures program (jointly owned generation and transmission projects). The power generation company is owned by its member municipalities. AMP member utilities serve some 635,000 customers.

	Annual Growth	12/18	12/19	12/20	12/21	12/22
Sales ($mil.)	1.7%	–	1,170.0	1,091.4	1,137.3	1,229.5
Net income ($ mil.)	–	–	5.3	2.5	14.4	(2.0)
Market value ($ mil.)	–	–	–	–	–	–
Employees	–	–	–	–	–	229

AMERICAN NATURAL ENERGY CORP

4849 GRNVLLE AVE STE 1250
DALLAS, TX 75206
Phone: 918 481-1440
Fax: –
Web: –

CEO: –
CFO: –
HR: –
FYE: December 31
Type: Private

American Natural Energy Corp. is not selling organic food and dietary supplements to boost metabolism, it is tapping into that other American natural energy source -- hydrocarbons. Doing business as ANEC, the company is an oil and natural gas exploration and production company which focuses its operations on a property in St. Charles Parish, Louisiana. ANEC works in tandem with partner Exxon Mobil to develop this Louisiana project. In 2007 the company sold 75% of ANEC's development rights in this project to Dune Energy.

AMERICAN NOBLE GAS INC

15612 College Blvd
Lenexa, KS 66219
Phone: 913 955-0532
Fax: –
Web: www.amnoblegas.com

NBB: AMNI
CEO: Thomas Heckman
CFO: Thomas Heckman
HR: –
FYE: December 31
Type: Public

Maybe nothing lasts forever, but Infinity Energy Resources hopes that US demand for fossil fuels won't go away for a long, long time. The company focuses its oil exploration and production operations in the Fort Worth Basin of Texas, in the Rocky Mountain region in the Greater Green River Basin in Wyoming, and the Sand Wash and Piceance Basins in Colorado. It is also pursuing an opportunity in offshore Nicaragua. The company has proved reserves of 7.8 billion cu. ft. of natural gas equivalent. Infinity Energy Resources has exited the oil services business.

	Annual Growth	12/18	12/19	12/20	12/21	12/22
Sales ($mil.)	–	–	–	–	0.0	0.1
Net income ($ mil.)	–	(0.3)	1.8	5.6	(1.6)	(3.9)
Market value ($ mil.)	29.9%	0.9	1.7	2.5	7.8	2.5
Employees	–	2	3	3	3	2

AMERICAN OUTDOOR PRODUCTS, INC.

6350 GUNPARK DR
BOULDER, CO 803013588
Phone: 303 581-0518
Fax: –
Web: www.backpackerspantry.com

CEO: –
CFO: –
HR: –
FYE: December 31
Type: Private

American Outdoor Products fills explorers' packs with gourmet goodies. The company manufactures freeze-dried and dehydrated meals, trail mixes, fruit snacks, and desserts (including freeze-dried ice cream) under the Backpacker's Pantry and Astronaut Foods brands. Its offerings are designed to stay fresh for up to three years. The firm also makes herb blends and meat rubs under the Colorado Spice brand, which does not use dyes, artificial colors, or MSG. American Outdoor Products sells its fare through its website and at outdoor specialty stores such as REI, Eastern Mountain Sports, and Academy Sports & Outdoors. Founded in 1951 by Ann Benedict, the company today is owned and operated by the Smith family.

	Annual Growth	12/15	12/16	12/17	12/18	12/22
Sales ($mil.)	0.1%	–	9.9	8.9	9.0	10.0
Net income ($ mil.)	0.7%	–	0.7	0.3	0.3	0.7
Market value ($ mil.)	–	–	–	–	–	–
Employees	–	–	–	–	–	50

AMERICAN PAYROLL INSTITUTE, INC.

660 N MAIN AVE STE 100
SAN ANTONIO, TX 782051217
Phone: 210 224-6406
Fax: -
Web: www.payroll.org

CEO: Daniel Maddux
CFO: -
HR: Hilary Camber
FYE: December 31
Type: Private

The American Payroll Association (APA) works to help the folks who help the rest of us get paid. The APA supports payroll administration professionals and people in related fields. It does so by providing seminars, publications, and certification. The organization also represents its members' interests in legislative and regulatory matters. The APA boasts about 22,000 members in some 150 chapters nationwide. The association operates from offices in Las Vegas; New York; San Antonio, Texas; and Washington, DC. The not-for-profit organization was established in 1982.

	Annual Growth	12/15	12/16	12/17	12/21	12/22
Sales ($mil.)	3.0%	-	9.5	11.3	12.0	11.4
Net income ($ mil.)	23.1%	-	1.5	1.7	5.1	5.1
Market value ($ mil.)	-	-	-	-	-	-
Employees	-	-	-	-	-	79

AMERICAN PET PRODUCTS ASSOCIATION, INC.

225 HIGH RIDGE RD STE 200
STAMFORD, CT 069053000
Phone: 203 532-0000
Fax: -
Web: www.americanpetproducts.org

CEO: -
CFO: -
HR: -
FYE: December 31
Type: Private

The American Pet Products Association (APPA) has a lot to bark, meow, and crow about. The group is a not-for-profit trade organization that comprises more than 1,000 pet products manufacturers and importers. The APPA promotes pet ownership and pet products and monitors legislation and regulation and responds to both. It also provides its members with services such as market and scientific research. The group's annual Pet Products Trade Show is the largest of its kind. In 2009 APPA teamed up with Pet Industry Distributors Association to host the first annual Global Pet Expo. The group was founded in 1958 as the American Pet Products Manufacturers Association.

AMERICAN PETROLEUM INSTITUTE INC

200 MASSACHUSETTS AVE NW STE 1100
WASHINGTON, DC 20001
Phone: 202 682-8000
Fax: -
Web: www.api.org

CEO: Jack N Gerard
CFO: -
HR: -
FYE: December 31
Type: Private

The American Petroleum Institute (API) is a trade association for the oil and natural gas industry. The group represents more than 625 corporate members, including such industry giants as BP and Exxon Mobil, as well as small independent companies, with offices in more than 20 state capitals and overseas. Besides serving as an advocate in legislative, regulatory, and media arenas, the API compiles data on industry operations. The organization's members come from several segments of the petroleum industry, including upstream (exploration and production), downstream (refining and marketing), pipeline operations, marine transportation, and oil field service. The API was founded in 1919.

	Annual Growth	12/06	12/07	12/08	12/09	12/13
Sales ($mil.)	1.9%	-	-	204.2	197.4	224.4
Net income ($ mil.)	-	-	-	(10.4)	19.0	1.0
Market value ($ mil.)	-	-	-	-	-	-
Employees	-	-	-	-	-	250

AMERICAN PLASTIC TOYS, INC.

799 LADD RD
WALLED LAKE, MI 483903025
Phone: 248 624-4881
Fax: -
Web: www.americanplastictoys.com

CEO: David B Littleton
CFO: -
HR: -
FYE: December 31
Type: Private

If your child spends hours applying pretend makeup at her Enchanted Beauty Salon, or hammering away at his Build & Play Tool Bench, or digging in the sand with her Castle Pail of Toys, you can thank American Plastic Toys for the much-needed break. The company manufactures plastic toys, including doll accessories (strollers, nurseries), children's furniture, role-playing items (kitchen sets, tool benches), riding toys (trikes, wagons), seasonal toys (pail and shovel sets), and vehicles (dump trucks, airplanes). Products are sold by such retailers as Wal-Mart, Kmart, and Toys "R" Us across the US, as well as in Canada, the Caribbean, Central and South America, and Mexico. The company was founded in 1962.

	Annual Growth	12/08	12/09	12/10	12/11	12/12
Sales ($mil.)	(0.1%)	-	-	51.1	45.4	51.0
Net income ($ mil.)	14.2%	-	-	4.0	(1.5)	5.2
Market value ($ mil.)	-	-	-	-	-	-
Employees	-	-	-	-	-	300

AMERICAN PODIATRIC MEDICAL ASSOCIATION, INCORPORATED

9312 OLD GEORGETOWN RD
BETHESDA, MD 208141621
Phone: 301 571-9200
Fax: -
Web: www.apma.org

CEO: Glenn Gastwirth
CFO: -
HR: -
FYE: May 31
Type: Private

Do you supposes their toeses smell like roses? The American Podiatric Medical Association (AMPA) is a professional organization of doctors of podiatric medicine practicing in the US. Among its public services, the AMPA conducts public education campaigns to raise awareness on a variety of topics relating to foot health, such as diabetes, foot fashion and health, and walking for exercise. Its Council on Podiatric Medical Education is the accrediting body for US podiatric medical schools. Founded in 1912, APMA has more than 50 chapters and a membership of some 12,000 foot and ankle specialists; membership fees provide 65% of the organization's revenue.

	Annual Growth	05/14	05/15	05/16	05/17	05/22
Sales ($mil.)	(0.2%)	-	13.7	14.5	13.7	13.5
Net income ($ mil.)	-	-	0.0	1.0	0.0	(0.2)
Market value ($ mil.)	-	-	-	-	-	-
Employees	-	-	-	-	-	60

AMERICAN POOLPLAYERS ASSOCIATION, INC.

1000 LAKE SAINT LOUIS BLVD STE 325
LAKE SAINT LOUIS, MO 633671387
Phone: 636 625-8611
Fax: -
Web: www.poolplayers.com

CEO: -
CFO: Olendia T Bell
HR: -
FYE: December 31
Type: Private

The American Poolplayers Association (APA) runs the amateur table. The group is the governing body for amateur pool in the US, Canada, and Japan. It has more than 260,000 members administered by a group of local franchise operators who conduct weekly tournaments. The APA produces three annual tournaments -- the APA National Team Championships, the APA National Singles Championships, and the US Amateur Championship -- which pay out more than $1 million a year. The APA also handles the handicap system, sells APA merchandise, publishes billiards rules, and spreads the word about amateur pool. The association was formed in 1979 as the National Pool League by professional pool players Terry Bell and Larry Hubbart.

	Annual Growth	12/10	12/11	12/12	12/13	12/14
Sales ($mil.)	0.7%	-	-	15.4	15.5	15.6
Net income ($ mil.)	4.6%	-	-	4.6	4.9	5.1
Market value ($ mil.)	-	-	-	-	-	-
Employees	-	-	-	-	-	61

AMERICAN POWER GROUP CORP
NBB: APGI

2503 East Poplar St
Algona, IA 50511
Phone: 781 224-2411
Fax: –
Web: www.americanpowergroupinc.com

CEO: Lyle Jensen
CFO: Charles E Coppa
HR: –
FYE: September 30
Type: Public

Wish your engine ran on natural gas instead of diesel? American Power Group Corporation (formerly GreenMan Technologies) makes and sells dual-fuel energy technology that allows for the easy conversion of diesel engines to liquid and compressed natural gas, as well as well-head gas or biomethane. This technology is specifically designed for aftermarket vehicular and diesel engines and diesel generators. The former GreenMan Technologies changed its name to American Power Group Corporation in mid-2012 after acquiring American Power Group in mid-2009.

	Annual Growth	09/14	09/15	09/16	09/22	09/23
Sales ($mil.)	(19.7%)	6.3	3.0	1.9	3.5	0.9
Net income ($ mil.)	–	(2.3)	0.5	(7.6)	0.3	(2.0)
Market value ($ mil.)	(26.2%)	650.9	314.6	184.4	14.2	42.1
Employees	–	–	21	19	20	–	–

AMERICAN PRODUCTIVITY & QUALITY CENTER, INC.

123 N POST OAK LN STE 300
HOUSTON, TX 770247718
Phone: 713 681-4020
Fax: –
Web: www.apqc.org

CEO: Lisa Higgins
CFO: Perry Wiggins
HR: Ashley White
FYE: December 31
Type: Private

Helping organizations live up to their potential is what the American Productivity & Quality Center (APQC) is all about. The not-for-profit APQC focuses on providing professional development, conducting and publishing research, and advising companies about maximizing productivity and improving quality. Members of the organization, including A.T. Kearney and Raytheon, have access to original research, journals and trade publications, discounted professional development conferences, and a directory of other members. Founded in 1977, the APQC was a force in the creation of the Malcolm Baldrige National Quality Award, an award given by the President of the United States to businesses for special achievement.

	Annual Growth	12/15	12/16	12/18	12/21	12/22
Sales ($mil.)	3.7%	–	15.9	15.2	18.2	19.7
Net income ($ mil.)	14.7%	–	2.1	1.8	3.9	4.7
Market value ($ mil.)	–	–	–	–	–	–
Employees	–	–	–	–	–	78

AMERICAN PSYCHOLOGICAL ASSOCIATION, INC.

750 1ST ST NE STE 605
WASHINGTON, DC 200028009
Phone: 202 336-5500
Fax: –
Web: www.apa.org

CEO: –
CFO: –
HR: –
FYE: December 31
Type: Private

The American Psychological Association (APA) works to advance mental health: yours and that of its members. The APA is the largest scientific and professional organization representing psychology in the US, as well as the world's largest association of psychologists. The association seeks to advance the study and practice of psychology in the US. It is also vocal about the role of psychological services in health care reform. It offers members career resources, insurance, and financial and other services. The APA has more than 134,000 members, including researchers, educators, clinicians, consultants, and students, as well some 55 professional divisions.

	Annual Growth	12/13	12/14	12/15	12/21	12/22
Sales ($mil.)	0.2%	–	130.4	117.8	143.9	133.0
Net income ($ mil.)	–	–	–	2.9	(12.2)	17.4	(3.6)
Market value ($ mil.)	–	–	–	–	–	–
Employees	–	–	–	–	–	550

AMERICAN PUBLIC EDUCATION INC
NMS: APEI

111 West Congress Street
Charles Town, WV 25414
Phone: 304 724-3700
Fax: –
Web: www.apei.com

CEO: Angela K Selden
CFO: Richard W Sunderland Jr
HR: Andrew Panzarella
FYE: December 31
Type: Public

American Public Education (APEI) provides online and campus-based postsecondary education and career learning to approximately 107,100 students through its subsidiary institutions. Its institutions offer purpose-built education programs and career learning designed to prepare individuals for productive contributions to their professions and society and to offer opportunities to advance students in their current professions or to help them prepare for their next career. It offers a total of about 185 degree programs, roughly 140 certificate programs, and nearly five diploma programs across a broad range of fields of study, including public service-focused fields such as nursing, national security, military studies, intelligence, and homeland security, as well as traditional academic fields such as business, health science, information technology, justice studies, education, and liberal arts.

	Annual Growth	12/19	12/20	12/21	12/22	12/23
Sales ($mil.)	20.3%	286.3	321.8	418.8	606.3	600.5
Net income ($ mil.)	–	10.0	18.8	17.8	(115.0)	(47.3)
Market value ($ mil.)	(23.0%)	482.2	536.6	391.7	216.4	169.9
Employees	33.3%	1,910	2,940	5,800	6,244	6,037

AMERICAN RAILCAR INDUSTRIES, INC.

100 CLARK ST
SAINT CHARLES, MO 633012075
Phone: 636 940-6000
Fax: –
Web: www.aitx.com

CEO: –
CFO: –
HR: –
FYE: December 31
Type: Private

American Industrial Transport (formerly known as American Railcar Industries) is as a leading railcar manufacturer dedicated to bringing the right railcars, as well as service and support to ensure that it delivers to customers day after day, every time. It provides solutions to freight shipping customers across railcar leasing, repair, and data. AITX also offers product specialties in industries such as energy, chemical, agriculture, and minerals. The company is part of ITE Management L.P., an asset manager targeting transportation and industrial assets and companies, and related industries and services.

AMERICAN REALTY INVESTORS, INC.
NYS: ARL

1603 Lyndon B. Johnson Freeway, Suite 800
Dallas, TX 75234
Phone: 469 522-4200
Fax: 469 522-4299
Web: www.americanrealtyinvest.com

CEO: Henry A Butler
CFO: Erik L Johnson
HR: –
FYE: December 31
Type: Public

American Realty Investors (ARI) invests in, develops, and operates commercial properties and land in growing suburban markets. The company's portfolio includes approximately 60 apartment communities, about 20 office buildings, and about five each of industrial, retail, and hotel properties. It also owns a trade show and exhibit hall, as well as undeveloped land. ARI has properties in about 20 states, but most of its holdings are located in Texas. The company is part of a complex web of ownership that includes Prime Income Asset Management, which manages ARI and owns about 15% of it. Through various entities, Texas real estate mogul Gene Phillips and his family control around three-quarters of ARI.

	Annual Growth	12/19	12/20	12/21	12/22	12/23
Sales ($mil.)	1.3%	48.0	59.0	42.0	37.5	50.5
Net income ($ mil.)	–	(16.0)	9.0	3.3	373.3	4.0
Market value ($ mil.)	0.4%	276.7	176.1	204.3	414.3	281.2
Employees	–	–	–	–	–	–

AMERICAN RED BALL TRANSIT COMPANY, INC

920 N SHADELAND AVE STE G3A
INDIANAPOLIS, IN 462194898
Phone: 703 226-3180
Fax: -
Web: www.redball.com

CEO: Bud Morrissette
CFO: Sang Han
HR: -
FYE: December 31
Type: Private

American Red Ball Transit provides household and corporate moving services throughout the US. The company specializes in corporate relocation services, in which a moving company contracts with a business to provide moving services and related offerings such as real estate transaction assistance for its employees. American Red Ball operates through a network of agents. (A separate company, American Red Ball International, handles overseas moves.) American Red Ball was founded in 1919. The company was acquired by its management team in 2001 from former owner Atlas World Group.

AMERICAN SCIENCE AND ENGINEERING, INC.

829 MIDDLESEX TPKE
BILLERICA, MA 018213907
Phone: 978 262-8700
Fax: -
Web: www.rapiscan-ase.com

CEO: Charles P Dougherty
CFO: Diane J Basile
HR: Tracy Griffith
FYE: March 31
Type: Private

American Science and Engineering (AS&E) makes X-ray detection systems for inspection and security at airports, border stations, military situations, shipping ports, high-security facilities, and law enforcement scenarios. Using a lower radiation dose than typical systems, AS&E's Z Backscatter technology detects organic materials such as illegal drugs, plastic explosives, and cigarettes. AS&E also makes scanning equipment for detecting contraband on persons, in aircraft, vehicles, and in luggage and packages. AS&E is a subsidiary of OSI Systems.

AMERICAN SERVICES TECHNOLOGY, INC.

1028 HARVIN WAY STE 120
ROCKLEDGE, FL 329553238
Phone: 321 631-8771
Fax: -
Web: www.americanservicestech.com

CEO: -
CFO: -
HR: -
FYE: December 31
Type: Private

American Services Technology (ASTI) provides contract facility management services to businesses and government organizations. Services provided by the company include pest control, logistics and transportation services, grounds maintenance, cost reduction consulting, and fleet vehicle maintenance. ASTI also offers its clients office products delivery services, usually by the next day. The company's clients have included Raytheon, Space Gateway Support, the US Department of Energy, NASA, and various branches of the US Armed Forces such as the US Army and Air Force.

AMERICAN SHARED HOSPITAL SERVICES
ASE: AMS

601 Montgomery, Suite 1112
San Francisco, CA 94111-2619
Phone: 415 788-5300
Fax: -
Web: www.ashs.com

CEO: Peter Gaccione
CFO: Robert Hiatt
HR: -
FYE: December 31
Type: Public

Business is brain surgery for American Shared Hospital Services (ASHS). The company owns 81% of GK Financing (GKF), which installs, finances, and services the Leksell Gamma Knife, a noninvasive surgical device that uses gamma rays to destroy brain tumors without harming surrounding tissue. Sweden-based Elekta, which makes the Gamma Knife, owns the other 19% of GKF. GKF usually leases the Gamma Knife units on a per-use basis to major urban medical centers; it has contracts for units installed in about 20 hospitals in the US; it markets the product in the US and Brazil.

	Annual Growth	12/18	12/19	12/20	12/21	12/22
Sales ($mil.)	-	19.7	20.6	17.8	17.6	19.7
Net income ($ mil.)	6.7%	1.0	0.7	(7.1)	0.2	1.3
Market value ($ mil.)	5.3%	14.7	15.1	13.7	14.7	18.1
Employees	24.7%	12	14	21	20	29

AMERICAN SOCIETY FOR TESTING AND MATERIALS

100 BARR HARBOR DR
CONSHOHOCKEN, PA 194282951
Phone: 610 832-9500
Fax: -
Web: www.astm.org

CEO: Taco Van Der Maten
CFO: -
HR: -
FYE: December 31
Type: Private

The American Society for Testing and Materials -- which does business as ASTM International -- is a not-for-profit standards organization focused on developing voluntary codes and regulations for technical materials, products, systems, and services. Established in 1898 to set standards for railroad steel, the organization also works in such areas as petroleum, medical devices, consumer products, and environmental assessment. ASTM International publishes its technical specifications in the Annual Book of ASTM Standards, a more than 70-volume set. Its income is derived from selling its publications and through annual administrative fees. The organization has more than 30,000 members in over 120 countries.

	Annual Growth	12/13	12/14	12/15	12/21	12/22
Sales ($mil.)	4.1%	-	68.9	84.7	135.7	94.8
Net income ($ mil.)	-	-	(9.0)	20.8	36.4	(23.7)
Market value ($ mil.)	-	-	-	-	-	-
Employees	-	-	-	-	-	230

AMERICAN SOFTWARE INC
NMS: AMSW A

470 East Paces Ferry Road, N.E.
Atlanta, GA 30305
Phone: 404 261-4381
Fax: -
Web: www.amsoftware.com

CEO: -
CFO: -
HR: -
FYE: April 30
Type: Public

American Software delivers an innovative technical platform that enables enterprises to accelerate their digital supply chain optimization from product concept to client availability via the Logility Digital Supply Chain Platform, a single platform spanning product, demand, inventory, network optimization, supply, and deployment aligned with integrated business planning and supply chain data management. The Company's software and services are designed to bring tangible business value to enterprises by supporting their global operations over cloud-based internet-architected solutions. Its software and services solutions are aligned with three business segments Supply Chain Management (SCM), Enterprise Resource Planning (ERP), and Information Technology (IT) Consulting. It also provides IT staffing and consulting services. The company's customers come from a wide range of industries worldwide, generating about 80% of its revenue from the US.

	Annual Growth	04/19	04/20	04/21	04/22	04/23
Sales ($mil.)	3.3%	108.7	115.5	111.4	127.6	123.7
Net income ($ mil.)	11.3%	6.8	6.7	8.1	12.8	10.4
Market value ($ mil.)	(2.0%)	442.1	562.6	706.4	583.8	407.6
Employees	2.8%	424	428	424	418	474

AMERICAN SOIL TECHNOLOGIES INC

9018 Balboa Ave., #558
Northridge, CA 91325
Phone: 818 899-4686
Fax: –
Web: www.americansoiltech.com

CEO: Carl P Ranno
CFO: Carl P Ranno
HR: –
FYE: September 30
Type: Public

American Soil Technologies works to make sure your farmland isn't dirt poor. The company manufactures agricultural chemicals that help retain water in soil, the direct benefit of which is manifold. In addition to minimizing the frequency of irrigation, the chemicals also decrease the likelihood of erosion and reduce other damage. Its products are used by agricultural, residential, and recreational clients. Subsidiary Smart World Organics gives American Soil entrance to the organic turf and horticultural markets. Though primarily operating in the US, it also distributes internationally to the Middle East, North Africa, and China. The family of the late chairman Louie Visco controls 30% of the company.

	Annual Growth	09/11	09/12	09/13	09/14	09/15
Sales ($mil.)	(61.5%)	0.1	0.0	0.0	0.0	0.0
Net income ($ mil.)	–	(0.7)	(0.6)	(0.5)	0.0	(0.6)
Market value ($ mil.)	(30.7%)	1.2	0.3	1.5	0.8	0.3
Employees		3	3	3	3	3

AMERICAN SPECTRUM REALTY, INC.

NBB: AQQS Q

2401 Fountain View, Suite 750
Houston, TX 77057
Phone: 713 706-6200
Fax: –
Web: www.americanspectrum.com

CEO: –
CFO: –
HR: –
FYE: December 31
Type: Public

American Spectrum Realty invests in and manages commercial real estate, primarily multitenant office and industrial space. The company and its subsidiaries own, manage, or lease 90 properties valued at more than $1 billion. Most properties are located in Texas, but it also owns assets in California and 20 other states. Since 2010 subsidiary American Spectrum Realty Management has owned the property and asset management assets of Evergreen Realty Group. The deal brought contracts for 80 properties ranging from storage units to student housing and has helped American Spectrum expand its third-party management and leasing capabilities across the US. CEO William Carden controls about 40% of the company.

	Annual Growth	12/09	12/10	12/11	12/12	12/13
Sales ($mil.)	6.4%	33.3	55.6	69.4	55.1	42.7
Net income ($ mil.)	–	(8.3)	(8.0)	4.0	1.4	(13.8)
Market value ($ mil.)	(46.5%)	82.5	64.9	18.0	12.7	6.7
Employees	(12.6%)	283	219	183	180	165

AMERICAN SPEECH-LANGUAGE-HEARING ASSOCIATION

2200 RESEARCH BLVD
ROCKVILLE, MD 208503289
Phone: 301 296-5700
Fax: –
Web: www.asha.org

CEO: –
CFO: –
HR: –
FYE: December 31
Type: Private

The American Speech-Language-Hearing Association (ASHA) helps the people helping people who have problems hearing or speaking. The organization is the professional, scientific, and credentialing association for audiologists, speech pathologists, and speech, language, and hearing scientists. It publishes professional journals, including the American Journal of Audiology and The ASHA Leader , and provides information on research, grants, practice management, and scientific data to its base of more than 182,000 members and affiliates. For the public, ASHA provides information on insurance coverage, hearing disorders, speech and language problems, and finding professional help. The organization was founded in 1925.

	Annual Growth	12/11	12/12	12/13	12/21	12/22
Sales ($mil.)	64.1%	–	0.5	64.6	71.0	68.1
Net income ($ mil.)	26.1%	–	0.3	13.6	8.9	2.7
Market value ($ mil.)	–	–	–	–	–	–
Employees	–	–	–	–	–	270

AMERICAN STAFFING ASSOCIATION

277 S WASHINGTON ST STE 200
ALEXANDRIA, VA 223143675
Phone: 703 253-2020
Fax: –
Web: www.americanstaffing.net

CEO: Richard Wahlquist
CFO: –
HR: –
FYE: December 31
Type: Private

The American Staffing Association (ASA) has a permanent interest in temporary staffing. The group promotes the business of staffing through such efforts as lobbying, improving public relations, setting ethical standards, and providing education. The ASA boasts more than 60 chapters in more than 40 states and the District of Columbia. The organization's members serve a variety of industries, especially health care, IT, clerical, professional, and industrial, from more than 15,000 offices across the US as temporary staff, recruiting and placement personnel, and outsourcing, training, and HR consultants. ASA was founded in 1966 as the Institute of Temporary Services.

	Annual Growth	12/16	12/17	12/19	12/21	12/22
Sales ($mil.)	1.4%	–	13.5	13.7	12.0	14.5
Net income ($ mil.)	(57.7%)	–	1.2	0.4	(1.0)	0.0
Market value ($ mil.)	–	–	–	–	–	–
Employees	–	–	–	–	–	30

AMERICAN STATES WATER CO

NYS: AWR

630 E. Foothill Boulevard
San Dimas, CA 91773-1212
Phone: 909 394-3600
Fax: –
Web: www.aswater.com

CEO: Robert J Sprowls
CFO: Eva G Tang
HR: –
FYE: December 31
Type: Public

American States Water Company (AWR) is the parent company of GSWC, Bear Valley Electric Service, Inc. (BVESI) and American States Utility Services, Inc. (ASUS). Through its water utility subsidiary, GSWC, the company provides water service to approximately 261,000 customer connections. GSWC is a public water utility engaged in the purchase, production, distribution and sale of water in ten counties in the state of California. AWR's regulated utilities served 262,770 water customers and 24,656 electric customers, or a total of 287,426 customers.

	Annual Growth	12/19	12/20	12/21	12/22	12/23
Sales ($mil.)	5.9%	473.9	488.2	498.9	491.5	595.7
Net income ($ mil.)	10.3%	84.3	86.4	94.3	78.4	124.9
Market value ($ mil.)	(1.8%)	3,204.0	2,940.3	3,825.3	3,422.6	2,974.0
Employees	(0.8%)	841	841	808	811	815

AMERICAN SUPERCONDUCTOR CORP.

NMS: AMSC

114 East Main Street
Ayer, MA 01432
Phone: 978 842-3000
Fax: –
Web: www.amsc.com

CEO: Daniel P McGahn
CFO: John W Kosiba Jr
HR: –
FYE: March 31
Type: Public

American Superconductor (AMSC) is a leading system provider of megawatt-scale power resiliency solutions that Orchestrate the Rhythm and Harmony of Power on the Grid, and protect and expand the capability of the Navy's fleet. The company manufactures products using two proprietary core technologies: PowerModule programmable power electronic converters and its Amperium high temperature superconductor (HTS) wires. These technologies and its system-level solutions are protected by a broad and deep intellectual property portfolio consisting of hundreds of patents and licenses worldwide. Customers in the US account for around 55% of the company's total revenue. Founded in 1987, AMSC has operations in Asia, Australia, Europe and North America.

	Annual Growth	03/19	03/20	03/21	03/22	03/23
Sales ($mil.)	17.2%	56.2	63.8	87.1	108.4	106.0
Net income ($ mil.)	–	26.8	(17.1)	(22.7)	(19.2)	(35.0)
Market value ($ mil.)	(21.4%)	379.9	161.9	560.1	224.8	145.0
Employees	8.9%	233	242	225	326	328

AMERICAN SYSTEMS CORPORATION

14151 PARK MEADOW DR STE 500
CHANTILLY, VA 20151
Phone: 703 968-6300
Fax: –
Web: www.americansystems.com

CEO: Peter L Smith
CFO: –
HR: Joseph Lightbody
FYE: December 31
Type: Private

American Systems provides government and commercial clients with IT management and consulting services, including custom engineering and application development. Its consulting division advises clients on such issues as network access and identity management, data security, and process optimization. The company also provides managed technical support and staffing. American Systems works with government customers to develop systems related to command and control, logistics, and national security functions. Its commercial-focused operations serve the energy, financial services, retail, and telecom industries, among others.

	Annual Growth	12/15	12/16	12/17	12/18	12/19
Sales ($mil.)	16.6%	–	–	275.0	–	373.9
Net income ($ mil.)	56.3%	–	–	4.4	–	10.8
Market value ($ mil.)	–	–	–	–	–	–
Employees	–	–	–	–	–	1,650

AMERICAN TERRAZZO COMPANY, LTD.

309 GOLD ST
GARLAND, TX 750426648
Phone: 972 272-8084
Fax: –
Web: www.americanterrazzo.com

CEO: –
CFO: Juliana Filippi
HR: –
FYE: December 31
Type: Private

If you walk all over American Terrazzo's handiwork, well, that's really kind of the point. The company installs mural-like terrazzo flooring in public, commercial, and residential facilities. Terrazzo, derived from the word for terraces in Italian, is made from discarded marble remnants or cement and is used in a wide range of applications including sidewalks, plazas, terraces, and stairways. American Terrazzo does most of its business in Texas, primarily in Dallas. The company's handiwork can be found anywhere from homes, schools, and churches to offices, airports, and arenas. Mattia "Mike" Flabiano founded the family-owned firm in 1931.

	Annual Growth	12/04	12/05	12/06	12/07	12/08
Sales ($mil.)	(89.0%)	–	–	666.0	9.2	8.0
Net income ($ mil.)	358.3%	–	–	0.0	0.1	0.3
Market value ($ mil.)	–	–	–	–	–	–
Employees	–	–	–	–	–	133

AMERICAN TIRE DISTRIBUTORS HOLDINGS, INC.

12200 HERBERT WAYNE CT STE 150
HUNTERSVILLE, NC 280786335
Phone: 704 992-2000
Fax: –
Web: www.atd.com

CEO: Stuart Schuette
CFO: Jason T Yaudes
HR: Charlomae Wathington
FYE: December 28
Type: Private

American Tire Distributors (ATD) is the largest independent tire and service distributor in North America. Its offerings include flagship brands Yokohama, Hankook, Continental, Nitto, Pirelli, Uniroyal, and Michelin, as well as budget brands and private-label tires. ATD also markets custom wheels and tire service equipment. Its network of over 130 distribution centers and mixing warehouses serve independent tire dealers, retail chains, and auto service centers across the US and Canada, and has approximately 1,500 deliver vehicles on the road across the nation. In addition to some 40 million delivery miles annually, the company provides access to over 4 million tires in every style and size from the top global brands in the industry.

	Annual Growth	12/09	12/10	12/11	12/12	12/13
Sales ($mil.)	12.2%	–	–	3,050.2	3,455.9	3,839.3
Net income ($ mil.)	–	–	–	0.1	(14.3)	(6.4)
Market value ($ mil.)	–	–	–	–	–	–
Employees	–	–	–	–	–	3,500

AMERICAN TOWER CORP (NEW)

116 Huntington Avenue
Boston, MA 02116
Phone: 617 375-7500
Fax: –
Web: www.americantower.com

NYS: AMT
CEO: –
CFO: –
HR: –
FYE: December 31
Type: Public

American Tower is one of the largest global real estate investment trust and a leading owner, operator and developer of multitenant communications real estate. The company rents space on towers and rooftop antenna systems to wireless carriers and radio and TV broadcasters who use the infrastructure to enable its services. It owns and operates more than a portfolio of more than 224,770 communications sites, including some 1,715 distributed antenna system (DAS) networks. American Tower also offers tower-related services such as site application, structural analysis to determine support for additional equipment, and zoning and permitting management services. Its customers include its tenants, licensees and other payers. American Tower generates most of its revenue in the US.

	Annual Growth	12/19	12/20	12/21	12/22	12/23
Sales ($mil.)	10.1%	7,580.3	8,041.5	9,356.9	10,711	11,144
Net income ($ mil.)	(5.9%)	1,887.8	1,690.6	2,567.7	1,765.8	1,483.3
Market value ($ mil.)	(1.6%)	107,164	104,665	136,392	98,789	100,664
Employees	0.9%	5,454	5,618	6,378	6,391	5,643

AMERICAN TRANSMISSION COMPANY, LLC

W234N2000 RIDGEVIEW PARKWAY CT
WAUKESHA, WI 531881022
Phone: 262 506-6700
Fax: –
Web: www.atcllc.com

CEO: Patricia Kampling
CFO: –
HR: Pam Kuhl
FYE: December 31
Type: Private

American Transmission Company is an entrepreneur in the US power grid business -- a for-profit, multi-state, transmission-only utility. Connecting electricity producers to distributors, American Transmission owns, operates, monitors, and maintains 9,480 miles of high-voltage electric transmission lines and 529 substations in portions of Illinois, Michigan, Minnesota, and Wisconsin. The company, a member of the Midwest Independent Transmission System Operator (MISO) regional transmission organization, operates the former transmission assets of some of its shareholders. About 30 utilities, municipalities, electric companies, and cooperatives in its service area have an ownership stake in American Transmission.

AMERICAN TRUCKING ASSOCIATIONS, INC.

80 M ST SE STE 800
WASHINGTON, DC 200033557
Phone: 703 838-1700
Fax: –
Web: www.trucking.org

CEO: Chrisopher Spear
CFO: Karla Hulett
HR: –
FYE: December 31
Type: Private

American Trucking Associations (ATA) aims to be heard over the roar of diesel engines on the interstate as the unified voice of the trucking industry. The group seeks to represent the national interests of truckers in legislation, regulation, the courts, and the media. It works closely with 50 state trucking associations and with groups concerned with segments of the trucking business and key industry issues, such as safety. ATA produces several publications and hosts seminars, meetings, and conventions. The organization was formed in 1933 and in 1944 adopted a federation structure comprising national, state and local, and special affiliated interests. ATA has more than 37,000 members.

	Annual Growth	12/14	12/15	12/16	12/21	12/22
Sales ($mil.)	1.8%	–	43.1	42.0	45.8	48.8
Net income ($ mil.)	–	–	(1.0)	(3.5)	1.6	(2.9)
Market value ($ mil.)	–	–	–	–	–	–
Employees	–	–	–	–	–	280

AMERICAN UNITED MUTUAL INSURANCE HOLDING COMPANY

1 AMERICAN SQ
INDIANAPOLIS, IN 462820020
Phone: 317 285-1877
Fax: –
Web: www.oneamerica.com

CEO: Dayton Molendorp
CFO: J S Davison
HR: –
FYE: December 31
Type: Private

There are 50 states, but only OneAmerica. American United Mutual Insurance Holding Company is primarily a life insurer whose operating units do business under the OneAmerica Financial Partners banner. The company offers individual life insurance, disability and long-term-care coverage, and annuities. For businesses the company offers employee benefits, retirement plans, and group life insurance. Its subsidiaries include American United Life Insurance, The State Life Insurance Company, OneAmerica Securities, OneAmerica Assets Management, and Pioneer Mutual Life Insurance. The company operates in 49 states and Washington, DC.

	Annual Growth	12/03	12/04	12/05	12/06	12/08
Assets ($mil.)	(96.5%)	–	–	12,123	18,491	0.5
Net income ($ mil.)	–	–	–	–	67.7	–
Market value ($ mil.)	–	–	–	–	–	–
Employees	–	–	–	–	–	13,840

AMERICAN UNIVERSITY

4400 MASSACHUSETTS AVE NW
WASHINGTON, DC 200168003
Phone: 202 885-1000
Fax: –
Web: www.american.edu

CEO: Gary Abramson
CFO: –
HR: Carol Edwards
FYE: April 30
Type: Private

American University is a student-centered research institution located in Washington, DC, with highly-ranked schools and colleges, internationally-renowned faculty, and a reputation for creating meaningful change in the world. The university was chartered by an Act of Congress in 1893 as a private, independent, co-educational institution under the auspices of the United Methodist Church. The university offers a broad range of undergraduate and graduate degree programs to approximately 13,855 students from over 100 countries. With more than 960 full-time faculty and more than 1,600 full-time staff, its student-teacher ratio is 11:1. American University has schools devoted to arts and sciences, business, communications, international service, public affairs, and law.

AMERICAN VANGUARD CORP.   NYS: AVD

4695 MacArthur Court
Newport Beach, CA 92660
Phone: 949 260-1200
Fax: –
Web: www.american-vanguard.com

CEO: Eric G Wintemute
CFO: David T Johnson
HR: Shirin Khosravi
FYE: December 31
Type: Public

American Vanguard Corporation (AVD) is a specialty chemical manufacturer that develops and markets products for agricultural, commercial and consumer uses. The company sells products to protect crops, turf and ornamental plants, as well as human and animal health. Products include insecticides, fungicides, herbicides, molluscicides, growth regulators, and soil fumigants. The company conducts its business through its principle operating subsidiaries, including AMVAC Chemical Corporation (AMVAC) for its domestic business and AMVAC Netherlands BV (AMVAC BV) for its international business. The company generates about 60% of its sales from the US.

	Annual Growth	12/19	12/20	12/21	12/22	12/23
Sales ($mil.)	5.5%	468.2	458.7	556.9	609.6	579.4
Net income ($ mil.)	(13.8%)	13.6	15.2	18.6	27.4	7.5
Market value ($ mil.)	(13.4%)	560.0	446.4	471.4	624.4	315.5
Employees	5.9%	671	771	804	822	845

AMERICAN WATER WORKS CO, INC.   NYS: AWK

1 Water Street
Camden, NJ 08102-1658
Phone: 856 955-4001
Fax: –
Web: www.amwater.com

CEO: M S Hardwick
CFO: John C Griffith
HR: –
FYE: December 31
Type: Public

American Water Works is the largest publicly-traded water utility in the US, providing water and wastewater services to over 14 million people in about 25 states through its regulated utilities. It also has market-based operations that include complementary home services primarily to residential and smaller commercial customers and water and wastewater services to the US government on military installations, as well as municipalities, utilities and industrial customers. Regulated operations account for over 95% of revenue. Subsidiary American Water Works Service provides support and operational services to the company and its affiliates.

	Annual Growth	12/19	12/20	12/21	12/22	12/23
Sales ($mil.)	4.1%	3,610.0	3,777.0	3,930.0	3,792.0	4,234.0
Net income ($ mil.)	11.0%	621.0	709.0	1,263.0	820.0	944.0
Market value ($ mil.)	1.8%	23,923	29,885	36,777	29,681	25,702
Employees	(1.1%)	6,800	7,000	6,400	6,500	6,500

AMERICAN WAY VAN AND STORAGE, INC.

1001 S BROWN SCHOOL RD STE A
VANDALIA, OH 453779632
Phone: 937 898-7294
Fax: –
Web: www.awvs.com

CEO: –
CFO: –
HR: –
FYE: December 31
Type: Private

An agent for National Van Lines, American Way Van & Storage provides moving and storage services for households and businesses throughout the US. The company manages local and interstate moves; it offers international relocation services through its affiliation with National Van Lines. American Way Van & Storage also provides transportation of trade show materials.

	Annual Growth	12/12	12/13	12/14	12/15	12/16
Sales ($mil.)	(5.1%)	–	5.2	5.2	4.9	4.5
Net income ($ mil.)	(5.4%)	–	0.0	0.0	0.0	0.0
Market value ($ mil.)	–	–	–	–	–	–
Employees	–	–	–	–	–	30

AMERICAN WHOLESALE MARKETERS ASSN, INC

2750 PROSPERITY AVE # 530
FAIRFAX, VA 220314312
Phone: 703 208-3358
Fax: –
Web: –

CEO: Scott Ramminger
CFO: –
HR: –
FYE: December 31
Type: Private

"I can get it for you wholesale" is more than a promise here. The American Wholesale Marketers Association (AWMA) provides research, education, and other services for convenience manufacturers, distributors and retailers. By way of clarification, convenience products include candy, snacks, tobacco, and general merchandise for convenience stores, drug stores, news stands, and gift shops. AWMA benefits include conferences and expos, government advocacy, and networking opportunities. It also publishes the monthly magazine Distribution Channels . The organization was founded in 1991 by the merger of the National Candy Wholesalers Association and the National Association of Tobacco Distributors.

	Annual Growth	12/00	12/01	12/12	12/13	12/22
Sales ($mil.)	(0.8%)	–	3.1	3.8	4.0	2.6
Net income ($ mil.)	–	–	3.7	0.3	0.4	(0.1)
Market value ($ mil.)	–	–	–	–	–	–
Employees	–	–	–	–	–	10

AMERICAN WOODMARK CORP.   NMS: AMWD

561 Shady Elm Road
Winchester, VA 22602
Phone: 540 665-9100
Fax: -
Web: www.americanwoodmark.com

CEO: M S Culbreth
CFO: Paul Joachimczyk
HR: -
FYE: April 30
Type: Public

American Woodmark offers a wide variety of products that fall into product lines including kitchen cabinetry, bath cabinetry, office cabinetry, home organization, and hardware. Its cabinetry products are available in a variety of designs, finishes and finish colors, and door styles. Styles vary by finish (plywood, cherry, beech lumber, hard maple) and door design. Brands include American Woodmark, Shenandoah Cabinetry, Timberlake, PCS, Allen + Roth, Hampton Bay, and Waypoint. Targeting the remodeling and new home construction markets, American Woodmark sells its lineup through home centers and independent dealers and distributors; it also sells directly to major builders. American Woodmark was established through a leveraged buyout of Boise Cascade's cabinet division.

	Annual Growth	04/19	04/20	04/21	04/22	04/23
Sales ($mil.)	5.9%	1,645.3	1,650.3	1,744.0	1,857.2	2,066.2
Net income ($ mil.)	2.9%	83.7	74.9	58.8	(29.7)	93.7
Market value ($ mil.)	-	-	-	-	-	-
Employees	-	9,300	9,900	10,000	10,000	-

AMERICARES FOUNDATION, INC.

88 HAMILTON AVE
STAMFORD, CT 069023105
Phone: 203 658-9500
Fax: -
Web: www.americares.org

CEO: Christine Squires
CFO: -
HR: Eric Cooper
FYE: June 30
Type: Private

AmeriCares Foundation provides emergency medical aid around the world. The not-for-profit charitable organization helps victims of natural disasters and supports long-term humanitarian programs by collecting medical supplies in the US and overseas and delivering them to places where they are needed. AmeriCares has provided aid in more than 90 countries worldwide. In the US, the organization offers medical assistance, runs a camp for kids with HIV/AIDS, and conducts HomeFront, a program that renovates housing for the needy in parts of Connecticut and New York. Robert C. Macauley founded AmeriCares in 1982.

	Annual Growth	06/14	06/15	06/19	06/20	06/22
Sales ($mil.)	9.2%	-	742.0	976.3	1,440.8	1,371.4
Net income ($ mil.)	-	-	101.5	(101.3)	192.8	(39.6)
Market value ($ mil.)	-	-	-	-	-	-
Employees	-	-	-	-	-	231

AMERICOLD REALTY TRUST INC   NYS: COLD

10 Glenlake Parkway, Suite 600, South Tower
Atlanta, GA 30328
Phone: 678 441-1400
Fax: -
Web: www.americold.com

CEO: George F Chappelle Jr
CFO: Marc J Smernoff
HR: -
FYE: December 31
Type: Public

Americold Realty Trust is the world's largest publicly traded REIT focused on the ownership, operation, acquisition and development of temperature-controlled warehouses. It is organized as a self-administered and self-managed REIT with proven operating, development and acquisition expertise. Americold operates a global network of over 240 temperature-controlled warehouses encompassing approximately 1.4 billion cubic feet, with around 195 warehouses in North America, more than 25 in Europe, nearly 20 warehouses in Asia-Pacific, and two warehouses in South America. In addition, it holds three minority interests in Brazilian-based joint ventures, one with SuperFrio, which operates about 40 temperature-controlled warehouses and one with Comfrio, which operates roughly 30 temperature-controlled warehouses. Majority of its revenue comes from North America.

	Annual Growth	12/18	12/19	12/20	12/21	12/22
Sales ($mil.)	16.1%	1,603.6	1,783.7	1,987.7	2,714.8	2,914.7
Net income ($ mil.)	-	48.0	48.2	24.5	(30.5)	(19.4)
Market value ($ mil.)	2.6%	6,891.1	9,459.7	10,072	8,847.2	7,638.5
Employees	8.9%	11,000	12,600	16,300	16,275	15,484

AMERICUS MORTGAGE CORPORATION

6110 PINEMONT DR STE 215
HOUSTON, TX 770923216
Phone: 713 684-0725
Fax: -
Web: -

CEO: -
CFO: James Hagen
HR: -
FYE: June 30
Type: Private

Need someone on your side while seeking a home loan? Americus Mortgage (formerly Allied Home Mortgage Capital) wants to be your ally. The company is a privately held mortgage banker and broker, with offices and representatives located throughout the US and the Virgin Islands. Through its history it has brokered a variety of mortgages including conventional loans, jumbo loans, reverse mortgages, FHA loans, and VA loans. At its peak (in 2003), Americus Mortgage originated more than $15 billion in loans in a single year; however, the company has had trouble in recent years following the housing crisis of 2008.

	Annual Growth	06/05	06/06	06/07	06/08	06/09
Assets ($mil.)	0.7%	-	-	16.4	15.6	16.6
Net income ($ mil.)	-	-	-	(2.5)	0.2	0.0
Market value ($ mil.)	-	-	-	-	-	-
Employees	-	-	-	-	-	2,500

AMERIPRISE FINANCIAL INC   NYS: AMP

1099 Ameriprise Financial Center
Minneapolis, MN 55474
Phone: 612 671-3131
Fax: -
Web: www.ameriprise.com

CEO: James M Cracchiolo
CFO: Walter S Berman
HR: Kelli A Hunter Petruzi
FYE: December 31
Type: Public

Ameriprise Financial is a leading diversified financial services company with over $1.2 trillion in assets under management and administration. Through its extensive wealth management and asset management capabilities, Ameriprise advises, manages and protects the assets and income of more than 2 million individual, small business and institutional clients. It markets and administers its products primarily through a network of over 10,000 financial advisors. Founded by John Tappan in 1894, Ameriprise Financial was spun off from American Express in 2005.

	Annual Growth	12/19	12/20	12/21	12/22	12/23
Sales ($mil.)	4.6%	12,967	11,899	13,431	14,271	15,535
Net income ($ mil.)	7.8%	1,893.0	1,534.0	2,760.0	2,559.0	2,556.0
Market value ($ mil.)	22.9%	16,687	19,467	30,218	31,191	38,049
Employees	2.5%	12,500	12,300	12,000	13,500	13,800

AMERIS BANCORP   NMS: ABCB

3490 Piedmont Road N.E., Suite 1550
Atlanta, GA 30305
Phone: 404 639-6500
Fax: -
Web: www.amerisbank.com

CEO: H P Proctor Jr
CFO: Nicole S Stokes
HR: -
FYE: December 31
Type: Public

Ameris Bancorp is a financial holding company whose business is conducted primarily through its wholly-owned banking subsidiary, Ameris Bank, which provides a full range of banking services to its retail and commercial customers who are primarily concentrated in select markets in Alabama, Georgia, North Carolina, South Carolina, and Florida. It operates some 165 full-service domestic banking offices. The company provides a broad range of commercial and retail lending services such as agricultural loans, commercial business loans, commercial and residential real estate construction and mortgage loans, consumer loans, revolving lines of credit, and letters of credit. Loans secured by commercial real estate and farmland accounted for nearly 40% of the company's loan portfolio. Ameris Bank opened its doors as an American Banking company in 1971.

	Annual Growth	12/19	12/20	12/21	12/22	12/23
Assets ($mil.)	8.4%	18,243	20,439	23,858	25,053	25,204
Net income ($ mil.)	13.6%	161.4	262.0	376.9	346.5	269.1
Market value ($ mil.)	5.7%	2,937.5	2,628.9	3,430.6	3,255.2	3,663.3
Employees	0.4%	2,722	2,671	2,865	2,847	2,765

AMERISAFE INC

2301 Highway 190 West
DeRidder, LA 70634
Phone: 337 463-9052
Fax: –
Web: www.amerisafe.com

NMS: AMSF
CEO: G J Frost
CFO: Anastasios Omiridi
HR: Barbara Morrison
FYE: December 31
Type: Public

AMERISAFE is a specialty provider of workers' compensation insurance for businesses in hazardous industries including agriculture, manufacturing, construction, logging and lumber, oil and gas, maritime, and trucking. Through its subsidiaries, American Interstate Insurance, Silver Oak Casualty, and American Interstate Insurance Company, the company writes coverage for more than 8,400 policyholders (mainly small and midsized firms). In addition, AMERISAFE offers worksite safety reviews, loss prevention, and claims management services. AMERISAFE sells its products in more than 45 states and the District of Columbia and the US Virgin Islands, in which Georgia accounts for the highest premiums.

	Annual Growth	12/19	12/20	12/21	12/22	12/23
Assets ($mil.)	(4.7%)	1,492.9	1,470.9	1,402.7	1,269.3	1,229.2
Net income ($ mil.)	(9.5%)	92.7	86.6	65.8	55.6	62.1
Market value ($ mil.)	(8.3%)	1,263.5	1,098.9	1,030.0	994.4	895.1
Employees	(4.4%)	434	395	379	366	362

AMERISERV FINANCIAL INC.

Main & Franklin Streets, P.O. Box 430
Johnstown, PA 15907-0430
Phone: 814 533-5300
Fax: –
Web: www.ameriserv.com

NMS: ASRV
CEO: Jeffrey A Stopko
CFO: Michael D Lynch
HR: –
FYE: December 31
Type: Public

AmeriServ Financial offers up a smorgasbord of banking services for Pennsylvanians. The company owns AmeriServ Financial Bank, which primarily serves the southwestern portion of the state through some 20 branches. Targeting individuals and local businesses, the bank offers standard services such as deposits, credit cards, and loans. Commercial mortgages account for more than half of its loan portfolio; other real estate loans, including residential mortgage and construction loans, make up about 30%. One of a handful of unionized banks in the US, AmeriServ also manages union pension funds through its AmeriServ Trust and Financial Services subsidiary, which provides trust and wealth management services as well.

	Annual Growth	12/18	12/19	12/20	12/21	12/22
Assets ($mil.)	4.1%	1,160.7	1,171.2	1,279.7	1,335.6	1,363.9
Net income ($ mil.)	(1.0%)	7.8	6.0	4.6	7.1	7.4
Market value ($ mil.)	(0.6%)	69.0	71.9	53.6	66.1	67.4
Employees	0.6%	321	328	314	319	329

AMERISTEEL CORP.

5100 W. Lemon Street
Tampa, FL 33609
Phone: 813 286-8383
Fax: –
Web: –

CEO: Peter J Campo
CFO: –
HR: –
FYE: December 31
Type: Public

Gerdau Ameristeel puts its stamp on the steel business in the US. The company is one of the largest minimill steelmakers in North America, with a capacity to produce about 12.4 million tons of finished steel annually. Through about 20 mills, Gerdau Ameristeel sells to the eastern two-thirds of North America. The company also operates scrap recycling operations, specialty processing centers, and rebar fabricating and coating plants. Its minimills produce beams, flat-rolled steel, merchant bar, rebar, and wire rod primarily used in the automotive, appliance, construction, machinery, and equipment industries. The company is owned by Brazilian steelmaker Gerdau.

	Annual Growth	03/98	03/99	03/00*	12/00	12/01
Sales ($mil.)	(4.3%)	–	–	706.8	503.1	647.4
Net income ($ mil.)	(41.7%)	–	–	29.3	2.3	10.0
Market value ($ mil.)	–	–	–	–	–	–
Employees	–	–	–	–	2,202	2,224

*Fiscal year change

AMERITYRE CORPORATION

1501 Industrial Road
Boulder City, NV 89005
Phone: 702 293-1930
Fax: –
Web: www.amerityre.com

NBB: AMTY
CEO: –
CFO: –
HR: –
FYE: June 30
Type: Public

Amerityre makes polyurethane foam tires, which are unable to go flat, for the bicycle and lawn equipment industries. The company also offers composite tires, pneumatic tires, and solid tires, along with tire-filling materials. Central Purchasing accounts for one-fifth of Amerityre's sales. In 2008 the company acquired the manufacturing assets of a competitor, KIK Technology International, and KIK went out of business.

	Annual Growth	06/19	06/20	06/21	06/22	06/23
Sales ($mil.)	12.2%	3.6	3.9	4.9	6.5	5.7
Net income ($ mil.)	94.3%	0.0	0.0	0.3	0.4	0.6
Market value ($ mil.)	19.7%	1.5	1.9	6.9	3.3	3.1
Employees	–	–	16	14	18	17	–

AMERY REGIONAL MEDICAL CENTER, INC.

265 GRIFFIN ST E
AMERY, WI 540011292
Phone: 715 268-8000
Fax: –
Web: www.amerymedicalcenter.org

CEO: –
CFO: –
HR: –
FYE: December 31
Type: Private

If your arteries have become a bit clogged from too much cheese eating, Amery Regional Medical Center in Amery, Wisconsin is here to help. The not-for-profit, community-owned hospital provides a range of medical services including emergency medicine, obstetrics, home and hospice care, physical therapy, surgery, and pain management. Amery Regional Medical Center also provides community services such as wellness classes, nutritional counseling, and support groups. Its affiliates include Clear Lake Clinic, Regions Hospital, and Luck Medical Clinic.

	Annual Growth	12/18	12/19	12/20	12/21	12/22
Sales ($mil.)	6.3%	–	64.1	58.7	68.5	77.0
Net income ($ mil.)	36.6%	–	2.1	3.7	3.7	5.5
Market value ($ mil.)	–	–	–	–	–	–
Employees	–	–	–	–	–	440

AMES CONSTRUCTION, INC.

2500 COUNTY ROAD 42 W
BURNSVILLE, MN 553376911
Phone: 952 435-7106
Fax: –
Web: www.amesconstruction.com

CEO: Raymond G Ames
CFO: Michael J Kellen
HR: Tanya Kesti
FYE: November 30
Type: Private

Ames Construction aims right for the heart of heavy construction. The company is a general contractor, providing heavy civil and industrial construction services to the transportation, mining, and power industries mainly in the West and Midwest. The family-owned company works on highways, airports, bridges, rail lines, mining facilities, power plants, and other infrastructure projects. Ames also performs flood control, environmental remediation, reclamation, and landfill work. Additionally, the firm builds golf courses and undertakes commercial and residential site development projects. Ames typically partners with other companies to perform the engineering and design portion of construction jobs.

	Annual Growth	11/14	11/15	11/16	11/19	11/20
Sales ($mil.)	4.1%	–	1,068.2	845.3	1,248.8	1,308.8
Net income ($ mil.)	52.5%	–	5.1	2.4	61.3	42.2
Market value ($ mil.)	–	–	–	–	–	–
Employees	–	–	–	–	–	2,500

AMES NATIONAL CORP.
NAS: ATLO

405 Fifth Street
Ames, IA 50010
Phone: 515 232-6251
Fax: 515 663-3033
Web: www.amesnational.com

CEO: John P Nelson
CFO: John L Pierschbacher
HR: –
FYE: December 31
Type: Public

This company aims to please citizens of Ames… and central Iowa. Ames National Corporation is the multi-bank holding company for flagship subsidiary First National Bank, Ames, Iowa, as well as Boone Bank & Trust, Reliance State, State Bank & Trust, and United Bank & Trust. Boasting over $1 billion in assets and 15 branches, the banks provide area individuals and businesses with standard services such as deposit accounts, IRAs, and credit and debit cards. Commercial-related loans account for about 50% of Ames' loan portfolio, while agricultural loans make up another 20%. The banks also write residential, construction, consumer, and business loans, and offer trust and financial management services.

	Annual Growth	12/19	12/20	12/21	12/22	12/23
Assets ($mil.)	5.5%	1,737.2	1,975.6	2,137.0	2,134.9	2,155.5
Net income ($ mil.)	(10.9%)	17.2	18.9	23.9	19.3	10.8
Market value ($ mil.)	(6.6%)	252.3	216.0	220.2	212.3	191.9
Employees	19.7%	133	265	281	270	273

AMETEK INC
NYS: AME

1100 Cassatt Road
Berwyn, PA 19312-1177
Phone: 610 647-2121
Fax: 610 647-0211
Web: www.ametek.com

CEO: David A Zapico
CFO: William J Burke
HR: –
FYE: December 31
Type: Public

AMETEK is a leading global manufacturer of electronic instruments and electromechanical devices. Its Electronic Instruments Group (EIG) makes monitoring, metering, and analytic devices for the aerospace, heavy equipment, and power generation markets, among others. Its Electromechanical Group (EMG) makes precision motion control solutions, thermal management systems, electrical interconnects, and specialty metals for the aerospace, mass transit, medical, and office products markets. AMETEK has manufacturing facilities throughout the world; about half of its sales are to customers outside the US.

	Annual Growth	12/19	12/20	12/21	12/22	12/23
Sales ($mil.)	6.3%	5,158.6	4,540.0	5,546.5	6,150.5	6,597.0
Net income ($ mil.)	11.1%	861.3	872.4	990.1	1,159.5	1,313.2
Market value ($ mil.)	13.4%	23,033	27,929	33,956	32,266	38,078
Employees	4.4%	18,100	16,500	18,500	19,600	21,500

AMEXDRUG CORP.
NBB: AXRX

6465 Corvette Street
Commerce, CA 90040
Phone: 323 725-3100
Fax: 323 725-3133
Web: www.amexdrug.com

CEO: Jack Amin
CFO: Jack Amin
HR: –
FYE: December 31
Type: Public

Amexdrug, through subsidiaries Allied Med and Dermagen, is a wholesale distributor of pharmaceuticals, nutritional supplements, and beauty products to pharmacies and other retailers. The company allows small pharmacies to get the lower prices that large pharmaceutical chains such as Walgreen and CVS enjoy. Its customers are primarily located in California. Part of Allied Med's growth strategy includes increasing its online traffic, so it is increasing its name recognition and branding efforts. Top executive Jack Amin and his wife own more than 90% of the company.

	Annual Growth	12/17	12/18	12/19	12/20	12/21
Sales ($mil.)	(17.5%)	10.4	10.5	7.7	6.4	4.8
Net income ($ mil.)	(9.7%)	0.1	0.2	0.2	0.2	0.0
Market value ($ mil.)	(11.1%)	40.7	18.8	9.8	13.4	25.4
Employees		–	–	–	–	–

AMGEN INC
NMS: AMGN

One Amgen Center Drive
Thousand Oaks, CA 91320-1799
Phone: 805 447-1000
Fax: 805 447-1010
Web: www.amgen.com

CEO: Robert A Bradway
CFO: Peter H Griffith
HR: –
FYE: December 31
Type: Public

Amgen is among the most significant biotechnology companies committed to unlocking biology's potential for patients suffering from serious illnesses by discovering, developing, manufacturing and delivering innovative human therapeutics. Its main products with the most significant annual commercial sales, are ENBREL, Prolia, Neulasta, Otezla, XGEVA, Aranesp, KYPROLIS, and Repatha. Amgen focuses on six commercial areas: inflammation, oncology/hematology, bone health, CV disease, nephrology and neuroscience, and it conducts discovery research primarily in three therapeutic areas: inflammation, oncology/hematology and CV/metabolic diseases. Amgen's products are marketed worldwide, with the US market accounting for about 70% of revenue.

	Annual Growth	12/19	12/20	12/21	12/22	12/23
Sales ($mil.)	4.8%	23,362	25,424	25,979	26,323	28,190
Net income ($ mil.)	(3.8%)	7,842.0	7,264.0	5,893.0	6,552.0	6,717.0
Market value ($ mil.)	4.5%	129,069	123,099	120,449	140,617	154,206
Employees	3.4%	23,400	24,300	24,200	25,200	26,700

AMICUS THERAPEUTICS INC
NMS: FOLD

3675 Market Street
Philadelphia, PA 19104
Phone: 215 921-7600
Fax: –
Web: www.amicusrx.com

CEO: John F Crowley
CFO: Daphne Quimi
HR: Karen Martini
FYE: December 31
Type: Public

Amicus Therapeutics is a global, patient-dedicated biotechnology company focused on discovering, developing, and delivering novel medicines for rare diseases. It has a portfolio of product opportunities including the first, oral monotherapy for Fabry disease. The lead biologics program of its pipeline is Amicus Therapeutics GAA (AT-GAA, also known as ATB200/AT2221, or cipaglucosidase alfa/miglustat), a novel, two-component, potential best-in-class treatment for Pompe disease. The company generates about 35% of its revenue from its domestic operations.

	Annual Growth	12/19	12/20	12/21	12/22	12/23
Sales ($mil.)	21.7%	182.2	260.9	305.5	329.2	399.4
Net income ($ mil.)	–	(356.4)	(276.9)	(250.5)	(236.6)	(151.6)
Market value ($ mil.)	9.9%	2,859.6	6,779.1	3,391.0	3,584.8	4,166.1
Employees	(3.0%)	584	483	496	484	517

AMKOR TECHNOLOGY INC.
NMS: AMKR

2045 East Innovation Circle
Tempe, AZ 85284
Phone: 480 821-5000
Fax: –
Web: www.amkor.com

CEO: Giel Rutten
CFO: Megan Faust
HR: –
FYE: December 31
Type: Public

Amkor Technology Inc. is one of the world's leading providers of outsourced semiconductor packaging and test services making sure that chips are ready to go for smartphones, tablets, computers, high-performance gaming systems, automobiles, IoT wearable, and network systems. The company's customers worldwide include many of the largest semiconductor companies around the world. Although Amkor is a public company, founder and chairman James Kim and his family control the firm. Some 55% of revenue is from US customers. The company traces its roots back to 1935.

	Annual Growth	12/19	12/20	12/21	12/22	12/23
Sales ($mil.)	12.5%	4,052.7	5,050.6	6,138.3	7,091.6	6,503.1
Net income ($ mil.)	31.3%	120.9	338.1	643.0	765.8	359.8
Market value ($ mil.)	26.5%	3,196.5	3,708.0	6,095.6	5,896.4	8,180.7
Employees	(0.8%)	29,650	29,050	30,400	31,300	28,700

AMN HEALTHCARE SERVICES INC   NYS: AMN

2999 Olympus Boulevard, Suite 500
Dallas, TX 75019
Phone: 866 871-8519
Fax: –
Web: www.amnhealthcare.com

CEO: Susan R Salka
CFO: Jeffrey R Knudson
HR: –
FYE: December 31
Type: Public

Operating under such brands as American Mobile Healthcare, NurseChoice, NursesRx, Med Travelers, Staff Care, and O'Grady-Peyton International, AMN Healthcare Services is one of the leading talent solutions for the healthcare sector in the US. It places nurses, technicians, and therapists for 13-week stints at hospitals, clinics, and schools across the US. AMN total talent solutions include managed services programs, clinical and interim healthcare leaders, temporary staffing, executive search solutions, vendor management systems, recruitment process outsourcing, predictive modeling, language interpretation services, revenue cycle solutions, credentialing and other services. The majority of temporary assignments for its clients are at acute-care hospitals. Substantially all of the company's revenue comes from the US.

	Annual Growth	12/19	12/20	12/21	12/22	12/23
Sales ($mil.)	14.3%	2,222.1	2,393.7	3,984.2	5,243.2	3,789.3
Net income ($ mil.)	16.6%	114.0	70.7	327.4	444.1	210.7
Market value ($ mil.)	4.7%	2,355.9	2,580.5	4,625.3	3,887.6	2,831.2
Employees	2.6%	3,236	3,000	3,800	4,230	3,585

AMNEAL PHARMACEUTICALS INC   NMS: AMRX

400 Crossing Boulevard
Bridgewater, NJ 08807
Phone: 908 947-3120
Fax: –
Web: www.amneal.com

CEO: Paul M Bisaro
CFO: Bryan M Reasons
HR: –
FYE: December 31
Type: Public

Impax Laboratories is betting that its pharmaceuticals will make a positive impact on the world's health. The company makes specialty generic pharmaceuticals, which it markets through its Impax Generics division and through marketing alliances with other pharmaceutical firms. It concentrates on controlled-release versions of various generic versions of branded and niche pharmaceuticals that require difficult-to-obtain raw materials or specialized expertise. Additionally, the company's branded pharmaceuticals business (Impax Specialty Pharma) is developing and improving upon previously approved drugs that target Parkinson's disease, multiple sclerosis, and other central nervous system disorders. In 2018 Impax merged with Amneal Pharmaceuticals to create a top generics firm.

	Annual Growth	12/18	12/19	12/20	12/21	12/22
Sales ($mil.)	7.4%	1,663.0	1,626.4	1,992.5	2,093.7	2,212.3
Net income ($ mil.)	–	(169.7)	(361.9)	91.1	10.6	(130.0)
Market value ($ mil.)	(38.1%)	4,107.8	1,463.4	1,387.5	1,454.3	604.2
Employees	6.1%	6,000	5,500	6,000	7,000	7,600

AMPCO SERVICES, L.L.C.

16945 NORTHCHASE DR STE 1950
HOUSTON, TX 770602135
Phone: 281 872-8324
Fax: –
Web: www.atlanticmethanol.com

CEO: –
CFO: –
HR: –
FYE: December 31
Type: Private

Atlantic Methanol Production Company (AMPCO) must have adopted "Waste not, want not" as its motto. It tries not to waste the natural gas that is a by-product of its parent companies' production processes. A joint venture between Noble Energy (45% ownership), Marathon Oil (45%), and SONAGAS, the National Gas Company of Equatorial Guinea (10%), the company operates one of the largest methanol plants in the world. The plant, off the coast of Equatorial Guinea, produces about 1 million tons of methanol annually -- 2% of the global market. AMPCO also distributes using three vessels and five terminals in Europe and US, where it sells most of its production.

	Annual Growth	12/05	12/06	12/07	12/08	12/10
Sales ($mil.)	(43.4%)	–	–	1,405.6	341.1	254.2
Net income ($ mil.)	10372.8%	–	–	0.0	122.0	65.5
Market value ($ mil.)	–	–	–	–	–	–
Employees	–	–	–	–	–	500

AMPCO-PITTSBURGH CORP.   NYS: AP

726 Bell Avenue, Suite 301
Carnegie, PA 15106
Phone: 412 456-4400
Fax: 412 456-4404
Web: www.ampcopittsburgh.com

CEO: J B McBrayer
CFO: Michael G McAuley
HR: –
FYE: December 31
Type: Public

Steel giant Ampco-Pittsburgh keeps its worth by never losing its temper. Among the leaders in steel producers, the company divides its work in two segments: The Forged and Engineered Cast Products segment -- comprising subsidiaries Union Electric Steel and Union Electric Steel UK -- makes forged hardened-steel rolling mill rolls and cast rolls for steel and aluminum manufacturers. The Air and Liquid Processing unit has three divisions: Buffalo Pumps, which makes centrifugal pumps for refrigeration, marine defense, and power generation industries; Aerofin, highly-engineered heat-exchange coils, and Buffalo Air Handling, air-handling systems for defense, power generation, and construction customers.

	Annual Growth	12/18	12/19	12/20	12/21	12/22
Sales ($mil.)	(1.8%)	419.4	397.9	328.5	344.9	390.2
Net income ($ mil.)	–	(69.3)	(21.0)	8.0	(12.7)	3.4
Market value ($ mil.)	(5.1%)	60.2	58.4	106.3	97.0	48.7
Employees	(5.0%)	1,922	1,673	1,533	1,485	1,565

AMPHASTAR PHARMACEUTICALS INC (DE)   NMS: AMPH

11570 6th Street
Rancho Cucamonga, CA 91730
Phone: 909 980-9484
Fax: –
Web: www.amphastar.com

CEO: –
CFO: –
HR: –
FYE: December 31
Type: Public

Amphastar Pharmaceuticals is a bio-pharmaceutical company focusing primarily on developing, manufacturing, marketing, and selling technically challenging generic and proprietary injectable, inhalation, intranasal, and insulin API products. Its more than 20 products include Primatene Mist (an over-the-counter epinephrine inhalation product) and Enoxaparin (an injectable form of low molecular weight heparin), but the company might be best known for making Naloxone, which reverses the dangerous effects of opioids like painkillers and other narcotics. The company has over candidates in its pipeline, including generic ANDAs, biosimilar product candidates and proprietary product candidates. Vast majority of its revenue comes from its domestic operation.

	Annual Growth	12/19	12/20	12/21	12/22	12/23
Sales ($mil.)	18.9%	322.4	349.8	437.8	499.0	644.4
Net income ($ mil.)	29.5%	48.9	1.4	62.1	91.4	137.5
Market value ($ mil.)	33.8%	927.2	966.7	1,119.5	1,346.9	2,973.1
Employees	(3.5%)	2,027	1,980	1,761	1,615	1,761

AMPHENOL CORP.   NYS: APH

358 Hall Avenue
Wallingford, CT 06492
Phone: 203 265-8900
Fax: 203 265-8746
Web: www.amphenol.com

CEO: R A Norwitt
CFO: Craig A Lampo
HR: Sarah Dwyer
FYE: December 31
Type: Public

Amphenol Corporation designs, manufactures and markets electrical, electronic and fiber optic connectors and interconnect systems, antennas, sensors and sensor-based products and coaxial and high-speed specialty cable. Amphenol designs, manufactures and assembles its products at facilities in the Americas, Europe, Asia, Australia and Africa and sells its products through its own global sales force, independent representatives and a global network of electronics distributors. Amphenol has a diversified presence as a leader in high-growth areas of the interconnect market including automotive, broadband communications, commercial aerospace, industrial, information technology and data communications, military, mobile devices and mobile networks. Over 65% of its sales come from outside the US.

	Annual Growth	12/19	12/20	12/21	12/22	12/23
Sales ($mil.)	11.2%	8,225.4	8,598.9	10,876	12,623	12,555
Net income ($ mil.)	13.7%	1,155.0	1,203.4	1,590.8	1,902.3	1,928.0
Market value ($ mil.)	(2.2%)	64,819	78,318	52,380	45,600	59,369
Employees	6.4%	74,000	80,000	90,000	91,000	95,000

AMPIO PHARMACEUTICALS INC
ASE: AMPE

9800 Mount Pyramid Court, Suite 400
Englewood, CO 80112
Phone: 720 437-6500
Fax: -
Web: www.ampiopharma.com

CEO: Michael Macaluso
CFO: Dan Stokely
HR: -
FYE: December 31
Type: Public

With hopes one day of taking in revenues somewhere between ample and copious, Ampio Pharmaceuticals is a development-stage company that focuses on repositioning existing drugs for new uses. Drugs in formulation for new indications include candidates for treating eye and kidney disorders, inflammatory conditions, and metabolic disease. In addition, the company is working on diagnostic devices for measuring levels of oxidation in the bloodstream. Ampio is conducting clinical trials for two drugs: Ampion (for osteoarthritis of the knee) and Optina (for diabetic macular edema). In late 2013 it announced plans to spin off its sexual dysfunction business (Zertane and Zertane-ED).

	Annual Growth	12/18	12/19	12/20	12/21	12/22
Sales ($mil.)	-	-	-	-	-	-
Net income ($ mil.)	-	34.0	(13.6)	(15.9)	(17.1)	(16.3)
Market value ($ mil.)	(13.1%)	0.3	0.4	1.2	0.4	0.2
Employees	(22.3%)	22	23	18	21	8

AMPLIFY ENERGY CORP (NEW)
NYS: AMPY

500 Dallas Street, Suite 1700
Houston, TX 77002
Phone: 713 490-8900
Fax: -
Web: www.amplifyenergy.com

CEO: Martyn Willsher
CFO: James Frew
HR: Jason W Moore
FYE: December 31
Type: Public

Midstates Petroleum Company knows there's much more to Louisiana than Creoles, crawfish, and alligators. An independent oil and gas exploration and production company, Midstates operates on some 64,700 net acres in the central Louisiana portion of the Upper Gulf Coast Tertiary. The company's assets consist primarily of mature oilfields discovered in the 1940s and '50s that continue to show production potential when developed with modern techniques. The company routinely uses such techniques and technologies to produce oil, including hydraulic fracturing and 3D seismic data. In 2013 Midstates reported proved reserves of 127.8 million barrels of oil equivalent. If filed for bankruptcy protection in 2016.

	Annual Growth	12/19	12/20	12/21	12/22	12/23
Sales ($mil.)	2.8%	275.6	202.1	342.9	458.5	307.6
Net income ($ mil.)	-	(35.2)	(464.0)	(32.1)	57.9	392.8
Market value ($ mil.)	(2.7%)	258.8	51.3	121.7	344.1	232.1
Employees	(1.8%)	230	189	210	208	214

AMPLIFY ENERGY HOLDINGS LLC
NBB: AMPY

500 Dallas Street, Suite 1700
Houston, TX 77002
Phone: 713 490-8900
Fax: -
Web: www.memorialpp.com

CEO: -
CFO: -
HR: -
FYE: December 31
Type: Public

Memorial Production Partners was birthed as a limited partnership in April 2011 to own and acquire oil and natural gas properties in North America. With estimated proved reserves of about 325 billion cu. ft. of natural gas equivalent, it will own and operate properties in South and East Texas, mainly consisting of mature, onshore oil and natural gas reservoirs. They were acquired by predecessor entities from the likes of Forest Oil and BP America Production Company. Formed and controlled by Memorial Resource Development LLC, Memorial Production Partners is managed by a general partner and conducts operations. It went public in 2011. The company filed for Chapter 11 bankruptcy protection in 2017.

	Annual Growth	12/15	12/16*	05/17*	12/17	12/18
Sales ($mil.)	(1.7%)	358.1	284.6	109.2	205.5	340.1
Net income ($ mil.)	-	(395.9)	(540.4)	(91.0)	1.3	54.6
Market value ($ mil.)	-	-	-	-	225.1	193.0
Employees	-	-	289	-	281	222

*Fiscal year change

AMREP CORP.
NYS: AXR

850 West Chester Pike, Suite 205
Havertown, PA 19083
Phone: 610 487-0905
Fax: -
Web: www.amrepcorp.com

CEO: Christopher V Vitale V
CFO: -
HR: -
FYE: April 30
Type: Public

Mailing magazines and developing land in New Mexico keep AMREP hopping. About 80% of the company's sales come from newsstand distribution and subscription and product fulfillment services it provides through its Kable Media Services and Palm Coast Data subsidiaries. The units serve about 200 publishing clients by managing subscriptions and mailing 900-plus magazine titles. Through its AMREP Southwest subsidiary, the company develops its Rio Rancho property (roughly 17,300 acres) as well as certain parts of Sandoval County outside Albuquerque, New Mexico. AMREP was founded in 1961. Its largest shareholder in 2010 scrapped plans to take AMREP private and merge it with another firm.

	Annual Growth	04/19	04/20	04/21	04/22	04/23
Sales ($mil.)	39.6%	12.8	18.8	40.1	62.5	48.7
Net income ($ mil.)	94.4%	1.5	(5.9)	7.4	15.9	21.8
Market value ($ mil.)	25.6%	29.3	25.4	56.2	67.6	73.0
Employees	26.3%	11	16	20	22	28

AMRON INTERNATIONAL, INC.

1380 ASPEN WAY
VISTA, CA 920818349
Phone: 760 208-6500
Fax: -
Web: www.amronintl.com

CEO: -
CFO: -
HR: -
FYE: December 31
Type: Private

Talk about being under pressure. Amron International is a manufacturer and supplier of high quality signature underwater communication systems, commercial diving equipment, hyperbaric chamber applications, and tactical gear throughout the world. Its underwater products include helium unscramblers, oxygen treatment panels and hoods, chamber conditioning systems, diver communication systems, and vulcanized rubber dry suits. The company also distributes tactical and outdoor gear from such brands as Analox, Kirby Morgan, AVOX Systems, Stanley Hydraulic Tools, and Suunto. Amron International also sells its products to military and government agencies. Other customers include commercial business, with many in the oil industry. The company has facilities in Vista, California, and in Virginia Beach, Virginia. Amron International was founded in 1978 by Norma Ockwig.

	Annual Growth	12/04	12/05	12/06	12/07	12/08
Sales ($mil.)	33.3%	-	-	44.7	63.4	79.4
Net income ($ mil.)	35.7%	-	-	2.5	3.1	4.6
Market value ($ mil.)	-	-	-	-	-	-
Employees	-	-	-	-	-	75

AMRYT PHARMACEUTICALS INC.

160 FEDERAL ST FL 21
BOSTON, MA 021101700
Phone: 877 764-3131
Fax: -
Web: www.amrytpharma.com

CEO: Joe Wiley
CFO: Gregory Perry
HR: -
FYE: December 31
Type: Private

Bad cholesterol, beware! Aegerion Pharmaceuticals is hot on your trail. The biopharmaceutical company develops cholesterol-lowering drugs for the treatment of cardiovascular and metabolic disease, specifically targeting elevated LDL (low-density lipoprotein, also known as "bad" cholesterol) levels. Aegerion's first approved drug is Juxtapid (lomitapide, branded Lojuxta in Europe), a protein inhibitor that blocks cholesterol production in the liver and intestine. The firm is working on getting Juxtapid approved in Japan and for children and teens. Aegerion also markets Myalept, a treatment for leptin deficiency. In November 2016, Aegerion was acquired by Canada's QLT (which then renamed itself Novelion Therapeutics).

AMS HEALTH SCIENCES, INC.

711 NE 39TH ST
OKLAHOMA CITY, OK 731057219
Phone: 866 758-7222
Fax: –
Web: –

CEO: –
CFO: –
HR: –
FYE: December 31
Type: Private

Combine green algae, ionized silver, shark cartilage, and pomegranate juice and you might find the fountain of youth, or at least the ingredients for a multi-level marketing company like AMS Health Sciences. The company's 60 products consist of dietary supplements, weight management products, and hair and skin care products -- all of which are manufactured by third parties. A network of 7,000 independent distributors sell the products in Canada and the US. Its products are sold under the Advantage, AMS, Prime One, and ToppFast brands. The company also markets and sells promotional material to its distributors. AMS has restructured and emerged from Chapter 11 bankruptcy protection.

AMSTED INDUSTRIES INCORPORATED

180 N STETSON AVE # 1800
CHICAGO, IL 606016710
Phone: 312 645-1700
Fax: –
Web: www.amsted.com

CEO: Steven R Smith
CFO: Tomas Bergmann
HR: Erica Zawadzki
FYE: September 30
Type: Private

Amsted Industries is a diversified manufacturer serving several industries including rail, automotive and commercial vehicle, building markets, and construction. Through its Amsted Rail subsidiary, the company makes freight car and locomotive components including axles, wheels, brakes, and bearings. Amsted Automotive Group is the synergy of Burgess-Norton, Means Industries, and SMW manufacturing?experts in high efficiency mechatronic clutch designs, electrified torque management systems, advanced metal-forming, powdered metallurgy, soft magnetic composites, precision-bearing components, and engineering and manufacturing. The Construction and Industrial segment offers evaporative condensers and cooling towers used for climate control in commercial, industrial, and institutional buildings. The company has been operating under the Amsted Industries umbrella since 1962.

	Annual Growth	09/05	09/06	09/07	09/08	09/09
Sales ($mil.)	(0.3%)	–	–	–	57.4	57.3
Net income ($ mil.)	92.2%	–	–	–	0.1	0.2
Market value ($ mil.)	–	–	–	–	–	–
Employees	–	–	–	–	–	16,000

AMTECH SYSTEMS, INC.

NMS: ASYS

131 South Clark Drive
Tempe, AZ 85288
Phone: 480 967-5146
Fax: –
Web: www.amtechsystems.com

CEO: –
CFO: –
HR: –
FYE: September 30
Type: Public

Amtech Systems furnishes fabs with furnaces and more. The company operates through four subsidiaries: Tempress Systems makes diffusion furnaces for semiconductor and solar cell fabrication, as well as for precision thermal processing (annealing, brazing, silvering, sealing, and soldering) of electronic devices, including optical components and photovoltaic (PV) solar cells. P.R. Hoffman Machine Products makes equipment used to polish items such as silicon wafers, precision optics, ceramic components, and disk media. Bruce Technologies makes horizontal diffusion furnace systems, and R2D Automation makes wafer automation and handling equipment for the solar and semiconductor sectors and is based in France.

	Annual Growth	09/19	09/20	09/21	09/22	09/23
Sales ($mil.)	7.4%	85.0	65.5	85.2	106.3	113.3
Net income ($ mil.)	–	(5.2)	(15.7)	1.5	17.4	(12.6)
Market value ($ mil.)	9.5%	75.2	69.4	162.1	120.6	108.1
Employees	(0.6%)	415	296	296	327	405

AMX INTERNATIONAL, INC.

346 GRAND LOOP STE 100
REXBURG, ID 834404944
Phone: 208 356-4167
Fax: –
Web: –

CEO: –
CFO: –
HR: –
FYE: December 31
Type: Private

AMX International can hook you up, no matter what state you're in or what systems you're running. The company provides a variety of software and services used to integrate enterprise software with existing systems. It specializes in implementing and adapting enterprise software applications from Oracle and J.D. Edwards. AMX's clients come from industries such as manufacturing, financial services, energy and utilities, and the public sector. Its 800-plus customers include Amgen, Bank of America, Boeing, Coca-Cola, Lockheed Martin, and the Montgomery County government in Maryland. AMX International was founded in 1989 by Jay Price, president and CEO, who owns the company.

AMYRIS INC

NBB: AMRS Q

5885 Hollis Street, Suite 100
Emeryville, CA 94608
Phone: 510 450-0761
Fax: –
Web: www.amyris.com

CEO: Han Kieftenbeld
CFO: Han Kieftenbeld
HR: –
FYE: December 31
Type: Public

Amyris is a biotechnology company delivering sustainable, science-based ingredients and consumer products that are better than incumbent options for people and the planet. It creates, manufactures, and commercializes consumer products and ingredients that reach more than 300 million consumers. The largest component of revenue is derived from marketing and selling Clean Beauty, Personal Care, and Health & Wellness consumer products through its direct-to-consumer e-commerce platforms and a growing network of retail partners. Its proprietary sustainable ingredients are sold in bulk to industrial leaders who serve Flavor & Fragrance, Nutrition, Food & Beverage, among other end markets. Around 75% of its sales are generated domestically.

	Annual Growth	12/18	12/19	12/20	12/21	12/22
Sales ($mil.)	43.5%	63.6	152.6	173.1	341.8	269.8
Net income ($ mil.)	–	(230.2)	(242.8)	(331.0)	(271.0)	(528.5)
Market value ($ mil.)	(17.7%)	1,218.2	1,127.1	2,252.3	1,973.3	558.1
Employees	33.5%	503	561	595	980	1,598

ANACOR PHARMACEUTICALS, INC.

66 HUDSON BLVD E
NEW YORK, NY 100012189
Phone: 212 733-2323
Fax: –
Web: www.pfizer.com

CEO: –
CFO: –
HR: –
FYE: December 31
Type: Private

Anacor is hardcore about curing skin conditions. The company is developing boron-based drug compounds for use as topical treatments of bacterial, fungal, and inflammatory conditions. Its lead candidates aim to treat onychomycosis (a kind of toenail fungus), psoriasis, and hospital-acquired bacterial infections. Anacor has focused on topical treatments for the time being because they are relatively easy to develop and market, but it believes its boron chemistry can produce drugs in therapeutic fields such as viral and parasitic infections and rare infectious diseases. The company went public in 2010; it was then acquired by Pfizer for $5.2 billion in 2016.

ANALOG DEVICES INC   NMS: ADI

One Analog Way
Wilmington, MA 01887
Phone: 781 935-5565
Fax: -
Web: www.analog.com

CEO: Vincent Roche
CFO: Richard C Puccio Jr
HR: -
FYE: October 28
Type: Public

Analog Devices Inc. (ADI) is a leading maker of mixed-signal, analog and digital integrated circuits (ICs) that convert real-world phenomena such as pressure, temperature, and sound into digital signals. Its devices include converters, amplifiers, power management products, and digital signal processors (DSPs). The company's chips are used in industrial process controls, medical and scientific instruments, defense/aerospace, communications gear, computers, automobiles, and consumer electronics. ADI claims has operations around the world with around two- thirds of its revenue from customers outside the US.

	Annual Growth	11/19*	10/20	10/21	10/22	10/23
Sales ($mil.)	19.7%	5,991.1	5,603.1	7,318.3	12,014	12,306
Net income ($ mil.)	24.9%	1,363.0	1,220.8	1,390.4	2,748.6	3,314.6
Market value ($ mil.)	10.1%	54,276	58,822	86,096	71,898	79,685
Employees	12.2%	16,400	15,900	24,700	24,450	26,000

*Fiscal year change

ANALOGIC CORPORATION

8 CENTENNIAL DR
PEABODY, MA 019607987
Phone: 978 326-4000
Fax: -
Web: www.analogic.com

CEO: Thomas Ripp
CFO: Will Rousmaniere
HR: Debbie Marino
FYE: July 31
Type: Private

Founded in 1967, Analogic Corporation is a global leader in the design, development, manufacturing, and support of technically-advanced and cost-effective imaging & detection and power & automation solutions for security, healthcare, and other high-end industrial markets. The company is a leading designer and manufacturer of computed tomography (CT) systems and subsystems; magnetic resonance imaging (MRI) power systems; and selenium-based direct digital 2D and 3D mammography detectors sold to OEMs around the world. Its subsystems are used in half of all the CT and MRI scanners installed worldwide. It also designs and manufactures high-precision solutions motion control, and power amplifiers used in various industrial applications, such as factory automation, autonomous guide vehicles (AVG), semiconductor manufacturing, and defense.

ANALOGIX SEMICONDUCTOR, INC.

2350 MISSION COLLEGE BLVD STE 1100
SANTA CLARA, CA 950541566
Phone: 408 988-8848
Fax: -
Web: www.analogix.com

CEO: Kewei Yang
CFO: Mike Seifert
HR: -
FYE: December 31
Type: Private

Analogix Semiconductor sees the logic in making analog and mixed-signal integrated circuits. Its interconnect chips are designed to enable computer systems to communicate over copper wires at fiber-optic speeds. Analogix also targets multimedia applications with its DisplayPort and HDMI receiver and transmitter devices. The fabless semiconductor company was founded in 2002. Analogix's senior executives previously worked at such companies as Agilent Technologies and Mindspeed Technologies. The company has offices in China, Japan, Taiwan, and the US.

	Annual Growth	12/17	12/18	12/19	12/20	12/21
Sales ($mil.)	33.9%	-	-	73.3	93.8	131.4
Net income ($ mil.)		-	-	(0.8)	2.5	14.2
Market value ($ mil.)		-	-	-	-	-
Employees		-	-	-	-	24

ANCHIN, BLOCK & ANCHIN LLP

3 TIMES SQ
NEW YORK, NY 100366564
Phone: 212 840-3456
Fax: -
Web: www.anchin.com

CEO: -
CFO: -
HR: Janice Strain
FYE: December 31
Type: Private

Einstein knew that logic will get you from A to B, and Anchin, Block & Anchin is no exception. The regional accounting and consulting firm concentrates on serving privately held businesses in a number of industries. It offers audits, financial statements, reviews and compilations, tax preparation, and other advisory services. Its Anchin Wealth Management unit serves wealthy clients with investment, estate, and other financial services, while Anchin Capital Advisors specializes in mergers and acquisitions. Anchin, Block & Anchin, which was founded in 1923 as a three-man partnership, has grown to number more than 55 partners and principals.

ANCHORAGE, MUNICIPALITY OF (INC)

632 W 6TH AVE STE 810
ANCHORAGE, AK 995016312
Phone: 907 343-6610
Fax: -
Web: www.muni.org

CEO: -
CFO: -
HR: -
FYE: December 31
Type: Private

Anchorage is Alaska's largest city in both size and population. The city encompasses almost 2,000 sq. mi. of land -- almost the size of Delaware. Anchorage had a 2010 population of about 290,000 residents, or about a quarter of the state's population. Anchorage is located in the south central part of the state and sits on the Gulf of Alaska.

	Annual Growth	12/17	12/18	12/19	12/20	12/21
Sales ($mil.)	11.2%	-	740.2	800.8	956.5	1,018.3
Net income ($ mil.)		-	-	26.4	21.7	272.3	(22.1)
Market value ($ mil.)		-	-	-	-	-
Employees		-	-	-	-	3,680

ANDALAY SOLAR INC

2721 Shattuck Avenue, #305
Berkeley, CA 94705
Phone: 408 402-9400
Fax: -
Web: www.andalaysolar.com

CEO: -
CFO: -
HR: -
FYE: December 31
Type: Public

Ask anyone at Akeena about their company's name, and they'll tell you Akeena was the mistress of the Greek sun god Apollo. The company (which does business under the Westinghouse Solar name as the result of a 2010 partnership agreement) designs, markets, and sells solar power systems for residential and small commercial customers. Akeena was founded in 2001, and by early 2009 had installed more than 3,000 solar power systems at schools, wineries, restaurants, housing developments, and other locations. However, the company exited the installation business in 2009 to concentrate on manufacturing and distribution. Previously limited to six states, the company now distributes in some 34 states and in Canada.

	Annual Growth	12/10	12/11	12/12	12/13	12/14
Sales ($mil.)	(37.9%)	8.7	11.4	5.2	1.1	1.3
Net income ($ mil.)		(12.9)	(4.6)	(8.6)	(2.8)	(1.9)
Market value ($ mil.)	(55.9%)	131.9	89.4	12.6	6.1	5.0
Employees	(26.4%)	34	31	7	9	10

ANDEAVOR LLC

19100 RIDGEWOOD PKWY
SAN ANTONIO, TX 782591828
Phone: 210 626-6000
Fax: –
Web: www.stellar.bank

CEO: Gary R Heminger
CFO: Steven M Sterin
HR: –
FYE: December 31
Type: Private

Andeavor Corporation does its best to turn crude oil into something useful for its customers. The independent oil refiner and marketer operates seven US refineries that produce nearly 900,000 barrels per day of gasoline, jet fuel, diesel fuel, fuel oil, liquid asphalt, and other fuel products. It has refineries in Alaska, California (two), North Dakota (two), Utah, and Washington. Andeavor markets fuel to nearly 2,5000 branded retail gas stations (including Shell and USA Gasoline brands), primarily in Alaska and the Western US. It owns 36% of Andeavor Logistics LP (ALLP). In 2017 Andeavor (then called Tresoro) acquired all segments of Western Refining except its logistics arm in a $6.4 billion deal. The combined Tesoro-Western company changed its name to Andeavor.

ANDERSEN CORPORATION

100 4TH AVE N
BAYPORT, MN 550031096
Phone: 651 264-5150
Fax: –
Web: www.andersenwindows.com

CEO: Chris Galvin
CFO: Philip E Donaldson
HR: –
FYE: December 31
Type: Private

Andersen Corporation is a maker of wood-clad windows and patio doors in North America and Europe. Andersen offers window designs from bay and bow, single and double-hung, gliding, and pass-through. Its Renewal by Andersen subsidiary provides start-to-finish window renewal services in more than 100 markets in the US. MQ windows and doors designs draw inspiration from the company's Italian and French heritage offering many product styles including contemporary, European, classical, traditional, historic, and rustic. The company was founded in 1903 as Andersen Lumber Company.

ANDERSON AND DUBOSE, INC.

5300 TOD AVE SW
WARREN, OH 444819767
Phone: 440 248-8800
Fax: –
Web: www.a-d.us

CEO: –
CFO: –
HR: Gregory Lytle
FYE: December 30
Type: Private

You might say this company keeps the Big Mac big and the Happy Meals happy. Anderson-DuBose Pittsburgh is a leading wholesale distributor that supplies food and non-food items to McDonald's and Chipotle fast-food restaurants in Ohio, Pennsylvania, New York, and West Virginia. It serves about 500 Golden Arches locations with frozen meat and fish, dairy products, and paper goods and packaging, as well as toys for Happy Meals. One of the largest black-owned companies in the US, Anderson-DuBose was started in 1991 by Warren Anderson and Stephen DuBose, who purchased control of a McDonald's distributorship from Martin-Brower. Anderson became sole owner in 1993 when he bought out his partner's stake in the business.

	Annual Growth	12/18	12/19	12/20	12/21	12/22
Sales ($mil.)	8.2%	–	599.0	–	676.5	758.7
Net income ($ mil.)	(2.5%)	–	4.4	–	4.6	4.1
Market value ($ mil.)	–	–	–	–	–	–
Employees	–	–	–	–	–	100

ANDERSONS INC

NMS: ANDE

1947 Briarfield Boulevard
Maumee, OH 43537
Phone: 419 893-5050
Fax: –
Web: www.andersonsinc.com

CEO: Patrick E Bowe
CFO: Brian A Valentine
HR: Katie Huss
FYE: December 31
Type: Public

Agribusiness giant The Andersons operates in a variety of areas, including trade, and plant nutrients, and rail. It operates grain elevators located in the US and Canada. The company purchases and sells ethanol, offers facility operations, risk management, and ethanol and corn oil marketing services to the ethanol plants it invests in and operates. The Anderson's Plant Nutrient segment makes and sells fertilizers, crop protection chemicals, and related products, and the company leases grain handling and storage facilities, ethanol storage terminals, warehouse space, railcars, office space, machinery and equipment, and vehicles and IT equipment. It operates primarily in the US where more than 70% of the company's total revenue is generated from.

	Annual Growth	12/19	12/20	12/21	12/22	12/23
Sales ($mil.)	15.9%	8,170.2	8,208.4	12,612	17,325	14,750
Net income ($ mil.)	53.3%	18.3	7.7	104.0	131.1	101.2
Market value ($ mil.)	22.8%	854.3	828.3	1,308.2	1,182.5	1,944.5
Employees	0.2%	2,320	2,359	2,371	2,283	2,334

ANDES CHEMICAL, LLC

11125 NW 29TH ST
DORAL, FL 331725011
Phone: 305 591-5601
Fax: –
Web: www.andeschem.com

CEO: –
CFO: George Perez
HR: –
FYE: December 31
Type: Private

Andes Chemical sells its products in the Andes, and elsewhere. The company exports raw chemical materials and equipment to more than 300 clients throughout Latin America and the Caribbean. It distributes additives, monomers, plasticizers and other ingredients for use by the paints, inks, concrete and masonry additives, adhesives, pharmaceuticals, cosmetics, and personal care product industries. The house paint industry accounts for most of the company's sales. Suppliers include Akzo Nobel, Arkema, Kemira, and Ferro. Andes Chemical was founded in 1986 by president and CEO Fernando Espinosa.

	Annual Growth	12/03	12/04	12/05	12/06	12/09
Sales ($mil.)	2.0%	–	–	32.4	34.8	35.0
Net income ($ mil.)	(4.0%)	–	–	2.5	2.7	2.1
Market value ($ mil.)	–	–	–	–	–	–
Employees	–	–	–	–	–	29

ANDREA ELECTRONICS CORP.

NBB: ANDR

620 Johnson Avenue, Suite 1-B
Bohemia, NY 11716
Phone: 631 719-1800
Fax: –
Web: –

CEO: Douglas J Andrea
CFO: Corisa L Guiffre
HR: –
FYE: December 31
Type: Public

Andrea Electronics wants to make a big noise with its Anti-Noise technology. The company's Anti-Noise products include software that increases voice clarity and reduces background noise, plus headsets that enhance audio in high-noise environments. Andrea Electronics also offers voice recognition products for voice-activated computing applications, such as word processing. The company designs its products for audio- and videoconferencing, call centers, in-vehicle communications, and personal computing. Andrea Electronics sells directly and through distributors, software publishers, ISPs, and other resellers. The company gets most of its sales in the US.

	Annual Growth	12/18	12/19	12/20	12/21	12/22
Sales ($mil.)	7.6%	1.5	1.9	1.4	1.7	2.0
Net income ($ mil.)	–	(0.9)	(0.5)	(0.8)	(0.4)	(0.3)
Market value ($ mil.)	(14.8%)	3.9	1.4	2.5	2.0	2.0
Employees	–	8	9	9	9	8

ANGELO IAFRATE CONSTRUCTION COMPANY

26300 SHERWOOD AVE
WARREN, MI 480914168
Phone: 586 756-1070
Fax: –
Web: www.iafrate.com

CEO: –
CFO: –
HR: –
FYE: December 31
Type: Private

Angelo Iafrate Construction Company spends most of its time on the road. The company specializes in highway and road construction and is qualified by the US Department of Transportation to work in more than half of the states across the country. Angelo Iafrate provides preconstruction, construction, and project management services for both the public and private sector. The heavy construction contractor targets clients in the commercial, transportation, utilities, manufacturing, health care, and education industries. Angelo Iafrate also sells used equipment. The company is owned and managed by the Iafrate family.

	Annual Growth	12/10	12/11	12/12	12/13	12/14
Sales ($mil.)	167.1%	–	–	–	34.4	92.0
Net income ($ mil.)	372.9%	–	–	–	0.7	3.1
Market value ($ mil.)	–	–	–	–	–	–
Employees	–	–	–	–	–	350

ANGELO STATE UNIVERSITY

2601 W AVENUE N
SAN ANGELO, TX 769095099
Phone: 325 942-2555
Fax: –
Web: www.angelo.edu

CEO: –
CFO: Angela Wright
HR: Kurtis Neal
FYE: August 31
Type: Private

Out in the West Texas town of San Angelo (a community of 100,000), more than 6,000 students attend Angelo State University (ASU). The school offers approximately 45 undergraduate programs of study at its College of Liberal and Fine Arts, College of Education, College of Business, and College of Sciences. ASU also has a School of Graduate Studies that offers nearly 30 master's degree programs. It also offers one doctorate program. With more than 330 faculty members, its student-teacher ratio is 20:1. ASU is part of the Texas Tech University System.

	Annual Growth	08/12	08/13	08/14	08/19	08/22
Sales ($mil.)	0.9%	–	64.7	60.9	74.6	70.0
Net income ($ mil.)	2.4%	–	12.1	5.2	0.9	15.0
Market value ($ mil.)	–	–	–	–	–	–
Employees	–	–	–	–	–	550

ANGELS BASEBALL LP

2000 E GENE AUTRY WAY
ANAHEIM, CA 928066143
Phone: 714 940-2000
Fax: –
Web: www.mlb.com

CEO: –
CFO: –
HR: –
FYE: December 31
Type: Private

Los Angeles' other baseball team actually resides in Anaheim, California. Angels Baseball owns and operates the Los Angeles Angels of Anaheim professional baseball franchise. The team, originally owned by cowboy actor Gene Autry, joined Major League Baseball as an expansion franchise in 1960 and has boasted such Hall of Fame talent as Rod Carew and Nolan Ryan. However, Angels fans had to wait until 2002 for the team to win its first American League pennant and World Series title. Phoenix businessman Arturo Moreno, who has owned the team since 2003, was the first Hispanic to own a major sports franchise in the US.

ANGI INC

NMS: ANGI

3601 Walnut Street
Denver, CO 80205
Phone: 303 963-7200
Fax: –
Web: www.angihomeservices.com

CEO: Jeffrey W Kip
CFO: Andrew Russakoff
HR: –
FYE: December 31
Type: Public

Angi Inc., formerly ANGI Homeservices Inc., connects quality home service professionals with consumers across more than 500 different categories, from repairing and remodeling homes to cleaning and landscaping. Over 220,000 domestic service professionals actively sought consumer leads, completed jobs or advertised work through Angi Inc. platforms. Additionally, consumers turned to at least one of its brands to find a service professional for approximately 29 million projects. About 95% of Angi revenue comes from the US.

	Annual Growth	12/19	12/20	12/21	12/22	12/23
Sales ($mil.)	0.6%	1,326.2	1,467.9	1,685.4	1,891.5	1,358.7
Net income ($ mil.)	–	–	34.8	(6.3)	(71.4)	(128.5)	(40.9)
Market value ($ mil.)	(26.4%)	4,270.8	6,653.3	4,643.9	1,184.9	1,255.5
Employees	(6.6%)	5,000	5,100	5,200	4,600	3,800

ANGIE'S LIST, INC.

1030 E WASHINGTON ST
INDIANAPOLIS, IN 462023953
Phone: 866 843-5478
Fax: –
Web: www.angieslist.com

CEO: –
CFO: –
HR: –
FYE: December 31
Type: Private

Angi's got a list and over six million households a year check it for information on service providers, from roofers and plumbers to dentists and doctors. From repairs and renovations to products and financing, Angi is transforming every touch point in the customer journey. With over 25 years of experience and a network of over 200,000 pros, the company have helped more than 150 million people with their home needs. The company's top cities have included New York, Houston, Chicago, Indianapolis, Boston, Atlanta, and Cincinnati, among others. Founded in 1995, Angie's List is a leading online ratings and reviews platform that provides trusted reviews and information to help millions of consumers make smart hiring decisions.

ANGIODYNAMICS INC

NMS: ANGO

14 Plaza Drive
Latham, NY 12110
Phone: 518 795-1400
Fax: –
Web: www.angiodynamics.com

CEO: –
CFO: –
HR: –
FYE: May 31
Type: Public

AngioDynamics, Inc. is a leading and transformative medical technology company focused on restoring healthy blood flow in the body's vascular system, expanding cancer treatment options, and improving quality of life for patients. It designs, manufactures, and sells a wide range of medical, surgical, and diagnostic devices used by professional healthcare providers for the treatment of peripheral vascular disease, vascular access and for use in oncology and surgical settings. Its devices are generally used in minimally invasive, image-guided procedures. Products include laser systems that ablate varicose veins, angiographic catheters that deliver drugs and contrast agents for imaging, dialysis catheters for those with renal failure, abscess drainage devices, and radiofrequency ablation devices that help destroy tumors. The US market accounts for about 85% of total revenue. AngioDynamics was founded in 1988.

	Annual Growth	05/19	05/20	05/21	05/22	05/23
Sales ($mil.)	5.8%	270.6	264.2	291.0	316.2	338.8
Net income ($ mil.)	–	61.3	(166.8)	(31.5)	(26.5)	(52.4)
Market value ($ mil.)	(15.8%)	744.3	404.4	915.8	777.6	374.7
Employees	2.1%	750	800	800	760	815

ANI PHARMACEUTICALS INC

NMS: ANIP

210 Main Street West
Baudette, MN 56623
Phone: 218 634-3500
Fax: –
Web: www.anipharmaceuticals.com

CEO: Nikhil Lalwani
CFO: Stephen P Carey
HR: –
FYE: December 31
Type: Public

ANI Pharmaceuticals is a diversified bio-pharmaceutical company serving patients in need by developing, manufacturing, and marketing high quality branded and generic prescription pharmaceuticals, including for diseases with high unmet medical need. Some of its branded products are Apexicon, Cortenema, Purified Cortrophin Gel, Cortrophin-Zinc, Inderal LA, Inderal XL, InnoPran XL, Lithobid, Reglan, Vancocin, and Veregen. The company's currently markets include controlled substances, oncology products, hormones and steroids, injectables, and complex formulations, including extended release and combination products. The vast majority of its revenue comes from the US.

	Annual Growth	12/19	12/20	12/21	12/22	12/23
Sales ($mil.)	23.9%	206.5	208.5	216.1	316.4	486.8
Net income ($ mil.)	32.5%	6.1	(22.5)	(42.6)	(47.9)	18.8
Market value ($ mil.)	(2.8%)	1,262.9	594.7	943.6	823.8	1,129.1
Employees	17.4%	338	369	601	600	642

ANIKA THERAPEUTICS INC.

NMS: ANIK

32 Wiggins Avenue
Bedford, MA 01730
Phone: 781 457-9000
Fax: –
Web: www.anika.com

CEO: Cheryl R Blanchard
CFO: Michael L Levitz
HR: Karen S Connolly Sphr
FYE: December 31
Type: Public

Founded in 1992, Anika Therapeutics is a global joint preservation company that creates and delivers meaningful advancements in early intervention orthopedic care. The company uses hyaluronic acid (HA), a natural polymer extracted from rooster combs and other sources, to make products that treat bone, cartilage, and soft tissue. Its proprietary technologies for modifying the HA molecule allow product properties to be tailored specifically to multiple uses, including enabling longer residence time to support OA pain management and creating a solid form of HA called Hyaff, which is a platform utilized in its regenerative solutions portfolio. The US accounts for more than 75% of the company's total revenue.

	Annual Growth	12/19	12/20	12/21	12/22	12/23
Sales ($mil.)	9.8%	114.6	130.5	147.8	156.2	166.7
Net income ($ mil.)	–	27.2	(24.0)	4.1	(14.9)	(82.7)
Market value ($ mil.)	(18.7%)	760.1	663.5	525.3	433.9	332.2
Employees	23.4%	154	277	297	345	357

ANIXA BIOSCIENCES INC

NAS: ANIX

3150 Almaden Expressway, Suite 250
San Jose, CA 95118
Phone: 408 708-9808
Fax: –
Web: www.anixa.com

CEO: Amit Kumar
CFO: Michael J Catelani
HR: –
FYE: October 31
Type: Public

CopyTele has an original take on display and communications technology. The company licenses technology used in thin, low-voltage phosphor displays. A licensing agreement with Videocon Industries allows the India-based consumer electronics company to develop televisions utilizing CopyTele's technology. CopyTele also provides secure communications products. Its stand-alone devices provide encryption for secure voice, fax, and data communication. Boeing, the exclusive distributor for many of the company's security products, uses CopyTele's encryption products on the Thuraya satellite communications network, which is employed by the US military.

	Annual Growth	10/19	10/20	10/21	10/22	10/23
Sales ($mil.)	(4.3%)	0.3	–	0.5	–	0.2
Net income ($ mil.)	–	(11.6)	(10.0)	(13.0)	(13.6)	(9.8)
Market value ($ mil.)	(4.9%)	120.5	64.2	148.6	174.4	98.4
Employees	(11.1%)	8	4	5	5	5

ANMED HEALTH SERVICES, INC.

800 N FANT ST
ANDERSON, SC 296215708
Phone: 864 512-1170
Fax: –
Web: www.anmed.org

CEO: William Manson III
CFO: Jerry Parrish
HR: Teresa Threlkeld
FYE: December 31
Type: Private

Whether Peach or Palmetto, AnMed Health system can meet your health care needs. The health care organization serves residents of western South Carolina and northeast Georgia with more than 30 health care sites. Its flagship facility is the 460-bed acute care AnMed Health Medical Center. The system also features a 70-bed all private-room Women's and Children's Hospital and a 40-bed Rehabilitation Hospital. Specialties include cancer care, general and specialized diagnostic, surgical, and treatment services. The organization also provides emergency and trauma care. Founded in 1908, AnMed has affiliations agreements with Cannon Memorial Hospital and Carolinas HealthCare System.

ANN & HOPE, INC.

24 HEMINGWAY DR
RIVERSIDE, RI 029152224
Phone: 401 722-1000
Fax: –
Web: www.vermontcountrystore.com

CEO: –
CFO: –
HR: –
FYE: December 31
Type: Private

Ann & Hope's ship has come in through the form of sales of discounted curtain rods and canopies. Ann & Hope sells discounted window and shower curtains, blinds, shades, rugs, and other bath and window accessories at about 10 Curtain & Bath Outlet locations in Connecticut, Massachusetts, and Rhode Island. The company also operates an e-commerce site. The regional curtain and bath retailer buys in bulk and sells its merchandise at 20% to 50% off department store prices. Founded in 1953, Ann & Hope was named after a ship that was lost at sea off the coast of Block Island, Rhode Island, in 1806.

ANN & ROBERT H. LURIE CHILDREN'S HOSPITAL OF CHICAGO

225 E CHICAGO AVE
CHICAGO, IL 606112991
Phone: 312 227-4000
Fax: –
Web: www.luriechildrens.org

CEO: Thomas Shanley
CFO: Paula Noble
HR: –
FYE: August 31
Type: Private

When it comes to caring for kids, Ann & Robert H. Lurie Children's Hospital of Chicago has the Windy City covered. Founded in 1882, the not-for-profit hospital provides a full range of pediatric services with acute and specialty care. Lurie Children's provides services through its main hospital campus with about 300 beds and outpatient centers in Chicago's Lincoln Park neighborhood and through more than a dozen suburban outpatient centers and outreach partner locations in the greater Chicago area. A leader in pediatric research, the hospital operates the Children's Hospital of Chicago Research Center and is the pediatric teaching facility of Northwestern University's Feinberg School of Medicine.

	Annual Growth	08/07	08/08	08/09	08/10	08/13
Sales ($mil.)	6.8%	–	–	534.0	599.3	694.2
Net income ($ mil.)	–	–	–	(5.2)	53.0	28.8
Market value ($ mil.)	–	–	–	–	–	–
Employees	–	–	–	–	–	2,800

ANNALY CAPITAL MANAGEMENT INC
NYS: NLY

1211 Avenue of the Americas
New York, NY 10036
Phone: 212 696-0100
Fax: 212 696-9809
Web: www.annaly.com

CEO: -
CFO: -
HR: -
FYE: December 31
Type: Public

A real estate investment trust (REIT), Annaly Capital Management is a leading diversified capital manager with investment strategies across mortgage finance. It primarily manages a portfolio of mortgage-backed securities, including mortgage pass-through certificates, collateralized mortgage obligations, credit risk transfer (CRT) securities, other securities representing interests in or obligations backed by pools of mortgage loans, residential mortgage loans, mortgage servicing rights (MSR) and corporate debt. The REIT has three investment groups ? Annaly Agency, Annaly Residential Credit, and Annaly Middle Market Lending Group. Founded in 1996 as Annaly Mortgage Management Inc. and became public in 1997.

	Annual Growth	12/19	12/20	12/21	12/22	12/23
Assets ($mil.)	(8.0%)	130,295	88,455	76,764	81,851	93,227
Net income ($ mil.)	-	(2,162.9)	(891.2)	2,389.9	1,725.3	(1,643.2)
Market value ($ mil.)	19.7%	4,710.8	4,225.7	3,910.6	10,542	9,686.6
Employees	1.7%	175	180	171	161	187

ANNAMS SYSTEMS CORPORATION

2420 CAMINO RAMON STE 130
SAN RAMON, CA 945834320
Phone: 925 355-0700
Fax: -
Web: www.sunflowersystems.com

CEO: -
CFO: -
HR: -
FYE: December 31
Type: Private

Annams Systems offers a variety of database technology services, from installation to data migration to systems integration, as well as broader enterprise information management services used in business intelligence applications. It also provides related consulting, training, support, and maintenance services. Clients come from fields such as manufacturing, financial services, and electronics. The company's Sunflower Systems unit provides asset management products and services to corporate customers and government agencies. Annams Systems was founded by CEO Naeem Raza in 1992.

	Annual Growth	12/13	12/14	12/15	12/16	12/17
Sales ($mil.)	6.3%	-	10.1	9.3	10.8	12.1
Net income ($ mil.)	(4.8%)	-	2.7	0.7	1.8	2.4
Market value ($ mil.)	-	-	-	-	-	-
Employees	-	-	-	-	-	39

ANR PIPELINE COMPANY

700 LOUISIANA ST STE 700
HOUSTON, TX 770022702
Phone: 832 320-2000
Fax: -
Web: www.anrpl.com

CEO: Lee G Hobbs
CFO: -
HR: -
FYE: December 31
Type: Private

ANR Pipeline keeps natural gas in line, a pipeline that is. The company operates one of the largest interstate natural gas pipeline systems in the US. A subsidiary of TransCanada Corp., ANR controls about 10,350 miles of pipeline and delivers more than 1 trillion cu. ft. of natural gas per year. The company primarily serves customers in the Midwest, but through its network is capable of connecting to all major gas basins in North America. In tandem with its ANR Storage and Blue Lake Gas Storage subsidiaries, ANR Pipeline also provides natural gas storage services and has ownership interests in more than 250 billion cu. ft. of underground natural gas storage capacity.

	Annual Growth	12/04	12/05	12/06	12/16	12/17
Sales ($mil.)	2.7%	-	548.0	540.0	686.3	758.2
Net income ($ mil.)	(0.4%)	-	147.0	152.0	54.7	139.9
Market value ($ mil.)	-	-	-	-	-	-
Employees	-	-	-	-	-	1,000

ANSYS INC.
NMS: ANSS

2600 ANSYS Drive
Canonsburg, PA 15317
Phone: 844 462-6797
Fax: -
Web: www.ansys.com

CEO: Ajei S Gopal
CFO: Nicole Anasenes
HR: Kathleen Weslock
FYE: December 31
Type: Public

ANSYS develops and globally markets engineering simulation software and services widely used by engineers, designers, researchers and student across a broad spectrum of industries and academia, including aerospace and defense, automotive, electronics, semiconductors, energy, consumer products, healthcare and more. The company focus on development and flexible solutions that enable users to analyze and designs directly to desktop, providing a common platform for fast, efficient and cost-conscious product development, from design concept to final-stage testing and validation. The company products consist of platform, structures, fluids, electronics, semiconductors, embedded software, and more.

	Annual Growth	12/19	12/20	12/21	12/22	12/23
Sales ($mil.)	10.6%	1,515.9	1,681.3	1,906.7	2,065.6	2,269.9
Net income ($ mil.)	2.6%	451.3	433.9	454.6	523.7	500.4
Market value ($ mil.)	9.0%	22,370	31,616	34,860	20,996	31,536
Employees	10.9%	4,100	4,800	5,100	5,600	6,200

ANTERO MIDSTREAM CORP
NYS: AM

1615 Wynkoop Street
Denver, CO 80202
Phone: 303 357-7310
Fax: -
Web: www.anteromidstream.com

CEO: Paul M Rady
CFO: Brendan E Krueger
HR: -
FYE: December 31
Type: Public

Antero Midstream GP LP owns the general partner and all the incentive distribution rights (IDRs) in Antero Midstream Partners LP, a master limited partnership that owns, operates, and develops midstream energy infrastructure primarily to service Antero Resource Corporation's oil and gas production activity in the Appalachian Basin. Antero Midstream GP LP's only source of income are payouts from the Antero Midstream Partners LP IDRs. It does not own or operate tangible assets. Parent company Antero Resources said late in 2018 that it would eliminate Antero Midstream Partners LP (AM), by merging the partnership with Antero Midstream GP LP (AMGP). AMGP will acquire AM, and the combined company will be converted into a corporation and renamed Antero Midstream Corp. Antero Resources will be the largest shareholder of the new company at 31%.

	Annual Growth	12/19	12/20	12/21	12/22	12/23
Sales ($mil.)	7.1%	792.6	900.7	898.2	920.0	1,041.8
Net income ($ mil.)	-	(355.1)	(122.5)	331.6	326.2	371.8
Market value ($ mil.)	13.4%	3,641.0	3,698.6	4,643.6	5,176.1	6,010.8
Employees	2.5%	547	522	519	586	604

ANTERO RESOURCES CORP
NYS: AR

1615 Wynkoop Street
Denver, CO 80202
Phone: 303 357-7310
Fax: -
Web: www.anteroresources.com

CEO: Paul M Rady
CFO: Michael N Kennedy
HR: K Hughes
FYE: December 31
Type: Public

Antero Resources is engaged in the development, production, exploration and acquisition of natural gas, NGLs and oil properties located in the Appalachian Basin. It helps approximately 504,000 net acres of natural gas, NGLs and oil properties located in the Appalachian Basin primarily in West Virginia and Ohio. It reports proved reserves of over 17.5 trillion cu. ft. consisting of some 10 Tcf of natural gas equivalent. The company maintains its daily output of natural gas equivalent by deploying horizontal drilling and advanced fracturing stimulation technologies. It focuses on unconventional reservoirs, typically fractured shale formations. Subsidiary Antero Midstream owns, operates, and develops Antero's energy infrastructure.

	Annual Growth	12/19	12/20	12/21	12/22	12/23
Sales ($mil.)	1.5%	4,408.7	3,491.7	4,619.4	7,138.4	4,682.0
Net income ($ mil.)	-	(340.1)	(1,267.9)	(186.9)	1,898.8	242.9
Market value ($ mil.)	68.0%	865.1	1,654.3	5,312.0	9,406.8	6,884.4
Employees	2.5%	547	522	519	586	604

ANTHERA PHARMACEUTICALS INC

NBB: ANTH

25801 Industrial Boulevard, Suite B
Hayward, CA 94545
Phone: 510 856-5600
Fax: –
Web: www.anthera.com

CEO: Craig Thompson
CFO: –
HR: –
FYE: December 31
Type: Public

Anthera Pharmaceuticals is involved in some very complicated sounding (not to mention hard to say) drug development. Its lead product, varespladib methyl, is in late stage clinical trials to treat acute coronary syndrome. Other candidates include A-623 to treat lupus and varespladib sodium to treat acute chest syndrome. Varespladib is designed to inhibit an enzyme called sPLA 2 that is implicated in a variety of acute inflammatory conditions, such as cardiovascular disease, sickle cell disease, and coronary artery disease. Since its founding in 2004, Anthera's operations have consisted primarily of research and development activities. The company went public in early 2010 in an IPO worth about $37 million.

	Annual Growth	12/13	12/14	12/15	12/16	12/17
Sales ($mil.)	–	–	–	3.2	0.1	–
Net income ($ mil.)	–	(30.9)	(29.6)	(35.2)	(55.5)	(26.9)
Market value ($ mil.)	(14.4%)	42.5	21.9	64.3	9.0	22.9
Employees	(4.3%)	25	20	25	33	21

ANTHONY FOREST PRODUCTS COMPANY, LLC

309 N WASHINGTON AVE
EL DORADO, AR 717305614
Phone: 870 862-3414
Fax: –
Web: www.anthonyforest.com

CEO: Aubra H Anthony Jr
CFO: –
HR: Kim Winfrey
FYE: April 24
Type: Private

Anthony Forest Products first logged on well before the computer age. The company, which began in 1916, obtains its timber from more than 90,000 acres, maintained according to Sustainable Forestry Initiative policy, in Arkansas, Louisiana, and Texas. Anthony Forest Products then processes the timber into lumber and wood chips at mills located in the same three states. The company operates engineered wood laminating plants in Arkansas and Georgia, and, through a joint venture with Domtar, it produces I-joists under the Power Joist name at a plant in Canada. Anthony's Power Log products are used for log-home construction. Anthony Forest Products is owned by the fourth generation of the Anthony family.

	Annual Growth	04/06	04/07	04/08	04/09	04/10
Sales ($mil.)	–	–	–	(1,423.0)	91.4	98.3
Net income ($ mil.)	31511.1%	–	–	0.0	(5.8)	49.3
Market value ($ mil.)	–	–	–	–	–	–
Employees	–	–	–	–	–	470

ANTI-DEFAMATION LEAGUE

605 3RD AVE FL 9B
NEW YORK, NY 101581300
Phone: 212 885-7919
Fax: –
Web: www.adl.org

CEO: –
CFO: –
HR: Britney B Shrmcp
FYE: December 31
Type: Private

The Anti-Defamation League (ADL) is a not-for-profit foundation dedicated to combating anti-Semitism and other forms of bigotry. Among its awareness-raising initiatives are educational programs for high school and college students and juvenile intervention community programs. The ADL advocates for Israel, fights hate crimes and hate groups, forms interfaith groups, promotes civil rights for all people, and works with the Organization for Security and Cooperation in Europe to combat anti-Semitism in Europe. It also works with the Vatican to strengthen Catholic-Jewish relations. The ADL operates a network of about 30 offices in the US and abroad. Chicago lawyer Sigmund Livingston founded the organization in 1913.

ANTS SOFTWARE INC.

4514 CHAMBLEE DUNWOODY RD # 188
DUNWOODY, GA 303386272
Phone: 404 216-2783
Fax: –
Web: –

CEO: Rik Sanchez
CFO: Elise Vetula
HR: –
FYE: December 31
Type: Private

ANTs software hopes to help your data march about in perfect order, with no locking up. The company develops and markets software used to improve the performance of database-driven enterprise applications. ANTs' technology is designed to process and manipulate data with no database locking. Its primary product is its ANTs Compatibility Server, which enables customers to move software applications from one company's database product to another. ANTs markets its products to information technology departments, application developers, and database architects. The company also provides professional services such as consulting, training, support, implementation, and maintenance.

ANYWHERE REAL ESTATE GROUP LLC

175 Park Avenue
Madison, NJ 07940
Phone: 973 407-2000
Fax: –
Web: www.realogy.com

CEO: Ryan M Schneider
CFO: Charlotte C Simonelli
HR: –
FYE: December 31
Type: Public

Anywhere Real Estate (formerly known as Realogy Holdings Corp.) is the leading and most integrated provider of US residential real estate services, encompassing franchise, brokerage, relocation, and title and settlement businesses as well as a mortgage joint venture, supporting 1.2 million home transaction in 2022. Its brands include Better Homes and Gardens Real Estate,?CENTURY 21,?Coldwell Banker,?Coldwell Banker Commercial,?Corcoran,?ERA, and?Sotheby's International Realty. In addition to franchising, the company owns and operates about 680 brokerage offices under those brands and the Corcoran Group. Anywhere's affiliated brokerages operate around the world with approximately 195,000 independent sales agents in the US and approximately 142,400 independent sales agents in about 120 other countries and territories. Almost 100% of the company's revenue were from the US.

	Annual Growth	12/19	12/20	12/21	12/22	12/23
Sales ($mil.)	0.2%	5,598.0	6,221.0	7,983.0	6,908.0	5,636.0
Net income ($ mil.)	–	(188.0)	(360.0)	343.0	(287.0)	(97.0)
Market value ($ mil.)	–	–	–	–	–	–
Employees	(5.5%)	10,150	9,435	9,830	9,025	8,090

AOXING PHARMACEUTICAL CO INC

NBB: AOXG

1098 Foster City Blvd., Suite 106-810
Foster City, CA 94404
Phone: 646 367-1747
Fax: –
Web: www.aoxingpharma.com

CEO: –
CFO: –
HR: –
FYE: June 30
Type: Public

Narcotics are the name of the game for Aoxing Pharmaceutical, which makes Naloxone and oxycodone products. Opioids are relatively new to China and the company has one of the only government-sanctioned manufacturing facilities; it is also the largest. Like many pharma companies, Aoxing operates through many joint ventures and partnerships including a JV with pharmaceutical ingredient maker Johnson Matthey Plc and strategic alliances with American Oriental Bioengineering, QRxPharma, and Phoenix PharmaLabs. In addition to narcotics, the company offers OTC pain relievers, some based on traditional Chinese medicine. Aoxing, which traces its roots to 1600, became a public company in 2006 through a reverse merger.

	Annual Growth	06/12	06/13	06/14	06/15	06/16
Sales ($mil.)	41.2%	8.1	10.8	12.7	25.5	32.3
Net income ($ mil.)	–	(15.8)	(16.8)	(8.2)	5.5	2.1
Market value ($ mil.)	18.9%	24.8	16.4	24.4	133.4	49.5
Employees	(2.0%)	375	589	481	339	346

APA CORP

NMS: APA

One Post Oak Central, 2000 Post Oak Boulevard, Suite 100
Houston, TX 77056-4400
Phone: 713 296-6000
Fax: -
Web: www.apachecorp.com

CEO: John J Christmann IV
CFO: Stephen J Riney
HR: -
FYE: December 31
Type: Public

Apache Corporation, an oil and gas exploration and production company, has onshore and offshore operations in major oil patches around the world, including in the US, Egypt, and the UK's North Sea oil fields. In the US, it is active in the Permian Basin in West Texas and New Mexico, including the Permian sub-basins: Midland Basin, Central Basin Platform/Northwest Shelf, and Delaware Basin. The company boasts worldwide estimated proved reserves of about 915 million barrels of oil equivalent. Most of the company's sales is generated in the US at about 60%. In 2021, Apache and APA announced completion of the previously announced holding company structure, making APA the parent holding company of Apache. APA replaces Apache as the public company trading on the Nasdaq stock market under the ticker symbol "APA."

	Annual Growth	12/19	12/20	12/21	12/22	12/23
Sales ($mil.)	6.3%	6,411.0	4,308.0	7,928.0	12,132	8,192.0
Net income ($ mil.)	-	(3,553.0)	(4,860.0)	973.0	3,674.0	2,855.0
Market value ($ mil.)	8.8%	7,768.5	4,307.7	8,163.2	14,171	10,892
Employees	(7.9%)	3,163	2,272	2,253	2,273	2,271

APACHE CONSTRUCTION COMPANY, INC.

1932 COORS BLVD SW
ALBUQUERQUE, NM 871214309
Phone: 505 877-7978
Fax: -
Web: www.valleyfencecompany.com

CEO: Mariano Chavez Jr
CFO: -
HR: -
FYE: December 31
Type: Private

This company wants to fence you in. Apache Construction Company, Inc., provides residential and industrial fence construction in New Mexico, Arizona, and Nevada. The company, doing business as Valley Fence Company, builds and installs fencing for residential and commercial customers -- including prisons, schools, sports facilities, and parks -- and guardrails for highways and bridges. The company is ranked as one of the 500 largest Hispanic-owned companies in the US. Apache Construction was incorporated in 1981 by its officers and is owned by members of the Chavez family, including CEO Mariano Chavez Jr. and president Paul Chavez.

APARTMENT INCOME REIT, L.P.

4582 S ULSTER ST STE 1700
DENVER, CO 802372641
Phone: 303 757-8101
Fax: -
Web: www.aimco.com

CEO: Terry Considine
CFO: Ernest M Freedman
HR: -
FYE: December 31
Type: Private

AIMCO Properties' aim is true. The company is the operating arm of multifamily real estate giant Apartment Investment and Management Company (AIMCO), which owns and/or manages some 500 apartment properties (with nearly 94,000 individual units) throughout the US. AIMCO Properties holds most of AIMCO's assets and manages its day-to-day operations, including property management and asset management. Its portfolio includes suburban apartment communities, urban high-rise properties, and government-subsidized affordable housing properties. Investment management operations include management of its own portfolio as well as services for affiliated partnerships. AIMCO controls more than 90% of AIMCO Properties.

APARTMENT INVESTMENT & MANAGEMENT CO

NYS: AIV

4582 South Ulster Street, Suite 1450
Denver, CO 80237
Phone: 303 224-7900
Fax: 303 759-3226
Web: www.aimco.com

CEO: Wesley W Powell
CFO: H C Lynn Stanfield
HR: -
FYE: December 31
Type: Public

Apartment Investment and Management Company (Aimco) is a self-administered and self-managed real estate investment trust (REIT). Through a wholly-owned subsidiary, Aimco is the general partner and directly is the special limited partner of the Aimco Operating Partnership. It conducts all of its business and owns all of its assets through the Aimco Operating Partnership. Its portfolio of operating properties includes about 25 operating apartment communities (some 20 consolidated properties with approximately 5,640 apartment homes and four unconsolidated properties), diversified by both geography and price point, in eight major US markets.

	Annual Growth	12/19	12/20	12/21	12/22	12/23
Sales ($mil.)	(32.8%)	914.3	151.5	169.8	190.3	187.0
Net income ($ mil.)	-	474.1	(5.0)	(5.9)	75.7	(166.2)
Market value ($ mil.)	(37.6%)	7,260.8	742.2	1,085.2	1,000.9	1,100.7
Employees	(49.7%)	950	52	62	62	61

APEX DATA SERVICES, INC.

198 VAN BUREN ST STE 200
HERNDON, VA 201705338
Phone: 703 709-3000
Fax: -
Web: -

CEO: Shashikant Gupta
CFO: -
HR: -
FYE: December 31
Type: Private

Apex CoVantage provides outsourced project management and consulting services in a number of areas such as engineering design and back office processes. Its Apex Publishing unit provides digital content services (building digital libraries and databases); Apex also handles print production for publishing companies and offers in-bound and out-bound teleservices. Through its ProField branded technology product, its TPS (Technology Products and Solutions) group offers testing and field management services. Apex serves clients in a number of industries, including construction, telecommunications, manufacturing, education, and utilities. Owning more than 10 offices throughout India, Apex was established in 1988.

APEX GLOBAL BRANDS INC.

5990 SEPULVEDA BLVD STE 600
SHERMAN OAKS, CA 914112500
Phone: 818 908-9868
Fax: -
Web: -

CEO: Henry Stupp
CFO: Steven Brink
HR: -
FYE: February 02
Type: Private

Apex Global Brands (formerly Cherokee Global Brands) owns several trademarks, including Cherokee, Liz Lange, Sideout, Tony Hawk, and Everyday California, and licenses them to retailers and wholesalers of apparel, footwear, and accessories. The main idea behind Apex's business is that large retailers can source merchandise more efficiently than individual brand owners and that licensed brands can sell better for retailers than private labels. In addition to licensing its own brands, Apex helps other brand owners gain licensing contracts. Target, the company's largest customer, accounts for more than half of Apex's revenue; other licensees include Tesco (in Europe) and TJ Maxx. The company changed its name from Cherokee Global Brands to Apex Global Brands in 2019 to reflect its expanded brand portfolio, marketing, and design services.

APEX OIL COMPANY, INC.

8235 FORSYTH BLVD STE 400
SAINT LOUIS, MO 631051644
Phone: 314 889-9600
Fax: –
Web: www.apexoil.com

CEO: Ed Wahl
CFO: John L Hank Jr
HR: Beverly Wessels
FYE: December 31
Type: Private

Apex Oil provides wholesale sales, storage, and distribution of petroleum products including asphalt, kerosene, fuel oil, diesel fuel, heavy oil, gasoline, and marine bunker sales with terminals throughout the US including the East Coast, Gulf Coast, California and throughout the Midwest, with service to international destinations. The company's assets and subsidiaries include Apex Towing (a tugboat and barge cargo business); Petroleum Fuel and Terminal (owner and operator of bulk materials); Enjet (specializing in carbon black and heavy petroleum products); Shanty Creek Resorts, and Clark Oil Trading (specializing in #6 Oil and other heavy petroleum products). Apex Oil was founded in 1932.

API GROUP LIFE SAFETY USA LLC

7026 S TUCSON WAY
CENTENNIAL, CO 801123921
Phone: 303 792-0022
Fax: –
Web: www.wsfp.com

CEO: Joe Depriest
CFO: –
HR: –
FYE: December 31
Type: Private

Western States Fire Protection (WSFP) is sprinkling its own brand of safety west of the Mississippi. The company, a division of APi Group, installs water-based fire sprinklers and other fire suppression systems for the commercial, residential, and industrial markets primarily in the western US. It designs, installs, and maintains fire protection systems at defense, gaming, high-tech, institutional, medical, processing, and sports facilities. Specific projects include installing systems at the Colorado Convention Center and Microsoft's data storage facility in Washington. WSFP also manufactures fire sprinklers at its own fabrication workshops. The company was founded in 1985.

	Annual Growth	12/13	12/14	12/15	12/16	12/17
Sales ($mil.)	5.9%	–	–	274.1	292.6	307.6
Net income ($ mil.)	17.7%	–	–	31.8	40.8	44.0
Market value ($ mil.)	–	–	–	–	–	–
Employees	–	–	–	–	–	2,500

API GROUP, INC.

1100 OLD HIGHWAY 8 NW
NEW BRIGHTON, MN 551126447
Phone: 651 636-4320
Fax: –
Web: www.apigroupinc.com

CEO: –
CFO: –
HR: –
FYE: December 31
Type: Private

Holding company APi Group has a piece of the action in two main sectors: fire protection systems and industrial and specialty construction services. APi boasts about 40 subsidiaries, which operate as independent companies across the US (nearly half of them in Minnesota), the UK, and Canada. Services provided by the company's construction subsidiaries include HVAC and plumbing system installation; electrical, industrial, and mechanical contracting; industrial insulation; and garage door installation. Safety-focused units install a host of fire sprinkler, detection, security, and alarm systems. The family-owned company was founded in 1926 by Reuben Anderson, father of chairman Lee Anderson.

	Annual Growth	12/14	12/15	12/16	12/17	12/18
Sales ($mil.)	15.1%	–	2,448.7	2,608.5	3,046.1	3,730.3
Net income ($ mil.)	5.0%	–	106.2	104.0	112.7	122.9
Market value ($ mil.)	–	–	–	–	–	–
Employees	–	–	–	–	–	4,237

API TECHNOLOGIES CORP.

8061 AVONIA RD
FAIRVIEW, PA 164152829
Phone: 814 474-2207
Fax: –
Web: www.apitech.com

CEO: Rich Sorelle
CFO: Mark McClanahan
HR: Kathy Jividen
FYE: November 30
Type: Private

Spectrum Controls, formerly known as APITech, is a leading global company that specializes in managing and controlling the electromagnetic spectrum. The company has the ability to make the invisible electromagnetic spectrum visible and controllable, which is made possible by its cutting-edge capabilities. Spectrum Control's products are used by customers worldwide in various industries such as defense, industrial, and commercial. These products are essential for critical applications like electronic warfare, radar, C4ISR, space exploration, missile defense, commercial aerospace, wireless communications, medical, oil and gas, and harsh environments. The company has a rich history that dates back to 1981.

APICS, INC.

8430 W BRYN MAWR AVE STE 1000
CHICAGO, IL 606313417
Phone: 773 867-1777
Fax: –
Web: www.ascm.org

CEO: Abe Eshkenazi
CFO: –
HR: –
FYE: December 31
Type: Private

APICS helps its members pick a better way to run their businesses. APICS The Association for Operations Management helps companies and individuals learn how best to develop, produce, and distribute their products. The group provides education and certification programs designed to improve business processes related to inventory, logistics, materials management, production, purchasing, and the supply chain. It counts about 41,000 members from some 15,000 companies worldwide. APICS was founded in 1957 and is composed of more than 200 chapters throughout North America. The name stands for American Production and Inventory Control Society.

	Annual Growth	12/14	12/15	12/17	12/21	12/22
Sales ($mil.)	4.0%	–	24.5	26.9	30.8	32.1
Net income ($ mil.)	–	–	0.3	1.3	2.1	(2.8)
Market value ($ mil.)	–	–	–	–	–	–
Employees	–	–	–	–	–	80

APOGEE 21 HOLDINGS INC

NBB: APHD

80 Broad Street, 5th Floor
New York, NY 10004
Phone: 212 962-4400
Fax: –
Web: www.30dcinc.com

CEO: Henry Pinskier
CFO: Theodore A Greenberg
HR: –
FYE: June 30
Type: Public

30DC offers digital marketing platforms, tools, services, and training through four business units. Its original product was a free 30 day challenge (30DC) training program for Internet marketers. The company also offers digital publishing and marketing tools with MagCast, a platform that enables online content to be published and delivered via Apple's Newstand application, and Market ProMax, a comprehensive online marketing platform that aids in the creation of digital products and e-commerce sites. Formerly a business development company named Infinity Capital Group, the company completed a reverse merger with 30DC in 2010 and adopted its name, business, and management team.

	Annual Growth	06/11	06/12	06/13	06/14	06/15
Sales ($mil.)	(21.0%)	1.9	2.9	2.0	2.8	0.7
Net income ($ mil.)	–	(1.4)	0.0	(0.4)	0.0	(1.6)
Market value ($ mil.)	(50.8%)	0.0	0.0	0.0	0.0	0.0
Employees	2.4%	10	10	14	11	11

APOGEE ENTERPRISES INC   NMS: APOG

4400 West 78th Street, Suite 520   CEO: Ty R Silberhorn
Minneapolis, MN 55435   CFO: Andrew Cox
Phone: 952 835-1874   HR: –
Fax: –   FYE: February 25
Web: www.apog.com   Type: Public

Apogee Enterprises is a leading provider of architectural products and services for enclosing buildings, and high-performance glass and acrylic products used in applications for preservation, protection, and enhanced viewing. Its architectural products and services segment design, engineer, fabricate and install custom glass and aluminum windows, curtainwall, storefront, and entrance systems. It also offers high-performance thermal framing systems, energy-efficient glass coatings, and sun control products. Its large-scale optical (LSO) technologies segment manufactures anti-reflective, UV-protected glass and acrylic under the Tru Vue brand. Tru Vue products are sold through national and regional retail chains. The company generates the majority of its revenue in the US.

	Annual Growth	03/19*	02/20	02/21	02/22	02/23
Sales ($mil.)	0.7%	1,402.6	1,387.4	1,230.8	1,314.0	1,440.7
Net income ($ mil.)	22.9%	45.7	61.9	15.4	3.5	104.1
Market value ($ mil.)	6.2%	800.7	671.0	831.2	1,011.9	1,019.7
Employees	(8.5%)	7,000	7,200	6,100	5,500	4,900

*Fiscal year change

APOGEE TECHNOLOGY, INC.

129 Morgan Drive   CEO: Herbert M Stein
Norwood, MA 02062   CFO: Paul J Murphy
Phone: 781 551-9450   HR: –
Fax: –   FYE: December 31
Web: www.apogeebio.com   Type: Public

Apogee Technology hopes that a combination of nanotechnology and drugs will produce a profitable business. The company is developing its PyraDerm drug delivery system, which uses nanotechnology to deliver drugs and medicine through contact with the skin, avoiding the need for painful injections. Prior to focusing on its PyraDerm product the company had developed and manufactured high-end loudspeakers; Apogee sold that business to SigmaTel in order to move into the nanotechnology market.

	Annual Growth	12/06	12/07	12/08	12/09	12/10
Sales ($mil.)	(56.9%)	1.9	0.2	0.0	–	0.0
Net income ($ mil.)	–	(3.0)	(3.2)	(4.0)	(2.2)	(1.6)
Market value ($ mil.)	(26.4%)	17.5	6.7	8.6	13.8	5.1
Employees	(15.9%)	12	14	13	8	6

APOLLO COMMERCIAL REAL ESTATE FINANCE INC.   NYS: ARI

c/o Apollo Global Management, Inc., 9 West 57th Street, 42nd Floor   CEO: Stuart A Rothstein
New York, NY 10019   CFO: Anastasia Mironova
Phone: 212 515-3200   HR: –
Fax: –   FYE: December 31
Web: www.apolloreit.com   Type: Public

Apollo Commercial Real Estate Finance thinks the sky is the limit for commercial property loans. The New York-based mortgage real estate investment trust (REIT) originates, acquires, and invest performing US commercial first mortgage loans, subordinate financings and other commercial real estate-related debt investments. About 85%40% of its about $6.4 billion investment portfolio is made up of commercial mortgage loans, while another about 15% is made up of subordinate loans. Formed in 2009 by Apollo Global Management, the REIT is externally managed by ACREFI Management (an indirect subsidiary of Apollo Global Management).

	Annual Growth	12/19	12/20	12/21	12/22	12/23
Assets ($mil.)	7.8%	6,888.4	6,940.0	8,416.7	9,568.4	9,296.7
Net income ($ mil.)	(29.1%)	230.2	18.4	223.5	265.2	58.1
Market value ($ mil.)	(10.5%)	2,585.4	1,579.0	1,860.3	1,521.0	1,659.6
Employees		–	–	–	–	–

APOLLO EDUCATION GROUP, INC.

4035 S RIVERPOINT PKWY   CEO: Gregory W Cappelli
PHOENIX, AZ 850400723   CFO: Gregory J Iverson
Phone: 480 966-5394   HR: Corey Milley
Fax: –   FYE: August 31
Web: www.apollo.edu   Type: Private

Apollo's creed could be that we all deserve the chance to advance. The for-profit Apollo Education Group provides educational programs through a number of subsidiaries, including online stalwart University of Phoenix. The largest private university in the US, the University of Phoenix accounts for the majority of Apollo's sales; it offers degree programs ranging from associate's to doctoral. Other schools include Western International University (graduate and undergraduate courses, this entity is being wound down), South Africa's MBA-grantor Milpark Education, and UK-based BPP Holdings, a provider of legal and financial professional training. Apollo was founded in 1973.

APOLLO GLOBAL MANAGEMENT INC (NEW)   NYS: APO

9 West 57th Street, 42nd Floor   CEO: –
New York, NY 10019   CFO: –
Phone: 212 515-3200   HR: –
Fax: –   FYE: December 31
Web: –   Type: Public

Founded in 1990, Apollo Asset Management is a high-growth, global alternative asset manager. It raise, invest and manage funds on behalf of some of the world's most prominent pension, endowment and sovereign wealth funds, as well as other institutional and individual investors. Apollo has some $497.6 billion of assets under management spread among credit, private equity, and real assets. It specializes in buying distressed businesses and believes that the long-term capital it manages also leaves it well-positioned during economic downturns. The company has offices in the US, Europe, and Asia.

	Annual Growth	12/19	12/20	12/21	12/22	12/23
Sales ($mil.)	82.7%	2,931.8	2,354.0	5,951.0	10,968	32,644
Net income ($ mil.)	56.4%	843.2	156.6	1,839.0	(3,213.0)	5,047.0
Market value ($ mil.)	18.2%	27,088	27,809	41,123	36,218	52,910
Employees	36.1%	1,421	1,729	–	2,540	4,879

APOLLO RESIDENTIAL MORTGAGE, INC.

9 W 57TH ST FL 43   CEO: –
NEW YORK, NY 100192700   CFO: –
Phone: 212 515-3200   HR: –
Fax: –   FYE: December 31
Web: www.apolloresidentialmortgage.com   Type: Private

The gods at Apollo Global Management are trying their luck with the residential mortgage market. The alternative asset manager formed Apollo Residential Mortgage to invest in residential mortgage-backed securities (MBS) and collateralized mortgage obligations (CMOs) guaranteed by Fannie Mae, Freddie Mac, and Ginnie Mae. A real estate investment trust, the company is externally managed by ARM Manager, an indirect subsidiary of Apollo Global Management. Formed in March 2011, Apollo Residential Mortgage went public later that year via a $205 million initial public offering (IPO).

APOLLO THEATRE FOUNDATION INC

253 W 125TH ST
NEW YORK, NY 100274408
Phone: 212 531-5300
Fax: –
Web: www.apollotheater.org

CEO: –
CFO: –
HR: –
FYE: June 30
Type: Private

Once again it's showtime at the Apollo Theater. The Apollo Theater Foundation was created to manage and operate the historic building, considered by many to be the spiritual home of African-American music in New York. The foundation has reinvented the former music hall as an arts center with plays and musicals being responsible for about 80% of its revenue. As part of a historic renovation project, New York governor David Paterson's Downstate Revitalization Fund will help to restore, enhance, and sustain the Apollo Theater. Improvements include work above the auditorium, work on the building's western wall, roof and wall repair, asbestos abatement, and heating and cooling system replacement.

	Annual Growth	06/09	06/10	06/11	06/12	06/14
Sales ($mil.)	3.2%	–	14.2	12.8	13.9	16.1
Net income ($ mil.)	(13.3%)	–	4.2	2.6	3.9	2.4
Market value ($ mil.)	–	–	–	–	–	–
Employees	–	–	–	–	–	145

APP WINDDOWN, LLC

747 WAREHOUSE ST
LOS ANGELES, CA 900211106
Phone: 213 488-0226
Fax: –
Web: –

CEO: Chelsea Grayson
CFO: –
HR: –
FYE: December 31
Type: Private

American Apparel wants you to be hip and comfortable inside and out. It makes and sells logo-free T-shirts, tanks, yoga pants, and more for men, women, and children -- and does it all from its California factory, rather than exporting labor overseas. Its 235-plus retail stores in 20 countries carry the company's Classic Girl, Standard American, Classic Baby, and Sustainable Edition brands, among others. Known for its fair treatment of factory workers but also for alleged sexual harassment of staff by its CEO, American Apparel has seen its share of troubles. In late 2016 the company filed for Chapter 11 bankruptcy protection for the second time in just over a year. It had emerged earlier in 2016 from Chapter 11 bankruptcy protection, which was filed in October 2015.

APPALACHIAN POWER CO.

1 Riverside Plaza
Columbus, OH 43215-2373
Phone: 614 716-1000
Fax: –
Web: www.aep.com

CEO: Nicholas K Akins
CFO: Brian X Tierney
HR: –
FYE: December 31
Type: Public

When they're not out enjoying the scenery, Virginians and West Virginians count on Appalachian Power to keep indoor temperatures stable. A subsidiary of American Electric Power, Appalachian Power serves about 960,000 residential and business customers in southwestern Virginia and southern West Virginia, and a small portion of northwestern Tennessee. The electric utility operates about 53,300 miles of distribution and transmission lines. It operates coal-fired, gas-fired and hydroelectric plants that give it about 8,020 MW of capacity, and it markets power to wholesale customers in the region.

	Annual Growth	12/18	12/19	12/20	12/21	12/22
Sales ($mil.)	4.4%	2,967.5	2,924.7	2,796.2	3,105.2	3,519.9
Net income ($ mil.)	1.7%	367.8	306.3	369.7	348.9	394.2
Market value ($ mil.)	–	–	–	–	–	–
Employees	(2.1%)	1,797	1,699	1,652	1,617	1,650

APPALACHIAN REGIONAL COMMISSION INC

1666 CONNECTICUT AVE NW STE 700
WASHINGTON, DC 200091068
Phone: 202 884-7700
Fax: –
Web: www.arc.gov

CEO: –
CFO: –
HR: Allison Thiriez
FYE: September 30
Type: Private

With 23 million people, nearly half of them rural, spread across 200 thousand square miles in the Appalachian mountains, Appalachia needs help shedding its backwoods image. That's where the federal-state partnership Appalachian Regional Commission (ARC) comes in. Its Area Development Program and Highway Program are designed to increase jobs and per capita income, improve economic competition, develop infrastructure, and reduce isolation in the region. Projects include improving local water and sewer systems, increasing health care access, creating jobs, and providing community strategic planning assistance. The forerunner to ARC was created by President Kennedy in 1963. It became official in 1965.

APPALACHIAN REGIONAL HEALTHCARE, INC.

2260 EXECUTIVE DR
LEXINGTON, KY 405054808
Phone: 859 226-2440
Fax: –
Web: www.arh.org

CEO: Jerry W Haynes
CFO: Byron Gabbard
HR: –
FYE: June 30
Type: Private

Under-the-weather coal miners (and their daughters) can turn to Appalachian Regional Healthcare (ARH) for medical services. The not-for-profit health system serves residents of eastern Kentucky and southern West Virginia through a dozen hospitals with more than 1,000 beds, as well as dozens of clinics, home health care agencies, HomeCare Stores, and retail pharmacies. Its largest hospital in Hazard, Kentucky, has 310 beds and features an inpatient psychiatric unit that serves as the state mental health facility. Several of the system's hospitals are Critical Access Hospitals, a federal government designation for rural community hospitals that operate in medically underserved areas.

	Annual Growth	06/18	06/19	06/20	06/21	06/22
Sales ($mil.)	13.5%	–	760.3	868.6	993.9	1,112.3
Net income ($ mil.)	–	–	1.2	23.2	275.6	(10.5)
Market value ($ mil.)	–	–	–	–	–	–
Employees	–	–	–	–	–	4,520

APPALACHIAN STATE UNIVERSITY INC

438 ACADEMY ST RM 340
BOONE, NC 286080001
Phone: 828 262-2000
Fax: –
Web: www.appstate.edu

CEO: Alice G Roess
CFO: –
HR: Tracy Espy
FYE: June 30
Type: Private

Appalachian State University, located in the heart of North Carolina's Blue Ridge Mountains, has a student enrollment of about 17,000 graduate and undergraduate students. The school has a student-teacher ratio of 17:1. Part of the University of North Carolina system, the university offers roughly 140 degree programs and 1,500 courses. Appalachian State was founded in 1899 as Watauga Academy by Blanford B. Dougherty and his brother Dauphin D. Dougherty to educate teachers for the mountains of northwestern North Carolina. It became known as Appalachian State Teachers College in 1929 and adopted its current name in 1967.

	Annual Growth	06/14	06/15	06/16	06/17	06/18
Sales ($mil.)	4.3%	–	194.6	204.6	217.0	220.5
Net income ($ mil.)	100.3%	–	7.3	20.7	21.1	58.5
Market value ($ mil.)	–	–	–	–	–	–
Employees	–	–	–	–	–	3,390

APPIAN CORP
NMS: APPN

7950 Jones Branch Drive
McLean, VA 22102
Phone: 703 442-8844
Fax: -
Web: www.appian.com

CEO: -
CFO: -
HR: -
FYE: December 31
Type: Public

Appian Corporation provides a process automation platform that helps organizations unleash digital innovation and drive efficiency. Appian is one of the only enterprise software vendors that offer Workflow, Artificial Intelligence, or AI, Robotic Process Automation, or RPA, Data Fabric, and Process Mining in one fully integrated low-code platform. Its platform allows organizations to deliver excellent customer experiences, maximize operational efficiency, and effortlessly ensure compliance with laws and regulations. It provides a unified platform with the capabilities its customers need to quickly achieve process excellence. The McLean, Virginia-based company has about 925 customers, of which over 710 were commercial and roughly 215 were government customers. It makes the majority of its revenue from its domestic markets. Appian was founded in 1999.

	Annual Growth	12/19	12/20	12/21	12/22	12/23
Sales ($mil.)	20.3%	260.4	304.6	369.3	468.0	545.4
Net income ($ mil.)	-	(50.7)	(33.5)	(88.6)	(150.9)	(111.4)
Market value ($ mil.)	(0.4%)	2,803.3	11,892	4,784.2	2,388.8	2,763.0
Employees	15.2%	1,275	1,460	1,798	2,307	2,243

APPLE AMERICAN GROUP LLC

6200 OAK TREE BLVD STE 250
INDEPENDENCE, OH 441316943
Phone: 216 525-2775
Fax: -
Web: www.flynn.com

CEO: -
CFO: -
HR: -
FYE: December 27
Type: Private

This company must really enjoy casual dining in its neighborhood. Apple American Group is the largest franchisee of Applebee's with about 450 Applebee's Neighborhood Grill & Bar locations in about two dozen states. The #1 casual dining chain in the US, Applebee's restaurants offer a full-service menu of beef, chicken, and seafood entrees, along with a wide selection of appetizers. Apple American's restaurants are found from coast to coast with large concentrations in the Midwest (Ohio, Indiana, Pennsylvania) and on the West Coast (California, Washington). Founded in 1998 by CEO Greg Flynn, Apple American is controlled by private equity firm Weston Presidio Service.

	Annual Growth	12/05	12/06	12/07	12/08	12/09
Sales ($mil.)	19.0%	-	-	339.0	431.1	479.8
Net income ($ mil.)	13783.8%	-	-	0.0	9.9	19.3
Market value ($ mil.)	-	-	-	-	-	-
Employees	-	-	-	-	-	5,500

APPLE INC
NMS: AAPL

One Apple Park Way
Cupertino, CA 95014
Phone: 408 996-1010
Fax: 408 974-2483
Web: www.apple.com

CEO: Timothy D Cook
CFO: Lucca Maestri
HR: -
FYE: September 30
Type: Public

Apple designs, manufactures and markets smartphones, personal computers, tablets, wearables and accessories. The company also offers and sells a variety of related services. Apple products include its famous iPhone, which is the company's line of smartphones basing on its iOS operating system. The company recently released its iPhone 14 product line last year. Other apple products also include Mac computers and iPad tablets Apple Music, the Apple Watch, and other wearable devices. Its' services include AppleCare, Cloud Services, Digital content, and Payment services (ApplePay). Apple has entered entertainment with the Apple TV+ streaming service. More than 60% of Apple's revenue comes from outside the Americas.

	Annual Growth	09/19	09/20	09/21	09/22	09/23
Sales ($mil.)	10.2%	260,174	274,515	365,817	394,328	383,285
Net income ($ mil.)	15.1%	55,256	57,411	94,680	99,803	96,995
Market value ($ mil.)	(5.9%)	3,402.66 4	1,745,961	2,284,615	2,339,196	2,662,326
Employees	4.1%	137,000	147,000	154,000	164,000	161,000

APPLIED CARD SYSTEMS INC.

5401 BROKEN SOUND BLVD NW
BOCA RATON, FL 334873512
Phone: 561 995-8820
Fax: -
Web: www.appliedcard.com

CEO: Rocco A Abessinio
CFO: -
HR: -
FYE: December 31
Type: Private

Applied Card Systems is the servicing arm for Applied Bank, a subprime consumer lender that issues secured and unsecured credit cards to customers with little or no credit history. Applied Card Systems processes payments from and provides customer service to more than 500,000 holders of subprime Visa and MasterCard accounts. Applied Card Systems also services credit card accounts for third-party issuers, primarily small and midsized financial institutions. Rocco Abessinio is the founder of both Applied Card Bank and Applied Card Systems, which was formed in 1987. The company has offices in Florida and Pennsylvania.

	Annual Growth	12/05	12/06	12/07	12/08	12/09
Sales ($mil.)	(24.3%)	-	-	282.4	251.2	162.0
Net income ($ mil.)	(61.1%)	-	-	144.0	145.4	21.8
Market value ($ mil.)	-	-	-	-	-	-
Employees	-	-	-	-	-	126

APPLIED DIGITAL CORP
NBB: ADIG

3811 Turtle Creek, Blvd., Suite 2100
Dallas, TX 75219
Phone: 214 556-2465
Fax: -
Web: -

CEO: Wes Cummins
CFO: David Rench
HR: -
FYE: May 31
Type: Public

Applied Science Products (ASP, formerly Flight Safety Technologies) has its sights set on another atmosphere. Through its Advanced Plasma Products unit, ASP develops products using glow discharge plasma technology, which uses electricity to purify air at standard pressure and room temperature. Its TriClean Pro stand-alone air purifier removes bacteria, viruses, allergens, molds, and other contaminants in settings where air quality is an issue, such as hospitals, schools, and nursing homes. Other products in development include a disinfectant chamber to rid surfaces of microbial contamination, and the PlasmaGen DNA sample preparation unit. Funding issues forced Flight Safety to change its name and direction in 2009.

	Annual Growth	05/07	05/08	05/21	05/22	05/23
Sales ($mil.)	25.1%	1.5	0.3	-	8.5	55.4
Net income ($ mil.)	-	(2.8)	(3.3)	(0.6)	(23.5)	(44.6)
Market value ($ mil.)	-	-	-	-	-	-
Employees	15.5%	12	7	-	55	121

APPLIED DNA SCIENCES INC
NAS: APDN

50 Health Sciences Drive
Stony Brook, NY 11790
Phone: 631 240-8800
Fax: -
Web: www.adnas.com

CEO: James A Hayward
CFO: Beth M Jantzen
HR: -
FYE: September 30
Type: Public

Counterfeiters needn't apply here. Applied DNA Sciences makes anti-counterfeiting and product authentication solutions. Its products are encoded with botanical DNA sequences that can distinguish counterfeits from the genuine article. The DNA markers (which hold the SigNature DNA brand) can be employed in ink, glue, holograms, microchips, and paint, and are then used to tag documents, currency, event tickets, and clothing labels. The company applies its SigNature markers to art and collectibles, fine wine, consumer products, digital recording media, pharmaceuticals, and homeland security products.

	Annual Growth	09/19	09/20	09/21	09/22	09/23
Sales ($mil.)	25.5%	5.4	1.9	9.0	18.2	13.4
Net income ($ mil.)	-	(8.6)	(13.0)	(14.3)	(8.3)	(9.9)
Market value ($ mil.)	52.5%	3.1	105.6	73.6	15.4	16.5
Employees	1.9%	51	61	101	69	55

APPLIED ENERGETICS INC — NBB: AERG

9070 S. Rita Road, Suite 1500
Tucson, AZ 85747
Phone: 520 628-7415
Fax: –
Web: www.aergs.com

CEO: Gregory J Quarles
CFO: –
HR: –
FYE: December 31
Type: Public

Bullets?!! We don't need no stinkin' bullets -- not with the Buck Rogers technology of Applied Energetics. The company is developing Laser Guided Energy and Laser Induced Plasma Channel directed-energy weapons for sale to the US government. In plain English? Laser-guided, man-made lightning! Applied Energetics is developing more compact laser sources and field testing its technology for mobile platforms such as tanks, Humvees, and personnel carriers. Depending on the military situation, the charge can be set to stun or kill people, or to disable vehicles. Applied Energetics also develops technology for neutralizing car bombs and other explosives.

	Annual Growth	12/19	12/20	12/21	12/22	12/23
Sales ($mil.)	–	–	0.2	–	1.3	2.6
Net income ($ mil.)	–	(5.6)	(3.2)	(5.4)	(5.8)	(7.4)
Market value ($ mil.)	61.0%	69.7	63.4	507.0	414.0	467.9
Employees	–	1	2	7	14	–

APPLIED INDUSTRIAL TECHNOLOGIES, INC. — NYS: AIT

One Applied Plaza
Cleveland, OH 44115
Phone: 216 426-4000
Fax: –
Web: www.applied.com

CEO: Neil A Schrimsher
CFO: David K Wells
HR: –
FYE: June 30
Type: Public

Applied Industrial Technologies leading distributor and solutions provider of industrial motion, power, control, and automation technologies. It offers a selection of more than 8.8 million stock-keeping units with a focus on industrial bearings, power transmission products, fluid power components, and systems, specialty flow control, and advanced factory automation solutions. Customers are concentrated across the maintenance, repair, and operations (MRO) and original equipment manufacturer (OEM) markets. The company markets its products with a set of service solutions including inventory management, engineering, design, repair, assembly, and systems integration, as well as customized mechanical, fabricated rubber, and shop services. Applied Industrial Technologies traces its historical roots back to 1923. Its largest market is the US, which generates nearly 90% of its revenue.

	Annual Growth	06/19	06/20	06/21	06/22	06/23
Sales ($mil.)	6.2%	3,472.7	3,245.7	3,235.9	3,810.7	4,412.8
Net income ($ mil.)	24.6%	144.0	24.0	144.8	257.4	346.7
Market value ($ mil.)	23.9%	2,378.6	2,411.8	3,520.1	3,717.6	5,598.7
Employees	(1.7%)	6,650	6,200	5,947	6,100	6,200

APPLIED MATERIALS, INC. — NMS: AMAT

3050 Bowers Avenue, P.O. Box 58039
Santa Clara, CA 95052-8039
Phone: 408 727-5555
Fax: –
Web: www.appliedmaterials.com

CEO: Gary E Dickerson
CFO: Brice Hill
HR: –
FYE: October 29
Type: Public

Applied Materials is the leading producer of machines for semiconductor, display, and related industries. The company's semiconductor systems segment handles the complex processes of making chips, from laying down patterns on silicon at the beginning to packaging them for shipment at the end. Its display business produces equipment for manufacturing liquid crystal displays (LCDs), organic light-emitting diodes (OLEDs), and other display technologies for TVs, personal computers, and smart phones. The services business offers manufacturing consulting and automation software. Asian customers account for about 80% of revenue.

	Annual Growth	10/19	10/20	10/21	10/22	10/23
Sales ($mil.)	16.1%	14,608	17,202	23,063	25,785	26,517
Net income ($ mil.)	26.2%	2,706.0	3,619.0	5,888.0	6,525.0	6,856.0
Market value ($ mil.)	23.9%	46,415	50,771	113,829	74,737	109,373
Employees	11.5%	22,000	24,000	27,000	33,000	34,000

APPLIED MICRO CIRCUITS CORP

4555 GREAT AMERICA PKWY # 6
SANTA CLARA, CA 950541243
Phone: 408 542-8600
Fax: –
Web: www.macom.com

CEO: –
CFO: –
HR: –
FYE: March 31
Type: Private

For Applied Micro Circuits, X marks the spot for its chips. The company's lines of chips bearing the "X" are aimed at data centers, scientific and high-performance computing, and enterprise applications. The X-Gene and X-Weave families of chips, based on the ARM architecture, provide computing power and high-speed connectivity for telecommunications applications while operating on a low-level of energy. The company outsources manufacturing to TSMC and UMC. Its top customers include Avnet (26% of sales) and Wintec (20%). Applied Micro gets 57% of its sales from outside the US.

APPLIED MINERALS INC — NBB: AMNL

1200 Silver City Road, P.O. Box 432
Eureka, UT 84628
Phone: 435 433-2059
Fax: –
Web: www.appliedminerals.com

CEO: Mario Concha
CFO: Christopher T Carney
HR: –
FYE: December 31
Type: Public

Applied Minerals (formerly Atlas Mining) develops the Dragon mine in Utah. The 230-acre site contains a deposit of halloysite clay, a substance used as an intermediate ingredient in chemicals manufacturing as well as in making bone china, fine china, and porcelain. The mine is believed to be the only source of halloysite clay in the Western Hemisphere suitable for large-scale commercial production. In addition to halloysite, the Dragon mine contains other clays, including kaolinite, ilite, and smectite, as well as iron oxide ores such as hematite, goethite, and manganese. The Dragon property contains a measured resource of nearly 600,000 tons of clay and more than 2 million tons of iron ore.

	Annual Growth	12/17	12/18	12/19	12/20	12/21
Sales ($mil.)	(12.9%)	2.4	4.9	0.5	0.9	1.4
Net income ($ mil.)	–	(14.9)	(3.3)	(6.0)	(3.3)	(3.3)
Market value ($ mil.)	(33.2%)	12.0	10.9	1.4	8.0	2.4
Employees	(14.3%)	13	13	11	10	7

APPLIED OPTOELECTRONICS INC — NMS: AAOI

13139 Jess Pirtle Blvd.
Sugar Land, TX 77478
Phone: 281 295-1800
Fax: –
Web: www.ao-inc.com

CEO: Chih-Hsiang Lin
CFO: Stefan J Murry
HR: –
FYE: December 31
Type: Public

Applied Optoelectronics is a leading, vertically integrated provider of fiber-optic networking products, primarily for four networking end-markets: internet data center, cable television, (CATV), telecommunications, (telecom) and fiber-to-the-home (FTTH). The company designs and manufactures a range of optical communications products at varying levels of integration, from components, subassemblies and modules to complete turn-key equipment. Applied Optoelectronics designs, manufactures and integrates its own analog and digital lasers using proprietary Molecular Beam Epitaxy (MBE) and Metal Organic Chemical Vapor Deposition (MOCVD) fabrication process. About 95% of sales are generated from customers in Taiwan and China.

	Annual Growth	12/19	12/20	12/21	12/22	12/23
Sales ($mil.)	3.3%	190.9	234.6	211.6	222.8	217.6
Net income ($ mil.)	–	(66.0)	(58.5)	(54.2)	(66.4)	(56.0)
Market value ($ mil.)	12.9%	453.2	324.6	196.1	72.1	737.0
Employees	(8.9%)	3,115	2,682	2,534	2,213	2,149

APPLIED RESEARCH ASSOCIATES, INC.

4300 SAN MATEO BLVD NE STE A220
ALBUQUERQUE, NM 871101229
Phone: 505 883-3636
Fax: –
Web: www.ara.com

CEO: –
CFO: –
HR: –
FYE: September 30
Type: Private

Applied Research Associates, Inc. (ARA) offers science and engineering research to solve problems of national importance. ARA delivers leading-edge products and innovative solutions for national defense, energy, homeland security, aerospace, healthcare, transportation, and manufacturing. With locations in the US and Canada, ARA offers a broad range of technical expertise in defense technologies, civil engineering, computer software and simulation, systems analysis, biomedical engineering, environmental technologies, and blast testing and measurement. Founded in 1979, the company is owned by its employees.

	Annual Growth	09/09	09/10	09/11	09/12	09/13
Sales ($mil.)	(4.0%)	–	–	232.1	226.8	213.7
Net income ($ mil.)	1.3%	–	–	6.0	2.8	6.1
Market value ($ mil.)	–	–	–	–	–	–
Employees	–	–	–	–	–	1,650

APPLIED TRUST ENGINEERING, INC.

1033 WALNUT ST STE 300
BOULDER, CO 803025114
Phone: 303 245-4524
Fax: –
Web: www.flexential.com

CEO: Trent R Hein
CFO: –
HR: –
FYE: December 31
Type: Private

Applied Trust Engineering is ready to be the trusty sidekick on the glory road of IT services. The consulting firm provides information technology expertise focused on the areas of security, performance, availability, incident management, and ecoinfrastructure. The company is vendor neutral, offering advice on the best hardware and software solutions to enhance security, improve performance, and ensure critical system availability. Incident management services help clients investigate and respond to suspected security breaches. The firm's ecoinfrastructure services help clients reduce energy costs, decrease data center footprint, and reduce operational costs through environmentally conscious technology choices.

	Annual Growth	12/06	12/07	12/08	12/09	12/10
Sales ($mil.)	7.6%	–	–	2.9	3.1	3.4
Net income ($ mil.)	89.2%	–	–	0.0	0.0	0.1
Market value ($ mil.)	–	–	–	–	–	–
Employees	–	–	–	–	–	22

APPLIED VISUAL SCIENCES INC.

NBB: APVS

525K East Market Street, #116
Leesburg, VA 20176
Phone: 703 539-6190
Fax: –
Web: www.appliedvs.com

CEO: William J Donovan
CFO: Gregory E Hare
HR: –
FYE: December 31
Type: Public

Applied Visual Sciences sees a new future for itself. Formerly Guardian Technologies, the company changed its name and restructured its operations in July 2010. It primarily operates through two subsidiaries: Guardian Technologies (homeland security and defense technology) and Signature Mapping Medical Sciences (health care technology). Its security and defense products include threat identification and screening software for airlines, while its health care offerings include medical image processing applications.

	Annual Growth	12/10	12/11	12/12	12/13	12/14
Sales ($mil.)	–	0.1	0.0	–	–	–
Net income ($ mil.)	–	(3.7)	(1.2)	(1.8)	(2.4)	(0.8)
Market value ($ mil.)	(44.6%)	34.6	3.7	2.6	8.4	3.2
Employees	(28.1%)	15	7	7	7	4

APPLIEDINFO PARTNERS, INC.

28 WORLDS FAIR DR
SOMERSET, NJ 088731391
Phone: 732 507-7300
Fax: –
Web: www.appliedinfo.com

CEO: Betty Lau
CFO: –
HR: –
FYE: December 31
Type: Private

Appliedinfo Partners provides interactive training, software solutions, and digital communications services. The company's DIF platform that lets users collaborate to create interactive courseware. It integrates into video, 2D and 3D graphics, and UNITY game-based simulations. In digital marketing, AppliedInfo's DivTRAK a a leading supplier diversity management software. It provides digital agency services serving B2B, B2C, and non-profit organizations. Betty and John Lau, who are married, established Appliedinfo and own the company. It was founded in 1990.

	Annual Growth	12/03	12/04	12/05	12/06	12/18
Sales ($mil.)	(2.4%)	–	10.2	11.9	10.6	7.3
Net income ($ mil.)	(14.3%)	–	0.9	1.2	0.4	0.1
Market value ($ mil.)	–	–	–	–	–	–
Employees	–	–	–	–	–	59

APPLOVIN CORP

NMS: APP

1100 Page Mill Road
Palo Alto, CA 94304
Phone: 800 839-9646
Fax: –
Web: www.applovin.com

CEO: –
CFO: –
HR: –
FYE: December 31
Type: Public

AppLovin is a leading growth platform for developers. Through AppLovin's technologies and scaled distribution, developers are able to manage, optimize, and analyze their marketing investments, and improve the monetization of their apps. The key elements of its solutions are delivered through the AppLovin Core Technologies and AppLovin Software Platform. Its Core Technologies consist of its AXON machine-learning recommendation engine, App Graph, and elastic cloud infrastructure. AppLovin Software Platform is a comprehensive suite of tools for developers to get their mobile apps discovered and downloaded by the right users, optimize return on marketing spend, and maximize monetization of engagement. Its Software Platform is comprised of three solutions ? AppDiscovery, Adjust and MAX. With nearly 20 offices around the world, AppLovin earns around 60% of its revenue in the US.

	Annual Growth	12/19	12/20	12/21	12/22	12/23
Sales ($mil.)	34.8%	994.1	1,451.1	2,793.1	2,817.1	3,283.1
Net income ($ mil.)	31.6%	119.0	(125.2)	35.4	(192.7)	356.7
Market value ($ mil.)	–	–	–	32,038	3,579.0	13,544
Employees	–	–	902	1,594	1,707	1,734

APPROACH RESOURCES INC.

7924 BROADWAY ST STE 104
PEARLAND, TX 775817933
Phone: 817 989-9000
Fax: –
Web: –

CEO: Sergei Krylov
CFO: –
HR: –
FYE: December 31
Type: Private

Approach Resources takes a different approach to natural gas and oil exploration, development, and production. Specializing in finding and exploiting unconventional reservoirs, the company operates primarily in West Texas' Permian Basin. It also has operations in East Texas. The company's unconventional designation results from a focus on developing natural gas reserves in tight gas sands and shale areas, necessitating a reliance on advanced completion, fracturing, and drilling techniques. In 2012 Approach Resources reported proved reserves of 95.5 million barrels of oil equivalent.

APPTECH CORP

2002 TIMBERLOCH PL # 200　　　　　　　　　　　　CEO: Luke D'Angelo
THE WOODLANDS, TX 773801171　　　　　　　　　　CFO: Gary Wachs
Phone: 281 296-5778　　　　　　　　　　　　　　　HR: –
Fax: –　　　　　　　　　　　　　　　　　　　　　FYE: December 31
Web: –　　　　　　　　　　　　　　　　　　　　　Type: Private

When nutritional supplements didn't transform its fortunes, AppTech decided to apply itself elsewhere. Formerly known as Natural Nutrition, the company it lost its primary customer in 2009 and switched its focus to mobile device applications. AppTech plans to create an online marketplace for not just Apple apps, but apps that will run on Motorola Mobility's Android, the BlackBerry, Palm smartphones, and China Mobile's new OPhone. The company plans to act a middleman for US-based app developers and mobile users in the emerging markets of Brazil, China, India. The company will translate English-based apps and sell them to wireless carriers overseas.

APPTIX, INC.

13461 SUNRISE VALLEY DR STE 300　　　　　　　　CEO: –
HERNDON, VA 201713283　　　　　　　　　　　　　CFO: –
Phone: 703 890-2800　　　　　　　　　　　　　　　HR: –
Fax: –　　　　　　　　　　　　　　　　　　　　　FYE: December 31
Web: www.apptix.com　　　　　　　　　　　　　　　Type: Private

Apptix has an appetite for e-mail. The company provides hosted communications services including Microsoft Exchange e-mail, mobile e-email, SharePoint collaboration, VoIP (Voice over Internet Protocol) phone services, Web conferencing, website hosting, online backup, and other services. In addition to Microsoft, the company counts Mozy, Global Relay, PARALLELS, and BlackBerry among its technology partners. Its channel partners include Bell Canada, Fujitsu, IBM Global Services, and SAVVIS. Once a provider of services to small businesses, Apptix has added midsized and large enterprise subscribers. The company operates in the US.

APPVION, INC.

825 E WISCONSIN AVE　　　　　　　　　　　　　　CEO: –
APPLETON, WI 549113873　　　　　　　　　　　　　CFO: –
Phone: 920 734-9841　　　　　　　　　　　　　　　HR: –
Fax: –　　　　　　　　　　　　　　　　　　　　　FYE: December 31
Web: www.appvion.com　　　　　　　　　　　　　　Type: Private

Appvion (formerly Appleton Papers) has an app for that -- paper. The company manufactures specialty coated paper products, including carbonless and security papers, and thermal papers. It is the world's #1 producer of carbonless paper. Sold under the NCR Paper brand, carbonless paper is used in multi-part business forms (such as invoices). Appvion makes security papers for government documents and coated products for point-of-sale displays. Its thermal papers are used in coupons, gaming and transportation tickets, and medical charts. Its Encapsys segment makes microencapsulation (a microscopic wall around a substance) materials. Appvion is the primary operating subsidiary of Paperweight Development Corp.

APRIA HEALTHCARE GROUP LLC

7353 COMPANY DR　　　　　　　　　　　　　　　　CEO: Daniel J Stark
INDIANAPOLIS, IN 462379274　　　　　　　　　　　CFO: Debra L Morris
Phone: 949 639-2000　　　　　　　　　　　　　　　HR: Jodee Mountain
Fax: –　　　　　　　　　　　　　　　　　　　　　FYE: December 31
Web: www.apria.com　　　　　　　　　　　　　　　Type: Private

Apria Healthcare Group is one of the nation's largest providers of home healthcare equipment and related services. The company provides supplemental oxygen, ventilators, nebulizers, glucose monitors and support, and sleep monitoring equipment and medication to patients with emphysema, diabetes, sleep apnea, negative pressure wound therapy (NPWT), and other respiratory conditions. Serving approximately 2 million patients from its approximately 280 locations, Apria also delivers home medical equipment such as walkers, hospital beds, and wound therapy devices.

APTARGROUP INC.

265 Exchange Drive, Suite 301　　　　　　　　　　NYS: ATR
Crystal Lake, IL 60014　　　　　　　　　　　　　CEO: Stephan B Tanda
Phone: 815 477-0424　　　　　　　　　　　　　　　CFO: Robert Kuhn
Fax: 815 477-0481　　　　　　　　　　　　　　　　HR: Grainne O'meara
Web: www.aptar.com　　　　　　　　　　　　　　　FYE: December 31
　　　　　　　　　　　　　　　　　　　　　　　　Type: Public

AptarGroup is a known leader in the design and manufacturing of a broad range of drug delivery, consumer product dispensing, and active material science solutions and services for the pharmaceutical, beauty, personal care, home care, food, and beverage markets. The company's primary products are dispensing pumps, closures, aerosol valves, elastomeric primary packaging components, active material science solutions, and digital health solutions. The company has operations in about 20 countries, including countries from Europe, Asia, and Latin America. The majority of the company's sales are generated internationally.

	Annual Growth	12/19	12/20	12/21	12/22	12/23
Sales ($mil.)	5.1%	2,859.7	2,929.3	3,227.2	3,322.2	3,487.5
Net income ($ mil.)	4.1%	242.2	214.0	244.1	239.3	284.5
Market value ($ mil.)	1.7%	7,619.4	9,021.1	8,071.4	7,247.7	8,146.6
Employees	(0.4%)	14,000	13,000	13,000	13,500	13,800

APX, INC.

2150 N 1ST ST STE 200　　　　　　　　　　　　　CEO: Joseph Varnas
SAN JOSE, CA 951312020　　　　　　　　　　　　　CFO: Kent Liang
Phone: 408 517-2100　　　　　　　　　　　　　　　HR: –
Fax: –　　　　　　　　　　　　　　　　　　　　　FYE: December 31
Web: www.apx.com　　　　　　　　　　　　　　　　Type: Private

APX facilitates transactions and information trading for the power and environmental markets. Its software helps manage such tradable environmental commodities as renewable energy, energy efficiency, and conservation certificates, as well as carbon offset credits. The company also provides consulting and related services to the wholesale power market, as well as hosted services for energy users, including power scheduling, generation control, real-time information, and settlement. Customers include the major regional renewable energy markets in North America and the international Voluntary Carbon Standard Registry. APX is owned by NYSE Blue, a subsidiary of NYSE Euronext and NYSE's Parisian subsidiary, Bluenext.

APYX MEDICAL CORP
NMS: APYX

5115 Ulmerton Road
Clearwater, FL 33760
Phone: 727 384-2323
Fax: –
Web: www.apyxmedical.com

CEO: Charles D Goodwin
CFO: Matthew Hill
HR: Laresa Colvin
FYE: December 31
Type: Public

Surgeons don't think about Bovie Medical during surgery, but Bovie thinks about them. Bovie makes electrosurgical generators and disposable electrosurgical products (including desiccators, electrodes, electrosurgical pencils, and other devices) for cutting and cauterizing tissue. These are mainly used for outpatient surgical procedures in doctors' offices, surgery centers, and hospitals. Bovie also makes battery-operated cauteries (to stop bleeding), physician penlights and other medical lighting instruments, and nerve locator simulators (used in hand and facial reconstruction) to identify motor nerves. Bovie markets and distributes worldwide under its own Aaron, ICON, and IDS brands and under private labels.

	Annual Growth	12/19	12/20	12/21	12/22	12/23
Sales ($mil.)	16.7%	28.2	27.7	48.5	44.5	52.3
Net income ($ mil.)	–	(19.7)	(11.9)	(15.2)	(23.2)	(18.7)
Market value ($ mil.)	(25.4%)	293.1	249.4	444.1	81.1	90.8
Employees	(1.3%)	266	266	272	276	252

AQUIS COMMUNICATIONS GROUP, INC
NBB: AQIS

1719A Route 10, Suite 300
Parsippany, NJ 07054
Phone: 973 560-8000
Fax: 973 560-8004
Web: www.aquiscommunications.com

CEO: –
CFO: –
HR: –
FYE: December 31
Type: Public

Aquis Communications Group offers paging and wireless messaging products and services in the mid-Atlantic and northeastern US. It provides one-way and two-way messaging with local, regional, and national connections, as well as cellular, long-distance, voice-over-Internet-protocol (VoIP), and data services. Aquis serves clients in such industries as health care and education, as well as the public sector; customers have included Solaris Health Systems and the City of Richmond, Virginia. The company operates from offices in Georgia, New Jersey, Pennsylvania, Tennessee, and Virginia. Aquis is a subsidiary of ComSoft.

	Annual Growth	12/99	12/00	12/01	12/02	12/03
Sales ($mil.)	(21.8%)	31.2	28.7	18.9	13.9	11.6
Net income ($ mil.)	–	(10.9)	(23.7)	(11.8)	18.8	(1.8)
Market value ($ mil.)	(67.0%)	303.1	23.3	3.2	0.4	3.6
Employees	–	–	88	64	53	43

ARADIGM CORPORATION

1613 LYON ST
SAN FRANCISCO, CA 941152414
Phone: 510 265-9000
Fax: –
Web: www.aradigm.com

CEO: –
CFO: –
HR: –
FYE: December 31
Type: Private

Aradigm helps the medicine go down for people who swoon at the sight of a needle. Aradigm develops orally inhaled drug delivery systems that treat respiratory diseases. Its lead delivery technology, AERx (an aerosol created from liquid drug formulations), is being adapted to deliver a variety of drugs to treat pulmonary diseases. Aradigm has focused its efforts on developing respiratory treatments for conditions such as cystic fibrosis, bronchiectasis, inhaled anthrax, smoking cessation, and asthma. Aradigm typically elects to reformulate already-approved drugs (such as antibiotic ciprofloxacin) and combine them with its inhalation delivery technologies in order to speed up the regulatory process. Aradigm filed for Chapter 11 bankruptcy protection in February 2019.

ARAMARK
NYS: ARMK

2400 Market Street
Philadelphia, PA 19103
Phone: 215 238-3000
Fax: –
Web: www.aramark.com

CEO: Sasha Day
CFO: James Tarangelo
HR: –
FYE: September 29
Type: Public

Founded in 1959, ARAMARK is a leading global provider of food, facilities and uniform services to education, healthcare, business & industry, and sports, leisure & corrections clients. The company offers corporate dining services and operates concessions at sports arenas and other entertainment venues. The firm is the third top companies in the food and facilities services and second in uniform services in North America. Through ARAMARK Uniform and Career Apparel, the company supplies uniforms for manufacturing, transportation, and service industries. The US customers generate about three-quarters of the company's revenue.

	Annual Growth	09/19*	10/20	10/21*	09/22	09/23
Sales ($mil.)	3.8%	16,227	12,830	12,096	16,327	18,854
Net income ($ mil.)	10.7%	448.5	(461.5)	(90.8)	194.5	674.1
Market value ($ mil.)	(5.2%)	11,248	7,203.0	9,354.7	8,157.3	9,072.3
Employees	(1.9%)	283,500	247,900	248,300	273,875	262,550

*Fiscal year change

ARAVIVE INC
NMS: ARAV

River Oaks Tower, 3730 Kirby Drive, Suite 1200
Houston, TX 77098
Phone: 936 355-1910
Fax: –
Web: www.aravive.com

CEO: Gail McIntyre
CFO: Rudy Howard
HR: –
FYE: December 31
Type: Public

Aravive Biologics (formerly Versartis) is a clinical-stage biotech focused on developing treatments designed to halt the progression of life-threatening diseases, including cancer and fibrosis. Its lead candidate AVB-500 is an ultrahigh-affinity, decoy protein for platinum-resistant recurrent ovarian cancer. The drug is also being evaluated as a potential treatment for a number of tumor types in addition to ovarian cancer and ccRCC, triple negative breast cancer, acute myeloid leukemia, and pancreatic cancer. It is also considering conducting studies in non-oncology indications such as lung or liver fibrosis in addition to the clinical trial with patients with IgAN.

	Annual Growth	12/18	12/19	12/20	12/21	12/22
Sales ($mil.)	60.7%	1.4	4.8	5.7	7.4	9.1
Net income ($ mil.)	–	(76.3)	(18.2)	(30.5)	(39.2)	(76.3)
Market value ($ mil.)	(21.7%)	210.7	818.1	337.5	131.1	79.0
Employees	13.2%	14	17	17	23	23

ARBITECH, LLC

64 FAIRBANKS
IRVINE, CA 926181602
Phone: 949 376-6650
Fax: –
Web: www.arbitech.com

CEO: –
CFO: David Walker
HR: –
FYE: December 31
Type: Private

There's nothing arbitrary about Arbitech's business model. Arbitech sells a variety of new and used computer equipment made by such companies as Avaya, Cisco Systems, Hewlett-Packard, IBM, Microsoft, Nortel, and VMware. The company's wide range of products include PCs, networking equipment, servers, storage systems, components, memories, and software. In addition to new equipment, the company deals in open-box, discontinued, and refurbished inventory, a niche typically not served by other large distributors and resellers of computer products. Arbitech was co-founded in 2000 by CEO Torin Pavia and one of the company's partners, William Poovey.

	Annual Growth	12/03	12/04	12/05	12/08	12/09
Sales ($mil.)	5.7%	–	–	153.3	180.3	191.4
Net income ($ mil.)	–	–	–	8.4	–	–
Market value ($ mil.)	–	–	–	–	–	–
Employees	–	–	–	–	–	74

ARBOR REALTY TRUST INC — NYS: ABR

333 Earle Ovington Boulevard, Suite 900
Uniondale, NY 11553
Phone: 516 506-4200
Fax: –
Web: www.arbor.com

CEO: Ivan Kaufman
CFO: Paul Elenio
HR: Corlene Orffeo
FYE: December 31
Type: Public

Money doesn't grow on trees, so Arbor Realty Trust invests in real estate-related assets. The real estate investment trust (REIT) buys structured finance assets in the commercial and multifamily real estate markets. It primarily invests in bridge loans (short-term financing) and mezzanine loans (large and usually unsecured loans), but also invests in discounted mortgage notes and other assets. The REIT targets lending and investment opportunities where borrowers seek interim financing until permanent financing is attained. Arbor Realty Trust is managed by financing firm Arbor Commercial Mortgage, though in early 2016 the REIT agreed to buy Arbor Commercial Mortgage for $250 million to expand into the government-sponsored, multi-family real estate loan origination business.

	Annual Growth	12/19	12/20	12/21	12/22	12/23
Sales ($mil.)	32.0%	535.8	603.7	799.2	1,176.7	1,624.2
Net income ($ mil.)	30.4%	128.6	170.9	339.3	325.8	371.4
Market value ($ mil.)	1.4%	2,705.1	2,673.6	3,453.4	2,486.4	2,861.5
Employees	5.0%	532	522	579	630	647

ARBUTUS BIOPHARMA CORP — NMS: ABUS

701 Veterans Circle
Warminster, PA 18974
Phone: 267 469-0914
Fax: 604 419-3201
Web: www.arbutusbio.com

CEO: –
CFO: –
HR: –
FYE: December 31
Type: Public

Tekmira Pharmaceuticals is giving diseases the silent treatment. The biopharmaceutical company is attempting to develop therapies that inhibit or "silence" certain disease-causing genes through ribonucleic acid interference (RNAi), a mechanism that disrupts the production of proteins that can lead to cancer, metabolic, and infectious diseases. Tekmira's lead candidates are being developed to treat tumors and high cholesterol. It also partners with other pharmaceutical companies, such as Alnylam Pharmaceuticals and Pfizer, to advance additional RNAi products using Tekmira's stable nucleic acid-lipid particles (SNALP) RNAi drug delivery technology.

	Annual Growth	12/19	12/20	12/21	12/22	12/23
Sales ($mil.)	31.8%	6.0	6.9	11.0	39.0	18.1
Net income ($ mil.)	–	(153.7)	(63.7)	(76.2)	(69.5)	(72.8)
Market value ($ mil.)	(2.6%)	472.2	603.0	660.8	395.8	424.7
Employees	(2.3%)	80	78	87	98	73

ARC DOCUMENT SOLUTIONS, INC. — NYS: ARC

12657 Alcosta Blvd., Suite 200
San Ramon, CA 94583
Phone: 925 949-5100
Fax: –
Web: www.e-arc.com

CEO: –
CFO: –
HR: –
FYE: December 31
Type: Public

Founded in 1988, ARC Document Solutions, also known as ARC, provides large-format document reproduction services, mainly to architectural, engineering, building owner/operator, and construction firms. It operates more than 130 service centers under a variety of local brands and offers on-site managed print services at some 10,500 locations. Adapting to the shift to digital, the company offers a number of applications, such as SKYSITE, Planwell, and Abacus that offer digital documentation management. ARC's network of facilities extends beyond the US into Canada, China, India, UAE, and the UK. The company generates about 90% of sales in the US.

	Annual Growth	12/19	12/20	12/21	12/22	12/23
Sales ($mil.)	(7.4%)	382.4	289.5	272.2	286.0	281.2
Net income ($ mil.)	28.6%	3.0	6.2	9.1	11.1	8.2
Market value ($ mil.)	23.9%	59.5	63.3	149.7	125.4	140.3
Employees	(4.7%)	2,300	1,750	1,700	1,800	1,900

ARCA BIOPHARMA INC — NAS: ABIO

10170 Church Ranch Way, Suite 100
Westminster, CO 80021
Phone: 720 940-2200
Fax: –
Web: www.arcabiopharma.com

CEO: Michael R Bristow
CFO: C J Dekker
HR: –
FYE: December 31
Type: Public

ARCA biopharma is using genes to treat your heart. The biopharmaceutical company's lead candidate, Gencaro, is a beta-blocker being developed to treat chronic heart failure and other cardiovascular diseases. Having identified common genetic variations in the cardiac nervous system, ARCA biopharma believes those variations may help predict how well patients will respond to Gencaro. Pending regulatory approval, Gencaro may be marketed directly by the company or through partnerships. If approved, it will be the first genetically-targeted heart failure treatment. ARCA biopharma is also collaborating with LabCorp to develop a companion genetic diagnostic test for Gencaro.

	Annual Growth	12/19	12/20	12/21	12/22	12/23
Sales ($mil.)	–	–	–	–	–	–
Net income ($ mil.)	–	(5.5)	(9.7)	(19.3)	(9.9)	(5.3)
Market value ($ mil.)	(26.1%)	82.8	58.1	31.2	34.4	24.7
Employees	(25.5%)	13	14	19	6	4

ARCADIS INC.

2101 L ST NW STE 200
WASHINGTON, DC 200371558
Phone: 410 537-6000
Fax: –
Web: www.callisonrtkl.com

CEO: Kelly Farrell
CFO: –
HR: Kristina Livingston
FYE: December 31
Type: Private

RTKL Associates has a global appetite for architecture and engineering projects. Ranked among the top providers of architecture and engineering services to the public sector, RTKL also caters to the hospitality, retail and entertainment, health care, and academic markets. The firm offers a variety of services such as planning and urban design, interior architecture, historic preservation, structural engineering, and mechanical and electrical engineering. to clients in the Americas, Europe, and the Middle East. Other services include graphic design, landscape design, and information technology planning. RTKL was founded in 1946 and is owned by Dutch consulting and engineering firm ARCADIS.

	Annual Growth	12/10	12/11	12/12	12/13	12/16
Sales ($mil.)	7.8%	–	201.9	202.8	205.4	294.1
Net income ($ mil.)	0.8%	–	9.3	11.0	10.4	9.7
Market value ($ mil.)	–	–	–	–	–	–
Employees	–	–	–	–	–	1,236

ARCBEST CORP — NMS: ARCB

8401 McClure Drive
Fort Smith, AR 72916
Phone: 479 785-6000
Fax: 479 785-6004
Web: www.arcb.com

CEO: Judy R McReynolds
CFO: David R Cobb
HR: Lindsay Fuchs
FYE: December 31
Type: Public

ArcBest is a multibillion-dollar logistics company that leverages technology and a full suite of shipping and logistics solutions to meet its customers' needs and help keep the global supply chain moving. Subsidiary ABF Freight System specializes in less-than-truckload (LTL) shipments of general commodities (no hazardous waste or dangerous explosives). It also offers ground expedite solutions under Panther Premium Logistics, household moving via U-Pack, and vehicle maintenance under FleetNet America. ArcBest was founded in Arkansas in 1923 (its name was shortened from Arkansas Best in 2014) and has grown to serve all US states, plus Canada and Puerto Rico through about 240 service centers.

	Annual Growth	12/19	12/20	12/21	12/22	12/23
Sales ($mil.)	10.3%	2,988.3	2,940.2	3,980.1	5,324.1	4,427.4
Net income ($ mil.)	48.7%	40.0	71.1	213.5	298.2	195.4
Market value ($ mil.)	44.5%	650.4	1,005.5	2,824.1	1,650.4	2,832.6
Employees	3.6%	13,000	13,000	14,000	15,700	15,000

ARCH RESOURCES INC (DE)
NYS: ARCH

One CityPlace Drive, Suite 300
St. Louis, MO 63141
Phone: 314 994-2700
Fax: –
Web: www.archcoal.com

CEO: Paul A Lang
CFO: Matthew C Giljum
HR: Bradley Allbritten
FYE: December 31
Type: Public

Arch Resources is one of the world's largest coal producers and a premier producer of metallurgical coal, selling approximately 73 million tons of coal, including some 0.1 million tons of coal it purchased from third parties coming from seven active mining complexes spread across all the major coal-producing regions of the US. The company sells its metallurgical coal to five North American customers and exports to nearly 35 customers overseas in roughly 20 countries. North America generates almost 40% of the company's total revenue.

	Annual Growth	12/19	12/20	12/21	12/22	12/23
Sales ($mil.)	8.2%	2,294.4	1,467.6	2,208.0	3,724.6	3,145.8
Net income ($ mil.)	18.7%	233.8	(344.6)	337.6	1,330.9	464.0
Market value ($ mil.)	23.3%	1,317.1	803.6	1,676.6	2,621.6	3,046.7
Employees	(2.1%)	3,700	3,200	3,300	3,404	3,400

ARCH VENTURE CORPORATION

8755 W HIGGINS RD STE 1025
CHICAGO, IL 606312778
Phone: 773 380-6600
Fax: –
Web: www.archventure.com

CEO: –
CFO: –
HR: –
FYE: December 31
Type: Private

ARCH Venture Partners wants to catch companies on the upward curve of their development. The firm invests in startup and seed-stage companies, particularly those concentrating on information technology, life sciences, and physical sciences. The company also specializes in the commercialization of technologies originating from academic and research institutions. ARCH launched its first fund in 1989 and now manages seven funds totaling some $1.5 billion. It has invested in more than 130 companies since its founding. Portfolio holdings include AmberWave Systems, Impinj, Nanosys, Surface Logix, and Xtera Communications.

ARCHER DANIELS MIDLAND CO.
NYS: ADM

77 West Wacker Drive, Suite 4600
Chicago, IL 60601
Phone: 312 634-8100
Fax: –
Web: www.adm.com

CEO: Juan R Luciano
CFO: –
HR: –
FYE: December 31
Type: Public

Archer-Daniels-Midland (ADM) is one of the world's leading agricultural supply chain managers and human and animal nutrition providers in over 190 countries. From staple foods, such as flour, oils, and sweeteners, to innovative alternatives like plant-based meat and dairy, ADM offers the industry's broadest portfolio of food and beverage solutions. It is also a leader in health and well-being, with an industry-leading range of probiotics, enzymes, supplements, and more to meet the needs of consumers looking for new ways to live healthier lives. Almost 45% of its sales come from the US.

	Annual Growth	12/19	12/20	12/21	12/22	12/23
Sales ($mil.)	9.8%	64,656	64,355	85,249	101,556	93,935
Net income ($ mil.)	26.1%	1,379.0	1,772.0	2,709.0	4,340.0	3,483.0
Market value ($ mil.)	11.7%	23,778	25,860	34,674	47,632	37,049
Employees	2.3%	38,100	39,000	41,000	42,001	41,802

ARCHON CORP
NBB: ARHN

2200 Casino Drive
Laughlin, NV 89029
Phone: 702 732-9120
Fax: –
Web: www.archoncorp.com

CEO: Paul W Lowden
CFO: –
HR: –
FYE: September 30
Type: Public

Archon is banking on gamblers to follow the trail of the Pioneer. Formerly Santa Fe Gaming, the embattled company owns and operates one casino, the Pioneer Hotel & Gambling Hall, in Laughlin, Nevada. The Pioneer features more than 410 guest rooms and gaming operations that consist of approximately 730 slot machines, six blackjack tables, one craps table, one roulette wheel, and five other gaming tables. The hotel includes two restaurants and bars, a special events area, banquet rooms, and a swimming pool and spa. Chairman and CEO Paul Lowden controls the company. Archon has been the subject of a number of unsuccessful takeover bids in recent years.

	Annual Growth	09/06	09/07	09/08	09/09	09/10
Sales ($mil.)	(15.1%)	45.2	45.2	43.2	32.0	23.5
Net income ($ mil.)	–	(3.4)	0.6	58.8	(1.5)	1.2
Market value ($ mil.)	(19.2%)	198.0	284.3	186.9	85.8	84.3
Employees	(11.0%)	512	556	471	365	321

ARCHROCK INC
NYS: AROC

9807 Katy Freeway, Suite 100
Houston, TX 77024
Phone: 281 836-8000
Fax: –
Web: www.archrock.com

CEO: D B Childers
CFO: Douglas S Aron
HR: Karin Buenger
FYE: December 31
Type: Public

Archrock has a rock solid compression game going. The US based company is a leading natural gas contract operator and compression service provider to the oil & gas producers and midstream companies. In addition, the company provides aftermarket services to compression equipment owners. The company owns about 4,320 compression units, providing an aggregate roughly 4.0 million horsepower. Archrock's business supports a must-run service that is essential to the production, processing, transportation and storage of natural gas.

	Annual Growth	12/19	12/20	12/21	12/22	12/23
Sales ($mil.)	0.6%	965.5	875.0	781.5	845.6	990.3
Net income ($ mil.)	1.9%	97.3	(68.4)	28.2	44.3	105.0
Market value ($ mil.)	11.3%	1,565.9	1,350.6	1,166.6	1,400.6	2,401.8
Employees	(10.3%)	1,700	1,250	1,100	1,100	1,100

ARCHROCK PARTNERS, L.P.

9807 KATY FWY STE 100
HOUSTON, TX 770241276
Phone: 281 836-8000
Fax: –
Web: www.archrock.com

CEO: D B Childers
CFO: David S Miller
HR: –
FYE: December 31
Type: Private

Archrock Partners (formerly Exterran Partners) is the largest operator of contract compression equipment in the US. Its services include designing, installing, operating, repairing, and maintaining compression equipment. The company operates a fleet of more than 3,950 compressor units, comprising almost 1.6 million horsepower. Archrock, a global leader in full-service natural gas compression equipment and services, controls Archrock Partners. Archrock Partners and Archrock (formerly Exterran Holdings) manage their respective US compression fleets as one pool of compression equipment in order to more easily fulfill their respective customers' needs.

ARCONIC CORPORATION

201 ISABELLA ST STE 200
PITTSBURGH, PA 152125872
Phone: 412 992-2500
Fax: –
Web: www.arconic.com

CEO: Chris Ayers
CFO: Erick R Asmussen
HR: –
FYE: December 31
Type: Private

Arconic is a global leader in manufacturing aluminum sheet, plate, extrusions and architectural products and systems, serving primarily the ground transportation, aerospace, building and construction, industrial, and packaging end markets. The company maintains a leadership position in its targeted markets through its global footprint of more than 20 primary manufacturing facilities, as well as various sales and service facilities, located across North America, Europe, the UK, and China. The company manages its business operations through three reportable segments ? Rolled Products, Building and Construction Systems, and Extrusions. The US accounts for more than 65% of total revenue. In late 2023, Apollo Funds completed its previously announced acquisition of Arconic at an enterprise value of approximately $5.2 billion.

ARCTIC CAT INC.

600 BROOKS AVE S
THIEF RIVER FALLS, MN 567012735
Phone: 218 681-8558
Fax: –
Web: arcticcat.txtsv.com

CEO: Christopher T Metz
CFO: Christopher J Eperjesy
HR: –
FYE: March 31
Type: Private

Arctic Cat designs, engineers, manufactures, and markets all-terrain vehicles (ATVs), side-by-side, and snowmobile models. Its four-wheel recreational and utility ATVs, side-by-side, and snowmobiles are marketed under the Arctic Cat, Wildcat, Prowler, and Alterra names. Arctic Cat also supplies replacement parts, and Arctic Cat-branded protective clothing and riding gear to foster its drivers' experience and loyalty. The company also sells parts to other vehicle OEMs. Products are sold through a network of independent dealers and representatives of dealers worldwide. Arctic Cat was formed by Edgar Hetteen in 1962. As part of the Textron family, the company is connected to a global network of brands that build everything from helicopters to aircraft to military machinery.

ARCTIC SLOPE REGIONAL CORPORATION

3900 C ST STE 801
ANCHORAGE, AK 995035963
Phone: 907 339-6000
Fax: –
Web: www.asrc.com

CEO: Rex A Rock Sr
CFO: Kristin Mellinger
HR: Amanda Cascio
FYE: December 31
Type: Private

The In~upiat-owned Arctic Slope Regional Corporation (ASRC) is a locally owned and operated business in Alaska. It gets the bulk of its sales from energy services (ASRC Energy Services) and petroleum refining and marketing unit (Petro Star). Other operations include construction (ASRC Construction Holding), governmental services (ASRC Federal Holding), industrial services (ASRC Industrial Services), local services (Eskimos, Inc.) and tourism (Tundra Tours). ASRC, along with its family of companies, is the largest Alaskan-owned company, with operation across Alaska and the Lower 48 states.

	Annual Growth	12/04	12/05	12/06	12/07	12/08
Sales ($mil.)	13.6%	–	1,566.5	1,700.5	1,777.5	2,297.3
Net income ($ mil.)	5.8%	–	127.5	206.3	207.7	151.2
Market value ($ mil.)	–	–	–	–	–	–
Employees	–	–	–	–	–	6,700

ARCTURUS THERAPEUTICS HOLDINGS INC

NMS: ARCT

10628 Science Center Drive, Suite 250
San Diego, CA 92121
Phone: 858 900-2660
Fax: –
Web: www.arcturusrx.com

CEO: –
CFO: –
HR: –
FYE: December 31
Type: Public

If it were that easy to treat ADHD, Alcobra would wave a magic wand and say "Abracadabra!" Instead, the Israeli company is developing a new type of drug to treat ADHD (Attention Deficit Hyperactivity Disorder). The drug candidate, MG01CI, differs from traditional pharmaceuticals prescribed to manage ADHD in that it is not a stimulant like its well-known counterparts Adderall and Ritalin. MG01CI aims to be a safer alternative for patients who cannot tolerate the side effects, such as insomnia and high blood pressure, associated with stimulantsAlcobra plans to merge with private biotech Arcturus Therapeutics the combined firm will focus on developing RNA medicines to treat rare liver diseases, non-alcoholic steatohepatitis (NASH), cystic fibrosis, infectious diseases, and other therapeutic areas.

	Annual Growth	12/19	12/20	12/21	12/22	12/23
Sales ($mil.)	68.3%	20.8	9.5	12.4	206.0	166.8
Net income ($ mil.)	–	(26.0)	(72.1)	(203.7)	9.3	(29.7)
Market value ($ mil.)	30.5%	291.6	1,163.8	992.9	455.0	845.9
Employees	19.6%	88	118	177	170	180

ARDELYX INC

NMS: ARDX

400 Fifth Avenue, Suite 210
Waltham, MA 02451
Phone: 510 745-1700
Fax: –
Web: www.ardelyx.com

CEO: Michael Raab
CFO: Justin Renz
HR: –
FYE: December 31
Type: Public

Ardelyx is a biopharmaceutical company founded with a mission to discover, develop and commercialize innovative first-in-class medicines that meet significant unmet medical needs. The company has developed a portfolio of novel products to address unmet medical needs across gastrointestinal and cardiorenal therapeutic areas. The company products are for adult patients with irritable bowel syndrome with constipation (IBS-C), adult patients with chronic kidney disease (CKD) on dialysis suffering from elevated serum phosphorus, or hyperphosphatemia; and adult patients with CKD and/or heart failure with elevated serum potassium, or hyperkalemia. It is also advancing its small molecule potassium secretagogue program, RDX013 for the potential treatment of hyperkalemia. Hyperkalemia is a common problem in patients with heart and kidney disease.

	Annual Growth	12/19	12/20	12/21	12/22	12/23
Sales ($mil.)	120.3%	5.3	7.6	10.1	52.2	124.5
Net income ($ mil.)	–	(94.9)	(94.3)	(158.2)	(67.2)	(66.1)
Market value ($ mil.)	(4.7%)	1,744.6	1,504.0	255.7	662.5	1,441.2
Employees	32.0%	88	129	86	133	267

ARENA 3D HOLDINGS, INC.

291 EVANS WAY
BRANCHBURG, NJ 088763766
Phone: 908 429-1200
Fax: –
Web: www.dancker.com

CEO: Steven Lang
CFO: Bill Hendry
HR: –
FYE: March 31
Type: Private

Dancker, Sellew & Douglas (DS&D) is a furniture dealership serving the New York City metropolitan area, upstate New York and New Jersey. It specializes in providing furniture to businesses, with clients including AT&T and Coldwell Banker. DS&D offers chairs, desks, lighting, and storage from a variety of manufacturers, including Peter Pepper Products, Steelcase and Teknion. The company also offers furniture rental and warehousing, along with design consulting, inventory management, and refurbishment services. DS&D also caters to hospitals and universities, and provides lab furniture and equipment to pharmaceutical companies. The firm was founded in 1829 as the T.G. Seller Company, making roll-top desks.

	Annual Growth	03/02	03/03	03/04	03/06	03/07
Sales ($mil.)	(10.2%)	–	111.8	97.9	135.8	72.8
Net income ($ mil.)	–	–	(1.7)	(0.8)	0.5	(0.4)
Market value ($ mil.)	–	–	–	–	–	–
Employees	–	–	–	–	–	170

ARENA GROUP HOLDINGS INC DEL

NBB: MVEN D

200 Vesey Street, 24th Floor
New York, NY 10281
Phone: 212 321-5002
Fax: -
Web: -

CEO: -
CFO: Douglas B Smith
HR: -
FYE: December 31
Type: Public

Integrated Surgical Systems (ISS) wanted to be the hippest company around with its ROBODOC Surgical Assistant System, a computer-controlled robot used in hip and knee replacements. However, ISS ceased operations in mid-2005 because of lawsuits and lack of funding, and it sold its ROBODOC assets to Novatrix Biomedical in 2007. Using those assets, Novatrix has set up a new company called Curexo Medical to continue development of ROBODOC, which is sold in Europe, Asia, and other regions and received FDA approval in 2008. Meanwhile, ISS used the money from the asset sale to pay its debtors and is looking for acquisition opportunities.

	Annual Growth	12/18	12/19	12/20	12/21	12/22
Sales ($mil.)	149.5%	5.7	53.3	128.0	189.1	220.9
Net income ($ mil.)	-	-	(26.1)	(38.5)	(89.2)	(89.9)	(70.9)
Market value ($ mil.)	116.8%	8.8	14.6	11.0	11.7	194.2
Employees	-	-	-	299	328	364	400

ARES COMMERCIAL REAL ESTATE CORP

NYS: ACRE

245 Park Avenue, 42nd Floor
New York, NY 10167
Phone: 212 750-7300
Fax: -
Web: www.arescre.com

CEO: Bryan P Donohoe
CFO: Tae S Yoon
HR: -
FYE: December 31
Type: Public

Ares Commercial Real Estate Corporation is primarily engaged in commercial real estate loans and related investments. The company is externally managed by Ares Commercial Real Estate Management LLC (ACREM), a subsidiary of Ares Management Corporation a leading global alternative investment manager with approximately $165 billion of assets under management. The company target borrowers whose capital needs are not being suitably met by traditional bank or capital markets sources by offering these borrowers customized financing solutions. The company was formed in late 2011.

	Annual Growth	12/19	12/20	12/21	12/22	12/23
Assets ($mil.)	6.3%	1,784.1	1,929.5	2,631.8	2,523.0	2,279.8
Net income ($ mil.)	-	-	37.0	21.8	60.5	29.8	(38.9)
Market value ($ mil.)	(10.1%)	857.7	644.9	787.3	557.2	561.0
Employees	23.6%	1,200	1,450	2,100	2,550	2,800

ARES MANAGEMENT CORP

NYS: ARES

2000 Avenue of the Stars, 12th Floor
Los Angeles, CA 90067
Phone: 310 201-4100
Fax: -
Web: www.aresmgmt.com

CEO: Michael J Arougheti
CFO: Jarrod Phillips
HR: -
FYE: December 31
Type: Public

Ares Management Corporation is a leading global alternative investment manager offering clients complementary primary and secondary investment solutions across the credit, private equity, real estate, and infrastructure asset classes. Subsidiary Ares Capital Corporation (ARCC) specializes in providing direct loans and other investments to private middle-market companies in the US. With approximately $378.0 billion of assets under management and over 2,600 employees in more than 40 offices in over 15 countries, Ares offers its investors a range of investment strategies and seeks to deliver attractive performance to an investor base that includes over 1,900 direct institutional relationships and a significant retail investor base across its publicly-traded and sub-advised funds.

	Annual Growth	12/19	12/20	12/21	12/22	12/23
Sales ($mil.)	19.8%	1,765.4	1,764.0	4,212.1	3,055.4	3,631.9
Net income ($ mil.)	33.6%	148.9	152.1	408.8	167.5	474.3
Market value ($ mil.)	35.1%	10,978	14,472	24,997	21,051	36,578
Employees	24.1%	1,200	1,450	2,100	2,550	2,850

ARETEC GROUP, INC.

405 PARK AVE FL 12
NEW YORK, NY 100224405
Phone: 866 904-2988
Fax: -
Web: www.rcscapital.com

CEO: -
CFO: -
HR: -
FYE: December 31
Type: Private

Aretec Group is a holding company with a hand in a variety of financial services businesses, namely securities brokering, investment banking, and securities record-keeping services. Its Cetera Financial Group is a combination of some 10 brokerages with more than 9,000 financial advisors. RCS Advisory Services is a company that provides financing and consulting to clients served by the brokerage. Finally, American National Stock Transfer, among other services, registers the securities with the SEC. RCS Capital filed for Chapter 11 bankruptcy in January 2016 to reduce its debt; it emerged in May 2016 as Aretec Group.

ARGAN INC

NYS: AGX

One Church Street, Suite 201
Rockville, MD 20850
Phone: 301 315-0027
Fax: -
Web: www.arganinc.com

CEO: David H Watson
CFO: Richard H Deily
HR: -
FYE: January 31
Type: Public

Argan makes sure its customers stay all juiced up. The holding company owns subsidiaries that provide power services and products for the government, telecommunications, power, and personal health care industries. Its main subsidiary, Gemma Power Systems, designs, builds, and maintains power plants including traditional and alternate fuel plants. The company's Southern Maryland Cable unit provides inside-premise wiring and also performs splicing and underground and aerial telecom infrastructure construction services to carriers, government entities, service providers, and electric utilities. Argan's power industry segment accounts for more than 95% of its total revenues.

	Annual Growth	01/19	01/20	01/21	01/22	01/23
Sales ($mil.)	(1.4%)	482.2	239.0	392.2	509.4	455.0
Net income ($ mil.)	(10.7%)	52.0	(42.7)	23.9	38.2	33.1
Market value ($ mil.)	(2.0%)	567.5	566.0	581.1	499.4	524.1
Employees	(9.8%)	1,487	1,154	1,473	1,358	985

ARGO INTERNATIONAL CORPORATION

160 CHUBB AVE STE 102
LYNDHURST, NJ 070713526
Phone: 201 561-7017
Fax: -
Web: www.argointl.com

CEO: -
CFO: -
HR: -
FYE: December 31
Type: Private

Argo International is naut about Jason and the Golden Fleece, but it does have a stimulating story to tell. The company distributes electrical (fuses, generators, motors), mechanical (cable reels, pumps, thrusters), and marine (controls, gauges, valves) equipment to industrial users in the mining, oil, utility, marine, petroleum, and refining industries. Argo has more than 20 offices and warehouses throughout Asia, Europe, the Middle East, and North and South America. The company, which was established in 1952, is a subsidiary of New York-based Delcal Enterprises, Inc.

ARGOS THERAPEUTICS, INC.

4233 TECHNOLOGY DR
DURHAM, NC 277042173
Phone: 919 287-6300
Fax: –
Web: www.argostherapeutics.com

CEO: Jeffrey D Abbey
CFO: Richard D Katz
HR: –
FYE: December 31
Type: Private

Argos aimed to be a faithful servant of those fighting cancer and infectious diseases. The pharmaceutical firm's proprietary Arcelis platform uses biological components from the patient to create a white blood cell that triggers that patient's particular immune response. Its most promising candidate targets metastatic renal cell carcinoma, the most common kidney cancer. Argos also has an HIV treatment, a lupus antibody, and a treatment for psoriasis in the pipeline. Argos filed for Chapter 11 bankruptcy protection in November 2018. It plans to sell its assets to Cellscript.

ARIAD PHARMACEUTICALS, INC.

40 LANDSDOWNE ST
CAMBRIDGE, MA 021394234
Phone: 617 494-0400
Fax: –
Web: www.ariad.com

CEO: Harvey J Berger
CFO: Manmeet S Soni
HR: Curtis Demick
FYE: December 31
Type: Private

ARIAD Pharmaceuticals is exploring the myriad possibilities for new cancer treatments. The firm has a handful of candidates being studied for the treatment of various types of cancer. Its drug Iclusig (ponatinib), a treatment for two rare forms of leukemia, is already approved in the US and Europe though the company is seeking approvals for additional indications. ARIAD is also developing brigatinib for the treatment of crizotinib-resistant lung cancer. ARIAD's drug candidates are in varying stages of preclinical research and clinical trials. In early 2017, Japan's Takeda Pharmaceutical acquired ARIAD in a $5.2 billion transaction.

ARISTA INVESTORS CORP.

116 John St.
New York, NY 10038
Phone: 212 964-2150
Fax: –
Web: –

CEO: –
CFO: –
HR: –
FYE: December 31
Type: Public

Arista Investors has given itself a makeover. The company sold its disability insurance portfolio to Guardian Life Insurance, with whom it already had an existing relationship providing third-party administrative services. The company continues to perform such services for Guardian, whose main line of business is group accident and health insurance, and Highmark Life. Arista performs services such as pricing of risk, underwriting new and renewal business, calculation and payment of claims, and maintenance of records. The company then receives a percentage of premiums.

	Annual Growth	12/97	12/98	12/99	12/00	12/01
Sales ($mil.)	52.5%	0.7	2.0	3.7	4.0	4.0
Net income ($ mil.)	–	(1.2)	0.4	(0.0)	0.1	(0.1)
Market value ($ mil.)	(11.9%)	5.5	7.7	2.9	3.1	3.3
Employees	(3.0%)	43	43	41	46	38

ARISTA NETWORKS INC

NYS: ANET

5453 Great America Parkway
Santa Clara, CA 95054
Phone: 408 547-5500
Fax: –
Web: www.arista.com

CEO: –
CFO: –
HR: –
FYE: December 31
Type: Public

Arista Networks is an industry leader in data-driven, client-to-cloud networking for next-generation data center and campus workspace environments. The company has developed a highly scalable cloud networking platform that uses software to address the needs of large-scale internet companies, cloud service providers, and large enterprises, including financial services organizations, government agencies, and media and entertainment companies, including AI, virtualization, big data, and low-latency applications. EOS supports such virtual networks as Ansible, CFEngine, Chef, Puppet, virtual network orchestration applications, and third-party management tools. Customers in the Americas account for nearly 80% of revenue. Arista was founded in 2008 by industry luminaries Andy Bechtolsheim, Ken Duda, and David Cheriton.

	Annual Growth	12/19	12/20	12/21	12/22	12/23
Sales ($mil.)	24.9%	2,410.7	2,317.5	2,948.0	4,381.3	5,860.2
Net income ($ mil.)	24.8%	859.9	634.6	840.9	1,352.4	2,087.3
Market value ($ mil.)	3.7%	63,511	90,729	44,885	37,891	73,537
Employees	15.0%	2,300	2,613	2,993	3,612	4,023

ARIZONA PROFESSIONAL BASEBALL LP

401 E JEFFERSON ST
PHOENIX, AZ 850042438
Phone: 602 462-3430
Fax: –
Web: www.mlb.com

CEO: –
CFO: –
HR: –
FYE: December 31
Type: Private

These serpents strike at the baseball diamond. Arizona Professional Baseball owns and operates the Arizona Diamondbacks baseball franchise. The team joined Major League Baseball as a National League expansion franchise in 1998 and enjoyed early success, reaching the postseason in its second year and winning the World Series in 2001. The Diamondbacks play host at the state-of-the-art Chase Field, which features a retractable roof, air-conditioning, and a swimming pool in the outfield stands. A group led by former computer industry executive and Datatel founder Ken Kendrick has controlled the team since 2004.

	Annual Growth	12/14	12/15	12/16	12/17	12/18
Sales ($mil.)	1.0%	–	–	–	233.1	235.4
Net income ($ mil.)	–	–	–	–	77.9	(44.1)
Market value ($ mil.)	–	–	–	–	–	–
Employees	–	–	–	–	–	150

ARIZONA PUBLIC SERVICE CO.

400 North Fifth Street, P.O. Box 53999
Phoenix, AZ 85072-3999
Phone: 602 250-1000
Fax: –
Web: www.apsc.com

CEO: Donald E Brandt
CFO: Andrew Cooper
HR: –
FYE: December 31
Type: Public

Arizona Public Service (APS), a subsidiary of Pinnacle West Capital, distributes power to about 1.3 million customers in about 10 of 15 Arizona counties, making it the largest electric utility in the state. Its transmission facilities consist of about 5,830 pole miles of overhead lines and some 85 miles of underground lines. APS's distribution facilities consist of some 11,275 miles of overhead lines and over 23,080 miles of underground primary cable, all of which are located in Arizona. It owns and leases around 6,340 MW of regulated generation capacity and holds a mix of both long-term and short-term purchased power agreements for additional capacity, including a variety of agreements for the purchase of renewable energy.

	Annual Growth	12/19	12/20	12/21	12/22	12/23
Sales ($mil.)	7.8%	3,471.2	3,587.0	3,803.8	4,324.4	4,696.0
Net income ($ mil.)	(0.8%)	565.3	568.0	632.3	524.9	547.3
Market value ($ mil.)	–	–	–	–	–	–
Employees	(0.3%)	6,111	5,933	5,776	5,772	6,045

ARIZONA STATE UNIVERSITY

300 E UNIVERSITY DR STE 410
TEMPE, AZ 852812061
Phone: 480 965-2100
Fax: -
Web: www.asu.edu

CEO: -
CFO: Carol Campbell
HR: -
FYE: June 30
Type: Private

Arizona State University (ASU) is a comprehensive public research university that offers more than 850 degree programs for undergraduate and degree pursuing a master's degree or doctoral program. The university offers more than 550 undergraduate and graduate degree programs and certificates are also offered 100% online. With a student to faculty ratio of 19:1, the ASU has approximately 144,800 students enrolled. ASU is ranked top 10 nationally for best online bachelor's programs by US News & World Report. It offers nearly 300 online degree and certificate programs taught by award-winning ASU faculty. The university has students from all 50 states and more than 130 nations. ASU was founded in 1885.

	Annual Growth	06/18	06/19	06/20	06/21	06/22
Sales ($mil.)	6.7%	-	2,048.6	2,180.6	2,220.8	2,492.0
Net income ($ mil.)	41.9%	-	85.4	6.7	248.0	243.9
Market value ($ mil.)	-	-	-	-	-	-
Employees	-	-	-	-	-	8,000

ARK RESTAURANTS CORP

NMS: ARKR

85 Fifth Avenue
New York, NY 10003
Phone: 212 206-8800
Fax: 212 206-8845
Web: www.arkrestaurants.com

CEO: Michael Weinstein
CFO: Anthony J Sirica
HR: -
FYE: September 30
Type: Public

You might say this company floats the boat of fine dining fans. Ark Restaurants owns and manages about 20 chic eateries in New York City, Las Vegas, and Washington, DC, including the Bryant Park Grill, Center Caf', and V-Bar. It also operates locations under the names America and Sequoia. In addition, Ark Restaurants manages food courts, banquet facilities, and room services at several casino resorts, including the New York-New York Hotel & Casino (owned by MGM Resorts International), the Venetian Casino Resort (Las Vegas Sands), and the Foxwoods Resorts Casino (Mashantucket Pequot Tribal Nation). Founder and CEO Michael Weinstein owns about 30% of the company.

	Annual Growth	09/19*	10/20	10/21	10/22*	09/23
Sales ($mil.)	3.3%	162.4	106.5	131.9	183.7	184.8
Net income ($ mil.)	-	-	2.7	(4.7)	12.9	9.3	(5.9)
Market value ($ mil.)	(7.0%)	73.3	41.5	55.9	67.0	54.9
Employees	(1.8%)	2,145	1,262	1,741	1,901	1,993

*Fiscal year change

ARKANSAS CHILDREN'S HOSPITAL

1 CHILDRENS WAY
LITTLE ROCK, AR 722023500
Phone: 501 364-1100
Fax: -
Web: www.archildrens.org

CEO: -
CFO: Gena G Wingfield
HR: -
FYE: June 30
Type: Private

Arkansas Children's Hospital (ACH) is a pediatric hospital with a Level I Trauma Center, that's located in Little Rock, Arkansas. It is among the largest pediatric hospitals in the US and serves children from birth to age 21. ACH is the state's only Level IV neonatal intensive care unit; the state's only pediatric intensive care unit; the state's only pediatric surgery program with Level 1 verification from the American College of Surgeons (ACS); the state's only magnetoencephalography (MEG) system for neurosurgical planning and cutting-edge research; and the state's only nationally recognized pediatric transport program. ACH is affiliated with the University of Arkansas for Medical Sciences and is a teaching hospital with the UAMS College of Medicine's Department of Pediatrics. ACH staff consists of more than 505 physicians, 200 residents, and 4,400 support staff. The hospital includes 336 beds and offers three intensive care units.

ARKANSAS DEPARTMENT OF CORRECTIONS

6814 PRINCETON PIKE
WHITE HALL, AR 716029411
Phone: 870 267-6999
Fax: -
Web: doc.arkansas.gov

CEO: -
CFO: -
HR: -
FYE: June 30
Type: Private

The Arkansas Department of Correction (ADC) oversees the state's prisons and work-release centers and provides rehabilitation and support services for the incarcerated and their families. Inmate programs include job training, substance abuse programs, anger management classes, and college courses. A voluntary boot camp offers male and female first-time offenders opportunities for personal growth through military discipline. Qualifying inmates help encourage others to stay on the straight and narrow path by speaking to schools, church groups, and other organizations. ADC is led by seven governor-appointed board members.

	Annual Growth	06/17	06/18	06/19	06/20	06/21
Sales ($mil.)	10.9%	-	-	-	49.1	54.5
Net income ($ mil.)	69.4%	-	-	-	15.4	26.1
Market value ($ mil.)	-	-	-	-	-	-
Employees	-	-	-	-	-	3,688

ARKANSAS ELECTRIC COOPERATIVE CORP.

1 Cooperative Way, P.O. Box 194208
Little Rock, AR 72219-4208
Phone: 501 570-2200
Fax: 501 570-2900
Web: www.aecc.com

CEO: -
CFO: -
HR: Sarah Littleton
FYE: October 31
Type: Public

Having access to power is the natural state in the Natural State, thanks to Arkansas Electric Cooperative Corporation (AECC), the sole wholesale power provider for 17 Arkansas electric distribution cooperatives. The company operates power plants with 3,418 MW of generating capacity, owns transmission assets, and buys wholesale power to meet its members' demands. Affiliate Arkansas Electric Cooperatives, Inc. (AECI) provides administrative and maintenance services to the distribution companies. The distribution utilities serve about 500,000 customers in more than 60% of Arkansas. AECC and AECI, along with the state's 17 electric distribution cooperatives, are known as the Electric Cooperatives of Arkansas.

	Annual Growth	10/01	10/02	10/03	10/04	10/05
Sales ($mil.)	0.9%	499.4	381.2	412.4	414.7	517.8
Net income ($ mil.)	(32.9%)	38.2	17.9	13.5	7.8	7.7
Market value ($ mil.)	-	-	-	-	-	-
Employees	-	-	-	-	193	-

ARKANSAS HEART HOSPITAL, LLC

1701 S SHACKLEFORD RD
LITTLE ROCK, AR 722114335
Phone: 501 219-7000
Fax: -
Web: www.arheart.com

CEO: -
CFO: -
HR: -
FYE: September 30
Type: Private

You won't be leaving your heart in Little Rock. At least not with help of Arkansas Heart Hospital, which specializes in the diagnosis and treatment of heart disease. With more than 110 beds, the hospital provides inpatient and outpatient cardiac care, as well as 24-hour emergency services. Arkansas Heart Hospital also has six catheterization labs and offers pharmacy, radiology, and respiratory services. The hospital also offers advanced wound healing services through its Wound Care and Hyperbaric Oxygen Therapy Clinic. Former parent MedCath held 70% of the Arkansas Heart Hospital before selling its stake to another shareholder, physician-owned entity AR-MED, in 2011.

	Annual Growth	09/16	09/17	09/18	09/20	09/21
Sales ($mil.)	0.2%	-	184.0	197.8	174.7	185.8
Net income ($ mil.)	10.4%	-	12.1	16.5	16.1	17.9
Market value ($ mil.)	-	-	-	-	-	-
Employees	-	-	-	-	-	414

ARKANSAS STATE UNIVERSITY

2105 AGGIE RD
JONESBORO, AR 72401
Phone: 870 972-2400
Fax: –
Web: www.astate.edu

CEO: –
CFO: Bradley Johnson
HR: Clemetta Hood
FYE: June 30
Type: Private

Arkansas State University (A-State) is home to more than 14,000 students, or Red Wolves. The university has more than 10 colleges that offer more than 140 undergraduate and graduate academic programs; classes are also offered at technical sites and in partnership with community colleges. It offers doctoral degrees in educational leadership, environmental science, heritage studies, and molecular biosciences. In additional to its flagship campus in Jonesboro, the ASU system offers courses at regional campuses in Beebe, Mountain Home, and Newport. The university has a 17:1 student-teacher ratio; and approximately 600 international students came from more than 60 countries. A-State was founded in 1909.

	Annual Growth	06/15	06/16	06/17	06/18	06/19
Sales ($mil.)	(0.1%)	–	–	136.0	137.9	135.7
Net income ($ mil.)	37.1%	–	–	6.5	(2.6)	12.2
Market value ($ mil.)	–	–	–	–	–	–
Employees	–	–	–	–	–	2,690

ARKANSAS TECH UNIVERSITY

1605 COLISEUM DR
RUSSELLVILLE, AR 728018819
Phone: 479 968-0300
Fax: –
Web: www.atu.edu

CEO: –
CFO: –
HR: Carla Barkley
FYE: June 30
Type: Private

Technically, Arkansas Tech University is more than a tech college. The state-supported, four-year institution of higher education offers undergraduate and graduate degrees in a variety of disciplines, including science, business, arts and humanities, engineering, and computer science. The school employs more than 400 faculty members and has an average enrollment of more than 11,000 students. Based in Russellville, Arkansas, it also operates a small satellite campus in the town of Ozark. Arkansas Tech was founded in 1909 as the Second District Agricultural School. The school's purpose and name were changed in 1925 when it became Arkansas Polytechnic College; it was renamed Arkansas Tech University in 1976.

	Annual Growth	06/14	06/15	06/16	06/17	06/21
Sales ($mil.)	(0.6%)	–	77.4	80.7	81.2	74.8
Net income ($ mil.)	(17.4%)	–	7.4	5.1	2.0	2.4
Market value ($ mil.)	–	–	–	–	–	–
Employees	–	–	–	–	–	1,039

ARKO CORP

8565 Magellan Parkway, Suite 400
Richmond, VA 23227-1150
Phone: 804 730-1568
Fax: –
Web: www.arkocorp.com

NAS: ARKO
CEO: Arie Kotler
CFO: Donald Bassell
HR: –
FYE: December 31
Type: Public

ARKO is a leading independent convenience store operator and is the sixth largest convenience store chain in the US ranked by store count, operating about 1,405 retail convenience stores. Its highly recognizable family of community brands offers delicious, prepared foods, beer, snacks, candy, hot and cold beverages, and multiple popular quick serve restaurant brands. Its high value fast REWARDS loyalty program offers exclusive savings on merchandise and gas. The company operates in four reportable segments: retail, which includes convenience stores selling fuel products and other merchandise to retail customers; wholesale, which supplies fuel to independent dealers and consignment agents; GPM Petroleum, which sells and supplies fuel to its retail and wholesale sites; and fleet fueling, which operates proprietary cardlock locations, manages third-party cardlock locations, and markets fuel cards that give customers access to a nationwide network of fueling sites.

	Annual Growth	12/19	12/20	12/21	12/22	12/23
Sales ($mil.)	22.9%	4,128.7	3,910.7	7,417.4	9,142.8	9,412.7
Net income ($ mil.)	–	–	(43.5)	13.2	59.2	71.7	34.4
Market value ($ mil.)	–	–	–	1,045.5	1,018.8	1,006.0	958.4
Employees	7.5%	10,102	10,380	11,236	12,223	13,481

ARLINGTON INDUSTRIES, INC.

1 STAUFFER INDUSTRIAL PARK
SCRANTON, PA 185179620
Phone: 570 562-0270
Fax: –
Web: www.aifittings.com

CEO: –
CFO: –
HR: –
FYE: December 31
Type: Private

Thank goodness for zinc's abundance; the element has enabled Arlington Industry's dominance in manufacturing individual zinc die-cast line items. Arlington manufactures and distributes a slew of metallic and non-metallic fittings and connectors. Its lineup includes bushings, cable connectors, concrete pipe sleeves, conduit bodies, gaskets, and screw couplings used in the electrical and construction markets. The company operates a sole plant in Scranton, Pennsylvania. Since 2003 the privately-held manufacturing company has introduced more than 400 new products.

ARMANINO FOODS OF DISTINCTION, INC.

5976 West Las Positas Blvd, Suite 200
Pleasanton, CA 94588
Phone: 510 441-9300
Fax: –
Web: www.armaninofoods.com

NBB: AMNF
CEO: Tim Anderson
CFO: Edgar Estonina
HR: Rita Rupp
FYE: December 31
Type: Public

Armanino Foods would tell us: "You're too skinny! Eat!" Armanino Foods of Distinction makes upscale frozen and refrigerated Italian-style food. Its flagship product is pesto and it makes half a dozen varieties. The company also manufactures frozen filled pastas and frozen meatballs. It counts other US food manufacturers, restaurants, and foodservice vendors among its customers, as well as club stores and major retail food chains. Near its headquarters in Hayward, California, Armanino Foods operates pesto and pasta production facilities. The firm processes its meat in nearby Stockton, California. It has branch offices in San Francisco, Sacramento, Los Angeles, Las Vegas, Boston, and Sioux City, Iowa.

	Annual Growth	12/18	12/19	12/20	12/21	12/22
Sales ($mil.)	8.4%	41.8	42.6	31.8	43.8	57.9
Net income ($ mil.)	1.3%	6.3	6.5	2.0	5.7	6.6
Market value ($ mil.)	5.9%	91.4	112.2	81.4	105.8	115.1
Employees	(5.1%)	42	42	37	35	34

ARMATA PHARMACEUTICALS INC

5005 McConnell Avenue
Los Angeles, CA 90066
Phone: 310 665-2928
Fax: –
Web: www.armatapharma.com

ASE: ARMP
CEO: Todd R Patrick
CFO: Steve R Martin
HR: –
FYE: December 31
Type: Public

AmpliPhi Biosciences (formerly called Targeted Genetics) is amping up the fight against bacterial infections. The drug developer focuses on anti-bacterial (bacteriophage) therapeutics. It was after the 2011 acquisition of Biocontrol that AmpliPhi reorganized itself; going from being focused on developing DNA-based gene therapies to encourage (or sometimes inhibit) the production of proteins associated with disease to its current focus of treatments for antibiotic-resistant bacterial infections. The field for anti-infective treatments is receiving great attention these days with the spread of antibiotic-resistant infections such as the deadly methicillin-resistant Staphylococcus aureus aka MRSA.

	Annual Growth	12/19	12/20	12/21	12/22	12/23
Sales ($mil.)	–	–	0.8	4.5	5.5	4.5
Net income ($ mil.)	–	(19.5)	(22.2)	(23.2)	(36.9)	(69.0)
Market value ($ mil.)	(0.1%)	117.4	107.8	198.0	44.8	117.0
Employees	–	38	62	71	75	–

ARMCO METALS HOLDINGS INC

1730 S Amphelt Blvd, #230
San Mateo, CA 94402
Phone: 650 212-7620
Fax: –
Web: www.armcometals.com

CEO: –
CFO: –
HR: –
FYE: December 31
Type: Public

Steel is important to China's growth and iron ore is important to steel. That's where China Armco Metals comes in. The company imports ores for sale to steel mills and other heavy industry. Its iron, copper, chrome, and nickel ore, as well as coal, come from South America and Asia. Armco's largest customers include Lianyungang Jiaxin Resources Import & Export, Sundial Metals and Minerals, and China-Base Ningbo Foreign Trade, together about two-thirds of sales. The company also imports and recycles scrap metal, a cheaper replacement for iron ore in steel production. Armco was incorporated in 2001 in China as Armco & Metawise; it went public in 2008 through a reverse merger with US firm Cox Distributing.

	Annual Growth	12/10	12/11	12/12	12/13	12/14
Sales ($mil.)	15.9%	68.8	106.2	106.6	128.7	124.2
Net income ($ mil.)	–	(2.2)	(3.3)	(2.6)	(4.1)	1.9
Market value ($ mil.)	(50.8%)	21.8	1.6	2.7	1.7	1.3
Employees	(20.2%)	131	115	98	58	53

ARMED FORCES BENEFIT ASSOCIATION

909 N WASHINGTON ST
ALEXANDRIA, VA 223141555
Phone: 703 549-4455
Fax: –
Web: www.afba.com

CEO: –
CFO: –
HR: A J Hoover
FYE: December 31
Type: Private

Taking risks that might scare off other commercial insurance companies, Armed Forces Benefit Association (AFBA) provides group life insurance products for military personnel, government employees, police officers and firefighters, and defense department contractors. The not-for-profit membership association was established in 1947 and has some 300,000 members; its policies contain no war or terrorism restrictions. It sells property/casualty policies through affiliate Armed Forces Insurance. AFBA's for-profit 5Star Financial division, founded in 1989, sells to the general public, offering individual life insurance, supplemental health insurance, and other financial services such as banking and mutual funds.

	Annual Growth	12/03	12/04	12/05	12/21	12/22
Sales ($mil.)	(0.3%)	–	141.1	129.4	157.9	134.7
Net income ($ mil.)	–	–	10.0	1.7	(19.2)	(21.1)
Market value ($ mil.)	–	–	–	–	–	–
Employees	–	–	–	–	–	210

ARMOUR RESIDENTIAL REIT INC.   NYS: ARR

3001 Ocean Drive, Suite 201
Vero Beach, FL 32963
Phone: 772 617-4340
Fax: –
Web: www.armourreit.com

CEO: Scott J Ulm
CFO: James R Mountain
HR: –
FYE: December 31
Type: Public

ARMOUR Residential hopes to protect its investments with the strength of the US government. A real estate investment trust, or REIT, ARMOUR Residential invests in single-family residential mortgage-backed securities issued or guaranteed by Fannie Mae, Freddie Mac, and Ginnie Mae. The company's investments include fixed-rate, adjustable-rate, and hybrid adjustable-rate mortgages (hybrid mortgages start off with fixed rates that may eventually increase as the loan matures). To a lesser extent, the company also invests in government-issued bonds, unsecured notes, and other debt. Formed in 2008, ARMOUR Residential is externally managed by ARMOUR Residential Management LLC.

	Annual Growth	12/19	12/20	12/21	12/22	12/23
Assets ($mil.)	(1.8%)	13,272	5,524.5	5,277.3	9,437.0	12,344
Net income ($ mil.)	–	(249.9)	(215.1)	15.4	(229.9)	(67.9)
Market value ($ mil.)	2.0%	872.0	526.5	478.7	274.7	942.8
Employees	–	–	–	–	–	–

ARMSTRONG ENERGY INC

7733 Forsyth Boulevard, Suite 1625
St. Louis, MO 63105
Phone: 314 721-8202
Fax: –
Web: www.armstrongenergyinc.com

CEO: –
CFO: –
HR: –
FYE: December 31
Type: Public

Armstrong Energy is strong on coal. The company produces coal from Kentucky's Illinois Basin with proved and probable reserves of 319 million tons; it sells about 7 million tons of coal per year to utilities. In addition to six mines, the company also owns three coal processing plants along the Green River with access to river, rail, and truck transportation. Armstrong Energy uses a variety of coal seams and processing techniques to deliver custom blends to its energy plant customers. The company leases the land its mine are on from its sister firm, real estate management company Armstrong Resource Partners. Both are owned by investors Yorktown Partners.

	Annual Growth	12/12	12/13	12/14	12/15	12/16
Sales ($mil.)	(9.7%)	382.1	415.3	441.8	360.9	253.9
Net income ($ mil.)	–	(18.0)	(25.1)	(28.8)	(162.1)	(58.8)
Market value ($ mil.)	–	–	–	–	–	–
Employees	–	–	1,046	980	751	637

ARMSTRONG WORLD INDUSTRIES INC   NYS: AWI

2500 Columbia Avenue
Lancaster, PA 17603
Phone: 717 397-0611
Fax: –
Web: www.armstrong.com

CEO: Victor D Grizzle
CFO: Christopher P Calzaretta
HR: Michelle Bloxham
FYE: December 31
Type: Public

Armstrong World Industries (AWI) is a leading producer of ceiling systems for use in the construction and renovation of commercial and residential buildings. It designs, manufactures and sells ceiling and wall systems (primarily mineral fiber, fiberglass wool, metal, wood, wood fiber, glass-reinforced-gypsum and felt). Among the company's brands are Armstrong, Calla, Cirrus, Dune, HumiGuard, Total Acoustics, and WoodWorks. AWI makes its products in over 15 plants in the US and Canada. Most of AWI's sales are to distributors. The US accounts for over 90% of the company's sales. The company was founded in 1860.

	Annual Growth	12/19	12/20	12/21	12/22	12/23
Sales ($mil.)	5.7%	1,038.1	936.9	1,106.6	1,233.1	1,295.2
Net income ($ mil.)	1.1%	214.5	(99.1)	183.2	202.9	223.8
Market value ($ mil.)	1.1%	4,125.5	3,265.9	5,097.9	3,011.2	4,316.5
Employees	5.5%	2,500	2,700	2,800	3,000	3,100

ARMY & AIR FORCE EXCHANGE SERVICE

3911 S WALTON WALKER BLVD
DALLAS, TX 752361598
Phone: 214 312-2011
Fax: –
Web: www.shopmyexchange.com

CEO: –
CFO: –
HR: –
FYE: January 28
Type: Private

The Army and Air Force Exchange Service (the Exchange) is a joint non-appropriated fund instrumentality (NAFI) of the US organized under the Departments of the US Army and the US Air Force. The Exchange provides retail services (including e-commerce) to soldiers, airmen, and their families through a network of stores located on US Government installations in the US, Europe, the Pacific Rim, and the Middle East. Middle East services operating in Afghanistan and Iraq primarily provide support for Operation Freedom Sentinel (OFS) and Operation Inherent Resolve (OIR). Its presence ranges from tents to shopping centers, including 580 convenience and retail stores, more than 1,600 fast-food outlets, more than 50 movie theaters, 3,470-plus mall stores and kiosks, including barbershops, wellness services such as dentistry and optometry, and some 250 gas stations dispensing more than 390 million gallons of fuel in 2021.

ARNET PHARMACEUTICAL CORPORATION

2525 DAVIE RD STE 330
DAVIE, FL 333177403
Phone: 954 236-9053
Fax: –
Web: www.arnetusa.com

CEO: –
CFO: Adam Friedman
HR: –
FYE: December 31
Type: Private

Arnet Pharmaceutical manufactures private-label nutritional supplements. Its products range from daily vitamins and herbal extracts to minerals and amino acids. The company's capabilities include making tablet, capsule, powder, and chewable products. As a contract manufacturer, Arnet will work from customer-provided formulations or formulate products themselves. It also produces blended products such as Osteoporex, a calcium blend to address osteoporosis, and Gluthatione, an antioxidant supplement to increases energy and reduces stress. Founded in 1972, Arnet's customers span across more than 50 countries.

ARNOLD & PORTER KAYE SCHOLER LLP

601 MASSACHUSETTS AVE NW
WASHINGTON, DC 200015369
Phone: 202 942-5000
Fax: –
Web: www.arnoldporter.com

CEO: –
CFO: –
HR: –
FYE: December 31
Type: Private

Arnold & Porter Kaye Scholer's lawyers practice in more than 40 practice areas across the litigation, regulatory, and transactional spectrum to help clients with complex needs stay ahead of the global market, anticipate opportunities and address issues that impact the very value of their businesses. The firm's global reach, experience and deep knowledge allow it to work across geographic, cultural, technological, and ideological borders, to offer clients forward-looking, results-oriented solutions that resolve their US, international and cross-border legal need. The firm has about 15 Offices in the US, Europe, and Asia.

	Annual Growth	12/18	12/19	12/20	12/21	12/22
Sales ($mil.)	(37.1%)	–	–	–	1.3	0.8
Net income ($ mil.)	(94.2%)	–	–	–	0.8	0.0
Market value ($ mil.)	–	–	–	–	–	–
Employees	–	–	–	–	–	1,500

ARNOLD MACHINERY COMPANY

2975 W 2100 S
SALT LAKE CITY, UT 841191273
Phone: 801 972-4000
Fax: –
Web: www.arnoldmachinery.com

CEO: –
CFO: Jon Pugmire
HR: Samantha Luna
FYE: September 24
Type: Private

Arnold Machinery, through its four divisions, distributes construction, mining, industrial, and material handling equipment, as well as farm machinery throughout the US. The company's General Implement Distributors is a wholesale distributor of short-line farm implements supplying local farm implement dealers through the Intermountain Area and the Pacific Northwest. Arnold Machinery serve industries such as agriculture, farm implement dealers, construction, fabrication, government agencies, mining and warehousing. The company is headquartered in Salt Lake City, Utah, with a full-service branch facilities located throughout Idaho, Utah, Wyoming, Nevada, Colorado, and Arizona. It was established in 1929.

	Annual Growth	09/17	09/18	09/19	09/20	09/21
Sales ($mil.)	4.3%	–	363.5	367.0	399.5	413.0
Net income ($ mil.)	3.3%	–	18.1	18.3	20.4	19.9
Market value ($ mil.)	–	–	–	–	–	–
Employees	–	–	–	–	–	600

ARO LIQUIDATION, INC.

125 CHUBB AVE
LYNDHURST, NJ 070713504
Phone: 201 508-5576
Fax: –
Web: www.aeropostale.com

CEO: –
CFO: –
HR: –
FYE: January 31
Type: Private

The company is a specialty retailer of casual apparel and accessories principally serving young woman and men through its A ropostale stores and the company's ecommerce site, Aeropostale.com. Operating in Europe, the Middle East, Asia, and America, it stocks the usual teen outerwear (jeans, T-shirts, accessories), mostly under the A ropostale and A ro names. A ropostale maintains control over its proprietary brands by designing, sourcing, marketing and selling all of its own merchandise. The history of the name dates back to the 1920's.

AROTECH CORPORATION

1229 OAK VALLEY DR
ANN ARBOR, MI 481089675
Phone: 800 281-0356
Fax: –
Web: www.arotech.com

CEO: Dean M Krutty
CFO: –
HR: –
FYE: December 31
Type: Private

Arotech has broadened its horizon from making batteries and chargers in 1990 to military training simulators, and aviation and vehicle armor. Subsidiary FAAC supplies simulators, related software, and training for the US military, and various government and private industry clients. MDT Protective Industries and MDT Armor produce lightweight armor and ballistic glass for vehicles, as well as aircraft armor kits under the Armour of America name. Arotech also makes lithium batteries and charging systems for military and homeland security markets via Electric Fuel Battery and Epsilor Electronic Industries. The US government (through its military branches) is Arotech's #1 customer, representing about 40% of sales.

ARPIN MOVING, INC.

99 JAMES P MURPHY IND HWY
WEST WARWICK, RI 028932382
Phone: 800 343-3500
Fax: –
Web: www.arpinintl.com

CEO: David Arpin
CFO: Michael Killoran
HR: –
FYE: December 31
Type: Private

From the fairway to the highway and home again, Arpin Van Lines provides a wide range of moving services for residential, business, and government customers, which have included the LPGA. The company, formerly known as Paul Arpin Van Lines, operates through a network of independent agents throughout North America. (The agents handle local moves within assigned geographic territories; Arpin Van Lines coordinates interstate moves.) Arpin Van Lines' fleet includes some 700 trucks. The company, which is run by members of the founding Arpin family, is a division of Arpin Group, which also includes Arpin International Group and Arpin Moving Systems (Canada). The original Arpin moving company was founded in 1900.

	Annual Growth	12/05	12/06	12/07	12/09	12/10
Sales ($mil.)	(2.3%)	–	–	113.5	105.8	105.7
Net income ($ mil.)	(14.9%)	–	–	0.6	1.1	0.4
Market value ($ mil.)	–	–	–	–	–	–
Employees	–	–	–	–	–	79

ARQ INC
NMS: ARQ

8051 E. Maplewood Ave, Suite 210
Greenwood Village, CO 80111
Phone: 720 598-3500
Fax: -
Web: www.advancedemissionssolutions.com

CEO: -
CFO: -
HR: -
FYE: December 31
Type: Public

Advanced Emissions Solutions wants to make "clean coal" more than just a marketing term. The company makes environmental technology systems and specialty chemicals to reduce emissions at coal-burning power plants. It offers integrated mercury control systems, as well as flue gas conditioning and combustion aid chemicals. Advanced Emissions Solutions provides consulting and testing services and mercury measurement equipment. It also has a joint venture with NexGen Refined Coal to market technology that reduces emissions of nitrogen oxides and mercury from some treated coals. The company has three reportable segments: Refined Coal, Emission Control, and CO2 Capture.

	Annual Growth	12/19	12/20	12/21	12/22	12/23
Sales ($mil.)	9.1%	70.1	61.6	100.3	103.0	99.2
Net income ($ mil.)	-	35.5	(20.3)	60.4	(8.9)	(12.2)
Market value ($ mil.)	(27.0%)	348.3	182.5	219.6	80.6	98.9
Employees	6.8%	133	136	139	147	173

ARQULE, INC.

1 WALL ST STE 603
BURLINGTON, MA 018034769
Phone: 781 994-0300
Fax: -
Web: www.arqule.com

CEO: -
CFO: -
HR: -
FYE: December 31
Type: Private

ArQule is pursuing drug research in the molecular biology field, with a focus on cancer cell termination. The biotechnology firm works independently and with other drugmakers to discover new potential drug compounds based on its cancer-inhibiting technology platform. ArQule is developing a portfolio of oncology drugs, with a handful of anti-cancer compounds undergoing clinical trials. Its lead product candidate, in Phase 2 and Phase 3 clinical development together with development and commercialization partner, Daiichi Sankyo, is tivantinib, an oral, selective inhibitor of the c-MET receptor tyrosine kinase.

ARRAY NETWORKS, INC.

1371 MCCARTHY BLVD
MILPITAS, CA 950357432
Phone: 408 240-8700
Fax: -
Web: www.arraynetworks.com

CEO: -
CFO: -
HR: -
FYE: December 31
Type: Private

Array Networks attacks the problems of application performance and network security. The company makes networking equipment that companies use to securely manage and deliver applications. Its products include virtual private network (VPN) and application server appliances. Utilizing its direct sales force and reseller partners, the company markets to banks, telecom services providers, and other large enterprises worldwide. Its customers have included Amdocs, CNN, Humana, and Vodafone. Founded in 2000, the company counts H&Q Asian Pacific and U.S. Venture Partners among its investors.

	Annual Growth	12/04	12/05	12/06	12/16	12/17
Sales ($mil.)	4.0%	-	12.3	14.2	16.8	19.7
Net income ($ mil.)	-	-	(2.0)	(4.6)	(2.1)	(2.7)
Market value ($ mil.)	-	-	-	-	-	-
Employees	-	-	-	-	-	32

ARRIS GROUP, INC.

3871 LAKEFIELD DR STE 300
SUWANEE, GA 300241292
Phone: 678 473-2907
Fax: -
Web: www.arris.com

CEO: -
CFO: -
HR: -
FYE: December 31
Type: Private

ARRIS brings the idea of broadband home. The company makes communications equipment and components used to enable broadband voice and data transmission and to build television broadcast networks. Products include cable network headend gear, Internet protocol switching systems, modems, and other consumer premises products. It also sells such related hardware as cable, connectors, and other supplies used for mounting and installation. ARRIS primarily markets to large cable-network operators. In 2016, ARRIS acquired Pace, a telecom equipment maker based in the UK for $2.1 billion.

ARROW ELECTRONICS, INC.
NYS: ARW

9201 East Dry Creek Road
Centennial, CO 80112
Phone: 303 824-4000
Fax: -
Web: www.arrow.com

CEO: Sean J Kerins
CFO: Rajesh K Agrawal
HR: -
FYE: December 31
Type: Public

Arrow Electronics is a global distributor of electronic components and enterprise computing solutions. It sells semiconductors, passive components, interconnect products, computing and memory and computer peripherals to more than 220,000 equipment and contract manufacturers, resellers, and other commercial customers. The company's Global ECS' portfolio of computing solutions includes datacenter, cloud, security, and analytics solutions. Arrow Electronics, which generates about 70% of revenue outside the US, serves about 210,000 customers over 90 countries. The company was incorporated in New York in 1946.

	Annual Growth	12/19	12/20	12/21	12/22	12/23
Sales ($mil.)	3.4%	28,917	28,673	34,477	37,124	33,107
Net income ($ mil.)	-	(204.1)	584.4	1,108.2	1,426.9	903.5
Market value ($ mil.)	9.6%	4,559.9	5,235.8	7,225.2	5,627.0	6,578.4
Employees	3.4%	19,300	19,600	20,700	22,300	22,100

ARROW FINANCIAL CORP.
NMS: AROW

250 Glen Street
Glens Falls, NY 12801
Phone: 518 745-1000
Fax: -
Web: www.arrowfinancial.com

CEO: David S Demarco
CFO: Edward J Campanella
HR: Sally Costello
FYE: December 31
Type: Public

Arrow Financial has more than one shaft in its quiver. It's the holding company for two banks: $2 billion-asset Glens Falls National Bank operates 30 branches in eastern upstate New York, while $400 million-asset Saratoga National Bank and Trust Company has around 10 branches in Saratoga County. Serving local individuals and businesses, the banks offer standard deposit and loan products as well as retirement, trust, and estate planning services and employee benefit plan administration. Its subsidiaries include: McPhillips Insurance Agency and Upstate Agency, which offer property and casualty insurance; Capital Financial Group, which sells group health plans; and North Country Investment Advisors, which provides financial planning services.

	Annual Growth	12/19	12/20	12/21	12/22	12/23
Assets ($mil.)	7.0%	3,184.3	3,688.6	4,028.0	3,969.5	4,169.9
Net income ($ mil.)	(5.4%)	37.5	40.8	49.9	48.8	30.1
Market value ($ mil.)	(7.3%)	640.4	506.7	596.9	574.4	473.4
Employees	0.8%	520	517	512	502	537

ARROW RESOURCES DEVELOPMENT, INC.　　　　　　　NBB: ARWD

Carnegie Hall Tower, 152 W. 57th Street, 27th Floor　　　CEO: Peter J Frugone
New York, NY 10019　　　　　　　　　　　　　　　　　　CFO: –
Phone: 212 262-2300　　　　　　　　　　　　　　　　　　HR: –
Fax: –　　　　　　　　　　　　　　　　　　　　　　　　FYE: December 31
Web: www.arrowrd.com　　　　　　　　　　　　　　　　Type: Public

Arrow Resources Development may have found its bullseye. After stints in wireless equipment, merchant banking, and real estate, the company is targeting natural resources. Arrow provides corporate, marketing, sales, and other services for regional companies that exploit timber, oil, and other natural resources in Indonesia. Working to restore areas that have been illegally deforested, the company combines tree farms (primarily eucalyptus, for the paper products industries) with farming operations (mostly corn), while using organic fertilizers and renewable energy sources and focusing on environmental and wildlife issues. Indonesian financier Hans Karundeng's Arrow Pacific Resources Group owns 53% of the firm.

	Annual Growth	12/08	12/09	12/10	12/11	12/12
Sales ($mil.)	–	0.0	–	–	–	–
Net income ($ mil.)	–	(5.4)	(6.5)	(8.9)	(8.8)	(8.6)
Market value ($ mil.)	(36.1%)	69.1	21.6	49.9	12.3	11.5
Employees	–	–	–	–	–	–

ARROWHEAD PHARMACEUTICALS INC　　　　　　　NMS: ARWR

177 E. Colorado Blvd., Suite 700　　　　　　　　CEO: Christopher Anzalone
Pasadena, CA 91105　　　　　　　　　　　　　　CFO: Kenneth A Myszkowski
Phone: 626 304-3400　　　　　　　　　　　　　　HR: –
Fax: –　　　　　　　　　　　　　　　　　　　　　FYE: September 30
Web: www.arrowheadpharma.com　　　　　　　　Type: Public

Arrowhead Pharmaceuticals develops drugs that silence disease-causing genes in the body. Its RNA interference (RNAi) platform, named Targeted RNAi Molecule or TRiM, utilizes ligand-mediated delivery and is designed to enable tissue-specific targeting while being structurally simple. The company's JNJ-3989 (formerly ARO-HBV) drug is in clinical trials for the treatment of hepatitis B. Arrowhead has other RNA assets that are being explored to work in combination with ARO-HBV to treat various diseases. In late 2016 the company stopped developing its intravenously delivered dynamic polyconjugate delivery vehicle programs in order to focus on its TRiM technology. Arrowhead was originally incorporated in 1989.

	Annual Growth	09/19	09/20	09/21	09/22	09/23
Sales ($mil.)	9.3%	168.8	88.0	138.3	243.2	240.7
Net income ($ mil.)	–	68.0	(84.6)	(140.8)	(176.1)	(205.3)
Market value ($ mil.)	(1.2%)	3,024.1	4,620.9	6,699.5	3,546.7	2,883.5
Employees	48.1%	109	232	329	397	525

ARROWHEAD REGIONAL MEDICAL CENTER

400 N PEPPER AVE　　　　　　　　　　　　　　　CEO: –
COLTON, CA 923241801　　　　　　　　　　　　　CFO: –
Phone: 909 580-1000　　　　　　　　　　　　　　HR: –
Fax: –　　　　　　　　　　　　　　　　　　　　　FYE: June 30
Web: www.arrowheadregional.org　　　　　　　　Type: Private

Find yourself dehydrated after searching the Inland Empire deserts for arrowheads? Arrowhead Regional Medical Center (ARMC) can fix you up. The San Bernardino County owned and operated hospital provides a range of health services, from general medical and surgical care to emergency services, rehabilitation, inpatient psychiatric care, pediatric, and women's health services. It also serves as a Level II trauma center, a regional burn center, and medical training facility. ARMC, with some 460 beds (370 inpatient and 90 behavioral), opened in 1999 to replace the aging San Bernardino County Hospital. The hospital also offers outpatient services on its main campus and at area clinics.

	Annual Growth	06/02	06/03	06/04	06/09	06/15
Sales ($mil.)	3.4%	–	313.5	439.1	225.0	469.0
Net income ($ mil.)	–	–	(1.1)	3.7	25.4	74.3
Market value ($ mil.)	–	–	–	–	–	–
Employees	–	–	–	–	–	2,500

ART CENTER COLLEGE OF DESIGN INC

1700 LIDA ST　　　　　　　　　　　　　　　　　　CEO: –
PASADENA, CA 911031999　　　　　　　　　　　　CFO: –
Phone: 626 396-2200　　　　　　　　　　　　　　HR: Dave D Raddo
Fax: –　　　　　　　　　　　　　　　　　　　　　FYE: June 30
Web: www.artcenter.edu　　　　　　　　　　　　　Type: Private

Art Center College of Design (ACCD) is designing a future of creativity for its students. The college offers undergraduate and graduate degrees in such fields as advertising, film, fine art media, graphic design, illustration, photography, industrial design, product design, and transportation design. Degrees offered include 11 Bachelor of Fine Arts and Bachelor of Science programs and six Master of Fine Arts and Master of Science programs. ACCD, which has an enrollment of about 1,700 full-time students, is ranked among top design schools in the US.

	Annual Growth	06/13	06/14	06/15	06/20	06/22
Sales ($mil.)	0.4%	–	121.1	94.1	136.2	124.7
Net income ($ mil.)	–	–	2.8	(5.5)	(0.6)	(19.2)
Market value ($ mil.)	–	–	–	–	–	–
Employees	–	–	–	–	–	400

ART VAN FURNITURE, LLC

2301 E EVESHAM RD　　　　　　　　　　　　　　CEO: –
VOORHEES, NJ 080434501　　　　　　　　　　　　CFO: –
Phone: 586 939-2100　　　　　　　　　　　　　　HR: –
Fax: –　　　　　　　　　　　　　　　　　　　　　FYE: September 30
Web: www.artvan.com　　　　　　　　　　　　　　Type: Private

Art Van Furniture is one of the leading furniture and mattress retailers in the US with some 190 locations in nine states (primarily the Midwest). Its stores, which operate under several Art Van, Levin, and Wolf banners, offer a full range of upscale furniture for the home from national brands such as La-Z-Boy, Simmons, Cindy Crawford, Serta, Beautyrest, and Magnolia Home. Most stores are company-owned, although Art Van Furniture does franchise some locations. The late Art Van Elslander founded the company with an East Detroit store in 1959. It is now owned by private equity firm Thomas H. Lee Partners.

ARTECH L.L.C.

360 MOUNT KEMBLE AVE STE 3　　　　　　　　　CEO: –
MORRISTOWN, NJ 079606662　　　　　　　　　　CFO: –
Phone: 973 998-2500　　　　　　　　　　　　　　HR: Manisha Ganguly
Fax: –　　　　　　　　　　　　　　　　　　　　　FYE: December 31
Web: www.artechinfo.com　　　　　　　　　　　　Type: Private

Artech Information Systems comes to the rescue for the technically unsavvy. The minority- and woman-owned company specializes in providing IT staffing and consulting, project management, and business process outsourcing (BPO) services. Artech Information Systems serves clients in the financial services, pharmaceutical, telecommunications, and technology industries, among others. The company, which operates from more than 30 locations in China, India, Mexico, and the US, also works with federal and state government agencies. It provides its services 24 hours a day, seven days a week.

ARTEL, LLC

13665 DULLES TECHNOLOGY DR STE 300　　　　　CEO: Paul Domorski
HERNDON, VA 201714607　　　　　　　　　　　　　CFO: -
Phone: 703 620-1700　　　　　　　　　　　HR: Karen Randolph
Fax: -　　　　　　　　　　　　　　　　　　FYE: December 31
Web: www.artelllc.com　　　　　　　　　　　　Type: Private

Information technology is the name of the game for ARTEL. The company provides a range of managed network and IT systems integration services for government and corporate clients. Its areas of specialty include strategic planning, database management, and telecom network management. ARTEL also offers systems engineering services that enable federal, state, and local government agencies to provide online services and information to constituents. The company's communications services are made possible through partnerships with network operators such as AT&T, KDDI, and Eutelsat. Customers have included the US Nuclear Regulatory Commission and SES World Skies. ARTEL was founded in 1986 by CEO Abbas Yazdani.

ARTESIAN RESOURCES CORP.　　　　　　　　NMS: ARTN A

664 Churchmans Road　　　　　　　　　　　　CEO: Dian C Taylor
Newark, DE 19702　　　　　　　　　　　　　CFO: David B Spacht
Phone: 302 453-6900　　　　　　　　　　　　HR: Kathy Thaeder
Fax: -　　　　　　　　　　　　　　　　　　FYE: December 31
Web: www.artesianwater.com　　　　　　　　　Type: Public

All's well that ends in wells for Artesian Resources. Operating primarily through regulated utility Artesian Water, the company provides water in parts of Delaware, Maryland, and Pennsylvania (about 76,300 metered customers). It serves residential, commercial, industrial, municipal, and utility customers; residential customers account for about 55% of the utility's water sales. Artesian pumps nearly 2 billion gallons of water annually from its wells, then sends it to customers through approximately 1,300 miles of mains. The company also provides wastewater services in Delaware, Pennsylvania, and Maryland.

	Annual Growth	12/19	12/20	12/21	12/22	12/23
Sales ($mil.)	4.3%	83.6	88.1	90.9	98.9	98.9
Net income ($ mil.)	2.8%	14.9	16.8	16.8	18.0	16.7
Market value ($ mil.)	2.7%	382.7	381.4	476.5	602.5	426.3
Employees	1.2%	239	235	245	252	251

ARTISAN PARTNERS ASSET MANAGEMENT INC　　　NYS: APAM

875 E. Wisconsin Avenue, Suite 800　　　　　　　CEO: Eric R Colson
Milwaukee, WI 53202　　　　　　　　　　　CFO: Charles J Daley Jr
Phone: 414 390-6100　　　　　　　　　　　　HR: -
Fax: -　　　　　　　　　　　　　　　　　　FYE: December 31
Web: www.artisanpartners.com　　　　　　　　Type: Public

These artisans are into making bread. Artisan Partners Asset Management is an institutional investment manager with $64 billion in assets under management. The firm manages a dozen funds, from small- and mid-cap growth and value funds to foreign and emerging markets funds. It acts as the investment adviser to Artisan Funds mutual funds, which account for about 55% of its assets under management. The remainder is made up of separate accounts for institutional investors, including pension plans, trusts, endowments, foundations, not-for-profit organizations, government entities, and private companies. Founded in 1994, Artisan Partners Asset Management went public in 2013.

	Annual Growth	12/19	12/20	12/21	12/22	12/23
Sales ($mil.)	5.1%	799.0	899.6	1,227.2	993.3	975.1
Net income ($ mil.)	9.2%	156.5	212.6	336.5	206.8	222.3
Market value ($ mil.)	8.1%	2,586.1	4,027.9	3,811.9	2,376.4	3,535.1
Employees	6.8%	440	453	498	549	573

ARTISANAL BRANDS INC.

483 Tenth Avenue　　　　　　　　　　　　　CEO: Daniel W Dowe
New York, NY 10018　　　　　　　　　　　　CFO: -
Phone: 212 871-3150　　　　　　　　　　　　HR: -
Fax: -　　　　　　　　　　　　　　　　　　FYE: May 31
Web: www.artisanalcheese.com　　　　　　　　Type: Public

Artisanal Brands, which does business as Artisanal Cheese, aspires to be the big cheese. Formerly a building supply marketing firm, the company is now active in the marketing of private-label foods. In 2007 it acquired specialty food company Artisanal Premium Cheese for about $4.5 million. At the same time, the company sold its building material assets for approximately $1 million. Artisanal Cheese markets and sells specialty and handmade cheeses to upscale restaurants and retailers. In addition to wholesale and foodservice distribution, the company sells products in supermarkets, through catalogs, and on its Web site.

	Annual Growth	05/08	05/09	05/10	05/11	05/12
Sales ($mil.)	(14.5%)	-	5.7	4.2	4.6	3.6
Net income ($ mil.)	-	-	(1.6)	(2.3)	(2.5)	(4.3)
Market value ($ mil.)	(46.3%)	-	8.1	3.4	4.8	1.3
Employees	-	-	-	23	30	34

ARTIVION INC　　　　　　　　　　　　　　NYS: AORT

1655 Roberts Boulevard NW　　　　　　　　　CEO: J P Mackin
Kennesaw, GA 30144　　　　　　　　　　　CFO: Lance A Berry
Phone: 770 419-3355　　　　　　　　　　　　HR: -
Fax: 770 426-0031　　　　　　　　　　　　　FYE: December 31
Web: www.artivion.com　　　　　　　　　　　Type: Public

Artivion (formerly known as CryoLife) is a leader in the manufacturing, processing, and distribution of medical devices and implantable human tissues used in cardiac and vascular surgical procedures for patients with aortic disease. The company has four major product families: aortic stent grafts, surgical sealants, On-X mechanical heart valves and related surgical products, and implantable cardiac and vascular human tissues. Aortic stents and stent grafts include E-vita Open NEO, the Ascyrus Medical Dissection Stent (AMDS) hybrid prosthesis, and the NEXUS endovascular stent graft system. Surgical sealants include BioGlue Surgical Adhesive (BioGlue) products. In addition to these four major product families, it sells or distributes PhotoFix bovine surgical patches, CardioGenesis cardiac laser therapy, and PerClot hemostatic powder (prior to the sale to a subsidiary of Baxter.. Half of its comes from the US.

	Annual Growth	12/19	12/20	12/21	12/22	12/23
Sales ($mil.)	6.4%	276.2	253.2	298.8	313.8	354.0
Net income ($ mil.)	-	1.7	(16.7)	(14.8)	(19.2)	(30.7)
Market value ($ mil.)	(9.9%)	1,112.9	969.9	836.0	497.9	734.5
Employees	5.7%	1,200	1,200	1,300	1,300	1,500

ARTS WAY MANUFACTURING CO INC　　　　　　NAS: ARTW

5556 Highway 9　　　　　　　　　　　　　CEO: David A King
Armstrong, IA 50514　　　　　　　　　　　CFO: Michael W Woods
Phone: 712 208-8467　　　　　　　　　　　　HR: -
Fax: 712 864-3154　　　　　　　　　　　　　FYE: November 30
Web: www.artsway-mfg.com　　　　　　　　　Type: Public

Sinatra did it his way, but farmers have been doing it Art's way since 1956. Art's-Way Manufacturing makes an assortment of machinery under its own label and its customers' private labels. Art's-Way equipment includes custom animal-feed processing machines, high-bulk mixing wagons, mowers and stalk shredders, and equipment for harvesting sugar beets and potatoes. Its private-label OEM customers include CNH Global, for whom Art's-Way makes and supplies hay blowers. Equipment dealers throughout the US sell Art's-Way products. Steel truck bodies are also manufactured under the Cherokee Truck Bodies name. Art's-Way owns subsidiaries Art's-Way Vessels and Art's-Way Scientific.

	Annual Growth	11/19	11/20	11/21	11/22	11/23
Sales ($mil.)	7.2%	22.9	22.4	25.0	28.4	30.3
Net income ($ mil.)	-	(1.4)	(2.1)	0.2	0.0	0.3
Market value ($ mil.)	2.9%	9.2	12.5	17.7	9.7	10.3
Employees	4.7%	103	126	139	149	124

ARTSQUEST

25 W 3RD ST STE 300
BETHLEHEM, PA 180151238
Phone: 610 332-1300
Fax: –
Web: www.artsquest.org

CEO: Kassie Hilgert
CFO: –
HR: –
FYE: December 31
Type: Private

ArtsQuest looks for ways to celebrate art in Bethlehem, Pennsylvania. The not-for-profit group promotes performing and visual arts through classes, after-school programs, and, mainly through its three signature venues. Banana Factory is an arts center with two galleries and about 25 studios offering classes, lectures, and touring works from around the world. It is funded by Christkindlmarkt, ArtsQuest's European-themed Christmas arts and crafts fair with more than 150 vendors. Musikfest, the organization's original program, features more than 300 musical performers in an annual week long festival that attracts more than a million people each year. ArtsQuest began in 1963 as the Bethlehem Musikfest Association.

	Annual Growth	12/12	12/13	12/15	12/17	12/19
Sales ($mil.)	(22.0%)	–	14.1	17.8	17.3	3.2
Net income ($ mil.)	–	–	(1.8)	(0.1)	(4.5)	3.0
Market value ($ mil.)	–	–	–	–	–	–
Employees	–	–	–	–	–	150

ARUBA NETWORKS, INC.

6280 AMERICA CENTER DR
SAN JOSE, CA 950022563
Phone: 408 941-4300
Fax: –
Web: www.hpe.com

CEO: –
CFO: Jon Faust
HR: –
FYE: July 31
Type: Private

Aruba Networks, a unit of Hewlett Packard Enterprise (HPE), has been recognized by third party analysts as a leader in Wi-Fi 6, switching, SD-Branch, and a visionary in Data Center networking. The world's largest companies rely on the company to provide a secure, AI-powered edge services platform that spans across campus, branch, data center, and remote working environments. Products include gateways and controllers, access points, and switches as well as security functions. The company also offers location products and services including beacons, tags, and applications. Customers include DropBox, KEMET, Verisk, US Department of Defense, among others.

ARVIN SANGO, INC.

2905 WILSON AVE
MADISON, IN 472503834
Phone: 812 265-2888
Fax: –
Web: www.arvinsango.com

CEO: –
CFO: –
HR: –
FYE: December 31
Type: Private

Arvin Sango is the North American intersection where Japanese auto parts maker SANGO and carmaker Toyota merge together. The SANGO/ Meritor joint venture supplies automotive components, primarily for Toyota Motor North America's assembly plants. Arvin Sango's products include exhaust system assemblies, body panel stampings, door impact beams, and tubular manifolds. Its facilities use Pokayok, a defect protection technology. The company supplies about 75% of Toyota's exhaust systems in North America. Other customers include Nissan and Subaru.

ASA ELECTRONICS LLC

2602 MARINA DR
ELKHART, IN 465148642
Phone: 574 264-3135
Fax: –
Web: www.asaelectronics.com

CEO: –
CFO: –
HR: –
FYE: November 30
Type: Private

It's likely that more than just a few family road trips may have been saved by Audiovox Specialized Applications (ASA). The 50%-owned subsidiary of Audiovox distributes entertainment systems and video observation units designed for use in mobile applications. The company's brands include Audiovox, Aquatronics, Flexvision, Jensen (flat-panel TVs, marine stereos and speakers), and Voyager (back-up cameras, observation systems). ASA's products can be found in RVs, trucks, family vans, tractors, marine, and construction machinery. The company originated in 1977 as a regional distributor of Audiovox products and is set up with Audiovox having a non-controlling 50% ownership interest.

ASA INTERNATIONAL LTD.

10 SPEEN ST STE 9
FRAMINGHAM, MA 017014661
Phone: 508 626-2727
Fax: –
Web: www.asa-international.com

CEO: –
CFO: –
HR: –
FYE: December 31
Type: Private

ASA International treads a path through a variety of industries. Through its operating divisions, the company provides software, systems, and services to tire dealers and retreaders, systems integrators, law firms, and manufacturing and distribution companies. ASA Tire Systems builds network systems for the tire and automotive aftermarket industries and operates online marketplace eTireLink. Khameleon Software provides e-business management tools for systems integrators. ASA's Rainmaker Software division develops accounting and practice management applications for law firms, and Verticent offers enterprise software for manufacturers and distributors.

	Annual Growth	12/03	12/04	12/05	12/06	12/07
Sales ($mil.)	8.7%	–	16.7	21.0	19.8	21.4
Net income ($ mil.)	(43.6%)	–	1.2	(0.2)	(0.8)	0.2
Market value ($ mil.)	–	–	–	–	–	–
Employees	–	–	–	–	–	110

ASAP SOLUTIONS GROUP, LLC

2400 MEADOWBROOK PKWY
DULUTH, GA 300964635
Phone: 770 246-1718
Fax: –
Web: www.myasap.com

CEO: Nancy A Williams
CFO: Tamar A Harari
HR: –
FYE: December 31
Type: Private

Companies that need IT professionals on the double can go to ASAP Staffing for help. The company provides contract and permanent information technology personnel in a variety of fields, including project management, programming, and technical support. It also provides sale, marketing, and training staff for IT companies. ASAP supports organizations such as American Red Cross, United Way Tocqueville Leadership, Junior Achievement, and C5 Georgia, among others. The company operates in Georgia, Texas, New York and India.

	Annual Growth	12/02	12/03	12/04	12/05	12/17
Sales ($mil.)	5.5%	–	27.1	31.3	34.2	57.5
Net income ($ mil.)	(0.3%)	–	1.5	1.9	2.0	1.4
Market value ($ mil.)	–	–	–	–	–	–
Employees	–	–	–	–	–	740

ASARCO LLC

5285 E WILLIAMS CIR STE 2000
TUCSON, AZ 857117711
Phone: 520 798-7500
Fax: –
Web: www.asarco.com

CEO: –
CFO: –
HR: Debbie McMorrow
FYE: December 31
Type: Private

Copper is king for ASARCO. A subsidiary of diversified mining firm Grupo M xico, ASARCO (American Smelting and Refining Company) operates mining and copper smelting activities, primarily in the Southwestern US. Each year its mines produce from 350 million to 400 million pounds of copper, as well as silver and gold as by-products of copper production. It produces copper cathode, rod, and cake. The company's three mines and a 720,000 tons per year smelter are located in Arizona. It also operates a copper refinery with a 279.5 million pounds per year production capacity in Amarillo, Texas.

ASBURY AUTOMOTIVE GROUP INC   NYS: ABG

2905 Premiere Parkway NW, Suite 300
Duluth, GA 30097
Phone: 770 418-8200
Fax: –
Web: www.asburyauto.com

CEO: David W Hult
CFO: Michael Welch
HR: –
FYE: December 31
Type: Public

Car dealership giant Asbury Automotive Group oversees some 185 new vehicle franchises, representing approximately 140 dealership locations, in some 15 states including the Carolinas, Florida, Texas, and Virginia. The dealerships sell around 30 different brands of US-made and imported new and used vehicles. Asbury also offer parts, servicing, and collision repair from over 30 repair centers as well as financing, insurance, and warranty and service contracts. The auto dealer has grown by acquiring large, locally-branded dealership groups throughout the US. Toyota vehicles account for approximately 50% of Asbury's new car sales.

	Annual Growth	12/19	12/20	12/21	12/22	12/23
Sales ($mil.)	19.7%	7,210.3	7,131.8	9,837.7	15,434	14,803
Net income ($ mil.)	34.4%	184.4	254.4	532.4	997.3	602.5
Market value ($ mil.)	19.1%	2,273.1	2,963.4	3,512.2	3,644.8	4,574.4
Employees	15.3%	8,500	7,900	14,200	13,000	15,000

ASCENDIUM EDUCATION GROUP, INC.

2401 INTERNATIONAL LN
MADISON, WI 537043121
Phone: 608 246-1800
Fax: –
Web: www.ascendiumeducation.org

CEO: Richard D George
CFO: Nancy Seifert
HR: Dennis Cottrell
FYE: December 31
Type: Private

Allying with Great Lakes Higher Education Corporation may be a Superior way to pay for college. The corporation is one of the nation's largest student loan servicers and is the designated student loan guarantor for Minnesota, Ohio, Wisconsin, South Dakota, Iowa, Puerto Rico, and the US Virgin Islands. The company works with the US Department of Education, 1,100 US lenders, and more than 6,000 colleges, universities, and schools. Great Lakes Higher Education Corporation does not originate loans, but guarantees them and collects on them on behalf of lenders. Its Loan Services unit acts as a service provider and Great Lakes Higher Education Guaranty serves as its affiliated guarantor.

	Annual Growth	12/02	12/03	12/04	12/05	12/17
Assets ($mil.)	–	–	–	249.0	326.8	894.7
Net income ($ mil.)	(15.0%)	–	46.6	60.9	80.4	4.8
Market value ($ mil.)	–	–	–	–	–	–
Employees	–	–	–	–	–	900

ASCENSION BORGESS HOSPITAL

1521 GULL RD
KALAMAZOO, MI 490481640
Phone: 269 226-7000
Fax: –
Web: www.borgess.com

CEO: –
CFO: –
HR: –
FYE: June 30
Type: Private

Borgess Medical Center is part of the Borgess Health Alliance, which is a member of the Ascension Health network. The general acute care facility, which serves residents of southwestern Michigan, houses more than 420 beds. It has a comprehensive offering of medical and surgical services, including specialty care in areas such as cancer, heart disease, neuroscience, and orthopedics. Borgess Medical Center also serves as a Level II trauma center and features a research institute, a sleep disorders clinic, a weight loss surgery center, no-wait emergency room, and outpatient facilities. The hospital was founded in 1889 by a local priest.

	Annual Growth	06/13	06/14	06/15	06/16	06/21
Sales ($mil.)	(6.8%)	–	850.1	382.8	394.2	519.1
Net income ($ mil.)	378.6%	–	0.0	28.2	60.7	35.1
Market value ($ mil.)	–	–	–	–	–	–
Employees	–	–	–	–	–	2,200

ASCENSION GENESYS HOSPITAL

1 GENESYS PKWY
GRAND BLANC, MI 484398065
Phone: 810 606-5000
Fax: –
Web: healthcare.ascension.org

CEO: Christopher J Palazzolo
CFO: David Carrol
HR: –
FYE: June 30
Type: Private

Genesys Regional Medical Center generates health care services for residents of a six-county region in eastern Michigan. The integrated medical center features a 410-bed hospital providing general medical and surgical care, as well as specialty care in areas such as heart disease (through the Genesys Heart Institute). Additionally, Genesys Regional includes family medicine, outpatient diagnostic, and rehabilitative care centers. It also operates a women and children's center, and in cooperation with Flint's Hurley Medical Center, it runs the Genesys Hurley Cancer Institute. Genesys Regional is a member the Genesys Health System, which is part of Catholic hospital operator Ascension Health.

	Annual Growth	06/12	06/13	06/14	06/21	06/22
Sales ($mil.)	0.1%	–	415.1	417.6	437.9	419.4
Net income ($ mil.)	–	–	1.8	0.2	31.1	(19.9)
Market value ($ mil.)	–	–	–	–	–	–
Employees	–	–	–	–	–	3,739

ASCENSION HEALTH

4600 EDMUNDSON RD
SAINT LOUIS, MO 631343806
Phone: 314 733-8000
Fax: –
Web: www.ascensionhealth.org

CEO: Joseph R Impicciche
CFO: Anthony J Speranzo
HR: Tandala Cook
FYE: June 30
Type: Private

As one of the leading non-profit and Catholic health systems in the US, Ascension provides approximately $2.3 billion in care of persons living in poverty and other community benefit programs. Ascension includes some 139,000 associates and approximately 36,000 aligned providers. Ascension provides a variety of services including clinical and network services, venture capital investing, investment management, biomedical engineering, facilities management, risk management, and contracting through Ascension's own group purchasing organization. Ascension Health was created in 1999 from a union of the Daughters of Charity National Health System and the Sisters of St. Joseph Health System.

	Annual Growth	06/06	06/07	06/08	06/10	06/15
Sales ($mil.)	(44.2%)	–	–	13,489	14,773	227.8
Net income ($ mil.)	–	–	–	351.0	1,230.9	(18.0)
Market value ($ mil.)	–	–	–	–	–	–
Employees	–	–	–	–	–	109,000

ASCENSION PROVIDENCE HOSPITAL

16001 W 9 MILE RD
SOUTHFIELD, MI 480754818
Phone: 248 849-3000
Fax: –
Web: www.pulmccmprov.org

CEO: Brant Russell
CFO: –
HR: –
FYE: June 30
Type: Private

Providence Hospital and Medical Centers provides health care in the Motor City and surrounding areas. The main Providence Hospital is a 408-bed teaching facility that has been recognized for its cardiology program and clinical expertise in behavioral medicine. It offers a variety of other services ranging from cancer treatment and neurosurgery to orthopedics and women's health. The network also includes dozens of affiliated general practice and specialty health clinics. The not-for-profit medical center, founded in 1845 as St. Vincent's Hospital in Detroit by the Daughters of Charity, is part of Catholic health ministry St. John Health (itself a subsidiary of Ascension Health).

	Annual Growth	06/13	06/14	06/15	06/16	06/21
Sales ($mil.)	4.8%	–	659.5	654.1	703.6	913.7
Net income ($ mil.)	9.3%	–	53.2	25.5	21.6	98.9
Market value ($ mil.)	–	–	–	–	–	–
Employees	–	–	–	–	–	4,700

ASCENSION PROVIDENCE ROCHESTER HOSPITAL

1101 W UNIVERSITY DR
ROCHESTER, MI 483071863
Phone: 248 652-5000
Fax: –
Web: www.crittenton.com

CEO: Lynn C Orfgen
CFO: Donna Kopinski
HR: Margo Naiol
FYE: June 30
Type: Private

Crittenton Hospital Medical Center treats patients in the western counties of the suburban Detroit area. The not-for-profit hospital has 290 beds for acute care, but also provides primary and specialist care. Crittenton offers such services as urgent pediatric care, rehabilitative therapy, inpatient psychiatric care, joint replacement, and sleep analysis. It is a fully accredited teaching campus and partners with area universities and medical providers. It also operates outpatient facilities including surgery, imaging, and therapy centers. With a heritage that reaches back to the early 1900s, Crittenton Hospital Medical Center opened its doors in 1967.

	Annual Growth	12/14	12/15*	06/19	06/20	06/21
Sales ($mil.)	4.0%	–	188.3	212.6	223.9	238.1
Net income ($ mil.)	–	–	(48.2)	4.0	9.7	6.0
Market value ($ mil.)	–	–	–	–	–	–
Employees	–	–	–	–	–	1,515

*Fiscal year change

ASCENSION VIA CHRISTI HEALTH, INC.

2622 W CENTRAL AVE STE 200
WICHITA, KS 672034969
Phone: 316 858-4900
Fax: –
Web: www.viachristi.org

CEO: –
CFO: –
HR: –
FYE: June 30
Type: Private

How do the sick become well? Via Christi Health, of course. Via Christi Health is a Catholic, not-for-profit health care system that provides a range of medical services to residents of Kansas and northern Oklahoma through a network of hospitals, medical centers, and health service organizations. The system's facilities include four hospitals, about a dozen senior living communities, nearly 20 medical clinics, and specialized facilities for behavioral health and rehabilitative care. The system is affiliated with Marian Health System and Ascension Health. Via Christi Health was formed in 1995 when the Sisters of the Sorrowful Mother and the Sisters of St. Joseph of Wichita merged their health care ministries.

	Annual Growth	06/12	06/13	06/14	06/15	06/19
Sales ($mil.)	(25.7%)	–	–	131.6	149.6	29.9
Net income ($ mil.)	–	–	–	(23.5)	(31.0)	8.7
Market value ($ mil.)	–	–	–	–	–	–
Employees	–	–	–	–	–	11,970

ASCENT CAPITAL GROUP, INC.

5251 DTC PKWY STE 1000
GREENWOOD VILLAGE, CO 801112739
Phone: 303 628-5600
Fax: –
Web: www.ascentcapitalgroupinc.com

CEO: William E Niles
CFO: Fred A Graffam
HR: –
FYE: December 31
Type: Private

Ascent Capital Group, through subsidiary Monitronics International (MONI), provides security alarm monitoring services in the US, Canada, and Puerto Rico. Its offerings include home monitoring and automation services featuring interactive voice communication between its customers and its monitoring center. The firm serves more than 1 million residential and commercial customers. MONI subsidiary LiveWatch Security provides do-it-yourself home security products and services. In 2018 the company entered into a trademark licensing agreement with armored car giant Brink's through which it rebranded MONI and LiveWatch as BRINKS Home Security.

ASCENT INDUSTRIES CO

NMS: ACNT

1400 16th Street, Suite 270
Oak Brook, IL 60523
Phone: 630 884-9181
Fax: –
Web: www.synalloy.com

CEO: Christopher G Hutter
CFO: William Steckel
HR: –
FYE: December 31
Type: Public

Synalloy brings stainless steel and specialty chemicals together under one company. Operating through Bristol Metals and Ram-Fab, the company manufactures welded pipe and fabricates piping systems from stainless steel and other alloys, or carbon and chrome alloy. Its customers, who require corrosion resistance or high purity, are chiefly engaged in the chemical, petrochemical, water and waste water treatment, and paper industries. Steel pipe, branded Brismet, is sold to distributors and directly to end-users. Synalloy's chemicals business, Manufacturers Chemicals, produces specialty chemicals and dyes (defoamers, surfactants, softening agents) for the textile, chemical, paper, mining, and metals industries.

	Annual Growth	12/18	12/19	12/20	12/21	12/22
Sales ($mil.)	10.2%	280.8	305.2	256.0	334.7	414.1
Net income ($ mil.)	13.9%	13.1	(3.0)	(27.3)	20.2	22.1
Market value ($ mil.)	(15.0%)	183.9	143.1	86.5	182.1	96.1
Employees	3.6%	607	606	526	707	698

ASCENT SOLAR TECHNOLOGIES INC

NAS: ASTI

12300 Grant Street
Thornton, CO 80241
Phone: 720 872-5000
Fax: –
Web: www.ascentsolar.com

CEO: Paul Warley
CFO: Jin Jo
HR: –
FYE: December 31
Type: Public

As long as that sun keeps ascending in the eastern skies every day, there will be ventures trying to tap its enormous energy resources. Ascent Solar Technologies is a development-stage company working on photovoltaic modules for use in consumer applications as well as satellites and spacecraft. The firm aspires to make such gear smaller, lighter, and more flexible than existing solar cells for use in space by utilizing a thin-film absorbing layer on top of a polyimide substrate. The thin-film layer on top of the high-temperature plastic is made up of copper, indium, gallium, and selenium, which is why the technology is called CIGS. Norsk Hydro has a 39% stake in the company.

	Annual Growth	12/19	12/20	12/21	12/22	12/23
Sales ($mil.)	(8.0%)	0.6	0.0	0.6	1.2	0.5
Net income ($ mil.)	–	(4.9)	1.6	(6.0)	(19.8)	(17.1)
Market value ($ mil.)	865.8%	0.0	0.0	0.0	5.8	3.1
Employees	(3.8%)	21	29	54	62	18

ASG TECHNOLOGIES GROUP, INC.

77 4TH AVE FL 3
WALTHAM, MA 024517567
Phone: 239 435-2200
Fax: –
Web: www.rocketsoftware.com

CEO: David Reibel
CFO: Ernie Scheidemann
HR: –
FYE: December 31
Type: Private

ASG Technologies Group, Inc. (ASG) is a Global Enterprise Software vendor providing solutions for some of the world's largest businesses. ASG is the only solutions provider for both Information Management and IT Systems Management. Its information management solutions capture, manage, govern, and enable companies to understand and support all types of information, while its IT systems management solutions, ensure that the systems and infrastructure supporting that information lifecycle are always available and performing as expected. Customers have included Oney, Clemson, Postbank, and Primerica.

	Annual Growth	12/06	12/07	12/08	12/09	12/17
Sales ($mil.)	(1.9%)	–	–	300.1	276.5	252.4
Net income ($ mil.)		–	–	(12.6)	(11.5)	15.7
Market value ($ mil.)		–	–	–	–	–
Employees						600

ASGN INC   NYS: ASGN

4400 Cox Road, Suite 110
Glen Allen, VA 23060
Phone: 888 482-8068
Fax: –
Web: www.asgn.com

CEO: Theodore S Hanson
CFO: Marie L Perry
HR: –
FYE: December 31
Type: Public

ASGN Incorporated is a leading provider of information technology (IT) services and professional solutions, including technology and creative digital marketing, across the commercial and government sectors. The firm offers its services to both commercial and federal government customers. Its largest segment caters to companies in Fortune 1000 clients as well as mid-market companies. The company has over 130 branch offices across the US, the UK, Canada, and Spain.

	Annual Growth	12/19	12/20	12/21	12/22	12/23
Sales ($mil.)	3.2%	3,923.9	3,950.6	4,009.5	4,581.1	4,450.6
Net income ($ mil.)	5.8%	174.7	200.3	409.9	268.1	219.3
Market value ($ mil.)	7.9%	3,314.3	3,900.9	5,762.8	3,805.1	4,491.1
Employees	(51.6%)	67,700	55,200	56,800	54,000	3,700

ASH STEVENS LLC

18655 KRAUSE ST
RIVERVIEW, MI 481934260
Phone: 734 282-3370
Fax: –
Web: www.piramalpharmasolutions.com

CEO: Stephen A Munk
CFO: –
HR: –
FYE: September 30
Type: Private

Ash Stevens is the active type -- active ingredients, that is. The company, a contract pharmaceutical manufacturer, develops and manufactures active pharmaceutical ingredients (APIs) for other pharmaceutical companies. It also supports clinical drug trials and helps others navigate the FDA's regulatory maze. Its customers include the federal government and commercial pharmaceutical firms. The company's portfolio includes about a dozen FDA-approved drug components. It was founded in 1962 to provide chemical research for the government and later branched out into the private sector. Pharmaceutical firm Piramal Pharma Solutions is buying Ash Stevens for $53 million.

ASHFORD HOSPITALITY TRUST INC   NYS: AHT

14185 Dallas Parkway, Suite 1200
Dallas, TX 75254
Phone: 972 490-9600
Fax: 972 980-2705
Web: www.ahtreit.com

CEO: J R Hays III
CFO: Deric S Eubanks
HR: Laura Simmons
FYE: December 31
Type: Public

A self-administered real estate investment trust (REIT), Ashford Hospitality Trust owns about 100 hotel properties representing some 22,315 rooms throughout the US. It holds some 80 condominium units at WorldQuest Resort in Orlando, Florida; 15.1% ownership in OpenKey with a carrying value of $2.1 million; 32.5% ownership in 815 Commerce Managing Member with a carrying value of $8.5 million, and an investment in an entity with a carrying value of approximately $9.0 million. Most of its properties operate under the upscale and upper upscale Hilton, Marriott, Hyatt, and Intercontinental Hotels Group brands. The company also provides other products and services including design and construction services, debt placement and related services, audio visual services, real estate advisory services, insurance claims services, hypoallergenic premium rooms, broker-dealer services and mobile key technology.

	Annual Growth	12/19	12/20	12/21	12/22	12/23
Sales ($mil.)	(2.3%)	1,502.8	508.2	805.4	1,240.9	1,367.5
Net income ($ mil.)		(113.6)	(543.9)	(267.0)	(139.8)	(178.5)
Market value ($ mil.)	(8.7%)	104.4	96.9	359.3	167.3	72.6
Employees	(2.5%)	116	–	–	–	105

ASHLAND INC (NEW)   NYS: ASH

8145 Blazer Drive
Wilmington, DE 19808
Phone: 302 995-3000
Fax: –
Web: www.ashland.com

CEO: Guillermo Novo
CFO: J K Willis
HR: –
FYE: September 30
Type: Public

Ashland is a leading provider of specialty ingredients and other chemical solutions that improve the formulation and performance of a host of products. It generates the most revenue from cellulosics and Polyvinylpyrrolidones (PVP) that improve toothpaste, cleaning supplies, paint, medications, and food, among other items. The company's offerings are also used in electronics and plastic products. Ashland's customers operate in a variety of industries, including adhesives, architectural coatings, construction, energy, food and beverage, nutraceuticals, personal care and pharmaceutical. With approximately 3,900 employees worldwide, Ashland serves customers in more than 100 countries. It generates most of its revenue outside the US.

	Annual Growth	09/19	09/20	09/21	09/22	09/23
Sales ($mil.)	(3.2%)	2,493.0	2,326.0	2,111.0	2,391.0	2,191.0
Net income ($ mil.)	(22.9%)	505.0	(308.0)	220.0	927.0	178.0
Market value ($ mil.)	1.5%	3,929.6	3,616.9	4,545.1	4,843.5	4,165.7
Employees	(5.2%)	4,700	4,500	4,100	3,900	3,800

ASHLAND LLC

50 E RIVERCENTER BLVD # 16
COVINGTON, KY 410111683
Phone: 859 815-3333
Fax: –
Web: www.ashland.com

CEO: –
CFO: –
HR: –
FYE: September 30
Type: Private

Ashland's three business units are built on chemicals and cars. Ashland Performance Materials makes specialty resins, polymers, and adhesives. Specialty Ingredients makes cellulose ethers, vinyl pyrrolidones and biofunctionals. It offers industry-leading products, technologies and resources for solving formulation and product-performance challenges. Consumer Markets, led by subsidiary Valvoline, runs an oil-change chain in the US and sells Valvoline oil and Zerex antifreeze. The company's Ashland Specialty Ingredients unit produces polymers and additives for the food, personal care, pharmaceutical, and other industries. In 2016 Ashland spun off Valvoline.

ASI COMPUTER TECHNOLOGIES INC

48289 FREMONT BLVD
FREMONT, CA 945386510
Phone: 510 226-8000
Fax: –
Web: www.asipartner.com

CEO: Christine Liang
CFO: –
HR: Mu Lay
FYE: December 31
Type: Private

ASI Computer Technologies is a national distributor of IT software and hardware products. It offers more than 10,000 products, including PCs, scanners, security, surveillance, and data storage devices. The company has rapidly grown to become the partner of choice for over 10,000 VARs throughout North America. Its vendor partners include companies the likes of AMD, Intel, Micron, Samsung, and Viewsonic. ASI's services include custom systems integration. Furthermore, it caters to various industries such as retail and the SMB market. The company was established in 1987 by president and owner Cristine Liang.

	Annual Growth	12/01	12/02	12/03	12/04	12/13
Sales ($mil.)	6.6%	–	865.6	982.5	1,057.1	1,746.9
Net income ($ mil.)	4.9%	–	10.4	13.1	12.2	17.6
Market value ($ mil.)	–	–	–	–	–	–
Employees	–	–	–	–	–	76

ASIS INTERNATIONAL, INC.

1625 PRINCE ST
ALEXANDRIA, VA 223142882
Phone: 703 519-6200
Fax: –
Web: www.asisonline.org

CEO: Michael J Stack
CFO: –
HR: Jeremy Ornstein
FYE: June 30
Type: Private

ASIS International wants to know if you packed your own bags, and if you've seen anything suspicious. The group, formerly the American Society for Industrial Security, is a nonprofit association for security professionals. It serves nearly 40,000 members through more than 200 chapters worldwide with educational programs, conferences, and publications, including Security Management magazine. ASIS works with corporations and governments (including the US Department of Homeland Security) to set up security systems and emergency contingency plans. It also represents the industry before the media and government groups. ASIS was founded in 1955 by five security directors working on DOD contract manufacturing.

	Annual Growth	12/15	12/16	12/17*	06/21	06/22
Sales ($mil.)	(3.9%)	–	27.6	31.4	13.1	21.7
Net income ($ mil.)	–	–	(5.8)	0.5	(5.0)	1.7
Market value ($ mil.)	–	–	–	–	–	–
Employees	–	–	–	–	–	85

*Fiscal year change

ASPEN AEROGELS INC

30 Forbes Road, Building B
Northborough, MA 01532
Phone: 508 691-1111
Fax: –
Web: www.aerogel.com

NYS: ASPN
CEO: Donald R Young
CFO: John F Fairbanks
HR: Lisa Studholme
FYE: December 31
Type: Public

Aspen Aerogels' insulation products -- which look like thin, flexible blankets -- represent a new breed of thermal insulation. Its two product lines, Cryogel and Pyrogel, are used by industrial companies to keep pipes and storage tanks at certain temperatures and protect equipment from water and fire damage. Customers have included ADM, Chevron, Exelon, Exxon Mobil, NextEra Energy, Petrobras, and Shell. Its Spaceloft brand insulation, develop with BASF's Construction Chemicals division, is used by the building and construction market to insulate walls and roofs. Aspen held an IPO in mid-2014.

	Annual Growth	12/19	12/20	12/21	12/22	12/23
Sales ($mil.)	14.4%	139.4	100.3	121.6	180.4	238.7
Net income ($ mil.)	–	(14.6)	(21.8)	(37.1)	(82.7)	(45.8)
Market value ($ mil.)	19.4%	593.7	1,276.8	3,809.1	902.0	1,207.2
Employees	15.9%	304	290	418	533	548

ASPEN SKIING COMPANY, L.L.C.

117 ASPEN AIRPORT BUSINESS CTR
ASPEN, CO 816112502
Phone: 970 925-1220
Fax: –
Web: www.aspensnowmass.com

CEO: –
CFO: –
HR: Jeff Hembury
FYE: December 31
Type: Private

Aspen Skiing Company says, "let it snow, let it snow, let it snow." The company owns and operates four ski resorts in Colorado, including Aspen Highlands, Aspen Mountain, Buttermilk, and Snowmass. In addition to skiing, the resorts offer accommodations, restaurants, and tours, as well as such summer activities as gondola rides, hiking, mountain biking, and naturalist programs. Aspen Skiing also operates the Ski & Snowboard Schools of Aspen/Snowmass. Chicago industrialist Walter Paepcke started the company in 1946 with the help of Austrian skier Friedl Pfeifer.

ASPIRA WOMENS HEALTH INC

12117 Bee Caves Road, Building III, Suite 100
Austin, TX 78738
Phone: 512 519-0400
Fax: –
Web: www.aspirawh.com

CEO: Valerie B Palmieri
CFO: Robert Beechey
HR: –
FYE: December 31
Type: Public

Vermillion is enabling the next step in biotechnology -- deciphering proteins. The company is bio-analytical products and services company that helps physicians diagnose, treat, and improve gynecologic health outcomes for women. Vermillion, along with its prestigious scientific collaborators, has diagnostic programs in gynecologic disease. The company's lead diagnostic in the US, OVA1, is a blood test for pre-surgical assessment of ovarian tumors for malignancy, using an innovative algorithmic approach and is available through Vermillion's wholly owned subsidiary, ASPiRA LABS.

	Annual Growth	12/18	12/19	12/20	12/21	12/22
Sales ($mil.)	28.0%	3.1	4.5	4.7	6.8	8.2
Net income ($ mil.)	–	(11.4)	(15.2)	(17.9)	(31.7)	(27.2)
Market value ($ mil.)	2.6%	2.5	6.7	55.7	14.7	2.8
Employees	18.6%	43	53	69	108	85

ASPIRUS, INC.

2200 WESTWOOD DR
WAUSAU, WI 544017806
Phone: 715 847-2121
Fax: –
Web: www.aspirus.org

CEO: Matthew Heywood
CFO: Jerry Yang
HR: Hardesty Jon
FYE: June 30
Type: Private

Aspirus is a non-profit, community-directed health system based in Wausau, Wisconsin. The health system provides a comprehensive range of health and medical services to communities through four hospitals in Upper Michigan and about 15 hospitals in Wisconsin, some 75 clinics, home health and hospice care, pharmacies, critical care and air-medical transport, medical goods, nursing homes and a broad network of physicians. In addition to its four hospitals in Michigan, Aspirus operates the Aspirus Wausau Hospital, a 325-bed and staffed by 350 physicians in 35 specialties. With approximately 15,000 admissions per year, outpatient visits exceed 50,000 and there are also more than 24,000 annual emergency department visits.

	Annual Growth	06/17	06/18	06/19	06/20	06/22
Sales ($mil.)	16.7%	–	911.4	996.5	1,090.7	1,687.8
Net income ($ mil.)	(18.2%)	–	78.2	102.7	169.1	35.0
Market value ($ mil.)	–	–	–	–	–	–
Employees	–	–	–	–	–	7,100

ASPYRA INC — NBB: APYI

4360 Park Terrace Drive, Suite 220
Westlake Village, CA 91361
Phone: 818 880-6700
Fax: 818 880-4397
Web: www.aspyra.com

CEO: Rodney W Schutt
CFO: Anahita Villafane
HR: –
FYE: December 31
Type: Public

Aspyra aspires to keep folks around the globe healthy. The company, a provider of clinical and diagnostic information solutions for the health care industry, specializes in enterprise-wide systems for hospitals, multi-specialty clinics, clinical laboratories, imaging departments and centers, orthopedic environments, and pharmacies. CEO Rodney Schutt resigned in 2009 after about a year in the job, quitting the company's board, as well. COO Ademola Lawal was promoted to CEO to succeed Schutt. Aspyra was formed from the 2005 merger of Creative Computer Applications (CCA), a provider of clinical information systems, and StorCOMM, a provider of clinical image management systems.

	Annual Growth	12/04	12/05	12/06	12/07	12/08
Sales ($mil.)	37.4%	2.4	7.2	12.7	10.3	8.5
Net income ($ mil.)	–	(0.3)	(2.5)	(3.6)	(4.2)	(5.2)
Market value ($ mil.)	(53.1%)	43.8	31.7	22.6	21.8	2.1
Employees	–	–	105	101	70	71

ASSEMBLY BIOSCIENCES INC — NMS: ASMB

331 Oyster Point Blvd., Fourth Floor
South San Francisco, CA 94080
Phone: 833 509-4583
Fax: –
Web: www.assemblybio.com

CEO: –
CFO: –
HR: –
FYE: December 31
Type: Public

Assembly Biosciences is a development-stage drug company focused specifically on anal disorders (such as difficile-associated diarrhea, or CDAD) and the treatment of hepatitis B infections. Its primary product is a diltiazem cream for pain associated with anal fissures while a secondary product is a phenylephrine gel for fecal incontinence. Assembly has licensed intellectual property associated with an oral drug delivery system that targets sites within the intestines. Assembly Biosciences is the result of a 2014 merger between Ventrus Biosciences and Assembly Pharmaceuticals.

	Annual Growth	12/19	12/20	12/21	12/22	12/23
Sales ($mil.)	(18.2%)	16.0	79.1	6.3	–	7.2
Net income ($ mil.)	–	(97.6)	(62.2)	(129.9)	(93.1)	(61.2)
Market value ($ mil.)	(55.3%)	112.2	33.2	12.8	7.1	4.5
Employees	(13.3%)	115	139	102	68	65

ASSERTIO HOLDINGS INC — NAS: ASRT

100 South Saunders Road, Suite 300
Lake Forest, IL 60045
Phone: 224 419-7106
Fax: –
Web: www.assertiotx.com

CEO: –
CFO: –
HR: –
FYE: December 31
Type: Public

Assertio Therapeutics (formerly Depomed) is a pharmaceutical firm with a focus on neurology, orphan, and specialty medicines. The company works to discover, develop, and license new drugs; it has three products on the market in the US. Gralise is used to treat nerve pain, CAMBIA is a non-steroidal anti-inflammatory drug for the acute treatment of migraine attacks in adults, and Zipsor is used for pain relief in adults. In late 2017, the firm granted Collegium Pharmaceutical the commercialization rights for its Nucynta franchise of pain medications, for which it will receive royalty payments. In mid-2018 Depomed changed its name to Assertio in reference to its confident, assertive, and entrepreneurial activities.

	Annual Growth	12/19	12/20	12/21	12/22	12/23
Sales ($mil.)	(9.8%)	229.5	106.3	111.0	156.2	152.1
Net income ($ mil.)	–	(217.2)	(28.1)	(1.3)	109.6	(331.9)
Market value ($ mil.)	(3.8%)	118.3	33.9	206.4	407.1	101.3
Employees	(19.3%)	125	27	19	30	53

ASSET ACQUISITION AUTHORITY, INC.

1660 BLAKE ST
DENVER, CO 802021324
Phone: 303 628-9000
Fax: –
Web: www.rtd-denver.com

CEO: Debra Johnson
CFO: –
HR: –
FYE: December 31
Type: Private

The Regional Transportation District (RTD) offers mass transit services via bus and light rail in the Denver area. The agency services over 3 million people across six counties, covering approximately 2,340 square miles. The agency's bus system operates a fleet of approximately 9,000 buses. It provides more than 70 park-n-ride facilities to riders. RTD's light rail system includes more than 50 stations. The agency's service territory encompasses all of Boulder, Broomfield, Denver and Jefferson counties, along with parts of Adams, Arapahoe, Weld, and Douglas counties. The agency was established by the Colorado legislature in 1969.

	Annual Growth	12/14	12/15	12/16	12/17	12/18
Sales ($mil.)	6.2%	–	125.9	140.4	147.4	150.8
Net income ($ mil.)	(35.0%)	–	182.2	145.4	91.2	50.0
Market value ($ mil.)	–	–	–	–	–	–
Employees	–	–	–	–	–	2,700

ASSET PROTECTION & SECURITY SERVICES, LP

5502 BURNHAM DR STE C
CORPUS CHRISTI, TX 784133855
Phone: 361 906-1552
Fax: –
Web: www.asset-security-pro.com

CEO: –
CFO: Thelma Mandel
HR: –
FYE: December 31
Type: Private

Asset Protection & Security Services is a leading provider of patrol and security guard services in the US. It offers both armed and unarmed guard services, as well as specialized services such as executive protection, movie production security, and mobile command centers. In addition, Asset Protection provides investigative services (computer security, internal investigations, loss prevention) and electronic surveillance and security, as well as security consulting and training services. The company was founded in 1994 by CEO Charles Mandel.

ASSOCIATED BANC-CORP — NYS: ASB

433 Main Street
Green Bay, WI 54301
Phone: 920 491-7500
Fax: –
Web: www.associatedbank.com

CEO: Philip B Flynn
CFO: Christopher D Moral-Niles
HR: –
FYE: December 31
Type: Public

Associated Banc-Corp is a bank holding company of Associated Bank. Through Associated Bank and various nonbanking subsidiaries, it provides a broad array of banking and nonbanking products and services to individuals and businesses through nearly 230 facilities, including more than 200 branches in Wisconsin, Illinois, and Minnesota. Catering to consumers and local businesses, it offers deposit accounts, loans, mortgage banking, credit and debit cards, and leasing. The bank serves more than 100 communities and has approximately 1.3 million customer accounts. Commercial loans, including commercial and industrial, real estate construction, CRE loans, and ABL & equipment finance loans, make up over 60% of the bank's loan portfolio. The bank also writes residential mortgages, consumer loans, and home equity loans.

	Annual Growth	12/19	12/20	12/21	12/22	12/23
Assets ($mil.)	6.1%	32,386	33,420	35,104	39,406	41,016
Net income ($ mil.)	(13.5%)	326.8	306.8	351.0	366.1	183.0
Market value ($ mil.)	(0.7%)	3,328.8	2,575.2	3,411.9	3,487.4	3,230.7
Employees	(3.2%)	4,669	4,100	4,000	4,118	4,100

ASSOCIATED CATHOLIC CHARITIES INC.

320 CATHEDRAL ST STE 2
BALTIMORE, MD 212014421
Phone: 410 561-6363
Fax: -
Web: www.catholiccharities-md.org

CEO: William E Lori
CFO: -
HR: Diane M Polk
FYE: June 30
Type: Private

Catholic Charities of Baltimore (CCB) provides people in the greater Baltimore area, including about a dozen Maryland counties, with a wide variety of social services. The not-for-profit, religious organization runs 80 programs that focus on children and families, the elderly, and people with developmental disabilities; offerings include adoption services, child abuse prevention, food, immigration assistance, residential facilities, and services for homeless people. It serves more than 160,000 people of all religions each year. Money for its operations comes mainly from government contracts and grants. In addition, CCB relies on a network of about 15,000 volunteers. CCB was founded in 1923.

	Annual Growth	06/04	06/05	06/06	06/08	06/09
Sales ($mil.)	6.6%	-	92.3	108.6	115.8	119.4
Net income ($ mil.)	-	-	-	9.7	(8.0)	(11.0)
Market value ($ mil.)	-	-	-	-	-	-
Employees	-	-	-	-	-	2,000

ASSOCIATED ELECTRIC COOPERATIVE, INC.

2814 S GOLDEN AVE
SPRINGFIELD, MO 658073213
Phone: 417 881-1204
Fax: -
Web: www.aeci.org

CEO: David Tudor
CFO: David W McNabb
HR: Becca Stapleton
FYE: December 31
Type: Private

Associated Electric Cooperative makes the connection between power and cooperatives. The utility provides transmission and generation services to its six member/owner companies, which in turn provide power supply services to 51 distribution cooperatives in three Midwest states. (The distribution cooperatives have a combined customer count of about 875,000 member homes, farms, and businesses.) Associated Electric operates 9,937 miles of power transmission lines and has about 5,895 MW of generating capacity from interests in primarily coal- and gas-fired power plants and from wholesale energy transactions with other regional utilities.

	Annual Growth	12/12	12/13	12/14	12/20	12/21
Sales ($mil.)	3.5%	-	1,129.8	1,142.3	-	1,484.4
Net income ($ mil.)	2.7%	-	41.8	40.1	-	52.0
Market value ($ mil.)	-	-	-	-	-	-
Employees	-	-	-	-	-	658

ASSOCIATED EQUIPMENT DISTRIBUTORS

650 E ALGONQUIN RD # 305
SCHAUMBURG, IL 601733846
Phone: 630 574-0650
Fax: -
Web: www.aednet.org

CEO: -
CFO: -
HR: -
FYE: December 31
Type: Private

If you need something built, torn down, moved, or dug up, AED knows who to call. Associated Equipment Distributors is a not-for-profit trade group that supports more than 800 heavy equipment manufacturers and service providers in the construction, mining, agricultural, and power generation industries. AED provides research, training, advocacy, networking, and business management support. It also publishes Construction Equipment Distribution magazine and offers research, analysis and information from economic and business trends to labor issues.

	Annual Growth	12/13	12/14	12/17	12/18	12/19
Sales ($mil.)	52.6%	-	0.1	0.6	5.2	1.1
Net income ($ mil.)	(5.7%)	-	0.1	(0.2)	0.3	0.0
Market value ($ mil.)	-	-	-	-	-	-
Employees	-	-	-	-	-	25

ASSOCIATED FOOD STORES, LLC

1850 W 2100 S
SALT LAKE CITY, UT 841191304
Phone: 801 973-4400
Fax: -
Web: www.afstores.com

CEO: -
CFO: Travis Boman
HR: -
FYE: March 31
Type: Private

This business makes sure there's plenty of grub for the Wild West. Associated Food Stores (AFS) is a leading regional cooperative wholesale distributor that supplies groceries and other products to some 500 independent supermarkets in about eight Western states. It also offers support services for its member-owners, including market research, real estate analysis, store design, technology procurement, and training. In addition, AFS owns a stake in Western Family Foods, a grocery wholesalers' partnership that produces Western Family private-label goods. The co-op, formed in 1940, also operates 40-plus corporate stores in Utah under five different banners, including Fresh Market.

	Annual Growth	03/08	03/09	03/10	03/11	03/12
Sales ($mil.)	6.1%	-	-	1,785.6	1,954.0	2,011.3
Net income ($ mil.)	-	-	-	(2.1)	(6.5)	5.9
Market value ($ mil.)	-	-	-	-	-	-
Employees	-	-	-	-	-	5,629

ASSOCIATED GROCERS OF NEW ENGLAND, INC.

11 COOPERATIVE WAY
PEMBROKE, NH 032753251
Phone: 603 223-6710
Fax: -
Web: www.agne.com

CEO: Mike Violette
CFO: Steven N Murphy
HR: -
FYE: March 28
Type: Private

AGNE gets the products you want on to grocers' shelves. Associated Grocers of New England (AGNE) is a leading wholesale grocery distributor. The retailer-owned organization supplies more than 650 independent grocers and convenience stores in six New England states, and the Upstate New York and Albany area. AGNE supplies customers with baked goods, fresh produce, and meat, as well as general grocery items and other merchandise. The grocery distributor also offers such retail support services as advertising, marketing, and merchandising. AGNE's retail arm operates about a half a dozen supermarkets under the Harvest Market, Sully's Superette, and Vista Foods banners. The cooperative was formed in 1946.

	Annual Growth	03/05	03/06	03/07	03/08	03/09
Sales ($mil.)	-	-	-	(1,996.9)	315.8	340.3
Net income ($ mil.)	3701.4%	-	-	0.0	0.2	0.7
Market value ($ mil.)	-	-	-	-	-	-
Employees	-	-	-	-	-	625

ASSOCIATED GROCERS OF THE SOUTH, INC.

3600 VANDERBILT RD
BIRMINGHAM, AL 352174256
Phone: 205 841-6781
Fax: -
Web: www.agsouth.com

CEO: -
CFO: Jackie Plott
HR: -
FYE: March 29
Type: Private

Associated Grocers of the South is a grocery wholesale cooperative serving more than 300 independently-owned supermarkets in Alabama, Florida, Georgia, Mississippi, and Tennessee. In addition to supplying more than 16,000 products under the Shurfine brand (from Topco Associates) and other labels, the cooperative provides its members with accounting, advertising, merchandising and other support services. Associated Grocers of the South was formed in Birmingham, Alabama, by a group of a dozen neighborhood stores in 1927.

ASSOCIATED GROCERS, INC.

8600 ANSELMO LN
BATON ROUGE, LA 708101209
Phone: 225 444-1000
Fax: –
Web: www.agbr.com

CEO: Manard M Lagasse Jr
CFO: –
HR: Logan Thibodeaux
FYE: May 31
Type: Private

Associated Grocers is a leading grocery wholesale cooperative that distributes broadline grocery products to over 200 independent retailers in Louisiana, Mississippi and Texas. It supplies member stores with food and non-food items under a host of brands, including Food Club, Simply Done, FullCircle, and Top Care, among others. In addition, the cooperative offers such services as retail accounting, advertising, marketing, retail services, procurement and merchandising, printing services. Associated Grocers was founded in 1950 by over 15 founding member stores.

ASSOCIATED MATERIALS, LLC

3773 STATE RD
CUYAHOGA FALLS, OH 442232603
Phone: 330 929-1811
Fax: –
Web: www.associatedmaterials.com

CEO: James Drexinger
CFO: Scott F Stephens
HR: Angela Casida
FYE: January 03
Type: Private

Associated Materials is the parent company of several North American manufacturing and distribution operations. The company serves the needs of the contractors, remodelers, and architects through its company-owned wholesale stores and select independent distributer partners throughout the US and Canada. Operates about 10 manufacturing facilities, the company offers vinyl siding, trim and decorative accents, and metal building products, among others. Associated Materials also operates about 130 supply centers across the US and Canada under the Alside and Gentek brands. The company was founded in 1947 as Alside, an aluminum siding company. In early 2022, SVPGLOBAL completed the acquisition of Associated Materials.

ASSOCIATED WHOLESALE GROCERS, INC.

5000 KANSAS AVE
KANSAS CITY, KS 661061135
Phone: 913 288-1000
Fax: –
Web: www.awginc.com

CEO: Dan Funk
CFO: Gary Koch
HR: Michelle S Uzee
FYE: December 31
Type: Private

Associated Wholesale Grocers (AWG) is one of the largest grocery wholesalers in the US and the nation's oldest grocery cooperative. AWG supplies more than 1,100 member companies and over 3,400 locations throughout some 30 states. In addition to its cooperative wholesale grocery operations, AWG also offers a variety of business services to its members, including certain real estate and supermarket development services, print and digital marketing services, health and beauty care, general merchandise, pharmaceutical products, specialty foods, and natural and organic products. AWG was founded by a group of independent grocers in 1924.

	Annual Growth	12/12	12/13	12/14	12/15	12/17
Sales ($mil.)	3.7%	–	8,380.2	8,934.2	8,935.9	9,703.8
Net income ($ mil.)	0.8%	–	192.5	226.9	198.9	199.1
Market value ($ mil.)	–	–	–	–	–	–
Employees	–	–	–	–	–	2,997

ASSOCIATION FOR CREATIVE INDUSTRIES

330 N WABASH AVE STE 2000
CHICAGO, IL 606117621
Phone: 201 835-1200
Fax: –
Web: www.namta.org

CEO: Mark Hill
CFO: –
HR: –
FYE: December 31
Type: Private

The Craft & Hobby Association (CHA) has been a model association since its beginning. The organization was founded in 1940 as the Model Industry Association and currently consists of about 5,500 member companies involved in the manufacturing, distribution, and sale of craft and hobby products. Formerly known as Hobby Industry Association, in 2004 the organization joined with the Association of Crafts & Creative Industries (ACCI) to form CHA. Together they conduct consumer research, put on industry trade fairs, host elementary school craft projects, and publish newsletters and other materials for members. Its members also receive discounts on shipping and related services.

	Annual Growth	12/02	12/03	12/04	12/08	12/18
Sales ($mil.)	(2.3%)	–	5.5	6.2	9.1	3.9
Net income ($ mil.)	–	–	(0.3)	0.1	–	(0.2)
Market value ($ mil.)	–	–	–	–	–	–
Employees	–	–	–	–	–	17

ASSOCIATION FOR FINANCIAL PROFESSIONALS, INC.

12345 PARKLAWN DR FL 2
ROCKVILLE, MD 208527702
Phone: 301 907-2862
Fax: –
Web: www.afponline.org

CEO: Anthony Scaglione
CFO: –
HR: –
FYE: June 30
Type: Private

The Association for Financial Professionals (AFP) knows where the money is. Or at least its members do. The organization represents more than 16,000 individuals in the corporate treasury and financial management fields. It provides training, certification, career counseling, and other professional development services and hosts an annual four-day conference. AFP is an advocate for financial professionals and lobbies for improved industry standards and systems. The organization also publishes AFP Exchange, a bi-monthly magazine. Its Committee on Investment of Employee Benefit Assets represents executives who oversee investment funds of pension and benefit plans. AFP was founded in 1980 and operates in the US, Canada, and Puerto Rico.

	Annual Growth	06/09	06/10	06/14	06/21	06/22
Sales ($mil.)	1.3%	–	17.5	23.4	15.1	20.4
Net income ($ mil.)	–	–	(0.0)	(1.0)	(2.4)	0.0
Market value ($ mil.)	–	–	–	–	–	–
Employees	–	–	–	–	–	72

ASSOCIATION FOR INTELLIGENT INFORMATION MANAGEMENT

8403 COLESVILLE RD # 1100
SILVER SPRING, MD 209106331
Phone: 301 587-8202
Fax: –
Web: www.aiim.org

CEO: Peggy Winton
CFO: –
HR: –
FYE: December 31
Type: Private

AIIM International can't improve the way you look, but it can help with your image management. The nonprofit (whose name stands for Association for Information and Image Management) connects users with suppliers who can help them apply document and content technologies to improve their internal processes via the enterprise content management system. It also offers professional development, networking, and vendor services. In addition, AIIM International publishes magazines, hosts conferences, and lobbies government on behalf of its members. The organization was founded in 1943 as the National Microfilm Association.

	Annual Growth	12/13	12/14	12/17	12/18	12/21
Sales ($mil.)	(10.5%)	–	5.8	4.8	4.5	2.7
Net income ($ mil.)	–	–	(0.9)	0.0	0.0	0.2
Market value ($ mil.)	–	–	–	–	–	–
Employees	–	–	–	–	–	28

ASSOCIATION OF UNIVERSITIES FOR RESEARCH IN ASTRONOMY, INC.

950 N CHERRY AVE
TUCSON, AZ 857194933
Phone: 520 318-8000
Fax: –
Web: www.aura-astronomy.org

CEO: –
CFO: Barbara Lam
HR: –
FYE: September 30
Type: Private

There is nothing quasi-scientific about this aura. The Association of Universities for Research in Astronomy (AURA) is a consortium of universities and not-for-profit organizations devoted to the study of space. The organization was founded to create astronomical observing facilities for use by qualified researchers, and to serve the community by offering public outreach, education, and dissemination of information. AURA was founded in 1957 and operates astronomical observatories at 34 US institutions and six international affiliates, including Harvard University, Ohio State University, and the University of Toronto.

	Annual Growth	09/12	09/13	09/14	09/19	09/20
Sales ($mil.)	5.9%	–	238.4	264.4	369.9	357.0
Net income ($ mil.)	–	–	2.1	1.0	1.8	(3.9)
Market value ($ mil.)	–	–	–	–	–	–
Employees	–	–	–	–	–	1,000

ASSURANCEAMERICA CORP

5500 Interstate North Parkway, Suite 600
Atlanta, GA 30328
Phone: 770 952-0200
Fax: –
Web: www.assuranceamerica.com

CEO: Joseph J Skruck
CFO: Daniel J Scruggs
HR: Peter Weprinsky
FYE: December 31
Type: Public

AssuranceAmerica can assure you that the missing space in its name is not the result of a name fender-bender. Through its two operating subsidiaries, the company offers nonstandard (high-risk) auto insurance products to customers in 10 southeastern states. Its AssuranceAmerica Insurance subsidiary writes the policies, while its Managing General Agency markets the products and provides services through a network of 2,700 independent agencies. The company sold its TrustWay Insurance Agencies (retail nonstandard auto insurance agencies) in Florida, Alabama, and Georgia in 2011.

	Annual Growth	12/07	12/08	12/09	12/10	12/11
Assets ($mil.)	(3.6%)	125.3	131.5	141.1	127.8	108.0
Net income ($ mil.)	–	0.3	(3.2)	0.4	0.9	(11.6)
Market value ($ mil.)	–	–	–	–	–	–
Employees	(14.9%)	282	257	263	251	148

ASSURANT INC

NYS: AIZ

260 Interstate North Circle SE
Atlanta, GA 30339
Phone: 770 763-1000
Fax: –
Web: www.assurant.com

CEO: Keith W Demmings
CFO: Keith Meier
HR: –
FYE: December 31
Type: Public

Assurant, Inc. is a leading global provider of lifestyle and housing solutions that support, protect and connect major consumer purchases. The company provides a diverse range of specialty insurance products such as extended service contracts for electronics, appliances, and vehicles; mobile device protection; manufactured home coverage; renters insurance; and voluntary homeowners insurance. Assurant's products are distributed through sales offices and independent agents across North America, Latin America, Europe, and the Asia/Pacific region. The US accounts for more than 80% of revenue.

	Annual Growth	12/19	12/20	12/21	12/22	12/23
Assets ($mil.)	(6.6%)	44,291	44,650	33,912	33,124	33,635
Net income ($ mil.)	13.8%	382.6	441.8	1,372.4	276.6	642.5
Market value ($ mil.)	6.5%	6,810.4	7,077.4	8,097.9	6,497.6	8,754.1
Employees	(1.1%)	14,200	14,100	15,600	13,700	13,600

ASTA FUNDING, INC.

210 SYLVAN AVE
ENGLEWOOD CLIFFS, NJ 076322532
Phone: 201 567-5648
Fax: –
Web: www.astafunding.com

CEO: –
CFO: –
HR: –
FYE: September 30
Type: Private

Say Hasta luego to unpaid receivables. Asta Funding buys, services, and collects unpaid credit card debts and consumer loans. The company buys delinquent accounts at a discount directly from the credit grantors, as well as indirectly through auctions, brokers, and other third parties. It targets credit card charge-offs from banks, finance companies, and other issuers of Visa, MasterCard, and private-label cards, as well as telecom and other industry charge-offs. The company then collects on its debt balances either internally or through an outsourced agency. Asta Funding also invests in semi-performing and non-delinquent receivables. Subsidiary VATIV Recovery Solutions services bankrupt and deceased accounts.

ASTEC INDUSTRIES, INC.

NMS: ASTE

1725 Shepherd Road
Chattanooga, TN 37421
Phone: 423 899-5898
Fax: 423 899-4456
Web: www.astecindustries.com

CEO: Jaco Van Der Merwe
CFO: David C Silvious
HR: Mickenzie Swentik
FYE: December 31
Type: Public

Astec Industries designs, engineers, manufactures and markets equipment and components used primarily in road building and related construction activities. Its products are used in each phase of road building, from quarrying and crushing the aggregate to application of the road surface for both asphalt and concrete. It also manufactures certain equipment and components unrelated to road construction, including equipment for the mining, quarrying, construction, demolition, land clearing and recycling industries among others. Its products are marketed both domestically and internationally primarily to asphalt producers; highway and heavy equipment contractors; utility contractors; sand and gravel producers; construction, demolition, recycle and crushing contractors; forestry and environmental recycling contractors; mine and quarry operators; port and inland terminal authorities; power stations and domestic and foreign government agencies. The US generates some 80% of the company's total revenue.

	Annual Growth	12/19	12/20	12/21	12/22	12/23
Sales ($mil.)	3.4%	1,169.6	1,024.4	1,097.2	1,274.5	1,338.2
Net income ($ mil.)	10.7%	22.3	46.9	17.8	(0.1)	33.5
Market value ($ mil.)	(3.0%)	955.1	1,316.2	1,575.2	924.6	846.0
Employees	2.8%	3,866	3,537	4,041	4,291	4,322

ASTELLAS INSTITUTE FOR REGENERATIVE MEDICINE

9 TECHNOLOGY DR
WESTBOROUGH, MA 015811794
Phone: 800 727-7003
Fax: –
Web: www.astellascareers.jobs

CEO: –
CFO: Edward Myles
HR: –
FYE: December 31
Type: Private

No need to choose between embryonic and adult stem cells -- Ocata Therapeutics (formerly Advanced Cell Technology) works with both to develop therapies to regenerate human tissue. The firm has developed three product platforms based on stem-cell technology: retinal pigment epithelial therapy for the treatment of degenerative retinal disease; myoblast stem cell therapy to treat chronic heart failure and other heart problems; and the hemangioblast platform for the treatment of blood and cardiovascular diseases. Though Ocata is focused on bringing the clinical-stage technologies to market, it also conducts research for other regenerative medicine treatments. Astellas Pharma acquired Ocata for $379 million in 2016.

ASTRON WIRELESS TECHNOLOGIES INC.

22560 GLENN DR STE 114
STERLING, VA 201644440
Phone: 703 450-5517
Fax: –
Web: www.astronwireless.com

CEO: James L Jalbert
CFO: –
HR: –
FYE: December 31
Type: Private

Astron Wireless Technologies designs, manufactures, and installs communications antennas for rooftop, in-building, mobile, and tower applications. The company provides custom product design and development services for larger equipment makers and it manufactures its own electronic goods primarily for military and commercial use. Astron specializes in antennas used for wireless data and voice networking, portable communications, and satellite transmission among other applications. Astron Wireless has served such clients as the US Army. The company also offers electronic tagging and barcoding systems used to automate data collection activities related primarily to manufacturing and distribution.

	Annual Growth	12/02	12/03	12/04	12/05	12/07
Sales ($mil.)	11.7%	–	4.4	5.1	6.2	6.9
Net income ($ mil.)	(16.1%)	–	1.6	0.4	0.5	0.8
Market value ($ mil.)	–	–	–	–	–	–
Employees	–	–	–	–	–	40

ASTRONAUTICS CORPORATION OF AMERICA

135 W FOREST HILL AVE
OAK CREEK, WI 531542901
Phone: 414 449-4000
Fax: –
Web: www.astronautics.com

CEO: Ronald E Zelazo Dr
CFO: Stephen Givant
HR: Donna McSorley
FYE: May 31
Type: Private

Astronautics Corporation of America is a global leader in the design and manufacture of avionics equipment and systems for commercial and military aerospace. The company's key product areas include electronic primary flight displays, engine displays, mission computers, electronic flight bags and certified servers for airborne applications. Its customers have included Commercial Transport, Defense and Helicopter markets. It also provides system integration and custom software for critical applications. The company was founded in 1959 by Nathaniel Zelazo, and Norma Paige.

	Annual Growth	05/04	05/05	05/06	05/07	05/08
Sales ($mil.)	8.2%	–	–	201.2	233.0	235.7
Net income ($ mil.)	12.8%	–	–	15.4	20.7	19.6
Market value ($ mil.)	–	–	–	–	–	–
Employees	–	–	–	–	–	1,550

ASTRONICS CORP

NMS: ATRO

130 Commerce Way
East Aurora, NY 14052
Phone: 716 805-1599
Fax: –
Web: www.astronics.com

CEO: Peter J Gundermann
CFO: David C Burney
HR: Anita Porter
FYE: December 31
Type: Public

Astronics Corporation is a leading provider of advanced technologies to the global aerospace, defense, and other mission-critical industries. Its products and services include advanced, high-performance electrical power generation, distribution and seat motion systems, lighting and safety systems, avionics products, systems and certification, aircraft structures, and automated test systems. The company serves customers across commercial, general aviation, military, communications, aerospace and defense, and mass transit industries. Astronics operates subsidiaries including Astronics Advanced Electronic Systems, Astronics Ballard Technology, Astronics Luminescent Systems Inc., and Astronics DME, among others. Nearly 80% of the sales were generated from the US.

	Annual Growth	12/19	12/20	12/21	12/22	12/23
Sales ($mil.)	(2.8%)	772.7	502.6	444.9	534.9	689.2
Net income ($ mil.)	–	52.0	(115.8)	(25.6)	(35.7)	(26.4)
Market value ($ mil.)	(11.1%)	964.9	456.7	414.3	355.6	601.4
Employees	(2.8%)	2,800	2,200	2,100	2,400	2,500

ASTRONOVA INC

NMS: ALOT

600 East Greenwich Avenue
West Warwick, RI 02893
Phone: 401 828-4000
Fax: –
Web: www.astronovainc.com

CEO: Gregory A Woods
CFO: David S Smith
HR: –
FYE: January 31
Type: Public

AstroNova designs, develops, manufactures, and distributes a broad range of specialty printers and data acquisition and analysis systems, including both hardware and software. Its target markets for its products include aerospace, apparel, automotive, avionics, chemicals, computer peripherals, communications, distribution, food and beverage, general manufacturing, packaging, and transportation. The company's PI segment includes specialty printing systems and related supplies sold under the brand names QuickLabel, GetLabels, TrojanLabel, and GetLabels. The T&M segment include its line of aerospace printers, ethernet-networking products, and test and measurement data acquisition systems sold under the AstroNova brand name. AstroNova generates almost 65% of total sales from its home country, the US.

	Annual Growth	01/19	01/20	01/21	01/22	01/23
Sales ($mil.)	1.1%	136.7	133.4	116.0	117.5	142.5
Net income ($ mil.)	(17.4%)	5.7	1.8	1.3	6.4	2.7
Market value ($ mil.)	(9.8%)	146.5	91.2	78.8	100.8	97.2
Employees	1.3%	374	365	327	339	394

ASTROTECH CORP

NAS: ASTC

2105 Donley Drive, Suite 100
Austin, TX 78758
Phone: 512 485-9530
Fax: –
Web: www.astrotechcorp.com

CEO: Thomas B Pickens III
CFO: Jaime Hinojosa
HR: –
FYE: June 30
Type: Public

Astrotech is the muscle on the ground prior to satellite launch countdown. Formerly SPACEHAB, the company offers services and products that aid the US government and commercial customers in preparing satellites and cargo payloads for space launch. Its Astrotech Space Operations (ASO) business unit is a contractor that provides such services as ground transportation, hardware integration, fueling, and launch pad delivery. It also fabricates launch equipment and hardware. Astrotech's much smaller Spacetech unit is focused on using space-based technologies to develop commercial products in the chemical and biotechnology sectors. About 75% of Astrotech's revenues are made from NASA and US government contracts.

	Annual Growth	06/19	06/20	06/21	06/22	06/23
Sales ($mil.)	55.9%	0.1	0.5	0.3	0.9	0.8
Net income ($ mil.)	–	(7.5)	(8.3)	(7.6)	(8.3)	(9.6)
Market value ($ mil.)	54.3%	4.2	4.8	2.2	0.7	23.8
Employees	(7.5%)	30	27	12	14	22

ASURA DEVELOPMENT GROUP, INC

101 California Street, Suite 2450
San Francisco, CA 94111
Phone: 415 946-8828
Fax: –
Web: www.iaglobalinc.com

CEO: –
CFO: –
HR: –
FYE: March 31
Type: Public

IA Global has made the call to the Pacific Rim region. The holding company is focused on growing its existing businesses and making strategic acquisitions in Asia. Its primary holdings revolve around Global Hotline, a Japanese business process outsourcing (BPO) company that owns two call centers and offers telemarketing services, medical insurance, and other products to customers in Japan. IA Global also owns call center operations in the Philippines, along with parts of Japanese firms GPlus Media (online media), Slate Consulting (executive search), Taicom Securities (financial services), and Australian Secured Financial Limited (private loans and real estate investment). IA Global was formed in 1998.

	Annual Growth	12/06	12/07*	03/08	03/09	03/10
Sales ($mil.)	–	19.1	29.1	16.0	57.1	–
Net income ($ mil.)	–	(3.8)	(8.3)	0.4	(20.2)	(0.3)
Market value ($ mil.)	(54.7%)	0.9	1.8	1.8	0.3	0.0
Employees	(69.0%)	469	841	–	907	14

*Fiscal year change

ASURE SOFTWARE INC.

NAS: ASUR

405 Colorado Street, Suite 1800
Austin, TX 78701
Phone: 512 437-2700
Fax: –
Web: www.asuresoftware.com

CEO: Patrick Goepel
CFO: John Pence
HR: Andy Gray
FYE: December 31
Type: Public

Asure Software wants to guaranty a more organized workplace. The company develops Web-based business administration software through its NetSimplicity and iEmployee divisions. NetSimplicity's offerings include Meeting Room Manager, which lets users reserve meeting rooms and schedule equipment and resources. NetSimplicity also provides an asset management tool called Visual Asset Manager that tracks and manages fixed and mobile IT assets. The company's iEmployee division offers tools for managing time and attendance, benefits, payroll, and expense information. Asure primarily sells its products directly in North America; it uses resellers for customers outside the US and for federal government sales.

	Annual Growth	12/19	12/20	12/21	12/22	12/23
Sales ($mil.)	13.0%	73.2	65.5	76.1	95.8	119.1
Net income ($ mil.)	–	30.0	(16.3)	3.2	(14.5)	(9.2)
Market value ($ mil.)	3.9%	204.5	177.5	195.7	233.5	238.0
Employees	8.3%	423	482	517	501	581

AT&T INC

NYS: T

208 S. Akard St.
Dallas, TX 75202
Phone: 210 821-4105
Fax: –
Web: www.att.com

CEO: John T Stankey
CFO: Pascal Desroches
HR: –
FYE: December 31
Type: Public

AT&T is a leading provider of telecommunications, media and technology services globally. The company offers wireless, wireline, and satellite, as well as strategic data services including Virtual Private Networks (VPN), AT&T Dedicated Internet (ADI), and Ethernet and broadband services. In North America, AT&T's network covers over 440 million people with 4G LTE and over 285million with 5G technology. The company classify its subscribers as either postpaid, prepaid, connected device or reseller. In 2022, it served 217 million Mobility subscribers, including 85 million postpaid (70 million phone), 19 million prepaid, 6 million reseller and 107 million connected devices. The US supplies the majority of the company's revenue.

	Annual Growth	12/19	12/20	12/21	12/22	12/23
Sales ($mil.)	(9.3%)	181,193	171,760	168,864	120,741	122,428
Net income ($ mil.)	0.9%	13,903	(5,176.0)	20,081	(8,524.0)	14,400
Market value ($ mil.)	(19.1%)	279,424	205,636	175,892	131,633	119,978
Employees	–	246,000	230,000	203,000	160,700	–

ATALANTA CORPORATION

1 ATALANTA PLZ
ELIZABETH, NJ 072062186
Phone: 908 351-8000
Fax: –
Web: www.atalantacorp.com

CEO: George Gellert
CFO: Tom Decarll
HR: Carly Beim
FYE: December 31
Type: Private

Atalanta Corporation helps customers outfit any wine and cheese soir e. The company is a top specialty food importer that markets 3,000 different products, such as gourmet cheeses, deli and canned meats, and frozen seafood. Its menu of products also includes pastas, rices, and grains, as well as coffee and a line of kosher foods. Atalanta's brands include Casa, Diva, Celebrity, Zerto, Del Destino, Maria Brand, Martel, and Atalanta. Importing products from Europe, Asia, and South America, Atalanta sells primarily to restaurants and other foodservice operators, grocery stores, and specialty food retailers. Founded in 1945, the company is controlled by the Gellert family and led by CEO George Gellert.

	Annual Growth	12/04	12/05	12/06	12/07	12/09
Sales ($mil.)	–	–	–	(1,092.3)	348.8	384.9
Net income ($ mil.)	14310.1%	–	–	0.0	10.8	9.0
Market value ($ mil.)	–	–	–	–	–	–
Employees	–	–	–	–	–	220

ATALIAN US NORTHEAST, LLC

525 WASHINGTON BLVD STE 25
JERSEY CITY, NJ 07310
Phone: 212 889-6353
Fax: –
Web: www.gdi.com

CEO: Christopher Hughes
CFO: –
HR: –
FYE: September 30
Type: Private

Temco Service Industries provides temps, trees, and tidiness. The company offers facility management services, including building management, cleaning, maintenance, landscaping, and temporary personnel staffing. It also provides temperature control, HVAC systems, mechanical equipment, building automation systems, lighting, fire, and security services. To address varied client needs, the company runs its business through three divisions that offer support services to commercial properties; education facilities, including public school systems and universities; and corporate, manufacturing, and industrial properties. Temco was founded in 1917.

	Annual Growth	09/96	09/97	09/98	09/05	09/07
Sales ($mil.)	7.7%	–	–	172.3	306.3	334.7
Net income ($ mil.)	47.8%	–	–	1.2	1.2	40.7
Market value ($ mil.)	–	–	–	–	–	–
Employees	–	–	–	–	–	2,000

ATC GROUP SERVICES LLC

5750 JOHNSTON ST STE 400
LAFAYETTE, LA 705035334
Phone: 337 234-8777
Fax: –
Web: www.oneatlas.com

CEO: –
CFO: –
HR: –
FYE: February 28
Type: Private

ATC Group Services likes to take take on the tough jobs -- the bigger the better. The company helps clients design and execute large-scale projects that can have a variety of construction, environmental, health, safety, and technical applications. The firm, which does business as ATC Associates, often can coordinate services to save money. (ATC stands for Assess, Test, and Consult). Companies in sectors such as petroleum, manufacturing, construction, retail, and government have used ATC to plan the removal of mold and asbestos, treatment of sewage, and testing of construction and construction materials. The company is a subsidiary of Australia-based professional services group Cardno.

ATC VENTURE GROUP INC

NBB: ATCV

5929 Baker Road, Suite 400
Minnetonka, MN 55345
Phone: 952 215-3100
Fax: 952 215-3129
Web: www.cyclecountry.com

CEO: –
CFO: –
HR: –
FYE: September 30
Type: Public

Cycle Country Accessories turns ATVs into beasts of burden. The company makes all-terrain vehicle (ATV) accessories, such as snowplow blades, lawnmowers, spreaders, sprayers, tillage equipment, winch mounts, utility boxes, and wheel covers for Honda, Yamaha, Kawasaki, Suzuki, Polaris, Arctic Cat, and other ATV models. Cycle Country also makes hubcaps for golf carts, riding lawnmowers, and light-duty trailers. Its products are sold through 20 distributors in the US and more than 30 other countries. The company also makes pull-behind implements and other accessories for riding mowers under the Weekend Warrior brand, and offers contract manufacturing services. Cycle Country makes most of its sales in the US.

	Annual Growth	09/07	09/08	09/09	09/10	09/11
Sales ($mil.)	(37.2%)	14.2	17.5	10.3	12.1	2.2
Net income ($ mil.)	–	0.4	(0.4)	(6.8)	(1.7)	(3.9)
Market value ($ mil.)	(35.2%)	11.3	7.4	4.4	2.5	2.0
Employees	(3.0%)	104	104	72	105	92

ATCO RUBBER PRODUCTS, INC.

7101 ATCO DR
FORT WORTH, TX 761187029
Phone: 817 595-2894
Fax: –
Web: www.atcoflex.com

CEO: –
CFO: Randall Calaway
HR: –
FYE: December 31
Type: Private

ATCO Rubber Products is the worldwide leader in flexible ducts systems used in commercial and residential heating, cooling, and ventilation systems. Its products include both insulated and uninsulated sleeves, sheet metal, aluminum and special purpose items. ATCO operates around 10 manufacturing sites across the US and international sites in Europe, the Middle East, and India. All of ATCO's products are developed and manufactured to meet the most stringent national and international standards.

ATEECO, INC.

600 E CENTRE ST
SHENANDOAH, PA 179761825
Phone: 570 462-2745
Fax: –
Web: www.mrstspierogies.com

CEO: –
CFO: –
HR: Angela Kelley
FYE: December 31
Type: Private

Ateeco, doing business as Mrs. T's Pierogies, produces more than 600 million frozen pierogies a year. Its customers include industries such as commercial restaurants, colleges and universities, as well as US military commissaries worldwide. Mrs. T's pierogies come in more than a dozen varieties, including potato and cheddar; sauerkraut; and potato, sour cream, and chives. Its frozen pierogies are perfect quick meals, sides, and snacks. The family-owned and -managed company was founded by Ted Twardzik in 1952; the product was named after his mother, Mary Twardzik.

ATHENA ENGINEERING, INC.

456 E FOOTHILL BLVD
SAN DIMAS, CA 917731205
Phone: 909 599-0947
Fax: –
Web: www.athenaengineering.com

CEO: Jane Chiera
CFO: –
HR: –
FYE: December 31
Type: Private

The goddess of construction and engineering? Not quite, but close. Athena Engineering specializes in the installation and design of heating, cooling, ventilation, lighting, building automation, and other systems services for the commercial, food processing, health, and telecommunications industries. Athena also offers general construction, energy management, and environmental systems services. The company mostly works for both public and private entities in Southern California. In addition to being privately owned, Athena Engineering is one of the top women/minority-owned companies in the region. Athena Engineering was founded in 1984.

	Annual Growth	12/07	12/08	12/11	12/20	12/21
Sales ($mil.)	1.1%	–	18.1	7.0	12.9	20.8
Net income ($ mil.)	16.5%	–	0.6	(2.8)	2.8	4.4
Market value ($ mil.)	–	–	–	–	–	–
Employees	–	–	–	–	–	32

ATHENAHEALTH, INC.

80 GUEST ST
BOSTON, MA 021352071
Phone: 617 402-1000
Fax: –
Web: www.athenahealth.com

CEO: Robert E Segert
CFO: John Hofmann
HR: John Marshall
FYE: December 31
Type: Private

athenahealth, Inc. is a leading provider of network-enabled software and services for medical groups and health systems nationwide. athenahealth partners with more than 140,000 ambulatory care providers, throughout all 50 states and across more than 120 specialties, to accelerate the pace of healthcare innovation and support the delivery of leading clinical and financial outcomes. athenahealth's athenaOne cloud platform addresses the critical aspects of a physician's practice - with modules spanning patient engagement, revenue cycle, telehealth, payments, population health, and value-based care management. athenahealth delivers this suite of capabilities to customers by combining powerful SaaS technology with the expert services and data-driven insights that come from the country's largest single connected network. In 2022, athenahealth was acquired by Bain Capital and Hellman & Friedman from Veritas Capital and Evergreen Coast Capital for $17 billion.

ATHERSYS INC

3201 Carnegie Avenue
Cleveland, OH 44115-2634
Phone: 216 431-9900
Fax: –
Web: www.athersys.com

NBB: ATHX Q
CEO: William Lehmann Jr
CFO: Ivor Macleod
HR: Cynthia Burge
FYE: December 31
Type: Public

Biotechnology is all the RAGE at Athersys. The development-stage company uses its Random Activation of Gene Expression (RAGE) technology to scan the human genome, identify proteins with specific biological functions, and link those protein functions with gene structures (functional genomics). It is also developing therapies for oncology and vascular applications based on its MultiStem technology, which uses stem cells from adult bone marrow. The firm plans to leverage its technologies by partnering with other biotechs and drugmakers, but it also aims to develop its own proprietary drugs. It counts Bristol-Myers Squibb and Angiotech Pharmaceuticals among its partners.

	Annual Growth	12/18	12/19	12/20	12/21	12/22
Sales ($mil.)	(31.6%)	24.3	5.6	1.4	5.5	5.3
Net income ($ mil.)	–	(24.3)	(44.6)	(78.8)	(87.0)	(72.5)
Market value ($ mil.)	(12.6%)	25.9	22.1	31.5	16.2	15.1
Employees	(24.8%)	75	83	97	104	24

ATI INC (NEW)

2021 McKinney Avenue
Dallas, TX 75201
Phone: 800 289-7454
Fax: –
Web: www.atimetals.com

NYS: ATI
CEO: –
CFO: –
HR: –
FYE: December 31
Type: Public

ATI, formerly Allegheny Technologies Incorporated, is a global manufacturer of technically advanced specialty materials and complex components. ATI is a market leader in manufacturing differentiated products that require its materials science capabilities and unique process technologies, including its new product development competence. The company's product focuses are maximizing aero-engine materials and components growth; and delivering high-value flat products primarily to the energy, aerospace, and defense end-markets. The US customers generate almost 60% of the company's total revenue.

	Annual Growth	12/19	12/20	12/21	12/22	12/23
Sales ($mil.)	0.3%	4,122.5	2,982.1	2,799.8	3,836.0	4,173.7
Net income ($ mil.)	12.4%	257.6	(1,572.6)	(38.2)	130.9	410.8
Market value ($ mil.)	21.8%	2,621.3	2,127.8	2,021.2	3,788.6	5,769.2
Employees	(2.6%)	8,100	6,500	6,300	6,700	7,300

ATKORE INC

NYS: ATKR

16100 South Lathrop Avenue
Harvey, IL 60426
Phone: 708 339-1610
Fax: –
Web: www.atkore.com

CEO: –
CFO: –
HR: –
FYE: September 30
Type: Public

Atkore is a leading manufacturer of Electrical products primarily for the non-residential construction and renovation markets, as well as residential markets, and Safety & Infrastructure products for the construction and industrial markets. It offers products and services under various brands including Allied Tube & Conduit, AFC Cable Systems, Kaf-Tech, Heritage Plastics, Unistrut, Power-Strut, Cope, US Tray, FRE Composites, United Poly Systems, Calbond and Calpipe. The company has operational presence in the US, the UK, Belgium, Canada, China, Australia and New Zealand. About 90% of its revenue were sold to customers located in the US.

	Annual Growth	09/19	09/20	09/21	09/22	09/23
Sales ($mil.)	16.4%	1,916.5	1,765.4	2,928.0	3,913.9	3,518.8
Net income ($ mil.)	49.2%	139.1	152.3	587.9	913.4	689.9
Market value ($ mil.)	48.9%	1,132.6	848.2	3,243.7	2,903.7	5,567.5
Employees	9.5%	3,900	3,700	4,000	5,000	5,600

ATKORE INTERNATIONAL HOLDINGS INC.

16100 LATHROP AVE
HARVEY, IL 604266021
Phone: 708 225-2051
Fax: –
Web: www.atkore.com

CEO: –
CFO: –
HR: –
FYE: September 28
Type: Private

Atkore International's Electrical and Infrastructure arm makes conduits and cables, and cable management systems. An Engineered Products and Services segment produces pipes and tubes, as well as fence framework and structural steel sheets, all in various sizes. Atkore sells its lineup under brands Allied Tube & Conduit, AFC Cable Systems, and others, through retailers, electrical and plumbing distributors, OEMs, and general contractors in North America, Brazil, the UK, France, Australia, and New Zealand. Late in 2010, Tyco spun off a 51% stake in the company to Clayton, Dubilier & Rice. (Tyco sold its remaining interest in Atkore in 2014.)

ATLANTA CLARK UNIVERSITY INC

223 JAMES P BRAWLEY DR SW
ATLANTA, GA 303144385
Phone: 404 880-8000
Fax: –
Web: www.cau.edu

CEO: Colton Brown Dr
CFO: Lucille Mauge
HR: Michael Lacour
FYE: June 30
Type: Private

Clark Atlanta University (CAU) is a historically African-American liberal arts college that enrolls about 3,500 students. The private school, which is affiliated with the United Methodist Church, offers undergraduate and graduate degrees through its four schools: Arts and Sciences, Business Administration, Education, Social Work. It also offers professional programs and certificates. CAU is a member of the Atlanta University Center, a consortium of educational institutions that includes Spelman College and Morehouse College. Clark Atlanta University was formed by the 1988 merger of two colleges founded in the 1860s -- Clark College and Atlanta University.

	Annual Growth	06/17	06/18	06/19	06/21	06/22
Sales ($mil.)	17.6%	–	111.9	113.3	177.0	214.3
Net income ($ mil.)	15.0%	–	23.3	10.9	38.8	40.8
Market value ($ mil.)	–	–	–	–	–	–
Employees	–	–	–	–	–	1,150

ATLANTA HARDWOOD CORPORATION

5596 RIVERVIEW RD SE
MABLETON, GA 301262914
Phone: 404 792-2290
Fax: –
Web: www.hardwoodweb.com

CEO: James W Howard Jr
CFO: Paul Harris
HR: Carolyn Carlin
FYE: December 31
Type: Private

Atlanta Hardwood Corporation carves out its living from the trees of the Appalachian Mountains. Through its various divisions, Atlanta Hardwood supplies hardwood products, including lumber, plywood, veneer, moulding, and flooring, made from some 75 varieties of wood. It specializes in processing, distributing, and exporting products made from Appalachian wood, including Ash, Maple, Poplar, and White Oak. It also imports Mahogany, Teak, European Beech, and several other types of wood from international sources. Other offerings include custom product services that cater to architects, designers, and fabricators. Founded in 1952 by James Howard, Sr., Atlanta Hardwood is today headed by Howard's son, Jim Howard.

	Annual Growth	12/04	12/05	12/06	12/07	12/08
Sales ($mil.)	(17.2%)	–	–	34.0	27.3	23.3
Net income ($ mil.)	–	–	–	0.7	0.6	(0.3)
Market value ($ mil.)	–	–	–	–	–	–
Employees	–	–	–	–	–	243

ATLANTA NATIONAL LEAGUE BASEBALL CLUB, LLC

755 BATTERY AVE SE
ATLANTA, GA 303393017
Phone: 404 614-2300
Fax: –
Web: www.mlb.com

CEO: Terence F McGuirk
CFO: Chip Moore
HR: –
FYE: December 31
Type: Private

America may be the land of the free, but Atlanta is the home of these baseball Braves. Atlanta National League Baseball Club owns and operates the Atlanta Braves Major League Baseball franchise, which boasts three World Series championships, its last in 1995. A charter member of the National League, the team was formed as the Boston Red Stockings in 1871 (it became the Braves in 1912) and moved to Milwaukee in the 1950s before settling in Atlanta in 1966. Under the ownership of media mogul Ted Turner, the Braves won five pennants during the 1990s. John Malone's Liberty Media has owned the team since 2007.

	Annual Growth	12/18	12/19	12/20	12/21	12/22
Sales ($mil.)	15.1%	–	–	–	4.2	4.8
Net income ($ mil.)	–	–	–	–	(0.4)	1.7
Market value ($ mil.)	–	–	–	–	–	–
Employees	–	–	–	–	–	1,700

ATLANTIC AMERICAN CORP.

NMS: AAME

4370 Peachtree Road, N.E.
Atlanta, GA 30319
Phone: 404 266-5500
Fax: –
Web: www.atlam.com

CEO: Hilton H Howell Jr
CFO: J R Franklin
HR: –
FYE: December 31
Type: Public

Baseball, apple pie, and... insurance! Atlantic American sells a mix of property/casualty, health, and life insurance throughout the US. Its Bankers Fidelity Life Insurance subsidiary provides life and supplemental health insurance offerings, with income primarily coming from sales of Medicare supplement policies. Its American Southern subsidiary offers commercial and personal property/casualty products including automobile insurance products targeted at large motor pools and fleets owned by local governments. The unit also offers general commercial liability coverage and surety bonds catering to niche markets such as school bus transportation and subdivision construction.

	Annual Growth	12/18	12/19	12/20	12/21	12/22
Assets ($mil.)	1.6%	344.3	377.6	405.2	402.3	367.1
Net income ($ mil.)	–	(0.7)	(0.4)	12.2	4.3	1.5
Market value ($ mil.)	(0.7%)	49.2	40.2	42.0	50.0	47.8
Employees	(3.1%)	161	155	153	140	142

ATLANTIC CITY ELECTRIC CO

500 North Wakefield Drive
Newark, DE 19702-5440
Phone: 202 872-2000
Fax: -
Web: www.atlanticcityelectric.com

CEO: David M Velazquez
CFO: Frederick J Boyle
HR: -
FYE: December 31
Type: Public

Atlantic City Electric makes America's favorite playground shine in the nighttime. The Pepco Holdings' utility generates, transmits, and distributes electricity to 547,000 homes and businesses in southern New Jersey. Atlantic City Electric operates more than 11,000 miles of transmission and distribution lines in its 2,700 sq. ml., 8-county service area. Atlantic City Electric's electricity delivery operations are regulated by the New Jersey Board of Public Utilities. As part of the 2016 acquisition of Pepco Holdings, Atlantic City Electric joined the Exelon family of utilities.

	Annual Growth	12/19	12/20	12/21	12/22	12/23
Sales ($mil.)	5.3%	1,240.0	1,245.0	1,388.0	1,431.0	1,522.0
Net income ($ mil.)	4.9%	99.0	112.0	146.0	148.0	120.0
Market value ($ mil.)	-	-	-	-	-	-
Employees	(0.7%)	639	650	633	621	621

ATLANTIC DIVING SUPPLY, INC.

621 LYNNHVEN PKWY STE 160
VIRGINIA BEACH, VA 23452
Phone: 757 481-7758
Fax: -
Web: www.adsinc.com

CEO: -
CFO: -
HR: -
FYE: December 31
Type: Private

Atlantic Diving Supply (doing business as ADS) is a leading value-added logistics and supply chain solutions provider that proudly serves all branches of the US Military, federal, state, and local government organizations, law enforcement agencies, first responders, partner nations, and the defense industry. The company provides tactical equipment, procurement, logistics, government contracts, and supply chain solutions. The company is focused on solving customers' challenges by providing the best product and service offerings, the broadest array of procurement and contract options, world-class support and legendary customer service. The company has grown to be a #1 DLA Supplier, #17 GSA Contractor, and #22 Federal Government Contractor.

	Annual Growth	12/06	12/07	12/08	12/09	12/10
Sales ($mil.)	42.8%	-	-	650.8	938.9	1,327.2
Net income ($ mil.)	38.7%	-	-	40.2	54.4	77.3
Market value ($ mil.)	-	-	-	-	-	-
Employees	-	-	-	-	-	517

ATLANTIC HEALTH SYSTEM INC.

475 SOUTH ST
MORRISTOWN, NJ 079606459
Phone: 973 660-3100
Fax: -
Web: www.atlantichealth.org

CEO: Brian Gragnolati
CFO: Barbara Cerame
HR: Amy Duncan
FYE: December 31
Type: Private

The not-for-profit Atlantic Health System (AHS) operates about dozen urgent care hospitals providing general medical and surgical services to residents of northern New Jersey. Its flagship Morristown Medical Center is a nationally-recognized leader in cardiology, orthopedics, nursing, critical care and geriatrics. AHS is a member of AllSpire Health Partners ? an alliance of five hospital systems that addresses quality, population health management, best practices and medical research in the Northeast region. Atlantic Health System also has medical school affiliation with the Sidney Kimmel Medical College at Thomas Jefferson University, and is the official health care partner of the New York Jets.

ATLANTIC POWER CORPORATION

3 ALLIED DR STE 155
DEDHAM, MA 020266101
Phone: 617 977-2400
Fax: -
Web: www.atlanticpower.com

CEO: James J Moore Jr
CFO: Terrence Ronan
HR: Erica Maginn
FYE: March 31
Type: Private

Atlantic Power, a Canadian independent power producer, owns 21 power generation projects in eleven US states and two provinces of Canada. The company has a generation capacity of more than 1,300 MW, about 85% of which is generated in the US. Its primarily sells natural gas, biomass, and hydro-power, under long-term fuel supply agreements to utilities and other parties. The company also partners with Heorot Power Management and Purenergy LLC to provide operations, maintenance and repair services. Nearly three-quarters of Atlantic Power's revenue comes from the US.

	Annual Growth	12/17	12/18	12/19	12/20*	03/21
Sales ($mil.)	(36.6%)	-	282.3	281.6	272.0	72.0
Net income ($ mil.)	(65.0%)	-	37.2	(43.8)	73.5	1.6
Market value ($ mil.)	-	-	-	-	-	-
Employees	-	-	-	-	-	261

*Fiscal year change

ATLANTIC UNION BANKSHARES CORP   NYS: AUB

1051 East Cary Street, Suite 1200
Richmond, VA 23219
Phone: 804 633-5031
Fax: -
Web: www.atlanticunionbank.com

CEO: John C Asbury
CFO: Robert M Gorman
HR: Kimberly Helie
FYE: December 31
Type: Public

Atlantic Union Bankshares (formerly Union Bankshares Corporation) is a financial holding company and a bank holding company committed to the delivery of financial services through its subsidiary Atlantic Union Bank and non-bank financial services affiliates. The bank also provides banking, trust, and wealth management services through some 115 branches and approximately 130 ATMs located throughout Virginia, and portions of Maryland and North Carolina. Certain non-bank affiliates include Atlantic Union Equipment Finance, Inc., which provides equipment financing; Atlantic Union Financial Consultants LLC, which provides brokerage services; and Union Insurance Group, LLC, which offers various lines of insurance products. The company was incorporated in 1991 and it completed its bank holding company formation in 1993.

	Annual Growth	12/19	12/20	12/21	12/22	12/23
Assets ($mil.)	4.8%	17,563	19,628	20,065	20,461	21,166
Net income ($ mil.)	1.1%	193.5	158.2	263.9	234.5	201.8
Market value ($ mil.)	(0.7%)	2,817.1	2,471.3	2,797.6	2,636.3	2,741.4
Employees	(2.4%)	1,989	1,879	1,876	1,877	1,804

ATLANTICARE HEALTH SYSTEM INC.

6550 DELILAH RD STE 301A
EGG HARBOR TOWNSHIP, NJ 082345102
Phone: 609 407-2300
Fax: -
Web: www.atlanticare.org

CEO: Michael J Charlton
CFO: -
HR: Nilda Mahrer
FYE: December 31
Type: Private

AtlantiCare Health System won't gamble with your health. The not-for-profit health system operates AtlantiCare Regional Medical Center (ARMC), home to roughly 570 beds at two campuses (Atlantic City and Mainland). The hospital's specialty departments include a Level II Trauma center, heart institute, center for childbirth, weight loss clinic, cancer center, and joint and spine institutes. Other facilities include child care centers (AtlantiCare Kids), behavioral health facilities, and urgent care centers. The company also operates a PPO (AtlantiCare Health Plans) and offers home health and hospice services.

	Annual Growth	06/18	06/19	06/20*	12/21	12/22
Sales ($mil.)	1.4%	-	-	84.0	84.1	86.3
Net income ($ mil.)	(44.7%)	-	-	1.2	2.0	0.4
Market value ($ mil.)	-	-	-	-	-	-
Employees	-	-	-	-	-	5,000

*Fiscal year change

ATLANTICUS HOLDINGS CORP

NMS: ATLC

Five Concourse Parkway, Suite 300
Atlanta, GA 30328
Phone: 770 828-2000
Fax: –
Web: www.atlanticus.com

CEO: Jeffrey A Howard
CFO: William R McCamey
HR: –
FYE: December 31
Type: Public

Atlanticus is a financial technology company powering more inclusive financial solutions for everyday Americans. The company leverages data, analytics, and innovative technology to unlock access to financial solutions for the millions of Americans who would otherwise be underserved. Using its infrastructure and technology, Atlanticus provides loan servicing, including risk management and customer service outsourcing, for third parties. Also through its CaaS segment, the company engages in testing and limited investment in consumer finance technology platforms as it seeks to capitalize on its expertise and infrastructure. In auto finance segment, Atlanticus purchase auto loans at a discount and with dealer retentions or holdbacks that provide risk protection. It also provides certain installment lending products in addition to its traditional loans secured by automobiles.

	Annual Growth	12/19	12/20	12/21	12/22	12/23
Sales ($mil.)	26.0%	458.2	563.4	748.1	1,046.9	1,155.9
Net income ($ mil.)	40.4%	26.4	94.1	177.9	135.6	102.8
Market value ($ mil.)	43.9%	131.6	359.7	1,041.5	382.6	564.7
Employees	4.9%	319	327	331	357	386

ATLAS AIR WORLDWIDE HOLDINGS, INC.

1 N LEXINGTON AVE
WHITE PLAINS, NY 106011712
Phone: 914 701-8000
Fax: –
Web: www.atlasair.com

CEO: Michael T Steen
CFO: Artem Gonopolskiy
HR: Denise Cambone
FYE: December 31
Type: Private

Atlas Air Worldwide Holdings (AAWW) is a global leader in outsourced aircraft and aviation operating services. It leases cargo planes to customers, mainly airlines, under long-term ACMI (aircraft, crew, maintenance, and insurance) contracts. AAWW operates the world's largest fleet of Boeing 747 freighters and offers its customers a broad array of 747, 777, 767, and 737 aircraft for domestic, regional, and international cargo and passenger applications. It also offers dry leasing (aircraft and engines only) via its Titan division. In addition, affiliates Atlas Air and around 50% economic interest and some 75% voting interest in Polar Air Cargo. In 2022, AAWW was acquired by an investor group led by funds managed by affiliates of Apollo Global Management, Inc., together with investment affiliates of J.F. Lehman & Company and Hill City Capital, for $5.2 billion.

	Annual Growth	12/18	12/19	12/20	12/21	12/22
Sales ($mil.)	18.4%	–	2,739.2	3,211.1	4,030.8	4,549.1
Net income ($ mil.)	–	–	(293.1)	360.3	493.3	355.9
Market value ($ mil.)	–	–	–	–	–	–
Employees	–	–	–	–	–	4,061

ATLAS INDUSTRIAL CONTRACTORS, L.L.C.

5275 SINCLAIR RD
COLUMBUS, OH 432295042
Phone: 614 841-4500
Fax: –
Web: www.atlascos.com

CEO: –
CFO: –
HR: –
FYE: December 31
Type: Private

You won't need to consult your big book of maps to discover that Atlas Industrial Holdings provides such specialty contracting services as machinery and equipment rigging and steel fabricating, as well as piping, transportation, and electrical services. It also offers plant relocation and maintenance services. The company, which serves clients throughout the US, Mexico, and Canada, has performed such projects as rigging work for a Valero oil refinery and an electrical furnace upgrade for Owens Corning. Clients, which are mostly in the automotive, cement, power, and food and beverage industries, have included Anheuser-Busch, LafargeHolcim, and Honda of America.

	Annual Growth	12/11	12/12	12/13	12/15	12/16
Sales ($mil.)	9.1%	–	–	107.5	–	140.1
Net income ($ mil.)	–	–	–	4.0	–	(0.5)
Market value ($ mil.)	–	–	–	–	–	–
Employees	–	–	–	–	–	450

ATLAS WORLD GROUP, INC.

1212 SAINT GEORGE RD
EVANSVILLE, IN 477112364
Phone: 812 424-2222
Fax: –
Web: www.atlasworldgroupinc.com

CEO: John P Griffin
CFO: Donald R Breivogel Jr
HR: Bret Hartman
FYE: December 31
Type: Private

Willing to carry the weight of a moving world, agent-owned Atlas World Group is the holding company for Atlas Van Lines, one of the largest moving companies in the US. Atlas Van Lines' more than 500 agents transport household goods domestically and between the US and Canada; it also offers specialized transportation of items such as trade show exhibits, fine art, and electronics. Atlas Van Lines International provides international corporate relocation and freight forwarding services. Its Atlas Canada unit moves household goods in that country while American Red Ball International specializes in military relocations and serves van lines outside Atlas' network.

	Annual Growth	12/17	12/18	12/19	12/20	12/21
Sales ($mil.)	2.6%	–	900.5	906.4	806.0	973.6
Net income ($ mil.)	18.8%	–	10.0	9.6	8.0	16.8
Market value ($ mil.)	–	–	–	–	–	–
Employees	–	–	–	–	–	726

ATLASSIAN CORP

NMS: TEAM

350 Bush Street, 13th Floor
San Francisco, CA 94104
Phone: 415 701-1110
Fax: –
Web: www.atlassian.com

CEO: –
CFO: –
HR: –
FYE: June 30
Type: Public

This company is hardcore about software. More than 51,000 large and small organizations use Atlassian's tracking, collaboration, communication, service management, and software development products. The company serves customers in a wide variety of industries, helping developers collaborate with non-developer teams involved in software innovation. Atlassian's products include include JIRA for team planning and project management, Confluence for team content creation and sharing, HipChat for team messaging and communications, Bitbucket for team code sharing and management, and JIRA Service Desk for team services and support applications. Founded in 2002, the company went public in 2015.

	Annual Growth	06/19	06/20	06/21	06/22	06/23
Sales ($mil.)	30.7%	1,210.1	1,614.2	2,089.1	2,802.9	3,534.6
Net income ($ mil.)	–	(637.6)	(350.7)	(696.3)	(614.1)	(486.8)
Market value ($ mil.)	6.4%	33,700	46,432	66,159	48,268	43,222
Employees	31.2%	3,616	4,907	6,433	8,813	10,726

ATMEL CORPORATION

1600 TECHNOLOGY DR
SAN JOSE, CA 951101382
Phone: 408 735-9110
Fax: –
Web: www.microchip.com

CEO: –
CFO: –
HR: –
FYE: December 31
Type: Private

Atmel is a leading maker of microcontrollers, which are used in a wide range of products, from computers and mobile devices (smartphones, tablets, e-readers) to automobile motor control systems, television remote controls, and solid-state lighting. In addition, the company offers touchscreen controllers and sensors, nonvolatile memory devices, and radio frequency (RF) and wireless components. Its chips are used worldwide in consumer, communications, industrial, military, and networking applications. Most of Atmel's sales come from customers outside the US. In mid-2016 the company was bought by Microchip, a chip maker, for $3.6 billion.

	Annual Growth	12/10	12/11	12/12	12/13	12/14
Sales ($mil.)	(0.7%)	–	–	1,432.1	1,386.4	1,413.3
Net income ($ mil.)	7.5%	–	–	30.4	(22.1)	35.2
Market value ($ mil.)	–	–	–	–	–	–
Employees	–	–	–	–	–	5,200

ATMOS ENERGY CORP.   NYS: ATO

1800 Three Lincoln Centre, 5430 LBJ Freeway
Dallas, TX 75240
Phone: 972 934-9227
Fax: 972 855-3075
Web: www.atmosenergy.com

CEO: J K Akers
CFO: Christopher T Forsythe
HR: -
FYE: September 30
Type: Public

Atmos Energy is the country's largest natural-gas-only distributor based on number of customers. The company safely delivers reliable, affordable, efficient and abundant natural gas through regulated sales and transportation arrangements to approximately 3.3 million residential, commercial, public authority and industrial customers in eight states located primarily in the South. Atmos Energy also operates one of the largest intrastate pipelines in Texas based on miles of pipe.

	Annual Growth	09/19	09/20	09/21	09/22	09/23
Sales ($mil.)	10.2%	2,901.8	2,821.1	3,407.5	4,201.7	4,275.4
Net income ($ mil.)	14.7%	511.4	601.4	665.6	774.4	885.9
Market value ($ mil.)	(1.8%)	16,912	14,194	13,097	15,124	15,730
Employees	1.2%	4,776	4,694	4,684	4,791	5,019

ATN INTERNATIONAL INC   NMS: ATNI

500 Cummings Center, Suite 2450
Beverly, MA 01915
Phone: 978 619-1300
Fax: -
Web: www.atni.com

CEO: Michael T Prior
CFO: Justin D Benincasa
HR: Mary E Fairbairn
FYE: December 31
Type: Public

ATN provides digital infrastructure and communications services in the US and internationally, including in the Caribbean region, with a focus on smaller markets. Through its operating subsidiaries, the company primarily provide: carrier and enterprise communications services, such as terrestrial and submarine fiber optic transport, and communications tower facilities; and fixed and mobile telecommunications connectivity to residential, business, and government customers, including a range of high-speed internet and data services, fixed and mobile wireless solutions, and video and voice services. ATN owns and operates almost 320 towers and roughly 295 fiber connected tower. About 50% of the company's revenue comes from the US.

	Annual Growth	12/19	12/20	12/21	12/22	12/23
Sales ($mil.)	14.8%	438.7	455.4	602.7	725.7	762.2
Net income ($ mil.)	-	(10.8)	(14.1)	(22.1)	(5.6)	(14.5)
Market value ($ mil.)	(8.4%)	854.2	644.0	616.1	698.7	601.0
Employees	7.8%	1,700	1,700	2,300	2,400	2,300

ATOS SYNTEL INC.

525 E BIG BEAVER RD STE 300
TROY, MI 480831367
Phone: 248 619-2800
Fax: -
Web: www.syntelinc.com

CEO: Rakesh Khanna
CFO: Anil Agrawal
HR: -
FYE: December 31
Type: Private

In 2018, Syntel joined forces with Atos to form Atos/Syntel that provides infrastructure and data management, big data, cybersecurity, high performance computing, digital workplace, global delivery model and core and digital service powered by automation. Atos Syntel's digital platform, ATOM, helps customers build the next generation of smart business applications with ready-to-use solution building blocks that improve developer productivity and time to market by 20-40%.

ATRICURE INC   NMS: ATRC

7555 Innovation Way
Mason, OH 45040
Phone: 513 755-4100
Fax: -
Web: www.atricure.com

CEO: Michael H Carrel
CFO: M A Wade
HR: -
FYE: December 31
Type: Public

AtriCure is a leading innovator in treatments for atrial fibrillation (Afib), left atrial appendage (LAA) management and post-operative pain. Afib affects more than 37 million people worldwide. AtriCure's Isolator Synergy Ablation System is the first medical device to receive FDA approval for the treatment of persistent Afib. AtriCure's AtriClip Left Atrial Appendage Exclusion System products and is the most widely sold LAA management devices worldwide. AtriCure's Hybrid AF Therapy is a minimally invasive procedure that provides a lasting solution for long-standing persistent Afib patients. AtriCure's cryoICE cryoSPHERE probe is cleared for temporary ablation of peripheral nerves to block pain, providing pain relief in cardiac and thoracic procedures. Its US markets account for about 85% of revenue.

	Annual Growth	12/19	12/20	12/21	12/22	12/23
Sales ($mil.)	14.7%	230.8	206.5	274.3	330.4	399.2
Net income ($ mil.)	-	(35.2)	(48.2)	50.2	(46.5)	(30.4)
Market value ($ mil.)	2.4%	1,545.1	2,645.8	3,304.5	2,109.2	1,696.2
Employees	13.2%	730	750	875	1,050	1,200

ATRION CORP.   NMS: ATRI

One Allentown Parkway
Allen, TX 75002
Phone: 972 390-9800
Fax: -
Web: www.atrioncorp.com

CEO: David A Battat
CFO: Cindy Ferguson
HR: -
FYE: December 31
Type: Public

Atrion Corporation is a leading manufacturer of medical devices and components that makes a wide range of products for specific niche markets, including soft contact lens disinfection cases, clamps for IV sets, vacuum relief valves, surgical loops used in minimally invasive surgery, and check valves. As an extension of its expertise in valve design and manufacturing, Atrion also is the leading manufacturer of valves and inflation devices for the marine and aviation markets, supplying valves used in safety products such as life vests, and inflatable boats. About 60% of company's revenue comes from the US customers.

	Annual Growth	12/19	12/20	12/21	12/22	12/23
Sales ($mil.)	2.2%	155.1	147.6	165.0	183.5	169.3
Net income ($ mil.)	(14.8%)	36.8	32.1	33.1	35.0	19.4
Market value ($ mil.)	(15.7%)	1,322.6	1,130.3	1,240.6	984.6	666.7
Employees	3.7%	616	636	667	722	712

ATRION, INC.

659 SOUTH COUNTY TRL
EXETER, RI 028223412
Phone: 401 736-6400
Fax: -
Web: www.atrion.com

CEO: Oscar T Hebert
CFO: Marianne Caserta
HR: -
FYE: June 30
Type: Private

Atrion Networking helps companies in the northeastern US develop and operate their communications networks. The company provides network integration and consulting services; implements virtual private networks (VPNs) and corporate telephone systems; and protects networks from spam, viruses, and hackers. Atrion also resells business telecommunications services, including voice, data colocation, and Internet access, from such carriers as AT&T, Qwest and Verizon. The company has served such customers as KB Toys, Polaroid, and the government of Ghana. The company was being acquired by Carousel Industries in 2016.

	Annual Growth	06/02	06/03	06/05	06/06	06/07
Sales ($mil.)	17.6%	-	17.5	24.9	26.2	33.4
Net income ($ mil.)	15.9%	-	0.2	0.3	0.2	0.4
Market value ($ mil.)	-	-	-	-	-	-
Employees	-	-	-	-	-	200

ATRIUS HEALTH, INC.

275 GROVE ST STE 3300
AUBURNDALE, MA 024662274
Phone: 617 559-8444
Fax: –
Web: www.atriushealth.org

CEO: Steven Strongwater
CFO: Leland J Stacy
HR: –
FYE: December 31
Type: Private

Atrius Health, an innovative nonprofit healthcare leader, delivers an effective system of connected care for adult and pediatric patients at some 30 medical practice locations in eastern Massachusetts. Atrius Health's physicians and primary care providers, along with additional clinicians, work in close collaboration with hospital partners, community specialists and skilled nursing. Atrius Health provides high-quality, patient-centered, coordinated, cost effective care to every patient it serves. Atrius Health was founded in 2004 by medical groups including Dedham Medical Associates and Harvard Vanguard Medical Associates; Granite Medical Group joined a short time later in 2005.

	Annual Growth	12/13	12/14	12/15	12/17	12/19
Sales ($mil.)	137.6%	–	28.6	1,577.0	1,873.0	2,167.7
Net income ($ mil.)	–	–	(0.2)	(28.5)	39.5	5.7
Market value ($ mil.)	–	–	–	–	–	–
Employees	–	–	–	–	–	3,906

ATRIX INTERNATIONAL, INC.

1350 LARC INDUSTRIAL BLVD
BURNSVILLE, MN 553371412
Phone: 800 222-6154
Fax: –
Web: www.atrix.com

CEO: Shane Vail
CFO: –
HR: –
FYE: June 30
Type: Private

Atrix International manufactures fine particulate vacuum cleaners and related products and accessories for use in industrial, hospital, office, restaurant, and HAZMAT applications. Atrix also makes copier control, management, and tracking products. Its Omega vacuum cleaner can be used to make cleanrooms for manufacturing semiconductors and other precision components even cleaner. The Omega line guards against electrostatic discharges (ESD), and is shielded against electromagnetic and radio-frequency interference. The company also offers the Windows-based ATRAX network monitoring software. Atrix was established in 1981. Steve Riedel, the company's president, is the majority shareholder.

ATRM HOLDINGS, INC.

5215 GERSHWIN AVE N
OAKDALE, MN 551281326
Phone: 651 704-1800
Fax: –
Web: www.atrmholdings.com

CEO: David Noble
CFO: Stephen Clark
HR: –
FYE: December 31
Type: Private

ATRM Holdings makes modular building units and engineered wood products for residential and commercial construction projects. Subsidiary KBS Builders makes modular housing units for projects including apartments, office buildings, and hospitals. Subsidiary EdgeBuilder makes structural wall panels, wood foundation systems, and other engineered materials. Formerly named Aetrium, the company sold its semiconductor testing equipment manufacturing operations in 2014 and changed its name and business model. ATRM Holdings agreed to be acquired by Digirad in 2019.

ATTORNEY GENERAL, TEXAS

300 W 15TH ST
AUSTIN, TX 787011649
Phone: 512 475-4375
Fax: –
Web: www.texasattorneygeneral.gov

CEO: –
CFO: Greg Herbert
HR: –
FYE: August 31
Type: Private

The Office of the Attorney General of Texas defends the state Constitution, represents the state in litigation, and approves public bond issues. The office is legal counsel to state government boards and agencies and issues legal opinions when requested by the Governor and agency heads. The Attorney General also sits as an ex-officio member of state committees and commissions and defends state laws and suits against agencies and state employees. Other roles include enforcing health, safety, and consumer regulations; protecting elderly and disabled residents' rights; collecting court-ordered child support; and administering the Crime Victims' Compensation Fund. Greg Abbott was elected Attorney General in 2002.

ATTRONICA COMPUTERS, INC.

15867 GAITHER DR
GAITHERSBURG, MD 208771403
Phone: 301 417-0070
Fax: –
Web: www.attronica.net

CEO: Atul Thakkar
CFO: –
HR: –
FYE: December 31
Type: Private

Attronica hopes to offer an alternative to chunking your old, outdated computers out the window. The company provides a variety of information technology (IT) services, including network and systems integration, product consulting, and hardware procurement to middle-market businesses in the mid-Atlantic states. Attronica also offers such services as network security support, inventory management, and training. The company's customers come from a wide range of industries including financial services, health care, manufacturing, retail, consumer goods, and transportation. It operates from four offices in Maryland and Virginia. Attronica was co-founded by CEO Atul Tucker in 1983.

	Annual Growth	12/17	12/18	12/20	12/21	12/22
Sales ($mil.)	4.7%	–	69.6	103.7	80.0	83.5
Net income ($ mil.)	44.9%	–	0.6	2.7	3.8	2.5
Market value ($ mil.)	–	–	–	–	–	–
Employees	–	–	–	–	–	70

ATWELL, LLC

2 TOWNE SQ STE 700
SOUTHFIELD, MI 480763737
Phone: 248 447-2000
Fax: –
Web: www.atwell-group.com

CEO: –
CFO: –
HR: –
FYE: December 31
Type: Private

Atwell provides real estate and development consulting encompassing civil engineering, land planning, surveying, and environmental services. Spanning the commercial, residential, corporate real estate, and institutional development markets, the company helps clients manage real estate development projects and navigate local regulations and planning requirements. The company's consulting services include feasibility studies and economic viability analysis. Atwell's more technical services consist of surveying, civil engineering, landscape architecture as well as expertise covering environmental impact, water and wastewater systems, and water resource management.

	Annual Growth	12/11	12/12	12/13	12/15	12/17
Sales ($mil.)	8.3%	–	–	64.7	86.3	88.9
Net income ($ mil.)	(10.7%)	–	–	2.2	2.0	1.4
Market value ($ mil.)	–	–	–	–	–	–
Employees	–	–	–	–	–	436

ATWOOD OCEANICS, INC.

5847 SAN FELIPE ST # 3300
HOUSTON, TX 770573195
Phone: 281 749-7800
Fax: –
Web: www.atwd.com

CEO: George S Dotson
CFO: Mark W Smith
HR: –
FYE: September 30
Type: Private

Atwood Oceanics was an offshore oil and gas drilling contractor, headquartered in Houston, Texas. In October 2017, Ensco acquired Atwood. Ensco has a modern fleet of ultra-deepwater rig fleets and premium jackup, with presence in all the strategic offshore basins across the world. Before being bought out, Atwood operated a dozen rigs and drilled offshores in the Gulf of Mexico, Southeast Asia, West Africa, Australia, and in the Mediterranean. Customers included Noble Energy, Royal Dutch Shell, Woodside Petroleum, Chevron Corporation, and Kosmos Energy.

AU MEDICAL CENTER, INC.

1120 15TH ST FY100
AUGUSTA, GA 309120004
Phone: 706 721-6569
Fax: –
Web: www.augustahealth.org

CEO: –
CFO: Dennis R Roemer
HR: –
FYE: June 30
Type: Private

This health system isn't directed by the famous Hollywood director McG, but it will direct you to good health. MCGHealth System is an integrated organization serving east-central Georgia and areas of South Carolina. Its facilities include the nearly 500-bed MCGHealth Medical Center, an ambulatory care center with more than 80 outpatient practice sites, a specialized care center with a Level I trauma unit, and the MCGHealth Children's Medical Center. The health system also includes a variety of dedicated centers and units, such as the MCGHealth Sports Medicine Center. MCGHealth System is directly affiliated with Georgia Health Sciences University and is a part of its academic training programs.

	Annual Growth	06/03	06/04	06/06	06/08	06/21
Sales ($mil.)	(4.4%)	–	336.9	30.7	1.4	157.0
Net income ($ mil.)	–	–	–	–	1.4	(28.7)
Market value ($ mil.)	–	–	–	–	–	–
Employees	–	–	–	–	–	3,095

AUBURN NATIONAL BANCORP, INC.

NMS: AUBN

100 N. Gay Street
Auburn, AL 36830
Phone: 334 821-9200
Fax: –
Web: www.auburnbank.com

CEO: Robert W Dumas
CFO: David A Hedges
HR: –
FYE: December 31
Type: Public

War Eagle! Auburn National Bancorporation is the holding company for AuburnBank, which operates about 10 branches and a handful of loan offices in and around its headquarters in the eastern Alabama home of Auburn University. With offices in area grocery stores and Wal-Mart locations, AuburnBank offers traditional retail banking services such as checking and savings accounts and CDs. It uses funds from deposits to fund residential mortgages and other loans for individuals and businesses. Auburn Bank was founded in 1907.

	Annual Growth	12/19	12/20	12/21	12/22	12/23
Assets ($mil.)	4.2%	827.9	956.6	1,105.2	1,023.9	975.3
Net income ($ mil.)	(38.5%)	9.7	7.5	8.0	10.3	1.4
Market value ($ mil.)	(20.4%)	185.2	145.6	112.8	80.4	74.3
Employees	(1.6%)	159	152	152	150	149

AUBURN UNIVERSITY

107 SAMFORD HALL
AUBURN, AL 368490001
Phone: 334 844-4650
Fax: –
Web: www.auburn.edu

CEO: –
CFO: Kelli Shomaker
HR: –
FYE: September 30
Type: Private

Most of us bleed red, but students and alumni of this university bleed auburn. One of the largest schools in the South, Auburn University has an enrollment of more than 30,000 students on two campuses and offers bachelors, master's, and doctoral degrees in more than 140 different fields of study through about a dozen colleges and schools. Fields of study include agriculture, business, education, construction, forestry, and mathematics and science, as well as medical fields including nursing, pharmacy, and veterinary medicine. Auburn has 1,200 faculty members and a student-to-teacher ratio of 18:1.

	Annual Growth	09/19	09/20*	12/20*	09/21	09/22
Sales ($mil.)	6.9%	–	888.1	5.0	975.2	1,015.3
Net income ($ mil.)	–	–	109.1	0.3	226.0	(49.5)
Market value ($ mil.)	–	–	–	–	–	–
Employees	–	–	–	–	–	6,000

*Fiscal year change

AUDACY INC

NBB: AUDA Q

2400 Market Street, 4th Floor
Philadelphia, PA 19103
Phone: 610 660-5610
Fax: –
Web: www.audacyinc.com

CEO: David J Field
CFO: –
HR: Lynnette Hollins
FYE: December 31
Type: Public

Audacy is a leading, multi-platform audio content and entertainment company. As a leading creator of live, original, local, premium audio content in the US and the nation's leader in local sports radio and news, the company is home to the nation's most influential collection of podcasts, digital and broadcast content, and premium live events. Through its multi-channel platform, Audacy engage its consumers each month with highly immersive content and experiences. Available in every US market, the company delivers compelling live and on-demand content and experiences from voices and influencers its communities trust. Its nationwide footprint of radio stations includes positions in all of the top 15 markets and 21 of the top 25 markets.

	Annual Growth	12/19	12/20	12/21	12/22	12/23
Sales ($mil.)	(5.9%)	1,489.9	1,060.9	1,219.4	1,253.7	1,168.9
Net income ($ mil.)	–	(420.2)	(242.2)	(3.6)	(140.7)	(1,136.9)
Market value ($ mil.)	(53.6%)	23.2	12.4	12.9	1.1	1.1
Employees	(8.8%)	7,055	6,037	4,882	4,969	4,870

AUDIO-TECHNICA U.S., INC.

1221 COMMERCE DR
STOW, OH 442241760
Phone: 330 686-2600
Fax: –
Web: www.audio-technica.com

CEO: K Matsushita
CFO: –
HR: Carla Fitzpatrick
FYE: December 31
Type: Private

Audio-Technica US designs, distributes, and manufactures problem-solving audio equipment. The company's products include high-performance microphones, headphones, wireless microphone systems, turntables, phonograph cartridges, and electronic products for home and professional use. Audio-Technica US is a subsidiary of Japan's Audio-Technica Corporation. The company has authorized resellers such as 3 Pillars Music, Absolute USA, Alamo Music, American Music Supply, Big Dudes Music City, Broadcasters General Store, Campbell Resources, Clearwing Productions, among others. Matsushita founded Audio-Technica in 1962.

AUDUBON METALS LLC

3055 OHIO DR
HENDERSON, KY 424204394
Phone: 270 830-6622
Fax: –
Web: www.audubonmetals.com

CEO: –
CFO: –
HR: –
FYE: December 31
Type: Private

Audubon Metals provides innovative separation and refinement solutions to its customers. It delivers high-quality metal units in whatever specification and form the marketplace requires. The company is the only heavy media separator and secondary specification aluminum alloy producer under one roof in the US. Started in 1996 as a single furnace operation, the company has grown to a multi-site, seven-furnace operation that processes and recycles over half a billion pounds of non-ferrous scrap metals per year. In its system, automobile shredder residue (Zorba) is processed, dried, melted, alloyed to customer specification, and delivered to diecasters within the domestic and international markets. The company is owned by Koch Enterprises.

AUGUSTA UNIVERSITY

1120 15TH ST
AUGUSTA, GA 309120004
Phone: 706 721-0011
Fax: –
Web: www.augustahealth.org

CEO: –
CFO: –
HR: –
FYE: June 30
Type: Private

Georgia Regents University (GRU) is home to the Medical College of Georgia, one of the oldest continuously operating medical schools in the nation. GRU operates nine colleges in fields including medicine, dentistry, nursing, education, mathematics, business, humanities, sciences, and graduate studies. It awards 110 undergraduate and graduate degrees as well as one-year and advanced certificates. The university has 10,000 students and about 1,000 full-time faculty members. GRU was formed through the merger of Augusta State University (ASU) and Georgia Health Sciences University (GHSU) in 2013.

	Annual Growth	06/16	06/17	06/18	06/19	06/21
Sales ($mil.)	(88.5%)	–	–	–	682.7	9.0
Net income ($ mil.)	(94.4%)	–	–	–	146.3	0.5
Market value ($ mil.)	–	–	–	–	–	–
Employees	–	–	–	–	–	5,000

AUGUSTANA COLLEGE

639 38TH ST
ROCK ISLAND, IL 612012296
Phone: 309 794-3377
Fax: –
Web: www.augustana.edu

CEO: –
CFO: David English
HR: Ashley Osborn
FYE: June 30
Type: Private

Augustana College is a private liberal arts college located near the Mississippi River in northwestern Illinois. The school offers undergraduate degrees in some 50 areas of study plus pre-professional programs in fields including dentistry, law, medicine, and veterinary medicine. It enrolls approximately 2,500 students. The Swenson Center, a national archive dedicated to the study of Swedish immigration to the US, is housed on the Augustana campus. Augustana College is associated with the Evangelical Lutheran Church.

	Annual Growth	06/15	06/16	06/17	06/18	06/19
Sales ($mil.)	1.4%	–	75.1	76.4	78.5	78.3
Net income ($ mil.)	–	–	(2.5)	29.9	16.0	9.1
Market value ($ mil.)	–	–	–	–	–	–
Employees	–	–	–	–	–	650

AUGUSTANA UNIVERSITY ASSOCIATION

2001 S SUMMIT AVE
SIOUX FALLS, SD 571970001
Phone: 605 274-4116
Fax: –
Web: www.augie.edu

CEO: –
CFO: –
HR: Amanda Olson
FYE: July 31
Type: Private

Augustana College is a liberal arts college affiliated with the Evangelical Lutheran Church. It enrolls about 1,800 students in more than 50 academic fields. The college focuses on its five shared core values: Christian, Liberal Arts, Excellence, Community, and Service. Augustana College was founded in 1860 in Chicago and moved to four other sites in the Midwest before settling in its current home of Sioux Falls, South Dakota in 1918.

	Annual Growth	07/11	07/12	07/13	07/14	07/15
Sales ($mil.)	(8.9%)	–	–	58.2	55.1	48.3
Net income ($ mil.)	(67.1%)	–	–	13.4	9.2	1.5
Market value ($ mil.)	–	–	–	–	–	–
Employees	–	–	–	–	–	510

AULT ALLIANCE INC

11411 Southern Highlands Pkwy #240
Las Vegas, NV 89141
Phone: 949 444-5464
Fax: –
Web: www.ault.com

ASE: AULT
CEO: Amos Kohn
CFO: Amos Kohn
HR: –
FYE: December 31
Type: Public

Digital Power is a real switch hitter. The company makes power supplies, such as AC/DC switchers and DC/DC converters, for OEMs in the industrial, medical, military, and telecommunications markets. Its products protect electronic components and circuits from power surges while converting a single input voltage into different output voltages. Most of Digital Power's products, which can be easily modified to meet the specific needs of its 400 customers, are made by subcontractors in China and Mexico. UK-based subsidiary Digital Power Limited, doing business as Gresham Power Electronics, makes AC/DC power supplies, uninterruptible power supplies, and power inverters; it accounts for more than half of sales.

	Annual Growth	12/18	12/19	12/20	12/21	12/22
Sales ($mil.)	49.1%	27.2	26.5	23.9	52.4	134.3
Net income ($ mil.)	–	(32.2)	(32.9)	(32.7)	(24.2)	(181.8)
Market value ($ mil.)	4.6%	0.1	1.5	5.5	1.5	0.2
Employees	25.5%	248	210	154	323	615

AULTMAN HEALTH FOUNDATION

2600 6TH ST SW
CANTON, OH 447101702
Phone: 330 452-9911
Fax: –
Web: www.aultman.org

CEO: Christopher Remark
CFO: –
HR: Jean Lescallett
FYE: December 31
Type: Private

The Aultman Health Foundation provides health care and health insurance in Ohio's Stark County. The health organization operates Aultman Hospital, which has more than 800 beds and 575 physicians and was founded in 1892. As Stark County's largest hospital, it offers specialty services in such areas as cancer therapy, neurosurgery, orthopedics, and cardiovascular care. The health care system also includes clinics, 25-bed urgent care facility Aultman Orrville Hospital, and Aultman Woodlawn, a skilled nursing and rehabilitation facility with 90 beds that also provides home health and hospice services. Established in 1985, the foundation's AultCare affiliate provides managed care health plans to more than 530,000 participants.

	Annual Growth	12/12	12/13	12/19	12/21	12/22
Sales ($mil.)	3.8%	–	55.6	55.1	64.5	77.5
Net income ($ mil.)	–	–	12.7	(0.7)	(4.5)	(0.1)
Market value ($ mil.)	–	–	–	–	–	–
Employees	–	–	–	–	–	7,200

AURA MINERALS INC (BRITISH VIRGIN ISLANDS) — TSX: ORA

255 Giralda Ave, Suite 6W102
Coral Gables, FL 33134
Phone: 305 239-9499
Fax: –
Web: www.auraminerals.com

CEO: –
CFO: –
HR: –
FYE: December 31
Type: Public

Aura Minerals digs deep to make a profit. The mid-tier producer of gold and copper owns operating projects in Honduras, Mexico, and Brazil. The company's diversified portfolio of precious metal assets include the San Andres producing gold mine in Honduras, the Sao Francisco producing gold mine in Brazil, and the copper-gold-silver Aranzazu mine in Mexico (where operations were temporarily suspended in late 2015 due to disruptions caused by unauthorized persons entering the company mine). Aura Minerals' core development asset is the copper-gold-iron Serrote project in Brazil. In early 2018, the company acquired fellow gold miner Rio Novo.

	Annual Growth	12/18	12/19	12/20	12/21	12/22
Sales ($mil.)	25.6%	157.7	226.2	299.9	444.6	392.7
Net income ($ mil.)	6.4%	52.0	24.9	68.5	43.5	66.5
Market value ($ mil.)	–	–	–	–	–	–
Employees	7.4%	863	863	1,102	1,225	1,149

AURA SYSTEMS INC — NBB: AUSI

20431 North Sea Circle
Lake Forest, CA 92630
Phone: 310 643-5300
Fax: –
Web: www.aurasystems.com

CEO: Cipora Lavut
CFO: Gary Campbell
HR: –
FYE: February 28
Type: Public

Aura Systems is charging ahead with its AuraGen electric generator, which can produce 8,500 watts of power from an idling car engine. Companies in the telecommunications, utilities, and oil and gas industries use the AuraGen to generate mobile power; the military version of the AuraGen is marketed as the VIPER. RV maker Country Coach announced plans in 2004 to install the AuraGen on its Prevost model. Aura Systems also is entitled to royalties from Daewoo Electronics for use of electro-optical technology found in projection TVs. The company gets about 80% of its sales in the US.

	Annual Growth	02/19	02/20	02/21	02/22	02/23
Sales ($mil.)	16.0%	0.0	0.8	0.1	0.1	0.0
Net income ($ mil.)	–	(4.5)	(2.6)	0.8	(4.0)	(3.4)
Market value ($ mil.)	(16.3%)	48.3	18.9	33.1	38.8	23.7
Employees	12.5%	5	7	9	10	8

AURARIA HIGHER EDUCATION CENTER

1068 9TH STREET PARK
DENVER, CO 80204
Phone: 303 556-3291
Fax: –
Web: www.ahec.edu

CEO: Dean W Wolf
CFO: –
HR: –
FYE: June 30
Type: Private

The Auraria Higher Education Center supports high learning in the Mile High City. On its campus, the company offers non-academic services such as facilities management, child care, and human resources support for the Community College of Denver, Metropolitan State College of Denver, and the University of Colorado at Denver and Health Sciences Center's Downtown Denver Campus. It runs the student union, events center, childcare facilities, and all parking facilities. The combined enrollment for all three institutions on the Auraria campus totals about 40,000 students.

	Annual Growth	06/18	06/19	06/20	06/21	06/22
Sales ($mil.)	(3.3%)	–	62.9	73.2	45.3	56.8
Net income ($ mil.)	52.7%	–	3.3	24.3	15.4	11.9
Market value ($ mil.)	–	–	–	–	–	–
Employees	–	–	–	–	–	380

AURORA FLIGHT SCIENCES CORP

9950 WAKEMAN DR
MANASSAS, VA 201102702
Phone: 703 369-3633
Fax: –
Web: www.aurora.aero

CEO: Mike Caimona
CFO: –
HR: Jeanine Boyle
FYE: September 30
Type: Private

Aurora Flight Sciences, a Boeing Company, specializes in creating advanced aircraft through the development of versatile and intuitive autonomous systems, in addition to advanced composite manufacturing. Operating at the intersection of technology and robotic aviation, Aurora leverages the power of autonomy to make manned and unmanned flight safer and more efficient. Customers have included sectors such as government, commercial, AeroSystems. As a subsidiary of Boeing, Aurora's innovation and Boeing's size and strength were combined to create an unprecedented opportunity to advance the future of flight. The company's Applied Research and Development division specializes in the technologies of autonomy, electric propulsion, and human machine integration. Aurora Flight Sciences traces its roots in 1989 as a small garage shop in Alexandria to utilize UAS for atmospheric research.

	Annual Growth	09/06	09/07	09/08	09/09	09/10
Sales ($mil.)	–	–	–	(1,111.2)	65.1	62.7
Net income ($ mil.)	1064.5%	–	–	0.0	(1.6)	0.1
Market value ($ mil.)	–	–	–	–	–	–
Employees	–	–	–	–	–	794

AURORA ORGANIC DAIRY CORP.

1919 14TH ST STE 300
BOULDER, CO 803025321
Phone: 720 564-6296
Fax: –
Web: www.auroraorganic.com

CEO: Scott McGinty
CFO: –
HR: Martha Treto
FYE: December 31
Type: Private

Aurora Organic Dairy suspects you've never heard of its herd. That's why the cow-to-carton company is aiming to change that situation by becoming a leader in the US organic dairy market. Aurora Organic specializes in private-label and store-brand milk and butter, cream, and non-fat dry milk for large grocery retailers and natural food stores. It also supplies industrial customers with bulk milk, cream, butter, and non-fat dry milk. The company has agreements with Colorado and Texas farmers who operate 50,000 acres of organic farmland and supply Aurora with organic feed and pasture for its cows. With its clean-living herds, Aurora works to make organic dairy products widespread and affordable.

	Annual Growth	12/05	12/06	12/07	12/08	12/09
Sales ($mil.)	16.2%	–	77.5	111.3	125.9	121.6
Net income ($ mil.)	183.5%	–	0.8	(12.4)	(1.8)	18.1
Market value ($ mil.)	–	–	–	–	–	–
Employees	–	–	–	–	–	700

AURORA WHOLESALERS, LLC

31000 AURORA RD
SOLON, OH 441392769
Phone: 440 248-5200
Fax: –
Web: www.themazelcompany.com

CEO: –
CFO: –
HR: –
FYE: December 31
Type: Private

Aurora Wholesalers (dba The Mazel Company) buys a broad range of name-brand closeout consumer products from some 700 global suppliers and sells the items at below-wholesale prices. It also offers such proprietary goods as candles, party goods, tableware, batteries, and light bulbs. The company operates from offices and a warehouse distribution facility in Solon, Ohio. It has buyers in Solon and in New York City, and sales and marketing representation in Boston, Chicago, New York, Philadelphia, and in Solon and Columbus, Ohio. CEO Reuven Dessler and EVP Jacob "Jake" Koval founded The Mazel Company as a wholesaler of closeout merchandise in 1975.

	Annual Growth	12/07	12/08	12/09	12/12	12/13
Sales ($mil.)	(56.8%)	–	–	1,827.7	61.2	63.7
Net income ($ mil.)	646.9%	–	–	0.0	0.0	1.1
Market value ($ mil.)	–	–	–	–	–	–
Employees	–	–	–	–	–	87

AUSTIN COLLEGE

900 N GRAND AVE
SHERMAN, TX 750904400
Phone: 903 813-2000
Fax: –
Web: www.austincollege.edu

CEO: –
CFO: –
HR: –
FYE: June 30
Type: Private

Located in the North Texas city of Sherman rather than in Austin, Austin College is a small private liberal arts college. The educational institution sits on an 85-acre campus and draws an enrollment of about 1,350 full-time undergraduate students, including graduate students working on a Master of Arts in Teaching. It's nationally known for its focus on international education, pre-professional training, and leadership studies. Tuition and fees at Austin College run about $26,500 and housing costs are typically $8,600 per year. Affiliated with the Presbyterian Church, Austin College was founded in 1849 by missionary Daniel Baker. It plans to open its new IDEA Center in fall 2013.

	Annual Growth	06/17	06/18	06/20	06/21	06/22
Sales ($mil.)	19.4%	–	41.1	79.4	90.7	83.5
Net income ($ mil.)	–	–	20.0	(0.8)	13.0	(1.9)
Market value ($ mil.)	–	–	–	–	–	–
Employees	–	–	–	–	–	325

AUSTIN COMMUNITY COLLEGE

5930 MIDDLE FISKVILLE RD
AUSTIN, TX 787524390
Phone: 512 223-7000
Fax: –
Web: www.austincc.edu

CEO: Richard M Rhodes
CFO: –
HR: –
FYE: August 31
Type: Private

It may not be the most well known school in Austin, Texas, but Austin Community College (ACC) does have its fans. ACC provides technical certificate programs (50 fields), associate's degrees (30 university transfer majors), and continuing education courses to central Texas students through about a dozen campuses. The school, which has an enrollment of more than 70,000 students, also offers honors programs, college prep classes for high school students, and Tech-Prep courses that allow high school students to earn credits toward an ACC technical certificate. The school serves as a primary feeder for students transferring to the University of Texas, one of the nation's largest universities. ACC was founded in 1973.

	Annual Growth	08/18	08/19	08/20	08/21	08/22
Sales ($mil.)	4.9%	–	96.4	94.6	91.4	111.1
Net income ($ mil.)	44.6%	–	17.6	6.0	17.9	53.3
Market value ($ mil.)	–	–	–	–	–	–
Employees	–	–	–	–	–	4,200

AUSTIN TASK, INC.

7305B BURLESON RD
AUSTIN, TX 787443207
Phone: 512 389-3333
Fax: –
Web: www.austintask.com

CEO: –
CFO: –
HR: –
FYE: December 31
Type: Private

As long as companies keep building their databases, Austin Task will be there to provide secure data destruction. The non-profit organization was originally founded to provide janitorial services (dedicated to employing people with disabilities) to businesses in the Austin, Texas area. In 2005 it added secure data destruction services, including document shredding for businesses and the general public. The addition of these services soon overshadowed the company's janitorial services and eventually became the organization's primary business. The company now specializes in secure data destruction offering consulting, witness destruction, off-site destruction and secure pick-up services.

	Annual Growth	12/08	12/09	12/10	12/11	12/15
Sales ($mil.)	(1.0%)	–	3.8	4.7	4.1	3.5
Net income ($ mil.)	–	–	(0.3)	0.1	0.1	0.0
Market value ($ mil.)	–	–	–	–	–	–
Employees	–	–	–	–	–	145

AUTO BRAKES, INC.

6179 E BROADWAY BLVD
TUCSON, AZ 857114028
Phone: 520 512-0000
Fax: –
Web: www.brakemasters.com

CEO: –
CFO: –
HR: Terry Christopherson
FYE: December 31
Type: Private

Brake Masters handles master cylinders and slave cylinders too. The company offers a wide range of automotive services on just about every make and model vehicle. Its services include tire rotation, transmission fluid and belt replacement, and battery and air conditioning service. Brake Masters boasts ASE-certified technicians at its more than 80 franchises in Arizona, California, Nevada, New Mexico, and Texas. Brake Master employees are not paid based on parts and services they sell, leading the company to claim it offers only what's needed. Brothers Eric and Shalom Laytin, natives of Israel, co-own Brake Masters, which first opened in Tucson, Arizona, in 1983.

	Annual Growth	12/01	12/02	12/03	12/04	12/07
Sales ($mil.)	8.1%	–	26.9	29.2	32.7	39.8
Net income ($ mil.)	12.4%	–	1.6	1.7	4.0	2.8
Market value ($ mil.)	–	–	–	–	–	–
Employees	–	–	–	–	–	90

AUTODESK INC

One Market Street, Ste. 400
San Francisco, CA 94105
Phone: 415 507-5000
Fax: –
Web: www.autodesk.com

NMS: ADSK
CEO: Andrew Anagnost
CFO: Deborah L Clifford
HR: –
FYE: January 31
Type: Public

Autodesk is a global leader in 3D design, engineering, and entertainment software and services, offering customers productive business solutions through powerful technology products and services. The AutoCAD, AutoCAD Civil3D, and Revit software programs are used by architects, engineers, and structural designers to design, draft, and make models of products, buildings, and other objects. The company also provides product and manufacturing software for manufacturers in automotive, transportation, industrial machinery, consumer products, and building product industries with comprehensive digital design, engineering, manufacturing, and production solutions. The company's digital media and entertainment products provide tools for digital sculpting, modeling, animation, effects, rendering, and compositing for design visualization, visual effects, and game production. Customers in the US account for nearly 40% of sales.

	Annual Growth	01/19	01/20	01/21	01/22	01/23
Sales ($mil.)	18.1%	2,569.8	3,274.3	3,790.4	4,386.4	5,005.0
Net income ($ mil.)	–	(80.8)	214.5	1,208.2	497.0	823.0
Market value ($ mil.)	10.0%	31,648	42,323	59,647	53,705	46,259
Employees	9.3%	9,600	10,100	11,500	12,600	13,700

AUTOLIV ASP, INC.

3350 AIRPORT RD
OGDEN, UT 844051563
Phone: 801 629-9800
Fax: –
Web: –

CEO: –
CFO: William Campbell
HR: –
FYE: December 31
Type: Private

Autoliv ASP, the North American subsidiary of Sweden-based Autoliv Inc., designs and manufactures automobile safety restraint systems, such as airbags and airbag inflators (the highest-cost item in making an airbag module), seat belts, night vision systems, radar sensors, gas generators, and other airbag modules. It is credited with the invention of the side-impact airbag, the Inflatable Curtain (for head protection), the Anti-Whiplash Seat, and night vision systems. It also provides testing of automotive safety products for vehicle manufacturers, as well as engineering design of products at its technical center and test laboratory.

AUTOMATIC DATA PROCESSING INC.   NMS: ADP

One ADP Boulevard
Roseland, NJ 07068
Phone: 973 974-5000
Fax: 973 974-5390
Web: www.adp.com

CEO: Maria Black
CFO: Don McGuire
HR: –
FYE: June 30
Type: Public

Automatic Data Processing (ADP) is one of the largest payroll and tax filing processors in the world, serving over 920,000 clients and pay more than 39 million workers in approximately 140 countries and territories. Employer services (payroll services, benefits administration, talent management, HR management, workforce management, compliance services, insurance services and retirement services) account for majority of the company's sales, and its PEO (Professional Employer Organization) services are provided through ADP TotalSource. Other offerings include HR management, benefits administration, payroll, background checking services. The US accounts for about 90% of the company's revenue.

	Annual Growth	06/19	06/20	06/21	06/22	06/23
Sales ($mil.)	6.2%	14,175	14,590	15,005	16,498	18,012
Net income ($ mil.)	10.4%	2,292.8	2,466.5	2,598.5	2,948.9	3,412.0
Market value ($ mil.)	7.4%	68,132	61,358	81,851	86,557	90,575
Employees	2.1%	58,000	58,000	56,000	60,000	63,000

AUTOMATIC STEEL , INC.

4990 GRAND AVE
PITTSBURGH, PA 152251324
Phone: 412 865-4444
Fax: –
Web: www.frontiersteel.com

CEO: –
CFO: –
HR: –
FYE: December 31
Type: Private

Frontier Steel processes and distributes plate and flat-rolled steel products. The company maintains its own burning equipment; other steel processing services, such as bending, powder-coating, punching, and rolling, are provided by subcontractors. Customers of Frontier Steel include manufacturers of rail cars, power generating equipment, and other industrial equipment. President John Matig founded Frontier Steel at the turn of this century.

	Annual Growth	12/05	12/06	12/07	12/08	12/09
Sales ($mil.)	(76.9%)	–	–	569.4	57.4	30.4
Net income ($ mil.)	22188.5%	–	–	0.0	3.1	1.3
Market value ($ mil.)	–	–	–	–	–	–
Employees	–	–	–	–	–	60

AUTOMATION ALLEY

2675 BELLINGHAM DR
TROY, MI 480832044
Phone: 248 457-3200
Fax: –
Web: www.automationalley.com

CEO: –
CFO: –
HR: –
FYE: December 31
Type: Private

Automation Alley wants to speed up business development in the Motor City. The membership organization helps technology-related companies in Detroit and surrounding counties in southeast Michigan expand their businesses and find new opportunities. It does this by organizing business development seminars and workforce development events, offering small business mentoring to entrepreneurs, providing exporting assistance, and hosting an online job board to recruit new talent. Founded in 1999, Automation Alley counts more than 1,000 educational institutions, government entities, and not-for-profit organizations as members.

	Annual Growth	12/16	12/17*	08/18*	12/18	12/19
Sales ($mil.)	441.1%	–	0.0	5.0	0.0	0.0
Net income ($ mil.)	–	–	(0.0)	0.3	0.0	0.0
Market value ($ mil.)	–	–	–	–	–	–
Employees	–	–	–	–	–	32

*Fiscal year change

AUTOMOTIVE FINANCE CORPORATION

11299 ILLINOIS ST
CARMEL, IN 460328887
Phone: 317 815-9645
Fax: –
Web: www.autofinance.com

CEO: John Hammer
CFO: –
HR: –
FYE: December 31
Type: Private

Automotive Finance Corp. (AFC) is where auto dealers go to make a deal. The firm finances floor planning, or inventory purchases, for independent used car dealers that buy vehicles from sister company ADESA Auctions, as well as independent auctions, auctions affiliated with other networks, and non-auction purchases. Through more than 80 North American offices (about half of which are located at ADESA sites) AFC provides short-term (30- to 60-day) loans; it sells most of its finance receivables to subsidiary, AFC Funding Corp., which then sells them to a bank conduit facility. Proceeds from the revolving sale of receivables are used to fund new loans. AFC is a subsidiary of KAR Auction Services.

	Annual Growth	12/04	12/05	12/06	12/07	12/08
Assets ($mil.)	2704.9%	–	–	0.9	975.2	720.2
Net income ($ mil.)	–	–	–	0.0	41.9	(149.0)
Market value ($ mil.)	–	–	–	–	–	–
Employees	–	–	–	–	–	488

AUTONATION, INC.   NYS: AN

200 SW 1st Avenue
Fort Lauderdale, FL 33301
Phone: 954 769-6000
Fax: –
Web: www.autonation.com

CEO: Michael Manley
CFO: Thomas Szlosek
HR: –
FYE: December 31
Type: Public

AutoNation is the largest automotive retailer in the US. The company owns and operates almost 345 new vehicle franchises about 245 stores located in almost 20 US states, predominantly in major metropolitan markets in the Sunbelt region. Its stores sell roughly 35 different new vehicle brands. The core brands of new vehicles that the company sells, representing almost 90% of the new vehicles that it sold in 2022, are manufactured by Toyota (including Lexus), Honda, Ford, General Motors, Stellantis, Mercedes-Benz, BMW, and Volkswagen (including Audi and Porsche). In addition, the company also owns and operates more than 55 AutoNation-branded collision centers, nearly 15 AutoNation USA used vehicle stores, four AutoNation-branded automotive auction operations, three parts distribution centers, and an auto finance company.

	Annual Growth	12/19	12/20	12/21	12/22	12/23
Sales ($mil.)	6.0%	21,336	20,390	25,844	26,985	26,949
Net income ($ mil.)	22.7%	450.0	381.6	1,373.0	1,377.4	1,021.1
Market value ($ mil.)	32.6%	2,025.2	2,906.4	4,866.2	4,468.5	6,254.2
Employees	0.3%	25,000	21,600	22,200	23,600	25,300

AUTOSCOPE TECHNOLOGIES CORP   NBB: AATC

1115 Hennepin Avenue
Minneapolis, MN 55403
Phone: 612 438-2363
Fax: –
Web: www.autoscope.com

CEO: Chad A Stelzig
CFO: –
HR: –
FYE: December 31
Type: Public

If you're stuck in traffic, you can't blame Image Sensing Systems (ISS). ISS's Autoscope vehicle detection system converts video images into digitized traffic data for traffic management. Unlike traditional embedded wire loop detectors, which are buried in the pavement, Autoscope enables wide-area detection using video cameras, a microprocessor, software, and a PC. The systems help users to design roads, manage traffic signals, and determine the environmental impact of gridlock. Royalty income from traffic management company Econolite Control Products accounts for nearly half of sales. The company gets three-quarters of its sales in North America.

	Annual Growth	12/18	12/19	12/20	12/21	12/22
Sales ($mil.)	(3.9%)	14.6	14.7	13.2	13.2	12.4
Net income ($ mil.)	(10.3%)	1.9	7.0	1.1	2.3	1.2
Market value ($ mil.)	(5.4%)	24.4	24.6	24.3	34.1	19.5
Employees	(9.9%)	53	55	46	36	35

AUTOTRADER.COM, INC.

3003 SUMMIT BLVD FL 200
BROOKHAVEN, GA 303191469
Phone: 404 568-8000
Fax: –
Web: –

CEO: Victor A Perry IV
CFO: –
HR: Brian Jones
FYE: December 31
Type: Private

AutoTrader Group gives the Internet its very own Motor Mile. The company operates the AutoTrader.com and KBB.com websites, which work to connect online buyers with those who have cars to sell. AutoTrader.com publishes extensive listings as well as vehicle reviews, warranty information, insurance, and financing. In addition to used cars and trucks, the site offers listings for motorcycles and classic cars for collectors (at AutoTrader Classics), as well as some new cars. Its kbb.com website provides consumers with a ballpark car value when they set out to shop. Autotrader claims it attracts more than 14 million qualified buyers each month. AutoTrader is majority-owned by Cox Enterprises.

AUTOWEB, INC.

400 N ASHLEY DR STE 300
TAMPA, FL 336024313
Phone: 949 225-4500
Fax: –
Web: www.autoweb.com

CEO: –
CFO: –
HR: –
FYE: December 31
Type: Private

AutoWeb (formerly Autobytel) puts cars on the information superhighway. Using the company's websites, a potential car buyer can research make, model, and vehicle price, and more than complete an online request form for the desired new or used car. The form is forwarded to local auto dealers and manufacturers. Car buyers can also research insurance, financing, and other related services. AutoWeb generates its revenue through lead generation and website traffic it charges dealers and manufacturers (car buyers pay no fees). In mid-2022, AutoWeb was acquired by One Planet Group LLC (One Planet Group), a closely held private equity firm that owns a suite of online technology and media businesses.

AUTOZONE, INC.

NYS: AZO

123 South Front Street
Memphis, TN 38103
Phone: 901 495-6500
Fax: –
Web: www.autozone.com

CEO: Phil Daniele
CFO: Jamere Jackson
HR: –
FYE: August 26
Type: Public

AutoZone is the leading distributor of automotive replacement parts and accessories in the Americas. The company operate some 6,170 stores in the US, about 705 stores in Mexico and more than 70 stores in Brazil. Each store carries an extensive product line for cars, sport utility vehicles, vans and light trucks, including new and remanufactured automotive hard parts, maintenance items, accessories and non-automotive products. AutoZone also has commercial programs in all stores in Mexico and Brazil. The company also sells the ALLDATA brand automotive diagnostic, repair and shop management software through www.alldata.com. Additionally, AutoZone sells automotive hard parts, maintenance items, accessories and non-automotive products through www.autozone.com, and its commercial customers can make purchases through www.autozonepro.com.

	Annual Growth	08/19	08/20	08/21	08/22	08/23
Sales ($mil.)	10.1%	11,864	12,632	14,630	16,252	17,457
Net income ($ mil.)	11.8%	1,617.2	1,733.0	2,170.3	2,429.6	2,528.4
Market value ($ mil.)	22.2%	19,673	21,234	27,651	38,625	43,810
Employees	5.5%	96,000	100,000	100,000	112,000	119,000

AUVIL FRUIT COMPANY, INC.

21902 STATE HIGHWAY 97
ORONDO, WA 988459759
Phone: 509 784-1033
Fax: –
Web: www.auvilfruit.com

CEO: –
CFO: –
HR: –
FYE: March 31
Type: Private

Auvil Fruit Company's products are "auvilly" tasty. The company grows apples in the US's cool, misty Northwest, whose climate would do Johnny Appleseed proud. Auvil markets its crops under the brand names Elite, Gee Whiz, and Topaz. Granny Smith, Fuji, Gala, and Pink Lady apples are grown on one of three Auvil ranches (some 1,350 acres) and sold at grocery stores throughout the US and Canada. Auvil also sells Rainier and Bing cherries. Its retail food customers include Raley's and Stop & Shop. The company was founded in 1928 by Grady Auvil, who introduced the Granny Smith apple to state of Washington.

	Annual Growth	03/07	03/08	03/09	03/10	03/11
Sales ($mil.)	11.7%	–	–	32.6	36.0	40.6
Net income ($ mil.)	92.1%	–	–	1.9	5.4	7.2
Market value ($ mil.)	–	–	–	–	–	–
Employees	–	–	–	–	–	575

AV HOMES, INC.

6730 N SCOTTSDALE RD # 150
SCOTTSDALE, AZ 852534415
Phone: 480 214-7400
Fax: –
Web: www.avhomesinc.com

CEO: –
CFO: –
HR: –
FYE: December 31
Type: Private

AV Homes (formerly Avatar Holdings) aspires to be the embodiment of stylish retirement living. The company develops active adult and primary residential communities and builds homes in Florida, Arizona, and North Carolina. Its Joseph Carl Homes unit builds homes for people of all ages in Florida and Phoenix. AV Homes owns some 23,000 acres of developed and developable land. AV Homes also operates a title insurance agency and manages the day-to-day operations of its communities' amenities. The company gets nearly 90% of its revenue from homebuilding developments, while the remainder comes from land sales.

AVALON CORRECTIONAL SERVICES, INC.

13401 Railway Drive
Oklahoma City, OK 73114
Phone: 405 752-8802
Fax: 405 752-8852
Web: www.avaloncorrections.com

CEO: Donald Smith
CFO: Michael Bradley
HR: –
FYE: December 31
Type: Public

Avalon Correctional Services benefits from its captive market. The company manages about 10 community corrections facilities in four states: Colorado, Oklahoma, Texas, and Wyoming. Its facilities have a total capacity of some 2,600 beds. Avalon Correctional Services provides a variety of programs for offenders, who usually are within a few months of freedom. The company's services include drug abuse treatment, work release programs, family and individual counseling, and educational and vocational training. The company was founded in 1985 by CEO Donald E. Smith.

	Annual Growth	12/07	12/08	12/09	12/10	12/11
Sales ($mil.)	(3.0%)	29.9	22.6	23.1	26.0	26.5
Net income ($ mil.)	0.5%	1.2	(2.7)	6.8	6.4	1.2
Market value ($ mil.)	2.1%	0.0	0.0	0.0	0.0	0.0
Employees						

AVALON HOLDINGS CORP. ASE: AWX

One American Way
Warren, OH 44484-5555
Phone: 330 856-8800
Fax: –
Web: www.avalonholdings.com

CEO: –
CFO: –
HR: –
FYE: December 31
Type: Public

The magical promise of this Avalon is waste management services and golf courses. Through its American Waste Management Services subsidiary, Avalon Holdings helps customers manage and dispose of wastes. Services include hazardous and nonhazardous waste brokerage and management services and captive landfill management services -- management of landfills used exclusively by their owners. The company also operates two golf courses near its headquarters. The golf operations include the management of dining and banquet facilities and a travel agency. Chairman Ronald Klingle controls a 67% voting stake in Avalon Holdings.

	Annual Growth	12/19	12/20	12/21	12/22	12/23
Sales ($mil.)	4.2%	68.4	58.7	70.4	81.2	80.5
Net income ($ mil.)	–	(0.5)	0.0	2.0	(0.6)	(1.8)
Market value ($ mil.)	5.6%	7.5	10.1	14.1	10.7	9.3
Employees	9.7%	521	482	611	796	755

AVALONBAY COMMUNITIES, INC. NYS: AVB

4040 Wilson Blvd., Suite 1000
Arlington, VA 22203
Phone: 703 329-6300
Fax: 703 329-9130
Web: www.avalonbay.com

CEO: Benjamin W Schall
CFO: Kevin P O'Shea
HR: Lauren Gill
FYE: December 31
Type: Public

Real estate investment trust (REIT) AvalonBay Communities develops, redevelops, acquires, owns and operates multifamily apartment communities in New England, the New York/New Jersey metro area, the Mid-Atlantic, the Pacific Northwest, and Northern and Southern California, as well as in its expansion markets of Raleigh-Durham and Charlotte, North Carolina, Southeast Florida, Dallas and Austin, Texas, and Denver, Colorado. AvalonBay operates its apartment communities under four core brands Avalon, AVA, Eaves by Avalon, and Kanso. The REIT holds direct or indirect ownership interests in about 275 operating apartment communities containing approximately 82,410 apartment homes. It also has roughly 20 properties under construction, and owns rights to develop almost 40 additional communities.

	Annual Growth	12/19	12/20	12/21	12/22	12/23
Sales ($mil.)	4.5%	2,324.6	2,301.3	2,294.9	2,593.4	2,767.9
Net income ($ mil.)	4.3%	786.0	827.6	1,004.3	1,136.8	928.8
Market value ($ mil.)	(2.8%)	29,783	22,785	35,874	22,940	26,590
Employees	–	3,122	3,090	2,927	2,947	–

AVANGRID INC NYS: AGR

180 Marsh Hill Road
Orange, CT 06477
Phone: 207 629-1190
Fax: –
Web: www.avangrid.com

CEO: Robert Kump
CFO: Patricia Cosgel
HR: Carolee Sargent
FYE: December 31
Type: Public

Avangrid (formerly Iberdrola USA) is an energy and utility company with holdings in regulated utilities, electricity generation, and natural gas storage. It distributes electricity and natural gas to more than 3 million customers in the US northeast through Central Maine Power, New York State Electric & Gas, and Rochester Gas and Electric. Avangrid is also active in electricity generation via wind power and owns or operates natural gas storage and hub service facilities, primarily in the southern and western US. The former Iberdrola USA was combined with UIL Holdings in late 2015 and spun off by Iberdrola as Avangrid.

	Annual Growth	12/19	12/20	12/21	12/22	12/23
Sales ($mil.)	7.0%	6,338.0	6,320.0	6,974.0	7,923.0	8,309.0
Net income ($ mil.)	2.9%	700.0	581.0	707.0	881.0	786.0
Market value ($ mil.)	(10.8%)	19,787	17,579	19,292	16,623	12,535
Employees	4.9%	6,597	7,031	7,348	7,579	7,999

AVANOS MEDICAL INC NYS: AVNS

5405 Windward Parkway, Suite 100 South
Alpharetta, GA 30004
Phone: 844 428-2667
Fax: –
Web: www.avanos.com

CEO: Joseph F Woody
CFO: Michael C Greiner
HR: –
FYE: December 31
Type: Public

Avanos Medical is a medical technology with two areas of focus: pain management and chronic care. Its products include non-opioid pain therapies such as cooled radiofrequency treatments and cold and compression therapy systems, enteral feeding tubes, and closed suction catheters. Avanos conducts its business in one operating and reportable segment that provides its medical device products to healthcare providers and patients in more than 90 countries with manufacturing facilities in the US and Mexico. North America generates some 80% of Avanos' total revenue.

	Annual Growth	12/19	12/20	12/21	12/22	12/23
Sales ($mil.)	(0.9%)	697.6	714.8	744.6	820.0	673.3
Net income ($ mil.)	–	(45.9)	(27.2)	5.2	50.5	(61.8)
Market value ($ mil.)	(9.7%)	1,556.1	2,118.5	1,600.9	1,249.5	1,035.7
Employees	(5.4%)	4,700	5,380	4,555	4,044	3,771

AVANTOR INC NYS: AVTR

Radnor Corporate Center, Building One, Suite 200, 100 Matsonford Road
Radnor, PA 19087
Phone: 610 386-1700
Fax: –
Web: www.avantorsciences.com

CEO: Michael Stubblefield
CFO: R B Jones
HR: –
FYE: December 31
Type: Public

Avantor is a leading global provider of mission-critical products and services to customers in the biopharma, healthcare, education & government, and advanced technologies & applied materials industries. It serves as a one-stop shop, providing scientists with all they need to conduct their research: materials & consumables, equipment & instrumentation, and services & specialty procurement. The company's broad portfolio of approximately six million products and services, fully integrated business model and world-class supply chain enable the company to support its customers' journey every step of the way. Avantor, Inc. was incorporated in Delaware in May 2017 in anticipation of the VWR acquisition. The company serves more than 300,000 customer locations in more than 180 countries around the world. Its largest market is the US with more than 55% of its revenue.

	Annual Growth	12/19	12/20	12/21	12/22	12/23
Sales ($mil.)	3.6%	6,040.3	6,393.6	7,386.1	7,512.4	6,967.2
Net income ($ mil.)	70.7%	37.8	116.6	572.6	686.5	321.1
Market value ($ mil.)	5.9%	12,280	19,046	28,512	14,269	15,447
Employees	4.8%	12,000	12,400	13,500	14,500	14,500

AVAX TECHNOLOGIES, INC. NBB: AVXT

2000 Hamilton Street, Suite 204
Philadelphia, PA 19130
Phone: 215 241-9760
Fax: –
Web: www.avax-tech.com

CEO: –
CFO: –
HR: –
FYE: December 31
Type: Public

AVAX Technologies wants to turn cancer cells into cancer fighters. The company is developing vaccines created by extracting a patient's own cancer cells and chemically treating them to induce an immune system response. The technology used to create the vaccines (called AC Vaccine) is licensed from Thomas Jefferson University. AVAX's lead vaccine candidate MVax is intended as a treatment for late-stage melanoma. The company is also developing vaccine candidates to fight ailments such as ovarian cancer (OVax) and non-small cell lung cancer (LungVax).

	Annual Growth	12/03	12/04	12/05	12/06	12/07
Sales ($mil.)	(9.8%)	0.9	1.7	1.6	0.7	0.6
Net income ($ mil.)	–	(3.3)	(3.5)	(3.7)	(5.4)	(6.4)
Market value ($ mil.)	(13.7%)	25.5	43.9	35.4	18.4	14.2
Employees	14.3%	17	20	22	24	29

AVAYA HOLDINGS CORP

NBB: AVYA Q

2605 Meridian Parkway, Suite 200
Durham, NC 27713
Phone: 908 953-6000
Fax: –
Web: www.avaya.com

CEO: William D Watkins
CFO: Kieran J McGrath
HR: –
FYE: September 30
Type: Public

Avaya provides software and equipment for contact centers, unified communications, and workflow automation. The company's software, offered via the cloud, and hardware products provide workers with one place for communicating with colleagues and customers. Avaya's customers range from small and medium-sized businesses and organizations to Fortune 100 companies in financial services, hospital, government, and other industries. More than half of its sales are to customers in the US. A descendant company of the old AT&T, Avaya still sells phones, but has shifted to sell mostly software and services.

	Annual Growth	12/17*	09/18	09/19	09/20	09/21
Sales ($mil.)	48.9%	604.0	2,247.0	2,887.0	2,873.0	2,973.0
Net income ($ mil.)	–	2,977.0	287.0	(671.0)	(680.0)	(13.0)
Market value ($ mil.)	–	–	1,862.3	860.5	1,278.6	1,664.6
Employees	–	–	8,100	7,900	8,266	8,063

*Fiscal year change

AVAYA LLC

350 MOUNT KEMBLE AVE
MORRISTOWN, NJ 079606635
Phone: 908 953-6000
Fax: –
Web: www.avaya.com

CEO: Alan Masarek
CFO: –
HR: Mary Trimmer
FYE: September 30
Type: Private

Avaya provides software and equipment for contact centers, unified communications, and workflow automation. The company's software, offered via the cloud, and hardware products provide workers with one place for communicating with colleagues and customers. Avaya's customers range from small and medium-sized businesses and organizations to Fortune 100 companies in financial services, hospital, government, and other industries. More than half of its sales are to customers in the US. A descendant company of the old AT&T, Avaya still sells phones, but has shifted to sell mostly software and services.

AVE MARIA UNIVERSITY, INC.

5050 AVE MARIA BLVD
AVE MARIA, FL 341429505
Phone: 239 280-2500
Fax: –
Web: www.avemaria.edu

CEO: –
CFO: Eugene Munin
HR: Kathleen Phelps
FYE: June 30
Type: Private

Ave Maria University offers four-year bachelor's degrees with majors and minors in biology and chemistry, classics and early Christian literature, economics, history, literature, mathematics and physics, philosophy, politics, sacred music, and theology. The university also offers a Masters of Arts degree in Theology. In addition to its main campus has a branch campus in San Marcos, Nicaragua. Ave Maria University, which opened in 2003, was the first new Catholic institution of higher learning to open in the US in 40 years. Ave Maria is Latin for Hail Mary.

	Annual Growth	06/14	06/15	06/16	06/21	06/22
Sales ($mil.)	9.6%	–	–	43.7	61.7	75.5
Net income ($ mil.)	–	–	–	(4.2)	6.9	9.0
Market value ($ mil.)	–	–	–	–	–	–
Employees	–	–	–	–	–	195

AVENUE GROUP INC

405 Lexington Avenue, 26th Floor
New York, NY 10174
Phone: 888 612-4188
Fax: 347 952-3683
Web: www.avenuegroup.com

CEO: –
CFO: –
HR: –
FYE: December 31
Type: Public

Avenue Group, once solely located in the world of cyberspace, is now traveling along the down and dirty pathways of the oil and gas industry. Chairman and CEO Levi Mochkin formed the company in 1999 to invest in Internet, e-commerce, and related IT ventures, but the company is now focusing on the oil and gas sector though the formation of its Avenue Energy subsidiary. It explores for oil and gas in the Appalachian Basin through its Avenue Appalachia 2006-LP unit. Subsidiary Avenue Energy Israel LTD, is the license holder of the Heletz-Kokhav field. The most prolific oil field in Israel, Heletz-Kokhav has produced more than 17.2 million barrels of oil equivalent. Mochkin owns 28% of Avenue Group.

	Annual Growth	12/04	12/05	12/06	12/07	12/08
Sales ($mil.)	6.7%	0.0	0.0	0.0	0.0	0.1
Net income ($ mil.)	–	(13.7)	(6.0)	(0.5)	(1.5)	(3.6)
Market value ($ mil.)	(21.5%)	12.8	12.8	4.9	3.9	4.9
Employees	–	–	3	5	4	5

AVEO PHARMACEUTICALS, INC.

1 MARINA PARK DR FL 12
BOSTON, MA 022101832
Phone: 857 400-0101
Fax: –
Web: www.aveooncology.com

CEO: Michael P Bailey
CFO: Erick J Lucera
HR: –
FYE: December 31
Type: Private

AVEO Pharmaceuticals' models don't pout, strut, or even turn heads -- unless you're a cancer drug researcher. Operating as AVEO Oncology, the biotech firm develops cancer models to uncover how genes mutate into tumors and how tumors progress through additional mutations. AVEO then builds genetic profiles of such tumors and applies them to antibody (protein) drug candidates in preclinical and clinical development to help predict actual human responses. In addition to its own pipeline of potential drugs, AVEO has partnered with other pharmaceutical developers to apply its Human Response Platform to their drug candidates.

AVERA HEALTH

3900 W AVERA DR STE 100
SIOUX FALLS, SD 571085721
Phone: 605 322-4700
Fax: –
Web: www.avera.org

CEO: –
CFO: –
HR: Ellen Deneui
FYE: June 30
Type: Private

Avera Health provides health care services to eastern South Dakota as well as parts of Iowa, Minnesota, Nebraska, and North Dakota. The health care system operates an extensive network of facilities across approximately 315 locations including community hospitals, primary care clinics, nursing homes, hospices, urgent care clinics, and home health offices. Avera Health is sponsored by the Benedictine Sisters of Yankton, South Dakota, and the Presentation Sisters of Aberdeen, South Dakota. The Avera Health Plans and DAKOTACARE cover more than 84,500 members.

	Annual Growth	06/14	06/15	06/20	06/21	06/22
Sales ($mil.)	14.7%	–	169.4	295.6	323.6	441.7
Net income ($ mil.)	34.0%	–	19.3	28.9	(9.6)	149.4
Market value ($ mil.)	–	–	–	–	–	–
Employees	–	–	–	–	–	2,450

AVERA ST. MARY'S

801 E SIOUX AVE
PIERRE, SD 575013323
Phone: 605 224-3100
Fax: –
Web: –

CEO: Paul Ebmeier
CFO: Tom Wagner
HR: –
FYE: June 30
Type: Private

St. Mary's Healthcare Center, consisting of a 60-bed acute-care hospital, a 105-bed long-term-care hospital, and 58-unit senior-living apartments, provides health care services in central South Dakota. The health care center offers both inpatient and outpatient care, including surgery, children's health, home and hospice care, and rehabilitation services. St. Mary's got its start in the nineteenth century; in the 1920s, it became one of the first hospitals in South Dakota to become accredited.

	Annual Growth	06/14	06/15	06/16	06/21	06/22
Sales ($mil.)	5.1%	–	77.7	80.1	115.5	109.8
Net income ($ mil.)	–	–	(2.3)	(2.8)	10.3	(5.4)
Market value ($ mil.)	–	–	–	–	–	–
Employees	–	–	–	–	–	450

AVERITT EXPRESS, INC.

1415 NEAL ST
COOKEVILLE, TN 385014328
Phone: 931 526-3306
Fax: –
Web: www.averitt.com

CEO: Gary Sasser
CFO: Johnny Fields
HR: Ashley McCormick
FYE: December 31
Type: Private

Averitt Express is a leading provider of freight transportation and supply chain management with international reach to more than 100 countries. Averitt's less-than-truckload (LTL), truckload, dedicated, distribution and fulfillment, and integrated services provide shippers access to a wide array of services and customized solutions that cover every link in the supply chain. The company offers import and export services to all major ports and airports around the globe ? from the US, Canada, and Mexico, to Asia and beyond. Its PortSide solutions offer quick access to container drayage, transloading and processing, warehousing and storage, and inland transportation and distribution services. The company was founded by Thurman Averitt in 1958.

	Annual Growth	12/15	12/16	12/18	12/20	12/21
Sales ($mil.)	7.1%	–	1,088.4	1,292.7	1,204.9	1,531.0
Net income ($ mil.)	26.0%	–	45.0	77.0	77.3	143.0
Market value ($ mil.)	–	–	–	–	–	–
Employees	–	–	–	–	–	16,708

AVERY DENNISON CORP

8080 Norton Parkway
Mentor, OH 44060
Phone: 440 534-6000
Fax: –
Web: www.averydennison.com

NYS: AVY
CEO: Mitchell R Butier
CFO: Gregory S Lovins
HR: –
FYE: December 30
Type: Public

Avery Dennison is a materials science and digital identification solutions company that provides branding and information labeling solutions to industries including home and personal care, apparel, e-commerce, logistics, food and grocery, pharmaceuticals, and automotive. Avery's material group is a manufacturer of pressure-sensitive label materials and performance tapes products, including Fasson, JAC, and Mactac. While Avery's solution group offers RFID solutions, branding and embellishment solutions, data management and identification solutions, and pricing and productivity solutions. With facilities in more than 50 countries, Avery Dennison generates about 30% of its sales from the US. The company traces its roots back to 1990 when Avery International merged with Dennison Manufacturing.

	Annual Growth	12/19*	01/21	01/22*	12/22	12/23
Sales ($mil.)	4.3%	7,070.1	6,971.5	8,408.3	9,039.5	8,364.3
Net income ($ mil.)	13.5%	303.6	555.9	740.1	757.1	503.0
Market value ($ mil.)	11.3%	10,594	12,486	17,433	14,570	16,273
Employees	3.9%	30,000	32,000	36,000	36,000	35,000

*Fiscal year change

AVERY DESIGN SYSTEMS INC

1565 MAIN ST STE 207
TEWKSBURY, MA 018764766
Phone: 978 851-3627
Fax: –
Web: www.avery-design.com

CEO: –
CFO: –
HR: –
FYE: December 31
Type: Private

Avery Design Systems provides Verilog-based functional verification software for simulating chip designs. Verilog is a hardware description language used by semiconductor developers to shorten the design cycle. The company specializes in verifying designs for Parallel ATA/Serial ATA components and for PCI Express communications interfaces. Customers have included Attansic and NextIO. Avery Design was founded in 1998 by CEO Chilai Huang, who owns the company.

AVI SYSTEMS, INC.

9675 W 76TH ST STE 130
EDEN PRAIRIE, MN 553443762
Phone: 952 949-3700
Fax: –
Web: www.avisystems.com

CEO: Jeff Stoebner
CFO: Christopher Mounts
HR: –
FYE: March 31
Type: Private

AVI Systems, is an employee-owned company that delivers next-generation visual collaboration solutions built with a people-first approach. Its unique four-step planning process delivers better adoption. Its PRO Development phase lays the foundation for exceptional user adoption. Its PRO Design applies engineering best practices to develop the standards that help organizations scale its workflows and optimize its investment. Its PRO Integration ensures that the project is completed on time, on budget, and meets high expectations. Its PRO Support supplements IT departments, enabling customers' team to focus on more strategic priorities. AVI runs around 30 regional business units, with local delivery in over 50 countries. AVI was founded in 1974 by Joe Stoebner.

	Annual Growth	03/15	03/16	03/17	03/18	03/22
Sales ($mil.)	–	–	(1,318.3)	196.5	219.6	264.5
Net income ($ mil.)	690.7%	–	0.0	9.7	9.0	11.0
Market value ($ mil.)	–	–	–	–	–	–
Employees	–	–	–	–	–	650

AVIAT NETWORKS, INC.

200 Parker Drive, Suite C100A
Austin, TX 78728
Phone: 408 941-7100
Fax: –
Web: www.aviatnetworks.com

NMS: AVNW
CEO: Peter Smith
CFO: David M Gray
HR: Wendell F Sherrell
FYE: June 30
Type: Public

Aviat Networks designs, manufactures, and sells wireless networking products, solutions and services. Its products utilize microwave and millimeter wave technologies to create point to point wireless links for short, medium and long-distance interconnections. It also provides software tools and applications to enable deployment, monitoring, network management and optimization of its systems as well as to automate network design and procurement. It sources, qualifies, supplies and supports third party equipment such as antennas, routers, optical transmission equipment and other equipment necessary to build and deploy a complete telecommunications transmission network. Aviat's customers include Communications Service Providers (CSPs) and private network operators.

	Annual Growth	06/19*	07/20	07/21	07/22*	06/23
Sales ($mil.)	9.2%	243.9	238.6	274.9	303.0	346.6
Net income ($ mil.)	4.3%	9.7	0.3	110.1	21.2	11.5
Market value ($ mil.)	24.9%	157.8	214.1	367.2	289.0	384.4
Employees	(1.2%)	738	674	687	712	704

*Fiscal year change

AVID BIOSERVICES INC

NAS: CDMO

14191 Myford Road
Tustin, CA 92780
Phone: 714 508-6100
Fax: –
Web: www.avidbio.com

CEO: Nicholas S Green
CFO: Daniel R Hart
HR: Gabriel Montoya
FYE: April 30
Type: Public

Peregrine Pharmaceuticals is spreading its wings and taking flight to attack and kill its prey: cancer and viral infections. While nearly all its revenue comes from its Avid Bioservices subsidiary, which provides contract antibody and protein manufacturing to drug companies, Peregrine is focused on shepherding its own candidates through clinical trials. Up first is bavituximab, a monoclonal antibody candidate being tested to treat lung, pancreatic, and liver cancers, as well as for other oncology and infectious disease applications. Next is Cotara, being tested to treat glioblastoma multiforme, a deadly brain cancer. The company also has development programs for potential diagnostic imaging agents.

	Annual Growth	04/19	04/20	04/21	04/22	04/23
Sales ($mil.)	29.2%	53.6	59.7	95.9	119.6	149.3
Net income ($ mil.)	–	(4.2)	(10.5)	11.2	127.7	0.6
Market value ($ mil.)	–	–	–	–	–	–
Employees	–	215	227	257	327	–

AVIENT CORP

NYS: AVNT

Avient Center, 33587 Walker Road
Avon Lake, OH 44012
Phone: 440 930-1000
Fax: –
Web: www.avient.com

CEO: Robert M Patterson
CFO: Jamie A Beggs
HR: Idalia Montejano
FYE: December 31
Type: Public

Avient Corporation (formerly PolyOne Corporation), a top North American plastics compounder and resins distributor, has a single focus ? providing specialized polymer products and services. Its products include specialty engineered materials, advanced composites, color and additive systems and polymer distribution. The company is also a highly specialized developer and manufacturer of performance enhancing additives, liquid colorants, and fluoropolymer and silicone colorants. The company is one of the biggest makers of plastic materials and color and additive systems in both the US and Europe, with a growing presence in Asia and South America. The US and Canada account for approximately 40% of revenue.

	Annual Growth	12/19	12/20	12/21	12/22	12/23
Sales ($mil.)	2.4%	2,862.7	3,242.1	4,818.8	3,396.9	3,142.8
Net income ($ mil.)	(40.1%)	588.6	131.6	230.8	703.1	75.7
Market value ($ mil.)	3.1%	3,355.2	3,673.5	5,102.6	3,078.9	3,791.2
Employees	13.5%	5,600	8,400	8,700	9,700	9,300

AVINTIV SPECIALTY MATERIALS INC.

9335 HARRIS CORNERS PKWY STE 300
CHARLOTTE, NC 28269
Phone: 704 697-5100
Fax: –
Web: www.berryglobal.com

CEO: J J Hackney Jr
CFO: Dennis Norman
HR: Jorge Martinezbazua
FYE: December 28
Type: Private

Avintiv's business is interwoven with nonwovens. Formerly known as the Polymer Group, the company is a leading developer and maker of nonwoven textiles and other engineered materials used by consumer and industrial product manufacturers. Its absorbent and disposable fabrics go into baby wipes, diapers, and other hygiene and medical products. On the industrial side, they are incorporated into filtration, insulation, and automotive acoustics products. The company operates more than 20 manufacturing and converting facilities worldwide. Avintiv was acquired by Berry Plastics in the summer of 2015 for almost $2.5 billion.

AVIS BUDGET GROUP INC

NMS: CAR

6 Sylvan Way
Parsippany, NJ 07054
Phone: 973 496-4700
Fax: –
Web: www.avisbudgetgroup.com

CEO: Joseph A Ferraro
CFO: Brian J Choi
HR: –
FYE: December 31
Type: Public

Avis Budget Group (ABG) is a leading global provider of mobility solutions through its three most recognized brands, Avis, Budget, and Zipcar. Its brands offer a range of options, from car and truck rental to car sharing. The company and its licensees operate their brands in approximately 180 countries in North America, Europe, and Australia. Its rental fleet totaled approximately 655,000 vehicles and it completed more than 36 million vehicle rental transactions worldwide. ABG's brands and mobility solutions have an extended global reach with nearly 10,250 rental locations, including approximately 3,900 locations operated by their licensees. Its Budget Truck rental business is one of the leading local and one-way truck and cargo van rental businesses in the US. The company generates most of its sales in the US.

	Annual Growth	12/19	12/20	12/21	12/22	12/23
Sales ($mil.)	7.0%	9,172.0	5,402.0	9,313.0	11,994	12,008
Net income ($ mil.)	52.5%	302.0	(684.0)	1,285.0	2,764.0	1,632.0
Market value ($ mil.)	53.1%	1,144.5	1,324.2	7,361.6	5,819.5	6,292.7
Employees	(4.9%)	30,000	20,000	21,000	24,500	24,500

AVISTA CORP

NYS: AVA

1411 East Mission Avenue
Spokane, WA 99202-2600
Phone: 509 489-0500
Fax: 509 482-4361
Web: www.avistacorp.com

CEO: Dennis P Vermillion
CFO: Kevin Christie
HR: Dan Kolbet
FYE: December 31
Type: Public

Incorporated in the territory of Washington in 1889, Avista enjoys quite a wide vista when it comes to its service area. This electric and natural gas utility primarily serves the Pacific Northwest through Avista Utilities, and some customers in Juneau, Alaska through electric utility AEL&P (Alaska Electric Light and Power). Through its subsidiaries, Avista also engages in sheet metal fabrication, venture fund investments, real estate and capital investments. The company has a net capability of about 2,000 MW, of which over 50% come from hydroelectric and over 40% is thermal. It serves more than 775,000 electric and natural gas customers.

	Annual Growth	12/19	12/20	12/21	12/22	12/23
Sales ($mil.)	6.8%	1,345.6	1,321.9	1,438.9	1,710.2	1,751.6
Net income ($ mil.)	(3.4%)	197.0	129.5	147.3	155.2	171.2
Market value ($ mil.)	(7.2%)	3,754.6	3,133.9	3,317.4	3,461.8	2,790.4
Employees	(0.8%)	1,920	–	1,809	1,767	1,858

AVISTAR COMMUNICATIONS CORP

NBB: AVSR

1875 South Grant Street, 10th Floor
San Mateo, CA 94402
Phone: 650 525-3300
Fax: –
Web: www.avistar.com

CEO: Robert F Kirk
CFO: Elias A Murraymetzger
HR: –
FYE: December 31
Type: Public

If geography prevents you from concluding business with a firm handshake, Avistar Communications is ready to furnish the next-best thing. The company provides communication software and hardware used to equip communications networks with video capabilities. Its systems enable videoconferencing, content creation, video broadcasting, and data sharing between users over telephony networks and the Internet. Avistar markets its products primarily to corporations in the financial services industry, including UBS Investment Bank, Deutsche Bank, and JPMorgan Chase.

	Annual Growth	12/07	12/08	12/09	12/10	12/11
Sales ($mil.)	(9.7%)	12.0	8.8	8.8	19.7	7.9
Net income ($ mil.)	–	(2.9)	(6.4)	(4.0)	4.4	(6.4)
Market value ($ mil.)	9.6%	14.7	35.9	18.2	19.1	21.2
Employees	(15.3%)	74	50	49	51	38

AVNET INC

NMS: AVT

2211 South 47th Street
Phoenix, AZ 85034
Phone: 480 643-2000
Fax: –
Web: www.avnet.com

CEO: Philip R Gallagher
CFO: Kenneth A Jacobson
HR: –
FYE: July 1
Type: Public

Avnet is one of the world's top distributors of electronic components (including IP&E components and semiconductors), Inductors, and storage products, and software, with competitors such as Arrow Electronics and World Peace Group, among others. It works with suppliers in major technology segments, serving more than 2.1 million customers and more than 1,400 suppliers in more than 140 countries. Customers include startups, small and mid-sized businesses, and big companies that produce electronics. Avnet has operations globally and makes most of its sales to international customers with Asia/Pacific generating about 40% of revenue. Semiconductors and related products comprise about 80% of Avnet's revenue. The company was founded in 1921 by Charles Avnet.

	Annual Growth	06/19	06/20*	07/21	07/22	07/23
Sales ($mil.)	8.0%	19,519	17,634	19,535	24,311	26,537
Net income ($ mil.)	44.6%	176.3	(31.1)	193.1	692.4	770.8
Market value ($ mil.)	2.7%	4,142.4	2,382.8	3,662.9	3,867.9	4,616.4
Employees	0.5%	15,500	14,600	14,500	15,300	15,800

*Fiscal year change

AVON PRODUCTS, INC.

1 AVON PL
SUFFERN, NY 109015691
Phone: 845 369-2000
Fax: –
Web: www.avon.com

CEO: Sherilyn S McCoy
CFO: James S Scully
HR: Ann Chung
FYE: December 31
Type: Private

"Avon calling" -- calling for a younger crowd, overseas reps, and improved global operational efficiencies. Avon Products, the world's top direct seller of cosmetics and beauty-related items, is busy building a global brand and enticing more consumers to buy its products. Direct selling remains its modus operandi ; sales also come from catalogs and a website. Its lineup includes cosmetics, fragrances, toiletries, apparel, home furnishings, and more. Avon boasts more than 6 million independent representatives worldwide, and has sales and distribution operations in approximately 70 countries. In 2015, Avon sold its North American operations to private equity firm Cerberus Capital Management.

AWARE INC. (MA)

NMS: AWRE

76 Blanchard Road
Burlington, MA 01803
Phone: 781 276-4000
Fax: –
Web: www.aware.com

CEO: Robert A Eckel
CFO: David B Barcelo
HR: Lindsey Savarino
FYE: December 31
Type: Public

Aware is mindful of both the physical and intellectual aspects of its business. The company provides biometrics and imaging software to capture and verify fingerprint, facial, and iris images for identification purposes. The software is primarily used in law enforcement, border control, access control, and national defense applications. Aware also offers imaging software used to process and display medical images and data. While DSL service assurance systems were once its largest product line, Aware discontinued its DSL hardware business, opting to focus on DSL software, used by broadband service providers to manage DSL networks. The company also has a small intellectual property (IP) licensing business.

	Annual Growth	12/19	12/20	12/21	12/22	12/23
Sales ($mil.)	10.6%	12.2	11.3	16.9	16.0	18.2
Net income ($ mil.)	–	(8.3)	(7.6)	(5.8)	(1.7)	(7.3)
Market value ($ mil.)	(16.2%)	70.6	73.6	66.2	35.9	34.9
Employees	0.7%	71	90	81	82	73

AXCELIS TECHNOLOGIES INC

NMS: ACLS

108 Cherry Hill Drive
Beverly, MA 01915
Phone: 978 787-4000
Fax: 978 787-3000
Web: www.axcelis.com

CEO: Russell J Low
CFO: Kevin J Brewer
HR: –
FYE: December 31
Type: Public

Axcelis Technologies designs, manufactures and services ion implantation and other processing equipment used in the fabrication of semiconductor chips. The company believes that its Purion family of products offers the most innovative implanters available on the market today. Axcelis Technologies markets its products and services to leading semiconductor chip manufacturers worldwide. The company provides extensive aftermarket lifecycle products and services, including used tools, spare parts, equipment upgrades, maintenance services, and customer training. While the company sells its products around the world, the US accounts for almost 70% of sales. Axcelis' business commenced in 1978.

	Annual Growth	12/19	12/20	12/21	12/22	12/23
Sales ($mil.)	34.7%	343.0	474.6	662.4	920.0	1,130.6
Net income ($ mil.)	95.0%	17.0	50.0	98.7	183.1	246.3
Market value ($ mil.)	52.3%	787.5	951.8	2,437.0	2,593.9	4,238.9
Employees	14.0%	1,009	1,004	1,195	1,485	1,704

AXEL JOHNSON INC.

155 SPRING ST FL 6
NEW YORK, NY 100125254
Phone: 646 291-2445
Fax: –
Web: www.axeljohnson.com

CEO: Antonia A Johnson
CFO:
HR: –
FYE: December 31
Type: Private

The Johnson family of Stockholm, Sweden, has an investment arm that stretches across the ocean. Axel Johnson owns and operates North American businesses on behalf of the Johnson dynasty. The investment firm focuses on several industries, such as energy, medical device manufacturing, and water treatment. Its portfolio includes Sprague Energy, Parkson Corp., and Kinetico Incorporated. Axel Johnson's companies boast about $4 billion in annual revenues. Axel Johnson, along with Axel Johnson AB, and AXFast are all affiliated with Sweden-based Axel Johnson Group but are independent. Established in 1873, the Johnson family of companies is in its fourth generation of family ownership.

	Annual Growth	12/06	12/07	12/08	12/09	12/10
Assets ($mil.)	(4.5%)	–	–	1,207.2	1,066.3	1,101.1
Net income ($ mil.)	35.5%	–	–	8.2	11.9	15.0
Market value ($ mil.)	–	–	–	–	–	–
Employees	–	–	–	–	–	1,200

AXESSTEL INC

6815 Flanders Drive, Suite 210
San Diego, CA 92121
Phone: 858 625-2100
Fax: –
Web: www.axesstel.com

CEO: Patrick Gray
CFO: Patrick Gray
HR: –
FYE: December 31
Type: Public

Axesstel can soup up that old phone on your desk. The company designs and manufactures fixed wireless voice and broadband data systems that link stationary office phones to the communications network via cellular connections. Axesstel's products include fixed wireless telephones, transmission terminals, and wireless modems. The company mostly sells its products to telecommunications companies in developing countries that then resell the products to consumers. Axesstel has shifted its engineering and design operations to China in an effort to reduce operating expenses.

	Annual Growth	12/08	12/09	12/10	12/11	12/12
Sales ($mil.)	(14.1%)	109.6	50.8	45.4	54.1	59.7
Net income ($ mil.)	32.1%	1.4	(10.1)	(6.3)	1.1	4.3
Market value ($ mil.)	50.6%	8.5	3.1	2.4	7.5	43.5
Employees	(11.8%)	71	22	34	39	43

AXIS CONSTRUCTION CORP.

125 LASER CT
HAUPPAUGE, NY 117883911
Phone: 631 243-5970
Fax: –
Web: www.theaxisgroup.com

CEO: –
CFO: –
HR: –
FYE: December 31
Type: Private

Axis Construction revolves around building health care facilities, from operating suites and emergency rooms to outpatient treatment centers and medical imaging facilities. About 80% of the company's business comes from the health care industry, but Axis also constructs commercial and retail buildings, modular structures, and educational and intuitional facilities. The company provides general contracting, construction management, design/build, consulting, and renovation services to clients throughout New York. Its list of clients include Brookhaven National Lab, Northrop Grumman, and Este Lauder. Axis Construction was founded in 1993 by company leaders Robert Wihlborg and Roy and Ralph Lambert.

	Annual Growth	12/03	12/04	12/05	12/07	12/08
Sales ($mil.)	13.4%	–	31.9	43.2	47.5	52.8
Net income ($ mil.)	5.7%	–	0.3	0.9	0.5	0.4
Market value ($ mil.)	–	–	–	–	–	–
Employees	–	–	–	–	–	45

AXOGEN INC

13631 Progress Blvd., Suite 400
Alachua, FL 32615
Phone: 386 462-6800
Fax: –
Web: www.axogeninc.com

NAS: AXGN
CEO: –
CFO: –
HR: –
FYE: December 31
Type: Public

AxoGen, formerly known as LecTec, is an intellectual property licensing and holding company. It licenses topical patches that deliver over-the-counter drugs through the skin. Its patents, used by pharmaceutical companies, include adhesive patches, wound dressings, and inhalation therapies. AxoGen licenses its technology to Novartis for that company's Triaminic Vapor Patch, a cough suppressant for adults and children, and is pursuing additional licensing agreements with Novartis. After acquiring AxoGen Corporation in 2011, LecTec changed its name to AxoGen, Inc., and became the parent of AxoGen Corporation, which develops and sells peripheral nerve reconstruction and regeneration products.

	Annual Growth	12/19	12/20	12/21	12/22	12/23
Sales ($mil.)	10.5%	106.7	112.3	127.4	138.6	159.0
Net income ($ mil.)	–	(29.1)	(23.8)	(27.0)	(28.9)	(21.7)
Market value ($ mil.)	(21.4%)	771.5	771.9	404.1	430.4	294.5
Employees	–	394	368	451	396	–

AXON ENTERPRISE INC

17800 North 85th Street
Scottsdale, AZ 85255
Phone: 480 991-0797
Fax: –
Web: www.axon.com

NMS: AXON
CEO: Patrick W Smith
CFO: –
HR: –
FYE: December 31
Type: Public

Axon Enterprise is well known for designing and manufacturing various non-lethal TASER lines of stun guns. These conducted energy devices (CEDs) are geared at the law enforcement, corrections, military, and private security markets, as well as consumers. The company also offers AXON wearable video cameras for officers and a hosted product called Evidence.com that allows digital evidence to be viewed, shared, and managed from a Web browser. Products are sold worldwide through a direct sales force, distribution partners, and online store and third-party resellers. The US generates almost 85% of the company's total revenue.

	Annual Growth	12/19	12/20	12/21	12/22	12/23
Sales ($mil.)	31.0%	530.9	681.0	863.4	1,189.9	1,563.4
Net income ($ mil.)	274.9%	0.9	(1.7)	(60.0)	147.1	174.2
Market value ($ mil.)	37.0%	5,518.1	9,226.7	11,822	12,495	19,453
Employees	22.1%	1,916	2,548	2,992	3,734	4,260

AXOS FINANCIAL INC

9205 West Russell Road, Suite 400
Las Vegas, NV 89148
Phone: 858 649-2218
Fax: –
Web: www.axosfinancial.com

NYS: AX
CEO: Gregory Garrabrants
CFO: Derrick K Walsh
HR: –
FYE: June 30
Type: Public

Formerly BofI Holding, Axos Financial is the holding company for Axos Bank, which provides consumers and businesses a variety of deposit and loan products via the internet. It has designed its online banking platform and its workflow processes to handle traditional banking functions with elimination of duplicate and unnecessary paperwork and human intervention. Axos Bank has deposit and loan customers nationwide including consumer and business checking, savings and time deposit accounts and financing for single family and multifamily residential properties, small-to-medium size businesses in target sectors, and selected specialty finance receivables. Founded in 2000, the company holds over $17.4 billion in assets, and a total portfolio of net loans and leases of about $14 billion.

	Annual Growth	06/19	06/20	06/21	06/22	06/23
Assets ($mil.)	16.0%	11,220	13,852	14,266	17,401	20,348
Net income ($ mil.)	18.6%	155.1	183.4	215.7	240.7	307.2
Market value ($ mil.)	9.7%	1,606.2	1,301.5	2,734.4	2,113.1	2,324.7
Employees	9.6%	1,007	1,099	1,165	1,335	1,455

AXT INC

4281 Technology Drive
Fremont, CA 94538
Phone: 510 438-4700
Fax: –
Web: www.axt.com

NMS: AXTI
CEO: Morris S Young
CFO: Gary L Fischer
HR: –
FYE: December 31
Type: Public

For applications in which plain silicon would get the ax, AXT offers fancier fare. AXT makes semiconductor substrates from compounds such as gallium arsenide (GaAs) and indium phosphide (InP), and from single elements such as germanium. Manufacturers use AXT's substrates to make high-performance semiconductors for products -- including fiber-optic devices, satellite solar cells, and wireless handsets -- for which standard silicon microchips are not adequate. Most of its customers -- and its employees -- are in China. International customers include Soitec of France and IQE Group of the UK.

	Annual Growth	12/19	12/20	12/21	12/22	12/23
Sales ($mil.)	(2.3%)	83.3	95.4	137.4	141.1	75.8
Net income ($ mil.)	–	(2.6)	3.2	14.6	15.8	(17.9)
Market value ($ mil.)	(13.8%)	192.4	423.4	389.7	193.8	106.2
Employees	18.8%	731	784	1,008	1,559	1,456

AYRO INC

900 E. Old Settlers Boulevard, Suite 100
Round Rock, TX 78664
Phone: 512 994-4917
Fax: –
Web: www.wpcs.com

NAS: AYRO
CEO: Rodney C Keller Jr
CFO: David E Hollingsworth
HR: –
FYE: December 31
Type: Public

WPCS International provides the engineering behind communications networks. Through subsidiaries, the company designs and installs broadband wireless, video security systems, and specialty communications systems. Services include product integration, fiber-optic cabling, project management, and technical support. The company also provides engineering services to support wireless networks. Its specialty communication systems division offers support for telematics and telemetry systems, as well as networks designed for asset tracking. WPCS serves the enterprise, government, and education sectors. Clients have included Amtrak, the Jacksonville Jaguars, and Wake Forest University Baptist Medical Center.

	Annual Growth	12/18	12/19	12/20	12/21	12/22
Sales ($mil.)	(16.2%)	6.1	–	1.6	2.7	3.0
Net income ($ mil.)	–	(18.7)	(4.9)	(10.8)	(33.1)	(22.9)
Market value ($ mil.)	16.3%	1.0	4.1	28.3	7.5	1.8
Employees	(17.1%)	93	6	26	32	44

AZEK CO INC (THE)   NYS: AZEK

1330 W Fulton Street, Suite 350
Chicago, IL 60607
Phone: 877 275-2935
Fax: –
Web: www.azekco.com

CEO: Jesse Singh
CFO: Ralph Nicoletti
HR: Taysha Allen
FYE: September 30
Type: Public

When it comes to CPG's building products, appearance is key. Through its AZEK, Scranton, and Vycom operating segments, CPG is a leading manufacturer of synthetic building products and other materials used in residential remodeling and construction, as well as by commercial and industrial clients, in the US and Canada. Its core AZEK unit manufactures PVC-based residential products such as trim, deck, rail, moulding, and porch materials made to look like wood and other natural materials. CPG's Scranton unit makes polyurethane bathroom partitions and lockers for commercial and institutional end-users, while Vycom makes PVC plastic sheeting for industrial uses. CPG's TimberTech unit makes decking and railings.

	Annual Growth	09/19	09/20	09/21	09/22	09/23
Sales ($mil.)	14.6%	794.2	899.3	1,179.0	1,355.6	1,370.3
Net income ($ mil.)	–	(20.2)	(122.2)	93.2	75.2	68.0
Market value ($ mil.)	–	–	5,141.4	5,395.5	2,454.8	4,392.6
Employees	9.8%	1,540	1,663	2,072	2,182	2,236

AZENTA INC   NMS: AZTA

200 Summit Drive 6th Floor
Burlington, MA 01803
Phone: 978 262-2626
Fax: –
Web: www.brooks.com

CEO: Stephen S Schwartz
CFO: Herman Cueto
HR: –
FYE: September 30
Type: Public

Azenta, formerly Brooks Automation, is a leading provider of life sciences solutions worldwide. The company provides precision robotics, integrated automation systems, and contamination control solutions to semiconductor fabrications plants and original equipment manufacturers worldwide. In the life sciences market, it offers a full suite of services and solutions for analyzing, managing, and storing biological and chemical compound samples to advance research and development for clinical, pharmaceutical, and other scientific endeavors. Azenta has sales operations in more than 80 countries and generates around 65% from its domestic customers.

	Annual Growth	09/19	09/20	09/21	09/22	09/23
Sales ($mil.)	(3.9%)	780.8	897.3	513.7	555.5	665.1
Net income ($ mil.)	–	437.4	64.9	110.7	2,132.9	(14.3)
Market value ($ mil.)	7.9%	2,141.5	2,675.3	5,919.1	2,478.7	2,902.6
Employees	4.1%	2,984	3,159	2,800	3,100	3,500

AZURE DYNAMICS CORP.   NBB: AZDD Q

14925 West Eleven Mile Road
Oak Park, MI 48237-1013
Phone: 248 298-2403
Fax: 248 298-2410
Web: www.azuredynamics.com

CEO: –
CFO: –
HR: –
FYE: December 31
Type: Public

Azure Dynamics (AZD) has a blue-sky vision for how to make heavy vehicles run in an ecologically friendly way. The development-stage company designs energy management systems for use in commercial vehicles. AZD's hybrid electric vehicle (HEV) control systems include both vehicle management software and controllers used with a variety of drive components. Customers and partners include Canada Post, the US Postal Service, Federal Express, and Purolator Courier. As part of efforts to build a US battery supply base and infrastructure support for hybrid electric vehicles, AZD signed a five-year agreement with lithium-ion suppliers Johnson Controls-SAFT (a joint venture) in early 2009.

	Annual Growth	12/06	12/07	12/08	12/09	12/10
Sales ($mil.)	45.1%	5.0	2.9	6.2	9.0	22.0
Net income ($ mil.)	–	(20.1)	(30.8)	(31.7)	(26.5)	(28.2)
Market value ($ mil.)	(18.9%)	11.3	5.8	0.6	2.9	4.9
Employees	9.8%	112	127	148	119	163

AZURE MIDSTREAM PARTNERS LP

8451 HIGHWAY 175
GRAND CANE, LA 710326125
Phone: 972 674-5200
Fax: –
Web: www.azuremidstream.com

CEO: –
CFO: –
HR: –
FYE: December 31
Type: Private

Marlin Midstream Partners knows how to capture and prepare the biggest of energy fish. An oil and gas company, Marlin gathers, transports, and processes natural gas and crude oil for energy companies. It operates two natural gas facilities in East Texas with an aggregate 65 miles of natural gas pipelines, a gathering capacity of 200 million cu. ft. of gas per day (MMcf/d), and a 300 MMcf/d processing capacity. It also operates crude oil transloading facilities in Wyoming and Colorado. Marlin's core customer base comprises Anadarko and Associated Energy Services. The company was formed in 2013 and went public that year, using its $137.5 million in proceeds to repay debt. In 2017 the company filed for Chapter 11 bankruptcy protection.

AZUSA PACIFIC UNIVERSITY

901 E ALOSTA AVE
AZUSA, CA 917022701
Phone: 626 969-3434
Fax: –
Web: www.apu.edu

CEO: Jon R Wallace
CFO: Bob Johansen
HR: –
FYE: June 30
Type: Private

An evangelical Christian institution, Azusa Pacific University (APU) has an enrollment of more than 7,120 undergraduate, graduate, and doctoral students. It offers about 70 bachelor's degrees, about 45 master's degrees, about 25 certificates, eight credentials, and nine doctoral programs. In addition to its main campus, APU also maintains seven off-site regional locations throughout Southern California, including in the High Desert, Inland Empire, Monrovia, Murrieta, Orange County, and San Diego, as well as many online programs. With more than 945 teaching faculty, the university has a 13:1 student-to-faculty ratio. Founded in 1899 as the Training School for Christian Workers, APU continues to be recognized annually as one of America's Best Colleges by US News and World Report.

	Annual Growth	06/17	06/18	06/19	06/20	06/22
Sales ($mil.)	0.7%	–	265.9	239.2	298.1	273.1
Net income ($ mil.)	–	–	(5.7)	5.5	(6.5)	(0.9)
Market value ($ mil.)	–	–	–	–	–	–
Employees	–	–	–	–	–	1,545

AZZ INC   NYS: AZZ

One Museum Place, Suite 500, 3100 West 7th Street
Fort Worth, TX 76107
Phone: 817 810-0095
Fax: –
Web: www.azz.com

CEO: Thomas E Ferguson
CFO: Philip A Schlom
HR: Amy Caster
FYE: February 28
Type: Public

AZZ is a global provider of galvanizing and a variety of metal coating solutions, welding solutions, specialty electrical equipment and highly engineered services to a broad range of markets, including, but not limited to, the power generation, transmission, distribution, refining, and industrial markets. The company has two business segments: Metal Coatings and Infrastructure Solutions. AZZ's Metal Coatings segment provides metal finishing solutions for corrosion protection, including galvanizing, powder coating, anodizing, and plating to North American steel fabrication and other industries. Its Infrastructure Solutions segment delivers safe and reliable transmission of power from generation sources to end customers, and automated weld overlay solutions for corrosion and erosion mitigation to critical infrastructure in energy and waste management markets worldwide. More than 95% of the company's revenue comes from its domestic market. The company was established in 1956 and incorporated under the laws of the state of Texas.

	Annual Growth	02/19	02/20	02/21	02/22	02/23
Sales ($mil.)	9.3%	927.1	1,061.8	838.9	902.7	1,323.6
Net income ($ mil.)	–	51.2	48.2	39.6	84.0	(53.0)
Market value ($ mil.)	(3.1%)	1,146.5	919.0	1,272.8	1,226.4	1,012.7
Employees	(0.3%)	3,884	4,343	3,883	3,885	3,837

B & G FOOD ENTERPRISES, LLC

1430 SANDRA ST
MORGAN CITY, LA 703802136
Phone: 985 384-3333
Fax: –
Web: www.bgfood.com

CEO: –
CFO: –
HR: –
FYE: December 22
Type: Private

B&G Food Enterprises brings diversity to the otherwise seafood-heavy fare of the coastal US. Not to be confused with food seasoning and condiment company B&G Foods, B&G Food is a franchise that operates more than 90 KFC fast-food restaurants, primarily Taco Bell, but also a handful of KFC, and Long John Silver's outlets. The company operates primarily in Louisiana, Mississippi, and Texas. B&G Food was founded by Brenda and Gregory Hamer in 1982 after the couple acquired their first Taco Bell restaurant in Morgan City, Louisiana. Privately owned by the Hamer family, the company is Louisiana's largest Taco Bell franchisee.

	Annual Growth	12/03	12/04	12/05	12/06	12/09
Sales ($mil.)	7.6%	–	25.9	27.7	29.7	37.2
Net income ($ mil.)	28.7%	–	1.2	2.3	0.8	4.2
Market value ($ mil.)	–	–	–	–	–	–
Employees		–	–	–	–	2,300

B&G FOODS INC

NYS: BGS

Four Gatehall Drive
Parsippany, NJ 07054
Phone: 973 401-6500
Fax: –
Web: www.bgfoods.com

CEO: Kenneth C Keller
CFO: Bruce C Wacha
HR: Michelle Magoon
FYE: December 30
Type: Public

B&G Foods makes, markets, and distributes a wide variety of shelf-stable foods, frozen foods, and household goods throughout the US. Many of B&G's products are regional or national best-sellers, including B&M and B&G (beans, condiments), Clabber Girl (baking), Green Giant (frozen and canned foods), Spice Islands (seasonings), McCann's (oatmeal), Ortega (Mexican foods), Grandma's and Brer Rabbit (molasses), Snackwell's (snacks), and Underwood (meat spread). They are sold through B&G's subsidiaries to supermarkets, mass merchants, warehouse clubs, and drug store chains, as well as institutional and food service operators in the US, Canada, and Puerto Rico.

	Annual Growth	12/19*	01/21	01/22*	12/22	12/23
Sales ($mil.)	5.6%	1,660.4	1,967.9	2,056.3	2,163.0	2,062.3
Net income ($ mil.)	–	76.4	132.0	67.4	(11.4)	(66.2)
Market value ($ mil.)	(12.9%)	1,432.5	2,180.3	2,416.1	876.7	825.6
Employees	0.1%	2,899	3,207	2,847	3,085	2,912

*Fiscal year change

B. L. HARBERT INTERNATIONAL, L.L.C.

820 SHADES CREEK PKWY STE 3000
BIRMINGHAM, AL 352094564
Phone: 205 802-2800
Fax: –
Web: www.blharbert.com

CEO: Billy Harbert
CFO: R A Hall
HR: Arianit Pasha
FYE: December 31
Type: Private

My way or the highway? For Harbert, it's my way and the highway. B. L. Harbert International Group provides highway and heavy construction services for commercial, industrial, and public projects throughout the world, but primarily in the Southeast US. The design/build company's portfolio includes commercial and institutional buildings, research facilities, hotels and condominiums, water and wastewater treatment plants, dams and highways, and pipelines. B. L. Harbert International has offices in the US and Dubai. CEO Billy Harbert, Jr., leads the family-owned company, which traces its roots to the 1949 founding of Harbert Construction by brothers Bill and John Harbert.

B/E AEROSPACE, INC.

150 OAK PLAZA BLVD STE 200
WINSTON SALEM, NC 271051482
Phone: 336 747-5000
Fax: –
Web: www.collinsaerospace.com

CEO: –
CFO: –
HR: Sean Cromie
FYE: December 31
Type: Private

A leading maker of cabin components for commercial, business jets and military aircraft, B/E Aerospace makes aircraft seats, coffeemakers, lighting, refrigeration equipment, galley structures, and emergency oxygen systems. B/E aftermarket operations represent about 40% of its revenue. Operating through two business segments (commercial aircraft, and business jet), B/E sells its products to most major airlines and aviation OEMs. The company also provides oil field equipment and services. In late 2016, B/E Aerospace agreed to be acquired by rival Rockwell Collins in a transaction valued at $6.4 billion plus the assumption of $1.9 billion in debt.

BAB INC

NBB: BABB

500 Lake Cook Road, Suite 475
Deerfield, IL 60015
Phone: 847 948-7520
Fax: –
Web: –

CEO: –
CFO: –
HR: –
FYE: November 30
Type: Public

Bagels, muffins, and coffee are fueling this company. BAB operates a chain of about 110 franchised coffee and baked goods outlets under the brand names Big Apple Bagels and My Favorite Muffin. The stores offer several varieties of bagels and spreads, muffins, sandwiches, soups, salads, and gourmet coffee. The company also markets a proprietary java brand, Brewster's Coffee. BAB has coffee shops in more than 25 states, as well as in the United Arab Emirates. An investment group controlled by CEO Michael Evans and VP Michael Murtaugh owns nearly 40% of the company.

	Annual Growth	11/19	11/20	11/21	11/22	11/23
Sales ($mil.)	3.4%	3.1	2.4	3.1	3.3	3.5
Net income ($ mil.)	1.0%	0.4	(0.1)	0.7	0.4	0.5
Market value ($ mil.)	(3.5%)	6.0	4.0	5.8	5.3	5.2
Employees	(4.1%)	13	12	13	12	11

BABCOCK & JENKINS, INC.

1233 NW 12TH AVE STE 100
PORTLAND, OR 972092986
Phone: 503 382-8500
Fax: –
Web: www.bnj.com

CEO: William Babcock
CFO: –
HR: –
FYE: December 31
Type: Private

Babcock & Jenkins (B&J) provides direct and relationship marketing services. Through its products and services, B&J offers clients the ability to qualify leads online, automate lead distribution, profile potential clients, and warehouse the relevant information. The firm also provides B2B marketing information such as targeting, acquiring, and converting services. B&J has expanded its expertise in data, analytics, marketing automation, sales enablement, pipeline acceleration, brand strategy. The firm has offices in Portland, Oregon and London, UK.

	Annual Growth	12/99	12/00	12/01	12/02	12/11
Sales ($mil.)	(6.3%)	–	17.1	10.4	7.9	8.3
Net income ($ mil.)	(15.1%)	–	1.3	(0.8)	0.0	0.2
Market value ($ mil.)	–	–	–	–	–	–
Employees		–	–	–	–	42

BABCOCK LUMBER COMPANY

2220 PALMER ST
PITTSBURGH, PA 152182603
Phone: 412 310-6291
Fax: –
Web: www.babcocklumber.com

CEO: Carl W Borntraeger
CFO: –
HR: –
FYE: December 31
Type: Private

Founded in Pittsburgh in 1889, Babcock Lumber produces hardwood lumber products (dimension lumber, plywood, flooring, logs, and other millwork), custom laminate and solid surface countertops, and floor and roof trusses. Babcock Lumber operates five hardwood manufacturing plants in Alabama, Pennsylvania, and West Virginia. It also distributes building materials such as siding, insulation, doors, and windows, as well as kitchen and bath fixtures, sinks, and cabinets, through ten facilities in Florida, Illinois, New York, Ohio, Pennsylvania, and West Virginia.

BABSON COLLEGE

231 FOREST ST
BABSON PARK, MA 02457
Phone: 781 235-1200
Fax: –
Web: www.babson.edu

CEO: Joseph Winn
CFO: Philip Shapiro
HR: Henry Deneault
FYE: June 30
Type: Private

Babson students could babble on and on about business management. With an enrollment of more than 3,000 students, Babson College is lauded as one of the nation's leading business schools. The school's undergraduate programs combine liberal arts with business curriculum; it also grants master's degrees in business administration, entrepreneurship, and other fields. Babson students in their first year receive the practical experience of creating for-profit ventures. Babson's entrepreneurship program has been ranked at the top of such programs in publications including Entrepreneur and U.S. News & World Report.

	Annual Growth	06/12	06/13	06/15	06/21	06/22
Sales ($mil.)	3.0%	–	177.6	232.5	206.6	231.4
Net income ($ mil.)	(18.6%)	–	43.3	11.9	225.0	6.8
Market value ($ mil.)	–	–	–	–	–	–
Employees						750

BADGER METER INC

4545 W. Brown Deer Road
Milwaukee, WI 53223
Phone: 414 355-0400
Fax: –
Web: www.badgermeter.com

NYS: BMI
CEO: Kenneth C Bockhorst
CFO: Robert A Wrocklage
HR: Sheryl L Hopkins
FYE: December 31
Type: Public

Badger Meter is a leading innovator, manufacturer, and marketer of products incorporating flow measurement, quality, control, and other system solutions serving markets worldwide. Badger Meter offers Advanced Metering Infrastructure (AMI) and Automated Meter Reading (AMR) communication options as part of the ORION product family, including mobile and cellular solutions. It also offers a wide range of instrumentation devices that can be mounted directly to a meter. Its flow instrumentation business product line includes meters, valves, and other sensing instruments for industrial markets including HVAC, water and wastewater, and heating. Badger meter serves water utilities, municipalities, and commercial and industrial customers worldwide. The Majority of its sales come from the US.

	Annual Growth	12/19	12/20	12/21	12/22	12/23
Sales ($mil.)	13.5%	424.6	425.5	505.2	565.6	703.6
Net income ($ mil.)	18.4%	47.2	49.3	60.9	66.5	92.6
Market value ($ mil.)	24.2%	1,905.5	2,760.4	3,127.3	3,199.7	4,530.3
Employees	8.1%	1,567	1,602	1,837	1,976	2,140

BAER'S FURNITURE CO., INC.

1589 NW 12TH AVE
POMPANO BEACH, FL 330691734
Phone: 954 582-4200
Fax: –
Web: www.baers.com

CEO: Jerome Baer
CFO: –
HR: Sue Scovin
FYE: December 31
Type: Private

Having assembled a furniture portfolio full of big-name brands, Baer's Furniture counts the likes of Lexington Home Brands and Bernhardt as family. Family-owned Baer's Furniture operates about 15 mid-priced to high-end retail furniture showrooms and two warehouses in South Florida. The company offers furnishings (living room, dining room, bedroom, and office furniture), bedding, rugs, and accessories made by popular manufacturers that are designed to fit the budgets of shoppers who have a little cash tucked away. The chain was founded in 1945 by Melvin and Lucile Baer in South Bend, Indiana. Their sons Robert, now the company's CEO, and Allan, company president, moved the business to Florida in 1968.

BAIN CAPITAL, LP

200 CLARENDON ST
BOSTON, MA 021165021
Phone: 617 516-2000
Fax: –
Web: www.baincapital.com

CEO: –
CFO: –
HR: –
FYE: December 31
Type: Private

Bain Capital is one of the world's leading private multi-asset alternative investment firms with approximately $160 billion in assets under management that creates lasting impact for its investors, teams, businesses and the communities. The private equity and venture capital investor acquires and owns interests in companies in the business services, retail and consumer products, communications, healthcare, hospitality, financial services, industrials, and technology sectors in the US, Europe, and Asia. Bain's private equity portfolio holds stakes in companies like Aveanna Healthcare, Auto Distribution, Blue Nile, Camp Australia, Central Square Technologies, and Kestra Medical Technologies. Bain Capital was founded in 1984.

BAKER & HOSTETLER LLP

127 PUBLIC SQ STE 2000
CLEVELAND, OH 441141214
Phone: 216 621-0200
Fax: –
Web: www.bakerlaw.com

CEO: –
CFO: Kevin L Cash
HR: Denise Kaston
FYE: December 31
Type: Private

Baker & Hostetler is one of the nation's largest law firms that represents clients worldwide. The firm's nearly 1,000 lawyers practice from over 15 offices in the US, from New York to Los Angeles. Besides baseball and other sports and entertainment enterprises, the firm's roster of clients includes leading companies in the energy, media, manufacturing, healthcare, financial services and insurance, consumer products and hospitality. Among Baker & Hostetler's major practice groups are teams devoted to digital assets and data management, intellectual property, business, employment and labor, and tax and litigation. The firm was founded in 1916, when its three founding partners each deposited approximately $500 into a firm account.

	Annual Growth	12/18	12/19	12/20	12/21	12/22
Sales ($mil.)	(1.8%)	–	–	0.3	0.5	0.3
Net income ($ mil.)	59.7%	–	–	0.0	0.3	0.2
Market value ($ mil.)	–	–	–	–	–	–
Employees		–	–	–	–	1,771

BAKER BOOK HOUSE COMPANY

6030 FULTON ST E
ADA, MI 493019156
Phone: 616 676-9185
Fax: –
Web: www.bakerpublishinggroup.com

CEO: Dwight Baker
CFO: –
HR: Rachael Kehr
FYE: April 30
Type: Private

Baker Publishing Group has a spirit in its step. The Christian publisher publishes books through seven market-focused divisions: Baker Books, Baker Academic, Bethany House Publishers, Brazos Press, Cambridge University Press, Chosen Books, and Revell. Its Baker Books division includes titles for pastors and church leaders, featuring books on worship, preaching, counseling, and leadership. Its Cambridge division focuses on bible publishing. Other imprints publish Christian fiction and self-help titles, as well as books on subjects such as theology, discipleship, and Christian living. The company was founded in 1939 by Herman Baker.

	Annual Growth	04/12	04/13	04/14	04/15	04/16
Sales ($mil.)	4.0%	–	53.2	56.4	54.5	59.9
Net income ($ mil.)	5.3%	–	4.0	4.7	1.4	4.7
Market value ($ mil.)	–	–	–	–	–	–
Employees		–	–	–	–	215

BAKER HUGHES COMPANY

NMS: BKR

17021 Aldine Westfield
Houston, TX 77073-5101
Phone: 713 439-8600
Fax: –
Web: www.bakerhughes.com

CEO: Lorenzo Simonelli
CFO: Nancy Buese
HR: –
FYE: December 31
Type: Public

Baker Hughes Co (Baker Hughes) is an energy technology company with a diversified portfolio of technologies and services that span the energy and industrial value chain. The company's portfolio of products includes drilling equipment, subsea production systems, compressors, pipe systems, generators, and storage systems, regulators, control systems, pumps, valves and process control technologies. It also offers digital solutions such as non-destructive technologies, measurement, sensing, and pipeline solutions. It serves independent oil and natural gas companies and national or state-owned oil companies. The company has operations in the Americas, Europe, the Middle East, Africa, and Asia. Majority of its sales were generated outside US.

	Annual Growth	12/19	12/20	12/21	12/22	12/23
Sales ($mil.)	1.7%	23,838	20,705	20,502	21,156	25,506
Net income ($ mil.)	97.4%	128.0	(9,940.0)	(219.0)	(601.0)	1,943.0
Market value ($ mil.)	7.5%	25,571	20,802	24,005	29,462	34,102
Employees	(3.9%)	68,000	55,000	54,000	55,000	58,000

BAKER HUGHES HOLDINGS LLC

17021 Aldine Westfield
Houston, TX 77073-5101
Phone: 713 439-8600
Fax: 713 439-8699
Web: www.bakerhughes.com

CEO: Lorenzo Simonelli
CFO: Brian Worrell
HR: –
FYE: December 31
Type: Public

Baker Hughes is a leading provider of services and equipment for drilling, extracting, moving, processing, and refining oil and natural gas. Its offerings range from tools for drilling wells and producing hydrocarbons to deepwater drilling equipment, subsea production systems, flexible pipe systems, and mechanical-drive, compression, and power-generation applications as well as hardware and software for digitizing some operations. The company has worldwide reach, operating in more than 120 countries. About 70% of Baker Hughes' revenue is from international customers. In 2019, General Electric sold its controlling interest in the company, making Baker Hughes a majority publicly held company.

	Annual Growth	12/18	12/19	12/20	12/21	12/22
Sales ($mil.)	(1.9%)	22,877	23,838	20,705	20,502	21,156
Net income ($ mil.)		120.0	241.0	(15,825.0)	(372.0)	(526.0)
Market value ($ mil.)	–	–	–	–	–	–
Employees	(4.5%)	66,000	68,000	55,000	54,000	55,000

BALCHEM CORP.

NMS: BCPC

5 Paragon Drive
Montvale, NJ 07645
Phone: 845 326-5600
Fax: –
Web: www.balchem.com

CEO: Theodore L Harris
CFO: Martin Bengtsson
HR: Brent Tignor
FYE: December 31
Type: Public

Balchem develops, manufactures, distributes and markets specialty performance ingredients and products for the nutritional, food, pharmaceutical, animal health, medical device sterilization, plant nutrition and industrial markets. The company reports three business segments: Human Nutrition & Health; Animal Nutrition & Health; and Specialty Products. The Human Nutrition & Health segment delivers customized food and beverage ingredient systems, as well as key nutrients into a variety of applications across the food, supplement and pharmaceutical industries. The Animal Nutrition & Health segment manufactures and supplies choline chloride to the poultry, pet and swine industries. Through Specialty Products, Balchem distributes performance gases and chemicals primarily for various uses by its customers, and also provides chelated minerals to the micronutrient agricultural market to produce high value crops. Over 70% of company's total revenue comes from US.

	Annual Growth	12/19	12/20	12/21	12/22	12/23
Sales ($mil.)	9.4%	643.7	703.6	799.0	942.4	922.4
Net income ($ mil.)	8.0%	79.7	84.6	96.1	105.4	108.5
Market value ($ mil.)	10.0%	3,278.0	3,716.4	5,438.1	3,938.6	4,797.9
Employees	(2.2%)	1,424	1,342	1,317	1,340	1,302

BALDWIN TECHNOLOGY COMPANY, INC.

8027 FORSYTH BLVD
SAINT LOUIS, MO 631051734
Phone: 314 726-2152
Fax: –
Web: www.baldwintech.com

CEO: Joe Kline
CFO: Ivan R Habibe
HR: –
FYE: June 30
Type: Private

Baldwin Technology Company is a leading global manufacturer and supplier of innovative process automation, equipment, parts service and consumables for a number of industries. It manufactures printing press equipment and control systems, used for press cleaning, ink control, drying, water-regulation, spray dampening, and UV and LED curing. Baldwin conceptualizes, engineers and manufactures solutions for leading industrial companies and OEMs around the world, in segments from printing and textile production to film extrusion and the manufacturing of electronics. Baldwin is a member of Barry-Wehmiller family of companies.

BALFOUR BEATTY CONSTRUCTION GROUP, INC.

3100 MCKINNON ST 10TH FL
DALLAS, TX 752017007
Phone: 214 451-1000
Fax: –
Web: www.balfourbeattyus.com

CEO: Mark Layman
CFO: Richard Jaggers
HR: Annalisa Brown
FYE: December 31
Type: Private

Balfour Beatty Construction is deep in the heart of Texas -- and beyond. The company provides start-to-finish project management, pre-construction, and related services for commercial construction projects. Offerings include site evaluation and analysis, general contracting, cost consulting, process equipment installation, turnkey medical facility development, capital equipment planning, and closeout services. The company works on a range of facilities including hotels, office buildings, civic centers, airports, hospitals, schools, public buildings, and retail locations. UK firm Balfour Beatty plc acquired the company, then named Centex Construction, from Centex Corp. in 2007.

	Annual Growth	12/11	12/12	12/13	12/14	12/15
Sales ($mil.)	3.7%	–	3,459.0	3,816.9	3,933.0	3,852.8
Net income ($ mil.)		–	19.2	24.8	17.5	(14.7)
Market value ($ mil.)	–	–	–	–	–	–
Employees		–	–	–	–	2,495

BALFOUR BEATTY INFRASTRUCTURE, INC.

600 GALLERIA PKWY SE STE 1500
ATLANTA, GA 303395994
Phone: 707 427-8900
Fax: –
Web: www.balfourbeattyus.com

CEO: Ray Bond
CFO: Mark Birch
HR: –
FYE: December 31
Type: Private

Balfour Beatty is an industry-leading provider in the US of general contracting, at-risk construction management and design-build services for public and private sector clients across the nation. Performing heavy civil and vertical construction, it builds the unique structures and infrastructure that play an important role in how people live, work, learn and play in their communities. Consistently ranked among the nation's largest building contractors, by Engineering News-Record, its US business is a subsidiary of London-based Balfour Beatty plc. Its portfolio have included buildings, rails, highways and bridges, and water. Beyond stand-alone projects, it is involved in multiple joint ventures, and works on some of the nation's largest public works projects, including the design and construction of the $1.1 billion Texas State Highway 130 toll road.

	Annual Growth	12/11	12/12	12/13	12/14	12/15
Sales ($mil.)	0.8%	–	–	509.3	555.6	517.8
Net income ($ mil.)	–	–	–	9.5	9.9	(3.4)
Market value ($ mil.)	–	–	–	–	–	–
Employees	–	–	–	–	–	1,100

BALL CORP

NYS: BALL

9200 West 108th Circle
Westminster, CO 80021
Phone: 303 469-3131
Fax: –
Web: www.ball.com

CEO: Daniel W Fisher
CFO: Scott C Morrison
HR: Sharon Romero
FYE: December 31
Type: Public

The Ball Corporation is one of the world's leading suppliers of aluminum packaging for the beverage, personal care and household products industries. Its largest product line is aluminum beverage containers and it also produces extruded aluminum aerosol containers, aluminum slugs and aluminum cups. Its aerospace business produces spacecraft, instruments and sensors, radio frequency systems and components, data exploitation solutions and a variety of advanced technologies and products. Ball Corporation operates in North and Central America, the EMEA, and South America, with the US its largest market at more than 50% of the total sales. The company was founded in 1880.

	Annual Growth	12/19	12/20	12/21	12/22	12/23
Sales ($mil.)	5.2%	11,474	11,781	13,811	15,349	14,029
Net income ($ mil.)	5.7%	566.0	585.0	878.0	719.0	707.0
Market value ($ mil.)	(2.9%)	20,416	29,416	30,391	16,144	18,158
Employees	3.5%	18,300	21,500	24,300	21,000	21,000

BALL HORTICULTURAL COMPANY

622 TOWN RD
WEST CHICAGO, IL 601852698
Phone: 630 231-3600
Fax: –
Web: www.ballhort.com

CEO: Anna C Ball
CFO: Jacco Kuipers
HR: Jennifer Peck
FYE: December 31
Type: Private

Ball Horticultural is a leader in all facet of horticulture and sells commercial seed for flowers and perennials, roses, and shrubs. Its global family of breeding, distribution, and research teams has a global presence on six continents in more than 20 countries, including subsidiaries and joint ventures PanAmerican Seed and Ball Seed. The company sells through its own sales force. Founded in 1905 by George Ball, Ball Horticultural remains family owned and is run by Anna Caroline Ball, third-generation leader of the company.

BALL STATE UNIVERSITY

2000 W UNIVERSITY AVE
MUNCIE, IN 473060002
Phone: 765 289-1241
Fax: –
Web: www.bsu.edu

CEO: –
CFO: –
HR: Jennifer Eber
FYE: June 30
Type: Private

Ball State University (BSU) has an enrollment of about 20,320 undergraduate and graduate students. It offers approximately 120 undergraduate majors, more than 100 graduate programs in seven academic colleges. It has a Teachers College, as well as colleges of health; architecture and planning; business; communication, information, and media; fine arts; and sciences and humanities. BSU has a student-to-faculty ratio of 14:1. Notable alumni include late night talk show host David Letterman, and Jay Williams, founder of Legion Creative Group and former senior vice president of creative content for Walt Disney Co. and Disneyland Resort.

	Annual Growth	06/03	06/04	06/05	06/06	06/07
Sales ($mil.)	3.4%	–	–	209.7	219.7	224.1
Net income ($ mil.)	35.6%	–	–	23.6	24.5	43.4
Market value ($ mil.)	–	–	–	–	–	–
Employees	–	–	–	–	–	6,426

BALLET MAKERS, INC.

1 CAMPUS RD
TOTOWA, NJ 075121296
Phone: 973 595-9000
Fax: –
Web: www.centerstagedancesupplies.com

CEO: Marc Terlizzi
CFO: Ron Koesterich
HR: –
FYE: December 31
Type: Private

Ballet Makers, doing business as Capezio, has been operating for more than a century. It makes dance apparel and footwear, including ballet "pointe" shoes, figure skating tights, and ballroom dancing apparel. It also markets accessories such as bags, bunheads, socks shoe accessories, and socks. Its products are sold online through capezio.com. In addition, the brand of choice for athletes and performers across the globe also sells its products through its store locations worldwide. The company was established in 1887 and run by the family of founder Salvatore Capezio, a cobbler who made a name for himself with performers at the neighborhood's Metropolitan Opera House.

BALLISTIC RECOVERY SYSTEMS, INC.

NBB: BRSI

300 Airport Road
South St. Paul, MN 55075-3541
Phone: 651 457-7491
Fax: 651 457-8651
Web: www.airplaneparachutes.com

CEO: –
CFO: –
HR: –
FYE: September 30
Type: Public

Ballistic Recovery Systems (doing business as BRS Aerospace) lets you down easy with its rocket-deployed emergency recovery parachute system, which has been credited with saving over 200 lives. BRS is unique in its fabrication of whole-aircraft canopies designed to bring recreational, general and light sport aircraft, including the Cessna 172/182 and Cirrus SR20/SR22, safely to the ground. BRS is partnered with CIMSA Ingenieria de Sistemas (Spain) to expand its share in civil and military markets worldwide. Wholly owned subsidiary Advanced Tactical Fabrication (ATF) produces personal safety equipment, such as high-visibility apparel, components, trims, and emergency lighting systems under the Head Lites brand.

	Annual Growth	09/03	09/04	09/05	09/06	09/07
Sales ($mil.)	9.5%	6.5	6.9	8.1	9.2	9.4
Net income ($ mil.)	–	0.5	0.5	(1.1)	0.0	(1.7)
Market value ($ mil.)	8.9%	13.1	24.9	25.4	17.5	18.4
Employees	72.4%	24	22	47	50	212

BALLSTON SPA BANCORP INC
NBB: BSPA

87 Front Street
Ballston Spa, NY 12020
Phone: 518 363-8150
Fax: –
Web: www.bsnb.com

CEO: Christopher R Dowd
CFO: –
HR: –
FYE: December 31
Type: Public

Ballston Spa Bancorp is the holding company for Ballston Spa National Bank, which serves Saratoga County in New York from about 10 branches. It offers traditional deposit products including checking and savings accounts, IRAs, and CDs. The bank also offers investment products, wealth and estate planning, insurance, and trust services. Residential mortgages account for about two-thirds of the company's loan portfolio; the company also writes commercial mortgages, consumer loans, and business loans. Ballston Spa National Bank was established in 1838.

	Annual Growth	12/02	12/03	12/04	12/08	12/09
Assets ($mil.)	4.8%	263.3	284.3	303.0	356.6	365.8
Net income ($ mil.)	24.9%	0.5	1.3	0.9	2.2	2.3
Market value ($ mil.)	(5.0%)	27.1	21.0	28.2	26.7	18.9
Employees		–	–	–	–	–

BALTIMORE GAS AND ELECTRIC COMPANY

110 W FAYETTE ST
BALTIMORE, MD 212013708
Phone: 410 234-5000
Fax: –
Web: www.bge.com

CEO: Calvin G Butler Jr
CFO: Carim V Khouzami V
HR: David Vosvick
FYE: December 31
Type: Private

Baltimore Gas and Electric (BGE), a subsidiary of Exelon, provides electricity and natural gas services to the Monument City and surrounding areas. The company not only provides services in Baltimore, but to all or parts of 10 surrounding central Maryland counties as well in a service area of 2,300 square miles. The company's regulated power transmission and distribution system consists of almost 25,320 circuit miles of distribution lines, and 1,300 circuit miles of transmission lines, and serves more than 1.2 million customers; its gas system of more than 13,360 miles of gas mains serves more than 655,000 homes and businesses in an 800 square-mile service area.

BALTIMORE RAVENS LIMITED PARTNERSHIP

1 WINNING DR
OWINGS MILLS, MD 211174776
Phone: 410 547-8100
Fax: –
Web: www.baltimoreravens.com

CEO: –
CFO: –
HR: –
FYE: December 31
Type: Private

Named in honor of the Edgar Allan Poe poem, the Baltimore Ravens Limited Partnership owns and operates Baltimore's National Football League franchise, which won its first Super Bowl following the 2000 season and its second championship after the 2012 campaign. The team was created in 1996 when former Cleveland Browns owner Art Modell relocated his franchise to Maryland. As part of the deal, Modell agreed to give up all rights to the Browns' name, colors, and history. The team plays host at M&T Bank Stadium. Stephen Bisciotti, a local businessman who founded staffing firm Allegis Group, acquired control of the team from Modell in 2004.

BANC OF CALIFORNIA INC
NYS: BANC

3 MacArthur Place
Santa Ana, CA 92707
Phone: 855 361-2262
Fax: –
Web: www.bancofcal.com

CEO: Jared M Wolff
CFO: Joseph Kauder
HR: Alicia Schlensker
FYE: December 31
Type: Public

Banc of California delivers comprehensive products and solutions for businesses, business owners, and individuals through nearly 30 branches from San Diego to Santa Barbara. The company offers a variety of financial products and services designed around its clients to serve their banking and financial needs. Customers enjoy checking, savings, and money market accounts, certificates of deposit, retirement accounts, and safe deposit boxes. Additional products and services leverage other technology and include automated bill payment, cash and treasury management, master demand accounts, foreign exchange, interest rate swaps, card payment services, remote and mobile deposit capture, automated clearing house origination, wire transfer, and direct deposit. In addition to its branches, the $9.2 billion-asset Banc of California operates around loan production offices.

	Annual Growth	12/19	12/20	12/21	12/22	12/23
Assets ($mil.)	49.0%	7,828.4	7,877.3	9,393.7	9,197.0	38,534
Net income ($ mil.)	–	23.8	12.6	62.3	120.9	(1,899.1)
Market value ($ mil.)	(6.0%)	2,701.9	2,313.4	3,085.6	2,505.3	2,112.1
Employees	36.7%	660	611	673	685	2,304

BANCFIRST CORP. (OKLAHOMA CITY, OKLA)
NMS: BANF

100 N. Broadway Ave.
Oklahoma City, OK 73102-8405
Phone: 405 270-1086
Fax: 405 270-1089
Web: www.bancfirst.bank

CEO: David R Harlow
CFO: Kevin Lawrence
HR: –
FYE: December 31
Type: Public

BancFirst Corporation is the holding company for BancFirst, a super-community bank that emphasizes decentralized management and centralized support. BancFirst operates about 110 branches in roughly 60 Oklahoma communities. It serves individuals and small to midsized businesses, offering traditional deposit services including checking accounts, Negotiable Order of Withdrawal (NOW) accounts, savings accounts, money market accounts, sweep accounts, club accounts, individual retirement accounts and certificates of deposit. Commercial real estate lending (including farmland and multifamily residential loans) makes up more than 60% of the bank's loan portfolio, while commercial and agricultural non-real estate generated some 20%.

	Annual Growth	12/19	12/20	12/21	12/22	12/23
Assets ($mil.)	9.6%	8,565.8	9,212.4	9,405.6	12,388	12,372
Net income ($ mil.)	12.0%	134.9	99.6	167.6	193.1	212.5
Market value ($ mil.)	11.7%	2,056.3	1,933.2	2,323.8	2,904.0	3,205.4
Employees	2.0%	1,948	2,036	1,948	2,051	2,109

BANCROFT CONSTRUCTION COMPANY

1300 N GRANT AVE STE 101
WILMINGTON, DE 198062456
Phone: 302 655-3434
Fax: –
Web: www.bancroftconstruction.com

CEO: Greg Sawka
CFO: Casey McCabe
HR: –
FYE: December 31
Type: Private

Bancroft Homes likes people who like custom homes, and you can take that to the bank. The company custom-builds new homes and luxury townhomes, develops communities, and provides renovation and addition work on existing homes, working primarily in Delaware and Pennsylvania's Delaware Valley. Sister company Bancroft Construction is active in construction management for commercial, academic, and government projects, including offices, retail spaces, health care facilities, and university buildings. Bancroft Homes entered the homebuilding industry in 1975.

	Annual Growth	12/99	12/00	12/01	12/02	12/21
Sales ($mil.)	3.7%	–	–	60.8	101.5	125.8
Net income ($ mil.)		–	–	–	0.4	2.5
Market value ($ mil.)		–	–	–	–	–
Employees		–	–	–	–	140

BANDWIDTH INC
NMS: BAND

2230 Bandmate Way
Raleigh, NC 27607
Phone: 800 808-5150
Fax: –
Web: www.bandwidth.com

CEO: David A Morken
CFO: Daryl E Raiford
HR: –
FYE: December 31
Type: Public

Bandwidth is the universal communications platform that simplifies how businesses deliver integrated global experiences. Its solutions include a broad range of software Application Programming Interfaces (APIs) for voice, messaging and emergency services. Its sophisticated and easy-to-use software APIs allow enterprises to enhance their products and services by incorporating advanced, global connectivity for voice, messaging and emergency services communications capabilities. Its customers currently include some of the largest hyperscale tech companies, well-recognized enterprise customers, as well as small and medium-sized businesses. Bandwidth's clients have included Google, Genesys and RingCentral. Bandwidth was founded in 1999 by CEO David Morken. Majority of its sales were generated in the US.

	Annual Growth	12/19	12/20	12/21	12/22	12/23
Sales ($mil.)	26.8%	232.6	343.1	490.9	573.2	601.1
Net income ($ mil.)	–	2.5	(44.0)	(27.4)	19.6	(16.3)
Market value ($ mil.)	(31.1%)	1,675.8	4,020.6	1,877.5	600.5	378.6
Employees	50.9%	212	216	1,100	1,100	1,100

BANK OF AMERICA CORP
NYS: BAC

Bank of America Corporate Center, 100 N. Tryon Street
Charlotte, NC 28255
Phone: 704 386-5681
Fax: –
Web: www.bankofamerica.com

CEO: Brian T Moynihan
CFO: Alastair M Borthwick
HR: –
FYE: December 31
Type: Public

Bank of America Corporation is one of the world's largest financial institutions with a network of approximately 4,200 financial centers and approximately 16,000 ATMs. The bank's core services include consumer and small and middle-market businesses, institutional investors, large corporations and governments with a full range of banking, investing, asset management, and other financial and risk management products and services. Its online banking operation counts more than 41 million active users, including approximately 33 million active mobile users. Its US operations account for the vast majority of sales.

	Annual Growth	12/19	12/20	12/21	12/22	12/23
Assets ($mil.)	6.9%	2,434,079	2,819,627	3,169,495	3,051,375	3,180,151
Net income ($ mil.)	(0.8%)	27,430	17,894	31,978	27,528	26,515
Market value ($ mil.)	(1.1%)	278,078	239,311	351,269	261,498	265,840
Employees	0.6%	208,000	213,000	208,000	217,000	213,000

BANK OF HAWAII CORP
NYS: BOH

130 Merchant Street
Honolulu, HI 96813
Phone: 888 643-3888
Fax: –
Web: www.boh.com

CEO: Peter S Ho
CFO: Dean Y Shigemura
HR: –
FYE: December 31
Type: Public

Bank of Hawaii Corporation is the holding company for Bank of Hawaii (the bank), which has about 55 branches and more than 305 ATMs throughout Hawaii and the Pacific Islands, e-Bankoh (online banking service), a customer service center, and a mobile banking service. Founded in 1897, the bank operates through three business segments: Consumer Banking, Commercial Banking, and Treasury and Other. The bank provides a broad range of financial products and services, including loan, deposit and insurance products; corporate banking, commercial real estate loans, commercial lease financing, auto dealer financing, and deposit products and corporate asset and liability management activities. Some of its subsidiaries include Bank of Hawaii Leasing, Inc., Bankoh Investment Services, Inc., and Pacific Century Life Insurance Corporation.

	Annual Growth	12/19	12/20	12/21	12/22	12/23
Assets ($mil.)	7.0%	18,095	20,604	22,785	23,607	23,733
Net income ($ mil.)	(6.7%)	225.9	153.8	253.4	225.8	171.2
Market value ($ mil.)	(6.6%)	3,782.9	3,045.9	3,329.7	3,083.3	2,880.5
Employees	(2.8%)	2,124	2,022	2,056	2,076	1,899

BANK OF MARIN BANCORP
NAS: BMRC

504 Redwood Boulevard, Suite 100
Novato, CA 94947
Phone: 415 763-4520
Fax: –
Web: www.bankofmarin.com

CEO: Russell A Colombo
CFO: Tani Girton
HR: –
FYE: December 31
Type: Public

Bank of Marin supports the wealthy enclave of Marin County, north of San Francisco. The bank operates more than 20 branches in the posh California counties of Marin, Sonoma, and Napa, as well as in San Francisco and Alameda counties. Targeting area residents and small to midsized businesses, the bank offers standard retail products as checking and savings accounts, CDs, credit cards, and loans. It also provides private banking and wealth management services to high net-worth clients. Commercial mortgages account for the largest portion of the company's loan portfolio, followed by business, construction, and home equity loans.

	Annual Growth	12/19	12/20	12/21	12/22	12/23
Assets ($mil.)	8.9%	2,707.3	2,911.9	4,314.2	4,147.5	3,803.9
Net income ($ mil.)	(12.7%)	34.2	30.2	33.2	46.6	19.9
Market value ($ mil.)	(16.4%)	727.9	554.9	601.6	531.3	355.8
Employees	1.8%	306	290	328	313	329

BANK OF NEW YORK MELLON CORP
NYS: BK

240 Greenwich Street
New York, NY 10286
Phone: 212 495-1784
Fax: –
Web: www.bnymellon.com

CEO: Robin A Vince
CFO: Dermot McDonogh
HR: –
FYE: December 31
Type: Public

The Bank of New York Mellon (BNY Mellon) is a New York state-chartered bank, which houses the Securities Services businesses, including Asset Servicing, and Issuer Services, and certain Market and Wealth Services businesses, including Treasury Services, Clearance and Collateral Management, as well as the bank-advised business of Investment Management. The firm boasts some $46.7 trillion in assets under custody and administration, and some $2.4 trillion in assets under management. BNY Mellon N.A. also offers wealth management services. Alexander Hamilton, a founding father of the US and icon of the US $10 bill, helped establish in 1784. The Bank of New York, which merged in 2007 with Pittsburgh's Mellon Financial to form BNY Mellon. Majority of its sales were generated from its domestic markets.

	Annual Growth	12/19	12/20	12/21	12/22	12/23
Assets ($mil.)	1.8%	381,508	469,633	444,438	405,783	409,953
Net income ($ mil.)	(7.3%)	4,441.0	3,617.0	3,759.0	2,573.0	3,286.0
Market value ($ mil.)	0.8%	38,218	32,227	44,103	34,565	39,524
Employees	2.5%	48,400	48,500	49,100	43,700	53,400

BANK OF SOUTH CAROLINA CORP
NBB: BKSC

256 Meeting Street
Charleston, SC 29401
Phone: 843 724-1500
Fax: –
Web: www.banksc.com

CEO: Fleetwood S Hassell
CFO: Eugene H Walpole IV
HR: –
FYE: December 31
Type: Public

What, were you expecting something different? The Bank of South Carolina Corporation is the holding company for The Bank of South Carolina, which was founded in 1987. It operates four branches in and around Charleston. Targeting individuals and small to midsized business customers, the bank offers such standard retail services as checking and savings accounts, credit cards, and money market and NOW accounts. Real estate loans make up more than 70% of the The Bank of South Carolina's loan portfolio, which also includes commercial loans (around 20%) and to a lesser extent, personal loans. President and CEO Hugh Lane and his family control about 12% of the company.

	Annual Growth	12/18	12/19	12/20	12/21	12/22
Assets ($mil.)	11.1%	429.1	445.0	532.5	679.2	653.3
Net income ($ mil.)	(1.0%)	6.9	7.3	6.5	6.7	6.7
Market value ($ mil.)	(2.6%)	101.1	104.3	89.0	113.8	91.1
Employees	0.3%	79	79	76	81	80

BANK OF THE JAMES FINANCIAL GROUP INC
NAS: BOTJ

828 Main Street
Lynchburg, VA 24504
Phone: 434 846-2000
Fax: –
Web: www.bankofthejames.bank

CEO: Thomas W Pettyjohn Jr
CFO: –
HR: –
FYE: December 31
Type: Public

Bank of the James Financial Group is the holding company for Bank of the James, a financial institution serving central Virginia from about 10 branch locations. Catering to individuals and small businesses, the bank offers standard retail products and services including checking and savings accounts, CDs, and IRAs. Funds from deposits are mainly used to originate residential mortgages, which make up about half of the bank's loan portfolio, and commercial and consumer loans. Subsidiary BOTJ Investment Group offers bank customers brokerage services, annuities, and related investment products through a third-party broker-dealer.

	Annual Growth	12/18	12/19	12/20	12/21	12/22
Assets ($mil.)	8.3%	674.9	725.4	851.4	987.6	928.6
Net income ($ mil.)	14.0%	5.3	5.6	5.0	7.6	9.0
Market value ($ mil.)	(2.2%)	60.2	70.7	56.1	71.6	55.1
Employees	2.3%	158	160	146	158	173

BANK OF THE WEST (SAN FRANCISCO, CA)

180 Montgomery Street
San Francisco, CA 94104
Phone: 415 765-4800
Fax: 415 397-8354
Web: –

CEO: –
CFO: –
HR: –
FYE: December 31
Type: Public

Bank of the West is one of the largest banks headquartered in California and the 33rd largest commercial bank in the US by assets, boasting more than $94.5 billion in assets and 500-plus banking offices in almost 25 states. The bank is the third-largest agriculture production loans bank lender, and a leading bank lender in the RV/Marine and religious institution sectors. Through digital channels, the bank provides financial tools and resources to individuals, families and businesses. It also offer investment and insurance services through its subsidiary, BancWest Investment Services, a registered broker/dealer. Bank of the West is owned by French bank BNP Paribas.

	Annual Growth	12/95	12/96	12/97	12/01	12/02
Assets ($mil.)	29.0%	4,382.0	5,071.5	5,643.1	13,412	26,050
Net income ($ mil.)	38.5%	32.1	44.0	63.1	140.4	312.9
Market value ($ mil.)	–	–	–	–	–	–
Employees	–	–	–	–	–	6,000

BANK OZK
NMS: OZK

18000 Cantrell Road
Little Rock, AR 72223
Phone: 501 978-2265
Fax: 501 978-2224
Web: www.ozk.com

CEO: –
CFO: –
HR: –
FYE: December 31
Type: Public

Bank of the Ozarks is the holding company for the bank of the same name, which has about 260 branches in Alabama, Arkansas, California, the Carolinas, Florida, Georgia, New York, and Texas. Focusing on individuals and small to midsized businesses, the $12-billion bank offers traditional deposit and loan services, in addition to personal and commercial trust services, retirement and financial planning, and investment management. Commercial real estate and construction and land development loans make up the largest portion of Bank of the Ozarks' loan portfolio, followed by residential mortgage, business, and agricultural loans. Bank of the Ozarks grows its loan and deposit business by acquiring smaller banks and opening branches across the US.

	Annual Growth	12/19	12/20	12/21	12/22	12/23
Assets ($mil.)	9.8%	23,556	27,163	26,530	27,657	34,237
Net income ($ mil.)	12.9%	425.9	291.9	579.0	564.1	690.8
Market value ($ mil.)	13.1%	3,451.6	3,538.2	5,264.8	4,532.7	5,638.2
Employees	(0.3%)	2,774	2,652	2,542	2,646	2,744

BANKFINANCIAL CORP
NMS: BFIN

60 North Frontage Road
Burr Ridge, IL 60527
Phone: 800 894-6900
Fax: –
Web: www.bankfinancial.com

CEO: F M Gasior
CFO: Paul A Cloutier
HR: –
FYE: December 31
Type: Public

If you need a BankNow to handle your BankBusiness, try BankFinancial. The bank serves individuals and businesses through about 20 branches in Cook, DuPage, Lake, and Will counties in northeastern Illinois, including parts of Chicago. It offers standard products such as checking and savings accounts, credit cards, and loans; services such as account management are available online. Multifamily residential mortgage loans make up 40% of its loan portfolio, while another 40% is made up of commercial leases and non-residential mortgage loans. The bank also writes one-to-four family residential mortgages and home equity loans and lines of credit, business loans, and construction and land loans.

	Annual Growth	12/19	12/20	12/21	12/22	12/23
Assets ($mil.)	–	1,488.0	1,596.8	1,700.7	1,575.1	1,487.4
Net income ($ mil.)	(5.3%)	11.7	9.2	7.4	10.5	9.4
Market value ($ mil.)	(5.9%)	163.2	109.5	133.1	131.4	128.0
Employees	(1.7%)	242	230	243	224	226

BANKUNITED INC.
NYS: BKU

14817 Oak Lane
Miami Lakes, FL 33016
Phone: 305 569-2000
Fax: –
Web: www.bankunited.com

CEO: –
CFO: –
HR: –
FYE: December 31
Type: Public

BankUnited, with total consolidated assets of $35.9 billion, is a bank holding company with one direct wholly-owned subsidiary, BankUnited. BankUnited, a national banking association, provides a full range of commercial lending and both commercial and consumer deposit services through banking centers located in Florida, the New York metropolitan area, and Dallas, Texas. The bank also provides certain commercial lending and deposit products through national platforms and certain consumer deposit products through an online channel. Deposit offerings include checking and savings accounts, treasury management services, and certificates of deposit. Through the Bank's two commercial lending subsidiaries, Pinnacle and Bridge, it provides municipal, equipment, and franchise financing on a national basis.

	Annual Growth	12/19	12/20	12/21	12/22	12/23
Assets ($mil.)	2.1%	32,871	35,010	35,815	37,027	35,762
Net income ($ mil.)	(13.1%)	313.1	197.9	415.0	285.0	178.7
Market value ($ mil.)	(3.0%)	2,719.4	2,586.7	3,146.7	2,526.4	2,411.9
Employees	1.7%	1,511	1,495	1,495	1,636	1,616

BANNER CORP.
NMS: BANR

10 South First Avenue
Walla Walla, WA 99362
Phone: 509 527-3636
Fax: –
Web: www.bannerbank.com

CEO: –
CFO: –
HR: –
FYE: December 31
Type: Public

Banner is the holding company for Banner Bank (the bank), a Washington-chartered commercial bank that conducts business from its main office in Walla Walla, Washington. It has about 150 branches and around 20 loan production offices in Washington, Oregon, California and Idaho. The bank offer standard products such as deposit accounts, credit cards, and business and consumer loans. Commercial loans, including business, agriculture, construction, and multifamily real estate, account for about 95% of the company's portfolio. Bank subsidiary Community Financial writes residential mortgage and construction loans. Banner has total consolidated assets of $16.80 billion and total deposits of $14.33 billion.

	Annual Growth	12/19	12/20	12/21	12/22	12/23
Assets ($mil.)	5.6%	12,604	15,032	16,805	15,833	15,670
Net income ($ mil.)	5.8%	146.3	115.9	201.0	195.4	183.6
Market value ($ mil.)	(1.4%)	1,943.8	1,600.3	2,083.9	2,170.8	1,839.7
Employees	(2.8%)	2,198	2,116	1,935	1,977	1,966

BANNER HEALTH

2901 N CENTRAL AVE STE 160
PHOENIX, AZ 850122702
Phone: 602 747-4000
Fax: -
Web: www.bannerhealth.com

CEO: Peter S Fine
CFO: Dan Weinman
HR: Eric Pickney
FYE: December 31
Type: Private

Banner Health is one of the largest, secular nonprofit health care systems in the country. In addition to 30 acute-care hospitals, Banner also operates an academic medicine division, Banner ? University Medicine, and Banner MD Anderson Cancer Center, a partnership with one of the world's leading cancer programs, MD Anderson Cancer Center. Banner's array of services includes a health insurance division, employed physician groups, outpatient surgery centers, urgent care locations, home care and hospice services, retail pharmacies, stand-alone imaging centers, physical therapy and rehabilitation, behavioral health services, a research division and a nursing registry.

	Annual Growth	12/16	12/17	12/18	12/19	12/22
Sales ($mil.)	10.3%	-	-	-	9,426.6	12,656
Net income ($ mil.)		-	-	-	753.8	(447.5)
Market value ($ mil.)		-	-	-	-	-
Employees		-	-	-	-	35,000

BANNER-UNIVERSITY MEDICAL CENTER TUCSON CAMPUS LLC

1501 N CAMPBELL AVE
TUCSON, AZ 857240001
Phone: -
Fax: -
Web: www.uahealth.ixt.com

CEO: -
CFO: -
HR: -
FYE: June 30
Type: Private

Banner - University Medicine (formerly The University of Arizona Health Network) heals Arizonans and trains Wildcats. It operates three academic medical centers in Phoenix and Tucson, serving as the primary teaching hospital for the University of Arizona (UA) and offering medical treatment, research, and education services. The not-for-profit center provides cancer, cardiology, geriatric, respiratory, transplant, and dialysis care, as well as general practice and home health services. Specialty services include burn care, behavioral health, integrative medicine, sports medicine, and level I trauma care. The network merged with Banner Healthcare in 2015.

	Annual Growth	06/03	06/04	06/05	06/08	06/09
Sales ($mil.)	(6.5%)	-	-	708.8	512.2	541.5
Net income ($ mil.)		-	-	0.0	27.1	-
Market value ($ mil.)		-	-	-	-	-
Employees		-	-	-	-	3,000

BANTAM ELECTRONICS, INC.

4616 W HOWARD LN
AUSTIN, TX 787286300
Phone: 512 402-9696
Fax: -
Web: www.bantamelectronics.com

CEO: -
CFO: -
HR: -
FYE: December 31
Type: Private

Bantam Electronics does custom manufacturing of electronics products for such clients as AMD, Crossroads Systems, NetQoS, and Wayport. The company also distributes a variety of computer systems and electronics, including software, motherboards, monitors, cables, and accessories. Bantam provides various IT services, as well, such as network installation and management, and server room analysis and design. The company was founded by Λ. W. Scott in 1969 as Tinkertronics. The manufacturer and distributor changed its name to Bantam Electronics in 2002. A. W. Scott retired in 2000. His son, EVP Cliff Scott, owns 60% of the company, while brother Trey Scott (VP) owns 40%.

BAPTIST HEALTH

9601 BAPTIST HEALTH DR STE 109
LITTLE ROCK, AR 722056323
Phone: 501 202-2000
Fax: -
Web: www.baptist-health.com

CEO: -
CFO: -
HR: Cheri Glass
FYE: December 31
Type: Private

For those seeking medical salvation, Baptist Health may be the answer to their prayers. The organization provides health services through about 175 points of care scattered throughout in Arkansas. Its facilities include seven hospitals and a number of rehabilitation facilities, family clinics, and therapy and wellness centers. Arkansas Health Group, a division of Baptist Health, runs more than 20 physician clinics across the state. Specialized services include cardiology, women's health, orthopedics, rehabilitation, and home and hospice care. Baptist Health's Parkway Village is a 90-acre retirement community for active seniors located close to Baptist Health Medical Center - Little Rock.

	Annual Growth	12/17	12/18	12/20	12/21	12/22
Sales ($mil.)	11.8%	-	1,215.9	1,650.6	1,872.5	1,900.0
Net income ($ mil.)		-	(45.1)	155.2	98.1	(77.8)
Market value ($ mil.)		-	-	-	-	-
Employees		-	-	-	-	7,000

BAPTIST HEALTH CARE CORPORATION

1000 W MORENO ST
PENSACOLA, FL 325012316
Phone: 850 434-4080
Fax: -
Web: www.ebaptisthealthcare.org

CEO: -
CFO: -
HR: -
FYE: September 30
Type: Private

Baptist Health Care strives for coastal health excellence. The firm operates hospitals, clinics, and a home health agency in northern and western Florida, as well as southern Alabama. Founded in 1951, the Pensacola, Florida-based not-for-profit health care system operates three hospital, four medical parks, child protective services, work placement for persons with disabilities, including Baptist Hospital and Gulf Breeze Hospital. Baptist Health Care, in conjunction with its affiliates, provides a wide variety of services such as home health care, rehabilitation services, and behavioral health services. Lakeview Center is a network of behavioral health, vocational and child protective services, and the Andrews Institute provides sports medicine services.

	Annual Growth	09/07	09/08	09/09	09/14	09/15
Sales ($mil.)	(24.2%)	-	340.9	36.5	43.7	49.2
Net income ($ mil.)	(39.2%)	-	2.1	(1.0)	(4.7)	0.0
Market value ($ mil.)		-	-	-	-	-
Employees		-	-	-	-	5,200

BAPTIST HEALTH SOUTH FLORIDA, INC.

6855 SW 57TH AVE
SOUTH MIAMI, FL 331433647
Phone: 305 596-1960
Fax: -
Web: www.baptisthealth.net

CEO: Alexandra Villoch
CFO: Matthew Arsenault
HR: Diana Montenegro
FYE: September 30
Type: Private

Baptist Health South Florida (BHSF) is the largest healthcare organization in the region, with over 10 hospitals, more than 26,000 employees, 4,000 physicians and 200 outpatient centers, urgent care facilities and physician practices spanning across Miami-Dade, Monroe, Broward and Palm Beach Counties. Baptist Health has internationally-renowned centers of excellence in cancer, cardiovascular care, orthopedics and sports medicine, and neurosciences. In addition, it includes Baptist Health Medical Group; Baptist Health Quality Network; and Baptist Health Care On Demand, a virtual health platform. The health system has more than 1.8 million patients every year.

	Annual Growth	09/16	09/17	09/19	09/21	09/22
Sales ($mil.)	24.3%	-	608.3	1,294.0	2,027.9	1,802.8
Net income ($ mil.)	14.3%	-	244.3	598.5	832.1	477.1
Market value ($ mil.)		-	-	-	-	-
Employees		-	-	-	-	16,000

BAPTIST HEALTH SYSTEM, INC.

841 PRUDENTIAL DR STE 1802
JACKSONVILLE, FL 322078329
Phone: 904 202-2000
Fax: –
Web: www.baptistjax.com

CEO: Michael Mayo
CFO: Michael Lukaszewski
HR: –
FYE: September 30
Type: Private

Founded in 1955, Baptist Health is the largest non-profit health system in Northeast, Florida. With about 1,325 beds, the health system, operates five hospitals (Baptist Jacksonville, Baptist Beaches, Baptist Nassau, Baptist South, and Wolfson Children's Hospital) with about 331,920 emergency room visits and performs 46,700 surgeries. Baptist Health is the region's first and largest primary care network, with more than 160 physicians in over 55 offices. It has four satellite emergency centers in Clay, Northside, St. Johns Town Center, and Oakleaf, including three comprehensive medical campuses. Baptist Health is part of Coastal Community Health, an affiliation with Southeast Georgia Health System, to create a contiguous health network spanning from Brunswick to Jacksonville.

	Annual Growth	09/18	09/19	09/20	09/21	09/22
Sales ($mil.)	8.8%	–	1,923.2	2,022.2	2,408.3	2,480.4
Net income ($ mil.)	–	–	176.8	95.8	570.3	(198.2)
Market value ($ mil.)	–	–	–	–	–	–
Employees	–	–	–	–	–	7,000

BAPTIST HEALTHCARE SYSTEM, INC.

2701 EASTPOINT PKWY
LOUISVILLE, KY 402234166
Phone: 502 896-5000
Fax: –
Web: www.baptisthealth.com

CEO: Gerard Colman
CFO: Stephen R Oglesby
HR: Lynette Walker
FYE: August 31
Type: Private

Baptist Health is a full-spectrum health system dedicated to improving the health of the communities it serves. Baptist Health's eight owned hospitals include more than 2,300 licensed beds in Corbin, Elizabethtown, La Grange, Lexington, Louisville, Paducah, Richmond and New Albany, Indiana. Baptist Health also operates the 410-bed Baptist Health Deaconess Madisonville in Madisonville, Kentucky in a joint venture with Deaconess Health System based in Evansville, Indiana. Baptist Health employs more than 23,000 people in Kentucky and surrounding states. The Baptist Health family consists of nine hospitals, employed and independent physicians, and more than 400 points of care, including outpatient facilities, physician practices and services, urgent care clinics, outpatient diagnostic and surgery centers, home care, fitness centers, and occupational medicine and physical therapy clinics. The health system was founded in 1924.

	Annual Growth	08/18	08/19	08/20	08/21	08/22
Sales ($mil.)	11.8%	–	2,878.7	2,994.6	3,886.0	4,023.3
Net income ($ mil.)	–	–	122.0	199.5	373.8	(150.7)
Market value ($ mil.)	–	–	–	–	–	–
Employees	–	–	–	–	–	12,601

BAPTIST HOSPITAL OF MIAMI, INC.

8900 N KENDALL DR
MIAMI, FL 331762197
Phone: 786 596-1960
Fax: –
Web: www.baptisthealth.net

CEO: –
CFO: Ralph Lawson
HR: –
FYE: September 30
Type: Private

Baptist Hospital of Miami can treat many vices for Miami residents. The flagship facility of the Baptist Health South Florida health system provides residents of the city with a full range of health care services, including pediatric, cancer, home health, rehabilitation, neurology, and cardiovascular care. The hospital has more than 680 beds and includes the Baptist Children's Hospital, which offers a pediatric emergency room and a neonatal intensive care unit. Baptist Hospital of Miami also includes the Baptist Cardiac & Vascular Institute, a regional cancer program, and a diabetes care center. Baptist Hospital of Miami was founded in 1960.

	Annual Growth	09/18	09/19	09/20	09/21	09/22
Sales ($mil.)	6.2%	–	1,717.7	1,310.9	1,532.9	2,057.8
Net income ($ mil.)	(1.2%)	–	282.2	161.2	291.5	272.0
Market value ($ mil.)	–	–	–	–	–	–
Employees	–	–	–	–	–	4,200

BAPTIST MEMORIAL HEALTH CARE SYSTEM, INC.

350 N HUMPHREYS BLVD
MEMPHIS, TN 381202177
Phone: 901 227-5117
Fax: –
Web: www.bmhcc.org

CEO: Jason Little
CFO: –
HR: –
FYE: September 30
Type: Private

Baptist Memorial Health Care is one of the country's largest not-for-profit health care systems and the largest provider of Medicaid in the region. Baptist offers a full continuum of care to communities throughout the Mid-South and consistently ranks among the top integrated health care networks in the nation. The health care system comprises more than 20 affiliate hospitals in West Tennessee, North and Central Mississippi and East Arkansas; more than 5,400 affiliated physicians; Baptist Medical Group, a multispecialty physician group with more than 900 providers; home, hospice and psychiatric care; minor medical centers and clinics; a network of surgery, rehabilitation and other outpatient centers; and an education system highlighted by Baptist Health Sciences University (formerly Baptist College of Health Sciences).

	Annual Growth	09/08	09/09	09/10	09/12	09/15
Sales ($mil.)	8.2%	–	124.1	136.2	161.9	199.5
Net income ($ mil.)	–	–	(3.5)	(1.5)	1.3	(10.0)
Market value ($ mil.)	–	–	–	–	–	–
Employees	–	–	–	–	–	9,877

BAPTIST MEMORIAL HOSPITAL

6019 WALNUT GROVE RD
MEMPHIS, TN 381202113
Phone: 901 226-5000
Fax: –
Web: www.baptistonline.org

CEO: Jason Little
CFO: Don Pounds
HR: –
FYE: September 30
Type: Private

When most of us think of Memphis, we think of Elvis Presley. When doctors think of Memphis, they think of Elvis and Baptist Memorial Hospital-Memphis. As the flagship facility of Baptist Memorial Health Care, the 710-bed hospital, often simply called Baptist Memphis, offers patients the full spectrum of health care services, including cancer treatment, orthopedics, surgical services, and neurology. The campus also features the Baptist Heart Institute for cardiovascular care and research, a pediatric emergency room, a skilled nursing facility, and the Plaza Diagnostic Pavilion for outpatient health care. Baptist Memphis, established in 1979, is one of the state's highest volume hospitals.

	Annual Growth	09/12	09/13	09/14	09/15	09/21
Sales ($mil.)	5.2%	–	504.3	663.5	691.0	759.3
Net income ($ mil.)	(3.7%)	–	17.4	(47.8)	(1.2)	12.9
Market value ($ mil.)	–	–	–	–	–	–
Employees	–	–	–	–	–	6,000

BAPTIST/ST. ANTHONY'S HEALTH SYSTEM

1600 WALLACE BLVD
AMARILLO, TX 791601799
Phone: 806 212-2000
Fax: –
Web: www.bsahs.org

CEO: Bob Williams
CFO: –
HR: Amy Rambo
FYE: December 31
Type: Private

Baptist St. Anthony's Health System (BSA Health System) serves the residents of the Texas Panhandle through its medical facilities in Amarillo. The organization's main hospital facility, BSA Hospital, has 445 beds and more than 450 physicians and offers acute care and specialty services such as imaging, oncology, and orthopedics. BSA Health System also operates outpatient clinics that provide diagnostic imaging, family medicine, urgent care, and surgery services, as well as hospice and home health divisions. The health system traces its roots to 1901 and is operated through a partnership between majority owner Ardent Health Services and regional senior services provider Baptist Community Services.

BAR HARBOR BANKSHARES
ASE: BHB

PO Box 400, 82 Main Street
Bar Harbor, ME 04609-0400
Phone: 207 288-3314
Fax: —
Web: www.barharbor.bank

CEO: Curtis C Simard
CFO: Josephine Iannelli
HR: Barbara Scarpino
FYE: December 31
Type: Public

Bar Harbor Bankshares which holds Bar Harbor Bank & Trust, is a Maine -stay. Boasting $1.6 billion in assets, the bank offers traditional deposit and retirement products, trust services, and a variety of loans to individuals and businesses through 15 branches in the state's Hancock, Knox, and Washington counties. Commercial real estate and residential mortgages loans make up nearly 80% of the bank's loan portfolio, though it also originates business, construction, agricultural, home equity, and other consumer loans. About 10% of its loans are to the tourist industry, which is associated with nearby Acadia National Park. Subsidiary Bar Harbor Trust Services offers trust and estate planning services.

	Annual Growth	12/19	12/20	12/21	12/22	12/23
Assets ($mil.)	2.0%	3,669.1	3,725.8	3,709.2	3,909.8	3,970.9
Net income ($ mil.)	18.7%	22.6	33.2	39.3	43.6	44.9
Market value ($ mil.)	3.7%	385.2	342.7	438.9	486.1	445.5
Employees	0.1%	460	531	489	486	462

BARCLAYS BANK DELAWARE

100 S WEST ST
WILMINGTON, DE 198015015
Phone: 302 255-8000
Fax: —
Web: cards.barclaycardus.com

CEO: Barry Rodrigues
CFO: —
HR: —
FYE: December 31
Type: Private

Barclays Bank Delaware (doing business as Barclays US) is a leading co-branded credit card issuer and financial services partner in the US that creates highly customized programs to drive customer loyalty and engagement for some of the country's most successful travel, entertainment, retail and affinity institutions. The company, a division of Barclays, issues Visa and MasterCard credit cards, in addition to co-branded credit cards through partnerships with over 25 top companies, including Priceline, Choice Privileges, Carnival World, and JetBlue. Founded as Juniper Financial in 2000; it became a part of Barclays in 2004.

	Annual Growth	12/06	12/07	12/08	12/13	12/14
Assets ($mil.)	18.8%	—	7,470.3	12,418	19,056	25,013
Net income ($ mil.)	—	—	—	20.6	331.6	239.8
Market value ($ mil.)	—	—	—	—	—	—
Employees	—	—	—	—	—	349

BARD COLLEGE

30 CAMPUS RD
ANNANDALE ON HUDSON, NY 125049800
Phone: 845 758-7518
Fax: —
Web: www.bard.edu

CEO: —
CFO: —
HR: —
FYE: June 30
Type: Private

Although Shakespeare might appreciate the curriculum, Bard College is not named for the Bard of Avon but for founder John Bard. The institution of higher learning is an independent, nonsectarian, residential, coeducational, four-year college of the liberal arts and sciences. Bard's total enrollment of 1,900 includes some 600 graduate students. First-year students are required to take a three-week Workshop in Language and Thinking that emphasizes the connection between expression and thought. Students must also complete a year-long senior project that is reviewed by faculty members.

	Annual Growth	06/15	06/16	06/17	06/18	06/22
Sales ($mil.)	13.1%	—	189.6	184.9	197.8	396.7
Net income ($ mil.)	—	—	(21.6)	18.9	(11.2)	72.7
Market value ($ mil.)	—	—	—	—	—	—
Employees	—	—	—	—	—	525

BARNES & NOBLE EDUCATION INC
NYS: BNED

120 Mountain View Blvd.
Basking Ridge, NJ 07920
Phone: 908 991-2665
Fax: —
Web: www.bned.com

CEO: Michael P Huseby
CFO: Kevin Watson
HR: Joann Magill
FYE: April 29
Type: Public

Barnes & Noble Education serves more than 6 million students and faculty members through more than 1,365 physical, virtual, and custom bookstores in the US (aimed at both K-12 and college levels). The company offers direct-to-student products through Textbooks.com, which is one of the largest e-commerce sites for new, used, and digital textbooks. It provides product and service offerings designed to address the most pressing issues in higher education, including equitable access, enhanced convenience, and improved affordability through innovative course material delivery models. Barnes & Noble is also one of the largest textbook wholesalers, inventory management hardware and software providers, and a leading provider of digital education solutions. The company began in 1965 when founder Leonard Riggio opened his first bookstore in New York City's Greenwich Village.

	Annual Growth	04/19*	05/20	05/21*	04/22	04/23
Sales ($mil.)	(6.7%)	2,034.6	1,851.1	1,433.9	1,531.4	1,543.2
Net income ($ mil.)	—	(24.4)	(38.3)	(131.8)	(68.9)	(101.9)
Market value ($ mil.)	(22.8%)	231.5	88.9	416.1	159.9	82.1
Employees	(8.3%)	6,000	5,500	4,095	4,870	4,250

*Fiscal year change

BARNES & NOBLE, INC.

122 5TH AVE FL 2
NEW YORK, NY 100115634
Phone: 212 633-3300
Fax: —
Web: stores.barnesandnoble.com

CEO: James Daunt
CFO: Allen W Lindstorm
HR: Amy Willis
FYE: April 28
Type: Private

Barnes & Noble is one of the largest bookstore chains in the US operating more than 600 Barnes & Noble bookstores in all 50 states, and one of the web's premier e-commerce sites, BN.com. Carrying about 3,000 magazine titles and more than 400 newspaper titles, the company sold more than 190 million physical books between its retail stores and online operations annually. In addition, Barnes & Noble has approximately 1 million unique physical book titles sold per year. The company's NOOK brand, develops, supports, and creates digital content and products for the digital reading and digital education markets. Founded in 1971 by bookseller Leonard Riggio, Barnes & Noble is now owned by Elliott Advisors (UK) Limited.

	Annual Growth	04/14	04/15	04/16	04/17	04/18
Sales ($mil.)	(6.2%)	—	—	4,163.8	3,894.6	3,662.3
Net income ($ mil.)	—	—	—	(24.4)	22.0	(125.5)
Market value ($ mil.)	—	—	—	—	—	—
Employees	—	—	—	—	—	15,557

BARNES GROUP INC.
NYS: B

123 Main Street
Bristol, CT 06010
Phone: 860 583-7070
Fax: —
Web: www.barnesgroup.inc

CEO: Thomas J Hook
CFO: Julie K Streich
HR: —
FYE: December 31
Type: Public

Barnes Group is a global provider of highly engineered products, differentiated industrial technologies, and innovative solutions, serving a wide range of end markets and customers. The company provides highly-engineered, high-quality precision components, products, and systems for critical applications serving a diverse customer base in end-markets such as mobility, industrial equipment, automation, personal care, packaging, electronics, and medical devices. Its Aerospace Aftermarket business supplements jet engine OEMs' maintenance, repair, and overhaul capabilities. Customers benefit from its integrated hardware and software capabilities focused on improving the processing, control, service, and sustainability of engineered plastics, factory automation technologies, and precision components. Barnes Group generates about half of its sales from the Americas. Barnes was founded in 1857 and headquartered in Bristol, Connecticut.

	Annual Growth	12/19	12/20	12/21	12/22	12/23
Sales ($mil.)	(0.7%)	1,491.1	1,124.4	1,258.8	1,261.9	1,450.9
Net income ($ mil.)	(43.6%)	158.4	63.4	99.9	13.5	16.0
Market value ($ mil.)	(14.8%)	3,140.5	2,569.3	2,361.5	2,070.5	1,653.9
Employees	3.1%	5,749	4,952	5,100	5,200	6,500

BARNWELL INDUSTRIES, INC.
ASE: BRN

1100 Alakea Street, Suite 500
Honolulu, HI 96813
Phone: 808 531-8400
Fax: –
Web: www.brninc.com

CEO: Kenneth S Grossman
CFO: Russell M Gifford
HR: –
FYE: September 30
Type: Public

Barnwell Industries has more than a barnful of assets, which range from oil and gas production, contract well drilling, and Hawaiian land and housing investments. Barnwell Industries explores for and produces oil and natural gas primarily in Alberta. In 2009 it reported proved reserves of 1.3 million barrels of oil and 20.6 billion cu. ft. of gas. Subsidiary Water Resources International drills water and geothermal wells and installs and repairs water pump systems in Hawaii. The company also owns a 78% interest in Kaupulehu Developments, which owns leasehold rights to more than 1,000 acres in Hawaii, and is engaged in other real estate activities.

	Annual Growth	09/19	09/20	09/21	09/22	09/23
Sales ($mil.)	20.3%	12.1	18.3	18.1	28.5	25.3
Net income ($ mil.)	–	(12.4)	(4.8)	6.3	5.5	(1.0)
Market value ($ mil.)	49.9%	5.2	8.5	30.3	26.4	26.3
Employees	–	43	43	36	35	–

BARRACUDA NETWORKS, INC.

3175 WINCHESTER BLVD
CAMPBELL, CA 950086557
Phone: 408 342-5400
Fax: –
Web: www.barracuda.com

CEO: Hatem Naguib
CFO: Dustin Driggs
HR: –
FYE: February 29
Type: Private

Barracuda provides easy, comprehensive and affordable solutions for email protection, application protection, network protection, and data protection. More than 200,000 global customers trust Barracuda to safeguard their employees, data, and applications from a wide range of threats. The company works with more than 5,000 channel partners worldwide. Barracuda enables managed service providers to offer multi-layered security and data protection services to their customers through its products and a purpose-built MSP platform. The company serves businesses in industries such as banking and finance, government, healthcare, manufacturing, physical and virtual appliances, retail, software, technology, travel and entertainment, and consumer goods.

BARRETT BUSINESS SERVICES, INC.
NMS: BBSI

8100 NE Parkway Drive, Suite 200
Vancouver, WA 98662
Phone: 360 828-0700
Fax: 360 828-0701
Web: www.barrettbusiness.com

CEO: –
CFO: –
HR: –
FYE: December 31
Type: Public

Barrett Business Services (BBSI) offers professional employment organization (PEO) services to some 7,200 small and mid-sized businesses and their approximately 200,000 employees. Its PEO services business provides outsourced human resource services, such as payroll management, benefits administration, and other administrative functions. The company also offers temporary and long-term staffing services, such as on-demand or short-term staffing, on-site management, contract staffing, direct placement. Established in 1965, BBSI operates through about 65 branch offices in more than 10 US states. More than 75% of revenue comes from clients in California.

	Annual Growth	12/19	12/20	12/21	12/22	12/23
Sales ($mil.)	3.2%	942.3	880.8	955.2	1,054.3	1,069.3
Net income ($ mil.)	1.2%	48.3	33.8	38.1	47.3	50.6
Market value ($ mil.)	6.4%	594.5	448.3	453.9	613.0	761.0
Employees	0.7%	127,085	115,075	121,660	127,141	130,513

BARRY UNIVERSITY, INC.

11300 NE 2ND AVE
MIAMI, FL 331616695
Phone: 305 899-3000
Fax: –
Web: www.barry.edu

CEO: –
CFO: –
HR: Myra Jackson
FYE: June 30
Type: Private

Barry University is a Catholic institution of Dominican heritage based in South Florida. With a student-faculty ratio of about 14:1, the liberal arts university annually enrolls about 3,000 undergraduate students and some 4,000 graduate students. The university's academic division includes two colleges (the College of Arts and Sciences and the College of Health Sciences) and seven schools. It offers more than 100 specializations and programs for undergraduate, graduate, and doctoral studies. Barry University also offers about 35 non-degree and certificate programs. Barry University was founded by the Adrian Dominican Sisters in 1940.

	Annual Growth	06/18	06/19	06/20	06/21	06/22
Sales ($mil.)	3.8%	–	192.7	201.3	207.5	215.7
Net income ($ mil.)	–	–	(0.4)	1.6	7.3	10.1
Market value ($ mil.)	–	–	–	–	–	–
Employees	–	–	–	–	–	1,407

BARRY-WEHMILLER GROUP, INC.

8020 FORSYTH BLVD
SAINT LOUIS, MO 631051707
Phone: 314 862-8000
Fax: –
Web: www.barrywehmiller.com

CEO: Kyle Chapman
CFO: Michael Monarchi
HR: –
FYE: September 30
Type: Private

Barry-Wehmiller is a diversified global supplier of highly engineered capital equipment and consulting services for a wide variety of industries. It manufactures and supplies packaging, corrugating, paper converting, filling, and labeling automation equipment for a broad range of industries. It conducts business around the world through some 20 operating companies such as Accraply (labeling machinery), Design Group (automation and control systems), Winkler and Dunnebier (postage services and tissue and hygiene), and Synerlink (ultra-clean packaging for milk products and desserts). Other divisions manufacture paper converting machinery and offer engineering/IT consulting services. Berry-Wehmiller is privately owned by the Chapman family, who took over from Fred Wehmiller in 1963.

	Annual Growth	09/09	09/10	09/11	09/18	09/19
Sales ($mil.)	11.2%	–	1,097.5	1,241.0	3,037.9	2,856.3
Net income ($ mil.)	–	–	–	–	85.0	77.9
Market value ($ mil.)	–	–	–	–	–	–
Employees	–	–	–	–	–	4,500

BARTLETT AGRI ENTERPRISES, INC.

4900 MAIN ST STE 1200
KANSAS CITY, MO 641122807
Phone: 816 753-6300
Fax: –
Web: www.bartlett-grain.com

CEO: –
CFO: –
HR: –
FYE: December 31
Type: Private

When the cows come home, Bartlett and Company will be ready. The company's primary business is grain merchandising, but it also runs cattle feedlots, mills flour, and sells feed and fertilizer. Bartlett operates grain storage facilities, terminal elevators, and country elevators in the Midwestern US, including locations in Kansas, Iowa, Missouri, and Nebraska. Bartlett also operates flour mills and feed stores in the Midwest, as well as along the East Coast. Its cattle operations are based in Texas and reach to Kansas. Bartlett and Company Grain Charitable Foundation makes financial gifts to local causes. Founded in 1907 as Bartlett Agri Enterprises, the company is still owned by the founding Bartlett family.

BARTON MALOW COMPANY

26500 AMERICAN DR
SOUTHFIELD, MI 480342252
Phone: 248 436-5000
Fax: –
Web: www.bartonmalow.com

CEO: –
CFO: Lars Luedeman
HR: Heather Cunningham
FYE: March 31
Type: Private

Barton Malow is a union contractor leveraging an integrated, self-perform approach that includes civil, concrete, steel, equipment setting, general trades, and boilermaker work. Barton Malow builds automotive, energy, and industrial projects throughout North America. Projects include McLaren Greater Lansing Replacement Hospital, Outdoor Event and Tailgate Park; Peppa Pig Theme Park Florida; Munn Ice Arena Addition and Renovation; SeaWorld Park and Entertainment Mako Rollercoaster; Meridian Wind Park; Truist Park; Ohio Stadium Renovations: and American Legion Memorial Stadium; among others. Carl Osborn Barton founded the employee-owned firm as C.O. Barton Company in 1924.

	Annual Growth	03/15	03/16	03/17	03/18	03/19
Sales ($mil.)	(16.8%)	–	–	2,361.9	2,502.2	1,634.1
Net income ($ mil.)	354.5%	–	–	0.4	11.1	8.2
Market value ($ mil.)	–	–	–	–	–	–
Employees	–	–	–	–	–	1,600

BASIC ENERGY SERVICES INC

801 Cherry Street, Suite 2100
Fort Worth, TX 76102
Phone: 817 334-4100
Fax: –
Web: www.basices.com

NBB: BASX Q
CEO: –
CFO: –
HR: –
FYE: December 31
Type: Public

Basic Energy Services make wells flow. It provides onshore well-site services to the domestic oil & natural gas industry across the US. This includes completion and remedial services, water logistics, well servicing, and manufacturing and rig servicing was realigned with Well Servicing segment. The company has significant presence in liquids-rich basins, including the Permian Basin and the Bakken, Eagle Ford, Haynesville, and Denver-Julesburg. Customers include a motley of some 2,000 oil and gas companies.

	Annual Growth	12/16	12/17	12/18	12/19	12/20
Sales ($mil.)	(6.9%)	547.5	864.0	964.7	567.3	411.4
Net income ($ mil.)	–	(123.4)	(96.7)	(144.6)	(181.9)	(268.2)
Market value ($ mil.)	(76.8%)	880.2	584.4	95.6	6.6	2.6
Employees	(7.4%)	3,800	4,100	4,100	3,000	2,800

BASIN ELECTRIC POWER COOPERATIVE

1717 East Interstate Avenue
Bismarck,, ND 58503
Phone: 701 223-0441
Fax: –
Web: www.basinelectric.com

CEO: Paul M Sukut
CFO: Steve Johnson
HR: –
FYE: December 31
Type: Public

Basin Electric Power Cooperative is a not-for-profit generation and transmission cooperative incorporated in 1961 to provide supplemental power to a consortium of rural electric cooperative. As do other electric-powered items in nine states including Montana, Iowa, Colorado, Minnesota, Nebraska, North Dakota, South Dakota, Wyoming and New Mexico. The consumer-owned power generation and transmission co-op provides power to about 140 rural electric member systems, which serve some 3 million people. It has a generating capacity of almost 5,220 MW of wholesale electric generating capability and has nearly 7,385 MW of capability within its resource portfolio. Other subsidiaries have included Dakota Coal, Basin Cooperative Services, Montana Limestone, and Souris Valley Pipeline.

	Annual Growth	12/11	12/12	12/13	12/14	12/15
Sales ($mil.)	(7.1%)	–	–	–	2,248.8	2,089.0
Net income ($ mil.)	(83.7%)	–	–	–	49.7	8.1
Market value ($ mil.)	–	–	–	–	–	–
Employees	–	–	–	–	–	2,300

BASSETT FURNITURE INDUSTRIES, INC

3525 Fairystone Park Highway
Bassett, VA 24055
Phone: 276 629-6000
Fax: 276 629-6332
Web: www.bassettfurniture.com

NMS: BSET
CEO: Robert H Spilman Jr
CFO: –
HR: –
FYE: November 25
Type: Public

Bassett Furniture Industries is a leading retailer, manufacturer, and marketer of branded home furnishings. The company, founded in 1902, makes wooden and upholstered furniture for home use, featuring bedroom and dining suites furniture. Bassett sells its products primarily through a network of nearly 60 company-owned and licensee-owned branded stores under the Bassett Home Furnishings (BHF) name, with additional distribution through other wholesale channels including multi-line furniture stores, many of which feature Bassett galleries or design centers. Texas is the largest market among some 25 states in which Bassett operates.

	Annual Growth	11/19	11/20	11/21	11/22	11/23
Sales ($mil.)	(3.6%)	452.1	385.9	486.5	485.6	390.1
Net income ($ mil.)	–	(1.9)	(10.4)	18.0	65.3	(3.2)
Market value ($ mil.)	2.2%	133.5	145.3	147.2	163.3	145.8
Employees	(14.3%)	2,579	2,071	2,219	1,561	1,389

BATH & BODY WORKS INC

Three Limited Parkway
Columbus, OH 43230
Phone: 614 415-7000
Fax: –
Web: www.lb.com

NYS: BBWI
CEO: Gina Boswell
CFO: Eva C Boratto
HR: Ad Hernandez
FYE: February 3
Type: Public

Bath & Body Works, Inc. (BBW) is a specialty retailer of home fragrances, body care products, and soaps and sanitizer products. Through the Bath & Body Works, White Barn and other brand names, the company sells merchandise through approximately 1,800 company-operated specialty retail stores and e-commerce sites in the US and Canada, and through over 425 stores and around 30 e-commerce sites in more than 45 other countries operating under franchise, license and wholesale arrangements.

	Annual Growth	02/20*	01/21	01/22	01/23*	02/24
Sales ($mil.)	(12.9%)	12,914	11,847	7,882.0	7,560.0	7,429.0
Net income ($ mil.)	–	(366.0)	844.0	1,333.0	800.0	878.0
Market value ($ mil.)	17.0%	5,211.0	9,171.0	12,296	10,046	9,776.3
Employees	(11.8%)	94,400	92,300	56,900	57,200	57,157

*Fiscal year change

BATON ROUGE GENERAL MEDICAL CENTER

3600 FLORIDA ST
BATON ROUGE, LA 708063889
Phone: 225 387-7000
Fax: –
Web: www.brgeneral.org

CEO: Milton Sietman
CFO: –
HR: Faye Nettles
FYE: September 30
Type: Private

The first hospital founded in Louisiana's capital, Baton Rouge General Medical Center is a not-for-profit, full-service community hospital offering patients general medical and surgical care. Through the hospital's two locations, Bluebonnet and Mid City, Baton Rouge General also provides specialty services for cancer, heart, and neonatal care. In addition, the nearly 530-bed health care facility provides services in areas such as burn treatment, diabetes, sleep disorders, and behavioral health. Baton Rouge General Medical Center is the flagship facility of General Health System.

BATTALION OIL CORP

ASE: BATL

3505 West Sam Houston Parkway North, Suite 300
Houston, TX 77043
Phone: 832 538-0300
Fax: –
Web: www.battalionoil.com

CEO: Matthew B Steele
CFO: –
HR: –
FYE: December 31
Type: Public

Battalion Oil Corporation, formerly known as Halcon Resources Corporation, is an independent energy company focused on the acquisition, production, exploration, and development of onshore liquids-rich oil and natural gas properties currently focusing on the Delaware Basin in Texas. The company has working interests in over 40, 375 net acres in the Delaware Basin in Pecos, Reeves, Ward, and Winkler Counties, Texas. Its primary targets in this area are the Wolfcamp and Bone Spring formations. It has roughly 105 operated wells producing about 15,440 average barrels of oil equivalent per day in this area. It has oil and gas reserves of approximately 90 MMBoe. The company's three largest customers collectively represent about 80% of its total revenue.

	Annual Growth	10/19*	12/19	12/20	12/21	12/22
Sales ($mil.)	31.2%	159.1	65.6	148.3	285.2	359.1
Net income ($ mil.)	–	(1,156.1)	(10.5)	(229.7)	(28.3)	18.5
Market value ($ mil.)	–	–	–	135.7	160.2	158.7
Employees	–	–	69	60	58	63

*Fiscal year change

BATTELLE MEMORIAL INSTITUTE INC

505 KING AVE
COLUMBUS, OH 432012681
Phone: 614 424-6424
Fax: –
Web: www.battelle.org

CEO: Lewis V Thaer
CFO: Chris Boynton
HR: Angie Snyder
FYE: September 30
Type: Private

The not-for-profit Battelle Memorial Institute is one of the largest research enterprises, with more than 40,000 scientists, engineers, and staff serving corporate and government clients. Research areas include national security, health and life sciences, and energy and environment. Battelle owns facilities in the US and Europe and manages about nine Department of Energy-sponsored labs, including Brookhaven National Laboratory, Los Alamos National Laboratory, and Pacific Northwest National Laboratory. The institute was established by the family of steel industry pioneer Gordon Battelle in 1923.

BATTLE CREEK FARMERS COOPERATIVE, NON-STOCK

83755 HIGHWAY 121
BATTLE CREEK, NE 687155004
Phone: 402 675-2375
Fax: –
Web: www.farmerspridecoop.com

CEO: Dean Thernes
CFO: –
HR: Molly Brozek
FYE: November 30
Type: Private

From crop aggregation to fuel supply, Battle Creek Farmers Cooperative provides its members with an arsenal of farm supplies and services. The co-op serves some 900 northeastern Nebraskan farmers. Its offerings include grain marketing, soil nutrient inputs, pest-control products, seed, animal feed, transportation, and energy (gasoline, ethanol, diesel, kerosene, propane, and lubricants). The co-op processes soybeans and offers soybean meal and oil under the NewMaSoy brand. In addition to its administrative offices in Battle Creek, Nebraska, it operates 10 service centers. Battle Creek Farmers Cooperative was established in 1929.

	Annual Growth	11/08	11/09	11/10	11/11	11/12
Sales ($mil.)	29.0%	–	–	120.6	188.5	200.8
Net income ($ mil.)	2.9%	–	–	6.2	7.5	6.5
Market value ($ mil.)	–	–	–	–	–	–
Employees	–	–	–	–	–	90

BAUER BUILT, INC.

1111 W PROSPECT ST
DURAND, WI 547361061
Phone: 715 672-8300
Fax: –
Web: www.bauerbuilt.com

CEO: Jerome M Bauer
CFO: Sean P Brant
HR: Chelsea Schneider
FYE: December 31
Type: Private

Bauer Built ensures its customers are well-treaded. The company owns about 30 automotive tire and service centers throughout the Midwest, more than 10 wholesale distribution centers, seven tire retread plants, and three rim and wheel reconditioning centers. It delivers petroleum products (including gasoline, ethanol, biodiesel, and kerosene) throughout eastern Minnesota and western Wisconsin, as well as operates a car wash in Durand, Wisconsin. Bauer Built was founded in 1944 by Sam Bauer, the father of president Jerome "Jerry" Bauer, as Bauer Oil Co. It got into the retread business in 1950. Employees own about 30% of the company; the Bauer family holds the remainder.

	Annual Growth	12/03	12/04	12/05	12/06	12/08
Sales ($mil.)	4.3%	–	161.6	182.1	171.8	191.0
Net income ($ mil.)	6.7%	–	2.7	2.9	2.6	3.5
Market value ($ mil.)	–	–	–	–	–	–
Employees	–	–	–	–	–	450

BAXLEY & APPLING COUNTY HOSPITAL AUTHORITY

163 E TOLLISON ST
BAXLEY, GA 315130120
Phone: 912 367-9841
Fax: –
Web: www.ahcs.org

CEO: Randy Crawford
CFO: John C Graham
HR: Carla McLendon
FYE: August 31
Type: Private

Administering medical care to Georgia Peaches is the Appling HealthCare System. The not-for-profit provides a variety of health care services to the residents in southeastern Georgia through a 40-bed community hospital (of which half the beds are slated for geriatric behavioral care), a long-term acute-cute care facility with about 100 beds, and an emergency medical services unit. The system is also home to a number of primary and specialty care practices such as Appling Pediatrics, Appling Medical Group, and the South Georgia Medical Group. Appling HealthCare System is governed by the Baxley-Appling County Hospital Board Authority.

	Annual Growth	06/97	06/98	06/01	06/02*	08/19
Sales ($mil.)	4.5%	–	11.5	–	20.3	28.9
Net income ($ mil.)	–	–	(1.5)	–	0.0	(1.1)
Market value ($ mil.)	–	–	–	–	–	–
Employees	–	–	–	–	–	400

*Fiscal year change

BAXTER COUNTY REGIONAL HOSPITAL, INC.

624 HOSPITAL DR
MOUNTAIN HOME, AR 726532955
Phone: 870 508-1000
Fax: –
Web: www.baxterhealth.org

CEO: Ron Peterson
CFO: Ivan Holleman
HR: Natalie Amato
FYE: December 31
Type: Private

Hark! If you trip in the Ozarks, rest assured that Baxter Regional Medical Center (BRMC) will be there to help. The not-for-profit acute care hospital provides services to residents of north central Arkansas and south central Missouri and has about 270 all-private rooms. BRMC provides general and advanced medical-surgical care in more than 30 medical specialties, including cardiology, oncology, orthopedics, women's health, and physical rehabilitation. BRMC also runs several primary care and specialty clinics and a home health and hospice agency. The hospital started in 1963 with about 40 beds and four doctors.

	Annual Growth	12/18	12/19	12/20	12/21	12/22
Sales ($mil.)	8.9%	–	–	–	280.5	305.4
Net income ($ mil.)	44.6%	–	–	–	8.1	11.7
Market value ($ mil.)	–	–	–	–	–	–
Employees	–	–	–	–	–	1,358

BAXTER INTERNATIONAL INC NYS: BAX

One Baxter Parkway
Deerfield, IL 60015
Phone: 224 948-2000
Fax: 847 948-2964
Web: www.baxter.com

CEO: Jose E Almeida
CFO: Brian C Stevens
HR: Jeanne K Mason
FYE: December 31
Type: Public

Baxter International Inc., through its subsidiaries, provides a broad portfolio of essential healthcare products, including acute and chronic dialysis therapies; sterile intravenous (IV) solutions; infusion systems and devices; parenteral nutrition therapies; inhaled anesthetics; generic injectable pharmaceuticals; and surgical hemostat and sealant products. Baxter manufactures its products in over 20 countries and sold them in more than 100 countries. The company generates around 50% of its revenue from the US. Drs. Ralph Falk and Don Baxter launched the Don Baxter Intravenous Products Corporation, the first commercial manufacturer of prepared IV solutions in 1931.

	Annual Growth	12/19	12/20	12/21	12/22	12/23
Sales ($mil.)	6.9%	11,362	11,673	12,784	15,113	14,813
Net income ($ mil.)	27.6%	1,001.0	1,102.0	1,284.0	(2,433.0)	2,656.0
Market value ($ mil.)	(17.5%)	42,448	40,732	43,575	25,874	19,625
Employees	4.7%	50,000	50,000	60,000	60,000	60,000

BAY CITIES PAVING & GRADING, INC.

1450 CIVIC CT BLDG B
CONCORD, CA 945207950
Phone: 925 687-6666
Fax: –
Web: www.baycities.us

CEO: Ben L Rodriguez
CFO: –
HR: –
FYE: September 30
Type: Private

Up among the tall trees or down by the bay, Bay Cities Paving & Grading is on the job. The company provides highway and street construction services for private and public projects, primarily in Northern California. Bay Cities Paving also performs road improvements, renovations, and extensions on existing roads. The company has provided work for such clients as the cities of Elk Grove, Brentwood, and Pleasant Hill and the school district of West Contra Costa. Bay Cities Paving & Grading is one of the largest Hispanic-owned firms in the US.

	Annual Growth	09/05	09/06	09/07	09/08	09/09
Sales ($mil.)	17.3%	–	73.9	100.3	96.2	119.1
Net income ($ mil.)	48.2%	–	1.5	7.7	9.4	4.9
Market value ($ mil.)	–	–	–	–	–	–
Employees	–	–	–	–	–	250

BAY COUNTY HEALTH SYSTEM, LLC

615 N BONITA AVE
PANAMA CITY, FL 324013623
Phone: 850 769-1511
Fax: –
Web: bay.floridahealth.gov

CEO: Steve Grubbs
CFO: Chris Brooks
HR: –
FYE: December 31
Type: Private

Bay Medical Center is a 320-bed regional hospital located in the Florida panhandle. the center provides general medical and surgical services. The hospital's specialized services and programs include an open-heart surgery program, a cancer center, women's and children's health, and emergency care. It also operates centers for sleep disorder and childhood communication disorders. Bay Medical Center has a staff of more than 300 physicians. The hospital also operates outpatient facilities for primary care and diagnostics. Bay Medical Center is operated by a joint venture between Sacred Heart Health System and LHP Hospital Group.

BAYCARE HEALTH SYSTEM, INC.

2985 DREW ST
CLEARWATER, FL 337593012
Phone: 727 820-8200
Fax: –
Web: www.baycare.org

CEO: –
CFO: –
HR: –
FYE: December 31
Type: Private

BayCare Health System is the leading, not-for-profit healthcare system that connects individuals and families to a wide range of services at hundreds of locations in the Tampa Bay and West Central Florida regions. The health system offer a variety of specialty services ranging from orthopedics to cancer care to women's services. Established in 1997, the health system operates around 15 hospitals, nearly 40 outpatient imaging facilities, and about 20 urgent care centers.

	Annual Growth	12/13	12/14	12/19	12/21	12/22
Sales ($mil.)	7.2%	–	464.0	818.6	1,143.3	810.0
Net income ($ mil.)	(2.0%)	–	163.6	228.4	493.5	138.8
Market value ($ mil.)	–	–	–	–	–	–
Employees	–	–	–	–	–	27,739

BAYLOR SCOTT & WHITE HEALTH

301 N WASHINGTON AVE
DALLAS, TX 752461754
Phone: 214 820-3151
Fax: –
Web: www.bswhealth.com

CEO: Jim Hinton
CFO: Penny Cermak
HR: –
FYE: June 30
Type: Private

As the largest not-for-profit health system in the state of Texas, Baylor Scott & White was born from the 2013 combination of Baylor Health Care System and Scott & White Healthcare. It is committed to making quality care more accessible, convenient and affordable through its integrated delivery network, which includes the Baylor Scott & White Health Plan, Baylor Scott & White Research Institute, the Baylor Scott & White Quality Alliance and its leading digital health platform ? MyBSWHealth. Through some 50 hospitals and more than 1,100 access points, including flagship academic medical centers in Dallas, Fort Worth and Temple, the system offers the full continuum of care, from primary to award-winning specialty care. Founded as a Christian ministry of healing more than a century ago, Baylor Scott & White serves more than three million Texans.

	Annual Growth	06/17	06/18	06/19	06/20	06/21
Sales ($mil.)	245.1%	–	–	982.5	416.3	11,704
Net income ($ mil.)	–	–	–	(17.2)	51.9	1,814.0
Market value ($ mil.)	–	–	–	–	–	–
Employees	–	–	–	–	–	49,000

BAYLOR UNIVERSITY

700 S UNIVERSITY PARKS DR STE 670
WACO, TX 767061003
Phone: 254 710-1561
Fax: –
Web: www.baylor.edu

CEO: Robert Sloan PHD
CFO: –
HR: –
FYE: May 31
Type: Private

Don't mess with Texas, and don't mess around at Baylor University. The world's largest Baptist institution of higher learning requires its more than 15,000 students to follow a strict code of conduct. The university has approximately 150 undergraduate degree programs, as well as about 75 masters and more than 30 doctoral programs. With a student-to-faculty ratio of 15:1, the private, co-educational university also offers degrees from its law school (juris doctor) and theological seminary (master of divinity and doctor of ministry), as well as extensive research programs. Founded in 1845, the college is affiliated with the Baptist General Convention of Texas.

	Annual Growth	05/18	05/19	05/20	05/21	05/22
Sales ($mil.)	9.2%	–	710.3	791.7	920.5	925.1
Net income ($ mil.)	142.2%	–	19.8	142.4	524.1	281.6
Market value ($ mil.)	–	–	–	–	–	–
Employees	–	–	–	–	–	2,500

BAYLOR UNIVERSITY MEDICAL CENTER

2001 BRYAN ST STE 2200
DALLAS, TX 752013024
Phone: 214 820-3151
Fax: –
Web: www.bswhealth.com

CEO: –
CFO: –
HR: –
FYE: June 30
Type: Private

Baylor University Medical Center at Dallas is the flagship institution of the Baylor Health Care System. The medical center (known as Baylor Dallas) serves more than 300,000 patients annually with more than 1,000 inpatient beds and some 1,200 physicians. It offers general medical and surgical services to specialty care in a wide range of fields, including oncology, cardiovascular disease, and neuroscience. The hospital also features a Level I trauma center, neonatal ICU, and organ transplantation center. Founded in 1903, the Baylor Dallas campus includes the Charles A. Sammons Cancer Center and the Baylor Research Institute, which conducts basic and clinical research across numerous medical specialties.

	Annual Growth	06/08	06/09	06/15	06/21	06/22
Sales ($mil.)	4.1%	–	1,072.7	1,394.6	1,552.6	1,805.5
Net income ($ mil.)	–	–	–	379.0	434.1	536.5
Market value ($ mil.)	–	–	–	–	–	–
Employees	–	–	–	–	–	5,003

BAYOU CITY EXPLORATION, INC.

923 COLLEGE ST STE 200
BOWLING GREEN, KY 421012120
Phone: 270 282-8544
Fax: –
Web: www.bycex.net

CEO: Stephen C Larkin
CFO: Stephen C Larkin
HR: –
FYE: December 31
Type: Private

An affiliate of the Blue Ridge Group, Bayou City Exploration is engaged in oil and gas exploration primarily in Texas and Louisiana. It conducts its activities through partnerships and the acquisition of direct stakes in oil and gas properties, and in exploratory and development wells. In 2008 the company reported proved reserves of about 1.1 billion cu. ft. of natural gas equivalent. The Blue Ridge Group owns 14% of Bayou City Exploration. Shifting its exploration focus from Appalachia to the Gulf Coast, in 2005 Blue Ridge Energy, the exploration and production unit of Blue Ridge Group, renamed itself Bayou City Exploration. To raise cash, in 2010 the company sold its stakes in two wells in Texas.

BAYSIDE FUEL OIL DEPOT CORP

1776 SHORE PKWY
BROOKLYN, NY 112146546
Phone: 718 372-9800
Fax: –
Web: www.baysidedepot.com

CEO: –
CFO: –
HR: –
FYE: December 31
Type: Private

A tree isn't the only thing that has grown in Brooklyn. So has Bayside Fuel Oil Depot, which provides heating oil to customers in New York through its own four Brooklyn terminals, and from two other locations, the 149th Street terminal in the Bronx and the Western Nassau terminal in Nassau County. The company was founded in 1937 as a retail distributor of heating oil, by Sergio Allegretti, In 1965 Bayside Fuel became a wholesale oil terminal operator. It sold its retail business in 2001. Vincent Allegretti, the grandson of the company's founder, runs the business.

	Annual Growth	12/02	12/03	12/04	12/05	12/12
Sales ($mil.)	7.4%	–	146.0	152.8	195.5	276.5
Net income ($ mil.)	–	–	0.7	1.1	1.2	(3.3)
Market value ($ mil.)	–	–	–	–	–	–
Employees	–	–	–	–	–	36

BAYSTATE HEALTH INC.

759 CHESTNUT ST
SPRINGFIELD, MA 011991001
Phone: 413 794-0000
Fax: –
Web: www.baystatehealth.org

CEO: Mark A Keroack
CFO: Dennis W Chalke
HR: Shelly Phillips
FYE: September 30
Type: Private

Baystate Medical Center, the flagship facility of the not-for-profit Baystate Health System, is a 746-bed, 57- bassinet academic medical center in Springfield, Massachusetts. Baystate Medical Center Emergency & Trauma Center is the busiest single-site emergency department in Massachusetts providing the most comprehensive surgical care to the most seriously injured and ill patients 24/7, and the region's only Level 1 Trauma Center serving over 105,000 adult and pediatric patients. The Baystate Medical Center campus includes Baystate Children's Hospital is the region's only pediatric IC and neonatal IC units. It is the only accredited full-service children's hospital in western Massachusetts. Other Baystate Medical Center operations include specialty programs in endocrinology, cardiac care, cancer, and neurology.

	Annual Growth	09/18	09/19	09/20	09/21	09/22
Sales ($mil.)	(26.3%)	–	28.9	40.1	30.2	11.5
Net income ($ mil.)	–	–	(0.5)	5.4	(1.9)	(10.5)
Market value ($ mil.)	–	–	–	–	–	–
Employees	–	–	–	–	–	11,000

BAYSTATE HEALTH SYSTEM HEALTH SERVICES, INC.

280 CHESTNUT ST
SPRINGFIELD, MA 011991000
Phone: 413 794-9939
Fax: –
Web: –

CEO: –
CFO: –
HR: –
FYE: September 30
Type: Private

Patients in need of medical care can dock at this bay. Not-for-profit Baystate Health is the largest health care services provider in western Massachusetts. The system operates five acute-care and specialty hospitals with a total of approximately 1,000 beds, including the flagship Baystate Medical Center, which operates a Level 1 Trauma Center and a specialized children's hospital. Baystate Health also offers ancillary medical services such as cancer care, respiratory care, infusion therapy, visiting nurse, and hospice services through its regional clinics and agencies. The system controls for-profit health plan provider Health New England, as well as clinical pathology firm Baystate Reference Laboratories.

BAYVIEW ELECTRIC COMPANY, LLC

12230 DIXIE
REDFORD, MI 482392480
Phone: 313 255-5252
Fax: –
Web: www.bayelectric.com

CEO: Robert J Davies
CFO: –
HR: –
FYE: October 31
Type: Private

Bayview Electric Company provides electrical contracting and construction services ranging from the installation of electrical, data, and communication systems to audio/visual interactive systems to plant renovations. The company serves industrial, commercial, service, and maintenance customers from two offices in the Detroit area. Projects have included Ford Field (home of the NFL's Detroit Lions), MotorCity Casino, the baggage handling system at Detroit Metropolitan Airport's North Terminal, and work for the Big Three automakers (Ford, GM, and Chrysler).

	Annual Growth	10/05	10/06	10/07	10/08	10/09
Sales ($mil.)	(30.9%)	–	–	26.6	30.4	12.7
Net income ($ mil.)	–	–	–	0.5	0.0	(0.0)
Market value ($ mil.)	–	–	–	–	–	–
Employees	–	–	–	–	–	75

BAZAARVOICE, INC.

10901 STONELAKE BLVD
AUSTIN, TX 787595749
Phone: 512 551-6000
Fax: –
Web: www.bazaarvoice.com

CEO: Keith Nealon
CFO: –
HR: –
FYE: April 30
Type: Private

Bazaarvoice brings a people-first approach to advanced technology, connecting thousands of brands and retailers to the voices of their customers. Its extensive global retail, social, and search syndication network, product-passionate community, and enterprise-level technology provide the tools brands and retailers need to create smarter shopper experiences. The company offers visual and social content and social commerce, among others. It has over 1.3 billion monthly shoppers, and more than 55 million authentic reviews. It counts over 12,000 brand and retail websites in its network. The company was founded in 2005.

BDP INTERNATIONAL, INC.

510 WALNUT ST STE 14
PHILADELPHIA, PA 191063619
Phone: 215 629-8900
Fax: –
Web: www.psabdp.com

CEO: Mike Andaloro
CFO: Katherine Harper
HR: Nina Olatoke
FYE: December 31
Type: Private

BDP International, a member of the PSA Group, is a leading provider of global, integrated supply chain, transportation and logistics solutions. It serves more than 5,000 customers and provides a range of services, including lead logistics (LLP) and fourth-party logistics (4PL) solutions; ocean, air and ground transportation; origin management, export freight forwarding; import customs clearance and regulatory compliance; trade compliance, analytics and optimization solutions; project logistics; warehousing, and supply chain visibility and predictive ETA tracking through its proprietary technology BDP Smart. In 2022, BDP International was acquired by PSA International Pte Ltd (PSA), a leading global port group and trusted partner to cargo stakeholders.

BBX CAPITAL CORPORATION

201 E LAS OLAS BLVD STE 1900
FORT LAUDERDALE, FL 333014442
Phone: 954 940-4000
Fax: –
Web: www.bbxcapital.com

CEO: Jarett S Levan
CFO: Ray S Lopez
HR: –
FYE: December 31
Type: Private

BBX Capital is a diversified holding company that invests in real estate and development projects, confectioneries, manufacturers and other businesses. Its BBX Asset Management subsidiary manages the commercial loan portfolio and real estate properties. Renin Holdings manufacturers building supplies and home improvement products. Florida Asset Resolution (FAR) provides asset liquidation services for tax certificates, loans, and real estate properties. BBX Sweet Holdings owns confectioneries including Hoffman's Chocolates, Boca Bons, S&F Good Fortunes, Williams & Bennett, Jer's, Helen Grace, and Anastasia. Formerly the owner of BankAtlantic, BBX sold the struggling bank to BB&T in 2012.

BEACHBODY CO INC (THE)   NYS: BODI

400 Continental Blvd, Suite 400
El Segundo, CA 90245
Phone: 310 883-9000
Fax: –
Web: www.spacroadone.com

CEO: Carl Daikeler
CFO: Sue Collyns
HR: –
FYE: December 31
Type: Public

Beachbody is considered a worldwide leader in health and fitness. As part of The Beachbody Company, the company offers a comprehensive approach to at-home health. It combines world-class fitness, nutrition, and support ? a proven formula that has helped millions of people completely transform their lives ? physically, mentally, and financially. Beachbody offers clinically-proven nutritionals that are developed by top scientists and fitness and nutrition experts. All fitness and nutrition programs are available through Beachbody On Demand streaming service which includes hundreds of hours of premium content along with customized nutrition guides, workout calendars and the exclusive FIXATE cooking show featuring healthy recipes from Autumn & Bobby Calabrese. The company was founded in 1998 by Carl Daikeler and Jon Congdon.

BCB BANCORP INC   NMS: BCBP

104-110 Avenue C
Bayonne, NJ 07002
Phone: 201 823-0700
Fax: –
Web: www.bcb.bank

CEO: Michael A Shriner
CFO: Jawad Chaudhry
HR: Jacqueline Cabrera
FYE: December 31
Type: Public

BCB Bancorp be the holding company for BCB Community Bank, which opened its doors in late 2000. The independent bank serves Hudson County and the surrounding area from about 15 offices in New Jersey's Bayonne, Hoboken, Jersey City, and Monroe. The bank offers traditional deposit products and services, including savings accounts, money market accounts, CDs, and IRAs. Funds from deposits are used to originate mortgages and loans, primarily commercial real estate and multi-family property loans (which together account for more than half of the bank's loan portfolio). BCB agreed to acquire IA Bancorp in a $20 million deal in 2017.

	Annual Growth	12/19	12/20	12/21	12/22	12/23
Assets ($mil.)	7.1%	2,907.5	2,821.0	2,967.5	3,546.2	3,832.4
Net income ($ mil.)	8.8%	21.0	20.9	34.2	45.6	29.5
Market value ($ mil.)	(1.7%)	233.1	187.1	260.8	304.1	217.2
Employees	(7.6%)	365	302	292	301	266

BEACON MEDICAL GROUP, INC.

615 N MICHIGAN ST
SOUTH BEND, IN 466011033
Phone: 574 647-1000
Fax: –
Web: www.beaconhealthsystem.org

CEO: Philip A Newbold
CFO: –
HR: –
FYE: December 31
Type: Private

When you're on a fishing trip in northern Indiana and feel a little green around the gills, you can rely on Memorial to help you get back in the swim. The health network provides wellness services in northern Indiana and southern Michigan. The Memorial Hospital of South Bend has some 620 acute care beds; it also operates a network of outpatient care and specialty clinics. Other divisions include Memorial Medical Group (physician practice organization), Memorial MedFlight (emergency air transportation), and Memorial Home Care (visiting nurse association). Memorial is part of regional care organization Beacon Health System, along with Elkhart General.

	Annual Growth	12/17	12/18	12/19	12/20	12/21
Assets ($mil.)	7.8%	–	93.2	90.5	102.8	116.8
Net income ($ mil.)	63.7%	–	2.7	(3.5)	3.6	11.9
Market value ($ mil.)	–	–	–	–	–	–
Employees	–	–	–	–	–	1,900

BEACON ROOFING SUPPLY INC
NMS: BECN

505 Huntmar Park Drive, Suite 300
Herndon, VA 20170
Phone: 571 323-3939
Fax: -
Web: www.becn.com

CEO: -
CFO: -
HR: -
FYE: December 31
Type: Public

Beacon Roofing Supply (BRS) is the leading publicly traded distributor of roofing materials and complementary building products in North America. Along with roofing products, BRS distributes complementary building materials such as siding, windows, and weatherproofing systems. The company operates approximately 480 branches across all 50 US states and six Canadian provinces. BRS carries more than 130,000 stock keeping units (SKUs) available for around 100,000 customers, including contractors, home builders, building owners, and other resellers. Most of BRS's business involves new construction projects as well as the repair or remodeling of residential and non-residential properties. The company generates the majority of its sales in the US.

	Annual Growth	09/20	09/21*	12/21	12/22	12/23
Sales ($mil.)	9.5%	6,943.9	6,642.0	1,754.9	8,429.7	9,119.8
Net income ($ mil.)	-	(80.9)	(45.5)	68.0	458.4	435.0
Market value ($ mil.)	41.0%	1,966.7	3,023.2	3,630.3	3,341.6	5,508.4
Employees	2.1%	7,582	6,676	-	7,478	8,063

*Fiscal year change

BEACON TECHNOLOGIES, INC

1441 DONELSON PIKE
NASHVILLE, TN 372172957
Phone: 615 301-5020
Fax: -
Web: www.beacontech.net

CEO: Karl R Montgomery
CFO: -
HR: Angela Harris
FYE: December 31
Type: Private

Beacon Technologies holds a torch for telephony in Nashville. The company designs, installs, and supports business telephone systems and related equipment, video teleconferencing systems, communications systems cabling, and video security surveillance systems. Other services include computer telephony integration, Internet and intranet services, and consulting. Serving businesses, state agencies, and schools, the company resells, integrates, and services equipment from such information technology product vendors as 3Com and Vodavi. Beacon Technologies' customers have included the Tennessee Valley Authority, the Nashville public school system, and Vanderbilt Law School.

BEALL'S, INC.

700 13TH AVE E
BRADENTON, FL 342082624
Phone: 800 683-8039
Fax: -
Web: www.beallsinc.com

CEO: Robert M Beall III
CFO: Alison Smith
HR: Cheryl Woeltjen
FYE: August 01
Type: Private

Residents of the Sun Belt have been known to leave their homes with Beall's on. The retail holding company operates through subsidiaries Beall's Department Stores, Beall's Outlet, and Burke's Outlet Stores in a dozen states. The multi-brand retailer has more than 530 department and outlet stores (about 200 are in Florida) located throughout states in the southern and western US, including Arizona, California, Georgia, Louisiana, and Texas. Products range from off-price clothing and footwear for men and women to cosmetics, gifts, and housewares. Each chain has its own online shopping destination. The family-owned company was founded in 1915 by the grandfather of chairman Robert Beall (pronounced "bell").

	Annual Growth	07/09	07/10	07/11	07/12*	08/15
Sales ($mil.)	3.2%	-	-	1,166.8	1,232.2	1,321.9
Net income ($ mil.)	12.8%	-	-	15.5	14.2	25.0
Market value ($ mil.)	-	-	-	-	-	-
Employees	-	-	-	-	-	10,179

*Fiscal year change

BEARING DISTRIBUTORS, INC.

8000 HUB PKWY
CLEVELAND, OH 441255788
Phone: 216 642-9100
Fax: -
Web: www.bdtroy.com

CEO: -
CFO: Dan Maisonville
HR: -
FYE: December 31
Type: Private

Bearing Distributors, Inc. (BDI) began as a regional Midwestern distributor of replacement parts to OEMs. Among the world's largest industrial suppliers today, the company also provides maintenance and repair services, as well as training and inventory management. Its offerings include bearings, electrical power products, material handling systems, and motion control products, hydraulic and pneumatic systems, and fluid power components. BDI serves customers in automotive to power generation industries, and from mining to food and beverage, paper processing, and package handling operations. Founded in 1935, the company, a unit of Forge Industries, has locations dotting North America, Europe, and Asia.

BEASLEY BROADCAST GROUP INC
NMS: BBGI

3033 Riviera Drive, Suite 200
Naples, FL 34103
Phone: 239 263-5000
Fax: 239 263-8191
Web: www.bbgi.com

CEO: Caroline Beasley
CFO: Marie Tedesco
HR: -
FYE: December 31
Type: Public

Beasley Broadcast Group is a leading radio broadcaster with some 52 stations operating in about a dozen large and mid-sized markets in seven states, primarily Florida, Georgia, and North Carolina. The company's stations (serving 7.7 million listeners per week) broadcast a variety of formats, including news, sports, and talk radio, as well as Top 40, Urban, Oldies and other music formats. Most of its stations operate as part of a cluster within a specific market, allowing the company to combine certain business functions between those stations and achieve greater operating efficiencies. Beasley Broadcast Group was founded by George Beasley in 1961.

	Annual Growth	12/19	12/20	12/21	12/22	12/23
Sales ($mil.)	(1.4%)	261.6	206.1	241.4	256.4	247.1
Net income ($ mil.)	-	13.5	(17.8)	(1.4)	(42.1)	(75.1)
Market value ($ mil.)	(27.0%)	93.7	45.2	57.6	27.9	26.6
Employees		1,438	1,135	1,160	1,093	

BEAUFORT MEMORIAL HOSPITAL

955 RIBAUT RD
BEAUFORT, SC 299025454
Phone: 843 522-5200
Fax: -
Web: www.bmhsc.org

CEO: -
CFO: Jeff White
HR: -
FYE: September 30
Type: Private

Beaufort Memorial Hospital provides medical, surgical, and therapeutic services in southern South Carolina. As the largest hospital between Savannah, Georgia, and Charleston, South Carolina, the not-for-profit community hospital is a regional referral center providing inpatient acute care and outpatient services. The about 200-bed facility offers specialties in areas including cancer treatment, cardiology, emergency medicine, mental health, rehabilitation, and obstetrics/gynecology. With Beaufort Memorial Hospital's Keyserling Cancer Center, clients have access to medical oncology, radiation oncology, cancer surgeries, and lab, imaging, infusion and breast health services. It also partners with the Medical University of South Carolina. The system also offers education and support services, oncology-certified nurses, dietitians, and social workers. The medical center opened its doors in 1944.

	Annual Growth	09/16	09/17	09/18	09/20	09/21
Sales ($mil.)	6.0%	-	207.1	222.3	235.3	261.2
Net income ($ mil.)	-	-	(10.1)	7.6	5.1	12.9
Market value ($ mil.)	-	-	-	-	-	-
Employees	-	-	-	-	-	1,300

BEAUMONT HEALTH

3601 W 13 MILE RD
ROYAL OAK, MI 480736712
Phone: 248 898-5000
Fax: –
Web: www.beaumont.org

CEO: –
CFO: John Keuten
HR: Marybeth Zook
FYE: December 31
Type: Private

Beaumont Health is an eight-hospital regional health system in southeastern Michigan. The health system boasts about 3,400 hospital beds, 150 outpatient sites, and 5,000 affiliated physicians. Outpatient facilities include community medical centers, nursing homes, a home health agency, a research institute, and primary and specialty care clinics, as well as rehabilitation, cardiology, and cancer centers. Beaumont is the exclusive clinical teaching site for the Oakland University William Beaumont School of Medicine; it also has affiliations with Michigan State University College of Osteopathic Medicine and Wayne State University School of Medicine. In 2019 it agreed to acquire Ohio hospital operator Summa Health.

	Annual Growth	12/17	12/18	12/19	12/20	12/21
Sales ($mil.)	0.3%	–	4,659.9	4,703.3	4,580.8	4,695.7
Net income ($ mil.)	52.1%	–	142.1	401.1	318.4	500.1
Market value ($ mil.)	–	–	–	–	–	–
Employees	–	–	–	–	–	35,000

BEAUMONT PRODUCTS INCORPORATED

1560 BIG SHANTY DR NW
KENNESAW, GA 301447040
Phone: 800 451-7096
Fax: –
Web: www.beaumontproducts.com

CEO: Henry M Picken Jr
CFO: –
HR: Karen Picken
FYE: December 31
Type: Private

Orange you glad you know Beaumont Products? The company is a manufacturer and distributor of 100% natural, citrus-based air fresheners, disinfectants, natural household cleaners, fruit and vegetable washes, personal care items, and pet care products. Its brand names include Citrus Magic, Citrus II, Veggie Wash, Clearly Natural, and Natural Causes. The company's products are sold through retailers nationwide, including Albertson's, King Sooper, Target, and Whole Foods. Beaumont Products acquired Clearly Natural Products in early 2006 to expand its personal care products niche.

BEAVER DAM COMMUNITY HOSPITALS, INC.

707 S UNIVERSITY AVE
BEAVER DAM, WI 539163027
Phone: 920 887-7181
Fax: –
Web: www.bdch.com

CEO: Kim Miller
CFO: Donna Hutchinson
HR: –
FYE: December 31
Type: Private

Beaver Dam Community Hospitals (BDCH) provides medical services for the residents of south central Wisconsin. The non-profit medical center includes the 60-bed Beaver Dam Community Hospital as well as its Hillside Manor skilled nursing facility. Other facilities include an assisted living retirement center, community-based residential facilities, home health care services, and a wellness center. BDCH also operates FastCare clinics in two towns and a dialysis center. BDCH has invested in an electronic medical records system and upgrades to its dialysis services.

	Annual Growth	06/18	06/19	06/20*	12/21	12/22
Sales ($mil.)	(5.5%)	–	115.2	109.3	106.9	97.3
Net income ($ mil.)	–	–	3.3	(2.5)	0.2	(29.8)
Market value ($ mil.)	–	–	–	–	–	–
Employees	–	–	–	–	–	900

*Fiscal year change

BEAVER STREET FISHERIES, INC.

1741 W BEAVER ST
JACKSONVILLE, FL 322097570
Phone: 904 354-8533
Fax: –
Web: www.beaverstreetfisheries.com

CEO: Hans Frisch
CFO: –
HR: Andrea Favarelli
FYE: May 28
Type: Private

After more than 60 years of fishing, Beaver Street Fisheries can tell a tale or two of the one that got away. It's a top supplier of fish and other seafood products to wholesalers, retailers, and food service operators. Sourcing its products from more than 50 countries, family-owned Beaver Street Fisheries offers one of the largest selections of seafood in the US. It boasts a variety of fresh and frozen seafood -- including octopus, shrimp, and turtle -- sold under its flagship Sea Best brand, as well as the HF's and Island Queen names. Beaver Street Fisheries also imports lamb from New Zealand and sells Silver Fern-brand pork and beef via its Florida-New Zealand Lamb & Meat unit.

	Annual Growth	05/07	05/08	05/09	05/10	05/11
Sales ($mil.)	(1.9%)	–	–	468.2	442.9	450.7
Net income ($ mil.)	(11.8%)	–	–	17.2	19.6	13.4
Market value ($ mil.)	–	–	–	–	–	–
Employees	–	–	–	–	–	350

BEAZER HOMES USA, INC.

2002 Summit Boulevard NE, 15th Floor
Atlanta, GA 30319
Phone: 770 829-3700
Fax: –
Web: www.beazer.com

NYS: BZH

CEO: Allan P Merrill
CFO: David I Goldberg
HR: –
FYE: September 30
Type: Public

Beazer Homes USA is a geographically diversified homebuilder which, its homes are designed to appeal to homeowners at different price points across various demographic segments and are generally offered for sale in advance of their construction. Building homes with an average price of about $484,100, the company courts the entry-level, move-up, and active adult markets. Beazer Homes focuses on high-growth regions in over a dozen states across the East, Southeast, and West; it tends to close around 4,755 homes each year. Like most large homebuilders, Beazer relies on subcontractors to build its homes.

	Annual Growth	09/19	09/20	09/21	09/22	09/23
Sales ($mil.)	1.4%	2,087.7	2,127.1	2,140.3	2,317.0	2,206.8
Net income ($ mil.)	–	(79.5)	52.2	122.0	220.7	158.6
Market value ($ mil.)	13.7%	467.1	413.8	540.8	303.2	781.0
Employees	(3.0%)	1,205	1,063	1,052	1,129	1,067

BEBE STORES INC

552 Wisconsin Street
San Francisco, CA 94107
Phone: 415 251-3355
Fax: –
Web: www.bebe.com

NBB: BEBE

CEO: Manny Mashouf
CFO: Walter Parks
HR: –
FYE: July 1
Type: Public

Retailer bebe stores offered apparel in two main sizes: slim and none. bebe (pronounced "beebee") designed and sold contemporary women's career, evening, and casual clothing and accessories under the bebe banner through more than 180 stores in the US, Canada, and Puerto Rico, abroad through licensees, and online. The company targeted hip, "body-conscious" (some say skinny) 21- to 34-year-olds. bebe also licensed its name for items such as eyewear and swimwear. The majority of bebe's products were designed in-house and produced by contract manufacturers. Owner and former chairman and CEO Manny Mashouf founded bebe in 1976. In 2017, after an extended period of revenue and cash flow decline, the company closed all of its stores and ceased its retail operations.

	Annual Growth	07/19	07/20	07/21	07/22	07/23
Sales ($mil.)	–	–	–	30.9	54.1	56.9
Net income ($ mil.)	–	7.0	7.3	6.9	21.5	(0.6)
Market value ($ mil.)	(16.1%)	70.0	46.3	68.9	77.6	34.8
Employees	–	–	–	231	332	312

BECHTEL GROUP, INC.

12011 SUNSET HILLS RD STE 110
RESTON, VA 201905918
Phone: 734 205-9093
Fax: –
Web: www.bechtel.com

CEO: –
CFO: –
HR: –
FYE: December 31
Type: Private

Global engineering, construction, and project management firm Bechtel Group serves sectors including oil, gas and chemical, infrastructure, metals, nuclear, environmental, mining, and security. The company conducts all project activities?from initial planning and investment to start-up and operations. Operating out of offices in some 35 countries, Bechtel has completed more than 25,000 projects in roughly 160 countries on all seven continents. Founded in 1898, the contractor may be best known for building the Hoover Dam and its containment work at the Chernobyl nuclear plant.

BECK SUPPLIERS, INC.

1000 N FRONT ST
FREMONT, OH 434201921
Phone: 800 232-5645
Fax: –
Web: www.becksuppliers.com

CEO: Daryl Becker
CFO: Loren Owens
HR: –
FYE: December 31
Type: Private

More than willing to be at the beck and call of its customers, Beck Suppliers provides its clients in Ohio with fuel oil, diesel, gasoline, kerosene, and propane. The company annually delivers more than 170 million gallons of fuel at Sunoco, Marathon, and other gas stations in northwestern Ohio. Beck Suppliers also operates 20 Friendship Food Stores. The company's truck fleet delivers diesel, fuel oil, gasoline, kerosene, and propane for farm, construction, and industrial purposes, as well as home heating oil and propane for residential use. Beck Suppliers also operates car washes and has a construction division that builds convenience stores, gas stations, and car washes.

	Annual Growth	12/05	12/06	12/07	12/08	12/09
Sales ($mil.)	(7.3%)	–	–	293.3	316.6	252.3
Net income ($ mil.)	14.6%	–	–	1.0	0.8	1.4
Market value ($ mil.)	–	–	–	–	–	–
Employees	–	–	–	–	–	250

BECTON, DICKINSON & CO

NYS: BDX

1 Becton Drive
Franklin Lakes, NJ 07417-1880
Phone: 201 847-6800
Fax: –
Web: www.bd.com

CEO: Thomas E Polen
CFO: Christopher J Delorefice
HR: –
FYE: September 30
Type: Public

Becton, Dickinson and Company (BD) is a global medical technology company that develops, manufactures, and sells a broad range of medical supplies, devices, laboratory equipment and diagnostic products. These products are used and offered to healthcare institutions, physicians, life science researchers, clinical laboratories, the pharmaceutical industry and the general public. The company provides innovative solutions that help advance medical research and genomics, enhance the diagnosis of infectious disease and cancer, improve medication management, promote infection prevention, equip surgical and interventional procedures and support the management of diabetes. The company's domestic operations accounts for about 55% of the total revenue.

	Annual Growth	09/19	09/20	09/21	09/22	09/23
Sales ($mil.)	2.9%	17,290	17,117	20,248	18,870	19,372
Net income ($ mil.)	4.7%	1,233.0	874.0	2,092.0	1,779.0	1,484.0
Market value ($ mil.)	0.5%	73,458	67,568	71,384	64,708	75,075
Employees	1.0%	70,093	72,000	75,000	77,000	73,000

BED, BATH & BEYOND, INC.

NBB: BBBY Q

650 Liberty Avenue
Union, NJ 07083
Phone: 908 688-0888
Fax: 908 810-8813
Web: www.bedbathandbeyond.com

CEO: Sue E Gove
CFO: Holly Etlin
HR: Alyssa Addimando
FYE: February 25
Type: Public

Bed Bath & Beyond sells a wide assortment of merchandise in the Home, Baby, and Beauty & Wellness markets and operates under the names Bed Bath & Beyond (BBB), buybuy BABY (BABY), and Harmon, Harmon Face Values or Face Values. It also operates Decorist, an online interior design platform that provides personalized home design services. The company also operates about 955 retail stores, consisting of around 770 BBB stores in all 50 states, the District of Columbia, Puerto Rico and Canada, some 130 BABY stores in more than 35 states and Canada and over 50 Harmon stores in six states.

	Annual Growth	03/19*	02/20	02/21	02/22	02/23
Sales ($mil.)	(18.4%)	12,029	11,159	9,233.0	7,867.8	5,344.7
Net income ($ mil.)	–	(137.2)	(613.8)	(150.8)	(559.6)	(3,498.8)
Market value ($ mil.)	(45.0%)	4,323.3	2,800.1	6,957.6	4,188.6	396.3
Employees	(24.6%)	62,000	55,000	37,600	32,000	20,000

*Fiscal year change

BEEBE MEDICAL CENTER, INC.

424 SAVANNAH RD
LEWES, DE 199581462
Phone: 302 645-3300
Fax: –
Web: www.beebehealthcare.org

CEO: David Tam
CFO: –
HR: –
FYE: June 30
Type: Private

Sea shells on the sea shore can be found near Beebe Medical Center. The health care provider offers emergency, inpatient, long-term care, women's health, and other medical services to residents of Sussex County, Delaware. The hospital is located in the town of Lewes, near Rehoboth Beach. It has approximately 210 beds and offers specialized services including cardiology, orthopedic, rehabilitation, and oncology treatments. Beebe Medical Center offers outpatient services including wound care, diabetes management, surgery, radiology, and sleep disorder diagnosis. It also operates senior care centers, home health agencies, medical laboratories, and a nursing school.

	Annual Growth	06/18	06/19	06/20	06/21	06/22
Sales ($mil.)	9.1%	–	447.8	450.8	500.4	582.0
Net income ($ mil.)	27.7%	–	21.2	(8.2)	65.7	44.2
Market value ($ mil.)	–	–	–	–	–	–
Employees	–	–	–	–	–	1,606

BEL FUSE INC

NMS: BELF B

300 Executive Drive, Suite 300
West Orange, NJ 07052
Phone: 201 432-0463
Fax: –
Web: www.belfuse.com

CEO: Daniel Bernstein
CFO: Farouq Tuweiq
HR: –
FYE: December 31
Type: Public

Bel Fuse Inc. designs, manufactures, and markets a broad array of products that power, protect and connect electronic circuits. These products are primarily used in the networking, telecommunications, computing, general industrial, high-speed data transmission, military, commercial aerospace, transportation, and eMobility industries. Its magnetic products include discrete components, power transformers, and MagJack connector modules. It also offers power conversion modules for a variety of applications. Bel Fuse's circuit protection products include board-level fuses (miniature, micro, and surface-mounted), and Polymeric PTC (Positive Temperature Coefficient) devices, designed for the global electronic and telecommunication markets. The company also makes passive jacks, plugs, and cable assemblies. Majority of the company's sales were generated from North America.

	Annual Growth	12/19	12/20	12/21	12/22	12/23
Sales ($mil.)	6.8%	492.4	465.8	543.5	654.2	639.8
Net income ($ mil.)	–	(8.7)	12.8	24.8	52.7	73.8
Market value ($ mil.)	34.3%	261.6	191.8	165.0	420.1	852.1
Employees	(6.7%)	6,935	6,400	6,300	7,000	5,260

BELCAN GOVERNMENT SOLUTIONS, INC.

8300 GREENSBORO DR STE 600
MC LEAN, VA 221023605
Phone: 571 267-2937
Fax: -
Web: www.belcan.com

CEO: -
CFO: -
HR: -
FYE: December 31
Type: Private

Telesis provides a variety of information technology services, including systems integration, document control and records management, analysis and testing, and network design. The company also offers network security monitoring, technical support services, and custom software development. Telesis caters primarily to IT service needs of the defense, government, and the health care sectors in the eastern US. The company's customers have included the Food and Drug Administration, the Federal Aviation Administration, the Department of Agriculture, Lockheed Martin, and the US Army. Telesis was founded in 1998.

	Annual Growth	12/13	12/14	12/15	12/16	12/17
Sales ($mil.)	33.6%	-	-	29.8	37.1	53.3
Net income ($ mil.)	101.4%	-	-	1.7	3.2	6.8
Market value ($ mil.)	-	-	-	-	-	-
Employees	-	-	-	-	-	550

BELCAN, LLC

10151 CARVER RD STE 105
BLUE ASH, OH 452424760
Phone: 513 891-0972
Fax: -
Web: www.belcan.com

CEO: Lance H Kwasniewski
CFO: Beth Ferris
HR: -
FYE: December 31
Type: Private

Belcan is a global supplier of design, software, manufacturing, supply chain, information technology, and digital engineering solutions to the aerospace, defense, space, government services, automotive, and industrial markets. The company has more than 10,000 professionals serving approximately 900 active customers worldwide. Belcan engineers better outcomes for customers ? from jet engines, airframe, and avionics to heavy vehicles, automobiles, and cybersecurity. Family-owned Belcan, founded in 1958 by Ralph Anderson, operates some 60 offices primarily in the US.

BELDEN & BLAKE CORPORATION

1001 FANNIN ST STE 800
HOUSTON, TX 770026707
Phone: 713 659-3500
Fax: -
Web: -

CEO: Mark A Houser
CFO: James M Vanderhider
HR: -
FYE: December 31
Type: Private

It may sound like a law firm, but Belden & Blake is in fact an energy company that obeys the laws of supply and demand in the oil and gas market. It acquires properties, explores for and develops oil and gas reserves, and gathers and markets natural gas in the Appalachian and Michigan basins. In 2010 Belden & Blake reported interests in 1,216 gross wells and leases on more than 1.1 million gross acres, and it owned and operated 1,600 miles of gas gathering lines. That year the company reported estimated proved reserves of 202.4 billion cu. ft. of gas equivalent. Belden & Blake is controlled by Capital C Energy Operations, itself controlled by EnerVest Ltd.

	Annual Growth	12/06	12/07	12/08	12/09	12/10
Sales ($mil.)	(80.8%)	-	-	1,792.0	-	66.4
Net income ($ mil.)	26118.9%	-	-	0.0	-	40.1
Market value ($ mil.)	-	-	-	-	-	-
Employees	-	-	-	-	-	6

BELDEN INC

NYS: BDC

1 North Brentwood Boulevard, 15th Floor
St. Louis, MO 63105
Phone: 314 854-8000
Fax: 314 854-8001
Web: www.belden.com

CEO: Ashish Chand
CFO: Jeremy Parks
HR: -
FYE: December 31
Type: Public

Belden designs and manufactures cable, connectivity, and networking products for the transmission of data, sound, and video signals. The company's segments are organized around two global businesses, Enterprise Solutions and Industrial Solutions. It also makes fiber and copper connectors and networking products such as Ethernet switches. Products are used in industrial (robotics), programmable controllers, operator interfaces, motor drivers, sensors, printers, and other devices. Customers in the US account for about 70% of Belden's sales. The company's roots going back to its founding in 1902 by Joseph Belden.

	Annual Growth	12/19	12/20	12/21	12/22	12/23
Sales ($mil.)	4.2%	2,131.3	1,862.7	2,408.1	2,606.5	2,512.1
Net income ($ mil.)	-	(377.0)	(55.2)	63.9	254.7	242.8
Market value ($ mil.)	8.9%	2,262.0	1,723.2	2,703.3	2,957.0	3,177.1
Employees	2.7%	7,200	6,400	-	8,000	8,000

BELKIN INTERNATIONAL, INC.

555 S AVIATION BLVD STE 180
EL SEGUNDO, CA 90245
Phone: 310 751-5100
Fax: -
Web: www.belkin.com

CEO: Steven Malony
CFO: Jasjit J Singh
HR: Ada Wang
FYE: September 29
Type: Private

Belkin is an accessories market leader delivering power, protection, productivity, connectivity, audio, security and home automation solutions for a broad range of consumer electronics and enterprise environments. Belkin also provides security, infrastructure, and server-room products that include Keyboard-Video-Mouse (KVM) switches, dock and hubs, cables and adapters, among others. Belkin products include award-winning lines such as the Store and Charge Go business solution, SOUNDFORM audio portfolio, BOOSTCHARGE mobile power collection, and SCREENFORCE screen protection.

BELL INDUSTRIES INC (DE)

8888 Keystone Crossing, Suite 1700
Indianapolis, IN 46240
Phone: 317 704-6000
Fax: 317 575-9410
Web: www.bellind.com

CEO: Clinton J Coleman
CFO: -
HR: -
FYE: December 31
Type: Public

Bell Industries is nothing if not diverse. The holding company operates through two separate business units that specialize in technology consulting and recreational vehicle products. Its Bell Techlogix unit (formerly Technology Solutions Group) offers IT systems integration services, including network assessment and design, project management, software procurement, technical and customer support, and training throughout the US, primarily in the East and Midwest. It is one of Apple's largest service providers in North America. Bell's Recreational Products Group is a wholesale distributor of more than 50,000 aftermarket parts for motorcycles, boats, snowmobiles, and recreational vehicles.

	Annual Growth	12/05	12/06	12/07	12/08	12/09
Sales ($mil.)	(6.4%)	130.9	120.3	119.9	101.9	100.6
Net income ($ mil.)	-	(0.8)	(2.9)	(15.2)	(4.9)	(1.9)
Market value ($ mil.)	(20.4%)	0.0	0.0	0.0	0.0	0.0
Employees	(7.8%)	850	1,150	936	785	615

BELL PARTNERS INC.

300 N GREENE ST STE 1000
GREENSBORO, NC 274012173
Phone: 336 232-1900
Fax: –
Web: www.bellpartnersinc.com

CEO: Lili F Dunn
CFO: John E Tomlinson
HR: Laurie McLain
FYE: December 31
Type: Private

If someone's ringing you up about a real estate deal, it might be Bell Partners. One of the largest apartment operators in the US, the firm buys, sells, and manages multifamily residential real estate. Bell Partners' $4-billion-plus portfolio includes apartment communities with more than 63,000 individual units across 15 states. It invests on behalf of individuals and institutional investors. The firm targets markets in cities throughout the Northeast, Southeast, and Southwest. The privately-owned company also offers property management services. Bell Partners has exited the commercial and senior-living markets to focus on apartments.

BELLEHARVEST SALES, INC.

11900 FISK RD
BELDING, MI 488099413
Phone: 616 794-0320
Fax: –
Web: www.belleharvest.com

CEO: Milton Fuehrer
CFO: Tony Kramer
HR: Julia Willer
FYE: June 30
Type: Private

BelleHarvest Sales wants to be the belle of the ball in the produce market. The company sells fresh vegetables and fruits to global customers; it primarily operates in the eastern US. BelleHarvest Sales, formed by a group of Michigan growers in 1957, provides storage, packing, delivery, and marketing services. Its products include apples, peaches, plums, and asparagus. BelleHarvest Sales is the sales and marketing arm of parent Belding Fruit Storage. It is also the exclusive marketer of produce from Umlor Orchards, Roossinck Fruit Storage, Gavin Orchards, and Timpson Orchards.

	Annual Growth	06/99	06/00	06/01	06/02	06/07
Sales ($mil.)	11.6%	–	–	–	1.6	2.8
Net income ($ mil.)		–	–	–	0.2	–
Market value ($ mil.)		–	–	–	–	–
Employees		–	–	–	–	12

BELOIT COLLEGE

700 COLLEGE ST
BELOIT, WI 535115509
Phone: 608 363-2000
Fax: –
Web: www.beloit.edu

CEO: –
CFO: –
HR: –
FYE: June 30
Type: Private

Beloit College, home of the famed Beloit Poetry Journal, is a liberal arts and sciences college with an enrollment of about 1,300 students. The school offers more than 50 majors in nearly 30 departments and has some 100 full-time faculty members. Academic fields include anthropology, health and society, and philosophy. Beloit College also offers pre-professional programs in medicine, law, engineering, and environmental management. The town of Beloit (population 36,500) is home to a Frito-Lay cheese powder plant and incoming freshman are warned about the "cheese breeze" prevalent in winter months.

	Annual Growth	06/16	06/17	06/18	06/20	06/22
Sales ($mil.)	11.7%	–	49.4	47.3	–	86.2
Net income ($ mil.)	(33.4%)	–	16.6	10.2	–	2.2
Market value ($ mil.)		–	–	–	–	–
Employees		–	–	–	–	450

BELOIT HEALTH SYSTEM, INC.

1969 W HART RD
BELOIT, WI 535112298
Phone: 608 364-5011
Fax: –
Web: www.beloithealthsystem.org

CEO: –
CFO: –
HR: –
FYE: December 31
Type: Private

Beloit, Wisconsin: Home of the world's largest can of chili, the Beloit Snappers, and... Beloit Health System. Its Beloit Memorial Hospital acute care facility provides medical care to the city's residents and surrounding areas. Specialty services include emergency medicine, cardiology, home care, and occupational health. Its NorthPointe integrative medicine campus provides traditional and alternative medical approaches including massage, Tai Chi, and yoga. Beloit Health also provides primary care and specialized services through numerous outreach medical centers and operates an assisted living complex called Riverside Terrace. Beloit Health is affiliated with the University of Wisconsin Hospital and Clinics.

	Annual Growth	12/13	12/14	12/17	12/19	12/21
Sales ($mil.)	3.5%	–	211.3	247.0	262.0	269.6
Net income ($ mil.)	6.3%	–	9.3	10.6	10.7	14.2
Market value ($ mil.)		–	–	–	–	–
Employees		–	–	–	–	1,400

BEMIS MANUFACTURING COMPANY INC

300 MILL ST
SHEBOYGAN FALLS, WI 530851807
Phone: 920 467-4621
Fax: –
Web: www.bemismfg.com

CEO: Jeff Lonigro
CFO: Francisco Zarate
HR: Michael Klein
FYE: December 31
Type: Private

Bemis Manufacturing Company is a family-owned business that traces its roots back to 1901. One of the top largest manufacturers of toilet seats, the company has five divisions including Toilet Seats, Bio Bidet, Contract Group, Health Care Products, and Kelch. The company distributes its products under the Bemis, Bio Bidet by Bemis, Flow by Bemis and Mayfair by Bemis brands through retail and wholesale channels. Bemis is also one of North America's top non-automotive producers of contract plastic components serving consumer, commercial, medical and industrial markets worldwide.

BEN E. KEITH COMPANY

601 E 7TH ST
FORT WORTH, TX 761025501
Phone: 817 877-5700
Fax: –
Web: www.benekeith.com

CEO: John H Hallam
CFO: Gordon Crow
HR: Blanca Torres
FYE: December 31
Type: Private

Ben E. Keith is a leader in fine food and premium beverage distribution. Through its food division, the company offers thousands of fresh and frozen goods (including meats, seafood, produce, and dairy) as well as restaurant equipment and supplies. It distributes products under well-known national brands and its exclusive brands, including Admiral of the Fleet, Bellacibo, Ceylon Tea Gardens, Elite World Imports, Golden Harvest, Rancher's Legacy, Platinum Harvest, and more. Ben E. Keith's beverage division serves more than 60 Texas counties, and it is one of the largest Anheuser-Busch InBev distributors in the nation. Founded in 1906, Ben E. Keith began selling Anheuser-Busch beers in 1933.

BENCHMARK ELECTRONICS, INC.   NYS: BHE

56 South Rockford Drive
Tempe, AZ 85288
Phone: 623 300-7000
Fax: -
Web: www.bench.com

CEO: -
CFO: -
HR: -
FYE: December 31
Type: Public

Benchmark Electronics provides advanced manufacturing services (electronic manufacturing services (EMS) and precision technology (PT) services), which includes design and engineering services and technology solutions. Customers include manufacturers of computers and related products for business enterprises, industrial equipment, medical devices, telecommunications equipment, semi-cap equipment and equipment for the A&D industries. Around 50% of Benchmark's sales are from customers in the US, while its 10 largest customers account for 50% of sales. The company was founded in 1979.

	Annual Growth	12/19	12/20	12/21	12/22	12/23
Sales ($mil.)	5.8%	2,268.1	2,053.1	2,255.3	2,886.3	2,839.0
Net income ($ mil.)	28.7%	23.4	14.1	35.8	68.2	64.3
Market value ($ mil.)	(5.3%)	1,225.4	963.3	966.5	951.9	985.8
Employees	4.6%	10,600	11,234	10,900	11,873	12,703

BENCO DENTAL SUPPLY CO.

295 CENTERPOINT BLVD
PITTSTON, PA 186406136
Phone: 570 602-7781
Fax: -
Web: www.benco.com

CEO: -
CFO: -
HR: -
FYE: January 04
Type: Private

Benco Dental Supply is a one-stop shop for the tooth doc. Through regional showrooms and distribution centers, Benco provides dental and dentistry supplies to more than 30,000 dental professionals throughout the US. Its offerings include dental hand pieces, furniture, and disposable supplies. Its BencoNET division develops and distributes custom computers and proprietary programming and networking systems for dentists. Other services include dental office design, practice consulting, financing and real estate planning, wealth management, and equipment repairs.

	Annual Growth	12/05	12/06	12/07	12/12*	01/14
Sales ($mil.)	6.9%	-	-	389.2	600.8	620.4
Net income ($ mil.)	8.5%	-	-	5.0	7.4	8.9
Market value ($ mil.)	-	-	-	-	-	-
Employees	-	-	-	-	-	1,600

*Fiscal year change

BEND THE ARC A JEWISH PARTNERSHIP FOR JUSTICE

330 7TH AVE STE 1902
NEW YORK, NY 100015241
Phone: 212 213-2113
Fax: -
Web: www.bendthearc.us

CEO: Stosh Cotler
CFO: -
HR: Amanda Gilmore
FYE: June 30
Type: Private

The Jewish Funds for Justice (JFJ) leaves anti-defamation to the other guys and just concentrates on poverty, which it considers the greatest injustice. The not-for-profit organization has helped more than 500 grassroots groups that assist people of all religions in areas such as health care, education, employment, and housing. It supports the Jewish values of community (kehilah) and hope (tikvah) and seeks to educate Jewish people about social justice and issues related to poverty. The JFJ was formed in 2006 through a merger of The Shefa fund and the Jewish Fund for Justice. In mid-2011 JFJ merged with another group: The Progressive Jewish Alliance. The merged organization plans to expand nationally.

	Annual Growth	06/15	06/16	06/18	06/20	06/22
Sales ($mil.)	6.4%	-	4.0	5.6	6.1	5.8
Net income ($ mil.)	10.2%	-	0.2	1.9	0.6	0.4
Market value ($ mil.)	-	-	-	-	-	-
Employees	-	-	-	-	-	41

BENEDICT COLLEGE

1600 HARDEN ST
COLUMBIA, SC 292041086
Phone: 803 256-4220
Fax: -
Web: www.benedict.edu

CEO: -
CFO: Sharron T Burnett
HR: -
FYE: June 30
Type: Private

Benedict College is a private, Baptist-affiliated liberal arts college in an urban environment. It has an annual enrollment of about 3,140 students from across the US and abroad and its student-faculty ratio is 18:1. Students may choose from 29 majors offered through a dozen academic departments, including business, education, social sciences, technology, and more. Benedict College is also part of the NCAA II athletic conference. The historically black school began in 1870, when the American Baptist Home Mission Society created Benedict Institute, setting as its goal to train emancipated slaves to teach and preach. The school name was changed to Benedict College in 1894.

	Annual Growth	06/11	06/12	06/13	06/14	06/22
Sales ($mil.)	0.4%	-	69.6	62.6	56.3	72.3
Net income ($ mil.)	5.2%	-	2.6	(0.3)	(3.3)	4.3
Market value ($ mil.)	-	-	-	-	-	-
Employees	-	-	-	-	-	600

BENEDICTINE COLLEGE

1020 N 2ND ST
ATCHISON, KS 660021402
Phone: 913 367-5340
Fax: -
Web: www.benedictine.edu

CEO: -
CFO: -
HR: Charol Kelley
FYE: June 30
Type: Private

Benedictine College is a Roman Catholic liberal arts school that provides instruction to nearly 1,200 students. It offers bachelor's degrees in nearly 40 major fields, as well as three graduate degree programs. The school's Atchison, Kansas campus overlooks the Missouri River. The college, which opened its doors in 1859, is sponsored by brothers and sisters of the Benedictine monastic order.

	Annual Growth	06/15	06/16	06/17	06/20	06/21
Sales ($mil.)	(1.2%)	-	74.1	78.2	89.0	69.9
Net income ($ mil.)	34.0%	-	3.6	2.6	2.6	15.5
Market value ($ mil.)	-	-	-	-	-	-
Employees	-	-	-	-	-	184

BENEDICTINE HEALTH SYSTEM

1001 KENWOOD AVE
DULUTH, MN 558112370
Phone: 218 786-2370
Fax: -
Web: www.benedictineliving.org

CEO: Gerald Carley
CFO: Kevin Rymanowski
HR: Bonnie Kingsley
FYE: June 30
Type: Private

The Benedictine Health System (BHS) is a peaceful provider of senior care services across the Midwest. The health system mostly serves rural and smaller communities in seven states. It owns or operates about 40 long-term care facilities including nursing homes, assisted-living centers, and independent senior housing developments. Other offerings include adult day-care, transitional care, and outpatient rehabilitation. Many of its facilities are integrated campuses that provide a spectrum of services. BHS was founded in 1892 and took its present form in 1985. It is sponsored by the Benedictine Sisters of St. Scholastica Monastery.

	Annual Growth	06/15	06/16	06/17	06/18	06/22
Sales ($mil.)	(26.4%)	-	-	266.3	272.2	57.3
Net income ($ mil.)	-	-	-	3.4	6.2	(3.8)
Market value ($ mil.)	-	-	-	-	-	-
Employees	-	-	-	-	-	8,000

BENEVOLENT AND PROTECTIVE ORDER OF ELKS

2750 N LAKEVIEW AVE
CHICAGO, IL 606142256
Phone: 773 755-4700
Fax: –
Web: www.elks.org

CEO: –
CFO: –
HR: –
FYE: May 31
Type: Private

The Elks are dear to those they help. The Benevolent and Protective Order of Elks (BPOE) dispenses millions of dollars annually by way of its philanthropic works. The organization has about 1 million members and more than 2,000 lodges throughout the US. Its programs include veterans' events, athletic programs (Little League, Special Olympics), patriotic events (Flag Day, constitutional awareness raising), drug education (schools, doctor offices, hospitals), youth programs (Boy Scouts, Girl Scouts), and other community service. Founded in 1868, the BPOE began as a social drinking club of actors before deciding to put their fraternity to benevolent and protective uses.

	Annual Growth	05/09	05/10	05/11	05/19	05/22
Sales ($mil.)	1.8%	–	29.1	28.6	28.3	35.9
Net income ($ mil.)	–	–	(0.3)	(1.8)	(1.3)	2.1
Market value ($ mil.)	–	–	–	–	–	–
Employees	–	–	–	–	–	100

BENNETT COLLEGE

900 E WASHINGTON ST
GREENSBORO, NC 274013298
Phone: 336 273-4431
Fax: –
Web: www.bennett.edu

CEO: –
CFO: George Latter
HR: –
FYE: June 30
Type: Private

No boys allowed. Bennett College for Women is a women's university with annual enrollment of about 600 students, primarily of African-American descent, from the US and abroad. The school awards the bachelor of art, science, arts and sciences in interdisciplinary studies, fine arts, and social work degrees. Originally founded as a coeducational institution in 1873, Bennett College's first classes assembled in the basement of St. Matthew's Methodist Church. The Freedmen's Aid and Southern Education Society of the Methodist Episcopal Church assumed responsibility for support of the school a year later. In 1926 Bennett was reorganized, becoming a school exclusively for women.

	Annual Growth	06/13	06/14	06/16	06/17	06/20
Sales ($mil.)	(3.3%)	–	18.8	18.4	16.6	15.3
Net income ($ mil.)	–	–	(2.0)	(1.1)	(1.0)	(3.5)
Market value ($ mil.)	–	–	–	–	–	–
Employees	–	–	–	–	–	200

BENNINGTON COLLEGE CORPORATION

1 COLLEGE DR
BENNINGTON, VT 052016004
Phone: 802 442-5401
Fax: –
Web: www.bennington.edu

CEO: –
CFO: –
HR: Audry Herbig
FYE: June 30
Type: Private

Bennington College offers bachelor's and master's degrees in areas such as the humanities, social sciences, mathematics, and visual and performing arts. The liberal arts college enrolls some 725 students, about 20% of which are graduate students. It has a student-faculty ratio of 8 to 1. Tuition and fees for undergraduates is more than $41,000 per year. Bennington College was founded in 1932.

	Annual Growth	06/14	06/15	06/20	06/21	06/22
Sales ($mil.)	4.0%	–	55.6	73.7	83.2	73.1
Net income ($ mil.)	–	–	2.2	6.2	16.7	(5.1)
Market value ($ mil.)	–	–	–	–	–	–
Employees	–	–	–	–	–	265

BENT GRASS HOLDINGS, INC.

1923 BOMAR AVE
FORT WORTH, TX 761032102
Phone: 817 339-1400
Fax: –
Web: www.mmwholesale.com

CEO: –
CFO: –
HR: –
FYE: December 31
Type: Private

This M&M is sweet on pawn shops. M&M Merchandisers is a wholesale supplier of electronics, musical instruments, and accessories, primarily to pawn shops in Texas and Georgia. It has expanded to serve several other industries, including smaller music retailers, and specializes in mobile audio, video game accessories, music, surveillance, tools and hardware, sporting goods, and jewelers supplies. The company distributes monthly newsletters and a semiannual catalog featuring its product offerings. M&M got its start in 1976 as a value added distributor with 150 SKUs; today it offers some 6,000 SKUs. The business was founded by CEO Marty Stenzler and his father Mitch (hence the company name, M&M).

	Annual Growth	12/04	12/05	12/06	12/07	12/08
Sales ($mil.)	(3.6%)	–	–	23.2	20.6	21.6
Net income ($ mil.)	–	–	–	(0.2)	(0.2)	0.8
Market value ($ mil.)	–	–	–	–	–	–
Employees	–	–	–	–	–	52

BENTLEY UNIVERSITY

175 FOREST ST
WALTHAM, MA 024524713
Phone: 781 891-2000
Fax: –
Web: www.bentley.edu

CEO: –
CFO: Maureen Forrester
HR: –
FYE: June 30
Type: Private

Bentley University is not the Rolls-Royce of universities, but is fairly prestigious nevertheless. It offers undergraduate, graduate, and doctoral degree programs to its nearly 5,670 enrolled students from 82 countries. The university also offers professional development and certificate programs for executives and corporations. The focus at Bentley is on business; the school was a pioneer in integrating information technology into the business curriculum. In the belief that businesspeople need a broad education, Bentley requires a liberal arts core of classes in behavioral and social sciences, English, and other subjects in the humanities, as well as math and natural sciences.

	Annual Growth	06/14	06/15	06/20	06/21	06/22
Sales ($mil.)	2.9%	–	288.1	316.6	292.3	351.9
Net income ($ mil.)	5.7%	–	18.7	9.4	5.6	27.5
Market value ($ mil.)	–	–	–	–	–	–
Employees	–	–	–	–	–	911

BEREA COLLEGE

101 CHESTNUT ST
BEREA, KY 404031516
Phone: 859 985-3000
Fax: –
Web: www.berea.edu

CEO: –
CFO: –
HR: –
FYE: June 30
Type: Private

Berea College is a Christian school that provides a private, tuition-free, liberal arts education to about 1,600 students each year, most of whom come from Kentucky and the Appalachian region. In lieu of tuition, Berea has a work program that requires its students to work in on-campus jobs for at least 10 hours each week in their choice of some 130 different departments. Berea offers about 30 majors leading to Bachelor of Arts and Bachelor of Science degrees, and each student is required to attend seven convocations (guest lectures, concerts, or other cultural events) each term. It also offers 15 teacher education programs.

	Annual Growth	06/18	06/19	06/20	06/21	06/22
Sales ($mil.)	4.2%	–	140.0	151.0	139.8	158.3
Net income ($ mil.)	–	–	43.4	25.6	347.7	(166.3)
Market value ($ mil.)	–	–	–	–	–	–
Employees	–	–	–	–	–	550

BERGELECTRIC CORP.

3182 LIONSHEAD AVE
CARLSBAD, CA 920104701
Phone: 760 638-2374
Fax: –
Web: www.bergelectric.com

CEO: –
CFO: –
HR: –
FYE: January 31
Type: Private

One of the nation's top electrical contractors, Bergelectric provides design/build and design/assist services on projects that include office buildings, public-sector facilities, bioscience labs, entertainment complexes, hotels, data centers, and hospitals. Its projects also consist of parking garages, water treatment plants, residential towers, and correctional facilities. The company boasts expertise in building information modeling, fire alarms and security, and telecommunications and data infrastructure. Bergelectric operates mainly in the western and southeastern US from about a dozen offices.

	Annual Growth	01/13	01/14	01/20	01/21	01/22
Sales ($mil.)	3.8%	–	525.2	521.4	667.7	705.0
Net income ($ mil.)	4.9%	–	5.0	6.1	9.2	7.3
Market value ($ mil.)	–	–	–	–	–	–
Employees	–	–	–	–	–	2,600

BERGEN COMMUNITY COLLEGE

400 PARAMUS RD STE A
PARAMUS, NJ 076521508
Phone: 201 447-7100
Fax: –
Web: www.bergen.edu

CEO: –
CFO: –
HR: Patti Bonomolo
FYE: June 30
Type: Private

Bergen Community College offers academic degree programs, as well as adult and continuing education. Its students work to earn Associate in Arts, Associate in Science, and Associate in Applied Science degrees, as well as to complete certificate and continuing education programs. It has an enrollment of approximately 17,000 students at its main campus in Paramus, New Jersey, as well as at two satellite campuses. The college offers courses in more than 100 areas of study. More than half of its students are able to transfer to four-year institutions in New Jersey and nationwide. Bergen Community College was founded in 1965.

	Annual Growth	06/07	06/08	06/16	06/17	06/18
Sales ($mil.)	51.3%	–	1.1	69.6	68.1	66.8
Net income ($ mil.)	18.4%	–	0.5	1.8	(1.2)	2.7
Market value ($ mil.)	–	–	–	–	–	–
Employees	–	–	–	–	–	1,054

BERGEN PINES COUNTY HOSPITAL INC

230 E RIDGEWOOD AVE
PARAMUS, NJ 076524142
Phone: 800 730-2762
Fax: –
Web: –

CEO: –
CFO: Connie Magdangal
HR: Kim Cox
FYE: December 31
Type: Private

Bergen Regional Medical Center (BRMC) is not just the biggest hospital in Paramus, New Jersey -- it's one of the biggest in the state. BRMC provides acute care, long-term care, and behavioral health care services to the residents of northeastern New Jersey. The not-for-profit medical center, with approximately 1,190 beds, also offers specialized services including orthopedics, cardiology, neurology, emergency medicine, and surgery, as well as substance abuse treatment and hospice services. About half of the facility is devoted to long-term nursing care; and about 325 beds serve behavioral health patients.

	Annual Growth	12/06	12/07	12/08	12/15	12/21
Sales ($mil.)	(38.0%)	–	–	146.2	207.5	0.3
Net income ($ mil.)	–	–	–	(78.9)	(8.4)	(0.1)
Market value ($ mil.)	–	–	–	–	–	–
Employees	–	–	–	–	–	2,700

BERGSTROM INC.

2390 BLACKHAWK RD
ROCKFORD, IL 611093602
Phone: 815 874-7821
Fax: –
Web: www.bergstrominc.com

CEO: Dan Giovannetti
CFO: –
HR: –
FYE: December 31
Type: Private

Bergstrom is the leading designer and manufacturer of cab climate-control systems for commercial trucks and buses, off-highway machinery, and specialty vehicles. Customers include Navistar, AB Volvo's Mack, PACCAR's Peterbilt, and Kenworth Truck. It also developed a strong understanding of the unique climate control challenges in many different industries, including heavy-duty trucking, construction, agriculture, military, mining, and more. Bergstrom has regional operations that cover North America, Europe, and Asia/Pacific. The company was founded in 1949.

BERKLEE COLLEGE OF MUSIC, INC.

1140 BOYLSTON ST
BOSTON, MA 022153693
Phone: 617 266-1400
Fax: –
Web: www.berklee.edu

CEO: –
CFO: –
HR: –
FYE: May 31
Type: Private

If you get accepted to this school, you've no doubt hit a high note in your musical career. Berklee College of Music is one of the largest independent music college in the world, offers bachelor's degrees in a dozen majors including film scoring, jazz composition, music education, music production and engineering, performance, and songwriting. Located in Boston, the school has some 6,440 students and some 940 faculty members. Berklee has a student-to-faculty ratio of 12:1. Notable alumni include Branford Marsalis, Quincy Jones, Charlie Puth, Steely Dan vocalist Donald Fagen. Pianist Lawrence Berk founded the college in 1945. The school was named after his son, Lee Berk, who served as Berklee president from 1979 to 2004.

	Annual Growth	05/14	05/15	05/17	05/20	05/22
Sales ($mil.)	5.8%	–	259.6	276.0	368.6	384.6
Net income ($ mil.)	(11.3%)	–	12.6	107.9	27.1	5.4
Market value ($ mil.)	–	–	–	–	–	–
Employees	–	–	–	–	–	716

BERKLEY (WR) CORP

NYS: WRB

475 Steamboat Road
Greenwich, CT 06830
Phone: 203 629-3000
Fax: –
Web: www.wrberkley.com

CEO: W R Berkley Jr
CFO: Richard M Baio
HR: Nancy Micale
FYE: December 31
Type: Public

Holding company W. R. Berkley offers an assortment of niche commercial property/casualty insurance across two segments ? Insurance and Reinsurance and Monoline Excess. The Insurance segment, comprising about 60 operating companies, underwrites commercial insurance coverage including excess and surplus lines and admitted lines. The Reinsurance and Monoline Excess segment allows insurance companies to pool their risks in order to reduce their liability. Founded in 1967, Berkley serves customers in more than 60 countries in the Americas, Europe, and the Asia/Pacific region.

	Annual Growth	12/19	12/20	12/21	12/22	12/23
Assets ($mil.)	8.7%	26,643	28,607	32,086	33,861	37,202
Net income ($ mil.)	19.3%	681.9	530.7	1,022.5	1,381.1	1,381.4
Market value ($ mil.)	0.6%	17,727	17,040	21,137	18,617	18,143
Employees	–	7,493	7,495	7,681	8,186	–

BERKSHIRE HATHAWAY ENERGY COMPANY

666 GRAND AVE STE 500
DES MOINES, IA 503092511
Phone: 515 242-4300
Fax: –
Web: www.brkenergy.com

CEO: –
CFO: –
HR: –
FYE: December 31
Type: Private

Berkshire Hathaway Energy (BHE), a subsidiary of Berkshire Hathaway, is a global energy company with subsidiaries and affiliates that generate, transmit, store, distribute and supply energy. A major player in the US brokerage industry, BHE also manages the largest residential real estate firm in the country. BHE's energy businesses report some 29,400 MWs of collective generation capacity and approximately 27,700 miles of transmission lines. The company's locally managed businesses are organized as separate operating units. BHE's domestic regulated energy interests are comprised of four regulated utility companies serving approximately 5.2 million retail customers, five interstate natural gas pipeline companies with approximately 21,100 miles of operated pipeline having a design capacity of approximately 21 billion cubic feet of natural gas per day and ownership interests in electricity transmission businesses.

BERKSHIRE HATHAWAY INC

NYS: BRK A

3555 Farnam Street
Omaha, NE 68131
Phone: 402 346-1400
Fax: –
Web: www.berkshirehathaway.com

CEO: Warren E Buffett
CFO: Marc D Hamburg
HR: –
FYE: December 31
Type: Public

Berkshire Hathaway is the holding company where Warren Buffett, one of the world's richest men, makes his money and spreads his risk. The company invests in a variety of industries. The most important of these are insurance businesses conducted on both a primary basis and a reinsurance basis, a freight rail transportation business and a group of utility and energy generation and distribution businesses. Its core insurance subsidiaries include GEICO, National Indemnity, and reinsurance giant General Re. The company currently owns a 91.1% ownership interest in Berkshire Hathaway Energy Company (BHE), a global energy company with subsidiaries and affiliates that generate, transmit, store, distribute, and supply energy. BHE's domestic regulated utility interests include PacifiCorp, MidAmerican Energy Company (MEC), and NV Energy. In late 2022, Berkshire Hathaway acquired Alleghany Corporation for approximately $11.6 billion.

	Annual Growth	12/19	12/20	12/21	12/22	12/23
Assets ($mil.)	7.0%	817,729	873,729	958,784	948,452	1,069,978
Net income ($ mil.)	4.3%	81,417	42,521	89,795	(22,819.0)	96,223
Market value ($ mil.)	12.4%	445,246.3	456,030.432	590,876.145	614,540.678	711,451.527
Employees	0.3%	391,500	360,000	372,000	383,000	396,500

BERKSHIRE HEALTH SYSTEMS, INC.

725 NORTH ST
PITTSFIELD, MA 012014109
Phone: 413 447-2000
Fax: –
Web: www.berkshirehealthsystems.org

CEO: David E Phelps
CFO: Sean Fitzpatrick
HR: –
FYE: September 30
Type: Private

Berkshire Health Systems serves the residents of Massachusetts and surrounding regions. The system operates two acute-care hospitals: Berkshire Medical Center with 300 beds, and Fairview Hospital with 25 beds. Berkshire Medical Center is a teaching hospital affiliated with the University of Massachusetts' medical school. It also operates the Berkshire Visiting Nurse Association (home health care), a family health center (BMC Hillcrest), and several outpatient clinics and physician practices. In addition, affiliate Berkshire Healthcare runs about 20 long-term care facilities in Massachusetts, Ohio, and Pennsylvania. Not-for-profit Berkshire Health Systems was founded in 1983.

	Annual Growth	09/13	09/14	09/15	09/21	09/22
Sales ($mil.)	(16.1%)	–	–	0.0	0.0	0.0
Net income ($ mil.)	(16.1%)	–	–	0.0	0.0	0.0
Market value ($ mil.)	–	–	–	–	–	–
Employees	–	–	–	–	–	3,000

BERKSHIRE HILLS BANCORP INC

NYS: BHLB

60 State Street
Boston, MA 02109
Phone: 800 773-5601
Fax: –
Web: www.berkshirebank.com

CEO: Nitin J Mhatre
CFO: –
HR: –
FYE: December 31
Type: Public

Berkshire Hills Bancorp is the holding company for Berkshire Bank (the bank). The company offers a wide range of deposit, lending, insurance, and wealth management products to retail and commercial customers in its market areas. Berkshire Bank has $11.3 billion in assets and operates some 105 banking offices primarily in New England and New York.

	Annual Growth	12/19	12/20	12/21	12/22	12/23
Assets ($mil.)	(1.5%)	13,216	12,838	11,555	11,663	12,431
Net income ($ mil.)	(8.1%)	97.5	(533.0)	118.7	92.5	69.6
Market value ($ mil.)	(6.8%)	1,430.3	744.7	1,236.7	1,300.7	1,080.1
Employees	(3.6%)	1,550	1,505	1,319	1,310	1,340

BERKSHIRE INCOME REALTY, INC.

1 BEACON ST
BOSTON, MA 021083107
Phone: 617 523-7722
Fax: –
Web: –

CEO: Charles B Leitner III
CFO: David E Doherty
HR: –
FYE: December 31
Type: Private

If you enjoy attractive landscaping and swimming pools, but can't stand the upkeep and maintenance, Berkshire Income Realty might have just the spot for you. The real estate investment trust (REIT) invests and operates apartment communities. It owns 10 multi-family properties in major cities in Texas, Georgia, Colorado, California, Washington, Massachusetts, and Pennsylvania. The company often acquires neglected properties and then rehabilitates them. Affiliate Berkshire Property Advisors provides day-to-day management and business operations services to the company. The company went private in 2015.

BERKSHIRE PRODUCTION SUPPLY LLC

40333 W 14 MILE RD
NOVI, MI 483771609
Phone: 586 755-2200
Fax: –
Web: www.pts-tools.com

CEO: –
CFO: –
HR: –
FYE: December 31
Type: Private

Production Tool Supply totes the tools of the trade -- and it distributes them to customers worldwide. With nine showrooms in Michigan and Ohio, the company (PTS) distributes brand-name discount industrial tools and machinery. It markets approximately 235,000 products through a 1,700-page catalog, on the Internet, and through independent distributors. Products include cutting tools, carbide tools, abrasives, measuring tools, clamps and vises, power tools, tool safety products, and power machinery by blue chip OEMs, such as Bosch, Porter-Cable, and Sandvik. D. Dan Kahn founded PTS in 1951 to serve small factories and shops in the Detroit area. The Kahn family still controls the company.

	Annual Growth	10/07	10/08	10/09	10/10*	12/13
Sales ($mil.)	18.2%	–	–	117.2	129.1	228.5
Net income ($ mil.)	21.7%	–	–	10.7	15.0	23.5
Market value ($ mil.)	–	–	–	–	–	–
Employees	–	–	–	–	–	357

*Fiscal year change

BERMELLO, AJAMIL & PARTNERS, INC.

4711 S LE JEUNE RD
CORAL GABLES, FL 331461884
Phone: 305 859-2050
Fax: –
Web: www.bermelloajamil.com

CEO: –
CFO: –
HR: –
FYE: December 31
Type: Private

Bermello, Ajamil & Partners provides architectural, engineering, planning, interior design, and landscape services for commercial, public, and institutional clients around the world. It was worked on projects including high-rise residential towers, ports and other maritime structures, airport terminals, bridges, and educational facilities. The company operates globally from offices in California, Florida, and New York, as well as Dubai (where it worked on the design of resort island The World). Bermello, Ajamil & Partners was founded in 1939.

BERNATELLO'S PIZZA, INC.

200 CONGRESS ST W
MAPLE LAKE, MN 553583525
Phone: 320 963-6191
Fax: –
Web: www.bernatellos.com

CEO: William Ramsay
CFO: –
HR: –
FYE: June 30
Type: Private

This company feeds your frozen pizza amore . Bernatello's Pizza is a leading frozen-pizza maker in the US's Northeast, Midwest, and Rocky Mountain regions, marketing its pies under the Bernatello's and Roma brands. Its product line (pumping out 100,000 pizzas every day) offers a variety of different pizzas, such as pan-style, sausage and pepperoni, Mexican-style, four-cheese, half-pounder, and thin-and-crispy. The company also produces pizza-related frozen items such as garlic cheese bread, mozzarella sticks, and jalape o snappers (Bernie's Bites). In addition, Bernatello's provides manufacturing services for private-label customers. The family-owned company is controlled by food-industry veteran Bill Ramsay.

	Annual Growth	06/02	06/03	06/04	06/05	06/07
Sales ($mil.)	2.7%	–	42.4	40.2	45.7	47.1
Net income ($ mil.)	–	–	11.5	(0.7)	0.0	(0.0)
Market value ($ mil.)	–	–	–	–	–	–
Employees	–	–	–	–	–	470

BERNER FOOD & BEVERAGE, LLC

2034 E FACTORY RD
DAKOTA, IL 610189736
Phone: 815 563-4222
Fax: –
Web: www.bernerfoodandbeverage.com

CEO: Stephen A Kneubuehl
CFO: Bill Marchido
HR: –
FYE: September 30
Type: Private

Berner Food & Beverage is burning up with dairy fever. The company is a producer of natural cheese (Swiss, cheddar, American), processed cheese (shelf-stable dips, spreads, aerosols, and jars), and salsa con queso sauce, well as energy, coffee and specialty beverages. Berner contract-manufactures products for private-label customers, including supermarkets, drug stores, club, membership, and dollar stores, food distributors, and foodservice companies. It also sells products under its own Berner labels. The company was founded in 1943 by the Kneubuehl family. It is still owned and operated by the family.

	Annual Growth	12/06	12/07	12/08*	09/12	09/14
Sales ($mil.)	12.9%	–	–	65.4	74.8	135.5
Net income ($ mil.)	–	–	–	(1.3)	3.2	6.0
Market value ($ mil.)	–	–	–	–	–	–
Employees	–	–	–	–	–	300

*Fiscal year change

BERRY COMPANIES, INC.

2402 E 37TH ST N
WICHITA, KS 672193538
Phone: 316 832-0171
Fax: –
Web: www.berrycompaniesinc.com

CEO: Fred F Berry Jr
CFO: Greg Joerg
HR: –
FYE: March 31
Type: Private

Savoring the fruit of its labor, Berry Companies makes a living bulldozing big jobs. The employee-owned business runs eight divisions; each independently sells and rents new and used construction and material handling equipment. Berry Cos. specialize in graders, tractors, loaders, excavators, cranes, rollers, construction and woodworking supplies, concrete equipment, and small tools. The company's five distribution dealerships include White Star Machinery (Kansas); Bobcat of Dallas and Houston (Texas); K.C. Bobcat (Missouri); and Bobcat of the Rockies (Colorado). Berry Cos. also operates Berry Tractor and Equipment, Berry Material Handling, and Superior Broom (makes self-propelled road construction brooms).

	Annual Growth	03/05	03/06	03/07	03/08	03/09
Sales ($mil.)	–	–	–	(1,240.6)	203.6	178.6
Net income ($ mil.)	9168.5%	–	–	0.0	2.6	0.6
Market value ($ mil.)	–	–	–	–	–	–
Employees	–	–	–	–	–	556

BERRY CORP (BRY)

NMS: BRY

16000 Dallas Parkway, Suite 500
Dallas, TX 75248
Phone: 661 616-3900
Fax: –
Web: www.bry.com

CEO: Fernando Araujo
CFO: Michael Helm
HR: –
FYE: December 31
Type: Public

Berry Corporation (bry) ? formerly Berry Petroleum Corporation -- is a western United States independent upstream energy company with a focus on onshore, low geologic risk, long-lived, oil reserves in conventional reservoirs. Most of its assets are located in the oil-rich reservoirs in California which focus on conventional, shallow oil reservoirs, the drilling and completion of resource plays. The company has also assets in Utah and Colorado. In 2019, Berry had estimated total proved reserves of 138 million barrels of oil equivalent and an average production of about 30 thousand barrels of oil equivalent daily.

	Annual Growth	12/19	12/20	12/21	12/22	12/23
Sales ($mil.)	12.7%	559.4	523.8	545.0	918.3	903.5
Net income ($ mil.)	(3.7%)	43.5	(262.9)	(15.5)	250.2	37.4
Market value ($ mil.)	(7.1%)	713.5	278.5	637.1	605.3	531.9
Employees	37.9%	355	347	1,224	1,372	1,282

BERRY GLOBAL FILMS, LLC

95 CHESTNUT RIDGE RD
MONTVALE, NJ 076451801
Phone: 201 641-6600
Fax: –
Web: www.berryglobal.com

CEO: Tom Salmon
CFO: Mark W Miles
HR: Renee Porcile
FYE: October 31
Type: Private

Making plastic cling is this company's thing. AEP Industries manufactures plastic packaging films -- more than 15,000 types -- including stretch wrap for industrial pallets, packaging for foods and beverages, and films for agricultural uses, such as wrap for hay bales. AEP also makes dispenser-boxed plastic wraps, which are sold to consumers as well as institutions ranging from schools to hospitals. Other industries courted by AEP are packaging, transportation, food, autos, chemicals, textiles, and electronics. The company operates in the US and in Canada. In the summer of 2016, AEP agreed to be acquired by rival Berry Plastics Group.

	Annual Growth	10/11	10/12	10/13	10/14	10/15
Sales ($mil.)	(0.1%)	–	–	1,143.9	1,193.0	1,141.4
Net income ($ mil.)	63.8%	–	–	10.7	(5.5)	28.8
Market value ($ mil.)	–	–	–	–	–	–
Employees	–	–	–	–	–	2,600

BERRY GLOBAL GROUP INC   NYS: BERY

101 Oakley Street
Evansville, IN 47710
Phone: 812 424-2904
Fax: –
Web: www.berryplastics.com

CEO: Kevin J Kwilinski
CFO: Mark W Miles
HR: –
FYE: September 30
Type: Public

Berry Global Group is a leading maker of injection-molded plastic products. Its lineup includes drink cups, bottles, closures, tubes and prescription containers, stretch films, plastic sheeting, tapes, and housewares. Customers include a mix of leading global, national, mid-sized regional and local specialty businesses. The company has about 250 manufacturing facilities in North America, Europe, the Middle East, and Asia, as well as extensive distribution capabilities. North America is its largest market, which generates about 55% of the company's net sales.

	Annual Growth	09/19	09/20*	10/21	10/22*	09/23
Sales ($mil.)	9.3%	8,878.0	11,709	13,850	14,495	12,664
Net income ($ mil.)	10.8%	404.0	559.0	733.0	766.0	609.0
Market value ($ mil.)	12.0%	4,541.5	5,478.2	7,080.2	5,374.2	7,150.6
Employees	(2.2%)	48,000	47,000	47,000	46,000	44,000

*Fiscal year change

BERRY PETROLEUM COMPANY, LLC

11117 RIVER RUN BLVD
BAKERSFIELD, CA 933118957
Phone: 661 616-3900
Fax: –
Web: www.bry.com

CEO: Trem Smith
CFO: –
HR: Lisa Rodriguez
FYE: December 31
Type: Private

It may be a small fruit in the giant petroleum industry, but Berry Petroleum delivers the juice. The company buys properties with heavy crude and other oil reserves for exploitation and sale to refining companies. Berry Petroleum's core properties are in California (Kern, Los Angeles, and Ventura counties), Colorado, Texas, and Utah. It has proved reserves of crude oil, condensate, natural gas liquids, and natural gas. Berry Petroleum also owns three gas-fired cogeneration plants in its California fields. The former Linn Energy subsidiary emerged from Chapter 11 bankruptcy protection in 2017.

BEST BUY INC   NYS: BBY

7601 Penn Avenue South
Richfield, MN 55423
Phone: 612 291-1000
Fax: –
Web: www.investors.bestbuy.com

CEO: Corie S Barry
CFO: Matthew Bilunas
HR: –
FYE: February 3
Type: Public

Best Buy operates an omnichannel platform that sells both products and services through almost 1,140 stores in the US and Canada, under the Best Buy, Best Buy Ads, Best Buy Business, Best Buy Health, CST, Current Health, Geek Squad, Lively, Magnolia, Pacific Kitchen and Home, and Yardbird brands. Its stores sell a variety of electronic gadgets and wearables, digital imaging, health and fitness products, home theater, portable audio, tablets, movies, music, drones, computers, mobile phones, and appliances. On the services side, it offers consultation, delivery, design, health-related services, installation, memberships, repair, set-up, technical support, and warranty-related services. The US accounts for approximately 90% of the company's total revenue.

	Annual Growth	02/20*	01/21	01/22	01/23*	02/24
Sales ($mil.)	(0.1%)	43,638	47,262	51,761	46,298	43,452
Net income ($ mil.)	(5.3%)	1,541.0	1,798.0	2,454.0	1,419.0	1,241.0
Market value ($ mil.)	(2.8%)	18,242	23,440	21,032	18,348	16,304
Employees	(9.2%)	125,000	102,000	105,000	90,000	85,000

*Fiscal year change

BEST WESTERN INTERNATIONAL, INC.

6201 N 24TH PKWY
PHOENIX, AZ 850162023
Phone: 602 957-4200
Fax: –
Web: www.bestwestern.com

CEO: David Kong
CFO: Mark Straszynski
HR: John Kongkalai
FYE: November 30
Type: Private

Founded in 1946 by M.K. Guertin, Best Western is a privately-held hotel brand with more than 4,500 independently-owned and -operated hotels in over 100 countries and territories. Its WorldHotels Collection is a curated global offering of the finest independent hotels and resorts around the world. The SureStay Hotel Group offers value-oriented travelers an exceptional experience at an affordable price. Comprised of four distinct brands, SureStay Hotel Group offers traditional and longer stay travelers comfort and value while away from home.

	Annual Growth	11/03	11/04	11/05	11/06	11/07
Sales ($mil.)	5.4%	–	–	198.8	205.5	220.9
Net income ($ mil.)	–	–	–	(1.3)	2.5	(3.0)
Market value ($ mil.)	–	–	–	–	–	–
Employees	–	–	–	–	–	1,015

BETH ISRAEL DEACONESS MEDICAL CENTER, INC.

330 BROOKLINE AVE
BOSTON, MA 022155400
Phone: 617 667-7000
Fax: –
Web: www.bidmc.org

CEO: Kevin Tabb
CFO: Steve Fischer
HR: –
FYE: September 30
Type: Private

Beth Israel Deaconess Medical Center (BIDMC) is part of Beth Israel Lahey Health, a new health care system that brings together academic medical centers and teaching hospitals, community and specialty hospitals with more than 4,000 physicians and 35,000 employees. BIDMC has about 47,780 emergency department visits and around 803,000 outpatient visits. It delivers around 5,095 child births. It also provides a full range of emergency services, including a Level 1 Trauma Center and roof-top heliport. BIDMC a patient care, teaching and research affiliate of Harvard Medical School. The health system traces its roots to Deaconess Hospital, founded in 1896, and Beth Israel Hospital, established in 1916.

	Annual Growth	09/18	09/19	09/20	09/21	09/22
Sales ($mil.)	7.9%	–	1,945.1	1,359.6	1,890.2	2,446.0
Net income ($ mil.)	(6.5%)	–	68.0	100.0	181.4	55.7
Market value ($ mil.)	–	–	–	–	–	–
Employees	–	–	–	–	–	6,500

BETH ISRAEL MEDICAL CENTER

281 1ST AVE
NEW YORK, NY 100032925
Phone: 212 420-2000
Fax: –
Web: www.mountsinai.org

CEO: Kenneth L Davis
CFO: Donald Scanlon
HR: –
FYE: December 31
Type: Private

Mount Sinai Beth Israel (formerly Beth Israel Medical Center) is a member of Mount Sinai Health System. It is notable for its unique approach to combining medical excellence with clinical innovation in Manhattan's Lower East Side. It emphasizes its services in heart disease, cancer, neurology, and orthopedics. It also continues its long tradition of excellence in medical specialties, including gastrointestinal disease, chemical dependency, psychiatric disorders, pain management and palliative care, and HIV/AIDS research and treatment. It also significantly advanced its commitment to community-based ambulatory care and expanding patient access to primary and specialty care. The company traces its roots back in 1889.

	Annual Growth	12/07	12/08	12/09	12/21	12/22
Sales ($mil.)	0.7%	–	932.4	1,256.6	774.7	1,024.0
Net income ($ mil.)	–	–	(59.7)	15.2	(154.4)	(152.8)
Market value ($ mil.)	–	–	–	–	–	–
Employees	–	–	–	–	–	8,100

BETHESDA HOSPITAL, INC.

4750 WESLEY AVE
CINCINNATI, OH 452122244
Phone: 513 569-6100
Fax: –
Web: www.trihealth.com

CEO: –
CFO: Craig Rucker
HR: –
FYE: June 30
Type: Private

From modest beginnings as a informal cottage hospital, Bethesda North Hospital has grown into the fourth largest medical center in Cincinnati, Ohio. Bethesda North is a full-service acute care hospital with some 360 beds for adults and 60 for children. It provides comprehensive medical and surgical care, including maternity and fertility services, emergency care, and diagnostic imaging. The hospital joined with fellow Cincinnati health care provider Good Samaritan Hospital in 1995 to form TriHealth. Together, the two hospitals offer care at some 80 locations, including primary care offices, fitness centers, and occupational health facilities.

	Annual Growth	06/18	06/19	06/20	06/21	06/22
Sales ($mil.)	9.3%	–	624.1	643.1	744.5	815.3
Net income ($ mil.)	–	–	32.6	(37.0)	67.0	(2.5)
Market value ($ mil.)	–	–	–	–	–	–
Employees	–	–	–	–	–	3,000

BETHUNE-COOKMAN UNIVERSITY INC.

640 DR MARY MCLEOD BETHUNE BLVD
DAYTONA BEACH, FL 321143012
Phone: 386 481-2000
Fax: –
Web: www.cookman.edu

CEO: –
CFO: –
HR: –
FYE: June 30
Type: Private

Founded by educator Dr. Mary McLeod Bethune as a school for African-American women, Bethune-Cookman University (B-CU) is in the top tier of Historically Black Colleges & Universities (HBCUs) in the US. The Daytona, Florida-based university has about 3,600 students enrolled in undergraduate and graduate programs in some 40 majors. Approximately 54% of the school's students live in on-campus residential housing. B-CU has about 200 full-time faculty members and faculty/student ratio of 1:17. The university also offers a NCAA Division One athletic program. B-CU charges some $14,410 in annual tuition and fees.

	Annual Growth	06/13	06/14	06/20	06/21	06/22
Sales ($mil.)	4.5%	–	92.0	94.7	117.7	130.7
Net income ($ mil.)	–	–	(0.3)	(0.9)	36.3	19.1
Market value ($ mil.)	–	–	–	–	–	–
Employees	–	–	–	–	–	600

BEXIL CORP

3814 Route 44
Millbrook, NY 12545
Phone: 212 785-0900
Fax: 212 785-0400
Web: www.bexil.com

NBB: BXLC
CEO: –
CFO: –
HR: –
FYE: December 31
Type: Public

Bexil Corporation is on a quest to seek out new business ventures. The shell corporation has left the insurance business behind and is hoping to acquire another promising business. The holding company's primary operation had been a 50% stake in York Insurance Services Group, which provided independent adjustment and third-party administration services to insurance companies and self-insured groups. In 2006, however, Bexil sold its stake in York to Odyssey Investment Partners and began seeking other opportunities for investment.

	Annual Growth	12/18	12/19	12/20	12/21	12/23
Assets ($mil.)	7.9%	19.3	23.1	23.0	27.2	28.3
Net income ($ mil.)	–	–	(1.3)	4.5	1.0	6.5	3.2
Market value ($ mil.)	23.5%	7.2	11.1	10.6	17.3	20.6
Employees	–	–	–	–	–	–

BEYOND INC

799 West Coliseum Way
Midvale, UT 84047
Phone: 801 947-3100
Fax: –
Web: www.overstock.com

NYS: BYON
CEO: David J Nielsen
CFO: Adrianne Lee
HR: –
FYE: December 31
Type: Public

Overstock.com offers a broad range of price-competitive products, including furniture, décor, area rugs, bedding and bath, home improvement, outdoor, and kitchen and dining items, among others. The company sells its products and services through its Internet websites located at www.overstock.com, www.o.co, www.overstock.ca, and www.overstockgovernment.com and through its mobile app. It offers millions of products which about 100% are in-line products (products in active production). In addition to Overstock's nearly 1,290 facilities, the company's supply chain allows it to ship directly to customers from its suppliers or from its warehouses. Started in 1999, Dr. Patrick M. Byrne acquired the company Discounts Direct and rebranded it as Overstock.com.

	Annual Growth	12/19	12/20	12/21	12/22	12/23
Sales ($mil.)	1.7%	1,459.4	2,549.8	2,756.4	1,929.3	1,561.1
Net income ($ mil.)	–	(121.8)	56.0	389.4	(35.2)	(307.8)
Market value ($ mil.)	40.8%	320.2	2,178.5	2,679.9	879.2	1,257.5
Employees	(15.3%)	1,613	1,750	1,350	1,050	830

BG MEDICINE INC

303 Wyman Street, Suite 300
Waltham, MA 02451
Phone: 781 890-1199
Fax: –
Web: www.bg-medicine.com

NBB: BGMD
CEO: Paul R Sohmer
CFO: Stephen P Hall
HR: –
FYE: December 31
Type: Public

BG Medicine wants to fill big gaps in diagnostic medicine. The biosciences researcher specializes in developing biomarkers (substances used to detect disease at a molecular level) that enable research into the causes of disease and the effectiveness of drugs used to treat them. Products in commercialization, development, and discovery stages include molecular diagnostic tests for heart disease, neurological disorders, and immune-system ailments. BG Medicine also provides drug research and development services to global pharmaceutical makers, US government agencies, and other health care organizations. The company, built through venture capital backing, held its IPO in 2011.

	Annual Growth	12/11	12/12	12/13	12/14	12/15
Sales ($mil.)	(1.1%)	1.6	2.8	4.1	2.8	1.6
Net income ($ mil.)	–	(17.6)	(23.8)	(15.8)	(8.1)	(5.3)
Market value ($ mil.)	(47.3%)	53.4	26.1	11.8	5.2	4.1
Employees	(40.2%)	39	30	23	7	5

BGC GROUP INC

499 Park Avenue
New York, NY 10022
Phone: 212 610-2200
Fax: –
Web: www.bgcpartners.com

NMS: BGC
CEO: Howard W Lutnick
CFO: Jason W Hauf
HR: Evelyn Tan
FYE: December 31
Type: Public

BGC Partners is a leading global brokerage and financial technology company. Through brands including BGC, Fenics, GFI, Sunrise Brokers, Poten & Partners, and RP Martin, among others, the company's businesses specialize in the brokerage of a broad range of products, including fixed income such as government bonds, corporate bonds, and other debt instruments, as well as related interest rate derivatives and credit derivatives. Additionally, it provides brokerage products across FX, Equities, Energy and Commodities, Shipping and Futures and Options. Its businesses also provide a wide variety of services, including trade execution, connectivity solutions, brokerage services, clearing, trade compression and other post-trade services, information, and other back-office services to a broad assortment of financial and non-financial institutions. The majority of the company's revenue comes from international markets.

	Annual Growth	12/19	12/20	12/21	12/22	12/23
Sales ($mil.)	(1.0%)	2,104.2	2,056.7	2,015.4	1,795.3	2,025.4
Net income ($ mil.)	(10.2%)	55.7	48.9	124.0	48.7	36.3
Market value ($ mil.)	5.0%	2,967.3	1,998.2	2,322.9	1,883.3	3,606.7
Employees	(7.0%)	5,200	5,000	3,920	3,818	3,895

BGR GOVERNMENT AFFAIRS, LLC

601 13TH ST NW
WASHINGTON, DC 200053807
Phone: 202 661-6351
Fax: –
Web: www.bgrdc.com

CEO: Lanny Griffith
CFO: –
HR: –
FYE: December 31
Type: Private

BGR wasn't elected by the people, but it is still instrumental in shaping public policy. Founded in 1991 by Haley Barbour, who later became a two-term Governor of Mississippi, the firm employs lawyers, policy specialists, and other professionals to represent the interests of its clients at the federal level. The lobbyist firm has counted such heavyweights as Bristol-Myers Squibb, Lockheed Martin, and the University of Florida as clients. Its units include BGR Government Affairs, BGR Asset Management, and BGR Business Advisors. BGR Public Relations focuses on issues management and crisis communications, while BGR Gabara, a London-based public affairs firm, caters to the European market.

BH MEDIA, INC.

491 DUTTON ST STE 1
LOWELL, MA 018544292
Phone: 617 426-3000
Fax: –
Web: www.bostonherald.com

CEO: –
CFO: Jeff Magram
HR: –
FYE: March 31
Type: Private

Beantown news hounds aren't locked into one source thanks to this company. Boston Herald Inc. publishes the Boston Herald newspaper, which competes for readers with The Boston Globe (owned by The New York Times Company). The paper, which boasts a weekday circulation of more than 160,000, also publishes news online. The Boston Herald traces its roots back to 1846 when the city saw the first copy of The Herald published . After numerous incarnations, Rupert Murdoch's News Corporation bought The Herald American in 1982, changing its name back to the Boston Herald . Publisher Patrick Purcell later acquired the paper in 1994; it operates today as a subsidiary of his Herald Media company.

	Annual Growth	03/02	03/03	03/04	03/05	03/16
Sales ($mil.)	(51.0%)	–	–	–	0.0	0.0
Net income ($ mil.)	–	–	–	–	0.0	(0.0)
Market value ($ mil.)	–	–	–	–	–	–
Employees	–	–	–	–	–	375

BI-RITE RESTAURANT SUPPLY CO., INC.

123 S HILL DR
BRISBANE, CA 940051203
Phone: 415 656-0187
Fax: –
Web: www.birite.com

CEO: William Barulich
CFO: Zachary Barulich
HR: –
FYE: December 31
Type: Private

Bi-Rite Restaurant Supply, which does business as BiRite Foodservice Distributors, is a leading food service supplier serving the San Francisco Bay area and Northern California. The company distributes a full line of food, equipment, and supplies, including meat and dairy items, seafood, frozen foods, dry groceries, cleaning supplies, china, kitchen equipment, and disposables. Its customers include restaurant operators, hotels, universities, and hospitals. The company's international arm supplied food to the Middle East and Asia. A member of the UniPro Foodservice cooperative, the family-owned company was founded in 1966 by cousins Victor and John Barulich.

	Annual Growth	12/14	12/15	12/16	12/17	12/18
Sales ($mil.)	0.3%	–	321.6	305.6	314.8	324.0
Net income ($ mil.)	50.6%	–	8.5	12.2	13.3	29.2
Market value ($ mil.)	–	–	–	–	–	–
Employees	–	–	–	–	–	300

BIDDEFORD INTERNET CORP.

43 LANDRY ST
BIDDEFORD, ME 040054348
Phone: 866 494-2020
Fax: –
Web: www.gwi.net

CEO: Fletcher Kittredge
CFO: Fred Diehl
HR: –
FYE: December 31
Type: Private

Great Works Internet feels that connecting to the Web is no small matter. The company, known as GWI, provides Internet services to customers in Maine and areas of New Hampshire. The company serves more than 60,000 residential and business customers with dial-up and broadband connection services. GWI offers other residential services including Internet telephony, while providing such business-oriented services as Web site, email, and data server hosting, as well as online access for local cable operators. The company was founded in 1994 as Biddeford Internet.

BIG 5 SPORTING GOODS CORP

2525 East El Segundo Boulevard
El Segundo, CA 90245
Phone: 310 536-0611
Fax: –
Web: www.big5sportinggoods.com

NMS: BGFV
CEO: Steven G Miller
CFO: Barry D Emerson
HR: –
FYE: December 31
Type: Public

Big 5 Sporting Goods, which started with five army surplus shops in California in 1955, is a leading sporting goods retailer in the western US with more than 430 stores in which more than half of the stores are located in California. The company sells brand-name and private-label equipment, apparel, and footwear for indoor and outdoor activities such as camping, hunting, fishing, tennis, golf, and winter and summer recreation among others. Big 5 provides a full-line product offering in a traditional sporting goods store format that averages approximately 12,000 square feet. It supplements its traditional sports merchandise mix with an assortment of other products that the company purchase through opportunistic buys of vendor over-stock or close-out merchandise.

	Annual Growth	12/19*	01/21	01/22	01/23*	12/23
Sales ($mil.)	(2.9%)	996.5	1,041.2	1,161.8	995.5	884.7
Net income ($ mil.)	–	8.4	55.9	102.4	26.1	(7.1)
Market value ($ mil.)	20.4%	67.8	229.1	426.6	198.1	142.3
Employees	(2.7%)	8,800	8,400	7,800	8,700	7,900

*Fiscal year change

BIG BROTHERS BIG SISTERS OF AMERICA CORPORATION

2502 N ROCKY POINT DR STE 550
TAMPA, FL 336071421
Phone: 813 720-8778
Fax: –
Web: www.bbbs.org

CEO: Artis Stevens
CFO: Tim Midkiff
HR: –
FYE: June 30
Type: Private

These siblings wrote the book on youth mentoring. Big Brothers Big Sisters of America establishes and supervises mentoring relationships between adults and children ages five to 18. Its network of some 400 local agencies serves more than 250,000 youths. It pairs at-risk youth with adults for casual interactions like going to movies, sporting events, parks, and just being together. Adults, or "Bigs," are interviewed, screened, trained, and approved by the parent or guardian of the "Littles." Agency staff makes matches and a caseworker stays in touch with the pair to make sure everything works well. The group is funded by federal, state, and local government, as well as individuals, foundations, and companies.

	Annual Growth	06/13	06/14	06/15	06/16	06/21
Sales ($mil.)	57.8%	–	1.0	15.0	20.3	23.3
Net income ($ mil.)	42.8%	–	0.1	2.4	0.0	1.8
Market value ($ mil.)	–	–	–	–	–	–
Employees	–	–	–	–	–	85

BIG BUCK BREWERY & STEAKHOUSE, INC. NBB: BBUC Q

550 South Wisconsin Street
Gaylord, MI 49734
Phone: 989 731-0401
Fax: –
Web: www.bigbuck.com

CEO: Mark S Provenzano
CFO: –
HR: –
FYE: December 29
Type: Public

Big Buck Brewery & Steakhouse operates a casual dining spot in northern Michigan that offers handcrafted microbrews and a menu featuring steaks, chicken, seafood, and pasta dishes. It produces a variety of beers under such labels as Big Buck Beer and Buck Naked, as well as seasonal and specialty varieties. William Rolinski started the restaurant business in 1994.

	Annual Growth	01/99	01/00*	12/00	12/01	12/02
Sales ($mil.)	1.3%	15.6	13.9	16.6	17.5	16.4
Net income ($ mil.)	–	(1.4)	(1.3)	(3.2)	(2.2)	(3.6)
Market value ($ mil.)	(46.3%)	2.8	1.5	0.5	0.4	0.2
Employees	(4.0%)	443	397	568	419	376

*Fiscal year change

BIG HEART PET BRANDS, INC.

1 MARITIME PLZ FL 2
SAN FRANCISCO, CA 941113407
Phone: 415 247-3000
Fax: –
Web: –

CEO: Richard K Smucker
CFO: Mark R Belgya
HR: –
FYE: April 28
Type: Private

If you are feeding your pet anything other than table scraps, you've likely come across Big Heart Pet Brands. Formerly Del Monte Corporation, the company is the leading provider of branded pet food and snacks in the US; its portfolio includes Milk-Bone, Meow Mix, Natural Balance, Kibbles 'n Bits, and Gravy Train, among others. Its products are available through grocery stores, club stores, mass merchandisers, specialty pet stores, and supercenters primarily in the US. In early 2014 the company sold its canned fruit, vegetables, and broths business and changed its name from Del Monte to Big Heart Pet Brands. In early 2015 it was acquired by The J. M. Smucker Company.

BIG JACK ULTIMATE HOLDINGS LP

124 W OXMOOR RD
BIRMINGHAM, AL 352096303
Phone: 205 945-8167
Fax: –
Web: www.jacksfamilyfund.org

CEO: –
CFO: –
HR: –
FYE: December 31
Type: Private

It's the hamburgers that bring the customers back to Jack's. Jack's Family Restaurants operates a chain of more than 100 burger joints across the Southeast, many of which are located in Alabama. The eateries offer a menu of hamburgers, cheeseburgers, and chicken sandwiches, along with sides, salads, and breakfast items. Most Jack's locations are company-owned; a handful of units in Alabama are franchised. The chain was started in Homewood, Alabama, in 1960 by Jack Caddell, an entrepreneur who was impressed by the early success of McDonald's. Former franchisee Benny LaRussa bought the business in 1989.

	Annual Growth	12/16	12/17	12/18	12/19	12/20
Sales ($mil.)	(5.3%)	–	–	–	0.5	0.5
Net income ($ mil.)	(74.0%)	–	–	–	0.1	0.0
Market value ($ mil.)	–	–	–	–	–	–
Employees	–	–	–	–	–	1,966

BIG LOTS, INC. NYS: BIG

4900 E. Dublin-Granville Road
Columbus, OH 43081
Phone: 614 278-6800
Fax: 614 278-6666
Web: www.biglots.com

CEO: Bruce K Thorn
CFO: Jonathan E Ramsden
HR: –
FYE: January 28
Type: Public

Big Lots is a community retailer operating approximately 1,425 stores across the US. It sells a variety of brand-name products that include food, decor, consumables, furniture, housewares, hosiery, seasonal items, electronics, toys, and accessories, among others. Furniture represents the company's largest product line, accounting for almost 25% of sales. The company also offers products via e-commerce platforms, including some items only available online. The majority of its merchandise offerings are processed for retail sale and distributed to its stores from five regional distribution centers.

	Annual Growth	02/19	02/20*	01/21	01/22	01/23
Sales ($mil.)	1.1%	5,238.1	5,323.2	6,199.2	6,150.6	5,468.3
Net income ($ mil.)	–	156.9	242.5	629.2	177.8	(210.7)
Market value ($ mil.)	(14.3%)	907.0	783.6	1,728.3	1,154.6	488.2
Employees	(2.5%)	35,600	34,000	37,000	36,200	32,200

*Fiscal year change

BIG ROCK SPORTS, LLC

1141 JAY LN
GRAHAM, NC 272532619
Phone: 252 808-3500
Fax: –
Web: www.bigrocksports.com

CEO: –
CFO: –
HR: –
FYE: December 31
Type: Private

If you want muscles like big rocks, perhaps Big Rock Sports can be of assistance. The company wholesales sporting goods, specializing in fishing and hunting equipment, to more than 15,000 retail outlets throughout the US, the Caribbean, and about 10 other countries. Some of the brands carried by its stores include Calcutta, Cabin Creek, Federal Ammunition, and Winchester. Big Rock operates five distribution centers in California (as AWR Sports), Minnesota (CSI Sports), Montana (MT Sports), North Carolina (Henry's), and Oregon (All Sports), as well as a sales office in Pennsylvania. Big Rock Sports' management team owns the company.

BIG WEST OIL, LLC

333 W CENTER ST
NORTH SALT LAKE, UT 840542805
Phone: 801 624-1000
Fax: –
Web: www.bigwestoil.com

CEO: –
CFO: –
HR: –
FYE: January 31
Type: Private

Big West Oil keeps the wagon trains rolling across the big West -- at least the station wagons. The company is in the oil processing and products business, centered around its 35,000 barrels-a-day refinery in North Salt Lake, Utah, to its fleet of tanker trucks that gather crude oil from the refinery and other purchases and deliver to wholesale customers and gas station/convenience stores in seven Western states, including Colorado, Idaho, Nevada, Utah, and Wyoming. The company's refinery processes crude oil produced in Utah, Wyoming and Canada. Big West Oil is a subsidiary of FJ Management.

	Annual Growth	01/04	01/05	01/06	01/07	01/08
Sales ($mil.)	60.7%	–	735.6	2,014.1	2,399.5	3,053.3
Net income ($ mil.)	55.6%	–	50.8	102.9	89.0	191.1
Market value ($ mil.)	–	–	–	–	–	–
Employees	–	–	–	–	–	460

BIG-D CONSTRUCTION CORP.

404 W 400 S
SALT LAKE CITY, UT 841011108
Phone: 801 415-6000
Fax: –
Web: www.big-d.com

CEO: Rob Moore
CFO: –
HR: Kaitlyn McKenna
FYE: December 31
Type: Private

Founded in 1967 by Dee Livingood (who carried the nickname "Big-Dee"), the family-run construction firm offers design/build services to customers in nine states from Minnesota to California. Known for its work on projects in the food and beverage sector, Big-D also works on light commercial, office and retail properties, manufacturing, health care, and hospitality projects, among others. Other owned affiliates include Martin Harris in Las Vegas and Reno, Nevada; Dovetail Construction in Bozeman, Montana; McAlvain Companies Inc. in Boise, Idaho; and CFC Construction in Golden, Colorado.

	Annual Growth	12/08	12/09	12/10	12/11	12/12
Sales ($mil.)	44.4%	–	–	259.8	554.8	541.6
Net income ($ mil.)	–	–	–	–	–	–
Market value ($ mil.)	–	–	–	–	–	–
Employees	–	–	–	–	–	1,384

BILL & MELINDA GATES FOUNDATION

500 5TH AVE N
SEATTLE, WA 981094636
Phone: 206 709-3100
Fax: –
Web: www.gatesfoundation.org

CEO: Mark Suzman
CFO: –
HR: Brena Cole
FYE: December 31
Type: Private

Bill & Melinda Gates Foundation is nonprofit fighting poverty, disease, and inequity around the world. In developing countries, the foundation focuses on improving people's health and giving them the chance to lift themselves out of hunger and extreme poverty. Based in Washington, Bill & Melinda Gates Foundation is led by CEO Mark Suzman, under the direction of co-chairs Bill Gates and Melinda French Gates and the board of trustees. With a charitable support of approximately $7.0 billion, the company have about 1,970 grants from over 1,215 grantees.

	Annual Growth	12/14	12/15	12/16	12/21	12/22
Sales ($mil.)	4.8%	–	–	5,281.0	6,739.0	6,988.0
Net income ($ mil.)	–	–	–	(457.2)	1,334.7	(280.3)
Market value ($ mil.)	–	–	–	–	–	–
Employees	–	–	–	–	–	1,376

BILLING SERVICES GROUP LTD.

7411 John Smith Drive, Suite 1500
San Antonio, TX 78229
Phone: 210 949-7000
Fax: 210 949-7101
Web: www.bsgclearing.com

CEO: Norman M Phipps
CFO: –
HR: –
FYE: December 31
Type: Public

The idea behind Billing Services Group (doing business as BSG Clearing Solutions) is simple: Leave the bills to someone else. The company provides outsourced bill processing and settlement to telecommunications companies around the world. Its technology platform tracks direct long-distance calls, as well as operator-assisted and calling-card calls, and enables authentication, invoicing, collection, and settlement. Originally a subsidiary of U.S. Long Distance, the company (then Billing Concepts) was spun off as a public company in 1996. ABRY Partners took the company private in 2003 and merged it with ACI Billing Services the next year to form parent Billing Services Group, which is domiciled in Bermuda.

	Annual Growth	12/14	12/15	12/16	12/17	12/18
Sales ($mil.)	(21.5%)	42.4	36.4	30.2	21.1	16.1
Net income ($ mil.)	–	2.1	8.7	10.9	(6.7)	(7.8)
Market value ($ mil.)	–	–	–	–	–	–
Employees	–	–	–	–	–	–

BILLINGS CLINIC

2800 10TH AVE N
BILLINGS, MT 591010703
Phone: 406 657-4000
Fax: –
Web: www.colstripclinic.com

CEO: Clint Seger
CFO: Priscilla Needham
HR: –
FYE: June 30
Type: Private

Through a group of more than 450 doctors and other providers, Billings Clinic caters a vast region covering much of Montana, Wyoming and the western Dakotas. It offers more than 80 specialties, such as emergency and trauma, cancer, orthopedics, birthing, cardiovascular, neurosciences, dialysis, and pediatrics. Its operations include a more than 300-bed hospital and the organization's main clinic. Additionally, Billings Clinic has more than 15 regional partnerships, including management agreements with about a dozen of Critical Access Hospitals and one outpatient clinic. The not-for-profit health care system is owned by the community.

	Annual Growth	06/14	06/15	06/16	06/21	06/22
Sales ($mil.)	9.0%	–	565.5	586.8	922.6	1,036.6
Net income ($ mil.)	3.2%	–	30.3	(2.4)	40.8	37.8
Market value ($ mil.)	–	–	–	–	–	–
Employees	–	–	–	–	–	3,300

BIO-KEY INTERNATIONAL INC

NAS: BKYI

3349 Highway 138, Building A, Suite E
Wall, NJ 07719
Phone: 732 359-1100
Fax: –
Web: –

CEO: Michael W Depasquale
CFO: Cecilia Welch
HR: –
FYE: December 31
Type: Public

BIO-key International has its finger securely on the pulse of biometrics. The company develops biometric security software and technology designed to secure access to enterprise applications and mobile devices. Its products incorporate biometric technology to scan and analyze fingerprints in order to grant or deny user access to wireless and enterprise data. BIO-key licenses its technology to original equipment manufacturers, systems integrators, and application developers. End users of its technology include corporations, government agencies, and other organizations concerned about the theft or misuse of sensitive data.

	Annual Growth	12/18	12/19	12/20	12/21	12/22
Sales ($mil.)	14.8%	4.0	2.3	2.8	5.1	7.0
Net income ($ mil.)	–	(6.9)	(14.6)	(9.7)	(5.1)	(11.9)
Market value ($ mil.)	(6.0%)	0.4	0.3	1.8	1.1	0.3
Employees	37.1%	15	22	36	55	53

BIO-RAD LABORATORIES INC

NYS: BIO

1000 Alfred Nobel Drive
Hercules, CA 94547
Phone: 510 724-7000
Fax: –
Web: www.bio-rad.com

CEO: Norman Schwartz
CFO: Ilan Daskal
HR: Ashley Moelter
FYE: December 31
Type: Public

Bio-Rad Laboratories is a multinational manufacturer and worldwide distributor of its own life science research and clinical diagnostics products. Bio-Rad's clinical diagnostics segment leverages a broad range of technologies and delivers high-value clinical information in the blood transfusion, diabetes monitoring, autoimmune, and infectious disease testing markets. Its life science segment provides instruments, software, consumables, reagents, and content for the areas of cell biology, gene expression, protein purification, protein quantitation, drug discovery and manufacture, food safety, and science education. Bio-Rad's customers include prominent universities, research institutions, hospitals, commercial laboratories, diagnostic manufacturers, and companies in the biotechnology, pharmaceutical, chemical, and food industries. The US generates about 40% of total sales.

	Annual Growth	12/19	12/20	12/21	12/22	12/23
Sales ($mil.)	3.7%	2,311.7	2,545.6	2,922.5	2,802.2	2,671.3
Net income ($ mil.)	–	1,758.7	3,806.3	4,245.9	(3,627.5)	(637.3)
Market value ($ mil.)	(3.3%)	10,553	16,625	21,548	11,992	9,208.3
Employees	(0.3%)	8,120	8,000	7,900	8,200	8,030

BIO-TECHNE CORP   NMS: TECH

614 McKinley Place N.E.
Minneapolis, MN 55413
Phone: 612 379-8854
Fax: –
Web: www.bio-techne.com

CEO: Charles Kummeth
CFO: James T Hippel
HR: Emma Hall
FYE: June 30
Type: Public

Bio-Techne develops, manufactures, and sells life science reagents, instruments and services for the research, diagnostics, and bioprocessing markets worldwide. With its broad product portfolio and application expertise, it sells integral components of scientific investigations into biological processes and molecular diagnostics, revealing the nature, diagnosis, etiology, and progression of specific diseases. The company's products aid in drug discovery efforts and provide the means for accurate clinical tests and diagnoses. It also makes hematology controls and calibrators for blood analysis systems and sells them to equipment makers. The US accounts the largest for more than 55% of total revenue.

	Annual Growth	06/19	06/20	06/21	06/22	06/23
Sales ($mil.)	12.3%	714.0	738.7	931.0	1,105.6	1,136.7
Net income ($ mil.)	31.3%	96.1	229.3	140.4	272.1	285.3
Market value ($ mil.)	(20.9%)	32,867	41,629	70,980	54,645	12,868
Employees	1.6%	2,250	2,300	2,600	3,000	2,400

BIOCARDIA INC   NAS: BCDA

320 Soquel Way
Sunnyvale, CA 94085
Phone: 650 226-0120
Fax: –
Web: www.biocardia.com

CEO: –
CFO: –
HR: –
FYE: December 31
Type: Public

A healthy ticker really makes BioCardia (formerly Tiger X Medical) tick. The biopharma and diagnostics firm is exploring a stem cell therapy system to treat heart failure. Its CardiAMP therapy, derived from a patients' bone marrow, is in phase III clinical trials for the treatment of those who have already had a heart attack. The therapy is enabled by BioCardia's Helix delivery system, through which treatments are injected into the walls of the heart. The firm has other regenerative biologic therapies under development for cardiovascular disease. The biotech was established in October 2016 after private company BioCardia conducted a reverse merger with publicly traded medical device shell company Tiger X Medical.

	Annual Growth	12/19	12/20	12/21	12/22	12/23
Sales ($mil.)	(9.5%)	0.7	0.1	1.0	1.4	0.5
Net income ($ mil.)	–	(14.7)	(15.0)	(12.6)	(11.9)	(11.6)
Market value ($ mil.)	(34.8%)	87.1	81.9	45.9	49.5	15.7
Employees	(4.5%)	24	29	35	36	20

BIOCEPT INC   NAS: BIOC

9955 Mesa Rim Road
San Diego, CA 92121
Phone: 858 320-8200
Fax: –
Web: www.biocept.com

CEO: –
CFO: –
HR: –
FYE: December 31
Type: Public

The concept at Biocept is to make cancer tumor identification quicker and more accurate. The company's products detect circulating tumor cells (CTCs) in a standard blood sample. Only one test is in production, OncoCEE-BR, for breast cancer. Its pipeline contains tests for lung, gastric, colorectal, prostate, and skin cancers; it plans to launch five new tests by 2017. Biocept collaborates with doctors and researchers at The University of Texas M.D. Anderson Cancer Center and the Dana-Farber Cancer Institute. The company was formed in 1997 and went public in 2014. It raised $18.8 million that it plans to use for sales and marketing, R&D and development of tests, and scaling up its production capabilities.

	Annual Growth	12/18	12/19	12/20	12/21	12/22
Sales ($mil.)	67.9%	3.3	5.5	27.5	61.2	25.9
Net income ($ mil.)	–	(24.6)	(25.1)	(17.8)	(2.8)	(32.1)
Market value ($ mil.)	(11.4%)	0.5	0.2	2.5	2.1	0.3
Employees	(13.1%)	91	95	134	192	52

BIOCOM INSTITUTE

10996 TORREYANA RD # 200
SAN DIEGO, CA 921211159
Phone: 858 455-0300
Fax: –
Web: www.biocom.org

CEO: Joseph D Panetta
CFO: –
HR: Aileen Gipson
FYE: December 31
Type: Private

BIOCOM puts biology and commerce together. The group is a trade association for the life science industry in Southern California. Its goal is to promote favorable public policy, education, and business networking though its membership and to seek funding for the advancement of life sciences. BIOCOM represents more than 575 member biotech, medical technology, and pharmaceutical companies and accepts members on several different levels; benefits range from member discounts and event announcements to committee participation and group purchasing discounts. BIOCOM was formed in 1995 by the merger of San Diego Biocommerce Association and Biotechnology Industry Council.

	Annual Growth	12/11	12/12	12/13	12/18	12/19
Sales ($mil.)	(13.1%)	–	4.0	4.6	1.0	1.5
Net income ($ mil.)	(4.7%)	–	0.0	0.0	(0.2)	0.0
Market value ($ mil.)	–	–	–	–	–	–
Employees	–	–	–	–	–	14

BIOCRYST PHARMACEUTICALS INC   NMS: BCRX

4505 Emperor Blvd., Suite 200
Durham, NC 27703
Phone: 919 859-1302
Fax: 919 859-1314
Web: www.biocryst.com

CEO: Jon P Stonehouse
CFO: Anthony J Doyle
HR: –
FYE: December 31
Type: Public

BioCryst Pharmaceuticals is a commercial-stage biotechnology company that discovers novel, oral, small-molecule medicines. It focuses on oral treatments for rare diseases in which significant unmet medical needs exist and an enzyme plays the key role in the biological pathway of the disease. BioCryst's peramivir is a treatment for acute influenza that was developed with funding from the Department of Health and Human Services (HHS). RAPIVAB (Peramivir) is marketed in Japan by Shionogi under the commercial name Rapiacta; in Korea, it is marketed by Green Cross Corporation under the name PeramiFlu. Additional development programs include ORLADEYO (Berotralstat), is an oral, once-daily therapy discovered, and developed by the company for the prevention of hereditary angioedema (HAE) attacks.

	Annual Growth	12/19	12/20	12/21	12/22	12/23
Sales ($mil.)	61.4%	48.8	17.8	157.2	270.8	331.4
Net income ($ mil.)	–	(108.9)	(182.8)	(184.1)	(247.1)	(226.5)
Market value ($ mil.)	14.8%	709.9	1,533.0	2,849.9	2,362.3	1,232.6
Employees	39.9%	140	246	358	531	536

BIOGEN INC   NMS: BIIB

225 Binney Street
Cambridge, MA 02142
Phone: 617 679-2000
Fax: –
Web: www.biogen.com

CEO: Christopher A Viehbacher
CFO: Michael R McDonnell
HR: –
FYE: December 31
Type: Public

Biogen is a global biopharmaceutical company focused on discovering, developing and delivering innovative therapies for people living with serious neurological and neurodegenerative diseases as well as related therapeutic adjacencies. Biogen's marketed products include TECFIDERA, VUMERITY, AVONEX, PLEGRIDY, TYSABRI and FAMPYRA for the treatment of multiple sclerosis (MS); SPINRAZA for the treatment of spinal muscular atrophy (SMA); ADUHELM for the treatment of Alzheimer's disease; and FUMADERM for the treatment of severe plaque psoriasis. Biogen, which serves customers around the world, gets majority of its revenue from the US.

	Annual Growth	12/19	12/20	12/21	12/22	12/23
Sales ($mil.)	(9.1%)	14,378	13,445	10,982	10,173	9,835.6
Net income ($ mil.)	(33.4%)	5,888.5	4,000.6	1,556.1	3,046.9	1,161.1
Market value ($ mil.)	(3.4%)	42,996	35,480	34,764	40,126	37,496
Employees	0.6%	7,400	9,100	9,610	8,725	7,570

BIOGENEX LABORATORIES

48810 KATO RD STE 200
FREMONT, CA 945387311
Phone: 510 824-1400
Fax: –
Web: www.biogenex.com

CEO: Krishan L Kalra
CFO: –
HR: –
FYE: December 31
Type: Private

BioGenex Laboratories isn't slacking when it comes to helping researchers unfold the mysteries contained in tissues and cells. The company develops technologies that perform automated analyses useful in drug discovery and development, life science research, and cellular and molecular diagnostics. The firm's products include antibodies, probes, imaging systems, labeling, and staining systems; reagents; and detection kits. It sells primarily to biotechnology and pharmaceutical companies, reference labs, hospitals, cancer treatment centers, and academic medical institutions.

	Annual Growth	12/06	12/07	12/08	12/12	12/14
Sales ($mil.)	22.1%	–	16.9	14.5	9.1	68.0
Net income ($ mil.)	5.1%	–	2.8	0.5	0.6	3.9
Market value ($ mil.)	–	–	–	–	–	–
Employees	–	–	–	–	–	25

BIOJECT MEDICAL TECHNOLOGIES INC

20245 SW 95th Avenue
Tualatin, OR 97062
Phone: 503 692-8001
Fax: –
Web: www.bioject.com

CEO: Tony K Chow
CFO: –
HR: –
FYE: December 31
Type: Public

Bioject Medical Technologies wants to give the medical community a shot in the arm. Its Biojector 2000 jet injection system delivers injectable medication without a needle (and thus without needle-associated risks) by using a fine, high-pressure stream that goes through the skin; the injector is powered by CO 2 disposable cartridges or tanks. The accompanying vial adapter device allows the Biojector system to be filled without a needle. The company also markets Vitajet, a spring-powered, needle-free self-injection device that has been cleared for administering injections of insulin. Investment firm Signet Healthcare Partners and affiliates own one-third of Bioject.

	Annual Growth	12/06	12/07	12/08	12/09	12/10
Sales ($mil.)	(15.2%)	10.8	8.3	6.5	6.7	5.6
Net income ($ mil.)	–	(7.0)	(4.0)	(3.0)	(1.1)	(1.5)
Market value ($ mil.)	(47.5%)	17.5	10.2	1.3	2.4	1.3
Employees	(18.4%)	81	37	33	32	36

BIOLA UNIVERSITY, INC.

13800 BIOLA AVE
LA MIRADA, CA 906390001
Phone: 562 903-6000
Fax: –
Web: www.biola.edu

CEO: –
CFO: –
HR: Judith Rood
FYE: June 30
Type: Private

Biola University is a nationally-ranked Christian university in the heart of Southern California. The private evangelical Christian institution of higher learning provides more than 300 academic programs through nine schools. The non-denominational school offers bachelor's, master's, and doctoral degrees, and has an enrollment of over 5,385 students at the La Mirada campus, online, and in distance programs throughout the world. Biola University was founded as the Bible Institute in 1908 and its campuses rest on the border of Orange and Los Angeles counties. With esteemed professors that hold doctorates from some of the world's leading research universities, such as Cambridge, Caltech, Cornell, Stanford, and Oxford, Biola has a 14:1 student-faculty ratio that allows students to receive personal attention and mentoring.

	Annual Growth	06/14	06/15	06/16	06/20	06/22
Sales ($mil.)	1.4%	–	161.5	165.3	260.7	178.4
Net income ($ mil.)	–	–	29.1	10.6	32.9	(24.9)
Market value ($ mil.)	–	–	–	–	–	–
Employees	–	–	–	–	–	3,914

BIOLARGO INC

NBB: BLGO

14921 Chestnut St.
Westminster, CA 92683
Phone: 888 400-2863
Fax: –
Web: www.biolargo.com

CEO: Dennis P Calvert
CFO: Charles K Dargan II
HR: –
FYE: December 31
Type: Public

After morphing identities several times over the past few years, BioLargo (formerly NuWay Medical) hopes that it has found its way. The company went from car dealership and casino ownership to being a medical device maker and application service provider (ASP). It believes it has found its future in designing sanitizing chemicals for specialty packaging (such as pads, protective liners, and surgical drapes) used for shipping blood, biohazardous materials, meat and poultry, and other items requiring sanitary containment. Consultant Kenneth Code controls 56% of BioLargo.

	Annual Growth	12/18	12/19	12/20	12/21	12/22
Sales ($mil.)	44.1%	1.4	1.9	2.4	2.5	5.9
Net income ($ mil.)	–	(10.2)	(10.7)	(8.4)	(7.1)	(4.5)
Market value ($ mil.)	(5.0%)	66.7	60.1	34.3	59.1	54.3
Employees	7.2%	25	25	27	27	33

BIOLASE INC

NAS: BIOL

27042 Towne Centre Drive, Suite 270
Lake Forest, CA 92610
Phone: 949 361-1200
Fax: –
Web: www.biolase.com

CEO: John R Beaver
CFO: Jennifer Bright
HR: –
FYE: December 31
Type: Public

BioLase is causing dentists to drop the knife and pick up the laser. The company develops, manufactures, and sells laser-based systems for use primarily in dental applications. BioLase's surgical cutting system, Waterlase, uses laser pulses to turn water droplets into high-speed particles that can cut both hard and soft tissues and bones in the mouth. Waterlase is used in procedures traditionally performed with dental drills and scalpels. The company's Diode laser systems are used to perform soft tissue and cosmetic dental procedures, as well as non-dental procedures. BioLase markets its products in more than 60 countries.

	Annual Growth	12/19	12/20	12/21	12/22	12/23
Sales ($mil.)	6.8%	37.8	22.8	39.2	48.5	49.2
Net income ($ mil.)	–	(17.9)	(16.8)	(16.2)	(28.6)	(20.6)
Market value ($ mil.)	19.4%	1.9	1.4	1.3	2.2	3.8
Employees	2.3%	157	135	161	192	172

BIOLIFE SOLUTIONS INC

NAS: BLFS

3303 Monte Villa Parkway, Suite 310
Bothell, WA 98021
Phone: 425 402-1400
Fax: –
Web: www.biolifesolutions.com

CEO: Michael Rice
CFO: Troy Wichterman
HR: Sarah Aebersold
FYE: December 31
Type: Public

BioLife Solutions makes sure your tissues and organs don't get freezer burn. The company has designed liquid media technologies for frozen (cryogenic) storage and cold (hypothermic) storage of biological products including cells, tissues, and organs. Its HypoThermosol and CryoStor products minimize the damage done to these biological products during refrigeration and freezing, making them viable for transplant or experimentation for longer periods. The company sells its products directly to academic institutions, companies, and laboratories conducting clinical research.

	Annual Growth	12/19	12/20	12/21	12/22	12/23
Sales ($mil.)	51.3%	27.4	48.1	119.2	161.8	143.3
Net income ($ mil.)	–	(1.7)	2.7	(7.6)	(139.8)	(66.4)
Market value ($ mil.)	0.1%	730.8	1,801.7	1,683.4	822.0	734.0
Employees	27.2%	158	199	437	467	414

BIOMARIN PHARMACEUTICAL INC   NMS: BMRN

770 Lindaro Street   CEO: Jean-Jacques Bienaime
San Rafael, CA 94901   CFO: Brian R Mueller
Phone: 415 506-6700   HR: –
Fax: –   FYE: December 31
Web: www.bmrn.com   Type: Public

BioMarin Pharmaceuticals develops drugs with a focus on rare disease treatments. Its portfolio consists of several commercial products and multiple clinical and preclinical product candidates for the treatment of various diseases. The company's Vimizim, Naglazyme, and Aldurazyme drugs treat versions of the life-threatening genetic condition mucopolysaccharidosis (MPS), caused by a rare enzyme deficiency that prevents patients from metabolizing certain complex carbohydrates. Another drug, Kuvan, is approved to treat enzyme deficiency phenylketonuria (PKU). Additional medicines include Brineura, and Palynziq. More than 30% of the company's revenue comes from the US.

	Annual Growth	12/19	12/20	12/21	12/22	12/23
Sales ($mil.)	9.2%	1,704.0	1,860.5	1,846.3	2,096.0	2,419.2
Net income ($ mil.)	–	(23.8)	859.1	(64.1)	141.6	167.6
Market value ($ mil.)	3.3%	15,946	16,538	16,663	19,518	18,185
Employees	3.2%	3,001	3,059	3,045	3,082	3,401

BIOMED REALTY TRUST, INC.

4570 EXECUTIVE DR STE 400   CEO: Alan D Gold
SAN DIEGO, CA 921213074   CFO: Greg N Lubushkin
Phone: 858 207-2513   HR: Susan Green
Fax: –   FYE: December 31
Web: www.biomedrealty.com   Type: Private

BioMed Realty, a Blackstone portfolio company, is a leading provider of real estate solutions to the life science and technology industries. BioMed owns and operates high quality life science real estate comprising approximately 16.3 million square feet concentrated in leading innovation markets throughout the US and UK, including Boston/Cambridge, San Francisco, San Diego, Seattle, Boulder, and Cambridge, UK. In addition, BioMed maintains a premier in process development platform with about 4.6 million square feet of Class A properties in active construction and approximately 5.6 million square feet of future development platform in these core innovation markets to meet the growing demand of the life science and technology industries.

BIOMEDICAL TECHNOLOGY SOLUTIONS HOLDINGS, INC.

12741 East Caley Avenue,, Unit 140   CEO: –
Centennial , CO 80111   CFO: –
Phone: 303 653-0100   HR: –
Fax: –   FYE: December 31
Web: www.bmtscorp.com   Type: Public

BioMedical Technology Solutions (BMTS) takes the hazard out of hazardous medical waste. Its flagship product is the Demolizer, a desktop device that uses dry heat to sterilize medical waste and to destroy sharps (needles, lancets, scalpel blades, etc.). The resulting waste can then be disposed of as common, solid waste. This allows smaller facilities to dispose of waste on site, rather than through third-party collection and treatment providers. The company's primary markets are health care facilities, including medical offices, nursing homes, veterinary hospitals. Additional markets include less commonly considered places where medical waste can collect including hotels, cruise ships, and field clinics

	Annual Growth	12/06	12/07	12/08	12/09	12/10
Sales ($mil.)	(29.2%)	3.0	2.1	1.2	1.0	0.7
Net income ($ mil.)	–	(0.3)	(1.3)	(1.2)	(1.7)	(1.5)
Market value ($ mil.)	(6.5%)	12.1	1.9	15.7	13.8	9.3
Employees	23.6%	3	1	16	9	7

BIOMERICA INC   NAS: BMRA

17571 Von Karman Avenue   CEO: Zackary Irani
Irvine, CA 92614   CFO: Gary Lu
Phone: 949 645-2111   HR: –
Fax: –   FYE: May 31
Web: www.biomerica.com   Type: Public

God bless Biomerica. The firm makes diagnostic tests for use worldwide in hospitals and other clinical laboratories, as well as in doctors' offices and homes. Its clinical laboratory products are immunoassay tests for conditions such as food allergies, diabetes, infectious diseases, and hyperthyroidism. Its point-of-care product portfolio, which includes products that produce rapid results, provides tests for prostate cancer, pregnancy, cat allergies, and drugs of abuse. Biomerica has manufacturing facilities in the US and in Mexico. It once owned a minority interest in Lancer Orthodontics, a maker of orthodontic products such as arch wires, lingual attachments, and buccal tubes, but it sold its stake in 2008.

	Annual Growth	05/19	05/20	05/21	05/22	05/23
Sales ($mil.)	0.7%	5.2	6.7	7.2	18.9	5.3
Net income ($ mil.)	–	(2.4)	(2.3)	(6.5)	(4.5)	(7.1)
Market value ($ mil.)	(11.7%)	37.8	108.8	61.4	58.9	23.0
Employees	12.3%	39	45	49	64	62

BION ENVIRONMENTAL TECHNOLOGIES INC   NBB: BNET

9 East Park Court, Old Bethpage   CEO: William O'Neill
New York, NY 11804   CFO: Mark A Smith
Phone: 516 586-5643   HR: –
Fax: –   FYE: June 30
Web: www.bionenviro.com   Type: Public

A "moo moo" here and an "oink oink" there are music to the ears of Bion Environmental Technologies. The company provides waste stream remediation for animal operations, primarily for large dairy and hog farms. To reduce pollution caused by animal waste, Bion Environmental uses organic nutrients, bacteria, and other microbes to treat the waste before disposal. The treatment creates organic soil and fertilizer products, which the company markets for use on athletic fields, gardens, and golf courses. The company is working closely with government bodies and universities in Pennsylvania to address the major problem of animal waste run-off from farms into the Chesapeake Bay.

	Annual Growth	06/19	06/20	06/21	06/22	06/23
Sales ($mil.)	–	–	–	–	–	–
Net income ($ mil.)	–	(2.7)	(4.5)	(3.4)	8.3	(3.2)
Market value ($ mil.)	17.5%	30.8	27.5	63.9	55.9	58.7
Employees	7.5%	6	6	6	7	8

BIOSYNERGY, INC.

1940 East Devon Avenue   CEO: Fred K Suzuki
Elk Grove Village, IL 60007   CFO: Laurence Mead
Phone: 847 956-0471   HR: –
Fax: 847 956-6050   FYE: April 30
Web: www.biosynergyinc.com   Type: Public

Biosynergy does its part to keep the good blood good. Biosynergy makes blood monitoring devices, most of which are used in blood banks to keep blood healthy and at the right temperature. Its products are disposable cholesteric (asymmetrical) liquid crystal devices that cool, heat, and monitor blood and other lab materials or samples. The company also distributes some third-party products. In addition, Biosynergy is developing antibacterial compounds for use in food and other products. The company sells its products to hospitals, laboratories, product dealers, and clinical end-users. Chairman, president, and CEO Fred Suzuki controls about 35% of the company, which was founded in 1976.

	Annual Growth	04/17	04/18	04/19	04/20	04/21
Sales ($mil.)	(2.4%)	1.3	1.2	1.3	1.2	1.2
Net income ($ mil.)	(38.0%)	0.1	0.0	0.0	0.0	0.0
Market value ($ mil.)	–	0.0	0.0	–	–	–
Employees	(4.5%)	6	6	6	6	5

BIOVERATIV INC.

225 2ND AVE
WALTHAM, MA 024511122
Phone: 781 663-4400
Fax: –
Web: www.bioverativ.com

CEO: Olivier Brandicourt
CFO: –
HR: –
FYE: December 31
Type: Private

Bioverativ is a biotechnology firm focused on discovering, developing, and commercializing treatments for hemophilia and other rare blood disorders. It has two products on the market -- Eloctate and Alprolix for hemophilia; they are sold in the US, Canada, the European Union, and Japan, and the company plans to launch them in new geographic markets. Both drugs utilize Fc fusion technology, whereby clotting factors are fused to a certain portion of protein found in the body to prolong circulation and the amount of time the therapy remains in the body. Pipeline products include programs in hemophilia A and B, sickle cell disease, and beta thalassemia. Bioverativ was spun off from Biogen in early 2017; it is now being acquired by France-based drug maker Sanofi for $11.6 billion.

BIOVEST INTERNATIONAL, INC.

8500 EVERGREEN BLVD NW
MINNEAPOLIS, MN 554336016
Phone: 763 786-0302
Fax: –
Web: www.cellculturecompany.com

CEO: Christiaan Engstrom
CFO: –
HR: –
FYE: September 30
Type: Private

BioVest International is invested in biotechnology. BioVest offers cell culture products, instruments, and related contract services to research institutions, biotech firms, and pharmaceutical companies. The company is also developing a therapeutic cancer vaccine for follicular non-Hodgkin's lymphoma that is customized for individual patient use. The candidate, dubbed BiovaxID, is in late stages of development. Its AutovaxID product is a cell culture instrument designed to ease use of BiovaxID. BioVest was established in 1981.

BIRDS EYE FOODS INC

90 Linden Oaks, P.O. Box 20670
Rochester, NY 14602-0670
Phone: 585 383-1850
Fax: –
Web: www.birdseyefoods.com

CEO: Neil Harrison
CFO: Chris Puma
HR: –
FYE: June 24
Type: Public

The view at Birds Eye Foods is on vegetables and a healthy bottom line. The company's namesake packaged frozen vegetables, whether boxed and bagged, are the #1 brand in the US frozen vegetable industry -- a more than $2 billion market in terms of retail sales. The company is also the #2 producer of frozen complete bagged meals that provide a protein, starch, and vegetable. Birds Eye also makes such staples as bottled salad dressings and canned pie fillings and chili. It supplies US retail food retailers, as well as foodservice and industrial food customers. Birds Eye operates as a division of diversified foods producer Pinnacle Foods, itself owned by investment giant The Blackstone Group.

	Annual Growth	06/02	06/03	06/04	06/05	06/06
Sales ($mil.)	(2.1%)	1,010.5	779.0	843.4	858.7	927.8
Net income ($ mil.)	–	(130.7)	20.8	31.9	18.6	14.7
Market value ($ mil.)	–	–	–	–	–	–
Employees	(10.3%)	5,484	3,900	3,650	3,700	3,550

BIRMINGHAM-SOUTHERN COLLEGE INC

900 ARKADELPHIA RD
BIRMINGHAM, AL 352540002
Phone: 205 226-4600
Fax: –
Web: www.bsc.edu

CEO: –
CFO: –
HR: –
FYE: May 31
Type: Private

Birmingham-Southern College is a private liberal arts college affiliated with the United Methodist Church. The school offers bachelor's degrees in more than 50 fields of study, including art history, math, physics, and religion. It has an enrollment of approximately 1,300 students. In addition to core curriculum in areas of arts, fine arts, music, and science, the college has study abroad, independent study, research, honors, interdisciplinary study, and internship programs. Birmingham-Southern College is the result of the 1918 merger between Southern University (founded in 1856) and Birmingham College (founded in 1898).

	Annual Growth	05/14	05/15	05/16	05/20	05/22
Sales ($mil.)	(6.2%)	–	66.6	70.5	47.2	42.7
Net income ($ mil.)	–	–	(4.1)	(4.4)	(8.5)	(37.9)
Market value ($ mil.)	–	–	–	–	–	–
Employees	–	–	–	–	–	299

BIRNER DENTAL MANAGEMENT SERVICES, INC.

1777 S HARRISON ST STE 1400
DENVER, CO 802103937
Phone: 720 897-1526
Fax: –
Web: www.perfectteeth.com

CEO: –
CFO: –
HR: –
FYE: December 31
Type: Private

Rocky Mountain Dental Services (formerly Birner Dental Management Services) hopes to leave its customers smiling. The company acquires, develops, and manages dental practice networks, freeing dentists of their administrative duties by providing management services such as billing, accounting, and marketing. Rocky Mountain Dental manages about 60 offices under the Perfect Teeth brand name; more than 40 of the practices are located in Colorado, and the rest are in Arizona and New Mexico. Some locations offer special services such as orthodontics, oral surgery, and periodontics. In early 2019 Mid-Atlantic Dental Partners bought Birner, which it then renamed Rocky Mountain Dental.

BIT MINING LTD

428 South Seiberling Street
Akron, OH 44306
Phone: 346 204-8537
Fax: (86) 755 83796070
Web: www.500.com

NYS: BTCM
CEO: –
CFO: –
HR: –
FYE: December 31
Type: Public

Could you be a winner? Check out 500.com. The company runs online lotteries and sports betting services in China. Operating under the brand 500wan (which translates to "5 million" in Chinese, the typical top prize amount), the company is only one of two authorized by the Ministry of Finance to provide online lotteries. More than 18 million people are registered users with 500wan (only about 800,000 are active users, in a country with 1.3 billion people), but 500.com plans to boost its user base by offering mobile betting services. 500.com went public in the US in 2013. It raised $75 million and plans to use the proceeds to grow its business with investments in sales and marketing, R&D, and technology improvement.

	Annual Growth	12/18	12/19	12/20	12/21	12/22
Sales ($mil.)	144.0%	18.3	5.7	3.3	1,328.9	650.2
Net income ($ mil.)	–	(65.7)	(93.6)	(34.1)	(60.5)	(155.4)
Market value ($ mil.)	(32.4%)	8,063.7	9,148.8	9,574.3	6,531.8	1,680.8
Employees	–	282	171	138	153	–

BJ'S RESTAURANTS INC
NMS: BJRI

7755 Center Avenue, Suite 300
Huntington Beach, CA 92647
Phone: 714 500-2400
Fax: –
Web: www.bjsrestaurants.com

CEO: –
CFO: –
HR: –
FYE: January 2
Type: Public

BJ's Restaurants (BJ's) owns and operates some 215 restaurants located in 30 other states. BJ's more than 100 menu includes a wide variety of offerings and has something for everyone: slow-roasted entrees, like prime rib; BJ's EnLIGHTened Entrees including Cherry Chipotle Glazed Salmon; signature deep dish pizza; and the world-famous Pizookie dessert. The company takes pride in serving BJ's award-winning proprietary handcrafted beers, brewed on its own brewing facilities and certain third party craft brewers using its proprietary recipes. It offers best-in-class service, hospitality, and enjoyment, in a high-energy, welcoming, and approachable atmosphere. The first BJ's opened in California in 1978.

	Annual Growth	12/19	12/20	12/21*	01/23	01/24
Sales ($mil.)	3.5%	1,161.5	778.5	1,087.0	1,283.9	1,333.2
Net income ($ mil.)	(18.8%)	45.2	(57.9)	(3.6)	4.1	19.7
Market value ($ mil.)	(1.8%)	880.1	880.8	827.7	622.5	817.9
Employees	(1.7%)	22,500	17,000	21,000	22,000	21,000

*Fiscal year change

BJ'S WHOLESALE CLUB HOLDINGS INC
NYS: BJ

350 Campus Drive
Marlborough, MA 01752
Phone: 774 512-7400
Fax: –
Web: www.bjs.com

CEO: Robert W Eddy
CFO: Laura L Felice
HR: –
FYE: February 3
Type: Public

BJ's Wholesale Club is a leading warehouse club operator concentrated primarily on the east coast of the US. The company provides a curated assortment focused on perishable products, continuously refreshed general merchandise, gasoline and other ancillary services, coupons, and promotions. It has grown its footprint to over 235 large-format, high-volume warehouse clubs, and 165 gas stations spanning nearly 20 states. In addition to shopping in its clubs, members can shop through its website, www.bjs.com, and its highly rated mobile app, which allows them to use the company's buy-online-pickup-in-club service, curbside delivery, same-day home delivery or traditional ship-to-home service, as well as through the DoorDash and Instacart marketplaces. Its two private-label brands include Wellsley Farms and Berkley Jensen.

	Annual Growth	02/20*	01/21	01/22	01/23*	02/24
Sales ($mil.)	10.9%	13,191	15,430	16,667	19,315	19,969
Net income ($ mil.)	29.3%	187.2	421.0	426.7	513.2	523.7
Market value ($ mil.)	33.2%	2,724.4	5,585.5	7,691.3	9,253.9	8,564.9
Employees	5.7%	27,231	32,000	34,000	34,000	34,000

*Fiscal year change

BJT, INC.

2233 CAPITAL BLVD
RALEIGH, NC 276041421
Phone: 919 828-3842
Fax: –
Web: www.mutualdistributing.com

CEO: William Kennedy
CFO: –
HR: Suette Strod
FYE: December 31
Type: Private

A wholesaler of Southern comfort, Mutual Distributing distributes alcoholic and nonalcoholic beverages in North Carolina. The company, started in 1946, operates from seven locations across the state. Alcoholic beverage brands handled by Mutual Distributing include domestic and imported wine labels by Wyndham Estate, Robert Mondavi, Moet & Chandon, and Folie a Deux, and beers by Anchor, Tecate, Heineken, and Sapporo. The company distributes bottled waters, too, such as Evian, Perrier, San Pellegrino, and Fiji. Mutual Distributing caters to retail customers (supermarkets, convenience stores and specialty package outlets, restaurants, and hotels) in every county in North Carolina.

	Annual Growth	12/04	12/05	12/06	12/08	12/09
Sales ($mil.)	6.1%	–	158.3	172.7	192.0	200.4
Net income ($ mil.)	17.8%	–	3.2	4.2	7.8	6.2
Market value ($ mil.)	–	–	–	–	–	–
Employees	–	–	–	–	–	650

BK TECHNOLOGIES CORP
ASE: BKTI

7100 Technology Drive
West Melbourne, FL 32904
Phone: 321 984-1414
Fax: –
Web: www.bktechnologies.com

CEO: John M Suzuki
CFO: William P Kelly
HR: –
FYE: December 31
Type: Public

RELM Wireless spreads communications across the land. The company makes portable land mobile radio (LMR) products used for mobile handheld and vehicle communications. In addition to radios, its products include base stations, repeaters, and related subsystems. The US government and public safety agencies account for the vast majority of RELM's sales, but the company also markets to hotels, construction firms, schools, and transportation service providers. RELM Wireless sells its radio communications systems under the BK Radio, RELM, and RELM/BK brands.

	Annual Growth	12/19	12/20	12/21	12/22	12/23
Sales ($mil.)	16.6%	40.1	44.1	45.4	51.0	74.1
Net income ($ mil.)	–	(2.6)	0.2	(1.7)	(11.6)	(2.2)
Market value ($ mil.)	40.9%	11.1	10.8	8.6	11.9	43.7
Employees	6.9%	111	95	113	148	145

BKF CAPITAL GROUP INC
NBB: BKFG

1 Jenner, Suite 200
Irvine, CA 92618
Phone: 949 504-4424
Fax: –
Web: www.bkfcapital.com

CEO: Steven N Bronson
CFO: David S Burnett
HR: –
FYE: December 31
Type: Public

Wanted: business opportunity for former investment firm. Contact BKF Capital Group. BKF is evaluating strategic alternatives including a possible merger, acquisition, or other business combination. The company has no operations and only a small revenue stream (more like a trickle) from its days as an asset manager and broker dealer; it is no longer a registered investment advisor and has also surrendered its broker license. Its primary subsidiary is BKF Asset Management, but as the company itself points out, it has no operations either. BKF Capital's search for a new raison d'etre was put on hold when it was named in a class action shareholder lawsuit, but the suit was dropped in 2007 and the search resumed.

	Annual Growth	12/17	12/18	12/19	12/20	12/21
Sales ($mil.)	–	–	–	–	–	0.1
Net income ($ mil.)	–	0.1	(0.1)	(0.2)	(0.4)	(0.2)
Market value ($ mil.)	(5.4%)	8.7	6.6	7.0	7.0	7.0
Employees	–	–	–	–	–	–

BLACK & VEATCH CORPORATION

11401 LAMAR AVE
OVERLAND PARK, KS 662111598
Phone: 913 458-2000
Fax: –
Web: www.bv.com

CEO: –
CFO: –
HR: –
FYE: December 31
Type: Private

Black & Veatch (BV) is one of the world's top global engineering, procurement, consulting, and construction companies specializing in infrastructure development for the energy, oil and gas, water, environmental, and telecommunications industries and governments. BV offers micro consulting experts on demand, engineering consulting, and management consulting. In addition to data analytics, master planning and construction, the company also offers federal design and integrated solutions, land services and acquisition, civil works, integrated water solutions, and advisory services. The employee-owned contractor has offices in roughly 25 countries around the world. The company was founded by engineers Ernest Bateman (E.B.) Black and Nathan Thomas (N.T.) Veatch in 1915.

	Annual Growth	12/06	12/07	12/08	12/09	12/20
Sales ($mil.)	(40.9%)	–	1,287.3	1,267.3	1,163.0	1.4
Net income ($ mil.)	(33.3%)	–	33.5	16.9	58.2	0.2
Market value ($ mil.)	–	–	–	–	–	–
Employees	–	–	–	–	–	6,375

BLACK HILLS CORPORATION
NYS: BKH

7001 Mount Rushmore Road
Rapid City, SD 57702
Phone: 605 721-1700
Fax: –
Web: www.blackhillscorp.com

CEO: Linden R Evans
CFO: Richard W Kinzley
HR: Bret Atkins
FYE: December 31
Type: Public

The Black Hills Corporation is a customer-focused, growth-oriented utility company with a mission of Improving Life with Energy for more than 1.3 million customers and over 800 communities it serves. The company conducts natural gas utility operations through its Arkansas, Colorado, Iowa, Kansas, Nebraska, and Wyoming subsidiaries. Its Gas Utilities transport and distribute natural gas through its distribution network and provide non-regulated services to its regulated customers. Its Electric Utilities segment conducts operations through its Colorado, South Dakota, and Wyoming subsidiaries. Its electric generating facilities and power purchase agreements provide for the supply of electricity principally to its retail customers.

	Annual Growth	12/19	12/20	12/21	12/22	12/23
Sales ($mil.)	7.7%	1,734.9	1,696.9	1,949.1	2,551.8	2,331.3
Net income ($ mil.)	7.1%	199.3	227.6	236.7	258.4	262.2
Market value ($ mil.)	(9.0%)	5,356.2	4,190.7	4,812.7	4,797.0	3,679.2
Employees	(0.6%)	2,944	3,011	2,884	2,982	2,874

BLACK HILLS POWER INC.

7001 Mount Rushmore Road
Rapid City, SD 57702
Phone: 605 721-1700
Fax: –
Web: www.blackhillspower.com

CEO: David R Emery
CFO: Richard W Kinzley
HR: –
FYE: December 31
Type: Public

Mount Rushmore is a monument to the powerful in the Black Hills of South Dakota. Black Hills Power, formed in 1941, the same year the Mount Rushmore was completed, gets power to the people. It generates, transmits, and distributes electricity to 66,000 customers. Its 9,300 sq.ml. service area encompasses western South Dakota, northeastern Wyoming, and southeastern Montana. The utility became a subsidiary of Black Hills Corporation in 2000. Its five electric power plants are fueled by low-sulphur Wyoming coal, mined by Black Hills Corp.'s unit Wyodak Resource Development Corp.

	Annual Growth	12/15	12/16	12/17	12/18	12/19
Sales ($mil.)	1.2%	277.9	267.6	288.4	298.1	291.2
Net income ($ mil.)	0.9%	45.2	45.1	51.3	45.6	46.9
Market value ($ mil.)	–	–	–	–	–	–
Employees	–	–	–	–	–	217

BLACK KNIGHT, INC.

601 RIVERSIDE AVE
JACKSONVILLE, FL 322042946
Phone: 904 854-5100
Fax: –
Web: www.blackknightinc.com

CEO: Joseph M Nackashi
CFO: Kirk T Larsen
HR: –
FYE: December 31
Type: Private

Black Knight is a premier provider of integrated, innovative, mission-critical, high-performance software solutions, data and, analytics to the US mortgage and real estate markets. The Black Knight ecosystem stretches across four core "pillar" verticals: mortgage loan servicing, mortgage loan origination, real estate and capital markets; with its data and analytics flowing throughout the interconnected ecosystem of solutions. In 2022, Black Knight agreed to be acquired by Intercontinental Exchange, Inc, a leading global provider of data, technology, and market infrastructure, for a market value of about $13.1 billion.

BLACK RAVEN ENERGY, INC.

1331 Seventeenth Street, Suite 350
Denver, CO 80202
Phone: 303 308-1330
Fax: –
Web: www.prbtrans.com

CEO: Robert Watson Jr
CFO: Douglas Wright
HR: –
FYE: December 31
Type: Public

Black Raven Energy (formerly PRB Energy) is engaged in coal-bed methane production in the Rocky Mountains. The company focuses on natural gas gathering and exploration and production. Its exploration and gathering and processing operations are primarily located in the Powder River Basin. In 2007 PRB Energy was targeting reserves of about 100 billion cu. ft. of natural gas equivalent, before deteriorating finances hurt its expansion plans. The company filed for Chapter 11 bankruptcy protection in 2008. In preparation to emerge from bankruptcy it reorganized as Black Raven Energy in 2009.

	Annual Growth	12/06	12/07	12/08	12/09	12/10
Sales ($mil.)	(44.2%)	4.8	3.1	2.4	0.5	0.5
Net income ($ mil.)	–	(8.7)	(30.4)	(12.1)	20.7	(3.3)
Market value ($ mil.)	–	55.5	4.7	0.0	–	–
Employees	(30.7%)	26	–	6	6	6

BLACK STONE MINERALS LP
NYS: BSM

1001 Fannin Street, Suite 2020
Houston, TX 77002
Phone: 713 445-3200
Fax: –
Web: www.blackstoneminerals.com

CEO: Thomas L Carter Jr
CFO: Jeffrey P Wood
HR: –
FYE: December 31
Type: Public

One of the largest owners of oil and natural gas mineral interests in the US, Black Stone Minerals holds an average of 48.1% ownership interest in mineral assets in 14.5 million acres. It also own nonparticipating royalty interests in 1.2 million acres and overriding royalty interests in 1.4 million acres. It also has ownership in 40,000 producing wells. Black Stone Minerals' mineral and royalty interests are located in 41 states and in 62 onshore basins. The breadth of its asset base and the long-lived, non-cost-bearing nature of the company's mineral and royalty interests allows it to add production and reserves from new and existing plays without investing more capital. The company went public in 2015.

	Annual Growth	12/19	12/20	12/21	12/22	12/23
Sales ($mil.)	5.0%	487.8	342.8	359.3	663.6	592.2
Net income ($ mil.)	18.5%	214.4	121.8	182.0	476.5	422.5
Market value ($ mil.)	5.8%	2,671.1	1,402.7	2,169.2	3,542.6	3,351.5
Employees	(1.6%)	115	101	108	108	108

BLACKBAUD, INC.
NMS: BLKB

65 Fairchild Street
Charleston, SC 29492
Phone: 843 216-6200
Fax: 843 216-6100
Web: www.blackbaud.com

CEO: Michael P Gianoni
CFO: Anthony W Boor
HR: –
FYE: December 31
Type: Public

Serving nonprofits, higher education institutions, K?12 schools, healthcare organizations, faith communities, arts and cultural organizations, foundations, companies and individual change agents, Blackbaud connects and empowers organizations and individuals to increase their impact through cloud software, services, data intelligence, and expertise. The Blackbaud's tailored portfolio of software and services has grown to support the unique needs of vertical markets, with solutions for fundraising and CRM, marketing, advocacy, peer-to-peer fundraising, corporate social responsibility (CSR) and environmental, social and governance (ESG), school management, ticketing, grant-making, financial management, payment processing and analytics.

	Annual Growth	12/19	12/20	12/21	12/22	12/23
Sales ($mil.)	5.3%	900.4	913.2	927.7	1,058.1	1,105.4
Net income ($ mil.)	(37.5%)	11.9	7.7	5.7	(45.4)	1.8
Market value ($ mil.)	2.2%	4,268.6	3,086.7	4,235.3	3,156.4	4,649.3
Employees	(4.5%)	3,611	3,100	3,600	3,200	3,000

BLACKFOOT TELEPHONE COOPERATIVE, INC.

1221 N RUSSELL ST
MISSOULA, MT 598081898
Phone: 406 541-2121
Fax: –
Web: www.blackfoot.com

CEO: Bill Squires
CFO: Theodore Otis
HR: –
FYE: December 31
Type: Private

Blackfoot Telecommunications Cooperative provides phone services to rural communities along the Blackfoot River in western Montana and central Idaho. Founded in 1954, it is the first of the Blackfoot Communications Group of companies, which includes competitive local-exchange carrier (CLEC) Blackfoot Communications, Blackfoot.net Internet services provider, and telecom software maker TeleSphere. The company's services include local and long-distance phone service, dial-up and DSL Internet access, and PCS wireless. It also owns a stake in video conferencing specialist Vision Net.

	Annual Growth	12/05	12/06	12/07	12/08	12/09
Sales ($mil.)	0.6%	–	31.6	33.1	33.9	32.1
Net income ($ mil.)	10.5%	–	2.9	2.9	3.7	3.9
Market value ($ mil.)	–	–	–	–	–	–
Employees	–	–	–	–	–	214

BLACKHAWK BANCORP INC

400 Broad Street
Beloit, WI 53511
Phone: 608 364-8911
Fax: 608 363-6186
Web: www.blackhawkbank.com

NBB: BHWB
CEO: –
CFO: –
HR: –
FYE: December 31
Type: Public

This Blackhawk's mission is to increase your bottom line. Blackhawk Bancorp is the holding company for Blackhawk State Bank (aka Blackhawk Bank), which has nearly 10 locations in south-central Wisconsin and north-central Illinois. Serving area consumers and businesses, the bank offers standard financial services, such as checking, savings, and money market accounts, CDs, credit cards, and wealth management. It also caters to the Hispanic community by offering bilingual services at some of its branches. Blackhawk Bank maintains a somewhat diverse loan portfolio, with residential mortgages, commercial and industrial loans, and commercial real estate loans accounting for the bulk of its lending activities.

	Annual Growth	12/18	12/19	12/20	12/21	12/22
Assets ($mil.)	12.8%	817.3	963.9	1,141.6	1,341.2	1,321.8
Net income ($ mil.)	13.8%	8.1	9.6	10.8	13.6	13.6
Market value ($ mil.)	2.8%	76.3	79.8	80.3	99.6	85.3
Employees	–	–	–	–	–	–

BLACKLINE INC

21300 Victory Boulevard, 12th Floor
Woodland Hills, CA 91367
Phone: 818 223-9008
Fax: –
Web: www.blackline.com

NMS: BL
CEO: Owen Ryan
CFO: Mark Partin
HR: –
FYE: December 31
Type: Public

BlackLine created its comprehensive cloud-based accounting software platform designed to transform and modernize accounting and finance operations for organizations of all types and sizes. The company's secure, scalable platform supports critical accounting processes such as the financial close, account reconciliations, intercompany accounting, and controls assurance. BlackLine's customers include multinational corporations, large domestic enterprises and mid-market companies across a broad array of industries. It empowers its customers to improve the integrity of their financial reporting, increase efficiency in their accounting and finance processes and enhance real-time visibility into their results and operations. The US generates more than 70% of the company's total sales.

	Annual Growth	12/19	12/20	12/21	12/22	12/23
Sales ($mil.)	19.5%	289.0	351.7	425.7	522.9	590.0
Net income ($ mil.)	–	(32.5)	(46.9)	(115.2)	(29.4)	52.8
Market value ($ mil.)	4.9%	3,171.7	8,204.9	6,369.3	4,138.1	3,841.0
Employees	13.5%	1,055	1,325	1,557	1,814	1,750

BLACKROCK INC

50 Hudson Yards
New York, NY 10001
Phone: 212 810-5300
Fax: –
Web: www.blackrock.com

NYS: BLK
CEO: Laurence D Fink
CFO: Martin Small
HR: –
FYE: December 31
Type: Public

With about 8.6 trillion in assets under management, BlackRock is a leading public investment management firm. It specializes in equity and fixed income products, as well as alternative and money market instruments, which it invests in on behalf of institutional and retail investors worldwide. Clients include pension plans, governments, insurance companies, financial institutions, endowments, foundations, charities, third party fund sponsors and retail investors. BlackRock also provides technology products and services through its Aladdin, Aladdin Wealth, eFront, and Cachematrix. The company has offices in more than 30 countries who serve clients in over 100 countries across the globe. The company's largest geographical market is the Americas with more than 65% of the total revenue.

	Annual Growth	12/19	12/20	12/21	12/22	12/23
Sales ($mil.)	5.3%	14,539	16,205	19,374	17,873	17,859
Net income ($ mil.)	5.3%	4,476.0	4,932.0	5,901.0	5,178.0	5,502.0
Market value ($ mil.)	12.7%	74,651	107,149	135,961	105,232	120,552
Employees	5.1%	16,200	16,500	18,400	19,800	19,800

BLACKSTONE INC

345 Park Avenue
New York, NY 10154
Phone: 212 583-5000
Fax: –
Web: www.blackstone.com

NYS: BX
CEO: Stephen A Schwarzman
CFO: Michael S Chae
HR: –
FYE: December 31
Type: Public

Blackstone is one of the world's largest real estate, private equity, and alternative asset managers in the world, with more than $974.7 billion in assets under management. Its real estate investment holdings constitute more than $326.1 billion, making Blackstone one of the world's largest real estate investors. The firm manages investment vehicles including real estate, private equity, public debt and equity, growth equity, opportunistic, non-investment grade credit, real assets and secondary funds, all on a global basis. Blackstone's clients include more than 31 million pensioners in the US and millions more globally. In 2023, Blackstone agreed to acquire Cvent Holding Corp. (Cvent), an industry-leading meetings, events and hospitality technology provider, for an enterprise value of approximately of $4.6 billion.

	Annual Growth	12/19	12/20	12/21	12/22	12/23
Sales ($mil.)	2.3%	7,338.3	6,101.9	22,577	8,517.7	8,022.8
Net income ($ mil.)	(9.2%)	2,049.7	1,045.4	5,857.4	1,747.6	1,390.9
Market value ($ mil.)	23.7%	40,241	46,622	93,078	53,369	94,178
Employees	13.0%	2,905	3,165	3,795	4,695	4,735

BLACKSTONE MORTGAGE TRUST INC

345 Park Avenue, 24th Floor
New York, NY 10154
Phone: 212 655-0220
Fax: –
Web: www.blackstonemortgagetrust.com

NYS: BXMT
CEO: Michael B Nash
CFO: Anthony F Marone Jr
HR: Lorena Cohen
FYE: December 31
Type: Public

Capital Trust thinks investing in commercial mortgages is a capital idea. The self-managed real estate investment trust (REIT) originates, underwrites, and invests in commercial real estate assets on its own behalf and for other investors. Its portfolio includes first mortgage and bridge loans, mezzanine loans, and collateralized mortgage-backed securities. Subsidiary CT Investment Management, which the company is selling, manages five private equity funds and a separate account for third parties. Most Capital Trust's assets are related to US properties, but the REIT does make occasional investments in international instruments.

	Annual Growth	12/18	12/19	12/20	12/21	12/22
Sales ($mil.)	15.4%	756.1	882.7	779.6	854.7	1,339.0
Net income ($ mil.)	(3.4%)	285.1	305.6	137.7	419.2	248.6
Market value ($ mil.)	(9.7%)	5,470.2	6,390.5	4,726.8	5,257.3	3,634.8
Employees	–	–	–	–	–	–

BLARNEY CASTLE OIL CO.

12218 WEST ST
BEAR LAKE, MI 496149453
Phone: 231 864-3111
Fax: –
Web: www.blarneycastleoil.com

CEO: –
CFO: –
HR: –
FYE: March 31
Type: Private

While kissing the Blarney stone has a reputation for reliably making people loquacious, Blarney Castle Oil and Propane has a reputation for reliably supplying its customers with fuels. The family-owned company transports petroleum products to customers through about 10 office locations in Michigan. Its products include agricultural and commercial fuels (diesel and gasoline), commercial and industrial lubricants and coolants, home heating oil, fuel oil, and propane. Blarney Castle Oil and Propane also operates 90 convenience stores under the EZ Mart brand name.

	Annual Growth	03/09	03/10	03/11	03/12	03/13
Sales ($mil.)	11.2%	–	–	415.3	501.5	513.6
Net income ($ mil.)	42.7%	–	–	3.0	4.0	6.0
Market value ($ mil.)	–	–	–	–	–	–
Employees		–	–	–	–	700

BLESSING HOSPITAL

BROADWAY AT 11TH ST
QUINCY, IL 62301
Phone: 217 223-1200
Fax: –
Web: www.blessinghealth.org

CEO: Maureen A Kahn
CFO: –
HR: –
FYE: September 30
Type: Private

Blessing Hospital is a not-for-profit acute care medical center that provides a wide range of health services to residents in areas of western Illinois, northeast Missouri, and southeast Iowa. Through its main campus location, it provides primary and emergency care, as well as specialty services including diagnostics and surgery. The hospital is home to centers of excellence in the treatment of cancer, heart and cardiovascular ailments, wound care, and women's health issues. Blessing Hospital provides outpatient and behavioral health services at a nearby campus. It also operates family practice centers and provides home and hospice care services. It is part of the Blessing Health System.

	Annual Growth	09/07	09/08	09/12	09/15	09/16
Sales ($mil.)	5.1%	–	238.4	289.1	316.3	355.2
Net income ($ mil.)	–	–	(2.2)	14.8	15.2	52.6
Market value ($ mil.)	–	–	–	–	–	–
Employees	–	–	–	–	–	2,500

BLISH-MIZE CO.

223 S 5TH ST
ATCHISON, KS 660022801
Phone: 913 367-1250
Fax: –
Web: www.blishmize.com

CEO: Jonathan Mize
CFO: Tom Hottovy
HR: –
FYE: December 31
Type: Private

Hardware supplier Blish-Mize distributes more than 52,000 products to hardware stores, home centers, lumberyards, and paint stores in a dozen states in the heartland of the US. Its catalog includes hand and power tools, lawn equipment, hardware, paint, heating and cooling products, housewares, plumbing and electrical supplies, and sporting goods. The company has distribution centers in Colorado and Kansas. Aside from its wholesaling business, Blish-Mize operates toolmaker Hardware House with House-Hasson. Brothers-in-law David Blish, Edward Mize, and Jack Silliman founded the firm in 1871 to outfit wagon trains. President and CEO John Mize, Jr., represents the fourth generation of the family-owned company.

	Annual Growth	12/05	12/06	12/07	12/08	12/09
Sales ($mil.)	(2.8%)	–	–	64.1	64.0	60.5
Net income ($ mil.)	(33.6%)	–	–	1.6	1.8	0.7
Market value ($ mil.)	–	–	–	–	–	–
Employees	–	–	–	–	–	175

BLISTEX INC.

1800 SWIFT DR
OAK BROOK, IL 605231574
Phone: 630 571-2870
Fax: –
Web: www.blistex.com

CEO: David C Arch
CFO: –
HR: –
FYE: December 31
Type: Private

As one of the nation's largest lip-care product makers, Blistex intends to gloss over its competition. The company is best known for its slew of slick lip treatments and treats sold under the Blistex name. Products range from medicated berry balm to a lip massage or infusion. Dipping into other personal care niche markets, Blistex product lines include Stridex acne medication, Foille first aid ointment, Kank-A which provided solutions tailored to specific oral pain needs, and Ivarest, a skin care brand. Blistex sells its products primarily through supermarkets such as Kroger and drug and beauty stores the likes of Ulta worldwide. The founding Arch family owns and operates Blistex.

BLOCK (H & R), INC.

NYS: HRB

One H&R Block Way
Kansas City, MO 64105
Phone: 816 854-3000
Fax: –
Web: www.hrblock.com

CEO: Jeffrey J Jones II
CFO: Tony G Bowen
HR: –
FYE: June 30
Type: Public

H&R Block is one of the largest providers of tax return preparation solutions and electronic filing services in the US, Canada, and Australia with 23.4 million returns filed by or through H&R Block in fiscal year 2023 via more than 12,000 offices and its virtual tax preparation services, mobile applications, and online and desktop DIY solutions. The company offers customers the options of filing taxes online or in person and doing their own taxes or having them done by an H&R Block professional. Through Block Advisors and Wave, the company helps small business owners with an online solution to manage their finances, including payment processing, payroll, and bookkeeping services. H&R was founded in 1955 by brothers Henry and Richard Bloch.

	Annual Growth	04/20	04/21*	06/21	06/22	06/23
Sales ($mil.)	9.6%	2,639.7	3,414.0	466.1	3,463.3	3,472.2
Net income ($ mil.)	–	(7.5)	583.8	89.6	553.7	553.7
Market value ($ mil.)	24.2%	2,433.4	3,253.3	3,431.6	5,162.0	4,657.8
Employees	4.6%	3,500	3,600	–	–	4,000

*Fiscal year change

BLOCK COMMUNICATIONS, INC.

405 MADISON AVE STE 2100
TOLEDO, OH 436041224
Phone: 419 724-6212
Fax: –
Web: www.blockcommunications.com

CEO: Allan J Block
CFO: –
HR: Jodi L Miehs
FYE: December 31
Type: Private

If your block happens to be in Toledo, Ohio, or Pittsburgh, you can thank this company for delivering the daily news. Block Communications (BCI) is a family-owned regional media company that operates two major newspapers, The Blade (Toledo) and the Pittsburgh Post-Gazette. It also owns and operates TV stations: Wand; NBC Lima; WDRB Fox, WMYOTV, as well as cable television systems serving subscribers in Toledo and Sandusky, Ohio. Its Telesystem provides communication solutions across more than 17,000 addresses in some 45 states, DC and four foreign countries. Block family patriarch Paul Block started the family fortune when he acquired The Blade in 1927.

BLOCK INC   NYS: SQ

1455 Market Street, Suite 600
San Francisco, CA 94103
Phone: 415 375-3176
Fax: -
Web: www.squareup.com

CEO: -
CFO: -
HR: -
FYE: December 31
Type: Public

Block is a global technology company with a focus on financial services. Made up of Square, Cash App, Spiral, TIDAL, and TBD, Block build tools to help more people access the economy. Square helps sellers run and grow their businesses with its integrated ecosystem of commerce solutions, business software, and banking services. With Cash App, anyone can easily send, spend, or invest their money in stocks or Bitcoin. Spiral builds and funds free, open-source Bitcoin projects. Artists use TIDAL to help them succeed as entrepreneurs and connect more deeply with fans. TBD is building an open developer platform to make it easier to access Bitcoin and other blockchain technologies without having to go through an institution. Almost 95% of total revenue comes from the US.

	Annual Growth	12/19	12/20	12/21	12/22	12/23
Sales ($mil.)	46.8%	4,713.5	9,497.6	17,661	17,532	21,916
Net income ($ mil.)	(59.8%)	375.4	213.1	166.3	(540.7)	9.8
Market value ($ mil.)	5.4%	38,526	134,027	99,461	38,698	47,634
Employees	35.6%	3,835	5,477	8,521	12,428	12,985

BLONDER TONGUE LABORATORIES, INC.   NBB: BDRL

One Jake Brown Road
Old Bridge, NJ 08857
Phone: 732 679-4000
Fax: -
Web: www.blondertongue.com

CEO: Edward R Grauch
CFO: Eric S Skolnik
HR: -
FYE: December 31
Type: Public

Blonder Tongue Laboratories isn't involved in genetic modification -- it makes equipment for acquiring and distributing cable TV signals. Founded by Isaac Blonder and Ben Tongue, the company's offerings center on analog and digital video products for headend facilities (television signal-receiving centers), such as encoders, receivers, and modulators, as well as hybrid fiber-coax (HFC) distribution products, which deliver the signal to the viewer. Blonder Tongue mainly serves cable operators, TV broadcasters, the lodging and hospitality sector, and institutional facilities such as schools, hospitals, stadiums, airports, and prisons.

	Annual Growth	12/18	12/19	12/20	12/21	12/22
Sales ($mil.)	(4.4%)	21.7	19.8	16.4	15.8	18.1
Net income ($ mil.)	-	(1.3)	(0.7)	(7.5)	0.0	(2.9)
Market value ($ mil.)	(35.5%)	14.8	10.1	17.8	7.9	2.6
Employees	(13.0%)	117	93	85	84	67

BLOODWORKS

921 TERRY AVE
SEATTLE, WA 981041239
Phone: 206 292-6500
Fax: -
Web: www.bloodworksnw.org

CEO: -
CFO: -
HR: -
FYE: June 30
Type: Private

Residents of the Emerald City can go here to give red. Bloodworks Northwest (formerly Puget Sound Blood Center) is a not-for-profit blood and tissue bank serving nearly 90 hospitals and clinics in the Pacific Northwest. The blood center collects and processes donated blood through about a dozen donation centers and several mobile units; it also registers bone marrow donors, provides testing and training services to patients with hemophilia, and collects cord blood for use in stem cell transplantation. Bloodworks Northwest Research Institute conducts research on improving transfusion and transplantation medicine. The organization was formed in 1944.

	Annual Growth	06/18	06/19	06/20	06/21	06/22
Sales ($mil.)	(27.7%)	-	-	-	185.8	134.3
Net income ($ mil.)	-	-	-	-	12.3	(2.1)
Market value ($ mil.)	-	-	-	-	-	-
Employees	-	-	-	-	-	750

BLOOM ENERGY CORP   NYS: BE

4353 North First Street
San Jose, CA 95134
Phone: 408 543-1500
Fax: -
Web: www.bloomenergy.com

CEO: K R Sridhar
CFO: Gregory Cameron
HR: -
FYE: December 31
Type: Public

Bloom Energy is one of the most advanced electricity and hydrogen-producing technologies on the market today. It created the first large-scale, commercially viable solid oxide fuel-cell-based power generation platform that empowers businesses, essential services, critical infrastructure, and communities to responsibly take charge of their energy. Its fuel-flexible Bloom Energy Servers can use biogas, hydrogen, natural gas, or a blend of fuels, to create resilient, sustainable, and cost-predictable power at electricity at significantly higher efficiencies than traditional, combustion-based resources. Its enterprise customers include some of the largest multinational corporations in the world. It also has strong relationships with some of the largest utility companies in the US and Korea. The company's largest market in terms of revenue is the Republic of Korea.

	Annual Growth	12/19	12/20	12/21	12/22	12/23
Sales ($mil.)	14.2%	785.2	794.2	972.2	1,199.1	1,333.5
Net income ($ mil.)	-	(304.4)	(157.6)	(164.2)	(301.7)	(302.1)
Market value ($ mil.)	18.6%	1,678.6	6,440.4	4,928.1	4,296.6	3,325.8
Employees	11.9%	1,518	1,711	1,719	2,530	2,377

BLOOMIN' BRANDS INC   NMS: BLMN

2202 North West Shore Boulevard, Suite 500
Tampa, FL 33607
Phone: 813 282-1225
Fax: -
Web: www.bloominbrands.com

CEO: David J Deno
CFO: Christopher Meyer
HR: -
FYE: December 31
Type: Public

Bloomin' Brands is one of the largest casual dining restaurant companies in the world with a portfolio of leading, differentiated restaurant concepts. The company owns nearly 1,200 restaurants in more than 45 US states, Guam and roughly 15 countries. It also franchises around 320 restaurants. Bloomin' Brands has four founder-inspired concepts: Outback Steakhouse, Carrabba's Italian Grill, Bonefish Grill and Fleming's Prime Steakhouse & Wine Bar. The company's restaurant concepts range in price point and degree of formality from casual (Outback Steakhouse and Carrabba's Italian Grill) to upscale casual (Bonefish Grill) and fine dining (Fleming's Prime Steakhouse & Wine Bar). OSI Restaurant Partners, LLC (OSI), a wholly-owned subsidiary of Bloomin' Brands, is its primary operating entity. The US accounts for about 90% of the company's revenue.

	Annual Growth	12/19	12/20	12/21	12/22	12/23
Sales ($mil.)	3.1%	4,139.4	3,170.6	4,122.4	4,416.5	4,671.5
Net income ($ mil.)	17.3%	130.6	(158.7)	215.6	101.9	247.4
Market value ($ mil.)	6.7%	1,885.5	1,648.1	1,822.0	1,822.9	2,448.2
Employees	(1.9%)	94,000	77,000	82,000	87,000	87,000

BLOUNT INTERNATIONAL, INC.

4909 SE INTERNATIONAL WAY
PORTLAND, OR 972224679
Phone: 503 653-8881
Fax: -
Web: www.blount.com

CEO: -
CFO: -
HR: -
FYE: December 31
Type: Private

Oregon Tool (formerly known as Blount International) is a global, premium-branded, aftermarket-driven precision cutting-tool platform. The company's portfolio of brands specializes in professional grade precision cutting tools for forestry, lawn and garden; farming, ranching and agriculture; and concrete cutting and finishing. Oregon Tool sells its products in more than 110 countries under the Oregon, Woods, ICS, Pentruder, Merit, Carlton, and SpeeCo brands. The company is the world's #1 manufacturer of saw chain and guide bars for chainsaws and diamond saw chain for concrete and pipe, a leading manufacturer of agricultural tractor attachments, and the leading OEM supplier of first-fit and replacement parts. Oregon Tool was founded in 1947 as Oregon Saw Chain Company by Joe Cox.

	Annual Growth	12/11	12/12	12/13	12/14	12/15
Sales ($mil.)	(3.7%)	-	927.7	900.6	944.8	828.6
Net income ($ mil.)	-	-	39.6	4.8	36.6	(49.9)
Market value ($ mil.)	-	-	-	-	-	-
Employees	-	-	-	-	-	4,000

BLOUNT MEMORIAL HOSPITAL, INCORPORATED

907 LAMAR ALEXANDER PKWY
MARYVILLE, TN 378045015
Phone: 865 983-7211
Fax: –
Web: www.blountmemorial.org

CEO: Don Heinemann
CFO: –
HR: –
FYE: June 30
Type: Private

Blount Memorial Hospital provides health care services in eastern Tennessee. Founded in 1947, the hospital offers area communities cardiopulmonary care, cancer care, radiology, women's health, and laboratory services. As part of its operations, Blount Memorial boasts satellite clinics devoted to family care, diagnostic imaging, occupational health services, and outpatient rehabilitation. The hospital serves seniors through its focus on specialty services, including senior care, home health care, hospice, home life assistance, occupational health, and wellness care.

	Annual Growth	06/02	06/03	06/05	06/06	06/15
Sales ($mil.)	4.3%	–	131.9	0.5	0.2	218.9
Net income ($ mil.)	(47.7%)	–	14.3	(0.0)	0.2	0.0
Market value ($ mil.)	–	–	–	–	–	–
Employees	–	–	–	–	–	2,060

BLUBUZZARD INC

13134 Route 62
Salem, OH 44460
Phone: 440 439-9480
Fax: –
Web: www.giantcorporate.com

NBB: BZRD
CEO: Russell A Haehn
CFO: –
HR: –
FYE: December 31
Type: Public

Giant Motorsports believes in thinking big when it comes to fun. The company is a leading motorsports dealer in the US that specializes in Suzuki models, but also peddles Yamaha, Honda, Ducati, Kawasaki, and Polaris brands. The company sells new and used motorcycles, ATVs, motor scooters, and personal watercraft, as well as related parts and accessories. It operates through two subsidiaries, W. W. Cycles (which does business in Ohio as Andrews Cycles) and Chicago Cycles. It also owns and operates two superstores: one in Salem, Ohio, and one as Chicago. Giant has been expanding and updating showrooms in hopes of becoming a shopping destination for those in the market for big, noisy toys.

	Annual Growth	12/04	12/05	12/06	12/07	12/08
Sales ($mil.)	2.3%	80.0	105.6	100.8	98.7	87.5
Net income ($ mil.)	(55.0%)	1.0	(0.0)	(0.2)	0.8	0.0
Market value ($ mil.)	(51.5%)	224.1	85.9	27.4	31.1	12.5
Employees	(5.9%)	112	154	134	118	88

BLUE BEACON, INC.

500 GRAVES BLVD
SALINA, KS 674014306
Phone: 785 825-2221
Fax: –
Web: www.bluebeacon.com

CEO: –
CFO: –
HR: Darcy Campbell
FYE: September 30
Type: Private

RV and truck drivers can follow the beacon to get a clean rig. Blue Beacon operates approximately 110 truck and RV washing locations in about 40 US states and in Ontario, Canada, more than any of its competitors. Its washes are open 24 hours and usually found at truck stops (including Pilot Flying J and Petro Stopping Centers) or close by. A crew completes the "touchless" wash in about 15 minutes. The company also offers fleet programs to help trucking firms keep vehicles clean and shiny while controlling costs and tracking spending. Blue Beacon prides itself on being in compliance with all environmental regulations and therefore doesn't franchise its washes. The company was founded in 1973.

BLUE BIRD CORP

3920 Arkwright Road, 2nd Floor
Macon, GA 31210
Phone: 478 822-2801
Fax: –
Web: www.blue-bird.com

NMS: BLBD
CEO: Philip Horlock
CFO: Razvan Radulescu
HR: –
FYE: September 30
Type: Public

Blue Bird is the leading independent designer and manufacturer of school buses. It produces three types of buses: Type C school buses, Type D school buses, and specialty buses. Specialty buses include school buses that are converted to suit applications required by the US Government, state and local governments, and various customers for commercial and export markets. School buses vary in size, capacities, power choices, and engine types. It also provides financing services through a financing product maintained by an independent third party, Huntington Distribution Finance, Inc. Most of the company's revenue is generated from the US.

	Annual Growth	09/19*	10/20	10/21	10/22*	09/23
Sales ($mil.)	2.7%	1,018.9	879.2	684.0	800.6	1,132.8
Net income ($ mil.)	(0.5%)	24.3	12.2	(0.3)	(45.8)	23.8
Market value ($ mil.)	2.9%	612.7	387.9	685.8	268.6	686.7
Employees	(5.6%)	2,300	1,736	1,790	1,596	1,830

*Fiscal year change

BLUE BUFFALO PET PRODUCTS, INC.

11 RIVER RD STE 103
WILTON, CT 068976011
Phone: 203 762-9751
Fax: –
Web: www.bluebuffalo.com

CEO: –
CFO: –
HR: –
FYE: December 31
Type: Private

Blue Buffalo makes natural dog and cat food using whole meats, fruits, and vegetables with no by-products or artificial ingredients; some products are also grain-free. The company's products undergo a robust formulation, manufacturing and testing process to ensure they are safe, effective and compliant with all nutrient requirements outlined by AAFCO and the Global Nutrition Committee of the World Small Animal Veterinary Association (WSAVA). BLUE's highly digestible carbohydrate sources that provide essential phytonutrients, antioxidants, and enzymes ? plus natural vitamins, minerals, and fibers to promote overall health. Blue Buffalo started in 2003.

	Annual Growth	12/13	12/14	12/15	12/16	12/17
Sales ($mil.)	11.4%	–	–	1,027.4	1,149.8	1,274.6
Net income ($ mil.)	47.1%	–	–	89.4	130.2	193.5
Market value ($ mil.)	–	–	–	–	–	–
Employees	–	–	–	–	–	1,800

BLUE CROSS & BLUE SHIELD ASSOCIATION

225 N MICHIGAN AVE FL 5
CHICAGO, IL 606017658
Phone: 312 297-6000
Fax: –
Web: www.bcbs.com

CEO: Kim A Keck
CFO: –
HR: Sue Rosinski
FYE: December 31
Type: Private

The Blue Cross and Blue Shield Association is a national federation of about 35 independent, community-based and locally-operated Blue Cross and Blue Shield companies that collectively provide health care coverage for one in three Americans across all 50 US states, the District of Columbia and Puerto Rico. The association owns and manages the Blue Cross and Blue Shield trademarks and names in more than 170 countries. In addition, the BCBS Federal Employee Program insures over 5.6 million federal employees, retirees and their families. The company traces its roots back to 1929.

	Annual Growth	12/04	12/05	12/06	12/17	12/21
Sales ($mil.)	6.7%	–	275.4	320.5	592.0	780.0
Net income ($ mil.)	14.8%	–	8.2	14.5	(1.4)	74.6
Market value ($ mil.)	–	–	–	–	–	–
Employees	–	–	–	–	–	1,880

BLUE CROSS AND BLUE SHIELD OF ARIZONA, INC.

8220 N 23RD AVE
PHOENIX, AZ 850214872
Phone: 602 864-4100
Fax: –
Web: www.azblue.com

CEO: Pam Kehaly
CFO: Mark El-Tawil
HR: Keisha Toppa
FYE: December 31
Type: Private

Blue Cross Blue Shield of Arizona (BCBSAZ) provides health insurance products and services to more than 2 million Arizonans. The not-for-profit company offers a variety of managed care plans to small and large employer groups, individuals, and families, including PPO, HMO, and high-deductible health plans. It also provides dental, vision, and prescription drug coverage, as well as supplemental health plans for Medicare beneficiaries. Founded in 1933, the company is an independent licensee of the Blue Cross and Blue Shield Association.

	Annual Growth	12/05	12/06	12/07	12/08	12/09
Assets ($mil.)	8.6%	–	–	–	975.9	1,059.5
Net income ($ mil.)	(9.9%)	–	–	–	71.7	64.6
Market value ($ mil.)	–	–	–	–	–	–
Employees	–	–	–	–	–	1,278

BLUE CROSS BLUE SHIELD OF NORTH DAKOTA

4510 13TH AVE S
FARGO, ND 581211000
Phone: 701 282-1100
Fax: –
Web: www.bcbsnd.com

CEO: Tim Huckle
CFO: –
HR: Kelsey Roth
FYE: December 31
Type: Private

Noridian Mutual Insurance Company (doing business as Blue Cross Blue Shield of North Dakota (BCBSND)) provides health care administration and support services in all 50 US states. As a member-owned, not-for-profit independent licensee of the Blue Cross and Blue Shield Association (BCBSA), BCBSND is committed to transforming care and health across the state to improve outcomes, lower cost trends and make it easier to shop, buy and use health care coverage. Members have access to unmatched local service and to a comprehensive network of health care providers across the state, the nation and in 200 countries. BCBSND was founded in 1940.

	Annual Growth	12/18	12/19	12/20	12/21	12/22
Sales ($mil.)	(0.1%)	–	–	–	16.5	16.5
Net income ($ mil.)	–	–	–	–	(12.6)	(17.3)
Market value ($ mil.)	–	–	–	–	–	–
Employees	–	–	–	–	–	16,000

BLUE DOLPHIN ENERGY CO.

NBB: BDCO

801 Travis Street, Suite 2100
Houston, TX 77002
Phone: 713 568-4725
Fax: –
Web: www.blue-dolphin-energy.com

CEO: Jonathan P Carroll
CFO: –
HR: –
FYE: December 31
Type: Public

Blue Dolphin Energy is trying to stay afloat in the waters of the Gulf of Mexico. The company's primary asset is its 40-mile-long Blue Dolphin Pipeline System, which includes an offshore platform for separation, metering, and compression; the onshore Buccaneer oil pipeline; onshore facilities including 85,000 barrels of surface tankage, separation and dehydration facilities; 360 acres of land; and a barge-loading terminal. Blue Dolphin Energy owns interests in three producing blocks in the High Island area in the Gulf of Mexico and has two exploratory prospects for sale. In 2010 the company reported estimated proved reserves of 155.5 cu. ft. of natural gas and 134,122 barrels of oil.

	Annual Growth	12/18	12/19	12/20	12/21	12/22
Sales ($mil.)	9.4%	340.8	309.3	174.8	300.8	487.5
Net income ($ mil.)	–	(0.5)	7.4	(14.5)	(12.8)	32.9
Market value ($ mil.)	7.1%	17.9	6.9	4.8	4.4	23.6
Employees	–	–	–	–	–	–

BLUE NILE, INC.

135 W 50TH ST
NEW YORK, NY 100201201
Phone: 206 336-6700
Fax: –
Web: www.bluenile.com

CEO: Sean Kell
CFO: Bill Koefoed
HR: Anita McGraw
FYE: January 04
Type: Private

The Blue Nile is a leader in handcrafted engagement rings and beautiful fine jewelry. The company offers luxury-grade jewelry, diamonds, settings, and engagement rings, as well as non-bridal jewelry made of gold, platinum, and silver set with diamonds, emeralds, rubies, and sapphires. The Blue Nile proudly offers handcrafted engagement rings that are made and quadruple-checked in Dublin. It only purchases ethically-sourced diamonds through the largest and most respected suppliers who adhere to and enforce the standards established by the Kimberley Process. The company was founded in 1999.

BLUE RIDGE ENERGY MEMBERS FOUNDATION

1216 BLOWING ROCK BLVD
LENOIR, NC 286453619
Phone: 828 758-2383
Fax: –
Web: www.blueridgeenergy.com

CEO: Douglas W Johnson
CFO: Katie Woodle
HR: –
FYE: December 31
Type: Private

Keeping the lights on in the Blue Ridge Mountains, Blue Ridge Electric Membership transmits and distributes electricity in the mountains and valleys of North Carolina. The utility provides power to about 73,390 customers, who are also its member-owners, in all or parts of seven counties (Alleghany, Ashe, Caldwell, and Watauga, and parts of Alexander, Avery and Wilkes counties). The electric cooperative's Blue Ridge Energies, LLC for-profit subsidiary sells propane, commercial gasoline, and other heating fuels to customers in the same service area.

	Annual Growth	12/05	12/06	12/08	12/09	12/14
Sales ($mil.)	(52.0%)	–	134.1	0.2	0.2	0.4
Net income ($ mil.)	(58.4%)	–	4.7	–	(0.0)	0.0
Market value ($ mil.)	–	–	–	–	–	–
Employees	–	–	–	–	–	402

BLUE RIDGE HEALTHCARE HOSPITALS, INC.

2201 S STERLING ST
MORGANTON, NC 286554044
Phone: 828 580-5000
Fax: –
Web: www.unchealthblueridge.org

CEO: Kathy C Bailey
CFO: Patricia Moll
HR: Debbie Kale
FYE: December 31
Type: Private

Perhaps it is a lack of grace that lands patients in the Grace Hospital emergency room? Whether treatment for a broken ankle or more serious cancer care is needed, Grace Hospital provides general medical services for the residents of Burke County, North Carolina. The 200-bed, not-for-profit hospital also serves as the anchor of Blue Ridge HealthCare Systems. Specialty services include cancer and cardiac care, behavioral health, rehabilitation, senior services, and home health care. Other services include advanced imaging, Level 2 neonatology, and pediatrics.

	Annual Growth	12/13	12/14	12/19	12/20	12/21
Sales ($mil.)	3.9%	–	191.0	253.1	212.5	249.3
Net income ($ mil.)	1.9%	–	28.8	47.1	59.7	32.9
Market value ($ mil.)	–	–	–	–	–	–
Employees	–	–	–	–	–	1,400

BLUE RIDGE HEALTHCARE SYSTEM, INC..

2201 S STERLING ST
MORGANTON, NC 286554044
Phone: 828 580-5000
Fax: –
Web: www.unchealthblueridge.org

CEO: Kathy Bailey
CFO: –
HR: Lorinnsa Bridges-Kee
FYE: December 31
Type: Private

Blue Ridge HealthCare wants to keep you as far from the thin blue line as possible. Blue Ridge HealthCare provides health care services to Burke County, North Carolina and the surrounding area via two acute-care hospitals (Grace Hospital and Valdese Hospital, with nearly 350 beds between the two), and several outpatient facilities (behavioral health care, rehabilitation, cancer care, senior care, and wellness services). Blue Ridge HealthCare also provides senior living services, including in-house medical care and hospice services through its Grace Ridge retirement community. The company is an affiliate of the Carolinas HealthCare System.

	Annual Growth	12/13	12/14	12/16	12/18	12/19
Sales ($mil.)	(1.6%)	–	7.4	263.1	271.3	6.8
Net income ($ mil.)	–	–	(0.4)	16.6	(7.6)	(0.6)
Market value ($ mil.)	–	–	–	–	–	–
Employees	–	–	–	–	–	1,200

BLUE RIVER BANCSHARES, INC.

29 East Washington Street
Shelbyville, IN 46176
Phone: 317 398-9721
Fax: –
Web: –

CEO: Russell Breeden III
CFO: Sarita S Grace
HR: –
FYE: December 31
Type: Public

Linda Ronstadt took "Blue Bayou" to the bank, but the folks in the Hoosier State take their green to Blue River Bancshares. The firm is the holding company for SBC Bank (also known as Shelby County Bank), which has a handful of branches in Shelby County, Indiana. The bank offers a variety of deposit products such as checking, savings, NOW, and money market accounts; CDs; and IRAs. With funds raised from deposits, it primarily originates one- to four-family residential mortgage loans, commercial mortgages, home equity and other consumer loans, and business loans. Blue River sold the Paramount Bank division of SBC Bank in Lexington, Kentucky, to Porter Bancorp in 2008.

	Annual Growth	12/02	12/03	12/04	12/05	12/06
Assets ($mil.)	24.2%	95.1	198.8	206.6	221.2	226.5
Net income ($ mil.)	–	(4.5)	0.0	(0.3)	1.6	0.6
Market value ($ mil.)	9.1%	15.1	21.9	18.2	18.2	21.4
Employees	13.0%	43	63	68	71	70

BLUE TEE CORP.

387 PARK AVE S FL 5
NEW YORK, NY 100161495
Phone: 212 598-0880
Fax: –
Web: www.bluetee.com

CEO: William M Kelly
CFO: David P Alldian
HR: –
FYE: December 31
Type: Private

Handling a variety of steel products and scrap materials suits Blue Tee to a tee. The holding company, which operates through two primary subsidiaries, distributes steel building materials and scrap metal. Blue Tee's Brown-Strauss Steel subsidiary is one of the largest distributors of wide flange beam and structural steel products (beams, pipe, and tubing) in North America. The metal distributor's other primary business is Azcon, a leading scrap processor, broker, and mill services management company which handles scrap metal sales, rail cars, and other steel parts.

	Annual Growth	12/06	12/07	12/08	12/09	12/10
Sales ($mil.)	(27.7%)	–	–	1,549.3	564.6	809.8
Net income ($ mil.)	(34.4%)	–	–	33.2	(10.1)	14.3
Market value ($ mil.)	–	–	–	–	–	–
Employees	–	–	–	–	–	900

BLUEBIRD BIO INC

NMS: BLUE

455 Grand Union Boulevard
Somerville, MA 02145
Phone: 339 499-9300
Fax: –
Web: www.bluebirdbio.com

CEO: –
CFO: –
HR: –
FYE: December 31
Type: Public

bluebird bio is ready to fly in the faces of rare genetic diseases. The company is using gene therapy to develop orphan drugs for two rare diseases. Its lead drug candidate, Lenti-D, is being developed to treat childhood cerebral adrenoleukodystrophy (CCALD), a rare neurological disorder that affects boys. Its second drug candidate, LentiGlobin, is being developed to treat the blood disorders beta-thalassemia major and sickle cell disease. Both drugs will begin studies by 2014. In addition, bluebird bio partnered with Celgene to develop gene therapies for cancer. Founded in 1992 as Genetix Pharmaceuticals, the company changed its name to bluebird bio in 2010 and filed an IPO in 2013.

	Annual Growth	12/18	12/19	12/20	12/21	12/22
Sales ($mil.)	(49.3%)	54.6	44.7	250.7	3.7	3.6
Net income ($ mil.)	–	(555.6)	(789.6)	(618.7)	(819.4)	(266.6)
Market value ($ mil.)	(48.6%)	8,226.0	7,276.5	3,588.1	828.4	573.8
Employees	(19.4%)	764	1,090	1,213	518	323

BLUEBONNET ELECTRIC COOPERATIVE, INC.

155 ELECTRIC AVE
BASTROP, TX 78602
Phone: 800 842-7708
Fax: –
Web: www.bluebonnet.coop

CEO: Matt Bentke
CFO: Christina Martinez
HR: Rachel Meinke
FYE: December 31
Type: Private

Bluebonnet Electric Cooperative's mission has echoes of the late Lady Bird Johnson's quest to spread bluebonnets and other wildflower seeds along Texas' highways. In this case the cooperative spreads power to homes and businesses in rural central and southeast Texas. One of the largest power distribution cooperatives in the state, Bluebonnet Electric serves more than 81,000 customers in 14 counties (a service area of more than 3,800 square miles). The member-owned company, which was formed in 1939, operates approximately 11,000 miles of transmission and distribution lines, and 19 substations. It purchases its wholesale power supply at 21 Lower Colorado River Authority-owned substations.

	Annual Growth	12/18	12/19	12/20	12/21	12/22
Sales ($mil.)	11.3%	–	221.1	225.4	246.3	304.6
Net income ($ mil.)	(59.1%)	–	29.0	32.4	32.4	2.0
Market value ($ mil.)	–	–	–	–	–	–
Employees	–	–	–	–	–	265

BLUEBONNET NUTRITION CORPORATION

12915 DAIRY ASHFORD RD
SUGAR LAND, TX 774783101
Phone: 281 240-3332
Fax: –
Web: www.bluebonnetnutrition.com

CEO: –
CFO: –
HR: –
FYE: September 30
Type: Private

This company really has a bee in its bonnet for good nutrition. Bluebonnet Nutrition Corp. makes and markets vitamins and other dietary supplements, including amino acids and herbs, under the Bluebonnet brand name. It provides its supplements in multiple forms, such as capsules, soft gels, powders, and liquids. Lead products include Super Earth Phytonutrient Soy Protein Powder and Multi-Action Whey of Life Protein Powder. The family-owned company sells its products in health and natural food stores throughout the US, as well as in Europe and Asia, to retailers that include Whole Foods Market. Bluebonnet, which manufactures the majority of its products at its facility in Texas, was founded in 1991.

BLUELINX HOLDINGS INC

NYS: BXC

1950 Spectrum Circle, Suite 300
Marietta, GA 30067
Phone: 770 953-7000
Fax: –
Web: www.bluelinxco.com

CEO: Shyam K Reddy
CFO: R A Wamser Jr
HR: –
FYE: December 30
Type: Public

BlueLinx is a leading wholesale distributor of residential and commercial building products in the US with a broad portfolio of both branded and private-label SKUs, and a broad distribution footprint servicing 50 US states. Products include plywood, oriented strand board, rebar and remesh, lumber, engineered wood products, moulding, siding, cedar, metal products and insulation. Distributes a comprehensive range of products from more than 750 suppliers, BlueLinx serves approximately 15,000 national, regional, and local dealers, specialty distributors, national home centers, pro dealers, and residential and commercial builders, contractors, and remodelers in their respective geographic areas and local markets. It was established as a division of Georgia-Pacific in 1954.

	Annual Growth	12/19*	01/21	01/22*	12/22	12/23
Sales ($mil.)	4.4%	2,637.3	3,097.3	4,277.2	4,450.2	3,136.4
Net income ($ mil.)	–	(17.7)	80.9	296.1	296.2	48.5
Market value ($ mil.)	71.3%	113.7	253.1	828.3	615.1	980.1
Employees	(2.4%)	2,200	2,100	2,055	2,100	2,000

*Fiscal year change

BLUEPRINT MEDICINES CORP

NMS: BPMC

45 Sidney Street
Cambridge, MA 02139
Phone: 617 374-7580
Fax: –
Web: www.blueprintmedicines.com

CEO: Jeffrey W Albers
CFO: Michael Landsittel
HR: –
FYE: December 31
Type: Public

Blueprint Medicines is a precision therapy company that is inventing life-changing medicines for people with cancer and blood disorders and creates therapies that selectively target genetic drivers, with the goal of staying one step ahead across stages of the disease. Its pipeline of drug candidates includes Avapritinib for the treatment of systemic Mastocytosis (SM), is a rare disorder that causes an overproduction of mast cells and other organs, which can lead to a wide range of debilitating symptoms and organ dysfunction and failure. It also includes BLU-263 for the treatment of indolent SM and other mast cell disorders. To develop and commercialize its product, Blueprint Medicines partnered with Roche, Zai Lab, Clementia, and CStone.

	Annual Growth	12/19	12/20	12/21	12/22	12/23
Sales ($mil.)	39.2%	66.5	793.7	180.1	204.0	249.4
Net income ($ mil.)	–	(347.7)	313.9	(644.1)	(557.5)	(507.0)
Market value ($ mil.)	3.6%	4,898.5	6,857.7	6,549.5	2,678.9	5,640.2
Employees	–	383	429	495	641	

BLUESCOPE CONSTRUCTION, INC.

1540 GENESSEE ST
KANSAS CITY, MO 641021069
Phone: 816 245-6000
Fax: –
Web: www.bluescopeconstruction.com

CEO: –
CFO: –
HR: –
FYE: June 30
Type: Private

Steel fabrication and construction is within the scope of BlueScope Construction (BSC). The company is the US-based construction subsidiary of Australian steel maker BlueScope Steel. BSC receives its steel materials directly from 10 BlueScope mills in the US. As a design/build general contractor, BSC plans, develops, and builds pre-engineered shells for large structures. Company divisions handle government projects and offer concrete services. BSC usually builds commercial and industrial facilities such as distribution centers, airplane hangars, arenas, manufacturing plants, offices, and warehouses. Customers have included Toys "R" Us, Best Buy, and FedEx Ground.

BLUM CAPITAL PARTNERS T, L.P.

909 MONTGOMERY ST STE 400
SAN FRANCISCO, CA 941334652
Phone: 415 645-0092
Fax: –
Web: www.himalayan-foundation.org

CEO: Richard C Blum
CFO: –
HR: –
FYE: December 31
Type: Private

Investment firm Blum Capital Partners targets small and middle-market US firms, providing capital for such transactions as share repurchases, acquisitions and divestitures, and privatizations. The partnership invests in a relatively small number of public or private companies (usually around five per year), but typically takes a substantial position either by acquiring a strategic block of the company's shares, or through a negotiated transaction. Blum Capital often takes an active role in management. It oversees investments for wealthy families, corporations, and university and philanthropic endowment funds, as well as its own account. Chairman Richard Blum founded the company in 1975.

BLUMENTHAL DISTRIBUTING, INC.

1901 S ARCHIBALD AVE
ONTARIO, CA 917618548
Phone: 909 930-2000
Fax: –
Web: www.officestar.net

CEO: Richard Blumenthal
CFO: Richard Blumenthal
HR: Esther Magallanes
FYE: November 30
Type: Private

Office Star Products isn't as into being a star in the office as it is into being a star furnishing firm. The company makes ready-to-assemble (RTA) furniture (chairs and seating alternatives, tables, filing cabinets, and decorative shelving) primarily for home offices and waiting rooms. Office Star's brand names include Pro-Line II, Work Smart, OSP Designs, and SPACE. The company's products are sold throughout the US at retail and wholesale chains, as well as regional home furnishings dealers. The company has manufacturing and warehousing facilities in the state of California. In April 2009, Office Star Products acquired the assets of Avenue Six.

BMC HOLDINGS, INC.

1914 RANDOLPH DR
BRYAN, OH 435062253
Phone: 419 636-1194
Fax: –
Web: www.bardhvac.com

CEO: –
CFO: –
HR: –
FYE: December 31
Type: Private

All the world's a stage for Bard Manufacturing -- if that world revolved around heating, ventilation, and air conditioning. Founded in 1914, the fourth-generation family-owned company manufactures wall-mounted climate-control products and sells them through a global network of distributors. Its products include air conditioners, heat pumps, oil furnaces and electric heaters, and control and ventilation systems, including thermostats, energy monitors, and dehumidifiers. Bard's products are used in residential homes, mobile homes, offices, schools, and telecommunications facilities. With headquarters in Ohio, the company has manufacturing and production plants in Georgia and Mexico.

BNCCORP INC

NBB: BNCC

322 East Main Avenue
Bismarck, ND 58501
Phone: 701 250-3040
Fax: 701 222-3653
Web: www.bnccorp.com

CEO: Daniel Collins
CFO: -
HR: -
FYE: December 31
Type: Public

BNCCORP is the holding company for BNC National Bank, which has about 20 branches in Arizona, North Dakota, and Minnesota. Serving individuals and small and midsized businesses, the bank offers deposit accounts, credit cards, and wealth management services. It also has residential mortgage banking operations in Iowa, Kansas, and Missouri. Real estate loans account for nearly half of the company's portfolio; commercial, industrial, construction, agricultural, and consumer loans make up most of the remainder. BNCCORP sold BNC Insurance Services to Hub International in 2007 for more than $37 million. It arranged to sell some of its operations in Arizona and Minnesota to Alerus Financial in 2010.

	Annual Growth	12/18	12/19	12/20	12/21	12/22
Assets ($mil.)	(0.7%)	971.0	966.8	1,074.1	1,047.4	943.3
Net income ($ mil.)	(1.3%)	6.8	10.2	44.6	22.0	6.5
Market value ($ mil.)	9.8%	73.0	123.3	161.1	158.4	105.9
Employees	–	–	–	–	–	–

BOARD OF REGENTS OF THE UNIVERSITY OF NEBRASKA

3835 HOLDREGE ST
LINCOLN, NE 685031435
Phone: 402 472-3906
Fax: –
Web: www.nebraska.edu

CEO: –
CFO: –
HR: Kim Morrison
FYE: June 30
Type: Private

The University of Nebraska is the state's only public university system, made up of four campuses ? an R1 flagship land-grant university, the University of Nebraska Lincoln (UNL); an academic medical center, the University of Nebraska Medical Center (UNMC); a metropolitan university, the University of Nebraska at Omaha (UNO); and a regional undergraduate university, the University of Nebraska at Kearney (UNK). The UNK offers roughly 120 undergraduate majors, about 20 pre-professional programs, and more than 25 graduate programs. The campus is a model for undergraduate research, with over 30% of UNK students doing research outside of the classroom and presenting at academic conferences. The University of Nebraska has more than 49,000 students and approximately 16,000 faculty and staff who serve the state, nation, and world through education, research, and outreach.

	Annual Growth	06/12	06/13	06/14	06/15	06/16
Sales ($mil.)	4.3%	–	1,313.5	1,333.6	1,405.0	1,491.0
Net income ($ mil.)	(5.4%)	–	254.8	222.6	221.3	215.5
Market value ($ mil.)	–	–	–	–	–	–
Employees	–	–	–	–	–	15,200

BOARD OF TRUSTEES OF COMMUNITY COLLEGE DISTRICT 508 (INC)

1900 W JACKSON BLVD # 212
CHICAGO, IL 606123111
Phone: 312 553-2752
Fax: –
Web: www.ccc.edu

CEO: Gery Chico
CFO: –
HR: –
FYE: June 30
Type: Private

City Colleges of Chicago (CCC) is one of the largest urban community college systems in the US. It includes seven separately accredited schools -- Daley College, Kennedy-King College, Malcolm X College, Olive-Harvey College, Truman College, Washington College, and Wright College. CCC offers associate degrees, continuing education, IT certifications, industry training, GED and ESL classes, and other programs to some 120,000 students each year. Other institutions under the CCC umbrella include the French Pastry School, the Washburne Culinary Institute, three learning centers, and the public television station, WYCC-TV. City Colleges of Chicago was founded in 1911 as Crane Junior College.

	Annual Growth	06/17	06/18	06/19	06/21	06/22
Sales ($mil.)	(11.9%)	–	49.7	41.3	32.7	29.9
Net income ($ mil.)	–	–	(15.1)	(37.1)	10.1	20.5
Market value ($ mil.)	–	–	–	–	–	–
Employees	–	–	–	–	–	3,500

BOARD OF TRUSTEES OF ILLINOIS STATE UNIVERSITY

302 HOVEY HALL
NORMAL, IL 617900001
Phone: 309 438-2111
Fax: –
Web: www.illinoisstate.edu

CEO: –
CFO: –
HR: –
FYE: June 30
Type: Private

Normal doesn't quite describe it. Illinois State University (ISU), in Normal-Bloomington, provides advanced education courses in more than 150 academic fields, including business, fine arts, education, and science, nursing, and technology. The school has a student body of more than 19,920 graduate and undergraduate students; about 95% are Illinois residents. ISU's facilities include a public planetarium, 490-acre arboretum, two primary laboratory schools, and the Milner Library with more than 1.6 million volumes. The university is governed by a board of trustees selected by the Illinois governor.

BOARDRIDERS, INC.

5600 ARGOSY AVE STE 100
HUNTINGTON BEACH, CA 926491063
Phone: 714 889-5404
Fax: –
Web: www.boardriders.com

CEO: –
CFO: –
HR: –
FYE: October 31
Type: Private

Boardriders (formerly known as Quiksilver) is a leading action sports and lifestyle company that designs, produces, and distributes branded apparel, footwear, and accessories for board riders around the world. The company caters to the young and athletic with surf wear, snowboard wear, sportswear, and swimwear sold under the Quiksilver, Billabong, Element, RVCA, VonZipper, and Roxy names, among others. It also owns the DC Shoes brand of footwear and apparel for young men and juniors. It sells its apparel, footwear, and accessories in specialty and department stores worldwide, as well as through its own network of approximately 570 retail stores. In early 2023, Boardriders, owned by Oaktree Capital Management, is nearing a deal to be acquired by Authentic Brands Group for approximately $1.3 billion.

	Annual Growth	10/10	10/11	10/12	10/13	10/14
Sales ($mil.)	(11.7%)	–	–	2,013.2	1,810.6	1,570.4
Net income ($ mil.)	–	–	–	(9.7)	(233.5)	(320.1)
Market value ($ mil.)	–	–	–	–	–	–
Employees	–	–	–	–	–	600

BOB EVANS FARMS, INC.

8200 WALTON PKWY
NEW ALBANY, OH 430547687
Phone: 614 492-7700
Fax: –
Web: www.bobevansgrocery.com

CEO: Mark Delahanty
CFO: Mark E Hood
HR: Jill McFarland
FYE: April 28
Type: Private

Bob Evans Farms is a leading manufacturer of farm-fresh refrigerated sides and breakfast products. The company is proud to be the number one selling refrigerated dinner sides, including many varieties of mashed potatoes and macaroni and cheese. It is also a leading producer and distributor of more than 60 varieties of sausage and bacon products, egg whites, frozen handheld breakfast items, and other convenience foods. In addition to its flagship Bob Evans brand, its product portfolio includes Simply Potatoes, Egg Beaters and Owens Sausage. Founded in 1953, Bob Evans Farms has delivered delicious, quick-to-table, farm-inspired food that makes mealtime a little bit easier and a lot more delicious. The company is owned by Post Holdings, a consumer-packaged goods holding company.

BOB ROSS BUICK, INC.

85 LOOP RD
DAYTON, OH 454592199
Phone: 937 433-0990
Fax: –
Web: www.bobrossbuickgmc.com

CEO: –
CFO: –
HR: Emily Crowley
FYE: December 31
Type: Private

The Bob Ross Group sells new and used cars made by Buick, for sure, as well as by GMC, Alfa Romeo, Fiat, and Mercedes Benz in Centerville, Ohio. Bob Ross also provides financing, parts, service, and collision repair. The company's bobrossauto.com Web site allows customers to search new and used inventory as well as schedule service, order parts, and apply for financing. Bob Ross ranks near the top of many categories (Buick sales, customer satisfaction, GMC truck sales) for Buick dealerships in Ohio. The company was founded in 1979 by the late Bob Ross, Sr. and his wife Norma Ross (daughter Jenell is now the owner). It was the first African-American owned Mercedes-Benz dealership in the world.

	Annual Growth	12/11	12/12	12/13	12/14	12/15
Sales ($mil.)	7.7%	–	–	66.8	72.8	77.5
Net income ($ mil.)	17.2%	–	–	0.5	0.5	0.6
Market value ($ mil.)	–	–	–	–	–	–
Employees	–	–	–	–	–	100

BODDIE-NOELL ENTERPRISES, INC.

1021 NOELL LN
ROCKY MOUNT, NC 278041761
Phone: 252 937-2000
Fax: –
Web: www.hardees.com

CEO: Bill Boddie
CFO: W C Worthy
HR: Cassie Webb
FYE: December 30
Type: Private

Boddie-Noell Enterprises (BNE) is a hearty competitor in the fast-food business. The company is one of the largest franchise operators of Hardee's, a fast-food chain owned by CKE Restaurants, with about 330 locations the four southeastern states of Kentucky, North Carolina, South Carolina, and Virginia. In addition, the company owns The Highway Diner restaurant concept. BNE is also involved in real estate development through BNE Land & Development. The family owned company was started in 1962 by Carleton Noell and his nephews Nick and Mayo Boddie.

	Annual Growth	12/09	12/10	12/11	12/12	12/13
Sales ($mil.)	(3.3%)	–	–	395.3	395.3	369.9
Net income ($ mil.)	–	–	–	(9.6)	14.0	16.6
Market value ($ mil.)	–	–	–	–	–	–
Employees	–	–	–	–	–	12,000

BOEHRINGER INGELHEIM CORPORATION

900 RIDGEBURY RD
RIDGEFIELD, CT 068771058
Phone: 203 798-9988
Fax: –
Web: www.boehringer-ingelheim.com

CEO: –
CFO: Stefan Rinn
HR: Gunter Damian
FYE: December 31
Type: Private

As the US headquarters of German drug maker, Boehringer Ingelheim, Boehringer Ingelheim Corporation (Boehringer Ingelheim Pharmaceuticals, Inc.) is a research-driven group of companies dedicated to the discovery, development, manufacture and marketing of innovative health care products. The company focuses primarily on the therapeutic areas of cardiovascular disease, respiratory diseases, diseases of the central nervous system, metabolic diseases, virological diseases and oncology.

BOEHRINGER INGELHEIM PHARMACEUTICALS, INC.

900 RIDGEBURY RD
RIDGEFIELD, CT 068771058
Phone: 203 798-9988
Fax: –
Web: www.bi-animalhealth.com

CEO: Paul Fonteyne
CFO: –
HR: Barbara Koger
FYE: December 31
Type: Private

Boehringer Ingelheim Pharmaceuticals brings a little German drugmaking know-how to the USA. The firm is the pharmaceuticals unit of Boehringer Ingelheim Corporation, which is the US headquarters of Germany's Boehringer Ingelheim. It sells a range of drugs in the US market, including prescription products (respiratory treatment Spiriva, high blood pressure medication Micardis, enlarged prostate treatment Flomax, Parkinson's disease drug Mirapex, and HIV/AIDS product Aptivus) and over-the-counter products (heartburn aid Zantac and constipation drug Ducolax). It is also an R&D center for Boehringer Ingelheim, specializing in immunology, inflammatory conditions, and cardiovascular disease.

	Annual Growth	12/18	12/19	12/20	12/21	12/22
Sales ($mil.)	33.6%	–	–	–	800.2	1,068.8
Net income ($ mil.)	(29.5%)	–	–	–	38.4	27.1
Market value ($ mil.)	–	–	–	–	–	–
Employees	–	–	–	–	–	1,796

BOEING CAPITAL CORP

500 Naches Ave. S.W., 3rd Floor
Renton, WA 98057
Phone: 425 965-4000
Fax: –
Web: www.boeing.com

CEO: Gregory D Smith
CFO: Kelvin E Council
HR: Greg Lim
FYE: December 31
Type: Public

Need financing for that 747? Boeing Capital, a major subsidiary of Boeing, provides asset-backed leasing and lending services through two divisions: Aircraft Financial Services offers financing and leasing services for airlines and governmental customers interested in Boeing aircraft; Space & Defense Financial Services offers similar services for Boeing's Integrated Defense Systems customers. AirTran is Boeing Capital's biggest customer, followed by American Airlines, Hawaiian Airlines, and Continental Airlines. Boeing Capital was founded in 1968 as McDonnell Douglas Finance, and changed its name when Boeing acquired McDonnell Douglas in 1997.

	Annual Growth	12/08	12/09	12/10	12/11	12/12
Sales ($mil.)	(11.3%)	703.0	660.0	639.0	532.0	436.0
Net income ($ mil.)	(20.5%)	120.0	57.0	92.0	83.0	48.0
Market value ($ mil.)	–	–	–	–	–	–
Employees	(2.3%)	160	161	150	146	146

BOEING CO. (THE)

929 Long Bridge Drive
Arlington, VA 22202
Phone: 703 414-6338
Fax: –
Web: www.boeing.com

NYS: BA
CEO: David L Calhoun
CFO: Brian J West
HR: –
FYE: December 31
Type: Public

Boeing is one of the world's largest aerospace company that designs, develops, and manufactures the sale, service and support of commercial jetliners, military aircraft, satellites, missile defense, human space flight and launch systems and services. The company is one of the two major manufacturers of 100-plus seat airplanes. Its commercial jet aircraft models include 737, 767, 777 and 787 families of airplanes and the Boeing Business Jet range. New product development efforts include the 737-7 and 737-10, and the 777X program. The company generates about 60% of its revenue domestically.

	Annual Growth	12/19	12/20	12/21	12/22	12/23
Sales ($mil.)	0.4%	76,559	58,158	62,286	66,608	77,794
Net income ($ mil.)	–	(636.0)	(11,873.0)	(4,202.0)	(4,935.0)	(2,222.0)
Market value ($ mil.)	(5.4%)	198,556	130,473	122,708	116,107	158,876
Employees	1.5%	161,100	141,000	142,000	156,000	171,000

BOINGO WIRELESS, INC.

10960 WILSHIRE BLVD FL 23
LOS ANGELES, CA 900243809
Phone: 310 586-5180
Fax: –
Web: www.boingo.com

CEO: Mike Finley
CFO: Peter Hovenier
HR: Laurie Shikhman
FYE: December 31
Type: Private

Boingo simplifies complex wireless challenges to connect people, business and things. It designs, builds and manages converged, neutral host public and private networks at major venues around the world. Boingo's vast footprint of distributed antenna systems (DAS), Wi-Fi, small cells and macro towers securely powers innovation and connectivity in airports, transit stations, stadiums, military bases, hospitals, commercial properties and enterprises worldwide. The company is leading the way to pioneer many firsts to connect people, businesses and things, from 5G to CBRS to Wi-Fi 6 to whatever comes next.

BOISE CASCADE CO. (DE) — NYS: BCC

1111 West Jefferson Street, Suite 300
Boise, ID 83702-5389
Phone: 208 384-6161
Fax: –
Web: www.bc.com

CEO: Nathan R Jorgensen
CFO: Kelly E Hibbs
HR: –
FYE: December 31
Type: Public

Boise Cascade is one of the largest producers of engineered wood products (EWP) and plywood in North America and a leading US wholesale distributor of building products. Its products are used in the construction of new residential housing, including single-family, multi-family, and manufactured homes, the repair-and-remodeling of existing housing, the construction of light industrial and commercial buildings, and industrial applications. The company has a broad base of national and local customers, which includes a diverse mix of dealers, home improvement centers, leading wholesalers, specialty distributors, and industrial converters. Boise Cascade was formed in 2004.

	Annual Growth	12/19	12/20	12/21	12/22	12/23
Sales ($mil.)	10.2%	4,643.4	5,474.8	7,926.1	8,387.3	6,838.2
Net income ($ mil.)	56.4%	80.9	175.0	712.5	857.7	483.7
Market value ($ mil.)	37.2%	1,444.4	1,890.0	2,815.2	2,715.2	5,114.9
Employees	–	6,010	6,040	6,110	6,780	–

BOISE STATE UNIVERSITY FOUNDATION, INC.

1910 UNIVERSITY DR
BOISE, ID 837250001
Phone: 208 426-1000
Fax: –
Web: www.boisestate.edu

CEO: Bob Kustra
CFO: Martin Schimpf
HR: –
FYE: June 30
Type: Private

Boise State University (BSU) provides higher education in the shadows of the Rocky Mountains. BSU has an enrollment of approximately 23,000 students and a faculty and staff of more than 2,400. The university offers about 200 undergraduate, graduate, and technical fields of study through seven colleges: Arts and Sciences, Business and Economics, Education, Engineering, Health Sciences, Social Sciences and Public Affairs, and Graduate Studies. In addition to its main campus in Boise, Idaho, it operates a satellite campus in Nampa (Boise State West), which offers academic, non-credit, and applied technology courses. BSU also has three centers elsewhere in the state, as well as online learning programs.

	Annual Growth	06/18	06/19	06/20	06/21	06/22
Sales ($mil.)	5.7%	–	275.0	286.5	273.5	324.4
Net income ($ mil.)	22.5%	–	28.9	32.6	28.5	53.2
Market value ($ mil.)	–	–	–	–	–	–
Employees	–	–	–	–	–	1,879

BOJANGLES', INC.

9432 SOUTHERN PINE BLVD
CHARLOTTE, NC 282735553
Phone: 704 527-2675
Fax: –
Web: www.bojangles.com

CEO: –
CFO: –
HR: –
FYE: December 31
Type: Private

Bojangles', Inc. is a highly differentiated and growing restaurant operator and franchisor dedicated to serving customers high-quality, craveable food made from our Southern recipes, including breakfast served All Day, Every Day. It serves menu items such as made-from-scratch biscuit breakfast sandwiches, delicious hand-breaded bone-in chicken, flavorful fixins (sides) and Legendary Iced Tea. It was founded in 1977 in Charlotte, North Carolina.

BOK FINANCIAL CORP — NMS: BOKF

Bank of Oklahoma Tower, Boston Avenue at Second Street
Tulsa, OK 74192
Phone: 918 588-6000
Fax: –
Web: www.bokf.com

CEO: Stacy C Kymes
CFO: Steven E Nell
HR: Jeff Reid
FYE: December 31
Type: Public

BOK Financial began in 1910 as a regional source of capital for the energy industry. It has eight principal banking divisions in Oklahoma, Texas, New Mexico, Arkansas, Colorado, Arizona, Kansas, and Missouri. Its primary focus is to provide a comprehensive range of nationally competitive financial products and services in a personalized and responsive manner. Products and services include loans and deposits, cash management services, fiduciary and insurance services, mortgage banking and brokerage, and trading services to middle-market businesses, financial institutions, and consumers. About 40% of the total loan portfolio is in Texas, while Oklahoma has around 25%.

	Annual Growth	12/19	12/20	12/21	12/22	12/23
Assets ($mil.)	4.3%	42,172	46,671	50,249	47,791	49,825
Net income ($ mil.)	1.5%	500.8	435.0	618.1	520.3	530.7
Market value ($ mil.)	(0.5%)	6,694.3	5,245.1	8,079.8	7,949.6	6,560.2
Employees	(0.7%)	5,107	4,915	4,711	4,791	4,966

BOKER USA, INC.

1550 BALSAM ST
LAKEWOOD, CO 802145917
Phone: 303 462-0662
Fax: –
Web: www.bokerusa.com

CEO: –
CFO: –
HR: –
FYE: December 31
Type: Private

Boker USA distributes high-end hunting and sporting knives, as well as kitchen cutlery, sharpeners, and watches through US retail outlets and its own catalogs. Many of the products it sells are made by sister company Heinr. Boker Baumwerk in Germany. Other items include bags, self-defense videos, and flashlights. The company sells its products through independent dealers, catalogs, and its Web site. The earliest manifestation of the company began in Germany with Herman and Robert Boeker when they began making sabers in 1829. Boker USA was founded in Colorado in 1986.

BOLLORE LOGISTICS USA INC.

1412 BROADWAY RM 402
NEW YORK, NY 100183551
Phone: 281 209-4676
Fax: –
Web: www.sdvusa.com

CEO: Thomas Duplan
CFO: –
HR: Angela Lotito
FYE: December 31
Type: Private

SDV (USA) aims to arrange the transportation of its customers' freight PDQ. The company, which provides international air and ocean freight forwarding and logistics services, specializes in serving customers from industries such as in aerospace, high technology, manufacturing, and oil and gas. (As a freight forwarder, SDV (USA) buys transportation capacity from carriers and resells it to customers.) The company operates from more than a dozen offices in major US trade gateways. SDV (USA) is a unit of France-based SDV International Logistics, which itself is a unit of the diversified Bollor group.

	Annual Growth	12/05	12/06	12/07	12/09	12/13
Sales ($mil.)	5.2%	–	–	239.6	211.8	324.6
Net income ($ mil.)	12.7%	–	–	4.3	5.5	8.8
Market value ($ mil.)	–	–	–	–	–	–
Employees	–	–	–	–	–	480

BOLNER'S FIESTA PRODUCTS, INC.

426 MENCHACA ST
SAN ANTONIO, TX 782071230
Phone: 210 734-6404
Fax: –
Web: www.fiestaspices.com

CEO: –
CFO: –
HR: –
FYE: December 31
Type: Private

If you can't make it down to San Antonio for the annual fiesta celebration, you can at least get a taste of Texas flavor with Bolner's Fiesta Products. The company makes dry herbs, rubs, and spices for enhancing the flavor of fajitas or hamburgers. Although it specializes in Cajun, Mexican, and Southwestern flavors, the company imports spices from some 60 countries to make its more than 600 products. Bolner's Fiesta Products sells its items in grocery and discount stores throughout the US, including such retailers as Albertson's, Kroger, Randall's, Winn-Dixie, Fiesta, Kmart, and Wal-Mart. The Bolner family owns and operates the company.

BON SECOURS - RICHMOND COMMUNITY HOSPITAL, INCORPORATED

1500 N 28TH ST
RICHMOND, VA 232235332
Phone: 804 225-1700
Fax: –
Web: www.bonsecours.com

CEO: Mark Gordon
CFO: –
HR: –
FYE: August 31
Type: Private

Part of the Bon Secours Health System, Bon Secours-Richmond Community Hospital is a 100-bed facility that provides general medical and surgical care to the residents of Richmond, Virginia. Located in the city's historic Church Hill neighborhood, the hospital provides inpatient care, as well as emergency services, diagnostic imaging services, and outpatient rehabilitation. The hospital also features an inpatient psychiatric unit and provides primary health care services at a medical office building next door. Bon Secours-Richmond Community Hospital was founded in 1903 by a husband-and-wife duo of African American doctors, Sarah and Miles Jones.

	Annual Growth	08/02	08/03	08/05	08/09	08/16
Sales ($mil.)	15.1%	–	21.6	31.0	49.6	134.3
Net income ($ mil.)	–	–	(4.6)	(3.7)	(3.2)	41.3
Market value ($ mil.)	–	–	–	–	–	–
Employees	–	–	–	–	–	189

BON SECOURS MERCY HEALTH, INC.

1701 MERCY HEALTH PL
CINCINNATI, OH 452376147
Phone: 513 956-3729
Fax: –
Web: www.bonsecours.com

CEO: John M Starcher Jr
CFO: –
HR: Danielle J Ellis
FYE: December 31
Type: Private

From hospitals and free standing emergency departments, to specialty and primary care locations, lab facilities and imaging centers ? Bon Secours Mercy Health is one of the largest and most expansive health care systems in the country. The ministry's quality, compassionate care is provided by more than 60,000 associates serving communities in Florida, Kentucky, Maryland, New York, Ohio, South Carolina, Virginia, and throughout Ireland. Bon Secours Mercy Health established through merger of Bon Secours Health System in 2018.

BON-TON STORES INC

2801 East Market Street
York, PA 17402
Phone: 717 757-7660
Fax: –
Web: www.bonton.com

NBB: BONT Q
CEO: William X Tracy
CFO: Michael G Culhane
HR: –
FYE: January 28
Type: Public

Age wasn't enough to protect Bon-Ton Stores from major shifts in the department store industry. Founded in 1898 by the Grumbacher family, the company filed for Chapter 11 bankruptcy in early 2018 and later that year sold its inventory and assets to liquidators. All of its stores will close. Amid a decline in mall traffic and overall harsh retail environment, Bon-Ton struggled with falling revenue and debt, which limited its ability to invest in all-important e-commerce operations.

	Annual Growth	02/13	02/14*	01/15	01/16	01/17
Sales ($mil.)	(2.7%)	2,978.8	2,834.1	2,822.9	2,789.5	2,674.4
Net income ($ mil.)	–	(21.6)	(3.6)	(7.0)	(57.1)	(63.4)
Market value ($ mil.)	(44.2%)	282.8	232.1	118.3	36.7	27.4
Employees	(3.5%)	26,900	25,800	25,200	24,100	23,300

*Fiscal year change

BONITZ, INC.

645 ROSEWOOD DR
COLUMBIA, SC 292014699
Phone: 803 799-0181
Fax: –
Web: www.bonitz.com

CEO: –
CFO: Doug Dozier
HR: –
FYE: December 31
Type: Private

Bonitz is a veteran US acoustical ceiling and drywall contractor. Founded by chairman Bill Rogers in 1954, the company got a humble start in South Carolina and has grown to operate in more than a dozen US locations primarily in the Southeast, including Alabama, Colorado, Georgia, Tennessee, Virginia, and the Carolinas. Through its operating divisions, Bonitz also offers commercial and residential flooring contracting, roofing contracting, and manufacturing of prefabricated, light gage metal wall panels and trusses for educational, institutional, and commercial buildings. Its clients include architects, interior designers, general contractors, and building owners. Bonitz is employee owned.

	Annual Growth	12/11	12/12	12/13	12/14	12/15
Sales ($mil.)	11.6%	–	129.0	143.9	178.8	179.2
Net income ($ mil.)	26.0%	–	3.9	6.7	6.1	7.8
Market value ($ mil.)	–	–	–	–	–	–
Employees	–	–	–	–	–	850

BONNEVILLE POWER ADMINISTRATION

905 NE 11TH AVE
PORTLAND, OR 972324169
Phone: 503 230-3000
Fax: –
Web: www.bpa.gov

CEO: John Hairston
CFO: Claudia Andrews
HR: Brian Carter
FYE: September 30
Type: Private

Bonneville Power Administration (BPA) keeps the lights on in the Pacific Northwest. The US Department of Energy power marketing agency operates a transmission grid (with more than 15,000 miles of high-voltage lines). The electricity that BPA wholesales is generated primarily by around 30 federal hydroelectric dams (operated by the US Army Corp of Engineers) and one nonfederal nuclear facility and several small nonfederal power plants. In all, BPA markets about a third of the electricity consumed in the Northwest and operates three-quarters of the region's high-voltage transmission grid.

	Annual Growth	09/06	09/07	09/08	09/09	09/10
Sales ($mil.)	0.3%	–	–	3,036.6	2,870.3	3,055.1
Net income ($ mil.)	–	–	–	264.8	(101.1)	(127.6)
Market value ($ mil.)	–	–	–	–	–	–
Employees	–	–	–	–	–	3,100

BOOKING HOLDINGS INC

800 Connecticut Avenue
Norwalk, CT 06854
Phone: 203 299-8000
Fax: 203 595-0160
Web: www.bookingholdings.com

NMS: BKNG
CEO: Glenn D Fogel
CFO: David I Goulden
HR: Heather Royce
FYE: December 31
Type: Public

Booking Holdings (formerly The Priceline Group) operates six of the world's leading online travel tools. Booking.com is its namesake and top brand that offers online reservation services for approximately 2.3 million properties ? including hotels, motels, resorts, apartments, and homes ? across over 220 countries. The holding company also owns Priceline, which features discount bookings for hotels, cars, airline tickets, cruises, and vacation packages; other brands include Agoda, KAYAK, RentalCars, and OpenTable. Booking Holdings generates revenues from credit card processing rebates and customer processing fees, advertising services, restaurant reservations and management services, and various other services, such as travel-related insurance. It was founded in 1997 and generates more than 85% of sales outside the US.

	Annual Growth	12/19	12/20	12/21	12/22	12/23
Sales ($mil.)	9.1%	15,066	6,796.0	10,958	17,090	21,365
Net income ($ mil.)	(3.1%)	4,865.0	59.0	1,165.0	3,058.0	4,289.0
Market value ($ mil.)	14.6%	70,643	76,613	82,528	69,321	122,016
Employees	(2.8%)	26,400	20,300	20,300	21,600	23,600

BOOKS-A-MILLION, INC.

402 INDUSTRIAL LN
BIRMINGHAM, AL 352114465
Phone: 205 942-3737
Fax: –
Web: www.booksamillion.com

CEO: –
CFO: –
HR: –
FYE: January 31
Type: Private

Books-A-Million (BAM) has grown to become the premier book retailing chain in the Southeastern US, and the second largest book retailer in the nation. The company operates more than 260 stores in some 30 states and the District of Columbia and sells books online. In addition to its primary retail component, the corporation includes a book wholesale and distribution subsidiary, American Wholesale Book Company, an e-commerce division operating as BOOKSAMILLION.COM, and an internet development and services company, NetCentral, in Nashville, Tennessee. Its offerings include books, eBooks, Kids-A-Million, teen, bargain books, entertainment, toys, and fandom items. Some Books-A-Million stores also feature the Joe Muggs Caf ? a full line coffee and espresso bar offering a wide selection of gourmet coffees, teas, desserts and brewing supplies.

	Annual Growth	01/18	01/19	01/20	01/21	01/22
Sales ($mil.)	(34.4%)	–	–	0.1	0.0	0.0
Net income ($ mil.)	(34.4%)	–	–	0.0	0.0	0.0
Market value ($ mil.)	–	–	–	–	–	–
Employees	–	–	–	–	–	5,400

BOONE HOSPITAL CENTER

1600 E BROADWAY
COLUMBIA, MO 652015897
Phone: 573 815-8000
Fax: –
Web: www.boone.health

CEO: –
CFO: –
HR: –
FYE: December 31
Type: Private

If you're torn apart by tigers, you might end up here. Boone Hospital Center is a 390-bed, full-service hospital that serves St. Louis and a 25-county area in central Missouri. Boone provides a range of programs and services, including emergency care and emergency transportation. The hospital offers specialized care in the areas of cardiology, neurology, oncology, surgery, and obstetrics. It also operates outreach clinics and provides home health care services through Boone Hospital Home Care. Its Wellaware center focuses on behavioral and occupational medicine. Boone Hospital is part of the BJC HealthCare network.

	Annual Growth	12/15	12/16	12/17	12/18	12/21
Sales ($mil.)	1.8%	–	299.5	288.8	286.8	327.4
Net income ($ mil.)	36.1%	–	6.3	(10.9)	(16.4)	29.5
Market value ($ mil.)	–	–	–	–	–	–
Employees	–	–	–	–	–	3,150

BOOZ ALLEN HAMILTON HOLDING CORP.

8283 Greensboro Drive
McLean, VA 22102
Phone: 703 902-5000
Fax: –
Web: www.boozallen.com

NYS: BAH
CEO: –
CFO: –
HR: –
FYE: March 31
Type: Public

Booz Allen Hamilton is a leading provider of management and technology consulting, analytics, engineering, digital solutions, mission operations, and cyber services to US and international governments, major corporations, and not-for-profit organizations. The company, which acts as prime contractor in nearly every instance, generates billions in sales each year from the delivery of highly technical skills to the Department of Defense, the National Security Agency, the IRS, and nearly every cabinet-level US Government department. It increasingly works with foreign governments and commercial clients as well. Investment company, The Carlyle Group owns a majority interest in the consulting company, which was founded in 1914.

	Annual Growth	03/19	03/20	03/21	03/22	03/23
Sales ($mil.)	8.4%	6,704.0	7,463.8	7,858.9	8,363.7	9,258.9
Net income ($ mil.)	(10.2%)	418.5	482.6	609.0	466.7	271.8
Market value ($ mil.)	12.4%	7,653.4	9,035.6	10,601	11,563	12,201
Employees	5.1%	26,100	27,200	27,700	29,300	31,900

BORGESS HEALTH ALLIANCE, INC.

1521 GULL RD
KALAMAZOO, MI 490481640
Phone: 269 226-7000
Fax: –
Web: www.borgess.com

CEO: Paul A Staude
CFO: Rich Felbinger
HR: Kandi Torres
FYE: June 30
Type: Private

Borgess Health Alliance operates hospitals and related health care facilities. The alliance serves more than 1 million people through owned or affiliated hospitals and satellite facilities in more than a dozen cities in southwest Michigan. Its main location, Borgess Medical Center, has about 420 beds and offers a variety of specialty services such as emergency, orthopedic, cancer, radiology, neurology, rehabilitation, and women's health. Other Borgess Health Alliance facilities and services include Borgess-Lee Memorial Hospital, Borgess-Pipp Hospital, a nursing home, physician offices, emergency clinics, home health care, and air ambulance services. Borgess Health Alliance is a subsidiary of Ascension Health.

	Annual Growth	06/16	06/17	06/18	06/21	06/22
Sales ($mil.)	(5.3%)	–	9.0	8.2	6.9	6.9
Net income ($ mil.)	–	–	(55.6)	(44.8)	(12.8)	(15.3)
Market value ($ mil.)	–	–	–	–	–	–
Employees	–	–	–	–	–	4,000

BORGWARNER INC   NYS: BWA

3850 Hamlin Road   CEO: Frederic B Lissalde
Auburn Hills, MI 48326   CFO: Kevin A Nowlan
Phone: 248 754-9200   HR: Julie Curtin
Fax: –   FYE: December 31
Web: www.borgwarner.com   Type: Public

BorgWarner is a global product leader in clean and efficient technology solutions for combustion, hybrid and electric vehicles. Products include turbochargers, timing chain systems, emissions and thermal systems, control modules, fuel rail assemblies, and fuel injection, among others. Together, automakers Ford and Volkswagen account for about 15% of sales. Other customers include Ford, Stellantis, and General Motors. In addition to automotive customers, BorgWarner also serves OEMs of commercial and off-highway vehicles. The company gets some 70% of its sales from outside the US.

	Annual Growth	12/19	12/20	12/21	12/22	12/23
Sales ($mil.)	8.7%	10,168	10,165	14,838	15,801	14,198
Net income ($ mil.)	(4.3%)	746.0	500.0	537.0	944.0	625.0
Market value ($ mil.)	(4.7%)	9,968.0	8,878.8	10,356	9,248.8	8,237.7
Employees	8.3%	29,000	49,700	49,300	52,700	39,900

BORGWARNER MASSACHUSETTS INC.

100 OTIS ST   CEO: Matthew Boyle
NORTHBOROUGH, MA 015322463   CFO: Paul N Farquhar
Phone: 508 281-5500   HR: –
Fax: –   FYE: September 30
Web: www.borgwarner.com   Type: Private

You might say that Tech/Ops Sevcon prevents electric vehicles from becoming speed demons. The company makes Sevcon solid-state controllers, which regulate motor speed and acceleration in battery-powered vehicles, such as forklifts and coal mining equipment. Through a UK-based subsidiary, Tech/Ops Sevcon also makes metalized film capacitors for power electronics, signaling, and audio equipment applications. Targeting manufacturers of aerial lifts, forklift trucks, and underground mining vehicles, Tech/Ops sells directly and through a network of independent dealers in Asia, Europe, and the US. About 60% of sales are to customers outside the US.

BORN FREE USA, UNITED WITH ANIMAL PROTECTION INSTITUTE

2300 WISCONSIN AVE NW 100B   CEO: Angela Grimes
WASHINGTON, DC 200071842   CFO: –
Phone: 202 450-3168   HR: –
Fax: –   FYE: December 31
Web: www.bornfreeusa.org   Type: Private

Born Free USA (formerly Animal Protection Institute) advocates the protection of animals from exploitation and cruelty. The not-for-profit group employs public education, governmental lobbying, litigation, and grassroots organizing to prevent the keeping of exotic pets, protect animals used in entertainment, control the international wildlife trade, and abolish trapping and the use of fur in fashion. Its primate sanctuary in Texas cares for animals rescued from labs, roadside zoos, and private ownership. Founded in 1968, API merged with Born Free USA (the US arm of the UK's Born Free Foundation, formed by the stars of the film Born Free) to form Born Free USA United with Animal Protection Institute in 2007.

	Annual Growth	12/15	12/16	12/19	12/20	12/21
Sales ($mil.)	(9.4%)	–	2.8	2.1	2.4	1.7
Net income ($ mil.)	–	–	(1.1)	(0.4)	0.0	(0.4)
Market value ($ mil.)	–	–	–	–	–	–
Employees	–	–	–	–	–	20

BOSS HOLDINGS, INC.   NBB: BSHI

1221 Page Street   CEO: G L Graziadio III
Kewanee, IL 61443   CFO: –
Phone: 309 852-2131   HR: –
Fax: –   FYE: December 31
Web: www.bossgloves.com   Type: Public

Boss Holdings would rather take orders (for its gloves, boots, and rainwear) than give them. Its primary subsidiary Boss Manufacturing Company (BMC) imports and markets gloves and protective wear that it sells through mass merchandisers, hardware stores, and other retailers in North America. The company also sells its products directly to commercial users in industries such as agriculture and automotive. The holding company's Boss Pet Products markets pet supplies to US retailers while its Galaxy Balloons subsidiary sells latex balloons. Boss Holdings was founded in 1893 as a manufacturer of work gloves. Today, gloves and protective gear account for a majority of annual sales.

	Annual Growth	12/15	12/16	12/20	12/21	12/22
Sales ($mil.)	(63.0%)	67.9	62.2	0.0	0.0	0.0
Net income ($ mil.)	–	2.0	1.6	(0.0)	0.0	(0.0)
Market value ($ mil.)	6.4%	23.9	26.1	36.4	49.1	36.9
Employees	–	–	–	–	–	–

BOSTON BEER CO INC (THE)   NYS: SAM

One Design Center Place, Suite 850   CEO: David A Burwick
Boston, MA 02210   CFO: Frank H Smalla
Phone: 617 368-5000   HR: Cheryl Fisher
Fax: 617 368-5500   FYE: December 30
Web: www.bostonbeer.com   Type: Public

The Boston Beer Company, Inc. began in 1984 brewing Samuel Adams beer, and the Samuel Adams brand is currently recognized as one of the largest and most respected craft beer brands. Its hard seltzers, beers, and hard ciders are primarily positioned in the market for high-end beer occasions. The company's brands include Truly Hard Seltzer, Twisted Tea, Samuel Adams, Angry Orchard, Dogfish Head brand, and Jim Beam Kentucky Coolers, as well as other craft beer brands from Angel City Brewery and Coney Island Brewing. Boston Beer produces alcoholic beverages, including hard seltzer, malt beverages (beers), and hard cider at company-owned breweries and its cidery and under contract arrangements at other brewery locations.

	Annual Growth	12/19	12/20	12/21	12/22	12/23
Sales ($mil.)	12.6%	1,249.8	1,736.4	2,057.6	2,090.3	2,008.6
Net income ($ mil.)	(8.8%)	110.0	192.0	14.6	67.3	76.3
Market value ($ mil.)	(2.3%)	4,583.4	12,282	6,351.6	3,987.6	4,182.1
Employees	7.0%	2,128	2,423	2,543	2,679	2,793

BOSTON MEDICAL CENTER CORPORATION

1 BOSTON MEDICAL CTR PL STE 1   CEO: Monica Watson
BOSTON, MA 021182999   CFO: –
Phone: 617 414-5000   HR: –
Fax: –   FYE: September 30
Web: www.bmc.org   Type: Private

Boston Medical Center (BMC) offers a full spectrum of healthcare services, from prenatal care and obstetrics to surgery and rehabilitation. It offers world-class trauma and emergency services and operates the busiest center for these services in New England. The not-for-profit hospital boasts around 515 licensed beds and about 880 physicians. It is the founding partner of the Boston Medical Center Health System, which provides world-class care to all. BMC Health System includes BMC and five other major entities serving patients and health plan members in Massachusetts and New Hampshire. BMC is the primary teaching hospital of Boston University's School of Medicine.

	Annual Growth	09/14	09/15	09/17	09/21	09/22
Sales ($mil.)	11.4%	–	1,004.7	1,089.4	1,975.4	2,141.1
Net income ($ mil.)	7.4%	–	7.6	12.8	59.0	12.6
Market value ($ mil.)	–	–	–	–	–	–
Employees	–	–	–	–	–	4,200

BOSTON PROPERTIES INC   NYS: BXP

Prudential Center, 800 Boylston Street, Suite 1900
Boston, MA 02199-8103
Phone: 617 236-3300
Fax: –
Web: www.bxp.com

CEO: Owen D Thomas
CFO: Michael E Labelle
HR: –
FYE: December 31
Type: Public

Boston Properties is a fully integrated, self-administered and self-managed real estate investment trust (REIT) and is one of the largest publicly traded office REITs that owns, develops, and manages mostly Class A office buildings in large US cities. Its core markets are Boston, Los Angeles, New York, San Francisco, and Washington, DC. As one of the nation's largest office owners and developers, Boston Properties owns about 175 office properties with some 54.1 million rentable square feet. Its largest tenants include the US government, Salesforce.com, Arnold & Porter Kaye Scholer, and Biogen. The REIT also owns a handful of retail, hotel, and residential properties. The company's chairman Mort Zuckerman was the co-founder of Boston Properties in 1970.

	Annual Growth	12/19	12/20	12/21	12/22	12/23
Sales ($mil.)	2.5%	2,960.6	2,765.7	2,888.6	3,108.6	3,273.6
Net income ($ mil.)	(22.3%)	521.5	872.7	505.2	848.9	190.2
Market value ($ mil.)	(15.5%)	21,636	14,836	18,076	10,606	11,013
Employees	2.4%	760	750	743	780	836

BOSTON SAND & GRAVEL CO.   NBB: BSND

100 North Washington Street, 2nd Floor
Boston, MA 02114
Phone: 617 227-9000
Fax: 617 523-7947
Web: –

CEO: Dean M Boylan Sr
CFO: –
HR: –
FYE: December 31
Type: Public

Boston Sand & Gravel's shovel is full of aggregates and concrete. The company operates concrete and ready-mix cement plants in eastern Massachusetts; it also has a sand and gravel facility in New Hampshire. The construction materials business operates a fleet of more than 250 mixer trucks that deliver concrete to its customers (including home builders, developers, and contractors in the New England region) and it operates a short-line railroad that transports aggregate products from the New Hampshire facility to the greater Boston area. Founded in 1914, Boston Sand & Gravel has supplied concrete for major projects such as Boston's Central Artery/Tunnel, known as The Big Dig.

	Annual Growth	12/02	12/03	12/04	12/05	12/06
Sales ($mil.)	(6.6%)	92.1	73.7	66.6	63.8	70.2
Net income ($ mil.)	2.6%	0.0	(2.6)	(2.0)	(0.9)	0.1
Market value ($ mil.)	8.1%	44.6	43.2	44.6	44.6	60.8
Employees		–	–	–	–	–

BOSTON SCIENTIFIC CORP.   NYS: BSX

300 Boston Scientific Way
Marlborough, MA 01752-1234
Phone: 508 683-4000
Fax: –
Web: www.bostonscientific.com

CEO: Michael F Mahoney
CFO: Daniel Brennan
HR: Ana Correa
FYE: December 31
Type: Public

Boston Scientific Corporation is a global developer, manufacturer, and marketer of medical devices that are used in a broad range of interventional medical specialties. The company develops cardiovascular and cardiac rhythm management (CRM) products, including imaging catheters, imaging system and guidewires. It also makes devices used for electrophysiology, endoscopy, pain management (neuromodulation), urology, and pelvic health, including laser systems, hydrogel systems and brain stimulation systems. Boston Scientific markets its products in about 130 countries, but the US generates about 60% of revenue.

	Annual Growth	12/19	12/20	12/21	12/22	12/23
Sales ($mil.)	7.3%	10,735	9,913.0	11,888	12,682	14,240
Net income ($ mil.)	(23.7%)	4,700.0	(82.0)	1,041.0	698.0	1,593.0
Market value ($ mil.)	6.3%	66,279	52,692	62,263	67,818	84,733
Employees	7.5%	36,000	38,000	41,000	45,000	48,000

BOSTON SYMPHONY ORCHESTRA, INC.

301 MASSACHUSETTS AVE
BOSTON, MA 021154511
Phone: 617 838-5026
Fax: –
Web: www.bso.org

CEO: Mark Volpe
CFO: –
HR: –
FYE: August 31
Type: Private

If you want to venture out for some live music but are not in the mood for rock or pop, then a performance by The Boston Symphony Orchestra (BSO) might strike the right chord with you. Featuring compositions by composers like Beethoven, Mozart, and Stravinsky, the BSO performs more than 100 concerts during the regular season at Symphony Hall. The BSO also performs during the summer at the Tanglewood music center; other BSO-related performances are given by the smaller and lighter Boston Pops orchestra. One of the more prominent orchestras in the US, the BSO was founded in 1881 by businessman Henry Lee Higginson. Current music director James Levine is the BSO's first America-born conductor.

BOTTOMLINE TECHNOLOGIES, INC.

325 CORPORATE DR
PORTSMOUTH, NH 038016847
Phone: 603 436-0700
Fax: –
Web: www.bottomline.com

CEO: Craig Saks
CFO: Richard D Booth
HR: –
FYE: June 30
Type: Private

Bottomline Technologies is a leading provider of financial technology that makes complex business payments simple, smart and secure. Corporations and banks rely on Bottomline for domestic and international payments, efficient cash management, automated workflows for payment processing and bill review, and fraud detection, behavioral analytics and regulatory compliance solutions. Thousands of corporations around the world benefit from Bottomline solutions. In 2022, Bottomline Technologies announced the completion of its acquisition by Thoma Bravo, a leading software investment firm, in an all-cash transaction valued at approximately $2.6 billion.

BOULDER BRANDS, INC.

1600 PEARL ST STE 100
BOULDER, CO 803025453
Phone: 303 652-0521
Fax: –
Web: www.boulderbrands.com

CEO: –
CFO: –
HR: –
FYE: December 31
Type: Private

Trying to reach the pinnacle of healthy eating? Boulder Brands may help; its growing portfolio of food brands target the health conscious and those with health problems, such as diabetes and gluten allergies. The company makes Smart Balance buttery spreads and other alternative food products, including peanut butter, popcorn, and cooking oils. As the company has grown, its Smart Balance business has been outweighed by its Natural foods segment, including the Glutino, Gluten-Free Pantry, Udi's, Earth Balance, and the EVOL brands of shelf-stable and frozen products. Boulder Brands' products are sold by food retailers throughout North America. Founded in 2005, the company was acquired by Pinnacle Foods in January 2016.

BOURNS, INC.

1200 COLUMBIA AVE
RIVERSIDE, CA 925072129
Phone: 951 781-5500
Fax: -
Web: www.bourns.com

CEO: Gordon Bourns
CFO: James Heiken
HR: Christina Brysacz
FYE: November 30
Type: Private

Bourns, Inc., is a manufacturer and supplier of position and speed sensors, circuit protection solutions, magnetic components, microelectronic modules, panel controls and resistors, among others. Bourns is recognized as a global leading supplier of reliable circuit protection solutions based on innovative technologies such as TBU HSPs, TCS, mini-breaker TCOs and GMOV hybrid protection components. Bourns full line of Trimpot trimming potentiometers help fine-tune board components to achieve optimal performance in applications that must be calibrated before being shipped. Founded in 1947, Bourns serves automotive, consumer, industrial, communications markets.

BOWDOIN COLLEGE

255 MAINE ST
BRUNSWICK, ME 040113343
Phone: 207 725-3000
Fax: -
Web: www.bowdoin.edu

CEO: -
CFO: -
HR: Jessica Depaiva
FYE: June 30
Type: Private

Bowdoin College churns out graduates from its campus on the coast of Maine. The private, liberal arts school serves some 1,800 students, offering undergraduate degrees in about 40 fields of study, including English, psychology, history, mathematics, and biology. It has about 200 faculty members and a student-to-teacher ratio of 9:1. Most classes are conducted on the main campus in Brunswick, Maine; Bowdoin also includes a Coastal Studies Center some eight miles from campus on Orr's Island. Notable alumni include writers Nathanial Hawthorne and Henry Wadsworth Longfellow, as well as former president Franklin Pierce. Established in 1794, Bowdoin is Maine's oldest college.

	Annual Growth	06/18	06/19	06/20	06/21	06/22
Sales ($mil.)	4.3%	-	177.9	183.5	176.8	202.1
Net income ($ mil.)	-	-	116.8	61.6	936.8	(252.2)
Market value ($ mil.)	-	-	-	-	-	949
Employees	-	-	-	-	-	-

BOWEN ENGINEERING CORPORATION

8802 N MERIDIAN ST STE X
INDIANAPOLIS, IN 462605319
Phone: 219 661-9770
Fax: -
Web: www.bowenengineering.com

CEO: A D Bowen III
CFO: Scot Evans Sr
HR: Misha Kennedy
FYE: September 30
Type: Private

Bowen Engineering understands the elements of earth, wind, and water. The company provides engineering and construction services for water, wastewater, earthwork, concrete, industrial, power, and underground utility projects. It operates through three divisions: Power and industrial; private water; and public works. The company, which has offices in Indiana, Tennessee, and Ohio, offers design/build, general contracting, and construction management services to public and private clients. Bowen Engineering was founded in 1967 by Robert Bowen. The Bowen family continues to lead the company.

	Annual Growth	09/05	09/06	09/07	09/08	09/09
Sales ($mil.)	26.5%	-	-	228.2	288.9	365.2
Net income ($ mil.)	2.8%	-	-	15.3	17.5	16.2
Market value ($ mil.)	-	-	-	-	-	-
Employees	-	-	-	-	-	700

BOWFLEX INC

17750 S.E. 6th Way
Vancouver, WA 98683
Phone: 360 859-2900
Fax: -
Web: www.nautilusinc.com

NBB: BFXX Q

CEO: James Barr IV
CFO: Aina E Konold
HR: -
FYE: March 31
Type: Public

Nautilus is a global leader in innovative home fitness solutions. Its products include cardio products (bikes, line, and treadmills) and strength products (dumbbells, kettlebells and barbells and a range of home gyms) that are sold under the popular brand names Bowflex, Nautilus, Schwinn, and JRNY. Nautilus sells its fitness equipment directly to consumers primarily through websites and through a network of independent retail companies to reach consumers in the home use markets in the US and internationally. The company operates in the US, Europe, Asia, and Canada. The company generates the majority of its sales in the US.

	Annual Growth	12/19	12/20*	03/21	03/22	03/23
Sales ($mil.)	(2.5%)	309.3	552.6	206.1	589.5	286.8
Net income ($ mil.)	-	(92.8)	59.8	30.4	(22.4)	(105.4)
Market value ($ mil.)	(8.5%)	55.7	577.7	498.1	131.2	42.7
Employees	(1.7%)	434	412	-	521	412

*Fiscal year change

BOWLIN TRAVEL CENTERS INC

150 Louisiana N.E.
Albuquerque, NM 87108
Phone: 505 266-5985
Fax: -
Web: www.bowlintc.com

NBB: BWTL

CEO: Michael L Bowlin
CFO: Nina J Pratz
HR: -
FYE: January 31
Type: Public

Dotting the desert with gas pumps and gifts, Bowlin Travel Centers (BTC) operates about 10 full-service, southwestern-themed travel centers along desolate stretches of interstates I-10 and I-40 in arid Arizona and New Mexico. Its travel centers offer snacks, souvenirs provided by Native American tribes or imported from Mexico, gas (Shell and ExxonMobil brands), and restaurants (Dairy Queen at five locations). It also sells gasoline wholesale. BTC traces its roots to 1912 when founder, Claude Bowlin, started trading goods and services with Native Americans in New Mexico. Today, BTC is controlled by its chairman, president, and CEO Michael Bowlin and his family.

	Annual Growth	01/18	01/19	01/20	01/21	01/22
Sales ($mil.)	12.3%	27.4	29.9	30.7	29.4	43.7
Net income ($ mil.)	39.9%	0.5	0.2	0.3	0.8	1.8
Market value ($ mil.)	24.2%	8.3	9.7	11.5	11.9	19.8
Employees	-	-	-	-	-	-

BOWLING GREEN STATE UNIVERSITY

110 MCFALL CTR
BOWLING GREEN, OH 434034402
Phone: 419 372-2311
Fax: -
Web: www.bgsu.edu

CEO: -
CFO: -
HR: Sandy Heck
FYE: June 30
Type: Private

Bowling Green State University (BGSU) prepares young adults to live vibrant lives. The university is home to more than 20,000 students at its flagship campus and at its BGSU Firelands satellite campus. It offers some 200 undergraduate majors and programs, nearly 50 master's degree programs, and more than 15 doctoral degree programs, as well as certificate programs, associate degrees, and a specialist degree in education. It also has more than 40 study abroad programs. Established in 1910 to educate teachers, BGSU has not strayed far from its original mission; it is among the top producers of teachers in the US.

BOWMAN CONSULTING GROUP LTD

NMS: BWMN

12355 Sunrise Valley Drive, Suite 520
Reston, VA 20191
Phone: 703 464-1000
Fax: –
Web: www.bowman.com

CEO: –
CFO: –
HR: –
FYE: December 31
Type: Public

Bowman Consulting is in tune with land development. The firm provides civil engineering, environmental assessment, land planning, and surveying services to businesses and government agencies interested in land development. Projects include residential communities, hotels, retail centers, industrial parks, recreational facilities, and schools. Bowman also provides environmental services that range from asbestos surveys to wetland delineation. Formerly active primarily in the DC area, the firm has been expanding into new markets such as the Southwest (which it entered by acquiring Phoenix-based Vantage Resources and DEI Professional Services in 2011). President Gary Bowman formed his namesake firm in 1995.

	Annual Growth	12/19	12/20	12/21	12/22	12/23
Sales ($mil.)	32.1%	113.7	122.0	150.0	261.7	346.3
Net income ($ mil.)	–	1.5	1.0	0.3	5.0	(6.6)
Market value ($ mil.)	–	–	–	320.7	329.8	536.1
Employees	–	–	750	1,000	1,600	2,000

BOWTIE, INC.

500 N BRAND BLVD STE 600
GLENDALE, CA 912034704
Phone: 213 385-2222
Fax: –
Web: www.merlenorman.com

CEO: –
CFO: –
HR: –
FYE: December 31
Type: Private

BowTie, formerly Fancy Publications, knows people fancy their pets. Publisher of Dog Fancy, Cat Fancy, Ferrets, and Bird Talk, the company publishes more than 70 trade titles, most of which are aimed at pet-loving consumers, veterinarians, breeders, and pet stores. It also offers lifestyle titles such as Hobby Farms, transportation titles such as Auto Restorer, and Web sites such as AnimalNetwork.com. In addition, the company operates the distribution unit Global Distribution Services, and publishes equine and lifestyle books from BowTie Press and Kennel Club Books, as well as reptile care books from Advanced Vivarium Systems.

BOX INC

NYS: BOX

900 Jefferson Ave.
Redwood City, CA 94063
Phone: 877 729-4269
Fax: –
Web: www.box.com

CEO: Aaron Levie
CFO: Dylan Smith
HR: –
FYE: January 31
Type: Public

Box, Inc. is the Content Cloud: a single, secure, cloud-native platform for managing the entire content journey. Content from blueprints to wireframes, videos to documents, proprietary formats to PDFs ? is the source of an organization's unique value. With a platform available in approximately 25 languages, Box's customers include nearly 70% of the Fortune 500. Its Content Cloud enables its customers to securely manage the entire content lifecycle, from the moment a file is created or ingested to when it's shared, edited, published, approved, signed, classified, and retained. The company has more than 100,000 paying organizations, including industries in the healthcare and life sciences, government, legal, and financial services sectors. Box has operations in the US, Europe, and Asia.

	Annual Growth	01/20	01/21	01/22	01/23	01/24
Sales ($mil.)	10.5%	696.3	770.8	874.3	990.9	1,037.1
Net income ($ mil.)	–	(144.3)	(43.4)	(41.5)	26.8	129.0
Market value ($ mil.)	14.7%	2,169.6	2,503.1	3,771.9	4,617.9	3,750.3
Employees	5.5%	2,046	1,934	2,172	2,487	2,530

BOY SCOUTS OF AMERICA

1325 W WALNUT HILL LN
IRVING, TX 750383096
Phone: 972 580-2000
Fax: –
Web: www.scouting.org

CEO: Roger Krone
CFO: –
HR: Alicia Wesseling
FYE: December 31
Type: Private

Boy Scouts of America (BSA) provides the nation's foremost youth program of character development and values-based leadership training. It is composed of approximately 2.2 million members between the ages of 5 and 21 and 800,000 volunteers in local councils through the US and territories. In addition to traditional scouting programs (Cub, and Boy Scouts), BSA offers the Venturing program for boys and girls ages 14-20. The organization was founded in 1910, and since then, its youth programs was participated by more than 130 million young men and women, while over 35 million adult volunteers have helped carry out the BSA's mission.

BOYD GAMING CORP.

NYS: BYD

6465 South Rainbow Boulevard
Las Vegas, NV 89118
Phone: 702 792-7200
Fax: –
Web: www.boydgaming.com

CEO: Keith E Smith
CFO: Josh Hirsberg
HR: Randee Dalton
FYE: December 31
Type: Public

Boyd Gaming operates about 30 wholly-owned casino properties in Nevada and nine other US states. Most of its properties that offer casino spaces, slot machines, table games, hotel rooms, and hotels. The company also has a partnership with digital gaming company FanDuel Group through which it uses FanDuel's technology for its own online and mobile gambling and sports betting services. In addition to its casinos, Boyd owns and operates a travel agency and a travel insurance company in Hawaii. Founded in 1975, the company generates more than 65% of revenue from Midwest & South.

	Annual Growth	12/19	12/20	12/21	12/22	12/23
Sales ($mil.)	3.0%	3,326.1	2,178.5	3,369.8	3,555.4	3,738.5
Net income ($ mil.)	40.8%	157.6	(134.7)	463.8	639.4	620.0
Market value ($ mil.)	20.3%	2,899.2	4,156.0	6,349.3	5,280.3	6,062.7
Employees	(9.7%)	24,300	13,583	15,114	15,771	16,129

BOYD LACONIA, LLC

1 AAVID CIR
LACONIA, NH 03246
Phone: 603 528-3400
Fax: –
Web: www.boydcorp.com

CEO: –
CFO: David Wall
HR: –
FYE: December 31
Type: Private

Aavid Thermalloy is a fan of fans and other cooling devices. The company makes heat sinks, fans, heat spreaders, liquid cooling products, cooling assemblies, and other devices used to manage temperature in computer, networking, and industrial electronic systems. It also makes interface materials including insulating films and thermal greases, as well as insulating covers. Aavid offers consulting and systems analysis services for data center operators looking to improve the efficiency of their facilities. The company's Aavid Design subsidiary provides product design, testing, and prototyping services related to thermal, mechanical, electronic, and industrial design.

BOYDS COLLECTION LTD

NBB: BYDC

350 South Street
McSherrystown, PA 17344
Phone: 717 633-9898
Fax: –
Web: www.boydsstuff.com

CEO: –
CFO: –
HR: –
FYE: December 31
Type: Public

In the forest of collectibles, The Boyds Collection bears are watching. The company sold resin, porcelain, and plush renditions of bears and other animals, including its Bearstones figurines and its J.B. Bean & Associates line of fully-jointed bears and other animals. It also sold other collectibles and home décor items, such as stationery and picture frames. Boyds has licensed products via deals with NASCAR and Coca-Cola. Its products were sold primarily in US gift shops and department stores, as well as through catalogs and trade shows. The company is owned by Enesco, which put the bear-making company into hibernation in late 2014, citing poor market conditions.

	Annual Growth	12/01	12/02	12/03	12/04	12/05
Sales ($mil.)	(15.4%)	153.5	131.3	113.0	103.7	78.6
Net income ($ mil.)	–	35.8	31.4	10.9	5.4	(181.8)
Market value ($ mil.)	–	–	–	–	–	–
Employees	11.8%	269	437	419	520	420

BOYS & GIRLS CLUBS OF AMERICA

1275 PEACHTREE ST NE STE 500
ATLANTA, GA 303093576
Phone: 404 487-5700
Fax: –
Web: www.bgca.org

CEO: James Clark
CFO: –
HR: –
FYE: December 31
Type: Private

The Boys & Girls Clubs of America (BGCA) runs after-school programs nationwide to give children and teenagers a safe and supervised environment. Operating through local affiliates, BGCA boasts nearly 4,740 locations that serve approximately 4.6 million youth. Members engage in sports, recreation, and fitness activities, as well as in programs centered on character development, leadership, and life skills. BGCA alumni include Bill Clinton, Jackie Joyner-Kersee, Martin Sheen, Michael Jordan, and Queen Latifah. Boys & Girls Clubs of America had its beginnings in 1860.

	Annual Growth	12/17	12/18	12/19	12/21	12/22
Sales ($mil.)	(5.0%)	–	158.3	138.0	217.7	129.0
Net income ($ mil.)	–	–	(10.1)	(18.2)	16.8	15.5
Market value ($ mil.)	–	–	–	–	–	–
Employees	–	–	–	–	–	360

BOZZUTO'S, INC.

275 SCHOOLHOUSE RD
CHESHIRE, CT 064101257
Phone: 203 272-3511
Fax: –
Web: www.bozzutos.com

CEO: Michael A Bozzuto
CFO: –
HR: Bonnie N Sirois
FYE: September 27
Type: Private

Bozzuto's is a leading wholesale grocery distribution company that supplies food and household products to retailers in New Jersey, New York, Pennsylvania, and in New England. The company distributes a full line of grocery items, including meat products, produce and floral, grocery, dairy and frozen food, bakery and deli, fresh meat and seafood, as well as seasonal and GM/HBC and specialty and organics. It carries goods sold under both the IGA and Hy-Top labels, in addition to national brands. Bozzuto's also owns about five distribution centers in Connecticut and Pennsylvania. The company was founded in 1945.

	Annual Growth	09/04	09/05	09/06	09/07	09/08
Sales ($mil.)	(96.4%)	–	–	955.449	1,180.7	1,244.0
Net income ($ mil.)	–	–	–	0.2	(0.4)	(5.9)
Market value ($ mil.)	–	–	–	–	–	–
Employees	–	–	–	–	–	3,100

BPZ RESOURCES, INC.

10497 TOWN AND COUNTRY WAY
HOUSTON, TX 770241117
Phone: 281 556-6200
Fax: –
Web: –

CEO: Manuel P Zuniga-Pflucker
CFO: Richard S Menniti
HR: –
FYE: December 31
Type: Private

BPZ Resources was committed to exploring for oil and gas resources in South America. The company operated through its BPZ Energy subsidiary and that unit's BPZ Energy International Holdings subsidiary. BPZ Resources owned 2.2 million acres of oil and gas properties in northwest Peru. It also held acreage in Ecuador, where it held a 10% stake in a producing block. In 2012 the company reported proved reserves of 16.4 million barrels of oil equivalent (of which 13.4 million barrels were in the Corvina field and 3 million barrels in the Albacora field, both of which are located offshore northwest Peru). BPZ Resources filed for Chapter 11 bankruptcy in early 2015.

BRADFORD WHITE CORPORATION

725 TALAMORE DR
AMBLER, PA 190021873
Phone: 215 641-9400
Fax: –
Web: www.bradfordwhite.com

CEO: R B Carnevale
CFO: –
HR: Jillian Fournier
FYE: December 31
Type: Private

Bradford White Corporation helps folks get in -- and stay in -- hot water. The company makes and markets water heaters for residential, commercial, and industrial heating applications. It makes oil-fired products, gas power burners, and indirect-fired units. Through a pair of subsidiaries, Bradford White-Canada and LAARS Heating Systems, it also makes products, such as pool heaters, oil burners, and air handlers. Bradford White wholesales its products through a network of plumbing and heating professionals. Subsidiary Niles Steel Tank produces custom steel tanks for companies in the automotive, petrol-chemical, pharmaceutical, and refrigeration industries. Bradford White Corporation was founded in 1881.

BRADLEY COMPANY, LLC

W142N9101 FOUNTAIN BLVD
MENOMONEE FALLS, WI 530512348
Phone: 262 251-6000
Fax: –
Web: www.bradleycorp.com

CEO: Bryan Mullett
CFO: Mark Umhoefer
HR: John H Morrow
FYE: December 31
Type: Private

Bradley Corporation manufactures commercial washroom accessories and plumbing fixtures, including faucets, hand wash fountains, Skid systems, wall and pedestal-mounted eyewash stations, group showers, and related valves and parts. Its washroom accoutrements include baby changers, hand dryers, medicine cabinets, shower seats, soap dispensers, toilet paper dispensers, towel holders, and waste receptacle. The company also makes Lenox-brand plastic locker systems and Mills brand washroom partitions. Some of its clients are Boeing, Walmart, O'Hare Airport, Starbucks, Johns Hopkins Medical Center, and more. The company was founded in 1921.

BRADLEY UNIVERSITY

1501 W BRADLEY AVE
PEORIA, IL 616250003
Phone: 309 676-7611
Fax: –
Web: www.bradley.edu

CEO: –
CFO: –
HR: –
FYE: May 31
Type: Private

Bradley University is a private university offering a wide breadth of higher education opportunitites. The school provides 100 undergraduate programs in fields ranging from art, science, and education to business, media, and health. Bradley also confers graduate degrees in more than 30 academic fields, including a Doctorate of Physical Therapy. With a student-to-teacher ratio of 12:1, the university has an enrollment of approximately 6,000 students -- more than 5,000 of whom are undergraduates -- that receive instruction from some 350 full-time faculty members.

	Annual Growth	05/15	05/16	05/20	05/21	05/22
Sales ($mil.)	(3.1%)	–	194.8	238.6	147.4	160.9
Net income ($ mil.)	–	–	7.0	5.8	108.7	(34.6)
Market value ($ mil.)	–	–	–	–	–	–
Employees	–	–	–	–	–	1,000

BRADY CORP

6555 West Good Hope Road
Milwaukee, WI 53233
Phone: 414 358-6600
Fax: –
Web: www.bradyid.com

NYS: BRC
CEO: Russell R Shaller
CFO: Ann E Thornton
HR: –
FYE: July 31
Type: Public

Brady Corporation makes a diversified array of industrial identification and workplace safety products. The company's ID products include label printing systems, lockout/tagout devices, wire markers and tags, hospital and entertainment wristbands, ID badges, and safety compliance software and services. Other products include safety and compliance signs, tags, and labels; informational signage; compliance posters; asset tracking labels; and first aid products. Brady operates in about 40 manufacturing and distribution across the globe. The US accounts for around 55% of the company's sales.

	Annual Growth	07/19	07/20	07/21	07/22	07/23
Sales ($mil.)	3.5%	1,160.6	1,081.3	1,144.7	1,302.1	1,331.9
Net income ($ mil.)	7.4%	131.3	112.4	129.7	150.0	174.9
Market value ($ mil.)	(0.1%)	2,511.4	2,231.7	2,654.6	2,323.0	2,504.1
Employees	(2.1%)	6,100	5,400	5,700	5,700	5,600

BRAINWORKS SOFTWARE DEVELOPMENT CORPORATION

320 CARLETON AVE STE 3000
CENTRAL ISLIP, NY 117224500
Phone: 631 563-5000
Fax: –
Web: www.brainworks.com

CEO: –
CFO: –
HR: –
FYE: December 31
Type: Private

Brainworks Software develops newspaper software designed to manage all aspects of advertising, including layout, billing, and sales force automation. The company's software includes tools for circulation management, editorial story selection and production, classified and display advertising, contract management, and pagination. More than 700 North American newspapers use Brainworks' software. Customers include Tyler Morning Telegraph, The Tribune Review, and Chesapeake Publishing. Brainworks was founded in 1988.

BRAKEBUSH BROTHERS, INC.

N4993 6TH DR
WESTFIELD, WI 539648200
Phone: 608 296-2121
Fax: –
Web: www.brakebush.com

CEO: –
CFO: Thomas Ludwig
HR: Anna Kassouf
FYE: December 31
Type: Private

It should be pointed out that chickens don't start out with fingers, but Brakebush Brothers produces plenty of 'em. The company manufactures processed value-added chicken products (wings, nuggets, patties, fingers, and strips) for sale through retail grocery and foodservice operators. Its subsidiary, Squawkers, is a branded, restaurant-concept family of products marketed to the foodservice industry; Brakebush Transportation distributes the company's products to destinations in the 48 contiguous US states. Brakebush Brothers, a family-owned company, was founded by William and Otto Brakebush in 1925.

	Annual Growth	12/18	12/19	12/20	12/21	12/22
Sales ($mil.)	(2.4%)	–	–	–	17.0	16.6
Net income ($ mil.)	–	–	–	–	(0.1)	0.9
Market value ($ mil.)	–	–	–	–	–	–
Employees	–	–	–	–	–	400

BRAMMO, INC.

300 W VALLEY VIEW RD
TALENT, OR 975409629
Phone: 541 482-9555
Fax: –
Web: www.brammo.com

CEO: –
CFO: –
HR: –
FYE: December 31
Type: Private

Brammo's electric bikes are gearing up for a little eco-friendly competition. The startup specialty vehicle manufacturer has developed the Enertia, a plug-in electric motorcycle being marketed to city commuters as a greener alternative to traditional gas-powered motorcycles, scooters, and cars. Scheduled to begin production in 2009, the lightweight Enertia exceeds 50 mph and gets up to 45 miles per charge. The company claims it is at least two times more energy efficient than all-electric and hybrid automobiles. Founded in 2002, Brammo is privately held. It is controlled by CEO Craig Bramscher, Best Buy Capital, and Chrysalix Energy Venture Capital.

BRANCH BUILDS, INC.

5732 AIRPORT RD NW
ROANOKE, VA 240121122
Phone: 540 989-5215
Fax: –
Web: www.branch-associates.com

CEO: –
CFO: –
HR: –
FYE: December 31
Type: Private

Branch & Associates is no twig in the Branch Group family tree. The employee-owned subsidiary offers general contracting, design/build, and construction management services for commercial and industrial construction projects in the Carolinas, Tennessee, Virginia, and West Virginia. The company builds retail, health care, educational, multi-unit residential, government, hospitality, and industrial facilities. Billy Branch founded the company in 1963. It was reorganized and became Branch Associates under the Branch Group in 1985. Other Branch Group subsidiaries include Branch Highways, E.V. Williams, and G.J. Hopkins.

	Annual Growth	12/16	12/17	12/18	12/19	12/20
Sales ($mil.)	23.2%	–	121.9	177.7	268.6	227.7
Net income ($ mil.)	–	–	–	–	–	–
Market value ($ mil.)	–	–	–	–	–	–
Employees	–	–	–	–	–	90

BRANDEIS UNIVERSITY

298 CRESCENT ST
WALTHAM, MA 024533803
Phone: 781 736-8318
Fax: –
Web: www.brandeis.edu

CEO: –
CFO: –
HR: Lori Dougherty
FYE: June 30
Type: Private

Brandeis University offers about 45 undergraduate majors and around 50 minors programs in the creative arts, humanities, sciences and social sciences. Located in Waltham, it comprises the College of Arts and Sciences, the Graduate School of Arts and Sciences, the International Business School, the Heller School for Social Policy and Management, and the Rabb School of Continuing Studies. The university has an enrollment of about 5,560 students; the student/faculty ratio is 10-to-1. A non-sectarian Jewish community-sponsored institution named after the late Justice Louis Brandeis of the US Supreme Court, Brandeis University was founded in 1948.

	Annual Growth	06/08	06/09	06/10	06/15	06/16
Sales ($mil.)	0.5%	–	–	323.3	508.9	333.7
Net income ($ mil.)	–	–	–	(24.1)	80.1	(64.7)
Market value ($ mil.)	–	–	–	–	–	–
Employees	–	–	–	–	–	1,200

BRANDYWINE COMMUNICATIONS

2921 DAIMLER ST
SANTA ANA, CA 927055810
Phone: 714 755-1050
Fax: –
Web: www.brandywinecomm.com

CEO: –
CFO: –
HR: Kelli Commeville
FYE: September 30
Type: Private

Brandywine Communications makes precision time and frequency products, including computer plug-in boards, network time servers, oscillators, and time displays, for the aerospace, financial services, government, military, telecommunications, and utility markets. Customers include Argonne National Laboratory, Boeing, Caltech, General Electric, Lawrence Livermore National Laboratory, Lockheed Martin, NASA, QUALCOMM, the US Air Force, and the US Army. The company was founded in 1995 and is owned by its officers. Brandywine has offices in California and Virginia, with sales representatives around the world.

	Annual Growth	09/08	09/09	09/10	09/11	09/12
Sales ($mil.)	18.5%	–	–	6.5	8.5	9.1
Net income ($ mil.)	15.4%	–	–	0.3	(0.3)	0.4
Market value ($ mil.)	–	–	–	–	–	–
Employees	–	–	–	–	–	70

BRANDYWINE REALTY TRUST

2929 Arch Street, Suite 1800
Philadelphia, PA 19104
Phone: 610 325-5600
Fax: –
Web: www.brandywinerealty.com

NYS: BDN
CEO: Gerard H Sweeney
CFO: Howard Sipzner
HR: –
FYE: December 31
Type: Public

If the thought of making it big in real estate intoxicates you, look into Brandywine. A self-managed real estate investment trust (REIT), Brandywine buys, leases, sells, and manages commercial properties. It owns more than 200 office properties, about 20 industrial properties, a handful of mixed-use properties, and some 500 acres of undeveloped land. Its portfolio comprises more than 25 million sq. ft. of rentable space, located mainly in urban and suburban areas of the mid-Atlantic region, as well as California and Texas. Jerry Sweeney, who founded Brandywine in 1986, remains president and CEO of the company.

	Annual Growth	12/19	12/20	12/21	12/22	12/23
Sales ($mil.)	(3.0%)	580.4	534.9	486.8	506.1	514.7
Net income ($ mil.)	–	34.3	305.5	12.3	53.8	(196.8)
Market value ($ mil.)	(23.5%)	2,710.5	2,049.7	2,309.6	1,058.4	929.3
Employees	(0.4%)	337	341	324	336	331

BRASFIELD & GORRIE, L.L.C.

3021 7TH AVE S
BIRMINGHAM, AL 352333502
Phone: 205 328-4000
Fax: –
Web: www.brasfieldgorrie.com

CEO: M J Gorrie
CFO: Randall J Freeman
HR: –
FYE: December 31
Type: Private

Brasfield & Gorrie is one of the largest privately-held construction firms in the nation. The company provides construction management, general contracting, and design and build services for commercial, industrial, federal, municipal, infrastructure, healthcare, and institutional projects, mostly in the southeastern US. Established in 1964, the company generates about $5.0 billion in annual revenue.

BRAVO GROUP, INC.

20 N 2ND ST FL 2
HARRISBURG, PA 171011634
Phone: 717 214-2200
Fax: –
Web: www.bravogroup.us

CEO: Chris Bravacos
CFO: –
HR: –
FYE: June 30
Type: Private

No need for applause, Bravo Group is content to let its clients get all the attention. Not to be confused with the giant multicultural advertising agency The Bravo Group, this Bravo Group offers public relations services in the areas of public affairs and strategic communications, specializing in high profile clients and issues. Services include branding and identity program development, speechwriting, newsletter and print collateral development, event marketing, and employee training. The company's government affairs operations provides lobbying, Internet advocacy services, issue management, and event planning services.

BRAZOS ELECTRIC POWER COOPERATIVE, INC.

7616 BAGBY AVE
WACO, TX 767126924
Phone: 254 750-6500
Fax: –
Web: –

CEO: –
CFO: –
HR: Debra Wendrock
FYE: December 31
Type: Private

Brazos means "arms" in Spanish, and the generation and transmission arms of Brazos Electric Power Cooperative reach across 68 Texas counties. It serves 16 member/owner distribution cooperatives and one municipality in Northern and Central Texas. Brazos Electric Power annually generates (through its four power stations) and/or accesses from other power marketers some 3,655 MW of electric power. The cooperative's members include Comanche Electric Cooperative Association, Heart of Texas Electric Co-op (McGregor), Mid-South Synergy (Navasota), United Coop Services (Cleburne), and Wise Electric (Decatur).

	Annual Growth	12/97	12/98	12/99	12/09	12/17
Sales ($mil.)	6.2%	–	–	307.4	963.4	905.3
Net income ($ mil.)	12.6%	–	–	6.9	56.6	58.8
Market value ($ mil.)	–	–	–	–	–	–
Employees	–	–	–	–	–	366

BRAZOS HIGHER EDUCATION SERVICE CORPORATION, INC.

5609 CROSSLAKE PKWY
WACO, TX 767125500
Phone: 254 753-0915
Fax: –
Web: www.studentloans.com

CEO: Ben Litle
CFO: Ricky Turman
HR: –
FYE: June 30
Type: Private

Beginning in the 1920s, the Brazos River basin produced more than 18 million barrels of oil a year. Today, the area is churning out student loans under Brazos Higher Education Service Corp., a group of primarily non-for-profit companies that originates and services student loans for US lending institutions. It is one of the nation's largest student loan holders with assets totaling more than $5 billion. In addition to financial aid, the group helps undergraduate and graduate students find grants, scholarships, and work-study programs. Founded in 1975, Brazos Higher Education Service Corp. operates offices in Texas, Arkansas, California, Florida, and Virginia.

	Annual Growth	06/16	06/17	06/18	06/19	06/22
Assets ($mil.)	–	–	–	68.0	71.4	152.7
Net income ($ mil.)	(38.4%)	–	56.6	2.9	3.2	5.0
Market value ($ mil.)	–	–	–	–	–	–
Employees	–	–	–	–	–	30

BRC MERGER SUB, LLC

1300 17TH ST N STE 1400
ARLINGTON, VA 222093807
Phone: 703 312-9500
Fax: –
Web: –

CEO: Richard J Hendrix
CFO: Bradley J Wright
HR: –
FYE: December 31
Type: Private

Don't confuse FDR and FBR: One was a beloved US president, while the other loves dead presidents. FBR & Co. provides investment banking and institutional brokerage services for institutional and corporate clients and wealthy individuals. It also conducts equities research, manages mutual funds, and invests its own capital in merchant banking transactions alongside its clients. The company focuses on the consumer, industrials, energy, financial services, health care, real estate, media, telecommunications, and technology markets Crestview Partners. Its principal operating subsidiaries are FBR Capital Markets & Co. and FBR Fund Advisers.

BREAD FINANCIAL HOLDINGS INC

NYS: BFH

3095 Loyalty Circle
Columbus, OH 43219
Phone: 614 729-4000
Fax: –
Web: www.alliancedata.com

CEO: Ralph J Andretta
CFO: Perry S Beberman
HR: –
FYE: December 31
Type: Public

Bread Financial (formerly known as Alliance Data Systems) is a leading provider of simple, personalized payment, lending and saving solutions. Its partner base of more than 700 companies and online merchants consists of large consumer-based businesses, including well-known brands such as Victoria's Secret, Signet, Ulta, Toyota, Petco and Big Lots, as well as small- and medium-sized businesses. Through omnichannel touch points and a comprehensive product suite that includes credit card products and Bread digital payment solutions, the company helps its partners drive revenue growth and customer loyalty, while giving customers greater payment choices. It also offers credit and savings products directly to consumers through its proprietary products, including its Comenity-branded financial services.

	Annual Growth	12/19	12/20	12/21	12/22	12/23
Assets ($mil.)	(3.3%)	26,495	22,547	21,746	25,407	23,141
Net income ($ mil.)	26.8%	278.0	213.7	801.0	223.0	718.0
Market value ($ mil.)	(26.4%)	5,531.5	3,653.1	3,281.9	1,856.6	1,623.9
Employees	(4.7%)	8,500	8,000	6,000	7,500	7,000

BREAD FOR THE WORLD, INC.

425 3RD ST SW STE 1200
WASHINGTON, DC 200243234
Phone: 202 639-9400
Fax: –
Web: www.bread.org

CEO: –
CFO: –
HR: –
FYE: December 31
Type: Private

Bread for the World wants Congress to break the cycle of world hunger. The not-for-profit Christian organization with 50,000 members strives to end hunger through political action and volunteering. Its membership spans 2,500 churches in 45 denominations. The organization's partner group, Bread for the World Institute, performs education and research on hunger issues and publishes an annual hunger report. Bread for the World serves as the secretariat for the Alliance to End Hunger, a group of religious groups, foundations, labor unions, business leaders, and other charities. Bread for the World began in 1972 with a plan to bring faith-based organizations together to influence policies on hunger.

	Annual Growth	12/18	12/19	12/20	12/21	12/22
Sales ($mil.)	(5.4%)	–	6.6	5.9	5.9	5.6
Net income ($ mil.)	–	–	(1.6)	(1.5)	(0.6)	0.4
Market value ($ mil.)	–	–	–	–	–	–
Employees	–	–	–	–	–	60

BREAKING GROUND HOUSING DEVELOPMENT FUND CORPORATION

14 E 28TH ST LBBY PH
NEW YORK, NY 100167448
Phone: 212 471-0800
Fax: –
Web: www.breakingground.org

CEO: Brenda Rosen
CFO: –
HR: –
FYE: December 31
Type: Private

Common Ground gives some New Yorkers a second chance. The not-for-profit buys dilapidated or abandoned resident hotels and converts them into housing for homeless and low-income adults. In addition to modernizing units, Common Ground restores the buildings' historic ornamentation and reopens ground-floor retail space. Common Ground manages about a half-dozen housing properties in New York and Connecticut; the organization also develops new properties. Common Ground subsists on rents and management fees, government grants and contracts, and donations. Former president Rosanne Haggerty, who stepped down in 2011 to focus on housing initiatives beyond New York City, founded the organization in 1990.

BREEZE-EASTERN LLC

35 MELANIE LN
WHIPPANY, NJ 079811638
Phone: 973 602-1001
Fax: –
Web: www.breeze-eastern.com

CEO: –
CFO: –
HR: Edward Chestnut
FYE: March 31
Type: Private

Does your cargo need a lift? Breeze-Eastern makes electric and hydraulic rescue hoist systems for helicopters, as well as cargo winches and tie-downs, hook systems, and weapons handling systems. Its external helicopter cargo hook systems range in capacity from 1,500 pounds to 36,000 pounds. The company's weapons-handling systems include hoists for missiles, and gearboxes for specialty weapons applications. It also offers overhaul/repair and engineering sales services. Breeze-Eastern caters mainly to the US government in addition to major aerospace manufacturers and airlines. In 2016 Breeze-Eastern was acquired by TransDigm Group, a maker of components for commercial and military aircraft.

BREG, INC.

2885 LOKER AVE E
CARLSBAD, CA 920106626
Phone: 760 599-3000
Fax: –
Web: www.breg.com

CEO: Brad Lee
CFO: Aaron Heisler
HR: –
FYE: December 31
Type: Private

BREG is in the business of broken bones -- and sprained ankles and wounded ACLs and all kinds of other injuries to bones, joints, and ligaments that afflict athletes and non-athletes alike. A maker of orthopedic braces and other devices, BREG's product line includes soft goods, functional braces, and post-operative immobilizers for joints and body parts from shoulder to foot. The sports medicine company also makes devices for rehabilitation and pain management, such as home physical therapy kits and cold therapy products. In mid-2012 former parent Orthofix International sold BREG to private equity firm Water Street Healthcare Partners for $157.5 million.

BREITBURN ENERGY PARTNERS LP

707 WILSHIRE BLVD # 4600
LOS ANGELES, CA 900173612
Phone: 213 225-5900
Fax: –
Web: www.mavresources.com

CEO: –
CFO: –
HR: –
FYE: December 31
Type: Private

Oil and gas futures burn brightly for BreitBurn Energy Partners, one of California's largest independent exploration and production companies. With assets in Antrim Shale (Michigan), the Los Angeles Basin, the Wind River and Big Horn Basins (both in Wyoming), the Sunniland Trend (Florida), the New Albany Shale (Indiana and Kentucky), and the Permian Basin (West Texas), in 2011 the company reported estimated proved reserves of 151.1 million barrels of oil equivalent (65% of which was natural gas). That year 49% of its reserves were in Michigan, 29% in Wyoming, 14% in California, 7% in Florida, and 1% in Indiana and Kentucky. The company filed for Chapter 11 bankruptcy protection in 2016.

BREMER FINANCIAL CORP.

445 Minnesota St., Suite 2000
St. Paul, MN 55101-2107
Phone: 651 227-7621
Fax: 651 312-3750
Web: www.bremer.com

CEO: Stan K Dardis
CFO: Robert B Buck
HR: –
FYE: December 31
Type: Public

Bremer Financial Corporation, founded in 1943 by Otto Bremer, is the holding company for Bremer Bank, which operates more than 100 branches across Minnesota, North Dakota, and Wisconsin. The bank offers traditional retail banking services, such as checking and savings accounts, certificates of deposit, and credit cards. Altogether, commercial real estate loans, business loans, and residential mortgages account for the bulk of the company's lending activities. The $8.7 billion bank is also a prominent agricultural lender. In addition to its traditional bank products, Bremer Bank provides private banking, wealth management, financial planning, insurance, and trust services.

	Annual Growth	12/01	12/02	12/03	12/04	12/05
Assets ($mil.)	6.5%	5,094.1	5,259.5	5,671.3	6,141.5	6,555.9
Net income ($ mil.)	8.7%	51.6	61.6	61.1	64.2	72.0
Market value ($ mil.)	–	–	–	–	–	–
Employees	0.1%	1,671	1,649	1,632	1,625	1,680

BRENDAN TECHNOLOGIES INC

2236 Rutherford Road, Suite 107
Carlsbad, CA 92008
Phone: 760 929-7500
Fax: 760 929-7504
Web: www.brendan.com

CEO: –
CFO: –
HR: –
FYE: June 30
Type: Public

Brendan Technologies software is used to manage immunoassay testing in agricultural, biopharmaceutical, clinical, research, and veterinary laboratories. Applications include automating of immunoassay testing, data management, quality assurance, and regulatory complicance. Its products can be installed across single or multiple workstations and include the ability to upload worklists and download results to spreadsheets, databases, and laboratory information management systems.

	Annual Growth	06/03	06/04	06/05	06/06	06/07
Sales ($mil.)	(59.8%)	20.0	19.2	21.0	0.7	0.5
Net income ($ mil.)	–	0.4	0.3	(0.6)	(0.8)	(2.1)
Market value ($ mil.)	(10.8%)	14.2	25.6	33.2	6.2	9.0
Employees	(48.2%)	194	216	216	12	14

BRENDEN THEATRE CORPORATION

1985 WILLOW PASS RD STE C
CONCORD, CA 945202533
Phone: 925 677-0462
Fax: –
Web: www.brendentheatres.com

CEO: –
CFO: –
HR: –
FYE: December 31
Type: Private

Brenden Theatres has one foot in the future of movies and one in the past. The company operates seven theaters with more than 90 screens in California, Nevada, and Arizona. Brenden Theatres prides itself on being state-of-the-art, offering stadium seating, glass "Behind the Scenes" projection booths, Internet ticket ATMs, and express concession stands; its Vegas location has a five-story high IMAX theater. The company is owned by founder, president, and CEO John Brenden whose grandfather, Ted Mann, built and ran what is now the Mann Theatres chain in Los Angeles, including Grauman's Chinese Theatre (built in 1926), where the hand and foot prints of Hollywood stars can be found in the cement out front.

BRENTWOOD INDUSTRIES, INC.

500 SPRING RIDGE DR
READING, PA 196101069
Phone: 610 374-5109
Fax: –
Web: www.brentwoodindustries.com

CEO: –
CFO: –
HR: Christa Yergey
FYE: September 30
Type: Private

Brentwood Industries is a second-generation family business that specializes in thermoplastic molding and engineered plastic systems. The company manufactures a variety of plastic products, including wheelbarrows, cooling towers, wastewater treatment systems, and thermoplastic molding services. Its Polychem sludge collectors have become the industry standard for high performance and reliability. They feature plastic parts that provide a lightweight alternative to metallic components and have been engineered to function efficiently as part of any water or wastewater treatment system. The company was founded in 1965.

	Annual Growth	09/09	09/10	09/11	09/12	09/13
Sales ($mil.)	(76.3%)	–	–	1,953.8	110.2	110.2
Net income ($ mil.)	16326.4%	–	–	0.0	6.4	4.5
Market value ($ mil.)	–	–	–	–	–	–
Employees	–	–	–	–	–	700

BRESCIA UNIVERSITY

717 FREDERICA ST
OWENSBORO, KY 423013019
Phone: 270 685-3131
Fax: –
Web: www.brescia.edu

CEO: –
CFO: –
HR: –
FYE: May 31
Type: Private

Brescia University is a Catholic institution offering associate, undergraduate, and two graduate degrees rooted in the liberal arts. It also offers Bachelor of Science degrees in professional fields such as business, education, computer science, and ministry. The school has an enrollment of about 750 students and a 14:1 faculty/student radio. It's accredited by the Commission on Colleges of the Southern Association of Colleges and Schools. Brescia University was founded in 1950 by the Ursuline Sisters of Mount Saint Joseph.

	Annual Growth	05/15	05/16	05/19	05/20	05/22
Sales ($mil.)	4.3%	–	18.5	21.7	22.1	23.8
Net income ($ mil.)	–	–	0.3	0.1	0.2	(0.9)
Market value ($ mil.)	–	–	–	–	–	–
Employees	–	–	–	–	–	135

BRETFORD MANUFACTURING, INC.

11000 SEYMOUR AVE
FRANKLIN PARK, IL 601311230
Phone: 847 678-2545
Fax: –
Web: www.bretford.com

CEO: –
CFO: –
HR: –
FYE: December 31
Type: Private

Bretford designs furniture with technology in mind. The company makes and markets technologically-enabled furniture for offices, schools and universities, the government, and other markets. The modern look of its furniture is designed for the Digital Age and collaborative workspaces that the company promotes, and its line of mobile chairs, tables, and partitions keep office spaces flexible. Bretford boasts more than 240 furniture models that are GREENGUARD Indoor Air Quality (IAQ) Certified by the GREENGUARD Environmental Institute. The company also sells carts and furniture dedicated to Apple products, including the iPad and iMac. Bretford Manufacturing was founded in 1948 by brothers Russ and Edward Petrick.

	Annual Growth	12/18	12/19	12/20	12/21	12/22
Sales ($mil.)	(1.2%)	–	–	–	2.1	2.1
Net income ($ mil.)	–	–	–	–	(0.0)	(0.0)
Market value ($ mil.)	–	–	–	–	–	–
Employees	–	–	–	–	–	450

BRG SPORTS, INC.

1700 E HIGGINS RD STE 500
DES PLAINES, IL 600183800
Phone: 224 585-5200
Fax: –
Web: content.riddell.com

CEO: Dan Arment
CFO: Mark A Tripp
HR: –
FYE: December 29
Type: Private

BRG Sports is a corporate holding company of leading brands that design, develop and market innovative sports equipment, smart helmet technology, team apparel, and accessories. The company's Riddell brand is a premier designer and developer of football helmets, protective sports equipment, head impact monitoring technologies, apparel and related accessories. A recognized leader in helmet technology and innovation, Riddell is the leading manufacturer of football helmets and shoulder pads, and a top provider of reconditioning services (cleaning, repairing, repainting and recertifying existing equipment).

	Annual Growth	01/09	01/10	01/11*	12/11	12/12
Sales ($mil.)	7.0%	–	–	772.8	834.9	827.2
Net income ($ mil.)	–	–	–	8.1	10.0	(3.4)
Market value ($ mil.)	–	–	–	–	–	–
Employees	–	–	–	–	–	2,370

*Fiscal year change

BRIDGELINE DIGITAL INC

100 Sylvan Road, Suite G700
Woburn, MA 01801
Phone: 781 376-5555
Fax: –
Web: www.bridgeline.com

NAS: BLIN
CEO: –
CFO: –
HR: –
FYE: September 30
Type: Public

Bridgeline Digital believes the Web is the causeway to the customer. The company develops and sells Web application creation and management software. Its iAPPS product suite offers tools for content and relationship management, e-commerce, website creation, and analytics. Bridgeline also offers usability engineering, search engine optimization, and rich media development services. Bridgeline's target markets are financial services, technology, health services and life sciences, retailers, transportation and storage, foundations and associations, and the US government. Its customers have included Honeywell, John Hancock, AARP, Budget Rent A Car, and the Washington Redskins. Bridgeline operates in the US and India.

	Annual Growth	09/19	09/20	09/21	09/22	09/23
Sales ($mil.)	12.4%	10.0	10.9	13.3	16.8	15.9
Net income ($ mil.)	–	(9.5)	0.3	(6.7)	2.1	(9.4)
Market value ($ mil.)	(18.7%)	19.8	19.4	42.8	13.6	8.7
Employees	(6.5%)	72	39	60	50	55

BRIDGEPORT HOSPITAL & HEALTHCARE SERVICES INC

267 GRANT ST
BRIDGEPORT, CT 066102805
Phone: 203 384-3000
Fax: –
Web: www.bridgeporthospital.org

CEO: –
CFO: –
HR: –
FYE: September 30
Type: Private

Serving as a bridge to wellness and a port in the stormy waters of health care is the 425-bed Bridgeport Hospital. Part of the Yale New Haven Health System, the facility offers acute care and specialized services to residents of Bridgeport, Connecticut and surrounding counties. The hospital operates a cancer center, a burn treatment center, a heart center, and a rehabilitation therapy center. Its medical staff includes nearly 600 physicians representing more than 60 specialties. Founded in 1878 as Fairfield County's first hospital, Bridgeport Hospital has grown into a nearly $350 million regional health care organization.

	Annual Growth	09/07	09/08	09/09	09/10	09/13
Sales ($mil.)	(14.7%)	–	–	0.3	380.0	0.1
Net income ($ mil.)	–	–	–	0.2	13.9	(0.1)
Market value ($ mil.)	–	–	–	–	–	–
Employees	–	–	–	–	–	150

BRIDGFORD FOODS CORP.

1707 South Good-Latimer Expressway
Dallas, TX 75226
Phone: 214 428-1535
Fax: –
Web: www.bridgford.com

NMS: BRID
CEO: Michael W Bridgford
CFO: Cindy Matthews-Morale
HR: –
FYE: November 3
Type: Public

Bridgford Foods manufactures, markets, and distributes a slew of frozen, refrigerated, and snack foods. Its lineup ranges from biscuits and bread dough to deli meats, dry sausage, and beef jerky. Bridgford adds to its offerings by buying for resale some snacks and refrigerated foods made by other processors. The company primarily sells its products to food service (restaurants and institutions) and retailers (supermarkets, mass merchandise, and convenience stores) in 50 US states through distributors, brokers, and a direct store delivery network. Bridgford traces its roots back to 1932, when its founder Hugh H. Bridgford (1908-1992) opened a retail meat market in San Diego, California.

	Annual Growth	11/19*	10/20	10/21	10/22*	11/23
Sales ($mil.)	7.4%	188.8	198.0	240.4	265.9	251.6
Net income ($ mil.)	(14.4%)	6.5	7.3	(5.5)	45.1	3.5
Market value ($ mil.)	(19.7%)	228.7	165.7	106.5	112.9	95.3
Employees	4.4%	564	563	699	705	671

*Fiscal year change

BRIGGS & STRATTON CORPORATION

12301 W WIRTH ST
WAUWATOSA, WI 532222110
Phone: 414 259-5333
Fax: –
Web: www.briggsandstratton.cn

CEO: –
CFO: –
HR: –
FYE: July 02
Type: Private

Briggs & Stratton is one of the world's largest manufacturers of gasoline engines for lawn mowers. It designs, makes, markets, and services these engines primarily for lawn and garden OEMs worldwide, including Husqvarna, MTD Products, and Deere & Company. It is also a top North American manufacturer of portable generators and pressure washers and a leading maker of lawn mowers, garden tillers, and related service parts and accessories sold through retailers and independent dealers. Briggs & Stratton, which has offices and manufacturing facilities in North America, Europe, Asia, and Australia, gets 75% of its revenue from the US.

BRIGHAM YOUNG UNIVERSITY

A-41 ASB
PROVO, UT 846029901
Phone: 801 422-1211
Fax: –
Web: music.byu.edu

CEO: –
CFO: –
HR: Cali O'Connell
FYE: December 31
Type: Private

Brigham Young University (BYU) is founded, supported, and guided by The Church of Jesus Christ of Latter-Day Saints (also known as the Mormon Church). Through around 15 colleges, the Mormon-owned university offers bachelor's degrees in some 195 undergraduate majors, approximately 110 undergraduate minors, master's in almost 100, and doctorates of some 30. BYU's enrollment includes over 34,735 students representing all 50 states in more than 100 countries. With more than 1,620 international students, most of the university's students are from the US.

BRIGHTCOVE INC   NMS: BCOV

281 Summer Street
Boston, MA 02210
Phone: 888 882-1880
Fax: –
Web: www.brightcove.com

CEO: Marc Debevoise
CFO: Robert Noreck
HR: –
FYE: December 31
Type: Public

Brightcove is a leading global provider of cloud-based services for video. The company sells five core video products, which include Brightcove Video Cloud and Brightcove Live, which helps its customers use video to further their businesses in meaningful ways. It has some 2,845 customers, including media companies, broadcasters, publishers, sports and entertainment companies, fashion and hospitality brands, faith-based institutions, retail and e-commerce platforms, and hi-tech organizations, as well as governments, educational institutions and non-profit organizations. Brightcove delivers an average of about 3.77 billion streams a month. The majority of the company's sales were generated in North America.

	Annual Growth	12/19	12/20	12/21	12/22	12/23
Sales ($mil.)	2.2%	184.5	197.4	211.1	211.0	201.2
Net income ($ mil.)	–	(21.9)	(5.8)	5.4	(9.0)	(22.9)
Market value ($ mil.)	(26.1%)	379.7	804.1	446.6	228.5	113.2
Employees	2.4%	610	623	687	725	671

BRIGHTHOUSE FINANCIAL INC   NMS: BHF

11225 North Community House Road
Charlotte, NC 28277
Phone: 980 365-7100
Fax: –
Web: www.brighthousefinancial.com

CEO: Eric T Steigerwalt
CFO: Edward A Spehar
HR: –
FYE: December 31
Type: Public

Brighthouse Financial, Inc. (Brighthouse Financial) is a provider of annuity products and life insurance in the US with over 2.5 million annuity contracts and insurance policies in force. The company also offers a range of life insurance products which includes term life, universal life, whole life and variable life products. The company offers its products and services through multiple independent distribution channels and marketing arrangements with an extensive network of distribution partners. Brighthouse Financial's run-off business includes operations related to products that are not actively sold and separately managed. Brighthouse Financial traces its roots back to 1863 as Travelers Insurance Company, and was founded in Hartford, Connecticut.

	Annual Growth	12/19	12/20	12/21	12/22	12/23
Assets ($mil.)	1.0%	227,259	247,869	259,840	225,580	236,340
Net income ($ mil.)	–	(740.0)	(1,061.0)	(108.0)	5.0	(1,112.0)
Market value ($ mil.)	7.8%	2,491.2	2,299.1	3,289.5	3,255.8	3,360.6
Employees	3.1%	1,330	1,400	1,500	1,500	1,500

BRIGHTLAND HOMES, LTD.

15725 DALLAS PKWY STE 300
ADDISON, TX 750013850
Phone: 972 383-4300
Fax: –
Web: www.brightlandhomes.com

CEO: –
CFO: –
HR: –
FYE: December 31
Type: Private

They say everything is bigger in Texas, and for Gehan Homes that hopefully applies to the number of homes sold. Gehan Homes builds single-family houses in about 60 communities in and around Austin, Dallas, Fort Worth, Houston, and San Antonio. Its houses range in price from the low $100,000s to the low $300,000s. Gehan Homes owns the land it builds on and provides mortgage brokerage through majority-owned Suburban Mortgage. Through cutting costs and slowing down production, the homebuilder is working to stay afloat in a market that has caused several competitors to file for bankruptcy or shut down operations. John Gehan founded the family-owned company in the 1960s.

	Annual Growth	11/99	11/00	11/01	11/02*	12/07
Sales ($mil.)	7.4%	–	–	–	150.5	214.6
Net income ($ mil.)	(21.8%)	–	–	–	13.8	4.0
Market value ($ mil.)	–	–	–	–	–	–
Employees	–	–	–	–	–	577

*Fiscal year change

BRIGHTVIEW HOLDINGS INC   NYS: BV

980 Jolly Road
Blue Bell, PA 19422
Phone: 844 235-7778
Fax: –
Web: www.brightview.com

CEO: Dale A Asplund
CFO: Brett Urban
HR: –
FYE: September 30
Type: Public

BrightView Holdings, Inc. provides commercial landscaping services in the US, with revenues approximately 7 times those of its next largest commercial landscaping competitor. It provides commercial landscaping services, ranging from landscape maintenance and enhancements to tree care and landscape development. It operates through a differentiated and integrated national service model which systematically delivers services at the local level by combining its network of over 290 branches with a qualified service partner network. Its branch delivery model underpins its position as a single-source end-to-end landscaping solution provider to a diverse customer base.

	Annual Growth	09/19	09/20	09/21	09/22	09/23
Sales ($mil.)	4.0%	2,404.6	2,346.0	2,553.6	2,774.6	2,816.0
Net income ($ mil.)	–	44.4	(41.6)	46.3	14.0	(7.7)
Market value ($ mil.)	(18.0%)	1,605.2	1,067.0	1,381.5	743.2	725.4
Employees	0.1%	21,500	19,700	20,500	21,000	21,600

BRINKER INTERNATIONAL, INC.   NYS: EAT

3000 Olympus Blvd.
Dallas, TX 75019
Phone: 972 980-9917
Fax: –
Web: www.brinker.com

CEO: Kevin D Hochman
CFO: Joseph G Taylor
HR: Brooke Burgiel
FYE: June 28
Type: Public

Brinker International, Inc. owns, develops, operates, and franchises the Chili's Grill & Bar and Maggiano's Little Italy restaurant brands, as well as certain virtual brands including It's Just Wings and Maggiano's Italian Classics. Chili's is a recognized leader in the casual dining industry and the flagship brand of the company. It enjoys a global presence with restaurants in the Us, around 30 countries and two US territories. Maggiano's is a full-service, national, polished casual restaurant brand offering Italian-American cuisine. It's Just Wings is a no-frills offering that consists of chicken wings available in a variety of different sauces and rubs, curly fries, ranch dressing and hand pies for a value price. Maggiano's Italian Classics offers a select group of items inspired by the menu at Maggiano's Little Italy, including several appetizers, salads, pastas, entrées and hand pies.

	Annual Growth	06/19	06/20	06/21	06/22	06/23
Sales ($mil.)	6.5%	3,217.9	3,078.5	3,337.8	3,804.1	4,133.2
Net income ($ mil.)	(9.8%)	154.9	24.4	131.6	117.6	102.6
Market value ($ mil.)	(1.4%)	1,708.6	1,049.4	2,758.5	999.5	1,614.5
Employees	3.5%	56,147	62,200	59,491	62,025	64,323

BRINKS CO (THE)   NYS: BCO

1801 Bayberry Court
Richmond, VA 23226-8100
Phone: 804 289-9600
Fax: –
Web: www.brinks.com

CEO: Mark Eubanks
CFO: Kurt B McMaken
HR: –
FYE: December 31
Type: Public

The Brink's Company is a leading global provider of cash and valuables management, digital retail solutions, and ATM managed services. Its customers include financial institutions, retailers, government agencies, mints, jewelers, and other commercial operations around the world and serves customers in more than 100 countries. It also have controlling ownership interests in companies in roughly 55 countries and agency relationships with companies in additional countries. Its operations include approximately 1,300 facilities and about 16,300 vehicles. The company's largest geographic market is the US, which generates about 30% of the company's total revenue.

	Annual Growth	12/19	12/20	12/21	12/22	12/23
Sales ($mil.)	7.3%	3,683.2	3,690.9	4,200.2	4,535.5	4,874.6
Net income ($ mil.)	31.9%	29.0	16.0	105.2	170.6	87.7
Market value ($ mil.)	(0.8%)	4,035.3	3,204.0	2,917.9	2,390.1	3,913.8
Employees	1.4%	64,600	76,500	74,500	72,200	68,200

BRISTOL HOSPITAL INCORPORATED

41 BREWSTER RD
BRISTOL, CT 060105141
Phone: 860 585-3000
Fax: –
Web: www.bristolhealth.org

CEO: –
CFO: –
HR: Stacy Roberge
FYE: September 30
Type: Private

Bristol Hospital bristles with health care services for central Connecticut residents. The health care facility has more than 130 beds and offers a range of services including counseling, diagnostic imaging, inpatient and outpatient care, surgery, home health, and physical therapy. Specialty services include oncology, obstetrics, neurology, pediatrics, and orthopedic care. Its wellness center is dedicated to cardiac and pulmonary rehabilitation, diabetes care, health education, health screenings, nutrition, fitness, and pain management. Bristol Hospital also operates Ingraham Manor, a skilled nursing residence for seniors.

	Annual Growth	09/17	09/18	09/19	09/20	09/21
Sales ($mil.)	1.7%	–	143.5	150.4	151.7	151.0
Net income ($ mil.)	–	–	8.7	(18.2)	2.3	(1.5)
Market value ($ mil.)	–	–	–	–	–	–
Employees	–	–	–	–	–	1,600

BRISTOL MYERS SQUIBB CO.   NYS: BMY

Route 206 & Province Line Road
Princeton, NJ 08543
Phone: 609 252-4621
Fax: 212 546-4020
Web: www.bms.com

CEO: Giovanni Caforio
CFO: David V Elkins V
HR: –
FYE: December 31
Type: Public

Bristol-Myers Squibb (BMS) is one of the leading biopharmaceutical company. The company offers drugs such as Eliquis for stroke prevention, cancer treatment Opdivo, and rheumatoid arthritis treatment Orencia. BMS has significant biologics, cell therapy and pharmaceutical manufacturing facilities are located in the US, Puerto Rico, Ireland, and Switzerland. Most of its revenues come from products in the following therapeutic classes: hematology, oncology, cardiovascular and immunology. The US accounts for about 70% of revenue.

	Annual Growth	12/19	12/20	12/21	12/22	12/23
Sales ($mil.)	14.5%	26,145	42,518	46,385	46,159	45,006
Net income ($ mil.)	23.6%	3,439.0	(9,015.0)	6,994.0	6,327.0	8,025.0
Market value ($ mil.)	(5.4%)	128,252	123,936	124,575	143,756	102,517
Employees	3.3%	30,000	30,250	32,200	34,300	34,100

BRISTOW GROUP INC (DE)   NYS: VTOL

3151 Briarpark Drive, Suite 700
Houston, TX 77042
Phone: 713 267-7600
Fax: –
Web: www.bristowgroup.com

CEO: Christopher S Bradshaw
CFO: Jennifer Whalen
HR: –
FYE: December 31
Type: Public

Bristow Group (formerly known as Era Group) is a global provider of vertical flight solutions. The company primarily provides aviation services to a broad base of major integrated, national and independent energy companies. It also provides commercial search and rescue services in multiple countries and public sector SAR services in the United Kingdom on behalf of the Maritime & Coastguard Agency. Additionally, it offers fixed wing transportation and other aviation related solutions. Its oil and gas customers charter its helicopters primarily to transport personnel to, from and between onshore bases and offshore production platforms, drilling rigs and other installations.

	Annual Growth	03/20	03/21	03/22*	12/22	12/23
Sales ($mil.)	27.8%	485.8	1,178.1	1,185.2	922.6	1,297.4
Net income ($ mil.)	–	139.2	(56.1)	(15.8)	13.5	(6.8)
Market value ($ mil.)	51.8%	150.9	732.7	1,049.7	768.1	800.3
Employees	–	–	3,167	2,916	3,138	3,298

*Fiscal year change

BRIXMOR PROPERTY GROUP INC   NYS: BRX

450 Lexington Avenue
New York, NY 10017
Phone: 212 869-3000
Fax: –
Web: www.brixmor.com

CEO: James M Taylor Jr
CFO: Angela Aman
HR: Donna Colliluori
FYE: December 31
Type: Public

Brixmor Property Group hopes you swing by the grocery store more than once a week. The internally-managed real estate investment trust (REIT) owns a portfolio of about 520 strip mall-style shopping centers across 38 states. Its properties are situated in high-traffic commercial areas anchored by grocery store chains such as Ahold, Kroger, Publix, Safeway, and Wal-Mart. Besides the main grocery store tenant, its shopping centers offer a mix of smaller retailers such as Dollar Tree or other big box stores such as Best Buy, Kmart, and TJX Cos. Altogether Brixmor Property Group owns some 87 million sq. ft. of leasable space; each shopping center averages about 166,100 sq. ft. The trust went public in 2013.

	Annual Growth	12/19	12/20	12/21	12/22	12/23
Sales ($mil.)	1.6%	1,168.3	1,053.3	1,152.3	1,218.1	1,245.0
Net income ($ mil.)	2.7%	274.8	121.2	270.2	354.2	305.1
Market value ($ mil.)	1.9%	6,495.9	4,974.9	7,638.2	6,814.5	6,994.9
Employees	1.8%	477	480	501	502	513

BROADCOM INC (DE)   NMS: AVGO

3421 Hillview Avenue
Palo Alto, CA 94304
Phone: 650 427-6000
Fax: –
Web: www.broadcom.com

CEO: –
CFO: –
HR: –
FYE: October 29
Type: Public

Broadcom Limited's products cover a broad range of semiconductors. The products include chips for wireless and wired communications as well as optoelectronics, radio-frequency and microwave components, power amplifiers, and application-specific integrated circuits (custom chips). The company's thousands of products are used in a wide range of applications, including mobile phones, data networking and telecommunications equipment, consumer appliances, displays, printers, servers and storage networking gear, and factory automation. Broadcom Limited was created with Avago Technologies acquired Broadcom Inc. The company took the Broadcom Limited name when the deal closed in early 2016.

	Annual Growth	11/19	11/20*	10/21	10/22	10/23
Sales ($mil.)	12.2%	22,597	23,888	27,450	33,203	35,819
Net income ($ mil.)	50.8%	2,724.0	2,960.0	6,736.0	11,495	14,082
Market value ($ mil.)	29.7%	122,788	144,747	220,111	195,781	347,081
Employees	1.3%	19,000	21,000	20,000	20,000	20,000

*Fiscal year change

BROADRIDGE FINANCIAL SOLUTIONS INC   NYS: BR

5 Dakota Drive
Lake Success, NY 11042
Phone: 516 472-5400
Fax: –
Web: www.broadridge.com

CEO: Timothy C Gokey
CFO: Edmund L Reese
HR: –
FYE: June 30
Type: Public

Broadridge Financial Solutions is a global financial technology leader providing investor communications and technology-driven solutions to banks, broker-dealers, asset and wealth managers, public companies, investors and mutual funds. Through its proprietary ProxyEdge system, Broadridge processes and distributes proxy materials, voting instructions for institutional investors, processing over 7 billion investor and customer communications per year. It also offers related services, such as marketing and customer communications and virtual shareholder meetings. The US accounts for about 85% of total revenue.

	Annual Growth	06/19	06/20	06/21	06/22	06/23
Sales ($mil.)	8.6%	4,362.2	4,529.0	4,993.7	5,709.1	6,060.9
Net income ($ mil.)	6.9%	482.1	462.5	547.5	539.1	630.6
Market value ($ mil.)	6.7%	15,079	14,903	19,077	16,835	19,561
Employees	7.5%	11,000	12,000	13,704	14,300	14,700

BROADSOFT, INC.

9737 WASHINGTONIAN BLVD STE 350
GAITHERSBURG, MD 208787337
Phone: 301 977-9440
Fax: –
Web: –

CEO: Michael Tessler
CFO: –
HR: –
FYE: December 31
Type: Private

BroadSoft hopes to remove some of the hard work from the process of supplying voice and data services. The company develops software that more than 500 fixed-line, mobile, and cable telecommunications service providers use to deliver voice and data services. Its BroadWorks software enables carriers to offer their subscribers unified communications services such as video calling, hosted multimedia communications, business telephone systems, and collaboration tools. A hosted program is sold under the BroadCloud platform. Customers include Alteva, Axiom, Broadconnect Telecom, and Birch Telecom. In 2017 BroadSoft agreed to be bought by Cisco Systems for $1.9 billion.

BROADVIEW INSTITUTE, INC.

8147 GLOBE DR
WOODBURY, MN 551253742
Phone: 651 332-8000
Fax: –
Web: www.broadviewinstitute.com

CEO: Jeffrey D Myhre
CFO: Kenneth J McCarthy
HR: –
FYE: March 31
Type: Private

Broadview Institute isn't narrow-minded about education. The company owns and operates C Square Educational Enterprises, dba Utah Career College or UCC, which offers career vocational training programs in the Salt Lake City area to about 1,000 students. Its degree programs span four growing industries: business and accounting, health sciences (including veterinary studies), information technology, and legal science. Classes are offered at three campuses in Utah and through online and accelerated programs. Chairman Terry Myhre owns about 65% of Broadview. Additionally, Myhre has controlling interest in two other post-secondary career colleges, Globe University and Minnesota School of Business.

BROADWAY BANCSHARES, INC. (TX)   NBB: BRDW

1177 N.E. Loop 410, P.O. Box 17001
San Antonio, TX 78217
Phone: 210 283-6500
Fax: 210 283-6676
Web: www.broadwaybank.com

CEO: –
CFO: –
HR: –
FYE: December 31
Type: Public

Broadway Bancshares is the holding company for Broadway National Bank (dba Broadway Bank) and its Eisenhower Bank division. The former is a community-oriented financial institution with about 30 branches in San Antonio and Central Texas; the latter has seven offices on military bases throughout the Lone Star State and serves military personnel worldwide. The banks offer traditional deposit products such as checking and savings accounts, IRAs, and CDs. Both originate various personal, consumer, construction, and commercial loans, as well as commercial and residential mortgages. The banks also provide private banking, trust, investment management, and wealth advisory services.

	Annual Growth	12/98	12/99	12/00	12/01	12/02
Assets ($mil.)	6.8%	1,079.0	1,113.9	1,165.0	1,276.8	1,402.9
Net income ($ mil.)	15.4%	14.9	17.4	17.7	20.5	26.3
Market value ($ mil.)	–	–	–	–	–	–
Employees	–	–	–	–	–	–

BROADWAY FINANCIAL CORP. (DE)

4601 Wilshire Boulevard, Suite 150
Los Angeles, CA 90010
Phone: 323 634-1700
Fax: –
Web: www.broadwayfederalbank.com

CEO: –
CFO: –
HR: –
FYE: December 31
Type: Public

This company won't quit 'til it's a star! Broadway Financial is the holding company for Broadway Federal Bank, a savings and loan that serves the low- and moderate-income minority neighborhoods of central and south central Los Angeles and nearby Inglewood. Through about a half-dozen branches and loan offices, the bank primarily originates multi-family (about 40% of its loan portfolio) and commercial real estate loans (another 40%). These loans are secured primarily by multi-family dwellings and properties used for business and religious purposes. Deposit products include CDs and savings, checking, money market, and NOW accounts.

	Annual Growth	12/18	12/19	12/20	12/21	12/22
Assets ($mil.)	30.4%	409.4	440.4	483.4	1,093.5	1,184.3
Net income ($ mil.)	62.2%	0.8	(0.2)	(0.6)	(4.1)	5.6
Market value ($ mil.)	(1.0%)	9.6	14.1	17.0	21.2	9.3
Employees	6.6%	65	64	64	80	84

BROADWIND INC

3240 S. Central Avenue
Cicero, IL 60804
Phone: 708 780-4800
Fax: –
Web: www.bwen.com

NAS: BWEN
CEO: Eric B Blashford
CFO: Jason L Bonfigt
HR: –
FYE: December 31
Type: Public

If you're a wind energy producer, Broadwind Energy wants to be the wind beneath your wings. The company serves the wind power generation industry with wind turbine towers and gear systems along with engineering, repair, and logistics services. Its gear systems are also used by other energy and mining companies. Broadwind's logistics segment specializes in transporting the oversize and overweight components used in constructing wind power generation facilities. The company's locations are spread across North America in areas where wind energy production is heavy.

	Annual Growth	12/19	12/20	12/21	12/22	12/23
Sales ($mil.)	3.4%	178.2	198.5	145.6	176.8	203.5
Net income ($ mil.)	–	(4.5)	(1.5)	2.8	(9.7)	7.6
Market value ($ mil.)	13.7%	35.8	171.0	40.5	38.6	59.7
Employees	(3.9%)	521	512	493	499	444

BROCADE COMMUNICATIONS SYSTEMS LLC

1320 RIDDER PARK DR
SAN JOSE, CA 951312313
Phone: 408 333-8000
Fax: –
Web: www.broadcom.com

CEO: –
CFO: –
HR: –
FYE: October 29
Type: Private

Brocade Communications Systems maintains silky smooth computer network operations. A leading supplier of data center networking products, Brocade makes Fibre Channel switches and related software for connecting corporate storage systems and servers. Its products are used in storage area networks (SANs), which pool storage resources across enterprises for easier management and more efficient asset use. Brocade's products support internet connectivity and enterprise mobility, as well as key technologies such as software defined networking (SDN), network function virtualization (NFV), and cloud computing. It generates about half of its sales in the US. Brocade was bought by Broadcom for about $5.5 billion in 2017.

BROCKTON HOSPITAL, INC.

680 CENTRE ST
BROCKTON, MA 023023395
Phone: 508 941-7000
Fax: –
Web: www.signature-healthcare.org

CEO: Kim Hollon
CFO: –
HR: –
FYE: September 30
Type: Private

Signature Healthcare Brockton Hospital is a not-for-profit, acute medical facility that serves southeastern Massachusetts. The hospital has 245 beds, including about 30 beds in its skilled nursing unit. Its emergency department sees more than 62,000 patients per year. Specialized services include radiation oncology, cardiac care, pediatrics, orthopedics and joint replacement, and inpatient and outpatient psychiatry. It is a community-based teaching hospital and part of the Signature Healthcare network. Brockton Hospital also formed a clinical affiliation with Beth Israel Deaconess Medical Center in 2013.

BRODER BROS., CO.

6 INTERPLEX DR
FEASTERVILLE TREVOSE, PA 190536964
Phone: 800 523-4585
Fax: –
Web: www.alphabroder.com

CEO: Norman Hullinger
CFO: –
HR: Grace O'Farril
FYE: December 26
Type: Private

Selling clothes had been in the genes of sportswear distributor Broder Bros. for years. Begun as a haberdashery in 1919, the company evolved from making hats and gloves into a leading distributor of imprintable sportswear, distributing 40,000-plus SKUs across more than 40 retail brands, including adidas Golf, Champion, Russell Athletic, alternative, Dickies, and private labels. It operates under the Broder, Alpha, and NES divisions. Private labels include Devon & Jones, Chestnut Hill, and Harriton. Customers, mostly small US retailers, order merchandise through seasonal catalogs or online. Private investment firm Bain Capital has held a majority interest in the company since 2000, when the Broder family sold the company.

	Annual Growth	12/05	12/06	12/07	12/08	12/09
Sales ($mil.)	(12.9%)	–	–	929.1	926.1	705.2
Net income ($ mil.)	–	–	–	(124.1)	(68.9)	(13.2)
Market value ($ mil.)	–	–	–	–	–	–
Employees	–	–	–	–	–	3,101

BROMBERG & COMPANY, INC.

123 20TH ST N
BIRMINGHAM, AL 352033694
Phone: 205 969-1776
Fax: –
Web: www.brombergs.com

CEO: Frank H Bromberg Jr
CFO: –
HR: –
FYE: June 30
Type: Private

Bromberg and Co. is a jeweler and high-end retailer that sells china, crystal, jewelry, and sterling flatware through four Bromberg's stores in Alabama. Its fine offerings come from such makers as David Yurman, Mikimoto, Rolex, and Wedgwood. The company also operates an online bridal registry. In 2004 brothers Billy and John Bromberg, formerly part of the company's management, sold their stake in Bromberg and Co. to other family members (including chairman Frank Bromberg Jr.) and left to form their own jewelry store. Bromberg and Co. was originally founded by the Bromberg family in 1836.

BRONSON BATTLE CREEK HOSPITAL

300 NORTH AVE
BATTLE CREEK, MI 490173396
Phone: 269 966-8000
Fax: –
Web: –

CEO: –
CFO: –
HR: –
FYE: December 31
Type: Private

Bronson Battle Creek Hospital fights against injury and disease in residents of south central Michigan. The hospital is located on two campuses with a total of some 220 beds; it also operates a mental health facility (Fieldstone Center), a variety of outpatient clinics, and a home health care and hospice network (Lifespan). The health care provider's hospital and outpatient facilities house general and specialty care clinics including a wound healing center, a diagnostic imaging center, a sleep center, and cardiac and cancer care centers. Its Employer Health Services program features two occupational health and therapy clinics. Bronson Battle Creek is part of the Bronson Health Care Group.

	Annual Growth	12/16	12/17	12/18	12/21	12/22
Sales ($mil.)	5.4%	–	244.9	227.0	248.0	319.1
Net income ($ mil.)	–	–	(16.4)	(26.4)	(6.5)	(21.7)
Market value ($ mil.)	–	–	–	–	–	–
Employees	–	–	–	–	–	1,882

BRONSON HEALTH CARE GROUP, INC.

301 JOHN ST
KALAMAZOO, MI 490075295
Phone: 269 341-6000
Fax: –
Web: www.mygnp.com

CEO: –
CFO: Kenneth L Taft
HR: Leah Warwick
FYE: December 31
Type: Private

Bronson Health Care Group has a strong presence as a provider of a wide range of medical services in southern Michigan and northern Indiana. The company operates several regional hospitals and health clinics, including Bronson Methodist Hospital (some 400 beds), Bronson Battle Creek (220 beds), and Bronson Lakeview Hospital (35 beds). The not-for-profit health care system's facilities provide general and specialty services including trauma, stroke, burn, cancer, and cardiac care, as well as emergency medicine, pediatrics, obstetrics, rehabilitation, and home health care.

	Annual Growth	12/08	12/09	12/16	12/17	12/19
Sales ($mil.)	11.0%	–	119.6	1,136.1	1,233.9	338.8
Net income ($ mil.)	–	–	16.5	28.7	63.5	(39.1)
Market value ($ mil.)	–	–	–	–	–	–
Employees	–	–	–	–	–	4,180

BRONSON METHODIST HOSPITAL INC

601 JOHN ST STE E-012
KALAMAZOO, MI 490075346
Phone: 269 341-7654
Fax: –
Web: –

CEO: –
CFO: Mary Meitz
HR: Krista Selent
FYE: December 31
Type: Private

From your leg bone to your knee bone; your neck bone to your head bone, Bronson Methodist Hospital has the specialists to cure what ails you. The 435-bed hospital is the flagship facility of the Bronson Healthcare Group, a not-for-profit health care system. Bronson Methodist provides care in just about every specialty including orthopedics, surgery, and oncology. The hospital also contains specialist units for critical care (level I trauma center), neurology (primary stroke center), cardiology (Chest pain emergency center), women's health (BirthPlace), and pediatrics (children's hospital).

	Annual Growth	12/17	12/18	12/19	12/21	12/22
Sales ($mil.)	9.0%	–	864.3	952.8	1,050.6	1,219.9
Net income ($ mil.)	21.9%	–	26.9	2.7	186.1	59.3
Market value ($ mil.)	–	–	–	–	–	–
Employees	–	–	–	–	–	2,861

BRONXCARE HEALTH SYSTEM

1276 FULTON AVE
BRONX, NY 104563467
Phone: 718 590-1800
Fax: –
Web: www.bronxcare.org

CEO: Miguel Fuentes
CFO: –
HR: –
FYE: December 31
Type: Private

Bronx-Lebanon Hospital Center cares for patients in the central and south Bronx, no doubt while rooting for the Yankees a few blocks away. The health care provider maintains more than 970 beds across its two campuses, as well as psychiatric and nursing home facilities. Hospital specialty units include chest pain, orthopedic, cancer, and women's health centers. Bronx-Lebanon also manages a network of about 70 owned and affiliated medical practices (under the BronxCare brand). This network includes primary care doctors and specialty clinics, as well as rehabilitation facilities. The hospital is also a primary teaching hospital for the Albert Einstein College of Medicine.

	Annual Growth	12/15	12/16	12/17	12/21	12/22
Sales ($mil.)	6.8%	–	641.1	750.8	760.7	951.0
Net income ($ mil.)	49.9%	–	6.5	12.1	61.6	73.8
Market value ($ mil.)	–	–	–	–	–	–
Employees	–	–	–	–	–	4,000

BROOKDALE SENIOR LIVING INC

111 Westwood Place, Suite 400
Brentwood, TN 37027
Phone: 615 221-2250
Fax: –
Web: www.brookdale.com

NYS: BKD
CEO: Lucinda M Baier
CFO: Steven E Swain
HR: Josephine Munoz
FYE: December 31
Type: Public

Brookdale Senior Living operates assisted and independent living centers and retirement communities for middle- and upper-income elderly clients. The US largest senior living provider, Brookdale owns, leases, or manages about 675 communities offering studio, one-bedroom, and two-bedroom units in some 40 states. It has the capacity to serve about 60,000 residents. Services for its residents include health assessments, meals, 24-hour emergency response, personal care, housekeeping, concierge services, transportation, and recreational activities. Brookdale's continuing care retirement centers include skilled nursing units and operates memory care units for Alzheimer's and dementia patients.

	Annual Growth	12/19	12/20	12/21	12/22	12/23
Sales ($mil.)	(7.1%)	4,057.1	3,540.2	2,758.3	2,825.4	3,015.8
Net income ($ mil.)	–	(267.9)	82.0	(99.3)	(238.4)	(189.0)
Market value ($ mil.)	(5.4%)	1,368.6	834.0	971.4	513.9	1,095.6
Employees	(11.4%)	58,400	45,000	33,000	36,000	36,000

BROOKFIELD OAKTREE HOLDINGS LLC

333 South Grand Avenue, 28th Floor
Los Angeles, CA 90071
Phone: 213 830-6300
Fax: –
Web: www.oaktreecapital.com

NYS: OAK PRB
CEO: Jay S Wintrob
CFO: Daniel D Levin
HR: Madeline Horton
FYE: December 31
Type: Public

Oaktree is a leader among global investment managers specializing in alternative investments. Oaktree emphasizes an opportunistic, value-oriented and risk-controlled approach to investments in credit, private equity, real assets and listed equities. Founded in 1995, Oaktree Capital boasts about $172.0 billion in assets under management on behalf of institutional investors such as pension plans, insurance companies, endowments, foundations and sovereign wealth funds. The company operates through its single reporting segment of investment management and has offices in the US, Asia, and Europe. Brookfield Asset Management holds 64% of shares in Oaktree Business.

	Annual Growth	12/18	12/19	12/20	12/21	12/22
Sales ($mil.)	(22.8%)	1,386.1	929.0	429.1	1,454.4	492.6
Net income ($ mil.)	(2.3%)	223.4	154.8	165.7	631.7	203.6
Market value ($ mil.)	(1.7%)	3,670.5	4,308.9	4,408.1	4,270.5	3,422.5
Employees	3.9%	978	988	1,018	1,056	1,140

BROOKLINE BANCORP INC (DE)

131 Clarendon Street
Boston, MA 02116
Phone: 617 425-4600
Fax: –
Web: www.brooklinebancorp.com

NMS: BRKL
CEO: Paul A Perrault
CFO: –
HR: –
FYE: December 31
Type: Public

Boston-based Brookline Bancorp is the holding company for Brookline Bank, Bank Rhode Island (BankRI), and its subsidiaries, Brookline Securities Corp. and Clarendon Private, LLC (Clarendon Private), which together operate some full-service banking offices and two lending offices in the greater Boston metropolitan area. Commercial and multifamily mortgages backed by real estate such as apartments, condominiums, and office buildings account for the largest portion of the company's loan portfolio, followed by equipment financing, commercial and residential mortgage. Established in 1997 as Brookline Savings Bank, the bank went public five years later and changed its name to Brookline Bank in 2003.

	Annual Growth	12/19	12/20	12/21	12/22	12/23
Assets ($mil.)	9.7%	7,856.9	8,942.4	8,602.6	9,185.8	11,382
Net income ($ mil.)	(3.8%)	87.7	47.6	115.4	109.7	75.0
Market value ($ mil.)	(9.8%)	1,475.5	1,079.3	1,451.3	1,268.5	978.0
Employees	5.8%	811	813	826	852	1,018

BROOKLYN ACADEMY OF MUSIC INC

30 LAFAYETTE AVE
BROOKLYN, NY 112171430
Phone: 718 636-4100
Fax: –
Web: www.bam.org

CEO: –
CFO: –
HR: –
FYE: June 30
Type: Private

The Brooklyn Academy of Music (better known as BAM) is famous for its progressive nature. The urban arts center is America's oldest operating performing arts center and brings international performing arts, media, and film to Brooklyn, New York. In addition, the academy annually hosts the Next Wave Festival (featuring avant-garde music, dance, theater, and opera) and houses a four-screen cineplex to draw young audiences. BAM's resident orchestra produces an annual season of concerts. BAM was founded in Brooklyn Heights in 1861.

BROOKLYN HOSPITAL CENTER

121 DEKALB AVE
BROOKLYN, NY 112015493
Phone: 718 250-8000
Fax: –
Web: www.tbh.org

CEO: Carlos P Naudon
CFO: –
HR: –
FYE: December 31
Type: Private

The Brooklyn Hospital Center has been taking care of ailing Kings County residents since before Brooklyn was a borough. Established in 1845 (before Brooklyn became part of New York City), the hospital houses some 460 beds and is a member of the NewYork-Presbyterian Healthcare System. It provides general medical and surgical care, as well as a wide variety of specialty medical services including dialysis, pediatrics, obstetrics, and cardiovascular care. The Brooklyn Hospital Center is affiliated with Weill Medical College of Cornell University. The hospital also operates a network of outpatient clinics providing primary and specialty care throughout the borough.

	Annual Growth	12/15	12/16	12/17	12/19	12/21
Sales ($mil.)	0.1%	–	349.6	347.5	404.6	352.0
Net income ($ mil.)	–	–	4.0	(10.0)	(24.5)	(22.7)
Market value ($ mil.)	–	–	–	–	–	–
Employees	–	–	–	–	–	3,300

BROOKLYN INSTITUTE OF ARTS AND SCIENCES

200 EASTERN PKWY
BROOKLYN, NY 112386052
Phone: 718 638-5000
Fax: –
Web: www.brooklynmuseum.org

CEO: Robert S Rubin
CFO: –
HR: Nancy Currey
FYE: June 30
Type: Private

Brooklyn Museum is the second-largest art museum in New York City (after the Metropolitan Museum of Art) and one of the oldest and largest in the US. Its permanent collection includes more than a million works of art and artifacts from all over the world. Brooklyn Museum is making a push to attract more visits from Brooklynites, with exhibitions and events geared toward local families. The museum has been abandoning its traditional structure of organizing curators by specialties (such as African, Asian, and Egyptian art) in favor of two main functional groups: collections and exhibitions. The Museum is part of a complex of parks and gardens that also includes Prospect Park and the Brooklyn Botanic Garden.

BROOKLYN NAVY YARD DEVELOPMENT CORPORATION

141 FLUSHING AVE BLDG 77
BROOKLYN, NY 112051338
Phone: 718 237-6740
Fax: –
Web: www.brooklynnavyyard.org

CEO: David Ehrenberg
CFO: Dan Conlon
HR: –
FYE: December 31
Type: Private

After the federal government closed the military facilities at Brooklyn Navy Yard in 1966, the property on the East River was taken over and converted into commercial real estate by The City of New York. Brooklyn Navy Yard Development Corporation is in charge of the management and development of the old Navy Yard, which contains about 4 million sq. ft. of leasable office and industrial space. Located near the Brooklyn Bridge, the Navy Yard is home to about 250 tenants, including small businesses, high-tech startups, and film and television studios. Since 2006, the company has been managing a Mayor Bloomberg-sanctioned expansion of the yard, including some 1.7 million sq. ft. of new industrial space.

	Annual Growth	06/13	06/14	06/15	06/16*	12/19
Assets ($mil.)	(13.8%)	–	422.7	453.7	553.7	200.9
Net income ($ mil.)	15.8%	–	9.6	12.3	58.6	20.0
Market value ($ mil.)	–	–	–	–	–	–
Employees	–	–	–	–	–	165

*Fiscal year change

BROOKLYN NETS, LLC

168 39TH ST UNIT 7
BROOKLYN, NY 112322714
Phone: 718 933-3000
Fax: –
Web: www.nba.com

CEO: –
CFO: –
HR: –
FYE: June 30
Type: Private

National Basketball Association professional basketball team the Brooklyn Nets aren't really new kids on the NBA block. The team was previously known as the New Jersey Nets, a storied franchise with a rich history. Russian billionaire Mikhail Prokhorov purchased majority control of the New Jersey Nets from New York real estate developer Bruce Ratner back in 2010. Following the 2011-12 season, the team moved to New York City borough Brooklyn and changed its name to the Brooklyn Nets. The team's ownership group includes media mogul Jay-Z, who helped design the Brooklyn Nets logo and merchandise.

BROOKMOUNT EXPLORATIONS INC

NBB: BMXI

1 East Liberty, Suite 600
Reno, NV 89501
Phone: 775 525-6012
Fax: –
Web: www.brookmountcorp.com

CEO: –
CFO: –
HR: –
FYE: November 30
Type: Public

Brookmount Explorations hopes it has the Midas touch. Formed in 1999, the exploration-stage mining company is engaged in the exploration of precious metal resource properties located Peru and Canada. Its primary project is the Mercedes 100 gold/silver/lead/zinc property in Peru. The company is also on the lookout for potential acquisitions in Canada and elsewhere in South America. President Peter Flueck controls approximately 40% of Brookmount Explorations, having joined the company when he sold his ownership interests in the Mercedes property to Brookmount in 2005.

	Annual Growth	11/17	11/18	11/19	11/20	11/21
Sales ($mil.)	–	–	6.0	7.0	11.0	14.1
Net income ($ mil.)	–	(0.1)	2.0	2.8	5.7	6.7
Market value ($ mil.)	134.7%	0.2	0.2	0.1	13.6	6.2
Employees	–	–	–	–	–	–

BROOKS TROPICALS HOLDING, INC.

18400 SW 256TH ST
HOMESTEAD, FL 330311892
Phone: 305 247-3544
Fax: –
Web: www.brookstropicals.com

CEO: Greg Smith
CFO: Janice Kolar
HR: –
FYE: December 31
Type: Private

Brooks Tropicals offers exotic tastes with every bite. The company is a producer, importer, and supplier of tropical fruits and vegetables. Brooks product line consists of about 25 fruits and vegetables -- some familiar, some virtually unknown to American palates. They include avocados, boniato, calabaza, chayote, coconut, ginger, key lime, kumquat, lime, malanga, mamey sapote, mango, papaya, Scotch bonnet pepper, star fruit, sugar cane, and yuca. Brooks' produce is grown on its more than 6,000 acres located in Florida, as well as growing operations in Belize. The company was founded in 1928 by J.R. Brooks and is still owned and managed by his son and company president, Neal (Pal) Brooks.

	Annual Growth	12/06	12/07	12/08	12/09	12/10
Sales ($mil.)	3.8%	–	–	44.8	42.1	48.3
Net income ($ mil.)	–	–	–	(1.7)	(2.0)	2.9
Market value ($ mil.)	–	–	–	–	–	–
Employees	–	–	–	–	–	250

BROTHER INTERNATIONAL CORPORATION

200 CROSSING BLVD FL 1
BRIDGEWATER, NJ 088072861
Phone: 908 704-1700
Fax: –
Web: www.brother-usa.com

CEO: Tadashi Ishiguro
CFO: –
HR: –
FYE: March 31
Type: Private

Brother International is a leading supplier of innovative products for the home sewing and crafting enthusiast. A subsidiary of Japan-based Brother Industries, Brother International sells a host of products ? including inkjet and laser printers, fax machines, scanners, typewriters, sewing machines, gear motors, and machine tools ? manufactured by its parent company. Its products are marketed to consumers and businesses in North America and across Latin America. Through its subsidiaries, Brother International operates production and sales facilities in more than 30 countries worldwide, and it serves customers in over 100 countries. The business was formed in 1954.

	Annual Growth	03/12	03/13	03/14	03/15	03/18
Sales ($mil.)	(1.0%)	–	–	1,826.4	1,852.7	1,751.5
Net income ($ mil.)	6.1%	–	–	26.8	3.8	34.0
Market value ($ mil.)	–	–	–	–	–	–
Employees	–	–	–	–	–	2,000

BROTHERS PRODUCE, INCORPORATED

3173 PRODUCE ROW
HOUSTON, TX 770235813
Phone: 713 924-4196
Fax: –
Web: www.brothersproduce.com

CEO: Martin Erenwert
CFO: –
HR: –
FYE: March 31
Type: Private

Brothers Produce is a leading supplier of fresh fruits and vegetables serving both retailers and foodservice customers in and around Dallas and Houston. It distributes a wide variety of fresh produce, including such specialty items as Maitake mushrooms, passion fruit, and purple asparagus. The company operates two distribution facilities and a fleet of more than 75 refrigerated trucks. A family-owned business, Brothers Produce was started in 1980.

BROWN & BIGELOW, INC.

1400 CORPORATE CENTER CURV STE 100
SAINT PAUL, MN 55121
Phone: 651 293-7000
Fax: –
Web: www.brownandbigelow.com

CEO: William Smith
CFO: Garry Hoden
HR: –
FYE: December 31
Type: Private

Brown & Bigelow can help keep your company's name on the minds (and walls) of all of your customers. The company distributes corporate promotional products, including calendars, pens, USB flash drives, apparel, and related items. Brown & Bigelow sells its wares through a network of 250 sales executives located throughout the country, supported by more than 15 full-service offices. Brown & Bigelow was founded in 1896 by calendar salesman Herbert Bigelow and financier Hiram Brown. The firm is known for having commissioned works by renowned artists such as Norman Rockwell and Cassius Coolidge (who created the paintings of those famous poker-playing, cigar-smoking dogs).

	Annual Growth	12/12	12/13	12/14	12/15	12/16
Sales ($mil.)	(2.3%)	–	61.3	65.9	60.0	57.3
Net income ($ mil.)	12.3%	–	0.0	0.0	0.2	0.0
Market value ($ mil.)	–	–	–	–	–	–
Employees	–	–	–	–	–	450

BROWN & BROWN INC

300 North Beach Street
Daytona Beach, FL 32114
Phone: 386 252-9601
Fax: –
Web: www.bbinsurance.com

NYS: BRO
CEO: J P Brown
CFO: R A Watts
HR: –
FYE: December 31
Type: Public

The insurance agency Brown & Brown is one of largest independent insurance brokerages in the US. It markets and sells insurance products and services, primarily in the property, casualty and employee benefits areas. The company provides its customers with quality, non-investment insurance contracts, as well as other targeted, customized risk management products and services. The company operates a write-your-own flood insurance carrier, Wright National Flood Insurance Company (WNFIC). WNFIC's underwriting business consists of policies written pursuant to the National Flood Insurance Program (NFIP), the program administered by the Federal Emergency Management Agency (FEMA) to which premiums and underwriting exposure are ceded and excess flood and private flood policies which are fully reinsured in the private market. With more than 500 locations, Brown & Brown generates some 95% of its total revenue in the US.

	Annual Growth	12/19	12/20	12/21	12/22	12/23
Sales ($mil.)	15.5%	2,392.2	2,613.4	3,051.4	3,573.4	4,257.1
Net income ($ mil.)	21.6%	398.5	480.5	587.1	671.8	870.5
Market value ($ mil.)	15.8%	11,232	13,488	19,995	16,208	20,231
Employees	12.5%	10,083	11,136	12,023	15,201	16,152

BROWN & HALEY

3500 20TH ST E STE C
FIFE, WA 984241718
Phone: 253 620-3067
Fax: –
Web: www.brown-haley.com

CEO: Pierson E Clair III
CFO: Clarence Guimond
HR: –
FYE: June 30
Type: Private

Brown & Haley is a Tacoma, Washington Food Company that has been making Almond Roca and Mountain bars since 1923. Its Almond Roca is the largest exported gift candy in the US. It also operates two factory outlet stores in Tacoma, Washington and Fife, Washington. The confectioner sells its products in roughly 65 countries worldwide through retailers and its website. Brown & Haley is growing domestically and internationally, with about 50% of its business in export markets. Brown & Haley continues to innovate new products with a focus on sustainability.

BROWN RUDNICK LLP

1 FINANCIAL CTR
BOSTON, MA 021112621
Phone: 617 330-9000
Fax: –
Web: www.brownrudnick.com

CEO: –
CFO: –
HR: –
FYE: December 31
Type: Private

Brown Rudnick Berlack Israels is an international law firm with 200 attorneys in seven locations (Boston; Hartford, Connecticut; London; New York; Providence, Rhode Island; Washington, DC; and Dublin). The full-service law firm provides legal guidance for companies of all sizes, municipalities, and not-for-profit organizations. Founded in 1948, the firm offers legal expertise in more than 30 practice areas including banking and finance, corporate, real estate, litigation, tax, and government law and strategies.

BROWN UNIVERSITY

1 PROSPECT ST
PROVIDENCE, RI 029129127
Phone: 401 369-0294
Fax: –
Web: www.brown.edu

CEO: Christina Paxson
CFO: –
HR: Elizabeth Scotto
FYE: June 30
Type: Private

Brown University is a leading research university distinct for its student-centered learning and deep sense of purpose. The university's academic programs include undergraduate, graduate and professional, schools and colleges, academic departments, centers and institutes, libraries and collections, global education, medical school, as well as non-degree programs. It is a private, not-for-profit, nonsectarian, co-educational institution of higher education with over 7,220 undergraduate students and approximately 3,515 graduate and medical students. Its student-to-faculty ratio is 6:1. The university, founded in 1764, is located in Providence, Rhode Island ? Brown's home for more than two and a half centuries.

	Annual Growth	06/09	06/10	06/11	06/12	06/13
Sales ($mil.)	4.8%	–	–	666.5	704.9	732.1
Net income ($ mil.)	(10.2%)	–	–	359.4	(69.1)	289.6
Market value ($ mil.)	–	–	–	–	–	–
Employees	–	–	–	–	–	5,121

BROWN-FORMAN CORP NYS: BF B

850 Dixie Highway
Louisville, KY 40210
Phone: 502 585-1100
Fax: 502 774-7876
Web: www.brown-forman.com

CEO: Lawson E Whiting
CFO: Jane C Morreau
HR: Alesha Frazier
FYE: April 30
Type: Public

Distiller Brown-Forman primarily manufactures, distills, bottles, imports, exports, markets, and sells a wide variety of beverage alcohol products under recognized brands. The company's portfolio of mid-priced to super-premium alcoholic beverages includes such well-known brands as Jack Daniel's, el Jimador, Finlandia, and Woodford Reserve. Its wine labels include Sonoma-Cutrer and Korbel champagnes. Jack Daniel's Tennessee Whiskey is the company's signature brand and the largest-selling American whiskey in the world (by volume). Offering more than 40 brands, the company sells its beverages in more than 170 countries across the globe; sales outside the US account for about half of the revenue. Incorporated in 1933, more than half of the company's voting stock is owned by the Brown family.

	Annual Growth	04/19	04/20	04/21	04/22	04/23
Sales ($mil.)	6.2%	3,324.0	3,363.0	3,461.0	3,933.0	4,228.0
Net income ($ mil.)	(1.6%)	835.0	827.0	903.0	838.0	783.0
Market value ($ mil.)	5.1%	25,543	29,813	36,562	32,325	31,199
Employees	4.5%	4,700	4,800	4,700	5,200	5,600

BRT APARTMENTS CORP NYS: BRT

60 Cutter Mill Road
Great Neck, NY 11021
Phone: 516 466-3100
Fax: –
Web: www.brtapartments.com

CEO: Jeffrey A Gould
CFO: George E Zweier
HR: –
FYE: December 31
Type: Public

BRT Realty is a real estate investment trust (REIT) that originates and holds senior and junior mortgage loans for income-producing commercial property. Most are high-yield short-term mortgages or bridge loans secured by shopping centers, office buildings, hotels and apartments that are being converted into condominiums, and other multifamily residential properties. The REIT also invests in real estate joint ventures and in stock of other real estate companies. BRT Realty's loan portfolio consists of approximately 40 mortgages on properties in about a dozen states, mainly New York, New Jersey, and Florida. Chairman Fredric Gould and his family control about a quarter of BRT Realty.

	Annual Growth	12/19	12/20	12/21	12/22	12/23
Sales ($mil.)	35.5%	27.8	28.1	32.1	70.5	93.6
Net income ($ mil.)	45.8%	0.9	(19.9)	29.1	50.0	3.9
Market value ($ mil.)	2.3%	297.6	266.5	420.7	344.4	326.0
Employees	(6.3%)	13	9	9	10	10

BRTRC FEDERAL SOLUTIONS, INC.

12930 WORLDGATE DR # 600
HERNDON, VA 201706011
Phone: 703 204-9277
Fax: –
Web: –

CEO: Robert Olsen
CFO: –
HR: Susie Seal
FYE: December 31
Type: Private

Baum, Romstedt Technology Research, or BRTRC, wants to B irreplaceable to its clients. The firm offers a variety of technical and professional support services to federal agencies including US Army, FBI, and the Department of Defense. Its on- and off-site services include program management (strategy development, program assessment, and research and analysis), project engineering, and IT services (web design and software development). Its BRTRC Institute develops training programs on commercial contracting, privatization, contract law, and other topics. BRTIRC also provides marketing, communications, and event-planning services. It was founded in 1985 and has offices in Maryland, Michigan, Missouri, and Virginia.

	Annual Growth	12/11	12/12	12/13	12/14	12/15
Sales ($mil.)	(7.2%)	–	46.6	43.2	3.1	37.2
Net income ($ mil.)	–	–	0.2	1.2	(0.8)	(0.0)
Market value ($ mil.)	–	–	–	–	–	–
Employees	–	–	–	–	–	280

BRUCE OAKLEY, INC.

3400 GRIBBLE ST
NORTH LITTLE ROCK, AR 721146406
Phone: 501 945-0875
Fax: –
Web: www.bruceoakley.com

CEO: –
CFO: Tim Cummins
HR: Leslie Jenkins
FYE: September 25
Type: Private

From little acorns, mighty Oakleys grow. Bruce Oakley provides road and river (barge) transportation of dry bulk commodities, as well as grain storage and bulk fertilizer sales. The company's trucking division, which uses both end-dump and pneumatic tank trailers, serves the continental US and Canada. Overall Bruce Oakley operates some 450 trailers. It maintains about half a dozen ports in Arkansas, Louisiana, and Missouri on the Arkansas, Mississippi, and Red rivers, and the company's river barge transportation unit operates on those and other inland and intracoastal waterways. Grain storage services are available in five ports in Arkansas. Bruce Oakley was founded in 1968.

	Annual Growth	09/04	09/05	09/06	09/07	09/08
Sales ($mil.)	66.3%	–	–	419.5	526.8	1,160.1
Net income ($ mil.)	53.6%	–	–	13.6	11.8	32.0
Market value ($ mil.)	–	–	–	–	–	–
Employees	–	–	–	–	–	800

BRUKER CORP   NMS: BRKR

40 Manning Road
Billerica, MA 01821
Phone: 978 663-3660
Fax: –
Web: www.bruker.com

CEO: Frank H Laukien
CFO: Gerald N Herman
HR: –
FYE: December 31
Type: Public

Bruker develops, manufactures and distributes an array of high-performance scientific analysis instruments and diagnostic tools for life science and clinical research, pharmaceutical, biotech, industrial, academic, and government customers. Many of the company's products are used to detect, measure and visualize structural characteristics of chemical, biological and industrial material samples. Its platforms include magnetic resonance, mass spectrometry, X-ray, atomic force microscopy, fluorescence optical microscopy, and infrared technologies. The company operates through four business units: BSI BioSpin, BSI CALID, BSI Nano, and BEST. About 30% of Bruker's revenue comes from Europe.

	Annual Growth	12/19	12/20	12/21	12/22	12/23
Sales ($mil.)	9.4%	2,072.6	1,987.5	2,417.9	2,530.7	2,964.5
Net income ($ mil.)	21.3%	197.2	157.8	277.1	296.6	427.2
Market value ($ mil.)	9.6%	7,399.1	7,857.8	12,181	9,922.0	10,667
Employees	7.6%	7,230	7,400	7,765	8,525	9,707

BRUNSWICK CORP.   NYS: BC

26125 N. Riverwoods Blvd., Suite 500
Mettawa, IL 60045-3420
Phone: 847 735-4700
Fax: –
Web: www.brunswick.com

CEO: David M Foulkes
CFO: Ryan M Gwillim
HR: –
FYE: December 31
Type: Public

Incorporated in 1907, Brunswick Corporation is a global designer, manufacturer, and marketer of recreational marine products including marine engines, boats, and parts and accessories for those products. The propulsion segment makes a full range of outboard, sterndrive, and inboard engines, as well as propulsion-related controls, rigging, and propellers. The company also makes pleasure craft, offshore fishing boats, and pontoons. Through its Brunswick Financial Services Corporation subsidiary, the company owns 49% stake in marine financing company Brunswick Acceptance Company; a Wells Fargo subsidiary holds the other 51%. It generates over 70% of sales in the US.

	Annual Growth	12/19	12/20	12/21	12/22	12/23
Sales ($mil.)	11.7%	4,108.4	4,347.5	5,846.2	6,812.2	6,401.4
Net income ($ mil.)	–	(131.0)	372.7	593.3	677.0	420.4
Market value ($ mil.)	12.7%	4,092.3	5,201.6	6,872.5	4,917.8	6,601.0
Employees	6.7%	12,828	14,382	18,582	19,000	16,608

BRYAN CAVE LEIGHTON PAISNER LLP

1 METROPOLITAN SQ 211N
SAINT LOUIS, MO 631022711
Phone: 314 259-2000
Fax: –
Web: www.bclplaw.com

CEO: –
CFO: –
HR: Alicia Kuhn
FYE: December 31
Type: Private

Formed in 2018, Bryan Cave Leighton Paisner focuses on corporate transactions and litigation; specialties include agribusiness, entertainment, environmental, health care, intellectual property, real estate, and tax law. By combining the practice experience, industry knowledge and market connections of more than 1,200 lawyers across around 30 offices in North America, Europe, the Middle East, and Asia, with its recognized leadership in applying legal service and technology innovation, it delivers commercial advantage to clients. Approximately 35% of the Fortune 500 companies rely on the firm to protect their interests and make their business ambitions become business realities.

	Annual Growth	12/18	12/19	12/20	12/21	12/22
Sales ($mil.)	(51.7%)	–	–	–	0.2	0.0
Net income ($ mil.)	–	–	–	–	0.0	(0.0)
Market value ($ mil.)	–	–	–	–	–	–
Employees	–	–	–	–	–	2,559

BRYAN MEDICAL CENTER

1600 S 48TH ST
LINCOLN, NE 685061283
Phone: 402 481-1111
Fax: –
Web: www.bryanhealth.com

CEO: Kim Russel
CFO: Russell Gronewold
HR: Arnie Christensen
FYE: December 31
Type: Private

Bryan Medical Center is the centerpiece of a not-for-profit health care system serving residents of Lincoln, Nebraska, and surrounding communities. The medical center, which operates as part of Bryan Health, features two acute-care hospitals (Bryan East and Bryan West) housing a combined 670 beds. In addition to providing general medical and surgical care, it serves as a regional trauma center and provides specialty care in areas such as cancer, orthopedics, and cardiology. The Bryan Health organization also includes a rural hospital and several outpatient clinics, and it provides medical training, home health care services, and wellness programs.

	Annual Growth	12/16	12/17	12/19	12/21	12/22
Sales ($mil.)	7.4%	–	606.4	785.7	839.6	865.5
Net income ($ mil.)	4.0%	–	74.7	129.4	(51.4)	90.8
Market value ($ mil.)	–	–	–	–	–	–
Employees	–	–	–	–	–	3,970

BRYN MAWR COLLEGE

101 N MERION AVE
BRYN MAWR, PA 190102899
Phone: 610 526-5000
Fax: –
Web: www.brynmawr.edu

CEO: Hannah H Gray
CFO: –
HR: –
FYE: May 31
Type: Private

These Mawrters aren't sacrificing anything, especially when it comes to their education. Bryn Mawr is a college for women, often referred to as Mawrters, who hail from 60 countries. Its undergraduate programs, including biology, English, math, political science, and psychology, enroll 1,300 students. Bryn Mawr also offers degrees through its co-educational Graduate School of Arts and Sciences and Graduate School of Social Work and Social Research, which enrolls some 425 students. The college pools resources with Haverford, Swarthmore, and The University of Pennsylvania. Founded in 1885, Bryn Mawr is one of the nation's oldest women's colleges and the first to offer women an education through the Ph.D. level.

	Annual Growth	05/13	05/14	05/15	05/20	05/22
Sales ($mil.)	4.4%	–	200.5	225.0	204.1	282.0
Net income ($ mil.)	11.0%	–	43.7	67.3	31.7	100.4
Market value ($ mil.)	–	–	–	–	–	–
Employees	–	–	–	–	–	777

BSA BUSINESS SOFTWARE ALLIANCE, INC

20 F ST NW STE 800
WASHINGTON, DC 200016708
Phone: 202 872-5500
Fax: –
Web: www.bsa.org

CEO: Victoria Espinel
CFO: Joe Desalvio
HR: Asia Collins
FYE: September 30
Type: Private

The Business Software Alliance (BSA) or Software Alliance is the leading advocate for the global software industry before governments and in the international marketplace. It also tries to keep the digital world safe by working on cyber security and other Internet-related concerns and operating hotlines around the world where people can report piracy or ask questions. The BSA, which focuses its efforts on emerging markets, operates in more than 30 countries. Members include Adobe Systems, Oracle, IBM, and Microsoft, which it represents before government bodies and to the public.

BSD MEDICAL CORPORATION

391 S CHIPETA WAY STE F
SALT LAKE CITY, UT 841081206
Phone: 801 972-5555
Fax: –
Web: www.pyrexar.com

CEO: –
CFO: –
HR: –
FYE: August 31
Type: Private

BSD Medical has developed equipment to provide hyperthermia treatment, specifically for treating cancer (including melanoma, breast cancer, brain cancer, and cervical cancer). Its systems are used in tandem with chemotherapy and radiation therapy or as a stand-alone treatment. BSD Medical was the first to develop an approvable hyperthermia system, which uses focused radio frequencies and microwaves to heat cancer cells until they die. The company's devices are designed to target superficial tumors, as well as tumors located deep within a patient's body. Its products are sold to clinics, hospitals, and other cancer-treatment institutions through its sales force and external distributors.

BTD MANUFACTURING, INC.

1111 13TH AVE SE
DETROIT LAKES, MN 565013736
Phone: 866 562-3986
Fax: –
Web: www.btdmfg.com

CEO: Paul Gintner
CFO: –
HR: Brittany Nordick
FYE: December 31
Type: Private

What started in 1979 as Bismarck Tool & Die didn't die at all; it lives on today as BTD Manufacturing. The company provides metal fabrication services for custom machine parts and metal components through stamping, tool and die, machining, tube bending, welding, and assembly. BTD offers design, engineering, prototyping, and short-run functions. It serves customers in the agricultural machinery, appliance, health and fitness, lawn and garden equipment, and recreational vehicle industries, mainly in the Midwest. Major clients include snowmobile maker Arctic Cat, agricultural equipment manufacturer AGCO, and power plant construction firm Siemens Energy. BTD is a wholly-owned subsidiary of Otter Tail Corporation.

BUCHANAN TECHNOLOGIES, INC.

1026 TEXAN TRL STE 200
GRAPEVINE, TX 760513703
Phone: 972 869-3966
Fax: –
Web: www.buchanan.com

CEO: James Buchanan
CFO: Doug Hansen
HR: –
FYE: December 31
Type: Private

Buchanan Technologies hopes that you come to associate it with good service. The company provides a variety of IT services, such as consulting, application development, managed network services, network design and implementation, systems integration, training, and support. Buchanan Associates also resells and distributes a variety of computer hardware and software. Clients come from fields such as education, electronics, financial services, government, health care, manufacturing, retail, and transportation. CEO Jim Buchanan founded Buchanan Associates in 1988.

	Annual Growth	12/04	12/05	12/06	12/09	12/10
Sales ($mil.)	3.5%	–	–	38.3	36.1	44.0
Net income ($ mil.)		–	–	7.2	1.6	(1.3)
Market value ($ mil.)		–	–	–	–	–
Employees		–	–	–	–	347

BUCHBINDER TUNICK & COMPANY L.L.P

1 PENN PLZ STE 3500
NEW YORK, NY 101193601
Phone: 212 629-8744
Fax: –
Web: www.weaver.com

CEO: –
CFO: –
HR: –
FYE: December 31
Type: Private

Buchbinder Tunick & Company helps clients hold onto their hard-earned bucks. The firm provides primarily midsized, privately-held and non-profit companies with assurance, business advisory and valuation, forensics, and tax services. It also assists individuals with estate and financial planning, and tax preparation. The firm advises benefit plan trustees and administrators in the execution of employee benefit plans such as 401(k), medical, and ownership plans. It also specializes in providing nonprofit clients such as charities, religious organizations, and schools, with accounting, grant writing, and grant auditing. The firm, which traces its roots to the 1940s, operates offices in New York and Maryland.

BUCKEYE PARTNERS, L.P.

4200 WESTHEIMER RD STE 975
HOUSTON, TX 770274428
Phone: 832 615-8600
Fax: –
Web: www.buckeye.com

CEO: Todd Russo
CFO: Gary Bohnsack Jr
HR: –
FYE: December 31
Type: Private

Buckeye Partners, L.P. owns and operates a diversified global network of integrated assets providing midstream logistic solutions, primarily consisting of the transportation, storage, processing and marketing of liquid petroleum products. Buckeye is one of the largest independent liquid petroleum products pipeline operators in the US in terms of volumes delivered, with approximately 5,000 miles of pipeline. Buckeye's Gulf Coast regional hub, Buckeye Texas Partners, offers world-class marine terminalling, storage and processing capabilities. Buckeye is also a wholesale distributor of refined petroleum products in certain areas served by its pipelines and terminals. Buckeye Partners traces its roots to March 1886, when The Buckeye Pipe Line Company was incorporated as a subsidiary of the Standard Oil Company.

BUCKEYE PIPE LINE COMPANY, L P

6161 HAMILTON BLVD
ALLENTOWN, PA 181069767
Phone: 610 904-4000
Fax: –
Web: –

CEO: –
CFO: –
HR: –
FYE: December 31
Type: Private

It's the octane in fuel in the pipes of Buckeye Pipe Line that gets engines to buck up. A partnership subsidiary of Buckeye Partners, the company operates an interstate common carrier refined petroleum pipeline that runs some 2,643 miles from Massachusetts to Illinois. The refined petroleum products carried include gasoline, turbine fuel, diesel fuel, heating oil and kerosene. The company serves major population centers in nine states. It is also the major jet engine fuel provider to John F. Kennedy International Airport, LaGuardia Airport, Newark International Airport and a number of other airports within the territory served by the pipeline operator.

	Annual Growth	12/01	12/02	12/03	12/04	12/16
Sales ($mil.)	4.6%	–	179.9	196.3	323.5	335.5
Net income ($ mil.)	8.5%	–	55.7	14.1	83.0	173.6
Market value ($ mil.)		–	–	–	–	–
Employees		–	–	–	–	504

BUCKEYE POWER, INC.

6677 BUSCH BLVD
COLUMBUS, OH 432291101
Phone: 614 781-0573
Fax: -
Web: www.ohioec.org

CEO: Anthony J Ahern
CFO: -
HR: -
FYE: June 30
Type: Private

It has cost a few bucks to generate power, but the effort has been well worth it for Buckeye Power, an electricity generation and transmission cooperative that provides electricity to 24 distribution companies in Ohio and one in Michigan. Together they serve about 400,000 homes and businesses in 77 of Ohio's 88 counties. The company was established by Ohio's rural electric co-ops to produce and transmit electric power for member systems throughout the state. Buckeye Power contracts with other Ohio electric companies to use their transmission systems to transmit power to its member electric distribution cooperatives.

	Annual Growth	06/15	06/16	06/17	06/18	06/22
Sales ($mil.)	3.6%	-	-	-	708.2	814.4
Net income ($ mil.)	(5.5%)	-	-	-	45.9	36.6
Market value ($ mil.)	-	-	-	-	-	-
Employees	-	-	-	-	-	300

BUCKLE, INC. (THE)
NYS: BKE

2407 West 24th Street
Kearney, NE 68845-4915
Phone: 308 236-8491
Fax: -
Web: www.buckle.com

CEO: -
CFO: -
HR: -
FYE: January 28
Type: Public

The Buckle is a retailer of medium to better-priced casual apparel, footwear, and accessories for fashion-conscious young men and women. With approximately 440 mostly mall-based stores in more than 40 states, the Buckle sells fashion-conscious 15- to 30-year-olds the clothes they've just got to have. The company retails a variety of clothing items, including mid- to higher-priced casual apparel (pants, tops, and outerwear), shoes, and accessories. Its products portfolio boasts such brands as Oakley, Fox, Hurley, Billabong, Fossil, and American Fighter. The Buckle operates under the names Buckle and The Buckle; it also has an online store. Born in Nebraska in 1948 under the name Mills Clothing, the company has expanded into the South and West.

	Annual Growth	02/19	02/20*	01/21	01/22	01/23
Sales ($mil.)	11.0%	885.5	900.3	901.3	1,294.6	1,345.2
Net income ($ mil.)	27.7%	95.6	104.4	130.1	254.8	254.6
Market value ($ mil.)	25.7%	870.6	1,222.6	1,969.6	1,829.4	2,171.5
Employees	5.3%	7,400	7,000	7,200	8,300	9,100

*Fiscal year change

BUCKNELL UNIVERSITY

1 DENT DR
LEWISBURG, PA 178372029
Phone: 570 577-2000
Fax: -
Web: www.bucknell.edu

CEO: -
CFO: -
HR: Andrea Reiner
FYE: June 30
Type: Private

Just getting into Bucknell University is an accomplishment. The highly selective private liberal arts school accepts only about 10% of applicants each year. Students who do get in, some 3,600 of them from around the world, have the option to specialize in more than 50 majors and 60 minors. Bucknell confers both undergraduate and master's degrees in the liberal arts, sciences, engineering, and music. It also offers programs in pre-law and pre-med. Bucknell tuition and fees total more than $58,000; more than half of the student body typically receives financial aid. The school's student-to-faculty ratio is 10-to-1.

	Annual Growth	06/18	06/19	06/20	06/21	06/22
Sales ($mil.)	5.3%	-	247.2	247.7	253.3	288.9
Net income ($ mil.)	-	-	22.6	(23.3)	282.6	(46.1)
Market value ($ mil.)	-	-	-	-	-	-
Employees	-	-	-	-	-	1,300

BUFFALO WILD WINGS, INC.

5500 WAYZATA BLVD STE 1600
MINNEAPOLIS, MN 554161241
Phone: 952 593-9943
Fax: -
Web: www.buffalowildwings.com

CEO: Sally J Smith
CFO: Alexander H Ware
HR: -
FYE: December 27
Type: Private

Buffalo Wild Wings is the largest sports bar brand in the US and operates a chain of more than 1,255 Buffalo Wild Wings Grill & Bar quick-casual dining spots that specialize in serving Buffalo-style chicken wings in around 10 countries. A part of Roark Capital under Inspire Brands, the company features an immersive sports restaurant experience and a variety of boldly flavored menu items, including buffalo-style chicken wings spun in over 20 signature sauces and seasonings. Buffalo Wild Wings is founded in 1982 by Jim Disbrow and Scott Lowery in Minneapolis.

BUILD-A-BEAR WORKSHOP INC
NYS: BBW

415 South 18th St.
St. Louis, MO 63103
Phone: 314 423-8000
Fax: 314 423-8188
Web: www.buildabear.com

CEO: Sharon John
CFO: Voin Todorovic
HR: -
FYE: January 28
Type: Public

The Build-A-Bear Workshop (BBW) is a multi-channel retailer offering a "make their own stuffed animal" interactive retail-entertainment experience. Located mainly in malls, the company's stores allow kids to design their own teddy bears and other stuffed animals complete with clothing, shoes, and a barrage of accessories. Build-A-Bear, founded by Maxine Clark in 1997, boasts about 350 corporately-managed locations, including some 310 stores in the US and Canada, nearly 40 stores in the UK and Ireland and about 70 franchised stores operating internationally under the Build-A-Bear Workshop brand. Most of the company's revenue comes from North America.

	Annual Growth	02/19	02/20*	01/21	01/22	01/23
Sales ($mil.)	8.6%	336.6	338.5	255.3	411.5	467.9
Net income ($ mil.)	-	(17.9)	0.3	(23.0)	47.3	48.0
Market value ($ mil.)	51.1%	68.5	61.9	83.0	256.5	357.6
Employees	(0.6%)	4,300	4,300	3,700	3,700	4,200

*Fiscal year change

BUILDERS FIRSTSOURCE INC.
NYS: BLDR

2001 Bryan Street, Suite 1600
Dallas, TX 75201
Phone: 214 880-3500
Fax: 214 880-3599
Web: www.bldr.com

CEO: David E Rush
CFO: Peter M Jackson
HR: -
FYE: December 31
Type: Public

Builders FirstSource is a leading supplier and manufacturer of building materials, manufactured components, and construction services to professional homebuilders, sub-contractors, remodelers, and consumers. It also offers construction-related services. The company's products and services ? which manufactured products include the factory-built roof and floor trusses, wall panels and stairs, vinyl windows, custom millwork and trim, as well as engineered wood ? are offered through about 570 locations across more than 40 US states. Homebuilders such as Pulte Homes and Lennar are among its largest customers. Builders FirstSource's residential building products industry is driven by the level of activity in both the US residential new construction market and the US residential repair and remodeling market.

	Annual Growth	12/19	12/20	12/21	12/22	12/23
Sales ($mil.)	23.8%	7,280.4	8,558.9	19,894	22,726	17,097
Net income ($ mil.)	62.3%	221.8	313.5	1,725.4	2,749.4	1,540.6
Market value ($ mil.)	60.1%	3,096.4	4,973.0	10,444	7,906.1	20,343
Employees	16.4%	15,800	26,000	28,000	29,000	29,000

BUILDING MATERIALS CORP. OF AMERICA

1361 Alps Road
Wayne, NJ 07470
Phone: 973 628-3000
Fax: –
Web: www.gaf.com

CEO: John Altmeyer
CFO: John F Rebele
HR: Carlee Hongskula
FYE: December 31
Type: Public

Building Materials Corporation of America (BMCA), doing business as GAF Materials, wants to keep your roof looking spiffy. BMCA, which deals primarily in shingles and roofing systems, also makes flashing, vents, decorative stone for fireplaces, decking, and wrought iron balusters. Its GAF-Elk products include Timberline- and Sovereign-brand residential shingles and GAF CompositeRoof for commercial roofing. Customers include contractors, distributors, property owners, and retail outlets like The Home Depot. Founded in 1886, GAF is one of North America's largest manufacturers of commercial and residential roofing. It is a subsidiary of G-I Holdings, which is controlled by the family of the late Samuel Heyman.

	Annual Growth	12/04	12/05	12/06	12/07	12/08
Sales ($mil.)	11.6%	1,773.4	1,955.8	1,969.2	2,310.1	2,748.9
Net income ($ mil.)	(1.6%)	54.9	61.0	38.8	(134.5)	51.4
Market value ($ mil.)	–	–	–	–	–	–
Employees	–	3,700	3,700	3,600	4,200	3,700

BULOVA TECHNOLOGIES GROUP, INC

1501 Lake Avenue SE
Largo, FL 33771
Phone: 727 536-6666
Fax: –
Web: www.bulovatechgroup.com

CEO: –
CFO: –
HR: –
FYE: September 30
Type: Public

Bulova Technologies Group believes defense, manufacturing, and technology is a recipe for business success. Bulova operates in three primary segments: defense, contract manufacturing, and technologies. Its defense operations provide the DoD with explosive simulators, ammunition, and pyrotechnic devices, as well as integration services. Bulova's contract manufacturing division assembles printed circuit boards and cable assemblies. It sold its BulovaTech Labs, which developed and licensed applications for the defense, energy, and health care markets, to Growth Technologies International in 2010. Bulova completed a reverse merger with 3Si Holdings in late 2009 in order to become a publicly traded company.

	Annual Growth	09/13	09/14	09/15	09/16	09/17
Sales ($mil.)	40.6%	6.4	3.2	1.8	18.7	25.2
Net income ($ mil.)	(53.1%)	11.2	(3.8)	(5.3)	(8.1)	0.5
Market value ($ mil.)	124.8%	0.0	14.0	36.5	1.4	1.6
Employees	–	–	–	–	–	–

BUNGE GLOBAL SA

NYS: BG

1391 Timberlake Manor Parkway
Chesterfield, MO 63017
Phone: 314 292-2000
Fax: –
Web: www.bunge.com

CEO: –
CFO: –
HR: –
FYE: December 31
Type: Public

Bunge's businesses stretch from the farm field to your local supermarket shelf. A leading integrated agribusiness and food company, Bunge produces, stores, and sells agricultural products such as oilseeds and grains, which it turns into vegetable oils and protein meals. Customers include animal feed, poultry, and aquaculture producers. The agribusiness markets vegetable oils used in the biodiesel industry. The company's edible oil products segment sells packaged oils, like shortening and margarine under brands Bunge Pro, Floriol, and Olek. A sugar and bioenergy unit produces sugar and ethanol, which are sold primarily in Brazil. Bunge also mixes and distributes crop fertilizers to farmers in South America.

	Annual Growth	12/18	12/19	12/20	12/21	12/22
Sales ($mil.)	10.1%	45,743	41,140	41,404	59,152	67,232
Net income ($ mil.)	56.7%	267.0	(1,280.0)	1,145.0	2,078.0	1,610.0
Market value ($ mil.)	–	–	–	–	–	–
Employees	(7.2%)	31,000	24,000	23,000	22,000	23,000

BUNGE NORTH AMERICA, INC.

1391 TIMBERLAKE MANOR PKWY
CHESTERFIELD, MO 630176058
Phone: 314 292-2000
Fax: –
Web: www.bunge.com

CEO: Todd Bastean
CFO: George P Allard
HR: –
FYE: December 31
Type: Private

Bunge North America (BNA) is an agribusiness and food ingredient company dedicated to improving the global food supply chain. BNA buys and sells raw agricultural commodities such as corn, soybeans, canola, wheat, and rice. The food and ingredients business makes edible oils, such as sunflower oil, butter alternatives, batter, and shortening. BNA's facilities across the US, Canada, and Mexico include grain stores, oilseed processing plants, edible oil refineries, packaging facilities, and mills. Value-add processing includes animal feed mixes, biodiesel, and lubricants. Customers include food manufacturers, foodservice operators, and retail outlets in North America. BNA is the North American arm of Bunge Limited.

BURKE HERBERT FINANCIAL SERVICES CORP

NAS: BHRB

100 South Fairfax Street
Alexandria, VA 22314
Phone: 703 837-3747
Fax: 703 836-5591
Web: www.burkeandherbert.com

CEO: E H Burke
CFO: Jeffrey Stryker
HR: –
FYE: December 31
Type: Public

Founded in 1852, Burke & Herbert Bank & Trust is one of the oldest banks in Virginia. Placing an emphasis on personal service, it operates about 25 branches in the northern part of the state, including part of the Washington, DC, metropolitan area. The bank offers standard products such as checking and savings accounts, money market accounts, CDs, IRAs, and debit cards. Its loan portfolio is primarily made up of residential and commercial mortgages, while construction, business, and consumer loans round out its lending activities. Burke & Herbert Bank & Trust also offers trust and financial planning services. The company is owned by members of the founding Burke and Herbert families.

	Annual Growth	12/02	12/19	12/20	12/21	12/22
Assets ($mil.)	6.2%	1,078.4	2,865.9	3,432.6	3,621.7	3,562.9
Net income ($ mil.)	4.1%	19.6	17.0	26.5	36.2	44.0
Market value ($ mil.)	–	–	–	–	–	–
Employees	–	–	–	–	–	–

BURKE REHABILITATION HOSPITAL

785 MARINAC AVE
WHITE PLAINS, NY 10605
Phone: 914 597-2500
Fax: –
Web: www.burke.org

CEO: –
CFO: –
HR: –
FYE: December 31
Type: Private

Founded in 1915, Burke Rehabilitation Hospital is a stalwart provider of rehabilitation services in White Plains, New York, and surrounding areas. The 150-bed hospital provides inpatient rehabilitation services to patients suffering from physical disabilities resulting from illness, injury, or surgery. Inpatient services include cardiac, orthopedic, and spinal cord therapy. It also operates outpatient clinics that offer such services as arthritis, cognitive, occupational, speech, and sports medicine therapy. In addition, Burke Rehabilitation Hospital conducts research in areas such as head injuries, neurological disorders, and Alzheimer's disease through its Burke Medical Research Institute.

BURKE, INC.

500 W 7TH ST
CINCINNATI, OH 452031543
Phone: 513 241-5663
Fax: –
Web: www.burke.com

CEO: Micheal H Baumgardner
CFO: –
HR: Julie O 'donnell
FYE: September 25
Type: Private

Nearly 100% of survey respondents agree: Burke provides strategic consulting and research services to both consumer-oriented and business-to-business companies. With expertise in serving health care clients, the independent firm collects data from about 20 centers across the US and offers market research in such areas as branding and product development; it also implements customer satisfaction and loyalty, as well as employee engagement and retention measurement systems. Additionally, Burke offers public seminars and in-house training on market research through The Burke Institute. Founded in 1931 by Alberta Burke as a data collection firm named Burke Marketing Research, the company is 100% employee-owned.

BURKHART DENTAL SUPPLY CO.

2502 S 78TH ST
TACOMA, WA 984099053
Phone: 253 474-7761
Fax: –
Web: www.burkhartdental.com

CEO: –
CFO: –
HR: –
FYE: December 31
Type: Private

Burkhart Dental Supply is dedicated to supplying dentists with the tools they need. The family-owned company provides dental equipment and supplies to more than 5,000 dentists throughout the midwestern, southwestern, and western US. The company also offers a variety of technical services, equipment repairs, office management software, continuing education, financing, and consulting services, such as office design and equipment planning. It distributes products made by some 100 manufacturers including Dentsply Sirona and Kimberly Clark. Its operating subsidiaries include ADC Group Financial Services, Burkhart Consulting, and Summit Dental Study Group.

	Annual Growth	12/05	12/06	12/07	12/08	12/09
Sales ($mil.)	1.0%	–	–	140.1	157.1	142.8
Net income ($ mil.)	14.6%	–	–	1.3	2.1	1.7
Market value ($ mil.)	–	–	–	–	–	–
Employees	–	–	–	–	–	400

BURLINGTON NORTHERN & SANTA FE RAILWAY CO. (THE)

2650 Lou Menk Drive
Fort Worth, TX 76131-2830
Phone: 800 795-2673
Fax: –
Web: www.bnsf.com

CEO: Kathryn Farmer
CFO: Julie A Piggott
HR: –
FYE: December 31
Type: Public

BNSF Railway is one of North America's leading freight transportation companies. A wholly-owned subsidiary of Burlington Northern Santa Fe, itself is a unit of Berkshire Hathaway, the company provides freight transportation over a network of approximately 32,500 route miles of track across nearly 30 US states and three provinces in Canada. BNSF Railway owns or leases a fleet of about 8,000 locomotives. It also has some 25 intermodal facilities that help to transport agricultural, consumer, and industrial products, as well as coal. In addition to major cities and ports, BNSF Railway is one of the top transporters of the products and materials that help feed, clothe, supply and power communities throughout America and the world.

	Annual Growth	12/13	12/14	12/15	12/16	12/17
Sales ($mil.)	(0.9%)	21,552	22,714	21,401	19,278	20,747
Net income ($ mil.)	29.8%	4,271.0	4,397.0	4,915.0	4,260.0	12,119
Market value ($ mil.)	–	–	–	–	–	–
Employees	(1.2%)	43,000	48,000	44,000	41,000	41,000

BURLINGTON NORTHERN SANTA FE, LLC

2650 LOU MENK DR
FORT WORTH, TX 761312830
Phone: 800 795-2673
Fax: –
Web: www.bnsf.com

CEO: –
CFO: –
HR: –
FYE: December 31
Type: Private

Burlington Northern Santa Fe (BNSF) is a holding company that conducts no operating activities and owns no significant assets other than through its interests in its subsidiaries. Through its primary subsidiary, BNSF Railway, the company is one of the leading railroad operators in the US. BNSF makes tracks through about 30 states in the US and three Canadian provinces. The company operates its trains over a system of about 32,500 route miles. BNSF is owned by Warren Buffett's Berkshire Hathaway. The company traces its roots back in 1849 when the 12-mile Aurora Branch Railroad was founded in Illinois.

BURLINGTON STORES INC

NYS: BURL

2006 Route 130 North
Burlington, NJ 08016
Phone: 609 387-7800
Fax: –
Web: www.burlingtoninvestors.com

CEO: Michael O'Sullivan
CFO: –
HR: –
FYE: February 3
Type: Public

Burlington Stores (Burlington) is a nationally recognized off-price retailer of high-quality, branded apparel at everyday low prices. The clothing retailer, which made its name selling coats, operates over 925 no-frills retail stores offering off-price current, brand-name clothing in approximately 45 states Puerto Rico. Although it is one of the nation's largest coat sellers, the stores also sell a full wardrobe of products, including children's apparel, bath items, furniture, gifts, jewelry, linens, and shoes. Sister chain was the higher-priced Cohoes Fashions shops. Burlington was founded in 1972.

	Annual Growth	02/20*	01/21	01/22	01/23*	02/24
Sales ($mil.)	7.5%	7,286.4	5,764.0	9,322.3	8,702.6	9,727.5
Net income ($ mil.)	(7.6%)	465.1	(216.5)	408.8	230.1	339.6
Market value ($ mil.)	(2.5%)	13,910	15,921	14,730	14,480	12,584
Employees	10.9%	47,000	55,959	62,395	61,166	71,049

*Fiscal year change

BURNS MOTOR FREIGHT, INC.

18750 SENECA TRL
MARLINTON, WV 249546899
Phone: 304 799-6106
Fax: –
Web: www.burnsmotorfreight.com

CEO: Fred C Burns Jr
CFO: Sam McNeel
HR: Michael Burns
FYE: December 31
Type: Private

Truckload carrier Burns Motor Freight hauls wood products and other cargo in the eastern half of the US and into eastern Canada. Serving timber producers in Appalachia, the company operates from three terminals in West Virginia. Burns Motor Freight is owned and run by members of the Burns family. Fred Burns Sr. founded the company with a single used tractor in 1949.

BURTON LUMBER & HARDWARE CO.

1170 S 4400 W
SALT LAKE CITY, UT 841044413
Phone: 801 952-3700
Fax: –
Web: www.burtonlumber.com

CEO: –
CFO: –
HR: –
FYE: December 31
Type: Private

Family-owned-and-run Burton Lumber & Hardware designs, makes, and installs truss and floor packages, wall panels, and doors (interior and exterior) from its facility in Salt Lake City. It also sells and installs Heatilator-brand fireplaces and building materials made by Trex, James Hardie, and other companies. Burton Lumber & Hardware operates half a dozen locations in Utah and offers delivery services throughout the state. Its customers have included contractors, home builders, and government agencies. The company was founded in 1911 by Willard C. Burton.

	Annual Growth	12/13	12/14	12/15	12/16	12/17
Sales ($mil.)	13.0%	–	131.2	137.5	167.7	189.5
Net income ($ mil.)	26.3%	–	8.8	9.1	13.4	17.7
Market value ($ mil.)	–	–	–	–	–	–
Employees	–	–	–	–	–	520

BUSCHMAN CORPORATION

4100 PAYNE AVE STE 1
CLEVELAND, OH 441032340
Phone: 216 431-6633
Fax: –
Web: www.buschman.com

CEO: Tom Buschman
CFO: –
HR: –
FYE: December 31
Type: Private

Buschman makes wire-wound rods used in coating applications by the paper and converting industries. The company controls all stages of manufacturing for its products, which include wire-wound metering rods, custom-engineered grooved metering and sizing rods, roll-formed rods, smoothing rods, holders, headbox sheets, and tapes for paper machinery and coating applications, as well as customized rods for specific machines. It also provides spare parts and accessories. Customers include 3M, Avery Dennison, Cascades, Hewlett Packard, RockTenn CP, and Temple Inland, among others. The company operates through representatives and distributors located worldwide.

	Annual Growth	12/96	12/97	12/98	12/99	12/19
Sales ($mil.)	(26.6%)	–	4.5	4.5	–	0.0
Net income ($ mil.)	–	–	–	–	–	0.0
Market value ($ mil.)	–	–	–	–	–	–
Employees	–	–	–	–	–	19

BUSINESS FOR SOCIAL RESPONSIBILITY

220 MONTGOMERY ST STE 1700
SAN FRANCISCO, CA 941043402
Phone: 415 984-3200
Fax: –
Web: www.bsr.org

CEO: Aron Cramer
CFO: –
HR: Kelli Pacicco
FYE: December 31
Type: Private

Business for Social Responsibility (BSR) seeks to promote business ethics, including respect for people, communities, and the environment. Companies such as General Motors, Microsoft, and Wal-Mart are among BSR's more than 250 members. The nonprofit organization provides advisory services, training, and networking, as well as several libraries and databases. BSR helps its members learn to engage stakeholders and develop workable ethics guidelines. In addition, BSR works with corporate social responsibility organizations outside the US. The organization has received support from the US Department of State and the EPA, as well as from several private foundations and member companies.

	Annual Growth	12/14	12/15	12/16	12/21	12/22
Sales ($mil.)	12.1%	–	–	21.2	33.7	42.0
Net income ($ mil.)	–	–	–	(1.9)	3.3	5.4
Market value ($ mil.)	–	–	–	–	–	–
Employees	–	–	–	–	–	130

BUSKEN BAKERY, INC.

2675 MADISON RD
CINCINNATI, OH 452081389
Phone: 513 871-2114
Fax: –
Web: www.busken.com

CEO: D P Busken
CFO: –
HR: –
FYE: December 26
Type: Private

Fans of schnecken can make a connection at these bakery stores. Busken Bakery operates a dozen bakery stores in the Cincinnati area known for schnecken, a kind of cinnamon roll that is a regional favorite and occasionally served by the bakery. The bakeries also make cookies, coffee cakes, and pies, as well as donuts, muffins, several varieties of bread, and custom-made cakes. Its products are also sold through Remke Markets, a regional supermarket chain. In addition, Busken Bakery offers catering services and provides baked goods for fundraising efforts. Joe Busken Sr. started the family-owned company in 1928.

	Annual Growth	12/04	12/05	12/06	12/08	12/09
Sales ($mil.)	0.8%	–	–	10.2	10.7	10.4
Net income ($ mil.)	(42.5%)	–	–	0.4	0.0	0.0
Market value ($ mil.)	–	–	–	–	–	–
Employees	–	–	–	–	–	175

BUSY BEAVER BUILDING CENTERS, INC.

3130 WILLIAM PITT WAY BLDG A-6
PITTSBURGH, PA 152381360
Phone: 412 828-2323
Fax: –
Web: www.busybeaver.com

CEO: Frank Filmelk
CFO: Nicholas Demao
HR: –
FYE: December 30
Type: Private

They're busy as, well, you know what kind of animals at Busy Beaver Building Centers. The company has 16 stores in Ohio, Pennsylvania, and West Virginia selling ceilings, flooring, lumber, plumbing fixtures, and other building materials, along with garden supplies, hardware, power equipment, and tools. Busy Beaver serves the professional contractor as well as the do-it-yourselfer. The regional home improvement center chain was founded in 1962. A management group led by chairman and former CEO Charles Bender acquired the company in 1988 and now owns about one-quarter of Busy Beaver, which is facing heavyweight competition from big-box chains, such as Home Depot and Lowe's.

	Annual Growth	12/08	12/09	12/10	12/11	12/12
Sales ($mil.)	(1.3%)	–	–	41.5	40.8	40.4
Net income ($ mil.)	(8.4%)	–	–	0.4	0.4	0.3
Market value ($ mil.)	–	–	–	–	–	–
Employees	–	–	–	–	–	350

BUTLER HEALTH SYSTEM, INC.

1 HOSPITAL WAY
BUTLER, PA 160014670
Phone: 724 283-6666
Fax: –
Web: www.butlerhealthsystem.org

CEO: Ken Defurio
CFO: Anne Krebs
HR: –
FYE: June 30
Type: Private

Butler Health System (BHS) ushers in health care services for Pennsylvania residents. The not-for-profit provider operates a network of inpatient and outpatient health care facilities. Its primary location is the 300-bed Butler Memorial Hospital, which provides general surgical and medical care and specialty programs for the treatment of women's health, behavioral health, cancer, pain management, and other conditions. Other BHS locations include diagnostic, family practice, urgent care, and specialist facilities.

	Annual Growth	06/18	06/19	06/20	06/21	06/22
Sales ($mil.)	185.1%	–	0.2	0.1	4.8	5.6
Net income ($ mil.)	740.7%	–	0.0	(0.0)	4.6	3.3
Market value ($ mil.)	–	–	–	–	–	–
Employees	–	–	–	–	–	3,000

BUTLER MANUFACTURING COMPANY INC

1540 GENESSEE ST
KANSAS CITY, MO 641021069
Phone: 816 968-3000
Fax: -
Web: www.butlermfg.com

CEO: -
CFO: -
HR: -
FYE: June 30
Type: Private

Need an eight-story building fast? Not a problem for Butler Manufacturing, maker of pre-engineered buildings, structural systems, and roof and wall systems for nonresidential construction. Its leading brands include Butler and Varco Pruden. A subsidiary of Australia-based BlueScope Steel, Butler produces pre-engineered and custom-designed steel structures used in a range of projects, from offices to schools to shopping centers. Through its BUCON and Butler Heavy Structures units, the company provides general contracting services for large-scale projects. Butler also offers real estate development services. It distributes its products throughout North America.

BUTLER NATIONAL CORP.

One Aero Plaza
New Century, KS 66031
Phone: 913 780-9595
Fax: -
Web: www.butlernational.com

NBB: BUKS

CEO: Christopher J Reedy
CFO: Tad M McMahon
HR: -
FYE: April 30
Type: Public

This Butler is at the service of aircraft operators. Butler National's Avcon subsidiary (over half of sales) provides aircraft modification services, including the conversion of passenger planes to freighters. The company works mainly on Learjet models; it also modifies Beechcraft, Cessna, and Dassault Falcon aircraft. It adds aerial photography capability to aircraft and offers stability enhancements. The company's avionics unit makes airborne electronic switching components. Other Butler National businesses provide remote water and wastewater monitoring (SCADA Systems) and architectural services (BCS Design), as well as gaming management services to Indian tribes (Butler National Service Corporation; BNSC).

	Annual Growth	04/19	04/20	04/21	04/22	04/23
Sales ($mil.)	6.4%	58.7	65.9	61.5	73.5	75.2
Net income ($ mil.)	4.0%	3.9	4.2	1.4	10.4	4.5
Market value ($ mil.)	14.6%	30.8	39.2	46.1	71.4	53.0
Employees	(25.6%)	349	114	118	112	107

BVSN, LLC

401 CONGRESS AVE STE 2650
AUSTIN, TX 787013708
Phone: 512 524-6149
Fax: -
Web: -

CEO: Scott Brighton
CFO: -
HR: -
FYE: December 31
Type: Private

BroadVision gives companies a peek into the world of customer self-service. The company develops software that enables businesses to offer their customers personalized self-service via the Internet. Its software suite includes tools for integrating business processes with self-service operations; managing the sales process, including lead generation, execution, and customer service; connecting customers to personalized online views of content; and managing content from creation through distribution. BroadVision serves such industries as travel, retail, health care, and entertainment. Clients have included Canon, Oreck, PETCO, Vodafone, and the US Air Force. Founder and CEO Pehong Chen owns 37% of BroadVision.

BWMB, LLC

3787 MARTINEZ BLVD
MARTINEZ, GA 309072665
Phone: 706 863-6191
Fax: -
Web: www.maner.com

CEO: -
CFO: -
HR: -
FYE: December 31
Type: Private

You can build a manor house with what Maner Builders Supply Company can offer. It sells and distributes building supplies such as deck and railing, designed closets, doors, engineered lumber, fencing materials, glass, gypsum, masonry, roofing, and premium windows. The company offers industry-leading sales and support, delivery and logistics options, design expertise, and special. Maner Builders Supply carries products from manufacturers such as Bradley, Masonite, Ceco Door, Makita, and Atlantic. It was founded in 1951 as the Maner Hardware & Supply Company. In late 2020, the company was acquired by US LBM, a leading distributor of specialty building materials in the US.

	Annual Growth	12/10	12/11	12/14	12/15	12/16
Sales ($mil.)	8.2%	-	44.2	55.0	60.0	65.4
Net income ($ mil.)	45.0%	-	0.6	2.5	3.4	4.0
Market value ($ mil.)	-	-	-	-	-	-
Employees	-	-	-	-	-	325

BWX TECHNOLOGIES INC

800 Main Street, 4th Floor
Lynchburg, VA 24504
Phone: 980 365-4300
Fax: -
Web: www.bwxt.com

NYS: BWXT

CEO: -
CFO: -
HR: -
FYE: December 31
Type: Public

BWX Technologies is a specialty manufacturer of nuclear components, a developer of nuclear technologies and a service provider with an operating history of more than 100 years. Its core businesses focus on the design, engineering and manufacture of precision naval nuclear components, reactors and nuclear fuel for the US government. It also provides precision manufactured components, nuclear fuel and services to the commercial nuclear industry and provides special nuclear materials processing, environmental site restoration services, and a variety of products and services to customers in the critical medical radioisotopes and radiopharmaceuticals industries. The US government agencies are its largest customers. Additionally, the US is responsible for more than 80% of the sales.

	Annual Growth	12/19	12/20	12/21	12/22	12/23
Sales ($mil.)	7.1%	1,894.9	2,123.5	2,124.1	2,232.8	2,496.3
Net income ($ mil.)	0.2%	244.1	278.7	305.9	238.2	245.8
Market value ($ mil.)	5.4%	5,682.0	5,517.3	4,382.4	5,315.9	7,022.9
Employees	4.9%	6,450	6,700	6,600	7,000	7,800

BYCOR GENERAL CONTRACTORS, INC.

6490 MARINDUSTRY DR
SAN DIEGO, CA 921215297
Phone: 858 587-1901
Fax: -
Web: www.bycor.com

CEO: Scott Kaats
CFO: -
HR: -
FYE: December 31
Type: Private

Bycor General Contractors provides construction services for a variety of commercial, retail, institutional, civic, and leisure facilities in the San Diego area. Its offerings include tenant improvements, shell construction, build-to-suit, and LEED-certified services, and projects range from church sanctuaries to auto dealerships. The company has served clients including Western University of Health Sciences, Northrop Grumman, and San Diego National Bank. President Rich Byer, CEO Scott Kaats, and Van Smith founded co-founded Bycor General Contractors in 1981.

BYLINE BANCORP INC

NYS: BY

180 North LaSalle Street, Suite 300
Chicago, IL 60601
Phone: 773 244-7000
Fax: –
Web: www.bylinebancorp.com

CEO: Roberto R Herencia
CFO: Lindsay Corby
HR: –
FYE: December 31
Type: Public

Byline Bancorp is the holding for the full service Byline Bank, which serves small- and medium-sized businesses, financial sponsors, and consumers. The bank has been a community partner in its neighborhoods for over 100 years and operates more than 50 full service branch locations throughout the Chicago and Milwaukee metropolitan areas. Byline offers commercial and retail banking products and services and is one of the Top 10 Small Business Administration lenders in the US.

	Annual Growth	12/19	12/20	12/21	12/22	12/23
Assets ($mil.)	12.6%	5,521.8	6,390.7	6,696.2	7,362.9	8,882.0
Net income ($ mil.)	17.3%	57.0	37.5	92.8	88.0	107.9
Market value ($ mil.)	4.7%	856.5	676.2	1,196.9	1,005.3	1,031.1
Employees	1.3%	1,001	931	970	977	1,055

C & F FINANCIAL CORP.

NMS: CFFI

3600 La Grange Parkway
Toano, VA 23168
Phone: 804 843-2360
Fax: 804 843-3017
Web: www.cffc.com

CEO: Larry G Dillon
CFO: Jason E Long
HR: –
FYE: December 31
Type: Public

C&F Financial Corporation is the holding company for C&F Bank (aka Citizens and Farmers Bank), which operates about 20 branches in eastern Virginia. The bank targets individuals and local businesses, offering such products and services as checking and savings accounts, CDs, credit cards, and trust services. Commercial, industrial, and agricultural loans account for the largest portion of the company's loan portfolio (about 40%), which also includes residential mortgages, consumer auto loans, and consumer and construction loans.

	Annual Growth	12/19	12/20	12/21	12/22	12/23
Assets ($mil.)	10.1%	1,657.4	2,086.3	2,264.5	2,332.3	2,438.5
Net income ($ mil.)	5.8%	18.9	22.1	28.7	29.2	23.6
Market value ($ mil.)	5.4%	186.7	125.2	172.7	196.6	230.1
Employees	(2.0%)	643	697	650	613	594

C & K MARKET, INC.

850 OHARE PKWY STE 100
MEDFORD, OR 975047720
Phone: 541 469-3113
Fax: –
Web: www.ckmarket.com

CEO: –
CFO: –
HR: –
FYE: December 31
Type: Private

Family-owned C&K Market operates more than 40 supermarkets in southern Oregon and northern California, mostly under the name Ray's Food Place, but also under Shop Smart and C&K banners. The Shop Smart warehouse-style stores focus on value-priced groceries and household goods. Most of C&K's stores are situated in small, rural communities. C&K Market was founded in 1957 by Raymond "Ray" Nidiffer. Stung by competition from large national discounters, including Wal-Mart and Costco, the regional chain filed for bankruptcy in late 2013 and closed 15 supermarkets and sold 15 pharmacies. It emerged from bankruptcy in 2014.

	Annual Growth	12/05	12/06	12/07	12/09	12/10
Sales ($mil.)	(1.6%)	–	–	479.3	467.0	457.1
Net income ($ mil.)	245.6%	–	–	0.0	5.2	3.5
Market value ($ mil.)		–	–	–	–	–
Employees		–	–	–	–	2,000

C&S WHOLESALE GROCERS, LLC

7 CORPORATE DR
KEENE, NH 034315042
Phone: 603 354-7000
Fax: –
Web: www.cswg.com

CEO: –
CFO: –
HR: Jason Pineda
FYE: December 31
Type: Private

C&S Wholesale Grocers is an industry leader in supply chain solutions and wholesale grocery supply in the US. C&S now services customers of all sizes, supplying more than 7,700 independent supermarkets, chain stores, military bases, and institutions with over 137,000 different products. It provides access to multiple banner programs and more than 3,000 private label high-quality products. Its market-leading brands include Best Yet, That's Smart!, Exceptional Value, Piggly Wiggly, IGA, TopCare, and Simply Done. The company also provides a full range of services that range from the weekly newspaper or mailbox insert advertisements to in-store media promotions. Israel Cohen started the company with Abraham Siegel in 1918.

C. G. SCHMIDT, INC.

11777 W LAKE PARK DR
MILWAUKEE, WI 532243047
Phone: 414 577-1177
Fax: –
Web: www.cgschmidt.com

CEO: Richard L Schmidt Jr
CFO: –
HR: –
FYE: December 31
Type: Private

You can salute C. G. Schmidt as one of the top general contractors and construction managers in the Midwest. The company also offers design/build services. Markets include health care, senior living, commercial, education, industrial, parking structure, and municipal projects. C. G. Schmidt has completed projects for customers such as American Express, Ball Corporation, and The University of Wisconsin. The firm, founded in 1920 as Charles Schmidt & Sons Construction, is now in its fourth generation of family ownership and leadership with president and CEO Richard Schmidt, Jr.

C. OVERAA & CO.

200 PARR BLVD
RICHMOND, CA 948011120
Phone: 510 234-0926
Fax: –
Web: www.overaa.com

CEO: Jerry Overaa
CFO: –
HR: –
FYE: December 31
Type: Private

For more than a century, C. Overaa & Co. has been making its mark in Northern California. Norwegian immigrant and carpenter Carl Overaa founded the company in 1907 in order to help rebuild San Francisco after a major earthquake struck. Today the family-owned company builds institutional, commercial, industrial, public, and housing projects primarily in San Francisco's East Bay. It provides preconstruction, design/build, construction, sustainable building, and contracting services. The company's customers have included Courtyard by Marriott, the John Muir Medical Center, the US Postal Service, YMCA, and the University of California, Berkeley.

C. R. BARD, INC.

1 BECTON DR
FRANKLIN LAKES, NJ 074171815
Phone: 201 847-6800
Fax: –
Web: www.crbard.com

CEO: Timothy Ring
CFO: Christopher S Holland
HR: Mary Leib
FYE: December 31
Type: Private

CABLE ONE INC

210 E. Earll Drive
Phoenix, AZ 85012
Phone: 602 364-6000
Fax: –
Web: www.sparklight.com

NYS: CABO
CEO: Julia M Laulis
CFO: Steven S Cochran
HR: Kelly Gorman
FYE: December 31
Type: Public

Cable ONE is a leading broadband communications providers committed to connecting customers and communities. The company, through its fiber-rich infrastructure, provides residential customers with a wide portfolio of connectivity and entertainment services, including Gigabit speeds, advanced Wi-Fi, and video. Its core service areas include Arizona, Idaho, Mississippi, Missouri, Oklahoma, South Carolina, and Texas. Approximately 2.7 million subscribers receive data services, some 180,000 subscribers to video services, and around 132,000 subscribers to voice services. The company also offers voice-over-Internet-protocol (VoIP) computer telephony and digital video services. Quarter-fifth of revenue comes from Residential.

	Annual Growth	12/19	12/20	12/21	12/22	12/23
Sales ($mil.)	9.5%	1,168.0	1,325.2	1,605.8	1,706.0	1,678.1
Net income ($ mil.)	10.6%	178.6	304.4	291.8	234.1	267.4
Market value ($ mil.)	(21.8%)	8,360.7	12,513	9,905.3	3,998.5	3,126.4
Employees	2.1%	2,751	2,716	3,628	3,132	2,993

C.D. SMITH CONSTRUCTION, INC.

125 CAMELOT DR
FOND DU LAC, WI 549358038
Phone: 920 924-2900
Fax: –
Web: www.cdsmith.com

CEO: –
CFO: Robert Seibel
HR: –
FYE: September 30
Type: Private

One of the Midwest's top contractors, C.D. Smith Construction works on commercial, institutional, and industrial projects. It builds manufacturing, retail, correctional, health care, and education facilities, as well as water treatment plants. The company offers general contracting and design/build services and also provides specialty contracting services such as steel erection, masonry and concrete work, carpentry, and demolition. Charles D. Smith, grandfather of president Gary Smith, founded the company in 1936.

CABLEVISION SYSTEMS CORPORATION

1111 STEWART AVE
BETHPAGE, NY 117143581
Phone: 516 803-2300
Fax: –
Web: www.cablevision.com

CEO: –
CFO: –
HR: –
FYE: December 31
Type: Private

Altice USA (formerly Cablevision Systems) is a leading provider of digital television, phone, and internet services in the New York City and Long Island area. All told, the company delivers broadband, pay television, telephony services, Wi-Fi hotspot access, proprietary content, and advertising services to about 4.9 million residential and business customers in more than 20 states. The company, which is the US business of international media and communications group Altice N.V., went public in 2017.

C.R. ENGLAND, INC.

4701 W 2100 S
SALT LAKE CITY, UT 841201223
Phone: 800 421-9004
Fax: –
Web: www.crengland.com

CEO: Chad England
CFO: Tj McGeean
HR: Eugene England
FYE: December 31
Type: Private

C.R. England is one of North America's largest and long-running transportation companies. C.R. England services include OTR, and Mexico/Cross-Border Truckload services in addition to Dedicated and Intermodal services. The family-owned company's fleet includes more than 4,000 tractors, over 6,000 trailers, and some 1,500 containers. England Logistics, a wholly owned subsidiary of C.R. England, is one of the nation's top third-party logistics firms. The company is a privately-owned, family-run business since its founding in 1920.

	Annual Growth	12/05	12/06	12/07	12/11	12/12
Sales ($mil.)	13.7%	–	–	829.8	1,315.3	1,579.3
Net income ($ mil.)	6.2%	–	–	41.8	55.9	56.5
Market value ($ mil.)	–	–	–	–	–	–
Employees	–	–	–	–	–	6,500

CABOT CORP.

Two Seaport Lane, Suite 1400
Boston, MA 02210
Phone: 617 345-0100
Fax: –
Web: www.cabotcorp.com

NYS: CBT
CEO: Sean D Keohane
CFO: Erica McLaughlin
HR: –
FYE: September 30
Type: Public

Cabot is a global specialty chemicals and performance materials company. The company is a leading maker of carbon black, a compound that strengthens tires, hoses, belts, and molded products. It also makes specialty carbons and metal oxides used in automotive, construction, infrastructure, and energy applications. Cabot's activated carbon products are used to purify air and water and food and beverages. One of the few carbon black manufacturers with a worldwide presence, Cabot's biggest market is China. The company goes back to 1882 when Godfrey and Samuel Cabot opened a carbon black plant in Pennsylvania.

	Annual Growth	09/19	09/20	09/21	09/22	09/23
Sales ($mil.)	4.2%	3,337.0	2,614.0	3,409.0	4,321.0	3,931.0
Net income ($ mil.)	29.8%	157.0	(238.0)	250.0	209.0	445.0
Market value ($ mil.)	11.2%	2,503.6	1,990.4	2,768.8	3,529.5	3,826.7
Employees	(1.3%)	4,500	4,500	4,500	4,200	4,268

CABRAL ROOFING & WATERPROOFING CORPORATION

675 W TERRACE DR
SAN DIMAS, CA 917732917
Phone: 909 305-0063
Fax: –
Web: www.cabralroofing.com

CEO: –
CFO: –
HR: –
FYE: December 31
Type: Private

Mansard roofs, gabled, flat, A-frame, or otherwise -- Cabral Roofing & Waterproofing has them covered. The company offers roofing installation, maintenance, and repair services for mostly commercial buildings in Southern California. Its clients include architects and engineers, churches, government facilities, hospitals, industrial operators, school districts, and universities. Clients have included Bed, Bath, & Beyond, Pepsi, County of Los Angeles, and UCLA. Founded in 1997, Cabral Roofing & Waterproofing is owned by president Andrew Cabral and the Cabral family.

CACHE VALLEY ELECTRIC COMPANY

875 N 1000 W
LOGAN, UT 843217800
Phone: 435 752-6405
Fax: –
Web: www.cve.com

CEO: –
CFO: Brett Heggi
HR: –
FYE: August 31
Type: Private

Family-owned Cache Valley Electric (CVE) is one of the largest electrical contractors in the West. With operations in Utah, Oregon, Arkansas, Hawaii, and Texas, CVE installs power and lighting systems in commercial, industrial, and government facilities. The company is a provider of ground-to-cloud solutions that include transmission lines and substations; power distribution; signals and utilities; heavy industrial; service and maintenance; electrical construction; teledata, multimedia, and distributed antenna systems; systems integration as well as network and physical security; network infrastructure; and cloud computing. Cache Valley Electric was founded in 1915 by Henry F. Laub.

	Annual Growth	12/02	12/03	12/04	12/05*	08/20
Sales ($mil.)	(35.9%)	–	76.3	91.9	107.6	0.0
Net income ($ mil.)	–	–	7.6	4.1	9.0	(0.1)
Market value ($ mil.)	–	–	–	–	–	–
Employees	–	–	–	–	–	1,000

*Fiscal year change

CACI INTERNATIONAL INC

12021 Sunset Hills Road
Reston, VA 20190
Phone: 703 841-7800
Fax: 703 841-7882
Web: www.caci.com

NYS: CACI
CEO: John S Mengucci
CFO: Jeffrey D Maclauchlan
HR: –
FYE: June 30
Type: Public

CACI International Inc. (CACI) is a leading provider of Expertise and Technology to Enterprise and Mission customers in support of national security missions and government modernization/transformation in the intelligence, defense, and federal civilian sectors, both domestically and internationally. It provides modernize business systems, command and control, communications, cyber security, intelligence services, enterprise information technology, and investigation and litigation support. CACI serves the US Department of Defense (DoD), departments of the US government, various state and local government agencies, foreign governments, and commercial enterprises. The company operates through offices and subsidiaries in North America and Europe. The majority of the company's sales were generated in the US.

	Annual Growth	06/19	06/20	06/21	06/22	06/23
Sales ($mil.)	7.7%	4,986.3	5,720.0	6,044.1	6,202.9	6,702.5
Net income ($ mil.)	9.7%	265.6	321.5	457.4	366.8	384.7
Market value ($ mil.)	13.6%	4,664.0	4,944.2	5,816.0	6,423.7	7,770.1
Employees	1.0%	22,100	22,900	22,000	22,000	23,000

CADDO INTERNATIONAL INC

202 N. Thomas, Suite 4
Shreveport, LA 71107-6539
Phone: 318 424-6396
Fax: –
Web: –

CEO: –
CFO: –
HR: –
FYE: December 31
Type: Public

Caddo International (formerly Petrol Industries), a small-time player in the petroleum sector, provides oil and gas exploration and production support and services in Louisiana and Texas. The independent's oil field services include well servicing, connections, and lease maintenance. Caddo is focusing on providing contracting services in Caddo, Desoto, Bossier, and Claiborne Parishes, as well as certain areas in East Texas. As a way to increase shareholder value, in 2009 the company spun off subsidiary, Petrolind Drilling Company, a drilling operation with a fully equipped drilling rig. In 2010 the company agreed to be acquired by oil and gas and lighting concern EGPI Firecreek.

	Annual Growth	12/00	12/01	12/02	12/03	12/04
Sales ($mil.)	0.2%	0.8	0.5	0.4	0.8	0.8
Net income ($ mil.)	–	–	(0.0)	(0.2)	(0.2)	(0.0)	0.0
Market value ($ mil.)	(7.9%)	0.0	0.0	0.0	0.0	0.0
Employees	6.8%	10	13	13	13	13

CADENCE DESIGN SYSTEMS INC

2655 Seely Avenue, Building 5
San Jose, CA 95134
Phone: 408 943-1234
Fax: –
Web: www.cadence.com

NMS: CDNS
CEO: Anirudh Devgan
CFO: John M Wall
HR: –
FYE: December 31
Type: Public

Cadence Design Systems is a leader in electronic system design, building upon more than 30 years of computational software expertise. Customers use Cadence products to design integrated circuits (ICs), systems-on-chip (SoCs), printed circuit boards (PCBs), smartphones, laptop computers, gaming systems, and more. Cadence offers software, hardware, services and reusable IC design blocks, which are commonly referred to as intellectual property (IP). The company also provides technical support and maintenance to facilitate customer's use of its software, hardware and IP solutions. International customers account for nearly 55% of the company's sales.

	Annual Growth	12/19*	01/21	01/22*	12/22	12/23
Sales ($mil.)	15.0%	2,336.3	2,682.9	2,988.2	3,561.7	4,090.0
Net income ($ mil.)	1.3%	989.0	590.6	696.0	849.0	1,041.1
Market value ($ mil.)	40.3%	19,098	37,069	50.632	43,647	74,005
Employees	8.4%	8,100	8,800	9,300	10,200	11,200

*Fiscal year change

CADENCE MCSHANE CONSTRUCTION COMPANY LLC

5057 KELLER SPRINGS RD STE 500
ADDISON, TX 750016231
Phone: 972 239-2336
Fax: –
Web: www.cadencemcshane.com

CEO: James A McShane
CFO: –
HR: –
FYE: September 30
Type: Private

With a certain cadence, Cadence McShane Construction has been right in step with the top contractors in the US. A part of development and construction group The McShane Companies, it provides general construction, construction management, and design/build services for commercial, institutional, and industrial projects in Texas and the central US. The firm is known for its school and community projects throughout Texas. It also provides services to the manufacturing, office, multi-family residential, government, hospitality, and retail markets. Cadence McShane was founded in 1995.

	Annual Growth	09/05	09/06	09/07	09/09	09/10
Sales ($mil.)	(12.7%)	–	–	237.5	259.2	158.2
Net income ($ mil.)	(45.9%)	–	–	7.8	4.9	1.2
Market value ($ mil.)	–	–	–	–	–	–
Employees	–	–	–	–	–	225

CADIZ INC
NMS: CDZI

550 South Hope Street, Suite 2850
Los Angeles, CA 90071
Phone: 213 271-1600
Fax: -
Web: www.cadizinc.com

CEO: Scott S Slater
CFO: Stanley E Speer
HR: -
FYE: December 31
Type: Public

Cadiz hopes to strike gold with water. The land and water resource development firm owns some 45,000 acres of land -- and the groundwater underneath it -- in eastern San Bernardino County, California near the Colorado River Aqueduct and in the eastern Mojave Desert. Cadiz is betting on its groundwater storage and distribution project as water supplies become increasingly scarce in Southern California and as the state aims to increase its renewable energy production levels. Cadiz is also looking into commercial and residential development of its land. It has some agricultural assets that are leased as lemon groves and grape vineyards.

	Annual Growth	12/19	12/20	12/21	12/22	12/23
Sales ($mil.)	45.8%	0.4	0.5	0.6	1.5	2.0
Net income ($ mil.)	-	(29.5)	(37.8)	(31.2)	(24.8)	(31.4)
Market value ($ mil.)	(29.0%)	735.2	710.5	257.5	166.8	186.8
Employees	18.9%	9	10	10	9	18

CAESARS ENTERTAINMENT INC (NEW)
NMS: CZR

100 West Liberty Street, 12th Floor
Reno, NV 89501
Phone: 775 328-0100
Fax: -
Web: www.eldoradoresorts.com

CEO: Thomas R Reeg
CFO: Bret Yunker
HR: Jennifer Jennings
FYE: December 31
Type: Public

Caesars Entertainment is a geographically diversified gaming and hospitality company that was founded in 1973 by the Carano family with the opening of the Eldorado Hotel Casino. Its primary source of revenue generates by gaming operations and utilizes its hotels, restaurants, bars, entertainment, racing, retail shops, and other services to attract customers to its properties. It has some 20 casinos owned and around 25 casinos leased in the US. It currently owned, leased, or managed an aggregate of over 50 domestic properties in around 15 states with approximately 52,800 slot machines, VLTs, and e-tables; approximately 2,800 table games, and approximately 47,200 hotel rooms.

	Annual Growth	12/19	12/20	12/21	12/22	12/23
Sales ($mil.)	46.1%	2,528.2	3,474.0	9,570.0	10,821	11,528
Net income ($ mil.)	76.5%	81.0	(1,757.0)	(1,019.0)	(899.0)	786.0
Market value ($ mil.)	(5.8%)	12,870	16,028	20,184	8,977.3	10,117
Employees	34.7%	15,500	54,000	49,000	49,000	51,000

CAI INTERNATIONAL, INC.

1 MARKET PLZ STE 2400
SAN FRANCISCO, CA 941051102
Phone: 415 788-0100
Fax: -
Web: www.capps.com

CEO: Timothy B Page
CFO: Timothy B Page
HR: -
FYE: December 31
Type: Private

CAI International (CAI) one of the world's leading transportation finance companies. It is a global transportation company offering intermodal container leasing and sales and has grown into a leading expert in transportation operations and finance. With offices around the world and a broad network of agents and depots, CAI serves hundreds of the world's leading shipping lines, container operators, and logistics providers. The company was founded in 1989 and is a group company of Mitsubishi HC Capital Inc.

CAJUN INDUSTRIES HOLDINGS, LLC

15635 AIRLINE HWY
BATON ROUGE, LA 708177318
Phone: 225 753-5857
Fax: -
Web: www.cajunusa.com

CEO: Todd Grigsby
CFO: Shane Recile
HR: -
FYE: September 30
Type: Private

Offering a mixed gumbo of services, Cajun Industries builds oil refineries, power plants, process plants, water-treatment plants, and other industrial and infrastructure projects, primarily in Louisiana and Texas. Subsidiary Cajun Constructors provides a full range of services from design/build to maintenance; Cajun Deep Foundations offers drilling, piles installation, and related services. Cajun Maritime focuses on marine, coastal, and oilfield services including construction, repair, and power distribution. Cajun Equipment Services manages a fleet of trucks and trailers that transport heavy and specialized loads. Chairman and owner Lane Grigsby founded the company as Cajun Contractors and Engineers in 1973.

	Annual Growth	09/17	09/18	09/19	09/20	09/21
Sales ($mil.)	(15.4%)	-	515.8	478.8	429.3	312.7
Net income ($ mil.)	(1.2%)	-	19.8	5.9	14.3	19.1
Market value ($ mil.)	-	-	-	-	-	-
Employees	-	-	-	-	-	1,500

CAL-MAINE FOODS INC
NMS: CALM

1052 Highland Colony Pkwy, Suite 200
Ridgeland, MS 39157
Phone: 601 948-6813
Fax: 601 969-0905
Web: www.calmainefoods.com

CEO: Adolphus B Baker
CFO: Max P Bowman
HR: -
FYE: June 3
Type: Public

Cal-Maine Foods is the nation's largest fresh shell egg producer and marketer with egg products processing facilities capable of producing approximately 43,140 lbs. per hour. Its total flock consists of approximately 42.2 million layers and 11.5 million pullets and breeders. It is also one of the top suppliers of specialty shell eggs, such as Omega-3 enhanced and organic eggs, marketed under the Egg-Land's Best, Land O' Lakes, and 4-Grain brands. Cal-Maine's operations consist of hatching chicks, growing and maintaining flocks of pullets, layers, and breeders, making feed, and producing, processing, packaging and distributing shell eggs. Customers include national and regional grocery stores, supermarkets, club stores, and foodservice distributors and consumers of egg products.

	Annual Growth	06/19*	05/20	05/21	05/22*	06/23
Sales ($mil.)	23.3%	1,361.2	1,351.6	1,349.0	1,777.2	3,146.2
Net income ($ mil.)	93.4%	54.2	18.4	2.1	132.7	758.0
Market value ($ mil.)	6.5%	1,813.4	2,182.7	1,710.0	2,359.1	2,329.7
Employees	(3.9%)	3,490	3,636	3,286	2,985	2,976

*Fiscal year change

CALAMOS ASSET MANAGEMENT, INC.

2020 CALAMOS CT OFC
NAPERVILLE, IL 605632796
Phone: 630 245-7200
Fax: -
Web: www.calamos.com

CEO: John S Koudounis
CFO: -
HR: -
FYE: December 31
Type: Private

Calamos Asset Management wants to make the most of your assets. Through its subsidiaries, the company provides money management and investment advice to institutional and individual investors. The firm manages more than 30 mutual funds, closed-end funds, separately managed portfolios, private funds, exchange-traded funds and UCITS funds representing a range of investment strategies and risk levels. Calamos has nearly $25 billion of assets under management, with most of it invested in US and global equities, though it also employs fixed income, convertible, and alternative investment strategies. The firm mainly distributes its products through large broker-dealers. Calamos was taken private by top management in 2017.

CALAMP CORP

NMS: CAMP

15635 Alton Parkway, Suite 250
Irvine, CA 92618
Phone: 949 600-5600
Fax: –
Web: www.calamp.com

CEO: Jason Cohenour
CFO: Jikun Kim
HR: –
FYE: February 28
Type: Public

CalAmp is a globally connected intelligence company that leverages a data-driven solutions ecosystem to help people and organizations improve operational performance. It solves complex problems for customers within the market verticals of transportation and logistics, commercial and government fleets, industrial equipment, K12 fleets, and consumer vehicles by providing solutions that track, monitor, and protect their vital assets with real-time visibility into a user's vehicles, assets, drivers, and cargo, giving organizations greater understanding and control of their operations. It provides asset tracking units, mobile telematics devices, fixed and mobile wireless gateways, and routers for mobile resource management (MRM) and original equipment manufacturers (OEM). CalAmp keeps track of it all through cloud-based telematics and applications offered through Software & Subscription Services. It generates Nearly 65% of revenue in the US.

	Annual Growth	02/19	02/20	02/21	02/22	02/23
Sales ($mil.)	(5.1%)	363.8	366.1	308.6	295.8	294.9
Net income ($ mil.)	–	18.4	(79.3)	(56.3)	(28.0)	(32.5)
Market value ($ mil.)	(25.6%)	22.6	15.6	18.2	11.5	6.9
Employees	(8.8%)	931	1,090	983	887	644

CALATLANTIC GROUP, INC.

1100 WILSON BLVD STE 2100
ARLINGTON, VA 222092295
Phone: 240 532-3806
Fax: –
Web: www.lennar.com

CEO: Larry T Nicholson
CFO: Jeff J McCall
HR: –
FYE: December 31
Type: Private

CalAtlantic builds homes from California to the Atlantic Coast. Targeting entry level, move-up, and luxury market homebuyers, the builder constructs homes in upwards of 40 metropolitan markets across 17 states in the West, Southwest, Southeast, and North. Its houses typically range in size from 1,100 sq. ft. to more than 6,000 sq. ft., with prices ranging from $165,000 to more than $2 million and averaging around $480,000 each. It also builds townhomes and condominiums, and buys and develops tracts of high-quality land (both alone and through joint ventures). CalAtlantic, the fourth largest homebuilder in the US, offers home loans to its customers in all of its markets as well. In 2018, larger rival Lennar Homes acquired CalAtlantic for $6 billion.

CALAVO GROWERS, INC.

NMS: CVGW

1141-A Cummings Road
Santa Paula, CA 93060
Phone: 805 525-1245
Fax: 805 921-3223
Web: www.calavo.com

CEO: Lecil Cole
CFO: Shawn Munsell
HR: –
FYE: October 31
Type: Public

Calavo Growers is a global leader in the avocado industry and a provider of value-added fresh food. The company is expert in marketing and distributing avocados, prepared avocados, and other perishable foods, which allows the company to deliver a wide array of fresh and prepared food products to retail grocery, food service, club stores, mass merchandisers, food distributors, and wholesalers on a worldwide basis. Calavo procures avocados from California, Mexico, and other growing regions around the world. Its products are marketed under the Garden Highway Fresh Cut, Garden Highway, Garden Highway Chef Essentials, El Dorado, Fresh Ripe, Select, and Taste of Paradise brands, among others. Calavo distributes its products both domestically and internationally. Calavo was founded in 1924 to market California avocados.

	Annual Growth	10/19	10/20	10/21	10/22	10/23
Sales ($mil.)	(5.0%)	1,195.8	1,059.4	1,055.8	1,191.1	971.9
Net income ($ mil.)	–	36.6	(13.6)	(11.8)	(6.2)	(8.3)
Market value ($ mil.)	(26.5%)	1,540.4	1,192.3	714.0	614.4	450.1
Employees	(4.3%)	3,657	3,971	3,676	3,266	3,064

CALCOT, LTD.

3701 PEGASUS DR
BAKERSFIELD, CA 933086842
Phone: 661 395-6866
Fax: –
Web: www.calcot.com

CEO: Paul Bush
CFO: Roxanne Wang
HR: –
FYE: August 31
Type: Private

With cotton-producing members in Arizona, California, New Mexico, and Texas, Calcot is one of the top cotton-marketing cooperatives in the US. Members of the co-op primarily grow premium-grade Far Western cottons, including California Upland, Pima, and San Joaquin Acala (SJV Acala). The company operates three warehousing locations which can store 600,000 bales of cotton per year. Calcot has gained and maintained a highly-regarded reputation among cotton producers, textile mills and the entire cotton industry.

	Annual Growth	08/09	08/10	08/11	08/12	08/13
Sales ($mil.)	(30.0%)	–	–	399.6	306.2	195.7
Net income ($ mil.)	61.5%	–	–	0.6	5.3	1.6
Market value ($ mil.)	–	–	–	–	–	–
Employees	–	–	–	–	–	43

CALERES INC

NYS: CAL

8300 Maryland Avenue
St. Louis, MO 63105
Phone: 314 854-4000
Fax: –
Web: www.caleres.com

CEO: John W Schmidt
CFO: Jack P Calandra
HR: –
FYE: January 28
Type: Public

Caleres is a global footwear company that operates retail shoe stores and e-commerce websites, and designs, develops, sources, manufactures and distributes footwear for people of all ages. It operates over 965 value-priced family footwear stores under the Famous Footwear, Sam Edelman, Naturalizer, and Allen Edmonds banners in the US, Canada, China, and Guam. The company also sells shoes online and licenses Dr. Scholl's, LifeStride, Franco Sarto, Ryk , and Blowfish Malibu-branded footwear, among others. It distributes footwear worldwide through approximately 4,600 retailers, including independent retailers, chain (DSW), department stores (Nordstrom), catalogs, and online retailers. The company was originally founded as Brown Shoe Company in 1878.

	Annual Growth	02/19	02/20*	01/21	01/22	01/23
Sales ($mil.)	1.2%	2,834.8	2,921.6	2,117.1	2,777.6	2,968.1
Net income ($ mil.)	–	(5.4)	62.8	(439.1)	137.0	181.7
Market value ($ mil.)	(4.0%)	1,057.5	626.8	539.7	824.3	897.2
Employees	(5.2%)	11,500	11,400	8,400	9,200	9,300

*Fiscal year change

CALGON CARBON CORPORATION

3000 GSK DR
MOON TOWNSHIP, PA 151081381
Phone: 412 787-6700
Fax: –
Web: www.calgoncarbon.com

CEO: Stevan R Schott
CFO: Robert Fortwangler
HR: Kimberly Bruce
FYE: December 31
Type: Private

Calgon Carbon is a global leader in activated carbons and purification systems. It offers purification and a variety of industrial and commercial manufacturing processes. Services include ballast water treatment, ultraviolet light disinfection, and advanced ion-exchange technologies used in the treatment of drinking water, wastewater, odor control, pollution abatement, and a variety of industrial and commercial manufacturing processes. With more than 240 patents, its products find usage in more than 700 discrete market applications including air, drinking water, foods, and pharmaceuticals purification, and the removal of mercury emissions from coal-powered electrical plants.

	Annual Growth	12/13	12/14	12/15	12/16	12/17
Sales ($mil.)	3.7%	–	555.1	535.0	514.2	619.8
Net income ($ mil.)	(24.7%)	–	49.4	43.5	13.8	21.1
Market value ($ mil.)	–	–	–	–	–	–
Employees	–	–	–	–	–	1,334

CALHOUN ENTERPRISES, INC.

4155 LOMAC ST STE G
MONTGOMERY, AL 361062864
Phone: 334 272-4400
Fax: –
Web: www.calhounent.com

CEO: –
CFO: –
HR: –
FYE: December 31
Type: Private

Calhoun Enterprises operates a handful of supermarkets under the Calhoun Foods banner in central Alabama. The Alabama grocer locates its stores in buildings vacated by national chains, such as Winn-Dixie, and in areas the larger national chains avoid. The family-run company is one of the largest African-American-owned and -run businesses in the South. Calhoun Enterprises was founded by president and CEO Gregory Calhoun (who started his food industry career as a package clerk at a local supermarket when he was 14 years old) in 1984. The company also runs subsidiaries involved in telecommunications, warehousing, consulting, investments, and food brokering and distribution.

	Annual Growth	12/04	12/05	12/06	12/08	12/09
Sales ($mil.)	(16.1%)	–	–	36.0	–	21.3
Net income ($ mil.)	(26.9%)	–	–	1.0	–	0.4
Market value ($ mil.)	–	–	–	–	–	–
Employees	–	–	–	–	–	352

CALIBER IMAGING & DIAGNOSTIC INC

NBB: LCDX

50 Methodist Hill Drive, Suite 1000
Rochester, NY 14623
Phone: 585 239-9800
Fax: –
Web: www.caliberid.com

CEO: L M Hone
CFO: John Sprague
HR: –
FYE: December 31
Type: Public

Lucid, Inc. hopes to have a clear understanding of skin cancer. The company's medical imaging device, the VivaScope, cuts down on the ouch factor for skin biopsies. The VivaScope takes a microscopic-resolution picture of a skin lesion, a less painful alternative to the traditional method of cutting out a portion of the lesion to ship off to the lab. Lucid, Inc. has also developed a complementary network called VivaNet that allows immediate transfer of the images over the Internet for pathologists to diagnose melanoma and give patients same-day results. The VivaScope is cleared for sale and use in Australia, China, the European Union, and the US. Lucid, Inc. filed a modest $28.75 million IPO in April 2011.

	Annual Growth	12/09	12/10	12/11	12/12	12/13
Sales ($mil.)	8.3%	–	2.6	3.6	2.4	3.3
Net income ($ mil.)	–	–	(4.3)	(9.1)	(9.8)	(5.5)
Market value ($ mil.)	–	–	–	–	12.8	4.7
Employees	–	–	–	28	27	26

CALIBRE SYSTEMS, INC.

6361 WALKER LN STE 1100
ALEXANDRIA, VA 223103284
Phone: 703 797-8500
Fax: –
Web: www.calibresys.com

CEO: Richard Y Pineda
CFO: Craig College
HR: Cortney Meador
FYE: February 28
Type: Private

When it comes to information technology, CALIBRE aims to please. The employee-owned company provides information technology and management services to government and commercial clients in the US. It specializes in data analytics, modeling and simulation, financial and cost management, land management, logistics, and strategic planning, among other areas. The company serves clients in the public and private sectors: Defense, Federal / Civil, National Security, and Commercial. To expand its capabilities, the company partners with academia, large and small businesses, and has entered a joint venture with VC Solutions. CALIBRE operates from a handful of US offices, as well as on-site at customer facilities.

	Annual Growth	02/06	02/07	02/08	02/09	02/11
Sales ($mil.)	16.8%	–	–	99.0	109.0	157.9
Net income ($ mil.)	25.4%	–	–	5.2	6.2	10.3
Market value ($ mil.)	–	–	–	–	–	–
Employees	–	–	–	–	–	707

CALIFORNIA BEER AND BEVERAGE DISTRIBUTORS

1415 L ST STE 890
SACRAMENTO, CA 958143964
Phone: 916 441-5402
Fax: –
Web: www.cbbd.com

CEO: –
CFO: –
HR: –
FYE: December 31
Type: Private

Dude, do you know where the keg party is? The California Beer and Beverage Distributors does! The nonprofit trade organization comprises more than 100 independent beer distributors, brewers, and vendors. It offers members a software system for keeping track of liquor licenses and, thereby, avoiding fines from the California Alcohol Beverage Control, educates the public about small beer distributors, sponsors responsible alcohol consumption programs, lobbies the California legislature, and hosts an annual convention. California Beer and Beverage Distributors was formed in 1947.

	Annual Growth	12/15	12/16	12/17	12/21	12/22
Sales ($mil.)	(3.1%)	–	3.2	3.1	2.7	2.7
Net income ($ mil.)	(16.1%)	–	0.4	0.3	0.5	0.1
Market value ($ mil.)	–	–	–	–	–	–
Employees	–	–	–	–	–	8

CALIFORNIA CEDAR PRODUCTS COMPANY

2385 ARCH AIRPORT RD # 50
STOCKTON, CA 952064403
Phone: 209 932-5002
Fax: –
Web: www.calcedar.com

CEO: Charles Berolzheimer
CFO: Susan Macintyre
HR: –
FYE: December 31
Type: Private

Pencil pushers everywhere are beholden to California Cedar Products Company. Founded in 1919, family-owned CalCedar is a leading supplier of wooden slats used in making wood-cased pencils, including art and cosmetic varieties. The company also makes its own brand of pencils (California Republic Stationers, EcoSlat, and ForestChoice) and pencils for other customers. CalCedar's products are sold worldwide. It also operates its business overseas; the company moved its slat production plant from California to China and boasts a factory in Thailand. CalCedar sold its Duraflame log business, which it invented in 1969, to Clorox in 1978 and has exited the supply siding and decking business.

CALIFORNIA CENTER FOR THE ARTS, ESCONDIDO, FOUNDATION

340 N ESCONDIDO BLVD
ESCONDIDO, CA 920252600
Phone: 760 839-4138
Fax: –
Web: www.artcenter.org

CEO: –
CFO: –
HR: –
FYE: June 30
Type: Private

The California Center For The Arts, Escondido, promotes musical acts, performers, and art exhibitions for educational and entertainment purposes. Its performing arts center showcases musicians and performers of various genres, ranging from classical pianists and country vocalists to traveling tango troupes and Chinese acrobats. The museum plays constant host to touring and original art exhibits and lecturers. In addition to presentations, the center offers public education programs, which are funded through government and foundation grants, corporate sponsorships, private gifts, admissions, and ticket sales. It also operates a conference center for meetings and banquets and provides catering services.

	Annual Growth	06/16	06/17	06/18	06/20	06/21
Sales ($mil.)	0.3%	–	5.2	5.8	6.4	5.2
Net income ($ mil.)	(1.4%)	–	0.2	(0.0)	(0.5)	0.2
Market value ($ mil.)	–	–	–	–	–	–
Employees	–	–	–	–	–	185

CALIFORNIA COASTAL COMMUNITIES, INC.

6 EXECUTIVE CIR STE 250
IRVINE, CA 926146732
Phone: 949 250-7700
Fax: –
Web: www.hearthside-homes.com

CEO: Raymond J Pacini
CFO: Sandra G Sciutto
HR: –
FYE: December 31
Type: Private

The tide is turning for California Coastal Communities. Through operating subsidiaries Hearthside Homes and Signal Landmark, the company builds homes and develops residential communities in Southern California. Long wrapped up in a battle over land development rights, California Coastal Communities has begun development of its Brightwater project, some 215 acres (about half of which is undevelopable land) situated near important wetlands in Bolsa Chica, the last undeveloped strip of coastal property in Orange County. Besides the controversial parcels, the company has homebuilding operations in Los Angeles County. California Coastal Communities emerged from Chapter 11 bankruptcy in March 2011.

CALIFORNIA COMMUNITY FOUNDATION

221 S FIGUEROA ST STE 400
LOS ANGELES, CA 900123760
Phone: 213 413-4130
Fax: –
Web: www.calfund.org

CEO: Antonia Hernandez
CFO: Steve Cobb
HR: Sandra Gayle
FYE: June 30
Type: Private

California Community Foundation supports not-for-profit organizations and public institutions in the Los Angeles area. The organization performs its function by offering funding for health and human services, affordable housing, early childhood education, and community arts and culture. The 24th Street Theatre, Antelope Valley Hospital, and Community Arts Partnership are among the organizations to have received the foundation's grant funding. In times of emergency, it has also pitched in to help groups in other areas. California Community Foundation was founded in 1915.

	Annual Growth	06/08	06/09	06/10	06/11	06/12
Assets ($mil.)	(1.3%)	–	–	1,120.5	1,242.4	1,092.0
Net income ($ mil.)	(9.0%)	–	–	85.4	139.6	70.7
Market value ($ mil.)	–	–	–	–	–	–
Employees	–	–	–	–	–	60

CALIFORNIA DEPARTMENT OF WATER RESOURCES

715 P ST
SACRAMENTO, CA 958146400
Phone: 916 653-9394
Fax: –
Web: water.ca.gov

CEO: –
CFO: –
HR: –
FYE: June 30
Type: Private

The California Department of Water Resources knows that water is gold. The agency is dedicated to managing the state's water resources in partnership with other agencies. Its core areas include designing the State Water Project (which supplies water to some 25 million farms, businesses, and residents), providing legislative guidance, creating recreational opportunities, educating the public, and offering technical and financial support for local planning and regional water management. The department also provides flood control and dam safety services, as well as plans for future water needs for the state.

CALIFORNIA FIRST LEASING CORP

NBB: CFNB

5000 Birch Street, Suite 500
Newport Beach, CA 92660
Phone: 949 255-0500
Fax: 949 255-0501
Web: www.calfirstlease.com

CEO: Patrick E Paddon
CFO: S L Jewett
HR: –
FYE: June 30
Type: Public

California First National Bancorp (CFNB) is a leasing company and a bank. Its California First Leasing (CalFirst Leasing) subsidiary leases equipment for a wide variety of industries including computers and software. Other leases include retail point-of-sale systems, office furniture, and manufacturing, telecommunications, and medical equipment. The bank holding company also operates California First National Bank (CalFirst Bank), a branchless FDIC-insured retail bank that conducts business mainly over the Internet, but also by mail and phone. About three-quarters of its revenue comes from interest.

	Annual Growth	06/19	06/20	06/21	06/22	06/23
Assets ($mil.)	(7.1%)	304.9	267.8	242.9	216.5	227.4
Net income ($ mil.)	23.1%	7.3	(2.4)	36.2	(12.7)	16.9
Market value ($ mil.)	(2.4%)	153.3	148.5	177.7	168.8	139.2
Employees	–	–	–	–	–	–

CALIFORNIA INDEPENDENT SYSTEM OPERATOR CORPORATION

250 OUTCROPPING WAY
FOLSOM, CA 956308773
Phone: 916 351-4400
Fax: –
Web: www.caiso.com

CEO: –
CFO: –
HR: –
FYE: December 31
Type: Private

The California Independent System Operator (California ISO) manages nearly 26,000-mile power transmission system (about 80% of California's power grid), balancing wholesale supply to meet retail demand. The enterprise maintains reliability on one of the largest and most modern power grids in the world, and operates a transparent, accessible wholesale energy market. The California ISO provides open and non-discriminatory access to the bulk of the state's wholesale transmission grid, supported by a competitive energy market and comprehensive infrastructure planning efforts. It also operates a competitive wholesale power market designed to promote a broad range of resources at lower prices. The ISO opened its two California control centers in 1998 as the state restructured its wholesale electricity industry.

CALIFORNIA INSTITUTE OF TECHNOLOGY

1200 E CALIFORNIA BLVD
PASADENA, CA 911250001
Phone: 626 395-6811
Fax: –
Web: www.caltech.edu

CEO: –
CFO: –
HR: –
FYE: September 30
Type: Private

The California Institute of Technology (Caltech) is a world-renowned science and engineering institute that marshals some of the world's brightest minds and most innovative tools to address fundamental scientific questions and pressing societal challenges. The institute enrolls over 2,395 students and offers about 30 majors across six academic divisions focused on biology, chemistry, engineering, geology, humanities, and physics. Caltech's academic offering includes undergraduate studies, graduate studies, online education, executive education, and teaching, learning, and outreach. Caltech has a very low student-teacher ratio of 3:1. Caltech operates the Jet Propulsion Laboratory (JPL), which supervises robotic Mars exploration programs and other interplanetary missions, under contract to NASA. The school was founded in 1891.

	Annual Growth	09/18	09/19	09/20	09/21	09/22
Sales ($mil.)	(1.2%)	–	3,434.1	3,354.4	3,146.0	3,309.8
Net income ($ mil.)	–	–	(11.2)	82.7	1,103.0	(618.3)
Market value ($ mil.)	–	–	–	–	–	–
Employees	–	–	–	–	–	6,567

CALIFORNIA PHARMACISTS ASSOCIATION

4030 LENNANE DR
SACRAMENTO, CA 958341987
Phone: 916 779-1400
Fax: –
Web: www.cpha.com

CEO: Carlo Michelotti
CFO: –
HR: –
FYE: December 31
Type: Private

You turn to your pharmacists for advice, but who can they count on for support? In California, it's the California Pharmacists Association (CPhA). Founded in 1869, the organization serves pharmacists by advocating for them before Congress and several private boards (including the Academy of Hospital Pharmacists, Academy of Long Term Care, and Academy of Employee Pharmacists). CPhA also offers continuing education opportunities and discounts on insurance and books. In addition, the group publishes journals and newsletters for its members.

	Annual Growth	12/16	12/17	12/18	12/21	12/22
Sales ($mil.)	(2.4%)	–	2.9	3.1	2.9	2.6
Net income ($ mil.)	–	–	(0.1)	(0.4)	0.2	0.0
Market value ($ mil.)	–	–	–	–	–	–
Employees	–	–	–	–	–	30

CALIFORNIA POLYTECHNIC STATE UNIVERSITY

1 GRAND AVE 1R
SAN LUIS OBISPO, CA 934079000
Phone: 805 756-1111
Fax: –
Web: foundation.calpoly.edu

CEO: –
CFO: –
HR: Joyce Haratani
FYE: June 30
Type: Private

Cal Poly students have more than one option, actually they have many. More formally known as California Polytechnic State University, the school offers about 65 undergraduate degree programs and 30 graduate programs. Founded in 1901, it offers courses in agriculture, architecture and environmental design, business, education, engineering, liberal arts, and science and mathematics. Some 19,000 students attend the university, which also is one of the largest land-holding schools in the California State University System. The not-for-profit Cal Poly Corporation runs the school's non-academic businesses such as bookstores, dining halls, and even a campus market.

	Annual Growth	06/99	06/00	06/05	06/19	06/22
Sales ($mil.)	(28.6%)	–	191.8	0.4	44.1	0.1
Net income ($ mil.)	–	–	(6.0)	0.0	8.7	(0.1)
Market value ($ mil.)	–	–	–	–	–	–
Employees	–	–	–	–	–	2,500

CALIFORNIA RESOURCES CORP NYS: CRC

1 World Trade Center, Suite 1500
Long Beach, CA 90831
Phone: 888 848-4754
Fax: –
Web: www.crc.com

CEO: Francisco J Leon
CFO: Manuela Molina
HR: –
FYE: December 31
Type: Public

California Resources is an independent oil and gas exploration and production company operating properties exclusively within California. The company provides affordable and reliable energy in a safe and responsible manner, to support and enhance the quality of life of Californians and the local communities in which we operate. The company does this through the development of its broad portfolio of assets while adhering to its commitment to create shareholder value. The company has proved reserves of nearly 415 million barrels of oil equivalent and average daily production of some 90 million barrels of oil equivalent.

	Annual Growth	10/20*	12/20	12/21	12/22	12/23
Sales ($mil.)	25.8%	1,407.0	152.0	1,889.0	2,707.0	2,801.0
Net income ($ mil.)	(33.2%)	1,889.0	(123.0)	612.0	524.0	564.0
Market value ($ mil.)	59.8%	920.5	1,620.5	2,933.9	2,988.9	3,756.2
Employees	–	–	1,000	970	1,060	970

*Fiscal year change

CALIFORNIA STATE POLYTECHNIC UNIVERSITY OF POMONA

3801 W TEMPLE AVE
POMONA, CA 917682557
Phone: 909 869-7659
Fax: –
Web: www.cpp.edu

CEO: –
CFO: –
HR: –
FYE: June 30
Type: Private

California State Polytechnic University, Pomona (Cal Poly Pomona) offers bachelor's, graduate, and doctoral degrees, as well as certificate and credential programs, in a variety of disciplines in the industrial arts and applied sciences. The university has nine colleges, nearly 100 degree programs, and more than 1,200 faculty members. Cal Poly Pomona has an enrollment of some 24,000 students. Areas of study include agriculture, business, education, engineering, hospitality, arts, and sciences. The university operates on a system of four quarters per year, each quarter being 11 weeks long.

	Annual Growth	06/06	06/07	06/08	06/20	06/22
Sales ($mil.)	(25.5%)	–	–	6.4	0.0	0.1
Net income ($ mil.)	(8.5%)	–	–	0.2	0.0	0.0
Market value ($ mil.)	–	–	–	–	–	–
Employees	–	–	–	–	–	40

CALIFORNIA STATE UNIVERSITY EAST BAY

25800 CARLOS BEE BLVD
HAYWARD, CA 945423000
Phone: 510 885-3000
Fax: –
Web: www.csueastbay.edu

CEO: –
CFO: –
HR: Violeta Morales-Solis
FYE: June 30
Type: Private

California State University, East Bay (Cal State East Bay) has more than 14,700 students at its three campuses on the east side of San Francisco Bay. Students can choose from about 50 bachelor's and nearly 55 minors, and approximately 35 master's degrees as well as about 25 credentials and certificates from fields of study including liberal arts, science, and business on its one main academic campuses. It also offers continuing-education programs at the Professional Development and Conference Center, and it offers some programs and services via the Internet. The school is part of the California State University System.

	Annual Growth	06/11	06/12	06/15	06/16	06/22
Sales ($mil.)	1.9%	–	13.4	17.3	15.6	16.3
Net income ($ mil.)	–	–	1.4	1.3	1.1	(1.0)
Market value ($ mil.)	–	–	–	–	–	–
Employees	–	–	–	–	–	1,600

CALIFORNIA STATE UNIVERSITY SYSTEM

401 GOLDEN SHORE
LONG BEACH, CA 908024210
Phone: 562 951-4000
Fax: –
Web: www.calstate.edu

CEO: –
CFO: –
HR: –
FYE: June 30
Type: Private

California State University System turns students into teachers. The university, known simply as CSU, traces its roots to the state's teaching colleges and trains the majority of California's teachers and staff. CSU is neck-and-neck with the State University of New York (SUNY) as the nation's largest university system. And it's growing. CSU's enrollment has ballooned to about 450,000. Those students, along with 44,000 faculty and staff members, are spread out among CSU's roughly two dozen campuses in cities such as Bakersfield, Los Angeles, San Francisco, and San Jose. CSU awards bachelor's and master's degrees in more than 380 subject areas, including education, business, psychology, and social work.

	Annual Growth	06/02	06/03	06/04	06/05	06/08
Sales ($mil.)	(88.5%)	–	–	2,899.5	1.1	0.5
Net income ($ mil.)	(86.5%)	–	–	306.1	0.0	0.1
Market value ($ mil.)	–	–	–	–	–	–
Employees	–	–	–	–	–	45,000

CALIFORNIA STATE UNIVERSITY, FRESNO

5241 N MAPLE AVE
FRESNO, CA 937400001
Phone: 559 278-4240
Fax: –
Web: www.fresnostate.edu

CEO: –
CFO: –
HR: Glenda Harada
FYE: June 30
Type: Private

California State University, Fresno -- commonly known as Fresno State -- is one of 23 member institutions in the California State University System, one of the largest higher education systems in the world. It enrolls some 23,000 students and has more than 1,200 faculty members. The university offers 60 undergraduate and 50 graduate degrees in dozens of subject areas through 10 academic schools and divisions: agricultural sciences and technology, arts and humanities, business, education and human development, engineering, health and human services, science and math, social sciences, global and continuing education, and graduate studies. Fresno State was founded in 1911 as Fresno State Normal School.

CALIFORNIA STATE UNIVERSITY, LOS ANGELES

5151 STATE UNIVERSITY DR
LOS ANGELES, CA 900324226
Phone: 323 343-3000
Fax: –
Web: www.calstatela.edu

CEO: –
CFO: –
HR: –
FYE: June 30
Type: Private

With such notable accomplishments as its first place-winning solar cars and first-ever fuel cell plane, California State Los Angeles has made a scientific name for itself in the crowded Southern California university landscape. The university boasts more than 20,000 students working toward undergraduate and graduate degrees and vocational certificate programs through six colleges. Areas of study include arts, business, economics, education, engineering, computer science, technology, health and human services, and natural and social sciences. Founded in 1947 as the Los Angeles State College, Cal State Los Angeles is part of the California State University system, which includes more than 20 campuses.

	Annual Growth	06/06	06/07	06/08	06/09	06/21
Sales ($mil.)	0.7%	–	–	33.3	0.4	36.3
Net income ($ mil.)	–	–	–	(3.3)	(0.2)	6.0
Market value ($ mil.)	–	–	–	–	–	–
Employees	–	–	–	–	–	2,201

CALIFORNIA STATE UNIVERSITY, MONTEREY BAY

100 CAMPUS CTR
SEASIDE, CA 939558000
Phone: 831 582-3330
Fax: –
Web: www.csumb.edu

CEO: –
CFO: –
HR: –
FYE: June 30
Type: Private

For students who want to study and hit the beach, there's California State University, Monterey Bay (CSUMB). A member of the California State University System CSUMB is located on 1,400 acres on the grounds of the US Army's former Fort Ord, between the coastal cities of Monterey and Santa Cruz. Its undergraduate and graduate programs include business administration, education, information technology, marine science, performing arts, and psychology degrees. The staff includes more than 250 faculty members, and some 5,600 students are enrolled at CSUMB.

	Annual Growth	06/05	06/06	06/07	06/08	06/11
Sales ($mil.)	(32.2%)	–	–	–	39.5	12.3
Net income ($ mil.)	–	–	–	–	(0.2)	11.9
Market value ($ mil.)	–	–	–	–	–	–
Employees	–	–	–	–	–	400

CALIFORNIA STATE UNIVERSITY, NORTHRIDGE

18111 NORDHOFF ST
NORTHRIDGE, CA 913300001
Phone: 818 677-1200
Fax: –
Web: www.csun.edu

CEO: –
CFO: –
HR: Melissa Billeter
FYE: June 30
Type: Private

Valley girls (and boys) who want to stick close to home for school can totally get the education they need at California State University, Northridge (CSUN). The school, part of the California State University System, enrolls some 36,000 students and is situated in the heart of Los Angeles' San Fernando Valley. Founded in 1958, CSUN offers bachelor's and master's degree programs in a various fields of study. The Michael D. Eisner College of Education leads the state in the number of teachers it graduates and offers specialty credential programs. The university's Mike Curb College of Arts, Media, and Communication has turned out a collection of notable performers such as Paula Abdul and actress Debra Winger.

	Annual Growth	06/06	06/07	06/08	06/11	06/12
Sales ($mil.)	(10.8%)	–	–	17.0	243.0	10.8
Net income ($ mil.)	(34.3%)	–	–	11.7	55.2	2.2
Market value ($ mil.)	–	–	–	–	–	–
Employees	–	–	–	–	–	82

CALIFORNIA STATE UNIVERSITY, SACRAMENTO

6000 J ST STE 2200
SACRAMENTO, CA 958192605
Phone: 916 278-6011
Fax: –
Web: www.csus.edu

CEO: –
CFO: –
HR: –
FYE: June 30
Type: Private

Hornet's nests aren't the only things getting stirred up at California State University, Sacramento. Also known as Sacramento State or Sac State, the school's mascot is a hornet. Sacramento State has some 29,000 students at its 300-acre campus. Academic offerings at the university's seven colleges include about 60 undergraduate and 40 graduate programs in majors including business, nursing, and criminal justice. Sacramento State was founded as Sacramento State College in 1947 and today is one of about two-dozen schools in the California State University System.

CALIFORNIA STATE UNIVERSITY, SAN MARCOS

333 S TWIN OAKS VALLEY RD
SAN MARCOS, CA 920960001
Phone: 760 750-4000
Fax: –
Web: www.csusm.edu

CEO: –
CFO: –
HR: Michelle Buth
FYE: June 30
Type: Private

California State University San Marcos is a public university that offers undergraduate and graduate programs in a variety of disciplines, including arts and sciences, education, and business administration. It grants bachelor's and master's degrees as well as doctorates in education and teaching credentials. Campus enrollment is more than 9,200 students with faculty numbering about 650. The university is supported by the CSU San Marcos Foundation through grants and contracts administration, financial management, and commercial enterprises. The school was founded in 1989 as the first of a new generation of Cal State campuses.

	Annual Growth	06/08	06/09	06/10	06/11	06/22
Sales ($mil.)	(20.5%)	–	–	–	78.9	6.3
Net income ($ mil.)	(6.1%)	–	–	–	3.1	1.5
Market value ($ mil.)	–	–	–	–	–	–
Employees	–	–	–	–	–	1,680

CALIFORNIA STEEL INDUSTRIES, INC.

14000 SAN BERNARDINO AVE
FONTANA, CA 923355259
Phone: 909 350-6300
Fax: –
Web: www.californiasteel.com

CEO: Marcelo Botelho
CFO: –
HR: –
FYE: December 31
Type: Private

California Steel Industries (CSI) doesn't use forensic evidence, but its work does involve a steel slab. The company uses steel slab produced by third parties to manufacture steel products such as hot-rolled and cold-rolled steel, galvanized coils and sheets, and electric resistance weld (ERW) pipe. Its customers include aftermarket automotive manufacturers, oil and gas producers, roofing makers, tubing manufacturers, and building suppliers. CSI serves the western region of the US. The company operates slitting, shearing, coating, and single-billing services for third parties. Japan's JFE Holdings and Brazilian iron ore miner Vale SA each own 50% of CSI.

	Annual Growth	12/05	12/06	12/07	12/08	12/09
Sales ($mil.)	(63.5%)	–	–	–	1,510.6	551.8
Net income ($ mil.)	–	–	–	–	13.3	(13.1)
Market value ($ mil.)	–	–	–	–	–	–
Employees	–	–	–	–	–	1,095

CALIFORNIA WATER SERVICE GROUP (DE)

NYS: CWT

1720 North First Street
San Jose, CA 95112
Phone: 408 367-8200
Fax: –
Web: www.calwatergroup.com

CEO: Martin A Kropelnicki
CFO: James P Lynch
HR: –
FYE: December 31
Type: Public

California Water Service Group is a holding company with seven operating subsidiaries: California Water Service Company (Cal Water), New Mexico Water Service Company, Washington Water Service Company, Hawaii Water Service Company, Inc., TWSC, Inc., and CWS Utility Services and HWS Utility Services LLC. The business provides utility services to approximately two million people. he bulk of the business consists of the production, purchase, storage, treatment, testing, distribution and sale of water for domestic, industrial, public and irrigation uses, and the provision of domestic and municipal fire protection services. Cal Water was the original operating company and began operations in 1926.

	Annual Growth	12/19	12/20	12/21	12/22	12/23
Sales ($mil.)	2.7%	714.6	794.3	790.9	846.4	794.6
Net income ($ mil.)	(4.8%)	63.1	96.8	101.1	96.0	51.9
Market value ($ mil.)	0.1%	2,976.2	3,118.8	4,148.0	3,500.4	2,994.1
Employees	1.2%	1,207	1,192	1,182	1,225	1,266

CALIFORNIA WELLNESS FOUNDATION

515 S FLOWER ST STE 1100
LOS ANGELES, CA 900712213
Phone: 818 702-1900
Fax: –
Web: www.calwellness.org

CEO: Debra Nakatomi
CFO: –
HR: –
FYE: December 31
Type: Private

Health is wealth for The California Wellness Foundation. Its primary mission is to improve the health of the people of California. The foundation extends grants for health promotion, wellness education, and disease prevention. It focuses on underserved populations, including such groups as the poor, minority groups, and rural residents. On average, the foundation grants about $40 million a year toward programs in such areas as environmental health, healthy aging, mental health, teen pregnancy prevention, violence prevention, and women's health. The California Wellness Foundation was established in 1992 when Health Net (a health maintenance organization) converted to for-profit status.

	Annual Growth	12/12	12/13	12/14	12/15	12/16
Assets ($mil.)	(2.6%)	–	–	941.1	870.2	892.6
Net income ($ mil.)	–	–	–	13.7	1.2	(11.8)
Market value ($ mil.)	–	–	–	–	–	–
Employees	–	–	–	–	–	41

CALIX INC

NYS: CALX

2777 Orchard Parkway
San Jose, CA 95134
Phone: 408 514-3000
Fax: –
Web: www.calix.com

CEO: Michael Weening
CFO: Cory Sindelar
HR: –
FYE: December 31
Type: Public

Calix develops, market, and sell the Calix platform (cloud, software, and systems) and managed services that enable service providers of all types and sizes to innovate and transform their business. The company's Calix platform, which includes Calix Cloud, Revenue EDGE, and Intelligent Access EDGE, gathers, analyzes, and applies machine learning to deliver real-time insights seamlessly to each key business function. Its customers utilize these data and insights to simplify network operations, marketing, and customer support and deliver experiences that excite their subscribers. Held about 115 US patents and nearly 10 pending US patent applications, the company generates the majority of its revenue in the US. Calix was founded in 1999.

	Annual Growth	12/19	12/20	12/21	12/22	12/23
Sales ($mil.)	25.1%	424.3	541.2	679.4	867.8	1,039.6
Net income ($ mil.)	–	(17.7)	33.5	238.4	41.0	29.3
Market value ($ mil.)	52.9%	520.4	1,935.9	5,202.2	4,451.5	2,842.1
Employees	23.2%	763	785	954	1,426	1,760

CALL NOW INC.

1 Retama Parkway
Selma, TX 78154
Phone: 210 651-7145
Fax: –
Web: www.retamapark.com

CEO: Thomas R Johnson
CFO: –
HR: –
FYE: December 31
Type: Public

Call Now operates the Retama Park horse racing facility in Selma, Texas, through its 80%-owned subsidiary, Retama Entertainment Group. The track, which opened in 1995, offers both live and simulcast thoroughbred racing. Call Now purchased rights to operate the racetrack a year later (the actual land and facility are owned by Retama Development Corporation, which is a division of the city of Selma). Retama Park's grandstand features a dining room and sports bar. Private club facilities also are on site.

	Annual Growth	12/06	12/07	12/08	12/09	12/10
Sales ($mil.)	(5.1%)	5.3	4.9	5.5	5.0	4.3
Net income ($ mil.)	–	0.1	(0.4)	(0.3)	(0.4)	(2.0)
Market value ($ mil.)	(43.3%)	30.2	34.2	2.2	3.0	3.1
Employees	6.0%	210	385	385	385	265

CALL2RECYCLE, INC.

1000 PARKWOOD CIR SE STE 200
ATLANTA, GA 303392131
Phone: 678 419-9990
Fax: –
Web: www.call2recycle.org

CEO: Leon Raudys
CFO: Gregory E Broe
HR: –
FYE: December 31
Type: Private

Call2Recycle (formerly known as Rechargeable Battery Recycling Corporation before adopting the name of its major business line) gathers used rechargeable batteries at more than 34,000 retail locations in the US and Canada and recycles them for further use. The company also recycles, refurbishes, and resells cell phones. Call2Recycle is funded by more than 350 makers and marketers of rechargeable batteries who license the Call2Recycle battery recycling seals to imprint on batteries and product packaging. The company has recycled about 100 million pounds of rechargeable batteries since 1996.

	Annual Growth	12/07	12/08	12/09	12/17	12/18
Sales ($mil.)	2.9%	–	12.8	10.3	13.8	17.1
Net income ($ mil.)	–	–	–	3.3	0.5	1.6
Market value ($ mil.)	–	–	–	–	–	–
Employees	–	–	–	–	–	15

CALLAHAN CHEMICAL COMPANY, LLC

BROAD ST & FILMORE AVE
PALMYRA, NJ 08065
Phone: 856 786-7900
Fax: –
Web: www.tilleydistribution.com

CEO: –
CFO: –
HR: –
FYE: December 31
Type: Private

Callahan Chemical carries chemicals to creators of coatings, cleaners, and cosmetics. The distribution company's chemicals are also used in inks, adhesives, personal care products, pharmaceuticals, and vitamin products. Product categories include antimicrobials, silicones, solvents, urethanes, surfactants, humectants, preservatives, and specialty resins. The company's suppliers include Dow Chemical, Eastman Chemical, Rhodia, and Stepan. Callahan transports products from four warehouses in the northeastern US and Puerto Rico; it also offers packaging and blending services. The family-owned company was formed in 1958 by James Callahan.

CALLIDUS SOFTWARE INC.

2700 CAMINO RAMON # 400
SAN RAMON, CA 945835004
Phone: 925 251-2200
Fax: –
Web: www.calliduscloud.com

CEO: –
CFO: –
HR: –
FYE: December 31
Type: Private

Callidus takes good care of office overachievers. The company provides enterprise incentive management software for managing employee compensation programs, including salaries, options, bonuses, and sales commissions. Its applications, grouped under the sobriquet Lead to Money, also help businesses align incentive programs with strategy and profit goals. The company's products are sold primarily under the CallidusCloud brand and include additional tools for managing sales hiring, coaching, training, marketing data analysis, social network marketing, search engine optimization, and web-based compensation reporting. Callidus agreed to be bought by SAP SE for $2.4 billion in 2018.

	Annual Growth	12/13	12/14	12/15	12/16	12/17
Sales ($mil.)	22.8%	–	136.6	173.1	206.7	253.1
Net income ($ mil.)	–	–	(11.6)	(13.1)	(19.0)	(20.3)
Market value ($ mil.)	–	–	–	–	–	–
Employees	–	–	–	–	–	1,113

CALLOWAY'S NURSERY, INC. NBB: CLWY

9003 Airport Freeway, Suite G350
North Richland Hills, TX 76180
Phone: 817 222-1122
Fax: –
Web: www.calloways.com

CEO: James C Estill
CFO: Dan Reynolds
HR: –
FYE: December 31
Type: Public

Calloway's Nursery babies its customers with green-thumb know-how -- about half of its employees are certified nursery professionals. The company owns and operates about 20 nurseries under the Calloway's name in the Dallas/Fort Worth area and San Antonio and under the Cornelius Nurseries banner in Houston. The company also sells plants online. Offerings include trees, shrubs, flowers, landscaping materials, soil, fertilizer, and Christmas goods. Christmas merchandise includes trees, poinsettias, wreaths, and garlands.

	Annual Growth	12/17	12/18	12/19	12/20	12/21
Sales ($mil.)	16.3%	55.4	56.6	58.7	73.8	101.5
Net income ($ mil.)	34.0%	5.1	4.4	3.0	9.8	16.3
Market value ($ mil.)	21.4%	64.1	61.8	47.1	74.4	139.1
Employees	–	–	–	–	–	–

CALLWAVE INC

136 West Canon Perdido Street, Suite C
Santa Barbara, CA 93101
Phone: 805 690-4100
Fax: –
Web: www.callwave.com

CEO: –
CFO: –
HR: –
FYE: June 30
Type: Public

FuzeBox, which considered itself dynamite at helping businesses handle incoming calls, is now setting light to its Web-conferencing wick. The company offers hosted conferencing and unified communications products, mainly through its Fuze Meeting product. Made for Apple's iPhone and iPad, Google's Android platform, and RIM's BlackBerry, it features include high definition video and audio conferencing, voicemail-to-text, and Internet fax and answering machine. Its Fuze Messenger is an enterprise-grade instant messaging (IM) application that consolidates various IM services. Customers include Amazon.com, CBS, eBay, Thomson Reuters, and Verizon Wireless.

	Annual Growth	06/04	06/05	06/06	06/07	06/08
Sales ($mil.)	(15.3%)	38.9	45.5	36.6	25.2	20.0
Net income ($ mil.)	–	11.5	11.6	(2.0)	(7.5)	(5.7)
Market value ($ mil.)	–	–	105.9	77.3	76.9	55.1
Employees	(14.8%)	93	103	91	113	49

CALMARE THERAPEUTICS INC NBB: CTTC

1375 Kings Highway East, Suite 400
Fairfield, CT 06824
Phone: 203 368-6044
Fax: –
Web: www.calmaretherapeutics.com

CEO: Conrad F Mir
CFO: Thomas P Richtarich
HR: Deborah McQuade
FYE: December 31
Type: Public

It doesn't matter how great your invention is if you can't get it to market -- that's where Competitive Technologies (CTT) comes in. The company helps individuals, corporations, government agencies, and universities commercialize their inventions. Clients such as Sony and the University of Illinois have used CTT's services, which include feasibility and marketability evaluations, as well as application for and enforcement of patents. CTT focuses on inventions in life and physical sciences as well as digital technologies. The company, established in 1971, also represents companies seeking to license technologies for commercial purposes.

	Annual Growth	12/12	12/13	12/14	12/15	12/16
Sales ($mil.)	2.2%	1.1	0.8	1.2	1.0	1.2
Net income ($ mil.)	–	(3.0)	(2.7)	(3.4)	(3.7)	(3.8)
Market value ($ mil.)	(26.2%)	18.5	9.3	4.5	5.1	5.5
Employees	8.8%	5	5	6	7	7

CALNET, INC.

12359 SUNRISE VALLEY DR STE 270
RESTON, VA 201913494
Phone: 703 547-6800
Fax: –
Web: www.calnet.com

CEO: Kaleem Shah
CFO: –
HR: –
FYE: December 31
Type: Private

CALNET, a privately held company, provides information technology (IT) consulting and services . The company's IT services include infrastructure services, managed services, cloud computing, cybersecurity and agile. In addition, CALNET provides intelligence analysis, including linguist services in a variety of languages, for the U.S Armed Forces. Additionally, it provides world-wide services in CONUS and OCONUS to include Afghanistan and Iraq. The company has an office in Reston, Virginia. CALNET was founded in 1989 by president Kaleem Shah.

	Annual Growth	12/18	12/19	12/20	12/21	12/22
Sales ($mil.)	8.6%	–	–	5.8	6.1	6.8
Net income ($ mil.)	(23.5%)	–	–	0.9	1.4	0.5
Market value ($ mil.)	–	–	–	–	–	–
Employees	–	–	–	–	–	50

CALPINE CORPORATION

717 TEXAS ST STE 1000
HOUSTON, TX 770022743
Phone: 713 830-2000
Fax: –
Web: www.calpine.com

CEO: John B Hill III
CFO: Zamir Rauf
HR: Carolyn Taylor
FYE: December 31
Type: Private

Calpine Corporation is America's largest generator of electricity from natural gas and geothermal resources with robust commercial, industrial and residential retail operations in key competitive power markets. Its fleet of around 75 power plants and three battery storage facilities, including one under construction, represents nearly 26,000 megawatts of generation capacity. Through wholesale power operations and its retail businesses, Calpine Energy Solutions and Champion Energy, it serve customers in over 20 states in the US, Canada, and Mexico. Calpine Corporation is owned by a consortium of investors that is led by Energy Capital Partners (ECP) and includes Access Industries and the Canada Pension Plan Investment Board.

CALUMET SPECIALTY PRODUCT PARTNERS LP   NMS: CLMT

2780 Waterfront Parkway East Drive, Suite 200
Indianapolis, IN 46214
Phone: 317 328-5660
Fax: –
Web: www.calumetspecialty.com

CEO: Todd Borgmann
CFO: Vincent Donargo
HR: Darrell Fox
FYE: December 31
Type: Public

Crude oil refiner Calumet Specialty Products Partners turns crude oil into specialty hydrocarbon products such as lubricating oils, solvents, petrolatums, and waxes under brands such as Royal Purple, Bel-Ray, and TruFuel. Additionally, it refines crude into fuels such as gasoline, diesel, and jet fuel; it also makes asphalt. The company's operations are scattered across the US, while it sells to both US and non-US customers. Calumet's products are used as a raw material component for basic industrial, consumer, and automotive goods.

	Annual Growth	12/19	12/20	12/21	12/22	12/23
Sales ($mil.)	4.9%	3,452.6	2,268.2	3,148.0	4,686.7	4,181.0
Net income ($ mil.)	–	(43.6)	(149.0)	(260.1)	(165.1)	48.1
Market value ($ mil.)	48.8%	291.9	250.3	1,055.6	1,349.8	1,429.0
Employees	–	–	1,500	1,400	1,450	1,530

CALVARY HOSPITAL, INC.

1740 EASTCHESTER RD
BRONX, NY 104612392
Phone: 718 518-2000
Fax: –
Web: www.calvaryhospital.org

CEO: Frank A Calamari
CFO: –
HR: Maryann Lane
FYE: December 31
Type: Private

Calvary Hospital rallies its doctors and nurses around advanced cancer patients, hoping to keep them as comfortable as possible. The facility specializes in palliative care, the practice of relieving the pain and symptoms associated with an illness (not curing the illness itself). Calvary Hospital offers both inpatient and outpatient services to adult patients in the advanced stages of cancer through two campuses; the main hospital has about 200 beds and a satellite location in Brooklyn has about 25 beds. In addition, the hospital operates home health and hospice agencies and provides case management and family support services. The not-for-profit organization is sponsored by the Archdiocese of New York.

	Annual Growth	12/13	12/14	12/15	12/17	12/21
Sales ($mil.)	1.2%	–	106.2	110.4	119.2	115.3
Net income ($ mil.)	–	–	(14.9)	(6.4)	(3.0)	(4.8)
Market value ($ mil.)	–	–	–	–	–	–
Employees	–	–	–	–	–	900

CALVERT COMPANY, INC.

218 N V ST
VANCOUVER, WA 986617701
Phone: 360 693-0971
Fax: –
Web: www.calvertglulam.com

CEO: –
CFO: –
HR: –
FYE: December 31
Type: Private

Strange as it may sound, this company makes glulams in Washougal. Calvert manufactures and supplies glulams, or pre-shaped glued-laminated lumber products, for use in decorative construction work, including arches, beams, bridges, domes, trusses, s-curves, columns, and even playground equipment. It uses species such as Douglas fir, Alaska yellow cedar, redwood, western red cedar, spruce pine fir, and more. The company manufactures glulams for export to Asia, Canada, and the Middle East, and provides container loading at its plants in Vancouver and Washougal, Washington. Calvert Company was founded by Ray Calvert and others in 1947.

CALVERTHEALTH MEDICAL CENTER, INC.

100 HOSPITAL RD
PRINCE FREDERICK, MD 206784017
Phone: 410 535-4000
Fax: –
Web: www.calverthealthmedicine.org

CEO: James J Xinis
CFO: Kirk Blandford
HR: Peter G Shrmsc
FYE: June 30
Type: Private

Calvert Memorial Hospital provides health care to Chesapeake Bay area residents in Southern Maryland. The medical facility, along with Dunkirk Medical Center, Solomons Medical Center, and a handful of specialty centers and clinics, comprise Calvert Health System. In addition to acute care, Calvert Memorial Hospital and its affiliates offer same-day surgery, outpatient behavioral health care, and diagnostic imaging. They also provide such alternative therapies as acupuncture, massage, and hypnotherapy. For long-term and critical care, Calvert Memorial Hospital partners with area facilities, including Washington Hospital Center, Children's National Medical Center, Johns Hopkins, and University of Maryland.

	Annual Growth	06/17	06/18	06/20	06/21	06/22
Sales ($mil.)	2.3%	–	138.5	142.5	153.3	151.6
Net income ($ mil.)	–	–	(1.3)	5.7	10.2	5.2
Market value ($ mil.)	–	–	–	–	–	–
Employees	–	–	–	–	–	1,000

CALYPTE BIOMEDICAL CORP

15875 SW 72nd Ave
Portland, OR 97224
Phone: 503 726-2227
Fax: –
Web: –

CEO: Adel Karas
CFO: Kartlos Edilashvili
HR: –
FYE: December 31
Type: Public

Fear of needles need not stop you from getting tested for HIV infection. Calypte Biomedical's line of HIV testing products includes several tests that use saliva rather than blood. These rapid-detection tests (sold under the Aware brand name) don't require sophisticated laboratory equipment, and Calypte hopes that such products will appeal to markets in developing countries where the incidence of HIV is high but health care infrastructure is lacking. The company has obtained regulatory approval for its Aware Rapid HIV tests in several foreign markets, including South Africa, India, and Russia. The company has also developed an Aware HIV blood test and an over-the-counter version of its oral test.

	Annual Growth	12/08	12/09	12/10	12/11	12/12
Sales ($mil.)	(25.0%)	0.7	1.0	0.4	0.6	0.2
Net income ($ mil.)	–	(9.2)	(3.6)	8.8	(0.7)	(1.1)
Market value ($ mil.)	(19.1%)	4.9	5.6	3.5	8.4	2.1
Employees	18.9%	4	11	10	9	8

CAMBER ENERGY INC
ASE: CEI

15915 Katy Freeway, Suite 450
Houston, TX 77094
Phone: 281 404-4387
Fax: 713 337-1510
Web: www.camber.energy

CEO: James A Doris
CFO: John McVicar
HR: –
FYE: December 31
Type: Public

Lucas Energy puts a good amount of energy into drilling. The independent crude oil and gas company owns and operates about 35 production wells and holds more than 1.5 million barrels of oil in proved reserves. Its operations are spread over some 11,000 acres primarily in the Austin Chalk region of Texas. The company leases its well-producing properties from local landowners and small operators and is building up its reserve base by acquiring and re-drilling older or underperforming wells that have been overlooked by larger oil and gas companies. Most of Lucas Energy's revenue comes from sales of crude oil to customers such as Gulfmart and Texon, with the remainder derived from natural gas sales.

	Annual Growth	03/19	03/20*	12/20	12/21	12/22
Sales ($mil.)	(31.7%)	2.7	0.4	0.2	0.4	0.6
Net income ($ mil.)	–	16.6	(3.9)	(52.0)	(169.7)	(107.7)
Market value ($ mil.)	51.6%	6.9	20.4	16.7	15.4	36.5
Employees	–	–	–	–	9	9

*Fiscal year change

CAMBIUM LEARNING GROUP, INC.

17855 DALLAS PKWY STE 400
DALLAS, TX 752876857
Phone: 214 932-9500
Fax: –
Web: www.cambiumlearning.com

CEO: John Campbell
CFO: Barbara Benson
HR: Paul Little
FYE: December 31
Type: Private

Cambium Learning Group is the education essentials company, providing award-winning education technology and services for K-12 markets. Operating through its Voyager Sopris Learning, Learning A-Z, Lexia Learning, Time4Learning, Explore Learning, Kurzweil Education and Cambium Assessment, the company provides comprehensive reading and math programs, as well as academic support services for pre-K through 12th grade students. Cambium is owned by Veritas Capital, a leading private equity firm that invests in companies that provide critical technology solutions to government and commercial customers around the world.

CAMBREX CORPORATION

1 MEADOWLANDS PLZ
EAST RUTHERFORD, NJ 070732214
Phone: 201 804-3000
Fax: –
Web: www.cambrex.com

CEO: Steven M Klosk
CFO: Dottie Donnelly-Brienz
HR: Dawn Moynihan
FYE: December 31
Type: Private

Cambrex is a leading global supplier of more than 100 generic APIs. It has more than 2,400 experts servicing global clients from its sites in North America and Europe. The company is also tried and trusted in branded and generic markets for API and finished dosage form development and manufacturing. With presence in over 15 locations globally, Cambrex is one of the leading global contract development and manufacturing organization that delivers drug substances, drug products, and analytical services across the entire drug lifecycle. Founded in 1981, the company has transformed from a fine chemical manufacturer to a leading CDMO with a singular focus on helping its customers advance life-improving therapies to the market.

CAMBRIDGE BANCORP
NAS: CATC

1336 Massachusetts Avenue
Cambridge, MA 02138
Phone: 617 876-5500
Fax: –
Web: www.cambridgetrust.com

CEO: Denis K Sheahan
CFO: Michael F Carotenuto
HR: –
FYE: December 31
Type: Public

Cambridge Bancorp is the nearly $2 billion-asset holding company for Cambridge Trust Company, a community bank serving Cambridge and the Greater Boston area through about a dozen branch locations in Massachusetts. It offers standard retail products and services including checking and savings accounts, CDs, IRAs, and credit cards. Residential mortgages, including home equity loans, account for about 50% of the company's loan portfolio, while commercial real estate loans make up more than 40%. The company also offers commercial, industrial, and consumer loans. Established in 1892, the bank also offers trust and investment management services.

	Annual Growth	12/19	12/20	12/21	12/22	12/23
Assets ($mil.)	17.4%	2,855.6	3,949.3	4,891.5	5,559.7	5,417.7
Net income ($ mil.)	7.8%	25.3	32.0	54.0	52.9	34.1
Market value ($ mil.)	(3.5%)	628.8	547.2	734.3	651.6	544.5
Employees	6.5%	321	383	389	447	413

CAMBRIDGE HEART INC.

100 Ames Pond Drive, Suite 100
Tewksbury, MA 01876
Phone: 978 654-7600
Fax: 978 654-4501
Web: www.cambridgeheart.com

CEO: Ali Haghighi-Mood
CFO: Vincenzo Licausi
HR: –
FYE: December 31
Type: Public

It's not just a heart -- it's a Cambridge heart. Cambridge Heart makes noninvasive tools for diagnosing cardiac arrest and ventricular arrhythmia. Its CH 2000 system conducts cardiac stress tests and measures extremely low levels of T-wave alternans, an irregularity in an electrocardiogram indicating the risk of sudden cardiac death. Another product, the Heartwave II System, allows T-wave alternans screenings to be performed with any stress test system. The company's Microvolt T-Wave Alternans technology can detect the smallest heartbeat variation, measuring from one-millionth of a volt. The company markets its products in the US through direct sales and representatives; it also has international distributors.

	Annual Growth	12/07	12/08	12/09	12/10	12/11
Sales ($mil.)	(31.6%)	10.1	4.2	3.2	2.8	2.2
Net income ($ mil.)	–	(9.2)	(10.0)	(7.3)	(5.2)	(5.4)
Market value ($ mil.)	(47.8%)	101.1	7.6	7.5	23.0	7.5
Employees	(9.9%)	47	44	32	30	31

CAMBRIDGE PUBLIC HEALTH COMMISSION

1493 CAMBRIDGE ST
CAMBRIDGE, MA 021391047
Phone: 617 665-1000
Fax: –
Web: www.challiance.org

CEO: Assaad Sayah MD
CFO: Jill Batty
HR: –
FYE: June 30
Type: Private

Cambridge Public Health Commission, doing business as Cambridge Health Alliance (CHA), is a vibrant, innovative health system dedicated to providing essential services to all members of the community. The health care system operates the Cambridge Public Health Department and collaborates with many local agencies and organizations to improve the health of local residents. It also provides a vital safety net for underserved populations facing barriers to care. CHA has a combined total of more than 275 inpatient beds. The system is a local provider of choice for primary care, specialty care, emergency services, hospital care, maternity care, bone density, dermatology, neurology, pediatrics, psychiatry, and dentistry. CHA is a teaching affiliate of Harvard Medical School, Harvard School of Public Health, Harvard School of Dental Medicine, and Tufts University School of Medicine.

	Annual Growth	06/02	06/03	06/05	06/09	06/22
Sales ($mil.)	(5.9%)	–	466.1	644.2	74.2	148.2
Net income ($ mil.)	–	–	(17.0)	6.1	–	–
Market value ($ mil.)	–	–	–	–	–	–
Employees	–	–	–	–	–	2,700

CAMDEN NATIONAL CORP. (ME)
NMS: CAC

2 Elm Street
Camden, ME 04843
Phone: 207 236-8821
Fax: 207 236-6256
Web: www.camdennational.com

CEO: Gregory A Dufour
CFO: Gregory A White
HR: Betsy Maguire
FYE: December 31
Type: Public

Camden National Corporation is the holding company for Camden National Bank, which boasts nearly 45 branches in about a dozen Maine counties and provides standard deposit products such as checking and savings accounts, CDs, and IRAs. Commercial mortgages and loans make up 50% of its loan portfolio, while residential mortgages make up another 40%, and consumer loans constitute the remainder. Subsidiary Acadia Trust provides trust, fiduciary, investment management, and retirement plan administration services, while Camden Financial Consultants offers brokerage and insurance services. The largest bank headquartered in Maine, Camden National Bank was founded in 1875 and once issued its own US currency.

	Annual Growth	12/19	12/20	12/21	12/22	12/23
Assets ($mil.)	6.6%	4,429.5	4,898.7	5,500.4	5,671.9	5,714.5
Net income ($ mil.)	(6.7%)	57.2	59.5	69.0	61.4	43.4
Market value ($ mil.)	(4.9%)	670.9	521.2	701.5	607.3	548.1
Employees	(1.6%)	639	609	623	630	600

CAMDEN PROPERTY TRUST
NYS: CPT

11 Greenway Plaza, Suite 2400
Houston, TX 77046
Phone: 713 354-2500
Fax: –
Web: www.camdenliving.com

CEO: Richard J Campo
CFO: Alexander J Jessett
HR: Rachel McKernan
FYE: December 31
Type: Public

Camden Property Trust and all its consolidated subsidiaries are primarily engaged in the ownership, management, development, redevelopment, acquisition, and construction of multifamily apartment communities. The real estate investment trust (REIT) has over 175 urban and suburban properties with about 60,650 apartment units. Around 15% of the REIT's properties are in Texas, while the rest are in top markets such as Florida, North Carolina, Georgia, California, and Washington, DC.

	Annual Growth	12/19	12/20	12/21	12/22	12/23
Sales ($mil.)	10.1%	1,061.9	1,069.6	1,169.7	1,411.3	1,561.8
Net income ($ mil.)	16.4%	219.6	123.9	303.9	653.6	403.3
Market value ($ mil.)	(1.6%)	11,552	10,879	19,454	12,181	10,811
Employees	(0.2%)	1,650	1,700	1,700	1,650	1,640

CAMERON INTERNATIONAL CORPORATION

1333 WEST LOOP S STE 1700
HOUSTON, TX 770279118
Phone: 713 939-2282
Fax: –
Web: www.slb.com

CEO: –
CFO: –
HR: –
FYE: December 31
Type: Private

Cameron International has been a Schlumberger company since 2016 that provides state-of-the-art wellhead, surface, and flow control products, systems, and services to oil, gas, and process companies around the world. It offers the industry's most complete portfolio of drilling and production systems backed by expertise in instrumentation, data processing, control software, and system integration. Cameron is committed to solving the industry's most sophisticated problems and is helping forge a new era of environmental stewardship and safety in an ever-evolving industry. It was founded in 1920 by Harry Cameron and James Abercrombie as Cameron Iron Works.

	Annual Growth	12/10	12/11	12/12	12/13	12/14
Sales ($mil.)	10.5%	–	–	8,502.1	9,838.4	10,381
Net income ($ mil.)	6.3%	–	–	750.5	724.2	848.0
Market value ($ mil.)	–	–	–	–	–	–
Employees	–	–	–	–	–	23,000

CAMPAGNA-TURANO BAKERY, INC.

6501 ROOSEVELT RD
BERWYN, IL 604021100
Phone: 708 788-9220
Fax: –
Web: www.turano.com

CEO: –
CFO: –
HR: –
FYE: December 31
Type: Private

The Campagna - Turano Bakery, doing business as the Turano Baking Company, manufactures delicious and authentic baked European-style artisan breads. The company offers a variety of products such as French baguettes, brioche rolls, soft sub rolls, and bambino rolls, as well as sweet baked goods, including cannoli, biscotti, muffins, cakes, and cookies. Operating bakeries in Illinois, Georgia, and Florida, Campagna - Turano Bakery serves customers in the restaurant, in-store bakery, and retail grocery markets. The company's products are can be found in Walmart, Jewel Osco, and Wholefoods. It was founded in 1962.

	Annual Growth	12/08	12/09	12/12	12/21	12/22
Sales ($mil.)	7.3%	–	5.3	7.0	13.5	13.2
Net income ($ mil.)	–	–	(0.7)	0.3	(0.1)	0.2
Market value ($ mil.)	–	–	–	–	–	–
Employees	–	–	–	–	–	470

CAMPBELL LODGING, INC.

1815 E HEIM AVE STE 101
ORANGE, CA 928653029
Phone: 714 256-2070
Fax: –
Web: www.campbelllodginginc.com

CEO: –
CFO: –
HR: –
FYE: December 31
Type: Private

Highways all over the west bear the stamp of Campbell Lodging. The company (formerly Campbell Motel Properties) builds, owns, and manages about 15 hotel properties under national franchised brands such as Holiday Inn Express, Marriott Fairfield Inn & Suites, Red Roof Inns, and Hampton Inn & Suites. Campbell Lodging has mid-range properties in six states in the Southwest (Arizona, California, Colorado, New Mexico, Nevada, and Texas), including locations near airports in Albuquerque and Denver. Campbell Lodging was founded in 1968 by CEO and president Jack Campbell. It is owned and run by the Campbell family.

CAMPBELL SOUP CO
NYS: CPB

1 Campbell Place
Camden, NJ 08103-1799
Phone: 856 342-4800
Fax: 856 342-3878
Web: www.campbellsoupcompany.com

CEO: Mark A Clouse
CFO: Carrie L Anderson
HR: –
FYE: July 30
Type: Public

Campbell Soup is a manufacturer and marketer of high-quality, branded food and beverage products. The company sells an array of soups, simple meals, cookies, fresh bakery and frozen products, potato chips, sauces, non-dairy beverages, pasta, beans, and popcorn, among others. Campbell's iconic brands include Campbell's, Cape Cod, Goldfish, Kettle Brand, Lance, Late July, Milano, Pace, Pacific Foods, Pepperidge Farm, Prego, Snyder's of Hanover, Swanson, and V8. Campbell operates with two reportable segments: meals and beverages and snacks, with meals and beverages accounting for the majority of the company's total revenue. Founded in 1869, Campbell has been connecting people through food they love.

	Annual Growth	07/19*	08/20	08/21*	07/22	07/23
Sales ($mil.)	3.6%	8,107.0	8,691.0	8,476.0	8,562.0	9,357.0
Net income ($ mil.)	42.0%	211.0	1,628.0	1,002.0	757.0	858.0
Market value ($ mil.)	3.1%	12,206	14,772	13,029	14,706	13,783
Employees	(6.5%)	19,000	14,500	14,100	14,700	14,500

*Fiscal year change

CAMPING WORLD HOLDINGS INC NYS: CWH

250 Parkway Drive, Suite 270
Lincolnshire, IL 60069
Phone: 847 808-3000
Fax: –
Web: www.campingworld.com
CEO: Marcus A Lemonis
CFO: Karin L Bell
HR: Gloria Baldonado
FYE: December 31
Type: Public

Camping World Holdings is America's largest retailers of new and used RVs, and related products and services. It also offers outdoor sports-related merchandise. The company's products are promoted via websites, digital, social, email, direct mail, print materials, traditional media, and around 195 retail locations in about 40 US states. Camping World also provides repair and collision services, such as fiberglass front and rear cap replacement, windshield replacement, interior remodel solutions, and paint and body work, and offers service and protection plans and Good Sam Club membership. The company also provides financing of new and used RVs, selling protection and insurance related services and plans for RVs.

	Annual Growth	12/19	12/20	12/21	12/22	12/23
Sales ($mil.)	6.2%	4,892.0	5,446.6	6,913.8	6,967.0	6,226.5
Net income ($ mil.)	–	(60.6)	122.3	278.5	136.9	31.0
Market value ($ mil.)	15.5%	1,245.3	2,200.9	3,413.2	1,885.7	2,218.6
Employees	0.9%	12,207	11,947	13,084	13,411	12,656

CAMPUS APARTMENTS, INC.

4043 WALNUT ST
PHILADELPHIA, PA 191043550
Phone: 215 243-7000
Fax: –
Web: www.campusapartments.com
CEO: Alan Horwitz
CFO: Jim Smith
HR: –
FYE: December 31
Type: Private

Campus Apartments teaches property management 101. One of the largest privately owned property management companies of its kind, Campus Apartments owns or manages more than 60 student apartment properties located near colleges and universities in 23 states. The company also offers design and development services, as well as construction management services to its clients. It has managed properties located on or near such universities as Notre Dame, LSU, Penn, and Ohio State; all in all, it has more than $1 billion in assets under management. Campus Apartments was founded in 1958.

CAN-AM CONSULTING SERVICES, INC

151 W PASSAIC ST
ROCHELLE PARK, NJ 076623105
Phone: 201 512-1414
Fax: –
Web: –
CEO: –
CFO: –
HR: –
FYE: December 31
Type: Private

Can Am Consulting Services has a can-do attitude toward IT. The company provides information technology services and products to small businesses, as well as larger corporate customers. Key services include consulting related to computer and network installation, support, purchasing, and systems administration. Its technical support services include disaster recovery, network security, maintenance, and inventory control. Can Am serves clients in such industries as financial services, real estate, and publishing. The company also offers support services tailored for residential users. Can Am was founded by CEO and owner Stanley M. Kuchar in 1990.

	Annual Growth	12/99	12/00	12/01	12/13	12/16
Sales ($mil.)	(52.4%)	–	8.5	18.6	0.0	0.0
Net income ($ mil.)	–	–	0.3	3.9	(0.0)	(0.0)
Market value ($ mil.)	–	–	–	–	–	–
Employees	–	–	–	–	–	98

CANAL CAPITAL CORP. NBB: COWP

4 Morris Street
Port Jefferson Station, NY 11776
Phone: 631 234-0140
Fax: –
Web: –
CEO: Michael E Schultz
CFO: Reginald Schauder
HR: –
FYE: October 31
Type: Public

Just as a canal has two different sides, Canal Capital has two different businesses. The company develops, manages, leases, and sells commercial, industrial, and retail real estate in five Midwestern states: Iowa, Minnesota, Missouri, Nebraska, and South Dakota. It develops or sells vacant land and manages properties such as offices, lumber yards, car shops, and meat-packing facilities. Capital also operates two public livestock stockyards. The company's stockyard operations (in St. Joseph, Missouri, and Sioux Falls, South Dakota) provide exchange markets for a variety of livestock and supplies. Chairman Asher Edelman owns some 44% of Canal Capital.

	Annual Growth	10/07	10/08	10/09	10/10	10/11
Sales ($mil.)	(13.6%)	3.6	4.4	4.5	4.3	2.0
Net income ($ mil.)	–	(0.9)	(0.1)	0.0	0.0	(0.7)
Market value ($ mil.)	(6.9%)	0.2	0.2	0.2	0.1	0.1
Employees	(24.0%)	75	50	30	25	25

CANAM STEEL CORPORATION

4010 CLAY ST
POINT OF ROCKS, MD 217772016
Phone: 301 874-5141
Fax: –
Web: www.cscsteelusa.com
CEO: –
CFO: –
HR: Alicia Ferkel
FYE: March 29
Type: Private

Canam Steel Corporation manufactures galvanized siding, steel joists, structural steel components, and decking. The company has steel fabrication plants in Florida, Maryland, Missouri, and Washington. Its materials have found their way into Montreal's Pierre Trudeau International Airport, New York's Citi Field, and the Cincinnati Zoo. In 2010 Canam Steel acquired a number of assets, including two manufacturing plants and the United Steel Deck brand name, from Commercial Metals Company. Canam Steel is a subsidiary of the Canadian steel fabricator Canam Group.

CANANDAIGUA NATIONAL CORP. NBB: CNND

72 South Main Street
Canandaigua, NY 14424
Phone: 585 394-4260
Fax: 585 394-4001
Web: www.cnbank.com
CEO: Frank H Hamlin III
CFO: Lawrence A Heilbronner
HR: –
FYE: December 31
Type: Public

Canandaigua National can undoubtedly stake its claim as the holding company for Canandaigua National Bank and Trust, which operates more than two dozen branches in the Finger Lakes region of upstate New York. In addition to traditional deposits and loans, the bank also offers online brokerage, insurance, and wealth management services, including corporate retirement plan management and individual financial planning. The company also owns Genesee Valley Trust Company and the recently formed Canandaigua National Trust Company of Florida. Canandaigua National's loan portfolio is composed largely of commercial mortgages, other business loans, and residential mortgages.

	Annual Growth	12/18	12/19	12/20	12/21	12/23
Assets ($mil.)	11.3%	2,862.5	3,015.7	3,635.4	4,160.4	4,883.8
Net income ($ mil.)	4.5%	35.9	39.2	42.3	44.7	44.7
Market value ($ mil.)	3.7%	324.4	374.9	348.5	435.6	389.3
Employees	3.7%	556	572	580	622	668

CANCER CARE, INC.

275 7TH AVE FL 22
NEW YORK, NY 100016754
Phone: 212 712-8400
Fax: –
Web: www.cancercare.org

CEO: Patricia J Goldsmith
CFO: John Rutigliano
HR: Margie Peguero
FYE: June 30
Type: Private

Cancer Care is a not-for-profit organization focused on helping cancer patients and those who care for them. The organization provides free counseling, support groups, educational tools, financial assistance, and other services to about 170,000 people every year. It serves anyone affected by cancer, including patients, caregivers, children, and the bereaved. Cancer Care also offers educational seminars and consulting services for health care professionals working with cancer patients. Founded in 1944, the organization has locations in Connecticut, New Jersey, and New York and provides services across the US.

	Annual Growth	06/16	06/17	06/20	06/21	06/22
Sales ($mil.)	4.3%	–	17.0	16.9	17.4	20.9
Net income ($ mil.)	62.8%	–	0.3	(1.6)	(1.0)	3.7
Market value ($ mil.)	–	–	–	–	–	–
Employees	–	–	–	–	–	120

CANCER RESEARCH FUND OF THE DAMON RUNYON-WALTER WINCHELL FOUNDATION

55 BROADWAY STE 302
NEW YORK, NY 100063720
Phone: 212 455-0500
Fax: –
Web: www.damonrunyon.org

CEO: –
CFO: –
HR: –
FYE: June 30
Type: Private

The Damon Runyon Cancer Research Foundation supports cancer research through grants to scientists in fields including cellular biology, genetics, immunology, and virology. It focuses on young scientists who will be able to provide a long career of advancements and discoveries. The Damon Runyon Fellowship, granted to medical doctors and new PhDs, is awarded to about 50 recipients annually. The group raises funds through donations, endowments, events, and its Broadway Tickets resale program. Established by radio broadcaster Walter Winchell in 1946, the foundation -- named for sportswriter Damon Runyon -- has invested some $275 million in cancer research and has funded over 3,420 young scientists.

	Annual Growth	06/13	06/14	06/15	06/17	06/18
Sales ($mil.)	6.6%	–	16.7	26.1	16.6	21.6
Net income ($ mil.)	–	–	(4.0)	8.3	(3.0)	0.4
Market value ($ mil.)	–	–	–	–	–	–
Employees	–	–	–	–	–	15

CANDID

32 OLD SLIP 24TH FLR
NEW YORK, NY 10005
Phone: 212 620-4230
Fax: –
Web: www.foundationcenter.org

CEO: –
CFO: –
HR: –
FYE: December 31
Type: Private

When it comes to information about the nonprofit sector, everyone should have a solid base. The Foundation Center researches US grants and philanthropy, and makes the results available through its website, libraries, and print and electronic publications. It also provides education and training on the grant seeking process. While the center offers all consumers free access to its information, it targets grant seekers, grant makers, researchers, and policymakers. Its Foundation Directory Online is an online subscription database that provides information about nearly 100,000 US foundations, corporate donors, and grantmaking public charities, and some 2.3 million grants. The Foundation Center was founded in 1956.

CANNABIS GLOBAL INC

520 S. Grand Avenue, Ste. 320
Los Angeles, CA 90071
Phone: 310 986-4929
Fax: –
Web: www.cannabisglobalinc.com

NBB: CBGL
CEO: Garry McHenry
CFO: Garry McHenry
HR: –
FYE: August 31
Type: Public

MicroChannel Technologies is trying to get on your nerves. The development-stage company is studying the use of stem cells to regenerate optical and bodily nerve damage caused by injury, diabetes, or post-surgical complications. The research involves scraping out tiny grooves in the damaged cells and filling them with stem cells (hence the micro channel) to accelerate new growth. The company was spun off from technology incubator Octillion in 2007, and up until mid-2008 it continued to fund studies conducted by the Research Foundation at Iowa State University. However, the project failed to find any commercially viable cells, and MicroChannel Technologies is now trying to find another commercial opportunity.

	Annual Growth	08/17	08/18	08/19	08/20	08/21
Sales ($mil.)	–	–	–	–	0.0	1.6
Net income ($ mil.)	–	(0.0)	(0.1)	(0.4)	(4.9)	(7.8)
Market value ($ mil.)	124.4%	0.1	1.7	3.8	10.2	3.0
Employees	–	–	–	–	–	–

CANNAE HOLDINGS INC

1701 Village Center Circle
Las Vegas, NV 89134
Phone: 702 323-7330
Fax: –
Web: www.cannaeholdings.com

NYS: CNNE
CEO: Richard N Massey
CFO: Bryan D Coy
HR: –
FYE: December 31
Type: Public

Cannae Holdings, Inc. primarily acquires interests in operating companies and is engaged in actively managing and operating a core group of those companies, which the company is committed to supporting for the long-term. From time to time, the company also seek to take meaningful majority or minority equity ownership stakes where the company can control or significantly influence quality companies, and it bring the strength of its operational expertise to each of our subsidiaries. Its primary assets include its ownership interests in Dun & Bradstreet Holdings, Inc. Ceridian HCM Holding, Inc. (Ceridian), Alight, Inc., and many more.

	Annual Growth	12/19	12/20	12/21	12/22	12/23
Sales ($mil.)	(14.6%)	1,070.0	585.7	742.2	662.1	570.0
Net income ($ mil.)	–	77.3	1,786.2	(287.0)	(428.1)	(313.4)
Market value ($ mil.)	(14.9%)	2,617.0	3,115.2	2,473.4	1,453.1	1,372.9
Employees	(23.4%)	22,482	14,509	12,938	11,988	7,741

CANO CONTAINER CORPORATION

3920 ENTERPRISE CT STE A
AURORA, IL 605048154
Phone: 630 585-7500
Fax: –
Web: www.canocontainer.com

CEO: –
CFO: –
HR: –
FYE: December 31
Type: Private

When it comes to customizing corrugated shipping containers, Cano Container can do! The company churns out a diversity of made to order cartons, trays, die cuts, and the like through its Aurora, Illinois, manufacturing facility. Through its Proactive Packaging & Display arm, Cano also provides point-of-sale displays, laminate printing services, and foam padding. A breadth of industries are served, from food and drink to high-tech, textile, retail, and government agencies. Procter & Gamble, General Mills, Kraft Foods, Pepsi, and McCormick & Company are a few of the company's regulars. Cano is owned by president Juventino Cano, who also operates California corrugated container company, Commander Packaging West.

	Annual Growth	12/06	12/07	12/08	12/09	12/10
Sales ($mil.)	34.0%	–	–	11.1	13.3	20.0
Net income ($ mil.)	–	–	–	0.5	0.8	(0.5)
Market value ($ mil.)	–	–	–	–	–	–
Employees	–	–	–	–	–	54

CANTALOUPE INC

NMS: CTLP

100 Deerfield Lane, Suite 300
Malvern, PA 19355
Phone: 610 989-0340
Fax: –
Web: www.cantaloupe.com

CEO: Ravi Venkatesan
CFO: Scott Stewart
HR: –
FYE: June 30
Type: Public

Since you can't get much from a vending machine with a quarter these days, USA Technologies decided to make them take plastic. Its ePort device attaches onto vending machines and its eSuds works on washing machines and clothes dryers to allow them to accept debit and credit cards. With the Business Express device, hotels, libraries, and universities can run their business centers as self-pay operations; customers simply swipe their cards to use a PC, fax machine, or copier. USA Technologies also sells energy-saving devices for such "always-on" appliances as vending machines and office equipment. Information from the company's remote devices is transmitted through the company's USALive network.

	Annual Growth	06/19	06/20	06/21	06/22	06/23
Sales ($mil.)	14.1%	143.8	163.2	166.9	205.2	243.6
Net income ($ mil.)	–	(32.0)	(40.6)	(8.7)	(1.7)	0.6
Market value ($ mil.)	1.7%	539.9	316.8	861.8	406.9	578.4
Employees	20.9%	126	147	185	225	269

CANTEL MEDICAL LLC

150 CLOVE RD STE 36
LITTLE FALLS, NJ 074242138
Phone: 973 890-7220
Fax: –
Web: www.steris.com

CEO: George L Fotiades
CFO: Shaun Blakeman
HR: Cora Gohmann
FYE: July 31
Type: Private

Cantel Medical is a leading global company dedicated to delivering innovative infection prevention products and services for patients, caregivers, and other healthcare providers which improve outcomes, enhance safety and help save lives. With a wide range of endoscopy, water purification, filtration, and healthcare disposables, Cantel offers top-quality infection prevention solutions and unmatched service. Every year, millions of patients worldwide benefit from Cantel's products and solutions. The company was founded in 1947.

CANTERBURY PARK HOLDING CORP (NEW)

NMS: CPHC

1100 Canterbury Road
Shakopee, MN 55379
Phone: 952 445-7223
Fax: –
Web: www.canterburypark.com

CEO: Randall D Sampson
CFO: Randy J Dehmer
HR: –
FYE: December 31
Type: Public

The tails of this Canterbury are connected to horses running around a track. The operator of the Canterbury Park racetrack in Shakopee, Minnesota, Canterbury Park Holding offers live pari-mutuel horse racing from May through September. The racetrack also offers year-round betting on simulcast races from racetracks such as Churchill Downs, Hollywood Park, and Belmont Park. When horses aren't dashing down the track, the company stages other events (snowmobile races, concerts, crafts shows, private parties) at Canterbury Park. It also offers gambling for card sharks at its on-site Card Club. Chairman Curtis Sampson owns more than 20% of the company.

	Annual Growth	12/19	12/20	12/21	12/22	12/23
Sales ($mil.)	0.9%	59.2	33.1	60.4	66.8	61.4
Net income ($ mil.)	40.4%	2.7	1.1	11.8	7.5	10.6
Market value ($ mil.)	13.3%	61.5	59.4	85.8	155.1	101.4
Employees	(4.8%)	930	610	769	753	765

CAPE COD HEALTHCARE, INC.

27 PARK ST
HYANNIS, MA 026015230
Phone: 508 862-5030
Fax: –
Web: www.capecodhealth.org

CEO: Michael K Lauf
CFO: Michael Connors
HR: –
FYE: September 30
Type: Private

Cape Cod Healthcare (CCHC) is a not-for-profit healthcare organization that operates two acute care hospitals (Cape Cod Hospital and Falmouth Hospital). Specializations include heart and vascular, women's health, bones and muscles, cancer care, and brain, spine, and nerves. CCHC also operates a home health services agency (Visiting Nurse Association of Cape Cod), more than 130-bed skilled nursing and rehabilitation facility (JML Care Center), and assisted living facility (Heritage at Falmouth). The health care system has affiliations with UMass Medical School, Boston University, University of New England and Cape Cod Community College. CCHC is the Cape's largest private employer with more than 5,300 staff members, 450 physicians and 790 volunteers.

	Annual Growth	09/18	09/19	09/20	09/21	09/22
Sales ($mil.)	(48.1%)	–	978.6	931.4	141.9	136.5
Net income ($ mil.)	(34.6%)	–	29.1	27.3	14.8	8.1
Market value ($ mil.)	–	–	–	–	–	–
Employees	–	–	–	–	–	1,850

CAPE COD HOSPITAL

27 PARK ST
HYANNIS, MA 026015203
Phone: 508 771-1800
Fax: –
Web: www.capecodhospitalauxiliary.org

CEO: Michael K Lauf
CFO: –
HR: Crystal Teixeira
FYE: September 30
Type: Private

Get too much sun or eat too much lobster while visiting Cape Cod? Never fear, Cape Cod Hospital can treat whatever ails you. Cape Cod Hospital, a subsidiary of Cape Cod Healthcare, is a 260-bed acute care hospital that serves the Cape Cod, Massachusetts area. Its specialty services include pediatrics, maternity care, cancer treatment, and infectious disease therapeutics. The not-for-profit Cape Cod Hospital also includes a specialty cardiovascular center, a psychiatry unit, a surgical pavilion, and a diagnostic imaging facility, as well as outpatient medical offices.

	Annual Growth	09/17	09/18	09/19	09/20	09/21
Sales ($mil.)	0.8%	–	564.0	599.3	569.8	578.3
Net income ($ mil.)	(9.1%)	–	46.6	26.0	12.3	35.0
Market value ($ mil.)	–	–	–	–	–	–
Employees	–	–	–	–	–	1,700

CAPE ENVIRONMENTAL MANAGEMENT INC.

500 PINNACLE CT STE 100
NORCROSS, GA 300713630
Phone: 770 908-7200
Fax: –
Web: www.cape-inc.com

CEO: Fernando J Rios
CFO: Les Flynn
HR: Cheryl Caviness
FYE: December 27
Type: Private

Cape Environmental Management offers a number of engineering and environmental services, including facility construction and demolition, remediation, and water and wastewater utility-related services. Clients include government agencies such as the US Air Force, and the US Army Corps of Engineers, and industrial clients in the petroleum, chemical, telecommunications, and transportation sectors. Specialty areas include engineering, scientific, construction, and industrial hygiene/safety. The company operates from 50 states. Cape Environmental Management was founded in 1985 and acquired by its executive team in 1991.

	Annual Growth	12/02	12/03	12/04	12/06	12/08
Sales ($mil.)	19.2%	–	–	46.1	117.7	92.9
Net income ($ mil.)	–	–	–	–	20.3	4.0
Market value ($ mil.)	–	–	–	–	–	–
Employees	–	–	–	–	–	315

CAPELLA EDUCATION COMPANY

225 S 6TH ST FL 9
MINNEAPOLIS, MN 554024309
Phone: 888 227-3552
Fax: –
Web: www.capella.edu

CEO: J K Gilligan
CFO: Steven L Polacek
HR: Peter M Ramstad
FYE: December 31
Type: Private

Capella Education is all about the digital age. The fast-growing company operates Capella University, an online school that offers more than 1,840 online courses, about 160 undergraduate and graduate degree programs with some 160 specializations. Its 37,000 students from the US and abroad are primarily composed of working adults, 72% of which are pursuing master's or doctoral degrees. Capella Education's faculty members are mostly part-time employees, typically teaching one to three courses per semester. The firm's programs range across a variety of subjects including business, health, human resources, information technology, and psychology. Capella Education merged with Strayer Education in a $1.9 billion transaction in mid-2018.

CAPILLARY BRIERLEY INC

6160 WARREN PKWY
FRISCO, TX 750346515
Phone: 214 743-5454
Fax: –
Web: www.brierley.com

CEO: Kats Murakami
CFO: David Mellinger
HR: Diane Brierley
FYE: December 31
Type: Private

Brierley & Partners wants to help its clients start (and keep) meaningful relationships. The direct marketing agency consults with corporate clients to develop and implement customer loyalty and customer relationship management (CRM) programs. The firm provides strategic planning, program design, and development of marketing technology that collects and analyzes information about customer habits and preferences. Brierley & Partners has developed programs such as Hilton HHonors, Hertz#1 Club Gold, and United Airlines' Mileage Plus. Founded in 1985 by "chief loyalty architect" Hal Brierley, the firm operates primarily in Europe and North America. WPP owns about 20% of Brierley & Partners.

CAPITAL CITY BANK GROUP, INC. NMS: CCBG

217 North Monroe Street
Tallahassee, FL 32301
Phone: 850 402-7821
Fax: –
Web: www.ccbg.com

CEO: William G Smith Jr
CFO: J K Davis
HR: Glenda Harrold
FYE: December 31
Type: Public

Capital City Bank Group is one of the largest publicly traded financial holding companies headquartered in Florida and has approximately $4.3billion in assets. The company provides a full range of banking services, including traditional deposit and credit services, mortgage banking, asset management, trust, merchant services, bankcards, securities brokerage services and financial advisory services, including the sale of life insurance, risk management and asset protection services. The bank has more than 55 banking offices and about 85 ATMs/ITMs in Florida, Georgia and Alabama. Through Capital City Home Loans, LLC, a Georgia limited liability company (CCHL), it has about 25 additional offices in the Southeast for its mortgage banking business.

	Annual Growth	12/19	12/20	12/21	12/22	12/23
Assets ($mil.)	8.6%	3,089.0	3,798.1	4,263.8	4,526.0	4,304.5
Net income ($ mil.)	14.1%	30.8	31.6	33.4	40.1	52.3
Market value ($ mil.)	(0.9%)	517.0	416.6	447.5	550.9	498.8
Employees	–	–	815	773	751	796

CAPITAL DIRECTIONS, INC.

322 South Jefferson Street
Mason, MI 48854-0130
Phone: 517 676-0500
Fax: 517 676-0528
Web: www.masonstate.com

CEO: –
CFO: –
HR: –
FYE: December 31
Type: Public

Capital Directions is the holding company for Mason State Bank, which offers traditional banking services from a handful of branches in Ingham County, Michigan. Residential mortgages make up the majority the bank's lending portfolio, which also includes commercial real estate, construction, and business operating loans. Other subsidiaries include Mason State Mortgage Company and Lakeside Insurance Services. Capital Directions is merging with Commercial National Financial Corporation, holding company of Commercial Bank. Mason State Bank will be merged into the 11-branch Commercial Bank.

	Annual Growth	12/00	12/01	12/02	12/03	12/04
Assets ($mil.)	3.0%	115.0	117.3	126.2	130.1	129.3
Net income ($ mil.)	(3.6%)	1.7	1.7	1.9	1.8	1.4
Market value ($ mil.)	9.6%	21.1	22.9	25.3	31.9	30.3
Employees	–	36	38	38	–	–

CAPITAL DISTRICT PHYSICIANS' HEALTH PLAN, INC.

500 PATROON CREEK BLVD
ALBANY, NY 122061057
Phone: 518 641-3700
Fax: –
Web: www.cdphp.com

CEO: John Bennett
CFO: Paul Kahlon
HR: Tricia Wendell
FYE: December 31
Type: Private

Capital District Physicians' Health Plan (CDPHP) is an independent, not-for-profit health plan serving some 448,000 members in two dozen New York counties. It offers employer-sponsored and individual managed care plans (including HMO, PPO, and consumer-directed plans), as well as a Medicare Advantage plan for seniors. The company's coverage include full coverage for some preventative medical services, as well as options for covering prescription drugs, dental work, and vision services. CDPHP also provides wellness programs that help members with weight loss, smoking cessation, and chronic disease management.

	Annual Growth	12/01	12/02	12/03	12/09	12/13
Assets ($mil.)	8.3%	–	–	237.1	457.8	526.3
Net income ($ mil.)	–	–	–	(1.8)	33.5	23.0
Market value ($ mil.)	–	–	–	–	–	–
Employees	–	–	–	–	–	700

CAPITAL HEALTH SYSTEM, INC.

750 BRUNSWICK AVE
TRENTON, NJ 086384143
Phone: 609 394-6000
Fax: –
Web: www.capitalhealth.org

CEO: Al Maghazehe
CFO: Shane Fleming
HR: –
FYE: December 31
Type: Private

Capital Health System (CHS) serves the residents of New Jersey's capital city through two hospitals. Together they have about 430 beds. The not-for-profit organization offers emergency, surgical, and acute health care, and it serves as a hands-on teaching facility to nursing and medical students. It also operates outpatient care facilities. CHS primarily serves residents of Mercer County and parts of Bucks County in central New Jersey. Capital Health System offers centers for maternal and pediatric health, neurology, emergency and trauma services, oncology, orthopedics, mental health, surgery, and sleep diagnostics.

CAPITAL METROPOLITAN TRANSPORTATION AUTHORITY

2910 E 5TH ST
AUSTIN, TX 787024895
Phone: 512 389-7400
Fax: –
Web: www.capmetro.org

CEO: –
CFO: –
HR: Virginia Keeling
FYE: September 30
Type: Private

Authority in the capital city of Texas might reside with the people's elected representatives, but when it comes to people-moving, Capital Metropolitan Transportation Authority takes charge. Capital Metro provides bus transportation services in the Austin, Texas, area. Funded mostly by a local sales tax, the agency transports about 113,000 passengers daily on more than 80 bus routes with its fleet of 400 vehicles. Capital Metro also contracts to provide shuttle bus services for the University of Texas at Austin. The agency provides park-and-ride services, special event shuttles, and special transit services for people with disabilities.

	Annual Growth	09/12	09/13	09/14	09/15	09/16
Sales ($mil.)	1.0%	–	–	28.3	28.8	28.8
Net income ($ mil.)	9.2%	–	–	31.8	39.0	37.9
Market value ($ mil.)	–	–	–	–	–	–
Employees	–	–	–	–	–	1,300

CAPITAL ONE FINANCIAL CORP   NYS: COF

1680 Capital One Drive
McLean, VA 22102
Phone: 703 720-1000
Fax: –
Web: www.capitalone.com

CEO: –
CFO: –
HR: –
FYE: December 31
Type: Public

Capital One Financial is one of the most recognizable issuers of Visa and MasterCard credit cards in the US. It offers credit and debit card products, auto loans and other consumer lending products in markets across the US. The company also offer products outside of the US principally through Capital One (Europe) plc (COEP) and through a branch of Capital One, National Association (CONA) in Canada. It offers a broad array of financial products and services to consumers, small businesses and commercial clients through digital channels, branch locations, cafés and other distribution channels.

	Annual Growth	12/19	12/20	12/21	12/22	12/23
Assets ($mil.)	5.2%	390,365	421,602	432,381	455,249	478,464
Net income ($ mil.)	(3.1%)	5,546.0	2,714.0	12,390	7,360.0	4,887.0
Market value ($ mil.)	6.2%	39,146	37,602	55,191	35,361	49,877
Employees	–	51,900	51,985	50,767	55,943	51,987

CAPITAL PROPERTIES, INC.   NBB: CPTP

5 Steeple Street, Unit 303
Providence, RI 02903
Phone: 401 435-7171
Fax: 401 435-7179
Web: www.capitalproperties.com

CEO: Robert H Eder
CFO: –
HR: –
FYE: December 31
Type: Public

Was it providence or clear foresight that led Capital Properties to buy land in what is now Capital Center, a downtown revitalization project in Providence, Rhode Island? The company owns and leases out about a dozen parcels of land totaling some 18 acres in the area, making it Capital Center's largest landowner. It leases parcels for the long term (at least 99 years) and leaves development and improvement to its tenants. Subsidiaries own and operate a petroleum storage facility in East Providence used by Global Partners, and lease land to Lamar Advertising for roadside billboards in Rhode Island and Massachusetts. Chairman and CEO Robert Eder and his wife Linda together own a majority of Capital Properties.

	Annual Growth	12/19	12/20	12/21	12/22	12/23
Sales ($mil.)	1.7%	5.2	4.6	4.8	5.1	5.5
Net income ($ mil.)	(1.6%)	2.5	2.0	1.8	1.8	2.3
Market value ($ mil.)	(6.0%)	101.6	81.5	82.8	72.6	79.2
Employees	–	3	3	3	3	3

CAPITOL FEDERAL FINANCIAL INC   NMS: CFFN

700 South Kansas Avenue
Topeka, KS 66603
Phone: 785 235-1341
Fax: –
Web: www.capfed.com

CEO: John B Dicus
CFO: Kent G Townsend
HR: –
FYE: September 30
Type: Public

Capitol Federal Financial is a leader in residential lending in Kansas and Missouri and boasts more than $9 billion in assets. In addition to single-family residential lending, the bank offers commercial loans, Small Business Loans and business banking services. Capitol Federal offers a variety of retail deposit accounts, including checking, savings, money market, IRA and certificates of deposit, as well as trust services. Capitol Federal Financial offers consumer lending that offers a variety of secured consumer loans, including home equity loans and lines of credit, home improvement loans, vehicle loans, and loans secured by savings deposits, as well as commercial lending. The savings bank serves metropolitan areas of the Topeka, Wichita, Lawrence, Manhattan, Emporia, and Salina, as well as Kansas City, Missouri, through a network of about 55 branches. The company was founded in 1893.

	Annual Growth	09/19	09/20	09/21	09/22	09/23
Assets ($mil.)	2.2%	9,340.0	9,487.2	9,631.2	9,624.9	10,177
Net income ($ mil.)	–	94.2	64.5	76.1	84.5	(101.7)
Market value ($ mil.)	(23.3%)	1,873.2	1,259.5	1,561.9	1,128.3	648.4
Employees	(2.8%)	773	793	750	733	689

CAPPS MANUFACTURING, INCORPORATED

2121 S EDWARDS AVE
WICHITA, KS 672131868
Phone: 316 942-9351
Fax: –
Web: www.cappsmfg.com

CEO: Barney L Capps
CFO: Ron L Capps
HR: –
FYE: December 31
Type: Private

This company only wears one hat -- manufacturer. Capps Manufacturing makes and assembles aircraft parts, including door assemblies, wings, components, and sheet metal pieces, at its 80,000 sq. ft. plant. Services include machining, roll forming, hydro forming, extrusion and skin stretch forming, component assembly, and heat treating. Customers include Boeing, Cessna, Raytheon, Northrop Grumman, and other major aircraft makers. Capps differentiates itself by doing assembly work few other companies have the desire to take on. Owner and president Barney Capps started Capps Manufacturing in 1983.

	Annual Growth	12/16	12/17	12/18	12/19	12/21
Sales ($mil.)	(10.4%)	–	27.3	27.4	29.6	17.6
Net income ($ mil.)	1.5%	–	5.4	4.0	6.5	5.7
Market value ($ mil.)	–	–	–	–	–	–
Employees	–	–	–	–	–	165

CAPRICOR THERAPEUTICS INC   NAS: CAPR

10865 Road to the Cure, Suite 150
San Diego, CA 92121
Phone: 858 727-1755
Fax: –
Web: www.capricor.com

CEO: Linda Marban
CFO: Anthony Bergmann
HR: –
FYE: December 31
Type: Public

While its operations are far from the Nile river, Nile Therapeutics makes products aimed at getting cardiovascular systems moving like a river. A biopharmaceutical company, Nile Therapeutics has a handful of candidates in development in its pipeline that are designed to treat acute heart failure. Its primary candidate, CD-NP, is a peptide (short, specialized amino acid chain) engineered to treat acute decompensated heart failure (ADHF), or the rapid degeneration of the heart resulting from a heart attack or other medical conditions. Nile's other prominent candidate is an early-stage peptide also designed to treat similar cardiovascular conditions.

	Annual Growth	12/19	12/20	12/21	12/22	12/23
Sales ($mil.)	123.7%	1.0	0.3	0.2	2.6	25.2
Net income ($ mil.)	–	(7.6)	(13.7)	(20.0)	(29.0)	(22.3)
Market value ($ mil.)	39.8%	39.9	106.8	91.3	120.2	152.3
Employees	58.5%	16	26	48	74	101

CAPSTEAD MORTGAGE CORPORATION

8401 N CNTL EXPY STE 800
DALLAS, TX 75225
Phone: 214 874-2323
Fax: –
Web: www.capstead.com

CEO: –
CFO: –
HR: –
FYE: December 31
Type: Private

Capstead Mortgage is a self-managed real estate investment trust (REIT) with holdings in mortgage-backed securities. It makes leveraged investments in single-family residential adjustable-rate mortgage securities issued and backed by government agencies such as Fannie Mae, Freddie Mac, and Ginnie Mae. It occasionally makes limited investments in credit-sensitive commercial mortgage assets, as well. The REIT typically funds its investment activities through short-term borrowings or equity offerings. Founded in 1985, Capstead is one of the oldest publicly traded mortgage REITs in the US and manages an investment portfolio worth nearly $1.17 billion.

CAPSTONE GREEN ENERGY CORP
NBB: CGRN Q

16640 Stagg Street
Van Nuys, CA 91406
Phone: 818 734-5300
Fax: –
Web: www.capstonegreenenergy.com

CEO: Robert C Flexon
CFO: John J Juric
HR: –
FYE: March 31
Type: Public

Capstone Green Energy (Capstone) is a provider of customized microgrid solutions, on-site resilient green Energy as a Service (EaaS) solutions, and on-site energy technology systems focused on helping customers around the globe meet their environmental, energy savings, and resiliency goals. The company makes the Capstone MicroTurbine, a power-generating system that produces environmentally friendly electricity and heat. The microturbines, which can operate on a stand-alone basis or be connected to the utility grid, run on a variety of liquid and gaseous fuels, such as natural gas, diesel, kerosene, biodiesel, landfill gas and biogas or digester gas. In the event of a power outage, customers can use microturbines to produce its own secure power for extended periods of time; microturbines can also be used as onboard battery chargers for hybrid electric vehicles. About 50% of the company's revenue comes from the US.

	Annual Growth	03/18	03/19	03/20	03/21	03/22
Sales ($mil.)	(4.2%)	82.8	83.4	68.9	67.6	69.6
Net income ($ mil.)	–	(10.0)	(16.7)	(21.9)	(18.4)	(20.2)
Market value ($ mil.)	37.7%	17.5	13.8	18.4	139.8	63.0
Employees	(2.9%)	151	154	112	123	134

CAPSTONE HOLDING CORP
NBB: CAPS

5141 W 122nd Street
Alsip, IL 60803
Phone: 708 371-0660
Fax: 708 371-0686
Web: www.capstonethx.com

CEO: –
CFO: Les M Taeger
HR: –
FYE: December 31
Type: Public

OrthoLogic, doing business as Capstone Therapeutics, is trying to make sense of scarred skin and damaged hearts with its biopharmaceutical products designed to repair the body's tissues. The biotechnology company is focused on a couple of synthetic peptide technologies that may accelerate healing. Its Chrysalin program has yielded several potential therapies, including TP508, which the company is evaluating as a treatment for vascular diseases, as well as diabetic foot ulcers. OrthoLogic acquired another candidate, AZX100, in 2006 and has begun clinical testing on the drug as a treatment for dermal scarring.

	Annual Growth	12/17	12/18	12/19	12/20	12/21
Sales ($mil.)	–	–	2.0	–	45.5	66.7
Net income ($ mil.)	–	(1.8)	(0.4)	(2.1)	10.5	3.9
Market value ($ mil.)	342.5%	0.0	0.0	1.2	2.7	1.4
Employees	–	–	–	–	56	60

CAPTECH VENTURES, INC.

7100 FOREST AVE STE 100
RICHMOND, VA 232263794
Phone: 804 545-1570
Fax: –
Web: www.captechconsulting.com

CEO: –
CFO: –
HR: –
FYE: December 31
Type: Private

CapTech Ventures provides management and IT consulting and related services to business and public sector clients primarily in the Mid-Atlantic region. The company specializes in providing technology services and products (covering big data, agile methodology, mobile app development, and digital strategies for top companies and government agencies). Areas of specialty include data warehousing, network design, systems integration, software interface design, training, and network security. CapTech serves retailers, health care providers, and financial services companies among others. Clients have included Campbell Soup Company, the Richmond, Virginia Chamber of Commerce, and the US Navy.

	Annual Growth	12/00	12/01	12/02	12/04	12/11
Sales ($mil.)	21.4%	–	–	8.7	14.4	49.8
Net income ($ mil.)	33.1%	–	–	0.2	0.0	2.3
Market value ($ mil.)	–	–	–	–	–	–
Employees	–	–	–	–	–	415

CARA THERAPEUTICS INC
NMS: CARA

4 Stamford Plaza, 107 Elm Street, 9th Floor
Stamford, CT 06902
Phone: 203 406-3700
Fax: –
Web: www.caratherapeutics.com

CEO: Christopher Posner
CFO: Ryan Maynard
HR: Rene Barron
FYE: December 31
Type: Public

Cara Therapeutics is a commercial-stage biopharmaceutical company leading a new treatment paradigm to improve the lives of patients suffering from pruritus. Its primary activities to date have been organizing and staffing the company, developing its lead product and product candidates, including conducting preclinical studies and clinical trials of difelikefalin-based product candidates and raising capital. The Company's KORSUVA (difelikefalin) injection is the first and only FDA-approved treatment for moderate-to-severe pruritus associated with chronic kidney disease in adults undergoing hemodialysis. The company also developing an oral formulation of difelikefalin and has Phase 3 programs ongoing for the treatment of pruritus in patients with advanced chronic kidney disease and atopic dermatitis. The company was founded in 2004.

	Annual Growth	12/19	12/20	12/21	12/22	12/23
Sales ($mil.)	1.3%	19.9	135.1	23.0	41.9	21.0
Net income ($ mil.)	–	(106.4)	8.4	(88.4)	(85.5)	(118.5)
Market value ($ mil.)	(53.7%)	877.7	824.3	663.6	585.1	40.5
Employees	–	67	80	84	106	–

CARBO CERAMICS INC.

5050 WESTWAY PARK BLVD STE 150
HOUSTON, TX 770412018
Phone: 281 921-6400
Fax: –
Web: www.carboceramics.com

CEO: Shannon Nelson
CFO: Ernesto Bautista III
HR: –
FYE: December 31
Type: Private

CARBO Ceramics is a global technology company that provides products and services to several markets, including oil and gas, industrial, agricultural and environmental markets. CARBO delivers products that are engineered to provide superior strength, hardness and uniform shape that result in a high resistance to particle attrition and compressive breakdown. This results in less equipment wear during milling, reduces final product contamination and lowers process costs. CARBO Ceramics also offers related software, fracture evaluation and consulting services.

	Annual Growth	12/14	12/15	12/16	12/17	12/18
Sales ($mil.)	43.0%	–	–	103.1	188.8	210.7
Net income ($ mil.)	–	–	–	(80.1)	(253.1)	(75.4)
Market value ($ mil.)	–	–	–	–	–	–
Employees	–	–	–	–	–	250

CARBONITE, INC.

8470 ALLISON POINTE BLVD STE 300
INDIANAPOLIS, IN 462504365
Phone: 617 587-1100
Fax: –
Web: www.carbonite.com

CEO: Stephen Munford
CFO: Anthony Folger
HR: Sheryl Loeffler
FYE: December 31
Type: Private

Carbonite provides to keep your data safe from the common causes of data loss. The company has primary products to protect your data from onsite, cloud and hybrid backup to high availability and document retention, and give powerful, secure and reliable protection for any type of data. Carbonite products such as Carbonite Endpoint, Carbonite Backup for Microsoft 365, Carbonite Server, Carbonite Migrate, Carbonite Availability and Carbonite Recover.

CARDENAS MARKETS LLC

2501 E GUASTI RD
ONTARIO, CA 917617657
Phone: 909 923-7426
Fax: –
Web: www.cardenasmarkets.com

CEO: Doug Sanders
CFO: Matt Holt
HR: Arlene Lassi
FYE: December 31
Type: Private

Cardenas Markets brings Mexico and Central and South America to Southern California and Nevada. Establishing its first supermarket in 1979, the regional grocer serves California's and Nevada's Hispanic population through a chain of nearly 30 grocery stores. The company specializes in sourcing and selling a wide variety of products from south of the border. Each store, which operates under the Cardenas Markets banner, offers customers meat and seafood, fruits and vegetables, baked breads and cakes, juices, and even tortillas from its in-store tortillerias. They also provide services such as bus passes, money orders, phone cards, check cashing, and money transfers.

	Annual Growth	12/00	12/01	12/02	12/21	12/22
Sales ($mil.)	(22.4%)	–	114.7	–	0.5	0.6
Net income ($ mil.)		–	3.7	–	0.0	(0.1)
Market value ($ mil.)		–	–	–	–	–
Employees		–	–	–	–	6,630

CARDIACASSIST, INC.

620 ALPHA DR
PITTSBURGH, PA 152382836
Phone: 412 963-8883
Fax: –
Web: www.livanova.com

CEO: –
CFO: –
HR: –
FYE: December 01
Type: Private

CardiacAssist's products get your blood pumping, for real. The company makes the TandemHeart pVAD (percutaneous ventricular assist device), which pumps blood through the bodies of patients suffering from heart failure. Unlike most cardiac-assist devices, TandemHeart is available as both an external pump and an implantable device; meaning it can be used by interventional cardiologists in a cath lab and by cardiac surgeons in an operating room to provide short-term circulatory support. The company supplies its device (and related accessories) to US hospitals through an in-house sales team and internationally through a network of European distributors. CardiacAssist was founded in 1996 by a group of investors.

CARDINAL HEALTH, INC.

NYS: CAH

7000 Cardinal Place
Dublin, OH 43017
Phone: 614 757-5000
Fax: –
Web: www.cardinalhealth.com

CEO: –
CFO: –
HR: –
FYE: June 30
Type: Public

Cardinal Health is a distributor of pharmaceuticals, a global manufacturer and distributor of medical and laboratory products, and a provider of performance and data solutions for healthcare facilities. Its pharmaceutical segment provides supply chain services including branded, generic, and specialty pharmaceutical and OTC drug distribution. Cardinal's medical division parcels out medical, laboratory, and surgical supplies. It sells manufactured products in the US, Canada, Europe, Asia, Latin America and other markets. Customers include retail pharmacies (including chain and independent drug stores and pharmacy departments of supermarkets and mass merchandisers), hospitals, health care systems, surgery centers, nursing homes, doctor's offices, clinical labs, and other health care businesses. The US accounts for the majority of Cardinal's revenue.

	Annual Growth	06/19	06/20	06/21	06/22	06/23
Sales ($mil.)	8.9%	145,534	152,922	162,467	181,364	205,012
Net income ($ mil.)	(33.8%)	1,363.0	(3,696.0)	611.0	(933.0)	261.0
Market value ($ mil.)	19.0%	11,822	13,100	14,330	13,120	23,737
Employees	(0.8%)	49,500	30,000	47,300	46,500	48,000

CARDIOVASCULAR BIOTHERAPEUTICS INC

1635 Village Center Circle, Suite 250
Las Vegas, NV 89134
Phone: 702 839-7200
Fax: –
Web: www.cvbt.com

CEO: Daniel C Montano
CFO: Mickael A Flaa
HR: –
FYE: December 31
Type: Public

Far from being a heartbreaker, Cardiovascular BioTherapeutics works to patch 'em up. The development-stage firm is working on a therapeutic regimen to treat patients with coronary artery disease. Its lead product candidates are based on a fibroblast growth factor protein that induces angiogenesis (blood vessel growth). When injected directly into the heart near affected arteries, the protein has been shown to help repair the artery and increase blood flow to the heart. The company hopes to prove that the protein technology will also help stroke victims and diabetes patients, as well as help heal vertebral injuries and assist in bone growth.

CARDIOVASCULAR SYSTEMS, INC.

1225 OLD HIGHWAY 8 NW
SAINT PAUL, MN 551126416
Phone: 651 259-1600
Fax: –
Web: www.csi360.com

CEO: –
CFO: –
HR: –
FYE: June 30
Type: Private

Cardiovascular Systems, Inc. (CSI) is a medical technology company leading the way in the effort to successfully treat patients suffering from peripheral and coronary artery diseases, including those with arterial calcium, the most difficult form of arterial disease to treat. Its Orbital Atherectomy Systems (OAS) treat calcified and fibrotic plaque in arterial vessels throughout the leg and heart in a few minutes of treatment time, and address many of the limitations associated with existing surgical, catheter and pharmacological treatment alternatives. CSI's Diamondback 360 and Stealth 360 products are minimally invasive catheter systems that help restore blood flow to the legs of patients with peripheral arterial disease (PAD), a condition that occurs when plaque builds up on limb arteries; and address the effects of coronary arterial disease (CAD). Vast majority of its revenue comes from its domestic operation.

CARDTRONICS, INC.

864 SPRING ST NW
ATLANTA, GA 303081007
Phone: 832 308-4000
Fax: –
Web: www.ncratleos.com

CEO: Edward H West
CFO: –
HR: –
FYE: December 31
Type: Private

Cardtronics provides convenient access to cash and financial services where they are needed most. It maintains more than 285,000 Automated Teller machines and multi functions financial service kiosk across four continents such as Europe, Asia Pacific, Africa, and North America. As the world's largest ATM operator, Cardtronics employs its substantial scale and innovation advantages to deliver more transactions to every ATM, to enhance consumer convenience around the corner and across continents, and to enable financial institutions to focus on their customers while Cardtronics manages their far flung ATM operations. Cardtronics also operates Allpoint, which is the largest surcharge-free ATM network with a global footprint.

CARE NEW ENGLAND HEALTH SYSTEM INC

4 RICHMOND SQ
PROVIDENCE, RI 029065117
Phone: 401 453-7900
Fax: –
Web: www.carenewengland.org

CEO: James Finale
CFO: –
HR: Elaine Medina
FYE: September 30
Type: Private

Care New England Health System take pains to ease its patients' pain. The system operates four hospitals: Kent Hospital, a general acute care facility with about 360 beds; the 290-bed Memorial Hospital of Rhode Island; psychiatric facility Butler Hospital; and Women & Infants Hospital of Rhode Island, which specializes in obstetrics, gynecology, and newborn pediatrics. All told, the system has more than 963 licensed beds. Care New England, formed in 1996 by three member hospitals, also operates a home health agency and outpatient care facilities. In late 2016 the system dropped its plans to merge with Southcoast Health. The following year it agreed to be acquired by Partners HealthCare, which is expanding outside of Massachusetts.

	Annual Growth	09/16	09/17	09/19	09/20	09/21
Sales ($mil.)	2.5%	–	1,132.6	1,146.4	1,123.8	1,248.3
Net income ($ mil.)	52.7%	–	21.9	(30.4)	(26.0)	119.1
Market value ($ mil.)	–	–	–	–	–	–
Employees	–	–	–	–	–	6,500

CAREADVANTAGE, INC.

485-A Route 1 South
Iselin, NJ 08830
Phone: 732 362-5000
Fax: –
Web: www.careadvantage.com

CEO: –
CFO: –
HR: –
FYE: December 31
Type: Public

Your health care provider will be happy for you to get a checkup, and management consulting firm CareAdvantage will be happy to give your health care provider a checkup. The firm aims to help its customers -- insurance plans, hospital systems, employers, and other health care providers -- serve patients as efficiently as possible. Much of its business comes from Blue Cross Blue Shield organizations. CareAdvantage operates through two main units: CareAdvantage Health Systems and Contemporary HealthCare Management. The company's signature offering is its RightPath Navigator software, which helps clients analyze the health status and care usage of member populations.

	Annual Growth	12/06	12/07	12/08	12/09	12/10
Sales ($mil.)	(5.8%)	4.4	4.4	3.8	4.1	3.5
Net income ($ mil.)	–	(0.2)	(0.1)	(0.8)	0.2	(0.2)
Market value ($ mil.)	(24.5%)	2.9	2.0	0.1	1.6	0.9
Employees	(10.3%)	17	15	13	14	11

CARECLOUD INC

7 Clyde Road
Somerset, NJ 08873
Phone: 732 873-5133
Fax: –
Web: www.carecloud.com

NMS: CCLD P
CEO: A H Chaudhry
CFO: Joseph C Dossantos
HR: Mehr Nisa
FYE: December 31
Type: Public

This company helps doctors and other medical professionals get paid for the services they provide. Medical Transcription Billing, Corp. (MTBC) is a healthcare information technology company that makes web-based billing software for healthcare providers. Its flagship offering, PracticePro, is a SaaS platform that includes practice management software, electronic health records (or EHR), total revenue cycle management (or RCM) services, and smartphone applications. The software suite helps healthcare providers navigate the Affordable Care Act and other legal and industry developments. MTBC went public in 2014.

	Annual Growth	12/19	12/20	12/21	12/22	12/23
Sales ($mil.)	16.1%	64.4	105.1	139.6	138.8	117.1
Net income ($ mil.)	–	(0.9)	(8.8)	2.8	5.4	(48.7)
Market value ($ mil.)	(21.8%)	64.5	144.0	100.4	44.6	24.1
Employees	7.5%	2,700	3,700	4,100	4,150	3,600

CAREDX INC

8000 Marina Boulevard, 4th Floor
Brisbane, CA 94005
Phone: 415 287-2300
Fax: 415 287-2450
Web: www.caredx.com

NMS: CDNA
CEO: Peter Maag
CFO: –
HR: –
FYE: December 31
Type: Public

Rejection hurts, but organ transplant rejection hurts worse, and CareDx wants to help. The company makes tests that monitor cellular rejection in heart and kidney transplant patients. Its FDA-approved AlloMap test measures gene expression in patients' blood samples to determine if a transplanted heart has been accepted. The company believes its tests will help reduce costs by decreasing the number of biopsies and drug therapies often used in evaluating transplants in patients. CareDx is also working on the development of AlloMap for kidney transplant patients, and it has other molecular (gene-based) diagnostic research programs in areas such as immunology. Founded in 1998, the company went public in 2014.

	Annual Growth	12/19	12/20	12/21	12/22	12/23
Sales ($mil.)	21.9%	127.1	192.2	296.4	321.8	280.3
Net income ($ mil.)	–	(22.0)	(18.7)	(30.7)	(76.6)	(190.3)
Market value ($ mil.)	(13.6%)	1,110.9	3,731.4	2,342.4	587.7	618.0
Employees	13.6%	386	475	645	738	643

CAREGROUP, INC.

375 LONGWOOD AVE FL 7
BOSTON, MA 022155395
Phone: 617 975-5000
Fax: –
Web: www.caregroup.org

CEO: –
CFO: –
HR: –
FYE: September 30
Type: Private

Thanks to CareGroup, there's well-bein' in Beantown. CareGroup serves Massachusetts residents through its flagship facility, the over 670-bed Beth Israel Deaconess Medical Center (BIDMC), and five other hospital campuses. With more than 1,200 beds total, the system provides a comprehensive range of general acute care, as well as specialty care in a number of areas including orthopedics, obstetrics, diabetes, and cardiovascular disease. In addition to its hospitals, CareGroup operates a network of outpatient clinics and physician practices in the Boston area. It is also heavily involved in biomedical research and medical education.

	Annual Growth	09/09	09/10	09/11	09/12	09/15
Sales ($mil.)	(62.6%)	–	2,311.1	2,380.1	2,448.8	16.9
Net income ($ mil.)	–	–	98.2	47.0	131.3	(0.1)
Market value ($ mil.)	–	–	–	–	–	–
Employees	–	–	–	–	–	12,000

CARETRUST REIT INC   NYS: CTRE

905 Calle Amanecer, Suite 300
San Clemente, CA 92673
Phone: 949 542-3130
Fax: –
Web: www.caretrustreit.com

CEO: –
CFO: –
HR: –
FYE: December 31
Type: Public

For CareTrust, the golden years are truly golden. A self-administered real estate investment trust (REIT), CareTrust owns, acquires, and leases senior health care properties. Spun off from senior care operator Ensign Group in mid-2014, CareTrust owns about 215 skilled nursing, assisted living, and independent living facilities with more than 11,905 operational beds and units. Its properties are largely located in the western US, with concentrations in Texas, Louisiana and California. The REIT is looking to expand its property portfolio, which it expects to lease to variety of health care providers.

	Annual Growth	12/19	12/20	12/21	12/22	12/23
Sales ($mil.)	7.4%	163.4	178.3	192.4	196.1	217.8
Net income ($ mil.)	3.8%	46.4	80.9	72.0	(7.5)	53.7
Market value ($ mil.)	2.1%	2,681.8	2,883.2	2,967.7	2,415.3	2,909.2
Employees	(24.4%)	52	15	16	15	17

CARHARTT, INC.

5750 MERCURY DR
DEARBORN, MI 481264167
Phone: 313 271-8460
Fax: –
Web: www.carhartt.com

CEO: Mark Valade
CFO: Susan Telang
HR: –
FYE: December 31
Type: Private

Carhartt is a global premium workwear brand that makes rugged overalls, flame-resistant workwear, outerwear, sweatshirts, sportswear, and pants favored by farmers, construction workers, and other hard-working people. Most of Carhartt's products, sold to men, women, and children, are made in the US factories. Preferred online retailers include Army Surplus For Less, Bass Pro Shops, Cabela's, Dungarees, Gempler's, Harrison's Workwear, and Tractor Supply Co., among others. In addition to Carhartt's global operations in the US, Mexico, and Europe, the company produces its products in four facilities located in Kentucky and Tennessee. It operates more than 35 Carhartt company stores nationwide. The family of founder Hamilton Carhartt owns the company, which was founded in 1889.

CARIBOU COFFEE COMPANY, INC.

3900 LAKE BREEZE AVE
MINNEAPOLIS, MN 554293921
Phone: 612 295-0707
Fax: –
Web: www.cariboucoffee.com

CEO: John Butcher
CFO: –
HR: Julie Droegemueller
FYE: December 31
Type: Private

Caribou Coffee is one of the leading coffee chains with stores in Minnesota and in in all 50 other states. Among the most successful coffee shops, the company operates coffeehouses across the US. In addition, it also operates in Asia, Africa, and the Middle East. The outlets offer fresh-brewed coffee along with specialty coffee drinks such as dark roast and flavored coffee. Caribou Coffee's stores also sell drinkware (tumblers, mugs and cold cups), apparel (shirts, outerwear and headwear), and more.

CARILION CLINIC

1906 BELLEVIEW AVE SE
ROANOKE, VA 240141838
Phone: 540 981-7900
Fax: –
Web: www.carilionclinic.org

CEO: Nancy H Agee
CFO: Don Lorton
HR: Jamie Ghypes
FYE: September 30
Type: Private

Carilion Clinic is not a profit health care organization with a comprehensive network hospitals, primary and specialty practices. Carilion Clinic specialized in adolescent medicine, allergy and immunology, breast surgery, cardiology, dermatology and more. Carilion Clinic (including its handful of affiliates) has more than 1,000 licensed beds and 60 neonatal ICU beds available. In addition to providing a range of medical treatments, Carilion Clinic provides continuing medical education through its affiliation with medical schools, including Virginia Tech Carilion School of Medicine and Research Institute (VTC).

CARISMA THERAPEUTICS INC   NAS: CARM

3675 Market Street, Suite 200
Philadelphia, PA 19104
Phone: 267 491-6422
Fax: –
Web: www.sesenbio.com

CEO: –
CFO: –
HR: –
FYE: December 31
Type: Public

After its EBI-005 treatment for dry eye disease failed in late-stage clinical trials, Eleven Biotherapeutics reinvented itself as a cancer fighter. The biologics firm acquired Canadian biotech Viventia Bio in September 2016, gaining that firm's roster of development programs targeting bladder cancer (Vicinium) and head and neck cancer (Proxinium). The new company is developing Targeted Protein Therapeutics (TPTs), some in combination with immunotherapy treatments. Eleven Bio went public in 2014 on the promise of its eye disease treatments but, once its most advanced candidate failed in trials, it cut 70% of its workforce. It began seeking new life in other fields and found hope with the purchase of Viventia Bio.Distancing itself from its troubled past, the company is now changing its name to Sesen Bio.

	Annual Growth	12/18	12/19	12/20	12/21	12/22
Sales ($mil.)	–	–	–	11.2	26.5	40.0
Net income ($ mil.)	–	(33.7)	(107.5)	(22.4)	(0.3)	(19.9)
Market value ($ mil.)	(19.1%)	14.4	10.5	13.7	8.3	6.2
Employees	(8.3%)	24	25	27	35	17

CARL BUDDIG AND COMPANY

950 W175 ST
HOMEWOOD, IL 604302027
Phone: 708 798-0900
Fax: –
Web: www.buddig.com

CEO: Thomas Buddig
CFO: –
HR: Danielle Hitterman
FYE: October 31
Type: Private

Carl Buddig & Company offers a large variety of affordable and packed-to-go lunchmeats that make lunch too delicious to be eaten just once a day. One of the largest-selling brands in lunchmeats, its Original Buddig brand comes in choices such as beef, chicken, ham, pastrami, and corned beef. It also offers the Old Wisconsin brand of smoked beef jerky sticks and snack bites, along with summer sausage, and hand-tied summer sausage. In addition, its Kingsford brand offers ribs and BBQ entrees to family dinners and cookouts. The company is owned by the founding Buddig family. The company was founded in 1943.

CARLE FOUNDATION HOSPITAL

611 W PARK ST
URBANA, IL 618012501
Phone: 217 326-2900
Fax: –
Web: www.carle.org

CEO: –
CFO: –
HR: –
FYE: December 31
Type: Private

The 453-bed Carle Foundation Hospital is a Level I Trauma Center and offers Level III perinatal services. It's certified as a Comprehensive Stroke Center and Level 3 Epilepsy Center. It has the largest emergency room in the region, offering comprehensive emergency services 24/7 to more than 90,000 patients each year. The Carle Foundation Hospital is the flagship hospital of Carle Health, an integrated system of healthcare services, which includes a five-hospital system, multi-specialty physician groups, as well as Carle Illinois College of Medicine and the Stephens Family Clinical Research Institute.

	Annual Growth	12/16	12/17	12/18	12/20	12/21
Sales ($mil.)	7.4%	–	900.8	937.8	1,038.8	1,197.5
Net income ($ mil.)	(2.9%)	–	247.6	216.5	182.0	219.7
Market value ($ mil.)	–	–	–	–	–	–
Employees	–	–	–	–	–	2,500

CARLETON COLLEGE

1 N COLLEGE ST
NORTHFIELD, MN 550574044
Phone: 507 222-4000
Fax: –
Web: www.carleton.edu

CEO: –
CFO: –
HR: –
FYE: June 30
Type: Private

Curiosity is key at Carleton College. In addition to providing a traditional undergraduate, liberal arts education, the school encourages critical thinking and creativity at its campus in southern Minnesota. It has an enrollment of some 2,000 students and a student-to-teacher ratio of 9:1. The college confers Bachelor of Arts degrees in more than 35 academic majors, with a focus on fields including biology, chemistry, physics, mathematics, and computer science. The school offers education and foreign language certification and pre-professional programs, as well. Carleton College was founded in 1866 by the Minnesota Conference of Congregational Churches under the name of Northfield College.

	Annual Growth	06/18	06/19	06/20	06/21	06/22
Sales ($mil.)	1.0%	–	154.1	240.3	151.0	158.5
Net income ($ mil.)	–	–	29.8	40.8	327.0	(69.8)
Market value ($ mil.)	–	–	–	–	–	–
Employees	–	–	–	–	–	650

CARLING TECHNOLOGIES, INC.

60 JOHNSON AVE
PLAINVILLE, CT 060621181
Phone: 860 793-9281
Fax: –
Web: www.carlingtech.com

CEO: –
CFO: –
HR: Abigail Richardson
FYE: June 30
Type: Private

Carling Technologies gives circuits a break. The company designs and manufactures a variety of electrical circuit breakers (hydraulic, magnetic, and thermal); electrical switches and assemblies; power distribution centers; digital switching systems; and electronic controls. It provides custom product design and tool-and-die fabrication, as well as technical and engineering services, to suit its clients' individual needs. Products are used by industrial and electronic makers for applications such as electronics, industrial controls, appliances, commercial food equipment, generators, HVAC equipment, security systems, and factory automation.

	Annual Growth	06/08	06/09	06/10	06/13	06/14
Sales ($mil.)	(81.5%)	–	–	736.2	1.5	0.9
Net income ($ mil.)	–	–	–	–	0.3	(0.3)
Market value ($ mil.)	–	–	–	–	–	–
Employees	–	–	–	–	–	2,600

CARLISLE COMPANIES INC.

16430 North Scottsdale Road, Suite 400
Scottsdale, AZ 85254
Phone: 480 781-5000
Fax: –
Web: www.carlisle.com

NYS: CSL
CEO: D C Koch
CFO: Kevin P Zdimal
HR: –
FYE: December 31
Type: Public

Carlisle Companies Incorporated is a global manufacturer of highly engineered products, including innovative building envelope products and energy-efficient solutions for customers creating sustainable buildings through its Carlisle Construction Materials (CCM) segment, and family of leading brands. High-performance waterproofing and moisture protection products for the building envelope sold through its Carlisle Weatherproofing Technologies (CWT). Interconnect products sold in the aerospace, medical technologies and general industrial markets through its Carlisle Interconnect Technologies (CIT) segment and finishing equipment and integrated system solutions through its Carlisle Fluid Technologies (CFT) segment. The company markets its products to original equipment manufacturers, distributors, and directly to end-users. The US accounts for around 85% of the company's total sales.

	Annual Growth	12/19	12/20	12/21	12/22	12/23
Sales ($mil.)	(1.2%)	4,811.6	4,245.2	4,810.3	6,591.9	4,586.9
Net income ($ mil.)	12.9%	472.8	320.1	421.7	924.0	767.4
Market value ($ mil.)	17.9%	7,719.8	7,449.8	11,835	11,241	14,903
Employees	(7.5%)	15,000	13,000	11,500	12,500	11,000

CARLYLE GROUP INC (THE)

1001 Pennsylvania Avenue, N.W.
Washington, DC 20004-2505
Phone: 202 729-5626
Fax: –
Web: www.carlyle.com

NMS: CG
CEO: Harvey M Schwartz
CFO: John C Redett
HR: –
FYE: December 31
Type: Public

A global investment firm, The Carlyle Group is a global alternative asset manager with more than $373 billion in assets under management. Through three business segments, the company invests in real estate, power, infrastructure, energy, distressed credit, energy credit, opportunistic credit, corporate mezzanine funds, aircraft financing and servicing, other closed-end credit funds, vehicles and corporate buyouts across numerous industries and regions. Carlyle has about 545 investment vehicles, and serve more than 2,900 active carry fund investors from around 90 countries. Most of the company's revenue comes from the Americas, which accounts for almost 60% of revenue.

	Annual Growth	12/19	12/20	12/21	12/22	12/23
Sales ($mil.)	(3.2%)	3,377.0	2,934.6	8,782.1	4,438.7	2,963.9
Net income ($ mil.)	–	380.9	348.2	2,974.7	1,225.0	(608.4)
Market value ($ mil.)	6.1%	11,591	11,360	19,837	10,782	14,702
Employees	5.5%	1,775	1,825	1,850	2,100	2,200

CARMA LABORATORIES, INC.

5801 W AIRWAYS AVE
FRANKLIN, WI 531329111
Phone: 414 421-7707
Fax: –
Web: www.mycarmex.com

CEO: Dave Kamm
CFO: –
HR: Beth Maloney
FYE: December 31
Type: Private

Carma Laboratories is a third-generation, family-owned company that manufactures and distributes all Carmex products. Carmex (now also in cherry and strawberry flavors) soothes lips in the US and in more than 60 countries and regions around the globe. Its product categories include Daily Care Minis, Daily Care, Comfort Care, Holiday, Cold Sore and Classic. The company was founded by Alfred Woelbing, who developed the formula for Carmex in 1937 as a treatment for his own cold sores.

	Annual Growth	12/03	12/04	12/05	12/07	12/09
Sales ($mil.)	9.4%	–	–	28.0	42.7	40.2
Net income ($ mil.)	5.3%	–	–	10.8	14.9	13.3
Market value ($ mil.)	–	–	–	–	–	–
Employees	–	–	–	–	–	70

CARMAX INC.   NYS: KMX

12800 Tuckahoe Creek Parkway   CEO: –
Richmond, VA 23238   CFO: –
Phone: 804 747-0422   HR: –
Fax: –   FYE: February 28
Web: www.carmax.com   Type: Public

CarMax is the US's largest used-car retailer that buys, reconditions, and sells cars through approximately 240 stores in almost 110 television markets. It offers customers a broad selection of makes and models of used vehicles, including domestic, imported, and luxury vehicles, as well as hybrid and electric vehicles, and sells about 807,825 used cars per year. The company is also one of the nation's largest operators of wholesale vehicle auctions, with about 585,070 vehicles sold annually. Additionally, it sells older vehicles with higher mileage in its auctions and Carmax also offers vehicle financing through its CarMax Auto Finance unit.

	Annual Growth	02/19	02/20	02/21	02/22	02/23
Sales ($mil.)	13.1%	18,173	20,320	18,950	31,900	29,685
Net income ($ mil.)	(12.9%)	842.4	888.4	746.9	1,151.3	484.8
Market value ($ mil.)	2.7%	9,816.7	13,802	18,892	17,283	10,914
Employees	4.2%	25,946	27,050	26,889	32,647	30,621

CARMIKE CINEMAS, LLC

11500 ASH ST   CEO: Adam M Aron
LEAWOOD, KS 662117804   CFO: Craig R Ramsey
Phone: 913 213-2000   HR: –
Fax: –   FYE: December 31
Web: www.amctheatres.com   Type: Private

At Carmike Cinemas, the show must go on. The movie exhibitor owns, operates, or has stakes in about 250 theaters with more than 2,500 screens in 35 states across the US. The company's theaters are located mostly in small to midsized communities where the chain hosts the only theater in town. Revenues come from the sale of admission tickets and concessions. Carmike also owns two Hollywood Connection family entertainment centers (one in Georgia and one in Utah), which feature multiplex theaters along with skating rinks, miniature golf, and arcades.

CARNEGIE INSTITUTION OF WASHINGTON

1530 P ST NW   CEO: –
WASHINGTON, DC 200051910   CFO: Cynthia Allen
Phone: 202 387-6400   HR: –
Fax: –   FYE: June 30
Web: www.carnegiescience.edu   Type: Private

The folks that work at the Carnegie Institution of Washington aren't exactly melon heads. The organization, known to the public as the Carnegie Institution for Science, supports scientific research in areas such as plant biology, developmental biology, Earth and planetary sciences, astronomy, and global ecology. It operates via six scientific departments on the East and West Coasts. The institution, funded primarily by an endowment of more than $530 million, was established in 1902 by steel magnate Andrew Carnegie (whose other philanthropic endeavors included the Carnegie Corporation of New York and Carnegie Mellon University).

	Annual Growth	06/17	06/18	06/19	06/20	06/22
Sales ($mil.)	5.2%	–	134.5	67.3	74.0	164.7
Net income ($ mil.)	13.7%	–	39.6	(34.1)	(20.0)	66.3
Market value ($ mil.)	–	–	–	–	–	–
Employees	–	–	–	–	–	500

CARNEGIE-MELLON UNIVERSITY

5000 FORBES AVE   CEO: –
PITTSBURGH, PA 152133890   CFO: Amir R Azar
Phone: 412 268-2000   HR: Beth Rupp
Fax: –   FYE: June 30
Web: www.cmu.edu   Type: Private

Carnegie Mellon University is a private, global research university, and one of the world's most renowned educational institutions. Carnegie Mellon enrolls approximately 15,800 students and granted some 5,150 bachelor's, master's, and doctoral degrees. About 80% of undergraduate students are from the US. International students comprise more than 20% of undergraduate, about 65% of master's, and nearly 55% of Ph.D. students. Carnegie Mellon was founded by philanthropist and industrialist Andrew Carnegie, who established the Carnegie Technical Schools in 1900 for the sons and daughters of Pittsburgh's blue-collar workers.

	Annual Growth	06/18	06/19	06/20	06/21	06/22
Sales ($mil.)	6.4%	–	1,363.1	1,850.1	1,672.7	1,642.7
Net income ($ mil.)	(13.4%)	–	207.5	411.6	1,525.8	134.9
Market value ($ mil.)	–	–	–	–	–	–
Employees	–	–	–	–	–	4,913

CARNIVAL CORP   NYS: CCL

3655 N.W. 87th Avenue   CEO: Josh Weinstein
Miami, FL 33178-2428   CFO: David Bernstein
Phone: 305 599-2600   HR: –
Fax: –   FYE: November 30
Web: www.carnivalcorp.com   Type: Public

Carnival Corporation is the largest global cruise company and among the largest leisure travel companies with a portfolio of world-class cruise lines. Carnival has a portfolio of nine leading cruise lines with a fleet of more than 90 ships visiting over 700 ports around the world under normal operations and with total lower berths of about 223,000. With operations in North America, Australia, Europe, and Asia, Carnival's portfolio features - AIDA Cruises, Carnival Cruise Line, Costa Cruises, Cunard, Holland America Line, Princess Cruises, P&O Cruises (Australia), P&O Cruises (UK) and Seabourn. A total of eight new ships are scheduled to be delivered to Carnival Corporation's brands through 2025. Carnival operates as a dual-listed company with UK-based Carnival plc, forming a single enterprise under a unified executive team.

	Annual Growth	11/19	11/20	11/21	11/22	11/23
Sales ($mil.)	0.9%	20,825	5,595.0	1,908.0	12,168	21,593
Net income ($ mil.)	–	2,990.0	(10,236.0)	(9,501.0)	(6,093.0)	(74.0)
Market value ($ mil.)	(24.0%)	56,981	25,255	22,272	12,552	19,036
Employees	3.6%	92,000	58,000	30,000	75,000	106,000

CAROLINA HANDLING, LLC

4835 SIRONA DR STE 100   CEO: –
CHARLOTTE, NC 282733253   CFO: –
Phone: 704 357-6273   HR: Emily Hunter
Fax: –   FYE: December 31
Web: www.carolinahandling.com   Type: Private

Founded in 1966, Carolina Handling is one of the Southeast's leading material handling solution providers and the exclusive Raymond Solutions and Support Center for North Carolina, South Carolina, Georgia, Alabama and Florida's Central time zone territory. The company provides lift trucks and automation solutions for warehouses and distribution centers, as well as parts, racking, storage, lighting and dock and door equipment.

	Annual Growth	12/04	12/05	12/06	12/07	12/08
Sales ($mil.)	(66.7%)	–	–	1,045.5	107.5	116.2
Net income ($ mil.)	33722.9%	–	–	0.0	4.3	4.1
Market value ($ mil.)	–	–	–	–	–	–
Employees	–	–	–	–	–	356

CAROLINAS MEDICAL CENTER-LINCOLN

433 MCALISTER RD
LINCOLNTON, NC 280924147
Phone: 980 212-2000
Fax: –
Web: www.carolinashealthcare.org/locations/carolinas-healthcare-system-lincoln

CEO: –
CFO: –
HR: –
FYE: December 31
Type: Private

Honestly, this Lincoln County hospital is there to care for all its citizens' health needs. Carolinas Medical Center-Lincoln (formerly Lincoln Medical Center) provides a host of medical services to Tar Heelers that range from general acute care to home health, imaging, surgery, and heart care. The 100-bed medical center also offers pain management services, rehabilitation, a birthing center, and comprehensive diabetes care. Carolinas Medical Center-Lincoln conducts research and clinical trials focused on a range of maladies including cardiology, oncology, and pediatric ailments. The hospital became part of the Carolinas HealthCare System (CHS) several years ago; it is led by CEO Michael Tarwater.

	Annual Growth	12/13	12/14	12/15	12/16	12/17
Sales ($mil.)	5.6%	–	105.2	116.4	116.4	124.1
Net income ($ mil.)	12.5%	–	14.0	24.0	17.0	20.0
Market value ($ mil.)	–	–	–	–	–	–
Employees	–	–	–	–	–	550

CAROMONT HEALTH, INC.

2525 COURT DR
GASTONIA, NC 280542140
Phone: 704 834-2000
Fax: –
Web: www.caromonthealth.org

CEO: Douglas Luckett
CFO: David O'Connor
HR: Melinda White
FYE: June 30
Type: Private

CaroMont Health is an independent not-for-profit health care system serving residents of North Carolina's Piedmont region. Anchoring CaroMont Health is Gaston Memorial Hospital, a 435-bed medical and surgical facility that features a birthing center, an inpatient psychiatric ward, and specialized facilities for heart disease, cancer, sleep disorders, diabetes, and wound care. Other operations include a nearly 100-bed nursing home, outpatient surgery and urgent care centers, and a network of primary and specialty medical practices. CaroMont Health also provides home health and hospice care services. CaroMont Health is governed by the North Carolina Medical Care Commission.

	Annual Growth	06/16	06/17	06/18	06/19	06/20
Sales ($mil.)	(64.8%)	–	552.4	602.7	510.6	24.2
Net income ($ mil.)	(36.7%)	–	80.6	63.3	54.3	20.4
Market value ($ mil.)	–	–	–	–	–	–
Employees	–	–	–	–	–	2,400

CARPARTS.COM INC (NEW)   NMS: PRTS

2050 W. 190th Street, Suite 400
Torrance, CA 90504
Phone: 424 702-1455
Fax: –
Web: www.carparts.com

CEO: –
CFO: –
HR: –
FYE: December 30
Type: Public

CarParts.com, Inc. is a leading online provider of aftermarket auto parts and accessories. The company offers a comprehensive selection of over 913,000 SKUs with detailed product descriptions, attributes, and photographs through its user-friendly website, and mobile-friendly platform. The company has developed a proprietary product database that maps its SKUs to product applications based on vehicle makes, models, and years to help ensure the right part for each specific vehicle is provided. Its inventory includes replacement parts, hard parts, and performance parts and accessories. The company's online sales channel and relationships with suppliers enable it to eliminate intermediaries in the traditional auto parts supply chain and to offer a broader selection of SKUs than can easily be offered by offline retailer competition.

	Annual Growth	12/19*	01/21	01/22*	12/22	12/23
Sales ($mil.)	24.6%	280.7	443.9	582.4	661.6	675.7
Net income ($ mil.)	–	(31.5)	(1.5)	(10.3)	(1.0)	(8.2)
Market value ($ mil.)	10.5%	122.0	713.2	644.7	360.4	181.9
Employees	19.1%	843	1,649	1,529	976	1,695

*Fiscal year change

CARPENTER CONTRACTORS OF AMERICA, INC.

3900 AVE D N W
WINTER HAVEN, FL 33880
Phone: 863 294-6449
Fax: –
Web: www.carpentercontractors.com

CEO: –
CFO: –
HR: –
FYE: February 03
Type: Private

Carpenter Contractors of America has been working with wood for more than half of a century. The company manufactures roof trusses and wall panels and supplies building materials through its manufacturing facilities in Florida. The company also has offices in North Carolina and Illinois, where it operates under the name R&D Thiel. The company's products and services are used in both residential and commercial construction. In 1955 brothers Robert and Donald Thiel founded the company as R&D Thiel in Belvidere, Illinois. Carpenter Contractors of America filed for Chapter 11 bankruptcy in 2010.

	Annual Growth	01/99	01/00*	02/01	02/02	02/07
Sales ($mil.)	12.1%	–	159.0	174.2	183.8	353.6
Net income ($ mil.)	13.6%	–	5.0	8.0	8.1	12.3
Market value ($ mil.)	–	–	–	–	–	–
Employees	–	–	–	–	–	1,000

*Fiscal year change

CARPENTER TECHNOLOGY CORP.   NYS: CRS

1735 Market Street, 15th Floor
Philadelphia, PA 19103
Phone: 610 208-2000
Fax: –
Web: www.carpentertechnology.com

CEO: Tony R Thene
CFO: Timothy F Lain
HR: –
FYE: June 30
Type: Public

Carpenter Technology (Carpenter) is a producer and distributor of premium specialty alloys, including titanium alloys, powder metals, stainless steels, alloy steels, and tool steels. The company primarily processes basic raw materials such as nickel, cobalt, titanium, manganese, chromium, molybdenum, iron scrap, as well as alloys specifically engineered for additive manufacturing processes and soft magnetics applications. Major customers operate in the aerospace, defense, medical, transportation, energy, industrial and consumer end-use markets. Carpenter's primary geographic market is the US (almost 65% of sales), but the company claims customers worldwide. It was founded in 1889.

	Annual Growth	06/19	06/20	06/21	06/22	06/23
Sales ($mil.)	1.7%	2,380.2	2,181.1	1,475.6	1,836.3	2,550.3
Net income ($ mil.)	(23.8%)	167.0	1.5	(229.6)	(49.1)	56.4
Market value ($ mil.)	4.0%	2,333.5	1,180.9	1,956.1	1,357.4	2,729.9
Employees	(3.1%)	5,100	4,600	3,900	4,100	4,500

CARRIAGE SERVICES, INC.   NYS: CSV

3040 Post Oak Boulevard, Suite 300
Houston, TX 77056
Phone: 713 332-8400
Fax: –
Web: www.carriageservices.com

CEO: Carlos R Quezada
CFO: Kian Granmayeh
HR: –
FYE: December 31
Type: Public

Carriage Services is a leading provider of funeral and cemetery services and merchandise in the US. The company runs approximately 170 funeral homes (owned and leased) in about 25 states and more than 30 cemeteries (owned and leased) operating in nearly a dozen states, mostly in California, Florida, and Texas. The company offers a complete range of services to meet a family's funeral needs, including consultation, the removal and preparation of remains, the sale of caskets and related funeral merchandise, the use of funeral home facilities for visitation and memorial services and transportation services. It also provides funeral and cemetery services and products on both an "atneed" (time of death) and "preneed" (planned prior to death) basis.

	Annual Growth	12/19	12/20	12/21	12/22	12/23
Sales ($mil.)	8.7%	274.1	329.4	375.9	370.2	382.5
Net income ($ mil.)	23.1%	14.5	16.1	33.2	41.4	33.4
Market value ($ mil.)	(0.6%)	384.0	469.8	966.6	413.1	375.1
Employees	(1.8%)	2,797	2,718	2,657	2,553	2,602

CARRIER ALLIANCE HOLDINGS INC
NBB: CAHI

120C Wilbur Place
Bohemia, NY 11776
Phone: 646 307-6911
Fax: –
Web: www.tildencarcare.com

CEO: –
CFO: –
HR: –
FYE: December 31
Type: Public

Providing customers with a full line of automotive repairs and services is what drives Tilden Associates. The company franchises about 50 Tilden Your Total Car Care Centers across the country, but most shops are located in New York, Florida, and Colorado. In addition to brake work, the stores offer oil changes, tune-ups, and general automotive repairs. The company's Tilden Equipment Corp. sells shop equipment to franchisees, and its real estate subsidiaries hold leases on store sites. The Tilden brand traces its history to a brake shop founded by Sydney G. Tilden in 1923.

	Annual Growth	12/07	12/08	12/09	12/10	12/11
Sales ($mil.)	(7.2%)	1.5	1.3	1.4	1.4	1.1
Net income ($ mil.)	–	(0.3)	(0.0)	(0.1)	(0.0)	(0.1)
Market value ($ mil.)	(25.2%)	0.0	0.0	0.0	0.0	0.0
Employees	–	–	3	4	4	3

CARRIER GLOBAL CORP
NYS: CARR

13995 Pasteur Boulevard
Palm Beach Gardens, FL 33418
Phone: 561 365-2000
Fax: –
Web: www.carrier.com

CEO: David Gitlin
CFO: Patrick Goris
HR: Latonya Reed
FYE: December 31
Type: Public

Carrier Global Corporation is a leading global provider of healthy, safe, sustainable, and intelligent building and cold chain solutions with a focus on providing differentiated, digitally-enabled lifecycle solutions to its customers. The company's portfolio includes industry-leading brands such as Carrier, Toshiba, Automated Logic, Carrier Transicold, Kidde, Edwards, and LenelS2 that offer innovative heating, ventilating, and air conditioning (HVAC), refrigeration, fire, security, and building automation technologies to help make the world safer and more comfortable. Carrier Global also provides a broad array of related building services, including audit, design, installation, system integration, repair, maintenance, and monitoring. The US is the company's largest market accounting for almost 60% of the company's revenue.

	Annual Growth	12/19	12/20	12/21	12/22	12/23
Sales ($mil.)	4.4%	18,608	17,456	20,613	20,421	22,098
Net income ($ mil.)	(10.6%)	2,116.0	1,982.0	1,664.0	3,534.0	1,349.0
Market value ($ mil.)	–	–	–	31,669	45,539	34,633	48,234
Employees	0.2%	52,635	56,000	58,000	52,000	53,000

CARRIO CABLING CORPORATION

2455 EXECUTIVE CIR
COLORADO SPRINGS, CO 809064182
Phone: 719 576-4571
Fax: –
Web: www.carriocabling.com

CEO: –
CFO: –
HR: –
FYE: December 31
Type: Private

Carrio Cabling Corporation carries on a simple but successful business tradition -- keep it simple. The company makes custom molded cable assemblies, coiled cords, and connectors to meet the specific needs of its various customers. Custom products go through a six-part process that includes sketching, designing, prototyping, tooling, testing and manufacturing before finally being delivered. It serves business customers in the broadcast, computer, industrial, military, and medical industries. Its products are manufactured in its 25,000 sq. ft. facility and headquarters in Colorado.

	Annual Growth	12/02	12/03	12/04	12/05	12/12
Sales ($mil.)	(66.9%)	–	5.2	4.5	6.2	0.0
Net income ($ mil.)	–	–	0.3	(0.2)	0.4	(0.0)
Market value ($ mil.)	–	–	–	–	–	–
Employees	–	–	–	–	–	48

CARRIX, INC.

1131 SW KLICKITAT WAY
SEATTLE, WA 981341108
Phone: 206 623-0304
Fax: –
Web: www.carrix.com

CEO: –
CFO: –
HR: –
FYE: December 31
Type: Private

Carrix is a Hall of Famer -- the Maritime Hall of Fame, that is. Holding company Carrix carries three transportation-related businesses on its books. The company's SSA Marine unit is a leading marine terminal operator. It loads and unloads ships and provides warehousing and distribution services. Overall, SSA Marine operates from about 120 locations worldwide. Other Carrix units include Rail Management Services (RMS), which operates more than 30 rail-yards in more than a dozen states. Thirdly, Tideworks Technology produces marine terminal management software.

CARROLS RESTAURANT GROUP INC
NMS: TAST

968 James Street
Syracuse, NY 13203
Phone: 315 424-0513
Fax: –
Web: www.carrols.com

CEO: Daniel T Accordino
CFO: Anthony E Hull
HR: Gerald J Digenova
FYE: January 1
Type: Public

Carrols Restaurant Group (also known as Carrols) is one of the leading quick-service restaurant operators and the world's largest Burger King franchisee, with around 1,025 locations in the US. As a franchisee of Burger King and Popeyes, the company also has contractual rights to use certain trademarks, service marks, and other intellectual property relating to the Burger King and Popeyes concepts. The company has no proprietary intellectual property other than the Carrols logo and trademark. In addition, almost all of the company's restaurants are freestanding. It has been operating Burger King restaurants since 1976.

	Annual Growth	12/18	12/19*	01/21	01/22	01/23
Sales ($mil.)	10.1%	1,179.3	1,462.8	1,547.5	1,652.4	1,730.4
Net income ($ mil.)	–	10.1	(31.9)	(29.5)	(43.0)	(75.6)
Market value ($ mil.)	(38.3%)	477.5	349.7	319.7	150.7	69.2
Employees	(0.2%)	24,500	31,500	26,500	25,500	24,300

*Fiscal year change

CARRY TRANSIT, LLC

711 JORIE BLVD STE 101N
OAK BROOK, IL 605232217
Phone: 630 573-2555
Fax: –
Web: www.superiorbulklogistics.com

CEO: –
CFO: –
HR: Yvania Sanchez
FYE: December 31
Type: Private

Superior Bulk Logistics, through subsidiaries Superior Carriers and Carry Transit, hauls liquid and dry bulk cargo, including both chemical and food-grade products. Overall, the trucking units of Superior Bulk Logistics operate a fleet of some 875 tractors and 2,000 trailers. The company's SuperFlo unit provides transloading services -- the transfer of cargo between railcars and trucks. Superior Bulk Logistics' Sanicare Wash Systems unit cleans tank truck trailers and other bulk containers used for food products. Superior Bulk Logistics offers service between Mexico and the US and Canada through a partnership with Transpormex, a division of Grupo Dexel.

	Annual Growth	12/04	12/05	12/06	12/07	12/09
Sales ($mil.)	(5.1%)	–	–	220.5	235.0	188.2
Net income ($ mil.)	(26.0%)	–	–	5.1	7.2	2.0
Market value ($ mil.)	–	–	–	–	–	–
Employees	–	–	–	–	–	2,201

CARSON TAHOE REGIONAL HEALTHCARE

1600 MEDICAL PKWY
CARSON CITY, NV 897034625
Phone: 775 445-8000
Fax: —
Web: www.carsontahoe.com

CEO: Michelle Joy
CFO: Ann Beck
HR: —
FYE: December 31
Type: Private

Carson Tahoe Regional Healthcare, which includes the Carson Tahoe Regional Medical Center (CTRMC), serves Nevada's Carson Valley and its surrounding areas. The not-for-profit CTRMC boasts about 220 beds and provides a wide range of services, such as acute general, surgical, specialty, and outpatient care. The medical center also includes a rehabilitation center, cardiovascular center, surgical unit, free-standing cancer center, emergency room, and women and children's center. Carson Tahoe Regional Healthcare also operates smaller urgent care, behavioral health, physical therapy, and outpatient care centers in Carson City and nearby communities.

	Annual Growth	12/17	12/18	12/19	12/21	12/22
Sales ($mil.)	4.3%	—	—	298.3	312.1	359.3	353.3
Net income ($ mil.)	—	—	—	7.9	31.5	11.1	(23.5)
Market value ($ mil.)	—	—	—	—	—	—
Employees	—	—	—	—	—	2,000

CARTER'S INC   NYS: CRI

Phipps Tower, 3438 Peachtree Road N.E., Suite 1800
Atlanta, GA 30326
Phone: 678 791-1000
Fax: —
Web: www.carters.com

CEO: Michael D Casey
CFO: Richard F Westenberger
HR: —
FYE: December 30
Type: Public

Carter's is the largest maker in the US of branded apparel exclusively for babies and young children. Primary products include newborn layette clothing, sleepwear, and playwear. It markets its items under the Carter's, OshKosh B'Gosh, and Skip Hop brands, as well as private labels Child of Mine, Just One You, and Simple Joys. With more than 40 international licensees who operated in more than 90 countries, Carter's distributes its products through multiple channels such as retail stores, e-commerce, and wholesale sales channels. Its channels include about 995 retail stores and approximately 19,350 wholesale locations. The company operates more than 755 retail stores in the US, over 185 in Canada, and around 50 in Mexico.

	Annual Growth	12/19*	01/21	01/22*	12/22	12/23
Sales ($mil.)	(4.4%)	3,519.3	3,024.3	3,486.4	3,212.7	2,945.6
Net income ($ mil.)	(3.1%)	263.8	109.7	339.7	250.0	232.5
Market value ($ mil.)	(9.2%)	4,022.8	3,438.4	3,699.7	2,727.1	2,737.3
Employees	(6.9%)	20,300	18,000	15,900	15,500	15,230

*Fiscal year change

CARTESIAN, INC.

6405 METCALF AVE STE 417
OVERLAND PARK, KS 662023930
Phone: 913 345-9315
Fax: —
Web: www.cartesian.com

CEO: Jim Serafin
CFO: —
HR: —
FYE: December 31
Type: Private

The Management Network Group, which does business as TMNG Global, helps its clients answer the call in the ever-changing communications industry. The company provides management, strategic, and operational consulting services to communications service providers, technology companies, and financial services firms. Its TMNG Marketing unit offers a full range of marketing and customer relationship management services, including product development, market research, and customer retention programs. The company's Ascertain suite of software products allows customers to manage billing services, analyze customer data, and monitor trends. Founded in 1990, TMNG Global serves clients primarily in the US and the UK.

CARVANA CO   NYS: CVNA

300 E. Rio Salado Parkway
Tempe, AZ 85281
Phone: 602 852-6604
Fax: —
Web: www.carvana.com

CEO: Ernest Garcia III
CFO: Mark Jenkins
HR: —
FYE: December 31
Type: Public

Carvana is a leading e-commerce platform for buying and selling used cars. Through subsidiary Carvana Group, Carvana operates an online platform for purchasing used cars that allows consumers to research and select a vehicle, view a 360-degree image of the vehicle, obtain financing and warranty coverage, and complete the purchase. Vehicles can then be delivered or picked up at one of vending machines throughout the US mostly southern and midwestern US states. The company targets more than 300 (and growing) metropolitan markets across the US and has a nationally pooled inventory of over 63,000 high-quality used vehicles.

	Annual Growth	12/19	12/20	12/21	12/22	12/23
Sales ($mil.)	28.6%	3,939.9	5,586.6	12,814	13,604	10,771
Net income ($ mil.)	—	(114.7)	(171.1)	(135.0)	(1,587.0)	450.0
Market value ($ mil.)	(12.9%)	18,397	47,874	46,325	947.3	10,580
Employees	16.9%	7,324	10,400	21,000	16,600	13,700

CARVER BANCORP INC.   NAS: CARV

75 West 125th Street
New York, NY 10027
Phone: 718 230-2900
Fax: —
Web: www.carverbank.com

CEO: Michael T Pugh
CFO: Christina L Maier
HR: Aida Goitia
FYE: March 31
Type: Public

Carver Bancorp, one of the largest minority-led financial institutions in the US, is the holding company for Carver Federal Savings Bank. The bank was founded in 1948 to provide community banking services to New York City's African-American and Caribbean-American population. From about 10 branches in mostly low- to moderate-income neighborhoods in Harlem, Brooklyn, and Queens, the thrift offers deposit accounts, insurance, and investment products. Carver Federal's lending activities are focused on housing (residential mortgages and multifamily real estate loans) and non-residential real estate (churches and commercial properties.) The latter makes up about 40% of Carver's loan portfolio.

	Annual Growth	03/19	03/20	03/21	03/22	03/23
Assets ($mil.)	6.4%	563.7	578.8	676.7	735.3	723.2
Net income ($ mil.)	—	(5.9)	(5.4)	(3.9)	(0.8)	(4.4)
Market value ($ mil.)	1.7%	16.0	8.1	39.0	30.1	17.1
Employees	(0.9%)	114	107	104	107	110

CARVIN CORP.

16262 W BERNARDO DR
SAN DIEGO, CA 921271879
Phone: 858 487-1600
Fax: —
Web: www.carvinaudio.com

CEO: Carson L Kiesel
CFO: —
HR: —
FYE: January 31
Type: Private

Carvin has put its guitars into the hands of musicians such as Frank Zappa, Steve Vai, and The Eagles. While Carvin's guitars aren't as well-known as Gibson and Fender, the firm has filled a value niche in the guitar market for more than 60 years. Carvin makes electric and acoustic guitars, electric basses, and a full line of amplifiers and PA equipment. It manufactures products at its factory showroom in San Diego and sells them at stores in San Diego, Sacramento, Hollywood, and Santa Ana, California, as well as via catalog and online. The guitar maker also distributes its instruments internationally. Carvin began in 1946 as L. C. Kiesel Co. The firm is still owned and managed by the Kiesel family.

CASCADE ENGINEERING, INC.

5175 36TH ST SE
GRAND RAPIDS, MI 495122009
Phone: 616 975-4800
Fax: –
Web: www.cascadeng.com

CEO: Christina Keller
CFO: Janice Oshinski
HR: John Huisinga
FYE: August 31
Type: Private

Ideas about plastic parts cascade down from Cascade Engineering's collection of companies, ending up as practical components for many applications. The company manufactures and markets, under the Cascade and other brands, plastic injection molded products as well as parts for OEMs in the automotive, truck, material handling, waste and recycling, and home and office industries. Its auto lineup includes interior and exterior trim, HVAC cases and ducts, and acoustical parts, along with heavy truck fairings, fenders, and grills. Catering to resource conservation markets, Cascade also makes and services an eco-lineup comprising building-mountable wind turbines, waste collection bins, and water filtration systems.

CASCADE FOREST CORPORATION

909 W BIRCH ST
SHELTON, WA 985841761
Phone: 360 426-5571
Fax: –
Web: www.cascadeforestcorporation.com

CEO: Allard Johnson
CFO: –
HR: –
FYE: December 31
Type: Private

If you're in the wholesale lumber business you might be trying to keep up with the Johnsons. Cascade Forest Corporation, formed in 1983 by the Johnson family, is a wholesale lumber brokerage that designs, produces, trades, and supplies wood products primarily in the western US. Its red cedar, douglas fir, and Chinese cedar are used to make fencing, porch and mailbox posts, construction framing, flooring, doors, and specialty outdoor structures, such as gazebos, arbors, and playground equipment. Cascade Forest also makes agricultural and industrial products, including fruit drying trays and bins used by farmers to dehydrate, sun dry, and transport crops.

CASCADIAN THERAPEUTICS, INC.

3101 WESTERN AVE STE 600
SEATTLE, WA 981213047
Phone: 206 801-2100
Fax: –
Web: www.seagen.com

CEO: –
CFO: –
HR: –
FYE: December 31
Type: Private

Beating cancer is Cascadian Therapeutics' sole goal. Formerly named Oncothyreon, the biotechnology company is developing synthetic vaccines and small-molecule (chemical) drugs that aim to battle the dread disease. Cascadian's vaccine candidates stimulate cancer-fighting elements in patients' immune systems. Lead candidate tucatinib is being studied for its ability to treat advanced HER2+ breast cancer. The company also has a couple of pre-clinical cancer treatments in development. Seattle Genetics acquired Cascadian Therapeutics for $614 million in 2018.

CASE WESTERN RESERVE UNIVERSITY

10900 EUCLID AVE
CLEVELAND, OH 441064901
Phone: 216 368-6062
Fax: –
Web: www.case.edu

CEO: –
CFO: Hossein Sadid
HR: –
FYE: June 30
Type: Private

Case Western Reserve University (CWRU) is an independent research school with an enrollment of about 12,201 students from all US states and more than 100 countries, more than half of whom are graduate and professional students. CWRU offers more than 260 undergraduate, graduate, and professional options, and more than 145 dual-degree programs from its eight colleges and schools ?management, engineering, law, arts and sciences, dentistry, social work, nursing, and medicine ? as well as a graduate school at its campus in Cleveland. The university has more than 4,155 full-time faculty and staff members and a student-to-teacher ratio of 11:1.

	Annual Growth	06/17	06/18	06/20	06/21	06/22
Sales ($mil.)	2.7%	–	1,016.3	1,075.6	1,101.1	1,132.3
Net income ($ mil.)	–	–	111.1	(49.2)	679.1	(140.5)
Market value ($ mil.)	–	–	–	–	–	–
Employees	–	–	–	–	–	6,599

CASELLA WASTE SYSTEMS, INC.

NMS: CWST

25 Greens Hill Lane
Rutland, VT 05701
Phone: 802 775-0325
Fax: –
Web: www.casella.com

CEO: –
CFO: –
HR: –
FYE: December 31
Type: Public

Casella Waste Systems is one of the largest recyclers and most experienced fully integrated resource management companies in the Eastern US. The company provides solid waste collection and disposal, transfer, recycling, and organics services to more than one million residential, commercial, municipal, institutional, and industrial customers and provides professional resource management services to over 10,000 customer locations in more than 40 states. It owned and/or operated about 50 solid waste collection operations, about 65 transfer stations, about 25 recycling facilities, nearly ten Subtitle D landfills, less than five landfill gas-to-energy facilities, and one landfill permitted to accept construction and demolition materials. The company was founded in 1975 as a single truck collection service.

	Annual Growth	12/19	12/20	12/21	12/22	12/23
Sales ($mil.)	14.2%	743.3	774.6	889.2	1,085.1	1,264.5
Net income ($ mil.)	(5.4%)	31.7	91.1	41.1	53.1	25.4
Market value ($ mil.)	16.7%	2,669.5	3,592.8	4,953.9	4,599.6	4,956.3
Employees	13.8%	2,500	2,500	2,900	3,200	4,200

CASEY INDUSTRIAL, INC.

890 W CHERRY ST STE 100
LOUISVILLE, CO 800273061
Phone: 541 926-8641
Fax: –
Web: www.caseyind.com

CEO: –
CFO: James W McHose
HR: –
FYE: December 31
Type: Private

Casey Industrial doesn't bat; it builds. Casey Industrial provides industrial construction and installation services for customers throughout the US, typically in about 20 states a year. It erects structural steel, forms concrete foundations, and installs machinery, process piping, and electrical power and control wiring. The company operates from principal offices in Albany, Oregon; Broomfield, Colorado; Garner, North Carolina; and Saltillo, Mississippi. Casey Industrial was founded in 1947. The company is owned by president and CEO Bart Wear and other senior management members.

CASEY'S GENERAL STORES, INC.   NMS: CASY

One SE Convenience Boulevard
Ankeny, IA 50021
Phone: 515 965-6100
Fax: –
Web: www.caseys.com

CEO: Darren M Rebelez
CFO: Stephen P Bramlage Jr
HR: –
FYE: April 30
Type: Public

Casey's General Stores is one of the largest convenience store chains in the country. Casey's owns more than 2,450 stores across about 15 states, primarily in the Midwest. Its stores, most of which operate in areas with fewer than 5,000 people, offer gasoline, prepared foods such as pizza and donuts, and other food and nonfood items traditionally found in convenience stores. In addition to Casey's and Casey's General Store locations, the company operates two stores selling primarily tobacco and nicotine products, one liquor-only store, and one grocery store. The company derives its revenue primarily from the retail sale of fuel.

	Annual Growth	04/19	04/20	04/21	04/22	04/23
Sales ($mil.)	12.7%	9,352.9	9,175.3	8,707.2	12,953	15,094
Net income ($ mil.)	21.7%	203.9	263.8	312.9	339.8	446.7
Market value ($ mil.)	14.7%	4,931.8	5,642.0	8,279.5	7,501.1	8,526.6
Employees	3.9%	36,841	–	37,205	42,481	42,982

CASH-WA DISTRIBUTING CO. OF KEARNEY, INC.

401 W 4TH ST
KEARNEY, NE 688457825
Phone: 308 237-3151
Fax: –
Web: web.cashwa.com

CEO: –
CFO: –
HR: –
FYE: November 28
Type: Private

This company keeps the Quik-E Marts in merchandise. Cash-Wa Distributing supplies food, produce, beverages, equipment, cleaning supplies, and more to foodservice operators and convenience stores throughout Nebraska and in all or parts of 10 surrounding states. It operates three distribution centers and serves more than 6,500 customers with an inventory of some 20,000 items. The family-owned and -operated company was formed in 1934 as a candy and tobacco wholesaler and was purchased by the Henning family in 1957. Cash-Wa Distributing is a member of the UniPro distribution cooperative.

CASPIAN SERVICES INC   NBB: CSSV

2319 Foothill Drive, Suite 160
Salt Lake City, UT 84109
Phone: 801 746-3700
Fax: –
Web: www.caspianservicesinc.com

CEO: –
CFO: –
HR: –
FYE: September 30
Type: Public

Caspian Services (formerly EMPS Corporation) provides geophysical and seismic data acquisition and interpretation services to the oil and gas industry operating in the Caspian Sea region. It also owns or leases a fleet of 15 shallow draft vessels that provide offshore marine services, including transportation, housing, and supplies for production personnel. Caspian Services' ships are chartered primarily to Agip KCO, a consortium of oil companies operating in the Caspian Sea, and CMOC/Shell joint venture. The company owns 56% of a joint venture that operates a desalinization plant and sells purified drinking water.

	Annual Growth	09/11	09/12	09/13	09/14	09/15
Sales ($mil.)	(23.9%)	49.1	24.9	33.1	29.9	16.4
Net income ($ mil.)	–	(9.7)	(14.0)	(11.5)	(16.6)	(28.0)
Market value ($ mil.)	(41.0%)	5.8	1.5	2.5	1.6	0.7
Employees	(14.7%)	757	516	574	509	400

CASS INFORMATION SYSTEMS INC   NMS: CASS

12444 Powerscourt Drive, Suite 550
St. Louis, MO 63131
Phone: 314 506-5500
Fax: –
Web: www.cassinfo.com

CEO: Eric H Brunngraber
CFO: P S Appelbaum
HR: –
FYE: December 31
Type: Public

Cass Information Systems provides payment and information processing services to large manufacturing, distribution, and retail companies across the US. Its offers include payment, and rating services, as well as bill processing and payments. Cass grew out of Cass Commercial Bank (now a subsidiary), which provides banking services to Its target markets, which include privately-owned businesses and faith-based ministries in the St. Louis metropolitan area as well as other selected cities in the US. Other major customer bases include Columbus, Ohio, and South Carolina.

	Annual Growth	12/19	12/20	12/21	12/22	12/23
Assets ($mil.)	8.9%	1,764.2	2,203.2	2,554.9	2,573.0	2,478.6
Net income ($ mil.)	(0.3%)	30.4	25.2	28.6	34.9	30.1
Market value ($ mil.)	(6.0%)	784.2	528.5	534.1	622.3	611.9
Employees	–	1,122	1,101	1,116	1,209	–

CASSAVA SCIENCES INC   NAS: SAVA

6801 N. Capital of Texas Highway, Suite 300
Austin, TX 78731
Phone: 512 501-2444
Fax: –
Web: www.cassavasciences.com

CEO: Remi Barbier
CFO: Eric Schoen
HR: –
FYE: December 31
Type: Public

Pain Therapeutics is changing its tune. A development-stage biopharmaceutical with a former focus on abuse-resistant painkillers, Pain Therapeutics announced a reorganization and strategy shift when its primary candidate Remoxy was rejected by the US FDA in mid-2018. The company will now concentrate on the development of Alzheimer's investigational treatment PTI-125 and related blood test PTI-125DX. PTI-125 is an oral, small-molecule drug that has shown promise in early clinical tests. The 2018 FDA rejection was the fourth for Remoxy, a development-stage alternative to frequently abused opioids, in the past decade.

	Annual Growth	12/19	12/20	12/21	12/22	12/23
Sales ($mil.)	–	–	–	–	–	–
Net income ($ mil.)	–	(4.6)	(6.3)	(32.4)	(76.2)	(97.2)
Market value ($ mil.)	44.2%	219.6	288.1	1,845.8	1,247.7	950.8
Employees	34.0%	9	11	24	26	29

CASTLE (AM) & CO   NBB: CTAM

1420 Kensington Road, Suite 220
Oak Brook, IL 60523
Phone: 847 455-7111
Fax: –
Web: www.castlemetals.com

CEO: Marec E Edgar
CFO: –
HR: Tanesha Watkins
FYE: December 31
Type: Public

Providing alloys for its allies, metals service company A. M. Castle distributes highly engineered metals and metal alloys to a broad range of industrial manufacturers. It sells steel (alloy, carbon, and stainless), nickel alloys, aluminum, copper, brass, cast iron, and titanium in bar, sheet, plate, and tube form. Its Transtar Metals unit distributes high-performance metals to the aerospace and defense markets. Through its Total Plastics unit, it distributes plastics in forms (such as plate, rod, and tube). A. M. Castle operates 47 steel service centers throughout North America, Europe, and Asia. It also holds 50% of steel distributor Kreher Steel. In 2017 the company filed for Chapter 11 bankruptcy protection.

	Annual Growth	08/17*	12/17	12/18	12/19	12/20
Sales ($mil.)	1.3%	353.9	164.9	582.0	559.6	368.3
Net income ($ mil.)	–	36.2	(13.3)	(37.1)	(38.5)	(40.7)
Market value ($ mil.)	–	–	26.9	20.6	12.0	22.1
Employees	–	–	930	979	873	681

*Fiscal year change

CASTLIGHT HEALTH, INC.

150 SPEAR ST STE 400
SAN FRANCISCO, CA 941051500
Phone: 415 829-1400
Fax: –
Web: www.mycastlighthealth.com

CEO: –
CFO: –
HR: –
FYE: December 31
Type: Private

Castlight pioneers digital head and offers the industry's most comprehensive navigation solution. The company provide individual to connect and engage in the right provider, benefit or virtual care solutions at the right time. It partners with Fortune 500 companies and health plans to transform employee and member benefits into one comprehensive health and wellbeing experience to deliver better health outcomes and maximize returns on healthcare investment. Castlight products are care guidance navigator, wellbeing navigator, complete health navigator and Castlight care guides. Castlight started in 2008 by integrating billions of health and wellbeing data points from thousands of sources to provide a deep understanding of members, providers, and benefit programs.

CATALENT INC

14 Schoolhouse Road
Somerset, NJ 08873
Phone: 732 537-6200
Fax: –
Web: www.catalent.com

NYS: CTLT
CEO: Alessandro Maselli
CFO: Ricky Hopson
HR: –
FYE: June 30
Type: Public

Catalent, through operating subsidiary Catalent Pharma Solutions, provides contract development and manufacturing of oral (soft and hardshell capsules), topical (ointment applicators), sterile (syringes), and inhaled (nasal sprays) drug delivery products to pharmaceutical and biotechnology companies. Catalent also provides packaging services, labeling, storage, distribution, and inventory management for clinical drug trials. Catalent operates more than 55 facilities across four continents. The company serves more than 1,200 customers in approximately 80 countries, with about 55% of the company's sales is generated in the US. Catalent traces its history to the 1933 founding of the R.P. Scherer Corporation, which developed the first rotary die machine for the manufacture of soft gelatin capsules, and assumed its current form in April 2007.

	Annual Growth	06/19	06/20	06/21	06/22	06/23
Sales ($mil.)	14.1%	2,518.0	3,094.3	3,998.0	4,828.0	4,263.0
Net income ($ mil.)	–	137.4	220.7	585.0	519.0	(256.0)
Market value ($ mil.)	(5.4%)	9,757.8	13,194	19,462	19,312	7,804.8
Employees	9.7%	12,300	13,900	17,300	19,000	17,800

CATALYST DIRECT, INC.

539 PINE GROVE AVE
ROCHESTER, NY 146173332
Phone: 585 453-8300
Fax: –
Web: www.catalystinc.com

CEO: Michael Osborn
CFO: Bob Scarciotta
HR: –
FYE: December 31
Type: Private

Catalyst (formerly Catalyst Direct) is nothing if not straightforward. The agency -- not to be confused with the not-for-profit organization with the same name-- specializes in direct marketing services that help clients identify, acquire, and retain customers. As a full-service marketing firm, Catalyst provides research, media planning, database development, creative, and evaluation services. Catalyst's clients have included such notable brands as Eastman Kodak, HSBC, and Oc N.V. Owners and managing directors Jeff Cleary and Mike Osborn founded the company in 1990.

	Annual Growth	12/04	12/05	12/06	12/07	12/08
Sales ($mil.)	22.8%	–	5.3	7.7	7.5	9.9
Net income ($ mil.)	(46.6%)	–	0.7	0.7	(0.0)	0.1
Market value ($ mil.)	–	–	–	–	–	–
Employees	–	–	–	–	–	85

CATALYST PHARMACEUTICALS INC

355 Alhambra Circle, Suite 801
Coral Gables, FL 33134
Phone: 305 420-3200
Fax: –
Web: www.catalystpharma.com

NAS: CPRX
CEO: Patrick J McEnany
CFO: Alicia Grande
HR: –
FYE: December 31
Type: Public

Catalyst Pharmaceutical, a development-stage biopharmaceutical firm, is developing treatments for rare neurological diseases such as Lambert-Eaton myasthenic syndrome (LEMS) and infantile spasms. Its amifampridine phosphate, named Firdapse, is under development for LEMS but also being tested for the treatment of other neuromuscular disorders; it was granted the breakthrough therapy designation by the FDA. Another candidate, CPP-115, is a GABA-aminotransferase inhibitor that is in studies for infantile spasms -- a rare form of epileptic seizures. It holds orphan drug designations in the US and Europe. Catalyst Pharma was previously engaged in developing drugs to treat addiction.

	Annual Growth	12/19	12/20	12/21	12/22	12/23
Sales ($mil.)	40.5%	102.3	119.1	140.8	214.2	398.2
Net income ($ mil.)	22.3%	31.9	75.0	39.5	83.1	71.4
Market value ($ mil.)	45.5%	401.7	357.8	725.2	1,992.5	1,800.7
Employees	–	–	76	74	76	82	–

CATALYST, INC.

120 WALL ST FL 15
NEW YORK, NY 100053905
Phone: 212 514-7600
Fax: –
Web: www.catalyst.org

CEO: Deborah Gillis
CFO: Jennifer Daniel-Davidson
HR: Afiya Wallace
FYE: August 31
Type: Private

Catalyst is dedicated to helping women succeed in business. The not-for-profit organization provides advisory services, speakers, and an information center that helps companies recruit and advance women in the workplace. It takes on such issues as diversity in the workplace, gender discrimination, flexible working arrangements, and women in management. Catalyst has more than 400 member corporations. It maintains offices in the US, Canada, and Switzerland. With the support of five women's college presidents, Felice Schwartz founded Catalyst in 1962 to help women enter the workplace. Ilene Lang acts as president and CEO of the organization, which is considered a leading source of information on women in business.

	Annual Growth	08/15	08/16	08/20	08/21	08/22
Sales ($mil.)	9.9%	–	12.4	27.2	22.2	21.9
Net income ($ mil.)	–	–	(1.6)	6.5	2.4	(0.7)
Market value ($ mil.)	–	–	–	–	–	–
Employees	–	–	–	–	–	85

CATAMOUNT CONSTRUCTORS, INC.

1527 COLE BLVD STE 100
LAKEWOOD, CO 804013421
Phone: 303 679-0087
Fax: –
Web: www.catamountinc.com

CEO: –
CFO: –
HR: –
FYE: December 31
Type: Private

A solid foundation is tantamount to Catamount's success. The company provides general contracting services for the construction of commercial, industrial, health care, institutional, and residential developments around the US. It offers services from conceptualization and design-build to construction management. Subsidiary CC Residential specializes in midrise multifamily residences including condominiums, apartments, and mixed-use developments. Catamount Constructors boasts a high customer return rate; it has provided services for such return clients as CarMax, Walgreen, and Chase Bank. CEO Geoff Wormer and other executives Kurt Kenchel, Jeff Sidwell, and Jeff Cochran founded the company in 1997.

	Annual Growth	12/04	12/05	12/06	12/07	12/08
Sales ($mil.)	–	–	–	(156.4)	183.4	226.2
Net income ($ mil.)	1499.4%	–	–	0.0	7.5	4.2
Market value ($ mil.)	–	–	–	–	–	–
Employees	–	–	–	–	–	142

CATCHMARK TIMBER TRUST, INC.

5 CONCOURSE PKWY STE 2650
ATLANTA, GA 303287104
Phone: 770 449-7800
Fax: –
Web: www.potlatchdeltic.com

CEO: Brian M Davis
CFO: –
HR: Kendra Emigh
FYE: December 31
Type: Private

Wood you be interested in investing in CatchMark Timber Trust? The real estate investment trust (REIT), which specializes in buying, owning, and selling commercial timberland, owns interests in about 435,000 acres of such property - mostly pine forest but also hardwood - across Alabama, Georgia, Florida, Louisiana, North Carolina, South Carolina, Tennessee, and Oregon. Unlike other landowning REITs, CatchMark only owns the land; it doesn't have logging operations or make wood products. Its largest customer is packaging manufacturer WestRock, which contributes around 15% to the REIT's annual revenues.

CATERPILLAR FINANCIAL SERVICES CORP

2120 West End Ave.
Nashville, TN 37203-0001
Phone: 615 341-1000
Fax: –
Web: www.caterpillar.com

CEO: –
CFO: –
HR: –
FYE: December 31
Type: Public

Cat Financial is a wholly owned finance subsidiary of Caterpillar, the world's leading manufacturer of construction and mining equipment, diesel and natural gas engines, industrial gas turbines, and diesel-electric locomotives. Cat Financial provides a wide range of financing solutions to customers and Cat dealers for machines, engines, Solar turbines, genuine Cat parts and services. It offers quality service throughout the life cycle of equipment including purchase, protect, manage and resell. A significant portion of Cat Financial's activity is conducted in North America, with additional offices and subsidiaries in Latin America, Asia/Pacific, Europe, Africa and the Middle East.

	Annual Growth	12/18	12/19	12/20	12/21	12/22
Sales ($mil.)	(1.0%)	2,847.0	2,966.0	2,550.0	2,562.0	2,734.0
Net income ($ mil.)	15.1%	305.0	410.0	293.0	505.0	535.0
Market value ($ mil.)	–	–	–	–	–	–
Employees	2.8%	1,877	1,973	2,000	2,100	2,100

CATERPILLAR INC.   NYS: CAT

5205 N. O'Connor Boulevard, Suite 100
Irving, TX 75039
Phone: 972 891-7700
Fax: –
Web: www.caterpillar.com

CEO: D J Umpleby III
CFO: Andrew R Bonfield
HR: –
FYE: December 31
Type: Public

Originally organized as Caterpillar Tractor Co. in 1925 and reorganized as Caterpillar Inc. in 1986, Caterpillar Inc. is a manufacturer of construction and mining equipment, which includes excavators, loaders, and tractors as well as forestry, paving, and tunneling machinery. It manufactures diesel and natural engines, industrial gas turbines and diesel-electric locomotives. Subsidiary Caterpillar Financial Services offers financing products and services for dealers and customers, wherein the company is able to be a top US exporter. It's Energy & Transportation segment supports customers in oil and gas, power generation, marine, rail and industrial applications, including Cat machines. The US supplies about more than 40% of revenue.

	Annual Growth	12/19	12/20	12/21	12/22	12/23
Sales ($mil.)	5.7%	53,800	41,748	50,971	59,427	67,060
Net income ($ mil.)	14.1%	6,093.0	2,998.0	6,489.0	6,705.0	10,335
Market value ($ mil.)	19.0%	73,748	90,897	103,241	119,631	147,651
Employees	2.6%	102,300	97,300	107,700	109,100	113,200

CATHAY GENERAL BANCORP   NMS: CATY

777 North Broadway
Los Angeles, CA 90012
Phone: 213 625-4700
Fax: –
Web: www.cathaybank.com

CEO: Chang M Liu
CFO: Heng W Chen
HR: –
FYE: December 31
Type: Public

Cathay General Bancorp is the holding company for Cathay Bank, which mainly serves Chinese and Vietnamese communities from more than 35 branches in California, and about 20 in New York, Washington, Illinois, Texas, Maryland, Massachusetts, Nevada, New Jersey. It also has a branch in Hong Kong, and offices in Beijing, Shanghai, and Taipei. Catering to small to medium-sized businesses and individual consumers, the bank offers standard deposit services and loans. Commercial mortgage loans account for about half of the bank's portfolio; residential mortgage loans comprise nearly 30%. The bank's Cathay Wealth Management unit offers stocks, bonds, mutual funds, insurance, annuities, and advisory services.

	Annual Growth	12/19	12/20	12/21	12/22	12/23
Assets ($mil.)	6.3%	18,094	19,043	20,887	21,948	23,082
Net income ($ mil.)	6.1%	279.1	228.9	298.3	360.6	354.1
Market value ($ mil.)	4.0%	2,765.1	2,339.2	3,124.0	2,964.2	3,238.9
Employees	0.5%	1,219	1,205	1,156	1,178	1,246

CATHOLIC CHARITIES USA

2050 BALLENGER AVE STE 400
ALEXANDRIA, VA 223146893
Phone: 703 549-1390
Fax: –
Web: www.catholiccharitiesusa.org

CEO: –
CFO: John Jackson
HR: –
FYE: December 31
Type: Private

Does this group help people in need? Is the Pope Catholic? Catholic Charities USA, one of the nation's largest not-for-profit groups, is a network of some 175 Catholic charity agencies nationwide that work to end poverty, support families, and strengthen communities. It helps more than 7 million people each year by providing disaster assistance, emergency financial aid, food services, health clinics, housing services, and mental health counseling. Catholic Charities spends about 90% of its income on program costs; most of its funding (60%) comes from the US government. Although the group was officially founded in 1910, it traces its roots to 1727 when French nuns started an orphanage in New Orleans.

	Annual Growth	12/04	12/05*	09/06*	06/16*	12/22
Sales ($mil.)	(7.2%)	–	147.9	28.1	18.3	41.2
Net income ($ mil.)	–	–	–	(25.5)	(11.4)	3.0
Market value ($ mil.)	–	–	–	–	–	–
Employees	–	–	–	–	–	50

*Fiscal year change

CATHOLIC HEALTH CARE SYSTEM

205 LEXINGTON AVE FL 3
NEW YORK, NY 100166022
Phone: 646 633-4700
Fax: –
Web: www.archcare.org

CEO: Scott Larue
CFO: –
HR: Barbara Munoz
FYE: December 31
Type: Private

New York's Catholic Healthcare System is dedicated to providing health care (rooted in the values of the Catholic Church) to people who need it, regardless of their religious affiliation or ability to pay. The Catholic Healthcare System includes seven large nursing care facilities and Calvary Hospital, which specializes in palliative cancer care. It also has affiliations with rehabilitation facilities and other medical centers (including non-Catholic institutions). Among its nursing facilities are Ferncliff Nursing Home, Kateri Residence, and St. Teresa's Nursing & Rehabilitation Center. The Catholic Healthcare System is sponsored by the Archdiocese of New York.

	Annual Growth	12/14	12/15	12/16	12/19	12/21
Sales ($mil.)	0.3%	–	–	94.5	111.3	96.0
Net income ($ mil.)	19.5%	–	–	4.1	3.7	10.1
Market value ($ mil.)	–	–	–	–	–	–
Employees	–	–	–	–	–	643

CATHOLIC HEALTH SYSTEM OF LONG ISLAND, INC.

992 N VILLAGE AVE
ROCKVILLE CENTRE, NY 115701002
Phone: 516 705-3700
Fax: –
Web: www.catholichealthli.org

CEO: Alan D Guerci MD
CFO: William Armstrong
HR: Maria Lerner
FYE: December 31
Type: Private

The long and the short of it is that Catholic Health Services of Long Island (CHS) provides health care to the residents of Long Island. Sponsored by the Diocese of Rockville Centre, CHS's operations consist of six hospitals and three nursing homes, as well as regional home care and hospice services. Within the CHS system, member organizations offer virtually any medical specialty or clinical service. The system's hospitals, which include Good Samaritan Hospital Medical Center, Mercy Medical Center, and St. Francis Hospital, house some 1,930 beds, more than 17,000 employees, and a medical staff of 4,600. CHS's MaryHaven Center provides services to people of all ages with disabilities.

	Annual Growth	12/03	12/04	12/05	12/06	12/13
Sales ($mil.)	49.3%	–	–	1.4	–	35.2
Net income ($ mil.)	96.3%	–	–	0.0	–	3.7
Market value ($ mil.)	–	–	–	–	–	–
Employees	–	–	–	–	–	13,500

CATHOLIC HEALTH SYSTEM, INC.

144 GENESEE ST FL 1
BUFFALO, NY 142031560
Phone: 716 685-4870
Fax: –
Web: www.chsbuffalo.org

CEO: –
CFO: –
HR: Christine Kukelka
FYE: December 31
Type: Private

The Catholic Health System gives residents of its home state even more reason to proclaim "I heart New York." The non-profit health care system, recognized for its cardiac services, serves residents of western New York through four hospitals and more than a dozen primary care centers, as well as long-term care facilities, diagnostic and treatment centers, and other health care sites. Catholic Health is also well-known for its women's health, cancer treatment, and rehabilitation services and is a leading provider of elderly care in the region. Its hospitals (including Kenmore Mercy, Sisters of Charity -- formerly St. Joseph's, Mercy Hospital of Buffalo, and St. Joseph's) have a capacity of about 825 beds.

	Annual Growth	12/08	12/09	12/13	12/21	12/22
Sales ($mil.)	6.4%	–	84.8	123.6	189.3	191.0
Net income ($ mil.)	–	–	(0.1)	–	–	(9.6)
Market value ($ mil.)	–	–	–	–	–	–
Employees	–	–	–	–	–	8,400

CATHOLIC MEDICAL CENTER

100 MCGREGOR ST
MANCHESTER, NH 031023770
Phone: 603 663-6888
Fax: –
Web: www.catholicmedicalcenter.org

CEO: Joseph Pepe
CFO: –
HR: –
FYE: September 30
Type: Private

Catholic Medical Center is a 330-bed hospital serving southern New Hampshire. Services include cancer treatment, surgery, rehabilitation, treatments for sleep disorders, and emergency medical services. Catholic Medical Center (CMC) offers about 40 medical specialties through divisions including The Mom's Place (a birthing facility) and the New England Heart Institute. CMC has partnered with its community to extend health care and dental care to the uninsured and the homeless, and has established a health clinic geared to help refugees being resettled in the area.

	Annual Growth	09/18	09/19	09/20	09/21	09/22
Sales ($mil.)	2.2%	–	490.5	423.7	493.6	523.3
Net income ($ mil.)	–	–	38.3	(58.1)	66.5	(6.0)
Market value ($ mil.)	–	–	–	–	–	–
Employees	–	–	–	–	–	1,500

CATO CORP.

NYS: CATO

8100 Denmark Road
Charlotte, NC 28273-5975
Phone: 704 554-8510
Fax: –
Web: www.catofashions.com

CEO: –
CFO: –
HR: –
FYE: February 3
Type: Public

The Cato operates approximately 1,280 fashion specialty stores in more than 30 states (primarily in the southeastern US) under the names Cato, Cato Fashions, Cato Plus, Versona, It's Fashion, and It's Fashion Metro. Its mostly private-label merchandise includes missy, juniors', girls', and plus-sized casual sportswear, career clothing, coats, shoes, and accessories. The Cato's stores are typically located in shopping centers anchored by a Walmart store or another major discounter or supermarket. Founded in 1946, the company is led by chairman John Cato, who beneficially owned about 50% of the combined voting power of the company's common stock.

	Annual Growth	02/20*	01/21	01/22	01/23*	02/24
Sales ($mil.)	(3.8%)	825.3	575.1	769.3	759.3	708.1
Net income ($ mil.)	–	35.9	(47.5)	36.8	0.0	(23.9)
Market value ($ mil.)	(19.1%)	329.9	233.8	332.1	208.1	141.5
Employees	(7.7%)	10,060	7,400	7,500	7,600	7,300

*Fiscal year change

CATO INSTITUTE, INC.

1000 MASSACHUSETTS AVE NW
WASHINGTON, DC 200015401
Phone: 202 842-0200
Fax: –
Web: www.cato.org

CEO: –
CFO: –
HR: –
FYE: March 31
Type: Private

The Cato Institute is a not-for-profit public policy research foundation that provides opinions and analysis in such areas as constitutional law, national security, civil liberties, and international trade. It publishes periodicals, books, and policy reports. The think tank has libertarian leanings, favoring limited government and free markets; its name comes from an 18th-century series of libertarian pamphlets that contributed to the philosophical arguments in favor of the American Revolution. Cato, which accepts no government funding, gets about 75% of its funding from individuals, and from foundations, corporations, and publication sales. The institute was established by president Edward H. Crane in 1977.

	Annual Growth	03/15	03/16	03/17	03/20	03/22
Sales ($mil.)	8.7%	–	27.9	36.9	32.5	45.9
Net income ($ mil.)	–	–	(1.3)	6.7	1.4	14.6
Market value ($ mil.)	–	–	–	–	–	–
Employees	–	–	–	–	–	105

CAVALIERS OPERATING COMPANY, LLC

1 CENTER CT
CLEVELAND, OH 441154001
Phone: 216 420-2000
Fax: –
Web: www.rocketmortgagefieldhouse.com

CEO: Len Komorski
CFO: –
HR: Farrell Finnin
FYE: December 31
Type: Private

This business hardly takes a carefree attitude towards roundball. Rocket Mortgage Fieldhouse, formely known as Cavaliers Operating Company owns and operates the Cleveland Cavaliers professional basketball team and its home court, Quicken Loans Arena. The Cavs joined the National Basketball Association in 1970 as part of an expansion that included the Portland Trail Blazers and Buffalo Braves (now the Los Angeles Clippers). Cleveland won its first NBA championship in 2016. Quicken Loans founder Dan Gilbert has controlled the team since 2005; the family of original owner Gordon Gund continues to have a minority stake in the Cavs. In early 2019, Cavaliers Operating change its name to Rocket Mortgage FieldHouse.

CAVCO INDUSTRIES INC (DE)

NMS: CVCO

3636 North Central Ave, Ste 1200
Phoenix, AZ 85012
Phone: 602 256-6263
Fax: –
Web: www.cavco.com

CEO: William C Boor
CFO: Allison K Aden
HR: –
FYE: April 1
Type: Public

Cavco Industries designs and produces factory-built housing products primarily distributed through a network of independent and company-owned retailers. It is one of the largest producers of manufactured and modular homes in the US, based on reported wholesale shipments. Its products are marketed under a variety of brand names including Cavco, Fleetwood, Palm Harbor, Nationwide, Fairmont, Friendship, Chariot Eagle, Destiny, Commodore, Colony, Pennwest, R-Anell, Manorwood, Solitaire, and MidCountry. It is also a leading producer of park model RVs, vacation cabins, and factory-built commercial structures. Its insurance subsidiary, Standard Casualty, provides property and casualty insurance to owners of manufactured homes. Cavco was founded in 1965.

	Annual Growth	03/19	03/20*	04/21	04/22	04/23
Sales ($mil.)	22.1%	962.7	1,061.8	1,108.1	1,627.2	2,142.7
Net income ($ mil.)	36.8%	68.6	75.1	76.6	197.7	240.6
Market value ($ mil.)	28.2%	1,018.4	1,286.5	2,013.9	2,113.0	2,753.3
Employees	10.8%	4,650	5,000	4,700	6,300	7,000

*Fiscal year change

CAVIUM, LLC

5488 MARVELL LN
SANTA CLARA, CA 950543606
Phone: 408 222-2500
Fax: –
Web: www.marvell.com

CEO: –
CFO: Jean Hu
HR: –
FYE: December 31
Type: Private

Cavium provides integrated circuits for use in networking equipment such as routers, switches, security appliances, gateway devices, and storage networking equipment. The company designs specialized microprocessors used in secure network transmissions based on ARM and MIPS architecture technologies. Manufacturing is contracted out to Taiwan Semiconductor Manufacturing and United Microelectronics, among others. Cavium also provides related software and services. Customers outside the US account for more than two-thirds of the company's sales. Marvell Technologies acquired Cavium for about $6 billion in 2018.

CAZENOVIA COLLEGE

547 HOWARD AVE
BROOKLYN, NY 112335057
Phone: 315 655-7000
Fax: –
Web: www.cazenovia.edu

CEO: –
CFO: Mark Edwards
HR: –
FYE: June 30
Type: Private

Students wanting individualized attention and a well-rounded education can apply to Cazenovia College. With a a student-faculty ratio of 15 to 1, the school focuses on liberal arts, offering bachelor's and associate degrees in more than 20 fields of study. The school has about 1,000 students and some 140 full- and part-time faculty members. Cazenovia College opened in 1824 in what had been the Madison County (New York) Courthouse. The school was founded as the Seminary of the Genesee Conference, the second Methodist seminary to be established in the US. Among its early notable alumni is Leland Stanford, who founded and endowed Stanford University.

	Annual Growth	06/10	06/11	06/20	06/21	06/22
Sales ($mil.)	5.0%	–	24.7	37.3	34.9	42.3
Net income ($ mil.)	(31.8%)	–	5.7	(3.4)	(4.3)	0.0
Market value ($ mil.)	–	–	–	–	–	–
Employees	–	–	–	–	–	369

CBIZ INC

NYS: CBZ

6801 Brecksville Rd., Door N.
Independence, OH 44131
Phone: 216 447-9000
Fax: 216 447-4809
Web: www.cbiz.com

CEO: –
CFO: –
HR: –
FYE: December 31
Type: Public

CBIZ, Inc. provides professional business services that help clients better manage their finances, employees and insurance needs. CBIZ provides its clients with financial services including accounting, tax, financial advisory, government healthcare consulting, risk advisory, and valuation services. Benefits and insurance services include group health benefits consulting, property and casualty insurance, retirement plan consulting, payroll, and HR consulting. As a leading provider of accounting, insurance and other professional consulting services to businesses throughout the US, the company's services are provided through more than 100 Company offices in more than 30 states. CBIZ generates most of its revenue in the US.

	Annual Growth	12/19	12/20	12/21	12/22	12/23
Sales ($mil.)	13.8%	948.4	963.9	1,104.9	1,412.0	1,591.2
Net income ($ mil.)	14.4%	70.7	78.3	70.9	105.4	121.0
Market value ($ mil.)	23.4%	1,343.0	1,325.6	1,948.7	2,333.8	3,117.9
Employees	8.7%	4,800	4,800	6,000	6,500	6,700

CBL & ASSOCIATES PROPERTIES INC

NYS: CBL

2030 Hamilton Place Blvd., Suite 500
Chattanooga, TN 37421
Phone: 423 855-0001
Fax: –
Web: www.cblproperties.com

CEO: Stephen D Lebovitz
CFO: Benjamin W Jaenicke
HR: –
FYE: December 31
Type: Public

CBL & Associates Properties is a self-managed real estate investment trust (REIT) owns, develops, manages, and finances shopping malls and other retail properties, primarily in the Southeast and Midwest US. In terms of number of stores, its largest tenants are Signet Jewelers, Hot Topic, Foot Locker, Genesco, and Luxottica Group. The company owns interests in some 90 properties, consisting of more than 45 malls, around 30 open-air centers, five outlet centers, five lifestyle centers and five other properties, including single-tenant and multi-tenant outparcels.

	Annual Growth	12/20*	10/21*	12/21	12/22	12/23
Sales ($mil.)	(2.4%)	575.9	468.0	108.8	563.0	535.3
Net income ($ mil.)	–	(295.1)	(470.6)	(151.5)	(93.5)	6.5
Market value ($ mil.)	–	–	–	997.6	738.0	780.8
Employees	(0.4%)	474	–	460	472	469

*Fiscal year change

CBOE BATS, LLC

8050 MARSHALL DR
LENEXA, KS 662141524
Phone: 913 815-7000
Fax: –
Web: –

CEO: –
CFO: –
HR: –
FYE: December 31
Type: Private

BATS could stand for Better Alternative Trading System since BATS Global Markets' mission is "making markets better." BATS is one of the largest US equity securities and options exchanges. Operating the BZX and BYX exchanges, the firm holds more than 10% of the US equity market. BATS's Chi-X Europe equity options exchange is a leading exchange in Europe, trading in 25 European indices with more than 20% of the market. Since the company owns and operates the technology at the core of its trading systems, it sees its technological expertise as the differentiating factor for its business. BATS was formed in 2005 as an alternative to NYSE. Chicago-based exchange firm CBOE Holdings bought BATS for some $3.2 billion.

CBOE GLOBAL MARKETS INC
BZX: CBOE

433 West Van Buren Street
Chicago, IL 60607
Phone: 312 786-5600
Fax: –
Web: www.cboe.com

CEO: –
CFO: –
HR: –
FYE: December 31
Type: Public

Cboe Global Markets, Inc., a leading provider of market infrastructure and tradable products, delivers cutting-edge trading, clearing, and investment solutions to market participants around the world. The company is committed to operating a trusted, inclusive global marketplace, and to providing leading products, technology and data solutions that enable participants to define a sustainable financial future. The company offers trading across a diverse range of products in multiple asset classes and geographies, including options, futures, US, Canadian, and European equities, exchange-traded products (ETPs), global foreign exchange (FX) and volatility products based on the Cboe Volatility Index (VIX Index), recognized as the world's premier gauge of US equity market volatility. In addition, the company operates one of the largest stock exchanges by value traded in Europe, and owns EuroCCP, a leading Pan-European equities clearing house.

	Annual Growth	12/19	12/20	12/21	12/22	12/23
Sales ($mil.)	10.9%	2,496.1	3,427.1	3,494.8	3,958.5	3,773.5
Net income ($ mil.)	19.4%	374.9	468.2	529.0	235.0	761.4
Market value ($ mil.)	10.4%	12,663	9,826.8	13,761	13,241	18,843
Employees	18.9%	823	1,010	1,196	1,543	1,647

CBRE GROUP INC
NYS: CBRE

2100 McKinney Avenue, Suite 1250
Dallas, TX 75201
Phone: 214 979-6100
Fax: –
Web: www.cbre.com

CEO: Robert E Sulentic
CFO: Emma E Giamartino
HR: –
FYE: December 31
Type: Public

As the largest commercial real estate services company, CBRE Group provides leasing, property sales, occupier outsourcing, and valuation businesses from about 655 offices worldwide. Subsidiaries Trammell Crow provides commercial real estate development services in the US, UK, and Continental Europe, and Telford Homes is a developer of residential multi-family properties in the UK. CBRE Investment Management provides investment management services to pension funds, insurance companies, sovereign wealth funds, foundations, endowments, and other institutional investors seeking to generate returns and diversification through investment in real assets such as real estate, infrastructure, master limited partnerships, and other assets. The company garners over 55% of its revenue from the US. CBRE Group was founded in San Francisco in 1906.

	Annual Growth	12/19	12/20	12/21	12/22	12/23
Sales ($mil.)	7.5%	23,894	23,826	27,746	30,828	31,949
Net income ($ mil.)	(6.4%)	1,282.4	752.0	1,836.6	1,407.4	986.0
Market value ($ mil.)	11.0%	18,687	19,123	33,084	23,464	28,382
Employees	6.8%	100,000	100,000	105,000	115,000	130,000

CCA INDUSTRIES, INC.
NBB: CAWW

500 Office Center Drive, Suite 400
Port Washington, PA 19034
Phone: 201 935-3232
Fax: 201 935-6784
Web: www.ccaindustries.com

CEO: Christopher Dominello
CFO: Stephen A Heit
HR: –
FYE: November 30
Type: Public

Consumers count on CCA Industries for health and beauty care. The company makes and markets health and beauty aids, each under its own brand name, including Plus+White (oral care), Bikini Zone (shave gels), Sudden Change (skin care), Solar Sense (sun protection), and Nutra Nail and Gel Perfect (nail care), among many. It also sells dietary supplements (tea and chewing gum) under the Mega-T label. CCA items are made under contract, and several, such as Hair-Off, Mega-T, and Kids Sense, are made and marketed under licensing agreements. The firm caters to food and drug retailers, such as Walgreens and CVS, mass merchandisers Wal-Mart and Target, warehouse club Sam's, and wholesale distributors, mainly in the US.

	Annual Growth	11/18	11/19	11/20	11/21	11/22
Sales ($mil.)	(6.2%)	16.6	17.1	14.1	13.8	12.8
Net income ($ mil.)	–	(3.3)	0.6	(0.1)	(0.6)	(0.1)
Market value ($ mil.)	(22.7%)	17.8	21.6	15.5	25.3	6.4
Employees	–	14	–	–	–	–

CCC GROUP, INC.

5797 DIETRICH RD
SAN ANTONIO, TX 782193599
Phone: 210 661-4251
Fax: –
Web: www.cccgroupinc.com

CEO: Joe Garza
CFO: –
HR: Chessia Brown
FYE: December 31
Type: Private

General contractor CCC Group is a nationally recognized industrial construction company. CCC specializes in industrial construction manufacturing and specialty engineering and design services. It performs a laundry list of construction services, including heavy hauling, rigging and lifting, structural steel erection, complex and intricate equipment setting, and many other structural items. CCC has a variety of specialized equipment including push boats, both impact and vibratory pile hammers, in addition to work-barges and spud-barges capable of carrying 250-ton cranes. The contractor is known for its work in the fertilizer industry, but also serves the power; oil, gas and chemical; mining and metal; and manufacturing industries. The employee ? owned company was founded in 1947 by Merl Huebner and George Guthrie.

CCC INTELLIGENT SOLUTIONS HOLDINGS INC
NMS: CCCS

167 N. Green Street, 9th Floor
Chicago, IL 60607
Phone: 800 621-8070
Fax: –
Web: www.dragoneergrowth.com

CEO: Githesh Ramamurthy
CFO: Andrew G Balbirer
HR: Christy Harris
FYE: December 31
Type: Public

CCC Information Services, now CCC Intelligent Solutions Inc. after changing its name in 2021, is a technology leader pioneering solutions that power insurers, automotive manufacturers, collision repairers, parts suppliers, lenders, fleet operators and more through its advanced cloud-based SaaS platform of digital and data services. It is trusted leader in AI, IoT, network management, customer experience, and digital workflows. Its solutions and big data insights are delivered through the powerful CCC ONE platform, which connects a vast network of 300-plus insurance companies, and more than 27,000 repair facilities, including the nation's top five multi-shop operators. CCC was founded in 1980.

	Annual Growth	07/20*	12/20	12/21	12/22	12/23
Sales ($mil.)	–	–	–	688.3	782.4	866.4
Net income ($ mil.)	–	(0.0)	(1.0)	(248.9)	38.4	(92.5)
Market value ($ mil.)	–	–	8,003.5	6,869.6	5,247.2	6,869.6
Employees	951.5%	2	2	2,250	2,375	2,325

*Fiscal year change

CCUR HOLDINGS INC
NBB: CCUR

6470 East Johns Crossing, Suite 490
Duluth, GA 30097
Phone: 770 305-6434
Fax: –
Web: www.ccurholdings.com

CEO: Wayne Barr
CFO: Warren Sutherland
HR: –
FYE: June 30
Type: Public

Watch a video on multiple devices? Simulate the performance of a car or aircraft part in real time? Such processes might be courtesy of Concurrent Computer. The company's video segment is mainly geared toward broadband and content providers worldwide to allow streaming video and collecting viewer data. The company also develops real-time products that allow manufacturers such as those in the aerospace and automotive industries to run their products through advanced computer simulations. The real-time computing products combine Linux and similar operating systems and software development tools with off-the-shelf hardware for time-critical applications.

	Annual Growth	06/16	06/17	06/18	06/19	06/20
Sales ($mil.)	(44.3%)	61.1	27.6	–	3.5	5.9
Net income ($ mil.)	–	(11.1)	28.4	16.1	0.7	12.2
Market value ($ mil.)	(11.5%)	0.0	0.0	0.0	0.0	0.0
Employees	(60.7%)	251	110	3	7	6

CD INTERNATIONAL ENTERPRISES INC

NBB: CDII Q

1333 S. University Drive, Suite 202
Plantation, FL 33342
Phone: 954 363-7333
Fax: –
Web: www.cdii.net

CEO: –
CFO: –
HR: –
FYE: September 30
Type: Public

China Direct Industries cuts out the middleman and goes directly to the source. The company invests in and manages Chinese companies that sell industrial metals and related products. Its portfolio includes controlling stakes in companies that produce and/or distribute magnesium, synthetic chemicals, steel, and other commodities. The company is increasingly focused on the production and distribution of pure magnesium, a high-demand commodity. China Direct provides its subsidiaries with management advisory services and strategic planning; its consulting segment specializes in providing services for US companies that primarily do business in China.

	Annual Growth	09/12	09/13	09/14	09/15	09/16
Sales ($mil.)	(83.6%)	114.1	2.0	1.7	0.4	0.0
Net income ($ mil.)	–	(41.7)	(24.7)	16.5	(3.1)	(20.4)
Market value ($ mil.)	(83.0%)	2.4	0.5	0.6	0.2	0.0
Employees	(66.2%)	610	25	10	9	8

CD WAREHOUSE INC

900 N. Broadway
Oklahoma City, OK 73102
Phone: 405 236-8742
Fax: –
Web: www.cdwarehouse.com

CEO: –
CFO: –
HR: –
FYE: December 31
Type: Public

Tired of relivin' "La Vida Loca"? Maybe CD Warehouse can take that Ricky Martin CD off your hands. CD Warehouse franchises (mostly) and owns music stores that sell, trade, and buy new and used CDs. The company sells through about 150 CD Warehouse, CD Exchange, Music Trader, and Disc Go Round stores located in more than 35 states. The company also has stores in Canada, Guatemala, France, Thailand, the UK, and Venezuela. Most stores are in strip shopping centers and offer between 10,000 and 16,000 CDs. The majority of sales are from used CDs; the company also sells DVDs, posters, and T-shirts. CD Warehouse is owned by Magnolia Entertainment.

	Annual Growth	12/97	12/98	12/99	12/00	12/01
Sales ($mil.)	31.3%	9.1	15.3	31.9	31.5	27.0
Net income ($ mil.)	–	0.4	0.8	(1.1)	(8.7)	(8.7)
Market value ($ mil.)	(37.0%)	14.0	47.1	11.9	1.5	2.2
Employees	38.3%	80	400	435	305	293

CDC SMALL BUSINESS FINANCE CORP.

2448 HISTORIC DECATUR RD STE 200
SAN DIEGO, CA 921066116
Phone: 619 291-3594
Fax: –
Web: www.cdcloans.com

CEO: Kurt Chilcott
CFO: –
HR: –
FYE: December 31
Type: Private

Securing a business loan can be as easy as A-B-CDC. Founded in 1978, the not-for-profit CDC Small Business Finance is one of the largest companies authorized by Congress to work with the US Small Business Administration (SBA) to provide capital to small businesses, with a focus on enterprises owned by women, veterans, and minorities in low- to moderate-income areas in California, Nevada, and Arizona. The company is partnered with more than 100 lenders such as Bank of America and Wells Fargo to provide fixed-rate SBA-504 loans, general business loans, and bridge loans to start a business or to purchase commercial real estate and office and industrial buildings.

	Annual Growth	09/14	09/15	09/19*	12/21	12/22
Assets ($mil.)	9.1%	–	50.5	86.4	123.4	92.7
Net income ($ mil.)	–	–	5.4	3.6	6.7	(1.3)
Market value ($ mil.)	–	–	–	–	–	–
Employees	–	–	–	–	–	75

*Fiscal year change

CDGJL, INC.

1900 WELLWORTH
JACKSON, MI 492036428
Phone: 517 787-2100
Fax: –
Web: www.comfortaire-hvac.com

CEO: Donald Peck
CFO: –
HR: –
FYE: December 31
Type: Private

Heat Controller keeps things warm and cozy or cool and breezy -- whatever you're in the mood for. The company makes and distributes the Comfort-Aire and Century brands of HVAC equipment for residential and light commercial use. Its products include central air conditioning units, gas and oil furnaces, portable units, and dehumidifiers; the company also makes air coils, heat pumps, and other unit elements. Heat Controller distributes its products in the US, while subsidiary Aitons' Equipment is active in Canada. Heat Controller was founded in Ohio in 1933 and moved its operations to Michigan in 1955.

CDI CONTRACTORS, LLC

3000 CANTRELL RD
LITTLE ROCK, AR 722022010
Phone: 501 666-4300
Fax: –
Web: www.cdicon.com

CEO: E L Garrison
CFO: Chris Johnson
HR: –
FYE: December 31
Type: Private

CDI Contractors means big buildings in Little Rock and beyond. The company has completed commercial, industrial, and institutional projects, including the William J. Clinton Presidential Library. Other areas of specialty include health care facilities, parking decks, condos, hotels, and educational institutions. CDI Contractors provides a range of services including pre-construction, scheduling, general contracting, and construction and project management. The company was founded in 1987 as a partnership between the late Bill Clark and Dillard's head Bill Dillard II. CDI has built several Dillard's department stores. Dillard's bought the remaining 50% of CDI it did not already own in 2008.

	Annual Growth	12/13	12/14	12/15	12/16	12/17
Sales ($mil.)	(2.0%)	–	213.2	284.5	261.0	200.8
Net income ($ mil.)	6.8%	–	2.0	4.7	4.2	2.4
Market value ($ mil.)	–	–	–	–	–	–
Employees	–	–	–	–	–	300

CDI CORP.

2 LOGAN SQ STE 300
PHILADELPHIA, PA 191032733
Phone: 215 569-2200
Fax: –
Web: www.cdiengineeringsolutions.com

CEO: –
CFO: –
HR: –
FYE: December 31
Type: Private

CDI Corp. is a multi-disciplinary organization offering a full range of integrated engineering design, project, procurement and management services to the energy and chemicals industry. It offers proven project management capabilities, mature systems and processes, a network of eight engineering centers and an incredible team of experts to deliver the most complex and challenging projects safely, on time, and on budget. Through its Technical Resourcing division, CDI provides short and long-term staff augmentation of skilled engineering and technical professionals for capital project requirements.

CDK GLOBAL, INC.

1950 HASSELL RD
HOFFMAN ESTATES, IL 601696308
Phone: 847 397-1700
Fax: –
Web: www.cdkglobal.com

CEO: Brian P Macdonald
CFO: –
HR: Amy Byrne
FYE: June 30
Type: Private

CDK Global is a leading provider of retail technology and software as a service (SaaS) solutions that help dealers and auto manufacturers run their businesses more efficiently, drive improved profitability and create frictionless purchasing and ownership experiences for consumers. The company provides technology, advertising, and marketing services for some 15,000 auto, truck, motorcycle, marine, recreational, and heavy equipment dealerships around the globe. The company also counts vehicle manufacturers and original equipment manufacturers (OEMs) as customers. In 2022, CDK Global has entered into a definitive agreement to be acquired by Brookfield Business Partners, together with institutional partners (collectively Brookfield), for a total enterprise value of $8.3 billion.

CDTI ADVANCED MATERIALS INC

1641 Fiske Place
Oxnard, CA 93033
Phone: 805 639-9458
Fax: –
Web: www.cdti.com

NBB: CDTI
CEO: –
CFO: –
HR: –
FYE: December 31
Type: Public

Clean Diesel Technologies (which operates as CDTi) has developed a few cool technologies to counteract global warming. The company is starting to commercialize its chemical fuel additives and other products for reducing diesel engine emissions and improving fuel economy. These include its platinum fuel catalysts, which are marketed in Europe and the US under the Platinum Plus brand. CDTi also manufactures and licenses nitrogen oxide reduction systems (under the brand name ARIS) and chemical fuel additives to help control diesel engine emissions. The company has a licensing deal with Mitsui to use the ARIS technology.

	Annual Growth	12/18	12/19	12/20	12/21	12/22
Sales ($mil.)	(0.2%)	9.8	8.8	5.0	6.4	9.7
Net income ($ mil.)	–	(4.4)	0.4	(1.0)	(0.4)	0.1
Market value ($ mil.)	(21.8%)	1.7	0.8	1.6	1.2	0.6
Employees	–	–	–	–	–	–

CDW CORP

200 N. Milwaukee Avenue
Vernon Hills, IL 60061
Phone: 847 465-6000
Fax: –
Web: www.cdw.com

NMS: CDW
CEO: Christine A Leahy
CFO: Albert J Miralles
HR: –
FYE: December 31
Type: Public

CDW is a leading multi-brand provider of information technology solutions to small, medium, and large business, government, education, and healthcare customers in the United States, the United Kingdom, and Canada. The company's broad array of offerings ranges from discrete hardware and software products to integrated IT solutions and services that include on-premise and cloud capabilities across hybrid infrastructure, digital experience, and security. Top brands include Adobe, APC, Apple, Cisco, Dell EMC, Hewlett-Packard, Microsoft, and VMware. Nearly 40% of its sales come from public-sector clients. About 90% of sales are generated in the US. CDW was founded in 1984 as Computer Discount Warehouse.

	Annual Growth	12/19	12/20	12/21	12/22	12/23
Sales ($mil.)	4.3%	18,032	18,468	20,821	23,749	21,376
Net income ($ mil.)	10.6%	736.8	788.5	988.6	1,114.5	1,104.3
Market value ($ mil.)	12.3%	19,155	17,673	27,461	23,948	30,484
Employees	178.8%	250	250	250	250	15,100

CEB INC.

1201 WILSON BLVD STE 1800
ARLINGTON, VA 222092342
Phone: 571 303-3000
Fax: –
Web: www.gartner.com

CEO: Thomas L Monahan III
CFO: Richard S Lindahl
HR: Divya Bhaskaran
FYE: December 31
Type: Private

Don't fear the competition; learn from it. So says CEB, a provider of business research and analysis services to more than 10,000 companies worldwide. Its program areas cover "best practices" in such topics as finance, human resources, information technology, operations, and sales and marketing. Unlike consulting firms, which engage with one client at a time, CEB operates on a membership-based business model. Members subscribe to one or more of the company's programs and participate in the research and analysis, thus sharing expertise with others. Besides reports on best practices, CEB offers seminars, customized research briefs, and decision-support tools.

	Annual Growth	12/12	12/13	12/14	12/15	12/16
Sales ($mil.)	5.0%	–	820.1	909.0	928.4	949.8
Net income ($ mil.)	–	–	32.0	51.2	92.5	(34.7)
Market value ($ mil.)	–	–	–	–	–	–
Employees	–	–	–	–	–	4,600

CECIL BANCORP INC

127 North Street, P.O. Box 568
Elkton, MD 21921
Phone: 410 398-1650
Fax: –
Web: www.cecilbank.com

NBB: CECL
CEO: Bill Knott
CFO: R L Whitehead
HR: –
FYE: December 31
Type: Public

Cecil Bancorp is the holding company for Cecil Federal Bank, which serves northeastern Maryland's Cecil and Harford counties through about a dozen branches. The bank offers standard deposit products such as checking and savings accounts, NOW and money market accounts, CDs, and IRAs. The bank focuses on real estate lending; commercial mortgages make up the largest portion of the bank's loan portfolio, followed by one- to four-family residential mortgages and construction loans. It offers investment and insurance services through an agreement with third-party provider Community Bankers Securities. First Mariner Bancorp acquired nearly 25% of Cecil Bancorp in 2012 through the collection of a defaulted loan.

	Annual Growth	12/08	12/09	12/10	12/11	12/12
Assets ($mil.)	(2.8%)	492.4	509.8	487.2	463.7	439.8
Net income ($ mil.)	–	1.9	(2.5)	1.1	(4.7)	(20.3)
Market value ($ mil.)	(46.3%)	0.5	0.3	0.2	0.0	0.0
Employees	(0.5%)	92	91	93	92	90

CECO ENVIRONMENTAL CORP.

14651 North Dallas Parkway, Suite 500
Dallas, TX 75254
Phone: 214 357-6181
Fax: –
Web: www.cecoenviro.com

NMS: CECO
CEO: Todd Gleason
CFO: –
HR: –
FYE: December 31
Type: Public

CECO Environmental makes industrial ventilation and pollution control systems, including air filters to improve air quality. The company serves customers in the automotive, chemical, electronics, refining, pharmaceutical, and aquaculture industries, among others. Its brands include Peerless, Emtrol-Buell, Fybroc, Adwest, and Busch International. CECO provides a wide spectrum of products and services including dampers and diverters, selective catalytic reduction and selective catalytic reduction systems, cyclonic technology, thermal oxidizers, filtration systems, scrubbers, water treatment and fluid handling equipment, and plant engineering services and engineered design build fabrication. CECO generates about 35% of revenue outside the US.

	Annual Growth	12/19	12/20	12/21	12/22	12/23
Sales ($mil.)	12.4%	341.9	316.0	324.1	422.6	544.8
Net income ($ mil.)	(7.6%)	17.7	8.2	1.4	17.4	12.9
Market value ($ mil.)	27.6%	266.8	242.5	217.0	406.9	706.5
Employees	9.7%	830	730	730	1,000	1,200

CEDAR FAIR LP

NYS: FUN

One Cedar Point Drive
Sandusky, OH 44870-5259
Phone: 419 626-0830
Fax: –
Web: www.cedarfair.com

CEO: Richard A Zimmerman
CFO: –
HR: Amanda Royer
FYE: December 31
Type: Public

Cedar Fair is one of the largest regional amusement park operators in the world with some 15 properties in its portfolio consisting of amusement parks, water parks and complementary resort facilities. It is formed in 1987 and managed by Cedar Fair Management, Inc., an Ohio corporation. Its parks are family-oriented, with recreational facilities for people of all ages, and provide clean and attractive environments with exciting rides and immersive entertainment. It generates revenue from sales of admission to amusement parks and water parks, from purchases of food, merchandise and games both inside and outside its parks, and from the sale of accommodations and other extra-charge products.

	Annual Growth	12/19	12/20	12/21	12/22	12/23
Sales ($mil.)	5.1%	1,474.9	181.6	1,338.2	1,817.4	1,798.7
Net income ($ mil.)	(7.8%)	172.4	(590.2)	(48.5)	307.7	124.6
Market value ($ mil.)	(8.0%)	2,828.2	2,006.9	2,553.7	2,108.9	2,030.3
Employees	0.9%	51,200	50,700	46,000	53,200	53,050

CEDAR REALTY TRUST INC

NYS: CDR PRC

2529 Virginia Beach Blvd.
Virginia Beach, VA 23452
Phone: 757 627-9088
Fax: –
Web: www.cedarrealtytrust.com

CEO: Bruce J Schanzer
CFO: Jennifer Bitterman
HR: Lauren Licausi
FYE: December 31
Type: Public

Cedar Realty Trust (formerly Cedar Shopping Centers) has tended its portfolio from a sapling to a full-grown evergreen. The self-managed real estate investment trust (REIT) owns, develops, and manages retail space, mainly supermarket-anchored strip centers from Washington, D.C. to Boston. It owns about 55 properties totaling more than 8.3 million sq. ft. of leasable space. Its portfolio spans eight states, with the heaviest concentration of shopping centers in Pennsylvania and Maryland. Major tenants include Giant Foods, LA Fitness, and Farm Fresh. The REIT usually redevelops or expands existing properties after it buys them.

	Annual Growth	12/19	12/20	12/21	12/22	12/23
Sales ($mil.)	(30.0%)	144.1	135.5	127.6	34.0	34.6
Net income ($ mil.)	16.9%	1.1	(1.1)	(45.1)	44.0	2.0
Market value ($ mil.)	(14.0%)	318.1	293.6	346.7	161.3	174.1
Employees	–	–	75	64	57	–

CEDARS-SINAI MEDICAL CENTER

8700 BEVERLY BLVD
WEST HOLLYWOOD, CA 900481804
Phone: 310 423-3277
Fax: –
Web: www.cedars-sinai.org

CEO: Thomas M Priselac
CFO: Edward M Pronchunas
HR: Michelle Bivans
FYE: June 30
Type: Private

Cedars-Sinai is a nonprofit academic healthcare organization serving the diverse Los Angeles community and beyond. It is consistently listed as a top-ranked hospital by US News & World Report in such specialties as cancer, cardiology, endocrinology, gastrointestinal disorders, gynecology, heart surgery, kidney disease, neurology, orthopedics, and respiratory disorders. Cedars-Sinai is a partner institution in the UCLA Clinical and Translational Science Institute (CTSI), an academic-clinical-community partnership and is engaged in hundreds of research programs in areas such as cancer, neuroscience, and genetics. In addition, Cedars-Sinai serves the community through its Medical Network, which includes the highly rated Cedars-Sinai Medical Group and Cedars-Sinai Health Associates.

	Annual Growth	06/18	06/19	06/20	06/21	06/22
Sales ($mil.)	8.8%	–	3,649.3	3,648.0	4,142.3	4,698.6
Net income ($ mil.)	24.4%	–	389.0	443.9	1,083.3	749.7
Market value ($ mil.)	–	–	–	–	–	–
Employees	–	–	–	–	–	8,000

CEL-SCI CORPORATION

ASE: CVM

8229 Boone Boulevard,, Suite 802
Vienna, VA 22182
Phone: 703 506-9460
Fax: 703 506-9471
Web: www.cel-sci.com

CEO: Geert R Kersten
CFO: Geert R Kersten
HR: –
FYE: September 30
Type: Public

CEL-SCI hopes to make L.E.A.P.S. and bounds in preventing and treating deadly diseases. Its L.E.A.P.S. (Ligand Epitope Antigen Presentation System) technology modulates T-cells and may lead to synthetic vaccines for herpes, viral encephalitis, smallpox, and other diseases; the National Institutes of Health is testing CEL-1000 (a compound developed using L.E.A.P.S. technology) as a potential avian flu vaccine. The firm's lead drug candidate, however, is Multikine, which might make tumors more susceptible to radiation therapy and help a patient's body produce tumor-fighting antibodies. Multikine is undergoing clinical trials for the treatment of head and neck tumors. The company was founded in 1983.

	Annual Growth	09/19	09/20	09/21	09/22	09/23
Sales ($mil.)	–	0.5	0.6	–	–	–
Net income ($ mil.)	–	(22.1)	(30.3)	(36.4)	(36.7)	(32.2)
Market value ($ mil.)	(38.9%)	424.0	604.6	521.2	146.5	59.3
Employees	–	–	–	–	–	–

CELADON GROUP INC

NBB: CGIP

9503 East 33rd Street, One Celadon Drive
Indianapolis, IN 46235-4207
Phone: 317 972-7000
Fax: –
Web: www.celadontrucking.com

CEO: Paul C Svindland
CFO: Vincent Donargo
HR: –
FYE: June 30
Type: Public

Celadon Group provides long-haul, dry van truckload service throughout North America via subsidiaries Celadon Trucking Services, Celadon Canada, and Mexico-based Jaguar. The group maintains a fleet of about 3,300 tractors and 8,700 trailers. Celadon also offers dedicated contract carriage, in which drivers and equipment are assigned to a customer long-term, as well as freight brokerage and warehousing services. Its clients have included large shippers with strict time-delivery requirements, such as Arconic, Procter & Gamble, Philip Morris, and Wal-Mart. Celadon Group filed Chapter 11 in late 2019.

	Annual Growth	06/12	06/13	06/14	06/15	06/16
Sales ($mil.)	15.5%	599.0	613.6	759.3	900.8	1,065.4
Net income ($ mil.)	(0.7%)	25.5	27.3	30.7	37.2	24.8
Market value ($ mil.)	(16.0%)	462.2	514.9	601.5	583.5	230.5
Employees	16.3%	3,982	4,351	4,876	7,606	7,286

CELANESE CORP (DE)

NYS: CE

222 W. Las Colinas Blvd., Suite 900N
Irving, TX 75039-5421
Phone: 972 443-4000
Fax: –
Web: www.celanese.com

CEO: Lori J Ryerkerk
CFO: Chuck Kyrish
HR: –
FYE: December 31
Type: Public

Celanese is a global chemical and specialty materials company. It produces engineered polymers that are used in a variety of high-value applications, as well as acetyl products, which are intermediate chemicals for nearly all major industries. Its product portfolio serves a diverse set of end-use applications including automotive, chemical additives, construction, consumer and industrial adhesives, consumer and medical, energy storage, filtration, food and beverage, paints and coatings, paper and packaging, performance industrial, and textiles. Its operations are primarily located in North America, Europe, and Asia and consist of about 60 global production facilities and an additional almost 20 strategic affiliate production facilities. Celanese gets about 25% of sales from the US.

	Annual Growth	12/19	12/20	12/21	12/22	12/23
Sales ($mil.)	14.8%	6,297.0	5,655.0	8,537.0	9,673.0	10,940
Net income ($ mil.)	23.2%	852.0	1,985.0	1,890.0	1,894.0	1,960.0
Market value ($ mil.)	6.0%	13,409	14,151	18,303	11,135	16,921
Employees	12.6%	7,714	7,658	8,529	13,263	12,410

CELL TECH INTERNATIONAL, INC.

565 Century Court
Klamath Falls, OR 97601
Phone: 541 882-5406
Fax: –
Web: www.celltech.com

CEO: –
CFO: –
HR: –
FYE: December 31
Type: Public

Simplexity Health is banking on pond scum for its health. More specifically, the company harvests Aphanizomenon flos-aquae, a type of blue-green algae, from Upper Klamath Lake in southern Oregon, which it uses to make nutritional supplements, body care products, and nutrition bars. Calling it Super Blue Green Algae, the company's product line includes digestive aids (for people and animals), weight loss supplements, and anti-aging lotions. Simplexity Health sells its products through a multi-level, direct marketing program using a network of independent associates who sell throughout the US, the UK, Mexico, and the UAE. Founded in 1974, the company's majority shareholder is Zubair Kazi, owner of Kazi Management.

	Annual Growth	12/99	12/00	12/01	12/02	12/03
Sales ($mil.)	(20.0%)	54.5	39.0	30.0	26.2	22.3
Net income ($ mil.)	–	(4.1)	(2.8)	(5.0)	(3.5)	(5.7)
Market value ($ mil.)	(38.2%)	19.2	2.8	2.8	2.8	2.8
Employees	–	–	84	87	85	75

CELLDEX THERAPEUTICS, INC.

Perryville III Building, 53 Frontage Road, Suite 220
Hampton, NJ 08827
Phone: 908 200-7500
Fax: –
Web: www.celldex.com

NAS: CLDX
CEO: Anthony S Marucci
CFO: Sam Martin
HR: Allison Dejesso
FYE: December 31
Type: Public

Celldex Therapeutics is a biopharmaceutical company dedicated to developing therapeutic monoclonal and bispecific antibodies that address diseases for which available treatments are inadequate. Its drug candidates include antibody-based therapeutics which have the ability to engage the human immune system and/or directly affect critical pathways to improve the lives of patients with inflammatory diseases and many forms of cancer. The company is focusing its efforts and resources on the continued research and development of barzolvolimab (also referred to as CDX-0159) and its next generation bispecific antibody platform to support pipeline expansion with additional candidates for inflammatory diseases and oncology.

	Annual Growth	12/19	12/20	12/21	12/22	12/23
Sales ($mil.)	17.8%	3.6	7.4	4.7	2.4	6.9
Net income ($ mil.)	–	(50.9)	(59.8)	(70.5)	(112.3)	(141.4)
Market value ($ mil.)	105.4%	124.6	979.1	2,159.3	2,490.7	2,216.3
Employees	5.3%	130	125	134	148	160

CELSIUS HOLDINGS INC

2424 N. Federal Highway, Suite 208
Boca Raton, FL 33431
Phone: 561 276-2239
Fax: –
Web: www.celsiusholdingsinc.com

NAS: CELH
CEO: John Fieldly
CFO: Jarrod Langhans
HR: –
FYE: December 31
Type: Public

Celsius Holdings wants consumers to enjoy the taste of burning calories. The company develops, markets, and distributes nutritional drinks that claim to burn calories, raise metabolism, and boost energy. Its first product, Celsius, is a canned sparkling beverage that comes in a variety of flavors and is marketed as an alternative to soda, coffee, and traditional energy drinks. Although it has undergone independent clinical studies, results have not been US FDA approved. Its products, which also include non-carbonated Celsius green tea drinks and single-serving powder mix packets that can be added to water, are manufactured by third-party co-packers. Celsius Holdings was founded in 2004 under the name Elite FX.

	Annual Growth	12/19	12/20	12/21	12/22	12/23
Sales ($mil.)	104.6%	75.1	130.7	314.3	653.6	1,318.0
Net income ($ mil.)	118.4%	10.0	8.5	3.9	(187.3)	226.8
Market value ($ mil.)	83.3%	1,119.5	11,661	17,284	24,115	12,637
Employees	58.9%	120	154	225	378	765

CELTIC INVESTMENT, INC.

268 S STATE ST STE 300
SALT LAKE CITY, UT 841115314
Phone: 801 320-6569
Fax: –
Web: –

CEO: –
CFO: –
HR: –
FYE: December 31
Type: Private

Celtic Investment is the holding company for Celtic Bank, an industrial loan corporation that primarily serves small businesses and individuals. As one of the nation's largest Small Business Administration (SBA) lenders, the bank offers a slew of commercial loans including working capital, commercial real estate, equipment leasing and financing, business acquisition, and construction loans, as well as consumer residential construction loans. It also offers traditional deposit accounts and online banking services, and has been recently expanding into renewable energy financing. The bank has a single branch in Salt Lake City, but provides its loans to companies throughout the US.

	Annual Growth	12/03	12/04	12/05	12/06	12/08
Sales ($mil.)	29.7%	–	–	6.1	9.0	13.4
Net income ($ mil.)	19.0%	–	–	0.7	2.0	1.3
Market value ($ mil.)	–	–	–	–	–	–
Employees	–	–	–	–	–	45

CEMEX DE PUERTO RICO, INC.

KM 2.7 CARRETERA 165 ZONA IND AMELIA
GUAYNABO, PR 00968
Phone: 787 783-3000
Fax: –
Web: www.cemexpuertorico.com

CEO: –
CFO: –
HR: –
FYE: December 31
Type: Private

CEMEX de Puerto Rico makes cement in Puerto Rico. Shocking, but true. Formerly Puerto Rican Cement Company (PRCC), the company operates a cement plant and about 20 ready-mix facilities, an aggregates quarry, and two land distribution centers in Puerto Rico. CEMEX de Puerto Rico serves cement customers throughout the island, but its ready-mix operations are concentrated in the eastern part of the island; it has an installed capacity of about 1.2 million tons a year. Its parent company, Mexico-based giant CEMEX, operates primarily in North America and Europe, but has customers throughout the world.

CENCORA INC

1 West First Avenue
Conshohocken, PA 19428-1800
Phone: 610 727-7000
Fax: 610 647-0141
Web: www.cencora.com

NYS: COR
CEO: Steven H Collis
CFO: James F Cleary Jr
HR: –
FYE: September 30
Type: Public

AmerisourceBergen is one of the largest global pharmaceutical sourcing and distribution services companies, helping both healthcare providers and pharmaceutical and biotech manufacturers improve patient access to products and enhance patient care. The company distributes a comprehensive offering of brand-name, specialty brand-name, and generic pharmaceuticals, over-the-counter healthcare products, home healthcare supplies and equipment, and related services to a wide variety of healthcare providers located in the US and select global markets. Additionally, it also offers data analytics, outcomes research, reimbursement and pharmaceutical consulting services, niche premium logistics services, inventory management, pharmacy automation, pharmacy management, and packaging solutions. In 2023, the company announced its intention to change its name to Cencora.

	Annual Growth	09/19	09/20	09/21	09/22	09/23
Sales ($mil.)	9.9%	179,589	189,894	213,989	238,587	262,173
Net income ($ mil.)	19.5%	855.4	(3,408.7)	1,539.9	1,698.8	1,745.3
Market value ($ mil.)	21.6%	16,533	19,463	23,987	27,176	36,141
Employees	17.5%	22,000	22,000	42,000	44,000	42,000

CENTAURI, LLC

15020 CONFRNCE CTR DR # 100
CHANTILLY, VA 201513868
Phone: 703 378-8672
Fax: –
Web: www.kbr.com

CEO: –
CFO: –
HR: –
FYE: December 31
Type: Private

The name is not for show -- Integrity Applications Incorporated (IAI) has the trust of the US Intelligence community. IAI provides engineering services and software applications development primarily for the US government with expertise in intelligence, national security, and defense. IAI's work extends to imagery and signals intelligence, geospatial intelligence, measurement and signature intelligence, and multi-intelligence collection, processing, and exploitation. AIA's products and services include geospatial analysis and consulting; modeling and simulations; systems engineering; and systems development. For commercial clients, the company offers risk mitigation tracking and security management tools.

CENTEGRA HEALTH SYSTEM

385 MILLENNIUM DR STE A
CRYSTAL LAKE, IL 600123761
Phone: 815 334-5050
Fax: –
Web: www.centegra.org

CEO: –
CFO: –
HR: –
FYE: June 30
Type: Private

Centegra Health System seeks integrity in the health care services realm. The health network serves residents of the greater McHenry County region in northern Illinois and southern Wisconsin. The company operates two main medical centers, Centegra Hospital-McHenry and Centegra Hospital-Woodstock, with a total of some 325 beds. They offer emergency and trauma care, as well as general medicine, surgery, and obstetrics services. Centegra has dedicated cancer, diabetes, and heart centers and also offers rehabilitation, behavioral health, and fitness services. In addition, the community-based health system operates a network of primary care and specialty outpatient clinics.

CENTENE CORP

NYS: CNC

7700 Forsyth Boulevard
St. Louis, MO 63105
Phone: 314 725-4477
Fax: 314 725-5180
Web: www.centene.com

CEO: Sarah M London
CFO: Andrew L Asher
HR: –
FYE: December 31
Type: Public

Centene is a leading healthcare enterprise committed to transforming the health of the community, one person at a time. The company offers affordable and high-quality products to nearly 1 in 15 individuals across the nation, including Medicaid and Medicare members (including Medicare Prescription Drug Plans) as well as individuals and families served by the Health Insurance Marketplace, and the TRICARE program. It also contracts with other healthcare and commercial organizations to provide a variety of specialty services focused on treating the whole person. Centene was founded in 1984 as a nonprofit Medicaid plan by a former hospital bookkeeper, Elizabeth "Betty" Brinn.

	Annual Growth	12/19	12/20	12/21	12/22	12/23
Sales ($mil.)	19.8%	74,639	111,115	125,982	144,547	153,999
Net income ($ mil.)	19.6%	1,321.0	1,808.0	1,347.0	1,202.0	2,702.0
Market value ($ mil.)	4.2%	33,603	32,085	44,041	43,833	39,664
Employees	4.6%	56,600	71,300	72,500	74,300	67,700

CENTENNIAL SPECIALTY FOODS CORP

400 Inverness Parkway, Suite 200
Englewood, CO 80112
Phone: 303 414-4613
Fax: 303 414-4614
Web: www.centennialspecialtyfoods.com

CEO: Jeffrey R Nieder
CFO: Doug Evans
HR: –
FYE: December 31
Type: Public

Centennial Specialty Foods (also known as Stokes - Ellis Foods) is a fiesta of fiery flavors. The company manufactures chili sauce. The 2003 acquisition of Stokes - Ellis added the Stokes brand to the company's brand roster. Both its two red and five green chili sauces, sold under the Stokes brand, are available in club, grocery, and superstores throughout the US, with a concentration in Arizona and Colorado. Centennial's customers include such food retailers as Wal-Mart, SAM'S CLUB, Costco, Safeway, IGA, Food 4 Less, Dillons, Albertsons, and Kroger. The company's products can also be ordered directly from its Web site.

	Annual Growth	12/00	12/01	12/02	12/03	12/04
Sales ($mil.)	(11.2%)	–	–	5.6	5.0	4.4
Net income ($ mil.)	–	–	–	0.2	0.0	(0.8)
Market value ($ mil.)	–	–	–	–	17.7	6.2
Employees	–	–	–	–	99	101

CENTER FOR CONSTITUTIONAL RIGHTS INC

666 BROADWAY FL 7
NEW YORK, NY 100122317
Phone: 212 614-6464
Fax: –
Web: www.ccrjustice.org

CEO: Robert Boehm
CFO: –
HR: –
FYE: June 30
Type: Private

Founded in 1966, the Center for Constitutional Rights (CCR) strives to protect human rights in the US. The non-profit legal and educational organization focuses on rights guaranteed by the US Constitution and the Universal Declaration of Human Rights. CCR uses litigation to protest government misconduct and racial, social, and economic injustice. For example, the group has sued a police department for arresting protesters the group says were protesting peacefully and lawfully. CCR also operates the Movement Support Resource Center, which serves the group's education and outreach work. CCR was founded in 1966 by civil rights attorneys Morton Stavis, Arthur Kinoy, Ben Smith, and Willaim Kunstler.

	Annual Growth	06/15	06/16	06/17	06/20	06/22
Sales ($mil.)	5.2%	–	9.8	22.7	13.6	13.3
Net income ($ mil.)	(7.6%)	–	2.4	12.2	2.9	1.5
Market value ($ mil.)	–	–	–	–	–	–
Employees	–	–	–	–	–	25

CENTER FOR CREATIVE LEADERSHIP

1 LEADERSHIP PL
GREENSBORO, NC 274109427
Phone: 336 288-7210
Fax: –
Web: www.ccl.org

CEO: Martin Schneider
CFO: Bradley E Shumaker
HR: Kathy Schaftlein
FYE: March 31
Type: Private

The Center for Creative Leadership (CCL) is a not-for-profit organization that provides coaching in management training to public, private, nonprofit, government, and education sectors worldwide. The center is headquartered in Greensboro, North Carolina, and offers its programs through open enrollment courses and customized training at its campuses and affiliates across North America, Europe, Africa, and Asia. Virtual learning through webinars, podcasts, and eBooks also is available. CCL serves some 20,000 individuals and 2,000 organizations each year with clients such as Wells Fargo, Time Warner Cable, and the US Army.

	Annual Growth	03/10	03/11	03/14	03/20	03/22
Sales ($mil.)	1.3%	–	92.6	113.7	117.5	106.7
Net income ($ mil.)	1.3%	–	3.8	0.5	(11.1)	4.3
Market value ($ mil.)	–	–	–	–	–	–
Employees	–	–	–	–	–	600

CENTER FOR VICTIMS OF TORTURE

2356 UNIVERSITY AVE W STE 430
SAINT PAUL, MN 551141860
Phone: 612 436-4800
Fax: –
Web: www.cvt.org

CEO: –
CFO: Karla Wetherby
HR: Heather Walton
FYE: September 30
Type: Private

The Center for Victims of Torture (CVT) works for the day when its services are no longer needed. Until then, the not-for-profit organization offers local, national, and international support to people who have survived government-sponsored torture. CVT provides direct services like medical and psychological care and referrals to support groups. It also conducts research on the effects of torture and treatment methods and trains those who work with survivors while advocating public policies to bring about healing and an end to torture worldwide. CVT was formed in 1985.

	Annual Growth	12/14	12/15*	09/19	09/20	09/22
Sales ($mil.)	9.2%	–	14.9	21.0	23.2	27.6
Net income ($ mil.)	–	–	(0.7)	(0.9)	0.2	0.0
Market value ($ mil.)	–	–	–	–	–	–
Employees	–	–	–	–	–	300

*Fiscal year change

CENTERPOINT ENERGY HOUSTON ELECTRIC LLC

1111 LOUISIANA ST STE 264
HOUSTON, TX 770020014
Phone: 713 207-1111
Fax: –
Web: www.centerpointenergy.com

CEO: –
CFO: –
HR: –
FYE: December 31
Type: Private

Houston, we don't have a problem. CenterPoint Energy Houston Electric's glow spreads across the fourth-largest US city and surrounding areas of the Texas Gulf Coast. The utility operates the regulated power transmission and distribution systems in the Houston metropolitan area. CenterPoint Energy Houston Electric, a subsidiary of utility holding company CenterPoint Energy, serves more than 2 million metered customers over its more than 48,230 miles of electric distribution lines and more than 230 substations; the utility's 3,780 miles of transmission lines are managed by the Electric Reliability Council of Texas (ERCOT).

CENTERPOINT ENERGY, INC

NYS: CNP

1111 Louisiana
Houston, TX 77002
Phone: 713 207-1111
Fax: –
Web: www.centerpointenergy.com

CEO: David J Lesar
CFO: Jason P Wells
HR: Shunda Gray
FYE: December 31
Type: Public

CenterPoint Energy is a public utility holding company. Its operating subsidiaries own and operate electric transmission, distribution, and generation facilities and natural gas distribution facilities and provide energy performance contracting and sustainable infrastructure services. Houston Electric is an indirect, wholly-owned subsidiary of CenterPoint Energy that provides electric transmission service to transmission service customers in the ERCOT region and distribution service to REPs serving the Texas gulf coast area that includes the city of Houston. Other subsidiaries also include CERC Corp, SIGECO, and its Energy Systems Group.

	Annual Growth	12/19	12/20	12/21	12/22	12/23
Sales ($mil.)	(8.3%)	12,301	7,418.0	8,352.0	9,321.0	8,696.0
Net income ($ mil.)	3.8%	791.0	(773.0)	1,486.0	1,057.0	917.0
Market value ($ mil.)	1.2%	17,214	13,660	17,618	18,930	18,034
Employees	(11.3%)	14,262	9,541	9,418	8,986	8,827

CENTERSPACE

NYS: CSR

3100 10th Street S.W., Post Office Box 1988
Minot, ND 58702-1988
Phone: 701 837-4738
Fax: –
Web: www.centerspacehomes.com

CEO: Anne Olson
CFO: Bhairav Patel
HR: –
FYE: December 31
Type: Public

Investors Real Estate Trust (IRET) is a self-advised umbrella partnership real estate investment trust (UPREIT) that invests in, develops, and maintains a portfolio of office, retail, and multifamily residential properties. IRET owns some 70 apartment communities composing nearly 12,000 individual units. More than 85% of its revenue comes from multi-family residential properties, while all others properties bring in nearly 15%.

	Annual Growth	12/19	12/20	12/21	12/22	12/23
Sales ($mil.)	8.9%	185.8	178.0	201.7	256.7	261.3
Net income ($ mil.)	(14.5%)	78.7	4.4	(0.0)	(14.1)	42.0
Market value ($ mil.)	(5.3%)	1,084.8	1,057.0	1,659.4	877.9	870.8
Employees	1.4%	392	365	462	471	414

CENTERWELL HEALTH SERVICES, INC.

3350 RIVERWOOD PKWY SE STE 1400
ATLANTA, GA 303396401
Phone: 770 951-6450
Fax: –
Web: www.gentivahs.com

CEO: David Causby
CFO: Eric R Slusser
HR: Adrianna Escamilla
FYE: December 31
Type: Private

CenterWell is one of the nation's largest providers of home care services. The company includes its pharmacy, provider services, and home solutions operations. CenterWell also includes its strategic partnerships with Welsh, Carson, Anderson & Stowe, or WCAS, to develop and operate senior-focused, payor-agnostic, primary care centers, as well as its minority ownership interest in hospice operations. CenterWell is a subsidiary of Humana, a leading health and well-being company committed to helping its millions of medical and specialty members achieve their best health.

	Annual Growth	12/18	12/19	12/20	12/21	12/22
Sales ($mil.)	58.1%	–	–	–	4.8	7.6
Net income ($ mil.)	–	–	–	–	1.0	(0.1)
Market value ($ mil.)	–	–	–	–	–	–
Employees	–	–	–	–	–	39,200

CENTIMARK CORPORATION

12 GRANDVIEW CIR
CANONSBURG, PA 153178533
Phone: 724 514-8700
Fax: –
Web: www.centimark.com

CEO: Edward B Dunlap
CFO: John L Heisey
HR: –
FYE: April 30
Type: Private

CentiMark is one of the largest commercial roofing and flooring company in North America. The company provides roof installation, inspection, repair, and emergency leak service. CentiMark typically works on flat roofs using EPDM rubber, thermoplastic, bitumen, metal, and coatings. Its QuestMark division offers commercial, industrial, and retail flooring, do-it-yourself (DIY) products, and floor maintenance and cleaning products. The family and employee owned company has more than 95 offices throughout US, Canada, and Mexico.

	Annual Growth	04/14	04/15	04/17	04/18	04/21
Sales ($mil.)	–	–	(817.2)	625.8	670.5	783.9
Net income ($ mil.)	952.3%	–	0.0	51.2	54.0	73.3
Market value ($ mil.)	–	–	–	–	–	–
Employees	–	–	–	–	–	3,500

CENTRA HEALTH, INC.

1920 ATHERHOLT RD
LYNCHBURG, VA 245011120
Phone: 434 200-3204
Fax: –
Web: www.centrahealth.com

CEO: Andrew Mueller
CFO: –
HR: Karen T Acker
FYE: December 31
Type: Private

Centra Health is a regional nonprofit healthcare system based in Lynchburg, Virginia. The company's four flagship facilities include the Lynchburg General Hospital (LGH) and Virginia Baptist Hospital (VBH), Southside Community Hospital (SCH), and Bedford Memorial Hospital (BMH). It also includes Centra Specialty Hospital, a long-term acute care hospital, a regional standalone emergency department, Centra Pearson Cancer Center, Centra College, and Piedmont Community Health Plan, Inc. Centra Health provides care to over 500,000 people throughout central and southern Virginia. It was founded on 1987 through the merger of the Lynchburg General Hospital (LGH) and Virginia Baptist Hospital (VBH).

	Annual Growth	12/18	12/19	12/20	12/21	12/22
Sales ($mil.)	0.6%	–	1,078.6	836.8	894.9	1,096.9
Net income ($ mil.)	–	–	8.5	285.8	78.0	(0.5)
Market value ($ mil.)	–	–	–	–	–	–
Employees	–	–	–	–	–	6,000

CENTRACARE HEALTH FOUNDATION

1406 6TH AVE N
SAINT CLOUD, MN 563031900
Phone: 320 240-2810
Fax: –
Web: www.centracare.com

CEO: –
CFO: –
HR: –
FYE: June 30
Type: Private

In north central Minnesota, CentraCare Health System is there when Aunt Judy's hot dish goes off or hockey practice turns ugly. CentraCare Health System includes St. Cloud, Long Prairie Memorial, and Melrose Area hospitals. In addition, CentraCare runs six assisted living and long-term care facilities, almost a dozen community clinics, and various specialty clinics. In total, CentraCare provides more than 550 hospital beds and more than 150 long-term care beds. The health care system offers services such as behavioral health, home care, rehabilitation, and surgery. The Catholic regional medical center was founded by the Sisters of St. Benedict in 1886.

CENTRAL CITY OPERA HOUSE ASSOCIATION

4875 WARD RD STE 100
WHEAT RIDGE, CO 800331943
Phone: 303 292-6500
Fax: –
Web: www.centralcityopera.org

CEO: Pelham Pearce
CFO: –
HR: –
FYE: December 31
Type: Private

It isn't just all about the music for the Central City Opera House Association. In addition to operating one of the oldest opera companies in the US (founded in 1932), the Central City Opera also owns and manages some 30 historic properties. These properties include its home, the historic Central City Opera House (built in 1878) and other buildings in the Central City National Historic Landmark District, known during the gold rush as "the richest square mile on earth," about an hour outside of Denver.

	Annual Growth	12/18	12/19	12/20	12/21	12/22
Assets ($mil.)	1.0%	–	3.5	5.0	4.0	3.6
Net income ($ mil.)	–	–	0.9	2.1	(0.2)	(1.0)
Market value ($ mil.)	–	–	–	–	–	–
Employees	–	–	–	–	–	21

CENTRAL DUPAGE HOSPITAL ASSOCIATION

25 N WINFIELD RD
WINFIELD, IL 601901379
Phone: 630 933-1600
Fax: –
Web: www.nm.org

CEO: –
CFO: James T Spear
HR: Karen Adams
FYE: June 30
Type: Private

Northwestern Medicine Central DuPage Hospital attends to the health needs of Windy City suburbanites. Located in DuPage County, just west of Chicago, the not-for-profit acute-care hospital has nearly 400 beds and provides general medical and surgical care, including specialty care in areas such as oncology, cardiovascular disease, neuroscience, behavioral health, and orthopedics. Its more than 1,100 physicians bring about 90 medical specialties to the facility. Central DuPage Hospital opened its doors in 1964 and today is part of Northwestern Memorial HealthCare.

CENTRAL GARDEN & PET CO

NMS: CENT A

1340 Treat Blvd., Suite 600
Walnut Creek, CA 94597
Phone: 925 948-4000
Fax: –
Web: www.central.com

CEO: Mary B Springer
CFO: Nicholas Lahanas
HR: Dana Brennion
FYE: September 30
Type: Public

Central Garden & Pet is among the leading US producers and distributors of consumer lawn, garden, and pet supplies, providing its products to retailers, home improvement centers, nurseries, and mass merchandisers. Central Garden & Pet operates approximately 45 manufacturing plants and nearly 65 sales and distribution centers throughout the US. The company sells private label brands as well as brands from other manufacturers. It offers product lines such as Aqueon, AMDRO fire ant bait, Comfort Zone, Four Paws animal products, Kaytee bird seed, Nylabone dog chews, and Farnam. The company was founded by Bill Brown in 1980 as Central Garden Supply.

	Annual Growth	09/19	09/20	09/21	09/22	09/23
Sales ($mil.)	8.6%	2,383.0	2,695.5	3,303.7	3,338.6	3,310.1
Net income ($ mil.)	7.9%	92.8	120.7	151.7	152.2	125.6
Market value ($ mil.)	9.4%	1,501.5	1,838.9	2,263.9	1,907.7	2,153.7
Employees	3.7%	5,800	6,300	7,000	7,000	6,700

CENTRAL GROCERS, INC.

2600 HAVEN AVE
JOLIET, IL 604338467
Phone: 815 553-8800
Fax: –
Web: www.central-grocers.com

CEO: –
CFO: –
HR: –
FYE: July 28
Type: Private

In a city of big stores, Central Grocers helps keep neighborhood markets stocked. Founded in 1917, the cooperative wholesale food distributor is owned by some 225 members. It supplies 40,000 food items and general merchandise to more than 400 independent grocery stores, serving several states such as Illinois, Indiana, Iowa, Michigan, and Wisconsin. Central Grocers distributes products under both national brands and its own Centrella brand, which is marketed exclusively to its member stores. The co-op also operates about 30 stores under a handful of banner names, including Strack & Van Til, Town & Country, Key Market, and the low-cost Ultra Foods chain. In 2017 the company filed for Chapter 11 bankruptcy protection.

	Annual Growth	07/03	07/04	07/05	07/06	07/07
Sales ($mil.)	4.5%	–	1,047.9	1,103.2	1,108.9	1,197.2
Net income ($ mil.)	–	–	3.2	4.8	5.5	(10.3)
Market value ($ mil.)	–	–	–	–	–	–
Employees	–	–	–	–	–	2,300

CENTRAL ILLINOIS LIGHT CO

300 Liberty Street
Peoria, IL 61602
Phone: 309 677-5271
Fax: –
Web: www.ameren.com

CEO: Richard J Mark
CFO: Michael L Moehn
HR: –
FYE: December 31
Type: Public

Ameren Illinois brings gas and electric services to customers across the Land of Lincoln. The Ameren subsidiary operates a rate-regulated electric and natural gas transmission and distribution business in Illinois, serving more than 1.2 million electricity and 806,000 natural gas customers in 85 of Illinois' 102 counties. The multi-utility has a service area of 43,700 square miles. Ameren Illinois operates 4,500 miles of transmission lines, 45,400 miles of power distribution lines, and 18,000 miles of gas transmission and distribution mains. It also has 12 underground natural gas storage fields.

	Annual Growth	12/05	12/06	12/07	12/08	12/09
Sales ($mil.)	9.9%	742.0	733.0	990.0	1,147.0	1,082.0
Net income ($ mil.)	51.0%	26.0	47.0	76.0	69.0	135.0
Market value ($ mil.)	(4.5%)	1,115.5	1,169.6	952.0	816.0	928.2
Employees	13.2%	721	408	598	626	1,183

CENTRAL IOWA POWER COOPERATIVE

1400 HIGHWAY 13
CEDAR RAPIDS, IA 524039060
Phone: 319 366-8011
Fax: –
Web: www.cipco.net

CEO: Dennis Murdock
CFO: –
HR: Morgan Dredge
FYE: December 31
Type: Private

Keeping a sharp eye out for the well-being of Iowa's citizens, Central Iowa Power Cooperative provides electricity transmission and generation services to 13 member distribution cooperatives (12 rural electric cooperatives and one municipal cooperative), which in turn serve about 320,000 residential and 7,000 industrial and commercial customers. Central Iowa Power's member distribution cooperatives deliver power to commercial businesses, farmsteads, industrial parks, manufacturers, urban residences, and other customers, in a service area that stretches 300 miles diagonally across the state from Shenandoah in the southwest to the Mississippi River in the east.

	Annual Growth	12/14	12/15	12/17	12/21	12/22
Sales ($mil.)	2.2%	–	188.4	188.0	189.2	219.3
Net income ($ mil.)	(14.3%)	–	7.0	3.2	(10.2)	2.4
Market value ($ mil.)	–	–	–	–	–	–
Employees	–	–	–	–	–	117

CENTRAL MAINE POWER CO.

83 Edison Drive
Augusta, ME 04336
Phone: 207 623-3521
Fax: –
Web: –

CEO: Stacy Dunham
CFO: –
HR: –
FYE: December 31
Type: Public

Central Maine Power (CMP) has electricity pumping through its veins (and transmission lines). The company, a subsidiary of utility holding firm Avangrid, itself a unit of Spanish powerhouse IBERDROLA, provides regulated power services to more than 612,700 residential and business customers (80% of Maine's population) in an 11,000 square mile area of southern and central Maine. CMP allows nonregulated retail electric providers to supply power to customers over its transmission and distribution grid. The utility caters to a peak demand of about 1,680 MW.

	Annual Growth	12/00	12/01	12/02	12/03	12/04
Sales ($mil.)	(4.5%)	–	–	653.5	610.6	596.3
Net income ($ mil.)	(5.0%)	–	–	54.9	49.8	49.6
Market value ($ mil.)	16.2%	–	–	2,255.0	2,543.7	3,043.1
Employees	–	–	–	–	–	1,148

CENTRAL MICHIGAN UNIVERSITY

1280 E CAMPUS DR
MOUNT PLEASANT, MI 488592033
Phone: 989 774-3015
Fax: –
Web: www.cmich.edu

CEO: –
CFO: –
HR: –
FYE: June 30
Type: Private

Academic advancement is central at Central Michigan University (CMU). The university offers more than 200 academic programs for undergraduate, graduate, and professional coursework through eight colleges, including business, communication and fine arts, medicine, and education and human services. The university enrolls more than 20,000 students at the main campus in Mt. Pleasant. The institution also enrolls another 7,000 students online and at 50 locations throughout North America. In addition, CMU offers study abroad programs in 40 countries.

	Annual Growth	06/18	06/19	06/20	06/21	06/22
Sales ($mil.)	(5.9%)	–	314.3	289.5	265.8	262.3
Net income ($ mil.)	–	–	2.3	(6.9)	102.3	(30.9)
Market value ($ mil.)	–	–	–	–	–	–
Employees	–	–	–	–	–	2,388

CENTRAL OHIO TRANSIT AUTHORITY

33 N HIGH ST
COLUMBUS, OH 432153076
Phone: 614 275-5800
Fax: –
Web: www.cota.com

CEO: W C Stitt
CFO: –
HR: Bryan Ware
FYE: December 31
Type: Private

There's no quota for COTA, but the more bus passengers, the better for the Central Ohio Transit Authority. With a fleet of about 280 buses, COTA provides bus transportation throughout Franklin County and parts of Delaware, Fairfield, and Licking counties on some 65 routes with 4,300 bus stops. COTA received about $14 million in federal stimulus money to repair facilities and replace older buses. One project that didn't receive funding was COTA's proposed light rail line to run from Columbus to Ohio State University. The agency also provides service for people with disabilities through Project Mainstream. COTA was created by local county and municipal governments and began operations in 1974.

	Annual Growth	12/01	12/02	12/03	12/05	12/09
Sales ($mil.)	–	–	13.8	13.0	12.1	13.8
Net income ($ mil.)	–	–	(7.6)	(4.1)	(5.9)	36.8
Market value ($ mil.)	–	–	–	–	–	–
Employees	–	–	–	–	–	750

CENTRAL PACIFIC FINANCIAL CORP

NYS: CPF

220 South King Street
Honolulu, HI 96813
Phone: 808 544-0500
Fax: 808 531-2875
Web: www.centralpacificbank.com

CEO: Paul K Yonamine
CFO: David S Morimoto
HR: –
FYE: December 31
Type: Public

When in the Central Pacific, do as the islanders do. This may include doing business with Central Pacific Financial, the holding company for Central Pacific Bank, which operates more than 35 branch locations and 110 ATMs across the Hawaiian Islands. Targeting individuals and local businesses, the $5 billion bank provides such standard retail banking products as checking and savings accounts, money market accounts, and CDs. About 70% of the bank's loan portfolio is made up of commercial real estate loans, residential mortgages and construction loans, though it also provides business and consumer loans.

	Annual Growth	12/19	12/20	12/21	12/22	12/23
Assets ($mil.)	6.2%	6,012.7	6,594.6	7,419.1	7,432.8	7,642.8
Net income ($ mil.)	0.1%	58.3	37.3	79.9	73.9	58.7
Market value ($ mil.)	(9.7%)	800.0	514.1	761.9	548.5	532.2
Employees	(3.6%)	854	822	820	781	737

CENTRAL REFRIGERATED SERVICE, LLC

5175 W 2100 S
WEST VALLEY CITY, UT 841201252
Phone: 801 924-7000
Fax: –
Web: –

CEO: –
CFO: –
HR: –
FYE: December 31
Type: Private

No matter the weather conditions, trucking company Central Refrigerated Service stays cool when it's on the move. The carrier provides temperature-controlled transportation and dry cargo services for major food suppliers and retailers across the US. It specializes in providing a wide array of offerings, from private fleet conversion to inner city and solo driver deliveries to long haul truckload transportation services. Central Refrigerated operates a fleet of about 1,800 tractors and 2,700 refrigerated trailers, or reefers. The company was acquired by truckload carrier Swift Transportation in mid-2013.

	Annual Growth	12/04	12/05	12/06	12/07	12/08
Sales ($mil.)	(27.6%)	–	–	775.6	361.9	406.9
Net income ($ mil.)	17487.7%	–	–	0.0	6.7	9.6
Market value ($ mil.)	–	–	–	–	–	–
Employees	–	–	–	–	–	1,650

CENTRAL STEEL AND WIRE COMPANY, LLC

3000 W 51ST ST
CHICAGO, IL 606322122
Phone: 773 471-3800
Fax: –
Web: www.centralsteel.com

CEO: Stephen E Fuhrman
CFO: Kevin G Powers
HR: –
FYE: December 31
Type: Private

When it comes to metal, service center Central Steel & Wire Company (CS&W) can shape up and ship out. CS&W distributes ferrous and nonferrous metals in a variety of shapes and forms, including bars, coils, plates, sheets, structurals, tubing, and wire. Among the company's processing services are annealing, blanking, computer numerical control (CNC) laser cutting, galvanizing, and structural fabrication. CS&W distributes its products throughout North America from five facilities that are located primarily in the Midwestern US. The company has metallurgical engineers on its staff to support customers with metal specifications and interpretation expertise.

	Annual Growth	12/10	12/11	12/12	12/13	12/14
Sales ($mil.)	(3.6%)	–	–	750.9	678.9	698.0
Net income ($ mil.)	–	–	–	10.6	2.2	(2.8)
Market value ($ mil.)	–	–	–	–	–	–
Employees	–	–	–	–	–	1,075

CENTRAL SUFFOLK HOSPITAL

1 HEROES WAY
RIVERHEAD, NY 119012058
Phone: 631 548-6000
Fax: –
Web: www.pbmchealth.org

CEO: –
CFO: –
HR: –
FYE: December 31
Type: Private

Central Suffolk Hospital (CSH--doing business as PBMC Health System) provides a sea of medical care services to residents of Long Island. The not-for-profit hospital covers a broad range of general and specialty care services including oncology, emergency medicine, general surgery, neurosurgery, orthopedics, and women's health care. With a medical staff of more than 200, the medical center has roughly 200 beds. PBMC also operates a 60-bed skilled nursing and rehabilitation center, a certified home health agency, a palliative care center, and a network of primary care centers. PBMC is affiliated with Stony Brook University Medical Center.

	Annual Growth	12/15	12/16	12/17	12/21	12/22
Sales ($mil.)	12.2%	–	165.8	175.9	261.7	331.1
Net income ($ mil.)	16.6%	–	3.5	3.4	0.3	8.9
Market value ($ mil.)	–	–	–	–	–	–
Employees	–	–	–	–	–	1,350

CENTRASTATE HEALTHCARE PARTNERS LIMITED LIABILITY COMPANY

901 W MAIN ST
FREEHOLD, NJ 077282537
Phone: 732 431-2000
Fax: –
Web: www.centrastate.com

CEO: John T Gribbin
CFO: John A Dellocono
HR: Caralee Zupa
FYE: December 31
Type: Private

Established in 1971, CentraState Healthcare System is a private, not-for-profit health organization dedicated to excellence, offering the full circle of health and wellness for its community. The health system operates CentraState Medical Center, an acute-care teaching hospital with almost 285 beds. The Rutgers Robert Wood Johnson Medical School Family Medicine Residency Program at CentraState Medical Center is a university-sponsored residency program located in the culturally diverse community of Freehold, New Jersey. Other CentraState Healthcare facilities include an ambulatory campus, three senior living communities, and a charitable foundation. It also offer a residency training program for family practice physicians and geriatric fellows in affiliation with the Rutgers Robert Wood Johnson Medical School.

	Annual Growth	12/15	12/16	12/17	12/18	12/19
Sales ($mil.)	4.6%	–	322.0	326.0	355.0	368.1
Net income ($ mil.)	36.3%	–	13.2	9.3	0.1	33.5
Market value ($ mil.)	–	–	–	–	–	–
Employees	–	–	–	–	–	2,527

CENTRE COLLEGE OF KENTUCKY

600 W WALNUT ST
DANVILLE, KY 404221394
Phone: 859 238-5200
Fax: –
Web: www.centre.edu

CEO: –
CFO: Robert Keasler
HR: –
FYE: June 30
Type: Private

Centre College's name reflects its location in the geographic center of Kentucky (near Lexington) as well as its founders' preponderance for British spellings. The private liberal arts school enrolls some 1,200 students majoring in about 30 academic areas. Some 85% of students participate in study-abroad opportunities, which cost little more than regular tuition. Centre boasts a fraternity that carries an oil portrait of alum former Supreme Court Chief Justice Fred Vinson (Dead Fred) to all home football games. Living alums seem to like the place too: The school is ranked #1 in the nation in terms of percentage of alumni making annual contributions. Centre College was founded in 1819 by Presbyterian leaders.

	Annual Growth	06/16	06/17	06/18	06/19	06/22
Sales ($mil.)	9.8%	–	70.2	66.3	71.8	111.8
Net income ($ mil.)	–	–	38.2	22.4	9.8	(3.6)
Market value ($ mil.)	–	–	–	–	–	–
Employees	–	–	–	–	–	340

CENTRIC BRANDS LLC

350 5TH AVE FL 6
NEW YORK, NY 101180700
Phone: 646 582-6000
Fax: –
Web: www.centricbrands.com

CEO: Jason Rabin
CFO: Anurup S Pruthi
HR: Julie Rosen
FYE: December 31
Type: Private

A pair of jeans that fit just right; Joe's Jeans gets us. The company designs, develops, and markets premium designer denim jeans under the Joe's, Hudson, and Else brands. Its Joe's line also includes men's jeans and pants, as well as shirts, sweaters, jackets, and accessories for both sexes. Newly-acquired Hudson targets a more fashion forward customers looking for a great fit. Joe's Jeans sells its lineup to US retailers, such as Saks, Nordstrom, and Macy's, boutiques, and through its namesake stores and website. It operates about 35 full-price retail and outlet stores in the US and now Canada. Founded in 1987, Joe's Jeans nearly doubled in size with the purchase of Hudson in 2013.

CENTRUS ENERGY CORP
ASE: LEU

6901 Rockledge Drive, Suite 800
Bethesda, MD 20817
Phone: 301 564-3200
Fax: −
Web: www.centrusenergy.com

CEO: Daniel B Poneman
CFO: Philip O Strawbridge
HR: Cindy Light
FYE: December 31
Type: Public

Centrus Energy (formerly USEC) beats radioactive swords into enriched uranium plowshares. The company processes used uranium -- about half of which comes from old Russian atomic warheads -- into enriched uranium, which it then supplies for commercial nuclear power plants. Centrus Energy is the radioactive recycler of choice for the "Megatons-to-Megawatts" program, a US-Russian agreement to convert uranium from warheads into nuclear fuel. In addition, Centrus Energy develops low-enriched uranium for the nuclear materials industry and also processes uranium for the US Department of Energy. The company filed for Chapter 11 bankruptcy protection in 2014 and emerged later the same year.

	Annual Growth	12/19	12/20	12/21	12/22	12/23
Sales ($mil.)	11.2%	209.7	247.2	298.3	293.8	320.2
Net income ($ mil.)	−	(16.5)	54.4	175.0	52.2	84.4
Market value ($ mil.)	67.7%	107.8	362.6	782.4	509.1	852.9
Employees	6.1%	230	267	266	275	292

CENTURY ALUMINUM CO.
NMS: CENX

One South Wacker Drive, Suite 1000
Chicago, IL 60606
Phone: 312 696-3101
Fax: −
Web: www.centuryaluminum.com

CEO: −
CFO: −
HR: −
FYE: December 31
Type: Public

Century Aluminum is a global producer of primary aluminum and operates aluminum reduction facilities, or smelters, in the US and Iceland. It operates three US aluminum smelters in Kentucky and South Carolina and one aluminum smelter in Iceland. Its primary aluminum reduction facilities produce standard-grade and value-added primary aluminum products. With an annual production capacity of approximately 1.02 million tonnes per year, the company produced approximately 771,000 tonnes of primary aluminum. Century Aluminum also owns a carbon anode production facility in Vlissingen, Netherlands. Glencore owns 42.9% of Century's outstanding common stock. Century Aluminum generates roughly 65% of the company's total revenue in the US.

	Annual Growth	12/19	12/20	12/21	12/22	12/23
Sales ($mil.)	4.4%	1,836.6	1,605.1	2,212.5	2,777.3	2,185.4
Net income ($ mil.)	−	(80.8)	(123.3)	(167.1)	(14.1)	(43.1)
Market value ($ mil.)	12.7%	696.6	1,022.4	1,534.9	758.2	1,125.3
Employees	9.0%	2,079	2,078	2,512	1,956	2,939

CENTURY CASINOS INC.
NAS: CNTY

455 E. Pikes Peak Ave., Suite 210
Colorado Springs, CO 80903
Phone: 719 527-8300
Fax: −
Web: www.cnty.com

CEO: Erwin Haitzmann
CFO: Margaret Stapleton
HR: −
FYE: December 31
Type: Public

In the 19th century, people rushed to Cripple Creek, Colorado, seeking their fortune in gold. Today, thanks to Century Casinos, they can do basically the same thing (but via midsized regional casinos, rather than through prospecting). The company's Womacks Casino & Hotel in Cripple Creek offers some 440 slot machines and video devices, as well as a handful of gaming tables. It also owns the Century Casino & Hotel in Central City, Colorado, and another Century Casino & Hotel in Edmonton, Canada. In addition, it operate four cruise ship casinos and is the casino concessionaire for cruise lines run by TUI Cruises, a joint venture between German travel operator TUI and #2 cruise ship operator Royal Caribbean.

	Annual Growth	12/19	12/20	12/21	12/22	12/23
Sales ($mil.)	26.0%	218.2	304.3	388.5	430.5	550.2
Net income ($ mil.)	−	(19.2)	(48.0)	20.6	8.0	(28.2)
Market value ($ mil.)	(11.4%)	240.5	194.0	369.8	213.4	148.2
Employees	4.3%	3,515	2,254	2,726	2,804	4,153

CENTURY COMMUNITIES INC
NYS: CCS

8390 East Crescent Parkway, Suite 650
Greenwood Village, CO 80111
Phone: 303 770-8300
Fax: −
Web: www.centurycommunities.com

CEO: Dale Francescon
CFO: David L Messenger
HR: −
FYE: December 31
Type: Public

Founded in 2002, Century Communities is engaged in the development, design, construction, marketing and sale of single-family attached and detached homes. Offering new homes under the Century Communities and Century Complete brands, Century is responsible for the entitlement and development of the underlying land, in addition to homebuilding. It also offers a wide range of buyer profiles including: entry-level, first and second time move-up, and lifestyle homebuyers, and provides its homebuyers with the ability to personalize their homes through certain option and upgrade opportunities. The company operates in about 20 states across the US and offers title, insurance, and lending services in select markets through its Parkway Title, IHL Home Insurance Agency, and Inspire Home Loan subsidiaries. The company delivers about 10,595 homes annually at an average selling price of approximately $414,700.

	Annual Growth	12/19	12/20	12/21	12/22	12/23
Sales ($mil.)	9.8%	2,535.9	3,161.2	4,216.3	4,505.9	3,692.2
Net income ($ mil.)	23.1%	113.0	206.2	498.5	525.1	259.2
Market value ($ mil.)	35.1%	869.0	1,391.1	2,598.8	1,589.0	2,895.9
Employees	3.1%	1,460	1,403	1,600	1,537	1,650

CERES SOLUTIONS, LLP

2112 INDIANAPOLIS RD
CRAWFORDSVILLE, IN 479333137
Phone: 765 362-6108
Fax: −
Web: www.keystonecoop.com

CEO: Jeff Troike
CFO: −
HR: −
FYE: July 31
Type: Private

Ceres Solutions is a growth business. The agricultural partnership provides farmers in about a dozen Indiana counties with crop farming support services and supplies. It sells, stores, and distributes such goods as fertilizers and fuel (gasoline, propane, home-heating). The company's agronomy services include field mapping, crop and pest management, soil sampling, and yield analysis. Ceres Solutions also offers crop-financing programs, sells crop insurance, and provides marketing services. Its Green Notes newsletter offers the state's farmers market and technical advice and analysis.

	Annual Growth	07/13	07/14	07/15	07/16	07/17
Sales ($mil.)	(9.1%)	−	412.2	368.1	299.7	309.9
Net income ($ mil.)	(14.4%)	−	22.2	16.5	10.7	13.9
Market value ($ mil.)	−	−	−	−	−	−
Employees	−	−	−	−	−	125

CERES, INC.

1535 RANCHO CONEJO BLVD
THOUSAND OAKS, CA 913201440
Phone: 805 376-6500
Fax: −
Web: www.foragegenetics.com

CEO: Richard Hamilton
CFO: Paul Kuc
HR: −
FYE: August 31
Type: Private

Imbued with the spirit of Ceres, the Roman goddess of agricultural fertility, Ceres, Inc. is an agricultural biotechnology firm that specializes in developing plant seeds used for bioenergy feedstock production. Its products, which include seeds to grow switchgrass, sweet and high-biomass sorghum, and miscanthus, have the potential as biomass feedstock to generate electric power and produce fuels like celluosic ethanol, butanol, and jet fuel. Ceres boasts that its grasses can be used with existing agricultural technologies and are suitable for cultivation on marginal crop land. (It claims its crops consume water and nitrogen more efficiently than corn and soybean crops.) Founded in 1996, Ceres went public in 2012. Food manufacturer Land O' Lakes agreed in 2016 to acquire Ceres; the transaction is valued at $17.2 million.

CERIDIAN CORPORATION

3311 E OLD SHAKOPEE RD
MINNEAPOLIS, MN 554251640
Phone: 952 853-8100
Fax: -
Web: www.ceridian.com

CEO: David Ossip
CFO: Lois M Martin
HR: Andre Lemay
FYE: December 31
Type: Private

Ceridian offers business services that can help. The company provides outsourced human resources services that cover payroll processing, tax filing, benefits administration, work-life balance coaching, and recruitment to employers. Offerings include Dayforce HCM, and PowerPay. Ceridian serves a host of industries around the world. Ceridian serves customers from more than 50 countries globally through its offices and employee centers located throughout the US. Outside of the US, the company also has a handful of facilities in Canada, EMEA, and the UK.

CERRITOS COMMUNITY COLLEGE DISTRICT

11110 ALONDRA BLVD
NORWALK, CA 906506203
Phone: 562 860-2451
Fax: -
Web: www.cerritos.edu

CEO: -
CFO: -
HR: Nancy Buvinger
FYE: June 30
Type: Private

Cerritos College provides comprehensive learning programs to communities in southeastern Los Angeles County. The public community college offers degrees and certificates in more than 200 fields of study through its nine divisions, including business education, fine arts, liberal arts, and technology. It also conducts vocational training programs, such as health-related programs for nurses, dental hygienists, pharmacy technicians, and physical therapy assistants. Cerritos College has more than 830 full- and part-time faculty members an enrollment of more than 23,650 students. Cerritos College was founded in 1955.

	Annual Growth	06/18	06/19	06/20	06/21	06/22
Sales ($mil.)	11.3%	-	41.5	43.5	49.9	57.2
Net income ($ mil.)	-	-	(17.8)	(0.8)	0.8	3.2
Market value ($ mil.)	-	-	-	-	-	-
Employees	-	-	-	-	-	2,005

CERTAINTEED GYPSUM PRODUCTS, INC.

12950 WORLDGATE DR STE 700
HERNDON, VA 201706001
Phone: 703 480-3800
Fax: -
Web: www.certainteed.com

CEO: James Bachmann
CFO: Dennis Schemm
HR: Greg Krizan
FYE: December 31
Type: Private

CertainTeed has helped shape the building products industry. Founded in 1904 as General Roofing Manufacturing Company, the company is North America's leading brand of exterior and interior building products, including roofing, siding, fence, decking, railing, trim, insulation, gypsum, and ceilings. A subsidiary of Saint-Gobain, one of the world's largest and oldest building products companies, CertainTeed and its affiliates have more than 60 manufacturing facilities throughout the US and Canada. Product lines include Easi-Lite, a lightweight product, and Mold Resistance, which protects against mildew.

CERTCO, INC.

5321 VERONA RD
FITCHBURG, WI 537116050
Phone: 608 271-4500
Fax: -
Web: www.certcoinc.com

CEO: Randy Simon
CFO: Amy Niemetscheck
HR: Deeanna Deane
FYE: April 30
Type: Private

Certco has built a business serving about 200 independent grocers in Minnesota, Wisconsin, Iowa, and Illinois. The food distribution cooperative offers customers an inventory of more than 57,000 items, including bakery goods, frozen foods, meat products, produce, and general merchandise. It distributes products under the Shurfine, Shurfresh, and Top Care labels. Additionally, Certco offers its member-operators such services as advertising, accounting, client data services, warehousing, merchandising, store planning and design, and other business support services. The cooperative was founded in 1930 as Central Wisconsin Cooperative Food Stores.

	Annual Growth	04/11	04/12	04/13	04/14	04/22
Sales ($mil.)	(0.5%)	-	1,027.3	607.3	640.5	980.6
Net income ($ mil.)	187.4%	-	0.0	5.5	5.6	4.6
Market value ($ mil.)	-	-	-	-	-	-
Employees	-	-	-	-	-	325

CERUS CORP.

1220 Concord Avenue, Suite 600
Concord, CA 94520
Phone: 925 288-6000
Fax: -
Web: www.cerus.com

NMS: CERS
CEO: William M Greenman
CFO: Kevin D Green
HR: Stephanie Dillon
FYE: December 31
Type: Public

Cerus Corporation is a biomedical products company focused on developing and commercializing the INTERCEPT Blood System to enhance blood safety. It develops and supplies vital technologies and pathogen-protected blood components to blood centers, hospitals, and ultimately patients who rely on safe blood. The INTERCEPT Blood System for platelets and plasma is available globally and remains the only pathogen reduction system with both CE mark and FDA approval for these two blood components. The INTERCEPT red blood cell system is under regulatory review in Europe, and in late-stage clinical development in the US. Also in the US, the INTERCEPT Blood System for Cryoprecipitation is approved for production of Pathogen Reduced Cryoprecipitated Fibrinogen Complex, a therapeutic product for the treatment and control of bleeding associated with fibrinogen deficiency, including massive hemorrhage. The US accounts for about 60% of revenue.

	Annual Growth	12/19	12/20	12/21	12/22	12/23
Sales ($mil.)	18.8%	93.8	114.2	159.5	188.3	186.8
Net income ($ mil.)	-	(71.2)	(59.9)	(54.4)	(42.8)	(37.5)
Market value ($ mil.)	(15.4%)	764.9	1,254.2	1,234.3	661.6	391.5
Employees	3.2%	254	270	294	309	288

CERVOMED INC

300 East Main Street, Suite 201
Charlottesville, VA 22902
Phone: 434 220-0718
Fax: -
Web: www.diffusionpharma.com

NAS: CRVO
CEO: John Alam
CFO: William Tanner
HR: -
FYE: December 31
Type: Public

This company wants you to get your head out of the clouds and into the bleachers. Stratus Media Group provides marketing and management services for live entertainment and sporting events, including action sports, automotive shows, and trade shows and expositions. The company makes money through corporate sponsorships, TV and broadcast fees, tickets, event merchandise, concessions, and consulting services. Specific events have included the Core Tour (action sports), the Freedom Bowl (college football), the Napa Jazz Festival, and the Long Beach Marathon. Stratus Media also offers talent representation services to athletes and is buying motor sports promoter Hot Import Nights.

	Annual Growth	12/18	12/19	12/20	12/21	12/22
Sales ($mil.)	-	-	-	-	-	-
Net income ($ mil.)	-	(18.4)	(11.8)	(14.2)	(24.1)	(15.6)
Market value ($ mil.)	26.3%	2.7	0.6	1.1	0.4	6.9
Employees	6.8%	10	10	13	12	13

CEVA INC
NMS: CEVA

15245 Shady Grove Road, Suite 400
Rockville, MD 20850
Phone: 240 308-8328
Fax: –
Web: www.ceva-dsp.com

CEO: Gideon Wertheizer
CFO: Yaniv Arieli
HR: Layla Bates
FYE: December 31
Type: Public

CEVA is the leading licensor of wireless connectivity and smart sensing technologies and a provider of chip design services. The company offers Digital Signal Processors, AI processors, short and long range connectivity solutions, 5G wireless platforms and complementary software for sensor fusion, image enhancement, computer vision, voice input and artificial intelligence, all of which are key enabling technologies for a smarter, more connected world. Its state-of-the-art technology is included in more than 15 billion chips shipped to date for a diverse range of end markets. In 2022, more than 1.7 billion CEVA-powered devices were shipped, equivalent to more than 50 devices every second. The US generates about 20% of CEVA's total revenue.

	Annual Growth	12/19	12/20	12/21	12/22	12/23
Sales ($mil.)	2.8%	87.2	100.3	122.7	134.6	97.4
Net income ($ mil.)	–	0.0	(2.4)	0.4	(23.2)	(11.9)
Market value ($ mil.)	(4.2%)	632.0	1,066.6	1,013.6	599.6	532.3
Employees	2.6%	382	404	476	485	424

CF BANKSHARES INC
NAS: CFBK

4960 E. Dublin Granville Road, Suite #400
Columbus, OH 43081
Phone: 614 334-7979
Fax: 614 334-7980
Web: www.cfbankonline.com

CEO: –
CFO: –
HR: –
FYE: December 31
Type: Public

Central Federal Corporation is the holding company for CFBank. Traditionally a retail-focused savings and loan, CFBank has added business banking, commercial real estate, and business lending to its foundation. It now serves not only local individuals, but also businesses through five branches in eastern Ohio and the state capital, Columbus. Its deposit products include checking, savings, NOW, and money market accounts, as well as CDs. Commercial, commercial real estate, and multifamily residential mortgages represent nearly 80% of the company's loan portfolio. Single-family mortgages make up about 13% of loans. CFBank traces its roots to 1892.

	Annual Growth	12/18	12/19	12/20	12/21	12/22
Assets ($mil.)	28.6%	665.0	880.5	1,477.0	1,495.6	1,820.2
Net income ($ mil.)	43.6%	4.3	9.6	29.6	18.5	18.2
Market value ($ mil.)	16.0%	75.9	90.6	114.9	133.4	137.6
Employees	7.1%	95	125	177	134	125

CF INDUSTRIES HOLDINGS INC
NYS: CF

4 Parkway North, Suite 400
Deerfield, IL 60015
Phone: 847 405-2400
Fax: –
Web: www.cfindustries.com

CEO: W A Will
CFO: Christopher D Bohn
HR: Anne Randhava
FYE: December 31
Type: Public

Owners of Terra Nitrogen Company, agricultural firm CF Industries manufactures and distributes nitrogen products, serving cooperatives, independent fertilizer distributors, traders, wholesalers, and industrial users. It serves its customers in North America through its production, storage, transportation and distribution network. Its core product is anhydrous ammonia (ammonia), which contains over 80% nitrogen and nearly 20% hydrogen. Its nitrogen products that are upgraded from ammonia are granular urea, urea ammonium nitrate solution (UAN) and ammonium nitrate (AN). Other nitrogen products include diesel exhaust fluid (DEF), urea liquor, nitric acid and aqua ammonia. The company also has nitrogen manufacturing complexes in Canada and the UK. Roughly, 75% of the company's revenue comes from the US.

	Annual Growth	12/19	12/20	12/21	12/22	12/23
Sales ($mil.)	9.6%	4,590.0	4,124.0	6,538.0	11,186	6,631.0
Net income ($ mil.)	32.6%	493.0	317.0	917.0	3,346.0	1,525.0
Market value ($ mil.)	13.6%	8,984.1	7,284.8	13,320	16,034	14,961
Employees	(2.6%)	3,000	3,000	3,000	2,700	2,700

CGB ENTERPRISES, INC.

1127 HIGHWAY 190 EAST SERVICE RD
COVINGTON, LA 704334929
Phone: 985 867-3500
Fax: –
Web: www.cgb.com

CEO: Eric Slater
CFO: Richard S Pemberton
HR: Dick Kendrick
FYE: May 31
Type: Private

CGB Enterprises is a leader in the grain and transportation industries. Located in Louisiana, the agricultural company provides US farmers with a range of services, including grain handling, storage, lending, and merchandising. It offers inland grain transportation by barge, rail, and truck and also markets and sells seeds, agricultural products, and insurance. CGB's Consolidated Terminals and Logistics Co. (CTLC) subsidiary provide transportation, logistics, and bulk commodity services for both agricultural and non-agricultural customers. The company operates about 115 locations across the US. Japanese trading conglomerates ITOCHU and ZEN-NOH own CGB.

	Annual Growth	05/18	05/19	05/20	05/21	05/22
Sales ($mil.)	29.4%	–	–	5,955.3	7,081.2	9,975.9
Net income ($ mil.)	54.8%	–	–	50.1	116.4	120.0
Market value ($ mil.)	–	–	–	–	–	–
Employees	–	–	–	–	–	3,250

CH2M HILL COMPANIES LTD

9191 South Jamaica Street
Englewood, CO 80112-5946
Phone: 303 771-0900
Fax: –
Web: –

CEO: –
CFO: –
HR: –
FYE: December 30
Type: Public

Engineering and construction firm CH2M HILL (named for its founders Cornell, Howland, Hayes, and Merryfield; dba CH2M) operates five divisions that offer up consulting, design, build, operations, and maintenance services. It is active across five markets: energy and industrial; environment and nuclear, transportation, water, and power. CH2M's top client is the US Government, and public sector clients include the US Department of Energy and the Department of Defense . CH2M also works for state and local governments building water and wastewater systems, airports, highways, and other transportation projects. Founded in 1946, the privately held company is owned by private equity firm Apollo Global Management .

	Annual Growth	12/12	12/13	12/14	12/15	12/16
Sales ($mil.)	(4.0%)	6,224.2	5,931.8	5,468.4	5,408.3	5,287.9
Net income ($ mil.)	(36.6%)	93.0	118.3	(181.5)	80.4	15.0
Market value ($ mil.)	–	–	–	–	–	–
Employees	–	–	–	25,000	22,000	20,000

CHA HOLLYWOOD MEDICAL CENTER LP

1300 N VERMONT AVE
LOS ANGELES, CA 900276005
Phone: 213 413-3000
Fax: –
Web: www.hollywoodpresbyterian.com

CEO: Jeff A Nelson
CFO: Galen Gorman
HR: –
FYE: December 31
Type: Private

As one might expect from a Hollywood hospital, the staff at Hollywood Presbyterian Medical Center (HPMC) includes bellmen, concierges, and parking valets in addition to nurses and doctors. HPMC aims to blur the lines between acute-care hospital and hotel, caring for the oft-pampered community of Hollywood, California. Its health care services include a cancer treatment center; physical, speech, and occupational therapy; and the Institute of Maternal Fetal Health, which performs fetal surgeries. Other services include community health outreach programs and The Chalet, a skilled nursing facility. The 430-plus-bed hospital with 500 physicians is part of CHA Health Systems.

	Annual Growth	12/12	12/13	12/14	12/15	12/16
Sales ($mil.)	10.9%	–	–	–	260.5	289.0
Net income ($ mil.)	83.0%	–	–	–	18.5	33.8
Market value ($ mil.)	–	–	–	–	–	–
Employees	–	–	–	–	–	1,500

CHADRON STATE COLLEGE

1000 MAIN ST
CHADRON, NE 693372667
Phone: 308 432-6000
Fax: –
Web: www.csc.edu

CEO: –
CFO: –
HR: –
FYE: June 30
Type: Private

Chadron State College (CSC) wants graduates to be home, home on the range. Its Agriculture & Range Management program educates students in domestic livestock, range management, soil and plant sciences, and wildlife management. But if ag isn't your thing CSC offers more than 50 other fields of study ranging from American Indian studies to chemistry, education, English, math, and music. The four-year college enrolls about 3,000 students. CSC also has one of the most extensive distance learning programs in the country with both off-campus, online, and self-study courses. Chadron State, which first opened for classes in 1911, is the only four-year and graduate-degree granting college in western Nebraska.

	Annual Growth	06/00	06/01	06/02	06/03	06/07
Sales ($mil.)	(33.2%)	–	32.8	9.3	9.5	2.9
Net income ($ mil.)	(2.2%)	–	1.8	2.6	2.0	1.6
Market value ($ mil.)	–	–	–	–	–	–
Employees	–	–	–	–	–	330

CHALLENGER INTERNATIONAL, INC.

1415 ELDRIDGE PKWY # 813
HOUSTON, TX 770771640
Phone: 713 896-4397
Fax: –
Web: www.challengerintl.com

CEO: –
CFO: –
HR: –
FYE: December 31
Type: Private

Challenger International meets the challenge of being a global player by being totally tubular. The oil services equipment company sells new and used drill pipe, down hole tubular products, and other drilling equipment to oil and gas customers worldwide. Its inventory is located at pipe yards and warehouses in Louisiana and Texas. Challenger International's services include external rust preventative coating, hard banding of tool joints, and internal plastic coating. The company was founded in 1992 by president and CEO George Dawley and Lawrence Woods (who retired from his senior management position in 2007).

	Annual Growth	12/04	12/05	12/07	12/08	12/09
Sales ($mil.)	(25.4%)	–	11.9	–	22.3	3.7
Net income ($ mil.)	–	–	0.0	–	0.0	(0.2)
Market value ($ mil.)	–	–	–	–	–	–
Employees	–	–	–	–	–	10

CHAMBER OF COMMERCE OF THE UNITED STATES OF AMERICA

1615 H ST NW
WASHINGTON, DC 200620001
Phone: 202 659-6000
Fax: –
Web: www.uschamber.com

CEO: Suzanne Clark
CFO: Stan M Harrell
HR: –
FYE: December 31
Type: Private

The Chamber of Commerce of The United States of America is all business. The organization, which aims to represent the interests of US business on national issues, counts among its members more than 3 million businesses, as well as thousands of state and local Chambers of Commerce and other business associations. It serves as an advocate before lawmakers, regulators, and courts; participates in public policy debates; and supports business-friendly candidates through its political arm. The organization also seeks to promote the interests of American firms overseas on issues such as trade and opportunity for US firms.

CHAMPION INDUSTRIES INC (WV)

2450-90 1st Avenue, P.O. Box 2968
Huntington, WV 25728
Phone: 304 528-2700
Fax: –
Web: www.champion-industries.com

NBB: CHMP
CEO: Marshall T Reynolds
CFO: Justin T Evans
HR: Justin Carpenter
FYE: October 31
Type: Public

This Champion hopes to win business in the printing and office supply fields. Through more than a dozen operating units, Champion Industries prints business cards, envelope, brochures, booklets, annual reports, flyers, and postcards. The company also offers banners, aluminum signs, yard signs, as well as apparel, bags, and accessories. Champion Industries operates primarily in West Virginia, Louisiana, and Indiana.

	Annual Growth	10/11	10/12	10/13	10/14	10/15
Sales ($mil.)	(16.9%)	128.5	104.4	72.3	63.5	61.3
Net income ($ mil.)	–	(4.0)	(22.9)	5.7	(1.1)	(1.2)
Market value ($ mil.)	(28.5%)	0.0	0.0	0.0	0.0	0.0
Employees	(16.8%)	660	550	330	330	316

CHAMPIONS ONCOLOGY INC

One University Plaza, Suite 307
Hackensack, NJ 07601
Phone: 201 808-8400
Fax: –
Web: www.championsoncology.com

NAS: CSBR
CEO: Ronnie Morris
CFO: David Miller
HR: –
FYE: April 30
Type: Public

Champions Oncology (formerly Champions Biotechnology) is hoping to win big in the field of cancer research. Its Champions Tumorgraft platform allows the company to implant human tumors of various cancer types into mice, allowing scientists to study the effects of investigational drugs on human cancers. The company uses the platform in its own research and also provides tumor-specific research to doctors, as well as the Tumorgraft platform to other drug developers. The company has licensed the rights to explore Irinophore, a nanoparticle in preclinical development.

	Annual Growth	04/19	04/20	04/21	04/22	04/23
Sales ($mil.)	18.8%	27.1	32.1	41.0	49.1	53.9
Net income ($ mil.)	–	0.1	(2.0)	0.4	0.5	(5.3)
Market value ($ mil.)	(14.2%)	123.0	104.6	145.3	104.0	66.6
Employees	18.9%	115	143	194	230	230

CHAMPIONX CORP

2445 Technology Forest Blvd., Building 4, 12th Floor
The Woodlands, TX 77381
Phone: 281 403-5772
Fax: –
Web: www.apergy.com

NMS: CHX
CEO: Sivasankaran Somasundaram
CFO: Kenneth M Fisher
HR: Jessica Bogenreif
FYE: December 31
Type: Public

ChampionX Corporation is a global leader in chemistry solutions, artificial lift systems, and highly engineered equipment and technologies that help companies drill for and produce oil and gas safely, efficiently, and sustainably around the world. Its products provide efficient and safe operations throughout the lifecycle of a well with a focus on the production phase of wells. Its business is organized into four reportable segments: Production Chemical Technologies, Production & Automation Technologies, Drilling Technologies, and Reservoir Chemical Technologies. The company generates around half of its revenue from the US. In 2020, the company and Ecolab completed a Reverse Morris Trust transaction in which they acquired the Chemical Technologies business. In association with the completion of the merger, the company changed its name from Apergy Corporation to ChampionX Corporation and its ticker symbol from APY to CHX.

	Annual Growth	12/19	12/20	12/21	12/22	12/23
Sales ($mil.)	35.0%	1,131.3	1,900.0	3,075.0	3,805.9	3,758.3
Net income ($ mil.)	56.7%	52.2	(743.9)	113.3	155.0	314.2
Market value ($ mil.)	(3.6%)	6,456.5	2,924.4	3,862.8	5,541.0	5,583.1
Employees	24.0%	3,000	6,600	7,000	7,300	7,100

CHANCELIGHT, INC.

5201 VIRGINIA WAY
BRENTWOOD, TN 370277668
Phone: 615 361-4000
Fax: –
Web: www.chancelight.com

CEO: Mark K Claypool
CFO: –
HR: –
FYE: July 31
Type: Private

ChanceLight (formerly Educational Services of America or ESA) partners with school districts and families as part of a continuum of services to intervene academically, behaviorally and socially to help students catch up with their peers. A provider of K-12 and post-secondary alternative and specialized education programs, ESA targets and teaches students with special needs, learning disabilities, and emotional and behavioral difficulties through four divisions. Its Ombudsman division provides alternative education programs for middle and high school students who have dropped out or who are at risk of dropping out of school.

	Annual Growth	12/05	12/06	12/07*	07/08	07/09
Sales ($mil.)	110.9%	–	8.6	74.9	85.1	80.7
Net income ($ mil.)	–	–	91.7	(8.6)	(10.6)	(12.8)
Market value ($ mil.)	–	–	–	–	–	–
Employees	–	–	–	–	–	2,600

*Fiscal year change

CHANGE HEALTHCARE HOLDINGS, INC.

424 CHURCH ST STE 1400
NASHVILLE, TN 372192367
Phone: 615 932-3000
Fax: –
Web: www.changehealthcare.com

CEO: Neil D Crescenzo
CFO: Bob A Newport Jr
HR: –
FYE: December 31
Type: Private

Change Healthcare (formerly Emdeon) wants to make MDs' lives a little easier by making the servicing of medical accounts more simple and efficient. The Blackstone portfolio company's offerings are designed to simplify and streamline health care billing for insurance companies, health care systems, and doctors. Change Healthcare offers discounted office supplies online, automated billing and document mailing services, and insurance card printing, and has products specifically for dental and pharmaceutical offices. It processes more than 6 billion health care-related transactions each year. Change Healthcare is merging with McKesson's Technology Solutions segment to create a new health care services firm.

CHANNELADVISOR CORPORATION

1010 SYNC ST
MORRISVILLE, NC 275609044
Phone: 919 228-4700
Fax: –
Web: www.channeladvisor.com

CEO: –
CFO: –
HR: –
FYE: December 31
Type: Private

ChannelAdvisor is a leading provider of cloud-based e-commerce solutions whose mission is to connect and optimize the world's commerce. Its multichannel commerce platform allows its customers to connect to hundreds of global channels, market to consumers on those channels, sell products, manage fulfillment processes, and analyze and optimize channel performance. The company offers software and support services for brands and retailer worldwide looking for greater product visibility and brand management in marketplaces (such as eBay, Amazon, and Google), comparison shopping sites (Google Shopping), search engines (Google and Bing), and their own Web stores. Founded in 2001, the company generates around 70% of sales domestically.

CHANNELL COMMERCIAL CORPORATION

1700 JUSTIN RD
ROCKWALL, TX 750874963
Phone: 214 304-7800
Fax: –
Web: www.channell.com

CEO: William H Channell Jr
CFO: Matthew R Van Steenhuyse
HR: –
FYE: December 31
Type: Private

Channell Commercial Corporation caters to companies that concentrate on communications. The company manufactures plastic and metal enclosures, copper wire connectors, fiber-optic cable management systems, and heat shrink products -- primarily for telecommunications applications. Its products can be used for data, power, video, and voice transmissions, as well as Internet connectivity. Channell Commercial serves such customers as Verizon Communications, Time Warner, Cox Communications, and Comcast. It also sells Bushman rainwater collection systems. The global company manufactures its products in Southern California and in Australia.

CHANNELLOCK, INC.

1306 S MAIN ST
MEADVILLE, PA 163353035
Phone: 814 337-9200
Fax: –
Web: www.channellock.com

CEO: William S De Arment
CFO: –
HR: –
FYE: April 30
Type: Private

Channellock has manufactured high-quality pliers on American soil. The company has over 350 dedicated associates who manufacture more than 130 different sizes and types of pliers. It sells its products to more than 4,000 wholesalers and retailers in some 45 countries. The signature color of the company's tool grips is trademarked as CHANNELLOCK BLUE. It holds several other trademarks, such as PERMALOCK, NUTBUSTER, and GRIPLOCK, among others. Channellock, founded in 1886 by blacksmith George B. DeArment as the Champion Bolt & Clipper Company, is now run by the fifth generation of the DeArment family.

	Annual Growth	06/00	06/01	06/02	06/03*	04/10
Sales ($mil.)	(81.6%)	–	–	–	54.0	0.0
Net income ($ mil.)	–	–	–	–	13.5	(0.0)
Market value ($ mil.)	–	–	–	–	–	–
Employees	–	–	–	–	–	400

*Fiscal year change

CHAPMAN UNIVERSITY

1 UNIVERSITY DR
ORANGE, CA 928661005
Phone: 714 997-6815
Fax: –
Web: www.chapman.edu

CEO: –
CFO: –
HR: –
FYE: May 31
Type: Private

Chapman University enrolls 7,000 students at campuses throughout California, as well as in Washington State. From its main campus in Orange, California, the university offers traditional undergraduate, graduate, and professional programs at seven colleges and schools. It also confers bachelor and master's degrees and teaching credentials to non-traditional students at its two-dozen satellite campuses. The university offers some 50 undergraduate majors and 40 graduate programs. It has 650 faculty members and a student-to-teacher ratio of 15:1. Chapman University includes Brandman University, a distance learning program for some 10,000 working adults that operates two dozen locations and offers online courses.

	Annual Growth	05/18	05/19	05/20	05/21	05/22
Sales ($mil.)	(4.8%)	–	530.8	461.4	446.9	458.5
Net income ($ mil.)	15.4%	–	70.9	90.7	230.7	108.9
Market value ($ mil.)	–	–	–	–	–	–
Employees	–	–	–	–	–	3,300

CHARGEPOINT, INC.

240 E HACIENDA AVE
CAMPBELL, CA 950086617
Phone: 408 841-4500
Fax: -
Web: www.chargepoint.com

CEO: -
CFO: Rex Jackson
HR: -
FYE: January 31
Type: Private

If you own an electric or hybrid car, ChargePoint (formerly Coulomb Technologies) products and services may get you charged up. The start-up company designs and builds charging stations for plug-in hybrid and electric vehicles. The company's branded charging stations are targeted to parking lot owners and municipalities and can be installed in areas like apartment and workplace parking lots as well as along public streets. The stations are linked together on a network and are tied into municipal electrical grids; drivers pay for access to ChargePoint's stations through subscription-based memberships. The company was co-founded in 2007 by CEO Richard Lowenthal and other company executives.

CHARGERS FOOTBALL COMPANY, LLC

3333 SUSAN ST
COSTA MESA, CA 926261632
Phone: 619 280-2121
Fax: -
Web: www.chargers.com

CEO: -
CFO: Jeanne Bonk
HR: Sandy Cordeau
FYE: December 31
Type: Private

This company energizes football fans in Southern California. Chargers Football owns and operates the Los Angeles Chargers professional football team, a charter member of the American Football League (AFL) and current member of the National Football League (NFL). Barron Hilton (the son of hotelier Conrad Hilton) founded the team in 1959 as the Los Angeles Chargers; it moved to San Diego in 1961 and won the AFL championship two years later. After 55 years as the San Diego Chargers, the team changed its name to the Los Angeles Chargers name and the team will move back to the Los Angeles area again starting with the 2017 season.

CHARLES & COLVARD LTD

170 Southport Drive
Morrisville, NC 27560
Phone: 919 468-0399
Fax: -
Web: www.charlesandcolvard.com

NAS: CTHR
CEO: Don O'Connell
CFO: -
HR: Lisa McDermott
FYE: June 30
Type: Public

Charles & Colvard hopes that it isn't just some shooting star. The company makes gemstones made from moissanite, a diamond substitute created in laboratories. Composed of silicon and carbon, moissanite (aka silicon carbide or SiC) is typically found in meteorites. Charles & Colvard makes its gemstones from SiC crystals purchased primarily from Cree, Inc., and Swedish company Norstel. Charles & Colvard markets its gemstones through two distributors (Stuller and Rio Grande) and jewelry manufacturers such as K&G Creations, Reeves Park, and Samuel Aaron International.

	Annual Growth	06/19	06/20	06/21	06/22	06/23
Sales ($mil.)	(1.8%)	32.2	29.2	39.2	43.1	29.9
Net income ($ mil.)	-	2.3	(6.2)	12.8	2.4	(19.6)
Market value ($ mil.)	(11.8%)	48.2	22.3	91.0	37.2	29.2
Employees	(6.1%)	63	48	51	60	49

CHARLES AND HELEN SCHWAB FOUNDATION INC

201 MISSION ST STE 1960
SAN FRANCISCO, CA 941051880
Phone: 415 795-4920
Fax: -
Web: www.schwabfoundation.org

CEO: Charles R Schwab
CFO: -
HR: -
FYE: December 31
Type: Private

The Charles and Helen Schwab Foundation (CHSF) provides grants for groups that target substance abuse, homelessness, poverty, and learning disabilities. Unsolicited grant requests aren't accepted; rather, the organization's staff identifies worthy not-for-profit organizations whose goals further the CHSF mission. CHSF was formed in 2001 from the merger of the Schwab Family Foundation and the Schwab Foundation for Learning. About half of the foundation's funding has gone toward its Schwab Learning program, which operated for more than 20 years until the CHSF transitioned it to a pair of nonprofit organizations in 2007.

	Annual Growth	12/14	12/15	12/16	12/21	12/22
Sales ($mil.)	-	-	42.4	13.6	120.0	42.6
Net income ($ mil.)	(7.5%)	-	27.8	(8.1)	49.6	16.2
Market value ($ mil.)	-	-	-	-	-	-
Employees	-	-	-	-	-	40

CHARLES C PARKS CO INC

500 N BELVEDERE DR
GALLATIN, TN 370665408
Phone: 615 452-2406
Fax: -
Web: www.charlescparks.com

CEO: -
CFO: -
HR: -
FYE: April 30
Type: Private

The Charles C. Parks Company is a grocery distributor that primarily supplies convenience stores in more than half a dozen Southern states. It distributes a variety of food items and dry goods, as well as beverages, cigarettes, candy, and general merchandise. The company also offers support programs for in-store delis and other quick-service food operations. Carl C. Parks, Jr., started the family-run business in 1934.

	Annual Growth	04/09	04/10	04/11	04/12	04/13
Sales ($mil.)	(2.0%)	-	292.3	264.3	268.3	275.5
Net income ($ mil.)	(32.8%)	-	1.5	0.3	(0.7)	0.4
Market value ($ mil.)	-	-	-	-	-	-
Employees	-	-	-	-	-	145

CHARLES REGIONAL MEDICAL CENTER FOUNDATION INC.

5 GARRETT AVE
LA PLATA, MD 206465960
Phone: 301 609-4000
Fax: -
Web: www.charlesregional.org

CEO: -
CFO: -
HR: -
FYE: June 30
Type: Private

Civista Health sees a civic vista wherever it looks. The organization brings medical care to the residents of Charles County and surrounding areas in southern Maryland. The regional, not-for-profit hospital system includes acute care facility Civista Medical Center, Civista Women's Health Center, Civista Surgery Center (an outpatient facility), and Civista OB/GYN Associates. Civista Health's services include emergency care, rehabilitation, surgery, and cancer treatment offered by more than 230 physicians. The system also offers a chronic pain program, radiology, and laboratory services. Nearly half the system's revenue comes from Medicare payments.

	Annual Growth	06/05	06/06	06/09	06/10	06/15
Sales ($mil.)	(50.8%)	-	318.4	0.0	102.7	0.5
Net income ($ mil.)	87.2%	-	0.0	-	1.8	0.2
Market value ($ mil.)	-	-	-	-	-	-
Employees	-	-	-	-	-	668

CHARLES RIVER LABORATORIES INTERNATIONAL INC.   NYS: CRL

251 Ballardvale Street
Wilmington, MA 01887
Phone: 781 222-6000
Fax: –
Web: www.criver.com

CEO: James C Foster
CFO: Flavia H Pease
HR: Mike Mikson
FYE: December 30
Type: Public

Charles River Laboratories International is a full service, leading, non-clinical global drug development partner.to pharmaceutical firms and other manufacturers and institutions. The company provides contract drug discovery services, including target identification and toxicology, through its Discovery and Safety Assessment (DRS) segment. Its Research Models and Services (RMS) segment is a leading global provider of research models (lab rats and mice) bred specifically for use in medical testing. The Manufacturing Support segment offers biologics testing and chicken eggs for vaccines. Charles River has operations in over 20 countries, but generates around 60% of revenue in the US. Charles River began operating in 1947 and went public in 2000.

	Annual Growth	12/19	12/20	12/21	12/22	12/23
Sales ($mil.)	12.0%	2,621.2	2,923.9	3,540.2	3,976.1	4,129.4
Net income ($ mil.)	17.1%	252.0	364.3	391.0	486.2	474.6
Market value ($ mil.)	11.7%	7,799.8	12,922	18,954	11,187	12,136
Employees	5.8%	17,100	18,400	20,000	21,400	21,400

CHARLESTON AREA MEDICAL CENTER, INC.

501 MORRIS ST
CHARLESTON, WV 253011326
Phone: 304 348-5432
Fax: –
Web: www.camc.org

CEO: –
CFO: –
HR: –
FYE: December 31
Type: Private

CAMC Health System is a catalyst for care in Charleston. The health network includes flagship facility Charleston Area Medical Center (CAMC), which is the largest hospital in West Virginia and consists of three campuses with some 840 beds total. The system also includes the CAMC Health Education and Research Institute, which coordinates education programs for medical students from West Virginia University. In addition, the health system operates smaller rural hospital CAMC Teays Valley and several urgent care and family practice clinics. CAMC Health System operates an online medical information system and physician services company Integrated Health Care Providers.

	Annual Growth	12/18	12/19	12/20	12/21	12/22
Sales ($mil.)	4.9%	–	1,273.4	2,439.4	1,257.5	1,471.7
Net income ($ mil.)	(39.9%)	–	40.8	1,236.2	60.0	8.8
Market value ($ mil.)	–	–	–	–	–	–
Employees	–	–	–	–	–	4,000

CHARLESTON HOSPITAL, INC.

333 LAIDLEY ST
CHARLESTON, WV 253011614
Phone: 304 347-6500
Fax: –
Web: www.wvumedicine.org

CEO: –
CFO: –
HR: –
FYE: September 30
Type: Private

If you get a little overzealous doing the Charleston while you're in Charleston, West Virginia, head to Charleston Hospital! Doing business as Saint Francis Hospital, the 155-bed facility provides a range of services that include the patching up of twisted ankles, inpatient surgery, nuclear medicine, and skilled nursing. Founded in 1913, Saint Francis Hospital is one-half of Thomas Health System (Thomas Memorial Hospital in South Charleston comprises the other half). Since acquiring Saint Francis Hospital a couple of years ago, Thomas Health System has invested about $8 million in St. Francis to provide it with updated equipment and a new pain management center.

	Annual Growth	09/18	09/19	09/20	09/21	09/22
Sales ($mil.)	(0.9%)	–	–	–	65.2	64.6
Net income ($ mil.)	(21.0%)	–	–	–	26.5	20.9
Market value ($ mil.)	–	–	–	–	–	–
Employees	–	–	–	–	–	570

CHARLIES HOLDINGS INC   NBB: CHUC

1007 Brioso Drive
Costa Mesa, CA 92627
Phone: 949 531-6855
Fax: –
Web: www.charliesholdings.com

CEO: Robert V Boerum
CFO: Matt Montesano
HR: –
FYE: December 31
Type: Public

True Drinks is focused on providing all-natural, healthy alternatives to sodas and other high-calorie beverages. Its flagship product is AquaBall Naturally Flavored Water, which is sweetened with all-natural stevia and infused with various vitamins. Marketed directly to children, it comes in a variety of fruit flavors and features Disney and Marvel characters on the bottles. True Drinks also makes and markets Bazi All Natural Energy, which is designed to boost energy through a combination of 12 vitamins and eight so-called super-fruits (such as jujube, goji berry, and acai). The products are sold primarily through mass-market retailers across the US.

	Annual Growth	12/18	12/19	12/20	12/21	12/22
Sales ($mil.)	91.9%	1.9	22.7	16.7	21.5	26.4
Net income ($ mil.)	–	(3.9)	(2.1)	(7.2)	4.8	(1.6)
Market value ($ mil.)	156.8%	0.5	0.4	0.6	24.7	23.8
Employees	143.2%	1	59	45	40	35

CHARLOTTE PIPE AND FOUNDRY COMPANY

2109 RANDOLPH RD
CHARLOTTE, NC 282071521
Phone: 704 372-5030
Fax: –
Web: www.charlottepipe.com

CEO: W F Dowd IV
CFO: William R Hutaff III
HR: Brett Henderson
FYE: December 31
Type: Private

Charlotte Pipe has been a trusted manufacturer of plumbing systems since 1901, and is the nation's top maker of cast iron and plastic pipe and fittings. The family-owned company's cast-iron and plastic pipes and fittings are used in commercial and residential plumbing under its ChemDrain and Quiet House system. The company runs a foundry in the Charlotte as well as a division in neighboring Monroe, North Carolina, that produces thermoplastic plumbing pipes and fittings.

CHART INDUSTRIES INC   NYS: GTLS

2200 Airport Industrial Drive, Suite 100
Ball Ground, GA 30107
Phone: 770 721-8800
Fax: –
Web: www.chartindustries.com

CEO: Jillian C Evanko
CFO: Joe Brinkman
HR: Alice Gong
FYE: December 31
Type: Public

Chart Industries is a leading independent global manufacturer of highly engineered cryogenic equipment servicing multiple applications in the industrial gas and clean energy markets. Its unique product portfolio is used in every phase of the liquid gas supply chain, including upfront engineering, service, and repair. Being at the forefront of the clean energy transition, Chart is a leading provider of technology, equipment, and services related to liquefied natural gas, hydrogen, biogas CO2 Capture, and water treatment, among other applications. Chart's customers are mainly large, multinational producers and distributors of hydrocarbon and industrial gases and their end-users. The company generates over 60% of its revenue in North America. In early 2023, Chart acquired Howden for approximately $4.4 billion in cash.

	Annual Growth	12/19	12/20	12/21	12/22	12/23
Sales ($mil.)	26.7%	1,299.1	1,177.1	1,317.7	1,612.4	3,352.5
Net income ($ mil.)	0.5%	46.4	308.1	59.1	24.0	47.3
Market value ($ mil.)	19.2%	2,834.1	4,946.4	6,697.5	4,838.9	5,725.0
Employees	19.3%	5,743	4,318	4,771	5,178	11,637

CHARTER COMMUNICATIONS INC (NEW)   NMS: CHTR

400 Washington Blvd.
Stamford, CT 06902
Phone: 203 905-7801
Fax: -
Web: www.charter.com

CEO: Christopher L Winfrey
CFO: Jessica M Fischer
HR: -
FYE: December 31
Type: Public

Charter Communications is a leading broadband connectivity company and cable operator serving more than 32 million customers in around 40 states through its Spectrum brand. Over an advanced high-capacity, two-way telecommunications network, it offers a full range of state-of-the-art residential and business services, including Spectrum Internet, TV, Mobile and Voice. For small and medium-sized companies, Spectrum Business delivers the same suite of broadband products and services coupled with special features and applications to enhance productivity, while for larger businesses and government entities, Spectrum Enterprise provides highly customized, fiber-based solutions. Its services for businesses include internet access, data networking, fiber connectivity, and telephone services. The company offers mobile phone service through a deal with Verizon Communications. The company was founded in 1993.

	Annual Growth	12/19	12/20	12/21	12/22	12/23
Sales ($mil.)	4.5%	45,764	48,097	51,682	54,022	54,607
Net income ($ mil.)	28.6%	1,668.0	3,222.0	4,654.0	5,055.0	4,557.0
Market value ($ mil.)	(5.4%)	70,446	96,074	94,683	49,246	56,446
Employees	1.5%	95,100	96,100	93,700	101,700	101,100

CHARTER MANUFACTURING COMPANY, INC.

12121 CORPORATE PKWY
MEQUON, WI 530923332
Phone: 262 243-4700
Fax: -
Web: www.chartermfg.com

CEO: -
CFO: John Couper
HR: Colleen McInnis
FYE: December 31
Type: Private

Charter Manufacturing's magna carta calls for it to make steel products. The family-owned company manufactures such steel products as special bar quality (SBQ) bar, rod, wire, and stainless steel rod. The company also supplies precision cold-rolled custom profiles and engineered components, including driveline, engine, and transmission parts, for the automotive industry. It operates primarily in the US, but also in Europe and Asia through subsidiaries Charter Steel (general steel products), Charter Wire (precision, cold-rolled custom profiles, flat wire and standard shapes), Charter Dura-Bar (cast iron bar and bronze alloys), and Charter Automotive (engineered components for automotive applications).

	Annual Growth	12/06	12/07	12/08	12/09	12/10
Sales ($mil.)	(4.8%)	-	-	996.1	517.8	903.3
Net income ($ mil.)	66.8%	-	-	26.8	2.2	74.6
Market value ($ mil.)	-	-	-	-	-	-
Employees	-	-	-	-	-	2,000

CHARTER OAK EQUITY, LP

10 WRIGHT ST STE 210
WESTPORT, CT 068803115
Phone: 203 221-4752
Fax: -
Web: www.charteroak-equity.com

CEO: -
CFO: -
HR: -
FYE: December 31
Type: Private

These little acorns might grow into mighty oaks too! Charter Oak Private Equity targets small and middle-market companies. Its investment vehicles, Charter Oak Capital Partners, Charter Oak Equity, and Charter Oak International Partners, invest in the health care, chemicals, consumer products, and industrial manufacturing industries. Investments include Daisy Manufacturing (the air rifle maker) and Aylward Enterprises (pharmaceuticals packaging). The company's Revere Industries holds several of its industrial manufacturing companies. Charter Oak Private Equity was founded as Charter Oak Partners by chairman Jerrold Fine in 1976. Charter Oak Partners still exists as a hedge fund manager focused on long/short equity.

CHARTER SOLUTIONS, INC.

3033 CAMPUS DR STE N160
PLYMOUTH, MN 554412695
Phone: 763 230-6100
Fax: -
Web: www.chartersolutions.com

CEO: William Leonard
CFO: -
HR: -
FYE: December 31
Type: Private

Charter Solutions wants to simplify IT for clients in Minnesota. The company's services include information technology and management consulting, systems design, software development and integration, and project management services. Its customers include small and midsized businesses in a variety of industries such as health care, manufacturing, transportation, financial services, retail, consumer goods, energy and utilities, and technology. Founded in 1997 by co-CEO's Bill Leonard and Dee Thibodeau, Charter primarily serves customers in and around the Twin Cities.

	Annual Growth	12/04	12/05	12/06	12/12	12/15
Sales ($mil.)	12.4%	-	3.2	5.5	9.2	10.3
Net income ($ mil.)	27.8%	-	0.0	0.3	0.4	0.5
Market value ($ mil.)	-	-	-	-	-	-
Employees	-	-	-	-	-	55

CHATHAM LODGING TRUST   NYS: CLDT

222 Lakeview Avenue, Suite 200
West Palm Beach, FL 33401
Phone: 561 802-4477
Fax: -
Web: www.chathamlodgingtrust.com

CEO: -
CFO: -
HR: -
FYE: December 31
Type: Public

Self-advised real estate investment trust (REIT) Chatham Lodging acquires upscale extended-stay hotels, including Residence Inn by Marriott, Homewood Suites by Hilton, and Hyatt House locations, To a lesser extent, the firm will also buy select-service and full-service hotels, such as Courtyard by Marriott, Hampton Inn, and Hilton Garden Inn. Chatham Lodging owns about 40 hotels with more than 6,090 rooms across about 15 US states. Through two joint ventures, it also has minority interests in more than 45 other hotels with nearly 5,950 rooms/suites.

	Annual Growth	12/19	12/20	12/21	12/22	12/23
Sales ($mil.)	(1.3%)	328.3	144.9	204.0	294.9	311.1
Net income ($ mil.)	(38.7%)	18.7	(76.0)	(18.4)	9.8	2.6
Market value ($ mil.)	(12.6%)	896.1	527.7	670.4	599.5	523.8
Employees	(18.7%)	39	23	17	17	17

CHATHAM UNIVERSITY

WOODLAND RD
PITTSBURGH, PA 15232
Phone: 412 365-1100
Fax: -
Web: www.chatham.edu

CEO: -
CFO: -
HR: Frank M Greco
FYE: June 30
Type: Private

Men need not apply to Chatham University, at least not for its undergraduate program. The university consists of Chatham College for Women, which offers bachelor's degrees to women only; Chatham College for Graduate Studies, which offers graduate degrees and teaching certificates to both men and women; and Chatham College for Continuing and Professional Studies, its co-educational online school. Undergraduate students can choose from more than 30 majors in such areas as the sciences, humanities, arts, environmental studies, and pre-professional studies. Chatham has an enrollment of more than 2,000 students. The private liberal arts school was founded in 1869 as Pennsylvania Female College.

	Annual Growth	06/15	06/16	06/17	06/21	06/22
Sales ($mil.)	9.4%	-	52.9	60.8	94.2	91.0
Net income ($ mil.)	-	-	(6.3)	(2.5)	6.3	(5.6)
Market value ($ mil.)	-	-	-	-	-	-
Employees	-	-	-	-	-	300

CHCA CONROE, L.P.

504 MEDICAL CENTER BLVD
CONROE, TX 773042808
Phone: 936 539-1111
Fax: –
Web: www.hcahoustonhealthcare.com

CEO: –
CFO: –
HR: –
FYE: December 31
Type: Private

CHCA Conroe operates its health care business under the Conroe Regional Medical Center name. Either way, the hospital is an acute care 360-bed facility serving the residents of Montgomery County, Texas, and surrounding areas. The medical center's Heart and Vascular Institute includes a cardiac care unit and catheterization laboratory. Conroe Regional Medical Center also provides wound, cancer, diabetes, diagnostic, sleep disorder, rehabilitation, trauma, and women's and children's care. Hospital operator HCA owns and manages the health care facility.

	Annual Growth	12/12	12/13	12/14	12/15	12/16
Sales ($mil.)	–	–	–	224.1	233.7	224.3
Net income ($ mil.)	–	–	–	17.2	9.6	(6.6)
Market value ($ mil.)	–	–	–	–	–	–
Employees	–	–	–	–	–	1,200

CHECKPOINT SYSTEMS, INC.

101 WOLF DR
WEST DEPTFORD, NJ 080862243
Phone: 800 257-5540
Fax: –
Web: www.checkpointsystems.com

CEO: George Babich
CFO: James M Lucania
HR: Leila Hajeri
FYE: December 27
Type: Private

Checkpoint Systems is a leading global supplier of RF and RFID hardware, software, labels, tags and connected solutions. As a global leader in Electronic Article Surveillance, Checkpoint's families of EAS antennas offer exceptional detection and have been create to meet retailer's product protection requirements across a wide range of applications. Checkpoint's range of technological solutions offers retailers and brands - from supermarkets to DIY, fashion to digital electronics, a connected approach to profitability and more seamless and engaging shopper experiences. Checkpoint Systems is a division of CCL Industries, a world leader in specialty label and packaging solutions for global corporations, small businesses, and consumers.

CHEESECAKE FACTORY INC. (THE)   NMS: CAKE

26901 Malibu Hills Road
Calabasas Hills, CA 91301
Phone: 818 871-3000
Fax: –
Web: www.thecheesecakefactory.com

CEO: David Overton
CFO: Matthew E Clark
HR: –
FYE: January 2
Type: Public

Originated in 1972, The Cheesecake Factory Incorporated is a leader in experiential dining. It owns and operates about 320s restaurants throughout the US and Canada under brands including The Cheesecake Factory, North Italia and a collection within its Fox Restaurant Concepts business. Internationally, about 30 The Cheesecake Factory restaurants operate under licensing agreements. Its bakery division operates two facilities that produce quality cheesecakes and other baked products for its restaurants, international licensees and third-party bakery customers.

	Annual Growth	12/19	12/20	12/21*	01/23	01/24
Sales ($mil.)	8.5%	2,482.7	1,983.2	2,927.5	3,303.2	3,439.5
Net income ($ mil.)	(5.5%)	127.3	(253.4)	72.4	43.1	101.4
Market value ($ mil.)	(3.0%)	1,968.3	1,873.1	2,008.9	1,638.6	1,740.4
Employees	0.9%	46,250	42,500	45,800	47,500	47,900

*Fiscal year change

CHEFS INTERNATIONAL, INC.

62 BROADWAY
POINT PLEASANT BEACH, NJ 087422699
Phone: 732 295-0350
Fax: –
Web: www.chefsinternationalnj.com

CEO: Robert M Lombardi MD
CFO: Martin W Fletcher
HR: –
FYE: January 28
Type: Private

These chefs are busy boiling seafood. Chefs International operates about a dozen casual dining restaurants in New Jersey and Florida mostly doing business under the Lobster Shanty name, such as Point Pleasant Lobster Shanty, Toms River Lobster Shanty, and its flagship Jack Baker's Lobster Shanty. Other locations include Jack Baker's Wharfside & Patio Bar and The Sunset Ballroom event and banquet hall. The restaurants serve a variety of seafood dishes in a casual setting. Jack Baker, a New Jersey fisherman, opened his first Jack Baker's Lobster Shanty in 1979. Chairman Robert Lombardi and his family control the company.

	Annual Growth	01/14	01/15	01/16	01/17	01/18
Sales ($mil.)	4.2%	–	31.0	30.1	28.7	35.2
Net income ($ mil.)	(20.7%)	–	2.7	2.0	0.5	1.4
Market value ($ mil.)	–	–	–	–	–	–
Employees	–	–	–	–	–	500

CHEFS' WAREHOUSE INC (THE)   NMS: CHEF

100 East Ridge Road
Ridgefield, CT 06877
Phone: 203 894-1345
Fax: –
Web: www.chefswarehouse.com

CEO: Christopher Pappas
CFO: James Leddy
HR: Cesar Garcia
FYE: December 29
Type: Public

A premier distributor of specialty food products, the Chefs' Warehouse sells such gourmet food items as artisan charcuterie, specialty cheeses, hormone-free protein, truffles, caviar, and chocolates, as well as basic food ingredients like cooking oils, flour, butter, milk, and eggs. The company provides more than 50,000 items sourced from 2,500 suppliers to a core customer base comprising chefs from independent restaurants, fine dining establishments, culinary schools, hotels, and country clubs. Its Allen Brothers subsidiary sells prime cuts direct-to-consumer via mail and online. The Chefs' Warehouse typically focuses on culinary hotbeds such as New York City, San Francisco, Los Angeles, and Washington, DC. Tracing its roots back to 1985, the Chefs' Warehouse went public in 2011.

	Annual Growth	12/19	12/20	12/21	12/22	12/23
Sales ($mil.)	21.2%	1,591.8	1,111.6	1,745.8	2,613.4	3,433.8
Net income ($ mil.)	9.3%	24.2	(82.9)	(4.9)	27.8	34.6
Market value ($ mil.)	(6.2%)	1,506.1	947.6	1,291.9	1,320.1	1,167.4
Employees	18.8%	2,447	2,221	2,712	4,124	4,873

CHEGG INC   NYS: CHGG

3990 Freedom Circle
Santa Clara, CA 95054
Phone: 408 855-5700
Fax: –
Web: www.chegg.com

CEO: Dan Rosensweig
CFO: Andrew Brown
HR: Janom Coleman
FYE: December 31
Type: Public

Chegg offers products and services that help students improve their outcomes throughout their educational journey. It also provides personal and professional development skills training. In addition to approximately 8.2 million individuals who paid for its products and services, the company's primary Subscription Services include Busuu, Chegg Study Pack, Chegg Study, Chegg Writing, and Chegg Math. Its mobile apps are built as hybrid applications leveraging the Chegg application programming interface (API). Formed in 2005, Chegg went public in 2013. The US generates approximately 85% of the company's revenue.

	Annual Growth	12/19	12/20	12/21	12/22	12/23
Sales ($mil.)	14.9%	410.9	644.3	776.3	766.9	716.3
Net income ($ mil.)	–	(9.6)	(6.2)	(1.5)	266.6	18.2
Market value ($ mil.)	(26.0%)	3,898.0	9,288.1	3,156.7	2,598.4	1,168.1
Employees	9.0%	1,401	1,941	1,736	2,071	1,979

CHEMED CORP
NYS: CHE

255 East Fifth Street, Suite 2600
Cincinnati, OH 45202
Phone: 513 762-6690
Fax: –
Web: www.chemed.com

CEO: Kevin J McNamara
CFO: Michael D Witzeman
HR: –
FYE: December 31
Type: Public

Chemed offers hospice care to terminally ill patients through its VITAS Healthcare subsidiary. VITAS employs doctors, nurses, and other professionals to provide at-home and inpatient services in care facilities. Chemed's better-known Roto-Rooter subsidiary was founded in 1935 and offers plumbing and drain-cleaning services for residential and commercial customers through company-owned, contractor-operated, and franchised locations. Roto-Rooter system offers services to more than 90% of the US population.

	Annual Growth	12/19	12/20	12/21	12/22	12/23
Sales ($mil.)	4.0%	1,938.6	2,079.6	2,139.3	2,135.0	2,264.4
Net income ($ mil.)	5.5%	219.9	319.5	268.6	249.6	272.5
Market value ($ mil.)	7.4%	6,604.2	8,007.7	7,954.0	7,674.2	8,791.6
Employees	(2.4%)	16,641	15,544	14,137	14,167	15,087

CHEMOURS CO (THE)
NYS: CC

1007 Market Street
Wilmington, DE 19801
Phone: 302 773-1000
Fax: –
Web: www.chemours.com

CEO: Mark E Newman
CFO: Jonathan S Lock
HR: –
FYE: December 31
Type: Public

The Chemours Company is a leading, global provider of performance chemicals that are key inputs in end-products and processes in a variety of industries. The company delivers customized solutions with a wide range of industrial and specialty chemicals products for markets, including coatings, plastics, refrigeration and air conditioning, transportation, semiconductor and consumer electronics, general industrial, and oil and gas. The company's principal products include titanium dioxide (TiO2) pigment, refrigerants, industrial fluoropolymer resins, sodium cyanide (prior to the Mining Solutions business sale), and performance chemicals and intermediates. The company's largest market is North America region with nearly 45% of its revenue.

	Annual Growth	12/18	12/19	12/20	12/21	12/22
Sales ($mil.)	0.6%	6,638.0	5,526.0	4,969.0	6,345.0	6,794.0
Net income ($ mil.)	(12.7%)	995.0	(52.0)	219.0	608.0	578.0
Market value ($ mil.)	2.1%	4,190.8	2,686.4	3,681.4	4,983.8	4,547.2
Employees	(1.5%)	7,000	7,000	6,500	6,400	6,600

CHEMUNG FINANCIAL CORP.
NMS: CHMG

One Chemung Canal Plaza
Elmira, NY 14901
Phone: 607 737-3711
Fax: –
Web: www.chemungcanal.com

CEO: Anders M Tomson
CFO: Karl F Krebs
HR: –
FYE: December 31
Type: Public

"Everybody Chemung Financial Tonight" probably wouldn't make much of a pop record. The firm is parent to Chemung Canal Trust Company, which provides bank and trust services from about 30 offices in upstate New York. The trust company offers such deposit services as savings, checking, and money market accounts; IRAs; and CDs. It also offers credit cards and originates a variety of loans, including personal, small business, and residential mortgage loans. Other services include retirement and estate planning, and tax services. Another Chemung Financial subsidiary, CFS Group, offers mutual funds, discount brokerage, and other financial services.

	Annual Growth	12/19	12/20	12/21	12/22	12/23
Assets ($mil.)	11.0%	1,787.8	2,279.5	2,418.5	2,645.6	2,710.5
Net income ($ mil.)	12.5%	15.6	19.3	26.4	28.8	25.0
Market value ($ mil.)	4.0%	201.3	160.8	220.1	217.3	235.9
Employees	(1.6%)	362	341	337	340	339

CHENEGA CORPORATION

3000 C ST STE 301
ANCHORAGE, AK 995033975
Phone: 907 277-5706
Fax: –
Web: www.chenega.com

CEO: Charles Totemoff
CFO: –
HR: Lashree Obee
FYE: September 30
Type: Private

An Alaska Native Corporation, Chenega Corporation has gone from landowner to business titan. Representing the Chenega people residing in the central Alaskan Prince William Sound region, it operates mostly through its subsidiaries. Chenega Integrated Systems and Chenega Technology Services offer information technology, security training, manufacturing, research and development, network engineering, and military operation support services. Chenega Corporation's clients have included the Department of Defense, Department of Homeland Security and EPA.

	Annual Growth	09/15	09/16	09/17	09/18	09/19
Sales ($mil.)	(0.3%)	–	–	875.9	829.9	871.0
Net income ($ mil.)	27.0%	–	–	12.2	19.3	19.6
Market value ($ mil.)	–	–	–	–	–	–
Employees	–	–	–	–	–	4,500

CHENIERE ENERGY INC.
NYS: LNG

700 Milam Street, Suite 1900
Houston, TX 77002
Phone: 713 375-5000
Fax: –
Web: www.cheniere.com

CEO: Jack A Fusco
CFO: Zach Davis
HR: Kathy Cassel
FYE: December 31
Type: Public

Cheniere Energy is a producer of liquefied natural gas (LNG) in the US, serving about 40 countries worldwide. The company purchases natural gas and processes it into LNG and offers customers the option to load the LNG onto their vessels at its terminals, or it delivers the LNG to regasification facilities around the world. The company has two terminals on the US Gulf Coast in various stages of development: its Sabine Pass liquefaction project in southwest Louisiana and its Corpus Christi liquefaction facility in South Texas. Around 85% of revenue comes from outside the US. Cheniere also has pipeline assets and operates an LNG and natural gas marketing business.

	Annual Growth	12/19	12/20	12/21	12/22	12/23
Sales ($mil.)	20.3%	9,730.0	9,358.0	15,864	33,428	20,394
Net income ($ mil.)	97.6%	648.0	(85.0)	(2,343.0)	1,428.0	9,881.0
Market value ($ mil.)	29.3%	14,474	14,227	24,037	35,541	40,458
Employees	1.2%	1,530	1,519	1,550	1,551	1,605

CHENIERE ENERGY PARTNERS L P
NYS: CQP

700 Milam Street, Suite 1900
Houston, TX 77002
Phone: 713 375-5000
Fax: –
Web: www.cheniere.com

CEO: Jack A Fusco
CFO: Zach Davis
HR: –
FYE: December 31
Type: Public

Cheniere Energy Partners, a subsidiary of Cheniere Energy, plans to be North America's biggest gas station -- natural gas, that is. The Sabine Pass LNG (liquefied natural gas) receiving terminal is one of North America's largest: It boasts 4 billion cu. ft. per day of regasification capacity as well as 17 billion cu. ft. of LNG storage capacity. The company provides clean, secure and affordable LNG to integrated energy companies, utilities and energy trading companies around the world. It aspires to conduct its business in a safe and responsible manner, delivering a reliable, competitive and integrated source of LNG to its customers.

	Annual Growth	12/19	12/20	12/21	12/22	12/23
Sales ($mil.)	9.0%	6,838.0	6,167.0	9,434.0	17,206	9,664.0
Net income ($ mil.)	37.9%	1,175.0	1,183.0	1,630.0	2,498.0	4,254.0
Market value ($ mil.)	5.8%	19,662	17,410	20,862	28,088	24,591
Employees	–	–	–	–	–	1,605

CHENIERE ENERGY PARTNERS LP HOLDINGS, LLC

700 LOUISIANA ST STE 1900
HOUSTON, TX 770022767
Phone: 713 375-5000
Fax: -
Web: www.cheniere.com

CEO: Jack A Fusco
CFO: Michael J Wortley
HR: -
FYE: December 31
Type: Private

Three's not a crowd for Cheniere Energy Partners LP Holdings. The LLC was formed by Cheniere Energy Partners to own a 55.9% stake in Cheniere Energy Partners, which operates the Sabine Pass LNG terminal in Louisiana. (Cheniere Energy Partners is itself an offshoot of Cheniere Energy.) By creating a stock-owning holding company, Cheniere Energy Partners reduces its risk to early-stage development projects and marketing activities. Shareholders of Cheniere Energy Partners LP Holdings are also entitled to quarterly cash dividends. Cheniere Energy Partners LP Holdings completed an IPO in 2013 and raised $720 million, which it will use to pay down debt and make a distribution to Cheniere Energy.

CHEROKEE NATION INDUSTRIES, L.L.C.

470739 HIGHWAY 51
STILWELL, OK 749609194
Phone: 918 696-3151
Fax: -
Web: www.cherokee.org

CEO: -
CFO: -
HR: -
FYE: September 30
Type: Private

Once relocated by US military forces, Cherokees today control a US military contractor. Cherokee Nation Industries (CNI), owned by the Cherokee Nation, assembles and distributes cable and wire harnesses for use in military aviation. Subsidiaries include Cherokee Nation CND (manufacturer of electric panels, racks, enclosures, and cable assemblies) and Cherokee Nation Metalworks (fabricated assemblies and components for commercial and military aircraft as well as missile and unmanned aerial vehicle programs). CNI also provides office products and document and print management services through Cherokee Nation Office Solutions. The company's customers have included heavy hitters Boeing, Lockheed Martin, and NASA.

	Annual Growth	06/02	06/03	06/04	06/05*	09/19
Sales ($mil.)	(11.8%)	-	49.8	85.5	85.5	6.6
Net income ($ mil.)	-	-	2.5	2.0	2.0	(1.0)
Market value ($ mil.)	-	-	-	-	-	-
Employees	-	-	-	-	-	387

*Fiscal year change

CHERRY BEKAERT LLP

200 S 10TH ST STE 900
RICHMOND, VA 232194064
Phone: 804 673-5700
Fax: -
Web: www.cbh.com

CEO: Michelle Thompson
CFO: Matthew Grossman
HR: -
FYE: April 30
Type: Private

Life's a bowl of accounting and consulting services at Cherry Bekaert (formerly Cherry, Bekaert & Holland). The firm provides financial and management consulting services in the southeastern US. It specializes in serving such sectors as government, financial services, not-for-profit, higher education, healthcare, retail, and manufacturing. In addition to tax and accounting services, Cherry Bekaert provides business valuations, litigation support, M&A advisory, and other services. It also has a wealth management arm for well-to-do families. The firm enjoys an international reach through its affiliation with Baker Tilly International.

CHERRY CENTRAL COOPERATIVE, INC.

1771 N US HIGHWAY 31 S
TRAVERSE CITY, MI 496858748
Phone: 231 946-1860
Fax: -
Web: www.cherrycentral.com

CEO: Melanie Laperriere
CFO: Catherine Collins
HR: -
FYE: April 30
Type: Private

Serving as a central hub for cherry pickers' crops, Cherry Central Cooperative is a fruit marketing co-operative that consists of more than a dozen member cooperatives representing hundreds of growers in Michigan, New York, Utah, Washington, Wisconsin, and Ontario. It processes cherries, cranberries, apples, and other fruit products, including the Indian Summer brand of apple and cherry juices and ciders. Its Oceana Foods unit makes dried fruit sold under the Traverse Bay label, while its Dunkley International subsidiary makes fruit-processing equipment. Cherry Central's products are sold to retail, foodservice, and ingredient customers. The cooperative was formed in 1973.

	Annual Growth	04/13	04/14	04/15	04/16	04/17
Sales ($mil.)	(3.2%)	-	-	167.7	150.6	157.2
Net income ($ mil.)	-	-	-	0.1	(0.8)	(0.2)
Market value ($ mil.)	-	-	-	-	-	-
Employees	-	-	-	-	-	308

CHERRY HILL MORTGAGE INVESTMENT CORP

NYS: CHMI

1451 Route 34, Suite 303
Farmingdale, NJ 07727
Phone: 877 870-7005
Fax: -
Web: www.chmireit.com

CEO: Jeffrey B Lown
CFO: Michael Hutchby
HR: -
FYE: December 31
Type: Public

Cherry Hill Mortgage Investment is interested in real estate assets that lie far beyond Cherry Hill, New Jersey. Formed in 2012, Cherry Hill is a real estate investment trust, or REIT, that looks to acquire, invest in, and manage real estate assets across the US. It plans to build a portfolio that comprises excess mortgage servicing rights (excess MSRs are servicing fees that exceed basic MSR servicing fees), agency residential mortgage-backed securities (secured by the government agencies like Fannie Mae and Freddie Mac), and other residential mortgage assets. The REIT is externally managed by Cherry Hill Mortgage Management, an affiliate of Freedom Mortgage. It went public in 2013.

	Annual Growth	12/19	12/20	12/21	12/22	12/23
Sales ($mil.)	61.4%	17.8	(18.4)	47.5	69.6	121.1
Net income ($ mil.)	-	(42.8)	(52.2)	12.3	21.7	(34.8)
Market value ($ mil.)	(27.5%)	438.0	274.4	248.3	174.1	121.3
Employees	-	5	15	12	12	-

CHESAPEAKE ENERGY CORP.

NMS: CHK

6100 North Western Avenue
Oklahoma City, OK 73118
Phone: 405 848-8000
Fax: -
Web: www.chk.com

CEO: Domenic J Dell'osso Jr
CFO: Mohit Singh
HR: -
FYE: December 31
Type: Public

Chesapeake Energy is an independent exploration and production company with oil and gas assets across the US. All of the company's operations are mainly done onshore in the US. The company owns interests in approximately 8,400 oil and natural gas wells. Chesapeake has exploration and production assets in Marcellus, Eagle Ford, and Haynesville shale plays, which accounts to about 3,800 gross acres. Its customer, Valero Energy Corporation, constitutes nearly 15% of the company's total revenues. In 2023, Chesapeake agreed to sell its portion of its Eagle Ford assets to WildFire Energy I LLC for $1.425 billion.

	Annual Growth	12/20*	02/21*	12/21	12/22	12/23
Sales ($mil.)	18.1%	5,296.0	260.0	5,549.0	11,743	8,721.0
Net income ($ mil.)	-	(9,734.0)	5,383.0	945.0	4,936.0	2,419.0
Market value ($ mil.)	-	-	-	8,438.6	12,343	10,063
Employees	(8.4%)	1,300	-	1,300	1,200	1,000

*Fiscal year change

CHESAPEAKE UTILITIES CORP. NYS: CPK

500 Energy Lane
Dover, DE 19901
Phone: 302 734-6799
Fax: –
Web: www.chpk.com

CEO: Jeffry M Householder
CFO: Beth W Cooper
HR: –
FYE: December 31
Type: Public

Chesapeake Utilities Corporation is an energy delivery company engaged in the distribution of natural gas, electricity and propane; the transmission of natural gas; the generation of electricity and steam, and in providing related services to its customers. Chesapeake's regulated natural gas distribution operations in central and southern Delaware, Maryland's eastern shore and Florida; regulated natural gas transmission operations on the Delmarva Peninsula, in Pennsylvania, Florida, and in Ohio; and regulated electric distribution operations serving customers in northeast and northwest Florida. On the unregulated side, the company also serves retail propane customers in Mid-Atlantic region, North Carolina, South Carolina and Florida, through Sharp Energy, Inc., Sharpgas, Inc., Diversified Energy, FPU, and Flo-gas.

	Annual Growth	12/19	12/20	12/21	12/22	12/23
Sales ($mil.)	8.7%	479.6	488.2	570.0	680.7	670.6
Net income ($ mil.)	7.6%	65.2	71.5	83.5	89.8	87.2
Market value ($ mil.)	2.5%	2,130.8	2,406.1	3,242.1	2,627.8	2,348.7
Employees	7.6%	955	947	1,007	1,034	1,281

CHESTER BANCORP INC. NBB: CNBA

1112 State Street
Chester, IL 62233
Phone: 618 826-5038
Fax: –
Web: –

CEO: –
CFO: –
HR: –
FYE: December 31
Type: Public

Chester Bancorp didn't grow big and strong eating spinach, like Chester, Illinois, native Popeye the Sailor Man would like you to believe. Instead, the holding company garners strength from its two subsidiary banks, Chester National Bank (formed in 1919) and Chester National Bank of Missouri (founded in 1996). The banks have approximately five branches serving rural southwestern Illinois and southeastern Missouri. They provide standard retail services such as savings, checking, and money market accounts, as well as certificates of deposit. These accounts are typically used to fund residential mortgage loans, and to a lesser extent business, construction, consumer, home equity, and lot loans.

	Annual Growth	12/98	12/99	12/00	12/01	12/02
Assets ($mil.)	(5.5%)	142.8	120.4	117.6	111.8	113.8
Net income ($ mil.)	(3.3%)	1.1	1.3	1.1	1.0	1.0
Market value ($ mil.)	9.0%	15.1	14.9	15.0	16.6	21.3
Employees	(2.9%)	36	35	30	31	32

CHEVRON CORPORATION NYS: CVX

6001 Bollinger Canyon Road
San Ramon, CA 94583-2324
Phone: 925 842-1000
Fax: 925 894-6017
Web: www.chevron.com

CEO: Michael K Wirth
CFO: Pierre R Breber
HR: –
FYE: December 31
Type: Public

Chevron manages its subsidiaries and affiliates and provides administrative, financial, management and technology to support US and international subsidiaries that engage in integrated energy and chemical operations. Its global operations explore for and produce oil and oil equivalents, refines them into various fuels and other end products, and sells them through gas stations, airport fuel depots, and industrial channels. Chevron boasts approximately 11.2 billion barrels of proved reserves. The company sells refined products branded under the Chevron, Texaco, and Caltex. Around 50% of its sales come from the US operations.

	Annual Growth	12/19	12/20	12/21	12/22	12/23
Sales ($mil.)	8.2%	146,516	94,692	162,465	246,252	200,949
Net income ($ mil.)	64.4%	2,924	(5,543.0)	15,625	35,465	21,369
Market value ($ mil.)	5.5%	224,829	157,554	218,934	334,865	278,280
Employees	(1.4%)	48,200	47,736	42,595	43,846	45,600

CHEVRON PHILLIPS CHEMICAL COMPANY LLC

10001 SIX PINES DR
THE WOODLANDS, TX 773801498
Phone: 832 813-4100
Fax: –
Web: www.cpchem.com

CEO: Mark Lashier
CFO: Carolyn Burke
HR: Maricela Caballero
FYE: December 31
Type: Private

Chevron Phillips Chemical (CPChem) is one of the top suppliers of polyethylene in the world today. It produces high-density (HDPE), medium-density (MDPE), low-density (LDPE), linear low-density (LLDPE), metallocene and masterbatches for a wide range of applications ? including pressure pipe, soap and detergent bottles, flexible packaging, coating and laminations, films, and more. Chevron Phillips Chemical also produces aromatics such as benzene and styrene, specialty chemicals for dozens of applications, from aerosols and fluid additives to textiles and water treatment products. CPChem is 50% owned by Chevron USA Inc., an indirect wholly-owned subsidiary of Chevron Corporation, and 50% by wholly-owned subsidiaries of Phillips 66.

	Annual Growth	12/12	12/13	12/14	12/15	12/16
Sales ($mil.)	(21.3%)	–	–	14,148	9,859.0	8,769.0
Net income ($ mil.)	(28.4%)	–	–	3,288.0	2,651.0	1,687.0
Market value ($ mil.)	–	–	–	–	–	–
Employees	–	–	–	–	–	6,472

CHEVRON PIPE LINE COMPANY

1500 LOUISIANA ST
HOUSTON, TX 770027308
Phone: 877 596-2800
Fax: –
Web: www.chevron.com

CEO: –
CFO: –
HR: –
FYE: December 31
Type: Private

Many US users of oil, petrochemicals, and natural gas rely on Chevron Pipe Line Company for delivery of these products. The pipeline company, a subsidiary of oil giant Chevron, transports crude oil, refined petroleum products, liquefied petroleum gas, natural gas, and chemicals. Through about 4,100 miles of pipeline, the company moves more than 1.3 million barrels of crude and other products across the US every day. Chevron Pipe Line also supplies other Chevron businesses with the supplies they need to run their operations efficiently. The company also makes use of joint ventures and third parties to move additional volumes.

	Annual Growth	12/13	12/14	12/15	12/16	12/17
Sales ($mil.)	(29.6%)	–	–	–	122.4	86.1
Net income ($ mil.)	20.8%	–	–	–	74.9	90.5
Market value ($ mil.)	–	–	–	–	–	–
Employees	–	–	–	–	–	715

CHEWY INC NYS: CHWY

7700 West Sunrise Boulevard
Plantation, FL 33322
Phone: 786 320-7111
Fax: –
Web: www.chewy.com

CEO: Sumit Singh
CFO: –
HR: –
FYE: January 28
Type: Public

Chewy is the largest pure-play pet e-tailer in the US, offering virtually every product a pet needs. It partners with more than 3,500 of the best and most trusted brands in the pet industry. Through the company's website and mobile applications, Chewy offers its customers more than 110,000 products, compelling merchandising, an easy and enjoyable shopping experience, and exceptional customer service. Leveraging the company's extensive infrastructure of its supply chain consisting of more than 15 fulfillment centers, Chewy serves more than 80% of the US population overnight and almost 100% in two days. It operates in a large and growing industry in the US, which consists of pet food and treats, pet supplies and pet medications, other pet-health products, and pet services.

	Annual Growth	02/20*	01/21	01/22	01/23	01/24
Sales ($mil.)	23.1%	4,846.7	7,146.3	8,890.8	10,099	11,148
Net income ($ mil.)	–	(252.4)	(92.5)	(73.8)	49.2	39.6
Market value ($ mil.)	(7.5%)	11,446	43,963	18,977	19,823	8,367.8
Employees	10.8%	12,000	18,500	21,300	19,400	18,100

*Fiscal year change

CHICAGO BEARS FOOTBALL CLUB, INC.

1920 FOOTBALL DR
LAKE FOREST, IL 600454829
Phone: 847 295-6600
Fax: –
Web: www.chicagobears.com

CEO: Michael McCaskey
CFO: –
HR: –
FYE: December 31
Type: Private

These Monsters of the Midway have been scaring opponents since the very beginning. Chicago Bears Football Club operates the storied Chicago Bears professional football team, which lays claim to nine National Football League titles (its last in Super Bowl XX at the end of the 1985 season). More than 25 Hall of Fame players have graced the roster of "Da Bears", including Red Grange, Dick Butkus, Gale Sayers, and Walter Payton. Loyal Chicago fans root on their team at venerable Soldier Field. The franchise, originally known as the Decatur Staleys, was a charter member of the NFL in 1920. Chairman Michael McCaskey (grandson of founder George "Papa Bear" Halas) and his family control the club.

CHICAGO BLACKHAWK HOCKEY TEAM, INC.

680 N LAKE SHORE DR STE 1900
CHICAGO, IL 606114546
Phone: 312 455-7000
Fax: –
Web: www.nhl.com

CEO: –
CFO: –
HR: –
FYE: June 30
Type: Private

When the Windy City turns cold, these Hawks start flying on the ice. One of the Original Six professional hockey franchises of the National Hockey League, the Chicago Blackhawks boast a long history that includes six Stanley Cup championships and a roster that has featured such Hall of Fame players as Phil and Tony Esposito, Bobby Hull, and Stan Mikita. The club won its most recent NHL championship titles in 2010, 2013, and 2015. Loyal fans support the team at Chicago's United Center. The Wirtz family has owned the Blackhawks franchise through their Wirtz Corporation since 1954.

CHICAGO COMMUNITY TRUST

33 S STATE ST STE 700
CHICAGO, IL 606032802
Phone: 312 616-8000
Fax: –
Web: www.cct.org

CEO: –
CFO: –
HR: Julianna Heger
FYE: September 30
Type: Private

You can trust this group to do the giving thing. The Chicago Community Trust gave more than $105 million in 2008 to not-for-profit organizations, such as social services agencies, schools, health centers, museums, and theaters in the Chicago area. The grant program targets groups working in arts and culture, basic human needs, community development, education, and health. Past projects have included after-school programs for impoverished children, funding a senior citizens center, and health services for people with AIDS. Chicago Community Trust gets its funds from corporate and private donations. It was founded in 1915.

	Annual Growth	09/13	09/14	09/15	09/16	09/19
Sales ($mil.)	14.1%	–	291.6	363.3	389.6	564.2
Net income ($ mil.)	12.9%	–	105.9	136.2	135.4	194.0
Market value ($ mil.)	–	–	–	–	–	–
Employees	–	–	–	–	–	100

CHICAGO PROFESSIONAL SPORTS CORPORATION

1901 W MADISON ST
CHICAGO, IL 606122459
Phone: 312 455-4000
Fax: –
Web: www.bulls.com

CEO: –
CFO: –
HR: Natalie Gamino
FYE: June 30
Type: Private

If you mess with these Bulls on the court, you might get the horns. Chicago Professional Sports owns and operates the Chicago Bulls professional basketball team, which boasts six NBA championships thanks to five-time MVP Michael Jordan. His charismatic presence not only set a high-water mark for Chicago between 1991 and 1998 but also helped increase the popularity of the league. The team was started by Dick Klein and joined the National Basketball Association in 1966. Real estate developer Jerry Reinsdorf has owned the Bulls since 1985. He also owns Chicago's United Center (along with Chicago Blackhawks owner the Wirtz Corporation) and the Chicago White Sox baseball team.

CHICAGO REVIEW PRESS INCORPORATED

814 N FRANKLIN ST STE 100
CHICAGO, IL 606103109
Phone: 312 337-0747
Fax: –
Web: www.chicagoreviewpress.com

CEO: Curtis Matthews Jr
CFO: –
HR: Jessie Winkler
FYE: December 31
Type: Private

You don't need to live in the windy city to enjoy books from Chicago Review Press. The independent book publisher and distributor has a catalog of more than 300 general nonfiction titles, including how-to, parenting, biography/memoir, and travel books. The company publishes titles under the Chicago Review Press, Lawrence Hill Books, A Cappella, and Zephyr Press imprints. It also publishes children's activity books under topics including art, math science, architecture, history, and literature. Chicago Review Press also owns book distributor Independent Publishers Group, which distributes and publicizes Chicago Review's and other independent publishers' books. Chicago Review Press was founded in 1973.

	Annual Growth	12/03	12/04	12/05	12/06	12/07
Sales ($mil.)	16.2%	–	30.7	32.8	39.1	48.1
Net income ($ mil.)	(8.2%)	–	0.0	(0.4)	(0.0)	0.0
Market value ($ mil.)	–	–	–	–	–	–
Employees	–	–	–	–	–	188

CHICAGO RIVET & MACHINE CO.

901 Frontenac Road
Naperville, IL 60563
Phone: 630 357-8500
Fax: –
Web: www.chicagorivet.com

ASE: CVR
CEO: Walter W Morrissey
CFO: –
HR: –
FYE: December 31
Type: Public

Rosie the Riveter might have used rivets made by Chicago Rivet & Machine. The company's main business is making fasteners, including rivets, screw machine products, and cold-formed fasteners. In addition to manufacturing assembly equipment, such as automatic rivet-setting equipment and rivet-working tools, it leases rivet-setting machines. Chicago Rivet sells its products through internal and independent sales representatives to US automotive and auto parts manufacturers. Major customers include Fisher & Company (accounting for about 20% of the company's sales) and TI Automotive (16% of sales).

	Annual Growth	12/19	12/20	12/21	12/22	12/23
Sales ($mil.)	(1.1%)	32.9	27.6	34.0	33.6	31.5
Net income ($ mil.)	–	0.5	0.0	1.1	2.9	(4.4)
Market value ($ mil.)	(9.9%)	24.9	22.1	25.4	27.7	16.4
Employees	(1.2%)	217	209	201	208	207

CHICAGO TRANSIT AUTHORITY (INC)

567 W LAKE ST STE 1150
CHICAGO, IL 606611405
Phone: 312 664-7200
Fax: –
Web: www.transitchicago.com

CEO: Lester L Barclay
CFO: –
HR: –
FYE: December 31
Type: Private

The Chicago Transit Authority (CTA) is the nation's second largest public transportation system in the US. On a typical weekday, CTA passengers take about 1.6 million rides on the agency's buses and trains, which travel in and around Chicago and about 35 suburbs. The CTA operates a fleet of about 1,865 buses on almost 130 routes. Its rail system includes eight rail lines with over 1,490 rail cars operating on 224 miles of track at some 145 stations. The agency, created by the Illinois legislature in 1947, is part of the state's Regional Transportation Authority, which also oversees Metra (commuter rail system) and Pace (suburban bus system).

	Annual Growth	12/18	12/19	12/20	12/21	12/22
Sales ($mil.)	(20.0%)	–	654.0	278.5	280.2	334.5
Net income ($ mil.)	–	–	(115.2)	17.1	(133.9)	1.0
Market value ($ mil.)	–	–	–	–	–	–
Employees	–	–	–	–	–	12,000

CHICAGO WHITE SOX, LTD.

333 W 35TH ST
CHICAGO, IL 606163621
Phone: 312 674-5404
Fax: –
Web: www.mlb.com

CEO: –
CFO: –
HR: –
FYE: December 31
Type: Private

In the summer in Chicago, you can either "root, root root for the Cubbies" or you can cheer on these southsiders. The venerable Chicago White Sox franchise is one of the oldest clubs in Major League Baseball, having joined the American League in 1900. The team boasts just three World Series championships, two from the early 1900s and it latest in 2005. (A World Series appearance in 1919 was marred by the "Black Sox" scandal that saw eight teammates banned from baseball for throwing the championship.) Playing host at US Cellular Field, the White Sox franchise is owned by real estate developer and chairman Jerry Reinsdorf, who also owns the Chicago Bulls basketball team.

	Annual Growth	12/10	12/11	12/12	12/13	12/17
Sales ($mil.)	26.9%	–	–	–	0.9	2.5
Net income ($ mil.)	–	–	–	–	(0.6)	0.5
Market value ($ mil.)	–	–	–	–	–	–
Employees	–	–	–	–	–	110

CHICKASAW HOLDING COMPANY

124 W VINITA AVE
SULPHUR, OK 730863821
Phone: 580 622-2111
Fax: –
Web: www.chickasawholding.com

CEO: RE Gauntt
CFO: –
HR: –
FYE: December 31
Type: Private

Chickasaw Holding's family of businesses keeps south central Oklahoma connected. The company's original business, Chickasaw Telephone Company, was founded in 1909 and offers local phone service to about 9,000 business and residential customers. Its other subsidiaries provide such services as long-distance (Chickasaw Long Distance), Internet access (BrightNet Oklahoma), wireless service (Chickasaw Cellular), and wholesale fiber-optic networking for business customers and other communications carriers (Indian Nations Fiber Optics). The group also installs telecommunications equipment, including private branch exchange (PBX) and voice mail systems through its Telco Supply Company subsidiary.

	Annual Growth	12/11	12/12	12/13	12/14	12/15
Assets ($mil.)	7.5%	–	–	202.4	132.8	233.9
Net income ($ mil.)	(4.8%)	–	–	24.6	21.2	22.3
Market value ($ mil.)	–	–	–	–	–	–
Employees	–	–	–	–	–	600

CHICO STATE ENTERPRISES

25 MAIN ST UNIT 203
CHICO, CA 959285388
Phone: 530 898-6811
Fax: –
Web: www.csuchico.edu

CEO: –
CFO: –
HR: –
FYE: June 30
Type: Private

A private non-profit corporation, Chico State Enterprises (formerly Chico Research Foundation) provides services and administrative support to the Chico campus of the California State University. It is responsible for fundraising and philanthropic endeavors on behalf of the University and also manages externally funded projects oriented towards research, education, or public service and provides a supplemental source of income and discretionary funds to support activities which cannot be met with State funds. Services include developing and administering of grants, managing property, and acting as a fiscal agent for campus programs. Chico State Enterprises is self-financed and receives no state appropriations.

	Annual Growth	06/18	06/19	06/20	06/21	06/22
Sales ($mil.)	9.3%	–	41.6	42.3	46.9	54.3
Net income ($ mil.)	(11.0%)	–	2.2	(0.3)	0.3	1.5
Market value ($ mil.)	–	–	–	–	–	–
Employees	–	–	–	–	–	2,000

CHIEF CONSOLIDATED MINING CO.

15988 Silver Pass Road, P.O. Box 51
Eureka, UT 84628
Phone: 435 433-6606
Fax: –
Web: www.chiefmines.com

CEO: –
CFO: –
HR: –
FYE: December 31
Type: Public

The chief asset of Chief Consolidated Mining is 16,000 acres of land near Eureka, Utah, that the company hopes will yield valuable minerals. The company has been working to develop the Burgin Mine (silver, plus lead and zinc) and the Trixie Mine (gold, silver, and copper). Environmental cleanup obligations associated with earlier mining operations on the property have delayed the company's progress, however. In 2008, Canadian investor Andover Ventures acquired 65% of Chief Consolidated from Genco Resources for about $5 million.

	Annual Growth	12/04	12/05	12/06	12/07	12/08
Sales ($mil.)	–	–	–	0.0	–	–
Net income ($ mil.)	–	(2.6)	(2.8)	(0.1)	(1.2)	(2.8)
Market value ($ mil.)	(9.6%)	15.8	14.7	26.3	15.8	10.5
Employees	–	–	–	–	–	–

CHIEF INDUSTRIES, INC.

3942 W OLD HIGHWAY 30
GRAND ISLAND, NE 688035051
Phone: 308 389-7200
Fax: –
Web: www.chiefind.com

CEO: Dj Eihusen
CFO: David Ostdiek
HR: Anastacia Glinsmann
FYE: June 30
Type: Private

When it comes serving the agriculture and transportation industries through its eclectic range of businesses, Chief Industries is the head honcho. Chief makes ethanol fuel and manufactures a host of supplies for agricultural, industrial, correctional, building, transportation, and wastewater treatment applications. Its agri/industrial unit makes grain-drying and storage bins, crop-drying fans, and aeration systems. Its transportation business makes rail car products, while division Chief Custom Homes makes modular homes and RVs. Chief offers services, including metal fabrication, powder coating, design/build general contracting, electrical/lighting design, and for-hire freight hauling.

	Annual Growth	06/98	06/99	06/00	06/01	06/08
Sales ($mil.)	(30.0%)	–	256.2	325.2	294.7	10.4
Net income ($ mil.)	–	–	6.9	6.0	1.6	(0.1)
Market value ($ mil.)	–	–	–	–	–	–
Employees	–	–	–	–	–	1,300

CHILD WELFARE LEAGUE OF AMERICA, INC.

727 15TH ST NW LBBY 1
WASHINGTON, DC 200052168
Phone: 202 642-9520
Fax: –
Web: www.cwla.org

CEO: Christine James-Brown
CFO: Nancy Mole
HR: –
FYE: September 30
Type: Private

The Child Welfare League of America (CWLA) puts children first. The not-for-profit group helps at-risk children and their families. Its 800 member agencies provide services in adolescent parenting and pregnancy prevention, child day care, child abuse prevention and treatment, and adoption to nearly 9 million children and their families each year. In addition to its headquarters in Washington, DC, CWLA has regional offices throughout the country. It publishes the periodicals Child Welfare Journal and Children's Voice Magazine as well as books and other materials under the Child & Family Press (general books) and CWLA Press (professional advocacy) imprints. The organization was founded in 1920.

	Annual Growth	09/10	09/11	09/13	09/14	09/15
Sales ($mil.)	(22.0%)	–	5.7	3.8	3.4	2.1
Net income ($ mil.)	–	–	(0.7)	(0.2)	0.0	0.2
Market value ($ mil.)	–	–	–	–	–	–
Employees	–	–	–	–	–	60

CHILDFUND INTERNATIONAL, USA

2821 EMERYWOOD PKWY
RICHMOND, VA 232943726
Phone: 804 756-2700
Fax: –
Web: www.childfund.org

CEO: –
CFO: James Tuite
HR: –
FYE: June 30
Type: Private

ChildFund International (CFI) serves the little ones. The worldwide non-profit organization provides education, medical care, food, and safe water to more than 13 million children -- of all faiths -- in about 30 countries in Africa, Asia, the Caribbean, Eastern Europe, Latin America, and the US. It works in areas of early childhood development, education, family income generation, nutrition, and sanitation. The group also tries to get child soldiers away from the military and reintegrated into daily life. Founded in 1938 as China's Children Fund, the group changed its name to Christian Children's Fund in 1951. In 2009 it again renamed itself ChildFund International.

	Annual Growth	06/13	06/14	06/19	06/20	06/22
Sales ($mil.)	(2.1%)	–	235.9	196.0	197.6	199.6
Net income ($ mil.)	(2.2%)	–	6.5	3.9	14.6	5.4
Market value ($ mil.)	–	–	–	–	–	–
Employees	–	–	–	–	–	160

CHILDREN'S HEALTH CARE

2525 CHICAGO AVE
MINNEAPOLIS, MN 554044518
Phone: 612 813-6000
Fax: –
Web: www.childrensmn.org

CEO: Robert Bonar
CFO: –
HR: –
FYE: December 31
Type: Private

Children's Hospitals and Clinics of Minnesota (also known as Children's Minnesota) is one of the largest pediatric health organizations in the US, with two full-service hospital campuses in St. Paul, and Minneapolis, as well as a number of specialty clinics in the region. It is the only health system and Level I Trauma Center in Minnesota to provide care exclusively to children from before birth through young adulthood. It specializes in diagnosing, treating, and researching diseases that afflict babies and children, including epilepsy, diabetes, cancers, and cystic fibrosis. Children's Minnesota is a member of Children's Health Network, Minnesota's largest pediatric health collaborative.

	Annual Growth	12/18	12/19	12/20	12/21	12/22
Sales ($mil.)	369.4%	–	10.2	740.2	885.9	1,057.3
Net income ($ mil.)	144.3%	–	2.6	35.2	153.0	37.6
Market value ($ mil.)	–	–	–	–	–	–
Employees	–	–	–	–	–	4,285

CHILDREN'S HEALTHCARE OF ATLANTA, INC.

1575 NORTHEAST EXPY NE
BROOKHAVEN, GA 303292401
Phone: 404 785-5437
Fax: –
Web: www.choa.org

CEO: –
CFO: –
HR: –
FYE: December 31
Type: Private

Children's Healthcare of Atlanta is a not-for-profit hospital system that specializes in pediatric health care, research, and education. Its three hospitals, Children's Healthcare of Atlanta at Egleston (on the Emory University campus), Hughes Spalding, and Scottish Rite, together, have more than 530 beds and manage some 850,000 patient visits a year. Children's also operates close to 25 health care facilities in the metro Atlanta area, including the Marcus Autism Center and the Sibley Heart Center Cardiology. Children's at Egleston, known for its pediatric services in cardiology, oncology, neonatal, orthopedics, rehabilitation, organ transplant, and general surgery, is Georgia's first Level 1 pediatric trauma center.

CHILDREN'S HEALTHCARE OF CALIFORNIA

1201 W LA VETA AVE
ORANGE, CA 928684203
Phone: 714 997-3000
Fax: –
Web: www.choc.org

CEO: Kimberly C Cripe
CFO: Kerri Ruppert
HR: Hanna Ngo
FYE: June 30
Type: Private

Children's Hospital of Orange County (aka CHOC) fights kid-sized ailments in southern California. The not-for-profit hospital's main campus in Orange has about 240 beds and provides a comprehensive range of care to young patients, including pediatric and neonatal intensive care. Its CHOC Mission facility (located within the Mission Hospital in Mission Viejo) has nearly 50 beds for pediatric patients, as well as neonatal and pediatric ICUs. CHOC also runs a handful of primary care community clinics and several mobile clinics. It also conducts research and educational programs. The hospital was founded in 1964.

	Annual Growth	06/18	06/19	06/20	06/21	06/22
Sales ($mil.)	(37.8%)	–	127.1	38.2	34.2	30.6
Net income ($ mil.)	(40.6%)	–	106.8	31.9	26.4	22.4
Market value ($ mil.)	–	–	–	–	–	–
Employees	–	–	–	–	–	1,800

CHILDREN'S HOSPITAL & MEDICAL CENTER

8200 DODGE ST
OMAHA, NE 681144113
Phone: 402 955-5400
Fax: –
Web: www.childrensnebraska.org

CEO: –
CFO: –
HR: –
FYE: December 31
Type: Private

Junior Cornhuskers can have their medical needs met at Children's Hospital & Medical Center. The not-for-profit center, Nebraska's only pediatric hospital (and a top US children's hospital), is a 145-bed facility offering pediatric in patient services. The Omaha hospital has neonatal and pediatric intensive care units, along with units dedicated surgery, child development, eating disorders, and conditions including asthma, allergies, cardiac care, diabetes, nephrology, and respiratory care. Children's serves as the teaching hospital for the University of Nebraska and Creighton University. It also operates urgent care and outreach clinics in the area.

	Annual Growth	12/15	12/16	12/17	12/21	12/22
Sales ($mil.)	9.4%	–	339.4	373.0	560.2	581.1
Net income ($ mil.)	(11.4%)	–	57.6	81.7	78.1	27.9
Market value ($ mil.)	–	–	–	–	–	–
Employees	–	–	–	–	–	1,400

CHILDREN'S HOSPITAL & RESEARCH CENTER AT OAKLAND

747 52ND ST
OAKLAND, CA 946091809
Phone: 510 428-3000
Fax: –
Web: www.ucsfbenioffchildrens.org

CEO: Harold Davis
CFO: Kathleen Cain
HR: Denise Jimenez
FYE: June 30
Type: Private

Children's Hospital & Research Center at Oakland (operating as Children's Hospital Oakland) does just what its name says, provides medical care for children and performs research to advance the treatment of pediatric diseases. The freestanding hospital has about 190 beds and a staff of some more than 200 hospital-based physicians professionals with more than 30 medical specialties. Its services include orthopedics, neurology, oncology, and cardiology, as well as surgery, trauma, neonatal, and intensive care. Additionally, the hospital operates several satellite outpatient clinics providing general and specialized care. Children's Hospital Oakland also conducts teaching and community outreach programs.

	Annual Growth	12/12	12/13*	06/15	06/20	06/22
Sales ($mil.)	3.2%	–	541.7	178.6	661.6	719.9
Net income ($ mil.)	1.2%	–	44.8	34.9	(8.2)	49.9
Market value ($ mil.)	–	–	–	–	–	–
Employees						2,000

*Fiscal year change

CHILDREN'S HOSPITAL AND HEALTH SYSTEM, INC.

8915 W CONNELL AVE
MILWAUKEE, WI 532293067
Phone: 414 266-2000
Fax: –
Web: www.childrenswi.org

CEO: –
CFO: Tim Birkenstock
HR: Linda Simatic
FYE: December 31
Type: Private

The Children's Hospital and Health System serves children and their families in Milwaukee and throughout the Great Lakes region. Its dozen entities dedicated to pediatric health care include the flagship 300-bed Children's Hospital of Wisconsin, which is also an affiliate of the Medical College of Wisconsin. Satellite facilities include the 42-bed Fox Valley pediatric hospital, as well as a surgical center, specialty care clinics in Wisconsin and Illinois, and research facilities. The organization also has a network of affiliated primary care pediatricians and manages an HMO that covers Medicaid recipients (children and adults) in several Wisconsin counties.

	Annual Growth	06/04	06/05*	12/13	12/21	12/22
Sales ($mil.)	(2.0%)	–	401.1	121.2	196.8	284.6
Net income ($ mil.)	–	–	–	(4.1)	(29.7)	2.6
Market value ($ mil.)	–	–	–	–	–	–
Employees						3,000

*Fiscal year change

CHILDREN'S HOSPITAL COLORADO

13123 E 16TH AVE
AURORA, CO 800457106
Phone: 720 777-1234
Fax: –
Web: www.childrenscolorado.org

CEO: Jena Hausemann
CFO: –
HR: –
FYE: December 31
Type: Private

Children's Hospital Colorado is a private, nonprofit pediatric healthcare network dedicated to caring for kids at all ages and stages of growth. With more than 3,000 pediatric specialists, the company provides comprehensive pediatric care at its hospital on Anschutz Medical Campus and several locations throughout the region. Children's Hospital Colorado also operates some 15 satellite locations in and around Denver that specialize in providing children with emergency and specialty care. Its affiliation with the University of Colorado School of Medicine means that its doctors are not only expert clinicians but also active researchers working toward better ways to care for kids.

	Annual Growth	12/17	12/18	12/19	12/21	12/22
Sales ($mil.)	13.4%	–	1,102.8	1,327.5	1,205.2	1,821.9
Net income ($ mil.)	(8.2%)	–	138.8	63.6	94.7	98.6
Market value ($ mil.)	–	–	–	–	–	–
Employees						2,200

CHILDREN'S HOSPITAL FOUNDATION

2924 BROOK RD
RICHMOND, VA 232201298
Phone: 804 228-5818
Fax: –
Web: www.chrichmond.org

CEO: –
CFO: –
HR: –
FYE: June 30
Type: Private

Crippled Children's Hospital provides medical care to children and adolescents throughout the southeastern region of the US. Operating as the Children's Hospital of Richmond, the medical center offers general pediatric care and specialized services including a dental program, orthopedics, rehabilitation, nutrition, infant care, occupational therapy, and psychological treatment. The hospital offers inpatient and outpatient services, as well as long-term care for patients needing extended nursing. It also operates satellite therapy clinics. The Crippled Children's Hospital was founded in 1917.

	Annual Growth	06/07	06/08	06/13	06/14	06/18
Sales ($mil.)	0.6%	–	29.6	36.0	33.5	31.5
Net income ($ mil.)	–	–	(1.3)	4.9	1.1	(1.8)
Market value ($ mil.)	–	–	–	–	–	–
Employees						300

CHILDREN'S HOSPITAL MEDICAL CENTER

3333 BURNET AVE
CINCINNATI, OH 452293039
Phone: 513 636-4200
Fax: –
Web: www.cincinnatichildrens.org

CEO: Steve Davis
CFO: Teresa Bowling
HR: David Schumann
FYE: June 30
Type: Private

Cincinnati Children's Hospital Medical Center is a nonprofit academic medical center established in 1883, is one of the oldest and most distinguished pediatric hospitals in the US. Cincinnati Children's Hospital offers specialty treatments for children and adolescents suffering from just about any ailments of the heart and liver, as well as blood diseases and cancer. Cincinnati Children's Hospital has more than 620 total registered beds, including some 110 registered inpatient psychiatric beds and about 30 registered residential psychiatric beds. Cincinnati Children's Hospital ranked No. 3 by US News & World Report.

	Annual Growth	06/19	06/20*	12/20*	06/21	06/22
Sales ($mil.)	5.7%	–	2,632.4	1.1	2,804.6	2,941.4
Net income ($ mil.)	(2.7%)	–	154.6	0.5	277.7	146.4
Market value ($ mil.)	–	–	–	–	–	–
Employees						18,000

*Fiscal year change

CHILDREN'S MEDICAL CENTER OF DALLAS

1935 MEDICAL DISTRICT DR
DALLAS, TX 752357701
Phone: 214 456-7000
Fax: –
Web: www.childrens.com

CEO: –
CFO: –
HR: –
FYE: December 31
Type: Private

Children's Medical Center of Dallas is one of the largest and most prestigious pediatric health care providers and the leading pediatric health system in North Texas. Through the academic affiliation with UT Southwestern, it is a leader in life changing treatments, innovative technology and groundbreaking research. Among the campus, Children's Health is licensed for around 600 beds, including some 490 beds at the main campus in the Southwestern Medical District and over 70 beds at Children's House facility in Dallas. Around 800 patients visits annually for 50 estates around the world. It was founded in 1913 when a group of nurses led by public health nurse May Forster Smith organized the Dallas Baby Camp.

	Annual Growth	12/07	12/08	12/13	12/14	12/15
Sales ($mil.)	(0.6%)	–	744.9	1,111.2	1,120.4	712.6
Net income ($ mil.)	–	–	(4.1)	166.7	135.4	(185.6)
Market value ($ mil.)	–	–	–	–	–	–
Employees						5,318

CHILDREN'S MIRACLE NETWORK

205 W 700 S
SALT LAKE CITY, UT 841012715
Phone: 801 214-7400
Fax: –
Web: www.childrensmiraclenetworkhospitals.org

CEO: Adrianna Karras
CFO: –
HR: –
FYE: December 31
Type: Private

The Children's Miracle Network (formerly known as The Osmond Foundation for the Children of the World) raises funds for more than 170 children's hospitals in the US and Canada. Network hospitals treat about 17 million children each year for everything from broken bones to AIDS. The not-for-profit organization raises money through a variety of methods including radio and television fund drives, corporate sponsorships, the sale of paper Miracle Balloons, and college dance marathons. It's assisted by 90 organizations and some 400 media partners. Singer and entertainer Marie Osmond founded the network in 1983 along with actor John Schneider (Dukes of Hazzard   ).

	Annual Growth	12/15	12/16	12/19	12/21	12/22
Sales ($mil.)	0.3%	–	45.2	49.5	48.4	46.2
Net income ($ mil.)	–	–	(1.4)	5.6	7.6	(0.2)
Market value ($ mil.)	–	–	–	–	–	–
Employees	–	–	–	–	–	180

CHILDREN'S NATIONAL MEDICAL CENTER

111 MICHIGAN AVE NW
WASHINGTON, DC 200102916
Phone: 202 476-5000
Fax: –
Web: www.childrensnational.org

CEO: –
CFO: –
HR: –
FYE: June 30
Type: Private

Children's National Hospital was established in 1870, has ranked as one of the top 10 pediatric hospitals in the nation ? with the #1 for the newborn care ? by US News & World Report for the fifth year in a row. The hospital is a Level 1 pediatric trauma center, with some 325 beds. It also has critical care transport program via ambulance, helicopter and fixed-wing airplane. Additionally, it operates roughly 15 specialty care centers spread throughout Maryland, Virginia and Washington DC, an ambulatory surgery center in Maryland, and two large emergency departments located at the main campus and on the United Medical Center campus. Children's National Health Network links more than 1,500 primary and specialty care physicians.

	Annual Growth	06/05	06/06	06/07	06/09	06/20
Sales ($mil.)	(10.3%)	–	574.0	694.6	516.6	126.1
Net income ($ mil.)	–	–	86.0	76.3	16.4	–
Market value ($ mil.)	–	–	–	–	–	–
Employees	–	–	–	–	–	6,000

CHILDREN'S PLACE INC (THE)

500 Plaza Drive
Secaucus, NJ 07094
Phone: 201 558-2400
Fax: –
Web: www.childrensplace.com

NMS: PLCE
CEO: Jane T Elfers
CFO: Sheamus Toal
HR: –
FYE: January 28
Type: Public

The Children's Place is the largest pure-play children's specialty apparel retailer in North America. It operates about 615 Children's Place stores throughout the US, Canada, and Puerto Rico, as well as its online stores. In addition, the company's five international partners operate around 210 international points of distribution in about 15 countries. It also sells apparel online. The Children's Place outfits children in its brand of value-priced apparel, shoes, and accessories, most of which are produced by contract manufacturers. The company also owns the Gymboree and Crazy 8 brands. Approximately 80% of its sales come from stores in the US.

	Annual Growth	02/19	02/20*	01/21	01/22	01/23
Sales ($mil.)	(3.1%)	1,938.1	1,870.7	1,522.6	1,915.4	1,708.5
Net income ($ mil.)	–	101.0	73.3	(140.4)	187.2	(1.1)
Market value ($ mil.)	(17.1%)	1,126.3	729.5	898.2	861.1	533.0
Employees	(11.8%)	18,700	15,400	13,300	11,900	11,300

*Fiscal year change

CHILDREN'S SPECIALIZED HOSPITAL INC

150 NEW PROVIDENCE RD
MOUNTAINSIDE, NJ 070922590
Phone: 888 244-5373
Fax: –
Web: www.rwjbh.org

CEO: Amy Mansue
CFO: –
HR: Denise Espinal
FYE: December 31
Type: Private

No grown-ups allowed! Children's Specialized Hospital (CSH) is the largest pediatric rehabilitation hospital in the US. The hospital provides rehabilitation, medical and developmental health care services to patients from infancy through young adulthood. CSH's areas of specialization include burn care, spinal cord and brain injury, and physical therapy. In addition, the hospital offers developmental care such as speech therapy, nutritional services, and audiology, and it operates a network of outpatient and care facilities throughout New Jersey. The hospital, an affiliate of the Robert Wood Johnson Health Network, also performs research in children's disorders. CSH, founded in 1892, is led by CEO Amy Mansue.

	Annual Growth	12/16	12/17	12/18	12/19	12/21
Sales ($mil.)	0.5%	–	141.9	146.5	158.4	144.6
Net income ($ mil.)	(12.9%)	–	9.4	6.0	1.8	5.4
Market value ($ mil.)	–	–	–	–	–	–
Employees	–	–	–	–	–	1,200

CHILDRENS HEALTH SYSTEM, INC.

601 CHILDRENS LN
NORFOLK, VA 235071910
Phone: 757 622-2134
Fax: –
Web: www.chkd.org

CEO: –
CFO: –
HR: –
FYE: June 30
Type: Private

You don't have to be royalty to be a patient at Children's Hospital of The King's Daughters (CHKD). CHKD is Virginia's only free-standing, full-service pediatric facility, and as such provides medical, dental, and therapeutic services to children and adolescents through the age of 21 years old. The 210-bed hospital has a staff of more than 500 physicians, and has the state's only dedicated pediatric emergency center, which gets more than 47,000 patient visits each year. CHKD also operates several outpatient pediatric centers throughout the state. The not-for-profit system was formed in 1961.

	Annual Growth	06/12	06/13	06/15	06/16	06/17
Sales ($mil.)	17.6%	–	12.7	30.1	33.2	24.3
Net income ($ mil.)	–	–	0.2	15.0	7.2	(6.2)
Market value ($ mil.)	–	–	–	–	–	–
Employees	–	–	–	–	–	1,905

CHILDRENS HOSPITAL MEDICAL CENTER OF AKRON

1 PERKINS SQ
AKRON, OH 443081063
Phone: 330 543-1000
Fax: –
Web: www.akronchildrens.org

CEO: William Considine
CFO: Spencer A Kowal
HR: Latonya Lewis
FYE: December 31
Type: Private

Akron Children's Hospital is the largest pediatric health care system in northeast Ohio. The health system operates through approximately 50 urgent, primary and specialty care locations scattered around the state. Among Children's specialized services are cardiology, orthopedics, rehabilitation, and home care. The main hospital's emergency department treats more than 88,600 patients each year. With about 330,575 urgent care visits, the health system also has around 547,360 specialty visits per year.

	Annual Growth	12/18	12/19	12/20	12/21	12/22
Sales ($mil.)	10.0%	–	1,014.5	853.4	999.5	1,349.4
Net income ($ mil.)	–	–	107.0	95.1	149.5	(38.2)
Market value ($ mil.)	–	–	–	–	–	–
Employees	–	–	–	–	–	4,763

CHILTON HOSPITAL

97 W PARKWAY
POMPTON PLAINS, NJ 074441647
Phone: 973 831-5000
Fax: –
Web: www.atlantichealth.org

CEO: Deborah K Zastocki
CFO: –
HR: –
FYE: December 31
Type: Private

Chilton Medical Center (formerly Chilton Memorial Hospital) serves the residents of northern New Jersey's Morris and Passaic counties. The acute-care facility has some 260 beds and provides emergency, diagnostic, inpatient, surgical, and outpatient care. The hospital operates with a staff of about 650 physicians who practice in 60 fields of health care. Chilton Medical Center offers such specialties as a cancer center, surgical weight-loss programs, occupational health, orthopedics, stroke care, pediatrics, and dialysis. Chilton Medical Center merged with Atlantic Health System in 2014.

	Annual Growth	12/03	12/04	12/05	12/08	12/14
Sales ($mil.)	3.6%	–	–	128.8	0.0	176.4
Net income ($ mil.)	46.3%	–	–	2.5	–	76.5
Market value ($ mil.)	–	–	–	–	–	–
Employees	–	–	–	–	–	1,188

CHIMERA INVESTMENT CORP

630 Fifth Avenue, Ste 2400
New York, NY 10111
Phone: 888 895-6557
Fax: –
Web: www.chimerareit.com

NYS: CIM
CEO: Phillip J Kardis II
CFO: Subramaniam Viswanathan
HR: –
FYE: December 31
Type: Public

This Chimera has the body of a mortgage real estate investment trust (REIT), but its head is that of its external manager, FIDAC (Fixed Income Discount Advisory Company), a fixed-income investment management firm wholly-owned by Annaly Capital Management. Formed in 2007, Chimera invests in residential mortgage loans; residential mortgage-backed securities (RMBS), such as those guaranteed by government agencies Fannie Mae and Freddie Mac; real estate-related securities; and other assets, including collateralized debt obligations, or CDOs. The REIT went public in 2007, shortly after it was formed.

	Annual Growth	12/19	12/20	12/21	12/22	12/23
Assets ($mil.)	(16.9%)	27,119	17,523	15,407	13,402	12,929
Net income ($ mil.)	(25.7%)	413.6	88.9	670.1	(513.1)	126.1
Market value ($ mil.)	(29.8%)	4,962.4	2,473.9	3,639.7	1,327.5	1,204.4
Employees	–	39	41	38	39	39

CHIMERIX INC.

2505 Meridian Parkway, Suite 100
Durham, NC 27713
Phone: 919 806-1074
Fax: –
Web: www.chimerix.com

NMS: CMRX
CEO: Michael A Sherman
CFO: Michelle Laspaluto
HR: Barbara Berg
FYE: December 31
Type: Public

All that shimmers isn't ? enhanced by lipid conjugate technology. Chimerix is a development-stage biopharmaceutical company, dedicated to accelerating the advancement of innovative for patients living with cancer and other serious diseases. Its two clinical-stage development programs include dociparstat sodium (DSTAT) and brincidofovir (BCV). DSTAT, is a glycosaminoglycan derivative of heparin with known anti-inflammatory properties and BCV is an oral antiviral in development for the treatment of smallpox.

	Annual Growth	12/19	12/20	12/21	12/22	12/23
Sales ($mil.)	(59.9%)	12.5	5.4	2.0	33.8	0.3
Net income ($ mil.)	–	(112.6)	(43.5)	(173.2)	172.2	(82.1)
Market value ($ mil.)	(17.0%)	180.5	429.5	571.8	165.4	85.6
Employees	13.8%	43	54	87	89	72

CHINA HUAREN ORGANIC PRODUCTS INC

c/o American Union Securities, Inc., 100 Wall Street, 15th Floor
New York, NY 10005
Phone: 212 232-0120
Fax: 314 997-1281
Web: –

CEO: Cao Yushu
CFO: Cao Yushu
HR: –
FYE: December 31
Type: Public

China Huaren Organic Products (dba Jilin Huaren) plays in a healthy arena. The company markets organic rice and grains, and grain-based products (biscuits, cakes, and crackers). It also makes organic nutritional supplements from ginkgo leaves and blue-green algae (spirulina). Jilin Huaren also offers organic cosmetics. All of its product manufacturing is outsourced. Aimed at the growing urban class in China, Jilin's products are available through a multilevel distribution network, made up of 90 branch units and 140 specialty stores, all of which are independently owned. Warner Technology & Investment owns 19% of the company; former officer Fang Jinzhong owns 16%; former officer Zhang Chengcai owns 10%.

	Annual Growth	12/04	12/05	12/06	12/07	12/08
Sales ($mil.)	–	4.0	0.8	2.2	7.4	–
Net income ($ mil.)	–	0.3	(5.9)	0.4	0.2	(7.4)
Market value ($ mil.)	(39.9%)	10.4	0.5	0.3	10.5	1.4
Employees	5.7%	8	8	40	40	10

CHINA NORTH EAST PETROLEUM HOLDINGS LIMITED

445 PARK AVE
NEW YORK, NY 100222606
Phone: 212 307-3568
Fax: –
Web: www.irpage.net

CEO: Jingfu LI
CFO: Shaohui Chen
HR: –
FYE: December 31
Type: Private

China North East Petroleum Holdings is engaged in the extraction and production of crude oil in a region of Northern China. Its current operations are focused on four oilfields located in China's Jilin province, where it operates about 250 producing wells. It operates in tandem with oil giant PetroChina to exploit a number of 20-year leases held by PetroChina. China North East Petroleum Holdings has proved reserves of approximately 5.5 million barrels of crude oil equivalent. Large-scale commercial drilling at the Jilin Quinan Oil Field started in 1986. The company also has exclusive exploration and drilling rights to the Durimu oilfield in Inner Mongolia.

CHIPOTLE MEXICAN GRILL INC

610 Newport Center Drive, Suite 1100
Newport Beach, CA 92660
Phone: 949 524-4000
Fax: –
Web: www.chipotle.com

NYS: CMG
CEO: Brian Niccol
CFO: John R Hartung
HR: –
FYE: December 31
Type: Public

The US restaurant chain Chipotle Mexican Grill owns and operates about 3,130 quick-casual eateries popular for burritos, tacos, burrito bowls, and salads. It also has about 55 international restaurants and five non-Chipotle restaurants. Chipotle offers a variety of menu that includes chicken, steak, carnitas, sofritas, barbecue, as well as beans, rice and various other veggies and salsas. The company claims that with extras, its menu offers thousands of choices. Chipotle restaurants also serve soft tacos, crispy tacos, chips and salsa, beer, and margaritas. Chipotle has about 25 independently owned and operated regional distribution centers. The company was founded in 1993 in Denver, Colorado.

	Annual Growth	12/19	12/20	12/21	12/22	12/23
Sales ($mil.)	15.3%	5,586.4	5,984.6	7,547.1	8,634.7	9,871.6
Net income ($ mil.)	36.9%	350.2	355.8	653.0	899.1	1,228.7
Market value ($ mil.)	28.6%	22,959	38,032	47,948	38,053	62,722
Employees	8.7%	83,000	88,000	97,660	104,958	116,068

CHIPPEWA VALLEY BEAN COMPANY, INC.

N2960 730TH ST
MENOMONIE, WI 547516615
Phone: 715 664-8342
Fax: –
Web: www.cvbean.com

CEO: –
CFO: –
HR: –
FYE: November 30
Type: Private

Chippewa Valley Bean has found its niche in the world through kidney beans. The company processes and wholesales dried light and dark red kidney beans. It grows and purchases beans grown on irrigated land in Wisconsin and three adjacent states. Chippewa Valley Bean's processing facility handles 40 million pounds of kidney beans every year. It exports its products to European and developing countries. The company also deals in pinto beans and dried green peas and sells prepackaged bean soups. Chippewa Valley Bean is a family-owned and -operated business.

	Annual Growth	11/07	11/08	11/09	11/10	11/11
Sales ($mil.)	(12.5%)	–	–	22.4	19.8	17.2
Net income ($ mil.)	(32.1%)	–	–	0.1	0.8	0.0
Market value ($ mil.)	–	–	–	–	–	–
Employees						15

CHIPTON-ROSS, INC.

420 CULVER BLVD
PLAYA DEL REY, CA 902937706
Phone: 310 414-7800
Fax: –
Web: www.chiptonross.com

CEO: –
CFO: –
HR: –
FYE: December 31
Type: Private

Founded in 1983, Chipton-Ross is a staffing firm, filling a variety of full service contract and permanent placement positions in the administrative, engineering, industrial, information technology, and professional sectors. Its client companies come from the aerospace, military, high tech, and entertainment industries. Chipton-Ross uses an online database of more than 100,000 potential employees to fulfill its clients' requests for qualified personnel. In addition to recruiting and hiring, it provides payroll and benefits processing, sometimes onsite. The company operates primarily in southern California, but also fills jobs in other locations throughout the US.

	Annual Growth	12/00	12/01	12/04	12/05	12/17
Sales ($mil.)	0.1%	–	8.9	9.5	2.3	9.0
Net income ($ mil.)	26.1%	–	0.0	0.1	0.0	0.9
Market value ($ mil.)	–	–	–	–	–	–
Employees	–	–	–	–	–	100

CHOATE CONSTRUCTION COMPANY

8200 ROBERTS DR STE 600
ATLANTA, GA 303504148
Phone: 678 892-1200
Fax: –
Web: www.choateco.com

CEO: William M Choate
CFO: David A Page
HR: Annette Conners
FYE: December 31
Type: Private

This firm has a Choate-hold on construction activities in the Southeast. Choate Construction provides design/build, preconstruction, and management services for the construction of commercial and public facilities. It has experience in a wide range of projects including automotive showrooms, manufacturing plants, office buildings, schools, and condominiums. Completed projects include a dormitory on The University of Georgia-East campus, golf clubhouses, and a distribution warehouse for Crate & Barrel. The company has offices in Georgia, North Carolina, and South Carolina and is licensed to build throughout the US.

CHOICE HOTELS INTERNATIONAL, INC.

NYS: CHH

1 Choice Hotels Circle
Rockville, MD 20850
Phone: 301 592-5000
Fax: –
Web: www.choicehotels.com

CEO: Patrick S Pacious
CFO: Scott E Oaksmith
HR: GM IA
FYE: December 31
Type: Public

Choice Hotels is a leading hotel franchisor with some 7,485 locations and almost 627,805 rooms throughout the US and approximately 50 other countries and territories. The company operates almost 25 brands which include Comfort Inn, Comfort Suites, Quality, Clarion, Clarion Pointe, Ascend Hotel Collection, Sleep Inn, Econo Lodge, Rodeway Inn, MainStay Suites, Suburban Studios, WoodSpring Suites, Everhome Suites, and Cambria Hotels. Additionally, through the Radisson Hotels Americas acquisition, its brands expanded to include Radisson Blu, Radisson RED, Radisson, Park Plaza, Country Inn & Suites by Radisson, Radisson Inn & SuitesSM, Park Inn by Radisson, Radisson Individuals, and Radisson Collection, which are located across the US, Canada, the Caribbean, and Latin America, collectively referred to for these markets as the "legacy Radisson brands".

	Annual Growth	12/19	12/20	12/21	12/22	12/23
Sales ($mil.)	8.5%	1,114.8	774.1	1,069.3	1,401.9	1,544.2
Net income ($ mil.)	3.8%	222.9	75.4	289.0	332.2	258.5
Market value ($ mil.)	2.3%	5,122.5	5,285.9	7,725.6	5,578.6	5,611.3
Employees	(0.1%)	1,807	1,498	1,460	1,789	1,800

CHOICEONE FINANCIAL SERVICES, INC.

NAS: COFS

109 East Division
Sparta, MI 49345
Phone: 616 887-7366
Fax: –
Web: www.choiceone.com

CEO: Kelly J Potes
CFO: Adom J Greenland
HR: –
FYE: December 31
Type: Public

One choice for a place to park your money is ChoiceOne Financial Services. The institution is the holding company for ChoiceOne Bank, which has more than a dozen offices in the western part of Michigan's Lower Peninsula. The bank serves consumers and area businesses, offering checking and savings accounts, CDs, investment planning, and other services. Real estate loans, including residential and commercial mortgages, constitute more than two-thirds of the company's loan portfolio. Agricultural, consumer, and business loans help to round out the bank's lending activities. ChoiceOne Financial Services sells life, health, and disability coverage through its ChoiceOne Insurance Agencies subsidiaries.

	Annual Growth	12/19	12/20	12/21	12/22	12/23
Assets ($mil.)	16.8%	1,386.1	1,919.3	2,366.7	2,385.9	2,576.7
Net income ($ mil.)	31.2%	7.2	15.6	22.0	23.6	21.3
Market value ($ mil.)	(2.1%)	241.2	232.6	200.0	218.9	221.2
Employees	–	339	359	386	402	–

CHORD ENERGY CORP

NMS: CHRD

1001 Fannin Street, Suite 1500
Houston, TX 77002
Phone: 281 404-9500
Fax: –
Web: www.chordenergy.com

CEO: –
CFO: –
HR: –
FYE: December 31
Type: Public

Chord Energy Corporation (formerly Oasis Petroleum), is an independent exploration and production company with quality and sustainable long-lived assets in the Williston Basin. The company's operations were focused in the North Dakota and Montana areas of the Williston Basin targeting the Middle Bakken and Three Forks formations. Chord Energy has net proved reserves of some 655.6 million barrels of oil equivalent and about 963,010 net leasehold acres of land holdings. The company also reported an average daily production of about 119,785 net barrels of oil per day. In 2022, the company merged with Whiting Petroleum, an independent oil and gas company engaged in the development, production, and acquisition of crude oil, NGLs, and natural gas primarily in the Rocky Mountains region of the US.

	Annual Growth	11/20*	12/20	12/21	12/22	12/23
Sales ($mil.)	59.3%	963.4	119.9	1,579.9	3,646.8	3,896.6
Net income ($ mil.)	–	(3,640.3)	(49.9)	319.6	1,856.2	1,023.8
Market value ($ mil.)	–	–	1,528.7	5,197.0	5,643.4	6,856.9
Employees	–	–	432	255	531	–

*Fiscal year change

CHRISTIAN HOSPITAL NORTHEAST - NORTHWEST

11133 DUNN RD
SAINT LOUIS, MO 631366163
Phone: 314 355-2300
Fax: -
Web: www.christianhospital.org

CEO: -
CFO: -
HR: Teri Bequette
FYE: December 31
Type: Private

Christian or heathen, if you're in the St. Louis area and need medical care, Christian Hospital wants to help. The not-for-profit hospital, which has some 485 beds, is part of BJC HealthCare. Established in 1903, it specializes in a range of treatment areas including diabetes and cancer care and cardiothoracic surgery. Its more than 430 physicians also offer services in 40 other specialties, from primary care to pulmonology. Christian Hospital offers a comprehensive mental health and substance abuse program that includes an inpatient option, as well as specialization in geriatric mental wellness. The hospital is headed by president Ron McMullen, a long-time health care administrator.

	Annual Growth	12/15	12/16	12/17	12/18	12/21
Sales ($mil.)	5.2%	-	253.1	253.5	262.8	326.4
Net income ($ mil.)	-	-	(20.0)	(45.6)	(35.1)	(13.0)
Market value ($ mil.)	-	-	-	-	-	-
Employees	-	-	-	-	-	2,493

CHRISTIANA CARE HEALTH SYSTEM, INC.

200 HYGEIA DR
NEWARK, DE 197132049
Phone: 302 733-1000
Fax: -
Web: www.christianacare.org

CEO: -
CFO: -
HR: -
FYE: June 30
Type: Private

Christiana Care Health System cares for the Brandywine Valley. The not-for-profit health care network serves patients in northern Delaware and surrounding areas of Pennsylvania, Maryland, and New Jersey. The company operates Christiana Hospital and Wilmington Hospital, which together have some 1,100 beds. The hospitals provide cardiac care, cancer treatment, women's health, pediatrics, rehabilitation, general medicine, and surgery. Other specialties include urology and gastroenterology. The system also operates area physician clinics and offers home health and adult day care services. In addition, Christiana Care conducts education, training, and research programs.

	Annual Growth	06/17	06/18	06/19	06/20	06/21
Sales ($mil.)	(32.2%)	-	-	3.8	3.5	1.7
Net income ($ mil.)	-	-	-	0.3	(2.2)	(2.9)
Market value ($ mil.)	-	-	-	-	-	-
Employees	-	-	-	-	-	8,500

CHRISTOPHER & BANKS CORP.

2400 Xenium Lane North
Plymouth, MN 55441
Phone: 763 551-5000
Fax: -
Web: www.christopherandbanks.com

NBB: CBKC Q
CEO: -
CFO: -
HR: -
FYE: February 1
Type: Public

Christopher & Banks is a Minneapolis-based specialty retailer featuring exclusively designed privately branded women's apparel and accessories. It offers a wide range of tops (knit, perfect tees, sweaters, blouses and shirts, camis and shells, jackets, vests, and kimonos and wraps), dresses and skirts, bottoms (jeans, pants, and capris, shorts), and more. In early 2021, the company filed voluntary petitions for relief under Chapter 11 of the Bankruptcy Code in the United States Bankruptcy Court for the District of New Jersey. It also filed a Form 15 with the US Securities and Exchange Commission to voluntarily deregister its common stock.

	Annual Growth	01/16	01/17*	02/18	02/19	02/20
Sales ($mil.)	(2.4%)	383.8	381.6	365.9	348.9	348.9
Net income ($ mil.)	-	(49.1)	(17.8)	(22.0)	(32.8)	(16.7)
Market value ($ mil.)	(27.4%)	66.4	50.7	47.6	22.0	18.4
Employees	(3.4%)	4,355	4,100	3,900	3,700	3,800

*Fiscal year change

CHRISTOPHER RANCH, LLC

305 BLOOMFIELD AVE
GILROY, CA 950209565
Phone: 408 847-1100
Fax: -
Web: www.christopherranch.com

CEO: -
CFO: -
HR: Richard Gutierrez
FYE: December 31
Type: Private

There are probably a lot of breath mints available at Christopher Ranch, the largest garlic producer in the US. Christopher Ranch sells dozens of types of fresh and jarred garlic, as well as specialty onions, sun-dried tomatoes, broccoli, dried chilies, herbs, and spices. Christopher Ranch, nestled in California's Santa Clara Valley, ships more than 60 million pounds of garlic every year to foodservice companies and grocery stores such as Kroger, Safeway, and Whole Foods. Its garlic is also exclusively used in Michael Angelo's frozen foods. Christopher Ranch was founded in 1953 by brothers Don and Art Christopher. Don's son Bill now runs the company.

	Annual Growth	12/05	12/06	12/07	12/08	12/09
Sales ($mil.)	(0.1%)	-	-	108.6	111.3	108.5
Net income ($ mil.)	(3.7%)	-	-	13.9	7.0	12.9
Market value ($ mil.)	-	-	-	-	-	-
Employees	-	-	-	-	-	200

CHRISTUS HEALTH

5101 N O CONNOR BLVD
IRVING, TX 750395714
Phone: 469 282-2000
Fax: -
Web: www.christushealth.org

CEO: Ernie Sadau
CFO: Jay Herron
HR: Becky Wilson
FYE: June 30
Type: Private

In CHRISTUS there is no east or west, but plenty of care nonetheless. The not-for-profit Catholic health care system operates about 350 medical facilities from its more than 60 hospitals, including general hospitals and long-term acute care facilities, to clinics and outpatient centers. It operates mostly in Louisiana and Texas, where its hospitals are, but also has facilities in Arkansas, Georgia, Iowa, Missouri, and New Mexico, and in six states in Mexico and one in Chile. In addition to its acute care facilities, CHRISTUS runs medical groups, home health and hospice agencies, and senior living facilities. Specialized services include oncology, pediatrics, rehabilitation, and women's and children's health care.

	Annual Growth	06/15	06/16	06/19	06/20	06/21
Sales ($mil.)	(36.2%)	-	4,212.4	736.5	415.2	446.3
Net income ($ mil.)	(25.1%)	-	149.7	(41.1)	30.8	35.2
Market value ($ mil.)	-	-	-	-	-	-
Employees	-	-	-	-	-	25,700

CHRISTUS HEALTH CENTRAL LOUISIANA

3330 MASONIC DR
ALEXANDRIA, LA 713013841
Phone: 318 487-1122
Fax: -
Web: www.christushealth.org

CEO: Stephen Wright
CFO: -
HR: -
FYE: June 30
Type: Private

CHRISTUS St. Frances Cabrini Hospital provides a wide range of medical services to the denizens of Alexandria, Louisiana. If you're ailing down south, there's not much the hospital can't do to help, especially in the area of cancer. Founded in 1950, the 240-bed St. Frances Cabrini Hospital has a staff of more than 320 physicians providing services that include emergency care, women's health, surgery, and cardiology. For the insomniacs among us, the hospital provides specialized care through its sleep center. St. Francis Cabrini's parent company is one of the nation's major hospital operators -- with about 50 facilities located around the country.

	Annual Growth	06/08	06/09	06/10	06/13	06/15
Sales ($mil.)	1.4%	-	217.4	219.5	222.3	236.9
Net income ($ mil.)	50.5%	-	1.6	(0.6)	5.0	18.4
Market value ($ mil.)	-	-	-	-	-	-
Employees	-	-	-	-	-	2,000

CHRISTUS SPOHN HEALTH SYSTEM CORPORATION

5802 SARATOGA BLVD STE 320
CORPUS CHRISTI, TX 784144253
Phone: 361 881-3000
Fax: –
Web: www.christushealth.org

CEO: Dominic Dominguez
CFO: Becky Rios
HR: Mary Lafrancios
FYE: June 30
Type: Private

CHRISTUS Spohn Health System, part of CHRISTUS Health, provides health care services to the residents and visitors of 15 counties across southern Texas. The medical system operates six acute care hospitals, including CHRISTUS Spohn Hospital Alice, CHRISTUS Spohn Hospital Beeville, and CHRISTUS Spohn Hospital Kleberg. Its flagship hospital, CHRISTUS Spohn Hospital in Corpus Christi, boasts three campuses, including its 557-bed Shoreline Hospital, which serves as the region's primary critical care center. The health system, which began in 1905, also operates about a dozen family practice and specialty health centers, and it offers mobile clinic services to rural and underserved communities.

	Annual Growth	06/01	06/02	06/03	06/05	06/22
Sales ($mil.)	2.8%	–	458.1	465.1	3.8	798.3
Net income ($ mil.)	–	–	15.4	15.0	3.0	(18.7)
Market value ($ mil.)	–	–	–	–	–	–
Employees	–	–	–	–	–	1,689

CHRISTUS-TRINITY MOTHER FRANCES FOUNDATION

800 E DAWSON ST
TYLER, TX 757012036
Phone: 903 531-5057
Fax: –
Web: www.christushealth.org

CEO: –
CFO: William Bellenfant
HR: Jessica McLean
FYE: June 30
Type: Private

Trinity Mother Frances Health System Foundation (dba Trinity Mother Frances Hospitals and Clinics) has a complicated name but a simple mission: to improve patient health. Consisting of three general hospitals, several specialist facilities, and a large physicians' group, Trinity Mother Frances serves northeastern Texas. Its largest acute-care facility is Mother Frances Hospital-Tyler with more than 400 beds, offering comprehensive medical, surgical, trauma, and cardiovascular care. Two smaller hospitals in Jacksonville and Winnsboro provide emergency, diagnostic, surgery, and select specialty services. The Trinity Clinic is a multi-specialty physician group that includes 300 doctors in 36 community clinics.

	Annual Growth	06/07	06/08	06/09	06/10	06/13
Sales ($mil.)	–	–	–	(901.2)	603.4	653.2
Net income ($ mil.)	1364.1%	–	–	0.0	19.9	21.5
Market value ($ mil.)	–	–	–	–	–	–
Employees	–	–	–	–	–	3,551

CHRISTY SPORTS L.L.C.

875 PARFET ST
LAKEWOOD, CO 802155507
Phone: 303 237-6321
Fax: –
Web: www.christysports.com

CEO: Matt Gold
CFO: Lindsay Goszulak
HR: –
FYE: April 30
Type: Private

Christy Sports isn't some girly group of ponytailed cheerleaders. It's the largest specialty ski and snowboard retailer in the Rocky Mountains. With more than 40 retail stores in skiing hot spots like Snowmass, Crested Butte, Steamboat Springs, and Vail, the company sells skiing, snowboarding, snowshoeing, mountain biking, and golf equipment along with shoes, shirts, gloves, and bags to carry it all. Stores also carry patio furniture, grills, hammocks, and other accessories for the outdoor life and rent skiing and snowboarding gear. Christy's staff are all serious skiers and snowboarders who use the equipment they sell. The company was founded in 1958 by avid skiers Ed and Gale Crist.

	Annual Growth	04/08	04/09	04/10	04/11	04/12
Sales ($mil.)	5.4%	–	–	50.4	56.5	56.0
Net income ($ mil.)	42.3%	–	–	0.7	2.4	1.5
Market value ($ mil.)	–	–	–	–	–	–
Employees	–	–	–	–	–	450

CHROMADEX CORP

10900 Wilshire Blvd., Suite 600
Los Angeles, CA 90024
Phone: 310 388-6706
Fax: –
Web: www.chromadex.com

NAS: CDXC
CEO: –
CFO: –
HR: –
FYE: December 31
Type: Public

ChromaDex can talk a blue streak about the health benefits of blueberries. The company markets pterostilbene, a plant-based chemical found in blueberries that is said to lower cholesterol and reduce the risk of cancer. Sold under the brand pTeroPure, the phytochemical is used in about 20 different nutritional supplements, including Nutraceutical's Solaray Super Resveratrol with Pterostilbene. ChromaDex also launched its own line of supplements in 2011 called BluScience that are sold at GNC and Walgreens. Biotech investor Philip Frost, the chairman of Teva Pharmaceuticals, owns almost 20% of ChromaDex.

	Annual Growth	12/19	12/20	12/21	12/22	12/23
Sales ($mil.)	15.9%	46.3	59.3	67.4	72.1	83.6
Net income ($ mil.)	–	(32.1)	(19.9)	(27.1)	(16.5)	(4.9)
Market value ($ mil.)	(24.1%)	323.2	359.9	280.4	126.0	107.2
Employees	(0.9%)	110	110	115	113	106

CHS ACQUISITION CORP.

211 E MAIN ST
CHICAGO HEIGHTS, IL 604114270
Phone: 708 756-5648
Fax: –
Web: www.chs.com

CEO: –
CFO: –
HR: Juan Avila
FYE: December 31
Type: Private

CHS Acquisition supplies its customers with steel strong enough to support a train. Operating as Chicago Heights Steel, it recycles steel train track rails into tee posts (for fences) and signposts (for roadsides). Chicago Heights Steel also uses rail steel to make components used in the agriculture, construction, energy, and transportation industries. It was founded in 1986 when CHS Acquisition acquired a plant Keystone Consolidated had decommissioned the year prior.

CHS INC

5500 Cenex Drive
Inver Grove Heights, MN 55077
Phone: 651 355-6000
Fax: –
Web: www.chsinc.com

NMS: CHSC N
CEO: Jay Debertin
CFO: Olivia Nelligan
HR: Mary Kaul-Hottinger
FYE: August 31
Type: Public

CHS is the leading integrated agricultural cooperative which provides grains, foods, and energy resources to businesses and consumers worldwide, owned by farmers and ranchers, as well as their member cooperatives across the US. The company provides products and services, ranging from initial agricultural inputs such as fuels, farm supplies, crop nutrients and protection products to agricultural outputs which include grains and oilseeds among others. CHS also operates petroleum refineries that sell Cenex-brand fuels, lubricants, and other energy products. The company does approximately 95% of its business in North America.

	Annual Growth	08/19	08/20	08/21	08/22	08/23
Sales ($mil.)	9.3%	31,900	28,406	38,448	47,792	45,590
Net income ($ mil.)	23.0%	829.9	422.4	554.0	1,678.8	1,900.4
Market value ($ mil.)	–	–	–	–	–	–
Employees	(0.2%)	10,703	10,493	9,941	10,014	10,609

CHUGACH ALASKA CORPORATION

3800 CENTERPOINT DR STE 1200
ANCHORAGE, AK 99503
Phone: 907 563-8866
Fax: -
Web: www.chugach.com

CEO: Sheri Buretta
CFO: -
HR: -
FYE: December 31
Type: Private

At the heart of Chugach Alaska Corporation is a vision of indigenous people running their own businesses on their own land. Chugach Alaska was formed following the activation of the Alaska Native Claims Settlement Act (which was passed by the US Congress in 1971), to provide land management services for the 928,000-acre Chugach region of Alaska. The company derives the bulk of its sales from oil and gas production, mining, commercial timber, and tourist activities that occur in the region and from its engagement in military base construction projects at more than 30 locations in Alaska, the US Pacific Northwest, and the Western Pacific. Chugach Alaska's shareholders consist of Aleut, Eskimo, and Indian natives.

	Annual Growth	12/13	12/14	12/15	12/16	12/17
Sales ($mil.)	387.6%	-	7.9	758.5	842.4	919.7
Net income ($ mil.)	-	-	(12.7)	22.7	35.7	20.8
Market value ($ mil.)	-	-	-	-	-	-
Employees	-	-	-	-	-	4,822

CHUGACH ELECTRIC ASSOCIATION, INC.

5601 Electron Drive
Anchorage, AK 99518
Phone: 907 563-7494
Fax: -
Web: www.chugachelectric.com

CEO: Lee D Thibert
CFO: Sherri Highers
HR: Amanda Romano
FYE: December 31
Type: Public

Deriving its name from an old Eskimo tribal word, Chugach Electric Association generates, transmits, distributes, and sells electricity in Alaska's railbelt region. This area extends from the coastal Chugach Mountains into central Alaska and includes the state's two largest cities (Anchorage and Fairbanks). The member-owned cooperative utility has 530 MW of generating capacity from its natural gas-fired and hydroelectric power plants. Serving 80,300 metered retail locations, Chugach Electric, the largest electric utility in Alaska, also sells wholesale power to other municipal and cooperative utilities in the region. In 2016 it agreed to buy Chicago-based Rex Electric and Technologies.

	Annual Growth	12/15	12/16	12/17	12/18	12/19
Sales ($mil.)	(0.5%)	216.4	197.7	224.7	202.3	212.5
Net income ($ mil.)	(5.8%)	6.5	5.8	6.0	5.4	5.1
Market value ($ mil.)	-	-	-	-	-	-
Employees	0.3%	291	288	291	293	295

CHURCH & DWIGHT CO INC

NYS: CHD

500 Charles Ewing Boulevard
Ewing, NJ 08628
Phone: 609 806-1200
Fax: 609 497-7269
Web: www.churchdwight.com

CEO: Matthew T Farrell
CFO: Richard A Dierker
HR: Lori Woodward
FYE: December 31
Type: Public

Church & Dwight develops, manufactures, and markets a broad range of consumer household and personal care products and specialty products under the Arm & Hammer brand and about 15 other brands. The company's household products and specialty products include laundry detergent, fabric softener sheets, cat litter, antiperspirants, oral care products, depilatories, reproductive health products, oral analgesics, nasal saline moisturizers, and dietary supplements. Beyond Arm & Hammer, the company's top brands include XTRA and Oxiclean detergents, Nair depilatories, First Response pregnancy tests, Orajel toothpaste, L'il Critters and Vitafusion gummy vitamins, SpinBrush toothbrushes, Flawless hair removal products, and Trojan-brand condoms. About 85% of the company's sales come from customers in the US.

	Annual Growth	12/19	12/20	12/21	12/22	12/23
Sales ($mil.)	7.7%	4,357.7	4,895.8	5,190.1	5,375.6	5,867.9
Net income ($ mil.)	5.2%	615.9	785.9	827.5	413.9	755.6
Market value ($ mil.)	7.7%	17,103	21,210	24,923	19,601	22,993
Employees	3.7%	4,800	5,100	5,100	5,250	5,550

CHURCH LOANS & INVESTMENT TRUST

5305 W Interstate 40
Amarillo, TX 79106-4759
Phone: 806 358-3666
Fax: -
Web: www.churchloans.com

CEO: -
CFO: -
HR: -
FYE: March 31
Type: Public

If the cost of building a new steeple feels a bit too steep, Church Loans can help. The company does just what its name implies -- it makes loans to churches for the construction or purchase of new facilities; it also loans money to assisted living centers and other not-for-profit organizations. The company, founded in Amarillo, Texas in 1959, is organized as a real estate investment trust (REIT) and writes loans throughout the US. Most of Church Loans' investments are secured by first mortgages or deeds of trusts, but in recent years, the REIT has issued short-term loans for construction, the purchase of real estate, and refinancing.

	Annual Growth	03/05	03/06	03/07	03/08	03/09
Sales ($mil.)	6.6%	4.8	6.4	6.8	7.9	6.2
Net income ($ mil.)	4.6%	2.9	3.2	2.7	3.3	3.5
Market value ($ mil.)	-	-	-	-	-	-
Employees	(9.6%)	9	8	8	8	6

CHURCHILL DOWNS, INC.

NMS: CHDN

600 North Hurstbourne Parkway, Suite 400
Louisville, KY 40222
Phone: 502 636-4400
Fax: -
Web: www.churchilldownsincorporated.com

CEO: William C Carstanjen
CFO: Marcia A Dall
HR: -
FYE: December 31
Type: Public

Churchill Downs is most famous for owning its namesake horse racing track, online wagering, and gaming entertainment company anchored by its iconic flagship event ? the world-famous, Kentucky Derby. The gaming segment has approximately 13,980 slot machines and VLTs and some 360 table games located in eight states. It owns and operates three pari-mutuel gaming entertainment venues with approximately 6,810 historical racing machines (HRMs) in Kentucky. It also owns and operates TwinSpires, one of the largest and most profitable online wagering platforms for horse racing, sports and iGaming in the US and it has nine retail sportsbooks.

	Annual Growth	12/19	12/20	12/21	12/22	12/23
Sales ($mil.)	16.6%	1,329.7	1,054.0	1,597.2	1,809.8	2,461.7
Net income ($ mil.)	32.0%	137.5	(81.9)	249.1	439.4	417.3
Market value ($ mil.)	(0.4%)	10,221	14,512	17,947	15,752	10,052
Employees	0.7%	5,500	7,000	5,000	7,000	5,660

CHUY'S HOLDINGS INC

NMS: CHUY

1623 Toomey Rd.
Austin, TX 78704
Phone: 512 473-2783
Fax: -
Web: www.chuys.com

CEO: Steve Hislop
CFO: Jon Howie
HR: Jennifer Zion
FYE: December 31
Type: Public

Chuy's Holdings operates the Chuy's Tex-Mex casual dining restaurant chain, which serves up a menu of enchiladas, fajitas, tacos, burritos, combination platters and daily specials, complemented by a variety of appetizers, soups and salads, as well as a variety of homemade sauces, including Chuy's signature Hatch Green Chile, Boom-Boom and Creamy Jalape o sauces. Operates in over 15 states, each of the company's roughly 90 restaurants offers patrons a funky, upbeat, vibrant, and eclectic atmosphere. The company was founded in Austin, Texas in 1982.

	Annual Growth	12/19	12/20	12/21	12/22	12/23
Sales ($mil.)	2.0%	426.4	321.0	396.5	422.2	461.3
Net income ($ mil.)	50.1%	6.2	(3.3)	30.2	20.9	31.5
Market value ($ mil.)	10.3%	447.8	484.2	515.7	502.4	662.7
Employees	(4.8%)	9,000	6,100	6,700	7,400	7,400

CIANBRO CORPORATION

101 CIANBRO SQ
PITTSFIELD, ME 049676301
Phone: 207 487-3311
Fax: –
Web: www.cianbro.com

CEO: Peter A Vigue
CFO: Kyle K Holmstrom
HR: Chase McKenney
FYE: December 31
Type: Private

Cianbro is one of the highest-ranked contractors in the US and is one of the largest open-shop, 100% employee-owned construction companies. Cianbro and its subsidiaries have operational facilities in Maine, Massachusetts, Connecticut, Maryland, New Jersey, South Carolina, Illinois, Louisiana, Rhode Island, Texas, and Washington. Working with a fleet of 3,500-owned equipment units, Cianbro provides construction services from concept through implementation and works start-up, commissioned, and turn-key operations to markets such as building, industrial and manufacturing, infrastructure, and power and energy industries. Cianbro manages and self-performs civil, structural, mechanical, electrical, instrumentation, telecommunications, thermal, fabrication, and coating. The company was founded in 1949 by the Cianchette Brothers.

CIB MARINE BANCSHARES INC

19601 West Bluemound Road
Brookfield, WI 53045
Phone: 262 695-6010
Fax: 630 735-2841
Web: www.cibmarine.com

NBB: CIBH
CEO: J B Chaffin
CFO: Patrick J Straka
HR: –
FYE: December 31
Type: Public

CIB Marine Bancshares is semper fi to its banking strategy. The company owns CIBM Bank, which operates in the Indianapolis, Milwaukee, and Phoenix markets. Through some 20 branches, the bank caters to individuals and small- and midsized-business customers, offering checking and savings accounts, ATM and debit cards, CDs, and IRAs. The company's loan portfolio mainly consists of commercial mortgages, business loans, and commercial real estate construction loans. CIB Marine Bancshares emerged from Chapter 11 bankruptcy protection in early 2010.

	Annual Growth	12/17	12/18	12/19	12/20	12/21
Assets ($mil.)	3.0%	662.4	721.3	703.8	751.0	745.4
Net income ($ mil.)	(29.5%)	27.0	3.3	2.0	8.2	6.7
Market value ($ mil.)	129.1%	1.8	2.0	1.8	20.4	50.5
Employees	–	183	–	–	–	–

CIC GROUP, INC.

1509 OCELLO DR
FENTON, MO 630262406
Phone: 314 682-2900
Fax: –
Web: www.cicgroup.com

CEO: Donald H Lange
CFO: –
HR: –
FYE: November 30
Type: Private

CIC Group can see clearly that its future (like its present) is in heavy manufacturing and construction. Its group of commercial and industrial subsidiaries specialize in the manufacture, maintenance, and repair of equipment for the crude oil, natural gas, coal, and other energy industries. Its largest subsidiary is Nooter/Eriksen, which supplies heat recovery steam generators for combustion gas turbines worldwide. CIC's Nooter Construction is a construction contractor serving the refining, petrochemical, pulp and paper, and power industries, among others. The employee-owned holding company was formed in 2002.

	Annual Growth	11/06	11/07	11/08	11/10	11/11
Sales ($mil.)	(9.2%)	–	–	1,120.6	758.0	838.9
Net income ($ mil.)	–	–	–	–	–	–
Market value ($ mil.)	–	–	–	–	–	–
Employees	–	–	–	–	–	1,500

CIEE, INC.

600 SOUTHBOROUGH DR STE 104
SOUTH PORTLAND, ME 04106
Phone: 207 553-4066
Fax: –
Web: www.ciee.org

CEO: –
CFO: –
HR: Helen Lopez
FYE: August 31
Type: Private

Why work, study, or volunteer here when you can work, study, or volunteer over there? Council On International Educational Exchange (CIEE) is a non-profit international educational and cultural exchange program. It is composed of three independent entities based in Boston, Massachusetts; Portland, Maine; and Tokyo, Japan. CIEE runs more than 100 study-abroad programs and volunteer projects in about 35 host countries, as well as work programs in Australia, Canada, Ireland, and New Zealand and teaching programs in China and Thailand. It also brings foreign students to the US by finding host families and employers. The organization was founded in 1947 as the Council on Student Travel.

	Annual Growth	08/18	08/19	08/20	08/21	08/22
Sales ($mil.)	(66.0%)	–	169.7	91.7	4.2	6.7
Net income ($ mil.)	–	–	(1.5)	(26.7)	1.4	0.7
Market value ($ mil.)	–	–	–	–	–	–
Employees	–	–	–	–	–	600

CIENA CORP

7035 Ridge Road
Hanover, MD 21076
Phone: 410 694-5700
Fax: 410 694-5750
Web: www.ciena.com

NYS: CIEN
CEO: Gary B Smith
CFO: James E Moylan Jr
HR: –
FYE: October 28
Type: Public

Ciena is a networking systems, services and software company, providing solutions that enable a wide range of network operators to deploy and manage next-generation networks that deliver services to businesses and consumers. It provides provide hardware, software and services that support the delivery of video, data and voice traffic over core, metro, aggregation, and access communications networks. Users include communications service providers, cable and multiservice operators, web-scale providers, submarine network operators, governments, and enterprises across multiple industry verticals. In addition to its systems and software, Ciena also offer a broad range of services that help its customers build, operate and improve their networks and associated operational environments. These include network transformation, consulting, implementation, systems integration, maintenance, network operations center (NOC) management, and optimization services. Roughly 75% of sales are to North America customers.

	Annual Growth	10/19	10/20	10/21	10/22	10/23
Sales ($mil.)	5.3%	3,572.1	3,532.2	3,620.7	3,632.7	4,386.5
Net income ($ mil.)	0.1%	253.4	361.3	500.2	152.9	254.8
Market value ($ mil.)	2.5%	5,376.1	5,704.9	7,862.8	6,988.0	5,940.9
Employees	7.4%	6,383	7,032	7,241	8,079	8,483

CIFC CORP.

250 PARK AVE STE 400
NEW YORK, NY 101770502
Phone: 212 624-1200
Fax: –
Web: www.cifc.com

CEO: –
CFO: –
HR: –
FYE: December 31
Type: Private

CIFC is searching for a new world of investments. Through subsidiaries, the specialty finance company invests in and manages client assets such as asset-backed securities, bank loans, and government securities. It offers some 30 investment products, including separately managed accounts and a private investment fund. CIFC has some $14 billion of assets under management. Nearly 90% of its portfolio was once devoted to residential mortgage-backed securities (RMBS), but CIFC broadened its investment mix in the wake of the mortgage meltdown. Alternative investment platform F.A.B. Partners is buying CIFC for $333 million.

	Annual Growth	12/11	12/12	12/13	12/14	12/15
Assets ($mil.)	(71.4%)	–	10,505	11,600	13,148	244.6
Net income ($ mil.)	–	–	(240.3)	96.8	(12.3)	1.0
Market value ($ mil.)	–	–	–	–	–	–
Employees	–	–	–	–	–	82

CIGITAL, INC.

21351 RIDGETOP CIR # 400
DULLES, VA 201666561
Phone: 703 404-9293
Fax: -
Web: www.swsec.com

CEO: -
CFO: -
HR: -
FYE: December 31
Type: Private

Cigital offers software quality management (SQM) services and applications that help commercial and government clients assure software quality and improve software development processes. The resulting applications are more secure and reliable, the company asserts. The SQM products are driven by proprietary intellectual property generated by Cigital Labs, the company's research division. Cigital was founded in 1992 as Reliable Software Technologies (RST) and changed its name in 2000. The company has received venture backing from Mid-Atlantic Venture Funds, Blue Water Capital, and Washington Dinner Club LLC.

	Annual Growth	12/08	12/09	12/10	12/11	12/12
Sales ($mil.)	29.8%	-	-	21.3	28.1	35.9
Net income ($ mil.)	(34.6%)	-	-	3.0	0.3	1.3
Market value ($ mil.)	-	-	-	-	-	-
Employees	-	-	-	-	-	199

CIMARRON MORTGAGE COMPANY

2508 LAKELAND DR
FLOWOOD, MS 392329502
Phone: 601 709-0894
Fax: -
Web: www.origin.bank

CEO: -
CFO: -
HR: -
FYE: December 31
Type: Private

From Abbeville to Yazoo City, Cimarron Mortgage is helping Mississippians buy their homes. One of the largest mortgage providers based in the state, the company offers conventional, FHA, jumbo, and VA mortgages, as well as mortgage loans for those with less than stellar credit. It also services loans. The company offers borrowers online conveniences such as a one-page express pre-qualification form, and a detailed electronic loan application. Founded in 1993, the mortgage lender does business throughout the South, and operates offices in Atlanta; Jackson, Mississippi; and Clearwater, Florida.

	Annual Growth	12/05	12/06	12/07	12/09	12/10
Assets ($mil.)	(13.0%)	-	-	19.8	20.2	13.0
Net income ($ mil.)	-	-	-	(2.2)	0.8	0.1
Market value ($ mil.)	-	-	-	-	-	-
Employees	-	-	-	-	-	100

CINCINNATI BELL INC.

221 E 4TH ST
CINCINNATI, OH 452024118
Phone: 513 397-9900
Fax: -
Web: www.altafiber.com

CEO: Leigh R Fox
CFO: Joshua T Duckworth
HR: Andrew Brant
FYE: December 31
Type: Private

Cincinnati Bell is now doing business as "altafiber" in Ohio, Kentucky, and Indiana. The Company delivers integrated communications solutions to residential and business customers over its fiber-optic network including high-speed internet, video, voice and data. The company also provides service in Hawai'i under the brand Hawaiian Telcom. In addition, the company's enterprise customers across the US and Canada rely on CBTS and OnX, wholly-owned subsidiaries, for efficient, scalable office communications systems and end-to-end IT solutions.

CINCINNATI FINANCIAL CORP.

NMS: CINF

6200 S. Gilmore Road
Fairfield, OH 45014-5141
Phone: 513 870-2000
Fax: -
Web: www.cinfin.com

CEO: Steven J Johnston
CFO: Michael J Sewell
HR: -
FYE: December 31
Type: Public

Cincinnati Financial Corporation (CFC) provides property casualty insurance marketed through independent insurance agencies in around 45 states, primarily in the midwestern and southeastern US. Its flagship firm Cincinnati Insurance (operating through four subsidiaries) sells commercial property and casualty, liability, excess and surplus, auto, bond, and fire insurance. Personal lines include homeowners, auto, and other personal line products. The Cincinnati Insurance companies also sell life coverage and annuities. Other CFC subsidiaries include CFC Investment (leasing and financing services), CSU Producers Resources (excess and surplus lines brokerage), and Cincinnati Global Underwriting (global specialty insurance).

	Annual Growth	12/19	12/20	12/21	12/22	12/23
Assets ($mil.)	6.6%	25,408	27,542	31,387	29,736	32,769
Net income ($ mil.)	(2.0%)	1,997.0	1,216.0	2,946.0	(486.0)	1,843.0
Market value ($ mil.)	(0.4%)	16,509	13,717	17,887	16,075	16,243
Employees	1.3%	5,148	5,266	5,166	5,148	5,426

CINEMARK HOLDINGS INC

NYS: CNK

3900 Dallas Parkway
Plano, TX 75093
Phone: 972 665-1000
Fax: -
Web: www.cinemark.com

CEO: Sean Gamble
CFO: Melissa Thomas
HR: Ihsaana Gay
FYE: December 31
Type: Public

Cinemark Holdings is leader and one of the most geographically diverse operators in the motion picture exhibition industry with about 5,845 screens in roughly 520 theaters in the US and Latin America. Its significant and diverse presence in the US and Latin America has made the company an important distribution channel for movie studios and other content providers. As part of the Digital Cinema Distribution Coalition joint venture with certain exhibitors and distributors, Cinemark operates a satellite distribution network that distributes all digital content to US theatres via satellite. The company generates majority of its revenue domestically.

	Annual Growth	12/19	12/20	12/21	12/22	12/23
Sales ($mil.)	(1.7%)	3,283.1	686.3	1,510.5	2,454.7	3,066.7
Net income ($ mil.)	(0.4%)	191.4	(616.8)	(422.3)	(271.2)	188.2
Market value ($ mil.)	(19.7%)	4,116.0	2,117.0	1,960.1	1,053.0	1,713.3
Employees	5.1%	22,000	28,500	24,700	18,100	26,800

CINEVERSE CORP

NAS: CNVS

244 Fifth Avenue, Suite M289
New York, NY 10001
Phone: 212 206-8600
Fax: -
Web: www.cinedigm.com

CEO: Christopher J McGurk
CFO: Mark Lindsey
HR: -
FYE: March 31
Type: Public

Cinedigm Digital Cinema (formerly known as Access Integrated Technologies or AccessIT) hopes to make digital the new cinema paradigm. The company provides software and services for the managed storage and electronic delivery of digital content to movie theaters for major film studios. It also provides alternative digital content to customers such as museums and educational venues. Major customers include Warner Bros. and Universal Pictures. Cinedigm in 2011 sold its digital delivery assets to Technicolor. It kept assets in key areas related to alternative content and digital cinema operational software.

	Annual Growth	03/19	03/20	03/21	03/22	03/23
Sales ($mil.)	6.2%	53.5	39.3	31.4	56.1	68.0
Net income ($ mil.)	-	(16.2)	(14.7)	(62.8)	2.2	(9.7)
Market value ($ mil.)	(31.4%)	17.8	3.4	15.6	7.6	3.9
Employees	12.7%	104	72	72	146	168

CINTAS CORPORATION

NMS: CTAS

6800 Cintas Boulevard, P.O. Box 625737
Cincinnati, OH 45262-5737
Phone: 513 459-1200
Fax: 513 573-4030
Web: www.cintas.com

CEO: Todd M Schneider
CFO: J M Hansen
HR: –
FYE: May 31
Type: Public

Cintas is one of North America's leading providers of corporate identity uniforms through rental and sales programs, as well as a significant provider of related business services, including entrance mats, restroom cleaning services, and supplies, first aid and safety services, and fire protection products and services. It provides products and services to over one million businesses of all types through the company's nearly 475 facilities in nearly 340 cities. Besides offering rental and servicing of uniforms and other garments, the company also offers flame-resistant clothing, mats, mops and shop towels, and other ancillary items. Founded by Richard T. Farmer in 1968, Cintas generate around 90% of its revenue from its US operations.

	Annual Growth	05/19	05/20	05/21	05/22	05/23
Sales ($mil.)	6.3%	6,892.3	7,085.1	7,116.3	7,854.5	8,815.8
Net income ($ mil.)	11.1%	885.0	876.0	1,111.0	1,235.8	1,348.0
Market value ($ mil.)	20.8%	22,567	25,226	35,966	40,523	48,032
Employees	(0.3%)	45,000	40,000	40,000	43,000	44,500

CIPHERLOC CORPORATION

1291 GALLERIA DR STE 200
HENDERSON, NV 890148634
Phone: 702 818-9011
Fax: –
Web: www.cipherloc.net

CEO: –
CFO: –
HR: –
FYE: September 30
Type: Private

National Scientific keeps an eye on kids, and it doesn't mind riding the bus. The company makes location-tracking products that incorporate digital video recording (DVR) devices, Global Positioning System (GPS) technology, and software. Its Gotcha! radio device alerts parents when a child wanders too far away, while the Travado IBUS system provides position tracking and video monitoring of school buses. The company's Travado Mini product tracks the location of government and first responder vehicles. National Scientific has yet to be profitable. The company is owned by its executives and other shareholders.

	Annual Growth	09/05	09/06	09/07*	06/08*	09/14
Sales ($mil.)	11.5%	–	–	0.6	0.5	1.3
Net income ($ mil.)	–	–	–	(0.4)	(0.2)	(1.7)
Market value ($ mil.)	–	–	–	–	–	–
Employees	–	–	–	–	–	15

*Fiscal year change

CIRCUS AND ELDORADO JOINT VENTURE, LLC

407 N VIRGINIA ST
RENO, NV 895011138
Phone: 775 328-0100
Fax: –
Web: www.silverlegacyreno.com

CEO: –
CFO: –
HR: –
FYE: December 31
Type: Private

Circus and Eldorado Joint Venture knows there's gold and silver in the circuses of Reno, Nevada. The company owns and operates the Silver Legacy Resort Casino in Reno. The Silver Legacy, which features a 19th-century silver-mining theme, offers a more than 87,000-sq.-ft. casino with about 1,500 slot machines and more than 60 table games. The casino's hotel boasts some 1,500 guest rooms and suites. The company markets the Silver Legacy to a select group of patrons, including preferred casino customers, convention groups, and specialty Internet travel groups. Circus Circus Hotel and Casino owner MGM Resorts International and Eldorado Resorts each own 50% of the company.

CIRRUS LOGIC INC

NMS: CRUS

800 W. 6th Street
Austin, TX 78701
Phone: 512 851-4000
Fax: –
Web: www.cirrus.com

CEO: John M Forsyth
CFO: Thurman K Case
HR: –
FYE: March 25
Type: Public

Cirrus Logic is a leader in low-power, high-precision mixed-signal processing solutions that create innovative user experiences for the world's top mobile and consumer applications that are used in smartphones, laptops, and headsets among others. It also has an extensive portfolio of products, including "codecs" ? chips that integrate analog-to-digital converters (ADCs) and digital-to-analog converters (DACs) into a single integrated circuit (IC), smart codecs ? codecs with digital signal processing integrated, boosted amplifiers, as well as standalone digital signal processors (DSPs). Its SoundClear technology helps customers to differentiate its products by improving the user experience with features such as louder, high-fidelity sound, high-quality audio playback, voice capture, and hearing augmentation. About 65% of revenue comes from China. The company was incorporated in 1984 and became public in 1989, and reincorporated in 1999.

	Annual Growth	03/19	03/20	03/21	03/22	03/23
Sales ($mil.)	12.5%	1,185.5	1,281.1	1,369.2	1,781.5	1,897.6
Net income ($ mil.)	18.4%	90.0	159.5	217.3	326.4	176.7
Market value ($ mil.)	25.9%	2,318.0	3,411.7	4,573.7	4,831.5	5,817.8
Employees	2.3%	1,551	1,443	1,481	1,591	1,702

CIRTRAN CORP

NBB: CIRX

6360 S Pecos Road, Suite 8
Las Vegas, NV 89120
Phone: 801 963-5112
Fax: –
Web: www.cirtran.com

CEO: Iehab Hawatmeh
CFO: Iehab Hawatmeh
HR: –
FYE: December 31
Type: Public

CirTran provides contract electronics manufacturing services, through which it makes printed circuit boards and cables for customers in consumer electronics, networking equipment, the automotive industry, and other markets. The company has established an Asian subsidiary in Shenzhen, China, that undertakes manufacturing services for a wider variety of products, including cooking appliances, fitness equipment, and hair products. CirTran's Racore Technology subsidiary makes Ethernet adapter cards for PCs. Racore's customers include the Fire Department of New York City, Lear Siegler, Lockheed Martin, the US Air Force, and Walt Disney World.

	Annual Growth	12/18	12/19	12/20	12/21	12/22
Sales ($mil.)	–	–	–	1.7	2.9	1.7
Net income ($ mil.)	–	(1.1)	(1.2)	0.5	0.1	(1.5)
Market value ($ mil.)	–	–	0.0	0.1	0.2	0.1
Employees	71.6%	3	5	18	26	26

CISCO SYSTEMS INC

NMS: CSCO

170 West Tasman Drive
San Jose, CA 95134
Phone: 408 526-4000
Fax: –
Web: www.cisco.com

CEO: Charles H Robbins
CFO: R S Herren
HR: –
FYE: July 29
Type: Public

Cisco Systems designs and sells a broad range of technologies that power the Internet. The company is integrating its product portfolios across networking, security, collaboration, applications, and the cloud to create highly secure, intelligent platforms for its customers' digital businesses. These platforms are designed to help its customers manage more users, devices, and things connecting to customers' networks. Its offerings include among others switches, routers, Software-defined networking, controllers, access points, Internet of Things (IoT), servers, and software. The company offers its services to markets in the US, EMEA, and APJC. About half of its revenue comes from the Americas. Cisco's customers include businesses of all sizes, public institutions, governments, and service providers, including large webscale providers.

	Annual Growth	07/19	07/20	07/21	07/22	07/23
Sales ($mil.)	2.4%	51,904	49,301	49,818	51,557	56,998
Net income ($ mil.)	2.1%	11,621	11,214	10,591	11,812	12,613
Market value ($ mil.)	(2.0%)	229,851	188,662	225,134	184,474	211,798
Employees	2.8%	75,900	77,500	79,500	83,300	84,900

CITADEL ENTERPRISE AMERICAS LLC

131 S DEARBORN ST STE 200
CHICAGO, IL 606035563
Phone: 312 395-2100
Fax: –
Web: www.citadel.com

CEO: Kenneth C Griffin
CFO: Andrew Philipp
HR: –
FYE: December 31
Type: Private

Citadel is one of the largest alternative investment managers in the commodities markets. Citadel Energy Marketing (CEM) is a unique part of its business. CEM helps energy producers and consumers across North America manage their commodity and funding risks in markets including natural gas, power, environmental products and weather. In natural gas, CEM is one of the largest physical shippers in North America and helps more than 250 clients meet their energy needs. The firm is also a leading fixed-income and macro business. It focuses on rates (interest rate swaps, sovereign bonds, inflation), currencies, emerging markets, equities, commodities and credit. The firm was founded in 1990 by CEO Ken Griffin.

CITATION OIL & GAS CORP.

14077 CUTTEN RD
HOUSTON, TX 770692212
Phone: 281 891-1000
Fax: –
Web: www.cogc.com

CEO: Forrest E Harrell
CFO: Chris Phelps
HR: –
FYE: December 31
Type: Private

Citation Oil & Gas is writing its own ticket to prosperity in the petroleum industry. The oil and gas development and production company has interests in about 15,000 wells (in more than 480 separately designated fields) and reported 210 million barrels of proved oil equivalent reserves (91% oil) in 2012. Its oil fields are in the Mid-Continent, Illinois Basin, Permian Basin, and Rocky Mountain regions. Citation seeks out properties with high levels of crude oil, declining production with long reserve life, and low risk. The company uses a variety of techniques to recover oil and gas, including waterflood and infill drilling. Subsidiary Citation Crude Marketing sells the company's products to refiners.

	Annual Growth	12/14	12/15	12/16	12/17	12/18
Sales ($mil.)	25.6%	–	–	179.7	191.9	283.5
Net income ($ mil.)		–	–	(129.8)	74.1	125.9
Market value ($ mil.)		–	–	–	–	–
Employees		–	–	–	–	551

CITGO PETROLEUM CORP.

1293 Eldridge Parkway
Houston, TX 77077
Phone: 832 486-4000
Fax: –
Web: www.citgo.com

CEO: Carlos Jorda
CFO: John Zuklic
HR: Steve Bland
FYE: December 31
Type: Public

CITGO Petroleum is a refiner, transporter and marketer of motor fuels, lubricants, petrochemicals and other industrial products. It refines and markets petroleum products, including transportation fuels, lubricants, and petrochemicals. It markets CITGO branded gasoline through more than 4,200 independent retail outlets throughout the United States and internationally. CITGO Petroleum owns oil refineries in Illinois, Louisiana, and Texas. The company has the refining capacity to process approximately 807,000 barrels of crude oil per day. It markets an extensive line of finished agricultural, automotive, industrial and private label lubricants, oils and greases provide products for consumer, commercial and industrial customers.

	Annual Growth	12/00	12/01	12/02	12/03	12/04
Sales ($mil.)	27.5%	–	–	19,846	25,496	32,277
Net income ($ mil.)	86.3%	–	–	180.0	438.8	625.0
Market value ($ mil.)		–	–	–	–	–
Employees		–	–	–	–	4,000

CITI TRENDS INC

104 Coleman Boulevard
Savannah, GA 31408
Phone: 912 236-1561
Fax: –
Web: www.cititrends.com

NMS: CTRN
CEO: David N Makuen
CFO: Heather Plutino
HR: –
FYE: January 28
Type: Public

Citi Trends is a growing specialty value retailer of apparel, accessories, and home trends for way less spending, primarily for African American and multicultural families in the US. Its brand name includes Citi Steps, Citi Trends Fashion for Less, Lil Ms Hollywood, Red Ape, and Vintage Harlem among others. The company's product offering includes men's, women's, and children's clothing; shoes; fashion accessories; and housewares. Its high-quality and trend-right merchandise offerings at everyday low prices are designed to appeal to the fashion and trend preferences of value-conscious customers. Citi Trends operates more than 610 stores in nearly 35 states. The company was founded in 1946 and headquartered in Savannah.

	Annual Growth	02/19	02/20*	01/21	01/22	01/23
Sales ($mil.)	0.8%	769.6	781.9	783.3	991.6	795.0
Net income ($ mil.)	28.8%	21.4	16.5	24.0	62.2	58.9
Market value ($ mil.)	12.0%	170.3	194.6	492.9	399.2	268.3
Employees	(3.3%)	5,500	5,700	5,200	5,400	4,800

*Fiscal year change

CITIGROUP GLOBAL MARKETS HOLDINGS INC

388 Greenwich Street
New York, NY 10013
Phone: 212 816-6000
Fax: –
Web: –

CEO: James Forese
CFO: –
HR: –
FYE: December 31
Type: Public

Citigroup Global Markets Inc. (CGMI) is the US-based brokerage and securities arm of banking behemoth Citigroup. The company provides investment banking services to corporate, institutional, government, and retail clients. As a broker-dealer, CGMI offers clients access to the global markets in more than 100 countries. Services include underwriting, structuring, sales and trading across such asset classes as equities, corporate, government and agency bonds, and mortgage-backed securities. Through Citi Futures, it offers execution and clearing services.

	Annual Growth	12/11	12/12	12/13	12/14	12/15
Sales ($mil.)	9.1%	–	8,499.0	10,347	11,751	11,049
Net income ($ mil.)		–	(782.0)	(910.0)	(1,718.0)	2,022.0
Market value ($ mil.)		–	–	–	–	–
Employees		–	–	–	–	–

CITIGROUP GLOBAL MARKETS HOLDINGS INC

388 Greenwich Street
New York, NY 10013
Phone: 212 816-6000
Fax: 212 783-2400
Web: www.salomonsmithbarney.com

CEO: James Forese
CFO: –
HR: –
FYE: December 31
Type: Public

Citigroup Global Markets Inc. (CGMI) is the US-based brokerage and securities arm of banking behemoth Citigroup. The company provides investment banking services to corporate, institutional, government, and retail clients. As a broker-dealer, CGMI offers clients access to the global markets in more than 100 countries. Services include underwriting, structuring, sales and trading across such asset classes as equities, corporate, government and agency bonds, and mortgage-backed securities. Through Citi Futures, it offers execution and clearing services.

	Annual Growth	12/00	12/01	12/02	12/03	12/04
Sales ($mil.)	(7.0%)	30,772	27,374	21,250	20,722	23,065
Net income ($ mil.)		3,032.0	2,627.0	1,787.0	2,893.0	(1,441.0)
Market value ($ mil.)		–	–	–	–	–
Employees	(3.1%)	45,457	42,360	40,000	39,000	40,000

CITIGROUP INC
NYS: C

388 Greenwich Street
New York, NY 10013
Phone: 212 559-1000
Fax: –
Web: www.citigroup.com

CEO: Jane N Fraser
CFO: Mark A Mason
HR: –
FYE: December 31
Type: Public

Citigroup is a global diversified financial services holding company whose businesses provide consumers, corporations, governments and institutions with a broad, yet focused, range of financial products and services, including consumer banking and credit, corporate and investment banking, securities brokerage, trade and securities services and wealth management. Citi has approximately 200 million customer accounts and does business in more than 160 countries and jurisdictions. Citi has some $2.3 trillion in assets and some $1.3 trillion in deposits. Citigroup generates almost half of its sales from North America.

	Annual Growth	12/19	12/20	12/21	12/22	12/23
Assets ($mil.)	5.4%	1,951,158	2,260,090	2,291,413	2,416,676	2,411,834
Net income ($ mil.)	(17.0%)	19,401	11,047	21,952	14,845	9,228.0
Market value ($ mil.)	(10.4%)	152,040	117,346	114,929	86,078	97,896
Employees	4.6%	200,000	210,153	223,400	240,000	239,000

CITIZANT, INC.

5175 PARKSTONE DR STE 110
CHANTILLY, VA 201513816
Phone: 703 687-1703
Fax: –
Web: www.citizant.com

CEO: Alba M Alemn
CFO: Greg Gorgone
HR: –
FYE: December 31
Type: Private

Citizant brings IT to US citizens. Formerly known as Cairo Corporation, Citizant specializes in information technology services such as enterprise architecture, program management, and application development primarily for municipal, state, and federal clients. The company counts military and civilian agencies including the US Navy and NASA among its customers; it also serves state and municipal governments as well as such military contractors as General Dynamics. Citizant was founded in 1999 and rebranded itself in 2007.

	Annual Growth	12/14	12/15	12/16	12/17	12/18
Sales ($mil.)	11.3%	–	–	22.6	25.2	27.9
Net income ($ mil.)	96.7%	–	–	0.7	2.1	2.8
Market value ($ mil.)	–	–	–	–	–	–
Employees	–	–	–	–	–	150

CITIZEN SCHOOLS, INC.

308 CONGRESS ST LBBY 1
BOSTON, MA 022101016
Phone: 617 695-2300
Fax: –
Web: www.citizenschools.org

CEO: –
CFO: –
HR: –
FYE: June 30
Type: Private

If our nation was founded on the concept of citizen soldiers, Citizen Schools is like boot camp for citizen students. The non-profit organization offers real-life apprenticeships through after-school, Saturday, and summer programs for middle school students. They learn writing and Web design, publish newspapers, run sports tournaments, and most importantly gear up for a successful high school career. Some 3,800 students participate in an experiential curriculum that includes apprenticeships with about 2,300 adult volunteers. The program, which began at a single Boston elementary school in 1995, now partners with campuses in California, Massachusetts, New Jersey, New York, New Mexico, North Carolina, and Texas.

CITIZENS & NORTHERN CORP
NAS: CZNC

90-92 Main Street
Wellsboro, PA 16901
Phone: 570 724-3411
Fax: –
Web: www.cnbankpa.com

CEO: J B Scovill
CFO: –
HR: –
FYE: December 31
Type: Public

Citizens & Northern Corp. is the holding company for Citizens & Northern (C&N) Bank, Citizens & Northern Investment Corp., and Bucktail Life Insurance Company. Its primary business and largest subsidiary is C&N Bank, a community bank that serves individuals and commercial customers in Pennsylvania and New York. The bank operates more than 25 branches and offers online and telebanking services. The firm's other subsidiaries are Citizens & Northern Investment Corp., which provides investment services, and Bucktail Life Insurance, a provider of credit, life, and property/casualty reinsurance. The bank holding company has assets of more than $1.3 billion.

	Annual Growth	12/19	12/20	12/21	12/22	12/23
Assets ($mil.)	11.0%	1,654.1	2,239.1	2,327.6	2,454.3	2,515.6
Net income ($ mil.)	5.5%	19.5	19.2	30.6	26.6	24.1
Market value ($ mil.)	(5.6%)	432.1	303.5	399.5	349.6	343.1
Employees	4.7%	336	–	–	–	404

CITIZENS BANCORP (CORVALLIS, OR)
NBB: CZBC

275 SW Third Street, PO Box 30
Corvallis, OR 97339
Phone: 541 752-2261
Fax: –
Web: www.citizensebank.com

CEO: –
CFO: Lark Wysham
HR: –
FYE: December 31
Type: Public

Citizens Bancorp is the holding company for Citizens Bank, which offers traditional banking services through about a dozen branches in western Oregon. Its retail offerings include regular savings and checking accounts, money market and NOW accounts, CDs, IRAs, and home mortgages. The bank also offers safe-deposit boxes and online banking and bill payment. It is mainly a business lender, with commercial mortgages making up the largest portion of its loan portfolio. Loans to farmers for land, operations, and equipment are a growing part of Citizens Bank's business.

	Annual Growth	12/05	12/06	12/07	12/20	12/21
Assets ($mil.)	7.4%	338.9	359.0	360.8	983.6	1,067.3
Net income ($ mil.)	4.2%	5.3	5.5	6.1	4.1	10.3
Market value ($ mil.)	(0.1%)	95.9	99.8	106.9	87.2	94.5
Employees		131	127	140	–	–

CITIZENS BANCSHARES CORP. (GA)
NBB: CZBS

230 Peachtree Street, NW, Suite 2700
Atlanta, GA 30303
Phone: 678 406-4000
Fax: –
Web: www.ctbconnect.com

CEO: Cynthia N Day
CFO: Samuel J Cox
HR: –
FYE: December 31
Type: Public

One of the largest minority-led financial institutions in the US, Citizens Bancshares is the holding company for Citizens Trust Bank, which serves the Atlanta and Columbus, Georgia and Birmingham and Eutaw, Alabama communities from about 10 branch offices. The bank provides standard services such as checking and savings accounts, CDs, IRAs, credit cards, financial planning, and investments. Its lending portfolio mainly consists of loans secured by one- to four-family residences, multifamily dwellings, or commercial or industrial real estate. Former chairman and Atlanta-area entrepreneur and philanthropist Herman J. Russell owns about 30% of Citizens Bancshares' stock.

	Annual Growth	12/17	12/18	12/19	12/20	12/21
Assets ($mil.)	11.7%	429.1	410.6	417.8	571.9	668.9
Net income ($ mil.)	26.0%	1.6	4.0	3.7	5.2	4.1
Market value ($ mil.)	(7.2%)	33.6	25.3	27.5	24.5	24.9
Employees		–	–	–	–	–

CITIZENS COMMUNITY BANCORP INC (MD)   NMS: CZWI

2174 EastRidge Center
Eau Claire, WI 54701
Phone: 715 836-9994
Fax: –
Web: www.ccf.us

CEO: Stephen M Bianchi
CFO: James S Broucek
HR: –
FYE: December 31
Type: Public

Citizens Community Bancorp is the holding company for Citizens Community Federal, a community bank with about 20 branches in Wisconsin, southern Minnesota, and northern Michigan. Serving consumers and businesses, the bank offers standard deposit services such as savings, checking, money market, and retirement accounts, as well as a variety of loan products. The bank focuses its lending activities on one- to four-family mortgages, which represent more than half of its loan portfolio. The bank also offers consumer loans such as auto and personal loans; it does not routinely make commercial loans. Founded in 1938, Citizens Community was a state-chartered credit union until 2001.

	Annual Growth	12/19	12/20	12/21	12/22	12/23
Assets ($mil.)	4.9%	1,531.2	1,649.1	1,739.6	1,816.4	1,851.4
Net income ($ mil.)	8.4%	9.5	12.7	21.3	17.8	13.1
Market value ($ mil.)	(1.1%)	127.6	113.7	143.8	125.6	122.3
Employees	–	288	251	248	236	–

CITIZENS ENERGY GROUP

2020 N MERIDIAN ST
INDIANAPOLIS, IN 462021306
Phone: 317 924-3341
Fax: –
Web: info.citizensenergygroup.com

CEO: Jeffrey Harrison
CFO: –
HR: Jodi Underwood
FYE: September 30
Type: Private

Hoosiers are happy to have their homes provided with gas and water services by Public Utilities of the City of Indianapolis (dba Citizens Energy, and CWA Authority, public charitable trusts). Its Citizens Water unit provides water and wastewater services to 300,000 customers in Indianapolis; Citizens Gas serves more than 266,000 gas customers. Citizens Energy also provides steam heating and chilled water cooling services to about 250 customers through Citizens Thermal Energy. The regional utility also has a small oil production unit (Citizens Oil Division). Its Citizens Resources unit has joint venture stakes in some companies not regulated by the Indiana Utility Regulatory Commission, such as ProLiance Energy.

	Annual Growth	09/08	09/09	09/10	09/11	09/12
Sales ($mil.)	25.7%	–	–	440.7	463.6	696.4
Net income ($ mil.)	–	–	–	(1.8)	32.4	(11.8)
Market value ($ mil.)	–	–	–	–	–	–
Employees	–	–	–	–	–	1,100

CITIZENS FINANCIAL CORP. (KY)   NBB: CFIN

12910 Shelbyville Road, Suite 300
Louisville, KY 40243
Phone: 502 244-2420
Fax: 502 244-2439
Web: www.citizensfinancialcorp.com

CEO: Darrell R Wells
CFO: Len E Schweitzer
HR: Carla Ritzie
FYE: December 31
Type: Public

From life to the passing, Citizens Financial offers a variety of life and health insurance through subsidiary Citizens Security Life Insurance Company. Founded in 1965, Citizens Security Life offers individual whole life and annuities products, as well as pre-need and final-expense products (life policies linked with funeral expenses). Through its CS Group Benefits unit, Citizens Security offers group benefits including employer-paid and voluntary life insurance policies, as well as supplemental dental and vision insurance. Products are sold by independent agents in about 20 states in the southern, midwestern, and northeastern US. CEO and chairman Darrell Wells owns a controlling stake in the company.

	Annual Growth	12/03	12/04	12/05	12/06	12/07
Assets ($mil.)	(2.1%)	158.9	157.3	153.3	147.3	145.9
Net income ($ mil.)	(10.3%)	0.7	0.3	0.3	(0.8)	0.5
Market value ($ mil.)	(6.3%)	0.0	0.0	0.0	0.0	0.0
Employees	–	–	70	63	68	69

CITIZENS FINANCIAL CORP. (WV)   NBB: CIWV

213 Third Street
Elkins, WV 26241
Phone: 304 636-4095
Fax: 304 636-6924
Web: www.cnbelkins.com

CEO: Robert J Schoonover
CFO: –
HR: –
FYE: December 31
Type: Public

The proletariat should not confuse Citizens Financial with Citizens Financial Corporation (in Kentucky), Citizens Financial Group (Rhode Island), or Citizens Financial Services (Pennsylvania). This Citizens Financial is the holding company of Citizens National Bank, which has about a half-dozen offices in central and eastern West Virginia. Citizens National Bank offers savings and checking accounts, consumer and commercial loans, trust services, and other financial services and products. Real estate loans -- including mortgages, home equity loans, and construction loans -- account for some 80% of the bank's lending portfolio.

	Annual Growth	12/06	12/07	12/08	12/13	12/14
Assets ($mil.)	(1.2%)	243.0	246.6	282.5	208.7	220.8
Net income ($ mil.)	0.1%	2.1	1.0	0.9	1.5	2.1
Market value ($ mil.)	(10.5%)	35.3	20.4	12.7	12.2	14.5
Employees	–	91	88	84	–	–

CITIZENS FINANCIAL GROUP INC (NEW)   NYS: CFG

One Citizens Plaza
Providence, RI 02903
Phone: 203 900-6715
Fax: –
Web: www.citizensbank.com

CEO: Bruce V Saun
CFO: John F Woods
HR: –
FYE: December 31
Type: Public

Citizens Financial Group offers a broad range of retail and commercial banking products and services to individuals, small businesses, middle-market companies, large corporations, and institutions. The company's products and services are offered through approximately 1,100 branches in around 15 states and the District of Columbia, and nearly 125 retail and commercial non-branch offices, though certain lines of business serve national markets. It has total assets of $226.7 billion, total deposits of $180.7 billion, and total stockholders' equity of $23.7 billion. The bank's branches offer standard retail and commercial services including loans, leases, trade financing, deposits, cash management, commercial cards, foreign exchange and others.

	Annual Growth	12/19	12/20	12/21	12/22	12/23
Assets ($mil.)	7.6%	165,733	183,349	188,409	226,733	221,964
Net income ($ mil.)	(2.7%)	1,791.0	1,057.0	2,319.0	2,073.0	1,608.0
Market value ($ mil.)	(5.0%)	18,941	16,679	22,038	18,363	15,457
Employees	(0.6%)	18,000	17,584	17,463	18,889	17,570

CITIZENS FINANCIAL SERVICES INC   NAS: CZFS

15 South Main Street
Mansfield, PA 16933
Phone: 570 662-2121
Fax: –
Web: www.firstcitizensbank.com

CEO: Randall E Black
CFO: Stephen J Guillaume
HR: –
FYE: December 31
Type: Public

Citizens Financial Services is an upstanding resident of the financial community. The holding company for First Citizens National Bank serves north-central Pennsylvania's Tioga, Potter, and Bradford counties and southern New York. Through some 15 branches, the bank offers checking, savings, time, and deposit accounts as well as real estate, commercial, industrial, residential, and consumer loans. Residential mortgage loans account for more than half of the bank's total loan portfolio. The Trust and Investment division offers investment advice and employee benefits coordination, as well as estate and retirement planning services. Insurance is offered through the First Citizen's Insurance Agency subsidiary.

	Annual Growth	12/19	12/20	12/21	12/22	12/23
Assets ($mil.)	19.4%	1,466.3	1,891.7	2,143.9	2,333.4	2,975.3
Net income ($ mil.)	(2.2%)	19.5	25.1	29.1	29.1	17.8
Market value ($ mil.)	1.3%	289.5	263.6	285.7	361.1	304.6
Employees	12.4%	268	306	306	328	428

CITIZENS HOLDING CO

NBB: CIZN

521 Main Street
Philadelphia, MS 39350
Phone: 601 656-4692
Fax: –
Web: www.thecitizensbankphila.com

CEO: Greg L McKee
CFO: Phillip R Branch
HR: –
FYE: December 31
Type: Public

Citizens Holding Company has taken the proletariat approach to banking. The firm is the holding company for The Citizens Bank of Philadelphia, Mississippi, which operates some 20 locations in the eastern part of the state. Founded in 1908, the bank targets individuals and local businesses, offering products such as checking and savings accounts, money market accounts, CDs, IRAs, and trust services. Lending activities consist mostly of real estate loans (about 70% of the loan portfolio) and commercial, industrial, and agricultural loans (more than 10%). Citizens Holding offers discount brokerage services through an agreement with First Tennessee Bank. Subsidiary Title Services offers title insurance.

	Annual Growth	12/18	12/19	12/20	12/21	12/22
Assets ($mil.)	8.4%	958.6	1,195.4	1,450.7	1,361.3	1,324.0
Net income ($ mil.)	9.6%	6.7	5.9	6.9	7.5	9.6
Market value ($ mil.)	(10.1%)	117.7	122.6	117.4	105.1	76.8
Employees	1.1%	259	290	289	274	271

CITIZENS, INC. (AUSTIN, TX)

NYS: CIA

11815 Alterra Pkwy, Suite 1500
Austin, TX 78758
Phone: 512 837-7100
Fax: –
Web: www.citizensinc.com

CEO: Gerald W Shields
CFO: Jeffery P Conklin
HR: Lisa Gould
FYE: December 31
Type: Public

Citizens is an insurance holding company serving the life insurance needs of individuals in the United States since 1969 and internationally since 1975. Through its insurance subsidiaries, the company provides insurance benefits to residents in about 30 US states and more than 70 different countries. The company operates in two segment ? Life Insurance and Home Service Insurance. Through its Life Insurance, it issues life insurance in US dollars to wealthy individuals in Latin America and Pacific Rim. Its Home Service segment sells life insurance to middle and lower-income individuals in a Louisiana, Mississippi and Arkansas, through employee and independent agents in its home service distribution channel and through funeral homes. The company has about $1.9 billion of assets and approximately $4.2 billion of insurance in force.

	Annual Growth	12/19	12/20	12/21	12/22	12/23
Assets ($mil.)	(1.1%)	1,744.9	1,843.4	1,854.5	1,570.0	1,668.9
Net income ($ mil.)	–	–	(1.4)	(11.0)	36.8	(6.6)	24.4
Market value ($ mil.)	(20.5%)	334.5	283.9	263.1	105.6	133.3
Employees	(12.7%)	400	245	215	224	232

CITRIN COOPERMAN & COMPANY, LLP

529 5TH AVE FL 2
NEW YORK, NY 100174667
Phone: 212 697-1000
Fax: –
Web: www.citrincooperman.com

CEO: –
CFO: –
HR: Jacqueline Weinstein
FYE: July 31
Type: Private

Citrin Cooperman is one of the nation's largest professional services firms, helping companies and high net worth individuals find smart solutions. It targets closely-held businesses in such industries as healthcare, entertainment, franchising, professional services, real estate, construction, technology, and financial services. Citrin Cooperman Wealth Management, LP (CCWM) offers clients in-depth and independent personal financial planning and fee-based investment advisory services. The firm was founded in 1979.

	Annual Growth	12/95	12/96	12/97	12/99*	07/21
Sales ($mil.)	(3.6%)	–	–	1.0	15.4	0.4
Net income ($ mil.)	–	–	–	0.0	1.2	(0.8)
Market value ($ mil.)	–	–	–	–	–	–
Employees	–	–	–	–	–	214

*Fiscal year change

CITRIX SYSTEMS, INC.

851 NW 62ND ST
FORT LAUDERDALE, FL 333092040
Phone: 954 267-3000
Fax: –
Web: www.citrix.com

CEO: Thomas Krause
CFO: Thomas Berquist
HR: –
FYE: December 31
Type: Private

Citrix builds secure, unified digital workspace technology that helps organizations unlock human potential and deliver a consistent workspace experience wherever work needs to get done. With Citrix, users get seamless work experience, and IT has a unified platform to secure, manage, and monitor diverse technologies in complex cloud environments. Its product line includes, Digital workspace solutions, DaaS and VDI, Secure Access solutions, Zero Trust Network Access (ZTNA) solutions, and Citrix Analytics solutions. In late 2022, Citrix was acquired by affiliates of Vista Equity Partners and Evergreen Coast Capital Corporation, an affiliate of Elliott Investment Management L.P., in an all-cash transaction valued at $16.5 billion, including the assumption of Citrix debt.

CITRUS COMMUNITY COLLEGE DISTRICT

1000 W FOOTHILL BLVD
GLENDORA, CA 917411899
Phone: 626 963-0323
Fax: –
Web: www.citruscollege.edu

CEO: –
CFO: –
HR: Kai Wattree-Jackson
FYE: June 30
Type: Private

Citrus College doesn't want you to get a lemon of an education. The community college has an annual enrollment of some 13,000 students in California. Citrus College offers about 50 associate degree programs in disciplines such as nursing, performing arts, foreign language, and behavioral sciences. The school also issues 40-plus technical certificates in programs that include automotive repair, public works, and drafting. In addition, the school offers online, continuing, and distance education programs. Citrus College employs about 350 full- and part-time faculty members.

	Annual Growth	06/18	06/19	06/20	06/21	06/22
Sales ($mil.)	10.5%	–	31.9	30.8	34.0	42.9
Net income ($ mil.)	–	–	(4.4)	6.0	3.9	36.9
Market value ($ mil.)	–	–	–	–	–	–
Employees	–	–	–	–	–	1,414

CITRUS WORLD, INC.

20205 HWY 27
LAKE WALES, FL 338533080
Phone: 863 676-1411
Fax: –
Web: www.floridasnatural.com

CEO: Stephen M Caruso
CFO: William Hendry
HR: David Barker
FYE: August 31
Type: Private

Citrus World works to squeeze out pulpy profits. One of the nation's largest citrus juice sellers, the cooperative is ranked among the country's two giant brand names: PepsiCo's Tropicana and Coca-Cola's Minute Maid. Some 1,000 farmer/members across more than a dozen grower associations harvest 60,000-plus acres of citrus groves for the co-op's products. Its portfolio includes frozen concentrated and not-from-concentrate juices, such as orange, grapefruit, lemonade, apple, and fruit blends. The group's brands include Florida's Natural, Growers Pride, Bluebird, and Donald Duck, among others. Organized in 1933, it also provides juice to customers in the foodservice, retail food, and vending industries.

	Annual Growth	08/04	08/05	08/10	08/21	08/22
Sales ($mil.)	(37.7%)	–	373.9	–	0.3	0.1
Net income ($ mil.)	–	–	–	–	0.0	(0.2)
Market value ($ mil.)	–	–	–	–	–	–
Employees	–	–	–	–	–	800

CITY & COUNTY OF HONOLULU

530 S KING ST RM 300
HONOLULU, HI 968133019
Phone: 808 768-4141
Fax: -
Web: www.honolulu.gov

CEO: -
CFO: -
HR: -
FYE: June 30
Type: Private

With a population of almost 1 million people, Honolulu County, located on the island of Oahu, is the largest city and county in Hawaii. The city and county are governed by a mayor and a nine-member legislative council. Honolulu's largest industry is tourism, but the city is also the financial center of Hawaii.

	Annual Growth	06/18	06/19	06/20	06/21	06/22
Sales ($mil.)	6.3%	-	2,013.9	2,211.4	2,557.1	2,417.3
Net income ($ mil.)	(13.3%)	-	315.1	336.2	231.8	205.5
Market value ($ mil.)	-	-	-	-	-	-
Employees	-	-	-	-	-	8,000

CITY & COUNTY OF SAN FRANCISCO

1 CARLTON B GOODLETT PL STE 316
SAN FRANCISCO, CA 941024604
Phone: 415 554-7500
Fax: -
Web: www.sf.gov

CEO: -
CFO: -
HR: Michael Brown
FYE: June 30
Type: Private

The City of San Francisco is the 14th largest in the US, and its dense population, geographic detachment, and cultural diversity have made San Francisco a favorite with both tourists and residents. San Francisco's government is a consolidated city-county bureaucracy, with both entities led by an elected mayor. The government includes an executive branch led by the mayor and consisting of other elected officials and city departments, and a legislative branch consisting of an 11-member Board of Supervisors. The city is also home to several federal institutions, including the Federal Reserve Bank and the US Mint.

	Annual Growth	06/16	06/17	06/18	06/19	06/20
Sales ($mil.)	5.8%	-	-	6,411.4	7,561.9	7,181.4
Net income ($ mil.)	-	-	-	1,172.5	563.3	(100.7)
Market value ($ mil.)	-	-	-	-	-	-
Employees	-	-	-	-	-	30,000

CITY CAPITAL CORP

3100 Smoke Tree Lane
Raleigh, NC 27616
Phone: 877 367-1463
Fax: -
Web: www.justwebit.com

NBB: CTCC
CEO: -
CFO: -
HR: -
FYE: December 31
Type: Public

City Capital Corporation finds making capital a capital idea. The investment management firm targets the alternative energy technology and services industries and, in 2011, launched solar roofing builder ERX Energy. City Capital was formerly engaged in the purchase and rehabilitation of distressed assets, but it had limited luck in the economic recession and began liquidating or selling its holdings (which include a gaming machine distributor and juice bars). The company changed gears in 2011 to concentrate on alternative energy services and is restructuring most of its debt.

	Annual Growth	12/05	12/06	12/07	12/08	12/09
Sales ($mil.)	-	-	-	0.2	0.2	2.8
Net income ($ mil.)	-	(0.5)	(0.9)	(7.0)	(2.6)	(6.3)
Market value ($ mil.)	(1.6%)	14.5	12.7	136.2	0.6	13.6
Employees	-	-	-	-	18	28

CITY HARVEST, INC.

6 E 32ND ST FL 5
NEW YORK, NY 100165415
Phone: 646 412-0600
Fax: -
Web: www.cityharvest.org

CEO: -
CFO: -
HR: Latoya Ellis
FYE: June 30
Type: Private

The folks at City Harvest have found a way to harvest food straight from the asphalt of New York City streets. City Harvest is a not-for-profit organization that delivers food to soup kitchens, food pantries, and community food programs in New York. The organization distributes almost 110 million pounds of good food each year. Founded by Helen verDuin Palit in 1982, City Harvest works with nearly 2,500 food donors such as Blue Apron, Baldor, PRET, Vita Coco, Whole Foods Market as well as financial supporters, to bring food to the city streets.

	Annual Growth	06/16	06/17	06/18	06/19	06/20
Sales ($mil.)	19.2%	-	123.6	136.7	142.4	209.4
Net income ($ mil.)	312.5%	-	0.5	0.5	0.2	36.4
Market value ($ mil.)	-	-	-	-	-	-
Employees	-	-	-	-	-	140

CITY HOLDING CO.

25 Gatewater Road
Charleston, WV 25313
Phone: 304 769-1100
Fax: -
Web: www.bankatcity.com

NMS: CHCO
CEO: Charles R Hageboeck
CFO: David L Bumgarner
HR: Beverly Blake
FYE: December 31
Type: Public

City Holding conducts its principal activities through its wholly-owned subsidiary City National Bank of West Virginia. City National offers full range of commercial banking services to corporation and other business customers, and provides banking services to consumers, including checking, savings and money market accounts as well as certificates of deposit and individual retirement accounts. It also provides mortgage banking services and offers specialized services and expertise in the areas of wealth management, trust, investment and custodial services for commercial and individual customers. City National operates about 95 branches along the I-64 corridor from Lexington, Kentucky through Lexington, Virginia and along the I-81 corridor through the Shenandoah Valley from Lexington, Virginia to Martinsburg, West Virginia.

	Annual Growth	12/19	12/20	12/21	12/22	12/23
Assets ($mil.)	5.3%	5,018.8	5,758.6	6,003.7	5,878.1	6,168.1
Net income ($ mil.)	6.4%	89.4	89.6	88.1	102.1	114.4
Market value ($ mil.)	7.7%	1,215.5	1,031.6	1,213.1	1,380.7	1,635.4
Employees	1.5%	918	926	905	909	973

CITY NATIONAL BANCSHARES CORP. (NEWARK, N.J.)

900 Broad Sreet
Newark, NJ 07102
Phone: 973 624-0865
Fax: -
Web: www.citynatbank.com

NBB: CYNB
CEO: Preston D Pinkett III
CFO: Edward R Wright
HR: -
FYE: December 31
Type: Public

City National Bancshares is far from stingy. The community development enterprise is the holding company for City National Bank (CNB), which has a handful of branches in underserved minority and low- to middle-income urban neighborhoods in New Jersey (Paterson and Newark) and New York City (Harlem and Brooklyn). The bank offers standard deposit products and services, including checking and savings accounts, IRAs, money market accounts, and CDs. CNB's mostly makes commercial real estate loans, but it also offers residential mortgages, construction loans, small- and medium-business loans, and consumer loans. Founded in 1971, the minority-owned bank is not to be confused with Los Angeles-based City National Corporation.

	Annual Growth	12/09	12/10	12/11	12/12	12/13
Assets ($mil.)	(11.6%)	466.3	387.3	358.4	331.0	285.4
Net income ($ mil.)	-	(7.8)	(7.5)	(3.7)	(6.3)	(8.0)
Market value ($ mil.)	-	-	-	-	-	-
Employees	-	103	89	86	-	-

CITY OF AKRON

166 S HIGH ST RM 502
AKRON, OH 443081622
Phone: 330 375-2720
Fax: –
Web: www.akronohio.gov

CEO: –
CFO: –
HR: –
FYE: December 31
Type: Private

Akron, Ohio, once known as the "Rubber Capital of the World" is the fifth-largest city in Ohio. It is located about 40 miles south of Cleveland in the north-central part of the state. Akron's largest corporation is the Goodyear Tire & Rubber Company (founded 1898); it's also home to the University of Akron. Akron was founded in 1825. Its population in 2015 was about 200,000 people.

	Annual Growth	12/16	12/17	12/18	12/19	12/20
Sales ($mil.)	9.6%	–	330.9	359.8	384.6	436.2
Net income ($ mil.)	–	–	(36.2)	(1.4)	(20.2)	13.2
Market value ($ mil.)	–	–	–	–	–	–
Employees	–	–	–	–	–	2,866

CITY OF ALBUQUERQUE

400 MARQUETTE AVE NW
ALBUQUERQUE, NM 871022117
Phone: 505 768-3000
Fax: –
Web: www.cabq.gov

CEO: –
CFO: Sanjay Bhakta
HR: Mona Plasse
FYE: June 30
Type: Private

Albuquerque is by far New Mexico's largest city, with a 2015 estimated population of 561,380 (about 970,680 in the greater metropolitan area). Albuquerque is located in the central part of the state and is home to The University of New Mexico. While Pueblo Indians lived in the general area for several centuries, Spanish explorers arrived in the 16th century. The city of Albuquerque was founded in 1706 and named after the Spanish town of Albuquerque (with an extra "r"). The City of Albuquerque is administered by a Mayor and a nine-person City Council.

	Annual Growth	06/18	06/19	06/20	06/21	06/22
Sales ($mil.)	8.5%	–	825.1	913.3	1,040.9	1,053.0
Net income ($ mil.)	6.2%	–	20.6	209.7	47.4	24.7
Market value ($ mil.)	–	–	–	–	–	–
Employees	–	–	–	–	–	6,500

CITY OF ALEXANDRIA

301 KING ST
ALEXANDRIA, VA 223143211
Phone: 703 746-4000
Fax: –
Web: www.alexandriava.gov

CEO: –
CFO: –
HR: Avis Hunter
FYE: June 30
Type: Private

Historically a wartime victim of occupying forces, modern Alexandria is home to many Defense Department contractors and employees. It uses a council-manager form of government wherein the mayor is part of the six-member city council (all elected at large), which determines city policy. The city manager works to carry out the policy and run the day-to-day operations of Alexandria. In addition to the city manager, the council also appoints the city attorney, city clerk, and members of various commissions and boards. Alexandria's more than 30 departments operate on an annual budget of about $400 million and serve about 130,000 citizens. The city was founded in 1749.

	Annual Growth	06/18	06/19	06/20	06/21	06/22
Sales ($mil.)	4.2%	–	880.9	911.0	924.6	997.4
Net income ($ mil.)	–	–	(8.3)	167.7	(76.0)	137.9
Market value ($ mil.)	–	–	–	–	–	–
Employees	–	–	–	–	–	2,375

CITY OF ANAHEIM

200 S ANAHEIM BLVD
ANAHEIM, CA 928053820
Phone: 714 765-5162
Fax: –
Web: www.anaheim.net

CEO: –
CFO: –
HR: Deidre Braun
FYE: June 30
Type: Private

Anaheim is a city in sunny southern Orange County, California. The state's 10th largest city is home to Disneyland Resort, one of Walt Disney Parks and Resorts' theme parks. The city also features a number of professional sports franchises, such as the Anaheim Ducks hockey team and the Angels baseball team. Anaheim was founded in 1857.

	Annual Growth	06/17	06/18	06/19	06/20	06/21
Sales ($mil.)	(1.1%)	–	566.2	592.7	574.9	547.1
Net income ($ mil.)	48.9%	–	27.7	12.9	(100.4)	91.3
Market value ($ mil.)	–	–	–	–	–	–
Employees	–	–	–	–	–	3,100

CITY OF ARLINGTON

101 W ABRAM ST
ARLINGTON, TX 760107102
Phone: 817 275-3271
Fax: –
Web: www.arlingtontx.gov

CEO: –
CFO: –
HR: Jeffrey Ross
FYE: September 30
Type: Private

This City of Arlington is in Texas, though it's named for the one in Virginia. Established in 1876, Arlington was named for Confederate General Robert E. Lee's Arlington House in Arlington, Virginia. The city, which is between Dallas and Fort Worth, is the seventh-largest city in Texas and home to about 380,000 people. Its most popular attraction is the Six Flags Over Texas theme park. It also plays host to the Texas Rangers Major League Baseball team and the Dallas Cowboys AT&T Stadium. The city also boasts the second largest unit of the University of Texas System, UT Arlington and a General Motors assembly plant built in 1954.

	Annual Growth	09/13	09/14	09/15	09/16	09/17
Sales ($mil.)	3.5%	–	338.0	355.1	405.9	374.8
Net income ($ mil.)	–	–	15.1	6.4	48.9	(9.4)
Market value ($ mil.)	–	–	–	–	–	–
Employees	–	–	–	–	–	2,477

CITY OF ATLANTA

55 TRINITY AVE SW STE 3900
ATLANTA, GA 303033543
Phone: 404 330-6100
Fax: –
Web: www.atlantaga.gov

CEO: –
CFO: Mohamed Balla
HR: Angelia Ratliff
FYE: June 30
Type: Private

City of Atlanta leaders have a dream to improve Atlantans' quality of life. The birthplace of civil rights activist Martin Luther King, Jr., Atlanta is run by a mayor and a 16-member council. With a metropolitan population of more than 5 million, Atlanta is the most populous city in Georgia. It's also the state capital and home to such major companies as The Coca-Cola Company, The Home Depot, and UPS. In addition, Atlanta has a number of professional sports franchises, namely the Atlanta Braves, Hawks, and Falcons.

	Annual Growth	06/13	06/14	06/15	06/17	06/22
Sales ($mil.)	5.2%	–	883.3	920.2	1,044.6	1,324.8
Net income ($ mil.)	47.3%	–	9.1	274.1	146.2	202.8
Market value ($ mil.)	–	–	–	–	–	–
Employees	–	–	–	–	–	8,885

CITY OF AUSTIN

301 W 2ND ST
AUSTIN, TX 787014652
Phone: 512 974-2000
Fax: -
Web: www.austintexas.gov

CEO: -
CFO: -
HR: Stephanie Menendez
FYE: September 30
Type: Private

Deep in the heart of Texas you'll find Austin, the capital of the state and self-proclaimed Live Music Capital of the World. The city, covering more than 300 square miles, follows the council/manager model where the mayor and six city council members, all elected to three-year terms, enact policy and the city manager carries it out. The manager's office oversees about 30 departments/offices, the municipal court system, city utilities, and the city's airport. Austin has a city population of more than 820,000 and a greater metro population of more than 1.8 million. Stephen F. Austin brought the first Anglo settlers to the area in 1821.

	Annual Growth	09/18	09/19	09/20	09/21	09/22
Sales ($mil.)	11.1%	-	1,352.9	1,449.5	1,712.5	1,855.4
Net income ($ mil.)	64.8%	-	33.7	(34.9)	(25.9)	151.0
Market value ($ mil.)	-	-	-	-	-	-
Employees	-	-	-	-	-	10,922

CITY OF BAKERSFIELD

1600 TRUXTUN AVE 5TH FL
BAKERSFIELD, CA 933015140
Phone: 661 326-3000
Fax: -
Web: www.bakersfieldcity.us

CEO: -
CFO: -
HR: Anthony Gonzales
FYE: June 30
Type: Private

Californians can enjoy sunny weather with fewer crowds in the City of Bakersfield. With a population of about 350,000, Bakersfield is the 9th largest city in the state. Governed by the mayor and seven city council members (elected for four-year terms), the City of Bakersfield operates through 15 departments, including water resources, animal services, and recreation and parks. Bakersfield was founded in 1858 and named after early settler Colonel Thomas Baker. The city is home to the Bakersfield Panthers, California State University, and the Rabobank Arena.

	Annual Growth	06/18	06/19	06/20	06/21	06/22
Sales ($mil.)	13.0%	-	359.9	448.8	572.9	519.7
Net income ($ mil.)	24.0%	-	12.7	27.1	143.7	24.2
Market value ($ mil.)	-	-	-	-	-	-
Employees	-	-	-	-	-	1,570

CITY OF BALTIMORE

100 HOLLIDAY ST STE 250
BALTIMORE, MD 212023459
Phone: 410 396-3835
Fax: -
Web: www.baltimorecity.gov

CEO: -
CFO: -
HR: Catherine Burns
FYE: June 30
Type: Private

Although it is the birthplace of the National Anthem, home to the first commercial ice cream factory in the US, and among the nation's oldest cities, Baltimore is more than an asterisk to history. With a population of about 620,000, the city -- Maryland's largest -- supports a major seaport, and is part of the Baltimore-Washington metropolis. The city's economy is founded on shipping, transportation, auto manufacturing, and steel processing. It is, however, shifting to a diverse service base attractive to tourists. Baltimore is home to two professional sports teams, the Baltimore Orioles and the Baltimore Ravens.

	Annual Growth	06/18	06/19	06/20	06/21	06/22
Sales ($mil.)	3.8%	-	2,413.1	2,391.8	2,436.4	2,701.0
Net income ($ mil.)	(23.4%)	-	133.1	(6.0)	(54.0)	59.7
Market value ($ mil.)	-	-	-	-	-	-
Employees	-	-	-	-	-	26,400

CITY OF BATON ROUGE

222 SAINT LOUIS ST RM 301
BATON ROUGE, LA 708025832
Phone: 225 389-3000
Fax: -
Web: www.brla.gov

CEO: -
CFO: -
HR: -
FYE: December 31
Type: Private

The capital of Louisiana sits along the Mississippi River about 80 miles upstream from New Orleans. Baton Rouge (which means "red stick" in French) counts a population of about 230,000. The city is home to a number of companies in the oil, gas, and chemical industries; it also has a thriving film industry. The Louisiana State University System and its beloved LSU Tigers football team are also located in Baton Rouge.

	Annual Growth	12/16	12/17	12/18	12/21	12/22
Sales ($mil.)	6.8%	-	583.0	559.5	692.1	809.4
Net income ($ mil.)	47.5%	-	11.5	35.9	20.6	80.3
Market value ($ mil.)	-	-	-	-	-	-
Employees	-	-	-	-	-	4,400

CITY OF BELLEVUE

450 110TH AVE NE
BELLEVUE, WA 980045514
Phone: 425 452-6800
Fax: -
Web: www.bellevuewa.gov

CEO: -
CFO: -
HR: -
FYE: December 31
Type: Private

The pretty view from the City of Bellevue, Washington is of its larger neighbor across Lake Washington, the City of Seattle. The bedroom community boasts a population of more than 130,000 and a council-manager form of government where the post of mayor is mostly ceremonial. The seven-member council serves staggered four-year terms and chooses the mayor from its ranks. Day-to-day operations are carried out by the city manager, city attorney, and city clerk. Bellevue sits right next to Microsoft hometown Redmond, Washington and the Lake Washington "Gold Coast" where Bill Gates and other technology millionaires make their homes. Bellevue was founded in 1869.

	Annual Growth	12/18	12/19	12/20	12/21	12/22
Sales ($mil.)	6.3%	-	379.1	392.2	448.9	455.9
Net income ($ mil.)	83.2%	-	12.4	32.2	101.7	76.4
Market value ($ mil.)	-	-	-	-	-	-
Employees	-	-	-	-	-	1,175

CITY OF BERKELEY

2120 MILVIA ST
BERKELEY, CA 947041113
Phone: 510 981-7300
Fax: -
Web: www.berkeleyca.gov

CEO: -
CFO: -
HR: David Abel
FYE: June 30
Type: Private

Situated on the eastern shore of San Francisco Bay, the City of Berkeley has a population of more than 100,000 within the confines of roughly 18 square miles. It is home to the University of California, Berkeley, considered the flagship institution of the California higher education system. Since 1823, the city has operated under the council-manager form of government. Eight council members (elected by separate districts) and the mayor are responsible for decisions regarding the city's economic development, health and human services, housing, public works, and transportation.

	Annual Growth	06/18	06/19	06/20	06/21	06/22
Sales ($mil.)	10.1%	-	334.5	332.7	347.5	445.9
Net income ($ mil.)	42.4%	-	36.6	24.1	45.3	105.8
Market value ($ mil.)	-	-	-	-	-	-
Employees	-	-	-	-	-	1,520

CITY OF BIRMINGHAM

710 20TH ST N STE 600
BIRMINGHAM, AL 352032281
Phone: 205 254-2000
Fax: –
Web: www.birminghamal.gov

CEO: –
CFO: –
HR: –
FYE: June 30
Type: Private

Birmingham is the largest city in Alabama with a city population of more than 242,000 people and a metro population of more than 1 million. The namesake University of Alabama at Birmingham is located in Birmingham, as is one Fortune 500 company, Regions Financial.

	Annual Growth	06/18	06/19	06/20	06/21	06/22
Sales ($mil.)	–	–	–	539.2	595.8	658.8
Net income ($ mil.)	7.0%	–	50.2	11.5	112.7	61.5
Market value ($ mil.)	–	–	–	–	–	–
Employees	–	–	–	–	–	4,000

CITY OF BOSTON

1 CITY HALL SQ STE 242
BOSTON, MA 022011020
Phone: 617 635-4545
Fax: –
Web: www.boston.gov

CEO: –
CFO: –
HR: Vivian Leonard
FYE: June 30
Type: Private

Boston's legacy includes a famous Tea Party, Paul Revere's Ride, and clam chowder. With about 625,000 residents, Boston has been called the economic and cultural hub of New England. The Greater Boston metro area is home to about 4.6 million people, making it the 10th largest city in the US. Boston also boasts world class educational institutions (Harvard, Massachusetts Institute of Technology), champion sports teams (Red Sox, Celtics, Patriots), and a rich cultural and historical identity. Boston is also the capital of Massachusetts.

	Annual Growth	06/14	06/15	06/16	06/17	06/21
Sales ($mil.)	(67.1%)	–	3,278.1	3,393.1	3,542.4	4.2
Net income ($ mil.)	–	–	79.3	139.0	93.9	(0.1)
Market value ($ mil.)	–	–	–	–	–	–
Employees	–	–	–	–	–	18,760

CITY OF BROCKTON

45 SCHOOL ST
BROCKTON, MA 023014063
Phone: 508 580-7123
Fax: –
Web: www.brockton.ma.us

CEO: –
CFO: Troy Clarkson
HR: Maureen Cruise
FYE: June 30
Type: Private

Owing to the success of native boxers Rocky Marciano and "Marvelous" Marvin Hagler, the City of Brockton has been hailed "The City of Champions." With a population of more than 90,000, the city covers 22 square miles in southeastern Massachusetts. It is primarily urban in nature and is situated along the Salisbury River, which once fueled the city's many shoe factories. During the American Civil War, Brockton was the largest producer of shoes in the country. Incorporated in 1881, its city government today consists of the mayor (elected to a two-year term) and 11 city council members.

	Annual Growth	06/05	06/06	06/12	06/13	06/14
Sales ($mil.)	3.2%	–	294.2	361.2	368.9	379.7
Net income ($ mil.)	–	–	(4.6)	(9.4)	(10.1)	2.4
Market value ($ mil.)	–	–	–	–	–	–
Employees	–	–	–	–	–	30,000

CITY OF BROWNSVILLE

1001 E ELIZABETH ST STE 234
BROWNSVILLE, TX 785205142
Phone: 956 542-2064
Fax: –
Web: www.brownsvilletn.gov

CEO: –
CFO: –
HR: Skip Keller
FYE: September 30
Type: Private

This city's motto -- "On the Border by the Sea" -- says it all. The City of Brownsville is situated on the US-Mexico border and is the southernmost city in the state of Texas. Mexican city Matamoros is located just across the Rio Grande River. With a population of more than 165,000, the city covers 83 square miles. Its city government consists of the mayor, six city commissioners (serving staggered four-year terms), and a city manager. Departments include building inspections, engineering, health, planning and community development, and purchasing. Brownsville is one of "America's greenest cities," according to Forbes magazine.

	Annual Growth	09/13	09/14	09/15*	12/20*	09/21
Sales ($mil.)	3.0%	–	–	137.4	0.3	164.3
Net income ($ mil.)	39.1%	–	–	5.1	0.0	37.2
Market value ($ mil.)	–	–	–	–	–	–
Employees	–	–	–	–	–	1,162

*Fiscal year change

CITY OF BUFFALO

65 NIAGARA SQ
BUFFALO, NY 142023392
Phone: 716 851-4200
Fax: –
Web: www.buffalony.gov

CEO: –
CFO: –
HR: –
FYE: June 30
Type: Private

Buffalo, New York is the second-largest city in the state (behind New York City, of course). Located in the western part of the state of the state by Lake Erie, Buffalo is home to more than 260,000 people. The greater metropolitan area, including the famed Niagara Falls, is home to more 1.2 million people. It also has two professional sports franchises, the Buffalo Bills football team and the Sabres hockey team.

	Annual Growth	06/18	06/19	06/20	06/21	06/22
Sales ($mil.)	(89.4%)	–	525.9	504.9	587.7	0.6
Net income ($ mil.)	–	–	(19.3)	(18.2)	59.1	(3.8)
Market value ($ mil.)	–	–	–	–	–	–
Employees	–	–	–	–	–	3,426

CITY OF CAMBRIDGE

795 MASSACHUSETTS AVE
CAMBRIDGE, MA 021393219
Phone: 617 349-4260
Fax: –
Web: www.cambridgema.gov

CEO: –
CFO: –
HR: Gallagher Mark
FYE: June 30
Type: Private

The City of Cambridge houses an abundance of prominent minds. Part of the Greater Boston area, it is home to prestigious universities Harvard and the Massachusetts Institute of Technology (MIT). With a population of more than 100,000, the city covers just seven square miles. Most of its commercial districts are major street intersections (which act as neighborhood centers), which has given rise to its nickname "City of Squares." They include: Central, Harvard, Inman, Kendall, Lechmere, and Porter Squares. Cambridge's city government is a bit unusual. The city manager (appointed by its nine city council members), rather than the mayor (also elected by the council), serves as the chief executive of the city.

	Annual Growth	06/18	06/19	06/20	06/21	06/22
Sales ($mil.)	4.9%	–	754.7	782.3	825.5	870.3
Net income ($ mil.)	(15.0%)	–	38.2	25.7	31.3	23.5
Market value ($ mil.)	–	–	–	–	–	–
Employees	–	–	–	–	–	2,000

CITY OF CHANDLER

175 S ARIZONA AVE
CHANDLER, AZ 852257526
Phone: 480 782-2000
Fax: -
Web: www.chandleraz.gov

CEO: -
CFO: -
HR: Jasmine Kelly
FYE: June 30
Type: Private

Chandler, Arizona is just one of the many popular cities located in Maricopa County. This suburb of Phoenix has a population of more than 240,000 residents, but don't call it a bedroom community -- Chandler is home to a number of high tech companies, including an Intel plant that makes semiconductors. The city is named after Dr. Alexander Chandler, a veterinarian who moved to the area in the late 19th century.

	Annual Growth	06/18	06/19	06/20	06/21	06/22
Sales ($mil.)	6.2%	-	330.3	376.9	373.2	395.7
Net income ($ mil.)	103.0%	-	5.9	49.5	7.8	49.7
Market value ($ mil.)	-	-	-	-	-	-
Employees	-	-	-	-	-	1,498

CITY OF CHARLOTTE

600 E 4TH ST
CHARLOTTE, NC 282022816
Phone: 704 336-7600
Fax: -
Web: www.charlottenc.gov

CEO: -
CFO: -
HR: -
FYE: June 30
Type: Private

You can bank on Charlotte ... the nation's second-largest banking center (behind New York City). The City of Charlotte delivers public services and promotes safety and health among residents. Policies are set by a mayor and 11 council members elected for two-year terms. The day-to-day operations are handled by a city manager. Charlotte has a population of more than 750,000 and covers about 280 square miles. It's home to a handful of Fortune 500 companies, including Bank of America, Family Dollar, and Duke Energy, as well as the Carolina Panthers and Charlotte Motor Speedway. It also boasts some 700 places of worship, earning it the nickname "The City of Churches."

	Annual Growth	06/18	06/19	06/20	06/21	06/22
Sales ($mil.)	4.4%	-	1,065.6	1,102.5	1,219.7	1,212.0
Net income ($ mil.)	8.3%	-	148.6	(83.4)	(215.4)	189.0
Market value ($ mil.)	-	-	-	-	-	-
Employees	-	-	-	-	-	5,011

CITY OF CHESAPEAKE

306 CEDAR RD
CHESAPEAKE, VA 233225597
Phone: 757 382-6586
Fax: -
Web: www.cityofchesapeake.net

CEO: -
CFO: -
HR: -
FYE: June 30
Type: Private

The City of Chesapeake attracts both beachcombers and history buffs. Located about 20 miles from Virginia Beach, Chesapeake was established in 1963 through the merging of the city of South Norfolk and Norfolk County, which was created in 1691. The first English settlement in the area began around 1620 along the banks of the Elizabeth River. The mayor, vice mayor, and seven city council members (elected for four-year terms) govern the city, which has a population of more than 233,370. The third-largest city in Virginia, Chesapeake is home to the College of William and Mary and Hampton University.

	Annual Growth	06/15	06/16	06/20	06/21	06/22
Sales ($mil.)	4.2%	-	621.9	703.0	775.8	797.9
Net income ($ mil.)	29.4%	-	15.0	54.1	90.7	70.2
Market value ($ mil.)	-	-	-	-	-	-
Employees	-	-	-	-	-	2,893

CITY OF CHICAGO

121 N LA SALLE ST RM 700
CHICAGO, IL 606021246
Phone: 312 744-6558
Fax: -
Web: www.cityofchicago.org

CEO: -
CFO: -
HR: -
FYE: December 31
Type: Private

It may be the windy city, or even the "Second City," but Chicago has much more going for it than memorable nicknames. With a population of almost 3 million packed into more than 230 square miles, Chicago has grown from its roots as a transportation and business hub into a world class city with a rich cultural and historical background. The city government is led by a mayor and 50 aldermen (all of them elected to four-year terms), as well as the officials appointed by the mayor to oversee the various administrative city departments. The city clerk and the treasurer round out the city's elected officials. Chicago was first incorporated as a municipality in 1833.

CITY OF CHULA VISTA

276 FOURTH AVE
CHULA VISTA, CA 919102699
Phone: 619 691-5137
Fax: -
Web: www.chulavistaca.gov

CEO: -
CFO: -
HR: -
FYE: June 30
Type: Private

Chula Vista (which means "beautiful view" in Spanish) is a suburb of city of San Diego. With a population of nearly 250,000, Chula Vista is governed by a mayor and four city council members. As a bedroom community, the city's largest employers are the local school districts.

	Annual Growth	06/18	06/19	06/20	06/21	06/22
Sales ($mil.)	7.3%	-	276.7	278.1	305.9	341.6
Net income ($ mil.)	5.9%	-	31.7	10.6	18.7	37.7
Market value ($ mil.)	-	-	-	-	-	-
Employees	-	-	-	-	-	942

CITY OF CINCINNATI

801 PLUM ST RM 246
CINCINNATI, OH 452025704
Phone: 513 352-3221
Fax: -
Web: www.cincinnati-oh.gov

CEO: -
CFO: -
HR: -
FYE: June 30
Type: Private

Founded in 1788, Cincinnati is home to almost 300,000 people and covers roughly 80 square miles. It is the third-largest city in Ohio, trailing behind Columbus and Cleveland. The city's government consists of the mayor and nine city council members (elected at large). Council committees deal with a wide range of issues including public education, health, economic concerns, and community development. The city is also home to two major-league sports franchises -- baseball's Cincinnati Reds and football's Cincinnati Bengals.

	Annual Growth	06/17	06/18	06/19	06/21	06/22
Sales ($mil.)	6.1%	-	729.0	769.2	998.5	925.3
Net income ($ mil.)	-	-	(22.2)	25.3	218.4	126.4
Market value ($ mil.)	-	-	-	-	-	-
Employees	-	-	-	-	-	5,964

CITY OF CLEVELAND

601 LAKESIDE AVE E RM 210
CLEVELAND, OH 441141015
Phone: 216 664-2000
Fax: –
Web: www.clevelandohio.gov

CEO: –
CFO: –
HR: –
FYE: December 31
Type: Private

It's only rock and roll, but Cleveland residents like it. The City of Cleveland, Ohio (C-Town), is home to the Rock and Roll Hall of Fame, and is the nation's 45th largest city and Ohio's second largest (behind Columbus). C-Town, with more than 390,000 residents, is run by a mayor-council form of government. The legislative branch consists of a 21-member council and the executive branch comprises the mayor, his adjunct offices, advisors, and the city's administrative departments. The mayor is the city's CEO and is elected to enforce its charter, ordinances, and state laws. The Village of Cleveland was incorporated in 1814.

	Annual Growth	12/16	12/17	12/19	12/20	12/21
Sales ($mil.)	5.0%	–	801.3	839.5	816.9	972.7
Net income ($ mil.)	27.4%	–	75.9	31.0	8.9	200.2
Market value ($ mil.)	–	–	–	–	–	–
Employees	–	–	–	–	–	8,073

CITY OF COLORADO SPRINGS

107 N NEVADA AVE
COLORADO SPRINGS, CO 809031305
Phone: 719 385-5900
Fax: –
Web: www.coloradosprings.gov

CEO: –
CFO: –
HR: –
FYE: December 31
Type: Private

There may not be much gold in them thar hills anymore, but Colorado Springs is still a glitzy place to live. With more than 415,000 residents, it's the second-largest city in Colorado, behind Denver. (Colorado Springs is located about 70 miles south of Denver along Interstate 25.) The city was incorporated in 1871, chosen for its scenic location in the valley of Pikes Peak and the Rocky Mountains.

	Annual Growth	12/11	12/12	12/13	12/14	12/15
Sales ($mil.)	5.1%	–	272.6	279.1	304.6	316.8
Net income ($ mil.)	(55.1%)	–	17.3	(2.2)	2.8	1.6
Market value ($ mil.)	–	–	–	–	–	–
Employees	–	–	–	–	–	7,000

CITY OF COLUMBUS

90 W BROAD ST RM B33
COLUMBUS, OH 432159061
Phone: 614 645-7671
Fax: –
Web: new.columbus.gov

CEO: –
CFO: –
HR: Jennifer Suliksdieringer
FYE: December 31
Type: Private

So what if European explorer Christopher Columbus didn't sail the Scioto River? Columbus, the capital of Ohio, is located smack dab in the middle of the state. With a population of almost 836,000 people, Columbus is the largest city in the Buckeye State. (Cleveland and Cincinnati, however, have larger populations in their greater metropolitan areas.) Columbus is home to a handful of Fortune 500 companies, including Nationwide Insurance and retailer L Brands. While the area had been home to European fur trappers since the 1700s and Native Americans for centuries, Columbus became a city in 1812.

	Annual Growth	12/18	12/19	12/20	12/21	12/22
Sales ($mil.)	4.1%	–	1,630.7	1,805.7	1,727.8	1,841.2
Net income ($ mil.)	78.5%	–	29.2	(73.0)	105.5	166.5
Market value ($ mil.)	–	–	–	–	–	–
Employees	–	–	–	–	–	8,385

CITY OF CORPUS CHRISTI

1201 LEOPARD ST
CORPUS CHRISTI, TX 784012120
Phone: 361 880-3000
Fax: –
Web: www.cctexas.com

CEO: –
CFO: –
HR: –
FYE: September 30
Type: Private

Corpus Christi (which means "body of Christ" in Latin) is a port city that sits on the Gulf of Mexico in south Texas. With a population of more than 305,000, it's the eighth-largest city in Texas. Its Port of Corpus Christi is one of the top 10 ports in the country.

	Annual Growth	09/14	09/15	09/16	09/18	09/20
Sales ($mil.)	2.3%	–	340.5	348.9	372.8	381.7
Net income ($ mil.)	(6.0%)	–	95.2	12.0	13.7	69.8
Market value ($ mil.)	–	–	–	–	–	–
Employees	–	–	–	–	–	3,518

CITY OF DALLAS

1500 MARILLA ST
DALLAS, TX 752016390
Phone: 214 670-3146
Fax: –
Web: www.dallascityhall.com

CEO: –
CFO: –
HR: –
FYE: September 30
Type: Private

Big D, with a population of 1.2 million, is actually Texas' third-largest city (behind Houston and San Antonio) and the nation's ninth largest. The city operates through 14 districts, each represented by a council member, and about 40 city departments, including the Trinity River Corridor Project and the CityDesign Studio. The city is home to Southern Methodist University, the Dallas Market Center, and the Dallas Cowboys.

	Annual Growth	09/17	09/18	09/19	09/20	09/22
Sales ($mil.)	6.3%	–	1,802.7	1,898.6	2,067.4	2,301.1
Net income ($ mil.)	(58.4%)	–	258.0	147.1	45.2	7.7
Market value ($ mil.)	–	–	–	–	–	–
Employees	–	–	–	–	–	13,000

CITY OF DAYTON

101 W 3RD ST
DAYTON, OH 454021859
Phone: 937 333-3333
Fax: –
Web: www.daytonohio.gov

CEO: Jacquelyn Y Powell
CFO: –
HR: Angie Pennington
FYE: December 31
Type: Private

If you "heart" nerds, The City of Dayton, Ohio, is the place for you. Dayton boasts one of the highest concentrations of engineers and patents in the US, with aerospace and high tech bolstering its economy. Dayton is run by a commission, comprised of the mayor and four commissioners who are elected for four-year terms. The commission passes ordinances and resolutions, adopts regulations, and appoints the city manager. The manager oversees the day-to-day workings of about 20 departments that provide such services as water supply and treatment, police protection, and street and bridge maintenance. Dayton covers nearly 60 square miles, has more than 166,000 residents, and an annual budget of about $155 million.

	Annual Growth	12/18	12/19	12/20	12/21	12/22
Sales ($mil.)	6.2%	–	236.3	256.5	273.6	283.1
Net income ($ mil.)	104.2%	–	6.3	27.0	43.6	53.5
Market value ($ mil.)	–	–	–	–	–	–
Employees	–	–	–	–	–	2,000

CITY OF DENTON

215 E MCKINNEY ST
DENTON, TX 762014229
Phone: 940 349-8200
Fax: –
Web: www.cityofdenton.com

CEO: –
CFO: –
HR: –
FYE: September 30
Type: Private

Texans who prefer a more laid-back atmosphere than Dallas or Houston can find a home in the City of Denton. The mayor and six city council members (elected for two-year terms) govern the city, which has a population of about 120,000. Founded in 1857 by lawyer and preacher, John Denton, the city is home to the University of North Texas (third-largest in the state with 40,000 students) and Texas Woman's University. Denton, which operates with an annual budget of about $550 million, has about 20 public schools, some 30 parks, and a public library with three branches.

	Annual Growth	09/17	09/18	09/19	09/20	09/21
Sales ($mil.)	2.7%	–	192.0	193.8	204.0	207.9
Net income ($ mil.)	(3.1%)	–	40.1	(0.6)	10.0	36.5
Market value ($ mil.)	–	–	–	–	–	–
Employees	–	–	–	–	–	1,000

CITY OF EL PASO

300 N CAMPBELL ST
EL PASO, TX 799011402
Phone: 915 212-0000
Fax: –
Web: www.elpasotexas.gov

CEO: –
CFO: –
HR: –
FYE: August 31
Type: Private

Out in the West Texas Town of El Paso, the sprawling metropolis is administered by the City of El Paso. The sixth-largest city in Texas with a population of about 650,000 (2.5 million in the region, including Ciudad Juárez, Mexico), El Paso is built around the base of the Franklin Mountains, across the Rio Grande from Juárez. Its city government consists of the mayor and eight council members (elected to four-year terms), along with a hired city manager. US Army post Fort Bliss and The University of Texas at El Paso are among the city's largest employers.

	Annual Growth	08/18	08/19	08/20	08/21	08/22
Sales ($mil.)	7.1%	–	–	679.7	827.8	780.0
Net income ($ mil.)	37.4%	–	–	83.2	121.0	156.9
Market value ($ mil.)	–	–	–	–	–	–
Employees	–	–	–	–	–	6,500

CITY OF FONTANA

8353 SIERRA AVE
FONTANA, CA 923353528
Phone: 909 350-7605
Fax: –
Web: www.fontanaca.gov

CEO: –
CFO: –
HR: Kimberly Clayton
FYE: June 30
Type: Private

Historic Route 66 runs through the heart of Fontana making it a major Southern California thoroughfare. Formerly an agricultural community, then a steel town, the city serves as a transportation hub with heavy industrial facilities and warehousing/distribution centers serving railroad and truck operations. Fontana supports a growing population of 150,000 by offering some of the most affordable housing in the area. It is governed by an elected mayor and four city council members. They appoint a city manager who runs four main departments, which oversee human resources, information technology, public works, and community development. The city's annual budget tops $200 million.

	Annual Growth	06/17	06/18	06/19	06/20	06/21
Sales ($mil.)	15.0%	–	220.7	233.1	241.2	335.7
Net income ($ mil.)	110.3%	–	10.1	29.7	8.8	94.2
Market value ($ mil.)	–	–	–	–	–	–
Employees	–	–	–	–	–	1,300

CITY OF FORT WAYNE

200 E BERRY ST STE 425
FORT WAYNE, IN 468022739
Phone: 260 427-1111
Fax: –
Web: www.cityoffortwayne.org

CEO: –
CFO: –
HR: –
FYE: December 31
Type: Private

Fort Wayne, Indiana, is the state's second-largest city after Indianapolis. Located in the northeast part of Indiana near the borders of Michigan and Ohio, and covering more than 110.7 square miles, the city counts more than 258,500 residents. The city has more than 1,380 miles of water lines and 1,302 miles of streets. As part of America's "Rust Belt," Fort Wayne has one Fortune 500 company, metal maker Steel Dynamics. Other major employers include insurance company Lincoln National and branches of defense contractors BAE Systems, Exelis, and Raytheon.

	Annual Growth	12/18	12/19	12/20	12/21	12/22
Sales ($mil.)	6.0%	–	298.3	371.9	332.7	355.5
Net income ($ mil.)	48.5%	–	15.9	29.1	38.3	52.1
Market value ($ mil.)	–	–	–	–	–	–
Employees	–	–	–	–	–	1,910

CITY OF FREMONT

3300 CAPITOL AVE
FREMONT, CA 945381514
Phone: 510 284-4000
Fax: –
Web: www.fremont.gov

CEO: –
CFO: –
HR: Tina Gallegos
FYE: June 30
Type: Private

Fremont, California, is a city located on the southeast side of San Francisco Bay about 25 miles south of Oakland. Fremont is home to about 215,000 residents. It is overseen by a mayor, an appointed city manager, and four elected city council members. Situated near Silicon Valley, Fremont is home to a number of tech companies. Major employers include Lam Research and branches of Tesla Motors and Western Digital.

	Annual Growth	06/18	06/19	06/20	06/21	06/22
Sales ($mil.)	4.0%	–	350.4	382.8	372.6	393.6
Net income ($ mil.)	4.0%	–	36.1	35.0	31.2	40.6
Market value ($ mil.)	–	–	–	–	–	–
Employees	–	–	–	–	–	1,000

CITY OF FRESNO

2600 FRESNO ST
FRESNO, CA 937213620
Phone: 559 621-7001
Fax: –
Web: www.fresno.gov

CEO: –
CFO: –
HR: –
FYE: June 30
Type: Private

Fresno (which means "ash" or "ash tree" in Spanish) is California's fifth-largest city. Located in the fertile San Joaquin Valley, Fresno counts about 500,000 residents in the city and about 940,000 residents across Fresno County. The City's residents represent more than 80 different nationalities. Centrally located, Fresno is the financial, industrial, trade, and commercial capital of the Central San Joaquin Valley. The area is home to many agricultural concerns, including Sun-Maid Raisins, Valley Fig Growers, and Zacky Farms. Fresno was founded by the Central Pacific Railroad Company in 1872.

	Annual Growth	06/18	06/19	06/20	06/21	06/22
Sales ($mil.)	15.4%	–	436.2	462.6	573.4	670.3
Net income ($ mil.)	23.6%	–	22.3	23.1	35.5	42.2
Market value ($ mil.)	–	–	–	–	–	–
Employees	–	–	–	–	–	2,600

CITY OF GARLAND

200 N 5TH ST
GARLAND, TX 750406314
Phone: 972 205-2000
Fax: –
Web: www.gpltexas.org

CEO: –
CFO: –
HR: Denise Fletcher
FYE: September 30
Type: Private

Garland is a city in North Texas considered part of the Dallas/ Fort Worth Metroplex. With a population of almost 230,000 people, the city is governed by a mayor, an appointed city manager, and eight city council members. Garland was incorporated in 1891 and is named after 19th century US Attorney General Augustus Hill Garland. Its top employer is military contractor Raytheon.

	Annual Growth	09/18	09/19	09/20	09/21	09/22
Sales ($mil.)	8.2%	–	227.5	256.5	258.5	288.0
Net income ($ mil.)	–	–	(6.1)	22.9	0.7	17.0
Market value ($ mil.)	–	–	–	–	–	–
Employees	–	–	–	–	–	2,000

CITY OF GLENDALE

141 N GLENDALE AVE FL 2
GLENDALE, CA 912064975
Phone: 818 548-2085
Fax: –
Web: www.glendaleca.gov

CEO: –
CFO: –
HR: –
FYE: June 30
Type: Private

Glendale, California (not to be confused with Glendale, Arizona) is a suburb of Los Angeles. The city encompasses about 30 square miles of land, and with a population of more than 190,000, it's the third-largest city in Los Angeles County. Mostly a bedroom community, Glendale's two largest employers are hospitals, Glendale Adventist and Glendale Memorial.

	Annual Growth	06/18	06/19	06/20	06/21	06/22
Sales ($mil.)	2.4%	–	363.1	354.6	374.4	390.2
Net income ($ mil.)	(12.7%)	–	62.9	3.8	39.2	41.8
Market value ($ mil.)	–	–	–	–	–	–
Employees	–	–	–	–	–	2,000

CITY OF GLENDALE

5850 W GLENDALE AVE FL 4
GLENDALE, AZ 853012599
Phone: 623 930-2000
Fax: –
Web: www.glendaleaz.com

CEO: –
CFO: –
HR: –
FYE: June 30
Type: Private

There are more than a dozen cities in the US named Glendale, but Glendale, Arizona, is the largest. A suburb of Phoenix, Glendale has more than 250,000 residents, and is one of the many cities that make up Maricopa County. The city is governed by a mayor, an appointed city manager, and six city council members. Glendale was settled in the late 1800s after a canal was built.

	Annual Growth	06/18	06/19	06/20	06/21	06/22
Sales ($mil.)	4.3%	–	331.5	376.1	406.7	376.1
Net income ($ mil.)	–	–	(6.4)	24.0	73.8	24.0
Market value ($ mil.)	–	–	–	–	–	–
Employees	–	–	–	–	–	1,000

CITY OF GREENSBORO

300 W WASHINGTON ST
GREENSBORO, NC 274012624
Phone: 336 373-2002
Fax: –
Web: www.greensboro-nc.gov

CEO: –
CFO: –
HR: Anne Howerton
FYE: June 30
Type: Private

Greensboro is the third-largest city in North Carolina (behind Charlotte and Raleigh), with a population of about 275,000 people. The city government is organized in the style of council-manager, where the city manager heads executive affairs and the mayor and eight council members make up the legislative body. Greensboro is home to two Fortune 1000 companies -- apparel manufacturer V.F. Corporation and tobacco maker Lorillard.

	Annual Growth	06/18	06/19	06/20	06/21	06/22
Sales ($mil.)	7.1%	–	327.0	342.4	376.8	401.2
Net income ($ mil.)	–	–	77.6	6.2	(23.2)	(27.7)
Market value ($ mil.)	–	–	–	–	–	–
Employees	–	–	–	–	–	2,650

CITY OF HENDERSON

240 S WATER ST
HENDERSON, NV 890157227
Phone: 702 267-2323
Fax: –
Web: www.cityofhenderson.com

CEO: –
CFO: –
HR: Christine Scott
FYE: June 30
Type: Private

Henderson, Nevada, may be a suburb of Las Vegas, but it's a far cry from Sin City, with its focus on arts, galleries, recreational venues, and a host of family friendly activities. With a population of more than 277,400, Henderson is the state's second-largest city. It is governed by a mayor and four city council members. Situated more than a mile high, the high desert city gets less than six inches of rainfall per year. Founded in 1941 Henderson quickly became a main supplier of magnesium to the US military through its Basic Magnesium Plant (which closed after WWII). The City of Henderson was founded in 1953.

	Annual Growth	06/18	06/19	06/20	06/21	06/22
Sales ($mil.)	8.1%	–	368.0	358.8	418.3	464.8
Net income ($ mil.)	19.4%	–	42.2	75.8	(17.7)	71.8
Market value ($ mil.)	–	–	–	–	–	–
Employees	–	–	–	–	–	3,775

CITY OF HIALEAH

501 PALM AVE
HIALEAH, FL 330104719
Phone: 305 883-8075
Fax: –
Web: www.hialeahfl.gov

CEO: –
CFO: –
HR: Dayli Mesa
FYE: September 30
Type: Private

Hialeah, a suburb of Miami, is located in Miami-Dade County and is Florida's fifth-largest city. Its population of more than 235,000 residents lives in only 20 sq. mi. of land. Hialeah is governed by a mayor and seven city council members. While Native Americans lives in the area for centuries, the city of Hialeah was incorporated in 1925.

	Annual Growth	09/15	09/16	09/17	09/18	09/19
Sales ($mil.)	6.0%	–	179.6	185.3	200.2	213.9
Net income ($ mil.)	(29.6%)	–	32.7	5.7	9.7	11.4
Market value ($ mil.)	–	–	–	–	–	–
Employees	–	–	–	–	–	1,800

CITY OF HOUSTON

901 BAGBY ST
HOUSTON, TX 770022049
Phone: 201 581-6104
Fax: –
Web: www.houstontx.gov

CEO: –
CFO: Tantri Emo
HR: Ceasar De La Rosa
FYE: June 30
Type: Private

It is bigger in Texas when you consider the City of Houston. As the largest city in the state and one of the largest cities nationwide, Houston is more than an oil town. Founded in 1836 and home to Rice University and the Astros, it also has a noteworthy museum district and operates the Texas Medical Center, one of the world's largest health care facilities. While a mayor oversees Houston's management, 14 council members (elected for two-year terms) have the power to enact and enforce city ordinances. With a population of more than 2 million, Houston operates through some 20 departments, including health and human services, police, and parks and recreation. It has an annual budget of about $2 billion.

	Annual Growth	06/16	06/17	06/18	06/19	06/22
Sales ($mil.)	51.3%	–	494.0	3,110.5	3,253.3	3,920.8
Net income ($ mil.)	2.8%	–	128.1	52.3	98.4	146.9
Market value ($ mil.)	–	–	–	–	–	–
Employees	–	–	–	–	–	23,235

CITY OF INDEPENDENCE

111 E MAPLE AVE
INDEPENDENCE, MO 640503066
Phone: 816 325-7000
Fax: –
Web: www.independencemo.gov

CEO: –
CFO: –
HR: –
FYE: June 30
Type: Private

The City of Independence is the fourth-largest city in Missouri with a population of about 115,000. Governed by the mayor and six city council members, the city operates through some 20 departments, including health, tourism, and water pollution control. The city of Independence, founded by Missouri's General Assembly in 1827, has an annual budget of about $66 million. In the early 1830s, 2,000 Mormon settlers followed leader Joseph Smith to live in Independence, which he considered the site of Zion. Residents of the city forced the Mormons to leave by 1833.

	Annual Growth	06/17	06/18	06/19	06/20	06/21
Sales ($mil.)	3.8%	–	106.5	105.9	106.3	119.1
Net income ($ mil.)	175.5%	–	0.1	2.2	23.6	2.4
Market value ($ mil.)	–	–	–	–	–	–
Employees	–	–	–	–	–	1,100

CITY OF IRVING

825 W IRVING BLVD
IRVING, TX 750602860
Phone: 972 721-2600
Fax: –
Web: www.cityofirving.org

CEO: –
CFO: Jeff Spivey
HR: Sotelo Miguel
FYE: September 30
Type: Private

This city makes up the Dallas-Plano-Irving metropolitan division, which is part of the larger Dallas-Fort Worth Metroplex. With a population of more than 220,000, the City of Irving covers approximately 68 square miles. It contains Las Colinas, a developed area founded in 1972 by cattle ranching millionaire Ben H. Carpenter. Las Colinas is known for its landmark office towers, luxury hotels, private country clubs, and gated residencies. Irving's city government consists of its mayor, eight council members (serving three-year terms), and a city manager.

	Annual Growth	09/18	09/19	09/20	09/21	09/22
Sales ($mil.)	6.2%	–	342.3	329.2	365.6	410.4
Net income ($ mil.)	–	–	(30.8)	(11.4)	34.5	109.0
Market value ($ mil.)	–	–	–	–	–	–
Employees	–	–	–	–	–	1,635

CITY OF JACKSONVILLE

117 W DUVAL ST
JACKSONVILLE, FL 322023700
Phone: 904 630-1776
Fax: –
Web: www.coj.net

CEO: –
CFO: –
HR: –
FYE: September 30
Type: Private

In Jacksonville, residents and visitors can enjoy the Florida wilderness. The city, which offers some 57,000 acres of parks, provides more land for recreation than any other city in the US. Its 19 city council members (five at-large members and 14 representing geographic districts) enact the legislation for the Jacksonville. Elected for four-year terms, the mayor oversees the administration of the central government and appoints directors for its 10 departments. The 14th-largest city in the US, Jacksonville has a population of more than 850,000 residents.

	Annual Growth	09/14	09/15	09/16	09/17	09/18
Sales ($mil.)	4.2%	–	1,414.1	1,493.3	1,560.4	1,599.4
Net income ($ mil.)	8.7%	–	50.3	33.7	12.8	64.7
Market value ($ mil.)	–	–	–	–	–	–
Employees	–	–	–	–	–	7,908

CITY OF JERSEY CITY

280 GROVE ST
JERSEY CITY, NJ 073023610
Phone: 201 547-5000
Fax: –
Web: www.jerseycitynj.gov

CEO: –
CFO: –
HR: –
FYE: December 31
Type: Private

Sitting on the western bank of the Hudson River, Jersey City has a population of more than 262,000 and covers approximately 21 square miles. New Jersey's second-largest city (behind Newark) and part of the larger New York metropolitan area, it is a commercial and industrial center, as well as a port of entry. Historic Ellis Island is situated within its borders and is jointly managed by the states of New Jersey and New York. Jersey City boasts communities of Jewish, Italian, Cuban, Filipino, Polish, Indian, Irish, Puerto Rican, Dominican, African, Arab, and Asian decent. City government consists of a mayor and nine city council members.

CITY OF LAREDO

1110 HOUSTON ST
LAREDO, TX 780408019
Phone: 956 791-7308
Fax: –
Web: www.cityoflaredo.com

CEO: –
CFO: –
HR: Linda Teniente
FYE: September 30
Type: Private

Laredo is Texas' 10 th -largest city. Located right across the Rio Grande River from Nuevo Laredo, Mexico, the city has a population of more than 235,000. Due to its location along the border, Laredo is a major point of entry for trade between Mexico and the US. The area's major employers are government agencies, such as those with the local school district, city, Webb County, and US Border Patrol.

	Annual Growth	09/15	09/16	09/17	09/18	09/20
Sales ($mil.)	2.3%	–	280.4	281.8	291.9	306.9
Net income ($ mil.)	4.6%	–	14.0	(8.6)	17.7	16.8
Market value ($ mil.)	–	–	–	–	–	–
Employees	–	–	–	–	–	2,100

CITY OF LAS VEGAS

495 S MAIN ST
LAS VEGAS, NV 891012986
Phone: 702 229-6321
Fax: –
Web: www.lasvegasnevada.gov

CEO: –
CFO: –
HR: –
FYE: June 30
Type: Private

Some 585,000 people call Sin City home. Las Vegas, Nevada's largest city, is the gaming capital of the US. The city is overseen by a mayor, an appointed city manager, and six elected city council members. Its largest industry is tourism; the casino resorts attract visitors seeking business and pleasure -- Las Vegas hosts almost 20,000 conventions every year.

	Annual Growth	06/18	06/19	06/20	06/21	06/22
Sales ($mil.)	5.9%	–	857.7	999.2	967.3	1,020.1
Net income ($ mil.)	36.6%	–	58.9	(95.0)	55.3	150.0
Market value ($ mil.)	–	–	–	–	–	–
Employees	–	–	–	–	–	2,500

CITY OF LINCOLN

555 S 10TH ST RM B115
LINCOLN, NE 685082803
Phone: 402 441-7511
Fax: –
Web: lincoln.ne.gov

CEO: –
CFO: –
HR: Gail Anderson
FYE: August 31
Type: Private

Welcome to Cornhusker nation. Lincoln is Nebraska's second-largest city (behind Omaha) with a population of more than 255,000 people. Of course, the University of Nebraska is located in Lincoln. The city is also the state capital, and the state of Nebraska is the city's top employer. Other government agencies, such as the school system, the city, and the federal government, are also major employers.

	Annual Growth	08/18	08/19	08/20	08/21	08/22
Sales ($mil.)	7.9%	–	349.9	365.4	423.4	439.4
Net income ($ mil.)	–	–	(23.6)	7.4	92.9	22.5
Market value ($ mil.)	–	–	–	–	–	–
Employees	–	–	–	–	–	2,000

CITY OF LONG BEACH

1800 E WARDLOW RD
LONG BEACH, CA 908074931
Phone: 562 570-6450
Fax: –
Web: www.longbeach.gov

CEO: –
CFO: –
HR: Vickie Gordon
FYE: September 30
Type: Private

It's a city, it's a port, it's Long Beach. The City of Long Beach boasts the Port of Long Beach, one of the busiest ports in the nation. With a population of more than 460,000, Long Beach is part of the greater Los Angeles metropolitan area. The city uses a charter form of government with an elected mayor and city council, as well as an appointed city manager. It's also known for its large oil reserves managed by the Long Beach Gas & Oil Department.

	Annual Growth	09/16	09/17	09/18	09/19	09/20
Sales ($mil.)	6.9%	–	–	779.1	864.6	889.8
Net income ($ mil.)	(13.8%)	–	–	26.6	36.8	19.8
Market value ($ mil.)	–	–	–	–	–	–
Employees	–	–	–	–	–	5,028

CITY OF LOS ANGELES

200 N SPRING ST STE 303
LOS ANGELES, CA 900123239
Phone: 213 978-0600
Fax: –
Web: www.lacity.org

CEO: –
CFO: –
HR: –
FYE: June 30
Type: Private

Los Angeles may be a Mecca for the rich and famous, but there is little glamour in running a city of more than 4 million people. Governing responsibilities are shared among the city's mayor and city council, while various commissions, departments, and bureaus see to the daily operations that keep the wheels spinning. Elected every four years, the mayor appoints most commission members (subject to approval by the city council) and serves as the city's executive officer. The City of Los Angeles is located in the County of Los Angeles.

	Annual Growth	12/06	12/07	12/08*	06/09	06/16
Sales ($mil.)	217.6%	–	–	0.7	6,281.3	7,196.2
Net income ($ mil.)	–	–	–	–	(285.4)	231.1
Market value ($ mil.)	–	–	–	–	–	–
Employees	–	–	–	–	–	41,000

*Fiscal year change

CITY OF LUBBOCK

1314 AVENUE K
LUBBOCK, TX 794014051
Phone: 806 775-2016
Fax: –
Web: ci.lubbock.tx.us

CEO: –
CFO: –
HR: Freddy Chavez
FYE: September 30
Type: Private

Lubbock or leave it! Famous as the home to Texas Tech and rock and roll legend Buddy Holly, the City of Lubbock is located in northwest Texas at the center of the area known as the South Plains. Main industries within the region include agriculture (primarily cotton), ranching, oil and gas mining, and manufacturing. Lubbock has a population of about 238,000 and is governed by a council-manager system consisting of a seven- person city council headed by the mayor and its city manager. The City was formed in 1890 and named after a former Texas Ranger and Confederate officer.

	Annual Growth	09/18	09/19	09/20	09/21	09/22
Sales ($mil.)	11.2%	–	254.1	298.8	317.1	349.4
Net income ($ mil.)	–	–	36.0	6.0	22.9	(17.1)
Market value ($ mil.)	–	–	–	–	–	–
Employees	–	–	–	–	–	2,700

CITY OF MADISON

210 MARTIN LUTHER KING JR BLVD
MADISON, WI 537033341
Phone: 608 266-4671
Fax: –
Web: www.cityofmadison.com

CEO: –
CFO: –
HR: –
FYE: December 31
Type: Private

Named for the forth president of the United States, James Madison, Madison, Wisconsin is located in the southern part of the state. It is the second largest city in Wisconsin, behind Milwaukee, and is the state's capital. The City of Madison is governed by a mayor and city council composed of 20 alders that each represents a district. The city was incorporated in 1856.

	Annual Growth	12/17	12/18	12/19	12/20	12/21
Sales ($mil.)	5.0%	–	383.6	408.0	398.0	443.9
Net income ($ mil.)	–	–	(22.7)	(14.4)	57.0	28.5
Market value ($ mil.)	–	–	–	–	–	–
Employees	–	–	–	–	–	2,918

CITY OF MEMPHIS

125 N MAIN ST STE 628
MEMPHIS, TN 381032032
Phone: 901 676-6657
Fax: –
Web: www.memphistn.gov

CEO: –
CFO: Shirley Ford
HR: Hubert Mays
FYE: June 30
Type: Private

Home to Graceland and Beale Street, Memphis has both feet entrenched in the world of music. With a population of more than 670,000, it is located in the southwestern corner of the state and stretches over 300 square miles. Serving the largest urban population in Tennessee, it is run by a mayor and 13 city council members (elected from nine districts). City government is responsible for economic development, public education, housing, public utilities, homeland security, and landmark preservation. Set atop the eastern bank of the Mississippi River and named after the ancient capital of Egypt, Memphis was founded in 1820.

	Annual Growth	06/12	06/13	06/14	06/15	06/16
Sales ($mil.)	2.3%	–	845.8	840.9	863.4	906.5
Net income ($ mil.)		–	–	(25.0)	26.6	1.4	8.0
Market value ($ mil.)		–	–	–	–	–
Employees		–	–	–	–	6,000

CITY OF MESA

20 E MAIN ST
MESA, AZ 852017425
Phone: 480 644-2011
Fax: –
Web: www.mesaaz.gov

CEO: –
CFO: –
HR: –
FYE: June 30
Type: Private

This city, which literally covers a "mesa" or plateau, stands roughly 100 feet higher than Phoenix and spreads across 130 square miles. With a population of more than 468,000, the City of Mesa is the third-largest city in Arizona, behind Phoenix and Tucson. Its city government consists of the mayor, six city council members (elected to four-year terms), and a city manager. Mesa is also home to the Chicago Cubs baseball team during spring training. The city was founded in 1878 by Mormon (Latter-day Saint or LDS) pioneers, who gave it its name; Mesa still has a large Mormon population. It was incorporated in 1883.

	Annual Growth	06/18	06/19	06/20	06/21	06/22
Sales ($mil.)	14.7%	–	539.1	646.2	725.8	814.5
Net income ($ mil.)	6.8%	–	50.1	89.6	176.0	61.1
Market value ($ mil.)	–	–	–	–	–	–
Employees	–	–	–	–	–	4,068

CITY OF MIAMI

3500 PAN AMERICAN DR FL 2
MIAMI, FL 331335595
Phone: 305 250-5300
Fax: –
Web: www.miamigov.com

CEO: –
CFO: –
HR: Angela V Roberts V
FYE: September 30
Type: Private

Thankfully, the City of Miami is much more than Dolphins, sound-machines, and vice cops. With a population of more than 400,000 the city has little trouble attracting tourists and residents alike to the bustling international hub of business, entertainment, and culture. Thanks to its status as a transportation hub and the businesses that make the city home to international operations, the city is also known as the Gateway to Latin America. The city government consists of its elected mayor, five commissioners, a city manager, and the heads of Miami's various public services departments.

	Annual Growth	09/07	09/08	09/09	09/12	09/15
Sales ($mil.)	2.3%	–	–	691.3	675.2	792.7
Net income ($ mil.)	–	–	–	(30.2)	(18.6)	(1.7)
Market value ($ mil.)	–	–	–	–	–	–
Employees	–	–	–	–	–	3,000

CITY OF MINNEAPOLIS

350 S 5TH ST
MINNEAPOLIS, MN 554151316
Phone: 612 673-3000
Fax: –
Web: www.minneapolismn.gov

CEO: –
CFO: –
HR: –
FYE: December 31
Type: Private

One half of Minnesota's famed Twin Cities, Minneapolis is a combination of the Sioux word for water with the Greek word for city. With 20 lakes and wetlands plus the Mississippi River waterfront and many creeks and streams, the City of Minneapolis is known as the City of Lakes. It is governed by a mayor and city council with 13 members representing the city's wards. The mayor appoints the chief of police but has little other power. Independent boards oversee public housing, the tax office, and public parks and libraries. The city's more than 80 parks serve as a model for city park systems nationwide. Formed in 1856, Minneapolis is now home to a population of almost 400,000.

	Annual Growth	12/17	12/18	12/19	12/20	12/21
Sales ($mil.)	(1.6%)	–	858.1	916.4	903.3	817.3
Net income ($ mil.)	–	–	84.0	85.5	(21.4)	(22.9)
Market value ($ mil.)	–	–	–	–	–	–
Employees	–	–	–	–	–	5,000

CITY OF MODESTO

1010 10TH ST STE 5200
MODESTO, CA 953540869
Phone: 209 577-5387
Fax: –
Web: www.modestogov.com

CEO: –
CFO: –
HR: Dawn Kelley
FYE: June 30
Type: Private

With a population of 210,000, Modesto is a modest-sized city in California. Located about 90 miles east of San Francisco in central California, Modesto has many agricultural companies due to its prime spot in the fertile San Joaquin Valley. Major employers include the world's largest family-owned winemaker, E&J Gallo, as well as branches of Del Monte and Seneca Foods.

	Annual Growth	06/18	06/19	06/20	06/21	06/22
Sales ($mil.)	13.4%	–	190.5	236.0	260.2	278.0
Net income ($ mil.)	–	–	(2.6)	17.0	27.0	22.8
Market value ($ mil.)	–	–	–	–	–	–
Employees	–	–	–	–	–	1,200

CITY OF MONTGOMERY

103 N PERRY ST
MONTGOMERY, AL 361043728
Phone: 334 625-2025
Fax: –
Web: www.montgomeryal.gov

CEO: –
CFO: –
HR: –
FYE: September 30
Type: Private

Montgomery is the state capital of Alabama, and with a population of about 205,000, it's the second-largest city (behind Birmingham). Government jobs with the state and the public school system employ many residents, but the city's largest employer is the Maxwell Air Force Base. Montgomery is also home to Hyundai Motor Manufacturing Alabama, the Korean automaker's only US plant.

	Annual Growth	09/18	09/19	09/20	09/21	09/22
Sales ($mil.)	5.2%	–	277.7	284.3	311.7	323.7
Net income ($ mil.)	139.5%	–	1.8	10.8	77.9	24.6
Market value ($ mil.)	–	–	–	–	–	–
Employees	–	–	–	–	–	2,895

CITY OF NEW ORLEANS

1300 PERDIDO ST BSMT W05
NEW ORLEANS, LA 701122112
Phone: 504 658-4900
Fax: –
Web: www.nola.gov

CEO: –
CFO: –
HR: Charles Goldsborough
FYE: December 31
Type: Private

New Orleans is a city with a story. The city was founded in 1718 and became famous for its architecture, music, food, and parties. The city is home to a major port, the New Orleans Saints, the French Quarter, and is the regarded as the birthplace of jazz. Devastated by Hurricane Katrina and the flooding which ensued in 2005, the city has undertaken a massive rebuilding and recovery effort utilizing state and federal assistance. The city of New Orleans is governed by a city council consisting of seven members and an elected mayor.

CITY OF NEW YORK

CITY HALL PARK
NEW YORK, NY 10007
Phone: 212 788-3000
Fax: –
Web: www.nyc.gov

CEO: –
CFO: –
HR: –
FYE: June 30
Type: Private

The City That Never Sleeps, the Big Apple, Gotham -- NYC by any name is a unique place. With a population of 8.2 million packed into more than 300 square miles, New York City is run by the mayor and 51 city council members (elected to four-year terms) along with the public advocate, comptroller, and presidents of the five boroughs. The city government is responsible for welfare services, public education, water supply/sanitation, correctional institutions, recreational facilities, public safety, and libraries. It uses about $65 to $70 billion a year to manage those departments. First settled by Europeans around 1614, New York took its current name when the English conquered it in 1664.

	Annual Growth	06/16	06/17	06/18	06/20	06/22
Sales ($mil.)	4.9%	–	–	90,569	98,236	109,744
Net income ($ mil.)	–	–	–	1,348.6	819.9	(147.4)
Market value ($ mil.)	–	–	–	–	–	–
Employees	–	–	–	–	–	310,000

CITY OF NEWPORT NEWS

2400 WASHINGTON AVE
NEWPORT NEWS, VA 236074300
Phone: 757 926-8411
Fax: –
Web: www.newportnewshistory.org

CEO: –
CFO: –
HR: –
FYE: June 30
Type: Private

There are nearly as many theories on where the unusual city name came from as there are citizens of Newport News, Virginia. Whether it was founded on land chosen by Sir William Newce or the point where Captain Newport delivered good news to early settlers, Newport News today boasts a population of some 193,000. The mayor and six-member city council (representing three districts) work together to serve residents and visitors backed by an annual budget of about $750 million. The council sets up city policies and controls funding while the city manager, attorney, and clerk carry out the day-to-day administration of Newport News. The city, which was settled around 1621, is well known as a military shipbuilding hub.

	Annual Growth	06/18	06/19	06/20	06/21	06/22
Sales ($mil.)	5.3%	–	603.0	598.6	653.1	703.4
Net income ($ mil.)	(4.8%)	–	50.4	(30.6)	99.6	43.5
Market value ($ mil.)	–	–	–	–	–	–
Employees	–	–	–	–	–	5,000

CITY OF NEWTON

1000 CMMWL AVE NEWTON CTR
NEWTON, MA 02459
Phone: 617 796-1200
Fax: –
Web: www.newtonma.gov

CEO: –
CFO: –
HR: –
FYE: June 30
Type: Private

It takes more than a village to comprise Newton, Massachusetts. A suburb of Boston, Newton Massachusetts consists of 13 villages home to about 84,000 residents. The area was settled in 1630 and after a number of name changes the city finally named newton in 1766 (it was actually incorporated in 1873). The city's biggest claim to fame (arguably) is the fact that the fig newton was named for the city by the Kennedy Biscuit Company. The city government consists of a city council, called the Board of Aldermen and the elected mayor. The Board of Aldermen is made up of 24 members who are elected every two years.

	Annual Growth	06/11	06/12	06/13	06/14	06/16
Sales ($mil.)	3.8%	–	368.0	389.0	–	427.5
Net income ($ mil.)	–	–	(1.7)	3.0	7.3	31.1
Market value ($ mil.)	–	–	–	–	–	–
Employees	–	–	–	–	–	3,000

CITY OF NORFOLK

810 UNION ST STE 508
NORFOLK, VA 235108048
Phone: 757 664-7300
Fax: –
Web: www.norfolk.gov

CEO: –
CFO: –
HR: Kiwania Dennis
FYE: June 30
Type: Private

You could say that the City of Norfolk, Virginia, is at home on the water. The second-largest city in Virginia with a population of more than 245,400, Norfolk sports miles of lake, river, and bay front as well as a bustling international port and the world's largest naval base. The city was founded in 1682 and offers such attractions as the battleship USS Wisconsin , the National Maritime Center, and Old Dominion University. Norfolk Southern Railway's corporate headquarters are also located in the city. Norfolk city government consists of its seven-member city council and mayor. The city manager serves as the city's COO and is appointed by the city council.

	Annual Growth	06/18	06/19	06/20	06/21	06/22
Sales ($mil.)	6.5%	–	751.1	749.5	835.8	906.5
Net income ($ mil.)	(1.6%)	–	162.4	(16.0)	28.3	154.9
Market value ($ mil.)	–	–	–	–	–	–
Employees	–	–	–	–	–	4,364

CITY OF OAKLAND

1 FRANK H OGAWA PLZ
OAKLAND, CA 946121904
Phone: 510 238-3280
Fax: –
Web: www.oaklandca.gov

CEO: –
CFO: –
HR: Lisette D Pino
FYE: June 30
Type: Private

Joining San Francisco and San Jose, Oakland makes up one-third of Northern California's Golden Triangle . Founded in 1852, Oakland boasts of a diverse population, numbering more than 390,000 residents, a Mediterranean climate and thriving hip arts scene. The city is a hub for the port of San Francisco Bay, as well as for the business elite and the higher educated. Environmental policies have helped propel Oakland to stand among the top green economies in the US. The city is served by a mayor and eight council members, who oversee a budget of almost $1 billion. It is home to the NBA's Golden State Warriors, NFL's Oakland Raiders and national landmark, Lake Merritt.

	Annual Growth	06/18	06/19	06/20	06/21	06/22
Sales ($mil.)	6.7%	–	1,211.7	1,239.9	1,401.1	1,470.0
Net income ($ mil.)	116.8%	–	28.2	163.1	(13.1)	288.0
Market value ($ mil.)	–	–	–	–	–	–
Employees	–	–	–	–	–	4,000

CITY OF OKLAHOMA CITY

100 N WALKER AVE
OKLAHOMA CITY, OK 731022230
Phone: 405 297-2506
Fax: -
Web: www.okc.gov

CEO: -
CFO: -
HR: -
FYE: June 30
Type: Private

Oklahoma City was born overnight as a boomtown named Oklahoma Station in 1889 during the celebrated land rush in Oklahoma Territory. It became in time the state capital and largest city (with a population approaching 600,000) and is headquarters of oil and gas companies Chesapeake Energy and Devon Energy as well as electric utility OGE Energy and service station operator Love's Truck Stops. City government is headed by a mayor and council members representing eight wards. The city captured its first top-rank sports franchise when the Oklahoma City Thunder NBA team began play in 2008.

	Annual Growth	06/16	06/17	06/18	06/21	06/22
Sales ($mil.)	5.6%	-	806.1	865.8	1,031.4	1,056.7
Net income ($ mil.)	-	-	(21.6)	112.4	157.4	103.5
Market value ($ mil.)	-	-	-	-	-	-
Employees	-	-	-	-	-	4,500

CITY OF OMAHA

1819 FARNAM ST RM 300
OMAHA, NE 681831000
Phone: 402 444-5000
Fax: -
Web: www.cityofomaha.org

CEO: -
CFO: -
HR: -
FYE: December 31
Type: Private

Owing it name to one the tribes living in the area, the City Omaha was once bypassed by the Lewis and Clark expedition. Founded in 1854, Omaha has become the 42nd largest city in the U.S. with a population of almost 409,000 in an area measuring little more than 130 square miles. The city is ruled by a mayor-council consisting of of an "at-large" mayor and 7 district councilmembers. The City of Omaha is home for megacompanies Berkshire Hathaway, ConAgra, Peter Kiewit Sons, Mutual of Omaha, TD Ameritrade, Union Pacific, West Corporation, Valmont Industries, and Werner Enterprises.

	Annual Growth	12/17	12/18	12/19	12/20	12/21
Sales ($mil.)	10.7%	-	593.4	636.3	707.8	805.7
Net income ($ mil.)	-	-	(29.1)	1.3	4.8	44.2
Market value ($ mil.)	-	-	-	-	-	-
Employees	-	-	-	-	-	2,800

CITY OF ORLANDO

1 CITY CMMONS 400 S ORNGE
ORLANDO, FL 32801
Phone: 407 246-2121
Fax: -
Web: www.orlando.gov

CEO: -
CFO: -
HR: -
FYE: September 30
Type: Private

The City of Orlando offers its own fountain of youth for tourists from around the globe. The young and the young at heart all flock to Orlando, home to Disney World and other popular theme parks. The fast-growing Orlando, which is in the geographic center of Florida, offers a wide variety of attractions for kids of all ages, including Sea World, Universal Studios, and Epcot. The mayor and six city commissioners (elected for four-year terms) make up its city council, which enacts policy for Orlando. Warm and sunny year-round, the city has over 240,000 residents. Incorporated in 1885, the City of Orlando, which operates through some 50 departments, has an annual budget of more than $950 million.

	Annual Growth	09/14	09/15	09/16	09/17	09/21
Sales ($mil.)	8.0%	-	493.7	556.6	567.7	783.2
Net income ($ mil.)	-	-	77.3	26.7	17.5	(9.1)
Market value ($ mil.)	-	-	-	-	-	-
Employees	-	-	-	-	-	3,000

CITY OF OXNARD

300 W 3RD ST
OXNARD, CA 930305729
Phone: 805 385-7803
Fax: -
Web: www.oxnard.org

CEO: -
CFO: -
HR: -
FYE: June 30
Type: Private

If California is truly full of fruits and nuts, then Oxnard supplies much of the former. The City of Oxnard's economy is driven by agricultural (including a huge annual strawberry crop), as well as international trade, defense, manufacturing, and tourism. It has a council-manager form of government. The city council -- comprised of a mayor, mayor pro tem, and three council members -- establishes city policies. The city manager supports the needs of the council, implements council directives, and manages the day-to-day operations of some 15 departments. Incorporated in 1903, Oxnard is the largest city in Ventura County. It's located some 60 miles northwest of Los Angeles and has a population of about 200,000.

	Annual Growth	06/18	06/19	06/20	06/21	06/22
Sales ($mil.)	11.1%	-	219.4	209.1	252.9	301.0
Net income ($ mil.)	88.9%	-	8.3	3.3	(12.3)	56.0
Market value ($ mil.)	-	-	-	-	-	-
Employees	-	-	-	-	-	1,100

CITY OF PEORIA

8401 W MONROE ST
PEORIA, AZ 853456560
Phone: 623 773-7148
Fax: -
Web: www.peoriaaz.gov

CEO: -
CFO: -
HR: Carol Johnson
FYE: June 30
Type: Private

Peoria, Arizona was established in the 1880s based on the vision of William J. Murphy to use water from the Salt River to create fertile farm lands in Arizona. After the completion of the Arizona Canal, Murphy went east to sell his vision eventually convincing four families from Peoria, Illinois to make the move and establish the farming community. Now considered a suburb of Phoenix, Peoria has a population of about 120,000 and is growing steadily. The ninth largest city in Arizona, Peoria's six-person city council and mayor set policy and serve the legislative role for the city, the City Manager oversees daily operations and acts as the city's CEO.

	Annual Growth	06/18	06/19	06/20	06/21	06/22
Sales ($mil.)	8.2%	-	231.3	259.6	269.8	292.7
Net income ($ mil.)	13.0%	-	36.6	(16.0)	18.1	52.8
Market value ($ mil.)	-	-	-	-	-	-
Employees	-	-	-	-	-	1,600

CITY OF PHILADELPHIA

215 CITY HALL
PHILADELPHIA, PA 191073214
Phone: 215 686-2181
Fax: -
Web: www.phila.gov

CEO: -
CFO: -
HR: Joan Wilson
FYE: June 30
Type: Private

Known as the City of Brotherly Love, Philadelphia is the fifth largest city in the nation, with a population of more than 1.5 million. The city, which covers 135 square miles, operates through some 50 departments, boards, offices, and other units that include emergency medical services, sanitation services, and street maintenance. Founded in 1682 by William Penn, Philadelphia has a mayor, 10 districts and 17 council members. The city, which hosts millions of tourists each year, is home to the Phillies, the Eagles, the Flyers, the 76ers, Bryn Mawr College, the Liberty Bell, and the National Constitution Center. The City of Philadelphia has an annual budget of more than $3.5 billion.

	Annual Growth	06/13	06/14	06/15	06/16	06/17
Sales ($mil.)	3.8%	-	5,947.1	6,070.8	6,264.8	6,646.5
Net income ($ mil.)	-	-	(10.1)	(92.2)	(65.0)	20.8
Market value ($ mil.)	-	-	-	-	-	-
Employees	-	-	-	-	-	29,862

CITY OF PHOENIX

200 W WASHINGTON ST FL 11
PHOENIX, AZ 850031611
Phone: 602 262-7111
Fax: –
Web: www.phoenix.gov

CEO: –
CFO: –
HR: Courtney Rogers
FYE: June 30
Type: Private

Phoenix, the capital of Arizona, has a population of about 1.4 million and is the sixth largest city in the US. Located in the south-central portion of the state, Phoenix covers a sprawling 500 square miles and is geographically larger than Los Angeles. The City of Phoenix operates through some 30 departments, including street transportation, water services, human services, and public transit. Eight city council members (representing eight districts) and the mayor make up the city council, which develop laws and policy for governing the city. Phoenix was incorporated in 1881.

	Annual Growth	06/18	06/19	06/20	06/21	06/22
Sales ($mil.)	11.1%	–	2,588.3	2,786.5	3,384.1	3,551.3
Net income ($ mil.)	(59.5%)	–	54.4	27.8	260.0	3.6
Market value ($ mil.)	–	–	–	–	–	–
Employees	–	–	–	–	–	14,000

CITY OF PITTSBURGH

414 GRANT ST
PITTSBURGH, PA 152192409
Phone: 412 255-2640
Fax: –
Web: www.pittsburghpa.gov

CEO: –
CFO: –
HR: Denise Demarco
FYE: December 31
Type: Private

Take one look at the skyline and it's no wonder Pittsburgh's been nicknamed "The City of Bridges." With more than 440 bridges, 150 skyscrapers, and a countless number of steel behemoths, Pittsburgh is Pennsylvania's second largest city (behind Philadelphia) with a population of more than 305,700. The city is composed of nine districts, each represented by a council member, while the mayor rounds out the executive side. Its annual budget goes toward enhancements to health care and retirement as well as hiring police and fire prevention personnel; most of its revenue comes from real estate taxes. Pittsburgh was founded in 1758.

	Annual Growth	12/17	12/18	12/19	12/21	12/22
Sales ($mil.)	(81.3%)	–	635.6	651.7	705.9	0.8
Net income ($ mil.)	(53.9%)	–	2.0	48.1	62.9	0.0
Market value ($ mil.)	–	–	–	–	–	–
Employees	–	–	–	–	–	3,500

CITY OF PLANO

1520 AVE K
PLANO, TX 75074
Phone: 972 941-7121
Fax: –
Web: www.plano.gov

CEO: –
CFO: –
HR: Shante Akafia
FYE: September 30
Type: Private

Plano isn't located deep in the heart of Texas, but it is, nonetheless, a proud Texas city. Part of the Dallas-Fort Worth metropolitan area, Plano is located in the northeastern region of the state, just north of Dallas. It is the ninth-largest city in Texas and is governed by a city council made up of a mayor and seven city council members. Incorporated in 1873, the City of Plano comprises large suburban areas and boasts safe neighborhoods and high-performing schools.

	Annual Growth	09/18	09/19	09/20	09/21	09/22
Sales ($mil.)	0.4%	–	409.4	404.2	407.1	413.7
Net income ($ mil.)	(7.0%)	–	31.1	16.4	19.0	25.0
Market value ($ mil.)	–	–	–	–	–	–
Employees	–	–	–	–	–	2,000

CITY OF PORTLAND

1221 SW 4TH AVE RM 340
PORTLAND, OR 972041900
Phone: 503 823-4120
Fax: –
Web: www.portland.gov

CEO: –
CFO: –
HR: Sukho Viboolsittiseri
FYE: June 30
Type: Private

"A rose by any other name would smell as sweet" may be only way to tell this city from 18 other Portlands in the US. Portland has been known as the City of Roses since 1888 and has hosted an annual rose festival since 1905.

	Annual Growth	06/18	06/19	06/20	06/21	06/22
Sales ($mil.)	7.1%	–	1,604.8	1,648.9	1,768.1	1,969.4
Net income ($ mil.)	16.1%	–	138.7	269.4	(9.7)	216.8
Market value ($ mil.)	–	–	–	–	–	–
Employees	–	–	–	–	–	5,684

CITY OF RALEIGH

222 W HARGETT ST
RALEIGH, NC 276011316
Phone: 919 996-3000
Fax: –
Web: www.raleighnc.gov

CEO: –
CFO: –
HR: –
FYE: June 30
Type: Private

Raleigh offers the culture of a city with the character of a small town. As North Carolina's capital, it boasts a variety of arts, parks, and historic sites. It joins Durham and Chapel Hill to form Research Triangle Park , the nation's largest hub for research and economic development. A city council, comprising seven members and a mayor (elected for two-year terms), sets policy and enacts ordinances for its 400,000 residents. The City of Raleigh, whose operations are directed by a city manager, has an annual budget of about $860 million. Founded in 1792, Raleigh is home to the NHL's Carolina Hurricanes and NC State. Notable residents include former US president Andrew Johnson and US senator Jesse Helms.

CITY OF RICHMOND

900 E BROAD ST STE 201
RICHMOND, VA 232191907
Phone: 804 646-7970
Fax: –
Web: www.rva.gov

CEO: –
CFO: –
HR: –
FYE: June 30
Type: Private

Music legends Joan Baez and Jerry Garcia both sang about seeing Richmond fall but these days Richmond is rising. The city, which made its living on tobacco and slave trading early in its history, now thrives on business, law, and the research center at the Virginia Biotechnology Research Park. Richmond is home to several major corporations including CarMax, Dominion Resources, Genworth Financial, and MeadWestvaco. It's also home to more than 200,000 people, who are governed by a city council representing nine districts along with an at-large mayor. The city follows a council-manager system and the mayor is not part of the council. Richmond, which was founded in 1737, has an annual budget of about $1.4 billion.

	Annual Growth	06/18	06/19	06/20	06/21	06/22
Sales ($mil.)	4.2%	–	800.8	824.7	878.2	906.2
Net income ($ mil.)	(17.2%)	–	72.2	(6.2)	65.5	40.9
Market value ($ mil.)	–	–	–	–	–	–
Employees	–	–	–	–	–	5,315

CITY OF RICHMOND

450 CIVIC CENTER PLAZA
RICHMOND, CA 948041661
Phone: 510 620-6727
Fax: -
Web: ci.richmond.ca.us

CEO: -
CFO: -
HR: -
FYE: June 30
Type: Private

In the shadows of San Francisco's East Bay, the City of Richmond stands on the shoulders of its shipbuilding past. Richmond's shipyards, home of Rosie the Riveter Museum, broke records building American ships for WWII. The city government uses a council-manager system, with nine at-large members and a mayor, all elected to four-year terms. Major employers include Chevron USA and HMO Kaiser Permanente (originally the medical system for the shipyard workers); the Port of Richmond does a brisk business importing automobiles. With a population of nearly 104,000, Richmond has a budget of about $315 million. It was incorporated in 1905 and in 2007 became the largest city in the nation with a Green Party mayor.

	Annual Growth	06/18	06/19	06/20	06/21	06/22
Sales ($mil.)	3.2%	-	242.8	235.5	252.3	266.9
Net income ($ mil.)	26.3%	-	13.4	8.1	17.5	27.0
Market value ($ mil.)	-	-	-	-	-	-
Employees	-	-	-	-	-	1,158

CITY OF RIVERSIDE

3900 MAIN ST FL 7
RIVERSIDE, CA 925220002
Phone: 951 826-5311
Fax: -
Web: www.riversideca.gov

CEO: -
CFO: Paul Sundeen
HR: -
FYE: June 30
Type: Private

This city's cup will likely not runneth over. The City of Riverside, California, is home to the World's Largest Paper Cup (68 feet tall), set in front of a former Dixie cup plant. Riverside operates under a council-manager form of government with a seven-member council presided over by a mayor. The council passes ordinances, appoints committees, and hires the city manager, attorney, and clerk. Its city manager carries out the council's policies and ordinances and oversees city day-to-day operations. Incorporated in 1883, Riverside planted the seeds for the US navel orange-growing industry. It is located about 60 miles east of Los Angeles, occupies about 80 square miles, and has a population of some 300,000.

	Annual Growth	06/17	06/18	06/19	06/20	06/21
Sales ($mil.)	8.1%	-	318.4	338.6	338.1	402.5
Net income ($ mil.)	(18.3%)	-	41.3	71.3	10.5	22.6
Market value ($ mil.)	-	-	-	-	-	-
Employees	-	-	-	-	-	2,700

CITY OF ROCHESTER

30 CHURCH ST
ROCHESTER, NY 146141206
Phone: 585 428-6755
Fax: -
Web: www.cityofrochester.gov

CEO: -
CFO: -
HR: Dawn Bartoccidowd
FYE: June 30
Type: Private

Known as "The World's Image Center," the City of Rochester, situated on the south of Lake Ontario, encompasses some 37 sq. mi. The city, incorporated in 1703, was one of the first "boomtowns" in the US due to a large number of flour mills. Rochester is now a center of higher education, medical and technological research with University of Rochester, Rochester Institute of Technology, Bausch & Lomb, and Kodak calling it home. Xerox still has a large presence in the city. A population of over 200,000 makes the city the third largest in the state. The government is a "strong mayor" style with 4 district and 5 at-large council members. Previously known as "The Flower City," it hosts an annual lilac festival.

	Annual Growth	06/18	06/19	06/20	06/21	06/22
Sales ($mil.)	(89.6%)	-	577.4	559.6	645.8	0.7
Net income ($ mil.)	-	-	(3.9)	(44.5)	6.2	0.0
Market value ($ mil.)	-	-	-	-	-	-
Employees	-	-	-	-	-	3,200

CITY OF SACRAMENTO

915 I ST FL 5
SACRAMENTO, CA 958142622
Phone: 916 808-5300
Fax: -
Web: www.cityofsacramento.org

CEO: -
CFO: -
HR: -
FYE: June 30
Type: Private

With its Mediterranean climate and location at the foot of the Sierra Nevadas, living in the city of Sacramento is no sacrifice. Founded in 1849, Sacramento is the oldest incorporated city in the state, and its seventh most populated comprising about 470,000 residents. California's capital city uses a council-manager form of government, with council members from eight districts elected to four-year terms. The council sets up city policies, approves contracts and a budget of nearly $800 million, as well as hears appeals of city decisions. The four council-appointed officers that carry out the city's business are the city manager, attorney, treasurer, and clerk. A Legislative Affairs Unit supports the council.

	Annual Growth	06/15	06/16	06/17	06/18	06/19
Sales ($mil.)	5.7%	-	709.9	694.4	723.9	838.2
Net income ($ mil.)	(1.9%)	-	91.4	46.5	2.0	86.5
Market value ($ mil.)	-	-	-	-	-	-
Employees	-	-	-	-	-	4,500

CITY OF SAINT PAUL

15 KELLOGG BLVD W STE 390
SAINT PAUL, MN 551021615
Phone: 651 266-8500
Fax: -
Web: www.stpaul.gov

CEO: -
CFO: -
HR: Dan Ferralez
FYE: December 31
Type: Private

In a Pig's Eye once referred to the City of Saint Paul. Founded in 1849 in the Territory of Minnesota, the city of 285,000 has gone through a few other name changes, finally settling on its current name in 1854. Saint Paul is located on the east bank of the Mississippi River and with its twin city Minneapolis forms the 16th largest metropolis in the US. The mayor-council government consists of an "at large" mayor and seven ward councilmembers. Minnesota's capital, Saint Paul is home to professional sports teams Minnesota Wild of the NHL and Minnesota Swarm of the National Lacrosse League (NLL).

	Annual Growth	12/17	12/18	12/19	12/20	12/21
Sales ($mil.)	3.5%	-	488.4	509.1	544.3	542.1
Net income ($ mil.)	-	-	(24.1)	36.5	(41.6)	45.9
Market value ($ mil.)	-	-	-	-	-	-
Employees	-	-	-	-	-	3,358

CITY OF SAINT PETERSBURG

175 5TH ST N
SAINT PETERSBURG, FL 337013708
Phone: 727 893-7111
Fax: -
Web: www.golfstpete.com

CEO: -
CFO: -
HR: Delores Raigns
FYE: September 30
Type: Private

Luckily for all those Midwesterners escaping snowy weather, St. Pete is nothing like its Russian namesake. The city of St. Petersburg, known almost universally as St. Pete, is surrounded by warm Gulf water and boasts nearly 360 days of sunshine per year. Along with Tampa and Clearwater, it makes up the Tampa Bay Area on Florida's west coast. St. Pete's mayor-council government includes eight council members each representing their home district. The first deputy mayor oversees the city's daily operations. Tourism and marine research are major industries with about a dozen oceanographic institutes in the area. St. Pete, founded in 1892, spends about $500 million each year on a population of about 400,000.

	Annual Growth	09/16	09/17	09/18	09/19	09/20
Sales ($mil.)	9.2%	-	-	309.6	336.3	368.8
Net income ($ mil.)	-	-	-	(49.9)	(16.9)	32.3
Market value ($ mil.)	-	-	-	-	-	-
Employees	-	-	-	-	-	2,800

CITY OF SALINAS

200 LINCOLN AVE
SALINAS, CA 939012639
Phone: 831 758-7489
Fax: –
Web: www.cityofsalinas.org

CEO: –
CFO: –
HR: –
FYE: June 30
Type: Private

It isn't known as the "Salad Bowl of America" for nothing; Salinas Valley is responsible for more than 80% of the lettuce grown in the US. With a population of more than 140,000, the City of Salinas' economy is primarily based on agriculture. Many major vegetable producers are headquartered in the city, and the area is well known for fruits and vegetables, including broccoli, carrots, lettuce, spinach, strawberries, and watermelons. The city's government consists of the mayor (two-year term) and six city council members (four-year terms). Salinas is also the hometown of famed writer and Nobel price laureate John Steinbeck.

	Annual Growth	06/17	06/18	06/19	06/20	06/21
Sales ($mil.)	5.8%	–	161.8	171.6	171.9	191.4
Net income ($ mil.)	–	–	(7.8)	59.4	7.7	(5.4)
Market value ($ mil.)	–	–	–	–	–	–
Employees	–	–	–	–	–	735

CITY OF SAN ANTONIO

100 W HOUSTON ST FL 8
SAN ANTONIO, TX 782051414
Phone: 210 207-6000
Fax: –
Web: www.sanantonio.gov

CEO: –
CFO: –
HR: Erica Granado
FYE: September 30
Type: Private

When you "Remember the Alamo," don't forget San Antonio! The second-largest Texas city (behind Houston), with a population of about 1.5 million, San Antonio was the site of the Battle of the Alamo. Today, it's home to major tourist attractions like the River Walk, SeaWorld, and Six Flags Fiesta Texas, as well as the San Antonio Spurs NBA franchise and more than 50 golf courses. It has a huge military presence, with three major Army and Air Force bases. San Antonio is run by a mayor and 10 district representatives who pass laws and establish policies for the city. Its city manager oversees day-to-day operations, including nearly 40 departments. San Antonio has an annual budget of more than $2 billion.

	Annual Growth	09/17	09/18	09/19	09/20	09/22
Sales ($mil.)	6.8%	–	2,056.6	2,150.0	2,168.0	2,677.3
Net income ($ mil.)	(8.6%)	–	284.1	192.7	(15.8)	198.3
Market value ($ mil.)	–	–	–	–	–	–
Employees	–	–	–	–	–	12,000

CITY OF SAN DIEGO

202 C ST
SAN DIEGO, CA 921013860
Phone: 619 236-6330
Fax: –
Web: www.sandiego.gov

CEO: –
CFO: –
HR: –
FYE: June 30
Type: Private

The City of San Diego offers more than just warm weather and beautiful beaches. The second-largest city in California (with a population of more than 1.3 million), known as Telecom Valley, is also one of the centers in the US for technological manufacturing. Its council members each represent one of its nine districts. Founded in 1769, San Diego is the home to 3 universities as well as professional sports teams Padres of MLB and Chargers of the NFL. The city operates through some 50 programs and departments, including environmental services, homeland security, parks and recreation, and the commission for arts and culture. The City of San Diego has an annual budget of approximately $3 billion.

	Annual Growth	06/18	06/19	06/20	06/21	06/22
Sales ($mil.)	5.4%	–	2,283.5	2,237.5	2,362.8	2,674.2
Net income ($ mil.)	12.0%	–	62.2	(103.4)	113.5	87.4
Market value ($ mil.)	–	–	–	–	–	–
Employees	–	–	–	–	–	11,200

CITY OF SAN JOSE

200 E SANTA CLARA ST 13TH FL
SAN JOSE, CA 951131905
Phone: 408 535-3500
Fax: –
Web: www.sanjoseca.gov

CEO: –
CFO: –
HR: Carissa Bertelli
FYE: June 30
Type: Private

Do you know the way to San Jos ? If so, you're probably a high tech worker, and hopefully one with a salary to match its real estate prices. The city is known for its Silicon Valley location and technology-driven economy. More than 500 tech firms are the major employers in the area, which is also known for its premium home prices (median $495,000). San Jos was founded in 1777 and incorporates some 180 square miles. 950,000 residents make San Jos the third largest city in the state. The city government uses the council/manager model wherein the council, made up of the mayor (elected at large) and the 10 council members (one from each district), sets policy and the council-appointed city manager carries it out.

	Annual Growth	06/18	06/19	06/20	06/21	06/22
Sales ($mil.)	7.3%	–	1,731.6	1,868.7	1,894.1	2,141.1
Net income ($ mil.)	38.8%	–	135.0	309.9	3.9	360.7
Market value ($ mil.)	–	–	–	–	–	–
Employees	–	–	–	–	–	7,500

CITY OF SANTA ANA

20 CIVIC CENTER PLZ FL 8
SANTA ANA, CA 927014058
Phone: 714 647-5400
Fax: –
Web: www.santa-ana.org

CEO: –
CFO: –
HR: –
FYE: June 30
Type: Private

The area was named by a Spanish army sergeant in 1810, and the city of Santa Ana was founded in 1869 by William Spurgeon. The city encompasses 27.5 sq. mi. and, coupled with a population of almost 330,000, is the fourth most densely populated city in the US. Santa Ana is home for Behr Paint, CoreLogic, Corinthian Colleges, Ingram Micro, and Rickenbacker with regional headquarters for T-Mobile, Ultimate Software, and Xerox. A Mediterranean climate and proximity to Disneyland, Knotts Berry Farm, and Huntington and Newport beaches offer residents and visitors with ample recreational activities. The city is governed by a council-manager system consisting of a mayor and six councilmembers elected to 4-year terms.

	Annual Growth	06/18	06/19	06/20	06/21	06/22
Sales ($mil.)	13.4%	–	381.1	422.7	514.4	555.6
Net income ($ mil.)	22.1%	–	16.7	14.5	36.0	30.4
Market value ($ mil.)	–	–	–	–	–	–
Employees	–	–	–	–	–	2,044

CITY OF SEATTLE

700 5TH AVE STE 5500
SEATTLE, WA 981041916
Phone: 206 684-7999
Fax: –
Web: www.seattle.gov

CEO: –
CFO: –
HR: Bobby Humes
FYE: December 31
Type: Private

In the Emerald City, it's not just the name that's green. The City of Seattle is known for rain-fed lush greenery but also for its environmentalism. It uses a charter form of government, which features an elected mayor and city council along with a city attorney. The nine council members are elected at large annually. Among some 25 other departments, Seattle has an Office of Sustainability and Environment, it's restoring salmon habitat, and it celebrates Earth Month rather than just Earth Day. The city serves a population of more than 600,000 with an annual budget of around $4 billion. It was first settled by Europeans in 1851, and takes its name from Chief Seattle, a local tribal leader.

CITY OF SHREVEPORT

505 TRAVIS ST STE 600
SHREVEPORT, LA 711013042
Phone: 318 423-5611
Fax: -
Web: www.shreveportla.gov

CEO: -
CFO: -
HR: Canisha Tisby
FYE: December 31
Type: Private

As industry goes in the Ark-La-Tex, so it goes in the City of Shreveport, located on the banks of the Red River. The third largest city in Louisiana and ranked 108th in the US, Shreveport has a population of nearly 200,000 encompassing almost 118 sq. mi. Founded in 1805 by the Shreve Town Company and later incorporated in 1893, Shreveport along with its neighbor Bossier City boast a thriving service economy. The elected mayor and seven district councilmembers run the city government.

	Annual Growth	12/18	12/19	12/20	12/21	12/22
Sales ($mil.)	6.6%	-	260.4	425.8	291.6	315.6
Net income ($ mil.)	-	-	(8.4)	(18.3)	42.2	39.3
Market value ($ mil.)	-	-	-	-	-	-
Employees	-	-	-	-	-	3,000

CITY OF ST. LOUIS

1200 MARKET ST RM 212
SAINT LOUIS, MO 631032805
Phone: 314 622-3201
Fax: -
Web: www.stlouis-mo.gov

CEO: -
CFO: -
HR: -
FYE: June 30
Type: Private

"The Gateway to the West" is bordered by the Mississippi River on the east and occupies approximately 62 square miles with a population of more than 300,000. The government of the City of St. Louis is comprised of the city's mayor and a Board of Aldermen (made up of 28 elected members, in addition to the board president). Unlike most city governments, the mayor shares executive authority with other independent citywide elected officials, such as the treasurer and comptroller. During the 21st century, St. Louis has transitioned from a manufacturing and industrial economy to one heavily dependent on medicine, biotechnology, and other sciences. It is home to MLB's St. Louis Cardinals and NFL's St. Louis Rams.

	Annual Growth	06/18	06/19	06/20	06/21	06/22
Sales ($mil.)	3.7%	-	870.1	863.3	899.9	969.8
Net income ($ mil.)	(8.4%)	-	111.1	8.8	121.5	85.5
Market value ($ mil.)	-	-	-	-	-	-
Employees	-	-	-	-	-	4,500

CITY OF STOCKTON

425 N EL DORADO ST
STOCKTON, CA 952021997
Phone: 209 937-8212
Fax: -
Web: www.stocktonca.gov

CEO: -
CFO: -
HR: Pamela Summerville
FYE: June 30
Type: Private

Tuleburg, Fat City and Mudville were just a few of the early names for the City of Stockton. A German immigrant and gold miner, founding father Captain Charles Webber settled on Stockton in honor of Commodore Robert Stockton, a leader in the capture of California in the Mexican-American War. A population of over 290,000 is packed into an area of almost 65 sq. mi. Historically a farming community for asparagus, cherries, tomatoes, walnuts, and almonds, Stockton is home to the University of the Pacific and Diamond Foods.

	Annual Growth	06/18	06/19	06/20	06/21	06/22
Sales ($mil.)	11.3%	-	369.8	371.3	441.5	509.9
Net income ($ mil.)	37.0%	-	39.5	30.8	48.8	101.4
Market value ($ mil.)	-	-	-	-	-	-
Employees	-	-	-	-	-	2,200

CITY OF SYRACUSE

233 E WASHINGTON ST STE 231
SYRACUSE, NY 132021423
Phone: 315 448-8005
Fax: -
Web: www.syr.gov

CEO: -
CFO: -
HR: -
FYE: June 30
Type: Private

Syracuse, New York is located in the center of the state but it is a world apart from the "Big Apple". Named after the Sicilian city of Syracuse, the city owes much of its growth and history to two things-- salt and the Erie Canal. Although neither is as important as it once was to the city, Syracuse is still a regional transportation hub and the city has managed to weather the economic trends supplanting a salt-centric economy with industrial manufacturing, before evolving to a service industry centered economy. The city has a population of about 150,000 and is governed by its mayor and a ten-person Common Council.

	Annual Growth	06/15	06/16	06/17	06/18	06/19
Sales ($mil.)	2.3%	-	-	741.5	758.8	775.9
Net income ($ mil.)	61.2%	-	-	6.2	122.8	16.0
Market value ($ mil.)	-	-	-	-	-	-
Employees	-	-	-	-	-	6,456

CITY OF TAMPA

306 E JACKSON ST
TAMPA, FL 336025223
Phone: 813 274-8211
Fax: -
Web: www.tampa.gov

CEO: -
CFO: -
HR: Carrie Ortolano
FYE: September 30
Type: Private

Disregarded by its first owners, the Spanish in 1517 and the British in 1763, Tampa is now a thriving city on the Gulf Coast of Florida. It joins Clearwater and St. Petersburg in forming the Tampa Bay Area. The city uses a mayor-council form of government with seven council members, one from each of four districts and three at-large. The mayor and council members are elected to four year terms. They set policy and the chief of staff carries it out by running the day-to-day operations of the city. In addition to tourism and the port of Tampa, major area industry includes agriculture, construction, health care, and military operations. Tampa, which has a population of about 350,000, was incorporated in 1855.

	Annual Growth	09/17	09/18	09/19	09/20	09/21
Sales ($mil.)	7.7%	-	558.8	610.2	652.2	698.4
Net income ($ mil.)	4.3%	-	64.5	33.8	43.8	73.1
Market value ($ mil.)	-	-	-	-	-	-
Employees	-	-	-	-	-	4,500

CITY OF TOLEDO

1 GOVERNMENT CTR STE 2050
TOLEDO, OH 436042281
Phone: 419 245-1050
Fax: -
Web: toledo.oh.gov

CEO: Paula Hicks-Hudson
CFO: -
HR: Michael Niedzielski
FYE: December 31
Type: Private

Known as the Glass City because of its strong presence in the glass and auto manufacturing industry, the City of Toledo is by no means fragile. The city, incorporated in Ohio in 1837, is situated in the northwestern part of the state along the Michigan border. It is the fourth most populous city in Ohio. Toledo's heavy dependence on manufacturing has made it particularly susceptible to the country's economic lows, but the city has bounced back each time through revitalization and redevelopment efforts. The City of Toledo is governed by a mayor and a 12-member city council.

	Annual Growth	12/16	12/17	12/18	12/19	12/21
Sales ($mil.)	3.9%	-	328.3	338.9	360.5	383.3
Net income ($ mil.)	-	-	16.9	12.1	13.8	(15.5)
Market value ($ mil.)	-	-	-	-	-	-
Employees	-	-	-	-	-	3,000

CITY OF TRENTON

319 E STATE ST
TRENTON, NJ 086081809
Phone: 609 989-3030
Fax: –
Web: www.trentonnj.org

CEO: –
CFO: –
HR: –
FYE: June 30
Type: Private

Trenton, New Jersey is a city with a lot of history. The first settlement in the area dates to 1679 with the town adopting the name "Trent-towne" in 1719. Eventually shortened to Trenton, the city became famous for the Battle of Trenton in which Washington crossed the Delaware on December 26 to defeat the Hessian troops stationed there. The city was also briefly the capital of the United States. Although it is no longer the nation's capital, the city is the capital of New Jersey sporting a population of about 85,000. Trenton's city government consists of a seven-member city council and its elected mayor.

	Annual Growth	06/10	06/11	06/12	06/13	06/15
Sales ($mil.)	(1.1%)	–	–	300.3	307.0	290.9
Net income ($ mil.)	(6.0%)	–	–	14.9	8.1	12.3
Market value ($ mil.)	–	–	–	–	–	–
Employees	–	–	–	–	–	13,000

CITY OF TUCSON

255 W ALAMEDA ST
TUCSON, AZ 857011362
Phone: 520 791-4561
Fax: –
Web: www.tucsonaz.gov

CEO: –
CFO: –
HR: Angela Scott
FYE: June 30
Type: Private

There's no such thing as too much sun in Tucson. The City of Tucson, Arizona, enjoys 360 sunny days a year, is divided into six wards, each represented by a council member. Together with the mayor, the members form the Tucson City Council, which sets city policies; a city manager leads all departments in implementing these policies. Tucson has about half a million residents and a culture that blends Native American and Mexican influences. It's home to The University of Arizona, Davis-Monthan Air Force Base, and The National Optical Astronomy Observatories. The Arizona Diamondbacks are based in Tucson and the Chicago White Sox hold spring training here. The city has an annual budget of greater than $2 billion.

	Annual Growth	06/13	06/14	06/15	06/16	06/19
Sales ($mil.)	4.4%	–	728.7	723.8	763.5	903.6
Net income ($ mil.)	12.8%	–	31.7	(16.3)	19.4	58.0
Market value ($ mil.)	–	–	–	–	–	–
Employees	–	–	–	–	–	5,900

CITY OF TULSA

175 E 2ND ST STE 15129
TULSA, OK 741033201
Phone: 918 596-2100
Fax: –
Web: www.cityoftulsa.org

CEO: –
CFO: –
HR: –
FYE: June 30
Type: Private

Named for the Tulsa Lochapokas indian tribe, the City of Tulsa was incorporated in 1898. The finding of oil in 1901 resulted in rapid growth and still links Tulsa to the US oil industry. The city, with a population of over 395,000, straddles the Arkansas River and maintains a temperate climate. AAON, Mazzios, Nordam Group, ONEOK, and The Williams Companies headquarter in Tulsa. The University of Tulsa, Oral Roberts University, and Rogers State University form the base of the 15 institutions in the city.

	Annual Growth	06/13	06/14	06/15	06/16	06/17
Sales ($mil.)	1.4%	–	467.2	469.0	478.4	487.5
Net income ($ mil.)	97.0%	–	21.5	45.2	15.2	164.4
Market value ($ mil.)	–	–	–	–	–	–
Employees	–	–	–	–	–	3,897

CITY OF VIRGINIA BEACH

2401 COURTHOUSE DR STE 9001
VIRGINIA BEACH, VA 234569120
Phone: 757 385-3111
Fax: –
Web: www.vbgov.com

CEO: –
CFO: –
HR: Monica McNeal-Kopin
FYE: June 30
Type: Private

Whether you're looking for seaside peace and seclusion or bustling boardwalk adventure, Virginia Beach is the spot. With nearly 40 miles of Chesapeake Bay and Atlantic Ocean coastline, the city's economy thrives largely on travel and tourism and supports a population of more than 435,000 people. Virginia Beach's city council consists of 11 elected members (including its mayor) and is responsible for legislative duties including levying taxes, adopting an annual budget, and appointing a city manager. The city manager carries out executive and administrative tasks in this city's Council-Manager government.

	Annual Growth	06/18	06/19	06/20	06/21	06/22
Sales ($mil.)	3.9%	–	1,379.5	1,412.5	1,463.6	1,548.9
Net income ($ mil.)	–	–	(70.2)	156.8	(12.5)	30.6
Market value ($ mil.)	–	–	–	–	–	–
Employees	–	–	–	–	–	7,500

CITY OF YONKERS

40 S BROADWAY
YONKERS, NY 107013715
Phone: 914 377-6000
Fax: –
Web: www.yonkersny.gov

CEO: –
CFO: –
HR: –
FYE: June 30
Type: Private

The city of Jonk Herr (Dutch for young gentleman) has gone through many changes since its founding in 1670. Incorporated in 1872, the City of Yonkers now has a population of almost 200,000 nestled into an area of about 20 sq. mi. overlooking the Hudson River. Home to Sarah Lawrence College, Yonkers' mayor/council style of government is run by an "at large" mayor and seven district councilmembers.

	Annual Growth	06/18	06/19	06/20	06/21	06/22
Sales ($mil.)	(89.6%)	–	1,263.1	–	1,299.3	1.4
Net income ($ mil.)	–	–	(41.1)	–	75.6	0.1
Market value ($ mil.)	–	–	–	–	–	–
Employees	–	–	–	–	–	2,500

CITY PUBLIC SERVICES OF SAN ANTONIO

500 MCCULLOUGH AVE
SAN ANTONIO, TX 782152104
Phone: 210 353-2222
Fax: –
Web: www.cpsenergy.com

CEO: Paula Gold-Williams
CFO: Delores Lenzy-Jones
HR: Leon Bilewitz
FYE: January 31
Type: Private

Established in 1860, CPS Energy is the nation's largest public power, natural gas, and electric company, providing safe, reliable, and competitively-priced service to electric and natural gas customers in San Antonio and portions of seven adjoining counties. CPS Energy's customers' combined energy bills rank among the lowest of the nation's 20 largest cities ? while generating $9 billion in revenue for the City of San Antonio for 80 years. CPS Energy is among the top public power wind energy buyers in the nation and number one in Texas for solar generation.

	Annual Growth	01/08	01/09	01/10	01/11	01/12
Sales ($mil.)	8.1%	–	–	1,930.9	2,068.7	2,258.4
Net income ($ mil.)	(55.5%)	–	–	107.6	78.8	21.3
Market value ($ mil.)	–	–	–	–	–	–
Employees	–	–	–	–	–	3,100

CITY UTILITIES OF SPRINGFIELD MO

301 E CENTRAL ST
SPRINGFIELD, MO 658023834
Phone: 417 863-9000
Fax: –
Web: www.cityutilities.net

CEO: –
CFO: Amy Derdall
HR: Baoling Wengbrandon
FYE: September 30
Type: Private

City Utilities of Springfield, Missouri springs to action with multiple services and products. The multi-utility supplies electricity, natural gas, and water for residents and businesses in the southwestern Missouri town. It has about 1,870 miles of power lines and 1,260 miles of natural gas mains, serves about 110,000 electric customers, 82,000 natural gas customers, and 81,000 water customers. It also operates the municipal bus system, which has 25 regular street buses and five demand/response buses, and serves about 790 broadband contracts through SpringNet Telecommunications. City Utilities of Springfield has a service region of 320 sq. ml. and serves a base population of 229,000.

	Annual Growth	09/16	09/17	09/18	09/19	09/20
Sales ($mil.)	(0.2%)	–	432.8	459.7	457.7	429.8
Net income ($ mil.)	20.5%	–	34.9	61.0	66.9	60.9
Market value ($ mil.)	–	–	–	–	–	–
Employees	–	–	–	–	–	980

CITYSERVICEVALCON, LLC

640 W MONTANA ST
KALISPELL, MT 599013834
Phone: 406 755-4321
Fax: –
Web: www.cityservicevalcon.com

CEO: –
CFO: –
HR: –
FYE: September 30
Type: Private

You don't have to live in the city to get the services of CityServiceValcon, which markets and distributes petroleum products throughout the Inland Northwest, and Rocky Mountain regions of the US, as well as in the adjacent Plains states. Its products include gasoline, diesel, aviation fuels, lubricants, propane, and heating oil. The company has diesel, gasoline, and heating oils for delivery through its network of bulk plants. CityServiceValcon also operates cardlock fueling facilities under the Pacific Pride brand name. Regional independent petroleum marketers City Service and Valcon merged their operations in 2003 to form CityServiceValcon.

	Annual Growth	09/04	09/05	09/06	09/07	09/08
Sales ($mil.)	16.6%	–	–	459.5	490.1	625.1
Net income ($ mil.)	(8.0%)	–	–	4.7	3.0	4.0
Market value ($ mil.)	–	–	–	–	–	–
Employees	–	–	–	–	–	50

CIVEO U.S. HOLDINGS LLC

333 CLAY ST STE 4980
HOUSTON, TX 770024101
Phone: 713 510-2400
Fax: –
Web: www.civeo.com

CEO: Bradley J Dodson
CFO: Frank C Steininger
HR: –
FYE: December 31
Type: Private

Housing natural resources workers in the Great White North and the Land Down Under is Civeo Corporation's calling. The company is a leading provider of workforce accommodations with prominent market positions in the Canadian oil sands and the Australian natural resource markets. Civeo offers comprehensive provides housing hundreds or thousands of workers with its long-term and temporary accommodations and also provides catering, facility management, water systems and logistics services. Civeo owns a total of eighteen lodges and villages in operation in Canada and Australia, with an aggregate of more than 21,000 rooms. The company was spun off from Oil States International in 2014.

CIVISTA BANCSHARES INC

100 East Water Street
Sandusky, OH 44870
Phone: 419 625-4121
Fax: –
Web: –

NAS: CIVB
CEO: Dennis G Shaffer
CFO: –
HR: –
FYE: December 31
Type: Public

First Citizens Banc Corp. is the holding company for The Citizens Banking Company and its Citizens Bank and Champaign Bank divisions, which together operate more than 30 branches in northern Ohio. The banks offer such deposit products as checking and savings accounts and CDs, in addition to trust services. They concentrate on real estate lending, with residential mortgages and commercial mortgages each comprising approximately 40% of the company's loan portfolio. The Citizens Banking Company's Citizens Wealth Management division provides financial planning, brokerage, insurance, and investments through an agreement with third-party provider UVEST (part of LPL Financial).

	Annual Growth	12/19	12/20	12/21	12/22	12/23
Assets ($mil.)	13.7%	2,309.6	2,762.9	3,012.0	3,537.8	3,861.4
Net income ($ mil.)	6.1%	33.9	32.2	40.5	39.4	43.0
Market value ($ mil.)	(6.4%)	376.7	275.1	383.0	345.5	289.4
Employees	3.9%	457	459	441	530	532

CIVITAS RESOURCES INC

555 17th Street, Suite 3700
Denver, CO 80202
Phone: 303 293-9100
Fax: –
Web: www.civitasresources.com

NYS: CIVI
CEO: –
CFO: –
HR: –
FYE: December 31
Type: Public

Bonanza Creek Energy searches for a treasure of black gold. The independent oil and natural gas company has exploration and production assets in Arkansas, California, Colorado, and Texas. Unlike many in the industry, it operates nearly all of its projects and has an 89% working interest in its holdings. The company reported a 32% increase in proved reserves in 2013 to 69.8 million barrels of oil equivalent, resulting primarily from the development of the Wattenberg Field in Colorado. Most of the company's proved reserves are in its Rocky Mountains (Niobara oil shale) and Arkansas (Cotton Valley sands) holdings. Bonanza Creek Energy filed for and emerged from Chapter 11 bankruptcy protection in 2017.

	Annual Growth	12/19	12/20	12/21	12/22	12/23
Sales ($mil.)	82.6%	313.2	218.1	930.6	3,791.4	3,479.2
Net income ($ mil.)	84.9%	67.1	103.5	178.9	1,248.1	784.3
Market value ($ mil.)	30.8%	2,188.7	1,812.7	4,592.2	5,432.4	6,412.3
Employees	42.5%	125	109	322	353	516

CK CONSTRUCTION GROUP INC.

6245 WESTERVILLE RD
WESTERVILLE, OH 430814041
Phone: 614 901-8844
Fax: –
Web: www.ckbuilds.com

CEO: Lori M Gillett
CFO: –
HR: –
FYE: March 31
Type: Private

Corna Kokosing provides general contracting services for commercial, industrial, institutional, and health care construction projects, primarily in central Ohio. Services include construction management, design/build, and finance services for new construction and renovations. The company also performs construction services ranging from carpentry and drywall installation to metal building erection and demolition. Stonemason Al Corna and carpenter Joe DiCesare co-founded the company in 1956. Midwest heavy construction group Kokosing Construction acquired Corna Kokosing 40 years later.

CKHS, INC.

100 W SPROUL RD
SPRINGFIELD, PA 190642033
Phone: 610 338-8200
Fax: –
Web: www.crozerhealth.org

CEO: Kevin Spiegel
CFO: Arthur Anderson
HR: –
FYE: June 30
Type: Private

Crozer-Keystone Health System provides a full range of health care in the Philadelphia metropolitan area. The health system's facilities include five acute care hospitals, four outpatient care centers, and a sports science and technology center. Combined, its not-for-profit member hospitals have about 840 beds. The hospitals' specialty units include trauma, cardiac, cancer, orthopedic, wound healing, obesity, sleep disorder, and women's and children's health centers. The system also operates family, occupational, and diagnostic health clinics, as well as home health and hospice agencies. In 2016 the company was acquired by for-profit hospital operator Prospect Medical Holdings.

	Annual Growth	06/12	06/13	06/14	06/15	06/16
Sales ($mil.)	21.5%	–	–	–	42.8	52.0
Net income ($ mil.)	–	–	–	–	(4.5)	(2.4)
Market value ($ mil.)	–	–	–	–	–	–
Employees	–	–	–	–	–	7,100

CKX LANDS INC

2417 Shell Beach Drive
Lake Charles, LA 70601
Phone: 337 493-2399
Fax: –
Web: www.ckxlands.com

ASE: CKX
CEO: –
CFO: –
HR: –
FYE: December 31
Type: Public

Revenues come naturally to CKX Lands. The company owns or has stakes in about 14,000 acres in Louisiana that contain oil and gas wells, mines, timber, and agricultural operations. Formed in 1930, the company does not perform any of these operations and is not involved in oil and gas exploration. Instead, it generates revenues through royalties from the natural resources produced on its land. Originally set up to receive mineral royalties spun off by a bank to its shareholders, CKX Lands' growth strategy is built around acquiring land in southwestern Louisiana. Its largest customers, Mayne and Mertz and Cox & Perkins, account for nearly 40% of sales.

	Annual Growth	12/18	12/19	12/20	12/21	12/22
Sales ($mil.)	(1.9%)	1.2	0.8	0.7	0.7	1.1
Net income ($ mil.)	–	1.1	0.2	0.3	0.8	(1.3)
Market value ($ mil.)	(0.9%)	20.4	18.4	18.8	22.1	19.6
Employees	18.9%	1	1	1	1	2

CLAFLIN UNIVERSITY

400 MAGNOLIA ST
ORANGEBURG, SC 291156815
Phone: 803 535-5628
Fax: –
Web: www.claflin.edu

CEO: –
CFO: –
HR: –
FYE: June 30
Type: Private

Independent liberal arts institution Claflin University offers higher education in South Carolina. It provides 40 undergraduate, graduate programs, internships, and other career-focused and continuing education programs for about 2,000 in-state and out-of-state students. The university offers more than 30 undergraduate degree programs in fields including education, humanities, natural science, math, and music. Masters programs include biotechnology and business administration programs. Claflin University is affiliated with the United Methodist Church.

	Annual Growth	06/14	06/15	06/16	06/20	06/22
Sales ($mil.)	7.8%	–	53.4	–	–	90.5
Net income ($ mil.)	40.6%	–	2.5	–	–	27.6
Market value ($ mil.)	–	–	–	–	–	–
Employees	–	–	–	–	–	340

CLARCOR INC.

840 CRESCENT CENTRE DR # 600
FRANKLIN, TN 370674687
Phone: 615 771-3100
Fax: –
Web: www.parker.com

CEO: –
CFO: –
HR: –
FYE: November 30
Type: Private

CLARCOR cleans up with filters. The company's industrial and environmental filtration unit makes air and antimicrobial filters for commercial, industrial, and residential buildings, along with filters used in industrial processes. Brands include Airguard, Facet, ATI, Transweb, UAS, Keddeg, MKI, TFS, and Purolator. Companies in CLARCOR's engine and mobile filtration business make products under brands such as Baldwin, Hastings Filters, and Clark that filter the air, oil, fuel, coolant, and hydraulic fluids. In 2017, in order to expand its filtration portfolio, Parker-Hannifin acquired CLARCOR for about $4.3 billion.

	Annual Growth	11/12	11/13	11/14	11/15	11/16
Sales ($mil.)	7.1%	–	1,130.8	1,512.9	1,481.0	1,389.6
Net income ($ mil.)	5.6%	–	118.4	144.2	134.9	139.4
Market value ($ mil.)	–	–	–	–	–	–
Employees	–	–	–	–	–	5,773

CLARE ROSE, INC.

100 ROSE EXECUTIVE BLVD
EAST YAPHANK, NY 119671524
Phone: 631 475-2337
Fax: –
Web: www.clarerose.com

CEO: Sean Rose
CFO: Karen Cermak
HR: –
FYE: December 31
Type: Private

Clare Rose has risen to the top with help from The King of Beers. The company, a top beer wholesaler in the US, primarily markets Anheuser-Busch products, including Budweiser, Michelob, Bacardi, and Busch branded products. Clare Rose dominates distribution of the US beer maker's brands on New York's Long Island and Staten Island. The firm also carries other products, including those of Heineken, Redhook Ale and Widmer Brothers (both owned by Craft Brewers Alliance), Kona Brewing, China's Harbin, and Japan's Kirin. Founded in 1936 by Clare Rose, the company is still owned and operated by the Rose family.

	Annual Growth	12/09	12/10	12/11	12/12	12/13
Sales ($mil.)	0.5%	–	–	199.8	209.9	202.0
Net income ($ mil.)	(11.4%)	–	–	8.4	9.5	6.6
Market value ($ mil.)	–	–	–	–	–	–
Employees	–	–	–	–	–	267

CLAREMONT GRADUATE UNIVERSITY

150 E 10TH ST
CLAREMONT, CA 917115909
Phone: 909 607-8632
Fax: –
Web: www.cgu.edu

CEO: Deborah Freund
CFO: –
HR: Alejandra Gaytan
FYE: June 30
Type: Private

Claremont Graduate University (CGU) offers sunshine as well as strong academics to students. About 35 miles from Los Angeles, the university provides master's and doctoral degrees in 22 disciplines including education, mathematics, and psychology. A member of the Claremont University Consortium, the university is made up of nine academic schools including arts and humanities, educational studies, and politics and economics. The Peter F. Drucker Graduate School of Management also is housed on the Claremont Graduate University campus. The relatively small university, with an enrollment of about 2,000, focuses on giving its students individualized attention. CGU was founded in 1925.

	Annual Growth	06/18	06/19	06/20	06/21	06/22
Sales ($mil.)	16.5%	–	77.9	87.8	94.6	123.3
Net income ($ mil.)	–	–	(7.1)	(3.5)	16.4	39.5
Market value ($ mil.)	–	–	–	–	–	–
Employees	–	–	–	–	–	250

CLAREMONT MCKENNA COLLEGE FOUNDATION

500 E 9TH ST
CLAREMONT, CA 917115929
Phone: 909 621-8088
Fax: –
Web: www.cmc.edu

CEO: –
CFO: –
HR: –
FYE: June 30
Type: Private

Claremont McKenna College (CMC) is an coeducational, undergraduate liberal arts college with an annual enrollment of some 1,250 students. It offers 33 majors and 8 sequences (programs of related courses). Double, dual, individualized, off campus majors, and more than 2,000 courses available for cross registration across a network of CMC and six affiliated schools. CMC is also home to nearly a dozen research centers, including The Keck Center for International and Strategic Studies and The Center for Human Rights Leadership. The college is managed by the Claremont University Consortium, which supports seven independent Claremont colleges, and is modeled after the University of Oxford.

	Annual Growth	06/12	06/13	06/14	06/15	06/21
Sales ($mil.)	0.9%	–	–	–	155.1	164.1
Net income ($ mil.)	(11.9%)	–	–	–	27.0	12.6
Market value ($ mil.)	–	–	–	–	–	–
Employees	–	–	–	–	–	370

CLARIENT, INC.

31 COLUMBIA
ALISO VIEJO, CA 926561460
Phone: 949 445-7300
Fax: –
Web: www.neogenomics.com

CEO: Cynthia Collins
CFO: George A Cardoza
HR: –
FYE: December 31
Type: Private

Clarient can help provide clarity for cancer patients and their physicians. The firm is a specialized diagnostic services provider, offering a collection of advanced tests that detect and monitor the progression of various types of cancer. In addition to testing materials, Clarient provides pathology lab services and delivers the test results via its PATHSiTE Web portal. The company's principal customers include pathologists, oncologists, hospitals and biopharmaceutical companies that outsource all or most of their specialized testing functions. Founded in 1993, Clarient was acquired by NeoGenomics from GE Healthcare in late 2015.

CLARK CONSTRUCTION GROUP, LLC

7500 OLD GEORGETOWN RD
BETHESDA, MD 208146800
Phone: 301 272-8100
Fax: –
Web: www.clarkconstruction.com

CEO: Robert D Moser Jr
CFO: Sameer Bhargava
HR: Brittany Pile
FYE: December 31
Type: Private

Clark Construction Group is a leading provider of general contracting, design-build, construction management, and specialty contracting services for building and infrastructure assets. Some of its projects include The Paramount, Twinbrook Quarter, National Desert Storm and Desert Shield Memorial, JHU Hopkins Student Center, Pinnacle Office Tower, West Falls Condominium, Century City Center, and Willis Tower Renovations, among others. The company traces its roots back to 1906 as George Hyman Construction Company founded by George Hyman.

CLARK DUBIN & COMPANY INC

323 NEWBURY ST
BOSTON, MA 021152710
Phone: 203 629-2030
Fax: –
Web: www.dubinclark.com

CEO: –
CFO: Michelle Cummings
HR: –
FYE: December 31
Type: Private

Dubin Clark & Company is in the business of buying businesses. The private equity firm targets small and middle-market companies for its long-term investments. The firm partners with management and supplies the capital necessary for its investments to grow. Dubin Clark is choosy when it comes to making investments and intentionally limits amount of companies in its portfolio. Over the years the firm has invested in companies such as CompUSA, which experienced a period of rapid growth and an IPO. More recent investments include B&M Racing & Performance Products which makes high-performance auto parts, and Tulsa Power, a material handling equipment maker. Dubin Clark was founded in 1984.

CLARK ENTERPRISES, INC.

7500 OLD GEORGETOWN RD FL 15
BETHESDA, MD 208146195
Phone: 301 657-7100
Fax: –
Web: www.clarkenterprises.com

CEO: Lawrence Nussdorf
CFO: James J Brinkman
HR: –
FYE: December 31
Type: Private

Clark Enterprises, Inc. (CEI) is a private investment firm with diverse investments in real estate, financial markets, and venture capital. CEI is based in Bethesda, Maryland. Founded in 1972 by A. James Clark.

CLARK, SCHAEFER, HACKETT & CO.

1 E 4TH ST STE 1200
CINCINNATI, OH 452024294
Phone: 513 241-3111
Fax: –
Web: www.cshco.com

CEO: –
CFO: –
HR: Jenni R Rossi
FYE: June 30
Type: Private

There might be no accounting for taste, but you'd better believe there's accounting for corporate financial practices. CPA firm Clark, Schaefer, Hackett & Co. provides accounting, tax, and business services for business and consumer clients in Ohio, Kentucky, and Indiana. Operating from five offices throughout Ohio, the firm specializes in core industries including manufacturing and distributions, health care, manufacturing, financial institutions, and legal services as well as government entities and not-for-profit organizations. Clark, Schaefer, Hackett & Co. was founded in 1938.

	Annual Growth	06/07	06/08	06/09	06/10	06/11
Sales ($mil.)	1.4%	–	–	43.6	43.2	44.8
Net income ($ mil.)	6.6%	–	–	0.7	0.5	0.8
Market value ($ mil.)	–	–	–	–	–	–
Employees	–	–	–	–	–	245

CLARKSON UNIVERSITY

8 CLARKSON AVE
POTSDAM, NY 136761402
Phone: 315 268-6400
Fax: -
Web: www.clarkson.edu

CEO: -
CFO: James Fish
HR: -
FYE: June 30
Type: Private

Clarkson University knows that quality research never sleeps in The Empire State. The research institution confers bachelor's, master's, and doctoral degrees in more than 95 fields of study, including engineering, business, science, liberal arts, and health sciences. It also has well-regarded programs in advanced materials, biotech, environment and energy, entrepreneurship, and global supply chain management. The university employs around 870 faculty and staff catering to more than 4,300 students. Clarkson University was founded in 1896 as a memorial to Thomas Clarkson, a businessman from Potsdam, New York, where the primary campus is located. Its Capital Region satellite is located in Schenectady.

	Annual Growth	06/17	06/18	06/19	06/20	06/22
Sales ($mil.)	1.7%	-	132.8	135.3	247.2	141.9
Net income ($ mil.)	-	-	(7.0)	17.4	9.2	(17.4)
Market value ($ mil.)	-	-	-	-	-	-
Employees	-	-	-	-	-	700

CLAROCITY CORP

3115 Melrose Drive, Suite 130
Carlsbad, CA 92010
Phone: 403 984-9246
Fax: 403 770-8780
Web: www.clarocity.com

NBB: CLRY F
CEO: -
CFO: -
HR: -
FYE: December 31
Type: Public

How much is your home sweet home worth? Zaio -- short for Zone Appraisal and Imaging Operations -- aims to provide instant access (through its Web site) to property information on almost every residential property in the 250 largest US cities. Its proprietary GeoScore property rating system uses comprehensive property data including real estate appraisals and property photos provided by contracted independent appraisers and photographers to calculate an estimated valuation. Revenues are generated by selling geographic zones to appraisers and photographers and property information to customers including mortgage companies, county tax assessors, investors, and property owners.

	Annual Growth	12/13	12/14	12/15	12/16	12/17
Sales ($mil.)	-	-	-	2.3	4.7	10.6
Net income ($ mil.)	-	(6.4)	(4.7)	(9.4)	(7.3)	(11.6)
Market value ($ mil.)	(21.2%)	35.0	47.2	16.0	17.8	13.5
Employees	-	-	-	-	-	-

CLARUS CORP (NEW)

2084 East 3900 South
Salt Lake City, UT 84124
Phone: 801 278-5552
Fax: -
Web: -

NMS: CLAR
CEO: John C Walbrecht
CFO: Michael J Yates
HR: -
FYE: December 31
Type: Public

Black Diamond caters to expert skiers, snowboarders, rock and ice climbers, and other hardy-outdoor types. The company makes and distributes climbing and mountaineering equipment (carabiners, harnesses, helmets), backpacks, tents, trekking poles, headlamps and lanterns, gloves and mittens, skis, bindings, boots, avalanche safety equipment, mountain biking gear, and more under the Black Diamond and PIEPS brands. Black Diamond sells its products across more than 5,000 retail locations. The US account for almost 50% of its sales.

	Annual Growth	12/19	12/20	12/21	12/22	12/23
Sales ($mil.)	5.7%	229.4	224.0	375.8	448.1	286.0
Net income ($ mil.)	-	19.0	5.5	26.1	(69.8)	(10.1)
Market value ($ mil.)	(15.6%)	517.3	587.5	1,057.5	299.1	263.0
Employees	-	500	600	950	900	500

CLAY ELECTRIC COOPERATIVE, INC.

225 W WALKER DR
KEYSTONE HEIGHTS, FL 326567617
Phone: 352 473-8000
Fax: -
Web: www.clayelectric.com

CEO: Richard K Davis
CFO: -
HR: -
FYE: December 31
Type: Private

Clay Electric Cooperative covers a lot of ground in Florida. The utility distributes electricity to 14 counties in the northeastern part of the state, including the suburbs of Jacksonville and Gainesville. It delivers power to about 170,000 residential, commercial, and industrial members over more than 13,000 miles of distribution and transmission lines. The consumer-owned utility offers electronic funds transfer, average billing, and a seniors' payment plan to residential customers, and backup diesel power generation and special rate plans to businesses. The consumer-owned utility has a stake in Seminole Electric Cooperative, which provides generation services to Clay Electric and nine other cooperatives.

	Annual Growth	12/17	12/18	12/19	12/20	12/22
Sales ($mil.)	5.8%	-	373.2	364.7	371.7	468.3
Net income ($ mil.)	4.6%	-	22.3	19.4	22.3	26.8
Market value ($ mil.)	-	-	-	-	-	-
Employees	-	-	-	-	-	444

CLAYCO, INC.

35 E WACKER DR STE 1300
CHICAGO, IL 606012110
Phone: 312 658-0747
Fax: -
Web: www.claycorp.com

CEO: Russ Burns
CFO: Anthony Schofield
HR: -
FYE: December 31
Type: Private

Clayco is a top US general building contractor that offers real estate, architecture, design, engineering, and construction services. The privately owned company serves a range of industries with a focus on industrial, corporate, government, residential, institutional, and financial facilities. Projects include distribution and logistics centers, industrial facilities, and food and beverage industry warehouses and plants. Clayco also has constructed headquarters and operation centers, call and data centers, sports and education facilities, and retail centers. Its Clayco Realty Group provides land development, site selection, and project financing.

	Annual Growth	12/08	12/09	12/10	12/11	12/12
Sales ($mil.)	(6.0%)	-	-	443.2	511.3	391.3
Net income ($ mil.)	(26.2%)	-	-	4.4	2.4	2.4
Market value ($ mil.)	-	-	-	-	-	-
Employees	-	-	-	-	-	2,600

CLEAN ENERGY FUELS CORP

4675 MacArthur Court, Suite 800
Newport Beach, CA 92660
Phone: 949 437-1000
Fax: -
Web: www.cleanenergyfuels.com

NMS: CLNE
CEO: Andrew J Littlefair
CFO: Robert M Vreeland
HR: Lupe Portillo
FYE: December 31
Type: Public

Clean Energy Fuels is a leading renewable energy company focused on the procurement and distribution of renewable natural gas (RNG) and conventional natural gas, in the form of compressed natural gas (CNG) and liquefied natural gas (LNG), for the US and Canadian transportation markets. The company owns, operates, or supplies about 570 fueling stations in the US and about 25 in Canada. These enable Clean Energy's over 1,000 fleet customers to tank up their more than 50,000 fleet vehicles with CNG or LNG. Clean Energy also helps customers buy natural gas vehicles and apply for federal, state, and local grant programs. Most of the company's revenue comes from the US.

	Annual Growth	12/19	12/20	12/21	12/22	12/23
Sales ($mil.)	5.4%	344.1	291.7	255.6	420.2	425.2
Net income ($ mil.)	-	20.4	(9.9)	(93.1)	(58.7)	(99.5)
Market value ($ mil.)	13.1%	521.9	1,753.0	1,367.2	1,159.7	854.2
Employees	8.3%	412	465	482	496	566

CLEAN HARBORS INC
NYS: CLH

42 Longwater Drive
Norwell, MA 02061-9149
Phone: 781 792-5000
Fax: -
Web: www.cleanharbors.com

CEO: Alan S McKim
CFO: Michael L Battles
HR: Tyler Tatman
FYE: December 31
Type: Public

Clean Harbors is one of the leading providers of environmental, energy and industrial services throughout North America. It is also the largest re-refiner and recycler of used oil in the world and the largest provider of parts cleaning and related environmental services to commercial, industrial and automotive customers in North America. Services include end-to-end hazardous waste management, emergency response, industrial cleaning and maintenance and recycling services. It has an annual collection capacity of about 230 million gallons of waste oil and some 570 service locations across the US and parts of Canada, Puerto Rico, and Mexico. Nearly 90% of its revenue comes from the US.

	Annual Growth	12/19	12/20	12/21	12/22	12/23
Sales ($mil.)	12.2%	3,412.2	3,144.1	3,805.6	5,166.6	5,409.2
Net income ($ mil.)	40.2%	97.7	134.8	203.2	411.7	377.9
Market value ($ mil.)	19.4%	4,624.5	4,104.1	5,380.6	6,154.5	9,411.3
Employees	9.9%	14,400	14,000	19,100	20,260	21,021

CLEANNET U.S.A., INC.

8300 BOONE BLVD STE 500
VIENNA, VA 221822681
Phone: 410 720-6444
Fax: -
Web: www.cleannetusa.com

CEO: -
CFO: -
HR: Kelly Wiseman
FYE: December 31
Type: Private

If Mr. Clean himself can't make a personal appearance at your office building, CleanNet USA will happily come to your rescue. The company provides commercial building cleaning services to clients nationwide through franchises in at more than 35,000 locations, totaling more than 160 million square feet across the US. Its clients' properties include commercial and retail buildings and facilities including banks, airports, entertainment venues, convention centers, restaurants, and medical facilities, as well as places of worship. Its trained personnel are uniformed and carry identification badges. CleanNet USA was founded in 1987 by president Mark Salek.

	Annual Growth	12/16	12/17	12/20	12/21	12/22
Sales ($mil.)	7.0%	-	68.8	114.6	93.4	96.4
Net income ($ mil.)	9.3%	-	4.4	13.3	9.6	6.9
Market value ($ mil.)	-	-	-	-	-	-
Employees	-	-	-	-	-	150

CLEAR CHANNEL OUTDOOR HOLDINGS INC (NEW)
NYS: CCO

4830 North Loop 1604 West, Suite 111
San Antonio, TX 78249
Phone: 210 547-8800
Fax: -
Web: www.clearchanneloutdoor.com

CEO: Scott R Wells
CFO: Brian D Coleman
HR: -
FYE: December 31
Type: Public

Clear Channel Outdoor Holdings is a leading display advertising operator, with over 500,000 displays in more than 25 countries across Asia, Europe, Latin America and North America. Besides billboards, Clear Channel Outdoor Holdings sells advertising on buses and trains and on street furniture such as bus stops and information kiosks in metropolitan markets. The company sells advertising space in airports and malls and on the sides of high-profile buildings, and also creates displays that feature video and moving parts. More than 50% of the company's revenue comes from Americas operation.

	Annual Growth	12/19	12/20	12/21	12/22	12/23
Sales ($mil.)	(5.6%)	2,683.8	1,854.6	2,241.1	2,481.1	2,127.1
Net income ($ mil.)	-	(363.3)	(582.7)	(433.8)	(96.6)	(310.9)
Market value ($ mil.)	(10.7%)	1,381.5	797.0	1,598.9	507.2	879.2
Employees	(9.8%)	5,900	4,800	4,600	4,700	3,900

CLEARDAY INC
NBB: CLRD

8800 Village Drive, Suite 106
San Antonio, TX 78217
Phone: 210 451-0839
Fax: -
Web: www.suptech.com

CEO: James T Walesa
CFO: Randall Hawkins
HR: Casey May
FYE: December 31
Type: Public

Superconductor Technologies Inc. (STI) can cool even the most heated conversation. The company uses high-temperature superconducting (HTS) technology in its line of communications products, which combine low-noise amplifiers and filters, are designed to improve the quality of radio-frequency (RF) transmissions between cellular base stations and mobile devices in wireless networks. It also makes cryogenic cooling devices used to cool HTS materials. STI relies on government contracts to fund its R&D operations; on the commercial side the company serves such top wireless network operators as AT&T, Verizon Wireless, Sprint Nextel, and T-Mobile.

	Annual Growth	12/18	12/19	12/20	12/21	12/22
Sales ($mil.)	68.3%	1.6	0.5	0.2	12.9	12.5
Net income ($ mil.)	-	(8.1)	(9.2)	(3.0)	(19.7)	(14.3)
Market value ($ mil.)	(18.8%)	26.8	3.8	16.4	42.9	11.7
Employees	73.2%	25	7	3	225	225

CLEARFIELD HOSPITAL

809 TURNPIKE AVE
CLEARFIELD, PA 168301243
Phone: 814 768-2470
Fax: -
Web: www.clearfieldhosp.org

CEO: Robert Murray
CFO: Dave M Connell
HR: -
FYE: June 30
Type: Private

Clearly, if you are looking for health care in Clearfield, Pennsylvania, the place to go is Clearfield Hospital. Operated by Clearfield Area Health Services, the rural acute care hospital has about 100 beds and provides emergency, surgical, diagnostic, and general inpatient services. Specialized care centers focus on pediatrics, obstetrics, cardiac care, wound healing, cancer treatment, rehabilitation, and home care. Clearfield Hospital -- which operates a number of rural primary and specialty care clinics -- also provides educational programs, classes, and community outreach testing and screening services.

	Annual Growth	06/13	06/14	06/15	06/16	06/21
Sales ($mil.)	1.9%	-	43.0	42.6	40.7	49.2
Net income ($ mil.)	-	-	(4.0)	(3.9)	(1.2)	5.9
Market value ($ mil.)	-	-	-	-	-	-
Employees	-	-	-	-	-	700

CLEARFIELD INC
NMS: CLFD

7050 Winnetka Avenue North, Suite 100
Brooklyn Park, MN 55428
Phone: 763 476-6866
Fax: -
Web: www.seeclearfield.comwww.seeclearfield.com

CEO: Cheryl Beranek
CFO: Daniel R Herzog
HR: -
FYE: September 30
Type: Public

Clearfield designs, manufactures and distributes fiber protection, fiber management and fiber delivery solutions to enable rapid and cost-effective fiber-fed deployment throughout the broadband service provider space across North America. Products include a series of panels, cabinets, wall boxes and other enclosures that house the Clearfield components; optical components integrated for signal coupling, splitting, termination, and multiplexing among others for a seamless integration within their fiber management platform; fiber management and fiber pathway and protection method. More than 95% of Clearfield's revenue comes from customers in the US.

	Annual Growth	09/19	09/20	09/21	09/22	09/23
Sales ($mil.)	33.3%	85.0	93.1	140.8	270.9	268.7
Net income ($ mil.)	63.4%	4.6	7.3	20.3	49.4	32.5
Market value ($ mil.)	24.7%	180.8	307.7	673.5	1,596.3	437.2
Employees	13.6%	240	230	250	407	400

CLEARONE INC

NAS: CLRO

5225 Wiley Post Way, Suite 500
Salt Lake City, UT 84116
Phone: 801 975-7200
Fax: –
Web: www.clearone.com

CEO: Zeynep Hakimoglu
CFO: –
HR: –
FYE: December 31
Type: Public

ClearOne is a global company that designs, develops and sells conferencing, collaboration, and AV networking solutions for voice and visual communications. The company provides audio conferencing systems to small and large enterprises, educational institutions, churches, and government agencies largely in the US. It also sells related products including microphones and equipment carts. ClearOne's conferencing systems connect large venues such as auditoriums and board rooms, as well as desktops and small conference rooms. The company markets its products worldwide, selling primarily through distributors who, in turn, sell to systems integrators and resellers. Customers in the US account for about 50% of revenue.

	Annual Growth	12/18	12/19	12/20	12/21	12/22
Sales ($mil.)	(2.7%)	28.2	25.0	29.1	29.0	25.2
Net income ($ mil.)	–	(16.7)	(8.4)	0.5	(7.7)	20.6
Market value ($ mil.)	5.0%	29.9	39.8	54.4	30.9	36.4
Employees	(10.9%)	130	127	126	107	82

CLEARPOINT NEURO INC

NAS: CLPT

120 S. Sierra Ave., Suite 100
Solana Beach, CA 92075
Phone: 888 287-9109
Fax: –
Web: www.clearpointneuro.com

CEO: –
CFO: –
HR: –
FYE: December 31
Type: Public

SurgiVision designs products with surgical focus. A medical devices company, SurgiVision develops imaging technologies and precision instruments (i.e. needles that deliver radiation) designed for surgeons performing minimally invasive procedures by way of MRI (magnetic resonance imaging) scanners. The company received FDA approval for its first commercial product, the ClearPoint system for use in neurological procedures, in 2010. It also has candidates in earlier stages of development, including its ClearTrace and SafeLead products, which are designed for cardiac procedures. SurgiVision was established in 1998; it filed to go public through an IPO in 2009.

	Annual Growth	12/19	12/20	12/21	12/22	12/23
Sales ($mil.)	20.9%	11.2	12.8	16.3	20.6	24.0
Net income ($ mil.)	–	(5.5)	(6.8)	(14.4)	(16.4)	(22.1)
Market value ($ mil.)	9.1%	118.3	391.7	276.6	208.8	167.4
Employees	–	49	67	80	108	–

CLEARSIGN TECHNOLOGIES CORP

NAS: CLIR

8023 East 63rd Place, Suite 101
Tulsa, OK 74133
Phone: 918 236-6461
Fax: –
Web: www.clearsign.com

CEO: Colin J Deller
CFO: Brent Hinds
HR: –
FYE: December 31
Type: Public

Improved energy efficiency and lower emissions? Clearsign believes it has found a way to do what many said couldn't be done. The company's proprietary Electrodynamic Combustion Control (ECC) system uses a computer connected to electrodes inside a combustion system to electrostatically control the process. ECC uses existing ions to manipulate chemical combustion thereby reducing pollution and directing the heat transfer for greater efficiency. The process, which can be part of new construction or a retrofit, works in combustion power generation (from coal, natural gas, and other fuels), in petrochemical refining, and in other industrial heat processes. Formed in 2008, Clearsign filed to go public in 2011.

	Annual Growth	12/18	12/19	12/20	12/21	12/22
Sales ($mil.)	(8.3%)	0.5	–	–	0.6	0.4
Net income ($ mil.)	–	(9.5)	(8.5)	(6.9)	(7.9)	(5.8)
Market value ($ mil.)	(14.9%)	38.8	29.0	111.4	52.5	20.4
Employees	(2.9%)	18	15	15	12	16

CLEARWATER PAPER CORP

NYS: CLW

601 West Riverside, Suite 1100
Spokane, WA 99201
Phone: 509 344-5900
Fax: –
Web: www.clearwaterpaper.com

CEO: Arsen S Kitch
CFO: Sherri Baker
HR: Gina Ciampaglio
FYE: December 31
Type: Public

Clearwater Paper is a manufacturer and supplier of quality consumer tissue, parent roll tissue, and bleached paperboard. It supplies bleached paperboard to quality-conscious printers and packaging converters and offers services that include custom sheeting, slitting, and cutting. It supplies private label tissue to major retailers and wholesale distributors, including groceries, clubs, mass merchants, and discount stores. It uses a variety of chemicals in its manufacturing processes, including petroleum-based polyethylene and certain petroleum-based latex chemicals. Vast majority of Clearwater's revenue is made in the US. The company traces its roots back to 1926.

	Annual Growth	12/19	12/20	12/21	12/22	12/23
Sales ($mil.)	4.3%	1,761.5	1,868.6	1,772.6	2,080.1	2,082.8
Net income ($ mil.)	–	(5.6)	77.1	(28.1)	46.0	107.7
Market value ($ mil.)	14.0%	352.1	622.3	604.5	623.3	595.4
Employees	(1.5%)	3,290	3,340	3,000	3,000	3,100

CLEARWAY ENERGY INC

NYS: CWEN

300 Carnegie Center, Suite 300
Princeton, NJ 08540
Phone: 609 608-1525
Fax: –
Web: www.nrgyield.com

CEO: Christopher S Sotos
CFO: Sarah Rubenstein
HR: –
FYE: December 31
Type: Public

Clearway Energy is one of the largest renewable energy owners in the US with over 5,500 net MW of installed wind and solar generation projects. The company is a publicly-traded energy infrastructure investor with a focus on investments in clean energy and owner of modern, sustainable, and long-term contracted assets across North America. The company's over 8,000 net MW of assets includes approximately 2,500 net MW of environmentally-sound, highly efficient natural gas-fired generation facilities. The company is sponsored by GIP and TotalEnergies through the portfolio company, Clearway Energy Group LLC, or CEG, which became equally owned by GIP and TotalEnergies.

	Annual Growth	12/19	12/20	12/21	12/22	12/23
Sales ($mil.)	6.2%	1,032.0	1,199.0	1,286.0	1,190.0	1,314.0
Net income ($ mil.)	–	(11.0)	25.0	51.0	582.0	79.0
Market value ($ mil.)	8.3%	4,031.5	6,452.4	7,281.0	6,440.3	5,543.1
Employees	(33.2%)	307	301	304	58	61

CLEARY UNIVERSITY

3750 CLEARY DR STE 1
HOWELL, MI 488438542
Phone: 517 338-3320
Fax: –
Web: www.cleary.edu

CEO: –
CFO: –
HR: Kait Conahan
FYE: June 30
Type: Private

Cleary University helps students navigate the murky waters of business education. The school offers associate, bachelor's, and master's degrees in business administration. Cleary University focuses on adult undergraduate students, first-time college students wanting to begin a business career, and senior managers seeking to advance their careers through a graduate degree. It has two campuses (Howell and Ann Arbor) and three extension sites (Flint, Garden City, and Warren) in Michigan. The school also offers distance learning courses online through its eCleary program. Patrick Roger Cleary founded the school as The Cleary School of Penmanship in 1883.

	Annual Growth	06/18	06/19	06/20	06/21	06/22
Sales ($mil.)	5.1%	–	16.2	15.5	17.0	18.8
Net income ($ mil.)	–	–	1.7	(0.4)	0.2	(1.3)
Market value ($ mil.)	–	–	–	–	–	–
Employees	–	–	–	–	–	200

CLECO CORPORATE HOLDINGS LLC

2030 DONAHUE FERRY RD
PINEVILLE, LA 713605226
Phone: 318 484-7400
Fax: –
Web: www.cleco.com

CEO: William G Fontenot
CFO: Kristin Guillory
HR: –
FYE: December 31
Type: Private

Down in the Louisiana bayous, Cleco comes alive with the click of a light switch. The holding company's utility unit, Cleco Power, generates, transmits, and distributes electricity to approximately 290,000 residential and business customers. Cleco Power has a net generating capacity of over 3,000 MW from its interests in nine fossil-fueled power plants. It also purchases power from other utilities and energy marketers and sells some excess power to wholesale customers. Cleco Cajun is an unregulated electric utility that owns about 15 generating assets with a rated capacity of 3,3380 MW and supplies wholesale power and capacity in Arkansas, Louisiana, and Texas.

	Annual Growth	12/18	12/19	12/20	12/21	12/22
Sales ($mil.)	10.9%	–	1,639.6	1,498.1	1,745.9	2,239.1
Net income ($ mil.)	7.3%	–	152.7	122.3	208.1	188.8
Market value ($ mil.)	–	–	–	–	–	–
Employees	–	–	–	–	–	1,204

CLEVELAND BROWNS FOOTBALL COMPANY LLC

76 LOU GROZA BLVD
BEREA, OH 440171269
Phone: 440 891-5000
Fax: –
Web: www.clevelandbrowns.com

CEO: –
CFO: –
HR: –
FYE: December 31
Type: Private

The Dawg Pound is the place to be for football fans in Cleveland. The Cleveland Browns Football Company owns and operates the Cleveland Browns, one of the more storied franchises in the National Football League. Started in 1944 by Arthur McBride as part of the All-American Football Conference, the club joined the NFL in 1949 and boasts four championship titles, its last in 1964. The present team was awarded to the late Alfred Lerner and former 49ers president Carmen Policy after Art Modell relocated the original Browns to Baltimore in 1996. (A deal struck with the NFL allowed Cleveland to retain the team name, colors, and history.) Lerner's family, led by son Randy, continues to control the team.

	Annual Growth	12/05	12/06	12/07	12/08	12/19
Sales ($mil.)	9.6%	–	–	–	0.6	1.7
Net income ($ mil.)	–	–	–	–	–	0.7
Market value ($ mil.)	–	–	–	–	–	–
Employees	–	–	–	–	–	150

CLEVELAND CLINIC MERCY HOSPITAL

1320 MERCY DR NW
CANTON, OH 447082614
Phone: 330 489-1000
Fax: –
Web: www.cantonmercy.org

CEO: –
CFO: –
HR: –
FYE: December 31
Type: Private

Mercy Medical Center keeps patients doing the cancan in Canton. The facility is a 480-bed acute care hospital serving residents of five counties in southeastern Ohio. The Catholic medical center has 700 physicians and provides a comprehensive range of care including inpatient, outpatient, and rehabilitative services. It operates specialty care centers for cardiac, vascular, stroke, and cancer treatment, as well as trauma, chest pain, and rehabilitation units. Mercy Medical Center also operates outpatient health centers in the communities surrounding Canton, Ohio. The facility is part of the Sisters of Charity Health System (SCHS), a not-for-profit ministry of the Sisters of Charity of St. Augustine.

	Annual Growth	12/16	12/17	12/18	12/19	12/20
Sales ($mil.)	6.9%	–	–	–	299.8	320.5
Net income ($ mil.)	–	–	–	–	–	(5.2)
Market value ($ mil.)	–	–	–	–	–	–
Employees	–	–	–	–	–	3,320

CLEVELAND CONSTRUCTION, INC.

8620 TYLER BLVD
MENTOR, OH 440604348
Phone: 440 255-8000
Fax: –
Web: www.clevelandconstruction.com

CEO: –
CFO: –
HR: –
FYE: December 31
Type: Private

Cleveland Construction, Inc. (CCI) is a family-owned national commercial contractor specializing in Construction Management, General Contracting, and Interior Specialty Contracting. Beyond general contractor work, the company provides design build, and self-performing walls & ceilings services. Also a top interior contractor in the US, the contractor installs finishes such as metal stud framing and drywall, acoustical and specialty ceilings, and prefabricated panels. Its projects have included hospitals, universities, correctional facilities, hotels, convention centers, sports complexes, retail outlets (including Wal-Mart stores), and public projects such as Charlotte Douglas International Airport and Offutt Air Force Base. Richard G. Small and his sons founded Cleveland Construction, Inc. in December of 1980 as commercial drywall contractors.

	Annual Growth	12/05	12/06	12/07	12/08	12/09
Sales ($mil.)	(2.4%)	–	–	228.0	186.5	217.0
Net income ($ mil.)	25.2%	–	–	16.4	24.0	25.7
Market value ($ mil.)	–	–	–	–	–	–
Employees	–	–	–	–	–	800

CLEVELAND ELECTRIC ILLUMINATING CO

c/o FirstEnergy Corp., 76 South Main Street
Akron, OH 44308
Phone: 800 736-3402
Fax: –
Web: –

CEO: –
CFO: Mark T Clark
HR: –
FYE: December 31
Type: Public

The Cleveland Electric Illuminating Company (CEI) has a glowing reputation. The utility, commonly referred to as The Illuminating Company, distributes electricity to a base population of about 1.8 million inhabitants in a 1,600 sq. mi. area of northeastern Ohio. CEI has 33,210 miles of distribution lines. In 2010 the utility met 4,420 MW of hourly maximum generating demand from interests in fossil-fueled and nuclear power plants (which are operated by fellow FirstEnergy subsidiaries). It also engages in wholesale energy transactions with other power companies. CEI is also a competitive retail electric service provider in Ohio alongside sister companies Ohio Edison and Toledo Edison.

	Annual Growth	12/07	12/08	12/09	12/10	12/11
Sales ($mil.)	(16.7%)	1,822.9	1,815.9	1,676.1	1,221.4	876.8
Net income ($ mil.)	(28.9%)	276.4	284.5	(12.7)	71.7	70.6
Market value ($ mil.)	–	–	–	–	–	–
Employees	7.5%	672	1,010	873	916	897

CLEVELAND STATE UNIVERSITY

2121 EUCLID AVE
CLEVELAND, OH 441152226
Phone: 216 687-2000
Fax: –
Web: www.csuohio.edu

CEO: Lee Fisher
CFO: –
HR: –
FYE: June 30
Type: Private

Cleveland State University offers a well-rounded education in the land of the Buckeyes. The university provides some 1,000 courses in the arts and sciences, business administration, law, engineering, and other areas. The school, which enrolls more than 17,000 students, offers undergraduate and graduate degrees in 200 fields of study through eight colleges and two academic divisions. The university has more than 570 faculty members on its staff. Tuition for undergraduate residents is about $7,900. Its Maxine Goodman Levin College of Urban Affairs is nationally recognized for its public administration programs. Established in 1964, Cleveland State merged with Cleveland-Marshall College of Law in 1969.

	Annual Growth	06/17	06/18	06/19	06/20	06/22
Sales ($mil.)	1.3%	–	199.4	191.9	185.4	209.6
Net income ($ mil.)	(29.8%)	–	73.4	9.4	(10.3)	17.8
Market value ($ mil.)	–	–	–	–	–	–
Employees	–	–	–	–	–	2,600

CLEVELAND-CLIFFS INC (NEW)   NYS: CLF

200 Public Square
Cleveland, OH 44114-2315
Phone: 216 694-5700
Fax: –
Web: www.clevelandcliffs.com

CEO: Lourenco Goncalves
CFO: Celso Goncalves
HR: –
FYE: December 31
Type: Public

Cleveland-Cliffs is the largest flat-rolled steel and iron ore pellets producer in North America. Its fully integrated portfolio includes custom-made pellets and HBI; flat-rolled carbon steel, stainless, electrical, plate, tinplate, and long steel products; as well as carbon and stainless steel tubing, hot and cold stamping, and tooling. Cleveland-Cliffs' operations, including Tilden Mine, Northshore, Minorca, Hibbing, and United Taconite mines, produce some 28 million tons of iron ore pellets annually. The company sells its ore primarily in North America. The majority of its sales were generated in the US. The company traces its roots back to 1847.

	Annual Growth	12/19	12/20	12/21	12/22	12/23
Sales ($mil.)	82.3%	1,989.9	5,354.0	20,444	22,989	21,996
Net income ($ mil.)	8.0%	292.8	(122.0)	2,988.0	1,335.0	399.0
Market value ($ mil.)	24.9%	4,241.0	7,351.2	10,991	8,133.7	10,310
Employees	85.4%	2,372	25,000	26,000	27,000	28,000

CLICKER INC

1111 Kane Concourse, Suite 304
Bay Harbor Islands, FL 33154
Phone: 786 309-5190
Fax: –
Web: www.clickercorporate.com

CEO: –
CFO: –
HR: –
FYE: August 31
Type: Public

This company is much more interested in the mouse than the remote control. Clicker operates a network of websites focused around such topics as celebrity news, classified advertising, investing, and sports. Its online properties include the ForWant (classified ads), Sippin' It (celebrity news and gossip), and Wall Street Network (investment community). Most of its sites include social networking functions to help foster interactivity and generate revenue through advertising and rewards programs. Chairman and CEO Albert Aimers owns nearly 45% of Clicker.

	Annual Growth	08/08	08/09	08/10	08/11	08/12
Sales ($mil.)	(86.4%)	7.8	1.3	0.8	0.0	0.0
Net income ($ mil.)	–	(2.9)	(3.3)	(7.5)	(4.1)	(1.8)
Market value ($ mil.)	(25.5%)	0.3	0.0	0.2	0.0	0.0
Employees	(53.8%)	22	9	6	1	1

CLIENT SERVICES, INC.

3451 HARRY S TRUMAN BLVD
SAINT CHARLES, MO 633014047
Phone: 636 947-2321
Fax: –
Web: www.clientservices.com

CEO: Brad Franta
CFO: –
HR: –
FYE: October 31
Type: Private

This CSI investigates debt. Client Services, Inc. (CSI) is a collections agency that provides accounts receivable management and customer care services nationwide. CSI markets its services to banks and credit card companies, utilities, and other government and commercial clients. It performs a range of services from pre-collection consultation to skiptracing, debt purchasing, and recovery consulting. Debtors can also make payments on the company's website. However, call centers are the heart of its daily operations. CSI has four call centers that are staffed 24/7 and can handle 10,000 calls per day. The company was founded in 1987.

CLIF BAR & COMPANY, LLC

1451 66TH ST
EMERYVILLE, CA 946081004
Phone: 510 596-6300
Fax: –
Web: www.clifbar.com

CEO: Sally Grimes
CFO: Hari Avula
HR: Lindsey Young
FYE: December 31
Type: Private

Launched in 1992, Clif Bar & Company is one of the leading makers of natural energy, nutrition, and snack bars. Its high-carb CLIF and LUNA bars aim to refuel sports enthusiasts and others and are distributed in bike shops, outdoor stores, and natural food markets, as well as grocery stores, convenience stores, and other retail outlets nationwide. Customers can also order via the company's ecommerce site. Additionally, Clif Bar offers various iterations of its products, including Builder's bars, along with children's versions called ZBar. The family- and employee-owned company also sells CLIF Shot ? energy drinks and gels fortified with electrolytes. In mid-2022, the company was acquired by Mondelez International for approximately $2.9 billion.

CLIFTONLARSONALLEN LLP

220 S 6TH ST STE 300
MINNEAPOLIS, MN 554021418
Phone: 612 376-4500
Fax: –
Web: www.claconnect.com

CEO: Denny Schleper
CFO: Heidi Hillman
HR: Angie Ross
FYE: December 04
Type: Private

CliftonLarsonAllen (CLA) exists to create opportunities for its clients, its people, and its communities through industry-focused wealth advisory, outsourcing, audit, tax, and consulting services. CLA is a network member of CLA Global, an international organization of independent accounting and advisory firms. The firm has operations in more than 130 locations across the US.

	Annual Growth	12/11	12/12	12/13	12/14	12/15
Sales ($mil.)	7.5%	–	–	563.0	598.7	650.7
Net income ($ mil.)	5.1%	–	–	154.8	163.3	170.8
Market value ($ mil.)	–	–	–	–	–	–
Employees	–	–	–	–	–	4,786

CLIMB GLOBAL SOLUTIONS INC   NMS: CLMB

4 Industrial Way West, Suite 300
Eatontown, NJ 07724
Phone: 732 389-8950
Fax: –
Web: www.waysidetechnology.com

CEO: Dale Foster
CFO: Andrew Clark
HR: –
FYE: December 31
Type: Public

Wayside Technology connects developers with users of IT products. A leading reseller for software developers, the firm's TechXtend (formerly Programmer's Paradise) business markets software, hardware, and services to IT professionals, government agencies, and educational institutions in the US and Canada. Wayside's Lifeboat Distribution subsidiary provides software to resellers, consultants, and systems integrators worldwide. (Software accounts for about 95% of the company's sales.) Wayside Technology sells products through its catalogs and e-commerce sites, and its suppliers include Quest Software, Intel, Flexera, TechSmith, and Vmware, among others.

	Annual Growth	12/19	12/20	12/21	12/22	12/23
Sales ($mil.)	14.0%	208.8	251.6	282.6	304.3	352.0
Net income ($ mil.)	16.1%	6.8	4.5	9.2	12.5	12.3
Market value ($ mil.)	35.6%	74.1	87.4	160.5	144.2	250.8
Employees	26.6%	142	275	269	300	365

CLINCH VALLEY MEDICAL CENTER, INC.

6801 GOVERNOR GC PEERY HWY
RICHLANDS, VA 246412194
Phone: 276 596-6000
Fax: –
Web: www.clinchvalleyhealth.com

CEO: –
CFO: –
HR: –
FYE: November 30
Type: Private

Clinch Valley Medical Center oversees southwestern Virginia's acute medical needs. The regional hospital provides medical and emergency care services in about a dozen counties around Richlands, Virginia. Clinch Valley Medical Center offers cancer care, cardiac catheterization, diagnostic imaging, laboratory services, women's services, pediatrics, physical rehabilitation services, sleep studies, and surgical services. The medical center has a 200-bed capacity and is part of the LifePoint Health network. The hospital's medical staff represent 33 medical specialties.

	Annual Growth	11/17	11/18	11/19	11/20	11/21
Sales ($mil.)	19.0%	–	–	–	96.9	115.2
Net income ($ mil.)	68.2%	–	–	–	6.4	10.7
Market value ($ mil.)	–	–	–	–	–	–
Employees	–	–	–	–	–	715

CLOROX CO (THE) NYS: CLX

1221 Broadway
Oakland, CA 94612-1888
Phone: 510 271-7000
Fax: –
Web: www.thecloroxcompany.com

CEO: Linda Rendle
CFO: Kevin B Jacobsen
HR: –
FYE: June 30
Type: Public

The Clorox Company is a leading multinational manufacturer and marketer of consumer and professional products. Its products are sold primarily through mass retailers; grocery outlets; warehouse clubs; dollar stores; home hardware centers; drug, pet, and military stores; third-party and owned e-commerce channels; and distributors. It sells bleach, cleaning and disinfecting products (Clorox) as well as dressings, dips, seasonings, and sauces (Hidden Valley), grilling products (Kingsford), home care products (Glad), and cat litters (Fresh Step). Other items include filtration systems (Brita), vitamins, minerals, and supplements (Rainbow Light, RenewLife, NeoCell, Natural Vitality), and natural personal care products (Burt's Bees), among many other products and brands. Clorox makes and sells its products worldwide. The US market accounts for about 85% of its net sales.

	Annual Growth	06/19	06/20	06/21	06/22	06/23
Sales ($mil.)	4.4%	6,214.0	6,721.0	7,341.0	7,107.0	7,389.0
Net income ($ mil.)	(34.7%)	820.0	939.0	710.0	462.0	149.0
Market value ($ mil.)	1.0%	18,958	27,162	22,276	17,456	19,692
Employees	(0.3%)	8,800	8,800	9,000	9,000	8,700

CLOUD PEAK ENERGY INC.

606 POST RD E # 624
WESTPORT, CT 068804540
Phone: 307 687-6000
Fax: –
Web: –

CEO: Todd Myers
CFO: Heath Hill
HR: Jeanie Fox
FYE: December 31
Type: Private

Cloud Peak Energy owns and operates three surface coal mines in the Powder River Basin of Montana and Wyoming. One of the largest producers of coal in the US, it sells mainly to utilities and industrial customers and accounts for about 3% of the electricity generated in the US. Formerly part of Rio Tinto, it sells about 60 million tons of coal annually and controls almost 1.1 billion tons in proved and probable reserves. Cloud Peak supplies coal to more than 45 domestic and foreign electric utilities. The company was formed in 1993 as Kennecott Coal.

CLOVIS ONCOLOGY INC NMS: CLVS

5500 Flatiron Parkway, Suite 100
Boulder, CO 80301
Phone: 303 625-5000
Fax: –
Web: www.clovisoncology.com

CEO: Patrick J Mahaffy
CFO: Daniel W Muehl
HR: Katie Messimer
FYE: December 31
Type: Public

Clovis Oncology is a biopharmaceutical company that acquires, develops, and commercializes innovative anti-cancer agents in the United States, Europe and additional international markets. Its first marketed product, Rubraca, is approved by the FDA for the treatment of adult patients with deleterious BRCA (human genes associated with the repair of damaged DNA) mutation (germline and/or somatic)-associated epithelial ovarian, fallopian tube, or primary peritoneal cancer. The company target its development programs for the treatment of specific subsets of cancer populations, and simultaneously develop, with partners, for those indications that require them, diagnostic tools intended to direct a compound in development to the population that is most likely to benefit from its use. Clovis also works with partners to develop companion diagnostics for its treatment drugs. The company was founded in 2009.

	Annual Growth	12/17	12/18	12/19	12/20	12/21
Sales ($mil.)	27.9%	55.5	95.4	143.0	164.5	148.8
Net income ($ mil.)	–	(346.4)	(368.0)	(400.4)	(369.2)	(264.5)
Market value ($ mil.)	(55.3%)	8,779.4	2,318.8	1,346.0	619.7	349.9
Employees	3.5%	360	468	484	429	413

CLUBCORP HOLDINGS, INC.

3030 LYNDON B JOHNSON FWY STE 600
DALLAS, TX 752347744
Phone: 972 243-6191
Fax: –
Web: www.invitedclubs.com

CEO: Eric L Affeldt
CFO: Andrew Lacko
HR: –
FYE: December 29
Type: Private

ClubCorp, which changed its name to Invited Club in 2022, is the largest owner and operator of golf courses and private clubs, with more than 200 facilities in some 30 states (mostly in the fair weather states of California, Florida, and Texas). Invite Club properties include: Firestone Country Club (Akron, Ohio); Mission Hills Country Club (Rancho Mirage, California); The Woodlands Country Club (The Woodlands, Texas); and The Metropolitan in Chicago. Invite Club is founded by Robert H. Dedman Sr. in 1957.

CME GROUP INC NMS: CME

20 South Wacker Drive
Chicago, IL 60606
Phone: 312 930-1000
Fax: –
Web: www.cmegroup.com

CEO: –
CFO: –
HR: –
FYE: December 31
Type: Public

CME Group owns the Chicago Mercantile Exchange, the Chicago Board of Trade (CBOT), the New York Mercantile Exchange (NYMEX), and the Commodity Exchange (COMEX). The exchanges provide marketplaces for agricultural commodities, energy, and metals as well as for interest rate-sensitive instruments, equity, and foreign exchange futures. It also offers cash and repo fixed income trading via BrokerTec, and cash and OTC FX trading via EBS. Easily the world's largest futures exchange, CME owns 27% in S&P/Dow Jones Indices LLC (S&P/DJI) and accounts for its investment in S&P/DJI using the equity method of accounting. CME was founded in 1898 as a not-for-profit corporation.

	Annual Growth	12/19	12/20	12/21	12/22	12/23
Sales ($mil.)	3.5%	4,868.0	4,883.6	4,689.7	5,019.4	5,578.9
Net income ($ mil.)	11.1%	2,116.5	2,105.2	2,636.4	2,691.0	3,226.2
Market value ($ mil.)	1.2%	72,105	65,399	82,071	60,409	75,655
Employees	(4.9%)	4,360	4,370	3,480	3,460	3,565

CMS ENERGY CORP
NYS: CMS

One Energy Plaza
Jackson, MI 49201
Phone: 517 788-0550
Fax: –
Web: www.cmsenergy.com

CEO: Garrick J Rochow
CFO: Rejji P Hayes
HR: –
FYE: December 31
Type: Public

CMS Energy is an energy company operating primarily in Michigan. It is the parent holding company of several subsidiaries, including Consumers, an electric and gas utility, and NorthStar Clean Energy, primarily a domestic independent power producer and marketer. Consumers serve individuals and businesses operating in the alternative energy, automotive, chemical, food, and metal products industries, as well as a diversified group of other industries. NorthStar Clean Energy, through its subsidiaries and equity investments, is engaged in domestic independent power production, including the development and operation of renewable generation, and the marketing of independent power production.

	Annual Growth	12/19	12/20	12/21	12/22	12/23
Sales ($mil.)	2.2%	6,845.0	6,680.0	7,329.0	8,596.0	7,462.0
Net income ($ mil.)	6.9%	680.0	755.0	1,353.0	837.0	887.0
Market value ($ mil.)	(2.0%)	18,500	17,961	19,151	18,644	17,096
Employees	(1.3%)	8,789	8,837	9,122	9,073	8,356

CMTSU LIQUIDATION INC
NBB: CBRI

6312 South Fiddler's Green Circle, Suite 600E
Greenwood Village, CO 80111
Phone: 303 220-0100
Fax: 303 220-7100
Web: www.ciber.com

CEO: Michael Boustridge
CFO: Christian Mezger
HR: –
FYE: December 31
Type: Public

CIBER (Consultants in Business, Engineering, and Research) is a global IT consultancy that provides enterprise systems integration through consulting practices, specializing in such software systems as Lawson, Microsoft, Oracle, SAP, and Salesforce.com, as well as custom software development. It serves corporate customers in such industries as communications, financial services, manufacturing, health care, and education, as well as not-for-profits. Its diverse client list includes Boeing, The University of Texas System, Duke Energy, and Disney. CIBER filed for Chapter 11 bankruptcy in april 2917. The company was bought by HTC Global Services for more than $90 million in 2017.

	Annual Growth	12/11	12/12	12/13	12/14	12/15
Sales ($mil.)	(5.3%)	976.9	884.4	877.3	863.6	787.0
Net income ($ mil.)	–	(67.3)	(14.6)	(14.5)	(19.6)	3.3
Market value ($ mil.)	(2.3%)	308.9	267.3	331.3	284.1	280.9
Employees	(2.0%)	6,500	6,700	6,500	6,500	6,000

CNA FINANCIAL CORP
NYS: CNA

151 N. Franklin
Chicago, IL 60606
Phone: 312 822-5000
Fax: 312 822-6419
Web: www.cna.com

CEO: Dino E Robusto
CFO: Albert J Miralles
HR: Elizabeth Aguinaga
FYE: December 31
Type: Public

CNA Financial is an umbrella organization for a wide range of insurance providers, including Continental Casualty, Continental Insurance, Western Surety Company, CNA Insurance Company Limited, Hardy Underwriting Bermuda Limited and its subsidiaries (Hardy), and CNA Insurance Company (Europe). CNA also sells specialty insurance including professional liability (real estate agents, lawyers, architects) and vehicle warranty service contracts. Its insurance products primarily include commercial property and casualty coverages, including surety. Its services include warranty, risk management information services and claims administration. Holding company Loews owns 90% of CNA.

	Annual Growth	12/19	12/20	12/21	12/22	12/23
Assets ($mil.)	1.6%	60,612	64,026	66,639	60,927	64,711
Net income ($ mil.)	4.8%	1,000.0	690.0	1,202.0	894.0	1,205.0
Market value ($ mil.)	(1.4%)	12,138	10,554	11,940	11,453	11,461
Employees	1.7%	5,900	5,800	5,600	6,100	6,300

CNB CORP (MI)
NBB: CNBZ

303 North Main Street
Cheboygan, MI 49721
Phone: 231 627-7111
Fax: –
Web: www.cnbismybank.com

CEO: Susan A Eno
CFO: –
HR: Trisha Dobias
FYE: December 31
Type: Public

CNB Corporation is the holding company for Citizens National Bank of Cheboygan, which serves individuals and local businesses through more than five branches in the northern reaches of Michigan's Lower Peninsula. Serving the counties of Cheboygan, Emmet, and Presque Isle, the bank offers standard fare such as checking, savings, and money market accounts, CDs, and IRAs. CNB Mortgage, a subsidiary of the bank, handles residential mortgage lending activities, which account for approximately half of the company's loan portfolio; commercial mortgages make up most of the remainder. Bank affiliate CNB Financial Services provides insurance and financial planning. Citizens National Bank was founded in 1931.

	Annual Growth	12/10	12/11	12/12	12/13	12/14
Assets ($mil.)	(0.1%)	255.1	250.1	260.9	247.7	253.9
Net income ($ mil.)	56.0%	0.3	(2.7)	1.4	2.7	1.9
Market value ($ mil.)	10.2%	11.5	7.9	12.4	13.3	17.0
Employees	–	78	79	–	–	–

CNB FINANCIAL CORP. (CLEARFIELD, PA)
NMS: CCNE

1 South Second Street, P.O. Box 42
Clearfield, PA 16830
Phone: 814 765-9621
Fax: –
Web: www.cnbbank.bank

CEO: Joseph B Bower Jr
CFO: Tito L Lima
HR: BJ Sterndale
FYE: December 31
Type: Public

CNB Financial is the holding company for CNB Bank, ERIEBANK, and FCBank. The banks and subsidiaries provide traditional deposit and loan services as well as wealth management, merchant credit card processing, and life insurance through nearly 30 CNB Bank- and ERIEBANK-branded branches in Pennsylvania and nine FCBank branches in central Ohio. Commercial, industrial, and agricultural loans make up more than one-third of the bank's loan portfolio, while commercial mortgages make up another one-third. It also makes residential mortgages, consumer, and credit card loans. The company's non-bank subsidiaries include CNB Securities Corporation, Holiday Financial Services Corporation, and CNB Insurance Agency.

	Annual Growth	12/19	12/20	12/21	12/22	12/23
Assets ($mil.)	11.2%	3,763.7	4,729.4	5,328.9	5,475.2	5,753.0
Net income ($ mil.)	9.7%	40.1	32.7	57.7	63.2	58.0
Market value ($ mil.)	(8.8%)	682.9	444.9	553.8	497.1	472.1
Employees	9.4%	559	651	703	759	801

CNO FINANCIAL GROUP INC
NYS: CNO

11825 N. Pennsylvania Street
Carmel, IN 46032
Phone: 317 817-6100
Fax: –
Web: www.cnoinc.com

CEO: Gary C Bhojwani
CFO: Paul H McDonough
HR: –
FYE: December 31
Type: Public

CNO Financial Group is a holding company for a group of insurance companies operating throughout the US that develops, markets and administers health insurance, annuity, individual life insurance and other insurance products. The company serves middle-income pre-retiree and retired Americans. It centralizes certain functional areas, including marketing, business unit finance, sales training and support, and agent recruiting, among others. CNO markets its insurance products under Bankers Life, Washington National and Colonial Penn. CNO has approximately $33.3 billion in total assets.

	Annual Growth	12/19	12/20	12/21	12/22	12/23
Assets ($mil.)	1.1%	33,631	35,340	36,204	33,339	35,103
Net income ($ mil.)	(9.3%)	409.4	301.8	441.0	396.8	276.5
Market value ($ mil.)	11.4%	1,982.7	2,431.0	2,607.1	2,498.8	3,051.1
Employees	1.5%	3,300	3,400	3,350	3,400	3,500

CNX RESOURCES CORP

NYS: CNX

CNX Center, 1000 Horizon Vue Drive
Canonsburg, PA 15317-6506
Phone: 724 485-4000
Fax: –
Web: www.cnx.com

CEO: Nicholas J Deiuliis
CFO: Alan K Shepard
HR: –
FYE: December 31
Type: Public

CNX Resources is a premier independent natural gas and midstream company engaged in the exploration, development, production and acquisition of natural gas properties in the Appalachian Basin. The company explores for, develops, produces, gathers, acquires, and processes natural gas found in unconventional shale formations, primarily the Marcellus Shale and Utica Shale, covering parts of Pennsylvania, West Virginia, and Ohio. It also operates and develops Coal Bed Methane properties in Virginia. CNX has an average daily production of around 1.6 Mcfe and boasts approximately 9.6 Tcfe of proved reserves.

	Annual Growth	12/19	12/20	12/21	12/22	12/23
Sales ($mil.)	15.6%	1,922.4	1,258.0	756.8	1,261.2	3,434.9
Net income ($ mil.)	–	(80.7)	(483.8)	(498.6)	(142.1)	1,720.7
Market value ($ mil.)	22.6%	1,366.3	1,667.3	2,122.8	2,599.8	3,087.7
Employees	0.2%	467	451	441	466	470

CO HOLDINGS, LLC

452 WINCHESTER ST
KEENE, NH 034313918
Phone: 603 352-0001
Fax: –
Web: www.deadriver.com

CEO: –
CFO: –
HR: –
FYE: October 31
Type: Private

Cheshire Oil is confident that the smile it has put on customers' faces in Southern New Hampshire and Vermont won't suddenly disappear. The company's services (under the Cheshire Oil and T-Bird Fuel brands) to residential and commercial clients include heating oil delivery, oil and propane furnace and boiler installation, service, and repair, fleet fueling, and central air-conditioning installation and repair. Cheshire Oil also operates gas stations and convenience stores under the T-Bird Mini-Marts moniker. It also offers storage rental services through Keene Mini Storage. Cheshire Oil is owned and managed by members of the founding Robertson family.

	Annual Growth	10/07	10/08	10/09	10/10	10/11
Sales ($mil.)	15.1%	–	–	70.0	77.4	92.7
Net income ($ mil.)	(1.4%)	–	–	0.7	0.2	0.7
Market value ($ mil.)	–	–	–	–	–	–
Employees	–	–	–	–	–	175

COAST CITRUS DISTRIBUTORS

7597 BRISTOW CT
SAN DIEGO, CA 921547419
Phone: 619 661-7950
Fax: –
Web: www.coasttropical.com

CEO: –
CFO: –
HR: –
FYE: December 28
Type: Private

Coast Citrus Distributors is a leading wholesale distributor of fresh fruits and vegetables in Mexico and the US. The company supplies a variety of produce, including bananas, lettuce, limes, and potatoes, to retail grocers and other food customers. It distributes under the names Coast Citrus, Coast Tropical, Olympic Fruit and Vegetable, and Importadora y Exportadora. Coast Citrus Distributors operates half a dozen distribution facilities in California, Texas, and Florida. It also has about five locations in Mexico. The late Roberto Alvarez founded the family-owned business in 1950.

	Annual Growth	12/15	12/16	12/17	12/18	12/19
Sales ($mil.)	5.0%	–	290.2	293.4	306.9	335.6
Net income ($ mil.)	64.6%	–	1.7	2.0	3.7	7.7
Market value ($ mil.)	–	–	–	–	–	–
Employees	–	–	–	–	–	320

COAST ELECTRIC POWER ASSOCIATION

18020 HIGHWAY 603
KILN, MS 395568487
Phone: 228 363-7000
Fax: –
Web: www.coastelectric.coop

CEO: Robert J Occhi
CFO: John Holston
HR: Marilyn Sefton
FYE: December 31
Type: Private

There's no coasting for the Coast Electric Power Association when it comes to providing residents in three southern Mississippi counties with electricity. The utility uses a 6,400-mile distribution network to serve its more than 76,000 members (the great majority or which are residential customers) in Hancock, Pearl River, and Harrison counties. Coast offers electronic fund transfer and average monthly payment plans and rebates on energy efficient home improvements. The utility's power is generated by South Mississippi Electric Power, an association of Coast and 10 other cooperatives. It partners with Touchstone Energy Cooperatives.

	Annual Growth	12/16	12/17	12/18	12/21	12/22
Sales ($mil.)	4.3%	–	187.6	200.2	205.4	232.0
Net income ($ mil.)	–	–	9.5	9.6	–	–
Market value ($ mil.)	–	–	–	–	–	–
Employees	–	–	–	–	–	238

COASTAL CAROLINA UNIVERSITY ALUMNI ASSOCIATION, INC.

642 CENTURY CIR
CONWAY, SC 295268279
Phone: 843 347-3161
Fax: –
Web: www.coastal.edu

CEO: –
CFO: –
HR: –
FYE: June 30
Type: Private

It's hard for students at Coastal Carolina University not to be cocky. The university (whose rooster mascot, Chanticleer, appears in Chaucer's Canterbury Tales) offers bachelor's degrees in about 60 fields of study through schools of science, humanities, education, and business. It also offers about 10 master's degrees in fields including business administration, education, and coastal marine and wetland studies. Coastal Carolina University has an enrollment of more than 9,000 students and about 1,000 faculty members. Its student-to-teacher ratio is 17:1.

	Annual Growth	06/09	06/10	06/11	06/12	06/13
Sales ($mil.)	10.0%	–	–	117.0	128.8	141.6
Net income ($ mil.)	(3.0%)	–	–	29.5	29.8	27.7
Market value ($ mil.)	–	–	–	–	–	–
Employees	–	–	–	–	–	900

COASTAL PACIFIC FOOD DISTRIBUTORS, INC.

1015 PERFORMANCE DR
STOCKTON, CA 952064925
Phone: 909 947-2066
Fax: –
Web: www.cpfd.com

CEO: –
CFO: –
HR: –
FYE: December 29
Type: Private

Coastal Pacific Food Distributors (CPF) fuels the military forces from facility to fork. The company is one of the top wholesale food distributors that primarily serves the US armed forces across the Western US and in the Far East. As part of its business, CPF provides a full line of groceries to military bases run by the US Army, Navy, Air Force, and Marines. It delivers a variety of products from distribution centers located in California, Washington, and Hawaii. CPF also offers information system programming services for its customers to track sales and shipping, as well as procurement and logistics through partnerships in Iraq, Kuwait, and Saudi Arabia. The company was founded in 1986.

	Annual Growth	01/09	01/10	01/11*	12/11	12/12
Sales ($mil.)	8.9%	–	–	1,113.6	1,162.7	1,213.0
Net income ($ mil.)	(14.6%)	–	–	17.7	25.2	15.1
Market value ($ mil.)	–	–	–	–	–	–
Employees	–	–	–	–	–	459

*Fiscal year change

COATES INTERNATIONAL LTD

2100 Highway 34
Wall Township, NJ 07719
Phone: 732 449-7717
Fax: –
Web: www.coatesengine.com

CEO: George J Coates
CFO: Barry C Kaye
HR: –
FYE: December 31
Type: Public

Coates International Ltd. (CIL) may be sparking the next industrial revolution. CEO George J. Coates founded CIL to develop his many patents, the most noteworthy being the Coates Spherical Rotary Valve (CSRV). The CSRV is designed to replace the century-old technology of the internal combustion engine's camshaft and poppet valve system. An engine equipped with the CSRV can run on different fuels while reducing emissions and increasing efficiency; the need for maintenance is also reduced. CIL licenses its CSRV engine technology to makers of heavy-duty vehicles, automobiles, and industrial engines. Major customer Almont Energy (Canada) took first delivery of CSRV engines in 2010.

	Annual Growth	12/13	12/14	12/15	12/16	12/17
Sales ($mil.)	–	0.0	0.0	0.0	0.0	0.0
Net income ($ mil.)	–	(2.8)	(12.8)	(10.2)	(8.4)	(8.4)
Market value ($ mil.)	(13.5%)	1.2	0.3	0.0	0.0	0.7
Employees	(13.1%)	7	6	5	5	4

COBANK ACB

NBB: CBKP P

6340 South Fiddlers Green Circle
Greenwood Village, CO 80111
Phone: 303 740-4000
Fax: –
Web: www.cobank.com

CEO: Robert B Engel
CFO: David P Burlage
HR: Dona Snader
FYE: December 31
Type: Public

CoBank is one of the largest private providers of credit to the US rural economy. The bank delivers loans, leases and other financial services to agribusiness, rural infrastructure and Farm Credit customers in all 50 states. Primary products and services include term loans, trade finance, capital markets services, as well as risk management, cash management, leasing and investment products. It also offers non-credit products and services including cash management, online banking, mobile banking and commercial credit card solutions. Its Farm Credit Banking has some 20 affiliated associations operating in about 25 states serving the Northwest, West, Southwest, Rocky Mountains, Mid-Plains, and Northeast regions of the US. Formed in 1989, CoBank merged with US AgBank in early 2012.

	Annual Growth	12/18	12/19	12/20	12/21	12/23
Sales ($mil.)	16.8%	4,320.8	4,689.0	3,594.2	3,068.1	9,392.0
Net income ($ mil.)	4.8%	1,190.8	1,091.2	1,263.0	1,314.2	1,507.0
Market value ($ mil.)	–	4,100.7	4,289.6	4,343.0	4,187.7	–
Employees	2.7%	1,050	1,115	1,136	1,077	1,199

COBB ELECTRIC MEMBERSHIP CORPORATION

1000 EMC PKWY NE
MARIETTA, GA 300607908
Phone: 770 429-2100
Fax: –
Web: www.cobbemc.com

CEO: –
CFO: –
HR: –
FYE: December 31
Type: Private

Cobb Electric Membership Corporation (Cobb EMC) makes sure that Cobb County, Georgia residents can cook corn on the cob (and anything else) using either electric power or natural gas. The utility distributes electricity to more than 200,000 meters (more than 177,000 residential, commercial, and industrial members) in Cobb County and four other north metro Atlanta counties. Cobb EMC operates about 10,000 miles of power lines. The company's Gas South unit markets natural gas to customers who receive their service on Atlanta Gas & Light's natural gas distribution pipelines in Georgia.

	Annual Growth	04/17	04/18*	12/20	12/21	12/22
Sales ($mil.)	(13.7%)	–	849.7	802.4	448.6	472.1
Net income ($ mil.)	(16.7%)	–	25.4	49.2	11.2	12.2
Market value ($ mil.)	–	–	–	–	–	–
Employees	–	–	–	–	–	548

*Fiscal year change

COBORN'S, INCORPORATED

1921 COBORN BLVD
SAINT CLOUD, MN 563012100
Phone: 320 252-4222
Fax: –
Web: www.cobornsinc.com

CEO: Christopher Coborn
CFO: James Shaw
HR: –
FYE: December 28
Type: Private

Coborn's operates some 200 stores across the Midwest of the US under Coborn's, Cash Wise, Captain Jack's, Marketplace Foods and Hornbacher's. Coborn's operates its central bakery, fuel and convenience division, pharmacy division, in-house grocery warehouse, distribution center and top cleaners. Along with its grocery stores, the firm owns and operates pharmacies and convenience, and liquor stations. The company manages the delivery logistics of hundreds of grocery products for its entire family of stores throughout the upper Midwest. Founded in 1921, Coborn's is a fourth-generation business managed by its CEO Chris Coborn.

	Annual Growth	12/09	12/10	12/11	12/12	12/13
Sales ($mil.)	2.1%	–	–	–	1,220.5	1,246.7
Net income ($ mil.)	(5.0%)	–	–	–	32.4	30.8
Market value ($ mil.)	–	–	–	–	–	–
Employees	–	–	–	–	–	7,200

COCA-COLA CO (THE)

NYS: KO

One Coca-Cola Plaza
Atlanta, GA 30313
Phone: 404 676-2121
Fax: 404 676-6792
Web: www.coca-colacompany.com

CEO: James B Robert Quincey
CFO: John Murphy
HR: –
FYE: December 31
Type: Public

The Coca-Cola Company is home to numerous beverage brands, including five of the world's top six nonalcoholic sparkling soft drink brands: Coca-Cola, Sprite, Fanta, Coca-Cola Zero Sugar, and Diet Coke/Coca-Cola Light. In addition to soft drinks, it markets water, sports, coffee, and tea; juice, value-added dairy, and plant-based beverages; and emerging beverage. Other top brands include BODYARMOR, Minute Maid, Powerade, Dasani, glac au vitaminwater, and glac au smartwater. With 32.7 billion unit cases of products sold, Coca-Cola reaches thirsty consumers in more than 200 countries. Nearly 65% of its sales come from outside the US.

	Annual Growth	12/19	12/20	12/21	12/22	12/23
Sales ($mil.)	5.3%	37,266	33,014	38,655	43,004	45,754
Net income ($ mil.)	4.7%	8,920.0	7,747.0	9,771.0	9,542.0	10,714
Market value ($ mil.)	1.6%	238,448	236,251	255,077	274,032	253,870
Employees	(2.1%)	86,200	80,300	79,000	82,500	79,100

COCA-COLA CONSOLIDATED INC

NMS: COKE

4100 Coca-Cola Plaza
Charlotte, NC 28211
Phone: 980 392-8298
Fax: –
Web: www.cokeconsolidated.com

CEO: J F Harrison III
CFO: F S Anthony
HR: James L Matte
FYE: December 31
Type: Public

As the largest Coca-Cola bottler in the US, Coca-Cola Consolidated, Inc. (formerly Coca-Cola Bottling Co. Consolidated) distributes, markets, and manufactures nonalcoholic beverages to approximately 60 million consumers across nearly 15 states and the District of Columbia. It offers a range of nonalcoholic beverage products and flavors, principally the products of The Coca-Cola Company, which account for about 85% of total sales. Other beverages bottled and distributed by Coca-Cola Consolidated include Dr. Pepper and Monster Energy drinks. In addition to bottles and cans, the company also sells products to other bottlers and offers post-mix products that enable fountain retailers to sell finished products to consumers.

	Annual Growth	12/19	12/20	12/21	12/22	12/23
Sales ($mil.)	8.4%	4,826.5	5,007.4	5,562.7	6,201.0	6,653.9
Net income ($ mil.)	144.8%	11.4	172.5	189.6	430.2	408.4
Market value ($ mil.)	33.3%	2,752.6	2,495.9	5,804.1	4,802.7	8,702.5
Employees	0.1%	16,900	15,800	16,000	17,000	17,000

CODALE ELECTRIC SUPPLY, INC.

5225 W 2400 S
SALT LAKE CITY, UT 841201264
Phone: 801 975-7300
Fax: –
Web: www.codale.com

CEO: –
CFO: –
HR: –
FYE: December 31
Type: Private

Codale Electric Supply distributes lighting fixtures, electrical supplies, and datacomm products to wholesale customers through 11 locations in Nevada, Utah, Idaho, and Wyoming. It stocks products from such manufacturers as Brad Harrison, Chromalox, Greenlee, Philips Lighting, Southwire, and Western Tube & Conduit. The company sells to the aerospace, construction, mining, healthcare, schools, government, and utility markets. Codale Electric also offers consulting and training, energy and safety audits, and inventory management services. The company was founded in 1975 by CEO Dale Holt, who owns nearly all of Codale Electric's equity.

CODEXIS INC

NMS: CDXS

200 Penobscot Drive
Redwood City, CA 94063
Phone: 650 421-8100
Fax: –
Web: www.codexis.com

CEO: John J Nicols
CFO: Ross Taylor
HR: Eve Lai
FYE: December 31
Type: Public

The pharmaceutical and the biodiesel industries don't seem like they have much in common, but they both use the chemicals produced by Codexis. The company develops biocatalysts -- chemicals used to manufacture other chemicals in a way that's easy on the environment. Its technology is used to make the active ingredients in pharmaceuticals and produce biofuel from plant material. Codexis has a research agreement with Shell to develop new ways of converting biomass to biofuel; Shell accounts for more than half of Codexis' sales. The company is also working within other markets to use its technology to manage carbon emissions from coal-fired power plants and treat wastewater.

	Annual Growth	12/19	12/20	12/21	12/22	12/23
Sales ($mil.)	0.6%	68.5	69.1	104.8	138.6	70.1
Net income ($ mil.)	–	(11.9)	(24.0)	(21.3)	(33.6)	(76.2)
Market value ($ mil.)	(33.9%)	1,117.8	1,526.0	2,185.9	325.8	213.2
Employees	2.0%	161	181	261	248	174

CODORUS VALLEY BANCORP, INC.

NMS: CVLY

105 Leader Heights Road
York, PA 17403
Phone: 717 747-1519
Fax: –
Web: www.peoplesbanknet.com

CEO: Larry J Miller
CFO: –
HR: –
FYE: December 31
Type: Public

Codorus Valley Bancorp is a people-oriented business. The firm is the holding company for PeoplesBank, which operates about 20 branches in southeastern Pennsylvania's York County and Hunt Valley and Bel Air, Maryland. The bank offers the standard fare, including checking and savings accounts and CDs. It uses funds from deposits to write a variety of loans, primarily commercial loans and commercial real estate loans but also residential mortgages and consumer installment loans. Bank subsidiary Codorus Valley Financial Advisors offers investment products, while SYC Settlement Services provides real estate settlement services.

	Annual Growth	12/19	12/20	12/21	12/22	12/23
Assets ($mil.)	3.9%	1,886.5	2,162.2	2,418.6	2,195.1	2,194.8
Net income ($ mil.)	7.6%	18.6	8.4	14.7	20.1	25.0
Market value ($ mil.)	2.8%	222.1	163.5	207.5	229.5	247.8
Employees	(1.6%)	363	346	345	339	341

COE COLLEGE

1220 1ST AVE NE
CEDAR RAPIDS, IA 524025092
Phone: 319 399-8000
Fax: –
Web: www.coe.edu

CEO: –
CFO: –
HR: Jennifer Boettger
FYE: June 30
Type: Private

Coe College is a private liberal arts college with a residential campus in Cedar Rapids, Iowa. The school offers more than 40 academic majors and grants undergraduate degrees (Bachelor of Arts, Bachelor of Music, and Bachelor of Science in Nursing), as well as a Master of Arts in Teaching. Coe College's has an annual enrollment of more than 1,400 students (from across more than 30 US states and more than 15 other countries) who are required to participate in an internship, student research project, practicum, or study abroad program as they matriculate. Approximately half of the school's students go on to post-graduate studies.

	Annual Growth	06/15	06/16	06/17	06/21	06/22
Sales ($mil.)	4.3%	–	70.6	73.9	86.1	91.2
Net income ($ mil.)	–	–	(0.3)	(0.3)	0.8	1.5
Market value ($ mil.)	–	–	–	–	–	–
Employees	–	–	–	–	–	272

COEUR MINING INC

NYS: CDE

200 South Wacker Drive Suite 2100
Chicago, IL 60606
Phone: 312 489-5800
Fax: –
Web: www.coeur.com

CEO: Mitchell J Krebs
CFO: Thomas S Whelan
HR: Lindsay Tripp
FYE: December 31
Type: Public

Coeur Mining (formerly Coeur d'Alene Mines) is primarily a gold and silver producer with operating assets located in the US and Mexico and an exploration project in Canada. The company also has interests in other precious metals exploration projects in North America, other mineral interests, strategic equity investments, among other items. The dor produced at the Palmarejo complex and Rochester mine, as well as the concentrate product produced by the Wharf mine, is refined by a geographically diverse group of third-party refiners into gold and silver bullion according to benchmark standards set by the London Bullion Market Association. It has proven and probable reserves of approximately 245.7 million ounces of silver and over 3.4 million ounces of gold. The US accounts for more than 60% of the company's revenue.

	Annual Growth	12/19	12/20	12/21	12/22	12/23
Sales ($mil.)	3.6%	711.5	785.5	832.8	785.6	821.2
Net income ($ mil.)	–	(341.2)	25.6	(31.3)	(78.1)	(103.6)
Market value ($ mil.)	(20.3%)	3,121.2	3,998.0	1,946.9	1,297.9	1,259.3
Employees	(1.0%)	2,155	1,959	2,105	2,107	2,074

COFFEE HOLDING CO INC

NAS: JVA

3475 Victory Boulevard
Staten Island, NY 10314
Phone: 718 832-0800
Fax: –
Web: www.coffeeholding.com

CEO: –
CFO: Andrew Gordon
HR: –
FYE: October 31
Type: Public

Coffee Holding in integrated wholesale coffee roaster and dealer in the US and one of the few coffee companies that offers a broad array of coffee products across the entire spectrum of consumer tastes, preferences and price points. Its products are divided into three categories: Wholesale Green Coffee, Private Label Coffee, and Branded Coffee. The company's private label and branded coffee products are sold throughout the US, Canada, and abroad to supermarkets, wholesalers, and individually owned and multi-unit retail customers. Its unprocessed green coffee, which includes over 90 specialty coffee offerings, is primarily sold to specialty gourmet roasters in the US, Canada, and multiple international countries. Established in 1972, Coffee Holding has operated under the leadership of the founding Gordon family, including Andrew Gordon and David Gordon who have both worked with the company for more than 35 years.

	Annual Growth	10/19	10/20	10/21	10/22	10/23
Sales ($mil.)	(5.8%)	86.5	74.3	63.9	65.7	68.2
Net income ($ mil.)	–	(0.1)	(0.1)	1.3	(3.7)	(0.8)
Market value ($ mil.)	(34.4%)	21.6	21.7	25.3	13.1	4.0
Employees	5.0%	79	82	75	79	96

COGENT COMMUNICATIONS HOLDINGS, INC.   NMS: CCOI

2450 N Street N.W.
Washington, DC 20037
Phone: 202 295-4200
Fax: –
Web: www.cogentco.com

CEO: –
CFO: –
HR: –
FYE: December 31
Type: Public

Cogent Communications offers fiber-optic data network that serves customers in North America, Europe, and Asia. It offers dedicated Internet access and data transport services to businesses through Ethernet connections that link its nearly 35 data center facilities directly to customer office buildings. Clients include financial services companies, law firms, ad agencies, and other professional services businesses including Cloudhelix, Cadwalader, Chartright air group, and CHF industries. Cogent also sells access to its network and provides colocation management services to ISPs, hosting companies, and other high-volume bandwidth users. Cogent serves almost 210 markets in more than 45 countries globally.

	Annual Growth	12/19	12/20	12/21	12/22	12/23
Sales ($mil.)	14.6%	546.2	568.1	589.8	599.6	940.9
Net income ($ mil.)	141.4%	37.5	6.2	48.2	5.1	1,273.4
Market value ($ mil.)	3.7%	3,198.9	2,910.2	3,557.2	2,774.6	3,697.2
Employees	16.7%	1,051	1,083	1,001	1,076	1,947

COGENTIX MEDICAL, INC.

5420 FELTL RD
MINNETONKA, MN 553437982
Phone: 952 426-6140
Fax: –
Web: www.laborie.com

CEO: Michael Frazzette
CFO: –
HR: –
FYE: December 31
Type: Private

Even those outside California know Cogentix Medical's products are totally tubular. The firm (formerly named Vision-Sciences) makes endoscopic tools -- tubular instruments that let doctors see into the body and perform procedures without invasive surgery. It makes traditional endoscopes and the EndoSheath System, which consists of a disposable sterile sheath covering the reusable endoscope. The system allows health care providers to save money by avoiding costly cleaning and repairs and reduces the risk of cross-contamination. Subsidiary Machida makes flexible borescopes, endoscope-like tools used in industrial applications. In 2018 Cogentix agreed to be acquired by Laborie Medical Technologies for $239 million.

	Annual Growth	03/14	03/15*	12/15	12/16	12/17
Sales ($mil.)	45.7%	–	–	26.5	36.6	51.9	56.3
Net income ($ mil.)	–	–	–	(7.7)	(7.0)	(22.1)	(0.9)
Market value ($ mil.)	–	–	–	–	–	–	–
Employees	–	–	–	–	–	–	181

*Fiscal year change

COGENTRIX ENERGY, INC.

9405 Arrowpoint Blvd.
Charlotte, NC 28273-8110
Phone: 704 525-3800
Fax: –
Web: www.cogentrix.com

CEO: –
CFO: S M Rudolph
HR: Linda Okowita
FYE: December 31
Type: Public

Cogentrix is an industry-leading power generation organization delivering expert management and superior performance to its clients. It has stood out for its ability to execute acquisitions, financings, operations and asset improvements. Cogentrix provides a complete service offering to those looking to succeed in power plant operations and investments, including outstanding technical, commercial, and financial capabilities. Cogentrix is a subsidiary of the asset manager, The Carlyle Group.

	Annual Growth	12/98	12/99	12/00	12/01	12/02
Sales ($mil.)	11.8%	411.5	447.6	551.1	568.1	642.9
Net income ($ mil.)	(8.1%)	37.0	43.4	51.5	67.5	26.4
Market value ($ mil.)	–	–	–	–	–	–
Employees	3.6%	463	524	541	562	533

COGNEX CORP   NMS: CGNX

One Vision Drive
Natick, MA 01760-2059
Phone: 508 650-3000
Fax: –
Web: www.cognex.com

CEO: Robert J Willett
CFO: Paul D Todgham
HR: –
FYE: December 31
Type: Public

Cognex is a leading worldwide provider of machine vision products and solutions that improve efficiency and quality in a wide range of businesses across attractive industrial end markets. Its solutions blend physical products and software to capture and analyze visual information, allowing for the automation of manufacturing and distribution tasks for customers worldwide. It offers a full range of machine vision systems and sensors, vision software, and industrial image-based barcode readers designed to meet customer needs at different performance and price points. Sales to customers based in the Americas account for almost 40% of sales.

	Annual Growth	12/19	12/20	12/21	12/22	12/23
Sales ($mil.)	3.7%	725.6	811.0	1,037.1	1,006.1	837.5
Net income ($ mil.)	(13.7%)	203.9	176.2	279.9	215.5	113.2
Market value ($ mil.)	(7.1%)	9,616.4	13,777	13,344	8,084.0	7,162.5
Employees	7.2%	2,267	2,055	2,257	2,441	2,992

COGNITION FINANCIAL CORPORATION

200 CLARENDON ST LBBY 3
BOSTON, MA 021165079
Phone: 617 638-2000
Fax: –
Web: www.cognitionfinancial.com

CEO: Daniel Meyers
CFO: Alan Breitman
HR: –
FYE: June 30
Type: Private

With a Harvard education costing six figures, that government student loan just isn't going to cut it anymore. Enter First Marblehead. The firm provides underwriting and risk management services for lenders and schools who offer private student loans for undergraduate, graduate, and professional education, and to a lesser extent, continuing education and study abroad programs. First Marblehead also provides marketing and processing services. In response to deteriorating economic conditions and upheaval in the private student loan industry, it also offers such fee-based services as tuition planning, portfolio management, and asset servicing. Canadian investment firm FP Resources USA took the firm private in mid-2016.

COGNIZANT TECHNOLOGY SOLUTIONS CORP.   NMS: CTSH

300 Frank W. Burr Blvd.
Teaneck, NJ 07666
Phone: 201 801-0233
Fax: 201 801-0243
Web: www.cognizant.com

CEO: Ravi S Kumar
CFO: –
HR: –
FYE: December 31
Type: Public

Cognizant Technology Solutions is one of the world's leading professional services companies, engineering modern business for the digital era. To help customers make the switch, the information technology outsourcing company provides intelligent systems, automation, cloud technologies, and cyber security tools. Cognizant also offers digital services and solutions, consulting, application development, systems integration, application testing, application maintenance, infrastructure services and business process services. The company targets companies in financial services, healthcare, manufacturing, retail, and logistics as well as communications and media. Most of the company's revenue is generated in North America.

	Annual Growth	12/19	12/20	12/21	12/22	12/23
Sales ($mil.)	3.6%	16,783	16,652	18,507	19,428	19,353
Net income ($ mil.)	3.6%	1,842.0	1,392.0	2,137.0	2,290.0	2,126.0
Market value ($ mil.)	5.1%	30,886	40,811	44,183	28,481	37,614
Employees	4.4%	292,500	289,500	330,600	355,300	347,700

COHEN & COMPANY INC (NEW)   ASE: COHN

Cira Centre, 2929 Arch Street, Suite 1703 — CEO: Lester R Brafman
Philadelphia, PA 19104 — CFO: Joseph W Pooler Jr
Phone: 215 701-9555 — HR: –
Fax: – — FYE: December 31
Web: www.cohenandcompany.com — Type: Public

Institutional Financial Markets Inc. (IFMI) believes in the institution of the markets. Formerly a real estate investment trust named Alesco Financial (and later Cohen & Company), the company now manages and trades financial investments, specializing in credit-related fixed income assets. The company serves institutional investors. IFMI's asset management arm offers funds, separately managed accounts, collateralized debt obligations, international hybrid securities, and other investment products; it manages some $10 billion in assets. The firm also has a capital markets division, which sells, trades, and issues corporate and securitized products. IFMI has about 10 offices in the US and London.

	Annual Growth	12/19	12/20	12/21	12/22	12/23
Sales ($mil.)	13.7%	49.7	130.1	146.4	44.4	83.0
Net income ($ mil.)	–	(2.1)	14.2	11.3	(13.4)	(5.1)
Market value ($ mil.)	13.9%	7.5	30.9	28.0	15.8	12.6
Employees	5.8%	94	87	118	121	118

COHEN & STEERS INC   NYS: CNS

280 Park Avenue — CEO: Robert H Steers
New York, NY 10017 — CFO: Matthew S Stadler
Phone: 212 832-3232 — HR: Alison Digena
Fax: 212 832-3622 — FYE: December 31
Web: www.cohenandsteers.com — Type: Public

Cohen & Steers (CNS), founded in 1986, is a global investment manager specializing in liquid real assets, including real estate securities, listed infrastructure and natural resource equities, as well as preferred securities and other income solutions. The company offers strategies through a variety of investment vehicles, including US and non-US registered funds and other commingled vehicles, separate accounts, and subadvised portfolios. CNS has more than $80.4 billion of assets under management. The majority of its sales come from North America.

	Annual Growth	12/19	12/20	12/21	12/22	12/23
Sales ($mil.)	4.5%	410.8	427.5	583.8	566.9	489.6
Net income ($ mil.)	(1.1%)	134.6	76.6	211.4	171.0	129.0
Market value ($ mil.)	4.8%	3,085.0	3,652.2	4,547.4	3,173.5	3,722.5
Employees	5.4%	328	347	354	388	405

COHERENT CORP   NYS: COHR

375 Saxonburg Boulevard — CEO: Vincent D Mattera Jr
Saxonburg, PA 16056 — CFO: Mary J Raymond
Phone: 724 352-4455 — HR: –
Fax: – — FYE: June 30
Web: www.ii-vi.com — Type: Public

II-VI develops, manufactures, and markets engineered materials, optoelectronic components, and devices for use in optical communications, industrial, aerospace and defense, consumer electronics, semiconductor capital equipment, life sciences, and automotive applications and markets. The company products are deployed in a variety of applications, including optical, data, and wireless communications products; laser cutting, welding, and marking operations; 3D sensing consumer applications; aerospace and defense applications including intelligence, surveillance, and reconnaissance; semiconductor processing tools; and thermoelectric cooling and power-generation solutions. Customers have included Coherent Inc., Nikon Corporation, Aurubis AG, and Apple Inc., among others. The North America is its largest market accounting for about 55% of sales.

	Annual Growth	06/19	06/20	06/21	06/22	06/23
Sales ($mil.)	39.5%	1,362.5	2,380.1	3,105.9	3,316.6	5,160.1
Net income ($ mil.)	–	107.5	(67.0)	297.6	234.8	(259.5)
Market value ($ mil.)	8.7%	5,103.2	6,591.1	10,132	7,111.8	7,116.0
Employees	20.8%	12,487	22,969	23,000	24,000	26,622

COHESANT INC.

3601 GREEN RD STE 308 — CEO: –
BEACHWOOD, OH 441225719 — CFO: –
Phone: 216 910-1700 — HR: –
Fax: – — FYE: November 30
Web: www.cohesant.com — Type: Private

Cohesant, which forms one coherent water-protection company from four subsidiaries, believes in repair over replacement. Cohesant Materials produces specialty coatings used in protecting, renewing, and repairing pipes and other infrastructure. CuraFlo Franchising operates about a dozen North American CuraFlo franchises selling proprietary equipment and coatings for repairing water pipes. CuraFlo Services owns two of the franchises and provides training and support for the franchisees. RLS Solutions offers Cohesant's Raven Engineered System of coatings and epoxies used in municipal water and waste water systems. The company has manufacturing facilities in Ohio and Oklahoma as well as in Vancouver, Canada.

COHU INC   NMS: COHU

12367 Crosthwaite Circle — CEO: Luis A Muller
Poway, CA 92064-6817 — CFO: Jeffrey D Jones
Phone: 858 848-8100 — HR: Donna Schmidt
Fax: – — FYE: December 30
Web: www.cohu.com — Type: Public

Cohu is a leading supplier of semiconductor test and inspection automation systems (handlers), micro-electromechanical system (MEMS) test modules, test contactors, thermal sub-systems, and semiconductor automated test equipment used by global semiconductor manufacturers and test subcontractors. Its DI-Core software provides real-time online performance monitoring and process control to improve utilization, manage predictive maintenance, and link semiconductor tester, handler, and test contactor data. Cohu's differentiated and broad product portfolio is designed to optimize semiconductor manufacturing yield and productivity, accelerating customers' time-to-market. Customers include semiconductor integrated device manufacturers, fabless design houses, and test subcontractors around the world. China is the California-based company's single biggest market. Cohu was founded in 1947 as Kalbfell Lab, Inc., later renamed to Kay Lab in 1954, and eventually became Cohu, Inc in 1972.

	Annual Growth	12/19	12/20	12/21	12/22	12/23
Sales ($mil.)	2.2%	583.3	636.0	887.2	812.8	636.3
Net income ($ mil.)	–	(69.7)	(13.8)	167.3	96.8	28.2
Market value ($ mil.)	12.2%	1,102.3	1,915.4	1,878.8	1,584.2	1,749.3
Employees	0.5%	3,200	3,250	3,240	3,218	3,259

COINBASE GLOBAL INC   NMS: COIN

c/o The Corporation Trust Company, 1209 Orange Street — CEO: Brian Armstrong
Wilmington, DE 19801 — CFO: Alesia J Haas
Phone: 302 777-0200 — HR: –
Fax: – — FYE: December 31
Web: www.coinbase.com — Type: Public

Coinbase Global is a leading provider of end-to-end financial infrastructure and technology for the cryptoeconomy. It builds safe, trusted, easy-to-use technology and financial infrastructure products and services that enable any person or business with an internet connection to discover, transact, and engage with crypto assets and decentralized applications. The company's products provide access to the cryptoeconomy in more than 100 countries and serve as a critical infrastructure layer to Web3, a broad category of crypto-powered technologies including self-custody wallets, decentralized apps and services, and open community engagement platforms. Coinbase is trusted by about 245,000 ecosystem partners worldwide. The company's largest market is the US with about 85% of its revenue. Coinbase Global was incorporated in 2014 to act as the holding company of Coinbase, Inc. and its other subsidiaries.

	Annual Growth	12/19	12/20	12/21	12/22	12/23
Sales ($mil.)	55.3%	533.7	1,277.5	7,839.4	3,194.2	3,108.4
Net income ($ mil.)	–	(30.4)	322.3	3,624.1	(2,624.9)	94.9
Market value ($ mil.)	–	–	–	61,086	8,566.1	42,097
Employees	–	–	1,249	3,730	4,510	3,416

COINSTAR, LLC

330 120TH AVE NE STE 100
BELLEVUE, WA 980053014
Phone: 425 943-8000
Fax: –
Web: www.coinstar.com

CEO: James H Gaherity
CFO: Kevin McColly
HR: Anindita Banerjee
FYE: December 31
Type: Private

Outerwall (formerly Coinstar) takes its name from the previously underutilized "fourth wall" area between the cash registers and the front door in retail stores. The company aimed to create an easy and convenient way for people to turn their loose change into spending money without having to sort, roll, and take it to the bank. The company was founded in 1991, and installed its first kiosk in San Francisco the next year. The kiosk provider changed its name to Outerwall in 2013 to reflect its evolution from coin counting to an operator of various automated retail businesses.

COLAVITA USA L.L.C.

1 RUNYONS LN
EDISON, NJ 088172219
Phone: 732 404-8300
Fax: –
Web: www.colavita.com

CEO: Giovanni Colavita
CFO: Simon Boltuch
HR: Terry Rodrigues
FYE: December 31
Type: Private

This company helps bring Italian flavors to American palates. Colavita USA is a leading importer and distributor of Italian foods, notably olive oil, pastas, sauces, and vinegars sold under the Colavita label. It supplies products to retail grocery store chains, specialty food stores, and wholesale distributors, as well as restaurants, caterers, and other foodservice operators. The company was started by John J. Profaci, who struck a distribution agreement with Italy's Colavita family in 1978. Rome-based Colavita S.p.A owns 80% of the US importer.

COLD JET, LLC

455 WARDS CORNER RD
LOVELAND, OH 451409033
Phone: 513 831-3211
Fax: –
Web: www.coldjet.com

CEO: Eugene L Cooke III
CFO: –
HR: –
FYE: December 31
Type: Private

Cold Jet is the global leader in innovative dry ice technologies. It makes dry ice blasting equipment used in industrial cleaning applications. Dry ice blasting can remove ink, nonwoven die, mold, and asphalt from industrial equipment. The company, which operates in Europe, Asia, the Middle East, Canada, and Australia, uses recycled carbon dioxide to eliminate the need for solvents or chemicals in the cleaning process. In addition to its cleaning products, Cold Jet makes dry ice production equipment sold worldwide. It has about 15 service centers located in 10 countries around the world and the largest install base of human technical resources. The company was established in 1986, in conjunction with the creation of the first patent-protected dry ice blasting product.

	Annual Growth	12/11	12/12	12/13	12/14	12/15
Sales ($mil.)	14.5%	–	–	34.0	37.4	44.6
Net income ($ mil.)	20.5%	–	–	3.4	3.9	5.0
Market value ($ mil.)	–	–	–	–	–	–
Employees	–	–	–	–	–	254

COLEMAN UNIVERSITY

8888 BALBOA AVE
SAN DIEGO, CA 921231506
Phone: 858 499-0202
Fax: –
Web: www.coleman.edu

CEO: –
CFO: –
HR: –
FYE: June 30
Type: Private

Coleman College prepares students for careers in information technology. The school offers associates and bachelors degree programs in network security, graphic design, programming, networking, and bioinformatics. It also offers a Master of Science in Information Technology and a Master of Science in Business and Technology Management. Coleman has two campuses (La Mesa and San Marcos) in California and was founded in 1963.

	Annual Growth	06/12	06/13	06/14	06/15	06/17
Sales ($mil.)	(9.8%)	–	14.5	12.1	10.4	9.6
Net income ($ mil.)	(32.1%)	–	1.8	(4.1)	(3.0)	0.4
Market value ($ mil.)	–	–	–	–	–	–
Employees	–	–	–	–	–	200

COLGATE UNIVERSITY

13 OAK DR
HAMILTON, NY 133461386
Phone: 315 228-1000
Fax: –
Web: www.colgate.edu

CEO: –
CFO: –
HR: –
FYE: June 30
Type: Private

Colgate University is located in upstate New York. The university is a liberal arts college with an enrollment of about 3,000 students. Most students are undergrads, though the school has a small graduate program that offers master's degrees in arts and teaching. Colgate offers some 50 major fields of study, plus about 15 minor study programs. Its most popular programs include business, communications, finance, education, medicine, law, and technology. The university has about 300 full-time faculty members.

	Annual Growth	06/18	06/19	06/20	06/21	06/22
Sales ($mil.)	22.1%	–	226.1	307.5	378.1	411.7
Net income ($ mil.)	26.1%	–	52.7	35.7	104.5	105.7
Market value ($ mil.)	–	–	–	–	–	–
Employees	–	–	–	–	–	1,014

COLGATE-PALMOLIVE CO.

NYS: CL

300 Park Avenue
New York, NY 10022
Phone: 212 310-2000
Fax: 212 310-3284
Web: www.colgatepalmolive.com

CEO: Noel R Wallace
CFO: Stanley J Sutula III
HR: –
FYE: December 31
Type: Public

Colgate-Palmolive is a global leader in oral, personal, and home care products. The company also offers pet nutrition products through subsidiary Hill's Pet Nutrition, which makes Science Diet and Prescription Diet pet foods. Many of its oral care products fall under the Colgate brand and include toothbrushes and mouthwashes. Its Oral Care segment also includes pharmaceutical products for dentists and other oral health professionals. Personal Care and Home Care items include Ajax brand household cleaner, Palmolive bar soap and dishwashing liquid, Softsoap shower gel, and Sanex deodorant and soap, as well as Speed Stick deodorants. Colgate-Palmolive sells its products in more than 200 countries and generates most of its sales outside North America.

	Annual Growth	12/19	12/20	12/21	12/22	12/23
Sales ($mil.)	5.5%	15,693	16,471	17,421	17,967	19,457
Net income ($ mil.)	(0.7%)	2,367.0	2,695.0	2,166.0	1,785.0	2,300.0
Market value ($ mil.)	3.7%	56,546	70,239	70,099	64,719	65,475
Employees	(0.2%)	34,300	34,200	33,800	33,800	34,000

COLLECTORS UNIVERSE, INC.

1610 E SAINT ANDREW PL
SANTA ANA, CA 927054931
Phone: 949 567-1234
Fax: -
Web: www.collectors.com

CEO: Joseph J Orlando
CFO: Joseph J Wallace
HR: -
FYE: June 30
Type: Private

Collectors Universe, now Collectors Holdings Inc., after changing its name in 2022, helps collectors pursue their passion through industry-leading grading and authentication, tools to help collectors research and find the next big thing and marketplaces to buy and sell. The company provides authentication, grading, and information services for sellers and buyers of trading cards, event tickets, vintage autographs, and other memorabilia. The company's brands include leading authentication and grading services PSA (trading cards and memorabilia), PCGS (coins and currency), and WATA (video games and pop culture), as well as online collectibles marketplace, Goldin. Collectors Holdings also publishes price guides, market reports, rarity reports, and other information in print form, as well as on its website.

COLLEGE ENTRANCE EXAMINATION BOARD

250 VESEY ST
NEW YORK, NY 102811052
Phone: 212 713-8000
Fax: -
Web: www.collegeboard.org

CEO: -
CFO: Tho Higgins
HR: Brian D Vogel
FYE: December 31
Type: Private

The College Board is a not-for-profit association that owns and administers the Scholastic Assessment Test (SAT), College-Level Examination Program (CLEP), and the Advanced Placement Program (AP) at high schools across the US. Its research interests span academic preparation, career readiness, college access, admissions, affordability, collegiate outcomes, and education policy. Founded in 1900, College Board members include more than 6,000 of the world's leading schools, colleges, universities, and other educational institutions. There are six College Board offices throughout the US, located in New York, Virginia, Puerto Rico, Pennsylvania, Iowa, and Washington, D.C.

COLLEGE OF SAINT BENEDICT

37 COLLEGE AVE S
SAINT JOSEPH, MN 563742099
Phone: 320 363-5011
Fax: -
Web: www.csbsju.edu

CEO: -
CFO: -
HR: Carol Abell
FYE: June 30
Type: Private

The College of Saint Benedict (CSB) is an all-female, Catholic liberal arts college with an enrollment of more than 2,000 students, about 70% of which are Catholic (though students of all faith are welcome). Saint John's University (SJU), located six miles from from CSB in central Minnesota, is the school's male counterpart. SJU and CSB share a common curriculum and students from both institutions attend classes together. The schools offer some 60 areas of study with more than 35 majors. CSB was incorporated when it separated from the Saint Benedict's Monastery in 1961.

	Annual Growth	06/18	06/19	06/20	06/21	06/22
Sales ($mil.)	(1.3%)	-	70.6	62.9	61.3	67.9
Net income ($ mil.)	-	-	8.8	1.7	24.2	(8.3)
Market value ($ mil.)	-	-	-	-	-	-
Employees	-	-	-	-	-	431

COLLEGE OF THE HOLY CROSS (INC)

1 COLLEGE ST
WORCESTER, MA 016102395
Phone: 508 793-2011
Fax: -
Web: www.holycross.edu

CEO: -
CFO: -
HR: Donna Wrenn
FYE: June 30
Type: Private

College of The Holy Cross has some real Crusaders. The Jesuit-founded college, with sports teams nicknamed the Crusaders, is a liberal arts undergraduate institution in central Massachusetts with more than 2,900 students. Some of the school's more popular areas of study include liberal arts' favorites such as English, history, and political science, but also multidisciplinary concentrations and specialty programs including biochemistry, Latin American studies, and women's studies. The co-educational school has more than 300 full- and part-time faculty, with a 10:1 student-to-faculty ratio. Holy Cross is the oldest Catholic college in New England.

	Annual Growth	06/18	06/19	06/20	06/21	06/22
Sales ($mil.)	3.9%	-	200.7	193.4	177.9	225.3
Net income ($ mil.)	-	-	10.5	(14.7)	292.2	(41.5)
Market value ($ mil.)	-	-	-	-	-	-
Employees	-	-	-	-	-	949

COLLEGIUM PHARMACEUTICAL INC

100 Technology Center Drive
Stoughton, MA 02072
Phone: 781 713-3699
Fax: -
Web: www.collegiumpharma.com

NMS: COLL
CEO: -
CFO: -
HR: -
FYE: December 31
Type: Public

Collegium Pharmaceutical is a specialty pharmaceutical company committed to being the leader in responsible pain management. Its first product, Xtampza ER, is an abuse-deterrent form of oxycodone for the management of severe pain. The company commercializes its pain portfolio, consisting of Xtampza ER, Nucynta ER, and Nucynta IR (collectively the Nucynta Products), Belbuca, and Symproic, in the US. Nucynta ER is for the management of severe pain and Nucynta IR is for the management of acute adult severe pain. The company do not own any manufacturing facilities, it only relies to contract manufacturers, as well as other vendors to formulate, test, supply, store, and distribute its products.

	Annual Growth	12/19	12/20	12/21	12/22	12/23
Sales ($mil.)	17.6%	296.7	310.0	276.9	463.9	566.8
Net income ($ mil.)	-	(22.7)	26.8	71.5	(25.0)	48.2
Market value ($ mil.)	10.6%	655.9	638.3	595.3	739.4	980.9
Employees	(6.2%)	255	234	152	207	197

COLLIN COUNTY COMMUNITY COLLEGE DISTRICT

3452 SPUR 399
MCKINNEY, TX 750698742
Phone: 972 599-3100
Fax: -
Web: www.collin.edu

CEO: -
CFO: Ken Lynn
HR: Floyd Nickerson
FYE: August 31
Type: Private

North Texans looking for an education beyond high school turn to Collin College. Collin County Community College District, known simply as Collin College, offers more than 100 associate degree and technical certification programs. Founded in 1985, the community college has an enrollment of more than 46,000 credit and continuing education students and about 700 staff members. It offers courses at about half a dozen campus locations in North Texas, as well as via the Internet. It works with local employers and government agencies to design training and workforce development programs. Collin has dual-admissions agreements with Texas universities such as Baylor, UNT, UTD, SMU, Texas Tech, and Texas A&M.

	Annual Growth	08/17	08/18	08/19	08/21	08/22
Sales ($mil.)	9.9%	-	44.2	48.5	59.5	64.5
Net income ($ mil.)	-	-	34.9	38.1	(11.5)	(22.6)
Market value ($ mil.)	-	-	-	-	-	-
Employees	-	-	-	-	-	2,650

COLOMBIA ENERGY RESOURCES INC.   NBB: CERX

One Embarcadero Center, Suite 500
San Francisco, CA 94111
Phone: 415 460-1165
Fax: –
Web: www.colombiaenergyresources.com

CEO: –
CFO: –
HR: –
FYE: December 31
Type: Public

Freedom Resources Enterprises is a development stage company. It developed a series of eight self-help, self-improvement workshops. Each self-taught workshop consisted of an audio tape and a workbook, which Freedom Resources marketed over the Internet. The company's workshops did not generated expected revenue, and Freedom Resources has announced plans to pursue other business opportunities.

	Annual Growth	12/07	12/08	12/09	12/10	12/11
Sales ($mil.)	–	–	–	–	–	–
Net income ($ mil.)	–	(0.0)	(0.0)	(0.0)	(2.2)	(13.0)
Market value ($ mil.)	130.0%	0.1	0.1	0.1	5.7	4.1
Employees	–	–	–	–	9	133

COLONIAL METALS CO.

217 LINDEN ST
COLUMBIA, PA 175121179
Phone: 717 684-2311
Fax: –
Web: www.colonialmetalsco.com

CEO: –
CFO: –
HR: –
FYE: June 30
Type: Private

It may be based in one of the early American colonies, but Colonial Metals is a modern nonferrous metals smelting company. The company primarily produces brass and bronze ingots from purchased copper and from scrap and recycled materials. It recycles about 90 million pounds annually, producing more than 60 million pounds of brass and bronze ingots. Other products include specialty alloys (chrome-copper and nickel-based). Colonial Metals sells its products mainly to makers of defense, housing, and industrial equipment. The company handles all of its production at its Pennsylvania headquarters.

COLONIAL PIPELINE COMPANY

1000 LAKE ST
ALPHARETTA, GA 300093904
Phone: 678 762-2200
Fax: –
Web: www.colpipe.com

CEO: Joseph A Blount Jr
CFO: –
HR: –
FYE: December 31
Type: Private

Colonial Pipeline is the largest refined products pipeline in the US, transporting more than 100 million gallons or 2.5 million barrels per day. Colonial transports approximately 45% of all fuel consumed on the East Coast, providing refined products to more than 50 million Americans. The company delivers refined petroleum products such as gasoline, diesel, jet fuel, home heating oil, and fuel for the US Military. More than 250 shippers and 270 terminals use the Colonial Pipeline system to transport refined petroleum products to locations in about 15 states. Founded in 1962, Colonial Pipeline is owned by a consortium of companies, including Koch, KKR-Keats Pipeline Investors, L.P., CDPQ Colonial Partners, L.P., IFM (US) Colonial Pipeline 2, and Shell Midstream Operating.

COLONY BANKCORP, INC.   NMS: CBAN

115 South Grant Street
Fitzgerald, GA 31750
Phone: 229 426-6000
Fax: –
Web: www.colonybank.com

CEO: T H Fountain
CFO: Derek Shelnutt
HR: Becky Robertson
FYE: December 31
Type: Public

Colony Bankcorp seems to be colonizing Georgia. The multibank holding company owns seven financial institutions doing business under variations of the Colony Bank name throughout central and southern portions of the state. The banks operate more than 25 branches in all. They offer traditional fare such as checking and savings accounts, NOW and IRA accounts, and CDs. Real estate loans, including residential and commercial mortgages and construction and farmland loans, make up the largest portion of the company's loan portfolio, at more than 80%. The banks also issue business and consumer loans.

	Annual Growth	12/19	12/20	12/21	12/22	12/23
Assets ($mil.)	19.1%	1,515.3	1,764.0	2,691.7	2,936.6	3,053.4
Net income ($ mil.)	20.8%	10.2	11.8	18.7	19.5	21.7
Market value ($ mil.)	(5.2%)	289.8	257.3	299.8	222.9	233.6
Employees	5.2%	370	376	502	522	453

COLONY BRANDS, INC.

1112 7TH AVE
MONROE, WI 535661364
Phone: 608 328-8400
Fax: –
Web: www.colonybrands.com

CEO: Robert Erb
CFO: –
HR: –
FYE: December 31
Type: Private

Colony Brands is one of the largest direct marketers in the US. It offers a diverse assortment of merchandise and credit through a number of retail brands. Through its flagship Swiss Colony unit, the company makes, markets, and distributes seasonal and special-occasion food gift products through its mail-order catalogs and websites. Swiss Colony's products include candies, cheeses, cookies and pastries, nut mixes, and sausages. The company also offers apparel, electronics, furniture, housewares, and gift items through a dozen other merchant units, such as Country Door, Ginny's, Midnight Velvet, and Montgomery Ward; its Tender Filet unit markets restaurant-quality steaks and seafood, desserts, and wine gifts. Colony Brands is owned by the founding Kubly family.

COLONY CAPITAL, INC.

515 S FLOWER ST FL 44
LOS ANGELES, CA 900712201
Phone: 310 282-8820
Fax: –
Web: –

CEO: –
CFO: –
HR: –
FYE: December 31
Type: Private

When most real estate investors are heading for the nearest exit, Colony Capital (formerly Colony Financial) is knocking on the doors of opportunity. The real estate investment and finance company, which formed in 2009 and immediately filed for an initial public offering, was established to acquire, originate, and manage commercial mortgage loans and other commercial real estate related debts. The firm's portfolio also includes real estate equity, including single- and multifamily homes. It also has an interest in about 100 hotels acquired through foreclosure. In 2015 Colony Financial acquired affiliate Colony Capital, LLC, and changed its name to Colony Capital, Inc.

COLONY RESORTS LVH ACQUISITIONS, LLC

3000 PARADISE RD
LAS VEGAS, NV 891091287
Phone: 702 732-5111
Fax: -
Web: www.lvhilton.com

CEO: -
CFO: -
HR: -
FYE: December 31
Type: Private

Vegas, baby! Vegas! Colony Resorts LVH Acquisition is behind the famed Las Vegas Hilton, a hotel near the Strip with some 3,000 rooms and a 74,000 square-foot casino with games of chance. In addition to the casino, the hotel features more than a dozen restaurants, the Hilton Theater showroom, and a variety of wedding chapels. The Las Vegas Hilton is adjacent to the Las Vegas Convention Center, one of the largest convention facilities in the world. The hotel-casino was sold in 2012 to a joint venture between Gramercy Capital and Goldman Sachs for about $310 million.

COLOR ME MINE ENTERPRISES INC

2121 N CAUSEWAY BLVD
MANDEVILLE, LA 704711806
Phone: 818 291-5900
Fax: -
Web: www.colormemine.com

CEO: -
CFO: -
HR: -
FYE: December 31
Type: Private

Color Me Mine Enterprises brings out the Picasso in you. The company has some 150 franchise locations open or under development in about two dozen US states, as well as in Australia, France, Kuwait, the Netherlands, the Philippines, Saudi Arabia, and Taiwan. Customers can choose from more than 400 pieces of pottery and paint it on site, either solo or as part of a party package for birthdays, bridal showers, and other events. Color Me Mine To Go brings the pottery and paint to the party when you can't make it to the store. Some locations also offer workshops catering to students in kindergarten through sixth grades and home-school art certification.

	Annual Growth	12/04	12/05	12/06	12/07	12/08
Sales ($mil.)	(12.5%)	-	-	3.3	3.3	2.5
Net income ($ mil.)	(0.8%)	-	-	0.3	0.0	0.3
Market value ($ mil.)		-	-	-	-	-
Employees		-	-	-	-	15

COLORADO COLLEGE

14 E CACHE LA POUDRE ST
COLORADO SPRINGS, CO 809033243
Phone: 719 389-6000
Fax: -
Web: www.coloradocollege.edu

CEO: -
CFO: -
HR: -
FYE: June 30
Type: Private

Colorado College does things a little differently, but it shares its mission with other institutions of higher learning. The private liberal arts and sciences college in 1970 adopted the Block Plan, which divides the school year into eight three-and-a-half week blocks. Students take one course per three-and-a-half week block, allowing them to focus on a single subject at a time. Its class size averages about 15 students with most classes capped at 25. Colorado College's 12,000 students can choose from more than 40 majors and 30-plus minors. They are required to live on campus the first three years. Established in 1874, the Colorado Springs school boasts a 10:1 student-faculty ratio.

	Annual Growth	06/17	06/18	06/19	06/20	06/21
Sales ($mil.)	(3.2%)	-	160.7	169.5	166.4	145.9
Net income ($ mil.)	100.8%	-	23.9	40.9	48.2	193.7
Market value ($ mil.)		-	-	-	-	-
Employees		-	-	-	-	800

COLORADO INTERSTATE GAS CO.

1001 Louisiana Street, Suite 1000
Houston, TX 77002
Phone: 713 369-9000
Fax: -
Web: -

CEO: -
CFO: David P Michels
HR: -
FYE: December 31
Type: Public

Colorado Interstate Gas knows that there is no fuel like an old fuel -- natural gas. The company, an indirect subsidiary of Kinder Morgan, transports natural gas from fields in the Rocky Mountains and the Anadarko Basin to customers in the Rocky Mountains, Midwest, Southwest, Pacific Northwest, and California. All told, Colorado Interstate Gas has some 4,300 miles of pipeline that can carry more than 4.6 billion cu. ft. per day. It has 38 billion cu. ft. of storage capacity in facilities in Colorado and Kansas. It also has a 50% stake in WYCO Development LLC, a joint venture with an affiliate of Xcel Energy, which owns and operates an intrastate gas pipeline.

	Annual Growth	12/10	12/11	12/12	12/13	12/14
Sales ($mil.)	(0.4%)	410.0	415.0	398.0	397.0	404.0
Net income ($ mil.)	5.5%	143.0	144.0	156.0	170.0	177.0
Market value ($ mil.)		-	-	-	-	-
Employees		-	-	-	-	-

COLORADO MESA UNIVERSITY

1100 NORTH AVE
GRAND JUNCTION, CO 815013122
Phone: 970 248-1020
Fax: -
Web: www.coloradomesa.edu

CEO: -
CFO: -
HR: Barbara King
FYE: June 30
Type: Private

Colorado Mesa University is a small liberal arts university with an enrollment of more than 10,600 students and a student-to-faculty ratio of 22:1. The school has three campuses in Colorado: the main campus in Grand Junction; another campus in Grand Junction that houses two-year affiliate Western Colorado Community College; and a third campus located in nearby Montrose. Colorado Mesa University offers more than 70 liberal arts and sciences programs and a limited number of professional, technical, and graduate programs. It was founded as Grand Junction State Junior College in 1925.

	Annual Growth	06/17	06/18	06/19	06/21	06/22
Sales ($mil.)	5.4%	-	120.0	130.2	117.6	148.2
Net income ($ mil.)		-	(12.0)	19.8	29.6	37.1
Market value ($ mil.)		-	-	-	-	-
Employees		-	-	-	-	850

COLORADO ROCKIES BASEBALL CLUB, LTD.

2001 BLAKE ST
DENVER, CO 802052060
Phone: 303 292-0200
Fax: -
Web: www.mlb.com

CEO: Charles K Monfort
CFO: Harold R Roth
HR: Elizabeth Stecklein
FYE: December 31
Type: Private

Rockies fans have mile-high hopes of a World Series championship. The Colorado Rockies Baseball Club joined the ranks of Major League Baseball as an expansion team in 1993. Thanks to the rarefied air in Denver, the franchise's Coors Field home has developed a reputation as a hitter-friendly park where even ordinary pop-ups can drift into the bleachers. Colorado earned its first National League pennant in 2007. CEO Charlie Monfort and his brother Dick have controlled the team since 2005. FOX Sports Net also owns a 14% interest in the franchise, as does brewer Molson Coors.

	Annual Growth	12/05	12/06	12/07	12/08	12/15
Sales ($mil.)	22.6%	-	-	-	0.0	0.4
Net income ($ mil.)		-	-	-	0.0	(0.2)
Market value ($ mil.)		-	-	-	-	-
Employees		-	-	-	-	1,000

COLORADO SPRINGS UTILITIES

121 S TEJON ST STE 200
COLORADO SPRINGS, CO 809032187
Phone: 719 448-4800
Fax: -
Web: www.csu.org

CEO: Travas Deal
CFO: Tristan Gearhart
HR: -
FYE: December 31
Type: Private

Even one of the country's most scenic areas needs creature comforts, and that's where utilities come in. Community-owned Colorado Springs Utilities is a multi-utility company that provides natural gas, electric, water and wastewater services in the Pikes Peak region. Colorado Springs Utilities' service territories include Colorado Springs, Manitou Springs, and several of the suburban residential areas surrounding the city. The City of Colorado Springs is the only customer of the streetlight system and is responsible for all streetlight service charges. The military installations of Fort Carson, Peterson Air Force Base, and the US Air Force Academy are also serviced by the multi-utility.

COLORADO STATE UNIVERSITY

6003 CAMPUS DELIVERY
FORT COLLINS, CO 805236003
Phone: 970 491-1372
Fax: -
Web: www.colostate.edu

CEO: -
CFO: -
HR: Stephen Cramer
FYE: June 30
Type: Private

Colorado State University (CSU) got its start as an agricultural college in 1870, six years before Colorado was even a state. The school still has agricultural and forestry programs, as well as a veterinary medicine school, but it also offers degrees in liberal arts, business, engineering, and the sciences. True to its roots as a land-grant college, CSU engages the larger community in research and outreach through statewide Cooperative Extension programs and centers like the Colorado Agricultural Experiment Station. More than 30,000 students are enrolled at CSU, about 80% of whom are Colorado residents. It employs about 1,500 faculty members and has a student-to-teacher ratio of 19:1.

	Annual Growth	06/03	06/04	06/05	06/06	06/08
Sales ($mil.)	14.7%	-	-	-	562.9	740.3
Net income ($ mil.)	-	-	-	-	26.4	(44.5)
Market value ($ mil.)	-	-	-	-	-	-
Employees	-	-	-	-	-	6,701

COLORADO STATE UNIVERSITY-PUEBLO FOUNDATION

2200 BONFORTE BLVD
PUEBLO, CO 810014901
Phone: 719 549-2100
Fax: -
Web: www.csupueblo.edu

CEO: -
CFO: -
HR: Karen Abernathy
FYE: June 30
Type: Private

Colorado State University-Pueblo offers a colorful educational experience in a rugged atmosphere. Some 5,000 students are enrolled at CSU-Pueblo, which is part of the Colorado State University System along with the larger Colorado State University in Denver. The school's 275-acre campus is located at the foot of the Greenhorn Mountains in southern Colorado. While it offers traditional majors and courses of study in the liberal arts, sciences, and technical fields, CSU-Pueblo also emphasizes professional and career-oriented programs. It boasts more than 30 undergraduate programs and offers nine graduate degrees, with a 1-to-18 faculty/student ratio.

	Annual Growth	05/04	05/05*	06/08	06/09	06/22
Sales ($mil.)	10.6%	-	1.5	3.3	2.1	8.1
Net income ($ mil.)	-	-	(0.4)	0.5	(0.5)	0.2
Market value ($ mil.)	-	-	-	-	-	-
Employees	-	-	-	-	-	1,534

*Fiscal year change

COLORADO STRUCTURES, INC.

540 ELKTON DR STE 202
COLORADO SPRINGS, CO 809073587
Phone: 719 522-0500
Fax: -
Web: www.csigc.com

CEO: -
CFO: -
HR: -
FYE: October 31
Type: Private

When retailers want to build stores, Colorado Structures Inc. (CSI) wants to be on the scene. CSI provides general contracting, design, development, and construction management services; the company focuses on retail projects, but it also takes on other types of commercial and non-commercial jobs such as industrial facilities, office buildings, and multi-family residential projects. CSI's customers have included Wal-Mart, Home Depot, and Trammell Crow Company. The firm primarily serves the western US from offices in California, Colorado, and Oregon. Founded in 1978, CSI is controlled by president Tim Phelan.

COLOREDGE, INC.

190 JONY DR
CARLSTADT, NJ 070722411
Phone: 212 594-4800
Fax: -
Web: www.coloredge.com

CEO: Donald R Uzzi
CFO: -
HR: -
FYE: December 31
Type: Private

Merisel is graphically inclined. The company provides an array of digital imaging services, including customized printing, production, and design, through its ColorEdge business. It also operates a prototype division, Comp 24 Group, that develops mockups and packaging samples used for market testing and focus groups, sales samples, examples in corporate presentations, and as props for print and TV advertising. Clients include advertising agencies, consumer packaged goods manufacturers, and retailer firms. The company has office and production facilities in California, Georgia, New Jersey, New York, and Oregon.

COLQUITT ELECTRIC MEMBERSHIP CORPORATION

15 ROWLAND DR
MOULTRIE, GA 317684169
Phone: 229 985-3620
Fax: -
Web: www.colquittemc.com

CEO: -
CFO: -
HR: -
FYE: December 31
Type: Private

There's no quit in the electric service to Colquitt and surrounding counties in Georgia, thanks to Colquitt Electric Membership Corporation (Colquitt EMC). The consumer-owned non-profit utility distributes electricity to more than 41,000 members in Berrien, Brooks, Colquitt, Cook, Lowndes, Tift, and Worth counties. Colquitt EMC distributes electricity via more than 8,020 miles of power line. In 1976 the cooperative changed its name from Colquitt County Rural Electric Company to Colquitt EMC. The utility is the largest EMC in south Georgia with some of the lowest electric rates in the state.

	Annual Growth	12/18	12/19	12/20	12/21	12/22
Sales ($mil.)	7.0%	-	137.0	129.2	136.1	167.9
Net income ($ mil.)	(20.7%)	-	8.5	5.4	2.7	4.3
Market value ($ mil.)	-	-	-	-	-	-
Employees	-	-	-	-	-	164

COLSA CORPORATION

6728 ODYSSEY DR NW
HUNTSVILLE, AL 358063305
Phone: 256 964-5361
Fax: –
Web: www.colsa.com

CEO: Francisco J Collazo
CFO: –
HR: Dana Perez
FYE: December 31
Type: Private

COLSA doesn't mind being called a little defensive. The company provides advanced technology systems and services to US government agencies such as the Missile Defense Agency and NASA. COLSA, which specializes in radar and guidance system technology, offers services including engineering and testing, developing war games simulations, analyzing radar technology, and virtual prototyping. Its information systems services include integration, maintenance, and administration for large computer centers. COLSA also offers a software system for nuclear power plants and a gateway for sending simulation data to remote systems. COLSA was founded in 1980.

	Annual Growth	12/15	12/16	12/17	12/18	12/19
Sales ($mil.)	24.0%	–	190.1	–	336.1	362.7
Net income ($ mil.)	15.7%	–	15.2	–	16.5	23.6
Market value ($ mil.)	–	–	–	–	–	–
Employees	–	–	–	–	–	1,100

COLSON & COLSON CONSTRUCTION CO

2260 MCGILCHRIST ST SE # 100
SALEM, OR 973021147
Phone: 503 586-7401
Fax: –
Web: www.colson-colson.com

CEO: –
CFO: –
HR: –
FYE: December 31
Type: Private

Colson & Colson is the general contractor so good they named it twice. The company develops, builds, and operates retirement communities throughout the US, Canada, and the UK. It has built or managed more than 300 retirement communities since it was founded in 1963. Colson & Colson primarily develops properties for former affiliate Holiday Retirement (HRC), the #1 owner and manager of retirement homes in the US and Canada. It provides site selection, rezoning, construction, and finance services. Prior to focusing exclusively on retirement facilities, Colson & Colson developed single-family residential, commercial, and retail properties as well. The Colson family owns the majority of Colson & Colson.

	Annual Growth	12/03	12/04	12/05	12/06	12/07
Sales ($mil.)	2.1%	–	1.9	1.9	2.0	2.1
Net income ($ mil.)	408.4%	–	2.7	10.8	15.0	357.5
Market value ($ mil.)	–	–	–	–	–	–
Employees	–	–	–	–	–	22

COLT DEFENSE LLC

547 NEW PARK AVE
WEST HARTFORD, CT 061101336
Phone: 860 232-4489
Fax: –
Web: www.colt.com

CEO: Dennis Veilleux
CFO: Richard Harris
HR: –
FYE: December 31
Type: Private

Today's soldier needs more than just a horse and a Colt .45-caliber handgun, and to its benefit Colt Defense has changed with the times. The company has been providing quality firearms for the US military and law enforcement agencies. Products include military rifles (M4 carbine rifles and M16 rifles), auxiliary weapon systems (M203 grenade launchers), law enforcement firearms, and spare parts and replacement kits. In addition it also offers pistols such as defender series, commander, series, traditional series, and competition series, as well as, Revolvers, such as King Cobra series, Python, Cobra, and Single Action Army series. The company began in 1836 when Samuel Colt is issued the US Patent for the first Colt firearm and builds his first factory.

COLUMBIA BANKING SYSTEM INC

1301 A Street
Tacoma, WA 98402-2156
Phone: 253 305-1900
Fax: –
Web: www.columbiabank.com

NMS: COLB
CEO: –
CFO: –
HR: –
FYE: December 31
Type: Public

Columbia Banking System (CBS) is the holding company for Columbia Bank and the Columbia Trust. The regional community bank has more than 150 branches in Washington, Oregon, Idaho and California, offering a full range of financial services to these areas. Targeting retail and small to medium-sized business customers, the bank offers standard retail services such as checking and savings accounts, CDs, IRAs, credit cards, loans, and mortgages. Its business loans comprise of agricultural loans, asset-based loans, builder and other commercial real estate loans. CBS was established in 1993.

	Annual Growth	12/19	12/20	12/21	12/22	12/23
Assets ($mil.)	38.7%	14,080	16,585	20,945	20,266	52,174
Net income ($ mil.)	15.7%	194.5	154.2	202.8	250.2	348.7
Market value ($ mil.)	(10.0%)	8,486.3	7,488.2	6,824.9	6,284.7	5,565.0
Employees	24.0%	2,162	2,091	2,260	2,093	5,114

COLUMBIA COLLEGE CHICAGO

600 S MICHIGAN AVE
CHICAGO, IL 606051996
Phone: 312 663-1600
Fax: –
Web: www.colum.edu

CEO: –
CFO: –
HR: –
FYE: August 31
Type: Private

Columbia College Chicago revels in its creative reputation. Specializing in arts and media, the private not-for-profit school offers undergraduate and graduate degrees in the visual, performing, media, and communication arts. The college offers more than 120 academic programs, including architecture and interior design, photography, dance, television, theater, film, music composition, journalism, and marketing communications. Comedian Andy Richter and Wheel of Fortune host Pat Sajak are among the school's notable alumni. Founded in 1890 as the Columbia School of Oratory, the college is located in several buildings in downtown Chicago and has about 12,000 students. Average teacher to student ratio is 20:1.

	Annual Growth	08/15	08/16	08/19	08/21	08/22
Sales ($mil.)	(4.0%)	–	210.8	226.2	156.7	164.6
Net income ($ mil.)	–	–	6.3	1.4	12.4	(72.8)
Market value ($ mil.)	–	–	–	–	–	–
Employees	–	–	–	–	–	1,000

COLUMBIA FOREST PRODUCTS, INC.

7900 MCCLOUD RD STE 200
GREENSBORO, NC 274093234
Phone: 336 605-0429
Fax: –
Web: www.columbiaforestproducts.com

CEO: –
CFO: –
HR: –
FYE: December 31
Type: Private

Contrary to the proverb, Columbia Forest Products can see the forest for the trees. The company has become North America's biggest producer of plywood and veneer made from hardwood, such as oak, ash, birch, maple, hickory, and pine. Its plywood panels and decorative veneers are hammered into fine cabinets and furniture, commercial fixtures, architectural millwork, and other carpentry for homes and commercial buildings. The company also imports hardwood plywood from Asia, Africa, Russia, and South America. Columbia's lineup is sold through OEMs, wholesale distributors, and mass merchandisers. Founded in 1957, the employee-owned company has grown to a dozen plants located in forest regions of the US and Canada.

	Annual Growth	12/04	12/05	12/19	12/21	12/22
Sales ($mil.)	(35.5%)	–	859.9	0.3	0.5	0.5
Net income ($ mil.)	(14.3%)	–	4.3	(0.0)	0.2	0.3
Market value ($ mil.)	–	–	–	–	–	–
Employees	–	–	–	–	–	2,500

COLUMBIA GAS OF OHIO, INC.

290 W NATIONWIDE BLVD UNIT 114
COLUMBUS, OH 432151082
Phone: 614 460-6000
Fax: –
Web: –

CEO: –
CFO: –
HR: –
FYE: December 31
Type: Private

Columbia Gas of Ohio takes pride in the fact that it can deliver gas first class, en masse, without impasse to the working class, the middle class, and the upper class. The utility is the largest natural gas utility in the state, serving 1.4 million customers (including about 1.3 million residential, 112,000 commercial, and 2,600 industrial customers in more than 1,030 communities in more than 60 of Ohio's 88 counties). The NiSource subsidiary offers a customer choice program, which allows customers to choose their energy suppliers while Columbia Gas of Ohio continues to deliver the gas.

	Annual Growth	12/13	12/14	12/15	12/16	12/17
Sales ($mil.)	(3.0%)	–	993.9	872.2	854.1	908.2
Net income ($ mil.)	(1.9%)	–	102.8	113.1	114.8	96.9
Market value ($ mil.)	–	–	–	–	–	–
Employees	–	–	–	–	–	2,500

COLUMBIA GULF TRANSMISSION, LLC

700 LOUISIANA ST
HOUSTON, TX 770022700
Phone: 713 623-0124
Fax: –
Web: –

CEO: Glen Kettering
CFO: –
HR: –
FYE: December 31
Type: Private

Gas, many people need it, and Columbia Gulf Transmission likes to pass it. The company operates a 3,400 mile pipeline that delivers natural gas to customers in Louisiana, Mississippi, Kentucky, and Tennessee. Its transportation services unit moves gas from the Gulf of Mexico to pipelines in southern Louisiana. The company also provides electric power services for power generation plants. Through its affiliate, Columbia Gas Transmission Company, it provides markets in the East, Mid-Atlantic, Midwest, and Northeast US. Columbia Gulf Transmission, founded in 1954, is a subsidiary of NiSource.

	Annual Growth	12/13	12/14	12/15	12/16	12/17
Sales ($mil.)	(7.1%)	–	–	–	171.2	159.0
Net income ($ mil.)	414.2%	–	–	–	10.6	54.3
Market value ($ mil.)	–	–	–	–	–	–
Employees	–	–	–	–	–	1,300

COLUMBIA HOSPITAL (PALM BEACHES) LIMITED PARTNERSHIP

2201 45TH ST
WEST PALM BEACH, FL 334072047
Phone: 561 842-6141
Fax: –
Web: www.hcafloridahealthcare.com

CEO: Dana C Oaks
CFO: Leah Hess
HR: –
FYE: June 30
Type: Private

From vicious sunburn to sprained surfer's ankle, West Palm Hospital (formerly Columbia Hospital) is there to help. The 250-bed acute care hospital serves Florida's Palm Beach County, just up the coast from Miami. It is also a teaching hospital affiliated with Nova Southeastern University. Specialist services include pain management, orthopedics, and women's health. The Pavilion, the hospital's onsite psychiatric facility, has nearly 90 beds and is the largest such facility in the county. West Palm Hospital is part of nationwide hospital operating group HCA.

COLUMBIA OGDEN MEDICAL CENTER, INC.

5475 S 500 E
OGDEN, UT 844056905
Phone: 801 479-2111
Fax: –
Web: www.mountainstar.com

CEO: Mark Adams
CFO: –
HR: –
FYE: May 31
Type: Private

Ogden Regional Medical Center is a nearly 240-bed hospital in Ogden, Utah. The regional hospital offers general medical and acute care services. It operates specialty units for the treatment of alcoholism, cancer, and heart ailments, as well as blood collection, women's health, and radiology. The hospital employs more than 300 medical staff members. Ogden Regional Medical Center is part of HCA's MountainStar Healthcare Network, a group of hospitals and regional health clinics in Utah and Idaho.

	Annual Growth	06/05	06/06*	12/08*	05/15	05/16
Sales ($mil.)	10.5%	–	75.0	–	192.8	204.0
Net income ($ mil.)	–	–	–	–	70.8	74.0
Market value ($ mil.)	–	–	–	–	–	–
Employees	–	–	–	–	–	950

*Fiscal year change

COLUMBIA PIPELINE GROUP, INC.

5151 SAN FELIPE ST STE 2500
HOUSTON, TX 770563603
Phone: 713 386-3701
Fax: –
Web: www.tcenergy.com

CEO: –
CFO: Nathaniel A Brown
HR: –
FYE: December 31
Type: Private

Columbia Pipeline Group was formed in 2015 as a fee-based, growth-oriented limited partnership by NiSource to own, operate and develop pipelines, storage, and related midstream assets. Its operating company, Columbia OpCo, is a partnership between NiSource subsidiary Columbia Energy Group (CEG), and Columbia Pipeline Partners. Columbia OpCo owns CEG's natural gas transmission and storage assets (15,000 miles of interstate pipelines extending from New York to the Gulf of Mexico and one of the nation's largest underground natural gas storage systems). In 2014, 94% of Columbia OpCo's revenues came from firm revenue contracts. Columbia Pipeline Group went public as an independent company in July 2015. A year later it was acquired by TransCanada.

COLUMBIA PIPELINE PARTNERS LP

5151 SAN FELIPE ST STE 2500
HOUSTON, TX 770563607
Phone: 713 386-3701
Fax: –
Web: www.tcenergy.com

CEO: Robert C Skaggs Jr
CFO: Stephen P Smith
HR: –
FYE: December 31
Type: Private

Columbia Pipeline Partners was formed in 2015 as a fee-based, growth-oriented limited partnership by NiSource to own, operate and develop pipelines, storage, and related midstream assets. Its operating company, Columbia OpCo, is a partnership between NiSource subsidiary Columbia Energy Group (CEG), and Columbia Pipeline Partners. Columbia OpCo owns CEG's natural gas transmission and storage assets (15,000 miles of interstate pipelines extending from New York to the Gulf of Mexico and one of the nation's largest underground natural gas storage systems). In 2016 TransCanada announced that it would buy the Columbia Pipeline Group for $10.2 billion.

COLUMBIA SPORTSWEAR CO.　　　　　　　　　　NMS: COLM

14375 Northwest Science Park Drive　　　　　　CEO: Timothy P Boyle
Portland, OR 97229　　　　　　　　　　　　　　CFO: Jim A Swanson
Phone: 503 985-4000　　　　　　　　　　　　　　HR: –
Fax: –　　　　　　　　　　　　　　　　　　　　FYE: December 31
Web: www.columbia.com　　　　　　　　　　　　Type: Public

Columbia Sportswear connects active people with their passions through its portfolio of well-known brands, making it a global leader in upscale outdoor, active and lifestyle apparel, footwear, accessories and equipment products. Its key brands include Columbia, Mountain Hardwear, Sorel, and prAna. In addition to its products which are designed to be used during a wide variety of activities, such as skiing, hiking, mountaineering, camping, and hunting, among others, the company's footwear products include lightweight hiking boots, trail running shoes, rugged cold weather boots, sandals and shoes, and function-first fashion footwear and casual shoes. It operates around the world, but generates about 65% of sales in US. The company was founded as a hat distributor in 1938 in Oregon.

	Annual Growth	12/19	12/20	12/21	12/22	12/23
Sales ($mil.)	3.5%	3,042.5	2,501.6	3,126.4	3,464.2	3,487.2
Net income ($ mil.)	(6.6%)	330.5	108.0	354.1	311.4	251.4
Market value ($ mil.)	(5.6%)	6,011.0	5,242.5	5,846.0	5,254.4	4,772.1
Employees	3.1%	8,900	7,275	8,325	9,450	10,070

COLUMBIA SUSSEX CORPORATION

740 CENTRE VIEW BLVD　　　　　　　　　　　　CEO: –
CRESTVIEW HILLS, KY 410172750　　　　　　　　CFO: Chris Ballad
Phone: 859 578-1100　　　　　　　　　　　　　　HR: David Diehl
Fax: –　　　　　　　　　　　　　　　　　　　　FYE: December 31
Web: www.columbiasussex.com　　　　　　　　　Type: Private

If you're looking for some hospitality, no need to travel to a South American country or a historic county in England. Columbia Sussex develops and manages about 50 upscale and midscale hotels in the US. The company is a franchisee for national hotel brands, with hotels operating under established banners such as Hilton, Marriott, Doubletree, and Starwood Hotel's Westin brand. Properties include the Las Vegas Westin, the Williamsburg Marriott in Virginia, and the Doubletree Cincinnati Airport. CEO William Yung and his family own Columbia Sussex. Yung founded the firm in 1972.

COLUMBIA VALLEY HEALTHCARE SYSTEM, L.P.

100A E ALTON GLOOR BLVD　　　　　　　　　　CEO: Art Garza
BROWNSVILLE, TX 785263346　　　　　　　　　　CFO: –
Phone: 956 350-7000　　　　　　　　　　　　　　HR: Elizabeth Sanchez
Fax: –　　　　　　　　　　　　　　　　　　　　FYE: September 30
Web: www.valleyregionalmedicalcenter.com　　　　Type: Private

The Brownsville-Valley Regional Medical Center provides health care to residents of Brownsville, Texas, and the surrounding region (generally called "the Valley"). The acute care facility has about 215 beds and offers primary and emergency care services. Its operations include a specialty center devoted to women's care, a minor and major trauma center, and community outreach programs. It also provides neonatal, neurology, cardiology, and orthopedic care. Founded in 1975, Brownsville-Valley Regional Medical Center is part of the HCA healthcare system.

COLUMBUS MCKINNON CORP. (NY)　　　　　　NMS: CMCO

13320 Ballantyne Corporate Place, Suite D　　　　CEO: David J Wilson
Charlotte, NC 28277　　　　　　　　　　　　　　CFO: Gregory P Rustowicz
Phone: 716 689-5400　　　　　　　　　　　　　　HR: Huan MA
Fax: –　　　　　　　　　　　　　　　　　　　　FYE: March 31
Web: www.columbusmckinnon.com　　　　　　　Type: Public

Columbus McKinnon is a leading worldwide designer, manufacturer and marketer of intelligent motion solutions that move the world forward and improve lives by efficiently and ergonomically moving, lifting, positioning and securing materials. Key products include hoists, crane components, precision conveyor systems, rigging tools, light rail workstations and digital power and motion control systems. The company is focused on commercial and industrial applications that require the safety, reliability and quality provided by its superior design and engineering know-how. Well known in the marketplace, its brand names include Coffing, Duff-Norton, Shaw-Box, and Yale, among others. In addition to OEMs, the company sells to hardware distributors and mass merchandiser outlets. Approximately 65% of its revenue comes from domestic customers.

	Annual Growth	03/19	03/20	03/21	03/22	03/23
Sales ($mil.)	1.7%	876.3	809.2	649.6	906.6	936.2
Net income ($ mil.)	3.3%	42.6	59.7	9.1	29.7	48.4
Market value ($ mil.)	2.0%	982.8	715.3	1,509.6	1,213.1	1,063.2
Employees	2.0%	3,128	2,997	2,651	3,224	3,392

COLUMBUS REGIONAL HEALTHCARE SYSTEM, INC

707 CENTER ST　　　　　　　　　　　　　　　　CEO: Scott Hill
COLUMBUS, GA 319011575　　　　　　　　　　　CFO: Allen Holladay
Phone: 706 571-1495　　　　　　　　　　　　　　HR: Virginia Korcha
Fax: –　　　　　　　　　　　　　　　　　　　　FYE: June 30
Web: www.crhealthcare.org　　　　　　　　　　　Type: Private

Columbus Regional Healthcare System is a not-for-profit system serving communities in Alabama and Georgia. The 730-bed system includes two Columbus, Georgia acute-care hospitals (The Medical Center and the Doctors Hospital), an orthopedic facility (Hughston Hospital), a rehabilitation center, and long-term care nursing facilities. The Children's Hospital is located within The Medical Center. Columbus Regional Healthcare System also operates a cancer center, women's health centers, urgent care centers, and physician practices. Other specialty services include neurology, critical care, radiology, and respiratory care.

	Annual Growth	06/12	06/13	06/14	06/15	06/17
Sales ($mil.)	239.2%	–	–	–	37.4	430.6
Net income ($ mil.)	–	–	–	–	(4.4)	(11.0)
Market value ($ mil.)	–	–	–	–	–	–
Employees	–	–	–	–	–	2,400

COMARCO INC.

28202 Cabot Road, Suite 300　　　　　　　　　　CEO: Thomas W Lanni
Laguna Niguel, CA 92677　　　　　　　　　　　　CFO: –
Phone: 949 599-7400　　　　　　　　　　　　　　HR: –
Fax: 800 792-0250　　　　　　　　　　　　　　　FYE: January 31
Web: www.comarco.com　　　　　　　　　　　　Type: Public

Comarco develops universal power supplies that charge various portable devices. Operating solely through wholly owned subsidiary Comarco Wireless Technologies, the company's flagship product is its ChargeSource line of adapters that recharge consumer electronic devices, such as notebooks, mobile phones, and music players. Comarco sells directly to consumers through its chargesource.com retail website and to notebook OEMs such as Lenovo, who brand the accessories and sell them in conjunction with their notebooks. Comarco was spun off from Genge Industries in 1971. Elkhorn Partners Limited Partnership holds a 49% stake in Comarco.

	Annual Growth	01/13	01/14	01/15	01/16	01/17
Sales ($mil.)	–	6.3	4.4	–	–	–
Net income ($ mil.)	–	(5.6)	(2.1)	6.0	(1.3)	0.8
Market value ($ mil.)	(18.7%)	2.3	2.6	2.0	1.6	1.0
Employees	(43.8%)	10	1	1	1	1

COMBIMATRIX CORPORATION

310 GODDARD STE 150
IRVINE, CA 926184601
Phone: –
Fax: –
Web: www.combimatrix.com

CEO: –
CFO: –
HR: –
FYE: December 31
Type: Private

CombiMatrix works to untangle the complicated matrix of genetic profiles. The company develops and sells diagnostic testing supplies and provides related laboratory services. Through its CombiMatrix Molecular Diagnostics subsidiary, it provides molecular diagnostic testing assays and other genetic analysis products. The tests evaluate a patient's DNA to find genetic irregularities, which can then help to diagnose health conditions or predict disease susceptibility. CombiMatrix markets its products and services to physician practices, hospitals, and other health care centers.In 2017 CombiMatrix agreed to be acquired by genetic information firm Invitae Corporation for $33 million.

COMCAST CORP
NMS: CMCS A

One Comcast Center
Philadelphia, PA 19103-2838
Phone: 215 286-1700
Fax: –
Web: www.comcastcorporation.com

CEO: Brian L Roberts
CFO: Jason S Armstrong
HR: Chris Winton
FYE: December 31
Type: Public

Comcast Corporation is a global media and technology company with three primary businesses: Comcast Cable, NBCUniversal, and Sky. It offers broadband services over its hybrid fiber-optic and coaxial (HFC) cable network to nearly 30 million customers. Its other business interests consist primarily of the operations of Comcast Spectacor, which owns the Philadelphia Flyers and the Wells Fargo Center arena in Philadelphia, Pennsylvania, and other business initiatives. This is on top of the millions of customers they serve for its video, voice, and wireless services. The company generates the majority of its revenue domestically.

	Annual Growth	12/19	12/20	12/21	12/22	12/23
Sales ($mil.)	2.8%	108,942	103,564	116,385	121,427	121,572
Net income ($ mil.)	4.2%	13,057	10,534	14,159	5,370.0	15,388
Market value ($ mil.)	(0.6%)	178,925	208,487	200,251	139,137	174,469
Employees	(0.5%)	190,000	168,000	189,000	186,000	186,000

COMENITY BANK

12921 S VISTA STATION BLVD STE 400
DRAPER, UT 840202377
Phone: 614 729-4000
Fax: –
Web: www.breadfinancial.com

CEO: –
CFO: –
HR: –
FYE: December 31
Type: Private

World Financial Network National Bank (WFNNB) will take credit for the credit it extends. The company is the private-label and co-branded credit card banking subsidiary of Alliance Data Systems. Along with affiliate World Financial Capital Bank, the company underwrites cards on behalf of more than 85 businesses. The company's largest clients include apparel retailers L Brands and Redcats USA. WFNNB oversees about 120 million cardholder accounts and roughly $4 billion in receivables. Private equity giant Blackstone planned to acquire parent Alliance Data Systems for more than $6 billion, but that deal was terminated in 2008.

	Annual Growth	12/02	12/03	12/05	12/13	12/14
Assets ($mil.)	26.8%	–	672.1	332.6	7,453.2	9,149.2
Net income ($ mil.)	14.4%	–	88.8	10.8	350.0	389.3
Market value ($ mil.)	–	–	–	–	–	–
Employees	–	–	–	–	–	200

COMERICA, INC.
NYS: CMA

Comerica Bank Tower, 1717 Main Street, MC 6404
Dallas, TX 75201
Phone: 214 462-6831
Fax: –
Web: www.comerica.com

CEO: Curtis C Farmer
CFO: James J Herzog
HR: –
FYE: December 31
Type: Public

Comerica is the holding company for Comerica Bank, which operates primarily in five US states (Texas, California, Michigan, Arizona, and Florida), Canada, and Mexico. The company is organized into three main business segments: The Commercial Bank offers commercial loans and lines of credit, deposits, and capital markets products, among others, to small- and middle-market businesses, multinational corporations, and government clients. The Retail Bank serves consumers, while the Wealth Management provides fiduciary services, investment management and advisory, and retirement services, among others. Comerica categorizes its securities portfolio and asset and liability management under an additional Finance segment. The company boasts total assets of approximately $85.4 billion, total deposits of approximately $71.4 billion, total loans of approximately $53.4 billion, and shareholders' equity of approximately $5.2 billion.

	Annual Growth	12/19	12/20	12/21	12/22	12/23
Assets ($mil.)	4.0%	73,402	88,129	94,616	85,406	85,834
Net income ($ mil.)	(7.4%)	1,198.0	474.0	1,168.0	1,151.0	881.0
Market value ($ mil.)	(6.1%)	9,463.7	7,367.8	11,475	8,817.4	7,361.2
Employees	(0.3%)	7,948	7,870	7,611	7,649	7,863

COMERTON CORP
NBB: COCM

6554-44th Street, Suite #1004
Pinellas Park, FL 33781
Phone: 727 877-6747
Fax: –
Web: www.comertoncorp.com

CEO: –
CFO: –
HR: –
FYE: December 31
Type: Public

Spearhead, formerly known as First Aid Direct, is out of the first-aid business. The company had used a system of mobile vans and sales people to wholesale first-aid supplies to first-aid distributors. But Spearhead has changed channels and is growing through acquisitions into an information technology consulting firm serving companies in Canada and the U.S. The company offers services such as consulting, network design, systems integration, application development, legacy migration, support, and training. Officers and directors own about 25% of Spearhead.

	Annual Growth	12/13	12/14	12/15	12/16	12/17
Sales ($mil.)	–	–	–	–	–	–
Net income ($ mil.)	–	(0.0)	(0.0)	(0.0)	(0.0)	(0.1)
Market value ($ mil.)	136.4%	0.0	0.0	0.0	0.0	0.0
Employees	–	–	–	–	–	–

COMFORT SYSTEMS USA INC
NYS: FIX

675 Bering Drive, Suite 400
Houston, TX 77057
Phone: 713 830-9600
Fax: 713 830-9696
Web: www.comfortsystemsusa.com

CEO: Brian E Lane
CFO: William George
HR: –
FYE: December 31
Type: Public

Established in 1997, Comfort Systems USA builds, installs, maintains, repairs and replaces mechanical, electrical and plumbing (MEP) systems throughout its more than 40 operating units with about 170 locations in around 130 cities throughout the US. The company operates primarily in the commercial, industrial and institutional MEP markets and perform most of its services, including mechanical, electrical, process piping, modular construction and building automation controls in industrial, healthcare, education, office, technology, retail and government facilities. Substantially all of its revenue is generated in the US.

	Annual Growth	12/19	12/20	12/21	12/22	12/23
Sales ($mil.)	18.8%	2,615.3	2,856.7	3,073.6	4,140.4	5,206.8
Net income ($ mil.)	29.7%	114.3	150.1	143.3	245.9	323.4
Market value ($ mil.)	42.5%	1,778.9	1,879.2	3,530.6	4,106.6	7,339.3
Employees	7.1%	12,000	11,100	13,200	14,100	15,800

COMMERCE BANCSHARES INC
NMS: CBSH

1000 Walnut
Kansas City, MO 64106
Phone: 816 234-2000
Fax: 816 234-2369
Web: www.commercebank.com

CEO: John W Kemper
CFO: Charles G Kim
HR: Michelle Sacks
FYE: December 31
Type: Public

Commerce Bancshares owns bank branch operator Commerce Bank. The financial institution boasts a network of approximately 275 locations across several US states, including Missouri, Kansas, Illinois, Oklahoma, and Colorado. The company focuses on retail and commercial banking services, such as deposit accounts, mortgages, loans, and credit cards. Commerce Bank also runs a wealth management division that offers asset management, trust, private banking, brokerage, and estate planning services, and also manages proprietary mutual funds. As part of its operations, the company has subsidiaries devoted to insurance, leasing, securities brokerage, and private equity investments. In addition, the company has consolidated assets of $31.9 billion, loans of $16.3 billion, deposits of $26.2 billion, and equity of $2.5 billion.

	Annual Growth	12/19	12/20	12/21	12/22	12/23
Assets ($mil.)	5.0%	26,066	32,923	36,689	31,876	31,701
Net income ($ mil.)	3.2%	421.2	354.1	530.8	488.4	477.1
Market value ($ mil.)	(5.8%)	8,863.0	8,570.8	8,967.3	8,879.9	6,967.5
Employees	(0.6%)	4,835	4,588	4,537	4,598	4,728

COMMERCE ENERGY GROUP INC
NBB: CMNR

600 Anton Boulevard, Suite 2000
Costa Mesa, CA 92626
Phone: 714 259-2500
Fax: –
Web: www.commerceenergy.com

CEO: –
CFO: –
HR: –
FYE: July 31
Type: Public

Commerce Energy works for the good of customer choice and greater commerce by marketing electricity and natural gas (in tandem with its parent Just Energy Group) to 1.8 million residential and commercial customers in the US and Canada. The competitive green energy retailer's primary residential, small business, commercial and industrial customers are in California, Georgia, Maryland, New Jersey, and Pennsylvania. Since 2007 Commerce Energy and its parent have invested $14 million in carbon emission reduction projects and more than $32 million in renewable energy projects (wind, solar, and other). The company is a subsidiary of the Canada-based energy retailer Just Energy.

	Annual Growth	07/04	07/05	07/06	07/07	07/08
Sales ($mil.)	21.6%	210.6	253.9	247.1	371.6	459.8
Net income ($ mil.)	–	(21.7)	(6.1)	(2.2)	5.5	(31.8)
Market value ($ mil.)	(9.6%)	51.4	46.4	43.0	65.4	34.3
Employees	3.4%	175	160	176	255	200

COMMERCE GROUP CORP.
NBB: CGCO

6001 North 91st Street
Milwaukee, WI 53225-1795
Phone: 414 462-5310
Fax: 414 462-5312
Web: www.commercegroupcorp.com

CEO: Edward A Machulak
CFO: –
HR: –
FYE: March 31
Type: Public

Commerce Group owns El Salvador's San Sebastian Gold Mine, which contains some 1.5 million ounces of gold reserves. Production at the mine has been suspended since 1999, however, while the company works to raise money to upgrade the facility's gold-processing equipment. Commerce Group also explores for other gold and silver mining opportunities in El Salvador. In 2009, the Commerce Group filed a motion for arbitration hearings with the government of El Salvador, which revoked the company's permits to explore the San Sebastian Gold Mine in 2006. The company has postponed all business activity pending the outcome of the arbitration.

	Annual Growth	03/06	03/07	03/08	03/09	03/10
Sales ($mil.)	–	–	–	–	–	–
Net income ($ mil.)	–	(0.2)	(0.2)	(3.1)	(30.0)	(4.9)
Market value ($ mil.)	(30.1%)	6.5	4.3	9.8	2.2	1.5
Employees	(18.4%)	45	55	40	30	20

COMMERCIAL ENERGY OF MONTANA INC.

7677 OAKPORT ST
OAKLAND, CA 946211929
Phone: 406 873-3300
Fax: –
Web: www.commercialenergy.net

CEO: –
CFO: C F Jackson
HR: –
FYE: December 31
Type: Private

Montana (and California) businesses can get their commercial energy from Commercial Energy of Montana. The company purchases, transmits, and distributes natural gas and electricity to customers that include businesses, school districts, universities, and government agencies. Commercial Energy's ROC Gathering unit acquires gas gathering systems and producing wells. Commercial Energy of Montana was created to sell natural gas from family-owned Ranck Oil Company, which was founded in 1957. Today, it owns and gathers natural gas at more than 150 producing wells located primarily in California and Montana.

	Annual Growth	12/03	12/04	12/05	12/06	12/07
Sales ($mil.)	36.6%	–	19.4	16.7	28.8	49.3
Net income ($ mil.)	137.0%	–	0.1	0.9	0.4	1.4
Market value ($ mil.)	–	–	–	–	–	–
Employees	–	–	–	–	–	21

COMMERCIAL METALS CO.
NYS: CMC

6565 North MacArthur Boulevard
Irving, TX 75039
Phone: 214 689-4300
Fax: 214 689-5886
Web: www.cmc.com

CEO: Peter R Matt
CFO: Paul J Lawrence
HR: –
FYE: August 31
Type: Public

Commercial Metals (CMC) manufactures, recycles, and fabricates steel and metal products, related materials, and services through a network of facilities that includes seven electric arc furnace (EAF) mini mills, two EAF micro mills, two rerolling mills, steel fabrication, and processing plants, construction-related product warehouses, and metal recycling facilities in the US and Poland. Through its Tensar operations, the company provides innovative ground and soil stabilization solutions selling into more than 80 national markets through two major product lines: Tensar geogrids and Geopier foundation systems. CMC operates through two reportable segments: North America and Europe. The US accounts for about 75% of sales.

	Annual Growth	08/19	08/20	08/21	08/22	08/23
Sales ($mil.)	10.8%	5,829.0	5,476.5	6,729.8	8,913.5	8,799.5
Net income ($ mil.)	44.3%	198.1	279.5	412.9	1,217.3	859.8
Market value ($ mil.)	37.7%	1,825.8	2,431.7	3,800.7	4,720.0	6,558.7
Employees	3.1%	11,524	11,297	11,089	12,483	13,022

COMMERCIAL NATIONAL FINANCIAL CORP. (PA)
NBB: CNAF

900 Ligonier Street, P.O. Box 429
Latrobe, PA 15650
Phone: 724 539-3501
Fax: 724 539-1137
Web: www.cnbthebank.com

CEO: Gregg E Hunter
CFO: Thomas D Watters
HR: Charles Taylor
FYE: December 31
Type: Public

Commercial National Financial is the holding company for Commercial Bank & Trust of PA, which serves individuals and local businesses through more than five branches in western Pennsylvania's Westmoreland County. Founded in 1934, the bank offers standard deposit services like checking and savings accounts, money market investments, CDs, and IRAs, as well as trust and asset management services. Commercial Bank & Trust of PA's loan portfolio consists mostly of residential mortgages and commercial mortgages, in addition to business, construction, consumer, and municipal loans.

	Annual Growth	12/18	12/19	12/20	12/21	12/22
Assets ($mil.)	(0.7%)	419.6	419.6	425.4	472.0	408.4
Net income ($ mil.)	(2.6%)	4.3	4.7	5.7	4.9	3.9
Market value ($ mil.)	(13.4%)	60.2	58.4	47.2	51.8	33.9
Employees	–	–	98	46	80	–

COMMERCIAL VEHICLE GROUP INC   NMS: CVGI

7800 Walton Parkway
New Albany, OH 43054
Phone: 614 289-5360
Fax: –
Web: www.cvgrp.com

CEO: James Ray
CFO: Christopher H Bohnert
HR: Chris Peters
FYE: December 31
Type: Public

Commercial Vehicle Group (CVG) is a global provider of systems, assemblies and components to the global commercial vehicle market, the electric vehicle market, and the industrial automation markets. Products include seat and seating systems, plastic assemblies and components, cab structures and interior parts, wire harness and cable harness assemblies, aftermarket and accessories, electrical systems, control panel, and electro-mechanical assemblies. CVG offers various products which are sold into many end markets such as internal combustion commercial vehicles, electric vehicles, construction equipment, power sports, industrial automation, and military. CVG generates some three-quarters of total revenue from its home country, the US.

	Annual Growth	12/19	12/20	12/21	12/22	12/23
Sales ($mil.)	2.5%	901.2	717.7	971.6	981.6	994.7
Net income ($ mil.)	33.0%	15.8	(37.0)	23.7	(22.0)	49.4
Market value ($ mil.)	2.5%	211.6	288.2	268.6	226.9	233.6
Employees	1.2%	7,347	7,740	7,600	8,000	7,700

COMMODORE APPLIED TECHNOLOGIES, INC.   NBB: CXIA

507 Knight Street, Suite B
Richland, WA 99352
Phone: 509 943-2565
Fax: –
Web: www.commodore.com

CEO: –
CFO: –
HR: –
FYE: December 31
Type: Public

Commodore Applied Technologies has SET its sights on cleaning up the environment. The company's SET (solvated electron technology) is a non-thermal process that removes PCBs, pesticides, dioxins, radioactivity, and other contaminants from water and soil. Commodore is working to commercialize SET; in the meantime, the company gets more than 90% of its sales from its Commodore Advanced Sciences unit, which provides waste containment, remediation, and removal management services, mainly for government agencies. Projects undertaken by Commodore Advanced Sciences have included US government radioactive waste sites in Oak Ridge, Tennessee, and Rocky Flats, Colorado.

	Annual Growth	12/04	12/05	12/06	12/07	12/08
Sales ($mil.)	43.0%	0.7	10.3	7.3	3.2	3.1
Net income ($ mil.)	–	(2.4)	(2.7)	(1.8)	(2.0)	(2.4)
Market value ($ mil.)	14.1%	0.1	1.4	1.2	0.9	0.2
Employees	(3.1%)	34	38	33	34	30

COMMONSPIRIT HEALTH

444 W LAKE ST STE 2500
CHICAGO, IL 606060097
Phone: 312 741-7000
Fax: –
Web: www.commonspirit.org

CEO: –
CFO: –
HR: –
FYE: June 30
Type: Private

Formed in 2019 through the merger of Catholic hospital systems Catholic Health Initiatives and Dignity Health, CommonSpirit Health is a not-for-profit organization with more than 140 hospitals in about 20 states. Its hospitals range from large urban medical centers (many with educational and research programs) to small hospitals in rural areas. The company also operates clinics, long-term care, assisted-living, and senior residential facilities (totaling more than 2,200 care sites) and provides home-based care services.

	Annual Growth	06/17	06/18	06/19	06/21	06/22
Sales ($mil.)	(78.2%)	–	14,982	7,170.0	33,253	33.9
Net income ($ mil.)	–	–	222.1	9,008.0	8,303.0	(1.8)
Market value ($ mil.)	–	–	–	–	–	–
Employees	–	–	–	–	–	72,500

COMMONWEALTH EDISON COMPANY

10 S DEARBORN ST 52ND FL
CHICAGO, IL 606032398
Phone: 312 394-4321
Fax: –
Web: www.comed.com

CEO: Anne R Pramaggiore
CFO: Joseph R Trpik Jr
HR: Elizabeth Bailey
FYE: December 31
Type: Private

Commonwealth Edison (ComEd) is the largest electric utility in Illinois. ComEd, a subsidiary of utility holding company Exelon, distributes electricity to more than 4 million customers across Northern Illinois, representing 70% of population of the state. The utility owns manages more than 90,000 miles of lines in an 11,400-square-mile territory. ComEd works with regional operator PJM Interconnection, which manages wholesale activities on the utility's transmission grid.

COMMONWEALTH EQUITY SERVICES, LLC

29 SAWYER RD STE 2
WALTHAM, MA 024533483
Phone: 781 736-7980
Fax: –
Web: www.commonwealth.com

CEO: –
CFO: –
HR: Holly Sivec
FYE: December 31
Type: Private

Commonwealth Equity Services, doing business as Commonwealth Financial Network, is a member of FINRA/SIPC, and a Registered Investment Adviser which provides financial advisors with holistic, integrated solutions that support business evolution, growth acceleration, and operational efficiency The company is dually registered as both an investment adviser and a broker/dealer. This means it supervises and processes the investment business of the more than 2,000 financial professionals who have affiliated with them. These professionals, whom was called advisors, are independent business owners who provide financial guidance to clients looking for assistance. Commonwealth functions as the unseen back office that processes client transactions for them. Founded in 1979, Commonwealth now manages roughly $200 billion in client account assets.

	Annual Growth	12/99	12/00	12/01	12/02	12/19
Assets ($mil.)	(12.9%)	–	15.4	15.7	17.6	1.1
Net income ($ mil.)	4.6%	–	0.0	0.2	0.4	0.2
Market value ($ mil.)	–	–	–	–	–	–
Employees	–	–	–	–	–	827

COMMONWEALTH HEALTH CORPORATION, INC.

800 PARK ST
BOWLING GREEN, KY 421012347
Phone: 270 745-1500
Fax: –
Web: www.medcenterhealth.org

CEO: Connie Smith
CFO: –
HR: Lynn Williams
FYE: March 31
Type: Private

For care in Kentucky, Bluegrass Staters can turn to Commonwealth Health Corporation. The holding company houses a full spectrum of health care facilities and services including The Medical Center, a 415-bed regional health care system comprised of four hospitals, long-term health care providers, and senior care, among other services. Commonwealth's outpatient offerings include nutrition therapy, a women's center, diabetes programs, and adult day care. The corporation's Center Care Health Benefits Program supplies employers with products and services to support the distribution and administration of employee benefits and healthcare services.

	Annual Growth	03/14	03/15	03/19	03/20	03/21
Sales ($mil.)	43.5%	–	68.7	–	531.7	598.4
Net income ($ mil.)	94.9%	–	2.7	–	18.5	150.6
Market value ($ mil.)	–	–	–	–	–	–
Employees	–	–	–	–	–	2,700

COMMSCOPE HOLDING CO INC
NMS: COMM

1100 CommScope Place, SE
Hickory, NC 28602
Phone: 828 324-2200
Fax: –
Web: www.commscope.com

CEO: –
CFO: –
HR: –
FYE: December 31
Type: Public

CommScope is a global provider of infrastructure solutions for communication and entertainment networks. Its solutions for wired and wireless networks enable service providers including cable, telephone and digital broadcast satellite operators and media programmers to deliver media, voice, Internet Protocol (IP) data services and Wi-Fi to their subscribers and allow enterprises to experience constant wireless and wired connectivity across complex and varied networking environments. The company's major brands are Andrew, SYSTIMAX, NETCONNECT, and Uniprise. The company serves customers in over 150 countries. The US is the largest market accounting for over 60% of the company's total sales.

	Annual Growth	12/19	12/20	12/21	12/22	12/23
Sales ($mil.)	(8.7%)	8,345.1	8,435.9	8,586.7	9,228.1	5,789.2
Net income ($ mil.)	–	(929.5)	(573.4)	(462.6)	(1,286.9)	(1,450.9)
Market value ($ mil.)	(33.2%)	3,009.8	2,842.3	2,341.7	1,559.0	598.1
Employees	(9.6%)	30,000	30,000	30,000	30,000	20,000

COMMUNICATIONS TEST DESIGN, INC.

1373 ENTERPRISE DR
WEST CHESTER, PA 193805959
Phone: 610 436-5203
Fax: –
Web: www.ctdi.com

CEO: –
CFO: –
HR: –
FYE: December 31
Type: Private

Communications Test Design (CTDI) is a full-service, global engineering, repair, and logistics company that provides best-cost solutions to the communications industry. CTDI provides a dynamic business model to global customers that are comprised of five divisions: STB / CPE Division, Mobile & Consumer Electronics, Mobility Product Solutions, Network Services, and Product / Supply. CTDI has earned a solid reputation in the communications service industry as a world-class company with a genuine employee-focused approach to business. Partners with Fortune 100 Companies around the world, the company was founded in 1975 by chairman Jerry Parsons, his father Donald, and his brother Dick. CTDI is owned and led by the Parsons family.

	Annual Growth	12/06	12/07	12/08	12/09	12/15
Sales ($mil.)	(60.8%)	–	861.3	761.9	740.5	0.5
Net income ($ mil.)	(38.8%)	–	22.4	15.5	24.0	0.4
Market value ($ mil.)	–	–	–	–	–	–
Employees	–	–	–	–	–	7,880

COMMUNICATIONS WORKERS OF AMERICA, AFL-CIO, CLC

501 3RD ST NW
WASHINGTON, DC 200012760
Phone: 202 434-1100
Fax: –
Web: www.cwa-union.org

CEO: –
CFO: –
HR: –
FYE: May 31
Type: Private

CWA knows how to get its message across. Communications Workers of America is a labor union representing more than 700,000 employees in the communications and media industries. Members work in a variety of sectors including telecommunications, journalism, publishing, manufacturing, and customer service. With about 1,200 locals across the US, Canada, and Puerto Rico, CWA is one of the most geographically diverse unions. It holds more than 2,000 collective bargaining agreements guaranteeing wages, benefits, and good working conditions for members. The group is affiliated with the AFL-CIO, the Canadian Labour Congress, and Union Network International.

	Annual Growth	05/10	05/11	05/13	05/16	05/22
Sales ($mil.)	(0.3%)	–	155.3	146.0	164.8	150.7
Net income ($ mil.)	2.7%	–	2.0	(4.2)	(13.5)	2.7
Market value ($ mil.)	–	–	–	–	–	–
Employees	–	–	–	–	–	510

COMMUNITY ASPHALT CORP.

9675 NW 117TH AVE STE 108
MEDLEY, FL 331781244
Phone: 305 884-9444
Fax: –
Web: www.ohla-usa.com

CEO: Daniel R Andujar
CFO: Jose Parra
HR: Mario Rosales
FYE: December 31
Type: Private

Community Asphalt provides paving services for the road more traveled. The company's services include grading and paving, pavement milling, surveying, excavation, on- and off-road hauling, drainage, utilities, base finishing, and highway sweeping. It also provides engineering contracting and design/build services; projects include parking lots, industrial and retail complexes, auto race tracks, and airport runways. Formed in 1980, Community Asphalt has three asphalt plants in southeastern Florida. It also operates a limestone quarry, and a fleet of dump trucks. In 2006 Community Asphalt and Spain's Obrasc n Huarte Lain (OHL) made a stock purchase agreement, which gave OHL a controlling interest in the company.

	Annual Growth	12/08	12/09	12/10	12/11	12/12
Sales ($mil.)	(14.1%)	–	–	330.7	260.8	243.9
Net income ($ mil.)	(70.6%)	–	–	27.7	3.1	2.4
Market value ($ mil.)	–	–	–	–	–	–
Employees	–	–	–	–	–	640

COMMUNITY BANCORP. (DERBY, VT)
NBB: CMTV

4811 U.S. Route 5
Derby, VT 05829
Phone: 802 334-7915
Fax: –
Web: www.communitybancorpvt.com

CEO: Kathryn M Austin
CFO: –
HR: –
FYE: December 31
Type: Public

Winters may be cold in Vermont, but Community Bancorp. hopes to warm the hearts of its customers with its hometown banking services. It is the holding company for Community National Bank, which has been serving Vermont since 1851. Through nearly 20 branches, the bank offers such products and services as checking and savings accounts, CDs, IRAs, residential and commercial mortgages, and business, consumer, and other loans. In conjunction with two other regional banks, the company is part of Community Financial Services Group, which offers trust and investment planning services. At the end of 2007 Community Bancorp. acquired LyndonBank, which added about a half-dozen branches to its network.

	Annual Growth	12/18	12/19	12/20	12/21	12/22
Assets ($mil.)	10.0%	720.3	738.0	918.2	1,019.1	1,056.0
Net income ($ mil.)	13.1%	8.4	8.8	10.8	13.1	13.7
Market value ($ mil.)	4.3%	89.7	87.0	80.7	112.0	106.0
Employees	(0.9%)	135	136	136	134	130

COMMUNITY BANK SYSTEM INC
NYS: CBU

5790 Widewaters Parkway
DeWitt, NY 13214-1883
Phone: 315 445-2282
Fax: –
Web: www.communitybankna.com

CEO: Mark E Tryniski
CFO: Joseph E Sutaris
HR: –
FYE: December 31
Type: Public

Community Bank System is a diversified financial services company focused on four main business lines ? banking, benefits administration, insurance services, and wealth management with total assets of $15.1 billion. Its banking subsidiary, Community Bank is among the country's 100 largest banking institutions. In addition to a full range of retail, business, and municipal banking services, the company offers comprehensive financial planning, trust administration, and wealth management services through its Community Bank Wealth Management operating unit. The company's Benefit Plans Administrative Services, Inc. subsidiary is a leading provider of employee benefits administration, trust services, collective investment fund administration, and actuarial consulting services to customers on a national scale. The Company's OneGroup NY, Inc. subsidiary is a top 100 US insurance agency.

	Annual Growth	12/19	12/20	12/21	12/22	12/23
Assets ($mil.)	8.1%	11,410	13,931	15,553	15,836	15,556
Net income ($ mil.)	(6.0%)	169.1	164.7	189.7	188.1	131.9
Market value ($ mil.)	(7.4%)	3,783.0	3,322.8	3,971.8	3,356.9	2,778.9
Employees	(1.6%)	3,038	3,047	2,927	3,026	2,849

COMMUNITY CAPITAL BANCSHARES INC

NBB: ALBY

2815 Meredyth Drive, P.O. Drawer 71269
Albany, GA 31708-1269
Phone: 229 446-2265
Fax: 229 446-7030
Web: www.comcapbancshares.com

CEO: Luke Flatt
CFO: David J Baranko
HR: –
FYE: December 31
Type: Public

Community Capital Bancshares has taken hometown to heart. The bank holding company owns Albany Bank & Trust, a community bank serving southwestern Georgia through three branches. It also includes AB&T National Bank, which operates two branches in Alabama. The banks offer standard deposit products and services including checking and savings accounts, money market accounts, CDs, and IRAs. The company mainly uses these deposits to fund residential and commercial construction loans and mortgages, as well as business and consumer loans. Real estate loans comprise about 80% of the company's loan book. The company plans to combine all of its banks under the AB&T National Bank name.

	Annual Growth	12/17	12/18	12/19	12/20	12/21
Assets ($mil.)	9.3%	180.3	194.2	195.6	281.8	257.2
Net income ($ mil.)	–	(1.4)	1.2	1.5	1.8	2.0
Market value ($ mil.)	48.8%	3.4	11.8	14.5	14.2	16.4
Employees	–	–	–	–	–	–

COMMUNITY CHOICE FINANCIAL INC

6785 Bobcat Way, Suite 200
Dublin, OH 43016
Phone: 888 513-9395
Fax: –
Web: www.ccfi.com

CEO: –
CFO: –
HR: –
FYE: December 31
Type: Public

Dire Straits may have gotten their money for nothing, but the rest of us sometimes need to hit up payday lenders like Community Choice Financial. Formed in 2011, the company issues unsecured short-term consumer loans of up to $5,000, charging fees from $8 to $15 per $100 borrowed in addition to interest rates, which vary by state but typically range from 60% to 120% APR. Its stores, operated under the CheckSmart and California Check Cashing Stores brands, also issue title loans, prepaid MasterCard debit cards, and offer check cashing, money transfers, bill payments, and money orders in 9 US states.

	Annual Growth	12/13	12/14	12/15	12/16	12/17
Sales ($mil.)	(4.6%)	439.2	518.3	527.4	402.3	364.1
Net income ($ mil.)	–	8.2	(51.8)	(70.0)	(1.5)	(180.9)
Market value ($ mil.)	–	–	–	–	–	–
Employees	(5.3%)	3,523	3,831	3,356	2,819	2,829

COMMUNITY ENERGY, INC.

THREE RADNOR CORPORATE CENTER 100 MATSONFORD ROAD
RADNOR, PA 190874545
Phone: 484 654-1877
Fax: –
Web: www.communityenergyinc.com

CEO: R B Alderfer
CFO: –
HR: –
FYE: December 31
Type: Private

Community Energy is working to create greener communities in the northeastern and midwestern US. Through supply agreements with alternative energy generation companies and sales agreements with electricity distribution utilities, Community Energy, a unit of industry leader IDERBROLA RENEWABLES, offers green energy solutions to major businesses and governments as well as to more than 110,000 residential and small-business customers. The company is also involved in the development of wind farms and supplies power directly to end-users. Community Energy, which operates under the NewWind Energy brand, purchases power primarily from wind-powered generation facilities; it also markets solar and hydroelectric energy.

COMMUNITY HEALTH CHARITIES

1240 N PITT ST STE 300
ALEXANDRIA, VA 223145601
Phone: 703 528-1007
Fax: –
Web: www.chcimpact.org

CEO: –
CFO: –
HR: Amanda Williams
FYE: June 30
Type: Private

If you gave at the office, Community Health Charities probably collected. The not-for-profit is a federation of about 50 health groups that raise money in the workplace. Community Health Charities receives some $69 million annually from employee donation campaigns at major employers like American Express, Accenture, McDonald's Corporation, and from government employees. The group's Web site includes a corporate resource center, a real-time online donation center, and a list of organizations that need volunteers. Charities supported by Community Health Charities include AIDS Research Foundation, American Lung Association, and American Diabetes Association.

	Annual Growth	06/07	06/08	06/09	06/10	06/22
Sales ($mil.)	(1.3%)	–	25.2	25.0	25.6	20.9
Net income ($ mil.)	13.9%	–	0.3	–	0.2	1.7
Market value ($ mil.)	–	–	–	–	–	–
Employees	–	–	–	–	–	9

COMMUNITY HEALTH GROUP

2420 FENTON ST STE 100
CHULA VISTA, CA 919143516
Phone: 800 224-7766
Fax: –
Web: www.chgsd.com

CEO: Norma A Diaz
CFO: William Rice
HR: Eric Bearden
FYE: December 31
Type: Private

Community Health Group is the oldest and one of the largest locally based HMOs in San Diego. Founded in 1982, the not-for-profit HMO provides health insurance products and related services to more than 270,000 members. Community Health Group's product offerings include its California's Healthy Families program, which provides low-cost health, dental, and vision coverage to children. The company also provides other managed care services to California communities, such as Medi-Cal low-income coverage and Medicare Advantage Special Needs plans, as well as third-party administration services.

	Annual Growth	12/01	12/02	12/03	12/05	12/09
Sales ($mil.)	(15.5%)	–	–	110.2	79.3	40.0
Net income ($ mil.)	–	–	–	(4.1)	1.2	2.2
Market value ($ mil.)	–	–	–	–	–	–
Employees	–	–	–	–	–	140

COMMUNITY HEALTH NETWORK, INC.

1500 N RITTER AVE
INDIANAPOLIS, IN 462193027
Phone: 317 355-1411
Fax: –
Web: www.ecommunity.com

CEO: Kristin Sherman
CFO: Kyle Fisher
HR: –
FYE: December 31
Type: Private

As a non-profit health system with more than 200 sites of care and affiliates throughout Central Indiana, Community's full continuum of care integrates hundreds of physicians, specialty and acute care hospitals, surgery centers, home care services, MedChecks, behavioral health and employer health services. Its state-of-the-art emergency departments are open 24/7 to treat emergency medical conditions, including stroke, head trauma, heart attack, chest pain, broken bones, wounds and more. Community Health has partnership with Marian University's College of Osteopathic Medicine. Community Health has been deeply committed to the communities it serves since opening its first hospital, Community Hospital East, in 1956.

	Annual Growth	12/12	12/13	12/14	12/19	12/21
Sales ($mil.)	(5.5%)	–	1,763.4	1,942.1	1,645.9	1,125.1
Net income ($ mil.)	4.4%	–	179.1	(0.9)	413.4	253.1
Market value ($ mil.)	–	–	–	–	–	–
Employees	–	–	–	–	–	5,000

COMMUNITY HEALTH SYSTEMS, INC.   NYS: CYH

4000 Meridian Boulevard
Franklin, TN 37067
Phone: 615 465-7000
Fax: –
Web: www.chs.net

CEO: Tim L Hingtgen
CFO: Kevin J Hammons
HR: Beverly Ray
FYE: December 31
Type: Public

Community Health Systems (CHS) is one of the nation's largest healthcare companies. The company owns or leases about 80 hospitals in around 15 states. Its hospitals with roughly 12,830 beds, is comprised of some 80 general acute care hospitals. Healthcare services are also provided in more than 1,000 outpatient facilities, including affiliated physician practices, urgent care centers, freestanding emergency departments, occupational medicine clinics, imaging centers, cancer centers and ambulatory surgery centers. Services provided through its hospitals and outpatient facilities include general acute care, emergency room, general and specialty surgery, critical care, internal medicine, obstetrics, diagnostic, psychiatric and rehabilitation services.

	Annual Growth	12/19	12/20	12/21	12/22	12/23
Sales ($mil.)	(1.4%)	13,210	11,789	12,368	12,211	12,490
Net income ($ mil.)	–	(675.0)	511.0	230.0	46.0	(133.0)
Market value ($ mil.)	1.9%	396.6	1,016.2	1,820.5	590.9	428.1
Employees	(1.9%)	80,000	70,000	66,000	66,000	74,000

COMMUNITY HEALTHCARE TRUST INC   NYS: CHCT

3326 Aspen Grove Drive, Suite 150
Franklin, TN 37067
Phone: 615 771-3052
Fax: –
Web: www.chct.reit

CEO: David H Dupuy
CFO: William G Monroe IV
HR: –
FYE: December 31
Type: Public

Healthcare real estate company Community Healthcare Trust was formed in 2015 to acquire and own properties that are leased to hospitals, doctors, healthcare systems, and other healthcare service providers outside of urban areas. It invests in real estate that is diversified across healthcare provider, geography, facility type, and industry segment. Following the completion of its 2015 IPO, the company's initial 35 properties amounted to 623,000 leasable square feet in 18 US states. At the end of March, 2015, Community Healthcare's initial properties were 94% leased to 69 separate tenants.

	Annual Growth	12/19	12/20	12/21	12/22	12/23
Sales ($mil.)	16.7%	60.8	75.7	90.6	97.7	112.8
Net income ($ mil.)	(2.0%)	8.4	19.1	22.5	22.0	7.7
Market value ($ mil.)	(11.2%)	1,183.5	1,300.8	1,305.3	988.5	735.6
Employees	10.3%	25	28	30	31	37

COMMUNITY HOSPITAL OF ANDERSON AND MADISON COUNTY, INCORPORATED

1515 N MADISON AVE
ANDERSON, IN 460113453
Phone: 765 298-4242
Fax: –
Web: www.ecommunity.com

CEO: Beth Tharp
CFO: –
HR: –
FYE: December 31
Type: Private

The folks of Madison County, Indiana needn't race south to Indianapolis to find medical care. Community Hospital Anderson is an acute care facility with some 200 beds. Departments and services include a sleep analysis lab, ECG (electrocardiogram) tests for cardiopulmonary conditions, and specialized treatment for cancer and diabetes, among other conditions. Community Hospital Anderson operates four intermediate and supervised care facilities in the area. The hospital is part of Community Hospitals of Indiana (also known as Community Health Network), a not-for-profit health care system that serves the health care needs of patients in Indiana.

	Annual Growth	12/14	12/15	12/19	12/21	12/22
Sales ($mil.)	4.0%	–	167.5	214.0	205.7	220.7
Net income ($ mil.)	(4.9%)	–	23.8	(10.2)	5.5	16.7
Market value ($ mil.)	–	–	–	–	–	–
Employees	–	–	–	–	–	1,250

COMMUNITY HOSPITAL OF SAN BERNARDINO

1805 MEDICAL CENTER DR
SAN BERNARDINO, CA 924111217
Phone: 909 887-6333
Fax: –
Web: www.dignityhealth.org

CEO: –
CFO: Ed Sorenson
HR: Deena Marano
FYE: June 30
Type: Private

You really don't have to feel deserted in the desert: CHSB will make you realize you aren't alone when you're illin'. The Community Hospital of San Bernardino is an acute care facility with more than 320 beds. Special health care services available at the hospital include pediatric and adult behavioral health, neurological care, surgery, laboratory testing, a long-term care unit for children, and home health care. Serving the city and its surrounding areas since 1908, Community Hospital of San Bernardino is a member of Catholic Healthcare West.

	Annual Growth	06/12	06/13	06/16*	12/21*	06/22
Sales ($mil.)	3.6%	–	193.2	244.8	293.9	266.3
Net income ($ mil.)	–	–	(22.5)	(11.0)	15.3	(19.3)
Market value ($ mil.)	–	–	–	–	–	–
Employees	–	–	–	–	–	1,400

*Fiscal year change

COMMUNITY HOSPITAL OF THE MONTEREY PENINSULA

23625 HOLMAN HWY
MONTEREY, CA 939405902
Phone: 831 624-5311
Fax: –
Web: –

CEO: Steven J Packer
CFO: Matthew Morgan
HR: –
FYE: December 31
Type: Private

Community Hospital of the Monterey Peninsula has a sunny disposition when it comes to medical care. The not-for-profit health care facility provides general medical and surgical services to residents of Monterey, California. It has about 235 acute care and skilled nursing beds and offers specialty services including cardiac and cancer care, obstetrics, orthopedics, and rehabilitation. In addition to its main facility, the hospital operates several ancillary centers, including a mental health clinic, an inpatient hospice, medical laboratory branches, and several outpatient centers offering diagnostic imaging, diabetes care, and other services.

	Annual Growth	12/14	12/15	12/16	12/21	12/22
Sales ($mil.)	5.5%	–	560.7	526.9	739.9	813.4
Net income ($ mil.)	–	–	66.7	72.0	110.5	(145.3)
Market value ($ mil.)	–	–	–	–	–	–
Employees	–	–	–	–	–	1,947

COMMUNITY HOSPITALS OF CENTRAL CALIFORNIA

2823 FRESNO ST
FRESNO, CA 937211324
Phone: 559 459-6000
Fax: –
Web: www.communitymedical.org

CEO: Tim A Joslin
CFO: Joseph Nowicki
HR: Ginny R Burdick
FYE: August 31
Type: Private

Community Health System is a locally owned, not-for-profit, public-benefit organization based in Fresno, California. It is the region's largest healthcare provider and private employer and operate a residency program with one of the nation's top medical schools ? the University of California, San Francisco. The Community Health System is made up of three entities. Community Medical Centers includes four hospitals, a cancer institute and several long-term care, outpatient and other healthcare facilities. This network is known for its Level I Trauma Center, comprehensive burn care, long-standing medical education partnership with UCSF Fresno, and as the place to deliver babies. Its Community Care Health plan is now one of the largest HMOs in the region, offering local businesses medical insurance for their employees.

	Annual Growth	08/18	08/19	08/20	08/21	08/22
Sales ($mil.)	6.2%	–	1,813.2	1,857.2	2,016.1	2,169.6
Net income ($ mil.)	–	–	117.7	100.4	94.2	(138.9)
Market value ($ mil.)	–	–	–	–	–	–
Employees	–	–	–	–	–	6,200

COMMUNITY INVESTORS BANCORP, INC
NBB: CIBN

119 South Sandusky Avenue, P.O. Box 749
Bucyrus, OH 44820
Phone: 419 562 7055
Fax: 800 222-4955
Web: www.ffcb.com

CEO: –
CFO: –
HR: –
FYE: June 30
Type: Public

You won't find these investors on Wall Street or in Omaha. You'll find Community Investors Bancorp, the holding company for First Federal Community Bank of Bucyrus, in north central Ohio's Crawford County. The bank provides traditional deposit options like CDs, checking and savings accounts, money market accounts, and NOW accounts. First Federal's lending activities include residential and nonresidential real estate mortgages, commercial loans, construction loans, and land loans. Its consumer loan options include automobile and home equity loans. Community Investors Bancorp plans to become private after a reverse stock split transaction.

	Annual Growth	06/17	06/20	06/21	06/22	06/23
Assets ($mil.)	11.3%	143.4	206.9	222.4	233.8	271.9
Net income ($ mil.)	7.8%	0.5	1.5	2.3	1.7	0.7
Market value ($ mil.)	1.9%	12.0	12.3	15.1	13.5	13.5
Employees	–	–	–	–	–	–

COMMUNITY MEDICAL CENTER, INC.

99 ROUTE 37 W
TOMS RIVER, NJ 087556423
Phone: 732 557-8000
Fax: –
Web: www.rwjbh.org

CEO: –
CFO: Mark Ostrander
HR: Vanessa Smith
FYE: December 31
Type: Private

When Garden Staters in Ocean County get sick, they look to the community for help. Community Medical Center (CMC), that is. Part of the Saint Barnabas Health Care System, CMC is a full-service 590-bed acute care hospital that provides a range of health services including primary and emergency care, obstetrics and maternity care, pediatrics, diabetes and cancer treatment, surgery, senior care, and rehabilitative care. CMC's community wellness centers provide ambulatory health services, diagnostic services, and primary care, as well as prevention and wellness education, to the communities they serve. CMC is one of New Jersey's largest non-teaching hospitals.

	Annual Growth	12/16	12/17	12/18	12/19	12/21
Sales ($mil.)	3.9%	–	380.7	391.7	395.2	443.2
Net income ($ mil.)	–	–	25.8	19.4	(13.4)	(4.2)
Market value ($ mil.)	–	–	–	–	–	–
Employees	–	–	–	–	–	2,500

COMMUNITY TRUST BANCORP, INC.
NMS: CTBI

346 North Mayo Trail, P.O. Box 2947
Pikeville, KY 41502
Phone: 606 432-1414
Fax: –
Web: www.ctbi.com

CEO: Mark A Gooch
CFO: Kevin J Stumbo
HR: Amy Breault
FYE: December 31
Type: Public

Community Trust Bancorp is the holding company for Community Trust Bank, one of the largest Kentucky-based banks. It operates 70-plus branches throughout the state, as well as in northeastern Tennessee and southern West Virginia. The bank offers standard services to area businesses and individuals, including checking and savings accounts, credit cards, and CDs. Loans secured by commercial properties and other real estate account for nearly 70% of the bank's portfolio, which also includes business, consumer, and construction loans. Subsidiary Community Trust and Investment Company provides trust, estate, retirement, brokerage, and insurance services through a handful of offices in Kentucky and Tennessee.

	Annual Growth	12/19	12/20	12/21	12/22	12/23
Assets ($mil.)	7.2%	4,366.0	5,139.1	5,418.3	5,380.3	5,769.7
Net income ($ mil.)	4.9%	64.5	59.5	87.9	81.8	78.0
Market value ($ mil.)	(1.5%)	839.5	666.9	785.0	826.7	789.5
Employees	(0.8%)	1,000	998	974	985	967

COMMUNITY WEST BANCSHARES
NMS: CWBC

445 Pine Avenue
Goleta, CA 93117
Phone: 805 692-5821
Fax: 805 692-5835
Web: www.communitywest.com

CEO: Martin E Plourd
CFO: Richard Pimentel
HR: –
FYE: December 31
Type: Public

Community West Bancshares is the holding company for Community West Bank, which serves individuals and small to midsized businesses through five branches along California's Central Coast. Services include checking and savings accounts and CDs, as well as health savings accounts. Approximately 40% of the bank's loan portfolio is secured by manufactured housing loans; real estate mortgages account for more than 30%. A preferred Small Business Administration lender, Community West also writes SBA loans through offices in about a dozen other states.

	Annual Growth	12/18	12/19	12/20	12/21	12/22
Assets ($mil.)	5.6%	877.3	913.9	975.4	1,157.1	1,091.5
Net income ($ mil.)	16.1%	7.4	8.0	8.2	13.1	13.4
Market value ($ mil.)	10.5%	88.2	97.7	79.9	118.0	131.7
Employees	–	–	139	133	128	126	139

COMMVAULT SYSTEMS INC
NMS: CVLT

1 Commvault Way
Tinton Falls, NJ 07724
Phone: 732 870-4000
Fax: –
Web: www.commvault.com

CEO: –
CFO: –
HR: –
FYE: March 31
Type: Public

Commvault Systems is a global leader in cloud data protection. Its intelligent data services protect customers' data in a difficult world. The company provides its customers with a data protection platform that helps them secure, defend and recover their most precious asset, their data. Its data protection offerings are delivered via self-managed software, software-as-a-service (SaaS), integrated appliances, or managed by partners. Commvault Backup and Recovery provides backup, verifiable recovery, and cost-optimized cloud workload mobility, helping to ensure data availability and granular recovery, even across multiple clouds. Commvault serves a diverse array of industries such as financial services, healthcare, technology manufacturing, utilities, and energy, as well as the public sector. Nearly 55% of its revenue comes from US customers.

	Annual Growth	03/19	03/20	03/21	03/22	03/23
Sales ($mil.)	2.5%	711.0	670.9	723.5	769.6	784.6
Net income ($ mil.)	–	3.6	(5.6)	(31.0)	33.6	(35.8)
Market value ($ mil.)	(3.2%)	2,857.6	1,786.8	2,847.0	2,928.7	2,504.5
Employees	2.1%	2,559	2,533	2,671	2,848	2,779

COMPANION PROFESSIONAL SERVICES LLC

1301 GERVAIS ST STE 1700
COLUMBIA, SC 292013367
Phone: 803 765-1431
Fax: –
Web: www.tmfloyd.com

CEO: –
CFO: –
HR: Jennifer McCormack
FYE: December 31
Type: Private

Companion Professional Services (which does business as TM Floyd & Company) targets customers that need a friend when it comes to information technology. The company provides IT consulting primarily to clients in the insurance industry. Its areas of specialty include health, property, and casualty insurance. TM Floyd offers executive consulting, product integration, IT staffing, and project management services among others. The company helps clients upgrade their software systems, identify administrative inefficiencies, and improve billing methods. It was founded in 1976 by managing partner Terry M. Floyd.

	Annual Growth	12/05	12/06	12/07	12/08	12/09
Sales ($mil.)	(17.7%)	–	–	30.3	23.5	20.6
Net income ($ mil.)	(59.0%)	–	–	4.5	1.6	0.8
Market value ($ mil.)	–	–	–	–	–	–
Employees	–	–	–	–	–	300

COMPASS DIVERSIFIED
NYS: CODI

301 Riverside Avenue, Second Floor
Westport, CT 06880
Phone: 203 221-1703
Fax: -
Web: www.compassdiversifiedholdings.com

CEO: Elias J Sabo
CFO: Ryan J Faulkingham
HR: -
FYE: December 31
Type: Public

Compass Diversified Holdings helps niche companies navigate their way toward profitability. The holding company owns controlling stakes in and manages promising middle-market businesses throughout North America. Its strategy is two-fold: help its portfolio firms grow and increase their profits, and increase the size of its own portfolio. Compass invests in niche businesses across a variety of industries, including furniture maker AFM Holdings (sold in 2015) and home and gun safes maker Liberty Safe and Security Products. Its arsenal includes helping its holdings make strategic acquisitions, enter new business arenas, or improve operations to increase profitability.

	Annual Growth	12/19	12/20	12/21	12/22	12/23
Sales ($mil.)	9.2%	1,450.3	1,560.8	1,841.7	2,264.0	2,058.9
Net income ($ mil.)	(5.0%)	301.9	22.8	114.6	36.4	246.3
Market value ($ mil.)	(2.5%)	1,871.2	1,464.0	2,301.8	1,372.2	1,689.8
Employees	(8.0%)	3,456	4,598	3,211	5,055	2,480

COMPASS INC
NYS: COMP

90 Fifth Avenue, 3rd Floor
New York, NY 10011
Phone: 212 913-9058
Fax: -
Web: www.compass.com

CEO: Robert Reffkin
CFO: Kalani Reelitz
HR: -
FYE: December 31
Type: Public

Compass is a technology-enabled brokerage that provides an end-to-end platform of software, services, and support to empower its residential real estate agents to deliver exceptional service to seller and buyer clients. Compass' platform includes an integrated suite of cloud-based software for customer relationship management, marketing, client service, and other critical functionality, all custom-built for the real estate industry and enabling its core brokerage services. The platform also uses proprietary data, analytics, artificial intelligence, and machine learning to deliver high-value recommendations and outcomes for Compass agents and their clients. Real estate agents are themselves business owners, and Compass agents utilize the platform to grow their respective businesses, save time, and manage their businesses more effectively.

	Annual Growth	12/19	12/20	12/21	12/22	12/23
Sales ($mil.)	19.6%	2,386.0	3,720.8	6,421.0	6,018.0	4,885.0
Net income ($ mil.)	-	-	(388.0)	(270.2)	(494.1)	(601.5)	(321.3)
Market value ($ mil.)	-	-	-	4,407.7	1,129.8	1,823.2
Employees	-	-	2,702	4,775	3,191	2,549

COMPASS MINERALS INTERNATIONAL INC
NYS: CMP

9900 West 109th Street, Suite 100
Overland Park, KS 66210
Phone: 913 344-9200
Fax: -
Web: www.compassminerals.com

CEO: Edward C Dowling Jr
CFO: Lorin Crenshaw
HR: -
FYE: September 30
Type: Public

Compass Minerals is a leading provider of essential minerals focused on safely delivering where and when it matters to help solve nature's challenges for customers and communities. Its salt products help keep roadways safe during winter weather and are used in numerous other consumer, industrial, chemical and agricultural applications. Its plant nutrition products help improve the quality and yield of crops, while supporting sustainable agriculture. Highway deicing salt ? generally sold to states, provinces, counties, municipalities, and road maintenance contractors. Compass Minerals has about 10 production- and packaging facilities and operates a number of salt mines in Canada, the UK, and the US. The US accounts for some 70% of sales.

	Annual Growth	12/19	12/20*	09/21	09/22	09/23
Sales ($mil.)	(5.2%)	1,490.5	1,373.5	836.5	1,244.1	1,204.7
Net income ($ mil.)	(29.4%)	62.5	59.5	(213.3)	(25.1)	15.5
Market value ($ mil.)	(17.7%)	2,509.1	2,540.4	2,650.7	1,585.9	1,150.4
Employees	(10.8%)	3,131	3,229	2,223	1,954	1,981

*Fiscal year change

COMPUMED INC
NBB: CMPD

5777 West Century Blvd., Suite 360
Los Angeles, CA 90045
Phone: 310 258-5000
Fax: 310 645-5880
Web: www.compumedinc.com

CEO: -
CFO: -
HR: -
FYE: September 30
Type: Public

CompuMed won't comp your meds, but it might interpret your ECG. Through its CardioGram software, the telemedicine company provides online analyses of ECGs (electrocardiograms) for more than 1,000 hospitals, clinics, and other health care facilities throughout the US. The firm's ECG services are available 24 hours a day. CompuMed also rents and, to a lesser extent, sells ECG equipment. The company's additional product, OsteoGram, monitors osteoporosis by analyzing bone density; the test involves taking a hand X-ray and can be performed using standard X-ray equipment.

	Annual Growth	09/18	09/19	09/20	09/21	09/22
Sales ($mil.)	16.0%	3.5	5.0	5.3	6.3	6.4
Net income ($ mil.)	23.0%	0.2	1.0	0.3	1.1	0.5
Market value ($ mil.)	127.7%	0.2	0.3	0.3	0.6	6.7
Employees	-	-	-	-	-	-

COMPUNET CLINICAL LABORATORIES, LLC

2308 SANDRIDGE DR
MORAINE, OH 454391856
Phone: 937 296-0844
Fax: -
Web: www.compunetlab.com

CEO: Ed Doucette
CFO: Jan Wooles
HR: Jennifer Gossett
FYE: December 31
Type: Private

If you're a Daytonian in need of a cholesterol check, CompuNet Clinical Laboratories has a vial with your name on it. The company provides comprehensive laboratory testing services to physicians, patients, hospitals, and managed care companies in and around Dayton, Ohio. It draws blood (and takes other patient samples) at some 30 specimen collection centers throughout its service area and processes them at one of its various laboratory locations including at its headquarters in Dayton and at Miami Valley Hospital. Founded in 1986, the company is a joint venture owned by Miami Valley Hospital, Quest Diagnostics, and a local pathology group.

COMPUTER AID, INC.

1390 RIDGEVIEW DR STE 300
ALLENTOWN, PA 181049065
Phone: 610 530-5000
Fax: -
Web: www.cai.io

CEO: Anthony J Salvaggio
CFO: Andrew McIntyre
HR: Cydney Comfort
FYE: December 31
Type: Private

Computer Aid Inc. (CAI) is a privately held company with a global footprint. Its over 8,500 associates have the freedom and the focus to do what's right for its clients, colleagues, and communities. The company specializes in digital transformation services, including application management, strategy and consulting, intelligent automation, contingent workforce solutions, IT service management, and business analytics. Its strategic consulting encompasses legacy application support, intelligent automation, agile development and IT service management address. It has a partnership with ServiceNow. CAI also offers application maintenance. It serves such markets as financial, utilities, health care, and retail, as well as the public sector. It has offices throughout the US and the Asia-Pacific region.

	Annual Growth	12/16	12/17	12/18	12/19	12/20
Sales ($mil.)	20.4%	-	-	603.4	733.6	874.8
Net income ($ mil.)	-	-	-	-	-	-
Market value ($ mil.)	-	-	-	-	-	-
Employees	-	-	-	-	-	1,411

COMPUTER ENTERPRISES INC

1000 OMEGA DR
PITTSBURGH, PA 152055001
Phone: 412 341-3541
Fax: –
Web: www.ceiamerica.com

CEO: –
CFO: –
HR: –
FYE: December 31
Type: Private

Computer Enterprises (CEI) helps customers tackle IT issues. Founded in 1992, CEI provides application development and customization, technical staffing services, database and Internet consulting, and computer security assessment and implementation. The company serves such industries as media, health care, and manufacturing. Clients have included National Public Radio, PPG Industries, and Roche Diagnostics. CEI has offices in Woodland Hills, CA; Indianapolis; and Pittsburgh. The company also has an offshore software development facility in India. CEI was founded in 1992 by CEO and director D. Raja and director Barry Zungre.

	Annual Growth	12/02	12/03	12/05	12/06	12/09
Sales ($mil.)	(3.9%)	–	30.4	35.8	38.7	24.0
Net income ($ mil.)	(30.8%)	–	6.2	2.1	(0.2)	0.7
Market value ($ mil.)	–	–	–	–	–	–
Employees	–	–	–	–	–	371

COMPUTER SCIENCES CORPORATION

20408 BASHAN DR STE 231
ASHBURN, VA 201475553
Phone: 855 716-0853
Fax: –
Web: www.dxc.com

CEO: J M Lawrie
CFO: Paul N Saleh
HR: –
FYE: March 31
Type: Private

Computer Sciences Corporation (CSC) has been one of the world's leading providers of systems integration and other information technology services. It offers application development, data center management, communications and networking development, IT systems management, and business consulting. It also provides business process outsourcing (BPO) services in such areas as billing and payment processing, customer relationship management (CRM), and human resources. CSC boasts 2,500 clients in more than 70 countries. In 2017 CSC merged with the Enterprise Services segment of Hewlett-Packard Enterprise to form DXC Technology Co. This report is based on CSC's last year as an independent company.

	Annual Growth	03/13	03/14*	04/15	04/16*	03/17
Sales ($mil.)	(16.4%)	–	12,998	12,173	7,106.0	7,607.0
Net income ($ mil.)	–	–	690.0	7.0	263.0	(100.0)
Market value ($ mil.)	–	–	–	–	–	–
Employees	–	–	–	–	–	66,000

*Fiscal year change

COMPX INTERNATIONAL, INC.

5430 LBJ Freeway, Suite 1700
Dallas, TX 75240-2620
Phone: 972 448-1400
Fax: –
Web: www.compx.com

ASE: CIX
CEO: Scott C James
CFO: Amy A Samford
HR: –
FYE: December 31
Type: Public

CompX International tries to keep the workday smooth, theft-free, and painless. Through CompX's three operating divisions -- security products, furniture components, and marine components -- the company makes ball bearing slides, cabinet locks, and ergonomic computer support systems. The company's primary customers are office furniture makers, but its components are used in recreational marine vehicles, ignition systems, vending equipment, mailboxes, appliances, and computer equipment. CompX International believes that it is a North American market leader in the manufacture and sale of cabinet locks and other locking mechanisms. The company is majority-owned by NL Industries.

	Annual Growth	12/19	12/20	12/21	12/22	12/23
Sales ($mil.)	6.7%	124.2	114.5	140.8	166.6	161.3
Net income ($ mil.)	9.0%	16.0	10.3	16.6	20.9	22.6
Market value ($ mil.)	14.7%	179.7	175.2	276.7	227.6	311.3
Employees	0.4%	547	513	570	609	555

COMSCORE INC

11950 Democracy Drive, Suite 600
Reston, VA 20190
Phone: 703 438-2000
Fax: –
Web: www.comscore.com

NMS: SCOR
CEO: Jonathan Carpenter
CFO: John Green
HR: Wesley Slater
FYE: December 31
Type: Public

comScore, Inc. is a global information and analytics company that measures advertising, content, and the consumer audiences of each, across media platforms. The company creates its products using a global data platform that combines information on digital platforms (connected (Smart) televisions, mobile devices, tablets, and computers), television (TV), direct-to-consumer applications, and movie screens with demographics and other descriptive information. Its ability to unify behavioral and other descriptive data enables the company to provide audience ratings, advertising verification, and granular consumer segments that describe hundreds of millions of consumers. Comscore allows media buyers and sellers to quantify their multiscreen behavior and make business decisions with confidence. The company was established in 1999. The US accounts for about 90% of its revenue.

	Annual Growth	12/19	12/20	12/21	12/22	12/23
Sales ($mil.)	(1.1%)	388.6	356.0	367.0	376.4	371.3
Net income ($ mil.)	–	(339.0)	(47.9)	(50.0)	(66.6)	(79.4)
Market value ($ mil.)	35.6%	23.5	11.8	15.9	5.5	79.4
Employees	(2.5%)	1,300	1,340	1,500	1,382	1,175

COMSTOCK HOLDING COMPANIES, INC

1900 Reston Metro Plaza, 10th Floor
Reston, VA 20190
Phone: 703 230-1985
Fax: –
Web: www.comstock.com

NAS: CHCI
CEO: Christopher Clemente
CFO: Christopher Guthrie
HR: –
FYE: December 31
Type: Public

While people take stock of their lives, Comstock takes stock of its portfolio. The homebuilder develops land and builds single-family homes, townhouses, and mid- and high-rise condominiums in and around Washington, DC. The company annually delivers some 200 homes with an average price of approximately $289,000. Its customer base includes first-time homebuyers, buyers looking to move up, empty nesters, and active retirees. The company also rents resdential properties under the Comstock Communities name. Average rent is appoximately $1,500 a month.

	Annual Growth	12/19	12/20	12/21	12/22	12/23
Sales ($mil.)	15.3%	25.3	28.7	31.1	39.3	44.7
Net income ($ mil.)	71.8%	0.9	2.1	13.6	7.3	7.8
Market value ($ mil.)	22.7%	18.9	30.6	46.9	41.1	42.8
Employees	16.4%	109	147	161	170	200

COMSTOCK RESOURCES INC

5300 Town and Country Blvd., Suite 500
Frisco, TX 75034
Phone: 972 668-8800
Fax: –
Web: www.comstockresources.com

NYS: CRK
CEO: M J Allison
CFO: Roland O Burns
HR: Anja Vukich
FYE: December 31
Type: Public

Comstock Resources' stock in trade is exploring for and producing natural gas and oil. In 2012 the midsized independent oil and gas company reported proved reserves of 711.9 trillion cu. ft. of natural gas equivalent (67% natural gas, 33% oil) on its properties primarily located in three major areas -- East Texas/North Louisiana, South Texas, and West Texas. Comstock Resources operates more than 960 of the 1,640 producing wells in which it holds an interest. The company has grown through the drill bit (by exploiting existing reserves) and through complementary acquisitions.

	Annual Growth	12/19	12/20	12/21	12/22	12/23
Sales ($mil.)	19.5%	768.7	858.2	1,850.7	3,628.1	1,565.1
Net income ($ mil.)	21.5%	96.9	(52.4)	(241.7)	1,140.9	211.1
Market value ($ mil.)	1.8%	2,291.5	1,216.7	2,252.5	3,817.3	2,464.1
Employees	4.9%	207	204	205	244	251

COMTECH TELECOMMUNICATIONS CORP. NMS: CMTL

68 South Service Road, Suite 230
Melville, NY 11747
Phone: 631 962-7000
Fax: 631 962-7001
Web: www.comtech.com

CEO: Ken Peterman
CFO: Michael A Bondi
HR: David Castelblanco
FYE: July 31
Type: Public

Comtech is a leading global provider of next-generation 911 emergency systems (NG-911) and secure wireless and satellite communications technologies. The company sees these two end-markets as part of what Comtech has identified as the "Failsafe Communications Market." This includes the critical communications infrastructure that people, businesses, and governments rely on when durable, trusted connectivity is required from armed conflict to a natural disaster. Comtech makes equipment used largely by the US government and related defense contractors. Other customers include satellite systems integrators, communications service providers, and oil companies. Its transmission equipment includes modems, frequency converters, very-small-aperture terminal (VSAT) satellite transceivers and antennas, and microwave radios. It was founded in 1967. The US generated majority of its sales.

	Annual Growth	07/19	07/20	07/21	07/22	07/23
Sales ($mil.)	(4.9%)	671.8	616.7	581.7	486.2	550.0
Net income ($ mil.)	–	25.0	7.0	(73.5)	(33.1)	(26.9)
Market value ($ mil.)	(23.6%)	835.2	460.8	700.7	326.1	285.1
Employees	(3.9%)	2,013	2,034	2,038	1,993	1,718

COMTEX NEWS NETWORK INC NBB: CMTX

625 North Washington Street, Suite 301
Alexandria, VA 22314
Phone: 703 820-2000
Fax: –
Web: www.comtex.com

CEO: Kan Devnani
CFO: –
HR: –
FYE: June 30
Type: Public

Comtex News Network is a leading distributor of electronic news and alerts that specializes in the business and financial markets. The company gathers news and content from more than 10,000 national and international news agencies and publications, including PR Newswire, United Press International, and The Associated Press, and packages those feeds into several different product offerings. In addition to individual and institutional customers, Comtex supplies news to such information distributors as MarketWatch, Dow Jones' Factiva, and Thomson Financial.

	Annual Growth	06/05	06/06	06/07	06/08	06/09
Sales ($mil.)	(5.3%)	8.0	7.7	7.1	7.1	6.4
Net income ($ mil.)	(40.4%)	0.7	(0.5)	(0.1)	0.7	0.0
Market value ($ mil.)	(3.8%)	0.0	0.0	0.0	0.0	0.0
Employees	4.3%	22	25	21	29	26

CONAGRA BRANDS INC NYS: CAG

222 West Merchandise Mart Plaza, Suite 1300
Chicago, IL 60654
Phone: 312 549-5000
Fax: –
Web: www.conagrabrands.com

CEO: Sean M Connolly
CFO: David S Marberger
HR: –
FYE: May 28
Type: Public

Conagra Brands is one of North America's leading branded food companies. The company makes and markets name-brand packaged and frozen foods that are sold widely across the US, including in Walmart stores. Conagra's cornucopia of America's best-known brands includes Duncan Hines, Birds Eye, Slim Jim, Reddi-Wip, Vlasic, Angie's BOOMCHICKAPOP, Duke's, Earth Balance, Gardein, Frontera, Healthy Choice, and Marie Callender's. Its roughly 40 domestic manufacturing facilities are located in Arkansas, California, Illinois, Kentucky, Maryland, Michigan, Nebraska, and Ohio, among others. Conagra began as a flour-milling company in Nebraska in 1919, and over the decades transformed into a consumer goods company.

	Annual Growth	05/19	05/20	05/21	05/22	05/23
Sales ($mil.)	6.5%	9,538.4	11,054	11,185	11,536	12,277
Net income ($ mil.)	0.2%	678.3	840.1	1,298.8	888.2	683.6
Market value ($ mil.)	4.8%	13,753	16,596	18,175	15,813	16,619
Employees	0.8%	18,000	16,500	18,600	18,000	18,600

CONCENTRIC CONSUMER MARKETING, INC.

101 W WORTHINGTON AVE STE 108
CHARLOTTE, NC 282030063
Phone: 704 731-5100
Fax: –
Web: www.getconcentric.com

CEO: –
CFO: –
HR: –
FYE: December 31
Type: Private

Concentric Consumer Marketing is centered on building emerging and middle-market brands. The advertising and marketing agency -- which does business by the shortened Concentric Marketing name -- specializes in branding, design, promotion, direct marketing, and creative ad services for clients ready to break from the pack. It helps clients build better brands across all forms of media, whether it be print, radio, television, or the Internet. In addition, Concentric Marketing offers online articles and blogs featuring the latest industry trends and developments in the world of advertising. Founded in 2000, the company has worked with clients such as Big Brothers Big Sisters, Continental Tire, and Unilever.

	Annual Growth	08/05	08/06	08/07*	12/08	12/09
Sales ($mil.)	30.3%	–	–	1.3	2.2	2.3
Net income ($ mil.)	–	–	–	0.0	0.0	(0.0)
Market value ($ mil.)	–	–	–	–	–	18
Employees	–	–	–	–	–	–

*Fiscal year change

CONCHO RESOURCES INC.

600 W ILLINOIS AVE ONE CONCHO CENTER
MIDLAND, TX 79701
Phone: 432 683-7443
Fax: –
Web: www.conocophillips.com

CEO: Timothy A Leach
CFO: Brenda R Schroer
HR: Karen Willis
FYE: December 31
Type: Private

Fracking company Concho Resources (Concho) explores, develops and extracts oil and gas assets in the Permian Basin, the hottest energy resource region on US shores. It has about 549,000 net acres to its name, along with over 255 net wells, primarily underground, in Southeastern New Mexico and West Texas. Its over 1,000 million barrels of proved reserves is split between crude oil and natural gas. Concho produces roughly 330 million barrels of oil equivalent each day, ranking it among the region's top producers and the only companies operating exclusively in the Permian.

CONCORD HOSPITAL, INC.

250 PLEASANT ST
CONCORD, NH 033012598
Phone: 603 227-7000
Fax: –
Web: www.concordhospital.org

CEO: Robert Steigmeyer
CFO: Bruce R Burns
HR: Nancy Seibert
FYE: September 30
Type: Private

Concord Hospital is agreeably an acute care regional hospital serving central New Hampshire. The hospital has some 300 licensed beds and provides general inpatient and outpatient medical care, as well as specialist centers for cardiology, orthopedics, cancer care, urology, and women's health. Concord Hospital operates other medical facilities either on its main campus or nearby, including surgery, imaging, diagnostic, hospice, and rehabilitation facilities, as well as physician practice locations. With roots reaching back to 1884, Concord Hospital is part of the Capital Region Health Care system, which also offers mental health and home health care services.

	Annual Growth	09/18	09/19	09/20	09/21	09/22
Sales ($mil.)	13.9%	–	528.8	516.1	657.3	780.8
Net income ($ mil.)	–	–	9.4	10.0	90.9	(30.9)
Market value ($ mil.)	–	–	–	–	–	–
Employees	–	–	–	–	–	2,000

CONCORD LITHO GROUP LLC

92 OLD TURNPIKE RD
CONCORD, NH 033017305
Phone: 603 224-1202
Fax: –
Web: www.concorddirect.com

CEO: Peter Cook
CFO: Marlin Kaufman
HR: Paula Kukas
FYE: December 31
Type: Private

Concord Litho Group is all about the commercially printed word. The company specializes in producing promotional and marketing materials of all sizes for retailers, publishers, ad agencies, and consumer products brands. It prints catalogs, brochures, calendars, greeting cards, and maps, as well as point-of-purchase displays, art prints, and other large-format items. Concord Litho Group also offers product and program development services. Clients have included Macy's, Rodale, Dunkin' Donuts, Publishers Clearing House, Prudential Financial, and TV Guide . Concord Litho Group was founded in 1958.

	Annual Growth	12/08	12/09	12/10	12/11	12/12
Sales ($mil.)	13.5%	–	–	39.0	44.7	50.3
Net income ($ mil.)	144.7%	–	–	0.3	1.1	1.9
Market value ($ mil.)	–	–	–	–	–	–
Employees	–	–	–	–	–	200

CONCORDIA COLLEGE - NEW YORK FOUNDATION, INC.

171 WHITE PLAINS RD
BRONXVILLE, NY 107081923
Phone: 914 337-9300
Fax: –
Web: www.concordia-ny.org

CEO: –
CFO: –
HR: –
FYE: June 30
Type: Private

Concordia College is a four-year, co-educational liberal arts college offering bachelor's degrees in areas such as business, education, behavioral science, English, biology, and social work. The school also has a one-year accelerated degree program for working adults. Pre-professional studies are offered in law and medicine. Concordia enrolls about 700 students and has a 16-to-1 student-to-teacher ratio. Annual tuition and fees at the private school total about $30,000; more than 95% of students receive some form of financial assistance. Concordia is a religious institution, backed by The Lutheran Church - Missouri Synod, and offers a pre-seminary program. The college was founded in 1881.

CONCURRENT TECHNOLOGIES CORPORATION

100 CTC DR
JOHNSTOWN, PA 159041935
Phone: 800 282-4392
Fax: –
Web: www.ctc.com

CEO: Edward J Sheehan Jr
CFO: –
HR: Crystal Vaarvik
FYE: June 30
Type: Private

Concurrent Technologies Corporation (CTC) helps customers keep pace with all the current technologies. The not-for-profit research and development organization provides IT services to public and private sectors, although it primarily serves the needs of the Department of Defense and about 20 other federal departments. CTC provides training, rapid prototyping, studies and analysis, network design, project management, design and development, and systems integration. It serves clients in advanced materials and manufacturing, IT, healthcare, energy, environmental sustainability, training, and intelligence, among others. CTC has about 50 locations across the US and one in Canada.

	Annual Growth	06/11	06/12	06/13	06/14	06/15
Sales ($mil.)	(20.4%)	–	–	219.7	140.0	139.1
Net income ($ mil.)	–	–	–	1.2	(0.0)	(2.6)
Market value ($ mil.)	–	–	–	–	–	–
Employees	–	–	–	–	–	450

CONDOR HOSPITALITY TRUST INC

ASE: CDOR

P.O. Box 153
Battle Creek, NE 68715
Phone: 301 861-3305
Fax: –
Web: www.condorhospitality.com

CEO: Jill Burger
CFO: Jill Burger
HR: –
FYE: December 31
Type: Public

Condor Hospitality (formerly Supertel Hospitality) wants to help business and leisure travelers have a super overnight stay. The self-administered real estate investment trust (REIT) owns some 39 limited-service and midscale hotels operated by third parties. The hotels are located in 18 primarily midwestern and eastern states and operate under such franchised brand names as Super 8, Comfort Inn, Holiday Inn Express, Days Inn, Hampton Inn, and Sleep Inn. The hotels are leased to the REIT's taxable subsidiaries. Condor Hospitality also develops hotel properties on a limited basis.

	Annual Growth	12/17	12/18	12/19	12/20	12/21
Sales ($mil.)	(3.6%)	55.5	65.1	61.1	35.2	47.8
Net income ($ mil.)	101.1%	2.9	5.4	(5.0)	(19.1)	47.1
Market value ($ mil.)	–	146.5	101.4	162.5	58.0	–
Employees	(48.3%)	14	14	14	6	1

CONDUENT INC

NMS: CNDT

100 Campus Drive, Suite 200
Florham Park, NJ 07932
Phone: 844 663-2638
Fax: –
Web: www.conduent.com

CEO: Clifford Skelton
CFO: Stephen Wood
HR: –
FYE: December 31
Type: Public

Conduent is one of the largest business process services companies in the world that delivers mission-critical services and solutions on behalf of businesses and governments. The company's services include a range of innovative solutions such as Medicaid management, Medicaid business intelligence, pharmacy benefits management, eligibility and enrollment support, and contract center services, among others. Conduent is also a leader in government payment disbursements for federally sponsored programs, including Supplemental Nutrition Assistance Program (SNAP), formerly known as food stamps and Women, Infant and Children (WIC), as well as government-initiated cash disbursements. Approximately 90% of revenue comes from the US. Conduent caters to about 80% of Fortune 100 companies and over 600 government and transportation entities.

	Annual Growth	12/19	12/20	12/21	12/22	12/23
Sales ($mil.)	(4.5%)	4,467.0	4,163.0	4,140.0	3,858.0	3,722.0
Net income ($ mil.)	–	(1,934.0)	(118.0)	(28.0)	(182.0)	(296.0)
Market value ($ mil.)	(12.4%)	1,311.4	1,015.2	1,129.5	856.6	772.0
Employees	(3.1%)	67,000	63,000	60,000	62,000	59,000

CONEMAUGH HEALTH COMPANY, LLC

1086 FRANKLIN ST
JOHNSTOWN, PA 159054305
Phone: 814 534-9000
Fax: –
Web: www.conemaugh.org

CEO: –
CFO: –
HR: –
FYE: June 30
Type: Private

Medical provider Conemaugh Health System serves the residents of western Pennsylvania through three hospitals and a rehabilitation center. Its operations include Memorial Medical Center, Meyersdale Medical Center, Miners Medical Center, and Crichton Rehabilitation Center. Altogether, its facilities boast more than 600 beds. Conemaugh Health System also operates a network of community health care facilities. It offers such services as regional cancer, cardiovascular, and neurosciences centers; home health care and home medical equipment; general care facilities; and specialized facilities for managing pain and wounds. The system was acquired by Duke LifePoint Healthcare in 2014.

	Annual Growth	06/12	06/13	06/14	06/21	06/22
Sales ($mil.)	4.7%	–	–	8.8	11.5	12.6
Net income ($ mil.)	–	–	–	(2.5)	10.3	8.8
Market value ($ mil.)	–	–	–	–	–	–
Employees	–	–	–	–	–	2,626

CONGOLEUM CORP (NEW)

3500 Quakerbridge Road
Mercerville, NJ 08619
Phone: 609 584-3000
Fax: 609 584-3522
Web: www.congoleum.com

CEO: Christopher Oconnor
CFO: -
HR: -
FYE: December 31
Type: Public

For more than a century, Congoleum has taken a pounding. The company has four manufacturing facilities where it makes hard-surface flooring products for residential and commercial use, including resilient sheet flooring (linoleum or vinyl flooring), do-it-yourself vinyl tile, and commercial-grade flooring. Its lineup is used in new construction, as well as remodeling, manufactured housing, and commercial applications. Congoleum markets its products via a distributor network and directly to mass market retailers in North America. It has three manufacturing plants in the US.

	Annual Growth	12/05	12/06	12/07	12/08	12/09
Sales ($mil.)	(13.2%)	237.6	219.5	204.3	172.6	134.9
Net income ($ mil.)	–	(21.6)	0.7	(0.7)	(14.6)	(15.2)
Market value ($ mil.)	(72.6%)	21.9	13.7	4.2	0.0	0.1
Employees	(11.0%)	833	823	753	613	523

CONMED CORP

11311 Concept Blvd.
Largo, FL 33773
Phone: 727 392-6464
Fax: 315 797-0321
Web: www.conmed.com

NYS: CNMD
CEO: Curt R Hartman
CFO: Todd W Garner
HR: John Ferrell
FYE: December 31
Type: Public

CONMED is a medical technology company that provides devices and equipment for surgical procedures. The company's products are used by surgeons and other healthcare professionals in a variety of specialties including orthopedics, general surgery, gynecology, thoracic surgery and gastroenterology. The company develops and manufactures a wide range of electronic instruments such as electrosurgical systems, powered surgical instruments, and endomechanical devices. Its arthroscopic (joint surgery) products include reconstruction tools, scopes, implants, and fluid management systems. The company sells its products in more than 100 countries but generates about 55% of revenue in the US market.

	Annual Growth	12/19	12/20	12/21	12/22	12/23
Sales ($mil.)	6.8%	955.1	862.5	1,010.6	1,045.5	1,244.7
Net income ($ mil.)	22.5%	28.6	9.5	62.5	(80.6)	64.5
Market value ($ mil.)	(0.5%)	3,440.5	3,445.7	4,361.3	2,727.0	3,369.1
Employees	4.9%	3,300	3,400	3,800	4,100	4,000

CONNECTICUT CHILDREN'S MEDICAL CENTER

282 WASHINGTON ST
HARTFORD, CT 061063322
Phone: 860 545-9000
Fax: -
Web: www.connecticutchildrens.org

CEO: Thomas Barnes
CFO: Gerald Boisvert
HR: -
FYE: September 30
Type: Private

Connecticut Children's is the only health system in Connecticut dedicated to children, providing more than 30 pediatric specialties along with community-based programs. The 187-bed not-for-profit children's hospital is one of the best children's hospitals in the nation. It fosters a patient- and family-centered environment with a focus on research, education and advocacy. Connecticut Children's serves as the primary pediatric teaching hospital for the UConn School of Medicine, has a teaching partnership with the Frank H. Netter MD School of Medicine at Quinnipiac University and is a research partner of The Jackson Laboratory. Connecticut Children's is now one of only two freestanding children's hospitals in New England and the only freestanding children's hospital in Connecticut.

	Annual Growth	09/13	09/14	09/19	09/20	09/21
Sales ($mil.)	6.0%	–	256.4	393.9	339.0	384.7
Net income ($ mil.)	–	–	(1.6)	37.9	41.3	53.4
Market value ($ mil.)	–	–	–	–	–	–
Employees	–	–	–	–	–	1,117

CONNECTICUT COLLEGE

270 MOHEGAN AVE
NEW LONDON, CT 063204150
Phone: 860 447-1911
Fax: -
Web: www.conncoll.edu

CEO: -
CFO: -
HR: Cheryl Miller
FYE: June 30
Type: Private

With its picturesque campus overlooking Long Island Sound, Connecticut College (CC) strives to be the quintessential New England college. It is a private co-educational liberal arts college in New London, which is close to Providence, Hartford, and New Haven. The college offers approximately 55 majors, has an enrollment of 1,900, and a reputation as one of the most selective schools in the nation. Top majors include biology, English, government, international relations, and psychology. CC is known for its interdisciplinary studies. The school has a 9-to-1 student-faculty ratio. The comprehensive fee (tuition, room, board, and fees) for the 2009-10 academic year is just over $51,000. CC was founded in 1911.

	Annual Growth	06/14	06/15	06/16	06/21	06/22
Sales ($mil.)	1.3%	–	162.7	148.9	97.0	177.6
Net income ($ mil.)	–	–	18.5	2.2	141.9	(0.8)
Market value ($ mil.)	–	–	–	–	–	–
Employees	–	–	–	–	–	1,216

CONNECTICUT DEPARTMENT OF LABOR

200 FOLLY BROOK BLVD
WETHERSFIELD, CT 061091153
Phone: 860 263-6000
Fax: -
Web: www.ct.gov

CEO: -
CFO: Robert Merola
HR: -
FYE: December 31
Type: Private

The Connecticut Department of Labor is a friend of the workers. The agency strives to help employees, as well as job seekers, displaced workers, students, and employers. Through its wide variety of programs, the department offers career guidance, consulting, assessment, and veterans services. The agency also provides education and training, including apprenticeships and its welfare-to-work program, and support for people with disabilities. In addition, the department helps businesses find qualified employees and develop the skills of their workforce.

	Annual Growth	12/13	12/14	12/15	12/16	12/17
Sales ($mil.)	(2.0%)	–	–	–	0.4	0.4
Net income ($ mil.)	92.7%	–	–	–	0.0	0.0
Market value ($ mil.)	–	–	–	–	–	–
Employees	–	–	–	–	–	800

CONNECTICUT LIGHT & POWER CO

107 Selden Street
Berlin, CT 06037-1616
Phone: 800 286-5000
Fax: -
Web: www.eversource.com

NBB: CNLH N
CEO: Werner J Schweiger
CFO: Philip J Lembo
HR: -
FYE: December 31
Type: Public

Northeast utility Connecticut Light and Power Company (CL&P) keeps the folks in the Constitution State connected. CL&P provides electric utility services to 1.2 million customers in nearly 150 Connecticut communities. The electric utility, a subsidiary of Eversource Energy, has 225 substations and more than 288,400 transformers, and owns and operates regulated transmission and distribution assets in its 4,400-sq.-mile service territory. It has more than 22,800 miles of distribution lines and more than 1,770 miles of transmission lines. CL&P's transmission assets are monitored by ISO New England.

	Annual Growth	12/19	12/20	12/21	12/22	12/23
Sales ($mil.)	9.1%	3,232.6	3,547.5	3,637.4	4,817.7	4,578.8
Net income ($ mil.)	6.0%	410.9	457.9	401.7	532.9	518.7
Market value ($ mil.)	(9.2%)	295.7	303.6	295.7	236.6	200.7
Employees	3.3%	1,343	1,381	1,382	1,444	1,529

CONNECTICUT STATE UNIVERSITY SYSTEM

61 WOODLAND ST
HARTFORD, CT 061052345
Phone: 860 493-0000
Fax: –
Web: www.ct.edu

CEO: Lawrence D McHugh
CFO: Pamela J Kedderis
HR: –
FYE: June 30
Type: Private

The Connecticut State University System (CSUS) is the largest public university system in Connecticut and consists of four universities -- Central Connecticut State University, Eastern Connecticut State University, Southern Connecticut State University, and Western Connecticut State University. CSUS has an enrollment of more than 36,000 students and its schools offer undergraduate and graduate degrees in some 180 subjects. Programs include courses in liberal arts, sciences (including meteorology), business, nursing, education, and technology. CSUS traces its roots to 1849 when Central Connecticut State University was founded. It is part of the broader Connecticut State Colleges & Universities (ConnSCU) system.

	Annual Growth	06/10	06/11	06/17	06/19	06/20
Sales ($mil.)	(0.2%)	–	428.0	429.2	438.5	419.3
Net income ($ mil.)	–	–	55.5	(55.2)	(38.1)	(195.6)
Market value ($ mil.)	–	–	–	–	–	–
Employees	–	–	–	–	–	2,800

CONNECTON, INC.

4925 INDEPENDENCE PKWY STE 400
TAMPA, FL 336347552
Phone: 813 935-7100
Fax: –
Web: www.connecton.com

CEO: David Bellini
CFO: –
HR: Katherine Davis
FYE: December 31
Type: Private

ConnectWise is hip to the notion that IT services are only improved by greater connectivity. The company's so-called "professional service automation" software is used by businesses in the IT industry to automate and integrate such functions as help desk service, project management, and customer relationship management. Its core product enables centralized scheduling, tracking, invoicing, and reporting for IT departments as they manage a variety of projects. ConnectWise also develops applications to support inventory tracking and wireless invoicing for mobile technicians. The Bellini brothers, CEO Arnie and president David, founded ConnectWise in 1982. In 2019, the Thoma Bravo private equity firm bought ConnectWise.

	Annual Growth	12/05	12/06	12/07	12/08	12/09
Sales ($mil.)	(53.2%)	–	–	15.3	20.7	3.3
Net income ($ mil.)	(61.6%)	–	–	6.3	7.9	0.9
Market value ($ mil.)	–	–	–	–	–	–
Employees	–	–	–	–	–	96

CONNECTONE BANCORP INC (NEW)

NMS: CNOB

301 Sylvan Avenue
Englewood Cliffs, NJ 07632
Phone: 201 816-8900
Fax: –
Web: www.centerbancorp.com

CEO: Frank Sorrentino III
CFO: William S Burns
HR: –
FYE: December 31
Type: Public

ConnectOne Bancorp (formerly Center Bancorp) is the holding company for ConnectOne Bank, which operates some two dozen branches across New Jersey. Serving individuals and local businesses, the bank offers such deposit products as checking, savings, and money market accounts; CDs; and IRAs. It also performs trust services. Commercial loans account for about 60% of the bank's loan portfolio; residential mortgages account for most of the remainder. It also has a subsidiary that sells annuities and property/casualty, life, and health coverage. The former Center Bancorp acquired rival community bank ConnectOne Bancorp in 2014 and took that name.

	Annual Growth	12/19	12/20	12/21	12/22	12/23
Assets ($mil.)	12.4%	6,174.0	7,547.3	8,129.5	9,644.9	9,855.6
Net income ($ mil.)	4.3%	73.4	71.3	130.4	125.2	87.0
Market value ($ mil.)	(2.9%)	990.7	762.3	1,260.0	932.6	882.5
Employees	–	–	413	438	515	499

CONNECTRIA, LLC

10845 OLIVE BLVD STE 300
SAINT LOUIS, MO 631417762
Phone: 314 587-7000
Fax: –
Web: www.connectria.com

CEO: –
CFO: –
HR: –
FYE: December 31
Type: Private

Businesses around the world hook up with Connectria for their information technology needs. The company is a leading global technology solutions provider. In addition to over 1,000 IBM i LPARs under management, Connectria is trusted by more than 1,000 clients around the world. Connectria also provides managed hosting, cloud migration services and security & compliance, among others. The company operates hosting facilities in St. Louis, Missouri, Pennsylvania, and Philadelphia as well as Texas. Connectria's customers are represented by companies of all sizes in over 30 countries around the world. Connectria was founded in 1996 by Richard Waidmann.

	Annual Growth	12/06	12/07	12/08	12/09	12/10
Sales ($mil.)	16.6%	–	–	17.7	21.1	24.0
Net income ($ mil.)	54.4%	–	–	0.7	1.3	1.6
Market value ($ mil.)	–	–	–	–	–	–
Employees	–	–	–	–	–	150

CONNEXUS ENERGY

14601 RAMSEY BLVD NW
RAMSEY, MN 553036775
Phone: 763 323-2600
Fax: –
Web: www.connexusenergy.com

CEO: Mike Rajala
CFO: Michael Bash
HR: –
FYE: December 31
Type: Private

Connexus Energy connects more Minnesotans to electricity than any other cooperative. The member-owned organization distributes power to more than 127,000 customers in the northern suburbs of Minneapolis-St. Paul. Connexus buys its power from generation and transmission cooperative Great River Energy and distributes it through more than 8,880 miles of overhead and underground power lines. It also operates 47 electrical substations. Residential customers account for the bulk of sales. The cooperative is governed by a board of directors, elected by its members.

	Annual Growth	12/17	12/18	12/19	12/21	12/22
Sales ($mil.)	(0.7%)	–	273.9	246.8	274.0	266.9
Net income ($ mil.)	–	–	21.7	–	–	–
Market value ($ mil.)	–	–	–	–	–	–
Employees	–	–	–	–	–	250

CONNOR CO.

2800 NE ADAMS ST
PEORIA, IL 616032806
Phone: 309 688-1068
Fax: –
Web: www.connorco.com

CEO: –
CFO: –
HR: Julie Driscoll
FYE: December 31
Type: Private

Goldilocks would like Connor Co. If it's too hot or too cold, the heating and A/C company can make it just right. Through about 20 locations in Illinois and one in St. Louis, the company distributes heating and air conditioning equipment along with boilers, fittings, furnaces, pipes, pumps, valves, wells, and other industrial equipment. The company also conducts its business online. Connor Co. boasts sheet metal fabrication and valve automation facilities and peddles Kohler products within its showrooms in many locations. The company was founded as Kinsey & Mahler, a brass valve manufacturer, in 1850. It became Connor Co. in 1936.

	Annual Growth	12/03	12/04	12/05	12/06	12/07
Sales ($mil.)	6.2%	–	91.5	100.6	106.0	109.5
Net income ($ mil.)	12.0%	–	4.5	4.8	6.9	6.4
Market value ($ mil.)	–	–	–	–	–	–
Employees	–	–	–	–	–	276

CONNS INC
NMS: CONN

2445 Technology Forest Blvd., Suite 800
The Woodlands, TX 77381
Phone: 936 230-5899
Fax: –
Web: www.conns.com

CEO: Norman L Miller
CFO: George L Bchara
HR: Connie Davis
FYE: January 31
Type: Public

Conn's is a leading specialty retailer that offers a broad selection of quality, branded durable consumer goods and related services in addition to proprietary credit solutions for its core consumers. It sells consumer electronics, home appliances, home office, furniture, and mattresses through nearly 170 stores located in some 15 states, including Texas (accounting for nearly 45% of the company's number of stores), Florida, Arizona, Louisiana, and North Carolina. It also trades online. Conn's markets its products under brands such as Corinthian (furniture and mattresses), Samsung, LG, General Electric, and Frigidaire (home appliances and consumer electronics), and HP, Apple, and Microsoft (home office, including computers, printers, and accessories). Originally a plumbing and heating business, Conn's has been around for about 135 years.

	Annual Growth	01/19	01/20	01/21	01/22	01/23
Sales ($mil.)	(3.5%)	1,549.8	1,543.7	1,386.0	1,590.0	1,342.5
Net income ($ mil.)	–	73.8	56.0	(3.1)	108.2	(59.3)
Market value ($ mil.)	(18.1%)	502.0	210.0	377.1	581.9	225.6
Employees	(3.2%)	4,475	4,425	4,260	4,200	3,930

CONOLOG CORP

5 Columbia Road
Somerville, NJ 08876
Phone: 908 722-8081
Fax: 908 722-5461
Web: www.conolog.com

CEO: –
CFO: –
HR: –
FYE: July 31
Type: Public

Conolog makes small electronic and electromagnetic components that military, industrial, and utilities customers use for microwave, radio, and telephone transmission. Its products include transducers, receivers, electromagnetic-wave filters, and signal-processing equipment. Its products for commercial customers, electrical and industrial utilities in particular, are carried under the INIVEN brand name, taken from a company Conolog acquired in 1981. Leading customers include the US military and power utilities Bonneville Power Administration, NSTAR, and Tucson Electric Power.

	Annual Growth	07/08	07/09	07/10	07/11	07/12
Sales ($mil.)	(9.2%)	1.2	1.5	1.2	1.7	0.8
Net income ($ mil.)	–	(7.0)	(2.4)	(24.9)	(4.3)	(1.8)
Market value ($ mil.)	(45.2%)	19.2	23.1	18.4	1.7	1.7
Employees	(1.7%)	15	16	15	15	14

CONRAD INDUSTRIES INC
NBB: CNRD

1100 Brashear Avenue, Suite 200
Morgan City, LA 70380
Phone: 985 702-0195
Fax: 985 702-1126
Web: www.conradindustries.com

CEO: John P Conrad Jr
CFO: Carl A Hebert Jr
HR: Joyce Blanchette
FYE: December 31
Type: Public

Like the story of Noah's Ark, Conrad Industries starts anew by rescuing the things its likes. Conrad Industries builds, converts, and repairs small to midsized vessels for commercial and government customers. More than half of the company's work is in constructing barges, liftboats, towboats, and tugboats. Its boat-conversion projects mainly involve lengthening vessel mid-bodies or modifying vessels to perform different functions. Conrad Industries operates shipyards along the Gulf Coast, in Louisiana and Texas. Conrad also offers fabrication of modular components, used on offshore drilling rigs, as well as storage and offloading of vessels. Established in 1948, the company is led by the founding Conrad family.

	Annual Growth	12/18	12/19	12/20	12/21	12/22
Sales ($mil.)	1.5%	182.3	207.4	158.7	191.2	193.9
Net income ($ mil.)	–	0.2	0.0	(4.0)	6.5	(17.4)
Market value ($ mil.)	6.2%	66.0	56.9	57.6	72.6	84.1
Employees	(2.0%)	442	489	432	409	408

CONSERVATION INTERNATIONAL FOUNDATION

2011 CRYSTAL DR STE 600
ARLINGTON, VA 222023715
Phone: 703 341-2400
Fax: –
Web: www.conservation.org

CEO: Peter N Seligman
CFO: Barbara Dipietro
HR: –
FYE: December 31
Type: Private

Conservation International (CI) is dedicated to protecting the environment and its inhabitants. The not-for-profit organization has helped protect some 2.3 million square miles of land and sea across 70-plus countries. Its projects focus on areas such as climate change, agriculture, fresh water, hotspots, seascapes, and wildlife poaching. CI, which has offices in around 25 countries, has a worldwide network of thousands of partners. It generates revenue primarily through contributions and grants and contracts and has total assets of some $380.6 million. The not-for-profit organization was formed in 1987.

	Annual Growth	06/18	06/19	06/20	06/22*	12/22
Sales ($mil.)	(23.5%)	–	140.4	159.5	290.5	62.8
Net income ($ mil.)	–	–	(7.5)	9.2	78.2	4.3
Market value ($ mil.)	–	–	–	–	–	–
Employees	–	–	–	–	–	454

*Fiscal year change

CONSOLIDATED COMMUNICATIONS HOLDINGS INC
NMS: CNSL

2116 South 17th Street
Mattoon, IL 61938-5973
Phone: 217 235-3311
Fax: –
Web: www.consolidated.com

CEO: C R Udell Jr
CFO: Steven L Childers
HR: Christine Edwards
FYE: December 31
Type: Public

Consolidated Communications is a broadband and business communications provider offering a wide range of communication solutions to consumer, commercial and carrier customers by leveraging its advanced fiber network, which spans approximately 57,800 fiber route miles across many rural areas and metro communities. It offers residential high-speed internet, video, phone and home security services as well as multi-service residential and small business bundles. Its business product suite includes data and internet solutions, voice, data center services, security services, managed and IT services, and an expanded suite of cloud services. It also provides wholesale solutions to wireless and wireline carriers and other service providers including data, voice, network connections, and custom fiber builds and last mile connections.

	Annual Growth	12/19	12/20	12/21	12/22	12/23
Sales ($mil.)	(4.5%)	1,336.5	1,304.0	1,282.2	1,191.3	1,110.1
Net income ($ mil.)	–	(20.4)	37.0	(107.1)	140.1	(250.5)
Market value ($ mil.)	2.9%	450.7	568.1	869.0	415.9	505.4
Employees	(1.7%)	3,400	3,200	3,200	3,200	3,180

CONSOLIDATED CONTRACTING SERVICES, INC.

181 AVENIDA LA PATA STE 200
SAN CLEMENTE, CA 92673
Phone: 949 498-7500
Fax: –
Web: www.consolidatedcontracting.com

CEO: Jose A Elias-Calles
CFO: Scott Eaton
HR: –
FYE: January 31
Type: Private

Consolidated Contracting Services has consolidated a large offering of general contracting and specialty contracting services. Focusing on the new construction and renovation of commercial buildings in Southern California, the firm provides construction management and other construction services Consolidated Contracting has worked with a variety of clients to build cleanrooms, storage units, banks, churches, recreation areas, and restaurants. Specialty services include soft demolition, drywall framing and taping, acoustical ceiling and door installation, wood framing, and concrete work. Cuban-born cofounders Tony Elias-Calles and Joe Troya own Consolidated Contracting Services, which was incorporated in 1983.

CONSOLIDATED EDISON CO. OF NEW YORK, INC.

4 Irving Place
New York, NY 10003
Phone: 212 460-4600
Fax: –
Web: www.coned.com

CEO: Timothy P Cawley
CFO: Robert Hoglund
HR: –
FYE: December 31
Type: Public

Consolidated Edison Company of New York (CECONY) distributes electricity to approximately 3.6 million customers in all of New York City and most Westchester County. It also delivers natural gas to about 1.1 million customers in Manhattan, Bronx, parts of Queens and most part of Westchester County. The utility also provides steam services to some 1,530 customers in parts of Manhattan. CECONY owns and operates about 37,490 miles of overhead distribution lines and 98,435 miles of underground distribution lines. CECONY is a subsidiary of Consolidated Edison.

	Annual Growth	12/18	12/19	12/20	12/21	12/22
Sales ($mil.)	5.6%	10,680	10,821	10,647	11,716	13,268
Net income ($ mil.)	3.8%	1,196.0	1,250.0	1,185.0	1,344.0	1,390.0
Market value ($ mil.)	–	–	–	–	–	–
Employees	1.1%	13,685	14,890	12,477	12,325	14,319

CONSOLIDATED EDISON INC

NYS: ED

4 Irving Place
New York, NY 10003
Phone: 212 460-4600
Fax: –
Web: www.conedison.com

CEO: Timothy P Cawley
CFO: Robert Hoglund
HR: Randall Sowder
FYE: December 31
Type: Public

Consolidated Edison (Con Edison) is a holding company that owns Consolidated Edison Company of New York, the company's main subsidiary that distributes electricity to some 3.6 million residential and business customers in some 660-mile service territory centered on New York City. It delivers natural gas to approximately 1.1 million customers and operates the country's largest steam distribution service to deliver energy to parts of Manhattan. Subsidiary Orange and Rockland Utilities serves approximately 0.3 million electric and gas customers in New York and New Jersey. Con Edison also owns or operates renewable energy facilities and advises large clients on energy efficiency programs.

	Annual Growth	12/19	12/20	12/21	12/22	12/23
Sales ($mil.)	3.9%	12,574	12,246	13,676	15,670	14,663
Net income ($ mil.)	17.0%	1,343.0	1,101.0	1,346.0	1,660.0	2,519.0
Market value ($ mil.)	0.1%	31,250	24,963	29,471	32,922	31,422
Employees	(0.5%)	14,890	14,071	13,871	14,319	14,592

CONSOLIDATED HEALTH SYSTEMS, INC.

5000 KY ROUTE 321
PRESTONSBURG, KY 416539113
Phone: 606 886-9558
Fax: –
Web: –

CEO: Burl W Spurlock
CFO: Jack Blackwell
HR: Susan Ellis
FYE: June 30
Type: Private

If you get banged up while floating down the Big Sandy River, Consolidated Health Systems can fix you right up. Doing business as Highlands Health System, the health care provider offers a range of specialties including cardiology, family practice, obstetrics, orthopedics, and pediatrics. It operates a full-service acute care hospital called Highland Regional Medical Center with about 185 beds, as well as several clinics throughout Floyd, Johnson, Martin, and Magoffin counties in rural eastern Kentucky (aka the Big Sandy Region). Highlands Health System is merging with fellow eastern Kentucky care provider Appalachian Regional Healthcare.

	Annual Growth	06/14	06/15	06/16	06/19	06/20
Sales ($mil.)	44.3%	–	15.2	15.8	11.4	94.7
Net income ($ mil.)	–	–	(1.9)	(2.1)	(1.3)	21.8
Market value ($ mil.)	–	–	–	–	–	–
Employees	–	–	–	–	–	450

CONSOLIDATED PIPE & SUPPLY COMPANY, INC.

1205 HILLTOP PKWY
BIRMINGHAM, AL 352045002
Phone: 205 323-7261
Fax: –
Web: www.consolidatedpipe.com

CEO: –
CFO: –
HR: –
FYE: December 31
Type: Private

Consolidated Pipe and Supply lives up to its name: Its nine divisions supply pipe and pipeline materials to a swath of industries, from energy to water and waste treatment, chemical, mining, nuclear, oil and gas, and pulp and paper. Its industrial unit specializes in carbon and stainless alloy pipe, valves, and fittings. Vulcan makes all types of PVC. Corrosion resistant coatings are offered by a Line Pipe and Tubular unit, and liquid applied coatings by Specialty Coatings. Its Consolidated Power Supply is the largest in the business of safety related metallic materials for commercial nuclear generation. Another unit caters to utilities. Consolidated also provides engineering services and inventory systems.

	Annual Growth	12/13	12/14	12/15	12/16	12/18
Sales ($mil.)	12.1%	–	–	575.7	550.7	810.7
Net income ($ mil.)	81.3%	–	–	7.4	17.9	44.0
Market value ($ mil.)	–	–	–	–	–	–
Employees	–	–	–	–	–	900

CONSTANT CONTACT, INC.

1601 TRAPELO RD STE 329
WALTHAM, MA 024517357
Phone: 781 472-8100
Fax: –
Web: www.constantcontact.com

CEO: Frank Vella
CFO: Michael Pellegrino
HR: Matthew Montoya
FYE: December 31
Type: Private

Constant Contact is a digital marketing platform trusted by millions of small businesses and nonprofits worldwide with powerful tools that simplify and amplify digital marketing. Whether it's driving sales, growing a customer base, or engaging an audience, Constant Contact delivers the performance and guidance to build strong connections and generate powerful results. Constant Contact is owned by Endurance International. In 1995, its mission was to give small businesses a way to level the playing field against their larger competitors. What started simply as email marketing has grown into a robust digital marketing solution with all the tools small businesses need to grow and thrive.

CONSTANTIN ASSOCIATES, LLP

20 W 55TH ST FL 7
NEW YORK, NY 100195373
Phone: 212 744-2565
Fax: –
Web: www.constantin.com

CEO: –
CFO: –
HR: –
FYE: December 31
Type: Private

It's not a Roman emperor, but perhaps its services will reign supreme. Constantin Associates is an international network of financial audit and consulting firms that help both large and small clients file financial statements and comply with major accounting standards in the US and Europe. It is a member of the Forum of Firms, an association of international networks of accounting firms that specialize in performing audits across national borders. Constantin Associates also offers special accounting work for companies, investment banks, and governments preparing for a listing, transaction, or reorganization. It maintains offices in the US, Canada, France, and Asia.

	Annual Growth	12/99	12/00	12/01	12/02	12/19
Sales ($mil.)	(22.4%)	–	–	–	4.3	0.0
Net income ($ mil.)	–	–	–	–	0.0	(0.0)
Market value ($ mil.)	–	–	–	–	–	–
Employees	–	–	–	–	–	26

CONSTELLATION BRANDS INC

NYS: STZ

207 High Point Drive, Building 100
Victor, NY 14564
Phone: 585 678-7100
Fax: –
Web: www.cbrands.com

CEO: William A Newlands
CFO: Garth Hankinson
HR: –
FYE: February 28
Type: Public

Constellation Brands is a leading wine, beer, and spirits company in North America. The company is the world's largest premium wine producer, offering more than 100 brands sourced from the world's premier wine-growing regions; brands include Robert Mondavi, Corona Extra, and Meiomi. On the beer front, Constellation holds the exclusive license to produce, import, and sell Mexican beer giant Grupo Modelo's Corona and Modelo brand in the US; it also owns a number of small-scale craft beer brands. Spirits, the company's smallest business, includes the premium spirits Casa Noble and SVEDKA vodka. The company was founded by the late Marvin Sands in 1945. The majority of the company's revenue is generated from the US.

	Annual Growth	02/19	02/20	02/21	02/22	02/23
Sales ($mil.)	3.9%	8,116.0	8,343.5	8,614.9	8,820.7	9,452.6
Net income ($ mil.)	–	–	3,435.9	(11.8)	1,998.0	(40.4)	(71.0)
Market value ($ mil.)	7.2%	30,994	31,584	39,235	39,506	40,987
Employees	2.2%	9,800	9,000	9,300	10,000	10,700

CONSULIER ENGINEERING, INC.

2391 PRESIDENT BARACK OBA
RIVIERA BEACH, FL 334045456
Phone: 561 842-2492
Fax: –
Web: www.moslerauto.com

CEO: Warren B Mosler
CFO: –
HR: –
FYE: December 31
Type: Private

Consulier Engineering has designs on all sorts of markets. Consulier holds a 51% stake in Systems Technologies, LLC; Systems Technologies in turn owns 75% of Patient Care Technology Systems (PCTS), a provider of medical software for hospital emergency departments, including passive tracking technologies for emergency departments and operating rooms. Consulier also has a 40% stake in environmentally safe products maker BioSafe Systems, which develops alternatives to traditionally toxic pesticides. Warren Mosler owns about 80% of Consulier Engineering, which he formed in 1985.

CONSUMER PORTFOLIO SERVICES, INC.

NMS: CPSS

3800 Howard Hughes Parkway, Suite 1400
Las Vegas, NV 89169
Phone: 949 753-6800
Fax: 949 753-6805
Web: www.consumerportfolio.com

CEO: Charles E Bradley Jr
CFO: Jeffrey P Fritz
HR: –
FYE: December 31
Type: Public

Consumer Portfolio Services (CPS) buys, sells, and services auto loans made to consumers who probably don't have portfolios. The company finances vehicles for subprime borrowers who can't get traditional financing due to poor or limited credit; these loans typically carry a higher interest rate than prime loans. CPS purchases contracts from both new car and independent used car dealers in more than 45 states; the company then securitizes (bundles and sells) them on the secondary market. Its total managed portfolio comprises some $900 million in contracts. The bulk of the contracts CPS acquires finance used vehicles. The company has servicing operations in California, Florida, Illinois, and Virginia.

	Annual Growth	12/19	12/20	12/21	12/22	12/23
Sales ($mil.)	0.4%	345.8	271.2	267.8	329.7	352.0
Net income ($ mil.)	70.2%	5.4	21.7	47.5	86.0	45.3
Market value ($ mil.)	29.1%	71.4	89.8	250.9	187.4	198.4
Employees	(3.1%)	1,010	787	739	792	890

CONSUMER PRODUCT DISTRIBUTORS, LLC

705 MEADOW ST
CHICOPEE, MA 010134820
Phone: 413 592-4141
Fax: –
Web: www.thencd.com

CEO: Jeff Polep
CFO: Bill Fitzsimmons
HR: –
FYE: September 29
Type: Private

Consumer Product Distributors helps convenience stores provide convenient services to their customers. The company, which operates as J. Polep Distribution Services, is a leading wholesale supplier serving more than 4,000 convenience retailers in New York, Pennsylvania, and the New England states. J. Polep distributes a variety of products, including cigarettes and other tobacco items, candy, dairy products, frozen foods, snack items, and general merchandise, as well as alcohol and other beverages. As part of its business, J. Polep provides merchandising, sales and marketing, and technology services. The family-owned company was founded as Polep Tobacco in 1898 by Charles Polep.

	Annual Growth	10/14	10/15	10/16*	09/17	09/18
Sales ($mil.)	8.8%	–	968.9	1,005.3	1,101.8	1,249.0
Net income ($ mil.)	(14.4%)	–	2.5	5.5	5.9	1.5
Market value ($ mil.)	–	–	–	–	–	–
Employees	–	–	–	–	–	400

*Fiscal year change

CONSUMER REPORTS, INC.

101 TRUMAN AVE
YONKERS, NY 107031044
Phone: 914 378-2000
Fax: –
Web: www.consumerreports.org

CEO: Marta L Tellado
CFO: –
HR: Tony Bilangino
FYE: May 31
Type: Private

Consumer Reports (CR) inspires both trust and fear. CR is an independent, nonprofit member organization that works side by side with consumers for truth, transparency, and fairness in the marketplace. CR is the publisher of Consumer Reports, ConsumerReports.org, as well as other periodicals, publications, and consumer services. It conducts consumer advocacy and education programs for public health and safety. Print products include subscription or newsstand sales of Consumer Reports Magazine, a Health based newsletter, and special interest publications. CR derives revenue from the subscription sale of Consumer Reports and other services, and non-commercial contributions, subscriptions, newsstands, and other. CR traces its roots to 1936 when consumers had very few options to gauge the value, quality, or authenticity of goods and services.

	Annual Growth	05/18	05/19	05/20	05/21	05/22
Sales ($mil.)	2.6%	–	241.7	245.4	262.3	261.0
Net income ($ mil.)	–	–	–	(0.5)	9.4	111.8	1.4
Market value ($ mil.)	–	–	–	–	–	–
Employees	–	–	–	–	–	480

CONSUMER TECHNOLOGY ASSOCIATION

1919 S EADS ST STE LL
ARLINGTON, VA 222023028
Phone: 703 907-7600
Fax: –
Web: www.cta.tech

CEO: Gary J Shapiro
CFO: Glenda Macmullin
HR: Beth Singh
FYE: December 31
Type: Private

What's the next hot gadget going to be? Members of this group probably know. The Consumer Electronics Association (CEA) researches and reports trends in the $223-billion-plus US consumer electronics market. It also provides its members with educational programs, technical training, market research, forecasts, and networking opportunities. CEA boasts about 2,000 corporate members who receive marketing exposure, representation before Congress and other government bodies, and invitations to participate in the technology tradeshow, International CES (North America's largest consumer electronics show). The annual show attracts more than 150,000 buyers, distributors, and manufacturers from about 150 nations.

	Annual Growth	12/14	12/15	12/16	12/17	12/21
Sales ($mil.)	(32.2%)	–	–	–	120.4	25.5
Net income ($ mil.)	–	–	–	–	16.9	(27.0)
Market value ($ mil.)	–	–	–	–	–	–
Employees	–	–	–	–	–	150

CONSUMERS BANCORP, INC. (MINERVA, OH)

NBB: CBKM

614 East Lincoln Way, P.O. Box 256
Minerva, OH 44657
Phone: 330 868-7701
Fax: –
Web: www.consumers.bank

CEO: –
CFO: –
HR: –
FYE: June 30
Type: Public

You don't have to be a consumer to do business with Consumers -- it's happy to serve businesses, as well. Consumers Bancorp is the holding company for Consumers National Bank, which has about 10 branches in eastern Ohio. The bank offers standard services, such as savings and checking accounts, CDs, and NOW accounts. Business loans make up more than half of the bank's loan portfolio; real estate, consumer, and construction loans round out its lending activities. CNB Investment Services, a division of the bank, offers insurance, brokerage, financial planning, and wealth management services through a third-party provider, UVEST. Chairman Laurie McClellan owns more than 20% of Consumers Bancorp.

	Annual Growth	06/19	06/20	06/21	06/22	06/23
Assets ($mil.)	17.6%	553.9	740.8	833.8	977.3	1,060.0
Net income ($ mil.)	17.7%	5.6	5.5	9.0	11.2	10.7
Market value ($ mil.)	(0.7%)	57.3	43.9	60.4	59.4	55.7
Employees	7.7%	144	172	176	187	194

CONSUMERS ENERGY CO.

NYS: CMS PRB

One Energy Plaza
Jackson, MI 49201
Phone: 517 788-0550
Fax: –
Web: www.consumersenergy.com

CEO: Garrick J Rochow
CFO: Rejji P Hayes
HR: Anthony Chipkewich
FYE: December 31
Type: Public

Consumers Energy Company is a subsidiary of CMS Energy, which owns and operates electric generation and distribution facilities and gas transmission, storage, and distribution facilities. The company's customer base consists of a mix of primarily residential, commercial, and diversified industrial customers in Michigan's lower peninsula. The company was founded in 1886.

	Annual Growth	12/19	12/20	12/21	12/22	12/23
Sales ($mil.)	3.0%	6,376.0	6,189.0	7,021.0	8,151.0	7,166.0
Net income ($ mil.)	3.9%	743.0	816.0	868.0	945.0	867.0
Market value ($ mil.)	(6.8%)	9,209.0	9,171.1	9,176.2	7,299.9	6,938.3
Employees	(1.8%)	8,762	8,738	9,583	8,879	8,144

CONTAINER STORE GROUP, INC

NYS: TCS

500 Freeport Parkway
Coppell, TX 75019
Phone: 972 538-6000
Fax: –
Web: www.containerstore.com

CEO: Satish Malhotra
CFO: Jeffrey A Miller
HR: –
FYE: April 1
Type: Public

The Container Store (TCS) is the original and leading specialty retailer of organizing solutions, custom spaces, and in-home organizing services in the US and the only national retailer solely devoted to these categories. It provides a collection of creative, multifunctional, and customizable storage and organization solutions that are sold in its stores and online through a high-service, differentiated shopping experience. Its merchandise ranges from hanging storage bags to pantry organizers. The company operates about 95 stores in almost 35 states and the District of Columbia. It also runs an e-commerce site. The company offers free shipping on orders over $75 and same-day home delivery in select markets. Stores offer over 10,000 products designed to provide customers solutions that simplify their lives and maximize their spaces within their homes; the company's Elfa brand of wire shelving (made in Sweden) accounts for nearly 5% of its sales.

	Annual Growth	03/19	03/20*	04/21	04/22	04/23
Sales ($mil.)	4.0%	895.1	916.0	990.1	1,094.1	1,047.3
Net income ($ mil.)	–	21.7	14.5	58.3	81.7	(158.9)
Market value ($ mil.)	(21.0%)	432.8	156.4	807.6	399.4	168.7
Employees	–	5,110	5,100	5,100	5,200	5,100

*Fiscal year change

CONTI ENTERPRISES INC.

2045 STATE ROUTE 27
EDISON, NJ 088173334
Phone: 732 528-1250
Fax: –
Web: www.thecontigroup.com

CEO: Gerard Maurer
CFO: Marc Hesse
HR: –
FYE: December 31
Type: Private

Conti Civil (formerly known as Conti Enterprises) is a fourth-generation, privately-owned construction leader specializing in building Heavy Civil projects. The company provides construction management, general contracting, and design/build services for a range of projects, including commercial and industrial buildings, power plants, environmental remediation, physical security upgrades, and infrastructure such as dams, roads, bridges, and rail systems. Conti Civil is a member of The Conti Group, a creator, builder, and operator of businesses.

	Annual Growth	12/03	12/04	12/05	12/08	12/09
Sales ($mil.)	11.4%	–	115.4	123.4	198.2	198.2
Net income ($ mil.)	–	–	0.2	–	–	–
Market value ($ mil.)	–	–	–	–	–	–
Employees	–	–	–	–	–	500

CONTINENTAL MATERIALS CORP.

440 South La Salle Street, Suite 3100
Chicago, IL 60605
Phone: 312 541-7200
Fax: –
Web: www.continental-materials.com

CEO: James G Gidwitz
CFO: Paul A Ainsworth
HR: –
FYE: December 28
Type: Public

Continental Materials provides construction and heating, ventilation, and air conditioning (HVAC) services. Its HVAC segment, which sccounts for a majority of sales, makes wall furnaces, console heaters, and fan coils through Williams Furnace and evaporative air coolers through Phoenix Manufacturing. Customers include wholesale distributors and retail home centers in the Southwest. The construction products segment produces ready-mix concrete and aggregates through three subsidiaries and metal doors from McKinney Door and Hardware. Contractors, government entities, and consumers in Colorado are the segment's primary customers. CEO James Gidwitz and family own more than 60% of Continental Materials.

	Annual Growth	01/16*	12/16	12/17	12/18	12/19
Sales ($mil.)	(4.6%)	136.8	151.6	152.8	164.0	113.3
Net income ($ mil.)	–	1.4	3.7	1.8	(5.9)	(13.9)
Market value ($ mil.)	(15.8%)	25.6	41.0	32.6	19.2	12.9
Employees	(4.9%)	563	590	590	612	460

*Fiscal year change

CONTINENTAL RESOURCES, INC.

175 MIDDLESEX TPKE STE 1
BEDFORD, MA 017301469
Phone: 781 275-0850
Fax: –
Web: www.conres.com

CEO: Mary Nardella
CFO: James M Bunt
HR: Michelle Varga
FYE: December 31
Type: Private

Continental Resources is a family-owned global IT solutions provider that offers a broad range of technologies and services you'd expect from a distributor, combined with the personalized touch and flexibility you'd expect from a family business. Also known as ConRes, the company designs, procures, implements, and manages IT solutions that solve business-specific problems. The company's managed services include service desk and end user support, cloud, and managed backup services. Professional services use a multi-vendor solution approach coupled with extensive technical expertise that consistently develops long-term client relationships. To provide multi-vendor solutions, ConRes partners with industry leaders that include Apple, Brocade, Citrix Systems, Dell Technologies, F5 Networks, IBM, McAfee, and many more.

	Annual Growth	12/14	12/15	12/16	12/18	12/19
Sales ($mil.)	(4.0%)	–	479.1	455.6	547.2	407.1
Net income ($ mil.)	(19.3%)	–	8.4	6.2	7.8	3.6
Market value ($ mil.)	–	–	–	–	–	–
Employees	–	–	–	–	–	300

CONTINENTAL RESOURCES, INC.

20 N BROADWAY
OKLAHOMA CITY, OK 731029213
Phone: 405 234-9000
Fax: -
Web: www.clr.com

CEO: William B Berry
CFO: John D Hart
HR: -
FYE: December 31
Type: Private

Continental Resources is an independent crude oil and natural gas company formed in 1967 engaged in the exploration, development, management, and production of crude oil and natural gas and associated products with properties primarily located in four leading basins in the United States ? the Bakken field of North Dakota and Montana, the Anadarko Basin of Oklahoma, the Permian Basin of Texas, and the Powder River Basin of Wyoming. Additionally, the company has leading positions in two major plays near its home-base of Oklahoma?the SCOOP (South Central Oklahoma Oil Province) and STACK (Sooner Trend Anadarko Canadian Kingfisher). Continental Resources maintains around 1,865 MMboe of proved reserves, some 55% is crude oil. It reports a production average of over 401,800 Boe per day.

	Annual Growth	12/18	12/19	12/20	12/21	12/22
Sales ($mil.)	26.9%	-	4,631.9	2,586.5	5,719.3	9,473.7
Net income ($ mil.)	73.5%	-	774.5	(605.6)	1,666.4	4,046.1
Market value ($ mil.)	-	-	-	-	-	-
Employees	-	-	-	-	-	1,254

CONTRACTORS STEEL COMPANY

48649 SCHOONER ST
VAN BUREN TWP, MI 481115370
Phone: 734 464-4000
Fax: -
Web: www.upgllc.com

CEO: -
CFO: -
HR: -
FYE: April 30
Type: Private

When you contract with Contractors Steel, you get steel products delivered to you. Steel service center operator Contractors Steel provides products such as bars (cold-rolled and hot-rolled), pipe, plate, sheet, structural members (angles, beams, and channels), and tubing. The company's fabricating and processing services include burning, grinding, plasma cutting, sawing, and shearing. Contractors Steel operates from facilities in Michigan, Indiana, Arizona and Ohio. Chairman, president, and CEO Donald Simon founded Contractors Steel in 1960.

	Annual Growth	10/07	10/08	10/09	10/10*	04/16
Sales ($mil.)	(5.7%)	-	-	153.1	101.2	101.2
Net income ($ mil.)	-	-	-	(24.1)	0.8	0.8
Market value ($ mil.)	-	-	-	-	-	-
Employees	-	-	-	-	-	439

*Fiscal year change

CONTROL CHIEF HOLDINGS, INC.

P.O. Box 141, 200 Williams Street
Bradford, PA 16701
Phone: 814 368-4132
Fax: 814 368-4133
Web: www.controlchief.com

CEO: Douglas S Bell
CFO: -
HR: -
FYE: December 31
Type: Public

Crane operators arguing over the remote? Could be . . . if it's one made by Control Chief. Control Chief develops and manufactures wireless remote controls for pneumatic, hydraulic, and electronic machines, from heavy-duty cranes to trains, shipyard, mining, and farm equipment. Its remote control lineup, including brands Communicator, Raymote, and MU&Go, is held to increase safety by allowing workers to drive machinery from a distance. Microprocessors, operated by radio or infrared waves, are used in its remote control systems. The company markets its products through independent sales representatives, as well as directly, and through distributors and private-label licenses and agreements, across the Americas.

	Annual Growth	06/98	06/99	06/00*	12/00	12/01
Sales ($mil.)	(13.0%)	8.8	7.7	7.4	3.4	5.1
Net income ($ mil.)	(57.5%)	0.6	0.5	0.4	0.4	0.0
Market value ($ mil.)	(13.8%)	0.0	0.0	0.0	0.0	0.0
Employees	(12.1%)	72	58	52	49	43

*Fiscal year change

CONTROL4 CORPORATION

11734 S ELECTION RD
DRAPER, UT 840206802
Phone: 801 523-3100
Fax: -
Web: www.control4.com

CEO: John Heyman
CFO: -
HR: JD Ellis JD
FYE: December 31
Type: Private

Control4 is a leading automation system for homes and businesses, offering a personalized and unified smart home system to automate and control connected devices, including lighting, audio, video, climate control, intercom, and security. Control4 systems are only sold through authorized dealers who install the hardware and configure and customize the software to unify and personalize the homeowner's technology. Founded in 2003 by Eric Smith, Will West, and Mark Morgan, Control4 debuted at the 2004 CEDIA Expo home technology trade show.

CONVAID PRODUCTS LLC

2830 CALIFORNIA ST
TORRANCE, CA 905033908
Phone: 310 618-0111
Fax: -
Web: www.etac.com

CEO: Chris Braun
CFO: -
HR: -
FYE: December 31
Type: Private

Convaid makes lightweight, compact-folding wheelchairs that are made for clients with orthopedic conditions and limited upper body control. The company also offers accessories such as travel bags, canopies, footplates, incontinence liners, and torso support vests. Convaid sells the wheelchairs to the pediatric, adult, and geriatric markets. The company was founded in 1976.

CONVERGENT OUTSOURCING, INC.

800 SW 39TH ST STE 100
RENTON, WA 980574927
Phone: 206 322-4500
Fax: -
Web: www.tsico.com

CEO: -
CFO: -
HR: -
FYE: December 31
Type: Private

Companies send their ailing accounts receivable to Convergent Outsourcing. A subsidiary of Convergent Resources (CRI), one of the largest collections companies in the US, Convergent Outsourcing (formerly ER Solutions) provides receivables collections services to creditors in the retail, telecommunications, utilities, and financial services industries. Utilizing a mixture of state-of-the-art technology and old-fashioned diplomacy, the company tracks down delinquent customers and encourages voluntary repayment of debt. It also provides customer service both for outbound communications (contacting customers to remind them of their debt and payment options), and inbound customer relations.

	Annual Growth	12/06	12/07	12/08	12/10	12/11
Sales ($mil.)	5.4%	-	-	81.2	86.2	95.0
Net income ($ mil.)	6.4%	-	-	8.6	8.7	10.4
Market value ($ mil.)	-	-	-	-	-	-
Employees	-	-	-	-	-	730

CONVERGINT TECHNOLOGIES LLC

1 COMMERCE DR
SCHAUMBURG, IL 601735302
Phone: 847 620-5000
Fax: –
Web: www.convergint.com

CEO: –
CFO: –
HR: –
FYE: December 31
Type: Private

Convergint Technologies is a global, industry-leading systems integrator that designs, installs, and services electronic security, cybersecurity, fire and life safety, building automation, and audio-visual systems. Its vertical expertise understands specific business and service needs, and the company offers a suite of tools for consistency of execution and unparalleled service delivery. Convergint started in 2001.

	Annual Growth	12/07	12/08	12/09	12/12	12/14
Sales ($mil.)	19.9%	–	–	164.8	96.8	408.2
Net income ($ mil.)	(17.0%)	–	–	13.6	(7.4)	5.4
Market value ($ mil.)	–	–	–	–	–	–
Employees	–	–	–	–	–	7,800

CONWAY REGIONAL MEDICAL CENTER, INC.

2302 COLLEGE AVE
CONWAY, AR 720346297
Phone: 501 329-3831
Fax: –
Web: www.conwayregional.org

CEO: Matt Troup
CFO: Bill Pack
HR: –
FYE: December 31
Type: Private

Ailing Arkansans have a health services provider in Conway Regional Health System. The health system is composed of not-for-profit 154-bed acute care hospital Conway Regional Medical Center, as well as four health clinics, a home health agency, a health and fitness center, and an inpatient rehabilitation hospital. Conway Regional provides specialized cardiovascular, neurology, oncology, orthopedics, physical therapy, and women's services (including obstetrics and gynecology). Its facilities serve the health needs of residents of several central Arkansas counties, including Cleburne, Conway, Faulkner, Perry, and Van Buren.

	Annual Growth	12/18	12/19	12/20	12/21	12/22
Sales ($mil.)	11.9%	–	200.5	232.1	273.5	280.6
Net income ($ mil.)	–	–	12.7	7.0	15.5	(19.8)
Market value ($ mil.)	–	–	–	–	–	–
Employees	–	–	–	–	–	1,200

COOK CHILDREN'S HEALTH CARE SYSTEM

801 7TH AVE
FORT WORTH, TX 761042733
Phone: 682 885-4000
Fax: –
Web: www.cookchildrens.org

CEO: Russell Tolman
CFO: Stephen W Kimmel
HR: –
FYE: September 30
Type: Private

Cook Children's Health Care System is one of the largest freestanding pediatric health care systems in the country with a complete network of care, including a medical center, pediatric surgery centers, specialty clinics, pediatrician offices, urgent care centers, and an emergency department. It encompasses the Cook Children's Medical Center, Cook Children's Home Health, and Cook Children's Health Plan. Cook Children's treats children from virtually every state in the nation and in more than 30 countries. Specialties include behavioral health/psychology/psychiatry, endocrinology, hematology/oncology, bone marrow and stem cell transplant, and pain management and trauma services. Cook's Life After Cancer Program is funded by the Livestrong Foundation and helps people manage and survive cancer.

	Annual Growth	09/06	09/07	09/09	09/15	09/21
Sales ($mil.)	(4.0%)	–	500.8	75.8	140.6	282.2
Net income ($ mil.)	(10.4%)	–	59.9	(1.5)	2.0	12.9
Market value ($ mil.)	–	–	–	–	–	–
Employees	–	–	–	–	–	2,000

COOKEVILLE REGIONAL MEDICAL CENTER

1 MEDICAL CENTER BLVD
COOKEVILLE, TN 385014294
Phone: 931 528-2541
Fax: –
Web: www.crmchealth.org

CEO: Paul Korth
CFO: Tommye R Wells
HR: Bruce Boyer
FYE: June 30
Type: Private

Cookeville Regional Medical Center (CRMC) serves east-central potions of Tennessee. Specialty units include The Heart Center (cardiac rehabilitation), The Cancer Center (cancer treatment), and The Spine Center (spinal surgery). Other services include rehabilitation, orthopedics, diagnostics, neurology, critical care, surgery, and women's health. Tracing its roots to 1921, the community hospital has about 250 inpatient beds and more than 150 physicians with 40 specialties on its medical staff. CRMC also operates the nearby Cumberland River Hospital and a 30-bed behavioral health unit. The Foundation at CRMC provides fundraising and charity programs; CRMC also has an affiliated physician practice organization.

	Annual Growth	06/13	06/14	06/15	06/16	06/19
Sales ($mil.)	(8.9%)	–	–	–	0.0	0.0
Net income ($ mil.)	–	–	–	–	0.0	(0.0)
Market value ($ mil.)	–	–	–	–	–	–
Employees	–	–	–	–	–	2,300

COOLSYSTEMS, INC.

5405 WINDWARD PKWY STE 100
ALPHARETTA, GA 300044668
Phone: 888 426-3732
Fax: –
Web: www.gameready.com

CEO: –
CFO: Steven Voskuil
HR: Laura Elders
FYE: December 31
Type: Private

Many sports injuries put players on RICE (Rest, Ice, Compression, Elevation) and CoolSystems helps serve up two portions. The company's Game Ready products provide active compression and adjustable cold therapy to treat bruises, sprains, and other muscular injuries. The device consists of a control unit that pumps cold water to a fabric wrap that provides intermittent pressure to injured areas. Used by professional and school sports teams, the system is also used for post-surgical recovery and has been adapted for veterinary use. CoolSystems is also marketing the ReBound heat therapy system developed by ReGear Life Sciences. NASA spacesuit designer Bill Elkins founded the company in 1998. Medical device firm Avanos Medical acquired CoolSystems for $65 million in mid-2018.

COOPER COMMUNITIES, INC.

903 N 47TH ST
ROGERS, AR 727569660
Phone: 479 246-6500
Fax: –
Web: www.coopercommunitiesinc.com

CEO: –
CFO: –
HR: –
FYE: December 31
Type: Private

Feeling cooped up in your cookie-cutter house with its bare minimum of surrounding green space? Cooper Communities develops master-planned communities and resorts in the southeastern US. Some properties feature golf courses and lakes, with 20-30% of their land set aside for natural landscape. Subsidiaries include custom builder Cooper Homes, Cooper Land Development, and Escapes!, which sells timeshare options for Cooper's resorts. Cooper Realty Investments acquires and manages commercial properties. The largest homebuilder in Arkansas, Cooper Communities also has developments in eight other states. Cooper Communities was founded by John Cooper in 1954, and builds about 1,300 new homes each year.

	Annual Growth	12/05	12/06	12/07	12/08	12/10
Sales ($mil.)	(24.5%)	–	–	139.5	91.1	60.1
Net income ($ mil.)	–	–	–	14.1	(29.5)	(65.4)
Market value ($ mil.)	–	–	–	–	–	–
Employees	–	–	–	–	–	400

COOPER COMPANIES, INC. (THE)   NMS: COO

6101 Bollinger Canyon Road, Suite 500
San Ramon, CA 94583
Phone: 925 460-3600
Fax: 925 460-3648
Web: www.coopercos.com

CEO: -
CFO: -
HR: -
FYE: October 31
Type: Public

The Cooper Companies specializes in eye care and, to a lesser extent, lady care. The global company makes specialty medical devices in two niche markets: vision care and gynecology. Its CooperVision subsidiary makes specialty contact lenses, including toric lenses for astigmatism, multifocal lenses for presbyopia, and cosmetic lenses. The company also offers spherical lenses for more common vision problems such as nearsightedness and farsightedness. Subsidiary CooperSurgical specializes in women's health care; its wide range of products that are based on the point of health care delivery used in medical office and surgical procedures primarily by Obstetricians/Gynecologists (OB/GYN) as well as fertility products and genetic testing services used primarily in fertility clinics and laboratories. Cooper's products are sold in more than 130 countries. The company primarily earns about 55% of sales from its US operations.

	Annual Growth	10/19	10/20	10/21	10/22	10/23
Sales ($mil.)	7.9%	2,653.4	2,430.9	2,922.5	3,308.4	3,593.2
Net income ($ mil.)	(10.9%)	466.7	238.4	2,944.7	385.8	294.2
Market value ($ mil.)	1.7%	57,618	63,172	82,550	54,131	61,727
Employees	5.7%	12,000	12,000	12,000	14,000	15,000

COOPER-STANDARD HOLDINGS INC   NYS: CPS

40300 Traditions Drive
Northville, MI 48168
Phone: 248 596-5900
Fax: -
Web: www.cooperstandard.com

CEO: Jeffrey S Edwards
CFO: Jonathan P Banas
HR: Denise Austin
FYE: December 31
Type: Public

Cooper-Standard Holdings is a leading manufacturer of sealing, fuel and brake delivery, and fluid transfer systems. Its products are primarily for use in passenger vehicles and light trucks that are manufactured by global automotive original equipment manufacturers (OEMs) and replacement markets. Its sealing products protect interiors from noise, dust, and weather. Its fuel and brake delivery systems deliver and control fluid and fluid vapors. Fluid transfer systems deliver and control fluids to fuel and brake systems and HVAC systems. The company sells to virtually every global OEMs, although Ford, GM, and Stellantis combined generate almost 60% of sales. Cooper-Standard also generates about 55% of its sales in North America.

	Annual Growth	12/19	12/20	12/21	12/22	12/23
Sales ($mil.)	(2.4%)	3,108.4	2,375.4	2,330.2	2,525.4	2,815.9
Net income ($ mil.)	-	-	67.5	(267.6)	(322.8)	(215.4)	(202.0)
Market value ($ mil.)	(12.4%)	570.3	596.2	385.4	155.8	336.0
Employees	(4.8%)	28,000	25,000	22,600	23,000	23,000

COOPERATIVE ELEVATOR CO.

7211 E MICHIGAN AVE
PIGEON, MI 487555202
Phone: 989 453-4500
Fax: -
Web: www.coopelev.com

CEO: Kurt Ewald
CFO: -
HR: Corinne Schornack
FYE: January 31
Type: Private

Cooperative Elevator represents and serves northern Michigan bean and grain farmers. The agricultural cooperative is made up of approximately 900 member/owners. It operates storage facilities and processing plants, offers crop marketing and agronomy services, and provides farm supplies to its members, including seed, feed, fertilizer, herbicides, fuel, and agricultural chemicals. The co-op's bean farmers grow black, red, pinto, and navy beans, which are distributed in bulk throughout the US, as well as in Africa and the Caribbean. Cooperative Elevator's grain farmers produce wheat, soy, corn, barley, and oats and the co-op provides storage and market services such as price updates for these commodities.

	Annual Growth	01/12	01/13	01/14	01/15	01/16
Sales ($mil.)	(13.0%)	-	-	277.1	216.6	209.9
Net income ($ mil.)	(24.3%)	-	-	10.0	8.3	5.7
Market value ($ mil.)	-	-	-	-	-	-
Employees	-	-	-	-	-	164

COOPERATIVE FOR ASSISTANCE AND RELIEF EVERYWHERE, INC. (CARE)

151 ELLIS ST NE
ATLANTA, GA 303032420
Phone: 404 681-2552
Fax: -
Web: www.care.org

CEO: Michelle Nunn
CFO: Vickie J Barrow-Klien
HR: Emilly Babirye
FYE: June 30
Type: Private

The Cooperative for Assistance and Relief Everywhere (CARE) strives to be the beginning of the end of poverty. The organization works to reduce poverty in about 85 countries by helping communities in areas such as health, education, economic development, emergency relief, and agriculture. CARE supports more than 1,100 projects to combat poverty. It also operates a small economic activity development (SEAD) unit that supports moneymaking activities. Through SEAD, CARE provides technical training and savings and loans programs to help people -- particularly women -- open or expand small businesses. CARE was founded in 1945 to give aid to WWII survivors.

	Annual Growth	06/17	06/18	06/19	06/20	06/22
Sales ($mil.)	10.0%	-	604.5	621.0	609.3	886.1
Net income ($ mil.)	45.8%	-	15.6	16.5	(38.0)	70.6
Market value ($ mil.)	-	-	-	-	-	-
Employees	-	-	-	-	-	10,000

COOPERATIVE REGIONS OF ORGANIC PRODUCER POOLS

1 ORGANIC WAY
LA FARGE, WI 546396604
Phone: 608 625-2602
Fax: -
Web: www.organicvalley.coop

CEO: Bob Kirchoff
CFO: Michael Bedessem
HR: -
FYE: December 31
Type: Private

Cooperative Regions of Organic Producers Pool (CROPP) is America's largest cooperative of organic family farmers. The cooperative's more than 1,600 farmers/members produce the co-op's Organic Valley Family of Farms and Organic Prairie brands of fluid and shelf-stable milk, along with cheese, butter, and cream. Beyond the dairy barn, the cooperative also offers produce, eggs, meats, poultry, and feeds. CROPP's Organic Valley is one of the nation's leading organic brands, and its products are featured in mainstream and natural grocery stores in all 50 states. Wisconsin-headquartered CROPP's farmers/members are located throughout North America. The co-op was founded in 1988.

	Annual Growth	12/05	12/06	12/07	12/08	12/10
Sales ($mil.)	12.7%	-	-	432.6	527.8	619.7
Net income ($ mil.)	24.6%	-	-	6.2	3.8	12.1
Market value ($ mil.)	-	-	-	-	-	-
Employees	-	-	-	-	-	764

COPART INC   NMS: CPRT

14185 Dallas Parkway, Suite 300
Dallas, TX 75254
Phone: 972 391-5000
Fax: -
Web: www.copart.com

CEO: -
CFO: -
HR: -
FYE: July 31
Type: Public

Copart is one of the leading global providers of online auctions and vehicle remarketing services. It takes those vehicles and auctions them for insurers as well as auto dealers, fleet operations, vehicle rental companies, and individuals. The buyers are mostly rebuilders, licensed dismantlers, repair licensees, used vehicle dealers, exporters, and the general public. The company has replaced live auctions with internet auctions using a platform known as Virtual Bidding Third Generation (VB3). It also provides services such as towing and storage to buyers and other salvage companies. Copart serves customers in the US, Canada, the UK, Brazil, Ireland, Germany, Finland, the UAE, Oman, Bahrain, and Spain, although the US accounts for more than 80% of its revenue.

	Annual Growth	07/19	07/20	07/21	07/22	07/23
Sales ($mil.)	17.3%	2,042.0	2,205.6	2,692.5	3,500.9	3,869.5
Net income ($ mil.)	20.3%	591.7	699.9	936.5	1,090.1	1,237.7
Market value ($ mil.)	3.3%	74,223	89,272	140,730	122,636	84,620
Employees	8.6%	7,327	7,600	8,600	9,500	10,200

COPT DEFENSE PROPERTIES   NYS: CDP

6711 Columbia Gateway Drive, Suite 300   CEO: –
Columbia, MD 21046   CFO: –
Phone: 443 285-5400   HR: –
Fax: 443 285-7650   FYE: December 31
Web: www.copt.com   Type: Public

A real estate investment trust (REIT), Corporate Office Properties Trust owns and manages some 185 properties totaling some 21.1 million sq. ft. of leasable space. The REIT focuses on large suburban business parks near federal government hubs and military installations. More than 45% of its office space is located in the Fort Meade/ BW Corridor regions; other major markets include Northern Virginia, Lackland Air Force Base, and Redstone Arsenal. Subsidiaries provide property management, construction and development services primarily for its properties bus also for third parties. The REIT's largest tenants are the US Government and defense information technology concerns.

	Annual Growth	12/19	12/20	12/21	12/22	12/23
Sales ($mil.)	1.7%	641.2	609.4	664.4	739.0	685.0
Net income ($ mil.)	–	191.7	97.4	76.5	173.0	(73.5)
Market value ($ mil.)	(3.4%)	3,306.9	2,935.4	3,148.2	2,919.7	2,884.8
Employees	1.0%	394	406	405	395	410

CORASCLOUD, INC.

7918 JONES BRANCH DR STE 800   CEO: –
MC LEAN, VA 221023337   CFO: –
Phone: 703 797-1881   HR: Robin Mugaas
Fax: –   FYE: December 31
Web: www.coras.com   Type: Private

CorasWorks develops software used to build Web-based business applications. The company's modular software components are designed to work primarily with Microsoft's SharePoint application. Corporate, non-profit, and government customers in about 20 countries worldwide use Coras' technology to connect, share, and aggregate data and workflows originating in their IT, finance, marketing, and sales processes. The company serves commercial clients in such industries as aerospace, health care, transportation, and manufacturing. Customers have included Boeing, Rockwell Collins, and Pfizer. CorasWorks was founded by director William Rogers.

CORCENTRIC, LLC

62861 COLLECTIONS CENTER DRIVE 606   CEO: Douglas Clark
CHICAGO, IL 606930001   CFO: Mark Joyce
Phone: 800 608-0809   HR: –
Fax: –   FYE: December 31
Web: www.nationalease.com   Type: Private

AmeriQuest Business Services makes money helping its clients save money. The company provides products and services focused on procurement (group purchasing, spend management), asset management (asset financing, remarketing), and financial process automation (centralized processing, accounts payable). Its clients hail from a broad range of industries, from construction to healthcare to retail. In addition, it offers a host of transportation services -- fleet management, fleet maintenance, truck leasing, materials handling, and logistics, among them. It has more than 1,500 customers, mostly middle-market companies, across North America.

CORCEPT THERAPEUTICS INC   NAS: CORT

149 Commonwealth Drive   CEO: Joseph K Belanoff
Menlo Park, CA 94025   CFO: Atabak Mokari
Phone: 650 327-3270   HR: Lenore Ockerberg
Fax: –   FYE: December 31
Web: www.corcept.com   Type: Public

Corcept Therapeutics is a pharmaceutical company engaged in the discovery, development and commercialization of drugs that treat severe metabolic, oncologic and psychiatric disorders by modulating the effects of the stress hormone cortisol. Corcept has a large portfolio of proprietary compounds that selectively modulate the effects of cortisol but not progesterone. Corcept owns extensive United States and foreign intellectual property covering the composition of its selective cortisol modulators and the use of cortisol modulators to treat a wide variety of serious disorders.

	Annual Growth	12/19	12/20	12/21	12/22	12/23
Sales ($mil.)	12.0%	306.5	353.9	366.0	401.9	482.4
Net income ($ mil.)	3.0%	94.2	106.0	112.5	101.4	106.1
Market value ($ mil.)	28.0%	1,251.2	2,705.1	2,047.4	2,100.2	3,358.6
Employees	14.3%	206	236	238	299	352

CORE & MAIN INC   NYS: CNM

1830 Craig Park Court   CEO: Stephen O Leclair
St. Louis , MO 63146   CFO: Mark R Witkowski
Phone: 314 432-4700   HR: –
Fax: –   FYE: January 28
Web: www.coreandmain.com   Type: Public

Core & Main is a leading specialized distributor of water, wastewater, storm drainage and fire protection products, and related services, to municipalities, private water companies, and professional contractors across municipal, non-residential, and residential end markets nationwide. Core & Main specialty products and services are used in the maintenance, repair, replacement, and new construction of water, wastewater, storm drainage, and fire protection infrastructure. With more than 320 branch locations in nearly 50 US states, the company provides its customers with local expertise backed by a national supply chain. Core & Main's 4,500 associates are committed to helping its communities thrive with safe and reliable infrastructure. Core & Main was established in 2017 and went public in 2021.

	Annual Growth	02/20*	01/21	01/22	01/23	01/24
Sales ($mil.)	18.6%	3,388.6	3,642.3	5,004.0	6,651.0	6,702.0
Net income ($ mil.)	73.2%	41.2	44.5	166.0	366.0	371.0
Market value ($ mil.)	–	–	–	4,720.3	4,362.0	8,162.5
Employees	–	–	3,700	4,100	4,500	5,000

*Fiscal year change

CORE CONSTRUCTION, INC.

3036 E GREENWAY RD   CEO: –
PHOENIX, AZ 850324414   CFO: –
Phone: 602 494-0800   HR: –
Fax: –   FYE: December 31
Web: www.coreconstruction.com   Type: Private

CORE Construction fits into the core clique of contractors in the southwestern US. The company, formerly Targent General, is one of the top contractors in the region; it also has offices in Florida and Illinois. CORE offers construction management, general contracting, and design/build services for municipal, educational, health care, office, residential, retail, sports, institutional, and industrial projects. It has worked on projects as diverse as Phoenix's Chase Field Ballpark, Dodge Theatre, and Lower Buckeye Jail. German immigrant Otto Baum founded the company in 1937.

	Annual Growth	12/16	12/17	12/18	12/19	12/21
Sales ($mil.)	8.7%	–	223.8	262.6	194.8	313.0
Net income ($ mil.)	–	–	–	3.9	5.0	9.5
Market value ($ mil.)	–	–	–	–	–	–
Employees	–	–	–	–	–	60

CORE LABORATORIES INC
NYS: CLB

6316 Windfern Road
Houston, TX 77040
Phone: 713 328-2673
Fax: 713 328-2150
Web: www.corelab.com

CEO: –
CFO: –
HR: –
FYE: December 31
Type: Public

The core of Core Laboratories' mission is to enable oil exploration and production companies to get the most out of their aging petroleum reservoirs. The company, which has 70 offices in more than 50 countries, analyzes petroleum reservoir rock and fluids, helping oil companies determine how much gas or oil is present in their reservoirs and how quickly it can be extracted. After oil and gas well analysis, Core Laboratories offers hydraulic fracturing and field flooding (forcing water, carbon dioxide, or hydrocarbon gases into a well to push out oil and gas and boost production). The company also provides reservoir management services.

	Annual Growth	12/19	12/20	12/21	12/22	12/23
Sales ($mil.)	(6.5%)	668.2	487.3	470.3	489.7	509.8
Net income ($ mil.)	(22.6%)	102.0	(97.6)	19.7	19.5	36.7
Market value ($ mil.)	(17.3%)	1,765.1	1,242.2	1,045.4	949.8	827.5
Employees	(4.3%)	4,300	3,700	3,700	3,600	3,600

CORE MOLDING TECHNOLOGIES INC
ASE: CMT

800 Manor Park Drive
Columbus, OH 43228-0183
Phone: 614 870-5000
Fax: –
Web: www.coremt.com

CEO: –
CFO: –
HR: –
FYE: December 31
Type: Public

The core business of Core Molding Technologies is fiberglass reinforced plastic and sheet molding composite materials. Through compression molding, sprayup, hand layup, and vacuum-assisted resin infusion molding, the company makes truck components (air deflectors, fenders, hoods) and personal watercraft parts (decks, hulls, and engine hatches). It divides its operations into two segments: Products and Tooling. Navistar International accounts for one-third sales, and other major customers include heavy-duty truck manufacturers Volvo and PACCAR. The company's sales are confined to North America.

	Annual Growth	12/19	12/20	12/21	12/22	12/23
Sales ($mil.)	5.9%	284.3	222.4	307.5	377.4	357.7
Net income ($ mil.)	–	(15.2)	8.2	4.7	12.2	20.3
Market value ($ mil.)	54.5%	28.1	121.9	73.7	112.4	160.4
Employees	0.5%	1,821	1,617	1,584	1,986	1,857

CORECARD CORP
NYS: CCRD

One Meca Way
Norcross, GA 30093
Phone: 770 381-2900
Fax: –
Web: www.corecard.com

CEO: J L Strange
CFO: Matthew A White
HR: –
FYE: December 31
Type: Public

Intelligent Software Solutions (ISS) is no dummy when it comes to software development and IT systems analysis. The privately-held company develops and integrates custom software for data visualization and analysis, pattern detection, and mission planning for the aerospace, defense, and maritime industries. Its products include a software tool that counters improvised explosive devices (Dfuze) and public safety management software tool (WebTAS). The company provides on-site product and development support and training. Customers include government military, intelligence agencies, and local law enforcement in the US and abroad.

	Annual Growth	12/19	12/20	12/21	12/22	12/23
Sales ($mil.)	13.0%	34.3	35.9	48.2	69.8	56.0
Net income ($ mil.)	(25.4%)	11.0	8.2	9.0	13.9	3.4
Market value ($ mil.)	(23.3%)	331.3	332.7	321.9	240.3	114.7
Employees	–	–	530	570	800	1,200

CORECIVIC INC
NYS: CXW

5501 Virginia Way
Brentwood, TN 37027
Phone: 615 263-3000
Fax: –
Web: www.corecivic.com

CEO: Damon T Hininger
CFO: David M Garfinkle
HR: Blake Changnon
FYE: December 31
Type: Public

CoreCivic is the nation's largest owner of partnership correctional, detention, and residential reentry facilities and one of the largest prison operators in the US. Through its CoreCivic Safety segment, it has around 45 correctional and detention facilities which it owns or manages for federal, state, and local government agencies. Federal clients account for about 55% of sales. The company also own properties for lease to third parties and used by government agencies through CoreCivic Properties and provides a number of non-residential correctional alternative services, including electronic monitoring and case management services through CoreCivic Community.

	Annual Growth	12/19	12/20	12/21	12/22	12/23
Sales ($mil.)	(1.1%)	1,980.7	1,905.5	1,862.6	1,845.3	1,896.6
Net income ($ mil.)	(22.7%)	188.9	54.2	(51.9)	122.3	67.6
Market value ($ mil.)	(4.4%)	1,959.3	738.4	1,123.9	1,303.2	1,638.0
Employees	(5.6%)	14,075	12,415	10,348	10,653	11,194

CORENERGY INFRASTRUCTURE TRUST INC
NBB: CORR Q

1100 Walnut, Ste. 3350
Kansas City, MO 64106
Phone: 816 875-3705
Fax: –
Web: www.corenergy.reit

CEO: David J Schulte
CFO: Robert L Waldron
HR: –
FYE: December 31
Type: Public

A closed-end investment management firm, CorEnergy Infrastructure Trust (formerly Tortoise Capital Resources) invests in privately held and public micro-cap energy companies, including midstream and downstream oil and gas companies and coal companies. The firm typically makes equity or debt investments in low-risk, established energy companies that will generate steadily increasing returns on its investments over the long term. CorEnergy, which has more than $90 million in assets under management, is managed by Tortoise Capital Advisors, a fund manager with five other publicly traded funds under management.

	Annual Growth	12/18	12/19	12/20	12/21	12/22
Sales ($mil.)	10.6%	89.2	85.9	11.3	128.1	133.6
Net income ($ mil.)	–	43.7	4.1	(306.1)	(11.5)	(12.8)
Market value ($ mil.)	(16.5%)	374.5	404.2	288.0	326.7	181.7
Employees	63.2%	22	16	21	155	156

CORENET GLOBAL, INC.

133 PEACHTREE ST NE STE 3000
ATLANTA, GA 303031804
Phone: 404 589-3200
Fax: –
Web: www.corenetglobal.org

CEO: Angela Cain
CFO: Dino S Piccini
HR: –
FYE: March 31
Type: Private

CoreNet Global's core competency is real estate. The organization provides programs and services to about 7,000 corporate real estate professionals organized into more than 50 chapters worldwide. CoreNet's offerings include educational programs, research, networking, and executive development. Headquartered in the US, the company also has international offices in Canada and across Europe, the Middle East, and the Asia/Pacific region. CoreNet was formed from the merger of International Development Research Council and The International Association of Corporate Real Estate Executives in 2002.

	Annual Growth	03/11	03/12	03/16	03/17	03/22
Sales ($mil.)	(4.7%)	–	16.4	13.8	13.4	10.1
Net income ($ mil.)	(6.1%)	–	1.7	0.9	0.8	0.9
Market value ($ mil.)	–	–	–	–	–	–
Employees	–	–	–	–	–	43

CORESITE REALTY CORPORATION

1001 17TH ST STE 500
DENVER, CO 802022461
Phone: 866 777-2673
Fax: –
Web: www.coresite.com

CEO: –
CFO: –
HR: –
FYE: December 31
Type: Private

CoreSite Realty is a real estate investment trust (REIT) which owns, develops, and operates these specialized facilities, which require enough power, security, and network interconnection to handle often complex IT operations. Its property portfolio includes about 25 operating data center facilities, with additional space under development. These properties comprise around 4.6 million rentable sq. ft. Tenants include enterprise organizations, communications service providers, media and content companies, and government agencies. CoreSite Realty started in 2001 as CRG West, a portfolio company of The Carlyle Group.

COREWELL HEALTH

100 MICHIGAN ST NE
GRAND RAPIDS, MI 495032560
Phone: 866 989-7999
Fax: –
Web: www.corewellhealth.org

CEO: –
CFO: –
HR: Jane Jahn
FYE: December 31
Type: Private

Corewell Health (formerly Spectrum Health) is a not-for-profit health system that provides health care and coverage with an exceptional team of more than 60,000 dedicated people?including more than 11,500 physicians and advanced practice providers and more than 15,000 nurses offering services in over 20 hospitals, around 300 outpatient locations and several post-acute facilities?and Priority Health, a provider-sponsored health plan serving over 1.2 million members.

	Annual Growth	06/18	06/19*	12/20	12/21	12/22
Sales ($mil.)	26.1%	–	6,884.4	8,299.8	9,179.1	13,805
Net income ($ mil.)	95.8%	–	332.6	714.2	599.2	2,498.1
Market value ($ mil.)	–	–	–	–	–	–
Employees	–	–	–	–	–	51,996

*Fiscal year change

CORIUM, LLC

11 FARNSWORTH ST FL 4
BOSTON, MA 022101210
Phone: 855 253-2407
Fax: –
Web: www.corium.com

CEO: Mark Sirgo
CFO: Robert S Breuil
HR: –
FYE: September 30
Type: Private

At its core, Corium International is all about transdermal (through the skin) and transmucosal (through the mucous membranes) drug delivery. Its development platforms enable transdermal delivery of large molecules (including vaccines, peptides and proteins) as well as small molecules difficult to deliver in a standard transdermal dosage form. With partners, the firm has already developed six marketed products in the prescription drug/consumer market, including four Crest Advanced Seal Whitestrips products. Corium is being acquired by health care fund Gurnet Point Capital, which is backed by Switzerland's richest person Ernesto Bertarelli.

CORMEDIX INC

300 Connell Drive, Suite 4200
Berkeley Heights, NJ 07922
Phone: 908 517-9500
Fax: 908 429-4307
Web: www.cormedix.com

NMS: CRMD
CEO: Matthew David
CFO: –
HR: –
FYE: December 31
Type: Public

CorMedix is a commercial-stage biopharmaceutical company which seeks to in-license, develop, and commercialize therapeutic products for the prevention and treatment of cardiac, renal, and infectious diseases. Its first commercial product in Europe is Neutrolin, a catheter lock for the prevention of catheter related bloodstream infections and maintenance of catheter patency in tunneled, cuffed, central venous catheters used for vascular access in hemodialysis, oncology, critical care, and other patients. CorMedix, controlled by a group of its officers, went public in early 2010.

	Annual Growth	12/19	12/20	12/21	12/22	12/23
Sales ($mil.)	–	0.3	0.2	0.2	0.0	–
Net income ($ mil.)	–	(16.4)	(22.0)	(28.2)	(29.7)	(46.3)
Market value ($ mil.)	(15.2%)	400.0	408.2	250.0	231.8	206.6
Employees	–	30	35	30	41	–

CORNELL UNIVERSITY

260 DAY HALL
ITHACA, NY 148532801
Phone: 607 254-4636
Fax: –
Web: www.cornell.edu

CEO: –
CFO: –
HR: Kathy Carpenter
FYE: June 30
Type: Private

Cornell is the federal land-grant institution of New York State, a private endowed university, a member of the Ivy League/Ancient Eight, and a partner of the State University of New York. The Ivy League school's some 25,900 students can select undergraduate, graduate, and professional courses from more than 15 colleges and schools. In addition to its Ithaca, New York, campus, the university has medical and professional programs in New York City and Doha, Qatar. Cornell's faculty includes about 2,865 of regular and part-time employee. It was founded in 1865 by Ezra Cornell and Andrew Dickson White.

	Annual Growth	06/10	06/11	06/12	06/16	06/17
Sales ($mil.)	5.2%	–	2,955.8	2,956.8	3,809.2	4,013.9
Net income ($ mil.)	3.2%	–	814.0	(342.0)	(442.4)	985.6
Market value ($ mil.)	–	–	–	–	–	–
Employees	–	–	–	–	–	12,207

CORNERSTONE AGENCY INC.

71 W 23RD ST 13TH FL
NEW YORK, NY 100104102
Phone: 212 741-7100
Fax: –
Web: www.cornerstoneagency.com

CEO: –
CFO: Anthony Holland
HR: –
FYE: December 31
Type: Private

Cornerstone Promotion is a marketing and branding firm that serves the music, film, technology, and fashion industries by specializing in urban and alternative lifestyles. The firm uses viral marketing and other nontraditional marketing disciplines to influence the cool trendsetters and early adopters. Cornerstone Promotion has provided brand consulting, radio promotion, field marketing, digital marketing, and event marketing services for such clients as Levi Strauss & Co., Coca-Cola, Converse, and Proctor & Gamble. Music industry veterans Rob Stone and Jon Cohen launched the firm in 1996, with Sprite as a major customer. Cornerstone Promotion operates from offices in Chicago, Los Angeles, and New York.

	Annual Growth	12/12	12/13	12/14	12/15	12/16
Sales ($mil.)	21.5%	–	–	–	0.3	0.3
Net income ($ mil.)	–	–	–	–	(0.0)	0.0
Market value ($ mil.)	–	–	–	–	–	–
Employees	–	–	–	–	–	30

CORNERSTONE BUILDING BRANDS, INC.

5020 WESTON PKWY STE 400
CARY, NC 275132322
Phone: 866 419-0042
Fax: –
Web: www.cornerstonebuildingbrands.com

CEO: Rose Lee
CFO: Jeffrey S Lee
HR: –
FYE: December 31
Type: Private

Cornerstone Building Brands is a leading North American integrated manufacturer of external building products, including vinyl windows, vinyl siding, stone veneer installation, metal accessories, metal roofing/wall systems, insulated metal panels, and a top-three position in engineered metal building systems for the commercial, residential, and repair and remodel construction industries. Its collection of leading brands include Ply Gem, Simonton, Atrium, American Craftsman, Silver Line, Great Lakes Window, and North Star. About 95% of total revenue comes from the US. In 2022, Cornerstone Building Brands was acquired by Clayton, Dubilier & Rice (CD&R) in an all-cash transaction with an enterprise value of approximately $5.8 billion, including the assumption of debt.

	Annual Growth	12/18	12/19	12/20	12/21	12/22
Sales ($mil.)	(17.5%)	–	4,889.7	4,617.4	5,583.1	2,744.1
Net income ($ mil.)	–	–	(15.4)	(482.8)	665.9	(63.5)
Market value ($ mil.)	–	–	–	–	–	–
Employees	–	–	–	–	–	21,700

CORNERSTONE ONDEMAND, INC.

1601 CLOVERFIELD BLVD STE 620S
SANTA MONICA, CA 904044178
Phone: 310 752-0200
Fax: –
Web: www.cornerstoneondemand.com

CEO: Himanshu Palsule
CFO: Chirag Shah
HR: Naomi Barrons
FYE: December 31
Type: Private

Cornerstone powers the future-ready workforce with adaptive HR solutions designed to unite technology, data, and content and inspire a work environment of growth, agility and success for all. With an AI-powered, skills-forward, experiential system designed for the contemporary workforce, Cornerstone helps organizations modernize their learning and development experience, deliver the most relevant content from anywhere, accelerate talent, and career mobility, and establish skills as the universal language of growth and success across their business. Cornerstone serves over 7,000 customers and 90 million users and is available in 180 countries and 50 languages.

CORNING INC

NYS: GLW

One Riverfront Plaza
Corning, NY 14831
Phone: 607 974-9000
Fax: –
Web: www.corning.com

CEO: Wendell P Weeks
CFO: Edward A Schlesinger
HR: Samantha Garcia
FYE: December 31
Type: Public

Corning Incorporated makes a diverse range of glass and ceramic products for optical communications, mobile consumer electronics, display technology, automotive, and life sciences markets. Its products include damage-resistant cover glass for mobile devices, precision glass for advanced displays, optical fiber, and automotive emissions control products, to name a few. Corning's signature Gorilla Glass is a chemically strengthened thin glass designed specifically to function as a cover, or back-enclosure glass, for mobile consumer electronic devices such as mobile phones, tablets, laptops, and smartwatches. The company operates about 125 manufacturing and processing facilities in around 15 countries but generates over 45% of its revenue in the Asia Pacific region. It was founded in 1936.

	Annual Growth	12/19	12/20	12/21	12/22	12/23
Sales ($mil.)	2.3%	11,503	11,303	14,082	14,189	12,588
Net income ($ mil.)	(11.8%)	960.0	512.0	1,906.0	1,316.0	581.0
Market value ($ mil.)	1.1%	23,870	29,520	30,529	26,191	24,969
Employees	0.2%	49,500	50,110	61,200	57,500	49,800

CORNING NATURAL GAS CORP

330 W WILLIAM ST
CORNING, NY 148302152
Phone: 607 936-3755
Fax: –
Web: www.corninggas.com

CEO: Michael I German
CFO: Firouzeh Sarhangi
HR: Nicole Astolfi
FYE: September 30
Type: Private

Corning Natural Gas has cornered the market for natural gas supply in Corning, New York. The company is a regulated transmission and distribution utility serving 14,500 residential and business customers in Corning and surrounding areas; the company also sells gas wholesale to two nearby communities (Elmira and Bath). It has about 586,000 decatherms of natural gas storage capacity, and 400 miles of gas distribution pipelines and 15,000 miles of service pipelines in its service area. In 2009 Corning Natural Gas had four major customers, venerable industrial concern Corning Incorporated, New York State Electric & Gas, Bath Electric, Gas & Water Systems, and Fortuna Energy.

CORPLAY INC

NYS: CPAY

3280 Peachtree Road, Suite 2400
Atlanta, GA 30305
Phone: 770 449-0479
Fax: –
Web: www.fleetcor.com

CEO: Ronald F Clarke
CFO: Charles R Freund
HR: –
FYE: December 31
Type: Public

FLEETCOR is a leading global provider of digital payment solutions that enables businesses to control purchases and make payments more effectively and efficiently. FLEETCOR's wide range of digitized solutions generally provides control, reporting, and automation benefits over the payment methods businesses often use, such as cash, paper checks, general purpose credit cards, as well as employee pay and reclaim processes.. The company now serves hundreds of thousands of business customers with millions of cardholders making payments to millions of vendors around the world.. The company's fuel partners include British Petroleum (BP), Arco, Speedway, Casey's and over 640 fuel marketers of all sizes. FLEETCOR generates about 60% of its revenue from domestic operations.

	Annual Growth	12/19	12/20	12/21	12/22	12/23
Sales ($mil.)	9.1%	2,648.8	2,388.9	2,833.7	3,427.1	3,757.7
Net income ($ mil.)	2.3%	895.1	704.2	839.5	954.3	981.9
Market value ($ mil.)	(0.4%)	20,634	19,566	16,053	13,173	20,268
Employees	4.8%	8,700	8,400	9,700	9,900	10,500

CORPORATE COMPUTER CENTERS, INC.

6990 CARROLL RD STE B
SAN DIEGO, CA 921213285
Phone: 858 597-0078
Fax: –
Web: www.hotchip.com

CEO: Christine R Roach
CFO: –
HR: –
FYE: December 31
Type: Private

Corporate Computer Centers builds custom workstations and servers and provides systems integration services. The company also resells computers, peripherals, networking equipment, and software from major manufacturers such as Hewlett-Packard and IBM. Corporate Computer Centers was founded in 1994; a predecessor, Hot Chip Computer, began operations in 1988.

CORPORATE FITNESS WORKS, INC.

1200 16TH ST N
SAINT PETERSBURG, FL 337051033
Phone: 727 522-2900
Fax: –
Web: www.corporatefitnessworks.com

CEO: –
CFO: –
HR: –
FYE: December 31
Type: Private

If working at a corporation leaves you less than fit, ask your boss to look up Corporate Fitness Works. The company provides consulting services to clients looking to create on-site physical fitness facilities. It also provides services such as design, development, and management training for customers ranging from government agencies to hospitals, office park developers, and retirement centers. Corporate Fitness Works manages some 45 locations for clients throughout the US, in states such as Washington, Maine, Texas, New York, Rhode Island, and Massachusetts. The company was founded in 1988 by CEO Sheila Drohan and president Brenda Loube.

CORPORATE TRAVEL CONSULTANTS, INC.

1717 N NAPER BLVD STE 300
NAPERVILLE, IL 605638839
Phone: 630 691-9100
Fax: –
Web: www.frosch.com

CEO: –
CFO: Gerry Lazar
HR: –
FYE: December 31
Type: Private

Corporate Travel Consultants (CorpTrav) brings order to the chaos of globetrotting go-getters and far-flung meetings on foreign soil. The company offers Internet-based booking, reporting, compliance, and management tools through CorpTrav On-line as well as meeting and incentive travel arrangements. Its online tools allow customers to check health advisories, travel alerts, and strike updates for planned destinations. CorpTrav has offices in Chicago, Dallas, New York, and San Francisco. The agency partners with GlobalStar to provide global support and service to travelers. CEO Bonnie Lorefice founded CorpTrav in 1976.

	Annual Growth	12/09	12/10	12/12	12/14	12/16
Sales ($mil.)	8.3%	–	135.8	209.4	222.4	219.6
Net income ($ mil.)	13.9%	–	0.5	1.9	1.6	1.1
Market value ($ mil.)	–	–	–	–	–	–
Employees	–	–	–	–	–	120

CORPORATE TRAVEL MANAGEMENT NORTH AMERICA, INC.

2120 S 72ND ST STE 450
OMAHA, NE 681242366
Phone: 402 399-4500
Fax: –
Web: us.travelctm.com

CEO: Bill Tech
CFO: –
HR: Christine Shimokawa
FYE: December 31
Type: Private

Travel and Transport can get you there and back. The company provides its business clients with travel management solutions such as air, hotel, vacation packages and meeting planning services. Its corporate travel services include travel policy development, vendor negotiation, analysis, and reporting. Travel and Transport is able to support international travel through its membership in RADIUS, a network of 90 US travel agencies with more than 3,300 offices worldwide. Travel and Transport also has a travel agent school and works with leisure travelers. The company, which was founded in 1946, is 100% owned by its employees.

CORPORATION FOR PUBLIC BROADCASTING

401 9TH ST NW STE 200
WASHINGTON, DC 200042129
Phone: 202 879-9600
Fax: –
Web: www.cpb.org

CEO: Laura G Ross
CFO: –
HR: –
FYE: September 30
Type: Private

This organization is made possible by a grant from the federal government and by support from viewers like you. The Corporation for Public Broadcasting (CPB) is a private, not-for-profit corporation created by the federal government that receives appropriations from Congress to help fund programming for more than 1,000 locally-owned public TV and radio stations. CPB-funded programs are distributed by the Public Broadcasting Service (PBS), National Public Radio (NPR), and Public Radio International (PRI). Funds are also used for research on media and education. CPB was created by Congress in 1967.

	Annual Growth	09/18	09/19	09/20	09/21	09/22
Sales ($mil.)	0.8%	–	498.3	570.5	678.6	510.9
Net income ($ mil.)	16.3%	–	17.2	29.6	(51.1)	27.1
Market value ($ mil.)	–	–	–	–	–	–
Employees	–	–	–	–	–	99

CORRELATE ENERGY CORP

220 Travis Street, Suite 501
Shreveport, LA 71101
Phone: 855 264-4060
Fax: –
Web: –

NBB: CIPI
CEO: –
CFO: –
HR: –
FYE: December 31
Type: Public

Frontier Oilfield Services (formerly TBX Resources) has switched from exploring for and producing natural gas to providing oilfield services to other companies that do. Frontier Oilfield Services now focuses on saltwater and drilling fluid disposal services for oil and gas producers and operators in East Texas. The company is targeting the Haynesville share area, where it believes as many as 35,000 additional wells will be drilled by 2023. Frontier currently manages the operations of Trinity Disposal and Trucking, which owns saltwater disposal wells and a fleet of trucks and trailers, and is seeking to buy the service. The company was formed in 2010.

	Annual Growth	12/18	12/19	12/20	12/21	12/22
Sales ($mil.)	31.6%	1.1	0.9	–	0.0	3.4
Net income ($ mil.)	–	(0.9)	(4.2)	(0.1)	(0.1)	(7.2)
Market value ($ mil.)	–	–	–	10.6	38.9	37.4
Employees	–	9	–	–	3	9

CORVEL CORP

5128 Apache Plume Road, Suite 400
Fort Worth, TX 76109
Phone: 817 390-1416
Fax: –
Web: www.corvel.com

NMS: CRVL
CEO: Michael G Combs
CFO: Brandon T O'Brien
HR: –
FYE: March 31
Type: Public

CorVel applies certain technology, including artificial intelligence, machine learning and natural language processing, to enhance the management of episodes of care and the related health-care costs. It partners with employers, TPAs, insurance companies and government agencies to assist its customers in managing the increasing medical cost of workers' compensation, group health and auto insurance, and in monitoring the quality of care provided to claimants. CorVel's diverse suite of solutions combines its integrated technologies with a human touch. Its services include claims management, bill review, preferred provider networks, utilization management, case management, pharmacy services, directed care, and Medicare services. Clients access CorVel's range of services through its CareMC web portal. Corvel was incorporated in 1987.

	Annual Growth	03/19	03/20	03/21	03/22	03/23
Sales ($mil.)	4.8%	595.7	592.2	552.6	646.2	718.6
Net income ($ mil.)	9.2%	46.7	47.4	46.4	66.4	66.4
Market value ($ mil.)	30.7%	1,120.1	935.9	1,761.4	2,892.0	3,267.0
Employees	3.3%	3,904	3,824	3,681	4,233	4,444

COSCO FIRE PROTECTION, INC.

29222 RANCHO VIEJO RD STE 205
SAN JUAN CAPISTRANO, CA 926751045
Phone: 714 974-8770
Fax: –
Web: www.coscofire.com

CEO: Keith R Fielding
CFO: –
HR: Max Hoynacki
FYE: December 31
Type: Private

COSCO Fire Protection designs, installs, and inspects automatic fire sprinkler systems, as well as fire alarm and detection systems. The company also designs and installs fire suppression systems. Its target customers include owners of office buildings and manufacturing facilities; hospitals and extended-care facilities; schools and universities; retail shopping malls; and government complexes and military facilities. COSCO operates in the western US (from offices in Alaska, California, Nevada, Oregon, and Washington). The company was founded in 1959 and is owned by Consolidated Fire Protection, which is itself a subsidiary of German fire protection firm Minimax.

	Annual Growth	12/13	12/14	12/15	12/16	12/17
Sales ($mil.)	12.8%	–	121.6	155.6	170.5	174.3
Net income ($ mil.)	33.7%	–	6.1	10.4	12.1	14.5
Market value ($ mil.)	–	–	–	–	–	–
Employees	–	–	–	–	–	601

COSI, INC.

200 SHEFFIELD ST STE 105
MOUNTAINSIDE, NJ 070922315
Phone: 866 580-2674
Fax: –
Web: www.getcosi.com

CEO: Mark Demilio
CFO: Edward Schatz
HR: –
FYE: December 28
Type: Private

Cosi's recipe calls for one part coffee house, one part sandwich shop, and one part cocktail bar. The company operates and franchises about 75 eclectic Cos caf s offering coffee and made-to-order sandwiches. Its menu also features breakfast items (including its bagel-inspired Squagels), salads, soups, and desserts. Most of the company's restaurants also offer dinner and drinks after 5 p.m., while its Cos Downtown units (primarily located in non-residential business districts) close in the evening. Cosi also offers delivery and catering services. About 45 of the locations are company-owned while the rest are franchised. In 2016 Cosi filed for Chapter 11 bankruptcy protection.

COSTAR GROUP, INC.

1331 L Street, N.W.
Washington, DC 20005
Phone: 202 346-6500
Fax: 877 739-0486
Web: www.costargroup.com

NMS: CSGP
CEO: Andrew C Florance
CFO: Scott T Wheeler
HR: –
FYE: December 31
Type: Public

CoStar is a leading provider of information, analytics, and online real estate marketplace services through its comprehensive, proprietary database of commercial real estate information in the US and the UK. Its highly complex database is comprised of hundreds of data fields, tracking such as location, ownership, site and zoning information, building characteristics, space and unit characteristics and availability, true ownership, sales and lease comparables, multi-family rents, vacancies and concessions, space requirements, retail locations, and tenant names among others. Clients include real estate brokers, agents, owners, developers, landlords, property managers, financial institutions, retailers, vendors, appraisers, investment banks, government agencies, and other parties involved in real estate. The company was founded in 1987. Majority of the company's sales were generated from North America.

	Annual Growth	12/19	12/20	12/21	12/22	12/23
Sales ($mil.)	15.1%	1,399.7	1,659.0	1,944.1	2,182.4	2,455.0
Net income ($ mil.)	4.4%	315.0	227.1	292.6	369.5	374.7
Market value ($ mil.)	(38.2%)	244,166	377,199	32,252	31,538	35,664
Employees	–	–	4,337	4,753	4,742	5,653

COSTCO WHOLESALE CORP

999 Lake Drive
Issaquah, WA 98027
Phone: 425 313-8100
Fax: –
Web: www.costco.com

NMS: COST
CEO: W C Jelinek
CFO: Richard A Galanti
HR: –
FYE: September 3
Type: Public

Operating nearly 840 membership warehouse stores, Costco is the nation's largest wholesale club operator. Primarily under the Costco Wholesale banner, it serves about 119 million cardholders in some 45 US states, Washington, DC, and Puerto Rico, and about 10 other countries. The company carries an average of approximately 4,000 active stock keeping units (SKUs) per warehouse in its core warehouse business, significantly less than other broadline retailers (many in bulk packaging), ranging from alcoholic beverages and appliances to fresh food, pharmaceuticals, and tires. Certain club memberships also offer products and services, such as car and home insurance, real estate services, and travel packages. Costco generates most of its sales in the US.

	Annual Growth	09/19*	08/20	08/21	08/22*	09/23
Sales ($mil.)	12.2%	152,703	166,761	195,929	226,954	242,290
Net income ($ mil.)	14.5%	3,659.0	4,002.0	5,007.0	5,844.0	6,292.0
Market value ($ mil.)	16.6%	130,518	154,256	199,407	235,486	240,990
Employees	5.6%	254,000	273,000	288,000	304,000	316,000

*Fiscal year change

COTERRA ENERGY INC

Three Memorial City Plaza, 840 Gessner Road, Suite 1400
Houston, TX 77024
Phone: 281 589-4600
Fax: 281 589-4653
Web: www.coterra.com

NYS: CTRA
CEO: Dan O Dinges
CFO: Scott C Schroeder
HR: –
FYE: December 31
Type: Public

Coterra Energy, Inc. is an independent oil and gas company engaged in the development, exploration and production of oil, natural gas, and NGLs. Coterra's assets are concentrated in areas with known hydrocarbon resources, which are conducive to multi-well, repeatable development programs. The company sells its products to a broad portfolio of customers, including industrial customers, local distribution companies, oil and gas marketers, major energy companies, pipeline companies, and power generation facilities. It operates in the Marcellus Shale in northeast Pennsylvania, the Permian Basin in west Texas and southeast New Mexico and the Anadarko Basin in the Mid-Continent region in Oklahoma.

	Annual Growth	12/19	12/20	12/21	12/22	12/23
Sales ($mil.)	30.1%	2,066.3	1,466.6	3,449.0	9,051.0	5,914.0
Net income ($ mil.)	24.3%	681.1	200.5	1,158.0	4,065.0	1,625.0
Market value ($ mil.)	10.0%	13,075	12,226	14,269	18,452	19,166
Employees	34.4%	274	503	936	981	894

COTIVITI HOLDINGS, INC.

1 GLENLAKE PKWY STE 1400
ATLANTA, GA 303283496
Phone: 770 379-2800
Fax: –
Web: www.cotiviti.com

CEO: –
CFO: –
HR: –
FYE: December 31
Type: Private

Cotiviti specializes in dotting i 's and crossing t 's. The company uses analytics technology to review health care claims and retail payments for accuracy, ensuring errors are minimized and correcting errors that have occurred. It counts among its clients some of the US' largest commercial, Medicare, and Medicaid managed health plans, as well as the US Centers for Medicare & Medicaid Services. The company also claims accuracy services to retailers, primarily in the US, Canada, and the UK. Cotiviti was created from the 2014 merger of Connolly and iHealth Technologies; the combined company went public in 2016.

COTTON INCORPORATED

6399 WESTON PKWY
CARY, NC 275132314
Phone: 919 678-2220
Fax: –
Web: www.cottoninc.com

CEO: –
CFO: –
HR: Jackie Cope
FYE: December 31
Type: Private

Cotton Incorporated battles both boll weevils and synthetic fibers. The organization bolsters the demand and profitability of the US cotton industry through its research and marketing efforts. To the public, Cotton Incorporated is known for its white-on-brown "Seal of Cotton" logo and its advertising slogan, "The fabric of our lives." Founded in 1970, Cotton Incorporated is funded by US growers of upland cotton, cotton importers, and cotton-product makers. Its board consists of representatives from each cotton-growing state -- all of whom are cotton producers -- and is overseen by the US Department of Agriculture.

	Annual Growth	12/12	12/13	12/14	12/15	12/19
Sales ($mil.)	(0.2%)	–	81.1	77.0	77.3	80.0
Net income ($ mil.)	–	–	5.5	(3.9)	0.3	(0.6)
Market value ($ mil.)	–	–	–	–	–	–
Employees						138

COTY, INC.

350 Fifth Avenue
New York, NY 10118
Phone: 212 389-7300
Fax: –
Web: www.coty.com

NYS: COTY
CEO: –
CFO: –
HR: –
FYE: June 30
Type: Public

Coty is one of the leading makers of fragrances, beauty, skin, and body care products for men and women across the globe. Its lineup ranges from moderately priced scents and cosmetics sold by mass retailers to prestige fragrances and premium skincare products found in hypermarkets, department stores, drugstores, and pharmacies. The company's nearly 35 owned or licensed brands include some of the world's most well-known, including COVERGIRL, Max Factor, philosophy, Escada, Calvin Klein, and Gucci. It generates most of its revenue outside North America. With a history that dates to 1904, Coty operates in more than 125 countries and territories.

	Annual Growth	06/19	06/20	06/21	06/22	06/23
Sales ($mil.)	(10.5%)	8,648.5	4,717.8	4,629.9	5,304.4	5,554.1
Net income ($ mil.)	–	(3,784.2)	(1,006.7)	(201.3)	259.5	508.2
Market value ($ mil.)	(2.1%)	11,428	3,812.0	7,965.2	6,830.9	10,481
Employees	(12.1%)	19,000	18,260	11,430	11,012	11,350

COUNCIL FOR ECONOMIC EDUCATION

122 E 42ND ST RM 1012
NEW YORK, NY 101681099
Phone: 212 730-7007
Fax: –
Web: www.councilforeconed.org

CEO: Nan J Morrison
CFO: –
HR: –
FYE: December 31
Type: Private

The Council for Economic Education (CEE, formerly the National Council on Economic Education) works to promote financial literacy by helping students develop economic and personal finance skills and knowledge. The not-for-profit organization provides training and supplementary materials for K-12 teachers through a network of state councils and university centers. Topics include saving and investing for retirement, credit card management, inflation and recession, and government spending. CEE programs annually reach more than 15 million students in the US and in some 30 other nations. The organization was founded in 1949.

	Annual Growth	12/13	12/14	12/15	12/21	12/22
Sales ($mil.)	5.0%	–	4.5	5.1	6.9	6.6
Net income ($ mil.)	–	–	(1.2)	(0.4)	1.2	(0.5)
Market value ($ mil.)	–	–	–	–	–	–
Employees						20

COUNCIL OF BETTER BUSINESS BUREAUS, INC.

4250 FAIRFAX DR STE 600
ARLINGTON, VA 222031665
Phone: 703 276-0100
Fax: –
Web: council.bbb.org

CEO: Stephen A Cox
CFO: Joseph E Dillon
HR: –
FYE: December 31
Type: Private

The Council of Better Business Bureaus (BBB) helps North American consumers and businesses know who's on the up-and-up. The non-profit organization comprises independent BBBs and branches in about 110 locations throughout North America, as well as some 200 national companies that have shown a commitment to business ethics. More than 300,000 companies that have demonstrated a similar commitment belong to local BBBs. The companies can promote their adherence to BBB standards; in return, they are subject to "reliability reports" that consist of any complaints clients or partners have had about them. BBBs work to resolve disputes between consumers and businesses and review companies' advertising.

	Annual Growth	12/07	12/08	12/09	12/11	12/15
Sales ($mil.)	4.3%	–	17.8	18.5	15.7	24.0
Net income ($ mil.)	–	–	(0.6)	(0.1)	(1.0)	1.5
Market value ($ mil.)	–	–	–	–	–	–
Employees						119

COUNCIL ON FOREIGN RELATIONS, INC.

58 E 68TH ST
NEW YORK, NY 100655953
Phone: 212 434-9400
Fax: –
Web: www.cfr.org

CEO: Carla Hills
CFO: –
HR: Antonia Martinez
FYE: June 30
Type: Private

The Council on Foreign Relations (CFR) was established in 1921, with support from the Rockefeller family, to provide a forum for government officials, corporate executives, journalists, students, and other interested parties to study and discuss world issues and the related impact on American foreign policy. The independent, nonpartisan council publishes Foreign Affairs, a magazine that comes out six times a year, along with books and studies by its own scholars. It also sponsors task forces and hosts meetings attended by world leaders, government officials, and diplomats. Prospective members must be US citizens (native-born or naturalized) and are nominated by an existing member. CFR currently has about 4,700 members.

	Annual Growth	06/15	06/16	06/18	06/19	06/22
Sales ($mil.)	3.6%	–	82.9	94.2	140.1	102.6
Net income ($ mil.)	32.3%	–	4.4	20.5	63.7	23.5
Market value ($ mil.)	–	–	–	–	–	–
Employees						200

COUNTERPART INTERNATIONAL INC

1919 PENNSYLVANIA AVE NW STE 425
WASHINGTON, DC 200063463
Phone: 571 447-5700
Fax: –
Web: www.counterpart.org

CEO: Jeffrey T Lariche
CFO: –
HR: Wendy R Bradford
FYE: September 30
Type: Private

Counterpart International finds perfect partners to work together in improving the quality of life for communities worldwide. The not-for-profit humanitarian relief organization provides food, medical supplies, disaster relief, technical and economic assistance, and training to countries in the former Soviet Union, Central Asian republics, Southeast Asia, Eastern Europe, and Africa. It helps to form coalitions of companies, governments, and grass roots organizations to build schools and hospitals, foster micro-businesses, and develop tourism in war-torn or disaster-affected areas. Counterpart was founded in 1965 as the Foundation for the Peoples of the South Pacific.

	Annual Growth	09/15	09/16	09/19	09/20	09/22
Sales ($mil.)	(8.3%)	–	62.3	60.6	39.9	37.1
Net income ($ mil.)	–	–	(0.3)	0.4	0.3	0.4
Market value ($ mil.)	–	–	–	–	–	–
Employees						45

COUNTRY CASUALTY INSURANCE CO. (BLOOMINGTON, IL)

1701 Towanda Avenue
Bloomington, IL 61701
Phone: 309 821-3000
Fax: –
Web: www.countryfinancial.com

CEO: Jim Jacobs
CFO: –
HR: Kristen Adams
FYE: December 31
Type: Public

COUNTRY Mutual Insurance sells property/casualty insurance in both rural and urban settings. A member of CC Services (also known as COUNTRY Financial, and part of the Illinois Agricultural Association), the company sells auto, home, farm, property, life and health and business insurance, as well as specialty products to individuals and businesses through approximately 2,000 financial representatives. The company provides policies in about 20 states in the midwestern, western, northeastern, and southeastern US. Founded in 1925, COUNTRY Mutual's subsidiaries include COUNTRY Preferred Insurance Company and COUNTRY Casualty Insurance Company.

	Annual Growth	12/97	12/98	12/99	12/00	12/01
Sales ($mil.)	7.7%	–	–	–	0.8	0.9
Net income ($ mil.)	28.1%	–	–	–	0.6	0.7
Market value ($ mil.)	–	–	–	–	–	–
Employees	–	–	–	–	–	–

COUNTRY INVESTORS LIFE ASSURANCE CO. (BLOOMINGTON, IL)

1701 Towanda Avenue
Bloomington, IL 61701
Phone: 309 821-3000
Fax: –
Web: www.countryfinancial.com

CEO: Jim Jacobs
CFO: –
HR: Kristen Adams
FYE: December 31
Type: Public

COUNTRY Mutual Insurance sells property/casualty insurance in both rural and urban settings. A member of CC Services (also known as COUNTRY Financial, and part of the Illinois Agricultural Association), the company sells auto, home, farm, property, life and health and business insurance, as well as specialty products to individuals and businesses through approximately 2,000 financial representatives. The company provides policies in about 20 states in the midwestern, western, northeastern, and southeastern US. Founded in 1925, COUNTRY Mutual's subsidiaries include COUNTRY Preferred Insurance Company and COUNTRY Casualty Insurance Company.

	Annual Growth	12/97	12/98	12/99	12/00	12/01
Assets ($mil.)	4.8%	905.5	946.6	1,006.7	1,020.9	1,092.5
Net income ($ mil.)	(27.7%)	8.5	10.1	8.4	8.9	2.3
Market value ($ mil.)	–	–	–	–	–	–
Employees	–	–	–	–	–	–

COUNTRY PRIDE COOPERATIVE, INC.

648 W 2ND ST
WINNER, SD 575801230
Phone: 605 842-2711
Fax: –
Web: www.countrypridecoop.com

CEO: –
CFO: –
HR: –
FYE: June 30
Type: Private

The Country Pride Cooperative has provided assistance to farmers in south central South Dakota since 1935. Country Pride offers it members an agronomy center, seed sales, grain storage and merchandising, a feed mill, and an equipment-rental center, as well as finance programs and farm supply stores an auto-service center and bulk refined fuel delivery. It also operates five convenience stores under the Cenex name. The co-op was created through the 2000 merger of two area cooperatives, Freeman Oil Cooperative (formed in 1935) and Dakota Pride Cooperative.

	Annual Growth	06/08	06/09	06/10	06/11	06/12
Sales ($mil.)	25.0%	–	–	109.4	139.6	170.8
Net income ($ mil.)	64.1%	–	–	1.3	2.3	3.4
Market value ($ mil.)	–	–	–	–	–	–
Employees	–	–	–	–	–	200

COUNTY OF ALAMEDA

1221 OAK ST STE 555
OAKLAND, CA 946124224
Phone: 510 272-6691
Fax: –
Web: www.acgov.org

CEO: Keith Carson
CFO: –
HR: Anna Montoya
FYE: June 30
Type: Private

Just east of San Francisco Bay lies Alameda County. Governed by a five-member board of supervisors, it includes 14 cities, among them Hayward, Oakland, and San Leandro. Nearly 60 departments handle services like behavioral health care, emergency medical, and human resources along with law enforcement, property tax assessment and collection, and community development for a population of more than 1.5 million. The county also serves as the keeper of birth, death, and marriage certificates and other public records. Its budget is more than $2.7 billion; most of it goes to public assistance, public protection, and health care. Alameda was incorporated in 1853 from parts of neighboring Contra Costa and Santa Clara counties.

	Annual Growth	06/11	06/12	06/13	06/14	06/15
Sales ($mil.)	4.1%	–	2,403.0	2,622.5	2,579.8	2,714.7
Net income ($ mil.)	–	–	(155.8)	65.7	203.0	(26.6)
Market value ($ mil.)	–	–	–	–	–	–
Employees	–	–	–	–	–	8,000

COUNTY OF LOS ANGELES

500 W TEMPLE ST STE 437
LOS ANGELES, CA 900122706
Phone: 213 974-1101
Fax: –
Web: www.lacounty.gov

CEO: Fesia Davenport
CFO: –
HR: Christian Martinez
FYE: June 30
Type: Private

The County of Los Angeles could easily be its own country; all it really needs is just an "r." It encompasses more than 4,000 square miles, 88 cities, two islands, and has a population of more than 10 million. The regional level of state government provides such services as law enforcement, property assessment, tax collection, public health protection, and other social services within its boundaries (sometimes sharing and often providing municipal services for unincorporated cities). The county's elected Board of Supervisors provide political direction, filling executive, legislative, and judicial roles, while the various departments manage daily operations. LA County has an annual budget of nearly $30 billion.

	Annual Growth	06/16	06/17	06/18	06/19	06/20
Sales ($mil.)	9.0%	–	–	21,191	23,511	25,198
Net income ($ mil.)	(10.4%)	–	–	403.5	915.5	324.0
Market value ($ mil.)	–	–	–	–	–	–
Employees	–	–	–	–	–	101,980

COUSINS PROPERTIES INC

NYS: CUZ

3344 Peachtree Road N.E., Suite 1800
Atlanta, GA 30326-4802
Phone: 404 407-1000
Fax: –
Web: www.cousins.com

CEO: M C Connolly
CFO: Gregg D Adzema
HR: Nataly McAlpin
FYE: December 31
Type: Public

Cousins Properties, a real estate investment trust (REIT) which buys, develops, and manages Class-A office properties mainly in high-growth markets in the Sunbelt region of the US. Its portfolio includes 18.3 million sq. ft. of office space and 620,000 square feet of mixed-use space in Atlanta, Austin, Dallas, Tampa, Nashville and Charlotte. The company conducts its operations through Cousins Properties, LP ("CPLP"). Its other subsidiary, Cousins TRS Services LLC ("CTRS"), also manages its own real estate portfolio and also provides real estate related services for other parties.

	Annual Growth	12/19	12/20	12/21	12/22	12/23
Sales ($mil.)	5.1%	657.5	740.3	755.1	762.3	802.9
Net income ($ mil.)	(13.8%)	150.4	237.3	278.6	166.8	83.0
Market value ($ mil.)	(12.3%)	6,254.1	5,085.3	6,114.5	3,839.0	3,696.3
Employees	(2.0%)	331	316	294	286	305

COVANTA HOLDING CORPORATION

445 SOUTH ST
MORRISTOWN, NJ 079606475
Phone: 862 345-5000
Fax: –
Web: www.covanta.com

CEO: Azeez Mohammed
CFO: Bradford J Helgeson
HR: John Atkinson
FYE: December 31
Type: Private

Covanta Holding Corporation is a leader in sustainable materials management providing environmental solutions to businesses and communities across North America. Through its network of facilities and state-of-the-art services, Covanta is a single-source partner in solving today's most complex environmental challenges. It treats and recycles municipal solid waste and operates Waste-to-Energy (WtE) facilities currently in commercial operation and processes approximately 21 million tons of solid waste annually. The company entered the waste business in the early 1980s.

COVENANT HEALTH

100 FORT SANDERS WEST BLVD
KNOXVILLE, TN 379223353
Phone: 865 531-5555
Fax: –
Web: www.covenanthealth.com

CEO: Jim Vandersteeg
CFO: John Geppi
HR: –
FYE: December 31
Type: Private

Covenant Health has made a pact to provide good health to the good people of Tennessee. The not-for-profit health care system, established in 1996, provides a variety of medical services through seven acute care hospitals, a psychiatric hospital and a number of specialty outpatient centers offering geriatrics, pediatric care, cancer services, weight management, and diagnostics. Covenant Health also operates home health and hospice agencies and a physician practice management company. Covenant Health provides staffing and medical management services to its affiliated facilities, and to make itself a really well-rounded health care provider, it operates the Covenant Health Federal Credit Union.

	Annual Growth	12/18	12/19	12/20	12/21	12/22
Sales ($mil.)	4.1%	–	1,407.0	1,470.1	1,572.4	1,589.2
Net income ($ mil.)	–	–	183.9	158.6	178.6	(200.4)
Market value ($ mil.)	–	–	–	–	–	–
Employees	–	–	–	–	–	10,000

COVENANT HEALTH SYSTEM

3615 19TH ST
LUBBOCK, TX 794101209
Phone: 806 725-1011
Fax: –
Web: www.covenanthealth.org

CEO: –
CFO: –
HR: –
FYE: December 31
Type: Private

Covenant Health System ties West Texas and Eastern New Mexico together with quality health care. The health services provider offers some 1,100 beds in its five primary acute-care and specialty hospitals; it also manages about a dozen affiliated community hospitals. Covenant Health System, part of Providence St. Joseph Health, also maintains a network of family health care and medical clinics. Covenant Health System's major facilities are Covenant Medical Center, Covenant Specialty Hospital, and Covenant Women's and Children's Hospital. The health system also includes some 20 clinics and 50 physician practices, and its extensive outreach programs target isolated rural communities with mobile services.

	Annual Growth	06/08	06/09	06/13	06/15*	12/21
Sales ($mil.)	(18.2%)	–	1,185.2	552.9	703.0	106.5
Net income ($ mil.)	–	–	(38.3)	35.7	76.3	8.2
Market value ($ mil.)	–	–	–	–	–	–
Employees	–	–	–	–	–	5,000

*Fiscal year change

COVENANT HOUSE

5 PENN PLZ FL 3
NEW YORK, NY 100011810
Phone: 212 613-0300
Fax: –
Web: www.covenanthouse.org

CEO: Kevin Ryan
CFO: –
HR: –
FYE: June 30
Type: Private

Young people rely on Covenant House to keep its promises. The not-for-profit group offers outreach and crisis centers for homeless and runaway youths. Its centers offer food, shelter, clothing, and medical and counseling services, as well as job skills and substance abuse and parenting programs. There are about 15 centers in the US, two in Canada, and one each in Mexico, Honduras, and Nicaragua. Its Rights of Passage Programs and Covenant House Crisis Shelters served more than 15,000 people and the entire organization reaches some 71,000 homeless kids annually. The group also operates the Nineline (1-800-999-9999) for runaways. Covenant House was founded in 1972 by Franciscan priest Father Bruce Ritter.

	Annual Growth	06/08	06/09	06/10	06/11	06/13
Sales ($mil.)	2.7%	–	–	54.3	56.7	58.7
Net income ($ mil.)	–	–	–	(10.2)	(5.5)	(7.4)
Market value ($ mil.)	–	–	–	–	–	–
Employees	–	–	–	–	–	1,860

COVENANT LOGISTICS GROUP INC

NMS: CVLG

400 Birmingham Hwy.
Chattanooga, TN 37419
Phone: 423 821-1212
Fax: 423 821-5442
Web: www.covenanttransport.com

CEO: David R Parker
CFO: –
HR: –
FYE: December 31
Type: Public

Covenant Logistics Group (formerly Covenant Transportation Group (CTG)) is a provider of expedited freight transportation, primarily using two-person driver teams in transcontinental lanes. The company operates a fleet of over 2,135 tractors and some 5,365 trailers, including both dry vans and temperature-controlled units. In addition to for-hire transportation, Covenant offers dedicated contract carriage and freight brokerage services. The company gets business from manufacturers, retailers, and food and beverage shippers. Covenant was founded in 1986 and has expanded its services to include a wide array of transportation and logistics services for its customers.

	Annual Growth	12/19	12/20	12/21	12/22	12/23
Sales ($mil.)	5.4%	894.5	838.6	1,046.0	1,216.9	1,103.6
Net income ($ mil.)	59.8%	8.5	(42.7)	60.7	108.7	55.2
Market value ($ mil.)	37.4%	168.9	193.6	345.5	451.9	601.8
Employees	–	5,850	5,100	4,659	4,753	–

COVENANT MEDICAL CENTER, INC.

1447 N HARRISON ST
SAGINAW, MI 486024727
Phone: 989 583-0000
Fax: –
Web: www.covenanthealthcare.com

CEO: Edward Bruff
CFO: Mark Gronda
HR: –
FYE: June 30
Type: Private

Covenant Medical Center (operating as Covenant HealthCare) has made a pact with Wolverine Staters to try to keep them in good health. The not-for-profit health care provider operates more than 20 inpatient and outpatient care facilities, including its two main Covenant Medical Center campuses. It serves residents in a 20-county area of east-central Michigan, with additional facilities in Bay City, Frankenmuth, and Midland. Specialized care services include cardiovascular health, cancer treatment, and obstetrics. The regional health care system has more about 650 beds.

	Annual Growth	06/14	06/15	06/16	06/21	06/22
Sales ($mil.)	5.6%	–	536.0	579.6	776.9	787.1
Net income ($ mil.)	–	–	31.3	40.3	(29.8)	(3.4)
Market value ($ mil.)	–	–	–	–	–	–
Employees	–	–	–	–	–	4,000

COVER-ALL TECHNOLOGIES INC.

412 MOUNT KEMBLE AVE 110C
MORRISTOWN, NJ 079606675
Phone: 973 461-5200
Fax: –
Web: www.cover-all.com

CEO: –
CFO: –
HR: –
FYE: December 31
Type: Private

Cover-All Technologies keeps insurers covered. The company offers software and services for carriers, agents, and brokers in the property/casualty insurance industry. Cover-All's software, which the company licenses and offers as a hosted application, automates insurance rating and policy issuance. Its My Insurance Center site, an Internet-based portal for insurance professionals, helps agents with policy quoting, rating, issuance, and billing; provides quick access to policy information; and offers applications for managing insurance agencies. The company also provides product customization, data integration, and other support services that keep the software up-to-date on industry information and regulations.

COVERALL NORTH AMERICA, INC.

350 SW 12TH AVE
DEERFIELD BEACH, FL 334423106
Phone: 561 922-2500
Fax: –
Web: www.coverall.com

CEO: –
CFO: Charlie Daniel
HR: Kathy Jones
FYE: December 31
Type: Private

Coverall North America, operating as Coverall Health-Based Cleaning System, has commercial cleaning covered. The company is a franchisor of commercial cleaning businesses. Through about 60 support centers and over 8,000 franchisees worldwide, the company offers franchises that provides janitorial services to fitness facilities, retail locations, office buildings, health care facilities, manufacturing and industrial plants, and educational facilities. The company's local Support Centers provide training, support, commercial cleaning and other programs to its Coverall Franchised Businesses. Headquartered in Deerfield Beach, Florida, the company was founded in 1985.

	Annual Growth	12/03	12/04	12/05	12/06	12/07
Assets ($mil.)	6.0%	–	–	50.1	53.4	56.3
Net income ($ mil.)	201.3%	–	–	1.5	6.7	13.2
Market value ($ mil.)	–	–	–	–	–	–
Employees	–	–	–	–	–	476

COVETRUS NORTH AMERICA, LLC

12 MOUNTFORT ST
PORTLAND, ME 041014307
Phone: 888 280-2221
Fax: –
Web: www.covetrus.com

CEO: –
CFO: –
HR: Marcedes Williams
FYE: December 31
Type: Private

Covetrus is a global animal-health technology and services company dedicated to supporting the companion, equine, and large-animal veterinary markets. The company develops, provides, and supports veterinary practices with a wide range of veterinary software systems. These technology solutions include practice management software, data-driven applications, client communications tools, and related services, which are designed to increase staff efficiency and improve business health, allowing veterinarians and their staff more time to provide patient care. It also offers solutions that integrate with its software platforms, including client communication services, reminders, data backup services, hardware sales and support, and credit card processing. Its main proprietary brands are Vi, Kruuse, SmartPak, and Calibra, along with Covetrus-branded products. Covetrus is to be acquired by Clayton, Dubilier & Rice and TPG at an enterprise valuation of approximately $4 billion. Revenue outside of the US was about 40% in 2021.

COVISINT CORPORATION

26533 EVERGREEN RD STE 500
SOUTHFIELD, MI 480764234
Phone: 248 483-2000
Fax: –
Web: www.opentext.com

CEO: –
CFO: –
HR: –
FYE: March 31
Type: Private

Covisint keeps things copacetic between buyers and suppliers, partners and customers with its enterprise and supply chain software. The company provides cloud-based systems for integrating business information and processes between links in the supply chain. The Compuware subsidiary offers industry-tailored products and services to customers in the automotive, energy, financial services, and health care sectors. Customers, which include a number of major car manufacturers, use its products to share applications with registered users, automate partner lifecycle administration and management, and create partner portals for information exchange and data messaging. Covisint agreed to sell to Open Text in 2017.

	Annual Growth	03/13	03/14	03/15	03/16	03/17
Sales ($mil.)	(10.9%)	–	–	88.5	76.0	70.2
Net income ($ mil.)	–	–	–	(38.6)	(14.9)	(12.7)
Market value ($ mil.)	–	–	–	–	–	–
Employees	–	–	–	–	–	382

COVISTA COMMUNICATIONS INC.

4803 Highway 58 North
Chattanooga, TN 37416
Phone: 423 648-9700
Fax: –
Web: www.covistacom.com

NBB: CVST
CEO: –
CFO: –
HR: –
FYE: January 31
Type: Public

Covista Communications offers alternative telecommunications services to business and residential customers, mostly in Georgia, New Jersey, New York, Pennsylvania, and Tennessee. Once primarily a long-distance provider, the company has added local service in some markets; it also provides Internet and data networking services. In addition to commercial and residential service, Covista sells wholesale termination services and colocation facilities to telecom carriers. The company operates its own switching facilities in Chattanooga, Tennessee; Dallas; and Minneapolis.

	Annual Growth	01/01	01/02	01/03	01/04	01/05
Sales ($mil.)	(18.1%)	133.2	95.3	101.0	84.1	59.9
Net income ($ mil.)	–	–	(8.6)	(12.0)	(9.4)	(0.9)	(5.3)
Market value ($ mil.)	4.7%	26.7	123.9	65.6	53.5	32.1
Employees	(6.5%)	212	243	263	238	162

COWAN SYSTEMS, LLC

4555 HOLLINS FERRY RD
BALTIMORE, MD 212274610
Phone: 410 247-0800
Fax: –
Web: www.cowansystems.com

CEO: Dennis Morgan
CFO: –
HR: Rose Maddox
FYE: December 31
Type: Private

Cowan Systems is a leader in the transportation industry. The company takes immense pride in the service that it provides to all of its customers. Working with a full scope of customers, including many Fortune 500 companies and small businesses, Cowan specializes in dedicated truckload, intermodal, warehousing, brokerage, and driver staffing. Cowan has about 2,000 tractors and over 6,000 trailers, as well as a fleet of nearly 2,000 power units Its warehousing division is a premier 3PL with warehousing facilities located throughout the Mid-Atlantic area. It offers 100% supply chain solutions, including local and long haul trucking in and out of Cowan facilities.

COX ENTERPRISES, INC.

6305 PEACHTREE DUNWOODY RD
ATLANTA, GA 303284535
Phone: 678 645-0000
Fax: –
Web: www.coxenterprises.com

CEO: Alex Taylor
CFO: Dallas Clement
HR: Marybeth N Leamer
FYE: December 31
Type: Private

Cox Enterprises is a private, family-owned holding company with cable fiber broadband networks and automobile listing services. Flagship subsidiary Cox Communications is the third largest US cable serving nearly 7 million customers in more than 30 states providing connections and advanced cloud and managed IT services. Cox Automotive has about 45,000 auto dealer clients across five continents and many other throughout the automotive industry it acts as a clearing house for buying and selling cars through platforms like Autotrader, Dealer.com, and Manheim (auto auctions). Cox is pushing beyond the boundaries of its core businesses with investments in adjacent industries and high growth potential markets, such as cleantech, healthcare, digital media and the public sector. Cox Enterprises was founded by James Middleton Cox in 1898.

	Annual Growth	12/96	12/97	12/98	12/99	12/19
Sales ($mil.)	(30.4%)	–	–	–	2,318.1	1.7
Net income ($ mil.)	(35.9%)	–	–	–	881.9	0.1
Market value ($ mil.)	–	–	–	–	–	–
Employees	–	–	–	–	–	55,000

COZEN O'CONNOR

1650 MARKET ST STE 2800
PHILADELPHIA, PA 191037325
Phone: 215 665-2053
Fax: –
Web: www.cozen.com

CEO: –
CFO: –
HR: –
FYE: December 31
Type: Private

Cozen O'Connor is a full-service North American law firm of more than 825 attorneys in approximately 30 cities across two continents. Through the firm's main practice areas of business litigation, construction law, and government relations, Cozen O'Connor provides legal assistance in everything from bankruptcy, insolvency and restructuring and other mass torts for large corporations and other companies. It serves as a trusted adviser and lead dealmaker on behalf of an impressive roster of national and international corporate clients. Cozen O'Connor's diverse client list includes global FORTUNE 500 companies, middle-market firms poised for growth, ambitious startups, and high-profile individuals.

	Annual Growth	12/17	12/18	12/19	12/21	12/22
Sales ($mil.)	(12.1%)	–	–	2.2	1.0	1.5
Net income ($ mil.)	–	–	–	0.4	(0.5)	(0.2)
Market value ($ mil.)	–	–	–	–	–	–
Employees	–	–	–	–	–	1,100

CPI AEROSTRUCTURES, INC.   ASE: CVU

91 Heartland Blvd.
Edgewood, NY 11717
Phone: 631 586-5200
Fax: –
Web: www.cpiaero.com

CEO: Dorith Hakim
CFO: Andrew L Davis
HR: –
FYE: December 31
Type: Public

To build an aircraft, some assembly is required, and CPI Aerostructures is ready. CPI Aero delivers contract production of structural aircraft subassemblies, chiefly for the US Air Force and other US military customers. Military products include skin panels, flight control surfaces, leading edges, wing tips, engine components, cowl doors, and nacelle and inlet assemblies. The lineup is used on military aircraft, such as the C-5A Galaxy and C-130 Hercules cargo jets, E-3 Sentry AWACs jet, and T-38 Talon jet trainer. As a subcontractor to OEMs, CPI Aero also makes aprons and engine mounts for commercial aircraft, such as business jets. Government prime and subcontracts represent a majority of CPI Aero's sales

	Annual Growth	12/18	12/19	12/20	12/21	12/22
Sales ($mil.)	(0.2%)	83.9	87.5	87.6	103.4	83.3
Net income ($ mil.)	42.7%	2.2	(4.5)	(1.3)	6.8	9.2
Market value ($ mil.)	(15.8%)	79.7	84.2	47.9	34.1	40.0
Employees	(7.2%)	281	258	267	249	208

CPI CARD GROUP INC   NMS: PMTS

10368 W. Centennial Road
Littleton, CO 80127
Phone: 720 681-6304
Fax: –
Web: www.cpicardgroup.com

CEO: John Lowe
CFO: Jeffrey Hochstadt
HR: Gayle Mines
FYE: December 31
Type: Public

CPI Card Group issues credit, debit, and prepaid debit cards on the large networks provided by Visa, MasterCard, American Express, and Discover in the US, and Interac in Canada. Beyond manufacturing roughly one billion debit and credit cards annually, it also provides card personalization services and tamper evident security packaging solutions to reduce prepaid debit card fraud. CPI mainly markets it products and services to card-issuing national, regional, and community banks; credit unions; and retailers selling prepaid debit cards; as well as managers of prepaid debit programs, group service providers, and card processors. CPI went public in 2015, and serves customers in the US, Canada, and Western Europe.

	Annual Growth	12/19	12/20	12/21	12/22	12/23
Sales ($mil.)	12.4%	278.1	312.2	375.1	475.7	444.5
Net income ($ mil.)	–	(4.5)	16.1	15.9	36.5	24.0
Market value ($ mil.)	114.9%	10.3	9.1	212.3	413.0	219.7
Employees	7.1%	1,100	1,000	1,150	1,375	1,448

CPP INTERNATIONAL, LLC

8616 STRIDER DR
CHARLOTTE, NC 282121519
Phone: 704 588-3190
Fax: –
Web: –

CEO: –
CFO: –
HR: –
FYE: December 31
Type: Private

CPP International has some bright ideas for school supplies and office essentials. The company, also known as Carolina Pad, makes notebooks, loose-leaf binders, files and folders, calendars, planners, pens and pencils, arts and crafts supplies, and other school and office accessories. Its products feature colorful, bold graphic designs. CPP sells its products through mass merchandisers, supermarkets, drugstores, and office supply retailers throughout the US, Canada, and Mexico. Founded in 1945 by Joseph Hall, the company originally manufactured and distributed supplies to schools in the Carolinas and Virginia.

CPS TECHNOLOGIES CORP   NAS: CPSH

111 South Worcester Street
Norton, MA 02766-2102
Phone: 508 222-0614
Fax: –
Web: www.cpstechnologysolutions.com

CEO: Francis J Hughes Jr
CFO: –
HR: –
FYE: December 30
Type: Public

CPS Technologies makes thermal management components for electronics using aluminum silicon carbide (ALSiC) metal matrix composites. Products include substrates, baseplates, and heat spreaders that are used by customers in motor controller and wireless communications component applications. CPS is working with the US Army on using its composite technology in armor for military vehicles. The company also licenses its technology to other manufacturers; revenue from licenses and royalties, however, has dwindled away to virtually nothing. CPS Technologies makes more than two-thirds of its sales to locations outside the US, although the majority of its customers are actually based in the US.

	Annual Growth	12/19	12/20	12/21	12/22	12/23
Sales ($mil.)	6.4%	21.5	20.9	22.4	26.6	27.6
Net income ($ mil.)	–	(0.6)	0.9	3.2	2.1	1.4
Market value ($ mil.)	22.3%	15.2	33.2	63.0	39.1	34.1
Employees	(9.9%)	152	104	90	86	100

CRA INTERNATIONAL INC

NMS: CRAI

200 Clarendon Street
Boston, MA 02116-5092
Phone: 617 425-3000
Fax: 617 425-3132
Web: www.crai.com

CEO: Paul Maleh
CFO: Daniel K Mahoney
HR: –
FYE: December 30
Type: Public

CRA International, doing business as Charles River Associates, employs about 940 consultants offering economic, financial, and management services to corporate clients, attorneys, government agencies, and other clients. Practices are organized into two areas. Litigation, Regulatory, and Financial Consulting advises on topics such as antitrust & competition, damages & valuation, financial accounting valuation, and insurance economics among others. Management Consulting focus areas include auctions and competitive bidding, corporate & business strategy, and enterprise risk management among others. Its consultants have backgrounds in a wide range of disciplines, including economics, business, corporate finance, materials sciences, accounting, and engineering. Most of its revenue comes from the US. CRA was founded in 1965.

	Annual Growth	12/19*	01/21	01/22*	12/22	12/23
Sales ($mil.)	8.4%	451.4	508.4	565.9	590.9	624.0
Net income ($ mil.)	16.7%	20.7	24.5	41.7	43.6	38.5
Market value ($ mil.)	16.6%	371.5	353.2	647.4	849.0	685.5
Employees	6.5%	779	831	861	939	1,004

*Fiscal year change

CRACKER BARREL OLD COUNTRY STORE INC

NMS: CBRL

305 Hartmann Drive
Lebanon, TN 37087-4779
Phone: 615 444-5533
Fax: –
Web: –

CEO: Sandra B Cochran
CFO: Craig A Pommells
HR: –
FYE: July 28
Type: Public

Cracker Barrel Old Country Store owns and operates about 665 of its flagship restaurants known for their rustic old country-store design offering a full-service restaurant menu that features home-style country food and a wide variety of decorative and functional items such as rocking chairs, holiday and seasonal gifts, toys, apparel, cookware and foods. It holds a non-controlling stake in entertainment venue chain Punch Bowl Social. The company was founded in 1969.

	Annual Growth	08/19*	07/20	07/21	07/22	07/23
Sales ($mil.)	2.9%	3,072.0	2,522.8	2,821.4	3,267.8	3,442.8
Net income ($ mil.)	(18.4%)	223.4	(32.5)	254.5	131.9	99.1
Market value ($ mil.)	(14.1%)	3,816.0	2,447.3	3,016.9	2,106.1	2,076.9
Employees	1.3%	73,000	55,000	70,000	73,000	77,000

*Fiscal year change

CRAIN COMMUNICATIONS, INC.

1155 GRATIOT AVE
DETROIT, MI 482072732
Phone: 313 446-6000
Fax: –
Web: www.crain.com

CEO: Keith E Crain
CFO: Bob Recchia
HR: Venetia Brna
FYE: December 31
Type: Private

Crain Communications is one of the oldest, privately held, family-owned media companies that produces trusted and relevant news across digital platforms, publications, lead generation, research and data products, digital platforms, custom publishing, and events with uncompromising integrity. Reaching approximately 78 million readers globally, the company's portfolio consists of almost 25 brands. Its portfolio covers such areas as the automotive industry (Automotive News and Automobilwoche), regional business publication (Crain's Business in Chicago, Cleveland, Detroit, New York, and Grand Rapids), and media (AdAge and Creativity). The family-owned company was started by G. D. Crain in 1916.

CRANE NXT CO

NYS: CXT

950 Winter Street, 4th Floor
Waltham, MA 02451
Phone: 610 430-2510
Fax: –
Web: www.craneco.com

CEO: Max H Mitchell
CFO: Richard A Maue
HR: –
FYE: December 31
Type: Public

Redco Corporation (formerly Crane Co.) is a diversified manufacturer of highly engineered industrial products. Founded in 1855, Crane provides products and solutions to customers in the chemicals, oil and gas, power, automated payment solutions, banknote design and production and aerospace and defense markets, along with a wide range of general industrial and consumer related end markets. The company operates through Process Flow Technologies, Payment & Merchandising Technologies, and Aerospace & Electronics segments. Redco, which operates in about 20 countries, spanning six continents, generates about 60% of total sales in the US.

	Annual Growth	12/18	12/19	12/20	12/21	12/22
Sales ($mil.)	0.2%	3,345.5	3,283.1	2,936.9	3,180.0	3,374.9
Net income ($ mil.)	4.6%	335.6	133.3	181.0	435.4	401.1
Market value ($ mil.)	8.6%	4,065.6	4,865.4	4,374.2	5,730.0	5,657.9
Employees	(2.2%)	12,000	13,000	11,000	11,000	11,000

CRAWFORD & CO.

NYS: CRD A

5335 Triangle Parkway
Peachtree Corners, GA 30092
Phone: 404 300-1000
Fax: –
Web: www.crawfordandcompany.com

CEO: Larry C Thomas
CFO: W B Swain Jr
HR: –
FYE: December 31
Type: Public

Crawford & Company is the world's largest publicly listed independent provider of claims management and outsourcing services for risk management and insurance companies as well as self-insured entities. Clients turn to Crawford for field investigation and the evaluation of property and casualty insurance claims. In addition to field investigation and claims evaluation, it also provides initial loss reporting services for its claimants, loss mitigation services such as medical bill review, medical case management and vocational rehabilitation, risk management information services, and loss fund administration to pay their claims. The company operates through a global network of service providers in more than 70 countries and generates more than 60% of its revenue in the US. Crawford was founded in 1941 by Jim Crawford.

	Annual Growth	12/19	12/20	12/21	12/22	12/23
Sales ($mil.)	5.9%	1,047.6	1,016.2	1,139.2	1,231.2	1,316.9
Net income ($ mil.)	25.1%	12.5	28.3	30.7	(18.3)	30.6
Market value ($ mil.)	3.5%	562.9	362.7	367.6	272.9	646.9
Employees	3.2%	9,000	8,985	9,400	10,400	10,200

CRAWFORD MEMORIAL FOUNDATION

1000 N ALLEN ST
ROBINSON, IL 624541114
Phone: 618 544-3131
Fax: –
Web: www.crawfordmh.org

CEO: Dough Florkauski
CFO: –
HR: –
FYE: April 30
Type: Private

It's not likely you'll come across a member of the Bush family at this Crawford. Crawford Memorial Hospital & Health Services provides acute care to residents of Crawford County in Illinois. Its hospital has about 25 acute care beds. Specialized services include cardiac rehabilitation, orthopedics, home health care, and emergency medicine. The hospital, founded in 1961, also offers a birthing center with prenatal education and breast-feeding classes. Crawford Memorial Hospital & Health Services operates a handful of rural health clinics staffed with physicians and physicians' assistants offering primary care to medically underserved areas.

	Annual Growth	04/09	04/10	04/12	04/13	04/16
Sales ($mil.)	(13.4%)	–	0.0	0.0	0.1	0.0
Net income ($ mil.)		–	–	(0.1)	(0.0)	0.0	(0.0)
Market value ($ mil.)		–	–	–	–	–
Employees		–	–	–	–	320

CRAWFORD UNITED CORP

NBB: CRAW A

10514 Dupont Avenue, Suite 200
Cleveland, OH 44108
Phone: 216 243-2614
Fax: –
Web: www.crawfordunited.com

CEO: Brian E Powers
CFO: Kelly J Marek
HR: Karen Walker
FYE: December 31
Type: Public

Like "Wild Bill" of Wild West lore, Hickok is quite comfortable shooting it out with competitors on its own measured road to success. The company manufactures testing equipment used by automotive technicians to repair cars. Hickok also makes instruments, indicators, and gauges for manufacturers of aircraft and locomotives. While Ford and General Motors traditionally were the company's largest customers, its biggest customer now is Environmental Systems Products (ESP), at 53% of sales. Hickok sells products primarily in the US. In 2019, Hickok bought Data Genomix, which develops social media marketing applications for political, legal, and recruiting campaigns. The companies are based in Cleveland, Ohio.

	Annual Growth	12/19	12/20	12/21	12/22	12/23
Sales ($mil.)	12.5%	89.7	85.1	104.2	127.8	143.9
Net income ($ mil.)	17.5%	7.0	5.8	5.7	6.6	13.3
Market value ($ mil.)	11.9%	69.3	65.8	105.3	48.6	108.9
Employees	10.6%	271	260	451	387	405

CRAYOLA LLC

1100 CHURCH LN
EASTON, PA 180405999
Phone: 610 253-6272
Fax: –
Web: www.crayola.com

CEO: Rich Wuerthele
CFO: Steve Hoff
HR: Frances Sciortino
FYE: December 31
Type: Private

Crayola offers a wide range of art materials and toys designed to spark children's creativity around the world. The world-famous producer of colored crayons (wax pencils) produces more than 3 billion crayons and some 700 million markers each year, as well as other Crayola art products for children and adults, such as paint, colored pencils, markers, chalk, light up toys, clay, watercolors, brushes, outdoor play toys, and craft and activity kits. The company's products, which are manufactured near its headquarters in Pennsylvania and at plants in Mexico, are packaged in multiple languages (English, Spanish, and French) and sold worldwide. Edwin Binney and C. Harold Smith produced the first box of eight crayons and sold them for 5 cents in 1903. Crayola is a subsidiary of Hallmark Cards.

CRAZY WOMAN CREEK BANCORP INC.

NBB: CRZY

106 Fort Street
Buffalo, WY 82834
Phone: 307 684-5591
Fax: 307 684-7854
Web: –

CEO: Paul Brunkhorst
CFO: Carolyn Kaiser
HR: –
FYE: September 30
Type: Public

Eat your heart out, Bank of America -- Crazy Woman Creek Bancorp officially has the best name of any bank holding company ever. The fabulously named company holds Buffalo Federal Savings Bank, which also operates as The Bank of Gillette, The Bank of Sheridan, and First Bank. Through four branches in northeastern Wyoming, the bank serves individuals and business customers. Services include savings and checking accounts. Lending activities consist mostly of residential mortgages and commercial real estate and agricultural loans. It also offers online banking.

	Annual Growth	09/00	09/01	09/02	09/04	09/05
Assets ($mil.)	9.0%	64.8	68.8	75.5	88.6	99.7
Net income ($ mil.)	(18.3%)	0.6	0.2	0.0	0.2	0.2
Market value ($ mil.)	5.4%	7.2	8.0	7.8	11.0	9.3
Employees	–	14	23	23	–	–

CREATION TECHNOLOGIES NEW YORK INC.

328 SILVER HILL RD
NEWARK, NY 145139185
Phone: 315 332-4220
Fax: –
Web: www.creationtech.com

CEO: Jeffrey T Schlarbaum
CFO: Thomas L Barbato
HR: –
FYE: September 30
Type: Private

IEC makes products you may never see. The company is a contract electronics manufacturer of printed circuit boards, system-level assemblies, extreme-condition cable and wire assemblies, and precision sheet metal components. Customers come from the aerospace, communications, medical, and military sectors. Like many contract electronics manufacturers, IEC also offers a variety of auxiliary services, including systems integration, design and prototyping, materials procurement and management, engineering, and testing.

CREATIVE GROUP, INC.

1500 N CALASOMA DR STE 201
APPLETON, WI 549138214
Phone: 920 739-8850
Fax: –
Web: www.creativegroupinc.com

CEO: Ronald Officer
CFO: Martin V Stippen
HR: –
FYE: September 30
Type: Private

Creative Group has devoted its energy towards business improvement. The company provides a variety of marketing services specializing in building and managing incentive programs, and planning corporate meetings and events. The company's incentive programs target sales, reseller, and employees, offering travel, merchandise, and gift certificates as rewards for good performance. Creative Group also offers personal travel services including travel planning and emergency services that benefit from the company's large corporate travel business. Clients have included Abbott Laboratories, Mutual of Omaha, and Johnson Controls. The company, which has offices in Wisconsin and Illinois, was founded in 1970.

CREATIVE MEDIA & COMMUNITY TRUST CORP

NMS: CMCT

17950 Preston Road, Suite 600
Dallas, TX 75252
Phone: 972 349-3200
Fax: –
Web: www.cimcommercial.com

CEO: David Thompson
CFO: Nathan D Debacker
HR: –
FYE: December 31
Type: Public

PMC Commercial Trust likes lending to little businesses. The real estate investment trust (REIT) makes small business loans, primarily to limited-service hotel franchisees. The loans, ranging from $100,000 to $4 million, are secured by first liens on real estate and written for hotel owner/operators of national franchises such as Comfort Inn and Holiday Inn Express. PMC Commercial Trust also lends to owners of convenience stores, restaurants, and other small businesses. About 20% of its loan portfolio is concentrated in Texas. Subsidiaries are active in Small Business Administration (SBA) lending and in investing (as small business investment companies, or SBICs). The company was founded in 1993.

	Annual Growth	12/18	12/19	12/20	12/21	12/22
Assets ($mil.)	(15.3%)	1,342.4	667.6	685.6	660.9	690.2
Net income ($ mil.)	51.6%	1.1	345.7	(15.0)	(0.9)	5.9
Market value ($ mil.)	(24.6%)	345.2	329.7	323.8	167.1	111.4
Employees	–	5	5	4	5	5

CREATIVE REALITIES INC
NAS: CREX

13100 Magisterial Drive, Suite 100
Louisville, KY 40223
Phone: 502 791-8800
Fax: -
Web: www.cri.com

CEO: -
CFO: -
HR: -
FYE: December 31
Type: Public

Wireless Ronin Technologies makes the signs of the time. The company's RoninCast electronic display products combine digital media players, video monitors, and wireless networking systems to enable the remote distribution of video marketing materials. Its digital signage is used for corporate logos and branding, promotional displays, interactive touchscreens, movie theater schedules, and restaurant menus. Wireless Ronin serves the automotive, financial services, gaming, restaurant, and retail industries, among others. Customers include Chrysler Canada, Carnival, Ford, KFC, Thomson Reuters, and Travelocity.

	Annual Growth	12/19	12/20	12/21	12/22	12/23
Sales ($mil.)	9.3%	31.6	17.5	18.4	43.4	45.2
Net income ($ mil.)	-	1.0	(16.8)	0.2	1.9	(2.9)
Market value ($ mil.)	11.4%	15.9	13.4	14.6	6.0	24.6
Employees	11.0%	100	75	105	120	152

CREDIT ACCEPTANCE CORP (MI)
NMS: CACC

25505 West Twelve Mile Road
Southfield, MI 48034-8339
Phone: 248 353-2700
Fax: -
Web: -

CEO: -
CFO: -
HR: -
FYE: December 31
Type: Public

Credit Acceptance Corporation offers financing programs that enable automobile dealers to sell vehicles to consumers. Working with approximately 60,000 independent and franchised automobile dealers in the US, the company provides financing programs through a nationwide network of automobile dealers who benefit from sales of vehicles to consumers who otherwise could not obtain financing; from repeat and referral sales generated by these same customers; and from sales to customers responding to advertisements for the company's financing programs. All of its revenues were derived from the US.

	Annual Growth	12/19	12/20	12/21	12/22	12/23
Sales ($mil.)	6.3%	1,489.0	1,669.3	1,856.0	1,832.4	1,901.9
Net income ($ mil.)	(18.7%)	656.1	421.0	958.3	535.8	286.1
Market value ($ mil.)	4.8%	5,539.0	4,334.5	8,611.4	5,940.6	6,671.1
Employees	2.6%	2,016	2,033	2,073	2,246	2,232

CREDIT SUISSE (USA) INC

Eleven Madison Avenue
New York, NY 10010
Phone: 212 325-2000
Fax: -
Web: -

CEO: Brady W Dougan
CFO: David C Fisher
HR: Mona Goh
FYE: December 31
Type: Public

Credit Suisse (USA) is one of the top US investment banks, offering advisory services on mergers and acquisitions, raising capital, securities underwriting and trading, research and analytics, and risk management products. Clients include corporations, governments, institutional investors such as hedge funds, and private individuals. The company provides asset management services through Credit Suisse Private Equity; while Credit Suisse Private Banking USA offers wealth services to the rich throughout the country. Credit Suisse (USA) is a wholly owned subsidiary of Swiss banking powerhouse Credit Suisse Group and part of Credit Suisse Americas, which includes North and South America and the Caribbean.

	Annual Growth	12/03	12/04	12/05	12/11	12/12
Sales ($mil.)	8.3%	4,993.0	6,341.0	7,025.0	6,738.0	10,232
Net income ($ mil.)	5.0%	1,329.0	787.0	127.0	(272.0)	2,063.0
Market value ($ mil.)	-	0.1	0.1	0.1	-	-
Employees	-	8,706	9,344	10,899	-	-

CREDITRISKMONITOR.COM, INC.
NBB: CRMZ

704 Executive Boulevard, Suite A
Valley Cottage, NY 10989
Phone: 845 230-3000
Fax: -
Web: www.creditriskmonitor.com

CEO: -
CFO: -
HR: -
FYE: December 31
Type: Public

Need to monitor credit risk? CreditRiskMonitor.com (also called CRMZ) provides online financial information and news about some 40,000 public companies worldwide, marketing the service to corporate credit managers who use the data to make credit decisions. Subscribers get access to such information as company background, financial statements, trend reports, and comparative analysis, in addition to proprietary credit scores. The firm also provides access to information on more than 6 million public and private US companies through affiliations with third-party providers. CreditRiskMonitor.com was formed in 1999 after buying Market Guide's credit information database.

	Annual Growth	12/19	12/20	12/21	12/22	12/23
Sales ($mil.)	6.9%	14.5	15.7	17.1	18.0	18.9
Net income ($ mil.)	67.1%	0.2	(0.0)	3.4	1.4	1.7
Market value ($ mil.)	10.4%	16.8	25.2	18.1	25.7	25.0
Employees	-	101	100	90	90	-

CREIGHTON UNIVERSITY

2500 CALIFORNIA PLZ
OMAHA, NE 681780002
Phone: 402 280-2900
Fax: -
Web: www.creighton.edu

CEO: -
CFO: -
HR: -
FYE: June 30
Type: Private

Consistently ranked among the top universities in the Midwest, Creighton University is a Jesuit Catholic university with an enrollment of approximately 8,000 undergraduate, graduate, and professional students. With a student-to-faculty ratio of 11:1, it offers more than 70 majors through nine schools and colleges, including institutions focused on arts and sciences, business, law, medicine, dentistry, pharmacy, and nursing. Its 130-acre campus is adjacent to the downtown business district of Omaha, Nebraska. Creighton University was founded in 1878 and named after Omaha businessman Edward Creighton.

	Annual Growth	06/18	06/19	06/20	06/21	06/22
Sales ($mil.)	8.5%	-	567.7	563.2	655.1	724.6
Net income ($ mil.)	33.8%	-	62.7	61.3	131.7	150.0
Market value ($ mil.)	-	-	-	-	-	-
Employees	-	-	-	-	-	5,000

CRESCENT ELECTRIC SUPPLY COMPANY

7750 TIMMERMAN DR
EAST DUBUQUE, IL 610251045
Phone: 815 747-3145
Fax: -
Web: www.crescentelectric.com

CEO: Scott Teerlinck
CFO: Kristi Dahlke
HR: -
FYE: December 31
Type: Private

Crescent Electric Supply Company is one of the nation's largest independent distributors of electrical hardware and supplies. The company has more than 150 branches in about 30 states, serving contractors, original equipment manufacturers (OEM) and the maintenance, repair and operations (MRO) needs of commercial, industrial, institutional, and utility customers. In addition to the Crescent Electric brand, customers are served by BA Supply in Missouri, Interstate Electric Supply in Idaho and Oregon, Mesco Electrical Supply in Ohio, National Electric Supply in New Mexico, Womack Electric Supply in Virginia and North Carolina, and Stoneway Electric in Washington and Idaho, and Lowe Electric in Georgia and South Carolina. Titus B. Schmid founded the company in 1919.

CREST OPERATIONS, LLC

4725 HIGHWAY 28 E
PINEVILLE, LA 713604730
Phone: 318 448-0274
Fax: –
Web: www.crestoperations.com

CEO: –
CFO: –
HR: –
FYE: December 31
Type: Private

Crest Operations, part of Crest Industries, distributes and installs electrical substations and transmission products for electric power generation and utility customers worldwide, through its DIS-TRAN and Beta Engineering subsidiaries. Other subsidiaries grow pine and hardwood trees in Louisiana and Texas (Crest Natural Resources), and make wooden utility poles and cross arms. Crest's Mid-State Supply Company subsidiary is a Louisiana-based distributor of electrical products that has showrooms for appliances and lighting. Crest Operations was founded in 1958.

	Annual Growth	12/17	12/18	12/19	12/20	12/21
Sales ($mil.)	14.2%	–	–	332.9	358.0	434.4
Net income ($ mil.)	9.9%	–	–	10.1	18.5	12.2
Market value ($ mil.)	–	–	–	–	–	–
Employees		–	–	–	–	1,222

CRESTWOOD MIDSTREAM PARTNERS LP

811 MAIN ST STE 3400
HOUSTON, TX 770026131
Phone: 832 519-2200
Fax: –
Web: www.crestwoodlp.com

CEO: Robert G Phillips
CFO: Robert T Halpin
HR: –
FYE: December 31
Type: Private

The middle of the oil and gas stream is best for Crestwood Midstream Partners (formerly Quicksilver Gas Services). The company gathers and processes natural gas and natural gas liquids from the Barnett Shale formation near Fort Worth, Texas. Crestwood Midstream Partners' assets include a pipeline and a processing plant with 200 million cu. ft. a day capacity, a processing unit at the existing plant, extensions to the existing pipeline, and pipelines in other drilling areas in Texas. In 2013 it merged with Inergy Midstream to become an $8 billion midstream entity.

CRETE CARRIER CORPORATION

400 NW 56TH ST
LINCOLN, NE 685288843
Phone: 800 998-4095
Fax: –
Web: www.cretecarrier.com

CEO: Tonn Ostergard
CFO: –
HR: Katie White
FYE: September 30
Type: Private

Holding company Crete Carrier Corporation's flagship business, Crete Carrier, provides dry van truckload freight transportation services in the 48 contiguous states. It operates from some two dozen terminals, mainly in the mid-western and southeastern US. The company's Shaffer Trucking unit transports temperature-controlled cargo, and Hunt Transportation (no relation to J.B. Hunt Transport Services) hauls heavy equipment and other cargo on flatbed trailers. Overall, the companies operate more than 5,400 tractors and 13,000 trailers. Family-owned Crete Carrier was founded in 1966 by chairman Duane Acklie; president and CEO Tonn Ostergard is his son-in-law.

	Annual Growth	09/13	09/14	09/15	09/16	09/18
Sales ($mil.)	2.7%	–	1,034.1	–	984.1	1,150.6
Net income ($ mil.)	2.3%	–	127.1	–	95.8	139.2
Market value ($ mil.)	–	–	–	–	–	–
Employees	–	–	–	–	–	6,000

CREXENDO INC

NAS: CXDO

1615 South 52nd Street
Tempe, AZ 85281
Phone: 602 714-8500
Fax: –
Web: www.crexendo.com

CEO: Jeffrey G Korn
CFO: Ron Vincent
HR: –
FYE: December 31
Type: Public

Crexendo (formerly iMergent) would like to help increase the volume on your e-commerce business. Catering to home-based, small, and medium-sized businesses, the company's cloud-based software helps merchants create, manage, and promote their e-commerce website and process orders. Premium services include site and logo design, supplier integration, and search engine optimization. The company has primarily used training seminars around the country to sell its products to aspiring e-commerce mavens, but hopes to open more sales channels. More than 90% of sales come from customers in North America (US and Canada). Chairman and CEO Steven Mihaylo, founder and former CEO of Inter-Tel, owns more than a third of Crexendo.

	Annual Growth	12/19	12/20	12/21	12/22	12/23
Sales ($mil.)	38.6%	14.4	16.4	28.1	37.6	53.2
Net income ($ mil.)	–	1.1	7.9	(2.4)	(35.4)	(0.4)
Market value ($ mil.)	3.4%	111.1	181.1	130.7	49.6	126.7
Employees	34.3%	56	58	121	181	182

CRIDER, INC.

1 PLANT AVE
STILLMORE, GA 30464
Phone: 912 562-4435
Fax: –
Web: www.criderfoods.com

CEO: W A Crider Jr
CFO: Abby Walden
HR: –
FYE: December 28
Type: Private

They may not know why the chicken crossed the road but the folks at Crider apparently have figured out how to get them to climb inside its cans. The company is a leading chicken canner in the US and makes a number of fresh and fully-cooked chicken offerings. It also cans turkey, beef, and ham. Crider's products are supplied to food retailers, including club stores nationwide under branded and private-labels. The Georgia company was founded in 1944 by Ahtee and Emma Lou Crider and is still owned and operated by the founders' descendants.

CRISTA MINISTRIES

19303 FREMONT AVE N
SHORELINE, WA 981333800
Phone: 206 546-7200
Fax: –
Web: www.crista.org

CEO: Robert Lonac
CFO: Brad Kirkpatrick
HR: Heidi Knapp
FYE: June 30
Type: Private

World Concern is concerned with the poorest of the poor around the world. The Christian not-for-profit helps about 4 million people a year in more than 30 nations. The group uses its own index of nine factors like economy, health issues, conflict, and food availability, along with prayer, to determine which nations most need assistance. World Concern provides emergency relief and community development, including small business loans, agriculture starter kits, prenatal education, Christian literature, village sanitation kits, and donated goods (clothing, plant seeds, bedding). Founded in 1973, the group uses about 1,300 volunteers throughout the world working from offices in the US, Bolivia, Kenya, and Thailand.

	Annual Growth	06/15	06/16	06/19	06/20	06/21
Sales ($mil.)	(8.7%)	–	115.2	117.3	108.5	73.1
Net income ($ mil.)	–	–	5.7	(6.8)	(9.9)	(5.1)
Market value ($ mil.)	–	–	–	–	–	–
Employees	–	–	–	–	–	1,200

CROCS INC
NMS: CROX

13601 Via Varra
Broomfield, CO 80020
Phone: 303 848-7000
Fax: –
Web: www.crocs.com

CEO: Andrew Rees
CFO: Anne Mehlman
HR: Aj Scordo
FYE: December 31
Type: Public

Crocs is one of the world's largest footwear companies. Crocs and its subsidiaries are engaged in the design, development, worldwide marketing, distribution, and sale of casual lifestyle footwear and accessories for women, men, and children. Jibbitz charms are the company's accessories for personalization. It reaches customers via about 345 owned stores, and company-operated and third party e-commerce marketplaces. Sold approximately 115.6 million pairs of shoes worldwide, the company has customers in more than 85 countries and earns most of its sales in the US. The vast majority of operations of its Crocs Brand production are in Vietnam and China.

	Annual Growth	12/19	12/20	12/21	12/22	12/23
Sales ($mil.)	34.0%	1,230.6	1,386.0	2,313.4	3,555.0	3,962.3
Net income ($ mil.)	60.5%	119.5	312.9	725.7	540.2	792.6
Market value ($ mil.)	22.2%	2,534.3	3,790.9	7,757.3	6,560.0	5,651.3
Employees	16.6%	3,803	4,600	5,770	6,680	7,030

CROGHAN BANCSHARES, INC.
NBB: CHBH

323 Croghan Street
Fremont, OH 43420
Phone: 419 332-7301
Fax: –
Web: www.croghan.com

CEO: Rick M Robertson
CFO: –
HR: –
FYE: December 31
Type: Public

Croghan Bancshares is helping to share the wealth in the Buckeye state. The firm is the holding company for Croghan Colonial Bank, which has about 10 branches in northern Ohio. Founded in 1888, the bank provides standard products and services, including checking and savings accounts, money market accounts, certificates of deposit, and credit cards, Its lending activities primarily consist of residential and commercial mortgages and, to a lesser extent, agricultural, business, construction, and consumer loans. In addition, the bank offers wealth management, investments, estate planning, private banking, and trust services.

	Annual Growth	12/19	12/20	12/21	12/22	12/23
Assets ($mil.)	6.3%	876.8	1,028.5	1,112.4	1,125.8	1,118.1
Net income ($ mil.)	(3.7%)	12.5	13.7	15.2	14.0	10.8
Market value ($ mil.)	(3.7%)	112.7	109.5	134.8	117.9	96.9
Employees	0.5%	207	199	203	205	211

CROSS BORDER RESOURCES INC.
NBB: XBOR

2515 McKinney Avenue, Suite 900
Dallas, TX 75201
Phone: 210 226-6700
Fax: –
Web: www.xbres.com

CEO: –
CFO: –
HR: –
FYE: December 31
Type: Public

Cross Border Resources is focusing its oil and gas exploration and development efforts on New Mexico and Texas. The company owns some 300,000 net acres primarily in New Mexico, with more than 30,000 of those acres located in the prolific Permian Basin in West Texas. Its properties consist of working, mineral, and royalty interests in various oil and gas wells and lease acreage located in the counties of Chaves, Eddy, Lea, and Roosevelt in New Mexico and the counties of Borden and Dawson in Texas. They produce more than 200 barrels of oil equivalent per day. Cross Border Resources formed in early 2011 following the business combination of Doral Energy and Pure Energy.

	Annual Growth	07/10*	12/11	12/12	12/13	12/14
Sales ($mil.)	65.1%	1.7	7.3	14.8	13.1	12.4
Net income ($ mil.)	–	(13.8)	(1.2)	(2.4)	3.4	(2.5)
Market value ($ mil.)	124.0%	0.5	28.8	15.6	6.4	13.5
Employees	–	–	2	5	–	–

*Fiscal year change

CROSS COUNTRY HEALTHCARE INC
NMS: CCRN

6551 Park of Commerce Boulevard, N.W.
Boca Raton, FL 33487
Phone: 561 998-2232
Fax: –
Web: www.crosscountryhealthcare.com

CEO: –
CFO: –
HR: –
FYE: December 31
Type: Public

Cross Country Healthcare (Cross Country) is one of the largest providers of workforce solutions and healthcare staffing in the US. The company offers strategic workforce solutions, contingent staffing, permanent placement, and other consultative services for healthcare clients. The company place highly qualified healthcare professionals in virtually every specialty on travel and per diem assignments, local short-term contracts, and permanent positions. It also places teachers, substitute teachers, and other education specialties at educational facilities, and healthcare leaders within nursing, allied, physician, and human resources at healthcare organizations. Subsidiaries and brands include Cross Country Nurses, Cross Country Allied, Cross Country Medical Staffing Network, Cross Country Search, Cross Country Workforce Solutions, and Cross Country Education.

	Annual Growth	12/19	12/20	12/21	12/22	12/23
Sales ($mil.)	25.2%	822.2	836.4	1,676.7	2,806.6	2,019.7
Net income ($ mil.)	–	(57.7)	(13.0)	132.0	188.5	72.6
Market value ($ mil.)	18.1%	399.6	305.0	954.5	913.6	778.5
Employees	58.9%	1,700	1,450	2,250	2,700	10,831

CROSS TECHNOLOGIES, INC.

4400 PIEDMONT PKWY
GREENSBORO, NC 274108121
Phone: 800 327-7727
Fax: –
Web: www.crossco.com

CEO: John King
CFO: Jerry Bohnsack
HR: –
FYE: November 30
Type: Private

Cross Company offers a wide range of products throughout its specialty groups. The Southeastern US-based automation technology company operates five divisions: Cross Automation Equipment, Cross Precision Measurement Equipment, Process Equipment, Cross Hose & Fittings, and Mobile Systems Integration products. It has operations across the US, as well as in Mexico. Division Cross Automation offers a range of products within primary areas of discipline such as robotics, pneumatics, and automation or motion control. Founded in 1954, Cross Company is a 100% employee-owned company.

	Annual Growth	11/99	11/00	11/01	11/02	11/20
Sales ($mil.)	3.4%	–	–	77.9	67.8	145.8
Net income ($ mil.)	–	–	–	(0.6)	(0.2)	0.2
Market value ($ mil.)	–	–	–	–	–	–
Employees	–	–	–	–	–	612

CROSS TIMBERS ROYALTY TRUST
NYS: CRT

c/o Corporate Trustee, Argent Trust Company, 3838 Oak Lawn Ave, Suite 1720
Dallas, TX 75219
Phone: 855 588-7839
Fax: –
Web: www.crt-crosstimbers.com

CEO: –
CFO: –
HR: –
FYE: December 31
Type: Public

Cross Timbers Royalty Trust distributes royalties from more than 2,900 oil and natural gas producing properties in Texas, Oklahoma, and New Mexico. The trust, which was formed in 1991, does not operate or control any of its properties. Instead, it owns stakes in wells located primarily in gas properties in the San Juan Basin of northwestern New Mexico. The trust's estimated proved reserves are 856,000 barrels of oil and 25.6 billion cu. ft. of gas. XTO Energy, which markets the trust's oil and gas, owns the underlying propeties and distributed all of its trust units as a dividend to its stockholders in 2003.

	Annual Growth	12/18	12/19	12/20	12/21	12/22
Sales ($mil.)	8.1%	9.2	6.0	5.3	7.4	12.5
Net income ($ mil.)	8.2%	8.6	5.3	4.7	6.7	11.7
Market value ($ mil.)	23.5%	65.5	52.4	49.4	68.8	152.6
Employees	–	–	–	–	–	–

CROSSAMERICA PARTNERS LP

NYS: CAPL

645 Hamilton Street, Suite 400
Allentown, PA 18101
Phone: 610 625-8000
Fax: –
Web: www.crossamericapartners.com

CEO: Jeremy L Bergeron
CFO: Evan W Smith
HR: –
FYE: December 31
Type: Public

CrossAmerica Partners (formerly Lehigh Gas Partners) is a leading wholesale distributor of motor fuels, operator of convenience stores, and owner and lessor of real estate used in the retail distribution of motor fuels. The company distributes branded and unbranded petroleum for motor vehicles to approximately 1,800 locations and owns or leases approximately 1,100 sites. Its geographic footprint covers nearly 35 states. CrossAmerica distributes branded motor fuel under the Exxon, Mobil, BP, Shell, Sunoco, Valero, Gulf, Citgo, Marathon, and Phillips 66 brands to its customers. More than 90% of motor fuels distributed yearly by CrossAmerica is branded. Its convenience store brands offer food, essentials, and car washes at more than 250 locations across about 10 states. The company was formed in 2012.

	Annual Growth	12/19	12/20	12/21	12/22	12/23
Sales ($mil.)	19.5%	2,149.4	1,932.3	3,579.3	4,967.4	4,386.3
Net income ($ mil.)	23.9%	18.1	107.5	21.7	63.7	42.6
Market value ($ mil.)	6.0%	685.6	652.2	724.0	753.2	866.0
Employees	–	–	203	215	228	244

CROSSLAND CONSTRUCTION COMPANY, INC.

833 S EAST AVE
COLUMBUS, KS 667252307
Phone: 620 429-1414
Fax: –
Web: www.crossland.com

CEO: –
CFO: –
HR: –
FYE: July 31
Type: Private

Crossland Construction has crossed the prairie, transitioning from a local player in Columbus, Kansas, to a firm with a strong regional presence. The company designs, builds, and manages construction of government, education, healthcare, retail, and other buildings from a handful of offices in Kansas, Missouri, Arkansas, Oklahoma, Colorado, and Texas. Customers have included Harley-Davidson, SAM'S CLUB, McCune Brooks Hospital, Embassy Suites, and a variety of school districts and municipalities. Crossland builds everything from office buildings and warehouses to veteran's memorials and airports. The company, which often works in partnership with PBA Architects, was founded by Ivan Crossland Sr. in 1978.

	Annual Growth	07/02	07/03	07/04	07/07	07/08
Sales ($mil.)	25.3%	–	–	176.3	336.1	434.2
Net income ($ mil.)	44.5%	–	–	2.3	11.4	10.2
Market value ($ mil.)	–	–	–	–	–	–
Employees	–	–	–	–	–	715

CROSSROADS IMPACT CORP

NBB: CRSS

4514 Cole Avenue, Suite 1600
Dallas, TX 75205
Phone: 214 999-0149
Fax: –
Web: www.crossroads.com

CEO: –
CFO: –
HR: –
FYE: October 31
Type: Public

Crossroads Systems sets up shop where business and information intersect. The company provides storage networking equipment and data archiving systems used to manage and protect critical data. Its products include StrongBox (network attached storage appliance that uses linear tape file system technology), RVA (monitoring tape media and the condition of disk drives), and SPHiNX (protecting data by working as a network attached storage device or virtual tape library). Crossroads Systems sells directly to manufacturers, such as HP (45% of sales) and EMC, and through distributors. The company was founded in 1996.

	Annual Growth	10/17	10/18	10/19	10/20	10/21
Sales ($mil.)	970.0%	0.0	28.4	37.7	36.6	930.6
Net income ($ mil.)	–	(1.7)	23.8	1.8	3.0	194.8
Market value ($ mil.)	54.1%	19.7	41.2	50.8	53.8	111.1
Employees	–	–	–	–	27	34

CROWDER CONSTRUCTION COMPANY INC

6425 BROOKSHIRE BLVD
CHARLOTTE, NC 282160301
Phone: 800 849-2966
Fax: –
Web: www.crowderusa.com

CEO: –
CFO: –
HR: –
FYE: March 31
Type: Private

Seeking to stand out from the crowd of US-based construction companies, Crowder Construction specializes in bridge and highway, civil, environmental, and industrial construction, serving a range of customers, primarily in the Southeast US. The specialty construction company's projects include parking decks, highway and bridge, water and sewer treatment plant construction. Projects that have been completed by its Crowder Electrical unit range from power substations to light rail facilities. The employee-owned company was founded in Charlotte, North Carolina in 1947 by W.T. and O. P. Crowder; it continues to be led by the Crowder family.

CROWELL & MORING LLP

1001 PENNSYLVANIA AVE NW
WASHINGTON, DC 200042543
Phone: 202 624-2500
Fax: –
Web: www.crowell.com

CEO: –
CFO: –
HR: –
FYE: December 31
Type: Private

Crowell & Morning is an international law firm and known for its work in antitrust, litigation, and government contracts, but the firm also offers expertise in other areas including employee benefits, tax, and white collar defense. The firm has about 750 lawyers practicing law through more than 10 offices in the US, Asia, and Europe. More than one-third of Fortune 100 companies turn to Crowell for their litigation and trial needs. Through its association with other law firms, Crowell & Moring advises clients on transactions, disputes, compliance, and other legal issues in Americas, London, China, Belgium, and Singapore. The firm was founded in 1979.

CROWLEY MARITIME CORPORATION

9487 REGENCY SQUARE BLVD
JACKSONVILLE, FL 322257800
Phone: 904 727-2200
Fax: –
Web: www.crowley.com

CEO: Thomas Crowley Jr
CFO: Dan Warner
HR: Francheska Bensan
FYE: December 31
Type: Private

Crowley, founded in 1892, is a privately-held, US-owned and operated logistics, government, marine and energy solutions company headquartered in Jacksonville, Florida. Crowley owns, operates and/or manages a fleet of more than 200 vessels, consisting of RO/RO (roll-on-roll-off) vessels, LO/LO (lift-on-lift-off) vessels, articulated tug-barges (ATBs), LNG-powered container/roll-on, roll-off ships (ConRos) and multipurpose tugboats and barges. Land-based facilities and equipment include port terminals, warehouses, tank farms, gas stations, office buildings, trucks, trailers, containers, chassis, cranes and other specialized vehicles.

	Annual Growth	12/04	12/05	12/06	12/07	12/08
Sales ($mil.)	18.0%	–	1,190.8	1,467.7	1,622.3	1,955.8
Net income ($ mil.)	30.3%	–	38.9	38.4	122.3	86.0
Market value ($ mil.)	–	–	–	–	–	–
Employees	–	–	–	–	–	4,329

CROWN BATTERY MANUFACTURING COMPANY

1445 MAJESTIC DR
FREMONT, OH 434209190
Phone: 419 334-7181
Fax: –
Web: www.crownbattery.com

CEO: –
CFO: Tim Hack
HR: Kristine Weiss
FYE: September 30
Type: Private

Crown Battery Manufacturing doesn't let its power go to its head. The company manufactures and sells industrial batteries and chargers, automotive batteries, and commercial battery products to clients across North America. Products serve clients in the marine, railroad, mining, and automotive industries; the company also offers products with deep-cycle and other heavy-duty applications. Other products include battery chargers and battery cleaners for industrial applications. The company was founded in 1926 by German immigrant William J. Koenig.

	Annual Growth	09/10	09/11	09/12	09/13	09/14
Sales ($mil.)	5.9%	–	–	191.1	196.2	214.2
Net income ($ mil.)	40.1%	–	–	6.1	10.8	12.0
Market value ($ mil.)	–	–	–	–	–	–
Employees		–	–	–	–	510

CROWN CASTLE INC
NYS: CCI

8020 Katy Freeway
Houston, TX 77024
Phone: 713 570-3000
Fax: –
Web: www.crowncastle.com

CEO: Jay A Brown
CFO: Daniel K Schlanger
HR: –
FYE: December 31
Type: Public

Crown Castle owns, operates and leases shared communications infrastructure that is geographically dispersed throughout the US. The company provides access, including space or capacity, lease, license, sublease and service agreements to communications infrastructure via long-term contracts. Wireless carrier customers including T-Mobile, AT&T, and Verizon Wireless are the company's largest tenants of Towers and Fiber segments. Crown Castle has about 40,000 tower sites (the most in the US), about 120,000 small cells on air or under contract, and some 85,000 miles of fiber, primarily supporting small cells and fiber solutions geographically dispersed throughout the US.

	Annual Growth	12/19	12/20	12/21	12/22	12/23
Sales ($mil.)	4.9%	5,763.0	5,840.0	6,340.0	6,986.0	6,981.0
Net income ($ mil.)	15.0%	860.0	1,056.0	1,096.0	1,675.0	1,502.0
Market value ($ mil.)	(5.1%)	61,693	69,088	90,593	58,868	49,992
Employees		–	5,100	4,900	5,000	5,000

CROWN CRAFTS, INC.
NAS: CRWS

916 South Burnside Avenue
Gonzales, LA 70737
Phone: 225 647-9100
Fax: –
Web: www.crowncrafts.com

CEO: Nanci Freeman
CFO: Craig J Demarest
HR: –
FYE: April 2
Type: Public

Prospects for new business opportunities keep Crown Crafts drooling. Operating through its subsidiaries, Hamco and Crown Crafts Infant Products, the company designs and sells textile products for infants and juveniles. Crown Crafts designs, makes, and markets baby bibs, burp cloths, bathing accessories, and bedding. The childcare products firm founded in 1957 has worked to regain profitability by selling or shuttering its US manufacturing operations and relying on foreign contractors, mainly in China, to make its goods. Crown Crafts' products are sold in department and specialty stores, mass retailers, catalog houses, and outlet stores.

	Annual Growth	03/19	03/20	03/21*	04/22	04/23
Sales ($mil.)	(0.4%)	76.4	73.4	79.2	87.4	75.1
Net income ($ mil.)	3.0%	5.0	6.6	6.1	9.9	5.7
Market value ($ mil.)	2.8%	52.4	48.2	78.0	66.0	58.5
Employees	1.4%	163	138	131	126	172

*Fiscal year change

CROWN EQUIPMENT CORPORATION

44 S WASHINGTON ST
NEW BREMEN, OH 458691288
Phone: 419 629-2311
Fax: –
Web: www.crown.com

CEO: James F Dicke II
CFO: –
HR: Pete Falk
FYE: March 31
Type: Private

Crown Equipment is a leader in the evolution of the material handling industry, earning more than 80 global design awards. From its smallest hand pallet truck to its highest lifting turret truck, Crown designs, manufactures, distributes, services and supports material handling products that provide customers with superior value. The company designs and manufactures up to 85% of its lift truck components, including motors, drive units, and electronic modules. Crown operates more than 20 manufacturing facilities and has more than 500 retail and service locations in around 85 countries. The Dicke family controls Crown.

CROWN HOLDINGS INC
NYS: CCK

14025 Riveredge Drive, Suite 300
Tampa, FL 33637
Phone: 215 698-5100
Fax: –
Web: www.crowncork.com

CEO: Timothy J Donahue
CFO: Kevin C Clothier
HR: Ingrid May
FYE: December 31
Type: Public

Crown Holdings is a leading global supplier of rigid packaging products to consumer marketing companies, as well as transit and protective packaging products, equipment and services to a broad range of end markets. The company's consumer packaging solutions primarily support the beverage and food industries, along with the personal care and household industries, through the development and sale of aluminum and steel cans. Its transit and protective packaging products include steel and plastic consumables and equipment, paper-based protective packaging, and plastic film consumables and equipment, which are sold into the metals, food and beverage, construction, agricultural, corrugated and general industries. Its roster of customers has included Anheuser-Busch InBev, Coca-Cola, SC Johnson, Unilever, FrieslandCampina, and Procter & Gamble. Crown traces its historical roots all the way back to 1892. Most of its sales are generated outside the US.

	Annual Growth	12/19	12/20	12/21	12/22	12/23
Sales ($mil.)	0.7%	11,665	11,575	11,394	12,943	12,010
Net income ($ mil.)	(3.1%)	510	579.0	(560.0)	727.0	450.0
Market value ($ mil.)	6.1%	8,751.5	12,089	13,346	9,918.2	11,110
Employees	(6.7%)	33,000	33,000	26,000	26,000	25,000

CROWN MEDIA HOLDINGS, INC.

12700 VENTURA BLVD STE 200
STUDIO CITY, CA 916042469
Phone: 888 390-7474
Fax: –
Web: www.hallmarkchannel.com

CEO: William J Abbott
CFO: Andrew Rooke
HR: –
FYE: December 31
Type: Private

All for the Family would be the name of a TV series about Crown Media Holdings. It owns and operates the Hallmark Channel, a cable network that specializes in family-oriented programming. It features third-party programs including such TV series as Golden Girls, Little House on the Prairie, and Matlock, as well as made-for-TV movies, feature films, and miniseries, which includes original programming. The channel reaches more than 87 million US homes through cable providers such as Comcast and Cox. Crown Media also operates the Hallmark Movies & Mysteries channel, a 24-hour channel that primarily offers feature films, miniseries, and lighter mysteries; it reaches nearly 64 million homes. Hallmark Cards, which already owned most of the company, acquired the rest in early 2016.

CRST INTERNATIONAL, INC.

201 1ST ST SE STE 400
CEDAR RAPIDS, IA 524011423
Phone: 319 396-4400
Fax: –
Web: www.crst.com

CEO: Hugh Ekberg
CFO: Wesley Brackey
HR: –
FYE: December 31
Type: Private

CRST International promises f-a-s-t freight transportation through its operating units. CRST Expedited provides standard dry van truckload transportation, primarily on long-haul routes, along with dedicated and expedited transportation services. CRST Malone hauls steel and other freight requiring flatbed trailers or trailers with removable sides, and CRST Logistics arranges freight transportation and provides other third-party logistics services. The family-owned business' other operations include CRST Dedicated Services and Specialized Transportation. Overall, the companies operate a fleet of about 4,500 tractors and 7,300 van trailers.

	Annual Growth	12/08	12/09	12/10	12/11	12/12
Sales ($mil.)	10.1%	–	–	–	1,143.1	1,258.0
Net income ($ mil.)	(7.8%)	–	–	–	81.6	75.3
Market value ($ mil.)	–	–	–	–	–	–
Employees	–	–	–	–	–	5,960

CRYO-CELL INTERNATIONAL INC

700 Brooker Creek Blvd.
Oldsmar, FL 34677
Phone: 813 749-2100
Fax: 813 723-0444
Web: www.cryo-cell.com

ASE: CCEL

CEO: David I Portnoy
CFO: Jill Taymans
HR: –
FYE: November 30
Type: Public

Cryo-Cell International freezes the ties that bind. The company collects and cryogenically stores umbilical cord blood stem cells, giving expectant parents some insurance in case disease (such as diabetes, heart disease, or stroke) should strike in the future. Specimens collected in the US are processed and stored at Cryo-Cell's facility in Oldsmar, Florida. The company also offers services through subsidiaries in certain countries in Asia, Europe, Latin America, and the Middle East. Cryo-Cell markets its services directly to consumers online through its website and by providing information and education to obstetricians, pediatricians, childbirth educators, and other health care providers.

	Annual Growth	11/19	11/20	11/21	11/22	11/23
Sales ($mil.)	(0.4%)	31.8	31.1	28.9	30.3	31.3
Net income ($ mil.)	–	2.3	3.6	2.1	2.8	(9.5)
Market value ($ mil.)	27.9%	16.6	16.6	102.6	36.2	44.3
Employees	(2.4%)	97	98	93	88	88

CRYSTAL FLASH, INC.

1754 ALPINE AVE NW
GRAND RAPIDS, MI 495042810
Phone: 616 363-4851
Fax: –
Web: www.crystalflash.com

CEO: –
CFO: –
HR: Krinn Vandersloot
FYE: December 31
Type: Private

Crystal Flash delivers propane, premium diesel, and other fuel products. The company's fleet of almost 205 trucks transport products to residential, agricultural, commercial, industrial, and government facilities throughout Michigan, Northern Indiana, and Northern Ohio. Crystal Flash moves fuels to homes, businesses, fleets and farms. It is a 100% employee-owned company that takes pride in treating its customers like family. John E. Fehsenfeld founded the company in 1932 with one old truck and a rented fuel storage facility in Indianapolis, Indiana.

	Annual Growth	12/07	12/08	12/09	12/10	12/11
Sales ($mil.)	26.4%	–	–	112.9	123.8	180.5
Net income ($ mil.)	123.8%	–	–	1.1	2.3	5.5
Market value ($ mil.)	–	–	–	–	–	–
Employees	–	–	–	–	–	240

CRYSTAL ROCK HOLDINGS, INC.

1050 BUCKINGHAM ST
WATERTOWN, CT 067956602
Phone: 860 945-0661
Fax: –
Web: www.crystalrock.com

CEO: –
CFO: –
HR: –
FYE: October 31
Type: Private

When co-workers gather around the water cooler or the coffeepot to discuss the Celtics, the Patriots, or the Red Sox (or even the Yankees), Crystal Rock wants to be there. The company delivers water and coffee to offices and homes throughout New England and in New York and New Jersey. Non-sparkling water, which the company bottles at facilities in Connecticut, Vermont, and New York, is offered under the Vermont Pure, Hidden Springs, and Crystal Rock brands, and private labels. Vermont Pure Holdings' coffee brands include Baronet Coffee and Green Mountain Coffee Roasters. Company president Peter Baker and his family own a majority of Crystal Rock.

CSG SYSTEMS INTERNATIONAL INC.

169 Inverness Dr W, Suite 300
Englewood, CO 80112
Phone: 303 200-2000
Fax: –
Web: www.csgi.com

NMS: CSGS

CEO: –
CFO: –
HR: –
FYE: December 31
Type: Public

CSG Systems International is a purpose-driven, SaaS platform company that enables global companies in a wide variety of industry verticals to tackle the ever-growing complexity of business in the digital age. Its cloud-first architecture and customer-centric approach help companies around the world acquire, monetize, engage, and retain their B2B (business-to-business), B2C (business-to-consumer), and B2B2X (business-to-business-to-consumer) customers. Its industry-leading solutions include revenue management and digital monetization, transformational customer experience, and payment solutions that help customers to deliver personalized, secure, and integrated customer experience solutions. The company serves primarily North American cable, satellite customers, and communication service providers (CSPs) such as Charter, AT&T, America Movil, and Comcast among many others. Majority of the company's sales were generated in the Americas.

	Annual Growth	12/19	12/20	12/21	12/22	12/23
Sales ($mil.)	4.1%	996.8	990.5	1,046.5	1,089.8	1,169.3
Net income ($ mil.)	(5.4%)	82.8	58.7	72.3	44.1	66.2
Market value ($ mil.)	0.7%	1,529.6	1,331.4	1,702.2	1,689.7	1,571.9
Employees	8.4%	4,339	4,807	5,200	5,700	6,000

CSI COMPRESSCO LP

1735 Hughes Landing Boulevard, Suite 200
The Woodlands, TX 77380
Phone: 832 365-2257
Fax: –
Web: www.csicompressco.com

NMS: CCLP

CEO: –
CFO: –
HR: –
FYE: December 31
Type: Public

Compressco Partners puts the pressure on before the natural gas and oil wells run dry. The company specializes in providing services to more than 400 natural gas and oil companies across 14 states to increase production and total recoverable reserves. The company offers compression, liquids separation, and gas metering services, as well as the GasJack units that perform these operations. It applies its services primarily to mature wells, but also on newer wells, which have declined in production. Compressco Partners, which was spun-off from TETRA Technologies in 2011, also provides well evaluations and well testing and monitoring services in Mexico.

	Annual Growth	12/19	12/20	12/21	12/22	12/23
Sales ($mil.)	(5.1%)	476.6	301.6	304.2	353.4	386.1
Net income ($ mil.)	–	(21.0)	(73.8)	(50.3)	(22.1)	(9.5)
Market value ($ mil.)	(12.0%)	385.5	150.5	169.0	188.9	231.5
Employees	(2.4%)	791	730	817	792	719

CSI LEASING, INC.

9990 OLD OLIVE STREET RD
SAINT LOUIS, MO 631415930
Phone: 314 997-7010
Fax: –
Web: www.csileasing.com

CEO: Steve Hamilton
CFO: Fred O'Neal
HR: –
FYE: June 30
Type: Private

CSI Leasing is an industry leader that provides lease financing in 50 countries. The company sees leasing as a way to gain the benefits of using equipment without many of the hassles, costs and limitations associated with ownership. It provides off-lease services through its EPC subsidiary, which helps hundreds of organizations around the world dispose of end-of-life IT and maximize their return in secondary markets. CSI serves clients in such industries as healthcare, government, and education. It is a wholly-owned subsidiary of Tokyo Century Corporation. The company was founded in 1972.

	Annual Growth	06/00	06/01	06/02	06/03	06/09
Sales ($mil.)	(5.6%)	–	576.5	502.4	531.3	362.1
Net income ($ mil.)	5.2%	–	11.0	13.7	14.4	16.4
Market value ($ mil.)	–	–	–	–	–	–
Employees	–	–	–	–	–	1,040

CSP INC

175 Cabot Street - Suite 210
Lowell, MA 01854
Phone: 978 954-5038
Fax: –
Web: www.cspi.com

NMS: CSPI
CEO: Victor Dellovo
CFO: Gary W Levine
HR: –
FYE: September 30
Type: Public

CSP knows IT. The company provides information technology services, including the resale and integration of computer hardware and software, through its Modcomp subsidiary. Modcomp serves clients in the UK, and the US. Its MultiComputer product line includes systems used for radar, sonar, and surveillance. The company generates most of its revenue in the Americas. CSP Inc. was incorporated in 1968 and is based in Lowell, Massachusetts.

	Annual Growth	09/19	09/20	09/21	09/22	09/23
Sales ($mil.)	(4.9%)	79.1	61.8	49.2	54.4	64.6
Net income ($ mil.)	–	(0.4)	(1.4)	0.7	1.9	10.1
Market value ($ mil.)	6.9%	126.9	81.6	84.4	68.0	165.5
Employees	(0.4%)	114	112	112	117	112

CSRA INC.

3170 FAIRVIEW PARK DR
FALLS CHURCH, VA 220424516
Phone: 703 641-2000
Fax: –
Web: www.csra.com

CEO: –
CFO: –
HR: –
FYE: April 01
Type: Private

CSRA provides IT services to the USA's public sector agencies. Formed in late 2015 through the combination of the North American Public Sector business of CSC and SRA International, CSRA is one of the nation's largest independent providers of IT services to the US federal government with customers from nearly every federal agency. The company's next-generation services are built around government priorities including: the migration to cloud infrastructure, application modernization, "as-a-service" delivery, big data services, health IT and informatics, cyber security, and mobility. CSRA operates two segments based on its customer type: Defense and Intelligence, and Civil. In 2018 CSRA was acquired by General Dynamics for a total of $9.7 billion in cash and debt.

CSS INDUSTRIES, INC.

450 PLYMOUTH RD STE 300
PLYMOUTH MEETING, PA 194621644
Phone: 610 729-3959
Fax: –
Web: www.dgamericas.com

CEO: Gideon Schlessinger
CFO: Keith W Pfeil
HR: Allison Davis
FYE: March 31
Type: Private

Design Group Americas designs, manufactures, sources, and distributes a broad variety of branded and private label consumer products in the seasonal, stationery, gift, craft and toy categories. It sells its products online and in store throughout North and South America, Europe and as far as Australia. It partners with many of the world's best retailers and focus its teams and business to support its customer partnerships. Some of its brands include Simplicity, PhotoFabric, Blokko, Pink Elephant, Eureka, Seastones, PaperCraft, C.R. Gibson, and BowGenius, among others. Design Group Americas is a part of IG Design Group PLC, a diverse group of companies operating across multiple regions, categories, seasons and brands.

CSSI, INC.

395 E ST SW STE 200
WASHINGTON, DC 200243281
Phone: 202 863-2175
Fax: –
Web: www.cssiinc.com

CEO: Cynthia Castillo
CFO: Christopher Giusti
HR: Poniesa Johnson
FYE: December 31
Type: Private

CSSI turns an eye toward R&D. A technology and engineering services company, the company specializes in air traffic management. Areas of expertise include decision support systems, safety management, and cost-benefit analysis. Its services include information management and custom software development, operational analysis and implementation, investment strategy and analysis, and systems engineering. CSSI's clients have included NASA, the US Department of Defense, the Federal Aviation Administration, and the airline industry. The company has satellite offices in Charleston, South Carolina; Landover, Maryland; and Northfield, New Jersey.

	Annual Growth	12/04	12/05	12/06	12/08	12/19
Sales ($mil.)	1.1%	–	22.4	21.4	31.2	26.2
Net income ($ mil.)	0.2%	–	1.3	20.1	1.9	1.3
Market value ($ mil.)	–	–	–	–	–	–
Employees	–	–	–	–	–	158

CST BRANDS, LLC

19500 BULVERDE RD STE 100
SAN ANTONIO, TX 782593701
Phone: 210 692-5000
Fax: –
Web: www.cstbrands.com

CEO: Kimberly S Bowers
CFO: Clayton E Killinger
HR: Ken Glascock
FYE: December 31
Type: Private

CST Brands is hoping to corner the market on convenience stores. The company operates some 1,300 gas stations/convenience stores in the US under the Corner Store/Corner Store Market moniker. Those operations also include wholesale gas supply businesses that sell fuel to the company's retail sites, primarily under the Valero and Diamond Shamrock brands. In addition, CST sells a host of other national gas brands to independent dealers and other customers. In 2017 the company was acquired by Canadian convenience store leader Alimentation Couche-Tard.

CSU FULLERTON AUXILIARY SERVICES CORPORATION

2600 NUTWOOD AVE STE 275
FULLERTON, CA 928313137
Phone: 657 278-4140
Fax: –
Web: www.csufasc.org

CEO: –
CFO: –
HR: –
FYE: June 30
Type: Private

CSU Fullerton Auxiliary Services (formerly California State University Fullerton Foundation) keeps an eye on auxiliary operations at Cal State. The organization administers research and education grants and oversees commercial operations, such as the Titan Shops (which stock textbooks, computers, gifts, and clothing) and franchise foodservices. It is also involved in real estate, providing affordable housing for sale and lease to the university's faculty and staff. A 25-member board governs CSU Fullerton Auxiliary Services Corporation, which was established in 1959.

	Annual Growth	06/07	06/08	06/09	06/10	06/12
Sales ($mil.)	(50.4%)	–	1,035.7	54.0	55.2	62.9
Net income ($ mil.)	–	–	0.0	(0.5)	2.3	(2.8)
Market value ($ mil.)	–	–	–	–	–	–
Employees	–	–	–	–	–	1,400

CSX CORP

500 Water Street, 15th Floor
Jacksonville, FL 32202
Phone: 904 359-3200
Fax: –
Web: www.csx.com

NMS: CSX
CEO: Joseph R Hinrichs
CFO: Sean R Pelkey
HR: –
FYE: December 31
Type: Public

Through its main subsidiary, CSX Transportation (CSXT), CSX Corporation operates a major rail system of around 20,000 route miles in the eastern US. The freight carrier links some 25 states, 70 ports, 240 short-line railroads, the District of Columbia, and two Canadian provinces (Ontario and Quebec). Freight hauled by the company includes a wide variety of merchandise (food and agricultural products, chemicals, and consumer goods among others), coal, and automotive products. CSX also transports via intermodal containers and trailers.

	Annual Growth	12/19	12/20	12/21	12/22	12/23
Sales ($mil.)	5.3%	11,937	10,583	12,522	14,853	14,657
Net income ($ mil.)	2.8%	3,331.0	2,765.0	3,781.0	4,166.0	3,715.0
Market value ($ mil.)	(16.8%)	141,712	177,727	73,637	60,672	67,899
Employees	2.3%	21,000	19,300	20,900	22,500	23,000

CTO REALTY GROWTH INC (NEW)

369 N. New York Avenue, Suite 201
Winter Park, FL 32789
Phone: 407 904-3324
Fax: –
Web: www.ctoreit.com

NYS: CTO
CEO: –
CFO: –
HR: –
FYE: December 31
Type: Public

From retail centers to hay farms, land developer CTO Realty Growth (formerly Consolidated-Tomoka) owns and manages, sometimes utilizing third-party property management companies, about 35 commercial real estate properties in more than 10 states in the United States. Its portfolio includes single- and multi-tenant retail properties (tenants include Wells Fargo, Big Lots, and Lowe's). Through its subsidiaries, it also holds subsurface oil, gas, and mineral interests on land throughout Florida. The company traces its roots to 1910 and change its name to CTO Realty Growth, Inc. from Consolidated-Tomoka Land Co. in mid-2020.

	Annual Growth	12/18	12/19	12/20	12/21	12/22
Sales ($mil.)	(1.3%)	86.7	44.9	56.4	70.3	82.3
Net income ($ mil.)	(46.0%)	37.2	115.0	78.5	29.9	3.2
Market value ($ mil.)	(23.2%)	1,199.9	1,378.6	963.6	1,403.7	417.8
Employees	16.7%	14	15	17	19	26

CTPARTNERS EXECUTIVE SEARCH INC

1166 Avenue of the Americas, 3rd Fl.
New York, NY 10036
Phone: 212 588-3500
Fax: –
Web: www.ctnet.com

NBB: CTPR
CEO: David C Nocifora
CFO: William J Keneally
HR: –
FYE: December 31
Type: Public

CTPartners finds the hidden treasures of senior management. The company performs CEO, board member, and senior-level executive management searches for both large and emerging companies worldwide. Operating through more than 20 global offices, it has special expertise in filling top-level technology positions, but also operates a number of other industry practices, including financial services, human resources, life sciences, media, and telecommunications. The company delivers talent within an average of about 100 days; it has placed executives with such companies as Sony, American Express, and RELX Group. CTPartners was founded in 1980.

	Annual Growth	12/10	12/11	12/12	12/13	12/14
Sales ($mil.)	108.3%	9.4	126.1	132.9	134.3	176.8
Net income ($ mil.)	–	(5.8)	(3.2)	(3.6)	(1.6)	3.3
Market value ($ mil.)	(0.9%)	114.5	38.6	33.2	40.7	110.4
Employees	17.1%	336	369	453	460	631

CTS CORP

4925 Indiana Avenue
Lisle, IL 60532
Phone: 630 577-8800
Fax: –
Web: www.ctscorp.com

NYS: CTS
CEO: Kieran M O'Sullivan
CFO: Ashish Agrawal
HR: –
FYE: December 31
Type: Public

CTS designs, manufactures, and sells a broad line of sensors, connectivity components, and actuators primarily to original equipment manufacturers (OEMs) and tier one suppliers for the aerospace and defense, industrial, telecommunications, information technology, medical, and transportation markets. The company is a global manufacturer of sensors, connectivity components, and actuators. These devices are categorized by their ability to Sense, Connect or Move. Sense products provide vital inputs to electronic systems. Connect products allow systems to function in synchronization with other systems. Move products ensure required movements are effectively and accurately executed. Customers have included industry leaders such as Cummins and Toyota. The US account for over 55% of the company's total sales. CTS was founded in 1896.

	Annual Growth	12/19	12/20	12/21	12/22	12/23
Sales ($mil.)	4.1%	469.0	424.1	512.9	586.9	550.4
Net income ($ mil.)	13.8%	36.1	34.7	(41.9)	59.6	60.5
Market value ($ mil.)	9.9%	925.0	1,058.2	1,131.9	1,215.1	1,348.3
Employees	3.4%	3,570	3,786	3,820	4,209	4,081

CTSC, LLC

10505 FURNACE RD STE 205
LORTON, VA 220792636
Phone: 703 493-9880
Fax: –
Web: –

CEO: Ken Ogden
CFO: –
HR: –
FYE: September 30
Type: Private

CTSC (Chenega Technology Services Corporation) is a certified Alaska Native Corporation (ANC) that provides support services to federal agencies. Its core competencies include base operations and facilities management, engineering, information technology, intelligence, support, logistics, and training. Partnering with prime government contractors and sub-contractors, CTSC offers information systems development, system integration, support to military operations, network engineering, and technical analysis. As an ANC, the company enjoys no-bid contracts with the government. CTSC is a subsidiary of Chenega Corporation.

CUBESMART, L.P.

1500 GATEWAY BLVD STE 190
BOYNTON BEACH, FL 334267233
Phone: 610 535-5700
Fax: -
Web: -

CEO: -
CFO: -
HR: -
FYE: December 31
Type: Private

CubeSmart is a real estate investment trust (REIT) that owns more than 605 self-storage facilities with about 43.6 million sq. ft. of rentable space in about 25 states and in the District of Columbia. The company also manages some 650 self-storage facilities for third parties. Its self-storage properties are designed to offer affordable and easily-accessible storage space for its residential and commercial customers. CubeSmart's customers rent storage cubes for their exclusive use, typically on a month-to-month basis. Additionally, some of its stores offer outside storage areas for vehicles and boats. Its stores are designed to accommodate both residential and commercial customers, with features such as wide aisles and load-bearing capabilities for large truck access.

CUBIC CORPORATION

9233 BALBOA AVE
SAN DIEGO, CA 921231513
Phone: 858 277-6780
Fax: -
Web: www.cubic.com

CEO: Stevan Slijepcevic
CFO: Travis Chester
HR: Jerald Raines
FYE: September 30
Type: Private

Cubic creates and delivers technology solutions in transportation that make people's lives easier by simplifying their daily journeys and defense capabilities that help promote mission success and safety for those who serve their nation. Cubic is also the leading integrator of payment and information solutions and related services for intelligent travel applications in the transportation industry. It delivers integrated systems for transportation and traffic management, providing tools for travelers to choose the smartest and easiest way to travel and pay for their journeys. Its C5ISR solutions provide information capture, assessment, exploitation, and dissemination in a secure network-centric environment. Cubic was founded in 1951.

CUISINE SOLUTIONS, INC.

NBB: CUSI

85 South Bragg Street, Suite 600
Alexandria, VA 22312
Phone: 703 270-2900
Fax: -
Web: -

CEO: Stanislas Vilgrain
CFO: -
HR: Donald Cajus
FYE: June 28
Type: Public

Whether you're traveling for pleasure or to serve your country, this company makes sure you get a good meal. Cuisine Solutions is a leading supplier of prepared meals for a variety of customers, such as travel and transportation providers, the military, hotels, and restaurants. Its client list has included Starwood Hotels & Resorts, Pei Wei, Panera Bread, and T.G.I. Friday's. The company also sells directly to consumers. Cuisine Solutions fully cooks and then freezes meals at its production facilities in the US, Chile, and France. Meals are distributed worldwide. The company, controlled by the family of chairman Jean-Louis Vilgrain, went private in 2009.

	Annual Growth	06/04	06/05	06/06	06/07	06/08
Sales ($mil.)	24.2%	36.7	46.2	64.1	80.3	87.5
Net income ($ mil.)	-	(1.0)	1.7	3.7	10.5	0.0
Market value ($ mil.)	2.7%	31.4	112.5	88.1	105.6	34.9
Employees	11.4%	230	263	302	354	354

CUIVRE RIVER ELECTRIC COOPERATIVE, INC.

1112 E CHERRY ST
TROY, MO 633791518
Phone: 636 528-8261
Fax: -
Web: www.cuivre.com

CEO: Doug Tracy
CFO: -
HR: Brittany Drones
FYE: December 31
Type: Private

Show me the power. Cuivre River Electric Cooperative provides power to four eastern counties in the "Show Me" state: Lincoln, Pike, St. Charles, and Warren. The membership utility, which is one of Missouri's largest cooperatives with more than 58,000 residential, commercial, and industrial customers, gets its wholesale power supply from the Associated Electric Cooperative and the Central Electric Power Cooperative. Cuivre River Propane, jointly owned and operated by Cuivre River Electric Cooperative and MFA Oil Company supplies propane to co-op members from four locations, Bowling Green, Elsberry, Troy, and Wright City.

	Annual Growth	12/13	12/14	12/15	12/21	12/22
Sales ($mil.)	2.7%	-	110.8	110.7	127.6	137.3
Net income ($ mil.)	(5.0%)	-	4.4	3.6	(0.2)	2.9
Market value ($ mil.)	-	-	-	-	-	-
Employees	-	-	-	-	-	138

CULINAIRE INTERNATIONAL, INC.

8303 ELMBROOK DR
DALLAS, TX 752474011
Phone: 214 754-1880
Fax: -
Web: www.culinaireintl.com

CEO: Richard N Gussoni
CFO: Buz Lafrano
HR: -
FYE: December 27
Type: Private

Culinaire International makes trips to the zoo, university food court, and music venue a little more palatable. The company is a leading contract foodservice operator that provides dining and hospitality services at entertainment venues, hotels and convention centers, and private clubs. Its foodservice and concessions operations include the Fort Worth Zoo, Sheraton properties, Hilton properties, Westin properties, Meyerson Symphony Center, and UT Southwestern. Culinaire International also offers catering and corporate dining services, and it operates Dallas area restaurants Ristorante Nicola, Sea Change, and Omaha Steakhouse.

CULLEN/FROST BANKERS, INC.

NYS: CFR

111 W. Houston Street
San Antonio, TX 78205
Phone: 210 220-4011
Fax: 210 220-5578
Web: www.frostbank.com

CEO: Phillip D Green
CFO: Jerry Salinas
HR: -
FYE: December 31
Type: Public

Cullen/Frost Bankers is a financial holding company and a bank holding company and one of the largest independent bank holding companies in Texas. The community-oriented bank serves individuals and local businesses. It offers commercial and consumer banking services, trust and investment management services, mutual funds, insurance, brokerage, leasing, treasury management, capital markets advisory, and item processing services. Subsidiaries include Frost Bank its principal operating subsidiary and sole banking subsidiary, Frost Insurance Agency, Frost Brokerage Services, Frost Investment Advisors, and investment banking arm Tri?Frost and Cullen/Frost Capital Trust II. Cullen/Frost serves a variety of industries including, among others, energy, manufacturing, services, construction, retail, telecommunications, healthcare, military, and transportation and has total assets of $52.9 billion.

	Annual Growth	12/19	12/20	12/21	12/22	12/23
Assets ($Mil.)	10.6%	34,027	42,391	50,878	52,892	50,845
Net income ($ mil.)	7.8%	443.6	331.2	443.1	579.2	598.0
Market value ($ mil.)	2.6%	6,276.0	5,598.9	8,091.8	8,581.6	6,963.5
Employees	4.2%	4,659	4,685	4,553	4,985	5,495

CULP INC
NYS: CULP

1823 Eastchester Drive
High Point, NC 27265-1402
Phone: 336 889-5161
Fax: –
Web: www.culp.com

CEO: Robert G Culp IV
CFO: Kenneth R Bowling
HR: –
FYE: April 30
Type: Public

Culp manufactures, sources, and markets mattress fabrics and sewn covers used for covering mattresses and foundations and other bedding products; and upholstery fabrics, including cut and sewn kits, primarily used in the production of upholstered furniture. Culp delivers fashion-conscious, stylish fabrics with broad appeal to some of the largest home furnishing retailers and manufacturers. Its upholstery fabrics include wovens (jacquards and dobbies), suedes, faux leathers, cut and sewn kits, and velvets (woven and tufted). Its fabrics are used in upholstering residential and commercial furniture such as recliners, sofas, chairs, sectionals, sofa beds, love seats, and office seating. Its mattress fabrics include Woven jacquards, Converted, Knitted fabric, and Sewn mattress covers used in the production of bedding products. About 70% of the company's revenue comes from the US.

	Annual Growth	04/19*	05/20	05/21	05/22*	04/23
Sales ($mil.)	(5.7%)	296.7	256.2	299.7	294.8	234.9
Net income ($ mil.)	–	–	5.7	(24.0)	3.2	(3.2)	(31.5)
Market value ($ mil.)	(28.4%)	255.7	85.2	174.4	79.6	67.3
Employees	(1.9%)	1,440	1,399	1,430	1,582	1,333

*Fiscal year change

CULVER FRANCHISING SYSTEM, LLC

1240 WATER ST
PRAIRIE DU SAC, WI 535781091
Phone: 608 643-7980
Fax: –
Web: www.culvers.com

CEO: Enrique Silva
CFO: –
HR: –
FYE: December 31
Type: Private

If you think ButterBurgers are better burgers, then you're probably a fan of Culver's. Culver Franchising System operates a chain of about 500 Culver's quick-service restaurants popular for their signature ButterBurgers (hamburgers served on a grilled buttered bun) and frozen custard. The chain's menu also includes chicken, fish, and pork sandwiches; salads; and dinner items such as shrimp and Norwegian cod. Nearly all of the restaurants are operated by franchisees. Chairman and CEO Craig Culver started the restaurant as a family business back in 1984.

CUMBERLAND COUNTY HOSPITAL SYSTEM, INC.

1638 OWEN DR
FAYETTEVILLE, NC 283043424
Phone: 910 609-4000
Fax: –
Web: www.capefearvalley.com

CEO: Michael Nagowski
CFO: Bret Johnson
HR: Brenda Hubbard
FYE: September 30
Type: Private

Don't fear for a lack of medical services at Cumberland County Hospital System (doing business as Cape Fear Valley Health System). The medical provider comprises five acute-care and specialty hospitals, with about 915 total beds, serving a six-county region of Southeastern North Carolina and more than 935,000 patients annually. The hospital system serves residents of coastal North Carolina, providing general and specialized medical services such as cancer treatment, open-heart surgery, psychiatric care, and rehabilitation. It also operates the HealthPlex fitness and wellness facility that has over 140 pieces of next-generation cardiovascular and strength-building equipment, and provides home health and hospice services. Among its medical facilities include Cape Fear Valley Medical Center, Highsmith-Rainey Specialty Hospital, Cape Fear Valley Rehabilitation Center, Bladen County Hospital and Hoke Hospital.

	Annual Growth	09/18	09/19	09/20	09/21	09/22
Sales ($mil.)	2.0%	–	1,149.4	779.6	1,117.1	1,220.4
Net income ($ mil.)	–	–	30.5	50.2	140.7	(59.3)
Market value ($ mil.)	–	–	–	–	–	–
Employees	–	–	–	–	–	5,000

CUMBERLAND PHARMACEUTICALS INC
NMS: CPIX

1600 West End Avenue, Suite 1300
Nashville, TN 37203
Phone: 615 255-0068
Fax: –
Web: www.cumberlandpharma.com

CEO: A J Kazimi
CFO: John Hamm
HR: Sasha Boustani
FYE: December 31
Type: Public

Cumberland Pharmaceuticals wants to make your search for the right drugs less cumbersome. The specialty pharmaceutical company focuses on acquiring, developing, and commercializing branded prescription drugs. Targeting the hospital acute care and gastroenterology segments, Cumberland's FDA-approved drugs include Acetadote for the treatment of acetaminophen poisoning; Kristalose, a prescription strength laxative; Vaprisol, for low sodium levels; and Caldolor (ne Amelior), the first injectable dosage form of ibuprofen. The company also has several projects in development. Acetadote and Kristalose are marketed through Cumberland's own hospital and gastroenterology sales forces. The company went public in a mid-2009 IPO.

	Annual Growth	12/19	12/20	12/21	12/22	12/23
Sales ($mil.)	(4.5%)	47.5	37.4	36.0	42.0	39.6
Net income ($ mil.)	–	(3.5)	(3.3)	(3.5)	(5.6)	(6.3)
Market value ($ mil.)	(23.2%)	72.7	41.7	65.9	31.8	25.3
Employees	(0.8%)	94	90	83	85	91

CUMMINS, INC.
NYS: CMI

500 Jackson Street, Box 3005
Columbus, IN 47202-3005
Phone: 812 377-5000
Fax: 812 377-4937
Web: www.cummins.com

CEO: Jennifer W Rumsey
CFO: Mark A Smith
HR: –
FYE: December 31
Type: Public

Cummins is a global power leader that designs, manufactures, distributes and services diesel, natural gas, electric and hybrid powertrains and powertrain-related components including filtration, aftertreatment, turbochargers, fuel systems, controls systems, air handling systems, automated transmissions, axles, drivelines, brakes, suspension systems, electric power generation systems, batteries, electrified power systems, electric powertrains, hydrogen production and fuel cell products. In addition to its flagship Engine segment, other business segments include Distribution (product distributors and servicing), Components (filtration products and fuel systems), Power Systems (vehicle and residential generators), and New Power (electric and hybrid powertrain systems). Cummins' major customers include OEMs Daimler, Ford, Komatsu, PACCAR, TRATON AG, Navistar, and Volvo, among others. Around 55% of the company's total sales come from the US. The company traces its historical roots back to 1919 as Cummins Engine Company.

	Annual Growth	12/19	12/20	12/21	12/22	12/23
Sales ($mil.)	9.6%	23,571	19,811	24,021	28,074	34,065
Net income ($ mil.)	(24.5%)	2,260.0	1,789.0	2,131.0	2,151.0	735.0
Market value ($ mil.)	7.6%	25,377	32,203	30,932	34,357	33,971
Employees	5.2%	61,615	57,825	59,900	73,600	75,500

CUMULUS MEDIA INC
NMS: CMLS

780 Johnson Ferry Road NE, Suite 500
Atlanta, GA 30342
Phone: 404 949-0700
Fax: –
Web: www.cumulusmedia.com

CEO: –
CFO: –
HR: –
FYE: December 31
Type: Public

Cumulus Media reigns over an empire of radio stations. The company is a radio station ownership group in the US (behind Clear Channel), with about 430 owned or operated stations in more than 85 markets throughout the country. In many of its markets, Cumulus provides advertisers with personal connections, local impact and national reach through on-air and on-demand digital, mobile, social, and voice-activated platforms, as well as integrated digital marketing services, powerful influencers, full-service audio solutions, industry-leading research and insights, and live event experiences. The company delivers nationally-syndicated sports, news, talk, and entertainment programming from iconic brands including the NFL, the NCAA, the Masters, the Olympics, the Academy of Country Music Awards, and many other world-class partners through Westwood One, an audio network in America.

	Annual Growth	12/19	12/20	12/21	12/22	12/23
Sales ($mil.)	(6.7%)	1,113.4	816.2	916.5	953.5	844.5
Net income ($ mil.)	–	61.3	(59.7)	17.3	16.2	(117.9)
Market value ($ mil.)	(25.8%)	290.8	144.3	186.2	102.8	88.0
Employees	(8.2%)	4,732	3,787	3,488	3,330	3,367

CURAEGIS TECHNOLOGIES INC

350 Linden Oaks
Rochester, NY 14625
Phone: 585 254-1100
Fax: -
Web: www.curaegis.com

CEO: Richard A Kaplan
CFO: Kathleen A Browne
HR: -
FYE: December 31
Type: Public

A development-stage company, Torvec hopes to bring its Torvec FTV (full-terrain vehicle) to the markets of developing nations. The FTV has the body of a truck, but has tracks similar to those of a tank. The tracks enable the FTV to venture where a mere wheeled vehicle would fear to tread. Several technologies developed by the late Vernon Gleasman and members of his family, including an infinitely variable transmission and a steering drive and suspension system for tracked vehicles, are being incorporated into the FTV. The company is working with Ford Motor to develop a version of the FTV to be manufactured and distributed in the US initially and then marketed globally.

	Annual Growth	12/15	12/16	12/17	12/18	12/19
Sales ($mil.)	-	-	0.0	0.0	0.0	0.0
Net income ($ mil.)	-	(2.7)	(4.2)	(5.4)	(6.3)	(4.3)
Market value ($ mil.)	(30.7%)	16.8	34.7	15.3	9.7	3.9
Employees	(14.3%)	13	24	24	15	7

CURIA GLOBAL, INC.

26 CORPORATE CIR
ALBANY, NY 122035121
Phone: 518 512-2000
Fax: -
Web: www.curiaglobal.com

CEO: John Ratliff
CFO: Felicia I Ladin
HR: Bridget Marlowe
FYE: December 31
Type: Private

Curia Global (formerly known as Albany Molecular Research) is a leading contract research, development and manufacturing organization providing products and services from R&D through commercial manufacturing to pharmaceutical and biopharmaceutical customers. Its services range from compound screening and other drug discovery services to the contract manufacturing of existing and experimental drugs and drug ingredients for clinical trials and commercial sale. The company has some 30 locations across the US, Europe, and Asia. Thomas E. D'Ambra, Ph.D., co-founded AMRI in 1991 and relaunched as Curia in 2021.

CURIS INC

128 Spring Street, Building C, Suite 500
Lexington, MA 02421
Phone: 617 503-6500
Fax: -
Web: www.curis.com

NAS: CRIS
CEO: James E Dentzer
CFO: William Steinkrauss
HR: Jennifer Wagner
FYE: December 31
Type: Public

Curis' cancer patients and Sega's gamers might one day have an unlikely hero in common: Sonic the Hedgehog. Drug development firm Curis is studying hedgehog signaling pathways (including the sonic hedgehog pathway, named after the Sega mascot) to find treatments for oncology ailments and other conditions. Its commercialize product, Erivedge is an orally bioavailable small molecule which is designed to selectively inhibit the Hedgehog signaling pathway by targeting a protein called Smoothened. Erivedge is FDA approved for treatment of adults with metastatic basal cell carcinoma. Its collaborating partner, Genentech (a member of the Roche Group) and Roche are responsible for the clinical development and global commercialization of Erivedge. The company also has internal development programs for cancer treatments using other signaling pathways.

	Annual Growth	12/19	12/20	12/21	12/22	12/23
Sales ($mil.)	-	10.0	10.8	10.6	10.2	10.0
Net income ($ mil.)	-	(32.1)	(29.9)	(45.4)	(56.7)	(47.4)
Market value ($ mil.)	65.5%	10.0	48.3	28.1	3.2	75.1
Employees	14.4%	28	28	60	51	48

CURRAN GROUP, INC.

286 MEMORIAL CT
CRYSTAL LAKE, IL 600146277
Phone: 815 455-5100
Fax: -
Web: www.currangroup.com

CEO: -
CFO: Todd Gierke
HR: -
FYE: December 31
Type: Private

The Curran Group knows how to get the show on the road. Through its Curran Contracting subsidiary, the company paves roads, as well as interstate highways and parking lots, throughout Northeastern Illinois for commercial, industrial, and county and municipal customers. Curran Contracting also provides contract excavation services, and operates five asphalt plants that produce a variety of hot-mix asphalt. Other businesses of the Group include porcelain stone tile manufacture and distribution (Crossville), rail welding equipment and services (Holland LP), and finishing and painting systems (Global Finishing Solutions).

CURTIS C. GUNN, INC.

227 BROADWAY ST
SAN ANTONIO, TX 782051923
Phone: 210 472-2501
Fax: -
Web: www.gunnauto.com

CEO: Curtis C Gunn Jr
CFO: Kelly Collins
HR: -
FYE: December 31
Type: Private

Business at Gunn Automotive is aimed straight at the heart of Texas. The company sells more than 12,000 new Acuras, Chevrolets, Dodges, Hondas, Infinitis, Nissans, and Pontiacs and about 5,500 used cars at eight automotive dealerships in San Antonio, Texas. Gunn Automotive also sells more than 110 Chevrolet commercial fleet units at a ninth location in San Antonio. It also provides financing, parts, and service, including collision repair. Car shoppers can browse for new and used cars on the group's Web site or apply for credit, order parts, and schedule service. Founded in 1956, Gunn Automotive is owned by the Gunn family.

	Annual Growth	06/03	06/04	06/05	06/06*	12/21
Sales ($mil.)	(23.4%)	-	500.8	549.2	547.8	5.3
Net income ($ mil.)	(19.3%)	-	4.4	11.3	12.3	0.1
Market value ($ mil.)	-	-	-	-	-	-
Employees	-	-	-	-	-	810

*Fiscal year change

CURTISS-WRIGHT CORP.

130 Harbour Place Drive, Suite 300
Davidson, NC 28036
Phone: 704 869-4600
Fax: -
Web: www.curtisswright.com

NYS: CW
CEO: Lynn M Bamford
CFO: K C Farkas
HR: -
FYE: December 31
Type: Public

Curtiss-Wright is a global integrated business that provides highly engineered products, solutions, and services mainly to aerospace & defense (A&D) markets, as well as critical technologies in demanding commercial power, process, and industrial markets. The company manufactures and services main coolant pumps, power-dense compact motors, generators, and secondary propulsion systems. Curtiss-Wright also provides embedded computing board level modules, integrated subsystems, flight testing systems, turret aiming, and weapons handling systems to defense customers. The company's manufacturing footprint spans over 145 facilities worldwide while it generates the majority of sales in the US.

	Annual Growth	12/19	12/20	12/21	12/22	12/23
Sales ($mil.)	3.4%	2,488.0	2,391.3	2,505.9	2,557.0	2,845.4
Net income ($ mil.)	3.6%	307.6	201.4	267.2	294.3	354.5
Market value ($ mil.)	12.1%	5,382.4	4,444.9	5,297.6	6,379.5	8,511.2
Employees	(1.4%)	9,100	8,200	7,800	8,100	8,600

CUSO FINANCIAL SERVICES, L.P.

10150 MEANLEY DR FL 1
SAN DIEGO, CA 921313007
Phone: 800 686-4724
Fax: –
Web: www.cusonet.com

CEO: Valorie Seyfert
CFO: Daniel J Kilroy
HR: Janine Holmes
FYE: December 31
Type: Private

For credit unions looking to expand their investment offerings, CUSO can do so. CUSO Financial Services (CFS) provides credit unions with online securities trading, retirement planning, wealth management, insurance, and other investment services from more than 300 providers that the credit unions can in turn offer to their members. Founded in 1996 by Valorie Seyfert and Amy Beattie (company president and COO, respectively), CFS serves about 100 credit unions throughout the US; more than 40 of them are limited partners that hold ownership stakes in the company.

	Annual Growth	12/04	12/05	12/06	12/07	12/08
Assets ($mil.)	0.8%	–	22.3	24.7	28.0	22.8
Net income ($ mil.)	(11.0%)	–	4.8	6.0	6.0	3.4
Market value ($ mil.)	–	–	–	–	–	–
Employees	–	–	–	–	–	20

CUSTOMERS BANCORP INC   NYS: CUBI

701 Reading Avenue
West Reading, PA 19611
Phone: 610 933-2000
Fax: –
Web: www.customersbank.com

CEO: Sam Sidhu
CFO: Carla A Leibold
HR: –
FYE: December 31
Type: Public

Boasting some $20.3 billion in assets, Customers Bancorp, is the bank holding company engaged in banking activities through its wholly owned subsidiary, Customers Bank, which operates about 10 branches across Florida, Illinois, Massachusetts, New Hampshire, New Jersey, New York, North Carolina, Pennsylvania, Rhode Island and Texas. It offers traditional loan and deposit banking products and financial services, and non-traditional products and services such as CBIT, to its commercial and consumer customers. Customers also offers traditional deposit products, including commercial and consumer checking accounts, non-interest-bearing demand accounts, MMDA, savings accounts, time deposit accounts and cash management services. Around 85% of the bank's loan portfolio is made up of commercial loans, while the rest consists of consumer loans.

	Annual Growth	12/19	12/20	12/21	12/22	12/23
Assets ($mil.)	16.6%	11,521	18,439	19,575	20,896	21,316
Net income ($ mil.)	33.3%	79.3	132.6	314.6	228.0	250.1
Market value ($ mil.)	24.7%	748.6	571.6	2,055.3	891.0	1,811.6
Employees	(4.7%)	867	830	641	668	714

CUSTOMINK, LLC

2910 DISTRICT AVE
FAIRFAX, VA 220312282
Phone: 703 434-3215
Fax: –
Web: www.customink.com

CEO: –
CFO: –
HR: Bo Bayer
FYE: December 31
Type: Private

CustomInk knows a T-shirt is not just a T-shirt. (It can also be an advertisement, a form of self-expression, or a fashion statement.) The firm provides screen printing and embroidery services for customers across the US through its online storefront. Customers pick the clothing type (short and long sleeve Ts, tank tops, sweats) and color, and then add text and graphics (picking from available graphics or designing their own). CustomInk team members -- or Inkers, as they call themselves -- then print and ship orders. The firm also offers anout 200 other customized products (pens, hats, drinkware). CustomInk was founded in 1999 by president Marc Katz and former classmates Mike Driscoll and Dave Christensen.

	Annual Growth	12/03	12/04	12/05	12/06	12/08
Sales ($mil.)	44.5%	–	13.7	–	34.0	59.6
Net income ($ mil.)	(1.0%)	–	4.8	–	3.8	4.6
Market value ($ mil.)	–	–	–	–	–	–
Employees	–	–	–	–	–	500

CUTCO CORPORATION

1116 E STATE ST
OLEAN, NY 147603814
Phone: 716 372-3111
Fax: –
Web: www.cutco.com

CEO: James E Stitt
CFO: Brent Driscoll
HR: –
FYE: December 31
Type: Private

CUTCO cuts up in the kitchen and on the battlefield. Founded in 1949, the company's CUTCO Cutlery subsidiary makes more than 100 kitchen cutlery items, such as butcher knives, paring knives, flatware, and other kitchen utensils. Its cutlery is sold in North America through CUTCO retail stores and home demonstrations by subsidiary Vector Marketing. CUTCO International markets the company's products outside North America. In addition, its KA-BAR Knives unit makes fighting and utility knives for the US military, along with hunting, fishing, and pocket knives that are sold by retailers worldwide. The company's Schilling Forge business provides precision forgings of medical instruments, hand tools, and cutlery.

CUTERA INC   NMS: CUTR

3240 Bayshore Blvd.
Brisbane, CA 94005
Phone: 415 657-5500
Fax: –
Web: www.cutera.com

CEO: Sheila Hopkins
CFO: Stuart Drummond
HR: Debbie Totah
FYE: December 31
Type: Public

Cutera was founded in 1998 and is a global provider of Face + Body laser, light, and other energy-based aesthetic systems. The company designs, develops, manufactures, and markets its platforms for use by physicians and other qualified practitioners enabling them to provide safe and effective aesthetic treatments to their customers. excel V, excel HR, xeo, enlighten, truSculpt, and Genesis Plus are the main product platforms sold globally for a wide range of aesthetic indications. The company sells both single and multi-application platforms, and all feature upgradability and customization to match customer needs. Cutera distributes its products globally through distributors in over 65 countries but generates about 50% of its revenue in North America.

	Annual Growth	12/18	12/19	12/20	12/21	12/22
Sales ($mil.)	11.6%	162.7	181.7	147.7	231.3	252.4
Net income ($ mil.)	–	(30.8)	(12.3)	(23.9)	2.1	(82.3)
Market value ($ mil.)	27.0%	334.8	704.3	474.2	812.7	869.7
Employees	7.7%	402	447	323	461	540

CVB FINANCIAL CORP   NMS: CVBF

701 North Haven Ave., Suite 350
Ontario, CA 91764
Phone: 909 980-4030
Fax: –
Web: www.cbbank.com

CEO: David A Brager
CFO: E A Nicholson
HR: –
FYE: December 31
Type: Public

CVB Financial is the holding company of Citizens Business Bank (CBB), which offers community banking services to primarily small and mid-sized businesses, but also to consumers through nearly 60 banking centers and office locations across central and southern California. Boasting more than $7.82 billion in assets, the bank offers checking, money market, CDs and savings accounts, trust and investment services, and a variety of loans. Commercial real estate loans account for about 75% of the bank's loan portfolio, which is rounded out by business, consumer, and construction loans; residential mortgages; dairy and livestock loans; and municipal lease financing.

	Annual Growth	12/19	12/20	12/21	12/22	12/23
Assets ($mil.)	9.2%	11,282	14,419	15,884	16,477	16,021
Net income ($ mil.)	1.6%	207.8	177.2	212.5	235.4	221.4
Market value ($ mil.)	(1.7%)	3,007.1	2,717.2	2,983.4	3,588.1	2,813.4
Employees	–	–	1,052	1,015	1,072	1,107

CVD EQUIPMENT CORP.
NAS: CVV

355 South Technology Drive
Central Islip, NY 11722
Phone: 631 981-7081
Fax: –
Web: www.cvdequipment.com

CEO: Emmanuel Lakios
CFO: Glen R Charles
HR: –
FYE: December 31
Type: Public

CVD Equipment has expanded well beyond the chemical vapor deposition (CVD) equipment that gave it its name. (During CVD, precise layers of chemicals are deposited onto semiconductor wafers during chip manufacturing.) The company's specialized equipment is also used in the development of nanotechnology -- namely solar cells, smart glass, carbon nanotubes, nanowires, LEDs, and micro-electromechanical systems (MEMS). CVD Equipment still makes custom-designed products for major semiconductor companies, but its newer technologies are used by universities, research labs, and startup companies. Its largest shareholder is Chairman and CEO Leonard A. Rosenbaum, who founded the company in 1982, and owns 29%.

	Annual Growth	12/19	12/20	12/21	12/22	12/23
Sales ($mil.)	5.3%	19.6	16.9	16.4	25.8	24.1
Net income ($ mil.)	–	(6.3)	(6.1)	4.7	(0.2)	(4.2)
Market value ($ mil.)	8.3%	22.0	24.8	28.2	37.6	30.2
Employees	(7.1%)	172	130	113	136	128

CVENT, INC.

1765 GREENSBORO STATION PL FL 7
TYSONS CORNER, VA 221023468
Phone: 703 226-3500
Fax: –
Web: www.cvent.com

CEO: Rajeev K Aggarwal
CFO: Cynthia Russo
HR: –
FYE: December 31
Type: Private

Cvent is a leading meetings, events, and hospitality technology provider with approximately 22,000 customers worldwide. Founded in 1999, the company delivers a comprehensive event marketing and management platform and offers a global marketplace where event professionals collaborate with venues to create engaging, impactful experiences. The comprehensive Cvent event marketing and management platform offers software solutions to event organizers and marketers for online event registration, venue selection, event marketing and management, virtual and onsite solutions, and attendee engagement. Cvent's suite of products automate and simplify the event management process and maximize the impact of in-person, virtual, and hybrid events. Hotels and venues use Cvent's supplier and venue solutions to win more group and corporate travel business through Cvent's sourcing platforms. The company's solutions is used by clients in about 130 countries. It generates almost 80% of revenue in North America.

CVR ENERGY INC
NYS: CVI

2277 Plaza Drive, Suite 500
Sugar Land, TX 77479
Phone: 281 207-3200
Fax: –
Web: www.cvrenergy.com

CEO: David L Lamp
CFO: Dane J Neumann
HR: –
FYE: December 31
Type: Public

Founded in 2006, CVR Energy refines and markets high value transportation fuels to retailers, railroads, and farm cooperatives and other refiners/marketers in Kansas, Oklahoma and Iowa. Located approximately 100 miles of Cushing, Oklahoma (a major crude oil trading and storage hub), it's two oil refineries?in Coffeyville, Kansas and Wynnewood, Oklahoma?represent close to a quarter of the region's refining capacity. Through a limited partnership, the company also produces and distributes ammonia and ammonium nitrate to farmers in Kansas and Illinois. As of 2022, it owned the general partner and over 35% of the outstanding common units representing limited partner interests in CVR Partners.

	Annual Growth	12/19	12/20	12/21	12/22	12/23
Sales ($mil.)	9.8%	6,364.0	3,930.0	7,242.0	10,896	9,247.0
Net income ($ mil.)	19.3%	380.0	(256.0)	25.0	463.0	769.0
Market value ($ mil.)	(7.0%)	4,064.5	1,497.9	1,689.9	3,150.6	3,046.1
Employees	1.3%	1,486	1,423	1,429	1,470	1,566

CVR PARTNERS LP
NYS: UAN

2277 Plaza Drive, Suite 500
Sugar Land, TX 77479
Phone: 281 207-3200
Fax: –
Web: www.cvrpartners.com

CEO: Mark A Pytosh
CFO: Dane J Neumann
HR: –
FYE: December 31
Type: Public

Farmers dreaming of fertile fields can turn to CVR Partners. The company makes nitrogen fertilizers. From its fertilizer manufacturing facility in Kansas, CVR Partners produces ammonia and urea ammonia nitrate (UAN). The company sells ammonia to agricultural and industrial customers such as Brandt Consolidated, Interchem and National Cooperative Refinery Association and provides UAN products to retailers and distributors. To lower production costs, CVR Partners uses petroleum coke instead of the more expensive natural gas. It obtains the majority of its petroleum coke from parent company CVR Energy, which founded CVR Partners in 2007. CVR Partners went public in April 2011, raising $307 million.

	Annual Growth	12/19	12/20	12/21	12/22	12/23
Sales ($mil.)	14.0%	404.2	350.0	532.6	835.6	681.5
Net income ($ mil.)	–	(35.0)	(98.2)	78.2	286.8	172.4
Market value ($ mil.)	114.4%	32.8	169.3	874.0	1,063.1	692.3
Employees	2.0%	286	287	296	300	310

CVS HEALTH CORPORATION
NYS: CVS

One CVS Drive
Woonsocket, RI 02895
Phone: 401 765-1500
Fax: 401 762-2137
Web: www.cvshealth.com

CEO: Karen S Lynch
CFO: Tom Cowhey
HR: –
FYE: December 31
Type: Public

CVS Health Corp. is a leading pharmacy benefits manager with approximately 110 million plan members as well as the nation's largest drugstore chain. It runs approximately 9,000 retail locations and more than 1,100 walk-in medical clinics. In addition to its standalone pharmacy operations, the company operates about 1,880 retail pharmacies within retail chains, as well as some 60 clinics inside Target stores and runs a panel of healthcare professionals, Caremark National Pharmacy and Therapeutics Committee. The company also offers walk-in health services through its retail network of MinuteClinics that are located in around 1,100 CVS stores. CVS Health also serves an estimated 35 million people through traditional, voluntary and consumer-directed health insurance products and related services.

	Annual Growth	12/19	12/20	12/21	12/22	12/23
Sales ($mil.)	8.6%	256,776	268,706	292,111	322,467	357,776
Net income ($ mil.)	5.9%	6,634.0	7,179.0	7,910.0	4,149.0	8,344.0
Market value ($ mil.)	1.5%	95,686	87,970	132,870	120,029	101,700
Employees	0.9%	290,000	300,000	300,000	300,000	300,000

CXTEC INC.

400 S SALINA ST STE 201
SYRACUSE, NY 132022423
Phone: 315 476-3000
Fax: –
Web: www.cxtec.com

CEO: –
CFO: –
HR: –
FYE: December 31
Type: Private

CABLExpress (dba CXtec) is hard wired for hardware. The company sells new and refurbished computer and communications equipment such as networking hardware, phone systems and accessories, storage products, cables, and media converters. It also provides such services as asset recovery, consulting, project management, systems integration, and technical support. CXtec distributes its products primarily in North America and serves various sectors, including education, financial services, government, and health care. The company sells products made by the likes of 3Com and Hewlett-Packard. CEO William Pomeroy founded the company from his home in 1978 as a distributor of used IBM mainframe cables and computer parts.

	Annual Growth	12/09	12/10	12/12	12/13	12/14
Sales ($mil.)	5.1%	–	61.7	68.2	75.3	75.3
Net income ($ mil.)	–	–	–	–	–	–
Market value ($ mil.)	–	–	–	–	–	–
Employees	–	–	–	–	–	355

CYANOTECH CORP.

NBB: CYAN

73-4460 Queen Kaahumanu Hwy. #102
Kailua-Kona, HI 96740
Phone: 808 326-1353
Fax: –
Web: www.cyanotech.com

CEO: –
CFO: –
HR: Miranda Watson
FYE: March 31
Type: Public

Cyanotech transforms the scum of the earth into health products. The majority of the company's sales come from Spirulina Pacifica, a nutritional supplement made from tiny blue-green vegetable algae and sold as powder, flakes, and tablets. The firm also produces BioAstin, an astaxanthin-based dietary supplement full of antioxidants. Cyanotech produces the microalgae used in its product lines at a 90-acre production facility on the Kona Coast of Hawaii. It sells them primarily to health food and dietary supplement makers. In order to focus on its nutritional supplement business, the company has discontinued some other product lines, including NatuRose, an algae-based pigmentation used to color farm-raised fish.

	Annual Growth	03/19	03/20	03/21	03/22	03/23
Sales ($mil.)	(6.4%)	30.2	31.9	32.3	36.0	23.2
Net income ($ mil.)	–	(3.6)	0.4	0.9	2.2	(3.4)
Market value ($ mil.)	(27.9%)	20.3	12.9	20.7	21.1	5.5
Employees	(5.8%)	109	95	96	95	86

CYBERTHINK, INC.

685 US HIGHWAY 202/206 STE 101
BRIDGEWATER, NJ 088071774
Phone: 908 429-8008
Fax: –
Web: www.cyberthink.com

CEO: –
CFO: –
HR: –
FYE: December 31
Type: Private

cyberThink wants businesses with technology needs to keep it mind. The company provides a range of outsourced information technology (IT) and technical staffing services from about 35 US offices and a software development facilities in India. cyberThink's IT services include web applications, enterprise solutions, data warehousing, systems integration, and network and infrastructure. It also provides custom application development for businesses from its offshore operation which specializes in design, programming, and testing. The company serves customers in such fields as financial services, pharmaceuticals, retail, and hospitality. cyberThink's clients have included Honeywell, Reed Elsevier, and Citigroup. cyberThink was founded in 1996.

CYCLACEL PHARMACEUTICALS INC

NAS: CYCC

200 Connell Drive, Suite 1500
Berkeley Heights, NJ 07922
Phone: 908 517-7330
Fax: –
Web: www.cyclacel.com

CEO: –
CFO: –
HR: –
FYE: December 31
Type: Public

Cyclacel Pharmaceuticals wants to stop the cycle of disease. The company's main focus is on cancer, but it is also working on treatments for inflammation, type II diabetes, and HIV/AIDS. Its cancer programs, which seek to halt cell cycles related to disease progression, target such ailments as leukemia and non-small cell lung cancer. Cyclacel's R&D operations are supported by commercial products sold through subsidiary ALIGN Pharmaceuticals, including Xclair cream for radiation-induced skin conditions and Numoisyn lozenge and liquid formulas for xerostomia (dry mouth, often related to chemotherapy).

	Annual Growth	12/19	12/20	12/21	12/22	12/23
Sales ($mil.)	–	–	–	–	–	0.4
Net income ($ mil.)	–	(7.8)	(8.4)	(18.9)	(21.2)	(22.6)
Market value ($ mil.)	41.3%	0.7	8.3	4.1	0.7	2.8
Employees	–	12	–	–	–	–

CYMER, INC.

17075 THORNMINT CT
SAN DIEGO, CA 921272413
Phone: 858 385-7300
Fax: –
Web: www.cymer.com

CEO: –
CFO: –
HR: –
FYE: December 31
Type: Private

Cymer operates with a laser-light focus. The company is a top maker of excimer lasers, light sources used by chip makers to pattern advanced semiconductors. Its products let semiconductor manufacturers produce smaller, faster microchips. Cymer supplies deep-ultraviolet (DUV) and extreme-ultraviolet (EUV) light sources to lithography tool manufacturers, who integrate the light sources into wafer steppers and scanners supplied to chip makers. Cymer also provides replacement parts and support through OnPulse, with sales based on the number of pulses used by customers on the light sources covered under the program. In 2013 the company was taken private by ASML Holding.

CYNERGISTEK, INC.

40 BURTON HILLS BLVD STE 200
NASHVILLE, TN 372155902
Phone: 512 402-8550
Fax: –
Web: www.cynergistek.com

CEO: –
CFO: –
HR: –
FYE: December 31
Type: Private

Hospitals count on AUXILIO to streamline their printing processes; you can print, copy, scan, and fax that. The company is a managed print services provider, meaning it does not sell printing equipment and related supplies. Rather, it is vendor neutral and procures different makes and models of equipment depending on the needs of its US health care industry clients, which include California Pacific Medical Center, Saddleback Memorial Medical Center, and St. Joseph Health System. Often working with IT departments, AUXILIO's consultants assess clients' print environments and assist them with plans to minimize costs on supplies that will maximize their productivity and also reduce unnecessary paper waste.

CYNOSURE, LLC

5 CARLISLE RD
WESTFORD, MA 018863601
Phone: 978 256-4200
Fax: –
Web: www.cynosure.com

CEO: Todd Tillemans
CFO: Timothy W Baker
HR: Anne Adams
FYE: December 31
Type: Private

Cynosure is a market leader in the medical aesthetics space with over 30 years developing, manufacturing, and marketing products for dermatologists, plastic surgeons, medical spas, and healthcare practitioners. With the aesthetic industry's most comprehensive product portfolio, its offerings span several categories including skin revitalization, body contouring, hair removal, and women's health. For patients who want to go deeper, its Smartlipo workstation allows cosmetic surgeons to perform a less-invasive procedure than conventional liposuction to target and reduce fat. The company's direct sales force and international distributors market and sell its products worldwide under such names as MonaLisa Touch, Apogee+, Cynergy, Elite, and PicoSure.

CYPRESS BIOSCIENCE, INC.

110 E 59TH ST FL 33
NEW YORK, NY 100221315
Phone: 858 452-2323
Fax: –
Web: –

CEO: Jay D Kranzler PHD
CFO: Sabrina M Johnson
HR: –
FYE: December 31
Type: Private

Cypress Bioscience searches for cures in the swampy waters surrounding neurological conditions. The biotech company is focused on researching and developing therapeutic candidates for central nervous system conditions such as schizophrenia and autism. Cypress Bioscience collaborated on the development of Savella (milnacipran) for fibromyalgia, a chronic functional condition marked by pain, stiffness, and fatigue that tends to affect adult women; the drug was approved by the FDA in 2009 and is marketed by former development partner Forest Laboratories. In early 2011 Cypress Bioscience was acquired by investors Ramius Capital and Royalty Pharma for roughly $255 million.

CYPRESS ENVIRONMENTAL PARTNERS LP

NBB: CELP Q

5727 South Lewis Avenue, Suite 300
Tulsa, OK 74105
Phone: 918 748-3900
Fax: –
Web: www.cypressenergy.com

CEO: Peter C Boylan III
CFO: Jeffrey A Herbers
HR: –
FYE: December 31
Type: Public

It's a dirty job, but someone's got to do it. After oil and gas companies drill wells, Cypress Energy Partners comes in and cleans up the mess. The company provides saltwater disposal and other water and environmental services to oil and natural gas companies that perform hydraulic fracturing, a process that pumps sand, water, and chemicals into shale reservoirs to release oil and gas. It owns and operates nine fluid management disposal facilities in North Dakota and Texas. It also provides independent pipeline inspection and integrity services to producers and pipeline companies through subsidiary Tulsa Inspection Resources. Cypress Energy Partners went public in early 2014.

	Annual Growth	12/17	12/18	12/19	12/20	12/21
Sales ($mil.)	(20.0%)	286.3	315.0	401.6	206.0	117.3
Net income ($ mil.)	–	(0.8)	11.4	16.0	(1.4)	(12.1)
Market value ($ mil.)	(34.3%)	74.2	69.5	113.7	28.4	13.8
Employees	–	–	–	–	–	63

CYRQ ENERGY, LLC

15 W SOUTH TEMPLE STE 1900
SALT LAKE CITY, UT 841011573
Phone: 801 765-1200
Fax: –
Web: www.cyrqenergy.com

CEO: –
CFO: –
HR: –
FYE: December 31
Type: Private

Cyrq Energy (formerly Raser Technologies) has two goals in mind: improvement of electric motors and development of alternative energy sources. With an emphasis on increasing power and energy efficiency, Cyrq has developed an electric motor technology (Symetron) that can be integrated with existing electric motors used in plug-in hybrid electric vehicles, hydraulic pumps, snowmobiles, and forklifts, as well as electric power generators. In addition to its electric motor technology business, Cyrq develops and operates geothermal-based power plants; the company typically earns revenue from its plants through the sale of electricity and tax incentives. In 2011 Cyrq filed for Chapter 11 bankruptcy protection; it was bought by two investment firms.

	Annual Growth	12/05	12/06	12/07	12/08	12/09
Sales ($mil.)	161.8%	–	–	0.3	0.2	2.2
Net income ($ mil.)	–	–	–	(15.7)	(45.5)	(20.9)
Market value ($ mil.)	–	–	–	–	–	–
Employees	–	–	–	–	–	110

CYS INVESTMENTS, INC.

500 TOTTEN POND RD FL 6
WALTHAM, MA 024511924
Phone: 888 444-0313
Fax: –
Web: www.twoharborsinvestment.com

CEO: Kevin E Grant
CFO: Jack Decicco
HR: –
FYE: December 31
Type: Private

CYS Investments (formerly Cypress Sharpridge Investments) is a real estate investment trust (REIT) that invests in residential mortgage-backed securities (RMBS) primarily collateralized by adjustable-rate mortgage loans and guaranteed by government agencies Fannie Mae, Freddie Mac, and Ginnie Mae. (As a REIT, CYS is exempt from paying federal income tax so long as it distributes dividends back to shareholders.) More than three-quarters of its portfolio is backed by hybrid adjustable-rate mortgages (ARMs) and 15-year fixed-rate single-family mortgages. The REIT's investment activities are usually financed through major commercial and investment banks.

CYSTIC FIBROSIS FOUNDATION

4550 MONTGOMERY AVE STE 1100
BETHESDA, MD 208145200
Phone: 301 951-4422
Fax: –
Web: www.cff.org

CEO: Michael Boyle
CFO: –
HR: –
FYE: December 31
Type: Private

The Cystic Fibrosis Foundation is is a donor-supported nonprofit organization and the world's leader in the search for a cure for cystic fibrosis (CF). It funds CF research and medical programs. Founded in 1955, the organization funds research, and drug development through matching funds, and offers CF-related information and educational materials. The Cystic Fibrosis Foundation Therapeutics Lab conducts groundbreaking CF research to rapidly advance new therapies. The foundation provides funding, training, and accreditation for more than 130 treatment centers in the US.

	Annual Growth	12/07	12/08	12/12	12/13	12/15
Sales ($mil.)	3.2%	–	138.5	297.7	405.5	173.1
Net income ($ mil.)	–	–	(2.1)	175.2	247.1	(134.9)
Market value ($ mil.)	–	–	–	–	–	–
Employees	–	–	–	–	–	550

CYTOKINETICS INC

NMS: CYTK

350 Oyster Point Blvd.
South San Francisco, CA 94080
Phone: 650 624-3000
Fax: –
Web: www.cytokinetics.com

CEO: Robert I Blum
CFO: Ching W Jaw
HR: –
FYE: December 31
Type: Public

Cytokinetics is a late-stage biopharmaceutical company focused on discovering, developing, and commercializing first-in-class muscle activators and best-in-class muscle inhibitors as potential treatments for people with debilitating diseases in which muscle performance is compromised and/or declining. Its clinical-stage drug candidates are omecamtiv mecarbil, a novel cardiac myosin activator, CK-136 (formerly known as AMG 594), a novel cardiac troponin activator, reldesemtiv, a novel FSTA and aficamten, a novel cardiac myosin inhibitor. Cytokinetics was founded in 1998 by pioneers in the field of muscle biology.

	Annual Growth	12/19	12/20	12/21	12/22	12/23
Sales ($mil.)	(27.2%)	26.9	55.8	70.4	94.6	7.5
Net income ($ mil.)	–	(121.7)	(127.3)	(215.3)	(389.0)	(526.2)
Market value ($ mil.)	67.5%	1,078.4	2,112.0	4,632.7	4,657.0	8,485.8
Employees	28.3%	156	184	367	576	423

D & A BUILDING SERVICES, INC.

321 GEORGIA AVE
LONGWOOD, FL 327504315
Phone: 407 831-5388
Fax: –
Web: www.dabuildingservices.com

CEO: Albert Sarabasa Jr
CFO: Kathy Sarabasa
HR: –
FYE: December 31
Type: Private

D & A Building Services is an indoor and outdoor facility maintenance company. The company provides carpet cleaning, construction clean-up, landscape management, janitorial services, pest control, and window cleaning for companies such as airports, government agencies, ports, and schools. It has four offices in Florida, as well as locations in Columbus, Ohio; Detroit, Michigan; and Kansas City, Missouri. President and CEO Albert Sarabasa, Jr. founded the company in 1985.

	Annual Growth	12/03	12/04	12/05	12/06	12/09
Sales ($mil.)	4.6%	–	–	13.3	16.1	16.0
Net income ($ mil.)	(3.5%)	–	–	0.1	1.2	0.1
Market value ($ mil.)	–	–	–	–	–	–
Employees	–	–	–	–	–	500

D W W CO., INC.

1400 N TUSTIN ST
ORANGE, CA 928673902
Phone: 714 516-3111
Fax: –
Web: www.toyota.com

CEO: –
CFO: –
HR: –
FYE: December 31
Type: Private

First Orange County, then the world -- or at least as far as Arizona and Mexico. Megadealer David Wilson Automotive Group has its roots in Orange County, California, with 16 branches that stretch to east to Scottsdale and now south to Puerto Vallarta, Mexico. David Wilson's Automotive locations sell new and used Acura, Ford, Honda, and Mazda cars as well as Toyota and Lexus brand vehicles. The group's dealerships also operate parts and service departments; some offer fleet services. Dealership Web sites allow customers to search inventory, schedule service appointments, and request quotes. David Wilson owns the company that bears his name

	Annual Growth	12/04	12/05	12/06	12/07	12/08
Sales ($mil.)	(8.8%)	–	214.6	229.9	199.9	162.8
Net income ($ mil.)	(9.2%)	–	10.0	12.0	7.6	7.5
Market value ($ mil.)	–	–	–	–	–	–
Employees	–	–	–	–	–	135

D. C. TAYLOR CO.

500 STICKLE DR NE
CEDAR RAPIDS, IA 524011021
Phone: 319 363-2073
Fax: –
Web: www.dctaylorco.com

CEO: William W Taylor
CFO: –
HR: Derik Gogg
FYE: December 31
Type: Private

D. C. Taylor is one of the largest commercial and industrial roofing contractors in the US, providing roof installation, repair, and maintenance services. It has some 60 service and roofing crews that operate from offices in Arizona, California, Georgia, Illinois, and Iowa. Dudley C. Taylor started Taylor Tuckpointing, a tuckpointing (cosmetic brick finishing commonly found on Federation houses and Californian bungalows) and masonry repair company, in Chicago in 1949; the company's name was changed to D. C. Taylor in 1954, and the firm was formally incorporated in 1960. Chairman and CEO Bill Taylor is the company's majority shareholder.

	Annual Growth	12/06	12/07	12/08	12/09	12/10
Sales ($mil.)	(15.3%)	–	–	56.3	8.4	40.4
Net income ($ mil.)	(9.5%)	–	–	2.3	1.2	1.9
Market value ($ mil.)	–	–	–	–	–	–
Employees	–	–	–	–	–	123

D.M. BOWMAN, INC.

10228 GOVERNOR LANE BLVD UNIT 3006
WILLIAMSPORT, MD 217954064
Phone: 301 223-6900
Fax: –
Web: www.dmbowman.com

CEO: –
CFO: –
HR: –
FYE: December 31
Type: Private

Trucking and logistics company D.M. Bowman wants to hit the target with a quiver full of service offerings. The company provides both short- and long-haul freight transportation with its fleet of tractors and trailers, including standard dry vans, flatbeds, and pneumatic tankers for dry bulk cargo. In addition, D.M. Bowman offers dedicated contract carriage, in which drivers and equipment are assigned to a customer long-term. The company's logistics services include freight brokerage, supply chain management, and short- and long-term warehousing. D.M. Bowman operates primarily in the eastern half of the US. Chairman Don Bowman owns the company, which he founded in 1959.

	Annual Growth	12/09	12/10	12/11	12/12	12/13
Sales ($mil.)	442.0%	–	–	–	0.0	0.3
Net income ($ mil.)	–	–	–	–	(0.1)	0.2
Market value ($ mil.)	–	–	–	–	–	–
Employees	–	–	–	–	–	600

D.R. SYSTEMS, INC.

10140 MESA RIM RD
SAN DIEGO, CA 921212914
Phone: 858 625-3344
Fax: –
Web: www.merge.com

CEO: –
CFO: –
HR: –
FYE: December 31
Type: Private

D.R. Systems envisions a world with better medical imaging and information management capabilities. The company develops and sells integrated picture archiving and communication systems (PACS) and information systems geared toward cardiology, mammography, pathology, and radiology all under its Unity platform. Other offerings include dictation, image processing, speech recognition, and transcription products. Among its services are consulting, data migration, project management, technical support, and training. D.R. Systems' enterprise products and services are targeted at health care networks, hospitals, and diagnostic imaging centers. The privately-held company was founded in 1992 by radiologists.

	Annual Growth	12/05	12/06	12/08	12/09	12/13
Sales ($mil.)	(15.1%)	–	137.3	62.8	43.2	43.7
Net income ($ mil.)	723.4%	–	0.0	21.3	11.8	10.3
Market value ($ mil.)	–	–	–	–	–	–
Employees	–	–	–	–	–	205

D/L COOPERATIVE INC.

5001 BRITTONFIELD PKWY
EAST SYRACUSE, NY 130579201
Phone: 315 233-1000
Fax: –
Web: www.dairylea.com

CEO: –
CFO: –
HR: –
FYE: March 31
Type: Private

Yes, the farmer takes a wife , then hi-ho , the dairy-o , the farmer takes membership in milk-marketing organizations such as Dairylea Cooperative. Owned by some 2,000 dairy farmers in the northeastern US, Dairylea processes and markets 6.3 billion pounds of milk for its farmers annually to dairy-product customers including food manufacturers. Its Agri-Services holding company provides members with a full range of financial and farm-management services, as well as insurance. Its Empire Livestock Marketing unit operates regional livestock auction locations. Dairylea, which was established in 1907 by New York dairy farmers, merged with the US's largest milk marketing coop, Dairy Farmers of America, in 2014.

	Annual Growth	03/07	03/08	03/09	03/10	03/11
Sales ($mil.)	25.1%	–	–	–	1,066.4	1,333.9
Net income ($ mil.)	7.6%	–	–	–	1.5	1.7
Market value ($ mil.)	–	–	–	–	–	–
Employees	–	–	–	–	–	107

DAC TECHNOLOGIES GROUP INTERNATIONAL INC.

NBB: DAAT

12120 Colonel Glenn Road, Suite 6200
Little Rock, AR 72210
Phone: 501 661-9100
Fax: –
Web: www.dactec.com

CEO: David A Collins
CFO: Robert C Goodwin
HR: –
FYE: December 31
Type: Public

This company's aim is to give gun owners a clean shot. DAC Technologies Group International manufactures more than 50 different GunMaster brand gun cleaning kits, as well as gun maintenance and safety products, such as trigger locks and gun safes. Its gun-related business rings up more than two-thirds of DAC's sales. The company also makes game processing equipment, aluminum camping tables and other items for the hunting and camping markets, as well as a line of household cleaning dusters. DAC also has a licensing agreement with Olin Corp. to market some of its gun cleaning items under the Winchester brand name for sale at Wal-Mart. (The retail giant accounts for about 55% of DAC's sales.)

	Annual Growth	12/05	12/06	12/07	12/08	12/09
Sales ($mil.)	2.4%	13.4	15.5	14.8	17.0	14.7
Net income ($ mil.)	(17.2%)	1.2	0.8	0.3	0.4	0.6
Market value ($ mil.)	(24.8%)	13.6	13.2	4.9	2.0	4.3
Employees	4.7%	10	11	11	12	12

DAEGIS INC.

600 LAS COLINAS BLVD E STE 1500
IRVING, TX 750395601
Phone: 214 584-6400
Fax: –
Web: www.opentext.com

CEO: Timothy P Bacci
CFO: Susan K Conner
HR: –
FYE: April 30
Type: Private

Daegis, formerly Unify Corporation, has a firm business plan. The company targets corporate law departments and law firms with products and services for the legal discovery process, including search, analysis, review, and production. Legal clients also use Daegis's archiving software to manage electronically stored information. The company additionally serves software value-added resellers, systems integrators, and independent software vendors, among others, with products that aid in the development and management of business applications and data. Services provided by Daegis include project management, maintenance, and consulting.

DAEMEN UNIVERSITY

4380 MAIN ST
AMHERST, NY 142263544
Phone: 716 839-3600
Fax: –
Web: www.daemen.edu

CEO: John Yurtchuk
CFO: –
HR: Samantha Maiarana
FYE: May 31
Type: Private

Daemen College is a private liberal arts university located in Amherst, New York. The college offers more than than three dozen undergraduate major programs, about 15 graduate and accelerated courses of study, and a handful of professional certifications. It has an enrollment of about 3,000 students and a student-faculty ratio of 15:1. The school was established in 1947 as Rosary Hill College by the Sisters of St. Francis of Penance and Christian Charity, whose founder was Magdalene Daemen, a Dutch woman dedicated to working with the poor. Originally a liberal arts college for women, Daemen became coeducational in 1971.

	Annual Growth	05/18	05/19	05/20	05/21	05/22
Sales ($mil.)	7.3%	–	47.5	49.5	53.0	58.7
Net income ($ mil.)	–	–	(4.4)	(0.5)	4.8	0.9
Market value ($ mil.)	–	–	–	–	–	–
Employees	–	–	–	–	–	500

DAILY EXPRESS, INC.

1072 HARRISBURG PIKE
CARLISLE, PA 170131615
Phone: 717 243-5757
Fax: –
Web: www.dailyexp.com

CEO: Todd Long
CFO: –
HR: –
FYE: December 31
Type: Private

Daily Express moves freight not seen every day. The trucking company carries mostly oversized loads (construction machinery, industrial equipment, even gigantic telescope mirrors) on various-sized trailers. Delivery of wind turbine components is a Daily Express specialty as the demand for alternative energy production surges globally. The company's fleet consists of more than 600 trailers. It operates throughout the US from a network of about 10 terminals. An affiliate, Plant Site Logistics, provides transportation management services.

DAILY JOURNAL CORPORATION

NAS: DJCO

915 East First Street
Los Angeles, CA 90012
Phone: 213 229-5300
Fax: 213 229-5481
Web: www.dailyjournal.com

CEO: Steven Myhill-Jones
CFO: Tu To
HR: –
FYE: September 30
Type: Public

Legal matters dominate in these papers. Daily Journal Corporation offers legal software and services to US courts and other justice agencies, including browser-based case processing systems (eCourt, eProsecutor, eDefender, and eProbation) and electronic filing and payment tools (eFile, ePayIt). The company is also a newspaper publisher with about a dozen papers serving markets primarily in California and Arizona. Its flagship papers include the Los Angeles Daily Journal and the San Francisco Daily Journal, which offer in-depth coverage of legal cases and court matters in addition to general interest news. Board members Charles Munger (who also serves as vice chairman of Berkshire Hathaway) and J.P. Guerin together control Daily Journal Corporation.

	Annual Growth	09/19	09/20	09/21	09/22	09/23
Sales ($mil.)	8.6%	48.7	49.9	49.4	54.0	67.7
Net income ($ mil.)	–	(25.2)	4.0	112.9	(75.6)	21.5
Market value ($ mil.)	4.4%	340.9	333.2	441.2	353.1	404.8
Employees	(1.7%)	385	320	300	325	360

DAILY NEWS, L.P.

4 NEW YORK PLZ
NEW YORK, NY 100042413
Phone: 212 210-2100
Fax: –
Web: www.nydailynews.com

CEO: William D Holiber
CFO: –
HR: –
FYE: December 31
Type: Private

This daily news might not always be fit to print, but it at least keeps New Yorkers entertained. Daily News, L.P. publishes New York City's Daily News, the big city tabloid that goes toe-to-toe with the New York Post (owned by Rupert Murdoch's News Corporation) by penning over-the-top headlines and sensational stories. The paper, founded in 1919, is distributed primarily in the Five Boroughs and boasts a circulation of more than 550,000. It also distributes news and features online through its website. The Daily News is owned by real estate magnate Mortimer Zuckerman, who also owns news magazine U.S. News & World Report.

DAIRY FARMERS OF AMERICA, INC.

1405 N 98TH ST
KANSAS CITY, KS 661111865
Phone: 816 801-6455
Fax: –
Web: www.dfamilk.com

CEO: –
CFO: –
HR: –
FYE: December 31
Type: Private

Dairy Farmers of America (DFA) is one of the world's largest dairy cooperatives, with more than 11,500 member farmers across the US. Along with fresh and shelf-stable fluid milk, the cooperative produces cheese, butter, powders, and sweetened condensed milk for industrial, wholesale, and retail customers. It also offers contract manufacturing services. Its brands include Borden and Cache Valley for consumer cheese; Keller's Creamery, Plugr, Breakstone's, Falfurrias, and Oakhurst Dairy; and other dairy products under Sport Shake (sports beverage), La Vaquita (queso), Kemps, Guida's, and Cass Clay. DFA was formed in 1998.

	Annual Growth	12/12	12/13	12/14	12/15	12/16
Sales ($mil.)	(13.0%)	–	–	17,856	13,803	13,528
Net income ($ mil.)	67.6%	–	–	48.6	98.3	136.6
Market value ($ mil.)	–	–	–	–	–	–
Employees	–	–	–	–	–	21,000

DAIRYLAND POWER COOPERATIVE

3200 EAST AVE S
LA CROSSE, WI 546017291
Phone: 608 788-4000
Fax: –
Web: www.dairylandpower.com

CEO: Brent Ridge
CFO: Phillip Moilien
HR: –
FYE: December 31
Type: Private

Dairyland Power Cooperative provides its customers with lots of juice in the land of lactose. The firm provides electricity generation (1,366 MW of generating capacity) and transmission services for 25 member distribution cooperatives and 16 municipal utilities in five states (including Wisconsin). The member cooperatives and municipal utilities in turn distribute electricity to almost 254,460 consumers. Dairyland Power generates 1,030 MW of capacity from its coal-fired power plants; it also operates more than 3,180 miles of transmission lines and 228 substations. The power cooperative also markets electricity and offers energy management services.

	Annual Growth	12/18	12/19	12/20	12/21	12/22
Sales ($mil.)	4.3%	–	470.6	442.4	463.6	533.8
Net income ($ mil.)	(46.4%)	–	18.3	14.7	19.9	2.8
Market value ($ mil.)	–	–	–	–	–	–
Employees	–	–	–	–	–	500

DAIS CORP

11552 Prosperous Drive
Odessa, FL 33556
Phone: 727 375-8484
Fax: –
Web: www.daisanalytic.com

NBB: DLYT
CEO: Timothy N Tangredi
CFO: –
HR: –
FYE: December 31
Type: Public

Dais Corporation develops nano polymers it hopes can be used to solve tough global problems like cleaning air and water and reducing harmful emissions. Its only current product is ConsERV, an energy recovery ventilator that uses nano technology to improve the efficiency of existing heating and cooling systems. Other Dais products in the development stage, including NanoAir, NanoClear, and NanoCap, use the same technology to cleaning air and water and storing energy more efficiently. Formed in 1993 as fuel cell developer Dais, the company bought fellow fuel cell firm Analytic in 1999 and changed its name. In 2002 it shifted focus to nano polymers.

	Annual Growth	12/18	12/19	12/20	12/21	12/22
Sales ($mil.)	(5.0%)	1.4	0.9	1.0	0.4	1.1
Net income ($ mil.)	–	(3.0)	(4.0)	(2.8)	(0.8)	(4.5)
Market value ($ mil.)	40.0%	0.3	2.3	3.0	72.2	1.0
Employees	15.0%	12	11	11	13	21

DAKOTA ELECTRIC ASSOCIATION

4300 220TH ST W
FARMINGTON, MN 550249583
Phone: 651 463-6212
Fax: –
Web: www.dakotaelectric.com

CEO: Greg Miller
CFO: –
HR: Christene Ratzlaff
FYE: December 31
Type: Private

The Dakota Electric Association delivers electricity to residents of southeastern Minnesota, the Gopher State, so they don't have to burrow underground to outlast those long, cold winters. The member-owned utility serves more than 103,000 customers in portions of Dakota, Goodhue, Rice, and Scott counties south of Minneapolis-St. Paul. The co-op gets its power wholesale from transmission cooperative Great River Energy and distributes it more than 4,010 miles of power lines, nearly two-thirds of which are buried. Dakota Electric is pushing energy efficiency programs and products to help save its customers money.

	Annual Growth	12/17	12/18	12/19	12/21	12/22
Sales ($mil.)	1.1%	–	210.5	207.9	228.8	219.7
Net income ($ mil.)	(8.5%)	–	5.1	4.6	9.4	3.6
Market value ($ mil.)	–	–	–	–	–	–
Employees	–	–	–	–	–	200

DAKOTA GASIFICATION COMPANY INC

420 60TH AVE SW
BEULAH, ND 58523
Phone: 701 873-2100
Fax: –
Web: www.dakotagas.com

CEO: Paul M Sukut
CFO: Steve Johnson
HR: Scott Fritz
FYE: December 31
Type: Private

A miracle on the prairie? A subsidiary of Basin Electric Power Cooperative, Dakota Gasification does not turn water into wine, but it does something pretty neat, anyway: It turns coal into natural gas. The Great Plains Synfuels Plant harnesses the abundant coal resources underlying the North Dakota prairie. The gasification process transforms more than 6 million tons of coal into more than 57 billion cu. ft. of natural gas annually, which is then used to supply the eastern US. In addition to natural gas, the company's Synfuels plant produces carbon dioxide, fertilizers, solvents, phenol, and other chemicals.

	Annual Growth	12/16	12/17	12/18	12/19	12/20
Sales ($mil.)	(6.0%)	–	337.2	381.4	345.6	279.7
Net income ($ mil.)	–	–	(87.2)	(397.8)	(70.5)	(94.9)
Market value ($ mil.)	–	–	–	–	–	–
Employees	–	–	–	–	–	725

DAKOTA STATE UNIVERSITY

820 N WASHINGTON AVE
MADISON, SD 570421735
Phone: 605 256-5127
Fax: –
Web: www.dsu.edu

CEO: –
CFO: –
HR: –
FYE: June 30
Type: Private

Dakota State University (DSU) was founded in 1881 as a teacher-training institute. The school changed its mission in 1984 and began specializing in programs in computer management and computer information systems. It also offers dozens of majors in business, science, and education, as well as graduate degrees in information systems and computer education and technology. DSU enrolls more than 2,300 students.

DAKOTA SUPPLY GROUP, INC.

2601 3RD AVE N
FARGO, ND 581024016
Phone: 701 237-9440
Fax: -
Web: www.dsgsupply.com

CEO: Paul Kennedy
CFO: Julianne Turk
HR: Kaylee Tran
FYE: December 31
Type: Private

Dakota Supply Group (DSG) distributes electrical, communications, and mechanical equipment to customers through more than a dozen branch locations in Minnesota, North Dakota, and South Dakota. The company stocks approximately 25,000 products. DSG carries products from 3Com, 3M, A. O. Smith, Buckingham Manufacturing, Corning, Emerson Electric, Ferraz Shawmut, General Electric, Honeywell, Hubbell, Moen, Schneider Electric, and Zurn Industries, among other manufacturers. The company was founded in 1898. An employee stock ownership plan holds nearly all of Dakota Supply.

	Annual Growth	12/13	12/14	12/15	12/16	12/17
Sales ($mil.)	(1.4%)	-	380.4	401.2	359.5	364.9
Net income ($ mil.)	(24.8%)	-	15.1	11.0	5.9	6.4
Market value ($ mil.)	-	-	-	-	-	-
Employees	-	-	-	-	-	909

DAKTRONICS INC.

NMS: DAKT

201 Daktronics Drive
Brookings, SD 57006
Phone: 605 692-0200
Fax: -
Web: www.daktronics.com

CEO: Reece A Kurtenbach
CFO: Sheila M Anderson
HR: -
FYE: April 29
Type: Public

Daktronics is an industry leader in designing and manufacturing electronic scoreboards, programmable display systems and large screen video displays for sporting, commercial and transportation applications. The company serves its customers by providing high quality standard display products as well as custom-designed and integrated systems. It offers a complete line of products, from small scoreboards and electronic displays to large multimillion-dollar video display systems as well as related control, timing, and sound systems. Daktronics is recognized as a technical leader with the capabilities to design, market, manufacture, install and service complete integrated systems displaying real-time data, graphics, animation and video. The company engages in a full range of activities: marketing and sales, engineering and product design and development, manufacturing, technical contracting, professional services and customer service and support. More than 85% of total revenue comes from the US operations. Daktronics was founded in 1968 by Drs. Aelred Kurtenbach and Duane Sander.

	Annual Growth	04/19*	05/20	05/21*	04/22	04/23
Sales ($mil.)	7.3%	569.7	608.9	482.0	611.0	754.2
Net income ($ mil.)	-	(1.0)	0.5	10.9	0.6	6.8
Market value ($ mil.)	(9.9%)	318.1	193.9	268.9	146.0	209.6
Employees	0.1%	2,722	2,671	2,117	2,477	2,734

*Fiscal year change

DALLAS BASKETBALL LIMITED

1333 N STEMMONS FWY # 10
DALLAS, TX 752073723
Phone: 214 658-7174
Fax: -
Web: www.dbabasketball.org

CEO: -
CFO: -
HR: Tarsha Lacour
FYE: June 30
Type: Private

The Dallas Mavericks professional basketball franchise joined the National Basketball Association in 1980. The Mavericks (also known as the Mavs) have struggled to find success for much of their history, but the team won its first NBA title in 2011, beating the Miami Heat in six games. Perennial All-Star forward Dirk Nowitzki led Dallas to the championship in his 13th season with the team. The Dallas Mavericks were formed by millionaire Donald Carter; Mark Cuban, an Internet billionaire, has controlled the team since 2000.

DALLAS COUNTY HOSPITAL DISTRICT

5200 HARRY HINES BLVD
DALLAS, TX 752357709
Phone: 214 590-8000
Fax: -
Web: www.parklandhealth.org

CEO: Frederick Cerise
CFO: John Moore
HR: -
FYE: September 30
Type: Private

Parkland Health & Hospital System (PHHS) is one of the largest public hospital systems and a level I Trauma Center and second largest civilian burn center in the U.S. and Level III Neonatal Intensive Care Unit. Parkland Memorial sits at the heart of the health system and is Dallas' only public hospital. PHHS also manages a network of about 20community clinics, as well as Parkland Community Health Plan, a regional HMO for Medicaid and CHIP (Children's Health Insurance Program) members. Additionally, the system offers Parkland Financial Assistance, a program to help residents of Dallas County pay for health care services. Founded in 1894.

	Annual Growth	09/18	09/19	09/20	09/21	09/22
Sales ($mil.)	10.1%	-	1,600.9	1,850.7	2,669.7	2,137.0
Net income ($ mil.)	4.2%	-	208.3	297.5	321.1	235.5
Market value ($ mil.)	-	-	-	-	-	-
Employees	-	-	-	-	-	11,000

DALLAS-FORT WORTH INTERNATIONAL AIRPORT FACILITY IMPROVEMENT CORPORATION

2400 AVIATION DR
DFW AIRPORT, TX 75261
Phone: 972 973-5400
Fax: -
Web: www.dfwairport.com

CEO: Jeff P Fegan
CFO: -
HR: -
FYE: September 30
Type: Private

Covering over 25 square miles, DFW is one of the world's largest airports by land mass. The facility includes seven runways, five terminals, and around 170 gates. Over 70 million passengers pass through DFW annually to destinations domestic and international. Aside from airport fare, DFW provides private warehouse and distribution centers to tenants and features Grand Hyatt and Hyatt Regency hotels. Opened in 1974, DFW is owned by the cities of Dallas and Fort Worth.

	Annual Growth	09/05	09/06	09/07	09/16	09/18
Sales ($mil.)	7.5%	-	389.0	567.6	745.6	929.4
Net income ($ mil.)	(7.6%)	-	140.9	28.5	(88.7)	54.7
Market value ($ mil.)	-	-	-	-	-	-
Employees	-	-	-	-	-	1,700

DALLASNEWS CORP

NAS: DALN

P.O. Box 224866
Dallas, TX 75222-4866
Phone: 214 977-8869
Fax: -
Web: www.ahbelo.com

CEO: Grant S Moise
CFO: Mary K Murray
HR: -
FYE: December 31
Type: Public

This company gives the Big D a helping of news with breakfast. A. H. Belo is a leading newspaper publisher with a portfolio of three daily newspapers anchored by The Dallas Morning News , one of the country's top papers with a circulation of about 260,000. It also owns The Press-Enterprise (Riverside, California). In addition to its flagship papers, A. H. Belo publishes the Denton Record-Chronicle (Texas) and several niche papers such as the Spanish-language paper Al Dia (Dallas), along with websites serving most of its publications. The company was spun off from TV station operator Belo Corp. in 2008.

	Annual Growth	12/19	12/20	12/21	12/22	12/23
Sales ($mil.)	(6.6%)	183.6	154.3	154.4	150.7	139.7
Net income ($ mil.)	-	9.3	(6.9)	(0.5)	(9.8)	(7.1)
Market value ($ mil.)	10.8%	15.1	8.1	38.6	20.7	22.7
Employees	(7.8%)	830	743	656	663	601

DANA INC
NYS: DAN

3939 Technology Drive
Maumee, OH 43537
Phone: 419 887-3000
Fax: 419 887-5200
Web: www.dana.com

CEO: James K Kamsickas
CFO: Timothy R Kraus
HR: –
FYE: December 31
Type: Public

Dana is a global leader in providing power-conveyance and energy-management solutions for vehicles and machinery. In addition to its core offerings, the company also offers driveline products (rear and front axles, driveshafts, transmissions), it provides power technologies (sealing and thermal-management products) and service parts. It makes products for vehicles in the light, medium/heavy (commercial), and off-highway markets that carry brand names such as Spicer and Victor Reinz, among others. Dana operates in roughly 90 facilities across the globe. It traces its historical roots back to 1904, when it introduced the automotive universal joint. About 50% of its sales comes from North America.

	Annual Growth	12/19	12/20	12/21	12/22	12/23
Sales ($mil.)	5.2%	8,620.0	7,106.0	8,945.0	10,156	10,555
Net income ($ mil.)	(36.0%)	226.0	(31.0)	197.0	(242.0)	38.0
Market value ($ mil.)	(5.3%)	2,627.8	2,818.4	3,294.9	2,184.6	2,109.5
Employees	3.6%	36,300	38,200	40,200	41,800	41,800

DANA-FARBER CANCER INSTITUTE, INC.

450 BROOKLINE AVE
BOSTON, MA 022155450
Phone: 617 632-3000
Fax: –
Web: www.dana-farber.org

CEO: Edward J Benz Jr
CFO: –
HR: Ivon Perezthornton
FYE: September 30
Type: Private

The Dana-Farber Cancer Institute fights cancer on two fronts: It provides treatment to cancer patients, young and old, and researches new cancer diagnostics, treatments, and preventions. The organization's scientists also research AIDS treatments and cures for a host of other deadly diseases. Patients receive treatment from Dana-Farber through its cancer centers operated in conjunction with Brigham and Women's Hospital, Boston Children's Hospital, and Massachusetts General Hospital. The institute is also a principal teaching affiliate of Harvard Medical School. Founded in 1947, Dana-Farber is funded by the National Cancer Institute, the National Institute of Allergy and Infectious Diseases, and private contributions.

	Annual Growth	09/13	09/14	09/19	09/20	09/21
Sales ($mil.)	12.8%	–	672.4	1,985.5	1,282.2	1,564.2
Net income ($ mil.)	37.8%	–	34.6	102.2	50.8	326.0
Market value ($ mil.)	–	–	–	–	–	–
Employees	–	–	–	–	–	3,000

DANAHER CORP
NYS: DHR

2200 Pennsylvania Avenue, N.W., Suite 800W
Washington, DC 20037-1701
Phone: 202 828-0850
Fax: 202 828-0860
Web: www.danaher.com

CEO: –
CFO: –
HR: –
FYE: December 31
Type: Public

Danaher is a global science and technology innovator committed to helping customers solve complex challenges and improving quality of life around the world. The company is comprised of more than 20 operating companies with leadership positions in the biotechnology, life sciences, diagnostics, environmental and applied sectors, organized under four segments (Biotechnology; Life Sciences; Diagnostics; and Environmental & Applied Solutions). It has facilities in more than 60 countries and generates about 45% of sales from customers in the US. Danaher was founded in 1984.

	Annual Growth	12/19	12/20	12/21	12/22	12/23
Sales ($mil.)	7.5%	17,911	22,284	29,453	31,471	23,890
Net income ($ mil.)	12.2%	3,008.2	3,646.0	6,433.0	7,209.0	4,764.0
Market value ($ mil.)	10.8%	113,452	164,206	243,204	196,198	171,007
Employees	1.2%	60,000	69,000	80,000	81,000	63,000

DANFOSS POWER SOLUTIONS INC.

2800 E 13TH ST
AMES, IA 500108600
Phone: 515 239-6000
Fax: –
Web: www.danfoss.com

CEO: Eric Alstrom
CFO: Jesper V Christensen V
HR: –
FYE: December 31
Type: Private

Danfoss Power Solutions (formerly known as Sauer-Danfoss) is one of the largest companies in the mobile hydraulics industry. It designs, manufactures and sells a complete range of engineered hydraulic, electronic and electric components and solutions. The mobile equipment manufacturers rely on its expertise for the most innovative, propel, control, work function and steering solutions around the world. Its solutions have included motors, pumps, valves, and software, among others. Danfoss Power Solutions is a wholly-owned subsidiary of Denmark-based industrial company Danfoss A/S.

	Annual Growth	12/07	12/08	12/09	12/10	12/11
Sales ($mil.)	33.2%	–	–	1,159.0	1,640.6	2,057.5
Net income ($ mil.)	–	–	–	(332.3)	246.3	259.8
Market value ($ mil.)	–	–	–	–	–	–
Employees	–	–	–	–	–	6,400

DANIEL F. YOUNG, INCORPORATED

1235 WESTLAKES DR STE 305
BERWYN, PA 193122412
Phone: 610 725-4000
Fax: –
Web: www.dfyoung.com

CEO: Aaron W Wyatt III
CFO: Denise Traynor
HR: –
FYE: December 31
Type: Private

Daniel F. Young provides air and ocean freight forwarding, customs brokerage, and logistics services to multinational businesses. The company, known as DF Young, also offers ground transportation, including full-truckload (FTL) and less-than-truckload (LTL) transportation, door to door service, and inter-coastal barge transportation. (Freight forwarding companies purchase transportation capacity from carriers and resell it to customers; LTL carriers consolidate freight from multiple shippers into a single trailer.) It operates in six main industry areas: automotive, Food & Beverage, Life Sciences, Aerospace, Government, Project & Custom Logisitics.

DANIEL J. EDELMAN, INC.

111 N CANAL ST STE 1100
CHICAGO, IL 606067219
Phone: 312 240-3000
Fax: –
Web: www.edelman.com

CEO: Richard Edelman
CFO: Fabien Fichaux
HR: Pankaj Suri
FYE: December 31
Type: Private

Daniel J. Edelman, which does business simply as Edelman, is a global communications company that partners with businesses and organizations evolve, promote, and protect their brands and reputations. With more than 60 offices worldwide, the company provides its services through almost 30 practice areas (including financial services, performance communications, predictive intelligence, start-up development, executive positioning, influencer marketing, and public affairs). The company's about 6,000 people delivers communications strategies that give its clients the confidence to lead and act with certainty, earning the trust of their stakeholders. The company was founded in 1952 by Daniel Edelman.

DANIS BUILDING CONSTRUCTION COMPANY

3233 NEWMARK DR
MIAMISBURG, OH 453425422
Phone: 937 228-1225
Fax: –
Web: www.danis.com

CEO: John Danis
CFO: Tim Carlson
HR: –
FYE: December 31
Type: Private

Danis Building Construction can reach from the Buckeye state to the Sunshine state. The company provides commercial and industrial construction services in Ohio, Indiana, Kentucky, Tennessee, North Carolina, Georgia, and Florida. The third-generation, family-owned company offers construction management, design/build, general construction, and build-to-suit lease-back services. It specializes in public and private building and industrial projects such as offices, health care facilities, retail complexes, hotels, cultural facilities, schools, and industrial plants. Its projects have included the Cincinnati Children's Hospital and a federal courthouse in Kentucky. B.G. Danis established the company in 1916.

DANONE US, INC.

12002 AIRPORT WAY
BROOMFIELD, CO 800212546
Phone: 303 635-4000
Fax: –
Web: www.danonenorthamerica.com

CEO: –
CFO: –
HR: –
FYE: December 31
Type: Private

Danone North America was formed in April 2017, when Danone acquired WhiteWave Foods and united two companies in North America with a shared commitment to purpose, growth, and good food. Its portfolio of brands includes Activia, DanActive, Danimals, Dannon, Horizon Organic, International Delight, Light + Fit, Oikos, Silk, So Delicious Dairy Free, SToK, Two Good, Vega, Wallaby Organic, and YoCrunch. Danone North America is a business unit of Danone and one of the top 15 food and beverage companies in the US.

	Annual Growth	12/11	12/12	12/13	12/14	12/15
Sales ($mil.)	23.3%	–	–	2,542.1	3,436.6	3,866.3
Net income ($ mil.)	30.4%	–	–	99.0	140.2	168.4
Market value ($ mil.)	–	–	–	–	–	–
Employees						500

DANVILLE REGIONAL MEDICAL CENTER, LLC

142 S MAIN ST
DANVILLE, VA 245412987
Phone: 434 799-2100
Fax: –
Web: www.lebanonshadyacres.com

CEO: Alan Larson
CFO: –
HR: –
FYE: December 31
Type: Private

If your name is Dan, you should feel right at home at Danville Regional Medical Center (DRMC) serving residents of the Dan River Region in Danville, Virginia. Founded in 1884 as the Ladies Benevolent Society Home for the Sick, the hospital provides a variety of health care services such as home care, cancer treatment, psychiatry, and rehabilitation. Outpatient options include endoscopy (for gastrointestinal care), imaging, neurosurgical treatments, and pain management. DRMC administers a range of senior care services such as skilled nursing and coordination of assisted and independent living options. The health system is owned by LifePoint Health.

	Annual Growth	06/08	06/09	06/15	06/16*	12/21
Sales ($mil.)	7.6%	–	153.4	172.2	172.2	371.4
Net income ($ mil.)	–	–	(12.0)	(2.9)	(3.6)	47.0
Market value ($ mil.)	–	–	–	–	–	–
Employees	–	–	–	–	–	1,400

*Fiscal year change

DARDEN RESTAURANTS, INC.

1000 Darden Center Drive
Orlando, FL 32837
Phone: 407 245-4000
Fax: –
Web: www.darden.com

NYS: DRI
CEO: –
CFO: –
HR: –
FYE: May 28
Type: Public

Darden Restaurants is a full-service restaurant company that has been fueled by its Olive Garden chain of more than 1,900 restaurants. These operating restaurants in the US and Canada (fully-owned and franchises). Other concepts include LongHorn Steakhouse, The Capital Grille (upscale steakhouse), Bahama Breeze (Caribbean food and drinks), Eddie V's (seafood), Yard House (American food), Seasons 52 (casual grill and wine bar), and Cheddar's Scratch Kitchen (meals from scratch). The company has about 70 restaurants by independent and third parties pursuant to area development and franchise segments.

	Annual Growth	05/19	05/20	05/21	05/22	05/23
Sales ($mil.)	5.4%	8,510.4	7,806.9	7,196.1	9,630.0	10,488
Net income ($ mil.)	8.3%	713.4	(52.4)	629.3	952.8	981.9
Market value ($ mil.)	7.6%	14,544	9,305.5	17,341	15,260	19,526
Employees	0.4%	184,514	177,895	156,883	178,956	187,384

DARE BIOSCIENCE INC

3655 Nobel Drive, Suite 260
San Diego, CA 92122
Phone: 858 926-7655
Fax: –
Web: www.darebioscience.com

NAS: DARE
CEO: William H Rastetter
CFO: –
HR: –
FYE: December 31
Type: Public

Dar Bioscience (formerly Cerulean Pharma) is a health care firm with a focus on women's reproductive health. It intends to develop and commercialize products that will address issues including fertility, contraception, vaginal health, and pain. Its primary candidate is Ovaprene, a non-hormonal contraceptive ring which can provide protection for multiple weeks. In 2016, oncology pharmaceutical Cerulean Pharma's CRLX101, a treatment for ovarian cancer, failed a phase 2 clinical trial in combination with Roche's Avastin. The following year, Cerulean merged with Dar Bioscience Operations to establish Dar Bioscience.

	Annual Growth	12/19	12/20	12/21	12/22	12/23
Sales ($mil.)	–	–	–	–	10.0	2.8
Net income ($ mil.)	–	(14.3)	(27.4)	(38.7)	(30.9)	(30.2)
Market value ($ mil.)	(21.7%)	82.0	134.0	199.9	83.0	30.9
Employees	9.6%	18	23	28	30	26

DARKPULSE INC

815 Walker Street, Suite 1155
Houston, TX 77002
Phone: 800 436-1436
Fax: –
Web: –

NBB: DPLS
CEO: Dennis M O'Leary
CFO: –
HR: –
FYE: December 31
Type: Public

Klever Marketing thinks it's pretty clever to advertise on a shopping cart. The company is developing advertising terminals that attach to the handlebars of shopping carts. Branded as the Giving Cart, the terminals provide advertisers with an opportunity to influence potential customers at the point of purchase. Using wireless technology and WiFi access points around the store, the terminals chime to alert customers when they approach a promoted product. Retailers that don't purchase the wireless capability can use the terminals to display two-second ads on selected products. So far, the company is still developing the Giving Cart and has not had any sales. CEO Paul Begum owns more than 60% of the company.

	Annual Growth	12/18	12/19	12/20	12/21	12/22
Sales ($mil.)	–	–	–	–	7.8	9.1
Net income ($ mil.)	–	(3.3)	(1.8)	(0.3)	(4.7)	(35.3)
Market value ($ mil.)	(29.8%)	257.1	0.6	4.5	385.6	62.3
Employees	–	–	–	1	167	182

DARLING INGREDIENTS INC
NYS: DAR

5601 N MacArthur Blvd.
Irving, TX 75038
Phone: 972 717-0300
Fax: –
Web: www.darlingii.com

CEO: Randall C Stuewe
CFO: Brad Phillips
HR: –
FYE: December 30
Type: Public

Darling Ingredients is a global developer and producer of sustainable natural ingredients from edible and inedible bio-nutrients, creating a wide range of ingredients and customized specialty solutions for customers in the pharmaceutical, food, pet food, animal feed, industrial, fuel, bioenergy, and fertilizer industries. The company collects and recycles animal by-products into specialty ingredients such as collagen, edible fats, animal proteins, plasma, fertilizers, fuel feedstocks, and natural casings. Darling Ingredients also recovers and converts used cooking grease and bakery waste and offers grease-trap cleaning services. It primarily collects animal by-products from slaughterhouses, butcher shops, grocery stores, and food service establishments. Darling Ingredients also produces yellow grease, tallow, and meat, bone, and blood meal. North America accounts for approximately 65% of the company's total sales.

	Annual Growth	12/19*	01/21	01/22*	12/22	12/23
Sales ($mil.)	19.2%	3,363.9	3,571.9	4,741.4	6,532.2	6,788.1
Net income ($ mil.)	20.0%	312.6	296.8	650.9	737.7	647.7
Market value ($ mil.)	15.5%	4,466.9	9,201.9	11,054	9,985.2	7,951.2
Employees	11.8%	10,100	10,000	9,900	14,600	15,800

*Fiscal year change

DARTMOUTH-HITCHCOCK CLINIC

1 MEDICAL CENTER DR
LEBANON, NH 037560001
Phone: 603 650-5000
Fax: –
Web: www.dartmouth-hitchcock.org

CEO: Nancy Sormella
CFO: Robin Mackey
HR: –
FYE: June 30
Type: Private

The New England Alliance for Health (NEAH) brings together health care facilities and professionals looking to improve health in the New England region. Members of the alliance include about 20 community hospitals, home health care agencies, and mental health centers in New Hampshire, Vermont, and Massachusetts. While the members collaborate on wellness, quality, and communication initiatives, each member of the alliance is an independently owned and operated not-for-profit organization with its own board of directors. Collaborative services provided by NEAH include procurement, staff training, information technology, quality control, and finance, as well as the coordination of facility policies and planning.

	Annual Growth	06/12	06/13	06/14	06/15	06/19
Sales ($mil.)	313.1%	–	–	–	6.5	1,888.0
Net income ($ mil.)	–	–	–	–	–	22.0
Market value ($ mil.)	–	–	–	–	–	–
Employees	–	–	–	–	–	7,999

DATA I/O CORP.
NAS: DAIO

6645 185th Avenue NE, Suite 100
Redmond, WA 98052
Phone: 425 881-6444
Fax: –
Web: www.dataio.com

CEO: Anthony Ambrose
CFO: Joel S Hatlen
HR: –
FYE: December 31
Type: Public

Data I/O knows the chip-programming business inside and out. The company makes programming systems used by electronics manufacturers to tailor their integrated circuits (ICs) to suit a broad range of products. Data I/O manufactures both manual and automated programming systems used to manufacture semiconductor components for wireless consumer electronics, automotive electronics, and flash memory cards. Data I/O sells its devices to manufacturers such as LG, Delphi, and Foxconn. The company does most of its business outside the US; in fact, Singapore-based Flextronics is its largest customer. Data I/O has locations in Brazil, Canada, China, Germany, Guam, and Hong Kong.

	Annual Growth	12/18	12/19	12/20	12/21	12/22
Sales ($mil.)	(4.6%)	29.2	21.6	20.3	25.8	24.2
Net income ($ mil.)	–	1.6	(1.2)	(4.0)	(0.6)	(1.1)
Market value ($ mil.)	(5.6%)	44.1	37.4	36.3	40.6	35.0
Employees	(1.8%)	102	96	96	95	95

DATA SYSTEMS ANALYSTS, INC.

8 NESHAMINY INTERPLEX DR STE 209
FEASTERVILLE TREVOSE, PA 190536980
Phone: 215 245-4800
Fax: –
Web: www.dsainc.com

CEO: –
CFO: John Foley
HR: Pam Lamaina
FYE: December 31
Type: Private

Data Systems Analysts (DSA) is an information technology services contractor to the US military and other organizations. Its services include sharepoint solutions, software development, data analysis, cyber security, and system engineering and integration. Among other programs, DSA has been responsible for securing the Pentagon's Defense Information System Network (DISN) in the US. The company also contracts with civilian government agencies, and has served clients in the fields of naval, educational institutions, and laboratories. Founded in 1963, the company has satellite offices in Maryland, New Jersey, and Virginia.

	Annual Growth	12/04	12/05	12/06	12/07	12/08
Sales ($mil.)	6.2%	–	–	30.9	28.6	34.9
Net income ($ mil.)	(0.5%)	–	–	1.3	1.0	1.3
Market value ($ mil.)	–	–	–	–	–	–
Employees	–	–	–	–	–	180

DATA2LOGISTICS, LLC

12631 WESTLINKS DR STE 3
FORT MYERS, FL 339138627
Phone: 239 936-2800
Fax: –
Web: www.data2logistics.com

CEO: Haywood Bower
CFO: Kevin Brown
HR: Callea Dolores
FYE: December 31
Type: Private

Shippers can leave the paperwork to Data2Logistics, which provides freight bill auditing and processing services, primarily for large companies. Processing more than 120 million freight bills each year, Data2Logistics handles shippers' bills from truckers, railroads, air and ocean carriers, and package delivery companies; it also manages transportation cost information for shippers. Its Web-based routing tool allows its customers to access carrier and transportation information. Data2Logistics was originally founded in 1935 as Barry & Lloyd; it ultimately became part of CorPay Solutions, which was acquired in 2002 by investment firm Platinum Equity Holdings.

	Annual Growth	12/03	12/04	12/05	12/06	12/07
Sales ($mil.)	2.1%	–	28.8	29.1	33.7	30.6
Net income ($ mil.)	–	–	(0.1)	2.3	2.0	0.7
Market value ($ mil.)	–	–	–	–	–	–
Employees	–	–	–	–	–	205

DATACON, INC.

10 ELIZABETH DR UNIT 8
CHELMSFORD, MA 018244145
Phone: 781 273-5800
Fax: –
Web: www.data-con.com

CEO: –
CFO: –
HR: –
FYE: December 31
Type: Private

What's a dataCon? No, it's not someone convicted of identity theft or of maliciously hacking into computer networks. dataCon is a supplier of contract electronics manufacturing services, making circuit card assemblies, backplanes, cables, and power supply interconnects for government systems and medical electronics. The company provides printed circuit board design services, using software tools from Cadence Design Systems and Mentor Graphics. dataCon also does integrated-circuit packaging repair and refurbishment services. Customers include Lockheed Martin and Raytheon. The company was founded in 1971. John Marshall, the company's president, owns dataCon.

	Annual Growth	12/14	12/15	12/16	12/17	12/21
Sales ($mil.)	2.2%	–	9.7	16.1	–	11.1
Net income ($ mil.)	47.6%	–	0.1	0.4	–	1.5
Market value ($ mil.)	–	–	–	–	–	–
Employees	–	–	–	–	–	45

DATALINK CORPORATION

10050 CROSSTOWN CIR # 500
EDEN PRAIRIE, MN 553443346
Phone: 800 448-6314
Fax: –
Web: www.datalink.com

CEO: –
CFO: –
HR: –
FYE: December 31
Type: Private

Datalink builds and implements high-end, custom-designed data storage systems for large corporations. Its storage systems include flash storage, disk- and tape-based storage devices, storage networking components, and data management software. The company employs an open-system standard, building networks from products made by leading manufacturers such as Brocade and Hitachi Data Systems. Datalink also provides ongoing support and maintenance services. The company markets its products directly to customers in the US. It has designed systems for clients including AT&T, Harris Corporation, NAVTEQ, and St. Jude Medical. It has about 35 locations across the US.

DATASITE GLOBAL CORPORATION

733 MARQUETTE AVE STE 600
MINNEAPOLIS, MN 554022357
Phone: 651 632-4000
Fax: –
Web: www.datasite.com

CEO: James R Wiley
CFO: Tom Donnelly
HR: Brenda Vail
FYE: January 31
Type: Private

Datasite is a leading SaaS provider for the M&A industry, empowering dealmakers around the world with the tools they need to succeed across the entire deal lifecycle. As the premiere virtual data room for M&A due diligence globally, Datasite is consistently recognized for breakthrough technologies like its AI/ML-enabled capabilities and automated redaction tools. Beyond due diligence, Datasite provides transaction and document management solutions for investment banks, corporate development, private equity, and law firms across industries.

	Annual Growth	01/13	01/14	01/15	01/16	01/17
Sales ($mil.)	(6.1%)	–	–	691.5	579.4	609.1
Net income ($ mil.)	(8.5%)	–	–	64.5	78.1	54.0
Market value ($ mil.)	–	–	–	–	–	–
Employees						6,010

DATATRAK INTERNATIONAL INC.   NBB: DTRK

3690 Orange Place, Suite 375
Beachwood, OH 44122
Phone: 440 443-0082
Fax: 440 442-3482
Web: www.datatrak.com

CEO: James R Ward
CFO: Julia Henderson
HR: Laura Stuebbe
FYE: December 31
Type: Public

Researchers rely on DATATRAK to keep tabs on their clinical data. The company develops online, hosted electronic data capture (EDC) software for the biotechnology, medical device, contract research, and pharmaceutical industries. Its software speeds up the process of gathering data during clinical trials by collecting and electronically transmitting trial data from remote research sites to sponsors. DATATRAK also offers project management, site assessment, training, and hosting services. Its products have been used to support hundreds of clinical trials involving patients in more than 50 countries.

	Annual Growth	12/18	12/19	12/20	12/21	12/22
Sales ($mil.)	(5.6%)	7.4	7.7	7.2	6.4	5.9
Net income ($ mil.)	–	0.2	0.4	(0.1)	(0.2)	(0.9)
Market value ($ mil.)	(39.6%)	8.2	17.6	16.0	24.2	1.1
Employees	–	–	–	–	–	–

DATS TRUCKING, INC.

321 N OLD HIGHWAY 91
HURRICANE, UT 847373194
Phone: 435 673-1886
Fax: –
Web: www.datstrucking.com

CEO: –
CFO: –
HR: –
FYE: December 31
Type: Private

DATS Trucking specializes in less-than-truckload (LTL) freight transportation in the western US, but that's not all there is to the company's operations. In addition to its LTL operations, in which freight from multiple shippers is combined into a single trailer, DATS Trucking provides truckload transportation. The company's tanker division, Overland Petroleum, transports gasoline, diesel fuel, and other petroleum products. Overall, DATS Trucking operates a fleet of about 500 tractors and 2,500 trailers. It offers LTL service outside its home territory via The Reliance Network, a group of regional carriers that covers the US and Canada. President and CEO Don Ipson founded DATS Trucking in 1988.

	Annual Growth	12/03	12/04	12/05	12/06	12/07
Sales ($mil.)	22.3%	–	391.7	600.1	658.9	717.3
Net income ($ mil.)	4.6%	–	1.6	1.2	7.8	1.8
Market value ($ mil.)	–	–	–	–	–	–
Employees	–	–	–	–	–	475

DAUBERT INDUSTRIES, INC.

700 S CENTRAL AVE
BURR RIDGE, IL 60527
Phone: 630 203-6800
Fax: –
Web: www.daubert.com

CEO: Matthew Puz
CFO: Tim Henderson
HR: –
FYE: December 31
Type: Private

For Daubert Industries, metal health is the top concern. Its three subsidiaries protect metals by different methods. Daubert Cromwell makes VCI (volatile corrosion inhibitors) protective coatings for almost every metal -- ferrous, nonferrous, and multi-metal. Its transparent coatings protect metal that is stored or shipped until it is unwrapped and the coatings break down. ECP (Entire Car Protection) offers paints, carpet dyes, detailing products, and under-the-hood cleaners for automobiles. Daubert Chemical focuses on developing corrosion prevention, industrial anti-skid, and sound-deadening coatings. Daubert Industries was formed in 1935 by George Daubert, whose decendants still control the company.

DAVCO RESTAURANTS, INC.

170 JENNIFER RD STE 150
ANNAPOLIS, MD 214017915
Phone: 410 721-3770
Fax: –
Web: www.wendys.com

CEO: Harvey Rothstein
CFO: –
HR: –
FYE: September 30
Type: Private

This company helps keep Dave's burger legacy alive. DavCo Restaurants is the #1 franchisee of Wendy's International, the fast-food empire founded by the late Dave Thomas. DavCo operates more than 150 burger joints mostly in the metro area around Baltimore and Washington, DC. Its Wendy's locations offer burgers and fries, along with alternative menu items such as chili, salads, and baked potatoes. The restaurants typically provide both drive-through and dine-in service. DavCo was started in 1969 by members of the Davenport family (founders of the Krystal chain) and began running Wendy's franchises in 1976.

	Annual Growth	09/01	09/02	09/03	09/05	09/07
Sales ($mil.)	1.2%	–	–	204.4	–	214.0
Net income ($ mil.)	–	–	–	2.7	–	(3.2)
Market value ($ mil.)	–	–	–	–	–	–
Employees	–	–	–	–	–	4,500

DAVE & BUSTER'S, INC.

1221 S BELT LINE RD STE 500
COPPELL, TX 750194957
Phone: 214 357-9588
Fax: –
Web: www.daveandbusters.com

CEO: Brian Jenkins
CFO: –
HR: –
FYE: February 03
Type: Private

Fun and games collide with food and drink at these nightspots. Dave & Buster's Entertainment owns and operates more than 60 entertainment complexes that offer casual dining, full bar service, and a cavernous game room. The adult fun centers feature the latest in video games and motion simulators, as well as games of skill played for prizes. For dining, Dave & Buster's offers a menu that features traditional American fare such as burgers, seafood, and steak. Partners David Corriveau and James "Buster" Corley opened the first Dave & Buster's in 1982. Private-equity firm Oak Hill Capital Partners acquired the company in 2010. Dave & Buster's cancelled plans for an IPO in 2012.

DAVE & BUSTERS ENTERTAINMENT INC — NMS: PLAY

1221 S. Beltline Rd., Suite 500
Coppell, TX 75019
Phone: 214 357-9588
Fax: –
Web: www.daveandbusters.com

CEO: Brian A Jenkins
CFO: Scott Bowman
HR: –
FYE: January 29
Type: Public

Dave & Buster's Entertainment owns and operates about 205 venues in North America that offer premier entertainment and dining experiences to its guests. It has over 150 Dave & Buster branded stores in over 40 states and offers guests the opportunity to "Eat Drink Play and Watch," all in one location. Each store offers a full menu of entrées and appetizers, a complete selection of alcoholic and non-alcoholic beverages, and an extensive assortment of entertainment attractions centered on playing games and watching live sports and other televised events. It also operates about 50 Main Event and three The Summit branded stores in over 15 states that offer food, drinks, and amusements, including bowling, laser tag, arcade games, and virtual reality. Dave & Buster's was founded in 1982.

	Annual Growth	02/19	02/20*	01/21	01/22	01/23
Sales ($mil.)	11.6%	1,265.3	1,354.7	436.5	1,304.1	1,964.4
Net income ($ mil.)	4.0%	117.2	100.3	(207.0)	108.6	137.1
Market value ($ mil.)	(5.1%)	2,485.4	2,137.8	1,646.9	1,709.4	2,013.9
Employees	9.0%	16,098	15,908	8,547	13,783	22,748

*Fiscal year change

DAVENPORT UNIVERSITY

6191 KRAFT AVE SE
GRAND RAPIDS, MI 495129396
Phone: 616 698-7111
Fax: –
Web: www.davenport.edu

CEO: –
CFO: –
HR: –
FYE: June 30
Type: Private

Couch potatoes need not apply to Davenport. A private, not-for-profit school, Davenport University offers its 9,000 students -- many of whom are working adults -- associate's, bachelor's, and master's degrees, as well as certification and diploma programs. Founded in 1866, Davenport offers more than 50 undergraduate majors in fields including business, health, and technology, plus an MBA and several other master's programs. With campuses across Michigan, online offerings, and a study abroad program, Davenport is a top independent university system in Michigan. Davenport University was founded by Union Army veteran Conrad Swensburg in 1866. It was originally named Grand Rapids Business College.

	Annual Growth	06/10	06/11	06/13	06/20	06/22
Sales ($mil.)	(0.5%)	–	137.2	126.8	124.3	130.0
Net income ($ mil.)	(19.1%)	–	9.4	(7.5)	(1.7)	0.9
Market value ($ mil.)	–	–	–	–	–	–
Employees	–	–	–	–	–	927

DAVEY TREE EXPERT CO. (THE) — NBB: DVTX

1500 North Mantua Street, P.O. Box 5193
Kent, OH 44240
Phone: 330 673-9511
Fax: –
Web: www.davey.com

CEO: Karl J Warnke
CFO: Joseph R Paul
HR: Craig Holcomb
FYE: December 31
Type: Public

The Davey Tree Expert Company's roots extend back to 1880 and provides a wide range of arboricultural, horticultural services, environmental and consulting services to residential, commercial, utility, and governmental entities throughout the US and Canada.. Davey's services include treatment, preservation, maintenance, and removal of trees, shrubs, and other plants; landscaping; grounds maintenance; tree surgery; tree feeding and tree spraying; the application of fertilizers, herbicides, and insecticides. It provides also natural resource management and consulting, forestry research and development, and environmental planning. Davey has been employee-owned since 1979. The US generates some 95% of Davey's total revenue.

	Annual Growth	12/18	12/19	12/20	12/21	12/22
Sales ($mil.)	10.2%	1,024.8	1,143.7	1,287.6	1,378.1	1,511.1
Net income ($ mil.)	21.7%	28.0	40.8	60.9	65.7	61.3
Market value ($ mil.)	–	–	–	–	–	–
Employees	4.0%	8,900	9,700	9,600	10,200	10,400

DAVID E. HARVEY BUILDERS, INC.

3663 BRIARPARK DR STE 101
HOUSTON, TX 770425205
Phone: 713 783-8710
Fax: –
Web: www.harveycleary.com

CEO: –
CFO: Rodney Finke
HR: –
FYE: December 31
Type: Private

Harvey-Cleary is a full-service general contractor. The company provides preconstruction, construction, technology, sustainability, and safety services. Projects include office buildings, condos, hotels and convention centers, retail stores, parking garages, hospitals, and research facilities. Harvey's customers have included University of Houston, Bassett Furniture Direct, Hotel Emma, Courtyard Marriott and Residence Inn. The company serves several industries, such as healthcare and research, industrial, oil, gas, and energy, corporate office, interiors, residential and hospitality, retail, non-profit, repositioning, education, and government. David E. Harvey, Sr. and Gerald D. Hines started Harvey Construction Company in 1957.

	Annual Growth	12/18	12/19	12/20	12/21	12/22
Sales ($mil.)	20.9%	–	–	–	1,353.8	1,636.8
Net income ($ mil.)	4.9%	–	–	–	39.3	41.3
Market value ($ mil.)	–	–	–	–	–	–
Employees	–	–	–	–	–	720

DAVID MONTOYA CONSTRUCTION, INC.

315 ALAMEDA BLVD NE STE A
ALBUQUERQUE, NM 871132155
Phone: 505 898-6330
Fax: –
Web: www.montoyaconstruction.com

CEO: –
CFO: –
HR: –
FYE: May 31
Type: Private

David Montoya Construction, a general contractor, provides civil and commercial construction services to customers in New Mexico. The company's portfolio includes such projects as site development (Big Rock Casino, Costco), bridges (High Street Bridge, Largo Bridge, Santa Fe Relief Route, Taos Bridge, and I-40 Moriarty Bridges), commercial development (Bureau of Land Management, Walgreen, and the Museum of Natural History), dams and canals (Agua Sarco Arroyo, La Cienega Dam, and Simms Reservoir), highway roads (Cerrillos Road/Santa Fe, and US Hwy. 371/Thoreau), and concrete paving work (Roswell Relief Route, Albuquerque International Airport/Cargo Parking). President David Montoya owns the company.

DAVID YURMAN ENTERPRISES LLC

24 VESTRY ST
NEW YORK, NY 100131903
Phone: 212 896-1550
Fax: –
Web: www.davidyurman.com

CEO: David Yurman
CFO: Victor Wong
HR: Heather Eisler
FYE: December 31
Type: Private

David Yurman, founder and owner of the namesake company, knows that while diamonds are a girl's best friend, she also can be pretty chummy with gold and silver pieces of well-crafted jewelry. The company makes classic bracelets, chains, earrings, necklaces, rings, jewel-encrusted watches, eyewear, and fragrances; it caters to a high-end clientele and celebrities the likes of Charlize Theron and Brad Pitt. Some 35 David Yurman jewelry boutiques stretch from New York City to Beverly Hills to Las Vegas to Houston. The jewelry retailer also sells its pieces on a website hosted by Neiman Marcus and through several catalogs. Its bridal collection features Yurman's signature cable accents.

DAVIDSON HOTEL COMPANY LLC

1 RAVINIA DR STE 1600
ATLANTA, GA 303462109
Phone: 678 349-0909
Fax: –
Web: www.davidsonhospitality.com

CEO: John Belden
CFO: –
HR: Joy French
FYE: December 31
Type: Private

Davidson Hotels & Resorts probably has room for you at the inn. One of the nation's top independent hotel management companies, it invests in, develops, renovates, and manages hospitality real estate throughout the US. The company owns and operates about 45 upscale hotel and resort properties under such brand names as Carlson, InterContinental, Hilton, Hyatt, Marriott, and Starwood. Altogether, its portfolio has approximately 13,500 rooms. Davidson also provides consulting and accounting support to the hospitality industry. The company is focused on growth and has been expanding its portfolio through acquisitions and third-party management deals.

DAVIESS COUNTY HOSPITAL

1314 E WALNUT ST
WASHINGTON, IN 475012132
Phone: 812 254-2760
Fax: –
Web: www.dchosp.org

CEO: David Dixler
CFO: Brad Hardcastle
HR: –
FYE: December 31
Type: Private

Daviess Community Hospital serves Daviess County in southwestern Indiana. The acute care facility has about 120 beds and offers behavioral health, cardiac rehabilitation, hospice, obstetric, physical therapy, and pediatric services. In addition, the hospital also has centers dedicated to women's health and diabetes management. Daviess Community Hospital opened its doors in 1915.

	Annual Growth	12/16	12/17	12/18	12/19	12/21
Sales ($mil.)	(28.5%)	–	248.5	291.8	299.2	65.1
Net income ($ mil.)	–	–	6.9	9.5	8.2	(1.9)
Market value ($ mil.)	–	–	–	–	–	–
Employees	–	–	–	–	–	550

DAVITA INC

2000 16th Street
Denver, CO 80202
Phone: 720 631-2100
Fax: –
Web: www.davita.com

NYS: DVA
CEO: –
CFO: –
HR: –
FYE: December 31
Type: Public

DaVita is a leading healthcare provider focused on transforming care delivery to improve quality of life for patients globally. The company is one of the US largest providers of dialysis -- its administrative services reach some 199,400 patients through about 2,725 outpatient centers across the US. It also offers home-based dialysis services, as well as inpatient dialysis in some 820 hospitals. Also, its US ancillary services and strategic initiatives provided integrated care and disease management services to 42,000 patients in risk-based integrated care arrangements and to an additional 15,000 patients in other integrated care arrangements. It operates one separately licensed and highly automated clinical laboratory that specializes in routine testing of dialysis patients and serve the company's network of clinics.

	Annual Growth	12/19	12/20	12/21	12/22	12/23
Sales ($mil.)	1.6%	11,388	11,551	11,619	11,610	12,140
Net income ($ mil.)	(3.9%)	811.0	773.6	978.5	560.4	691.5
Market value ($ mil.)	8.7%	6,664.5	10,428	10,105	6,632.5	9,305.2
Employees	1.9%	65,000	67,000	69,000	70,000	70,000

DAW TECHNOLOGIES INC.

2700 South 900 West
Salt Lake City, UT 84119
Phone: 801 977-3100
Fax: 801 973-6640
Web: www.dawtech.com

CEO: –
CFO: –
HR: –
FYE: December 31
Type: Public

Your clean room is ready. Daw Technologies (Daw Tech) makes, installs, and services ultraclean rooms and clean room components. Clean rooms enable biotech and microelectronics companies to control crucial environmental variables such as temperature, dust, and electromagnetic fields in their manufacturing facilities. The company also applies its clean room know-how to commercial and industrial air handling systems, and it offers high-precision contract manufacturing services for makers of electronic gear. Daw Tech's customers are principally in the US, and to a lesser extent in Europe. It has offices in Utah and Texas.

	Annual Growth	12/97	12/98	12/99	12/00	12/01
Sales ($mil.)	(6.3%)	52.5	53.1	45.2	52.6	40.5
Net income ($ mil.)	–	(2.3)	(3.9)	(7.6)	3.5	(8.0)
Market value ($ mil.)	(10.8%)	6.8	4.2	2.3	2.0	4.3
Employees	(12.7%)	370	357	302	215	215

DAWSON GEOPHYSICAL CO (NEW)

508 West Wall, Suite 800
Midland, TX 79701
Phone: 432 684-3000
Fax: –
Web: www.dawson3d.com

NMS: DWSN
CEO: Stephen C Jumper
CFO: James K Brata
HR: –
FYE: December 31
Type: Public

3-D technology has made Dawson Geophysical (formerly TGC Industries) one of the movers and shakers in the North American oil patch as it conducts seismic surveys for oil exploration companies. The company principally employs land surveys using Geospace Technologies and ARAM ARIES seismic systems, which obtain 3-D seismic data related to subsurface geological features. Employing radio-frequency telemetry and multi-channel recorders, the system enables the exploration of rivers, swamps, and inaccessible terrain. It also sells gravity information from its data bank to oil and gas exploration companies. In 2014 it was acquired by Dawson Operating, then known as Dawson Geophysical.

	Annual Growth	12/18	12/19	12/20	12/21	12/22
Sales ($mil.)	(29.8%)	154.2	145.8	86.1	24.7	37.5
Net income ($ mil.)	–	(24.4)	(15.2)	(13.2)	(29.1)	(20.5)
Market value ($ mil.)	(12.7%)	80.5	57.1	50.5	55.2	46.7
Employees	(21.1%)	582	455	219	190	226

DAWSON METAL COMPANY, INC.

825 ALLEN ST
JAMESTOWN, NY 147013998
Phone: 716 664-3811
Fax: –
Web: www.dawsonmetal.com

CEO: –
CFO: Guy F Lombardo
HR: –
FYE: December 31
Type: Private

Don't knock Dawson Metal's open-door policy. Dawson Metal (which does business as Dawson Doors) manufactures custom-made stainless steel, aluminum, and bronze doors for businesses and storefronts. The company also manufactures balanced doors, which open in an elliptical arch. It mainly serves US corporations and the construction industry, and makes doors for private residences, as well. Dawson Metal was established in Jamestown, New York, in 1946 as an industrial and architectural metal fabrication business by Axel Dawson and his son George. The Dawson family continues to own the company.

	Annual Growth	12/09	12/10	12/11	12/12	12/13
Sales ($mil.)	0.7%	–	–	14.6	12.9	14.8
Net income ($ mil.)	(22.1%)	–	–	0.5	0.2	0.3
Market value ($ mil.)	–	–	–	–	–	–
Employees	–	–	–	–	–	110

DAY KIMBALL HEALTHCARE, INC.

320 POMFRET ST
PUTNAM, CT 062601836
Phone: 860 928-6541
Fax: –
Web: www.daykimball.org

CEO: Robert Smanik
CFO: –
HR: –
FYE: September 30
Type: Private

With more than 100 beds, Day Kimball Hospital is a non-profit acute-care facility that caters primarily to Connecticut, with an extended reach into parts of Massachusetts and Rhode Island. The health care provider, founded in 1894, offers general medical and surgical care, along with the option of home care services. Logging an average of nearly 29,000 emergency department visits and 550 births, Day Kimball offers specialized services, such as pediatrics, gynecology, emergency medicine, and psychiatric health care. It also provides hospice and palliative care for terminally ill patients. Outpatient surgery and other medical services are provided through the facility's Ambulatory Care Unit.

	Annual Growth	09/18	09/19	09/20	09/21	09/22
Sales ($mil.)	2.2%	–	136.5	126.6	146.6	145.6
Net income ($ mil.)	–	–	(15.6)	(20.5)	15.9	8.3
Market value ($ mil.)	–	–	–	–	–	–
Employees	–	–	–	–	–	900

DAYFORCE INC

3311 East Old Shakopee Road
Minneapolis, MN 55425
Phone: 952 853-8100
Fax: –
Web: www.ceridian.com

NYS: CDAY
CEO: David D Ossip
CFO: Noemie C Heuland
HR: –
FYE: December 31
Type: Public

Ceridian Hcm Holding Inc. is a global human capital management (HCM) software company. Its flagship cloud HCM platform, Dayforce, provides human resources (HR), payroll, benefits, workforce management, and talent management functionality. In addition to Dayforce, it sells Powerpay, a cloud HR and payroll solution for the Canadian small business market, through both direct sales and established partner channels. Its platform is used by organizations, regardless of industry or size, to optimize management of the entire employee lifecycle, including attracting, engaging, paying, deploying, and developing their people. It also offers a broad portfolio of services aimed to ensure customer success and continues to increase its global reach in supporting and serving its customers. The company generated roughly 65% of revenue from the US.

	Annual Growth	12/19	12/20	12/21	12/22	12/23
Sales ($mil.)	16.4%	824.1	842.5	1,024.2	1,246.2	1,513.7
Net income ($ mil.)	(8.7%)	78.7	(4.0)	(75.4)	(73.4)	54.8
Market value ($ mil.)	(0.3%)	10,610	16,655	16,327	10,027	10,491
Employees	16.0%	5,011	5,974	7,462	8,526	9,084

DAYLIGHT DONUT FLOUR COMPANY LLC

11707 E 11TH ST
TULSA, OK 741284401
Phone: 918 438-0800
Fax: –
Web: www.daylightdonuts.com

CEO: John Bond
CFO: Jimmy Keeter
HR: –
FYE: December 31
Type: Private

Daylight Donut wants to tempt you whether it's day or night. The company sells a variety of sweet and savory pastries from nearly 1,000 Daylight Donuts locations in all 50 states plus single shops in Australia, China, Mexico, and Romania. It offers licenses instead of franchises, allowing owners to avoid franchise fees by agreeing to use company products in exchange for the use of the name and trademark. The products licensees agree to use include company-made dry mixes for the stores' signature donuts, bear claws, cinnamon rolls, sausage wraps, and other pastries as well as private-label coffee for use in-store and for resale. Formed in 1954, Daylight Donut is owned by John and Sheila Bond, husband and wife.

	Annual Growth	12/13	12/14	12/15	12/16	12/17
Sales ($mil.)	(0.2%)	–	15.1	15.3	15.0	15.0
Net income ($ mil.)	5.5%	–	2.1	2.4	2.5	2.5
Market value ($ mil.)	–	–	–	–	–	–
Employees	–	–	–	–	–	30

DBM GLOBAL INC

1841 West Buchanan Street
Phoenix, AZ 85007
Phone: 602 252-7787
Fax: –
Web: www.schuff.com

NBB: DBMG
CEO: –
CFO: –
HR: –
FYE: December 29
Type: Public

DBM Global (formerly Schuff International), and its collection of steel fabrication companies, comes on strong. Operating through Schuff Steel and other units, the integrated steel fabrication and erection company is one of the leading steel erectors in the US. It offers steel construction services including design/build, engineering, computer modeling, fabrication, joist and girder manufacturing, and project management. Its portfolio includes office buildings, sports arenas, hotels and casinos, hospitals, mines, bridges, and power plants. The group also fabricates water pipes, water storage tanks, and other equipment. DBM Global operates nine steel fabrication plants in Arizona, Texas, Kansas, Georgia, and Florida.

	Annual Growth	01/10	01/11	01/12*	12/12	12/13
Sales ($mil.)	(0.3%)	420.9	287.6	392.2	447.0	416.1
Net income ($ mil.)	(10.2%)	19.0	1.3	(5.0)	2.2	12.3
Market value ($ mil.)	4.7%	63.0	55.3	48.3	39.9	75.7
Employees	–	–	–	–	–	–

*Fiscal year change

DC GROUP INC.

1977 W RIVER RD STE 1
MINNEAPOLIS, MN 554113444
Phone: 612 529-9516
Fax: –
Web: www.dc-group.com

CEO: Jonathan Frank
CFO: –
HR: Heidi Solberg
FYE: December 31
Type: Private

If "knowledge is power," than DC Group is a force to reckon with. The company offers maintenance services for uninterruptible power supplies (UPS), such as backup power equipment for protecting computer systems, or for stationary batteries, air conditioning, and stand-by generators. The company alleviates concerns over electric brownouts or spikes, enabling clients to also cut costs by tightening internal service departments. Its roster of 6,300-plus clients, half of whom are Fortune 500s, ranges from data centers to telecommunications and government offices like Microsoft, Sprint Nextel, and the US Defense Department. Chairman Stephen Frank formed the privately held company in 1992, his son Jon Frank is CEO.

	Annual Growth	12/11	12/12	12/15	12/16	12/17
Sales ($mil.)	8.5%	–	23.2	32.4	30.8	35.0
Net income ($ mil.)	17.8%	–	2.2	3.6	5.2	5.0
Market value ($ mil.)	–	–	–	–	–	–
Employees	–	–	–	–	–	181

DCP MIDSTREAM LP
NYS: DCP PRB

6900 E. Layton Ave, Suite 900
Denver, CO 80237
Phone: 303 595-3331
Fax: –
Web: www.dcpmidstream.com

CEO: Don A Baldridge
CFO: –
HR: –
FYE: December 31
Type: Public

DCP Midstream is one of the natural gas gatherers in North America and a producer and marketer of natural gas liquids (NGLs). It also engages in natural gas compressing, treating, processing, transporting, and selling. DCP Midstream also transports and sells NGLs and distributes ethane, propane, and butane wholesale. The company operates natural gas gathering and transmission systems (some 48,000 miles of pipe) in some 35 plants. The company is a Delaware limited Partnership formed in 2005 by DCP Midstream, LLC to own, operate, acquire, and develop a diversified portfolio of complementary midstream energy assets.

	Annual Growth	12/18	12/19	12/20	12/21	12/22
Sales ($mil.)	11.2%	9,822.0	7,625.0	6,302.0	10,707	14,993
Net income ($ mil.)	37.1%	298.0	17.0	(306.0)	391.0	1,052.0
Market value ($ mil.)	3.1%	4,518.0	5,011.9	4,424.3	5,189.1	5,105.7
Employees		–	–	–	–	–

DEACONESS HEALTH SYSTEM, INC.

600 MARY ST
EVANSVILLE, IN 477101658
Phone: 812 450-5000
Fax: –
Web: www.deaconess.com

CEO: Shawn McCoy
CFO: Cheryl Wathen
HR: Katie Burnett
FYE: September 30
Type: Private

While it primarily presides over numerous health care facilities in the southwestern corner of Indiana, Deaconess Health System also serves residents in parts of southeastern Illinois and western Kentucky. The system consists of two general acute-care hospitals, as well as specialty hospitals for women's health, mental health, and medical rehabilitation. Its flagship Deaconess Hospital boasts 365 beds and serves as a regional referral center. Deaconess Health also operates a standalone cancer treatment center, medical group practice Deaconess Clinic, and about 20 outpatient and urgent care clinics. Its Deaconess Health Plans unit is a PPO network that contracts with various health insurers.

	Annual Growth	09/16	09/17	09/18	09/19	09/20
Sales ($mil.)	(76.3%)	–	930.9	1,058.4	16.2	12.5
Net income ($ mil.)		–	127.3	170.6	(61.5)	(75.8)
Market value ($ mil.)		–	–	–	–	–
Employees		–	–	–	–	9,000

DEACONESS HOSPITAL INC

600 MARY ST
EVANSVILLE, IN 477101674
Phone: 812 450-5000
Fax: –
Web: www.deaconess.com

CEO: Linda E White
CFO: Richard Stivers
HR: –
FYE: September 30
Type: Private

Deaconess Hospital provides benevolent medical assistance to residents of southern Indiana, western Kentucky, and southeastern Illinois. The not-for-profit hospital is a 365-bed acute care medical facility that is the flagship hospital of the Deaconess Health System. Specialized services include cardiovascular surgery, cancer treatment, orthopedics, neurological, and trauma care. The hospital also offers home health care, hospice services, and medical equipment rental, and it operates outpatient family practice, surgery, wellness, and community outreach centers. Founded in 1892, Deaconess Hospital is a teaching and research facility affiliated with the Indiana University School of Medicine.

	Annual Growth	09/18	09/19	09/20	09/21	09/22
Sales ($mil.)	5.8%	–	1,047.6	987.9	1,135.4	1,240.2
Net income ($ mil.)	(11.6%)	–	159.3	196.3	393.0	109.9
Market value ($ mil.)		–	–	–	–	–
Employees		–	–	–	–	5,300

DEALERS SUPPLY COMPANY, INC.

82 KENNEDY DR
FOREST PARK, GA 302972536
Phone: 404 361-6800
Fax: –
Web: www.dealerssupply.net

CEO: Richard E Laurens
CFO: Earl C Hunter
HR: –
FYE: March 31
Type: Private

Dealers Supply Company (DSC) strives to keep cool during those long Southern summers. Through about 15 locations in Georgia and North Carolina, the company distributes air conditioning and heating products to residential customers, contractors, and small businesses. Products include air conditioners, heaters, motors, insulation, lifts, sealants, and other items from such brands as Airgas, Honeywell, RUUD, Trion, and WeatherKing. DSC sells the tools needed to install and maintain all the heating and cooling equipment it sells, and it offers classes and reference guides. The company's Web site includes an online catalog and searchable database of licensed conditioned air contractors.

	Annual Growth	03/08	03/09	03/10	03/11	03/12
Sales ($mil.)	2.9%	–	–	38.5	41.0	40.8
Net income ($ mil.)	(4.5%)	–	–	0.6	0.7	0.5
Market value ($ mil.)		–	–	–	–	–
Employees		–	–	–	–	126

DEALERTRACK TECHNOLOGIES, INC.

3400 NEW HYDE PARK RD
NEW HYDE PARK, NY 110421226
Phone: 516 734-3600
Fax: –
Web: www.castagnarealty.com

CEO: Mark F O'Neil
CFO: Eric D Jacobs
HR: –
FYE: December 31
Type: Private

DealerTrack is the leading provider of integrated dealership technologies. From best-in-class Sales and F&I software that improves the customer experience to a Dealer Management System that boosts employee productivity, Dealertrack is committed to the growth and success of the customers' business. Superior product features are only a part of what makes Dealertrack DMS different. It is also the only provider of automotive retail solutions backed by the power of Cox Automotive. The company is controlled by Cox Automotive, a company with a strong reputation and track record for anticipating what's ahead in the industry.

DEAN FOODS COMPANY

2711 N HASKELL AVE STE 3400
DALLAS, TX 752042911
Phone: 214 303-3400
Fax: –
Web: www.dfamilk.com

CEO: –
CFO: –
HR: –
FYE: December 31
Type: Private

Dean Foods is one of the nation's largest milk processors. The company markets fluid milk, ice cream, and cultured dairy products as well as beverages (juices, teas, and bottled water). It operates under more than 25 local, regional, and private label brands, including DairyPure, Mayfield, Pet, Country Fresh, Meadow Gold, and TruMoo, a leading national flavored milk brand. Dean Foods owns and operates a number of smaller regional dairy companies, including Friendly's, and Garelick Farms. Its brands all share the same simple, farm-to-table attitude that you can feel good about, as well as being flavorful, enjoyable ways to feed a healthier lifestyle. In 2020, Dairy Farmers of America completed a $433 million acquisition of Dean Foods' properties after reaching an agreement with the US Department of Justice.

	Annual Growth	12/14	12/15	12/16	12/17	12/18
Sales ($mil.)	0.3%	–	–	7,710.2	7,795.0	7,755.3
Net income ($ mil.)		–	–	119.9	61.6	(327.4)
Market value ($ mil.)		–	–	–	–	–
Employees		–	–	–	–	14,500

DEBARTOLO, INC.

7620 MKT ST
YOUNGSTOWN, OH 445126076
Phone: 330 965-2000
Fax: –
Web: www.thedebartologroup.com

CEO: –
CFO: –
HR: –
FYE: December 31
Type: Private

Real estate holdings, gambling, a felony conviction, and warring siblings surrounded by a storied NFL franchise -- sounds like an old episode of Dallas. However, the story of The DeBartolo Corporation takes place in Youngstown, Ohio, via San Francisco. The family holding company controlled by Denise DeBartolo York and her husband John York owns the San Francisco 49ers professional football team, which was purchased in 1977. Family scion Edward J. DeBartolo Sr., who started the company in 1944, had a long career in both sports ownership and real estate development.

DEBT RESOLVE INC

1133 Westchester Ave., Suite S-223
White Plains, NY 10604
Phone: 914 949-5500
Fax: –
Web: www.debtresolve.com

CEO: William M Mooney Jr
CFO: –
HR: –
FYE: December 31
Type: Public

Debt Resolve isn't intimidated by mountains of debt. The company provides a hosted software service that allows credit card companies and collection agencies to collect money from consumers who are past due on their credit card bills. The online service, branded as DebtResolve, uses an Internet-based bidding system that allows debtors and creditors to agree on acceptable repayment schedules. Customers include banks and other credit originators, credit card issuers, and third-party collection agencies, as well as assignees and buyers of consumer debt.

	Annual Growth	12/12	12/13	12/14	12/15	12/16
Sales ($mil.)	124.0%	0.2	0.1	0.2	5.7	4.4
Net income ($ mil.)	–	(1.6)	(0.5)	(0.8)	(0.8)	(1.8)
Market value ($ mil.)	(22.2%)	3.6	2.5	0.8	1.1	1.3
Employees	(6.9%)	4	4	4	4	3

DECATUR MEMORIAL HOSPITAL

2300 N EDWARD ST
DECATUR, IL 625264192
Phone: 217 877-8121
Fax: –
Web: www.memorial.health

CEO: Ken Smithmier
CFO: –
HR: Ashley Patton
FYE: September 30
Type: Private

Not-for-profit Decatur Memorial Hospital (DMH) serves residents of Macon and neighboring counties in central Illinois. The 300-bed regional medical facility has a staff of 300 physicians who provide acute and tertiary care. DMH operates about a dozen Centers of Excellence in areas including cancer, heart and lung, women's health, birthing, allergy, orthopedic, and stroke care. Other health care services include preventive care through its DMH Wellness Center; home health and hospice programs, and local urgent care and primary care through centers in the surrounding area.

	Annual Growth	09/17	09/18	09/19	09/20	09/21
Sales ($mil.)	(3.8%)	–	296.3	–	257.6	264.0
Net income ($ mil.)	–	–	(18.6)	–	(2.0)	16.6
Market value ($ mil.)	–	–	–	–	–	–
Employees	–	–	–	–	–	1,311

DECIPHERA PHARMACEUTICALS INC

NMS: DCPH

200 Smith Street
Waltham, MA 02451
Phone: 781 209-6400
Fax: –
Web: www.deciphera.com

CEO: Steven L Hoerter
CFO: Thomas P Kelly
HR: –
FYE: December 31
Type: Public

Deciphera Pharmaceuticals is a clinical-stage biopharmaceutical with a focus on developing kinase inhibitors to treat a variety of cancers. Its proprietary kinase switch control inhibitor platform helps prevent cancer-related kinases from becoming active. Its FDA approved drug, QINLOCK, which commenced selling in May 2020 in the United States, is designed improve the treatment of GIST patients by inhibiting the full spectrum of the known mutations in KIT and PDGFRA. The company has a pipeline of novel research- and clinical-stage candidates, including tumor-targeting lead candidate DCC-2618, which is being studied for the treatment of stomach and small intestine cancers. Other programs include rebastinib, which is being tested in combination with chemotherapy for the treatment of advanced breast cancer, and DCC-3014, in studies for the treatment of solid tumors and hematological malignancies. Deciphera Pharmaceuticals serves biotechnology and pharmaceutical industries.

	Annual Growth	12/19	12/20	12/21	12/22	12/23
Sales ($mil.)	59.9%	25.0	42.1	96.1	134.0	163.4
Net income ($ mil.)	–	(192.3)	(266.5)	(300.0)	(178.9)	(194.9)
Market value ($ mil.)	(28.7%)	5,010.5	4,594.3	786.5	1,319.4	1,298.5
Employees	8.3%	258	350	280	300	355

DECISION DIAGNOSTICS CORP

NBB: DECN

2660 Townsgate Road, Suite 300
Westlake Village, CA 91361
Phone: 805 446-1973
Fax: 805 446-1983
Web: www.decisiondiagnostics.com

CEO: –
CFO: Keith Berman
HR: –
FYE: December 31
Type: Public

Decision Diagnostics Corp. (DDC) hopes IT plus pharmaceuticals will equal success. Previously focused on wireless systems for the health care and lodging markets, in 2005 the company added a pharmaceuticals distribution unit through its purchases of CareGeneration and the Pharmaceutical Solutions unit of Kelly Company. DDC drives customers to its pharmaceuticals business by providing wireless computing devices to doctors in clinics for the poor and uninsured; in return, doctors direct their patients to the company's discount mail-order prescription service. The company continues to sell its wireless PDA devices for the health care and lodging industries. Clearing company Cede & Co. owns 40% of DDC.

	Annual Growth	12/16	12/17	12/18	12/19	12/20
Sales ($mil.)	16.0%	1.1	1.9	2.2	2.4	2.0
Net income ($ mil.)	–	(3.2)	(3.0)	(2.2)	(3.1)	(29.7)
Market value ($ mil.)	(35.3%)	36.4	26.6	7.1	5.1	6.4
Employees	–	–	9	–	–	–

DECISIONPOINT SYSTEMS INC (NEW)

NBB: DPSI

1615 South Congress Avenue Suite 103
Delray Beach, FL 33445
Phone: 561 900-3723
Fax: –
Web: www.decisionpt.com

CEO: Steven Smith
CFO: Michael Roe
HR: –
FYE: December 31
Type: Public

When you need data to stay on point, this firm can help. DecisionPoint Systems is a provider of Enterprise Mobility and RFID software and hardware designed to make real-time interactive data accessible to workers. Data is accessed over wireless networks via handheld mobile devices and electronic tagging. The company markets its offerings to warehouse distribution and management customers, as well as retail, manufacturing, pharmaceutical, and telecommunications firms. Clients include Avis, G4S, and Celgene. DecisionPoint Systems was formed in 2011 through a reverse merger with desktop software firm Comamtech.

	Annual Growth	12/13	12/14	12/20	12/21	12/22
Sales ($mil.)	5.4%	60.7	64.5	63.4	65.9	97.4
Net income ($ mil.)	–	(5.2)	0.5	2.9	1.4	3.1
Market value ($ mil.)	–	–	–	–	–	60.1
Employees	2.6%	92	77	–	100	116

DECKERS OUTDOOR CORP.

NYS: DECK

250 Coromar Drive
Goleta, CA 93117
Phone: 805 967-7611
Fax: –
Web: www.deckers.com

CEO: David Powers
CFO: Steven J Fasching
HR: –
FYE: March 31
Type: Public

Deckers Outdoor is a global leader in designing, marketing, and distributing innovative footwear, apparel, and accessories developed for both everyday casual lifestyle use and high-performance activities. It designs and markets the iconic UGG brand of luxury sheepskin footwear in addition to Teva sports sandals ? a cross between a hiking boot and a flip-flop used for walking, hiking, and rafting, among other pursuits. Other product lines include Sanuk, HOKA UGGpure, and Koolaburra. Deckers Outdoor, which generates most of its revenue in the US, sells its footwear through about 160 retail stores worldwide, independent distributors, and e-commerce sites such as Amazon.com, Zappos.com, and Zalando.com.

	Annual Growth	03/19	03/20	03/21	03/22	03/23
Sales ($mil.)	15.8%	2,020.4	2,132.7	2,545.6	3,150.3	3,627.3
Net income ($ mil.)	18.3%	264.3	276.1	382.6	451.9	516.8
Market value ($ mil.)	32.2%	3,847.6	3,507.6	8,649.1	7,166.2	11,767
Employees	4.7%	3,500	3,600	3,400	4,000	4,200

DEEP FOODS INC.

1090 SPRINGFIELD RD
UNION, NJ 070838147
Phone: 908 810-7500
Fax: –
Web: www.deepfoods.com

CEO: –
CFO: –
HR: –
FYE: December 31
Type: Private

Deep Foods incorporates exotic flavors from the Far East into its recipes. The company manufactures and markets a range of dry, fresh, and frozen Indian food products, as well as Thai and Chinese entrees. Located in Union, New Jersey, Deep Foods sells its products primarily in specialty food emporiums throughout the US and Canada. The company's offerings, sold to food retailers and foodservice operators, under labels including Bansi, Bhagwati's, Mirch Masala, Reena's, Tandoor Chef, and Udupi, range from appetizers and meals to delicacies and desserts. The family-owned and -operated company was founded in 1977 by Bhagwati and Arvind Amin.

DEERE & CO.

NYS: DE

One John Deere Place
Moline, IL 61265
Phone: 309 765-8000
Fax: 309 765-9929
Web: www.deere.com

CEO: John C May
CFO: Joshua A Jepsen
HR: –
FYE: October 29
Type: Public

Deere & Co. is one of the world's largest makers of farm equipment and a major producer of construction, forestry, and commercial and residential lawn care equipment. Deere offers a portfolio of multiple brands to provide a full line of innovative solutions for its customers in a variety of production systems throughout the lifecycle of their machines. Some of its brands include Wirtgen, Hagie, Mazzotti, Monosem, Blue River Technology and Harvest Profit, among others. Deere, famous for its "Nothing Runs Like a Deere" slogan, sells John Deere and other brands through dealer networks and also sells lawn and garden products through home improvement retailers like The Home Depot and Lowes. Most of the company's revenue is generated in the US.

	Annual Growth	11/19	11/20*	10/21	10/22	10/23
Sales ($mil.)	11.8%	39,258	35,540	44,024	52,577	61,251
Net income ($ mil.)	33.0%	3,253.0	2,751.0	5,963.0	7,131.0	10,166
Market value ($ mil.)	19.7%	49,590	63,613	96,389	111,747	101,694
Employees	3.1%	73,489	69,634	75,550	82,239	83,000

*Fiscal year change

DEFENDER INDUSTRIES, INC.

42 GREAT NECK RD
WATERFORD, CT 063853334
Phone: 860 701-3400
Fax: –
Web: www.defender.com

CEO: –
CFO: –
HR: Paula Inglis
FYE: December 31
Type: Private

Defender Industries stays afloat selling supplies for power boats and sailboats to the people who love them. The marine outfitter offers inflatable rafts, depth sounders, navigation equipment, safety gear, and more than 50,000 other boating products and accessories through its catalog and Web site. It has more than 2,500 boats and motors in stock. Defender Industries aims to make boating easier and safer, offering books, DVDs, and VHS tapes on boat handling, safety tips, maintenance, and other topics every skipper needs to know. The company, founded in 1938 by CEO Sheldon Lance, is owned and run by the Lance family.

DEFENDERS OF WILDLIFE

1130 17TH ST NW STE 100
WASHINGTON, DC 200364607
Phone: 202 682-9400
Fax: –
Web: www.defenders.org

CEO: Jamie R Clark
CFO: –
HR: Daniel Ampuero
FYE: September 30
Type: Private

Defenders of Wildlife goes on the offensive for animals. The group is a national not-for-profit membership organization devoted to the preservation and protection of native wild animals and plants. In addition to species and habitat preservation, Defenders lobbies Congress for sound environmental policy development and has specific conservation programs for Alaska, California, Canada, and international locations. It also publishes Defenders , a quarterly magazine for members; an annual report on endangered lands; and state wildlife viewing guides. Founded in 1947 as Defenders of Furbearers, the group later changed its name and today boasts some 1 million members and other supporters worldwide.

	Annual Growth	09/16	09/17	09/19	09/20	09/22
Sales ($mil.)	4.8%	–	33.9	33.4	34.5	42.8
Net income ($ mil.)	3.5%	–	4.1	0.6	0.1	4.8
Market value ($ mil.)	–	–	–	–	–	–
Employees	–	–	–	–	–	165

DEFOE CORP.

800 S COLUMBUS AVE
MOUNT VERNON, NY 105505019
Phone: 914 699-7440
Fax: –
Web: www.defoecorp.com

CEO: John Amicucci
CFO: Dennis Brands
HR: –
FYE: December 31
Type: Private

DeFoe makes sure you can safely cross those proverbial bridges when you get to them. The heavy construction firm specializes in the design and construction of bridges, highways, airport terminals, railroads, and other transit projects throughout the New York Metropolitan and Tri-State area. Other areas of expertise include rehabilitation and reconstruction, foundations, and architectural concrete work. DeFoe, which was founded in 1946, often works for the New York State Department of Transportation as well as the The Port Authority of New York and New Jersey. President John Amicucci Sr., who is the son-in-law of former president Dario Cioti, owns the company.

	Annual Growth	12/11	12/12	12/13	12/17	12/18
Sales ($mil.)	6.2%	–	54.6	45.7	100.7	78.2
Net income ($ mil.)	–	–	(1.4)	(7.3)	6.1	1.4
Market value ($ mil.)	–	–	–	–	–	–
Employees	–	–	–	–	–	150

DEI HOLDINGS INC

One Viper Way
Vista, CA 92081
Phone: 760 598-6200
Fax: 760 598-6400
Web: www.directed.com

CEO: Kevin Duffy
CFO: Veysel Goker
HR: –
FYE: December 31
Type: Public

If you try to steal a car protected by DEI's Viper, you just might get bit. DEI Holdings is the holding company of several well-known consumer electronics brands in North America, including Directed Electronics' Viper, Python, and Clifford automobile security and remote start systems and Orion car audio systems. It is also a leading designer and manufacturer of premium home theater loudspeakers sold under the Polk Audio and Definitive Technology brands. DEI Holdings markets its products through several channels, including national retailers and specialty chains, among them Wal-Mart, Best Buy, and Sears. The company was acquired by private equity firm Charlesbank Capital Partners for about $305 million in 2011.

	Annual Growth	12/03	12/04	12/05	12/06	12/07
Sales ($mil.)	32.1%	131.8	189.9	304.6	437.8	401.1
Net income ($ mil.)	–	12.5	14.0	(5.1)	21.0	(140.0)
Market value ($ mil.)	–	–	–	365.8	291.1	42.2
Employees	–	–	248	236	513	581

DEKALB MEDICAL CENTER, INC.

2701 N DECATUR RD
DECATUR, GA 300335918
Phone: 404 501-1000
Fax: –
Web: www.dekalbmedical.org

CEO: –
CFO: –
HR: –
FYE: June 30
Type: Private

As far as DeKalb is concerned, da healthier, da better! Beginning as a rural hospital, DeKalb Regional Health System now serves all of the Atlanta metropolitan area. The health system, operating as DeKalb Medical, is home to two acute care hospitals -- DeKalb Medical at North Decatur and DeKalb Medical at Hillandale (with a combined total of about 550 beds). It also operates a 75-bed long-term rehabilitation hospital -- DeKalb Medical at Downtown Decatur. Specialty hospital services include oncology, cardiology, orthopedics, and diabetes care. The health system, which was founded in 1961, also operates primary, specialty, and mobile health care clinics, partly through the DeKalb Medical Physicians Group. DeKalb is merging with Emory Healthcare.

	Annual Growth	06/09	06/10	06/11	06/14	06/15
Sales ($mil.)	(5.3%)	–	397.1	422.9	524.8	303.0
Net income ($ mil.)	–	–	(15.0)	0.9	1.6	5.0
Market value ($ mil.)	–	–	–	–	–	–
Employees	–	–	–	–	–	2,700

DEL FRISCOS OF GEORGIA, LLC

671 N GLEBE RD STE 600
ARLINGTON, VA 222032123
Phone: 817 601-3421
Fax: –
Web: www.landrysinc.com

CEO: –
CFO: –
HR: –
FYE: December 26
Type: Private

Del Frisco's Restaurant Group operates two upscale steakhouse chains, Del Frisco's Double Eagle Steakhouse and Del Frisco's Grille. The group is a collection of approximately 30 restaurants across nearly 15 states and Washington DC. Del Frisco's Double Eagle Steakhouse has about 15 locations, and brings a modern twist on a classic American tradition ? the steakhouse, and with it, an unparalleled, elevated dining experience. Del Frisco's Grille elevates any night out with hand-crafted cocktails and a refreshing, modern menu at each of the nearly 25 locations. Both concepts serve premium cuts of beef along with seafood, lamb, and pork dishes, and both offer an extensive wine list. The group has an impeccable selection of more than 1,200 wines and exceptional hospitality.

DEL MONACO FOODS, LLC

18675 MADRONE PKWY STE 150
MORGAN HILL, CA 950372868
Phone: 408 500-4100
Fax: –
Web: –

CEO: –
CFO: –
HR: –
FYE: December 31
Type: Private

Del Monaco Specialty Foods makes products that any Tuscan, Roman, or Venetian mama would give her blessing to. The company cooks up and freezes Italian-style food items for the foodservice industry. Del Monaco's certified-organic food products include pastas, sauces, ravioli, tortellini, gnocchi, polenta, pestos, and desserts. It offers American-style foods as well, including barbecue sauce, pot pies and New England clam chowder. It makes its own Del Monaco products and also offers services such as recipe creation, duplication, and enhancement, plus the manufacture of custom products. The company was founded in 1964 by its namesakes, the late Mike Del Monaco and his wife Ernestine.

DEL WEST ENGINEERING, INC.

28128 LIVINGSTON AVE
VALENCIA, CA 913554115
Phone: 661 295-5700
Fax: –
Web: www.delwestengineering.com

CEO: –
CFO: –
HR: –
FYE: February 29
Type: Private

Del West Engineering started as an aerospace engineering firm, but found that racing was more its speed. These days the company makes highly engineered components for Formula One, CART, NASCAR and other race cars at its plants in California and Switzerland. Typical offerings include titanium and steel valves, valve spring systems, spring retainers, valve guides, and valve seat inserts. The company's research and development efforts include ceramic and film coatings to handle high wear or reduce friction on components.

	Annual Growth	02/03	02/04	02/05	02/06	02/08
Sales ($mil.)	9.9%	–	31.9	37.9	41.2	46.5
Net income ($ mil.)	(54.4%)	–	1.4	5.2	1.3	0.0
Market value ($ mil.)	–	–	–	–	–	–
Employees	–	–	–	–	–	135

DELAWARE RIVER BASIN COMMISSION

25 COSEY RD
EWING, NJ 086282438
Phone: 609 883-9500
Fax: –
Web: www.drb.net

CEO: –
CFO: –
HR: –
FYE: June 30
Type: Private

The Delaware River Basin Commission (DRBC) ensures that a river continues to run through its four-state jurisdiction. Established in 1961, the DRBC oversees the stewardship of the 330-mile Delaware River Basin, stretching through Delaware, New Jersey, Pennsylvania, and New York. Its programs include water quality protection, water supply, regulatory review, water conservation initiatives, watershed planning, drought management, flood control, and recreation. The commission is headed by the four basin state governors as well as a federal representative appointed by the President.

	Annual Growth	06/18	06/19	06/20	06/21	06/22
Sales ($mil.)	2.7%	–	5.0	4.9	4.9	5.4
Net income ($ mil.)	–	–	(0.0)	0.1	0.7	0.7
Market value ($ mil.)	–	–	–	–	–	–
Employees	–	–	–	–	–	41

DELAWARE RIVER PORT AUTHORITY

2 RIVERSIDE DR
CAMDEN, NJ 081031019
Phone: 856 968-2000
Fax: –
Web: www.drpa.org

CEO: John T Hanson
CFO: James M White
HR: –
FYE: December 31
Type: Private

The famous painting of George Washington crossing the Delaware would have lacked a good deal of its drama if the Delaware River Port Authority of Pennsylvania and New Jersey (DRPA) had been around in 1776. DRPA keeps commuters (and leaders of revolutionary armies) out of small boats by operating the Benjamin Franklin, Betsy Ross, Commodore Barry, and Walt Whitman toll bridges over the Delaware River, which divides Pennsylvania from New Jersey. Bridge operations account for 90% of the agency's revenue. Through its Port Authority Transit Corp. (PATCO) subsidiary, DRPA operates PATCO, a rail service that links Philadelphia with communities on the New Jersey side of the Delaware.

	Annual Growth	12/15	12/16	12/18	12/20	12/21
Sales ($mil.)	(2.0%)	–	354.7	371.8	287.2	321.1
Net income ($ mil.)	3.6%	–	66.9	124.0	57.0	79.7
Market value ($ mil.)	–	–	–	–	–	–
Employees	–	–	–	–	–	900

DELAWARE STATE UNIVERSITY

1200 N DUPONT HWY
DOVER, DE 199012202
Phone: 302 857-6060
Fax: –
Web: www.desu.edu

CEO: –
CFO: –
HR: Jasmine Passwaters
FYE: June 30
Type: Private

One of the top historically black colleges and universities in the US, Delaware State University (DSU) offers more than 50 bachelor's degree programs, 25 graduate degree programs, and five doctoral degree programs through more than 20 academic departments and five colleges. In addition to its main 400-acre campus in Dover, the university has satellite locations in Georgetown and Wilmington. The school began as a land-grant educational institution, founded in 1891 as the State College for Colored Students. It became known as Delaware State College in 1947 and gained university status in 1993. The university has a student-teacher ratio of 14:1 and enrolls more than 3,800 students each year.

	Annual Growth	06/18	06/19	06/20	06/21	06/22
Sales ($mil.)	15.1%	–	–	–	212.9	245.1
Net income ($ mil.)	184.5%	–	–	–	10.3	29.3
Market value ($ mil.)	–	–	–	–	–	–
Employees	–	–	–	–	–	918

DELAWARE VALLEY UNIVERSITY

700 E BUTLER AVE
DOYLESTOWN, PA 189012607
Phone: 215 345-1500
Fax: –
Web: www.delval.edu

CEO: –
CFO: –
HR: Paige Kraus
FYE: June 30
Type: Private

Delaware Valley College (DelVal) serves about 2,000 undergraduate and graduate students and boasts a student/faculty ratio of 15:1. The school offers associate's, bachelor's, and master's degrees in fields such as agriculture, biology, business administration, chemistry, environmental science, media, and secondary education; overall, it offers about two dozen undergraduate majors. DelVal's campus is located on 570 acres 30 miles north of Philadelphia. The college was founded in 1896 by activist rabbi Joseph Krauskopf.

	Annual Growth	06/18	06/19	06/20	06/21	06/22
Sales ($mil.)	16.8%	–	58.9	56.2	55.9	93.9
Net income ($ mil.)	–	–	(1.2)	(1.8)	8.7	1.9
Market value ($ mil.)	–	–	–	–	–	–
Employees	–	–	–	–	–	405

DELAWIE

1515 MORENA BLVD
SAN DIEGO, CA 921103731
Phone: 619 299-6690
Fax: –
Web: www.delawie.com

CEO: –
CFO: –
HR: –
FYE: December 31
Type: Private

Architects Delawie Wilkes Rodrigues Barker (A|DWRB) has designs on the Southern California market. A|DWRB provides design/build architectural services that range from analysis (including due diligence, code analysis, and site analysis of existing conditions to determine specific use suitability of a site or building) to master planning and interior design services. Its portfolio includes designs for biotech and advanced technology firms, educational facilities, and hospitality projects. A|DWRB, which was founded in 1961, focuses on projects in Southern California, but has also served clients around the globe.

	Annual Growth	12/05	12/06	12/07	12/08	12/09
Sales ($mil.)	(35.5%)	–	–	–	12.4	8.0
Net income ($ mil.)	–	–	–	–	(0.2)	(0.1)
Market value ($ mil.)	–	–	–	–	–	–
Employees	–	–	–	–	–	61

DELCATH SYSTEMS INC

1633 Broadway, Suite 22C
New York, NY 10019
Phone: 212 489-2100
Fax: –
Web: www.delcath.com

NAS: DCTH
CEO: Gerard Michel
CFO: –
HR: –
FYE: December 31
Type: Public

A cancer-stricken liver might be a lonely little organ, thanks to Delcath Systems. The company's technology allows blood infused with chemotherapy drugs to be pumped directly to the liver and then filtered before being returned into the circulation system. By isolating the liver, Delcath's proprietary Hepatic CHEMOSAT Delivery System is designed to protect other parts of the body from side effects and allow stronger doses of drugs to be used to treat liver cancer and malignant melanoma that has spread to the liver. The system, approved and available in Europe, is undergoing clinical trials to gain FDA approval. Delcath is also developing the system for use in treating other cancers and viral hepatitis.

	Annual Growth	12/19	12/20	12/21	12/22	12/23
Sales ($mil.)	6.9%	1.6	1.6	3.6	2.7	2.1
Net income ($ mil.)	–	(8.9)	(24.2)	(25.6)	(36.5)	(47.7)
Market value ($ mil.)	(33.5%)	483.7	407.9	176.4	81.9	94.7
Employees	–	33	36	55	52	–

DELEK LOGISTICS PARTNERS LP

310 Seven Springs Way, Suite 500
Brentwood, TN 37027
Phone: 615 771-6701
Fax: –
Web: www.deleklogistics.com

NYS: DKL
CEO: Ezra U Yemin
CFO: Assaf Ginzburg
HR: –
FYE: December 31
Type: Public

Oil is on the move at Delek Logistics Partners. An oil transportation and storage company, Delek Logistics owns and operates crude oil pipelines, storage and distribution facilities, and other assets in West Texas and the southeastern US. Core assets include 400 miles of crude oil transportation pipelines and a 600-mile crude oil gathering system. The company also offers wholesale marketing of refined petroleum products. The majority of Delek Logistics' operations serve oil company Delek US Holdings and the holding company's Texas and Arkansas-based refineries. The company was formed in 2012 when Delek US Holdings spun off its pipeline assets; Delek Logistics Partners subsequently went public.

	Annual Growth	12/19	12/20	12/21	12/22	12/23
Sales ($mil.)	15.0%	584.0	563.4	700.9	1,036.4	1,020.4
Net income ($ mil.)	6.9%	96.7	159.3	164.8	159.1	126.2
Market value ($ mil.)	7.8%	1,393.8	1,395.6	1,863.5	1,973.4	1,882.7
Employees	–	–	–	–	–	–

DELEK US ENERGY, INC.

310 SEVEN SPRINGS WAY STE 500
BRENTWOOD, TN 370275799
Phone: 615 771-6701
Fax: –
Web: www.delekus.com

CEO: Ezra U Yemin
CFO: Kevin L Kremke
HR: Jared P Serff
FYE: December 31
Type: Private

Delek US Holdings' US petroleum business is a delectable mix of crude oil refining and marketing. The company, a subsidiary of Israeli-based conglomerate Delek Group, sources crude oil from producers in Texas and Arkansas for refining into transportation fuels such as gasoline, distillate, and jet fuel. Some of its production also consists of residual products such as paving asphalt and roofing flux. Delek US' Tyler, Texas and El Dorado, Arkansas refineries have total production capacity of 155,000 barrels per day. Delek US Holdings' marketing segment sells refined products on a wholesale basis in west Texas through company-owned and third-party operated terminals. It sold off its gas station retail business in 2016.

DELEK US HOLDINGS INC (NEW)

310 Seven Springs Way, Suite 500
Brentwood, TN 37027
Phone: 615 771-6701
Fax: –
Web: www.delekus.com

NYS: DK

CEO: Avigal Soreq
CFO: Reuven Spiegel
HR: –
FYE: December 31
Type: Public

Delek US Holdings is an integrated downstream energy business focused on petroleum refining, the transportation, storage and wholesale distribution of crude oil, intermediate and refined products and convenience store retailing. Operating through its consolidated subsidiaries, Delek US Energy and Alon, Delek sources crude oil from producers in Texas and Arkansas for refining into transportation fuels such as gasoline, distillate, jet fuel and other petroleum-based products. Some of its production also consists of residual products such as paving asphalt and roofing flux. Delek's Tyler, Texas, Big Spring, Texas, Krotz Springs, Louisiana and El Dorado, Arkansas refineries have a total production capacity of about 302,000 barrels per day.

	Annual Growth	12/19	12/20	12/21	12/22	12/23
Sales ($mil.)	16.1%	9,298.2	7,301.8	10,648	20,246	16,917
Net income ($ mil.)	(49.8%)	310.6	(608.0)	(203.5)	257.1	19.8
Market value ($ mil.)	(6.3%)	2,144.7	1,027.9	958.8	1,727.0	1,650.3
Employees	(1.5%)	3,814	3,532	3,312	3,746	3,591

DELGADO COMMUNITY COLLEGE

615 CITY PARK AVE
NEW ORLEANS, LA 701194399
Phone: 504 671-5000
Fax: –
Web: www.dcc.edu

CEO: –
CFO: –
HR: Karen Laiche
FYE: June 30
Type: Private

Delgado Community College, a part of The Louisiana Community and Technical College System, is the state's largest and oldest community college. Nearly 13,500 students (about 50% of enrollment figure prior to Hurricane Katrina) are enrolled in the college through its five parish area. Delgado has five campuses: City Park Avenue, West Bank, Slidell, Northshore, and Charity School of Nursing. Since Katrina, the number of students taking online courses has grown from 4% to almost 30%. The college offers more than 70 areas of study. Its career training programs focus on five of New Orleans' top growth industry areas: health care; business and technology; maritime; hospitality and entertainment; and transportation.

	Annual Growth	06/08	06/09	06/18	06/19	06/21
Sales ($mil.)	42.8%	–	0.6	47.0	49.6	41.4
Net income ($ mil.)		–	–	2.1	15.1	3.6
Market value ($ mil.)		–	–	–	–	–
Employees		–	–	–	–	800

DELI MANAGEMENT, INC.

350 PINE ST STE 1775
BEAUMONT, TX 777012458
Phone: 409 838-1976
Fax: –
Web: www.jasonsdeli.com

CEO: –
CFO: –
HR: –
FYE: December 31
Type: Private

This company knows a good sandwich when serves one. Deli Management operates Jason's Deli, a chain of sandwich shops with more than 240 company-owned and franchised locations. The quick casual eateries specialize in deli-style sandwiches including such signature varieties as Bird to the Wise, The New York Yankee, and Rueben THE Great. The chain also serves panini and po'boy sandwiches, pasta dishes, soups, and salads. Many Jason's outposts provide delivery and catering services, as well as online ordering. President Joe Tortorice and partner Rusty Coco started the company in 1976.

	Annual Growth	12/04	12/05	12/06	12/08	12/19
Sales ($mil.)	(45.5%)	–	1,402.1	344.2	344.2	0.3
Net income ($ mil.)	32.4%	–	0.0	5.8	5.8	0.0
Market value ($ mil.)		–	–	–	–	–
Employees		–	–	–	–	6,000

DELL INC.

1 DELL WAY
ROUND ROCK, TX 786827000
Phone: 800 289-3355
Fax: –
Web: www.dell.com

CEO: Michael Dell
CFO: Thomas W Sweet
HR: –
FYE: January 30
Type: Private

Dell Technologies made its name as a supplier of built-to-order personal computers. Now, as a bigger, more mature company, Dell wants to build-to-order answers to its customers' IT needs. It remains a top PC company, #3 behind Lenovo and HP Inc., but Dell offers a wide range of IT products (hardware and software) and services for enterprise, government, small business, and consumer markets. It also markets third-party software and hardware. Dell expanded its offerings to include large computer storage systems with its $63 billion acquisition of EMC, which closed in September 2016. It changed its named to Dell Technologies to reflect the wider range of products and services.

DELL TECHNOLOGIES INC

One Dell Way
Round Rock, TX 78682
Phone: 800 289-3355
Fax: –
Web: www.delltechnologies.com

NYS: DELL

CEO: Michael S Dell
CFO: Yvonne McGill
HR: –
FYE: February 2
Type: Public

Dell Technologies, also known as Dell, helps organizations and individuals build their digital future and transform how they work, live, and play. The company provides customers with the industry's broadest and most innovative technology and services portfolio for the data era, spanning both traditional infrastructure and multi-cloud technologies. It also has a comprehensive portfolio of networking and storage systems through Dell EMC as well as cloud software from subsidiary VMware. Other brands include Alienware, Secureworks, Pivotal, and Virtustream. Dell operates in about 180 countries through about a 31,000-person sales force and a global network of about 240,000 channel partners.

	Annual Growth	01/20	01/21	01/22*	02/23	02/24
Sales ($mil.)	(1.0%)	92,154	94,224	101,197	102,301	88,425
Net income ($ mil.)	(8.7%)	4,616.0	3,250.0	5,563.0	2,442.0	3,211.0
Market value ($ mil.)	15.3%	34,383	51,387	39,649	29,779	60,856
Employees	(7.7%)	165,000	158,000	133,000	133,000	120,000

*Fiscal year change

DELMARVA POWER & LIGHT CO.

500 North Wakefield Drive
Newark, DE 19702-5440
Phone: 202 872-2000
Fax: –
Web: www.delmarva.com

CEO: David M Velazquez
CFO: –
HR: –
FYE: December 31
Type: Public

Delmarva Power & Light (DPL) has a delmarvellous proposition -- connecting people to an extensive energy supply network. The company is engaged in the transmission and distribution of electricity in Delaware and a portion of Maryland (the Eastern Shore); it delivers electricity to about 501,000 customers. DPL also provides natural gas (in northern Delaware) to more than 124,000 customers. DPL is an indirect subsidiary of Pepco Holdings, which owns two other utilities (Potomac Electric Power and Atlantic City Electric) as well as competitive energy generation, marketing, and supply businesses. As part of the 2016 acquisition of Pepco Holdings, Delmarva P&L joined the Exelon family of utilities.

	Annual Growth	12/19	12/20	12/21	12/22	12/23
Sales ($mil.)	6.6%	1,306.0	1,271.0	1,380.0	1,595.0	1,688.0
Net income ($ mil.)	4.8%	147.0	125.0	128.0	169.0	177.0
Market value ($ mil.)	–	–	–	–	–	–
Employees	–	–	936	936	910	891

DELPHAX TECHNOLOGIES INC

12301 Whitewater Drive, Suite 10
Minnetonka, MN 55343
Phone: 952 829-5700
Fax: 952 939-1151
Web: www.delphax.com

NBB: DLPX
CEO: –
CFO: –
HR: –
FYE: September 30
Type: Public

You don't have to be an oracle to know that Delphax Technologies doesn't like blank checks. The company makes digital print production systems based on its patented electron-beam imaging (EBI) technology for continuous roll-fed and cut-sheet printing applications. Its machines print addresses and numbers on checks, as well as print payroll and accounts payable checks with audit trail capabilities. Delphax's Imaggia II can print up to 300 pages per minute. Its Foliotronic finishing systems bind financial forms into books. Harland Clarke and RR Donnelly are the company's largest customers. While Delphax sells its products globally to more than 50 countries, about 80% of its sales are from the US.

	Annual Growth	09/07	09/19	09/20	09/21	09/22
Sales ($mil.)	(42.2%)	44.6	0.0	0.0	–	0.0
Net income ($ mil.)	–	(0.8)	5.5	0.3	(0.1)	(0.1)
Market value ($ mil.)	(14.0%)	6.2	0.0	0.0	1.0	0.7
Employees	–	286	–	–	–	–

DELTA AIR LINES INC (DE)

Post Office Box 20706
Atlanta, GA 30320-6001
Phone: 404 715-2600
Fax: –
Web: www.delta.com

NYS: DAL
CEO: Edward H Bastian
CFO: Daniel C Janki
HR: –
FYE: December 31
Type: Public

Delta Air Lines is one of the world's largest airlines by traffic and revenues. Through its regional carriers, the company serves over 800 destinations in about 130 countries, and it operates a mainline fleet of 1,200 aircraft, as well as maintenance, repair, and overhaul (MRO) and cargo operations. The company serves more than 200 million customers each year and offers more than 5,000 departures daily. Delta is a founding member of the SkyTeam marketing and code-sharing alliance, which includes carriers Aerom xico, Air France-KLM, China Eastern, Korean Air, and Virgin Atlantic. Customers from the US account for approximately 80% of sales.

	Annual Growth	12/19	12/20	12/21	12/22	12/23
Sales ($mil.)	5.4%	47,007	17,095	29,899	50,582	58,048
Net income ($ mil.)	(0.8%)	4,767.0	(12,385.0)	280.0	1,318.0	4,609.0
Market value ($ mil.)	(8.9%)	37,629	25,873	25,146	21,144	25,886
Employees	3.1%	91,224	74,000	83,000	95,000	103,000

DELTA APPAREL INC.

2750 Premiere Parkway, Suite 100
Duluth, GA 30097
Phone: 678 775-6900
Fax: –
Web: www.deltaappareinc.com

ASE: DLA
CEO: Robert W Humphreys
CFO: –
HR: –
FYE: September 30
Type: Public

Delta Apparel's wares are a wardrobe basic: the t-shirt. The company manufactures knitted cotton and polyester/cotton t-shirts, tank tops, sweatshirts, and caps for screen printers. Through subsidiary M.J. Soffe, Delta Apparel also designs, makes, and sells branded and private-label activewear apparel to mainly to US distributors, sporting goods and specialty stores, mass merchants, traditional and upscale department stores, the US military, college bookstores, and online. The company's garments are finished at plants in North Carolina, and abroad in Mexico, El Salvador, and Honduras. Delta entered the business of custom apparel design by acquiring Art Gun Technologies, and hats by taking over Gekko Brands.

	Annual Growth	09/19*	10/20	10/21	10/22*	09/23
Sales ($mil.)	(1.0%)	431.7	381.0	436.8	484.9	415.4
Net income ($ mil.)	–	8.2	(10.6)	20.3	19.7	(33.2)
Market value ($ mil.)	(26.8%)	161.4	102.8	192.2	97.9	46.4
Employees	(5.4%)	8,500	7,860	8,469	8,623	6,800

*Fiscal year change

DELTA COLLEGE FOUNDATION

1961 DELTA RD
UNIVERSITY CENTER, MI 487101002
Phone: 877 472-7677
Fax: –
Web: www.delta.edu

CEO: –
CFO: –
HR: Mary Gmeiner
FYE: June 30
Type: Private

This Delta can help ya prepare for a career. Delta College is a community college offering one-year certificate programs and two-year applied associate degree programs. In addition to its main campus, the college has satellite centers in Bay, Midland, and Saginaw counties in central Michigan. It also runs a public radio station, a public television station, a planetarium, and a small business and technology development center. Delta College has an enrollment of approximately 16,000; about two-thirds of students are 20 or older, and most of them take a combination of day and evening classes.

	Annual Growth	06/11	06/12	06/13	06/14	06/15
Sales ($mil.)	(2.0%)	–	–	36.7	35.4	35.2
Net income ($ mil.)	35.5%	–	–	3.8	7.6	7.1
Market value ($ mil.)	–	–	–	–	–	–
Employees	–	–	–	–	–	800

DELTA CORPORATE SERVICES, INC

129 LITTLETON RD STE 201
PARSIPPANY, NJ 070541869
Phone: 973 331-0148
Fax: –
Web: www.deltacorp.com

CEO: –
CFO: Sherry Silinger
HR: –
FYE: December 31
Type: Private

Just as the Greek delta symbol means change in the field of science, Delta Corporate Services wants to change companies in their business fields. Delta relies on information technology (IT) to improve its clients' operations. The company's services include management and strategy consulting, computer network upgrades, application integration, and ongoing IT support. It caters to large companies across the US, although its methods can be scaled down for smaller concerns. Owner and CEO Michael Iovino founded the company in 1991.

DELTA DENTAL PLANS ASSOCIATION

1515 W 22ND ST STE 450
OAK BROOK, IL 605238408
Phone: 630 574-6001
Fax: –
Web: www.deltadental.com

CEO: Steve Olson
CFO: –
HR: Stefany Currier
FYE: December 31
Type: Private

Delta Dental Plans Association (DDPA) is the leading provider of dental insurance in the US. DDPA is comprised of a network of about 40 independent Delta Dental companies. The not-for-profit organization provides dental benefits administration and related services to some 80 million Americans, protecting more smiles than any other dental benefits company, with a dental coverage in all 50 states, Puerto Rico, and other US territories, with a local presence across the country, providing groups and individuals with quality dental insurance and customer service. The company provides individual dental insurance products, senior dental insurance, and featured state dental insurance. Delta Dental Plans Association was founded in 1966.

	Annual Growth	12/18	12/19	12/20	12/21	12/22
Sales ($mil.)	18.6%	–	–	–	30.0	35.6
Net income ($ mil.)	(21.3%)	–	–	–	2.7	2.1
Market value ($ mil.)	–	–	–	–	–	–
Employees		–	–	–	–	30

DELTA HEALTH SYSTEM

1400 E UNION ST
GREENVILLE, MS 387033246
Phone: 662 378-3783
Fax: –
Web: www.deltahealthsystem.org

CEO: Scott Christensen
CFO: –
HR: Andrea Buchanan
FYE: September 30
Type: Private

If you're feeling bad down in the Lower Delta, Delta Regional Medical Center (DRMC) can help perk you up. The only full service hospital and Level III trauma center in northwest Mississippi, DRMC also serves as the tri-state Delta's safety-net hospital. The four medical centers provide heart and vascular care, a full service emergency room, diagnostics center, outpatient rehab, a sleep center, a wound healing center, maternal child center, and inpatient psychiatric care. Delta Medical Group includes about 15 clinics specializing in everything from gastroenterology to women's health. Founded as the Washington County General Hospital in 1953, the 358-bed DRMC serves more than 35,000 patients each year.

	Annual Growth	09/15	09/16	09/17	09/20	09/21
Sales ($mil.)	0.2%	–	123.1	120.0	110.9	124.1
Net income ($ mil.)	5.8%	–	4.2	1.2	2.5	5.6
Market value ($ mil.)	–	–	–	–	–	–
Employees		–	–	–	–	800

DELTA NATURAL GAS COMPANY, INC.

3617 LEXINGTON RD
WINCHESTER, KY 403919797
Phone: 859 744-6171
Fax: –
Web: www.deltagas.com

CEO: Glenn R Jennings
CFO: –
HR: –
FYE: June 30
Type: Private

Delta digs blue grass and natural gas. Delta Natural Gas provides gas to some 36,000 retail customers in central and southeastern Kentucky and has 2,500 miles of gathering, transmission, and distribution lines. It also provides transportation services to wholesale customers and operates an underground gas storage field. The regulated utility buys almost all of its gas supply from interstate gas marketers. Delta Natural Gas's production subsidiary, Enpro, has interests in 35 producing gas wells and it has proved developed reserves of 3 billion cu. ft. of natural gas. Other subsidiaries include Delta Resources and Delgasco. In 2017 Delta Natural Gas agreed to be acquired by Peoples Gas.

DELTA TUCKER HOLDINGS INC

1700 Old Meadow Road
McLean, VA 22102
Phone: 571 722-0210
Fax: –
Web: www.dyn-intl.com

CEO: –
CFO: –
HR: –
FYE: December 31
Type: Public

Through operating company DynCorp International (DI), Delta Tucker Holdings works behind the scenes to support military and diplomatic efforts on front lines. A US national security contractor, the company supports the US Departments of State and Defense by providing linguist services and international police force training, especially in Afghanistan and Iraq. It provides turnkey solutions for post-conflict countries to rebuild infrastructure, install utilities and telecommunications, provide security, transport equipment, and remove and dismantle weapons. About 40% the holding company's sales come from the US.

	Annual Growth	12/14	12/15	12/16	12/17	12/18
Sales ($mil.)	(1.2%)	2,252.3	1,923.2	1,836.2	2,004.4	2,148.3
Net income ($ mil.)	–	(269.8)	(132.6)	(54.1)	30.6	84.5
Market value ($ mil.)	–	–	–	–	–	–
Employees		–	12,000	10,700	13,100	13,200

DELUXE CORP

801 S. Marquette Ave.
Minneapolis, MN 55402-2807
Phone: 651 483-7111
Fax: 651 483-7337
Web: www.deluxe.com

NYS: DLX
CEO: Barry C McCarthy
CFO: Chip Zint
HR: Tina Tentis
FYE: December 31
Type: Public

Deluxe is a Trusted Business Technology company for enterprises, small businesses and financial institutions offering solutions to help customers manage and grow their businesses. Deluxe offers industry-leading programs in marketing services and data analytics, treasury management solutions, website development and hosting, promotional products and fraud solutions, as well as forms. The company is also a leading provider of checks and accessories sold directly to consumers. It has four million active small business customers and more than 4,000 financial institution clients. Most of its sales come from the US, but it also sells its products and services in Canada, and portions of Europe and South America.

	Annual Growth	12/19	12/20	12/21	12/22	12/23
Sales ($mil.)	2.2%	2,008.7	1,790.8	2,022.2	2,238.0	2,192.3
Net income ($ mil.)	–	(199.9)	8.8	62.6	65.4	26.1
Market value ($ mil.)	(19.0%)	2,183.7	1,277.3	1,404.6	742.8	938.3
Employees	(5.0%)	6,352	6,185	6,313	5,863	5,170

DEMANDWARE, LLC

5 WALL ST FL 2
BURLINGTON, MA 018034774
Phone: 888 553-9216
Fax: –
Web: www.salesforce.com

CEO: Thomas D Ebling
CFO: Timothy M Adams
HR: –
FYE: December 31
Type: Private

Consumers make a lot of demands on retailers and Demandware is there to provide demand satisfaction. The company's Demandware Commerce is an on-demand software-as-a-service (SaaS) platform that connects users to up-to-date tools for designing and maintaining websites, mobile apps, and other digital shopping avenues. It uses data centers to monitor customers' websites worldwide. Major customers include retailers Barneys New York, Crocs, Jones Group, and Columbia Sportswear. Demandware receives a share of the revenue its customers generate using the SaaS; it also collects subscription fees for platform use. Salesforce agreed to buy Demandware for $2.8 billion in 2016. The deal is expected to close in the July quarter.

DEMOCRASOFT, HOLDINGS INC

NBB: DEMO

1275 Fourth Street, #191
Santa Rosa, CA 95404
Phone: 707 541-3870
Fax: –
Web: www.burst.com

CEO: Richard Lang
CFO: Richard Lang
HR: –
FYE: December 31
Type: Public

Democrasoft (formerly known as Burst.com) wants to democratize the collaboration process. Its hosted Collaborize service allows associations, clubs, corporations, and other organizations to communicate, interact, and share information among employees and members engaged in a decision-making process. The company aims to put social networking to work on important topics. Founded in 1990, Democrasoft originally developed software for transmitting audio and video over computer networks. Developing a portfolio of intellectual property for multimedia transmission, the company licensed its patents to other parties over the past decade. It won big legal settlements from Apple and Microsoft after suing them.

	Annual Growth	12/00	12/01	12/05	12/06	12/07
Sales ($mil.)	53.4%	0.5	0.1	60.3	–	10.0
Net income ($ mil.)	–	(19.6)	(3.6)	35.0	(0.5)	3.4
Market value ($ mil.)	(31.4%)	219.9	1.5	40.9	44.0	15.7
Employees	(7.0%)	5	2	3	3	3

DENISON UNIVERSITY

100 W COLLEGE ST
GRANVILLE, OH 430231100
Phone: 740 587-0810
Fax: –
Web: www.denison.edu

CEO: –
CFO: David English
HR: –
FYE: June 30
Type: Private

Denizens of Denison University have a desire to dedicate themselves to higher learning. The small-town college is a private undergraduate school with an enrollment of about 2,200. It has some 220 faculty members and a low student-to-teacher ratio of about 10:1. Denison University offers some 60 majors, concentrations, and pre-professional programs. Its degrees range across a number of liberal arts and science fields, including a pre-medical program and an athletic training program, as well as social science and humanities programs.

	Annual Growth	06/18	06/19	06/20	06/21	06/22
Sales ($mil.)	4.2%	–	138.1	145.7	148.6	156.3
Net income ($ mil.)	–	–	50.1	20.0	312.6	(176.3)
Market value ($ mil.)	–	–	–	–	–	–
Employees	–	–	–	–	–	757

DENNY'S CORP

NAS: DENN

203 East Main Street
Spartanburg, SC 29319-0001
Phone: 864 597-8000
Fax: 864 597-8135
Web: www.dennys.com

CEO: John C Miller
CFO: Robert P Verostek
HR: –
FYE: December 27
Type: Public

Denny's is one of America's largest franchised full-service restaurant chains. Denny's is known as America's Diner, or in the case of international locations, "the local diner". Open 24/7 in most locations, the company provides guests with quality food. It offers a wide variety of entrées for breakfast, lunch, dinner and late-night dining as well as appetizers, desserts, and beverages including entrees, burgers, sandwiches, and salads. The company consists of almost 1,450 restaurants in the US and about 155 international restaurant locations, consisting of some 1,580 of which were franchised/licensed restaurants and almost 75 of which were company operated.

	Annual Growth	12/19	12/20	12/21	12/22	12/23
Sales ($mil.)	(3.8%)	541.4	288.6	398.2	456.4	463.9
Net income ($ mil.)	(35.8%)	117.4	(5.1)	78.1	74.7	19.9
Market value ($ mil.)	(14.3%)	1,057.8	737.1	820.2	470.2	569.9
Employees	(3.3%)	4,000	3,100	3,300	3,700	3,500

DENTON COUNTY ELECTRIC COOPERATIVE, INC.

7701 S STEMMONS FRWY
CORINTH, TX 76210
Phone: 940 321-7800
Fax: –
Web: www.coserv.com

CEO: Michael A Dreyspring
CFO: Donnie Clary
HR: Brenda Walker
FYE: December 31
Type: Private

Denton County Electric Cooperative makes a dent in the heat of a North Texas summer. Operating under the CoServ Electric name, the member-owned cooperative distributes power to more than 156,000 rural homes and businesses in North Texas. The second-largest member-owned co-op in Texas behind Pedernales Electric, it receives its wholesale electricity from Brazos Electric Power Cooperative. CoServ Electric also distributes natural gas to more than 70,000 customers through its CoServ Gas subsidiary. Through its affiliates the cooperative also provides infrastructure project management and construction services.

DENTSPLY SIRONA INC

NMS: XRAY

13320 Ballantyne Corporate Place
Charlotte, NC 28277-3607
Phone: 844 848-0137
Fax: –
Web: www.dentsplysirona.com

CEO: Donald M Casey Jr
CFO: Glenn Coleman
HR: Brittany Hoffman MBA Shr
FYE: December 31
Type: Public

Dentsply Sirona is the world's largest manufacturer of professional dental products and technologies. The company makes a range of dental tools and supplies, from artificial teeth, precious metal dental alloys, dental ceramics and crown and bridge materials. The company also manufactures dental equipment and supplies, including root canal instruments, ultrasonic polishers, imaging systems, CAD/CAM machines, and dentist chairs. It sells through distributors and directly to dentists, dental assistants, dental labs, and dental schools in more than 150 countries. In addition, Dentsply Sirona manufactures and sells healthcare consumable products for urological applications. About 35% of the company's total revenue come from customers in the US.

	Annual Growth	12/19	12/20	12/21	12/22	12/23
Sales ($mil.)	(0.4%)	4,029.2	3,342.0	4,251.0	3,922.0	3,965.0
Net income ($ mil.)	–	262.9	(83.0)	421.0	(950.0)	(132.0)
Market value ($ mil.)	(10.9%)	11,725	10,849	11,560	6,597.2	7,374.2
Employees	(0.3%)	15,200	15,000	15,000	15,000	15,000

DENVER BOARD OF WATER COMMISSIONERS

1600 W 12TH AVE
DENVER, CO 802043412
Phone: 303 893-2444
Fax: –
Web: www.denverwater.org

CEO: James Loughhead
CFO: Angela Bircmont
HR: Jonathan Tucker
FYE: December 31
Type: Private

Denver Water keeps the Broncos' troughs full. The Board of Water Commissioners, City and County of Denver, Colorado, which operates as Denver Water, distributes water to more than 1.5 million people in the Denver metropolitan area. The company serves about 319,230 customers for treated water, almost 168,675 is from inside city and county of Denver. The utility gets its water primarily from the Blue River, Fraser River watersheds, the South Platte River, and Williams Fork River. Denver Water is an independently operated division of the City and County of Denver. The utility was founded in 1918.

	Annual Growth	12/18	12/19	12/20	12/21	12/22
Sales ($mil.)	4.5%	–	317.2	357.2	336.0	362.4
Net income ($ mil.)	26.5%	–	68.1	119.1	97.3	137.8
Market value ($ mil.)	–	–	–	–	–	–
Employees	–	–	–	–	–	1,100

DENVER HEALTH AND HOSPITALS AUTHORITY INC

777 BANNOCK ST
DENVER, CO 802044597
Phone: 720 956-2580
Fax: –
Web: www.denverhealth.org

CEO: –
CFO: –
HR: –
FYE: December 31
Type: Private

Denver Health was founded as City Hospital in 1860 to serve the health care needs of the rapidly developing city of Denver. As a comprehensive, integrated organization, Denver Health provides hospital and emergency care to the public, regardless of ability to pay. The health system delivers preventative, primary, and acute care services including dental care, intensive care, kidney care, mental health, and cancer care, among others. Denver Health provides care services for nearly 25% of Denver's population annually. As Colorado's primary safety-net institution, Denver Health has provided billions of dollars in uncompensated care and serves as a model for other safety-net institutions across the nation.

	Annual Growth	12/17	12/18	12/19	12/21	12/22
Sales ($mil.)	3.5%	–	1,119.5	1,111.9	1,219.9	1,283.8
Net income ($ mil.)	–	–	62.6	127.2	14.7	(56.6)
Market value ($ mil.)	–	–	–	–	–	–
Employees	–	–	–	–	–	3,541

DEPAUL UNIVERSITY

1 E JACKSON BLVD
CHICAGO, IL 606042287
Phone: 312 362-8000
Fax: –
Web: www.depaul.edu

CEO: –
CFO: –
HR: –
FYE: June 30
Type: Private

One of the largest private, not-for-profit universities in the US, DePaul has more than 20,915 students attending classes at its Chicago-area campuses, and its increasing offerings of online learning courses. The university offers more than 300 undergraduate and graduate programs through ten colleges and schools, including the Driehaus College of Business and the College of Communication. It has a student teacher ratio of 16 to 1. One of the country's largest Catholic institutions of higher learning, DePaul was founded in 1898 by the Vincentian religious community and is named after 17th century French priest St. Vincent de Paul.

	Annual Growth	06/18	06/19	06/20	06/21	06/22
Sales ($mil.)	1.0%	–	580.7	595.2	569.0	597.7
Net income ($ mil.)	–	–	45.9	67.3	254.6	(125.4)
Market value ($ mil.)	–	–	–	–	–	–
Employees	–	–	–	–	–	3,895

DEPAUW UNIVERSITY

313 S LOCUST ST
GREENCASTLE, IN 461351736
Phone: 765 658-4800
Fax: –
Web: www.depauw.edu

CEO: David Greising
CFO: –
HR: Bruce Burking
FYE: June 30
Type: Private

DePauw University is a private, co-educational liberal arts university with an approximate enrollment of 2,300 students. Its campus boasts some 36 major buildings across nearly 700 acres, including a 520-acre nature preserve located 45 miles west of Indianapolis. The university offers undergraduate degrees from more than 30 academic departments and programs, as well as fellowships in media, management, and science. Prominent alumni include former US Vice President Dan Quayle, former US Rep. Lee Hamilton, and best-selling author Barbara Kingsolver. DePauw was founded in 1837 by the Methodist Church. The university's School of Music, founded in 1884, is one of the oldest in the US.

	Annual Growth	06/18	06/19	06/20	06/21	06/22
Sales ($mil.)	(6.7%)	–	128.2	115.8	115.3	104.2
Net income ($ mil.)	–	–	(13.4)	(51.9)	141.6	(57.8)
Market value ($ mil.)	–	–	–	–	–	–
Employees	–	–	–	–	–	652

DEPT OF EDUCATION ALABAMA

50 N RIPLEY ST 5114
MONTGOMERY, AL 361301001
Phone: 334 694-4900
Fax: –
Web: www.outdooralabama.com

CEO: –
CFO: –
HR: –
FYE: September 30
Type: Private

The Alabama Department of Education wants to prepare the state's workforce of tomorrow by providing safe schools, quality teachers, effective administrators, and challenging curricula. The state agency, along with the nine-member Alabama State Board of Education, oversees the state's public primary and secondary education system. The system is made up of more than 1,500 individual schools, nearly 750,000 elementary and secondary students, and about 48,000 teachers.

DERIVE TECHNOLOGIES LLC

40 WALL ST FL 20
NEW YORK, NY 100051374
Phone: 212 363-1111
Fax: –
Web: www.derivetech.com

CEO: –
CFO: –
HR: –
FYE: December 31
Type: Private

Derive Technologies gets its sense of purpose from solving enterprise IT problems. The company provides infrastructure development, maintenance, security implementation, and other network integration services in the New York metropolitan area. It also offers consulting services, with expertise in such areas as data storage, network virtualization, and wireless technologies. Derive serves the advertising, education, financial services, government, health care, legal, retail, and transportation sectors, among others. The company installs and maintains IT products from a variety of vendors, including Cisco, Citrix, Hewlett-Packard, Microsoft, and Symantec. Derive Technologies was founded in 1987 by CEO Kirit Desai.

DERMA SCIENCES, INC.

311 ENTERPRISE DR
PLAINSBORO, NJ 085363344
Phone: 609 514-4744
Fax: –
Web: –

CEO: Stephen T Wills
CFO: John E Yetter
HR: –
FYE: December 31
Type: Private

Time may eventually heal all wounds, but in the meantime there's Derma Sciences. The company operates in three segments: advanced wound care, traditional wound care, and pharmaceutical wound care products. Advanced wound care products include dressings, bandages, and ointments designed to promote wound healing and/or prevent infection. Traditional wound care products consist of commodity related dressings, ointments, gauze bandages, adhesive bandages, wound closer strips, catheter fasteners and skin care products. Integra Lifesciences, a manufacturer of specialty medical devices, reached an agreement to acquire Derma Sciences in early 2017.

DERMALOGICA, LLC

1535 BEACHEY PL
CARSON, CA 907464005
Phone: 310 900-4000
Fax: –
Web: www.dermalogica.com

CEO: –
CFO: –
HR: Ivette Figueroa
FYE: December 31
Type: Private

Whoever said beauty is only skin deep had the right idea, as far as Dermalogica is concerned. The personal care products company makes cleansers, toners, masques, exfoliants, and creams, as well as more specialized items, such as acne and under-eye treatments. Dermalogica's products are sold online and through International Dermal Institute-trained skin care professionals in more than 40 countries worldwide. These vendors can provide clients with Dermalogica's Face Mapping consultation, thermal back treatment, and touch therapies. Dermalogica was founded in 1986 by Jane Wurwand, who ceded control of operations in 2007. Dermalogica celebrated 25 years in business in 2011.

DESALES UNIVERSITY

2755 STATION AVE
CENTER VALLEY, PA 180349568
Phone: 610 282-1100
Fax: –
Web: www.desales.edu

CEO: –
CFO: Robert Snyder
HR: Margie Grandinetti
FYE: June 30
Type: Private

Named after scholar, writer, and Doctor of the Church, St. Francis de Sales, DeSales University prides itself on providing its students an education based on the philosophy of Christian humanism. The private, four-year Catholic university offers bachelor of arts (BA) and bachelor of science (BS) degrees in about 30 major fields of studies. It also administers graduate degrees in education, business, nursing, criminal justice, information systems, physical therapy, and physician assistant studies. Total enrollment is about 3,300 students, taught by more than 100 faculty members. DeSales University was founded in 1964.

	Annual Growth	06/14	06/15	06/20	06/21	06/22
Sales ($mil.)	4.9%	–	98.9	–	127.7	138.6
Net income ($ mil.)	2.6%	–	5.6	–	8.5	6.7
Market value ($ mil.)	–	–	–	–	–	–
Employees						580

DESCHUTES BREWERY, INC.

901 SW SIMPSON AVE
BEND, OR 977023118
Phone: 541 385-8606
Fax: –
Web: www.deschutesbrewery.com

CEO: –
CFO: Lisa Swanston
HR: Rick Kangail
FYE: December 31
Type: Private

Named for a nearby river, Deschutes Brewery goes with the flow of its craft beer. Among its stable of beers are the Black Butte Porter, Obsidian Stout, and Big Rig brands. Headquartered in Bend, Oregon, the company's beers are distributed to beverage retailers throughout the US's Pacific Northwest, as well as in California, Alaska, and Nevada. The brewery also operates two brew pubs -- one in Bend, another in Portland. They serve up the usual pub grub -- appetizers, soups, salads, and a bevy of burgers. And, of course, its craft beer is on tap. Deschutes Brewery, which was founded by company president Gary Fish in 1988, is also targeting expansion to the East Coast (Roanoke, Virginia).

	Annual Growth	12/03	12/04	12/05	12/06	12/07
Sales ($mil.)	8.3%	–	–	28.1	31.5	32.9
Net income ($ mil.)	39.6%	–	–	1.5	9.3	2.9
Market value ($ mil.)	–	–	–	–	–	–
Employees						270

DESERET GENERATION AND TRANSMISSION CO-OPERATIVE

10714 S JORDAN GTWY STE 300
SOUTH JORDAN, UT 840953922
Phone: 801 619-6500
Fax: –
Web: www.deseretgt.com

CEO: –
CFO: –
HR: –
FYE: December 31
Type: Private

Its service area may be dry but it is not a power desert, thanks to Deseret Generation and Transmission Cooperative (aka Deseret Power) which supplies wholesale electricity to its members (six retail distribution cooperatives) and other bulk energy customers in Arizona, Colorado, Nevada, Utah, and Wyoming. The member-owned utility operates 223 miles of transmission lines, and it has interests in two power generation facilities in Utah that give it 550 MW of capacity. Deseret Power also operates its own coal mine, which fuels its main power plant, through subsidiary Blue Mountain Energy; other operations include the transportation of coal by railroad and the development of a limestone extraction facility.

	Annual Growth	12/15	12/16	12/20	12/21	12/22
Sales ($mil.)	4.3%	–	221.5	228.0	235.4	285.9
Net income ($ mil.)	–	–	(3.5)	24.3	4.5	19.6
Market value ($ mil.)	–	–	–	–	–	–
Employees						250

DESIGNER BRANDS INC

810 DSW Drive
Columbus, OH 43219
Phone: 614 237-7100
Fax: –
Web: www.designerbrands.com

NYS: DBI
CEO: Douglas M Howe
CFO: Jared A Poff
HR: Akshay Asaithambi
FYE: February 3
Type: Public

Designer Brands (formerly known as DSW) is one of the world's largest designers, producers, and retailers of footwear and accessories. The company offers its products to men, women, and kids through around 640 stores and on e-commerce platforms. Its DSW banner stores average approximately 20,100 square feet and offer a wide assortment of brand name of dress, casual, and athletic shoes, as well as a complementary array of handbags, and accessories. Designer Brands designs and produces footwear and accessories through Camuto Group.

	Annual Growth	02/20*	01/21	01/22	01/23*	02/24
Sales ($mil.)	(3.1%)	3,492.7	2,234.7	3,196.6	3,315.4	3,075.0
Net income ($ mil.)	(25.5%)	94.5	(488.7)	154.5	162.7	29.1
Market value ($ mil.)	(10.3%)	814.9	701.0	731.9	600.9	527.0
Employees	(3.0%)	15,800	11,400	13,500	14,000	14,000

*Fiscal year change

DESKTOP SERVICE CENTER, INC.

111 N 17TH ST
RICHMOND, VA 232193609
Phone: 800 644-5737
Fax: –
Web: www.techead.com

CEO: Philise Conein
CFO: –
HR: –
FYE: December 31
Type: Private

Desktop Service Center, Inc. trading as TECHEAD can help you get the tech heads you need, whenever you need them. The company provides creative talent and information technology (IT) staffing services, as well web site design and development. It also offers graphic design software training. The company's staffing services include contract, contract to hire, and direct hire options. It has consultant partners and presence across the US. TECHEAD was started in 1988 by Phil and Philise Conein. The company has also expanded its cyber security workforce space.

DESTINATION MATERNITY CORP

232 Strawbridge Drive
Moorestown, NJ 08057
Phone: 856 291-9700
Fax: –
Web: www.destinationmaternitycorp.com

CEO: Marla Ryan
CFO: –
HR: Shari Orenstein
FYE: February 2
Type: Public

The destination for moms-to-be may be a store operated by Destination Maternity, a designer and seller of mid-priced to high-end maternity apparel. Its three chains (A Pea in the Pod, Destination Maternity, and Motherhood Maternity) occupy more than 2,000 retail locations, including more than 650 company-owned sites and about 1,400 leased spaces in department and specialty stores (Boscov's, Macys) in the US, Canada, and Puerto Rico. The company is also the exclusive supplier of maternity apparel to more than 1,100 Kohl's stores nationwide. Most of its merchandise is designed by the company and made by third-party contractors. The company was founded in 1982 as Mothers Work. The company filed for bankruptcy protection in 2019, citing a challenging retail environment. Destination Maternity agreed to be acquired by Marquee Brands in December 2019.

	Annual Growth	01/15	01/16	01/17*	02/18	02/19
Sales ($mil.)	23.4%	165.6	498.8	433.7	406.2	383.8
Net income ($ mil.)	–	(17.4)	(4.5)	(32.8)	(21.6)	(14.3)
Market value ($ mil.)	(33.7%)	220.7	96.4	81.3	34.5	42.5
Employees	–	–	4,200	4,000	3,700	3,400

*Fiscal year change

DESTINATION XL GROUP INC

555 Turnpike Street
Canton, MA 02021
Phone: 781 828-9300
Fax: –
Web: www.dxl.com

NMS: DXLG
CEO: –
CFO: –
HR: –
FYE: February 3
Type: Public

Destination XL is the largest specialty retailer of big and tall men's clothing and shoes. It sells moderately-priced, private-label, and name-brand casual wear, dress wear, and casual sportswear for big-and-tall men under the trade names of Destination XL, DXL, DXL Men's Apparel, DXL outlets, Casual Male XL and Casual Male XL outlets. Its DXL retail stores, e-commerce site, dxl.com, and mobile app offer its customers merchandise to fit a variety of lifestyles from casual to business, young to mature, in all price ranges, and all large sizes from XL and up. It has over 280 retail and outlet stores in about 45 US states. The company was founded in 1976 under the name Designs, Inc. It later changed its name to Casual Male Retail Group in 2002 and rebranded as Destination XL in 2010.

	Annual Growth	02/20*	01/21	01/22	01/23*	02/24
Sales ($mil.)	2.4%	474.0	318.9	505.0	545.8	521.8
Net income ($ mil.)	–	(7.8)	(64.5)	56.7	89.1	27.9
Market value ($ mil.)	39.1%	64.4	12.3	251.1	426.8	241.2
Employees	(11.6%)	2,353	1,316	1,353	1,480	1,439

*Fiscal year change

DETERMINE, INC.

200 LAKE DR E STE 200
CHERRY HILL, NJ 080021171
Phone: 800 608-0809
Fax: –
Web: www.corcentric.com

CEO: –
CFO: –
HR: –
FYE: March 31
Type: Private

Selectica's offerings are choice. Clients use Selectica's applications to sell complex goods and services over intranets, extranets, and the Internet. Selectica's software helps clients develop and deploy online sales channels that guide their customers through the selection, configuration, pricing, and fulfillment process for consumer goods, loans, and insurance. The cloud-based software also suggests optimum product configurations (based on sales objectives, marketing information, and product constraints). Selectica primarily serves clients from the manufacturing, retail, and consumer goods sectors.

DETROIT PISTONS BASKETBALL COMPANY

6201 2ND AVE
DETROIT, MI 482023405
Phone: 248 377-0100
Fax: –
Web: www.pistonsacademy.com

CEO: –
CFO: –
HR: Gabrielle Reed
FYE: June 30
Type: Private

Basketball fans get revved up thanks to these Pistons. Detroit Pistons Basketball Company owns and operates the Detroit Pistons professional basketball team, which boasts three National Basketball Association championships, its last coming in 2004. The team was formed in 1941 as the Fort Wayne (Indiana) Zollner Pistons by auto piston maker Fred Zollner, who moved the team to Detroit in 1957. The Pistons roster has included such stars as Joe Dumars, Bill Laimbeer, and Isiah Thomas. Karen Davidson, widow of the late William Davidson, controls the team. The family also owns Palace Sports & Entertainment, a holding company that owns Detroit's Palace of Auburn Hills arena.

DEVCON CONSTRUCTION INCORPORATED

690 GIBRALTAR DR
MILPITAS, CA 950356317
Phone: 408 942-8200
Fax: –
Web: www.devcon-const.com

CEO: Gary Filizetti
CFO: Brett Sisney
HR: –
FYE: December 31
Type: Private

Devcon Construction has built a sturdy business from building in the Bay Area. One of the area's top general building contractors, Devcon has constructed more than 30 million sq. ft. of office, industrial, and commercial space. Its focus is on Northern California, mainly in the San Francisco Bay Area and Silicon Valley. The company provides engineering, design/build, and interior design services. It specializes in high-tech projects, including data centers, and industrial research and development facilities. In addition to building company facilities and offices, Devcon works on such projects as hotels, restaurants, parking structures, retail stores, sports facilities, and schools.

	Annual Growth	12/10	12/11	12/12	12/13	12/14
Sales ($mil.)	23.1%	–	–	779.0	1,012.4	1,181.4
Net income ($ mil.)	138.8%	–	–	3.5	12.5	20.2
Market value ($ mil.)	–	–	–	–	–	–
Employees	–	–	–	–	–	550

DEVEREUX FOUNDATION

444 DEVEREUX DR
VILLANOVA, PA 190851932
Phone: 610 542-3057
Fax: –
Web: www.devereux.org

CEO: Carl E Clark II
CFO: –
HR: Ron Herget
FYE: June 30
Type: Private

Devereux Foundation endeavors to make a difference in the lives of people with behavioral, psychological, intellectual, or neurological problems. A not-for-profit organization, Devereux serves children, adolescents, and adults and their families through about 15 centers in about a dozen states. Its offerings include hospitalization, group homes, respite care, family counseling, and vocational training. Devereux also conducts behavioral health research and provides consulting services for other organizations with similar concerns. The group's work began in 1912 when Philadelphia educator Helena Devereux began working with three special education students in her parents' home.

	Annual Growth	06/07	06/08	06/11	06/12	06/22
Sales ($mil.)	2.1%	–	384.9	395.2	395.7	516.8
Net income ($ mil.)	–	–	5.3	17.9	(5.4)	(16.5)
Market value ($ mil.)	–	–	–	–	–	–
Employees	–	–	–	–	–	6,000

DEVON ENERGY CORP.   NYS: DVN

333 West Sheridan Avenue   CEO: Richard E Muncrief
Oklahoma City, OK 73102-5015   CFO: Jeffrey L Ritenour
Phone: 405 235-3611   HR: Sarah Fisher
Fax: –   FYE: December 31
Web: www.devonenergy.com   Type: Public

An independent energy company, Devon Energy explores for, develops, and produces oil, natural gas, and NGLs (natural gas liquids) assets onshore in the US. Its primary productive assets are in the Eagle Ford, Powder River Basin, Anadarko Basin, Williston Basin, and Delaware Basin. In total, Devon boasts proved developed and undeveloped reserves of about 220 million barrels of oil equivalent with about 4,040 net oil-producing wells. In addition, the company has more than 1,600 net natural gas wells. The company was founded in 1971 and has been publicly held since 1988.

	Annual Growth	12/19	12/20	12/21	12/22	12/23
Sales ($mil.)	25.1%	6,220.0	4,828.0	12,206	19,169	15,258
Net income ($ mil.)	–	(355.0)	(2,680.0)	2,813.0	6,015.0	3,747.0
Market value ($ mil.)	14.9%	16,509	10,050	28,003	39,102	28,797
Employees	1.4%	1,800	1,400	1,600	1,800	1,900

DEWEY ELECTRONICS CORP.   NBB: DEWY

27 Muller Road   CEO: John H Dewey
Oakland, NJ 07436   CFO: –
Phone: 201 337-4700   HR: –
Fax: –   FYE: June 30
Web: www.deweyelectronics.com   Type: Public

The Dewey Electronics Corporation powers the military and powders the slopes. The company's electronics segment, which accounts for nearly all of Dewey's sales, provides the US Army with diesel-operated tactical generator sets and produces underwater speed and distance measuring instrumentation for the US Navy. The US Department of Defense and its various agencies provide around 72% of sales. Dewey's HEDCO division designs, manufactures, and services the Snow Cub brand of snowmaking equipment, which it has sold to more than 300 ski resorts around the world. The family of late CEO Gordon Dewey owns about 37% of the company.

	Annual Growth	06/13	06/14	06/15	06/16	06/17
Sales ($mil.)	(20.3%)	8.3	6.5	6.6	5.8	3.3
Net income ($ mil.)	–	0.1	(0.1)	(0.1)	0.1	(1.0)
Market value ($ mil.)	(0.8%)	2.1	3.0	2.9	2.7	2.1
Employees	–	30	29	31	24	–

DEXCOM INC   NMS: DXCM

6340 Sequence Drive   CEO: Kevin R Sayer
San Diego, CA 92121   CFO: Jereme M Sylvain
Phone: 858 200-0200   HR: –
Fax: –   FYE: December 31
Web: www.dexcom.com   Type: Public

DexCom is a medical device company that develops and markets continuous glucose monitoring, or CGM, systems for the management of diabetes by patients, caregivers, and clinicians around the world. It develops and manufactures continuous glucose monitoring systems such as its G7, features are 60% reduction in size of the on-body wearable, fully disposable and reduced packaging. DexCom launched its latest generation system, the Dexcom G6 integrated Continuous Glucose Monitoring System, or G6, in 2018. DexCom's products are marketed to physicians, endocrinologists, and diabetes educators in the US and selected international markets. The company's largest geographic market is the US.

	Annual Growth	12/19	12/20	12/21	12/22	12/23
Sales ($mil.)	25.2%	1,476.0	1,926.7	2,448.5	2,909.8	3,622.3
Net income ($ mil.)	52.1%	101.1	493.6	154.7	341.2	541.5
Market value ($ mil.)	(13.2%)	84,302	142,490	206,941	43,643	47,824
Employees	16.6%	5,200	6,400	7,000	7,600	9,600

DFB PHARMACEUTICALS, LLC

3909 HULEN ST   CEO: –
FORT WORTH, TX 761077224   CFO: –
Phone: 817 900-4050   HR: –
Fax: –   FYE: December 31
Web: www.dfb.com   Type: Private

DFB Pharmaceuticals contributes to drug development and manufacturing processes by providing essential ingredients. The company produces various pharmaceutical ingredients for its own use and for other drug makers through its Phyton Biotech operating subsidiary. Phyton Biotech uses its plant cell culture technology to make APIs (active pharmaceutical ingredients). Phyton Biotech is a global provider of chemotherapeutic agents including paclitaxel and docetaxel APIs and taxane intermediates. Affiliate Phyton LTD. operates Phyton Biotech LLC, and Phyton Biotech, GmbH.

	Annual Growth	12/05	12/06	12/07	12/08	12/10
Sales ($mil.)	(44.8%)	–	–	1,916.0	318.7	322.4
Net income ($ mil.)	–	–	–	0.0	–	–
Market value ($ mil.)	–	–	–	–	–	–
Employees	–	–	–	–	–	700

DGO CORPORATION

229 LEE HWY   CEO: –
VERONA, VA 244822500   CFO: –
Phone: 540 438-9811   HR: –
Fax: –   FYE: June 30
Web: www.dixiegas.com   Type: Private

Far from looking away, local petroleum retailers look to Dixie Gas & Oil, a distributor of propane, heating oil, industrial lubricants, and other petroleum products to customers in Virginia and West Virginia. The company also operates gas stations and convenience stores and provides fleeting fueling services. In addition to propane and petroleum, Dixie Gas & Oil supplies CITGO- and Castrol-branded commercial and food grade lubricants; it also supplies some retailers with BP and Pure petroleum products. The company was founded as Dixie Bottled Gas Company in 1946. Dixie Gas & Oil's five gas stations/convenience stores offer BP fuels, Subway sandwiches and salads, as well as convenience food items.

	Annual Growth	06/15	06/16	06/17	06/18	06/19
Assets ($mil.)	(2.3%)	–	15.6	14.8	14.6	14.6
Net income ($ mil.)	75.9%	–	0.0	0.0	0.9	0.4
Market value ($ mil.)	–	–	–	–	–	–
Employees	–	–	–	–	–	115

DGT HOLDINGS CORP.

590 MADISON AVE FL 32   CEO: John J Quicke
NEW YORK, NY 100222524   CFO: Terry Gibson
Phone: 212 520-2300   HR: –
Fax: –   FYE: July 30
Web: www.steelpartners.com   Type: Private

Del Global Technologies can see the beauty of the inner you. And your pet. The firm's Medical Systems group makes medical and dental X-ray systems used by hospitals and doctors, dentists, and veterinarians. It sells its products through distributors worldwide under the Villa brand name; it also provides some of its products to OEMs under private-label agreements. Through its RFI subsidiary, Del Global Technologies' Power Conversion Group makes precision electronic components and sub-assemblies for makers of everything from weapons systems to satellites to MRI machines; brands include RFI, Filtron, Sprague, and Stanley. The company was formed in 1954.

DHI GROUP INC
NYS: DHX

6465 South Greenwood Plaza, Suite 400
Centennial, CO 80111
Phone: 212 448-6605
Fax: –
Web: www.dhigroupinc.com

CEO: Art Zeile
CFO: Raime Leeby
HR: –
FYE: December 31
Type: Public

DHI is a leading provider of artificial intelligence-powered software products, online tools, and services to deliver career marketplaces to candidates and employers globally. The company's three brands (Dice and ClearanceJobs) enable recruiters and hiring managers to efficiently search, match, and connect with highly skilled technologists in specialized fields, particularly technology, and those with active government security clearances. Most of DHI's revenue comes from the sale of recruitment packages, which allow customers to post jobs on its websites and source candidates through its resume databases. Recruitment packages are typically provided through contractual arrangements with annual, quarterly, or monthly terms.

	Annual Growth	12/19	12/20	12/21	12/22	12/23
Sales ($mil.)	0.4%	149.4	136.9	119.9	149.7	151.9
Net income ($ mil.)	(27.4%)	12.6	(30.0)	(29.7)	4.2	3.5
Market value ($ mil.)	(3.7%)	141.1	104.1	292.5	248.0	121.4
Employees	(4.8%)	559	524	470	530	460

DIAGNOSTIC LABORATORY SERVICES, INC.

99-859 IWAIWA ST
AIEA, HI 967013267
Phone: 808 589-5100
Fax: –
Web: www.dlslab.com

CEO: Mark Yamakawa
CFO: Rebecca S Roberts
HR: –
FYE: June 30
Type: Private

Diagnostic Laboratory Services (DLS) provides clinical laboratory and employee drug screening services in Hawaii and other Pacific islands. The company's toxicology department provides drug testing services for private companies, federal and state agencies, and health care providers. DLS' microbiology department provides infectious disease testing services. The company also provides provides diagnostic pathology lab services, including biopsy and pap smear analysis, through affiliate Hawaii Pathology Laboratory. DLS operates satellite locations throughout the Hawaiian Islands, Guam, and Saipan and has hospital-based laboratories including one at the affiliated Queen's Medical Center in Honolulu.

	Annual Growth	06/03	06/04	06/05	06/06	06/07
Sales ($mil.)	7.7%	–	55.9	60.2	65.0	69.8
Net income ($ mil.)	13.5%	–	4.0	6.7	7.3	5.9
Market value ($ mil.)	–	–	–	–	–	–
Employees	–	–	–	–	–	55

DIAKON

1 S HOME AVE
TOPTON, PA 195621317
Phone: 610 682-1262
Fax: –
Web: www.diakon.org

CEO: Mark T Pile
CFO: Richard Barger
HR: –
FYE: December 31
Type: Private

Taking its name from the Greek word for service, Diakon Lutheran Social Ministries offers a range of health and community services, including more than a dozen retirement communities, home health care, pregnancy and adoption services, hospice care, and counseling. The not-for-profit organization's Housing and Development subsidiary works to provide community planning, affordable housing, and property management. Diakon Lutheran also offers clinical pastoral education for seminary students. Its services cover tens of thousands of residents throughout Pennsylvania, Maryland, and Delaware. Diakon was established in 2000 through a merger of Lutheran Services Northeast and Tressler Lutheran Services.

	Annual Growth	12/18	12/19	12/20	12/21	12/22
Sales ($mil.)	(5.9%)	–	269.9	265.1	248.2	224.8
Net income ($ mil.)	–	–	(5.8)	11.6	73.9	0.0
Market value ($ mil.)	–	–	–	–	–	–
Employees	–	–	–	–	–	4,600

DIALYSIS CLINIC, INC.

1633 CHURCH ST STE 500
NASHVILLE, TN 372032948
Phone: 615 327-3061
Fax: –
Web: www.dciinc.org

CEO: H K Johnson
CFO: –
HR: –
FYE: September 30
Type: Private

Dialysis Clinic, Inc., or DCI, is dedicated to caring for patients with end-stage renal disease (ESRD). The not-for-profit company, which operates a network of more than 210 dialysis centers serving more than 14,000 patients in 27 states, also provides kidney transplant assistance services. Affiliate DCI Donor Services is an organ and tissue procurement agency. DCI also funds kidney-related research and educational programs and is affiliated with various universities and teaching hospitals throughout the US, including Tufts University, the University of Arizona, and Tulane University.

	Annual Growth	09/17	09/18	09/19	09/21	09/22
Sales ($mil.)	(77.4%)	–	760.1	739.1	2.5	2.0
Net income ($ mil.)	(49.5%)	–	5.5	7.8	0.5	0.4
Market value ($ mil.)	–	–	–	–	–	–
Employees	–	–	–	–	–	5,000

DIAMOND DISCOVERIES INTERNATIONAL CORP
NBB: DMDD

45 Rockefeller Plaza, Suite 2000
New York, NY 10111
Phone: 212 332-8016
Fax: –
Web: www.quebecdiscoveries.com

CEO: –
CFO: –
HR: –
FYE: December 31
Type: Public

Diamond Discoveries International: The name says it all. The company is a minerals exploration company that leases property in the Torngat fields in northern Quebec. The company is firmly in the exploration and development phase of the project, which will last at least through 2008. Former chairman and CEO Teodosia Pangia holds nearly 25% of Diamond Discoveries.

	Annual Growth	12/06	12/07	12/08	12/09	12/10
Sales ($mil.)	–	–	–	–	–	–
Net income ($ mil.)	–	–	(1.5)	(0.9)	(0.1)	(0.1)
Market value ($ mil.)	29.6%	–	1.6	3.9	2.0	3.4
Employees	–	–	–	–	1	1

DIAMOND HILL INVESTMENT GROUP INC.
NMS: DHIL

325 John H. McConnell Blvd., Suite 200
Columbus, OH 43215
Phone: 614 255-3333
Fax: –
Web: www.diamond-hill.com

CEO: Heather E Brilliant
CFO: Thomas E Line
HR: –
FYE: December 31
Type: Public

Diamond Hill Investment Group takes a shine to investment management. Operating through flagship subsidiary Diamond Hill Capital Management, the firm oversees some $11.5 billion in assets, most of it invested in mutual funds. Serving institutional and individual clients, the company administers several mutual funds and sells them mainly through independent investment advisers, broker-dealers, financial planners, investment consultants, and third-party marketing firms. The firm hews to a value-based investment philosophy and takes a long-term perspective to investing. Formed in 1990, Diamond Hill Investment Group also manages separate accounts and hedge funds.

	Annual Growth	12/19	12/20	12/21	12/22	12/23
Sales ($mil.)	–	136.6	126.4	182.2	154.5	136.7
Net income ($ mil.)	(6.4%)	55.0	38.7	74.2	40.4	42.2
Market value ($ mil.)	4.2%	396.5	421.4	548.3	522.3	467.5
Employees	–	129	126	128	129	129

DIAMOND OFFSHORE DRILLING INC (NEW)   NYS: DO

15415 Katy Freeway
Houston, TX 77094
Phone: 281 492-5300
Fax: 281 492-5316
Web: www.diamondoffshore.com

CEO: Bernie G Wolford Jr
CFO: Dominic A Savarino
HR: –
FYE: December 31
Type: Public

Diamond Offshore Drilling is a contract offshore oil and gas driller capable of descending in the deep blue to depths of 10,000 feet and deeper. Diamond Offshore has more than 10 offshore drilling rigs, including about four drillships, and eight semisubmersible rigs. This fleet enables the company to offer services in the floater market on a worldwide basis. A floater rig is a type of mobile offshore drilling rig that floats and does not rest on the seafloor. The US generates about 45% of the company's total sales. In 2021, Diamond Offshore emerged from their chapter 11 process after successfully completing a financial reorganization pursuant to their joint plan of reorganization.

	Annual Growth	12/20*	04/21*	12/21	12/22	12/23
Sales ($mil.)	12.9%	733.7	169.4	556.1	841.3	1,056.2
Net income ($ mil.)	–	(1,254.9)	(1,962.0)	(177.3)	(103.2)	(44.7)
Market value ($ mil.)	–	–	–	–	1,064.1	1,330.2
Employees	4.0%	1,900	–	1,900	2,100	2,140

*Fiscal year change

DIAMOND PARKING SERVICES, LLC

605 1ST AVE STE 600
SEATTLE, WA 981042209
Phone: 206 284-2732
Fax: –
Web: www.diamondparking.com

CEO: –
CFO: –
HR: –
FYE: December 31
Type: Private

Diamond Parking covers all facets of car lots. The company manages more than 1,500 parking locations, including Park N' Jets near airports, hospitals, sports arenas, multi-level garages, and surface locations. Besides management, Diamond Parking provides other parking-related services, including accounting, facility design, and financing. At its locations across western North America, the company will retrieve keys from locked cars, change flats, and jumpstart dead batteries for free. Customers include landlords, airports, property managers, and developers. Founded in 1922, Diamond Parking is owned by the Diamond family.

DIAMONDBACK ENERGY, INC.   NMS: FANG

500 West Texas Ave, Suite 100
Midland, TX 79701
Phone: 432 221-7400
Fax: –
Web: www.diamondbackenergy.com

CEO: Travis D Stice
CFO: Kaes V Hof
HR: Leo Guillen
FYE: December 31
Type: Public

Diamondback Energy, Inc. is an independent oil and natural gas company focused on the acquisition, development, exploration and exploitation of unconventional, onshore oil and natural gas reserves in the Permian Basin in West Texas. Its activities are primarily focused on horizontal development of the Spraberry and Wolfcamp formations of the Midland Basin and the Wolfcamp and Bone Spring formations of the Delaware Basin. These formations are characterized by a high concentration of oil and liquids rich natural gas, multiple vertical and horizontal target horizons, extensive production history, long-lived reserves and high drilling success rates.

	Annual Growth	12/19	12/20	12/21	12/22	12/23
Sales ($mil.)	20.7%	3,964.0	2,813.0	6,797.0	9,643.0	8,412.0
Net income ($ mil.)	90.2%	240.0	(4,517.0)	2,182.0	4,386.0	3,143.0
Market value ($ mil.)	13.7%	16,596	8,650.2	19,275	24,446	27,716
Employees	9.5%	712	732	870	972	1,023

DIAMONDHEAD CASINO CORP   NBB: DHCC

1013 Princess Street
Alexandria, VA 22314
Phone: 703 683-6800
Fax: –
Web: www.europacruises.com

CEO: Gregory A Harrison
CFO: Deborah A Vitale
HR: –
FYE: December 31
Type: Public

Diamondhead Casino Corporation owns more than 400 acres of land on Mississippi's St. Louis Bay, where it plans to develop a casino resort. The company previously owned and operated four "cruise-to-nowhere" casino gambling ships in Florida but sold the vessels between 1999 and 2001 to focus on its Diamondhead, Mississippi, casino plans. Currently Diamondhead Casino Corporation has no operations and four employees who are seeking the various permits, authorizations, and financing required to develop a casino. Chairman and CEO Deborah Vitale owns more than 10% of the company through an employee stock trust.

	Annual Growth	12/18	12/19	12/20	12/21	12/22
Sales ($mil.)	–	–	–	–	–	–
Net income ($ mil.)	–	–	(1.3)	(1.3)	(2.2)	(1.5)	(1.9)
Market value ($ mil.)	128.3%	0.5	0.5	7.6	9.1	13.8
Employees	–	1	1	1	1	–

DIAMONDROCK HOSPITALITY CO.   NYS: DRH

2 Bethesda Metro Center, Suite 1400
Bethesda, MD 20814
Phone: 240 744-1150
Fax: –
Web: www.drhc.com

CEO: Mark W Brugger
CFO: Jeffrey J Donnelly
HR: Kathy Johnson
FYE: December 31
Type: Public

Operating as an umbrella partnership real estate investment trust (UPREIT), DiamondRock Hospitality is a lodging-focused Maryland corporation with a portfolio of some 35 premium hotels and resorts that contain about 9,605 guest rooms located in almost 25 different markets in the US. Its hotels are concentrated in major urban market cities and in destination resort locations and the majority of its hotels are operated under a brand owned by one of the leading global lodging brand companies (Marriott International, Inc. (Marriott), Hilton Worldwide (Hilton), or IHG Hotels & Resorts).

	Annual Growth	12/19	12/20	12/21	12/22	12/23
Sales ($mil.)	3.5%	938.1	299.5	567.1	1,001.5	1,074.9
Net income ($ mil.)	(17.2%)	183.5	(394.4)	(194.6)	109.3	86.3
Market value ($ mil.)	(4.1%)	2,322.7	1,729.4	2,014.5	1,716.8	1,968.4
Employees	1.6%	31	29	28	30	33

DIASPARK INC.

515 PLAINFIELD AVE STE 1
EDISON, NJ 088172598
Phone: 732 248-8333
Fax: –
Web: www.diaspark.com

CEO: –
CFO: –
HR: Deepa Srikumar
FYE: December 31
Type: Private

Diaspark hopes to ignite its customers' information technology. The company primarily provides customized enterprise software development and related consulting services. Its areas of expertise include content delivery, customer service call centers, digital media management, and logistics. Diaspark serves such industries as entertainment, media, and publishing; clients have included ASCAP, Time Warner, and Viacom. The company also offers proprietary software (sold under the Jewel brand) used by jewelers to manage accounting, inventory, and manufacturing. It has regional sales offices in Chicago and New York, as well as a development facility in India. Diaspark was founded in 1995 by chairman Vinay Chhajlani.

	Annual Growth	12/04	12/05	12/06	12/07	12/08
Sales ($mil.)	18.3%	–	–	21.5	25.6	30.1
Net income ($ mil.)	9.9%	–	–	0.4	0.5	0.5
Market value ($ mil.)	–	–	–	–	–	–
Employees	–	–	–	–	–	210

DICERNA PHARMACEUTICALS, INC.

75 HAYDEN AVE
LEXINGTON, MA 024217979
Phone: 617 621-8097
Fax: –
Web: www.novonordisk-us.com

CEO: –
CFO: –
HR: Mafruha Haque
FYE: December 31
Type: Private

Dicerna Pharmaceuticals is trying to discern a viable treatment for rare diseases. The company is developing four drug candidates that aim to treat rare, inherited liver diseases and cancer. Its treatments are based on RNA interference (RNAi), a biological process where ribonucleic acid (RNA) molecules inhibit gene expression. Two of the drug candidates are being developed with Japanese pharmaceutical firm Kyowa Hakko Kirin (KHK). Formerly funded by Oxford Biosciences, the company went public in early 2014 and raised $90 million in its IPO. It plans to use the proceeds to fund preclinical and clinical trials of its drug candidates.

DICK'S SPORTING GOODS, INC

345 Court Street
Coraopolis, PA 15108
Phone: 724 273-3400
Fax: –
Web: www.dicks.com

NYS: DKS
CEO: Lauren R Hobart
CFO: Navdeep Gupta
HR: –
FYE: February 3
Type: Public

Dick's Sporting Goods is a leading omni-channel sporting goods retailer offering an extensive assortment of authentic, high-quality sports equipment, apparel, footwear and accessories. Aside from the company's over 850 stores across the US, its products are also sold through an eCommerce platform that is integrated with its store network. In addition to well-known brand names, Dick's carries exclusive brands such as Walter Hagen, Alpine Design, and Top-Flite. The company also operates about 100 Golf Galaxy, approximately 20 Field & Stream, around 15 Going Going Gone!, and seven Public Lands stores.

	Annual Growth	02/20*	01/21	01/22	01/23*	02/24
Sales ($mil.)	10.4%	8,750.7	9,584.0	12,293	12,368	12,984
Net income ($ mil.)	37.0%	297.5	530.3	1,519.9	1,043.1	1,046.5
Market value ($ mil.)	37.0%	3,556.4	5,388.1	9,101.4	10,150	12,540
Employees	7.5%	41,600	50,100	50,800	52,800	55,500

*Fiscal year change

DICKINSON COLLEGE

28 N COLLEGE ST
CARLISLE, PA 170132311
Phone: 717 245-1943
Fax: –
Web: www.dickinson.edu

CEO: –
CFO: –
HR: Kenneth Doman
FYE: June 30
Type: Private

Located in Carlisle, Pennsylvania, Dickinson College is a private liberal arts college with a penchant for international study. The small but selective college has an annual enrollment of some 2,400 students, half of which study abroad in programs that span 24 countries on six continents. The college offers more than 40 programs in arts and humanities (including a significant foreign language program), social sciences, and natural sciences. It also offers minors in fields including astronomy, creative writing, and film studies. Dickinson College traces its roots back to 1773; it is named for John Dickinson, who signed the US Constitution and was known as "The Penman of the [American] Revolution."

	Annual Growth	06/18	06/19	06/20	06/21	06/22
Sales ($mil.)	(6.1%)	–	147.9	113.3	256.3	122.5
Net income ($ mil.)	(56.4%)	–	17.9	(11.2)	148.2	1.5
Market value ($ mil.)	–	–	–	–	–	–
Employees	–	–	–	–	–	632

DIEBOLD NIXDORF INC

50 Executive Parkway, P.O. Box 2520
Hudson, OH 44236
Phone: 330 490-4000
Fax: –
Web: www.dieboldnixdorf.com

NYS: DBD
CEO: Octavio Marquez
CFO: James A Barna
HR: –
FYE: December 31
Type: Public

Diebold Nixdorf is the leading global producer of connected commerce through automated teller machines (ATMs) with that caters to millions of consumers every day. In addition, it offers remote teller systems, cash dispensers, and intelligent deposit terminals. The company's software encompasses front-end applications for consumer connection points as well as back-end platforms which manage channel transactions, operations and channel integration. The company is a partner to most of the world's top 100 financial institutions and top 25 global retailers. Diebold Nixdorf gets about three-quarters of its sales outside the US. The company has a presence in more than 100 countries with approximately 21,000 employees worldwide.

	Annual Growth	12/18	12/19	12/20	12/21	12/22
Sales ($mil.)	(6.8%)	4,578.6	4,408.7	3,902.3	3,905.2	3,460.7
Net income ($ mil.)	–	(568.7)	(341.3)	(269.1)	(78.8)	(581.4)
Market value ($ mil.)	–	–	–	–	–	–
Employees	(2.2%)	23,000	22,000	22,000	22,000	21,000

DIGERATI TECHNOLOGIES INC

8023 Vantage Dr, Suite 660
San Antonio, TX 78230
Phone: 210 614-7240
Fax: –
Web: www.digerati-inc.com

NBB: DTGI
CEO: Craig K Clement
CFO: Antonio Estrada Jr
HR: –
FYE: July 31
Type: Public

Digerati Technologies (formerly ATSI Communications) has its head in the clouds and its feet in the oil wells. Digerati is a diversified holding company with operating subsidiaries that specialize in cloud-based technology services, most notably Shift8 Technologies. Shift8 provides telecommunications solutions to commercial consumers. Digerati is also actively pursuing possible investments in the fossil fuels sector.

	Annual Growth	07/19	07/20	07/21	07/22	07/23
Sales ($mil.)	51.3%	6.0	6.3	12.4	24.2	31.6
Net income ($ mil.)	–	(4.5)	(3.4)	(16.7)	(8.0)	(8.3)
Market value ($ mil.)	(30.5%)	24.2	4.7	23.6	15.0	5.6
Employees	35.7%	23	22	46	90	78

DIGI INTERNATIONAL INC

9350 Excelsior Blvd., Suite 700
Hopkins, MN 55343
Phone: 952 912-3444
Fax: –
Web: www.digi.com

NMS: DGII
CEO: Ronald E Konezny
CFO: James J Loch
HR: –
FYE: September 30
Type: Public

Digi International is a global provider of business and mission-critical Internet of Things (IoT) connectivity products, services and solutions. The IoT Products & Services segment provides its customers with a device management platform and other professional services to enable customers to capture and manage data from devices they connect to networks. Digi serves over 81,000 customer including industries such as food service, retail, healthcare (primarily pharmacies) and supply chain. The company sells directly and through resellers and distributors. About 75% of company's total revenue comes from North America.

	Annual Growth	09/19	09/20	09/21	09/22	09/23
Sales ($mil.)	15.0%	254.2	279.3	308.6	388.2	444.8
Net income ($ mil.)	25.6%	10.0	8.4	10.4	19.4	24.8
Market value ($ mil.)	18.7%	491.2	563.7	758.1	1,246.8	973.8
Employees	10.9%	543	656	659	790	822

DIGICON CORPORATION

6319 EXECUTIVE BLVD
ROCKVILLE, MD 208523905
Phone: 703 621-1001
Fax: –
Web: www.digicon.com

CEO: –
CFO: –
HR: –
FYE: June 30
Type: Private

Digicon offers services for a digital age. The company provides outsourced information technology services to businesses and government agencies in the Washington, DC area. Services Web and network hosting, systems integration, consulting, and project management; other offerings include site architecture development, network management, and security monitoring. Digicon also provides computer telephony communications systems. Its commercial customers come from a such industries as telecommunications, financial services, health care, and retail. Clients have included Cisco Systems and the Federal Aviation Administration. Digicon was founded in 1985.

DIGIMARC CORP

NMS: DMRC

8500 S.W. Creekside Place
Beaverton, OR 97008
Phone: 503 469-4800
Fax: –
Web: www.digimarc.com

CEO: Riley McCormack
CFO: Charles Beck
HR: –
FYE: December 31
Type: Public

Digimarc is a global leader in product digitization, delivering business value across industries through unique identities and cloud-based solutions. The Digimarc Illuminate Platform is a distinctive software as a service that combines Digimarc's digital watermarks and/or Quick Response (QR) codes with product cloud technologies. By digitizing products using Digimarc's unique digital watermarks, QR codes, and/or other digital tags, products can connect with the web and interact with consumers and digital devices. Its licensees include AlpVision SA, Intellectual Ventures, Kantar SAS, and NexGuard Labs B.V., among others. The US generates about 35% of Digimarc's total revenue.

	Annual Growth	12/19	12/20	12/21	12/22	12/23
Sales ($mil.)	11.0%	23.0	24.0	26.5	30.2	34.9
Net income ($ mil.)	–	(32.8)	(32.5)	(34.8)	(59.8)	(46.0)
Market value ($ mil.)	1.9%	683.9	962.7	804.6	376.8	736.1
Employees	3.5%	216	203	228	277	248

DIGITAL ALLY INC (NEW)

NAS: DGLY

14001 Marshall Drive
Lenexa, KS 66215
Phone: 913 814-7774
Fax: –
Web: www.digitalallyinc.com

CEO: Stanton E Ross
CFO: Thomas J Heckman
HR: –
FYE: December 31
Type: Public

Digital video systems manufacturer Digital Ally is an ally to police and other law enforcement that want more than a paper record of their traffic stops. Targeted to city, state, and commercial law enforcement agencies, the company designs and manufactures specialized digital video cameras, including a rear-view mirror with a built-in digital video camera (used to capture video from inside police vehicles), as well as a portable digital video flashlight, which can be used to record routine traffic stops, sobriety tests, and other law enforcement/civilian interactions. The company also offers a version of their video camera that can be worn on law enforcement officers' uniforms. Digital Ally was formed in 2004.

	Annual Growth	12/18	12/19	12/20	12/21	12/22
Sales ($mil.)	34.6%	11.3	10.4	10.5	21.4	37.0
Net income ($ mil.)	–	(15.5)	(10.0)	(2.6)	25.5	(19.3)
Market value ($ mil.)	(45.7%)	7.3	2.8	6.4	2.9	0.6
Employees	20.6%	95	119	86	146	201

DIGITAL REALTY TRUST INC

NYS: DLR

5707 Southwest Parkway, Building 1, Suite 275
Austin, TX 78735
Phone: 737 281-0101
Fax: 415 738-6501
Web: www.digitalrealty.com

CEO: Andrew P Power
CFO: Matthew Mercier
HR: –
FYE: December 31
Type: Public

One of the largest publicly traded Real Estate Investment Trust (REIT), Digital Realty Trust owns or leases more than 315 data center and technology properties with around 50.8 million sq. ft. of rentable space. Active in around 55 metropolitan areas across some 30 countries on six continents, the company provides data center, colocation, and interconnection services for tenants in fields such as financial services, cloud and IT tech, manufacturing, energy, healthcare, and consumer products. It also holds some 60 properties with approximately 38.2 million rentable square feet as investments. The company operates through Digital Realty Trust LP.

	Annual Growth	12/19	12/20	12/21	12/22	12/23
Sales ($mil.)	14.3%	3,209.2	3,903.6	4,427.9	4,691.8	5,477.1
Net income ($ mil.)	13.1%	579.8	356.4	1,709.3	377.7	948.8
Market value ($ mil.)	3.0%	37,312	43,472	55,114	31,245	41,936
Employees	24.0%	1,550	2,878	3,030	3,412	3,664

DIGITAL TURBINE INC

NAS: APPS

110 San Antonio Street, Suite 160
Austin, TX 78701
Phone: 512 387-7717
Fax: –
Web: www.digitalturbine.com

CEO: William G Stone III
CFO: Barrett Garrison
HR: –
FYE: March 31
Type: Public

When it comes to mobile digital content, Digital Turbine (formerly Mandalay Digital) doesn't play games (but it does make them). Through its Twistbox and AMV subsidiaries, the company develops content for 3G mobile phones, including games, images, chat services, and other products. Its content is targeted to users aged 18 to 40 and covers a variety of themes, including mature entertainment. The company distributes its products in 40 European, North American, Latin American, and Asian countries through agreements with major mobile phone operators, including Verizon, Virgin Mobile, T-Mobile, and Vodafone.

	Annual Growth	03/19	03/20	03/21	03/22	03/23
Sales ($mil.)	59.2%	103.6	138.7	313.6	747.6	665.9
Net income ($ mil.)	–	(6.0)	13.9	54.9	35.5	16.7
Market value ($ mil.)	37.1%	348.1	428.7	7,992.5	4,357.3	1,229.3
Employees	48.2%	161	207	280	844	777

DIGITALBRIDGE GROUP INC

NYS: DBRG

750 Park of Commerce Drive, Suite 210
Boca Raton, FL 33487
Phone: 561 570-4644
Fax: –
Web: www.clns.com

CEO: Marc C Ganzi
CFO: Jacky Wu
HR: –
FYE: December 31
Type: Public

With $53 billion of assets under management (AUM), DigitalBridge Group is a leading global-scale digital infrastructure manager, deploying and managing capital across the digital ecosystem, including data centers, cell towers, fiber networks, small cells, and edge infrastructure. Its diverse global investor base includes public and private pensions, sovereign wealth funds, asset managers, insurance companies, and endowments. The company currently owns interests in two companies, DataBank, an edge colocation data center business (11% DBRG ownership); and Vantage SDC, a stabilized hyperscale data center business (13% DBRG ownership).

	Annual Growth	12/19	12/20	12/21	12/22	12/23
Sales ($mil.)	(22.9%)	2,326.4	1,236.6	965.8	1,144.6	821.4
Net income ($ mil.)	–	(1,048.8)	(2,675.8)	(310.1)	(321.8)	185.3
Market value ($ mil.)	38.6%	776.0	785.8	1,360.9	1,787.3	2,865.6
Employees	(6.9%)	400	350	250	300	300

DIGNITY HEALTH

185 BERRY ST STE 200
SAN FRANCISCO, CA 941071777
Phone: 415 438-5500
Fax: –
Web: www.dignityhealth.org

CEO: Lloyd Dean
CFO: Michael Blaszyk
HR: David Schnitzer
FYE: June 30
Type: Private

Dignity Health is the largest hospital provider in California and the fifth largest health system in the US. The not-for-profit healthcare provider operates a network of more than 400 care centers, including nearly 40 hospitals, urgent and occupational care, imaging and surgery centers, home health, and primary care clinics in more than 20 states. With more than 60,000 caregivers and staff who deliver excellent care to diverse communities, the company has more than 10,000 active physicians.

	Annual Growth	06/07	06/08	06/09	06/19	06/21
Sales ($mil.)	1.0%	–	–	8,957.9	9,916.6	10,102
Net income ($ mil.)	–	–	–	(799.1)	119.3	1,120.7
Market value ($ mil.)	–	–	–	–	–	–
Employees	–	–	–	–	–	55,494

DILLARD UNIVERSITY

2601 GENTILLY BLVD
NEW ORLEANS, LA 701223043
Phone: 504 283-8822
Fax: –
Web: www.dillard.edu

CEO: –
CFO: Ralph Johnson
HR: –
FYE: June 30
Type: Private

Dillard University is diligent about providing a quality liberal arts education for its students. The historically black institution is named after James Hardy Dillard, the former president of Tulane University, who played a role in the education of African Americans in the South. The New Orleans-based university enrolls some 850 students. Enrollment fell in the wake of Hurricane Katrina, which flooded the university in 2005. The damage forced Dillard to suspend operations for a semester and lay off staff and faculty. The university resumed operations at a temporary campus in Spring 2006. Classes resumed on campus later that same year. Dillard has been busy rebuilding facilities and recruiting new students.

	Annual Growth	06/18	06/19	06/20	06/21	06/22
Sales ($mil.)	(10.6%)	–	–	–	59.1	52.8
Net income ($ mil.)	(89.5%)	–	–	–	18.6	2.0
Market value ($ mil.)	–	–	–	–	–	–
Employees	–	–	–	–	–	338

DILLARD'S INC.   NYS: DDS

1600 Cantrell Road
Little Rock, AR 72201
Phone: 501 376-5200
Fax: –
Web: www.dillards.com

CEO: William Dillard II
CFO: Chris B Johnson
HR: –
FYE: January 28
Type: Public

Dillard's is one of the nation's largest fashion apparel, cosmetics and home furnishing retailers that operates more than 275 locations in about 30 US states. It also operates some 30 clearance centers and an Internet store that offers a wide selection of merchandise including fashion apparel for women, men and children, accessories, cosmetics, home furnishings, and other consumer goods. Dillard's exclusive brand merchandise includes Antonio Melani, Gianni Bini, GB, Roundtree & Yorke and Daniel Cremieux. The company also operates a general contracting construction company, CDI Contractors, a portion of whose business includes constructing and remodeling stores for the company. The company was founded in 1938 by William T. Dillard.

	Annual Growth	02/19	02/20*	01/21	01/22	01/23
Sales ($mil.)	1.8%	6,503.3	6,343.2	4,433.2	6,624.3	6,996.2
Net income ($ mil.)	51.3%	170.3	111.1	(71.7)	862.5	891.6
Market value ($ mil.)	55.1%	1,124.2	1,040.4	1,504.6	4,301.2	6,505.3
Employees	(6.4%)	39,000	38,000	29,000	30,600	29,900

*Fiscal year change

DIME COMMUNITY BANCSHARES INC (NEW)   NMS: DCOM

898 Veterans Memorial Highway, Suite 560
Hauppauge, NY 11788
Phone: 631 537-1000
Fax: –
Web: www.bridgenb.com

CEO: Kevin M O'Connor
CFO: Avinash Reddy
HR: –
FYE: December 31
Type: Public

The Bridgehampton National Bank, which operates 40 branches on primary market areas of Suffolk and Nassau Counties on Long Island and the New York City boroughs. Founded in 1910, the bank offers traditional deposit services to area individuals, small businesses, and municipalities, including savings, money market accounts, and CDs. Deposits are invested primarily in mortgages, which account for some 80% of the bank's loan portfolio. Title insurance services are available through bank subsidiary Bridge Abstract. In addition, it offers merchant credit and debit card, ATMs, cash management services and individual retirement accounts through Bridge Financial Services LLC. Bridge Bancorp bought Hamptons State Bank in 2011 to fortify its presence on Long Island.

	Annual Growth	12/19	12/20	12/21	12/22	12/23
Assets ($mil.)	29.0%	4,921.5	6,434.3	12,066	13,190	13,636
Net income ($ mil.)	16.8%	51.7	42.0	104.0	152.6	96.1
Market value ($ mil.)	(5.3%)	1,301.7	938.7	1,365.0	1,235.7	1,045.5
Employees	14.4%	496	502	802	823	851

DIMENSIONS HEALTH CORPORATION

901 HARRY S TRUMAN DR N
LARGO, MD 207745477
Phone: 301 618-2000
Fax: –
Web: www.umms.org

CEO: –
CFO: –
HR: –
FYE: June 30
Type: Private

Dimensions Healthcare System takes care of the many, many facets of a human's dimensions. Dimensions Healthcare System operates a handful of medical facilities serving the residents in Prince George's County, Maryland, and the surrounding area. Acute care centers include Prince George's Hospital Center and Laurel Regional Hospital. Specialty services include rehabilitation, behavioral health, cardiology, emergency medicine, senior care, pediatrics, and a sleep disorders center. The not-for-profit health care system was established in 1982.

	Annual Growth	06/04	06/05	06/06	06/21	06/22
Sales ($mil.)	1.3%	–	338.3	367.0	386.9	422.5
Net income ($ mil.)	–	–	3.9	17.7	(29.0)	(45.4)
Market value ($ mil.)	–	–	–	–	–	–
Employees	–	–	–	–	–	2,800

DIMEO CONSTRUCTION COMPANY

75 CHAPMAN ST
PROVIDENCE, RI 029055496
Phone: 401 781-9800
Fax: –
Web: www.dimeo.com

CEO: –
CFO: Steven B Avery
HR: –
FYE: June 30
Type: Private

Dimeo Construction has built a reputation in New England. The company provides general contracting, design/build, and construction management services ranging from pre-planning to post-construction commissioning. It focuses on projects in the corporate, academic, health care, life sciences/R&D, public, commercial, and residential markets, working on schools, hospitals, corporate headquarters, research and development facilities, and shopping centers for clients including University of Rhode Island, National Elevator Industry Educational Program, and Washington Village. It also has worked on renovation projects such as Hasbro Children's Hospital Underway and Yale University ? Swartwout & Street Halls. Founded in 1930, the employee-owned firm is still run by the Dimeo family.

	Annual Growth	06/07	06/08	06/09	06/10	06/11
Sales ($mil.)	(27.2%)	–	–	567.8	356.1	300.9
Net income ($ mil.)	5.5%	–	–	8.4	9.6	9.3
Market value ($ mil.)	–	–	–	–	–	–
Employees	–	–	–	–	–	300

DINE BRANDS GLOBAL INC

NYS: DIN

10 West Walnut Street, 5th Floor
Pasadena, CA 91103
Phone: 818 240-6055
Fax: -
Web: www.dinebrands.com

CEO: -
CFO: -
HR: -
FYE: December 31
Type: Public

Dine Brands Global is one of the leading chain restaurant companies in the US with three flagship concepts, IHOP (the International House of Pancakes) concept in the midscale full-service restaurant segment within the family dining category of the restaurant industry; Applebee's Neighborhood Grill + Bar concept in the American full-serve restaurant segment within the casual dining category of the restaurant industry; and Fuzzy's Taco Shop concept in the Mexican limited-service restaurant segment within the fast-casual dining category of the restaurant industry. Most of its revenue is derived from domestic sources within its five operating segments, with roughly 75% of its total sales.

	Annual Growth	12/19	12/20	12/21	12/22	12/23
Sales ($mil.)	(2.2%)	910.2	689.3	896.2	909.4	831.1
Net income ($ mil.)	(1.8%)	104.3	(104.0)	97.9	81.1	97.2
Market value ($ mil.)	(12.2%)	1,281.6	890.0	1,163.3	991.3	761.9
Employees	(36.0%)	3,560	3,447	3,521	637	596

DINEWISE INC

NBB: DWIS

500 Bi-County Blvd., Suite 400
Farmingdale, NY 11735-3940
Phone: 631 694-1111
Fax: -
Web: www.dinewise.com

CEO: -
CFO: -
HR: -
FYE: December 30
Type: Public

For hungry Americans who would rather dial than cook, Colorado Prime and its sister company DineWise deliver meals directly to the door in 48 US states. The direct marketer serves up flash-frozen, chef-prepared meals for time-pressed cooks to microwave at home. Colorado Prime also offers diet meals, as well as meals tailored to fit special needs, including diabetic and low-sodium regimens. Complete meals include entrees, sides, and vegetables. Customers can order by phone, catalog, or online. Founded in 1959, the company acquired Home Bistro Foods, its largest direct competitor, in 2009.

	Annual Growth	12/03	12/04	12/05	12/06	12/07
Sales ($mil.)	(2.8%)	-	-	-	10.9	10.6
Net income ($ mil.)	-	-	-	-	(3.5)	(1.1)
Market value ($ mil.)	(92.0%)	-	-	-	23.3	1.9
Employees	-	-	-	-	-	16

DIODES, INC.

NMS: DIOD

4949 Hedgcoxe Road, Suite 200
Plano, TX 75024
Phone: 972 987-3900
Fax: -
Web: www.diodes.com

CEO: Keh-Shew Lu
CFO: Richard D White
HR: Cynthia Yanez
FYE: December 31
Type: Public

Diodes Incorporated is a leading global manufacturer and supplier of high-quality application-specific standard products within the broad discrete, logic, analog, and mixed-signal semiconductor markets. The company serves the consumer electronics, computing, communications, industrial, and automotive markets. Diodes' products include diodes, transistors, amplifiers, comparators, and rectifiers; they are used by computer and consumer electronics manufacturers in products such as notebooks, LCD monitors, smartphones, and game consoles. Other applications include power supplies, security systems, advanced driver assistance systems, and telematics. Majority of the company's total sales came from outside the US.

	Annual Growth	12/19	12/20	12/21	12/22	12/23
Sales ($mil.)	7.4%	1,249.1	1,229.2	1,805.2	2,000.6	1,661.7
Net income ($ mil.)	10.3%	153.3	98.1	228.8	331.3	227.2
Market value ($ mil.)	9.3%	2,589.5	3,238.7	5,044.5	3,497.7	3,699.0
Employees	4.4%	7,271	8,939	8,921	8,877	8,635

DIRECT MARKETING ASSOCIATION, INCORPORATED

1333 BROADWAY RM 301
NEW YORK, NY 100181170
Phone: 212 768-7277
Fax: -
Web: www.ana.net

CEO: Thomas Benton
CFO: -
HR: -
FYE: June 30
Type: Private

The Direct Marketing Association (DMA) knows how to reach you, your family, and your friends -- directly. The organization represents the interests of businesses and nonprofit enterprises engaged in direct marketing (selling their products through catalogs, the Internet, and other media). The DMA does so by offering training, conducting research, hosting conferences, and promoting the industry. The organization boasts thousands of members in the US and about 50 other countries. The DMA also endeavors to inform the general public about direct marketing, and it provides information about identity theft prevention and how to be removed from mailing and phone lists. The group was founded in 1917.

DIRECT RELIEF FOUNDATION

6100 BECKNELL RD
SANTA BARBARA, CA 931173265
Phone: 805 964-4767
Fax: -
Web: www.directrelief.org

CEO: -
CFO: -
HR: -
FYE: June 30
Type: Private

Direct Relief International wants to relieve the health problems of people around the world. The not-for-profit organization is dedicated to providing health care support and emergency relief to people in developing countries, as well as victims of disasters and war. Active in 50 US states and 70 countries, it gives medicine, supplies, and equipment through partnerships with local groups that make specific requests and coordinates distribution. The group also has partnered with nonprofit clinics and community health centers to provide medical care and medicine for homeless and low-income people in California. Direct Relief was founded in 1948 by Estonian immigrant William Zimdin.

	Annual Growth	06/18	06/19	06/20	06/21	06/22
Sales ($mil.)	367.3%	-	21.7	3.8	1,942.7	2,218.1
Net income ($ mil.)	-	-	10.3	(4.2)	20.1	(35.1)
Market value ($ mil.)	-	-	-	-	-	-
Employees	-	-	-	-	-	2

DIRECT SELLING ASSOCIATION (INC)

1667 K ST NW STE 1100
WASHINGTON, DC 200061660
Phone: 202 416-6400
Fax: -
Web: www.dsa.org

CEO: Ryan Napierski
CFO: -
HR: -
FYE: December 31
Type: Private

Direct Selling Association promotes the business interests of Avon ladies, Fuller Brush men, and Tupperware peddlers everywhere. The organization represents more than 200 companies that make and distribute a variety of goods and services directly to consumers including Discovery Toys, Herbalife, and The Longaberger Company. All member companies pledge to follow the group's code of ethics, which includes a ban on deceptive practices. Some 90% of direct sellers conduct their business on a part-time basis. DSA provides its members with a research center, publications, seminars, and an annual meeting. The group was formed as the Agents Credit Association in 1910.

	Annual Growth	12/09	12/10	12/18	12/21	12/22
Sales ($mil.)	0.3%	-	6.4	9.4	6.5	6.7
Net income ($ mil.)	5.6%	-	0.2	2.6	0.4	0.4
Market value ($ mil.)	-	-	-	-	-	-
Employees	-	-	-	-	-	28

DISABLED AMERICAN VETERANS

860 DOLWICK DR
ERLANGER, KY 410182774
Phone: 859 441-7300
Fax: –
Web: www.dav.org

CEO: J M Burgess
CFO: –
HR: –
FYE: December 31
Type: Private

Disabled American Veterans (DAV) helps ex-military men and women fight personal battles. The nonprofit group strives to improve the quality of life for some 200,000 wounded veterans and their families by helping them navigate the US Department of Veterans Affairs system to obtain benefits. DAV also represents the political interests of veterans and provides various outreach and volunteer programs. The group, which generates most of its revenue from tax-exempt contributions, has about 1.2 million members and boasts some 110 offices in the US and Puerto Rico. DAV was formed in 1920 and chartered by Congress in 1932. The organization has partnered with large corporations to help veterans get assistance.

	Annual Growth	12/18	12/19	12/20	12/21	12/22
Sales ($mil.)	0.5%	–	145.4	153.9	170.6	147.4
Net income ($ mil.)	–	–	1.4	21.4	30.5	(1.8)
Market value ($ mil.)	–	–	–	–	–	–
Employees	–	–	–	–	–	630

DISCOUNT DRUG MART, INC.

211 COMMERCE DR
MEDINA, OH 442561331
Phone: 330 725-2340
Fax: –
Web: www.discount-drugmart.com

CEO: Donald Boodjeh
CFO: Thomas McConnell
HR: Craig Kwasniewski
FYE: March 31
Type: Private

Drugs are merely part of the story at Discount Drug Mart. One of the largest drugstore chains in Ohio, the company offers pharmacy services, medical and home health care supplies, and over-the-counter medications. Stocking some 40,000 items, it also sells groceries, beauty aids, pet supplies, housewares, and hardware. As part of its business, Discount Drug Mart offers its customers video rentals and photo-developing services. Its 70-plus stores measure 25,000 sq. ft. on average -- about twice the size of its rivals' locations, but smaller and more convenient than its national big-box competitors Wal-Mart and Target. Chairman and CEO Parviz Boodjeh owns the company, which he founded in 1969.

DISCOVER FINANCIAL SERVICES

NYS: DFS

2500 Lake Cook Road
Riverwoods, IL 60015
Phone: 224 405-0900
Fax: –
Web: www.discover.com

CEO: John B Owen
CFO: John T Greene
HR: –
FYE: December 31
Type: Public

Discover Financial Services provides digital banking products and services and payment services through its subsidiaries. It offers credit card loans, private student loans, personal loans, home equity loans, and deposit products. Discover also licenses Diners Club which processes transactions for Discover-branded credit and debit cards, provides payment transaction processing and settlement services. The company also runs the PULSE Network ATM system, an electronic funds transfer network, providing financial institutions issuing debit cards on the PULSE network with access to ATMs domestically and internationally, as well as merchant acceptance throughout the US for debit card transactions. It was incorporated in Delaware in 1960.

	Annual Growth	12/19	12/20	12/21	12/22	12/23
Assets ($mil.)	7.4%	113,996	112,889	110,242	131,628	151,522
Net income ($ mil.)	(0.1%)	2,957.0	1,141.0	5,449.0	4,392.0	2,940.0
Market value ($ mil.)	7.3%	21,214	22,642	28,902	24,468	28,112
Employees	5.2%	17,200	17,600	16,700	20,200	21,100

DISH NETWORK CORP

NMS: DISH

9601 South Meridian Boulevard
Englewood, CO 80112
Phone: 303 723-1000
Fax: 303 723-1499
Web: www.dishnetwork.com

CEO: Hamid Akhavan
CFO: Paul W Orban
HR: –
FYE: December 31
Type: Public

DISH Network is a holding company that provides Pay-TV in the US, serving millions of subscribers as well as hotels, motels, and other commercial accounts. Its programming includes premium movies, on-demand streaming over-the-top, Latino video programming, specialty sports, local and international programming, and pay-per-view. Its relatively Sling TV offering provides streaming video over the internet. DISH Network generates almost all sales in the US. ADISH Network has approximately 9.8 million Pay-TV subscribers in the US, including 7.4 million DISH TV subscribers, and 2.3 million SLING TV subscribers.

	Annual Growth	12/18	12/19	12/20	12/21	12/22
Sales ($mil.)	5.2%	13,621	12,808	15,493	17,881	16,679
Net income ($ mil.)	10.0%	1,575.1	1,399.5	1,762.7	2,410.6	2,303.2
Market value ($ mil.)	(13.4%)	13,261	18,838	17,176	17,229	7,456.6
Employees	(2.9%)	16,000	16,000	13,500	14,500	14,200

DISNEY (WALT) CO. (THE)

NYS: DIS

500 South Buena Vista Street
Burbank, CA 91521
Phone: 818 560-1000
Fax: –
Web: www.disney.com

CEO: Robert A Iger
CFO: Hugh F Johnston
HR: –
FYE: September 30
Type: Public

The Walt Disney Company is one of the world's largest media conglomerate, with assets encompassing movies, television, streaming, publishing, and theme parks. Its TV holdings include the ABC TV network and around eight TV stations, as well as a portfolio of cable networks including Disney, ESPN, Freeform, FX, National Geographic, and a 50% equity investment in A+E. It produces films through the Walt Disney Pictures, Twentieth Century Studios, Marvel, Lucasfilm, Pixar, and Searchlight Pictures; and its Disney Parks and Resorts runs popular theme parks including Disney World and Disneyland. The company generates 80% of its revenue in Americas.

	Annual Growth	09/19*	10/20	10/21	10/22*	09/23
Sales ($mil.)	6.3%	69,570	65,388	67,418	82,722	88,898
Net income ($ mil.)	(32.1%)	11,054	(2,864.0)	1,995.0	3,145.0	2,354.0
Market value ($ mil.)	(11.1%)	231,459	218,262	313,474	168,002	144,350
Employees	0.2%	223,000	203,000	190,000	220,000	225,000

*Fiscal year change

DISTRIBUTION SOLUTIONS GROUP INC

NMS: DSGR

8770 W. Bryn Mawr Avenue, Suite 900
Chicago, IL 60631
Phone: 773 304-5050
Fax: –
Web: www.distributionsolutionsgroup.com

CEO: Cesar Lanuza
CFO: Ronald J Knutson
HR: Sue Eaglebarger
FYE: December 31
Type: Public

Distribution Solutions Group (DSG), formerly Lawson Products, offers roughly 120,000 different products from about 2,500 suppliers. Major product types include fasteners, cutting tools and abrasives, fluid power products, aftermarket automotive supplies, and safety equipment. DSG serves industrial, commercial, institutional, and government maintenance, repair and operations (MRO) markets. The company primarily operates as a one-stop solution provider as a global specialty distribution company. Sales are generated mainly in the US via about 1,000 sales representatives who also provide inventory management services.

	Annual Growth	12/19	12/20	12/21	12/22	12/23
Sales ($mil.)	43.5%	370.8	351.6	417.7	1,151.4	1,570.4
Net income ($ mil.)	–	7.2	15.1	9.4	7.4	(9.0)
Market value ($ mil.)	(11.8%)	2,436.1	2,380.5	2,560.0	1,723.5	1,475.7
Employees	(1.2%)	1,770	1,910	1,840	3,100	1,685

DITECH HOLDING CORPORATION

500 OFFICE CENTER DR STE 400
FORT WASHINGTON, PA 190343219
Phone: 844 714-8603
Fax: –
Web: www.ditechholding.com

CEO: Thomas F Marano
CFO: Gerald A Lombardo
HR: –
FYE: December 31
Type: Private

Walter Investment Management does its best to collect from the credit-challenged. The firm owns and services residential mortgages (particularly those of the subprime and nonconforming variety) for itself as well as for government sponsored entities, government agencies, third-party securitization trusts, and other credit owners. Operating through subsidiaries Walter Mortgage Company; Hanover Capital; Marix Servicing; Ditech; and third-party credit servicer Green Tree, Walter Investment Management services 2 million residential loan accounts with unpaid balances of $256 billion, making it one of the 10 largest mortgage servicers in the US. The firm also originates residential loans, including reverse loans.The firm filed for Chapter 11 bankruptcy in 2017 and is expected to emerged from it, less $800 million in debt overhang, in early 2018.

	Annual Growth	12/13	12/14	12/15	12/16	12/17
Sales ($mil.)	(19.2%)	–	–	1,274.3	995.7	831.3
Net income ($ mil.)	–	–	–	(263.2)	(529.2)	(426.9)
Market value ($ mil.)	–	–	–	–	–	–
Employees	–	–	–	–	–	3,800

DIVERSICARE HEALTHCARE SERVICES, INC.

1621 GALLERIA BLVD
BRENTWOOD, TN 370272926
Phone: 615 771-7575
Fax: –
Web: www.dvcr.com

CEO: James R McKnight Jr
CFO: Kerry D Massey
HR: Lori May
FYE: December 31
Type: Private

Diversicare Healthcare Services (formerly Advocat) provides a range of health and living services for the elderly through its nursing homes and assisted-living facilities, most of which are located in the southeastern and southwestern US. The company operates more than 75 nursing homes and assisted-living centers with about 8,500 beds. Diversicare, which focuses on rural areas, offers a range of health care services including skilled nursing, recreational therapy, and social services, as well as nutritional, respiratory, rehabilitative, and other specialized ancillary services.

DIVERSIFIED CHEMICAL TECHNOLOGIES, INC.

15477 WOODROW WILSON ST
DETROIT, MI 482381586
Phone: 313 867-5444
Fax: –
Web: www.dchem.com

CEO: –
CFO: –
HR: –
FYE: January 28
Type: Private

True to its name, Diversified Chemical Technologies manufactures a diverse range of specialty chemical products for a diverse range of customers. It serves a number of industries, but is best known for its process and maintenance chemicals for metalworking, and cleaning and sanitation chemicals for the food and beverage markets. Working through subsidiaries, it produces various adhesives (hot melt, pressure sensitive, and water-based adhesives), polymeric materials (including PVC seals, epoxies, acrylics, polyesters, and polyurethanes), custom-formulated specialty products, and recycled polymeric materials to make polyurethane foam for autos. It also offers office supplies through Detroit-based Paperworks.

	Annual Growth	01/07	01/08	01/09	01/10	01/11
Sales ($mil.)	0.9%	–	–	69.1	59.8	70.3
Net income ($ mil.)	–	–	–	(0.8)	1.0	7.1
Market value ($ mil.)	–	–	–	–	–	–
Employees	–	–	–	–	–	225

DIVERSIFIED COMMUNICATIONS

121 FREE ST
PORTLAND, ME 041013919
Phone: 207 842-5500
Fax: –
Web: www.divcom.com

CEO: –
CFO: Whit Mitchell
HR: –
FYE: December 31
Type: Private

For those who want to get a message out, Diversified Communications can help. The company has its hand in conventions, publishing, and television through offices in the US, Canada, the UK, Hong Kong, India, and Australia. Most of Diversified Communications' revenue comes from the more than 60 trade shows its business communications unit runs worldwide. It also publishes magazines on seafood, commercial fishing, and natural products . The company's broadcasting group handles two television stations in Maine and Florida. Diversified Communications is owned by the family of chairman Horace Hildreth, Jr., whose father founded the company in 1949 with a single radio station.

DIVERSIFIED HEALTHCARE TRUST   NMS: DHC

Two Newton Place, 255 Washington Street, Suite 300
Newton, MA 02458-1634
Phone: 617 796-8350
Fax: 617 796-8349
Web: www.dhcreit.com

CEO: –
CFO: Matthew Brown
HR: –
FYE: December 31
Type: Public

Diversified Healthcare Trust is real estate investment trust, or REIT, that owns medical office and life science properties, senior living communities and other healthcare related properties throughout the US. The company has some 380 wholly-owned properties, including eight closed senior living communities in about 35 states and Washington, DC. Its portfolio includes senior apartments, independent and assisted living facilities, nursing homes, medical office buildings, and gymnasiums.

	Annual Growth	12/19	12/20	12/21	12/22	12/23
Sales ($mil.)	7.9%	1,040.2	1,632.0	1,383.2	1,283.6	1,410.3
Net income ($ mil.)	–	(88.2)	(139.5)	174.5	(15.8)	(293.6)
Market value ($ mil.)	(18.4%)	2,029.2	990.5	742.9	155.5	899.2
Employees	–	–	–	–	–	–

DIXIE GROUP INC.   NMS: DXYN

475 Reed Road
Dalton, GA 30720
Phone: 706 876-5800
Fax: –
Web: www.thedixiegroup.com

CEO: Daniel K Frierson
CFO: Allen L Danzey
HR: Lisa Wise
FYE: December 30
Type: Public

The Dixie Group takes its business to the rug. Once a textile concern, the company has evolved into a maker of tufted broadloom carpets and custom rugs, and proprietary yarns used in manufacturing the soft floorcoverings. Its brands, Dixie Home, Masland Carpets, Fabrica International, and Candlewick Yarn, are differentiated by product price and styling. Dixie markets and sells carpets to high-end residential customers, including interior decorators, retailers, home builders, and motorhome and yacht OEMs. Less so, it supplies carpet for the specified (contract) market, such as architectural and commercial customers, as well as consumers through specialty floorcovering retailers.

	Annual Growth	12/19	12/20	12/21	12/22	12/23
Sales ($mil.)	(7.3%)	374.6	315.9	341.2	303.6	276.3
Net income ($ mil.)	–	15.3	(9.2)	1.6	(35.1)	(2.7)
Market value ($ mil.)	(10.3%)	17.9	40.5	87.4	12.2	11.6
Employees	(10.7%)	1,526	1,441	1,322	1,138	970

DIXON TICONDEROGA COMPANY

615 CRESCENT EXECUTIVE CT STE 500
LAKE MARY, FL 32746
Phone: 407 829-9000
Fax: –
Web: www.dixonwriting.com

CEO: Luca Pelosin
CFO: –
HR: Lillian Gonzalez
FYE: December 31
Type: Private

Dixon Ticonderoga is one of America's oldest corporations. The company makes classroom supplies, classroom learning, organization, dry erase, art and craft supplies, paper and board, bulletin board, papers, paper rolls, colors, brushes, clay, drawing and illustration, pencils, marking crayons, markers, chalks, reach, and writing instruments under the Bordette, Ticonderoga, Prang, Dixon, Pacon, and Oriole brands. Oriole pencils are perfect for schools, architects, engineers, contractors, or anyone who needs a dependable pencil. Dixon Ticonderoga is owned by F.I.L.A. S.p.A. of Milan, Italy.

	Annual Growth	12/06	12/07	12/08	12/09	12/12
Sales ($mil.)	13.2%	–	–	–	52.1	75.7
Net income ($ mil.)	(8.0%)	–	–	–	9.9	7.7
Market value ($ mil.)	–	–	–	–	–	–
Employees	–	–	–	–	–	1,403

DJSP ENTERPRISES, INC.

NBB: DJSP

900 South Pine Island Road, Suite 400
Plantation, FL 33324
Phone: 954 233-8000
Fax: 954 233-8570
Web: www.djspenterprises.com

CEO: –
CFO: –
HR: –
FYE: December 31
Type: Public

DJSP Enterprises is willing to do the paperwork on houses in foreclosure. Through a controlling interest in DAL LLC, the holding company provides mainly non-legal support services, such as document preparation and processing for mortgage lenders and servicers who are managing home foreclosures in Florida. DAL operating subsidiary DJS Processing prepares drafts of pleadings and other documentation in connection with residential foreclosures, bankruptcies, complex litigation, evictions, and sales of lender-owned real estate (REO) properties. In 2010 DJSP bought Timios, a provider of title insurance and settlement services throughout much of the US.

	Annual Growth	12/05	12/06	12/07	12/08	12/09
Sales ($mil.)	–	–	–	–	–	–
Net income ($ mil.)	–	–	–	–	(0.1)	(0.4)
Market value ($ mil.)	–	–	–	–	–	–
Employees	10.5%	–	–	–	860	950

DLA PIPER LLP (US)

650 S EXETER ST
BALTIMORE, MD 212024573
Phone: 410 580-3000
Fax: –
Web: www.dlapiper.com

CEO: –
CFO: –
HR: Melissa Westwood
FYE: December 31
Type: Private

DLA Piper is one of the world's largest law firms with lawyers located in more than 40 countries throughout the Americas, Europe, the Middle East, Africa, and Asia Pacific. The firm serves corporate clients through a broad range of practices divided into nearly 15 key groups; specialties include mergers and acquisitions, data protection, privacy, and cybersecurity, franchise, intellectual property, regulatory and government affairs, and technology and media. Gave more than 215,000 hours of free legal advice, the firm was formed in 2005 when Maryland-based Piper Rudnick merged with California-based Gray Cary Ware & Freidenrich and UK firm DLA.

	Annual Growth	12/03	12/04	12/06	12/08	12/12
Sales ($mil.)	(48.9%)	–	580.7	1,016.2	–	2.7
Net income ($ mil.)	(53.6%)	–	188.7	325.9	–	0.4
Market value ($ mil.)	–	–	–	–	–	–
Employees	–	–	–	–	–	3,323

DLH HOLDINGS CORP

NAS: DLHC

3565 Piedmont Road, Building 3, Suite 700
Atlanta, GA 30305
Phone: 770 554-3545
Fax: –
Web: www.dlhcorp.com

CEO: Zachary C Parker
CFO: Kathryn M Johnbull
HR: –
FYE: September 30
Type: Public

Dlh Holdings provides temporary and permanent medical, office administration, and technical staffing services to US government facilities nationwide. Its services on behalf of government agencies include case management, healthcare IT systems and tools, physical and behavioral health examinations; health and nutritional support for children and adults, biological research, disaster and emergency response staffing, among others. The company has contracts with the Department of Defense, Health and Human Services, and Veterans Affairs. It traces its roots back to 1969.

	Annual Growth	09/19	09/20	09/21	09/22	09/23
Sales ($mil.)	23.7%	160.4	209.2	246.1	395.2	375.9
Net income ($ mil.)	(27.6%)	5.3	7.1	10.1	23.3	1.5
Market value ($ mil.)	27.2%	62.2	101.1	171.6	171.2	162.8
Employees	13.9%	1,900	2,200	2,300	2,400	3,200

DLH SOLUTIONS, INC

3565 PIEDMONT RD NE BLDG 3-700
ATLANTA, GA 303058202
Phone: 770 554-3545
Fax: –
Web: www.teamstaffgs.com

CEO: –
CFO: –
HR: –
FYE: December 31
Type: Private

TeamStaff Government Solutions (formerly RS Staffing Services) offers contract staffing services to the federal government placing medical, administrative, and technical employees at more than 70 facilities. Clients can order services through multi-award contracts with the General Services Administration and the Department of Veterans Affairs. TeamStaff GS is a key subsidiary of TeamStaff, a provider of temporary and permanent medical and administrative staffing services.

DMC GLOBAL INC

NMS: BOOM

11800 Ridge Parkway, Suite 300
Broomfield, CO 80021
Phone: 303 665-5700
Fax: –
Web: www.dmcglobal.com

CEO: Michael Kuta
CFO: –
HR: –
FYE: December 31
Type: Public

Dynamic Materials Corporation (DMC) has an explosive personality when it comes to working with metal. Formerly Explosive Fabricators, the company uses explosives to metallurgically bond, or "clad," metal plates; the process usually joins a corrosion-resistant alloy with carbon steel -- metals that do not bond easily. Its clad metal plates are central to making heavy-duty pressure vessels and heat exchangers used in such industries as alternative energy and shipbuilding. Its Oilfield Products segment (operating as DYNAenergetics) makes explosive devices used to knock open oil and gas wells. Its AMK Welding unit machines and welds parts for commercial and military aircraft engines and power-generation turbines.

	Annual Growth	12/19	12/20	12/21	12/22	12/23
Sales ($mil.)	16.0%	397.6	229.2	260.1	654.1	719.2
Net income ($ mil.)	(6.3%)	34.0	(1.4)	(0.2)	12.2	26.3
Market value ($ mil.)	(19.6%)	888.8	855.4	783.4	384.5	372.2
Employees	24.8%	741	531	1,503	1,700	1,800

DMH REAL ESTATE HOLDINGS, INC.

900 N ROBERT AVE
ARCADIA, FL 342668712
Phone: 863 494-3535
Fax: –
Web: www.dmh.org

CEO: Vincent A Sica
CFO: Daniel Hogan
HR: Candy Kendrick
FYE: September 30
Type: Private

DMH Real Estate, doing business as DeSoto Memorial Hospital, provides health services to residents of DeSoto County, Florida. The 50-bed hospital offers services ranging from diagnostics and general medicine to emergency care, including pediatrics and maternity care, cardiac care, rehabilitative care, and surgery. DeSoto Memorial is involved in a number of health and wellness programs aimed at improving the health of the community through prevention and education.

	Annual Growth	09/12	09/13	09/14	09/20	09/21
Sales ($mil.)	3.6%	–	31.4	30.0	35.5	41.7
Net income ($ mil.)	–	–	(1.8)	(1.3)	0.5	6.3
Market value ($ mil.)	–	–	–	–	–	–
Employees	–	–	–	–	–	325

DMK PHARMACEUTICALS CORP

NBB: DMKP Q

11682 El Camino Real, Suite 300
San Diego, CA 92130
Phone: 858 997-2400
Fax: –
Web: www.adamispharmaceuticals.com

CEO: David J Marguglio
CFO: Seth Cohen
HR: –
FYE: December 31
Type: Public

Adamis Pharmaceuticals adamantly develops and markets specialty prescription drugs for respiratory ailments, allergies, viral infections, and other medical conditions. Subsidiary Adamis Labs develops and markets allergy, respiratory, and pediatric prescription medicines to physicians in the US. Its products include a pre-filled epinephrine syringe for severe allergic reactions dubbed Epi PFS. Adamis Viral Therapies is developing vaccine technologies for ailments such as influenza and hepatitis. The company is also developing other specialty pharmaceutical product candidates for the potential treatment of asthma and chronic obstructive pulmonary disease, bronchospasms, and allergic rhinitis.

	Annual Growth	12/18	12/19	12/20	12/21	12/22
Sales ($mil.)	(25.1%)	15.1	22.1	16.5	2.2	4.8
Net income ($ mil.)	–	(39.0)	(29.3)	(49.4)	(45.8)	(26.5)
Market value ($ mil.)	(47.6%)	4.8	1.5	1.0	1.3	0.4
Employees	(52.3%)	231	171	143	15	12

DNOW INC

NYS: DNOW

7402 North Eldridge Parkway
Houston, TX 77041
Phone: 281 823-4700
Fax: –
Web: www.dnow.com

CEO: David Cherechinsky
CFO: Mark Johnson
HR: –
FYE: December 31
Type: Public

NOW is a leading global supplier of energy and industrial solutions, products, and engineered equipment packages. Operating under the DistributionNOW and DNOW brands, the company is a distributor of energy products as well as products for industrial applications serving the upstream, midstream, and downstream energy and industrial sectors. It offers maintenance, repair, and operating (MRO) supplies, manual and automated pipe, valves, fittings flanges, gaskets, fasteners, electrical, instrumentation, artificial lift, pumping solutions, and modular process, production, measurement, and control equipment from approximately 170 locations worldwide. Customers include independent and national oil and gas companies, midstream operators, refineries, petrochemical, chemical, utilities, RNG facilities, and other downstream energy processors. NOW also offers warehouse and inventory management services. About 75% of the company's revenue is generated from the US.

	Annual Growth	12/19	12/20	12/21	12/22	12/23
Sales ($mil.)	(5.8%)	2,951.0	1,619.0	1,632.0	2,136.0	2,321.0
Net income ($ mil.)	–	(97.0)	(427.0)	5.0	128.0	247.0
Market value ($ mil.)	0.2%	1,194.3	762.9	907.4	1,349.5	1,202.8
Employees	(13.4%)	4,400	2,500	2,350	2,425	2,475

DO IT BEST CORP.

1626 BROADWAY STE 100
FORT WAYNE, IN 468020009
Phone: 260 748-5300
Fax: –
Web: www.doitbestonline.com

CEO: Dan Starr
CFO: –
HR: Nancy Harris
FYE: June 25
Type: Private

Do it Best is a member-owned wholesaler of hardware, lumber, builder supplies, and related products, operating as a wholesaler cooperative. Members are located principally in the US, with some member locations abroad. Only dealers in hardware, lumber, builder supplies, and related products are eligible to hold shares in the company. Besides the usual tools and building materials, merchandise includes automotive items, bicycles, camping gear, housewares, office supplies, and small appliances. Customers also can have products specially shipped to their local stores through Do it Best's e-commerce site. The company was founded in 1945.

	Annual Growth	06/08	06/09	06/10	06/11	06/16
Sales ($mil.)	4.1%	–	–	2,296.1	2,328.6	2,925.9
Net income ($ mil.)	(5.7%)	–	–	1.0	0.5	0.7
Market value ($ mil.)	–	–	–	–	–	–
Employees	–	–	–	–	–	1,519

DOCTOR'S ASSOCIATES INC.

1 CORPORATE DR STE 1000
SHELTON, CT 064846208
Phone: 203 877-4281
Fax: –
Web: order.subway.com

CEO: –
CFO: –
HR: –
FYE: December 31
Type: Private

Doctor's Associates owns the Subway chain of sandwich shops, the world's largest quick-service restaurant chain by number of locations, surpassing burger giant McDonald's. The company boasts more than 44,000 restaurants in greater than 110 countries. Virtually all Subway restaurants are franchised and offer such fare as hot and cold sub sandwiches, turkey wraps, and salads. The widely recognized eateries are in freestanding buildings, as well as in airports, convenience stores, sports facilities, and other locations.

	Annual Growth	12/05	12/06	12/07	12/08	12/10
Sales ($mil.)	10.4%	–	–	780.5	926.6	1,049.5
Net income ($ mil.)	9.8%	–	–	5.6	6.3	7.5
Market value ($ mil.)	–	–	–	–	–	–
Employees	–	–	–	–	–	650

DOCTORS HOSPITAL OF AUGUSTA, LLC

3651 WHEELER RD
AUGUSTA, GA 309096426
Phone: 706 651-3232
Fax: –
Web: www.doctors-hospital.net

CEO: Joanna Conley
CFO: –
HR: Frances Lester
FYE: March 31
Type: Private

Doctors Hospital of Augusta serves up physician care in eastern Georgia and western South Carolina. The general and acute health care facility has more than 350 beds and is part of hospital giant HCA. Its specialty units include the Joseph M. Still Advanced Wound and Burn Clinic and the Healthy Living Center. In addition, the hospital offers centers for cardiopulmonary health, digestive diseases, occupational medicine, orthopedics, cancer care, sleep disorders, stroke care, surgery, and women's health. Doctors Hospital of Augusta also operates freestanding surgical centers, diagnostic imaging centers, and Human Motion Institute rehabilitation clinics.

	Annual Growth	12/00	12/01	12/02*	03/09	03/17
Sales ($mil.)	–	–	(1,254.6)	162.8	271.6	392.9
Net income ($ mil.)	66.8%	–	0.0	28.1	89.6	121.9
Market value ($ mil.)	–	–	–	–	–	–
Employees	–	–	–	–	–	1,300

*Fiscal year change

DOCUMENT CAPTURE TECHNOLOGIES, INC.

41332 CHRISTY ST
FREMONT, CA 945383115
Phone: 408 436-9888
Fax: –
Web: www.docucap.com

CEO: –
CFO: –
HR: –
FYE: December 31
Type: Private

Like The Lorax , Document Capture Technologies speaks for the trees. The company makes digital scanners used to upload paper documents into electronic data. Its line of USB-powered portable image scanners, sold under the TravelScan and DocketPORT brand names, are used in bank note and check verification devices, ID card and passport scanners, barcode scanners, and business card readers. A handful of customers, including Brother Industries, NCR, and Newell Rubbermaid account for more than half of sales. Subsidiary Syscan, Inc. develops contact image sensor (CIS) modules used in fax machines and scanners. Investor Richard Dietl owns more than 35% of the company; Hong Kong-based Syscan Imaging Ltd. holds around 15%.

DOCUSIGN INC

221 Main St., Suite 1550
San Francisco, CA 94105
Phone: 415 489-4940
Fax: –
Web: www.docusign.com

NMS: DOCU
CEO: Allan Thygesen
CFO: Cynthia Gaylor
HR: –
FYE: January 31
Type: Public

DocuSign, Inc. offers the world's leading electronic signature product, enabling an agreement to be signed electronically on a wide variety of devices, from virtually anywhere in the world, securely. It offers the world's #1 e-signature product as the core part of the company's broader software platform that automates and connects the agreement process, the DocuSign Agreement Cloud. With more than 1.1 million customers and more than a billion users in over 180 countries, DocuSign Agreement Cloud includes more than 400 partner integrations with the world's most popular businesses. The company's customers range from the largest global enterprises to sole proprietorships and nonprofits, across virtually all industries and around the world. DocuSign generates the majority of its revenue in the US.

	Annual Growth	01/20	01/21	01/22	01/23	01/24
Sales ($mil.)	29.8%	974.0	1,453.0	2,107.2	2,515.9	2,761.9
Net income ($ mil.)	–	(208.4)	(243.3)	(70.0)	(97.5)	74.0
Market value ($ mil.)	(6.1%)	16,120	47,818	25,824	12,451	12,508
Employees	15.0%	3,909	5,630	7,461	7,336	6,840

DOLBY LABORATORIES INC

1275 Market Street
San Francisco, CA 94103-1410
Phone: 415 558-0200
Fax: –
Web: www.dolby.com

NYS: DLB
CEO: –
CFO: –
HR: –
FYE: September 29
Type: Public

Dolby Laboratories (Dolby) is the market leader in developing sound processing and noise reduction systems for use in professional and consumer audio and video equipment. Though it does make some of its own products, Dolby mostly licenses its technology to other manufacturers. The company has approximately 15,500 issued patents and approximately 1,400 trademarks worldwide. In film, the Dolby Digital format has become the de facto audio standard. Its systems equip movie screens around the globe. American engineer and physicist Ray Dolby and his family own the more than 55-year-old company. The company generates most of its sales internationally.

	Annual Growth	09/19	09/20	09/21	09/22	09/23
Sales ($mil.)	1.2%	1,241.6	1,161.8	1,281.3	1,253.8	1,299.7
Net income ($ mil.)	(5.8%)	255.2	231.4	310.2	184.1	200.7
Market value ($ mil.)	5.6%	6,108.5	6,223.4	8,854.9	6,238.7	7,589.9
Employees	0.6%	2,193	2,289	2,368	2,336	2,246

DOLLAR GENERAL CORP

100 Mission Ridge
Goodlettsville, TN 37072
Phone: 615 855-4000
Fax: 615 855-5527
Web: www.dollargeneral.com

NYS: DG
CEO: Jeffrey C Owen
CFO: Kelly M Dilts
HR: –
FYE: February 2
Type: Public

Dollar General is one of the largest discount retailers in the US by number of stores, with approximately 19,145 stores located in over 45 states, with the greatest concentration of stores in the southern, southwestern, midwestern and eastern US. It generates most of its sales from consumables (including paper and cleaning products; health and beauty aids; pet supplies; and refrigerated, shelf-stable, and perishable foods). The stores also offer seasonal items, cookware and small appliances, and apparel. The no-frills stores typically measure around 7,500 sq. ft. and approximately 80% of its stores are located in towns of 20,000 or fewer people.

	Annual Growth	01/20	01/21	01/22*	02/23	02/24
Sales ($mil.)	8.7%	27,754	33,747	34,220	37,845	38,692
Net income ($ mil.)	(0.8%)	1,712.6	2,655.1	2,399.2	2,416.0	1,661.3
Market value ($ mil.)	(2.9%)	33,699	42,749	44,884	50,103	29,909
Employees	–	143,000	158,000	163,000	170,000	

*Fiscal year change

DOLLAR TREE INC

500 Volvo Parkway
Chesapeake, VA 23320
Phone: 757 321-5000
Fax: –
Web: www.dollartree.com

NMS: DLTR
CEO: Richard W Dreiling
CFO: Jeffrey Davis
HR: –
FYE: February 3
Type: Public

Dollar Tree is a leading operator of discount variety stores with a solid history of growth and performance. The company operates approximately 16,340 Dollar Tree and Family Dollar discount stores across roughly 50 states and in five provinces in Canada. The stores carry a mix of durable housewares, toys, seasonal items, food, beverages, clothing, fashion accessories, pet supplies, health and beauty aids, and household paper and chemicals. At Dollar Tree shops, most goods are priced at $1.25 or less while Family Dollar merchandise generally range from $1.00 to $10.00.

	Annual Growth	02/20*	01/21	01/22	01/23*	02/24
Sales ($mil.)	6.7%	23,611	25,509	26,321	28,332	30,604
Net income ($ mil.)	–	827.0	1,341.9	1,327.9	1,615.4	(998.4)
Market value ($ mil.)	12.3%	18,973	22,152	27,999	32,767	30,226
Employees	2.3%	193,100	199,327	210,565	207,548	211,826

*Fiscal year change

DOMAIN ASSOCIATES L.L.C.

103 CARNEGIE CTR STE 300
PRINCETON, NJ 085406235
Phone: 609 683-5656
Fax: –
Web: www.domainvc.com

CEO: –
CFO: –
HR: –
FYE: December 31
Type: Private

Life science companies are the domain of Domain Associates. The venture capital firm invests in pharmaceutical, biotechnology, and other health care-related companies, preferring to participate in the first round of financing and taking an active role in the management and development of its portfolio companies. Domain Associates, which has approximately $2.5 billion in capital under management, also invests in small public companies in the health care industry and often forms new companies to in-license health care technologies and products. The firm's portfolio includes interests in Altea Therapeutics, Cadence Pharmaceuticals, and REVA Medical.

	Annual Growth	12/14	12/15	12/16	12/17	12/18
Assets ($mil.)	(1.1%)	–	17.1	14.8	20.2	16.6
Net income ($ mil.)	(31.2%)	–	12.9	10.4	10.5	4.2
Market value ($ mil.)	–	–	–	–	–	–
Employees	–	–	–	–	–	23

DOMINARI HOLDINGS INC
NAS: DOMH

725 5th Avenue, 22nd Floor
New York, NY 10022
Phone: 212 393-4540
Fax: -
Web: www.aikidopharma.com

CEO: Anthony Hayes
CFO: Anthony Hayes
HR: -
FYE: December 31
Type: Public

Spherix is sweet on health. The company's BioSpherix division is developing products from tagatose, a low-calorie sweetener, with possible applications for improving health. Approved for use in foods, the company sold the food-use rights for tagatose to Arla Foods but hung onto the non-food rights, which it then branded Naturlose. The product is in clinical trials as a possible treatment for Type 2 diabetes, although patient recruitment has been slower than expected. Spherix reported it will likely need a development partner to see the product through to market. To supplement its income, Spherix launched a Health Sciences division to provide regulatory and technical consulting services to other biotech firms.

	Annual Growth	12/18	12/19	12/20	12/21	12/22
Sales ($mil.)	-	0.0	0.0	-	-	-
Net income ($ mil.)	-	1.7	(4.2)	(12.3)	(7.2)	(22.1)
Market value ($ mil.)	50.3%	3.2	6.6	4.4	2.9	16.5
Employees	7.5%	6	3	5	5	8

DOMINION ENERGY INC (NEW)
NYS: D

120 Tredegar Street
Richmond, VA 23219
Phone: 804 819-2284
Fax: 804 775-5819
Web: www.dom.com

CEO: Robert M Blue
CFO: Steven Ridge
HR: Barrett Nichols
FYE: December 31
Type: Public

Dominion Energy is one of the nation's largest producers and distributors of energy. The company's portfolio of assets includes approximately 31.0 GW of electric generating capacity, 10,600 miles of electric transmission lines, 78,500 miles of electric distribution lines, and 93,500 miles of gas distribution mains and related service facilities, which are supported by 4,000 miles of gas transmission, gathering, and storage pipeline. It operates in 15 states and serves approximately 7 million customers. It currently expects approximately 90% of earnings from its primary operating segments to come from state-regulated electric and natural gas utility businesses.

	Annual Growth	12/19	12/20	12/21	12/22	12/23
Sales ($mil.)	(3.5%)	16,572	14,172	13,964	17,174	14,393
Net income ($ mil.)	10.1%	1,358.0	(401.0)	3,288.0	994.0	1,994.0
Market value ($ mil.)	(13.2%)	69,403	63,018	65,833	51,386	39,386
Employees	(1.9%)	19,100	17,300	17,100	17,200	17,700

DOMINION ENERGY QUESTAR CORPORATION

333 S STATE ST
SALT LAKE CITY, UT 841112302
Phone: 801 324-5900
Fax: -
Web: hwww.dominionenergy.com

CEO: -
CFO: Kevin W Hadlock
HR: -
FYE: December 31
Type: Private

Dominion Energy Questar is an integrated energy company engaged in natural gas production, transportation, and distribution. Public utility Questar Gas, its largest unit, distributes natural gas to about 1 million customers in Utah, southwestern Wyoming, and southeastern Idaho. Dominion Energy Questar Pipeline operates a 2,500-mile natural gas transportation system and gas storage facilities in Colorado, Utah, and Wyoming. Its exploration activities are led by its Dominion Energy Wexpro business. The company is a subsidiary of utility giant Dominion Energy.

DOMINION ENERGY SOUTH CAROLINA, INC.

400 OTARRE PKWY
CAYCE, SC 290333751
Phone: 804 819-2000
Fax: -
Web: www.dominionenergy.com

CEO: Diane Leopold
CFO: James R Chapman
HR: -
FYE: December 31
Type: Private

South Carolina Electric & Gas (SCE&G) is a regulated utility with 700,000 electricity and 350,000 natural gas customers in the Palmetto State. The utility, a subsidiary of SCANA, owns more than 25,000 miles of power distribution lines and almost 17,500 miles of gas transmission mains; it also operates fossil-fueled, nuclear, and hydroelectric power generation facilities with about 5,200 MW of capacity. Its power service area covers 16,000 square miles, and gas covers 23,000 square miles. SCE&G purchases additional power from other independent generators and utility companies, including SCANA-owned affiliate South Carolina Generating, and it sells wholesale power to other utilities and marketers.

DOMINION RESOURCES BLACK WARRIOR TRUST
NBB: DOMR

Royalty Trust Management, Southwest Bank, 2911 Turtle Creek Boulevard, Suite 850
Dallas, TX 75219
Phone: 855 588-7839
Fax: -
Web: www.dom-dominionblackwarriortrust.com

CEO: -
CFO: -
HR: -
FYE: December 31
Type: Public

Dominion Resources Black Warrior Trust knows that when the wells get old, financial warriors (aka shareholders) don't give up on the economic possibilities. The trust holds royalty interests in 532 natural gas producing wells and is set to terminate when these wells no longer produce enough gas to be profitable. The trust receives, then distributes to shareholders, 65% of the gross proceeds that Dominion Resources (via its subsidiary Dominion Black Warrior Basin) earns by selling the natural gas from its wells in the Black Warrior Basin of Alabama. In 2008 the trust had proved reserves of 22.6 billion cu. ft. of natural gas equivalent.

	Annual Growth	12/10	12/11	12/12	12/13	12/14
Sales ($mil.)	(8.8%)	10.2	8.4	5.3	6.4	7.1
Net income ($ mil.)	(10.7%)	9.2	7.4	4.2	5.4	5.8
Market value ($ mil.)	(22.1%)	121.3	62.7	23.2	43.7	44.7
Employees		-	-	-	-	-

DOMINOS PIZZA INC.
NYS: DPZ

30 Frank Lloyd Wright Drive
Ann Arbor, MI 48105
Phone: 734 930-3030
Fax: -
Web: www.dominos.com

CEO: Richard E Allison Jr
CFO: -
HR: Beth Bugnell
FYE: December 31
Type: Public

Domino's is a pizza company with about 19,800 locations in over 90 markets, and operates two distinct service models within its stores with a significant business in both delivery and carryout. Founded in 1960, its roots are in convenient pizza delivery, while a significant amount of its retail sales also come from carryout customers. It is highly recognized global brand, and it is focus on value while serving neighborhoods locally through its large worldwide network of franchise owners and US company-owned stores. Domino's Pizza is primarily a franchisor, with approximately 99% of Domino's stores currently owned and operated by its independent franchisees.

	Annual Growth	12/19*	01/21	01/22	01/23*	12/23
Sales ($mil.)	5.5%	3,618.8	4,117.4	4,357.4	4,537.2	4,479.4
Net income ($ mil.)	6.7%	400.7	491.3	510.5	452.3	519.1
Market value ($ mil.)	9.0%	10,151	13,316	19,597	12,029	14,315
Employees	(3.8%)	13,100	14,400	13,500	11,000	11,200

*Fiscal year change

DOMTAR CORPORATION

234 KINGSLEY PARK DR
FORT MILL, SC 297156468
Phone: 803 802-7500
Fax: –
Web: www.domtar.com

CEO: John D Williams
CFO: Daniel Buron
HR: Angel Huggins
FYE: December 31
Type: Private

Domtar Corp (Domtar) is an integrated manufacturer and marketer of uncoated freesheet papers. It designs, manufactures, markets and distributes a wide range of fine paper products for a variety of consumers including merchants, retail outlets, stationers, printers, publishers, converters, and end-users. It also manufactures paper grade, fluff and specialty pulp. Domtar offers communication papers, specialty and packaging papers, and absorbent hygiene products. Some of its brands are EarthChoice, Lynx, Ariva, Cougar, NovaThin, and Husky. The company generates more than 75% of its total revenue from the US operations.

	Annual Growth	12/17	12/18	12/19	12/20	12/22
Sales ($mil.)	(4.3%)	–	–	5,220.0	3,652.0	4,577.0
Net income ($ mil.)	59.2%	–	–	84.0	(127.0)	339.0
Market value ($ mil.)	–	–	–	–	–	–
Employees	–	–	–	–	–	10,000

DONALDSON CO. INC.

1400 West 94th Street
Minneapolis, MN 55431
Phone: 952 887-3131
Fax: –
Web: www.donaldson.com

NYS: DCI

CEO: Tod E Carpenter
CFO: Scott J Robinson
HR: Rob Santha
FYE: July 31
Type: Public

Donaldson is a global leader in technology-led filtration products and solutions, serving a broad range of industries and advanced markets. The company makes filtration systems designed to remove contaminants from air and liquids. Donaldson's engine products business makes air intake and exhaust systems, liquid-filtration systems, and replacement parts; products are sold to manufacturers of construction, mining, and transportation equipment, as well as parts distributors and fleet operators. The company's industrial products include dust, fume, and mist collectors and air filtration systems used in industrial gas turbines, computer disk drives, and manufacturers' clean rooms. Donaldson operates in more than 40 countries worldwide and has more than 100 technical laboratories. Donaldson generates about 45% of revenue from the US and Canada.

	Annual Growth	07/19	07/20	07/21	07/22	07/23
Sales ($mil.)	4.8%	2,844.9	2,581.8	2,853.9	3,306.6	3,430.8
Net income ($ mil.)	7.6%	267.2	257.0	286.9	332.8	358.8
Market value ($ mil.)	5.9%	6,049.7	5,854.7	8,016.6	6,589.8	7,609.6
Employees	(2.0%)	14,100	12,400	13,100	14,000	13,000

DONEGAL GROUP INC.

1195 River Road, P.O. Box 302
Marietta, PA 17547
Phone: 717 426-1931
Fax: –
Web: www.donegalgroup.com

NMS: DGIC A

CEO: Kevin G Burke
CFO: Jeffrey D Miller
HR: Chuck E Smith
FYE: December 31
Type: Public

Donegal Group is an insurance holding company whose insurance subsidiaries and affiliates offer property and casualty insurance in about 25 Mid-Atlantic, Midwestern, New England, Southern, and Southwestern states. Its insurance subsidiaries and Donegal Mutual provide their policyholders with a selection of insurance products and pursue profitability by adhering to a strict underwriting discipline, and also derives a substantial portion of their insurance business from smaller to mid-sized regional communities. The group's personal insurance offerings range from private passenger automobile and homeowners coverage; its commercial insurance products include business owners, multi-peril, and workers' compensation. Donegal Mutual Insurance controls approximately 70% of the group's voting stock.

	Annual Growth	12/19	12/20	12/21	12/22	12/23
Assets ($mil.)	4.2%	1,923.2	2,160.5	2,255.2	2,243.3	2,266.3
Net income ($ mil.)	(44.7%)	47.2	52.8	25.3	(2.0)	4.4
Market value ($ mil.)	(1.4%)	494.1	469.1	476.4	473.4	466.4
Employees	–	–	879	838	876	872

DONNELLEY FINANCIAL SOLUTIONS INC

35 West Wacker Drive
Chicago, IL 60601
Phone: 800 823-5304
Fax: –
Web: www.dfinsolutions.com

NYS: DFIN

CEO: Daniel N Leib
CFO: David A Gardella
HR: Annemarie Saidane
FYE: December 31
Type: Public

Donnelley Financial Solutions is a leading global risk and compliance solutions company. It provides regulatory filing and deal solutions via its software, technology-enabled services and print distribution to public and private companies, mutual funds and other regulated investment firms. It offers filing agent service, digital document creation, online content management tools, regulatory reporting, virtual data rooms, and more. Investment market customers include alternative investment and insurance investment companies, while language service customers include legal partnerships, life sciences firms, and corporations. Printing company R.R. Donnelley spin-off Donnelley Financial Solutions in 2016. Most of Donnelley Financial Solutions' revenue comes from the US.

	Annual Growth	12/19	12/20	12/21	12/22	12/23
Sales ($mil.)	(2.3%)	874.7	894.5	993.3	833.6	797.2
Net income ($ mil.)	21.6%	37.6	(25.9)	145.9	102.5	82.2
Market value ($ mil.)	56.2%	304.7	493.8	1,371.8	1,124.7	1,815.0
Employees	–	2,900	2,350	2,185	2,150	–

DOORDASH INC

303 2nd Street, South Tower, 8th Floor
San Francisco, CA 94107
Phone: –
Fax: 650 487-3970
Web: www.doordash.com

NMS: DASH

CEO: –
CFO: –
HR: –
FYE: December 31
Type: Public

DoorDash, Inc. is a technology company that connects consumers with their favorite local businesses in more than 25 countries across the globe. It offers on-demand food orders and door-to-door delivery services. The company allows consumers to place customized orders and track status through mobile or web applications. Through its Marketplace, DoorDash offers services such as customer acquisition, insights and analytics, delivery, merchandising, payment processing, and customer support. It allows merchants to operate online and connect them with millions of consumers. Merchants can fulfill these demands through delivery, facilitated by the company's local logistics platform, or in-person pickup by consumers. The company's operations span the US, Canada, Australia, Japan, and Germany. The US generates almost all of the company's revenue.

	Annual Growth	12/19	12/20	12/21	12/22	12/23
Sales ($mil.)	76.7%	885.0	2,886.0	4,888.0	6,583.0	8,635.0
Net income ($ mil.)	–	(667.0)	(461.0)	(468.0)	(1,365.0)	(558.0)
Market value ($ mil.)	–	–	57,561	60,041	19,686	39,875
Employees	55.8%	3,279	3,886	8,600	16,800	19,300

DORCHESTER MINERALS LP

3838 Oak Lawn Avenue, Suite 300
Dallas, TX 75219
Phone: 214 559-0300
Fax: –
Web: www.dmlp.net

NMS: DMLP

CEO: Bradley J Ehrman
CFO: –
HR: –
FYE: December 31
Type: Public

The stakeholders of Dorchester Minerals are enjoying the benefits of three natural resource exploitation enterprises which came together as one. The oil and gas exploration company was formed by the 2003 merger of oil trust Dorchester Hugoton with Republic Royalty and Spinnaker Royalty. Dorchester Minerals' holdings include about 141,600 net acres in Texas and 62,850 net acres in Montana. The company holds assets (producing and nonproducing mineral, royalty, overriding royalty, net profits, and leasehold interests) in properties in 574 counties in 25 states. In 2009 Dorchester Minerals reported proved reserves of 60.3 billion cu. ft. of natural gas and 3.3 million barrels of oil and condensate.

	Annual Growth	12/19	12/20	12/21	12/22	12/23
Sales ($mil.)	20.1%	78.8	46.9	93.4	170.8	163.8
Net income ($ mil.)	21.3%	52.8	21.9	70.2	130.6	114.1
Market value ($ mil.)	13.0%	772.3	431.9	783.3	1,184.7	1,259.9
Employees	–	–	34	24	24	26

DORMAN PRODUCTS INC
NMS: DORM

3400 East Walnut Street
Colmar, PA 18915
Phone: 215 997-1800
Fax: -
Web: www.dormanproducts.com

CEO: -
CFO: -
HR: -
FYE: December 31
Type: Public

Marketing approximately 129,000 unique parts, Dorman Products is one of the leading suppliers of replacement parts and fasteners for passenger cars and light-, medium-, and heavy-duty trucks in the automotive aftermarket industry. About 75% of the company's products are sold under brands that the company owns. Dorman sells to auto aftermarket retailers and warehouse distributors, as well as to parts manufacturers for resale under private labels. The company services more than 9,000 active accounts. Dorman distributes its products primarily in Canada, Mexico, Europe, the Middle East, and Australia. About 95% of the company's total sales come from the US.

	Annual Growth	12/19	12/20	12/21	12/22	12/23
Sales ($mil.)	18.1%	991.3	1,092.7	1,345.2	1,733.7	1,929.8
Net income ($ mil.)	11.5%	83.8	106.9	131.5	121.5	129.3
Market value ($ mil.)	2.7%	2,350.9	2,803.2	3,330.9	2,531.2	2,610.7
Employees	9.0%	2,742	2,681	3,360	3,786	3,872

DORSEY & WHITNEY LLP

50 S 6TH ST STE 1500
MINNEAPOLIS, MN 554021553
Phone: 612 340-2600
Fax: -
Web: www.dorsey.com

CEO: -
CFO: -
HR: Patrick Lutter
FYE: December 31
Type: Private

Dorsey & Whitney is an international law firm founded in 1912. The law firm has grown into a truly global practice operating in about 20 offices across the US, Canada, Europe, and Asia. Traditionally strong in matters of mergers and acquisitions, finance and restructuring, and litigation, the firm is focused on intellectual property, patent, and trademark issues in the international arena. In addition to its expertise in Canadian cross-border transactions, its India practice is supported by a network of Dorsey & Whitney lawyers in Hong Kong, London and North America.

DOSTER CONSTRUCTION COMPANY, INC.

2100 INTERNATIONAL PARK DR
BIRMINGHAM, AL 352434209
Phone: 205 443-3800
Fax: -
Web: www.dosterconstruction.com

CEO: Thomas E Doster III
CFO: -
HR: Susan Camp
FYE: November 30
Type: Private

Doster does what it takes to build its client list. Doster Construction provides construction, design, and project management services for multi-unit residential, health care, educational, and industrial construction projects. It has built distribution centers for Wal-Mart, and Chrysler, apartments in Alabama, and hospitals in Florida (about 50% of its construction is in the health care market). Doster performs most of its work in the southeastern US, although it also takes on projects in other regions. It operates from offices in Birmingham, Alabama, Orlando, Nashville, and Atlanta. Chairman Thomas Doster founded the family-controlled company in 1969, after returning from military service in Vietnam.

DOUGHERTY'S PHARMACY INC

5924 Royal Lane, Suite 250
Dallas, TX 75230
Phone: 972 250-0945
Fax: -
Web: www.ascendantsolutions.com

CEO: Stewart Edington
CFO: -
HR: Leigh Dillard
FYE: December 31
Type: Public

Ascendant Solutions holds stakes in companies involved in health care, retailing, real estate, and other sectors. It seeks out opportunities among corporate divestitures, distressed or bankrupt firms, and entrepreneurs looking to sell their companies. Its investments include Dallas-based specialty pharmacy Dougherty's and CRESA Partners, which provides tenant representation and lease management services. Ascendant Solutions also owns stakes in Ampco Safety Tools and Dallas-area mixed-use real estate development firm Frisco Square. In 2008 Ascendant Solutions sold its stake in the Medicine Man chain of pharmacies to a subsidiary of Medicine Shoppe.

	Annual Growth	12/14	12/15	12/16	12/17	12/18
Sales ($mil.)	6.1%	28.5	41.0	42.8	40.2	36.1
Net income ($ mil.)	-	0.5	(0.4)	(4.9)	(2.1)	(3.5)
Market value ($ mil.)	(50.5%)	6.0	5.2	4.7	3.2	0.4
Employees	-	-	-	-	105	99

DOUGLAS DYNAMICS, INC.
NYS: PLOW

11270 W. Park Place Ste. 300
Milwaukee, WI 53224
Phone: 414 354-2310
Fax: -
Web: www.douglasdynamics.com

CEO: -
CFO: -
HR: -
FYE: December 31
Type: Public

Douglas Dynamics is North America's premier manufacturer and upfitter of commercial work truck attachments and equipment. The company sells its lineup under brand names Western, Fisher, Snowex, Henderson, Turfex, Sweepex, Dejana, Brinextreme, and Blizzard. It also supplies related parts and accessories. End customers are mainly snowplowers in the business of removing snow and ice for commercial and residential areas in the Midwest, East, and Northeast US, as well as throughout Canada. Douglas Seaman creates Douglas Dynamics in 1977, which became the parent company for Western Products.

	Annual Growth	12/19	12/20	12/21	12/22	12/23
Sales ($mil.)	(0.2%)	571.7	480.2	541.5	616.1	568.2
Net income ($ mil.)	(16.7%)	49.2	(86.6)	30.7	38.6	23.7
Market value ($ mil.)	(14.3%)	1,264.1	983.0	897.8	831.1	682.2
Employees	3.0%	1,677	1,767	1,436	1,813	1,885

DOUGLAS EMMETT INC
NYS: DEI

1299 Ocean Avenue, Suite 1000
Santa Monica, CA 90401
Phone: 310 255-7700
Fax: -
Web: www.douglasemmett.com

CEO: Jordan L Kaplan
CFO: Peter D Seymour
HR: -
FYE: December 31
Type: Public

Douglas Emmett, a self-administered and self-managed real estate investment trust (REIT), invests in commercial real estate in Southern California and Hawaii. It owns about 70 Class A office properties (totaling 18.2 million sq. ft.), mostly in the heart of Hollywood and surrounding areas. Its office holdings account for more than 85% of its total revenue. The REIT also owns nearly 4,400 apartment units in tony neighborhoods of West Los Angeles and Honolulu. Douglas Emmett's portfolio includes some of the most notable addresses on the West Coast, including the famed Sherman Oaks Galleria, Burbank's Studio Plaza, and Beverly Hills. California accounts for the highest revenue by location which accounts for nearly 90%.

	Annual Growth	12/19	12/20	12/21	12/22	12/23
Sales ($mil.)	2.2%	936.7	891.5	918.4	993.7	1,020.5
Net income ($ mil.)	-	363.7	50.4	65.3	97.1	(42.7)
Market value ($ mil.)	(24.2%)	7,340.4	4,879.1	5,601.4	2,621.8	2,424.5
Employees	1.3%	713	700	700	750	750

DOVER CORP

NYS: DOV

3005 Highland Parkway
Downers Grove, IL 60515
Phone: 630 541-1540
Fax: –
Web: www.dovercorporation.com

CEO: Richard J Tobin
CFO: Brad M Cerepak
HR: Kimberly K Bors
FYE: December 31
Type: Public

Dover is a diversified global manufacturer and solutions provider delivering innovative equipment and components, consumable supplies, aftermarket parts, software and digital solutions, and support services through five operating segments: Engineered Products, Clean & Energy Fueling, Pumps & Process Solutions, Imaging & Identification and Refrigeration, and Climate & Sustainability Technologies. Dover serves industries such as chemical, hygienic, oil & gas, food and beverages, heating & cooling, and other end markets. It generates over 55% of revenue in the US. Dover traces its historical roots back to 1947.

	Annual Growth	12/19	12/20	12/21	12/22	12/23
Sales ($mil.)	4.3%	7,136.4	6,683.8	7,907.1	8,508.1	8,438.1
Net income ($ mil.)	11.7%	677.9	683.5	1,123.8	1,065.4	1,056.8
Market value ($ mil.)	7.5%	16,124	17,662	25,405	18,943	21,517
Employees	1.0%	24,000	23,000	25,000	25,000	25,000

DOVER MOTORSPORTS, INC.

1131 N DUPONT HWY
DOVER, DE 199012008
Phone: 302 883-6500
Fax: –
Web: www.dovermotorspeedway.com

CEO: Denis McGlynn
CFO: Timothy R Horne
HR: Janie Libby
FYE: December 31
Type: Private

This company makes its money when rubber meets the pavement at its racetrack. Dover Motorsports host more several auto racing events each year at its flagship Dover International Speedway in Delaware. The track hold events sponsored by all the major US racing leagues, including NASCAR, the Indy Racing League, and the National Hot Rod Association, though stock car racing accounts for 80% of sales. Dover Motorsports and Dover Downs Gaming & Entertainment were operating as one company before being separated in a spin-off in 2002. In 2014 the company sold off its Nashville area racetrack.

DOVER SADDLERY, INC.

525 GREAT RD
LITTLETON, MA 014606221
Phone: 978 952-8062
Fax: –
Web: www.doversaddlery.com

CEO: Brad Wolansky
CFO: David R Pearce
HR: –
FYE: December 31
Type: Private

Dover Saddlery is an upscale specialty retailer and direct marketer of equestrian products. The company's specialty is English-style riding gear, and its selection features riding apparel, tack, and stable supplies, as well as horse health care products. Its brand-name products include names such as Ariat, Grand Prix, Mountain Horse, Passier, and Prestige. Dover operates more than 20 retail stores, mostly on the East Coast and in Texas under the Dover Saddlery and Smith Brothers banners (Western-style gear), and it also markets products on its website and in catalogs. The company was founded in 1975 by US Equestrian Team members, including company directors Jim and Dave Powers.

DOW INC

NYS: DOW

2211 H.H. Dow Way
Midland, MI 48674
Phone: 989 636-1000
Fax: –
Web: www.dow.com

CEO: James R Fitterling
CFO: Howard I Ungerleider
HR: Lisa Bryant
FYE: December 31
Type: Public

Dow Inc. (Dow) is a material science company. The company operates its business through its wholly owned subsidiary, The Dow Chemical Co (TDCC). The company's product portfolio is comprised of plastics, performance materials, coatings and silicones and industrial intermediates. The company offers a range of products and solutions for customers in packaging, infrastructure, mobility and consumer care segments. Dow's products find application in various sectors including home and personal care, durable goods, adhesives and sealants, coatings, and food and specialty packaging. North America accounts for more than 35% of the company's total sales.

	Annual Growth	12/19	12/20	12/21	12/22	12/23
Sales ($mil.)	1.0%	42,951	38,542	54,968	56,902	44,622
Net income ($ mil.)	–	(1,359.0)	1,225.0	6,311.0	4,582.0	589.0
Market value ($ mil.)	0.1%	38,437	38,977	39,834	35,389	38,514
Employees	(0.4%)	36,500	35,700	35,700	37,800	35,900

DOWLING COLLEGE

150 IDLE HOUR BLVD
OAKDALE, NY 117691999
Phone: 631 244-3000
Fax: –
Web: www.dowling.edu

CEO: –
CFO: –
HR: –
FYE: June 30
Type: Private

Dowling College is private, but not exclusive. The college offers undergraduate and graduate educational opportunities from campuses in Oakdale, Shirley, and Melville, New York. Dowling enrolls about 6,500 students who can earn bachelors, masters, and doctoral degrees from four schools: Arts and Sciences, the Townsend School of Business, Education, and Aviation. Popular degrees include business administration, psychology, elementary education, and special education. Dowling's Aviation program includes a fleet of aircraft and offers flight simulation and air traffic control courses. Dowling College has a student/faculty ratio of 17:1.

DOYLESTOWN HOSPITAL HEALTH AND WELLNESS CENTER, INC.

595 W STATE ST
DOYLESTOWN, PA 189012597
Phone: 215 345-2200
Fax: –
Web: www.doylestownhealth.org

CEO: –
CFO: Dan Upton
HR: –
FYE: June 30
Type: Private

Doylestown Hospital is owned by the local women's civic organization Village Improvement Association (VIA). Founded in 1923, the hospital serves southeastern Pennsylvania and neighboring areas of New Jersey. With some 245 beds and a medical staff of more than 435 physicians in over 50 specialties, Doylestown Hospital provides a variety of acute and tertiary medical services. Specialties include cardiac surgery, cancer care (as part of the University of Pennsylvania Cancer Network), and orthopedics. Affiliated with the hospital are two Pine Run nursing and assisted-living centers. Doylestown Hospital the flagship facility of the Doylestown Health system.

	Annual Growth	06/18	06/19	06/20	06/21	06/22
Sales ($mil.)	7.5%	–	313.3	310.6	361.3	388.9
Net income ($ mil.)	(21.3%)	–	11.3	(18.3)	34.9	5.5
Market value ($ mil.)	–	–	–	–	–	–
Employees	–	–	–	–	–	2,853

DPL INC.

1065 WOODMAN DR
DAYTON, OH 454321438
Phone: 937 259-7215
Fax: –
Web: www.aes.com

CEO: –
CFO: Gustavo Garavaglia
HR: Jerry Mashburn
FYE: December 31
Type: Private

When it's dark in Dayton, DPL turns on the lights. The AES-owned holding company's main subsidiary, regulated utility Dayton Power and Light (DP&L), brightens the night for more than 513,000 electricity customers in west central Ohio. Nonregulated subsidiary DPL Energy operates DPL's power plants, which produce more than 3,800 MW of primarily coal-fired generating capacity. It also supplied power to energy marketing affiliate DPL Energy Resources (which it sold to IGS Energy in 2016) to meet the electric requirements of its 198,000 retail customers in Illinois and Ohio. Other activities include street lighting and financial support services.

DPR CONSTRUCTION, INC.

1450 VETERANS BLVD
REDWOOD CITY, CA 940632617
Phone: 650 474-1450
Fax: –
Web: www.dpr.com

CEO: –
CFO: Angela Floyd
HR: Alison Andres
FYE: December 31
Type: Private

DPR is one of the nation's leading general contractors and ranks among the top general contractors in the nation. The employee-owned firm provides general contracting and construction management services for the advanced technology/mission-critical life sciences, healthcare, higher education, and corporate office markets. The construction firm specializes in developing retail stores, hospitals, data centers, clean rooms, laboratories, manufacturing facilities, and green buildings. Altogether, DPR Construction boasts approximately 30 regional offices nationwide. Doug Woods, Peter Nosler, and Ron Davidowski founded the firm in 1990.

	Annual Growth	12/97	12/98	12/99	12/00	12/08
Sales ($mil.)	(0.8%)	–	–	–	1,958.1	1,836.1
Net income ($ mil.)	13.0%	–	–	–	25.7	68.5
Market value ($ mil.)	–	–	–	–	–	–
Employees	–	–	–	–	–	8,002

DRAKE UNIVERSITY

2507 UNIVERSITY AVE
DES MOINES, IA 503114505
Phone: 515 271-2011
Fax: –
Web: www.drake.edu

CEO: –
CFO: –
HR: –
FYE: June 30
Type: Private

You won't find duck, duck, goose as part of the curriculum at Drake University. The Des Moines, Iowa, school provides undergraduate and graduate education programs for some 5,500 students through its six colleges and schools: arts and sciences, business and public administration, education, journalism and mass communications, law, and pharmacy and health sciences. It has a 15:1 student-to-faculty ratio. A private school, Drake University was founded in 1881 with seed money from General Francis Marion Drake, a Civil War general and former Iowa governor, banker, railroad builder, and attorney. Drake University also hosts the Drake Relays, one of the largest track and field events in the US.

	Annual Growth	06/17	06/18	06/19	06/20	06/22
Sales ($mil.)	2.4%	–	144.5	150.1	222.3	159.0
Net income ($ mil.)	–	–	9.2	13.8	1.2	(20.2)
Market value ($ mil.)	–	–	–	–	–	–
Employees	–	–	–	–	–	830

DRAPER AND KRAMER, INCORPORATED

55 E MONROE ST STE 3900
CHICAGO, IL 606035701
Phone: 312 346-8600
Fax: –
Web: www.draperandkramer.com

CEO: Forrest D Bailey
CFO: James Hayes
HR: –
FYE: December 31
Type: Private

Draper and Kramer, a family-owned company that has been in business for more than a century, provides a full range of commercial and residential brokerage and financial services across the US and in Chile. The firm offerings include financing and mortgages, transactions, development services, risk management, insurance, property management, and leasing. Draper and Kramer also invests in such high-profile properties as Chicago's Palmolive Building, which it redeveloped into condominium space. Draper and Kramer was founded in 1893.

DRESS FOR SUCCESS WORLDWIDE

1040 AVENUE OF THE AMERICAS
NEW YORK, NY 100186816
Phone: 212 684-3611
Fax: –
Web: www.dressforsuccess.org

CEO: Joi Gordon
CFO: –
HR: –
FYE: December 31
Type: Private

While the clothes don't necessarily make the woman, it never hurts to dress for success. Dress for Success has assisted some 450,000 low-income women worldwide by providing each client with a suit to wear to a job interview and an additional suit after she lands the position. The not-for-profit organization also offers them support in developing their career skills and networking through a membership in the Professional Women's Group. Dress for Success, which relies on donations and volunteer help, operates from offices in about 90 cities. Former executive director Nancy Lublin founded the organization in 1997 with an inheritance from her great-grandfather, Poppy Max, an immigrant from Eastern Europe.

	Annual Growth	12/16	12/17	12/18	12/21	12/22
Sales ($mil.)	(12.0%)	–	22.6	20.5	14.1	12.0
Net income ($ mil.)	13.9%	–	0.2	(0.3)	1.1	0.5
Market value ($ mil.)	–	–	–	–	–	–
Employees	–	–	–	–	–	2

DREW UNIVERSITY

36 MADISON AVE
MADISON, NJ 079401434
Phone: 973 408-3000
Fax: –
Web: www.drew.edu

CEO: Lewis Andrews
CFO: –
HR: Maria Force
FYE: June 30
Type: Private

Drew University draws interest with its seminary. The school is a liberal arts college that offers both graduate school and as many as 30 undergraduate degrees, including master's and Ph.D. studies in religion from the Drew Theological School. It's the home of the Caspersen School of Graduate Studies. The educational institution's campus is located in Madison, New Jersey, on 186 wooded acres in the foothills of northern New Jersey. The school boasts an enrollment of about 2,370 students and has NCAA Division III teams playing as the Drew Rangers. With more than 150 faculty members, of which 98% hold terminal degrees, Drew University boasts a student/faculty ratio of 10:1 and an average class size of 17.

	Annual Growth	06/18	06/19	06/20*	12/21*	06/22
Sales ($mil.)	1.9%	–	73.0	73.2	59.2	77.2
Net income ($ mil.)	–	–	1.3	(30.1)	3.6	(12.5)
Market value ($ mil.)	–	–	–	–	–	–
Employees	–	–	–	–	–	550

*Fiscal year change

DREXEL UNIVERSITY

3141 CHESTNUT ST
PHILADELPHIA, PA 191042875
Phone: 215 895-2000
Fax: –
Web: www.drexel.edu

CEO: –
CFO: Jeff Eberly
HR: Carol Hetman
FYE: June 30
Type: Private

Drexel University is a comprehensive global R1-level research university with a unique model of experiential learning that combines academic rigor with one of the nation's premier cooperative education programs with an enrollment of about 22,345 undergraduate and graduate students and a student-teacher ratio of approximately 10:1. It operates approximately 15 schools and colleges in the US that offer an extensive range of degree program options at both the undergraduate and graduate levels. The Drexel University College of Medicine, one of the country's largest private medical schools, represents the consolidation of two venerable medical schools with rich and intertwined histories: Hahnemann Medical College and Woman's Medical College of Pennsylvania. Founded in 1891, Drexel runs a mandatory co-operative education program that helps students gain real-world experience while supplying local employers with trained workers.

	Annual Growth	06/14	06/15	06/16	06/17	06/22
Sales ($mil.)	6.5%	–	–	–	985.3	1,352.5
Net income ($ mil.)	(7.6%)	–	–	–	34.8	23.5
Market value ($ mil.)	–	–	–	–	–	–
Employees	–	–	–	–	–	2,868

DRIL-QUIP INC

NYS: DRQ

2050 West Sam Houston Parkway S., Suite 1100
Houston, TX 77042
Phone: 713 939-7711
Fax: –
Web: www.dril-quip.com

CEO: Blake T Deberry
CFO: Raj Kumar
HR: –
FYE: December 31
Type: Public

Dril-Quip designs, manufactures, sells and services the global deepwater oil and gas industry. The company specializes in deepwater, harsh-environment, and/or severe-condition equipment. Its products include drilling and production riser systems, subsea and surface wellheads and production trees, subsea control systems and manifolds, mudline hanger systems (which support the weight of each casing string at the mudline), and specialty connectors and pipe. Dril-Quip's offshore rig equipment includes drilling riser systems, wellhead connectors, diverters, safety valves and cement manifolds. The company also provides reconditioning and technical advisory services. The Western Hemisphere accounts the majority of sales with about two-thirds of sales.

	Annual Growth	12/19	12/20	12/21	12/22	12/23
Sales ($mil.)	0.6%	414.8	365.0	322.9	362.1	424.1
Net income ($ mil.)	(23.0%)	1.7	(30.8)	(128.0)	0.4	0.6
Market value ($ mil.)	(16.1%)	1,613.1	1,018.5	676.7	934.3	800.2
Employees	(2.2%)	1,814	1,424	1,342	1,356	1,659

DRINKS AMERICAS HOLDINGS, LTD.

NBB: DKAM

4101 Whiteside Street
Los Angeles, CA 90063
Phone: 323 266-8500
Fax: –
Web: www.drinksamericas.com

CEO: Leonard Moreno
CFO: –
HR: –
FYE: April 30
Type: Public

Image sells for Drinks Americas Holdings. The company markets and distributes alcoholic and nonalcoholic beverages bearing the face and name of such celebrities as Donald Trump (vodka), Willie Nelson (bourbon whiskey), and Paul Newman (fruit juice). It also makes ready-to-drink tea, beer, rum, tequila, and the first US-made ultrapremium sake. Subsidiary Drinks Global Imports offers premium European and Australian wines. Drinks Americas sells via a network of North American distributors for resale to supermarkets, and liquor and convenience stores. Southern Glazer's Wine and Spirits is its largest alcohol distributor. Worldwide Beverage Imports and Drinks America management own 49% and 35%, respectively, of the company.

	Annual Growth	04/09	04/10	04/11	04/12	04/13
Sales ($mil.)	8.9%	2.5	0.9	0.5	4.4	3.5
Net income ($ mil.)	–	(5.0)	(5.6)	(4.6)	(0.8)	(13.1)
Market value ($ mil.)	(32.6%)	4.6	0.4	0.0	31.3	1.0
Employees	31.6%	9	6	8	15	27

DRIVE SHACK INC

NBB: DSHK

10670 N. Central Expressway, Suite 700
Dallas, TX 75231
Phone: 646 585-5591
Fax: –
Web: www.driveshack.com

CEO: Mike Compton
CFO: Michael Nichols
HR: –
FYE: December 31
Type: Public

Drive Shack (formerly Newcastle Investment) owns and operates golf- and leisure-related assets. Its portfolio includes some 80 public, private, and managed golf properties in 13 states. The company is also developing a line of entertainment facilities that combine technology-enhanced golf and dining. Drive Shack is managed by Fortress Investment Group, which also owns a minority stake in the company. Newcastle transformed from a real estate investment trust (REIT) to a C-Corporation in 2017; now named Drive Shack, it still holds a portfolio of real estate securities, primarily Fannie Mae- or Freddie Mac-backed assets. .

	Annual Growth	12/18	12/19	12/20	12/21	12/22
Sales ($mil.)	0.9%	314.4	272.1	220.0	281.9	325.7
Net income ($ mil.)	–	(38.7)	(54.9)	(56.4)	(31.4)	(51.9)
Market value ($ mil.)	(54.5%)	362.1	338.1	219.9	132.1	15.5
Employees	0.9%	3,923	4,658	3,072	3,370	4,068

DRIVETIME AUTOMOTIVE GROUP INC

4020 East Indian School Road
Phoenix, AZ 85018
Phone: 602 852-6600
Fax: –
Web: www.drivetime.com

CEO: Ernest C Garcia II
CFO: Kurt Wood
HR: –
FYE: December 31
Type: Public

In this story the ugly duckling changes into DriveTime Automotive Group. Formerly known as Ugly Duckling, the company is a used-car dealership chain that primarily targets low-income customers and those with less-than-stellar credit. To cater to subprime clients, it's a "buy here-pay here" dealer, meaning it finances and services car loans, rather than using outside lenders. DriveTime operates more than 125 dealerships in 50 US metropolitan areas in 24 mostly southern and western states. The company provides customers with a comprehensive end-to-end solution for their automotive needs, including the sale, financing, and maintenance of their vehicle.

	Annual Growth	12/09	12/10	12/11	12/12	12/13
Sales ($mil.)	10.3%	946.3	1,025.7	1,121.3	1,222.9	1,400.9
Net income ($ mil.)	7.3%	186.1	221.0	216.9	237.7	247.1
Market value ($ mil.)	–	–	–	–	–	–
Employees	–	–	–	2,410	2,530	3,165

DROPBOX INC

NMS: DBX

1800 Owens Street
San Francisco, CA 94158
Phone: 415 857-6800
Fax: –
Web: www.dropbox.com

CEO: Andrew W Houston
CFO: Timothy Regan
HR: Monica Showrank
FYE: December 31
Type: Public

Dropbox is primarily known for offering a space for users to store documents in the cloud. However, the company also offers a variety of collaboration, creation, access and organization, sharing, and security. Dropbox has about 17 million are the paying subscribers. Basic storage services are offered for free; revenue comes from monthly or annual subscription plans, mainly purchased through the Dropbox app or website, offering collaboration tools and other services. Around half of the company's revenue comes from the US.

	Annual Growth	12/19	12/20	12/21	12/22	12/23
Sales ($mil.)	10.8%	1,661.3	1,913.9	2,157.9	2,324.9	2,501.6
Net income ($ mil.)	–	(52.7)	(256.3)	335.8	553.2	453.6
Market value ($ mil.)	13.3%	6,030.3	7,471.4	8,262.6	7,535.3	9,925.9
Employees	(1.0%)	2,801	2,760	2,667	3,118	2,693

DRX, LTD.

455 E REED ST
BRAIDWOOD, IL 604082090
Phone: 815 458-6104
Fax: –
Web: www.docsdrugs.com

CEO: –
CFO: –
HR: –
FYE: October 31
Type: Private

After visiting the doc, customers in northeastern Illinois can fill their prescriptions at Doc's Drugs. The regional drugstore chain operates more than 15 pharmacies under the Doc's Discount Drugs banner. In addition to dispensing prescription medications, Doc's Drugs sells medical equipment, collectibles, electronics, and toys, as well as offering in-store photo processing. Doc's Drugs also sells more than 100 products online. The company is remodeling many of its stores to focus on its pharmacy operation, which accounts for 80% of sales. To that end, it is eliminating hardware, liquor, and groceries from its shelves. Doc's Drugs was founded by Dave Sartoris, who runs the company with his son Tony.

	Annual Growth	10/10	10/11	10/12	10/13	10/14
Sales ($mil.)	4.6%	–	–	60.1	60.8	65.7
Net income ($ mil.)	49.2%	–	–	0.3	0.8	0.8
Market value ($ mil.)	–	–	–	–	–	–
Employees	–	–	–	–	–	210

DSS INC

275 Wiregrass Pkwy
Henrietta, NY 14586
Phone: 585 325-3610
Fax: –
Web: www.dsssecure.com

ASE: DSS
CEO: Frank D Heuszel
CFO: Todd D Macko
HR: –
FYE: December 31
Type: Public

Document Security Systems (DSS) caters to those who are insecure about their security, particularly on paper. The company develops anti-counterfeiting products. Its offerings include technology that prevents documents from being accurately scanned or copied and authentication coding that can be used in conjunction with a handheld reader to verify that a document is genuine. DSS also sells paper that displays words such as "void" or "unauthorized copy" if it goes through a copier, fax machine, or scanner. Customers include corporations, governments, and financial institutions. DSS is slated to merge with Lexington Technology Group (LTG) in 2013.

	Annual Growth	12/19	12/20	12/21	12/22	12/23
Sales ($mil.)	11.7%	19.4	17.4	20.3	47.3	30.3
Net income ($ mil.)	–	(2.9)	1.9	(31.0)	(59.8)	(80.6)
Market value ($ mil.)	(20.5%)	2.1	44.1	4.7	1.2	0.8
Employees	(1.3%)	100	93	113	119	95

DST SYSTEMS, INC.

333 W 11TH ST FL 5
KANSAS CITY, MO 641051628
Phone: 816 654-6067
Fax: –
Web: www.ssctech.com

CEO: William C Stone
CFO: Patrick J Pedonti
HR: Joy McCune
FYE: December 31
Type: Private

Financial firms and health institutions focus on making clients wealthy and healthy, respectively. So, they might be wise to turn to DST Systems to handle their information processing tasks. The company provides information processing software and services to the mutual fund, insurance, retirement, and healthcare industries. The company's financial services segment offers software and systems used to handle a wide range of tasks including shareowner recordkeeping, investment management, and business process management. Among the healthcare offerings are claims adjudication and benefit and care management. DST makes most of its sales to customers in the US. The company was acquired by SS&C Technologies Holdings in 2018.

	Annual Growth	12/13	12/14	12/15	12/16	12/17
Sales ($mil.)	(6.9%)	–	2,749.3	2,825.1	1,556.7	2,218.2
Net income ($ mil.)	(8.7%)	–	593.3	358.1	426.4	452.1
Market value ($ mil.)	–	–	–	–	–	–
Employees	–	–	–	–	–	15,700

DTE ELECTRIC COMPANY

One Energy Plaza
Detroit, MI 48226-1279
Phone: 313 235-4000
Fax: –
Web: www.dteenergy.com

CEO: –
CFO: Peter B Oleksiak
HR: –
FYE: December 31
Type: Public

Ford Motors is not the only powerhouse operating in Detroit -- DTE Electric is another. The utility (formerly known as Detroit Edison) generates and distributes electricity to 2.2 million customers in Michigan, mainly around Detroit with expansion north to Lake Huron and east to Ann Arbor. The company, a unit of regional power player DTE Energy, has more than 11,000 MW of generating capacity from its interests in primarily fossil-fueled, nuclear, and hydroelectric power plants. It operates more than 46,000 circuit miles of distribution lines and owns and operates more than 670 distribution substations.

	Annual Growth	12/19	12/20	12/21	12/22	12/23
Sales ($mil.)	2.7%	5,224.0	5,506.0	5,809.0	6,397.0	5,804.0
Net income ($ mil.)	1.9%	716.0	778.0	866.0	955.0	772.0
Market value ($ mil.)	–	–	–	–	–	–
Employees	(2.4%)	4,900	10,600	4,700	4,600	4,450

DTE ENERGY CO

One Energy Plaza
Detroit, MI 48226-1279
Phone: 313 235-4000
Fax: –
Web: www.dteenergy.com

NYS: DTE
CEO: Gerardo Norcia
CFO: David Ruud
HR: Heidi Daniels
FYE: December 31
Type: Public

DTE Energy is a diversified energy company involved in the development and management of energy-related businesses and services nationwide. DTE Energy is the parent company of DTE Electric and DTE Gas, regulated electric and natural gas utilities engaged primarily in the business of providing electricity and natural gas sales, distribution, and storage services. DTE Electric, distributes electricity to some 2.3 million customers in southeastern Michigan. The company's DTE Gas unit distributes natural gas to 1.3 million customers throughout Michigan. The DTE portfolio also includes non-utility businesses focused on industrial energy services, renewable natural gas, energy marketing, and trading that relates to DTE Vantage and Energy Trading segments.

	Annual Growth	12/19	12/20	12/21	12/22	12/23
Sales ($mil.)	0.1%	12,669	12,177	14,964	19,228	12,745
Net income ($ mil.)	4.6%	1,169.0	1,368.0	907.0	1,083.0	1,397.0
Market value ($ mil.)	(4.0%)	26,800	25,054	24,668	24,253	22,753
Employees	(1.8%)	10,700	10,600	10,300	10,250	9,950

DTS, INC.

5220 LAS VIRGENES RD
CALABASAS, CA 913021064
Phone: 818 436-1000
Fax: –
Web: www.dts.com

CEO: Jon E Kirchner
CFO: Melvin L Flanigan
HR: Christina Fernandez
FYE: December 31
Type: Private

DTS (formerly Digital Theater Systems) surrounds movie lovers with sound. The company is pioneering audio solutions for mobile devices, cinema, and home theater systems. DTS has licensing agreements with major consumer electronics manufacturers (Sony, Samsung, and Philips). It also provides DTS-encoded soundtracks in movies, TV shows, and music content. Since 1993, DTS has been dedicated to making the world sound better. It provides incredibly high-quality, immersive and engaging audio experiences to listeners everywhere. It was acquired by Tessera Technologies in late 2016.

DUCKS UNLIMITED, INC.

1 WATERFOWL WAY
MEMPHIS, TN 381202351
Phone: 901 758-3825
Fax: –
Web: www.ducks.org

CEO: Dale Hall
CFO: Randy L Graves
HR: –
FYE: June 30
Type: Private

If it walks like a duck and talks like a duck ... Ducks Unlimited wants to protect its habitat. The not-for-profit group works to conserve, manage, and restore wetlands and other waterfowl habitat through projects across North America and in more than 10 South American countries. With some 13 million acres under its care, DU's efforts are aimed at ducks but also benefit more than 900 other wildlife species. Most of the organization's members and volunteers are sport hunters, and DU puts out a magazine, cable TV show, and daily radio show for them. It also offers training in hunter ethics, firearm safety, and conservation and programs for children. DU was founded in 1937 and has more than 691,000 members.

	Annual Growth	06/13	06/14	06/15	06/20	06/22
Sales ($mil.)	8.4%	–	178.4	209.6	185.4	339.5
Net income ($ mil.)	39.6%	–	5.7	23.3	(24.3)	82.9
Market value ($ mil.)	–	–	–	–	–	–
Employees	–	–	–	–	–	500

DUCOMMUN INC. NYS: DCO

200 Sandpointe Avenue, Suite 700
Santa Ana, CA 92707-5759
Phone: 657 335-3665
Fax: –
Web: www.ducommun.com

CEO: Stephen G Oswald
CFO: Christopher D Wampler
HR: Jennifer Essex
FYE: December 31
Type: Public

Ducommun is a leading global provider of engineering and manufacturing services for high-performance products and high-cost-of-failure applications used primarily in the aerospace and defense (A&D), industrial, medical, and other industries (collectively, Industrial). Structural Systems designs, engineers, and manufactures various sizes of complex contoured aerostructure components and assemblies and supplies composite and metal bonded structures and assemblies, primarily used on commercial aircraft, military fixed-wing aircraft, and military and commercial rotary-wing aircraft. Electronic Systems products include sophisticated radar enclosures, aircraft avionics racks, shipboard communications, and control enclosures, printed circuit board assemblies, cable assemblies, wire harnesses and interconnect systems, lightning diversion strips, surge suppressors, conformal shields, and other high-level complex assemblies.

	Annual Growth	12/19	12/20	12/21	12/22	12/23
Sales ($mil.)	1.2%	721.1	628.9	645.4	712.5	757.0
Net income ($ mil.)	(16.3%)	32.5	29.2	135.5	28.8	15.9
Market value ($ mil.)	0.7%	737.8	784.1	682.9	729.5	760.1
Employees	(5.2%)	2,800	2,450	2,480	2,465	2,265

DUKE ENERGY CAROLINAS LLC

526 South Church Street
Charlotte, NC 28202-1803
Phone: 704 382-3853
Fax: –
Web: www.duke-energy.com

CEO: Lynn J Good
CFO: Steven K Young
HR: –
FYE: December 31
Type: Public

Duke Energy Carolinas is a regulated public utility primarily engaged in the generation, transmission, distribution and sale of electricity in portions of North Carolina and South Carolina. The company provides electricity services to about 2.8 million residential, commercial and industrial customers. Operating in a 24,000-square mile service territory, Duke Energy Carolinas has a net generating capacity of about 19,490 MW from interests in fossil-fueled, nuclear, renewables, and hydroelectric power plants. Duke Energy Carolinas is a subsidiary of Duke Energy.

	Annual Growth	12/18	12/19	12/20	12/21	12/22
Sales ($mil.)	1.9%	7,300.0	7,395.0	7,015.0	7,102.0	7,857.0
Net income ($ mil.)	10.6%	1,071.0	1,403.0	956.0	1,336.0	1,600.0
Market value ($ mil.)	–	–	–	–	–	–
Employees	–	–	–	–	–	–

DUKE ENERGY CORP NYS: DUK

526 South Church Street
Charlotte, NC 28202-1803
Phone: 704 382-3853
Fax: –
Web: www.duke-energy.com

CEO: Lynn J Good
CFO: Brian D Savoy
HR: –
FYE: December 31
Type: Public

Duke Energy is one of the top electric power holding companies in the US, serving about 8.2 million retail customers in North Carolina, South Carolina, Florida, Indiana, Ohio and Kentucky, and collectively own 50,000 megawatts of energy capacity. Its natural gas unit serves 1.6 million customers in North Carolina, South Carolina, Tennessee, Ohio and Kentucky.

	Annual Growth	12/19	12/20	12/21	12/22	12/23
Sales ($mil.)	3.8%	25,079	23,868	25,097	28,768	29,060
Net income ($ mil.)	(6.7%)	3,748.0	1,377.0	3,908.0	2,550.0	2,841.0
Market value ($ mil.)	1.6%	70,323	70,593	80,878	79,405	74,818
Employees	(1.6%)	28,793	27,535	27,605	27,859	27,037

DUKE ENERGY FLORIDA LLC

299 First Avenue North
St. Petersburg, FL 33701
Phone: 704 382-3853
Fax: –
Web: www.duke-energy.com

CEO: Lynn J Good
CFO: Steven K Young
HR: –
FYE: December 31
Type: Public

Sometimes the sunshine state just isn't bright enough, and that's when Florida Power (doing business as Progress Energy Florida) really shines. The utility transmits and distributes electricity to 1.6 million customers and oversees 10,025 MW of generating capacity from interests in 14 nuclear and coal-, oil-, and gas-fired power plants. Additionally, Florida Power purchases about 20% of the energy it provides. Florida Power operates 5,100 miles of transmission lines and 52,000 miles of overhead and 18,700 miles of underground distribution cable. It also has 500 electric substations. A subsidiary of holding company Duke Energy, the company also sells wholesale power to other utilities and marketers.

	Annual Growth	12/18	12/19	12/20	12/21	12/22
Sales ($mil.)	6.1%	5,021.0	5,231.0	5,188.0	5,259.0	6,353.0
Net income ($ mil.)	13.2%	554.0	692.0	771.0	738.0	909.0
Market value ($ mil.)	–	–	–	–	–	–
Employees	–	–	–	–	–	–

DUKE ENERGY INDIANA, INC.

1000 East Main Street
Plainfield, IN 46168
Phone: 704 382-3853
Fax: –
Web: www.duke-energy.com

CEO: Lynn J Good
CFO: Steven K Young
HR: –
FYE: December 31
Type: Public

Duke Energy Indiana helps to light up the Hoosier state. Indiana's largest utility, Duke Energy subsidiary Duke Energy Indiana transmits and distributes electricity to 69 of the state's 92 counties (approximately 790,000 customers). The utility also owns power plants (about 7,000 MW of primarily fossil-fueled capacity), which are operated by its parent's merchant energy division. Duke Energy Indiana's service area covers about 22,000 sq. miles with an estimated population of 2.4 million. The company operates about 31,000 miles of distribution lines and a 5,400-mile transmission system.

	Annual Growth	12/19	12/20	12/21	12/22	12/23
Sales ($mil.)	3.1%	3,004.0	2,795.0	3,174.0	3,922.0	3,399.0
Net income ($ mil.)	3.3%	436.0	408.0	481.0	137.0	497.0
Market value ($ mil.)	–	–	–	–	–	–
Employees	–	–	–	–	–	–

DUKE ENERGY OF KENTUCKY

125 East Fourth Street
Cincinnati, OH 45202
Phone: 513 421-9500
Fax: –
Web: –

CEO: James Rogers
CFO: –
HR: –
FYE: December 31
Type: Public

Duke Energy Kentucky (formerly Union Light, Heat and Power) helps to keep the citizens of the Bluegrass state in the light. The company, organized in 1901, provides electricity and gas to more than 134,000 industrial, commercial and residential customers across northern Kentucky. Duke Energy Kentucky, a direct subsidiary of Duke Energy Ohio, gets its fuel supply from a mix of nuclear, coal-fired, hydroelectric and combustion-turbine generation. Duke Energy acquired Union Light, Heat and Power's parent Cinergy in 2006, and subsequently merged it with Ohio power operations.

	Annual Growth	12/09	12/10	12/11	12/12	12/13
Sales ($mil.)	(0.6%)	462.1	488.1	456.1	431.0	451.5
Net income ($ mil.)	12.6%	28.1	43.3	24.3	28.2	45.1
Market value ($ mil.)	–	–	–	–	–	–
Employees		–	–	–	–	–

DUKE ENERGY OHIO, INC.

139 E 4TH ST
CINCINNATI, OH 452024034
Phone: 704 382-3853
Fax: –
Web: datacache.duke-energy.com

CEO: Lynn J Good
CFO: Steven K Young
HR: –
FYE: December 31
Type: Private

Duke Energy Ohio (formerly Cincinnati Gas & Electric) distributes electricity and natural gas in Cincinnati and surrounding areas, including portions of Indiana and Kentucky (through subsidiary Duke Energy Kentucky). The subsidiary of energy holding company Duke Energy has 830,000 transmission and distrtibution power customers and 500,000 gas customers. Duke Energy Ohio serves residential, commercial, and industrial customers over approximately 19,800 miles of distribution lines and a 2,500-mile transmission system in Indiana, Ohio, and Kentucky. The company's Commercial Power's assets are comprised of 6,835 MW of power generation primarily located in the Midwest. The unit sells wholesale power.

DUKE ENERGY PROGRESS, LLC

410 S WILMINGTON ST
RALEIGH, NC 276011849
Phone: 704 382-3853
Fax: –
Web: datacache.duke-energy.com

CEO: Lynn J Good
CFO: Steven K Young
HR: –
FYE: December 31
Type: Private

The Palmetto state and Tarheels both have Duke Energy Progress on their minds when they need some power. The company, which operates as Progress Energy Carolinas, transmits and distributes electricity to some 1.5 million homes and businesses in the Carolinas. The utility generates almost 12,600 MW of capacity from its fossil-fueled, nuclear, and hydroelectric power plants. Progress Energy Carolinas purchases about 5% of the power it distributes. The Duke Energy subsidiary also sells power to wholesale customers, primarily other utilities and energy marketers, including North Carolina Eastern Municipal Power Agency and North Carolina Electric Membership Corporation.

DUKE REALTY L.P.

8711 River Crossing Boulevard
Indianapolis, IN 46240
Phone: 317 808-6000
Fax: –
Web: www.dukerealty.com

CEO: James B Connor
CFO: –
HR: –
FYE: December 31
Type: Public

Duke Realty is a self-managed and self-administered real estate investment trust (REIT). It owns and develops industrial properties, primarily in major cities that are key logistics markets. In addition to about 550 properties totaling more than 162.7 million sq. ft. of rentable space, the company owns some 431 acres of land and control an additional 925 acres through purchase options. The REIT leases its properties to a variety of tenants including e-commerce, manufacturing, retail, wholesale, and distribution firms. Duke's service operations include construction and development, asset and property management, and leasing. The company was founded in 1972.

	Annual Growth	12/17	12/18	12/19	12/20	12/21
Sales ($mil.)	9.1%	780.9	947.9	973.8	993.2	1,105.9
Net income ($ mil.)	(15.0%)	1,649.6	387.3	432.7	302.6	861.2
Market value ($ mil.)	–	–	–	–	–	–
Employees	(4.0%)	400	400	400	350	340

DUKE REALTY LLC

8711 RIVER CROSSING BLVD
INDIANAPOLIS, IN 462402177
Phone: 317 808-6000
Fax: –
Web: www.prologis.com

CEO: James B Connor
CFO: –
HR: –
FYE: December 31
Type: Private

Duke Realty is a self-managed and self-administered real estate investment trust (REIT). It owns and develops industrial properties, primarily in major cities that are key logistics markets. In addition to about 550 properties totaling more than 162.7 million sq. ft. of rentable space, the company owns some 431 acres of land and control an additional 925 acres through purchase options. The REIT leases its properties to a variety of tenants including e-commerce, manufacturing, retail, wholesale, and distribution firms. Duke's service operations include construction and development, asset and property management, and leasing. The company was founded in 1972.

DUKE UNIVERSITY

324 BLACKWELL ST STE 800
DURHAM, NC 277013658
Phone: 919 684-8111
Fax: –
Web: www.duke.edu

CEO: –
CFO: Kenneth Morris
HR: Kathy Sparrow
FYE: June 30
Type: Private

Duke University, a North Carolina nonprofit corporation, is a private, coeducational institution located primarily in Durham, North Carolina, which owns and operates educational and research facilities (the University). Duke University Health System, Inc. (DUHS), a North Carolina nonprofit corporation, is a controlled affiliate of the University. The University's programs include undergraduate and graduate programs in Arts and Sciences, Engineering, Nursing, and Public Policy, and professional schools in Business, Divinity, Environment, Law, Medicine, and Nursing, as well as programs in Allied Health. The University has about 6,545 undergraduate students and more than 10,610 graduate and professional students. Duke University was created in 1924 by James Buchanan Duke as a memorial to his father, Washington Duke.

	Annual Growth	06/02	06/03	06/04	06/05	06/12
Sales ($mil.)	6.4%	–	–	2,806.8	1,832.9	4,611.9
Net income ($ mil.)		–	–	679.7	246.9	(508.0)
Market value ($ mil.)		–	–	–	–	–
Employees		–	–	–	–	8,852

DUKE UNIVERSITY HEALTH SYSTEM, INC.

2301 ERWIN RD
DURHAM, NC 277054699
Phone: 919 684-8111
Fax: –
Web: www.dukehealth.org

CEO: –
CFO: –
HR: Stephen Smith
FYE: June 30
Type: Private

Duke University Health System is a world-class hospital and health care network supported by outstanding and renowned clinical faculty, nurses and care teams. In addition to its hospitals, Duke Health has an extensive, geographically dispersed network of outpatient facilities that include primary care offices, urgent care centers, multi-specialty clinics and outpatient surgery centers. Its Duke Health & Well-Being includes a medically-based weight loss program, medically-based fitness, wellness and rehabilitation programs at the Duke Health & Fitness Center and Duke Integrative Medicine, which combines evidence-based treatment with proven complementary therapies.

	Annual Growth	06/18	06/19	06/20	06/21	06/22
Sales ($mil.)	5.3%	–	3,836.8	3,951.5	4,269.5	4,483.0
Net income ($ mil.)	(8.4%)	–	160.5	(296.6)	2,195.0	123.3
Market value ($ mil.)	–	–	–	–	–	–
Employees	–	–	–	–	–	2,400

DUN & BRADSTREET HOLDINGS INC   NYS: DNB

5335 Gate Parkway
Jacksonville, FL 32256
Phone: 904 648-6350
Fax: –
Web: www.dnb.com

CEO: Anthony M Jabbour
CFO: Bryan T Hipsher
HR: –
FYE: December 31
Type: Public

Dun & Bradstreet Holdings is primarily engaged in providing mercantile and consumer credit reporting services. Through its operating company The Dun & Bradstreet Corporation, the company helps companies around the world improve their business performance by transforming data into valuable business insights which are the foundation of its global solutions that clients rely on to make mission critical business decisions.

	Annual Growth	12/19	12/20	12/21	12/22	12/23
Sales ($mil.)	13.1%	1,413.9	1,738.1	2,165.6	2,224.6	2,314.0
Net income ($ mil.)	–	(674.0)	(175.6)	(71.7)	(2.3)	(47.0)
Market value ($ mil.)	–	–	10,927	8,992.0	5,380.3	5,134.5
Employees	12.3%	4,037	4,039	6,296	6,355	6,414

DUNCAN-WILLIAMS, INC.

6750 POPLAR AVE STE 300
MEMPHIS, TN 381387433
Phone: 901 260-6800
Fax: –
Web: www.southstateduncanwilliams.com

CEO: –
CFO: Frank Reid
HR: –
FYE: December 31
Type: Private

Duncan-Williams raises its capital by helping others raise theirs. An investment banking firm, Duncan-Williams offers research, sales, and trading of fixed income securities (bonds) and equities (stock) to individual and institutional investors, including banks, credit unions, corporations, and public entities (e.g. municipalities, housing authorities, school districts). Other services include underwriting, financial analysis, bond structuring for public entities, and equity capital market research of emerging growth companies in the health care and financial technology sectors. Founded in 1969 by the late A. Duncan Williams, the firm operates 16 offices across the eastern US and in Texas and California.

	Annual Growth	12/12	12/13	12/14	12/15	12/17
Sales ($mil.)	(7.5%)	–	36.5	30.1	33.5	26.7
Net income ($ mil.)	–	–	(3.8)	(1.0)	0.9	0.3
Market value ($ mil.)	–	–	–	–	–	–
Employees	–	–	–	–	–	85

DUNHAM & ASSOCIATES INVESTMENT COUNSEL, INC.

6256 GREENWICH DR STE 550
SAN DIEGO, CA 921225978
Phone: 858 964-0500
Fax: –
Web: www.dunham.com

CEO: Jeffrey A Dunham
CFO: Denise S Iverson
HR: Pamela Nichols
FYE: December 31
Type: Private

Dunham & Associates Investment Counsel administers about a dozen mutual funds that range in styles from a low-risk government and corporate bond fund to an emerging markets stock fund. Unlike most funds that charge investors flat fees, the company charges fees based upon the funds' performance (called fulcrum fees). Dunham & Associates also manages retirement plans; its Dunham Trust Company affiliate offers asset administration and other trust services. Clients include wealthy individuals and institutional investors. President and CEO Jeffrey Dunham founded Dunham & Associates in 1985.

	Annual Growth	12/99	12/00	12/01	12/08	12/11
Assets ($mil.)	8.0%	–	1.8	1.6	4.0	4.2
Net income ($ mil.)	11.4%	–	0.2	(0.5)	(0.3)	0.7
Market value ($ mil.)	–	–	–	–	–	–
Employees	–	–	–	–	–	40

DUNKIN' BRANDS GROUP, INC.

130 ROYALL ST
CANTON, MA 020211010
Phone: 781 737-3000
Fax: –
Web: www.dunkinbrands.com

CEO: –
CFO: –
HR: –
FYE: December 28
Type: Private

Dunkin' Brands Group is a leading quick service restaurant franchisor, operating both the Dunkin' and Baskin-Robbins chains with more than 21,000 locations in more than 60 countries. Dunkin' is the world's leading donut chain, boasting more than 13,000 units in about 40 countries (some 9,630 in US). Baskin-Robbins is a top ice cream and frozen snacks outlet with more than 8,100 locations in about 50 countries (more than 2,500 In US). Having divested all its company-operated restaurants, Dunkin' Brands counts royalty income and franchise fees as a key revenue source. The company ropped the "Donuts" from its name in 2019. It was founded in 1950. US operations accounts for about half of the company's revenue.

DUO-GARD INDUSTRIES, INC.

40442 KOPPERNICK RD
CANTON, MI 481874279
Phone: 734 207-9700
Fax: –
Web: www.duo-gard.com

CEO: Albert S Miller
CFO: –
HR: –
FYE: February 28
Type: Private

Duo-Gard Industries makes daylighting systems for windows, skylights, walls, and canopies. The company also makes modular shelters such as transit and bike shelters, kiosks, and toll booths. Duo-Gard integrates translucent, insulated polycarbonate panels with structural frames to create lighted structures that save energy. Its illumaWALL system uses programmable LEDs to add light to interior and exterior walls, ceilings, and custom signs. Duo-Gard offers in-house design, fabrication, and installation services for new construction and renovation of all types of facilities. Founded in 1984, the family-owned company works with architects, engineers, contractors, interior designers, and building owners.

	Annual Growth	02/14	02/15	02/17	02/18	02/19
Sales ($mil.)	(1.2%)	–	12.1	11.9	9.9	11.6
Net income ($ mil.)	(16.1%)	–	0.3	0.2	(0.6)	0.1
Market value ($ mil.)	–	–	–	–	–	–
Employees	–	–	–	–	–	68

DUPONT DE NEMOURS INC   NYS: DD

974 Centre Road, Building 730   CEO: Edward D Breen
Wilmington, DE 19805   CFO: Lori D Koch
Phone: 302 295-5783   HR: –
Fax: –   FYE: December 31
Web: www.investors.dupont.com   Type: Public

DuPont is a global innovation leader with technology-based materials and solutions that help transform industries and everyday life by applying diverse science and expertise to help customers advance their best ideas and deliver essential innovations in key markets including electronics, transportation, building and construction, healthcare and worker safety. The company has subsidiaries in about 60 countries worldwide and manufacturing operations in about 25 countries. The majority of the company's revenue comes from outside of the US.

	Annual Growth	12/19	12/20	12/21	12/22	12/23
Sales ($mil.)	(13.5%)	21,512	20,397	16,653	13,017	12,068
Net income ($ mil.)	(4.0%)	498.0	(2,951.0)	6,467.0	5,868.0	423.0
Market value ($ mil.)	4.6%	27,613	30,585	34,744	29,518	33,088
Employees	(9.0%)	35,000	34,000	28,000	23,000	24,000

DUPONT FABROS TECHNOLOGY, INC.

4 EMBARCADERO CTR # 3200   CEO: –
SAN FRANCISCO, CA 941114106   CFO: –
Phone: 202 728-0044   HR: –
Fax: –   FYE: December 31
Web: –   Type: Private

Digital Realty Trust's server farms corral a lot of data. The company owns, develops, operates, and manages about 225 data centers (including about 40 data centers held as investments in unconsolidated joint ventures), of which more than 145 are located in the United States, about 40 are located in Europe, nearly 20 are located in Latin America, some 10 are located in Asia, about 5 are located in Australia and less than 5 are located in Canada. Digital Realty Trust is exempt from paying federal income tax as long as it makes quarterly distributions to shareholders.

DUQUESNE LIGHT CO   NBB: DQUE N

411 Seventh Avenue   CEO: Kevin Walker
Pittsburgh, PA 15219   CFO: Mark E Kaplan
Phone: 412 393-6000   HR: Todd Faulk
Fax: 412 393-6517   FYE: December 31
Web: –   Type: Public

Duquesne Light is the first and last resort for light for many residential customers in the Keystone State. The utility company provides electricity to more than 588,000 customers (90% of which are residential) in southwestern Pennsylvania via an extensive transmission and distribution system. The utility, a subsidiary of Duquesne Light Holdings (formerly DQE) acts as a generation Provider of Last Resort (POLR) for customers who do not choose an alternative supplier. A consortium led by Macquarie Infrastructure Partners controls the company's parent.

	Annual Growth	12/02	12/03	12/04	12/05	12/06
Sales ($mil.)	(6.5%)	944.6	806.1	789.3	792.4	723.2
Net income ($ mil.)	(51.1%)	75.4	69.6	67.8	73.0	4.3
Market value ($ mil.)	–	–	–	0.0	0.0	0.0
Employees	3.7%	1,297	1,310	1,339	1,400	1,500

DUQUESNE LIGHT HOLDINGS, INC.

411 7TH AVE STE 3   CEO: Kevin Walker
PITTSBURGH, PA 152191905   CFO: –
Phone: 412 393-6000   HR: –
Fax: –   FYE: December 31
Web: www.duquesnelight.com   Type: Private

Venerable Duquesne Light Holdings spreads light to the people of the Keystone State. Its principal subsidiary, regulated utility Duquesne Light, distributes electricity to more than 588,000 customers in southwestern Pennsylvania. The utility serves as a generation Provider of Last Resort (POLR) for customers who do not choose an alternative supplier. Faced with declining margins due to unrecovered POLR payments to PJM Interconnection generators, Duquesne Light has a POLR plan to yield more reliable returns. Changes in Pennsylvania law regarding POLR costs and surcharges allowed Duquesne Light more certainty in terms of payments. The company is controlled by DQE Holdings, LLC.

DUQUESNE UNIVERSITY OF THE HOLY SPIRIT

600 FORBES AVE   CEO: –
PITTSBURGH, PA 152193016   CFO: –
Phone: 412 396-6000   HR: –
Fax: –   FYE: June 30
Web: www.duq.edu   Type: Private

Duquesne University of The Holy Spirit is the only Spiritan institution of higher education in the US. The Catholic university offers 80 undergraduate degree programs, and 90 master's, doctoral, and professional programs at about 10 schools, including ones devoted to business, education, law, liberal arts, health sciences, and music. Duquesne also offers more than 20 online programs. The college has an annual enrollment of more than 8,300 undergraduate, graduate, and professional students, and a student-faculty ratio of 14:1. Duquesne was founded in 1878 as the Pittsburgh Catholic College.

	Annual Growth	06/14	06/15	06/20	06/21	06/22
Sales ($mil.)	(3.2%)	–	400.4	434.2	296.0	319.6
Net income ($ mil.)	–	–	25.6	12.1	158.7	(40.0)
Market value ($ mil.)	–	–	–	–	–	–
Employees	–	–	–	–	–	3,601

DURA AUTOMOTIVE SYSTEMS INC

2791 Research Drive   CEO: –
Rochester Hills, MI 48309   CFO: –
Phone: 248 299-7500   HR: –
Fax: 248 299-7501   FYE: December 31
Web: www.duraauto.com   Type: Public

You wouldn't be able to keep the pedal to the metal without DURA Automotive Systems' driver control systems. The company is a leading supplier of pedal systems, parking brake mechanisms, manual and automatic transmission gear shifter systems, and auto cables. DURA also designs and makes engineered assemblies such as latches and seating adjustment controls, as well as structural door modules and exterior trim. The company sells to auto OEMs and many suppliers in the Americas, Europe, and Asia. In 2019, DURA's US operations filed Chapter 11.

	Annual Growth	12/03	12/04	12/05	12/06	12/07
Sales ($mil.)	(5.5%)	2,380.8	2,492.5	2,344.1	2,090.8	1,894.7
Net income ($ mil.)	–	22.3	11.7	1.8	(910.7)	(472.8)
Market value ($ mil.)	(80.2%)	245.4	204.7	42.3	9.3	0.4
Employees	(6.5%)	17,800	17,000	15,800	15,350	13,580

DURA COAT PRODUCTS, INC.

5361 VIA RICARDO
RIVERSIDE, CA 925092414
Phone: 951 341-6500
Fax: –
Web: www.axalta.com

CEO: Myung K Hong
CFO: –
HR: Raul Muytoy
FYE: December 31
Type: Private

Durability is fundamental to Dura Coat Products. The company specializes in high-performance coatings for metal surfaces. Dura Coat develops and makes coil-applied coatings to protect metal building exteriors and roofing, trim and sidewall, rain ware, and HVAC components. Coatings are also used on garage doors, appliances, hardware, and vehicles. Spray coatings protect aluminum extrusions such as window frames and storefronts. For galvanized tubing, its high-solids exterior and water-based interior coatings are made to meet mechanical and electrical tubing markets. Dura Coat operates manufacturing plants in Huntsville, Alabama, and Riverside, California.

DURECT CORP

NAS: DRRX

10260 Bubb Road
Cupertino, CA 95014
Phone: 408 777-1417
Fax: –
Web: www.durect.com

CEO: James E Brown
CFO: Timothy M Papp
HR: –
FYE: December 31
Type: Public

DURECT is a biopharmaceutical company advancing novel and potentially lifesaving investigational therapies derived from its Epigenetic Regulator Program. Larsucosterol (also known as DUR 928), a new chemical entity in clinical development, is the lead candidate in its Epigenetic Regulator Program. Its drug delivery technologies include SABER that uses a high viscosity base component, such as sucrose acetate isobutyrate (SAIB), to provide controlled release of a drug; CLOUD is a class of bioerodible injectable depot technology which generally does not contain SAIB but includes various other release rate modifying excipients and/or bioerodible polymers to achieve the delivery of drugs for periods of days to months from a single injection. The firm also sells absorbable polymers (LACTEL) and osmotic pumps (ALZET) to pharmaceutical and medical research firms. Its Europe markets account for the majority of revenue of the company.

	Annual Growth	12/18	12/19	12/20	12/21	12/22
Sales ($mil.)	1.0%	18.6	29.6	30.1	14.0	19.3
Net income ($ mil.)	–	(25.3)	(20.6)	(0.6)	(36.3)	(35.3)
Market value ($ mil.)	63.6%	11.0	86.6	47.2	22.5	78.8
Employees	–	–	90	81	79	79

DVL, INC.

NBB: DVLN

70 East 55th Street
New York, NY 10022
Phone: 212 350-9900
Fax: –
Web: www.dvlnet.com

CEO: Alan E Casnoff
CFO: Neil Koenig
HR: Christy Magee
FYE: December 31
Type: Public

As far as DVL is concerned, making money is all in the family. The commercial finance company owns and services commercial mortgages held by more than 40 affiliated limited partnerships (in which it is general partner). DVL's partnerships hold some 1.9 million sq. ft. of commercial, industrial, and office space; a percentage of its income comes from tenant rental payments. Retail giant Wal-Mart is its largest tenant. The company also owns residual interests in securitized portfolios and offers real estate asset management and administrative services for its partnerships.

	Annual Growth	12/05	12/06	12/07	12/08	12/09
Sales ($mil.)	0.5%	9.3	9.4	11.0	10.2	9.5
Net income ($ mil.)	(4.5%)	1.7	1.8	2.3	1.5	1.4
Market value ($ mil.)	(12.2%)	0.0	0.0	0.0	0.0	0.0
Employees	(2.4%)	11	11	11	11	10

DWA HOLDINGS, LLC

1000 FLOWER ST
GLENDALE, CA 912013007
Phone: 818 695-5000
Fax: –
Web: research.dreamworks.com

CEO: Jeffrey Katzenberg
CFO: Fazal Merchant
HR: –
FYE: December 31
Type: Private

While live action isn't a nightmare for DreamWorks Animation SKG, this company definitely prefers CGI. DreamWorks Animation has produced computer-animated family-friendly features -- including high-earning hits such as Shrek, Shrek 2, Kung Fu Panda, Trolls, and Madagascar. Its Shrek 2 is one of the highest-grossing films of all time at the domestic box office. DreamWorks Animation creates award-winning films for a global audience.

DXC TECHNOLOGY CO

NYS: DXC

20408 Bashan Drive, Suite 231
Ashburn, VA 20147
Phone: 703 972-7000
Fax: –
Web: www.dxc.technology

CEO: Raul Fernandez
CFO: Kenneth P Sharp
HR: –
FYE: March 31
Type: Public

DXC Technology Company is one of the world's providers of systems integration, cloud migration, and digitization services. The company offers analytics and engineering, applications, business process services, cloud and security, IT outsourcing and a modern workplace. Serving more than half of today's fortune 500 companies, DXC operates in approximately 70 countries and generates over 30% of its revenue from the US. DXC was formed in 2017 with the merger of Computer Sciences Corp. and the Enterprise Services segment of Hewlett Packard Enterprise.

	Annual Growth	03/19	03/20	03/21	03/22	03/23
Sales ($mil.)	(8.7%)	20,753	19,577	17,729	16,265	14,430
Net income ($ mil.)	–	1,257.0	(5,369.0)	(149.0)	718.0	(568.0)
Market value ($ mil.)	(20.6%)	13,809	2,802.2	6,712.3	7,006.5	5,488.4
Employees	–	130,000	138,000	134,000	130,000	130,000

DXP ENTERPRISES, INC.

NMS: DXPE

5301 Hollister
Houston, TX 77040
Phone: 713 996-4700
Fax: –
Web: www.dxpe.com

CEO: –
CFO: –
HR: –
FYE: December 31
Type: Public

DXP Enterprises (DXP) is a distributor of industrial maintenance, repair, and operations (MRO) products and services through its three main segments ? Service Centers, Innovative Pumping Solutions, and Supply Chain Services. The company's Service Centers segment offers more than one million items in the bearing, rotating equipment, fluid power, power transmission, and safety product categories. It also provides technical design and logistics services. DXP serves the oil and gas, agriculture, chemical, construction, food and beverage, mining, and transportation markets. It operates from some 180 locations throughout the US and Canada as well as in Mexico and Dubai.

	Annual Growth	12/19	12/20	12/21	12/22	12/23
Sales ($mil.)	7.3%	1,267.2	1,005.3	1,113.9	1,480.8	1,678.6
Net income ($ mil.)	17.6%	36.0	(28.7)	16.5	48.2	68.8
Market value ($ mil.)	(4.1%)	644.0	359.6	415.3	445.7	545.2
Employees	15.6%	1,586	2,550	2,490	1,651	2,837

DYADIC INTERNATIONAL INC

NAS: DYAI

140 Intracoastal Pointe Drive, Suite 404
Jupiter, FL 33477
Phone: 561 743-8333
Fax: 561 743-8343
Web: www.dyadic.com

CEO: Mark A Emalfarb
CFO: Ping W Rawson
HR: –
FYE: December 31
Type: Public

Dyadic International hopes to unlock biotechnology dynasties using its C1 technology. The company uses its C1 Expression System to develop biological and chemical substances for a variety of life sciences and industrial applications. The firm's enzyme business makes enzymes and other products for commercial and industrial uses employing C1 know-how. Industries served include textiles, agriculture, and paper mills. Dyadic's biopharma division uses the expression system to make therapeutic proteins for drugmakers. The company is also developing its enzymes for bioenergy applications including biofuels.

	Annual Growth	12/18	12/19	12/20	12/21	12/22
Sales ($mil.)	22.6%	1.3	1.7	1.6	2.4	2.9
Net income ($ mil.)	–	(5.7)	(8.3)	(9.3)	(13.1)	(9.7)
Market value ($ mil.)	(10.2%)	54.0	148.0	153.7	129.1	35.1
Employees	–	8	9	6	7	–

DYAX CORP.

300 SHIRE WAY
LEXINGTON, MA 024212101
Phone: 617 349-0200
Fax: –
Web: www.shire.com

CEO: –
CFO: –
HR: –
FYE: December 31
Type: Private

Dyax has two ways to make a difference -- by developing its own drugs or by licensing its proprietary discovery technology to help others discover and develop drugs. The biopharmaceutical firm's phage display technology rapidly identifies proteins, peptides, and antibodies useful in treating disease. Its first commercial drug, Kalbitor, is approved in the US to treat hereditary angioedema (HAE, a condition causing tissue swelling) and enjoys orphan drug designation in patients 12 years of age and older. The firm is also investigating the drug for use in treating other types of angioedema and working to obtain regulatory approval for the drug in overseas markets. UK-based Shire is buying Dyax for $5.9 billion.

DYCOM INDUSTRIES, INC.

NYS: DY

11780 US Highway 1, Suite 600
Palm Beach Gardens, FL 33408
Phone: 561 627-7171
Fax: 561 627-7709
Web: www.dycomind.com

CEO: Steven E Nielsen
CFO: H A Deferrari
HR: –
FYE: January 27
Type: Public

Dycom Industries is a leading provider of specialty contracting services to the telecommunications infrastructure and utility industries throughout the US. Operating through a nationwide network of more than 40 subsidiaries, Dycom supplies telecommunications providers with a comprehensive portfolio of specialty services such as program management, planning, and engineering and design, among others. Dycom provides engineering services including the planning and design of aerial, underground, and buried fiber optic, copper, and coaxial cable systems that extend from the telephone company hub location, or cable operator headend, to a consumer's home or business. It also plans and designs wireless networks in connection with the deployment of new and enhanced macro cell and new small cell sites. Most of the company's revenue comes from major telecommunications companies. Dycom was incorporated in 1969.

	Annual Growth	01/20	01/21	01/22	01/23	01/24
Sales ($mil.)	5.7%	3,339.7	3,199.2	3,130.5	3,808.5	4,175.6
Net income ($ mil.)	39.9%	57.2	34.3	48.6	142.2	218.9
Market value ($ mil.)	26.8%	1,294.9	2,360.5	2,459.1	2,697.6	3,350.7
Employees	0.6%	15,230	14,276	15,024	15,410	15,611

DYNA GROUP INTERNATIONAL, INC.

NBB: DGIX

1661 South Seguin Street
New Braunfels, TX 78130
Phone: 830 620-4400
Fax: 830 620-8430
Web: www.gap1.com

CEO: Roger R Tuttle
CFO: –
HR: –
FYE: December 31
Type: Public

Pewter is like gold to Dyna Group. Through wholly-owned subsidiary Great American Products, the company produces pewter products, mostly collectibles, that are centrifugally cast in rubber molds. The company's products include belt buckles, key chains, picture frames, magnets, glassware and bar accessories, as well as keepsake boxes. Dyna Group has licensing agreements with NASCAR, the NFL, MLB, the NBA, the NHL, and other sports leagues. Dyna Group maintains a manufacturing facility in New Braunfels, Texas, but also outsources some manufacturing to companies in Mexico. CEO Roger Tuttle founded the company in 1972.

	Annual Growth	12/00	12/01	12/02	12/03	12/04
Sales ($mil.)	9.1%	10.7	12.8	13.2	13.3	15.2
Net income ($ mil.)	19.8%	0.5	0.6	0.2	0.6	1.1
Market value ($ mil.)	12.5%	4.0	6.0	4.9	4.1	6.4
Employees	6.8%	100	100	150	150	130

DYNACQ HEALTHCARE INC

4301 Vista Road
Pasadena, TX 77504
Phone: 713 378-2000
Fax: –
Web: www.dynacq.com

CEO: Eric K Chan
CFO: Hemant Khemka
HR: –
FYE: August 31
Type: Public

Dynacq Healthcare is a holding company that owns and operates acute-care specialty hospitals providing electively scheduled surgeries, such as bariatric (weight loss) and orthopedic surgeries and pain management procedures. Dynacq operates Vista Hospital in Garland, Texas, and Surgery Specialty Hospitals of America in Pasadena, Texas (suburbs of Dallas and Houston, respectively). Most of the Dynacq's revenues come from workers' compensation insurance and commercial insurers on an out-of-network basis. Chairman and CEO Chiu Moon Chan owns more than half of Dynacq.

	Annual Growth	08/11	08/12	08/13	08/14	08/15
Sales ($mil.)	–	(2.0)	5.5	6.1	10.2	7.0
Net income ($ mil.)	–	(19.2)	(12.2)	(3.3)	(3.8)	(3.8)
Market value ($ mil.)	(31.2%)	24.3	7.6	0.4	0.1	5.4
Employees	(2.1%)	137	111	127	131	126

DYNAMIX GROUP, INC

1905 WOODSTOCK RD STE 4150
ROSWELL, GA 300755625
Phone: 770 643-8877
Fax: –
Web: www.dynamixgroup.com

CEO: –
CFO: David A Delong
HR: –
FYE: December 31
Type: Private

Dynamix Group provides information technology (IT) products and services, including the implementation and configuration of software and hardware, as well as network systems maintenance and technical support from its offices throughout the southeastern US. The company offers a full range of products and services including top-of-the-line hardware, software and maintenance. With decades of combined experience and deep knowledge of IBM and Cisco products, the company has excellent client and technology partner relationships. Additional data network services include disaster recovery and storage management. The company targets the healthcare, retail, manufacturing as well as a variety of other industries. Dynamix was founded in 1995.

	Annual Growth	12/18	12/19	12/20	12/21	12/22
Sales ($mil.)	–	–	128.5	89.1	126.2	128.4
Net income ($ mil.)	3.2%	–	9.2	8.0	10.9	10.1
Market value ($ mil.)	–	–	–	–	–	–
Employees	–	–	–	–	–	97

DYNASIL CORP OF AMERICA

NBB: DYSL

313 Washington Street, Suite 403
Newton, MA 02458
Phone: 617 668-6855
Fax: –
Web: www.dynasil.com

CEO: Peter Sulick
CFO: Holly A Hicks
HR: –
FYE: September 30
Type: Public

Dynasil Corporation of America likes playing with the dynamics of silica. The company manufactures custom synthetic-fused silica and quartz products primarily used in industrial optical materials. Its products include filters, lenses, prisms, reflectors, windows, and mirrors. Customers use the company's fabricated optical products in lasers, aircraft, optical equipment, analytical instruments, semiconductors, and electronics. Manufacturers Corning, Schott Glass Technologies, and General Electric supply the company with some fused silica, fused quartz, and optical materials. Dynasil sells its products in the US and overseas.

	Annual Growth	09/15	09/16	09/17	09/18	09/19
Sales ($mil.)	1.9%	40.5	43.4	37.3	40.7	43.7
Net income ($ mil.)	–	(0.2)	0.7	2.2	1.8	(0.4)
Market value ($ mil.)	(16.8%)	28.7	14.7	18.5	19.1	13.8
Employees	(1.3%)	230	226	204	214	218

DYNATEM INC

23263 Madero, Suite C
Mission Viejo, CA 92691
Phone: 949 855-3235
Fax: 949 770-3481
Web: www.dynatem.com

CEO: Michael Horan
CFO: Belen Ramos
HR: –
FYE: May 31
Type: Public

Dynatem designs embedded computing systems based on Intel and Freescale microprocessor architectures. It also offers computer input/output boards. The company focuses on VMEbus-based products, VMEbus being a standard architecture for embedded electronics. Dynatem also supports the PCI and CompactPCI architectures. Among computer and real-time operating systems, Dynatem products support Linux, QNX, Solaris, VxWorks, and Windows.

	Annual Growth	05/02	05/03	05/04	05/05	05/06
Sales ($mil.)	6.2%	2.9	3.7	4.5	2.5	3.7
Net income ($ mil.)	(24.1%)	0.2	0.4	0.4	(0.7)	0.0
Market value ($ mil.)	7.7%	1.7	1.9	2.6	1.7	2.3
Employees	2.8%	17	19	20	20	19

DYNATRONICS CORP.

NAS: DYNT

1200 Trapp Road, Eagan
Eagan, MN 55121
Phone: 801 568-7000
Fax: 801 568-7711
Web: www.dynatronics.com

CEO: Brian Baker
CFO: Gabe Ellwein
HR: –
FYE: June 30
Type: Public

Dynatronics makes medical equipment to keep active people on the go. Its physical medicine products include electrotherapy, ultrasound, and infrared light therapy equipment; medical supplies such as wraps, braces, bandages, walking aids, and training equipment; and rehabilitation therapy tables. Dynatronics also sells aesthetic products under the Synergie brand, including the Synergie Aesthetic Massage System (AMS) for cosmetic weight loss and the Synergie Elite microdermabrasion device that reduces wrinkles. The company's products are sold directly through its own distributors and catalogs, as well as through independent dealers. Customers include physicians, surgeons, and physical therapists.

	Annual Growth	06/19	06/20	06/21	06/22	06/23
Sales ($mil.)	(10.2%)	62.6	53.4	47.8	44.3	40.6
Net income ($ mil.)	–	(0.9)	(3.4)	2.0	(4.0)	(5.0)
Market value ($ mil.)	(17.9%)	6.7	3.6	4.9	2.5	3.0
Employees	(13.9%)	284	195	175	197	156

DYNAVAX TECHNOLOGIES CORP

NMS: DVAX

2100 Powell Street, Suite 900
Emeryville, CA 94608
Phone: 510 848-5100
Fax: –
Web: www.dynavax.com

CEO: –
CFO: –
HR: –
FYE: December 31
Type: Public

Dynavax Technologies is a commercial stage biopharmaceutical company focused on developing and commercializing innovative vaccines. Its first marketed product, HEPLISAV-B (Hepatitis B Vaccine (Recombinant), Adjuvanted) is approved in the US and European Union for prevention of infection caused by all known subtypes of hepatitis B virus in adults age 18 years and older. We also manufacture and sell CpG 1018, the adjuvant used in HEPLISAV-B. The company is working to develop CpG 1018 as a premier vaccine adjuvant through research collaborations and partnerships. Current collaborations are focused on adjuvanted vaccines for COVID-19, plague, tetanus, diphtheria, and acellular pertussis (Tdap), seasonal influenza, universal influenza, and shingles. The US accounts for about 20% of company's total revenue.

	Annual Growth	12/19	12/20	12/21	12/22	12/23
Sales ($mil.)	60.3%	35.2	46.6	439.4	722.7	232.3
Net income ($ mil.)	–	(152.6)	(75.2)	76.7	293.2	(6.4)
Market value ($ mil.)	25.0%	740.9	576.4	1,822.5	1,378.2	1,810.8
Employees	15.3%	231	245	311	351	408

DYNEX CAPITAL INC

NYS: DX

4991 Lake Brook Drive, Suite 100
Glen Allen, VA 23060-9245
Phone: 804 217-5800
Fax: –
Web: www.dynexcapital.com

CEO: Byron L Boston
CFO: Stephen J Benedetti
HR: –
FYE: December 31
Type: Public

Dynex Capital is a real estate investment trust (REIT) that invests in loans and fixed-income securities backed by single-family residential and commercial mortgage loans. Its Investments consist primarily of Agency MBS including residential MBS (RMBS), commercial MBS (CMBS) and CMBS interest-only (IO) securities and non-Agency MBS, which consist mainly of CMBS IO. Agency MBS have an implicit guaranty of principal payment by an agency of the US government or a US government-sponsored entity (GSE) such as Fannie Mae and Freddie Mac. Non-Agency MBS are issued by non-governmental enterprises and do not have a guaranty of principal payment.

	Annual Growth	12/19	12/20	12/21	12/22	12/23
Sales ($mil.)	5.1%	170.2	96.5	60.1	86.7	207.5
Net income ($ mil.)	–	(152.7)	177.5	102.3	143.2	(6.1)
Market value ($ mil.)	(7.3%)	966.2	1,015.3	953.1	725.5	714.1
Employees	2.4%	20	19	19	19	22

DYONYX, L.P.

13430 NORTHWEST FWY STE 1000
HOUSTON, TX 770406051
Phone: 713 485-7000
Fax: –
Web: www.dyopath.com

CEO: –
CFO: –
HR: –
FYE: December 31
Type: Private

DYONYX offers management consulting and a slew of IT services that cover applications development, network management, risk management, security, systems design and integration, and training. It provides these services to both public and private sector clients, including companies in energy, financial services, health care, and transportation and US military and government agencies at the local, state, and federal levels. Among its clients are British Airways, Deloitte & Touche, and the US Department of Homeland Security. Founded in 1996, the privately-held DYONYX has offices in Texas and Washington, DC.

	Annual Growth	12/04	12/05	12/06	12/07	12/08
Sales ($mil.)	15.9%	–	–	16.5	20.9	22.1
Net income ($ mil.)	(21.4%)	–	–	1.0	1.7	0.6
Market value ($ mil.)	–	–	–	–	–	–
Employees	–	–	–	–	–	80

DZS INC
NAS: DZSI

5700 Tennyson Parkway, Suite 400
Plano, TX 75024
Phone: 469 327-1531
Fax: -
Web: www.zhone.com

CEO: -
CFO: -
HR: -
FYE: December 31
Type: Public

Zhone Technologies helps network service providers get into the SLMS zone. The company's all-IP Single Line Multi-Service (SLMS) platform uses existing local-loop infrastructures to deliver broadband services. Telecommunications service providers and wireless and cable operators use SLMS to offer their business and residential subscribers bundled broadband Internet access, local and long-distance voice, and broadcast video services. Its products are assembled at its plant in Florida using components manufactured in Asia. The company serves some 1,000 customers worldwide; about 70% of sales come from outside the US.

	Annual Growth	12/18	12/19	12/20	12/21	12/22
Sales ($mil.)	7.4%	282.3	306.9	300.6	350.2	375.7
Net income ($ mil.)	-	2.8	(13.5)	(23.1)	(34.7)	(37.4)
Market value ($ mil.)	(2.3%)	430.8	274.4	479.1	502.3	392.7
Employees	3.4%	670	789	830	840	765

E -PACIFIC I INC

150 W CREST ST
ESCONDIDO, CA 920251706
Phone: 760 294-7097
Fax: -
Web: www.iepacific.com

CEO: Diane Koester-Dion
CFO: -
HR: -
FYE: December 31
Type: Private

General contractor I.E.-Pacific provides general construction, engineering, and landscaping services to federal, state, and local agencies in the Southwest, primarily in California. The company performs new construction, renovations, alterations, revitalization, and repairs on projects that include industrial buildings, firing ranges, wastewater pre-treatment facilities, and housing. Many of its projects are military contracts. Clients have included the Navy, the Department of Labor, and Southern California Edison. President and owner Dianne Koester- Dion founded I.E.-Pacific in 1993.

	Annual Growth	12/98	12/99	12/00	12/11	12/12
Sales ($mil.)	5.7%	-	-	18.1	19.4	35.3
Net income ($ mil.)	13.8%	-	-	0.3	0.8	1.6
Market value ($ mil.)	-	-	-	-	-	-
Employees	-	-	-	-	-	20

E TRADE FINANCIAL CORPORATION

671 N GLEBE RD FL 15
ARLINGTON, VA 222032120
Phone: 646 521-4340
Fax: -
Web: us.etrade.com

CEO: -
CFO: -
HR: -
FYE: December 31
Type: Private

E*TRADE is the pioneer of online trading for retail investors and now part of Morgan Stanley, a leading global financial services firm renowned for the quality of its wealth management, investment advisory services, research, and market insights. Securities products and services are offered by E*TRADE Securities. Commodity futures and options on futures products and services are offered by E*TRADE Futures. Managed Account Solutions are offered through E*TRADE Capital Management, a Registered Investment Adviser. Bank products and services offered by E*TRADE Bank and E*TRADE Savings Bank, both federal savings banks and Members FDIC.

E Z LOADER BOAT TRAILERS, INC.

717 N HAMILTON ST
SPOKANE, WA 992022044
Phone: 574 266-0092
Fax: -
Web: www.ezloader.com

CEO: -
CFO: -
HR: Sheila Harris
FYE: December 31
Type: Private

Nine years after manufacturing its first boat trailer in 1953, EZ Loader invented the all-roller trailer and made loading boats easier for everyone. Its patented design has rubber rollers in key locations along the top of the trailer to allow boats to avoid damage and slide easily into place. The company's website includes an e-store that sells trailer kits for home assembly and replacement and spare parts. EZ Loader also sells its trailers through independent distributors located in the US, Japan, the Middle East, Asia, Australia, and Africa. The company has grown to include 10 divisions across the country. It is owned by Dave Thielman and president Randy Johnson.EZ Loader operates four manufacturing facilities and six distribution centers. About 60% of its trailers are made in Spokane, Washington; 30% in Midway, Arkansas; and the remaining 10% in Port St. Lucie, Florida.

	Annual Growth	12/02	12/03	12/04	12/06	12/08
Sales ($mil.)	(2.6%)	-	-	56.3	66.3	50.6
Net income ($ mil.)	-	-	-	-	0.5	(0.1)
Market value ($ mil.)	-	-	-	-	-	-
Employees	-	-	-	-	-	275

E-LYNXX CORPORATION

166 S MAIN ST
CHAMBERSBURG, PA 172012532
Phone: 717 709-0990
Fax: -
Web: www.elynxx.com

CEO: Nathan Rotz
CFO: -
HR: -
FYE: December 31
Type: Private

eLynxx offers cloud software for the marketing supply chain. The software is used for sourcing and managing direct mail, marketing, publications, packaging and print. eLynxx software enables collaboration to keep marketing projects on-spec and on-time, automating procurement task, and gaining transparency and reporting for finances.

	Annual Growth	12/03	12/04	12/05	12/06	12/07
Sales ($mil.)	(7.2%)	-	4.1	3.7	3.6	3.3
Net income ($ mil.)	(65.8%)	-	2.6	0.1	0.0	0.1
Market value ($ mil.)	-	-	-	-	-	-
Employees	-	-	-	-	-	23

E. & J. GALLO WINERY

600 YOSEMITE BLVD
MODESTO, CA 953542760
Phone: 209 341-3111
Fax: -
Web: www.gallo.com

CEO: Joseph E Gallo
CFO: -
HR: -
FYE: December 31
Type: Private

E. & J. Gallo Winery is a family-owned winemaker and is one of the most highly acclaimed wine and spirits companies in the world, having earned major awards from prestigious competitions in the US and internationally. The company owns more than a dozen wineries located in California and Washington. E. & J. Gallo Winery's team of world-class winemakers craft wines from the highest quality fruit, picked from vineyards. The company's range of offerings includes Apothic, Barefoot Wine, Black Box, J Vineyards and Winery, La Marca Prosecco, Orin Swift, New Amsterdam Vodka, RumChata, High Noon, along with partnerships with esteemed family-owned brands such as Allegrini, Argiano, The Dalmore, Don Fulano, and Gruppo Montenegro. E. & J. Gallo Winery was established in 1933 and is still owned and run by the family.

E. C. BARTON & COMPANY

2929 BROWNS LN
JONESBORO, AR 724017208
Phone: 870 932-6673
Fax: –
Web: www.ecbarton.com

CEO: –
CFO: –
HR: Allen Devereux
FYE: October 26
Type: Private

E.C. Barton & Company is a full-service lumber division that operates in Arkansas and Southeast Missouri. The stores carry everything homeowners and professionals need to build or remodel - from the lumber to the shingles and everything in-between. Its Home Outlet is a building materials retailer supplying homeowners/DIYers and professionals with expert advice and excellent customer service as they work to remodel or restore. Over 100 Home Outlet stores carry in-stock, quality kitchens, baths, flooring, windows, doors and more at the Guaranteed Lowest Price. E.C. Barton & Company's story began in 1885 at a grocery store in Jonesboro, Arkansas.

	Annual Growth	10/13	10/14	10/15	10/16	10/17
Sales ($mil.)	(1.4%)	–	–	304.5	–	296.2
Net income ($ mil.)	35867.7%	–	–	0.0	–	13.7
Market value ($ mil.)	–	–	–	–	–	–
Employees	–	–	–	–	–	881

E.DIGITAL CORP.

16870 West Bernardo Drive, Suite 120
San Diego, CA 92127
Phone: 858 304-3016
Fax: –
Web: www.edigital.com

CEO: –
CFO: –
HR: –
FYE: March 31
Type: Public

e.Digital believes that the future is digital. The company provides engineering services, product reference designs, and technology platforms to customers focusing on the digital video and audio markets. e.Digital, however, plans to focus future growth on selling its eVU mobile entertainment device, which features a 7-inch LCD screen, dual stereo headphone jacks, embedded credit card reader, and touch screen capabilities. The eVu is geared towards customers in the airline, health care, military, and travel and leisure industries.

	Annual Growth	03/12	03/13	03/14	03/15	03/16
Sales ($mil.)	(37.8%)	4.7	0.4	2.3	2.2	0.7
Net income ($ mil.)	–	1.2	(1.5)	0.0	(0.2)	(1.3)
Market value ($ mil.)	(1.0%)	11.8	49.5	20.3	31.2	11.3
Employees	(24.0%)	9	7	7	5	3

E.L.F. BEAUTY INC

NYS: ELF

570 10th Street
Oakland, CA 94607
Phone: 510 778-7787
Fax: –
Web: www.elfbeauty.com

CEO: Tarang Amin
CFO: Mandy Fields
HR: –
FYE: March 31
Type: Public

e.l.f. Beauty is a multi-brand beauty company that offers inclusive, accessible, clean and cruelty-free cosmetics and skincare products. With a focus on eyes, lips, and face, e.l.f. Beauty makes prestige-inspired makeup, including essentials like lipstick, mascara, blush, and foundation, for cost-conscious consumers. The company sells its cosmetics through Target, Walmart, and other national retailers, as well as through its e-commerce site. e.l.f. earns most of its sales in the US but sells internationally as well. Furthermore, the products are all formulated 100% vegan, cruelty-free, clean, and premium-quality.

	Annual Growth	03/19	03/20	03/21	03/22	03/23
Sales ($mil.)	72.0%	66.1	282.9	318.1	392.2	578.8
Net income ($ mil.)	–	(17.9)	17.9	6.2	21.8	61.5
Market value ($ mil.)	67.0%	570.0	529.1	1,442.7	1,388.9	4,428.0
Employees	–	–	–	217	288	303	339

E.N.M.R. TELEPHONE COOPERATIVE

7111 N PRINCE ST
CLOVIS, NM 881019730
Phone: 575 389-5100
Fax: –
Web: www.plateautel.com

CEO: Tom Phelps
CFO: David Robinson
HR: –
FYE: December 31
Type: Private

ENMR-Plateau Telecommunications is a telephone cooperative providing wireless and wired communications services in about two dozen communities in eastern New Mexico and western Texas. Mobile services are offered through its Plateau Wireless unit while Plateau Internet provides Internet access and other services including Web hosting. ENMR-Plateau has about 42,000 wireless accounts, 10,000 landline customers, and more than 13,000 internet subscribers. Area farmers, ranchers, and other residents founded the company in 1949 as Eastern New Mexico Rural Telephone Cooperative. It operates from offices in Roswell and Carlsbad, New Mexico, as well as in Levelland and Plainview, Texas among other cities.

	Annual Growth	12/08	12/09	12/10	12/11	12/12
Sales ($mil.)	(5.9%)	–	–	110.8	106.5	98.0
Net income ($ mil.)	55.7%	–	–	16.9	30.6	40.9
Market value ($ mil.)	–	–	–	–	–	–
Employees	–	–	–	–	–	270

EA ENGINEERING, SCIENCE, AND TECHNOLOGY, INC., PBC

225 SCHILLING CIR STE 400
HUNT VALLEY, MD 210311124
Phone: 410 584-7000
Fax: –
Web: www.eaest.com

CEO: –
CFO: Peter Ney
HR: –
FYE: December 31
Type: Private

EA Engineering, Science, and Technology wants to stop pollution before it starts by offering environmental consulting services. The company's specialties include brownfields and urban redevelopment, environmental compliance management, and natural resources management. Its more than 450 professionals have completed more than 100,000 environmental projects worldwide (more than $1 billion of services). Customers include government agencies and industrial manufacturers. EA Engineering operates from more than 25 offices -- 23 in the US (including facilities in Alaska and Hawaii) and one in Guam.

	Annual Growth	06/11	06/12	06/13*	12/15	12/16
Sales ($mil.)	22.4%	–	59.5	105.0	68.9	133.4
Net income ($ mil.)	(0.6%)	–	3.6	2.8	6.2	3.5
Market value ($ mil.)	–	–	–	–	–	–
Employees	–	–	–	–	–	440

*Fiscal year change

EACO CORP

NBB: EACO

5065 East Hunter Avenue
Anaheim, CA 92807
Phone: 714 876-2490
Fax: –
Web: www.eacocorp.com

CEO: Glen F Ceiley
CFO: –
HR: Stephanie Cuevas
FYE: August 31
Type: Public

EACO Corporation lost its appetite for the buffet business. For a half-dozen years after selling its restaurant operations to pursue a new line of business, the company generated revenues from a handful of rental properties including restaurant and industrial properties. (Tenant NES Rentals accounts for about half of its rental revenues.) In 2010 the company acquired Bisco Industries, which distributes electronics components in the US and Canada. EACO was once the sole franchisee of Ryan's Restaurant Group restaurants in Florida; it also owned a chain of 16 Whistle Junction and Florida Buffet locations. CEO Glen Ceiley owns 98.9% of EACO.

	Annual Growth	08/19	08/20	08/21	08/22	08/23
Sales ($mil.)	9.6%	221.2	225.2	238.0	292.6	319.4
Net income ($ mil.)	22.4%	9.4	7.8	8.4	21.3	21.2
Market value ($ mil.)	14.8%	95.0	84.5	94.8	94.8	165.3
Employees	3.5%	489	525	484	506	561

EAGLE BANCORP INC (MD)

NAS: EGBN

7830 Old Georgetown Road, Third Floor
Bethesda, MD 20814
Phone: 301 986-1800
Fax: –
Web: www.eaglebankcorp.com

CEO: Susan Riel
CFO: Charles D Levingston
HR: Courtney Michel
FYE: December 31
Type: Public

Eagle Bancorp serves as the bank holding company for EagleBank. The bank serves businesses and individuals through more than 15 branches in Maryland, Virginia, and Washington, DC, and its suburbs. Deposit products include checking, savings, and money market accounts; certificates of deposit; and IRAs. Commercial real estate loans represent about 65% of its loan portfolio, while construction loans make up another nearly 15%. The bank, which has significant expertise as a Small Business Administration lender, also writes business, consumer, and home equity loans. EagleBank offers insurance products through Eagle Insurance Services, LLC.

	Annual Growth	12/19	12/20	12/21	12/22	12/23
Assets ($mil.)	6.7%	8,988.7	11,118	11,847	11,151	11,665
Net income ($ mil.)	(8.4%)	142.9	132.2	176.7	140.9	100.5
Market value ($ mil.)	(11.3%)	1,455.3	1,235.9	1,745.9	1,318.8	902.0
Employees	(2.1%)	492	515	507	496	452

EAGLE BANCORP MONTANA, INC.

NMS: EBMT

1400 Prospect Avenue
Helena, MT 59601
Phone: 406 442-3080
Fax: –
Web: www.opportunitybank.com

CEO: Rick F Hays
CFO: Laura F Clark
HR: –
FYE: December 31
Type: Public

Eagle Bancorp Montana hopes to swoop down on every potential account holder in its home state. The holding company owns American Federal Savings Bank, a thrift that serves businesses and residents of southwestern Montana through six branches and seven ATMs. American Federal primarily writes mortgages on one- to four-family residences (these comprise almost half of its loan book); the rest of its portfolio consists of commercial mortgages (25%), home equity (about 20%), and consumer, business, and construction loans. The bank's deposit products include checking, money market, and savings accounts; CDs; IRAs; and Visa debit cards. Eagle Bancorp Montana is buying seven branches from Sterling Financial.

	Annual Growth	12/19	12/20	12/21	12/22	12/23
Assets ($mil.)	18.5%	1,054.3	1,257.6	1,435.9	1,948.4	2,075.7
Net income ($ mil.)	(1.9%)	10.9	21.2	14.4	10.7	10.1
Market value ($ mil.)	(7.3%)	171.5	170.1	184.2	129.6	126.6
Employees	8.1%	298	354	370	428	407

EAGLE BULK SHIPPING INC

NYS: EGLE

300 First Stamford Place, 5th Floor
Stamford, CT 06902
Phone: 203 276-8100
Fax: –
Web: www.eagleships.com

CEO: Gary Vogel
CFO: Frank D Costanzo
HR: –
FYE: December 31
Type: Public

Some eagles soar through the skies, but Eagle Bulk Shipping rides the waves. The company owns a fleet of 45 Handymax dry bulk carriers that it charters to customers, typically on one- to three-year contracts. Most of its vessels are classified as Supramaxes and range in capacity from 50,000 to 60,000 deadweight tons (DWT). Overall, the company's fleet has a carrying capacity of more than 1.1 million DWT. Cargo carried by charterers of Eagle Bulk Shipping's vessels includes cement, coal, fertilizer, grain, and iron ore. In mid-2014 Eagle Bulk Shipping filed for Chapter 11 bankruptcy protection and emerged in October of the same year.

	Annual Growth	12/19	12/20	12/21	12/22	12/23
Sales ($mil.)	7.7%	292.4	275.1	594.5	719.5	393.8
Net income ($ mil.)	–	(21.7)	(35.1)	184.9	248.0	22.7
Market value ($ mil.)	–	–	–	–	–	–
Employees	3.8%	974	900	1,000	1,000	1,130

EAGLE MATERIALS INC

NYS: EXP

5960 Berkshire Lane, Suite 900
Dallas, TX 75225
Phone: 214 432-2000
Fax: 214 432-2100
Web: www.eaglematerials.com

CEO: Michael R Haack
CFO: D C Kesler
HR: –
FYE: March 31
Type: Public

Eagle Materials is a leading manufacturer of heavy construction materials and light building materials in the US. The company produces ready-mix concrete, aggregates, and recycled paperboard sold to residential, commercial, and industrial construction customers throughout the US. It also produce and market other cementitious products, including slag cement and fly ash. Slag is used in concrete mix designs to improve the durability of concrete and reduce future maintenance costs. Fly ash is a by-product of a coal-fired power plant and acts as an extender of cement in concrete. Founded in 1963, Eagle Materials was spun off by homebuilder Centex Corporation in 2004.

	Annual Growth	03/19	03/20	03/21	03/22	03/23
Sales ($mil.)	11.4%	1,393.2	1,450.8	1,622.6	1,861.5	2,148.1
Net income ($ mil.)	60.9%	68.9	70.9	339.4	374.2	461.5
Market value ($ mil.)	14.9%	3,015.3	2,089.6	4,807.6	4,591.2	5,249.0
Employees	1.1%	2,300	2,400	2,200	2,200	2,400

EAGLE PHARMACEUTICALS, INC.

NMS: EGRX

50 Tice Boulevard, Suite 315
Woodcliff Lake, NJ 07677
Phone: 201 326-5300
Fax: –
Web: www.eagleus.com

CEO: Michael Graves
CFO: Brian Cahill
HR: –
FYE: December 31
Type: Public

Eagle Pharmaceuticals is a specialty pharmaceutical company working to advance safe and efficient injectable treatments for patients across oncology, critical care, and orphan diseases. The company has three FDA-approved products -- Ryanodex (dantrolene sodium, bendamustine ready-to-dilute (RTD) 500ml solution (Belrapzo), and rapidly infused bendamustine RTD (Bendeka). The company markets its products through marketing partners and its internal direct sales force. Eagle markets Ryanodex and Belrapzo, and Teva markets Bendeka through its subsidiary Cephalon, Inc. SymBio Pharmaceuticals Limited, or SymBio, markets Treakisym, a RTD product, in Japan. Reflecting further expansion of its oncology portfolio, in early 2020, the company received final FDA approval for Pemfexy, a branded alternative to Alimta for metastatic non-squamous non-small cell lung cancer and malignant pleural mesothelioma.

	Annual Growth	12/18	12/19	12/20	12/21	12/22
Sales ($mil.)	10.4%	213.3	195.9	187.8	171.5	316.6
Net income ($ mil.)	2.8%	31.9	14.3	12.0	(8.6)	35.6
Market value ($ mil.)	(7.7%)	524.4	782.0	606.2	662.8	380.5
Employees	8.7%	96	108	106	102	134

EALIXIR INC

NBB: EAXR

7500 College Blvd, Suite 500
Overland Park, KS 66210
Phone: 913 815-1570
Fax: –
Web: www.flinttelecomgroup.com

CEO: –
CFO: –
HR: –
FYE: June 30
Type: Public

Flint Telecom Group fans the flame of advanced communications. Through eight subsidiaries, the holding company provides a host of products and technologies to US and international communications service providers, including cable companies, ISPs, and telcos. It distributes advanced broadband, hosted digital phone, voice and data, and wireless products, as well as prepaid cellular and calling card products. The company's Digital Phone Solutions subsidiary offers VoIP services to independent cable companies, a niche that is showing strong market growth, particularly in the US.

	Annual Growth	03/08*	06/09	06/10	06/11	06/12
Sales ($mil.)	82.6%	1.0	34.3	34.1	15.8	10.7
Net income ($ mil.)	–	(2.1)	(14.6)	(28.9)	(9.3)	0.4
Market value ($ mil.)	(80.0%)	0.2	0.3	0.0	0.0	0.0
Employees	(38.5%)	14	21	7	–	2

*Fiscal year change

EARL G. GRAVES, LTD.

500 FASHION AVE FL 8A
NEW YORK, NY 100180818
Phone: 212 242-8000
Fax: –
Web: www.blackenterprise.com

CEO: Earl G Graves Jr
CFO: Jacques Jiha
HR: –
FYE: December 31
Type: Private

The eponymous Earl G. Graves Ltd. (founded in 1968 by chairman and publisher Earl G. Graves) publishes Black Enterprise, a business magazine aimed at African-American executives that reaches more than 4 million readers. The firm also has digital, broadcast, and event operations. Earl G. Graves Ltd. runs the online companion BlackEnterprise.com and organizes events for black entrepreneurs and professionals, such as The Black Enterprise Entrepreneurs Conference + Expo. In addition, the company produces two nationally syndicated television shows: Our World with Black Enterprise and the Black Enterprise Business Report.

	Annual Growth	12/00	12/01	12/02	12/03	12/08
Sales ($mil.)	(51.5%)	–	24.3	24.5	23.9	0.2
Net income ($ mil.)	–	–	(0.4)	(0.3)	(0.5)	0.0
Market value ($ mil.)	–	–	–	–	–	–
Employees	–	–	–	–	–	100

EARL L. HENDERSON TRUCKING COMPANY, LLC

8118 BUNKUM RD
CASEYVILLE, IL 622322104
Phone: 618 623-0057
Fax: –
Web: www.gotrekker.com

CEO: –
CFO: –
HR: –
FYE: December 31
Type: Private

This Earl aspires to hold a royal rank in the world of refrigerated transportation. Earl L. Henderson Trucking hauls food and other perishable products throughout the US. The company operates a fleet of some 400 tractors and 600 trailers, including about 500 refrigerated trailers. It offers long-haul service in the US and parts of Canada and regional service in the eastern half of the US. In addition to perishable products, Henderson Trucking transports time-sensitive printed matter. Company president John Kaburick owns Henderson Trucking, which was founded by Earl Henderson in 1978.

	Annual Growth	12/04	12/05	12/06	12/07	12/08
Sales ($mil.)	12.1%	–	–	79.5	94.9	100.0
Net income ($ mil.)	(45.8%)	–	–	1.8	93.0	0.5
Market value ($ mil.)	–	–	–	–	–	–
Employees	–	–	–	–	–	280

EARLHAM COLLEGE

801 NATIONAL RD W
RICHMOND, IN 473744095
Phone: 765 983-1200
Fax: –
Web: www.earlham.edu

CEO: –
CFO: –
HR: –
FYE: June 30
Type: Private

Earlham College is a private liberal arts college located in Richmond, Indiana. The venerable school, originally founded by Quakers, enrolls about 1,100 undergraduate students a year and offers 40 courses of study in the fine arts, humanities, natural sciences, and social sciences. Earlham also offers a three-year pre-professional course of study, as well as master's degree programs in teaching and education. The college's annual tuition is approximately $34,000. The affiliated Earlham School of Religion, established in 1960, offers graduate degrees in religion and ministry.

	Annual Growth	06/16	06/17	06/18	06/20	06/22
Sales ($mil.)	(2.6%)	–	63.1	67.9	67.0	55.3
Net income ($ mil.)	–	–	37.5	6.7	(26.6)	(29.3)
Market value ($ mil.)	–	–	–	–	–	–
Employees	–	–	–	–	–	365

EARNHARDT MANAGEMENT COMPANY

7300 W ORCHID LN
CHANDLER, AZ 852261000
Phone: 480 926-4000
Fax: –
Web: www.nobull.com

CEO: Hal J Earnhardt III
CFO: –
HR: Ramirez Willis
FYE: December 31
Type: Private

Using a "no bull" approach that US Southwesterners seem to like, Earnhardt Management, which does business as Earnhardt's Auto Centers, (and its bull-riding founder) sells thousands of new and used vehicles each month. The auto dealerships are located more than half a dozen Arizona cities, feature BMW, Dodge, Ford, Honda, Hyundai, Mazda, Nissan, Scion, and Toyota. Earnhardt's website allows customers to "build" their next car online: Shoppers can select from a complete list of options before submitting it online. Established in 1951 by Tex Earnhardt, the company is family-owned and -operated.

	Annual Growth	12/17	12/18	12/19	12/20	12/21
Sales ($mil.)	11.1%	–	9.1	9.1	10.6	12.4
Net income ($ mil.)	5.3%	–	1.0	0.8	1.0	1.2
Market value ($ mil.)	–	–	–	–	–	–
Employees	–	–	–	–	–	1,850

EARTH SEARCH SCIENCES INC.

306 Stoner Loop Road
Lakeside, MT 59922
Phone: 406 250-7750
Fax: –
Web: www.earthsearch.com

NBB: ESSE
CEO: –
CFO: –
HR: –
FYE: March 31
Type: Public

The technology used by Earth Search Sciences (ESSI) is rooted in the stars, not the ground. The company has developed remote sensing instruments (using what is called hyperspectral remote sensing technology) based on NASA's Airborne Visible and Infra-Red Imaging Spectrometer (AVIRIS). The instruments designed by ESSI collect and analyze data for use in oil and gas exploration, mining, hazardous material remediation, and ecosystem monitoring, among other things. The company has served customers in the private, military, and government sectors. Chairman and CEO Larry Vance owns 74% of the company.

	Annual Growth	03/11	03/12	03/13	03/14	03/15
Sales ($mil.)	–	–	–	–	–	–
Net income ($ mil.)	–	(1.9)	(1.7)	(1.1)	(0.7)	(1.5)
Market value ($ mil.)	(30.5%)	4.8	4.5	0.7	1.4	1.1
Employees	(24.0%)	3	3	1	1	1

EARTH SHARE

7735 OLD GEORGTWN RD # 9
BETHESDA, MD 208146130
Phone: 240 333-0300
Fax: –
Web: www.earthshare.org

CEO: –
CFO: –
HR: –
FYE: June 30
Type: Private

EarthShare wants to be sure our home planet gets its due. The group works to ensure that environmental organizations get their fair share of donations. The not-for-profit represents almost 600 local and national environmental and conservation groups and collects money primarily through payroll deduction campaigns at government and corporate offices in all 50 US states. EarthShare has affiliated offices in some 23 states. It strives to educate the public about environmental problems and their impacts on daily life through public service announcements on toxins in schools, childhood obesity, and the effects of mercury in the food chain.

	Annual Growth	06/14	06/15	06/17	06/18	06/20
Sales ($mil.)	(8.3%)	–	3.2	2.7	6.1	2.1
Net income ($ mil.)	(2.0%)	–	0.3	0.2	1.2	0.3
Market value ($ mil.)	–	–	–	–	–	–
Employees	–	–	–	–	–	2

EARTH SUN MOON TRADING COMPANY, INC.

111 N CENTER ST
GROVE CITY, PA 161271641
Phone: 724 458-1687
Fax: –
Web: www.earthsunmoon.com

CEO: –
CFO: Stephen Tessier
HR: Annette Oconner
FYE: December 31
Type: Private

Your T-shirt collection simply can't compare to the vast collection that Earth Sun Moon Trading has amassed. The company makes and sells screen-printed T-shirts and hats decorated with one-liners and nature-inspired themes (such as dogs and cats, gardening, sports, camping, and more). Its products are sold through more than 7,000 specialty retailers (including museums, aquariums, zoos, national parks, campgrounds, tourist attractions, and general gift shops) in the US and abroad. It also sells T-shirts online. Earth Sun Moon Trading began operations in 1996.

	Annual Growth	12/11	12/12	12/17	12/19	12/21
Sales ($mil.)	–	–	–	19.8	21.7	19.5
Net income ($ mil.)	3.7%	–	1.7	(0.0)	0.0	2.3
Market value ($ mil.)	–	–	–	–	–	–
Employees	–	–	–	–	–	100

EAST ALABAMA HEALTH CARE AUTHORITY

2000 PEPPERELL PKWY
OPELIKA, AL 368015452
Phone: 334 749-3411
Fax: –
Web: www.eastalabamahealth.org

CEO: Terry Andrus
CFO: –
HR: Kelli Truitt
FYE: September 30
Type: Private

The East Alabama Health Care Authority's flagship facility is East Alabama Medical Center (EAMC), a general acute-care hospital include services such as cancer center, surgery, maternity care, orthopaedic care, women's health, as well as hearth and vascular care. Other services have included eye care, HIV care and counseling, infectious disease, and more. The system also operates EAMC-Lanier, which offers a nursing home, emergency medicine, acute rehab unit and occupational medicine. The company traces its roots back in 1945.

	Annual Growth	09/16	09/17	09/18	09/19	09/21
Sales ($mil.)	31.1%	–	298.6	319.4	35.4	881.7
Net income ($ mil.)	168.0%	–	9.7	17.7	0.3	499.1
Market value ($ mil.)	–	–	–	–	–	–
Employees	–	–	–	–	–	2,250

EAST BAY MUNICIPAL UTILITY DISTRICT, WATER SYSTEM

375 11TH ST
OAKLAND, CA 946074246
Phone: 866 403-2683
Fax: –
Web: www.ebmud.com

CEO: –
CFO: –
HR: Gregory Konana
FYE: June 30
Type: Private

It is part of the job description of East Bay Municipal Utility District (EBMUD) to keep the mud out of the drinking water. The utility provides potable water to 1.3 million people in a 331-square-mile area (which includes the cities of Alameda, Berkeley, and Oakland). Its wastewater system serves about 650,000 people in an 88-square-mile area of Alameda and Contra Costa counties along San Francisco Bay's east shore. EBMUD operates a wastewater treatment plant that treats wastewater collected by nine East Bay cities and cleans it before discharge to the San Francisco Bay.

	Annual Growth	06/19	06/20	06/21*	09/21*	06/22
Sales ($mil.)	5.3%	–	693.7	625.0	228.0	769.5
Net income ($ mil.)	8.0%	–	244.1	212.8	94.8	284.7
Market value ($ mil.)	–	–	–	–	–	–
Employees	–	–	–	–	–	1,511

*Fiscal year change

EAST OF CHICAGO PIZZA INC

121 W HIGH ST FL 12
LIMA, OH 458014349
Phone: 419 225-7116
Fax: –
Web: www.eastofchicago.com

CEO: Anthony Collins
CFO: –
HR: –
FYE: December 31
Type: Private

Guess where East of Chicago Pizza Company operates? True to its name, its restaurants can be found to the East of the Windy City. East of Chicago Pizza operates a chain of about 100 franchised pizzerias in Ohio and Indiana. The restaurants offer a variety of specialty pizzas and toppings; crusts offered include pan, thin, crispy, and Chicago style. In addition to pizza, the menu offers sub sandwiches, salads, wings, and pasta dishes. The company was in Greenwich, Ohio founded by Scott Granneman in 1982 under the name Greenwich Pizza Barn. It was renamed East of Chicago Pizza in 1989.

EAST ORANGE GENERAL HOSPITAL (INC)

300 CENTRAL AVE
EAST ORANGE, NJ 070182897
Phone: 973 672-8400
Fax: –
Web: www.carewellhealth.org

CEO: –
CFO: Al Aboud
HR: Alicia Sobers
FYE: December 31
Type: Private

East Orange General Hospital pairs medical services with community action. Established in 1903, the not-for-profit hospital is the home of the first Candy Striper program in 1944 and continues with a number of community outreach programs. The 210-bed facility provides inpatient acute care in a wide range of specialties, including critical care, oncology, behavioral health, surgery, and intensive care. East Orange General Hospital also offers cardiology, physical rehabilitation, dialysis, respiratory care, diagnostic testing, and wound care, among other services. The hospital's Family Health Center provides primary and specialty care, as well as outpatient surgery. East Orange General Hospital is part of Essex Valley Healthcare.

	Annual Growth	12/07	12/08	12/09	12/10	12/11
Sales ($mil.)	–	–	–	(141.6)	112.5	118.2
Net income ($ mil.)	8297.4%	–	–	0.0	0.4	1.3
Market value ($ mil.)	–	–	–	–	–	–
Employees	–	–	–	–	–	801

EAST TENNESSEE CHILDREN'S HOSPITAL ASSOCIATION, INC.

2018 W CLINCH AVE
KNOXVILLE, TN 379162301
Phone: 865 541-8000
Fax: –
Web: www.etch.com

CEO: Matt Schaefer
CFO: –
HR: –
FYE: June 30
Type: Private

ETCH has made a permanent mark on the lives of countless children over the years. Knoxville-based East Tennessee Children's Hospital (ETCH), with more than 150 beds, provides a full range of health care services to children from eastern Tennessee and portions of surrounding states. Among its 30 specialized services are cardiology, neonatal care, orthopedics, and psychiatry, as well as cystic fibrosis and hearing impairment services. The hospital also offers support such as for families of children stricken by cancer. The hospital's roots are in the foundation of Knox County Crippled Children's Hospital in 1937, with less than 50 beds.

	Annual Growth	06/18	06/19	06/20	06/21	06/22
Sales ($mil.)	7.6%	–	210.6	220.4	234.8	262.1
Net income ($ mil.)	16.8%	–	11.4	22.7	21.3	18.2
Market value ($ mil.)	–	–	–	–	–	–
Employees	–	–	–	–	–	1,500

EAST TENNESSEE STATE UNIVERSITY

1276 GILBREATH DR
JOHNSON CITY, TN 376146503
Phone: 423 439-1000
Fax: –
Web: www.etsu.edu

CEO: –
CFO: –
HR: Deborah Frakes
FYE: June 30
Type: Private

East Tennessee State University (ETSU) is a public, coeducational member of the Tennessee Board of Regents' network of 45 postsecondary educational institutions. The university has 11 colleges and schools representing arts and sciences, business and technology, clinical and rehabilitative health sciences, education, medicine, nursing, pharmacy, public health, honors, as well as continuing and graduate studies. It offers approximately 125 undergraduate programs, 95 master's programs, and a dozen doctoral programs, as well as graduate certificates, teacher licensure, and specialist programs. Founded as East Tennessee State Normal School in 1911, ETSU has an enrollment of more than 15,000 students.

	Annual Growth	06/04	06/05	06/06	06/08	06/13
Sales ($mil.)	40.9%	–	–	16.3	14.7	179.7
Net income ($ mil.)	(4.3%)	–	–	8.8	7.6	6.4
Market value ($ mil.)	–	–	–	–	–	–
Employees	–	–	–	–	–	2,400

EAST TEXAS MEDICAL CENTER REGIONAL HEALTHCARE SYSTEM

1000 S BECKHAM AVE
TYLER, TX 757011908
Phone: 903 596-3267
Fax: –
Web: www.uthealtheasttexas.com

CEO: Elmer G Ellis
CFO: –
HR: Katrina Flores
FYE: October 31
Type: Private

East Texas Medical Center (ETMC) Regional Healthcare System works to meet the health care needs of residents of the Piney Woods. The not-for-profit health system operates more than a dozen hospitals across eastern Texas, along with behavioral, rehabilitation, and home health care businesses. Its flagship 450-bed Tyler location serves as the hub and referral center for satellite medical centers located in more rural locations. The system also runs numerous primary care and outpatient clinics throughout the region. Serving more than 300,000 patients each year, ETMC operates an emergency ambulance service subsidiary and a clinical laboratory, which provide services to the ETMC Regional Healthcare System.

	Annual Growth	10/04	10/05	10/06	10/07	10/08
Sales ($mil.)	1.5%	–	837.5	837.5	827.9	877.0
Net income ($ mil.)	20.4%	–	17.2	–	40.0	30.1
Market value ($ mil.)	–	–	–	–	–	–
Employees	–	–	–	–	–	7,600

EAST WEST BANCORP, INC

135 North Los Robles Ave., 7th Floor
Pasadena, CA 91101
Phone: 626 768-6000
Fax: –
Web: www.eastwestbank.com

NMS: EWBC
CEO: Dominic Ng
CFO: Christopher D Moral-Niles
HR: –
FYE: December 31
Type: Public

East West Bancorp is the holding company for East West Bank, which provides standard banking services and loans, operating in more than 120 locations in the US and China. Boasting $64.11 billion in assets, East West Bank focuses on making commercial real estate loans and commercial and industrial, which account for the majority of the company's loan portfolio. Catering to the Asian-American community, it also provides international banking and trade financing. The Bank provides services to its customers in English and over 10 other languages. The company commenced business in 1998 when pursuant to a reorganization, it acquired all of the voting stock of East West Bank, which became its principal asset.

	Annual Growth	12/19	12/20	12/21	12/22	12/23
Assets ($mil.)	12.0%	44,196	52,157	60,871	64,112	69,613
Net income ($ mil.)	14.6%	674.0	567.8	873.0	1,128.1	1,161.2
Market value ($ mil.)	10.2%	6,819.3	7,100.8	11,017	9,227.8	10,075
Employees	(0.7%)	3,300	3,200	3,100	3,155	3,206

EASTER SEALS, INC.

141 W JACKSON BLVD STE 1400A
CHICAGO, IL 606043508
Phone: 312 726-6200
Fax: –
Web: www.easterseals.com

CEO: Angela F Williams
CFO: –
HR: Jean Broach
FYE: December 31
Type: Private

A year round effort that has nothing to do with Easter, seals, or flowers, the National Easter Seal Society annually helps more than one million children and adults with disabilities through over 550 service centers in the US, Puerto Rico, Canada, and Australia. The organization offers medical rehabilitation, job training, child care, and adult day services. It began in 1907 as the National Society for Crippled Children and launched its first "seal" campaign around Easter in 1934. Supporters placed stickers or seals depicting the lily, a symbol of renewal, on letters and envelopes. The campaign was so successful and the symbol so associated with the organization that it changed its name in 1967.

	Annual Growth	12/08	12/09	12/13	12/14	12/19
Sales ($mil.)	(7.3%)	–	123.7	82.2	73.0	58.0
Net income ($ mil.)	4.9%	–	1.1	0.8	0.7	1.7
Market value ($ mil.)	–	–	–	–	–	–
Employees	–	–	–	–	–	120

EASTERLY GOVERNMENT PROPERTIES INC

2001 K Street NW, Suite 775
Washington, DC 20006
Phone: 202 595-9500
Fax: –
Web: www.easterlyreit.com

NYS: DEA
CEO: William C Trimble III
CFO: Meghan G Baivier
HR: –
FYE: December 31
Type: Public

Easterly Government Properties manages exactly what it's name states -- it provides office space to the government. The specialty real estate investment trust (REIT) owns 29 US properties spanning 2.1 million square feet of leasable space, including 26 that are leased primarily to federal government agencies such as the FBI, IRS, and Drug Enforcement Administration. While primarily focused on federal tenants, Easterly Government Properties also rents space to a few private tenants. Founded in 2011 as Easterly Partners LLC, the REIT went public on February 2015.

	Annual Growth	12/19	12/20	12/21	12/22	12/23
Sales ($mil.)	6.7%	221.7	245.1	274.9	293.6	287.2
Net income ($ mil.)	27.1%	7.2	12.0	30.1	31.5	18.8
Market value ($ mil.)	(13.2%)	2,396.1	2,287.0	2,314.3	1,440.9	1,357.1
Employees	10.9%	37	45	53	54	56

EASTERN BAG AND PAPER COMPANY, INCORPORATED

200 RESEARCH DR
MILFORD, CT 064602880
Phone: 203 878-1814
Fax: –
Web: www.imperialdade.com

CEO: Meredith Reuben
CFO: William J Donnell
HR: Remy Cooper
FYE: December 31
Type: Private

Eastern Bag and Paper Co. (dba EBP Supply) is a leading distributor of paper products in the northeastern US. In addition to disposable tableware and packaging, the company offers foodservice products (including china and glassware), restaurant equipment (can openers, refrigerators), personal care items (bath mats, roll towels), and cleansers and maintenance supplies (air fresheners, vacuums). Its name-brand products are used by the industrial, healthcare, foodservice, and janitorial industries. Founded in 1918 by Samuel Baum, the company is owned and run by CEO Meredith Baum Reuben.

	Annual Growth	12/16	12/17	12/18	12/19	12/20
Sales ($mil.)	1.3%	–	198.8	204.8	212.7	207.0
Net income ($ mil.)	10.7%	–	2.4	2.3	1.8	3.3
Market value ($ mil.)	–	–	–	–	–	–
Employees	–	–	–	–	–	285

EASTERN CO.

NMS: EML

3 Enterprise Drive, Suite 408
Shelton, CT 06484
Phone: 203 729-2255
Fax: –
Web: www.easterncompany.com

CEO: August M Vlak
CFO: Peter O'Hara
HR: Patti Miller
FYE: December 30
Type: Public

The Eastern Company has latched on to the security industry. The company's security products group makes coin acceptors used in laundry facilities, smart card payment systems, and keyless locks sold under such brands as Big Tag, Duo, Warlock, Searchalert, Sesamee, Prestolock, and Huski. It also manufactures industrial hardware, including latches, locks, and hinges, used by the transportation industry. Eastern owns a foundry that makes metal anchoring devices to support underground mine roofs, clamps for construction, and railroad brake system components. The company sells mainly to manufacturers, distributors, and locksmiths through its operations in North America, China, Mexico, and Taiwan.

	Annual Growth	12/19*	01/21	01/22*	12/22	12/23
Sales ($mil.)	2.1%	251.7	240.4	246.5	279.3	273.5
Net income ($ mil.)	(10.3%)	13.3	5.4	9.3	12.3	8.6
Market value ($ mil.)	(7.4%)	186.3	149.8	155.9	119.9	136.8
Employees	(3.8%)	1,399	1,323	1,191	1,191	1,199

*Fiscal year change

EASTERN GAS TRANSMISSION AND STORAGE, INC.

10700 ENERGY WAY
GLEN ALLEN, VA 230609243
Phone: 800 688-4673
Fax: –
Web: www.dominionenergy.com

CEO: Thomas F Farrell II
CFO: –
HR: –
FYE: December 31
Type: Private

Dominion Transmission knows how to dominate a market in order to keep its customers happy. The interstate gas transmission subsidiary of Dominion Energy operates one of the largest underground natural gas storage system in the US; it maintains 7,800 miles of pipeline in Maryland, New York, Ohio, Pennsylvania, Virginia, and West Virginia. Dominion Transmission also has links to other pipelines, which makes its gas available to markets in the Mid-Atlantic, Midwest, and Northeast regions of the US. Customers include public utilities and power plants. It also operates one of the largest liquefied natural gas (LNG) import terminals in the US, Dominion Cove Point LNG.

EASTERN KENTUCKY UNIVERSITY

521 LANCASTER AVE
RICHMOND, KY 404753102
Phone: 859 622-1791
Fax: –
Web: www.eku.edu

CEO: –
CFO: –
HR: –
FYE: June 30
Type: Private

Deep in the heart of bluegrass country, Eastern Kentucky University offers more than 100 degree programs, including some 30 masters degree programs, through its five colleges (Arts & Sciences, Business & Technology, Education, Health Sciences, and Justice & Safety). The school has an annual enrollment of some 16,000 students on eight campuses. It also offers online courses and degree programs. Eastern Kentucky University was founded in 1906 with a faculty of just seven; in 1909 the school's first graduating class consisted of 11 students. Originally Eastern Kentucky State Normal School, it gained university status in 1966 and began offering graduate degrees in fields other than education.

	Annual Growth	06/15	06/16	06/17	06/18	06/19
Sales ($mil.)	(3.2%)	–	–	183.9	180.3	172.4
Net income ($ mil.)	–	–	–	(21.4)	(27.0)	43.3
Market value ($ mil.)	–	–	–	–	–	–
Employees	–	–	–	–	–	2,100

EASTERN LIGHT CAPITAL INC

100 Pine Street, Suite 560
San Francisco, CA 94111
Phone: 415 693-9500
Fax: 415 693-9501
Web: www.caitreit.com

CEO: –
CFO: –
HR: –
FYE: December 31
Type: Public

Eastern Light Capital (ELC) is a real estate investment trust (REIT) focused on loans rather than properties. The company formerly originated and purchased (through mortgage banks and brokers) non-conforming first and second home mortgages and home equity loans collateralized mainly by properties in California. ELC suspended those operations in 2006, but continues to hold such investments in it portfolio, which consists primarily of loans that do not meet the purchasing standards set by Fannie Mae, Freddie Mac, and other government-sponsored housing enterprises. ELC is exploring investments in other REIT-compliant assets. Subsidiary WrenCap Funding invests in exchange-listed securities.

	Annual Growth	12/06	12/07	12/08	12/09	12/10
Sales ($mil.)	(48.6%)	2.5	1.1	0.7	0.4	0.2
Net income ($ mil.)	–	(1.6)	(2.9)	(0.6)	(2.8)	(1.4)
Market value ($ mil.)	(11.6%)	2.9	1.4	1.5	1.4	1.8
Employees	18.9%	1	4	3	4	2

EASTERN MAINE HEALTHCARE SYSTEMS

43 WHITING HILL RD STE 500
BREWER, ME 044121005
Phone: 207 973-7000
Fax: –
Web: www.northernlighthealth.org

CEO: –
CFO: Jennifer Goodrich
HR: David Wheaton
FYE: September 30
Type: Private

Eastern Maine Healthcare Systems (EMHS) keeps the folks in the Pine Tree State feeling fine. With more than a dozen member hospitals and multiple medical practices and clinics, the organization offers patients emergency, primary, mental-health, laboratory, and other specialty services. It primarily serves eastern, central, and northern portions of rural Maine. Some hospitals include Eastern Maine Medical Center (410 beds), Acadia Hospital (100 beds), Aroostook Medical Center (75 beds), and Inland Hospital (50 beds). The system also operates long-term care, hospice, and home health facilities, as well as emergency transportation and administrative services businesses.

	Annual Growth	09/17	09/18	09/19	09/20	09/21
Sales ($mil.)	7.8%	–	–	1,744.5	1,753.2	2,027.1
Net income ($ mil.)	168.6%	–	–	16.2	(77.4)	116.7
Market value ($ mil.)	–	–	–	–	–	–
Employees	–	–	–	–	–	8,175

EASTERN MICHIGAN UNIVERSITY

202 WELCH HALL
YPSILANTI, MI 481972214
Phone: 734 487-2031
Fax: –
Web: www.emich.edu

CEO: –
CFO: –
HR: –
FYE: June 30
Type: Private

Eastern Michigan University (known affectionately as just plain Eastern) has long been an affordable place to study your way into a better career. The university began as a teachers' college in 1849 and it still graduates one out of every four teachers in Michigan. Eastern has an enrollment of more than 23,000 students (90% are Michigan residents) who participate in undergraduate and graduate degree programs on its campus in the southeastern part of the state. Its 200 majors, minors, and concentrations are offered through colleges of arts and sciences, business, education, technology, and health and human services.

	Annual Growth	06/14	06/15	06/16	06/17	06/18
Sales ($mil.)	(1.5%)	–	–	–	244.3	240.7
Net income ($ mil.)	(29.2%)	–	–	–	9.7	6.9
Market value ($ mil.)	–	–	–	–	–	–
Employees	–	–	–	–	–	2,000

EASTERN VIRGINIA MEDICAL SCHOOL

735 FAIRFAX AVE STE 909C
NORFOLK, VA 235072007
Phone: 757 446-6052
Fax: –
Web: www.evms.edu

CEO: Richard C Zoretic
CFO: –
HR: –
FYE: June 30
Type: Private

Eastern Virginia Medical School (EVMS) sends graduated physicians down the Hampton Roads. The school offers medical and doctoral degrees, residencies, and specialty programs such as reproductive medicine. The community-oriented school does not have a teaching hospital but rather partners with about a dozen regional hospitals. Its main campus is part of the Eastern Virginia Medical Center, which is also home to Sentara Norfolk General Hospital and Children's Hospital of The King's Daughters, located in the Hampton Roads region of southeastern Virginia. The south campus hosts pediatric and diabetes research programs. EVMS also has research programs devoted to cancer, infectious diseases, and heart disease.

	Annual Growth	06/17	06/18	06/19	06/20	06/21
Sales ($mil.)	4.3%	–	255.8	336.5	294.5	289.9
Net income ($ mil.)	52.8%	–	26.0	71.8	54.8	92.8
Market value ($ mil.)	–	–	–	–	–	–
Employees	–	–	–	–	–	1,500

EASTERN WASHINGTON UNIVERSITY INC

307 SHOWALTER HALL
CHENEY, WA 990042445
Phone: 509 359-6200
Fax: –
Web: www.ewu.edu

CEO: –
CFO: Toni Havegger
HR: –
FYE: June 30
Type: Private

Eagles -- the mascot kind, at any rate -- soar around Eastern Washington University (EWU). The university serves about 13,000 undergraduate and graduate students in the area around metropolitan Spokane, Washington. Most students study at EWU's Cheney campus, but the school includes other learning centers around the state. EWU has 23:1 student-to-faculty ratio. About 140 fields of study are offered through four colleges: Arts, Letters, and Education; Business and Public Administration; Science, Health, and Engineering; and Social and Behavioral Sciences and Social Work. The school was founded in 1882 as the Benjamin P. Cheney Academy.

	Annual Growth	06/18	06/19	06/20	06/21	06/22
Sales ($mil.)	2.3%	–	154.0	152.6	149.3	164.8
Net income ($ mil.)	46.7%	–	13.2	38.1	46.1	41.7
Market value ($ mil.)	–	–	–	–	–	–
Employees	–	–	–	–	–	1,550

EASTGROUP PROPERTIES INC

NYS: EGP

400 W. Parkway Place, Suite 100
Ridgeland, MS 39157
Phone: 601 354-3555
Fax: –
Web: www.eastgroup.net

CEO: Marshall A Loeb
CFO: Brent W Wood
HR: –
FYE: December 31
Type: Public

EastGroup Properties is a self-administered real estate investment trust (REIT) invests in, develops, and manages industrial properties, with a particular emphasis on Florida, Texas, Arizona, North Carolina, and California. EastGroup's distribution space properties are typically multitenant buildings. Its distribution space for location sensitive customers ranges from about 20,000 to 100,000 sq. ft. in size, located near major transportation hubs. Its portfolio includes more than 485 industrial properties and an office building, totaling more than 58.7 million sq. ft. of leasable space.

	Annual Growth	12/19	12/20	12/21	12/22	12/23
Sales ($mil.)	14.6%	331.4	363.0	409.5	487.0	570.6
Net income ($ mil.)	13.3%	121.7	108.4	157.6	186.2	200.5
Market value ($ mil.)	8.5%	6,328.4	6,585.5	10,869	7,062.5	8,754.9
Employees	5.7%	77	80	82	87	96

EASTLAND MEMORIAL HOSPITAL DISTRICT

304 S DAUGHERTY AVE
EASTLAND, TX 764482609
Phone: 254 629-2601
Fax: –
Web: www.eastlandmemorial.com

CEO: Ted D Matthews
CFO: Jamie Hayden
HR: –
FYE: June 30
Type: Private

Eastland Memorial Hospital provides a variety of health care services to the residents of Eastland County, Texas. Specialized services include cardiac rehabilitation, emergency medicine, obstetrics, physical therapy, and radiology. Established in 1953, the hospital also has specialty clinics in areas such as oncology, orthopedics, neurology, hearing, and podiatry. Without government aid of any kind, Eastland Memorial Hospital was built back in the 1950s with Eastland citizens' voluntary time, as well as donated supplies.

	Annual Growth	06/06	06/07	06/08	06/09	06/14
Sales ($mil.)	3.9%	–	–	–	9.5	11.5
Net income ($ mil.)	63.6%	–	–	–	0.4	4.2
Market value ($ mil.)	–	–	–	–	–	–
Employees	–	–	–	–	–	264

EASTMAN CHEMICAL CO

NYS: EMN

200 South Wilcox Drive
Kingsport, TN 37662
Phone: 423 229-2000
Fax: –
Web: www.eastman.com

CEO: Mark J Costa
CFO: William T McLain Jr
HR: Linda Burchfield
FYE: December 31
Type: Public

Eastman Chemical Company is a chemical manufacturer with a focus on additives, chemical intermediates, advanced materials, and fibers. The company has about 35 manufacturing facilities and has equity interests in two manufacturing joint ventures in more than 10 countries that supply products to customers worldwide. Eastman's products wind up in scores of consumer and industrial products, including building materials, automotive paints, tires, personal and home care products, packaging, animal nutrition and crop protection products, water treatment, and health and wellness products. The company, founded in 1920, was once part of film giant Eastman Kodak. The US and Canada generate the largest sales with some 45%.

	Annual Growth	12/19	12/20	12/21	12/22	12/23
Sales ($mil.)	(0.2%)	9,273.0	8,473.0	10,476	10,580	9,210.0
Net income ($ mil.)	4.2%	759.0	478.0	857.0	793.0	894.0
Market value ($ mil.)	3.2%	9,296.6	11,762	14,182	9,552.3	10,535
Employees	(0.9%)	14,500	14,500	14,000	14,500	14,000

EASTMAN KODAK CO.

NYS: KODK

343 State Street
Rochester, NY 14650
Phone: 585 724-4000
Fax: –
Web: www.kodak.com

CEO: James V Continenza V
CFO: David E Bullwinkle
HR: –
FYE: December 31
Type: Public

Eastman Kodak is a global manufacturer focused on commercial print and advanced materials and chemicals. Committed to environmental stewardship, including industry leadership in developing sustainable solutions for print, the company provides industry-leading hardware, software, consumables and services primarily to customers in commercial printing, packaging, publishing, manufacturing and entertainment. With approximately 31,000 patents earned over 130 years of research and development, Kodak's innovative, award-winning products, combined with its customer-first approach, allow the company to attract customers worldwide. The company, which generates most of its sales outside the US, was founded in 1880 by George Eastman.

	Annual Growth	12/19	12/20	12/21	12/22	12/23
Sales ($mil.)	(2.6%)	1,242.0	1,029.0	1,150.0	1,205.0	1,117.0
Net income ($ mil.)	(10.3%)	116.0	(541.0)	24.0	26.0	75.0
Market value ($ mil.)	(4.3%)	370.1	647.9	372.5	242.8	310.4
Employees	(5.1%)	4,922	4,500	4,200	4,200	4,000

EASTON BANCORP, INC.
NBB: EASB

501 Idlewild Avenue
Easton, MD 21601
Phone: 410 819-0300
Fax: 410 819-8091
Web: www.eastonbankandtrust.com

CEO: –
CFO: –
HR: –
FYE: December 31
Type: Public

Go Easton, young Marylander! Easton Bancorp, that is. Easton Bancorp is the holding company for Easton Bank & Trust, which serves Talbot and Caroline counties on Maryland's eastern shore. From about a half dozen offices, the bank provides standard retail products and services, including checking and savings accounts, IRAs, and credit cards to local businesses and individuals. It uses funds from deposits to write mostly commercial and real estate loans; other offerings include consumer loans and agricultural loans. Easton Bank & Trust also operates under the names Denton Bank & Trust and Oxford Bank & Trust. Easton Bancorp is taking itself private.

	Annual Growth	12/99	12/00	12/01	12/02	12/03
Assets ($mil.)	16.2%	56.0	64.5	79.8	88.3	102.1
Net income ($ mil.)	3.7%	0.5	0.5	0.5	0.5	0.6
Market value ($ mil.)	19.8%	6.5	7.9	8.2	8.8	13.4
Employees	10.0%	28	32	35	40	41

EAU TECHNOLOGIES INC
NBB: EAUI

1890 Cobb International Blvd., Suite A
Kennesaw, GA 30152
Phone: 678 388-9492
Fax: –
Web: www.eau-x.com

CEO: Doug Kindred
CFO: Brian D Heinhold
HR: –
FYE: December 31
Type: Public

Of all the vowels, O is EAU's bread and butter (as in H 2 O). Using water electrolysis technology, EAU Technologies (formerly Electric Aquagenics Unlimited) makes equipment and process systems that clean and disinfect surfaces and foods. Its Empowered Water generators are sold and leased to companies in search of improved cleaning and sanitizing. The firm's water-based, non-toxic products reduce bacteria, viruses, spores, and molds in food processing, living surfaces, and other environments. Director Peter Ullrich, individually and through his Water Science firm, is EAU Technologies largest shareholder. Water Science is also EAU's biggest customer and it licenses EAU technology in Latin America.

	Annual Growth	12/10	12/11	12/12	12/13	12/14
Sales ($mil.)	9.2%	0.7	1.9	0.5	2.0	1.0
Net income ($ mil.)	–	2.4	(3.0)	(2.0)	(2.0)	(1.9)
Market value ($ mil.)	(41.4%)	4.9	5.7	0.6	1.1	0.6
Employees	(10.7%)	11	11	11	9	7

EBAY INC.
NMS: EBAY

2025 Hamilton Avenue
San Jose, CA 95125
Phone: 408 376-7108
Fax: –
Web: www.ebay.com

CEO: –
CFO: –
HR: –
FYE: December 31
Type: Public

eBay is a global commerce leader through its Marketplace platforms which connect millions of buyers and sellers in more than 190 markets around the world and boasts about 135 million users and over 1.5 billion listings globally. The platforms include its online marketplace located at www.ebay.com and its localized counterparts, including off-platform businesses in Japan, as well as eBay's suite of mobile apps. It generates revenue through final value fees, feature fees, including fees to promote listing and listing fees from sellers in its Marketplace. About half of eBay's revenue comes from the US.

	Annual Growth	12/19	12/20	12/21	12/22	12/23
Sales ($mil.)	(1.6%)	10,800	10,271	10,420	9,795.0	10,112
Net income ($ mil.)	11.6%	1,786.0	5,667.0	13,608	(1,269.0)	2,767.0
Market value ($ mil.)	4.8%	18,669	25,979	34,381	21,440	22,552
Employees	(1.9%)	13,300	12,700	10,800	11,600	12,300

EBIX INC
NMS: EBIX

1 Ebix Way
Johns Creek, GA 30097
Phone: 678 281-2020
Fax: –
Web: www.ebix.com

CEO: –
CFO: –
HR: –
FYE: December 31
Type: Public

Ebix Inc. is a leading international supplier of on-demand infrastructure exchanges to the insurance, financial services, travel, and healthcare industries. Its EbixCash Exchange (EbixCash) is primarily derived from the sales of prepaid gift cards and consideration paid by customers for financial transaction services, including services like transferring or exchanging money. It also offers several other services, including payment services and ticketing and travel services for which revenue is impacted by varying factors. Ebix also Software-as-a-Service (SaaS) enterprise solutions in the area of customer relationship management (CRM), front-end & back-end systems, outsourced administrative and risk compliance. The company has domestic and international operations spread across approximately 200 offices and serves thousands of customers in over 70 countries across six continents. Ebix generates the majority of its revenue in India.

	Annual Growth	12/18	12/19	12/20	12/21	12/22
Sales ($mil.)	20.5%	497.8	580.6	625.6	994.9	1,050.1
Net income ($ mil.)	(8.7%)	93.1	96.7	92.4	68.2	64.6
Market value ($ mil.)	(17.2%)	1,311.7	1,029.7	1,170.2	936.9	615.2
Employees	3.2%	9,263	7,975	9,802	10,030	10,521

EBY CORPORATION

2525 E 36TH CIR N
WICHITA, KS 672192303
Phone: 316 268-3500
Fax: –
Web: www.ebycorp.com

CEO: James R Greir III
CFO: –
HR: Karman Diehl
FYE: December 31
Type: Private

General contractor Eby Corporation, operating primarily through its Martin K. Eby Construction subsidiary, provides design-build, construction management, general contracting, and related services on projects such as office buildings, medical facilities, athletic facilities, and historical renovations. Eby serves major corporations, universities, hospitals, and state and local governments. Clients have included Disney, The University of Texas, Wichita State University, and The Salvation Army. Martin K. Eby Construction, named after the group's founder and the father of chairman Martin K. Eby Jr., was founded in 1937.

EBY-BROWN COMPANY, LLC

1415 W DIEHL RD STE 300N
NAPERVILLE, IL 605631153
Phone: 630 778-2800
Fax: –
Web: www.eby-brown.com

CEO: –
CFO: –
HR: Barry Bentley
FYE: October 02
Type: Private

Eby-Brown is one of the nation's leading convenience store suppliers, delivering innovative foodservice and merchandizing, along with valuable technology and insights to more than 11,000 c-store retail locations across North America. Eby-Brown operates ten distribution centers that supply such items as beverages, candy and snack foods, frozen and refrigerated foods, tobacco products, and general merchandise. The convenience store supplier also offers advertising and promotion services for its customers. Eby-Brown was founded in 1887 by the Wake family.

ECC CAPITAL CORP

NBB: ECRO

2600 East Coast Highway, Suite 250
Corona Del Mar, CA 92625
Phone: 949 955-8700
Fax: –
Web: www.ecccapital.com

CEO: Steven G Holder
CFO: Roque A Santi
HR: –
FYE: December 31
Type: Public

ECC Capital refused to conform -- to credit scoring criteria. The real estate investment trust (REIT) was formed to invest in non-conforming residential real estate loans. In the height of the subprime mortgage crisis, the REIT's revenues plummeted and ECC Capital was forced to close offices, reduce its workforce, and sell assets. In 2007 it sold wholesale mortgage banking arm Encore Credit to Bear Stearns; it also sold its portfolio of direct-to-consumer loans to ResCap. The REIT is seeking a buyer for the rest of its securitized assets. Subsidiary Performance Credit was formerly engaged in the origination of wholesale loans but now provides financing to ECC Capital's clients.

	Annual Growth	12/06	12/18	12/19	12/20	12/21
Sales ($mil.)	(2.1%)	30.7	1.7	(1.4)	5.1	22.4
Net income ($ mil.)	–	(134.6)	(2.7)	(4.8)	1.1	12.8
Market value ($ mil.)	(16.8%)	126.8	1.5	0.8	6.9	8.0
Employees	–	715	–	–	–	–

ECHELON CORPORATION

6024 SILVER CREEK VALLEY RD
SAN JOSE, CA 951381011
Phone: 408 938-5200
Fax: –
Web: www.adestotech.com

CEO: Ronald Sege
CFO: –
HR: –
FYE: December 31
Type: Private

Echelon Corp. has made the infrastructure that connected industrial devices into networks that morphed into the Internet of Things. The company's combination of computer chips, routers and controllers, network interfaces, and software have enabled connections for about 100 million devices for lighting, heating and cooling, security, manufacturing, lighting, and building automation around the world. Echelon is moving to develop networking resources for the Industrial Internet of Things (IIoT), providing the capability for things such as sensors inside jet engines to communicate their operating status. The company also develops and sells an array of lighting control systems, another portion of the Internet of Things.

ECHL INC.

830 BROAD ST STE 3
SHREWSBURY, NJ 077024216
Phone: 609 452-0770
Fax: –
Web: www.echl.com

CEO: Ray Harris
CFO: –
HR: –
FYE: June 30
Type: Private

East Coast Hockey League oversees an association of semi-professional hockey teams affiliated with National Hockey League and American Hockey League. Better known as ECHL, it has franchises in about 20 markets across the US and serves as a development league for the pro ranks. ECHL teams compete during a seven-month regular season for a chance to win the Kelly Cup championship. The league oversees team ownership, marketing, and promotional efforts for its confederation of local sports clubs. The ECHL was established in 1988.

	Annual Growth	06/12	06/13	06/18	06/19	06/22
Sales ($mil.)	6.4%	–	2.4	3.9	3.6	4.2
Net income ($ mil.)	–	–	(0.2)	(0.2)	(0.0)	(2.2)
Market value ($ mil.)	–	–	–	–	–	–
Employees	–	–	–	–	–	12

ECHO GLOBAL LOGISTICS, INC.

600 W CHICAGO AVE STE 725
CHICAGO, IL 606542522
Phone: 800 354-7993
Fax: –
Web: www.echo.com

CEO: Douglas R Waggoner
CFO: Peter M Rogers
HR: –
FYE: December 31
Type: Private

Echo Global Logistics is a leading Fortune 1000 provider of technology-enabled transportation and supply chain management services. Echo Global maintains a proprietary, web-based technology platform that compiles and analyzes data from its network of over 50,000 transportation providers to serve 35,000 clients across a wide range of industries and simplify the critical tasks involved in transportation management. It also offers intermodal services (which involves moving a shipment by rail and truck), small parcels, specialized/partial, and international transportation services. The company was founded in 2005.

ECHO THERAPEUTICS INC

99 Wood Avenue South, Suite 302
Iselin, NJ 08830
Phone: 732 201-4189
Fax: –
Web: www.echotx.com

CEO: Alan W Schoenbart
CFO: Alan W Schoenbart
HR: –
FYE: December 31
Type: Public

Echo Therapeutics tries not to scratch the surface. The company develops instruments for transdermal (through the skin) drug delivery and diagnostics. Its devices use gentle abrasion and ultrasound technologies to painlessly extract analytes or introduce drugs without breaking the skin. The firm's proprietary Prelude SkinPrep technology platform is being developed for use in glucose monitoring under the name Symphony. Echo is also developing a system to provide needle-free drug administration of lidocaine and other pharmaceuticals. Echo is also developing Azone, a transdermal technology used for reformulated drugs already on the market.

	Annual Growth	12/11	12/12	12/13	12/14	12/15
Sales ($mil.)	–	0.4	0.0	0.0	0.0	–
Net income ($ mil.)	–	(10.0)	(12.3)	(19.1)	(15.0)	(22.2)
Market value ($ mil.)	(11.0%)	25.1	11.6	34.9	15.0	15.8
Employees	(12.5%)	29	44	28	18	17

ECHOSTAR CORP

NMS: SATS

100 Inverness Terrace East
Englewood, CO 80112-5308
Phone: 303 706-4000
Fax: –
Web: www.echostar.com

CEO: Michael T Dugan
CFO: David J Rayner
HR: –
FYE: December 31
Type: Public

EchoStar Corporation is a premier global provider of satellite communication solutions and a pioneer in secure communications technologies through its Hughes Network Systems and EchoStar Satellite Services business segments. It provides internet services to consumer customers, which include home and small to medium-sized businesses, and satellite services. The company owns or leases around 10 GEO satellites. The company's Hughes unit has approximately 1.2 million business broadband subscribers. EchoStar is also an industry leader in both networking technologies and services, innovating to deliver the global solutions that power a connected future for people, enterprises and things everywhere. The North America region accounts for most of EchoStar's revenue.

	Annual Growth	12/19	12/20	12/21	12/22	12/23
Sales ($mil.)	73.3%	1,886.1	1,887.9	1,985.7	1,998.1	17,016
Net income ($ mil.)	–	(62.9)	(40.2)	72.9	177.1	(1,702.1)
Market value ($ mil.)	(21.4%)	11,759	5,753.1	7,154.1	4,528.6	4,498.8
Employees	60.6%	2,300	2,400	2,500	2,300	15,300

ECKERD COLLEGE, INC.

4200 54TH AVE S
SAINT PETERSBURG, FL 337114700
Phone: 727 867-1166
Fax: –
Web: www.eckerd.edu

CEO: Peter Armacost
CFO: –
HR: Liana Hemingway
FYE: June 30
Type: Private

What better place to study marine science than on nearly 200 acres of Florida waterfront? Eckerd College is a private, co-educational college located in St. Petersburg. The school has about 1,800 students and 160 faculty members, and it offers about 40 majors for students to earn bachelor of arts and bachelor of science degrees. Areas of study include marine science, psychology, economics, biology, biochemistry, international studies, literature, and art. The school also operates a Program for Experienced Learners where about 700 adult students can earn a bachelor's degree in about a dozen areas, as well as study abroad offerings. Eckerd College is affiliated with the Presbyterian Church (U.S.A.).

	Annual Growth	06/15	06/16	06/20	06/21	06/22
Sales ($mil.)	9.2%	–	74.1	127.9	134.8	125.3
Net income ($ mil.)	–	–	(6.7)	3.6	18.7	(12.0)
Market value ($ mil.)	–	–	–	–	–	–
Employees	–	–	–	–	–	377

ECKERD YOUTH ALTERNATIVES, INC.

100 N STARCREST DR
CLEARWATER, FL 337653224
Phone: 727 461-2990
Fax: –
Web: www.eckerd.org

CEO: –
CFO: –
HR: Tracy Willis
FYE: June 30
Type: Private

Eckerd Youth Alternatives (EYA) provides early intervention and prevention, wilderness education, residential and day treatment, and re-entry and aftercare programs for at-risk youths. The not-for-profit organization has worked to help more than 80,000 kids through its operations in about 10 states, located primarily in the eastern US. Many of EYA's some 40 programs are offered under contract with state juvenile justice agencies. EYA was established in 1968 by Jack Eckerd, the founder of the Eckerd drugstore chain, and his wife, Ruth Eckerd. During the past few years, the company has been focused on expanding its community-based support programs.

	Annual Growth	06/15	06/16	06/19	06/20	06/22
Sales ($mil.)	8.3%	–	193.2	236.5	284.7	312.3
Net income ($ mil.)	(6.9%)	–	4.6	3.2	2.1	3.0
Market value ($ mil.)	–	–	–	–	–	–
Employees	–	–	–	–	–	1,400

ECO2 PLASTICS, INC.

800 N HAVEN AVE STE 120
ONTARIO, CA 917644951
Phone: 209 848-3900
Fax: –
Web: www.eco2plastics.com

CEO: –
CFO: –
HR: –
FYE: December 31
Type: Private

Recycler ECO 2 Plastics wants to get the oil out. Using carbon dioxide and solvents rather than water, the company's Eco 2 Environmental System cleans plastic containers that have been used for motor oil and agricultural chemicals. The containers are then shredded into plastic flakes, which are used as raw materials by manufacturers of plastic containers. Technology for the system is licensed from Honeywell International and the US Department of Energy. ECO 2 Plastics market its system to recyclers. The company, which closed its doors and filed for Chapter 11 reorganization in 2009, emerged from bankruptcy in 2010 as a private company and restarted operations at its Melno Park, California, facility.

ECOLAB INC

NYS: ECL

1 Ecolab Place
St. Paul, MN 55102
Phone: 800 232-6522
Fax: –
Web: www.ecolab.com

CEO: Christophe Beck
CFO: Scott D Kirkland
HR: Laurie M Marsh
FYE: December 31
Type: Public

Ecolab is a global leader in water, hygiene and infection prevention solutions and services. It offers cleaning, sanitation, pest-elimination, and maintenance products and services to the energy, healthcare, hospitality, and industrial sectors, among others. Its cleaning and sanitizing operations serve hotels, schools, commercial and institutional laundries, and quick-service restaurants. It also makes chemicals used in water treatment for industrial processes, including in the paper and energy industries. The US is Ecolab's largest market, but also operates in other countries in Asia Pacific, Greater China, Western Europe, Latin America, and South Africa.

	Annual Growth	12/19	12/20	12/21	12/22	12/23
Sales ($mil.)	0.7%	14,906	11,790	12,733	14,188	15,320
Net income ($ mil.)	(3.1%)	1,558.9	(1,205.1)	1,129.9	1,091.7	1,372.3
Market value ($ mil.)	0.7%	55,089	61,760	66,963	41,550	56,619
Employees	(1.1%)	50,200	44,000	47,000	47,000	48,000

ECOLOGY AND ENVIRONMENT INC.

368 PLEASANT VIEW DR
LANCASTER, NY 140861316
Phone: 716 684-8060
Fax: –
Web: www.wsp.com

CEO: –
CFO: Peter F Sorci
HR: –
FYE: July 31
Type: Private

Every day is Earth Day at environmental consulting and testing company Ecology and Environment (E & E). The company, which has completed more than 50,000 projects in some 120 countries, provides engineering, permitting, and environmental support for all types of energy development, including offshore energy, power plants, pipelines, and renewables. Services include environmental impact assessments, air pollution control, wastewater analyses, and site-planning. It also consults on natural resource restoration programs, green initiatives, emergency planning, and hazardous waste projects. E & E, which generates most of its sales in the US, targets government, industrial, and engineering clients. The company has agreed to be acquired by Montreal-based consulting firm WSP Global.

ECOVYST INC

NYS: ECVT

300 Lindenwood Drive
Malvern, PA 19355
Phone: 484 617-1200
Fax: –
Web: www.pqcorp.com

CEO: Kurt J Bitting
CFO: Michael Feehan
HR: –
FYE: December 31
Type: Public

Ecovyst (formerly PQ Group Holdings) is a leading, integrated, and innovative global provider of specialty catalysts and services. The company provides sulfuric acid recycling services to North American refineries for the production of alkylate, an essential gasoline component for lowering vapor pressure and increasing octane to meet stringent gasoline specifications and fuel efficiency standards. It is also a producer of on-purpose virgin sulfuric acid for water treatment, mining, and industrial applications. Ecovyst generates almost 95% of sales in the US. The company traces its roots back to 1831.

	Annual Growth	12/19	12/20	12/21	12/22	12/23
Sales ($mil.)	(18.5%)	1,567.1	1,107.4	611.2	820.2	691.1
Net income ($ mil.)	(2.7%)	79.5	(278.8)	(139.9)	73.7	71.2
Market value ($ mil.)	(13.2%)	1,994.9	1,655.8	1,189.0	1,028.8	1,134.5
Employees	(27.4%)	3,279	2,274	883	890	911

ECS FEDERAL, LLC

2750 PROSPERITY AVE STE 600
FAIRFAX, VA 220314312
Phone: 703 270-1540
Fax: –
Web: www.ecstech.com

CEO: –
CFO: Thomas Weston
HR: Jim Lyons
FYE: December 31
Type: Private

Electronic Consulting Services (ECS) provides computer and telecommunications network consulting services primarily in the Eastern US. The company specializes in such areas as systems engineering, enterprise communications, project management, and program support. It also offers information assurance, help desk operations, and Web development services. ECS primarily serves government agencies and defense contractors. Customers have included Lockheed Martin, Titan, the US Department of Housing and Urban Development, and Advanced Technology Systems. The company has satellite offices in Florida, Missouri, North Carolina, Pennsylvania, and Washington, D.C. Electronic Consulting Services was founded in 1993.

	Annual Growth	12/08	12/09	12/10	12/11	12/12
Sales ($mil.)	36.0%	–	–	112.4	138.8	208.1
Net income ($ mil.)	21.4%	–	–	11.1	8.0	16.4
Market value ($ mil.)	–	–	–	–	–	–
Employees	–	–	–	–	–	3,500

EDD HELMS GROUP

17850 N.E. 5th Avenue
Miami, FL 33162-1008
Phone: 305 653-2520
Fax: –
Web: –

NBB: EDHD
CEO: Wade Helms
CFO: Dean Goodson
HR: –
FYE: May 31
Type: Public

Like a friend's sentiment in your junior high yearbook, the Edd Helms Group wants you to "stay cool." The contracting group provides electrical and HVAC maintenance and retrofitting services for commercial, marine (primarily private yachts), and residential customers in South Florida. It also offers temporary power and lighting installation for tradeshows and conventions; the group markets its temporary power services for emergency restoration in emergency situations such as hurricanes. Additionally, the group provides structural and radio frequency services for wireless and cellular towers. CEO and founder W. Edd Helms, Jr., owns 84% of the company.

	Annual Growth	05/04	05/05	05/06	05/07	05/08
Sales ($mil.)	7.5%	16.2	17.1	21.2	22.8	21.6
Net income ($ mil.)	–	(0.3)	0.2	0.8	0.9	(0.0)
Market value ($ mil.)	12.3%	0.0	0.0	0.0	0.0	0.0
Employees	4.6%	117	135	143	136	140

EDELBROCK, LLC

8649 HACKS CROSS RD
OLIVE BRANCH, MS 386543841
Phone: 310 781-2222
Fax: –
Web: www.edelbrock.com

CEO: Don Barry
CFO: Steve Zitkus
HR: Daisy Perez
FYE: June 30
Type: Private

Speed enthusiast Edelbrock makes performance-enhancing parts for race cars and motorcycles, recreational and passenger vehicles, light trucks, and watercraft. The short list includes carburetors, intake manifolds, cylinder heads, water pumps, air cleaners, camshafts, exhaust systems, an array of other aftermarket parts, and even some branded sportswear. Specifically for Harley-Davidson motorcycles, Edelbrock tailors a line of aftermarket engine parts. The company markets its products mainly through automotive chain stores, online dealers, mail-order houses, and warehouse distributors. The Edelbrock family -- led by company chairman, president, and CEO Vic Edelbrock Jr. -- runs the company.

EDELMAN FINANCIAL ENGINES, LLC

1050 ENTERPRISE WAY STE 300
SUNNYVALE, CA 940891415
Phone: 408 498-6000
Fax: –
Web: www.edelmanfinancialengines.com

CEO: Lawrence M Raffone
CFO: –
HR: –
FYE: December 31
Type: Private

Edelman Financial Engines is America's top independent wealth planning and workplace investment advisory firm. It provides financial advice, portfolio management, and retirement assessment services. The firm serves the US retirement-plan participants, sponsors, and service providers across a wide range of industries that includes more than 100 FORTUNE 500 companies and several of the largest retirement plan operators. Edelman Financial Engines serves approximately 1.3 million customers and boasts more than $242 billion client assets.

EDEN FOODS, INC.

701 TECUMSEH RD
CLINTON, MI 492369599
Phone: 517 456-7424
Fax: –
Web: store.edenfoods.com

CEO: Michael Potter
CFO: –
HR: –
FYE: December 31
Type: Private

Known for its Edensoy organic soymilk, Eden Foods offers more than 300 organic food items. It's North America's oldest natural and organic food company and the largest independent manufacturer of dry grocery organic foods. Products include canned beans and tomatoes, condiments, dry pasta, dried fruit and seeds, juices, oils, vinegars, teas, and spices. They're made using ingredients from more than 300 certified-organic North American farms. Eden Foods also imports sea salts from Europe and traditional Japanese miso and rice vinegar from Asia. Subsidiaries include American Soy Products, Eden Organic Pasta, Meridian Foods, and Sobaya. Family-owned, Eden Foods began in 1968 as a natural foods cooperative.

	Annual Growth	12/14	12/15	12/16	12/17	12/18
Sales ($mil.)	(4.5%)	–	49.0	47.4	43.9	42.7
Net income ($ mil.)	3.4%	–	5.7	2.9	3.8	6.3
Market value ($ mil.)	–	–	–	–	–	–
Employees	–	–	–	–	–	140

EDGEWAVE, INC

4225 EXECUTIVE SQ # 1600
LA JOLLA, CA 920371487
Phone: 800 782-3762
Fax: –
Web: www.edgewave.com

CEO: –
CFO: –
HR: –
FYE: December 31
Type: Private

Edgewave (formerly St. Bernard Software) rescues networks and data from the edge of disaster. The company provides security software and network appliances that guard against data loss, network attacks, unsolicited e-mail, and Internet abuse. Its 6,500 clients come from industries including financial services, electronics, manufacturing, health care, and telecommunications. EdgeWave also offers professional services such as consulting, installation, maintenance, training, and support. Founded in 1994, the company became a public company after a reverse merger with Sand Hill IT Security Acquisition in 2006. It rebranded as EdgeWave in January 2011 and changed its name later that year.

	Annual Growth	12/07	12/08	12/09	12/10	12/11
Sales ($mil.)	(0.9%)	–	–	18.4	18.1	18.0
Net income ($ mil.)	–	–	–	(0.3)	(3.6)	(4.6)
Market value ($ mil.)	–	–	–	–	–	–
Employees	–	–	–	–	–	100

EDGEWELL PERSONAL CARE CO
NYS: EPC

6 Research Drive
Shelton, CT 06484
Phone: 203 944-5500
Fax: –
Web: www.edgewell.com

CEO: Rod R Little
CFO: Daniel J Sullivan
HR: –
FYE: September 30
Type: Public

Edgewell Personal Care Company is one of the world's largest manufacturers and marketers of portfolio of personal care products includes razors, sunscreen, moist wipes, infant and pet care products, and feminine care products sold under brands such as Schick, Edge, Banana Boat, Hawaiian Tropic, Stayfree, Wet Ones, and Diaper Genie. The company distributes its products to consumers through numerous retail locations worldwide, including mass merchandisers and warehouse clubs, food, drug and convenience stores, and military stores. It operates in more than 20 countries and has a global footprint in more than 50 countries. The US accounts for about 60% of its total revenue.

	Annual Growth	09/19	09/20	09/21	09/22	09/23
Sales ($mil.)	1.3%	2,141.0	1,949.7	2,087.3	2,171.7	2,251.6
Net income ($ mil.)	–	(372.2)	67.6	117.0	98.6	114.7
Market value ($ mil.)	3.3%	1,628.4	1,397.3	1,819.3	1,874.4	1,852.4
Employees	3.2%	6,000	5,800	6,900	7,000	6,800

EDGIO INC
NAS: EGIO

11811 North Tatum Blvd., Suite 3031
Phoenix, AZ 85028
Phone: 602 850-5000
Fax: –
Web: www.edg.io

CEO: –
CFO: –
HR: –
FYE: December 31
Type: Public

Limelight Networks' goal is to provide clients with a productive, performant and protected environment to run their mission critical applications on the edge. The company provides edge services platform. Services include content delivery, web content management, online video publishing, video delivery, and cloud security. Limelight's global network infrastructure includes more than 140 points-of-presence, and is also directly interconnected with over 1,000 major internet service providers. It serves some 580 active customers worldwide and its biggest geographic market is the Americas.

	Annual Growth	12/18	12/19	12/20	12/21	12/22
Sales ($mil.)	14.7%	195.7	200.6	230.2	217.6	338.6
Net income ($ mil.)	–	9.8	(16.0)	(19.3)	(54.8)	(136.5)
Market value ($ mil.)	(16.6%)	13.0	22.7	22.2	19.1	6.3
Employees	14.9%	563	610	618	552	980

EDI SPECIALISTS, INC.

31 BELLOWS RD
RAYNHAM, MA 027671454
Phone: 800 821-4644
Fax: –
Web: www.edistaffing.com

CEO: –
CFO: –
HR: –
FYE: December 31
Type: Private

EDI Specialists' (EDI) specialty is providing information technology staffing and consulting services. It offers permanent and temporary staff in the areas of programming and troubleshooting, supply chain services, integrating applications, information technology, and e-commerce. EDI also deploys individual consultants or teams to conduct executive workshops, assist with strategy development, and implement IT system migrations, among other services. The company's consulting services assist customers with evaluating its current business processes and implementing a list of best practices. EDI was founded in 1994.

	Annual Growth	12/07	12/08	12/10	12/11	12/12
Sales ($mil.)	3.3%	–	15.4	11.5	14.6	17.6
Net income ($ mil.)	7.8%	–	0.3	0.6	0.7	0.4
Market value ($ mil.)	–	–	–	–	–	–
Employees	–	–	–	–	–	100

EDIBLE INTERNATIONAL, LLC

95 BARNES RD
WALLINGFORD, CT 064921800
Phone: 203 774-8000
Fax: –
Web: www.ediblearrangements.com

CEO: –
CFO: Amanda D Allen
HR: –
FYE: December 31
Type: Private

"Please don't eat the daisies" simply doesn't apply here. Edible Arrangements creates bouquets of hand-sculpted fresh fruit that are blooming with flower-shaped pineapples, shoots of melon slices, sprigs of skewered grapes, and an assortment of apple wedges, bananas, oranges, and strawberries. Customers can also add chocolate-dipped fruit to their arrangements. In addition to bouquets, the company offers smoothies and fruit salads at some shops. Fast-growing Edible Arrangements has more than 1,200 franchised locations throughout North America, Puerto Rico, the Middle East, Italy, Turkey, and Hong Kong. CEO Tariq Farid started Edible Arrangements in 1999 after doing software consulting for a similar business.

	Annual Growth	06/09	06/10	06/11*	12/12	12/13
Sales ($mil.)	46.3%	–	–	12.7	26.0	27.2
Net income ($ mil.)	36.9%	–	–	7.7	13.7	14.5
Market value ($ mil.)	–	–	–	–	–	180
Employees	–	–	–	–	–	–

*Fiscal year change

EDISON INTERNATIONAL
NYS: EIX

2244 Walnut Grove Avenue, P.O. Box 976
Rosemead, CA 91770
Phone: 626 302-2222
Fax: –
Web: www.edisoninvestor.com

CEO: Pedro J Pizarro
CFO: Maria Rigatti
HR: Bernice Crocchi
FYE: December 31
Type: Public

Edison International is a major power provider in California through its Southern California Edison (SCE) subsidiary, which distributes electricity to customers in a 50,000 square-mile area of central, coastal, and southern California. The distribution system, which takes power from substations to customers, includes about 40,000 line-miles of overhead lines, 31,000 line-miles of underground lines and approximately 730 substations, all of which are located in California. SCE also has about 7,000 MW of generating capacity and energy storage facilities, primarily located in California.

	Annual Growth	12/19	12/20	12/21	12/22	12/23
Sales ($mil.)	7.3%	12,347	13,578	14,905	17,220	16,338
Net income ($ mil.)	2.3%	1,284.0	739.0	819.0	824.0	1,407.0
Market value ($ mil.)	(1.3%)	28,952	24,118	26,203	24,425	27,447
Employees	2.6%	12,937	13,351	13,003	13,388	14,316

EDISONLEARNING, INC.

1 E BROWARD BLVD STE 1599
FORT LAUDERDALE, FL 333012040
Phone: 201 630-2600
Fax: –
Web: www.edisonlearning.com

CEO: Thomas Jackson
CFO: –
HR: –
FYE: June 30
Type: Private

Light bulbs switch on daily at EdisonLearning. The firm works with school districts and administrators to help improve school performance. It manages the operations of public and charter K-12 schools, ranging from curriculum decisions to community relations. EdisonLearning focuses on retaining quality teachers, engaging students and families, creating individualized instruction, and achievement-driven management. The company also provides online tutoring programs, hybrid instructional environments, and school design. EdisonLearning serves more than 450,000 students through partnerships with almost 400 schools in 20 US states, the UK and Abu Dhabi. The company was founded in 1992.

	Annual Growth	06/02	06/03	06/04	06/05	06/14
Sales ($mil.)	5.9%	–	–	–	8.7	14.6
Net income ($ mil.)	23.3%	–	–	–	0.3	1.6
Market value ($ mil.)	–	–	–	–	–	–
Employees	–	–	–	–	–	1,400

EDITAS MEDICINE INC

NMS: EDIT

11 Hurley Street
Cambridge, MA 02141
Phone: 617 401-9000
Fax: –
Web: www.editasmedicine.com

CEO: Gilmore O'Neill
CFO: Erick J Lucera
HR: –
FYE: December 31
Type: Public

The biotech firm Editas Medicine is one of a handful of companies that developed CRISPR technology -- a technique to edit genes with the potential to treat genetically defined diseases and continues to expand its capabilities. CRISPR uses a protein-RNA complex composed of an enzyme, including either Cas9 or Cas12a bound to a guide RNA molecule designed to recognize a particular DNA sequence. Once the complex binds to the DNA sequence it was designed to recognize, the complex makes a specific cut in the DNA. With the strategic research collaboration with AskBio, the firm also aims to develop a therapy to treat a neurological disease.

	Annual Growth	12/19	12/20	12/21	12/22	12/23
Sales ($mil.)	39.7%	20.5	90.7	25.5	19.7	78.1
Net income ($ mil.)	–	(133.7)	(116.0)	(192.5)	(220.4)	(153.2)
Market value ($ mil.)	(23.5%)	2,421.1	5,732.7	2,170.9	725.3	828.3
Employees	–	208	235	264	226	–

EDSI

22835 SAVI RANCH PKWY STE F
YORBA LINDA, CA 928874633
Phone: 951 272-8689
Fax: –
Web: www.edsi.com

CEO: –
CFO: –
HR: –
FYE: October 22
Type: Private

EDSI (Engineering Documentation Systems) offers a range of information technology (IT), logistics, and testing services primarily to the US armed forces and other government agencies. The company's IT services include data systems design, software engineering, and technical support. It also installs, tests, and maintains computer network systems. EDSI offers such logistics services as equipment maintenance, supply chain management, and equipment testing. The company's other testing activities involve the development and evaluation of a variety of operational systems, particulary related to weapons systems and combat vehicles. Customers have included the US Navy, DARPA, and the FAA.

	Annual Growth	03/01	03/02	03/03	03/04*	10/13
Sales ($mil.)	(35.7%)	–	2,070.0	17.9	20.3	16.0
Net income ($ mil.)	43.7%	–	0.0	0.4	0.8	0.9
Market value ($ mil.)	–	–	–	–	–	–
Employees	–	–	–	–	–	478

*Fiscal year change

EDUCATION MANAGEMENT CORP

NBB: EDMC Q

210 Sixth Avenue, 33rd Floor
Pittsburgh, PA 15222
Phone: 412 562-0900
Fax: 412 562-0598
Web: www.edmc.edu

CEO: –
CFO: –
HR: –
FYE: June 30
Type: Public

Education Management Corporation provides higher education to students in the arts, behavioral sciences, education, health sciences, and business fields. It operates five main branches with about 110 locations in more than 30 states and in Canada. The Art Institutes, Argosy University, South University, and Brown Mackie College offer degree programs from associate to postgraduate, and Western State University College of Law offers juris doctoral degrees. The company also offers online courses through three of its divisions. Education Management institutions boast a combined enrollment of approximately 91,000 students and some 17,400 faculty and staff. Education Management voluntarily delisted from the NASDAQ in 2014.

	Annual Growth	06/10	06/11	06/12	06/13	06/14
Sales ($mil.)	(2.4%)	2,508.5	2,887.6	2,761.0	2,498.6	2,272.7
Net income ($ mil.)	–	168.5	229.5	(1,515.7)	(268.0)	(663.9)
Market value ($ mil.)	(42.3%)	1,922.2	3,017.5	876.0	708.4	213.0
Employees	(1.7%)	22,300	16,900	24,700	23,400	20,800

EDUCATIONAL & INSTITUTIONAL COOPERATIVE SERVICE, INC.

2 JERICHO PLZ STE 309
JERICHO, NY 117531681
Phone: 800 283-2634
Fax: –
Web: –

CEO: Tom Fitzgerald
CFO: John D Orlando
HR: Jeannine Pozzo
FYE: December 31
Type: Private

Educational & Institutional Cooperative Service (E&I) is a not-for-profit buying cooperative that provides goods and services to its members at discounted prices. E&I seeks and enters contracts with athletic equipment, furniture, computer and electronics, maintenance, food service, office products, and transportation and delivery service suppliers. Established in 1934, the cooperative is owned by more than 1,600 tax-exempt organizations including colleges, universities, private schools, health care institutions, and hospitals.

	Annual Growth	12/03	12/04	12/05	12/06	12/07
Sales ($mil.)	0.7%	–	10.9	12.5	13.8	11.1
Net income ($ mil.)	–	–	0.8	1.4	1.9	(0.6)
Market value ($ mil.)	–	–	–	–	–	–
Employees	–	–	–	–	–	55

EDUCATIONAL DEVELOPMENT CORP.

NMS: EDUC

5402 South 122nd East Ave
Tulsa, OK 74146
Phone: 918 622-4522
Fax: –
Web: www.edcpub.com

CEO: Craig M White
CFO: Dan O'Keefe
HR: –
FYE: February 28
Type: Public

Educational Development Corporation (EDC) likes being in a bind, as long as the cover appeals to youngsters. The company is the exclusive US distributor of a line of about 1,500 children's books published by the UK's Usborne Publishing Limited. EDC's Home Business Division markets the books to individuals using independent sales reps who sell through personal websites, home parties, direct sales, and book fairs; this division also distributes books to public and school libraries. EDC's Publishing Division distributes the Usborne line to a network of book, toy, and other retail stores. EDC bought multi-cultural children's book publisher Kane/Miller in 2008 to complement its product offerings.

	Annual Growth	02/19	02/20	02/21	02/22	02/23
Sales ($mil.)	(7.3%)	118.8	113.0	204.6	142.2	87.8
Net income ($ mil.)	–	6.7	5.6	12.6	8.3	(2.5)
Market value ($ mil.)	(17.8%)	70.1	45.0	136.0	68.7	32.1
Employees	(6.2%)	178	201	214	166	138

EDUCATIONAL FUNDING OF THE SOUTH, INC.

12700 KINGSTON PIKE
KNOXVILLE, TN 379340917
Phone: 865 342-0684
Fax: –
Web: corp.elfi.com

CEO: Ron Gambill
CFO: –
HR: –
FYE: September 30
Type: Private

Reading is fundamental, but funding is crucial to higher education. That's where Educational Funding of the South comes in. Known as Edsouth, the not-for-profit, public benefit corporation provides student loan funding by purchasing loans from originators. Nearly 500 lending institutions participate in one or more of Edsouth's educational loan programs. Edsouth is one of the nation's largest holders of student loans. The organization was founded in 1988. Formerly known as Volunteer State Student Funding Corporation, it changed its name to Educational Funding of the South in 1996.

	Annual Growth	12/03	12/04	12/05	12/06*	09/12
Assets ($mil.)	(3.5%)	–	3,881.5	4,484.5	4,223.0	2,924.2
Net income ($ mil.)	–	–	30.6	26.1	252.2	(20.1)
Market value ($ mil.)	–	–	–	–	–	–
Employees	–	–	–	–	–	102

*Fiscal year change

EDUCATIONAL TESTING SERVICE

660 ROSEDALE RD
PRINCETON, NJ 085402218
Phone: 609 921-9000
Fax: –
Web: www.ets.org

CEO: Amit Sevak
CFO: Jack Hayon
HR: Michael Smith
FYE: September 30
Type: Private

ETS is the world's largest private educational testing and measurement organization. It offers tailored solutions for teacher certification, English language learning, and education at all levels, catering to individuals, educational institutions, and government agencies. Additionally, ETS conducts education research, analysis, and policy studies to better serve its customers. Founded in 1947, the company develops and administers more than 50 million achievements, admissions, academic, and professional tests a year at more than 9,000 locations in more than 180 countries.

	Annual Growth	09/18	09/19	09/20	09/21	09/22
Sales ($mil.)	(6.4%)	–	1,358.0	1,050.3	1,071.3	1,115.3
Net income ($ mil.)	–	–	(22.1)	(85.4)	168.7	5.1
Market value ($ mil.)	–	–	–	–	–	–
Employees	–	–	–	–	–	2,756

EDW. C. LEVY CO.

9300 DIX
DEARBORN, MI 481201528
Phone: 313 429-2200
Fax: –
Web: www.edwclevy.com

CEO: Evan Weiner
CFO: –
HR: Rachel M Hayes-Jenkins
FYE: December 31
Type: Private

When you say "slag off," Edw. C. Levy doesn't take offense, it gets to work. Operating as the Levy Group of Companies or Levy Company, the firm processes slag, an impurity that forms on the surface of molten metal from blast and steel furnaces. Each year the company processes more than 10 million tons of slag, which is made into aggregates for the construction industry. Levy Company boasts slag operations in about two dozen steel mills, located mostly in the Midwest but also in Australia and Thailand. As part of its business, the company also has asphalt, cement, and concrete products. Founded in 1918, the Levy Group is still controlled by the Levy family.

EDWARD D. JONES & CO., L.P.

12555 MANCHESTER RD
SAINT LOUIS, MO 631313710
Phone: 314 515-2000
Fax: –
Web: www.edwardjones.com

CEO: –
CFO: Steve Novik
HR: –
FYE: December 31
Type: Private

As the principal operating subsidiary of The Jones Financial Companies, retail brokerage Edward D. Jones & Co. (better known by trade name Edward Jones) operates around 15,525 branch offices. Of this total, the Partnership operated around 14,855 branch offices in the all 50 US states and roughly 670 branch offices in Canada. Edward Jones primarily derives revenues from fees for providing investment advisory and other account services to its clients, fees for assets held by clients, the distribution of mutual fund shares, and commissions for the purchase or sale of securities and the purchase of insurance products.

	Annual Growth	12/18	12/19	12/20	12/21	12/22
Sales ($mil.)	2.8%	–	53.2	53.3	58.5	57.7
Net income ($ mil.)	(57.6%)	–	12.1	9.7	7.6	0.9
Market value ($ mil.)	–	–	–	–	–	–
Employees	–	–	–	–	–	36,000

EDWARDS LIFESCIENCES CORP

NYS: EW

One Edwards Way
Irvine, CA 92614
Phone: 949 250-2500
Fax: –
Web: www.edwards.com

CEO: Bernard J Zovighian
CFO: Scott B Ullem
HR: –
FYE: December 31
Type: Public

Edwards Lifesciences Corporation is the global leader in patient-focused medical innovations for structural heart disease and critical care monitoring. The company is the world's leading manufacturer of heart valve systems and repair products used to replace or repair a patient's diseased or defective heart valve. It is also a global leader in hemodynamic and noninvasive brain and tissue oxygenation monitoring systems used to measure a patient's cardiovascular function in the hospital setting. Edwards Lifesciences markets its products worldwide but generates almost 60% of revenue from the US. Edward Lifesciences was founded in 1958 by Miles "Lowell" Edwards.

	Annual Growth	12/19	12/20	12/21	12/22	12/23
Sales ($mil.)	8.4%	4,348.0	4,386.3	5,232.5	5,382.4	6,004.8
Net income ($ mil.)	7.6%	1,046.9	823.4	1,503.1	1,521.9	1,402.4
Market value ($ mil.)	(24.4%)	140,231	54,838	77,873	44,848	45,834
Employees	9.2%	13,900	14,900	15,700	17,300	19,800

EEI HOLDING CORPORATION

3009 SINGER AVE
SPRINGFIELD, IL 627032136
Phone: 217 523-0108
Fax: –
Web: www.egiziielectric.com

CEO: Robert Egizii
CFO: John Hinkle
HR: –
FYE: December 31
Type: Private

Electricity comes easy for EEI Holding. The company owns Egizii Electric and other firms that provide electrical and general construction and contracting services throughout the US. It has expertise in utilities, medical facilities, infrastructure, telecommunications, data systems, and traffic control. The company also assists clients with site selection, budget development, and property lease-back transactions. EEI Holding began operations in the late 1940s. Chairman and CEO Robert Egizii is the firm's majority shareholder. The company has offices in Illinois and Florida.

	Annual Growth	12/98	12/99	12/00	12/01	12/09
Sales ($mil.)	(22.2%)	–	241.9	98.4	117.4	19.8
Net income ($ mil.)	(48.1%)	–	144.5	(2.4)	1.0	0.2
Market value ($ mil.)	–	–	–	–	–	–
Employees	–	–	–	–	–	500

EGAIN CORP

NAS: EGAN

1252 Borregas Avenue
Sunnyvale, CA 94089
Phone: 408 636-4500
Fax: –
Web: www.egain.com

CEO: Ashutosh Roy
CFO: Eric Smit
HR: Nikita Gurav
FYE: June 30
Type: Public

eGain Corporation is a leading knowledge platform for customer engagement. The company automates customer engagement with an innovative software as a service (SaaS) platform, powered by deep digital, artificial intelligence (AI), and knowledge capabilities. It sells mostly to large enterprises across financial services, telecommunications, retail, government, healthcare, and utilities. Leading brands use eGain's cloud software to improve customer satisfaction, empower agents, reduce service cost, and boost sales. North America generates nearly 80% of its revenue.

	Annual Growth	06/19	06/20	06/21	06/22	06/23
Sales ($mil.)	9.9%	67.2	72.7	78.3	92.0	98.0
Net income ($ mil.)	(15.7%)	4.2	7.2	7.0	(2.4)	2.1
Market value ($ mil.)	(2.1%)	256.3	349.8	361.4	306.9	235.8
Employees	5.7%	475	522	570	691	592

EGER HEALTH CARE AND REHABILITATION CENTER

140 MEISNER AVE
STATEN ISLAND, NY 103061236
Phone: 718 979-1800
Fax: –
Web: www.eger.org

CEO: William Preuss
CFO: Natale Falanga
HR: –
FYE: December 31
Type: Private

Eger Health Care Center provides hospice care, residential sub-acute care, specialized nursing services for the chronically ill, and adult day care services to the elderly and persons with disabilities. Edger Health Care Center also operates an on-site assisted living facility with about 75 beds. Eger Health Care Center was founded in 1916 and is affiliated the Evangelical Lutheran Church in America.

	Annual Growth	12/18	12/19	12/20	12/21	12/22
Sales ($mil.)	(1.2%)	–	52.9	44.7	43.9	51.1
Net income ($ mil.)	–	–	(1.0)	(5.3)	(7.2)	(2.4)
Market value ($ mil.)	–	–	–	–	–	–
Employees	–	–	–	–	–	620

EGPI FIRECREEK INC

NBB: EFIR

6564 Smoke Tree Lane
Scottsdale, AZ 85253
Phone: 480 948-6581
Fax: –
Web: www.egpifirecreek.com

CEO: Dennis R Alexander
CFO: Dennis R Alexander
HR: –
FYE: December 31
Type: Public

The fire in EGPI Firecreek's belly is for oil and gas exploration and production and traffic systems. Once dependent on the sale of private leisure and commercial vessels, EGPI Firecreek has refocused on US oil and gas activities. The company produces and sells oil and natural gas from wells in Sweetwater County, Wyoming, and Knox County, Texas. In 2009 in a diversification move, EGPI Firecreek subsidiary Asian Ventures Corp. acquired M3 Lighting as the company expanded into light and traffic fixture manufacturing. It picked up communications technology firm Terra Telecom in 2010. That year it moved to expand its assets by agreeing to acquire Caddo International, and by buying Arctic Solar Engineering in 2011

	Annual Growth	12/08	12/09	12/10	12/11	12/12
Sales ($mil.)	–	–	1.2	0.0	0.3	0.1
Net income ($ mil.)	–	3.3	(3.4)	(4.5)	(5.0)	(6.1)
Market value ($ mil.)	(80.3%)	1,142.6	1,104.5	99.0	40.0	1.7
Employees	–	–	–	–	–	–

EHEALTH INC

NMS: EHTH

2625 Augustine Drive, Suite 150
Santa Clara , CA 95054
Phone: 650 210-3150
Fax: –
Web: www.ehealth.com

CEO: Scott N Flanders
CFO: Christine Janofsky
HR: Rabeen Eddy
FYE: December 31
Type: Public

eHealth is a leading health insurance marketplace with a technology and service platform that provides consumer engagement, education, and health insurance enrollment solutions. The company created a marketplace that offers consumers a broad choice of insurance products that includes thousands of Medicare Advantage, Medicare Supplement, Medicare Part D prescription drugs, individual, family, small business, and other ancillary health insurance products. Licensed to sell insurance policies throughout the US, the company has partnerships with more than 200 health insurance carriers across all fifty states and the District of Columbia, for which it processes and delivers potential members' applications in return for a commission on policy sales. It lets consumers compare products online ? including health, dental, and vision insurance products. The company was founded in 1997.

	Annual Growth	12/19	12/20	12/21	12/22	12/23
Sales ($mil.)	(2.7%)	506.2	582.8	538.2	405.4	452.9
Net income ($ mil.)	–	66.9	45.5	(104.4)	(88.7)	(28.2)
Market value ($ mil.)	(45.1%)	2,750.7	2,021.5	730.0	138.6	249.6
Employees	6.1%	1,500	1,960	2,379	1,515	1,903

EIDE BAILLY LLP

4310 17TH AVE S
FARGO, ND 581033339
Phone: 701 239-8500
Fax: –
Web: www.eidebailly.com

CEO: –
CFO: –
HR: –
FYE: April 30
Type: Private

Eide Bailly is how the West was audited. The company, which was founded in 1917, provides clients with audit, accounting, tax, and consulting services from more than 20 offices in nearly a dozen western and central US states. Eide Bailly's target industries include construction, agricultural processing, oil and gas, real estate, renewable energy, government, financial services, manufacturing, health care, and not-for-profit organizations. Additional services are provided by subsidiaries and affiliates, including Eide Bailly Technology Consulting. International services are provided through Eide Bailly's affiliation with HLB International. The accounting firm serves some 44,000 clients annually.

	Annual Growth	04/18	04/19	04/20	04/21	04/22
Sales ($mil.)	18.0%	–	–	–	455.5	537.6
Net income ($ mil.)	–	–	–	–	–	–
Market value ($ mil.)	–	–	–	–	–	–
Employees	–	–	–	–	–	2,500

EIDP, INC.

9330 ZIONSVILLE RD
INDIANAPOLIS, IN 462681053
Phone: 833 267-8382
Fax: –
Web: www.dupont.com

CEO: Charles V Magro V
CFO: David J Anderson
HR: –
FYE: December 31
Type: Private

Du Pont de Nemours (DuPont) is a top US maker of chemicals and materials that serves a global community of consumers, businesses, governments, and industrial companies. DuPont's businesses serve a diverse set of markets including aerospace, automotive, sports nutrition, semiconductors, medical, construction, and renewable energy. Using its expertise in science-based development, it offers products, materials, and services that are applied in everything from solar cells to Kevlar vests to biofuels to nutritional probiotics. Other DuPont brands include Tyvek, Corian, and Styrofoam. The company operates hundreds of plants worldwide. In 2019, DuPont was spun out as an independent company from DowDuPont.

EIGER BIOPHARMACEUTICALS INC

NMS: EIGR

2155 Park Boulevard
Palo Alto, CA 94306
Phone: 650 272-6138
Fax: –
Web: www.eigerbio.com

CEO: –
CFO: –
HR: –
FYE: December 31
Type: Public

Celladon is a clinical-stage biotechnology firm working in the field of calcium dysregulation, a cause of heart failure. It is targeting enzymes that play an integral part in the regulation of intra-cellular calcium in all human cells. The company's therapeutic portfolio includes both gene therapies and small molecule compounds. In 2015 its most advanced product candidate, MYDICAR (which uses gene therapy to target SERCA2a, an enzyme that becomes deficient in patients with heart failure) failed a mid-stage trial, prompting the company to cut its workforce by about half. Celladon is now seeking a buyer; if unable to find one, it will possibly liquidate itself.

	Annual Growth	12/18	12/19	12/20	12/21	12/22
Sales ($mil.)	–	–	–	–	12.1	13.5
Net income ($ mil.)	–	(52.4)	(70.3)	(65.1)	(33.9)	(96.8)
Market value ($ mil.)	(41.6%)	14.9	21.9	18.1	7.6	1.7
Employees	32.8%	18	24	28	43	56

EILEEN FISHER, INC.

2 BRIDGE ST STE 230
IRVINGTON, NY 105331595
Phone: 914 591-5700
Fax: –
Web: locations.eileenfisher.com

CEO: Lisa Williams
CFO: Vincent Phelan
HR: Ann M Piazza
FYE: December 31
Type: Private

EILEEN FISHER designs women's clothing that embraces simplicity, sustainability, and timeless design. The company is committed to responsible business practices that create positive change ? giving to causes that support women and girls, building a more sustainable fashion industry, and creating a more responsible supply chain. The company makes and sells upscale women's business and casual clothing (tops, jackets, pants, skirts, and dresses) made mostly from organic cotton or naturally dyed silk, EILEEN FISHER operates nearly 50 stores in the US and Canada. It also offers personal shopping services for US customers. Additionally, After working in the fields of graphic arts and interior design, Eileen Fisher founded the company in 1984.

	Annual Growth	12/04	12/05	12/06	12/07	12/08
Sales ($mil.)	(55.2%)	–	–	1,361.8	253.8	272.9
Net income ($ mil.)	5435.0%	–	–	0.0	7.4	2.7
Market value ($ mil.)		–	–	–	–	–
Employees		–	–	–	–	1,000

EISENHOWER MEDICAL CENTER

39000 BOB HOPE DR
RANCHO MIRAGE, CA 922703221
Phone: 760 340-3911
Fax: –
Web: www.eisenhowerhealth.org

CEO: G A Serfling
CFO: Kimberly Osborne
HR: Terry Coulson
FYE: June 30
Type: Private

As the valley's only not-for-profit hospital, Eisenhower Health has provided high quality, compassionate care for more than 45 years through a full range of state-of-the-art diagnostic, treatment and emergency facilities. With primary care, urgent care centers, multi-specialty health centers, and specialized programs across the valley, the hospital now offers comprehensive health care support, from education and prevention to diagnosis, treatment and rehabilitation. It provides customized care in Men's Health, Women's Health, LGBTQ services, HIV care, and much more. And added physicians, online access, and community events to enhance convenience and access for all of its patient. In addition to the 437-bed Eisenhower Hospital located on the Rancho Mirage campus. numerous health centers are located throughout the Valley offering a broad array of outpatient services.

	Annual Growth	06/16	06/17	06/18	06/19	06/20
Sales ($mil.)	(37.3%)	–	–	–	6.1	3.8
Net income ($ mil.)		–	–	–	0.3	(0.7)
Market value ($ mil.)		–	–	–	–	–
Employees		–	–	–	–	3,000

EISNERAMPER LLP

733 3RD AVE FL 9
NEW YORK, NY 100173242
Phone: 212 949-8700
Fax: –
Web: www.eisneramper.com

CEO: –
CFO: Korhan Kivanc
HR: Ria Saviolakis
FYE: January 31
Type: Private

EisnerAmper is one of the largest accounting, tax and business advisory firms in the US, serving more than 300 US public companies as well as with family offices and high net worth individuals. Most EisnerAmper clients are based in the US, or comprised of US business interests of foreign entities. To serve domestically-based clients with interests in financial services opportunities overseas, it offers the resources of offices in the UK, Israel, India and EisnerAmper Global, with offices in the Cayman Islands, Singapore, and Ireland; as well as the services of Allinial Global.

	Annual Growth	01/10	01/11	01/12	01/13	01/14
Sales ($mil.)	35.8%	–	–	230.7	247.6	425.6
Net income ($ mil.)	(1.0%)	–	–	59.7	55.7	58.5
Market value ($ mil.)		–	–	–	–	–
Employees		–	–	–	–	4,000

EL DORADO FURNITURE CORP

4200 NW 167TH ST
MIAMI GARDENS, FL 330546112
Phone: 305 624-9700
Fax: –
Web: www.eldoradofurniture.com

CEO: Luis E Capo
CFO: –
HR: Gretchen Lopez
FYE: December 31
Type: Private

The road to El Dorado Furniture is covered in sand. The company sells home furnishings in South Florida through about a dozen retail showrooms and a pair of outlets located in Broward, Miami-Dade, Palm Beach, and Lee counties. El Dorado Furniture stores offer wood, upholstered, and leather furniture for every room in the house, as well as mattresses, bedding, and decorative accessories. Its stores are designed to look like small towns, with building fa ades situated along a boulevard; some locations also feature caf s. Founded in 1967 and run by the Cap family, El Dorado Furniture has become the nation's largest Hispanic-owned retail enterprises.

	Annual Growth	12/15	12/16	12/17	12/18	12/22
Sales ($mil.)	(13.8%)	–	668.3	219.7	233.8	274.5
Net income ($ mil.)		–	–	38.7	36.8	51.9
Market value ($ mil.)		–	–	–	–	–
Employees		–	–	–	–	705

EL PASO COUNTY HOSPITAL DISTRICT

4815 ALAMEDA AVE
EL PASO, TX 799052705
Phone: 915 544-1200
Fax: –
Web: www.umcelpaso.org

CEO: James N Valenti
CFO: Michael Nunez
HR: Gilbert Blancas
FYE: September 30
Type: Private

University Medical Center is a community, not-for-profit health care system serving West Texas and southern New Mexico. The network includes the 330-bed University Medical Center of El Paso (formerly also known as Thomason General Hospital), several neighborhood primary care clinics, and the El Paso First Health Plans HMO. The hospital is an acute-care teaching hospital affiliated with Texas Tech. It specializes in emergency/trauma care, obstetrics, pediatric medicine, and orthopedics. The hospital district, through its affiliates, provides a range of outpatient services including physical rehabilitation, speech therapy, family planning, dental care, cancer treatment, diagnostics, and pharmacy services.

	Annual Growth	09/18	09/19	09/20	09/21	09/22
Sales ($mil.)	17.5%	–	679.6	769.5	918.2	1,103.0
Net income ($ mil.)		–	(10.9)	30.9	63.8	20.0
Market value ($ mil.)		–	–	–	–	–
Employees		–	–	–	–	1,898

EL PASO ELECTRIC COMPANY

100 N STANTON ST
EL PASO, TX 799011407
Phone: 915 543-5711
Fax: –
Web: www.epelectric.com

CEO: Mary E Kipp
CFO: Richard Ostberg
HR: Victor Rueda
FYE: December 31
Type: Private

El Paso Electric (EPE) is a regional energy provider that is engaged in generation, transmission, and distribution service to approximately 460,000 residential, commercial, industrial, and wholesale customers in a 10,000 square mile area of the Rio Grande valley in west Texas and Southern New Mexico and extends its service territory to Hatch, New Mexico to Van Horn, Texas. The company's generation portfolio is 100% coal-free and contains 115 Megawatts (MW) of solar capacity. El Paso was founded in 1901 as the El Paso Electric Railway Company, which provides transportation via mule-drawn streetcars, which were replaced in 1902 with electric streetcars.

EL POLLO LOCO HOLDINGS INC
NMS: LOCO

3535 Harbor Blvd., Suite 100
Costa Mesa, CA 92626
Phone: 714 599-5000
Fax: –
Web: www.elpolloloco.com

CEO: Michael G Maselli
CFO: Laurance Roberts
HR: –
FYE: December 27
Type: Public

El Pollo Loco Holdings operates and franchises some 490 restaurants, comprised of about 190 company-operated and more than 300 franchised restaurants operating under the El Pollo Loco banner. It offers high-quality food typical of fast casual restaurants while providing the speed, convenience, and value typical of traditional quick-service restaurants (QSRs). Specializing fire-grilling citrus-marinated chicken in a wide variety of contemporary Mexican and LA-style chicken dishes including specialty chicken burritos, chicken quesadillas, chicken tostada salads, chicken tortilla soup, variations on its Pollo Bowl, Pollo Salads and its Pollo Fit entrees. Most El Pollo Loco outlets are found in the Los Angeles area and other markets in California. Pancho Ochoa started the chain in Mexico in 1975 and went public in 2014.

	Annual Growth	12/19	12/20	12/21	12/22	12/23
Sales ($mil.)	1.5%	442.3	426.1	454.4	470.0	468.7
Net income ($ mil.)	0.7%	24.9	24.5	29.1	20.8	25.6
Market value ($ mil.)	(11.9%)	471.9	570.9	439.3	312.3	283.7
Employees	(3.4%)	5,005	4,711	4,626	4,931	4,362

ELAH HOLDINGS INC
NBB: ELLH

4514 Cole Avenue, Suite 1600
Dallas, TX 75205
Phone: 805 435-1255
Fax: –
Web: www.elahholdings.com

CEO: Michael J Hobey
CFO: –
HR: –
FYE: December 31
Type: Public

Elah Holdings Inc., formerly known as Real Industry, Inc., is a holding company that is continuing to execute its longstanding business strategy of seeking to acquire profitable businesses in the commercial, industrial, financial and other markets. Elah seeks transaction partners with established businesses or assets to generate sustainable profitability and cash flows to unlock the value of its considerable tax assets. Its acquisition approach uses win-win deal structures to meet the particular exit or growth needs of business owners, position the acquired businesses for continued success, reduce risk, and ultimately create long-term value for its shareholders. Further, Elah Holdings is committed to supporting the performance of such acquisitions post-closing, seeking new opportunities, and managing its legacy assets.

	Annual Growth	12/17	12/18	12/19	12/20	12/21
Sales ($mil.)	(93.1%)	1,346.4	0.1	0.1	0.2	0.0
Net income ($ mil.)	–	(121.7)	73.6	(0.2)	(1.7)	(1.9)
Market value ($ mil.)	–	–	44.3	45.3	60.6	65.0
Employees	–	1,850	–	–	–	–

ELAMEX, S.A. DE C.V. (MEXICO)
NBB: ELAM F

1800 Northwestern Drive
El Paso, TX 79912
Phone: 915 298 3061
Fax: 915 298 3065
Web: www.elamex.com

CEO: –
CFO: Sam L Henry
HR: –
FYE: December 31
Type: Public

It may sound nutty, but Elamex has a sweet tooth for candy. The company manufactures candy and packaged nuts through its subsidiary, Mount Franklin Foods. Mount Franklin operates Sunrise Confections in Juarez, Mexico, and Azar Nut Company in El Paso, Texas. Sunrise makes Sunrise and private-label branded sugar-based candies, including starlight mints, orange slices, spice drops, jelly beans, and gummies, which are sold at grocery store, drug store, mass merchandising, convenience store, and foodservice operators. Azar offers walnuts, pecans, almonds, sunflower seeds, and trail mixes in packaged and bulk form to the retail food and foodservice sectors.

	Annual Growth	12/02	12/03	12/04	12/05	12/06
Sales ($mil.)	(6.0%)	134.3	157.3	97.6	111.7	105.0
Net income ($ mil.)	–	(6.0)	(34.6)	(5.2)	1.0	(2.3)
Market value ($ mil.)	(37.2%)	33.8	18.8	17.3	11.3	5.3
Employees	–	2,039	794	820	–	–

ELANCO ANIMAL HEALTH INC
NYS: ELAN

2500 Innovation Way
Greenfield, IN 46140
Phone: 877 352-6261
Fax: –
Web: www.elanco.com

CEO: Jeffrey N Simmons
CFO: Todd S Young
HR: –
FYE: December 31
Type: Public

Elanco Animal Health Incorporated is a global leader in animal health dedicated to innovating and delivering products and services to prevent and treat disease in farm animals and pets, creating value for farmers, pet owners, veterinarians, stakeholders, and society as a whole. With a presence in more than 90 countries, its diverse, durable portfolio serves animals across the company's core species consisting of: dogs and cats (collectively, pet health) and cattle, poultry, swine, sheep, and aqua (collectively, farm animal). With a heritage dating back to 1954, Elanco is committed to helping its customers improve the health of animals in their care, while also making a meaningful impact on its local and global communities. The company generates the majority of its revenue outside the US.

	Annual Growth	12/19	12/20	12/21	12/22	12/23
Sales ($mil.)	9.5%	3,071.0	3,273.3	4,765.0	4,411.0	4,417.0
Net income ($ mil.)	–	67.9	(560.1)	(472.0)	(78.0)	(1,231.0)
Market value ($ mil.)	(15.7%)	14,514	15,116	13,987	6,022.6	7,343.4
Employees	12.7%	6,080	10,200	9,800	9,740	9,800

ELCOM INTERNATIONAL, INC.
NBB: ELCO

10 Oceana Way
Norwood, MA 02062
Phone: 781 501-4000
Fax: –
Web: –

CEO: William Lock
CFO: David Elliott
HR: –
FYE: December 31
Type: Public

If only sales were as easy for Elcom to procure as the products bought and sold with its software. Elcom International's PECOS (Professional Electronic Commerce Online System) software enables clients to automate procurement functions such as pricing, invoicing, and payment. Its application suite, which Elcom offers as either a licensed or hosted application, includes tools for managing the order cycle, creating rapid requisitions, and building electronic marketplaces to conduct online transactions with suppliers and distributors. Elcom also provides integration services for suppliers and buyers to help them manage catalog information and other content.

	Annual Growth	12/03	12/04	12/05	12/06	12/07
Sales ($mil.)	9.1%	3.8	4.6	3.3	3.2	5.4
Net income ($ mil.)	–	(5.5)	(3.3)	(5.8)	(6.8)	(3.8)
Market value ($ mil.)	(65.0%)	0.1	0.0	0.0	0.0	0.0
Employees	(0.7%)	35	37	35	46	34

ELDERHOSTEL, INC.

20 PARK PLZ
BOSTON, MA 021164303
Phone: 800 454-5768
Fax: –
Web: www.roadscholar.org

CEO: –
CFO: –
HR: –
FYE: June 30
Type: Private

No, it's not a cheap place for older folks to stay whilst backpacking around the world. But Elderhostel does provide a wide variety of educational travel programs to adults ages 55 and over. The not-for-profit entity offers 5,500 Road Scholar educational tours throughout the US and in more than 150 countries, from Africa to Antarctica. Programs are taught by professors, local scholars, and museum professionals and include lectures, field trips, and hands-on activities. Participants experience and learn about art, literature, music, nature, and traditional cultures. Elderhostel was founded in 1975 by world traveler and social activist Marty Knowlton and University of New Hampshire administrator David Bianco.

	Annual Growth	06/17	06/18	06/19	06/20	06/22
Sales ($mil.)	39.5%	–	41.5	389.9	254.3	157.1
Net income ($ mil.)	–	–	(3.1)	3.5	(23.8)	(1.0)
Market value ($ mil.)	–	–	–	–	–	–
Employees	–	–	–	–	–	480

ELDORADO ARTESIAN SPRINGS INC

1783 DOGWOOD ST
LOUISVILLE, CO 800273085
Phone: 303 499-1316
Fax: -
Web: www.eldoradosprings.com

CEO: -
CFO: Cathleen M Shoenfeld
HR: -
FYE: March 31
Type: Private

If Cortez had sought a wealth of water instead of streets of gold, he might have headed for Eldorado Artesian Springs. The company bottles water from springs it owns in the foothills of the Rocky Mountains. The bulk of its sales come from home and office delivery of three and five gallon bottles of its natural spring water (and water cooler rentals); it also supplies smaller bottles to wholesalers and distributors for retail sale. Eldorado's water is distributed primarily in Colorado but also in regions of bordering states. In addition to its bottled water business, the company owns and operates a resort on its property.

	Annual Growth	03/10	03/11	03/12	03/13	03/14
Sales ($mil.)	11.0%	-	-	9.2	9.9	11.4
Net income ($ mil.)	108.6%	-	-	0.1	0.5	0.5
Market value ($ mil.)	-	-	-	-	-	-
Employees	-	-	-	-	-	75

ELECTRIC & GAS TECHNOLOGY, INC.

3233 W. Kingsley Road
Garland, TX 75041
Phone: 972 840-3223
Fax: 972 271-8925
Web: -

NBB: ELGT
CEO: -
CFO: -
HR: -
FYE: July 31
Type: Public

Oil and water may not mix, but electric and metal does -- in the business plan of Electric & Gas Technology (EGTI). EGTI operates as a holding company. Its subsidiary Logic Metals Technology offers contract precision sheet metal fabrication of electronic metal enclosures and equipment panels. The company caters to communications and electronics industries, as well as a variety of aesthetic design applications. The father and son team, Chairman S. Mort Zimmerman and CEO Daniel Zimmerman control the company.

	Annual Growth	07/02	07/03	07/04	07/05	07/06
Sales ($mil.)	6.9%	9.7	13.6	6.4	8.5	12.7
Net income ($ mil.)	-	(2.5)	(1.2)	(3.0)	0.1	(1.5)
Market value ($ mil.)	54.3%	1.5	12.4	1.7	6.2	8.4
Employees	11.8%	78	115	72	78	122

ELECTRIC ENERGY, INC.

P.O. Box 165
Joppa, IL 62953
Phone: 618 543-7531
Fax: 618 543-7420
Web: -

CEO: -
CFO: -
HR: -
FYE: December 31
Type: Public

It does not take a genius to figure out what business Electric Energy (EEI) is involved in. The company generates 1,000 MW of electric capacity at its coal-fired power plant in Joppa, Illinois (which began operating in 1953), and 74 MW at it natural gas-fired facility (which commenced operations in 2000) at the same location. The independent producer sells its power output to its shareholders. The Missouri-based utility holding company Ameren holds an 80% stake in EEI; Kentucky Utilities (a subsidiary of LG&E Energy) owns the remaining 20% of the company.

	Annual Growth	12/00	12/01	12/02	12/03	12/04
Sales ($mil.)	(0.5%)	211.9	178.8	265.9	227.2	207.3
Net income ($ mil.)	3.7%	11.0	10.6	34.1	17.6	12.7
Market value ($ mil.)	-	-	-	-	-	-
Employees	(1.5%)	273	261	258	262	257

ELECTRIC POWER BOARD OF CHATTANOOGA

10 MARTIN LUTHER KING BLVD
CHATTANOOGA, TN 374021832
Phone: 423 756-2706
Fax: -
Web: www.epb.com

CEO: Harold D Priest
CFO: Greg Eaves
HR: Sheryl Jenkins
FYE: June 30
Type: Private

Pardon me .... is that the Electric Power Board (EPB) of Chattanooga? EPB keeps on choo-chooin' along by providing electricity to more than 167,410 residents and businesses. The utility (a non-profit agency of the City of Chattanooga) distributes energy in a 600 sq.-ml. area that includes greater Chattanooga, as well as parts of surrounding counties in Georgia and Tennessee. It gets its wholesale power supply from the Tennessee Valley Authority. EPB also provides telecommunications (telephone and Internet) services to area homes and businesses through its EPB Fiber Optics unit.

	Annual Growth	06/17	06/18	06/19	06/21	06/22
Sales ($mil.)	1.6%	-	729.7	741.7	721.5	776.7
Net income ($ mil.)	14.4%	-	43.8	36.9	47.9	74.9
Market value ($ mil.)	-	-	-	-	-	-
Employees	-	-	-	-	-	400

ELECTRIC POWER BOARD OF THE METROPOLITAN GOVERNMENT OF NASHVILLE & DAVIDSON COUNTY

1214 CHURCH ST
NASHVILLE, TN 372460001
Phone: 615 736-6900
Fax: -
Web: www.nespower.com

CEO: Teresa Broyles-Aplin
CFO: -
HR: Cheryl Cole
FYE: June 30
Type: Private

The Electric Power Board of the Metropolitan Government of Nashville and Davidson County is a mouthful. Its operating name, Nashville Electric Service (NES), sounds much better. And talking of sound, the legendary "Nashville Sound" would be hard to hear without the resources of this power distributor, which serves more than 360,000 customers in central Tennessee. NES is one of the largest government-owned utilities in the US. The company is required to purchase all its power from another government-owned operator, the Tennessee Valley Authority (TVA).

	Annual Growth	06/14	06/15	06/16	06/18	06/19
Sales ($mil.)	1.9%	-	1,246.6	1,203.5	380.7	1,342.2
Net income ($ mil.)	12.7%	-	55.8	28.6	94.2	90.0
Market value ($ mil.)	-	-	-	-	-	-
Employees	-	-	-	-	-	950

ELECTRIC POWER RESEARCH INSTITUTE, INC.

3420 HILLVIEW AVE
PALO ALTO, CA 943041338
Phone: 650 855-2000
Fax: -
Web: www.epri.com

CEO: Arshad Mansoor
CFO: -
HR: Melissa Barnhill
FYE: December 31
Type: Private

The Electric Power Research Institute (EPRI) is an independent non-profit energy research, development, and deployment organization, with three specialized labs. EPRI also maintains an employee presence in more than a dozen countries in Europe/Middle East/Africa, as well as Asia, and the Americas through its subsidiary EPRI International and its Ireland-based research arm, EPRI Europe DAC. It conducts research, development, and demonstration projects for the benefit of the public in the US and internationally. The company collaborates with more than 450 companies in some 45 countries, driving innovation to ensure the public has clean, safe, reliable, affordable, and equitable access to electricity worldwide. Its portfolio of research programs is defined and guided by advisors from both industry and public stakeholders. Over 1,400 leaders and technical experts from the electricity sector, academia, and government help EPRI develop and conduct its research, deliver results, and provide for technology transfer and the application of research findings. EPRI was founded in 1972.

	Annual Growth	12/18	12/19	12/20	12/21	12/22
Sales ($mil.)	3.6%	-	396.6	420.2	404.2	441.4
Net income ($ mil.)	-	-	(0.6)	17.7	2.6	(18.3)
Market value ($ mil.)	-	-	-	-	-	-
Employees	-	-	-	-	-	1,123

ELECTRIC RELIABILITY COUNCIL OF TEXAS, INC.

8000 METROPOLIS DR BLD E STE 100
AUSTIN, TX 787443149
Phone: 512 225-7000
Fax: –
Web: www.ercot.com

CEO: Bill Magness
CFO: Sean Taylor
HR: Donna Montgomery
FYE: December 31
Type: Private

The Electric Reliability Council of Texas (ERCOT) manages the flow of electric power to approximately 26 million Texas customers ? representing about 90% of the state's electric load. As the independent system operator for the region, ERCOT schedules power on an electric grid that connects more than 52,700 miles of transmission lines and more than 1,030 generation units. It also performs financial settlement for the competitive wholesale bulk-power market and administers retail switching for nearly 8 million premises in competitive choice areas. The nonprofit organization is regulated by the Public Utility Commission of Texas and the Texas Legislature. Its members include consumers, cooperatives, generators, power marketers, retail electric providers, investor-owned electric utilities, transmission and distribution providers, and municipally owned electric utilities.

	Annual Growth	12/09	12/10	12/11	12/15	12/21
Sales ($mil.)	(0.7%)	–	272.5	279.8	181.4	252.6
Net income ($ mil.)	–	–	19.1	(2.0)	(2.1)	(4.7)
Market value ($ mil.)	–	–	–	–	–	–
Employees	–	–	–	–	–	625

ELECTRICAL APPARATUS SERVICE ASSOCIATION INC

1331 BAUR BLVD
SAINT LOUIS, MO 631321913
Phone: 314 993-2220
Fax: –
Web: www.easa.com

CEO: –
CFO: –
HR: –
FYE: August 31
Type: Private

It's easy to get more charge from your electromechanical sales with EASA. The Electrical Apparatus Service Association is a membership trade organization comprised of more than 2,150 electromechanical sales and service companies in about 50 countries. The group provides engineering and educational programs, engineering consulting services, networking opportunities, and other tools to keep members ahead of the competition. EASA was established as the National Industrial Service Association as part of the National Recovery Act in 1933. The act was declared unconstitutional in 1935 but the group remained together to network and problem solve. It became the Electrical Apparatus Service Association in 1962.

	Annual Growth	08/15	08/16	08/17	08/19	08/22
Sales ($mil.)	(0.1%)	–	4.1	4.0	4.1	4.1
Net income ($ mil.)	(25.7%)	–	0.3	0.3	0.0	0.0
Market value ($ mil.)	–	–	–	–	–	–
Employees	–	–	–	–	–	14

ELECTRICAL GEODESICS, INC

500 East 4th Ave, Suite 200
Eugene, OR 97401
Phone: –
Fax: –
Web: –

CEO: Don Tucker
CFO: –
HR: –
FYE: December 31
Type: Public

Electrical Geodesics develops and sells medical equipment for use in medicine, psychology, and neuroscience research. To bring this research technology to clinical practice, Electrical Geodesics introduced clinical dense array electroencephalography (dEEG) systems for long-term monitoring for epilepsy evaluation. As with other applications of neurological assessment, the result is improved guidance of therapy (in this case, neurosurgical intervention). Its EEG measurement and analysis systems are used in laboratories throughout the US, Europe, and Asia for research in areas such as neonatal sleep monitoring, stroke evaluation, dementia, and infant language comprehension. The company was founded in 1992.

	Annual Growth	12/12	12/13	12/14	12/15	12/16
Sales ($mil.)	6.9%	12.5	11.6	13.8	15.1	16.3
Net income ($ mil.)	–	–	0.2	(2.2)	(4.3)	(2.8)	(2.8)
Market value ($ mil.)	–	–	–	–	–	–
Employees	–	–	–	90	–	–

ELECTRO-MATIC VENTURES, INC.

23409 INDUSTRIAL PARK CT
FARMINGTON HILLS, MI 483352849
Phone: 248 478-1182
Fax: –
Web: www.electro-matic.com

CEO: James C Baker Jr
CFO: –
HR: –
FYE: September 30
Type: Private

Electro-Matic Products are not "as seen on TV." The company distributes industrial automation equipment and electrical supplies to customers in the industrial, chemical, pharmaceutical, utility, and automotive industries. Products include cables, connectors, sensors, fuses, and control devices, along with automation tools, indoor and outdoor LED displays, and industrial computer hardware. Electro-Matic stocks products from Littelfuse, Molex, Rittal Corporation, Siemens, and Woodhead Industries, among other vendors. Founded in 1969, the company sells worldwide through sales, engineering, and support offices in Michigan and Ohio. Electro-Matic established an employee stock ownership plan in 2007.

	Annual Growth	09/06	09/07	09/08	09/10	09/11
Sales ($mil.)	8.3%	–	–	64.5	53.9	81.9
Net income ($ mil.)	57.1%	–	–	0.7	0.3	2.8
Market value ($ mil.)	–	–	–	–	–	–
Employees	–	–	–	–	–	199

ELECTRO-SENSORS, INC.

NAS: ELSE

6111 Blue Circle Drive
Minnetonka, MN 55343-9108
Phone: 952 930-0100
Fax: –
Web: www.electro-sensors.com

CEO: David L Klenk
CFO: David L Klenk
HR: –
FYE: December 31
Type: Public

Electro-Sensors supports the manufacturing process with sensitive loving care. The company's Product Monitoring Division, which accounts for the bulk of sales, makes computerized systems that monitor and regulate the production speed of industrial machinery. Products are sold worldwide. Electro-Sensors also has an AutoData Systems unit, which makes software that reads hand-printed characters, check marks, and bar code information from scanned or faxed forms. The unit has an exclusive license to use a neural network algorithm developed by PPT Vision. Its software sells mostly in North America and Western Europe. Electro-Sensors director and secretary Peter Peterson and his family own 38% of the company.

	Annual Growth	12/19	12/20	12/21	12/22	12/23
Sales ($mil.)	0.9%	8.3	7.6	8.6	9.0	8.6
Net income ($ mil.)	10.1%	0.2	(0.1)	0.4	0.1	0.3
Market value ($ mil.)	1.2%	12.4	16.5	21.5	15.5	13.0
Employees	(3.3%)	40	37	35	35	35

ELECTROMED, INC.

ASE: ELMD

500 Sixth Avenue N.W.
New Prague, MN 56071
Phone: 952 758-9299
Fax: –
Web: www.electromed.com

CEO: –
CFO: –
HR: –
FYE: June 30
Type: Public

Electromed aims to clear the way for patients suffering from respiratory ailments. A medical device maker, the company manufactures respiratory products designed to treat patients with cystic fibrosis, chronic obstructive pulmonary disease (COPD), and other ailments that affect respiratory systems. Its FDA-approved SmartVest System is a vest worn by patients that helps loosen lung congestion. A self-administered therapy, the vest works by administering high frequency pulsations that compress and release the patient's chest area. Electromed sells its SmartVest and related products primarily in the US to patients, home health care professionals, and hospitals. Founded in 1992, the company went public in 2010.

	Annual Growth	06/19	06/20	06/21	06/22	06/23
Sales ($mil.)	11.3%	31.3	32.5	35.8	41.7	48.1
Net income ($ mil.)	12.6%	2.0	4.2	2.4	2.3	3.2
Market value ($ mil.)	18.4%	46.6	131.7	96.6	82.5	91.6
Employees	9.3%	119	120	132	156	170

ELECTRONIC ARTS, INC.   NMS: EA

209 Redwood Shores Parkway   CEO: Andrew Wilson
Redwood City, CA 94065   CFO: Stuart Canfield
Phone: 650 628-1500   HR: –
Fax: –   FYE: March 31
Web: www.ea.com   Type: Public

Electronic Arts (EA) is a global leader in digital interactive entertainment which develops, markets, publishes and delivers games, content and services that can be played and watched on game consoles, PCs, mobile phones and tablets. Its leading titles are Madden NFL, FIFA, and Star Wars, all of which it licenses from other companies, and its own Battlefield, and The Sims. While EA generates increasing sales for games on mobile devices, it still makes most of its revenue from games played on consoles from Sony and Microsoft and on personal computers. EA gets majority of revenue from international customers. The company was founded in 1982.

	Annual Growth	03/19	03/20	03/21	03/22	03/23
Sales ($mil.)	10.7%	4,950.0	5,537.0	5,629.0	6,991.0	7,426.0
Net income ($ mil.)	(5.8%)	1,019.0	3,039.0	837.0	789.0	802.0
Market value ($ mil.)	4.3%	27,736	27,338	36,944	34,526	32,872
Employees	8.4%	9,700	9,800	11,000	12,900	13,400

ELECTRONIC CONTROL SECURITY INC.   NBB: EKCS

65 Kingsland Avenue   CEO: Arthur Barchenko
Clifton, NJ 07015   CFO: Daryl Holcomb
Phone: 973 574-8555   HR: –
Fax: 973 574-8562   FYE: June 30
Web: www.ecsiinternationalgov.com   Type: Public

Electronic Control Security (ECSI) is a leading provider of integrated security systems for government and commercial facilities worldwide. Its products include command and control, intrusion detection, and sensing and surveillance systems used at airports, military bases, ports, and other sensitive facilities such as embassies and power plants. ECSI also provides risk assessment and other security consulting services. Its customers include a number of government agencies, such as the US Department of Energy and the Department of Defense. In addition to offices in the US, the company has operations in the Middle East and Latin America.

	Annual Growth	06/18	06/19	06/20	06/21	06/22
Sales ($mil.)	(8.1%)	1.0	1.8	0.6	0.8	0.7
Net income ($ mil.)	–	(0.1)	0.2	(0.3)	0.2	0.1
Market value ($ mil.)	(2.6%)	2.0	1.1	2.0	11.5	1.8
Employees	–	–	–	–	–	–

ELECTRONIC INSTRUMENTATION AND TECHNOLOGY, LLC

309 KELLYS FORD PLZ SE   CEO: –
LEESBURG, VA 201755442   CFO: –
Phone: 703 478-0700   HR: –
Fax: –   FYE: December 31
Web: www.eit.com   Type: Private

Electronic Instrumentation and Technology (EIT) provides engineering and design and contract manufacturing services to OEMs (original equipment manufacturers) in the medical, communications, industrial process control, analytical instrument, and defense markets, among others. The company's engineering and design services include prototyping, electronic design, printed circuit board layout, and mechanical and process engineering. It also offers electronic manufacturing services, as well as assembly, cabling, and machining. Customers are located in some 30 countries. EIT was founded in 1977 by chairman and CTO Joe T. May.

	Annual Growth	12/04	12/05	12/06	12/07	12/08
Sales ($mil.)	(4.0%)	–	–	37.2	36.1	34.3
Net income ($ mil.)	(53.4%)	–	–	7.8	1.5	1.7
Market value ($ mil.)	–	–	–	–	–	–
Employees	–	–	–	–	–	270

ELECTRONIC KNOWLEDGE INTERCHANGE INC

33 W MONROE ST STE 1050   CEO: Robert Blackwell
CHICAGO, IL 606035323   CFO: –
Phone: 312 236-0903   HR: –
Fax: –   FYE: December 31
Web: www.eki-digital.com   Type: Private

Electronic Knowledge Interchange (EKI) believes that technological know-how should flow throughout every enterprise. The company, also known as EKI Consulting, provides a variety of IT services, including compliance and risk management, custom software development, and systems integration. EKI installs and maintains IT products from vendors such as Adobe Systems, BroadVision, IBM, and Oracle. Clients hail from a variety of industries such as financial services, manufacturing, health care, retail, and consumer goods. Customers have included Abbott Laboratories, Deluxe Corporation, FMC, and Morton's of Chicago.

	Annual Growth	12/99	12/00	12/01	12/06	12/07
Sales ($mil.)	12.5%	–	–	7.1	17.1	14.3
Net income ($ mil.)	(9.7%)	–	–	3.0	2.7	1.6
Market value ($ mil.)	–	–	–	–	–	–
Employees	–	–	–	–	–	48

ELECTRONIC SYSTEMS TECHNOLOGY, INC.   NBB: ELST

415 North Roosevelt St. Ste. B1   CEO: –
Kennewick, WA 99336   CFO: Michael W Eller
Phone: 509 735-9092   HR: –
Fax: –   FYE: December 31
Web: www.esteem.com   Type: Public

Electronic Systems Technology (EST) makes wireless modems that it markets under the ESTeem brand. EST targets the modems for applications in industrial automation, the military, and public safety. The ESTeem line includes Ethernet radios that can be used for handling video and voice over Internet protocol (VoIP) transmissions. EST buys parts from Hitachi, Intersil, Integrated Microelectronics, Mitsubishi, Murata Manufacturing, Rakon, and Toko America for its products. Assembly of EST's products is farmed out to Manufacturing Services.

	Annual Growth	12/19	12/20	12/21	12/22	12/23
Sales ($mil.)	2.3%	1.4	1.2	1.5	1.9	1.5
Net income ($ mil.)	–	(0.2)	(0.2)	0.0	0.1	(0.2)
Market value ($ mil.)	(5.8%)	2.0	1.4	1.5	1.2	1.6
Employees	(2.9%)	9	8	9	8	8

ELECTRONIC TELE-COMMUNICATIONS, INC.   NBB: ETCI A

1915 MacArthur Road   CEO: Dean W Danner
Waukesha, WI 53188   CFO: –
Phone: 262 542-5600   HR: –
Fax: –   FYE: December 31
Web: www.etcia.com   Type: Public

So you've dialed the wrong number and it looks like it might rain. At least products from Electronic Tele-Communications (ETC) will give you the bad news in a pleasant voice. ETC's interactive voice information and call processing systems let service providers provide enhanced services such as changed-number announcements, wake-up calls, call return, and time and temperature information over phone networks. For corporate customers, it offers professional voice recording services used to create outgoing voicemail and on-hold messages. The company was founded in 1980 by George Danner, father of president and CEO Dean Danner.

	Annual Growth	12/03	12/04	12/05	12/06	12/07
Sales ($mil.)	(6.5%)	3.0	3.7	2.7	2.3	2.3
Net income ($ mil.)	–	(0.7)	(0.0)	(1.4)	(0.4)	(0.1)
Market value ($ mil.)	(28.5%)	1.2	0.5	0.4	0.3	0.3
Employees	–	–	39	–	–	–

ELECTRONICS FOR IMAGING, INC.

12 INNOVATIION WAY
LONDONDERRY, NH 030532052
Phone: 650 357-3500
Fax: –
Web: www.efi.com

CEO: Frank Pennisi
CFO: Grant Fitz
HR: Lindsay Goyette
FYE: December 31
Type: Private

Electronics For Imaging (EFI) is leading the transformation from analog to digital imaging with scalable, digital, award-winning products. The company develops breakthrough technologies for the manufacturing of signage, packaging, textiles, ceramic tiles, and personalized documents, with a wide range of printers, inks, digital front ends, and a comprehensive business and production workflow suite that transforms and streamlines the entire production process. EFI's Fiery line includes print servers, as well as print engines and applications, and more. EFI was founded in 1988 by Efraim "Efi" Arazi and opens its first office in San Francisco, California.

ELEGANT ILLUSIONS INC

542 Lighthouse Ave., Suite 5
Pacific Grove, CA 93950
Phone: 831 649-1814
Fax: –
Web: www.elegantillusions.com

CEO: James C Cardinal
CFO: Gavin M Gear
HR: –
FYE: December 31
Type: Public

You can't believe all you see at Elegant Illusions, but you can believe in some of it. The jewelry company operates eight stores in a handful of US states and on St. Croix, US Virgin Islands. Most locations sell copies of fine jewelry, although a couple sell the real deal. Elegant Illusions also boasts art galleries in Louisiana, Colorado, and California. Its faux jewelry includes different styles of rings, earrings, and pendants featuring lab-created emeralds, rubies, sapphires, and opals in 14-carat gold and white gold settings. The company was founded by executives James Cardinal and Gavin and Tamara Gear. The Gears started the company at a former hot dog stand on Cannery Row in San Francisco.

	Annual Growth	12/97	12/98	12/99	12/00	12/01
Sales ($mil.)	2.5%	8.4	9.7	10.6	9.6	9.3
Net income ($ mil.)	(47.9%)	0.6	0.3	0.1	(0.0)	0.0
Market value ($ mil.)	(9.0%)	2.7	3.2	6.1	6.1	1.8
Employees	0.2%	123	172	149	124	124

ELEMENT SOLUTIONS INC
NYS: ESI

500 East Broward Boulevard, Suite 1860
Fort Lauderdale, FL 33394
Phone: 561 207-9600
Fax: –
Web: www.elemetsolutionsinc.com

CEO: Benjamin Gliklich
CFO: Carey J Dorman
HR: –
FYE: December 31
Type: Public

Element Solutions (formerly known as Platform Specialty Products) is a leading global specialty chemicals company whose businesses supply a broad range of solutions that enhance the performance of products people use every day. Its offerings include electronic assembly materials, and hydraulic control fluids for the electronics, automotive, oil and gas, and consumer packaged goods, among others. The company's businesses provide products that are consumed by customers as part of their production process, providing customers with reliable and recurring revenue streams as the products are replenished in order to continue production. Element Solutions was incorporated in 2014. Approximately 75% of sales were generated outside the US.

	Annual Growth	12/19	12/20	12/21	12/22	12/23
Sales ($mil.)	6.2%	1,835.9	1,853.7	2,399.8	2,549.4	2,333.2
Net income ($ mil.)	6.4%	92.2	75.7	203.5	187.2	118.1
Market value ($ mil.)	18.6%	2,821.1	4,282.4	5,864.5	4,393.5	5,589.1
Employees	4.8%	4,400	4,400	5,300	5,300	5,300

ELEVANCE HEALTH INC
NYS: ELV

220 Virginia Avenue
Indianapolis, IN 46204
Phone: 833 401-1577
Fax: –
Web: www.elevancehealth.com

CEO: Gail K Boudreaux
CFO: John E Gallina
HR: –
FYE: December 31
Type: Public

Health benefits provider Elevance Health (formerly known as Anthem), through a number of subsidiaries, provides health coverage to approximately 47.5 million members in the US. One of the nation's largest health insurers, Elavance Health is a Blue Cross and Blue Shield Association licensee in more than a dozen states (where it operates as Anthem Blue Cross, Anthem Blue Cross and Blue Shield, and Empire Blue Cross Blue Shield or Empire Blue Cross) and provides non-BCBS plans under the Unicare, Amerigroup, CareMore, Simply Healthcare, HealthSun, HealthLink, and other brands in numerous states across the US. The company provides services to the federal government in connection with its Federal Health Products & Services business, which administers the Federal Employees Health Benefits (FEHB) Program. In 2022, the company changed its name to Elevance Health.

	Annual Growth	12/19	12/20	12/21	12/22	12/23
Sales ($mil.)	13.2%	104,213	121,867	138,639	156,595	171,340
Net income ($ mil.)	5.6%	4,807.0	4,572.0	6,104.0	6,025.0	5,987.0
Market value ($ mil.)	11.8%	70,394	74,837	108,038	119,558	109,907
Employees	10.4%	70,600	83,400	98,200	102,300	104,900

ELEVATE TEXTILES, INC.

121 W TRADE ST STE 1700
CHARLOTTE, NC 282021154
Phone: 336 379-6220
Fax: –
Web: www.elevatetextiles.com

CEO: Per-Olof Loof
CFO: Gail A Kuczkowski
HR: Arturo Bahena
FYE: December 31
Type: Private

Elevate Textiles is a collection of distinguished global textile brands including American & Efird, Burlington, Cone Denim, G termann, and Safety Components. With a global array of premium fabric and thread solutions focused on innovation, sustainability, and quality craftsmanship, Elevate and its portfolio brands provide products that surround people every day and in all facets of life. The company offers advanced, high-quality products and mission-critical textile solutions across vast industries including fashion and functional apparel, footwear, military, fire, medical, athletic, automotive, aerospace, outdoor, and other specialty sectors. Elevate Textiles has about 25,000 customers across some 100 countries.

ELGIN SEPARATION SOLUTIONS INDUSTRIALS LLC

10050 CASH RD
STAFFORD, TX 774774407
Phone: 281 261-5778
Fax: –
Web: www.elginseparationsolutions.com

CEO: –
CFO: –
HR: –
FYE: December 31
Type: Private

No stuck-in-the mud company, KEM-TRON Technologies is credited with developing a line of dewatering systems used in zero liquid discharge/closed loop mud systems. The company designs, manufactures, and distributes equipment for solids separation and polymer applications. Its multifunctional linear motion shaker/mud cleaner, used in mobile mud systems, touts simultaneous flow line running with hydro-cyclone underflow cleaning. Other products include a jet shearing and mixing system, integral to drilling rigs, and a vacuum degasser, to separate gases. KEM-TRON units are installed in some 30 countries. Founded in 1990, the company operates a facility in Texas, and a service and maintenance hub in Russia.

	Annual Growth	12/09	12/10	12/11	12/12	12/13
Sales ($mil.)	11.5%	–	–	–	21.7	24.2
Net income ($ mil.)		–	–	–	(0.7)	1.1
Market value ($ mil.)		–	–	–	–	–
Employees		–	–	–	–	50

ELITE PHARMACEUTICALS INC
NBB: ELTP

165 Ludlow Avenue
Northvale, NJ 07647
Phone: 201 750-2646
Fax: –
Web: www.elitepharma.com

CEO: Nasrat Hakim
CFO: Carter J Ward
HR: –
FYE: March 31
Type: Public

Elite Pharmaceuticals isn't above peddling generics. Subsidiary Elite Laboratories develops generic versions of existing controlled-release drugs whose patents are about to expire. Its commercial products include allergy therapeutics Lodrane 24 and Lodrane 24D, which are marketed by ECR Pharmaceuticals. Products in various stages of testing and preclinical development include oxycodone pain medications, anti-infectives, and treatments for gastrointestinal disorders. Elite Laboratories also provides contract research and development services for other drugmakers.

	Annual Growth	03/19	03/20	03/21	03/22	03/23
Sales ($mil.)	45.8%	7.6	18.0	25.4	32.3	34.2
Net income ($ mil.)	–	(9.3)	(2.2)	5.1	8.9	3.6
Market value ($ mil.)	(26.4%)	100.4	73.0	61.8	35.4	29.4
Employees	10.9%	35	43	43	43	53

ELIXIR INDUSTRIES

24800 CHRISANTA DR # 210
MISSION VIEJO, CA 926914833
Phone: 949 860-5000
Fax: –
Web: –

CEO: –
CFO: –
HR: –
FYE: December 31
Type: Private

Elixir Industries is a diversified manufacturer of aluminum extrusions, aluminum fabrication, and custom metal fabrication products. Its portfolio of offerings includes doors, siding and roofing, window guards, recreational vehicle products, cargo trailers, and aluminum painted coil. It also makes a variety of coatings, sealants, and tapes. The company operates from about a dozen locations in half a dozen states, serving clients across the US as well as in selected international markets. Roland Sahm founded what is now Elixir Industries in 1948.

	Annual Growth	12/02	12/03	12/04	12/05	12/11
Sales ($mil.)	(6.7%)	–	–	–	221.0	146.0
Net income ($ mil.)	–	–	–	–	–	14.4
Market value ($ mil.)	–	–	–	–	–	–
Employees	–	–	–	–	–	64

ELKHART GENERAL HOSPITAL, INC.

600 EAST BLVD
ELKHART, IN 465142499
Phone: 574 294-2621
Fax: –
Web: www.beaconhealthsystem.org

CEO: Gregory W Lintjer
CFO: Kevin Higdon
HR: Amanda Flick
FYE: December 31
Type: Private

From Nappanee to Edwardsburg, Elkhart General serves residents of northern Indiana and southwestern Michigan. The community-owned Elkhart General Hospital has about 325 beds. The system also operates about ten general practice clinics throughout its region, and provides home care, rehabilitation, and occupational health services. The system's Michiana Linen unit provides linen and laundry services to other hospitals, clinics, and physician offices in the region. Its hospital staff includes about 300 physicians representing about 30 medical specialties. Elkhart General is affiliated with Memorial Hospital of South Bend through the Beacon Health System organization.

	Annual Growth	12/18	12/19	12/20	12/21	12/22
Sales ($mil.)	4.3%	–	300.1	301.6	333.5	340.9
Net income ($ mil.)	56.1%	–	7.8	(21.9)	(1.2)	29.7
Market value ($ mil.)	–	–	–	–	–	–
Employees	–	–	–	–	–	1,900

ELKINS CONSTRUCTORS, INC.

701 W ADAMS ST
JACKSONVILLE, FL 322041600
Phone: 904 353-6500
Fax: –
Web: www.elkinsllc.com

CEO: Barry L Allred
CFO: –
HR: –
FYE: December 31
Type: Private

Elkins Constructors builds it all. The company, one of Florida's largest privately held construction companies, works on commercial, industrial, multi-family residential, institutional, and retail projects mainly in the Southeast. It offers general contracting, design/build, and construction management services, and its retail market clients have included Lowe's, British Airways, and Castleton Beverage. Other projects include the America Online call center and headquarters for PGA Tour Productions. Elkins also has been named one of the top green contractors in the US by Engineering News-Record. Founded in 1955 by Martin Elkins, the company was acquired in 1984 by CEO Barry Allred and a team of investors.

	Annual Growth	12/04	12/05	12/06	12/07	12/08
Sales ($mil.)	117.0%	–	–	60.8	231.7	286.0
Net income ($ mil.)	2391.3%	–	–	0.0	8.1	10.2
Market value ($ mil.)	–	–	–	–	–	–
Employees	–	–	–	–	–	55

ELLINGTON FINANCIAL INC
NYS: EFC

53 Forest Avenue
Old Greenwich, CT 06870
Phone: 203 698-1200
Fax: –
Web: www.ellingtonfinancial.com

CEO: Laurence Penn
CFO: –
HR: –
FYE: December 31
Type: Public

Mortgage-related assets are music to Ellington Financial's ears. The specialty finance company manages a portfolio of primarily non-agency residential mortgage-backed securities, valued at more than $366 million. It also seeks to acquire other target assets, such as residential whole mortgage loans, commercial mortgage-backed securities, commercial real estate debt, and asset-backed securities. Riskier residential whole mortgage loans, which are generally not guaranteed by the US government, include subprime, non-performing, and sub-performing mortgage loans. Founded in 2007, Ellington Financial went public in 2010 in hopes of taking advantage of the current credit environment.

	Annual Growth	12/19	12/20	12/21	12/22	12/23
Sales ($mil.)	18.5%	45.4	72.1	172.7	161.4	89.5
Net income ($ mil.)	9.8%	57.9	25.0	133.5	(70.0)	84.1
Market value ($ mil.)	(8.7%)	1,521.4	1,231.7	1,418.5	1,026.7	1,054.9
Employees	27.8%	150	150	170	170	400

ELLINGTON RESIDENTIAL MORTGAGING REAL ESTATE INVESTMENT TRUST
NYS: EARN

53 Forest Avenue
Old Greenwich, CT 06870
Phone: 203 698-1200
Fax: –
Web: www.earnreit.com

CEO: Laurence Penn
CFO: Lisa Mumford
HR: –
FYE: December 31
Type: Public

Ellington Financial LLC is ready to double its money. The investment firm formed Ellington Residential Mortgage REIT, a real estate residential trust (REIT), to invest in agency residential mortgage-backed securities (Agency RMBS), or those guaranteed by federally sponsored entities Fannie Mae, Freddie Mac, and Ginnie Mae. (Agency RMBS carry less risk than privately issued mortgage securities.) The trust's portfolio is balanced out with about 10% non-Agency RMBS such as residential whole mortgage loans, mortgage servicing rights (MSRs), and residential real properties. (Non-Agency RMBS carry more risk but might offer better returns.) The trust went public in 2013.

	Annual Growth	12/19	12/20	12/21	12/22	12/23
Assets ($mil.)	(10.7%)	1,489.1	1,194.8	1,598.5	1,053.6	945.7
Net income ($ mil.)	(32.7%)	22.3	20.1	(6.3)	(30.2)	4.6
Market value ($ mil.)	(13.3%)	201.8	242.6	193.3	127.6	114.0
Employees	–	–	150	170	170	170

ELLIOT HOSPITAL OF THE CITY OF MANCHESTER

1 ELLIOT WAY
MANCHESTER, NH 031033502
Phone: 603 669-5300
Fax: –
Web: www.elliothospital.org

CEO: Douglas Dean
CFO: Richard Elwell
HR: –
FYE: June 30
Type: Private

Elliot Health System provides medical care to southern New Hampshire. The health care organization operates Elliot Hospital, an acute care hospital with nearly 300 beds that is home to a regional cancer center, a designated regional trauma center, and a level III neonatal intensive care unit (NICU). In addition to general and surgical care, the hospital offers rehabilitation, behavioral health, obstetrics, cardiology, and lab services. The system also operates the Elliot Physician Network, which operates primary care centers, specialty clinics, and surgery centers in various regional communities. Elliot Hospital was founded in 1890.

	Annual Growth	06/18	06/19	06/20	06/21	06/22
Sales ($mil.)	6.3%	–	560.2	549.4	621.6	672.5
Net income ($ mil.)	–	–	(4.7)	(27.7)	139.9	9.8
Market value ($ mil.)	–	–	–	–	–	–
Employees	–	–	–	–	–	2,000

ELLIS HOSPITAL

1101 NOTT ST
SCHENECTADY, NY 123082489
Phone: 518 243-4000
Fax: –
Web: www.ellishospital.org

CEO: James W Connolly
CFO: –
HR: Tricia Boeri
FYE: December 31
Type: Private

Schenectady-based Ellis Hospital (dba Ellis Medicine) serves the residents of New York's capital area as part of Ellis Medicine, a 438-bed community and teaching health care system. The hospital provides emergency, inpatient medical/surgical and psychiatric care including diagnostic, primary, and rehabilitative care. The hospital is also home to centers of excellence in the treatment of and care for heart and cardiovascular ailments, cancer, women's health issues, stroke-related problems, and behavioral health concerns. It also operates the Ellis Center the Bellvue Woman's Center, the satellite outpatient clinic Ellis Health Center, and recently-constructed Medical Center of Clifton Park.

	Annual Growth	12/16	12/17	12/18	12/21	12/22
Sales ($mil.)	(0.7%)	–	401.8	401.4	375.6	387.9
Net income ($ mil.)	–	–	1.5	11.0	(0.1)	(63.1)
Market value ($ mil.)	–	–	–	–	–	–
Employees	–	–	–	–	–	3,000

ELLSWORTH COOPERATIVE CREAMERY

232 WALLACE ST
ELLSWORTH, WI 540113500
Phone: 715 273-4311
Fax: –
Web: www.ellsworthcheese.com

CEO: Paul Bauer
CFO: –
HR: –
FYE: December 31
Type: Private

Ellsworth Cooperative Creamery processes and markets the cream of its members' crops, which in this instance are dairy cows. The creamery manufactures and distributes butter, cheese, whey powder, cheese curds, and other dairy foods. Founded in 1908 (as the Milton Dairy Company and taking its current name in 1910), the cooperative processes 1.5 million pounds of milk daily. The co-op has more than 500 farmer/members, whose dairy operations are located in Minnesota and Wisconsin. It is known for its cheddar cheese curds; the company was officially nicked-named the "Cheese Curd Capital of the World" by (former) Wisconsin's governor, Anthony Earl.

	Annual Growth	12/03	12/04	12/05	12/06	12/07
Sales ($mil.)	21.8%	–	–	98.2	92.2	145.7
Net income ($ mil.)	21.7%	–	–	2.3	2.8	3.5
Market value ($ mil.)	–	–	–	–	–	–
Employees	–	–	–	–	–	60

ELLUCIAN INC.

2003 EDMUND HALLEY DR # 500
RESTON, VA 201911108
Phone: 703 968-9000
Fax: –
Web: www.ellucian.com

CEO: Laura K Ipsen
CFO: Harshan Bhangdia
HR: –
FYE: December 31
Type: Private

Ellucian (formerly Datatel+SGHE) is the market leader charting the digital future of higher education with a portfolio of cloud-ready technology solutions and services. It serves over 2,900 higher education institutions in more than 50 countries, improves operations and enhancing the user experience for their faculties, staff, and over 22 million students. With more than 5 billion data transactions on the Ellucian platform, it is a connected and fully optimized technology environment and has data-driven insights that drive innovation and problem-solving. In addition, Ellucian supports more than 2,900 customers around the world, improving operations and bettering outcomes for faculty, staff, and over 28 million students.

	Annual Growth	12/18	12/19	12/20	12/21	12/22
Sales ($mil.)	(41.4%)	–	–	–	0.5	0.3
Net income ($ mil.)	–	–	–	–	(0.1)	(0.4)
Market value ($ mil.)	–	–	–	–	–	–
Employees	–	–	–	–	–	3,090

ELMA ELECTRONIC INC.

44350 S GRIMMER BLVD
FREMONT, CA 945386385
Phone: 510 656-3400
Fax: –
Web: www.elma.com

CEO: Fred Ruegg
CFO: –
HR: Pramane Phommachit
FYE: December 31
Type: Private

Elma Electronic thinks your electronics equipment should be contained, not your enthusiasm. The US subsidiary of Elma Electronic AG manufactures and distributes an array of electronic enclosures, backplanes, and server racks. It also makes passive electronic components, from rotary switches to knobs and light-emitting diodes. Elma Electronic's slate of services includes component customization, design, engineering, manufacture, systems integration, and verification. Subsidiary Elma Bustronic offers custom backplane applications, and Optima EPS makes electronic enclosures. The company courts industries worldwide in telecommunications, medical electronics, industrial control, defense, and aerospace.

	Annual Growth	12/14	12/15	12/16	12/17	12/18
Sales ($mil.)	(89.8%)	–	66.7	66.0	73.2	0.0
Net income ($ mil.)	(89.0%)	–	2.8	2.5	2.3	0.0
Market value ($ mil.)	–	–	–	–	–	–
Employees	–	–	–	–	–	280

ELME COMMUNITIES

1775 Eye Street, N.W., Suite 1000
Washington, DC 20006
Phone: 202 774-3200
Fax: –
Web: www.writ.com

NYS: ELME
CEO: Paul T McDermott
CFO: Steven M Freishtat
HR: –
FYE: December 31
Type: Public

Elme Communities is a self-administered equity real estate investment trust. Its business primarily consists of the ownership of apartment communities in the greater Washington, DC metro and Sunbelt regions. Elme owns around 8,900 residential apartment homes in the Washington, DC metro and Sunbelt regions. It also owns approximately 300,000 square feet of commercial space in the Washington, DC metro region. In late 2022, the company changed its name from Washington Real Estate Investment Trust to Elme Communities to reflect the company's transition into a focused multifamily company, and subsequent geographic expansion into Sunbelt markets.

	Annual Growth	12/19	12/20	12/21	12/22	12/23
Sales ($mil.)	(7.3%)	309.2	294.1	169.2	209.4	227.9
Net income ($ mil.)	–	383.6	(15.7)	16.4	(30.9)	(53.0)
Market value ($ mil.)	(15.9%)	2,564.0	1,900.6	2,271.4	1,564.0	1,282.9
Employees	–	125	112	53	102	–

ELMHURST MEMORIAL HOSPITAL INC

155 E BRUSH HILL RD
ELMHURST, IL 601265658
Phone: 331 221-9003
Fax: -
Web: www.eehealth.org

CEO: Mary L Mastro
CFO: James Doyle
HR: -
FYE: June 30
Type: Private

Elmhurst Memorial Healthcare operates Elmhurst Memorial Hospital, an acute care facility located in DuPage County, Illinois, in the western suburbs of Chicago. Founded in 1926, the hospital provides a comprehensive range of medical services -- from emergency care to specialty cancer and orthopedics care to behavioral health services. In addition to the 310-bed main hospital, Elmhurst Memorial Healthcare operates several facilities, such as doctors' offices, outpatient centers, occupational health programs, and other ancillary health care operations. Elmhurst Memorial Healthcare is part of Edward-Elmhurst Healthcare after it merged with Edward Hospital & Health Services and Linden Oaks.

	Annual Growth	06/06	06/07	06/08	06/09	06/15
Sales ($mil.)	1.3%	-	341.8	345.8	305.7	379.8
Net income ($ mil.)	-	-	43.3	(22.1)	20.1	(9.9)
Market value ($ mil.)	-	-	-	-	-	-
Employees	-	-	-	-	-	2,444

ELOXX PHARMACEUTICALS INC

NBB: ELOX

480 Arsenal Way
Watertown, MA 02472
Phone: 781 577-5300
Fax: -
Web: www.eloxxpharma.com

CEO: Sumit Aggarwal
CFO: Daniel Geffken
HR: Lori Lavoie
FYE: December 31
Type: Public

Senesco Technologies wants to find the fountain of youth for melons, tomatoes, bananas, and lettuce. The company does research surrounding new plant gene technologies for use in combating senescence, or cell aging in fruits, vegetables, and flowers. Its research activities are geared toward developing plants whose crops will have longer shelf-lives and higher yields. Senesco Technologies' research work is performed by third parties, primarily researchers at the University of Waterloo in Ontario, Canada. The company is also investigating some of its technologies for use as treatments for inflammatory diseases and/or to delay or inhibit apoptosis, i.e. , cell aging in humans (for possible use in cancer treatment).

	Annual Growth	12/18	12/19	12/20	12/21	12/22
Sales ($mil.)	-	-	-	-	-	-
Net income ($ mil.)	-	-	(47.2)	(50.9)	(34.6)	(66.7)	(36.1)
Market value ($ mil.)	(37.6%)	26.0	15.9	8.6	1.5	3.9
Employees	(15.2%)	29	29	25	25	15

ELWYN OF PENNSYLVANIA AND DELAWARE

111 ELWYN RD
MEDIA, PA 190634622
Phone: 610 891-2000
Fax: -
Web: www.elwyn.org

CEO: Charles McLister
CFO: Cindy Bertrando
HR: Tom Colgan
FYE: June 30
Type: Private

Elwyn isn't a character out of Harry Potter or Lord of the Rings . It's a not-for-profit organization that serves more than 13,000 disabled and disadvantaged people of all ages at multiple sites through education, rehabilitation, and vocational counseling. The organization also operates residential communities, including more than 80 group homes and apartments, and provides a variety of health care services for persons with developmental, physical, and emotional disabilities. The group also publishes training materials and hosts conferences and seminars for human services professionals. Founded in 1852 as a school for children with mental retardation, Elwyn is one of the oldest organizations of its kind in the US.

	Annual Growth	06/14	06/15	06/17	06/21	06/22
Sales ($mil.)	1.1%	-	218.2	314.6	222.0	236.3
Net income ($ mil.)	-	-	-	2.5	19.5	(4.3)	(1.0)
Market value ($ mil.)	-	-	-	-	-	-
Employees	-	-	-	-	-	2,500

EMANATE HEALTH MEDICAL GROUP

210 W SAN BERNARDINO RD
COVINA, CA 917231515
Phone: 626 331-7331
Fax: -
Web: www.emanatehealth.org

CEO: Robert Curry
CFO: Lois Conyers
HR: -
FYE: December 31
Type: Private

Citrus Valley Health Partners is a 660-bed hospital system that serves the residents of California's San Gabriel Valley region located between Los Angeles and San Bernardino. It operates through four health care facilities: Citrus Valley Medical Center (CVMC) Queen of the Valley Campus, CVMC Inter-Community Campus, Foothill Presbyterian Hospital, and Citrus Valley Hospice. Citrus Valley Health Partners also operates a home health care provider that offers nursing and rehabilitation care. The hospital system boasts several areas of specialty, including diabetes care, cancer treatment, palliative care, wound care, and cardiac therapy.

	Annual Growth	12/16	12/17	12/18	12/19	12/22
Sales ($mil.)	3.3%	-	64.4	606.3	75.4	75.6
Net income ($ mil.)	-	-	2.5	21.1	0.7	(2.3)
Market value ($ mil.)	-	-	-	-	-	-
Employees	-	-	-	-	-	2,800

EMBREE CONSTRUCTION GROUP, INC.

4747 WILLIAMS DR
GEORGETOWN, TX 786333799
Phone: 512 819-4700
Fax: -
Web: www.embreegroup.com

CEO: -
CFO: -
HR: -
FYE: December 31
Type: Private

The Embree Construction Group develops, designs, and builds free-standing buildings for business chains across the US. The group serves as a general contractor or construction manager, primarily for major national companies. It is active throughout the US. Ground-up and remodeling projects include retail properties, restaurants, gas stations, convenience stores, automotive service centers, and correctional facilities. Operating companies include Embree Healthcare Group, which develops assisted-living and specialty medical projects, and Embree Asset Group, which develops build-to-suit single-tenant buildings and leases them back to clients. Owner and chairman Jim Embree founded the firm in 1979 in Kansas City.

	Annual Growth	12/13	12/14	12/15	12/16	12/17
Sales ($mil.)	16.2%	-	140.9	190.4	177.0	220.9
Net income ($ mil.)	57.3%	-	2.8	8.9	9.8	11.0
Market value ($ mil.)	-	-	-	-	-	-
Employees	-	-	-	-	-	175

EMBRY-RIDDLE AERONAUTICAL UNIVERSITY, INC.

1 AEROSPACE BLVD
DAYTONA BEACH, FL 321143910
Phone: 386 226-6000
Fax: -
Web: www.erau.edu

CEO: -
CFO: -
HR: Andrea R Hooper
FYE: June 30
Type: Private

Embry-Riddle Aeronautical University (ERAU) helps students solve the mysteries of space and flying. The not-for-profit corporation teaches aviation, aerospace, and engineering to about 30,000 students a year (and a student-teacher ratio of about 13:1). ERAU, which offers hands-on training through a fleet of 90 instructional aircraft, has residential campuses in Daytona Beach, Florida and Prescott, Arizona. Its Embry-Riddle Worldwide program provides learning through more than 150 teaching centers and online training in the US, Canada, Europe, and Middle East. It offers bachelor's, master's, and doctoral degrees in 35 areas.

EMCOR GROUP, INC.

NYS: EME

301 Merritt Seven
Norwalk, CT 06851-1092
Phone: 203 849-7800
Fax: –
Web: www.emcorgroup.com

CEO: Anthony J Guzzi
CFO: Mark A Pompa
HR: –
FYE: December 31
Type: Public

EMCOR Group is an electrical and mechanical construction specialist and facilities services company. Its electrical and mechanical construction services primarily involve the design, integration, installation, start-up, operation and maintenance, and provision of services relating to electrical power transmission and distribution systems, lighting, water and wastewater treatment, voice and data communications, fire protection, plumbing, and heating, ventilation, and air-conditioning (HVAC). EMCOR also provides facilities services, including management and maintenance support. Through some 100 subsidiaries, the company serves a range of commercial, industrial, institutional, healthcare, and utility customers. EMCOR's domestic operations account for most of its revenue.

	Annual Growth	12/19	12/20	12/21	12/22	12/23
Sales ($mil.)	8.2%	9,174.6	8,797.1	9,903.6	11,076	12,583
Net income ($ mil.)	18.1%	325.1	132.9	383.5	406.1	633.0
Market value ($ mil.)	25.7%	4,060.2	4,302.9	5,993.4	6,968.2	10,135
Employees	1.6%	36,000	33,000	34,000	35,500	38,300

EMCORE CORP.

NMS: EMKR

2015 W. Chestnut Street
Alhambra, CA 91803
Phone: 626 293-3400
Fax: –
Web: www.emcore.com

CEO: Jeffrey Rittichier
CFO: Tom Minichiello
HR: –
FYE: September 30
Type: Public

EMCORE Corporation (also known as EMCORE) is a leading provider of sensors for navigation in the aerospace and defense market as well as a manufacturer of lasers and optical subsystems for use in the Broadband and Cable TV (CATV) industries. The company pioneered the linear fiber optic transmission technology that enabled the world's first delivery of CATV directly on fiber. Its best-in-class components and systems support a broad array of applications including navigation and inertial sensing, defense optoelectronics, broadband communications, optical sensing, and specialty chips for telecom and data center applications. The company makes around 85% of its revenue from companies based in the US and Canada.

	Annual Growth	09/19	09/20	09/21	09/22	09/23
Sales ($mil.)	2.9%	87.3	110.1	158.4	124.1	97.7
Net income ($ mil.)	–	(36.0)	(7.0)	25.6	(24.3)	(75.4)
Market value ($ mil.)	(37.3%)	236.7	250.6	576.8	128.8	36.7
Employees	(4.5%)	420	387	365	439	350

EMERALD DAIRY INC

11990 Market Street, Suite 205
Reston, VA 20190
Phone: 703 867-9247
Fax: –
Web: www.emeralddairy.com

CEO: –
CFO: –
HR: –
FYE: December 31
Type: Public

Emerald Dairy's formula for success is turning milk into milk powder. The company produces milk powder (infant formula and enriched milk powders for children and adults), as well as rice and soybean powders. Its product line includes two brands: Xing An Ling, which is marketed to low-end customers, and Yi Bai, which is marketed to middle and high-end customers. Producing more than 9,000 tons of milk powder annually, the dairy distributes its products to more than 5,800 retail stores located in 20 of China's 30 provinces. Emerald Dairy gets its milk supply through contracting with local dairy farmers. Chairman and CEO Yong Shan Yang owns 47% of Emerald, John Winfield owns 10%, and Farallon Partners owns 9%.

	Annual Growth	03/07*	12/07	12/08	12/09	12/10
Sales ($mil.)	–	–	29.6	44.3	44.7	55.3
Net income ($ mil.)	–	(0.0)	3.6	2.3	4.2	3.1
Market value ($ mil.)	–	–	408.4	23.8	61.3	43.2
Employees	17.2%	767	867	1,110	1,376	1,449

*Fiscal year change

EMERALD HOLDING INC

NYS: EEX

100 Broadway, 14th Floor
New York, NY 10005
Phone: 949 226-5700
Fax: –
Web: www.emeraldexpositions.com

CEO: Herve Sedky
CFO: David Doft
HR: –
FYE: December 31
Type: Public

Emerald is a leading operator of business-to-business trade shows in the US. Sectors served include retail, design and construction, equipment, safety, and technology. In addition to organizing its trade shows, conferences and other events, the company also operates content and content-marketing websites and related digital products and produce publications, each of which is aligned with a specific event sector. It also offers B2B ecommerce and digital merchandising solutions, serving the needs of manufacturers and retailers, through its recently-acquired Elastic Suite platform.

	Annual Growth	12/19	12/20	12/21	12/22	12/23
Sales ($mil.)	1.2%	367.0	234.4	222.9	508.7	385.6
Net income ($ mil.)	–	(50.0)	(633.6)	(78.1)	130.8	(8.2)
Market value ($ mil.)	(13.2%)	663.8	341.0	249.8	222.7	376.2
Employees	5.3%	548	542	600	759	673

EMERALD OIL, INC.

200 COLUMBINE ST STE 500
DENVER, CO 802064736
Phone: 303 595-5600
Fax: –
Web: www.emeraldoil.com

CEO: McAndrew Rudisill
CFO: Ryan Smith
HR: –
FYE: December 31
Type: Private

Emerald Oil (formerly Voyager Oil & Gas) is involved in energy exploration and production in the northern US. It has oil and gas rights in properties Colorado, Montana, and North Dakota, primarily in the Bakken and Three Forks formations in the Williston Basin. Growing its assets in the Rockies, in 2012 Voyager Oil & Gas acquired fellow oil and gas exploration and production company Emerald Oil and assumed that company's name. That year, the company reported proved reserves of approximately 5.35 million barrels of oil equivalent, all of which were located in the Williston Basin.

EMERGE ENERGY SERVICES LP

5600 Clearfork Main Street, Suite 400
Fort Worth, TX 76109
Phone: 817 618-4020
Fax: –
Web: www.emergelp.com

CEO: –
CFO: Deborah Deibert
HR: Kara Dahm
FYE: December 31
Type: Public

Emerge Energy Services is ready to come into being. The company formed in April 2012 by an investment firm, Insight Equity, to take over three of its portfolio investments -- Allied Energy Company LLC; Direct Fuels Partners, L.P.; and Superior Silica Sands LLC. Allied Energy and Direct Fuels distribute petroleum products, including ethanol and biodiesel, while Superior Silica Sands owns three processing plants that supply sand to natural gas production companies. (Sand is one of the key components in hydraulic fracturing.) When Emerge Energy Services went public in March 2013, it took ownership of the three companies. Emerge Energy Services filed Chapter 11 in 2019.

	Annual Growth	12/14	12/15	12/16	12/17	12/18
Sales ($mil.)	(27.1%)	1,111.3	711.6	128.4	364.3	313.6
Net income ($ mil.)	–	89.1	(9.4)	(72.8)	(6.8)	(128.5)
Market value ($ mil.)	(58.9%)	1,680.2	144.1	383.0	223.7	47.9
Employees	–	–	–	–	–	–

EMERGENT BIOSOLUTIONS INC
NYS: EBS

400 Professional Drive, Suite 400
Gaithersburg, MD 20879
Phone: 240 631-3200
Fax: –
Web: www.emergentbiosolutions.com

CEO: Robert G Kramer Sr
CFO: Richard S Lindahl
HR: Amy Linkous
FYE: December 31
Type: Public

Emergent BioSolutions a global life sciences company focused on providing innovative preparedness and response solutions addressing accidental, deliberate and naturally occurring public health threats (PHTs). The company's solutions include a product portfolio, a product development portfolio, and a contract development and manufacturing (CDMO) services portfolio. Primary product BioThrax is the only FDA-approved anthrax vaccine. Its commercial business line includes, Vivotif (typhoid fever), and Vaxchora (cholera); and opioid overdose drug Narcan. The company has centralized research and development (R&D) organization and an enterprise-wide governance approach to managing its portfolio of R&D projects. Emergent generates some 80% of its revenue from the US.

	Annual Growth	12/19	12/20	12/21	12/22	12/23
Sales ($mil.)	(1.3%)	1,106.0	1,555.4	1,792.7	1,120.9	1,049.3
Net income ($ mil.)	–	54.5	305.1	230.9	(223.8)	(760.5)
Market value ($ mil.)	(54.1%)	2,816.2	4,677.1	2,269.1	616.5	125.3
Employees	(3.4%)	1,834	700	2,416	2,500	1,600

EMERSON COLLEGE

120 BOYLSTON ST
BOSTON, MA 021164624
Phone: 617 824-8500
Fax: –
Web: www.emerson.edu

CEO: Ted Benard-Cutler
CFO: –
HR: Candace Carter-Smalley
FYE: June 30
Type: Private

Emerson College specializes in teaching subjects in the fields of communication and the arts in a liberal arts context. Areas of study include journalism; marketing; organizational and political communication; performing arts; visual and media arts; and writing, literature, and publishing. Its also has an acclaimed communication sciences and disorders program. The college enrolls about 3,200 full-time undergraduates and 1,000 full and part-time graduate students on its Boston-based campus. Among its alumni are producer Norman Lear, talk show host Jay Leno, and journalist Morton Dean. The college has additional facilities in Los Angeles and in the Netherlands. Emerson was founded in 1880 as a school of oratory.

	Annual Growth	06/16	06/17	06/20	06/21	06/22
Sales ($mil.)	11.8%	–	189.8	281.1	275.7	331.2
Net income ($ mil.)	2.3%	–	20.7	11.0	0.5	23.2
Market value ($ mil.)	–	–	–	–	–	–
Employees	–	–	–	–	–	425

EMERSON ELECTRIC CO.
NYS: EMR

8000 W. Florissant Avenue, P.O. Box 4100
St. Louis, MO 63136
Phone: 314 553-2000
Fax: –
Web: www.emerson.com

CEO: Surendralal L Karsanbhai
CFO: Michael J Baughman
HR: –
FYE: September 30
Type: Public

Emerson Electric is a global leader that designs and manufactures products and delivers services that bring technology and engineering together to provide innovative solutions for customers in a wide range of industrial, commercial, and consumer markets around the world. The company operates globally in the Americas, Europe, Asia, and the Middle East & Africa. The company offers its products through its segments, such as automation solutions that manufacture products and integrated solutions, which include measurement and analytical instrumentation. Its Tools & Home Products segment include brands such as Emerson, Emerson Professional Tools, Badger, Greenlee, Grind2Energy, InSinkErator, Klauke, ProTeam, and RIDGID. About 55% of total sales come from the Americas region.

	Annual Growth	09/19	09/20	09/21	09/22	09/23
Sales ($mil.)	(4.7%)	18,372	16,785	18,236	19,629	15,165
Net income ($ mil.)	54.7%	2,306.0	1,965.0	2,303.0	3,231.0	13,219
Market value ($ mil.)	9.6%	38,244	37,506	53,882	41,882	55,238
Employees	(6.6%)	88,000	83,500	86,700	85,500	67,000

EMERSON HOSPITAL

133 OLD ROAD TO 9 ACRE COR
CONCORD, MA 017424169
Phone: 978 369-1400
Fax: –
Web: www.emersonhospital.org

CEO: –
CFO: –
HR: –
FYE: September 30
Type: Private

Emerson Hospital is a regional medical center that provides a wide range of advanced medical services to more than 300,000 people in about 25 towns. With about 179-bed hospital, Emerson Hospital has about 300 primary care doctors and specialists. Emerson Hospital is well known for its outstanding nursing care and patient-centered specialty facilities, including the Mass General Cancer Center at Emerson Hospital ? Bethke, the Dr. Robert C. Cantu Concussion Center, the Clough Surgical Center and the Clough Birthing Center, home to the area's only special care level 2 nursery for moderately ill newborns.

	Annual Growth	09/18	09/19	09/20	09/21	09/22
Sales ($mil.)	8.9%	–	272.1	245.2	300.9	351.5
Net income ($ mil.)	6.2%	–	3.7	(4.8)	42.4	4.4
Market value ($ mil.)	–	–	–	–	–	–
Employees	–	–	–	–	–	1,450

EMERSON RADIO CORP.
ASE: MSN

959 Route 46 East, Suite 210
Parsippany, NJ 07054
Phone: 973 428-2000
Fax: –
Web: www.emersonradio.com

CEO: Christopher Ho
CFO: Richard LI
HR: –
FYE: March 31
Type: Public

Emerson Radio is tuned to the crowd that thinks a new television or microwave oven shouldn't cost an arm and a leg. The company designs, imports, sells, and licenses housewares and audio and video products under the Emerson, H.H. Scott, and Olevia brand names. Its products are sold primarily by mass merchants in the US. (Wal-Mart and Target account for more than 85% of the company's sales.) Emerson's products include microwave ovens, compact refrigerators, wine openers and coolers, clock radios, televisions, and other audio and video products. Its products are sourced from foreign suppliers, primarily in China. Emerson Radio was founded in 1948.

	Annual Growth	03/19	03/20	03/21	03/22	03/23
Sales ($mil.)	(5.5%)	9.0	6.3	7.4	8.2	7.2
Net income ($ mil.)	–	(2.4)	(4.3)	(4.0)	(3.6)	(1.4)
Market value ($ mil.)	(19.7%)	27.4	14.7	26.9	16.2	11.4
Employees	(1.1%)	23	22	24	22	22

EMI HOLDING, INC.

21250 HAWTHORNE BLVD STE 800
TORRANCE, CA 905035506
Phone: 310 214-0065
Fax: –
Web: www.emmausmedical.com

CEO: –
CFO: –
HR: –
FYE: December 31
Type: Private

Emmaus is ready to find a glut of uses for glutamine. The pharmaceutical firm has one prescription-strength dosage of the amino acid L-glutamine on the market and one in development. NutreStore is a powder form of L-glutamine used to treat short bowel syndrome, while the company has also been testing L-glutamine to treat sickle cell disease. In 2017 its Endari treatment was approved by the FDA to treat sickle cell disease in adults and children five years of age and older. Subsidiary Newfield Nutrition sells L-glutamine as a nutritional supplement under the brand AminoPure at stores in the US and through importers and distributors in Japan and Taiwan. In early 2019, Emmaus agreed to be acquired by MYnd Analytics.

EMJ CORPORATION

6148 LEE HWY
CHATTANOOGA, TN 374212941
Phone: 423 855-1550
Fax: –
Web: www.emjcorp.com

CEO: –
CFO: –
HR: –
FYE: March 07
Type: Private

EMJ does it all for the mall. Founded in 1968 by namesake Edgar M. Jolley, the company specializes in building and renovating retail outlets and shopping centers throughout the US. It is also known for other building projects, such as offices, warehouses, churches, hotels, multifamily residences, hospitals, and wind farms. Working from five offices nationwide, EMJ provides general construction and construction management. The company's pre-construction services include creating detailed budgets and construction schedules and coordinating permitting, utility companies, and municipal requirements. To track a project's progress and monitor costs, EMJ offers quality control and safety and warranty management.

	Annual Growth	12/06	12/07	12/08	12/11*	03/17
Sales ($mil.)	–	–	959.2	821.8	437.5	960.3
Net income ($ mil.)	(7.1%)	–	10.2	7.9	0.4	4.9
Market value ($ mil.)	–	–	–	–	–	–
Employees	–	–	–	–	–	210

*Fiscal year change

EMKAY, INC.

805 W THORNDALE AVE
ITASCA, IL 601431355
Phone: 630 250-7400
Fax: –
Web: www.emkay.com

CEO: Gary Tepas
CFO: –
HR: –
FYE: February 28
Type: Private

Emkay is an ehiclevay easerlay. Or for the Pig Latin challenged: Emkay is a vehicle leaser. One of the oldest and largest fleet leasing and management companies in the nation, it leases and manages some 75,000 cars, trucks, and electric vehicles to more than 500 corporate clients. The employee-owned company offers open- and closed-end leasing programs, as well as assistance with fleet purchase and disposal. Other services include maintenance and fuel management. It also operates Emkay Motors, a retail used vehicle outlet in Illinois. Founded in 1946, Emkay has 10 US offices and is active in Canada, Mexico, and the Caribbean. It operates Unico CarLease in Europe.

EMMET, MARVIN & MARTIN, LLP

120 BROADWAY FL 32
NEW YORK, NY 102713291
Phone: 212 238-3000
Fax: –
Web: www.emmetmarvin.com

CEO: –
CFO: –
HR: –
FYE: April 30
Type: Private

Emmet, Marvin & Martin can bring the weight of institutional knowledge to bear on a variety of legal problems. The firm, founded in 1805, has represented some of its clients for more than 150 years. The firm has more than 50 lawyers practicing in areas such as banking and finance (including bankruptcy, commercial lending, creditors rights, private equity, and venture capital), corporate (including securities), litigation, real estate, tax and employee benefits, and trusts and estates. Clients have included Citibank and Webster Bank. Emmet, Marvin & Martin has offices in New York, Connecticut and New Jersey. Former US President Franklin Roosevelt was a partner in the firm from 1920 to 1924.

EMMIS CORP

One Emmis Plaza, 40 Monument Circle, Suite 700
Indianapolis, IN 46204
Phone: 317 266-0100
Fax: –
Web: www.emmis.com

NBB: EMMS
CEO: –
CFO: –
HR: –
FYE: February 29
Type: Public

Emmis Communications is into communicating -- whether it's through the radio or magazines. The company operates two radio stations in New York through a local marketing agreement with ESPN Radio (WLIB 1190 AM and WEPN 98.7 FM). It also owns four radio stations in Indianapolis. In addition, Emmis has a controlling interest in Digonex, a dynamic pricing company, and Indianapolis Monthly, a city regional magazine. Significantly smaller than it once was, Emmis has been busy as of late selling off radio and publishing properties in order to pay off debt.

	Annual Growth	02/16	02/17	02/18	02/19	02/20
Sales ($mil.)	(35.6%)	231.4	214.6	148.5	114.1	39.7
Net income ($ mil.)	121.1%	2.1	13.1	82.1	23.4	50.5
Market value ($ mil.)	61.6%	7.1	37.0	55.7	51.3	48.2
Employees	(21.5%)	1,085	830	620	560	412

EMPIRE ENERGY CORP INTERNATIONAL

4500 College Blvd, Suite 240
Leawood, KS 66211
Phone: 913 663-2310
Fax: –
Web: www.empireenergy.com

CEO: –
CFO: –
HR: –
FYE: December 31
Type: Public

Empire Energy Corporation International has put a lot of energy into the search for oil and gas in a once far-flung region of Her Majesty's former empire -- Australia. Oil and gas independent Empire Energy previously owned oil and gas interests in Texas, Wyoming, and Nicaragua. However, in 2005 the company acquired Australian oil and gas explorer Great South Land Minerals and began to focus on developing oil and gas assets in Tasmania. Empire Energy is investing in developing a potential 3-million-barrel oil deposit on 15,000 sq. km. of leasehold property. The company also controls 47% of Chinese food canner Pacific Rim Foods.

	Annual Growth	12/05	12/06	12/07	12/08	12/09
Sales ($mil.)	–	–	–	–	–	–
Net income ($ mil.)	–	(1.9)	(9.0)	(7.0)	(4.9)	(13.2)
Market value ($ mil.)	(24.5%)	30.1	22.6	22.3	16.7	9.8
Employees	–	3	2	1	1	–

EMPIRE RESORTS, INC.

204 STATE ROUTE 17B
MONTICELLO, NY 127013610
Phone: 845 807-0001
Fax: –
Web: www.empireresorts.com

CEO: Ryan Eller
CFO: Laurette J Pitts
HR: Eileen Cavanaugh
FYE: December 31
Type: Private

Empire Resorts has taken up permanent residence in New York's playground. The company owns and operates Resorts World Catskills.. The property, located 90 miles northwest of New York City includes a hotel and a casino with slot machines, a poker room, private gaming salons, and a sports lounge... The casino resort also offers more than 10 varied bar and restaurant experiences, which includes an Italian steakhouse created by celebrity chef Scott Conant. Empire also owns and operates Monticello Raceway, a harness horseracing facility in Monticello, New York. In 2019, Kien Huat Realty III Limited and Genting Malaysia Berhad will acquire all outstanding equity of Empire Resorts.

EMPIRE RESOURCES, INC.

80 E STATE RT 4 STE 205
PARAMUS, NJ 076522657
Phone: 201 944-2200
Fax: –
Web: www.empireresources.com

CEO: Johnny Hsieh
CFO: –
HR: –
FYE: December 31
Type: Private

When it comes to aluminum, Empire Resources is especially resourceful. The company distributes semi-finished aluminum products, including sheet, foil, wire, plate, and coil. Products are sold primarily to manufacturers of appliances, automobiles, packaging, and housing materials. Empire Resources provides a variety of related services, including sourcing of aluminum products, storage and delivery, and handling foreign exchange transactions. Company president and CEO Nathan Kahn and CFO Sandra Kahn, who are husband and wife, own some 40% of Empire Resources.

	Annual Growth	12/12	12/13	12/14	12/15	12/16
Sales ($mil.)	(1.7%)	–	482.7	582.3	521.7	458.9
Net income ($ mil.)	11.3%	–	2.4	3.7	2.8	3.3
Market value ($ mil.)	–	–	–	–	–	–
Employees	–	–	–	–	–	60

EMPIRE SOUTHWEST, LLC

1725 S COUNTRY CLUB DR
MESA, AZ 852106003
Phone: 480 633-4000
Fax: –
Web: www.empire-cat.com

CEO: Jeffrey S Whiteman
CFO: –
HR: Tina Lucero
FYE: October 31
Type: Private

Empire Southwest is a third-generation family-owned Cat Dealer that sells, rents and services heavy equipment, tractors, and power generation equipment to clients throughout Arizona and Southeastern California. One of the largest Caterpillar dealerships in the US, Empire Southwest operates through four divisions: hydraulic service, fluid labs, precision machining, and rebuilds. The company's equipment includes backhoe loaders, compactors, dozers, electric rope shovels, track loaders, pipelayers, telehandlers, and tractors. It also handles equipment used for mining and forestry projects. The company was founded by Jack Whiteman in 1950 as Empire Machinery, an Eastern Oregon Caterpillar dealer.

	Annual Growth	10/07	10/08	10/09	10/10	10/11
Sales ($mil.)	23.5%	–	–	448.2	528.5	683.9
Net income ($ mil.)	127.0%	–	–	7.4	22.5	38.0
Market value ($ mil.)	–	–	–	–	–	–
Employees	–	–	–	–	–	1,450

EMPIRE STATE REALTY OP LP

ARC: ESBA

111 West 33rd Street, 12th Floor
New York, NY 10120
Phone: 212 850-2600
Fax: –
Web: www.esrtreit.com

CEO: Anthony E Malkin
CFO: Christina Chiu
HR: Abigail Jones
FYE: December 31
Type: Public

If King Kong were around, he'd be an executive at Empire State Realty Trust. The self-administered and self-managed real estate investment trust (REIT) formed in mid-2011 to take over a portfolio of high-profile Manhattan properties from its previous owners, the Malkin family. Its flagship property is, of course, the 102-story Empire State Building, but the trust also owns more than a dozen other buildings in the greater New York area totaling almost 7.7 million sq. ft. of office and retail space. In addition, it plans to build a 340,000-sq.-ft. building at the train station in Stamford, Connecticut. Empire State Realty Trust went public in 2013, raising $929 million.

	Annual Growth	12/19	12/20	12/21	12/22	12/23
Sales ($mil.)	0.3%	731.3	609.2	624.1	727.0	739.6
Net income ($ mil.)	–	84.3	(22.9)	(13.0)	63.5	84.3
Market value ($ mil.)	(8.3%)	3,744.6	2,490.0	2,324.7	1,809.9	2,647.1
Employees	(5.4%)	831	755	693	667	666

EMPIRE STATE REALTY TRUST INC

NYS: ESRT

111 West 33rd Street, 12th Floor
New York, NY 10120
Phone: 212 850-2600
Fax: –
Web: www.empirestaterealtytrust.com

CEO: Anthony E Malkin
CFO: Christina Chiu
HR: Abigail Jones
FYE: December 31
Type: Public

If King Kong were around, he'd be an executive at Empire State Realty Trust. The self-administered and self-managed real estate investment trust (REIT) formed in mid-2011 to take over a portfolio of high-profile Manhattan properties from its previous owners, the Malkin family. Its flagship property is, of course, the 102-story Empire State Building, but the trust also owns more than a dozen other buildings in the greater New York area totaling almost 7.7 million sq. ft. of office and retail space. In addition, it plans to build a 340,000-sq.-ft. building at the train station in Stamford, Connecticut. Empire State Realty Trust went public in 2013, raising $929 million.

	Annual Growth	12/19	12/20	12/21	12/22	12/23
Sales ($mil.)	0.3%	731.3	609.2	624.1	727.0	739.6
Net income ($ mil.)	1.0%	51.2	(12.5)	(6.5)	40.6	53.2
Market value ($ mil.)	(8.7%)	2,276.1	1,519.6	1,451.1	1,098.9	1,579.9
Employees	(5.4%)	831	755	693	667	666

EMPLOYERS HOLDINGS INC

NYS: EIG

10375 Professional Circle
Reno, NV 89521
Phone: 888 682-6671
Fax: –
Web: www.employers.com

CEO: Katherine H Antonello
CFO: Michael S Paquette
HR: –
FYE: December 31
Type: Public

Employers Holdings is a holding company which provides workers' compensation services, including claims management, loss prevention consulting, and care management to small businesses in low-to-medium hazard industries including retailers and restaurants. The company provides workers' compensation through its Employer Insurance Company of Nevada (EICN) and Employers Compensation Insurance Company. Employers also operates Cerity Insurance Company, Employers Assurance and Employers Preferred Insurance Company, both of which also offer workers' compensation. The company operates throughout the US, with the exception of four states that are served exclusively by their state funds.

	Annual Growth	12/19	12/20	12/21	12/22	12/23
Assets ($mil.)	(3.0%)	4,004.1	3,922.6	3,783.2	3,716.7	3,550.4
Net income ($ mil.)	(6.9%)	157.1	119.8	119.3	48.4	118.1
Market value ($ mil.)	(1.4%)	1,059.2	816.7	1,049.8	1,094.2	999.6
Employees	0.5%	704	691	608	676	717

EMPORIA STATE UNIVERSITY

1 KELLOGG CIR
EMPORIA, KS 668015087
Phone: 620 341-1200
Fax: –
Web: www.emporia.edu

CEO: –
CFO: –
HR: –
FYE: June 30
Type: Private

Emporia State University (ESU) offers about 40 undergraduate and roughly 30 graduate degrees and programs, as well as certification programs, specialist degrees, and doctoral degrees. It has four schools and colleges: the School of Business, School of Library and Information Management, College of Liberal Arts and Sciences, and The Teachers College. Some 6,000 students are enrolled at the school, which employs more than 250 full-time faculty members. ESU is said to be the first and only university to offer a four-year degree in Engraving Arts. The school also offers more than 35 undergraduate and graduate degree programs online.

	Annual Growth	06/12	06/13	06/17	06/18	06/19
Sales ($mil.)	3.4%	–	42.3	50.8	49.3	51.8
Net income ($ mil.)	–	–	(0.7)	5.8	(7.4)	7.2
Market value ($ mil.)	–	–	–	–	–	–
Employees	–	–	–	–	–	1,700

EMULEX CORPORATION

5300 CALIFORNIA AVE
IRVINE, CA 926173038
Phone: 714 662-5600
Fax: –
Web: www.emulex.com

CEO: –
CFO: –
HR: –
FYE: June 29
Type: Private

Emulex sets an example in the data storage market. The company is a leading maker of host server products (HSP) and embedded storage products (ESP). Its LightPulse fibre channel host bus adapters (HBA) are used to connect storage devices in direct-attached storage configurations, as well as storage area network (SAN) and network-attached storage (NAS) systems. Emulex also develops HBAs based on the fibre channel over Ethernet protocol. The company primarily sells directly to equipment makers who incorporate Emulex components into their own storage platforms; its top customers have been IBM (29% of sales) and Hewlett-Packard (16%). Emulex was acquired by Broadcom Limited in mid-2015.

ENABLE HOLDINGS, INC.   NBB: ENAB

1140 W Thorndale Ave.
Itasca, IL 60143
Phone: 773 272-5000
Fax: –
Web: www.ubid.com

CEO: Patrick L Neville
CFO: –
HR: –
FYE: December 31
Type: Public

Enable Holdings (formerly uBid.com Holdings) is a multi-channel seller of refurbished and closeout merchandise that hosts both online and live auctions. In addition, its RedTag.com site offers merchandise at a fixed price, instead of through an auction process. Through its Dibu Trading Company, the company helps businesses sell entire inventories in a single transaction. Enable's merchandise includes computers, automobiles, and other consumer goods from some 200 product categories, and comes directly from manufacturers such as Hewlett-Packard, IBM, and Sony. As a result of the credit markets drying up, Enable Holdings was forced to file for Chapter 11 bankruptcy in September 2010.

	Annual Growth	12/05	12/06	12/07	12/08	12/09
Sales ($mil.)	(32.0%)	84.6	66.6	43.1	31.6	18.1
Net income ($ mil.)	–	(9.0)	(7.6)	(7.0)	(16.0)	(7.5)
Market value ($ mil.)	–	–	54.2	14.8	5.1	3.9
Employees	(18.9%)	95	78	79	72	41

ENACTUS

444 S CAMPBELL AVE
SPRINGFIELD, MO 658062054
Phone: 417 831-9505
Fax: –
Web: www.enactus.org

CEO: –
CFO: –
HR: Janice Goocher
FYE: December 31
Type: Private

Remember the kid who always sold the most candy bars for high school fund raisers? He probably joined Students In Free Enterprise in college. The group (doing business as Enactus) is a not-for-profit organization that helps university students develop skills to become socially responsible business leaders. Enactus is active with more than 1,300 universities in about 40 countries. Participating students form teams that partner with businesses, including Best Buy, Dell, and Wal-Mart, to sponsor outreach programs, community economic improvement projects, and competitions. Programs fall into one of four categories: business ethics, entrepreneurship, market economics, and personal finance. Enactus was founded in 1975.

	Annual Growth	12/16	12/17	12/19	12/21	12/22
Sales ($mil.)	(26.9%)	–	13.0	5.1	6.4	2.7
Net income ($ mil.)	–	–	(1.5)	(2.8)	1.1	(2.4)
Market value ($ mil.)	–	–	–	–	–	–
Employees	–	–	–	–	–	40

ENANTA PHARMACEUTICALS INC   NMS: ENTA

500 Arsenal Street
Watertown, MA 02472
Phone: 617 607-0800
Fax: –
Web: www.enanta.com

CEO: –
CFO: –
HR: –
FYE: September 30
Type: Public

Enanta Pharmaceuticals is a biotechnology company that uses its robust, chemistry-driven approach and drug discovery capabilities to become a leader in the discovery and development of small molecule drugs, with an emphasis on treatments for viral infections including hepatitis C (HCV), a virus that can lead to chronic liver diseases, such as cirrhosis, organ failure, and cancer. The company's first licensed product, which is licensed to AbbVie, is paritaprevir, a protease inhibitor for use against HCV. Enanta also develops the glecaprevir, the second of two protease inhibitors discovered and developed through its collaboration with AbbVie for the treatment of chronic infection with hepatitis C virus.

	Annual Growth	09/19	09/20	09/21	09/22	09/23
Sales ($mil.)	(21.2%)	205.2	122.5	97.1	86.2	79.2
Net income ($ mil.)	–	46.4	(36.2)	(79.0)	(121.8)	(133.8)
Market value ($ mil.)	(34.3%)	1,265.2	964.1	1,196.4	1,092.3	235.2
Employees	2.4%	132	141	155	160	145

ENCISION INC.   NBB: ECIA

6797 Winchester Circle
Boulder, CO 80301
Phone: 303 444-2600
Fax: –
Web: www.encision.com

CEO: Gregory J Trudel
CFO: –
HR: –
FYE: March 31
Type: Public

Encision enables doctors to make the cut during surgery. The company makes instruments for use in laparoscopic surgical procedures, including electrodes, graspers, monitors, and scissor inserts. Encision's products, sold under the brand name AEM Surgical Instruments, work like conventional electrosurgical instruments but incorporate proprietary technology that reduces the risk of accidental damage to surrounding tissues caused by stray electrosurgical energy. The company has been working to expand its marketing and distribution network, using independent distributors and sales representatives, as well as agreements with group purchasing organizations such as Novation and Premier.

	Annual Growth	03/19	03/20	03/21	03/22	03/23
Sales ($mil.)	(4.4%)	8.8	7.7	7.5	7.7	7.3
Net income ($ mil.)	–	(0.2)	(0.2)	0.6	(0.1)	(0.3)
Market value ($ mil.)	5.8%	3.9	6.1	8.0	11.8	4.9
Employees	(3.5%)	38	31	35	33	33

ENCOMPASS ENERGY SERVICES INC

914 North Broadway Avenue, Suite 220, P.O. Box 1218
Oklahoma City, OK 73101
Phone: 405 815-4041
Fax: –
Web: www.newsource-energy.com

CEO: Antranik Armoudian
CFO: –
HR: –
FYE: December 31
Type: Public

New Source Energy is actually looking for the same old energy source - oil and gas - but in a new way. The company, formed in July 2011, plans to comb over mature oil and natural gas reservoirs a second time to hunt for leftover deposits. Right away it bought the rights to working interests in about 54,000 net acres across the Hunton formation in Oklahoma. The company estimates the properties' net proved reserves to be 19 million barrels of oil equivalent, made up of about 60% oil and natural gas liquids and 40% natural gas. New Source Energy filed an IPO in 2011 but withdrew it in 2012.

	Annual Growth	12/09	12/10	12/11	12/12	12/13
Sales ($mil.)	–	–	–	–	–	–
Net income ($ mil.)	–	(0.1)	(0.1)	0.0	(0.3)	(0.3)
Market value ($ mil.)	–	–	2.0	2.1	1.2	1.0
Employees	(15.9%)	2	2	1	1	1

ENCOMPASS HEALTH CORP
NYS: EHC

9001 Liberty Parkway
Birmingham, AL 35242
Phone: 205 967-7116
Fax: –
Web: www.encompasshealth.com

CEO: Mark J Tarr
CFO: Douglas E Coltharp
HR: Anika Cornelese
FYE: December 31
Type: Public

Encompass Health is the nation's largest owner and operator of inpatient rehabilitation hospitals in terms of patients treated, revenues, and number of hospitals. Its national footprint spans across some 35 states and Puerto Rico, with about 155 inpatient rehabilitation hospitals. Its inpatient rehabilitation hospitals offer specialized rehabilitative care across an array of diagnoses and deliver comprehensive, high-quality, cost-effective patient care services. In 2022, Encompass Health completed its spin-off of 100% of Enhabit, Inc. (Enhabit), its home health and hospice business. Enhabit is now an independent public company.

	Annual Growth	12/19	12/20	12/21	12/22	12/23
Sales ($mil.)	1.0%	4,605.0	4,644.4	5,121.6	4,348.6	4,801.2
Net income ($ mil.)	(0.5%)	358.7	284.2	412.2	271.0	352.0
Market value ($ mil.)	(0.9%)	6,944.5	8,289.9	6,542.5	5,996.1	6,688.9
Employees	(5.4%)	31,570	43,178	43,362	34,519	25,308

ENCOMPASS HOLDINGS, INC.
NBB: ECMH

1005 Terminal Way, Suite 110
Reno, NV 89502-2179
Phone: 775 324-8531
Fax: –
Web: www.encompassholdings.com

CEO: –
CFO: –
HR: –
FYE: June 30
Type: Public

Surf's up at Encompass Holdings! The investment firm owns Aqua Xtremes, which makes water sports equipment including the XBoard brand of jet-powered surfboards. It also owns Nacio Systems, which provides outsourced IT services including e-commerce, customer relationship management, and software audits. Xtremes subsidiary Xtreme Engines and its majority-owned Rotary Engine Technologies are developing an engine for the XBoard. Encompass Holdings plans to spin off Nacio Systems (it will retain a stake) and continues to look for further investment opportunities in varied industries.

	Annual Growth	12/03	12/04*	06/05	06/06	06/07
Sales ($mil.)	–	0.0	–	1.3	4.4	–
Net income ($ mil.)	–	(4.6)	(4.2)	(5.4)	(4.7)	(9.5)
Market value ($ mil.)	(39.4%)	0.2	9.8	5.6	1.3	0.0
Employees	–	–	–	–	–	–

*Fiscal year change

ENCORE CAPITAL GROUP INC
NMS: ECPG

350 Camino De La Reina, Suite 100
San Diego, CA 92108
Phone: 877 445-4581
Fax: –
Web: www.encorecapital.com

CEO: –
CFO: –
HR: –
FYE: December 31
Type: Public

Encore Capital Group is an international specialty finance company that provides debt recovery solutions and other related services across a broad range of financial assets. Encore Capital purchases portfolios of defaulted consumer receivables at deep discounts to face value and manages them by working with individuals as they repay their obligations and work toward financial recovery. Defaulted receivables are consumers' unpaid financial commitments to credit originators, including banks, credit unions, consumer finance companies, and commercial retailers. Defaulted receivables may also include receivables subject to bankruptcy proceedings. The company also provides debt servicing and other portfolio management services to credit originators for non-performing loans in Europe. Around 70% of total revenue comes from the domestic operation.

	Annual Growth	12/19	12/20	12/21	12/22	12/23
Sales ($mil.)	(3.3%)	1,397.1	1,501.4	1,614.5	1,398.3	1,222.7
Net income ($ mil.)	–	167.9	211.8	350.8	194.6	(206.5)
Market value ($ mil.)	9.5%	832.6	917.1	1,462.4	1,128.7	1,194.9
Employees	0.3%	7,300	7,725	6,604	6,900	7,400

ENCORE NATIONWIDE, INC.

2447 PACIFIC COAST HWY FL 261
HERMOSA BEACH, CA 90254
Phone: 310 357-2848
Fax: –
Web: www.encorenationwide.com

CEO: –
CFO: –
HR: –
FYE: December 31
Type: Private

Encore Nationwide provides event staffing services for marketing and promotional campaigns. With a talent database of more than 12,000 people across the US, Encore can match the right person with appropriate event to create successful promotional events. The company can supply everything from promotional models and product demonstrators to emcees, tour managers, and all manner of casual laborers. Events include trade shows, bar and nightclub promotions, fashion shows, and guerilla marketing campaigns.

ENCORE WIRE CORP.
NMS: WIRE

1329 Millwood Road
McKinney, TX 75069
Phone: 972 562-9473
Fax: 972 562-4744
Web: www.encorewire.com

CEO: Daniel L Jones
CFO: Bret J Eckert
HR: –
FYE: December 31
Type: Public

A low-cost manufacturer of copper electrical building wire and cable, Encore Wire produces NM-B cable, a sheathed cable used to wire homes, apartments, and manufactured housing, and UF-B. Its inventory of stock-keeping units include THWN-2 cable, an insulated feeder, circuit, and branch wiring for commercial and industrial buildings, and other wires including SEU, SER, Photovoltaic, URD, tray cable, metal-clad and armored cable. The company's principal customers are wholesale electrical distributors that sells its products to electrical contractors. The company was founded in 1989.

	Annual Growth	12/19	12/20	12/21	12/22	12/23
Sales ($mil.)	19.1%	1,275.0	1,276.9	2,592.7	3,017.6	2,567.7
Net income ($ mil.)	59.1%	58.1	76.1	541.4	717.8	372.4
Market value ($ mil.)	38.9%	896.3	945.8	2,234.6	2,148.0	3,335.4
Employees	4.2%	1,380	1,289	1,440	1,672	1,629

ENDEAVOR HEALTH CLINICAL OPERATIONS

1301 CENTRAL ST
EVANSTON, IL 602011613
Phone: 847 570-2000
Fax: –
Web: www.northshore.org

CEO: JP Gallagher
CFO: –
HR: William R Luehrs
FYE: December 31
Type: Private

NorthShore University HealthSystem is an integrated healthcare delivery system. NorthShore operates six hospitals and a Medical Group with more than 1,000 primary and specialty care physicians. NorthShore's Evanston Hospital has teaching and research programs, as well as capabilities for trauma, cancer, and cardiology. NorthShore also includes Glenbrook Hospital, Highland Park Hospital, Swedish Hospital and Skokie Hospital. NorthShore is affiliated with the University of Chicago Pritzker School of Medicine. The NorthShore Research Institute focuses on clinical and translational research, including leadership in clinical trials and medical informatics.

	Annual Growth	09/18	09/19	09/20	09/21*	12/22
Sales ($mil.)	2.8%	–	1,883.0	1.5	1,730.8	2,043.7
Net income ($ mil.)	(41.0%)	–	172.2	0.3	1,334.0	35.4
Market value ($ mil.)	–	–	–	–	–	–
Employees	–	–	–	–	–	12,061

*Fiscal year change

ENDI CORP
NBB: ENDI

2400 Old Brick Road, Suite 115
Glen Allen, VA 23060
Phone: 434 336-7737
Fax: –
Web: www.endicorp.com

CEO: Steven L Kiel
CFO: Alea Kleinhammer
HR: –
FYE: December 31
Type: Public

Enterprise Diversified is primarily focused on partnering with alternative asset managers in addition to holding interests in companies associated with internet access. The company's internet operations are managed under Sitestar.net, which offers consumer and business-grade internet access, wholesale managed modem services, web hosting, and various ancillary services to customers in the US and Canada. Its asset management subsidiary, Willow Oak Asset Management, is passionate about growing a network of alternative asset managers who believe in the value investing framework. Through its Fund Management Services, Willow Oak partners with its affiliated firms, providing operational, marketing, and investor relations support to niche fund managers. In mid-2022, the company completed its previously announced business combination. As a result of the mergers, Enterprise Diversified and CrossingBridge will now operate as a wholly owned subsidiaries of ENDI Corp.

	Annual Growth	12/18	12/19	12/20	12/21	12/22
Sales ($mil.)	14.7%	4.4	3.6	5.2	5.9	7.6
Net income ($ mil.)	–	(3.8)	(5.4)	3.3	2.8	2.4
Market value ($ mil.)	(19.0%)	47.4	20.7	29.9	51.5	20.4
Employees	(4.0%)	20	7	7	6	17

ENDOLOGIX, INC.

2 MUSICK
IRVINE, CA 926181631
Phone: 949 595-7200
Fax: –
Web: www.endologix.com

CEO: John Onopchenko
CFO: Cindy Pinto
HR: Kimberly Stanley
FYE: December 31
Type: Private

Endologix LLC is a global medical device company dedicated to improving patients' lives by providing innovative therapies for the interventional treatment of vascular disease. Endologix has a therapeutic portfolio designed to treat diseases which currently have clinically relevant unmet needs. These products can treat a wide spectrum of vascular disease through abdominal aortic aneurysms to lower limb peripheral vascular disease. Excellent clinical outcomes are achieved through meticulous attention to product design, manufacturing, and training, all backed by industry-leading clinical evidence.

ENEL X NORTH AMERICA, INC.

101 SEAPORT BLVD FL 12
BOSTON, MA 022102149
Phone: 617 224-9900
Fax: –
Web: www.enelx.com

CEO: Enrico Viale
CFO: –
HR: Liz Lally
FYE: December 31
Type: Private

Enel X is Enel Group's global business line offering services that accelerate innovation and drive the energy transition. In North America, Enel X has around 4,500 business customers, spanning more than 35,000 sites and representing approximately $10.5 billion in energy spend under management. Enel X North America has approximately 4.7 GW of demand response capacity, over 140 battery storage projects that are operational and under contract, and more than 110,000 smart EV charging stations. Enel X advises large energy users on energy procurement, sustainability, and risk management, and has completed 65,000 energy procurement events including 3,500 MW of long-term renewable energy contracts.

ENER1, INC.

3619 W 73RD ST
ANDERSON, IN 460119608
Phone: 317 703-1800
Fax: –
Web: –

CEO: –
CFO: –
HR: –
FYE: December 31
Type: Private

Ener1 is on a quest to energize the world. The company develops and manufactures lithium-ion batteries and battery packs, primarily for grid energy storage, transportation, and small electronics applications. Its EnerDel unit makes lithium-ion batteries and battery cells in the US and South Korea. The subsidiary has an agreement with Norway-based Think Global to supply batteries for its Think City electric vehicle (EV). It is also developing batteries for the Volvo C30 EVs. Ener1's EnerFuel unit develops fuel cell components and its NanoEner subsidiary develops technology for depositing materials onto battery electrodes. Ener1 manufactures in the US and South Korea; more than half of sales come from its US operations.

ENERFAB, INC.

4430 CHICKERING AVE
CINCINNATI, OH 452321931
Phone: 513 641-0500
Fax: –
Web: www.enerfab.com

CEO: –
CFO: –
HR: –
FYE: September 30
Type: Private

Enerfab says "tanks, a lot" to customers who buy its products. The company manufactures fabricated metal products, including storage and brewery tanks, tank heads, and piping systems. Enerfab also operates as a boiler installation and maintenance contractor serving both the industrial and utility markets, and it offers material handling services including conveyors, rotary car dumpers, scales, and barge loaders. Customers include a range of companies in the chemical, food and beverage, pharmaceutical, and utility industries. Over the years, Enerfab has produced more than 400 million gallons of juice storage tanks in the US, Europe, and South America.

ENERGIZER HOLDINGS INC (NEW)
NYS: ENR

533 Maryville University Drive
St. Louis, MO 63141
Phone: 314 985-2000
Fax: –
Web: www.energizerholdings.com

CEO: Mark S Lavigne
CFO: John J Drabik
HR: –
FYE: September 30
Type: Public

Energizer is a global diversified household products leader in batteries, auto care and portable lights. Energizer is one of the world's largest manufacturers, marketers and distributors of household and specialty batteries; automotive appearance, performance, refrigerant and freshener products; and portable lights. It also makes handheld, headlights, lanterns, and area lights. In addition to the Energizer, Eveready and Rayovac brands, the company market its flashlights under the Hard Case, Dolphin, and WeatherReady sub-brands. Energizer operates in about 40 countries. About 65% of its revenue were from domestic operations.

	Annual Growth	09/19	09/20	09/21	09/22	09/23
Sales ($mil.)	4.4%	2,494.5	2,744.8	3,021.5	3,050.1	2,959.7
Net income ($ mil.)	28.8%	51.1	(93.3)	160.9	(231.5)	140.5
Market value ($ mil.)	(7.4%)	3,115.9	2,798.5	2,792.1	1,797.5	2,290.8
Employees	(9.3%)	7,500	5,900	6,000	5,500	5,080

ENERGOUS CORP

NAS: WATT

3590 North First Street, Suite 210
San Jose, CA 95134
Phone: 408 963-0200
Fax: –
Web: www.energous.com

CEO: Daniel W Fairfax
CFO: Mallorie Burak
HR: –
FYE: December 31
Type: Public

Energous is hoping to make power cords go the way of the VCR. The company is developing a device that can wirelessly power electronic devices from a distance. Its wireless recharging system, WattUp, is similar in size and shape to a Wi-Fi router. It's still in testing phase but has been shown to power devices as far as 15 feet away. Energous plans to license the technology for WattUp to other electronics makers who can incorporate it into their products. The company was founded in 2012 by CTO Michael Leabman, who holds a master's degree from MIT. It went public in 2014 and raised $24 million, which is plans to use to further fund product development and launch sales and marketing initiatives.

	Annual Growth	12/18	12/19	12/20	12/21	12/22
Sales ($mil.)	13.4%	0.5	0.2	0.3	0.8	0.9
Net income ($ mil.)	–	(50.8)	(38.4)	(31.8)	(41.4)	(26.3)
Market value ($ mil.)	(38.4%)	22.9	7.0	7.1	4.9	3.3
Employees	(11.2%)	69	51	54	38	43

ENERGY & ENVIRONMENTAL SERVICES INC

NBB: EESE

2601 NW Expressway, Suite 605W
Oklahoma, OK 73112
Phone: 405 843-8996
Fax: 405 843-0819
Web: www.eesokc.com

CEO: –
CFO: –
HR: –
FYE: December 31
Type: Public

Turning subterranean natural gas into a useful energy is the goal of exploration and development independent Energas Resources. Operating through its A.T. Gas Gathering Systems and TGC subsidiaries, the company is primarily focused on exploring and producing in the Arkoma Basin in Oklahoma, and the Powder River Basin in Wyoming. Energas Resources has proved reserves of 22,143 barrels of oil and 1.9 billion cu. ft. of natural gas. In 2007 the company sold most of its assets in the shallow Devonian Shale natural gas strata in the Appalachian Basin of Kentucky. President George Shaw owns about 24% of the company.

	Annual Growth	12/17	12/18	12/19	12/20	12/21
Sales ($mil.)	37.8%	3.8	7.2	8.6	8.5	13.7
Net income ($ mil.)	–	(2.4)	0.1	(0.3)	(1.7)	0.8
Market value ($ mil.)	(36.5%)	31.8	10.2	4.8	2.5	5.2
Employees	–	–	–	22	64	38	52

ENERGY FOCUS INC

NAS: EFOI

32000 Aurora Road, Suite B
Solon, OH 44139
Phone: 440 715-1300
Fax: –
Web: www.energyfocusinc.com

CEO: Jay Huang
CFO: –
HR: –
FYE: December 31
Type: Public

The Illuminator may be coming to a theater near you, but it isn't a movie--its what Energy Focus does. The company makes products such as energy-efficient fiber-optic, light-emitting diode, ceramic metal halide, and high-intensity discharge lighting systems. Serving the commercial/industrial and pool lighting markets, Energy Focus' systems illuminate cinemas, shopping malls, parking garages, performing arts centers, restaurants, pools/spas, and homes. Its lighting products include acrylic accent fixtures, downlight fixtures, spotlights, and display-case lighting. The company's Stones River Companies (SRC) unit concentrates on turnkey lighting projects and solar retrofit jobs.

	Annual Growth	12/19	12/20	12/21	12/22	12/23
Sales ($mil.)	(18.1%)	12.7	16.8	9.9	6.0	5.7
Net income ($ mil.)	–	(7.4)	(6.0)	(7.9)	(10.3)	(4.3)
Market value ($ mil.)	33.7%	2.1	17.5	18.6	1.4	6.6
Employees	(27.1%)	46	59	58	20	13

ENERGY FUTURE HOLDINGS CORP

1601 Bryan Street
Dallas, TX 75201-3411
Phone: 214 812-4600
Fax: –
Web: www.energyfutureholdings.com

CEO: Paul M Keglevic
CFO: Anthony R Horton
HR: –
FYE: December 31
Type: Public

Energy Future Holdings operates the largest nonregulated retail electric provider in Texas (TXU Energy) with more than 1.7 million customers, and its Luminant unit has a generating capacity of more than 13,700 MW in the state. Energy Future Holdings has regulated power transmission and distribution operations through 80%-owned Oncor Electric Delivery, which operates the largest regulated distribution and transmission system in Texas, providing power to more than 3.2 million electric delivery points over 120,000 miles of transmission and distribution lines. The company filed for bankruptcy protection in 2014 and expected to exit bankruptcy in 2016.

	Annual Growth	12/11	12/12	12/13	12/14	12/15
Sales ($mil.)	(6.5%)	7,040.0	5,636.0	5,899.0	5,978.0	5,370.0
Net income ($ mil.)	–	(1,913.0)	(3,360.0)	(2,218.0)	(6,406.0)	(5,342.0)
Market value ($ mil.)	–	–	–	–	–	–
Employees	(1.2%)	9,300	9,100	9,000	8,920	8,860

ENERGY NORTHWEST

P.O. Box 968
Richland, WA 99352
Phone: 509 372-5000
Fax: –
Web: www.energy-northwest.com

CEO: –
CFO: Brent Ridge
HR: –
FYE: June 30
Type: Public

Energy Northwest provides electricity to public utility districts (PUDs) and municipalities in Washington State. The company, which is owned by the utilities it serves, has interests in nuclear, hydroelectric, wind, and solar power generation. Energy Northwest is a joint operating agency comprised of more than 25 member public utilities from across the state of Washington, which collectively serve 1.5 million end-users. Its four electricity generating stations are Columbia Generating Station (nuclear), Nine Canyon Wind Project, Packwood Lake Hydroelectric Project, and the White Bluffs Solar Station. The company has a generating capacity of about 1,175 MW, primarily from its nuclear plant.

	Annual Growth	06/12	06/13	06/14	06/15	06/21
Sales ($mil.)	3.1%	425.7	569.9	470.8	542.3	560.7
Net income ($ mil.)	–	(0.2)	1.1	0.0	2.2	2.9
Market value ($ mil.)	–	–	–	–	–	–
Employees	–	–	–	–	–	1,100

ENERGY RECOVERY INC

NMS: ERII

1717 Doolittle Drive
San Leandro, CA 94577
Phone: 510 483-7370
Fax: –
Web: www.energyrecovery.com

CEO: –
CFO: –
HR: –
FYE: December 31
Type: Public

Desalination makes seawater potable; Energy Recovery (ERI) makes desalination practical. The company designs, develops, and manufactures energy recovery devices used in sea water reverse osmosis (SWRO) desalination plants. The SWRO process is energy intensive, using high pressure to drive salt water through membranes to produce fresh water. The company's main product, the PX Pressure Exchanger, helps recapture and recycle up to 98% of the energy available in the high-pressure reject stream, a by-product of the SWRO process. The PX can reduce the energy consumption of a desalination plant by up to 60% compared with a plant lacking an energy recovery device. Subsidiary Pump Engineering also makes high pressure pumps.

	Annual Growth	12/19	12/20	12/21	12/22	12/23
Sales ($mil.)	10.2%	86.9	119.0	103.9	125.6	128.3
Net income ($ mil.)	18.5%	10.9	26.4	14.3	24.0	21.5
Market value ($ mil.)	17.8%	556.9	775.9	1,222.4	1,165.5	1,071.6
Employees	9.4%	188	216	222	246	269

ENERGY SERVICES OF AMERICA CORP.
NAS: ESOA

75 West 3rd Ave.
Huntington, WV 25701
Phone: 304 522-3868
Fax: –
Web: www.energyservicesofamerica.com

CEO: Douglas V Reynolds V
CFO: Charles P Crimmel
HR: –
FYE: September 30
Type: Public

When energy companies don't want to get their hands dirty, they can call on Energy Services of America (ESA). The service company provides installation, repair, and maintenance work primarily for natural gas and electricity providers. It also installs water and sewer lines for government agencies. ESA operates mostly in the Mid Atlantic region; its customers include Spectra Energy, Hitachi, Columbia Gas Transmission, Toyota, MarkWest Energy, and American Electric Power. Typically the pipes, steel plates, wire, and fittings used by the company are supplied by their customer, keeping costs low. The company operates through subsidiaries ST Pipeline and C.J. Hughes Construction, which it purchased in 2008.

	Annual Growth	09/19	09/20	09/21	09/22	09/23
Sales ($mil.)	14.9%	174.5	119.2	122.5	197.6	304.1
Net income ($ mil.)	38.8%	2.0	2.4	9.1	3.9	7.4
Market value ($ mil.)	52.4%	12.4	13.6	27.5	47.4	67.0
Employees	27.6%	484	553	703	1,055	1,282

ENERGY SERVICES PROVIDERS, INC.

3700 LAKESIDE DR # 6
MIRAMAR, FL 330273264
Phone: 305 947-7880
Fax: –
Web: –

CEO: Douglas W Marcille
CFO: –
HR: –
FYE: December 31
Type: Private

Energy Services Providers, Inc. (ESPI) is an electricity and natural gas supplier dedicated to providing more efficient energy services in New York's deregulated power market. ESPI is one of about 20 energy service company (ESCOs) offered to customers of public utility Niagara Mohawk. ESPI also offers cost-saving services such as energy audits, energy-efficient lighting, HVAC, compressors, and controls. The company promises to save its customers some 7% of their electric bills through its energy-efficient offerings. ESPI was founded in 2002 by CEO Franklin Lewis. In 2009 the company was acquired by US Gas & Electric, a portfolio company of investment firm MVC Capital.

	Annual Growth	12/07	12/08	12/09	12/10	12/11
Sales ($mil.)	30.5%	–	–	–	73.9	96.5
Net income ($ mil.)	81.3%	–	–	–	4.1	7.4
Market value ($ mil.)	–	–	–	–	–	–
Employees	–	–	–	–	–	158

ENERGY TRANSFER LP
NYS: ET

8111 Westchester Drive, Suite 600
Dallas, TX 75175
Phone: 214 981-0700
Fax: –
Web: www.energytransfer.com

CEO: Marshall S McCrea III
CFO: Dylan A Bramhall
HR: –
FYE: December 31
Type: Public

Energy Transfer LP transfers natural gas and other energy resources through its massive network of US-based pipelines. The primary activities in which the company is engaged, which are in the US, and the operating subsidiaries through which it conducts those activities are natural gas midstream and intrastate transportation and storage, crude oil, NGL, and refined products transportation, terminalling services and acquisition and marketing activities, as well as NGL storage and fractionation services. In addition, Energy Transfer owns investments in other businesses, including Sunoco LP and USAC. Energy Transfer was formed in 1996 and became a publicly traded partnership in 2004.

	Annual Growth	12/19	12/20	12/21	12/22	12/23
Sales ($mil.)	9.7%	54,213	38,954	67,417	89,876	78,586
Net income ($ mil.)	2.3%	3,592.0	(648.0)	5,470.0	4,756.0	3,935.0
Market value ($ mil.)	1.8%	43,205	20,811	27,715	39,973	46,472
Employees	1.8%	12,812	11,421	12,558	12,565	13,786

ENERGYUNITED ELECTRIC MEMBERSHIP CORPORATION

567 MOCKSVILLE HWY
STATESVILLE, NC 286258269
Phone: 704 873-5241
Fax: –
Web: www.energyunited.com

CEO: –
CFO: –
HR: –
FYE: December 31
Type: Private

Electrical energy and propane energy come together, under the auspices of EnergyUnited Electric Membership. One of North Carolina's largest power utilities, EnergyUnited distributes electricity to more than 120,000 residential and business customers in 19 counties. The member-owned, not-for-profit cooperative also provides propane to 23,000 customers in 74 counties in North and South Carolina, and it also offers home security, bill management, and facility monitoring services. The third largest supplier of residential electricity in the state, its service territory includes three of the largest cities in North Carolina - Charlotte, Greensboro, and Winston-Salem.

	Annual Growth	12/16	12/17	12/19	12/20	12/21
Sales ($mil.)	(0.2%)	–	282.6	–	304.7	280.5
Net income ($ mil.)	(30.2%)	–	6.5	–	30.9	1.5
Market value ($ mil.)	–	–	–	–	–	–
Employees	–	–	–	–	–	185

ENERPAC TOOL GROUP CORP
NYS: EPAC

N86 W12500 Westbrook Crossing
Menomonee Falls, WI 53051
Phone: 262 293-1500
Fax: –
Web: www.enerpactoolgroup.com

CEO: Paul E Sternlieb
CFO: Anthony P Colucci
HR: –
FYE: August 31
Type: Public

Founded in 1910, Enerpac Tool Group (formerly Actuant) is a premier industrial tools and services company serving a broad and diverse set of customers in more than 100 countries. It provides engineering and manufacturing of high pressure hydraulic tools, controlled force products and solutions for precise positioning of heavy loads that help customers safely and reliably tackle some of the most challenging jobs around the world. The company generates approximately 40% of its revenue from the US.

	Annual Growth	08/19	08/20	08/21	08/22	08/23
Sales ($mil.)	(2.2%)	654.8	493.3	528.7	571.2	598.2
Net income ($ mil.)	–	(249.1)	0.7	38.1	15.7	46.6
Market value ($ mil.)	4.2%	1,221.3	1,143.8	1,383.5	1,066.8	1,440.7
Employees	(19.1%)	4,900	2,300	2,100	2,200	2,100

ENERSYS
NYS: ENS

2366 Bernville Road
Reading, PA 19605
Phone: 610 208-1991
Fax: –
Web: www.enersys.com

CEO: David M Shaffer
CFO: Andrea J Funk
HR: –
FYE: March 31
Type: Public

EnerSys is a world leader in stored energy solutions for industrial applications. The company manufactures, markets and distributes industrial batteries and related products such as chargers, outdoor cabinet enclosures, power equipment and battery accessories, and provides related after-market and customer-support services for its products. The battery manufacturer sells directly and through distributors to more than 10,000 customers in more than 100 countries. It serves distributors, warehouse operators, retailers, airports, and mine operators as well as customers in the telecom, electric utilities, emergency lighting, security systems, and space satellites markets.

	Annual Growth	03/19	03/20	03/21	03/22	03/23
Sales ($mil.)	7.2%	2,808.0	3,087.9	2,977.9	3,357.3	3,708.6
Net income ($ mil.)	2.3%	160.2	137.1	143.4	143.9	175.8
Market value ($ mil.)	7.5%	2,665.1	2,025.4	3,713.8	3,050.0	3,553.5
Employees	0.8%	11,000	11,400	11,100	11,400	11,350

ENERWISE GLOBAL TECHNOLOGIES, LLC DBA CPOWER

1001 FLEET ST STE 400
BALTIMORE, MD 212025123
Phone: 844 276-9371
Fax: –
Web: –

CEO: –
CFO: –
HR: –
FYE: December 31
Type: Private

Energy companies should definitely know where their power goes: Enerwise Global Technologies wouldn't have it any other way. The company provides energy management software and services for energy production and distribution companies. Enerwise's products and services are used for tasks such as demand response, energy consumption analysis, load management, allocation of utility costs, improvement planning, and asset maintenance. It also provides professional services such as consulting, support, and training. The company was acquired by Comverge in late 2007.

ENGELBERTH CONSTRUCTION, INC.

150 WATERTOWER CIR UNIT 100
COLCHESTER, VT 054461900
Phone: 802 655-0100
Fax: –
Web: www.engelberth.com

CEO: –
CFO: Thomas J Clavelle
HR: Gina Catanzarita
FYE: December 31
Type: Private

Engelberth Construction has spent more than thirty years building its business, but it doesn't take nearly as long in the business of building. Specializing in commercial construction the company offers construction management, design/build, general contracting, and additional services for educational, commericial, multi-family residential, and industrial clients. Engelberth Construction works primarily in the New England region (Vermont and New Hampshire) of the US. Otto Engelberth founded Engelberth Construction as a small two-person, home-based construction business in 1972.

	Annual Growth	12/14	12/15	12/16	12/17	12/18
Sales ($mil.)	15.4%	–	94.4	–	–	144.9
Net income ($ mil.)	–	–	1.1	–	–	–
Market value ($ mil.)	–	–	–	–	–	–
Employees	–	–	–	–	–	150

ENGHOUSE NETWORKS (US) INC.

333 N ALABAMA ST STE 240
INDIANAPOLIS, IN 462042151
Phone: 317 262-4666
Fax: –
Web: www.downtownindy.org

CEO: Manfred Hanuschek
CFO: Nathan Habegger
HR: –
FYE: December 31
Type: Private

Enghouse Networks helps telecommunications companies act on their transactions. The company provides software and services for billing, customer care, and telemanagement. Targeting service providers in the telecom, information technology, financial, cable, and health care industries, Enghouse Networks offers software that analyzes billing data, automates telecommunications spending, manages electronic invoicing, and handles call accounting. The company also offers professional services and outsourced call center management, output processing, training, support, and marketing services. In 2019, Enghouse acquired Espial Group, which develops a cloud platform for delivering video, bringing a new dimension to Enghouse's offerings.

ENGLEFIELD, INC.

447 JAMES PKWY
HEATH, OH 430561030
Phone: 740 928-8215
Fax: –
Web: www.englefieldoil.com

CEO: F W Englefield III
CFO: –
HR: Christopher Beem
FYE: December 31
Type: Private

Englefield Oil Company supplies fuel and lubricants and operates about 125 convenience stores under the Duchess Shoppes banner in Ohio and West Virginia. Many of the company's convenience stores sell BP, Marathon, and Valero brand gasoline. In addition, Englefield Oil operates several truck stops, as well as several Taco Bell, Long John Silvers, and Subway quick-serve restaurants, as well as a variety of other businesses across Ohio and West Virginia. As part of its business, Englefield operates more than a dozen Pacific Pride automated commercial fueling sites. Chairman F. W. "Bill" Englefield III founded the company in 1961 with three service stations and an office operating out of his basement.

ENGLEWOOD HOSPITAL AND MEDICAL CENTER FOUNDATION INC.

350 ENGLE ST
ENGLEWOOD, NJ 076311808
Phone: 201 894-3725
Fax: –
Web: www.englewoodhealthfoundation.org

CEO: Richard Lerner
CFO: –
HR: –
FYE: December 31
Type: Private

Englewood Hospital and Medical Center is a 520-bed acute care hospital serving New Jersey's Bergen County, which is part of the New York City metro area. The not-for-profit health care provider offers general medical and surgical care, along with specialty services in areas such as oncology, cardiovascular disease, wound care, women's health, joint replacement, and pediatrics. It also maintains a short-term inpatient behavioral health program for adults. The hospital is affiliated with the Mount Sinai School of Medicine and the Mount Sinai Consortium for Graduate Medical Education and provides residency programs to doctors from the Mount Sinai School of Medicine.

	Annual Growth	12/15	12/16	12/17	12/19	12/22
Sales ($mil.)	10.2%	–	552.8	11.5	770.3	988.0
Net income ($ mil.)	1.9%	–	19.2	7.7	45.0	21.4
Market value ($ mil.)	–	–	–	–	–	–
Employees	–	–	–	–	–	38

ENGLOBAL CORP.

NAS: ENG

11740 Katy Fwy. - Energy Tower III, 11th floor
Houston, TX 77079
Phone: 281 878-1000
Fax: –
Web: www.englobal.com

CEO: William A Coskey
CFO: Darren W Spriggs
HR: –
FYE: December 31
Type: Public

ENGlobal is engineering its way into the hearts of energy companies. A leading provider of engineering and automation services, the company provides engineering and systems services, procurement, construction management, inspection, and control system automation design, fabrication and implementation to the pipeline and process divisions of major oil and gas companies primarily in the US. Following a downturn in its business and heavy losses, ENGlobal has repositioned itself as a leaner operation by selling or discontinuing certain lines of business, including its Field Solutions and Electrical Services divisions, closing offices, and shedding about 75% of its workforce. ENGlobal was founded in 1994.

	Annual Growth	12/18	12/19	12/20	12/21	12/22
Sales ($mil.)	(7.1%)	54.0	56.6	64.4	36.4	40.2
Net income ($ mil.)	–	(5.7)	(1.5)	(0.6)	(5.7)	(18.5)
Market value ($ mil.)	3.5%	3.0	4.4	13.2	6.9	3.5
Employees	6.1%	238	251	241	198	302

ENHERENT CORP
NBB: ENHT

100 Wood Avenue South, Suite 116
Iselin, NJ 08830
Phone: 732 321-1004
Fax: –
Web: www.enherent.com

CEO: Pamela A Fredette
CFO: –
HR: Carol Anderson
FYE: December 31
Type: Public

Little "e," big on "IT." Information technology (IT) consultancy enherent provides software development and technical staffing. Its software integrates Web-enabled communication and transaction applications with legacy systems, as well as other enterprise information systems. Through its staffing business, enherent provides technical personnel and project management services. Targeting FORTUNE 1000 companies, enherent's customers come from industries such as financial services, health care, and manufacturing, and include AIG, Bank of America, New England Motor Freight, GlaxoSmithKline, and Wachovia Securities.

	Annual Growth	12/05	12/06	12/07	12/08	12/09
Sales ($mil.)	(20.8%)	27.3	30.1	30.7	27.4	10.8
Net income ($ mil.)	–	(0.7)	(0.3)	0.4	(0.4)	(1.3)
Market value ($ mil.)	(44.2%)	6.5	3.2	5.6	1.4	0.6
Employees	(30.7%)	269	272	213	119	62

ENIVA USA, INC.

2700 CAMPUS DR
PLYMOUTH, MN 554412601
Phone: 763 795-8870
Fax: –
Web: www.eniva.com

CEO: Andrew Baechler
CFO: –
HR: –
FYE: December 31
Type: Private

Prolonging youthfulness is big business for Eniva. The company researches, manufactures, and markets nutraceuticals (nutritional supplements produced under pharmaceutical standards of safety and quality) and skin care products. Its principal product is Vibe, a nutrient-infused energy drink that the company reports will slow the aging process and improve overall health. Eniva markets Vibe and some 100 other wellness products (for the heart, circulation, immune system, joint support, weight management, eye care, and sore-muscle relief) through a network of more than 120,000 independent distributors. Twin brothers Andrew and Benjamin Baechler started Eniva in 1998.

	Annual Growth	12/00	12/01	12/02	12/03	12/17
Sales ($mil.)	(1.2%)	–	9.7	11.6	11.4	8.0
Net income ($ mil.)	1.0%	–	0.2	9.6	0.2	0.2
Market value ($ mil.)	–	–	–	–	–	–
Employees	–	–	–	–	–	40

ENLINK MIDSTREAM LLC
NYS: ENLC

1722 Routh St., Suite 1300
Dallas, TX 75201
Phone: 214 953-9500
Fax: –
Web: www.enlink.com

CEO: Jesse Arenivas
CFO: Benjamin D Lamb
HR: –
FYE: December 31
Type: Public

EnLink Midstream, LLC is a US midstream energy company that transports, stores, and sells natural gas, NGLs, crude oil, and condensates to industrial end-users, utilities, marketers, and other pipelines. Its asset network includes approximately 13,600 miles of pipelines, about 25 natural gas processing plants, seven fractionators, barge and rail terminals, and product storage facilities. EnLink Midstream primarily focuses on gathering, compressing, treating, processing, fractioning, transporting, and stabilizing gasses. Generating all of its sales from the US, the company also offers purchasing and marketing capabilities, brine disposal wells, a crude oil trucking fleet, and equity investments in certain joint ventures.

	Annual Growth	12/19	12/20	12/21	12/22	12/23
Sales ($mil.)	3.3%	6,052.9	3,893.8	6,685.9	9,542.1	6,900.1
Net income ($ mil.)	–	(1,119.3)	(421.5)	22.4	361.3	206.2
Market value ($ mil.)	18.7%	2,768.4	1,675.5	3,111.6	5,554.9	5,491.6
Employees	(5.7%)	1,355	1,069	1,073	1,132	1,072

ENLINK MIDSTREAM PARTNERS, LP

1722 ROUTH ST STE 1300
DALLAS, TX 752012502
Phone: 214 953-9500
Fax: –
Web: www.enlink.com

CEO: –
CFO: –
HR: –
FYE: December 31
Type: Private

EnLink Midstream Partners, LP(ENLK) is a limited partnership energy company that transports, stores and sells natural gas, NGLs, crude oil and condensates to industrial end-users, utilities and other pipelines. Its asset network includes substantial pipelines, processing plants, fractionators, barge & rail terminals, storage and crude oil trucking services. Owned by Devon Energy Corporation, the company was sold to Global Infrastructure Partners in 2018.

ENNIS INC
NYS: EBF

2441 Presidential Pkwy.
Midlothian, TX 76065
Phone: 972 775-9801
Fax: 972 775-9820
Web: www.ennis.com

CEO: Keith S Walters
CFO: Vera Burnett
HR: –
FYE: February 28
Type: Public

Ennis is the largest provider of business forms, pressure-seal forms, labels, tags, envelopes, and presentation folders to independent distributors in the US. Its print units include Northstar Computer Forms, Witt Printing, and Adams McClure. Customers include fulfillment companies, payroll and accounts payable software companies, and advertising agencies, among others. About 95% of the business products it manufactures are custom and semi-custom products, constructed in a wide variety of sizes, colors, number of parts and quantities on an individual job basis, depending upon the customers' specifications. Founded in 1909, the company operates approximately 55 manufacturing plants in the US.

	Annual Growth	02/19	02/20	02/21	02/22	02/23
Sales ($mil.)	1.9%	400.8	438.4	358.0	400.0	431.8
Net income ($ mil.)	6.0%	37.4	38.3	24.1	29.0	47.3
Market value ($ mil.)	0.6%	546.7	518.3	511.1	484.3	560.9
Employees	(6.1%)	2,470	2,505	2,096	1,997	1,919

ENOVA INTERNATIONAL INC
NYS: ENVA

175 West Jackson Blvd.
Chicago, IL 60604
Phone: 312 568-4200
Fax: –
Web: www.enova.com

CEO: David A Fisher
CFO: Steven Cunningham
HR: John Pollak
FYE: December 31
Type: Public

Enova International is a leading technology and analytics company focused on providing online financial services. It offers or arranges loans or draws on lines of credit to consumers in more than 35 US states Brazil. It also offers financing to small businesses in all 50 US states and Washington DC. Enova uses its proprietary technology, analytics and customer service capabilities to quickly evaluate, underwrite and fund loans or provide financing, allowing the company to offer consumers and small businesses credit or financing. Enova has completed about 57.9 million customer transactions and collected approximately 60 terabytes of currently accessible consumer behavior data, allowing the company to better analyze and underwrite its specific customer base. Almost of its sales come from the US customers.

	Annual Growth	12/19	12/20	12/21	12/22	12/23
Sales ($mil.)	1.2%	1,174.8	1,083.7	1,207.9	1,736.1	1,229.9
Net income ($ mil.)	47.9%	36.6	377.8	256.3	207.4	175.1
Market value ($ mil.)	23.2%	699.9	720.5	1,191.5	1,116.2	1,610.4
Employees	6.0%	1,325	1,549	1,463	1,804	1,675

ENOVA SYSTEMS INC

2945 Columbia Street
Torrance, CA 90503
Phone: 650 346-4770
Fax: –
Web: www.enovasystems.com

CEO: –
CFO: –
HR: –
FYE: December 31
Type: Public

Enova Systems makes commercial digital power management systems for controlling and monitoring electric power in automobiles and stationary power generators. Products include hybrid-electric drive systems, electric drive motors, electric motor controllers, hybrid drive systems, battery care units, safety disconnect units, generator units, fuel cell management units, and fuel cell power conditioning units. The company counts EDO, First Auto Works of China, Ford Motor, Hyundai Motor, Navistar International, and Volvo/Mack among its customers. Enova gets more than half of its sales outside the US, primarily in China.

	Annual Growth	12/10	12/11	12/12	12/13	12/14
Sales ($mil.)	–	8.6	6.6	1.1	0.4	–
Net income ($ mil.)	–	(7.4)	(7.0)	(8.2)	(2.9)	(0.6)
Market value ($ mil.)	(72.3%)	82.7	10.7	1.0	0.5	0.5
Employees	(57.6%)	62	31	3	3	2

ENOVIS CORP

2711 Centerville Road, Suite 400
Wilmington, DE 19808
Phone: 302 252-9160
Fax: –
Web: www.enovis.com

NYS: ENOV
CEO: Matthew Trerotola
CFO: Christopher Hix
HR: –
FYE: December 31
Type: Public

novis Corporation (formerly known as Colfax Corporation) provides fabrication technology and medical technology products and services. The company offers a wide range of consumable products and equipment for use in the cutting, joining and automated welding of steels, aluminum and other metals and metal alloys. It also makes portable welding machines and large, customized and automated metal cutting and welding systems. The company is also a maker and distributor of medical devices with applications including orthopedic bracing, reconstructive implants, and physical therapy. Following the separation of Colfax and ESAB in 2022, the company changed its name to Enovis. Founded in 1995, Enovis generates almost 70% of the company's total revenue in the US.

	Annual Growth	12/19	12/20	12/21	12/22	12/23
Sales ($mil.)	(15.4%)	3,327.5	3,070.8	3,854.3	1,563.1	1,707.2
Net income ($ mil.)	–	(527.6)	42.6	71.7	(13.3)	(33.3)
Market value ($ mil.)	11.4%	1,986.2	2,087.8	2,509.8	2,922.0	3,058.5
Employees	(18.7%)	15,000	15,400	16,200	6,800	6,550

ENPHASE ENERGY INC.

47281 Bayside Parkway
Fremont, CA 94538
Phone: 877 774-7000
Fax: –
Web: www.enphase.com

NMS: ENPH
CEO: Badrinarayana Kothandaraman
CFO: Mandy Yang
HR: Debra Machado
FYE: December 31
Type: Public

Enphase Energy is a global energy technology company that designs, develops, manufactures, and sells home energy solutions that manage energy generation, energy storage, and control and communications on one intelligent platform. The company currently offers solutions targeting the residential and commercial markets in the US, Canada, Mexico, Europe, Australia, New Zealand, India, Brazil, the Philippines, Thailand, South Africa, and certain other Central American and Asian markets. Enphase Energy has shipped approximately 58 million microinverters, and over 3.0 million Enphase residential and commercial systems have been deployed in more than 145 countries. The company generates the majority of its revenue in the US.

	Annual Growth	12/19	12/20	12/21	12/22	12/23
Sales ($mil.)	38.4%	624.3	774.4	1,382.0	2,330.9	2,290.8
Net income ($ mil.)	28.5%	161.1	134.0	145.4	397.4	438.9
Market value ($ mil.)	50.0%	3,546.4	23,815	24,829	35,961	17,934
Employees	52.9%	577	850	2,260	2,821	3,157

ENPRO INC

5605 Carnegie Boulevard, Suite 500
Charlotte, NC 28209
Phone: 704 731-1500
Fax: –
Web: www.enproindustries.com

NYS: NPO
CEO: –
CFO: –
HR: –
FYE: December 31
Type: Public

EnPro is a US manufacturer of sealing systems, engineered products, and heavy-duty engines. The company has three principal business lines: Sealing Products (gaskets, dynamic seals, joints, compression packing, brake pads, milometers); and Advanced Surface Technologies segment (cleaning, coating, testing, refurbishment and verification services for critical components and assemblies). These serve the automotive, aerospace, chemical and petrochemical and food processing, power generation, and semiconductor industries. More than 60% of sales are generated in the US.

	Annual Growth	12/19	12/20	12/21	12/22	12/23
Sales ($mil.)	(3.2%)	1,205.7	1,074.0	1,141.8	1,099.2	1,059.3
Net income ($ mil.)	(12.7%)	38.3	184.4	177.2	205.1	22.2
Market value ($ mil.)	23.7%	1,398.4	1,579.0	2,301.4	2,272.5	3,277.2
Employees	(9.9%)	5,300	4,400	4,400	3,500	3,500

ENSERVCO CORP

14133 County Road 9 1/2
Longmont, CO 80504
Phone: 303 333-3678
Fax: –
Web: www.enservco.com

ASE: ENSV
CEO: –
CFO: –
HR: –
FYE: December 31
Type: Public

Aspen Exploration (which does business as ENSERVCO) is a leading provider of fluid-related services to the oil and gas production industry in the US. In 2008 Aspen Exploration announced that because of high expenses and rising debt it was pursuing strategic alternatives and subsequently sold its exploration and production oil and gas assets. In 2010 the shell company merged with oilfield services provider Dillco Fluid Service and reorganized under the ENSERVCO brand name. Its two operating subsidiaries (Dillco Fluid Services and Heat Wave Hot Oil) operate a fleet of 200 vehicles. Services include acidizing, water hauling and disposal, and well-site construction.

	Annual Growth	12/19	12/20	12/21	12/22	12/23
Sales ($mil.)	(15.4%)	43.0	15.7	15.3	21.6	22.1
Net income ($ mil.)	–	(7.7)	(2.5)	(8.1)	(5.6)	(8.5)
Market value ($ mil.)	7.9%	4.9	49.7	22.7	43.3	6.7
Employees	–	186	88	81	98	–

ENSIGN GROUP INC

29222 Rancho Viejo Road, Suite 127
San Juan Capistrano, CA 92675
Phone: 949 487-9500
Fax: –
Web: www.ensigngroup.net

NMS: ENSG
CEO: Barry R Port
CFO: Suzanne D Snapper
HR: –
FYE: December 31
Type: Public

The Ensign Group offers skilled nursing, senior living and rehabilitative care services through around 270 senior living facilities as well as other ancillary businesses (including mobile diagnostics and medical transportation), in about a dozen of states. In addition, it acquires, leases and owns healthcare real estate in addition to servicing the post-acute care continuum through accretive acquisition and investment opportunities in healthcare properties. Its transitional and skilled services companies provided skilled nursing care at around 260 operations, with more than 28,130 operational beds. It provides short and long-term nursing care services for patients with chronic conditions, prolonged illness, and the elderly.

	Annual Growth	12/19	12/20	12/21	12/22	12/23
Sales ($mil.)	16.3%	2,036.5	2,402.6	2,627.5	3,025.5	3,729.4
Net income ($ mil.)	17.3%	110.5	170.5	194.7	224.7	209.4
Market value ($ mil.)	25.4%	2,567.8	4,127.1	4,751.9	5,354.6	6,350.7
Employees	9.6%	24,500	24,400	25,900	29,900	35,300

ENSIGN-BICKFORD INDUSTRIES, INC.

999 17TH ST STE 900
DENVER, CO 802022701
Phone: 860 843-2000
Fax: –
Web: www.ensign-bickfordind.com

CEO: Caleb E White
CFO: Scott Deakin
HR: Michael J Butler
FYE: December 31
Type: Private

Finicky dog? Short fuse? Ensign-Bickford Industries' (EBI) potentially has a fix for both problems. Through its subsidiaries -- Aerospace & Defense (EBA&D), AFB International, EnviroLogix, DanChem, and Ensign-Bickford Realty Corporation -- the company manufactures one-shot systems for military demolition, combat explosives, and space (flight initiation and termination) applications, as well as taste enhancers (Optimizor brand) for pet foods. The company also provides agricultural diagnostic test kits to detect markers for genetically modified organisms (GMO), specialty chemical products, biomass wood pellets for energy and animal bedding, and real estate services.

ENSYNC INC
NBB: ESNC

N88 W13901 Main Street, Suite 200
Menomonee Falls, WI 53051
Phone: 262 253-9800
Fax: –
Web: www.ensync.com

CEO: Sandeep Gupta
CFO: William J Dallapiazza
HR: –
FYE: June 30
Type: Public

ZBB Energy makes and sells energy storage systems designed to store surplus energy for use at times when energy demand is higher than the utility company (or other generator) can provide. Its products -- based on the company's zinc-bromine battery technology -- also provide a source of power protection from voltage, current, or frequency deviations that can cause brownouts or power outages. While ZBB Energy markets its products primarily to utility companies and renewable energy generators in Australia, China, Europe, and North America, it has had only one customer to date, the California Energy Commission. ZBB Energy operates one manufacturing facility in Menomonee Falls, Wisconsin.

	Annual Growth	06/14	06/15	06/16	06/17	06/18
Sales ($mil.)	11.0%	7.9	1.8	2.1	12.5	11.9
Net income ($ mil.)	–	(8.9)	(12.9)	(17.9)	(4.1)	(13.0)
Market value ($ mil.)	(31.1%)	91.7	49.8	20.9	20.9	20.7
Employees	2.5%	58	59	78	66	64

ENTECH SALES AND SERVICE, LLC

3404 GARDEN BROOK DR
DALLAS, TX 752342496
Phone: 469 522-6000
Fax: –
Web: www.entechsales.com

CEO: Gale P Rucker
CFO: –
HR: –
FYE: December 31
Type: Private

Entech keeps Texans cool and safe. The company, which was founded in 1981, has business units that provide air-conditioning, heating, and refrigeration equipment and services in about a half-dozen cities across the Lone Star State. Entech also offers integrated-system building automation that syncs HVAC controls, access controls, security, closed-circuit television, alarms, and other automated systems. The company keeps its systems running by offering design, installation, maintenance, and repair of HVAC and refrigeration. Other products and services include rebuilt cooling towers and HVAC and power equipment rentals.

	Annual Growth	12/05	12/06	12/07	12/20	12/22
Sales ($mil.)	6.9%	–	52.4	56.8	122.7	152.3
Net income ($ mil.)	7.3%	–	5.1	6.8	6.1	15.6
Market value ($ mil.)	–	–	–	–	–	–
Employees	–	–	–	–	–	387

ENTECH SOLAR, INC

13301 Park Vista Blvd, Suite 100
Fort Worth, TX 76177
Phone: 817 224-3600
Fax: –
Web: www.entechsolar.com

CEO: David Gelbaum
CFO: Shelley Hollingsworth
HR: –
FYE: December 31
Type: Public

Entech Solar aims to shine brightly in the solar energy market. The company designs, makes, and markets solar energy systems that provide electricity and thermal energy for commercial, industrial, and utility applications. Its products include ThermoVolt System (a proprietary concentrating photovoltaic and thermal technology that produces both electricity and thermal energy), and Solar Volt System (which uses a concentrating photovoltaic technology that produces cost-competitive electricity). Entech Solar also makes energy-efficient skylights and provides engineering services. Venture capital firm Quercus Trust owns 54% of Entech Solar.

	Annual Growth	12/06	12/07	12/08	12/09	12/10
Sales ($mil.)	(65.5%)	17.3	18.5	30.8	2.2	0.2
Net income ($ mil.)	–	(8.2)	(14.4)	(29.3)	(35.5)	(18.3)
Market value ($ mil.)	(34.0%)	148.5	746.2	112.3	38.1	28.2
Employees	(20.5%)	45	93	57	26	18

ENTEGEE, INC.

4800 DEERWOOD CAMPUS PKWY UNIT 800
JACKSONVILLE, FL 322468317
Phone: 800 368-3433
Fax: –
Web: www.entegee.com

CEO: –
CFO: –
HR: –
FYE: December 31
Type: Private

When businesses need help with engineering and technical projects, Entegee is ready. The company's staffing division places engineering and technical professionals -- including assemblers, designers, drafters, programmers, and technical writers -- with clients such as defense contractors, government agencies, and manufacturing and engineering companies. In addition, Entegee offers consulting and project-based services and outsourced engineering and drafting. It operates throughout the US from a network of about 20 offices. Entegee was a unit of MPS Group, which was acquired by global staffing rival Adecco in 2010.

	Annual Growth	12/04	12/05	12/06	12/07	12/08
Sales ($mil.)	9.0%	–	245.7	277.2	306.8	318.1
Net income ($ mil.)	–	–	–	65.2	–	41.2
Market value ($ mil.)	–	–	–	–	–	–
Employees	–	–	–	–	–	2,629

ENTEGRIS INC
NMS: ENTG

129 Concord Road
Billerica, MA 01821
Phone: 978 436-6500
Fax: –
Web: www.entegris.com

CEO: Bertrand Loy
CFO: Gregory B Graves
HR: Christin Cunningham
FYE: December 31
Type: Public

Entegris is a leading supplier of advanced materials and process solutions for the semiconductor and other high-technology industries. It makes products integral to the manufacture of semiconductors and computer disk drives. The company makes more than 20,000 standard and custom products used to transport and protect semiconductor and disk drive materials during processing. Its products include filtration, wafer carriers, storage boxes, and chip trays as well as chemical delivery systems, such as pipes, fittings, and valves. Entegris gets more than 75% of revenue from international customers. The company expects its products to grow in the following years with the demand for semiconductors reaching $1 trillion by 2030.

	Annual Growth	12/19	12/20	12/21	12/22	12/23
Sales ($mil.)	22.0%	1,591.1	1,859.3	2,298.9	3,282.0	3,523.9
Net income ($ mil.)	(8.2%)	254.9	295.0	409.1	208.9	180.7
Market value ($ mil.)	24.4%	7,531.7	14,450	20,837	9,862.3	18,017
Employees	10.8%	5,300	5,800	6,850	10,000	8,000

ENTERGY ARKANSAS LLC

425 West Capitol Avenue
Little Rock, AR 72201
Phone: 501 377-4000
Fax: –
Web: www.entergy.com

CEO: Laura R Landreaux
CFO: Andrew S Marsh
HR: –
FYE: December 31
Type: Public

Entergy Arkansas is the largest power provider in the Natural State. The utility serves approximately 700,000 residential, commercial, industrial, and government customers in 63 eastern and central Arkansas counties. Residential customers account for about 84% of total clients. The Entergy subsidiary also has interests in fossil-fueled, nuclear, and hydroelectric power generation facilities with 5,200 MW of capacity, and it offers energy conservation and management programs.

	Annual Growth	12/18	12/19	12/20	12/21	12/22
Sales ($mil.)	6.7%	2,060.6	2,259.6	2,084.5	2,338.6	2,673.2
Net income ($ mil.)	4.1%	252.7	263.0	245.2	316.6	297.2
Market value ($ mil.)	–	–	–	–	–	–
Employees	(0.6%)	1,258	1,251	1,244	1,220	1,227

ENTERGY CORP

639 Loyola Avenue
New Orleans, LA 70113
Phone: 504 576-4000
Fax: –
Web: www.entergy.com

NYS: ETR
CEO: Leo P Denault
CFO: Andrew S Marsh
HR: –
FYE: December 31
Type: Public

Entergy is an integrated energy company engaged in electric power production, transmission and retail distribution operations. Entergy delivers electricity to 3 million utility customers in Arkansas, Louisiana, Mississippi and Texas. Entergy, owns power plants that have a combined generating capacity of about 25,000 MW, including approximately 5,000 MW of nuclear power. Entergy also provides ownership, operation, and decommissioning of nuclear power plants in the northern US and the sale of the electric power produced by its operating plants to wholesale customers. The company offer its services through its 12,000 employees.

	Annual Growth	12/19	12/20	12/21	12/22	12/23
Sales ($mil.)	2.8%	10,879	10,114	11,743	13,764	12,147
Net income ($ mil.)	17.1%	1,258.2	1,406.7	1,118.7	1,097.1	2,362.3
Market value ($ mil.)	(4.1%)	25,499	21,251	23,977	23,945	21,538
Employees	(2.8%)	13,635	13,400	12,369	11,707	12,177

ENTERGY GULF STATES LOUISIANA, L.L.C.

4809 JEFFERSON HWY
JEFFERSON, LA 701213126
Phone: 504 576-4000
Fax: –
Web: –

CEO: Phillip R May Jr
CFO: –
HR: –
FYE: December 31
Type: Private

Entergy Gulf States Louisiana keeps energy flowing in the Bayou State. The utility, a subsidiary of Entergy and an affiliate of Entergy Louisiana, provides electrical service to about 383,900 customers in the state of Louisiana; its customer base is comprised of residential, commercial, industrial, and governmental entities. The company owns or leases about 6,660 MW of generating capacity, including the River Bend Steam Electric Generation Station, a Louisiana-based 978 MW nuclear facility. Together, Entergy Louisiana and Entergy Gulf States Louisiana serve about 1 million electric customers in 58 parishes. Entergy Gulf States Louisiana also provides natural gas service to about 92,000 customers in Baton Rouge.

ENTERGY LOUISIANA LLC (NEW)

4809 Jefferson Highway
Jefferson, LA 70121
Phone: 504 576-4000
Fax: –
Web: www.entergy.com

CEO: Phillip R May Jr
CFO: Andrew S Marsh
HR: –
FYE: December 31
Type: Public

Entergy Louisiana energizes everything from fishing shacks and suburban enclaves to petroleum refineries and city infrastructure for the storm-weary citizens of the Bayou State. The utility serves electric customers in 58 parishes of northeast and south Louisiana. The company holds non-exclusive franchises to provide electric service in 116 incorporated Louisiana municipalities. It also supplies electric service in 45 Louisiana parishes in which it holds non-exclusive franchises. Of the Entergy subsidiary's almost 5,670 MW of generating capacity, about 4,900 MW comes from gas- and oil-fired power plants and almost 1,160 MW from nuclear power plants.

	Annual Growth	12/18	12/19	12/20	12/21	12/22
Sales ($mil.)	10.2%	4,296.3	4,285.2	4,069.9	5,068.4	6,338.8
Net income ($ mil.)	6.0%	675.6	691.5	1,082.4	654.0	854.5
Market value ($ mil.)	–	–	–	–	–	–
Employees	(0.9%)	1,656	1,670	1,654	1,656	1,597

ENTERGY MISSISSIPPI LLC

308 East Pearl Street
Jackson, MS 39201
Phone: 601 368-5000
Fax: –
Web: www.entergy.com

CEO: Haley R Fisackerly
CFO: –
HR: –
FYE: December 31
Type: Public

Entergy Mississippi keeps electricity flowing across the Magnolia state. With a physical presence in 45 of the state's 82 counties, the utility provides electricity to about 440,000 residential, business, and institutional customers (roughly 16% of electric customers in Mississippi) throughout the western half of its namesake state. Residential customers account for more than 90% of the company's client base. Entergy Mississippi is a subsidiary of the Louisiana-based utility holding company Entergy.

	Annual Growth	12/18	12/19	12/20	12/21	12/22
Sales ($mil.)	5.0%	1,335.1	1,323.0	1,247.9	1,406.3	1,624.2
Net income ($ mil.)	11.9%	126.1	119.9	140.6	166.8	197.6
Market value ($ mil.)	–	–	–	–	–	–
Employees	0.1%	713	745	750	741	716

ENTERGY NEW ORLEANS LLC

1600 Perdido Street
New Orleans, LA 70112
Phone: 504 670-3700
Fax: –
Web: www.entergy.com

CEO: –
CFO: –
HR: –
FYE: December 31
Type: Public

Entergy New Orleans lights up the path for the unsteady, libation-influenced patrons of Bourbon Street and others in the Crescent City. The regulated utility, a subsidiary of Entergy, distributes electricity to 200,000 residential, commercial, and industrial customers and natural gas to some 100,000 customers in Orleans Parish, Louisiana. It deactivated the Michoud power plant in 2016 and is considering building new power generating facilities on the same site.

	Annual Growth	12/18	12/19	12/20	12/21	12/22
Sales ($mil.)	8.6%	717.4	686.2	633.8	768.9	997.3
Net income ($ mil.)	4.8%	53.2	52.6	49.3	31.8	64.1
Market value ($ mil.)	–	–	–	–	–	–
Employees	1.6%	278	308	303	299	296

ENTERPRISE BANCORP, INC. (MA)
NMS: EBTC

222 Merrimack Street
Lowell, MA 01852
Phone: 978 459-9000
Fax: –
Web: www.enterprisebanking.com

CEO: –
CFO: –
HR: –
FYE: December 31
Type: Public

Enterprise Bancorp caters to more customers than just entrepreneurs. The holding company owns Enterprise Bank and Trust, which operates more than 20 branches in north-central Massachusetts and southern New Hampshire. The $2 billion-asset bank offers traditional deposit and loan products, specializing in lending to businesses, professionals, high-net-worth individuals, and not-for-profits. About half of its loan portfolio is tied to commercial real estate, while another one-third is tied to commercial and industrial and commercial construction loans. Subsidiaries Enterprise Investment Services and Enterprise Insurance Services provide investments and insurance geared to the bank's target business customers.

	Annual Growth	12/19	12/20	12/21	12/22	12/23
Assets ($mil.)	8.4%	3,235.0	4,014.3	4,447.8	4,438.3	4,466.0
Net income ($ mil.)	2.7%	34.2	31.5	42.2	42.7	38.1
Market value ($ mil.)	(1.2%)	415.7	313.6	551.3	433.2	395.9
Employees	1.5%	538	527	536	554	570

ENTERPRISE COMMUNITY PARTNERS, INC.

11000 BROKEN LAND PKWY STE 700
COLUMBIA, MD 210443541
Phone: 410 964-1230
Fax: –
Web: www.enterprisecommunity.org

CEO: Priscilla Almodovar
CFO: –
HR: Nina Wolf
FYE: December 31
Type: Private

Enterprise Community Partners (ECP) doesn't think affordable housing, safe streets, reliable child care, and access to jobs should remain an unattainable utopia for the majority of disadvantaged Americans. The organization provides grants, loans, and technical assistance to not-for-profit organizations that build and revitalize neighborhoods across the US. Its funding has helped to build or preserve more than 200,000 affordable homes. It also acquires HUD-owned, foreclosed homes at reduced rates in order to sell them to qualifying buyers. ECP has about 20 offices located throughout the US. The organization was founded in 1982 James and Patty Rouse as The Enterprise Foundation.

ENTERPRISE ELECTRIC, LLC

1300 FORT NEGLEY BLVD
NASHVILLE, TN 372034854
Phone: 615 350-7270
Fax: –
Web: www.enterprisellc.com

CEO: James C Seabury III
CFO: Lera Pendergrass
HR: –
FYE: December 31
Type: Private

Enterprise Electric welcomes the power hungry. The full service electrical firms specializes in construction and design of electrical systems for institutional, commercial, industrial, and services projects from planning through construction. The company completes projects large and small and has completed design and installation of wiring and electrical systems for health care, correctional, commercial, and industrial clients. Services include temporary power installations, voice, data, and fiber optic cabling systems, emergency generator and substation installations, maintenance services. Headquartered in Nashville, Tennessee, the company serves clients throughout the US.

	Annual Growth	12/09	12/10	12/11	12/12	12/13
Sales ($mil.)	2.6%	–	–	86.6	59.1	91.2
Net income ($ mil.)	(41.0%)	–	–	6.2	(2.9)	2.2
Market value ($ mil.)	–	–	–	–	–	–
Employees	–	–	–	–	–	400

ENTERPRISE FINANCIAL SERVICES CORP
NMS: EFSC

150 North Meramec
Clayton, MO 63105
Phone: 314 725-5500
Fax: –
Web: www.enterprisebank.com

CEO: –
CFO: –
HR: –
FYE: December 31
Type: Public

Enterprise Financial Services is the holding company for Enterprise Bank & Trust, a full-service financial institution offering banking and wealth management services to individuals and corporate customers primarily located in Arizona, California, Kansas, Missouri, Nevada, and New Mexico. Boasting $11.5 billion in assets and over 45 branches, Enterprise offers standard products such as checking, savings, and money market accounts and CDs. Commercial and industrial loans make up about 40$ of the company's lending activities, while real estate loans make up another 45%. The bank also writes consumer, and residential mortgage loans. Bank subsidiary Enterprise Trust offers wealth management services.

	Annual Growth	12/19	12/20	12/21	12/22	12/23
Assets ($mil.)	18.6%	7,333.8	9,751.6	13,537	13,054	14,519
Net income ($ mil.)	20.3%	92.7	74.4	133.1	203.0	194.1
Market value ($ mil.)	(1.9%)	1,803.8	1,307.7	1,761.9	1,831.9	1,670.6
Employees	11.0%	805	–	1,075	1,127	1,221

ENTERPRISE FINANCIAL SERVICES GROUP INC
NBB: EFSG

150 North Meramec
Clayton, MO 63105
Phone: 314 725-5500
Fax: –
Web: www.enterprisebankpgh.com

CEO: –
CFO: –
HR: –
FYE: September 30
Type: Public

Enterprise Financial Services is the holding company for Enterprise Bank & Trust, a full-service financial institution offering banking and wealth management services to individuals and corporate customers primarily located in Arizona, California, Kansas, Missouri, Nevada, and New Mexico. Boasting $11.5 billion in assets and over 45 branches, Enterprise offers standard products such as checking, savings, and money market accounts and CDs. Commercial and industrial loans make up about 40$ of the company's lending activities, while real estate loans make up another 45%. The bank also writes consumer, and residential mortgage loans. Bank subsidiary Enterprise Trust offers wealth management services.

	Annual Growth	09/14	09/19	09/20	09/21	09/22
Assets ($mil.)	5.7%	268.2	311.2	422.6	377.5	417.6
Net income ($ mil.)	12.0%	1.2	1.7	2.7	4.1	3.0
Market value ($ mil.)	8.8%	7.7	11.6	11.4	15.7	15.0
Employees	–	–	–	–	–	–

ENTERPRISE FLORIDA, INC.

800 N MAGNOLIA AVE STE 1100
ORLANDO, FL 328033252
Phone: 407 648-2463
Fax: –
Web: www.selectflorida.org

CEO: Gray Swoope
CFO: –
HR: –
FYE: June 30
Type: Private

Enterprise Florida, Inc., (EFI) is a not-for-profit partnership between state government and the private sector that is dedicated to boosting Florida's economic development. The partnership works to attract, retain, and grow businesses in Florida, focusing on such sectors as clean energy, life sciences, information technology, aerospace, defense, financial services, and manufacturing. EFI also assists small and midsize businesses expand international trade by providing information, consulting, networking opportunities, and financial assistance. EFI's marketing arm ensures that the state projects a pro-business image. The partnership was founded in 1996 by the Florida Legislature.

ENTERPRISE INFORMATICS INC
NBB: EINF

10052 Mesa Ridge Court, Suite 100
San Diego, CA 92121
Phone: 858 625-3000
Fax: 858 546-7671
Web: www.enterpriseinformatics.com

CEO: -
CFO: John W Low
HR: -
FYE: September 30
Type: Public

Forget bulky filing cabinets and snail mail. Enterprise Informatics' document, configuration, and records management software enables companies to scan and capture documents, then store the information or distribute it electronically. The company offers its eB software suite for documents ranging from letters and invoices to large-scale engineering drawings and multimedia files. eB also includes lifecycle management tools. Enterprise Informatics serves customers in a wide range of industries, but its primary markets include construction, energy, engineering, government, and procurement. In 2010 the company was acquired by Bentley Systems, which extended its portfolio into enterprise information management.

	Annual Growth	09/03	09/04	09/05	09/06	09/07
Sales ($mil.)	5.1%	7.4	9.0	5.8	7.0	9.0
Net income ($ mil.)	-	(3.0)	0.0	(3.5)	(1.0)	1.3
Market value ($ mil.)	(33.7%)	0.0	0.0	0.0	0.0	0.0
Employees	(5.3%)	46	46	38	33	37

ENTERPRISE MOBILITY

600 CORPORATE PARK DR
SAINT LOUIS, MO 631054204
Phone: 314 512-5000
Fax: -
Web: www.alamo.com

CEO: Christine B Taylor
CFO: -
HR: Charles Pugh
FYE: July 31
Type: Private

Enterprise Holdings is the most comprehensive service provider in the industry. It offers car and truck rental, vanpooling and car sharing services, car sales, fleet management, and much more. The company owns and operates the Enterprise Rent-A-Car, National Car Rental, and Alamo Rent A Car brands through an integrated global network of independent regional subsidiaries. The privately held company operates nearly 10,000 branches in more than 90 countries across North America, Central America, South America, the Caribbean and Europe, as well as parts of the Asia-Pacific and the Middle East. Enterprise began as a glimmer in the eye of an entrepreneur with a fleet of seven cars that turned out to be the world's largest rental car company. Founded in 1957, the company is owned by members of the founding Taylor family.

ENTERPRISE PARTNERS MANAGEMENT, LLC

2223 AVENIDA DE PLAYA 210
LA JOLLA, CA 92037
Phone: 858 731-0300
Fax: -
Web: -

CEO: -
CFO: -
HR: -
FYE: December 31
Type: Private

You guessed it -- Enterprise Partners Venture Capital seeks to partner with enterprising young companies. The firm invests in development-stage companies in the life sciences, technology, and communications sectors, specifically targeting firms located in California. It typically makes initial investments of between $3 million and $10 million and follows that up with additional infusions. Enterprise Partners has also begun investing in established companies, preferring to take the lead investor role. The firm has invested in more than 150 companies since it was founded in 1985; its current portfolio includes stakes in about 40 companies, including Muze, Calient Networks, and TargeGen.

ENTERPRISE PRODUCTS PARTNERS L.P.
NYS: EPD

1100 Louisiana Street, 10th Floor
Houston, TX 77002
Phone: 713 381-6500
Fax: -
Web: www.enterpriseproducts.com

CEO: -
CFO: -
HR: -
FYE: December 31
Type: Public

Enterprise Products Partners is one of the leading players in the North American provider of midstream energy services to producers and consumers of natural gas, NGLs, crude oil, petrochemicals, and refined products. Its fully integrated, midstream energy asset network or value chain links producers of natural gas, NGLs and crude oil from some of the largest supply basins in the US, Canada, and the Gulf of Mexico with domestic consumers and international markets. The company conducts substantially all of its business operations through EPO and its consolidated subsidiaries.

	Annual Growth	12/19	12/20	12/21	12/22	12/23
Sales ($mil.)	11.0%	32,789	27,200	40,807	58,186	49,715
Net income ($ mil.)	4.8%	4,591.3	3,775.6	4,637.7	5,490.0	5,532.0
Market value ($ mil.)	(1.6%)	61,058	42,476	47,615	52,298	57,133
Employees	-	-	-	-	-	7,447

ENTORIAN TECHNOLOGIES INC.

4030 W BRAKER LN STE 2-100
AUSTIN, TX 787595315
Phone: 512 334-0111
Fax: -
Web: www.entorian.com

CEO: Stephan B Godevais
CFO: W K Patterson
HR: -
FYE: December 31
Type: Private

Entorian Technologies knows all about the rugged side of computers. Through its Augmentix subsidiary, the company re-engineers and ruggedizes Dell notebooks and servers. Its products are used in environments where computers and other electronics are subjected to heavy wear and tear, including military applications, field service and sales, industrial manufacturing, and for emergency responders. Entorian sells its ruggedized notebooks directly to Dell, which in turn sells and markets them in North America and Europe. The company's ruggedized servers are sold directly to end users and channel partners.

	Annual Growth	12/05	12/06	12/07	12/08	12/09
Sales ($mil.)	-	-	-	(1,405.6)	55.9	45.1
Net income ($ mil.)	40887.8%	-	-	0.0	(42.6)	0.5
Market value ($ mil.)	-	-	-	-	-	-
Employees	-	-	-	-	-	507

ENTRAVISION COMMUNICATIONS CORP.
NYS: EVC

2425 Olympic Boulevard, Suite 6000 West
Santa Monica, CA 90404
Phone: 310 447-3870
Fax: -
Web: www.entravision.com

CEO: -
CFO: -
HR: -
FYE: December 31
Type: Public

Entravision Communications (Entravision) is a leading global advertising solutions, media and technology company. The company's operations encompass integrated, end-to-end advertising solutions across multiple media, comprised of digital, television and audio properties. Its digital segment, the company's largest by revenue, offers a full suite of end-to-end advertising services in 40 countries. It has commercial partnerships with Meta, Twitter, TikTok, and Spotify, and marketers can use its Smadex and other platforms to deliver targeted advertising to audiences around the globe. In the US, Entravision maintains a diversified portfolio of television and radio stations that target Hispanic audiences and complement its global digital services. Entravision remains the largest affiliate group of the Univision and UniM s television networks. The US accounts for about 25% of the company's total revenue.

	Annual Growth	12/19	12/20	12/21	12/22	12/23
Sales ($mil.)	41.8%	273.6	344.0	760.2	956.2	1,106.9
Net income ($ mil.)	-	(19.7)	(3.9)	29.3	18.1	(15.4)
Market value ($ mil.)	12.3%	234.5	246.1	606.8	429.6	373.2
Employees	10.7%	1,104	1,001	1,094	1,262	1,657

ENTRX CORPORATION

800 NICOLLET MALL # 2690
MINNEAPOLIS, MN 554027000
Phone: 612 333-0614
Fax: –
Web: –

CEO: –
CFO: –
HR: –
FYE: December 31
Type: Private

The raison d' tre of Entrx as of late has been to insulate and abate. The company provides insulation and asbestos abatement services through subsidiary Metalclad Insulation. Operating primarily in California, it installs insulation on pipes, ducts, furnaces, boilers, and other industrial equipment. It also maintains and removes insulation and sells specialty insulation products to public utilities, oil, petrochemical, and heavy construction companies. Metalclad's customers have included Jacobs Engineering Group and Southern California Edison.

	Annual Growth	12/05	12/06	12/07	12/08	12/09
Sales ($mil.)	(7.6%)	–	–	22.4	27.8	19.1
Net income ($ mil.)	–	–	–	0.6	0.3	(0.1)
Market value ($ mil.)	–	–	–	–	–	–
Employees	–	–	–	–	–	16

ENVELA CORP

ASE: ELA

1901 Gateway Drive, Ste. 100
Irving, TX 75038
Phone: 972 587-4049
Fax: 972 674-2596
Web: www.envela.com

CEO: John R Loftus
CFO: Bret A Pedersen
HR: –
FYE: December 31
Type: Public

Attracted to things gold and shiny? If so, DGSE is for you. The company buys and sells jewelry, bullion, rare coins, fine watches, and collectibles to retail and wholesale customers across the US through its various websites and 30-plus retail stores in California, Texas, and South Carolina. The company's eight e-commerce sites let customers buy and sell jewelry and bullion interactively, and obtain current precious-metal prices. In all, more than 7,500 items are available for sale on DGSE websites, including $2 million in diamonds. DGSE also owns Fairchild Watches, a leading vintage watch wholesaler, and the rare coin dealer Superior Galleries. The company sold its pair of pawn shops in Dallas in 2009.

	Annual Growth	12/19	12/20	12/21	12/22	12/23
Sales ($mil.)	20.3%	82.0	113.9	141.0	182.7	171.7
Net income ($ mil.)	26.6%	2.8	6.4	10.0	15.7	7.1
Market value ($ mil.)	37.7%	35.8	137.8	107.9	139.4	128.8
Employees	20.9%	135	152	256	257	288

ENVESTNET INC

NYS: ENV

1000 Chesterbrook Boulevard, Suite 250
Berwyn, PA 19312
Phone: 312 827-2800
Fax: 312 827-2801
Web: www.envestnet.com

CEO: William Crager
CFO: Joshua Warren
HR: –
FYE: December 31
Type: Public

Envestnet is a leader in helping transform wealth management, working towards its goal of building a holistic financial wellness ecosystem to improve the financial lives of millions of consumers. The company provides a financial network connecting technology, solutions and data, delivering better intelligence, and enabling its customers to drive better outcomes. Portfolio Management Consultants (Envestnet | PMC) provides consulting services to financial advisors and affords them access to managed accounts, multi manager-manager portfolios, fund strategist portfolios, as well over 950 proprietary products, such as quantitative portfolios and fund strategist portfolios. In addition, PMC offers portfolio overlay and tax optimization services. The company generates the majority of its revenue in the US.

	Annual Growth	12/19	12/20	12/21	12/22	12/23
Sales ($mil.)	8.5%	900.1	998.2	1,186.5	1,239.8	1,245.6
Net income ($ mil.)	–	(16.8)	(3.1)	13.3	(80.9)	(238.7)
Market value ($ mil.)	(8.2%)	3,813.9	4,507.3	4,345.7	3,379.5	2,712.4
Employees	(7.3%)	4,190	4,250	4,375	3,400	3,100

ENVIRI CORP

NYS: NVRI

Two Logan Square, 100-120 North 18th Street, 17th Floor
Philadelphia, PA 19103
Phone: 267 857-8715
Fax: –
Web: www.harsco.com

CEO: F N Grasberger III
CFO: Anshooman AGA
HR: Robert Field
FYE: December 31
Type: Public

Harsco is a market-leading, global provider of environmental solutions for industrial and specialty waste streams and innovative equipment and technology for the rail sector. The company serves about 70 customers at approximately 150 sites in roughly about 30 countries. The company offers resource recovery from iron, steel, and metals manufacturing as well as selling industrial abrasives. Other reprocessed materials are fertilizer, asphalt, and roofing granules. Harsco's railway business makes track maintenance equipment, collision avoidance and warning systems, and other equipment as well as provides rail maintenance services. About 70% of the company's revenue comes from the US.

	Annual Growth	12/19	12/20	12/21	12/22	12/23
Sales ($mil.)	8.3%	1,503.7	1,863.9	1,848.4	1,889.1	2,069.2
Net income ($ mil.)	–	503.9	(26.3)	(3.2)	(180.1)	(86.1)
Market value ($ mil.)	(20.9%)	1,837.0	1,435.4	1,334.0	502.2	718.5
Employees	5.5%	10,500	12,000	12,000	12,000	13,000

ENVIROMEDIA, INC.

2021 E 5TH ST STE 150
AUSTIN, TX 787024509
Phone: 512 476-4368
Fax: –
Web: www.enviromedia.com

CEO: Valerie S Davis
CFO: –
HR: –
FYE: December 31
Type: Private

EnviroMedia Social Marketing offers advertising, marketing, and public relations services for projects related to the environment, public health, and social issues. The firm's specialties include branding, broadcast production, interactive marketing, media relations, and media buying. EnviroMedia has counted among its clients the American Cancer Society, Dell, and the Texas Department of Transportation, for which the agency has overseen the "Don't Mess with Texas" anti-litter campaign. The agency -- which has offices in Austin, Texas and Portland, Oregon -- was founded in 1997 by CEO Valerie Davis and president Kevin Tuerff.

ENVIRONMENTAL DEFENSE FUND, INCORPORATED

257 PARK AVE S FL 17
NEW YORK, NY 100107386
Phone: 212 505-2100
Fax: –
Web: www.edfaction.org

CEO: –
CFO: –
HR: Sean Cook
FYE: September 30
Type: Private

Environmental Defense fights for those without a voice. The not-for-profit group works to protect the environment through programs in areas such as ecosystem restoration, environmental health, ocean protection, and global and regional air and energy. The organization, which has tripled in size since it was founded in 1967, boasts more than 500,000 members and employs some 300 scientists, attorneys, economists, and other professionals. In addition to its New York City headquarters, Environmental Defense maintains 10 regional offices nationwide and in Beijing. Environmental Defense initially funded its efforts from a battle won against the DDT pesticide, which had been harming wildlife.

	Annual Growth	09/12	09/13	09/14	09/15	09/16
Sales ($mil.)	18.3%	–	–	–	145.7	172.2
Net income ($ mil.)	–	–	–	–	–	7.2
Market value ($ mil.)	–	–	–	–	–	–
Employees	–	–	–	–	–	525

ENVIRONMENTAL HEALTH & ENGINEERING, INC.

180 WELLS AVE STE 200
NEWTON, MA 024593328
Phone: 781 247-4300
Fax: –
Web: www.eheinc.com

CEO: –
CFO: –
HR: –
FYE: December 31
Type: Private

Toxic mold and environmental air quality are just two of the concerns of Environmental Health & Engineering. The engineering and health and safety services firm offers consulting services geared towards creating healthier work environments in buildings -- ranging from large office complexes to suburban schools. Its services range from studies of the effects of pollutant exposure to human health, to risk assessments, to support the commissioning of research laboratories, to advice on federal compliance requirements. In 2009 it was contracted by the Consumer Product Safety Commission to study air quality in homes built using Chinese-made drywall. The group was founded in 1988 by Harvard lecturer Jack McCarthy.

	Annual Growth	12/12	12/13	12/14	12/16	12/17
Sales ($mil.)	4.7%	–	12.8	12.6	15.4	15.4
Net income ($ mil.)	5.8%	–	0.7	0.5	1.1	0.8
Market value ($ mil.)	–	–	–	–	–	–
Employees	–	–	–	–	–	70

ENVIRONMENTAL TECTONICS CORP.

125 James Way
Southampton, PA 18966
Phone: 215 355-9100
Fax: –
Web: www.etcusa.com

NBB: ETCC
CEO: –
CFO: –
HR: Carol Morgan
FYE: February 24
Type: Public

Environmental Tectonics Corporation (ETC) believes virtual environments can teach us a lot about real life. Through its Aerospace Solutions segment (formerly Training Services Group), the company makes software-driven aircrew training systems and disaster simulators. Through its Commercial/Industrial Systems segment (formerly Control Systems Group), it designs, manufactures, and sells industrial steam and gas sterilizers for the pharmaceutical, medical device, and animal research industries, hyperbaric chambers for the medical industry, and environmental testing products for the automotive and HVAC industries.

	Annual Growth	02/19	02/20	02/21	02/22	02/23
Sales ($mil.)	(14.1%)	48.4	40.6	16.3	19.1	26.3
Net income ($ mil.)	–	3.1	(4.0)	(7.5)	1.8	(1.6)
Market value ($ mil.)	(8.7%)	8.0	5.6	3.3	2.8	5.5
Employees	(4.9%)	270	234	17	203	221

ENVISION HEALTHCARE CORPORATION

1A BURTON HILLS BLVD
NASHVILLE, TN 372156100
Phone: 615 665-1283
Fax: –
Web: www.envisionhealth.com

CEO: James Rechtin
CFO: Kevin D Eastridge
HR: Allison Mercer
FYE: December 31
Type: Private

Envision Healthcare Corporation is a prominent medical group that offers physician and advanced practice provider services in emergency and hospitalist medicine, anesthesiology, radiology/teleradiology, and neonatology. AMSURG, a leader in ambulatory surgical care, has ownership in over 250 surgery centers across 40 states and the District of Columbia, specializing in various medical fields such as gastroenterology, ophthalmology, and orthopedics. With a national reach and local expertise, this medical group provides a range of clinical solutions to benefit health systems, payers, providers, and patients alike.

ENVIVA INC

7272 Wisconsin Ave., Suite 1800
Bethesda, MD 20814
Phone: 301 657-5560
Fax: –
Web: www.envivabiomass.com

NYS: EVA
CEO: Thomas Meth
CFO: Glenn Nunziata
HR: Lorie Burgess
FYE: December 31
Type: Public

Enviva Partners is wild about wood pellets. The company produces and supplies utility-grade wood pellets to major power customers. Its wood pellets are used as a substitute for coal in both converted and co-fired power generation and combined heat and power plants. They enable major power generators to generate electricity in a way that reduces the overall cost of compliance with mandatory greenhouse gas (GHG) emissions limits while also allowing them to diversify their sources of electricity supply. Enviva operates through roughly a half-dozen plants located within the Southern US. The company was established in 2010 and launched an IPO in 2015.

	Annual Growth	12/18	12/19	12/20	12/21	12/22
Sales ($mil.)	17.5%	573.7	684.4	875.1	1,041.7	1,094.3
Net income ($ mil.)	–	7.0	(2.9)	17.1	(122.1)	(168.3)
Market value ($ mil.)	17.5%	1,858.3	2,498.5	3,041.6	4,715.8	3,547.2
Employees	–	–	–	–	1,196	1,386

ENVIVIO, INC.

2795 AUGUSTINE DR
SANTA CLARA, CA 950542957
Phone: 650 243-2700
Fax: –
Web: www.mediakind.com

CEO: Julien Signes
CFO: Erik E Miller
HR: –
FYE: January 31
Type: Private

You could say Envivio is the middleman between content providers and consumers of video. The company designs and sells an Internet Protocol (IP) video processing and distribution product that helps deliver high-quality content, such as broadcast and on-demand video, to audiences via PCs, TVs, laptops, and mobile devices. The software-based system runs on industry-standard hardware and consists of encoders, transcoders, network media processors, and gateways. Envivio's customers include cable TV and mobile service providers in 50 countries. It sells through a direct sales force and a global distribution network of systems integrators like telecom equipment makers. Envivio went public in 2012 and in 2015 agreed to be acquired by Ericsson.

ENXNET INC.

7450 S. Winston Ave
Tulsa, OK 74136
Phone: 918 494-6663
Fax: –
Web: –

CEO: Ryan Corley
CFO: Stephen Hoelscher
HR: –
FYE: March 31
Type: Public

EnXnet licenses and markets emerging multimedia technologies, including video compression and content storage. It has acquired the licensing rights to a video compression technology called ClearVideo, used for distribution, downloading, and streaming of video and audio content over the Internet. Other technologies and products include DVDPlus, a media storage product that combines a CD and DVD on the same disc, gift cards, and CD/DVD anti-theft technologies. CEO Ryan Corley owns a majority stake in the company.

	Annual Growth	03/15	03/16	03/17	03/18	03/19
Sales ($mil.)	–	–	–	–	–	–
Net income ($ mil.)	–	(0.1)	(0.1)	(0.1)	(0.3)	(0.2)
Market value ($ mil.)	(7.8%)	0.8	0.4	3.6	1.5	0.6
Employees	10.7%	2	2	2	2	3

ENZO BIOCHEM, INC.   NYS: ENZ

81 Executive Blvd, Suite 3
Farmingdale, NY 11735
Phone: 631 755-5500
Fax: –
Web: www.enzo.com

CEO: –
CFO: –
HR: –
FYE: July 31
Type: Public

For Enzo Biochem, genomic research is the key to both diagnostic and therapeutic care. The biotech company is focused on the development and sale of gene-based tests and pharmaceuticals through its three operating divisions. The Enzo Clinical Labs unit provides diagnostic testing services in the New York City area, while Enzo Life Sciences makes reagents used in research by pharmaceutical firms, biotech companies, academic institutions. The third division, Enzo Therapeutics, is a development-stage firm working to treat ophthalmic conditions, gastrointestinal ailments, and other diseases.

	Annual Growth	07/19	07/20	07/21	07/22	07/23
Sales ($mil.)	(21.3%)	81.2	76.0	117.7	107.1	31.1
Net income ($ mil.)	69.0%	2.5	(28.5)	7.9	(18.3)	20.3
Market value ($ mil.)	(21.6%)	195.5	119.0	163.0	118.5	74.0
Employees	(21.5%)	500	448	514	520	190

ENZON PHARMACEUTICALS INC   NBB: ENZN

20 Commerce Drive (Suite 135)
Cranford, NJ 07016
Phone: 732 980-4500
Fax: 908 575-9157
Web: www.enzon.com

CEO: Richard L Feinstein
CFO: Richard L Feinstein
HR: –
FYE: December 31
Type: Public

Enzon Pharmaceuticals has PEGged its future on researching ways to fight cancer. The company has developed compounds using its PEGylation and Locked Nucleic Acid (LNA) technology platforms to improve the performance and deliverability of existing cancer drugs. PEGylation involves attaching polyethylene glycol (PEG) to a drug compound to make it more effective and less toxic for patients. However, in 2012 Enzon suspended clinical efforts and began reviewing strategic options; in 2013 it refocused on minimizing expenses and maximizing royalty revenue returns.

	Annual Growth	12/19	12/20	12/21	12/22	12/23
Sales ($mil.)	–	0.2	0.0	0.7	0.0	–
Net income ($ mil.)	–	(1.0)	(1.3)	(0.5)	(0.2)	1.4
Market value ($ mil.)	(17.9%)	15.3	18.4	25.4	18.3	6.9
Employees	–	–	–	–	–	–

EOG RESOURCES, INC.   NYS: EOG

1111 Bagby, Sky Lobby 2
Houston, TX 77002
Phone: 713 651-7000
Fax: –
Web: www.eogresources.com

CEO: Ezra Y Yacob
CFO: Tim K Driggers
HR: Keri White
FYE: December 31
Type: Public

EOG Resources explores for, develops, produces and markets crude oil, natural gas liquids (NGLs) and natural gas primarily in major producing basins in the US, The Republic of Trinidad and Tobago (Trinidad) and, from time to time, select other international areas. Of its approximately 4.2 million BOE reserves, EOG holds nearly 1.6 million barrels in crude oil and condensates, with an approximately 8.6 billion cubic feet of natural gas. The US is the company's largest market.

	Annual Growth	12/19	12/20	12/21	12/22	12/23
Sales ($mil.)	8.6%	17,380	11,032	18,642	25,702	24,186
Net income ($ mil.)	29.1%	2,734.9	(604.6)	4,664.0	7,759.0	7,594.0
Market value ($ mil.)	9.6%	48,653	28,968	51,598	75,233	70,255
Employees	1.3%	2,900	2,900	2,800	2,850	3,050

EOM PHARMACEUTICAL HOLDINGS INC   NBB: IMUC

30721 Russell Ranch Road, Suite 140
Westlake Village, CA 91362
Phone: 818 264-2300
Fax: –
Web: www.imuc.com

CEO: Irach B Taraporewala
CFO: Wayne I Danson
HR: –
FYE: December 31
Type: Public

ImmunoCellular Therapeutics primarily targets glioblastoma multiforme (GBM), which can hurt the brain just by trying to say or spell it. However, GBM is also regarded as the most aggressive brain cancer affecting humans. The development-stage company is also going after other cancers, such as those that attack the ovaries, pancreas, colon, and lungs. Its immunotherapy aims not only at normal tumor cells but also the stem cells where cancers grow and recur. ImmunoCellular has a partnership and licensing agreement with Los Angeles' Cedars-Sinai Medical Center to use the latter's technology in its research. The company was founded in 1987, took its current name in 2006, and went public in 2010.

	Annual Growth	12/16	12/17	12/20	12/21	12/22
Sales ($mil.)	–	–	–	–	–	–
Net income ($ mil.)	–	(22.1)	(14.3)	(0.5)	(2.7)	(2.6)
Market value ($ mil.)	(14.2%)	232.2	35.8	46.4	47.6	92.8
Employees	–	9	4	–	–	–

EP ENERGY CORP.

1001 Louisiana Street
Houston, TX 77002
Phone: 713 997-1000
Fax: –
Web: www.epenergy.com

CEO: –
CFO: –
HR: –
FYE: December 31
Type: Public

EP Energy is into the (E)xploration and (P)roduction of oil and gas. The company's primary operations are at the Eagle Ford Shale in South Texas, Northeastern Utah (NEU) in the Uinta basin, and the Permian basin in West Texas. It owns proved reserves of around 190 million barrels of oil equivalent, about 75% of which is oil and NGLs (natural gas liquids). In early 2020, EP Energy emerged from Chapter 11 bankruptcy protection. EP Energy was formed in 2012 when the former El Paso Corporation sold its exploration and production assets to an investment group for $7.2 billion.

	Annual Growth	12/15	12/16	12/17	12/18	12/19
Sales ($mil.)	(19.0%)	1,908.0	767.0	1,066.0	1,324.0	820.0
Net income ($ mil.)	–	(3,748.0)	(27.0)	(194.0)	(1,003.0)	(943.0)
Market value ($ mil.)	(83.3%)	1,118.2	1,672.2	602.5	178.7	0.9
Employees	(13.6%)	665	502	436	372	370

EPAM SYSTEMS, INC.   NYS: EPAM

41 University Drive, Suite 202
Newtown, PA 18940
Phone: 267 759-9000
Fax: –
Web: www.epam.com

CEO: Arkadiy Dobkin
CFO: Jason Peterson
HR: Sheryl Karczewski
FYE: December 31
Type: Public

EPAM is the global leading provider of digital platform engineering, and software development services to customers around the world, primarily in North America, Europe, and Asia. The company provides software development, product engineering services. Its key service offerings and solutions include five practice areas, such as engineering, operations, optimization, consulting, and design. The company has delivery locations in Belarus, Ukraine, Poland, India, and the US that employ approximately 52,850 delivery professionals. Approximately 60% of revenue come from North America. EPAM was founded in 1993.

	Annual Growth	12/19	12/20	12/21	12/22	12/23
Sales ($mil.)	19.6%	2,293.8	2,659.5	3,758.1	4,824.7	4,690.5
Net income ($ mil.)	12.4%	261.1	327.2	481.7	419.4	417.1
Market value ($ mil.)	8.8%	12,260	20,708	38,628	18,939	17,182
Employees	9.7%	36,739	41,168	58,824	59,300	53,150

EPI GROUP, LLC.

4020 STIRRUP CREEK DR
DURHAM, NC 277039410
Phone: 843 577-7111
Fax: –
Web: –

CEO: John P Barnwell
CFO: Ron Owens
HR: Paige Mollenkopf
FYE: December 31
Type: Private

Evening Post Publishing is a leading regional media company with newspapers and television stations in about 10 states. The company owns more than a dozen papers serving mostly small markets in North and South Carolina; its portfolio includes The Post and Courier in Charleston, South Carolina, with a circulation of almost 100,000. Evening Post Publishing's TV holdings include more than a dozen stations, including a group of CBS affiliates in Montana. The company also publishes Garden & Gun magazine and operates online news sites for most of its papers. The family-owned media business was started in 1894 by Robert Smith Manigault.

EPIQ SYSTEMS, INC.

11880 COLLEGE BLVD STE 200
OVERLAND PARK, KS 662102766
Phone: 770 390-2700
Fax: –
Web: www.epiqglobal.com

CEO: John Davenport Jr
CFO: –
HR: Rachel Noeth
FYE: December 31
Type: Private

Epiq, a global technology-enabled services leader to the legal industry and corporations, takes on large-scale, increasingly complex tasks for corporate counsel, law firms, and business professionals with efficiency, clarity, and confidence. The company provides case and document management software for bankruptcy, class action, mass tort, and other legal proceedings. Its software automates tasks including electronic discovery, legal notice, claims management, and government reporting. Epiq's software line includes products for Chapter 13 and 11 reorganizations. The company, which caters to law firms and bankruptcy trustees, also offers consulting and case management services.

EPITEC, INC.

26555 EVERGREEN RD STE 1700
SOUTHFIELD, MI 480764257
Phone: 248 353-6800
Fax: –
Web: www.epitec.com

CEO: –
CFO: –
HR: –
FYE: December 31
Type: Private

Epitec supports the idea that surrounding oneself with smart people is the key to a successful business. The company provides information technology staffing services to businesses across the US, although its primary market is the Detroit area. It offers contract, contract-to-hire, and direct hire placement of developers, analysts, architects, engineers, and other technical staff to companies in a wide range of industries. Epitec also provides on-site management services and related custom software development. It was founded by CEO Jerry Sheppard in 1978.

	Annual Growth	12/05	12/06	12/07	12/08	12/15
Sales ($mil.)	13.0%	–	–	–	28.5	67.0
Net income ($ mil.)	12.4%	–	–	–	0.8	1.8
Market value ($ mil.)	–	–	–	–	–	–
Employees	–	–	–	–	–	1,800

EPLUS INC

13595 Dulles Technology Drive
Herndon, VA 20171-3413
Phone: 703 984-8400
Fax: –
Web: www.eplus.com

NMS: PLUS
CEO: –
CFO: –
HR: –
FYE: March 31
Type: Public

ePlus is a leading provider of technology solutions and operates through two business segments that deal in technology sales and financing. Offerings include security, cloud, data center, networking, collaboration, artificial intelligence, and emerging solutions, to domestic, and foreign organizations across all industry segments. It offers IT hardware products, third-party software and maintenance contracts, its own and third-party advanced professional, and managed services, and its proprietary software. It also offers financing IT equipment, software, and related services. In addition, ePlus is an authorized reseller of over 1,500 vendors, including Arista Networks, Check Point, Cisco Systems, Dell EMC, F5 Networks, HPE, and NVIDIA, among others. Almost 95% of ePlus' revenue comes from the US.

	Annual Growth	03/19	03/20	03/21	03/22	03/23
Sales ($mil.)	10.8%	1,372.7	1,588.4	1,568.3	1,821.0	2,067.7
Net income ($ mil.)	17.2%	63.2	69.1	74.4	105.6	119.4
Market value ($ mil.)	(13.7%)	2,382.2	1,684.8	2,680.8	1,508.3	1,319.4
Employees	3.4%	1,537	1,579	1,560	1,577	1,754

EPR PROPERTIES

909 Walnut Street, Suite 200
Kansas City, MO 64106
Phone: 816 472-1700
Fax: 816 472-5794
Web: www.eprkc.com

NYS: EPR
CEO: Gregory K Silvers
CFO: Mark A Peterson
HR: Liz Grace
FYE: December 31
Type: Public

EPR Properties is a self-administered real estate investment trust (REIT) that owns some 170 theaters, around 55 eat & play properties, roughly 25, attraction properties, about 10 ski properties, seven experiential lodging properties, approximately 15 fitness & wellness properties, one gaming property, and three cultural properties around the US and Canada. Many of its theaters are leased to AMC Entertainment. Its Education portfolio, consisting of early childhood education centers and private schools, continues as a legacy investment and provides additional geographic and property diversity.

	Annual Growth	12/19	12/20	12/21	12/22	12/23
Sales ($mil.)	2.0%	652.0	414.7	531.7	658.0	705.7
Net income ($ mil.)	(3.8%)	202.2	(131.7)	98.6	176.2	173.0
Market value ($ mil.)	(9.0%)	5,321.5	2,448.3	3,577.5	2,841.5	3,649.9
Employees	(3.0%)	62	53	53	55	55

EPSILON SYSTEMS SOLUTIONS, INC.

9444 BALBOA AVE STE 100
SAN DIEGO, CA 921234351
Phone: 619 702-1700
Fax: –
Web: www.epsilonsystems.com

CEO: –
CFO: –
HR: –
FYE: December 31
Type: Private

Epsilon Systems Solutions is one of the largest professional and technical services company. The company provides total life cycle support to defense systems, such as basic research, concept development, system architecture, requirements definition and analysis, software development, integration and test, operational support, training, and maintenance and logistics. With a presence in more than 20 locations, Epsilon Systems' customers include the Department of Defense, Department of Energy, Department of Homeland Security and non-profit and commercial customers. The company was founded in 1998 by US Navy Veteran and Korean immigrant Bryan B. Min.

	Annual Growth	12/04	12/05	12/06	12/07	12/08
Sales ($mil.)	18.8%	–	–	66.4	94.1	93.8
Net income ($ mil.)	12.4%	–	–	1.3	1.7	1.7
Market value ($ mil.)	–	–	–	–	–	–
Employees	–	–	–	–	–	887

EQT CORP

NYS: EQT

625 Liberty Avenue, Suite 1700
Pittsburgh, PA 15222
Phone: 412 553-5700
Fax: –
Web: www.eqt.com

CEO: Toby Z Rice
CFO: David M Khani
HR: –
FYE: December 31
Type: Public

EQT Corporation (EQT) is a major US producer of natural gas, boasting proved reserves of about 25 trillion cubic feet equivalent of natural gas, natural gas liquids, and crude oil. Its assets are mainly in the Marcellus and Utica shale basin in Appalachia. The company has about 1.8 million gross acres in the Marcellus play. The company's customers include Appalachian-area utilities, such as natural gas and NGLs, and industrial customers, as well as natural gas marketers. In addition, the company also caters to markets that are accessible through the company's transportation portfolio, particularly in the Gulf Coast, Midwest, and Northeast US and Canada.

	Annual Growth	12/19	12/20	12/21	12/22	12/23
Sales ($mil.)	11.8%	4,416.5	3,058.8	3,064.7	7,497.7	6,908.9
Net income ($ mil.)	–	(1,221.7)	(967.2)	(1,155.8)	1,771.0	1,735.2
Market value ($ mil.)	37.2%	4,576.9	5,336.9	9,157.9	14,205	16,233
Employees	8.0%	647	624	693	744	881

EQUIFAX INC

NYS: EFX

1550 Peachtree Street, N.W.
Atlanta, GA 30309
Phone: 404 885-8000
Fax: –
Web: www.equifax.com

CEO: Mark W Begor
CFO: John W Gamble Jr
HR: Karen Wilkins
FYE: December 31
Type: Public

A global data, analytics and technology company, Equifax provides information solutions for businesses, governments and consumers, and provide human resources business process outsourcing services for employers. Its services are based on comprehensive databases of consumer and business information derived from numerous sources including credit, financial assets, telecommunications and utility payments, employment, income, educational history, criminal history, healthcare professional licensure and sanctions, demographic and marketing data. Clients include financial institutions, corporations, government agencies and individuals. Equifax operates around the world, but does most of its business in the US.

	Annual Growth	12/19	12/20	12/21	12/22	12/23
Sales ($mil.)	10.7%	3,507.6	4,127.5	4,923.9	5,122.2	5,265.2
Net income ($ mil.)	–	(398.8)	520.1	744.2	696.2	545.3
Market value ($ mil.)	15.3%	17,277	23,777	36,101	23,965	30,491
Employees	7.4%	11,200	11,400	12,700	14,000	14,900

EQUINIX INC

NMS: EQIX

One Lagoon Drive
Redwood City, CA 94065
Phone: 650 598-6000
Fax: –
Web: www.equinix.com

CEO: Charles Meyers
CFO: Keith D Taylor
HR: Robert Kraska
FYE: December 31
Type: Public

Equinix is a global digital infrastructure company. Platform Equinix combines a global footprint of International Business Exchange (IBX) data centers in the Americas, Asia-Pacific, and Europe, the Middle East and Africa regions, interconnection solutions, edge services, unique business and digital ecosystems and expert consulting and support. Its customers include telecommunications carriers, mobile and other network services providers, cloud and IT services providers, digital media and content providers, financial services companies, and global enterprise ecosystems in various industries. Altogether, Equinix operates more than 220 data centers around the world and gets some 55% of revenue outside the Americas region.

	Annual Growth	12/19	12/20	12/21	12/22	12/23
Sales ($mil.)	10.2%	5,562.1	5,998.5	6,635.5	7,263.1	8,188.1
Net income ($ mil.)	17.6%	507.5	369.8	500.2	704.3	969.2
Market value ($ mil.)	8.4%	55,148	67,475	79,914	61,887	76,093
Employees	11.9%	8,378	10,013	10,944	12,097	13,151

EQUINOR MARKETING & TRADING (US) INC.

600 WASHINGTON BLVD 8TH FL
STAMFORD, CT 06902
Phone: 203 978-6900
Fax: –
Web: –

CEO: –
CFO: –
HR: –
FYE: December 31
Type: Private

Check the stats. Oil. Hundreds of thousands of barrels of oil, gasoline, and more. Statoil Marketing & Trading is a wholesaler of oil and petroleum products. The company is the US trading arm of Statoil, the leading Scandinavian oil and gas enterprise. Statoil Marketing & Trading delivers about 600,000 barrels a day in the form of crude oil, gasoline, liquefied petroleum gas (LPG), propane, and butane to the North American market. In addition to supplying Norwegian crude, the company trades crude oil from Africa, South America, and North America. Statoil Marketing & Trading sells it oil products primarily to customers in Northeastern Canada, the US East Coast and Gulf Coast.

	Annual Growth	12/16	12/17	12/18	12/19	12/20
Sales ($mil.)	0.3%	–	9,874.2	14,852	13,595	9,959.5
Net income ($ mil.)	–	–	(28.8)	140.0	88.8	209.6
Market value ($ mil.)	–	–	–	–	–	–
Employees	–	–	–	–	–	5

EQUITABLE HOLDINGS INC

NYS: EQH

1290 Avenue of the Americas
New York, NY 10104
Phone: 212 554-1234
Fax: –
Web: www.axa.com

CEO: Mark Pearson
CFO: Robin M Raju
HR: –
FYE: December 31
Type: Public

Equitable Holdings is a financial services holding company comprised of two complementary and well-established principal franchises, Equitable and AllianceBernstein. Founded in 1859, Equitable provides advice, protection and retirement strategies to individuals, families and small businesses. AllianceBernstein is a global investment management firm that offers high-quality research and diversified investment services to institutional investors, individuals and private wealth clients in major world markets. Equitable Holdings has about $864 billion in assets under management and more than 5 million client relationships globally.

	Annual Growth	12/19	12/20	12/21	12/22	12/23
Assets ($mil.)	2.6%	249,870	275,397	292,262	253,468	276,814
Net income ($ mil.)	–	(1,733.0)	(648.0)	(439.0)	1,785.0	1,302.0
Market value ($ mil.)	7.7%	8,273.5	8,543.9	10,948	9,582.3	11,118
Employees	1.8%	7,900	7,900	7,800	8,200	8,500

EQUITRANS, L.P.

625 LIBERTY AVE STE 1700
PITTSBURGH, PA 152223114
Phone: 412 553-5700
Fax: –
Web: www.equitransmidstream.com

CEO: –
CFO: –
HR: –
FYE: December 31
Type: Private

Did someone order delivery? EQT Midstream Partners (formerly Equitrans), an indirect subsidiary of integrated natural gas behemoth EQT provides natural gas gathering, storage and transmission services through pipelines that connect to delivery points in Kentucky, Pennsylvania, and West Virginia. EQT formed EQT Midstream Partners to forge a new relationship between pipelines and their markets, where customers were active, discriminating buyers of energy services. The unit is expanding it operations in the lucrative Marcellus Shale play in West Virginia and Pennsylvania, to better serve growing natural gas demand in the Northeast. In 2012 EQT filed to take EQT Midstream Partners public.

EQUITY COMMONWEALTH
NYS: EQC

Two North Riverside Plaza, Suite 2100
Chicago, IL 60606
Phone: 312 646-2800
Fax: 617 332-2161
Web: www.eqcre.com

CEO: David Helfand
CFO: William H Griffiths
HR: –
FYE: December 31
Type: Public

Equity CommonWealth (formerly CommonWealth REIT) invests in office and industrial properties, primarily in the US, mainly located in suburbs of major metropolitan markets. Its portfolio includes about 40 properties, the majority of which are offices, comprising some 17 million sq. ft. of leasable space. Equity CommonWealth was one of the largest industrial private land owners in Oahu until it spun off those assets in 2012; other markets include Boston, Philadelphia, Southern California, and the District of Columbia. GlaxoSmithKline and Office Depot are among the REIT's largest tenants. The REIT has been selling off certain holdings; it has unloaded more than 1 billion sq. ft. since early 2016.

	Annual Growth	12/19	12/20	12/21	12/22	12/23
Sales ($mil.)	(17.1%)	127.9	66.3	58.0	63.1	60.5
Net income ($ mil.)	(34.4%)	492.7	451.3	(16.4)	37.3	91.2
Market value ($ mil.)	(12.6%)	3,507.8	2,914.8	2,767.3	2,668.0	2,051.5
Employees	(5.9%)	28	28	25	22	22

EQUITY LIFESTYLE PROPERTIES INC
NYS: ELS

Two North Riverside Plaza, Suite 800
Chicago, IL 60606
Phone: 312 279-1400
Fax: –
Web: www.equitylifestyleproperties.com

CEO: Marguerite Nader
CFO: Paul Seavey
HR: –
FYE: December 31
Type: Public

Snow birds and empty nesters flock to communities developed and owned by Equity LifeStyle Properties. The real estate investment trust (REIT) owns and operates lifestyle-oriented residential properties aimed at retirees, vacationers, and second home owners. Other properties provide affordable housing for families. Equity LifeStyle Properties leases lots for factory-built homes, cottages, cabins, and recreational vehicles. Available homes range in size and style. The REIT's portfolio includes more than 380 properties containing some 141,000 lots in about 30 states and Canada. Properties are similar to site-built residential subdivisions, with centralized entrances, utilities, gutters, curbs, and paved streets.

	Annual Growth	12/19	12/20	12/21	12/22	12/23
Sales ($mil.)	9.5%	1,037.3	1,091.4	1,271.7	1,447.1	1,489.4
Net income ($ mil.)	3.0%	279.1	228.3	262.5	284.6	314.2
Market value ($ mil.)	0.1%	13,123	11,812	16,342	12,043	13,151
Employees	–	4,200	4,000	4,100	4,200	–

EQUITY ONE, INC.

1 INDEPENDENT DR STE 114
JACKSONVILLE, FL 322025005
Phone: 212 796-1760
Fax: –
Web: –

CEO: –
CFO: –
HR: –
FYE: December 31
Type: Private

Equity One wants to be #1: the number one shopping center owner, that is. A real estate investment trust (REIT), Equity One acquires, develops, and manages shopping centers in urban areas across the US, targeting markets in California, the northeastern US, South Florida, Atlanta, and Washington DC. Its portfolio consists primarily of more than 120 properties, including shopping centers anchored by supermarkets, drug stores, and other specialty retail chains totaling about 14 million sq. ft. The REIT's top five tenants include Albertsons, Publix, LA Fitness, Food Emporium, and TJX Companies. Chairman Chaim Katzman controls the REIT through his Israeli real estate firm Gazit-Globe.

	Annual Growth	12/11	12/12	12/13	12/14	12/16
Assets ($mil.)	(0.1%)	–	3,502.7	3,354.7	3,262.2	3,494.6
Net income ($ mil.)	78.2%	–	7.2	88.7	61.1	72.8
Market value ($ mil.)	–	–	–	–	–	–
Employees	–	–	–	–	–	155

EQUITY RESIDENTIAL
NYS: EQR

Two North Riverside Plaza
Chicago, IL 60606
Phone: 312 474-1300
Fax: –
Web: www.equityapartments.com

CEO: Mark J Parrell
CFO: Robert A Garechana
HR: Erika Stephens
FYE: December 31
Type: Public

Equity Residential is one of the largest apartment owners in the US, actively investing in rental properties in the urban core of cities and in high density suburban areas near transit, entertainment, and cultural amenities. The company acquires, develops, and manages multifamily residential units in the form of garden-style, high-rise, and mid-rise properties. A real estate investment trust (REIT), Equity Residential owns about 310 multifamily communities composed of 79,600 rentable units in large metropolitan areas such as San Francisco, Seattle, and New York.

	Annual Growth	12/19	12/20	12/21	12/22	12/23
Sales ($mil.)	1.6%	2,701.1	2,571.7	2,464.0	2,735.2	2,874.0
Net income ($ mil.)	(3.7%)	970.4	913.6	1,332.9	776.9	835.4
Market value ($ mil.)	(6.8%)	30,692	22,484	34,326	22,378	23,197
Employees	(2.9%)	2,700	2,600	2,400	2,400	2,400

ERBA DIAGNOSTICS

14100 NW 57th Court
Miami Lakes, FL 33014
Phone: 305 324-2300
Fax: 305 324-2385
Web: www.erbadiagnostics.com

CEO: Hayden Jeffreys
CFO: –
HR: –
FYE: December 31
Type: Public

Using blood, sweat, or tears, ERBA Diagnostics (formerly IVAX Diagnostics) can tell if something is wrong. The company develops, manufactures, and distributes in vitro diagnostic products to identify autoimmune and infectious diseases, based upon samples of bodily fluids. It operates through three subsidiaries. Delta Biologicals develops and manufactures the MAGO and Aptus instrument systems, and distributes products to hospitals and medical laboratories in Italy. Diamedix makes and markets diagnostic test kits in the US. ImmunoVision develops, makes, and markets autoimmune reagents for use by clinical and research labs and other diagnostic manufacturers. ERBA Diagnostics Mannheim holds 72% of the company.

	Annual Growth	12/10	12/11	12/12	12/13	12/14
Sales ($mil.)	11.6%	17.0	16.8	19.3	28.3	26.4
Net income ($ mil.)	–	(4.2)	(3.3)	(1.6)	0.7	0.4
Market value ($ mil.)	53.6%	25.1	19.4	39.2	120.4	139.8
Employees	6.0%	106	87	99	135	134

ERGON ASPHALT PARTNERS, LP

2829 LAKELAND DR
FLOWOOD, MS 392329798
Phone: 601 933-3000
Fax: –
Web: www.ergonasphalt.com

CEO: D A Woodward
CFO: Matthew R Lewis
HR: –
FYE: December 31
Type: Private

Blueknight Energy Partners (formerly SemGroup Energy Partners) provides gathering, transporting, terminalling, and storage of crude oil in Oklahoma, Kansas, and Texas. It operates two pipeline systems (1,285 miles of pipeline) delivering crude oil to refineries, and provides storage services with a capacity of about 8.1 million barrels. It also provides asphalt services. Blueknight Energy Partners has about 7.4 million barrels of asphalt and residual fuel storage in 45 terminals located in 22 states. Blueknight Energy Partners' top customer is Netherlands-based natural resources group Vitol (54% of total revenues in 2010). Vitol and investment firm Charlesbank Capital Partners indirectly own the company.

ERHC ENERGY INC

NBB: ERHE

5444 Westheimer Road, Suite 1440
Houston, TX 77056
Phone: 713 626-4700
Fax: –
Web: www.erhc.com

CEO: Peter C Ntephe
CFO: –
HR: –
FYE: September 30
Type: Public

Oil, out of Africa, is the hope of ERHC Energy (formerly Environmental Remediation Holding Corporation), an independent oil and gas company whose sole assets are two West African oil and gas exploration concessions: in the Joint Development Zone between the Sao Tome and Nigeria; and in the Exclusive Economic Zone in Sao Tome. ERHC is teaming up with larger oil and gas companies (such as Noble Energy and Pioneer Natural Resources) to help it develop its holdings. The company is also hoping to acquire interests in high-potential non-producing international prospects in known oil producing areas. Former chairman and CEO Emeka Offor, the owner of Chrome Oil Services and Chrome Energy, controls about 40% of ERHC.

	Annual Growth	09/12	09/13	09/14	09/15	09/16
Sales ($mil.)	–	–	–	–	–	–
Net income ($ mil.)	–	(4.3)	(5.2)	(2.0)	(8.6)	(12.0)
Market value ($ mil.)	(50.7%)	6.4	2.9	2.4	0.0	0.4
Employees	15.8%	5	9	9	9	9

ERICKSON INCORPORATED

3100 WILLOW SPRINGS RD
CENTRAL POINT, OR 975029362
Phone: 503 505-5800
Fax: –
Web: www.ericksoninc.com

CEO: Barry Kohler
CFO: Stephen Wideman
HR: –
FYE: December 31
Type: Private

Erickson Incorporated is a trusted global provider of aviation services that specializes in aerial firefighting, civil protection, and defense. The company is the original equipment manufacturer (OEM) of the S-64 Air Crane heavy-lift helicopter and have modernized the global fleet of S-64 aircraft. Additionally, it offers vertically integrated manufacturing, Maintenance Repair and Overhaul (MRO), and augmented support to operators of various airframes across North America, South America, Europe, the Middle East, Africa, Asia Pacific, and Australia. The company was founded in 1971 by Jack Erickson.

ERIE INDEMNITY CO.

NMS: ERIE

100 Erie Insurance Place
Erie, PA 16530
Phone: 814 870-2000
Fax: –
Web: www.erieinsurance.com

CEO: Timothy G Necastro
CFO: Gregory J Gutting
HR: –
FYE: December 31
Type: Public

Founded in 1925 as an auto insurer, Erie Indemnity now provides management services that relate to the sales, underwriting, and issuance of policies of one customer: Erie Insurance Exchange. The Exchange is a reciprocal insurance exchange that pools the underwriting of several property/casualty insurance firms. The principal personal lines products are private passenger automobiles and homeowners. The principal commercial lines products are commercial multi-peril, commercial automobile and workers' compensation. Erie Indemnity charges a management fee of some 25% of all premiums written or assumed by the Exchange.

	Annual Growth	12/19	12/20	12/21	12/22	12/23
Assets ($mil.)	5.2%	2,016.2	2,117.1	2,242.1	2,239.5	2,472.0
Net income ($ mil.)	8.9%	316.8	293.3	297.9	298.6	446.1
Market value ($ mil.)	19.2%	7,667.8	11,345	8,899.3	11,489	15,470
Employees	3.4%	5,700	5,914	5,876	6,038	6,505

ERIN ENERGY CORP

NBB: ERIN Q

1330 Post Oak Blvd., Suite 2250
Houston, TX 77056
Phone: 713 797-2940
Fax: –
Web: www.camacenergy.com

CEO: –
CFO: –
HR: –
FYE: December 31
Type: Public

Erin Energy (formerly CAMAC Energy) likes to share the wealth, and the work. Rather than owning oil and gas assets outright, the company owns interests in production sharing contracts with a focus on West Africa and Asia. It has two producing wells at Oyo Field (75 miles off the coast of Nigeria) with plans for two more. Erin Energy shares the Nigerian oil profits with sister company Nigerian Agip Exploration Limited, which runs the operation. The company's total proved reserves of 5.2 billion barrels of oil, most of which is undeveloped, are all at Oyo. Its Chinese Zijinshan Project, an exploration-stage coal bed methane play, is shared with PetroChina CBM. Erin Energy was formed in 2005 to focus on energy projects in China.

	Annual Growth	12/13	12/14	12/15	12/16	12/17
Sales ($mil.)	89.3%	7.9	53.8	68.4	77.8	101.2
Net income ($ mil.)	–	(15.9)	(96.1)	(451.5)	(142.4)	(151.9)
Market value ($ mil.)	16.8%	318.3	79.6	688.3	656.0	591.5
Employees	6.7%	47	86	84	74	61

ERNST & YOUNG LLP

395 9TH AVE FL 1
NEW YORK, NY 100018604
Phone: 703 747-0049
Fax: –
Web: www.ey.com

CEO: Carmine Disibio
CFO: –
HR: –
FYE: June 30
Type: Private

Ernst & Young (EY) provides assurance, tax, consulting, and strategy and transaction services to public and private companies in the automotive, energy, chemicals, financial, health, real estate, retail, consumer, and entertainment industries in the US. The company also provides employee benefit plan and entrepreneurial services. With more than 700 office locations in more than 150 countries, the company serves more than 200,000 clients that range from start-ups to multinationals across all sectors.

	Annual Growth	06/18	06/19	06/20	06/21	06/22
Sales ($mil.)	1.1%	–	–	–	27.6	27.9
Net income ($ mil.)	–	–	–	–	(1.4)	6.0
Market value ($ mil.)	–	–	–	–	–	–
Employees	–	–	–	–	–	27,390

EROOM SYSTEM TECHNOLOGIES INC

150 Airport Road, Suite 1200
Lakewood, NJ 08701
Phone: 732 730-0116
Fax: 732 810-0380
Web: www.eroomsystem.com

CEO: David A Gestetner
CFO: David A Gestetner
HR: –
FYE: December 31
Type: Public

eRoomSystem Technologies is keeping tabs for hotels. The company provides computer-based refreshment centers for the hospitality industry. Its eRoomSystem products track beverage and other refreshment purchases and automatically charge lodgers' accounts. The eRoomSystem generates reports on sales statistics, inventory control, and restocking requirements. The company's other products include room safes that feature reprogrammable electronic combinations. Through revenue-sharing agreements the company installs its systems and takes a cut of the sales they generate.

	Annual Growth	12/11	12/12	12/13	12/14	12/15
Sales ($mil.)	3.0%	0.8	0.7	0.6	0.8	0.9
Net income ($ mil.)	–	(0.1)	(0.3)	(0.3)	0.1	0.0
Market value ($ mil.)	(24.1%)	0.0	0.0	0.0	0.0	0.0
Employees	–	15	17	19	15	15

EROS MEDIA WORLD PLC

NBB: EMWP F

3900 West Alameda Avenue, 32nd Floor
Burbank, CA 91505
Phone: 818 524-7000
Fax: –
Web: www.erosplc.com

CEO: –
CFO: –
HR: –
FYE: March 31
Type: Public

Entertainment distributor Eros International is there for moviegoers who reside outside of India yet yearn for a taste of Bollywood. The company operates under the goal of creating a global platform for Indian cinema. Its library of content includes more than 2,000 Indian films. Eros International also distributes Indian TV, DVDs, music, and digital content. It does so through its network of more than 500 distribution partners across some 50 countries. Eros has offices in India, the UK, the US, Dubai, Australia, Fiji, Isle of Man, and Singapore. Founded in 1977, the company was listed on the London Stock Exchange in 2006.

	Annual Growth	03/16	03/17	03/18	03/19	03/20
Sales ($mil.)	(13.2%)	274.4	253.0	261.3	270.1	155.5
Net income ($ mil.)	–	3.8	3.8	(22.6)	(423.9)	(419.0)
Market value ($ mil.)	–	–	–	–	–	–
Employees	(11.1%)	544	448	423	396	340

ERVIN INDUSTRIES, INC.

3893 RESEARCH PARK DR UPPR
ANN ARBOR, MI 481082267
Phone: 734 769-4600
Fax: –
Web: www.ervinindustries.com

CEO: –
CFO: Richard Conn
HR: –
FYE: December 31
Type: Private

Ervin Industries, founded in 1920, is the leading manufacturer of metal abrasives and its applications and technologies. It makes steel grit and steel shot ? sold under the AMACAST and AMASTEEL names ? for use in blast cleaning, cutting, and etching applications. Its Ervin Technologies focuses on the research and development of fine metal particles that lead to innovations in metal powder technologies. Its RSR (Rapid Solidification Rate) atomization process allows Ervin to develop a wide variety of Advanced Metal Powders for many industries and applications. It has locations in the US, as well as in Germany and the UK.

ESCALADE, INC.

NMS: ESCA

817 Maxwell Ave.
Evansville, IN 47711
Phone: 812 467-1358
Fax: –
Web: www.escaladeinc.com

CEO: Walter P Glazer Jr
CFO: Stephen Wawrin
HR: –
FYE: December 31
Type: Public

Escalade is the leader in tables for table tennis, residential in-ground basketball goals and in archery bows. Its other sporting goods include hockey and soccer tables, play systems, pickleball, water sports, archery, darts, and fitness and safety equipment. Products are sold under the STIGA, Ping-Pong, Goalrilla, Silverback, USWeight, and Woodplay, as well as private labels. The company manufactures, imports, and distributes widely recognized products through major sporting goods retailers, specialty dealers, key on-line retailers, traditional department stores and mass merchants. Escalade operates through eight manufacturing and distribution facilities across North America. Almost all of Escalade's revenue comes from the North America.

	Annual Growth	12/18	12/19	12/20	12/21	12/22
Sales ($mil.)	15.6%	175.8	180.5	273.6	313.6	313.8
Net income ($ mil.)	(3.1%)	20.4	7.3	25.9	24.4	18.0
Market value ($ mil.)	(2.9%)	155.5	133.1	294.9	213.3	138.4
Employees	2.8%	531	468	704	676	593

ESCALERA RESOURCES CO

1675 Broadway, Suite 2200
Denver, CO 80202
Phone: 303 794-8445
Fax: 303 794-8451
Web: www.escaleraresources.com

CEO: –
CFO: –
HR: –
FYE: December 31
Type: Public

It's double or nothing for Double Eagle Petroleum (formerly Double Eagle Petroleum and Mining), which gambles on hitting pay dirt as it explores for and produces oil and gas in the Rocky Mountains of Utah and Wyoming. Double Eagle owns interests in about 900 producing wells; natural gas accounts for more than 95% of the oil and gas independent's production and reserves. The company has proved reserves of more than 413,000 barrels of oil and 71.3 billion cu. ft. of natural gas, and leases acreage in seven states. Double Eagle sells its oil and gas on the spot market.

	Annual Growth	12/10	12/11	12/12	12/13	12/14
Sales ($mil.)	(5.4%)	55.0	64.7	38.2	35.3	44.1
Net income ($ mil.)	–	5.5	11.7	(10.3)	(13.1)	(7.6)
Market value ($ mil.)	(16.4%)	370.2	369.8	360.2	329.7	180.8
Employees	3.0%	24	24	24	22	27

ESCALON MEDICAL CORP

NBB: ESMC

435 Devon Park Drive, Suite 824
Wayne, PA 19087
Phone: 610 688-6830
Fax: 610 688-3641
Web: www.escalonmed.com

CEO: Richard J Depiano
CFO: Mark G Wallace
HR: –
FYE: June 30
Type: Public

Escalon Medical has an eye for ophthalmic instruments. The company develops, manufactures, markets, and distributes diagnostic and surgical devices for use in ophthalmology, specifically ultrasound, digital photography, and image management systems. Its subsidiary companies are branded and operate under the Sonomed Escalon name. Products include the PacScan Plus and Master-Vu ultrasound systems and AXIS image management system. Escalon Medical was founded in 1987. It divested its Escalon Clinical Diagnostics (ECD) business in 2012 to put more focus into growing its ophthalmic business.

	Annual Growth	06/19	06/20	06/21	06/22	06/23
Sales ($mil.)	6.1%	9.6	9.4	10.5	10.7	12.2
Net income ($ mil.)	–	(0.3)	(0.7)	(0.1)	0.0	0.5
Market value ($ mil.)	20.1%	0.9	0.9	1.6	0.9	1.9
Employees	–	38	38	41	41	38

ESCO TECHNOLOGIES, INC.

NYS: ESE

9900A Clayton Road
St. Louis, MO 63124-1186
Phone: 314 213-7200
Fax: –
Web: www.escotechnologies.com

CEO: Bryan H Sayler
CFO: Christopher L Tucker
HR: –
FYE: September 30
Type: Public

ESCO Technologies manufactures highly-engineered filtration and fluid control and integrated propulsion systems products for the aviation, navy, space, and process markets worldwide, as well as composite-based products and solutions for navy, defense, and industrial customers. Esco is the industry leader in RF shielding electromagnetic compatibility (EMC) test products. It provides diagnostic instruments, software, and services for the benefit of industrial power users and the electric utility and renewable energy industries. Subsidiaries include PTI, Doble, Crissair, Globe, Mayday, Westland, Altanova, Morgan Schaffer, NRG VACCO, and ETS-Lindgren. Its operating subsidiaries are engaged primarily in the research, development, manufacture, sale, and support of the products and systems. About 70% of revenue is to customers in the US.

	Annual Growth	09/19	09/20	09/21	09/22	09/23
Sales ($mil.)	4.1%	813.0	732.9	715.4	857.5	956.0
Net income ($ mil.)	3.4%	81.0	102.0	63.5	82.3	92.5
Market value ($ mil.)	7.0%	2,051.6	2,077.3	1,985.5	1,893.7	2,693.1
Employees	(0.3%)	3,239	2,844	2,822	2,922	3,195

ESPERION THERAPEUTICS INC (NEW)　　　　　　　　NMS: ESPR

3891 Ranchero Drive, Suite 150　　　　　　　　　　　　　　　CEO: –
Ann Arbor, MI 48108　　　　　　　　　　　　　　　　　　　　CFO: –
Phone: 734 887-3903　　　　　　　　　　　　　　　　　　　　HR: –
Fax: –　　　　　　　　　　　　　　　　　　　　　FYE: December 31
Web: www.esperion.com　　　　　　　　　　　　　　　　Type: Public

Esperion Therapeutics is a pharmaceutical company singularly focused on developing and commercializing accessible, oral, once-daily, non-statin medicines for patients struggling with elevated low-density lipoprotein cholesterol, or LDL-C. Its first two products were approved by the US. Food and Drug Administration (FDA), European Medicines Agency (EMA) and Swiss Agency for Therapeutic Products (Swissmedic), in 2020. Bempedoic acid and the bempedoic acid / ezetimibe combination tablet are oral, once-daily, non-statin, LDL-C lowering medicines for patients with atherosclerotic cardiovascular disease, or ASCVD, or heterozygous familial hypercholesterolemia, or HeFH.

	Annual Growth	12/19	12/20	12/21	12/22	12/23
Sales ($mil.)	(5.9%)	148.4	227.5	78.4	75.5	116.3
Net income ($ mil.)	–	(97.2)	(143.6)	(269.1)	(233.7)	(209.2)
Market value ($ mil.)	(52.7%)	7,048.9	3,073.5	591.1	736.5	353.4
Employees	5.6%	193	479	218	199	240

ESPEY MANUFACTURING & ELECTRONICS CORP.　　　ASE: ESP

233 Ballston Avenue　　　　　　　　　　　　　　　　CEO: David A O'Neil
Saratoga Springs, NY 12866　　　　　　　　　　　CFO: Katrina L Sparano
Phone: 518 245-4400　　　　　　　　　　　　　　　　　　　　HR: –
Fax: –　　　　　　　　　　　　　　　　　　　　　　　　FYE: June 30
Web: www.espey.com　　　　　　　　　　　　　　　　Type: Public

Espey is on a power trip. Espey Mfg. & Electronics makes electronic equipment for high-voltage applications, including specialized electronic power supplies, transformers, and electronic system components. Its transformers and electronic systems include high-power radar transmitters, antennas, and iron-core products such as magnetic amplifiers and audio filters. The company's products are used by industrial and military customers in radar, missile guidance and control, communications, aircraft navigation, and nuclear submarine control. Customers include General Electric, Lockheed Martin, Raytheon, and the US government. Exports account for more than 20% of Espey's sales.

	Annual Growth	06/19	06/20	06/21	06/22	06/23
Sales ($mil.)	(0.6%)	36.5	31.5	27.7	32.1	35.6
Net income ($ mil.)	11.9%	2.3	1.2	(0.2)	1.3	3.7
Market value ($ mil.)	(9.3%)	66.9	46.8	40.1	38.5	45.3
Employees	(1.1%)	160	151	150	150	153

ESSA BANCORP INC　　　　　　　　　　　　　　　　　NMS: ESSA

200 Palmer Street　　　　　　　　　　　　　　　　　　CEO: Gary S Olson
Stroudsburg, PA 18360　　　　　　　　　　　　　　　CFO: Allan A Muto
Phone: 570 421-0531　　　　　　　　　　　　　　　　　　　　HR: –
Fax: –　　　　　　　　　　　　　　　　　　　　FYE: September 30
Web: www.essabank.com　　　　　　　　　　　　　　　Type: Public

ESSA Bancorp is the holding company for ESSA Bank & Trust. Founded in 1916, the bank offers deposit and lending services to consumers and businesses through more than 25 branches located in eastern Pennsylvania's Lehigh, Monroe, and Northampton counties. One- to four-family residential mortgages dominate the bank's lending activities, representing more than 80% of its loan portfolio. Commercial real estate loans account for 10%, while home equity loans and lines of credit make up ESSA's other significant loan segments. The bank also offers financial and investment services through a third-party firm. ESSA Bancorp acquired First Star Bancorp in 2012, adding nine branches in Lehigh County.

	Annual Growth	09/19	09/20	09/21	09/22	09/23
Assets ($mil.)	6.3%	1,799.4	1,893.5	1,861.4	1,861.8	2,293.2
Net income ($ mil.)	10.1%	12.6	14.4	16.4	20.1	18.6
Market value ($ mil.)	(2.2%)	170.7	128.4	171.4	201.6	156.0
Employees	(1.1%)	262	252	251	250	251

ESSENDANT INC.

1 PARKWAY NORTH BLVD STE 100　　　　　　　　　　　　　　CEO: –
DEERFIELD, IL 600152559　　　　　　　　　　　　CFO: Janet Zelenka
Phone: 847 627-7000　　　　　　　　　　　　　　　HR: Thomas Grace
Fax: –　　　　　　　　　　　　　　　　　　　　　FYE: December 31
Web: www.essendant.com　　　　　　　　　　　　　Type: Private

Essendant is a diverse network of resellers, distributors, online retailers and national organizations across the US. Its more than 2 million products include janitorial and sanitation supplies; print, imaging, and other technology products; and traditional office supplies, as well as food service, safety supplies and tools, and office furniture. It serves customers, including office/workplace resellers and dealers, and more. The company was incorporated in 1922 under the name Utility Supply Company.

ESSENTIAL UTILITIES INC　　　　　　　　　　　　　　NYS: WTRG

762 W. Lancaster Avenue　　　　　　　　　　CEO: Christopher H Franklin
Bryn Mawr, PA 19010-3489　　　　　　　　　　CFO: Daniel J Schuller
Phone: 610 527-8000　　　　　　　　　　　　　　　　　　　　HR: –
Fax: –　　　　　　　　　　　　　　　　　　　　　FYE: December 31
Web: www.essential.co　　　　　　　　　　　　　　Type: Public

Essential Utilities (Essential), formerly Aqua America, provides water, wastewater, or natural gas services to an estimated five million customers in Pennsylvania, Ohio, Texas, Illinois, North Carolina, New Jersey, Indiana, Virginia, West Virginia, and Kentucky under the Aqua and Peoples brands. It is the holding company for several regulated utilities, the largest being Aqua Pennsylvania providing water or wastewater services. The Company also operates non-regulated market-based activities that are supplementary and complementary to its regulated utility businesses. Aqua Resources offers, through a third-party, water and sewer line protection solutions and repair services to households. Other non-regulated subsidiaries of Peoples provide utility service line protection services to households and operate gas marketing and production. The company was formed in 1968. Nearly 75% of Essential's total revenue comes from Pennsylvania.

	Annual Growth	12/19	12/20	12/21	12/22	12/23
Sales ($mil.)	23.3%	889.7	1,462.7	1,878.1	2,288.0	2,053.8
Net income ($ mil.)	22.0%	224.5	284.8	431.6	465.2	498.2
Market value ($ mil.)	(5.6%)	12,829	12,924	14,673	13,044	10,208
Employees	19.8%	1,583	3,180	3,211	3,178	3,258

ESSEX PROPERTY TRUST INC　　　　　　　　　　　　NYS: ESS

1100 Park Place, Suite 200　　　　　　　　　　CEO: Michael J Schall
San Mateo, CA 94403　　　　　　　　　　　　　　　　CFO: Barb Pak
Phone: 650 655-7800　　　　　　　　　　　　　　　　　　　　HR: –
Fax: –　　　　　　　　　　　　　　　　　　　　　FYE: December 31
Web: www.essex.com　　　　　　　　　　　　　　　Type: Public

Essex Property Trust acquires, develops, redevelops, and manages apartment communities, located along the West Coast of the US. The self-managed and self-administered real estate investment trust (REIT) owns more than 250 operating apartment communities aggregating some 62,145 apartment homes, excluding the company's ownership in preferred equity co-investments, loan investments, three operating commercial buildings, and a development pipeline comprised of one consolidated project and one unconsolidated joint venture project aggregating some 265 apartment homes.

	Annual Growth	12/19	12/20	12/21	12/22	12/23
Sales ($mil.)	3.4%	1,460.2	1,495.7	1,440.6	1,606.8	1,669.4
Net income ($ mil.)	(2.0%)	439.3	568.9	488.6	408.3	405.8
Market value ($ mil.)	(4.7%)	19,316	15,243	22,614	13,606	15,919
Employees	(1.0%)	1,822	1,799	1,757	1,772	1,750

ESSEX RENTAL CORP

1110 Lake Cook Road, Suite 220
Buffalo Grove, IL 60089
Phone: 847 215-6500
Fax: -
Web: www.essexrentalcorp.com

NBB: ESSX
CEO: Nicholas J Matthews
CFO: Kory M Glen
HR: -
FYE: December 31
Type: Public

Unless you employ construction workers who moonlight as super heroes, you may need to rent one of Essex Rental's cranes to hoist those steel beams and concrete pipes. Specializing in lattice-boom crawler cranes (large, heavy-duty cranes with dynamic lifting capabilities), Essex Rental rents a fleet of some 350 Manitowoc and Liebherr brand cranes and attachments to North American construction and industrial companies and municipalities. Its cranes are typically used in the construction of power plants, petrochemical plants, water treatment and purification facilities, as well as in commercial and infrastructure construction. Essex also sells used equipment and offers crane transportation and repair services.

	Annual Growth	12/10	12/11	12/12	12/13	12/14
Sales ($mil.)	25.6%	41.5	89.6	98.3	95.5	103.4
Net income ($ mil.)	-	(9.6)	(17.1)	(12.7)	(9.6)	(11.2)
Market value ($ mil.)	(30.0%)	136.5	73.2	84.9	81.2	32.8
Employees	(1.5%)	276	273	250	236	260

ESSILOR OF AMERICA, INC.

13555 N STEMMONS FWY
DALLAS, TX 752345765
Phone: 214 496-4000
Fax: -
Web: www.essilor.com

CEO: -
CFO: -
HR: Catherine Fraley
FYE: December 31
Type: Private

Essilor of America is one of the leading providers of eyeglass lenses worldwide. It works every day to bring good vision to approximately 4.5 billion people around the world in need of vision correction. It makes and distributes optical lenses under the Crizal, Eyezen, Transitions, Xperio UV, and Varilux brands, to name a few. The company's subsidiary, Laboratories of America, is the largest and most trusted optical lab network in the US and offers a wide range of products and services to eyecare professionals across the nation. Essilor of America is a subsidiary of Paris-based Essilor International.

ESSROC HOLDINGS LLC

3251 BATH PIKE
NAZARETH, PA 180648999
Phone: 610 837-6725
Fax: -
Web: www.heidelbergmaterials.us

CEO: Alex Car
CFO: Glenn R Dalrymple
HR: Craig C Becker
FYE: December 31
Type: Private

Essroc Cement likes to mix it up. The company operates about half a dozen cement plants and other facilities in the US, Canada, and Puerto Rico, and has an annual capacity of more than 6.5 million metric tons of cement. Essroc makes bulk and packaged cement products, including portland cement, ready mix concrete, and masonry cement. Its Axim Concrete Technologies subsidiary creates chemical admixtures used to improve the performance quality of cement. Essroc's brands include BRIXMENT, Saylor's PLUS, and VELVET masonry. Its BRAVO line includes masonry chemical products. Founded in 1866 by David Saylor as Coplay Cement, the company is part of Italian cement and building materials group, Italcementi.

ESTES EXPRESS LINES

3901 W BROAD ST
RICHMOND, VA 232303962
Phone: 804 353-1900
Fax: -
Web: www.estes-express.com

CEO: Robey W Estes Jr
CFO: -
HR: Amie Underwood
FYE: December 31
Type: Private

Estes Express is the largest, privately-owned freight shipping company in North America. Its fleet of over 9,700 tractors and some 37,000 trailers operates via a network of more than 270 terminals dotting the US. The company provides reliable Less Than Truckload (LTL) freight solutions to and from all 50 states, Canada, Mexico and the Caribbean, as well as asset-based and brokered Volume LTL and Truckload shipping to regional, national, international and offshore destinations. The company was founded in 1931 when W.W. Estes bought a used Chevrolet truck to haul livestock to market for his neighbors in rural Virginia.

	Annual Growth	12/16	12/17	12/18	12/19	12/20
Sales ($mil.)	9.2%	-	2,731.5	3,159.8	3,259.1	3,559.2
Net income ($ mil.)	28.9%	-	231.2	252.1	251.6	495.0
Market value ($ mil.)	-	-	-	-	-	-
Employees	-	-	-	-	-	14,000

ETERNA THERAPEUTICS INC

10355 Cambridge Street, Suite 18A
Cambridge, MA 02141
Phone: 212 582-1199
Fax: -
Web: www.eternatx.com

NAS: ERNA
CEO: Matt Angel
CFO: Andrew Jackson
HR: Amy Biondo
FYE: December 31
Type: Public

Brooklyn ImmunoTherapeutics is a clinical stage biopharmaceutical company committed to developing IRX-2, a novel hd-IL-2 -based therapy, to treat patients with cancer. IRX-2 delivers hd-IL-2 and other key cytokines to potentially restore immune function in the tumor microenvironment, enabling the immune system to attack cancer cells. The company is also exploring opportunities to advance oncology and blood disorder therapies using leading edge gene editing/cell therapy technology through the newly acquired license from Factor Bioscience and Novellus. Its headquarters, laboratories and manufacturing facilities are located in the historic Brooklyn Army Terminal.

	Annual Growth	12/19	12/20	12/21	12/22	12/23
Sales ($mil.)	(75.8%)	19.8	5.8	-	-	0.0
Net income ($ mil.)	-	(2.0)	(4.4)	(122.3)	(24.6)	(21.7)
Market value ($ mil.)	(5.0%)	11.9	12.1	22.6	17.4	9.7
Employees	(32.7%)	39	22	10	9	8

ETHAN ALLEN INTERIORS, INC.

25 Lake Avenue Ext.
Danbury, CT 06811-5286
Phone: 203 743-8000
Fax: -
Web: www.ethanallen.com

NYS: ETD
CEO: M F Kathwari
CFO: Matthew J McNulty
HR: -
FYE: June 30
Type: Public

Ethan Allen Interiors is a leading interior design company, manufacturer, and retailer in the home furnishings marketplace. A global luxury home fashion brand, the vertically integrated company boasts ten furniture factories, including four manufacturing plants, one sawmill, one rough mill and one kiln dry lumberyard in the US, two manufacturing plants in Mexico, and one manufacturing plant in Honduras. The company's products include case goods (wood furniture, such as beds, dressers, and tables), upholstery items (sofas, recliners), and accessories (wall decor, lighting). These products are sold through over 290 Ethan Allen stores located primarily in the US. More than half of its stores are operated by independent dealers who are required to deal exclusively in Ethan Allen products and follow company guidelines.

	Annual Growth	06/19	06/20	06/21	06/22	06/23
Sales ($mil.)	1.5%	746.7	589.8	685.2	817.8	791.4
Net income ($ mil.)	42.4%	25.7	8.9	60.0	103.3	105.8
Market value ($ mil.)	7.6%	534.0	300.0	699.8	512.4	717.1
Employees	(6.5%)	4,900	3,369	4,188	4,239	3,748

ETNA DISTRIBUTORS, LLC

4901 CLAY AVE SW
GRAND RAPIDS, MI 495483074
Phone: 616 245-4373
Fax: –
Web: www.etnasupply.com

CEO: David L Potgeter
CFO: –
HR: Julie Pardoe
FYE: December 31
Type: Private

Etna distributes equipment and supplies for residential and commercial plumbing, pipe, water meters, fire hydrants, and the related support services. It operates through more than 20 locations in Michigan, Wisconsin, Indiana, and Ohio. The company also offers related services, such as custom pipe flaring and threading, and welding services. Customers include contractors, engineers, architects, homeowners, residential, and commercial industries. The company works with market-leading brands such as Apollo, BASF, Copperhead, Dearborn, Ford, Kohler, and Wolverine, among others. Etna Supply was founded in 1965.

	Annual Growth	12/08	12/09	12/10	12/11	12/12
Sales ($mil.)	4.4%	–	–	130.2	132.8	141.8
Net income ($ mil.)	(51.8%)	–	–	2.9	0.8	0.7
Market value ($ mil.)	–	–	–	–	–	–
Employees	–	–	–	–	–	285

ETP LEGACY LP

8111 WESTCHESTER DR STE 600
DALLAS, TX 752256140
Phone: 214 981-0700
Fax: –
Web: –

CEO: Kelcy L Warren
CFO: Martin Salinas Jr
HR: –
FYE: December 31
Type: Private

Energy Transfer Partners transfers energy in the form of natural gas, natural gas liquids (NGLs) and crude oil across the US. The company operates more than 71,000 miles of intrastate and interstate natural gas, natural gas liquids, refined products, and crude oil pipelines pipelines and related storage assets. Energy Transfer Partners also operates gas gathering pipelines, gas processing plants and more than two dozen gas treating facilities. In 2017, parent company Energy Transfer Equity merged midstream assets of its Sunoco Logistics subsidiary into Energy Transfer Partners.

ETSY INC

117 Adams Street
Brooklyn, NY 11201
Phone: 718 880-3660
Fax: –
Web: www.etsy.com

NMS: ETSY
CEO: Josh Silverman
CFO: Rachel Glaser
HR: –
FYE: December 31
Type: Public

Etsy operates two-sided online marketplaces that connect millions of passionate and creative buyers and sellers worldwide. Its top six retail categories are homewares and home furnishings, jewelry and personal accessories, craft supplies, apparel, toys and games, and paper and party supplies, the company offers over 100 million items to a global community of approximately 95.1 million active buyers around the world. Its primary marketplace, Etsy.com, is the global destination for unique and creative goods made by independent sellers, its other marketplaces are Reverb, Depop, and Elo7. The company's six core geographic markets include the US, the UK, Canada, Australia, Germany, and France. Most of the company's revenue comes from the US.

	Annual Growth	12/19	12/20	12/21	12/22	12/23
Sales ($mil.)	35.4%	818.4	1,725.6	2,329.1	2,566.1	2,748.4
Net income ($ mil.)	33.8%	95.9	349.2	493.5	(694.3)	307.6
Market value ($ mil.)	16.3%	5,274.8	21,184	26,069	14,262	9,650.5
Employees	18.2%	1,240	1,414	2,402	2,790	2,420

EUGENE WATER & ELECTRIC BOARD

4200 ROOSEVELT BLVD
EUGENE, OR 974026520
Phone: 541 685-7000
Fax: –
Web: www.eweb.org

CEO: Frank Lawson
CFO: –
HR: Kira Hutchens
FYE: December 31
Type: Private

"Power (and water) to the people" is the the belief and practice of Eugene Water & Electric Board (EWEB), the source of power and water for residents and businesses in Eugene, Oregon. The utility is one of Oregon's largest municipal utilities. It has more than 89,000 electric customers, and about 52,000 water customers. EWEB generates 110 MW of capacity at its hydroelectric and fossil-fueled power plants; it gets the rest of its power supply from other generators, including the Bonneville Power Administration. The utility gets its water supply from the McKenzie River.

EURO GROUP OF COMPANIES INC

10 Midland Avenue
Port Chester, NY 10573
Phone: 914 937-3900
Fax: –
Web: www.eugro.com

CEO: –
CFO: –
HR: –
FYE: December 31
Type: Public

Eura gonna like the way Euro Group of Companies (formerly ICT Technologies) can help improve your communication, save gas, and keep you entertained. The company operates through three businesses: The EuroPhone division provides pre-paid mobile phone and calling services, as well as mobile hand sets under the EugroWorld SIM and Clear Choice brands; EuroSpeed manufactures motor scooters, ATVs, and motorcycles; and EuroKool makes consumer electronics (plasma TVs, laptops, digital cameras, power generators, etc.). Founded in 1999, the Euro Group of Companies has offices and manufacturing and distribution facilities in China, Greece, the US, and several European countries.

	Annual Growth	12/06	12/07	12/08	12/09	12/10
Sales ($mil.)	2.2%	0.2	0.1	2.7	0.2	0.2
Net income ($ mil.)	–	(0.4)	(1.3)	(1.4)	(1.1)	(1.8)
Market value ($ mil.)	(47.1%)	16.1	6.9	36.9	9.2	1.3
Employees	–	–	11	15	5	6

EUROFINS LANCASTER LABORATORIES, INC.

2425 NEW HOLLAND PIKE
LANCASTER, PA 176015946
Phone: 717 656-2300
Fax: –
Web: www.eurofinsus.com

CEO: Timothy S Oostdyk
CFO: –
HR: Margaret Stoltzfus
FYE: December 31
Type: Private

Don't buy those Bunsen burners. Let Lancaster Laboratories handle it. One of the largest contract laboratories in the country, it provides chemical and microbiological analytical, research, and testing services in the pharmaceutical and environmental sciences to commercial customers in several industries. Customers can access their analytical data around the clock on the Web through the company's LabAccess service. It also offers staffing services to clients involved in long-term projects through its Professional Scientific Staffing division. Founded in 1961, Lancaster Laboratories serves many global FORTUNE 500 companies. Thermo Fisher Scientific sold the company to Eurofins Scientific in 2011.

	Annual Growth	12/11	12/12	12/13	12/14	12/15
Sales ($mil.)	(7.7%)	–	–	146.9	153.7	125.1
Net income ($ mil.)	4.8%	–	–	11.4	16.1	12.6
Market value ($ mil.)	–	–	–	–	–	–
Employees	–	–	–	–	–	2,887

EURONAV MI II INC.

299 PARK AVE FL 2
NEW YORK, NY 101710299
Phone: 212 763-5600
Fax: –
Web: www.generalmaritimecorp.com

CEO: –
CFO: –
HR: –
FYE: December 31
Type: Private

Black gold on the deep blue generates the green for Gener8 Maritime (formerly General Maritime). A leading operator of mid-sized tankers, it transports crude oil and refined petroleum products, mainly in the Atlantic Basin but also in the Black Sea. Its fleet of 25 operational double-hull tankers includes 11 Suezmax, 4 Aframax, 2 Panamax, 1 Handymax, (totaling 4.5 million DWT) and 21 Very Large Crude Carriers (VLCCs) under contract to be built. Gener8 Maritime deploys its vessels on the spot market (short term/single voyage) and under long-term charter. Customers include major oil companies Chevron, ConocoPhillips, and Exxon Mobil. General Maritime merged with Navig8 Crude Tankers and went public in 2015.

EURONET WORLDWIDE INC.

NMS: EEFT

11400 Tomahawk Creek Parkway, Suite 300
Leawood, KS 66211
Phone: 913 327-4200
Fax: 913 327-1921
Web: www.euronetworldwide.com

CEO: –
CFO: –
HR: –
FYE: December 31
Type: Public

Euronet Worldwide is a leading electronic payments processing provider. The company offers ATM and POS services, prepaid mobile top-up, as well as cash-based and online global money transfer and payment services. It operates three primary businesses: epay (which sells prepaid mobile airtime and related products and services), EFT (electronic financial transaction processing, software, and ATM/POS management services); and consumer-to-consumer money transfer. Founded in 1994, Euronet operates in approximately 200 countries and its top markets are the US and Germany. It generates majority of its sales in Europe, but US is still its largest single market.

	Annual Growth	12/19	12/20	12/21	12/22	12/23
Sales ($mil.)	7.6%	2,750.1	2,482.7	2,995.4	3,358.7	3,688.0
Net income ($ mil.)	(5.2%)	346.7	(3.4)	70.7	231.0	279.7
Market value ($ mil.)	(10.4%)	7,212.8	6,634.1	5,455.4	4,320.5	4,646.0
Employees	6.8%	7,700	8,100	8,800	9,500	10,000

EVANGELICAL COMMUNITY HOSPITAL

1 HOSPITAL DR
LEWISBURG, PA 178379350
Phone: 570 522-2000
Fax: –
Web: www.evanhospital.com

CEO: John Meckley
CFO: Christine Martin
HR: Angela Hummel
FYE: June 30
Type: Private

Evangelical Community Hospital brings the good news of community health to residents in central Pennsylvania. The hospital provides a wide range of medical services to communities in the Susquehanna Valley. Among its specialized services are home health care and hospice, maternity, oncology, rehabilitation, and pediatrics. The hospital delivers more than 1,000 babies annually and treats more than 30,000 patients in its emergency department each year. Its outreach network includes family practice offices and other medical services. Despite its name, the hospital has no affiliation with any religious organization.

	Annual Growth	06/18	06/19	06/20	06/21	06/22
Sales ($mil.)	12.0%	–	211.0	205.3	278.6	296.8
Net income ($ mil.)	–	–	14.9	13.5	(0.4)	(11.9)
Market value ($ mil.)	–	–	–	–	–	–
Employees	–	–	–	–	–	1,360

EVANS & SUTHERLAND COMPUTER CORPORATION

770 S KOMAS DR
SALT LAKE CITY, UT 841081207
Phone: 801 588-1000
Fax: –
Web: www.es.com

CEO: Jonathan A Shaw
CFO: Paul L Dailey
HR: –
FYE: December 31
Type: Private

Evans & Sutherland Computer (E&S) makes products that can impartially be described as stellar. The company provides hardware and software used in digital planetariums and other theaters. Its products include laser projectors, domed projection screens, and complete planetarium packages. The company also produces planetarium content. E&S sells its visual systems to theaters and schools; its domes are additionally marketed to casinos, theme parks, and military contractors. The company counts Disney, Griffith Observatory, IMAX, Texas A&M University, and Universal Studios among its customers. E&S gets more than half of its sales in the US.

	Annual Growth	12/15	12/16	12/17	12/18	12/19
Sales ($mil.)	(5.6%)	–	32.9	30.5	37.2	27.7
Net income ($ mil.)	–	–	1.7	1.5	3.7	(1.6)
Market value ($ mil.)	–	–	–	–	–	–
Employees	–	–	–	–	–	96

EVANS BANCORP, INC.

ASE: EVBN

6460 Main Street
Williamsville, NY 14221
Phone: 716 926-2000
Fax: –
Web: www.evansbancorp.com

CEO: David J Nasca
CFO: –
HR: –
FYE: December 31
Type: Public

Evans National Bank wants to take care of Buffalo's bills. The subsidiary of Evans Bancorp operates about a dozen branches in western New York (including Buffalo). The bank primarily uses funds gathered from deposits to originate commercial and residential real estate loans (more than 70% of its loan portfolio) and to invest in securities. Subsidiaries include ENB Insurance Agency, which sells property/casualty insurance; ENB Associates, offering mutual funds and annuities to bank customers; and Evans National Leasing, which provides financing for business equipment throughout the US. In 2009 Evans Bancorp acquired the assets and single branch of the failed Waterford Village Bank in Clarence, New York.

	Annual Growth	12/19	12/20	12/21	12/22	12/23
Assets ($mil.)	9.6%	1,460.2	2,044.1	2,210.6	2,178.5	2,108.7
Net income ($ mil.)	9.6%	17.0	11.2	24.0	22.4	24.5
Market value ($ mil.)	(5.8%)	220.5	151.5	221.6	205.6	173.4
Employees	4.7%	250	309	378	379	300

EVENT NETWORK, LLC

9606 AERO DR STE 1000
SAN DIEGO, CA 921231869
Phone: 858 222-6100
Fax: –
Web: www.eventnetwork.com

CEO: –
CFO: –
HR: Courtney Fong
FYE: September 27
Type: Private

Event Network would like you to exit through the gift shop. The company (doing business as e|n) manages the retail gift shops on behalf of museums, zoos, aquariums, gardens, and other public cultural attractions. It designs and supplies stores with distinctive merchandise, such as apparel, toys and games, coffee mugs, key chains, jewelry, books, and art. e|n's partner network includes more than 70 cultural attractions, including the American Museum of Natural History in New York City, the Gettysburg National Battlefield Museum, the Philadelphia Zoo, and the Shedd Aquarium in Chicago. It also operates the e-commerce websites of more than 55 attractions. e|n was founded in 1998 by Larry Gilbert and Helen Sherman.

	Annual Growth	09/05	09/06	09/07	09/08	09/09
Sales ($mil.)	20.5%	–	–	73.5	92.5	106.7
Net income ($ mil.)	83.5%	–	–	1.7	2.8	5.6
Market value ($ mil.)	–	–	–	–	–	–
Employees	–	–	–	–	–	900

EVERBANK FINANCIAL CORP

501 RIVERSIDE AVE
JACKSONVILLE, FL 322024934
Phone: 904 281-6000
Fax: –
Web: –

CEO: –
CFO: –
HR: –
FYE: December 31
Type: Private

TIAA Bank, a division of TIAA, FSB, provides nationwide banking services to consumer, commercial and institutional clients through a variety of channels, including online and mobile applications, as well as its Florida-based financial centers.

EVERCORE INC
NYS: EVR

55 East 52nd Street
New York, NY 10055
Phone: 212 857-3100
Fax: 212 857-3101
Web: www.evercore.com

CEO: John S Weinberg
CFO: Timothy Lalonde
HR: –
FYE: December 31
Type: Public

Evercore is the leading independent investment banking advisory firm in the world based on the dollar volume of announced worldwide merger and acquisition (M&A) transactions. The company provides advisory services on mergers and mergers and acquisitions, strategic shareholder advisory, restructurings, and capital structure to corporate clients. Boasting some $10.5 billion in assets under management, the company's investment management business principally manages and invests capital for clients including institutional investors and private equity businesses. Evercore also makes private equity investments. Beyond the US, the company operates globally through subsidiaries such as Evercore Partners in the UK. Evercore was founded in 1995.

	Annual Growth	12/19	12/20	12/21	12/22	12/23
Sales ($mil.)	4.8%	2,008.7	2,263.9	3,289.5	2,762.0	2,425.9
Net income ($ mil.)	(3.7%)	297.4	350.6	740.1	476.5	255.5
Market value ($ mil.)	23.0%	2,824.0	4,141.5	5,131.6	4,120.4	6,461.2
Employees	3.7%	1,900	1,800	1,950	2,120	2,195

EVERGLADES STEEL CORPORATION

5901 NW 74TH AVE
MIAMI, FL 331663741
Phone: 305 591-9460
Fax: –
Web: www.evergladessteel.com

CEO: Orlando A Gomez
CFO: –
HR: –
FYE: December 31
Type: Private

Service center operator Everglades Steel processes and distributes steel products such as angles, channels, flat bars and strips, pipe fittings, stainless steel, and tubing. It also offers aluminum and various alloy products; services include galvanizing and shearing and sawing. Everglades Steel serves customers in the bridge construction, cement, metal fabrication, mining, and sugar mill industries.

	Annual Growth	12/09	12/10	12/11	12/12	12/13
Sales ($mil.)	(8.2%)	–	–	22.4	21.8	18.9
Net income ($ mil.)	(1.1%)	–	–	2.7	3.0	2.6
Market value ($ mil.)	–	–	–	–	–	–
Employees	–	–	–	–	–	22

EVERGREEN FS, INC

402 N HERSHEY RD
BLOOMINGTON, IL 617043546
Phone: 877 963-2392
Fax: –
Web: www.evergreen-fs.com

CEO: Dan Kelley
CFO: –
HR: –
FYE: August 31
Type: Private

Evergreen FS is an agricultural cooperative serving the needs of northern Illinois farmers. The co-op provides a full range of farm supplies and services including agronomy, feed, seed, fertilizer, fuel, financing, and marketing advice and products. The group also operates a handful of grain elevators as part of its operations. It specializes in the production of corn, soybeans, and wheat. The co-op boasts some 13,000 member/owners that operate businesses on farmland in the counties of McLean, Woodford, and Livingston. Evergreen FS is a member of the GROWMARK system.

	Annual Growth	08/05	08/06	08/07	08/09	08/10
Sales ($mil.)	6.4%	–	–	204.9	–	246.7
Net income ($ mil.)	26.5%	–	–	3.8	–	7.8
Market value ($ mil.)	–	–	–	–	–	–
Employees	–	–	–	–	–	240

EVERGREEN STATE COLLEGE

2700 EVERGREEN PKWY NW
OLYMPIA, WA 985050005
Phone: 360 867-6000
Fax: –
Web: www.evergreen.edu

CEO: –
CFO: –
HR: –
FYE: June 30
Type: Private

Puget Sounders can earn their sheepskins at The Evergreen State College. The public liberal arts and sciences college, the largest of its type in Washington state, offers a variety of undergraduate degrees as well as graduate-level programs in environmental studies, public administration, and education. Evergreen is known for its unusual approach to learning; students enroll in comprehensive programs rather than a series of separate classes and courses are taught by teams of two to four professors. Students then receive "narrative" evaluations rather than traditional letter grades. Tuition per year is $5,133 (residents) and $16,440 (non-residents).

	Annual Growth	06/04	06/05	06/06	06/07	06/08
Sales ($mil.)	–	–	–	(322.8)	56.5	56.7
Net income ($ mil.)	20379.1%	–	–	0.0	6.6	20.8
Market value ($ mil.)	–	–	–	–	–	–
Employees	–	–	–	–	–	580

EVERGY INC
NMS: EVRG

1200 Main Street
Kansas City, MO 64105
Phone: 816 556-2200
Fax: –
Web: www.evergyinc.com

CEO: David A Campbell
CFO: Kirkland B Andrews
HR: –
FYE: December 31
Type: Public

Evergy, Inc. is a public utility holding company which primarily operates through its wholly-owned direct subsidiaries Evergy Kansas Central, Evergy Metro, Evergy Missouri West, and Evergy Transmission Company. Evergy Kansas Central owns a 50% interest in Prairie Wind Transmission, LLC, which is a joint venture between Evergy Kansas Central and subsidiaries of AEP and Berkshire Hathaway Energy Company. Its subsidiaries are an integrated, regulated electric utility that conduct business in their respective service territories using the name Evergy. Joseph S. Chick, Lysander R. Moore and Judge William Holmes founded Evergy in 1881.

	Annual Growth	12/19	12/20	12/21	12/22	12/23
Sales ($mil.)	1.7%	5,147.8	4,913.4	5,586.7	5,859.1	5,508.2
Net income ($ mil.)	2.2%	669.9	618.3	879.7	752.7	731.3
Market value ($ mil.)	(5.4%)	14,953	12,752	15,762	14,457	11,992
Employees	(4.0%)	5,475	5,133	4,930	4,512	4,658

EVERI HOLDINGS INC — NYS: EVRI

7250 S. Tenaya Way, Suite 100
Las Vegas, NV 89113
Phone: 800 833-7110
Fax: –
Web: www.everi.com

CEO: Michael D Rumbolz
CFO: Randy L Taylor
HR: Mark Taylor
FYE: December 31
Type: Public

If you're losing your shirt at the casino tables, Global Cash Access can get you more money on the spot. The company provides such services as ATM cash withdrawals, credit- and debit-card advances, and check guarantee to the gaming industry in the US, Canada, Europe, Central America, the Caribbean, and Asia. The company provides services to some 1,000 casinos, such as Foxwoods Resort Casino. Global Cash Access also has developed cashless gaming systems including special ticket vouchers and systems that allow players to access funds without leaving their gaming machines. Other services include casino marketing and patron credit information through its QuikReports and CentralCredit database.

	Annual Growth	12/19	12/20	12/21	12/22	12/23
Sales ($mil.)	10.9%	533.2	383.7	660.4	782.5	807.8
Net income ($ mil.)	50.2%	16.5	(81.7)	152.9	120.5	84.0
Market value ($ mil.)	(4.3%)	1,124.6	1,156.4	1,787.8	1,201.6	943.7
Employees	12.0%	1,400	1,300	1,550	2,000	2,200

EVERSOURCE ENERGY — NYS: ES

300 Cadwell Drive
Springfield, MA 01104
Phone: 800 286-5000
Fax: –
Web: www.eversource.com

CEO: Joseph R Nolan Jr
CFO: John M Moreira
HR: Christine M Carmody
FYE: December 31
Type: Public

The largest energy delivery company in New England, Eversource Energy serves roughly 4.4 million customers in via its seven distinct utility companies in Connecticut, Massachusetts, and New Hampshire. Eversource delivers its energy through more than 60,000 overhead and underground lines and covers over 3,200 square miles of natural gas distribution. Its electricity-focused utility companies include Public Service Company of New Hampshire (PSNH), The Connecticut Light and Power Company, and NSTAR Electric Company. CL&P, NSTAR Electric and PSNH also serve New England customers through Eversource Energy's electric transmission business. Along with NSTAR Gas, EGMA and Yankee Gas, each is doing business as Eversource Energy in its respective service territory.

	Annual Growth	12/19	12/20	12/21	12/22	12/23
Sales ($mil.)	8.7%	8,526.5	8,904.4	9,863.1	12,289	11,911
Net income ($ mil.)	–	909.1	1,205.2	1,220.5	1,404.9	(442.2)
Market value ($ mil.)	(7.7%)	29,735	30,239	31,801	29,305	21,574
Employees	5.4%	8,234	9,299	9,227	9,626	10,171

EVERSOURCE ENERGY SERVICE COMPANY

56 PROSPECT ST
HARTFORD, CT 061032818
Phone: 800 286-5000
Fax: –
Web: www.eversource.com

CEO: James Judge
CFO: Philip Lembo
HR: Jane Bryggare
FYE: December 31
Type: Private

Northeast Utilities Service Company (NUSCO) provides support and reports for its cohorts. The company was created in 1966 to centralize corporate activities for Northeast Utilities (renamed Eversource Energy). NUSCO acts as an agent and offers centralized administrative services not only for its parent company, Northeast Utilities, but all of its subsidiaries (Connecticut Light and Power, Public Service Company of New Hampshire, Western Massachusetts Electric, and Yankee Gas Services Company) as well. NUSCO duties include accounting, financial, legal, operational, information technology, engineering, planning, and purchasing services.

EVERSPIN TECHNOLOGIES INC — NMS: MRAM

5670 W. Chandler Boulevard, Suite 130
Chandler, AZ 85226
Phone: 480 347-1111
Fax: –
Web: www.everspin.com

CEO: Sanjeev Aggarwal
CFO: Anuj Aggarwal
HR: –
FYE: December 31
Type: Public

EverSpin Technologies was spun off from Freescale Semiconductor in 2008 to provide magnetoresistive random-access memory (MRAM) chips. EverSpin will focus on finding new applications for MRAM, a relatively new technology that Freescale began producing in 2006. The company was given Freescale's MRAM R&D, intellectual property, and some 200 patents to continue making 1Mb, 2Mb, and 4Mb chips. EverSpin is backed by several venture capital firms -- Draper Fisher Jurvetson, Epic Ventures, Lux Capital, New Venture Partners, and Sigma Partners. Freescale will still own a portion of the new company. EverSpin is located in Freescale's 8-inch wafer manufacturing facility in Chandler, Arizona.

	Annual Growth	12/19	12/20	12/21	12/22	12/23
Sales ($mil.)	14.2%	37.5	42.0	55.1	60.0	63.8
Net income ($ mil.)	–	(14.7)	(8.5)	4.3	6.1	9.1
Market value ($ mil.)	14.5%	110.9	97.0	238.2	117.2	190.6
Employees	(1.5%)	88	89	75	74	83

EVERTEC, INC. — NYS: EVTC

Cupey Center Building, Road 176, Kilometer 1.3
San Juan, PR 00926
Phone: 787 759-9999
Fax: –
Web: www.evertecinc.com

CEO: –
CFO: –
HR: –
FYE: December 31
Type: Public

Evertec is a leading full-service transaction-processing business in Puerto Rico, Latin America and the Caribbean, providing a broad range of merchant acquiring, payment services and business process management services. Evertec owns and operates the ATH network, one of the leading personal identification number (PIN) debit networks in Latin America. It manages a system of electronic payment networks and offers a comprehensive suite of services for core banking, cash processing, and fulfillment in Puerto Rico, that process approximately 6 billion transactions annually. Founded in 1998, Evertec went public in the US in 2013. Serving some 25 countries, the company generates about 80% of its revenue in Puerto Rico.

	Annual Growth	12/19	12/20	12/21	12/22	12/23
Sales ($mil.)	9.3%	487.4	510.6	589.8	618.4	694.7
Net income ($ mil.)	(6.3%)	103.5	104.4	161.1	239.0	79.7
Market value ($ mil.)	4.7%	2,227.9	2,573.5	3,271.2	2,119.3	2,679.6
Employees	21.4%	2,300	2,500	2,500	2,700	5,000

EVERYDAY HEALTH, INC.

345 HUDSON ST RM 1600
NEW YORK, NY 100147120
Phone: 646 728-9500
Fax: –
Web: www.everydayhealth.com

CEO: –
CFO: –
HR: –
FYE: December 31
Type: Private

Everyday Health wants to be your virtual apple a day. The online health information provider operates websites that give free and subscription-based advice regarding fitness, nutrition, and treatment options to some 44 million monthly visitors. Its websites -- such as EverydayHealth.com, and JillianMichaels.com -- allow consumers to search health topics (including symptoms) and join online communities. It generates revenues primarily from advertising fees, sponsorships, and subscriptions. Everyday Health was acquired by J2 Global in 2016.

EVI INDUSTRIES INC
ASE: EVI

4500 Biscayne Blvd., Suite 340
Miami, FL 33137
Phone: 305 402-9300
Fax: –
Web: www.evi-ind.com

CEO: Henry M Nahmad
CFO: Robert H Lazar
HR: –
FYE: June 30
Type: Public

EnviroStar (formerly DRYCLEAN USA) is anything but hard pressed. The firm franchises and licenses more than 400 retail dry cleaners in three US states, the Caribbean, and Latin America through its DRYCLEAN USA unit. However, most of its sales are generated by subsidiary Steiner-Atlantic, which sells coin-operated laundry machines, steam boilers, and other laundry equipment; most are sold under the Aero-Tech, Green-Jet, and Multi-Jet names to some 750 customers and include independent dry cleaners, hotels, cruise lines, and hospitals. The company was founded in 1963 under the name Metro-Tel Corp. It changed its name to DRYCLEAN USA in 1999.

	Annual Growth	06/19	06/20	06/21	06/22	06/23
Sales ($mil.)	11.6%	228.3	235.8	242.0	267.3	354.2
Net income ($ mil.)	26.9%	3.7	0.8	8.4	4.1	9.7
Market value ($ mil.)	(12.9%)	481.3	273.1	357.2	125.6	276.7
Employees	10.4%	475	493	526	640	705

EVOFEM, INC.

12400 HIGH BLUFF DR # 600
SAN DIEGO, CA 921303077
Phone: 858 550-1900
Fax: –
Web: www.evofem.com

CEO: Saundra Pelletier
CFO: Justin File
HR: Katie Siegmund
FYE: December 31
Type: Private

Evofem (formerly Instead) hopes that women adopt its alternative to pads and tampons. Its primary product, the Instead Softcup, is a feminine hygiene product that sits inside a woman's body and collects, rather than absorbs, menstrual flow. Developed by a group of reproductive health scientists, the Softcup is sold in major US drugstores (including chain stores Wal-Mart and Target) and through its Web site. It's also distributed in Australia, Belgium, Canada, the Netherlands, Poland, and about a half-dozen other countries worldwide. Instead is also researching the possibility of using a version of its Softcup as a contraceptive device.

EVOKE PHARMA INC
NAS: EVOK

420 Stevens Avenue, Suite 230
Solana Beach, CA 92075
Phone: 858 345-1494
Fax: –
Web: www.evokepharma.com

CEO: David A Gonyer
CFO: –
HR: –
FYE: December 31
Type: Public

Who says nasal spray is just for sinus problems? Evoke Pharma is developing a nasal spray to treat gastrointestinal problems in women who also suffer from diabetes. It main drug candidate is designed to treat symptoms of gastroparesis, a common problem for diabetes patients, where the stomach takes too long to digest food. The nasal spray allows the drug to bypass the digestive system and directly enter the bloodstream to reduce symptoms such as bloating, nausea, and lack of appetite. Evoke Pharma bought the rights to the drug from Questcor in 2007; Phase III trials will begin by 2014. Evoke Pharma went public in 2013, raising $25 million in its IPO, which it will use to further fund drug development.

	Annual Growth	12/19	12/20	12/21	12/22	12/23
Sales ($mil.)	–	–	0.0	1.6	2.5	5.2
Net income ($ mil.)	–	(7.1)	(13.2)	(8.5)	(8.2)	(7.8)
Market value ($ mil.)	(10.3%)	5.4	8.6	1.8	9.0	3.5
Employees	(5.4%)	5	5	4	4	4

EVOLUTION PETROLEUM CORP
ASE: EPM

1155 Dairy Ashford Road, Suite 425
Houston, TX 77079
Phone: 713 935-0122
Fax: 713 935-0199
Web: www.evolutionpetroleum.com

CEO: Kelly W Loyd
CFO: Ryan Stash
HR: –
FYE: June 30
Type: Public

Just as petroleum and natural gas evolves from old living forms, Evolution Petroleum has evolved by producing these ancient hydrocarbons. The company operates oil and gas producing fields in Louisiana. One method it uses is gas flooding, which uses carbon dioxide to free up trapped oil deposits. Assets include a CO2 enhanced oil recovery -project in Louisiana's Delhi Field to extend the life and ultimate recoveries of wells with oil or associated water production. It reported more than 10 million barrels of oil equivalent proved reserves in fiscal 2019. The company was formed in 2003.

	Annual Growth	06/19	06/20	06/21	06/22	06/23
Sales ($mil.)	31.3%	43.2	29.6	32.7	108.9	128.5
Net income ($ mil.)	23.0%	15.4	5.9	(16.4)	32.6	35.2
Market value ($ mil.)	3.1%	237.7	93.1	164.9	181.5	268.3
Employees	28.8%	4	4	5	8	11

EVOLVE TRANSITION INFRASTRUCTURE LP
ASE: SNMP

1360 Post Oak Blvd, Suite 2400
Houston, TX 77056
Phone: 713 783-8000
Fax: –
Web: www.evolvetransition.com

CEO: Gerald F Willinger
CFO: Charles C Ward
HR: –
FYE: December 31
Type: Public

Constellation Energy Partners' domain is decidedly more terrestrial than stellar. A spin off from Constellation Energy, the company is a coalbed methane exploration and production company that operates in Alabama's Black Warrior Basin (one of the oldest and most lucrative coalbed methane basins in the US), the Cherokee Basin in Kansas and Oklahoma, and the Woodford Shale in the Arkoma Basin in Oklahoma. In 2010 Constellation Energy Partners reported proved reserves of 221 billion cu. ft. of natural gas equivalent. That year the company operated 87% of the more than 2,780 wells in which it held an interest.

	Annual Growth	12/18	12/19	12/20	12/21	12/22
Sales ($mil.)	(18.9%)	83.6	76.6	57.0	51.5	36.1
Net income ($ mil.)	–	15.7	(51.1)	(118.8)	(154.5)	(53.1)
Market value ($ mil.)	–	–	–	–	–	–
Employees	18.9%	6	9	13	15	12

EVOLVEWARE, INC.

4677 OLD IRONSIDES DR STE 240
SANTA CLARA, CA 950541825
Phone: 408 748-8301
Fax: –
Web: www.evolveware.com

CEO: –
CFO: –
HR: –
FYE: December 31
Type: Private

EvolveWare can help you with the evolution of your enterprise hardware and software. The company develops a wide array of software for its corporate clients, including e-commerce, data storage, financial, and networking applications. Its products are typically used to migrate legacy hardware and software to newer open-source applications providing discovery, extraction, analysis, and documentation of applications and databases. Clients include government agencies and companies of all sizes. EvolveWare was founded in 2001, and operates from Silicon Valley headquarters with operations in India.

	Annual Growth	12/03	12/04	12/05	12/12	12/13
Sales ($mil.)	57.2%	–	0.0	0.2	–	1.9
Net income ($ mil.)	76.8%	–	0.0	(0.4)	–	1.0
Market value ($ mil.)	–	–	–	–	–	–
Employees	–	–	–	–	–	78

EWING IRRIGATION PRODUCTS, INC.

3441 E HARBOUR DR
PHOENIX, AZ 850340908
Phone: 602 437-9546
Fax: –
Web: www.ewingoutdoorsupply.com

CEO: –
CFO: –
HR: –
FYE: June 25
Type: Private

Ewing Irrigation is the largest family-owned supplier of landscape and irrigation products in the country. The company supplies professional contractors with irrigation supplies, water efficient and sustainable solutions, landscape and turf products, agronomics and growing, hardscape and outdoor living, landscape lighting, water features, erosion control and more. The family-owned company also offers industry-leading training classes and events for professionals in the landscaping, sports field, golf and grower industries. The company was founded in 1922 when Atlas Lawn Sprinklers opens in San Francisco, California.

	Annual Growth	06/06	06/07	06/08	06/09	06/10
Sales ($mil.)	(7.8%)	–	–	306.7	278.9	260.8
Net income ($ mil.)	–	–	–	11.2	11.2	–
Market value ($ mil.)	–	–	–	–	–	–
Employees	–	–	–	–	–	850

EX-STUDENTS ASSOCIATION OF THE UNIVERSITY OF TEXAS

2110 SAN JACINTO BLVD
AUSTIN, TX 787121632
Phone: 512 840-4700
Fax: –
Web: www.texasexes.org

CEO: –
CFO: –
HR: –
FYE: June 30
Type: Private

All these Exes may have lived in Texas during college, but today they are spread throughout the world. The Ex-Students' Association is the alumni association for The University of Texas at Austin. The group has more than 83,000 members (Texas Exes) and some 140 chapters around the globe, though about half of those are in Texas. In addition to facilitating social gatherings for former students, the Ex-Students' Association offers career services and awards more than $2 million in scholarships annually. The group was established as the UT Alumni Association in 1885.

	Annual Growth	04/14	04/15*	06/20	06/21	06/22
Sales ($mil.)	9.6%	–	11.2	27.6	20.6	21.3
Net income ($ mil.)	17.2%	–	2.2	13.5	8.7	6.7
Market value ($ mil.)	–	–	–	–	–	–
Employees	–	–	–	–	–	38

*Fiscal year change

EXA CORPORATION

55 NETWORK DR
BURLINGTON, MA 018032765
Phone: 781 564-0200
Fax: –
Web: –

CEO: Stephen A Remondi
CFO: Richard F Gilbody
HR: Vishakha Mishra
FYE: January 31
Type: Private

Exa Corporation strives to be irresistible to its customers. A developer of engineering software for vehicle manufacturers, Exa makes digital simulation software used by engineers to enhance the performance of automobiles, trucks, trains, and off-road equipment. Its core product, PowerFLOW, can simulate structural and heating/cooling system fluid flow problems in vehicles, namely aerodynamics, thermal management, and aeroacoustics. (Aeroacoustics is the generation and transfer of sound by fluid flow.) The company sells PowerFLOW and related products in Japan, the US, and Europe through its direct sales force; it also sells in China and India through distributors. Exa went public in a 2012 IPO.

EXACT SCIENCES CORP.

NAS: EXAS

5505 Endeavor Lane
Madison, WI 53719
Phone: 608 535-8815
Fax: –
Web: www.exactsciences.com

CEO: Kevin T Conroy
CFO: Jeffrey T Elliott
HR: –
FYE: December 31
Type: Public

Exact Science is a leading, global, advanced cancer diagnostics company. It develops non-invasive tests for the early detection of colorectal cancer and precancerous lesions. Its flagship screening product, the Cologuard test, is a patient-friendly, non-invasive, stool-based DNA (sDNA) screening test that utilizes a multi-target approach to detect DNA and hemoglobin biomarkers associated with colorectal cancer and pre-cancer. Its Oncotype test is consist of its flagship line of Oncotype DX gene expression tests for breast, prostate and colon cancers. Its GEM ExTra test, one of the most comprehensive genomic (DNA) and transcriptomic (RNA) panels available that provides a complete biological picture of certain refractory, rare, or aggressive cancers. Almost all of its revenue comes from the US.

	Annual Growth	12/19	12/20	12/21	12/22	12/23
Sales ($mil.)	30.0%	876.3	1,491.4	1,767.1	2,084.3	2,499.8
Net income ($ mil.)	–	(84.0)	(848.5)	(595.6)	(623.5)	(204.1)
Market value ($ mil.)	(5.4%)	16,773	24,029	14,116	8,979.3	13,417
Employees	12.6%	4,110	5,000	6,500	6,400	6,600

EXACTECH, INC.

2320 NW 66TH CT
GAINESVILLE, FL 326531630
Phone: 352 377-1140
Fax: –
Web: www.exac.com

CEO: Darin Johnson
CFO: Tony Collins
HR: –
FYE: December 31
Type: Private

Exactech is a global medical device company that develops and markets joint replacement implants, surgical instruments and smart technologies that help surgeons worldwide make patients more mobile. Exactech is defining a new level of partnership in patient care with Active Intelligence(R), a powerful platform of technologies that helps surgeons engage with patients and peers, solve challenges with predictive tools and optimize the way they perform joint replacement surgery. The company has a presence in more than 30 countries. Exactech was founded in 1985 by Dr. Bill Petty, an orthopaedic surgeon, Dr. Gary Miller, a biomedical engineer and Betty Petty.

EXAR CORPORATION

1060 RINCON CIR
SAN JOSE, CA 951311325
Phone: 669 265-6100
Fax: –
Web: www.maxlinear.com

CEO: Ryan A Benton
CFO: Keith Tainsky
HR: –
FYE: March 27
Type: Private

Exar seeks excellence in the exacting world of integrated circuits. The fabless semiconductor company's digital, analog, and mixed-signal integrated circuits (ICs) are used in networking equipment -- especially telecom infrastructure gear -- as well as in video and imaging devices, such as handheld electronics, set-top boxes, and DVRs. It also makes ICs and subsystems for the power management and datacom and storage markets, including storage optimization and network security processors. Customers include Alcatel Lucent, EMC, Huawei, Teradata, and ZTE. The company gets about 85% of its sales outside the US. The company was acquired in 2017 by MaxLinear.

EXCEL INTERIOR CONSTRUCTION CORP.

330 W 38TH ST RM 511
NEW YORK, NY 100188634
Phone: 212 627-6319
Fax: –
Web: www.excelinteriorny.com

CEO: –
CFO: –
HR: –
FYE: June 30
Type: Private

Excel Interior Construction Corporation performs residential remodeling services in New York. The Hispanic-owned enterprise was founded by president Jose Mendez, who also serves on the advisory board of The Committee for Hispanic Children and Families, Inc. (New York). Hispanic Business magazine listed Excel Interior Construction Corporation as one of the "100 Fastest-Growing Companies" in 2001.

EXCEL RAILCAR CORPORATION

28367 DAVIS PKWY STE 300
WARRENVILLE, IL 605553037
Phone: 630 657-1100
Fax: –
Web: www.excelrailcar.com

CEO: –
CFO: –
HR: –
FYE: December 31
Type: Private

Excel Railcar leases equipment such as covered hopper cars and general purpose railcars to railroad operators. Its railcars are used to transport agriculture products (corn and soybeans) as well as building materials (floor tile), cement, chemicals (petcoke), paper, and plastic pellets. Excel Railcar also offers railcar equipment management and repair services. Excel Railcar operates through six subsidiaries, including a rail car leasing company based in Mexico. The company was founded in 1980.

	Annual Growth	12/08	12/09	12/10	12/11	12/12
Sales ($mil.)	0.2%	–	7.1	6.9	7.0	7.2
Net income ($ mil.)	–	–	1.3	0.2	0.0	(0.0)
Market value ($ mil.)	–	–	–	–	–	–
Employees	–	–	–	–	–	7

EXCELA HEALTH HOLDING COMPANY, INC.

532 W PITTSBURGH ST
GREENSBURG, PA 156012239
Phone: 724 832-4000
Fax: –
Web: www.excelahealth.org

CEO: Ken Defurio
CFO: –
HR: Chelsea Trout
FYE: June 30
Type: Private

Excela Health's hospital network hopes to rank as excellent health care providers to residents of southwestern Pennsylvania. Hospitals within the health system, which serves Pennsylvania's Westmoreland, Indiana, and Fayette counties, include Westmoreland Hospital, Latrobe Hospital, and Frick Hospital. Combined, they provide some 655 acute care beds. In addition to general medical and surgical care, the hospitals offer outpatient and specialty treatment in such areas as heart disease, cancer, and women's health. The system operates ancillary businesses as well, including a home health and hospice agency, surgery centers, primary and specialty care clinics, and an ambulance service.

	Annual Growth	06/02	06/03	06/06	06/20	06/21
Sales ($mil.)	(14.3%)	–	194.0	11.2	10.6	11.9
Net income ($ mil.)	–	–	(9.1)	3.7	5.9	5.1
Market value ($ mil.)	–	–	–	–	–	–
Employees	–	–	–	–	–	2,548

EXCHANGE BANK (SANTA ROSA, CA)

NBB: EXSR

545 Fourth Street
Santa Rosa, CA 95401
Phone: 707 524-3000
Fax: –
Web: www.exchangebank.com

CEO: Gary T Hartwick
CFO: Greg Jahn
HR: Cythia Conway
FYE: December 31
Type: Public

Exchange Bank serves personal and business customers from some 20 branch offices throughout Sonoma County, California. It also has a branch in nearby Placer County. The bank provides standard products, including checking and savings accounts, Visa credit cards, online banking, and a variety of real estate, business, and consumer loans. It also offers investment services, such as wealth management, personal trust administration, employee benefits plans, and individual retirement accounts. Effective early 2014 Exchange Bank is on its eighth president since its inception in 1890. The Doyle Trust, which was established by co-founder Frank Doyle, owns a majority of the bank.

	Annual Growth	12/17	12/18	12/19	12/20	12/21
Assets ($mil.)	8.2%	2,584.1	2,654.0	2,673.1	3,139.1	3,536.8
Net income ($ mil.)	16.9%	19.5	38.5	36.5	33.7	36.4
Market value ($ mil.)	0.6%	260.6	282.9	306.9	253.7	266.5
Employees	–	–	–	–	–	–

EXCO RESOURCES INC

NBB: EXCE

12377 Merit Drive, Suite 1700
Dallas, TX 75251
Phone: 214 368-2084
Fax: –
Web: www.excoresources.com

CEO: Harold L Hickey
CFO: Tyler Farquharson
HR: –
FYE: December 31
Type: Public

Exco Resources is an independent oil and natural gas company engaged in onshore oil and gas exploration exploitation, acquisition, development and production in the US. Its operations are primarily in Texas, Louisiana and the Appalachia region. The company's position in South Texas includes approximately 48,500 net acres, of which approximately 95% are held-by-production. It focuses on the exploitation and development of shale resources, targeting shale plays like Eagle Ford, Haynesville, and Marcellus, as well as leasing and acquisition opportunities. The company is headquartered in Dallas, Texas.

	Annual Growth	12/14	12/15	12/16	12/17	12/18
Sales ($mil.)	(12.1%)	660.3	328.3	271.0	283.6	394.0
Net income ($ mil.)	–	120.7	(1,192.4)	(225.3)	24.4	(182.7)
Market value ($ mil.)	(69.4%)	46.8	26.8	18.9	4.5	0.4
Employees	(27.6%)	558	315	183	168	153

EXELIXIS INC

NMS: EXEL

1851 Harbor Bay Parkway
Alameda, CA 94502
Phone: 650 837-7000
Fax: –
Web: www.exelixis.com

CEO: –
CFO: –
HR: –
FYE: December 29
Type: Public

Exelixis is an oncology-focused biotechnology company that strives to accelerate the discovery, development and commercialization of new medicines for difficult-to-treat cancers. Its flagship molecule, cabozantinib, is the origin of two commercial products, CABOMETYX, a tablets approved for advanced renal cell carcinoma and COMETRIQ, capsules approved for progressive, metastatic medullary thyroid cancer. It also include COTELLIC (cobimetinib), a treatment for advanced melanoma and marketed under a collaboration with Genentech. It also has other drug development candidates against multiple target classes for oncology, inflammation and metabolic diseases. The US accounts for about 90% of total revenue.

	Annual Growth	01/20	01/21*	12/21	12/22	12/23
Sales ($mil.)	17.3%	967.8	987.5	1,435.0	1,611.1	1,830.2
Net income ($ mil.)	(10.3%)	321.0	111.8	231.1	182.3	207.8
Market value ($ mil.)	9.0%	5,150.5	6,077.1	5,535.1	4,856.6	7,264.0
Employees	20.7%	617	773	954	1,223	1,310

*Fiscal year change

EXELON CORP

NMS: EXC

10 South Dearborn Street, P.O. Box 805379
Chicago, IL 60680-5379
Phone: 800 483-3220
Fax: –
Web: www.exeloncorp.com

CEO: Calvin Butler Jr
CFO: Jeanne Jones
HR: Jenn Webster
FYE: December 31
Type: Public

Exelon is the nation's largest utility company, serving more than 10 million customers through seven fully regulated transmission and distribution utilities. These includes Commonwealth Edison Company, PECO Energy Company, Baltimore Gas and Electric Company, Pepco Holdings LLC, Potomac Electric Power Company, Delmarva Power & Light company, and Atlantic City Electric Company. Exelon distributes electricity and gas to customers in Illinois, Maryland, the District of Columbia, Delaware, New Jersey, and Pennsylvania through its regulated utility companies.

	Annual Growth	12/19	12/20	12/21	12/22	12/23
Sales ($mil.)	(10.9%)	34,438	33,039	36,347	19,078	21,727
Net income ($ mil.)	(5.6%)	2,936.0	1,963.0	1,706.0	2,170.0	2,328.0
Market value ($ mil.)	(5.8%)	45,544	42,178	57,702	43,187	35,864
Employees	(11.6%)	32,713	32,340	31,518	19,063	19,962

EXELON GENERATION CO LLC

200 Exelon Way
Kennett Square, PA 19348-2473
Phone: 833 883-0162
Fax: –
Web: www.constellationenergy.com

CEO: Joseph Dominguez
CFO: Daniel Eggers
HR: –
FYE: December 31
Type: Public

Exelon Generation Company has built an excellent reputation by generating electricity. The company, a subsidiary of Exelon Corporation, is one of the largest electric wholesale and retail power generation companies in the US. In 2013 Exelon Generation had a generation capacity of more than 44,560 MW (primarily nuclear, but also fossil-fired and hydroelectric and other renewable energy-based plants). Subsidiary Exelon Nuclear operates the largest fleet of nuclear power plants in the US. Exelon Generation's Exelon Power unit oversees a fleet of more than 100 fossil- and renewable-fueled plants (more than 15,875 MW of capacity) in Illinois, Maryland, Massachusetts, Pennsylvania, and Texas.

	Annual Growth	12/18	12/19	12/20	12/21	12/22
Sales ($mil.)	4.6%	20,437	18,924	17,603	19,649	24,440
Net income ($ mil.)	–	370.0	1,125.0	589.0	(205.0)	(160.0)
Market value ($ mil.)	–	–	–	–	–	–
Employees	(1.3%)	14,110	13,082	12,482	11,696	13,370

EXETER HEALTH RESOURCES, INC.

5 ALUMNI DR
EXETER, NH 038332128
Phone: 603 778-7311
Fax: –
Web: www.exeterhospital.com

CEO: Kevin Callahan
CFO: Kevin J O'Leary
HR: –
FYE: September 30
Type: Private

Exeter Health Resources, through its operating subsidiaries, provides health care, education, and outreach services. Exeter Hospital is a 200-bed acute care hospital serving the residents of southeastern New Hampshire, and Exeter Healthcare is a nearby rehabilitation and therapy facility. The company has other operating health and wellness facilities including Rockingham Visiting Nurse Association and Hospice, which provides home health and terminal illness care, and Synergy Health & Fitness, a membership fitness center. It also has an affiliated network of doctors, Core Physicians, which operates 25 office locations in the area.

	Annual Growth	09/16	09/17	09/19	09/21	09/22
Sales ($mil.)	11.1%	–	13.6	18.7	15.8	23.0
Net income ($ mil.)	6.0%	–	3.3	3.3	2.2	4.4
Market value ($ mil.)	–	–	–	–	–	–
Employees	–	–	–	–	–	106

EXIDE TECHNOLOGIES

13000 Deerfield Parkway, Building 200
Milton, GA 30004
Phone: 678 566-9000
Fax: 678 566-9188
Web: www.exide.com

CEO: Timothy D Vargo
CFO: Lou Martinez
HR: Erin Lenius
FYE: March 31
Type: Public

Exide Technologies is one of the largest secondary recyclers in the world, and one of the few companies with the ability to provide Total Battery Management, also known as closed loop recycling. It designs, manufactures and markets today's and next-generation battery technologies used across a wide range of applications, from automotive and off-road to material handling, stationary, rail and defense. Exide Technologies serves the global markets. Exide is an original equipment manufacturer to leading automotive and industrial equipment manufacturers. Exide traces its roots back to 1888 by W.W. Gibbs.

	Annual Growth	03/10	03/11	03/12	03/13	03/14
Sales ($mil.)	1.5%	2,685.8	2,887.5	3,084.7	2,971.7	2,855.4
Net income ($ mil.)	–	(11.8)	26.4	56.7	(223.4)	(217.8)
Market value ($ mil.)	–	–	–	–	–	–
Employees	(3.5%)	10,349	10,027	9,988	9,628	8,986

EXLSERVICE HOLDINGS INC

NMS: EXLS

320 Park Avenue, 29th Floor
New York, NY 10022
Phone: 212 277-7100
Fax: –
Web: www.exlservice.com

CEO: Rohit Kapoor
CFO: Maurizio Nicolelli
HR: –
FYE: December 31
Type: Public

ExlService Holdings, known as EXL, offers business process management (BPM), research and analytics, and consulting services through its operating segments. EXL's BPM offerings, which generate most of its sales, include claims processing, clinical operations, and finance and accounting services. Customers come mainly from the banking, financial services, and insurance industries, as well as from the utilities and telecommunications sectors. It delivers data analytics and digital operations and solutions to its clients, driving enterprise-scale business transformation initiatives. EXL operates around the world but generates around 85% of its revenue from the US. The company was incorporated in 2002.

	Annual Growth	12/19	12/20	12/21	12/22	12/23
Sales ($mil.)	13.2%	991.3	958.4	1,122.3	1,412.0	1,630.7
Net income ($ mil.)	28.5%	67.7	89.5	114.8	143.0	184.6
Market value ($ mil.)	(18.4%)	11,480	14,070	23,927	28,003	5,098.8
Employees	14.2%	31,700	31,900	37,400	45,400	54,000

EXP WORLD HOLDINGS INC

NMS: EXPI

2219 Rimland Drive, Suite 301
Bellingham, WA 98226
Phone: 360 685-4206
Fax: –
Web: www.expworldholdings.com

CEO: –
CFO: –
HR: –
FYE: December 31
Type: Public

eXp World Holdings, Inc. owns and operates a cloud-based real estate brokerage platform, a Virbela business, and related affiliated services that support the development and success of agents, entrepreneurs, and businesses by leveraging innovative technologies and integrated services. Its North American and international real estate brokerage is now one of the largest and fastest-growing real estate brokerage companies, with more than 88,000 agents operating throughout the US, most of the Canadian provinces, and in over 20 other countries. The company and its businesses offer a full suite of brokerage and real estate tech solutions, including its innovative residential and commercial brokerage model, professional services, collaborative tools, and personal development. The cloud-based brokerage is powered by Virbela, an immersive 3D platform, enabling agents to be more connected and productive.

	Annual Growth	12/19	12/20	12/21	12/22	12/23
Sales ($mil.)	44.6%	979.9	1,798.3	3,771.2	4,598.2	4,281.1
Net income ($ mil.)	–	(9.5)	31.1	81.2	15.4	(9.0)
Market value ($ mil.)	8.2%	1,752.4	9,762.7	5,210.8	1,713.7	2,400.5
Employees	35.1%	634	900	1,669	2,016	2,114

EXPEDIA GROUP INC
NMS: EXPE

1111 Expedia Group Way W.
Seattle, WA 98119
Phone: 206 481-7200
Fax: –
Web: www.expediagroup.com

CEO: –
CFO: –
HR: –
FYE: December 31
Type: Public

Expedia, an online travel company, leverages its supply portfolio, platform, and technology capabilities across an extensive portfolio of consumer brands, and provides solutions to its business partners, to empower travelers to efficiently research, plan, book, and experience travel. It offers tools that allow users to book approximately 3 million lodging properties, including over 2 million online bookable alternative accommodations listings and approximately 900,000 hotels, over 500 airlines, packages, rental cars, cruises, insurance, as well as activities and experiences. Its travel products and services are offered through a diversified portfolio of brands, including Brand Expedia, Hotels.com, Expedia Partner Solutions, Vrbo, trivago, Orbitz, and Travelocity. Nearly 70% of total revenue comes from customers in the US.

	Annual Growth	12/19	12/20	12/21	12/22	12/23
Sales ($mil.)	1.6%	12,067	5,199.0	8,598.0	11,667	12,839
Net income ($ mil.)	9.0%	565.0	(2,612.0)	12.0	352.0	797.0
Market value ($ mil.)	8.8%	14,820	18,145	24,767	12,005	20,802
Employees	(9.4%)	25,400	19,100	14,800	16,500	17,100

EXPEDITORS INTERNATIONAL OF WASHINGTON, INC.
NYS: EXPD

1015 Third Avenue
Seattle, WA 98104
Phone: 206 674-3400
Fax: 206 674-3459
Web: www.expeditors.com

CEO: –
CFO: –
HR: –
FYE: December 31
Type: Public

Expeditors International of Washington is a third-party logistics provider offering a full suite of global services. The company purchases air and ocean cargo space on a volume basis and resells that space to its customers at lower rates than they could obtain directly. The company also acts as a customs broker for air and ocean freight shipped by its customers and offers supply chain management services. Customers include global businesses engaged in retailing and wholesaling, electronics, high technology, industrial and manufacturing. The company's estimated average airfreight consolidation weighs approximately 3,900 pounds and that a typical consolidation includes merchandise from several shippers. US accounts for about 30% of company's revenue.

	Annual Growth	12/19	12/20	12/21	12/22	12/23
Sales ($mil.)	3.3%	8,175.4	10,116	16,524	17,071	9,300.1
Net income ($ mil.)	6.3%	590.4	696.1	1,415.5	1,357.4	752.9
Market value ($ mil.)	13.0%	11,224	13,683	19,320	14,951	18,300
Employees	0.1%	18,000	17,480	19,000	19,900	18,100

EXPERIAN INFORMATION SOLUTIONS, INC.

475 ANTON BLVD
COSTA MESA, CA 926267037
Phone: 714 830-7000
Fax: –
Web: www.experian.com

CEO: Chris Callero
CFO: –
HR: Karen Whitney
FYE: March 31
Type: Private

Experian Information Solutions, a global leader in consumer and business credit reporting and marketing services, is the US-based arm of global credit reporting agency Experian plc. The unit's database represents approximately 220 million credit-active consumers nationwide with some 1.3 billion updates flowing through monthly. The company supports clients across many different markets, including financial services, direct-to-consumer, retail, telecommunications, and automotive, among others. It also provides such solutions as advanced analytics and modeling, cloud applications and services, data reporting and furnishing, employer services, fraud management, identity solutions, marketing solutions, and regulatory compliance.

EXPERIENCE LEARNING COMMUNITY

120 6TH AVE N STE 100
SEATTLE, WA 981095002
Phone: 206 770-2700
Fax: –
Web: www.mopop.org

CEO: –
CFO: –
HR: –
FYE: December 31
Type: Private

'Scuse me while I kiss this museum. Seattle's Experience Music Project (EMP) sprang from Microsoft co-founder Paul Allen's passion for all things Jimi Hendrix. Allen owned the world's largest collection of the guitar virtuoso's memorabilia, which he wanted to share with all music fans. The idea soon mushroomed to encompass all aspects of rock music, and EMP now boasts more than 80,000 music instruments and artifacts, ranging from Bob Dylan's first electric guitar to Gene Simmons' demon KISS costume, as well as an extensive archive of sound recordings, films, photographs, fanzines, and manuscript materials. EMP opened in 2000 and also features a variety of interactive exhibits, restaurants, and gift shops.

	Annual Growth	12/14	12/15	12/19	12/21	12/22
Sales ($mil.)	(0.3%)	–	20.1	20.9	23.5	19.8
Net income ($ mil.)	–	–	(3.2)	(2.7)	2.8	(4.2)
Market value ($ mil.)	–	–	–	–	–	–
Employees	–	–	–	–	–	131

EXPERIENCE WORKS, INC.

4401 WILSON BLVD STE 210
ARLINGTON, VA 222034194
Phone: 703 522-7272
Fax: –
Web: www.experienceworks.org

CEO: Sally A Boofer
CFO: –
HR: –
FYE: June 30
Type: Private

Experience Works makes experience pay. The not-for-profit organization helps low-income individuals 55 years of age and older find jobs. It provides training as well as community service and employment opportunities for more than 125,000 mature workers in 30 states and Puerto Rico. The group offers annual local, state, and national awards, computer and technology skills, services targeted to local markets, and Senior Community Service Employment Program funded by the Older Americans Act to help low-income seniors. Experience Works was created in 1965. The company was called Green Thumb before it was renamed in 2002.

	Annual Growth	06/13	06/14	06/15	06/20	06/21
Sales ($mil.)	(29.2%)	–	100.5	104.4	18.9	9.0
Net income ($ mil.)	–	–	(0.3)	(2.4)	0.3	(0.3)
Market value ($ mil.)	–	–	–	–	–	–
Employees	–	–	–	–	–	400

EXPONENT INC.
NMS: EXPO

149 Commonwealth Drive
Menlo Park, CA 94025
Phone: 650 326-9400
Fax: –
Web: www.exponent.com

CEO: Paul R Johnston
CFO: Richard L Schlenker Jr
HR: Priscilla Smith
FYE: December 29
Type: Public

Exponent is a science and engineering consulting firm that specializes in analyzing and solving complex problems and preventing disasters and product failures. It's cadre of scientists, physicians, engineers, and business consultants assess environmental risks, regulatory issues, and workplace hazards for government agencies and clients from such industries as transportation, construction, and manufacturing. It divides its more than 15 practices in two segments: Engineering and Other Scientific (Biomechanics, Civil Engineering, Human Factors, and Mechanical Engineering); and Environment and Health (Health Science and Chemical Regulation & Food Safety). Established in 1967, Exponent is active in US, Asia Pacific, Europe and generates the majority of revenue in the US.

	Annual Growth	01/20	01/21*	12/21	12/22	12/23
Sales ($mil.)	6.5%	417.2	399.9	466.3	513.3	536.8
Net income ($ mil.)	5.0%	82.5	82.6	101.2	102.3	100.3
Market value ($ mil.)	5.7%	3,563.4	4,553.1	5,903.4	5,011.3	4,452.4
Employees	2.4%	1,201	1,168	1,215	1,313	1,320

*Fiscal year change

EXPORT-IMPORT BANK OF THE UNITED STATES

811 VRMONT AVE NW RM 1138
WASHINGTON, DC 205710001
Phone: 202 565-3946
Fax: –
Web: www.exim.gov

CEO: Judith D Pryor
CFO: –
HR: –
FYE: September 30
Type: Private

Sure, the US is running a huge trade deficit, but don't blame the Export-Import Bank of the United States for that. The government agency (Ex-Im Bank for short) provides financing for the export of American goods and services, mainly to developing countries and regions. Ex-Im Bank, which assumes credit and country risks that private-sector lenders cannot or will not stomach, helps US small businesses (most of them with fewer than 100 employees) with operating credit and export credit insurance, and provides loans and loan guarantees to foreign buyers of US goods. President Franklin D. Roosevelt established Ex-Im Bank as part of the New Deal in 1934.

EXPRESS INC

1 Express Drive
Columbus, OH 43230
Phone: 614 474-4001
Fax: –
Web: www.express.com

NBB: EXPR
CEO: –
CFO: –
HR: –
FYE: January 28
Type: Public

Express is a fashion retail company whose business includes an omnichannel operating platform, physical and online stores, and a multi-brand portfolio that includes Express and UpWest. The company operates about 555 stores throughout the US, the District of Columbia and Puerto Rico that sell modern, versatile, dual gender apparel and accessories brand that helps people get dressed for every day and any occasion trendy. The chain's fashions ? which include everything from button-downs and dresses to jeans and pants to shoes, belts, and handbags ? are styled to have an international influence and modern appeal. Its stores are located primarily in malls, and Express also sells merchandise online and via mobile apps. Express was founded in 1980.

	Annual Growth	02/19	02/20*	01/21	01/22	01/23
Sales ($mil.)	(3.1%)	2,116.3	2,019.2	1,208.4	1,870.3	1,864.2
Net income ($ mil.)	135.0%	9.6	(164.4)	(405.4)	(14.4)	293.8
Market value ($ mil.)	(32.0%)	19.5	14.8	22.1	10.7	4.2
Employees	(8.5%)	15,700	14,000	10,000	10,000	11,000

*Fiscal year change

EXPRESS SCRIPTS HOLDING COMPANY

1 EXPRESS WAY
SAINT LOUIS, MO 631211824
Phone: 314 996-0900
Fax: –
Web: www.express-scripts.com

CEO: Timothy Wentworth
CFO: James Havel
HR: –
FYE: December 31
Type: Private

Express Scripts Holding is an online pharmacy and a pharmacy benefit manager serving more than 100 million Americans and delivers specialized care that puts patients first through a smarter approach to pharmacy services. The company is the country's largest pharmacy benefit manager and one of the largest pharmacies. The company delivers a wide range of services and solutions that expose opportunities in pharmacy, medical and beyond. The company traces its roots back in 1986 and is now part of Evernorth.

EXPRESS SERVICES, INC.

9701 BOARDWALK BLVD
OKLAHOMA CITY, OK 731626029
Phone: 405 840-5000
Fax: –
Web: www.expresspros.com

CEO: Arthur McColl
CFO: W A Bostwick
HR: Lance Turner
FYE: December 27
Type: Private

Express Services is a leading staffing provider helping job seekers find work with a wide variety of local businesses. Operating as Express Employment Professionals, the professional staffing company provides work at small-to-medium sized businesses for almost 580,000 employees globally each year. It operates on a franchise business model from a network of more than 850 employment agency offices across Canada, South Africa, Australia, New Zealand, and the US. In addition to temporary staffing, it offers professional search and contract staffing services in the accounting and finance, engineering, IT, sales and marketing, non-profit organizations, and HR sectors. The firm was founded in 1983 by William H. Stoller and Robert A. Funk, and James Gray.

	Annual Growth	12/11	12/12	12/13	12/14	12/15
Sales ($mil.)	–	–	–	–	–	2,648.7
Net income ($ mil.)	29.7%	–	–	58.9	55.9	99.2
Market value ($ mil.)	–	–	–	–	–	–
Employees	–	–	–	–	–	373,869

EXPRO GROUP HOLDINGS NV

1311 Broadfield Boulevard, Suite 400
Houston, TX 77084
Phone: 713 463-9776
Fax: –
Web: www.expro.com

NYS: XPRO
CEO: –
CFO: –
HR: –
FYE: December 31
Type: Public

Expro Group Holdings N.V. is a Netherlands limited liability company and includes the activities of Expro Group Holdings International Limited, Frank's International C.V. and their wholly owned subsidiaries. With roots dating to 1938, the company is a leading provider of energy services, offering cost-effective, innovative solutions and what the company considers to be best-in-class safety and service quality. The company's extensive portfolio of capabilities spans well construction, well flow management, subsea well access, and well intervention and integrity solutions. The company provides services in many of the world's major offshore and onshore energy basins, with operations in approximately 60 countries. The company's broad portfolio of products and services provides solutions to enhance production and improve recovery across the well lifecycle, from exploration through abandonment. The company generates nearly 40% of its revenue in the NLA.

	Annual Growth	12/19	12/20	12/21	12/22	12/23
Sales ($mil.)	27.1%	579.9	390.4	825.8	1,279.4	1,512.8
Net income ($ mil.)	–	(235.3)	(156.2)	(131.9)	(20.1)	(23.4)
Market value ($ mil.)	–	–	–	–	–	–
Employees	26.7%	3,100	2,400	7,200	7,600	8,000

EXTENDED STAY AMERICA, INC.

13024 BALLANTYNE CORPORATE PL
CHARLOTTE, NC 282772113
Phone: 980 345-1600
Fax: –
Web: www.extendedstayamerica.com

CEO: Greg Juceam
CFO: David Clarkson
HR: Rocedar Sellars
FYE: December 31
Type: Private

Guests at this hotel chain need not worry about wearing out their welcome. The company owns and operates some 680 Extended Stay hotels. Extended Stay brands include Extended Stay America, Extended Stay Canada, and Crossland Economy Studios. A hybrid between a hotel and an apartment, its lodgings offer all-suite accommodations targeting business and leisure travelers looking for a temporary place to call home. The rooms feature separate living and dining areas and fully-equipped kitchens. Extended Stay can charge lower rates than hotels by eliminating room service and daily maid services. The company went public in 2013.

	Annual Growth	12/15	12/16	12/17	12/18	12/19
Sales ($mil.)	(2.5%)	–	–	1,282.7	1,275.1	1,218.2
Net income ($ mil.)	(2.1%)	–	–	172.2	211.8	165.1
Market value ($ mil.)	–	–	–	–	–	–
Employees	–	–	–	–	–	8,400

EXTRA SPACE STORAGE INC NYS: EXR

2795 East Cottonwood Parkway, Suite 300
Salt Lake City, UT 84121
Phone: 801 365-4600
Fax: –
Web: www.extraspace.com

CEO: Joseph D Margolis
CFO: Nadine Stevenshendr
HR: –
FYE: December 31
Type: Public

Extra Space Storage is a self-administered and self-managed real estate investment trust (REIT) that owns roughly 2,390 self-storage properties, which comprise approximately 1.7 million units and approximately 180.0 million square feet of rentable storage space offering customers conveniently located and secure storage units across the country, including boat storage, RV storage, and business storage. Extra Space is the second largest owner and/or operator of self-storage properties in the US. Founded in 1977, Extra Space Storage went public in 2004.

	Annual Growth	12/19	12/20	12/21	12/22	12/23
Sales ($mil.)	18.3%	1,308.5	1,356.2	1,577.4	1,924.2	2,560.2
Net income ($ mil.)	17.6%	420.0	481.8	827.6	860.7	803.2
Market value ($ mil.)	11.0%	22,315	24,479	47,903	31,096	33,874
Employees	17.1%	4,048	4,013	4,309	4,781	7,618

EXTREME NETWORKS INC NMS: EXTR

2121 RDU Center Drive, Suite 300
Morrisville, NC 27560
Phone: 408 579-2800
Fax: –
Web: www.extremenetworks.com

CEO: –
CFO: –
HR: –
FYE: June 30
Type: Public

Extreme Networks is a leading provider of end-to-end, cloud-driven networking solutions and top-rated services and support. Providing a set of comprehensive solutions from the Internet of Things (IoT) edge to the cloud and Extreme designs, develops, and manufactures wired, wireless, and software-defined wide-area-network (SD-WAN) infrastructure equipment as well a leading cloud networking platform and application portfolio using cloud management, machine learning, and artificial intelligence to deliver network policy, analytics, security, and access controls. Extreme cloud-driven technologies provide flexibility and scalability in the deployment, management, and licensing of networks globally, and the global cloud footprint provides service to over 50,000 customers and over 10 million daily end users. Extreme, founded in 1996, generates about 45% of revenue from the US.

	Annual Growth	06/19	06/20	06/21	06/22	06/23
Sales ($mil.)	7.1%	995.8	948.0	1,009.4	1,112.3	1,312.5
Net income ($ mil.)	–	(25.9)	(126.8)	1.9	44.3	78.1
Market value ($ mil.)	41.7%	826.7	554.5	1,426.0	1,139.8	3,328.5
Employees	1.2%	2,713	2,584	2,441	2,643	2,849

EXXON MOBIL CORP NYS: XOM

22777 Springwoods Village Parkway
Spring, TX 77389-1425
Phone: 972 940-6000
Fax: 972 444-1505
Web: www.exxonmobil.com

CEO: Darren W Woods
CFO: Kathryn Mikells
HR: Adam Bond
FYE: December 31
Type: Public

Exxon Mobil Corporation's principal business involves exploration for, and production of, crude oil and natural gas; manufacture, trade, transport and sale of crude oil, natural gas, petroleum products, petrochemicals and a wide variety of specialty products; and pursuit of lower-emission business opportunities including carbon capture and storage, hydrogen and biofuels. Its vast portfolio holds about 18 billion barrels of oil equivalent of proved reserves, spread across six continents. The company's brands?ExxonMobil, Exxon, Esso, Mobil, and XTO? enjoy global recognition.

	Annual Growth	12/19	12/20	12/21	12/22	12/23
Sales ($mil.)	6.8%	264,938	181,502	285,640	413,680	344,582
Net income ($ mil.)	25.9%	14,340	(22,440.0)	23,040	55,740	36,010
Market value ($ mil.)	9.4%	277,096	163,685	242,985	438,001	397,021
Employees	(4.6%)	74,900	72,000	63,000	62,300	62,000

EXXONMOBIL PIPELINE COMPANY

22777 SPRINGWOODS VILLAGE PKWY
SPRING, TX 773891425
Phone: 888 804-4788
Fax: –
Web: www.exxonmobilpipeline.com

CEO: –
CFO: –
HR: –
FYE: December 31
Type: Private

This company makes its mark by sending its business down the tubes. Each day ExxonMobil Pipeline, the oil and gas transportation arm of Exxon Mobil, transports about 2.7 million barrels of crude oil, refined petroleum products, liquefied petroleum gases, natural gas liquids, and chemicals through 8,000 miles of pipeline that runs through 23 US states, Canada, and the Gulf of Mexico. The company also provides engineering and inspection services. Its joint interest pipelines include Mustang Pipeline, Plantation Pipe Line, and Wolverine Pipe Line. ExxonMobil Pipeline also owns a minority stake in The Trans-Alaska Pipeline System, Alaska's major vehicle for moving crude from Prudhoe Bay to the port of Valdez.

EZCORP, INC. NMS: EZPW

2500 Bee Cave Road, Bldg One, Suite 200
Rollingwood, TX 78746
Phone: 512 314-3400
Fax: 512 314-3404
Web: www.ezcorp.com

CEO: Lachlan P Given
CFO: Timothy K Jugmans
HR: –
FYE: September 30
Type: Public

EZCORP is a leading provider of pawn shops and associated loans in the US and Latin America. The company operates more than 515 EZPAWN and Value Pawn locations in the US; about 530 stores in Mexico under the Empe o F cil and Cash Apoyo Efectivo brand; and more than 130 pawn stores in Guatemala, El Salvador and Honduras (operating as GuatePrenda and MaxiEfectivo). In addition to its core pawn business in the US and Latin America, EZCORP owns about 43.7% in Cash Converters, which has operations in Australia and UK and 14.6% in Rich Data, a Singapore-based software-as-a-service company that utilizes global financial services expertise. Most of the company's revenue comes from its US operations.

	Annual Growth	09/19	09/20	09/21	09/22	09/23
Sales ($mil.)	5.5%	847.2	822.8	729.6	886.2	1,049.0
Net income ($ mil.)	97.2%	2.5	(68.5)	8.6	50.2	38.5
Market value ($ mil.)	6.3%	354.0	275.8	415.1	422.8	452.4
Employees	–	–	–	6,500	7,000	7,500

F & M BANK CORP. NBB: FMBM

P.O. Box 1111
Timberville, VA 22853
Phone: 540 896-8941
Fax: –
Web: www.fmbankva.com

CEO: Aubrey M Wilkerson
CFO: Lisa F Campbell
HR: –
FYE: December 31
Type: Public

F & M Bank has deep roots in Virginia's Shenandoah Valley. Founded in 1908, the holding company operates about 10 Farmers & Merchants Bank branches in the northern Virginia counties of Rockingham and Shenandoah. Farmers & Merchants caters to individuals and businesses. It provides typical deposit products, including checking and savings accounts, CDs, and IRAs. Some 40% of its loans are mortgages; it also writes agricultural, business, construction, and consumer loans. The company offers insurance, brokerage, and financial services through TEB Life Insurance and Farmers & Merchants Financial Services.

	Annual Growth	12/18	12/19	12/20	12/21	12/22
Assets ($mil.)	12.4%	780.3	814.0	966.9	1,219.3	1,245.9
Net income ($ mil.)	(2.2%)	9.1	4.5	8.8	10.7	8.3
Market value ($ mil.)	(6.6%)	103.7	100.2	79.5	99.4	79.0
Employees	(4.5%)	172	173	151	152	143

F&S PRODUCE COMPANY, INC.

500 W ELMER RD
VINELAND, NJ 083606314
Phone: 856 453-0316
Fax: –
Web: www.fsfreshfoods.com

CEO: –
CFO: –
HR: Melissa Garwood
FYE: December 31
Type: Private

F&S Produce is into slicing and dicing. The company is a supplier of processed fresh produce, including chunked, diced, and sliced fruits and vegetables and prepared fruit and vegetable salads and trays; it also makes brined and pickled products. Customers include food processors, food service distributors, and chain account representatives. F&S processes more than 75 million pounds of produce annually. Affiliate Pipco Transportation distributes the company's products through a fleet of approximately 30 trucks and 50 refrigerated trailers. The company is owned by president Sam Pipitone, who founded F&S in 1981.

	Annual Growth	12/17	12/18	12/19	12/20	12/21
Sales ($mil.)	21.0%	–	107.6	114.4	124.7	190.4
Net income ($ mil.)	–	–	(1.3)	4.6	16.6	13.8
Market value ($ mil.)	–	–	–	–	–	–
Employees	–	–	–	–	–	600

F5 INC

801 5th Avenue
Seattle, WA 98104
Phone: 206 272-5555
Fax: –
Web: www.f5.com

NMS: FFIV
CEO: –
CFO: –
HR: –
FYE: September 30
Type: Public

F5 is a multi-cloud application services and security provider. F5's portfolio of automation, security, performance, and insight capabilities empowers its customers to create, secure, and operate adaptive applications that reduce costs, improve operations, and better protect users. Its enterprise-grade application services are available as cloud-based, software-as-a-service, and software-only solutions optimized for multi-cloud environments. The company also offers such services as consulting, training, installation, maintenance, and other technical support services. F5 customers include large enterprise businesses, public sector institutions, governments, and service providers. More than half of its sales come from the US.

	Annual Growth	09/19	09/20	09/21	09/22	09/23
Sales ($mil.)	5.8%	2,242.4	2,350.8	2,603.4	2,695.8	2,813.2
Net income ($ mil.)	(2.0%)	427.7	307.4	331.2	322.2	394.9
Market value ($ mil.)	3.5%	8,313.8	7,268.8	11,769	8,569.0	9,540.6
Employees	5.2%	5,325	6,109	6,461	7,089	6,524

FA FINALE, INC.

24 PRIME PARK WAY STE 305
BOSTON, MA 02116
Phone: 617 226-7888
Fax: –
Web: –

CEO: –
CFO: –
HR: –
FYE: December 31
Type: Private

FA Finale wants to get lots of bang for its buck. It makes guitars, drums, and related accessories (microphones, music stands, pedals, strings, straps), as well as band and orchestral instruments. The company's products, which are sold through mass merchandisers (Wal-Mart and Target), specialty retailers, and club channels nationwide, are designed primarily for children, beginners, and school music programs. FA Finale's Global Design Studio makes handmade and one-of-a-kind instruments for professional musicians. It launched its Little First Act Discovery line of musical learning toys, geared toward infants and toddlers age 0 to 3, in late 2008.

FACTSET RESEARCH SYSTEMS INC.

45 Glover Avenue
Norwalk, CT 06850
Phone: 203 810-1000
Fax: 203 810-1001
Web: www.factset.com

NYS: FDS
CEO: F P Snow
CFO: Linda S Huber
HR: –
FYE: August 31
Type: Public

FactSet Research Systems is a global financial data and analytics company with an open and flexible digital platform that drives the investment community to see more, think bigger, and do its best work. FactSet has delivered expansive data, sophisticated analytics, and flexible technology used by global financial professionals to power their critical investment workflows. Its on- and off-platform solutions span the investment lifecycle to include investment research, portfolio construction and analysis, trade execution, performance measurement, risk management, and reporting. Revenues are derived from subscriptions to its multi-asset class data and solutions powered by its connected content (content refinery). The company's products and services include workstations, portfolio analytics, and enterprise solutions. The US generated majority of its sales.

	Annual Growth	08/19	08/20	08/21	08/22	08/23
Sales ($mil.)	9.8%	1,435.4	1,494.1	1,591.4	1,843.9	2,085.5
Net income ($ mil.)	7.3%	352.8	372.9	399.6	396.9	468.2
Market value ($ mil.)	12.5%	10,346	13,324	14,458	16,478	16,595
Employees	6.0%	9,681	10,484	10,892	11,203	12,237

FAEGRE DRINKER BIDDLE & REATH LLP

1 LOGAN SQ STE 2000
PHILADELPHIA, PA 191036909
Phone: 215 988-2700
Fax: –
Web: www.faegredrinker.com

CEO: Gina Kastel
CFO: Rich Ciccotto
HR: –
FYE: December 31
Type: Private

Founded in 1849, law firm Drinker Biddle & Reath, now operating as Faegre Drinker Biddle & Reath after its combination with Faegre Baker Daniels, employs over 1,200 experienced attorneys, consultants and professionals working out of around 20 locations. The firm maintains a broad range of practices, including litigation, corporate and securities, bankruptcy, government and regulatory affairs, health, intellectual property, private equity, and real estate. Its clients reside chiefly in the health care & life sciences, insurance, consumer products & retail, financial services, and food & agribusiness industries.

FAFCO, INC.

435 Otterson Drive
Chico, CA 95928
Phone: 530 332-2100
Fax: –
Web: www.fafco.com

NBB: FAFC
CEO: Freeman A Ford
CFO: Nancy I Garvin
HR: –
FYE: December 31
Type: Public

FAFCO is in hot water and wants others to jump in with it. The company makes solar swimming pool-heating systems, and thermal energy storage systems. In FAFCO's heating systems solar panels control water temperature of water. The company also manufactures IceStor -- a product that controls commercial cooling costs by storing energy at night during off-peak times, and then releasing it to cool buildings during the day. Customers include residential, hotels, and other industries. Its solar water heaters are marketed to homeowners. FAFCO was founded in 1969 by chairman Freeman Ford and Richard Rhodes.

	Annual Growth	12/98	12/99	12/00	12/01	12/02
Sales ($mil.)	7.4%	11.3	10.6	11.5	12.1	15.0
Net income ($ mil.)	(9.3%)	0.8	0.2	(0.1)	0.0	0.6
Market value ($ mil.)	–	–	–	–	–	–
Employees	6.3%	61	62	63	77	78

FAHLGREN, INC.

4030 EASTON STA STE 300
COLUMBUS, OH 432197012
Phone: 614 383-1500
Fax: –
Web: www.fahlgrenmortine.com

CEO: Neil Mortine
CFO: Brent Holbert
HR: Katie McGrath
FYE: December 31
Type: Private

An independent marketing communications agency, Fahlgren creates ad campaigns and provides design, event marketing, interactive, media buying, and strategy-related services. Public relations services are offered through the company's Fahlgren Mortine business unit (named after CEO Neil Mortine), which provides expertise in media relations, investor relations, and reputation management. Overall, Fahlgren maintains about 10 offices in the midwestern and southeastern US. Clients have included such high-profile brands as the American Heart Association, Cooper Tire, Kroger, McDonald's, and NAPA. Fahlgren was founded in 1962.

	Annual Growth	12/97	12/98	12/99	12/00	12/12
Sales ($mil.)	0.2%	–	22.3	20.6	21.5	23.0
Net income ($ mil.)	2.6%	–	0.6	0.0	(0.8)	0.9
Market value ($ mil.)	–	–	–	–	–	–
Employees	–	–	–	–	–	125

FAIR ISAAC CORP

5 West Mendenhall, Suite 105
Bozema, MT 59715
Phone: 406 982-7276
Fax: –
Web: www.fico.com

NYS: FICO
CEO: William J Lansing
CFO: Steven P Weber
HR: –
FYE: September 30
Type: Public

Fair Isaac, also known as FICO, is a company that provides credit scores and risk management tools for businesses worldwide, including banks, credit card issuers, mortgage and auto lenders, retailers, insurance firms, and health care providers. It also serve consumers through online services that enable people to access and understand their FICO Scores, the standard measure in the US of consumer credit risk, empowering them to manage their financial health. While the Americas accounts for some 80% of its revenue, the company operates globally in more than 120 countries. FICO was founded by Engineer Bill Fair and mathematician Earl Isaac in 1956.

	Annual Growth	09/19	09/20	09/21	09/22	09/23
Sales ($mil.)	6.9%	1,160.1	1,294.6	1,316.5	1,377.3	1,513.6
Net income ($ mil.)	22.3%	192.1	236.4	392.1	373.5	429.4
Market value ($ mil.)	30.1%	7,518.2	10,537	9,856.7	10,205	21,513
Employees	(3.6%)	4,009	4,003	3,662	3,404	3,455

FAIRCHILD SEMICONDUCTOR INTERNATIONAL, INC.

1272 BORREGAS AVE
SUNNYVALE, CA 940891310
Phone: 408 822-2000
Fax: –
Web: –

CEO: Keith D Jackson
CFO: Bernard Gutmann
HR: Tobin Cookman
FYE: December 27
Type: Private

One of the world's oldest chip makers, Fairchild Semiconductor makes semiconductors for tens of thousands of customers in the automotive, computer, consumer electronics, industrial, mobile, and communications markets. Its diversified product line includes logic chips, discrete power and signal components, optoelectronics, and many types of analog and mixed-signal chips. The company subcontracts a small amount of its fabrication, assembly, and test operations to companies that include TSMC, Amkor, and ASE, among others. In September 2016 the acquisition of Fairchild by On Semiconductor for $2.4 billion was concluded.

FAIRFIELD MEDICAL CENTER

401 N EWING ST
LANCASTER, OH 431303371
Phone: 740 687-8000
Fax: –
Web: www.fmchealth.org

CEO: Sky Gettys
CFO: Julie Grow
HR: –
FYE: December 31
Type: Private

Fairfield Medical Center is a more than 220-bed acute care hospital serving residents in southeastern and central Ohio. In addition to providing comprehensive medical and surgical care, Fairfield Medical Center offers specialty services including cancer, cardiovascular, women's and children's health, and rehabilitation services. The not-for-profit hospital also operates offsite facilities for physician practices, as well as specialty diagnostic and laboratory services. The Center employs more than 250 physicians, and is served by a number of volunteer organizations which help to support and operate it.

	Annual Growth	12/17	12/18	12/19	12/21	12/22
Sales ($mil.)	5.1%	–	282.4	280.0	349.1	344.6
Net income ($ mil.)	–	–	(21.1)	17.6	11.4	(28.6)
Market value ($ mil.)	–	–	–	–	–	–
Employees	–	–	–	–	–	2,200

FAIRFIELD UNIVERSITY

1073 N BENSON RD
FAIRFIELD, CT 068245195
Phone: 203 254-4000
Fax: –
Web: www.fairfield.edu

CEO: –
CFO: –
HR: –
FYE: June 30
Type: Private

Fairfield University is a private-only Jesuit catholic school with an enrollment of about 6,150 undergraduate and graduate students. It offers more than 50 undergraduate majors and minors and nearly 30 interdisciplinary minors, as well as about 55 graduate degree programs, more than 20 accelerated bachelor's/master's degree programs, and some 25 online graduate programs, through five schools and colleges: College of Arts and Sciences; Marion Peckham Egan School of Nursing & Health Studies; School of Engineering; Charles F. Dolan School of Business; and the School of Education and Human Development. With a 12:1 student-to-faculty ratio, Fairfield University has seven academic facilities and offers about 50 study-abroad programs across about 100 cities and 50 countries. The university was founded in 1942.

	Annual Growth	06/18	06/19	06/20	06/21	06/22
Sales ($mil.)	5.9%	–	238.4	227.7	242.7	283.3
Net income ($ mil.)	–	–	24.6	5.3	117.2	(12.6)
Market value ($ mil.)	–	–	–	–	–	–
Employees	–	–	–	–	–	883

FAIRLEIGH DICKINSON UNIVERSITY

1000 RIVER RD STE 1
TEANECK, NJ 076661939
Phone: 800 338-8803
Fax: –
Web: www.fdu.edu

CEO: –
CFO: –
HR: –
FYE: June 30
Type: Private

It's fair to say that Fairleigh Dickinson University (FDU) is the largest private university in New Jersey. It has an enrollment of approximately 12,000 students and 260 full-time faculty members. It has a student-teacher ratio of 14:1 and offers more than 100 undergraduate and graduate degree programs, as well as doctoral programs in clinical psychology and school psychology. In addition to its main Metropolitan Campus in Teaneck, New Jersey; the university also offers degree programs at the College at Florham in Madison, New Jersey; at FDU-Vancouver in Canada; and at Wroxton College in Oxfordshire, England. Fairleigh Dickinson was founded in 1942.

	Annual Growth	06/18	06/19	06/20	06/21	06/22
Sales ($mil.)	(4.2%)	–	222.1	210.2	187.6	195.1
Net income ($ mil.)	–	–	17.4	(0.9)	25.9	(30.9)
Market value ($ mil.)	–	–	–	–	–	–
Employees	–	–	–	–	–	1,505

FAIRPOINT COMMUNICATIONS, INC.

121 S 17TH ST
MATTOON, IL 619383915
Phone: 866 326-5789
Fax: –
Web: www.fairpoint.com

CEO: –
CFO: –
HR: –
FYE: December 31
Type: Private

FairPoint Communications provides local and long-distance phone services as well as broadband Internet access and cable TV to residential and business customers. It counts a total of more than 735,000 subscribers to its voice, broadband, and Ethernet services. It operates more than 30 local-exchange carriers in 17 US states. FairPoint concentrates on rural and small urban markets mainly in northern New England, but it also serves spots in the Midwest, South, and Northwest. In December 2016, FairPoint agreed to be bought by Consolidated Communications for $1.5 billion.

FAIRVIEW HEALTH SERVICES

1700 UNIVERSITY AVE W
SAINT PAUL, MN 551043727
Phone: 612 672-6300
Fax: –
Web: www.fairview.org

CEO: Rulon F Stacey
CFO: James M Fox
HR: Ann Sagendorf
FYE: December 31
Type: Private

It's fair to say that when it comes to health care, Fairview Health Services takes the long view. The not-for-profit system serves Minnesota's Twin Cities and nearby communities. Fairview Health is affiliated with the medical school of the University of Minnesota and counts among its 10 hospitals the University of Minnesota Medical Center. The hospitals house more than 2,500 beds and provide comprehensive medical and surgical services. The system also operates primary and specialty care clinics that provide preventive and wellness care. Additionally, it operates retail pharmacies and nursing homes and provides home health care and rehabilitation. Merger talks with University of Minnesota Physicians have stalled.

	Annual Growth	12/17	12/18	12/19	12/20	12/22
Sales ($mil.)	3.9%	–	5,709.2	6,049.8	6,123.8	6,661.8
Net income ($ mil.)	–	–	5.7	13.4	(18.4)	(469.0)
Market value ($ mil.)	–	–	–	–	–	–
Employees	–	–	–	–	–	18,000

FAIRWAY GROUP HOLDINGS CORP

2284 12th Avenue
New York, NY 10027
Phone: 646 616-8000
Fax: –
Web: www.fairwaymarket.com

CEO: Abel Porter
CFO: Erik Frederick
HR: –
FYE: March 29
Type: Public

Fairway Group Holdings Corp. keeps a well-stocked grocery cart for discerning Manhattan shoppers. The parent company of Fairway Market operates a growing chain of more than a dozen upscale grocery stores in the greater New York City metropolitan area. Three of those stores (in Connecticut, New Jersey, and New York) have adjacent liquor stores under the Fairway Wines & Spirits name. Fairway Markets feature fresh produce, meat, and seafood, as well as organic products, prepared foods, and hard-to-find specialty and gourmet products. Some Fairway Markets have on-site cafes that serve coffee, salads, and sandwiches, while other locations offer delivery. Fairway Group filed for Chapter 11 bankruptcy protection in June 2016 and left it a month later.

	Annual Growth	04/11	04/12*	03/13	03/14	03/15
Sales ($mil.)	13.2%	485.7	554.9	661.2	776.0	797.6
Net income ($ mil.)	–	(18.6)	(11.9)	(62.9)	(80.3)	(46.5)
Market value ($ mil.)	–	–	–	–	333.9	260.2
Employees	–	–	4,230	4,800	4,200	4,300

*Fiscal year change

FAITH TECHNOLOGIES, INC.

225 MAIN ST
MENASHA, WI 549523186
Phone: 920 738-1500
Fax: –
Web: www.faithtechnologies.com

CEO: –
CFO: –
HR: –
FYE: December 31
Type: Private

Keeping the faith in technology is a basic commitment of Faith Technologies, one of the largest privately held electrical and specialty systems contractors in the US. The company's specialties include electrical contracting and service, automated controls, lighting, security, technology, and preconstruction. It primarily serves clients in the commercial, government, industrial, institutional, health care, manufacturing, power, residential, retail, transportation, and data center sectors. The company has worked on a range of projects, such as airports, bridges, correctional facilities, government agencies, hospitals, restaurants, and shopping centers.

	Annual Growth	12/09	12/10	12/11	12/12	12/15
Sales ($mil.)	13.3%	–	228.3	248.6	260.2	425.9
Net income ($ mil.)	69.0%	–	2.3	4.6	10.0	31.8
Market value ($ mil.)	–	–	–	–	–	–
Employees	–	–	–	–	–	2,581

FALCON NORTHWEST COMPUTER SYSTEMS, INC.

2015 COMMERCE DR
MEDFORD, OR 975049744
Phone: 888 325-2661
Fax: –
Web: www.falcon-nw.com

CEO: –
CFO: –
HR: –
FYE: May 31
Type: Private

Falcon Northwest's PCs don't just compute -- they fly. Falcon Northwest Computer Systems manufactures customized, high-performance computers. Designed primarily for gaming enthusiasts, Falcon's desktop and notebook models features high-end components and unique form factors with colorful graphics. The company provides support services via telephone and e-mail. Falcon Northwest was founded in 1992 by president and CEO Kelt Reeves, who began building computers that specialized in flight simulation for fellow students and gamers at Embry-Riddle Aeronautical University in Florida. Kelt Reeves owns the company.

	Annual Growth	05/96	05/97	05/98	05/99	05/15
Sales ($mil.)	12.1%	–	1.4	1.0	2.7	10.7
Net income ($ mil.)	49.2%	–	0.0	0.1	0.0	0.5
Market value ($ mil.)	–	–	–	–	–	–
Employees	–	–	–	–	–	24

FALCONSTOR SOFTWARE INC

501 Congress Avenue, Suite 150
Austin, TX 78701
Phone: 631 777-5188
Fax: –
Web: www.falconstor.com

NBB: FALC
CEO: Todd Brooks
CFO: Vincent Sita
HR: –
FYE: December 31
Type: Public

FalconStor Software watches data like a hawk. The company provides hardware and software used in data storage, protection, and virtualization applications. Its IPStor software is used to manage storage provisioning and virtualization, data availability, replication, and disaster recovery functions in disk-based systems. Ranging from small and midsized businesses to large enterprises, the company's customers come from such fields as health care, insurance, financial services, education, telecommunications, and information technology. FalconStor sells predominantly through distributors, manufacturers, and resellers.

	Annual Growth	12/18	12/19	12/20	12/21	12/22
Sales ($mil.)	(13.4%)	17.8	16.5	14.8	14.2	10.1
Net income ($ mil.)	–	(0.9)	(1.8)	1.1	0.2	(1.8)
Market value ($ mil.)	115.4%	0.3	20.4	48.1	13.0	5.8
Employees	(11.4%)	86	71	44	61	53

FALKENBERG CONSTRUCTION CO., INC.

2435 109TH ST
GRAND PRAIRIE, TX 750501113
Phone: 214 324-4779
Fax: –
Web: www.falkenbergconstruction.com

CEO: –
CFO: –
HR: –
FYE: November 30
Type: Private

Falkenberg Construction Company provides general contracting and construction management services for commercial, light industrial, remodeling, and tenant finish-out projects. Its customers include banks, restaurants, hospitals, grocery stores, and government agencies. Projects include the Haltom City Recreation Center in Haltom City, Texas and the Kiest Athletic Complex in Dallas, as well as a variety of retail shopping complexes throughout Texas. The company was founded in 1983.

	Annual Growth	12/02	12/03*	11/13	11/14	11/15
Sales ($mil.)	6.6%	–	4.8	8.3	13.0	10.3
Net income ($ mil.)	–	–	(0.2)	0.0	0.4	0.0
Market value ($ mil.)	–	–	–	–	–	–
Employees	–	–	–	–	–	34

*Fiscal year change

FAMC SUBSIDIARY COMPANY

6100 TOWER CIR STE 600
FRANKLIN, TN 370671505
Phone: 615 778-1000
Fax: –
Web: www.franklinamerican.com

CEO: Daniel G Crockett
CFO: Scott J Tansil
HR: –
FYE: December 31
Type: Private

Franklin American Mortgage Company (FAMC) is flying as high as a kite. The private mortgage bank is one of the country's largest and fastest-growing mortgage brokers. Franklin American Mortgage operates through three loan production channels. The correspondent lending division services lenders nationwide, while the wholesale division funds and underwrites loans for mortgage brokers. The firm's retail division offers mortgages directly to individuals from about 20 offices (mostly located in the East and South). Founded in 1994, Franklin American Mortgage CEO Dan Crockett owns the company.

	Annual Growth	12/03	12/04	12/05	12/07	12/08
Assets ($mil.)	7.7%	–	–	238.3	206.8	298.1
Net income ($ mil.)	65.9%	–	–	5.6	5.5	25.7
Market value ($ mil.)	–	–	–	–	–	–
Employees	–	–	–	–	–	700

FAMILY EXPRESS CORPORATION

213 S STATE ROAD 49
VALPARAISO, IN 463837976
Phone: 219 531-6490
Fax: –
Web: www.familyexpress.com

CEO: –
CFO: –
HR: –
FYE: December 31
Type: Private

Convenience is all in the family at this Indiana chain. Family Express operates about 50 convenience store/gasoline stations in north central and northwestern Indiana (split almost evenly between city and rural locations). The chain's Cravin's Market in-house foodservice features fresh sandwiches, fruits, vegetables, salads and a selection of floral items. Family Express also has launched its own proprietary brands, including Java Wave gourmet coffees, Squeeze Freeze carbonated beverages, natural spring water, and bread and milk products. In addition, Family Express operates a small fleet of delivery trucks that say "moo." The company was founded in 1975.

	Annual Growth	12/05	12/06	12/07	12/09	12/10
Sales ($mil.)	0.2%	–	–	275.6	244.8	277.4
Net income ($ mil.)	(38.0%)	–	–	18.5	2.8	4.4
Market value ($ mil.)	–	–	–	–	–	–
Employees	–	–	–	–	–	500

FAMILY HEALTH INTERNATIONAL INC

359 BLACKWELL ST STE 200
DURHAM, NC 277012477
Phone: 919 544-7040
Fax: –
Web: www.fhiclinical.com

CEO: Albert J Siemens
CFO: Hubert C Graves
HR: Jessica Lamb
FYE: September 30
Type: Private

Known as FHI 360, Family Health International believes that health is wealth. From a handful of offices located in the US, Asia-Pacific, and South Africa, FHI 360 funds and manages public health programs, research, education, and other resources in more than 60 countries. Founded in 1971 as the International Fertility Research Program of the University of North Carolina at Chapel Hill, FHI 360 primarily focuses on and supports HIV/AIDS prevention research, reproductive health services, and maternal and neonatal health programs. The organization works with governments, private agencies, and non-governmental organizations to develop the most appropriate programs for different areas.

	Annual Growth	09/13	09/14	09/19	09/21	09/22
Sales ($mil.)	3.1%	–	653.7	781.6	764.8	834.9
Net income ($ mil.)	–	–	(3.4)	1.0	(15.3)	(54.0)
Market value ($ mil.)	–	–	–	–	–	–
Employees	–	–	–	–	–	4,000

FANNIE MAE

1100 15th Street, NW
Washington, DC 20005
Phone: 800 232-6643
Fax: –
Web: www.fanniemae.com

NBB: FNMA

CEO: Priscilla Almodovar
CFO: Chryssa C Halley
HR: –
FYE: December 31
Type: Public

The Federal National Mortgage Association, better known as Fannie Mae, is a government-sponsored enterprise (GSE) that provides liquidity and stability to the residential mortgage market and to promote access to mortgage credit. It is primarily driven by guaranty fees that the company receives for assuming the credit risk on loans underlying the mortgage-backed securities it issues. It does not originate loans or lend money directly to borrowers. Rather, it primarily works with lenders who originate loans to borrowers. Through its single-family and multifamily business segments, Fannie Mae provided over $684 billion in liquidity to the mortgage market, which enabled the financing of approximately 2.6 million home purchases, refinancing or rental units.

	Annual Growth	12/19	12/20	12/21	12/22	12/23
Assets ($mil.)	5.4%	3,503,319	3,985,749	4,229,166	4,305,288	4,325,437
Net income ($ mil.)	5.3%	14,160	11,805	22,176	12,923	17,408
Market value ($ mil.)	(23.5%)	3,613.2	2,767.8	949.7	409.3	1,239.2
Employees	1.9%	7,500	7,700	7,400	8,000	8,100

FANSTEEL INC.

1746 COMMERCE RD
CRESTON, IA 508018191
Phone: 641 782-8521
Fax: –
Web: www.fansteel.com

CEO: –
CFO: –
HR: –
FYE: December 31
Type: Private

Fansteel is a big fan of steel and other performance metals, such as tungsten carbide, titanium, special alloys, and other metals. The company's Advanced Structures segment (majority of sales) produces aluminum and magnesium sand castings, closed die forgings, and machined components. Its Metal Components segment makes powdered metal components, engineered investment castings, and custom assemblies. United Technologies and Navistar International are both major customers. Others customers include companies in the aerospace, automotive, defense, electrical appliances, heavy equipment, industrial hardware, and power tools industries.

FAR TECHNOLOGIES HOLDINGS, INC.

100 W MAIN ST
BOUND BROOK, NJ 088051972
Phone: 732 469-7760
Fax: –
Web: www.cpsperformancematerials.com

CEO: Jeremy Steinfink
CFO: Bob Nobile
HR: –
FYE: December 31
Type: Private

Cyalume Technologies Holdings believes in walking softly and carrying a big chemstick. Through two main subsidiaries, the company provides an array of tactical gear and training services to militaries and law enforcement agencies. Subsidiary Cyalume Technologies, Inc., makes chemical light sticks and other reflective items, as well as explosion simulation products. It also offers combat training. Customers include NATO and US militaries and Canadian and German defense procurement agencies. Subsidiary Cyalume Specialty Products makes specialty chemical products for military, pharmaceutical, and other markets. Cyalume, which has manufacturing plants in the US and France, filed a $5.8 million IPO in April 2012.

FAREWAY STORES, INC.

715 8TH ST
BOONE, IA 500362727
Phone: 515 432-2623
Fax: –
Web: www.farewaystores.com

CEO: –
CFO: Craig A Shepley
HR: –
FYE: January 27
Type: Private

Fareway Stores makes green through groceries. The regional grocery chain operates under the Fareway banner, primarily in Iowa but also in Minnesota, Nebraska, and several other Midwestern states. Fareway's 100-plus locations average about 25,000 sq. ft. Eschewing such amenities as video rentals and dry-cleaning services, Fareway Stores sticks to the basics -- lots of meat (all cut to order) and groceries only -- counting on low prices and customer service to compete with supercenter operators, such as Wal-Mart. Former Safeway workers Paul Beckwith and Fred Vitt founded Fareway in 1938; the Beckwith family controls the company. Because of the founders' biblical beliefs, the stores are closed on Sundays.

FARM AID INC

501 CAMBRIDGE ST STE 3
CAMBRIDGE, MA 021411104
Phone: 617 354-2922
Fax: –
Web: www.farmaid.org

CEO: Willie Nelson
CFO: –
HR: –
FYE: December 31
Type: Private

Willie Nelson, Neil Young, and John Mellencamp got together and...helped farmers? That's correct. Farm Aid helps farmers throughout the US. The organization gives grants for food and emergency aid, hotlines, and legal assistance, as well as for education, outreach, and research. The group also promotes sustainable farming techniques, advocates for fair pricing, and provides credit counseling. Farm Aid's celebrity founders hope to raise American awareness that family farms (as opposed to corporate agriculture) are safer, more healthy, better for local economies, and more environmentally sound. The first FARM AID concert, and founding of Farm Aid, took place in 1985.

	Annual Growth	12/16	12/17	12/18	12/21	12/22
Sales ($mil.)	15.1%	–	2.3	2.8	10.1	4.7
Net income ($ mil.)	79.1%	–	0.0	0.6	7.3	1.2
Market value ($ mil.)	–	–	–	–	–	–
Employees		–	–	–	–	23

FARM CREDIT BANK OF TEXAS

4801 PLAZA ON THE LK STE 1200
AUSTIN, TX 787461081
Phone: 512 465-0400
Fax: –
Web: www.farmcreditbank.com

CEO: Larry R Doyle
CFO: Thomas W Hill
HR: Steve Knowles
FYE: December 31
Type: Private

The largest member of the federal Farm Credit System, the Farm Credit Bank of Texas provides loans and financial services to about 20 lending cooperatives and financial institutions in Alabama, Louisiana, Mississippi, New Mexico and Texas. These include agricultural credit associations, which provide agricultural production loans, agribusiness financing, and rural mortgage financing; and federal land credit associations, which offer real estate loans on farms, ranches, and other rural property. Farm Credit Bank of Texas is owned by the lending cooperatives it serves.

	Annual Growth	12/06	12/07	12/12	12/13	12/16
Assets ($mil.)	5.1%	–	13,521	–	16,213	21,222
Net income ($ mil.)	11.2%	–	74.0	–	179.8	192.4
Market value ($ mil.)	–	–	–	–	–	–
Employees		–	–	–	–	200

FARM SERVICE COOPERATIVE

2308 PINE ST
HARLAN, IA 515371884
Phone: 712 755-2207
Fax: –
Web: www.fscoop.com

CEO: –
CFO: –
HR: –
FYE: August 31
Type: Private

Farm Service Cooperative (FSC) offers a big bushel basket full of products and services to farmers in west central Iowa. The agricultural co-op offers its members such farm-management supplies and services as grain elevator operations, grain marketing, equipment rental, tires, livestock feed and fertilizer sales, soil sampling, on-staff crop advisors, farm credit and financing, agronomy, and Cenex energy products (diesel, home-heating oil, propane, ethanol, gasoline) from its 10 locations.

	Annual Growth	08/03	08/04	08/05	08/06	08/07
Sales ($mil.)	17.0%	–	–	47.7	53.2	65.4
Net income ($ mil.)	334.8%	–	–	0.8	15.0	14.4
Market value ($ mil.)	–	–	–	–	–	–
Employees		–	–	–	–	110

FARMER BROS. CO.

NMS: FARM

1912 Farmer Brothers Drive
Northlake, TX 76262
Phone: 682 549-6600
Fax: –
Web: www.farmerbros.com

CEO: John Moore
CFO: Scott R Drake
HR: Amber Jefferson
FYE: June 30
Type: Public

Founded in 1912, Farmer Bros. is a national coffee roaster, wholesaler and distributor of coffee, tea and culinary products. The company roasts and packages coffee, and sells it mainly to institutional foodservice operators such as restaurants, gourmet coffee houses, hotels, and hospitals. It also distributes related coffee products such as filters, sugar, and creamers, as well as assorted teas and culinary products (spices, soup, gelatins, and mixes). In addition, Farmer Bros. provides private brand coffee programs nationwide to retail customers such as convenience and grocery stores. The company operates a large fleet of trucks and other vehicles to distribute and deliver its products through its DSD network, and it relies on 3PL service providers for its long-haul distribution.

	Annual Growth	06/19	06/20	06/21	06/22	06/23
Sales ($mil.)	(13.1%)	595.9	501.3	397.9	469.2	340.0
Net income ($ mil.)	–	(73.6)	(37.1)	(41.7)	(15.7)	(79.2)
Market value ($ mil.)	(35.9%)	329.7	147.8	255.6	94.5	55.8
Employees	(10.1%)	1,521	1,210	1,064	1,068	993

FARMERS CO-OPERATIVE SOCIETY, SIOUX CENTER, IOWA

317 3RD ST NW
SIOUX CENTER, IA 512501856
Phone: 712 722-2671
Fax: –
Web: www.farmerscoopsociety.com

CEO: –
CFO: –
HR: –
FYE: July 31
Type: Private

When farmers cooperate, society benefits. Through its seven centers in northwest Iowa, Farmers Cooperative Society offers its member/farmers a full range of agricultural growing and marketing products and services, including crop-storage facilities and business consulting. Its feedlot, with room for some 5,500 head of cattle, helps members buy and care for feeder cattle, and provides discounts on grain for members. The co-op also operates a member-only How-To Building Store in Sioux Center, Iowa, that sells hardware, lawn-care products, lumber, and paint, as well as brand-name home appliances. Farmers Cooperative Society has roots dating back to 1907.

	Annual Growth	07/12	07/13	07/14	07/15	07/16
Sales ($mil.)	(8.2%)	–	496.5	418.5	405.3	384.2
Net income ($ mil.)	21.7%	–	5.0	3.9	7.6	8.9
Market value ($ mil.)	–	–	–	–	–	–
Employees		–	–	–	–	160

FARMERS COOPERATIVE COMPANY

105 GARFIELD AVE
FARNHAMVILLE, IA 505386712
Phone: 515 817-2100
Fax: –
Web: www.farmerscoop.com

CEO: James Chism
CFO: –
HR: –
FYE: August 31
Type: Private

The importance of cooperation -- it's one of life's most important lessons. Dating back to the early 1900s, the Farmers Cooperative Company (FCC) learned that lesson early on. The 5,500-member-plus co-op offers agronomy and grain marketing services to its members, who oversee some 3 million acres of farmland in central and north central Iowa. The largest of its kind in Iowa, FCC operates 40 grain elevators and provides soil testing and mapping services. It sells supplies including seed, feed, and fertilizer to its members. The coop merged with another Iowa coop, West Central Cooperative in 2016 to form Landus Cooperative.

	Annual Growth	08/06	08/07	08/08	08/09	08/10
Sales ($mil.)	(12.8%)	–	–	–	894.5	779.6
Net income ($ mil.)	(19.9%)	–	–	–	13.0	10.4
Market value ($ mil.)	–	–	–	–	–	–
Employees		–	–	–	–	450

FARMERS NATIONAL BANC CORP. (CANFIELD, OH)   NAS: FMNB

20 South Broad Street
Canfield, OH 44406
Phone: 330 533-3341
Fax: –
Web: www.farmersbankgroup.com

CEO: Kevin J Helmick
CFO: –
HR: –
FYE: December 31
Type: Public

Farmers National Banc is willing to help even nonfarmers grow their seed income into thriving bounties of wealth. The bank provides commercial and personal banking from nearly 20 branches in Ohio. Founded in 1887, Farmers National Banc offers checking and savings accounts, credit cards, and loans and mortgages. Farmers' lending portfolio is composed of real estate mortgages, consumer loans, and commercial loans. The company also includes Farmers National Insurance and Farmers Trust Company, a non-depository trust bank that offers wealth management and trust services.

	Annual Growth	12/19	12/20	12/21	12/22	12/23
Assets ($mil.)	20.0%	2,449.2	3,071.1	4,142.7	4,082.2	5,078.4
Net income ($ mil.)	8.7%	35.8	41.9	51.8	60.6	49.9
Market value ($ mil.)	(3.0%)	612.0	497.7	695.7	529.5	541.9
Employees	10.3%	450	445	550	546	666

FARMERS NEW WORLD LIFE INSURANCE CO.

3003 77th Ave. S.E.
Mercer Island, WA 98040-2890
Phone: 206 232-8400
Fax: –
Web: www.farmers.com

CEO: –
CFO: Katherine P Cody
HR: –
FYE: December 31
Type: Public

Individuals hoping to reap the rich rewards of life may discover Farmers New World Life Insurance without crossing treacherous oceans. The company is the primary life insurance subsidiary of Farmers Group, a top provider of personal property/casualty insurance in the US. Farmers New World Life Insurance offers a range of individual life insurance products, including universal, term, and whole life policies, as well fixed and variable annuities. The products of Farmers New World Life Insurance (which operates under the Farmers Life brand) are marketed through the Farmers Group's agency force. The company was founded in 1910.

	Annual Growth	12/97	12/98	12/99	12/00	12/01
Assets ($mil.)	9.1%	3,974.8	4,301.1	4,736.6	5,099.8	5,628.0
Net income ($ mil.)	(27.3%)	122.9	98.8	114.9	134.8	34.4
Market value ($ mil.)	–	–	–	–	–	–
Employees		–	–	–	–	–

FARMERS PRIDE, INC.

520 CHESTNUT HILL RD
FREDERICKSBURG, PA 170269337
Phone: 717 865-6626
Fax: –
Web: www.bellandevans.com

CEO: J M Good
CFO: Daniel Chirico
HR: Iluminada Ythier
FYE: December 29
Type: Private

Why did the chicken cross the road? Answer: To become part of the portfolio of poultry products offered by Farmer's Pride. Doing business as Bell & Evans, the company produces fresh, organic chicken and a variety of ready-to-cook and fully-cooked entrees and snacks. Bell birds, touted as healthier fare, are raised sans antibiotics or growth hormones, and fed hexane-free soybean meal. Farmer's Pride also offers Cornish game hen, duck, and roaster chicken. Customers have included natural and national food retailers Whole Foods, Wild Oats, and Giant, as well as restaurants Chipotle Mexican Grill and Panera Bread. Founded in the 1890s by Howard Bell and Carlton Evans, the company is owned by Scott Sechler.

FARMERS TELECOMMUNICATIONS COOPERATIVE, INC.

144 MCCURDY AVE N
RAINSVILLE, AL 359864407
Phone: 256 638-2144
Fax: –
Web: www.farmerstel.com

CEO: –
CFO: Tyler Pair
HR: –
FYE: December 31
Type: Private

Farmers Telecommunications Cooperative (FTC) is a rural local telephone service provider for about 17,000 subscribers in DeKalb and Jackson counties in northeast Alabama. It connects callers in the communities of Higdon, Ider, Henagar, Pisgah, Fyffe, and Geraldine, among others. The member-owned co-op provides traditional phone services including local exchange access and long-distance, as well as business and data systems and broadband Internet access. It also provides digital cable television. Subsidiary Farmers Wireless offers cell phone service. FTC was founded in 1952.

	Annual Growth	12/05	12/06	12/15	12/21	12/22
Sales ($mil.)	(8.7%)	–	15.7	1.7	4.1	3.7
Net income ($ mil.)	(13.3%)	–	2.6	(0.4)	1.0	0.3
Market value ($ mil.)	–	–	–	–	–	–
Employees		–	–	–	–	100

FARMERS TELEPHONE COOPERATIVE, INC.

1101 E MAIN ST
KINGSTREE, SC 295564105
Phone: 843 382-2333
Fax: –
Web: www.ftc.net

CEO: Bradley Erwin
CFO: Jeffrey Lawrimore
HR: –
FYE: June 30
Type: Private

Farmers Telephone Cooperative (FTC) is the incumbent local-exchange carrier (ILEC) in Williamsburg, Lee, Sumter, Clarendon, and Florence counties in eastern South Carolina. Serving more than 60,000 customers in a 3,000 mile area, the company provides traditional phone services, including local-exchange access and long-distance, as well as dial-up and DSL Internet access. The company also offers wireless phone service through a partnership with AT&T Mobility, as well as security services and enterprise communications services. In operation since 1951, FTC claims to be the second-largest co-op in the US, and should not be confused with the Farmers Telephone Cooperative serving the Rainsville, Alabama area.

FARMINGTON FOODS, INC.

7419 FRANKLIN ST
FOREST PARK, IL 601301016
Phone: 708 771-3600
Fax: –
Web: www.farmingtonfoods.com

CEO: –
CFO: –
HR: –
FYE: December 29
Type: Private

Farmington Foods takes food from the farm, adds value, and sells the results. The company processes, markets, and distributes Value-added pork products, including pork loin, chops, and ribs. Its Lean N' Juicy product line consists of case-ready enhanced pork, such as bone-in or boneless loin chops, baby backribs, spareribs, pork shoulder, and tenderloin. Farmington also offers a variety of marinated pork products in flavors like Teriyaki, lemon pepper, and Italian. In addition to pork products, the company also sells pre-packaged kabobs made with beef, chicken and pork. Formerly known as the Farmington Meat Company, the family-owned company was established in 1972.

	Annual Growth	12/00	12/01	12/02	12/03	12/07
Sales ($mil.)	(4.6%)	–	90.1	67.5	73.8	68.0
Net income ($ mil.)	–	–	–	–	–	–
Market value ($ mil.)	–	–	–	–	–	–
Employees	–	–	–	–	–	310

FARMLAND MUTUAL INSURANCE CO

1963 Bell Avenue
Des Moines, IA 50315-1030
Phone: 515 245-8800
Fax: –
Web: www.farmlandins.com

CEO: –
CFO: –
HR: –
FYE: December 31
Type: Public

Whether you're in high cotton or riding out a 17-year locust outbreak, Nationwide Agribusiness Insurance (and affiliate Farmland Mutual Insurance) have your farm covered. The company is one of the leading providers of insurance for the US commercial agribusiness industry, food processors, and farm operators of all sizes. Products include commercial insurance (CommercialGard and AgriChoice), workers' compensation (ComPlus), cotton farmer and ginner coverage (CottonGard), and other specialized farm policies. Additionally, the company offers commercial auto, umbrella liability, and customized policies, as well as various insurance services. Nationwide Agribusiness is a subsidiary of insurance biggie Nationwide.

	Annual Growth	12/97	12/98	12/99	12/00	12/01
Assets ($mil.)	3.0%	–	179.0	188.3	190.1	195.6
Net income ($ mil.)	(21.5%)	–	5.6	0.9	0.9	2.7
Market value ($ mil.)	–	–	–	–	–	–
Employees	–	–	–	–	–	–

FARMLAND PARTNERS INC

NYS: FPI

4600 South Syracuse Street, Suite 1450
Denver, CO 80237-2766
Phone: 720 452-3100
Fax: –
Web: www.farmlandpartners.com

CEO: –
CFO: –
HR: –
FYE: December 31
Type: Public

Farmland Partners partners with farmland tenants to make money. It owns and buys primary row crop farmland across North America. Its initial portfolio includes 38 farms with 7,300 total acres (33 farms in Illinois, 4 in Nebraska, and 1 in Colorado) and 3 grain storage facilities. It plans to diversify its portfolio by geography, crop type, and tenant. Targeted crops include primary row crops (grains, and oilseeds), and forage crops. Future options include fresh produce, peanuts, and biofuel feedstocks. Farmland's farming tenants provide an ongoing revenue stream for the company. Following an April 2014 IPO (which raised $53.2 million to pay down debt and fund expansion), CEO Paul Pittman owned 30% of Farmland.

	Annual Growth	12/19	12/20	12/21	12/22	12/23
Sales ($mil.)	1.8%	53.6	50.7	51.7	61.2	57.5
Net income ($ mil.)	22.1%	13.9	7.1	10.0	11.7	30.9
Market value ($ mil.)	16.5%	325.5	417.6	573.6	598.1	599.1
Employees	17.8%	13	14	27	30	25

FARMVET.COM, INC.

1254 OLD HILLSBORO RD
FRANKLIN, TN 370699129
Phone: 615 377-2300
Fax: –
Web: www.farmvet.com

CEO: Christian B Currey
CFO: Allen Good
HR: –
FYE: December 31
Type: Private

Who has time to get veterinary supplies when you're tending to the farm? FarmVet.com understands and offers thousands of discounted name-brand animal-health products and farm supplies for livestock, horses, and pets throughout the US via its Web site. The company distributes more than 50,000 products, including dietary supplements, grooming supplies, insecticides, and tools, from its warehouse facility in Tennessee. It has separate category devoted to equine products. In addition to its online store, FarmVet also has a printed catalog, and operates mobile retail units that travel throughout the year to select horse show venues.

	Annual Growth	12/10	12/11	12/12	12/13	12/14
Sales ($mil.)	(7.6%)	–	–	–	0.0	0.0
Net income ($ mil.)	–	–	–	–	(0.0)	0.0
Market value ($ mil.)	–	–	–	–	–	–
Employees	–	–	–	–	–	20

FARO TECHNOLOGIES INC.

NMS: FARO

250 Technology Park
Lake Mary, FL 32746
Phone: 407 333-9911
Fax: –
Web: www.faro.com

CEO: Michael D Burger
CFO: Allen Muhich
HR: Audrey Anthony
FYE: December 31
Type: Public

FARO Technologies is a global technology company that designs, develops, manufactures, markets and supports software-driven, three dimensional (3D) measurement, imaging, and realization solutions for the 3D metrology, architecture, engineering and construction (AEC), operations and maintenance (O&M) and public safety analytics markets. Its FARO suite of 3D products and software solutions are used for inspection of components and assemblies, rapid prototyping, reverse engineering, documenting large volume or structures in 3D, surveying and construction, construction management, assembly layout, machine guidance as well as in investigation and reconstructions of crash and crime scenes. Customers located outside the Americas account for about 45% of its revenue.

	Annual Growth	12/19	12/20	12/21	12/22	12/23
Sales ($mil.)	(1.5%)	381.8	303.8	337.8	345.8	358.8
Net income ($ mil.)	–	(62.1)	0.6	(40.0)	(26.8)	(56.6)
Market value ($ mil.)	(18.2%)	955.0	1,339.6	1,328.1	557.8	427.3
Employees	(9.1%)	1,818	1,364	1,432	1,490	1,243

FAROUK SYSTEMS, INC.

250 PENNBRIGHT DR
HOUSTON, TX 770905905
Phone: 281 876-2000
Fax: –
Web: www.farouk.com

CEO: Rami Shami
CFO: Christopher Bryan
HR: Alison Hager
FYE: December 31
Type: Private

Farouk Systems makes and markets high-quality professional hair care products for the professional and consumer markets in about 145 countries. Its shampoos and conditioners, treatments, gels and foams, and implements (hair dryers, curling irons, clippers, and brushes) are available for both men and women under the industry-leading brands such as BioSilk, CHI, and Beyond Glow. Farouk Systems also provides educational support to professional hairdressers through partnerships with more than 500 schools and its own cosmetology school in Houston. The company was founded in 1986 by Farouk Shami.

FARREL CORPORATION

1 FARRELL BLVD
ANSONIA, CT 064011256
Phone: 203 736-5500
Fax: –
Web: www.farrel-pomini.com

CEO: Mark Meulbroek
CFO: Paul M Zepp
HR: Angela Dawley
FYE: December 31
Type: Private

Farrel is a global leader in the research, design and manufacture of compounding systems for the polymer processing industry, specializing in highly filled and temperature sensitive applications. Farrel is a solutions provider for protecting equipment investment and maximizing productivity with a full portfolio of consultative and aftermarket services. It provides long-term value, from making capital equipment decision to support the lifecycle of equipment. Farrel Corporation began in the 1840s during the Industrial Revolution of the US when the company operated as a foundry and equipment manufacturer for the rubber industry.

FASHION INSTITUTE OF TECHNOLOGY

227 W 27TH ST
NEW YORK, NY 100015992
Phone: 212 217-7999
Fax: –
Web: www.fitnyc.edu

CEO: –
CFO: –
HR: –
FYE: June 30
Type: Private

Fashionistas pay homage to the Fashion Institute of Technology (FIT). The school offers degrees and classes in a variety of disciplines (about 45) within the fashion and design industry as well as in business, technology, and communications. More than 10,000 students are enrolled at FIT; it has a student-teacher ratio of 17:1. The school also hosts The Museum at the Fashion Institute of Technology, which houses collections of costumes and textiles, with a focus on 20th-century fashion. Virginia Pope, fashion editor of The New York Times, was one of FIT's founders. FIT began in 1944 and was tuition-free until 1953; it is part of the State University of New York (SUNY) system.

	Annual Growth	06/16	06/17	06/19	06/20	06/22
Sales ($mil.)	10.6%	–	7.2	7.0	8.6	11.9
Net income ($ mil.)	40.7%	–	1.5	1.0	4.0	8.0
Market value ($ mil.)	–	–	–	–	–	–
Employees	–	–	–	–	–	1,212

FASTENAL CO.

2001 Theurer Boulevard
Winona, MN 55987-1500
Phone: 507 454-5374
Fax: 507 453-8049
Web: www.fastenal.com

NMS: FAST
CEO: Daniel L Florness
CFO: Holden Lewis
HR: –
FYE: December 31
Type: Public

Fastenal is an industrial and fastener distributor that sells products in more than nine major product lines, including threaded fasteners (such as screws, nuts, and bolts), which represent about 35% of overall sales. Other sales come from fluid-transfer parts for hydraulic and pneumatic power; janitorial, electrical, and welding supplies; material handling items; metal-cutting tool blades; and safety supplies. Founded in 1967 as a fastener shop, Fastenal now operates about 3,306 branches and on-site locations in all 50 US states and in Canada, Mexico, Asia, and Europe. Its customers include construction, manufacturing, and other industrial professionals.

	Annual Growth	12/19	12/20	12/21	12/22	12/23
Sales ($mil.)	8.3%	5,333.7	5,647.3	6,010.9	6,980.6	7,346.7
Net income ($ mil.)	9.9%	790.9	859.1	925.0	1,086.9	1,155.0
Market value ($ mil.)	15.1%	21,135	27,930	36,641	27,066	37,047
Employees	1.4%	21,948	20,365	20,507	22,386	23,201

FATE THERAPEUTICS INC

12278 Scripps Summit Drive
San Diego, CA 92131
Phone: 858 875-1800
Fax: –
Web: www.fatetherapeutics.com

NMS: FATE
CEO: J S Wolchko
CFO: Edward Dulac
HR: Anna Sevilla
FYE: December 31
Type: Public

Fate Therapeutics believes it's destined to treat orphan diseases. The biopharmaceutical company is developing stem cell-based treatments for hematologic malignancies such as leukemia and lymphoma, non-malignant orphan diseases such as lysosomal storage disorders, hemoglobinopathies such as sickle cell disease and beta-thalassemia, as well as anemia and other immune deficiencies. Its lead drug candidate, ProHema, uses umbilical cord blood to treat hematologic malignancies. The company was founded in 2007 by seven scientists who are not involved in its day-to-day operations. In 2013 it went public, raising $40 million in its IPO, which it will use toward R&D as well as clinical and preclinical drug development.

	Annual Growth	12/19	12/20	12/21	12/22	12/23
Sales ($mil.)	56.2%	10.7	31.4	55.8	96.3	63.5
Net income ($ mil.)	–	(98.1)	(173.4)	(212.2)	(281.7)	(160.9)
Market value ($ mil.)	(33.9%)	1,930.1	8,968.2	5,770.7	995.1	368.9
Employees	0.4%	178	279	449	551	181

FAYETTE COMMUNITY HOSPITAL, INC.

1255 HIGHWAY 54 W
FAYETTEVILLE, GA 302144526
Phone: 770 719-7000
Fax: –
Web: www.piedmont.org

CEO: James M Burnette
CFO: John Miles
HR: –
FYE: June 30
Type: Private

If you do too much boogying at the Fayetteville Bluegrass Blast or slip in the sleet at the Christmas in Fayetteville festival, Piedmont Fayette Hospital (PFH) is there to help. The acute care hospital is home to centers in cardiovascular medicine, diabetes treatment, sleep disorder therapy, women's health, fitness, and rehabilitative care. With more than 500 physicians on staff, the former Fayette Community Hospital has the ability to treat just about whatever comes through its doors -- from ear, nose, throat problems to pediatric dentistry. The about 155-bed hospital opened in 1997 and is part of the not-for-profit Piedmont Healthcare network.

	Annual Growth	06/13	06/14	06/16	06/21	06/22
Sales ($mil.)	8.9%	–	306.2	349.7	553.2	606.4
Net income ($ mil.)	13.5%	–	29.0	25.7	88.7	80.0
Market value ($ mil.)	–	–	–	–	–	–
Employees	–	–	–	–	–	1,045

FAYETTEVILLE PUBLIC WORKS COMMISSION

955 OLD WILMINGTON RD
FAYETTEVILLE, NC 283016357
Phone: 910 483-1382
Fax: –
Web: www.faypwc.com

CEO: Tim Bryant
CFO: J D Miller
HR: Bobby Russell
FYE: June 30
Type: Private

The taps, the toilets, and the plugs in Fayetteville are all the province of The Public Works Commission of the City of Fayetteville, North Carolina (PWC), which is responsible for operating, maintaining, and upgrading the municipal electric, water, and wastewater utility systems. PWC distributes electricity to about 79,000 residential, commercial, and industrial customers. The electric utility has 1,312 miles of distribution lines, 24,770 distribution line transformers and more than 46,880 poles. The water utility serves more than 83,150 customers and has 1,340 miles of mains; the wastewater unit serves about 79,180 customers and has about 1,340 miles of sewer line.

	Annual Growth	06/17	06/18	06/19	06/20	06/21
Sales ($mil.)	0.3%	–	334.1	346.7	342.5	337.1
Net income ($ mil.)	8.5%	–	43.0	50.0	44.9	55.0
Market value ($ mil.)	–	–	–	–	–	–
Employees	–	–	–	–	–	467

FAYGO BEVERAGES, INC.

3579 GRATIOT AVE
DETROIT, MI 482071892
Phone: 313 925-1600
Fax: –
Web: www.faygo.com

CEO: Nick A Caporella
CFO: –
HR: Rita A Shadhaya
FYE: April 27
Type: Private

Faygo Beverages believes in flavor. Old-fashioned flavor -- its products are made with cane sugar (rather than high-fructose corn syrup) and are packaged in gen u ine glass bottles. The company manufactures some 50 fruit-flavored sodas, cola, ginger ale, root beer, and creme soda under the Faygo name. It also makes Fago non-alcoholic mixers (club soda and tonic water). Although it is best known for its "pop," the beverage maker offers Ohana brand iced tea, lemonade, and fruit punch. The wide range of Faygo pop flavors include Blueberry, Vanilla Creme, Redpop, Dr. Faygo, Moon Mist, and Black Cherry. The company, whose products are available throughout the US, is a subsidiary of National Beverage Corp.

FB FINANCIAL CORP

NYS: FBK

1221 Broadway, Suite 1300
Nashville, TN 37203
Phone: 615 564-1212
Fax: –
Web: www.firstbankonline.com

CEO: Christopher T Holmes
CFO: Michael M Mettee
HR: –
FYE: December 31
Type: Public

First Banks is a bank holding company designated as a financial holding company. The holding company for First Bank, is owned by chairman James Dierberg and his family. The bank provides a comprehensive suite of commercial and consumer banking services to clients in select markets primarily in Tennessee, Alabama, Southern Kentucky, and North Georgia. First Bank has over 80 branches in California, Illinois, and Missouri, with a concentration in metropolitan markets such as Los Angeles, San Diego, San Francisco, Sacramento, and St. Louis. The bank offers standard services like deposits, mortgages, and business and consumer loans. Additional services include brokerage, insurance, trust, and private banking, as well as commercial treasury management and international trade services.

	Annual Growth	12/19	12/20	12/21	12/22	12/23
Assets ($mil.)	19.8%	6,124.9	11,207	12,598	12,848	12,604
Net income ($ mil.)	9.4%	83.8	63.6	190.3	124.6	120.2
Market value ($ mil.)	0.2%	1,854.7	1,627.1	2,052.9	1,693.1	1,866.9
Employees	3.3%	1,399	1,852	1,962	1,757	1,591

FEDERAL AGRICULTURAL MORTGAGE CORP

NYS: AGM

1999 K Street, N.W., 4th Floor
Washington, DC 20006
Phone: 202 872-7700
Fax: –
Web: www.farmermac.com

CEO: Bradford T Nordholm
CFO: Aparna Ramesh
HR: –
FYE: December 31
Type: Public

Farmer Mac (Federal Agricultural Mortgage Corporation) is stockholder-owned, federally chartered corporation that combines private capital and public sponsorship to serve a public purpose. The company provides a secondary market for a variety of loans made to borrowers in rural America. The company's market activities include purchasing eligible loans directly from lenders and more. Farmer Mac is an institution of the Farm Credit System (FCS) which is composed of the banks, associations, and related entities including Farmer Mac and its subsidiaries. Farmer Mac was chartered by Congress in 1987 and established under federal legislation first enacted in 1988.

	Annual Growth	12/19	12/20	12/21	12/22	12/23
Assets ($mil.)	8.0%	21,709	24,356	25,145	27,333	29,524
Net income ($ mil.)	16.2%	109.5	108.6	132.3	178.1	200.0
Market value ($ mil.)	23.0%	905.3	805.0	1,343.6	1,222.0	2,073.2
Employees	15.8%	103	121	153	158	185

FEDERAL DEPOSIT INSURANCE CORP.

550 17th Street, NW
Washington, DC 20429-9990
Phone: 202 942-3100
Fax: 202 942-3427
Web: www.fdic.gov

CEO: –
CFO: Steven O App
HR: –
FYE: December 31
Type: Public

The Federal Insurance Corporation (FDIC) is an independent agency created by Congress to maintain stability and public confidence in the nation's financial system. The FDIC insures deposits and retirement accounts in member accounts for up to $250,000, protecting depositors in the event of bank failure. It also examines and supervises financial institutions for safety, soundness, and consumer protection; makes large and complex financial institutions resolvable; and manages receiverships. The FDIC is funded by member bank premiums for deposit insurance coverage and from earnings on investments in US Treasury securities. It insures around $9.9 trillion of deposits, covering virtually every bank in the country. An independent federal agency, the FDIC was created in 1933 in response to bank runs during the Great Depression.

	Annual Growth	12/06	12/07	12/08	12/09	12/10
Sales ($mil.)	50.0%	2,643.5	3,196.2	7,306.3	24,706	13,380
Net income ($ mil.)	66.3%	1,739.2	2,105.3	(37,033.2)	(36,002.6)	13,305
Market value ($ mil.)	–	–	–	–	–	–
Employees	–	–	4,532	5,034	6,557	8,150

FEDERAL EXPRESS CORPORATION

3610 HACKS CROSS RD
MEMPHIS, TN 381258800
Phone: 901 369-3600
Fax: –
Web: www.fedex.com

CEO: Frederick Smith
CFO: Elise Jordan
HR: –
FYE: May 31
Type: Private

An operating company of air-express giant FedEx Corporation, Federal Express Corporation, which does business as FedEx Express, is the world's largest express transportation company, offering time-definite delivery to more than 220 countries and territories. It offers a wide range of US domestic and international shipping services for delivery of packages and freight, connecting markets that generate more than 99% of the world's gross domestic product through door-to-door, customs-cleared services. The company operates approximately 70,000 drop-off locations, a fleet of nearly 700 aircraft, and more than 82,000 vehicles in its global network. FedEx Express also provides time-critical shipment services through FedEx Custom Critical and cross-border enablement and technology solutions and e-commerce transportation solutions.

FEDERAL HOME LOAN BANK BOSTON

800 Boylston Street
Boston, MA 02199
Phone: 617 292-9600
Fax: –
Web: www.fhlbboston.com

CEO: Timothy J Barrett
CFO: Frank Nitkiewicz
HR: Meghan Baker
FYE: December 31
Type: Public

Federal Home Loan Bank of Boston (FHLB Boston) is banking on the continued support of other banks. The government-supported enterprise provides funds for residential mortgages and community development loans to its members, which consist of more than 440 financial institutions across New England, including banks, thrifts, credit unions, and insurance companies. The bank also lends to nonmember institutions the likes of state housing finance agencies primarily to promote the funding of low to moderate income housing in the region. FHLB Boston is one of 12 regional wholesale banks in the Federal Home Loan Bank System. Its region includes Connecticut, Maine, Massachusetts, New Hampshire, Rhode Island, and Vermont.

	Annual Growth	12/18	12/19	12/20	12/21	12/22
Sales ($mil.)	(3.8%)	1,447.4	1,487.3	794.7	378.7	1,240.6
Net income ($ mil.)	(4.0%)	216.8	190.7	120.3	69.5	184.2
Market value ($ mil.)	–	–	–	–	–	–
Employees	(1.5%)	200	194	196	183	188

FEDERAL HOME LOAN BANK CHICAGO

433 West Van Buren Street, Suite 501S
Chicago, IL 60607
Phone: 312 565-5700
Fax: –
Web: www.fhlbc.com

CEO: –
CFO: –
HR: –
FYE: December 31
Type: Public

Federal Home Loan Bank of Chicago (FHLB Chicago) is a government-sponsored enterprises that provides secured loans and other support services to about 760 members, including commercial banks, credit unions, insurance companies, thrifts, and community development financial institutions throughout Illinois and Wisconsin. It is cooperatively owned by its member institutions, who use advances from the bank to originate residential mortgages, invest in government or mortgage-related securities, and promote affordable housing and community development in their respective communities. FHLB Chicago is one of a dozen federal banks that comprise the Federal Home Loan Bank System that was established by Congress in 1932.

	Annual Growth	12/18	12/19	12/20	12/21	12/22
Sales ($mil.)	2.5%	2,323.0	2,723.0	1,525.0	802.0	2,565.0
Net income ($ mil.)	8.2%	303.0	300.0	374.0	275.0	415.0
Market value ($ mil.)	–	–	–	–	–	–
Employees	1.4%	468	488	474	466	495

FEDERAL HOME LOAN BANK INDIANAPOLIS

8250 Woodfield Crossing Blvd.
Indianapolis, IN 46240
Phone: 317 465-0200
Fax: –
Web: www.fhlbi.com

CEO: Cindy L Konich
CFO: Gregory L Teare
HR: Chris Dawson
FYE: December 31
Type: Public

Federal Home Loan Bank of Indianapolis (FHLB Indianapolis) is one of a dozen regional banks in the Federal Home Loan Bank System established by Congress in 1932. It provides funding for residential mortgages and community development loans to about 400 member financial institutions, including banks, credit unions, insurance companies, and thrifts in Indiana and Michigan. (Community development financial institutions are also eligibile to become members of FHLB Indianapolis.) It also provides support services such as risk management, securities safekeeping, and funds transfers. FHLB Indianapolis is a government-sponsored enterprise that is cooperatively owned by its member financial institutions.

	Annual Growth	12/18	12/19	12/20	12/21	12/22
Sales ($mil.)	(2.9%)	1,565.1	1,752.4	853.5	469.8	1,390.6
Net income ($ mil.)	(2.4%)	194.7	141.8	87.9	93.9	176.7
Market value ($ mil.)	–	–	–	–	–	–
Employees	0.9%	249	256	262	239	258

FEDERAL HOME LOAN BANK NEW YORK

101 Park Avenue
New York, NY 10178
Phone: 212 681-6000
Fax: –
Web: www.fhlbny.com

CEO: Jose R Gonzalez
CFO: Kevin M Neylan
HR: –
FYE: December 31
Type: Public

Federal Home Loan Bank of New York (FHLBNY) provides funds for residential mortgages and community development to more than 310 financial institutions in New York, New Jersey, Puerto Rico, and the US Virgin Islands. One of a dozen Federal Home Loan Banks in the US, it is cooperatively owned by its member institutions and supervised by the Federal Housing Finance Agency.

	Annual Growth	12/18	12/19	12/20	12/21	12/22
Assets ($mil.)	2.2%	144,381	162,062	136,996	105,358	157,391
Net income ($ mil.)	(7.1%)	560.5	472.6	442.4	265.5	417.4
Market value ($ mil.)	–	–	–	–	–	–
Employees	1.0%	314	342	354	340	327

FEDERAL HOME LOAN BANK OF ATLANTA

1475 PEACHTREE ST NE
ATLANTA, GA 303093037
Phone: 404 888-8000
Fax: –
Web: corp.fhlbatl.com

CEO: W W McMullan
CFO: Haig Kazazian
HR: Sara Kuhl
FYE: December 31
Type: Private

Federal Home Loan Bank of Atlanta, also known as FHLBank Atlanta, is a cooperative bank that offers competitively priced financing, community development grants, and other banking services. FHLBank Atlanta is one of the 11 district FHLBanks, which raises funds in the global financial markets and distributes the proceeds to members and local communities. Its membership totaled more than 810 financial institutions, comprised of about 445 commercial banks, 240 credit unions, 60 savings institutions, 55 insurance companies, and about 15 community development financial institutions (CDFIs). Organized in 1932, the bank's defined geographic district includes Alabama, Florida, Georgia, Maryland, North Carolina, South Carolina, Virginia, and the District of Columbia.

	Annual Growth	12/18	12/19	12/20	12/21	12/22
Assets ($mil.)	0.4%	–	149,857	92,295	78,746	151,622
Net income ($ mil.)	(20.6%)	–	367.0	255.0	133.0	184.0
Market value ($ mil.)	–	–	–	–	–	–
Employees	–	–	–	–	–	313

FEDERAL HOME LOAN BANK OF CINCINNATI

600 Atrium Two, P.O. Box 598
Cincinnati, OH 45201-0598
Phone: 513 852-7500
Fax: –
Web: www.fhlbcin.com

CEO: Andrew S Howell
CFO: Stephen J Sponaugle
HR: –
FYE: December 31
Type: Public

FHLB in Cincinnati doesn't have a Dr. Johnny Fever, but it may be just what the doctor ordered for home buyers and developers in its district. A government sponsored entity, Federal Home Loan Bank of Cincinnati (FHLB Cincinnati) provides funds for residential mortgages and community development loans to more than 700 member commercial banks, thrifts, credit unions, insurance companies, and community development financial institutions (CDFI) in Ohio, Kentucky, and Tennessee. FHLB Cincinnati is part of the Federal Home Loan Bank System, which consists of 12 district banks, a national network of approximately 8,000 financial institution members, the Federal Housing Finance Agency, and the Office of Finance.

	Annual Growth	12/18	12/19	12/20	12/21	12/22
Assets ($mil.)	2.3%	99,203	93,492	65,296	60,618	108,610
Net income ($ mil.)	(7.2%)	339.2	276.1	276.4	42.0	252.0
Market value ($ mil.)	–	–	–	–	–	–
Employees	1.2%	229	234	241	245	240

FEDERAL HOME LOAN BANK OF DALLAS

8500 Freeport Parkway South, Suite 600
Irving, TX 75063-2547
Phone: 214 441-8500
Fax: –
Web: www.fhlb.com

CEO: –
CFO: –
HR: –
FYE: December 31
Type: Public

One of 11 Federal Home Loan Banks in operation around the country, Federal Home Loan Bank of Dallas provides low-cost funding for residential mortgages, small businesses, community investment, and rural development to approximately 800 members and associated institutions, which include community banks, credit unions, and thrifts, plus insurance companies, and housing associations across Arkansas, Louisiana, Mississippi, New Mexico, and Texas. The bank, which has approximately $89.6 billion in assets, also provides deposit, wire transfer, securities safekeeping, and custody and collateral services to its members, which own the bank.

	Annual Growth	12/18	12/19	12/20	12/21	12/22
Assets ($mil.)	12.0%	72,773	75,382	64,913	63,488	114,349
Net income ($ mil.)	12.4%	198.8	227.3	198.7	164.4	317.2
Market value ($ mil.)	–	–	–	–	–	–
Employees	0.5%	197	203	203	197	201

FEDERAL HOME LOAN BANK OF DES MOINES

909 Locust Street
Des Moines, IA 50309
Phone: 515 412-2100
Fax: –
Web: www.fhlbdm.com

CEO: Kristina K Williams
CFO: Joelyn R Jensen-Marren
HR: –
FYE: December 31
Type: Public

Federal Home Loan Bank of Des Moines (FHLB Des Moines), part of the Federal Home Loan Bank System established by Congress in 1932, provides funding and other support services to member institutions that, in turn, promote housing and economic development in their communities by issuing residential and commercial mortgages, home equity loans, small business loans, and rural and agricultural loans. The co-op's members, who are also stockholders and customers, include more than 1,200 financial institutions in its five-state district of Iowa, Minnesota, Missouri, North Dakota, and South Dakota. Membership is primarily comprised of commercial banks (about 85%), but also thrifts, credit unions, and insurance agencies.

	Annual Growth	12/18	12/19	12/20	12/21	12/22
Assets ($mil.)	2.9%	146,515	129,603	87,691	85,852	164,169
Net income ($ mil.)	(1.7%)	460.0	384.0	362.0	206.0	430.0
Market value ($ mil.)	–	–	–	–	–	–
Employees	(1.0%)	372	379	386	368	357

FEDERAL HOME LOAN BANK OF PITTSBURGH

601 Grant Street
Pittsburgh, PA 15219
Phone: 412 288-3400
Fax: –
Web: www.fhlb-pgh.com

CEO: Winthrop Watson
CFO: David G Paulson
HR: Kelly Sullivan
FYE: December 31
Type: Public

The Federal Home Loan Bank of Pittsburgh helps revitalize neighborhoods and fund low-income housing in the City of Champions and beyond. One of a dozen banks in the Federal Home Loan Bank System, the government-sponsored entity (FHLB Pittsburgh for short) uses private capital and public sponsorships to provide low-cost funding for residential mortgages and community and economic development loans in Delaware, Pennsylvania, and West Virginia. It is cooperatively owned by about 300 member banks, thrifts, credit unions, and insurance companies in its three-state district. The bank also offers member banks correspondent banking services, such as depository, funds transfer, settlement, and safekeeping services.

	Annual Growth	12/18	12/19	12/20	12/21	12/22
Sales ($mil.)	(8.1%)	2,272.4	2,690.0	1,074.6	426.5	1,621.3
Net income ($ mil.)	(10.1%)	347.2	316.9	210.4	86.0	227.1
Market value ($ mil.)	–	–	–	–	–	–
Employees	0.2%	224	228	234	221	226

FEDERAL HOME LOAN BANK OF SAN FRANCISCO

333 Bush Street, Suite 2700
San Francisco, CA 94104
Phone: 415 616-1000
Fax: –
Web: www.fhlbsf.com

CEO: Greg Seibly
CFO: Kenneth C Miller
HR: Barbara Waite
FYE: December 31
Type: Public

The city by the bay is the home to the Federal Home Loan Bank of San Francisco, one of a dozen regional banks in the Federal Home Loan Bank System chartered by Congress in 1932 to provide credit to residential mortgage lenders. The government-sponsored enterprise is privately owned by its members, which include some 400 commercial banks, credit unions, industrial loan companies, savings and loans, insurance companies, and housing associates headquartered in Arizona, California, and Nevada. The bank links members to worldwide capital markets, which provide them with low-cost funding. Members then pass these advances along to their customers in the form of affordable home mortgage and economic development loans.

	Annual Growth	12/18	12/19	12/20	12/21	12/22
Assets ($mil.)	2.6%	109,326	106,842	68,634	54,121	121,056
Net income ($ mil.)	(2.7%)	360.0	327.0	335.0	287.0	323.0
Market value ($ mil.)	–	–	–	–	–	–
Employees	1.3%	282	282	305	297	297

FEDERAL HOME LOAN BANK TOPEKA

500 S.W. Wanamaker Road
Topeka, KS 66606
Phone: 785 233-0507
Fax: –
Web: www.fhlbtopeka.com

CEO: Mark E Yardley
CFO: –
HR: Darrin Kite
FYE: December 31
Type: Public

Don't worry, Toto, Federal Home Loan Bank of Topeka is in Kansas. The institution created by Congress provides funds for residential mortgages and community-development loans to almost 900 member banks, thrifts, credit unions, and insurance companies in Arizona, Colorado, Kansas, Nebraska, New Mexico, Oklahoma, and Wyoming. FHLBank Topeka also provides members with other financial services such as safekeeping, shelf funding, and wire transfer services. One of a dozen Federal Home Loan Banks in the US, FHLBank Topeka is cooperatively owned by its member institutions.

	Annual Growth	12/18	12/19	12/20	12/21	12/22
Sales ($mil.)	2.4%	1,257.0	1,488.8	741.1	463.7	1,381.3
Net income ($ mil.)	9.0%	170.3	185.2	118.1	160.6	240.7
Market value ($ mil.)	–	–	–	–	–	–
Employees	1.5%	234	233	239	237	248

FEDERAL PRISON INDUSTRIES, INC

320 1ST ST NW
WASHINGTON, DC 205340002
Phone: 202 305-3500
Fax: –
Web: www.unicor.gov

CEO: Steve V Schwalb V
CFO: –
HR: –
FYE: September 30
Type: Private

Federal Prison Industries (FPI), known by its trade name UNICOR, uses prisoners to make products and provide services, mainly for US government agencies. Nearly 2500 inmates are waiting employed to nearly 100 FPI factories in prisons across the US. UNICOR, which is part of the Justice Department's Bureau of Prisons, manufactures products such as office furniture, clothing, beds and linens, electronics equipment as well as signage and print products. It also offers services, including data entry, bindery services, call center solutions, electronic recycling, and distribution, warehousing and logistics services. Federal Prison Industries program was established in 1934.

FEDERAL REALTY INVESTMENT TRUST (NEW)

NYS: FRT

909 Rose Avenue, Suite 200
North Bethesda, MD 20852
Phone: 301 998-8100
Fax: –
Web: www.federalrealty.com

CEO: Donald C Wood
CFO: Daniel Guglielmone
HR: Laura Houser
FYE: December 31
Type: Public

Federal Realty Investment Trust is a real estate investment trust (REIT) which owns or has a majority interest in about 105 retail properties with approximately 25.1 million sq. ft. of leasable space, including community and neighborhood shopping centers and mixed-use complexes. Its key markets are densely populated, affluent areas in the Northeast and Mid-Atlantic regions of the US, California and South Florida. The REIT's real estate projects were some 95% leased properties and around 90% are occupied. Principal tenants include Giant Food, Barnes & Noble, Bed, Bath & Beyond, and Home Depot. One of the oldest publicly traded REITs in the US, Federal Realty was founded in 1962.

	Annual Growth	12/19	12/20	12/21	12/22	12/23
Sales ($mil.)	4.9%	935.8	835.5	951.2	1,074.4	1,132.2
Net income ($ mil.)	(9.5%)	353.9	131.7	261.5	385.5	237.0
Market value ($ mil.)	(5.4%)	10,656	7,045.8	11,284	8,363.6	8,530.0
Employees	–	313	311	315	322	–

FEDERAL RESERVE BANK OF ATLANTA, DIST. NO. 6

1000 Peachtree Street, N.E.
Atlanta, GA 30309-4470
Phone: 404 498-8500
Fax: –
Web: www.frbatlanta.org

CEO: Dennis P Lockhart
CFO: –
HR: Elizabeth Austin
FYE: December 31
Type: Public

The Federal Reserve Bank of Atlanta is part of the central bank of the US. One of 12 regional banks in the Federal Reserve System, the Federal Reserve Bank of Atlanta oversees Fed member banks and thrifts, and their holding companies throughout the Southeast, including Alabama, Florida, Georgia, and parts of Louisiana, Mississippi, and Tennessee. It has branches in Birmingham, Jacksonville, Miami, Nashville, and New Orleans. As part of the nation's central banking system, the bank participates in setting national monetary policy, supervises numerous commercial banks, and provides a variety of financial services to depository institutions and the US government. The bank also processes checks and acts as a clearing house for payments between banks. Fed Reserve Banks are independent arms within the government and return earnings (gleaned mostly from investments in government bonds) to the US Treasury.

	Annual Growth	12/17	12/18	12/19	12/20	12/21
Sales ($mil.)	2.9%	6,971.0	6,948.0	7,042.0	7,677.0	7,805.0
Net income ($ mil.)	–	48.0	(138.0)	(26.0)	(4.0)	(68.0)
Market value ($ mil.)	–	–	–	–	–	–
Employees	–	–	–	–	–	–

FEDERAL RESERVE BANK OF BOSTON, DIST. NO. 1

600 Atlantic Avenue
Boston, MA 02210
Phone: 617 973-3000
Fax: –
Web: www.bostonfed.org

CEO: Susan M Collins
CFO: –
HR: Joseph Cabral
FYE: December 31
Type: Public

One of 12 regional banks in the Federal Reserve System, the Federal Reserve Bank of Boston oversees more than 100 banks and bank holding companies in six New England states including Connecticut (except Fairfield County), Massachusetts, Maine, New Hampshire, Rhode Island, and Vermont. It conducts examinations and investigations of member institutions, distributes money, issues savings bonds and Treasury securities, and assists the Fed in setting monetary policy. The bank also processes checks and acts as a clearinghouse for payments between banks. Federal Reserve Banks are not-for-profit and return most of their earnings (primarily from investments in government bonds) to the US Treasury.

	Annual Growth	12/17	12/18	12/19	12/20	12/21
Sales ($mil.)	(4.0%)	2,544.0	2,213.0	2,119.0	2,529.0	2,161.0
Net income ($ mil.)	(31.1%)	31.0	(93.0)	54.0	(1.0)	7.0
Market value ($ mil.)	–	–	–	–	–	–
Employees	–	–	–	–	–	–

FEDERAL RESERVE BANK OF CHICAGO, DIST. NO. 7

230 South La Salle Street
Chicago, IL 60604-1413
Phone: 312 322-5322
Fax: –
Web: www.chicagofed.org

CEO: Charles L Evans
CFO: –
HR: –
FYE: December 31
Type: Public

The Federal Reserve Bank of Chicago (Chicago Fed) serve the Seventh District, an economically and demographically diverse region made up of Iowa, and portions of Michigan, Illinois, Indiana, and Wisconsin. As part of the Federal Reserve System, the United States' central bank, it contributes to the creation of national monetary policy, supervise and regulate banking organizations, and provide financial services to banks and similar institutions, as well as to the US government. The Chicago Fed is a non-governmental entity that conducts economic research, bank supervision, community outreach and education, and central bank services. It is one of the 12 Federal Reserve Banks (Reserve Banks) created by Congress, which are chartered by the federal government and possess a unique set of governmental, corporate, and central bank characteristics.

	Annual Growth	12/17	12/18	12/19	12/20	12/21
Sales ($mil.)	8.3%	4,902.0	5,752.0	5,520.0	5,751.0	6,747.0
Net income ($ mil.)	(25.0%)	41.0	(101.0)	19.0	40.0	13.0
Market value ($ mil.)	–	–	–	–	–	–
Employees	–	–	–	–	–	–

FEDERAL RESERVE BANK OF CLEVELAND, DIST. NO. 4

P.O. Box 6387
Cleveland, OH 44101-1387
Phone: 216 579-2000
Fax: –
Web: www.clevelandfed.org

CEO: Loretta J Mester
CFO: Jacqueline Dalton
HR: Nancy Dacek
FYE: December 31
Type: Public

One of 12 regional banks in the Federal Reserve System, the Federal Reserve Bank of Cleveland has offices in Cleveland, Cincinnati, and Pittsburgh, the company serve an area that comprises Ohio, western Pennsylvania, eastern Kentucky, and the northern panhandle of West Virginia. It provides short-term loans to depository institutions, distributes money, issues savings bonds and Treasury securities, and participates in setting monetary policy. Federal Reserve Banks is the nation's central bank to provide the nation with a safer, more flexible, and more stable monetary and financial system.

	Annual Growth	12/17	12/18	12/19	12/20	12/21
Sales ($mil.)	4.8%	3,525.0	3,224.0	3,015.0	3,344.0	4,250.0
Net income ($ mil.)	15.1%	62.0	(192.0)	88.0	32.0	109.0
Market value ($ mil.)	–	–	–	–	–	–
Employees	–	–	–	–	–	–

FEDERAL RESERVE BANK OF DALLAS, DIST. NO. 11

2200 North Pearl Street
Dallas, TX 75201-2272
Phone: 214 922-6000
Fax: –
Web: www.dallasfed.org

CEO: Richard W Fisher
CFO: –
HR: –
FYE: December 31
Type: Public

One of 12 regional banks in the Federal Reserve System, the Federal Reserve Bank of Dallas covers the state of Texas; more than 25 parishes in northern Louisiana; and nearly 20 counties in southern New Mexico. It conducts examinations and investigations of member institutions, distributes money, issues savings bonds and Treasury securities, and assists the Federal Reserve in setting monetary policy. The bank also processes checks and acts as a clearinghouse for payments between banks. Its head office is in Dallas and has branches in El Paso, Houston, and San Antonio.

	Annual Growth	12/17	12/18	12/19	12/20	12/21
Sales ($mil.)	5.6%	4,455.0	4,626.0	4,427.0	4,796.0	5,533.0
Net income ($ mil.)	19.5%	24.0	(23.0)	(3.0)	69.0	49.0
Market value ($ mil.)	–	–	–	–	–	–
Employees	–	–	–	–	–	–

FEDERAL RESERVE BANK OF KANSAS CITY, DIST. NO. 10

1 Memorial Drive
Kansas City, MO 64198
Phone: 816 881-2000
Fax: –
Web: www.kansascityfed.org

CEO: –
CFO: –
HR: –
FYE: December 31
Type: Public

One of 12 regional banks in the Federal Reserve System, the Federal Reserve Bank of Kansas City oversees system member banks and bank holding companies in Missouri, Nebraska, Kansas, Oklahoma, Wyoming, Colorado and northern New Mexico. The bank also has branch offices in Denver, Oklahoma, and Omaha. Considered the 10th District, it provides short-term loans to depository institutions, distributes money, issues savings bonds and treasury securities, and assists the Fed in setting monetary policy. The bank, established in 1914, also processes checks and acts as a clearinghouse for payments between banks.

	Annual Growth	12/17	12/18	12/19	12/20	12/21
Sales ($mil.)	1.2%	1,733.0	1,847.0	1,653.0	1,725.0	1,818.0
Net income ($ mil.)	–	19.0	(23.0)	30.0	18.0	(1.0)
Market value ($ mil.)	–	–	–	–	–	–
Employees	–	–	–	–	–	–

FEDERAL RESERVE BANK OF MINNEAPOLIS, DIST. NO. 9

90 Hennepin Avenue, P.O. Box 291
Minneapolis, MN 55408-0291
Phone: 612 204-5000
Fax: –
Web: www.minneapolisfed.org

CEO: Narayana Kocherlakota
CFO: –
HR: –
FYE: December 31
Type: Public

The Federal Reserve Bank of Minneapolis, one of the 12 regional banks in the Federal Reserve System, regulates banks and bank holding companies in the Ninth District in Minnesota, Montana, North Dakota, South Dakota, northern Wisconsin, and the Upper Peninsula of Michigan. It conducts investigations of member institutions, distributes money, issues savings bonds and Treasury securities, and assists the Fed in setting monetary policy. The bank also processes checks and acts as a clearinghouse for payments between banks. The Federal Reserve Bank of Minneapolis, like its 11 counterparts, returns its profits (earned largely from investments in government and federal agency securities) to the US Treasury.

	Annual Growth	12/17	12/18	12/19	12/20	12/21
Sales ($mil.)	3.9%	932.0	970.0	920.0	994.0	1,088.0
Net income ($ mil.)	–	11.0	(12.0)	17.0	19.0	(31.0)
Market value ($ mil.)	–	–	–	–	–	–
Employees	–	–	–	–	–	–

FEDERAL RESERVE BANK OF NEW YORK, DIST. NO. 2

33 Liberty Street
New York, NY 10045-0001
Phone: 212 720-5000
Fax: –
Web: www.newyorkfed.org

CEO: Denis Hughes
CFO: –
HR: Aliya Hussain
FYE: December 31
Type: Public

The Federal Reserve Bank of New York is one of the twelve regional Reserve Banks which, together with the Board of Governors in Washington, DC, make up the Federal Reserve System. It issues currency, clears checks drawn, and lends to banks in its district. In addition to the duties it shares with twelve other regional Federal Reserve Banks, the New York Fed trades US government securities to regulate the money supply, intervenes on foreign exchange markets, and stores monetary gold for foreign central banks and governments. The New York Fed represents the Federal Reserve's Second District, a dynamic region that includes New York state, northern New Jersey, southwestern Connecticut, as well as Puerto Rico and the US Virgin Islands.

	Annual Growth	12/17	12/18	12/19	12/20	12/21
Sales ($mil.)	1.0%	65,090	62,509	56,535	54,640	67,807
Net income ($ mil.)	–	(503.0)	(652.0)	226.0	1,317.0	(1,284.0)
Market value ($ mil.)	–	–	–	–	–	–
Employees	–	–	–	–	–	–

FEDERAL RESERVE BANK OF PHILADELPHIA, DIST. NO. 3

10 Independence Mall
Philadelphia, PA 19106-1574
Phone: 215 574-6000
Fax: 215 574-6030
Web: www.philadelphiafed.org

CEO: Phoebe A Haddon
CFO: Michael J Angelakis
HR: Candiss Casimirlittle
FYE: December 31
Type: Public

One of 12 regional banks in the Federal Reserve System, the Federal Reserve Bank of Philadelphia oversees system member banks and bank holding companies in eastern and central Pennsylvania, southern New Jersey, and Delaware. It provides short-term loans to depository institutions, distributes money, issues savings bonds and Treasury securities, and assists the Fed in setting monetary policy. The Bank also processes checks and acts as a clearinghouse for payments between banks in its region. Federal Reserve Banks are not-for-profit and return most of their income (primarily earned from investments in US government and federal agency securities) to the US Treasury.

	Annual Growth	12/17	12/18	12/19	12/20	12/21
Sales ($mil.)	(4.4%)	3,103.0	2,843.0	2,518.0	2,447.0	2,587.0
Net income ($ mil.)	(32.0%)	70.0	(119.0)	(123.0)	27.0	15.0
Market value ($ mil.)	–	–	–	–	–	–
Employees	–	–	–	–	–	–

FEDERAL RESERVE BANK OF RICHMOND, NO. 5

Post Office Box 27622
Richmond, VA 23261
Phone: 804 697-8000
Fax: –
Web: www.richmondfed.org

CEO: Jodie McLean
CFO: –
HR: David Reynolds
FYE: December 31
Type: Public

One of 12 regional banks in the Federal Reserve System, the Federal Reserve Bank of Richmond covers the states of Maryland, Virginia, North Carolina, and South Carolina; most of West Virginia; and the District of Columbia. It conducts examinations and investigations of member institutions, distributes money, issues savings bonds and Treasury securities, and assists the Federal Reserve System in setting monetary policy. The bank also processes checks and acts as a clearinghouse for payments between banks. It also conducts research which supports policymaking and thought leadership on issues important to the Federal Reserve and the Fifth District. Federal Reserve Banks return earnings (mostly from investments in government bonds) to the US Treasury. The bank was formed in 1913 by the Federal Reserve Act.

	Annual Growth	12/16	12/17	12/18	12/19	12/20
Sales ($mil.)	0.7%	6,604.0	7,217.0	6,602.0	6,232.0	6,792.0
Net income ($ mil.)	(12.1%)	67.0	165.0	(508.0)	135.0	40.0
Market value ($ mil.)	–	–	–	–	–	–
Employees	–	–	–	–	–	–

FEDERAL RESERVE BANK OF SAN FRANCISCO, DIST. NO. 12

101 Market Street
San Francisco, CA 94105
Phone: 415 974-2000
Fax: –
Web: www.frbsf.org

CEO: John C Williams
CFO: –
HR: Kirk Hieda
FYE: December 31
Type: Public

The Federal Reserve Bank of San Francisco (SF Fed) serves the public by promoting a healthy, sustainable economy, and supporting the nation's financial and payment systems. With offices in Los Angeles, Seattle, Salt Lake City, Portland and Phoenix, the Bank serves the Twelfth Federal Reserve District, which includes one-fifth of the nation's population and represents the world's fourth-largest economy. FRBSF inform monetary policy, regulate banks, administer certain consumer protection laws, and act as a financial partner to the US government.

	Annual Growth	12/17	12/18	12/19	12/20	12/21
Sales ($mil.)	(3.1%)	14,660	13,978	12,188	12,679	12,941
Net income ($ mil.)	(17.8%)	116.0	(330.0)	133.0	69.0	53.0
Market value ($ mil.)	–	–	–	–	–	–
Employees	–	–	–	–	–	–

FEDERAL RESERVE BANK OF ST. LOUIS, DIST. NO. 8

One Federal Reserve Bank Plaza, Broadway and Locust Street
St. Louis, MO 63102
Phone: 314 444-8444
Fax: –
Web: www.stlouisfed.org

CEO: James B Bullard
CFO: –
HR: Katy Merk
FYE: December 31
Type: Public

One of 12 regional banks in the Federal Reserve System, the Federal Reserve Bank of St. Louis regulates banks and bank holding companies in its region. Its territory encompasses eastern Missouri, southern Illinois, all of Arkansas, and portions of Indiana, Kentucky, Mississippi, and Tennessee. The bank, operating from four offices, conducts examinations and investigations of member institutions, distributes money, processes checks and payments between banks, issues savings bonds and Treasury securities, and assists the Fed in setting monetary policy. Federal Reserve Banks are not-for-profit and return almost all of their earnings (gleaned mostly from investments in government bonds) to the US Treasury.

	Annual Growth	12/17	12/18	12/19	12/20	12/21
Sales ($mil.)	2.2%	1,759.0	1,741.0	1,702.0	1,831.0	1,916.0
Net income ($ mil.)	(16.4%)	47.0	(26.0)	15.0	37.0	23.0
Market value ($ mil.)	–	–	–	–	–	–
Employees	–	–	–	–	–	–

FEDERAL RESERVE SYSTEM

20th Street and Constitution Avenue N.W.
Washington, DC 20551
Phone: 202 452-3245
Fax: 202 728-5886
Web: www.federalreserve.gov

CEO: –
CFO: –
HR: –
FYE: December 31
Type: Public

The Federal Reserve was created by an act of Congress in 1913, to provide the nation with a safer, more flexible, and more stable monetary and financial system. In establishing the Federal Reserve System, the United States was divided geographically into 12 Districts, each with a separately incorporated Reserve Bank. The Fed is the central bank of the United States. It conducts the nation's monetary policy to promote maximum employment, stable prices, and moderate long-term interest rates in the US economy, and promotes the stability of the financial system and seeks to minimize and contain systemic risks through active monitoring and engagement in the US and abroad.

	Annual Growth	12/17	12/18	12/19	12/20	12/21
Sales ($mil.)	1.2%	116,764	113,120	103,846	104,976	122,368
Net income ($ mil.)	–	133.0	(2,218.0)	565.0	1,662.0	(1,097.0)
Market value ($ mil.)	–	–	–	–	–	–
Employees	–	–	–	–	–	–

FEDERAL SCREW WORKS

NBB: FSCR

34846 Goddard Road
Romulus, MI 48174
Phone: 734 941-4211
Fax: –
Web: www.federalscrewworks.com

CEO: Thomas Zurschmiede
CFO: –
HR: –
FYE: June 30
Type: Public

Federal Screw Works (FSW) doesn't mind if you think of your car as a bucket of bolts. The Detroit native makes fasteners and related items, primarily for the automotive industry. The company produces high-volume lots to the specifications of manufacturers. Nonautomotive sales are mainly to makers of durable goods. FSW's products include locknuts, bolts, piston pins, studs, bushings, shafts, and other machined, cold-formed, hardened, and ground-metal parts. It maintains five manufacturing facilities, all of which are located in Michigan.

	Annual Growth	06/19	06/20	06/21	06/22	06/23
Sales ($mil.)	8.7%	73.4	60.0	69.6	85.2	102.4
Net income ($ mil.)	(29.6%)	4.2	(2.0)	7.0	(7.7)	1.0
Market value ($ mil.)	7.5%	10.1	6.9	8.7	9.7	13.5
Employees	1.1%	221	184	218	255	231

FEDERAL SIGNAL CORP.

NYS: FSS

1415 West 22nd Street
Oak Brook, IL 60523
Phone: 630 954-2000
Fax: 630 954-2030
Web: www.federalsignal.com

CEO: Jennifer L Sherman
CFO: Ian A Hudson
HR: –
FYE: December 31
Type: Public

Federal Signal designs, manufactures, and supplies a suite of products and integrated solutions for municipal, governmental, industrial, and commercial customers. Offerings include sewer cleaners, street sweepers, industrial vaccum loaders, vacuum- and hydro-excavation trucks, road-marking and line-removal equipment, water-blasting equipment, dump truck bodies, trailers, and safety and security systems, including technology-based products and solutions for the public safety market. In addition, the company engages in the sale of parts, service and repair, equipment rentals, and training as part of a comprehensive aftermarket offering to its customers. The company operates some 20 principal manufacturing facilities in five countries and provides products and integrated solutions to customers in all regions of the world. Federal Signal generates the majority of sales from the US market.

	Annual Growth	12/19	12/20	12/21	12/22	12/23
Sales ($mil.)	9.0%	1,221.3	1,130.8	1,213.2	1,434.8	1,722.7
Net income ($ mil.)	9.7%	108.5	96.2	100.6	120.4	157.4
Market value ($ mil.)	24.2%	1,967.3	2,023.4	2,643.7	2,834.7	4,681.1
Employees	5.7%	3,600	3,500	3,900	4,100	4,500

FEDERATED HERMES INC

NYS: FHI

1001 Liberty Avenue
Pittsburgh, PA 15222-3779
Phone: 412 288-1900
Fax: –
Web: www.federatedhermes.com

CEO: J C Donahue
CFO: Thomas R Donahue
HR: Cathy Perott
FYE: December 31
Type: Public

Federated Hermes is a global leader in active, responsible investment management, with $668.9 billion in assets under management. The company delivers investment solutions that help investors target a broad range of outcomes and provides offers a wide range of products and strategies, including money market, equity, fixed-income, alternative/private markets and multi-asset investments to more than 11,000 institutions and intermediaries worldwide. Its clients include corporations, government entities, insurance companies, foundations and endowments, banks and broker/dealers. The US accounts for some 80% of total revenue. Federated Hermes was founded in 1955 by John F. Donahue and Richard B. Fisher.

	Annual Growth	12/19	12/20	12/21	12/22	12/23
Sales ($mil.)	4.9%	1,326.9	1,448.3	1,300.4	1,445.8	1,609.6
Net income ($ mil.)	2.4%	272.3	326.4	270.3	239.5	299.0
Market value ($ mil.)	1.0%	2,765.3	2,451.3	3,188.7	3,080.9	2,873.0
Employees	2.6%	1,826	1,986	1,968	1,961	2,025

FEDERATED MUTUAL INSURANCE CO. (OWATONNA, MINN.)

121 East Park Square
Owatonna, MN 55060
Phone: 507 455-5200
Fax: 507 455-5651
Web: www.federatedinsurance.com

CEO: Jeffrey Fetters
CFO: –
HR: –
FYE: December 31
Type: Public

Federated Mutual Insurance, a member of the Federated Insurance Companies, which was founded in 1904. A.M. Best Company, one of the most widely recognized provider of insurance, includes Federal Mutual Insurance Company, Federal Service Insurance Company, Federal Reserve Insurance Company, and Granite Re, Inc.

	Annual Growth	12/97	12/98	12/99	12/00	12/01
Assets ($mil.)	2.6%	2,414.2	2,475.9	2,525.6	2,463.7	2,671.6
Net income ($ mil.)	–	89.4	74.8	63.4	49.4	(21.8)
Market value ($ mil.)	–	–	–	–	–	–
Employees	–	–	–	–	–	–

FEDERATED SERVICE INSURANCE CO. (OWATONNA, MN)

121 East Park Square
Owatonna, MN 55060
Phone: 507 455-5200
Fax: –
Web: –

CEO: Jeffrey Fetters
CFO: –
HR: Hjordi Churchill
FYE: December 31
Type: Public

Federated Insurance is a mutual firm with a clear focus. The company provides multiple lines of business insurance coverage and risk management to niche businesses including automotive repair and sales, building contractors, printers, funeral homes, and jewelers, among others. Its products and services include property, liability, and auto coverage, as well as workers' compensation, risk management, group life and health, and retirement planning. Federated Insurance markets its products across the US. Since its founding in 1904, the company has worked closely with trade associations to develop and endorse its insurance programs.

	Annual Growth	12/97	12/98	12/99	12/00	12/01
Assets ($mil.)	8.9%	–	–	–	2,614.4	2,847.5
Net income ($ mil.)	–	–	–	–	46.2	(32.7)
Market value ($ mil.)	–	–	–	–	–	–
Employees	–	–	–	–	–	–

FEDEX CORP

NYS: FDX

942 South Shady Grove Road
Memphis, TN 38120
Phone: 901 818-7500
Fax: –
Web: www.fedex.com

CEO: John A Smith
CFO: John W Dietrich
HR: –
FYE: May 31
Type: Public

Holding company FedEx Corporation operates through subsidiaries FedEx Express, FedEx Ground, and FedEx Freight, among others. Its FedEx Express unit is the world's largest express transportation provider to more than 220 countries and territories. It maintains a fleet of about 700 aircraft and more than 82,000 vehicles. To complement the express delivery business, FedEx Ground provides small-package ground delivery in North America, and less-than-truckload (LTL) carrier FedEx Freight hauls larger shipments. FedEx Office stores offer sales, marketing, information technology, communications, customer service, technical support, billing and collection services, and certain back-office functions for other FedEx units. About 70% of revenue is generated in the US.

	Annual Growth	05/19	05/20	05/21	05/22	05/23
Sales ($mil.)	6.6%	69,693	69,217	83,959	93,512	90,155
Net income ($ mil.)	64.7%	540.0	1,286.0	5,231.0	3,826.0	3,972.0
Market value ($ mil.)	9.0%	38,753	32,795	79,076	56,412	54,754
Employees	0.5%	239,000	245,000	289,000	249,000	244,000

FEDNAT HOLDING CO

NBB: FNHC Q

14050 N.W. 14th Street, Suite 180
Sunrise, FL 33323
Phone: 800 293-2532
Fax: –
Web: www.fednat.com

CEO: –
CFO: –
HR: –
FYE: December 31
Type: Public

Trashed trailer, crashed car, damaged dwelling? Federated National Holding Company has a policy to cover that. Through Federated National Insurance Company and other subsidiaries, it underwrites a variety of personal property/casualty insurance lines in Florida, Louisiana, Texas, South Carolina, Alabama, Georgia and Mississippi.. Products include homeowners, federal flood, liability, and other lines of insurance in Florida and other states.. Recently formed property insurance unit Monarch National (established in 2015) offers a complete homeowners policy multi-peril insurance product for Florida homeowners. The firm distributes its products through independent agents and its Insure-Link agency.

	Annual Growth	12/17	12/18	12/19	12/20	12/21
Assets ($mil.)	11.8%	904.9	925.4	1,179.0	1,428.5	1,412.7
Net income ($ mil.)	–	–	8.0	14.9	1.0	(78.2)	(103.1)
Market value ($ mil.)	(46.0%)	289.1	347.5	290.1	103.3	24.6
Employees	(5.0%)	419	318	357	377	341

FEED THE CHILDREN, INC.

333 N MERIDIAN AVE
OKLAHOMA CITY, OK 731076568
Phone: 405 942-0228
Fax: –
Web: www.feedthechildren.org

CEO: Travis Arnold
CFO: –
HR: Jessica Jean
FYE: June 30
Type: Private

Tuppence a bag might feed some birds, but it takes more to feed growing children. Feed The Children (FTC) is a not-for-profit Christian charity that distributes food, medicine, clothing, and other necessities. In the US, FTC accepts bulk contributions of surplus food from businesses, packages it in various ways at six main facilities nationwide, and distributes it to food banks, homeless shelters, churches, and other organizations that help feed the hungry. In more than 120 countries overseas FTC works with organizations such as schools, orphanages, and churches to provide food, medical supplies, clothing, and educational support to the needy. Larry and Frances Jones founded FTC in 1979.

	Annual Growth	06/12	06/13	06/14	06/20	06/22
Sales ($mil.)	(1.7%)	–	453.9	–	–	387.7
Net income ($ mil.)	–	–	42.3	–	–	(15.4)
Market value ($ mil.)	–	–	–	–	–	–
Employees	–	–	–	–	–	160

FEMINIST MAJORITY FOUNDATION

1600 WILSON BLVD STE 801
ARLINGTON, VA 222092513
Phone: 703 522-2214
Fax: –
Web: www.feminist.org

CEO: –
CFO: –
HR: –
FYE: December 31
Type: Private

"I am woman, hear me roar, in numbers too big to ignore". The old Helen Reddy song is the perfect anthem for The Feminist Majority Foundation (FMF). The not-for-profit organization is dedicated to fighting for women's equality and reproductive rights. Main focuses include protecting women's clinics from anti-abortion violence, helping Afghan women, publicizing women's issues, and opposing anti-abortion judges. FMF became the sole publisher of Ms. Magazine in 2001 and provides research resources for activists and students. The organization was founded in 1987 to fight for and protect women's rights in the US and globally.

FENNEC PHARMACEUTICALS INC

NAS: FENC

P.O. Box 13628, 68 T.W. Alexander Drive
Research Triangle Park, NC 27709
Phone: 919 636-4530
Fax: 919 890-0490
Web: www.fennecpharma.com

CEO: Rostislav Raykov
CFO: Robert Andrade
HR: –
FYE: December 31
Type: Public

Working nimbly with a very sticky subject, Adherex Technologies researches and develops cancer treatments. One of its lead drug candidates targets a tumor's blood supply and makes those blood vessels weak and leaky by disrupting a key protein. Other potential therapies could make cancer cells more vulnerable to anti-cancer drugs or help prevent hearing loss in children undergoing certain types of chemotherapy. Adherex Technologies' pipeline is strongly based on compounds that disrupt cadherins, proteins that adhere similar molecules together in cell adhesion. Southpoint Capital Advisors owns a controlling stake in the company.

	Annual Growth	12/18	12/19	12/20	12/21	12/22
Sales ($mil.)	–	–	–	0.2	–	1.5
Net income ($ mil.)	–	(9.9)	(12.8)	(18.1)	(17.3)	(23.7)
Market value ($ mil.)	10.8%	168.2	171.1	196.4	116.0	253.1
Employees	86.1%	3	4	9	10	36

FENTURA FINANCIAL INC
NBB: FETM

P.O. Box 725
Fenton, MI 48430-0725
Phone: 810 629-2263
Fax: –
Web: www.fentura.com

CEO: Ronald L Justice
CFO: James W Distelrath
HR: –
FYE: December 31
Type: Public

It just makes cents to say that Fentura Financial has its hands full. Fentura Financial is the holding company for Michigan community banks The State Bank, Davison State Bank, West Michigan Community Bank, and Community Bancorp. From about 20 branch locations, the banks provide commercial and consumer banking services and products, including checking and savings accounts and loans. Commercial loans account for some two-thirds of the bank's combined loan portfolio. The State Bank, Fentura's first subsidiary, traces its origins to 1898. Fentura acquired St. Charles-based Community Bancorp in late 2016.

	Annual Growth	12/18	12/19	12/20	12/21	12/22
Assets ($mil.)	16.2%	926.5	1,034.8	1,251.4	1,417.8	1,688.9
Net income ($ mil.)	10.2%	10.1	11.6	15.5	16.6	14.9
Market value ($ mil.)	1.4%	93.2	112.0	97.7	125.6	98.6
Employees	–	–	–	–	–	–

FENWAY PARTNERS, LLC

108 AIRPORT RD STE 202
WESTERLY, RI 028913436
Phone: 212 698-9400
Fax: –
Web: www.fenwaypartners.com

CEO: –
CFO: –
HR: –
FYE: December 31
Type: Private

No red socks here, but private equity firm Fenway Partners does boast an eclectic portfolio of midsized companies valued between $100 million and $600 million in the consumer products and logistics sectors, among others. Its holdings include stakes in Easton-Bell Sports (maker of official NFL helmets), scholastic memorabilia maker American Achievement, and temperature-controlled logistics provider Refrigerated Holdings. Upon making its investment in a company, Fenway Partners provides management and strategy advice to boost performance. Despite its name, the company has offices in New York and Los Angeles, but not in Boston, home of baseball's Fenway Park.

FERGUSON ENTERPRISES, LLC

751 LAKEFRONT CMNS
NEWPORT NEWS, VA 236063322
Phone: 757 969-4011
Fax: –
Web: www.ferguson.com

CEO: Kevin Murphy
CFO: Bill Brundage
HR: –
FYE: July 31
Type: Private

Ferguson Enterprises is one of the largest wholesale distributors of plumbing supplies, pipes, valves, and fittings in the US. It is also a major distributor of HVAC equipment for heating and cooling, waterworks (water hydrants and meters), kitchen and bath, lighting, safety equipment, appliances, and tools. The company's major brands include American Standard, KOHLER, Fujitsu, Delta, Jacuzzi, Samsung, Westcraft, and PROFLO, among others. Ferguson has greater than 1,500 locations and about 10 distribution centers serving customers across all 50 US states. Formed in 1953, Ferguson is a subsidiary of UK-based Ferguson plc (formerly Wolseley) and has more than 36,000 associates in some 1,720 locations.

	Annual Growth	07/18	07/19	07/20	07/21	07/22
Sales ($mil.)	19.8%	–	–	18,856	21,477	27,066
Net income ($ mil.)	42.2%	–	–	1,266.0	1,814.0	2,560.0
Market value ($ mil.)	–	–	–	–	–	–
Employees	–	–	–	–	–	27,065

FERRELLGAS PARTNERS LP
NBB: FGPR

One Liberty Plaza
Liberty, MO 64068
Phone: 816 792-1600
Fax: –
Web: www.ferrellgas.com

CEO: James E Ferrell
CFO: Michael E Cole
HR: –
FYE: July 31
Type: Public

Ferrellgas Partners is a leading distributor of propane and related equipment and supplies to customers in the US. It is also the second largest retail marketer of propane in the US and a leading national provider of propane by portable tank exchange. It serves residential, commercial, portable tank exchange, agricultural, wholesale and other customers in all 50 states, the District of Columbia, and Puerto Rico with propane delivery, Blue Rhino portable tank exchanges, and the sale of propane appliances and related parts and fittings, as well as other retail propane related services and consumer products under the Blue Rhino brand.

	Annual Growth	07/19	07/20	07/21	07/22	07/23
Sales ($mil.)	4.7%	1,684.4	1,497.8	1,754.3	2,114.5	2,026.5
Net income ($ mil.)	–	(64.2)	(82.5)	(68.4)	148.0	136.9
Market value ($ mil.)	75.1%	5.2	2.5	132.6	73.2	49.2
Employees	–	–	–	–	–	4,005

FERRIS STATE UNIVERSITY (INC)

1201 S STATE ST
BIG RAPIDS, MI 493072714
Phone: 231 591-2000
Fax: –
Web: www.ferris.edu

CEO: –
CFO: –
HR: –
FYE: June 30
Type: Private

Going to college is no carnival, but Ferris State University still hopes the experience is enjoyable. The career-oriented public university offers more than 180 degree programs, including associate's, bachelor's, master's, and doctoral degrees through the colleges of Allied Health Sciences, Arts and Sciences, Business, Education and Human Services, Optometry, Pharmacy, Technology, and Kendall College of Art and Design. The school has some 14,500 students on 21 campuses located across Michigan. Ferris State was founded in 1884 by Michigan educator and statesman Woodbridge N. Ferris.

	Annual Growth	06/14	06/15	06/16	06/17	06/19
Sales ($mil.)	(2.0%)	–	–	–	166.3	159.6
Net income ($ mil.)	(11.5%)	–	–	–	14.4	11.2
Market value ($ mil.)	–	–	–	–	–	–
Employees	–	–	–	–	–	1,200

FETCH LOGISTICS, INC.

25 NORTHPOINTE PKWY # 200
AMHERST, NY 142281891
Phone: 716 689-4556
Fax: –
Web: www.fitzmark.com

CEO: –
CFO: –
HR: –
FYE: November 30
Type: Private

Don't just throw this company a ball -- tell it you want a truckload of balls hauled to your customer's warehouse ASAP. Fetch Logistics provides freight transportation management services for businesses with items to ship throughout North America. The company doesn't own transportation assets; instead, by working through a network of more than 20,000 carriers, Fetch Logistics can arrange truckload, less-than-truckload, and intermodal freight hauling. It serves companies in the beverage, bottled water, building materials, consumer goods, food, paper, and plastics industries. Fetch Logistics was founded in 1997.

	Annual Growth	12/00	12/01	12/02*	11/09	11/10
Sales ($mil.)	10.1%	–	–	11.3	–	24.5
Net income ($ mil.)	7.0%	–	–	0.4	–	0.7
Market value ($ mil.)	–	–	–	–	–	–
Employees	–	–	–	–	–	47

*Fiscal year change

FFD FINANCIAL CORP
NBB: FFDF

321 North Wooster Avenue, P.O. Box 38
Dover, OH 44622
Phone: 330 364-7777
Fax: –
Web: www.firstfed.com

CEO: –
CFO: –
HR: –
FYE: June 30
Type: Public

FFD Financial is the holding company for First Federal Community Bank, which serves Tuscarawas County and contiguous portions of eastern Ohio through about five branches. Founded in 1898, the bank offers a full range of retail products, including checking and savings accounts, CDs, IRAs, and credit cards. The bank mainly uses these funds to originate one- to four-family residential mortgages, nonresidential real estate loans, and land loans. First Federal Community Bank also originates business, consumer, and multifamily residential real estate loans. In 2012, First Federal Community Bank converted its charter from a savings bank to a national commercial bank.

	Annual Growth	06/19	06/20	06/21	06/22	06/23
Assets ($mil.)	15.4%	414.0	522.3	591.5	652.9	733.5
Net income ($ mil.)	15.2%	6.3	7.0	8.8	9.1	11.1
Market value ($ mil.)	(11.0%)	155.9	183.6	214.8	103.6	97.7
Employees	–	–	–	–	–	–

FFW CORP.
NBB: FFWC

1205 North Cass Street
Wabash, IN 46992-1027
Phone: 260 563-3185
Fax: –
Web: www.crossroadsbanking.com

CEO: Roger K Cromer
CFO: –
HR: –
FYE: June 30
Type: Public

You can find this company at the intersection of Savings and Loans. FFW Corporation is the holding company for Crossroads Bank (formerly First Federal Savings Bank of Wabash), founded in 1920 as Home Loan Savings Association. Today, the bank has five branches in Columbia City, North Manchester, South Whitley, Syracuse, and Wabash, Indiana. Its deposit products include CDs and checking, savings, and NOW accounts. Lending activities consist mostly of residential mortgages (almost half of the company's loan portfolio), commercial mortgages, home equity and improvement loans, and auto loans; the bank also offers business, construction, manufactured home, and consumer loans.

	Annual Growth	06/13	06/14	06/15	06/16	06/17
Assets ($mil.)	2.1%	337.8	335.5	334.1	341.0	366.9
Net income ($ mil.)	14.9%	2.3	3.6	2.8	3.6	3.9
Market value ($ mil.)	23.5%	18.0	23.5	27.4	29.6	41.8
Employees	–	–	–	–	–	–

FGI INDUSTRIES LTD
NAS: FGI

906 Murray Road
East Hanover, NJ 07936
Phone: 973 428-0400
Fax: –
Web: www.fgi-industries.com

CEO: –
CFO: –
HR: –
FYE: December 31
Type: Public

Foremost Groups is a home furnishings manufacturer that markets and sells its products worldwide. The company produces a range of pieces for every room in the house, including home offices (computer desks, storage units), living rooms (ottomans, entertainment centers), and bathrooms (cabinets, vanities, shower enclosures, toilets). It also makes patio sets and food service equipment. Its furniture is manufactured under the Foremost, Foremost Casual, Contrac, Craft + Main, Veranda Classics, and CORE PRO COOKING brands, as well as private-label names for major retailers. The company was founded in 1987.

	Annual Growth	12/18	12/19	12/20	12/21	12/22
Sales ($mil.)	8.6%	–	126.3	134.8	181.9	161.7
Net income ($ mil.)	32.8%	–	1.6	4.7	7.9	3.7
Market value ($ mil.)	–	–	–	–	–	–
Employees	–	–	–	130	136	145

FHI SERVICES

500 HOSPITAL DR
WARRENTON, VA 201863027
Phone: 540 347-2550
Fax: –
Web: –

CEO: –
CFO: –
HR: Taylor Crystal
FYE: September 30
Type: Private

Fauquier Hospital takes care of the populace of rural northern Virginia. The multi-location system provides medical, surgical, outpatient, and home health care services to a four county area. With more than 85 beds, the facility is the only hospital in Fauquier, and also serves Culpeper, Prince William and Rappahannock Counties. Specialized services include emergency medicine, oncology, rehabilitation, and cardiac and pulmonary care. The hospital's emergency room has more than 30 private rooms and services about 30,000 patients each year. Fauquier Hospital partners with Prince William Hospital to operate the Cancer Center at Lake Manassas. Fauquier Hospital was founded in 1925.

	Annual Growth	09/04	09/05*	06/06*	09/09	09/16
Sales ($mil.)	(12.0%)	–	103.4	95.3	132.6	25.3
Net income ($ mil.)	9.4%	–	8.6	1.9	10.3	23.1
Market value ($ mil.)	–	–	–	–	–	–
Employees	–	–	–	–	–	700

*Fiscal year change

FIBERTOWER CORPORATION

8070 GEORGIA AVE STE 305
SILVER SPRING, MD 209104971
Phone: 202 223-9690
Fax: –
Web: –

CEO: –
CFO: –
HR: –
FYE: December 31
Type: Private

FiberTower is making some small waves to provide expanded wireless broadband connections. The company provides access to high frequency spectrum (24 GHz and 39 GHz bands) to telecommunications carriers, businesses, governments, and other customers. Employing millimeter wave bands, the company makes high-speed connection between a terminal such as a cell tower and a business's antenna. Millimeter waves are most effective over short, unobstructed distances. The technology can provide connections where wired lines are impractical. The technology can be deployed to make 'last mile' connections. FiberTower was founded in 2014, rising from a previous company that had declared bankruptcy.

FIBROCELL SCIENCE, INC.

405 EAGLEVIEW BLVD
EXTON, PA 193411117
Phone: 484 713-6000
Fax: –
Web: www.itsaboutmusic.com

CEO: –
CFO: –
HR: –
FYE: December 31
Type: Private

No cow collagen here -- Fibrocell Science (formerly Isolagen) lets you be your beautiful self, using your beautiful cells. The company's autologous cellular therapy process, used in its primary LAVIV product offering, extracts fibroblasts (collagen-producing cells) from a small tissue sample taken from behind a patient's ear. The cells reproduce over six to eight weeks and are then injected back into the patient, giving him or her a "natural" boost. The company gained FDA approval for LAVIV for use on wrinkle correction in 2011. It also hopes to gain approval for indications such as burn and acne scar treatment, and to regenerate tissue lost from periodontal disease.

FIBROGEN INC
NMS: FGEN

409 Illinois Street
San Francisco, CA 94158
Phone: 415 978-1200
Fax: –
Web: www.fibrogen.com

CEO: Thane Wettig
CFO: Juan Graham
HR: Dorothy Pacini
FYE: December 31
Type: Public

FibroGen re a leading biopharmaceutical company discovering, developing and commercializing a pipeline of first-in-class therapeutics. The company applies its pioneering expertise in hypoxia-inducible factor (HIF) biology, 2-oxoglutarate enzymology, and connective tissue growth factor (CTGF) biology to advance innovative medicines for the treatment of anemia, fibrotic disease, and cancer. Its product candidates Roxadustat is the most advanced therapeutic, is an oral small molecule inhibitor of hypoxia-inducible factor (HIF) prolyl hydroxylase, the enzyme that regulates HIF activity; and Pamrevlumab is a potential first-in-class antibody being developed by FibroGen to inhibit the activity of connective tissue growth factor (CTGF), a common factor in fibrotic and proliferative disorders characterized by persistent and excessive scarring that can lead to organ dysfunction and failure. The US accounts for about 20% of total revenue.

	Annual Growth	12/19	12/20	12/21	12/22	12/23
Sales ($mil.)	(12.9%)	256.6	176.3	235.3	140.7	147.8
Net income ($ mil.)	–	(77.0)	(189.3)	(290.0)	(293.7)	(284.2)
Market value ($ mil.)	(62.1%)	4,236.3	3,663.4	1,392.7	1,582.3	87.5
Employees	(2.2%)	531	599	566	592	486

FIDELITY D&D BANCORP INC
NMS: FDBC

Blakely & Drinker Street
Dunmore, PA 18512
Phone: 570 342-8281
Fax: –
Web: www.bankatfidelity.com

CEO: –
CFO: –
HR: –
FYE: December 31
Type: Public

Fidelity D & D Bancorp has loyal banking customers. The institution is the holding company for The Fidelity Deposit and Discount Bank, serving Lackawanna and Luzerne counties in northeastern Pennsylvania through about a dozen locations and about the same number of ATM locations. The bank attracts local individuals and business customers by offering such products and services as checking and savings accounts, certificates of deposit, investments, and trust services. Commercial real estate loans account for the bulk of the company's loan portfolio, followed by consumer loans, business and industrial loans, and residential mortgages. The bank also writes construction loans and direct financing leases.

	Annual Growth	12/19	12/20	12/21	12/22	12/23
Assets ($mil.)	25.5%	1,009.9	1,699.5	2,419.1	2,378.4	2,503.2
Net income ($ mil.)	12.0%	11.6	13.0	24.0	30.0	18.2
Market value ($ mil.)	(1.7%)	354.8	367.1	336.5	268.9	331.0
Employees	13.4%	189	265	319	320	313

FIDELITY FEDERAL BANCORP
NBB: FDLB

18 N.W. Fourth Steet
Evansville, IN 47708
Phone: 812 424-0921
Fax: 812 473-9786
Web: www.unitedfidelity.com

CEO: –
CFO: –
HR: –
FYE: December 31
Type: Public

Fidelity Federal is true to its community. It's the holding company for United Fidelity Bank (aka United Bank), which operates about a half-dozen branches in southern Indiana. In addition to traditional products like checking and savings accounts, CDs, and credit cards, the bank offers investments such as IRAs, heath savings accounts, education savings accounts, and savings bonds. One- to four-family residential mortgages account for the largest portion of the company's loan portfolio, followed by commercial real estate, construction and land development, and business loans. United Bank also offers private banking services.

	Annual Growth	12/00	12/01	12/02	12/03	12/04
Assets ($mil.)	4.8%	166.5	159.7	132.3	175.4	200.6
Net income ($ mil.)	–	(1.2)	0.2	(4.4)	0.2	0.5
Market value ($ mil.)	7.8%	1.3	2.2	1.4	1.4	1.7
Employees	(5.4%)	65	83	73	62	52

FIDELITY NATIONAL FINANCIAL INC
NYS: FNF

601 Riverside Avenue
Jacksonville, FL 32204
Phone: 904 854-8100
Fax: –
Web: www.fnf.com

CEO: Michael J Nolan
CFO: Anthony J Park
HR: –
FYE: December 31
Type: Public

Fidelity National Financial (FNF) is a leading provider of title insurance and transaction services to the real estate and mortgage industries. FNF is the nation's largest title insurance company through its title insurance underwriters - Fidelity National Title, Chicago Title, Commonwealth Land Title, Alamo Title and National Title of New York - that collectively issue more title insurance policies than any other title company in the US. In addition, the company retains an approximate 85% ownership stake in F&G Annuities & Life, Inc., a leading provider of insurance solutions, serving retail annuity and life customers and institutional clients.

	Annual Growth	12/19	12/20	12/21	12/22	12/23
Assets ($mil.)	65.8%	10,677	50,455	60,690	65,589	80,614
Net income ($ mil.)	(16.5%)	1,062.0	1,427.0	2,422.0	1,136.0	517.0
Market value ($ mil.)	3.0%	12,392	10,681	14,258	10,280	13,941
Employees	(2.9%)	25,063	27,058	28,290	21,759	22,293

FIDELITY NATIONAL INFORMATION SERVICES INC
NYS: FIS

347 Riverside Avenue
Jacksonville, FL 32202
Phone: 904 438-6000
Fax: –
Web: www.fisglobal.com

CEO: –
CFO: –
HR: –
FYE: December 31
Type: Public

Fidelity National Information Services (FIS) is a leading provider of technology solutions for financial institutions and businesses of all sizes and across any industry globally. The company's broad portfolio of solutions includes a wide range of flexible service arrangements, from managed processing arrangements, either at the client site or hosted at a FIS location, including data centers or its private cloud, to traditional license and maintenance approaches. For banks and other financing entities, the company's offerings address financial functions such as core processing software applications, retail and commercial applications, decision solutions, and card and retail payment technology solutions. North America accounts for about 75% of the company's total revenue.

	Annual Growth	12/19	12/20	12/21	12/22	12/23
Sales ($mil.)	(1.3%)	10,333	12,552	13,877	14,528	9,821.0
Net income ($ mil.)	–	298.0	158.0	417.0	(16,720.0)	(6,654.0)
Market value ($ mil.)	(18.9%)	81,089	82,471	63,634	39,557	35,021
Employees	2.2%	55,000	62,000	65,000	69,000	60,000

FIELD MUSEUM OF NATURAL HISTORY

1400 S LAKE SHORE DR
CHICAGO, IL 606052429
Phone: 312 922-9410
Fax: –
Web: www.fieldmuseum.org

CEO: –
CFO: Marivell Dominguez
HR: –
FYE: December 31
Type: Private

The Field Museum is one of the world's leading natural history museums. Founded as the Columbian Museum of Chicago in 1893, the institution adopted the Field name in 1905 in honor of major benefactor (and department store mogul) Marshall Field. The museum houses enormous biological and anthropological collections -- more than 40 million specimens in all. It is also home to Sue, the largest, most complete, and best preserved Tyrannosaurus rex fossil discovered to date. The Field Museum conducts basic research in anthropology and biology, as well as an extensive program of public education.

	Annual Growth	12/18	12/19	12/20	12/21	12/22
Sales ($mil.)	4.9%	–	68.5	68.5	77.4	79.1
Net income ($ mil.)	–	–	66.3	66.3	72.8	(86.4)
Market value ($ mil.)	–	–	–	–	–	–
Employees	–	–	–	–	–	600

FIELDALE FARMS CORPORATION

555 BROILER BLVD
BALDWIN, GA 305112064
Phone: 706 778-5100
Fax: –
Web: www.fieldale.com

CEO: Thomas A Arrendale III
CFO: David E Elrod
HR: –
FYE: December 31
Type: Private

Fieldale Farms Corporation is one of the largest independent poultry producers in the world. With several production plants, the poultry-processing company produces fresh and frozen chicken and chicken parts ? including skinless or skin-on, value-added, ready-to-cook, fully-cooked, pre-cooked, and breaded and marinated ? for sale in the US. It also ships internationally to more than 50 countries around the world and offers private-label chicken products, along with its namesake Fieldale Farms brand, for foodservice and retail food customers. These products are available as Ice-Pack, CVP, and CO2. Fieldale Farms is a family-owned and -operated company.

	Annual Growth	12/04	12/05*	09/08*	12/08	12/09
Sales ($mil.)	(1.9%)	–	0.4	2.0	0.5	0.4
Net income ($ mil.)	7.9%	–	0.0	(0.5)	–	0.0
Market value ($ mil.)	–	–	–	–	–	–
Employees						4,800

*Fiscal year change

FIELDPOINT PETROLEUM CORP   NBB: FPPP

609 Castle Ridge Road, Suite 335
Austin, TX 78746
Phone: 512 579-3560
Fax: –
Web: www.fppcorp.com

CEO: –
CFO: –
HR: –
FYE: December 31
Type: Public

Got oil and gas? FieldPoint Petroleum can point to its oil and gas fields and its interests in 480 productive oil and gas wells (96 net) in Louisiana, New Mexico, Oklahoma, Texas, and Wyoming. The independent oil and gas exploration company operates some 19 of these wells. About two-thirds of its gross productive oil wells are located in Oklahoma. FieldPoint Petroleum has proved reserves of more than 1.1 million barrels of oil and 1.9 billion cu. ft. of natural gas. Its business strategy is to expand its reserve base as well as its production and cash flow through the acquisition of producing oil and gas properties. However, low oil prices have forced the company to hold back on further acquisitions.

	Annual Growth	12/14	12/15	12/16	12/17	12/18
Sales ($mil.)	(30.4%)	9.2	4.0	2.8	3.0	2.2
Net income ($ mil.)	–	–	(1.9)	(11.0)	(2.5)	2.7	(3.3)
Market value ($ mil.)	(56.3%)	19.1	6.6	7.7	1.8	0.7
Employees	(6.9%)	4	3	3	3	3

FIFTH THIRD BANCORP (CINCINNATI, OH)   NMS: FITB

38 Fountain Square Plaza
Cincinnati, OH 45263
Phone: 800 972-3030
Fax: –
Web: www.53.com

CEO: Timothy N Spence
CFO: Bryan Preston
HR: Dede McNeal
FYE: December 31
Type: Public

Fifth Third Bancorp is the holding company of Fifth Third Bank which boasts assets of some $208.7 billion and operates nearly 1,100 full-service banking centers and over 2,100 Fifth Third branded ATMs in a dozen states in the Midwest and Southeast. The company operates three main businesses: Commercial Banking, Consumer and Small Business Banking, and Wealth & Asset Management. The company's subsidiaries provide a wide range of financial products and services to the commercial, financial, retail, governmental, educational, energy and healthcare sectors. This includes a variety of checking, savings and money market accounts, wealth management solutions, payments and commerce solutions, insurance services and credit products such as commercial loans and leases, mortgage loans, credit cards, installment loans and auto loans. The company started in 1975.

	Annual Growth	12/19	12/20	12/21	12/22	12/23
Assets ($mil.)	6.1%	169,369	204,680	211,116	207,452	214,574
Net income ($ mil.)	(1.7%)	2,512.0	1,427.0	2,770.0	2,446.0	2,349.0
Market value ($ mil.)	2.9%	20,938	18,779	29,663	22,348	23,492
Employees	(1.5%)	19,869	19,872	19,112	19,319	18,724

FIJI WATER COMPANY, LLC

11444 W OLYMPIC BLVD STE 250
LOS ANGELES, CA 900641534
Phone: 310 966-5700
Fax: –
Web: shop.fijiwater.com

CEO: Stewart A Resnick
CFO: Kim Katzenberger
HR: –
FYE: December 31
Type: Private

FIJI Water proves that it's hip to be square. The premium water, which is sourced from an artesian aquifer at the edge of a rainforest, is available in square bottles at retail food merchants and in luxury hotels, spas, and restaurants in 50 countries. Sourced and bottled on Viti Levu, the largest of the Republic of Fiji's islands, the water has garnered the attention of celebrity chefs and also made its way to the set of popular television programs and movies, including ABC's Desperate Housewives. The company, which sells genuine silver sleeves for the water bottles on its website, also offers home delivery of its water throughout the continental US. FIJI Water is part of Roll International's holdings.

FINANCIAL EXECUTIVES INTERNATIONAL

89 HEDQRTERS PLZ STE 1462
MORRISTOWN, NJ 07960
Phone: 973 765-1000
Fax: –
Web: www.financialexecutives.org

CEO: Andrej Suskavcevic
CFO: –
HR: –
FYE: June 30
Type: Private

Financial Executives International (FEI) is a professional association for CFOs, VPs of finance, treasurers, controllers, tax executives, and others in finance. It has 15,000 members throughout the US and Canada in about 85 branches. The association advocates the views of its members, notifies members of current issues, and promotes ethical conduct for financial executives. FEI also hosts conferences and networking opportunities for its members and publishes Financial Executive Magazine. The group was founded at the Controllers Institute of America in 1931.

	Annual Growth	06/17	06/18	06/19	06/21	06/22
Sales ($mil.)	(65.6%)	–	6.3	3.8	0.1	0.0
Net income ($ mil.)	(27.6%)	–	0.2	0.4	0.0	0.0
Market value ($ mil.)	–	–	–	–	–	–
Employees	–	–	–	–	–	30

FINANCIAL INDUSTRY REGULATORY AUTHORITY, INC.

1700 K ST NW
WASHINGTON, DC 200063817
Phone: 301 590-6500
Fax: –
Web: www.finra.org

CEO: Robert Cook
CFO: Todd Diganci
HR: Myrna Mitchell
FYE: December 31
Type: Private

FINRA is dedicated to protecting investors and safeguarding market integrity in a manner that facilitates vibrant capital markets. It is a not-for-profit organization that working under the supervision of the SEC actively engages with and provides essential tools for investors, member firms, and policymakers. Additionally, it is authorized by Congress to protect investors by making sure the broker-dealer industry operates fairly and honestly. FINRA oversees more than 624,000 brokers across the country and analyzes billion dollars of market events. It uses innovative AI and machine learning technologies to keep a close eye on the market and provide essential support to investors, regulators, policymakers, and other stakeholders. FINRA was formed in 2007 from the consolidation of the National Association of Securities Dealers and certain regulatory and enforcement elements of the NYSE.

	Annual Growth	12/18	12/19	12/20	12/21	12/22
Sales ($mil.)	22.6%	–	938.5	1,162.6	1,404.8	1,730.6
Net income ($ mil.)	–	–	(45.9)	19.8	218.8	(429.9)
Market value ($ mil.)	–	–	–	–	–	–
Employees	–	–	–	–	–	3,400

FINANCIAL INSTITUTIONS INC.
NMS: FISI

220 Liberty Street
Warsaw, NY 14569
Phone: 585 786-1100
Fax: –
Web: www.fiiwarsaw.com

CEO: Martin K Birmingham
CFO: –
HR: Allison Panowitz
FYE: December 31
Type: Public

Financial Institutions is a financial holding that offers a broad array of deposit, lending, and other financial services to individuals, municipalities and businesses in Western and Central New York through its wholly-owned New York-chartered banking subsidiary, Five Star Bank. Its indirect lending network includes relationships with franchised automobile dealers in Western and Central New York, the Capital District of New York and Northern and Central Pennsylvania. The company offers insurance services through its wholly-owned subsidiary, SDN Insurance Agency, LLC (SDN), a full-service insurance agency. It offers customized investment advice, wealth management, investment consulting and retirement plan services through its wholly-owned subsidiaries Courier Capital and HNP Capital, SEC-registered investment advisory and wealth management firms. In addition, the company offers Banking-as-a-Service (BaaS) and financial technology (FinTech) solutions through its wholly-owned subsidiary Corn Hill Innovation Labs, LLC (CHIL).

	Annual Growth	12/19	12/20	12/21	12/22	12/23
Assets ($mil.)	8.9%	4,384.2	4,912.3	5,520.8	5,797.3	6,160.9
Net income ($ mil.)	0.7%	48.9	38.3	77.7	56.6	50.3
Market value ($ mil.)	(9.7%)	494.6	346.7	490.0	375.3	328.2
Employees	(3.6%)	722	613	625	672	624

FINANCIALCONTENT INC

111 West Topa Topa Street
Ojai, CA 93023
Phone: 805 640-6468
Fax: –
Web: www.financialcontent.com

CEO: –
CFO: –
HR: –
FYE: June 30
Type: Public

It doesn't matter if it's a bear or bull market; FinancialContent puts financial data right in front of you. The company's software integrates financial data (including stock quotes, SEC filings, interest rates) and tools into Web sites, corporate intranets, and print media. Its products can be used as stand-alone products for internal use of financial data or integrated into products and offerings sold to third-parties. FinancialContent has content partnerships with companies such as Business Wire and PR Newswire and its customers have included Adobe, Bayer, and WR Hambrecht.

	Annual Growth	06/04	06/05	06/06	06/07	06/08
Sales ($mil.)	27.8%	1.0	1.3	1.8	2.8	2.6
Net income ($ mil.)	–	(1.6)	(0.9)	(0.5)	(1.4)	0.9
Market value ($ mil.)	(54.3%)	16.8	10.6	5.2	5.3	0.7
Employees	(49.2%)	15	14	13	14	1

FINDEX.COM, INC.

1313 South Killian Drive
Lake Park, FL 33403
Phone: 561 328-6488
Fax: –
Web: www.ecosmartsurfaces.com

CEO: Steven Malone
CFO: Steven Malone
HR: –
FYE: December 31
Type: Public

For churches needing more than divine inspiration, FindEx.com answers prayers. The company develops, publishes, and distributes software for churches, ministries, and other Christian organizations. Its primary product - making up almost 90% of sales - is QuickVerse, which is designed to facilitate biblical research. Other offerings include publishing software for Christian-themed printed materials, a program to assist pastors in developing sermons, children's Christian entertainment software, and language tutorials for Greek and Hebrew. In 2008 the company bought FormTool.com, which offers 800 form templates - its first non-Christian product. Director Gordon Landies controls more than 20% of FindEx.com.

	Annual Growth	12/14	12/15	12/16	12/17	12/18
Sales ($mil.)	17.3%	0.2	0.2	0.3	0.4	0.3
Net income ($ mil.)	–	(1.4)	(2.5)	(1.0)	(1.3)	(1.3)
Market value ($ mil.)	(33.1%)	7.1	6.1	7.1	5.7	1.4
Employees	3.4%	7	8	10	8	8

FINJAN HOLDINGS, INC.

234 MARSHALL ST STE 8
REDWOOD CITY, CA 940631550
Phone: 650 282-3228
Fax: –
Web: www.finjan.com

CEO: Philip Hartstein
CFO: Jevan Anderson
HR: –
FYE: December 31
Type: Private

Converted Organics is not a group of new and fervent farmers but a company that is religiously developing a process to turn food into fertilizer. The company uses organic food waste as raw material to make all-natural fertilizers that combine both disease suppression and nutritional characteristics. Its manufacturing process uses heat and bacteria to transform food waste into a high-value natural fertilizer. It sells its environmentally friendly products in the agribusiness, turf management, and retail markets. The company, which acquired vertical farming operation TerraSphere Systems in 2010, also has an industrial wastewater treatment unit. Converted Organics is restructuring to streamline operations.

FINWARD BANCORP
NAS: FNWD

9204 Columbia Avenue
Munster, IN 46321
Phone: 219 836-4400
Fax: –
Web: www.ibankpeoples.com

CEO: –
CFO: –
HR: –
FYE: December 31
Type: Public

NorthWest Indiana Bancorp is the holding company for Peoples Bank, which serves individuals and businesses customers through about 10 branches in northwest Indiana's Lake County. The savings bank offers traditional deposit services such as checking and savings accounts, money market accounts, and CDs. It primarily uses the funds collected to originate loans secured by single-family residences and commercial real estate; it also makes construction, consumer, and business loans. The bank's Wealth Management Group provides retirement and estate planning, investment accounts, land trusts, and profit-sharing and 401(k) plans.

	Annual Growth	12/18	12/19	12/20	12/21	12/22
Assets ($mil.)	17.2%	1,096.2	1,328.7	1,497.5	1,620.7	2,070.3
Net income ($ mil.)	12.7%	9.3	12.1	16.6	15.0	15.1
Market value ($ mil.)	(4.2%)	184.8	197.3	155.2	197.2	155.6
Employees	4.3%	276	290	263	280	326

FIORANO SOFTWARE, INC.

16192 COASTAL HWY
LEWES, DE 199583608
Phone: 650 326-1136
Fax: –
Web: www.fiorano.com

CEO: Atul Saini
CFO: Anjali Saini
HR: –
FYE: September 30
Type: Private

Fiorano Software wants to enable all your business processes to sing together in perfect harmony. The company provides business process integration and messaging applications. The company's clients use its products to deploy, manage, and track business processes across multiple platforms, applications, and partners. Fiorano also provides such services as consulting, support, and training. The company's clients come from industries such as aerospace, financial services, manufacturing, media, military contracting, retail, and technology; customers include Boeing, Lockheed Martin, Scottrade, and The Sports Authority. The company was founded in 1995 by CEO Atul Saini.

FIRECOM, INC.

3927 59TH ST
WOODSIDE, NY 113773435
Phone: 718 899-6100
Fax: -
Web: www.firecominc.com

CEO: -
CFO: -
HR: -
FYE: November 30
Type: Private

Firecom sparks feelings of security in its customers. The company designs, manufactures, tests, distributes, and services customizable fire safety and security systems. The firm sells its systems under the Firecom brand to residential, commercial, institutional, and industrial customers in the US. Firecom has installed its products in more than 350 facilities, protecting more than 3 million people. In addition, the company has a nearly 40% stake in alarm and safety products manufacturer Synergx Systems. Founded in 1963, Firecom was taken private in 2001 by an investment group led by chairman and CEO Paul Mendez.

	Annual Growth	04/97	04/98	04/99*	11/18	11/19
Sales ($mil.)	(30.4%)	-	14.1	17.4	-	0.0
Net income ($ mil.)	(20.3%)	-	0.6	1.1	-	0.0
Market value ($ mil.)	-	-	-	-	-	-
Employees		-	-	-	-	180

*Fiscal year change

FIRED UP, INC.

6705 W HIGHWAY 290 # 50296
AUSTIN, TX 787358400
Phone: 512 222-4090
Fax: -
Web: www.carinos.com

CEO: -
CFO: -
HR: -
FYE: December 31
Type: Private

Italian cooking and casual dining are two things that excite this company. Fired Up operates and franchises more than 140 Carino's Italian restaurants in more than 25 states. The full-service eateries offer pizza and freshly prepared pasta along with beef, chicken and pork dishes inspired by the cuisine of Southern Italy. The company owns about half the restaurants and franchises the rest; a handful of franchised Carino's units are located in Bahrain, Egypt, Kuwait, and UAE. Fired Up was founded in 1997 by partners and former Brinker International executives Norman Abdallah and Creed Ford. It is backed by private equity firm Rosewood Capital. In March 2014, it filed for Chapter 11 bankruptcy protection.

FIRELANDS REGIONAL HEALTH SYSTEM

1111 HAYES AVE
SANDUSKY, OH 448703323
Phone: 419 557-7485
Fax: -
Web: www.bellevuehospital.com

CEO: Martin E Tursky
CFO: Daniel Moncher
HR: -
FYE: December 31
Type: Private

Firelands Regional Health System primarily operates through its Firelands Regional Medical Center (FRMC). The center serves eight counties in northern Ohio. It operates two hospital campuses with a total of 400 beds, a medical office building, and outpatient clinics throughout the region. FRMC's medical staff of 225 represents more than 35 specialties. The center's broad range of services include cardiovascular care, home health care, mental health services, palliative care, dialysis, oncology care, and chemical dependency programs. It also has hospital network and teaching affiliations with several area hospitals, medical schools, and community colleges. The medical center is supported by a non-profit foundation.

	Annual Growth	12/16	12/17	12/18	12/19	12/22
Sales ($mil.)	1.1%	-	285.5	280.8	291.3	302.1
Net income ($ mil.)	-	-	27.3	(24.3)	20.5	(40.3)
Market value ($ mil.)	-	-	-	-	-	-
Employees	-	-	-	-	-	1,635

FIRST ACCEPTANCE CORP

NBB: FACO

3813 Green Hills Village Drive
Nashville, TN 37215
Phone: 615 844-2800
Fax: -
Web: www.acceptance.com

CEO: Kenneth D Russell
CFO: Brent J Gay
HR: -
FYE: December 31
Type: Public

First Acceptance sells car insurance to customers wanting to stay on the right side of the law. The personal auto insurer operates its business in a dozen states, specializing in providing non-standard auto insurance (insurance for drivers who have trouble getting coverage because of poor driving records or payment histories). As part of its business, First Acceptance sells its policies under the brand names Acceptance Insurance (in the Chicago area), Yale Insurance, and Insurance Plus brand. Altogether, the company operates about 350 retail offices staffed by employee agents and through independent agents at more than a dozen retail locations.

	Annual Growth	12/18	12/19	12/20	12/21	12/22
Assets ($mil.)	(2.2%)	389.1	356.4	341.0	322.6	355.9
Net income ($ mil.)	-	17.7	15.4	10.4	(1.2)	(17.5)
Market value ($ mil.)	(8.0%)	39.4	30.1	54.8	81.8	28.2
Employees	-	1,331	-	-	-	-

FIRST ADVANTAGE CORP (NEW)

NMS: FA

1 Concourse Parkway NE, Suite 200
Atlanta, GA 30328
Phone: 888 314-9761
Fax: -
Web: www.fadv.com

CEO: Scott Staples
CFO: David L Gamsey
HR: -
FYE: December 31
Type: Public

First Advantage is a leading global provider of employment background screening and verification solutions. The company delivers innovative services and insights that help its customers manage risk and hire the best talent. Enabled by its proprietary technology, its products help companies protect their brands and provide safer environments for their customers and their most important resources: employees, contractors, contingent workers, tenants, and drivers. The company's comprehensive product suite includes criminal background checks, drug/health screening, extended workforce screening, biometrics and identity, education/work verifications, resident screening, fleet/driver compliance, executive screening, data analytics, continuous monitoring, social media monitoring, and hiring tax incentives. First Advantage perform screens in over 200 countries and territories on behalf of its approximately 33,000 customers.

	Annual Growth	01/20*	12/20	12/21	12/22	12/23
Sales ($mil.)	113.5%	36.8	472.4	712.3	810.0	763.8
Net income ($ mil.)	-	(36.5)	(47.5)	16.1	64.6	37.3
Market value ($ mil.)	-	-	-	2,762.2	1,886.0	2,403.9
Employees	-	-	4,200	5,500	5,800	5,000

*Fiscal year change

FIRST AMERICAN FINANCIAL CORP

NYS: FAF

1 First American Way
Santa Ana, CA 92707-5913
Phone: 714 250-3000
Fax: 714 250-3151
Web: www.firstam.com

CEO: -
CFO: -
HR: -
FYE: December 31
Type: Public

First American Financial Corporation is a leading provider of title insurance, settlement services and risk solutions for real estate transactions. First American also provides title plant management services; title and other real property records and images; valuation products and services; home warranty products; banking, trust and wealth management services; and other related products and services. The company offers its products and services directly and through its agents throughout the US and abroad. First American Financial traces its heritage back to 1889.

	Annual Growth	12/19	12/20	12/21	12/22	12/23
Assets ($mil.)	9.9%	11,519	12,796	16,451	14,955	16,803
Net income ($ mil.)	(25.6%)	707.4	696.4	1,241.0	263.0	216.8
Market value ($ mil.)	2.5%	6,012.8	5,323.1	8,065.5	5,396.3	6,643.8
Employees	1.1%	18,412	19,597	22,233	21,153	19,210

FIRST BANCORP (NC)
NMS: FBNC

300 SW Broad St.
Southern Pines, NC 28387
Phone: 910 246-2500
Fax: –
Web: www.localfirstbank.com

CEO: Richard H Moore
CFO: Eric P Credle
HR: –
FYE: December 31
Type: Public

First BanCorp provides a wide range of financial services for retail, commercial and institutional clients. The corporation has two wholly-owned subsidiaries: FirstBank and FirstBank Insurance Agency. FirstBank is a Puerto Rico-chartered commercial bank, and FirstBank Insurance Agency is a Puerto Rico-chartered insurance agency. First Bank conducts its business through about 65 banking branches in Puerto Rico, eight banking branches in the USVI and the BVI, and around 10 banking branches in the state of Florida. First Bank focuses its lending on commercial loans, which account for more than 45% of its loan portfolio.

	Annual Growth	12/19	12/20	12/21	12/22	12/23
Assets ($mil.)	18.5%	6,143.6	7,289.8	10,509	10,625	12,115
Net income ($ mil.)	3.1%	92.0	81.5	95.6	146.9	104.1
Market value ($ mil.)	(1.9%)	1,640.7	1,390.8	1,879.5	1,761.2	1,521.5
Employees	6.8%	1,111	1,118	1,234	1,294	1,445

FIRST BANCORP INC (ME)
NMS: FNLC

223 Main Street
Damariscotta, ME 04543
Phone: 207 563-3195
Fax: –
Web: www.thefirstbancorp.com

CEO: Tony C McKim
CFO: Richard M Elder
HR: –
FYE: December 31
Type: Public

It may not actually be the first bank, but The First Bancorp (formerly First National Lincoln) was founded over 150 years ago. It is the holding company for The First, a regional bank serving coastal Maine from more than 15 branches. The bank offers traditional retail products and services, including checking and savings accounts, CDs, IRAs, and loans. Residential mortgages make up about 40% of the company's loan portfolio; business loans account for another 40%; and home equity and consumer loans comprise the rest. Bank subsidiary First Advisors offers private banking and investment management services. Founded in 1864, the bank now boasts more than $1.4 billion in assets.

	Annual Growth	12/19	12/20	12/21	12/22	12/23
Assets ($mil.)	9.2%	2,068.8	2,361.2	2,527.1	2,739.2	2,946.7
Net income ($ mil.)	3.7%	25.5	27.1	36.3	39.0	29.5
Market value ($ mil.)	(1.7%)	335.5	281.9	348.5	332.3	313.2
Employees	2.6%	245	255	269	279	271

FIRST BANCORP OF INDIANA INC
NBB: FBPI

5001 Davis Lant Drive
Evansville, IN 47715
Phone: 812 492-8104
Fax: –
Web: www.firstfedevansville.com

CEO: Michael H Head
CFO: George J Smith
HR: –
FYE: June 30
Type: Public

First Bancorp of Indiana wants to be second to none. It's the holding company for First Federal Savings Bank, which serves individuals and local businesses through nine branches in the Evansville, Indiana, area. The bank offers standard retail products and services like checking, savings, and money market accounts; certificates of deposit; and retirement savings plans. Its lending activities primarily consist of mortgage and consumer loans (approximately 50% and 40% of the company's loan portfolio, respectively). The bank also offers savings account loans and business loans.

	Annual Growth	06/19	06/20	06/21	06/22	06/23
Assets ($mil.)	10.0%	431.1	473.4	480.9	518.5	631.3
Net income ($ mil.)	7.9%	2.1	1.8	3.8	2.4	2.9
Market value ($ mil.)	(4.7%)	34.0	29.3	36.8	34.3	28.1
Employees		–	–	–	–	–

FIRST BANCSHARES INC (MS)
NMS: FBMS

6480 U.S. Highway 98 West, Suite A
Hattiesburg, MS 39402
Phone: 601 268-8998
Fax: –
Web: www.thefirstbank.com

CEO: M R Cole Jr
CFO: Donna T Lowery
HR: –
FYE: December 31
Type: Public

Hoping to be first in the hearts of its customers, The First Bancshares is the holding company for The First, a community bank with some two dozen branch locations in southern Mississippi's Hattiesburg, Alabama, and Louisiana. The company provides such standard deposit products as checking and savings accounts, NOW and money market accounts, and IRAs. Real estate loans account for about 80% of the bank's lending portfolio, including about equal portions of residential mortgages, commercial mortgages, and construction loans. The bank also writes business loans and consumer loans. The bank, which has expanded beyond Mississippi through several acquisitions, has approximately $970 million in assets.

	Annual Growth	12/19	12/20	12/21	12/22	12/23
Assets ($mil.)	19.4%	3,941.9	5,152.8	6,077.4	6,461.7	7,999.3
Net income ($ mil.)	14.6%	43.7	52.5	64.2	62.9	75.5
Market value ($ mil.)	(4.7%)	1,104.3	960.0	1,200.7	995.2	911.9
Employees	11.5%	697	744	797	870	1,078

FIRST BANCSHARES INC. (MO)
NBB: FBSI

142 East First Street, P.O. Box 777
Mountain Grove, MO 65711
Phone: 719 955-2800
Fax: 719 442-4330
Web: www.thestockmensbank.com

CEO: Robert M Alexander
CFO: Brady J Nachtrieb
HR: –
FYE: December 31
Type: Public

First Bancshares is the holding company for First Home Savings Bank, which has about a dozen locations serving south-central Missouri. First Home Savings offers a range of retail banking services, including checking and savings, as well as NOW accounts and CDs. Residential mortgages account for more than half of First Home Savings' lending portfolio; commercial real estate loans represent another quarter. First Home Savings Bank was founded in 1911 as Mountain Grove Building and Loan Association

	Annual Growth	12/18	12/19	12/20	12/21	12/22
Assets ($mil.)	8.1%	345.0	352.6	406.3	445.0	471.7
Net income ($ mil.)	15.4%	3.0	3.6	3.9	5.1	5.3
Market value ($ mil.)	8.4%	33.5	37.8	31.7	41.8	46.4
Employees		–	–	–	–	–

FIRST BANKS, INC. (MO)

135 North Meramec
Clayton, MO 63105
Phone: 314 854-4600
Fax: –
Web: www.firstbanks.com

CEO: Shelley Seifert
CFO: James Gordon
HR: Elaine Mintschenko
FYE: December 31
Type: Public

First Banks keeps it in the family. The holding company for First Bank, it is owned by chairman James Dierberg and his family; many of the bank's branches and ATMs are located in Dierbergs Markets, a Missouri-based grocery chain owned by relatives of the chairman. First Bank has about 130 branches in California, Florida, Illinois, and Missouri, with a concentration in metropolitan markets such as Los Angeles, San Diego, San Francisco, Sacramento, and St. Louis. The bank offers standard services like deposits, mortgages, and business and consumer loans. Additional services include brokerage, insurance, trust, and private banking, as well as commercial treasury management and international trade services.

	Annual Growth	12/10	12/11	12/12	12/13	12/14
Assets ($mil.)	(5.3%)	7,378.1	6,608.9	6,509.1	5,919.0	5,935.5
Net income ($ mil.)	–	(191.7)	(41.2)	26.3	241.7	21.7
Market value ($ mil.)		–	–	–	–	–
Employees	(4.1%)	1,380	1,171	1,177	1,147	1,167

FIRST BUSEY CORP
NMS: BUSE

100 W. University Avenue
Champaign, IL 61820
Phone: 217 365-4544
Fax: –
Web: www.busey.com

CEO: –
CFO: –
HR: –
FYE: December 31
Type: Public

First Busey conducts banking, related banking services, asset management, brokerage, and fiduciary services through its wholly-owned bank subsidiary, Busey Bank, which boasts approximately $12.9 billion in assets and about 60 branches across Illinois, Florida, Missouri, and Indiana. The bank offers a range of diversified financial products and services for consumers and businesses, including online and mobile banking capabilities. Its primary sources of income are interest and fees on loans and investments, wealth management fees and service fees. Subsidiary FirsTech provides retail payment processing services.

	Annual Growth	12/19	12/20	12/21	12/22	12/23
Assets ($mil.)	6.1%	9,695.7	10,544	12,860	12,337	12,283
Net income ($ mil.)	4.5%	103.0	100.3	123.4	128.3	122.6
Market value ($ mil.)	(2.5%)	1,519.2	1,190.5	1,498.2	1,365.6	1,371.2
Employees	(0.9%)	1,531	1,346	1,463	1,497	1,479

FIRST BUSINESS FINANCIAL SERVICES, INC.
NMS: FBIZ

401 Charmany Drive
Madison, WI 53719
Phone: 608 238-8008
Fax: –
Web: www.firstbusiness.com

CEO: Corey A Chambas
CFO: Edward G Sloane Jr
HR: –
FYE: December 31
Type: Public

First Business Financial Services is engaged in the commercial banking business through its wholly-owned bank subsidiary, First Business Bank. The bank operates as a business bank, delivering a full line of commercial banking products and services tailored to meet the specific needs of small and medium-sized businesses, business owners, executives, professionals, and high net worth individuals. The bank's products and services include those for business banking, private wealth, and bank consulting. Over 60% of the company's loan portfolio is made up of commercial real estate loans. Within its business banking, it offers commercial lending and asset-based lending, accounts receivable financing, commercial equipment financing and more.

	Annual Growth	12/19	12/20	12/21	12/22	12/23
Assets ($mil.)	13.7%	2,096.8	2,567.8	2,652.9	2,976.6	3,507.8
Net income ($ mil.)	12.2%	23.3	17.0	35.8	40.9	37.0
Market value ($ mil.)	11.1%	218.9	153.1	242.5	303.9	333.4
Employees	3.8%	301	301	312	345	349

FIRST CAPITAL INC.
NAS: FCAP

220 Federal Drive N.W.
Corydon, IN 47112
Phone: 812 738-2198
Fax: –
Web: www.firstharrison.com

CEO: –
CFO: –
HR: –
FYE: December 31
Type: Public

First Capital is the holding company for First Harrison Bank, which operates about a dozen branches in Clark, Floyd, Harrison, and Washington counties in southern Indiana. Targeting area consumers and small to midsized businesses, the bank offers standard deposit products such as checking and savings accounts, certificates of deposit, and individual retirement accounts. Residential mortgages make up nearly half of the company's loan portfolio; consumer loans and commercial mortgages are around 20% apiece. First Harrison Bank also offers access to investments such as stocks, bonds, and mutual funds.

	Annual Growth	12/18	12/19	12/20	12/21	12/22
Assets ($mil.)	9.7%	794.2	827.5	1,017.6	1,156.6	1,151.4
Net income ($ mil.)	6.5%	9.3	10.3	10.1	11.4	11.9
Market value ($ mil.)	(12.5%)	143.2	246.1	204.2	136.5	83.9
Employees	0.5%	210	214	214	221	214

FIRST CARE MEDICAL SERVICES

900 HILLIGOSS BLVD SE
FOSSTON, MN 565421542
Phone: 218 435-1133
Fax: –
Web: www.firstcare.org

CEO: –
CFO: Kim Bodensteiner
HR: –
FYE: June 30
Type: Private

First Care Medical Services doing business as Essentia Health-Fosston) helps keep the chill of northern Minnesota from getting the better of its residents. The hospital, part of Essentia Health, provides general medical and surgical health care services to the Polk County, Minnesota, area, including emergency, cardiovascular, rehabilitation, and cancer care. The not-for-profit hospital also operates regional health care clinics, assisted-living facilities, and nursing homes, and it provides home health and hospice services. Its TeleHomecare system helps monitor patients remotely using in-home technology. The hospital was founded in 1897 by Dr. C. J. Rosser and his family.

	Annual Growth	06/18	06/19	06/20	06/21	06/22
Sales ($mil.)	4.7%	–	29.4	30.7	31.9	33.8
Net income ($ mil.)	48.1%	–	1.0	3.8	4.9	3.3
Market value ($ mil.)	–	–	–	–	–	–
Employees	–	–	–	–	–	500

FIRST CITIZENS BANCSHARES INC (DE)
NMS: FCNC P

4300 Six Forks Road
Raleigh, NC 27609
Phone: 919 716-7000
Fax: –
Web: www.firstcitizens.com

CEO: Frank B Holding Jr
CFO: Craig L Nix
HR: –
FYE: December 31
Type: Public

First Citizens BancShares owns First-Citizens Bank, which operates about 580 branches in about 20 states throughout the Southeast, Mid-Atlantic, Midwest, and Western US. The $109.3 billion-asset bank provides standard services such as accepting deposits, cashing checks, and providing for consumer and commercial cash needs. The company provides various investment products and services through FCB's wholly owned subsidiaries, First Citizens Investor Services (FCIS) and First Citizens Asset Management (FCAM). As a registered broker, FCIS provides a full range of investment products, including annuities, discount brokerage services, and third-party mutual funds. As registered investment advisors, FCIS and FCAM provide investment management services and advice.

	Annual Growth	12/19	12/20	12/21	12/22	12/23
Assets ($mil.)	52.2%	39,824	49,958	58,308	109,298	213,758
Net income ($ mil.)	123.8%	457.4	491.7	547.5	1,098.0	11,466
Market value ($ mil.)	27.8%	7,727.8	8,338.5	12,049	11,011	20,604
Employees	22.2%	7,176	6,722	6,846	10,684	16,021

FIRST COMMONWEALTH FINANCIAL CORP (INDIANA, PA)
NYS: FCF

601 Philadelphia Street
Indiana, PA 15701
Phone: 724 349-7220
Fax: –
Web: www.fcbanking.com

CEO: Michael Price
CFO: James R Reske
HR: –
FYE: December 31
Type: Public

First Commonwealth Financial is the holding company for First Commonwealth Bank (the bank), which provides consumer and commercial banking services to about 120 bank offices throughout central and western Pennsylvania counties as well as in Columbus, Ohio. The bank's loan portfolio mostly consists of commercial and industrial loans, including real estate, operating, agricultural, and construction loans. It also issues consumer loans such as automobile, and home equity loans, and offers wealth management, insurance, financial planning, retail brokerage, and trust services. The bank also operates a network of about 135 automated teller machines, or ATMs, at various branch offices and offsite locations. The company has total assets of some $9.5 billion, total loans of $6.9 billion and total deposits of $8.0 billion.

	Annual Growth	12/19	12/20	12/21	12/22	12/23
Assets ($mil.)	8.4%	8,308.8	9,068.1	9,545.1	9,805.7	11,459
Net income ($ mil.)	10.5%	105.3	73.4	138.3	128.2	157.1
Market value ($ mil.)	1.6%	1,481.7	1,117.1	1,643.0	1,426.5	1,576.7
Employees	(1.1%)	1,571	1,393	1,471	1,477	1,504

FIRST COMMUNITY BANKSHARES INC (VA)   NMS: FCBC

P.O. Box 989
Bluefield, VA 24605-0989
Phone: 276 326-9000
Fax: –
Web: www.firstcommunitybank.com

CEO: William P Stafford II
CFO: David D Brown
HR: –
FYE: December 31
Type: Public

First Community Bancshares is a financial holding company founded in 1989. The company provides banking products and services to individual and commercial customers through its wholly-owned subsidiary First Community Bank, a Virginia-chartered banking institution founded in 1874. First Community Bank provides traditional services like checking and savings accounts, CDs, and credit cards and serves communities through about 50 branches across Virginia, West Virginia, North Carolina, and Tennessee. First Community Bancshares offers wealth management and investment advisory services through Trust Services and First Community Wealth Management.

	Annual Growth	12/19	12/20	12/21	12/22	12/23
Assets ($mil.)	4.0%	2,798.8	3,011.1	3,194.5	3,135.6	3,268.5
Net income ($ mil.)	5.5%	38.8	35.9	51.2	46.7	48.0
Market value ($ mil.)	4.6%	573.9	399.3	618.4	627.2	686.4
Employees	5.2%	527	635	625	631	645

FIRST COMMUNITY CORP (SC)   NAS: FCCO

5455 Sunset Boulevard
Lexington, SC 29072
Phone: 803 951-2265
Fax: –
Web: www.firstcommunitysc.com

CEO: Michael C Crapps
CFO: D S Jordan
HR: –
FYE: December 31
Type: Public

Putting first things first, First Community is the holding company for First Community Bank, which serves individuals and smaller businesses in central South Carolina. Through about a dozen offices, the bank, which was founded in 1995, offers such products and services as checking and savings accounts, money market accounts, CDs, IRAs, credit cards, insurance, and investment services. Commercial mortgages make up about 60% of First Community Bank's loan portfolio, which also includes residential mortgages and business, consumer, and construction loans. The company's First Community Financial Consultants division offers asset management and estate planning. First Community is merging with Cornerstone Bancorp, expanding its presence in upstate SC.

	Annual Growth	12/19	12/20	12/21	12/22	12/23
Assets ($mil.)	11.8%	1,170.3	1,395.4	1,584.5	1,672.9	1,827.7
Net income ($ mil.)	1.9%	11.0	10.1	15.5	14.6	11.8
Market value ($ mil.)	(0.1%)	164.4	129.2	158.8	166.5	163.8
Employees	3.9%	242	244	250	269	282

FIRST EAGLE PRIVATE CREDIT, LLC

500 BOYLSTON ST STE 1250
BOSTON, MA 021163891
Phone: 617 848-2500
Fax: –
Web: www.firsteagle.com

CEO: Timothy J Conway
CFO: John K Bray
HR: –
FYE: December 31
Type: Private

No hot air here: NewStar Financial is in the business of providing middle-market companies with the capital they need to create a spark. The commercial financier provides a variety of loans (primarily secured senior debt) for refinancing, acquisitions, consolidations, and commercial real estate and equipment purchases to clients in the retail and consumer, health care, media and information, and energy industries, among others. Its loans typically range from $10 million to $50 million. Newstar also offers investment advisory and asset management services to institutional investors through managed credit funds that invest in its originated loans.

FIRST ELECTRIC CO-OPERATIVE CORPORATION

1000 S JP WRIGHT LOOP RD
JACKSONVILLE, AR 720765264
Phone: 501 982-4545
Fax: –
Web: www.firstelectric.coop

CEO: Don Crabbe
CFO: Bruce Andrews
HR: Tracy Stell
FYE: December 31
Type: Private

First Electric Cooperative wasn't the first electric cooperative ever formed, but it was the first such entity created in its home state. The member-owned utility distributes power to more than 85,000 customers in 17 central and southeastern Arkansas counties. It also offers its members a range of energy products and value-added services, including energy efficient Marathon water heaters, surge and lightning protection equipment, and compact fluorescent light bulbs. Some 72% of the cooperative's revenues come from residential customers; commercial and industrial customers account for another 20%, and the rest comes from such sources as irrigation and street lighting.

	Annual Growth	12/14	12/15	12/18	12/21	12/22
Sales ($mil.)	6.2%	–	179.3	202.3	234.4	273.2
Net income ($ mil.)	–	–	–	–	(0.5)	(3.5)
Market value ($ mil.)	–	–	–	–	–	–
Employees	–	–	–	–	–	237

FIRST FINANCIAL BANCORP (OH)   NMS: FFBC

255 East Fifth Street, Suite 800
Cincinnati, OH 45202
Phone: 877 322-9530
Fax: –
Web: www.bankatfirst.com

CEO: Archie M Brown
CFO: James M Anderson
HR: –
FYE: December 31
Type: Public

The holding company's flagship subsidiary, First Financial Bank, operates over 130 banking centers in Ohio, Indiana, Kentucky, and Illinois. Founded in 1863, the banking services provided by the bank include commercial lending, real estate lending, and consumer financing. Real estate loans are loans secured by a mortgage lien on the real property of the borrower, which may either be residential property (one to four-family residential housing units) or commercial property (owner-occupied and/or investor income-producing real estate, such as apartments, shopping centers, or office buildings). In addition, First Financial offers deposit products that include interest-bearing and noninterest-bearing accounts, time deposits, and cash management services for commercial customers. First Financial Bancorp boasts some $17.0 billion in assets, including nearly $10.3 billion in loans.

	Annual Growth	12/19	12/20	12/21	12/22	12/23
Assets ($mil.)	4.8%	14,512	15,973	16,329	17,003	17,533
Net income ($ mil.)	6.6%	198.1	155.8	205.2	217.6	255.9
Market value ($ mil.)	(1.7%)	2,420.4	1,667.8	2,319.5	2,305.3	2,259.6
Employees	0.5%	2,123	2,107	2,010	2,108	2,165

FIRST FINANCIAL BANKSHARES, INC.   NMS: FFIN

400 Pine Street
Abilene, TX 79601
Phone: 325 627-7155
Fax: –
Web: www.ffin.com

CEO: F S Dueser
CFO: J B Hildebrand
HR: Lisa Roye
FYE: December 31
Type: Public

First Financial Bankshares is a financial holding company that through its subsidiary, First Financial Bank (the bank), operates multiple banking regions with around 80 locations in Texas. The bank provides general commercial banking services, which include accepting and holding checking, savings, and time deposits, making loans, offering automated teller machines (ATMs), drive-in and night deposit services, safe deposit facilities, remote deposit capture, internet banking, mobile banking, payroll cards, funds transfer, and performing other customary commercial banking services. The company also provides full-service trust and wealth management activities through its trust company, First Financial Trust & Asset Management. First Financial Bankshares is recognized as one of the nation's most financially secure banking institutions, with assets of about $13 billion.

	Annual Growth	12/19	12/20	12/21	12/22	12/23
Assets ($mil.)	12.2%	8,262.2	10,905	13,102	12,974	13,106
Net income ($ mil.)	4.8%	164.8	202.0	234.5	227.6	199.0
Market value ($ mil.)	(3.6%)	4,976.7	5,129.1	7,208.4	4,877.5	4,296.1
Employees	2.8%	1,345	1,500	1,500	1,501	1,500

FIRST FINANCIAL CORP. (IN)
NMS: THFF

One First Financial Plaza
Terre Haute, IN 47807
Phone: 812 238-6000
Fax: –
Web: www.first-online.com

CEO: Norman L Lowery
CFO: Rodger A McHargue
HR: –
FYE: December 31
Type: Public

Which came first, the First Financial in Indiana, Ohio, South Carolina, or Texas? Regardless, this particular First Financial Corporation is the holding company for First Financial Bank, which offers traditional banking deposit accounts and loans as well as trust, private banking, wealth management, and investment services through more than 70 branches in west-central Indiana and east-central Illinois. About 60% of its loan portfolio is tied to commercial loans while the rest is split between residential and consumer loans. Subsidiary Forrest Sherer sells personal and commercial insurance while subsidiary Morris Plan originates indirect auto loans through dealerships in the bank's market area.

	Annual Growth	12/19	12/20	12/21	12/22	12/23
Assets ($mil.)	4.8%	4,023.3	4,557.5	5,175.1	4,989.3	4,851.1
Net income ($ mil.)	5.6%	48.9	53.8	53.0	71.1	60.7
Market value ($ mil.)	(1.5%)	539.3	458.2	534.2	543.5	507.5
Employees	(2.6%)	957	917	883	900	861

FIRST FINANCIAL NORTHWEST INC
NMS: FFNW

201 Wells Avenue South
Renton, WA 98057
Phone: 425 255-4400
Fax: –
Web: –

CEO: Joseph W Kiley III
CFO: Richard P Jacobson
HR: Abbi Rudolph
FYE: December 31
Type: Public

Searching for green in The Evergreen State, First Financial Northwest is the holding company for First Financial Northwest Bank (formerly First Savings Bank Northwest). The small community bank offers deposit services like checking and savings accounts, and a variety of lending services to customers in western Washington. Almost 40% of First Savings Bank's loan portfolio consists of one- to four-family residential loans, while commercial real estate loans made up another 35%. Because the bank focuses almost exclusively on real estate loans, it writes very few unsecured consumer and commercial loans.

	Annual Growth	12/19	12/20	12/21	12/22	12/23
Assets ($mil.)	2.9%	1,341.9	1,387.7	1,426.3	1,502.9	1,505.1
Net income ($ mil.)	(11.7%)	10.4	8.6	12.2	13.2	6.3
Market value ($ mil.)	(2.5%)	137.1	104.6	148.4	137.5	123.7
Employees	(2.6%)	158	151	144	151	142

FIRST HARTFORD CORP
NBB: FHRT

149 Colonial Road
Manchester, CT 06042
Phone: 860 646-6555
Fax: 860 646-8572
Web: www.firsthartford.com

CEO: Neil H Ellis
CFO: –
HR: –
FYE: April 30
Type: Public

First Hartford puts real estate first. The company, operating through subsidiary First Hartford Realty, invests in and develops commercial and other real estate. Its portfolio is located primarily in the Northeast and includes shopping centers, a restaurant, and a business and technology school campus. First Hartford has also built single-family homes, public housing units, government facilities, and several industrial properties. It is a preferred developer for CVS Health in areas of Lousiana, New Jersey, New York, and Texas. The company's largest tenants include Stop & Shop, Big Y Foods, and Kmart. Subsidiary Lead Tech provides lead and asbestos inspection and remediation services.

	Annual Growth	04/19	04/20	04/21	04/22	04/23
Sales ($mil.)	(3.0%)	80.7	67.8	90.7	80.3	71.4
Net income ($ mil.)	4.5%	2.6	(4.6)	5.3	15.1	3.1
Market value ($ mil.)	37.2%	5.1	10.4	11.2	16.0	18.2
Employees	–	–	–	–	–	104

FIRST HAWAIIAN INC
NMS: FHB

999 Bishop Street, 29th Floor
Honolulu, HI 96813
Phone: 808 525-7000
Fax: –
Web: www.fhb.com

CEO: Robert S Harrison
CFO: Ravi Mallela
HR: –
FYE: December 31
Type: Public

Truly one of the archipelago's first and longest-surviving businesses, First Hawaiian (formerly BancWest) has served Hawaii since long before it joined the United States. The former wholly owned subsidiary of French banking group BNP Paribas is the holding company for First Hawaiian Bank. Founded in 1858, First Hawaiian has more than 60 branches in Hawaii plus a handful more in Guam and Saipan. The bank's services include residential and commercial real estate lending, commercial banking, consumer finance, credit cards, merchant processing, and wealth management. First Hawaiian Inc. went public in mid-2016, although BNP retained a controlling stake in the firm.

	Annual Growth	12/19	12/20	12/21	12/22	12/23
Assets ($mil.)	5.4%	20,167	22,663	24,992	24,577	24,926
Net income ($ mil.)	(4.7%)	284.4	185.8	265.7	265.7	235.0
Market value ($ mil.)	(5.7%)	3,681.8	3,009.3	3,487.8	3,323.2	2,917.4
Employees	(1.2%)	2,100	2,100	2,000	2,000	2,000

FIRST HORIZON CORP
NYS: FHN

165 Madison Avenue
Memphis, TN 38103
Phone: 901 523-4444
Fax: –
Web: www.firsthorizon.com

CEO: D B Jordan
CFO: Hope Dmuchowski
HR: –
FYE: December 31
Type: Public

First Horizon Corporation, a holding company that provides diversified financial services primarily through its principal subsidiary. Boasting some $79 billion in total assets, it offers traditional banking services like loans, deposit accounts, and credit cards, as well as trust, asset management, financial advisory, and investment services. It provides services through subsidiaries and divisions such as general banking services for consumers, businesses, financial institutions, and governments and fixed income sales and trading; underwriting of bank-eligible securities and other fixed-income securities eligible for underwriting by financial subsidiaries; loan sales; advisory services; and derivative sales. The bank was founded in 1864 as First National Bank of Memphis.

	Annual Growth	12/19	12/20	12/21	12/22	12/23
Assets ($mil.)	17.2%	43,311	84,209	89,092	78,953	81,661
Net income ($ mil.)	19.4%	440.9	845.0	999.0	900.0	897.0
Market value ($ mil.)	(3.8%)	9,254.4	7,130.8	9,125.8	13,692	7,913.2
Employees	10.1%	5,017	6,802	7,867	7,542	7,378

FIRST INDUSTRIAL REALTY TRUST INC
NYS: FR

One North Wacker Drive, Suite 4200
Chicago, IL 60606
Phone: 312 344-4300
Fax: 312 922-6320
Web: www.firstindustrial.com

CEO: Bruce W Duncan
CFO: Scott A Musil
HR: –
FYE: December 31
Type: Public

First Industrial Realty Trust is a self-administered and fully integrated real estate company which owns, manages, acquires, sells, develops, and redevelops industrial real estate. Its portfolio consists of about 415 industrial properties spanning approximately 62.9 million sq. ft. of leasable space in roughly 20 states. Most of the REIT's portfolio consists of light industrial properties but also includes bulk and regional warehouses. Tenants include e-commerce, third-party logistics and transportation, consumer and other manufactured products, retail and consumer services, food and beverage, lumber and building materials, wholesale goods, health services, governmental, and other businesses.

	Annual Growth	12/19	12/20	12/21	12/22	12/23
Sales ($mil.)	9.6%	426.0	448.0	476.3	539.9	614.0
Net income ($ mil.)	3.6%	238.8	196.0	271.0	359.1	274.8
Market value ($ mil.)	6.1%	5,491.3	5,573.3	8,757.5	6,384.3	6,967.7
Employees	0.2%	155	153	162	157	156

FIRST INTERNET BANCORP

NMS: INBK

8701 East 116th Street
Fishers, IN 46038
Phone: 317 532-7900
Fax: –
Web: www.firstinternetbancorp.com

CEO: David B Becker
CFO: Kenneth J Lovik
HR: –
FYE: December 31
Type: Public

First Internet Bancorp was formed in 2006 to be the holding company for First Internet Bank of Indiana (First IB). Launched in 1999, the bank was the first state-chartered, FDIC-insured institution to operate solely via the Internet. It now operates two locations in Indianapolis after adding one via its 2007 purchase of Landmark Financial (the parent of Landmark Savings Bank), a deal that also brought aboard residential mortgage brokerage Landmark Mortgage. First IB offers traditional checking and savings accounts in addition to CDs, IRAs, credit and check cards, consumer installment and residential mortgage loans, and lines of credit. It serves customers in all 50 states.

	Annual Growth	12/19	12/20	12/21	12/22	12/23
Assets ($mil.)	6.0%	4,100.1	4,246.2	4,211.0	4,543.1	5,167.6
Net income ($ mil.)	(24.0%)	25.2	29.5	48.1	35.5	8.4
Market value ($ mil.)	0.5%	205.0	248.4	406.6	209.9	209.1
Employees	5.6%	231	257	286	319	287

FIRST INTERSTATE BANCSYSTEM INC

NMS: FIBK

401 North 31st Street
Billings, MT 59101
Phone: 406 255-5311
Fax: –
Web: www.fibk.com

CEO: –
CFO: –
HR: –
FYE: December 31
Type: Public

First Interstate BancSystem (FIB) is a financial and bank holding company focused on community banking that operates over 305 banking offices, including detached drive-up facilities, in communities across nearly 15 states? Arizona, Colorado, Idaho, Iowa, Kansas, Minnesota, Missouri, Montana, Nebraska, North Dakota, Oregon, South Dakota, Washington, and Wyoming. Through the company's bank subsidiary, First Interstate Bank, it delivers a comprehensive range of banking products and services?including online and mobile banking?to individuals, businesses, municipalities, and others throughout their market areas. The company's principal business activity is lending to, accepting deposits from, and conducting financial transactions with and for individuals, businesses, municipalities, and other entities.

	Annual Growth	12/18	12/19	12/20	12/21	12/22
Assets ($mil.)	24.8%	13,300	14,644	17,649	19,672	32,288
Net income ($ mil.)	6.0%	160.2	181.0	161.2	192.1	202.2
Market value ($ mil.)	1.4%	3,818.4	4,378.2	4,258.1	4,247.7	4,036.7
Employees	12.9%	2,330	2,473	2,462	2,358	3,783

FIRST KEYSTONE CORP

NBB: FKYS

111 West Front Street
Berwick, PA 18603
Phone: 570 752-3671
Fax: –
Web: www.firstkeystonecorp.fkc.bank

CEO: Elaine A Woodland
CFO: Diane C Rosler
HR: –
FYE: December 31
Type: Public

First Keystone Corporation is the holding company for First Keystone Community Bank, which serves individuals and businesses from more 18 bank locations in northeastern and central Pennsylvania. The bank provides traditional deposit products including checking and savings accounts, debit cards, and CDs; it also offers trust and investment advisory services. It also operates 20 ATMs and offers online banking services. Commercial mortgages constitute more than half of the bank's loan portfolio; residential mortgages, business loans, and consumer installment loans make up the remainder. The bank was founded in 1864.

	Annual Growth	12/18	12/19	12/20	12/21	12/22
Assets ($mil.)	7.1%	1,012.0	1,007.2	1,179.0	1,320.4	1,329.2
Net income ($ mil.)	11.1%	9.2	10.2	11.8	14.7	14.0
Market value ($ mil.)	(0.8%)	126.1	149.0	123.9	144.9	122.1
Employees	0.4%	206	206	202	206	209

FIRST MANHATTAN CO

399 PARK AVE LBBY L2
NEW YORK, NY 100224614
Phone: 212 756-3300
Fax: –
Web: www.firstmanhattan.com

CEO: Zachary Wydra
CFO: Alvaro Spinola
HR: –
FYE: December 31
Type: Private

The first Manhattan was made in the 1870s using whiskey, vermouth, and a dash of bitters. However, this First Manhattan was made in 1964 of CFAs, MBAs, CPAs, and a dash of JDs. The company specializes in investment management services primarily for individuals, but also for institutional clients such as partnerships, pension plans, and trusts. Its customers typically have between $1 million and $100 million to invest. First Manhattan focuses on value-oriented equity investments with an eye toward long-term growth; its analysts follow a broad range of companies in industries such as banking, consumer products, health care, and oil. The company also manages investments in taxable and municipal bonds.

	Annual Growth	12/03	12/04	12/05	12/06	12/08
Assets ($mil.)	(63.2%)	–	55.5	56.6	70.1	1.0
Net income ($ mil.)	–	–	–	–	–	–
Market value ($ mil.)	–	–	–	–	–	–
Employees	–	–	–	–	–	115

FIRST MERCHANTS CORP

NMS: FRME

200 East Jackson Street
Muncie, IN 47305-2814
Phone: 765 747-1500
Fax: –
Web: www.firstmerchants.com

CEO: Mark K Hardwick
CFO: Michele M Kawiecki
HR: –
FYE: December 31
Type: Public

First Merchants is the holding company that owns First Merchants Bank, which operates some 120 branches in Indiana, Illinois, and western Ohio. Through its Lafayette Bank & Trust and First Merchants Private Wealth Advisors divisions, the bank provides standard consumer and commercial banking services, including checking and savings accounts, CDs, check cards, and consumer, commercial, agricultural, and real estate mortgage loans. First Merchants also provides trust and asset management services. Founded in 1982, First Merchants has nearly $9.4 billion worth of consolidated assets.

	Annual Growth	12/19	12/20	12/21	12/22	12/23
Assets ($mil.)	10.3%	12,457	14,067	15,453	17,938	18,406
Net income ($ mil.)	8.0%	164.5	148.6	205.5	222.1	223.8
Market value ($ mil.)	(2.8%)	2,471.4	2,223.1	2,489.3	2,442.9	2,203.4
Employees	3.4%	1,891	1,907	1,821	2,124	2,162

FIRST MID BANCSHARES INC

NMS: FMBH

1421 Charleston Avenue
Mattoon, IL 61938
Phone: 217 234-7454
Fax: 217 258-0485
Web: www.firstmid.com

CEO: Joseph R Dively
CFO: Matthew K Smith
HR: –
FYE: December 31
Type: Public

Money doesn't grow on trees, so when farmers in Illinois need a little cash, they turn to First Mid-Illinois Bank & Trust. The primary subsidiary of First Mid-Illinois Bancshares is a major supplier of farm credit (including real estate, machinery, and production loans; inventory financing; and lines of credit) in its market area. In addition to agricultural loans, the bank offers commercial, consumer, and real estate lending. It also provides deposit products such as savings and checking accounts, plus trust and investment services through a partnership with Raymond James. First Mid-Illinois Bank & Trust has about 40 branches. Other subsidiaries provide data processing services and insurance products and services.

	Annual Growth	12/19	12/20	12/21	12/22	12/23
Assets ($mil.)	18.6%	3,839.4	4,726.3	5,986.6	6,744.2	7,586.8
Net income ($ mil.)	9.5%	47.9	45.3	51.5	73.0	68.9
Market value ($ mil.)	(0.4%)	839.9	802.0	1,019.6	764.4	825.8
Employees	10.2%	827	824	994	1,043	1,219

FIRST MORTGAGE CORP

3230 Fallow Field Drive
Diamond Bar, CA 91765
Phone: 909 595-1996
Fax: -
Web: www.firstmortgage.com

CEO: -
CFO: -
HR: -
FYE: December 31
Type: Public

First Mortgage issues and purchases mortgage loans. Founded in 1975, the company originates loans for the purchase or refinancing of single-family residences. The company offers conventional, jumbo, and nonconforming loans, as well as loans backed by the Federal Housing Administration (FHA) and the Veterans Administration (VA). First Mortgage has more than 15 offices in California. The company is also an approved lender of the state's Public Employees' Retirement System, its State Teachers' Retirement System, and the state Housing Finance Agency.

	Annual Growth	03/03	03/04	03/05*	12/07	12/08
Sales ($mil.)	(10.2%)	47.6	21.3	16.8	14.7	25.0
Net income ($ mil.)	8.9%	2.8	(1.8)	(1.9)	(1.6)	4.7
Market value ($ mil.)	-	0.0	0.0	0.0	-	-
Employees	-	-	-	-	-	-

*Fiscal year change

FIRST NATIONAL BANK ALASKA

NBB: FBAK

101 West 36th Avenue, P.O. Box 100720
Anchorage, AK 99510-0720
Phone: 907 777-4362
Fax: 907 265-3528
Web: www.fnbalaska.com

CEO: Betsy Lawyer
CFO: -
HR: Henry Wiedle
FYE: December 31
Type: Public

First National Bank Alaska is a financial anchor in Anchorage. Founded in 1922, the bank is one of the state's oldest and largest financial institutions. With about 30 branches throughout The Last Frontier (and about 20 ATMs in rural communities), the bank offers traditional deposit products such as checking and savings accounts, CDs, and IRAs, as well as loans and mortgages, credit and debit cards, and trust and investment management services. The family of longtime president Daniel Cuddy owns a majority of First National Bank Alaska; he took the helm of the bank in 1951.

	Annual Growth	12/19	12/20	12/21	12/22	12/23
Assets ($mil.)	10.8%	3,808.3	4,695.3	5,581.3	5,337.7	5,730.8
Net income ($ mil.)	1.9%	55.6	57.5	58.4	58.2	60.0
Market value ($ mil.)	(4.9%)	769.6	588.7	734.6	737.8	629.9
Employees	-	-	-	-	-	-

FIRST NATIONAL CORP. (STRASBURG, VA)

NAS: FXNC

112 West King Street
Strasburg, VA 22657
Phone: 540 465-9121
Fax: -
Web: www.fbvirginia.com

CEO: Scott C Harvard
CFO: M S Bell
HR: -
FYE: December 31
Type: Public

First National Corporation knows that being number one is always good. The financial institution is the holding company for First Bank, which has about a dozen branches in northern Virginia's Shenandoah Valley. The bank provides community-oriented deposit products and services, including checking and savings accounts, IRAs, money market accounts, CDs, and NOW accounts. Mortgages account for about 60% of the company's loan portfolio; it also provides business, construction, and consumer loans. Additionally, First Bank provides trust and asset management services.

	Annual Growth	12/18	12/19	12/20	12/21	12/22
Assets ($mil.)	16.1%	753.0	800.0	950.9	1,389.4	1,369.4
Net income ($ mil.)	13.5%	10.1	9.6	8.9	10.4	16.8
Market value ($ mil.)	(3.1%)	121.5	134.1	105.9	144.1	107.3
Employees	7.7%	160	154	150	210	215

FIRST NATIONAL OF NEBRASKA, INC.

NBB: FINN

1620 Dodge Street
Omaha, NE 68197
Phone: 402 341-0500
Fax: -
Web: www.fnni.com

CEO: Bruce R Lauritzen
CFO: Michael A Summers
HR: Amy Brown
FYE: December 31
Type: Public

First National of Nebraska is a multi-state holding company headquartered in the heart of downtown Omaha. The First National Bank of Omaha, a subsidiary of First National of Nebraska, has set the standard for outstanding customer service coupled with some of the most innovative financial products in the industry. Altogether the company has more than 95 banking locations in seven states. It has some $26 billion in assets and nearly 5,000 employee associates and was founded in 1857.

	Annual Growth	12/18	12/19	12/20	12/21	12/22
Assets ($mil.)	-	-	22,624	24,817	26,892	28,351
Net income ($ mil.)	3.6%	280.1	292.9	296.1	493.4	322.5
Market value ($ mil.)	12.0%	2,259.5	2,925.6	3,053.6	3,691.7	3,553.0
Employees	-	-	-	-	-	-

FIRST NILES FINANCIAL INC.

NBB: FNFI

55 North Main Street
Niles, OH 44446
Phone: 330 652-2539
Fax: 330 652-0911
Web: -

CEO: -
CFO: -
HR: -
FYE: December 31
Type: Public

First Niles ain't a river in Egypt. It is the holding company for Home Federal Savings and Loan Association of Niles, a one-branch thrift serving its namesake town in northeastern Ohio. Founded in 1897, the association offers a variety of deposit products, including checking, savings, money market, and NOW accounts and CDs. With these funds, Home Federal primarily originates residential mortgages, which account for approximately 70% of its loan portfolio. The thrift also originates commercial mortgages, construction and development loans, and consumer loans.

	Annual Growth	12/18	12/19	12/20	12/21	12/22
Assets ($mil.)	7.8%	99.1	100.1	109.7	124.5	133.9
Net income ($ mil.)	3.6%	0.2	0.4	0.3	0.6	0.3
Market value ($ mil.)	-	10.7	10.7	10.7	10.7	-
Employees	-	-	-	-	-	-

FIRST NONPROFIT UNEMPLOYMENT ADMINISTRATION COMPANY, LLC

233 N MICHIGAN AVE # 1000
CHICAGO, IL 606015519
Phone: 800 526-4352
Fax: -
Web: -

CEO: -
CFO: -
HR: -
FYE: December 31
Type: Private

As its name suggests, First Nonprofit Insurance specializes in meeting the property/casualty insurance needs of not-for-profit organizations. The mutually-owned company writes automobile, workers' compensation, and umbrella policies as well as specialized products such as social workers liability and pastoral counseling lines. The company also offers loss control education and consultation services. In addition, it provides financial services and retirement products to groups around the US. Founded in 1978, First Nonprofit Insurance is a member of First Nonprofit Mutual Group. Its products are distributed by independent brokers and agents.

	Annual Growth	12/05	12/06	12/07	12/09	12/10
Assets ($mil.)	(20.2%)	-	46.0	108.0	14.5	18.7
Net income ($ mil.)	-	-	0.8	(0.5)	-	-
Market value ($ mil.)	-	-	-	-	-	-
Employees	-	-	-	-	-	7

FIRST NORTHERN COMMUNITY BANCORP
NBB: FNRN

195 N First Street
Dixon, CA 95620
Phone: 707 678-3041
Fax: –
Web: www.thatsmybank.com

CEO: Louise A Walker
CFO: Kevin Spink
HR: –
FYE: December 31
Type: Public

First Northern Community Bancorp is the holding company for First Northern Bank, which operates about 10 branches in the northern California counties of El Dorado, Placer, Sacramento, Solano, and Yolo. Founded in 1910, the bank offers community-oriented services such as checking, savings, and money market accounts, and certificates of deposit. It also offers electronic check depositing. Its loan products include real estate mortgages (which account for about half of the bank's portfolio), commercial and construction loans, and agricultural and installment loans. Investment products and services are available to customers via a pact with Raymond James Financial.

	Annual Growth	12/19	12/20	12/21	12/22	12/23
Assets ($mil.)	9.7%	1,292.6	1,655.4	1,899.1	1,871.4	1,871.8
Net income ($ mil.)	10.0%	14.7	12.2	14.2	15.9	21.6
Market value ($ mil.)	(6.2%)	178.0	156.4	158.7	125.4	138.1
Employees	(1.3%)	214	214	190	192	203

FIRST OF LONG ISLAND CORP
NAS: FLIC

275 Broadhollow Road
Melville, NY 11747
Phone: 516 671-4900
Fax: –
Web: www.fnbli.com

CEO: Christopher Becker
CFO: Jay P McConie
HR: Rita Quinn
FYE: December 31
Type: Public

When it comes to banking, The First of Long Island wants to be the first thing on Long Islanders' minds. The company owns The First National Bank of Long Island, which offers a variety of lending, investment, and deposit services through around 45 commercial and retail branches on New York's Long Island, and the boroughs of Manhattan and Queens. Residential and Commercial Mortgages (particularly tied to multifamily properties) make up more than 90% of the bank's loan portfolio, though the bank also writes revolving home equity, business, and consumer loans. Its two bank subsidiaries include insurance agency The First of Long Island Agency, and investment firm FNY Service.

	Annual Growth	12/19	12/20	12/21	12/22	12/23
Assets ($mil.)	0.8%	4,097.8	4,069.1	4,068.8	4,281.5	4,235.9
Net income ($ mil.)	(10.9%)	41.6	41.2	43.1	46.9	26.2
Market value ($ mil.)	(14.8%)	566.6	403.2	487.7	406.6	299.1
Employees	(4.1%)	341	350	318	303	288

FIRST PHYSICIANS CAPITAL GROUP INC
NBB: FPCG

433 North Camden Drive #810
Beverly Hills, CA 90210
Phone: 310 860-2501
Fax: –
Web: www.firstphysicianscapitalgroup.com

CEO: –
CFO: –
HR: –
FYE: September 30
Type: Public

First Physicians Capital Group (formerly Tri-Isthmus Group or TIGroup) is an investment and financing firm with an eye toward the health care industry. The group invests in and manages health care facilities, primarily rural critical access hospitals and ambulatory surgical centers. It owns or holds stakes in about a half-dozen medical facilities in Southern California and Oklahoma. In 2009 First Physicians Capital signed a letter of intent to acquire the assets of a hospital in southeastern Texas and to develop a new community hospital in the region. Oklahoma-based investor Carol Schuster owns more than 40% of the company's common stock. Director David Hirschhorn holds about 20%.

	Annual Growth	09/09	09/10	09/11	09/12	09/13
Sales ($mil.)	(16.1%)	39.1	39.5	6.7	16.2	19.4
Net income ($ mil.)	–	–	(10.1)	(9.5)	(0.5)	5.6	5.8
Market value ($ mil.)	(73.4%)	0.0	0.0	0.0	0.0	0.0
Employees	(19.6%)	424	4	174	174	177

FIRST REPUBLIC BANK (SAN FRANCISCO, CA)
NYS: FRC

111 Pine Street, 2nd Floor
San Francisco, CA 94111
Phone: 415 392-1400
Fax: –
Web: www.firstrepublic.com

CEO: –
CFO: –
HR: –
FYE: December 31
Type: Public

Founded in 1985, First Republic Bank offers private banking, real estate lending, wealth management, trust, and custody services for businesses and high-net-worth clients through nearly 95 offices. Its main geographic focus is on urban markets such as San Francisco, Los Angeles, New York, Portland, and San Diego, among others. The bank generates most of its revenue from commercial banking operations. It also offers investment advice and brokerage and trust services through its wealth management division. First Republic Bank has total assets of $181.1 billion, total deposits of $156.3 billion, total equity of $15.9 billion, and wealth management assets under management or administration of approximately $279.4 billion.

	Annual Growth	12/18	12/19	12/20	12/21	12/22
Assets ($mil.)	21.0%	99,205	116,264	142,502	181,087	212,639
Net income ($ mil.)	18.2%	853.8	930.3	1,064.2	1,478.0	1,665.0
Market value ($ mil.)	8.8%	15,924	21,523	26,925	37,843	22,336
Employees	12.6%	4,480	4,812	5,483	6,295	7,213

FIRST REPUBLIC PREFERRED CAPITAL CORP

111 Pine Street, 2nd Floor
San Francisco, CA 94111
Phone: 415 392-1400
Fax: –
Web: www.firstrepublic.com

CEO: –
CFO: Willis H Newton Jr
HR: –
FYE: December 31
Type: Public

First Republic Preferred Capital prefers mortgages to almost any other type of investment. The company is a real estate investment trust (REIT) that invests in conforming and nonconforming single-family residential mortgages originated by affiliate First Republic Bank and other lenders. Its portfolio of multifamily mortgages consists mainly of loans secured by urban properties in San Francisco and Los Angeles. California accounts for about 80% of its total portfolio. The company is also open to investing in commercial mortgages. Merrill Lynch, which acquired First Republic Preferred Capital and First Republic Bank in 2007, was bought by Bank of America in 2009.

	Annual Growth	12/08	12/09*	06/10*	12/10	12/11
Sales ($mil.)	4.3%	16.2	14.2	7.2	9.6	18.4
Net income ($ mil.)	3.0%	15.9	13.9	7.1	9.3	17.3
Market value ($ mil.)	18.7%	462.7	622.4	595.5	754.3	773.2
Employees		–	–	–	–	–

*Fiscal year change

FIRST ROBINSON FINANCIAL CORP.
NBB: FRFC

P.O. Box 8598, 501 East Main Street
Robinson, IL 62454
Phone: 618 544-8621
Fax: 618 544-7506
Web: www.frsb.net

CEO: Rick L Catt
CFO: Jamie E McReynolds
HR: –
FYE: March 31
Type: Public

If heaven holds a place for those who pay, hey, hey, hey, then here's to you, First Robinson! First Robinson Financial is the holding company for First Robinson Savings Bank, which provides traditional banking services to individuals and businesses through four locations in eastern Illinois' Crawford County. In 2008 the bank opened a division in Vincennes, Indiana, called First Vincennes Savings Bank. The banks' services include savings, checking, and NOW accounts; IRAs; and CDs. They use funds from deposits primarily to originate one- to four-family real estate loans (accounting for about half of the company's loan portfolio), and to a lesser extent, consumer, business, agricultural, and municipal loans.

	Annual Growth	03/19	03/20	03/21	03/22	03/23
Assets ($mil.)	8.8%	336.8	344.8	425.1	470.7	472.0
Net income ($ mil.)	2.6%	2.3	3.3	2.6	2.7	2.6
Market value ($ mil.)	(10.8%)	36.3	29.8	27.2	32.4	23.0
Employees	(2.2%)	81	80	75	76	74

FIRST SAVINGS FINANCIAL GROUP INC
NAS: FSFG

702 North Shore Drive, Suite 300
Jeffersonville, IN 47130
Phone: 812 283-0724
Fax: -
Web: www.fsbbank.net

CEO: Larry W Myers
CFO: Anthony A Schoen
HR: -
FYE: September 30
Type: Public

First Savings Financial Group was formed in 2008 to be the holding company for First Savings Bank, a community bank serving consumers and small businesses in southern Indiana. Through more than a dozen branches, the bank offers standard deposit services like savings, checking, and retirement accounts, as well as a variety of lending services. One- to four- family residential loans make up about 60% of First Savings Bank's loan portfolio; other loans in the bank's portfolio include commercial real estate, construction, consumer, and commercial business. In 2012 First Savings Financial expanded its footprint by acquiring the four Indiana branches of First Financial Service Corporation.

	Annual Growth	09/19	09/20	09/21	09/22	09/23
Assets ($mil.)	17.0%	1,222.6	1,764.6	1,720.5	2,057.7	2,288.9
Net income ($ mil.)	(15.7%)	16.2	33.4	29.6	16.4	8.2
Market value ($ mil.)	(30.5%)	434.1	373.2	192.0	157.8	101.1
Employees	(2.8%)	473	696	590	467	422

FIRST SOLAR INC
NMS: FSLR

350 West Washington Street, Suite 600
Tempe, AZ 85288
Phone: 602 414-9300
Fax: 602 414-9400
Web: www.firstsolar.com

CEO: Mark R Widmar
CFO: Alexander R Bradley
HR: Cong Tran
FYE: December 31
Type: Public

First Solar, one of the leading American solar technology company and global provider of PV solar energy solutions, designs, manufactures, and sells photovoltaic (PV) solar modules with an advanced thin film semiconductor technology that provide a high-performance, lower-carbon alternative to conventional crystalline silicon PV solar modules. The company is currently focusing on markets, including high insolation climates in which its modules provide superior temperature coefficient, humid environments in which its modules provide spectral response, and markets that favor the profile of its PV solar technology, in which its cadmium (CdTe) solar modules provide certain advantages over conventional crystalline silicon solar modules. The company generates almost 85% of its sales in the US.

	Annual Growth	12/19	12/20	12/21	12/22	12/23
Sales ($mil.)	2.0%	3,063.1	2,711.3	2,923.4	2,619.3	3,318.6
Net income ($ mil.)	-	(114.9)	398.4	468.7	(44.2)	830.8
Market value ($ mil.)	32.5%	5,979.2	10,569	9,312.8	16,005	18,408
Employees	0.4%	6,600	5,100	4,800	5,500	6,700

FIRST UNITED CORPORATION (MD)
NMS: FUNC

19 South Second Street
Oakland, MD 21550-0009
Phone: 800 470-4356
Fax: 301 334-8151
Web: www.mybank.com

CEO: Carissa L Rodeheaver
CFO: Tonya K Sturm
HR: -
FYE: December 31
Type: Public

First United is the holding company for First United Bank & Trust and other financial services subsidiaries. Founded in 1900, the bank operates about 25 branches in the panhandles of western Maryland and eastern West Virginia, as well as the Morgantown, West Virginia area. The bank provides standard services such as checking and savings accounts, money market accounts, and CDs, as well as retirement and trust services. Commercial loans make up the largest portion of the company's loan portfolio (more than 45%), followed by real estate mortgages (more than 35%), consumer installment loans, and construction loans.

	Annual Growth	12/19	12/20	12/21	12/22	12/23
Assets ($mil.)	7.2%	1,442.0	1,733.4	1,729.8	1,848.2	1,905.9
Net income ($ mil.)	3.5%	13.1	13.8	19.8	25.0	15.1
Market value ($ mil.)	(0.6%)	160.0	102.9	124.6	130.5	156.1
Employees	(1.2%)	319	319	303	336	304

FIRST US BANCSHARES INC
NAS: FUSB

3291 U.S. Highway 280
Birmingham, AL 35243
Phone: 205 582-1200
Fax: -
Web: www.firstusbank.com

CEO: James F House
CFO: Thomas S Elley
HR: -
FYE: December 31
Type: Public

First US Bancshares (formerly United Security Bancshares) is the holding company for First US Bank (formerly First United Security Bank), which has about 20 locations in central and western Alabama and eastern Mississippi. It serves area consumers and businesses, offering such standard retail services as savings, checking, and money market accounts, as well as CDs and credit and check cards. Real estate mortgages make up more than 70% of the bank's loan portfolio, which also includes business and consumer loans. Bank subsidiary Acceptance Loan Company primarily makes consumer loans through about two dozen offices in Alabama and Mississippi.

	Annual Growth	12/19	12/20	12/21	12/22	12/23
Assets ($mil.)	8.0%	788.7	890.5	958.3	994.7	1,072.9
Net income ($ mil.)	16.8%	4.6	2.7	4.5	6.9	8.5
Market value ($ mil.)	(2.9%)	66.6	51.7	60.6	49.8	59.1
Employees	(14.0%)	280	189	175	149	153

FIRSTCASH HOLDINGS INC
NMS: FCFS

1600 West 7th Street
Fort Worth, TX 76102
Phone: 817 335-1100
Fax: -
Web: www.firstcash.com

CEO: Rick L Wessel
CFO: R D Orr
HR: -
FYE: December 31
Type: Public

FirstCash operates some 2,590 pawnshops and cash advance stores in the US, Colombia, Mexico, El Salvador, and Guatemala. The company lends money secured by such personal property as jewelry, electronics, tools, sporting goods, and musical equipment. The company also melts certain quantities of scrap jewelry and sells gold, silver and diamonds in the commodity markets. Pawn stores provide a quick and convenient source of small, secured consumer loans, also known as pawn loans, to unbanked, under-banked and credit-constrained customers. Pawn loans are safe and affordable non-recourse loans for which the customer has no legal obligation to repay. The US operations generate around 75% of total revenue.

	Annual Growth	12/19	12/20	12/21	12/22	12/23
Sales ($mil.)	14.0%	1,864.4	1,631.3	1,699.0	2,728.9	3,151.8
Net income ($ mil.)	7.4%	164.6	106.6	124.9	253.5	219.3
Market value ($ mil.)	7.7%	3,637.1	3,159.4	3,374.5	3,920.3	4,889.3
Employees	(2.5%)	21,000	17,000	17,000	18,000	19,000

FIRSTENERGY CORP
NYS: FE

76 South Main Street
Akron, OH 44308
Phone: 800 736-3402
Fax: -
Web: www.firstenergycorp.com

CEO: John W Somerhalder II
CFO: K J Taylor
HR: -
FYE: December 31
Type: Public

FirstEnergy's and its subsidiaries are involved in the transmission, distribution, and generation of electricity. Its ten utility operating companies provide electricity to more than 6 million customers in the Midwest and the Mid-Atlantic. FirstEnergy controls about 24,000 miles of transmission lines. In addition, the company also has two regional transmission operation centers. Its' subsidiaries, Allegheny Generating company (AGC) and Monongahela Power Company (MP) control more than 3,500 MWs of total capacity. The Utilities' combined service areas cover about 65,000 square miles in states such as Ohio, Pennsylvania, West Virginia, Maryland, New Jersey, and New York.

	Annual Growth	12/19	12/20	12/21	12/22	12/23
Sales ($mil.)	3.9%	11,035	10,790	11,132	12,459	12,870
Net income ($ mil.)	4.8%	912.0	1,079.0	1,283.0	406.0	1,102.0
Market value ($ mil.)	(6.8%)	27,913	17,580	23,887	24,088	21,055
Employees	(0.6%)	12,316	12,153	12,395	12,335	12,042

FIRSTFLEET, INC.

202 HERITAGE PARK DR
MURFREESBORO, TN 371291556
Phone: 615 890-9229
Fax: –
Web: www.firstfleetinc.com

CEO: –
CFO: –
HR: Alisha Young
FYE: March 31
Type: Private

FirstFleet helps its customers move their freight -- not just by the truckload but by providing fleets of trucks. The company offers dedicated contract carriage, in which it supplies its customers with tractors and trailers and the drivers to operate them. In addition, FirstFleet provides related fleet management, logistics, and maintenance services. The company operates a fleet of about 1,450 trucks and tractors from facilities in some 30 states in the US, and it provides transportation services throughout the 48 contiguous states and in Canada and Mexico. FirstFleet began operations in 1986.

	Annual Growth	03/07	03/08	03/09	03/10	03/12
Sales ($mil.)	0.1%	–	288.1	274.6	259.4	288.7
Net income ($ mil.)	20.3%	–	1.3	0.1	0.5	2.8
Market value ($ mil.)	–	–	–	–	–	–
Employees	–	–	–	–	–	2,000

FIRSTHAND TECHNOLOGY VALUE FUND, INC.

150 ALMADEN BLVD STE 1250
SAN JOSE, CA 951132025
Phone: 408 886-7096
Fax: –
Web: www.firsthandtvf.com

CEO: Kevin Landis
CFO: Omar Billawala
HR: –
FYE: December 31
Type: Private

Firsthand Technology Value Fund has direct experience with successful investments. The externally managed, closed-end, non-diversified management investment fund mainly backs companies in the tech sector. The fund has around 12 companies in its portfolio, including Facebook and Twitter. It typically makes investments between $1 million and $10 million. Organized as a business development company (BDC), Firsthand doesn't have to pay corporate taxes as long as it distributes 90% of its profits back to shareholders. Firsthand Technology Value Fund is managed by Firsthand Capital Management.

FIRSTHEALTH OF THE CAROLINAS, INC.

155 MEMORIAL DR
PINEHURST, NC 283748710
Phone: 910 715-1000
Fax: –
Web: www.firsthealth.org

CEO: –
CFO: –
HR: –
FYE: September 30
Type: Private

FirstHealth of the Carolinas maintains a health care network that extends to 15 counties across the mid-Carolinas. The health network includes four hospitals -- Moore Regional, Richmond Memorial, Moore Regional - Hoke, and Montgomery Memorial -- that provide emergency, surgical, acute care, and diagnostic services and have a combined capacity of more than 580 beds. Moore Regional, its largest hospital, includes an inpatient rehabilitation center and a heart hospital. FirstHealth of the Carolinas also operates satellite facilities, including family practice clinics, fitness centers, and dental practices. The system's FirstCarolinaCare provides home health and hospice services, emergency care, medical transportation, and health insurance.

	Annual Growth	09/18	09/19	09/20	09/21	09/22
Sales ($mil.)	11.8%	–	793.3	768.7	–	1,109.5
Net income ($ mil.)	50.0%	–	35.9	83.1	–	120.9
Market value ($ mil.)	–	–	–	–	–	–
Employees	–	–	–	–	–	3,897

FISERV INC

NYS: FI

255 Fiserv Drive
Brookfield, WI 53045
Phone: 262 879-5000
Fax: 262 879-5013
Web: www.fiserv.com

CEO: Frank J Bisignano
CFO: Robert W Hau
HR: Jennifer Manchester
FYE: December 31
Type: Public

Fiserv is a leading global provider of payments and financial services technology solutions. The company provides account processing and digital banking solutions; card issuer processing and network services; payments; e-commerce; merchant acquiring and processing; and the Clover cloud-based point-of-sale (POS) solution and business management platform. Through its Fiserv Clearing Network, the company provides check clearing and image exchange services. Other products and services include image archive with online retrieval, in-clearings, exceptions and returns, statements, and fraud detection. Fiserv serves customers of all sizes, including banks, credit unions, other financial institutions, and merchants across the US and Canada; Europe, Middle East and Africa; Latin America; and Asia Pacific. About 85% of sales come from domestic operations.

	Annual Growth	12/19	12/20	12/21	12/22	12/23
Sales ($mil.)	17.0%	10,187	14,852	16,226	17,737	19,093
Net income ($ mil.)	36.1%	893.0	958.0	1,334.0	2,530.0	3,068.0
Market value ($ mil.)	3.5%	68,684	67,633	61,651	60,036	78,907
Employees	(1.2%)	44,000	44,000	44,000	41,000	42,000

FISHER PEN COMPANY

711 YUCCA ST
BOULDER CITY, NV 890051912
Phone: 702 293-3011
Fax: –
Web: www.spacepen.com

CEO: Cary Fisher
CFO: –
HR: –
FYE: December 31
Type: Private

If the man on the moon were inclined to pen a memoir, he'd likely reach for a Fisher Space writing instrument. Fisher Space Pen makes pens containing pressurized visco-elastic ink, which makes it possible to write upside down, underwater, in all temperatures, and in zero gravity. The company's pens have starred in space as the official pen of NASA and on TV in a Seinfeld sitcom episode. Urban legend has it that NASA spent millions to develop the pen. In July 2009 the company launched its limited edition AG7-40LE Space Pen to commemorate the Apollo 11 moon landing. The company was founded by brothers Paul Fisher and the late Robert Haydn Fisher.

	Annual Growth	12/08	12/09	12/10	12/11	12/13
Sales ($mil.)	(0.4%)	–	–	–	8.5	8.5
Net income ($ mil.)	(50.3%)	–	–	–	0.2	0.0
Market value ($ mil.)	–	–	–	–	–	–
Employees	–	–	–	–	–	80

FISK UNIVERSITY

1000 17TH AVE N
NASHVILLE, TN 372083051
Phone: 615 329-8555
Fax: –
Web: www.fisk.edu

CEO: –
CFO: –
HR: –
FYE: June 30
Type: Private

Fisk University is a predominantly African-American liberal arts university with an enrollment of around 1,000 students. Notable alumni include W. E. B. Du Bois and Booker T. Washington, as well as poets James Weldon Johnson and Nikki Giovanni (now a professor at Virginia Tech). It has 25 majors and pre-professional certification programs. The oldest university in Nashville, Fisk was founded in 1866 as an institution of higher learning committed to educating the country's newly freed slaves. It is affiliated with the United Church of Christ.

FIVE BELOW INC
NMS: FIVE

701 Market Street, Suite 300
Philadelphia, PA 19106
Phone: 215 546-7909
Fax: –
Web: www.fivebelow.com

CEO: –
CFO: –
HR: –
FYE: February 3
Type: Public

Five Below is a leading high-growth value retailer offering trend-right, high-quality products loved by tweens, teens, and beyond. It offers a dynamic, edited assortment of exciting products, most priced at $5 and below, including select brands and licensed merchandise across eight worlds: Style, Room, Sports, Tech, Create, Party, Candy, and New & Now. The company operates a total of 1,340 stores in over 40 states located within power, community, and lifestyle shopping centers across a variety of urban, suburban, and semi-rural markets; it also operates an e-commerce site. Five Below was founded in 2002.

	Annual Growth	02/20*	01/21	01/22	01/23*	02/24
Sales ($mil.)	17.8%	1,846.7	1,962.1	2,848.4	3,076.3	3,559.4
Net income ($ mil.)	14.5%	175.1	123.4	278.8	261.5	301.1
Market value ($ mil.)	12.5%	6,249.5	9,699.9	8,767.6	10,776	9,996.9
Employees	7.3%	16,600	19,000	20,200	21,900	22,000

*Fiscal year change

FIVE POINT HOLDINGS LLC
NYS: FPH

2000 FivePoint, 4th Floor
Irvine, CA 92618
Phone: 949 349-1000
Fax: –
Web: www.fivepoint.com

CEO: Daniel Hedigan
CFO: Kim Tobler
HR: –
FYE: December 31
Type: Public

Five Point Holdings is an owner and developer of mixed-use planned communities located in California that combine residential, commercial, retail, educational, and recreational elements with public amenities, including civic areas for parks and open space. Its existing communities have the general plan and zoning approvals necessary for the construction of thousands of home sites and millions of square feet of commercial space, and they represent a significant portion of the real estate available for development in three major markets in California?Los Angeles County, San Francisco County, and Orange County. Its communities are designed to include about 40,000 residential homes and some 23 million square feet of commercial space over a period of more than 10 years. The company was founded in 2009 as a limited liability company.

	Annual Growth	12/19	12/20	12/21	12/22	12/23
Sales ($mil.)	3.5%	184.4	153.6	224.4	42.7	211.7
Net income ($ mil.)	57.4%	9.0	(0.4)	6.6	(15.4)	55.4
Market value ($ mil.)	(18.5%)	1,031.6	810.4	970.8	345.9	455.7
Employees	(15.3%)	175	160	160	105	90

FIVE STAR COOPERATIVE

1949 N LINN AVE
NEW HAMPTON, IA 506599406
Phone: 641 394-3052
Fax: –
Web: www.fivestarcoop.com

CEO: –
CFO: –
HR: –
FYE: June 30
Type: Private

If Old MacDonald actually had a farm, he'd want to be a member of the Five Star Cooperative. Operating in north-central and northeast Iowa, Five Star has operations in more than 15 small to midsized towns in the Hawkeye State. The cooperative is divided into five divisions, according to the products and services offered -- agronomy, petroleum (diesel fuel and home heating oil), feed (for beef cattle and swine), grain, and hardware -- it operates a True Value hardware store in New Hampton that offers all the usual hardware products and services. Established in 1916, Five Star Cooperative provides a full complement for its member/farmers.

	Annual Growth	06/10	06/11	06/12	06/13	06/14
Sales ($mil.)	–	–	–	479.1	427.1	–
Net income ($ mil.)	(14.6%)	–	–	9.8	8.1	7.1
Market value ($ mil.)	–	–	–	–	–	–
Employees	–	–	–	–	–	190

FIVE9, INC
NMS: FIVN

3001 Bishop Drive, Suite 350
San Ramon, CA 94583
Phone: 925 201-2000
Fax: –
Web: www.five9.com

CEO: Rowan Trollope
CFO: Barry Zwarenstein
HR: Samantha Romero
FYE: December 31
Type: Public

Five9 is a leading pioneer provider of intelligent cloud software for contact centers. The company purpose is to build a highly scalable and secure Virtual Contact Center, or VCC, cloud platforms to delivers easy to used applications that enable breadth of contact center-related customer service, sales and marketing functions. The company develops cloud computing software that helps data collection centers manage client interactions across voice, chat, email, web, social media, and mobile channels. Its virtual contact center cloud platform matches each customer interaction with an agent resource and sends relative data to improve agent productivity. It also allows clients to adjust the number of contact center agent seats in response to changing business requirements. Five9 provides its software through a Software-as-a-Service (SaaS) model and generates most of its revenue through subscriptions. Majority of its sales were generated in the US.

	Annual Growth	12/19	12/20	12/21	12/22	12/23
Sales ($mil.)	29.1%	328.0	434.9	609.6	778.8	910.5
Net income ($ mil.)	–	(4.6)	(42.1)	(53.0)	(94.7)	(81.8)
Market value ($ mil.)	4.7%	4,808.1	12,786	10,068	4,975.3	5,769.3
Employees	22.0%	1,210	1,549	2,138	2,380	2,684

FLAGSTAFF MEDICAL CENTER, INC.

1200 N BEAVER ST
FLAGSTAFF, AZ 860013118
Phone: 928 779-3366
Fax: –
Web: www.nahealth.com

CEO: –
CFO: –
HR: Nina Ferguson
FYE: June 30
Type: Private

Flagstaff Medical Center serves northern Arizona's residents and those who are just passing through. Founded in 1936, the not-for-profit hospital is part of the Northern Arizona Healthcare family. It has some 270 beds and its medical staff includes about 210 physicians. The hospital offers cancer, heart, sports medicine, joint surgery, and women and infants' centers. Other medical services include behavioral health, audiology, diabetes care, home health, hospice, and ambulance and air flight transportation. In addition, Flagstaff Medical Center provides training courses for health care professionals. The hospital's emergency department treats about 40,000 patients each year.

	Annual Growth	06/08	06/09	06/15	06/16	06/22
Sales ($mil.)	2.9%	–	358.2	389.9	415.9	520.0
Net income ($ mil.)	–	–	–	53.7	55.3	52.2
Market value ($ mil.)	–	–	–	–	–	–
Employees	–	–	–	–	–	2,000

FLANDERS CORPORATION

531 FLANDERS FILTER RD
WASHINGTON, NC 278897805
Phone: 252 946-8081
Fax: –
Web: www.flanderscorp.com

CEO: –
CFO: –
HR: –
FYE: December 31
Type: Private

This Flanders handles flecks, fleas, flies, fluff, and other airborne flotsam. The company makes air filters under such brand names as Air Seal, Eco-Air, and Precisionaire. Its products include high-efficiency particulate air (HEPA) filters used in industrial cleanrooms, as well as standard residential and commercial heating, ventilation, and air-conditioning filters. Flanders makes most of its sales from aftermarket replacement filters that it sells directly to wholesalers, distributors, and retail outlets. Customers include the likes of Home Depot, Texas Instruments, and Wal-Mart. Japan-based air conditioner maker Daikin Industries agreed to buy Flanders for $434 million in February 2016.

	Annual Growth	12/05	12/06	12/07	12/08	12/09
Sales ($mil.)	(48.4%)	–	–	836.2	217.3	222.4
Net income ($ mil.)	19624.4%	–	–	0.0	(4.1)	7.0
Market value ($ mil.)	–	–	–	–	–	–
Employees	–	–	–	–	–	3,362

FLANIGAN'S ENTERPRISES, INC.   ASE: BDL

5059 N.E. 18th Avenue
Fort Lauderdale, FL 33334
Phone: 954 377-1961
Fax: –
Web: –

CEO: –
CFO: –
HR: –
FYE: September 30
Type: Public

Seafood and sauce are the catch of the day at Flanigan's Enterprises. The company operates and manages about 20 restaurants that do business as Flanigan's Seafood Bar and Grill, along with a chain of eight package liquor stores called Big Daddy's Liquors. (Four properties have combination liquor store/restaurant operations.) Six of its restaurants are franchised and owned primarily by family members of company executives. All the company's lounges and liquor stores are located in Florida. In addition, Flanigan's owns the Mardi Gras adult entertainment club in Atlanta, which is operated by a third party. The family of former chairman and CEO Joseph "Big Daddy" Flanigan owns more than 50% of the company.

	Annual Growth	09/19*	10/20	10/21	10/22*	09/23
Sales ($mil.)	10.7%	116.2	113.0	137.3	158.1	174.4
Net income ($ mil.)	2.3%	3.6	1.1	11.8	6.3	4.0
Market value ($ mil.)	11.6%	39.5	33.2	47.9	47.4	61.3
Employees	(0.2%)	1,870	1,804	1,555	1,766	1,855

*Fiscal year change

FLAVORX, INC.

9475 GERWIG LN STE A
COLUMBIA, MD 210463177
Phone: 800 884-5771
Fax: –
Web: www.flavorx.com

CEO: Stuart Amos
CFO: Colin Denney
HR: Randy Ennis
FYE: December 31
Type: Private

It takes a spoonful from FLAVORx to help the medicine go down. The company offers a medical flavoring system which makes medicine more palatable for children, (and some adults). The company doesn't neglect our furry friends either, as the product is also available to veterinarians. Using 42 flavors to sweeten some 600 human and nearly 400 animal medications, FLAVORx sells its products to about 35,000 pharmacies located in the US, as well as in Australia, the Bahamas, Canada, and New Zealand. CEO Kenny Kramm started the company out of the need to hide the bitter taste of his daughter's cerebral palsy medicine.

FLETCHER MUSIC CENTERS, INC.

12717 59TH WAY N
CLEARWATER, FL 337603908
Phone: 727 571-1088
Fax: –
Web: www.fletchermusic.com

CEO: John K Riley
CFO: –
HR: –
FYE: December 31
Type: Private

Yearning to learn to play -- and maybe own -- a home organ? Fletcher Music Centers would be a company to call. The firm sells a variety of Lowrey-brand organs and teaches aspiring organists to play. The company is one of the world's largest retailers of organs for home use. It boasts about 20 stores located in Arizona and Florida. Most of its locations offer lessons and the company plans special occasions, such as student concerts, parties, and potlucks. Fletcher Music Centers operates OrganFest, a three-day event featuring discussions, seminars, and professional concerts. Founded by Robert Fletcher in 1975, the company is still owned by the Fletcher family.

	Annual Growth	12/06	12/07	12/08	12/09	12/10
Sales ($mil.)	(5.9%)	–	18.4	19.6	14.4	15.3
Net income ($ mil.)	108.8%	–	0.0	0.8	(0.0)	0.2
Market value ($ mil.)	–	–	–	–	–	–
Employees	–	–	–	–	–	90

FLEXERA SOFTWARE LLC

300 PARK BLVD
ITASCA, IL 601432682
Phone: 502 617-0353
Fax: –
Web: www.flexera.com

CEO: Jim Ryan
CFO: David Zwick
HR: Brittney Zullo
FYE: December 31
Type: Private

Flexera is a global company with offices in North America, Europe, Australia and Asia. It delivers SaaS-based IT management solutions that enable enterprises to accelerate digital transformation and multiply the value of their technology investments. The company helps organizations inform their IT with unparalleled visibility into complex hybrid ecosystems. In addition, it helps them transform their IT with tools that deliver the actionable intelligence to effectively manage, govern and optimize their hybrid IT estate. Serving more than 50,000 customers around the world, six of the world's top ten largest and most renowned organizations rely on Flexera solutions (Walmart, Shell, Toyota, Volkswagen, Saudi Aramco, and BP).

	Annual Growth	12/10	12/11	12/12	12/13	12/14
Sales ($mil.)	5.8%	–	–	–	215.3	227.7
Net income ($ mil.)	–	–	–	–	–	(31.4)
Market value ($ mil.)	–	–	–	–	–	–
Employees	–	–	–	–	–	1,300

FLEXIINTERNATIONAL SOFTWARE, INC.   NBB: FLXI

Two Enterprise Drive
Shelton, CT 06484
Phone: 203 925-3040
Fax: –
Web: www.flexi.com

CEO: Stefan R Bothe
CFO: –
HR: –
FYE: December 31
Type: Public

FlexiInternational Software hopes to provide some flexibility for companies that deal with hard numbers every day. Founded in 1991, the company offers accounting and financial analysis software, primarily to midsized banks, insurance companies, and corporate accounting departments. Its software includes back-office applications for financials, payables, receivables, general ledger, asset tracking, and reporting. Flexi's applications manage financial information across different tax jurisdictions, currencies, and languages. The company also offers outsourced back-office accounting services.

	Annual Growth	12/99	12/00	12/01	12/02	12/03
Sales ($mil.)	(18.6%)	15.6	12.4	9.5	7.5	6.8
Net income ($ mil.)	–	(18.5)	0.2	(1.4)	1.2	0.8
Market value ($ mil.)	(27.1%)	12.6	2.0	1.4	1.2	3.6
Employees	(8.3%)	58	58	44	40	41

FLEXSTEEL INDUSTRIES, INC.   NMS: FLXS

385 Bell Street
Dubuque, IA 52001-0877
Phone: 563 556-7730
Fax: –
Web: www.flexsteel.com

CEO: Jerald K Dittmer
CFO: Alejandro Huerta
HR: Stacy M Kammes
FYE: June 30
Type: Public

Flexsteel Industries is one of the largest manufacturers, importers and online marketers of residential furniture and products in the US. It offers a wide variety of furniture such as sofas, loveseats, chairs, reclining rocking chairs, swivel rockers, sofa beds, convertible bedding units, occasional tables, desks, dining tables and chairs, kitchen storage, bedroom furniture, and outdoor furniture. A featured component in most of the upholstered furniture is a unique steel drop-in seat spring from which the name "Flexsteel" is derived. The company distributes its products throughout the US through its e-commerce channel and dealer network. Most of its upholstered products including recliners, rockers, and sofas incorporate a patented spring technology, Blue Steel Spring.

	Annual Growth	06/19	06/20	06/21	06/22	06/23
Sales ($mil.)	(2.9%)	443.6	366.9	478.9	544.3	393.7
Net income ($ mil.)	–	(32.6)	(26.8)	23.0	1.9	14.8
Market value ($ mil.)	2.9%	88.3	65.3	209.0	93.1	98.9
Employees	7.0%	1,295	636	665	1,800	1,700

FLINT ELECTRIC MEMBERSHIP CORPORATION

3 S MACON ST
REYNOLDS, GA 310763104
Phone: 478 847-3415
Fax: –
Web: www.flintenergies.com

CEO: Bob Ray
CFO: Anissa Derieux
HR: –
FYE: December 31
Type: Private

The Native American inhabitants of Georgia may have used flint to spark the fires that brought light to their dwellings. Central Georgians today rely on the Flint Electric Membership Corporation, which does business as Flint Energies, to light their homes. Flint Energies serves 250,000 residential, commercial, and industrial customers (through 82,500 meters) in 17 counties, Fort Benning, and the city of Warner Robins. The customer-owned cooperative operates more than 6,250 miles of distribution line and about 50 substations. Flint Energies first flicked the switch in 1937.

	Annual Growth	12/17	12/18	12/20	12/21	12/22
Sales ($mil.)	3.4%	–	220.1	218.0	228.5	251.7
Net income ($ mil.)	3.5%	–	6.9	8.3	8.6	7.9
Market value ($ mil.)	–	–	–	–	–	–
Employees	–	–	–	–	–	227

FLOOR & DECOR HOLDINGS INC

2500 Windy Ridge Parkway SE
Atlanta, GA 30339
Phone: 404 471-1634
Fax: –
Web: www.flooranddecor.com

NYS: FND
CEO: Thomas V Taylor Jr
CFO: Bryan Langley
HR: –
FYE: December 28
Type: Public

Floor & Decor is a hard-surface flooring and accessories retailer that operates about 190 warehouse-format stores, and six small design studios in nearly 35 states, as well as four distribution centers and an e-commerce site, including California, Florida, Texas, Georgia, and Illinois. The company stocks a selection of hardwood floors, flooring tiles (ceramic, granite, marble, porcelain, slate, and travertine), decorative bathroom items (sinks, glass, and wall tiles), and the tools necessary to perform flooring jobs (grout and moldings). The company provides business-building tools and awards points based on purchases through its Pro loyalty rewards program. Floor & Decor currently maintains a high level of inventory consisting of on average approximately 4,400 SKUs per store.

	Annual Growth	12/19	12/20	12/21	12/22	12/23
Sales ($mil.)	21.2%	2,045.5	2,425.8	3,433.5	4,264.5	4,413.9
Net income ($ mil.)	13.0%	150.6	195.0	283.2	298.2	246.0
Market value ($ mil.)	22.7%	5,368.9	9,910.6	13,874	7,577.3	12,156
Employees	15.0%	7,317	8,790	10,566	11,985	12,783

FLORIDA A & M UNIVERSITY

1601 S MRTN L KING JR BLV
TALLAHASSEE, FL 323070001
Phone: 850 599-3000
Fax: –
Web: www.famu.edu

CEO: –
CFO: Alan D Robertson
HR: –
FYE: December 31
Type: Private

If all the syllables in the name Florida Agricultural and Mechanical University start to rattle around in your mouth, just call it Florida A&M like everyone else -- or simply FAMU. With a student body of nearly 12,000, FAMU is known for its pharmacy, business, education, and engineering programs. The school has several satellite campuses in Miami, Jacksonville and Tampa. FAMU's College of Law is in Orlando. FAMU also gets a lot of attention for it Rattlers football team and its famous Marching "100," school band, which has performed numerous times at the NFL Super Bowl. It is part of Florida's State University System.

	Annual Growth	06/03	06/04*	12/05	12/07	12/20
Sales ($mil.)	(29.0%)	–	175.0	1.3	–	0.7
Net income ($ mil.)	(21.5%)	–	46.7	0.1	–	1.0
Market value ($ mil.)	–	–	–	–	–	–
Employees	–	–	–	–	–	1,700

*Fiscal year change

FLORIDA ATLANTIC UNIVERSITY

777 GLADES RD
BOCA RATON, FL 334316496
Phone: 561 297-3000
Fax: –
Web: www.fau.edu

CEO: –
CFO: –
HR: –
FYE: June 30
Type: Private

Who gives a hoot about tertiary education in Southeast Florida? About 30,000 "owls" enrolled at Florida Atlantic University (FAU) do. The Southeast Florida university's colleges offer more than 170 undergraduate and graduate degree programs in a range of academic fields including architecture, liberal arts, education, nursing, science, and engineering. The university has about a half-dozen locations in Boca Raton, Ft. Lauderdale, Port St. Lucie, Dania Beach, Jupiter, Fort Pierce, and Davie. FAU has a student to faculty ratio of 30:1

	Annual Growth	06/18	06/19	06/20	06/21	06/22
Sales ($mil.)	1.6%	–	288.9	301.2	287.7	303.0
Net income ($ mil.)	65.6%	–	20.2	24.8	19.1	91.7
Market value ($ mil.)	–	–	–	–	–	3,053
Employees	–	–	–	–	–	3,053

FLORIDA DEPARTMENT OF LOTTERY

250 MARRIOTT DR
TALLAHASSEE, FL 323012983
Phone: 850 487-7777
Fax: –
Web: www.flalottery.com

CEO: –
CFO: –
HR: –
FYE: June 30
Type: Private

The State of Florida Department of the Lottery runs instant-play scratch tickets and lotto games, including Florida Lotto, Mega Money, Fantasy 5, and Cash 3. In addition to its own games, Florida is part of the Multi-State Lottery Association, which operates the popular Powerball drawing. Proceeds from the games are contributed to Florida's Educational Enhancement Trust Fund, which provides funding for a variety of education programs from pre-kindergarten up to the state university level. The lottery has returned more than $19 billion to the state since starting in 1988.

	Annual Growth	06/18	06/19	06/20	06/21	06/22
Sales ($mil.)	9.2%	–	7,157.9	7,511.6	9,083.0	9,331.9
Net income ($ mil.)	–	–	36.3	4.1	(37.1)	(18.8)
Market value ($ mil.)	–	–	–	–	–	–
Employees	–	–	–	–	–	400

FLORIDA GAS TRANSMISSION COMPANY, LLC

1300 MAIN ST
HOUSTON, TX 770026803
Phone: 713 989-7000
Fax: –
Web: –

CEO: Marshall S McCrea III
CFO: Martin Salinas Jr
HR: –
FYE: December 31
Type: Private

Florida Gas Transmission gasses up the Gulf Coast. The company transports natural gas to cogeneration facilities, electric utilities, independent power producers, municipal generators, and local distribution companies through a 5,400-mile natural gas pipeline extending from south Texas to south Florida. It delivers 3.1 billion cu. ft. of natural gas a day to more than 250 delivery points consisting of more than 50 natural gas-fired electric generation facilities. Florida Gas Transmission is operated by Citrus Corp., which is a joint venture of Energy Transfer Partners and Kinder Morgan.

FLORIDA HEALTH SCIENCES CENTER, INC.

1 TAMPA GENERAL CIR
TAMPA, FL 336063571
Phone: 813 844-7000
Fax: –
Web: www.tgh.org

CEO: John Couris
CFO: Steve Short
HR: Alicia Gomez-Fuego
FYE: September 30
Type: Private

Florida Health Sciences Center, which does business as Tampa General Hospital (TGH), is a private, not-for-profit hospital and one of the most comprehensive medical facilities in Florida serving a dozen counties with a population in excess of four million. The hospital offers general medical and surgical care, as well as tertiary offerings including a Level 1 trauma center, a burn unit, a pediatric ward, women's and cardiovascular centers, and an organ transplant unit. The hospital has licensed for 1,040 beds, and with more than 8,000 team members, which specializes in helping patients recover from stroke, head or spine trauma, and other neuromuscular conditions. TGH is the primary teaching hospital for USF Health Morsani College of Medicine.

	Annual Growth	09/18	09/19	09/20	09/21	09/22
Sales ($mil.)	14.1%	–	1,447.2	1,590.8	1,840.6	2,150.5
Net income ($ mil.)	–	–	57.7	146.5	182.1	(85.2)
Market value ($ mil.)	–	–	–	–	–	–
Employees	–	–	–	–	–	8,000

FLORIDA HOSPITAL WATERMAN, INC.

1000 WATERMAN WAY
TAVARES, FL 327785266
Phone: 352 253-3333
Fax: –
Web: www.adventhealth.com

CEO: David Ottati
CFO: –
HR: Jennifer Ekas
FYE: December 31
Type: Private

Florida Hospital Waterman is a 270-bed community hospital serving the residents of Lake County, Florida, just north of Orlando. The hospital provides a full range of acute care services, including cardiac and cancer care, emergency services, obstetrics, pediatrics, and rehabilitation. It also offers outpatient surgery, diagnostic imaging, laboratory, and home health services. As part of its portfolio of services, Florida Hospital Waterman operates a primary care clinic. Established in 1938 and named after the philanthropic leader of the Waterman Fountain Pen Company, Florida Hospital Waterman has been part of the Adventist Health System since 1992.

	Annual Growth	12/15	12/16	12/17	12/20	12/21
Sales ($mil.)	7.7%	–	232.9	261.6	279.8	336.9
Net income ($ mil.)	13.2%	–	27.5	38.9	25.6	51.1
Market value ($ mil.)	–	–	–	–	–	–
Employees	–	–	–	–	–	1,200

FLORIDA HOUSING FINANCE CORP

227 N BRONOUGH ST STE 5000
TALLAHASSEE, FL 323011367
Phone: 850 488-4197
Fax: –
Web: www.floridahousing.org

CEO: –
CFO: Barb Goltz
HR: Jessica Cherry
FYE: December 31
Type: Private

Owning a home in Florida is just a bit easier thanks to Florida Housing Finance Corporation. Established in 1997 by the Florida Legislature as a public corporation, Florida Housing's mission is to help Floridians obtain safe, decent housing that might otherwise be unavailable to them. Florida Housing pursues its mission through a number of programs that provide financial assistance for first time homebuyers, and for developers of multifamily dwellings that serve elderly and low income Floridians. Florida Housing partners with various local, state, and federal agencies, as well as developers, and not-for-profit organizations to achieve its goals.

	Annual Growth	12/18	12/19	12/20	12/21	12/22
Assets ($mil.)	(2.9%)	–	5,373.5	5,701.3	5,816.7	4,912.2
Net income ($ mil.)	(43.4%)	–	224.9	332.6	40.7	40.7
Market value ($ mil.)	–	–	–	–	–	–
Employees	–	–	–	–	–	130

FLORIDA INTERNATIONAL UNIVERSITY

11200 SW 8TH ST
MIAMI, FL 331992516
Phone: 305 348-2494
Fax: –
Web: www.fiu.edu

CEO: –
CFO: Aime Martinez
HR: Ana Pineda
FYE: June 30
Type: Private

Florida International University (FIU) is a top public university that drives real talent and innovation in Miami and globally. FIU has more than more than 190 degree options including an extensive array of doctoral, master's and graduate-level certificate programs. FIU is a young, vibrant, and diverse university with an overall enrollment of over 56,000 students. It has an active Graduate Student Association and other avenues for graduate involvement on campus through the University Graduate School and other student services offices. Its academic community is composed of about 10 schools and colleges ? including its prestigious Honors College. It held its first classes in 1972.

FLORIDA MEMORIAL UNIVERSITY, INC.

15800 NW 42ND AVE
MIAMI GARDENS, FL 330546155
Phone: 305 626-3600
Fax: –
Web: www.fmuniv.edu

CEO: –
CFO: –
HR: Toni Clarke
FYE: June 30
Type: Private

Florida Memorial University (formerly Florida Memorial College) offers some 40 undergraduate and graduate programs to some 2,200 students in Miami-Dade County. A historically black college and Baptist institution, the school introduced its graduate studies in 2004 with programs in elementary education, special education, and reading. The school is known as the birthplace of the Negro National Anthem "Lift Every Voice and Sing." In 1900 the song was composed by brothers James Weldon Johnson and J. Rosamond Johnson, a former professor at the college. The school traces its roots to the 1879 founding of Florida Baptist Institute, which later merged with Florida Baptist Academy to form Florida Memorial University.

	Annual Growth	06/12	06/13	06/20	06/21	06/22
Sales ($mil.)	2.0%	–	38.0	–	39.0	45.4
Net income ($ mil.)	–	–	(2.9)	–	(5.5)	(5.1)
Market value ($ mil.)	–	–	–	–	–	–
Employees	–	–	–	–	–	300

FLORIDA MUNICIPAL POWER AGENCY

8553 COMMODITY CIR
ORLANDO, FL 328199002
Phone: 407 355-7767
Fax: –
Web: www.fmpa.com

CEO: Jacob Williams
CFO: –
HR: –
FYE: September 30
Type: Private

Unlike some politicians, Florida Municipal Power Agency (FMPA) doesn't believe in holding on to power. The non-profit public agency generates and supplies electric power to 31 county or municipally owned distribution utilities, which in turn serve 2 million Florida residents and businesses. Each of the distribution utilities appoints one representative to FMPA's board of directors, which governs the Agency's activities. The Agency is authorized to undertake joint power supply projects for its members and to issue tax-exempt bonds to finance the costs of such projects. It is also empowered to implement a pooled financing program for utility-related projects.

	Annual Growth	09/17	09/18	09/19	09/20	09/21
Sales ($mil.)	1.3%	–	604.3	620.5	582.8	629.0
Net income ($ mil.)	16.8%	–	32.1	0.4	(0.3)	51.0
Market value ($ mil.)	–	–	–	–	–	–
Employees	–	–	–	–	–	67

FLORIDA PANTHERS HOCKEY CLUB, LTD.

1 PANTHER PKWY
SUNRISE, FL 333235315
Phone: 954 835-7000
Fax: –
Web: www.nhl.com

CEO: Alan Cohen
CFO: –
HR: –
FYE: September 30
Type: Private

These Panthers are prowling the warmer climes in search of hockey fans. Florida Panthers Hockey Club operates the professional hockey team that represents the Miami area in the National Hockey League. The Panthers entered the NHL as an expansion franchise in 1993 and boasts a few playoff berths, including a Stanley Cup Finals appearance in 1996. (The team lost to the Colorado Avalanche that season.) Wayne Huizenga, who once owned the Miami Dolphins and the Florida Marlins, was awarded the franchise and later sold the team to a group of investors led by Alan Cohen in 2001. Cohen's Sunrise Sports & Entertainment controls the Panthers, as well as its BankAtlantic Center home arena.

FLORIDA POWER & LIGHT CO.

700 Universe Boulevard
Juno Beach, FL 33408
Phone: 561 694-4000
Fax: –
Web: www.fpl.com

CEO: Eric E Silagy
CFO: Terrell K Crews II
HR: –
FYE: December 31
Type: Public

Florida Power & Light (FPL) is the largest electric utility in the state of Florida and one of the largest electric utilities in the US. FPL has approximately 32,100 MW of net generating capacity, approximately 88,000 circuit miles of transmission and distribution lines and about 870 substations. FPL provides service to its electric customers through an integrated transmission and distribution system that links its generation facilities to its customers. FPL also owns a retail gas business, which serves approximately 119,000 residential and commercial natural gas customers in eight counties throughout southern Florida with some 3,795 miles of natural gas distribution pipelines. The company, a subsidiary of utility holding company NextEra Energy, serves more than 12 million electricity customers in eastern and southern Florida.

	Annual Growth	12/19	12/20	12/21	12/22	12/23
Sales ($mil.)	10.8%	12,192	11,662	14,102	17,282	18,365
Net income ($ mil.)	18.2%	2,334.0	2,650.0	3,206.0	3,701.0	4,552.0
Market value ($ mil.)	–	–	–	–	–	–
Employees	1.6%	8,900	9,100	9,700	9,300	9,500

FLORIDA STATE COLLEGE AT JACKSONVILLE

501 STATE ST W RM A
JACKSONVILLE, FL 322024030
Phone: 904 633-8100
Fax: –
Web: www.fscj.edu

CEO: –
CFO: –
HR: –
FYE: September 30
Type: Private

Offering more than just sunshine, the city of Jacksonville provides area residents with associate degrees, certificates, corporate training, continuing education, and high school completion programs from its Florida State College at Jacksonville. The college, previously known as Florida Community College at Jacksonville, nearly doubled its bachelor's degree programs in recent years by adding early childhood education, public safety management, and information technology management programs. It serves about 86,000 students through five campuses and seven educational centers in Florida's Duval and Nassau counties, as well as through online distance learning.

FLORIDA STATE UNIVERSITY

600 W COLLEGE AVE
TALLAHASSEE, FL 323061096
Phone: 850 644-5482
Fax: –
Web: www.fsu.edu

CEO: –
CFO: –
HR: Miranda Hacker
FYE: June 30
Type: Private

Home to the Florida State Seminoles, Florida State University offers more than 300 undergraduate, graduate, and professional programs, including M.D. (medicine) and J.D. (law) programs. The educational institution has 16 colleges dedicated to academic fields ranging from liberal arts, music, visual arts, and education, to criminology, engineering, social work, and information. A major research institution, the university is home to the National High Magnetic Field Laboratory, or "Mag Lab," the only national lab in Florida and the only such high-magnetic facility in the US. Florida State was founded in 1851 and is part of the 11-school State University System of Florida.

	Annual Growth	06/08	06/09	06/10	06/11	06/12
Sales ($mil.)	7.4%	–	–	567.1	607.3	654.7
Net income ($ mil.)	(42.4%)	–	–	121.3	188.3	40.2
Market value ($ mil.)	–	–	–	–	–	–
Employees	–	–	–	–	–	13,497

FLORSTAR SALES, INC.

1075 TAYLOR RD
ROMEOVILLE, IL 604464265
Phone: 815 836-2800
Fax: –
Web: www.florstar.com

CEO: Scott Rozmus
CFO: Greg Stirrett
HR: –
FYE: September 30
Type: Private

At FlorStar Sales, the floor is the star. The company distributes floor coverings to retailers throughout the Midwest from four locations in Illinois, Iowa, Michigan, and Minnesota. Florstar's product offerings include hardwoods, laminates, ceramic, porcelain, vinyl, rugs, and carpets from Armstrong, Interceramic, Milliken, Wilsonart, and Weyerhaeuser. From its four locations, the company serves nearly 5,000 customers in six additional Midwest states. In addition, it offers floor installation training and certification. FlorStar was part of Carson Pirie Scott & Co. until 1988, when management purchased the flooring division and created a separate company.

	Annual Growth	09/96	09/97	09/98	09/99	09/08
Sales ($mil.)	1.1%	–	95.2	120.3	130.9	107.9
Net income ($ mil.)	(0.2%)	–	0.7	0.8	2.6	0.7
Market value ($ mil.)	–	–	–	–	–	–
Employees	–	–	–	–	–	190

FLOTEK INDUSTRIES INC

NYS: FTK

8846 N. Sam Houston Parkway W.
Houston, TX 77064
Phone: 713 849-9911
Fax: –
Web: www.flotekind.com

CEO: Ryan Ezell
CFO: Bond Clement
HR: Andrea Berry
FYE: December 31
Type: Public

Flotek Industries, Inc. is a technology-driven, specialty chemistry and data company that serves customers across industrial, commercial and consumer markets. Flotek's Chemistry Technologies segment develops, manufactures, packages, distributes, delivers, and markets high-quality sanitizers and disinfectants for commercial, governmental and personal consumer use. Additionally, Flotek empowers the energy industry to maximize the value of their hydrocarbon streams and improve return on invested capital through its real-time data platforms and chemistry technologies. Flotek serves downstream, midstream and upstream customers, both domestic and international. The US generates more more than 90% of the Flotek's revenue.

	Annual Growth	12/19	12/20	12/21	12/22	12/23
Sales ($mil.)	12.0%	119.4	53.1	43.3	136.1	188.1
Net income ($ mil.)	–	(32.3)	(136.5)	(30.5)	(42.3)	24.7
Market value ($ mil.)	18.3%	59.3	62.6	33.5	33.2	116.3
Employees	(4.3%)	174	147	131	146	146

FLOWERS FOODS, INC.

1919 Flowers Circle
Thomasville, GA 31757
Phone: 229 226-9110
Fax: –
Web: www.flowersfoods.com

NYS: FLO
CEO: A R McMullian
CFO: R S Kinsey
HR: –
FYE: December 30
Type: Public

Flowers Foods is one of the largest producers and marketers of packaged bakery foods in the US. It bakes, markets, and distributes fresh breads, buns, rolls, snack cakes, and flour tortillas to retail food and foodservice customers across the nation. Currently operates about 240 such stores, Fresh baked foods' customers include mass merchandisers, supermarkets and other retailers, restaurants, quick-serve chains, food wholesalers, institutions, dollar stores, and vending companies. Flowers Foods' principal products are sold under a variety of brand names, including Nature's Own, Dave's Killer Bread, Wonder, Canyon Bakehouse, Tastykake, and Mrs. Freshley's. The company traces its roots to 1919.

	Annual Growth	12/19*	01/21	01/22*	12/22	12/23
Sales ($mil.)	5.4%	4,124.0	4,388.0	4,330.8	4,805.8	5,090.8
Net income ($ mil.)	(6.9%)	164.5	152.3	206.2	228.4	123.4
Market value ($ mil.)	0.9%	4,574.5	4,761.8	5,780.2	6,047.5	4,736.6
Employees	(1.0%)	9,700	9,200	8,900	9,200	9,300

*Fiscal year change

FLOWSERVE CORP

5215 N. O'Connor Blvd., Suite 700
Irving, TX 75039
Phone: 972 443-6500
Fax: 972 443-6800
Web: www.flowserve.com

NYS: FLS
CEO: R S Rowe
CFO: Amy Schwetz
HR: –
FYE: December 31
Type: Public

Flowserve is a manufacturer and aftermarket service provides of pumps, valves, and other flow control equipment. It makes highly-engineered custom and pre-configured pumps, mechanical seals, valves and actuators that control the flow of liquids and gases. Flowserve also provides services that include installation, diagnostics, repair, and retrofitting. Flowserve's customers are in the chemical, oil and gas, power generation, and water management industries, as well as some others. It operates in more than 50 countries, and manufactures more than 40 different active types of pumps and approximately 185 different models of mechanical seals and sealing systems. Over 40% of its sales are generated from the US.

	Annual Growth	12/19	12/20	12/21	12/22	12/23
Sales ($mil.)	2.3%	3,944.9	3,728.1	3,541.1	3,615.1	4,320.6
Net income ($ mil.)	(7.4%)	253.7	116.3	125.9	188.7	186.7
Market value ($ mil.)	(4.6%)	6,515.3	4,824.0	4,005.8	4,016.5	5,396.0
Employees	(1.5%)	17,000	16,000	16,000	16,000	16,000

FLOYD HEALTHCARE MANAGEMENT, INC.

304 TURNER MCCALL BLVD SW
ROME, GA 301655621
Phone: 706 509-5000
Fax: –
Web: www.floyd.org

CEO: Kurt Stuenkel
CFO: Clarice Cable
HR: Amy Simmons
FYE: December 31
Type: Private

If you need heart help in the Heart of Dixie, Floyd Healthcare Management is there for you. Its main hospital, Floyd Medical Center, has more than 300 beds and serves northwestern Georgia and northeastern Alabama with more than 40 medical specialties. In addition to medical, surgical, and emergency care (including a Level II trauma center and Level III neonatal intensive care unit), the hospital offers rehabilitation programs, hospice, and home health care. It also operates a 25-bed community hospital (Polk Medical Center) and the 53-bed Floyd Behavioral Health Center. Floyd Healthcare also operates outpatient centers including primary care, surgery, and urgent care locations. The organization was founded in 1942.

	Annual Growth	06/19	06/20	06/21*	12/21	12/22
Sales ($mil.)	24.9%	–	442.2	501.3	–	689.4
Net income ($ mil.)	52.3%	–	5.8	39.6	–	13.5
Market value ($ mil.)	–	–	–	–	–	–
Employees	–	–	–	–	–	2,400

*Fiscal year change

FLUOR CORP.

6700 Las Colinas Boulevard
Irving, TX 75039
Phone: 469 398-7000
Fax: –
Web: www.fluor.com

NYS: FLR
CEO: David E Constable
CFO: Joseph L Brennan
HR: Mallory Walden
FYE: December 31
Type: Public

Fluor is one of the world's largest international design, engineering, and contracting firms. Through subsidiaries, it provides engineering, procurement, construction (EPC), fabrication and modularization, operations, maintenance and asset integrity, as well as project management services for a variety of industrial sectors around the world. The company provides these services to its clients in a diverse set of industries worldwide, including oil and gas, chemicals and petrochemicals, mining and metals, infrastructure, life sciences, advanced manufacturing, and advanced technologies. Fluor is also a service provider to the US federal government and governments abroad. The company generates most of its revenue in North America.

	Annual Growth	12/19	12/20	12/21	12/22	12/23
Sales ($mil.)	1.9%	14,348	15,668	12,435	13,744	15,474
Net income ($ mil.)	–	(1,522.2)	(435.0)	(440.2)	145.0	139.0
Market value ($ mil.)	20.0%	3,217.3	2,721.4	4,220.9	5,906.3	6,674.8
Employees	(11.9%)	50,182	43,717	40,582	39,576	30,187

FLUSHING FINANCIAL CORP.

220 RXR Plaza
Uniondale, NY 11556
Phone: 718 961-5400
Fax: –
Web: www.flushingbank.com

NMS: FFIC
CEO: John R Buran
CFO: Susan K Cullen
HR: Russell Fleishman
FYE: December 31
Type: Public

Flushing Financial Corp. (FFC) is the holding company for Flushing Bank, which operates more than 15 branches in the New York City metropolitan area. The bank offers services catering to the sizable populations of Asians and other ethnic groups in Queens, where it has the most full-service offices. Deposit products include CDs and checking, savings, money market, and negotiable order of withdrawal (NOW) accounts. Mortgages secured by multifamily residential, commercial, and mixed-use real estate account for most of the company's $5.2 billion loan portfolio.

	Annual Growth	12/19	12/20	12/21	12/22	12/23
Assets ($mil.)	5.0%	7,017.8	7,976.4	8,045.9	8,422.9	8,537.2
Net income ($ mil.)	(8.7%)	41.3	34.7	81.8	76.9	28.7
Market value ($ mil.)	(6.5%)	623.6	480.3	701.4	559.4	475.7
Employees	4.4%	474	530	539	576	564

FLYERS ENERGY, LLC

2360 LINDBERGH ST
AUBURN, CA 956029562
Phone: 530 885-0401
Fax: –
Web: www.flyersenergy.com

CEO: Tom D Mercurio
CFO: –
HR: Michelle Shinault
FYE: December 31
Type: Private

Flyers Energy (formerly known as NELLA Oil) owns and operates about 40 convenience stores and gas stations, mostly in northern California, primarily under the Flyers and Olympian banners. The company is also a wholesale distributor to retail and wholesale customers for Valero, Chevron, and Shell. In Nevada Flyers Energy operates Western Energetix, a commercial fueling operation with more than 100 sites and about 10 bulk fueling plants located in Nevada and northern California. The company was originally founded as NELLA Oil in 1979 and is still run by four brothers -- David, Steve, Tom, and Walt Dwelle. NELLA was the name of their grandfather, Walter B. Allen (an oil industry veteran), spelled backwards.

	Annual Growth	12/03	12/04	12/05	12/06	12/07
Sales ($mil.)	(34.4%)	–	–	2.8	1.4	1.2
Net income ($ mil.)	–	–	–	(1.4)	(3.6)	(2.9)
Market value ($ mil.)	–	–	–	–	–	–
Employees	–	–	–	–	–	479

FMC CORP.
NYS: FMC

2929 Walnut Street
Philadelphia, PA 19104
Phone: 215 299-6000
Fax: 215 299-5998
Web: www.fmc.com

CEO: Mark A Douglas
CFO: Andrew D Sandifer
HR: Christina Joseph
FYE: December 31
Type: Public

FMC Corporation is a global agricultural sciences company dedicated to helping growers produce food, feed, fiber and fuel for an expanding world population while adapting to a changing environment. FMC's innovative crop protection solutions enable growers, crop advisers and turf and pest management professionals to address their toughest challenges economically without compromising safety or the environment. The company has five active ingredient plants, 16 formulation and packaging sites and sold products in approximately 120 countries. FMC dates back to 1883 when John Bean invented a piston pump for insecticides. It generates majority of its revenue from the US.

	Annual Growth	12/19	12/20	12/21	12/22	12/23
Sales ($mil.)	(0.7%)	4,609.8	4,642.1	5,045.2	5,802.3	4,486.8
Net income ($ mil.)	29.0%	477.4	551.5	736.5	736.5	1,321.5
Market value ($ mil.)	(10.9%)	12,454	14,339	13,710	15,570	7,866.2
Employees	0.8%	6,400	6,400	6,400	6,600	6,600

FMC TECHNOLOGIES, INC.

13460 LOCKWOOD RD
HOUSTON, TX 770446444
Phone: 281 591-4000
Fax: –
Web: www.technipfmc.com

CEO: Douglas J Pferdehirt
CFO: Alf Melin
HR: Jasmine Chua
FYE: December 31
Type: Private

FMC Technologies' name is a vestige of its early years as a food machinery maker, but today this company's bread and butter is oil and gas equipment. FMC Technologies offers subsea drilling and production systems for the exploration and production of oil and gas. It also offers similar equipment and services for onshore oil production. The company's energy infrastructure segment makes fluid control, measurement, marine loading, separation, material handling, blending systems, and other equipment. Its offerings are divided into three chief segments: subsea technologies, surface technologies, and energy infrastructure. In 2016 the company agreed to merge with Technip to form a $13 billion company, TechnipFMC.

FNB CORP
NYS: FNB

One North Shore Center, 12 Federal Street
Pittsburgh, PA 15212
Phone: 800 555-5455
Fax: –
Web: www.fnb-online.com

CEO: Vincent J Delie Jr
CFO: Vincent J Calabrese Jr
HR: –
FYE: December 31
Type: Public

F.N.B. Corporation is a bank holding company and a financial holding company. Through the company's largest subsidiary, it provides a full range of financial services, principally to consumers, corporations, governments, and small- to medium-sized businesses in its market areas through its subsidiary network. The company has nearly 350 banking offices throughout Pennsylvania, Ohio, Maryland, West Virginia, North Carolina, South Carolina, Washington, DC, and Virginia. In addition to community banking and consumer finance, FNB also has segments devoted to insurance and wealth management. It also offers leasing and merchant banking services through its F.N.B. Capital Corporation, LLC (FNBCC) subsidiary. The company has total assets of about $44 billion and about 1,350 ATMs conveniently located throughout a seven-state footprint and the District of Columbia.

	Annual Growth	12/19	12/20	12/21	12/22	12/23
Assets ($mil.)	7.5%	34,615	37,354	39,513	43,725	46,158
Net income ($ mil.)	5.8%	387.0	286.0	405.0	439.0	485.0
Market value ($ mil.)	2.0%	4,557.1	3,408.9	4,352.6	4,682.7	4,941.1
Employees	–	–	4,223	4,197	4,180	4,190

FNCB BANCORP INC
NAS: FNCB

102 E. Drinker St.
Dunmore, PA 18512
Phone: 570 346-7667
Fax: –
Web: www.fncb.com

CEO: –
CFO: –
HR: –
FYE: December 31
Type: Public

First National Community Bancorp is the holding company for First National Community Bank, which has about 20 offices in Lackawanna, Luzerne, Wayne and Monroe counties in northeastern Pennsylvania. The bank provides standard retail services such as checking and savings accounts, certificates of deposit, credit cards, mortgages, and other loans. It also offers wealth management services. The bank is mainly a business lender, with commercial mortgages accounting for more than 40% of its loan portfolio and operating loans comprising about another quarter. Chairman Louis DeNaples and his brother Dominick, who is vice chairman, each own around 10% of First National Community Bancorp.

	Annual Growth	12/19	12/20	12/21	12/22	12/23
Assets ($mil.)	11.8%	1,203.5	1,465.7	1,664.3	1,745.5	1,881.0
Net income ($ mil.)	4.1%	11.1	15.3	21.4	20.4	13.0
Market value ($ mil.)	(5.3%)	167.2	126.6	182.8	162.5	134.4
Employees	(0.2%)	224	214	227	230	222

FOGO DE CHAO, INC.

5908 HEADQUARTERS DR STE K200
PLANO, TX 75024
Phone: 972 960-9533
Fax: –
Web: www.fogodechao.com

CEO: Lawrence J Johnson
CFO: Anthony D Laday
HR: Terri Chatham
FYE: January 01
Type: Private

Fogo de Chão operates a chain of more than 20 restaurants across the US and in Brazil and Mexico specializing in Brazilian-style churrasco, a traditional way of slow-roasting meat. Customers at Fogo de Chão (pronounced fo-go-day-shou) can help themselves from unlimited servings of meat from the gaúcho chefs, who keep bringing food until guests turn over their serving card from green to red. Brothers Arri and Jair Coser opened their first Fogo de Chão in Brazil in 1979 and exported the concept to the US in 1997. The company went public in 2015.

	Annual Growth	01/13	01/14	01/15	01/16	01/17
Sales ($mil.)	6.1%	–	–	–	271.6	288.3
Net income ($ mil.)	(13.3%)	–	–	–	28.0	24.3
Market value ($ mil.)	–	–	–	–	–	–
Employees	–	–	–	–	–	3,154

FOLEY HOAG LLP

155 SEAPORT BLVD
BOSTON, MA 022102600
Phone: 617 832-1000
Fax: –
Web: www.foleyhoag.com

CEO: –
CFO: –
HR: Jillian Smerage
FYE: December 31
Type: Private

Founded in 1943, Foley Hoag employs more than 300 attorneys. With an office in the Boston metro area, one in Washington, DC, New York, Denver, and one in Paris, Foley Hoag has practices in a wide range of areas, including corporate, intellectual property, international litigation and arbitration, litigation and investigations, government and regulatory, and trending solutions. Clients come primarily from industries such as technology, energy and climate, life sciences, and health care.

FONAR CORP

NAS: FONR

110 Marcus Drive
Melville, NY 11747
Phone: 631 694-2929
Fax: –
Web: www.fonar.com

CEO: Timothy R Damadian
CFO: –
HR: –
FYE: June 30
Type: Public

SONAR finds objects hidden under the water using sound waves; FONAR uses magnetic resonance imaging (MRI) to find disease or injury hidden inside the body. The company was the first to market a commercial MRI scanner in 1980, and it is trying to stay at the forefront of the field. Its primary products include the Upright MRI, which scans patients in sitting, standing, or bending positions, and the FONAR 360, a room-sized MRI. Both systems do away with the claustrophobia-producing enclosed tubes of traditional machines. Additionally, FONAR's Health Management Corporation of America (HMCA) subsidiary provides management services to more than 20 diagnostic imaging centers, primarily in Florida and New York.

	Annual Growth	06/19	06/20	06/21	06/22	06/23
Sales ($mil.)	3.1%	87.2	85.7	89.9	97.6	98.6
Net income ($ mil.)	(11.5%)	15.3	8.2	10.2	12.4	9.4
Market value ($ mil.)	(5.6%)	147.0	146.0	120.8	103.8	116.9
Employees	2.9%	500	424	495	484	561

FONIX CORP. (DE)

387 South 520 West, Suite 110
Lindon, UT 84042
Phone: 801 553-6600
Fax: –
Web: www.fonix.com

CEO: –
CFO: –
HR: –
FYE: December 31
Type: Public

Fonix hopes to get speech down pat. The company develops text-to-speech and automated speech recognition applications that are integrated into a variety of products, enabling such services as voice-activated telephone menus. Marketing its products primarily to software developers, consumer electronics manufacturers, video game developers, and others who embed the software in their own products, Fonix also offers applications targeted to consumers.

	Annual Growth	12/04	12/05	12/06	12/07	12/08
Sales ($mil.)	(46.0%)	14.9	16.2	1.3	1.8	1.3
Net income ($ mil.)	–	(15.1)	(22.6)	(21.9)	15.0	(6.2)
Market value ($ mil.)	0.9%	0.7	0.0	0.0	0.0	0.7
Employees	–	–	–	–	–	–

FONON CORP

400 Rinehart Road
Lake Mary, FL 32746
Phone: 407 477-5618
Fax: –
Web: www.mabweminerals.com

CEO: Dmitriy Nikitin
CFO: Carlos Gonzalez
HR: –
FYE: December 31
Type: Public

Raptor Networks Technology preys on network latency. The company develops switching hardware and software for enterprise networks. Its core and edge switching products are designed specifically for high-bandwidth applications such as Internet Protocol television (IPTV) and Voice over Internet Protocol (VoIP). The company also offers network interface cards (NICs) for PCs and servers. It targets the education, financial services, government, health care, and telecommunications markets. Raptor sells directly and through resellers; the company is also pursuing an OEM channel strategy. The company has a systems integration partnership with government IT contractor CACI.

	Annual Growth	12/10	12/11	12/12	12/13	12/14
Sales ($mil.)	–	1.8	–	–	–	–
Net income ($ mil.)	–	(0.5)	(6.4)	5.6	(2.5)	(0.5)
Market value ($ mil.)	(28.9%)	1.4	0.0	1.4	1.2	0.4
Employees	(40.5%)	8	1	1	1	1

FOOD EXPORT U S A NORTH EAST

1617 JOHN F KENNEDY BLVD STE 420
PHILADELPHIA, PA 191031821
Phone: 215 829-9111
Fax: –
Web: www.foodexport.org

CEO: –
CFO: –
HR: –
FYE: December 31
Type: Private

Food Export USA Northeast, a not-for-profit organization, helps promote the exportation of agricultural and food products from companies located in the northeastern US. The organization facilitates trade between the region's food companies and importers around the world, offering information and networking opportunities to interested businesses. The organization also offers export promotion, customized export assistance, and a cost-share funding program.

	Annual Growth	12/16	12/17	12/19	12/21	12/22
Sales ($mil.)	7.3%	–	10.1	12.5	12.2	14.4
Net income ($ mil.)	(11.4%)	–	0.0	0.4	0.2	0.0
Market value ($ mil.)	–	–	–	–	–	–
Employees	–	–	–	–	–	7

FOOD FOR THE POOR, INC.

6401 LYONS RD
COCONUT CREEK, FL 330733602
Phone: 954 427-2222
Fax: –
Web: www.foodforthepoor.org

CEO: Ed Raine
CFO: Dennis North
HR: Judy Lady
FYE: December 31
Type: Private

Food For The Poor feeds spiritual and physical hunger. The Christian charity provides health, social, economic, and religious services for impoverished people in 17 countries in Latin America and the Caribbean. Food For The Poor believes its organization serves God by helping those most in need, distributing requested goods through local churches and charities. The group works through Caritas, the American-Nicaraguan Foundation, and others to provide vocational training, clinic and school construction, educational materials, feeding programs, and medical supplies. Food For The Poor has distributed more than $3 billion in goods since its 1982 inception; the group uses 96% of its funds on programs.

	Annual Growth	12/17	12/18	12/19	12/21	12/22
Sales ($mil.)	(15.0%)	–	942.6	914.5	856.6	491.3
Net income ($ mil.)	–	–	(10.5)	13.9	(8.2)	(9.9)
Market value ($ mil.)	–	–	–	–	–	–
Employees	–	–	–	–	–	418

FOOT LOCKER, INC.

NYS: FL

330 West 34th Street
New York, NY 10001
Phone: 212 720-3700
Fax: –
Web: www.footlocker.com

CEO: Mary N Dillon
CFO: Robert Higginbotham
HR: Amy Blaskowski
FYE: January 28
Type: Public

Foot Locker leads the celebration of sneaker and youth culture around the globe through a portfolio of brands including atmos, Foot Locker, Lady Foot Locker, Kids Foot Locker, Champs Sports, Eastbay, Footaction, Sidestep, and WSS. The company operates almost 2,715 primarily mall-based stores, as well as stores in high-traffic urban retail areas and high streets, in around 30 countries throughout the world. It also curates special product assortments and marketing content that supports its premium position, from leading global brands such as Nike, Jordan, Adidas, and Puma, as well as new and emerging brands in the athletic and lifestyle space. Foot Locker also sells via ecommerce sites, mobile devices, and catalogs. The US market accounts for about 70% of total revenue.

	Annual Growth	02/19	02/20*	01/21	01/22	01/23
Sales ($mil.)	2.5%	7,939.0	8,005.0	7,548.0	8,958.0	8,759.0
Net income ($ mil.)	(10.8%)	541.0	491.0	323.0	893.0	342.0
Market value ($ mil.)	(5.5%)	5,142.4	3,546.2	4,092.6	4,149.6	4,107.5
Employees	(1.3%)	49,331	50,999	51,252	49,933	46,880

*Fiscal year change

FOOTBALL NORTHWEST LLC

12 SEAHAWKS WAY
RENTON, WA 980561572
Phone: 425 203-8000
Fax: -
Web: www.seahawks.com

CEO: -
CFO: -
HR: Claire Penhale
FYE: December 31
Type: Private

The Northwest is a prime nesting spot for this football team. Football Northwest owns and operates the Seattle Seahawks professional football franchise. The team joined the National Football League during the league expansion of 1976 (the same year as the Tampa Bay Buccaneers) but suffered through mostly disappointing seasons until a resurgence beginning in the late 1990s. However, in 2014 the team won its first ever Super Bowl title. Founded by department store magnate Lloyd Nordstrom, the Seahawks franchise has been owned by Microsoft co-founder Paul Allen since 1997.

FORD MOTOR CREDIT COMPANY LLC

One American Road
Dearborn, MI 48126
Phone: 313 322-3000
Fax: -
Web: www.fordcredit.com

CEO: Cathy O'Callaghan
CFO: Eliane S Okamura
HR: -
FYE: December 31
Type: Public

Seems its trucks aren't the only things built Ford tough. The automaker's subsidiary, Ford Motor Credit, is proving to be pretty resilient, too. One of the world's largest auto financing companies, it funds autos for and through Ford and Lincoln dealerships in some 70 countries. It finances new, used, and leased vehicles, and provides wholesale financing, mortgages, and capital loans for dealers. The company also offers business fleet financing and insurance. Founded in 1959, Ford Motor Credit generates more than half of its revenue from operating leases, and more than 70% of revenue from the US.

	Annual Growth	12/18	12/19	12/20	12/21	12/22
Sales ($mil.)	(4.3%)	4,585.0	4,599.0	4,825.0	5,834.0	3,842.0
Net income ($ mil.)	(2.8%)	2,224.0	2,228.0	1,924.0	4,521.0	1,989.0
Market value ($ mil.)	-	-	-	-	-	-
Employees	(9.5%)	7,600	6,800	6,400	5,600	5,100

FORBES ENERGY SERVICES LTD
NBB: FLSS

3000 South Business Highway 281
Alice, TX 78332
Phone: 361 664-0549
Fax: -
Web: www.forbesenergyservices.com

CEO: -
CFO: -
HR: -
FYE: December 31
Type: Public

Forbes Energy Services (FES), an independent oilfield services company, offers well servicing and fluid management to onshore oil and gas drilling and production companies in Texas, Mississippi, and Pennsylvania. Its Fluid Logistics segment handles pumping, transport, and storage of fracking liquid, salt water, and other fluids used in drilling and extraction. FES's well-servicing segment provides well maintenance, repairs, cleanup, and plugging; the unit also offers pressure testing. Major customers have included Apache, Chesapeake Energy, ConocoPhillips, and EOG Resources.

	Annual Growth	12/16*	04/17*	12/17	12/18	12/19
Sales ($mil.)	17.5%	116.2	30.8	96.5	180.9	188.4
Net income ($ mil.)	-	(109.1)	27.2	(26.0)	(32.6)	(68.4)
Market value ($ mil.)	-	-	-	54.7	16.6	1.4
Employees	(1.6%)	825	-	843	1,178	786

*Fiscal year change

FORDHAM PREPARATORY SCHOOL

441 E FORDHAM RD
BRONX, NY 104585149
Phone: 718 367-7500
Fax: -
Web: www.fordhamprep.org

CEO: -
CFO: Carol Purcell
HR: -
FYE: June 30
Type: Private

When considering private schools, if you can't afford 'em don't apply to Fordham. A four-year, Catholic, college preparatory school, Fordham Prep's tuition will set you back nearly $11,000 annually. Located on the Rose Hill campus of Fordham University, "The Prep" was founded in the same year as the university, 1841. Priests from the Society of Jesus (the Jesuits) traditionally dominated the faculty of Fordham Prep, but most instructors now are not of the clergy. The student body, however, remains exclusively male. Nearly 100% of its graduates go on to college.

	Annual Growth	06/08	06/09	06/10	06/11	06/12
Sales ($mil.)	7.9%	-	-	16.4	18.2	19.1
Net income ($ mil.)	10.1%	-	-	0.9	3.6	1.1
Market value ($ mil.)	-	-	-	-	-	-
Employees	-	-	-	-	-	100

FORD MOTOR CO. (DE)
NYS: F

One American Road
Dearborn, MI 48126
Phone: 313 322-3000
Fax: -
Web: www.corporate.ford.com

CEO: Anning Chen
CFO: John T Lawler
HR: -
FYE: December 31
Type: Public

Ford Motor Company produces and sells automobiles designed and engineered by Henry Ford. Ford develops and delivers innovative, must-have Ford trucks, sport utility vehicles, commercial vans and cars, and Lincoln luxury vehicles, along with connected services. With its change in segments in 2023, Ford has three customer-centered business segments: Ford Blue, engineering iconic gas-powered and hybrid vehicles; Ford Model e, inventing breakthrough electric vehicles ("EVs") along with embedded software; and Ford Pro, helping commercial customers transform and expand their businesses. It generates majority of its revenue domestically.

FORDHAM UNIVERSITY

441 E FORDHAM RD
BRONX, NY 104589993
Phone: 718 817-1000
Fax: -
Web: www.fordham.edu

CEO: -
CFO: -
HR: -
FYE: June 30
Type: Private

Founded in 1841, Fordham is the Jesuit University of New York, offering exceptional education distinguished by the Jesuit tradition across nine schools. Fordham awards baccalaureate, graduate, and professional degrees to approximately 16,000 students from Fordham College at Rose Hill, Fordham College at Lincoln Center, the Gabelli School of Business (undergraduate and graduate), the School of Professional and Continuing Studies, the Graduate Schools of Arts and Sciences, Education, Religion and Religious Education, and Social Service, and the School of Law. With about 745 full-time instructors, the University has a 13:1 undergraduate student-to-faculty ratio.

	Annual Growth	12/19	12/20	12/21	12/22	12/23
Sales ($mil.)	3.1%	155,900	127,144	136,341	158,057	176,191
Net income ($ mil.)	210.1%	47.0	(1,279.0)	17,937	(1,981.0)	4,347.0
Market value ($ mil.)	7.0%	38,660	36,540	86,341	48,346	50,674
Employees	(1.8%)	190,000	186,000	183,000	173,000	177,000

	Annual Growth	06/18	06/19	06/20	06/21	06/22
Sales ($mil.)	4.6%	-	933.5	665.6	953.9	1,067.5
Net income ($ mil.)	(5.4%)	-	59.9	(20.6)	28.7	50.6
Market value ($ mil.)	-	-	-	-	-	-
Employees	-	-	-	-	-	4,070

FORESCOUT TECHNOLOGIES, INC.

300 SANTANA ROW STE 400
SAN JOSE, CA 951282424
Phone: 408 213-3191
Fax: –
Web: www.forescout.com

CEO: Wael Mohamed
CFO: Christopher Harms
HR: –
FYE: December 31
Type: Private

ForeScout Technologies is the industry innovator in providing an active defense for the Enterprise of Things. Forescout delivers automated cybersecurity across the digital terrain. The company empowers its customers to achieve continuous alignment of their security frameworks with their digital realities, across all asset types ? IT, IoT, OT and IoMT. Fortune 100 organizations and government agencies have trusted Forescout to provide automated cybersecurity at scale. The company's research team continuously finds new ways to ensure the company is delivering the world's best cybersecurity for any kind of networked device. ForeScout partners with Honeywell, ABB, Belden, IBM, Microsoft, VMware, and McAfee, among others.

FOREST BESSE PRODUCTS INC

933 N 8TH ST
GLADSTONE, MI 49837
Phone: 906 428-3113
Fax: –
Web: www.bessegroup.com

CEO: –
CFO: –
HR: –
FYE: December 31
Type: Private

Besse Forest Products Group is branching out and it wooden want it any other way. Consisting of about a dozen firms, the group manufactures and exports hardwood lumber, veneer, and plywood from nearly 20 species of trees. The group's manufacturing plants, including veneer cutting and splicing plants, rotary cutting mills, and sawmills, have the capacity to produce more than 850 million sq. ft. of veneer and some 40 million board feet of lumber annually. Besse Forest Products Group also exports lumber, logs, and veneer from its mills and warehouses in the US and Canada, with the bulk of its operations in Wisconsin and Michigan. Owned by the Besse family, the group was founded in 1966.

FOREST CITY ENTERPRISES, L.P.

127 PUBLIC SQ STE 3200
CLEVELAND, OH 441141229
Phone: 216 621-6060
Fax: –
Web: www.forestcityco.com

CEO: –
CFO: –
HR: –
FYE: January 31
Type: Private

Forest City Enterprises has grown from treeline to skyline. Founded in 1920 as a lumber dealer, the company now focuses on commercial and residential real estate development in metropolitan areas across the US. Forest City, which has more than $10.7 billion in assets, owns and develops commercial properties, including 44 retail centers and shopping malls, 47 office buildings, two hotels, and Brooklyn's Barclays Center in 15 states. The company's residential group owns and manages 115 upscale and middle-market apartments, condominiums, and senior housing properties, as well as more than 14,000 military housing units in over 20 states. Forest City converted into a real estate investment trust (REIT) in early 2015.

FORESTAR GROUP INC (NEW)

2221 E. Lamar Blvd., Suite 790
Arlington, TX 76006
Phone: 817 769-1860
Fax: –
Web: www.forestargroup.com

NYS: FOR
CEO: Daniel C Bartok
CFO: James D Allen
HR: –
FYE: September 30
Type: Public

A majority-owned subsidiary of D.R. Horton?which is one of the largest homebuilders in the US?residential lot development company Forestar Group owns or controls over 38,300 residential lots. Most of those are under contract are either under contract to sell to D.R. Horton or are assigned to D.R. Horton for right of first offer. The company owns approximately 4,400 developed lots. Forestar operates in about 50 markets across about 20 states, and while it sometimes develops land for commercial properties?including apartments, retail centers, and offices?Forestar primarily sells lots to homebuilders and developers for single-family homes.

	Annual Growth	09/19	09/20	09/21	09/22	09/23
Sales ($mil.)	35.3%	428.3	931.8	1,325.8	1,519.1	1,436.9
Net income ($ mil.)	50.0%	33.0	60.8	110.2	178.8	166.9
Market value ($ mil.)	10.2%	912.2	883.3	929.7	558.4	1,344.4
Employees	31.5%	78	143	250	291	233

FOREVERGREEN WORLDWIDE CORP

632 North 2000 West, Suite 101
Lindon, UT 84042
Phone: 801 655-5500
Fax: –
Web: www.forevergreen.org

CEO: Allen K Davis
CFO: John W Haight
HR: –
FYE: December 31
Type: Public

ForeverGreen Worldwide wants to give customers a piece of its mind, naturally. The holding company, through its ForeverGreen International subsidiary, offers a menu of whole foods, nutritional supplements, personal care products, and essential oils al sold via a network of independent distributors in the US and abroad. Company brands include LegaSea, O3World, Smart Food, and TRUessence Oils. Its products, which include energy bars, drinks, and snacks, body oils, creams, lotions, cleansers, and shampoos, claim to boost energy and mental acuity, shed pounds, ward off disease, and help forestall biological aging with ingredients such as marine phytoplankton and organic chocolate.

	Annual Growth	12/14	12/15	12/16	12/17	12/18
Sales ($mil.)	(35.4%)	58.3	67.1	40.3	18.5	10.2
Net income ($ mil.)	–		1.0	(2.6)	(5.9)	(2.2)	(2.7)
Market value ($ mil.)	(38.3%)	24.3	13.5	7.4	2.3	3.5
Employees	(37.3%)	97	103	65	39	15

FORGE INDUSTRIES, INC.

4450 MARKET ST
YOUNGSTOWN, OH 445121512
Phone: 330 960-2468
Fax: –
Web: –

CEO: William T James II
CFO: Dan Maisonville
HR: –
FYE: December 31
Type: Private

Forge Industries connects a diverse group of businesses. Operating via several subsidiaries, the family-owned private holding company distributes thousands of products, from industrial gears and bearings to asphalt and concrete construction equipment. Businesses include construction/landscape equipment maker Miller Spreader and sister companies Akron Gear & Engineering and Bearing Distributors (BDI), Forge's global product and service distributor. Forge's lineup includes curb builders and hand tools, as well as rebuild and repair gearboxes, redesign customer equipment, customize gear reducers, and machining services. Customers work in the automotive, package handling, food processing, and landscape industries.

	Annual Growth	12/04	12/05	12/06	12/07	12/08
Sales ($mil.)	9.9%	–	404.6	–	605.8	537.6
Net income ($ mil.)	(56.0%)	–	73.1	–	–	6.2
Market value ($ mil.)	–	–	–	–	–	–
Employees	–	–	–	–	–	2,000

FORMFACTOR BEAVERTON, INC.

9100 SW GEMINI DR
BEAVERTON, OR 970087127
Phone: 503 601-1000
Fax: -
Web: www.cascademicrotech.com

CEO: -
CFO: -
HR: -
FYE: December 31
Type: Private

Formfactor Beaverton, Inc. is a leading provider of essential test and measurement technologies along the full IC life cycle ? from characterization, modeling, reliability, and design de-bug, to qualification and production test offering a complete line of premium performance analytical probe stations supported by a software for on-wafer probing and board test. The company also offers additional products and programs that assists with equipment financing, educational savings, certifying a pre-owned equipment, trade-in/buy back and logistics services. The company serves markets data center, mobile and automotive and was founded in 1993.

FORMFACTOR INC

7005 Southfront Road
Livermore, CA 94551
Phone: 925 290-4000
Fax: -
Web: www.formfactor.com

NMS: FORM
CEO: Michael D Slessor
CFO: Shai Shahar
HR: -
FYE: December 30
Type: Public

FormFactor is a leading provider of test and measurement technologies. It provides a broad range of high-performance probe cards, analytical probes, probe stations, metrology systems, thermal systems, and cryogenic systems to both semiconductor companies and scientific institutions. Its products provide electrical and physical information from a variety of semiconductor and electro-optical devices and integrated circuits from early research, through development, to high-volume production. FormFactor designs probe cards to provide for a precise match with the thermal expansion characteristics of the wafer under test across the range of test operating temperatures. Its customers can use the same probe card for both low and high temperature testing. The majority of sales are to customers outside the US.

	Annual Growth	12/19	12/20	12/21	12/22	12/23
Sales ($mil.)	3.0%	589.5	693.6	769.7	747.9	663.1
Net income ($ mil.)	20.3%	39.3	78.5	83.9	50.7	82.4
Market value ($ mil.)	12.5%	2,014.9	3,294.7	3,444.0	1,720.1	3,227.4
Employees	3.6%	1,836	2,166	2,293	2,105	2,115

FORMOSA PLASTICS CORPORATION, U.S.A.

9 PEACH TREE HILL RD
LIVINGSTON, NJ 070395702
Phone: 973 716-7191
Fax: -
Web: www.fpcusa.com

CEO: -
CFO: -
HR: Roleo Marcelo
FYE: December 31
Type: Private

Formosa Plastics Corp, USA (Formosa Plastics) is one of the world's largest PVC (polyvinyl chloride) suppliers, it produces all manner of petrochemicals and plastic resins. Its product roster includes polyethylene, polypropylene, vinyl, and chlor alkali products like caustic soda. It also produces suspension and specialty PVC resins, the former for pipe and fencing, the latter for flooring and insect screening. Other Formosa Plastics' products are used for packaging and chemical processing. The vertically integrated company operates two manufacturing locations. Formosa Plastics was founded in 1978.

FORMS & SUPPLY, INC.

6410 ORR RD
CHARLOTTE, NC 282136332
Phone: 704 598-8971
Fax: -
Web: www.fsioffice.com

CEO: -
CFO: -
HR: -
FYE: December 31
Type: Private

Whether your boss needs a new mini-fridge for the office or you are just running low on staples, Forms & Supply can help out. The company, which does business as FSIoffice, carries more than 8,500 products, including office supplies, IT products, and furniture. It operates about 10 distribution centers in five states and maintains a fleet of some 75 trucks. FSIoffice is a GSA-certified vendor and offers national account services through its partnership with American Office Products Distributors. Customers can place their orders through the company's e-commerce site. FSIoffice was founded in 1962 by Jimmy Godwin.

	Annual Growth	05/12	05/13*	12/13	12/14	12/16
Sales ($mil.)	4.7%	-	74.5	-	78.9	85.6
Net income ($ mil.)	49.4%	-	0.7	-	1.0	2.2
Market value ($ mil.)		-	-	-	-	-
Employees		-	-	-	-	300

*Fiscal year change

FORREST COUNTY GENERAL HOSPITAL

6051 U S HIGHWAY 49
HATTIESBURG, MS 394017200
Phone: 601 288-7000
Fax: -
Web: -

CEO: -
CFO: Andy Woodard
HR: Tanisha Jones
FYE: September 30
Type: Private

Forrest General Hospital is the hub of health care in Hattiesburg, Mississippi. Founded in 1952, the regional medical center serves southern Mississippi and its "Hub City," so named for its importance to early rail and lumber interests in the Pine Belt area. With some 400 acute care beds, Forrest General offers general medical and surgical care, as well as specialty care in heart disease, cancer, and women's health. Other facilities include the 90-bed Pine Grove behavioral health center for psychiatric and substance abuse treatment, a 25-bed inpatient rehabilitation facility, and an outpatient surgery center. The hospital system also operates a home health care agency and two nearby community hospitals.

	Annual Growth	09/18	09/19	09/20	09/21	09/22
Sales ($mil.)	2.7%	-	546.3	556.2	595.4	592.0
Net income ($ mil.)	-	-	9.0	18.7	43.2	(42.5)
Market value ($ mil.)		-	-	-	-	-
Employees		-	-	-	-	4,030

FORRESTER RESEARCH INC.

60 Acorn Park Drive
Cambridge, MA 02140
Phone: 617 613-6000
Fax: -
Web: www.forrester.com

NMS: FORR
CEO: George F Colony
CFO: Michael A Doyle
HR: -
FYE: December 31
Type: Public

Forrester is one of the most influential research and advisory firms in the world. The firm help leaders across technology, customer experience, marketing, sales, and product functions use customer obsession to accelerate growth. Forrester gains powerful insights through its annual surveys of more than 700,000 consumers and business leaders, and technology leaders worldwide. The firm's portfolio of research services is designed to provide business and technology leaders with a proven path to growth through customer obsession. Through proprietary research, consulting, and events, leaders from around the globe are empowered to be bold at work, navigate change, and put their customers at the center of their leadership, strategy, and operations. Forrester was incorporated in Massachusetts on 1983 and reincorporated in Delaware in 1996. Most of its revenue comes from the US.

	Annual Growth	12/19	12/20	12/21	12/22	12/23
Sales ($mil.)	1.0%	461.7	449.0	494.3	537.8	480.8
Net income ($ mil.)	-	(9.6)	10.0	24.8	21.8	3.1
Market value ($ mil.)	(10.5%)	802.6	806.4	1,130.4	688.3	516.0
Employees	(0.7%)	1,795	1,798	1,781	2,033	1,744

FORSYTH MEDICAL CENTER FOUNDATION

3333 SILAS CREEK PKWY
WINSTON SALEM, NC 271033013
Phone: 336 277-1404
Fax: –
Web: www.novanthealth.org

CEO: Carl Armato
CFO: –
HR: –
FYE: December 31
Type: Private

Forsyth Medical Center learns from hindsight, but operates with foresight. One of the largest hospitals in North Carolina, Forsyth Medical Center (FMC) is a tertiary care hospital with about 960 beds. It provides Winston-Salem and Thomasville area patients with such health care services as behavioral health, emergency care, rehabilitation, and surgical procedures. The medical center also operates a network of community health centers including Medical Park Hospital (about 20 beds), Thomasville Medical Center (150 beds), and outpatient and physician clinics. Forsyth Medical Center became part of Novant Health in 1997.

	Annual Growth	12/15	12/16	12/17	12/18	12/22
Sales ($mil.)	20.0%	–	2.2	1.6	2.7	6.5
Net income ($ mil.)	(4.4%)	–	3.0	2.5	(7.0)	2.3
Market value ($ mil.)	–	–	–	–	–	–
Employees	–	–	–	–	–	3,995

FORT HAYS STATE UNIVERSITY FOUNDATION

1 TIGER PL
HAYS, KS 676013767
Phone: 785 628-5620
Fax: –
Web: foundation.fhsu.edu

CEO: –
CFO: –
HR: Lindsey S Murra
FYE: June 30
Type: Private

Fort Hays State University (FHSU) Foundation (formerly FHSU Endowment Association) is a not-for-profit organization that raises and manages money used to support FHSU students, staff, and alumni. The funds goes to student scholarships, co-curricular programs, graduate assistantships and fellowships, chairs, and professorships. Its Annual Giving Campaign raises more than $1 million each year for scholarships. Established in 1946, the foundation contacts donors and alumni, collects funds, and sees that the money is allocated according to donor wishes. FHSU has about $50 million in assets.

	Annual Growth	06/16	06/17	06/20	06/21	06/22
Sales ($mil.)	(2.8%)	–	23.6	18.9	16.6	20.5
Net income ($ mil.)	(7.5%)	–	16.0	6.3	6.6	10.9
Market value ($ mil.)	–	–	–	–	–	–
Employees	–	–	–	–	–	9

FORTH SMITH HMA, LLC

1001 TOWSON AVE
FORT SMITH, AR 729014921
Phone: 479 441-4000
Fax: –
Web: –

CEO: –
CFO: –
HR: –
FYE: December 31
Type: Private

Sparks Health System brings good health to western Arkansas and eastern Oklahoma. The not-for-profit health system operates Sparks Regional Medical Center, a nearly 500-bed community-based hospital, along with a broad range of health care programs and diagnostic facilities. With Arkansas' oldest hospital (founded in 1887) as part of its operations, Sparks boasts an impressive lists of "firsts," including the state's first heart institute (Stanley E. Evans Heart Institute) and the state's first ultrasound equipment. However, an expensive renovation and economic woes pinched the company and in 2009 it was acquired by health care giant Health Management Associates (HMA).

	Annual Growth	12/17	12/18	12/19	12/20	12/21
Sales ($mil.)	11.6%	–	–	–	234.8	262.0
Net income ($ mil.)	–	–	–	–	18.5	(13.9)
Market value ($ mil.)	–	–	–	–	–	–
Employees	–	–	–	–	–	2,350

FORTINET INC

NMS: FTNT

899 Kifer Road
Sunnyvale, CA 94086
Phone: 408 235-7700
Fax: 408 235-7737
Web: www.fortinet.com

CEO: Ken Xie
CFO: Keith Jensen
HR: –
FYE: December 31
Type: Public

Fortinet is a global leader in cybersecurity and networking solutions provided to a wide variety of organizations, including enterprises, communication and security service providers, government organizations and small businesses. Its cybersecurity solutions are designed to provide broad visibility and segmentation of the digital attack surface through our integrated cybersecurity platform products and services providing a mesh architecture, which feature automated protection, detection and response along with consolidated visibility across both Fortinet-developed solutions and a broad ecosystem of third-party solutions and technologies. The Fortinet operating system has an open architecture designed to integrate Fortinet solutions with third-party solutions in a single ecosystem, enabling automated detection and response across the attack surface. To support its broadly dispersed global channel and end-customer base, it has sales professionals in about 100 countries around the world. About 40% of the revenue comes from the US.

	Annual Growth	12/19	12/20	12/21	12/22	12/23
Sales ($mil.)	25.2%	2,156.2	2,594.4	3,342.2	4,417.4	5,304.8
Net income ($ mil.)	36.9%	326.5	488.5	606.8	857.3	1,147.8
Market value ($ mil.)	(14.0%)	81,244	113,031	273,503	37,205	44,541
Employees	17.6%	7,082	8,238	10,195	12,595	13,568

FORTIS CONSTRUCTION, INC.

1705 SW TAYLOR ST STE 200
PORTLAND, OR 972051922
Phone: 503 459-4477
Fax: –
Web: www.fortisconstruction.com

CEO: –
CFO: –
HR: –
FYE: December 31
Type: Private

Fortis Construction isn't afraid to get its hands dirty. The fast-growing US construction company offers general contracting, preconstruction, construction management, and environmentally-friendly green building services to customers primarily in Portland, Oregon and others in the Pacific Northwest. It specializes in remodeling and upgrading corporate offices, health care facilities, retail complexes, and schools; it also conducts seismic and structural upgrades. Customers have included Oregon State University, Portland State University, PPG Industries, and StanCorp.

	Annual Growth	12/12	12/13	12/14	12/15	12/16
Sales ($mil.)	66.6%	–	–	282.1	469.0	782.8
Net income ($ mil.)	48.0%	–	–	14.0	18.1	30.7
Market value ($ mil.)	–	–	–	–	–	–
Employees	–	–	–	–	–	175

FORTIVE CORP

NYS: FTV

6920 Seaway Blvd
Everett, WA 98203
Phone: 425 446-5000
Fax: –
Web: www.fortive.com

CEO: Patrick K Murphy
CFO: Charles E McLaughlin
HR: –
FYE: December 31
Type: Public

Fortive Corporation is a provider of essential technologies for connected workflow solutions across a range of attractive end-markets. Its businesses design, develop, manufacture, and service professional and engineered products, software, and services, building upon leading brand names, innovative technologies, and significant market positions. Among Fortive's brands are Accruent, Gordian, Intelex, Fluke, Pruftechnik, Industrial Scientific, and Servicechannel. The company operates facilities in more than 50 countries across North America, Asia Pacific, Europe, and Latin America. The US accounts for about 55% of Fortive's revenue.

	Annual Growth	12/19	12/20	12/21	12/22	12/23
Sales ($mil.)	(4.6%)	7,320.0	4,634.4	5,254.7	5,825.7	6,065.3
Net income ($ mil.)	4.0%	738.9	1,613.3	608.4	755.2	865.8
Market value ($ mil.)	(0.9%)	26,790	24,837	26,755	22,532	25,822
Employees	(7.9%)	25,000	17,000	18,000	18,000	18,000

FORTOVIA THERAPEUTICS, INC.

8540 COLONNADE CENTER DR # 1
RALEIGH, NC 276153052
Phone: 919 872-5578
Fax: –
Web: www.fortovia.com

CEO: Peter Melnyk
CFO: Ernest D Paolantonio
HR: –
FYE: December 31
Type: Private

Cancer patient? Midatech Pharma US (formerly DARA BioSciences) is looking to help. The drug development company is dedicated to providing healthcare professionals with a synergistic portfolio of medicines to help cancer patients adhere to their therapy and manage side effects arising from cancer treatments. Formerly called Point Therapeutics, the firm failed in its previous efforts to advance lead cancer drug talabostat and was forced to regroup and consider its options. The company turned to its preclinical pipeline, which included a potential diabetes drug, and then in 2008 executed a reverse merger with privately held DARA BioSciences. The company was acquired by UK-based Midatech Pharma in 2015.

FORTRESS INVESTMENT GROUP LLC

1345 AVENUE OF THE AMERICAS FL 46
NEW YORK, NY 10105
Phone: 212 798-6100
Fax: –
Web: www.fortress.com

CEO: Peter Briger Jr
CFO: –
HR: Jeevan Panesar
FYE: December 31
Type: Private

Fortress Investment Group is a leading, highly diversified global investment manager with approximately $44.2 billion of assets under management. Manages assets on behalf of approximately 1,900 institutional clients and private investors worldwide across a range of credit and real estate, private equity and permanent capital investment strategies, the company has a network of around 210 investment professionals around the world. Fortress's core competencies include asset-based, industry knowledge, operations management, corporate mergers and acquisitions, and capital markets. Additionally, Fortress is open to investments across a range of industries, including financial services, transportation, energy and infrastructure, and healthcare. The company was founded in 1998.

FORTUNE BRANDS INNOVATIONS INC

520 Lake Cook Road
Deerfield, IL 60015-5611
Phone: 847 484-4400
Fax: –
Web: www.fbhs.com

NYS: FBIN
CEO: Nicholas L Fink
CFO: Mark Warnsman
HR: Heidi Merrier
FYE: December 30
Type: Public

Formerly known as Fortune Brands Home & Security (FBHS), Fortune Brands Innovations is a leading home and security products company that competes in attractive long-term growth markets in its product categories. It manufactures, assembles and sells kitchen sinks and waste disposals, faucets, entry doors, and security products. Most of the company's products are the top sellers in its respective markets and are distributed via kitchen and bath dealers, wholesalers oriented toward builders or professional remodelers, industrial and locksmith distributors, "do-it-yourself" remodeling-oriented home centers, e-commerce and other retail outlets. With almost 30 manufacturing facilities worldwide, the company generates about 80% of sales in the US. In 2022, after its separation from its Cabinets business, MasterBrand, the company changed its name from "Fortune Brands Home & Security, Inc." to "Fortune Brands Innovations, Inc." and its stock ticker symbol changed from "FBHS" to "FBIN" to better reflect its focus on activities core to brands and innovation.

	Annual Growth	12/19	12/20	12/21	12/22	12/23
Sales ($mil.)	(5.4%)	5,764.6	6,090.3	7,656.1	4,723.0	4,626.2
Net income ($ mil.)	(1.6%)	431.9	553.1	772.4	686.7	404.5
Market value ($ mil.)	3.9%	8,251.6	10,825	13,500	7,212.3	9,615.5
Employees	(17.0%)	24,700	27,500	28,000	11,200	11,729

FORUM ENERGY TECHNOLOGIES INC

10344 Sam Houston Park Drive, Suite 300
Houston, TX 77064
Phone: 281 949-2500
Fax: –
Web: www.f-e-t.com

NYS: FET
CEO: Neal Lux
CFO: D L Williams
HR: Angela Pickering
FYE: December 31
Type: Public

Forum Energy Technologies (Forum) is a global company serving the oil, natural gas, industrial, and renewable energy industries. Forum provides value-added solutions aimed at improving the safety, efficiency, and environmental impact of its customers' operations. Its products include highly engineered capital equipment as well as consumable products. These consumable products are used in drilling, well construction, and completions activities and at processing centers and refineries. Its engineered capital products are directed at drilling rig equipment for constructing new or upgrading existing rigs, subsea construction and development projects, pressure pumping equipment, the placement of production equipment on new producing wells, downstream capital projects, and capital equipment for renewable energy projects. It also makes remote operating vehicles (ROVs) for subsea work. The US generates over 65% of sales. Forum was incorporated in 2005.

	Annual Growth	12/19	12/20	12/21	12/22	12/23
Sales ($mil.)	(6.3%)	956.5	512.5	541.1	699.9	738.9
Net income ($ mil.)	–	(567.1)	(96.9)	(82.7)	3.7	(18.9)
Market value ($ mil.)	90.6%	17.1	121.3	163.6	300.7	226.0
Employees	(8.7%)	2,300	1,400	1,400	1,500	1,600

FORWARD AIR CORP

1915 Snapps Ferry Road, Building N
Greeneville, TN 37745
Phone: 423 636-7000
Fax: –
Web: www.forwardaircorp.com

NMS: FWRD
CEO: Thomas Schmitt
CFO: Rebecca Garbrick
HR: –
FYE: December 31
Type: Public

Forward Air is a leading asset-light freight and logistics company. Forward Air provide less-than-truckload (LTL), final mile, truckload, and intermodal drayage services across the US and in Canada. It also offers premium services that typically require precision execution, such as expedited transit, delivery during tight time windows and special handling. It utilizes an asset-light strategy to minimize its investments in equipment and facilities and to reduce its capital expenditures. The company has around 6,725 trailers and roughly 275 owned and almost 645 leased tractors and straight trucks in its fleet. It also provides services such as warehousing, customs brokerage, and other handling.

	Annual Growth	12/19	12/20	12/21	12/22	12/23
Sales ($mil.)	(0.7%)	1,410.4	1,269.6	1,662.4	1,973.4	1,370.7
Net income ($ mil.)	17.7%	87.1	23.7	105.9	193.2	167.4
Market value ($ mil.)	(2.6%)	1,795.7	1,972.5	3,108.5	2,692.6	1,613.9
Employees	(6.2%)	5,480	4,144	4,327	4,427	4,251

FORWARD INDUSTRIES, INC.

700 Veterans Memorial Highway, Suite 100
Hauppauge, NY 11788
Phone: 631 547-3055
Fax: –
Web: www.forwardindustries.com

NAS: FORD
CEO: Terence Wise
CFO: Kathleen Weisberg
HR: –
FYE: September 30
Type: Public

Forward Industries knows how to make a good case. The company designs and markets carrying cases, bags, clips, hand straps, and related items for medical monitoring kits, bar code scanners, and a range of consumer products (such as cell phones, MP3 players, cameras, and firearms). Contractors in China manufacture most of the company's products, which are made of leather, nylon, vinyl, plastic, PVC, and other synthetic fibers. The products are primarily sold to original equipment manufacturers (OEMs). Forward's top three customers are makers of diabetic testing kits and generate more than 70% of revenues.

	Annual Growth	09/19	09/20	09/21	09/22	09/23
Sales ($mil.)	(0.5%)	37.4	34.5	39.0	42.3	36.7
Net income ($ mil.)	–	(3.6)	(1.8)	0.5	(1.4)	(3.7)
Market value ($ mil.)	(5.9%)	9.8	14.0	24.0	13.4	7.7
Employees	–	73	85	90	100	–

FOSSIL GROUP INC

NMS: FOSL

901 S. Central Expressway
Richardson, TX 75080
Phone: 972 234-2525
Fax: –
Web: www.fossilgroup.com

CEO: Kosta N Kartsotis
CFO: Sunil M Doshi
HR: –
FYE: December 30
Type: Public

Fossil is a design, innovation and distribution company specializing in consumer fashion accessories such as leather goods, handbags, sunglasses, and jewelry. A leading seller of mid-priced fashion watches in the US, its brands include company-owned Fossil and Relic watches and licensed names like Armani, Michael Kors, DKNY, and Kate Spade New York, to name a few. The company peddles its products through department stores, mass merchandisers, and specialty shops in some 140 countries, as well as online and at over 340 company-owned stores in the US and abroad. Its products are also sold on cruise ships and in airports. Around 45% of the company's revenue is generated in the US.

	Annual Growth	12/19*	01/21	01/22*	12/22	12/23
Sales ($mil.)	(10.7%)	2,217.7	1,613.3	1,870.0	1,682.4	1,412.4
Net income ($ mil.)	–	(52.4)	(96.1)	25.4	(44.2)	(157.1)
Market value ($ mil.)	(34.1%)	406.2	455.1	540.1	226.2	76.6
Employees	(12.1%)	10,200	7,500	6,900	6,900	6,100

*Fiscal year change

FOSTER (L.B.) CO

NMS: FSTR

415 Holiday Drive, Suite 100
Pittsburgh, PA 15220
Phone: 412 928-3400
Fax: –
Web: www.lbfoster.com

CEO: John F Kasel
CFO: William M Thalman
HR: –
FYE: December 31
Type: Public

L.B. Foster is a global technology solutions provider of engineered, manufactured products and services that builds and supports infrastructure. The company provides a full line of new and used rail, trackwork, and accessories to railroads, mines, and other customers in the rail industry as well as designs and produces insulated rail joints, power rail, track fasteners, concrete railroad ties, cover boards, and special accessories for mass transit and other rail systems. L.B. Foster also supplies pipe coatings for oil and natural gas pipelines and utilities, precision measurement systems for the oil and gas market, and produces threaded pipe products for industrial water well and irrigation markets as well as the oil and gas markets. The US is its largest market accounting for over 75% of sales. The company was established in 1902.

	Annual Growth	12/19	12/20	12/21	12/22	12/23
Sales ($mil.)	(4.5%)	655.1	497.4	513.6	497.5	543.7
Net income ($ mil.)	(56.9%)	42.6	7.6	3.6	(45.6)	1.5
Market value ($ mil.)	3.2%	208.0	161.5	147.6	103.9	236.0
Employees	(5.4%)	1,330	1,130	991	1,131	1,065

FOUNDATION BUILDING MATERIALS, INC.

2520 REDHILL AVE
SANTA ANA, CA 927055542
Phone: 714 380-3127
Fax: –
Web: www.fbmsales.com

CEO: Ruben Mendoza
CFO: John Gorey
HR: –
FYE: December 31
Type: Private

Foundation Building Materials (FBM) is a leading distributor of drywall, steel framing, acoustic ceiling, and construction supplies in the US. The company operates more than 250 branches across the North America, and has significant geographic reach into most major building materials markets. FBM supplies customers with products for use like construction tools, drywall hand tools, fasteners, and construction supplies for residential and commercial projects.

FOUNDATION FOR NATIONAL PROGRESS

222 SUTTER ST STE 600
SAN FRANCISCO, CA 941084457
Phone: 415 321-1700
Fax: –
Web: www.motherjones.com

CEO: –
CFO: Madeleine Buckingham
HR: –
FYE: June 30
Type: Private

The Foundation for National Progress (FNP) is full of words for its Mother . The non-profit foundation publishes and supports Mother Jones , a magazine devoted to environmental, social, political, and cultural issues. The bimonthly national magazine has a circulation of some 240,000). The FNP also runs the magazine's Web site, MotherJones.com. Revenues come from subscriptions and donors. The organization was founded in 1975 and the magazine started in 1976. The title refers to Mary Harris "Mother" Jones, a radical reformer who worked as a union organizer until her death in 1930.

	Annual Growth	06/15	06/16	06/17	06/19	06/20
Sales ($mil.)	5.8%	–	13.2	16.5	16.9	16.5
Net income ($ mil.)	–	–	(0.9)	2.9	0.1	(0.9)
Market value ($ mil.)	–	–	–	–	–	–
Employees	–	–	–	–	–	39

FOUNDATION HEALTHCARE, INC.

400 N SAINT PAUL ST # 600
DALLAS, TX 752016805
Phone: 800 783-0404
Fax: –
Web: www.fdnh.com

CEO: –
CFO: –
HR: –
FYE: December 31
Type: Private

Graymark Healthcare wants its businesses to help remedy the ills of small-town Americans. Through its operating subsidiaries, Graymark Healthcare acquires and operates independent pharmacies and sleep diagnostic centers, many of which are located in smaller US markets. Its ApothecaryRx subsidiary manages pharmacies doing business in a handful of central US states, and the company's Sleep Disorder Centers (SDC) subsidiary manages sleep diagnostics businesses in the South and Midwest. Formerly Graymark Productions (a film production firm), Graymark changed its name in 2008 following the acquisitions of ApothecaryRx and SDC. The company sold sell its ApothecaryRx stores to Walgreen in late 2010.

FOUNDATION MEDICINE, INC.

400 SUMMER ST
BOSTON, MA 022101717
Phone: 617 418-2200
Fax: –
Web: www.foundationmedicine.com

CEO: –
CFO: –
HR: –
FYE: December 31
Type: Private

Foundation Medicine is a leading company in cancer molecular profiling, dedicated to advancing the field of clinical care and research. The company partners with various stakeholders in the cancer community and aims to set the bar for scientific excellence, quality, and regulatory leadership. With a thorough grasp of cancer biology, Foundation Medicine equips physicians with the knowledge to make informed treatment decisions for their patients and empowers researchers to develop novel medicines. The company is committed to helping its partners find solutions and take action every day, in order to increase access to precision cancer care worldwide. The company was founded in 2010.

FOUNDATION OF NORTHERN NEW JERSEY INC.

150 RIVER ST
HACKENSACK, NJ 076017110
Phone: 201 646-4306
Fax: –
Web: www.northjersey.com

CEO: –
CFO: –
HR: –
FYE: December 31
Type: Private

When North Jersey Media Group reports on the news, it's for the record. Formerly Macromedia, the company is a leading newspaper publisher in New Jersey, with two daily newspapers (the Herald News and flagship publication The Record) and more than 40 weekly and bi-weekly community papers. North Jersey Media also publishes specialty monthly magazines (201) The Best of Bergen and Parent Paper . In addition, the company runs the NorthJersey.com website and other online properties, and has commercial printing operations. The Record was started as   The Evening Record   in 1895.

	Annual Growth	12/07	12/08	12/15	12/19	12/20
Sales ($mil.)	(33.6%)	–	1.7	0.2	0.0	0.0
Net income ($ mil.)	–	–	–	(0.0)	(0.0)	(0.1)
Market value ($ mil.)	–	–	–	–	–	–
Employees	–	–	–	–	–	1,431

FOUNDEVER OPERATING CORPORATION

600 BRICKELL AVE STE 3200
MIAMI, FL 331313089
Phone: 813 274-1000
Fax: –
Web: www.foundever.com

CEO: Charles E Sykes
CFO: John Chapman
HR: Dawn Dickenson
FYE: December 31
Type: Private

Sykes Enterprises is a leading full lifecycle provider of global customer experience management services, multichannel demand generation and digital transformation. The company provides differentiated full lifecycle customer experience management solutions and services primarily to Global 2000 companies and their end customers principally in the financial services, technology, communications, transportation & leisure and healthcare industries. Sykes operates in more than 65 locations in over 25 countries. The company provides services in many languages through phone, e-mail, social media, text messaging, chat, and digital self-service. In 2021, Sykes was acquired by Sitel for $2.2 billion.

FOUNTAIN POWERBOAT INDUSTRIES, INC.

1653 WHICHARDS BEACH RD
WASHINGTON, NC 27889
Phone: 252 975-2000
Fax: –
Web: www.fountainpowerboats.com

CEO: Reginald M Fountain Jr
CFO: Irving L Smith
HR: –
FYE: June 30
Type: Private

Fountain Powerboat Industries builds a range of sport boats, sport fishing boats, and express cruisers for aquatic speedracers with deep pockets. Overall, the company produces nearly a dozen Fountain-branded models, which range in length from 29 feet to more than 47 feet, and in speed from about 78 to 100-plus miles per hour. It offers, as well, several sports boats under its Baja brand acquired from rival Brunswick Corporation. For the US Navy, US Coast Guard, and other US and foreign government agencies, the company makes a line of interceptor boats. It is part of Iconic Marine Group.

FOUR B CORP.

5300 SPEAKER RD
KANSAS CITY, KS 661061050
Phone: 913 321-4223
Fax: –
Web: www.mypricechopper.com

CEO: –
CFO: –
HR: –
FYE: April 30
Type: Private

Four B likes to feather its nest with grocery stores. Doing business as Ball's Food Stores, the regional grocery company operates about a dozen Hen House Market stores and nearly 20 Price Chopper supermarkets in the Kansas City area. It serves a variety of customers. Upscale Hen House Markets are service-oriented establishments, while its Price Chopper outlets represent the firm's price-impact supermarket format. Services include lottery, Ticketmaster, Western Union, fax, money orders, and other. Founded in 1923 by Sidney and Mollie Ball, the grocery firm is run by their grandson David Ball, the company's chairman, president, and CEO. The grocery chain is a member of Associated Wholesale Grocers.

	Annual Growth	10/95	10/96	10/97*	12/08*	04/09
Sales ($mil.)	(42.7%)	–	436.7	455.1	–	0.3
Net income ($ mil.)	–	–	10.5	8.5	–	(0.0)
Market value ($ mil.)	–	–	–	–	–	–
Employees	–	–	–	–	–	4,000

*Fiscal year change

FOX BSB HOLDCO, INC.

1000 VIN SCULLY AVE
LOS ANGELES, CA 900122112
Phone: 323 224-1500
Fax: –
Web: www.mlb.com

CEO: Ron Wheeler
CFO: –
HR: –
FYE: December 31
Type: Private

These Dodgers try to be artful on the baseball diamond. Fox BSB Holdco, doing business as The Los Angeles Dodgers, operates one of the oldest and most storied franchises in Major League Baseball, boasting six World Series championships and 22 National League pennants. The team started in Brooklyn, New York in 1884 but moved west to Los Angeles in 1957. The Dodgers were the first team to break the color barrier with the signing of Jackie Robinson. The team plays home games at Dodger Stadium. In April 2012, a group led by former Los Angeles Lakers star Magic Johnson acquired the iconic Dodgers franchise from Frank McCourt for a record $2.15 billion.

FOX CORP

NMS: FOXA

1211 Avenue of the Americas
New York, NY 10036
Phone: 212 852-7000
Fax: –
Web: www.foxcorporation.com

CEO: Lachlan K Murdoch
CFO: Steven Tomsic
HR: –
FYE: June 30
Type: Public

Fox Corporation (Fox) is a media and entertainment company. It produces and licenses news and sports content. The company distributes content through traditional cable television systems, direct broadcast satellite operators and telecommunication companies, and online multi-channel video programming distributors. Fox's assets include the FOX News Media, FOX Entertainment, FOX Sports, and FOX Television Stations. It also acquires, markets, and distributes broadcast network programming and free advertising-supported video-on-demand (AVOD) services nationally under the Tubi and FOX brand. The company has ownership and operating interest in studios and other facilities in California, the US.

	Annual Growth	06/19	06/20	06/21	06/22	06/23
Sales ($mil.)	7.0%	11,389	12,303	12,909	13,974	14,913
Net income ($ mil.)	(6.1%)	1,595.0	999.0	2,150.0	1,205.0	1,239.0
Market value ($ mil.)	(1.9%)	18,264	13,369	18,509	16,031	16,948
Employees	7.8%	7,700	9,000	9,000	10,600	10,400

FOX FACTORY HOLDING CORP

NMS: FOXF

2055 Sugarloaf Circle, Suite 300
Duluth, GA 30097
Phone: 831 274-6500
Fax: –
Web: www.ridefox.com

CEO: Larry L Enterline
CFO: Scott Humphrey
HR: Dale Silvia
FYE: December 29
Type: Public

Fox Factory Holding Corp., designs, engineers, manufactures, and markets performance-defining products, and systems for customers worldwide. The company's premium brand, performance-defining products, and systems are used primarily on bicycles, side-by-side vehicles, on-road vehicles with and without off-road capabilities, off-road vehicles and trucks, all-terrain vehicles (ATVs), snowmobiles, specialty vehicles, and applications. Fox performance-defining products enhance vehicle performance across multiple consumer markets. Some of its products are specifically designed and marketed to some of the leading cyclings and powered vehicle original equipment manufacturers (OEMs), while others are distributed to consumers through a global network of dealers and distributors. Fox generates most of its sales from North American region.

	Annual Growth	01/20	01/21*	12/21	12/22	12/23
Sales ($mil.)	18.2%	751.0	890.6	1,299.1	1,602.5	1,464.2
Net income ($ mil.)	6.8%	93.0	90.7	163.8	205.3	120.8
Market value ($ mil.)	(0.8%)	2,927.6	4,435.0	7,136.4	3,827.5	2,831.1
Employees	13.4%	2,600	3,000	4,100	4,400	4,300

*Fiscal year change

FOX HEAD, INC.

16752 ARMSTRONG AVE
IRVINE, CA 926064912
Phone: 949 757-9500
Fax: –
Web: www.foxracing.com

CEO: Jeff McGuane
CFO: Tanya Fischesser
HR: Liz Laurel
FYE: December 31
Type: Private

Got a need for speed and big jumps? Fox Racing makes and distributes motocross and other extreme sport apparel, accessories, and protective gear, such as racewear pants, jerseys, gloves, boots, and helmets, emblazoned with its fox head graphic logo. The company also offers bicycle motocross (BMX) and mountain bike apparel, T-shirts, hats, jeans, hoodies and pullovers, and jackets. Line extensions include eyewear, footwear, and surf and wakeboard wear. Fox Racing sells its apparel through retail sporting goods and cycle and surf shops nationwide. International offices are located in Canada and the UK. Founded in 1974 by Geoff Fox, the company is family-owned and run by its second generation.

	Annual Growth	12/05	12/06	12/07	12/08	12/09
Sales ($mil.)	1.1%	–	–	211.7	244.0	216.3
Net income ($ mil.)	4.5%	–	–	18.7	24.4	20.4
Market value ($ mil.)	–	–	–	–	–	–
Employees	–	–	–	–	–	518

FOXWORTH-GALBRAITH LUMBER COMPANY

4965 PRESTON PARK BLVD # 400
PLANO, TX 750935141
Phone: 972 665-2400
Fax: –
Web: www.foxgal.com

CEO: –
CFO: –
HR: –
FYE: December 31
Type: Private

Foxworth-Galbraith Lumber Company is helping to build out the Southwest. The company sells hardware, lumber, paint, plumbing equipment, tools, and other building supplies through more than 20 locations across Texas, New Mexico, Arizona, and Colorado (versus about 70 stores in 2006). Foxworth-Galbraith's main customers are residential and commercial builders; other clients include do-it-yourselfers, specialty contractors, and federal and state agencies. Foxworth-Galbraith is still owned and operated by the families of W.L. Foxworth and H.W. Galbraith, who founded the company in Dalhart, Texas, in 1901, to take advantage of railroad construction.

	Annual Growth	12/08	12/09	12/10	12/11	12/12
Sales ($mil.)	13.0%	–	–	154.7	164.4	197.6
Net income ($ mil.)	–	–	–	(10.2)	(3.9)	0.8
Market value ($ mil.)	–	–	–	–	–	–
Employees	–	–	–	–	–	1,603

FP ACQUISITION COMPANY 3.5 LLC

745 5TH AVE FL 25
NEW YORK, NY 101512599
Phone: 855 650-6932
Fax: –
Web: www.fundamental.com

CEO: –
CFO: –
HR: –
FYE: December 31
Type: Private

Municipal Mortgage & Equity (MuniMae) invests in tax-free municipal bonds issued by state and local governments. Those bonds are typically used to build multifamily housing, including units for low-income families, students, and the elderly. The disruption in world credit markets, coupled with a deterioration in the tax-exempt bond market hurt MuniMae. The commercial real estate market also tanked, driving down the values of the company's assets. The company was forced to drastically reduce the size of its business, cut its workforce by 80%, and sell off assets at a loss in order to stay afloat. MuniMae continues to look for ways to reduce debt and raise capital.

FPB BANCORP INC

1301 SE Port St. Lucie Boulevard
Port St. Lucie, FL 34952
Phone: 772 225-5930
Fax: –
Web: www.1stpeoplesbank.com

CEO: David W Skiles
CFO: –
HR: –
FYE: December 31
Type: Public

FPB Bancorp is for the birds. Snow birds, that is. It's the holding company for First Peoples Bank, which targets retired winter visitors, as well as year-round residents and small to midsized businesses in southeastern Florida. The six-branch bank operates in Fort Pierce, Palm City, Port St. Lucie, Stuart, and Vero Beach, offering such standard deposit products as CDs and checking, savings, and money market accounts. Commercial real estate and business loans together account for about 85% of its loan portfolio; consumer loans make up most of the rest. The bank sells into the secondary market all of the fixed-rate residential mortgages that it writes. First Peoples Bank opened two new branches in 2008.

	Annual Growth	12/06	12/07	12/08	12/09	12/10
Assets ($mil.)	10.9%	153.4	196.8	239.2	248.2	232.4
Net income ($ mil.)	–	0.6	0.2	(3.0)	(9.2)	(8.0)
Market value ($ mil.)	(50.9%)	36.0	20.2	4.1	2.4	2.1
Employees	2.0%	71	81	73	78	77

FRANCHISE SERVICES, INC.

26722 PLAZA
MISSION VIEJO, CA 926918051
Phone: 949 348-5400
Fax: –
Web: www.franserv.com

CEO: Don F Lowe
CFO: Daniel J Conger
HR: Cathy Pilliod
FYE: December 31
Type: Private

Franchise Services is a holding company for the franchise operations of Sir Speedy, PIP Printing, Signal Graphics, and MultiCopy quick-printing chains. In addition to running the presses, the company manages TeamLogic IT, which provides computer maintenance and repair services to small and midsized businesses. It also operates Summit Marketing Communications, an advertising and marketing firm for the company's network of franchises. Franchise Services has more than 1,000 locations in the Americas, Asia, and Europe. It primarily targets corporate and business accounts.

	Annual Growth	12/13	12/14	12/15	12/17	12/18
Sales ($mil.)	1.6%	–	18.8	18.3	5.7	20.0
Net income ($ mil.)	25.0%	–	1.9	2.3	1.5	4.7
Market value ($ mil.)	–	–	–	–	–	–
Employees	–	–	–	–	–	300

FRANCIS SAINT MEDICAL CENTER

211 ST FRANCIS DR
CAPE GIRARDEAU, MO 637035049
Phone: 573 331-3000
Fax: –
Web: www.sfmc.net

CEO: Mary A Reese
CFO: David Prather
HR: Jason Snow
FYE: December 31
Type: Private

It may be guided by Catholic principles, but you don't have to be a saint to get medical care at Saint Francis Medical Center. The hospital serves a five-state region from Missouri (its home base) to Arkansas with about 285 beds. Services include emergency medicine, orthopedics, cancer, rehabilitation, and women's health care. It also offers heart and neurosciences institutes, as well as diabetes education and wound healing centers. The health care provider, which was established in 1875, partners with Poplar Bluff Medical Partners to provide outpatient care at Poplar Bluff Medical Complex. Services include family practice, OB-GYN, and pain management.

	Annual Growth	06/18	06/19*	12/20*	06/21*	12/21
Sales ($mil.)	(28.7%)	–	550.3	261.4	521.1	279.7
Net income ($ mil.)	(34.6%)	–	47.4	15.3	31.3	20.3
Market value ($ mil.)	–	–	–	–	–	–
Employees						1,500

*Fiscal year change

FRANCISCAN ALLIANCE, INC.

1515 W DRAGOON TRL
MISHAWAKA, IN 465444710
Phone: 574 256-3935
Fax: –
Web: www.franciscanhealth.org

CEO: Lori Price
CFO: –
HR: Ellen Page
FYE: December 31
Type: Private

Franciscan Alliance is a not-for-profit organization operating more than a dozen hospitals in Indiana and south suburban Chicago. It offers a variety of hospital-based services and programs, such as therapy pets and patient advocates, for patients and families at its hospitals. It also provides a full spectrum of behavioral and mental health services, including adult and adolescent treatments in psychiatric and psychological disorders, substance abuse and addiction, family conflicts, and more. Franciscan Alliance was founded and is sponsored by the Sisters of St. Francis of Perpetual Adoration.

	Annual Growth	12/14	12/15	12/18	12/21	12/22
Sales ($mil.)	3.0%	–	2,731.1	3,144.5	3,572.9	3,358.1
Net income ($ mil.)	–	–	250.7	14.2	572.8	(675.6)
Market value ($ mil.)	–	–	–	–	–	–
Employees						19,000

FRANCISCAN HEALTH SYSTEM

1717 S J ST
TACOMA, WA 984054933
Phone: 253 426-4101
Fax: –
Web: www.vmfh.org

CEO: –
CFO: –
HR: –
FYE: June 30
Type: Private

St. Francis himself may have hailed from Italy, but his followers look after the health of the residents of the South Puget Sound area through the Franciscan Health System. The not-for-profit system includes five full-service hospitals. The oldest and largest hospital is St. Joseph Medical Center in Tacoma, Washington, a 320-bed facility. Its facilities include community hospitals St. Clare Hospital (in Lakewood) and St. Francis Hospital (in Federal Way), as well as a hospice program, and numerous primary and specialty care clinics. Its St. Anthony Hospital is an 80-bed full service pharmacy and home medical equipment retail location at Gig Harbor.

	Annual Growth	06/18	06/19	06/20	06/21	06/22
Sales ($mil.)	4.3%	–	–	–	1,482.3	1,546.2
Net income ($ mil.)	–	–	–	–	133.1	(91.3)
Market value ($ mil.)	–	–	–	–	–	–
Employees						3,183

FRANCISCAN UNIVERSITY OF STEUBENVILLE

1235 UNIVERSITY BLVD
STEUBENVILLE, OH 439521792
Phone: 740 283-3771
Fax: –
Web: www.franciscan.edu

CEO: –
CFO: –
HR: –
FYE: May 31
Type: Private

Franciscan University of Steubenville is a Roman Catholic school that provides instruction to more than 2,300 students. It offers more than 30 undergraduate majors, as well as master's degrees in six separate fields. The college was established in 1946 when Steubenville, Ohio's first bishop, John King Mussio, invited Franciscan friars to establish a college to serve the needs of local students, especially veterans of WWII.

	Annual Growth	05/18	05/19	05/20	05/21	05/22
Sales ($mil.)	12.9%	–	76.1	121.4	105.1	109.5
Net income ($ mil.)	–	–	(0.9)	19.4	30.6	25.9
Market value ($ mil.)	–	–	–	–	–	–
Employees						375

FRANK CONSOLIDATED ENTERPRISES, INC.

666 GARLAND PL
DES PLAINES, IL 600164725
Phone: 847 699-7000
Fax: –
Web: www.wheels.com

CEO: –
CFO: –
HR: –
FYE: December 31
Type: Private

Frank Consolidated Enterprises works to keep the wheels turning. Frank Consolidated is a holding company for Wheels, which pioneered the auto leasing concept and provides fleet management services (including administrative, management, and financing assistance) to help clients maintain their vehicle fleets. The company operates in the US as Wheels and does business in other countries through Fleet Synergy International, an alliance of fleet management and leasing firms. Wheels manages more than 320,000 vehicles in North America and 1.5 million vehicles worldwide. It also purchases and remarkets some 120,000 vehicles annually. Established in 1939, Wheels is owned and led by the family of founder Zollie Frank.

FRANKLIN AND MARSHALL COLLEGE

415 HARRISBURG AVE
LANCASTER, PA 176032827
Phone: 717 291-3911
Fax: –
Web: www.fandm.edu

CEO: –
CFO: Eileen Austin
HR: Peggy Waddle
FYE: June 30
Type: Private

Franklin & Marshall College, named after Benjamin Franklin and John Marshall, is a private liberal arts institution serving about 2,400 students. It offers academic and research programs in about 60 fields including biology, chemistry, English, history, mathematics, political science, art, sociology, and environmental studies. It offers programs in 11 languages including Arabic and Greek. Franklin & Marshall College was created in 1853 through the merger of Franklin College (founded in 1787 with a contribution from Ben Franklin) and Marshall College (opened in 1836 and named after Chief Justice John Marshall).

	Annual Growth	06/16	06/17	06/20	06/21	06/22
Sales ($mil.)	5.3%	–	151.3	176.4	209.5	196.1
Net income ($ mil.)	(26.2%)	–	28.5	(17.6)	19.3	6.2
Market value ($ mil.)	–	–	–	–	–	–
Employees						800

FRANKLIN COMMUNITY HEALTH NETWORK

111 FRANKLIN HEALTH CMNS
FARMINGTON, ME 049386144
Phone: 207 779-2265
Fax: –
Web: www.mainehealth.org

CEO: Rebecca Ryder
CFO: –
HR: Judith M West
FYE: September 30
Type: Private

When it comes to providing health care, Franklin Community Health Network would rather rough it. The not-for-profit health care system serves mountainous rural areas in western Maine. Franklin Community Health Network consists of a 70-bed acute care hospital, a behavioral health facility, and several physician management groups. Its Franklin Memorial Hospital offers specialized services such as cardiology, orthopedics, emergency medicine, and occupational health care. The health network's unique Contract for Care program allows former patients to volunteer at the hospital if they do not have the means to pay all of their bill.

	Annual Growth	09/16	09/17	09/18	09/19	09/20
Sales ($mil.)	349.5%	–	1.0	82.8	84.6	94.9
Net income ($ mil.)	101.3%	–	0.7	(4.1)	(7.2)	6.1
Market value ($ mil.)	–	–	–	–	–	–
Employees	–	–	–	–	–	900

FRANKLIN COVEY CO

2200 West Parkway Boulevard
Salt Lake City, UT 84119-2099
Phone: 801 817-1776
Fax: –
Web: www.franklincovey.com

NYS: FC
CEO: Robert A Whitman
CFO: Stephen D Young
HR: –
FYE: August 31
Type: Public

Franklin Covey, publisher of the popular book The 7 Habits of Highly Effective People, The 4 Disciplines of Execution, and The 7 Habits. Targeted at individuals, teams, and organizations, the company is a global provider of training programs, consulting services, books, and planning products designed around five practice areas: leadership, execution, productivity, sales performance, and educational improvement. Franklin Covey's clients include the FORTUNE 100, the FORTUNE 500, and thousands of small and midsized businesses. In addition to companies, it serves government entities and educational institutions mostly in the US. The majority of the company's sales are from the Americas region.

	Annual Growth	08/19	08/20	08/21	08/22	08/23
Sales ($mil.)	5.6%	225.4	198.5	224.2	262.8	280.5
Net income ($ mil.)	–	(1.0)	(9.4)	13.6	18.4	17.8
Market value ($ mil.)	3.8%	481.3	258.2	568.7	622.3	558.2
Employees	5.4%	940	940	1,000	1,150	1,160

FRANKLIN CREDIT HOLDING CORPORATION

101 HUDSON ST FL 25
JERSEY CITY, NJ 073023984
Phone: 201 604-1800
Fax: –
Web: –

CEO: Thomas J Axon
CFO: Paul D Colasono
HR: –
FYE: December 31
Type: Private

Franklin Credit Holding is the holding company of mortgage servicer Franklin Credit Management. In 2009 the company entered into a restructuring agreement with The Huntington National Bank in which a large number (about 83%) of Franklin's subprime mortgages were transferred to the bank's real estate investment trust (REIT); in exchange, Franklin received a capital infusion of more than $13 million and services the mortgages transferred to the bank's books in order to generate fee income. Chairman and president Thomas Axon owns some 45% of Franklin Credit Holdings. Director Frank Evans more than 10%.

FRANKLIN ELECTRIC CO., INC.

9255 Coverdale Road
Fort Wayne, IN 46809
Phone: 260 824-2900
Fax: –
Web: www.franklin-electric.com

NMS: FELE
CEO: Gregg C Sengstack
CFO: Jeffery L Taylor
HR: –
FYE: December 31
Type: Public

Franklin Electric manufactures and distributes pumps and motors including submersible and specialty electric motors, electronic drives and controls, and related items. Its fueling systems products include electronic tank monitoring equipment, fittings, flexible piping, nozzles, and vapor recovery systems. Franklin Electric's products are used by OEMs for underground petroleum pumping systems, sewage pumps, vacuum pumping systems, and freshwater pumping systems. Some customers, such as independent distributors and repair shops, buy the company's products as replacement motors. Franklin Electric serves customers worldwide but generates more than 55% of sales from the US. The company was founded in 1944.

	Annual Growth	12/19	12/20	12/21	12/22	12/23
Sales ($mil.)	12.0%	1,314.6	1,247.3	1,661.9	2,043.7	2,065.1
Net income ($ mil.)	19.3%	95.5	100.5	153.9	187.3	193.3
Market value ($ mil.)	14.0%	2,640.6	3,188.3	4,356.1	3,673.8	4,452.4
Employees	4.3%	5,400	5,400	6,400	6,500	6,400

FRANKLIN FINANCIAL SERVICES CORP

1500 Nitterhouse Drive
Chambersburg, PA 17201-0819
Phone: 717 264-6116
Fax: 717 264-7129
Web: www.franklinfin.com

NAS: FRAF
CEO: Timothy G Henry
CFO: Mark R Hollar
HR: Levi Crouse
FYE: December 31
Type: Public

Ben Franklin said, "A penny saved is a penny earned," but Franklin Financial might be able to convert those pennies into dollars. It's the holding company for Farmers and Merchants Trust Company (F&M Trust), a community bank serving south-central Pennsylvania from more than 20 locations. Established in 1906, F&M Trust offers standard deposit products, including checking and savings accounts, IRAs, and CDs. It also provides discount brokerage, insurance, retirement planning, and other investment services. More than half of the company's lending portfolio is devoted to commercial, industrial, and agricultural loans; the bank also makes consumer, construction, and residential mortgage loans.

	Annual Growth	12/19	12/20	12/21	12/22	12/23
Assets ($mil.)	9.7%	1,269.2	1,535.0	1,773.8	1,699.6	1,836.0
Net income ($ mil.)	(4.2%)	16.1	12.8	19.6	14.9	13.6
Market value ($ mil.)	(5.0%)	169.1	118.2	144.7	157.8	137.9
Employees	2.0%	283	282	280	298	306

FRANKLIN HOSPITAL

900 FRANKLIN AVE
VALLEY STREAM, NY 115802190
Phone: 516 256-6000
Fax: –
Web: –

CEO: –
CFO: –
HR: –
FYE: December 31
Type: Private

Franklin Hospital is part of the North Shore-Long Island Jewish Health System. The medical center has more than 300 beds and provides emergency and specialty care services. Franklin Hospital includes the 120-bed Orzac Center, a long-term care rehabilitation unit, as well as a 21-bed psychiatric unit and an adult day care center. Franklin Hospital also provides outpatient care -- including pediatrics and women's health -- and home health services. Established in 1963 as a small community hospital, Franklin offers services and programs to the residents of Nassau and southeastern Queens Counties.

	Annual Growth	12/07	12/08	12/12	12/13	12/14
Sales ($mil.)	0.2%	–	169.5	175.3	192.0	171.1
Net income ($ mil.)	–	–	(3.8)	5.6	0.7	(0.7)
Market value ($ mil.)	–	–	–	–	–	–
Employees	–	–	–	–	–	1,300

FRANKLIN RESOURCES INC
NYS: BEN

One Franklin Parkway
San Mateo, CA 94403
Phone: 650 312-2000
Fax: 650 312-3655
Web: www.franklinresources.com

CEO: Jennifer M Johnson
CFO: Matthew Nicholls
HR: –
FYE: September 30
Type: Public

Operating as Franklin Templeton Investments, Franklin Resources manages mutual funds that invest in international and domestic stocks, taxable and tax-exempt money market instruments, and corporate, municipal, and US government bonds. Franklin also offers separately managed accounts, closed-end funds, insurance product funds, and retirement and college savings plans. The products are housed under the company's Franklin, Templeton, Legg Mason, Franklin Mutual Series, Franklin Bissett, Fiduciary Trust International, K2, Lexington Partners, and Martin Currie, among other brands. Franklin Resources and its subsidiaries boast roughly $1.3 billion in assets under management. The US is the company's largest market, accounting for about 75% of total revenue.

	Annual Growth	09/19	09/20	09/21	09/22	09/23
Sales ($mil.)	8.0%	5,774.5	5,566.5	8,425.5	8,275.3	7,849.4
Net income ($ mil.)	(7.3%)	1,195.7	798.9	1,831.2	1,291.9	882.8
Market value ($ mil.)	(3.9%)	14,313	10,092	14,739	10,673	12,190
Employees	(1.1%)	9,600	11,800	10,300	9,800	9,200

FRANKLIN SQUARE HOSPITAL CENTER, INC.

9000 FRANKLIN SQUARE DR
BALTIMORE, MD 212373901
Phone: 410 933-2777
Fax: –
Web: www.medstarhealth.org

CEO: –
CFO: Robert P Lally Jr
HR: –
FYE: June 30
Type: Private

Franklin Square Hospital Center has made a declaration to care for the residents of eastern Baltimore County, Maryland. The facility offers a wide range of specialties through some 700 doctors and about 380 beds. Since 1998 the hospital has been part of MedStar Health, the region's largest integrated health system. As a teaching hospital, Franklin Square offers a number of residency programs, including internal and family medicine, OB-GYN, and surgery. The not-for-profit hospital offers its medical services through half a dozen primary service lines: Medicine, Surgery, Women's and Children's Care, Oncology, Behavioral Health, and Community Health and Wellness.

	Annual Growth	06/15	06/16	06/20	06/21	06/22
Sales ($mil.)	1.3%	–	506.2	605.8	622.0	547.0
Net income ($ mil.)	–	–	10.8	56.0	8.0	(12.7)
Market value ($ mil.)	–	–	–	–	–	–
Employees	–	–	–	–	–	3,019

FRANKLIN STREET PROPERTIES CORP
ASE: FSP

401 Edgewater Place, Suite 200
Wakefield, MA 01880
Phone: 781 557-1300
Fax: –
Web: www.fspreit.com

CEO: –
CFO: –
HR: –
FYE: December 31
Type: Public

Franklin Street Properties acquires, finances, leases, and manages office properties in about a dozen states across the US. The real estate investment trust (REIT) owns more than 30 properties located mainly in suburban areas and manages about 5 others. Its top markets include Atlanta, Dallas, Denver, Houston, and Minneapolis. The company's FSP Investment unit is an investment bank and brokerage that organizes REITs that invest in single properties and raises equity for them through private placements. Another subsidiary, FSP Property Management, manages properties for Franklin Street, as well as for some of the REITs sponsored by FSP Investments.

	Annual Growth	12/19	12/20	12/21	12/22	12/23
Sales ($mil.)	(14.2%)	269.1	245.8	209.4	165.6	145.7
Net income ($ mil.)	–	6.5	32.6	92.7	1.1	(48.1)
Market value ($ mil.)	(26.0%)	885.4	452.0	615.6	282.4	264.8
Employees	–	–	37	37	34	28

FRANKLIN WIRELESS CORP
NAS: FKWL

9707 Waples Street, Suite 150
San Diego, CA 92121
Phone: 858 623-0000
Fax: 858 623-0050
Web: www.franklinwireless.com

CEO: Gary Nelson
CFO: Bill Bauer
HR: –
FYE: June 30
Type: Public

Franklin Wireless hopes lightning strikes with its wireless data products. The company makes high speed connectivity products for wireless devices. Its products include USB, embedded, and standalone modems, as well as modules, PC cards, and Wi-Fi hotspot routers. Customers use its products to connect their mobile computers to wireless broadband networks. Franklin Wireless primarily sells directly to wireless operators, but also through partners and distributors. The US is its largest market, but the Caribbean and South America have collectively grown to nearly 25% of sales. The company uses contract manufacturers such as South Korea-based shareholder (about 13%) C-Motech and Samsung Electro-Mechanics.

	Annual Growth	06/19	06/20	06/21	06/22	06/23
Sales ($mil.)	5.9%	36.5	75.1	184.1	24.0	45.9
Net income ($ mil.)	–	(1.3)	5.6	17.7	(3.8)	(2.9)
Market value ($ mil.)	11.1%	28.9	65.0	108.1	37.4	44.0
Employees	(0.7%)	71	71	74	76	69

FRASER/WHITE, INC.

1631 PONTIUS AVE
LOS ANGELES, CA 900253307
Phone: 310 319-3737
Fax: –
Web: www.frasercommunications.com

CEO: –
CFO: –
HR: –
FYE: December 31
Type: Private

Fraser/White speaks the languages of advertising and marketing. The agency -- which does business as Fraser Communications -- offers market research, media planning and buying, interactive (Web design), and public relations services. The company takes an approach it calls 360 Communications -- surrounding consumers with a client's message. Clients, which tend to come from such industries as automotive, consumer goods, financial services, and health care, have included Cedars-Sinai, Frederick's of Hollywood, and Toyota. President and CEO Renee Fraser founded Fraser Communications in 1992.

	Annual Growth	11/03	11/04	11/05*	12/06	12/08
Sales ($mil.)	38.6%	–	–	15.8	32.7	42.0
Net income ($ mil.)	(41.6%)	–	–	0.4	3.6	0.0
Market value ($ mil.)	–	–	–	–	–	–
Employees	–	–	–	–	–	14

*Fiscal year change

FRAZIER INDUSTRIAL COMPANY

91 FAIRVIEW AVE
LONG VALLEY, NJ 078533381
Phone: 908 876-3001
Fax: –
Web: www.frazier.com

CEO: William L Mascharka
CFO: Peter Acerra
HR: Sheri Goff
FYE: December 31
Type: Private

This company's racket is structural steel storage systems. Frazier Industrial Co. is a leading manufacturer of structural, as opposed to roll-formed, steel storage racks at nearly a dozen production centers located across the US, Canada, and Mexico. These facilities can adapt production to demand and receive just-in-time delivery of raw materials. Customers use Frazier Industrial's storage racks in warehouses, factories, farms, and other industrial and commercial facilities. Among the company's storage products is the Glide 'N Pick pallet cart that automatically rolls out for greater ease in retrieving items. Frazier Industrial is owned by CEO William Mascharka.

	Annual Growth	12/17	12/18	12/19	12/20	12/21
Sales ($mil.)	10.8%	–	281.2	336.8	288.6	382.8
Net income ($ mil.)	(7.6%)	–	21.6	25.6	19.2	17.1
Market value ($ mil.)	–	–	–	–	–	–
Employees	–	–	–	–	–	750

FRED JONES ENTERPRISES, L.L.C.

6200 SW 29TH ST
OKLAHOMA CITY, OK 731796800
Phone: 800 927-7845
Fax: –
Web: www.fred-jones.com

CEO: Al Dearmon
CFO: Kristi Edelman
HR: –
FYE: December 31
Type: Private

Fred Jones Enterprises' mission in life is to give power to the people. The company is an authorized distributor of Ford and Motorcraft remanufactured powertrain assemblies, including gasoline and diesel engines, transmissions, cylinder heads, crankshafts, fuel injectors, and water pumps. Warrants for the company's products range from 12 to 36 months. Fred Jones Enterprises operates from regional warehouses located in Florida, Georgia, Kentucky, Oklahoma, Tennessee, and Texas. A family-owned company, Fred Jones Enterprises was founded in 1938.

FRED USINGER, INC.

1030 N DR MARTIN LUTHER KING JR DR
MILWAUKEE, WI 532031300
Phone: 414 276-9100
Fax: –
Web: www.usinger.com

CEO: –
CFO: –
HR: Deanna Kutchenriter
FYE: December 31
Type: Private

A dedicated beer town like Milwaukee needs some sausage to "go with" and that's where Usinger's comes in. Fred Usinger, Inc., is a city institution known for its Old World sausage and other prepared meats. The company produces more than 70 kinds of sausage, including beerwurst, of course, as well as numerous varieties of bratwurst, knackwurst, summer sausage, and wieners. It also produces ham, bacon, and other smoked meats. Usinger's sells its products through retail food stores, as well as through its catalog and Web site. Usinger's also operates its landmark store in downtown Milwaukee. The family-owned company was founded in 1880 by German immigrant Fred Usinger.

FRED'S, INC.

4300 NEW GETWELL RD
MEMPHIS, TN 381186801
Phone: 901 365-8880
Fax: –
Web: www.discountoutlet.com

CEO: –
CFO: –
HR: –
FYE: February 02
Type: Private

With a quickly dwindling number of locations, discount retailer Fred's is wrapping up operations. In 2019 it filed for Chapter 11 bankruptcy and announced plans to liquidate all assets. The company formerly operated hundreds of discount stores and pharmacies, primarily in small- to medium-sized towns across the southeastern US. The stores carried more than 12,000 brand-name, off-brand, and private-label products, including pharmaceuticals, household goods, clothing and linens, food and tobacco items, health and beauty aids, and paper and cleaning supplies. Fred's traces its historical roots back to 1947.

FREDDIE MAC

NBB: FMCC

8200 Jones Branch Drive
McLean, VA 22102-3110
Phone: 703 903-2000
Fax: –
Web: www.freddiemac.com

CEO: Michael J Devito
CFO: Christian M Lown
HR: –
FYE: December 31
Type: Public

Government-sponsored enterprises (GSEs) Federal Home Loan Mortgage Corporation (Freddie Mac) was established to provide liquidity, stability, and affordability to the US housing market. Freddie Mac purchase single-family and multifamily residential mortgage loans from lenders and package these loans into guaranteed mortgage-related securities, which are sold in the global capital markets, and transfer interest-rate and liquidity risks to third-party investors. In addition, Freddie Mac transfer mortgage credit risk exposure to third-party investors through its credit risk transfer programs, which include securities- and insurance-based offerings. It also invests in mortgage loans and mortgage-related securities.

	Annual Growth	12/19	12/20	12/21	12/22	12/23
Assets ($mil.)	10.5%	2,203,623	2,627,415	3,025,586	3,208,333	3,280,976
Net income ($ mil.)	9.9%	7,214.0	7,326.0	12,109	9,327.0	10,538
Market value ($ mil.)	(29.7%)	7,703.2	5,694.5	1,865.7	1,319.6	1,885.2
Employees	–	6,912	6,939	7,318	7,839	–

FREDERICK HEALTH HOSPITAL, INC.

400 W 7TH ST
FREDERICK, MD 217014506
Phone: 240 566-3300
Fax: –
Web: www.frederickhealth.org

CEO: Thomas A Kleinhanzl
CFO: Michelle Nahan
HR: –
FYE: June 30
Type: Private

Frederick Health includes a network of providers offering primary care, family medicine and a wide range of specialty services in the form of the Frederick Health Medical Group. The system operates Frederick Health Hospital, an acute care facility in and around Frederick, Maryland. Specialty services include cardiology, oncology, pediatrics, and cancer. Other facilities in the system include Frederick Health Rose Hill, Frederick Health Crestwood, Frederick Health Emmitsburg, Kline Hospice House, James M Stockman Cancer Institute, Frederick Health ProMotion Fitness, and the Frederick Health Liberty.

	Annual Growth	06/17	06/18	06/19	06/21	06/22
Sales ($mil.)	4.3%	–	–	368.4	438.7	418.4
Net income ($ mil.)	–	–	–	(40.6)	54.2	12.3
Market value ($ mil.)	–	–	–	–	–	–
Employees	–	–	–	–	–	2,600

FREEDOM FROM HUNGER FOUNDATION

1400 K ST NW STE 550
WASHINGTON, DC 200052438
Phone: 530 758-6200
Fax: –
Web: www.freedomfromhunger.org

CEO: –
CFO: –
HR: –
FYE: June 30
Type: Private

Freedom from Hunger wants to give everybody just that. The not-for-profit organization strives to solve the problem of chronic hunger and poverty in 16 countries worldwide. The group provides self-help programs and training for more than 650,000 poor women to learn to better feed and tend the health of their families and turn a small enterprise into a sustaining business. Its main program, Credit With Education, is a microcredit program that provides loans to small groups of women who attend classes on nutrition, health, family planning, and sound business practices. Freedom From Hunger was founded in 1946 as Meals for Millions.

	Annual Growth	06/15	06/16	06/17	06/20	06/22
Sales ($mil.)	(32.5%)	–	5.0	4.2	0.4	0.5
Net income ($ mil.)	–	–	(0.6)	0.5	(0.3)	(0.1)
Market value ($ mil.)	–	–	–	–	–	–
Employees	–	–	–	–	–	45

FREEMAN HEALTH SYSTEM

1102 W 32ND ST
JOPLIN, MO 648043503
Phone: 417 347-1111
Fax: –
Web: www.freemanhealth.com

CEO: Paula Baker
CFO: Steven Graddy
HR: –
FYE: March 31
Type: Private

Freeman Health System (FHS) offers comprehensive health and behavioral health services to the residents of Arkansas, Kansas, Missouri, and Oklahoma through three hospitals with a total of more than 500 beds. Specialty facilities include a full-service cardiothoracic and vascular program at the Freeman Heart Institute, and behavioral health services through its Ozark Health Center. Community-owned, not-for-profit FHS also operates two urgent care centers, a separate sleep center, several doctors' office buildings, and serves as a teaching hospital with three residency programs (ear, nose, and throat; emergency medicine; and internal medicine). FHS employs more than 300 physicians in 60 specialties.

	Annual Growth	03/18	03/19	03/20	03/21	03/22
Sales ($mil.)	4.9%	–	624.4	562.1	676.5	721.7
Net income ($ mil.)	(1.0%)	–	57.3	16.9	164.7	55.5
Market value ($ mil.)	–	–	–	–	–	–
Employees	–	–	–	–	–	4,500

FREEPORT REGIONAL HEALTH CARE FOUNDATION

1045 W STEPHENSON ST
FREEPORT, IL 610324864
Phone: 815 599-6000
Fax: –
Web: www.fhn.org

CEO: –
CFO: –
HR: Brandi Zalaznik
FYE: December 31
Type: Private

FHN is a regional health care system serving residents in northwestern Illinois and southern Wisconsin. At its heart is the nearly 200-bed FHN Memorial Hospital, which provides general medical and surgical care, emergency services, and specialty care in areas such as sleep disorders, orthopedics, obstetrics, and cardiology. The health system also features a cancer center, home health care and hospice operations, and a network of satellite facilities providing primary medical and dental care, as well as occupational health, chiropractic, and counseling services. Its Northern Illinois Health Plan subsidiary supplies PPO health plans and third-party administrative services to the region's employers.

	Annual Growth	12/08	12/09	12/13	12/14	12/15
Sales ($mil.)	20.9%	–	55.0	53.1	–	171.6
Net income ($ mil.)	–	–	(16.1)	(23.1)	–	3.5
Market value ($ mil.)	–	–	–	–	–	–
Employees	–	–	–	–	–	1,500

FREEPORT-MCMORAN INC   NYS: FCX

333 North Central Avenue
Phoenix, AZ 85004-2189
Phone: 602 366-8100
Fax: –
Web: www.fcx.com

CEO: Richard C Adkerson
CFO: –
HR: Elizabeth Marquez
FYE: December 31
Type: Public

Freeport McMoran is one of the world's major mining companies with holdings in copper, molybdenum, and gold. It operates large, long-lived, geographically diverse assets with significant proven and probable mineral reserves of copper, gold and molybdenum. Its portfolio of assets includes the Grasberg minerals district in Indonesia, one of the world's largest copper and gold deposits; and significant mining operations in North America and South America, including the large-scale Morenci minerals district in Arizona and the Cerro Verde operation in Peru. With customers across the Americas, Europe, and Asia, the US is FCX's biggest market at over 30% of company revenue.

	Annual Growth	12/19	12/20	12/21	12/22	12/23
Sales ($mil.)	12.2%	14,402	14,198	22,845	22,780	22,855
Net income ($ mil.)	–	(239.0)	599.0	4,306.0	3,468.0	1,848.0
Market value ($ mil.)	34.2%	18,827	37,339	59,883	54,530	61,088
Employees	(20.5%)	68,100	58,300	46,900	74,500	27,200

FREESE AND NICHOLS, INC.

801 CHERRY ST STE 2800
FORT WORTH, TX 761026804
Phone: 949 753-8766
Fax: –
Web: www.freese.com

CEO: Brian Colpharp
CFO: Cynthia Milrany
HR: Janette Bridgewater
FYE: December 31
Type: Private

Freese and Nichols (FNI) keeps water in the Lone Star State flowing in the right direction. The consulting firm specializes in water management engineering but also offers architecture, environmental science, and construction management to clients in the Southwest, primarily Texas, and the Southeast. The company has designed more than 150 dams and reservoirs and also works on such projects as municipal waterworks, water treatment facilities, and highways. Freese and Nichols serves the private and public sectors; its clients include all levels of government. The company has offices in about 15 Texas cities and in North Carolina. It traces its roots to a Fort Worth firm founded in 1894 by John B. Hawley.

	Annual Growth	12/15	12/16	12/17	12/20	12/22
Sales ($mil.)	13.6%	–	129.7	150.7	228.1	279.4
Net income ($ mil.)	4.0%	–	1.9	2.9	7.9	2.4
Market value ($ mil.)	–	–	–	–	–	–
Employees	–	–	–	–	–	968

FREIGHTCAR AMERICA INC   NMS: RAIL

125 South Wacker Drive, Suite 1500
Chicago, IL 60606
Phone: 800 458-2235
Fax: –
Web: www.freightcaramerica.com

CEO: –
CFO: –
HR: –
FYE: December 31
Type: Public

FreightCar America is a diversified manufacturer of railcars and railcar components. The company designs and manufactures a broad variety of railcar types for transportation of bulk commodities and containerized freight products primarily in North America, including open top hoppers, covered hoppers, and gondolas along with intermodal and non-intermodal flat cars. FreightCar America rebuilds and converts railcars and sells forged, cast, and fabricated parts for all of the railcars it produces, as well as those manufactured by others. It also leases freight cars through its JAIX Leasing Company and FCA Leasing 1. Customers include financial companies, railroads, and shippers. The company has been making railcars since 1901.

	Annual Growth	12/19	12/20	12/21	12/22	12/23
Sales ($mil.)	11.7%	230.0	108.4	203.1	364.8	358.1
Net income ($ mil.)	–	(75.2)	(84.4)	(41.4)	(38.8)	(23.6)
Market value ($ mil.)	6.9%	37.1	43.1	66.1	57.3	48.3
Employees	42.1%	496	669	997	1,435	2,023

FREMONT CONTRACT CARRIERS, INC.

865 BUD BLVD
FREMONT, NE 680256270
Phone: 402 721-3020
Fax: –
Web: www.fcc-inc.com

CEO: Michael F Herre
CFO: –
HR: Suzie Radin
FYE: December 31
Type: Private

Truckload carrier Fremont Contract Carriers (FCC) hauls general and non-hazardous freight throughout the US and Canada. Its fleet consists of some 315 trucks, 700 high-cubed dry van trailers, and 100 flatbed, curtain-side, and step-deck trailers. The company's FCC Transportation Services unit provides freight brokerage and logistics services, in which customers' freight is matched with carriers' capacity. In addition to offering traditional trucking services, the company provides online load tracking and reporting on its Web site. The company transports food products, consumer products, retail products, construction and manufactured products as well as packaging and grocery goods. FCC was founded in 1966.

	Annual Growth	12/12	12/13	12/14	12/15	12/17
Sales ($mil.)	3.0%	–	73.1	75.0	70.7	82.4
Net income ($ mil.)	–	–	(0.4)	1.0	2.3	2.8
Market value ($ mil.)	–	–	–	–	–	–
Employees	–	–	–	–	–	91

FREMONT HEALTH

450 E 23RD ST
FREMONT, NE 680252387
Phone: 402 727-3795
Fax: –
Web: www.bestcare.org

CEO: Patrick Booth
CFO: –
HR: –
FYE: December 31
Type: Private

Fremont Area Medical Center's area of expertise is serving patients in Nebraska's Dodge County and surrounding areas. The non-profit healthcare facility has more than 200 beds, with about 112 beds dedicated to long-term care patients. Specialized services include cancer care, emergency medicine, rehabilitation, home health and hospice, and surgery. Fremont Area Medical Center is owned by Dodge County and its operations are funded by taxpayers. The institution is licensed by the Nebraska State Board of Health and maintains accreditation through the Joint Commission.

	Annual Growth	06/04	06/05	06/07*	12/19	12/21
Sales ($mil.)	3.4%	–	77.7	91.8	0.7	132.0
Net income ($ mil.)	10.6%	–	6.7	12.9	(0.3)	33.4
Market value ($ mil.)	–	–	–	–	–	–
Employees	–	–	–	–	–	900

*Fiscal year change

FREQUENCY ELECTRONICS INC

NMS: FEIM

55 Charles Lindbergh Blvd.
Mitchel Field, NY 11553
Phone: 516 794-4500
Fax: 516 794-4340
Web: www.frequencyelectronics.com

CEO: Stanton D Sloane
CFO: Steven L Bernstein
HR: –
FYE: April 30
Type: Public

Frequency Electronics, Inc. (FEI) lets the good times roll. The company makes quartz-, rubidium-, and cesium-based time and frequency control products, such as oscillators and amplifiers, used to synchronize voice, data, and video transmissions in satellite and wireless communications. The US military uses its products for navigation, communications, surveillance, and timing systems in aircraft, satellites, radar, and missiles. Though FEI has diversified into commercial markets, nearly half of its sales still come from the US government. Other top clients include AT&T, Lockheed Martin, Northrop Grumman, and Thales Alenia Space. The company was formed in 1961 as a time and frequency control R&D firm.

	Annual Growth	04/19	04/20	04/21	04/22	04/23
Sales ($mil.)	(4.7%)	49.5	41.5	54.3	48.3	40.8
Net income ($ mil.)	–	(2.5)	(10.0)	0.7	(8.7)	(5.5)
Market value ($ mil.)	(14.2%)	112.9	94.1	100.7	76.0	61.3
Employees	(8.5%)	280	220	240	197	196

FRESH MARK, INC.

1888 SOUTHWAY ST SW
MASSILLON, OH 446469429
Phone: 330 832-7491
Fax: –
Web: www.freshmark.com

CEO: Neil Genshaft
CFO: David Cochenour
HR: Carl Montalbano
FYE: January 01
Type: Private

Fresh Mark is one of the leading producers of smoked and processed pork products for the domestic and international retail and foodservice industries. From its four plants in Ohio, the company makes and markets such products as bacon (raw, par-cooked, and fully cooked), ham (fully cooked bone-in and boneless ham), pepperoni and salami (pizza, salad, sandwich, or charcuterie board), hot dogs, and sliced meats under the Sugardale and Superior's brands. Sugardale label is available in all 50 states and over 20 countries. The company also produces private-label processed meat products for others and supplies the foodservice industry through its Sugardale Food Service business. Founded in 1920, Ohio-based Fresh Mark is owned and operated by the Genshaft family.

	Annual Growth	12/04	12/05	12/06	12/07*	01/11
Sales ($mil.)	8.7%	–	481.5	481.5	534.6	795.7
Net income ($ mil.)	16.7%	–	23.5	21.7	31.0	59.5
Market value ($ mil.)	–	–	–	–	–	–
Employees	–	–	–	–	–	2,300

*Fiscal year change

FRESH TRACKS THERAPEUTICS INC

NBB: FRTX

2000 Central Avenue, Suite 100
Boulder, CO 80301
Phone: 720 505-4755
Fax: –
Web: www.ir.brickellbio.com

CEO: Robert B Brown
CFO: Albert N Marchio II
HR: –
FYE: December 31
Type: Public

Vical counts DNA as its main ally in tackling disease. The biopharmaceutical firm researches and develops vaccines based on its DNA delivery technology, which uses portions of the genetic code of a pathogen to induce an immune response. Faced with a number of failed trials, Vical announced cut around half of its workforce in early 2018. Later that year, it abandoned its lead program, a vaccine candidate for HSV-2. It then announced plans to focus on the development of antifungal candidate VL-2397, but put those plans on hold when it had problems finding trial participants. The company is now exploring its options, including possibly selling itself or its assets.

	Annual Growth	12/19	12/20	12/21	12/22	12/23
Sales ($mil.)	0.3%	7.9	1.8	0.4	6.9	8.0
Net income ($ mil.)	–	(23.9)	(20.9)	(39.5)	(21.1)	(5.7)
Market value ($ mil.)	(12.5%)	9.0	4.7	1.4	9.0	5.3
Employees	(28.1%)	15	13	16	13	4

FRICK COLLECTION

1 E 70TH ST
NEW YORK, NY 100214981
Phone: 212 288-0700
Fax: –
Web: www.frick.org

CEO: –
CFO: Michael Paccione
HR: –
FYE: June 30
Type: Private

The Frick Collection consists of hundreds of works of art, including paintings, sculpture, furniture and porcelains, clocks, and textiles, that are housed in a Manhattan mansion built by steel and railroad tycoon Henry Clay Frick. Upon his death in 1919, Frick bequeathed his vast collection of Western European art (from the Renaissance through the end of the 19th century) to the public. In addition to its permanent collection of more than 1,100 works of art and other exhibitions, The Frick Collection offers public programs, such as lectures and concerts. An affiliated facility, the Frick Art Reference Library, offers books and photographic materials for scholars.

	Annual Growth	06/14	06/15	06/17	06/20	06/22
Sales ($mil.)	8.7%	–	37.7	67.3	72.4	67.5
Net income ($ mil.)	32.4%	–	6.0	42.5	29.0	43.1
Market value ($ mil.)	–	–	–	–	–	–
Employees	–	–	–	–	–	240

FRIEDMAN INDUSTRIES, INC.

ASE: FRD

1121 Judson Road, Suite 124
Longview, TX 75601
Phone: 903 758-3431
Fax: –
Web: www.friedmanindustries.com

CEO: Michael J Taylor
CFO: Alex Larue
HR: –
FYE: March 31
Type: Public

Steel processor Friedman Industries operates in two business segments: coil products and tubular products. The company's Texas Tubular Products unit, the larger of Friedman Industries' segments, buys pipe and coil material and processes it for use in pipelines, oil and gas drilling, and piling and structural applications. Friedman Industries' coil products unit purchases hot-rolled steel coils and processes them into sheet and plate products. The company's XSCP unit sells surplus prime, secondary, and transition steel coils. Friedman Industries' processing facilities are located near mills operated by U.S. Steel and Nucor Corp. and work closely with both facilities.

	Annual Growth	03/19	03/20	03/21	03/22	03/23
Sales ($mil.)	30.8%	187.2	142.1	126.1	285.2	547.5
Net income ($ mil.)	43.0%	5.1	(5.2)	11.4	14.1	21.3
Market value ($ mil.)	10.3%	56.6	32.5	59.7	65.0	83.6
Employees	22.5%	104	103	94	76	234

FRIENDFINDER NETWORKS INC

6800 Broken Sound Parkway, Suite 200
Boca Raton, FL 33487
Phone: 561 912-7000
Fax: –
Web: www.ffn.cgellenom

CEO: –
CFO: –
HR: –
FYE: December 31
Type: Public

If you're looking for friendship, try knocking on some doors below the penthouse. FriendFinder Networks (publisher of the venerable adult magazine Penthouse , and producer of adult video content and images) now owns and operates some 38,000 social networking websites, including AdultFriendFinder.com, Amigos.com, AsiaFriendFinder.com, Cams.com, FriendFinder.com, BigChurch.com, and SeniorFriendFinder.com. In total, its sites are offered to about 528 million members in more than 200 countries. FriendFinder also distributes original pictorial and video content and engages in brand licensing. It emerged from Chapter 11 bankruptcy protection in late 2013, returning control to company founder Andrew Conru.

	Annual Growth	12/09	12/10	12/11	12/12	12/13
Sales ($mil.)	(4.6%)	327.7	346.0	331.3	314.4	271.4
Net income ($ mil.)	–	–	(41.2)	(43.2)	(31.1)	(49.4)	175.2
Market value ($ mil.)	–	–	–	–	–	–
Employees	–	–	–	407	692	342	–

FRISBIE MEMORIAL HOSPITAL

11 WHITEHALL RD
ROCHESTER, NH 038673297
Phone: 603 332-5211
Fax: –
Web: www.frisbiehospital.com

CEO: John Marzinzik
CFO: –
HR: –
FYE: September 30
Type: Private

Frisbie Memorial Hospital hopes to maintain a high-flying reputation as it serves southeastern New Hampshire and southern Maine. The acute-care facility has nearly 90 beds and about 250 physicians on staff. The not-for-profit community hospital offers patients a variety of services including emergency, radiology, cardiology, neurology, and respiratory and surgical care. Frisbie Memorial also operates outpatient and primary medical care facilities, and it provides oncology services through a partnership with the Dartmouth-Hitchcock Medical Center in Lebanon, New Hampshire.

	Annual Growth	09/14	09/15	09/16	09/17	09/18
Sales ($mil.)	1.0%	–	132.4	135.8	122.2	136.6
Net income ($ mil.)	–	–	(4.7)	3.2	(21.2)	(11.0)
Market value ($ mil.)	–	–	–	–	–	–
Employees	–	–	–	–	–	900

FROEDTERT MEMORIAL LUTHERAN HOSPITAL, INC.

9200 W WISCONSIN AVE
MILWAUKEE, WI 532263522
Phone: 414 805-3000
Fax: –
Web: www.froedtert.com

CEO: William Petasnick
CFO: –
HR: Cindy Daniels
FYE: June 30
Type: Private

The 711-bed Froedtert Memorial Lutheran Hospital (also known as Froedtert Hospital) is an academic medical center and a leading referral resource for advanced medical care. Froedtert Hospital also operates the region's only adult Level I Trauma Center. It is the primary adult teaching affiliate of the Medical College of Wisconsin, Froedtert Hospital is a major training facility for more than 1,000 medical, nursing and health technical students annually. Froedtert Hospital is part of the Froedtert & MCW health network, which includes 10 hospital locations, over 2,100 physicians and more than 45 health centers and clinics. It is also a respected research center, participating in some 2,000 research studies, including clinical trials, every year.

	Annual Growth	06/13	06/14	06/20	06/21	06/22
Sales ($mil.)	9.1%	–	1,164.8	1,958.7	2,165.4	2,334.1
Net income ($ mil.)	4.7%	–	92.4	143.6	186.2	133.1
Market value ($ mil.)	–	–	–	–	–	–
Employees	–	–	–	–	–	3,400

FRONT PORCH, INC.

27 S SHEPHERD ST
SONORA, CA 953704768
Phone: 209 288-5500
Fax: –
Web: www.frontporch.com

CEO: Zach Britton
CFO: Robert Hohne Jr
HR: –
FYE: March 31
Type: Private

Front Porch knows that providing Internet service is hard work, with little time to kick up your feet. The company, founded in 1998, provides advertising and content delivery systems for Internet services providers, annually serving millions of users in more than 30 countries. It offers products and services that ISPs use to insert and manage content and advertising into their offerings. ISPs use the company's products to redirect traffic and serve a variety of ads, including interstitials, pop-ups, and pop-under advertising. Front Porch also offers services for managing online advertising, customer service messaging, bill collection, and network reporting.

FRONTIER COMMUNICATIONS PARENT INC

401 Merritt 7
Norwalk, CT 06851
Phone: 972 445-0042
Fax: –
Web: www.frontier.com

NMS: FYBR
CEO: –
CFO: –
HR: –
FYE: December 31
Type: Public

Frontier Communications Parent formerly known as Frontier Communications Corporation is a leading communications and technology provider offering gigabit speeds that empower and connect about 2.8 million broadband subscribers in about 25 states. It offers data and internet, video, voice services, access services, and advanced hardware and network solutions for its consumer and commercial customers. It provides video services under the Frontier TV brand in portions of California, Indiana, Texas, and Florida and under the Vantage brand in portions of Connecticut, North Carolina, South Carolina, Illinois, New York, and Ohio. It also offers satellite TV video services under various agency relationships with satellite providers. Almost 50% of the company's revenue attributable to non-subsidy activities related to its copper products, with the other about 50% relating to fiber-optics products.

	Annual Growth	12/20*	04/21*	12/21	12/22	12/23
Sales ($mil.)	(7.0%)	7,155.0	2,231.0	4,180.0	5,787.0	5,751.0
Net income ($ mil.)	–	(402.0)	4,541.0	414.0	441.0	29.0
Market value ($ mil.)	556.6%	22.0	14.5	7,249.0	6,263.3	6,228.9
Employees	(6.4%)	16,200	–	15,600	14,700	13,300

*Fiscal year change

FRONTIER MERGER SUB LLC

1600 W 7TH ST
FORT WORTH, TX 761022504
Phone: 800 223-8738
Fax: –
Web: www.firstcash.com

CEO: T B Stuart
CFO: Thomas A Bessant Jr
HR: –
FYE: December 31
Type: Private

If cash is king, then Cash America International is king of pawns. As one of the largest pawn lenders in the US, Cash America operates more than 900 pawn and paycheck cashing stores in the US, including 825 lending locations under the Cash America Pawn, SuperPawn, Cash America Payday Advance, and Cashland brands in 20 states; and around 80 franchised check cashing centers under the Mr. Payroll banner in 12 states. The company's Mr. Payroll stores also offer money orders and money transfers. Founded in 1984, Cash America operates more than half of its stores in Texas, Ohio, and Florida. It exited Mexico after selling its 47 locations there in 2014. Cash America agreed to merge with First Cash Financial Services in April 2016.

FROZEN FOOD EXPRESS INDUSTRIES, INC.

3400 STONEWALL ST
LANCASTER, TX 751341536
Phone: 800 569-9200
Fax: –
Web: www.ffeinc.com

CEO: S R Stubbs
CFO: Steve Stedman
HR: –
FYE: December 31
Type: Private

The frozen assets of other companies mean big business for Frozen Food Express Industries, one of the largest temperature-controlled trucking companies in the US. Through its subsidiaries, which include FFE Transportation Services and Lisa Motor Lines, the company transports truckload and less-than-truckload (LTL) shipments in the US, Canada, and Mexico. Hauling temperature-sensitive cargo accounts for most of the company's sales. Frozen Food Express Industries also hauls dry freight, under the American Eagle Lines brand, and offers logistics services. Overall, the company maintains a fleet of about 1,260 tractors and 2,350 trailers. FFE traces its roots to 1946.

FRP HOLDINGS INC

200 West Forsyth Street, 7th Floor
Jacksonville, FL 32202
Phone: 904 396-5733
Fax: –
Web: www.frpholdings.com

NMS: FRPH

CEO: –
CFO: –
HR: –
FYE: December 31
Type: Public

Patriot Transportation Holding has plenty of tanks but hasn't fired a shot. The company's Transportation segment, comprising Florida Rock & Tank Lines subsidiary, transports liquid and dry bulk commodities, mainly petroleum (including ethanol) and chemicals, in tank trucks. Patriot Transportation's combined fleet of about 435 trucks and 530 trailers operates primarily in the southeastern and mid-Atlantic US. The company's Real Estate unit, comprising Florida Rock Properties and FRP Development, owns office and warehouse properties, as well as sand and gravel deposits on the East Coast that are leased to Vulcan Materials Company.

	Annual Growth	12/19	12/20	12/21	12/22	12/23
Sales ($mil.)	15.0%	23.8	23.6	31.2	37.5	41.5
Net income ($ mil.)	(24.3%)	16.2	12.7	28.2	4.6	5.3
Market value ($ mil.)	6.0%	472.4	432.0	548.2	510.8	596.4
Employees	5.7%	12	13	14	13	15

FRUIT GROWERS SUPPLY COMPANY INC

27770 ENTERTAINMENT DR STE 120
VALENCIA, CA 91355
Phone: 888 997-4855
Fax: –
Web: www.fruitgrowerssupply.com

CEO: Jim Phillips
CFO: Charles Boyce
HR: –
FYE: December 31
Type: Private

Shipping cartons are the real fruit of labor for Fruit Growers Supply (FSG). The non-profit cooperative association supplies affiliate Sunkist Growers and other agricultural businesses with packing materials, fertilizer, and related implements. Offerings include a range of equipment used to grow, pick, package, and transport many commodity cash crops. FSG also provides packing services and custom design and installation of irrigation systems. It owns and operates some 335,000 acres of timberland along the West coast (a source of box material and income), a carton manufacturing and supply plant, and seven retail operations centers. FGS is owned by 6,000-plus citrus growers and shippers in the US.

	Annual Growth	12/14	12/15	12/16	12/17	12/18
Sales ($mil.)	0.6%	–	218.8	214.5	220.7	222.6
Net income ($ mil.)	13.1%	–	5.1	0.9	(9.5)	7.4
Market value ($ mil.)	–	–	–	–	–	–
Employees	–	–	–	–	–	300

FRUTH, INC.

4016 OHIO RIVER RD
POINT PLEASANT, WV 255503257
Phone: 304 675-1612
Fax: –
Web: www.fruthpharmacy.com

CEO: Donald Pullin
CFO: Bob Messick
HR: Donald Stapleton
FYE: June 30
Type: Private

Fruth Pharmacy operates about 25 drugstores in southern Ohio and West Virginia. While prescriptions account for the majority of sales, Fruth pharmacies also sell gift items and computer supplies, and have floral departments and digital printing. The regional drugstore chain competes by constantly trying new things, such as participating in the Face2Face diabetes program and testing in-store dollar departments. It is countering Wal-Mart Stores's $4 generic offering with a discount generic drug program created by Cardinal Health. Founded in 1952 by its namesake -- the late Jack Fruth -- the company is family-owned and -operated.

	Annual Growth	06/05	06/06	06/07	06/08	06/09
Sales ($mil.)	1.3%	–	128.7	136.0	135.7	133.7
Net income ($ mil.)	–	–	4.7	0.3	0.9	(0.5)
Market value ($ mil.)	–	–	–	–	–	–
Employees	–	–	–	–	–	545

FS BANCORP INC (WASHINGTON)

6920 220th Street SW
Mountlake Terrace, WA 98043
Phone: 425 771-5299
Fax: –
Web: www.fsbwa.com

NAS: FSBW

CEO: Joseph C Adams
CFO: Matthew D Mullet
HR: –
FYE: December 31
Type: Public

FS Bancorp is the holding company for 1st Security Bank of Washington, which operates six branches in the Puget Sound region. The bank provides standard deposit products such as checking and savings accounts, CDs, and IRAs to area businesses and consumers. Its lending activities are focused on consumer loans (more than half of its portfolio), including home improvement, boat, and automobile loans. The bank also writes business and construction loans, and commercial and residential mortgages. FS Bancorp went public via in initial public offering in 2012.

	Annual Growth	12/19	12/20	12/21	12/22	12/23
Assets ($mil.)	14.8%	1,713.1	2,113.2	2,286.4	2,632.9	2,972.7
Net income ($ mil.)	12.2%	22.7	39.3	37.4	29.6	36.1
Market value ($ mil.)	(12.8%)	497.6	427.5	262.3	260.9	288.3
Employees	6.2%	452	506	538	537	574

FTAI AVIATION LTD

1345 Avenue of the Americas, 45th Floor
New York, NY 10105
Phone: 212 798-6100
Fax: –
Web: www.ftaiaviation.com

NMS: FTAI

CEO: Joseph P Adams Jr
CFO: Eun Nam
HR: –
FYE: December 31
Type: Public

If this firm could buy a flying fortress and lease it out with all the security equipment, it would. Fortress Transportation and Infrastructure Investors buys and owns vital infrastructure and related equipment needed to transport people and cargo globally, investing particularly in the aviation, energy, intermodal transport, and rail sectors. Boasting assets of $1.4 billion, the firm owns and leases railroads and related assets (including rail cars and locomotives), aviation property (including planes and aircraft engines), offshore oil and gas vessels, and shipping containers. Fortress has been externally managed by transport and infrastructure investor and affiliate FIG LLC since going public in 2015.

	Annual Growth	12/19	12/20	12/21	12/22	12/23
Sales ($mil.)	19.3%	578.8	366.5	455.8	708.4	1,170.9
Net income ($ mil.)	2.0%	225.1	(87.2)	(104.2)	(193.2)	243.8
Market value ($ mil.)	–	–	–	–	–	–
Employees	–	–	–	600	40	170

FTD COMPANIES, INC.

3113 WOODCREEK DR
DOWNERS GROVE, IL 605155420
Phone: 630 719-7800
Fax: –
Web: www.ftdcompanies.com

CEO: –
CFO: –
HR: –
FYE: December 31
Type: Private

Mercury, the Roman god of speed and commerce with winged feet, comes bearing flowers. FTD is a leader in the floral industry for over a century supported by the iconic Mercury Man logo displayed in more than 30,000 floral shops in over 125 countries. The company works with local florists to hand-craft floral arrangements available for same-day delivery on FTD.com and ProFlowers.com. In addition, the company provides technology, marketing, and digital services to members of its florist network. The company was founded by John A. Valentine in 1910.

	Annual Growth	12/14	12/15	12/16	12/17	12/18
Sales ($mil.)	(6.0%)	–	1,219.8	1,122.0	1,084.0	1,014.2
Net income ($ mil.)	–	–	(78.8)	(83.2)	(234.0)	(224.7)
Market value ($ mil.)	–	–	–	–	–	–
Employees	–	–	–	–	–	1,501

FTI CONSULTING INC.   NYS: FCN

555 12th Street NW
Washington, DC 20004
Phone: 202 312-9100
Fax: –
Web: www.fticonsulting.com

CEO: Steven H Gunby
CFO: Ajay Sabherwal
HR: –
FYE: December 31
Type: Public

FTI Consulting, Inc. is a global business advisory firm dedicated to helping organizations manage change, mitigate risk, and resolve disputes: financial, legal, operational, political & regulatory, reputational, and transactional. Individually, each of its segments and practices is staffed with experts recognized for the depth of their knowledge and a track record of making an impact. FTI Consulting professionals work closely with clients to help them anticipate, and overcome complex business challenges and make the most of opportunities. With operations in more than 30 countries, FTI Consulting generates roughly 65% of its sales in the US. The company was founded in 1982.

	Annual Growth	12/19	12/20	12/21	12/22	12/23
Sales ($mil.)	10.4%	2,352.7	2,461.3	2,776.2	3,028.9	3,489.2
Net income ($ mil.)	6.1%	216.7	210.7	235.0	235.5	274.9
Market value ($ mil.)	15.8%	3,930.8	3,968.4	5,449.6	5,640.7	7,074.0
Employees	9.5%	5,567	6,321	6,780	7,635	7,990

FTS INTERNATIONAL, INC.

777 MAIN ST STE 2900
FORT WORTH, TX 761025318
Phone: 817 862-2000
Fax: –
Web: www.profrac.com

CEO: –
CFO: –
HR: –
FYE: December 31
Type: Private

FTS International provides subject matter experts focused on independent analysis and mission support services. FTS attracts an elite workforce who deliver superior services for its customers in the fields of Engineering, Mission Operations, Intelligence, and Management Support. FTS maintains a broad range of customers and a large network across the IC, DoD, and industry. FTS International has provided the federal government with highly dedicated mission support personnel. John Fitzgerald, President and CEO, founded FTS International in 2005 with the purpose of providing unbiased and dedicated support to the US Government and Intelligence Community.

FUEL TECH INC   NAS: FTEK

27601 Bella Vista Parkway
Warrenville, IL 60555-1617
Phone: 630 845-4500
Fax: –
Web: www.ftek.com

CEO: Vincent J Arnone
CFO: Ellen T Albrecht
HR: –
FYE: December 31
Type: Public

Fuel Tech develops technologies and products so industrial plants and utilities around the world can run cleanly and efficiently. The company's air pollution control systems segment offers nitrogen oxide reduction products (such as NOxOUT and Over-Fire Air Systems), which reduce nitrogen oxide emissions from boilers, incinerators, furnaces, and other combustion sources. Fuel Tech's technologies are used on more than 700 combustion units, including utility, industrial and municipal solid waste applications. The company's FUEL CHEM segment develops chemical products used to reduce slag formation and corrosion. Each segment accounts for about half of the company's sales.

	Annual Growth	12/19	12/20	12/21	12/22	12/23
Sales ($mil.)	(2.9%)	30.5	22.6	24.3	26.9	27.1
Net income ($ mil.)	–	(7.9)	(4.3)	0.0	(1.4)	(1.5)
Market value ($ mil.)	2.5%	28.9	117.9	42.5	38.7	31.9
Employees	(3.2%)	82	73	73	66	72

FUELCELL ENERGY INC   NMS: FCEL

3 Great Pasture Road
Danbury, CT 06810
Phone: 203 825-6000
Fax: –
Web: www.fuelcellenergy.com

CEO: Jason B Few
CFO: Michael S Bishop
HR: –
FYE: October 31
Type: Public

FuelCell is a leading global manufacturer of proprietary fuel cell technology platforms. The company is a manufacturer of fuel cell clean power platforms delivering power and thermal energy and capable of delivering hydrogen, long-duration hydrogen energy storage, and carbon capture applications. Its product portfolio is based on two electrochemical platforms, carbonate and solid oxide. Its SureSource power plants produce power for various industries, such as commercial, industrial and government. FuelCell Energy generates majority of sales domestically. FuelCell Energy was founded in 1969 and became a publicly traded company in 1992.

	Annual Growth	10/19	10/20	10/21	10/22	10/23
Sales ($mil.)	19.4%	60.8	70.9	69.6	130.5	123.4
Net income ($ mil.)	–	(77.6)	(89.1)	(101.1)	(142.7)	(107.6)
Market value ($ mil.)	46.2%	107.4	901.3	3,600.5	1,406.0	491.2
Employees	20.2%	301	316	382	513	629

FUELSTREAM, INC.   NBB: FLST

11650 South State Street, Suite 240
Draper, UT 84020
Phone: 801 816-2510
Fax: –
Web: www.thefuelstream.com

CEO: Kenneth I Denos
CFO: Chene C Gardner
HR: –
FYE: December 31
Type: Public

Nutty about sports? SportsNuts is a sports management and marketing company that helps sports planners organize amateur sporting events and tournaments. The firm offers online event registration, merchandising, sponsorship, and promotion services. The SportsNuts Web site is a resource for events coordinators, coaches, athletes, and fans to post or obtain relevant information, such as schedules, statistics, and pictures. The company spun off its Web hosting and design subsidiary Synerteck and did the same with Secure Networks, which sold computer hardware.

	Annual Growth	12/10	12/11	12/12	12/13	12/14
Sales ($mil.)	–	–	–	1.1	0.0	0.7
Net income ($ mil.)	–	(5.6)	(2.5)	(19.7)	(4.1)	(3.2)
Market value ($ mil.)	(87.1%)	0.0	0.5	2.8	0.0	0.0
Employees	56.5%	1	2	6	6	6

FULL HOUSE RESORTS, INC. — NAS: FLL

One Summerlin, 1980 Festival Plaza Drive, Suite 680
Las Vegas, NV 89135
Phone: 702 221-7800
Fax: –
Web: www.fullhouseresorts.com

CEO: Daniel R Lee
CFO: Lewis A Fanger
HR: –
FYE: December 31
Type: Public

When it comes to gaming outside Sin City, nothing beats a Full House. Full House Resorts owns Stockman's Casino in Fallon, Nevada, featuring 260 slot and gaming machines, four table games, and keno. In addition, its Rising Star Casino Resort in Rising Son, Indiana includes a riverboat casino with 40,000 square feet of gaming space, a 200-room hotel, a theater, and several restaurants. The company also operates the Grand Lodge Casino at the Hyatt Regency Lake Tahoe Resort, Spa and Casino in Incline Village, Nevada through a five-year lease agreement with Hyat Hotels Corporationt.

	Annual Growth	12/19	12/20	12/21	12/22	12/23
Sales ($mil.)	9.9%	165.4	125.6	180.2	163.3	241.1
Net income ($ mil.)	–	(5.8)	0.1	11.7	(14.8)	(24.9)
Market value ($ mil.)	12.5%	115.9	135.9	418.9	260.1	185.7
Employees	–	1,585	1,151	1,158	1,540	–

FULLER (HB) COMPANY — NYS: FUL

1200 Willow Lake Boulevard
St. Paul, MN 55110-5101
Phone: 651 236-5900
Fax: 651 236-5161
Web: www.hbfuller.com

CEO: Celeste B Mastin
CFO: John J Corkrean
HR: –
FYE: December 2
Type: Public

H.B. Fuller is one of the world's top adhesive, sealant, and other specialty chemical manufacturers with sales operations in about 35 countries across the world. The company's core product, industrial adhesives, is used in the manufacturing process of a wide range of consumer and industrial goods like food, and beverage containers, disposable diapers, medical products, windows, doors and windows, appliances, multi-wall bags, water filtration products, insulation, textiles, marine products, solar energy systems, electronics and products for the aerospace and defense industries, and automobiles among others. The company's brands include H.B. Fuller, Swift, Advantra, Clarity, Earthic, Sesame, TEC, Foster, Rakoll, Rapidex, Full-Care, Thermonex, Silaprene, Eternabond, and Cilbond, among others. H.B. Fuller generates about 45% of its revenue from the US.

	Annual Growth	11/19	11/20	11/21*	12/22	12/23
Sales ($mil.)	4.9%	2,897.0	2,790.3	3,278.0	3,749.2	3,510.9
Net income ($ mil.)	2.6%	130.8	123.7	161.4	180.3	144.9
Market value ($ mil.)	11.4%	2,698.2	2,906.4	3,997.5	4,345.3	4,159.2
Employees	3.0%	6,400	6,428	6,500	7,000	7,200

*Fiscal year change

FULLER THEOLOGICAL SEMINARY

135 N OAKLAND AVE
PASADENA, CA 911820002
Phone: 626 584-5200
Fax: –
Web: www.fuller.edu

CEO: –
CFO: –
HR: –
FYE: June 30
Type: Private

Looking for a fuller life experience? Fuller Theological Seminary, one of the world's largest multidenominational seminaries, offers just that through its schools of theology, psychology, and intercultural studies. It offers about 20 master's and doctoral degree programs and about 10 certificate programs to more than 4,000 students from more than 80 countries. In addition to its main campus in Pasadena, California, the seminary operates eight campuses, as well as online classes. It also offers degree programs in Spanish and Korean. Fuller Theological Seminary was founded in 1947 by radio evangelist Charles E. Fuller and pastor Harold John Ockenga.

	Annual Growth	06/18	06/19	06/20	06/21	06/22
Sales ($mil.)	8.5%	–	53.0	48.9	74.7	67.6
Net income ($ mil.)	–	–	(13.8)	(14.1)	18.7	10.5
Market value ($ mil.)	–	–	–	–	–	–
Employees	–	–	–	–	–	550

FULLMER CONSTRUCTION

1725 S GROVE AVE
ONTARIO, CA 917614530
Phone: 909 947-9467
Fax: –
Web: www.fullmerco.com

CEO: –
CFO: –
HR: –
FYE: December 31
Type: Private

Fullmer Construction is full of ideas when it comes to commercial construction. The company, which does business as Fullmer Companies, provides commercial and industrial construction and reconstruction service in Southern California, including tenant improvements. Typical projects include industrial centers, airport facilities, and office/warehouse spaces. The company has built more than 2,000 buildings totaling about 98 million sq. ft. of space. Fullmer was founded in 1946; founder Leonard Fullmer still serves as a consultant to the family-controlled firm.

FULLNET COMMUNICATIONS INC — NBB: FULO

201 Robert S. Kerr Avenue, Suite 210
Oklahoma City, OK 73102
Phone: 405 236-8200
Fax: –
Web: www.fullnet.net; www.fulltel.com; www.callmultiplier.com

CEO: –
CFO: –
HR: –
FYE: December 31
Type: Public

FullNet Communications is trying to net as many Oklahoma Internet users as possible. Established in 1995, the company provides dial-up Internet access to the state's consumers and small to midsized businesses. It sells connectivity on a retail or wholesale basis, allowing other Internet service providers to resell the service under their own brand names. FullNet's wholly-owned FullTel subsidiary is a competitive local-exchange carrier (CLEC) that provides the company with the local phone numbers necessary to offer dial-up service.

	Annual Growth	12/18	12/19	12/20	12/21	12/22
Sales ($mil.)	19.8%	2.1	2.4	3.5	4.1	4.3
Net income ($ mil.)	26.0%	0.3	0.3	1.1	0.9	0.7
Market value ($ mil.)	79.7%	0.7	0.6	1.9	12.5	7.2
Employees	1.7%	14	15	15	16	15

FULTON FINANCIAL CORP. (PA) — NMS: FULT

One Penn Square, P.O. Box 4887
Lancaster, PA 17604
Phone: 717 291-2411
Fax: –
Web: www.fult.com

CEO: Curtis J Myers
CFO: Mark R McCollom
HR: –
FYE: December 31
Type: Public

Founded in 1982, Fulton Financial is a financial holding company with $25 billion in assets that delivers financial services within its five-state market areas of Pennsylvania, Maryland, Delaware, New Jersey, and Virginia. It operates through its wholly-owned banking subsidiary, Fulton Bank. The company offers standard products such as checking, savings, credit accounts, mortgages, and loans. Commercial lending products include commercial real estate loans, commercial and industrial loans, construction loans, and equipment lease financing loans. The company owns several non-banking units, including among others Fulton Insurance, an agency selling life insurance and related products; Fulton Financial Realty, which holds title to or leases certain properties; and FFC Penn Square, which owns TruPS issued by a subsidiary of Fulton Bank.

	Annual Growth	12/19	12/20	12/21	12/22	12/23
Assets ($mil.)	5.9%	21,886	25,907	25,796	26,932	27,572
Net income ($ mil.)	5.9%	226.3	178.0	275.5	287.0	284.3
Market value ($ mil.)	(1.4%)	2,855.1	2,083.6	2,784.6	2,756.8	2,696.2
Employees	(0.7%)	3,500	3,300	3,200	3,300	3,400

FUNDAMENTAL GLOBAL INC
NMS: FGF

104 S. Walnut Street, Unit 1A
Itasca, IL 60143
Phone: 847 773-1665
Fax: –
Web: www.fgfinancial.com

CEO: Larry G Swets Jr
CFO: Hassan R Baqar
HR: –
FYE: December 31
Type: Public

Property and casualty insurance company 1347 Property Insurance Holdings owns two subsidiaries: Maison Insurance (which offers property and casualty insurance to individuals in Louisiana) and Maison Managers (responsible for our marketing programs and other management services). The insurance unit is looking to offer coverage of wind and hail damage (a policy not offered by some other insurance firms in Louisiana in light of recent severe hurricane and flood damage). Parent Kingsway Financial Services (KSF) spun off 1347 Property in a 2014 IPO (for about $15 million) to gain additional capital and to create a public market for the stock. Following the offering KFS indirectly owned about 33% of the company.

	Annual Growth	12/18	12/19	12/20	12/21	12/22
Assets ($mil.)	(24.0%)	147.9	63.5	34.7	40.8	49.5
Net income ($ mil.)	7.9%	0.8	0.3	(22.5)	(8.5)	1.1
Market value ($ mil.)	1.1%	181.4	255.1	223.7	229.6	189.2
Employees	(34.0%)	37	2	3	9	7

FUNRISE, INC.

7811 LEMONA AVE
VAN NUYS, CA 914051139
Phone: 818 883-2400
Fax: –
Web: www.funrise.com

CEO: King Cheng
CFO: Kevin Stone
HR: –
FYE: December 31
Type: Private

Funrise Toy Corporation wants to make sure you have a blast from funrise to funset. And with toys like Doctor Dreadful's Demented Drink Lab and Gazillion Bubbles who wouldn't? The company creates, markets, and sells toys nationally through specialty toy shops as well as big-name retailers like Costco, KB Toys, Target, Toys "R" Us, and Wal-Mart. Funrise Toy's core products include Gazillion Bubbles (bubble machines and toys), Nylint (radio-controlled cars and trucks), Doctor Dreadful (freaky food and drink making kits), and Tub Town (bathtub toys). It makes products under licenses Tonka, Disney, Sesame Street, Marvel, and NASCAR. The company was acquired by investment firm Matrix Holding Limited in early 2008.

	Annual Growth	12/10	12/11	12/12	12/13	12/14
Sales ($mil.)	22.0%	–	–	5.6	7.1	8.4
Net income ($ mil.)	(31.7%)	–	–	1.1	0.5	0.5
Market value ($ mil.)	–	–	–	–	–	–
Employees	–	–	–	–	–	60

FURMAN FOODS, INC.

770 CANNERY RD
NORTHUMBERLAND, PA 178578615
Phone: 570 473-3516
Fax: –
Web: www.furmanos.com

CEO: David N Geise
CFO: Ted R Hancock
HR: Arnold Laila
FYE: March 28
Type: Private

Furman Foods has firm ideas about tomatoes and other food products. The Pennsylvania company has built a business producing a complete line of canned tomatoes and tomato products. It also offers canned beans; spaghetti, pasta, and pizza sauces; bean salads; vegetables; and ketchup and other condiments. The company's brand names include Furmano's, Conte, and Bella Vista. Furman Foods boasts customers in the foodservice (restaurants, schools, and hospitals), retail (supermarkets and grocery stores), export, branded, manufacturing, and private-label sectors along the US's East Coast. Furman Foods is a family-owned business founded in 1921 by J. W. Furman.

	Annual Growth	04/05	04/06*	03/07	03/08	03/09
Sales ($mil.)	9.2%	–	73.9	77.2	83.4	96.3
Net income ($ mil.)	–	–	(0.7)	13.8	1.2	1.7
Market value ($ mil.)	–	–	–	–	–	–
Employees	–	–	–	–	–	250

*Fiscal year change

FURMAN UNIVERSITY FOUNDATION, INC.

3300 POINSETT HWY
GREENVILLE, SC 296130002
Phone: 864 294-2000
Fax: –
Web: www.furman.edu

CEO: –
CFO: –
HR: –
FYE: June 30
Type: Private

The school's slogan could be, "Go Further than Furman." More than 70% of Furman University's graduates go on to law, medical, or other graduate schools. The private school offers an undergraduate liberal arts curriculum and a graduate program focused on teaching and education. Furman offers more than 40 majors through more than 25 departments to some 2,700 undergraduate and graduate students from US 46 states and 53 foreign countries. It also offers internship and study away programs. The university has 240 faculty members. The student-faculty ratio is 11:1. Its 750-acre campus features a lake, bell tower, amphitheater, and rose and Japanese gardens and is regarded as one of the most beautiful in the US.

	Annual Growth	06/09	06/10	06/11	06/12	06/15
Sales ($mil.)	(83.2%)	–	–	132.8	142.8	0.1
Net income ($ mil.)	–	–	–	83.3	(5.6)	(0.1)
Market value ($ mil.)	–	–	–	–	–	–
Employees	–	–	–	–	–	759

FURMANITE, LLC

10370 RICHMOND AVE STE 600
HOUSTON, TX 770424104
Phone: 713 634-7777
Fax: –
Web: www.teaminc.com

CEO: Jeffery G Davis
CFO: Robert S Muff
HR: –
FYE: December 31
Type: Private

Furmanite thrives under pressure. The specialty contractor provides a variety of technical services for petroleum refineries, chemical plants, nuclear power stations, and other clients in the power generation, manufacturing, and processing industries. Furmanite specializes in sealing leaks in valves, pipes, and other flow-process systems, often under emergency conditions involving exposure to high temperatures and pressures, potential contact with dangerous materials, explosion hazards, and environmental contamination. It also provides onsite machining and custom engineering services, as well as consulting and support services. Company rival Team Inc bought Furmanite in March 2016 for $335 million.

FUTURE FARMERS OF AMERICA INCORPORATED

6060 FFA DR
INDIANAPOLIS, IN 462781370
Phone: 317 802-4404
Fax: –
Web: www.ffa.org

CEO: W D Armstrong
CFO: –
HR: –
FYE: December 31
Type: Private

Known for the national-blue and corn-gold corduroy jackets worn by its members, The National FFA Organization (FFA) is a youth organization that promotes agricultural education through chartered chapters found mostly in high schools. FFA boasts more than 507,000 members aged 12-21 in all 50 states, Puerto Rico, and the Virgin Islands. The organization was founded in 1928 as Future Farmers of America; the name was changed in 1988 to reflect the growing diversity of agriculture and its membership. The organization incorporates classroom instruction and hands-on agricultural work experiences that range from raising animals or planting gardens to starting small businesses.

	Annual Growth	12/17	12/18	12/19	12/21	12/22
Sales ($mil.)	(5.8%)	–	39.0	30.4	26.3	30.8
Net income ($ mil.)	67.9%	–	0.4	0.3	3.2	3.0
Market value ($ mil.)	–	–	–	–	–	–
Employees	–	–	–	–	–	85

FUTURE TECH ENTERPRISE, INC.

500 E BROWARD BLVD STE 2400
FORT LAUDERDALE, FL 333943038
Phone: 631 472-5500
Fax: –
Web: www.ftei.com

CEO: –
CFO: –
HR: –
FYE: December 31
Type: Private

Future Tech Enterprise can help you realize the potential of all sorts of futuristic technologies. The company provides a variety of IT services, including network integration services, project management, systems integration, procurement, and call center support. Future Tech also resells computer systems, software, and peripherals. Its customers range from small businesses to enterprise organizations with complex technology needs; clients include Hofstra University, Honeywell, JetBlue, the New York Islanders, and Northrop Grumman. The company has configuration centers and product warehouses across the US. In 1996 Future Tech got its start in the basement of president and CEO Bob Venero.

	Annual Growth	12/18	12/19	12/20	12/21	12/22
Sales ($mil.)	17.3%	–	271.3	256.0	285.4	438.3
Net income ($ mil.)	0.6%	–	12.9	10.5	12.2	13.1
Market value ($ mil.)	–	–	–	–	–	–
Employees	–	–	–	–	–	143

FUTUREFUEL CORP

8235 Forsyth Blvd., Suite 400
St. Louis, MO 63105
Phone: 314 854-8352
Fax: –
Web: www.futurefuelcorporation.com

NYS: FF
CEO: Paul A Novelly
CFO: Rose M Sparks
HR: –
FYE: December 31
Type: Public

FutureFuel manufactures chemical products, biofuels, and bio-based specialty products for specific customers. Its annual biofuel production capacity is nearly 59 million gallons. Specialty products include laundry detergent additive, biocide and herbicide intermediates, chlorinated polyolefin adhesion promoters and antioxidant precursors. The company serves the cosmetics and personal care, specialty polymers, and the fuel industries. FutureFuel generates vast majority of its revenue in the US. FutureFuel Corp. was created in 2005.

	Annual Growth	12/19	12/20	12/21	12/22	12/23
Sales ($mil.)	15.7%	205.2	204.5	321.4	396.0	368.3
Net income ($ mil.)	(19.3%)	88.2	46.6	26.3	15.2	37.4
Market value ($ mil.)	(16.3%)	542.2	555.8	334.4	355.8	266.1
Employees	0.7%	500	470	470	472	515

FUTURES WITHOUT VIOLENCE

100 MONTGOMERY ST
SAN FRANCISCO, CA 94129
Phone: 415 678-5500
Fax: –
Web: www.futureswithoutviolence.org

CEO: Esta Soler
CFO: –
HR: –
FYE: December 31
Type: Private

The Family Violence Prevention Fund (FVPF) wants to stop the madness. The not-for-profit organization strives to end domestic abuse worldwide through educational and proactive programs. The group works with lawmakers, police, health care providers, employers, and others to address violence aimed at women and children. It publishes newsletters and educational materials for families and teens, campaigns for legislation to protect women, sponsors health care initiatives, and researches issues surrounding domestic abuse. FVPF works on a global scale by partnering with the United Nations and similar groups in China, India, Mexico, and Russia to address human trafficking and other forms of violence.

	Annual Growth	12/17	12/18	12/19	12/21	12/22
Sales ($mil.)	8.2%	–	13.2	20.1	17.4	18.1
Net income ($ mil.)	17.2%	–	1.8	7.7	(1.4)	3.5
Market value ($ mil.)	–	–	–	–	–	–
Employees	–	–	–	–	–	45

FX ENERGY, INC.

3006 S HIGHLAND DR STE 206
SALT LAKE CITY, UT 841064091
Phone: 801 486-5555
Fax: –
Web: –

CEO: David N Pierce
CFO: –
HR: –
FYE: December 31
Type: Private

FX Energy is not exactly fixated on energy in Poland, but it is in western Poland's Permian Basin where it is hoping to make its big breakthrough. The independent exploration and production company reports some proved reserves of 44.1 billion cu. ft. of natural gas equivalent in Poland, and 0.6 million barrels of oil equivalent in the US (from properties in Montana and Nevada). Partners include state-owned Polish Oil and Gas and CalEnergy Gas, which have served as operators for exploration wells in Poland. FX Energy holds about 2.7 million gross acres (2 million net) in western Poland.

G&P TRUCKING COMPANY, INC.

126 ACCESS RD
GASTON, SC 290539501
Phone: 803 791-5500
Fax: –
Web: –

CEO: –
CFO: –
HR: Greg Grubb
FYE: December 31
Type: Private

Founded in 1936, G&P Trucking provides truckload freight hauling and related logistics services. The company, which specializes in asset-based transportation, port drayage, and non-asset brokerage solutions, operates a fleet of more than 350 tractors and around 3,000 trailers from about a dozen terminals in the Carolinas, Georgia, Louisiana, Virginia, Tennessee, and Texas. Some of its business comes from handling cargo coming into and out of ports such as Chareston, Norfolk, and Savannah, it also arranges transportation to and from Mexico.

	Annual Growth	12/03	12/04	12/05	12/06	12/07
Sales ($mil.)	8.8%	–	76.9	84.7	93.4	99.2
Net income ($ mil.)	–	–	3.9	1.9	1.1	(5.1)
Market value ($ mil.)	–	–	–	–	–	–
Employees	–	–	–	–	–	700

G-III APPAREL GROUP LTD.

512 Seventh Avenue
New York, NY 10018
Phone: 212 403-0500
Fax: –
Web: www.g-iii.com

NMS: GIII
CEO: Morris Goldfarb
CFO: Neal S Nackman
HR: –
FYE: January 31
Type: Public

G-III Apparel Group designs, sources, and markets a wide range of men's and women's apparel under 30-plus licensed and proprietary brands, including global brands DKNY, Donna Karan, Calvin Klein, Tommy Hilfiger, and Karl Lagerfeld Paris. The company's offerings include outerwear, dresses, sports and performance wear, as well as handbags, shoes, leather goods, cold weather accessories, and luggage. It also has a team sports business with licenses from the NFL, NBA, MLB, NHL, and more than 150 US colleges and universities. The company also distributes its products through its retail stores and its digital channels and digital channel for its retail partners such as Macy's, Nordstrom, Amazon, and Fanatics. The US accounts for about 80% of sales.

	Annual Growth	01/20	01/21	01/22	01/23	01/24
Sales ($mil.)	(0.5%)	3,160.5	2,055.1	2,766.5	3,226.7	3,098.2
Net income ($ mil.)	5.2%	143.8	23.5	200.6	(133.1)	176.2
Market value ($ mil.)	2.5%	1,244.3	1,236.5	1,242.4	773.7	1,376.0
Employees	(7.9%)	6,400	3,300	3,600	4,700	4,600

G.E.C. ASSOCIATES, INC.

9487 NW 12TH ST
DORAL, FL 331722803
Phone: 305 994-2150
Fax: -
Web: www.gecassociates.com

CEO: -
CFO: -
HR: -
FYE: December 31
Type: Private

GEC Associates provides architectural, engineering, and construction management services for commercial, institutional, industrial, and government clients in Florida. The company performs mechanical, electrical, and plumbing services, as well as renovation, landscaping, painting, and HVAC work. The minority-owned firm has completed more than 220 major projects, including schools, hotels, federal government buildings, corporate facilities, restaurants, country clubs, parking lots, and a US Coast Guard air installation, since it was founded in 1989.

	Annual Growth	12/96	12/97	12/98	12/12	12/13
Sales ($mil.)	6.9%	-	1.7	2.2	-	4.8
Net income ($ mil.)	2.8%	-	0.2	0.2	-	0.3
Market value ($ mil.)	-	-	-	-	-	-
Employees	-	-	-	-	-	20

G.S.E. CONSTRUCTION COMPANY, INC.

7633 SUTHFRONT RD STE 160
LIVERMORE, CA 94551
Phone: 925 447-0292
Fax: -
Web: www.gseconstruction.com

CEO: Dennis Gutierrez
CFO: -
HR: -
FYE: December 31
Type: Private

GSE Construction Company provides heavy construction for government agencies, public utilities, and the private sector. The general engineering contractor specializes in building water and wastewater infrastructure. GSE provides services such as new construction, renovation work and upgrades, and construction labor. Projects range from retrofitting old systems and expanding capacity, to constructing storage tanks, treatment facilities, and pump stations. The company also often teams with fellow engineering firm Applied Technologies to complete waste-to-energy conversion projects. GSE performs most of its work in California and Nevada. President and CEO Orlando Gutierrez founded GSE Construction in 1980.

	Annual Growth	12/07	12/08	12/09	12/10	12/21
Sales ($mil.)	(31.9%)	-	76.2	69.8	63.3	0.5
Net income ($ mil.)	(28.9%)	-	3.8	2.1	0.3	0.0
Market value ($ mil.)	-	-	-	-	-	-
Employees	-	-	-	-	-	140

G1 THERAPEUTICS INC

700 Park Offices Drive, Suite 200
Research Triangle Park, NC 27709
Phone: 919 213-9835
Fax: -
Web: www.g1therapeutics.com

NMS: GTHX
CEO: John E Bailey Jr
CFO: Jennifer K Moses
HR: Ostra Jewell
FYE: December 31
Type: Public

G1 Therapeutics is a biopharmaceutical firm working to develop and delivery of next generation therapies that improve the lives of people affected by cancer. The company's first commercial product is COSELA (trilaciclib) which decreases the incidence of chemotherapy-induced myelosuppression. Another therapy the G1 offers is Rintodestrant, a selective estrogen receptor degrader (SERD) for the treatment of ER+ HER 2- breast cancer. G1 has a deep clinical pipeline evaluating targeted cancer therapies in a variety of solid tumors, including colorectal, breast, lung, and bladder cancers.

	Annual Growth	12/19	12/20	12/21	12/22	12/23
Sales ($mil.)	-	-	45.3	31.5	51.3	82.5
Net income ($ mil.)	-	(122.4)	(99.3)	(148.4)	(147.6)	(48.0)
Market value ($ mil.)	(41.7%)	1,372.4	934.2	530.2	282.0	158.4
Employees	(1.0%)	104	122	148	170	100

G4S SECURE INTEGRATION LLC

9140 W DODGE RD
OMAHA, NE 681143333
Phone: 402 233-7700
Fax: -
Web: www.g4s.com

CEO: John Kenning
CFO: -
HR: -
FYE: December 31
Type: Private

Adesta is adept at putting together communications and security systems. Specializing in systems integration and project management, the company brings together disparate components to create converged communications networks and security systems. Adesta provides design, construction, management, and maintenance of stand-alone or integrated communications networks, including long haul, last mile, mobile backhaul, and broadband networks. It serves clients in the energy, maritime, government, transportation, and broadband telecommunications industries. Adesta has completed projects in Asia, Central America, Europe, and the Middle East, in addition to the US. G4S plc acquired the company in late 2009.

G4S SECURE SOLUTIONS (USA) INC.

1395 UNIVERSITY BLVD
JUPITER, FL 334585289
Phone: 561 622-5656
Fax: -
Web: www.g4s.com

CEO: -
CFO: Joe Schwader
HR: Clare Leifels
FYE: December 31
Type: Private

G4S Secure Solutions (G4S) counters the perils of modern life by providing a full slate of security services to corporate, industrial, and government organizations. The company's offerings include armed guards, background investigations, program development, and security consulting. G4S also provides fire and rescue services, as well as specialized security for airports, nuclear power plants, and US embassies. The company markets security services to federal, state, and local government agencies via its Wackenhut Services subsidiary. Formerly known as Wackenhut Corporation, G4S is the US business unit of UK-based G4S plc, one of the world's largest security companies.

GA COMMUNICATIONS, INC.

2196 W PARK CT
STONE MOUNTAIN, GA 300873528
Phone: 770 498-4091
Fax: -
Web: www.purered.net

CEO: -
CFO: -
HR: -
FYE: September 30
Type: Private

GA Communications is in the business of transforming brands. The company produces advertising for retail clients which have included Lowe's, S.P. Richards Company, and Michaels. Also operating through its PureRed Creative subsidiary, it offers photography, prepress, print management, website design and development, set design and fabrication, visual merchandising, printing, and broadcast services. Established in 1967, employee-owned GA Communications has offices located in Atlanta, Charlotte, Dallas, Minneapolis, Philadelphia, Pittsburgh, and San Francisco.

	Annual Growth	09/02	09/03	09/04	09/05	09/09
Sales ($mil.)	11.4%	-	-	-	25.6	39.4
Net income ($ mil.)	(7.5%)	-	-	-	2.5	1.8
Market value ($ mil.)	-	-	-	-	-	-
Employees	-	-	-	-	-	430

GA TELESIS, LLC

1850 NW 49TH ST
FORT LAUDERDALE, FL 333093004
Phone: 954 676-3111
Fax: –
Web: www.gatelesis.com

CEO: –
CFO: –
HR: –
FYE: December 31
Type: Private

In the market for a big old jet airliner? GA Telesis brokers airplanes, engines, and parts to mid-sized and regional airlines around the world. The company sells and leases aircraft from its fleet of more than 30 planes from such makers as Airbus, Boeing, Bombardier, and Embraer. GA Telesis also maintains a large inventory of engines and replacement components from CFM International, GE, Honeywell, Pratt & Whitney, and Rolls-Royce. In addition, GA Telesis provides engine sales and marketing, parts inventory appraisal, dis-assembly, and technical support and logistics services.

GADSDEN PROPERTIES INC

15150 North Hayden Road, Suite 235
Scottsdale, AZ 85260
Phone: 480 750-8700
Fax: –
Web: www.photomedex.com

NBB: FCRE
CEO: Michael R Stewart
CFO: Michael R Stewart
HR: –
FYE: December 31
Type: Public

For PhotoMedex beauty is skin deep. The company manufactures and markets dermatological treatments for skin disorders such as acne, psoriasis, and vitiligo (loss of skin pigmentation). Other products include gels and creams intended to promote skin rejuvenation and hair growth. PhotoMedex also develops lasers and fiber-optic equipment for dermatological and surgical applications. Its FDA-approved XTRAC Excimer laser system is used for the treatment of psoriasis and eczema, and its VTRAC lamp system is sold outside the US to treat the same ailments. Customers in the US and overseas include consumers, dermatologists, cosmetic surgeons, and spas. PhotoMedex plans to sell its operations to Florida-based DS Healthcare.

	Annual Growth	12/14	12/15	12/16	12/17	12/18
Sales ($mil.)	(87.8%)	163.5	75.9	38.4	–	0.0
Net income ($ mil.)	–	(121.5)	(34.6)	(13.3)	(18.8)	(2.0)
Market value ($ mil.)	(53.1%)	40.8	12.0	58.6	24.2	2.0
Employees	(67.5%)	179	76	6	6	2

GADSDEN REGIONAL MEDICAL CENTER, LLC

1007 GOODYEAR AVE
GADSDEN, AL 359031195
Phone: 256 494-4000
Fax: –
Web: www.gadsdenregional.com

CEO: Stephen Pennington
CFO: Michael Cotton
HR: –
FYE: September 30
Type: Private

Located in northeastern Alabama, Gadsden Regional Medical Center is a general acute care hospital with about 350 beds and a medical staff of some 230 physicians. The hospital provides inpatient medical, surgical, and behavioral health care, as well as trauma care, ambulatory surgery, diagnostic imaging, and other outpatient services. Specialties include cardiology, oncology, neurology, orthopedics, and women's and children's care. Additionally, Gadsden Regional offers home health care and hospice services and runs a retail home medical equipment store. The health system is part of the Triad Hospitals group, which was acquired by Community Health Systems in 2007.

	Annual Growth	09/13	09/14	09/15	09/16	09/17
Sales ($mil.)	(9.5%)	–	243.8	240.9	190.6	180.6
Net income ($ mil.)	–	–	2.6	7.9	8.5	(4.8)
Market value ($ mil.)	–	–	–	–	–	–
Employees	–	–	–	–	–	1,300

GAIA INC (NEW)

833 West South Boulder Road
Louisville, CO 80027
Phone: 303 222-3600
Fax: –
Web: www.gaia.com

NMS: GAIA
CEO: James Colquhoun
CFO: Ned Preston
HR: –
FYE: December 31
Type: Public

If you're into living a healthy, sustainable lifestyle, Gaiam is your kind of company. The name Gaiam (pronounced "guy-um") is a combination of Gaia (the Earth goddess) and "I am." Most of the company's sales come from proprietary products and media for consumers interested in yoga, fitness, and wellness. Other merchandise includes organic cotton apparel, bedding, and personal care and home care products. Gaiam boasts a library of more than 7,000 DVD titles and a TV channel (which the company plans to spin off). It also owns a stake in Real Goods Solar, which designs and installs solar energy systems. Gaiam's offerings are sold through catalogs, its e-commerce site, and major retailers (including Target, and Whole Foods).

	Annual Growth	12/18	12/19	12/20	12/21	12/22
Sales ($mil.)	17.0%	43.8	54.0	66.8	79.6	82.0
Net income ($ mil.)	–	(33.8)	(18.2)	0.5	3.7	(3.1)
Market value ($ mil.)	(30.8%)	215.6	166.2	205.6	178.3	49.5
Employees	(7.3%)	150	135	123	150	111

GAINESVILLE REGIONAL UTILITIES

301 SE 4TH AVE
GAINESVILLE, FL 326016857
Phone: 352 334-3400
Fax: –
Web: www.gru.com

CEO: –
CFO: –
HR: –
FYE: September 30
Type: Private

Multi-service utility Gainesville Regional Utilities (GRU) started out small more than a century ago, but has been gaining ground ever since. The company (now the fifth largest municipal electric utility in Florida) is the sole utilities provider in Gainesville and surrounding areas in Alachua County. The municipal utility distributes electric, water, wastewater, natural gas and telecommunications services to approximately 93,000 retail and wholesale customers. GRU has interests in power generation facilities that give it more than 600 MW of capacity. It also offers internet and other communications services. GRU gets the bulk of its revenues from its electric utility operations.

	Annual Growth	09/05	09/06	09/07	09/08	09/09
Sales ($mil.)	12.0%	–	–	294.8	350.0	369.9
Net income ($ mil.)	32.6%	–	–	19.1	18.3	33.6
Market value ($ mil.)	–	–	–	–	–	–
Employees	–	–	–	–	–	850

GALE'S WILLOUGHBY HILLS GARDEN CENTER, INC.

2730 SOM CENTER RD
WILLOUGHBY HILLS, OH 440949122
Phone: 440 944-6066
Fax: –
Web: www.galeswilloughby.com

CEO: Gerald Silver
CFO: –
HR: –
FYE: December 31
Type: Private

Gale knows how to get your garden to grow. Through four locations in Ohio, Gale's Garden Centers sells flowering trees, shrubs, annuals, perennials, and houseplants. In addition to the usual garden items, Gale's locations offer wildlife feeders, pet supplies, seasonal yard decor, and outdoor furniture. Design centers at some locations carry exclusive gift collections, books on gardening and home decor, personal care items, and 300 lines of collectibles, as well as provide professional decorating and design assistance. The company's Willoughby location includes a glass conservatory to showcase plants year-round.

	Annual Growth	12/05	12/06	12/07	12/09	12/10
Sales ($mil.)	(7.5%)	–	–	6.4	5.6	5.1
Net income ($ mil.)	133.1%	–	–	0.0	0.1	0.2
Market value ($ mil.)	–	–	–	–	–	–
Employees	–	–	–	–	–	5

GALECTIN THERAPEUTICS INC
NAS: GALT

4960 Peachtree Industrial Blvd., Suite 240
Norcross, GA 30071
Phone: 678 620-3186
Fax: 617 928-3450
Web: www.galectintherapeutics.com

CEO: –
CFO: –
HR: –
FYE: December 31
Type: Public

Galectin Therapeutics has a knack for inhibiting galectin proteins. The drug developer is targeting galectin proteins as they play a key role in the development of a variety of diseases. It is developing such inhibitors to treat liver fibrosis, which is currently untreatable. Its GM-CT-01 drug candidate is being investigated for use targeting certain melanomas and in combination with another drug to improve its effectiveness in treating colorectal cancer. Galectin Therapeutics is focused on diseases with serious, life-threatening consequences and on diseases for which there is little to no current treatment available.

	Annual Growth	12/18	12/19	12/20	12/21	12/22
Sales ($mil.)	–	–	–	–	–	–
Net income ($ mil.)	–	(13.9)	(13.3)	(23.5)	(30.5)	(38.8)
Market value ($ mil.)	(24.2%)	203.8	170.0	133.1	123.0	67.2
Employees	18.9%	6	7	6	9	12

GALLAGHER (ARTHUR J.) & CO.
NYS: AJG

2850 Golf Road
Rolling Meadows, IL 60008
Phone: 630 773-3800
Fax: –
Web: www.ajg.com

CEO: J P Gallagher Jr
CFO: Douglas K Howell
HR: –
FYE: December 31
Type: Public

One of the world's largest insurance brokers, Arthur J. Gallagher (Gallagher) provides commercial insurance brokerage, consulting, and third-party property/casualty claims settlement and administration services to businesses and organizations around the world through a network of subsidiaries and agencies. It places (arranges directly with underwriters) traditional and niche/practice groups in addition to offering retirement solutions and managing employee benefits programs. Risk management services include claims management, insurance property appraisal services and loss control consulting. It also has investments in companies that own clean coal production facilities in the US. Most of Gallagher's revenue comes from the US.

	Annual Growth	12/19	12/20	12/21	12/22	12/23
Sales ($mil.)	8.8%	7,195.0	7,003.6	8,209.4	8,550.6	10,072
Net income ($ mil.)	9.7%	668.8	818.8	906.8	1,114.2	969.5
Market value ($ mil.)	24.0%	20,636	26,808	36,767	40,857	48,731
Employees	11.8%	33,300	32,401	39,000	44,000	52,000

GALLAUDET UNIVERSITY

800 FLORIDA AVE NE
WASHINGTON, DC 200023600
Phone: 202 651-5000
Fax: –
Web: www.gallaudet.edu

CEO: –
CFO: –
HR: Hollie Fallstone
FYE: September 30
Type: Private

Gallaudet University (GU) gives deaf and hard-of-hearing students the chance to be in the majority. Designed to accommodate hearing-impaired students, GU offers undergraduate and graduate degrees in more than 40 majors to about 2,000 students annually. The bilingual university, which uses both American Sign Language (ASL) and English, admits a small number of hearing, ASL-proficient students to each incoming freshman class. Through its Laurent Clerc National Deaf Education Center, GU provides training and support for teachers and parents of hearing impaired children and operates demonstration schools. Founded in 1864, GU was named for Thomas Hopkins Gallaudet, a pioneer in education for the deaf.

	Annual Growth	09/16	09/17	09/18	09/21	09/22
Sales ($mil.)	4.5%	–	183.6	187.8	205.7	229.1
Net income ($ mil.)	–	–	9.5	5.6	(7.5)	(4.8)
Market value ($ mil.)	–	–	–	–	–	–
Employees	–	–	–	–	–	1,200

GALLERY MODEL HOMES, INC.

6006 NORTH FWY
HOUSTON, TX 770764029
Phone: 713 694-5570
Fax: –
Web: www.galleryfurniture.com

CEO: –
CFO: –
HR: –
FYE: December 31
Type: Private

Gallery Furniture and its founder, Jim "Mattress Mac" McIngvale, have become something of a Houston institution. McIngvale's animated TV ads, promise they "really will save you money." With two locations, the firm has evolved into a leading regional furniture retailer, accounting for about 20% of Houston's market share. Gallery Furniture also ranks as one of the nation's top sellers in terms of sales per square foot. In addition to mattresses (Simmons Beautyrest and Tempur Sealy brands), it sells bedroom, dining room, home office, and living room furniture. The firm was founded in 1981. A fire in May 2009 destroyed its 100,000-sq.-ft. warehouse and damaged its North Freeway showroom.

	Annual Growth	12/03	12/04	12/05	12/06	12/07
Sales ($mil.)	(1.1%)	–	115.3	130.4	129.5	111.4
Net income ($ mil.)	–	–	(0.0)	0.5	1.0	3.6
Market value ($ mil.)	–	–	–	–	–	–
Employees	–	–	–	–	–	332

GALLUP, INC.

901 F ST NW STE 400
WASHINGTON, DC 200041419
Phone: 202 715-3030
Fax: –
Web: www.gallup.com

CEO: –
CFO: James R Krieger
HR: Ralinda Harter
FYE: December 31
Type: Private

Gallup is a global analytics and advice firm that helps leaders and organizations solve their most pressing problems. The company employs more than 2,000 professionals in approximately 30 offices around the world to provide analytics by knowing more than any other organization about "the will" of some 7 billion employees, customers, students, and citizens. In addition, the company serves over 1,000 education organizations with advice and analytics, including nearly half a million interviews with leaders and their teams and the perspectives of more than 6 million students and alumni captured by the Gallup Student Poll and Gallup Alumni Survey. The Gallup World Poll powers its independent research and metrics. George Gallup founded the company in 1935 as American Institute of Public Opinion.

	Annual Growth	12/07	12/08	12/09	12/11	12/12
Sales ($mil.)	1.4%	–	–	264.1	303.2	275.4
Net income ($ mil.)	48.8%	–	–	7.0	34.0	23.0
Market value ($ mil.)	–	–	–	–	–	–
Employees	–	–	–	–	–	2,000

GAMCO INVESTORS INC
NBB: GAMI

191 Mason Street
Greenwich, CT 06830
Phone: 203 629-2726
Fax: –
Web: www.gabelli.com

CEO: Mario J Gabelli
CFO: Diane M Lapointe
HR: –
FYE: December 31
Type: Public

GAMCO is a widely-recognized provider of investment advisory services to open-end funds, closed-end funds, actively managed semi-transparent exchange traded funds (ETFs), a soci t d'investissement capital variable (SICAV) and approximately 1,400 institutional and private wealth management (Institutional and PWM) investors principally in the US. GAMCO has approximately $35.0 billion in assets under management. GAMCO offers a wide range of solutions for clients across Value and Growth Equity, ESG, Convertibles, sector-focused strategies including Gold and Utilities, Merger Arbitrage, and Fixed Income. Its broker-dealer subsidiary, G.distributors acts and underwriter and distributor of its open-end funds.

	Annual Growth	12/18	12/19	12/20	12/21	12/22
Sales ($mil.)	(6.7%)	341.5	312.4	259.7	301.1	258.7
Net income ($ mil.)	(13.5%)	117.2	81.9	58.7	73.2	65.6
Market value ($ mil.)	(2.5%)	433.7	500.5	455.6	641.5	391.4
Employees	0.3%	172	189	178	168	174

GAMEFLY HOLDINGS, LLC

30 CORPORATE PARK STE 207
IRVINE, CA 926065121
Phone: 310 664-6400
Fax: –
Web: –

CEO: Jeff Walker
CFO: Shosannah Bacura
HR: –
FYE: December 31
Type: Private

GameFly is to gamers what Netflix is to movie lovers. The video game provider offers more than 8,000 titles for rent -- both newer releases and classics -- for entertainment systems such as Microsoft Xbox, Nintendo Wii, and Sony PlayStation, as well as handheld consoles. Some 334,000 members pay a monthly subscription fee to rent games with no due dates or late charges. To support this effort, GameFly maintains shipping centers in Austin, Los Angeles, Pittsburgh, Seattle, and Tampa. Through its Direct2Drive website, gamers can buy video games among 3,000 choices to download to PCs or Macs. Founded in 2002, GameFly counts among its backers venture firms Sequoia Capital and Tenaya Capital.

GAMESTOP CORP

NYS: GME

625 Westport Parkway
Grapevine, TX 76051
Phone: 817 424-2000
Fax: –
Web: www.gamestop.com

CEO: Ryan Cohen
CFO: Diana Saadeh-Jajeh
HR: Chris Toro
FYE: February 3
Type: Public

Established in 1996, GameStop is a retailer of new and pre-owned games and entertainment products through its e-commerce properties and thousands of stores. It boasts about 4,415 stores in the US, Australia, Canada, and Europe. GameStop's stores and e-commerce sites operate primarily under the names GameStop, EB Games, and Micromania. GameStop has a buy-sell-trade program, where gamers can trade-in video game consoles, games, and accessories, as well as consumer electronics for cash or in-store credit. Approximately 70% of the company's revenue comes from US operations.

	Annual Growth	02/20*	01/21	01/22	01/23*	02/24
Sales ($mil.)	(5.0%)	6,466.0	5,089.8	6,010.7	5,927.2	5,272.8
Net income ($ mil.)	–	(470.9)	(215.3)	(381.3)	(313.1)	6.7
Market value ($ mil.)	39.9%	1,173.9	99,353	29,931	6,976.1	4,503.0
Employees	(38.5%)	56,000	52,000	40,000	38,000	8,000

*Fiscal year change

GAMING COMMISSION, NEW YORK

1 BROADWAY CTR STE 600
SCHENECTADY, NY 123052533
Phone: 518 388-3415
Fax: –
Web: www.nylottery.org

CEO: –
CFO: –
HR: –
FYE: March 31
Type: Private

Winning the New York State Lottery could make you king of the hill, top of the heap. The New York State Lottery is one of the largest and oldest state lotteries in the US (only New Hampshire's lottery is older). It runs three jackpot, five daily, and about a dozen scratch-off games through retailers and online outlets. About a third of the lottery's revenue, or some $2 billion a year, goes to support New York State education. It also awards Leaders of Tomorrow scholarships to one eligible graduating senior from every public and private school in the state (provided they attend New York universities). The New York Lottery was established by the new state constitution passed in 1966.

GAMING PARTNERS INTERNATIONAL CORPORATION

3945 W CHEYENNE AVE STE 208
NORTH LAS VEGAS, NV 890328900
Phone: 702 384-2425
Fax: –
Web: www.angelplayingcards.com

CEO: –
CFO: –
HR: –
FYE: December 31
Type: Private

This company doesn't care if gamblers win or crap out, as long as they do it using its products. Gaming Partners International (GPI) is a leading manufacturer of casino gaming products, including dealing shoes, dice, gaming chips, playing cards, and roulette wheels. It also supplies table furniture and layouts for blackjack, poker, baccarat, craps, and other casino games. With manufacturing facilities in the US, Mexico, and France, the company markets its products under the brands Bourgogne et Grasset, Bud Jones, and Paulson to casino operators around the world. GPI is a subsidiary of playing card manufacturer Angel Holdings.

	Annual Growth	12/14	12/15	12/16	12/17	12/18
Sales ($mil.)	3.6%	–	78.2	82.1	80.6	87.0
Net income ($ mil.)	(18.8%)	–	6.9	5.2	3.6	3.7
Market value ($ mil.)	–	–	–	–	–	–
Employees	–	–	–	–	–	709

GAN LTD

NAS: GAN

400 Spectrum Center Drive, Suite 1900
Irvine, CA 92618
Phone: 833 565-0550
Fax: –
Web: www.gan.com

CEO: –
CFO: –
HR: –
FYE: December 31
Type: Public

GAN lets you play cards in the cloud. The company provides its in-house GameSTACK Internet Gaming System software to online and land-based casino gaming operators. It offers simulated gaming for its customers in the US alongside real money gaming in the rest of the world (as well as New Jersey) where online gaming with cash is legal. GAN also produces and brings to market online versions of classic games for desktop, tablet, and mobile devices. The UK-based company's key market is the US, where online gaming is slowly opening up. New Jersey was the first (and so far only) state to allow regulated real money internet-based casino gaming, while much of GAN's new business comes from land-based casinos. The company was founded in 2001 by David McDowell and Kevin O'Neal.

	Annual Growth	12/19	12/20	12/21	12/22	12/23
Sales ($mil.)	44.2%	30.0	35.2	124.2	141.5	129.4
Net income ($ mil.)	–	2.0	(20.2)	(30.6)	(197.5)	(34.4)
Market value ($ mil.)	–	–	–	–	–	–
Employees	49.4%	136	288	682	704	677

GANCEDO LUMBER CO., INC.

9300 NW 36TH AVE
MIAMI, FL 331472898
Phone: 305 836-7030
Fax: –
Web: www.gancedolumberco.net

CEO: Ignacio Perez Sr
CFO: –
HR: –
FYE: December 31
Type: Private

Gancedo Lumber never gets "board" when the subject is building in the Sunshine State. The company produces millwork and rebar; it serves customers in the state of Florida. The Perez family owns and runs the company, along with sister companies Florida Lumber and Gancedo Rebar Services. The family has been in the lumber business for five decades. In 1972 Ignacio Perez brought the family business from Cuba to establish Gancedo Lumber in the US.

	Annual Growth	12/14	12/15	12/16	12/17	12/18
Sales ($mil.)	2.3%	–	48.5	47.9	27.6	51.9
Net income ($ mil.)	(17.7%)	–	7.4	7.9	0.8	4.1
Market value ($ mil.)	–	–	–	–	–	–
Employees	–	–	–	–	–	110

GANNETT CO INC (NEW)   NYS: GCI

7950 Jones Branch Drive   CEO: Michael E Reed
McLean, VA 22107-0910   CFO: Douglas E Horne
Phone: 703 854-6000   HR: Donna Marshall
Fax: –   FYE: December 31
Web: www.gannett.com   Type: Public

Gannett Co., Inc. (formerly known as New Media Investment Group, Inc.) is a subscription-led and digitally focused media and marketing solutions company committed to empowering communities to thrive. The company aims to be the premiere source for clarity, connections, and solutions within its communities. The company's current portfolio of media assets includes USA TODAY, local media organizations in around 45 states in the US, and Newsquest, a wholly owned subsidiary operating in the United Kingdom with more than 150 local news media brands.

	Annual Growth	12/19	12/20	12/21	12/22	12/23
Sales ($mil.)	9.3%	1,867.9	3,405.7	3,208.1	2,945.3	2,663.6
Net income ($ mil.)	–	(119.8)	(670.5)	(135.0)	(78.0)	(27.8)
Market value ($ mil.)	(22.5%)	950.2	500.4	793.8	302.3	342.6
Employees	(14.9%)	24,455	18,141	16,300	14,200	12,800

GANNETT FLEMING, INC.

207 SENATE AVE   CEO: Robert Scaer
CAMP HILL, PA 170112316   CFO: Jon Kessler
Phone: 717 763-7211   HR: –
Fax: –   FYE: December 31
Web: www.gannettfleming.com   Type: Private

Engineering firm Gannett Fleming has waded through water, waste, and sludge for nearly a century. Gannett Fleming operates through more than a dozen subsidiaries that offer a variety of services that range from design/build, construction management, ground testing and soil strengthening, site remediation, structural rehabilitation, electrical and mechanical installation, geophysical mapping and surveying, and 3D visualization. Founded in 1915, Gannett Fleming serves the transportation, water and wastewater, facilities, energy, and environmental industries, working on projects around the world from more than 60 offices across North America and Middle East.

	Annual Growth	12/08	12/09	12/10	12/11	12/13
Sales ($mil.)	3.9%	–	–	–	286.5	309.5
Net income ($ mil.)	27.2%	–	–	–	4.5	7.2
Market value ($ mil.)	–	–	–	–	–	–
Employees	–	–	–	–	–	2,396

GARDNER DENVER INVESTMENTS, INC.

222 E ERIE ST STE 500   CEO: –
MILWAUKEE, WI 532026062   CFO: –
Phone: 217 222-5400   HR: –
Fax: –   FYE: December 31
Web: –   Type: Private

Located far from the Rocky Mountains, Milwaukee-based Gardner Denver designs and manufactures flow control and compression equipment. Products include compressors, pumps, vacuums, and blowers used in industrial and chemical manufacturing plants, oil and gas extraction and processing machinery, and medical and scientific laboratories. It also makes and sells aftermarket parts. The company markets its products under some 20 brands, including CompAir, Nash, Robuschi, and its Gardner Denver namesake. While the company sells in more than 175 countries, customers in North and South America comprise more the half of overall revenue. In 2017, the company went public through an IPO that raised $823 million in proceeds.

GARNEY HOLDING COMPANY

1700 SWIFT AVE STE 200   CEO: –
NORTH KANSAS CITY, MO 641163834   CFO: –
Phone: 816 741-4600   HR: –
Fax: –   FYE: December 31
Web: www.garney.com   Type: Private

Garney Holding Company has garnered more half a century of experience in the water infrastructure business. The company, which operates as Garney Construction, builds water and wastewater pipelines, pumping and storage facilities, and wastewater treatment plants for public and investor-owned utilities, as well as for industrial customers. The employee-owned firm, formed in 1961, has offices in Arizona, Colorado, Florida, Georgia, Kansas, Missouri, and Tennessee. Its subsidiaries include Garney Companies, Garney New Mexico, Grimm Construction Co., and Weaver Construction Management.

GARRETT MOTION INC.

47548 HALYARD DR   CEO: Olivier Rabiller
PLYMOUTH, MI 481703796   CFO: Sean Deason
Phone: 734 359-5901   HR: –
Fax: –   FYE: December 31
Web: www.garrettmotion.com   Type: Private

Garrett Motion Inc. is a global technology leader with significant expertise in delivering products for internal combustion engines (ICE) using gasoline, diesel, natural gas, and electrified powertrains (hybrid and fuel cell). The company designs, manufactures, and sells highly engineered turbochargers and electric-boosting technologies for light and commercial vehicle original equipment manufacturers (OEMs) and the global vehicle independent aftermarket as well as automotive software solutions. Additionally, With its large installed base, currently estimated at more than 120 million vehicles, the company operates through a distribution network of more than 250 distributors covering 165 countries. The company maintains a leading technology portfolio of approximately 1,700 patents and patents pending. Europe generates the majority of the company's revenue.

GARTNER INC   NYS: IT

P.O. Box 10212, 56 Top Gallant Road   CEO: –
Stamford, CT 06902-7700   CFO: –
Phone: 203 964-0096   HR: –
Fax: –   FYE: December 31
Web: www.gartner.com   Type: Public

Gartner helps clients understand the information technology (IT) industry and make informed decisions about IT products. It provides over 15,000 client organizations with competitive analysis reports, industry overviews, market trend data, and product evaluation reports. The company offers their products and services in about 90 countries across all major functions, in every industry and enterprise size. Gartner also offers technology and management consulting services, and produces conferences, seminars, and other events aimed at the technology sector. The US and Canada account for nearly two-thirds of the company's revenue.

	Annual Growth	12/19	12/20	12/21	12/22	12/23
Sales ($mil.)	8.6%	4,245.3	4,099.4	4,734.0	5,475.8	5,907.0
Net income ($ mil.)	39.5%	233.3	266.7	793.6	807.8	882.5
Market value ($ mil.)	30.8%	12,072	12,549	26,190	26,332	35,339
Employees	4.9%	16,724	15,600	16,600	19,500	20,237

GARY RABINE & SONS, INC.

900 NATIONAL PKWY STE 260
SCHAUMBURG, IL 601735117
Phone: 888 722-4633
Fax: –
Web: www.rabine.com

CEO: –
CFO: –
HR: –
FYE: December 31
Type: Private

Gary Rabine & Sons, known as The Rabine Group, provides the Chicago region with what any US metropolitan area at its latitude needs: paving, roofing, and snow removal. It specializes in paving roads, parking lots, driveways, and sidewalks. Rabine and its group of about a dozen companies also provide commercial and industrial roofing, including solar panel and gardentop installation. When winter arrives, it offers snow plowing, blowing, and rooftop shoveling. In addition, the company owns a fuel distribution business, hot mix asphalt plants, and an operation enabling televised views inside pipelines for maintenance crews. Rabine got its start in 1981 and was founded by Gary Rabine.

GAS TRANSMISSION NORTHWEST LLC

717 TEXAS ST STE 2400
HOUSTON, TX 770022834
Phone: 832 320-5000
Fax: –
Web: www.tcplus.com

CEO: Harold N Kvisle
CFO: Russell K Girling
HR: –
FYE: December 31
Type: Private

Gas Transmission Northwest (formerly PG&E Gas Transmission, Northwest) takes the phrase "pipe down" literally. The company pumps nearly 3 billion cu. ft. of gas a day through more than 610 miles of pipeline running from western Canada to the Pacific Northwest, California, and Nevada. Gas Transmission Northwest, a unit of TransCanada, provides firm and interruptible transportation services to more than 100 customers, including gas producers, marketers, and electric and gas utilities. Through Gas Transmission Northwest's pipeline, customers can also store, borrow, or sell their excess capacity.

	Annual Growth	12/13	12/14	12/15	12/16	12/17
Sales ($mil.)	2.8%	–	–	–	212.1	218.0
Net income ($ mil.)	(85.0%)	–	–	–	71.5	10.7
Market value ($ mil.)	–	–	–	–	–	–
Employees	–	–	–	–	–	6

GASCO ENERGY INC.

7979 E. Tufts Avenue, Suite 1150
Denver, CO 80237
Phone: 303 483-0044
Fax: 303 483-0011
Web: www.gascoenergy.com

CEO: –
CFO: –
HR: –
FYE: December 31
Type: Public

Gasco Energy is not your local gas company or energy provider. The exploration and production independent develops and explores for natural gas and crude petroleum primarily in the Rocky Mountains. The company's exploration activities are focused on Utah's Uinta Basin and Wyoming's Green River Basin. At the end of 2008, Gasco Energy's proved reserves stood at 53.1 billion cu. ft. of natural gas equivalent. It had working interests in 330,923 gross acres (214,483 net acres) located in California, Nevada, Utah, and Wyoming. That year it had stakes in 126 gross producing wells (77 net).

	Annual Growth	12/08	12/09	12/10	12/11	12/12
Sales ($mil.)	(32.1%)	41.9	21.1	20.3	18.3	8.9
Net income ($ mil.)	–	14.5	(50.2)	10.1	(7.3)	(22.2)
Market value ($ mil.)	(34.9%)	66.2	90.0	59.4	38.2	11.9
Employees	(9.3%)	37	28	25	25	25

GATE 1, LTD

455 MARYLAND DR
FORT WASHINGTON, PA 190342501
Phone: 215 572-7676
Fax: –
Web: www.gate1travel.com

CEO: –
CFO: –
HR: Melissa Picariello
FYE: December 31
Type: Private

Helen Reddy's I am Woman, Hear Me Roar could easily be the adopted theme song for this company. Gutsy Women Travel caters to women travelers almost exclusively, typically ages 30 to 80. Trips are specially designed for groups of up to 15 women with visits to markets and bazaars, tours of historic homes, and even cooking classes (pizza making in Italy, for example). In addition to the planned itinerary packages offered, the agency also can customize trips based on clients' requests. Packages offered include a variety of US and international destinations. President April Merenda was one of the founders of Gutsy Women, which opened in 2002. The agency is a division of Gate 1 Travel, an international tour operator.

	Annual Growth	12/94	12/95	12/96	12/97	12/20
Sales ($mil.)	(19.7%)	–	16.1	16.1	21.9	0.0
Net income ($ mil.)	–	–	(0.1)	(0.2)	2.6	(0.0)
Market value ($ mil.)	–	–	–	–	–	–
Employees	–	–	–	–	–	200

GATES INDUSTRIAL CORP PLC

1144 Fifteenth Street
Denver, CO 80202
Phone: 303 744-1911
Fax: –
Web: www.gates.com

NYS: GTES
CEO: Ivo Jurek
CFO: L B Mallard
HR: –
FYE: December 30
Type: Public

Gates Industrial Corporation is a global manufacturer of innovative, highly engineered power transmission and fluid power solutions. It offers a broad portfolio of products to diverse replacement channel customers, and to original equipment (first-fit) manufacturers as specified components, with the majority of its revenue coming from replacement channels. The company's products are used in applications across numerous end markets, including industrial off-highway end markets such as construction and agriculture, industrial on-highway end markets such as transportation, diversified industrial, energy and resources, automotive, and mobility and recreation. It sells its products globally under the Gates brand. The North America accounts for nearly 45% of the company's revenue.

	Annual Growth	12/19*	01/21	01/22*	12/22	12/23
Sales ($mil.)	3.7%	3,087.1	2,793.0	3,474.4	3,554.2	3,570.2
Net income ($ mil.)	(23.8%)	690.1	79.4	297.1	220.8	232.9
Market value ($ mil.)	–	–	–	–	–	–
Employees	–	–	14,700	14,300	15,050	15,000	14,700

*Fiscal year change

GATEWAY ENERGY CORPORATION

1415 LOUISIANA ST STE 4100
HOUSTON, TX 77002
Phone: 713 336-0844
Fax: –
Web: www.gatewayenergy.com

CEO: Frederick M Pevow Jr
CFO: –
HR: –
FYE: December 31
Type: Private

The door swings both ways for Gateway Energy, which serves as a go-between for natural gas producers and customers. It owns natural gas gathering, transportation, and distribution systems (totaling 280 miles of pipeline) in Texas, and in the Gulf of Mexico. Gateway Offshore Pipeline Company owns pipelines, and a related operating platform. Onshore Gateway Energy owns two active onshore pipeline system in Texas. The company gathers gas at the wellhead and transports it to distribution companies or its own processing facilities. It also operates a natural gas processing unit and and a gas marketing company.

GATX CORP
NYS: GATX

233 South Wacker Drive
Chicago, IL 60606-7147
Phone: 312 621-6200
Fax: –
Web: www.gatx.com

CEO: Brian A Kenney
CFO: Thomas A Ellman
HR: Craig Samuda
FYE: December 31
Type: Public

GATX Corporation, founded in 1898, is the leading global railcar lessor. Its wholly owned fleet of approximately 144,000 railcars is one of the largest railcar lease fleets in the world. It currently lease tank cars, freight cars, and locomotives in North America, tank cars and freight cars in Europe and Russia, and freight cars in India. In addition, jointly with Rolls-Royce plc, it owns one of the largest aircraft spare engine lease portfolios in the world. Almost 65% of company's total revenue comes from US operations.

	Annual Growth	12/19	12/20	12/21	12/22	12/23
Sales ($mil.)	0.3%	1,393.8	1,209.2	1,257.4	1,273.0	1,410.9
Net income ($ mil.)	5.3%	211.2	151.3	143.1	155.9	259.2
Market value ($ mil.)	9.8%	2,938.3	2,950.0	3,695.1	3,771.3	4,263.6
Employees	(1.7%)	2,165	1,904	1,863	1,904	2,020

GAUCHO GROUP HOLDINGS INC
NAS: VINO

112 NE 41st Street, Suite 106
Miami, FL 33137
Phone: 212 739-7700
Fax: –
Web: www.gauchogroup.com

CEO: Scott L Mathis
CFO: Maria I Echevarria
HR: –
FYE: December 31
Type: Public

Diversified Private Equity Corporation (DPEC) is a venture capital company that is focused on the biotechnology industry. The company's subsidiaries (InvestPrivate and InvestBio) offer brokerage transactions, investment advice, biotechnology publications, and a mutual fund. After withdrawing its plans for an IPO under investigation from the NASD for a number of fraudulent "self-offerings" held between 2000 and 2003, the company announced in late 2008 a letter of intent for a reverse merger with Mercari Communications Group, a transaction expected to provide DPEC with a public company platform.

	Annual Growth	12/18	12/19	12/20	12/21	12/22
Sales ($mil.)	(14.7%)	3.1	1.3	0.6	4.9	1.6
Net income ($ mil.)	–	(5.7)	(6.7)	(5.6)	(2.2)	(21.8)
Market value ($ mil.)	–	–	–	–	0.8	0.4
Employees	4.9%	66	65	69	80	80

GC SERVICES LIMITED PARTNERSHIP

6330 GULFTON ST
HOUSTON, TX 770811108
Phone: 713 777-4441
Fax: –
Web: www.gcserv.com

CEO: Frank A Taylor
CFO: Lourdes Barras
HR: Neva Rushing
FYE: December 31
Type: Private

GC Services considers it a Good Call when it Gets Cash. As one of the US' top collection agencies, the family-owned company provides a wide range of services, including customer relations and receivables management, to clients throughout North America from more than 30 call centers. Its customer care services division provides inbound and outbound call center management services, including general reception and operator services, billing and payment assistance, and back-office processing of accounts. Its receivables management division provides debt collection, data management, and other services. The company can take operator-assisted calls in various languages and handles about 20 million calls each month.

GCP APPLIED TECHNOLOGIES INC.

2325 LAKEVIEW PKWY
ALPHARETTA, GA 300097941
Phone: 617 876-1400
Fax: –
Web: www.gcpat.com

CEO: –
CFO: –
HR: –
FYE: December 31
Type: Private

GCP Applied Technologies is a global provider of construction products and technologies that include admixtures and additives for concrete and cement, the in-transit concrete monitoring and management system, high-performance waterproofing products and specialty construction products. Serving a diverse array of customers, including contractors, engineers, specialty distributors, home centers, developers and owners of industrial warehouses and manufacturing facilities, GCP operates in more than 30 countries. Among its key brands are CONCERA, PIERI, DUCTILCRETE, OPTEVA, PREPRUFE, VYCOR and MONOKOTE. North America generates about 55% of the total sales. In 2021, GCP agreed to be acquired by Saint-Gobain for a cash transaction valued at approximately $2.3 billion (approximately ?2.0 billion).

GCT SEMICONDUCTOR, INC.

2290 N 1ST ST STE 201
SAN JOSE, CA 951312017
Phone: 408 434-6040
Fax: –
Web: www.gctsemi.com

CEO: John Schlaefer
CFO: Gene Kulzer
HR: –
FYE: December 31
Type: Private

While not a household name, GCT Semiconductor enables activities most people are familiar with. The fabless semiconductor company's wireless communications chips include LTE-based radio-frequency (RF) transceivers for cell phones, WiMAX networking chips, and RF transceivers for WLAN equipment. Its single-chip LTE product for smartphones is used in mobile devices made by LG and sold by AT&T and Verizon, among others. Unlike many chip developers, GCT has its semiconductors fabricated with a CMOS silicon process. GCT was co-founded in 1998 by CEO Kyeongho Lee. The company filed an IPO in 2011 but withdrew it in 2014.

	Annual Growth	06/05	06/06	06/07	06/08*	12/13
Sales ($mil.)	(11.6%)	–	–	–	41.4	22.4
Net income ($ mil.)	–	–	–	–	(16.5)	(26.6)
Market value ($ mil.)	–	–	–	–	–	–
Employees	–	–	–	–	–	210

*Fiscal year change

GEE GROUP INC
ASE: JOB

7751 Belfort Parkway, Suite 150
Jacksonville, FL 32256
Phone: 630 954-0400
Fax: 630 954-0447
Web: www.geegroup.com

CEO: Derek E Dewan
CFO: Kim Thorpe
HR: –
FYE: September 30
Type: Public

The GEE Group Inc. is a provider of permanent and temporary professional, industrial and physician staffing and placement services near several major US cities. The company specializes in the placement of professionals in the information technology, engineering, medical and accounting field for either direct hire or contract staffing. It also offers temporary staffing services for its commercial clients. The company is able to provide these services through its subsidiaries, namely Access Data Consulting Corporation, Agile Resources, Inc., BMCH, Inc., Paladin Consulting, Inc., Scribe Solutions, Inc., SNI Companies, Inc., Triad Logistics, Inc., and Triad Personnel Services, Inc. The company operates in about 30 branches across eleven states.

	Annual Growth	09/19	09/20	09/21	09/22	09/23
Sales ($mil.)	0.1%	151.7	129.8	148.9	165.1	152.4
Net income ($ mil.)	–	(17.8)	(14.3)	0.0	19.6	9.4
Market value ($ mil.)	(5.6%)	83.1	111.5	51.8	70.3	66.0
Employees	(7.6%)	344	258	271	309	251

GEISINGER HEALTH

100 N ACADEMY AVE
DANVILLE, PA 178229800
Phone: 800 275-6401
Fax: –
Web: www.geisinger.org

CEO: Jaewon Ryu
CFO: –
HR: Amanda Bryan
FYE: June 30
Type: Private

Founded more than 100 years ago by Abigail Geisinger, Geisinger Health includes ten hospital campuses, a health plan with more than half a million members, a research institute and the Geisinger Commonwealth School of Medicine. With nearly 24,000 employees and more than 1,700 employed physicians, Geisinger Health offers women's health, sleep services, surgery, senior health, dental medicine, and addiction treatment, among others. Its Geisinger Health Plan is an integrated health system that provides its member and patients with exceptional healthcare. Geisinger Health System serves more than 1 million residents.

	Annual Growth	06/16	06/17	06/18	06/19	06/20
Sales ($mil.)	4.0%	–	6,337.4	6,536.6	7,145.6	7,121.7
Net income ($ mil.)	–	–	553.0	359.4	174.1	(190.3)
Market value ($ mil.)	–	–	–	–	–	–
Employees	–	–	–	–	–	13,030

GELBER GROUP, LLC

350 N ORLEANS ST FL N
CHICAGO, IL 606541975
Phone: 312 253-0005
Fax: –
Web: www.gelbergroup.com

CEO: –
CFO: –
HR: –
FYE: December 31
Type: Private

Gelber Group develops proprietary technology-based trading models for dealing in equities, cash, currencies, commodities, sovereign debt, futures, and related options markets. The company no longer has outside clients or investors; all of its trading activity is undertaken for its own account. Gelber Group, which previously provided electronic trading services to individual professional traders, was co-founded in 1982 by Brian Gelber (company chairman and president) and Frank Gelber (CFO). In addition to its Chicago Apparel Center headquarters, the company also boasts offices in Connecticut, New Jersey, and New York, as well as the UK.

	Annual Growth	12/01	12/02	12/03	12/04	12/07
Assets ($mil.)	65.9%	–	–	44.8	106.8	338.9
Net income ($ mil.)	33.3%	–	–	35.8	70.2	112.9
Market value ($ mil.)	–	–	–	–	–	–
Employees	–	–	–	–	–	300

GEMSTONE SOLUTIONS GROUP, INC

71 STEVENSON ST STE 2200
SAN FRANCISCO, CA 941052979
Phone: 415 278-7000
Fax: –
Web: www.gymboree.com

CEO: Daniel Griesemer
CFO: Liyuan Woo
HR: –
FYE: January 30
Type: Private

Gymboree sells clothes and accessories for kids in the US, Puerto Rico, and Canada. Its 950-plus locations include stores under the names Gymboree and Gymboree Outlet (colorful, fashionable playsuits and rompers), Janie and Jack (better newborn and toddler apparel), and Crazy 8 (bold styles meant to be mixed and matched). Gymboree's offerings -- tees & tops, jeans & pants, activewear, sleepwear, shoes -- cater to both girls and boys, from newborns through 14 years. The company is owned by a group of its former lenders, including Searchlight Capital, Oppenheimer, and others. It emerged from bankruptcy protection late in 2017 only to file again in early 2019; all Gymboree and Crazy 8 stores are being shuttered and Janie and Jack locations are expected to be sold at auction.

GEN DIGITAL INC

NMS: GEN

60 E. Rio Salado Parkway, Suite 1000
Tempe, AZ 85281
Phone: 650 527-8000
Fax: –
Web: www.symantec.com

CEO: Vincent Pilette
CFO: Natalie Derse
HR: Lynn Boyle
FYE: March 31
Type: Public

Gen Digital is a global company powering Digital Freedom with a family of trusted brands including Norton, Avast, LifeLock, Avira, AVG, ReputationDefender and CCleaner. The company provides products and services in Cyber Safety, covering security, privacy and identity protection to approximately 500 million users in more than 150 countries so they can live their digital lives safely, privately, and confidently today and for generations to come. Gen's Cyber Safety portfolio provides protection across three key categories in multiple channels and geographies, including security and performance, identity protection, and online privacy.

	Annual Growth	03/19*	04/20	04/21	04/22*	03/23
Sales ($mil.)	(8.3%)	4,731.0	2,490.0	2,551.0	2,796.0	3,338.0
Net income ($ mil.)	156.8%	31.0	3,887.0	554.0	836.0	1,349.0
Market value ($ mil.)	(7.1%)	14,714	11,706	13,709	17,242	10,982
Employees	(25.3%)	11,900	3,600	2,800	2,700	3,700

*Fiscal year change

GENASYS INC

NAS: GNSS

16262 West Bernardo Drive
San Diego, CA 92127
Phone: 858 676-1112
Fax: –
Web: www.genasys.com

CEO: Richard S Danforth
CFO: Dennis D Klahn
HR: –
FYE: September 30
Type: Public

High-tech sound may drive development for LRAD (formerly American Technology Corporation), but the firm is also banking on it to drive its bottom line. LRAD, whose past sales largely came from its portable radios, discontinued its portable consumer electronics division to make products that transmit sound over short and long distances. The company's Long Range Acoustic Devices generate the majority of revenues nowadays, and they have been deployed by the US military and used by public safety agencies worldwide. To strengthen its identity as a global provider of long-range acoustic technology systems, the company changed its name to LRAD in 2010.

	Annual Growth	09/19	09/20	09/21	09/22	09/23
Sales ($mil.)	6.0%	37.0	43.0	47.0	54.0	46.7
Net income ($ mil.)	–	2.8	11.9	0.7	(16.2)	(18.4)
Market value ($ mil.)	(12.0%)	124.7	228.8	192.8	103.1	74.8
Employees	22.5%	83	105	148	172	187

GENCO SHIPPING & TRADING LTD

NYS: GNK

299 Park Avenue, 12th Floor
New York, NY 10171
Phone: 646 443-8550
Fax: –
Web: www.gencoshipping.com

CEO: John C Wobensmith
CFO: Apostolos Zafolias
HR: –
FYE: December 31
Type: Public

Marine transportation company Genco Shipping & Trading transports dry cargo in a wet environment. The company maintains a fleet of about 50 oceangoing dry bulk carriers, which it charters mainly on long-term contracts to shippers of bulk commodities and marine transportation companies. Its fleet has an overall capacity of almost 4 million deadweight tons (DWT). Genco Shipping's vessels transport cargo such as coal, grain, iron ore, and steel products. More than half of its vessels are on time-charter contracts. Customers have included BHP Billiton, Lauritzen Bulkers, and NYK; clients Cargill and Pacific Basin Shipping make up about 10% of the company's revenues. Genco Shipping & Trading was founded in 2004.

	Annual Growth	12/19	12/20	12/21	12/22	12/23
Sales ($mil.)	(0.4%)	389.5	355.6	547.1	536.9	383.8
Net income ($ mil.)	–	(56.0)	(225.6)	182.0	158.6	(12.9)
Market value ($ mil.)	–	–	–	–	–	–
Employees	(5.8%)	1,255	960	1,027	1,086	990

GENCOR INDUSTRIES INC

ASE: GENC

5201 North Orange Blossom Trail
Orlando, FL 32810
Phone: 407 290-6000
Fax: –
Web: www.gencor.com

CEO: –
CFO: Eric E Mellen
HR: –
FYE: September 30
Type: Public

Gencor Industries is a leading manufacturer of heavy machinery used in the production of highway construction materials, and environmental control equipment. Subsidiary Bituma designs and manufactures hot-mix asphalt batch plants used in the production of asphalt paving materials. Subsidiary General Combustion engineers combustion systems, namely large burners that can transform almost any fuel into energy or burn multiple fuels simultaneously, and fluid heat transfer systems under the Hy-Way brand. Other companies include H&B (Hetherington & Berner), Thermotech Systems and Blaw-Knox. The company's products are manufactured in the US and sold through a combination of company sales representatives and independent dealers and agents located throughout the world.

	Annual Growth	09/19	09/20	09/21	09/22	09/23
Sales ($mil.)	6.6%	81.3	77.4	85.3	103.5	105.1
Net income ($ mil.)	9.5%	10.2	5.5	5.8	(0.4)	14.7
Market value ($ mil.)	5.0%	170.2	161.7	162.6	132.1	207.1
Employees	(1.3%)	334	316	380	367	317

GENE BIOTHERAPEUTICS INC

NBB: CRXM

11230 Sorrento Valley Rd., Suite 220
San Diego, CA 92121
Phone: 858 414-1477
Fax: –
Web: www.genbiotherapeutics.com

CEO: Christopher J Reinhard
CFO: James L Grainer
HR: –
FYE: December 31
Type: Public

At the heart of Cardium Therapeutics is a hope to hit it big with one of its assorted holdings. Its Cardium Biologics unit includes lead candidate Generx which is in development as a treatment for candidates ischemic heart disease (such as angina), and restoring heart functioning after a heart attack. Meanwhile its Tissue Repair Company business received FDA approval for Excellagen, a topical gel intended to promote healing diabetic foot ulcers and other wounds, in 2012. A third business, To Go Brands, develops and sells nutritional supplements and skin care products.

	Annual Growth	12/16	12/17	12/18	12/19	12/20
Sales ($mil.)	–	–	–	–	–	–
Net income ($ mil.)	–	–	(2.9)	(1.9)	(0.4)	0.9	(0.5)
Market value ($ mil.)	(29.3%)	6.1	4.0	2.1	7.5	1.5
Employees	(15.9%)	6	–	–	4	3

GENECA, L.L.C.

4138 WINDSWEPT DR
MONTGOMERY, TX 773565399
Phone: 630 599-0900
Fax: –
Web: www.geneca.com

CEO: Joel Basgall
CFO: –
HR: –
FYE: December 31
Type: Private

Geneca wants to be a source of good technology for its customers. The company develops customized enterprise software and provides a range of related information technology services such as consulting, application integration, project development, and risk assessment. Geneca serves customers in such industries as financial services, health care, retail, and consumer goods, as well as the public sector. The company markets its software development services under the Getting Predictable brand. Its clients have included FTD. The company was founded in 1998 by CEO Mark Hattas and president Joel Basgall.

GENELINK INC

NBB: GNLK Q

8250 Exchange Drive, Suite 120
Orlando, FL 32809
Phone: 407 680-1150
Fax: –
Web: www.genelink.info

CEO: –
CFO: –
HR: –
FYE: December 31
Type: Public

GeneLink has taken the science of molecular genetics and turned it into a way to sell face cream and vitamins. Although the promise of immortality is out of its reach, the biosciences company aims to improve one's health, beauty, and wellness with customized nutritional supplements and anti-aging skin care products based upon proprietary DNA assessments obtained from a cheek swab. Other consumer genomic products in development include products to predict how an individual's skin will age, or if an individual has a significant risk of developing cardiovascular disease, Alzheimer's, ADHD, or loss of bone density.

	Annual Growth	12/08	12/09	12/10	12/11	12/12
Sales ($mil.)	(23.9%)	6.4	8.6	7.8	4.7	2.1
Net income ($ mil.)	–	(2.6)	(2.7)	(2.4)	(3.8)	(3.1)
Market value ($ mil.)	(48.2%)	35.5	30.4	10.4	15.5	2.6
Employees	–	–	–	–	–	–

GENERAC HOLDINGS INC

NYS: GNRC

S45 W29290 Hwy. 59
Waukesha, WI 53189
Phone: 262 544-4811
Fax: –
Web: www.generac.com

CEO: Aaron P Jagdfeld
CFO: York A Ragen
HR: –
FYE: December 31
Type: Public

Generac Holdings is a leading global designer and manufacturer of a wide range of energy technology solutions. The company provides power generation equipment, energy storage systems, grid service solutions, and other power products serving the residential, light commercial and industrial markets. Generac's residential generator products provide emergency standby power for homes. The company's light-commercial standby generators and related transfer switches provide three-phase power sufficient for grocery stores, convenience stores, restaurants, gas stations, pharmacies, retail banks, small health care facilities, and other small-footprint retail applications. Other products include light towers, mobile energy storage systems, mobile heaters, mobile pumps, and related controllers for power generation equipment. The US accounts for some 85% of the company's sales.

	Annual Growth	12/19	12/20	12/21	12/22	12/23
Sales ($mil.)	16.2%	2,204.3	2,485.2	3,737.2	4,564.7	4,022.7
Net income ($ mil.)	(3.9%)	252.0	350.6	550.5	399.5	214.6
Market value ($ mil.)	6.5%	6,049.3	13,676	21,164	6,053.5	7,772.2
Employees	10.9%	5,689	6,797	9,540	9,500	8,600

GENERAL ATLANTIC LLC

677 WASHINGTON BLVD STE 800 # 8
STAMFORD, CT 069013716
Phone: 203 629-8600
Fax: –
Web: www.generalatlantic.com

CEO: William E Ford
CFO: Thomas J Murphy
HR: –
FYE: December 31
Type: Private

General Atlantic helps little fish become bigger fish in the world of business. The private equity firm provides both capital and strategic support to public and private growth companies. With about $17 billion in assets under management, General Atlantic focuses its investments on several sectors, such as Internet and technology, health care, and financial and business services. Typical investments range from $75 million to $400 million per transaction, and its average investment period lasts from five to 10 years. Established in 1980, General Atlantic has stakes in about 40 firms. Founded in 1980, the firm's current portfolio holdings include companies the likes of Tory Burch, Bazaarvoice, and Facebook.

	Annual Growth	12/18	12/19	12/20	12/21	12/22
Assets ($mil.)	33.9%	–	–	–	41.9	56.1
Net income ($ mil.)	(36.6%)	–	–	–	5.6	3.5
Market value ($ mil.)	–	–	–	–	–	–
Employees	–	–	–	–	–	536

GENERAL CABLE CORPORATION

4 TESSENEER DR
HIGHLAND HEIGHTS, KY 410769136
Phone: 859 572-8000
Fax: –
Web: www.generalcable.com

CEO: Michael T McDonnell
CFO: Matti M Masanovich
HR: Debra Eanes
FYE: December 31
Type: Private

General Cable is a leading designer, manufacturer and provider of the highest quality copper, aluminum, and fiber optic wire and cable products and system solutions. The company's customer base spans the globe, working in all areas of the energy, construction, industrial, specialty, and communications markets. It also magnifies the value of its products and technologies with expertise in distribution and logistics, marketing, sales, and technical and customer service. This creates a unique mix of products, technologies and services that makes General Cable a strong, important partner to customers striving to compete and expand globally, both in established and emerging markets. General Cable is a brand of Prysmian Group.

GENERAL CASUALTY CO. OF WISCONSIN (SUN PRAIRIE)

One General Drive
Sun Prairie, WI 53596-0001
Phone: 608 837-4440
Fax: 608 837-0583
Web: www.gencas.com

CEO: –
CFO: –
HR: –
FYE: December 31
Type: Public

Despite its name General Casualty Insurance Companies (GCIC) gets very specific about its property/casualty products. The company administers personal and commercial auto, homeowners, liability, and workers' compensation coverage through regional offices. GCIC's products are sold through more than 1,000 independent insurance agencies in all 50 states though it focuses on the northeastern and midwestern US. The company specializes in packages for large commercial accounts; it also serves niche and small business clients including golf courses and restaurants (read: niche). Its individual auto insurance segment includes nonstandard policies. GCIC is a subsidiary of QBE Regional Insurance.

	Annual Growth	12/97	12/98	12/99	12/00	12/01
Assets ($mil.)	9.0%	834.2	958.4	992.0	1,057.4	1,178.6
Net income ($ mil.)	–	31.6	36.1	35.2	13.1	(24.2)
Market value ($ mil.)	–	–	–	–	–	–
Employees	–	–	–	–	–	–

GENERAL DYNAMICS CORP

11011 Sunset Hills Road
Reston, VA 20190
Phone: 703 876-3000
Fax: –
Web: www.gd.com

NYS: GD
CEO: Phebe N Novakovic
CFO: Jason W Aiken
HR: –
FYE: December 31
Type: Public

General Dynamics is a global aerospace and defense company that specializes in high-end design, engineering and manufacturing to deliver state-of-the-art solutions to our customers. The company offers a broad portfolio of products and services in business aviation; ship construction and repair; land combat vehicles, weapons systems and munitions; and technology products and services. The company operates through four operating segments: Technologies, Marine Systems, Aerospace, and Combat Systems. Working with a network of global partners and through its about 40,000 employees, including technologists, engineers, mission experts and cleared personnel, General Dynamics offers a comprehensive support for more than 3,000 Gulfstream aircraft in service worldwide. More than 85% of the company's total sales come from North America.

	Annual Growth	12/19	12/20	12/21	12/22	12/23
Sales ($mil.)	1.8%	39,350	37,925	38,469	39,407	42,272
Net income ($ mil.)	(1.2%)	3,484.0	3,167.0	3,257.0	3,390.0	3,315.0
Market value ($ mil.)	10.2%	48,249	40,717	57,037	67,883	71,046
Employees	2.0%	102,900	100,700	103,100	106,500	111,600

GENERAL ELECTRIC CO

One Financial Center, Suite 3700
Boston, MA 02111
Phone: 617 443-3000
Fax: –
Web: www.ge.com

NYS: GE
CEO: H L Culp Jr
CFO: Carolina D Happe
HR: –
FYE: December 31
Type: Public

General Electric (GE) is an American multinational company. The company produces aircraft engines, locomotives and other transportation equipment, generators and turbines, lighting, and oil and gas exploration and production equipment. Its equipment and solutions are deployed in more than 64,000 commercial and military aircraft (including GE and its joint venture partners), 45,000 onshore wind turbines, 7,700 gas turbines, and more than four million healthcare installations. About 45% of GE's revenue comes from its US operations. GE was formed in 1892 by merging the Edison General Electric Company and the Thomson-Houston Company.

	Annual Growth	12/19	12/20	12/21	12/22	12/23
Sales ($mil.)	(8.1%)	95,214	79,619	74,196	76,555	67,954
Net income ($ mil.)	–	(4,979.0)	5,704.0	(6,520.0)	225.0	9,481.0
Market value ($ mil.)	83.9%	12,147	11,755	102,823	91,198	138,915
Employees	(11.6%)	205,000	174,000	168,000	172,000	125,000

GENERAL FINANCE CORPORATION

39 E UNION ST STE 206
PASADENA, CA 911033929
Phone: 626 584-9722
Fax: –
Web: www.unitedrentals.com

CEO: Jody E Miller
CFO: Charles E Barrantes
HR: –
FYE: June 30
Type: Private

General Finance Corporation wants to help you get your hands on some equipment. The investment holding company is building up a portfolio of specialty financing and equipment leasing companies in North America, Europe, and the Asia-Pacific. It made its first acquisition of RWA Holdings and its subsidiaries (collectively known as Royal Wolf) in 2007. Royal Wolf leases and sells portable storage containers, portable buildings, and freight containers to customers in the defense, mining, moving and storage, and road and rail markets in Australia. General Finance acquired Pac-Van, a provider of modular buildings and mobile offices, in 2008. CEO Ronald Valenta owns 20% of the company.

GENERAL HARDWARE AND BUILDERS SUPPLY, INC.

1100 INDUSTRIAL RD STE 7
SAN CARLOS, CA 940704131
Phone: 650 368-2885
Fax: –
Web: www.generalhardware.co

CEO: –
CFO: –
HR: –
FYE: March 31
Type: Private

General Hardware and Builder's Supply tells you right up front what they do. The company sells architectural and residential hardware and aluminum, steel, and wood doors and frames. Products include hollow metal doors and frames, seven-ply and five-ply architectural wood doors (manufactured by Algoma Hardwoods, Buell Door, Haley Lynden, Pacific Architetural, V.T. Industries, Western Oregon Door), Schlage locks, and Hager hinges.

	Annual Growth	03/03	03/04	03/05	03/08	03/09
Sales ($mil.)	8.8%	–	4.1	4.4	5.6	6.2
Net income ($ mil.)	(42.8%)	–	1.3	0.0	0.0	0.0
Market value ($ mil.)	–	–	–	–	–	–
Employees	–	–	–	–	–	12

GENERAL HEALTH SYSTEM

8585 PICARDY AVE
BATON ROUGE, LA 708093748
Phone: 225 387-7000
Fax: -
Web: www.brgeneral.org

CEO: Mark F Slyter
CFO: Kendall Johnson
HR: -
FYE: September 30
Type: Private

Injured? We're sending you to the General. General Health System provides a comprehensive range of health services to residents of southern Louisiana. The system's flagship facility is the not-for-profit, community-owned Baton Rouge General Medical Center, aka "the General". The medical center, founded in 1927, houses some 550 beds split between two campuses in Louisiana's capital. It provides general medical and surgical care, emergency services, and specialty care in a number of areas, including burn, cancer, and heart disease. General Health System is affiliated with Advanced Medical Concepts (a supplier of medical equipment) and First Care Physicians (a network of primary care physicians).

	Annual Growth	09/14	09/15	09/19	09/21	09/22
Sales ($mil.)	4.2%	–	86.9	101.9	106.1	115.9
Net income ($ mil.)	17.1%	–	3.9	8.3	9.5	11.8
Market value ($ mil.)	–	–	–	–	–	–
Employees	–	–	–	–	–	3,400

GENERAL INSURANCE COMPANY OF AMERICA

SAFECO Plaza
Seattle, WA 98185
Phone: 206 545-5000
Fax: -
Web: www.safeco.com

CEO: -
CFO: -
HR: -
FYE: December 31
Type: Public

While the name doesn't tell you much about the business, Safeco does sound secure, and with insurance that counts for a lot. Safeco Insurance offers personal property/casualty insurance including auto, homeowners, and fire coverage. In addition to its bread and butter standard products, it also offers specialty products including classic car insurance, rental property insurance, and personal umbrella coverage. Its policies are sold and maintained nationally through a network of independent agents and brokers. Safeco is a subsidiary of Liberty Mutual.

	Annual Growth	12/97	12/98	12/99	12/00	12/01
Assets ($mil.)	4.0%	1,845.1	2,109.6	2,231.2	2,006.9	2,158.6
Net income ($ mil.)	–	118.3	174.4	38.4	39.1	(19.9)
Market value ($ mil.)	–	–	–	–	–	–
Employees	–	–	–	–	–	–

GENERAL MILLS INC   NYS: GIS

Number One General Mills Boulevard
Minneapolis, MN 55426
Phone: 763 764-7600
Fax: 763 764-8330
Web: www.generalmills.com

CEO: Jeffrey L Harmening
CFO: Kofi A Bruce
HR: Taylor Behrman
FYE: May 28
Type: Public

General Mills is one of the leading global manufacturers and marketers of branded consumer foods with more than 100 brands in 100 countries. It offers a variety of human and pet food products that provide great taste, nutrition, convenience, and value for consumers around the world. Some of its market-leading brands include Betty Crocker, Gold Medal, Pillsbury, and Yoplait. While most of the company's sales come from the US, General Mills is working to extend the reach and position of its brands globally and has facilities across six major continents. In addition to its consolidated operations, the company has a 50% interest in two strategic joint ventures that manufacture and market food products sold in approximately 130 countries worldwide.

	Annual Growth	05/19	05/20	05/21	05/22	05/23
Sales ($mil.)	4.5%	16,865	17,627	18,127	18,993	20,094
Net income ($ mil.)	10.3%	1,752.7	2,181.2	2,339.8	2,707.3	2,593.9
Market value ($ mil.)	12.4%	30,978	36,979	36,874	40,997	49,380
Employees	(4.0%)	40,000	35,000	35,000	32,500	34,000

GENERAL MOLY, INC.

1726 COLE BLVD STE 115
LAKEWOOD, CO 804013213
Phone: 303 928-8599
Fax: -
Web: www.generalmoly.com

CEO: Ricardo M Campoy
CFO: -
HR: -
FYE: December 31
Type: Private

General Moly, reporting for molybdenum duty. The mineral development, exploration, and mining company (formerly Idaho General Mines) finds and exploits molybdenum oxide (moly), a mineral used primarily as an alloy in steel production. Steel makers create moly-enhanced pipes valued by the construction, aircraft manufacturing, and desalinization industries for their strength and resistance to heat and corrosion. Refiners use the pipes and employ the mineral to remove sulfur from diesel fuel and crude oil. General Moly owns two properties in Nevada, one (Mt. Hope) in an 80/20 joint venture with Korean steel company POSCO and one outright.

GENERAL MOTORS CO   NYS: GM

300 Renaissance Center
Detroit, MI 48265-3000
Phone: 313 667-1500
Fax: -
Web: www.gm.com

CEO: Mary T Barra
CFO: Paul A Jacobson
HR: -
FYE: December 31
Type: Public

General Motors (GM), one of the world's largest auto manufacturers, makes and sells trucks, crossovers, cars and automobile parts and provide software-enabled services and subscriptions worldwide under well-known brands such as Buick, Cadillac, Chevrolet, and GMC. Business divisions GM North America and GM International handle the automotive end of the business while General Motors Financial Co. provides financing services. Cruise segment responsible for the development and commercialization of autonomous vehicle technology. GM's biggest single market is the US, which accounts for about 80% of sales.

	Annual Growth	12/19	12/20	12/21	12/22	12/23
Sales ($mil.)	5.8%	137,237	122,485	127,004	156,735	171,842
Net income ($ mil.)	10.7%	6,732.0	6,427.0	10,019	9,934.0	10,127
Market value ($ mil.)	(0.5%)	42,252	48,071	67,684	38,835	41,467
Employees	(0.2%)	164,000	155,000	157,000	167,000	163,000

GENERAL MOTORS FINANCIAL CO INC

801 Cherry Street, Suite 3500
Fort Worth, TX 76102
Phone: 817 302-7000
Fax: -
Web: www.gmfinancial.com

CEO: Daniel E Berce
CFO: Susan Sheffield
HR: Terricka Brooks
FYE: December 31
Type: Public

General Motors Financial Company (better known as GM Financial), the wholly-owned captive finance subsidiary of General Motors Company (GM), is a global provider of automobile finance solutions. It works with GM dealers worldwide to offer new- and used-vehicle financing services (including auto leases) for consumers and dealerships through offices in the US and Canada, as well as in Europe and Latin America. Founded in 1992 as AmeriCredit, the company traditionally provided credit to customers with less-than-ideal credit histories. More than 90% of its revenue comes from the US customers.

	Annual Growth	12/18	12/19	12/20	12/21	12/22
Assets ($mil.)	2.8%	109,920	109,217	113,825	113,786	122,545
Net income ($ mil.)	18.4%	1,570.0	1,567.0	2,009.0	3,789.0	3,084.0
Market value ($ mil.)	–	–	–	–	–	–
Employees	(2.6%)	10,000	10,000	9,000	9,000	9,000

GENERAL SPORTS AND ENTERTAINMENT, L.L.C.

400 WATER ST STE 250
ROCHESTER, MI 483072091
Phone: 248 601-0003
Fax: –
Web: www.generalsportsworldwide.com

CEO: –
CFO: –
HR: –
FYE: December 31
Type: Private

General Sports & Entertainment provides sports teams with management consulting and executive placement services. The firm advises clients in sports marketing, hospitality programs, recruiting, and team management strategies. It facilitates corporate sponsorship deals, including the naming of sports facilities. Through its GSE Meetings and Events division, the company organizes meetings, conferences and events such as the Sports Executive Leadership Conference, an industry networking event. It owns an English soccer team, the Derby County Football Club, and provides management services for other teams. General Sports & Entertainment was founded in 1998 by owner, Chairman and CEO Andy Appleby.

GENEREX BIOTECHNOLOGY CORP (DE)

NBB: GNBT Q

10102 USA Today Way
Miramar, FL 33025
Phone: 416 364-2551
Fax: –
Web: www.generex.com

CEO: –
CFO: –
HR: –
FYE: July 31
Type: Public

Generex Biotechnology knows that needles can be a real pain for diabetics, so it has developed Oral-lyn, an oral insulin spray that allows the drug to be absorbed through the inside lining of the cheeks. Though the product has been approved for use in some developing countries, Oral-lyn is still undergoing clinical trials in the US. Generex also sells a line of over-the-counter energy and diet supplement glucose sprays available at retail stores and pharmacies in North America. The sprays are administered via Generex's handheld aerosol applicator RapidMist. Through its Antigen Express subsidiary, the company is developing vaccines for disease such as cancer, flu, and HIV.

	Annual Growth	07/16	07/17	07/18	07/19	07/20
Sales ($mil.)	–	–	–	0.7	6.2	2.7
Net income ($ mil.)	–	(3.2)	(70.0)	36.3	(9.3)	(33.3)
Market value ($ mil.)	183.5%	0.6	415.4	168.6	230.3	41.9
Employees	–	–	–	4	4	–

GENESCO INC.

NYS: GCO

535 Marriott Drive
Nashville, TN 37214
Phone: 615 367-7000
Fax: –
Web: www.genesco.com

CEO: Mimi E Vaughn
CFO: Thomas A George
HR: –
FYE: February 3
Type: Public

Genesco is a leading retailer and wholesaler of branded footwear, apparel, and accessories through some 1,410 shoe and accessory stores in the US, Canada, Puerto Rico, the UK, and the Republic of Ireland. Genesco's shoe operations include Journeys, upscale Johnston & Murphy, Schuh, as well as sales of licensed brands (Levi's, G.H. Bass and Dockers footwear). It also sells wholesale footwear through various brands. Through the use of youth-oriented decor and multi-channel media, Journeys retail footwear stores target customers in the 13-to-22-year age group. Founded in 1934 as a shoe retailer, Genesco expanded overseas with the purchase of Scotland's Schuh.

	Annual Growth	02/20*	01/21	01/22	01/23*	02/24
Sales ($mil.)	1.4%	2,197.1	1,786.5	2,422.1	2,384.9	2,324.6
Net income ($ mil.)	–	61.4	(56.4)	114.9	71.9	(16.8)
Market value ($ mil.)	(7.5%)	451.1	445.2	722.1	547.9	330.5
Employees	(4.9%)	22,050	19,000	18,000	19,000	18,000

*Fiscal year change

GENESEE & WYOMING INC.

20 WEST AVE
DARIEN, CT 068204401
Phone: 203 202-8900
Fax: –
Web: www.gwrr.com

CEO: –
CFO: –
HR: –
FYE: December 31
Type: Private

Genesee & Wyoming (G&W) owns or leases about 115 freight railroads with approximately 7,300 employees serving some 3,000 customers. The company's North American operations include some 110 short line and regional railroads that serve roughly 45 US states and five Canadian provinces over more than 13,000 track-miles, while its UK/Europe operations include the UK's largest rail-centric intermodal logistics franchise and the leading heavy haul freight rail provider, as well as regional rail services in Continental Europe. G&W subsidiaries and joint ventures also provide rail service at more than 30 major ports, rail-ferry service between the US Southeast and Mexico, transload services, and railcar switching and repair.

GENESEE VALLEY GROUP HEALTH ASSOCIATION

1425 PORTLAND AVE BLDG 1
ROCHESTER, NY 146213011
Phone: 585 338-1400
Fax: –
Web: www.rochesterregional.org

CEO: –
CFO: –
HR: –
FYE: December 31
Type: Private

Primary care is the primary concern of Lifetime Health Medical Group. The organization, a subsidiary of The Lifetime Healthcare Companies, offers up family practitioners, as well as internists, pediatricians, OB/GYNs, and specialists to about 100,000 patients in Upstate New York. Lifetime Medical operates about 10 family health centers in Buffalo and Rochester that offer diagnostic, therapeutic, and pharmacy services; the group also includes several affiliated physicians offices, a family medicine center for deaf patients, and a primary care practice staffed exclusively by female physicians. Lifetime Health Medical Group has been active in the Buffalo and Rochester communities since the 1970s.

	Annual Growth	12/03	12/04*	06/06*	12/09	12/12
Sales ($mil.)	0.2%	–	106.6	106.6	120.0	107.9
Net income ($ mil.)	(0.4%)	–	3.9	3.9	(2.1)	3.8
Market value ($ mil.)	–	–	–	–	–	–
Employees	–	–	–	–	–	576

*Fiscal year change

GENESIS CORP.

950 3RD AVE 26TH FL
NEW YORK, NY 100222705
Phone: 212 688-5522
Fax: –
Web: www.genesis10.com

CEO: Harley Lippman
CFO: Glenn Klein
HR: Lori Jenniges
FYE: December 31
Type: Private

Genesis Corp.'s raison d'etre is business and technology consulting. Focused on helping organizations streamline processes, manage employees, and minimize costs, the company (doing business as Genesis10) provides services in areas such as project management, application development, enterprise systems integration, staffing, and management support. The company's managed service program assists businesses in managing its workforce, as well as outsourced work. Genesis10, founded in 1999, also helps organizations with their hiring, compliance, and change management issues.

	Annual Growth	12/09	12/10	12/13	12/20	12/21
Sales ($mil.)	1.2%	–	173.6	175.1	159.7	197.6
Net income ($ mil.)	(0.4%)	–	10.6	2.0	4.5	10.1
Market value ($ mil.)	–	–	–	–	–	–
Employees	–	–	–	–	–	2,105

GENESIS ENERGY L.P.
NYS: GEL

811 Louisiana, Suite 1200
Houston, TX 77002
Phone: 713 860-2500
Fax: –
Web: www.genesisenergy.com

CEO: –
CFO: –
HR: –
FYE: December 31
Type: Public

Genesis Energy is a provider of an integrated suite of midstream services (primarily transportation, storage, sulfur removal, blending, terminaling, and processing) for a large area of the Gulf of Mexico and the Gulf Coast region of the crude oil and natural gas industry. The company is also one of the leading producers of natural soda ash (Na2CO3). Additionally, Genesis is one of the largest producers of sodium hydrosulfide (NaHS), a by-product derived from our refinery sulfur removal services process. Its largest customers include Shell, Exxon Mobil Corporation, Phillips 66, Occidental Petroleum Corporation (Occidental), and ANSAC.

	Annual Growth	12/19	12/20	12/21	12/22	12/23
Sales ($mil.)	6.4%	2,480.8	1,824.7	2,125.5	2,789.0	3,177.0
Net income ($ mil.)	5.2%	96.0	(416.7)	(165.1)	75.5	117.7
Market value ($ mil.)	(13.3%)	2,508.1	760.5	1,311.6	1,250.4	1,418.1
Employees	(0.7%)	2,200	1,914	1,903	2,109	2,137

GENESIS HEALTH SYSTEM

1227 E RUSHOLME ST
DAVENPORT, IA 528032459
Phone: 563 421-1000
Fax: –
Web: www.genesishealth.com

CEO: Doug Cropper
CFO: Mark Rogers
HR: Heidi K McMahon
FYE: June 30
Type: Private

Genesis Health System operates three acute care hospitals in Iowa and Illinois that have more than 660 beds total and employ some 700 doctors. Genesis Medical Center in Davenport, Iowa, with more than 500 beds, is the system's flagship facility; the hospital offers a range of general, surgical, and specialist health services. The system's Illini Campus in Silvis, Illinois, features an assisted-living center. The Genesis Medical Center Dewitt Campus serves that Iowa town and the surrounding area with its 13-bed hospital, nursing home, and related care facilities. Genesis Health System also operates physician practices, outpatient centers, and a home health agency.

	Annual Growth	06/18	06/19	06/20	06/21	06/22
Sales ($mil.)	3.7%	–	646.6	648.8	706.7	721.6
Net income ($ mil.)	–	–	–	13.8	4.9	74.0	(83.1)
Market value ($ mil.)	–	–	–	–	–	–
Employees	–	–	–	–	–	5,000

GENESIS HEALTH, INC.

3599 UNIVERSITY BLVD S STE 1
JACKSONVILLE, FL 322164259
Phone: 904 858-7600
Fax: –
Web: www.brooksrehab.org

CEO: Douglas M Baer
CFO: –
HR: –
FYE: December 31
Type: Private

Genesis Health helps people get back on their feet -- literally. The company (doing business as Brooks Rehabilitation) operates a 160-bed facility dedicated to helping patients recover from injury and illness. Rehab services include physical, occupational, speech, aquatic, and recreational therapy. The hospital also helps patients coping with chronic pain, cognitive disorders, and other long-term disabilities. Brooks Rehabilitation provides outpatient care through a network of more than two dozen clinics, a nursing home, and a home health care agency in northern Florida and southeastern Georgia.

	Annual Growth	12/10	12/11	12/13	12/14	12/22
Sales ($mil.)	(8.3%)	–	123.5	140.3	37.4	47.4
Net income ($ mil.)	–	–	(19.6)	20.6	15.2	7.1
Market value ($ mil.)	–	–	–	–	–	–
Employees	–	–	–	–	–	1,400

GENESIS HEALTHCARE INC
NBB: GENN

101 East State Street
Kennett Square, PA 19348
Phone: 610 444-6350
Fax: –
Web: www.genesishcc.com

CEO: Robert H Fish
CFO: Thomas Divittorio
HR: Jeanne Phillips
FYE: December 31
Type: Public

Genesis Healthcare is one of the nation's largest post-acute care providers with nearly 250 skilled nursing centers and senior living communities in more than 20 US states. The company offers inpatient services, rehabilitation and respiratory therapy services and a full complement of administrative services to its affiliated operators through its administrative services subsidiaries and management services to third-party operators with whom the company contract through its management services subsidiary. Genesis subsidiaries also supply rehabilitation therapy to approximately 1,100 locations in about 45 US states and the District of Columbia.

	Annual Growth	12/16	12/17	12/18	12/19	12/20
Sales ($mil.)	(9.1%)	5,732.4	5,373.7	4,976.7	4,565.8	3,906.2
Net income ($ mil.)	–	(64.0)	(579.0)	(235.2)	14.6	(59.0)
Market value ($ mil.)	(41.9%)	708.9	127.2	196.8	273.5	80.8
Employees	(14.4%)	82,000	68,700	61,300	55,000	44,000

GENESIS HEALTHCARE SYSTEM

2951 MAPLE AVE
ZANESVILLE, OH 437011406
Phone: 740 454-5000
Fax: –
Web: www.genesishcs.org

CEO: Matthew Perry
CFO: –
HR: –
FYE: December 31
Type: Private

Genesis HealthCare System is an integrated healthcare delivery system based in Zanesville, Ohio. The not-for-profit health care system consists of Genesis Hospital, is a network of more than 300 physicians, and multiple outpatient care centers throughout its six-country service region in southeastern Ohio. In addition to general medical, emergency, and surgical care, Genesis Hospital offers specialties such as open-heart surgery, trauma care, a Level II special care nursery, neurosurgery and comprehensive cancer services. The organization also operates a drug and alcohol recovery program.

	Annual Growth	12/08	12/09	12/10	12/19	12/21
Sales ($mil.)	3.2%	–	353.9	369.4	2.6	513.8
Net income ($ mil.)	11.4%	–	23.9	15.6	1.3	86.8
Market value ($ mil.)	–	–	–	–	–	–
Employees	–	–	–	–	–	3,500

GENESISCARE USA, INC.

1419 SE 8TH TER
CAPE CORAL, FL 339903213
Phone: 239 931-7333
Fax: –
Web: www.genesiscare.com

CEO: Kimberly C Tzoumakas
CFO: Todd Higgins
HR: –
FYE: December 31
Type: Private

21st Century Oncology operates almost 180 radiation treatment centers in several countries, including seven that involve hospital-based treatment centers and other groups. The company provides a wide variety of radiation therapy services, including image-guided radiation therapy, tomotherapy for treatment directly into affected areas, seed implantation for prostate cancer, and stereotactic radiosurgery for treating brain tumors. Its centers also participate in clinical research trials for cancer treatment.Faced with declining revenues, 21st Century Oncology filed for Chapter 11 bankruptcy protection in May 2017.

GENETHERA, INC.

3051 W. 105th Ave., #350251
Westminster, CO 80035
Phone: 720 587-5100
Fax: –
Web: www.genethera.net

NBB: GTHR
CEO: Antonio Milici
CFO: Tannya L Irizarry
HR: –
FYE: December 31
Type: Public

GeneThera does its part to protect the world's fauna. GeneThera, formerly called Hand Brand Distribution, develops genetic diagnostic assays for the agriculture and veterinary industries. The biotech company has developed assays that detect Chronic Wasting Disease in elk and deer, and Mad Cow Disease in cattle. The company is working on cancer detection tests for animals, as well as similar tests for humans, through its partnership with Xpention, a biotechnology company focused on oncology diagnostics. GeneThera is also developing vaccines for animal diseases, such as E. coli .

	Annual Growth	12/17	12/18	12/19	12/20	12/21
Sales ($mil.)	–	–	–	–	–	–
Net income ($ mil.)	–	(0.8)	(4.0)	(0.5)	(0.8)	(1.0)
Market value ($ mil.)	34.0%	0.3	0.3	0.2	0.5	1.1
Employees	–	2	2	2	2	2

GENICA CORPORATION

43195 BUSINESS PARK DR
TEMECULA, CA 925903629
Phone: 855 433-5747
Fax: –
Web: www.genica.com

CEO: –
CFO: –
HR: –
FYE: December 31
Type: Private

Think of Genica as computerdom's bargain basement. The company sells computer components, peripherals, and accessories -- mainly overstocks and closeouts -- over the Internet. It operates through two business units: Computer Geeks (which targets consumers through its geeks.com website) and Evertek Computer (which markets to small businesses and FORTUNE 500 firms via evertek.com). The company, which offers more than 3,000 brand-name products, was formed by the merger of online seller Computer Geeks with computer importer/distributor Evertek Computer and its Hong Kong-based sister firm Evertek Trading. Chairman and CEO Frank Segler owns a majority stake in Genica.

	Annual Growth	12/05	12/06	12/07	12/08	12/09
Sales ($mil.)	(49.4%)	–	–	672.7	164.7	172.5
Net income ($ mil.)	53932.2%	–	–	0.0	3.6	5.5
Market value ($ mil.)	–	–	–	–	–	–
Employees	–	–	–	–	–	334

GENIE ENERGY LTD

520 Broad Street
Newark, NJ 07102
Phone: 973 438-3500
Fax: –
Web: www.genie.com

NYS: GNE
CEO: –
CFO: –
HR: –
FYE: December 31
Type: Public

Genie Energy is a global provider of residential and commercial energy services. The company operates through two subsidiaries ? Genie Retail Energy (GRE) and Genie Renewables. GRE resells electricity and natural gas bought from the wholesale commodities markets, reselling those commodities to residential and small to large commercial customers throughout the US. Genie Renewables holds Genie Solar Energy, an integrated solar energy company, a 93.5% interest in CityCom Solar, a marketer of community solar energy solutions, Diversegy, an energy broker for commercial, and a 60% controlling interest in Prism Solar, a solar solutions company that is engaged in manufacturing of solar panels, solar installation design and solar energy project management. The majority of the company's revenue comes from the US.

	Annual Growth	12/19	12/20	12/21	12/22	12/23
Sales ($mil.)	8.0%	315.3	379.3	363.7	315.5	428.7
Net income ($ mil.)	47.1%	4.2	13.2	29.2	87.8	19.5
Market value ($ mil.)	38.1%	211.9	197.7	152.7	283.5	771.2
Employees	–	163	202	186	172	–

GENMARK DIAGNOSTICS, INC.

5964 LA PLACE CT STE 100
CARLSBAD, CA 920088829
Phone: 760 448-4300
Fax: –
Web: diagnostics.roche.com

CEO: –
CFO: –
HR: –
FYE: December 31
Type: Private

GenMark Diagnostics knows the secrets that DNA holds are just as helpful to doctors as they are to CSI detectives. The company makes molecular diagnostic equipment designed to detect diseases and determine the best medications for a person's genotype. Its XT-8 system is FDA-approved to test for cystic fibrosis and sensitivity to the blood thinner warfarin, and the company is seeking approval for other diagnostics including tests for viral respiratory infections and thrombosis. The XT-8 is compact and easy-to-use workstation and disposable test cartridges that supports a broad range of molecular tests for aiding in the diagnosis of certain infectious diseases and genetic conditions. GenMark Diagnostics was formed by Osmetech in 2010.

	Annual Growth	12/15	12/16	12/17	12/18	12/19
Sales ($mil.)	29.5%	–	–	52.5	70.8	88.0
Net income ($ mil.)	–	–	–	(61.9)	(50.5)	(47.4)
Market value ($ mil.)	–	–	–	–	–	–
Employees	–	–	–	–	–	618

GENOCEA BIOSCIENCES INC

100 Acorn Park Drive
Cambridge, MA 02140
Phone: 617 876-8191
Fax: –
Web: www.genocea.com

NBB: GNCA Q
CEO: William Clark
CFO: Diantha Duvall
HR: –
FYE: December 31
Type: Public

Genocea Biosciences seeks a panacea for human infection. It does this using its proprietary ATLAS technology that acts through T cells to target infectious diseases. The company's lead candidate is GEN-009, an adjuvanted peptide vaccine which will begin phase 1 clinical trials targeting a range of tumor types. Genocea believes its T-cell methodology allows it to develop vaccines more quickly than the traditional method, which uses B cells, or antibodies. It also thinks certain infections respond better to T cell treatments, which operate at the cellular level. Genocea is seeking to partner with others to develop general cancer vaccines as well as a vaccine that will target cancers caused by the Epstein-Barr Virus.

	Annual Growth	12/17	12/18	12/19	12/20	12/21
Sales ($mil.)	–	–	–	–	1.4	1.6
Net income ($ mil.)	–	(56.7)	(27.8)	(39.0)	(43.7)	(33.2)
Market value ($ mil.)	–	67.5	16.7	120.5	140.9	67.5
Employees	9.2%	52	61	59	72	74

GENTEX CORP.

600 N. Centennial
Zeeland, MI 49464
Phone: 616 772-1800
Fax: 616 772-7348
Web: www.gentex.com

NMS: GNTX
CEO: Steven R Downing
CFO: Kevin C Nash
HR: –
FYE: December 31
Type: Public

Gentex focuses on designing and manufacturing interior and exterior auto-dimming rearview mirrors and camera-based driver-assist systems for the automotive market. The company sells its products to OEM customers' sales through to Tier 1 suppliers such as Volkswagen, Toyota, and General Motors. To a lesser degree, Gentex also makes dimmable aircraft windows found on commercial aircraft (mainly for Boeing) and fire protection products (smoke detectors, fire alarms, and signaling devices), primarily for commercial buildings. Gentex serves customers worldwide, but about 30% of its sales are generated in the US.

	Annual Growth	12/19	12/20	12/21	12/22	12/23
Sales ($mil.)	5.5%	1,858.9	1,688.2	1,731.2	1,919.0	2,299.2
Net income ($ mil.)	0.2%	424.7	347.6	360.8	318.8	428.4
Market value ($ mil.)	3.0%	6,707.6	7,853.3	8,066.2	6,311.8	7,559.3
Employees	–	5,874	5,303	4,998	5,466	–

GENTHERM INC   NMS: THRM

21680 Haggerty Road   CEO: Phillip M Eyler
Northville, MI 48167   CFO: Matteo Anversa
Phone: 248 504-0500   HR: –
Fax: –   FYE: December 31
Web: www.gentherm.com   Type: Public

Gentherm is a global developer, manufacturer, and marketer of innovative thermal management technologies for a broad range of heating and cooling, and temperature control applications, as well as lumbar and massage comfort solutions, in the automotive and medical industries. It develops thermoelectric device (TED) technology for its climate-control seats (CCS) for vehicles. Its automotive products can be found on the vehicles of nearly every automotive manufacturer in North America, Europe, and several OEMs in Asia. The company's industrial segment also makes battery thermal management products, food or beverage cooling storage units, and hospital patient temperature management systems. The company sells its products worldwide, but the US represents its largest market that generates around 40% of the company's total sales.

	Annual Growth	12/19	12/20	12/21	12/22	12/23
Sales ($mil.)	10.9%	971.7	913.1	1,046.2	1,204.7	1,469.1
Net income ($ mil.)	1.8%	37.5	59.7	93.4	24.4	40.3
Market value ($ mil.)	4.2%	1,400.1	2,057.2	2,741.0	2,059.4	1,651.5
Employees	5.5%	11,726	11,519	10,474	14,568	14,504

GENUINE PARTS CO.   NYS: GPC

2999 Wildwood Parkway   CEO: Paul D Donahue
Atlanta, GA 30339   CFO: Carol B Yancey
Phone: 678 934-5000   HR: –
Fax: –   FYE: December 31
Web: www.genpt.com   Type: Public

Genuine Parts Company (GPC) is a global service organization engaged in the distribution of automotive and industrial replacement parts. The company is the sole member and majority owner of National Automotive Parts Association (NAPA), a voluntary trade association that distributes auto parts nationwide. GPC serves a diverse customer base through a network of more than 10,600 locations in more than 15 countries throughout North America, Australasia, and Europe. The majority of the company's sales were generated in the US. GPC was founded by Carlyle Fraser in 1928 with the purchase of Motor Parts Depot in Atlanta, Georgia.

	Annual Growth	12/19	12/20	12/21	12/22	12/23
Sales ($mil.)	4.5%	19,392	16,537	18,871	22,096	23,091
Net income ($ mil.)	20.7%	621.1	(29.1)	898.8	1,182.7	1,316.5
Market value ($ mil.)	6.9%	14,826	14,017	19,567	24,216	19,330
Employees	2.2%	55,000	50,000	52,000	58,000	60,000

GENVEC, INC.

910 CLOPPER RD STE 220N   CEO: –
GAITHERSBURG, MD 208781353   CFO: –
Phone: 240 632-0740   HR: –
Fax: –   FYE: December 31
Web: www.genvec.com   Type: Private

GenVec is all over the medical map. The clinical-stage biopharmaceutical firm develops gene-based drugs and vaccines for everything from cancer to HIV. GenVec has multiple vaccine candidates for contagious diseases, such as HIV, malaria, and foot-and-mouth, through grants and partnerships with several federal agencies including the US departments of Health and Human Services, Homeland Security, and Agriculture. The company's other drug research and development programs target cancers and hearing and balance disorders, mostly through collaborations with other drugmakers. Biotech research firm Intrexon bought GenVec in 2017 to expand its gene delivery platform; the price of the purchase was not disclosed.

GENWORTH FINANCIAL, INC. (HOLDING CO)   NYS: GNW

6620 West Broad Street   CEO: Rohit Gupta
Richmond, VA 23230   CFO: Jerome T Upton
Phone: 804 281-6000   HR: –
Fax: –   FYE: December 31
Web: www.genworth.com   Type: Public

Genworth Financial, through its principal insurance subsidiaries, offers mortgage and long-term care insurance products. Genworth Financial is the parent company of Enact Holdings, a leading provider of private mortgage insurance in the US through its mortgage insurance subsidiaries. Genworth Financial's US life insurance subsidiaries offer long-term care insurance and also manage in-force blocks of life insurance and annuity products which are no longer sold. The Runoff segment primarily includes variable annuity, variable life insurance and corporate-owned life insurance products, which have not been actively sold since 2011. Majority of its revenue comes from the US.

	Annual Growth	12/19	12/20	12/21	12/22	12/23
Assets ($mil.)	(2.7%)	101,342	105,747	99,171	86,442	90,817
Net income ($ mil.)	(31.4%)	343.0	178.0	904.0	609.0	76.0
Market value ($ mil.)	11.0%	1,966.0	1,689.0	1,809.6	2,363.7	2,984.8
Employees	(3.4%)	3,100	3,000	2,500	2,500	2,700

GEO GROUP INC (THE) (NEW)   NYS: GEO

4955 Technology Way   CEO: Jose Gordo
Boca Raton, FL 33431   CFO: Brian R Evans
Phone: 561 893-0101   HR: Kamerinn Tipp
Fax: –   FYE: December 31
Web: www.geogroup.com   Type: Public

The GEO Group specializes in the ownership, leasing, and management of secure facilities, processing centers, and reentry facilities and the provision of community-based services in the US, Australia, and South Africa. It owns, leases, and operates secure facilities, including maximum, medium, and minimum-security facilities, processing centers, as well as community-based reentry facilities. It provides technologies, monitoring services, and evidence-based supervision and treatment programs for community-based programs. It also provides secure transportation services domestically and in the UK through its joint venture GEOAmey. Worldwide operations include the management and ownership of approximately 82,000 beds at more than 100 facilities. About 90% of GEO's revenue derives from the US.

	Annual Growth	12/19	12/20	12/21	12/22	12/23
Sales ($mil.)	(0.7%)	2,477.9	2,350.1	2,256.6	2,376.7	2,413.2
Net income ($ mil.)	(10.4%)	166.6	113.0	77.4	171.8	107.3
Market value ($ mil.)	(10.1%)	2,094.3	1,117.1	977.2	1,380.7	1,365.5
Employees	(7.1%)	22,000	20,000	15,800	15,800	16,400

GEOBIO ENERGY INC

13110 NE 177th, PL #169   CEO: –
Woodinville, WA 98072   CFO: –
Phone: 425 402-3699   HR: –
Fax: –   FYE: September 30
Web: www.geobioenergyinc.com   Type: Public

GeoBio Energy used to think biodiesel was the way of the future, but lately it's decided that the oil and gas industry isn't going anywhere anytime soon. Though it acquired GeoAlgae Technologies, which develops low-cost, renewable feedstock used for the production of biodiesel, in 2008, GeoBio Energy has since switched directions. In 2009 it agreed to buy H&M Precision Products, which makes chemicals used in the drilling of oil and gas wells. In 2010 it also agreed to acquire a Colorado-based oil field site preparation and maintenance company.

	Annual Growth	09/08	09/09	09/10	09/11	09/12
Sales ($mil.)	–	–	–	–	–	–
Net income ($ mil.)	–	(18.5)	(1.2)	(2.8)	(2.9)	(1.9)
Market value ($ mil.)	(9.6%)	0.2	0.0	0.0	0.5	0.1
Employees	–	–	–	–	–	–

GEOKINETICS INC.

1500 CITYWEST BLVD # 800
HOUSTON, TX 770422300
Phone: 713 850-7600
Fax: –
Web: www.geokineticsinc.com

CEO: –
CFO: –
HR: –
FYE: December 31
Type: Private

Using kinetic energy to assess the Earth's hydrocarbon sources, Geokinetics is a global provider of geophysical services to the oil and gas industry. It acquires seismic data in North America and internationally and processes and interprets that data at processing centers in the US and the UK. The company's seismic crews work in a range of terrains, including land, marsh, swamp, shallow water, and difficult transition zones (between land and water). Not dependent on any one customer, its client base consists of international and national oil companies, as well as smaller independent oil and gas exploration and production companies.

	Annual Growth	12/07	12/08	12/09	12/10	12/11
Sales ($mil.)	22.3%	–	–	511.0	558.1	763.7
Net income ($ mil.)	–	–	–	(5.0)	(138.7)	(222.1)
Market value ($ mil.)	–	–	–	–	–	–
Employees	–	–	–	–	–	5,695

GEOPETRO RESOURCES CO

150 California Street, Suite 600
San Francisco, CA 94111
Phone: 415 398-8186
Fax: –
Web: www.geopetro.com

CEO: –
CFO: –
HR: –
FYE: December 31
Type: Public

You have to drill down deep to figure out exactly what GeoPetro Resources does. It's an oil and natural gas exploration and production company with projects in Canada, Indonesia, and the US. These sites cover about 1 million gross acres consisting of mineral leases, production-sharing contracts, and exploration permits. GeoPetro operates one cash-generating property in the Madisonville Project in Texas; almost all of the revenue from this project has been derived from natural gas sales to two clients: Luminant Energy and ETC Katy Pipeline. GeoPetro Resources also has a geographically diverse portfolio of oil and natural gas prospects. In 2013 the company agreed to be bought by fuel distributor MCW Energy Group.

	Annual Growth	12/09	12/10	12/11	12/12	12/13
Sales ($mil.)	–	4.1	3.1	1.0	0.4	–
Net income ($ mil.)	–	(25.8)	(4.9)	(1.5)	(3.9)	(2.9)
Market value ($ mil.)	(59.8%)	41.0	24.7	12.9	3.9	1.1
Employees	(33.1%)	20	14	14	6	4

GEORGE E. WARREN LLC

3001 OCEAN DR STE 203
VERO BEACH, FL 329631992
Phone: 772 778-7100
Fax: –
Web: www.gewarren.com

CEO: –
CFO: Michael George
HR: –
FYE: December 31
Type: Private

By barge, by pipeline, by tank truck, by George; George E. Warren is a major private wholesale distributor of refined petroleum products. It distributes by pipeline via the Buckeye, Colonial, Magellan, Nustar, and Explorer pipelines and by barges and vessels from facilities on the Gulf Coast, in the Mid Continent and New York Harbor area. It distributes a range of petroleum products including coal and heating oil to various industries.

	Annual Growth	12/12	12/13	12/14	12/15	12/16
Sales ($mil.)	(2.3%)	–	–	–	124.5	121.7
Net income ($ mil.)	(2.3%)	–	–	–	43.0	42.0
Market value ($ mil.)	–	–	–	–	–	–
Employees	–	–	–	–	–	35

GEORGE MASON UNIVERSITY

4400 UNIVERSITY DR
FAIRFAX, VA 220304444
Phone: 703 993-1000
Fax: –
Web: www.gmu.edu

CEO: Lanitra Berger
CFO: –
HR: –
FYE: March 31
Type: Private

George Mason University is the largest public research university in Virginia with campuses in Fairfax, Arlington, and Prince William counties, an international branch campus in Songdo, South Korea, and instructional sites in Loudoun County, Herndon, Lorton, Woodbridge, and Front Royal. It has grown to approximately 39,150 students from 130 countries and all 50 states. The school offers more than 200 degree and certificate programs in areas such as law, humanities, science, information technology, engineering, health, and human services, visual and performing arts, and education. It serves traditional and nontraditional students, including those looking to upskill/reskill.

	Annual Growth	06/14	06/15	06/16	06/17*	03/22
Sales ($mil.)	(69.1%)	–	–	–	663.9	1.9
Net income ($ mil.)	(61.7%)	–	–	–	124.9	1.0
Market value ($ mil.)	–	–	–	–	–	–
Employees	–	–	–	–	–	5,500

*Fiscal year change

GEORGE W. AUCH COMPANY

65 UNIVERSITY DR
PONTIAC, MI 483422359
Phone: 248 334-2000
Fax: –
Web: www.auchconstruction.com

CEO: David L Hamilton
CFO: Michael W Carroll
HR: –
FYE: March 31
Type: Private

This George Dubya has built a reputation in the construction industry. George W. Auch, a top contractor in the US, offers general contracting, design/build, and construction management services, primarily in Southeast Michigan. The commercial and institutional builder targets the medical/health care and educational markets. George W. Auch founded the company in 1908 as a family partnership, building homes and churches in the Detroit area.

GEORGETOWN MEMORIAL HOSPITAL

606 BLACK RIVER RD
GEORGETOWN, SC 294403368
Phone: 843 527-7000
Fax: –
Web: –

CEO: Bruce Bailey
CFO: –
HR: –
FYE: September 30
Type: Private

Georgetown Hospital System may be set amidst the Antebellum grace of the South, but its health care services are far from antiquated. The system on the southeast coast of South Carolina operates Georgetown Memorial Hospital, an acute-care facility with more than 130 beds, and Waccamaw Community Hospital, which operates with about 170 beds. Georgetown Memorial Hospital features ICU, cardiac and surgical services, labor and delivery, and a pediatric wing. Waccamaw Community Hospital, covering the northern part of the system's service area, provides 24-hour emergency services, rehabilitation, obstetrics, and inpatient and outpatient surgery.

	Annual Growth	09/17	09/18	09/20	09/21	09/22
Sales ($mil.)	11.8%	–	141.7	158.2	175.4	221.7
Net income ($ mil.)	17.9%	–	14.7	(2.2)	35.9	28.5
Market value ($ mil.)	–	–	–	–	–	–
Employees	–	–	–	–	–	1,300

GEORGIA FARM BUREAU MUTUAL INSURANCE COMPANY

1620 BASS RD
MACON, GA 312106500
Phone: 478 474-0679
Fax: –
Web: www.gfb.org

CEO: Vincent M Duvall
CFO: –
HR: –
FYE: December 31
Type: Private

You don't have to be a farmer to get insurance coverage here, but it helps. Georgia Farm Bureau Mutual Insurance Company (GFNMIC) and its subsidiaries offer a variety of commercial and individual property/casualty products to members of the Georgia Farm Bureau. Its products include farmowners, automobile, homeowners, marine, business owners, and personal liability insurance. The company specializes in writing lower-cost, preferred risk policies (policies for customers that are less likely to file claims). A network of nearly 500 agents and representatives market GFNMIC's products. The company, which was founded in 1959, is a part of the Georgia Farm Bureau. It is owned by its policyholders.

	Annual Growth	12/17	12/18	12/19	12/20	12/21
Assets ($mil.)	5.0%	–	687.4	738.0	768.8	795.8
Net income ($ mil.)	2.2%	–	21.5	37.5	33.9	22.9
Market value ($ mil.)	–	–	–	–	–	–
Employees	–	–	–	–	–	1,210

GEORGIA O'KEEFFE MUSEUM

217 JOHNSON ST
SANTA FE, NM 875011826
Phone: 505 946-1000
Fax: –
Web: www.okeeffemuseum.org

CEO: –
CFO: –
HR: –
FYE: December 31
Type: Private

American Modernist painter and sculptor Georgia O'Keeffe (1887-1986) is credited with saying "To create one's own world in any of the arts takes courage." O'Keeffe, a Wisconsin native, made the desert highlands near Abiquiu, New Mexico her adopted home, and is best known for her sensual paintings of flowers and the desert landscape. Carrying on that artistic legacy, the Georgia O'Keeffe Museum, which opened in 1997, houses the largest collection of O'Keeffe's works in the world. The collection contains more nearly 3,000 works, including more than 1,000 of her paintings, drawings, and sculptures; the museum is also home to a research center dedicated to the study of the American Modernist movement. In 2005, the Georgia O'Keeffe Foundation transferred all of its assets to the Georgia O'Keeffe Museum -- adding more than 1,000 O'Keeffe artworks and archival materials to the museum's collection. With the transaction, the museum also became steward of the artist's historic house in Abiquiu, New Mexico.

	Annual Growth	12/15	12/16	12/19	12/21	12/22
Sales ($mil.)	(2.4%)	–	11.7	17.2	16.3	10.1
Net income ($ mil.)	(20.1%)	–	3.8	7.6	8.5	1.0
Market value ($ mil.)	–	–	–	–	–	–
Employees	–	–	–	–	–	50

GEORGIA PORTS AUTHORITY

2 MAIN ST
GARDEN CITY, GA 314081403
Phone: 912 964-3811
Fax: –
Web: www.gaports.com

CEO: –
CFO: Michaela I Thompson
HR: Lise Marshall
FYE: June 30
Type: Private

A key gateway for international trade, the Georgia Ports Authority operates deepwater ports in Savannah and Brunswick and inland river ports at Bainbridge and Columbus. The Port of Savannah, one of the largest on the East Coast, includes the Garden City Terminal, a major container-handling facility. The port's Ocean Terminal is dedicated to breakbulk and roll-on/roll-off cargo. Cargo handled at the Brunswick terminals includes automobiles and agricultural and forest products. The Georgia Ports Authority is overseen by a thirteen-member board appointed by the governor of Georgia.

	Annual Growth	06/00	06/01	06/02	06/03	06/19
Sales ($mil.)	9.2%	–	97.8	–	121.5	473.6
Net income ($ mil.)	25.2%	–	3.5	–	27.6	197.3
Market value ($ mil.)	–	–	–	–	–	–
Employees	–	–	–	–	–	900

GEORGIA POWER CO

241 Ralph McGill Boulevard, N.E.
Atlanta, GA 30308
Phone: 404 506-6526
Fax: –
Web: www.georgiapower.com

CEO: Kimberly S Greene
CFO: Aaron P Abramovitz
HR: Jesse Owens
FYE: December 31
Type: Public

Georgia Power is the largest subsidiary of US utility holding company Southern Company. The regulated utility provides electricity to about 2.6 million residential, commercial, and industrial customers throughout most of Georgia. It has interests in about 10 gas/oil, nearly 15 solar one nuclear, and over 15 hydroelectric power plants that give it about 92,250 MW of generating capacity. Georgia Power also markets and sells outdoor lighting services and other customer-focused utility services. The utility also offers energy efficiency.

	Annual Growth	12/19	12/20	12/21	12/22	12/23
Sales ($mil.)	4.7%	8,408.0	8,309.0	9,260.0	11,584	10,118
Net income ($ mil.)	4.9%	1,720.0	1,575.0	584.0	1,813.0	2,080.0
Market value ($ mil.)	–	–	–	–	–	–
Employees	(1.2%)	6,938	6,700	6,500	6,600	6,600

GEORGIA REHABILITATION INSTITUTE, INC.

523 13TH ST
AUGUSTA, GA 309011005
Phone: 706 823-8505
Fax: –
Web: www.wrh.org

CEO: Dennis B Skelley
CFO: –
HR: Mary Campbell
FYE: June 30
Type: Private

Walton Rehabilitation Hospital provides rehabilitative care to people who have suffered catastrophic illness or injuries, primarily serving the central Savannah River area in Georgia. The hospital offers services for patients recovering from strokes, as well as brain, spinal cord, and orthopedic injuries. It also provides a pain center and independent living services. Walton Rehabilitation Hospital was founded in 1988.

	Annual Growth	06/16	06/17	06/18	06/21	06/22
Sales ($mil.)	12.0%	–	1.6	3.2	4.0	2.8
Net income ($ mil.)	–	–	(0.2)	1.8	2.3	0.9
Market value ($ mil.)	–	–	–	–	–	–
Employees	–	–	–	–	–	50

GEORGIA SOUTHERN UNIVERSITY

1582 SOUTHERN DR
STATESBORO, GA 30458
Phone: 912 478-4636
Fax: –
Web: www.georgiasouthern.edu

CEO: –
CFO: –
HR: Denise Gebara
FYE: June 30
Type: Private

Georgia Southern University shows students that higher education can be just peachy. Georgia Southern offers its student body more than 140 bachelor, master, and doctoral programs from eight colleges; academic fields include business, education, science, and public health. One of 26 colleges and universities in the University System of Georgia, it enrolls roughly 27,000 students, most of which hail from Georgia. The average class size of lower division courses is about 43, upper division 23, and graduate level 11. The student to faculty ratio is 22:1.

	Annual Growth	06/18	06/19	06/20	06/21	06/22
Sales ($mil.)	(0.9%)	–	257.9	233.9	233.3	250.7
Net income ($ mil.)	56.0%	–	27.8	(24.9)	(7.8)	105.6
Market value ($ mil.)	–	–	–	–	–	–
Employees	–	–	–	–	–	1,700

GEORGIA TRANSMISSION CORPORATION (AN ELECTRIC MEMBERSHIP CORPORATION)

2100 E EXCHANGE PL
TUCKER, GA 300845342
Phone: 770 270-7400
Fax: –
Web: www.gatransmission.com

CEO: –
CFO: –
HR: –
FYE: December 31
Type: Private

With Georgia on its mind, Georgia Transmission provides electric transmission services to power producers and distribution utilities. The company primarily transports power for its 39 member distribution cooperatives (out of Georgia's total of 42 coops) and their electricity supplier, Oglethorpe Power. Georgia Transmission owns 3,060 miles of transmission lines asn more that 640 substations. It jointly owns and plans the state's entire 17,500 miles of transmission lines through the Integrated Transmission System, in collaboration with Georgia Power, MEAG Power and Dalton Utilities.

	Annual Growth	12/18	12/19	12/20	12/21	12/22
Sales ($mil.)	4.5%	–	330.5	345.5	369.6	377.6
Net income ($ mil.)	12.5%	–	16.4	16.5	16.1	23.3
Market value ($ mil.)	–	–	–	–	–	–
Employees	–	–	–	–	–	285

GEORGIAN COURT UNIVERSITY

900 LAKEWOOD AVE
LAKEWOOD, NJ 087012600
Phone: 732 987-2200
Fax: –
Web: www.georgian.edu

CEO: –
CFO: –
HR: Dianna Sofo
FYE: June 30
Type: Private

If you've always dreamed of riding the Jersey Turnpike, here's your chance. Georgian Court University -- with campuses in Lakewood and Woodbridge, New Jersey -- is a Roman Catholic liberal arts school providing undergraduate and graduate education to more than 3,000 students. While the school focuses on educating women through its Women's College, it also offers coeducational learning through its evening, graduate, and professional studies programs. Georgian Court University was founded by the Sisters of Mercy in 1908. Formerly named Georgian Court College, the school became a university in 2004.

	Annual Growth	06/17	06/18	06/19	06/20	06/22
Sales ($mil.)	(1.0%)	–	42.5	44.0	44.7	40.8
Net income ($ mil.)	–	–	(1.5)	(3.1)	(1.4)	(10.2)
Market value ($ mil.)	–	–	–	–	–	–
Employees	–	–	–	–	–	854

GEOS COMMUNICATIONS, INC.

430 North Carroll Avenue, Suite 120
Southlake, TX 76092
Phone: 817 789-6000
Fax: –
Web: www.i2telecom.com

CEO: Andrew L Berman
CFO: Cynthia T Gordon
HR: –
FYE: December 31
Type: Public

Geos Communications (formerly known as i2 Telecom International) enables its customers to let their virtual fingers do the talking. The VoIP service and technology provider offers domestic and international long-distance calling over the Internet. The company has developed a software-based Internet phone device called VoiceStick, which plugs into any computer's USB port and allows phone calls over the Internet. Using the VoiceStick device and software, subscribers can call from their computers or from home and mobile phones through the company's service. The MyGlobalTalk application downloads to any cell phone and lets customers make international calls for a few cents per minute.

	Annual Growth	12/06	12/07	12/08	12/09	12/10
Sales ($mil.)	(42.5%)	0.8	0.9	0.6	0.3	0.0
Net income ($ mil.)	–	(5.8)	(9.1)	(2.9)	(12.6)	(12.2)
Market value ($ mil.)	(35.7%)	3.9	2.8	1.9	7.1	0.7
Employees	30.7%	12	14	19	76	35

GEOSPACE TECHNOLOGIES CORP

NMS: GEOS

7007 Pinemont
Houston, TX 77040
Phone: 713 986-4444
Fax: –
Web: www.geospace.com

CEO: Walter R Wheeler
CFO: Robert L Curda
HR: –
FYE: September 30
Type: Public

Geospace Technologies designs and manufactures seismic instruments and equipment. These seismic products are marketed to the oil and gas industry and used to locate, characterize and monitor hydrocarbon producing reservoirs. It also market its seismic products to other industries for vibration monitoring, border and perimeter security and various geotechnical applications. The company designs and manufactures other products of a non-seismic nature, including water meter products, imaging equipment, offshore cables, remote shutoff water valves and Internet of Things (IoT) platform and provide contract manufacturing services. The majority of the company's sales were generated from the US.

	Annual Growth	09/19	09/20	09/21	09/22	09/23
Sales ($mil.)	6.8%	95.8	87.8	94.9	89.3	124.5
Net income ($ mil.)	–	(0.1)	(19.2)	(14.1)	(22.9)	12.2
Market value ($ mil.)	(4.2%)	202.7	81.5	126.0	58.2	170.8
Employees	(3.5%)	786	651	649	650	681

GEOSYNTEC CONSULTANTS, INC.

900 BROKEN SOUND PKWY NW STE 200
BOCA RATON, FL 334873513
Phone: 561 995-0900
Fax: –
Web: www.geosyntec.com

CEO: Peter Zeeb
CFO: Jon Dickinson
HR: –
FYE: December 31
Type: Private

An environmental engineering and consulting firm, GeoSyntec Consultants provides services such as environmental management, geotechnical engineering, groundwater assessment and remediation, pollution prevention, and surface water management. The company operates from more than 75 offices, primarily in the US but also in Canada, Malaysia, and the UK. Its clients include Aerojet-General, AstraZeneca, Chevron, Delta Air Lines, FMC Corp., Georgia Power, Kimberly-Clark, Lockheed Martin, Pharmacia & Upjohn, and Shell Oil. The company has more than 1,000 engineers, scientists, and other specialists worldwide.

	Annual Growth	12/17	12/18	12/19	12/20	12/21
Sales ($mil.)	24.6%	–	225.7	314.3	394.2	437.0
Net income ($ mil.)	(9.0%)	–	11.7	7.7	4.0	8.8
Market value ($ mil.)	–	–	–	–	–	–
Employees	–	–	–	–	–	1,600

GERBER CHILDRENSWEAR LLC

7005 PELHAM RD STE D
GREENVILLE, SC 296155782
Phone: 864 987-5200
Fax: –
Web: www.gerberchildrenswear.com

CEO: Maria Montano
CFO: –
HR: Brandy Walters
FYE: January 29
Type: Private

Gerber Childrenswear may be one of the first companies to make kids brand-conscious. The company makes infant and toddler clothing sold under the licensed Gerber and Curity labels, as well as its own Onesies brand. Products include sleepwear, underwear, playwear, cloth diapers, footwear, and bibs. Through a licensing deal with Jockey International, Gerber Childrenswear also offers Jockey-branded underwear, sleepwear, and thermal items for children. The company sells its products primarily through national retailers (such as Wal-Mart, Kmart, and Toys "R" Us), department stores, and specialty shops. Gerber Childrenswear is a unit of Childrenswear, LLC, a portfolio company of investment firm Sun Capital Partners.

	Annual Growth	01/06	01/07	01/08	01/09	01/11
Sales ($mil.)	(9.1%)	–	–	–	193.8	160.1
Net income ($ mil.)	(12.0%)	–	–	–	6.6	5.1
Market value ($ mil.)	–	–	–	–	–	–
Employees	–	–	–	–	–	140

GERMAN AMERICAN BANCORP INC NMS: GABC

711 Main Street
Jasper, IN 47546
Phone: 812 482-1314
Fax: –
Web: www.germanamerican.com

CEO: Mark A Schroeder
CFO: –
HR: –
FYE: December 31
Type: Public

German American Bancorp is the holding company for German American Bank, which operates more than 75 branches in southern Indiana and Kentucky. Founded in 1910, German American offers such standard retail products as checking and savings accounts, certificates of deposit, and IRAs. It also provides trust services, while sister company German American Investment Services provides trust, investment advisory, and brokerage services. German American Bancorp also owns German American Insurance, which offers corporate and personal insurance products. Substantially all of the company's revenue derives from customers located in the US.

	Annual Growth	12/19	12/20	12/21	12/22	12/23
Assets ($mil.)	8.8%	4,397.7	4,977.6	5,608.5	6,156.0	6,152.2
Net income ($ mil.)	9.7%	59.2	62.2	84.1	81.8	85.9
Market value ($ mil.)	(2.3%)	1,053.8	979.0	1,153.2	1,103.5	958.8
Employees	0.7%	817	770	894	866	840

GERON CORP. NMS: GERN

919 East Hillsdale Boulevard, Suite 250
Foster City, CA 94404
Phone: 650 473-7700
Fax: –
Web: www.geron.com

CEO: John A Scarlett
CFO: Olivia K Bloom
HR: –
FYE: December 31
Type: Public

Geron is a clinical-stage biopharmaceutical is working to developing compounds able to treat various hematologic myeloid malignancies such as myelofibrosis, and myelodysplastic syndromes, and acute myelogenous leukemia. The company is developing pharmaceuticals based on protein inhibitor technologies that aim to demolish enzymes that feed cancer cells. The company's lead candidate, imetelstat, is an enzyme inhibitor being studied for its effectiveness in treating myelofibrosis and myelodysplastic syndromes.

	Annual Growth	12/19	12/20	12/21	12/22	12/23
Sales ($mil.)	(15.3%)	0.5	0.3	1.4	0.6	0.2
Net income ($ mil.)	–	(68.5)	(75.6)	(116.1)	(141.9)	(184.1)
Market value ($ mil.)	11.6%	741.1	866.4	664.8	1,318.7	1,149.8
Employees	32.3%	46	55	72	107	141

GERRITY'S SUPER MARKET, INC.

950 N SOUTH RD STE 5
SCRANTON, PA 185041430
Phone: 570 342-4144
Fax: –
Web: www.gerritys.com

CEO: –
CFO: –
HR: –
FYE: December 31
Type: Private

Gerrity's Super Market is not yet part of a matriarchal society but does boast that it's where Mom is "always in charge!" The regional grocery chain operates about 10 supermarkets under the Gerrity's Supermarket banner in Lackawanna and Luzerne counties in northeastern Pennsylvania. The regional chain also operates an online grocery order and home delivery service. Founded in 1895 by William Gerrity, the family-owned company is run by mother and son team Joyce ("Mom") and Joseph Fasula. Gerrity's Supermarkets is a member of the Shursave Supermarkets Co-op.

	Annual Growth	01/15	01/16	01/17*	12/17	12/18
Sales ($mil.)	0.8%	–	168.4	167.8	169.8	171.5
Net income ($ mil.)	(28.9%)	–	3.6	2.7	2.3	1.8
Market value ($ mil.)	–	–	–	–	–	–
Employees	–	–	–	–	–	1,100

*Fiscal year change

GETTY IMAGES HOLDINGS INC NYS: GETY

605 5th Ave South, Suite 400
Seattle, WA 98104
Phone: 206 925-5000
Fax: –
Web: www.gettyimages.com

CEO: –
CFO: –
HR: –
FYE: December 31
Type: Public

Getty Images is a preeminent global visual content creator and marketplace. Through Getty Images, iStock, and Unsplash, the company offers a full range of content solutions to meet the needs of any customer?no matter their size?around the globe, with over 520 million assets available through its industry-leading sites. The company has more than 835,000 purchasing customers, with customers from almost every country in the world with websites in nearly 25 languages bringing the world's best content to media outlets, advertising agencies, and corporations of all sizes and, increasingly, serving individual creators and prosumers. Getty Images was founded in 1995. In mid-2022, Getty Images and CC Neuberger Principal Holdings completed their business combination and are now trading on the NYSE under the symbols GETY and GETY WS.

GETTY REALTY CORP. NYS: GTY

292 Madison Avenue, 9th Floor
New York, NY 10017-6318
Phone: 646 349-6000
Fax: –
Web: www.gettyrealty.com

CEO: Christopher J Constant
CFO: Danion Fielding
HR: Eileen Marlow
FYE: December 31
Type: Public

Getty Realty, a self-administered real estate investment trust (REIT), owns or leases about 945 gas service stations, adjacent convenience stores, and petroleum distribution terminals in more than 30 US states and Washington, DC. Most of its properties are company-owned and located in the Northeast (about a third in New York). Major gas brands distributed at Getty properties include BP, Citgo, Conoco, Exxon, Getty, Shell, and Valero. The company's three most significant tenants by revenue -- which together occupy about 45% of its properties -- are petroleum distributors and gas station operators Global Partners, Apro, and Chestnut Petroleum.

	Annual Growth	12/19	12/20	12/21	12/22	12/23
Sales ($mil.)	7.2%	140.7	147.3	155.4	165.6	185.8
Net income ($ mil.)	4.9%	49.7	69.4	62.9	90.0	60.2
Market value ($ mil.)	(2.9%)	1,773.4	1,485.9	1,731.3	1,826.3	1,576.5
Employees	–	31	31	31	32	–

GETTYSBURG COLLEGE

300 N WASHINGTON ST
GETTYSBURG, PA 173251483
Phone: 717 337-6000
Fax: –
Web: www.gettysburg.edu

CEO: –
CFO: –
HR: –
FYE: May 31
Type: Private

Four score and many years ago, Gettysburg College opened its doors. The private, four-year liberal arts and sciences college offers about 65 academic programs and about 40 majors to 2,600 students who come from more than 40 states and 35 countries. Gettysburg's student-faculty ratio is 10:1. The campus is adjacent to the Gettysburg National Military Park in Pennsylvania. The college was founded in 1832; its first building, Pennsylvania Hall, served during and after the Battle of Gettysburg as a hospital for the wounded. In 1863 students and faculty of Gettysburg College walked from Pennsylvania Hall to the national cemetery in Gettysburg to hear President Lincoln deliver his legendary Gettysburg Address.

	Annual Growth	05/16	05/17	05/18	05/21	05/22
Sales ($mil.)	(7.8%)	–	196.8	138.2	113.3	131.1
Net income ($ mil.)	–	–	19.3	26.8	73.1	(1.6)
Market value ($ mil.)	–	–	–	–	–	–
Employees	–	–	–	–	–	108

GEVO INC

NAS: GEVO

345 Inverness Drive South, Building C, Suite 310
Englewood, CO 80112
Phone: 303 858-8358
Fax: –
Web: www.gevo.com

CEO: Patrick R Gruber
CFO: L L Smull
HR: –
FYE: December 31
Type: Public

Putting sugar in a gas tank is generally not a good idea, but Gevo has figured out a way to make it beneficial. A renewable chemical and biofuels company, Gevo produces isobutanol, a multi-purpose chemical derived from glucose and other cellulosic biomass extracted from plant matter. Its isobutanol can be used as a blendstock (additive used during the refining process) for gasoline and jet fuel production and as a chemical used in the production of plastics, fibers, and rubber. Gevo does not yet produce isobutanol on a commercial scale, but it is in the process of building its customer and partnership base in preparation of commencing production. In 2016 the company was seeking strategic alternatives.

	Annual Growth	12/19	12/20	12/21	12/22	12/23
Sales ($mil.)	(8.5%)	24.5	5.5	0.7	1.2	17.2
Net income ($ mil.)	–	(28.7)	(40.2)	(59.2)	(98.0)	(66.2)
Market value ($ mil.)	(15.8%)	555.6	1,022.1	1,029.3	456.9	279.0
Employees	15.9%	57	31	99	89	103

GF HEALTH PRODUCTS, INC.

1 GRAHAM FIELD WAY
ATLANTA, GA 303403140
Phone: 770 368-4700
Fax: –
Web: www.grahamfield.com

CEO: Kenneth Spett
CFO: –
HR: Terry Spector
FYE: April 30
Type: Private

GF Health Products helps patients gain ground. A leading maker of wheelchairs, the company (also known as Graham-Field) also manufactures and distributes medical and surgical supplies, diagnostics, rehabilitative and respiratory equipment, home safety products, pressure management equipment, specialized furnishings, and lifts and other mobility aids. Brands include Lumex, Grafco, Basic American, Lumiscope, Labtron, Hausted, John Bunn, and Everest & Jennings; it also distributes products from other manufacturers. GF's clients fall into four main categories: primary care, home care, long-term care (nursing homes), and acute care (hospitals).

	Annual Growth	03/12	03/13	03/14	03/15*	04/17
Sales ($mil.)	3.7%	–	–	–	79.9	85.8
Net income ($ mil.)	23.9%	–	–	–	2.1	3.3
Market value ($ mil.)	–	–	–	–	–	–
Employees	–	–	–	–	–	320

*Fiscal year change

GIANT EAGLE, INC.

101 KAPPA DR
PITTSBURGH, PA 152382833
Phone: 866 620-0216
Fax: –
Web: www.gianteagle.com

CEO: Bill Artman
CFO: David Burnworth
HR: Daniel Guevara
FYE: June 30
Type: Private

Giant Eagle is one of the nation's largest food retailers and distributors that operates approximately 175 company-owned stores and almost 55 operated supermarkets, as well as roughly 180 fuel and convenience stores, which feature fresh foods and sells gas at discounted prices. The regional chain also has stores in Ohio, Maryland, Indiana, and West Virginia. Many Giant Eagle stores feature video rental, banking, dry cleaning services, gift cards, and ready-to-eat meals. The company offers more than 10,000 Giant Eagle branded products. In 1931, the five families - Goldstein, Chait, Moravitz, and Weizenbaum - combine forces to form Giant Eagle.

GIBBS DIE CASTING CORPORATION

369 COMMUNITY DR
HENDERSON, KY 424204397
Phone: 270 827-1801
Fax: –
Web: www.gibbsdc.com

CEO: Kevin R Koch
CFO: Angela Phaup
HR: Dan Carr
FYE: December 31
Type: Private

There's plenty to die for at Gibbs Die Casting. The company manufactures aluminum and magnesium die-castings, such as air conditioning compressor, commercial refrigeration, and engine and viscous clutch parts. Its Comac Machining Division provides precision machining and assembly work. The Audubon Tool Division uses fused deposition modeling prototyping equipment and CNC electrical discharge machines to build die-casting tools. Gibbs Engineering offers on-site product design, prototype models, and production tooling services. Gibbs Die Casting serves industries, such as automobile and appliance manufacturing and alternative energy. The comopany is owned by Koch Enterprises.

GIBRALTAR INDUSTRIES INC

NMS: ROCK

3556 Lake Shore Road, P.O. Box 2028
Buffalo, NY 14219-0228
Phone: 716 826-6500
Fax: –
Web: www.gibraltar1.com

CEO: William T Bosway
CFO: Timothy F Murphy
HR: Barbara Woida
FYE: December 31
Type: Public

Gibraltar makes and distributes products for renewable energy, residential, agtech and infrastructure. The company's mission is to make life better for people and the planet, fueled by advancing the disciplines of engineering, science, and technology. Gibraltar is innovating to reshape critical markets in sustainable power, comfortable and efficient living, and productive growing throughout North America. Its building products are sold through a number of sales channel including major retail home centers, building material wholesalers, and building product distributors. The company generates the majority of sales from its domestic customers.

	Annual Growth	12/19	12/20	12/21	12/22	12/23
Sales ($mil.)	7.1%	1,047.4	1,032.6	1,339.8	1,390.0	1,377.7
Net income ($ mil.)	14.2%	65.1	64.6	75.6	82.4	110.5
Market value ($ mil.)	11.9%	1,535.4	2,189.9	2,029.8	1,396.6	2,404.2
Employees	2.2%	1,932	2,337	2,021	2,137	2,110

GIBSON OVERSEAS, INC.

2410 YATES AVE
COMMERCE, CA 900401918
Phone: 323 832-8900
Fax: –
Web: www.gibsonusa.com

CEO: –
CFO: –
HR: –
FYE: December 31
Type: Private

Not to be confused with the popular guitars under a similar name, this Gibson concentrates on place sets rather than music sets. Established in 1979, Gibson Overseas manufactures dinnerware, flatware, and glassware. The company makes and markets its products under the Cuisine Select, Gibson Everyday, Gibson Elite brand names, as well as under licenses Sunbeam and Oster. Gibson Overseas sells its wares (including combination sets, which put dinnerware, flatware, and glassware all in one box) to large retailers the likes of Pier 1 Imports and Crate & Barrel. The company is owned by the Gabbay family and today is run by founder Nejat Gabbay's three sons.

GIBSON, DUNN & CRUTCHER LLP

333 S GRAND AVE STE 4600
LOS ANGELES, CA 900713449
Phone: 213 229-7000
Fax: -
Web: www.gibsondunn.com

CEO: -
CFO: -
HR: Jennifer Wang
FYE: December 31
Type: Private

One of the top US corporate-transactions law firms, Gibson, Dunn & Crutcher also practices in such areas as litigation, public policy, real estate, tax, and white collar defense and investigations. The firm represents the majority of the Fortune 100 and more than half of the Fortune 500 companies ranging from some of the world's largest multinationals to start-up ventures and emerging growth companies. It also represents private equity firms, sovereign wealth funds, commercial and investment banks, other financial institutions, government entities, partnerships, and individuals. The firm has more than 1,800 lawyers working from almost 20 offices in the US, Europe, the Middle East, Asia, and South America. The firm was founded in 1890.

	Annual Growth	12/18	12/19	12/20	12/21	12/22
Sales ($mil.)	(4.1%)	-	-	-	2.1	2.0
Net income ($ mil.)	-	-	-	-	(1.0)	0.0
Market value ($ mil.)	-	-	-	-	-	-
Employees	-	-	-	-	-	1,900

GIGA-TRONICS INC

7272 E. Indian School Rd, Suite 540
Scottsdale, AZ 85251
Phone: 833 457-6667
Fax: -
Web: www.gigatronics.com

CEO: Jonathan Read
CFO: Lutz P Henckels
HR: -
FYE: December 31
Type: Public

Giga-tronics has a cool gig in electronics. Its three units -- Giga-tronics Instruments, Microsource, and ASCOR -- make test, measurement, and control equipment for both commercial and military customers. The units make synthesizers and power measurement instruments used in electronic warfare, radar, satellite, and telecommunications devices; switching systems for aircraft and automated test equipment; and oscillators and filters used in microwave instruments. Top customers include the US Department of Defense and its prime contractors. The majority of the company's business is done the US.

	Annual Growth	03/19	03/20	03/21	03/22*	12/22
Sales ($mil.)	28.4%	11.1	11.8	13.1	9.0	30.3
Net income ($ mil.)	-	(1.0)	(0.7)	(0.4)	(2.7)	(17.7)
Market value ($ mil.)	19.8%	2.0	14.5	24.9	16.4	4.0
Employees	49.9%	39	42	42	45	197

*Fiscal year change

GIGAMON INC.

3300 OLCOTT ST
SANTA CLARA, CA 950543005
Phone: 408 831-4000
Fax: -
Web: www.gigamon.com

CEO: Paul Hooper
CFO: -
HR: Anna Jackson
FYE: December 28
Type: Private

Gigamon offers a deep observability pipeline that harnesses actionable network-level intelligence to amplify the power of observability tools. The company's products make network traffic visible to operators and help it reach its destination. Gigamon's products such as the GigaVUE Visibility appliance deliver consistent into data that travels through network, network, including data centers and remote site. Besides keeping network traffic moving, the company's GigaSECURE Security Delivery Platform keeps an eye on security issues, helping detect, identify, and deal with network threats.

	Annual Growth	12/14	12/15	12/16	12/18	12/19
Sales ($mil.)	(79.9%)	-	222.0	310.9	-	0.4
Net income ($ mil.)	-	-	6.2	49.4	-	(0.1)
Market value ($ mil.)	-	-	-	-	-	-
Employees	-	-	-	-	-	684

GILBANE BUILDING COMPANY

7 JACKSON WALKWAY
PROVIDENCE, RI 029033694
Phone: 401 456-5800
Fax: -
Web: www.gilbaneco.com

CEO: -
CFO: -
HR: -
FYE: December 31
Type: Private

Gilbane Building Company provides construction services, consulting, subcontracting, and facilities management to commercial, institutional, and governmental markets. Operating as the construction arm of Gilbane, the company builds schools, hospitals, laboratories, and prisons, serving both the public and private sectors. Its completed projects include the Stroh Center at Bowling Green State University, Columbus Regional Airport Authority, and the National WWII Memorial in Washington, DC. Founded in 1870 as a carpentry and general contracting shop, the family-owned Gilbane Building Company operates from more than 45 offices around the world around the world and currently oversees more than 1,000 construction projects worldwide.

	Annual Growth	12/11	12/12	12/13	12/14	12/17
Sales ($mil.)	4.5%	-	-	4,100.7	3,840.7	4,899.2
Net income ($ mil.)	-	-	-	-	-	63.5
Market value ($ mil.)	-	-	-	-	-	-
Employees	-	-	-	-	-	2,500

GILBANE DEVELOPMENT COMPANY

7 JACKSON WALKWAY
PROVIDENCE, RI 029033638
Phone: 401 456-5800
Fax: -
Web: www.gilbaneco.com

CEO: Robert V Gilbane V
CFO: Matthew Lawrence
HR: Deb Francazio
FYE: December 31
Type: Private

Commercial property development is hardly the bane of Gilbane Development's existence; in fact, that's its forte. The development and ownership arm of its parent, construction giant Gilbane, it provides real estate development, property management, strategic planning, financing, and asset repositioning services to its clients. Its portfolio includes corporate build-to-suit and brownfield site redevelopment projects in Maryland, Ohio, Pennsylvania, Rhode Island, Vermont, and elsewhere. Gilbane Development (formerly Gilbane Properties) also has developed residential projects, ranging from condominiums to single-family-home developments, and has financed public school construction with lease-purchase arrangements.

GILBERT MAY, INC.

1125 LONGPOINT AVE
DALLAS, TX 752476809
Phone: 214 631-3331
Fax: -
Web: www.phillipsmay.com

CEO: -
CFO: -
HR: -
FYE: December 31
Type: Private

Gilbert May, which does business as the Phillips/May Corporation, provides general contracting services in the Dallas area. The company's projects include schools, libraries, and other institutional buildings and government projects, including work at the DFW International Airport. The firm, which was founded by president Gilbert May, ranks among the fastest-growing private companies in the Dallas area.

	Annual Growth	12/13	12/14	12/15	12/16	12/17
Sales ($mil.)	(16.7%)	-	-	-	74.9	62.4
Net income ($ mil.)	56.3%	-	-	-	0.8	1.2
Market value ($ mil.)	-	-	-	-	-	-
Employees	-	-	-	-	-	105

GILEAD SCIENCES INC

NMS: GILD

333 Lakeside Drive
Foster City, CA 94404
Phone: 650 574-3000
Fax: –
Web: www.gilead.com

CEO: Daniel P O'Day
CFO: Andrew D Dickinson
HR: –
FYE: December 31
Type: Public

Gilead Sciences is a biopharmaceutical company for infectious diseases, including hepatitis, HIV, and infections related to AIDS. The company's drug franchise includes Truvada, an oral formulation indicated in combination with other antiretroviral agents for the treatment of HIV-1 infection in certain patients. Other products on the market include AmBisome, an antifungal agent, for the treatment of serious invasive fungal infections caused by various fungal species in adults; and Letairis, an oral formulation of an endothelin receptor antagonist for the treatment of pulmonary arterial hypertension. Beyond HIV/AIDS, Gilead also markets Oncology medicines, including Yescarta CAR-T cell therapy for cancer. With operations in more than 35 countries worldwide, Gilead generates about 70% of its revenue from the US

	Annual Growth	12/19	12/20	12/21	12/22	12/23
Sales ($mil.)	4.8%	22,449	24,689	27,305	27,281	27,116
Net income ($ mil.)	1.3%	5,386.0	123.0	6,225.0	4,592.0	5,665.0
Market value ($ mil.)	5.7%	80,965	72,592	90,472	106,969	100,938
Employees	11.1%	11,800	13,600	14,400	17,000	18,000

GILLETTE CHILDREN'S SPECIALTY HEALTHCARE

200 UNIVERSITY AVE E
SAINT PAUL, MN 551012507
Phone: 651 291-2848
Fax: –
Web: www.gillettechildrens.org

CEO: –
CFO: –
HR: –
FYE: December 31
Type: Private

Caring for the Twin Cities' tiniest tykes and most truculent teens, Gillette Children's Specialty Healthcare provides diagnostic, therapeutic, and support services to children, adolescents, and young adults. Gillette Children's consists of a main campus in St. Paul, Minnesota, and eight clinics in the immediate and outlying areas of the city. The health system also provides adult services at its St. Paul-Phalen clinic. The main campus hospital (with about 345 beds) operates Centers of Excellence for cerebral palsy, craniofacial services, and pediatric neurosciences, among others. The not-for-profit hospital also provides outreach services through its mobile health care unit.

	Annual Growth	12/15	12/16	12/17	12/21	12/22
Sales ($mil.)	3.5%	–	244.2	244.7	251.1	300.6
Net income ($ mil.)	4.3%	–	16.7	8.0	22.6	21.5
Market value ($ mil.)	–	–	–	–	–	–
Employees	–	–	–	–	–	1,756

GIRL SCOUTS OF THE UNITED STATES OF AMERICA

420 5TH AVE FL 9
NEW YORK, NY 100182798
Phone: 212 852-8000
Fax: –
Web: www.girlscouts.org

CEO: Judith Batty
CFO: Angela Olden
HR: –
FYE: September 30
Type: Private

For the Girl Scouts of the United States of America, the calendar includes one month of cookie sales and 12 months of character-building. One of the largest groups devoted to girls, it has more than 2.5 million girl members, plus some 800,000 adult volunteers. Girl Scouts of the USA, founded in 1912, is open to girls between ages 5 and 17. It strives to develop character and leadership skills through projects using technology, sports, the environment, literacy, and the arts and sciences. Girl Scouts of the USA operates through 112 chartered regional councils. The US organization is part of the World Association of Girl Guides and Girl Scouts, which numbers some 10 million girls and adults in about 145 countries.

	Annual Growth	09/18	09/19	09/20	09/21	09/22
Sales ($mil.)	(0.5%)	–	122.1	112.2	130.7	120.2
Net income ($ mil.)	–	–	(8.0)	(10.5)	19.7	1.9
Market value ($ mil.)	–	–	–	–	–	–
Employees	–	–	–	–	–	500

GIRLS INCORPORATED OF NEW YORK CITY

120 WALL ST STE 1800
NEW YORK, NY 100053922
Phone: 212 509-2000
Fax: –
Web: www.girlsinc.org

CEO: Pamela Maraldo
CFO: –
HR: –
FYE: June 30
Type: Private

Girls Incorporated's going concern is giving girls a chance. Begun in 1864 during the Industrial Revolution, it's a national organization that supports the lives of girls and young women age 6 to 18 living in high-risk or underserved areas. Girls Incorporated is a not-for-profit group that provides educational programs for girls in areas such as math and science, sports, money management, and leadership. Its programs are implemented through partner entities, including schools and youth-service organizations nationwide. Programs encourage girls to master challenges while the group lobbies lawmakers to promote girls' needs. Girls Incorporated was formally founded in 1945 as Girls Clubs of America.

	Annual Growth	03/13	03/14	03/15	03/20*	06/21
Sales ($mil.)	(10.8%)	–	8.4	10.0	13.8	3.8
Net income ($ mil.)	25.1%	–	0.1	1.7	(0.9)	0.6
Market value ($ mil.)	–	–	–	–	–	–
Employees	–	–	–	–	–	189

*Fiscal year change

GIVE SOMETHING BACK, INC.

474 ROLAND WAY
OAKLAND, CA 946212013
Phone: 800 261-2619
Fax: –
Web: www.givesomethingback.com

CEO: Sean Marx
CFO: –
HR: –
FYE: December 31
Type: Private

Give Something Back lives up its company name. The organization was built around the idea of selling discounted office supplies (such products as paper clips and pens) directly to businesses through telephone sales and over the Internet. Give Something Back, founded by co-partners Sean Marx and Mike Hannigan and modeled after Newman's Own (the food company launched in 1982 by Paul Newman that donates its after-tax profits), awards more than half of its revenue to charitable organizations. Give Something Back's employees and some 13,000 customers assist in choosing the recipients of its grants.

GLACIER BANCORP, INC.

NYS: GBCI

49 Commons Loop
Kalispell, MT 59901
Phone: 406 756-4200
Fax: –
Web: www.glacierbancorp.com

CEO: Randall M Chesler
CFO: Ron J Copher
HR: Maggie Conry
FYE: December 31
Type: Public

Glacier Bancorp provides a full range of banking services to both individuals and businesses to about 220 locations in Montana, Idaho, Utah, Washington, Arizona, Colorado, and Wyoming. The bank offers retail banking, business banking, real estate, commercial, agriculture and consumer loans, as well as mortgage originating and loan servicing. The market area's economic base primarily focuses on tourism, construction, mining, energy, manufacturing, agriculture, service industry, and health care. The tourism industry is highly influenced by national parks, ski resorts, significant lakes and rural scenic areas.

	Annual Growth	12/19	12/20	12/21	12/22	12/23
Assets ($mil.)	19.3%	13,684	18,504	25,941	26,635	27,743
Net income ($ mil.)	1.4%	210.5	266.4	284.8	303.2	222.9
Market value ($ mil.)	(2.6%)	5,099.8	5,102.0	6,287.4	5,480.1	4,581.9
Employees	2.0%	3,046	3,032	3,559	3,552	3,294

GLADSTONE COMMERCIAL CORP — NMS: GOOD

1521 Westbranch Drive, Suite 100
McLean, VA 22102
Phone: 703 287-5800
Fax: 703 287-5801
Web: www.gladstonecommercial.com

CEO: David Gladstone
CFO: Gary Gerson
HR: -
FYE: December 31
Type: Public

Gladstone Commercial, a real estate investment trust (REIT), invests in and owns office and industrial real estate properties. The company owns more than 120 properties in more than 25 states with assets that include office buildings, medical office buildings, warehouses, retail stores, and manufacturing facilities. Gladstone generally provides net leases with terms between seven and 15 years for small to very large private and public companies. The business is managed by its external adviser, Gladstone Management, which is also headed by chairman and CEO David Gladstone. The company's largest revenue generating states are Texas and Florida.

	Annual Growth	12/19	12/20	12/21	12/22	12/23
Sales ($mil.)	6.6%	114.4	133.2	137.7	149.0	147.6
Net income ($ mil.)	(15.2%)	9.6	14.9	9.8	9.3	5.0
Market value ($ mil.)	(11.8%)	883.3	727.3	1,041.3	747.5	535.0
Employees	-	-	-	-	-	-

GLADSTONE LAND CORP — NMS: LAND

1521 Westbranch Drive, Suite 100
McLean, VA 22102
Phone: 703 287-5800
Fax: -
Web: www.gladstonefarms.com

CEO: David Gladstone
CFO: Lewis Parrish
HR: -
FYE: December 31
Type: Public

Gladstone Land buys farm properties in the US and rents them to corporate farming operations and medium-sized independent farmers through triple net leases, arrangements in which the tenant is responsible for maintaining the property. Gladstone Land is an externally managed real estate company that owns about a dozen row crop properties in California and Florida, which total more than 1,600 acres. It leases most of its properties to Dole Fresh Vegetables, a subsidiary of Dole Foods, which uses the farmland to grow annual fruit and vegetable crops like berries, melons, and lettuce, among others. Gladstone Land went public in early 2013 with an offering worth $50 million.

	Annual Growth	12/19	12/20	12/21	12/22	12/23
Sales ($mil.)	22.1%	40.7	57.0	75.3	89.2	90.4
Net income ($ mil.)	70.1%	1.7	4.9	3.5	4.7	14.6
Market value ($ mil.)	2.7%	464.8	524.7	1,209.9	657.6	517.9
Employees	-	-	-	-	-	69

GLASSBRIDGE ENTERPRISES INC — NBB: GLAE

18 East 50th Street, FL7
New York, NY 10022
Phone: 212 220-3300
Fax: -
Web: www.glassbridge.com

CEO: -
CFO: -
HR: -
FYE: December 31
Type: Public

GlassBridge (formerly Imation) owns and operates an asset management business through various subsidiaries. The company has established a full internal support infrastructure for its asset management business that can support additional strategies and assets growth. It expects its asset management business to earn revenues primarily by providing investment advisory services to third party investors through its managed funds, as well as separate managed accounts.

	Annual Growth	12/18	12/19	12/20	12/21	12/22
Sales ($mil.)	-	-	0.1	0.5	0.1	0.1
Net income ($ mil.)	-	4.1	20.2	(62.3)	29.0	(3.0)
Market value ($ mil.)	280.4%	0.0	6.3	1.3	0.0	0.8
Employees	-	-	5	17	-	-

GLATFELTER CORP — NYS: GLT

4350 Congress Street, Suite 600
Charlotte, NC 28209
Phone: 704 885-2555
Fax: 717 846-7208
Web: www.glatfelter.com

CEO: Thomas Fahnemann
CFO: Samuel L Hillard
HR: -
FYE: December 31
Type: Public

Glatfelter Corporation (formerly P. H. Glatfelter) is a leading global supplier of engineered materials. Its high-quality, innovative, and customizable solutions are found in tea and single-serve coffee filtration, and personal hygiene, as well as in many diverse packaging, home improvement, and industrial applications. Its Composite Fibers segment processes specialty long fibers, primarily from natural sources such as abaca, and other materials to create premium value-added products, while the Airlaid Materials segment makes nonwoven fabric-like materials used in feminine hygiene products and other hygiene products, and wipes. With customers in more than 100 countries, Glatfelter's operations utilize a variety of manufacturing technologies including airlaid, wetlaid, and spunlace with over 15 manufacturing sites located in the US, Canada, Germany, the UK, France, Spain, and the Philippines. The US is the company's largest single market, accounting for about 35% of total sales.

	Annual Growth	12/19	12/20	12/21	12/22	12/23
Sales ($mil.)	10.5%	927.7	916.5	1,084.7	1,491.3	1,385.5
Net income ($ mil.)	-	(21.5)	21.3	6.9	(194.2)	(79.1)
Market value ($ mil.)	(42.9%)	825.1	738.5	775.5	125.3	87.5
Employees	3.9%	2,557	2,415	3,235	3,250	2,980

GLEN BURNIE BANCORP — NAS: GLBZ

101 Crain Highway, S.E.
Glen Burnie, MD 21061
Phone: 410 766-3300
Fax: -
Web: www.thebankofglenburnie.com

CEO: Mark C Hanna
CFO: -
HR: -
FYE: December 31
Type: Public

Glen Burnie Bancorp has an interest in the Old Line State. The institution is the holding company for Bank of Glen Burnie, which has about 10 branches in central Maryland's Anne Arundel County, south of Baltimore. The bank offers such services as checking and savings accounts, money market and individual retirement accounts, CDs, and remote banking services. It focuses on real estate lending, with residential and commercial mortgages accounting for the largest portions of its loan portfolio. The bank also writes indirect automobile loans, which are originated through a network of about 50 area car dealers. Bank of Glen Burnie was founded in 1949.

	Annual Growth	12/19	12/20	12/21	12/22	12/23
Assets ($mil.)	(2.2%)	384.9	419.5	442.1	381.4	351.8
Net income ($ mil.)	(2.8%)	1.6	1.7	2.5	1.7	1.4
Market value ($ mil.)	(15.0%)	33.2	31.7	40.4	24.0	17.3
Employees	(4.7%)	102	90	85	89	84

GLEN ROSE PETROLEUM CORP

1210 West Clay Road, Suite 5
Houston, TX 77019
Phone: 281 974-1655
Fax: -
Web: www.glenrosepetroleum.com

CEO: Andrew Taylor-Kimmins
CFO: Theodore D Williams
HR: -
FYE: March 31
Type: Public

Glen Rose Petroleum is developing oil and gas prospects in South Texas. In 2006 the company, then known as United Heritage Corporation, was acquired by its largest shareholder, Lothian Oil, which holds a 71% stake. However, Lothian Oil filed for bankruptcy in 2007. In order to raise cash the company sold its New Mexico properties that year. Its remaining assets are two leaseholds in the Wardlaw Field in Edwards County, Texas. In 2008 United Heritage changed its name to Glen Rose Petroleum. In 2010 it acquired 5,400 acres in Edwards County, Texas, next to its existing leasehold property, bringing its total acreage to 15,900 acres.

	Annual Growth	03/07	03/08	03/09	03/10	03/11
Sales ($mil.)	2.1%	1.0	0.0	0.1	0.1	1.1
Net income ($ mil.)	-	(11.4)	(3.3)	(2.2)	(2.5)	(14.7)
Market value ($ mil.)	(10.4%)	24.1	22.0	4.7	10.9	15.5
Employees	21.8%	5	5	9	8	11

GLENDALE ADVENTIST MEDICAL CENTER INC

1509 WILSON TER
GLENDALE, CA 912064007
Phone: 818 409-8000
Fax: –
Web: www.adventisthealth.org

CEO: Kevin A Roberts
CFO: –
HR: Sandra Werner
FYE: December 31
Type: Private

Treating ladies from Pasadena and other patients throughout the suburbs of sunny Southern California, Glendale Adventist Medical Center (GAMC) is a stalwart community member. The hospital is part of Adventist Health, a not-for-profit group of about 20 hospitals and health care organizations in four western states. GAMC provides a range of specialty services including cancer treatment, cardiology, emergency medicine, neuroscience, home care, psychiatry, rehabilitation, and women's healthcare. It also provides medical training and residency programs. The 515-bed hospital was founded in 1905 by the Seventh-Day Adventist Church.

	Annual Growth	12/14	12/15	12/17	12/18	12/21
Sales ($mil.)	2.9%	–	408.4	–	502.0	486.1
Net income ($ mil.)	–	–	(15.2)	–	27.0	(48.2)
Market value ($ mil.)	–	–	–	–	–	–
Employees	–	–	–	–	–	2,600

GLENDALE COMMUNITY COLLEGE DIST

1500 N VERDUGO RD
GLENDALE, CA 912082894
Phone: 818 240-1000
Fax: –
Web: www.glendale.edu

CEO: –
CFO: Larry Serot
HR: –
FYE: June 30
Type: Private

Glendale Community College (GCC) offers post-high school education to some 25,000 Southern Californians. Located in the San Rafael Mountains north of Los Angeles, GCC offers college-credit courses to day and evening students, in addition to an adult education program and specialized job training programs from two campuses. Its areas of expertise include biotechnology, environment and energy, and supply chain management. GCC also offers contract instruction administered by the Montrose-located Professional Development Center, which provides businesses with customized training.

	Annual Growth	06/16	06/17	06/18	06/19	06/22
Sales ($mil.)	33.7%	–	13.5	34.8	38.3	57.9
Net income ($ mil.)	46.0%	–	0.5	(2.6)	(38.0)	3.4
Market value ($ mil.)	–	–	–	–	–	–
Employees	–	–	–	–	–	1,500

GLENDIVE MEDICAL CENTER, INC.

202 PROSPECT DR
GLENDIVE, MT 593301999
Phone: 406 345-3306
Fax: –
Web: www.gmc.org

CEO: Parker Powell
CFO: –
HR: Katherine Bosworth
FYE: June 30
Type: Private

Glendive Medical Center provides general medical and surgical care to residents in Glendive, Montana, and surrounding areas. Glendive Medical Center also offers assisted living, long-term care, and hospice facilities. Specialty services include behavioral health, pain management, orthopedics, occupational therapy, radiology, and cardiac rehabilitation.

	Annual Growth	06/17	06/18	06/19	06/20	06/22
Sales ($mil.)	6.1%	–	44.7	45.6	50.5	56.6
Net income ($ mil.)	–	–	(3.5)	(2.1)	0.6	(0.2)
Market value ($ mil.)	–	–	–	–	–	–
Employees	–	–	–	–	–	450

GLENN A. RICK ENGINEERING AND DEVELOPMENT CO.

5620 FRIARS RD
SAN DIEGO, CA 921102513
Phone: 619 291-0708
Fax: –
Web: www.rickengineering.com

CEO: –
CFO: Deborah B Ragione
HR: Alicia Wadsworth
FYE: December 31
Type: Private

Rick Engineering Company provides civil and transportation engineering, planning, and design services for government agencies, real estate companies, and other public and private institutions in the Southwest US. The company's offerings surveying and mapping, water resources modeling, aerial photogrammetry, legal support services, and specialized computer services. The company's urban design and planning division has overseen streetscape improvements, master planning and landscape architecture projects for municipalities and communities. Rick Engineering Company operates from eight offices in Southern California and in Arizona. The firm was founded as Glenn A. Rick Engineering and Development in 1955.

	Annual Growth	12/05	12/06	12/07	12/08	12/09
Sales ($mil.)	(31.7%)	–	–	46.2	36.1	21.6
Net income ($ mil.)	–	–	–	0.3	(1.9)	(1.5)
Market value ($ mil.)	–	–	–	–	–	–
Employees	–	–	–	–	–	224

GLENN O. HAWBAKER, INC.

1952 WADDLE RD STE 203
STATE COLLEGE, PA 168031649
Phone: 814 237-1444
Fax: –
Web: www.goh-inc.com

CEO: –
CFO: –
HR: Michele Foust
FYE: December 31
Type: Private

For Glenn O. Hawbaker (GOH), it's all about making the grade. Founded as an excavating and grading company, GOH provides heavy construction, concrete construction, utility work, asphalt production, and heavy equipment rentals and sales. From its home base in Pennsylvania, the company serves customers in the north-central portion of the state. As part of its business, GOH operates two dozen quarries and eight asphalt production facilities in Pennsylvania, New York, and eastern Ohio (since 2012). Its Hawbaker Engineering subsidiary provides civil engineering services and site designs. The family-owned company was founded in 1952 by Glenn and Thelma Hawbaker, the parents of president and CEO Daniel Hawbaker.

GLOBAL ACQUISITIONS CORP

6730 Las Vegas Boulevard
Las Vegas, NV 89119
Phone: 702 317-7302
Fax: –
Web: –

NBB: AASP
CEO: –
CFO: Ronald S Boreta
HR: –
FYE: December 31
Type: Public

If golf is your sport, then this company has a park for you. All-American SportPark operates Callaway Golf Center (CGC), a 42-acre golf practice facility located at the end of the famous Las Vegas Strip. Amenities include 110 driving stations in two tiers and a lighted nine-hole, par-three golf course called the Divine Nine. The center also features a restaurant and St. Andrews Golf Shop, where customers can buy golf equipment and related merchandise. The founding Boreta family owns more than 20% the company. Tennis pro Andre Agassi and partner Perry Rogers together also own almost 20% of All-American SportPark.

GLOBAL BROKERAGE INC   NBB: GLBR

55 Water Street, Floor 50
New York, NY 10041
Phone: 212 897-7660
Fax: –
Web: www.fxcm.com

CEO: –
CFO: –
HR: –
FYE: December 31
Type: Public

Money talks in more than a dozen different languages at FXCM. The online brokerage specializes in over-the-counter (OTC) foreign exchange (forex) trading for individual investors, or transactions that are bought in one currency and sold in another. FXCM operates through FXCM Holdings, which processes more than 300,000 trades per day for its 163,000 account holders. The firm's institutional trading segment, FXCM Pro, used by banks, hedge funds, and other financial service companies, accounts for less than 10% of revenue. More than three-quarters of the company's trading volume comes from outside the US. FXCM was founded in 1999 and went public in a 2010 initial public offering (IPO).

	Annual Growth	12/12	12/13	12/14	12/15	12/16
Sales ($mil.)	(9.2%)	417.3	489.6	463.8	402.3	284.1
Net income ($ mil.)	67.6%	9.0	14.8	17.2	(553.9)	70.6
Market value ($ mil.)	(8.5%)	61.9	109.6	101.8	102.8	43.3
Employees	(2.3%)	864	934	908	871	787

GLOBAL CONTACT SERVICES, LLC

118B S MAIN ST B
SALISBURY, NC 281444942
Phone: 704 647-9672
Fax: –
Web: www.gcsagents.com

CEO: Greg Alcorn
CFO: –
HR: Amy Lordan
FYE: June 30
Type: Private

Global Contact Services provides outsourced call center services for FORTUNE 500 companies. Making more than 2 million customer contacts each month, the company's services include inbound and outbound acquisition and inbound customer care, as well as market research and survey administration. Global Contact Services serves clients in such industries as insurance, financial services, telecommunications, and publishing. It has provided call center services for such notable clients as AIG, Bank of America, JP Morgan Chase, American Express, and Wells Fargo. The company owns a dozen call centers across the US.

GLOBAL DIVERSIFIED INDUSTRIES, INC.

450 COMMERCE AVE
ATWATER, CA 953019412
Phone: 559 665-5800
Fax: –
Web: www.gdvi.net

CEO: –
CFO: –
HR: –
FYE: April 30
Type: Private

Global Diversified Industries is the new mod squad. Through its Global Modular subsidiary, the company makes pre-fabricated portable modular buildings, mainly for use as classrooms. It also constructs permanent one- and two-story structures. Clients include public and private schools, universities, child-care facilities, and municipalities. The company is active throughout California. Global Diversified divested its MBS Construction subsidiary, which provided construction site management services, in 2006. Company president Phil Hamilton has voting control of more than 20% of Global Diversified's stock.

GLOBAL EXCHANGE

1446 MARKET ST
SAN FRANCISCO, CA 941026004
Phone: 415 255-7296
Fax: –
Web: www.globalexchange.org

CEO: –
CFO: –
HR: –
FYE: June 30
Type: Private

Free trade? Fair trade, man! Global Exchange is a member-driven human rights advocacy organization that lobbies on behalf of Third World artisans and small businesses. Besides influencing corporations like Starbucks to pay fairer prices to suppliers, the group also sells coffee beans, clothing, jewelry, and other products made in underdeveloped countries through retail stores in California and Oregon, as well as through a Web portal. The not-for-profit venture is also in the "reality tour" business, arranging travel to countries off the beaten path, including Cuba, which has led to legal conflicts with the US government. Global Exchange was founded in 1988.

	Annual Growth	12/07	12/08	12/09	12/10*	06/22
Sales ($mil.)	(8.4%)	–	5.1	4.8	4.7	1.5
Net income ($ mil.)	–	–	–	(0.1)	(0.4)	0.2
Market value ($ mil.)	–	–	–	–	–	51
Employees	–					

*Fiscal year change

GLOBAL GEAR & MACHINING LLC

2500 CURTISS ST
DOWNERS GROVE, IL 605154058
Phone: 630 969-9400
Fax: –
Web: www.globalgearllc.com

CEO: –
CFO: –
HR: Gabriela Lopez
FYE: December 29
Type: Private

When you need to get it in gear, you can get gears from Global Gear & Machining. The company is a supplier of various gears and precision mechanical components. Global Gear & Machining produces drilled, milled, and turned gears used in cam shafts, crank shafts, fuel pumps, oil pumps, and other engine parts, along with flywheel adaptors, belt drive pulleys, and sprockets. The company's products can be found in agricultural, construction, and mining equipment, as well as diesel engines designed for industrial, commercial, and marine applications. Global Gear was founded in 1991 and was acquired in late 2002 by IMS Companies, which is 70% owned by Dynagear and 30% owned by Navistar International.

GLOBAL GEOPHYSICAL SERVICES INC

13927 S GESSNER RD
MISSOURI CITY, TX 774891021
Phone: 713 972-9200
Fax: –
Web: www.globalgeophysical.com

CEO: –
CFO: –
HR: –
FYE: December 31
Type: Private

Global Geophysical builds its business from the ground down. It provides seismic data acquisition services to the oil and gas industry for locating potential reservoirs and studying known reserves. Global Geophysical transmits sound waves below the earth's surface to create images of the existing subsurface geology. Its integrated suite of seismic data solutions includes high-resolution RG-3D Reservoir Grade seismic data acquisition, microseismic monitoring, and seismic data processing and interpretation services. The firm's seismic crews have worked in a wide variety of terrains, including deserts, jungles, and swamps, in more than 100 countries. It emerged from Chapter 11 bankruptcy in early 2015.

GLOBAL INDUSTRIAL COMPANY — NYS: GIC

11 Harbor Park Drive
Port Washington, NY 11050
Phone: 516 608-7000
Fax: –
Web: www.investors.globalindustrial.com

CEO: –
CFO: –
HR: –
FYE: December 31
Type: Public

Global Industrial Company is a value-added industrial distributor of more than a million industrial and maintenance, repair and operation (MRO) products in North America going to market through a system of branded e-commerce websites and relationship marketers. Global Industrial also sells a wide array of industrial and maintenance, repair and operation products, markets the company has served since 1949. In addition, the company currently operates multiple e-commerce sites, including www.globalindustrial.com, www.globalindustrial.ca and www.industrialsupplies.com. Global Industrial was founded in 1949. Majority of the company's revenue (roughly 95%) comes from the US.

	Annual Growth	12/19	12/20	12/21	12/22	12/23
Sales ($mil.)	7.7%	946.9	1,029.0	1,063.1	1,166.1	1,274.3
Net income ($ mil.)	9.9%	48.5	65.4	103.3	78.8	70.7
Market value ($ mil.)	11.5%	958.0	1,366.5	1,557.2	895.9	1,478.8
Employees	6.9%	1,430	1,480	1,480	1,650	1,870

GLOBAL INFOTEK, INC.

1920 ASSOCIATION DR STE 100
RESTON, VA 20191
Phone: 703 652-1600
Fax: –
Web: www.globalinfotek.com

CEO: –
CFO: –
HR: –
FYE: December 31
Type: Private

Global InfoTek (GITI) doesn't stand for Governmental IT Inc., but it might as well. Established in 1996, the company primarily designs, builds, and tests information systems for governmental customers. GITI provides database and information management, systems engineering, network design, project management, custom software development, and technology integration services. The company also offers military data analysis software products, such as CMDR, that are designed to enable the transfer of information between other military software applications. Clients have included the US Air Force, Army, and Navy, as well as the Defense Advanced Research Projects Agency (DARPA).

	Annual Growth	12/11	12/12	12/13	12/19	12/21
Sales ($mil.)	24.5%	–	6.4	9.5	30.5	46.3
Net income ($ mil.)	–	–	(0.2)	0.4	1.2	2.6
Market value ($ mil.)	–	–	–	–	–	–
Employees	–	–	–	–	–	120

GLOBAL MARKET DEVELOPMENT CENTER

11201 QUIVAS LOOP
DENVER, CO 802342614
Phone: 719 576-4260
Fax: –
Web: www.gmdc.org

CEO: –
CFO: –
HR: –
FYE: December 31
Type: Private

Generally speaking, The General Merchandise Distributors Council (GMDC) gets beauty and health care manufacturers together with pharmacy and general merchandise suppliers for mutually beneficial buying and selling. GMDC hosts several conferences each year, bringing together wholesalers and retailers. Its education branch publishes studies and white papers and offers marketing training programs. GMDC also publishes weekly newsletters and helps its members connect to industry publications like Drug Store News and Chain Drug Review. The organization was founded in 1970.

	Annual Growth	12/13	12/14	12/15	12/16	12/17
Sales ($mil.)	(2.8%)	–	7.0	5.5	5.3	6.4
Net income ($ mil.)	(63.1%)	–	1.2	(0.4)	(0.9)	0.0
Market value ($ mil.)	–	–	–	–	–	–
Employees	–	–	–	–	–	19

GLOBAL PARTNERS LP — NYS: GLP

P.O. Box 9161, 800 South Street
Waltham, MA 02454-9161
Phone: 781 894-8800
Fax: –
Web: www.globalp.com

CEO: Eric Slifka
CFO: Gregory B Hanson
HR: –
FYE: December 31
Type: Public

Global Partners owns, controls or has access to one of the largest terminal networks of refined petroleum products and renewable fuels in the Northeast. The company wholesales heating oil, residual fuel oil, diesel oil, kerosene, distillates, and gasoline to commercial, retail, and wholesale customers in New England and New York. A major player in the regional home heating oil market, Global Partners operates storage facilities at around 25 bulk terminals, each with a storage capacity of more than 50,000 barrels, and with a collective storage capacity of some 10 million barrels. It also owns and supplies a network of gasoline stations. Wholesale revenues accounts for about 60% of the company's sales.

	Annual Growth	12/19	12/20	12/21	12/22	12/23
Sales ($mil.)	6.0%	13,082	8,321.6	13,248	18,878	16,492
Net income ($ mil.)	43.6%	35.9	102.2	60.8	362.2	152.5
Market value ($ mil.)	20.4%	687.7	567.0	801.3	1,186.1	1,443.3
Employees	(2.5%)	3,860	3,540	3,490	4,310	3,485

GLOBAL PAYMENT TECHNOLOGIES, INC. — NBB: GPTX

170 Wilbur Place
Bohemia, NY 11716
Phone: 631 563-2500
Fax: –
Web: www.gpt.com

CEO: Andre Soussa
CFO: –
HR: –
FYE: September 30
Type: Public

GPT's advice: Don't take any wooden nickels (or counterfeit dollar bills). Global Payment Technologies (GPT) makes systems that detect counterfeit paper currency. The gaming industry accounts for most of GPT's sales, but the company also makes products for vending machines, beverage dispensers, and other devices. GPT's basic currency validators accept, count, and store legal tender. Its advanced Generation II and Argus systems recognize coins and paper denominations from more than 50 countries, and incorporate bar-code readers, security sensors, and other features.

	Annual Growth	09/03	09/04	09/05	09/06	09/07
Sales ($mil.)	(18.3%)	26.1	24.4	25.9	14.3	11.6
Net income ($ mil.)	–	(5.7)	(1.7)	(0.6)	(4.1)	(5.6)
Market value ($ mil.)	(45.1%)	21.4	26.0	23.4	8.4	1.9
Employees	(9.5%)	106	114	102	82	71

GLOBAL PAYMENTS INC — NYS: GPN

3550 Lenox Road
Atlanta, GA 30326
Phone: 770 829-8000
Fax: –
Web: www.globalpaymentsinc.com

CEO: Jeffrey S Sloan
CFO: Paul M Todd
HR: Alix Orza
FYE: December 31
Type: Public

Global Payments is a leading payments technology company delivering innovative software and services to approximately 4 million merchant locations and more than 1,350 financial institutions across more than 170 countries throughout North America, Europe, Asia-Pacific and Latin America. The company also provides authorization services, settlement and funding services, customer support and help-desk functions, fraud solution services, prepaid debit and payroll cards, demand deposit accounts and other financial service solutions to the underbanked. It also provides a variety of value-added services, including specialty point-of-sale solutions, analytic and customer engagement tools, and payroll and human capital management services. Americas generate some 85% of Global Payments' revenue.

	Annual Growth	12/19	12/20	12/21	12/22	12/23
Sales ($mil.)	18.4%	4,911.9	7,423.6	8,523.8	8,975.5	9,654.4
Net income ($ mil.)	23.0%	430.6	584.5	965.5	111.5	986.2
Market value ($ mil.)	(8.7%)	47,535	56,092	35,199	25,861	33,069
Employees	3.0%	24,000	24,000	25,000	25,000	27,000

GLOBALFLUENCY, INC.

1494 HAMILTON AVE
SAN JOSE, CA 951254535
Phone: 408 677-5300
Fax: -
Web: www.globalfluency.com

CEO: -
CFO: -
HR: -
FYE: September 30
Type: Private

GlobalFluency (formerly Neale-May & Partners) offers services with some spin. The independent firm specializes in communications for high-tech companies but doesn't shy away from more traditional companies that need help sending a message. GlobalFluency provides its clients with such services as promotional marketing, crisis management, corporate and financial communication, strategic consulting, and event marketing. The company, which operates more than 70 offices in 40 nations worldwide, serves customers including Google, AT&T, and IBM. In 1987 Donovan Neale-May left his job at Ogilvy & Mather to establish the PR firm, which changed its name in 2008.

GLOBALSCAPE, INC.

6455 CITY WEST PKWY
EDEN PRAIRIE, MN 553443246
Phone: 210 308-8267
Fax: -
Web: www.fortra.com

CEO: -
CFO: -
HR: -
FYE: December 31
Type: Private

GlobalSCAPE is pretty cute, for a software company. With packages like CuteFTP and Enhanced File Transfer (EFT) Server, GlobalSCAPE provides managed file transfer software for businesses and individuals. The company also offers software used to collaborate, share, and backup data in real-time across multiple sites. Its software, which is also offered in hosted and managed versions, is sold primarily to small and midsized businesses and enterprise customers worldwide. GlobalSCAPE has counted Aon, Thomas Cook, Lone Star Bank, and the US Army among its clients. More than two-thirds of sales come from customers in the US.

GLOBALSTAR INC

1351 Holiday Square Blvd.
Covington, LA 70433
Phone: 985 335-1500
Fax: -
Web: www.globalstar.com

ASE: GSAT
CEO: Paul E Jacobs
CFO: Rebecca S Clary
HR: Michelle Hebert
FYE: December 31
Type: Public

Globalstar provides satellite voice and data service to remote areas where landlines and cell towers are few, if anywhere. Its network of satellites and ground stations provides service to approximately 769,000 subscribers worldwide. Customers include the US government as well as companies in the energy, maritime, agriculture, forestry, and mining industries. It also sells a handheld GPS navigation system called SPOT for adventure travelers or anyone needing a GPS device. Company's largest market was the United States with over 70% of total revenue.

	Annual Growth	12/19	12/20	12/21	12/22	12/23
Sales ($mil.)	14.2%	131.7	128.5	124.3	148.5	223.8
Net income ($ mil.)	-	15.3	(109.6)	(112.6)	(256.9)	(24.7)
Market value ($ mil.)	39.1%	975.8	637.0	2,182.2	2,502.0	3,649.5
Employees	0.9%	336	346	329	332	348

GLOBALWORKS GROUP LLC

220 5TH AVE FL 11
NEW YORK, NY 100018017
Phone: 212 867-8680
Fax: -
Web: -

CEO: -
CFO: -
HR: -
FYE: December 31
Type: Private

GlobalWorks is a marketing communications agency blending branding, culture, and technology for international clients. The agency's services include identity and logo design, product naming, broadcast and print ad development, direct mail, interactive advertising, and marketing communications which, when coupled with the agency's expertise in cultural adaptation, localization, and multilingual content development provide the backbone of global marketing campaigns. The company added specialist division HispanicWorks to serve clients interested in reaching the booming Hispanic population in the US. Clients have included Ernst & Young, IKEA, and Medtronic.

	Annual Growth	12/03	12/04	12/05	12/06	12/07
Sales ($mil.)	-	-	-	-	16.6	17.5
Net income ($ mil.)	405.7%	-	-	0.0	0.0	0.4
Market value ($ mil.)	-	-	-	-	-	-
Employees	-	-	-	-	-	11

GLOBE LIFE INC

3700 South Stonebridge Drive
McKinney, TX 75070
Phone: 972 569-4000
Fax: -
Web: www.globelifeinsurance.com

NYS: GL
CEO: Frank M Svoboda
CFO: Thomas P Kalmbach
HR: -
FYE: December 31
Type: Public

Globe Life specializes in providing individual life insurance and supplemental health insurance to middle-income families. Globe Life's subsidiaries, including American Income Life and Globe Life and Accident, offer whole and term life insurance policies and supplemental health insurance coverage including illness, accident, and Medicare Supplement policies. Globe Life sells its products through direct marketing efforts and a network of exclusive and independent agents. Substantially all of Globe Life's business is conducted in the US.

	Annual Growth	12/19	12/20	12/21	12/22	12/23
Assets ($mil.)	1.9%	25,977	29,047	29,768	25,537	28,051
Net income ($ mil.)	6.3%	760.8	731.8	745.0	739.7	970.8
Market value ($ mil.)	3.7%	9,871.5	8,906.4	8,790.1	11,307	11,416
Employees	3.3%	3,196	3,261	3,222	3,543	3,636

GLOBECOMM SYSTEMS INC.

200 EXECUTIVE DR STE G
EDGEWOOD, NY 117178322
Phone: 631 231-9800
Fax: -
Web: www.globecommsystems.com

CEO: -
CFO: -
HR: -
FYE: June 30
Type: Private

Globecomm Systems provides communications networking services, as well as network infrastructure design and installation. The company's services segment, its largest, includes data, voice, and video transport; hosted mobile switching; engineering consulting; and network installation, monitoring, and maintenance. The infrastructure segment involves the design, assembly, and installation of satellite earth stations, complete uplink centers, and media broadcast centers. Globecomm also builds Internet protocol-based communications networks. It is owned by a group of investors led by HPS Investment Partners and Tennenbaum Capital.

GLOBEIMMUNE, INC
NBB: GBIM

1450 Infinite Drive
Louisville, CO 80027
Phone: 303 625-2700
Fax: −
Web: www.globeimmune.com

CEO: Timothy C Rodell
CFO: −
HR: −
FYE: December 31
Type: Public

GlobeImmune would like to stop disease around the world. For now, it works on its proprietary Tarmogen method of stimulating cell-level immunity to cancer and other diseases. It has five cancer candidates targeting pancreatic, lung, colorectal, and thyroid cancers while the fifth addresses the metastasis mechanism in multiple tumors. GlobeImmune's current infectious disease candidates seek to permanently cure hepatitis B and C. The company, which produces its own products, works with Celgene and Gilead Sciences to develop and commercialize the cancer and infectious disease drugs, respectively. The company was formed in 1995 as Ceres Pharmaceutical and changed its name in 2001. It went public in 2014..

	Annual Growth	12/11	12/12	12/13	12/14	12/15
Sales ($mil.)	(23.9%)	−	14.6	22.5	6.0	6.5
Net income ($ mil.)	−	−	(2.0)	9.5	(16.3)	(2.8)
Market value ($ mil.)	−	−	−	−	43.7	22.3
Employees	−	−	−	−	22	2

GLOBUS MEDICAL INC
NYS: GMED

2560 General Armistead Avenue
Audubon, PA 19403-5214
Phone: 610 930-1800
Fax: 302 636-5454
Web: www.globusmedical.com

CEO: Daniel T Scavilla
CFO: Keith Pfeil
HR: −
FYE: December 31
Type: Public

Globus Medical makes procedural and therapeutic medical devices used during spinal surgery. Offerings range from screws and plates to disc replacement systems and bone void fillers. The company has two product segments: Musculoskeletal Solutions (implantable devices, biologics, surgical instruments, and accessories) and Enabling Technologies (imaging, navigation, and robotic-assisted surgery systems). With over 230 product launches across some 25 countries worldwide, the company generates some 85% of its revenue in the US markets. Globus Medical was founded in 2003.

	Annual Growth	12/19	12/20	12/21	12/22	12/23
Sales ($mil.)	18.9%	785.4	789.0	958.1	1,022.8	1,568.5
Net income ($ mil.)	(5.7%)	155.2	102.3	149.2	190.2	122.9
Market value ($ mil.)	(2.5%)	8,027.4	8,891.8	9,843.4	10,126	7,265.3
Employees	25.7%	2,000	2,200	2,400	2,600	5,000

GLORI ENERGY INC
NBB: GLRI

4315 South Drive
Houston, TX 77042
Phone: 713 237-8880
Fax: 713 237-8585
Web: www.glorienergy.com

CEO: Kevin Guilbeau
CFO: Victor M Perez
HR: −
FYE: December 31
Type: Public

Glory be. Oil will flow more freely for oil wells if Glori Energy has its way. The company's novel AERO System for oil recovery uses naturally occurring microbes to break down the barrier between oil and water, allowing more oil to flow from underground formations. It uses a three-step approach to create custom nutrient formulas for microbes at each well site and estimates that its technology, which uses existing pumps and pipelines, can increase oil recovery by up to 100%. While it sounds like something from a sci-fi movie, Shell, Husky, Merit Energy, and Citation Oil are all customers; it has about 10 projects in various stages.

	Annual Growth	03/13	03/14*	12/14	12/15	12/16
Sales ($mil.)	−	−	−	15.9	9.0	4.5
Net income ($ mil.)	−	(0.4)	(2.9)	(18.8)	(36.3)	(12.9)
Market value ($ mil.)	(69.6%)	239.6	248.0	130.1	10.9	2.0
Employees	−	5	5	42	35	−

*Fiscal year change

GLU MOBILE INC.

209 REDWOOD SHORES PKWY
REDWOOD CITY, CA 940651175
Phone: 415 800-6100
Fax: −
Web: www.glu.com

CEO: Nick Earl
CFO: Eric R Ludwig
HR: Sheila Ryan
FYE: December 31
Type: Private

Glu Mobile develops, publishes, and markets a portfolio of free-to-play mobile games designed to appeal to a broad cross section of users who download and make purchases within its games through direct-to-consumer digital storefronts, such as the Apple App Store, Google Play Store, and others. Glu's portfolio includes Cooking Dash, Covet Fashion, Deer Hunter, Design Home, and Diner DASH Adventures. The company has approximately 2.5 million daily active users and some 11.2 million active monthly users. The company gets around 80% of sales in the US. In 2021, Electronic Arts Inc., a global leader in interactive entertainment, completed the acquisition of Glu Mobile Inc. for $2.1 billion in enterprise value.

	Annual Growth	12/16	12/17	12/18	12/19	12/20
Sales ($mil.)	23.5%	−	286.8	366.6	411.4	540.5
Net income ($ mil.)	−	−	(97.6)	(13.2)	8.9	20.4
Market value ($ mil.)	−	−	−	−	−	−
Employees	−	−	−	−	−	715

GLY CONSTRUCTION, INC.

14432 SE EASTGATE WAY STE 300
BELLEVUE, WA 980076493
Phone: 425 451-8877
Fax: −
Web: www.gly.com

CEO: −
CFO: −
HR: −
FYE: September 30
Type: Private

General contracting firm GLY Construction specializes in TLC for commercial construction and sings its praises throughout Washington's Puget Sound region. The firm, which was founded in 1978, has built corporate facilities and distribution centers for the likes of Microsoft, Adobe, Nintendo, Overlake Hospital, and Boeing. The company's heating, ventilation, and air conditioning (HVAC) operations began in 1993 when one of its subcontractors entered into bankruptcy. GLY Construction is owned by its nine principals, including company president and CEO Lee Kilcup.

GLYCOMIMETICS INC
NMS: GLYC

9708 Medical Center Drive
Rockville, MD 20850
Phone: 240 243-1201
Fax: −
Web: www.glycomimetics.com

CEO: Rachel King
CFO: Brian Hahn
HR: Margot Mongold
FYE: December 31
Type: Public

Carbs are a good thing to GlycoMimetics. The biotechnology company uses carbohydrate chemistry to develop drug candidates for rare diseases. Its lead drug candidate is designed to treat vaso-occlusive crisis (VOC), a painful condition that affects people with sickle cell disease. If approved, it would be the first drug to treat the cause of VOC and potentially reduce dependence on narcotics for pain management. Pfizer bought the rights to develop and commercialize the VOC drug. In addition, the company is developing a drug to assist people with acute myeloid leukemia (AML) during chemotherapy. GlycoMimetics went public in 2014. It raised $56 million and plans to use the proceeds to further fund clinical trials.

	Annual Growth	12/18	12/19	12/20	12/21	12/22
Sales ($mil.)	−	−	−	10.2	1.2	0.0
Net income ($ mil.)	−	(48.3)	(57.9)	(51.0)	(63.4)	(46.7)
Market value ($ mil.)	(24.8%)	515.0	287.7	204.5	78.3	164.8
Employees	(6.0%)	50	57	54	52	39

GMS INC
NYS: GMS

100 Crescent Centre Parkway, Suite 800
Tucker, GA 30084
Phone: 800 392-4619
Fax: –
Web: www.gms.com

CEO: John C Turner Jr
CFO: Scott M Deakin
HR: Leigh Dobbs
FYE: April 30
Type: Public

GMS is a leading North American specialty building products distributor. The company operates a network of more than 300 distribution centers with extensive product offerings of wallboard, ceilings, steel framing and complementary construction products. It also operates more than 100 tool sales, rental and service centers. Through these operations, the company provides a comprehensive selection of building products and solutions for its residential and commercial contractor customer base across the US and Canada. Founded in 1971, the company generates about 90% of the total revenue is generated from the US.

	Annual Growth	04/19	04/20	04/21	04/22	04/23
Sales ($mil.)	14.4%	3,116.0	3,241.3	3,298.8	4,634.9	5,329.3
Net income ($ mil.)	56.2%	56.0	23.4	105.6	273.4	333.0
Market value ($ mil.)	34.7%	721.9	753.0	1,790.8	1,964.6	2,378.8
Employees	4.8%	5,800	5,308	5,843	5,475	7,007

GOLD RESERVE INC
TVX: GRZ

999 West Riverside Avenue, Suite 401
Spokane, WA 99201
Phone: 509 623-1500
Fax: 509 623-1634
Web: www.goldreserveinc.com

CEO: Rockne J Timm
CFO: Robert A McGuinness
HR: –
FYE: December 31
Type: Public

Gold Reserve's primary asset was the Brisas project in Venezuela, which contains estimated reserves of about 10 million ounces of gold and 1.4 billion pounds of copper. Gold Reserve had been developing Brisas since 1992. However, all activity on the mine ceased in late 2009 when the Venezuelan government canceled Gold Reserve's permits and seized the assets of the Brisas project. The company is pursuing an arbitration claim through the World Bank against the Venezuelan government in an effort to recoup its investment in the Brisas project. The company is restructuring its debt while it continues it $2.1 arbitration claim.

	Annual Growth	12/18	12/19	12/20	12/21	12/22
Sales ($mil.)	(69.2%)	51.6	1.6	0.3	0.0	0.5
Net income ($ mil.)	–	41.9	(13.1)	(11.5)	(10.6)	(8.6)
Market value ($ mil.)	(11.4%)	205.1	150.0	159.3	118.5	126.4
Employees	–	–	–	–	–	5

GODADDY INC
NYS: GDDY

2155 E. GoDaddy Way
Tempe, AZ 85284
Phone: 480 505-8800
Fax: –
Web: www.godaddy.com

CEO: Aman Bhutani
CFO: Mark McCaffrey
HR: –
FYE: December 31
Type: Public

GoDaddy provides cloud-based solutions, delivering simple, easy-to-use products, services and outcome-driven, personalized guidance to small businesses, individuals, organizations, developers, designers, and domain investors. The company is uniquely positioned to help customers with their evolution of e-commerce, social media, and consumer expectations of their online and in-person experience. The company has a global brand with high awareness and are one of the largest domain name providers, with nearly 84 million domains representing 24% of the approximately 350 million domain names registered worldwide as of September 30, 2022. The majority of GoDaddy's revenue are generated domestically.

	Annual Growth	12/19	12/20	12/21	12/22	12/23
Sales ($mil.)	9.2%	2,988.1	3,316.7	3,815.7	4,091.3	4,254.1
Net income ($ mil.)	78.0%	137.0	(495.1)	242.3	352.2	1,374.8
Market value ($ mil.)	11.8%	9,665.7	11,805	12,076	10,648	15,108
Employees	(3.2%)	7,024	6,621	6,611	6,910	6,159

GOLD RESOURCE CORP
ASE: GORO

7900 E. Union Ave., Suite 320
Denver, CO 80237
Phone: 303 320-7708
Fax: –
Web: www.goldresourcecorp.com

CEO: Allen Palmiere
CFO: Chet Holyoak
HR: –
FYE: December 31
Type: Public

Mining company Gold Resource aims to produce gold and other minerals from projects where operating costs are low. The company focuses on its El Aguila project in the southern Mexican state of Oaxaca. The El Aguila project, which began in 2010 at a shallow, open-pit mine, now includes an underground mine, La Arista. The deposit being mined at El Aguila includes not only gold and silver, but also copper, lead, and zinc. In addition to its primary operations, the company has interests in exploration properties in Oaxaca. Gold Resource was formed in 1998.

	Annual Growth	12/19	12/20	12/21	12/22	12/23
Sales ($mil.)	(7.8%)	135.4	90.7	125.2	138.7	97.7
Net income ($ mil.)	–	5.8	4.4	8.0	(6.3)	(16.0)
Market value ($ mil.)	(49.0%)	491.4	258.1	138.4	135.7	33.3
Employees	(6.2%)	630	581	10	16	488

GODDARD COLLEGE CORPORATION

123 PITKIN RD
PLAINFIELD, VT 056679432
Phone: 802 454-8311
Fax: –
Web: www.goddard.edu

CEO: –
CFO: –
HR: –
FYE: June 30
Type: Private

Goddard College offers progressive higher education based on the philosophies of educator John Dewey. Founded in 1938, the school offers bachelor's and master's degrees in areas such as creative writing, socially responsible business, consciousness studies, and transformative language arts. It also provides education studies leading to teaching certification. Most study is completed independently, with students attending the campus for intensive eight to 10 day sessions every six months. About two-thirds of Goddard's students are enrolled in graduate programs. Notable alumni include actor William H. Macy, author and playwright David Mamet, and poet Mark Doty.

	Annual Growth	06/17	06/18	06/20	06/21	06/22
Sales ($mil.)	(2.3%)	–	9.8	8.2	9.4	8.9
Net income ($ mil.)	–	–	(0.7)	(0.6)	1.5	0.1
Market value ($ mil.)	–	–	–	–	–	–
Employees	–	–	–	–	–	70

GOLD STAR CHILI, INC.

650 LUNKEN PARK DR
CINCINNATI, OH 452261800
Phone: 513 231-4541
Fax: –
Web: www.goldstarchili.com

CEO: Roger David
CFO: James Conover
HR: –
FYE: December 31
Type: Private

It's pretty easy to guess what the specialty of the house is at these restaurants. Gold Star Chili operates and franchises about 100 quick-service style eateries in Ohio, Indiana, and Kentucky that specialize in chili. Customers can have chili over fries, hot dogs, chips, or with garlic bread. The signature "3 Way" includes chili over spaghetti with grated cheese; more toppings can be added to make a four- or five-way. Gold Star, the official chili of the Cincinnati Bengals football team, also sells products through retail grocers and online. The Daoud family founded the company in 1965.

	Annual Growth	12/03	12/04	12/05	12/06	12/07
Sales ($mil.)	(6.3%)	–	25.5	20.1	20.1	20.9
Net income ($ mil.)	(55.7%)	–	25.1	2.5	2.3	2.2
Market value ($ mil.)	–	–	–	–	–	–
Employees	–	–	–	–	–	170

GOLD-EAGLE COOPERATIVE

415 LOCUST ST
GOLDFIELD, IA 505425092
Phone: 515 825-3161
Fax: –
Web: www.goldeaglecoop.com

CEO: –
CFO: –
HR: –
FYE: September 30
Type: Private

For Gold-Eagle Cooperative, service to its member/farmers is the golden rule. The firm is a member-owned agricultural co-op located in north central Iowa. It offers its members grain drying, custom crop spraying, feed, seed, fertilizer, and other bulk and packaged farm chemicals, storage and warehousing, as well as feed milling and marketing. The co-op runs a transportation fleet of grain-hoppers, feed-bottle trucks, and specialty trailers that take members' crops to and from its facilities. Gold-Eagle operates nine grain elevator/service center locations.

	Annual Growth	09/07	09/08	09/09	09/16	09/17
Sales ($mil.)	(0.8%)	–	–	302.7	309.7	284.1
Net income ($ mil.)	(1.8%)	–	–	10.0	10.0	8.7
Market value ($ mil.)	–	–	–	–	–	–
Employees	–	–	–	–	–	215

GOLDEN ENTERPRISES, INC.

1 GOLDEN FLAKE DR
BIRMINGHAM, AL 352053312
Phone: 205 458-7316
Fax: –
Web: www.utzsnacks.com

CEO: Dylan Lissette
CFO: Todd Staub
HR: –
FYE: May 29
Type: Private

Snackers who crave a taste for the South seek Golden Enterprises. Operating through subsidiary Golden Flake Snack Foods, the company makes and distributes a barbecue and other Southern flavored-varieties of potato chips, fried pork skins, corn chips, onion rings, and baked and fried cheese curls, among others. It also markets peanut butter, canned dips, dried meat snacks, pretzels, and nuts packed by other manufacturers under the Golden Flake brand. The Golden Flake lineup is sold through the company's sales force to commercial enterprises that sell food products across the Southeastern US, as well as through independent distributors. The company was founded in 1946 as Magic City Food Products. In 2016 snack food company Utz acquired the company for $135 million.

	Annual Growth	05/11	05/12	05/13	05/14	05/15
Sales ($mil.)	(2.1%)	–	–	137.3	135.9	131.7
Net income ($ mil.)	25.1%	–	–	1.1	0.9	1.8
Market value ($ mil.)	–	–	–	–	–	–
Employees	–	–	–	–	–	749

GOLDEN ENTERTAINMENT INC

NMS: GDEN

6595 S Jones Boulevard
Las Vegas, NV 89118
Phone: 702 893-7777
Fax: –
Web: www.goldenent.com

CEO: Blake L Sartini II
CFO: Charles H Protell
HR: Anne Lalama
FYE: December 31
Type: Public

Golden Entertainment is a gaming company. The company operates more than 12,000 slot machines and video lottery terminals, as well as approximately 30 table games in Nevada, Montana, and Maryland across four casino properties and more than 50 taverns. Its Golden Casino Group manages the Pahrump Nugget Hotel & Casino; Gold Town Casino and Lakeside Casino and RV Park and in Flintstone, Maryland; and the Rocky Gap Resort. All of the properties feature gaming, dining, and entertainment.

	Annual Growth	12/19	12/20	12/21	12/22	12/23
Sales ($mil.)	2.0%	973.4	694.2	1,096.5	1,121.7	1,053.1
Net income ($ mil.)	–	(39.5)	(136.6)	161.8	82.3	255.8
Market value ($ mil.)	20.1%	551.0	570.2	1,448.6	1,072.2	1,144.8
Employees	(7.7%)	8,000	6,700	6,300	6,400	5,800

GOLDEN GATE NATIONAL PARKS CONSERVANCY

201 FORT MASON
SAN FRANCISCO, CA 941231307
Phone: 415 561-3000
Fax: –
Web: www.parksconservancy.org

CEO: Greg Moore
CFO: –
HR: –
FYE: September 30
Type: Private

San Francisco, open your Golden Gate -- National Parks, that is. The Golden Gate National Parks Conservancy is dedicated to preserving and enhancing the national parks in the San Francisco Bay area. The not-for-profit organization is a cooperating association authorized by the US Congress to assist and support the National Park Service in operating almost 40 national park sites in and around the City by the Bay. The Golden Gate National Recreation Area includes such sites as Alcatraz Island, Fort Point, Muir Woods in nearby Marin County, and the Presidio of San Francisco (a former US Army base that was decommissioned in 1994). The conservancy was established in 1981.

	Annual Growth	09/17	09/18	09/19	09/21	09/22
Sales ($mil.)	(7.9%)	–	78.8	67.5	31.5	56.7
Net income ($ mil.)	–	–	25.2	8.6	(39.1)	(14.8)
Market value ($ mil.)	–	–	–	–	–	–
Employees	–	–	–	–	–	514

GOLDEN GRAIN ENERGY, LLC

1822 43RD ST SW
MASON CITY, IA 504017071
Phone: 641 423-8525
Fax: –
Web: www.ggecorn.com

CEO: Chad E Kuhlers
CFO: Brooke Peters
HR: –
FYE: October 31
Type: Private

The fruited plains with their golden grains have yielded Golden Grain Energy, an ethanol production company with a plant in Iowa that converts corn into ethanol, which is most commonly used as an additive to unleaded gasoline. Other uses include high octane fuel enhancer and a non-petroleum fuel substitute. Golden Grain Energy's plant has a production capacity of 110 million gallons of ethanol and 120,000 tons of distillers grains per year. The distillers grains are used to produce animal feed. In 2009, with raw material costs rising and selling prices falling, the company cut back production at the plant.

GOLDEN KRUST CARIBBEAN BAKERY INC.

399 KNOLLWOOD RD STE 115
WHITE PLAINS, NY 106031900
Phone: 718 655-7878
Fax: –
Web: www.goldenkrust.com

CEO: –
CFO: –
HR: Lorna Hawthorne
FYE: December 31
Type: Private

Golden Krust Caribbean Bakery & Grill operates a chain of about 120 franchised quick-service restaurants that specializes in jerk chicken dishes and Jamaican-style patties (pocket pastries filled with spiced chicken or beef). The eateries also serve such bakery items as pastries, cake, and sugar buns. Most Golden Krust Caribbean Bakery outlets are found in and around the New York City area; the chain has additional locations in Florida, New Jersey, and half a dozen other states in along the Eastern seaboard. In addition to the restaurants, the company sells its frozen Jamaican pastries at retail food stores throughout the US. CEO Lowell Hawthorne and his family started the business in 1989.

	Annual Growth	08/09	08/10	08/11*	12/12	12/16
Sales ($mil.)	16.6%	–	–	15.3	26.7	33.0
Net income ($ mil.)	(2.5%)	–	–	0.8	0.9	0.7
Market value ($ mil.)	–	–	–	–	–	–
Employees	–	–	–	–	–	200

*Fiscal year change

GOLDEN MINERALS CO
ASE: AUMN

350 Indiana Street, Suite 650
Golden, CO 80401
Phone: 303 839-5060
Fax: -
Web: www.goldenminerals.com

CEO: Warren M Rehn
CFO: Robert P Vogels
HR: -
FYE: December 31
Type: Public

Golden Minerals owns and operates a precious metals mine in Mexico, an exploration property in Argentina, and a portfolio of mining and exploration sites in parts of Mexico and South America. The company has been expanding its production at the Velarde a and Chicago mines in Mexico and is in the advanced evaluation stage at its El Quevar silver project in northwest Argentina. It sold most of its exploration properties in Peru in 2013. The company's strategy is focused on establishing itself as a mid-tier producer and expanding its precious metal operations in Mexico and Argentina. The company also has a joint venture with Golden Tag Resources in the San Diego silver project in Mexico.

	Annual Growth	12/19	12/20	12/21	12/22	12/23
Sales ($mil.)	11.6%	7.7	5.6	25.6	23.3	12.0
Net income ($ mil.)	-	(5.4)	(9.1)	(2.1)	(9.9)	(9.2)
Market value ($ mil.)	13.8%	4.4	10.7	4.9	3.9	7.3
Employees	3.4%	170	192	248	238	194

GOLDEN STAR ENTERPRISES LTD
NBB: GSPT

2803 Philadelphia Pike, Suite B #565
Claymont, DE 19703
Phone: 888 680-8033
Fax: -
Web: www.goldenstarenterprisesltd.com

CEO: -
CFO: -
HR: -
FYE: December 31
Type: Public

Terralene Fuels (formerly Golden Spirit Enterprises) has had many lives -- and many names. Founded in 1993 as Power Direct, an oil-and-gas exploration company, this development-stage firm has undergone several different incarnations. It took a gamble on online poker through its goldenspiritpoker.com site. After Congress passed the Unlawful Internet Gambling Enforcement Act of 2006, Golden Spirit again switched gears seeking to develop waste-recycled products. In 2010 the company launched its Terralene Fuel product, an alternative to ethanol-blended gasoline. It changed its name to Terralene Fuels in 2011 to reflect its core business.

	Annual Growth	12/17	12/18	12/19	12/20	12/21
Sales ($mil.)	29.8%	0.0	0.0	-	0.0	0.0
Net income ($ mil.)	-	(0.7)	(0.3)	(0.2)	(0.5)	(2.2)
Market value ($ mil.)	9.4%	10.7	11.7	2.9	1.4	15.3
Employees	-	-	-	-	-	-

GOLDEN STATE FOODS CORP.

18301 VON KARMAN AVE STE 1100
IRVINE, CA 926121009
Phone: 949 247-8000
Fax: -
Web: www.goldenstatefoods.com

CEO: -
CFO: -
HR: -
FYE: December 31
Type: Private

Golden State Foods (GSF) is a leading US food service company and a primary supplier for fast-food giant McDonald's. It processes and distributes liquid products (sauces, dressings, condiments, syrups and toppings, dairy-based beverages, and ice cream), meat and produce, and also provides logistics services such as Central Freight Management. The company services more than 100 leading brands and approximately 125,000 restaurants and stores from its more than 50 international locations across the globe. Founded in 1947 by the late Bill Moore, GSF is controlled by an investment group led by the company's chairman and CEO Mark Wetterau.

GOLDEN STATE HEALTH CENTERS, INC.

13347 VENTURA BLVD
SHERMAN OAKS, CA 914233979
Phone: 818 385-3200
Fax: -
Web: www.goldenstatehealth.com

CEO: Martin J Weiss
CFO: Ronald Mayer
HR: Jacob Lunger
FYE: March 31
Type: Private

Golden State Health Centers operates a network of long-term care facilities that serve southern California's elderly. The company's facilities include skilled nursing homes and assisted-living centers in the greater Los Angeles area. In addition to living and nursing care, Golden State Health Centers also provide psychiatric treatment, wound and respiratory care, physical therapy, and rehabilitation services. The company also has facilities that provide mental health services for younger patients, and it operates a center specializing in care for patients with Alzheimer's disease. The company was established in 1968.

	Annual Growth	11/99	11/00	11/01*	03/08	03/09
Sales ($mil.)	25.4%	-	-	58.7	-	359.7
Net income ($ mil.)	39.1%	-	-	4.3	-	59.9
Market value ($ mil.)	-	-	-	-	-	-
Employees	-	-	-	-	-	800

*Fiscal year change

GOLDEN STATE WARRIORS, LLC

1 WARRIORS WAY
SAN FRANCISCO, CA 941582250
Phone: 415 388-0100
Fax: -
Web: www.warriors.com

CEO: -
CFO: -
HR: -
FYE: June 30
Type: Private

These Warriors call the hardwood floor their battlefield. The Golden State Warriors professional basketball team has had a long and storied history since joining the Basketball Association of America (now the National Basketball Association) as a charter member in 1946. Originally formed as the Philadelphia Warriors by Eddie Gottlieb, the team moved to San Francisco in 1962 before relocating across the bay in 1971. Now playing host at Oracle Arena, the Warriors franchise boasts four NBA championships, its most recent in 2015. Former cable television system mogul Chris Cohan has controlled the franchise since 1995.

	Annual Growth	06/16	06/17	06/18	06/19	06/21
Sales ($mil.)	(18.3%)	-	-	-	4.6	3.1
Net income ($ mil.)	-	-	-	-	0.2	(1.4)
Market value ($ mil.)	-	-	-	-	-	-
Employees	-	-	-	-	-	100

GOLDMAN SACHS GROUP INC
NYS: GS

200 West Street
New York, NY 10282
Phone: 212 902-1000
Fax: 212 902-3000
Web: www.goldmansachs.com

CEO: David Solomon
CFO: Denis P Coleman III
HR: -
FYE: December 31
Type: Public

Goldman Sachs is a leading global financial institution that delivers a broad range of financial services across investment banking, securities, investment management and consumer banking to a large and diversified client base that includes corporations, financial institutions, governments and individuals. Goldman Sachs boasts some 2.5 trillion in assets under supervision covering all major asset classes. The firm was founded in 1869. The vast majority of its revenue comes from its Americas region.

	Annual Growth	12/19	12/20	12/21	12/22	12/23
Assets ($mil.)	13.4%	992,968	1,163,028	1,463,988	1,441,799	1,641,594
Net income ($ mil.)	0.1%	8,466.0	9,459.0	21,635	11,261	8,516.0
Market value ($ mil.)	13.8%	74,354	85,278	123,708	111,041	124,749
Employees	4.3%	38,300	40,500	43,900	48,500	45,300

GOLDRICH MINING CO

2525 E. 29th Ave. Ste. 10B-160
Spokane, WA 99223
Phone: 509 535-7367
Fax: –
Web: www.goldrichmining.com

NBB: GRMC
CEO: Steve Vincent
CFO: Ted R Sharp
HR: –
FYE: December 31
Type: Public

Goldrich Mining Company is looking in a remote area of northern Alaska to get rich off gold. The development-stage company is exploring a mining site in Chandalar, where gold was first discovered at the turn of the 20th century. Goldrich has mineral rights to 17,000 acres on land owned by the state of Alaska. The Chandalar property does not have any proved reserves, but the site did produce about 1,500 ounces of fine gold and 250 ounces of fine silver in 2010. However, its arctic climate creates a limited mining season; the company can only conduct business there for a few months every summer. Goldrich was incorporated in 1959 and has been public since 1970, buying its first mining claims in Chandalar in 1972.

	Annual Growth	12/18	12/19	12/20	12/21	12/22
Sales ($mil.)	–	–	–	–	–	–
Net income ($ mil.)	–	(3.8)	(2.6)	(2.2)	(1.8)	(1.1)
Market value ($ mil.)	10.5%	3.7	4.5	5.2	14.4	5.6
Employees	(57.4%)	61	2	2	2	2

GONZAGA UNIVERSITY

502 E BOONE AVE
SPOKANE, WA 992580001
Phone: 509 328-4220
Fax: –
Web: www.gonzaga.edu

CEO: –
CFO: –
HR: Kirk Wood-Gaines
FYE: May 31
Type: Private

Gonzaga University is a private liberal arts institution providing instruction to more than 7,800 undergraduate, graduate, doctoral, and law students. The school offers about 75 undergraduate majors, two dozen master's degree programs, and two leadership study doc at its six colleges and schools. The university offers a juris doctorate degree at its School of Law. The Roman Catholic university is run by the Society of Jesus -- the Jesuits -- and is named after a sixteenth-century Italian Jesuit, Aloysius Gonzaga, the patron saint of youth. The university was founded in 1887 as a men's college.

	Annual Growth	05/17	05/18	05/20	05/21	05/22
Sales ($mil.)	(0.4%)	–	232.0	242.0	228.6	228.6
Net income ($ mil.)	43.3%	–	30.3	12.9	127.6	127.6
Market value ($ mil.)	–	–	–	–	–	–
Employees	–	–	–	–	–	1,200

GOOD KARMA BROADCASTING LLC

100 BILL MCCOLLUM WAY
BEAVER DAM, WI 539161306
Phone: 608 758-9025
Fax: –
Web: www.goodkarmabrands.com

CEO: Craig Karmazin
CFO: –
HR: –
FYE: December 31
Type: Private

For those sports fans with rituals, lucky charms, and other superstitious methods of ensuring victory for their teams, Good Karma Broadcasting might just be the right place to listen to games. A local radio station broadcaster, GKB operates nine radio stations in small to large-sized markets in Wisconsin, Ohio, and Florida. Most of its stations are ESPN affiliates in mid-sized and large markets, including Cleveland; Madison (Wisconsin); and West Palm Beach. The Wisconsin-based broadcaster also operates a news station and a country station in its home town of Beaver Dam, as well as a rock station in Janesville. GKB was founded in 1997 by president and CEO Craig Karmazin.

GOOD SAMARITAN HOSPITAL

520 S 7TH ST
VINCENNES, IN 475911038
Phone: 812 882-5220
Fax: –
Web: www.gshvin.org

CEO: –
CFO: –
HR: Dean Wagoner
FYE: December 31
Type: Private

Good Samaritan Hospital provides a full slate of healthcare services to both southwest Indiana and southeast Illinois. Its services include cardiology, emergency care, orthopedics, women's health, and pediatrics, among others. The 230-bed hospital is located a few blocks from the Wabash River, which forms the border between the Hoosier and Prairies states. Good Samaritan operates specialty units, as well, including same-day surgery, breast care, behavioral health, radiology, sleep, cancer care, and rehabilitation centers. It also provides home health and hospice services. Established in 1908 with 25 beds, Good Samaritan was Indiana's first county hospital.

	Annual Growth	12/17	12/18	12/20	12/21	12/22
Sales ($mil.)	3.1%	–	323.3	324.7	339.4	364.7
Net income ($ mil.)	–	–	(12.0)	10.6	7.3	(13.0)
Market value ($ mil.)	–	–	–	–	–	–
Employees	–	–	–	–	–	1,900

GOOD SAMARITAN HOSPITAL

2222 PHILADELPHIA DR
DAYTON, OH 454061891
Phone: 937 278-2612
Fax: –
Web: www.montortho.net

CEO: –
CFO: –
HR: –
FYE: December 31
Type: Private

Good Samaritan Hospital offers a caring hand to the residents of Dayton, Ohio, and the surrounding areas. The hospital has some 560 beds and offers a mix of services, including primary and emergency care, pediatric specialties, and a family birthing center. Good Samaritan also runs the Samaritan North Health Center, an outpatient health center that offers outpatient surgery, rehab and sports medicine, diagnostic imaging, and cancer care, among other services. Other operations include the Maria-Joseph Living Care Center, a long-term care facility with some 400 beds, and Samaritan Family Care, a primary care physicians' network. Good Samaritan Hospital is part of Premier Health Partners.

	Annual Growth	12/02	12/03	12/05	12/06	12/15
Sales ($mil.)	1.1%	–	282.8	274.3	307.2	321.6
Net income ($ mil.)	(8.5%)	–	20.5	(5.2)	12.0	7.1
Market value ($ mil.)	–	–	–	–	–	–
Employees	–	–	–	–	–	2,000

GOOD SAMARITAN HOSPITAL MEDICAL CENTER

1000 MONTAUK HWY
WEST ISLIP, NY 117954927
Phone: 631 376-3000
Fax: –
Web: www.chsli.org

CEO: –
CFO: –
HR: –
FYE: December 31
Type: Private

The folks at Good Samaritan Hospital Medical Center have plenty of reasons to feel good about their efforts. The hospital is part of Catholic Health Services of Long Island (CHS) and serves the south shore community of West Islip, New York. The full-service medical center boasts 900 physicians and 440 acute care beds, offering a complete range of health care, counseling, and rehabilitation services. Good Samaritan provides emergency medicine and trauma care, in addition to oncology, cardiology, pediatric, woman's health, diagnostic, and surgical care. It also operates the Good Samaritan Nursing Home, a 100-bed skilled nursing facility, as well as satellite clinics and a home health care agency.

	Annual Growth	12/14	12/15	12/19	12/21	12/22
Sales ($mil.)	7.9%	–	505.1	725.2	735.1	858.7
Net income ($ mil.)	(4.6%)	–	28.8	20.1	28.1	20.7
Market value ($ mil.)	–	–	–	–	–	–
Employees	–	–	–	–	–	3,774

GOOD SAMARITAN HOSPITAL, L.P.

2425 SAMARITAN DR
SAN JOSE, CA 951243985
Phone: 408 559-2011
Fax: -
Web: www.goodsamsanjose.com

CEO: -
CFO: Darrel Neuenschwander
HR: Stacey Lawson
FYE: January 31
Type: Private

Good Samaritan Hospital lends a hand to help Silicon Valley's techies and their neighbors stay healthy. The facility, part of the HCA family of for-profit hospitals, administers care through campuses in San Jose (the main campus) and Los Gatos, California. Good Samaritan Hospital provides general acute care as well as a host of tertiary services that include cardiology and cardiovascular surgery; oncology; obstetrics and gynecology; and psychiatry (both inpatient and outpatient care). The main campus hospital has some 408 patient beds and 600 physicians, and the Los Gatos outpatient and short-stay facility houses approximately 100 beds.

GOOD TIMES RESTAURANTS INC.

651 Corporate Circle
Golden, CO 80401
Phone: 303 384-1400
Fax: -
Web: www.goodtimesburgers.com

NAS: GTIM
CEO: Ryan M Zink
CFO: Ryan M Zink
HR: -
FYE: September 26
Type: Public

Good Times Restaurants operates and franchises more than 50 Good Times Drive Thru fast-food eateries located primarily in the Denver area. The hamburger chain is made up mostly of double drive-through and walk-up eateries that feature a menu of burgers, fries, and frozen custard. A limited number of Good Times outlets also offer dine-in seating. More than 20 of the locations are operated by franchisees, while the rest are co-owned and co-operated under joint venture agreements. The family of director Geoffrey Bailey owns almost 30% of the company.

	Annual Growth	09/19	09/20	09/21	09/22	09/23
Sales ($mil.)	5.7%	110.8	109.9	124.0	138.2	138.1
Net income ($ mil.)	-	(5.1)	(13.9)	16.8	(2.6)	11.1
Market value ($ mil.)	15.5%	19.2	16.3	58.9	25.0	34.2
Employees	(3.0%)	2,535	2,318	2,230	2,411	2,245

GOOD360

675 N WASHINGTON ST STE 330
ALEXANDRIA, VA 223141934
Phone: 703 836-2121
Fax: -
Web: www.good360.org

CEO: Romaine Seguin
CFO: Ken Troshinsky
HR: -
FYE: December 31
Type: Private

Good360 (formerly Gifts in Kind International) helps companies find ways to be kind. The not-for-profit organization accepts gifts of products and services from corporate clients and distributes these donations to more than 150,000 community charities in the US and globally that directly help communities and people in need. About half of the FORTUNE 100 makes contributions through Good360, which has certified more than 200,000 charities as potential recipients. Good360 began operating in 1983 when 3M donated $12 million in new office equipment. The organization is known for its cost-efficiency, as more than 99% of its donations go directly to communities.

	Annual Growth	12/12	12/13	12/14	12/15	12/19
Sales ($mil.)	0.8%	-	310.0	314.5	382.9	325.0
Net income ($ mil.)	-	-	(12.7)	2.6	4.1	(13.5)
Market value ($ mil.)	-	-	-	-	-	-
Employees	-	-	-	-	-	36

GOODFELLOW BROS. LLC

135 N WENATCHEE AVE
WENATCHEE, WA 988012238
Phone: 509 662-7111
Fax: -
Web: www.goodfellowbros.com

CEO: Chad Goodfellow
CFO: Dan Reisenauer
HR: -
FYE: December 31
Type: Private

The good men at Goodfellow Bros. build everything from golf courses to runways, to dams and residences. The family-owned company specializes in heavy construction, infrastructure, transportation systems, and housing and recreation facilities in the western continental US and Hawaii. Goodfellow Bros. also offers earth moving and paving services. Its Blasting Technologies subsidiary blasts, drills, and demolishes rock and other structures. The company was founded in 1921 by brothers Jack, Bert, and Jim Sr. Their early business included the first excavation work on the Grand Coulee Dam in 1933. Now the company has a number of planned communities, public facilities, and other projects under its belt.

	Annual Growth	12/05	12/06	12/07	12/08	12/09
Sales ($mil.)	(32.0%)	-	-	519.9	-	240.2
Net income ($ mil.)	444829.9%	-	-	0.0	-	19.8
Market value ($ mil.)	-	-	-	-	-	-
Employees	-	-	-	-	-	800

GOODHEART-WILLCOX CO., INC.

18604 West Creek Drive
Tinley Park, IL 60477
Phone: 708 687-5000
Fax: 888 409-3900
Web: www.g-w.com

NBB: GWOX
CEO: John F Flanagan
CFO: -
HR: -
FYE: April 30
Type: Public

Goodheart-Willcox's educational textbooks run more toward HVAC than Homer. The company publishes textbooks, workbooks, computer software supplements, and instructor's guides for junior and senior high schools, vocational schools, technical and private trade schools, and colleges. Its titles cover industrial and technical topics (AutoCAD, drafting) and family and consumer topics (child care, nutrition). Apprentice trainers, educators, and do-it-yourselfers also use the company's books. Goodheart-Willcox hires authors and designs, edits, illustrates, and sells its books directly to schools or through bookstores. The company was founded in 1921.

	Annual Growth	04/11	04/19	04/20	04/21	04/22
Sales ($mil.)	5.7%	21.4	29.3	28.4	32.3	39.3
Net income ($ mil.)	12.5%	1.9	3.6	2.5	3.9	6.9
Market value ($ mil.)	6.6%	33.5	68.4	87.7	56.2	67.5
Employees	-	-	-	-	-	-

GOODMAN NETWORKS INCORPORATED

2801 NETWORK BLVD STE 300
FRISCO, TX 750341881
Phone: 972 406-9692
Fax: -
Web: -

CEO: John Goodman
CFO: John Debus
HR: Paulette Malone
FYE: December 31
Type: Private

Goodman Solutions builds the infrastructure for good end-to-end telecom networks. The family- and minority-owned company provides a variety of telecommunications services to the wireless industry, with services such as network design, engineering, deployment, integration, and maintenance. The company also offers staffing services as well as supply chain management services, such as materials management and logistics. Goodman Solutions specializes in providing equipment lifecycle services for telecom carriers and equipment manufacturers in the public and private sector.

GOODRICH PETROLEUM CORPORATION

801 LOUISIANA ST STE 700
HOUSTON, TX 770024936
Phone: 713 780-9494
Fax: –
Web: www.palomanaturalgas.com

CEO: –
CFO: –
HR: –
FYE: December 31
Type: Private

From deep in the good, rich hydrocarbon-impregnated rocks of ancient Mother Earth, Goodrich Petroleum brings forth oil and gas. The independent exploration and production company delves into formations in the Hayneville Shale play in Texas and Louisiana. The company also operates in the Eagle Ford Shale Trend in South Texas, the Tuscaloosa Marine Shale in Louisiana, and the Cotton Valley trend (in Texas and Louisiana). In the wake of a slump in oil prices, Goodrich Petroleum filed for Chapter 11 bankruptcy protection in 2016, in an attempt to shed some $400 million in debt.

	Annual Growth	12/12	12/13	12/14	12/15	12/16
Sales ($mil.)	(68.1%)	–	203.3	208.6	77.7	6.6
Net income ($ mil.)	–	–	(95.2)	(353.1)	(479.4)	(4.3)
Market value ($ mil.)	–	–	–	–	–	–
Employees	–	–	–	–	–	43

GOODWILL INDUSTRIES INTERNATIONAL, INC.

15810 INDIANOLA DR
ROCKVILLE, MD 208552674
Phone: 301 530-6500
Fax: –
Web: www.goodwill.org

CEO: Steven C Preston
CFO: –
HR: –
FYE: December 31
Type: Private

Goodwill Industries International supports the operations of more than 150 community-based, autonomous organizations in the US and Canada. While it's most well-known for its more than 3,200 goodwill stores, the group focuses on providing rehabilitation, job training, placement, coaching, treatment, and recovery services for people with disabilities and others. Goodwill is committed to providing employment, education, and skill-building opportunities to people worldwide. It is also honored to work with the nation's top brands to fight unemployment and underemployment.

	Annual Growth	12/18	12/19	12/20	12/21	12/22
Sales ($mil.)	0.5%	–	60.9	77.1	66.4	61.9
Net income ($ mil.)	–	–	0.2	24.8	11.1	(1.9)
Market value ($ mil.)	–	–	–	–	–	–
Employees	–	–	–	–	–	100

GOODWILL INDUSTRIES OF CENTRAL TEXAS

1015 NORWOOD PARK BLVD
AUSTIN, TX 787536608
Phone: 512 637-7100
Fax: –
Web: www.goodwillcentraltexas.org

CEO: –
CFO: –
HR: –
FYE: December 31
Type: Private

Deep in the heart of Texas there're some good folks doin' good things. Goodwill Industries of Central Texas is the Austin-area operating company for Goodwill Industries International. The organization serves people with barriers, like developmental, medical, psychiatric, and emotional problems, to employment. It also works with homeless people, at-risk youth, dislocated workers, and those over 50 seeking jobs. It operates about 20 retail outlets and two refurbished computer outlets. In 2008 the group partnered with area employers, not-for-profits, and community groups to help 10,000 needy individuals find jobs. It teamed with Dell and the City of Austin to form a computer-recycling program and computer museum.

	Annual Growth	12/07	12/08	12/14	12/15	12/17
Sales ($mil.)	6.4%	–	41.7	61.8	66.5	72.8
Net income ($ mil.)	–	–	(0.5)	0.7	(0.5)	0.8
Market value ($ mil.)	–	–	–	–	–	–
Employees	–	–	–	–	–	1,200

GOODYEAR TIRE & RUBBER CO.

NMS: GT

200 Innovation Way
Akron, OH 44316-0001
Phone: 330 796-2121
Fax: 330 796-4099
Web: www.goodyear.com

CEO: Mark Stewart
CFO: Christina L Zamarro
HR: –
FYE: December 31
Type: Public

Goodyear Tire & Rubber is one of the world's leading manufacturers of tires, engaging in operations in most regions of the world. The company sells tires under the Goodyear, Dunlop, Kelly, Fulda, Debica, and Sava brand names. It manufactures and sells its tires across the Americas, Europe, Middle East & Africa (EMEA), and the Asia Pacific region. Goodyear also makes and markets rubber-related chemicals for various applications. It operates approximately 950 tire and auto service centers where it offers its products for retail sale and provides automotive repair and other services. Goodyear has marketing operations in almost every country in the world, although the US generates about 55% of its revenue.

	Annual Growth	12/19	12/20	12/21	12/22	12/23
Sales ($mil.)	8.0%	14,745	12,321	17,478	20,805	20,066
Net income ($ mil.)	–	(311.0)	(1,254.0)	764.0	202.0	(689.0)
Market value ($ mil.)	(2.0%)	4,414.3	3,096.1	6,050.3	2,880.4	4,063.8
Employees	3.0%	63,000	62,000	72,000	74,000	71,000

GOPRO INC

NMS: GPRO

3025 Clearview Way
San Mateo, CA 94402
Phone: 650 332-7600
Fax: –
Web: www.gopro.com

CEO: Nicholas Woodman
CFO: Brian McGee
HR: –
FYE: December 31
Type: Public

GoPro helps the world capture and share itself in immersive and exciting ways. The company's cameras, mountable and wearable accessories, subscription services and software have generated substantially all of its revenue. Its products' small, lightweight, and durable designs allow for versatility when it comes to taking pictures. Flagship products include its Hero Black models as well as the 360-degree Fusion. Customers can transfer footage from cameras to mobile and desktop apps, such as GoPro Quik, for editing and sharing. With approximately 23,000 POP displays in retail outlets worldwide, the company sells its products in more than 90 countries. The US accounts for more than 50% of the company's total revenue.

	Annual Growth	12/19	12/20	12/21	12/22	12/23
Sales ($mil.)	(4.2%)	1,194.7	891.9	1,161.1	1,093.5	1,005.5
Net income ($ mil.)	–	(14.6)	(66.8)	371.2	28.8	(53.2)
Market value ($ mil.)	(5.4%)	650.6	1,241.1	1,545.4	746.5	520.1
Employees	0.1%	926	758	766	877	930

GORDON BROTHERS GROUP, LLC

101 HUNTINGTON AVE STE 1100
BOSTON, MA 021997728
Phone: 888 424-1903
Fax: –
Web: www.gordonbrothers.com

CEO: Norma Kuntz
CFO: –
HR: Karin Spychalski
FYE: October 31
Type: Private

Gordon Brothers Group can sell your assets in a flash. The company, founded in 1903, organizes the sale of retail inventories, equipment, real estate, accounts receivable, intellectual property, and other assets. Priding itself on discretion and speed, Gordon Brothers also facilitates mergers and acquisitions and manages closings of underperforming stores for top retailers. Its GB Merchant Partners affiliate provides debt financing to, and takes equity positions in, middle-market retail and consumer products firms for growth, acquisitions, or turnarounds. The firm has held stakes in such troubled companies as Linens 'N Things and Deb Shops. Gordon Brothers has about 25 offices in the US, Japan, and Europe.

GORDON COLLEGE

255 GRAPEVINE RD
WENHAM, MA 019841899
Phone: 978 927-2300
Fax: –
Web: www.gordon.edu

CEO: –
CFO: –
HR: James Graham
FYE: June 30
Type: Private

Gordon College, a New England non-denominational Christian liberal arts college, offers nearly 40 majors and has about 1,800 students. A demonstrated Christian commitment is required for admission. Undergraduate tuition is approximately $20,000. In 1985, Gordon merged with Barrington College, with the combined school retaining Gordon College's name. Gordon College was founded in 1889 by Reverend Dr. A.J. Gordon as a missionary training institute.

	Annual Growth	06/18	06/19	06/20	06/21	06/22
Sales ($mil.)	(13.0%)	–	116.7	92.8	107.4	76.9
Net income ($ mil.)	(69.9%)	–	49.1	1.6	17.9	1.3
Market value ($ mil.)	–	–	–	–	–	–
Employees	–	–	–	–	–	496

GORDON FOOD SERVICE, INC.

1300 GEZON PKWY SW
WYOMING, MI 495099302
Phone: 888 437-3663
Fax: –
Web: www.gfs.com

CEO: –
CFO: Jeff Maddox
HR: Amy Westphal
FYE: October 31
Type: Private

Gordon Food Service (GFS) is North America's largest family-owned broadline food service supplier. The company has about 15 distribution centers across the US and Canada. GFS's primary focus is distributing a range of food items, ingredients, and beverages to restaurants, schools, healthcare facilities, and institutional food service operators. In addition to its distribution operations, GFS also owns more than 170 wholesale stores under the GFS banner that are open to the public. Isaac Van Westenbrugge started the family-owned business in 1897 to deliver eggs and butter.

	Annual Growth	10/10	10/11	10/12	10/13	10/15
Sales ($mil.)	17.1%	–	–	–	64.9	89.0
Net income ($ mil.)	–	–	–	–	(1.2)	(0.2)
Market value ($ mil.)	–	–	–	–	–	–
Employees	–	–	–	–	–	14,000

GORDON REES SCULLY MANSUKHANI, LLP.

275 BATTERY ST STE 2000
SAN FRANCISCO, CA 941113327
Phone: 415 986-5900
Fax: –
Web: www.grsm.com

CEO: –
CFO: –
HR: –
FYE: December 31
Type: Private

Gordon Rees Scully Mansukhani is full-service firm focusing on complex litigation and sophisticated business transactions. It specializes in handling litigation and business transactions for clients in such industries as construction, health care, maritime, pharmaceutical, and real estate. The firm now stands as the 27th largest firm in the US comprising more than 1,000 lawyers and over 50 different practice and industry groups in more than 70 national offices located throughout the country. In 2014, the firm's name expanded to Gordon Rees Scully Mansukhani, LLP in order to recognize and honor the significant roles played by partners Miles Scully and Roger Mansukhani in contributing to its meteoric growth over the past decade.

GORMAN-RUPP COMPANY (THE)   NYS: GRC

600 South Airport Road
Mansfield, OH 44903
Phone: 419 755-1011
Fax: –
Web: www.gormanrupp.com

CEO: Jeffrey S Gorman
CFO: James C Kerr
HR: Barbara Woodman
FYE: December 31
Type: Public

Gorman-Rupp was founded in 1933 by engineers J. C. Gorman and H. E. Rupp. It designs, manufactures, and globally sells pumps and pump systems for use in water, wastewater, construction, dewatering, industrial, petroleum, original equipment, agriculture, fire protection, heating, ventilating and air conditioning (HVAC), military and other liquid-handling applications. Gorman-Rupp's pumps range in size from 1/4-inch (one gallon per minute) to nearly 15 feet and ranging in rated capacity from less than one gallon per minute to nearly one million gallons per minute. Smaller pumps are used for food processing, chemical processing, medical applications, and waste treatment, while large pumps include the ground refueling aircraft, fluid control in HVAC applications, and various agricultural purposes. The company generates most of its sales in its home country, the US.

	Annual Growth	12/19	12/20	12/21	12/22	12/23
Sales ($mil.)	13.4%	398.2	349.0	378.3	521.0	659.5
Net income ($ mil.)	(0.6%)	35.8	25.2	29.9	11.2	35.0
Market value ($ mil.)	(1.3%)	982.3	850.0	1,166.9	671.1	930.7
Employees	4.8%	1,200	1,150	1,150	1,420	1,450

GOTO GROUP, INC.

320 SUMMER ST STE 100
BOSTON, MA 022101701
Phone: 706 578-4964
Fax: –
Web: www.logmein.com

CEO: Rich Veldran
CFO: –
HR: Jo Deal
FYE: December 31
Type: Private

GoTo (formerly known as LogMeIn) has become one of the world's largest SaaS companies with tens of millions of active users. GoTo software is designed to support end-users' unified communications and collaboration (UCC) and IT management & support needs, and nearly 800,000 customers contribute to the more than one billion people joining meetings, classes, and webinars through GoTo's UCC products, and half a billion connections on the company's remote access and support tools. By building its secure, easy-to-use software, GoTo is committed to ensuring the time at work is well spent so that time outside of work is better spent.

GOTTLIEB MEMORIAL HOSPITAL

701 W NORTH AVE
MELROSE PARK, IL 601601612
Phone: 708 681-3200
Fax: –
Web: www.loyolamedicine.org

CEO: –
CFO: –
HR: –
FYE: June 30
Type: Private

Got health? Out in the western suburbs of Chicago, the staff at Gottlieb Memorial Hospital can help you find it. The not-for-profit community general hospital -- also known as Loyola Gottlieb -- boasts more than 250 beds, a staff of more than 300 physicians and dentists, 200 volunteers, a Level II trauma center with a heliport, heart and cancer care clinics, and a health and fitness center on site. The healthcare facility also offers rehabilitation services, a pharmacy, and a kidney dialysis center. Other Gottlieb Memorial Hospital services include outpatient clinics, hospice, and home health care. Gottlieb is part of Loyola University Health System.

	Annual Growth	06/14	06/15	06/20	06/21	06/22
Sales ($mil.)	1.5%	–	129.6	137.3	148.7	143.6
Net income ($ mil.)	–	–	(2.8)	5.1	17.1	(1.7)
Market value ($ mil.)	–	–	–	–	–	–
Employees	–	–	–	–	–	20

GOURMET SPECIALTIES, INC.

111 SOUTHWEST BLVD
KANSAS CITY, KS 661032132
Phone: 913 432-5228
Fax: –
Web: –

CEO: Joe R Polo Sr
CFO: –
HR: –
FYE: December 31
Type: Private

Original Juan Specialty Foods' creative product names include Pain is Good, Da' Bomb, Screamin' Wings, and the ever popular, Old Fart Baked Beans. In addition to fiery hot sauces and salsas, the company produces a large variety of other sauces, dips, and snack foods, including condiments, barbecue sauces, pasta sauces, salad dressings, drink mixes, microwave popcorn, and Amaretto-flavored or chocolate-flavored cheesecake-in-a-jar. Its most popular salsas and dips are sold under the Fiesta label. Original Juan's products are sold in retail stores and can also be ordered through the company's Web site. Founded in 1999, the company distributes its products worldwide.

	Annual Growth	12/08	12/09	12/10*	10/11*	12/14
Sales ($mil.)	17.7%	–	–	4.7	4.4	9.0
Net income ($ mil.)	–	–	–	(0.0)	0.7	0.2
Market value ($ mil.)	–	–	–	–	–	–
Employees	–	–	–	–	–	70

*Fiscal year change

GOUVERNEUR BANCORP INC MD

42 Church Street
Gouverneur, NY 13642
Phone: 315 287-2600
Fax: –
Web: www.gouverneurbank.com

NBB: GOVB
CEO: –
CFO: –
HR: –
FYE: September 30
Type: Public

Gouverneur Bancorp is the holding company for Gouverneur Savings and Loan, which serves upstate New York through two branches. Chartered in 1892, the thrift offers deposit products such as checking and savings accounts, NOW accounts, CDs, and money market accounts. Gouverneur Savings and Loan primarily uses funds from deposits to originate residential mortgages, which account for approximately 80% of its loan portfolio. It also offers commercial mortgages, business loans, and consumer loans (mostly automobile loans). Cambray Mutual Holding Company owns a majority of Gouverneur Bancorp.

	Annual Growth	09/03	09/04	09/05	09/06	09/07
Assets ($mil.)	10.2%	90.0	104.2	122.2	130.1	132.6
Net income ($ mil.)	12.3%	0.6	0.9	1.0	1.3	0.9
Market value ($ mil.)	–	–	–	–	28.4	32.3	25.9
Employees	1.5%	32	33	34	34	34

GOV NEW OPPTY REIT

7600 WISCONSIN AVE FL 11
BETHESDA, MD 208143657
Phone: 301 986-9200
Fax: –
Web: www.first-potomac.com

CEO: David M Blackman
CFO: Mark L Kleifges
HR: –
FYE: December 31
Type: Private

First Potomac Realty Trust is a self-managed real estate investment trust (REIT) whose largest tenants are the US government and government contracts. The company that acquires, owns, and manages a $1.6 billion portfolio of more than 130 single- and multi-tenant office and business park properties spanning some 8 million square feet of rentable space across the mid-Atlantic region, in Washington, DC, Maryland, and Virginia. More than 60% of the REIT's rental income comes from its office properties, while the rest comes from its business park and industrial properties.

GOVERNMENT NATIONAL MORTGAGE ASSN.

451 Seventh Street, S.W.
Washington, DC 20410
Phone: 202 401-2064
Fax: 202 708-5487
Web: www.ginniemae.gov

CEO: –
CFO: –
HR: –
FYE: September 30
Type: Public

Ginnie Mae is government-owned corporation operating within the US Department of Housing and Urban Development (HUD). More formally known as the Government National Mortgage Association, Ginnie Mae doesn't buy or sell loans or issue mortgage-backed securities. Rather, it manages the mortgage-backed securities program, providing liquidity, allowing lenders to obtain better prices for their loans on the secondary market, and lowering costs for homebuyers and renters throughout the nation, particularly low- to moderate-income Americans. Since its creation in 1968, Ginnie Mae has guaranteed more than $2.5 trillion in mortgage-backed securities and helped more than 34 million Americans secure affordable housing.

	Annual Growth	09/03	09/04	09/05	09/06	09/07
Sales ($mil.)	(0.3%)	799.6	815.5	786.5	849.3	791.3
Net income ($ mil.)	0.2%	731.5	737.7	705.2	789.3	738.3
Market value ($ mil.)	–	–	–	–	–	–
Employees	(4.2%)	76	66	–	66	64

GOVERNMENT OF DISTRICT OF COLUMBIA

441 4TH ST NW
WASHINGTON, DC 200012714
Phone: 202 727-0252
Fax: –
Web: www.dc.gov

CEO: –
CFO: Natawar Gandhi
HR: Naomi Chapman
FYE: September 30
Type: Private

Government of the District of Columbia manages ticket and tax payments, housing and property issues, children and youth services, and motor vehicles registration, among other duties for Washington, DC. More than 689,000 people live in Washington DC, and many more commute to the city every day to work for the federal government. Washington, DC is overseen by a mayor and a 13-member city council. It acquires contracts with more than 30 local government agencies. The Government of the District of Columbia was created in 1790 with donated land from Maryland and Virginia as part of the Residence Act.

	Annual Growth	09/14	09/15	09/16	09/20	09/22
Sales ($mil.)	7.1%	–	11,638	12,096	16,510	18,843
Net income ($ mil.)	19.4%	–	583.9	(78.4)	(504.1)	2,022.5
Market value ($ mil.)	–	–	–	–	–	–
Employees	–	–	–	–	–	34,600

GOYA FOODS, INC.

350 COUNTY RD
JERSEY CITY, NJ 073074503
Phone: 201 348-4900
Fax: –
Web: www.goya.com

CEO: –
CFO: –
HR: Edenia Garcia
FYE: December 31
Type: Private

The largest Hispanic-owned food company in the US, Goya Foods produces over 2,500 Hispanic and Caribbean grocery items, including canned grains and beans, canned meats, beverages, cooking oils and olives. Its product portfolio is available in wholesale clubs and other retailers. Goya sells many rice styles and a wide range of beans and peas under the Goya brand name. The company's beverages include cider, tropical fruit nectars, juices, tropical sodas, and coffee. Goya is owned and operated by the Unanue family, which founded the company in 1936. Overall, the company now boasts about 25 facilities throughout the US, Puerto Rico, Dominican Republic, and Spain.

GPM INVESTMENTS, LLC

8565 MAGELLAN PKWY STE 400
RICHMOND, VA 232271167
Phone: 276 328-3669
Fax: –
Web: www.gpminvestments.com

CEO: –
CFO: –
HR: Shannon Tierney
FYE: December 31
Type: Private

Convenience is key for GPM Investments, which operates or supplies fuel to more than 1,100 convenience stores in about 20 US states. The stores sell BP, Exxon, Marathon, and Valero brand gas, among others, as well as the usual beer, smokes, and snacks. Some locations also offer fresh, made-to-order salads, sandwiches, and other items, or offer branded food from Subway, Taco Bell, and others. The company, which primarily serves the Midwest and eastern US, operates or supplies stores under a host of names, including Fas Mart, Shore Stop, Jiffi Stop, Young's, and Roadrunner Markets.

	Annual Growth	12/04	12/05	12/06	12/07	12/08
Sales ($mil.)	40.2%	–	–	–	891.8	1,249.9
Net income ($ mil.)	–	–	–	–	3.2	(1.3)
Market value ($ mil.)	–	–	–	–	–	–
Employees	–	–	–	–	–	2,150

GRACELAND FRUIT, INC.

1123 MAIN ST
FRANKFORT, MI 496359341
Phone: 231 352-7181
Fax: –
Web: www.gracelandfruit.com

CEO: Alan Devore
CFO: Corey Geer
HR: Doug Rath
FYE: September 30
Type: Private

Graceland Fruit is a leading producer and global distributor of premium quality dried fruit ingredients for the food industry. The company makes dried, and frozen fruit and fruit ingredients for the food-manufacturing industry. Its product lines include infused dried fruit (cranberries, cherries, strawberries, and apple) and Soft-N-Frozen fruit. Its products are gluten-free, allergen-free, and Non-GMO verified. Its sells its products across the US and exports to about 15 countries. Furthermore, it has an office in China. It caters to food service manufacturers and distributors and consumer packaged foods manufacturers. The company was founded in 1973.

	Annual Growth	09/01	09/02	09/03	09/04	09/07
Sales ($mil.)	17.2%	–	–	29.7	33.5	56.1
Net income ($ mil.)	4.4%	–	–	0.8	0.0	0.9
Market value ($ mil.)	–	–	–	–	–	–
Employees	–	–	–	–	–	180

GRACO INC
NYS: GGG

88 - 11th Avenue N.E.
Minneapolis, MN 55413
Phone: 612 623-6000
Fax: 612 623-6777
Web: www.graco.com

CEO: Mark W Sheahan
CFO: David M Lowe
HR: Amie Burba
FYE: December 29
Type: Public

Graco, which was founded in 1926 as Gray Company, designs, manufactures, and markets systems and equipment used to move, measure, control, dispense, and spray fluid and powder materials. It supplies technology and expertise for the management of fluids and coatings in industrial and commercial applications. It specializes in providing equipment solutions for difficult-to-handle materials with high viscosities, abrasive or corrosive properties, and multiple component materials that require precise ratio control. Graco's customers include professional painters in the construction and maintenance industries, automotive, construction, and pharmaceutical, oil and natural gas, and fleet service centers among others. Graco primarily sells its products through independent third-party distributors worldwide. The US accounts for more than 50% of the total revenue.

	Annual Growth	12/19	12/20	12/21	12/22	12/23
Sales ($mil.)	7.5%	1,646.0	1,650.1	1,987.6	2,143.5	2,195.6
Net income ($ mil.)	10.2%	343.9	330.5	439.9	460.6	506.5
Market value ($ mil.)	13.6%	8,763.4	12,233	13,540	11,296	14,571
Employees	2.0%	3,700	3,700	3,800	4,000	4,000

GRAEBEL COMPANIES, INC.

16346 AIRPORT CIR
AURORA, CO 800111558
Phone: 303 214-6683
Fax: –
Web: www.graebel.com

CEO: Deborah Keeton
CFO: Bradley Siler
HR: –
FYE: December 31
Type: Private

Graebel offers both domestic and international household and commercial relocation services, most of the company's business comes from firms transferring employees, but it also provides individual household moving services and storage as well as freight forwarding. Graebel operates from service centers throughout the US and international forwarding offices at major ports. It provides transportation services in Asia, Europe, the Middle East, and Africa through hubs in Prague and Singapore and elsewhere in the world via a network of partners. Dave Graebel founded the family-run company in 1950.

	Annual Growth	12/17	12/18	12/19	12/20	12/21
Sales ($mil.)	1107.2%	–	–	–	91.0	1,098.8
Net income ($ mil.)	233.2%	–	–	–	7.4	24.6
Market value ($ mil.)	–	–	–	–	–	–
Employees	–	–	–	–	–	753

GRAFTECH INTERNATIONAL LTD
NYS: EAF

982 Keynote Circle
Brooklyn Heights, OH 44131
Phone: 216 676-2000
Fax: –
Web: www.graftech.com

CEO: –
CFO: –
HR: –
FYE: December 31
Type: Public

GrafTech International is a leading manufacturer of high-quality graphite electrode products essential to the production of electric arc furnace (EAF) steel and other ferrous and non-ferrous metals. GrafTech has the most competitive portfolio of low-cost ultra-high power (UHP) graphite electrode manufacturing facilities in the industry, including three of the highest capacity facilities in the world. It is the only large scale graphite electrode producer that is substantially vertically integrated into petroleum needle coke. Customers have included major steel producers and other ferrous and non-ferrous metal producers, which sell their products into the automotive, construction, appliance, machinery, equipment, and transportation industries. The majority of its sales were generated outside the US.

	Annual Growth	12/19	12/20	12/21	12/22	12/23
Sales ($mil.)	(23.3%)	1,790.8	1,224.4	1,345.8	1,281.3	620.5
Net income ($ mil.)	–	744.6	434.4	388.3	383.0	(255.3)
Market value ($ mil.)	(34.1%)	2,984.4	2,737.8	3,038.3	1,222.5	562.5
Employees	(1.9%)	1,346	1,285	1,353	1,347	1,249

GRAHAM CORP.
NYS: GHM

20 Florence Avenue
Batavia, NY 14020
Phone: 585 343-2216
Fax: –
Web: www.grahamcorp.com

CEO: Daniel J Thoren
CFO: Christopher J Thome
HR: –
FYE: March 31
Type: Public

Graham Corporation manufactures and sells critical equipment for the energy, marine, power generation, and chemical/petrochemical industries. For the defense industry, its equipment is used in nuclear and non-nuclear propulsion, power, fluid transfer, and thermal management systems. For the space industry, its equipment is used in propulsion, power and energy management systems and for life support systems. Graham supplies equipment for vacuum, heat transfer and fluid transfer applications used in energy and new energy markets including oil refining, cogeneration, and multiple alternative and clean power applications including hydrogen. For the chemical and petrochemical industries, its heat transfer equipment is used in fertilizer, ethylene, methanol and downstream chemical facilities. Graham sells its products worldwide with more than 80% of its revenue in the US.

	Annual Growth	03/19	03/20	03/21	03/22	03/23
Sales ($mil.)	14.4%	91.8	90.6	97.5	122.8	157.1
Net income ($ mil.)	–	(0.3)	1.9	2.4	(8.8)	0.4
Market value ($ mil.)	(9.7%)	208.8	137.2	151.4	82.0	139.1
Employees	12.4%	337	337	331	491	538

GRAHAM HOLDINGS CO.

NYS: GHC

1300 North 17th Street
Arlington, VA 22209
Phone: 703 345-6300
Fax: –
Web: www.ghco.com

CEO: Anne M Mulcahy
CFO: Wallace R Cooney
HR: –
FYE: December 31
Type: Public

Graham Holdings Company is a diversified education and media company whose operations include educational services, home health and hospice care, television broadcasting; online, print and local TV news, automotive dealerships, manufacturing, hospitality and consumer internet companies. The company's largest segment is education, conducted via Kaplan, which includes tutoring and test preparation services in the US and internationally. The company's other businesses include a consumer internet company that builds creator-driven brands in lifestyle, home and art design categories; restaurants; a custom framing company; a marketing solutions provider; a customer data and analytics software company; Slate and Foreign Policy magazines; an ad-free audio streaming service for children; and a daily local news podcast and newsletter company. The company generates about 20% of revenue outside the US.

	Annual Growth	12/19	12/20	12/21	12/22	12/23
Sales ($mil.)	10.8%	2,932.1	2,889.1	3,186.0	3,924.5	4,414.9
Net income ($ mil.)	(11.0%)	327.9	300.4	352.1	67.1	205.3
Market value ($ mil.)	2.2%	2,861.9	2,388.9	2,820.9	2,706.1	3,119.6
Employees	13.4%	12,053	16,661	18,000	19,527	19,900

GRAINGER (W.W.) INC.

NYS: GWW

100 Grainger Parkway
Lake Forest, IL 60045-5201
Phone: 847 535-1000
Fax: 847 535-0878
Web: www.grainger.com

CEO: Donald G Macpherson
CFO: Deidra C Merriwether
HR: –
FYE: December 31
Type: Public

W.W. Grainger is a broad line, distributor of maintenance, and repair and operating (MRO) products and services with operations primarily in North America, Japan, and the UK. The company offers material-handling and storage, safety and security supplies, pumps and plumbing equipment, cleaning and maintenance, metalworking and hand tools. Its more than 4.5 million customers are government, manufacturing, transportation, commercial, and contractors. Grainger sells through a network of branches, distribution centers, catalogs, sales and service representatives, and websites. About four-fifths of its revenue are generated from customers in the US.

	Annual Growth	12/19	12/20	12/21	12/22	12/23
Sales ($mil.)	9.4%	11,486	11,797	13,022	15,228	16,478
Net income ($ mil.)	21.2%	849.0	695.0	1,043.0	1,547.0	1,829.0
Market value ($ mil.)	25.1%	16,695	20,138	25,558	27,433	40,869
Employees	0.8%	25,300	23,100	24,200	26,000	26,100

GRAND CANYON EDUCATION INC

NMS: LOPE

2600 W. Camelback Road
Phoenix, AZ 85017
Phone: 602 247-4400
Fax: –
Web: www.gcu.edu

CEO: Brian E Mueller
CFO: Daniel E Bachus
HR: Danielle Espinosa
FYE: December 31
Type: Public

Grand Canyon Education (GCE) is a publicly traded education services company dedicated to serving colleges and universities. With more than 25 university partners, GCE has developed significant technological solutions, infrastructure, and operational processes to provide services to these institutions on a large scale. GCE's most significant university partner is Grand Canyon University (GCU), an Arizona non-profit corporation that operates a comprehensive regionally accredited university that offers graduate and undergraduate degree programs, emphases, and certificates across nine colleges both online and on the ground at its campus in Phoenix, Arizona and at four off-campus classroom and laboratory sites. GCE provided education services and support to more than 113,000 students with more than 108,600 students enrolled in GCU's programs, emphases, and certificates.

	Annual Growth	12/19	12/20	12/21	12/22	12/23
Sales ($mil.)	5.4%	778.6	844.1	896.6	911.3	960.9
Net income ($ mil.)	(5.7%)	259.2	257.2	260.3	184.7	205.0
Market value ($ mil.)	8.4%	2,869.2	2,788.9	2,567.3	3,164.8	3,955.0
Employees	14.3%	3,400	4,625	4,955	5,500	5,800

GRAND PIANO & FURNITURE CO.

4235 ELECTRIC RD STE 100
ROANOKE, VA 240188445
Phone: 540 776-7000
Fax: –
Web: www.grandhf.com

CEO: George B Cartledge Jr
CFO: –
HR: –
FYE: October 31
Type: Private

Grand Home Furnishings, formerly Grand Piano & Furniture, got its start as a piano and musical instrument store in Roanoke, Virginia. Several decades later, the company sells mattresses and home furnishings through more than 15 stores in Virginia, West Virginia, and Tennessee. The company stocks furniture from such manufacturers as Hooker, La-Z-Boy, Klaussner, Vaughan-Bassett, Meadowcraft, and Thomasville, and the mattresses come from Tempur Sealy, to name a few. Grand Home Furnishings was founded in 1910, and acquired in 1945 by the current owners, the Cartledge family. George Cartledge Jr. is the company's CEO.

GRAND RIVER DAM AUTHORITY

8142 S 412 B
CHOUTEAU, OK 74337
Phone: 918 256-5545
Fax: –
Web: www.grda.com

CEO: Dan Sullivan
CFO: Lorie Gudde
HR: Diana Martin
FYE: December 31
Type: Private

It took the dam authority of the State of Oklahoma to create the body that would dam the Grand River. The resulting power provider, the Grand River Dam Authority, is responsible for supplying wholesale electricity to municipal and cooperative utilities and industrial customers in its service territory, which encompasses 24 counties in northeastern Oklahoma. It also sells excess power to customers across a four-state region. The state-owned utility has 1,480 MW of generating capacity from hydroelectric and fossil-fueled power plants and operates a 2,090-mile transmission system. Grand River Dam Authority also manages two lakes and a total of 70,000 surface acres of water in Northeast Oklahoma.

	Annual Growth	12/18	12/19	12/20	12/21	12/22
Sales ($mil.)	16.3%	–	425.0	397.2	579.8	668.2
Net income ($ mil.)	6.5%	–	53.9	33.6	68.8	65.2
Market value ($ mil.)	–	–	–	–	–	–
Employees	–	–	–	–	–	468

GRAND STRAND REGIONAL MEDICAL CENTER, LLC

809 82ND PKWY
MYRTLE BEACH, SC 295724607
Phone: 843 692-1000
Fax: –
Web: www.mygrandstrandhealth.com

CEO: Mark Sims
CFO: –
HR: –
FYE: April 30
Type: Private

Grand Strand Regional Medical Center (GSRMC) is an acute care hospital serving Myrtle Beach, South Carolina, and surrounding Georgetown and Horry counties. The 220-bed hospital, a designated trauma center, is home to the only cardiac surgery program in those counties. GSRMC has a staff of more than 250 physicians representing a range of specializations including oncology, wound treatment and emergency care, women's health, pediatrics, rehabilitation, behavioral health, and treatment for sleeping disorders. Grand Strand Regional Medical Center includes the medical center and other satellite diagnostic, ambulatory care, and senior care facilities throughout the area.

	Annual Growth	04/07	04/08	04/09	04/13	04/15
Sales ($mil.)	294.8%	–	–	0.0	265.2	331.6
Net income ($ mil.)	284.3%	–	–	0.0	65.3	107.1
Market value ($ mil.)	–	–	–	–	–	–
Employees	–	–	–	–	–	1,000

GRAND VALLEY STATE UNIVERSITY

1 CAMPUS DR
ALLENDALE, MI 494019403
Phone: 616 331-5000
Fax: –
Web: www.gvsu.edu

CEO: –
CFO: –
HR: Alyssa Keith
FYE: June 30
Type: Private

Even the most average student can get a grand education at Grand Valley State University. The school operates five campuses in western Michigan. The main one is in Allendale; it has additional facilities in Grand Rapids, Holland, Muskegon, and Traverse City. Classes at the latter two locations are offered in conjunction with local community colleges. A public university with a liberal arts emphasis, Grand Valley State offers more than 200 fields of study, including about 80 undergraduate majors and more than 30 graduate programs. It has an enrollment of roughly 25,000 students and approximately 835 regular faculty members. Its student-teacher ratio is about 27:1.

	Annual Growth	06/17	06/18	06/19	06/21	06/22
Sales ($mil.)	(1.2%)	–	375.1	381.1	342.8	358.0
Net income ($ mil.)	2.2%	–	46.3	58.7	100.6	50.5
Market value ($ mil.)	–	–	–	–	–	–
Employees	–	–	–	–	–	3,630

GRAND VIEW HOSPITAL

700 LAWN AVE
SELLERSVILLE, PA 189601548
Phone: 215 453-4000
Fax: –
Web: www.gvh.org

CEO: Douglas Hughes
CFO: –
HR: –
FYE: June 30
Type: Private

Grand View Health (GVH), formerly Grand View Hospital, hopes to give patients a glimpse of great health care. The hospital provide emergency, inpatient, surgery, and specialty services including cardiology, orthopedics, sleep diagnostic, rehabilitation, women's and children's care, and other medical services to the Bucks County region of Pennsylvania. GVH's oncology program is affiliated with the Fox Chase Cancer Center in Philadelphia. The medical center also operates primary care and outpatient clinics in the region, and it provides home health, hospice, fitness, and community outreach programs. The hospital has about 200 beds.

	Annual Growth	06/15	06/16	06/20	06/21	06/22
Sales ($mil.)	4.1%	–	189.4	208.8	232.4	241.7
Net income ($ mil.)	–	–	10.1	(0.4)	(1.6)	(25.2)
Market value ($ mil.)	–	–	–	–	–	–
Employees	–	–	–	–	–	1,600

GRANDSOUTH BANCORPORATION   NBB: GRRB P

381 Halton Road
Greenville, SC 29607
Phone: 864 770-1000
Fax: –
Web: www.grandsouth.com

CEO: –
CFO: –
HR: –
FYE: December 31
Type: Public

GrandSouth Bancorporation likes to do things in a big way down past the Mason-Dixon line. The institution is the holding company for GrandSouth Bank, a local thrift serving the Greenville area of upstate South Carolina. The bank offers standard retail products and services including checking and savings accounts, IRAs, CDs, and money market accounts. Residential and commercial mortgages account for the majority of the bank's loan portfolio. GrandSouth Bank has offices in Anderson, Fountain Inn, and Greenville.

	Annual Growth	12/06	12/07	12/08	12/20	12/21
Assets ($mil.)	9.7%	300.3	345.1	375.0	1,089.8	1,203.7
Net income ($ mil.)	11.2%	3.3	2.8	1.3	8.6	16.1
Market value ($ mil.)	0.5%	129.2	55.6	28.4	78.6	139.6
Employees	7.7%	66	68	69	–	201

GRANDVIEW MANAGEMENT, INC.

613 N GRANDVIEW BLVD
WAUKESHA, WI 531882877
Phone: 262 547-9447
Fax: –
Web: www.zillihospitalitygroup.com

CEO: James Zilli
CFO: Kevin Zilli
HR: –
FYE: April 12
Type: Private

Grandview Management is a family-owned catering and dining company that provides an array of catering services through Ellen's Prestige Catering. The company also owns Zilli's Grandview Inn, a traditional upscale restaurant outside Milwaukee, as well as Coast, a contemporary fine-dining restaurant with a focus on bicoastal seafood dishes. Ellen Zilli and her late husband Angelo got started in the hospitality business in 1968 when they purchased a Tasti-Freeze ice cream outlet.

GRANITE BROADCASTING CORP   NBB: GRRP

767 Third Avenue, 34th Floor
New York, NY 10017
Phone: 212 826-2530
Fax: 212 826-2858
Web: www.granitetv.com

CEO: Don Cornwell
CFO: –
HR: –
FYE: December 31
Type: Public

Television really rocks the world of this company. Granite Broadcasting owns, jointly operates, or provides programming to more than 20 TV stations in about a dozen markets in about half a dozen states. Several of its stations are affiliated with major broadcast networks NBC and CBS, while others are affiliated with smaller networks The CW and MyNetworkTV. Granite Broadcasting also operates a number of independent stations, as well as online news and information portals serving its stations' viewers. Founded by former CEO W. Don Cornwell in 1988, the company is owned by private equity firm Silver Point Capital.

	Annual Growth	12/01	12/02	12/03	12/04	12/05
Sales ($mil.)	(6.6%)	113.1	135.3	108.5	113.8	86.2
Net income ($ mil.)	–	(76.7)	(79.6)	(46.9)	(83.3)	(99.4)
Market value ($ mil.)	–	–	–	–	–	–
Employees	(5.4%)	936	732	714	699	749

GRANITE CITY FOOD & BREWERY LTD   NBB: GCFB

3600 American Boulevard West, Suite 400
Bloomington, MN 55431
Phone: 952 215-0660
Fax: 952 215-0661
Web: www.gcfb.com

CEO: Richard H Lynch
CFO: James G Gilbertson
HR: –
FYE: December 25
Type: Public

Drinking and dining form the bedrock of this small restaurant chain. Granite City Food & Brewery owns and operates more than 25 casual dining brewpubs in about a dozen Midwestern states, mostly in Minnesota, Kansas, Illinois, Indiana, and Iowa. The restaurants offer a variety of handcrafted beers that are brewed on-site, including such varieties as Broad Axe Stout, Duke of Wellington (English ale), and Northern Light Lager. Granite City's broad food menu features chicken, steak, and seafood entrees, along with appetizers, burgers, sandwiches, and salads. The company also owns and operates five Cadillac Ranch All American Bar & Grill restaurants.

	Annual Growth	12/14	12/15	12/16	12/17	12/18
Sales ($mil.)	(0.4%)	136.2	150.6	150.3	141.2	133.8
Net income ($ mil.)	–	(3.1)	(0.3)	(4.7)	(9.1)	(7.4)
Market value ($ mil.)	(29.2%)	22.3	30.3	15.8	3.2	5.6
Employees	–	–	3,418	–	–	–

GRANITE CONSTRUCTION INC   NYS: GVA

585 W. Beach Street
Watsonville, CA 95076
Phone: 831 724-1011
Fax: –
Web: www.graniteconstruction.com

CEO: Kyle T Larkin
CFO: Elizabeth L Curtis
HR: Cara Burgess
FYE: December 31
Type: Public

In 1990, Granite Construction Incorporated was formed as the holding company for Granite Construction Company, a transportation and heavy construction contractor that works on public infrastructure projects, such as airports, bridges, highways, mass transit, dams, water-related facilities, utilities, and tunnels. Granite's private sector performs site preparation, mining services, and infrastructure services for residential development, energy development, commercial and industrial sites, and other facilities, as well as provides construction management professional services. In addition to construction services, Granite operates mines and processes aggregates and has plants that produce construction materials, such as asphalt concrete.

	Annual Growth	12/19	12/20	12/21	12/22	12/23
Sales ($mil.)	0.5%	3,445.6	3,562.5	3,010.1	3,301.3	3,509.1
Net income ($ mil.)	–	(60.2)	(145.1)	10.1	83.3	43.6
Market value ($ mil.)	16.4%	1,215.9	1,173.7	1,700.6	1,541.1	2,235.0
Employees	(21.7%)	5,600	5,400	3,300	3,800	2,100

GRANITE POINT MORTGAGE TRUST INC   NYS: GPMT

3 Bryant Park, Suite 2400A
New York, NY 10036
Phone: 212 364-5500
Fax: –
Web: www.gpmtreit.com

CEO: John A Taylor
CFO: Marcin Urbaszek
HR: –
FYE: December 31
Type: Public

Matthew famously advised to build your house on a rock; this company hopes you'll go to a rock for financing as well. Granite Point Mortgage Trust originates, investing in, and managing senior floating-rate commercial mortgage loans and other debt and debt-like commercial real estate investments. The REIT's portfolio consists of more than 120 commercial real estate with aggregate principal balance with a value of about $4.5 billion and additional about $750 million of potential future funding obligations. The company generally targets the top 25, and up to top 50, metropolitan statistical areas in the US, or MSAs. Northeast is the company's largest investment portfolio.

	Annual Growth	12/19	12/20	12/21	12/22	12/23
Assets ($mil.)	(10.6%)	4,460.9	4,219.6	3,988.5	3,454.1	2,846.9
Net income ($ mil.)	–	70.2	(40.4)	68.4	(40.8)	(63.2)
Market value ($ mil.)	(24.6%)	929.6	505.5	592.3	271.1	300.4
Employees	–	–	–	31	33	35	35

GRANITE TELECOMMUNICATIONS LLC

100 NEWPORT AVENUE EXT
QUINCY, MA 021712126
Phone: 617 933-5500
Fax: –
Web: www.granitenet.com

CEO: –
CFO: Richard Wurman
HR: –
FYE: December 31
Type: Private

Granite Telecommunications delivers advanced communications and technology solutions to businesses and government agencies throughout the US and Canada. The company serves more than two-thirds of Fortune 100 companies and has 1.75 million voice and data lines under management, supporting more than 650,000 locations. Founded in 2002, Granite has grown to be one of the largest competitive telecommunications carriers in the US by simplifying sourcing and management of voice, data and cellular service with a single point of contact and consolidated invoicing for all locations nationwide. Granite supports customers with a wide range of services, including access, UCaaS, mobile voice and data, and MSP solutions for SD-WAN, monitoring and network management.

	Annual Growth	12/08	12/09	12/10	12/11	12/12
Sales ($mil.)	19.3%	–	–	517.2	609.0	736.2
Net income ($ mil.)	31.0%	–	–	109.4	143.0	187.8
Market value ($ mil.)	–	–	–	–	–	–
Employees	–	–	–	–	–	2,116

GRAPHIC PACKAGING HOLDING CO   NYS: GPK

1500 Riveredge Parkway, Suite 100
Atlanta, GA 30328
Phone: 770 240-7200
Fax: –
Web: www.graphicpkg.com

CEO: –
CFO: –
HR: –
FYE: December 31
Type: Public

Graphic Packaging Holding Company (GPHC) is a provider of sustainable, paper-based packaging solutions for a wide variety of products to food, beverage, foodservice, and other consumer products companies. The company operates on a global basis, is one of the largest producers of folding cartons in the US, and holds leading market positions in coated-recycled paperboard (CRB), coated unbleached kraft paperboard (CUK), and solid bleached sulfate paperboard (SBS). The company operates seven paperboard mills across North America. It generates about 70% of its sales through US operations. Customers include such big names as Kraft Heinz, MillerCoors, Anheuser-Busch, General Mills, and various Coca-Cola, and Pepsi bottlers.

	Annual Growth	12/19	12/20	12/21	12/22	12/23
Sales ($mil.)	11.2%	6,160.1	6,559.9	7,156.0	9,440.0	9,428.0
Net income ($ mil.)	36.7%	206.8	167.3	204.0	522.0	723.0
Market value ($ mil.)	10.3%	5,095.9	5,184.6	5,968.1	6,809.8	7,544.3
Employees	6.9%	18,000	18,775	25,000	24,000	23,500

GRAY TELEVISION INC   NYS: GTN

4370 Peachtree Road, NE
Atlanta, GA 30319
Phone: 404 504-9828
Fax: –
Web: www.gray.tv

CEO: Hilton H Howell Jr
CFO: James C Ryan
HR: –
FYE: December 31
Type: Public

Gray Television is the nation's largest independent operator of TV stations in the US. It owns and operates local TV stations in nearly 115 markets, including ABC, NBC, CBS, and FOX. Its station portfolio reaches about 35% of total US TV households. The company also owns video production, marketing, and digital businesses including Raycom Sports, Tupelo Media Group, PowerNation Studios and Third Rail Studios. Revenue comes primarily from broadcast and internet ads and retransmission consent fees. Gray Television's roots begin in January 1891 with the creation of the Albany Herald in Albany, Georgia.

	Annual Growth	12/19	12/20	12/21	12/22	12/23
Sales ($mil.)	11.5%	2,122.0	2,381.0	2,413.0	3,676.0	3,281.0
Net income ($ mil.)	–	179.0	410.0	90.0	455.0	(76.0)
Market value ($ mil.)	(19.6%)	2,045.2	1,706.5	1,923.1	1,067.4	854.7
Employees	–	8,018	7,262	8,993	9,394	–

GRAYBAR ELECTRIC CO., INC.   NBB: GRBE

34 North Meramec Avenue
St. Louis, MO 63105
Phone: 314 573-9200
Fax: –
Web: www.graybar.com

CEO: –
CFO: –
HR: –
FYE: December 31
Type: Public

Graybar Electric Company (Graybar), a Fortune 500 company, specializes in supply chain management, and logistics services. The company is a leading North American distributor of electrical and communications and data networking products. Graybar products and services support new construction, infrastructure updates, building renovation, facility maintenance, repair and operations, and original equipment manufacturing. The employee-owned company serves approximately 146,000 customers through a network of about 325 distribution facilities across the US, Canada, and Puerto Rico. Graybar serves customers in the construction, industrial and utility vertical markets, and commercial, institutional and government (CIG). Graybar was founded in 1869 by inventor Elisha Gray and entrepreneur Enos Barton.

	Annual Growth	12/18	12/19	12/20	12/21	12/22
Sales ($mil.)	10.0%	7,202.5	7,523.9	7,265.7	8,767.3	10,534
Net income ($ mil.)	33.3%	143.3	144.5	121.8	262.4	452.9
Market value ($ mil.)	–	–	–	–	–	–
Employees	2.0%	8,700	9,100	8,200	8,800	9,400

GREAT AMERICAN BANCORP INC
NBB: GTPS

1311 S. Neil Street
Champaign, IL 61820
Phone: 217 356-2265
Fax: 217 356-2502
Web: www.greatamericanbancorp.com

CEO: -
CFO: -
HR: -
FYE: December 31
Type: Public

Great American Bancorp is the holding company for First Federal Savings Bank of Champaign-Urbana, which operates two branches in Champaign and one in Urbana, Illinois. Targeting individuals and local businesses, First Federal provides retail banking products such as checking, savings, and money market accounts, credit cards, and CDs. Lending activities consist primarily of residential mortgages, as well as commercial real estate, construction, business, and consumer loans. The bank was founded in 1908. Through a partnership with UMB Financial Corporation subsidiary UMB Financial Services, First Federal Savings Bank also offers investment services.

	Annual Growth	12/18	12/19	12/20	12/21	12/22
Assets ($mil.)	6.9%	167.4	172.7	203.7	230.1	218.9
Net income ($ mil.)	3.5%	1.0	1.5	1.2	0.4	1.1
Market value ($ mil.)	2.0%	11.4	13.2	12.1	13.6	12.4
Employees	-	-	-	-	-	-

GREAT AMERICAN INSURANCE CO.

580 Walnut St.
Cincinnati, OH 45202
Phone: 513 369-5000
Fax: -
Web: www.greatamericaninsurance.com

CEO: Carl H Lindner III
CFO: Annette D Gardner
HR: -
FYE: December 31
Type: Public

Great American Insurance Company is the flagship company of the Great American Insurance Group and is a subsidiary of American Financial Group (AFG). The company develop a diversified portfolio of businesses, which focused on specialty commercial, and casualty niches. The company provides insurance coverage to customers including industries such as healthcare, aviation, and construction, among others. It also provides risk management to public entities and equipment. Other products include crop insurance, marine insurance, professional liability coverage, and alternative markets. The company was founded in 1872.

	Annual Growth	12/96	12/97	12/99	12/00	12/01
Assets ($mil.)	0.9%	3,860.5	4,285.2	3,754.5	3,755.7	4,045.0
Net income ($ mil.)	-	81.5	122.6	67.2	76.6	(41.7)
Market value ($ mil.)	-	-	-	-	-	-
Employees	-	-	-	-	-	-

GREAT LAKES AVIATION LTD.
NBB: GLUX

1022 Airport Parkway
Cheyenne, WY 82001
Phone: 307 432-7000
Fax: -
Web: www.flygreatlakes.com

CEO: Douglas G Voss
CFO: -
HR: -
FYE: December 31
Type: Public

Great Lakes Aviation goes to great lengths to get people where they need to be, even if it's far from the big city. Flying as Great Lakes Airlines, the regional carrier transports passengers to more than 60 destinations in the western and midwestern US, mainly from Denver but also from markets such as Phoenix, Kansas City, and Ontario, California. It maintains code-sharing agreements with Frontier Airlines and United Airlines. (Code-sharing enables carriers to sell tickets on one another's flights and thus extend their networks.) Great Lakes operates a fleet of about 40 turboprop aircraft, consisting mostly of 19-passenger Beechcraft 1900Ds but also including 30-passenger Embraer Brasilia 120s.

	Annual Growth	12/10	12/11	12/12	12/13	12/14
Sales ($mil.)	(17.1%)	125.4	124.4	137.8	117.2	59.2
Net income ($ mil.)	-	5.1	10.7	2.9	(0.4)	(7.4)
Market value ($ mil.)	(29.9%)	15.3	6.7	17.9	10.9	3.7
Employees	(16.4%)	1,122	1,068	1,164	657	548

GREAT LAKES CHEESE CO., INC.

17825 GREAT LAKES PKWY
HIRAM, OH 442349677
Phone: 440 834-2500
Fax: -
Web: www.greatlakescheese.com

CEO: Gary Vanic
CFO: -
HR: Alysa Spangler
FYE: January 02
Type: Private

Great Lakes Cheese is one of the leading manufacturers and suppliers of high-quality cheese products. Each year the company makes hundreds of million pounds of cheese at eight facilities in the US. The company produces three categories of cheese: natural cheese, including cheddar, Swiss, mozzarella, provolone, and blue; processed cheese, such as American deluxe, cheese spread, and cheese product; and specialty cheese, such as blue-veined cheese for the retail and wholesale markets. Swiss immigrant Hans Epprecht founded the firm in 1958 as a Cleveland bulk-cheese distributor. The Epprecht family owns the company and has over 3,000 dedicated employees.

GREAT LAKES DREDGE & DOCK CORP
NMS: GLDD

9811 Katy Freeway, Suite 1200
Houston, TX 77024
Phone: 346 359-1010
Fax: -
Web: www.gldd.com

CEO: Lasse J Petterson
CFO: Mark W Marinko
HR: -
FYE: December 31
Type: Public

Founded in 1890, Great Lakes Dredge & Dock is of the largest provider of dredging services in the US. It also has a long history of performing significant international projects. Dredging involves enhancing or preserving waterways for navigability or protecting shorelines by removing or replenishing soil, sand, or rock. Great Lakes is involved in four major types of dredging work: capital (primarily port expansion projects), coastal protection (movement of sand from ocean floor to shoreline to alleviate erosion), rivers & lakes and maintenance (removal of silt and sediment from existing waterways and harbors).

	Annual Growth	12/19	12/20	12/21	12/22	12/23
Sales ($mil.)	(4.6%)	711.5	733.6	726.1	648.8	589.6
Net income ($ mil.)	(27.1%)	49.3	66.1	49.4	(34.1)	13.9
Market value ($ mil.)	(9.3%)	754.8	877.4	1,047.3	396.4	511.7
Employees	(23.2%)	1,047	437	1,241	1,181	364

GREAT NORTHERN IRON ORE PROPERTIES

801 E HOWARD ST
HIBBING, MN 557461719
Phone: 651 224-2385
Fax: -
Web: www.greatnorthernironbook.com

CEO: Joseph S Micallef
CFO: Thomas A Janochoski
HR: -
FYE: December 31
Type: Private

Great Northern Iron Ore Properties is the landlord of one big iron formation. The trust gets income from royalties on iron ore minerals (principally taconite) taken from its more than 67,000 acres on the Mesabi Iron Formation in Minnesota. The trust was formed in 1906 to own the properties of an affiliate of Burlington Northern Santa Fe (BNSF, formerly Great Northern Railway). The trust's beneficiaries were the heirs of railroad founder James Hill; however, the last survivor, his grandson Louis Hill, died in 1995. In 2015 (20 years after Louis Hill's death) the land will be transferred to a unit of ConocoPhillips, which acquired the BNSF assets in 2005.

GREAT PLAINS MANUFACTURING INCORPORATED

1525 E NORTH ST
SALINA, KS 674018562
Phone: 785 823-3276
Fax: –
Web: www.greatplainsmfg.com

CEO: –
CFO: –
HR: –
FYE: June 30
Type: Private

Great Plains Manufacturing goes to great pains to help farmers across the fruited plain to sow, grow, and harvest the fruits of their labor. Through its Great Plains division the company designs, manufactures, and sells agricultural planting, spraying, and cultivating equipment. Its Land Pride unit sells landscaping products, such as mowers and aerators. Great Plains Acceptance Corporation (GPAC) provides equipment financing, and Great Plains Trucking provides related trucking services in the US and Canada. In mid-2016, the company agreed to be acquired by Kubota Corporation, Japan's largest maker of tractors and farm equipment.

GREAT RIVER ENERGY

12300 ELM CREEK BLVD N
MAPLE GROVE, MN 553694718
Phone: 763 445-5000
Fax: –
Web: www.greatriverenergy.com

CEO: David Saggau
CFO: Larry Schmid
HR: Cynthia Schue
FYE: December 31
Type: Private

Great River Energy is not-for-profit wholesale electric power cooperative serving about 25 member-owner distribution cooperatives. It owns and operates nearly 4,800 miles of transmission line and owns or partly owns more than 100 transmission substations. Through its member-owners, Great River Energy serves two-thirds of Minnesota geographically and parts of Wisconsin. Its member cooperatives serve more than 685,000 member-consumers ? or about 1.7 million people. Great River Energy owns and operates some 10 power plants, plus the company purchase additional power from several wind farms and other generating facilities.

	Annual Growth	12/14	12/15	12/16	12/17	12/18
Sales ($mil.)	9.6%	–	983.0	1,022.1	1,270.2	1,295.9
Net income ($ mil.)	(17.8%)	–	15.2	21.5	18.2	8.5
Market value ($ mil.)	–	–	–	–	–	–
Employees	–	–	–	–	–	850

GREAT SOUTHERN BANCORP, INC.

NMS: GSBC

1451 E. Battlefield
Springfield, MO 65804
Phone: 417 887-4400
Fax: –
Web: www.greatsouthernbank.com

CEO: Joseph W Turner
CFO: –
HR: Matt Snyder
FYE: December 31
Type: Public

Despite its name, Great Southern Bancorp is firmly entrenched in the heartland. It is the holding company for nearly 200-year-old Great Southern Bank, which offers loans, deposit accounts, CDs, IRAs, and credit cards through more than 75 branches in Missouri, plus more than two dozen locations in Iowa, Kansas, Nebraska, Minnesota, and Arkansas. The firm's Great Southern Travel division is one of the largest travel agencies in Missouri. It serves both leisure and corporate travelers through about a dozen offices. Great Southern Insurance offers property/casualty and life insurance, while Great Southern Financial provides investment products and services through an agreement with Ameriprise.

	Annual Growth	12/19	12/20	12/21	12/22	12/23
Assets ($mil.)	3.8%	5,015.1	5,526.4	5,449.9	5,680.7	5,812.4
Net income ($ mil.)	(2.0%)	73.6	59.3	74.6	75.9	67.8
Market value ($ mil.)	(1.6%)	747.5	577.2	699.4	702.2	700.6
Employees	3.2%	1,191	1,156	1,105	1,124	1,352

GREAT WEST LIFE & ANNUITY INSURANCE CO - INSURANCE PRODUCTS

8515 East Orchard Road
Greenwood Village, CO 80111
Phone: 303 737-3000
Fax: –
Web: www.greatwest.com

CEO: Edmund F Murphy III
CFO: –
HR: –
FYE: December 31
Type: Public

Great-West Life & Annuity Insurance (GWL&A), a subsidiary of Canada's Great-West Lifeco and a member of the Power Financial family, represents the Great-West group's primary US operations. Through its Empower Retirement and Great-West Investments divisions, GWL&A provides retirement and investment management services. Parent Great-West Lifeco sold substantially all of GWL&A's individual life insurance and annuity operations to Protective Life Insurance for $1.2 billion in 2019. The divested business operated under the Great-West Financial brand. Its corporate headquarters is located in Greenwood Village, Colorado.

	Annual Growth	12/13	12/14	12/15	12/16	12/17
Assets ($mil.)	3.1%	55,324	58,348	57,900	60,309	62,461
Net income ($ mil.)	30.1%	128.7	317.4	190.5	231.1	369.1
Market value ($ mil.)	–	–	–	–	–	–
Employees	15.1%	3,300	4,500	5,400	5,800	5,800

GREATAMERICA FINANCIAL SERVICES CORPORATION

625 1ST ST SE STE 800
CEDAR RAPIDS, IA 524012031
Phone: 319 365-8000
Fax: –
Web: www.greatamerica.com

CEO: Tony Golobic
CFO: Joe Terfler
HR: Molly Hogan
FYE: May 31
Type: Private

GreatAmerica Financial Services (formerly GreatAmerica Leasing) takes pride in helping manufacturers, vendors, and dealers across the US provide lease financing for the equipment they sell. The company offers a variety of standard and custom leasing packages, with business units devoted to office equipment, communications and data providers, distributors, and health care equipment. It also provides portfolio management and servicing to manufacturers and financial institutions. GreatAmerica offers its services nationwide and in some US territories. Chairman and CEO Tony Golobic, formerly with GE Capital, founded the business in 1992; he and his wife Magda are the company's primary owners.

GREATER BALTIMORE MEDICAL CENTER, INC.

6701 N CHARLES ST
BALTIMORE, MD 212046808
Phone: 410 849-2000
Fax: –
Web: www.gbmc.org

CEO: John Chessare
CFO: Eric Melchior
HR: Brenee Palmer
FYE: June 30
Type: Private

Greater Baltimore Medical Center, also known as GBMC, operates an integrated health system for residents of Baltimore and surrounding counties. The 255-bed medical center provides surgery, women's health, oncology, cardiology, and other specialty and general medical services. In addition to inpatient and outpatient services, the medical center provides teaching services through an affiliation with Johns Hopkins University. GBMC also includes area clinics and physician practice locations. The GBMC Foundation coordinates fundraising for the health network.

	Annual Growth	06/19	06/20*	09/20*	06/21	06/22
Sales ($mil.)	6.3%	–	510.3	135.6	–	576.4
Net income ($ mil.)	–	–	1.9	11.0	–	(54.0)
Market value ($ mil.)	–	–	–	–	–	–
Employees	–	–	–	–	–	3,603

*Fiscal year change

GREATER LAFAYETTE HEALTH SERVICES, INC.

1501 HARTFORD ST
LAFAYETTE, IN 479042134
Phone: 765 423-6011
Fax: –
Web: –

CEO: –
CFO: –
HR: –
FYE: December 31
Type: Private

Part of Franciscan Alliance, St. Elizabeth Regional Health (operating as Franciscan Saint Elizabeth Health) operates three acute care hospitals that provide health services to residents of northwestern Indiana's Tippecanoe County. The facilities are full-service acute care hospitals providing primary, rehabilitative, and surgery care. Specialty units include centers for diabetes, cancer, wound, pulmonary, cardiac, and women's and children's care. The Franciscan St. Elizabeth Health-Lafayette East campus is home to a school of nursing. St. Elizabeth Regional Health also provides home health and hospice services and operates area poison control centers.

GREATER OMAHA PACKING CO., INC.

3001 L ST
OMAHA, NE 681071409
Phone: 402 731-1700
Fax: –
Web: www.greateromaha.com

CEO: Henry A Davis
CFO: –
HR: Barbra Jupina
FYE: December 31
Type: Private

Greater Omaha Packing turns great cattle into even greater beef. The company is a leading independent beef slaughterhouse in the US that processes some 15,000 head of cattle each week at its single plant in Omaha, Nebraska. Greater Omaha Packaging's packaged beef products are shipped to a variety of customers throughout the country and in some 50 international markets. The packaging company is one of a small number of US packing plants certified to ship non-hormone treated beef to Europe. The family-owned company -- which markets under the brands Omaha Natural Angus, Certified Angus Beef, Certified Hereford Beef, Halal Beef, and 1881 Omaha Hereford -- was started by Herman Cohen Davis in 1920.

GREATER ORLANDO AVIATION AUTHORITY

1 JEFF FUQUA BLVD
ORLANDO, FL 328274392
Phone: 407 825-2001
Fax: –
Web: www.goaa.org

CEO: –
CFO: –
HR: –
FYE: December 31
Type: Private

If your destination is Disney World and you're flying into Orlando, you might very well use one of the airports overseen by the Greater Orlando Aviation Authority (GOAA). The agency operates Orlando International Airport, which is one of Florida's largest, and Orlando Executive Airport, a general aviation facility. (Orlando Sanford International Airport is overseen by the Sanford Airport Authority, a separate agency.) GOAA is governed by a seven-member board that includes the mayor of Orlando, a member of the Orange County Commission, and five people appointed by the governor of Florida.

	Annual Growth	09/12	09/13	09/14	09/15*	12/15
Sales ($mil.)	6.4%	–	380.6	399.2	430.7	430.7
Net income ($ mil.)	8.2%	–	87.0	90.5	101.7	101.7
Market value ($ mil.)	–	–	–	–	–	–
Employees	–	–	–	–	–	670

*Fiscal year change

GREATER WASHINGTON EDUCATIONAL TELECOMMUNICATIONS ASSOCIATION, INC.

3939 CAMPBELL AVE
ARLINGTON, VA 222063440
Phone: 703 998-2600
Fax: –
Web: www.weta.org

CEO: Sharon P Rockefeller
CFO: –
HR: –
FYE: June 30
Type: Private

The Greater Washington Educational Telecommunications Association is a leading public broadcaster serving the Washington, DC, area with a television station and a radio station operating under the call letters WETA. It is also a leading producer of content for the Public Broadcasting Service, including PBS NewsHour (created in partnership with MacNeil/Lehrer Productions) and Washington Week. WETA has also co-produced several documentaries by Ken Burns, including The Civil War and Baseball. The not-for-profit organization was formed in 1953 and received a TV broadcast license in 1961.

	Annual Growth	06/18	06/19	06/20	06/21	06/22
Sales ($mil.)	3.3%	–	117.9	114.6	143.7	130.0
Net income ($ mil.)	(58.5%)	–	20.9	(7.5)	27.7	1.5
Market value ($ mil.)	–	–	–	–	–	–
Employees	–	–	–	–	–	236

GREEN BAY PACKERS, INC.

1265 LOMBARDI AVE
GREEN BAY, WI 543043997
Phone: 920 569-7500
Fax: –
Web: www.packers.com

CEO: Mark Murphy
CFO: –
HR: Chelsea Schettle
FYE: March 31
Type: Private

On the frozen tundra of Lambeau Field, the Green Bay Packers battle for pride in the National Football League. The not-for-profit corporation owns and operates the storied franchise, which was founded in 1919 by Earl "Curly" Lambeau and joined the NFL in 1921. Home to such icons as Bart Starr, Ray Nitschke, and legendary coach Vince Lombardi, Green Bay boasts a record 13 league titles including four Super Bowl victories. The team is also the only community-owned franchise in American professional sports with more than 250,000 shareholders. The shares do not increase in value nor pay dividends, and can only be sold back to the team.

	Annual Growth	03/00	03/01	03/02	03/03	03/22
Sales ($mil.)	(11.7%)	–	118.0	132.0	153.1	8.6
Net income ($ mil.)	0.3%	–	5.6	3.8	23.3	6.0
Market value ($ mil.)	–	–	–	–	–	–
Employees	–	–	–	–	–	160

GREEN BRICK PARTNERS INC

NYS: GRBK

2805 Dallas Parkway, Suite 400
Plano, TX 75093
Phone: 469 573-6755
Fax: –
Web: www.greenbrickpartners.com

CEO: James R Brickman
CFO: Richard A Costello
HR: Dawn McClintic
FYE: December 31
Type: Public

Green Brick Partners acquires and develops land and provides land and construction financing to its wholly owned and controlled builders. Also known as Green Brick, it is engaged in all aspects of the homebuilding process, including land acquisition and development, entitlements, design, construction, title and mortgage services, marketing and sales, and the creation of brand images at its residential neighborhoods and master planned communities. Based in Dallas, the company owns or controls over 12,000 prime home sites in high-growth sub-markets throughout the Dallas and Atlanta metropolitan areas, and the Vero Beach, Florida market.

	Annual Growth	12/19	12/20	12/21	12/22	12/23
Sales ($mil.)	22.4%	791.7	976.0	1,402.9	1,757.8	1,777.7
Net income ($ mil.)	48.4%	58.7	113.7	190.2	291.9	284.6
Market value ($ mil.)	45.8%	516.7	1,033.3	1,365.0	1,090.5	2,337.6
Employees	6.9%	460	440	540	550	600

GREEN DOT CORP
NYS: GDOT

114 W 7th Street, Suite 240
Austin, TX 78701
Phone: 626 765-2000
Fax: –
Web: www.greendot.com

CEO: Dan R Henry
CFO: George Gresham
HR: –
FYE: December 31
Type: Public

Bank holding company Green Dot offers prepaid debit cards through more than 90,000 retail locations in the US under brand names, including Green Dot, Go2Bank, MoneyPak, and TPG. Green Dot managed 67 million accounts to date and offers a broad set of financial services for consumers and businesses, including debit, checking, credit, prepaid and employer payroll cards, in addition to robust money processing services, tax refunds, cash deposits, disbursements, and more. The company's banking platform services (BaaS) division enables world-class partners to embed and deploy powerful, customized, scalable banking solutions designed to fuel engagement, trust, loyalty and value among customers. The company was founded in 1999.

	Annual Growth	12/19	12/20	12/21	12/22	12/23
Sales ($mil.)	7.9%	1,108.6	1,253.8	1,433.2	1,449.6	1,501.3
Net income ($ mil.)	(49.1%)	99.9	23.1	47.5	64.2	6.7
Market value ($ mil.)	(19.3%)	1,230.6	2,947.1	1,914.1	835.5	522.9
Employees	–	1,200	1,200	1,200	1,200	1,200

GREEN MILL RESTAURANTS, LLC

1342 GRAND AVE STE 1
SAINT PAUL, MN 551053569
Phone: 651 203-3100
Fax: –
Web: www.greenmill.com

CEO: Christopher Bangs
CFO: Mary Jule-Erickson
HR: –
FYE: December 31
Type: Private

Green Mill Restaurants is a leading regional restaurant company with about 30 company-owned and franchised Green Mill Restaurant and Bar locations in Minnesota, North Dakota, and Wisconsin. The casual dining chain is known for its signature pizza styles and pasta dishes. The eateries also serve appetizers, burgers, sandwiches, and salads, and they offer full bar service with happy hour specials. Myron Roth opened the first Green Mill location in St. Paul, Minnesota. CEO Chris Bangs along with two other partners acquired the business in 1975 and began franchising the chain in 1990.

	Annual Growth	12/03	12/04	12/05	12/06	12/07
Sales ($mil.)	(0.9%)	–	–	3.1	3.2	3.0
Net income ($ mil.)	2.7%	–	–	0.6	0.6	0.6
Market value ($ mil.)	–	–	–	–	–	–
Employees	–	–	–	–	–	101

GREEN MOUNTAIN POWER CORPORATION

163 ACORN LN
COLCHESTER, VT 054466611
Phone: 888 835-4672
Fax: –
Web: www.greenmountainpower.com

CEO: Mari McClure
CFO: Dawn D Bugbee
HR: –
FYE: September 30
Type: Private

Public utility Green Mountain Power (GMP) lights up the hills of Vermont, supplying electricity to more than 250,000 customers in the state. The utility also markets wholesale electricity in New England. The company operates several thousand miles of transmission and distribution lines and owns a minority stake in high-voltage transmission operator Vermont Electric Power (VELCO). About half of the generation capacity GMP taps is from hydroelectric and other renewable energy sources. GMP is an indirect subsidiary of Canada's GazMetro. The company absorbed Central Vermont Public Service's assets in 2012.

	Annual Growth	12/19	12/20*	09/21*	12/21*	09/22
Sales ($mil.)	6.8%	–	716.9	730.1	729.6	817.5
Net income ($ mil.)	(5.0%)	–	79.6	64.3	66.6	71.9
Market value ($ mil.)	–	–	–	–	–	–
Employees	–	–	–	–	–	510

*Fiscal year change

GREEN PLAINS INC.
NMS: GPRE

1811 Aksarben Drive
Omaha, NE 68106
Phone: 402 884-8700
Fax: –
Web: www.gpreinc.com

CEO: Todd A Becker
CFO: James E Stark
HR: –
FYE: December 31
Type: Public

Green Plains is one of the leading corn processors in the world which turns corn into ethanol at facilities in Illinois, Indiana, Iowa, Nebraska, Minnesota, and Tennessee. The company has annual ethanol production capacity of approximately 955 million gallons, primarily used as an auto fuel. It also sells ethanol produced by different types of grains. Co-products of the ethanol production process are used as mid-protein, high-energy animal feed and marketed to the dairy, beef, swine and poultry industries. It produces approximately 2.7 million tons of animal feed known as distiller grains, the primary co-product of ethanol production, as well as some 310 million pounds of corn oil, making it one of the largest ethanol producers in North America.

	Annual Growth	12/19	12/20	12/21	12/22	12/23
Sales ($mil.)	8.1%	2,417.2	1,923.7	2,827.2	3,662.8	3,295.7
Net income ($ mil.)	–	(166.9)	(108.8)	(66.0)	(127.2)	(93.4)
Market value ($ mil.)	13.1%	918.4	783.9	2,069.0	1,815.4	1,501.1
Employees	2.9%	820	839	859	902	921

GREEN ST. ENERGY, INC

123 Green St.
Tehachapi, CA 93561
Phone: 310 556-9688
Fax: –
Web: –

CEO: Anthony J Cataldo
CFO: –
HR: –
FYE: December 31
Type: Public

Green St. Energy (formerly known as M~Wave) got bored with boards and got into alternative energy. The company in early 2009 signed an agreement to purchase 160 acres of land in California that will be developed as a wind farm. Green St. Energy is negotiating to purchase another 4,840 acres of land in the same location. Senior executives of the company in 2008 offered to buy M~Wave's assets for $500,000 and the assumption of all operating liabilities; the transaction was completed in early 2009. M~Wave then changed its name to Green St. Energy.

	Annual Growth	12/04	12/05	12/06	12/07	12/08
Sales ($mil.)	–	17.5	16.6	9.8	11.6	–
Net income ($ mil.)	–	(0.3)	(5.4)	(3.2)	(1.5)	(1.4)
Market value ($ mil.)	(55.9%)	2.4	1.0	4.1	2.8	0.0
Employees	(39.9%)	23	20	21	21	3

GREENBRIER COMPANIES INC (THE)
NYS: GBX

One Centerpointe Drive, Suite 200
Lake Oswego, OR 97035
Phone: 503 684-7000
Fax: 503 684-7553
Web: www.gbrx.com

CEO: –
CFO: –
HR: –
FYE: August 31
Type: Public

The Greenbrier Companies is one of the leading designers, manufacturers, and marketers of railroad freight car equipment in North America, Europe, South America, and other geographies. It is also a leading provider of freight railcar wheel services, maintenance, and parts in North America. It offers railcar management, regulatory compliance services, and leasing services to railcar owners or other users of railcars. Through its primary Manufacturing segment, Greenbrier produces hopper cars; intermodal and conventional railcars; boxcars, center-partition, flat, and tank cars; and a full line of railcar equipment. Its maintenance services segment provides wheel and axle services and offers railcar repair, refurbishment, and parts for its railcars. Its Leasing & Services unit manages a fleet of more than 13,400 railcars. The US market generates most of its revenue.

	Annual Growth	08/19	08/20	08/21	08/22	08/23
Sales ($mil.)	6.8%	3,033.6	2,792.2	1,748.0	2,977.7	3,944.0
Net income ($ mil.)	(3.2%)	71.1	49.0	32.5	46.9	62.5
Market value ($ mil.)	16.3%	719.2	839.6	1,361.8	880.4	1,314.3
Employees	(5.2%)	17,100	10,600	10,300	14,400	13,800

GREENE COUNTY BANCORP INC
NAS: GCBC

302 Main Street
Catskill, NY 12414
Phone: 518 943-2600
Fax: –
Web: www.tbogc.com

CEO: –
CFO: –
HR: –
FYE: June 30
Type: Public

This company helps put the "green" in upstate New York. Greene County Bancorp is the holding company for The Bank of Greene County, serving New York's Catskill Mountains region from about a dozen branches. Founded in 1889 as a building and loan association, the bank offers traditional retail products such as savings, NOW, checking, and money market accounts; IRAs; and CDs. Real estate loans make up about 85% of the bank's lending activities; it also writes business and consumer loans. Through affiliations with Fenimore Asset Management and Essex Corp., Greene County Bancorp offers investment products. Subsidiary Greene County Commercial Bank is a state-chartered limited purpose commercial bank.

	Annual Growth	06/19	06/20	06/21	06/22	06/23
Assets ($mil.)	20.7%	1,269.5	1,676.8	2,200.3	2,571.7	2,698.3
Net income ($ mil.)	15.2%	17.5	18.7	23.9	28.0	30.8
Market value ($ mil.)	0.3%	500.9	379.7	478.8	771.1	507.4
Employees	6.0%	172	186	193	206	217

GREENE, TWEED & CO., INC.

1684 S BROAD ST
LANSDALE, PA 194465422
Phone: 215 256-9521
Fax: –
Web: www.gtweed.com

CEO: Magen Buterbaugh
CFO: Jeremy Midwinter
HR: Jennifer Perott
FYE: December 31
Type: Private

If Ralph Waldo Emerson were writing today, he might put to paper, "Build a better valve or gasket, and the world will beat a path to your door." Greene, Tweed & Co. (Greene, Tweed) manufactures next generation technology seals, gaskets, fiber optic connectors, and custom engineered plastic components for use in aerospace and defense, medical and pharmaceutical, nuclear, and chemical industries. The company's products are also at the heart of the petrochemical, oilfield OEM, industrial hydraulics, semiconductor, and solar markets. Greene, Tweed's facilities are located in the Americas, Asia, and Europe. It answers its door to customers such as Airbus, Boeing, Bayer, and the DoD, among others.

GREENLEAF BOOK GROUP, LLC

4005 BANISTER LN STE B
AUSTIN, TX 787048079
Phone: 512 891-6100
Fax: –
Web: www.greenleafbookgroup.com

CEO: –
CFO: –
HR: –
FYE: June 30
Type: Private

Greenleaf Book Group is a book publisher and distributor that specializes in developing independent authors.

GREENSHIFT CORP
NBB: GERS

1800 NE 135th Street
Oklahoma, OK 73131
Phone: 888 510-2392
Fax: –
Web: www.greenshift.com

CEO: Kevin Kreisler
CFO: Kevin Kreisler
HR: –
FYE: December 31
Type: Public

In a case of modern alchemy, GreenShift (formerly GS CleanTech) is working overtime to turn organic material into biodiesel. The company's proprietary technologies are used to produce biomass-derived end products, and at reduced cost and risk by extracting and refining raw materials that other producers cannot access or process. GreenShift owns and operates four proprietary corn oil extraction facilities, one biodiesel production facility, and one vegetable oilseed crushing plant. GreenShift claims that its technologies have the capability of extracting more than 6.5 million gallons of crude corn oil for every 100 million gallons of corn ethanol produced. The company also produces culinary oil.

	Annual Growth	12/17	12/18	12/19	12/20	12/21
Sales ($mil.)	(55.0%)	6.9	3.8	1.5	0.3	0.3
Net income ($ mil.)	–	(2.2)	0.4	0.4	(0.5)	0.2
Market value ($ mil.)	(14.8%)	4.8	0.9	1.0	1.6	2.5
Employees	–	–	–	–	–	–

GREENSTONE FARM CREDIT SERVICES ACA

3515 WEST RD
EAST LANSING, MI 488237312
Phone: 517 324-0213
Fax: –
Web: www.greenstonefcs.com

CEO: David B Armstrong
CFO: –
HR: Gayle Giddings
FYE: December 31
Type: Private

One of the largest associations in the Farm Credit System, GreenStone offers FARM CREDIT SERVICES (FCS) provides short, intermediate, and long-term loans; equipment and building leases; appraisal services; and life and crop insurance to farmers in Michigan and Wisconsin. It serves about 15,000 members and has nearly 40 locations. Through an alliance with AgriSolutions, a farm software and consulting company, Greenstone provides income tax planning and preparation services, farm business consulting, and educational seminars. FCS Mortgage provides residential loans for rural properties, as well as loans for home improvement, construction, and refinancing.

	Annual Growth	12/04	12/05	12/06	12/07	12/20
Assets ($mil.)	8.1%	–	–	3,691.3	4,317.3	10,967
Net income ($ mil.)	10.8%	–	–	63.9	69.6	270.2
Market value ($ mil.)	–	–	–	–	–	–
Employees	–	–	–	–	–	380

GREENVILLE UTILITIES COMMISSION

401 S GREENE ST
GREENVILLE, NC 278341977
Phone: 252 551-3315
Fax: –
Web: www.guc.com

CEO: –
CFO: –
HR: Lena Previll
FYE: June 30
Type: Private

For Greenville citizens the alternative to "YUK!" (no power, natural gas supply, potable water, or sanitation), is GUC. Greenville Utilities Commission (GUC) distributes electricity, natural gas, water, and wastewater services to residents and businesses in the city of Greenville, and 75% of Pitt County, in North Carolina, for a combined total of more than 143,000 customer connections. The utility receives wholesale power through its membership in the North Carolina Eastern Municipal Power Agency. One of 32 municipal members of the North Carolina Eastern Municipal Power Agency, GUC joined the Power Agency in 1982.

	Annual Growth	06/06	06/07	06/08	06/15	06/16
Sales ($mil.)	1.0%	–	225.5	–	272.0	247.2
Net income ($ mil.)	8.7%	–	11.8	12.8	13.2	24.9
Market value ($ mil.)	–	–	–	–	–	–
Employees	–	–	–	–	–	435

GREENWOOD MILLS, INC.

104 MAXWELL AVE
GREENWOOD, SC 296462641
Phone: 864 227-2121
Fax: -
Web: www.greenwoodmills.com

CEO: James C Self III
CFO: -
HR: Lisa McMillan
FYE: December 30
Type: Private

From garments to golf, Greenwood Mills has it covered. The company manufactures specialty fabrics for the apparel, home furnishings, and military markets. Greenwood Mills also produces garments, including jeans and other denim products, for retailers such as Levi Strauss and Abercrombie & Fitch through its SingleSource Apparel denim operations in Mexico. Greenwood Mills operates two plants in South Carolina. Through affiliated units, the company operates golf course, resort, and real estate developments. Founded in 1888 by James Self, Greenwood Mills is still owned and operated by the Self family.

GREIF INC

425 Winter Road
Delaware, OH 43015
Phone: 740 549-6000
Fax: -
Web: www.greif.com

NYS: GEF

CEO: Ole Rosgaard
CFO: Lawrence A Hilsheimer
HR: Eva Aguirre
FYE: October 31
Type: Public

Greif produces rigid industrial packaging products, including steel, plastic, and fibre drums and related closure systems. It sells corrugated products and containerboard for packaging home appliances, small machinery, and grocery and building products. Greif also makes flexible intermediate containers (based on polypropylene woven fabric) used to ship an array of bulk industrial and consumer goods. Additionally, the company owns approximately 175,000 acres of timber property used to provide the raw material for some of its products. Greif caters to a diverse group of industries such as chemicals, food and beverage, petroleum, agricultural, pharmaceuticals, and minerals. The company operates worldwide, however, it generates some 50% of revenue from US operations.

	Annual Growth	10/19	10/20	10/21	10/22	10/23
Sales ($mil.)	3.2%	4,595.0	4,515.0	5,556.1	6,349.5	5,218.6
Net income ($ mil.)	20.4%	171.0	108.8	390.7	376.7	359.2
Market value ($ mil.)	12.8%	1,833.4	1,899.8	3,027.4	3,099.0	2,972.1
Employees	(8.3%)	17,000	16,000	16,000	12,000	12,000

GRENADIER REALTY CORP.

168 39TH ST UNIT 2
BROOKLYN, NY 112322714
Phone: 718 642-8700
Fax: -
Web: www.grcrealty.com

CEO: Ryan Moorehead
CFO: Ebonie Nichols
HR: -
FYE: December 31
Type: Private

Once you find an available apartment in New York City, you just might find yourself acquainted with Grenadier Realty. Also known as GRC Realty, Grenadier Realty provides property and leasing management services for a wide variety of New York City residential communities through dozens of offices in the Big Apple. The company oversees such communities as government-assisted and public housing, fair-market housing, cooperatives, and condominiums. The company's service offerings include property maintenance, accounting administration, resident relations programs, and security. Grenadier Realty was founded in 1976.

	Annual Growth	12/05	12/06	12/07	12/08	12/09
Assets ($mil.)	969.4%	-	-	0.2	27.4	24.3
Net income ($ mil.)	-	-	-	0.0	3.1	-
Market value ($ mil.)	-	-	-	-	-	-
Employees	-	-	-	-	-	150

GREYSTONE LOGISTICS INC

NBB: GLGI

1613 East 15th Street
Tulsa, OK 74120
Phone: 918 583-7441
Fax: -
Web: www.greystonelogistics.com

CEO: -
CFO: -
HR: -
FYE: May 31
Type: Public

If you need plastic pallets, then Greystone Logistics is the logical choice for you. The company manufactures and sells plastic pallets for various commercial applications. Its products include the Greystone Beverage Pallet, Hawker Series fire-retardant plastic pallets, Tank picture frame pallets, and the Granada Series (including nestable and flat-deck plastic pallets). Greystone Logistics also offers multi-station plastic injection molding systems. The company uses a proprietary recycled resin mix and manufacturing process to produce its plastics. It serves customers in the pharmaceutical, beverage, and other industries, primarily in the US.

	Annual Growth	05/19	05/20	05/21	05/22	05/23
Sales ($mil.)	(3.8%)	71.1	76.2	64.9	74.2	60.8
Net income ($ mil.)	36.9%	1.8	4.7	3.4	4.3	6.3
Market value ($ mil.)	10.7%	15.8	25.7	35.6	22.2	23.7
Employees	(5.4%)	359	339	291	298	288

GREYSTONE POWER CORPORATION, AN ELECTRIC MEMBERSHIP CORPORATION

3400 HIRAM DOUGLASVILLE HWY
HIRAM, GA 301414924
Phone: 770 942-6576
Fax: -
Web: www.greystonepower.com

CEO: Gary Miller
CFO: -
HR: -
FYE: December 31
Type: Private

GreyStone's power helps to lift the grey and the darkness. GreyStone Power is an electric membership cooperative that provides transmission and distribution services to almost 116,000 residential, commercial, and industrial customers in eight counties west of Atlanta (Bartow, Carroll, Cobb, Coweta, Douglas, Fayette, Fulton, and Paulding). The utility operates about 3,500 miles of overhead power lines. GreyStone Power also offers natural gas services through a partnership with Gas South and offers banking, residential and commercial security, and surge protection operations.

	Annual Growth	08/14	08/15	08/16*	12/18	12/22
Sales ($mil.)	3.8%	-	-	270.0	305.1	337.5
Net income ($ mil.)	-	-	-	23.3	-	-
Market value ($ mil.)	-	-	-	-	-	-
Employees	-	-	-	-	-	260

*Fiscal year change

GRIFFIN HEALTH SERVICES CORPORATION

130 DIVISION ST
DERBY, CT 064181326
Phone: 203 735-7421
Fax: -
Web: www.griffinhealth.org

CEO: -
CFO: -
HR: Stephen Mordecai
FYE: September 30
Type: Private

Much as the mythical griffin is said to protect those it watches over, Griffin Health Services protects the well-being of residents in Connecticut. The company provides health services through its 160-bed Griffin Hospital, a not-for-profit, acute care hospital in Derby, Connecticut. The hospital is an affiliate of the Planetree organization, which works with its member facilities to create patient-centered environments. As a Planetree facility, Griffin Hospital allows patients access to their own charts, contains no restricted areas, and uses alternative therapies such as meditation and acupuncture. The hospital also operates an inpatient psychiatric unit with about two dozen beds serving adults and seniors.

	Annual Growth	09/17	09/18	09/19	09/21	09/22
Sales ($mil.)	20.0%	-	0.5	0.8	0.7	1.0
Net income ($ mil.)	-	-	(0.1)	0.3	0.0	0.3
Market value ($ mil.)	-	-	-	-	-	-
Employees	-	-	-	-	-	52

GRIFFITH FOODS GROUP INC.

1 GRIFFITH CTR
ALSIP, IL 608034701
Phone: 708 371-0900
Fax: -
Web: www.griffithfoods.com

CEO: -
CFO: Joseph R Maslick
HR: William McKee
FYE: September 30
Type: Private

A little pinch here, a little pinch there, pretty soon you have a business. Founded in 1919, Griffith Laboratories is a manufacturer of food ingredients with operations and customers worldwide. The company's clients include food manufacturers; food service operators, including restaurants, hotels, and cruise lines; and food retailers and wholesalers. Its products include seasonings, sauce and soup mixes, condiments, texturizers, and bakery blends. Griffith's subsidiaries include Custom Culinary (food bases and mixes) and Innova (meat and savory flavors). The company also offers customized ingredient services. Griffith Laboratories is family owned and run by third- and fourth-generation family members.

GRIFFON CORP.

712 Fifth Ave, 18th Floor
New York, NY 10019
Phone: 212 957-5000
Fax: -
Web: www.griffon.com

NYS: GFF
CEO: Ronald J Kramer
CFO: Brian G Harris
HR: -
FYE: September 30
Type: Public

Griffon Corporation is a diversified management and holding company that conducts business through wholly-owned subsidiaries. The company operates in two segments ? consumer and professional products, and home and building products. AMES, and ClosetMaid, Griffon's consumer and professional products subsidiaries, make wood and wire closet organizations, yard tools, cleaning and storage products. The home and building segment operates through Clopay, which has become the largest manufacturer and marketer of garage doors and rolling steel doors in North America. The US accounts for more than 80% of Griffon's total revenue.

	Annual Growth	09/19	09/20	09/21	09/22	09/23
Sales ($mil.)	5.0%	2,209.3	2,407.5	2,270.6	2,848.5	2,685.2
Net income ($ mil.)	20.1%	37.3	53.4	79.2	(191.6)	77.6
Market value ($ mil.)	17.3%	1,196.6	1,115.0	1,403.8	1,684.5	2,263.7
Employees	(6.0%)	7,300	7,400	6,700	6,200	5,700

GRILL CONCEPTS, INC.

6171 W CENTURY BLVD STE 360
LOS ANGELES, CA 900455310
Phone: 818 251-7000
Fax: -
Web: www.grillconcepts.com

CEO: Bob Spivak
CFO: Wayne Lipschitz
HR: -
FYE: December 30
Type: Private

You might say this company is cooking up some classics on a daily basis. Grill Concepts operates a chain of nearly 30 Daily Grill restaurants offering upscale casual dining in a setting reminiscent of a classic American grill during the 1930s and 1940s. Located primarily in California, the restaurants serve such fare as chicken pot pie, meatloaf, and cobbler, as well as steak, seafood, and pasta. In addition to its company-owned locations, Grill Concepts has a small number of licensed and managed units operating in shopping areas and hotels. The Daily Grill concept is based on the company's half dozen Grill on the Alley fine dining restaurants. Robert Spivak co-founded the Daily Grill chain in 1984.

GROCERY OUTLET HOLDING CORP

5650 Hollis Street
Emeryville, CA 94608
Phone: 510 845-1999
Fax: -
Web: www.groceryoutlet.com

NMS: GO
CEO: Robert J Sheedy Jr
CFO: Charles C Bracher
HR: -
FYE: December 30
Type: Public

Grocery Outlet is a high-growth, extreme-value retailer of quality, name-brand consumables, and fresh products sold through a network of independently operated stores. The company has about 440 stores in California, Washington, Oregon, Pennsylvania, Idaho, Nevada, Maryland, and New Jersey. An ever-changing assortment of "WOW!" deals, complemented by everyday staple products, generates customer excitement and encourages frequent visits from bargain-minded shoppers. Its flexible buying model allows the company to offer quality, name-brand opportunistic products at prices generally 40% to 70% below those of conventional retailers. Entrepreneurial independent operators (IOs) run their stores and create a neighborhood feel through personalized customer service and a localized product offering.

	Annual Growth	12/19*	01/21	01/22*	12/22	12/23
Sales ($mil.)	11.6%	2,559.6	3,134.6	3,079.6	3,578.1	3,969.5
Net income ($ mil.)	50.7%	15.4	106.7	62.3	65.1	79.4
Market value ($ mil.)	(5.3%)	3,321.0	3,894.5	2,806.1	2,896.3	2,675.1
Employees	4.2%	847	946	946	969	997

*Fiscal year change

GROEN BROTHERS AVIATION INC

2640 West California Avenue
Salt Lake City, UT 84104-4593
Phone: 801 973-0177
Fax: -
Web: -

CEO: David L Groen
CFO: David L Groen
HR: -
FYE: June 30
Type: Public

A centaur is part man, part horse; a griffin is part eagle, part lion; and a gyroplane is part helicopter, part airplane. Through its subsidiaries Groen Brothers Aviation (GBA) develops and manufactures gyroplane and gyrodyne rotor-wing aircraft. Its Hawk series gyroplane is designed to be safer in low and slow flight than either an airplane or a helicopter. Gyroplanes get lift from rotary blades and thrust from a propeller. Potential applications for the Hawk series include commercial surveying, fire patrol, law enforcement, and military surveillance. In 2012 GBA reached an agreement with its creditors to enter a period of financial restructuring and eliminate its debt of more than $170 million.

	Annual Growth	06/08	06/09	06/10	06/11	06/12
Sales ($mil.)	(78.8%)	5.9	1.1	0.0	0.0	0.0
Net income ($ mil.)	-	(19.8)	(16.1)	(19.4)	(23.3)	(25.8)
Market value ($ mil.)	(15.9%)	8.6	2.7	1.7	2.9	4.3
Employees	16.7%	7	9	11	12	13

GROOVE BOTANICALS INC

310 Fourth Avenue South, Suite 7000
Minneapolis, MN 55415
Phone: 952 746-9652
Fax: -
Web: www.avalonoilinc.com

NBB: GRVE
CEO: Kent Rodriguez
CFO: Kent Rodriguez
HR: -
FYE: March 31
Type: Public

Avalon Oil & Gas is looking for that legendary prize -- making consistent profits in the oil business. The company focuses on acquiring mature oil and gas wells in Kansas, Louisiana, Oklahoma, and Texas and in 2009 it reported proved reserves of about 45,650 barrels of oil equivalent. In addition to its oil and gas assets, Avalon Oil & Gas' technology segment (through majority-owned Oiltek) provides explorers with oil production enhancing technologies. To develop this segment the company has a strategic partnership with UK technology group Innovaro. In 2011 the company agreed to buy Oklahoma properties from Fossiltek. CEO Kent Rodriguez owns 46% of Avalon Oil & Gas.

	Annual Growth	03/13	03/14	03/15	03/16	03/17
Sales ($mil.)	(23.2%)	0.2	0.2	0.1	0.0	0.0
Net income ($ mil.)	-	(0.7)	(0.8)	0.1	(2.5)	(0.2)
Market value ($ mil.)	(40.4%)	2.9	1.5	0.8	0.3	0.4
Employees	(20.5%)	5	5	5	2	2

GROSSMONT HOSPITAL CORPORATION

5555 GROSSMONT CENTER DR
LA MESA, CA 919423077
Phone: 619 740-6000
Fax: –
Web: www.sharp.com

CEO: Dan Gross
CFO: –
HR: –
FYE: September 30
Type: Private

Residents of the eastern San Diego community of La Mesa, California, depend on Grossmont for medical care. Grossmont Hospital is a 540-bed, not-for-profit health care facility. The hospital, which opened in 1955, has a staff of about 700 physicians. The full-service acute care facility provides specialty services in the areas of cardiology, oncology, mental health, orthopedics, pediatrics, physical therapy, sleep therapy, hospice, and women's health care. The Grossmont Hospital Corporation is a subsidiary of Sharp HealthCare; it operates the Grossmont Hospital through a lease agreement with state-owned Grossmont Hospital District.

GROUP 1 AUTOMOTIVE, INC.   NYS: GPI

800 Gessner, Suite 500
Houston, TX 77024
Phone: 713 647-5700
Fax: 713 647-5858
Web: www.group1auto.com

CEO: Earl J Hesterberg
CFO: Daniel J McHenry
HR: Brooks O 'hara
FYE: December 31
Type: Public

Group 1 Automotive is a leading operator in the automotive retail industry. The company is a new and used car retailer with 200 dealerships, about 280 franchises across the US and the UK. The US is the company's biggest market (accounting for approximately 80% of the company's revenue), and the company is present in more than 15 US states. Group 1's largest concentration of dealerships is in its home state of Texas. The company also offers financing, provides maintenance and repair services, and sells replacement parts.

	Annual Growth	12/19	12/20	12/21	12/22	12/23
Sales ($mil.)	10.4%	12,044	10,852	13,482	16,222	17,874
Net income ($ mil.)	36.4%	174.0	286.5	552.1	751.5	601.6
Market value ($ mil.)	32.1%	1,368.4	1,794.5	2,671.4	2,468.2	4,170.1
Employees	1.1%	15,296	12,337	13,711	15,491	16,011

GROUP O, INC.

4905 77TH AVE E
MILAN, IL 612643250
Phone: 309 736-8100
Fax: –
Web: www.groupo.com

CEO: –
CFO: –
HR: Jennifer Bohler
FYE: December 31
Type: Private

The "O" in Group O stands for optimization. It also stands for Ontiveros, the family that leads this company. Founded by chairman Robert Ontiveros, Group O is one of the largest Hispanic-owned companies in the US. It helps big businesses improve their operations through three divisions: marketing, packaging, and supply chain. It offers everything from direct mail creation to shrink wrap procurement to warehousing and distribution, and business intelligence. It has served clients from various industries, including food and beverage (Kerry), consumer goods (P&G), manufacturing (Johnson Controls), pharmaceutical (Bristol-Myers Squibb), and telecommunications (AT&T).

	Annual Growth	12/02	12/03	12/04	12/05	12/13
Sales ($mil.)	11.4%	–	–	–	240.4	569.5
Net income ($ mil.)	0.9%	–	–	–	5.3	5.6
Market value ($ mil.)	–	–	–	–	–	–
Employees	–	–	–	–	–	1,066

GROUPON INC   NMS: GRPN

600 W. Chicago Avenue, Suite 400
Chicago, IL 60654
Phone: 312 334-1579
Fax: –
Web: www.groupon.com

CEO: Dusan Senkypl
CFO: Jiri Ponrt
HR: Livia Thomas
FYE: December 31
Type: Public

Groupon is a globally scaled two-sided marketplace that connects consumers to merchants. Consumers access its marketplace through its mobile applications and its websites. The company earns service revenue from transactions in which it earns commissions by selling goods or services on behalf of third-party merchants. Groupon also sells merchandise, such as electronics, toys, apparel, and household items, directly to customers. Customers access the company's platform through mobile apps and websites. Groupon has some 20 million active customers. North America is Groupon's largest market, accounting for nearly 75% of total revenue. Groupon was founded in 2008.

	Annual Growth	12/19	12/20	12/21	12/22	12/23
Sales ($mil.)	(30.6%)	2,218.9	1,416.9	967.1	599.1	514.9
Net income ($ mil.)	–	(22.4)	(287.9)	118.7	(237.6)	(55.4)
Market value ($ mil.)	52.2%	76.1	1,210.3	737.7	273.3	409.0
Employees	(1.6%)	2,358	4,159	3,675	2,904	2,213

GROWMARK, INC.

1705 TOWANDA AVE
BLOOMINGTON, IL 617012040
Phone: 309 557-6000
Fax: –
Web: www.growmark.com

CEO: Jim Spradlin
CFO: Wade Mittelstadt
HR: Ann Kafer
FYE: August 31
Type: Private

GROWMARK is an agricultural cooperative serving about 400,000 customers across North America. It provides agronomy, energy, facility engineering, and construction products and services, as well as grain marketing and risk management services. The company owns the FS trademark, which is used by member cooperatives. Handling more than 3.2 million tons of crop nutrients annually, GROWMARK also provides a host of services from warehousing and logistics to training and marketing support. The company has an extensive network of fertilizer terminals throughout the Midwest and Ontario. The GROWMARK began in 1927.

	Annual Growth	08/15	08/16	08/17	08/18	08/19
Sales ($mil.)	9.5%	–	–	7,291.2	8,522.4	8,745.2
Net income ($ mil.)	(19.0%)	–	–	115.4	65.8	75.7
Market value ($ mil.)	–	–	–	–	–	–
Employees	–	–	–	–	–	8,641

GRUMA CORPORATION

5601 EXECUTIVE DR STE 800
IRVING, TX 750382508
Phone: 972 232-5000
Fax: –
Web: www.missionfoods.com

CEO: –
CFO: –
HR: Carole Bastarrachea
FYE: December 31
Type: Private

Gruma Corporation is one of the main producers of tortillas and related products throughout the US as well as one of the main producers of nixtamalized corn flour in the US. Its tortilla business operates approximately 20 plants producing tortillas, tortilla chips, and other related products and the main brands include Mission, Guerrero, and Calidad. Through its corn flour business, GRUMA operates six plants and the main brand is Maseca. Its food service customers include major chain restaurants, food service distributors, schools, hospitals, and the military. The vast majority of nixtamalized corn flour produced by Azteca Milling in the US is sold to tortilla and tortilla chip manufacturers and is delivered directly from its plants to the customers' manufacturing facilities by third parties. Gruma is the American subsidiary of giant Mexican food company Gruma, S.A.B. de C.V.

	Annual Growth	12/14	12/15	12/16	12/19	12/21
Sales ($mil.)	3.7%	–	2,086.8	2,023.7	2,202.3	2,598.3
Net income ($ mil.)	9.7%	–	152.6	179.1	224.9	266.3
Market value ($ mil.)	–	–	–	–	–	–
Employees	–	–	–	–	–	7,000

GRUNLEY CONSTRUCTION CO., INC.

15020 SHADY GROVE RD STE 500
ROCKVILLE, MD 208503390
Phone: 240 399-2000
Fax: –
Web: www.grunley.com

CEO: Kenneth M Grunley
CFO: –
HR: –
FYE: December 31
Type: Private

Grunley gets it done, from the monumental to the mundane. Founded in 1955, Grunley Construction Company provides general contracting, engineering, architectural, and construction management services and specializes in the renovation, restoration, and modernization of historic buildings in the Washington, DC area. Its projects range from prestigious undertakings -- the Smithsonian Institution, the Washington Monument, and the US Treasury building -- to more pedestrian endeavors such as office buildings, apartment buildings, schools, and power plants. The company also has lent its services to the construction of embassies, airports, and military facilities.

	Annual Growth	12/09	12/10	12/11	12/15	12/16
Sales ($mil.)	5.6%	–	–	324.0	403.8	425.7
Net income ($ mil.)	–	–	–	–	–	6.3
Market value ($ mil.)	–	–	–	–	–	–
Employees	–	–	–	–	–	310

GSE SYSTEMS INC

NAS: GVP

6940 Columbia Gateway Dr., Suite 470
Columbia, MD 21046
Phone: 410 970-7800
Fax: –
Web: www.gses.com

CEO: Kyle J Loudermilk
CFO: Emmett A Pepe
HR: –
FYE: December 31
Type: Public

GSE Systems is into the appearance of power and control. The company provides simulation software to train power plant operators, engineers, and managers. Its systems, used primarily for the nuclear power, fossil energy, and chemical industries, can also be used to test new plant systems before they are installed. GSE Systems also offers training services through a partnership with General Physics. Customers include Slovenske electrarne, American Electric Power, Emerson Process Management, Statoil ASA, and Westinghouse Electric. With international offices in China, India, Sweden, and the UK, GSE Systems generates about 70% of sales from customers located outside the US.

	Annual Growth	12/18	12/19	12/20	12/21	12/22
Sales ($mil.)	(15.2%)	92.2	83.0	57.6	55.2	47.7
Net income ($ mil.)	–	(0.4)	(12.1)	(10.5)	10.6	(15.3)
Market value ($ mil.)	(23.5%)	4.7	3.7	3.0	3.8	1.6
Employees	(8.8%)	402	363	332	308	278

GSI TECHNOLOGY INC

NMS: GSIT

1213 Elko Drive
Sunnyvale, CA 94089
Phone: 408 331-8800
Fax: –
Web: www.gsitechnology.com

CEO: Lee-Lean Shu
CFO: Douglas Schirle
HR: –
FYE: March 31
Type: Public

GSI Technology makes very fast chips. The company's specialized SRAM (static random-access memory) integrated circuits are used in high-speed networking equipment. Marketed under the Very Fast brand, its chips allow routers, switches, and other gear from the likes of Alcatel-Lucent and Cisco Systems to retrieve data at the speeds needed for broadband transmission. The fabless semiconductor company does most of its business through contract manufacturers, such as Jabil Circuit (20% of sales) and Flextronics (9%), and through distributors such as Avnet (20%) and Nexcomm (11%). Other top customers include SMART Modular Technologies (11%), which buys memory chips for products it makes on behalf of Cisco.

	Annual Growth	03/19	03/20	03/21	03/22	03/23
Sales ($mil.)	(12.9%)	51.5	43.3	27.7	33.4	29.7
Net income ($ mil.)	–	0.2	(10.3)	(21.5)	(16.4)	(16.0)
Market value ($ mil.)	(31.4%)	191.8	171.8	165.1	94.5	42.5
Employees	(1.5%)	166	166	178	180	156

GSV INC

NBB: GSVI

191 Post Road West
Westport, CT 06880
Phone: 203 221-2690
Fax: –
Web: www.gsv.com; www.toolsforliving.com

CEO: –
CFO: –
HR: –
FYE: December 31
Type: Public

GSV (Grove Strategic Ventures) should know more about weeding out good and bad business plans since trashing its own. The firm operated consumer products e-tailers CyberShop.com and electronics.net. It opted out of those businesses and reinvented itself as an Internet startup incubator. Investments included Weema Technologies and Telephone.com. After the dot-com bust, the value of GSV's investments plummeted. GSV gets about half of its revenues from an interest in two Louisiana oil and gas wells. The company subletted offices in New Jersey. Since the tenant defaulted on the lease, insurance covered the payments, and GSV ceased those operations. Chairman Sagi Matza controls 77% of GSV.

	Annual Growth	12/04	12/05	12/06	12/07	12/08
Sales ($mil.)	18.7%	0.4	0.7	0.3	0.8	0.9
Net income ($ mil.)	–	(0.5)	(0.2)	(0.2)	0.2	(2.3)
Market value ($ mil.)	(26.0%)	2.3	1.1	0.8	1.3	0.7
Employees	–	1	1	1	1	1

GT ADVANCED TECHNOLOGIES INC.

5 WENTWORTH DR STE 1
HUDSON, NH 030514929
Phone: 603 883-5200
Fax: –
Web: www.onsemi.com

CEO: Gregory C Knight
CFO: Michele P Rayos
HR: –
FYE: December 31
Type: Private

GT Advanced Technologies (formerly GT Solar International) is a beacon on the path of the solar power supply chain. The company manufactures the equipment used by other companies to produce silicon wafers and solar cells. Key products include chemical vapor deposition (CVD) reactors used to produce polysilicon, the raw material in solar cells; and directional solidification systems (DSS), the furnaces used to transform polysilicon into ingots, which are sliced into silicon wafers to become solar cells. GT Advanced Technologies does most of its business in Asia, primarily in Malaysia. In 2014 the company filed for Chapter 11 bankruptcy protection. It left bankruptcy in 2016 after a financial restructuring.

GT BIOPHARMA INC

NAS: GTBP

8000 Marina Blvd., Suite 100
Brisbane, CA 94005
Phone: 415 919-4040
Fax: –
Web: www.gtbiopharma.com

CEO: Michael Breen
CFO: Manu Ohri
HR: –
FYE: December 31
Type: Public

GT Biopharma (formerly OXIS International) is an immuno-oncology biotech working with its proprietary platforms to develop innovative treatments for such cancers as lymphoma, leukemia, and solid tumors. Its TriKE and TetraKE platforms harness and promote the body's own natural killer (NK) cells. GT Biopharma's NK cell technology, which was created to treat solid and liquid tumors, is in early-stage clinical trials. The company's bi-specific Antibody Drug Conjugate (ADC) platform is being used to develop other product candidates. In mid-2017, OXIS International acquired Georgetown Translational Pharmaceuticals and changed its name to GT Biopharma. It also switched its focus from antioxidant nutritional and cosmeceutical products to immuno-oncology.

	Annual Growth	12/18	12/19	12/20	12/21	12/22
Sales ($mil.)	–	–	–	–	–	–
Net income ($ mil.)	–	(259.2)	(38.6)	(28.3)	(58.0)	(20.9)
Market value ($ mil.)	–	–	–	–	3.3	1.0
Employees	35.1%	3	2	3	8	10

GTC SYSTEMS INC.

504 W MISSION AVE STE 203
ESCONDIDO, CA 920251604
Phone: 858 560-5800
Fax: –
Web: www.gtcsystems.com

CEO: –
CFO: –
HR: –
FYE: June 30
Type: Private

GTC Systems offers information technology consulting, training, Web development, and technical staffing services. The company also provides software, computers, and networking products from such vendors as Citrix, Cisco, and VMware. GTC specializes in the implementation and customization of software from Citrix and Microsoft. The company serves clients in such industries as health care, education, and retail, as well as the public sector. Customers have included Salerno/Livingston Architects, the US Marine Corps, and San Diego State University. GTC was founded in 1995.

	Annual Growth	06/98	06/99	06/00	06/06	06/08
Sales ($mil.)	(20.4%)	–	44.6	12.2	4.9	5.7
Net income ($ mil.)	–	–	0.0	0.1	0.0	(0.0)
Market value ($ mil.)	–	–	–	–	–	–
Employees	–	–	–	–	–	30

GTS TECHNOLOGY SOLUTIONS, INC.

9211 WATERFORD CENTRE BLVD STE 275
AUSTIN, TX 787587679
Phone: 512 452-0651
Fax: –
Web: www.gts-ts.com

CEO: Laura Grant
CFO: –
HR: –
FYE: December 31
Type: Private

Nothing as archaic as ribbons and typewriters adorn the shelves at ARC (Austin Ribbon & Computer). The old-school name belies a modern firm offering IT products and services to state government, education, and health care customers throughout Texas. It sells more than 400 brands of computers, tablets, and peripherals -- including Dell, HP, EMC, Lenovo, and Cisco. (The company is the largest supplier of Dell computers to Texas government.) ARC also provides IT services from single computer fixes to office-wide system design, installation, and maintenance. Customers have included the Texas Lottery Commission, City of Dallas, The University of Texas at Austin, and University Health Systems San Antonio.

	Annual Growth	12/05	12/06	12/07	12/09	12/20
Sales ($mil.)	8.0%	–	56.4	72.2	–	164.8
Net income ($ mil.)	28.5%	–	0.3	4.0	–	9.8
Market value ($ mil.)	–	–	–	–	–	–
Employees	–	–	–	–	–	103

GTT COMMUNICATIONS, INC

7900 Tysons One Place, Suite 1450
McLean, VA 22102
Phone: 703 442-5500
Fax: –
Web: www.gtt.net

NBB: GTTN Q
CEO: Ed Morche
CFO: Johan Broekhuysen
HR: –
FYE: December 31
Type: Public

GTT Communications is a managed network and security services provider to global organizations. The design and deliver solutions that leverage advanced cloud, networking and security technologies. The company complements its solutions with a suite of professional services and exceptional sales and support teams in local markets around the world. It serves thousands of national and multinational companies with a portfolio that includes SD-WAN, security, Internet, voice and other connectivity options. Its services are uniquely enabled by its top-ranked, global, Tier 1 IP backbone, which spans more than 260 cities on six continents.

	Annual Growth	12/15	12/16	12/17	12/18	12/19
Sales ($mil.)	47.1%	369.3	521.7	827.9	1,490.8	1,727.8
Net income ($ mil.)	–	19.3	5.3	(71.5)	(243.4)	(105.9)
Market value ($ mil.)	(9.7%)	967.1	1,629.7	2,661.4	1,341.2	643.4
Employees	52.6%	572	662	1,257	3,200	3,100

GUADALUPE VALLEY TELEPHONE COOPERATIVE, INC.

36101 FM 3159
NEW BRAUNFELS, TX 781325900
Phone: 830 885-4411
Fax: –
Web: www.gvtc.com

CEO: Ritchie Sorrells
CFO: Mark J Gitter
HR: Kathy Young
FYE: December 31
Type: Private

Guadalupe Valley Telephone Cooperative (GVTC) offers telecommunications services to residential and business customers in the Hill Country area of south Texas. The cooperative local exchange carrier provides traditional local and long-distance telephone services, Internet access, digital cable television, high speed Fiber-To-The-Business (FTTB) service, and high-speed Fiber-To-The-Home (FTTH) converged service packages. GVTC also installs and monitors residential and commercial security systems, and provides additional enterprise services, such as its ID Vault information security service. Founded in 1951, GVTC also offers Web hosting, technical support, domain registration, and Web scam alert services.

	Annual Growth	12/16	12/17	12/18	12/19	12/20
Sales ($mil.)	5.2%	–	69.2	70.7	74.6	80.6
Net income ($ mil.)	19.7%	–	33.3	31.2	47.7	57.2
Market value ($ mil.)	–	–	–	–	–	–
Employees	–	–	–	–	–	229

GUARANTEE ELECTRICAL COMPANY

3405 BENT AVE
SAINT LOUIS, MO 631162601
Phone: 314 772-5400
Fax: –
Web: www.geco.com

CEO: Rich Ledbetter
CFO: Josh Voegtli
HR: Linda McGillis
FYE: September 30
Type: Private

Guarantee Electrical Company is one of the largest and oldest electrical contracting companies in the US. It has been a power in St. Louis since delivered on its "guarantee" to light up the 1904 World's Fair. Now a major US electrical contractor, the company offers commercial, institutional, and industrial services including pre-construction and construction, design/build, energy solutions, communications, data, security, life-safety systems, maintenance, and more. Guarantee Electrical partners with some of the biggest names and most successful enterprises in the hospitality field bringing creative flair and effective execution to new construction and renovations of hotels, restaurants, casinos, sports arenas, theaters, and conference/convention facilities. Among its projects are The Last Hotel, Belterra Park, River City Casino, SLU Macelwane Hall, Netrality Data Center, and BJC Alton Memorial Medical Office Building.

	Annual Growth	09/15	09/16	09/17	09/18	09/19
Sales ($mil.)	15.9%	–	–	152.6	152.2	205.0
Net income ($ mil.)	–	–	–	–	–	–
Market value ($ mil.)	–	–	–	–	–	–
Employees	–	–	–	–	–	700

GUARANTEED RATE, INC.

3940 N RAVENSWOOD AVE
CHICAGO, IL 606132420
Phone: 866 934-7283
Fax: –
Web: www.rate.com

CEO: Victor Ciardelli III
CFO: Suk Shah
HR: Kristen Johnson
FYE: December 31
Type: Private

Shopping around for the best rate so that you don't have to, Guaranteed Rate has grown to be the nation's eighth largest home loan company. The US mortgage company provides customers with a menu of loan products, including refinancing. It primarily serves first-time homebuyers and homeowners looking to reduce their monthly mortgage payments. Guaranteed Rate's retail division offers training and marketing support services to real estate agents and developers. Licensed to originate loans in all 50 states, the company boasts more than 170 offices nationwide, serving customers in person, online, or by phone. Since its founding in 2000, it has funded some $80 billion in loans.

GUARANTY BANCORP INC (NH)

1331 Seventeenth Street, Suite 300
Denver, CO 80202
Phone: 303 293-5563
Fax: -
Web: www.gbnk.com

CEO: -
CFO: -
HR: -
FYE: December 31
Type: Public

Guaranty Bancorp holds Colorado's Guaranty Bank and Trust, which operates 25-plus branches mostly in the metropolitan Denver and Front Range areas. Boasting $3.3 billion in assets, the bank offers traditional retail and commercial banking, including deposit accounts, loans, and trust services. Subsidiaries Private Capital Management and Cherry Hills Investment Advisors provide private banking, investment management, trust services, and other wealth management services. The bank mostly targets small to medium-sized businesses. Over 30% of the bank's loan portfolio is made up of commercial and residential real estate property loans, while another 15% consists of retail and industrial property loans.

GUARANTY BANCSHARES INC   NYS: GNTY

16475 Dallas Parkway, Suite 600
Addison, TX 75001
Phone: 888 572-9881
Fax: -
Web: www.gnty.com

CEO: Tyson T Abston
CFO: Shalene A Jacobson
HR: -
FYE: December 31
Type: Public

Guaranty Bancshares is the holding company for Guaranty Bond Bank, which operates about a dozen branches in northeast Texas and another in West Texas. Guaranty Bond Bank's deposit products and services include CDs and savings, checking, NOW, and money market accounts. Its lending activities include one- to four-family residential mortgages (more than a third of the company's loan portfolio) in addition to commercial mortgage, construction, business, agriculture, and personal loans. The company's GB Financial division provides wealth management, retirement planning, and trust services.

	Annual Growth	12/19	12/20	12/21	12/22	12/23
Assets ($mil.)	8.3%	2,318.4	2,740.8	3,086.1	3,351.5	3,184.8
Net income ($ mil.)	3.4%	26.3	27.4	39.8	40.4	30.0
Market value ($ mil.)	0.6%	379.5	345.6	433.7	399.8	388.0
Employees	1.1%	467	467	472	494	488

GUARDIAN GLASS COMPANY

2300 HARMON RD
AUBURN HILLS, MI 483261714
Phone: 248 340-1800
Fax: -
Web: www.guardian.com

CEO: Ron Vaupel
CFO: -
HR: -
FYE: December 31
Type: Private

Guardian Glass is a leading global manufacturer of commercial, residential, automotive, energy/solar, and technical glass. The company's glass products include InGlass (interior glass), SunGuard (advanced architectural glass), ClimaGuard (residential glass), EcoGuard (glass for solar energy systems), and technical glass for electronics, lighting, and commercial refrigeration. Its glass performs a variety of functions for buildings, such as insulate, reflect heat, save energy, and beautify. Guardian Glass is a subsidiary and one of three business units operated by privately held Guardian Industries.

	Annual Growth	12/98	12/99	12/00	12/21	12/22
Sales ($mil.)	0.7%	-	-	37.3	127.3	43.3
Net income ($ mil.)	-	-	-	(0.2)	58.9	(31.9)
Market value ($ mil.)	-	-	-	-	-	-
Employees	-	-	-	-	-	375

GUARDIAN LIFE INSURANCE CO. OF AMERICA (NYC)

7 Hanover Square, H-26-E
New York, NY 10004-2616
Phone: 212 598-8000
Fax: -
Web: www.guardianlife.com

CEO: -
CFO: -
HR: -
FYE: December 31
Type: Public

The Guardian Life Insurance Company of America is one of the largest mutual insurance companies in the US with $11 billion in capital and $1.7 billion in operating income and a leading provider of life, disability, dental, and other benefits for individuals. The company has $90.1 billion in assets under management and $833 billion in life insurance in force. With roots going back to 1860, the mutual company is owned by its policyholders.

	Annual Growth	12/02	12/03	12/04	12/11	12/12
Assets ($mil.)	1.0%	34,074	21,671	23,336	35,127	37,529
Net income ($ mil.)	-	(283.0)	218.0	286.0	196.0	253.0
Market value ($ mil.)	-	-	-	-	-	-
Employees	-	-	-	-	-	-

GUEST SERVICES, INC.

3055 PROSPERITY AVE
FAIRFAX, VA 220312290
Phone: 703 849-9300
Fax: -
Web: www.guestservices.com

CEO: Nico Foris
CFO: Daniel N Stoltzfus
HR: Danielle M Verderosa
FYE: December 31
Type: Private

Guest Services supplies hospitality management services across a wide variety of client sites including government and business dining facilities, museums, hotels, resorts, conference centers, luxury condominiums, senior living centers, health care systems, state and national parks, school and university dining facilities, specialty retail stores, and full-service restaurants. For leisure and resort facilities, Guest Services offers water recreation activities, golf, spa, and health club and range among other. It serves more than 35 million guests annually at over 250 facilities nationwide. Guest Services was founded in 1917 as a private company to serve governmental agencies.

	Annual Growth	12/18	12/19	12/20	12/21	12/22
Sales ($mil.)	8.8%	-	-	-	164.7	179.1
Net income ($ mil.)	-	-	-	-	(7.3)	(7.9)
Market value ($ mil.)	-	-	-	-	-	-
Employees	-	-	-	-	-	2,500

GUIDANCE SOFTWARE, INC.

1055 E COLORADO BLVD STE 400
PASADENA, CA 91106
Phone: 626 229-9191
Fax: -
Web: www.opentext.com

CEO: Patrick Dennis
CFO: Barry Plaga
HR: Cari Graham
FYE: December 31
Type: Private

Guidance Software could be the digital version of TV's CSI, only in real life. The company provides software that government authorities, police agencies, and corporate investigators use for digital forensic investigations, information auditing, e-discovery, and incident response. The company's EnCase software is a forensics platform that helps organizations respond to threats and analyze information, including court-validated forensics tools to conduct investigations. Guidance serves some two-thirds of FORTUNE 100 companies, such as Apple, Boeing, Coca-Cola, Facebook, Whole Foods, Yahoo!, government agencies such as the CIA and NASA, and international organizations such as NATO. In 2017 Guidance agreed to be bought by Open Text for about $240 million.

GUIDE DOG FOUNDATION FOR THE BLIND, INC.

371 E JERICHO TPKE
SMITHTOWN, NY 117872906
Phone: 631 265-2121
Fax: –
Web: www.guidedog.org

CEO: Wells B Jones
CFO: –
HR: Maureen Palmquist
FYE: June 30
Type: Private

The Guide Dog Foundation for the Blind helps people get around with the help of a four-footed friend. The not-for-profit organization offers guide dogs to the blind or visually impaired for free. The organization's cost of raising and training a guide dog (Labradors, Golden Retrievers, and mixes of the two) is $30,000. The foundation also provides instruction to the blind to handle their skilled guide dogs through a month-long training program. Classes, as well as dog breeding and training, are held at the Guide Dog Foundation's eight-acre facility in New York. Founded in 1946, the organization is supported solely by private donations.

	Annual Growth	06/15	06/16	06/17	06/20	06/22
Sales ($mil.)	4.1%	–	10.9	–	13.0	13.9
Net income ($ mil.)	20.7%	–	2.9	–	5.9	9.0
Market value ($ mil.)	–	–	–	–	–	–
Employees	–	–	–	–	–	78

GUIDED THERAPEUTICS INC

5835 Peachtree Corners East, Suite B
Norcross, GA 30092
Phone: 770 242-8723
Fax: –
Web: www.guidedinc.com

NBB: GTHP
CEO: Michael C James
CFO: Gene S Cartwright
HR: –
FYE: December 31
Type: Public

Guided Therapeutics (formerly SpectRx) can shed some light on your condition. The firm is developing diagnostic products, including a cervical cancer detection device, using its proprietary biophotonic technology known as LightTouch. The technology uses optics and spectroscopy to provide doctors with non-invasive diagnostic methods for finding cancer. In order to zero in on its diagnostic business, the company in 2007 sold its SimpleChoice line of insulin pumps, which diabetics use to control blood glucose levels, to ICU Medical; it changed its name to Guided Therapeutics the following year to reflect its new focus.

	Annual Growth	12/18	12/19	12/20	12/21	12/22
Sales ($mil.)	(30.9%)	0.0	0.0	0.1	0.0	0.0
Net income ($ mil.)	–	1.0	(1.9)	(0.3)	(2.1)	(4.3)
Market value ($ mil.)	462.3%	0.0	6.5	14.6	28.2	14.6
Employees	(5.4%)	10	8	8	8	8

GUIDEHOUSE INC.

1676 INTERNATIONAL DR STE 800
MCLEAN, VA 22102
Phone: 571 633-1711
Fax: –
Web: www.guidehouse.com

CEO: Scott McIntyre
CFO: –
HR: –
FYE: December 31
Type: Private

Professional services firm Navigant Consulting offers advisory, consulting, outsourcing, and technology services to clients. The firm specializes in consulting on business disputes, litigation, and regulatory compliance. It also offers operational, strategic, and technical management consulting services. Employing about 1,400 consultants, Navigant Consulting targets clients operating in regulated industries like energy, financial services, health care, and insurance and works with government agencies and companies involved in product liability cases. Navigant Consulting was formed in 1996 under the name The Metzler Group.

GUIDEWIRE SOFTWARE INC

970 Park Pl., Suite 200
San Mateo, CA 94403
Phone: 650 357-9100
Fax: 650 357-9101
Web: www.guidewire.com

NYS: GWRE
CEO: Michael Rosenbaum
CFO: Jeff Cooper
HR: –
FYE: July 31
Type: Public

Guidewire Software delivers a leading platform that property and casualty (P&C) insurers trust to engage, innovate, and grow efficiently. Guidewire's platform combines core operations, digital engagement, analytics, and artificial intelligence (AI) applications delivered as a cloud service or self-managed software. Its core operational services and products are InsuranceSuite Cloud, InsuranceNow, and InsuranceSuite for self-managed installations. These services and products are transactional systems of record that support the entire insurance lifecycle, including insurance product definition, distribution, underwriting, policyholder services, and claims management. Its customers range from some of the largest global insurance companies or their subsidiaries to predominantly national or local insurers that serve specific states and/or regions. The company generates the majority of its revenue in the Americas.

	Annual Growth	07/19	07/20	07/21	07/22	07/23
Sales ($mil.)	5.9%	719.5	742.3	743.3	812.6	905.3
Net income ($ mil.)	–	20.7	(27.2)	(66.5)	(180.4)	(111.9)
Market value ($ mil.)	(4.5%)	8,313.5	9,582.3	9,382.0	6,329.6	6,907.8
Employees	9.7%	2,355	2,690	2,942	3,376	3,415

GUILD MORTGAGE COMPANY

5898 COPLEY DR FL 4
SAN DIEGO, CA 921117916
Phone: 800 283-8823
Fax: –
Web: www.guildmortgage.com

CEO: –
CFO: –
HR: –
FYE: December 31
Type: Private

Guild Mortgage Company offers home mortgage financing and refinancing for both prime and sub-prime borrowers, and originates residential mortgages on a wholesale basis through third-party brokers. Originally founded in 1960 to provide mortgages to home buyers from American Housing Guild, the San Diego-based company is now a leading residential mortgage originator. Guild Mortgage Company is licensed and approved to serve borrowers in about 50 US states through its more than 250 branch and satellite offices. Guild Mortgage is privately owned by its senior management and private-equity firm McCarthy Capital.

	Annual Growth	12/03	12/04	12/05	12/06	12/07
Assets ($mil.)	8.1%	–	89.8	86.6	86.1	113.5
Net income ($ mil.)	–	–	(1.2)	2.8	3.0	(3.5)
Market value ($ mil.)	–	–	–	–	–	–
Employees	–	–	–	–	–	1,000

GUILDMASTER, INC.

1938 E PHELPS ST
SPRINGFIELD, MO 658022281
Phone: 417 447-1871
Fax: –
Web: –

CEO: –
CFO: –
HR: –
FYE: June 30
Type: Private

Rather than standardize, Decorize wants to spice things up in your living space. The company, founded in 2000, manufactures and wholesales imported home furnishings. In addition to furniture, Decorize imports accent pieces including lamps, frames, vases, mirrors, and baskets. It sources its wares directly to retailers from factories in China, Indonesia, the Philippines, and India. Decorize consolidated its brands in recent years. Products marketed to independent retailers (76% of 2008 revenue) maintain the GuildMaster brand, while products targeting large retailers (24% of 2008 revenue) are marketed under the Decorize brand name. Customers include Klaussner Furniture, Dillard's, OfficeMax, and Williams-Sonoma.

GUITAR CENTER HOLDINGS, INC.

5795 LINDERO CANYON RD
WESTLAKE VILLAGE, CA 913624013
Phone: 818 735-8800
Fax: –
Web: www.guitarcenter.com

CEO: Gabriel Dalporto
CFO: Tim Martin
HR: Mark Laughlin
FYE: December 31
Type: Private

Guitar Center is home to the world's guitars, basses, amplifiers, keyboards, workstations, drums, percussion, and pro-audio equipment operating in over 260 stores in the US. Major brands include Auralex, Gig Gear, and Marlin lesher, as well as Amsco, Yamaha, Cable Wrangler, Techra, and Vater. Stores also offer used and vintage instruments, computer hardware and software, and musician services. In addition, its Musician's Friend unit sells merchandise online and by catalog. Guitar Center was founded in 1959.

GULF COAST PROJECT SERVICES, INC.

5800 LAKEWOOD RNCH BLVD N
LAKEWOOD RANCH, FL 342408479
Phone: 941 921-6087
Fax: –
Web: www.dooleymack.com

CEO: –
CFO: –
HR: –
FYE: December 31
Type: Private

DooleyMack Constructors does the heavy lifting on big construction projects. The company provides design and planning, construction management and general contracting services for commercial, industrial, multifamily residential, and institutional projects. DooleyMack has built and renovated everything public schools, condos, and performance arts centers to waste disposal facilities and laboratories. The company mainly operates in the central and southeastern regions of the US and has several offices in Florida, as well as locations in Georgia, Texas, North Carolina and South Carolina. The privately-owned company was founded in 1977 by executives Bill Dooley and Ken Smith. CFO Wendy Mack later joined the firm.

	Annual Growth	12/04	12/05	12/06	12/07	12/08
Sales ($mil.)	14.8%	–	72.5	83.5	91.0	109.5
Net income ($ mil.)	81.3%	–	0.1	0.5	1.2	0.8
Market value ($ mil.)	–	–	–	–	–	–
Employees	–	–	–	–	–	93

GULF ISLAND FABRICATION, INC.

NMS: GIFI

2170 Buckthorne Place, Suite 420
The Woodlands, TX 77380
Phone: 713 714-6100
Fax: 985 876-5414
Web: www.gulfisland.com

CEO: Richard W Heo
CFO: Westley S Stockton
HR: –
FYE: December 31
Type: Public

Together with its subsidiaries, Gulf Island Fabrication (Gulf Island) is a leading fabricator of complex steel structures, modules, and a provider of project management, hookup, commissioning, repair, maintenance, scaffolding, coatings, welding enclosures, civil construction, and staffing services to the industrial and energy sectors. Products include jacket foundations, piles, and topsides for fixed production and utility platforms, as well as hulls and topsides for floating production platforms and utility platforms, and fabricates other complex steel structures and components. In 2022, roughly 50% of the total revenue was accounted for by two customers.

	Annual Growth	12/19	12/20	12/21	12/22	12/23
Sales ($mil.)	(16.0%)	303.3	251.0	93.5	142.3	151.1
Net income ($ mil.)	–	(49.4)	(27.4)	(22.2)	(3.4)	(24.4)
Market value ($ mil.)	(3.9%)	82.4	49.7	65.2	83.4	70.4
Employees	(2.9%)	944	875	960	874	839

GULF POWER CO

One Energy Place
Pensacola, FL 32520
Phone: 850 444-6111
Fax: –
Web: www.gulfpower.com

CEO: –
CFO: –
HR: –
FYE: December 31
Type: Public

Pensacola power users patronize Gulf Power. A subsidiary of Southern Company, Gulf Power is the largest energy provider in Northwest Florida, serving around half a million customers. The vertically-integrated company is engaged in the generation, transmission, distribution, and purchase of electricity, as well as selling electric service to some 70 towns, including Pensacola, Panama City, and Fort Walton Beach. In addition, the company has wholesale customers in Southeast Florida. NextEra Energy, Inc. announced the purchase of Gulf Power in May 2018 (purchase expected to close in 2019).

	Annual Growth	12/13	12/14	12/15	12/16	12/17
Sales ($mil.)	1.3%	1,440.3	1,590.5	1,483.0	1,485.0	1,516.0
Net income ($ mil.)	1.3%	132.1	149.2	157.0	140.0	139.0
Market value ($ mil.)	–	611.7	702.3	744.8	739.3	–
Employees	(2.2%)	1,410	1,384	1,391	1,352	1,288

GULF SOUTH PIPELINE COMPANY, LLC

9 GREENWAY PLZ STE 2800
HOUSTON, TX 770460926
Phone: 888 315-5005
Fax: –
Web: www.gulfsouthpl.com

CEO: –
CFO: –
HR: –
FYE: December 31
Type: Private

Although natural gas is known to rise, this company likes to keep it underground and flowing horizontally in the south. Gulf South Pipeline, a subsidiary of Boardwalk Pipeline Partners (itself a subsidiary of Loews), operates an interstate natural gas pipeline system that transports products from southern Texas to western Florida. Its system consists of about 7,700 miles of natural gas gathering systems and pipeline and about 40 compressor stations. The company also owns two natural gas storage fields in Louisiana and Mississippi capable (together) of holding approximately 131 billion cu. ft. of natural gas.

GULF UNITED ENERGY INC

P.O. Box 22165
Houston, TX 77227-2165
Phone: 713 942-6575
Fax: –
Web: www.gulfunitedenergy.com

CEO: John B Connally III
CFO: David C Pomerantz
HR: –
FYE: December 31
Type: Public

The Gulf of Mexico unites this company's headquarters with its operations. Houston-based oil and gas company Gulf United Energy holds oil and gas leases on one project in Colombia and three in Peru. The exploration and development stage company doesn't have any producing wells (or revenue) but it is working with Upland Oil and Gas and SK Energy to look for resources on nearly 44 million acres. Gulf United owns between two and 40 percent working interests on the four projects. The company, which was formed in 2003, exited the pipeline and liquefied natural gas business in 2010. John B. Connally III, grandson of former Texas governor John B. Connally, owns about 16% of Gulf United.

	Annual Growth	08/08	08/09	08/10	08/11*	12/11
Sales ($mil.)	–	–	–	–	–	–
Net income ($ mil.)	–	(0.4)	(1.4)	(2.3)	(14.6)	(1.3)
Market value ($ mil.)	3.2%	92.1	46.0	69.0	138.1	101.3
Employees	–	–	–	1	1	–

*Fiscal year change

GULFPORT ENERGY CORP.

NYS: GPOR

713 Market Drive
Oklahoma City, OK 73114
Phone: 405 252-4600
Fax: –
Web: www.gulfportenergy.com

CEO: John K Reinhart
CFO: William J Buese
HR: –
FYE: December 31
Type: Public

Gulfport is an independent natural gas-weighted exploration and production company with assets primarily located in the Appalachia and Anadarko basins. The company's principal properties are located in Eastern Ohio, where it targets development in what is commonly referred to as the Utica formation, and Central Oklahoma where Gulfport target development in the SCOOP Woodford and Springer formations. Additionally, Gulfport holds a sizeable acreage position in its interest in Grizzly Oil Sands ULC. The company reports proved reserves of approximately 18 million barrels of oil and 4.0 trillion cubic feet of natural gas.

	Annual Growth	12/19	12/20*	05/21*	12/21	12/22
Sales ($mil.)	(0.4%)	1,346.0	866.5	273.0	535.8	1,331.1
Net income ($ mil.)	–	(2,002.4)	(1,625.1)	251.0	(112.8)	494.7
Market value ($ mil.)	–	–	–	–	1,371.1	1,401.7
Employees	(9.2%)	298	256	–	212	223

*Fiscal year change

GULFSTREAM NATURAL GAS SYSTEM, L.L.C.

2701 N ROCKY POINT DR STE 1050
TAMPA, FL 336075554
Phone: 813 282-6600
Fax: –
Web: www.gulfstreamgas.com

CEO: –
CFO: –
HR: –
FYE: December 31
Type: Private

In the case of Gulfstream Natural Gas, the name says it all. The natural gas transportation and storage company delivers approximately 1.25 billion cu. ft. of natural gas per day from source areas on the Gulf Coast (in eastern Louisiana and Mississippi) to customers in Central and South Florida. Its system consists of some 745 miles of pipeline (including 294 miles of pipeline in Florida and 419 miles offshore). The company boasts the largest pipeline in the Gulf of Mexico. Gulfstream Natural Gas is a joint venture between The Williams Companies (through Williams Partners) and Spectra Energy and its Spectra Energy Partners unit.

GUNDERSEN LUTHERAN MEDICAL CENTER, INC.

1900 SOUTH AVE
LA CROSSE, WI 546015467
Phone: 608 782-7300
Fax: –
Web: www.gundersenhealth.org

CEO: Jeffery Thompson MD
CFO: –
HR: –
FYE: December 31
Type: Private

At the heart of the Gundersen Lutheran health system, Gundersen Lutheran Medical Center serves residents of nearly 20 counties that stretch across the upper Midwest. The clinical campus for the University of Wisconsin's medical and nursing schools operates a 325-bed teaching hospital with a Level II Trauma and Emergency Center. Focused on caring for patients in western Wisconsin, the hospital boasts several specialty services, such as bariatrics, behavioral health, cancer care, orthopedics, palliative care, pediatrics, rehabilitation, and women's health. The physician-led, not-for-profit medical center is affiliated with a group of regional clinics and specialty centers.

	Annual Growth	12/14	12/15	12/17	12/18	12/19
Sales ($mil.)	6.8%	–	980.7	1,071.2	1,073.8	1,275.9
Net income ($ mil.)	37.9%	–	60.0	112.1	117.0	216.9
Market value ($ mil.)	–	–	–	–	–	–
Employees	–	–	–	–	–	4,500

GURSEY, SCHNEIDER & CO. LLC

1888 CENTURY PARK E # 900
LOS ANGELES, CA 900671702
Phone: 310 552-0960
Fax: –
Web: www.gursey.com

CEO: –
CFO: –
HR: Crystal Fernandez
FYE: October 31
Type: Private

Gursey, Schneider is a Southern California accounting and business consulting firm catering to clients in the entertainment, real estate, sports, and financial services industries. The firm specializes in forensic accounting and litigation support for celebrity divorces. Other offerings include tax services, forensic technology consulting, and software development. Gursey, Schneider has offices in Century City and Torrance, California. Senior partner Stanley Schneider and the late Donald Gursey co-founded the company in 1964.

GUSTAVUS ADOLPHUS COLLEGE

800 W COLLEGE AVE
SAINT PETER, MN 560821498
Phone: 507 933-7508
Fax: –
Web: www.gustavus.edu

CEO: –
CFO: –
HR: –
FYE: May 31
Type: Private

You don't have to enter the Pearly Gates to get into this St. Peter, Minnesota, university. However, Gustavus Adolphus College is deeply rooted in its Evangelical Lutheran Church heritage. The private, liberal arts, coeducational school offers some 70 majors in about two dozen academic departments, including education, fine arts, humanities, and social sciences. It has a student population of about 2,500 and a student/faculty ratio of 12-to-1. Gustavus Adolphus College was founded in 1862 by Swedish Lutheran immigrant and pastor Eric Norelius. It is named after 17th-century Swedish king Gustav II Adolf.

	Annual Growth	05/18	05/19	05/20	05/21	05/22
Sales ($mil.)	28.9%	–	85.8	148.4	166.3	183.5
Net income ($ mil.)	(5.8%)	–	29.2	0.9	17.6	24.4
Market value ($ mil.)	–	–	–	–	–	–
Employees	–	–	–	–	–	700

GUTHRIE TOWANDA MEMORIAL HOSPITAL

91 HOSPITAL DR
TOWANDA, PA 188489702
Phone: 570 265-2191
Fax: –
Web: www.guthrie.org

CEO: –
CFO: –
HR: –
FYE: June 30
Type: Private

Memorial Hospital provides medical care to the residents of York, Pennsylvania. The 100-bed acute-care teaching hospital's services include emergency medicine, orthopedics, physical therapy, women's health, cardiac rehabilitation, and social services. The medical center also offers long-term care, home health services, a hospice program, and a wellness center. Construction of a new multispecialty physician medical complex and the 20-bed expansion of the 74-bed assisted living facility on the hospital's campus broke ground in fall 2012. Completion is expected in summer 2013. Memorial Hospital was founded in 1959.

	Annual Growth	06/14	06/15	06/16	06/18	06/20
Sales ($mil.)	0.3%	–	32.4	30.3	30.1	32.9
Net income ($ mil.)	–	–	0.0	(1.2)	(2.0)	(1.1)
Market value ($ mil.)	–	–	–	–	–	–
Employees	–	–	–	–	–	500

GUTHY-RENKER LLC

100 N PACIFIC COAST HWY STE 1600
EL SEGUNDO, CA 90245
Phone: 760 773-9022
Fax: –
Web: www.guthy-renker.com

CEO: –
CFO: –
HR: Nubia Ingham
FYE: December 31
Type: Private

What do Katy Perry, Cindy Crawford, Victoria Principal, and Tony Robbins have in common? Each has starred in a program produced by Guthy-Renker, one of the largest infomercial producers in the US. With distribution in nearly 70 countries, the electronic retailing company pursues marketing opportunities through direct TV, cable and satellite, mail, the Internet, and telemarketing. Its pitch people hawk a variety of goods and services, including skin care products and cosmetics such as Proactiv Solution (the company's primary category), fitness equipment, and motivational tapes. The company was founded in 1988 after being spun off from Guthy's Cassette Productions Unlimited (CPU).

GUTIERREZ-PALMENBERG, INC.

2922 W CLARENDON AVE
PHOENIX, AZ 850174609
Phone: 602 234-0696
Fax: –
Web: www.gpieng.com

CEO: –
CFO: –
HR: –
FYE: December 31
Type: Private

Gutierrez-Palmenberg (GPI) provides environmental management and consulting engineering services to customers in the government and commercial markets. The company provides engineering design, environmental and radioactive waste management, and IT services. Clients primarily hail from the government, military, and commercial sectors. Its revenue is equally divided between government prime contracts and private, commercial contracts. GPI was founded in 1980 and is owned by its officers.

	Annual Growth	12/08	12/09	12/10	12/11	12/12
Sales ($mil.)	(20.1%)	–	3.1	2.0	1.6	1.6
Net income ($ mil.)	–	–	(0.0)	0.0	(0.0)	(0.0)
Market value ($ mil.)	–	–	–	–	–	–
Employees	–	–	–	–	–	30

GWINNETT HEALTH SYSTEM, INC.

1000 MEDICAL CENTER BLVD
LAWRENCEVILLE, GA 300467694
Phone: 678 312-1000
Fax: –
Web: www.gwinnettmedicalcenter.org

CEO: –
CFO: –
HR: –
FYE: June 30
Type: Private

Gwinnett Health System provides a gamut of medical services in northern Georgia. The 553-bed hospital system consists of the Gwinnett Medical Center-Lawrenceville and the Gwinnett Medical Center-Duluth. Both hospitals are located northeast of Atlanta and offer acute care, day surgery, emergency care, and rehabilitation. The system also includes the Gwinnett Women's Pavilion (maternity and neonatal care) and the Gwinnett Extended Care Center. The Glancy Rehabilitation Center offers intensive inpatient and outpatient rehabilitation. Other facilities provide diagnostic imaging and general physician care. Gwinnett is merging with Atlanta's Northside Hospital.

GXO LOGISTICS INC

Two American Lane
Greenwich, CT 06831
Phone: 203 489-1287
Fax: –
Web: www.gxo.com

NYS: GXO
CEO: Malcolm Wilson
CFO: Baris Oran
HR: –
FYE: December 31
Type: Public

GXO Logistics, Inc. is the largest pure-play contract logistics provider in the world, and a foremost innovator in an industry propelled by strong secular tailwinds. The company provides its customers with high-value-added warehousing and distribution, order fulfillment, e-commerce, reverse logistics, and other supply chain services differentiated by its ability to deliver technology-enabled, customized solutions at scale. Operates in about 980 facilities worldwide, GXO serves a broad range of customers across a range of industries, such as e-commerce, omnichannel retail, technology and consumer electronics, food and beverage, and industrial and manufacturing, among others. The UK accounts for more than 35% of the company's revenue.

	Annual Growth	12/19	12/20	12/21	12/22	12/23
Sales ($mil.)	12.5%	6,094.0	6,195.0	7,940.0	8,993.0	9,778.0
Net income ($ mil.)	39.8%	60.0	(31.0)	153.0	197.0	229.0
Market value ($ mil.)	–	–	–	10,814	5,082.5	7,281.5
Employees	–	–	93,000	120,000	135,000	87,000

GYRE THERAPEUTICS INC

611 Gateway Blvd., Suite 710
South San Francisco, CA 94080
Phone: 650 871-0761
Fax: –
Web: www.catalystbiosciences.com

NAS: GYRE
CEO: Charles Wu
CFO: Ruoyu Chen
HR: –
FYE: December 31
Type: Public

Catalyst Biosciences (formerly Targacept) is a clinical-stage biopharmaceutical focused on developing products in the fields of hemostasis and inflammation. Its candidates treat such ailments as hemophilia and surgical bleeding, delayed graft function in kidney transplants, and dry age-related macular degeneration. The company's lead candidate is a next-generation coagulation Factor VIIa variant -- CB 813d -- which has completed Phase 1 clinical trials in severe hemophilia patients. The company was formed in 1997 and went public in 2006. Targacept was acquired by Catalyst Biosciences in a reverse merger mid-2015, after which the firm adopted the Catalyst moniker.

	Annual Growth	12/18	12/19	12/20	12/21	12/22
Sales ($mil.)	239.2%	0.0	–	20.9	7.3	0.8
Net income ($ mil.)	–	(30.1)	(55.2)	(56.2)	(87.9)	(8.2)
Market value ($ mil.)	(49.2%)	19.9	17.1	15.9	2.3	1.3
Employees	(24.0%)	21	34	56	45	7

H AND M CONSTRUCTION CO., INC.

50 SECURITY DR
JACKSON, TN 383053611
Phone: 731 660-3091
Fax: –
Web: www.hmcompany.com

CEO: –
CFO: –
HR: –
FYE: December 31
Type: Private

H and M Construction (which does business as H&M Company) is a provider of heavy industrial and manufacturing facility construction services. The group provides architectural, engineering, and construction services for manufacturing, distribution, power, and heavy industrial facilities around the US. It also offers construction management for educational and institutional projects and is a top school builder. In 1957 Charles "Chicken" Fite and Frank Warmath established the company, which became one of the first US contractors to use design/build project delivery.

H GROUP HOLDING, INC

67 DREXEL AVE
LA GRANGE, IL 605255845
Phone: 312 750-1234
Fax: –
Web: www.wyndhamhotels.com

CEO: –
CFO: –
HR: –
FYE: December 31
Type: Private

Owned and operated by Chicago's wealthy Pritzker family, H Group Holding is the investment holding company for a slowly dwindling number of assets. The Pritzkers once owned a vast empire (worth some $20 billion). However, since the death of Jay Pritzker in 1999, family squabbles over its vast fortune have led the Pritzkers to slowly break up the empire and sell billions of dollars worth of assets. Cofounder and brother Robert Pritzker died in 2011. The family still owns some 75% of luxury hotel operator Hyatt, which has more than 550 owned and franchised hotels worldwide. Other H Group holdings include property investor Pritzker Realty and a minority stake in the Royal Caribbean cruise ship line.

H MUNOZ AND COMPANY, INC.

723 S FLORES ST
SAN ANTONIO, TX 782041350
Phone: 210 349-1163
Fax: –
Web: www.alta-architects.com

CEO: Henry R Munoz III
CFO: –
HR: Alice Ramirez
FYE: November 30
Type: Private

H Mu oz and Company is very proud of that curly tilde above its name. As one of the largest minority-owned architectural firms in Texas, it often incorporates mestizo regionalism into designs to reflect the diverse history and culture of the Texas-Mexico border. H Mu oz has worked on public, corporate, and academic projects such as the San Antonio Convention Center, Six Flags Fiesta Texas, Trinity University, and SeaWorld. In addition to its architectural and planning services, the firm also offers logo design, branding, and interior design. Bartlett Cocke and John Kell Sr. co-founded Kell Mu oz Architects in 1927. Today the firm does business as H Mu oz and Company, led by entrepreneurs and activists Henry Mu oz III and Geoffrey Edwards.

H W D CASINGS, INC.

5010 INTERSTATE HWY 10 E
SAN ANTONIO, TX 782193300
Phone: 210 661-6161
Fax: –
Web: –

CEO: Howard W Dewied
CFO: –
HR: –
FYE: December 09
Type: Private

Stuff de wide end of the pork in this. DeWied International produces both natural (beef, sheep, and hog) and synthetic (cellulose, collagen, fibrous, and plastic) sausage casings. It is also the only North American distributor of HUKKI casings -- synthetic casings with built-in netting that can press unique patterns into sausages including diamond, daisy, and honeycomb shapes. The company has operations in Texas, Mexico, Australia, China, and the UK. Its customers include commercial meat processors and artisan and hobbyist sausage makers throughout the world. DeWied International was founded in 1932 and is owned and operated by the third generation of DeWieds.

H&E EQUIPMENT SERVICES INC

NMS: HEES

7500 Pecue Lane
Baton Rouge, LA 70809
Phone: 225 298-5200
Fax: –
Web: www.he-equipment.com

CEO: –
CFO: Leslie S Magee
HR: –
FYE: December 31
Type: Public

H&E Equipment Services primarily focus on providing rental equipment to its customers, it additionally provide used and new equipment sales, parts, repair, and maintenance functions to its customers. This approach provides the company with multiple points of customer contact, an effective method to manage its rental fleet through efficient maintenance and profitable distribution of used equipment and a mix of business activities that enables the company to operate effectively throughout economic cycles. The company's construction rental fleet is among the industry's youngest with an equipment mix comprised of aerial work platforms, earthmoving, material handling, and other general and specialty lines. The company had a network of some 120 branch facilities in almost 30 states in the US.

	Annual Growth	12/19	12/20	12/21	12/22	12/23
Sales ($mil.)	2.2%	1,348.4	1,169.1	1,062.8	1,244.5	1,469.2
Net income ($ mil.)	18.0%	87.2	(32.7)	102.5	132.2	169.3
Market value ($ mil.)	11.8%	1,218.5	1,086.6	1,613.6	1,654.8	1,907.0
Employees	3.3%	2,432	2,254	2,157	2,375	2,765

H. H. DOBBINS, INC.

99 WEST AVE
LYNDONVILLE, NY 140989744
Phone: 585 765-2271
Fax: –
Web: www.unitedapplesales.com

CEO: –
CFO: –
HR: –
FYE: June 30
Type: Private

Dobbins provides apples for bobbin', or just for eatin' -- whichever you please. H. H. Dobbins packages, stores, and ships apples under the Old Dobbin brand name. In addition to some 15 varieties of apples, including McIntosh, Crispin, and Empire, the company distributes sweet and tart cherries, grapes, peaches, pears, tomatoes, and other fruits and vegetables. Dobbins purchases produce from growers in New York state, as well as other areas of the US. It distributes its products to customers, including food processors and retailers, throughout the US and Canada; it also sells products overseas. H. H. Dobbins, which was founded in 1930, is owned by president Ward Dobbins.

	Annual Growth	06/13	06/14	06/15	06/18	06/19
Sales ($mil.)	17.0%	–	–	20.8	37.4	39.0
Net income ($ mil.)	23.4%	–	–	0.0	0.0	0.2
Market value ($ mil.)	–	–	–	–	–	–
Employees	–	–	–	–	–	70

H. J. RUSSELL & COMPANY

171 17TH ST NW STE 1600
ATLANTA, GA 303631235
Phone: 404 330-1000
Fax: –
Web: www.hjrussell.com

CEO: Michael B Russell
CFO: Ed Bradford
HR: Elaine Ubakanma
FYE: December 31
Type: Private

H.J. Russell & Company, one of the nation's largest minority-owned enterprises, helps shape southeastern cities. It's a general contractor, construction manager, property manager, and developer that specializes in affordable multifamily housing and mixed-use communities. It also has expertise in building airports, hospitals, office towers, retail stores, and schools. Its development arm, Russell New Urban Development, offers such services as feasibility analysis, land development, and asset management. H.J. Russell also manages more than 6,000 apartment and public housing units. The family-owned company was founded by chairman Herman J. Russell in 1952.

	Annual Growth	12/06	12/07	12/08	12/09	12/22
Sales ($mil.)	(24.5%)	–	233.3	222.2	170.9	3.4
Net income ($ mil.)	–	–	6.0	3.9	2.1	(1.1)
Market value ($ mil.)	–	–	–	–	–	–
Employees	–	–	–	–	–	733

H. LEE MOFFITT CANCER CENTER AND RESEARCH INSTITUTE HOSPITAL, INC.

12902 USF MAGNOLIA DR
TAMPA, FL 336129416
Phone: 813 745-4673
Fax: –
Web: www.moffitt.org

CEO: –
CFO: Yvette Tremonti
HR: –
FYE: June 30
Type: Private

The H. Lee Moffitt Cancer Center and Research Institute, founded in 1986, is a National Cancer Institute-designated Comprehensive Cancer Center located on the Tampa campus of the University of South Florida. The institute carries it out its stated mission of "contributing to the prevention and cure of cancer" through patient care, research, and education. It operates a 210-bed medical and surgical facility, as well as outpatient treatment programs and a blood and marrow transplant program. Its research programs include study in the areas of molecular oncology, immunology, risk assessment, health outcomes, and experimental therapeutics.

	Annual Growth	06/13	06/14	06/18	06/20	06/21
Sales ($mil.)	8.5%	–	855.2	1,020.9	1,353.5	1,516.0
Net income ($ mil.)	28.9%	–	50.2	167.2	288.0	296.0
Market value ($ mil.)	–	–	–	–	–	–
Employees	–	–	–	–	–	4,200

H.C. SCHMIEDING PRODUCE COMPANY, LLC

2330 N THOMPSON ST
SPRINGDALE, AR 727641709
Phone: 479 751-4517
Fax: –
Web: www.schmieding.com

CEO: –
CFO: –
HR: –
FYE: December 31
Type: Private

H. C. Schmieding Produce is a leading wholesale distributor of fresh fruits and vegetables. The company supplies primarily grocery store chains and independent retailers from two distribution centers in Arkansas and Florida. President Laurence Schmieding started the family-owned company in 1961 and heads a charitable organization called The Schmieding Foundation. Through their holding company, Schmieding Enterprises, the family also has interests in real estate.

	Annual Growth	12/14	12/15	12/16	12/17	12/18
Sales ($mil.)	11.3%	–	–	98.0	116.1	121.4
Net income ($ mil.)	–	–	–	3.2	2.7	(1.3)
Market value ($ mil.)	–	–	–	–	–	–
Employees	–	–	–	–	–	35

HABITAT FOR HUMANITY INTERNATIONAL, INC.

285 PEACHTREE CENTER AVE NE STE 2700
ATLANTA, GA 303031220
Phone: 800 422-4828
Fax: –
Web: www.hfhtkc.org

CEO: –
CFO: –
HR: –
FYE: June 30
Type: Private

Thanks to Habitat for Humanity, more than 5 million people worldwide know there's no place like home. The mission of the not-for-profit, ecumenical Christian organization is to provide adequate and affordable shelter. It has built or remodeled more than 800,000 houses at cost for families who demonstrate a need and are willing to invest "sweat equity" during construction. Homeowners make payments on no-interest mortgages; Habitat for Humanity funnels the funds back into the construction of homes for others. The group operates in all 50 states, the District of Columbia, Guam, and Puerto Rico, in addition to affiliates in nearly 80 countries. It was founded in 1976 by Linda Fuller and her late husband Millard.

	Annual Growth	06/13	06/14	06/16	06/19	06/20
Sales ($mil.)	0.3%	–	268.2	276.1	288.1	272.8
Net income ($ mil.)	(18.2%)	–	11.8	28.5	13.2	3.5
Market value ($ mil.)	–	–	–	–	–	–
Employees	–	–	–	–	–	1,500

HACKETT GROUP INC

NMS: HCKT

1001 Brickell Bay Drive, Suite 3000
Miami, FL 33131
Phone: 305 375-8005
Fax: –
Web: www.thehackettgroup.com

CEO: Ted A Fernandez
CFO: Robert A Ramirez
HR: –
FYE: December 29
Type: Public

The Hackett Group is an intellectual property-based digital transformation consultancy and leading enterprise benchmarking and best practices implementation firm serving global companies. It offers benchmarking, executive advisory, business transformation, and cloud enterprise application implementation. The group also provides dedicated expertise in business strategy, operations, finance, human capital management, strategic sourcing, procurement, and information technology. It has completed over 25,000 benchmarking and performance studies with major organizations, including more than 95% of the Dow Jones Industrials, about 95% of the Fortune 100, some 70% of the DAX 30 and around 50% of the FTSE 100. It generates more than 85% of sales from the US.

	Annual Growth	12/19*	01/21*	12/21	12/22	12/23
Sales ($mil.)	1.2%	282.5	239.5	278.8	293.7	296.6
Net income ($ mil.)	10.1%	23.3	5.5	41.5	40.8	34.2
Market value ($ mil.)	9.4%	433.5	392.4	559.8	555.4	620.9
Employees	4.2%	1,143	1,047	1,135	1,175	1,350

*Fiscal year change

HACKLEY HOSPITAL

1700 CLINTON ST
MUSKEGON, MI 494425591
Phone: 231 728-4950
Fax: –
Web: www.hackley-health.org

CEO: –
CFO: –
HR: –
FYE: June 30
Type: Private

Medical professionals at Hackley Hospital aim to heal. Operating as as Mercy Health Partners, Hackley Campus, the hospital is a 210-bed acute care facility that serves patients living in Muskegon, opposite the thumb on Michigan's shoreline. The teaching hospital offers such services as behavioral health care, a sleep analysis lab, a bariatric treatment center, a cancer center, stroke care, emergency medicine, and rehabilitation therapies. Mercy Health Partners, Hackley Campus, is part Mercy Health Partners Muskegon.

	Annual Growth	06/07	06/08	06/09	06/10	06/13
Sales ($mil.)	(36.1%)	–	1,673.5	144.4	151.0	177.8
Net income ($ mil.)	559.3%	–	0.0	(6.8)	(42.2)	5.6
Market value ($ mil.)	–	–	–	–	–	–
Employees	–	–	–	–	–	1,500

HAEMONETICS CORP.

NYS: HAE

125 Summer Street
Boston, MA 02110
Phone: 781 848-7100
Fax: –
Web: www.haemonetics.com

CEO: Christopher A Simon
CFO: James C D'Arecca
HR: –
FYE: April 1
Type: Public

Haemonetics is a global healthcare company dedicated to providing a suite of innovative medical products and solutions for customers, to help them improve patient care and reduce the cost of healthcare. The company develops and produces automated blood collection systems that collect and process whole blood, taking only the components (such as plasma or red blood cells) needed and returning the remainder to the donors. Typically these systems, sold under the Cell Saver and TEG, are bought and used by plasma centers and blood banks. Haemonetics' Hospital business has four product lines which include Hemostasis Management, Cell Salvage, Transfusion Management, and Vascular Closure. Haemonetics does business in more than 90 countries but generates most of its revenue in the US.

	Annual Growth	03/19	03/20*	04/21	04/22	04/23
Sales ($mil.)	4.8%	967.6	988.5	870.5	993.2	1,168.7
Net income ($ mil.)	20.3%	55.0	76.5	79.5	43.4	115.4
Market value ($ mil.)	(1.4%)	4,413.2	5,092.8	5,652.3	3,221.1	4,174.6
Employees	(1.4%)	3,216	3,004	2,708	2,821	3,034

*Fiscal year change

HAGERMAN CONSTRUCTION CORPORATION

510 W WASHINGTON BLVD
FORT WAYNE, IN 468022918
Phone: 260 424-1470
Fax: –
Web: www.thehagermangroup.com

CEO: Mark F Hagerman
CFO: –
HR: –
FYE: March 31
Type: Private

Hagerman Construction oversees just about everything but the kitchen sink. The company is part of The Hagerman Group, which performs general contracting services for commercial, retail, industrial, institutional, and medical and life sciences clients, mainly in the Midwest. The company's design-build services include construction, architectural and engineering design, masonry, carpentry, and building maintenance. It also provides financing and property management services. The family-owned company was founded in 1908 as Buesching Hagerman Construction by brothers-in-law William Hagerman and Frederick Buesching.

HAGGEN, INC.

2211 RIMLAND DR STE 300
BELLINGHAM, WA 982265699
Phone: 360 733-8720
Fax: –
Web: www.haggen.com

CEO: –
CFO: –
HR: –
FYE: December 31
Type: Private

Haggen showers shoppers in the Pacific Northwest with salmon, coffee, and other essentials. Formerly one of the area's largest independent grocers, Haggen operated some 130 supermarkets in Washington and Oregon, as well as California, Nevada, and Arizona. Most of the stores were acquired from Albertsons in late 2014. In late 2015 Haggen filed for Chapter 11 bankruptcy protection to allow it to reorganize around a reduced number of locations, and in 2016 the company agreed to sell its remaining core stores to Albertsons. The chain was founded in 1933 in Bellingham, Washington.

	Annual Growth	12/03	12/04	12/05	12/06	12/07
Sales ($mil.)	–	–	–	(164.8)	758.7	787.8
Net income ($ mil.)	20237.1%	–	–	0.0	6.5	8.6
Market value ($ mil.)	–	–	–	–	–	–
Employees	–	–	–	–	–	3,900

HAIN CELESTIAL GROUP INC
NMS: HAIN

4600 Sleepytime Drive
Boulder, CO 80301
Phone: 516 587-5000
Fax: –
Web: www.hain.com

CEO: Wendy P Davidson
CFO: Lee A Boyce
HR: Dana Perrino
FYE: June 30
Type: Public

The Hain Celestial Group is a leading manufacturer, marketer, and seller of natural and organic food, snacks, beverages, tea, and personal care and grocery products worldwide. Its vast pantry of "better-for-you" brands includes among others Celestial Seasonings (specialty teas), Terra and Garden of Eatin' (snacks), and Earth's Best (organic baby food). Hain's products are mainstays in natural foods stores and are increasingly available in mainstream supermarkets; club, mass-market, and drug stores; and grocery wholesalers. Hain is also a supplier of Avalon Organics, Alba Botanica, Live Clean, Queen Helene, and JASON grooming products. The US generates more than 55% of the group's revenue. The company was founded in 1993.

	Annual Growth	06/19	06/20	06/21	06/22	06/23
Sales ($mil.)	(6.0%)	2,302.5	2,053.9	1,970.3	1,891.8	1,796.6
Net income ($ mil.)	–	(183.3)	(80.4)	77.4	77.9	(116.5)
Market value ($ mil.)	(13.1%)	1,959.5	2,819.4	3,589.7	2,124.1	1,119.3
Employees	(15.0%)	5,441	4,287	3,087	3,078	2,837

HAJOCA CORPORATION

2001 JOSHUA RD
LAFAYETTE HILL, PA 194442431
Phone: 610 649-1430
Fax: –
Web: www.hajocagrandterrace.com

CEO: –
CFO: Kathleen Rusko
HR: –
FYE: December 31
Type: Private

Hajoca is the nation's largest privately held wholesale distributor of plumbing, heating, and industrial supplies. It offers an unparalleled selection of products to service the plumbing, heating and air conditioning, industrial pipe-valves-fittings, pool supply, and waterworks industries. The company stocks more than 100,000 products from over 500 suppliers. It operates under such names as Apex Supply, Cowan Supply, Decker's Plumbing Supply, Kohler Signature Store, The Majestic Bath, Richards Plumbing and Heating Supply, and Weinstein Supply. The company takes its current name from the last names of three visionaries who saw a demand for indoor plumbing (a relatively new concept in the 19th century): William H. Haines, Thomas J. Jones, and Joel Cadbury.

HALLADOR ENERGY CO
NAS: HNRG

1183 East Canvasback Drive
Terre Haute, IN 47802
Phone: 812 299-2800
Fax: –
Web: www.halladorenergy.com

CEO: –
CFO: –
HR: –
FYE: December 31
Type: Public

Hallador Energy puts most of its energy into selling coal from its Carlisle Mine in Indiana to three utilities in the Midwest and one in Florida. Hallador has recoverable coal reserves of 43.5 million tons (34.2 million tons proven, and 9.3 million tons probable). In addition to the Carlisle Mine it get coals from a mine in Clay County, Indiana, and has two inactive mines in Illinois. The company is exploring the possibility of other contracts with a number of coal purchasers. Additionally, Hallador has a 45% stake in Savoy Energy, L.P., an oil and gas company with operations in Michigan, and a 50% interest in Sunrise Energy, LLC, a private oil and gas exploration and production company with assets in Indiana.

	Annual Growth	12/19	12/20	12/21	12/22	12/23
Sales ($mil.)	18.3%	323.5	245.3	247.7	362.0	634.5
Net income ($ mil.)	–	(59.9)	(6.2)	(3.8)	18.1	44.8
Market value ($ mil.)	31.3%	101.1	50.1	83.8	340.2	301.0
Employees	0.6%	915	690	805	980	936

HALLIBURTON COMPANY
NYS: HAL

3000 North Sam Houston Parkway East
Houston, TX 77032
Phone: 281 871-2699
Fax: –
Web: www.halliburton.com

CEO: –
CFO: –
HR: –
FYE: December 31
Type: Public

Founded in 1919, Halliburton is one of the world's largest providers of products and services to the energy industry. It manufactures drill bits and other downhole and completion tools, provides pressure pumping services, locates hydrocarbons and manages geological data, drills new wells, and optimizes production once the well is operational. The company serves major, national, and independent oil and natural gas companies throughout the world. Halliburton operates in more than 70 countries around the world. North America accounts for about 50% of company sales.

	Annual Growth	12/19	12/20	12/21	12/22	12/23
Sales ($mil.)	0.7%	22,408	14,445	15,295	20,297	23,018
Net income ($ mil.)	–	(1,131.0)	(2,945.0)	1,457.0	1,572.0	2,638.0
Market value ($ mil.)	10.2%	21,754	16,802	20,331	34,982	32,137
Employees	(3.3%)	55,000	40,000	40,000	45,000	48,000

HALLMARK FINANCIAL SERVICES INC.

NBB: HALL

5420 Lyndon B., Johnson Freeway, Suite 1100
Dallas, TX 75240
Phone: 817 348-1600
Fax: –
Web: www.hallmarkgrp.com

CEO: Mark E Schwarz
CFO: Christopher J Kenney
HR: Irene Trevino
FYE: December 31
Type: Public

Hallmark Financial Services is an insurance holding company which, through its subsidiaries, engages in the sale of property/casualty insurance products to businesses and individuals. The company's business involves marketing, distributing, underwriting and servicing its insurance products, as well as providing other insurance-related services. It pursues its business activities primarily through subsidiaries whose operations are organized into business units and are supported by its insurance carrier subsidiaries. Its insurance company subsidiaries are American Hallmark Insurance Company of Texas (AHIC), Hallmark Insurance Company (HIC), Hallmark Specialty Insurance Company (HSIC), Hallmark County Mutual Insurance Company (HCM), Hallmark National Insurance Company (HNIC) and Texas Builders Insurance Company (TBIC).

	Annual Growth	12/18	12/19	12/20	12/21	12/22
Assets ($mil.)	5.0%	1,264.9	1,495.3	1,485.5	1,553.6	1,536.7
Net income ($ mil.)	–	10.3	(0.6)	(91.7)	9.0	(108.1)
Market value ($ mil.)	(51.7%)	19.4	32.0	6.5	7.9	1.1
Employees	(12.5%)	439	486	424	406	257

HALOZYME THERAPEUTICS INC

NMS: HALO

12390 El Camino Real
San Diego, CA 92130
Phone: 858 794-8889
Fax: –
Web: www.halozyme.com

CEO: –
CFO: –
HR: –
FYE: December 31
Type: Public

Halozyme Therapeutics is a biopharma technology platform company. Its Hylenex recombinant is used as an adjuvant for drug and fluid infusions. Most of Halozyme's products and candidates (including Hylenex) are based on rHuPH20, its patented recombinant human hyaluronidase enzyme. Halozyme partners with such pharmaceuticals as Roche, Pfizer, Janssen, Baxalta, and AbbVie for its ENHANZE drug delivery platform, which enables biologics and small molecule compounds to be delivered subcutaneously. The US generates most of the revenue which accounts for about 65%.

	Annual Growth	12/19	12/20	12/21	12/22	12/23
Sales ($mil.)	43.4%	196.0	267.6	443.3	660.1	829.3
Net income ($ mil.)	–	(72.2)	129.1	402.7	202.1	281.6
Market value ($ mil.)	20.2%	2,247.6	5,414.3	5,097.4	7,213.2	4,685.4
Employees	–	132	136	145	393	–

HAMAGAMI/CARROLL, INC.

2256 BARRY AVE
LOS ANGELES, CA 900641402
Phone: 310 458-7600
Fax: –
Web: www.hcassociates.com

CEO: –
CFO: –
HR: –
FYE: December 31
Type: Private

Hamagami/Carroll is a marketing services firm specializing in brand development and other identity enhancing services. With an eye for design, the company's services provide clients with expertise in visual communication across a variety of media from development to application. Services include research, messaging, style guide production, packaging design, visual merchandising, and advertising. Blockbuster, EA Games, and Mattel have all availed themselves of Hamagmi/Carroll's services. The agency was founded in 1989 by principals John Hamagami and Justin Carroll.

HAMILTON BEACH BRANDS HOLDING CO

NYS: HBB

4421 Waterfront Dr.
Glen Allen, VA 23060
Phone: 804 273-9777
Fax: –
Web: www.hamiltonbeachbrands.com

CEO: Gregory H Trepp
CFO: Michelle O Mosier
HR: –
FYE: December 31
Type: Public

Hamilton Beach designs, markets, and distributes a slew of branded, small electric household and specialty kitchenware appliances. The holding company primarily operates through its Hamilton Beach Brands (HBB) subsidiary, operating in the consumer, commercial and specialty small appliance markets. HBB's portfolio includes blenders, coffee makers, air purifiers, food processors, irons, and toasters, sold under the Hamilton Beach, Proctor Silex Commercial, Brightline, Professional, Weston, and TrueAir brands. Most of its products are sold through retailers and wholesale distributors in North America. The US accounts for approximately 80% of the company's revenue.

	Annual Growth	12/19	12/20	12/21	12/22	12/23
Sales ($mil.)	0.5%	612.8	603.7	658.4	640.9	625.6
Net income ($ mil.)	–	(3.5)	46.3	21.3	25.3	25.2
Market value ($ mil.)	(2.2%)	265.5	243.4	199.6	172.2	243.1
Employees	0.7%	680	700	700	700	700

HAMILTON CHATTANOOGA COUNTY HOSPITAL AUTHORITY

975 E 3RD ST
CHATTANOOGA, TN 374032173
Phone: 423 778-7000
Fax: –
Web: www.erlanger.org

CEO: –
CFO: Lynn Dejaco
HR: –
FYE: June 30
Type: Private

The Chattanooga-Hamilton County Hospital Authority (dba Erlanger Health System) offers a broad range of health service operations, including the T.C. Thompson Children's Hospital, a cancer treatment facility, and centers devoted to heart treatment, trauma, and eye care. The system comprises five hospital campuses in Tennessee with some 810 acute care beds, as well as 50 long-term care beds. A teaching center for the University of Tennessee College of Medicine, Erlanger provides tertiary care for a region that includes southeastern Tennessee, northern Georgia, northern Alabama, and western North Carolina.

	Annual Growth	06/17	06/18	06/20	06/21	06/22
Sales ($mil.)	4.4%	–	973.7	1,021.7	1,044.2	1,155.4
Net income ($ mil.)	(8.4%)	–	26.9	29.2	37.8	18.9
Market value ($ mil.)	–	–	–	–	–	–
Employees	–	–	–	–	–	4,700

HAMILTON COLLEGE

198 COLLEGE HILL RD
CLINTON, NY 133231295
Phone: 315 859-4727
Fax: –
Web: www.hamilton.edu

CEO: –
CFO: –
HR: –
FYE: June 30
Type: Private

Hamilton College is a private liberal arts school that serves some 1,800 students and employs about 180 faculty members. The school offers undergraduate programs in a variety of subjects, including economics, government, psychology, computer science, education, and English. Hamilton College, which has a 10-to-1 student/faculty ratio, is supported by a more than $500 million endowment. Located in the foothills of the Adirondack Mountains, the school is one of the oldest colleges in New York State. Hamilton College was founded in 1793 by Samuel Kirkland, missionary to the Oneida Indians; it was named for Alexander Hamilton, the first secretary of the US Treasury.

	Annual Growth	06/09	06/10	06/11	06/12	06/13
Sales ($mil.)	3.0%	–	–	112.7	116.8	119.6
Net income ($ mil.)	(22.2%)	–	–	142.9	(38.8)	86.4
Market value ($ mil.)	–	–	–	–	–	–
Employees	–	–	–	–	–	650

HAMILTON LANE INC
NMS: HLNE

110 Washington Street, Suite 1300
Conshohocken, PA 19428
Phone: 610 934-2222
Fax: –
Web: www.hamiltonlane.com

CEO: Christian Zimmermann
CFO: Jeffrey Armbrister
HR: Kristin Brandt
FYE: March 31
Type: Public

Hamilton Lane is a global private markets investment solutions provider with approximately $106 billion of assets under management (AUM), and approximately $795 billion of assets under advisement (AUA). Its clients are principally large, sophisticated, global investors that rely on its private markets expertise, deep industry relationships, differentiated investment access, risk management capabilities, proprietary data advantages and analytical tools to navigate the increasing complexity and opacity of private markets investing. It currently has approximately 530 employees, including some 180 investment professionals, operating across 20 global offices servicing its clients throughout the world. A significant majority of its employees has equity interests in Hamilton Lane. The US accounts for some 50% of total revenue. The company was founded in 1991.

	Annual Growth	03/19	03/20	03/21	03/22	03/23
Sales ($mil.)	20.3%	252.2	274.0	341.6	367.9	528.8
Net income ($ mil.)	34.3%	33.6	60.8	98.0	146.0	109.1
Market value ($ mil.)	14.1%	2,354.3	2,987.9	4,784.1	4,175.3	3,996.5
Employees	12.8%	370	400	450	530	600

HAMILTON PARTNERS, INC.

300 PARK BLVD STE 201
ITASCA, IL 601433106
Phone: 630 250-9700
Fax: –
Web: www.hamiltonpartners.com

CEO: –
CFO: –
HR: –
FYE: December 31
Type: Private

Hamilton Partners invests in, develops, leases, and manages commercial real estate in Chicago and Salt Lake City. The company has a portfolio of some 50 office and industrial properties totaling more than 20 million sq. ft. of space in and around the Windy City. The company also owns about five outdoor retail centers. Among its signature properties is the Riverwalk, a complex of two interconnected office towers with more than 500,000 sq. ft. of space in Chicago's suburbs. In addition, Hamilton Partners operates about a half-dozen mixed-use office and retail projects and an industrial property in Salt Lake City.

	Annual Growth	12/01	12/02	12/03	12/04	12/08
Assets ($mil.)	6.4%	–	–	1,719.0	1,798.1	2,340.6
Net income ($ mil.)	–	–	–	–	–	–
Market value ($ mil.)	–	–	–	–	–	–
Employees	–	–	–	–	–	160

HAMOT HEALTH FOUNDATION

201 STATE ST
ERIE, PA 165500002
Phone: 814 877-7020
Fax: –
Web: www.hamothealthfoundation.org

CEO: John T Malone
CFO: Stephen Danch
HR: –
FYE: June 30
Type: Private

Adventurous Frenchmen know the value of good medical care; Pierre S.V. Hamot felt absolutely "Erie" without it. Hamot Health Foundation (named for the wealthy immigrant merchant) is a not-for-profit health organization serving residents of northwestern Pennsylvania, western New York, and eastern Ohio. The flagship facility in this health system is UPMC Hamot, a tertiary-care hospital with about 450 beds located in Erie, Pennsylvania. Hamot has residency programs in a number of specialties, including schools run in cooperation with Gannon University and University of Pittsburgh. Hamot Health, also known as UPMC Hamot, is affiliated with the UPMC health network.

	Annual Growth	06/04	06/05	06/06	06/10	06/22
Sales ($mil.)	(21.6%)	–	332.3	353.6	6.8	5.3
Net income ($ mil.)	(14.6%)	–	11.2	24.8	4.4	0.8
Market value ($ mil.)	–	–	–	–	–	–
Employees	–	–	–	–	–	2,032

HAMPTON UNIVERSITY

200 WILLIAM R HARVEY WAY
HAMPTON, VA 236694561
Phone: 757 727-5000
Fax: –
Web: www.hamptonu.edu

CEO: –
CFO: –
HR: –
FYE: June 30
Type: Private

Hampton University is composed of six undergraduate schools, as well as a graduate college and a college of continuing education. It offers about 50 bachelor's degree programs, more than 20 master's degree programs, and several doctoral or professional degrees in nursing, physics, atmospheric and planetary science, physical therapy, and pharmacy. It also includes the Scripps Howard School of Journalism and Communications. The school has an enrollment of about 4,300 students. A historically black college, Hampton University was founded in 1868 during Reconstruction to educate newly-freed African Americans with the support of the Freedman's Bureau, Northern philanthropists, and religious groups.

HAMRICK MILLS

515 W BUFORD ST
GAFFNEY, SC 293411703
Phone: 864 489-4731
Fax: –
Web: www.hamrickmills.com

CEO: Wylie L Hamrick
CFO: –
HR: –
FYE: December 31
Type: Private

Hamrick Mills has not been milling around, but it has been around, milling, for more than a century. The company makes lightweight, greige-woven fabrics through two plants, Hamrick and Musgrove, in Gaffney, South Carolina. The lineup includes poly/cotton and 100% cotton blends. Hamrick Mills' fabrics are used in a diversity of applications, from home furnishings to apparel and support apparel (pockets to linings), and industrial goods (window shades to laminates for circuitry). The company makes yarn using the Murata Jet Spinning and Murata Vortex spinning machines. Common print cloth styles, along with special fabric construction weaves, are also produced. The founding Hamrick family owns and runs the company.

HANCOCK WHITNEY CORP
NMS: HWC

Hancock Whitney Plaza, 2510 14th Street
Gulfport, MS 39501
Phone: 228 868-4000
Fax: –
Web: www.hancockbank.com

CEO: John M Hairston
CFO: Michael Achary
HR: –
FYE: December 31
Type: Public

Hancock Whitney is the holding company of Hancock Whitney Bank, which has over 175 banking locations and around 225 ATMs throughout the Gulf South, from Florida to Texas. The community-oriented bank offers traditional and online products and services such as deposit accounts, treasury management and investment brokerage services, and loans to commercial, small business, and retail customers. The company also provides trust and investment management services to retirement plans, corporations, and individuals, as well as investment brokerage services, annuity and life insurance products, and consumer financing services. Formerly Hancock Holding Company, Hancock Whitney consolidated its two brands (Whitney Bank and Hancock Bank) in 2018 and changed its name.

	Annual Growth	12/19	12/20	12/21	12/22	12/23
Assets ($mil.)	3.8%	30,601	33,639	36,531	35,184	35,579
Net income ($ mil.)	4.6%	327.4	(45.2)	463.2	524.1	392.6
Market value ($ mil.)	2.6%	3,788.8	2,937.5	4,319.0	4,178.2	4,195.5
Employees	(3.5%)	4,136	3,986	3,486	3,627	3,591

HANDY & HARMAN LTD.

590 MADISON AVE FL 32
NEW YORK, NY 100222524
Phone: 212 520-2300
Fax: -
Web: www.handyharman.com

CEO: Jack L Howard
CFO: Douglas B Woodworth
HR: -
FYE: December 31
Type: Private

Handy & Harman (HNH) is the leading pioneer and global manufacturer dealing mainly as a refiner and a fabricator of precious metals, alloys, and electronic scraps. HNH's client base is fundamentally strong, with relationships and working with many international partners from America, United Kingdom, Australia and many Asian countries like China, Hong Kong, Indonesia, Japan, Malaysia, the Philippines, Sri Lanka, Taiwan, Thailand and many others worldwide. The company processes electronic & industrial scraps, as well as, plating, and jewellery. HNH was incorporated in the US as early as in 1867, and Handy & Harman Manufacturing (Singapore) Pte. Ltd. was established in Singapore since 1984.

HANESBRANDS INC

NYS: HBI

1000 East Hanes Mill Road
Winston-Salem, NC 27105
Phone: 336 519-8080
Fax: -
Web: www.hanes.com

CEO: Stephen B Bratspies
CFO: M S Lewis
HR: -
FYE: December 30
Type: Public

Hanesbrands Inc. is a leading marketer of everyday basic innerwear and activewear apparel in America, Australia, Europe, and Asia under the world-renowned brands such as Hanes, Champion, Bali, Just My Size, Bras N Things, Playtex, and Wonderbra. The lineup is sold to wholesalers, major retail chains (Walmart and Target), and through Hanesbrands' own outlet stores and Internet sites. Operations in the US account for almost 75% of the company's total sales.

	Annual Growth	12/19*	01/21	01/22*	12/22	12/23
Sales ($mil.)	(5.2%)	6,966.9	6,664.4	6,801.2	6,233.7	5,636.5
Net income ($ mil.)	-	-	600.7	(75.6)	77.2	(127.2)	(17.7)
Market value ($ mil.)	(25.9%)	5,192.5	5,105.0	5,854.3	2,226.9	1,561.6
Employees	(6.6%)	63,000	61,000	59,000	51,000	48,000

*Fiscal year change

HANGER, INC.

10910 DOMAIN DR STE 300
AUSTIN, TX 787587807
Phone: 512 777-3800
Fax: -
Web: corporate.hanger.com

CEO: Vinit K Asar
CFO: -
HR: -
FYE: December 31
Type: Private

Hanger ranks one of the leading US operators of orthotic and prosthetic (O&P) patient care centers, with more than 900 facilities in almost 50 states and the District of Columbia. The company operate through two segments - Patient Care and Products & Services. Patient Care segment is primarily comprised of Hanger Clinic, which specializes in comprehensive, outcomes-based design, fabrication, and delivery of custom O&P devices. The company's Products & Services segment provides therapeutic solutions, which develops specialized rehabilitation technologies and provides evidence-based clinical programs for post-acute rehabilitation to patients at approximately 4,000 skilled nursing and post-acute providers nationwide. In 2022, Hanger was acquired by Patient Square Capital, a dedicated health care investment firm, for about $1.25 billion

HANMI FINANCIAL CORP.

NMS: HAFC

900 Wilshire Boulevard, Suite 1250
Los Angeles, CA 90017
Phone: 213 382-2200
Fax: -
Web: www.hanmi.com

CEO: C G Kum
CFO: Romolo C Santarosa
HR: -
FYE: December 31
Type: Public

Hanmi Financial primarily operates through its primary subsidiary, Hanmi Bank, which serves California's Korean-American community and others in the multi-ethnic California, Colorado, Georgia, Illinois, New Jersey, New York, Texas, Virginia, and Washington. Hanmi Bank offers retail and small business banking, from some 35 full-service branches and eight loan production offices across some 10 US states, coast-to-coast. It specializes in real estate, commercial, SBA, and trade finance lending to small and middle-market businesses. The company is the first Korean-American bank established in 1982.

	Annual Growth	12/19	12/20	12/21	12/22	12/23
Assets ($mil.)	8.1%	5,538.2	6,201.9	6,858.6	7,378.3	7,570.3
Net income ($ mil.)	25.0%	32.8	42.2	98.7	101.4	80.0
Market value ($ mil.)	(0.8%)	607.2	344.4	719.1	751.6	589.2
Employees	(0.7%)	633	602	591	626	615

HANNA STEEL CORPORATION

4527 SOUTHLAKE PKWY
HOOVER, AL 352443238
Phone: 205 820-5200
Fax: -
Web: www.hannasteel.com

CEO: Pete M Hanna
CFO: -
HR: -
FYE: December 31
Type: Private

There's been no word on what happened to Barbera, but Hanna Steel specializes in steel tubing and painted steel products. Operating from facilities in Alabama and Illinois, the company makes mechanical and hollow structural steel tubing and provides heavy gauge coil coating and dry film lube processing services. The company's Hanna Truck Line division then delivers the steel shipments to customers. Hanna Steel was founded in 1954 by Gen. Walter "Crack" Hanna and is still family-owned. Pete Hanna, son of the company's founder, serves as chairman and CEO.

HANNON ARMSTRONG SUSTAINABLE INFRASTRUCTURE CAPITAL, INC.

One Park Place, Suite 200
Annapolis, MD 21401
Phone: 410 571-9860
Fax: -
Web: www.hannonarmstrong.com

CEO: Jeffrey W Eckel
CFO: Jeffrey A Lipson
HR: -
FYE: December 31
Type: Public

Hannon Armstrong Sustainable Infrastructure Capital invests in climate solutions developed or sponsored by leading companies in the energy efficiency, renewable energy and other sustainable infrastructure markets. It is one of the first US public companies solely dedicated to climate solution investments. Hannon Armstrong focuses on a wide variety of climate solutions including water distribution systems, combined heat and power systems, solar, electric distribution systems, clean fleet transportation, and other climate related technologies. The company manages approximately $9.8 billion in assets and operates mostly in the US.

	Annual Growth	12/19	12/20	12/21	12/22	12/23
Sales ($mil.)	22.6%	141.6	186.9	213.2	239.7	319.9
Net income ($ mil.)	16.2%	81.6	82.4	126.6	41.5	148.8
Market value ($ mil.)	(3.8%)	3,609.8	7,115.2	5,958.7	3,250.8	3,093.8
Employees	23.4%	60	73	99	124	139

HANOVER COLLEGE

517 BALL DR UNIT 302
HANOVER, IN 472439656
Phone: 812 866-7000
Fax: –
Web: www.hanover.edu

CEO: –
CFO: –
HR: –
FYE: June 30
Type: Private

Hanover College is a private coeducational liberal arts college affiliated with the Presbyterian Church. The school offers bachelor's degrees in about 30 areas of study. Students, who are required to take four classes each fall and winter term, as well as one class during the spring term, can design their own majors as well. The school also offers pre-professional programs in areas of study such as medicine, law, and dentistry. Hanover College has an enrollment of approximately 1,000. The oldest private college in Indiana, it was founded in 1827 by the Rev. John Finley Crowe.

	Annual Growth	06/17	06/18	06/19	06/21	06/22
Sales ($mil.)	10.5%	–	32.6	37.5	39.2	48.6
Net income ($ mil.)	–	–	1.1	3.3	40.2	(24.5)
Market value ($ mil.)	–	–	–	–	–	–
Employees	–	–	–	–	–	300

HANOVER HEALTH CORPORATION, INC.

300 HIGHLAND AVE
HANOVER, PA 173312297
Phone: 717 637-3711
Fax: –
Web: www.hanoverdocfinder.com

CEO: –
CFO: –
HR: –
FYE: June 30
Type: Private

Hanover HealthCare Plus operates the Hanover Hospital, plus a bunch of other health care facilities in south-central Pennsylvania. The not-for-profit health system's flagship facility, Hanover Hospital, is a 110-bed community hospital offering an array of inpatient and outpatient services including general medicine, emergency care, cardiovascular, women's health, and wellness services. The health care system, which was founded in 1926, also includes about two dozen family practice clinics, surgery and rehabilitation centers, and diagnostic and laboratory facilities.

	Annual Growth	06/03	06/04*	12/05*	06/08	06/12
Sales ($mil.)	(56.4%)	–	82.9	82.9	2.3	0.1
Net income ($ mil.)	(35.5%)	–	2.5	2.5	0.3	0.0
Market value ($ mil.)	–	–	–	–	–	–
Employees	–	–	–	–	–	1,000

*Fiscal year change

HANOVER INSURANCE GROUP INC

440 Lincoln Street
Worcester, MA 01653
Phone: 508 855-1000
Fax: 508 855-6332
Web: www.hanover.com

NYS: THG
CEO: –
CFO: –
HR: –
FYE: December 31
Type: Public

The Hanover Insurance Group is one of the oldest property/casualty insurance holding companies around. Through Hanover Insurance Company and Citizens Insurance Company of America (Citizens), the company provides personal and commercial automobile, homeowners, and workers' compensation coverage, as well as commercial multi-peril insurance and professional liability coverage. The company sells its products through a network of independent agents throughout the US. Hanover's Opus Investment Management subsidiary provides institutional investment management services. The company traces its roots back to as early as 1852, when The Hanover Fire Insurance Company was founded.

	Annual Growth	12/19	12/20	12/21	12/22	12/23
Assets ($mil.)	4.0%	12,491	13,444	14,254	13,997	14,613
Net income ($ mil.)	(46.3%)	425.1	358.7	418.7	116.0	35.3
Market value ($ mil.)	(2.9%)	4,892.8	4,185.7	4,691.9	4,837.7	4,346.8
Employees	2.8%	4,300	4,300	4,400	4,600	4,800

HANSEN MEDICAL, INC.

800 E MIDDLEFIELD RD
MOUNTAIN VIEW, CA 940434030
Phone: 650 404-5800
Fax: –
Web: www.boxingundefeated.com

CEO: Cary G Vance
CFO: Christopher P Lowe
HR: –
FYE: December 31
Type: Private

Hansen Medical helps doctors maneuver through matters of the heart. The firm develops medical devices designed to diagnose and treat common types of cardiac arrhythmia (irregular heartbeats), such as atrial fibrillation. Its core portable Sensei system (used along with its Artisan and Lynx catheters) incorporates robotics to assist in guiding the movement of flexible catheters in such places as the atria and ventricles. Sensei has received FDA and European regulatory approval for certain uses, including manipulation and control of catheters during procedures to detect irregular heartbeats by mapping the electrical impulses of the heart. Technology firm Auris Surgical Robotics is buying Hansen for some $80 million.

HARBOR BANKSHARES CORP.

25 West Fayette Street
Baltimore, MD 21201
Phone: 410 528-1800
Fax: –
Web: www.theharborbank.com

NBB: HRBK
CEO: –
CFO: –
HR: –
FYE: December 31
Type: Public

One of the largest minority-owned banks in the US, Harbor Bankshares is the holding company for The Harbor Bank of Maryland, which provides such services as checking and savings accounts, CDs, IRAs, and credit cards through seven branches in the Baltimore area. Commercial loans, including mortgages and operating loans, make up the majority of the bank's loan portfolio. Harbor Bank also originates residential mortgage, consumer, construction, land, and church loans. Subsidiary Harbor Financial Services offers brokerage, investment, insurance, and financial planning services.

	Annual Growth	12/01	12/02	12/03	12/04	12/05
Assets ($mil.)	8.3%	186.6	210.2	219.5	235.5	256.6
Net income ($ mil.)	26.7%	0.7	1.1	1.8	1.5	1.9
Market value ($ mil.)	–	–	–	–	14.1	17.2
Employees	(1.0%)	80	80	78	81	77

HARBOR HOSPITAL FOUNDATION, INC.

3001 S HANOVER ST
BALTIMORE, MD 212251233
Phone: 410 350-2563
Fax: –
Web: www.medstarhealth.org

CEO: L B Johnson
CFO: –
HR: –
FYE: June 30
Type: Private

When you're more than just water-logged, when you suffer from more than just salty seasickness, Harbor Health Center can pull you back into the swim of things. A subsidiary of MedStar Health, Harbor Hospital Center is a 220-bed hospital providing health care to Baltimore area residents. Founded in 1903, the hospital's present location overlooking the Patapsco River was built in 1968. Its specialty care units include the HarborView Cancer Center, as well as women's care and community outreach divisions. Harbor Hospital also operates outpatient primary care, surgery, and orthopedic clinics.

	Annual Growth	06/08	06/09	06/10	06/11	06/22
Sales ($mil.)	85.4%	–	0.1	0.9	1.2	324.4
Net income ($ mil.)	–	–	–	0.6	1.0	41.2
Market value ($ mil.)	–	–	–	–	–	–
Employees	–	–	–	–	–	1,220

HARBORQUEST, INC.

2750 W ROOSEVELT RD　　　　　　　　　　　　　　　　　CEO: -
CHICAGO, IL 606081094　　　　　　　　　　　　　　　　CFO: -
Phone: 312 612-7600　　　　　　　　　　　　　　　　　HR: -
Fax: -　　　　　　　　　　　　　　　　　　　　　　　FYE: June 30
Web: www.civicstaffing.com　　　　　　　　　　　　　Type: Private

Harborquest aims to be a port in the storm for those out of work in the Windy City. The Chicago-area, not-for-profit employment agency specializes in placing clients in transitional jobs and helping them reach those jobs each day. Harborquest also places some workers on a permanent basis. The agency's STRIVE/Chicago program provides intensive classroom job preparation, placement assistance, and retention services. Its 20/20 View service enables businesses to review job candidates' performance while they perform in the work environment. Founded in 1970 as Just Jobs, the agency changed its name to Harborquest in 2005.

	Annual Growth	06/14	06/15	06/16	06/17	06/18
Sales ($mil.)	(3.5%)	-	4.4	3.7	3.4	4.0
Net income ($ mil.)	-	-	(0.2)	(0.2)	0.1	0.2
Market value ($ mil.)	-	-	-	-	-	-
Employees	-	-	-	-	-	1,500

HARBOUR CONTRACTORS, INC.

23830 W MAIN ST　　　　　　　　　　　　　　　　　　CEO: Patrick C Harbour
PLAINFIELD, IL 605442120　　　　　　　　　　　　　　CFO: -
Phone: 815 230-3674　　　　　　　　　　　　　　　　HR: -
Fax: -　　　　　　　　　　　　　　　　　　　　　　　FYE: February 28
Web: www.harbour-cm.com　　　　　　　　　　　　　Type: Private

Harbour Contractors is no port in a storm but it could build one. One of the top construction companies in the Midwest and central US, it offers program management, design/build, and construction management services. It focuses on industrial facilities, distribution centers, transportation systems, food processing centers, and interior build-out and renovation. But it also builds shopping centers and sports facilities. Recent projects include several railway storage in transit facilities for Chevron Phillips and an upscale retail center. The family-owned firm was founded in 1959 by Irving Harbour. The company is now owned by CEO Patrick Harbour and VP Jonathan Harbour.

HARD AND SOFT FISHING, LLC

525 JEFFERSON ST　　　　　　　　　　　　　　　　　CEO: -
FORT ATKINSON, WI 535381824　　　　　　　　　　　CFO: Tony Jacobson
Phone: 920 563-2491　　　　　　　　　　　　　　　　HR: -
Fax: -　　　　　　　　　　　　　　　　　　　　　　　FYE: December 31
Web: -　　　　　　　　　　　　　　　　　　　　　　Type: Private

Uncle Josh Bait Company has pork rinds for you and your prey. The company makes a variety of pork rind fishing bait including pork frogs, strips, jigs, and spinner bait. It also sells preserved natural bait such as crawfish, crickets, maggots, and worms. The bait is sold in resealable bags or in pint jars of salt brine solution to help preserve the taste and texture, making it more attractive to fish. Uncle Josh's pork rind snacks (for humans) come in BBQ, Hot & Spicy, and Original flavors. Its products are sold online and in selected retailers. The company is owned by president Kurt Kellogg and investors Patrick McDevitt and Chris Miller, who purchased it from the founding Jones family in 2002.

HARD ROCK HEALS FOUNDATION, INC.

5701 STIRLING RD　　　　　　　　　　　　　　　　　CEO: Hamish Dodds
DAVIE, FL 333147429　　　　　　　　　　　　　　　　CFO: -
Phone: 954 585-5703　　　　　　　　　　　　　　　　HR: -
Fax: -　　　　　　　　　　　　　　　　　　　　　　　FYE: December 31
Web: www.hardrock.com　　　　　　　　　　　　　　Type: Private

You can rock hard, eat hard, buy merchandise hard, and even sleep hard with Hard Rock Cafe International. The company operates the Hard Rock Cafe chain of theme restaurants with more than 135 company-owned and franchised locations in about 55 countries. Offering a menu of mostly American fare, the eateries attract attention with a collection of rock music memorabilia and Hard Rock-branded merchandise. The company also licenses the Hard Rock name for use by more than a dozen hotels and casino resorts. Its collection of rock n' roll memorabilia boasts more than 70,000 items. Peter Morton and Isaac Tigrett opened the first Hard Rock Cafe in London in 1971. Today, the Seminole Tribe of Florida owns the chain.

HARDAWAY CONSTRUCTION CORP.

3011 ARMORY DR　　　　　　　　　　　　　　　　　　CEO: Stan H Hardaway
NASHVILLE, TN 372043746　　　　　　　　　　　　　CFO: Kerry P Sloan
Phone: 615 254-5461　　　　　　　　　　　　　　　　HR: Kristin Hawkins
Fax: -　　　　　　　　　　　　　　　　　　　　　　　FYE: December 31
Web: www.hardaway.net　　　　　　　　　　　　　　Type: Private

The hard work of Hardaway Construction is paying off all over the Southeast. The firm offers general contracting, construction management, and design/build services on both large and small projects. Known for the diversity of work it takes on, Hardaway has built everything from offices and schools to hospitals and industrial plants, among other commercial structures. Its Cumberland Builders unit focuses on the residential sector, building and remodeling condominiums and retirement facilities. The company's portfolio includes work on Vanderbilt University, the Gaylord Opryland Resort Hotel, and the Nashville International Airport. The family-owned company was founded in 1924 by the late L.H. Hardaway, Sr.

HARDINGE INC.

79 W PACES FERRY RD NW FL 2　　　　　　　　　　　CEO: Ryan Levenson
ATLANTA, GA 303051464　　　　　　　　　　　　　　CFO: Tina Mashiko
Phone: 607 734-2281　　　　　　　　　　　　　　　　HR: -
Fax: -　　　　　　　　　　　　　　　　　　　　　　　FYE: December 31
Web: www.hardinge.com　　　　　　　　　　　　　　Type: Private

Hardinge is a leading international provider of advanced metal-cutting solutions. The company provides a full spectrum of highly reliable CNC turning, milling, honing, and grinding machines. It also provides technologically advanced workholding and machine tool accessories. It makes industrial machine tools for small and midsized shops that create machined parts for the aerospace, agricultural, automotive, construction, consumer products, defense, energy, medical, technology, transportation, and other industries. Its T Series SP turning centers are the recognized market leader in super precision and hard turning applications. The company operates in the Americas, Europe, and Asia. The company traces its roots back in 1890s.

HARDWOOD FLOORING AND PANELING, INC.

15320 BURTON WINDSOR RD
MIDDLEFIELD, OH 440629785
Phone: 440 834-1710
Fax: –
Web: www.sheogaflooring.com

CEO: –
CFO: Barbara Titus
HR: –
FYE: December 31
Type: Private

Sheoga Hardwood Flooring and Paneling makes prefinished and unfinished flooring and paneling from hardwoods, including ash, beech, hard maple, walnut, hickory, and red and white oak harvested from the Appalachian region of the US. The company also offers dense Brazilian cherry prefinished hardwood flooring and wood paneling. Sheoga air-dries its lumber for several months and then kiln-dries it before milling it into hardwood products. The company began operations in 1982.

	Annual Growth	12/14	12/15	12/16	12/17	12/18
Sales ($mil.)	7.5%	–	14.3	16.4	15.9	17.7
Net income ($ mil.)	33.2%	–	1.2	2.7	2.2	2.8
Market value ($ mil.)	–	–	–	–	–	–
Employees	–	–	–	–	–	72

HARGROVE, LLC

1 HARGROVE DR
LANHAM, MD 207061804
Phone: 301 306-9000
Fax: –
Web: www.hargroveinc.com

CEO: Timothy McGill
CFO: –
HR: Kevin Waters
FYE: December 31
Type: Private

Hargrove has been in the background of every Presidential inauguration for more than 50 years. A trade show and special events company, Hargrove has a tradition of organizing the inaugural festivities as well as decorating the National Christmas Tree. The firm also organizes more than 1,200 trade shows and events annually in the US, providing design, production, installation, and management services. Hargrove also exercises its design and production capabilities by crafting parade floats that have appeared in Mardi Gras, Thanksgiving, and bowl game parades. The family-owned company was founded in 1949 by Earl Hargrove Jr. when he set the stage for Harry S Truman's presidential inaugural.

	Annual Growth	12/11	12/12	12/13	12/14	12/15
Sales ($mil.)	(8.8%)	–	100.8	67.6	75.3	76.5
Net income ($ mil.)	(11.7%)	–	3.4	1.8	2.6	2.3
Market value ($ mil.)	–	–	–	–	–	–
Employees	–	–	–	–	–	200

HARLAND M. BRAUN & CO., INC.

4010 WHITESIDE ST
LOS ANGELES, CA 900631617
Phone: 323 263-9275
Fax: –
Web: www.braunexp.com

CEO: –
CFO: –
HR: –
FYE: October 31
Type: Private

Hide (the raw material) and seek (find a buyer) are all in a day's work for Harland M. Braun & Co. Operating through its subsidiary Braun Export, the company supplies raw hide goods, primarily cattle hides and skins, and, to a lesser extent, pigskin and kipskins to tanners. A slate of services is provided for leather (wet blue and crust), hide and skin manufacturing, as well as brokering, exporting, and importing. Dotting the US, Braun & Co.'s processing facilities tie in with several suppliers of Holstein steer hides. Its partners include such meat packers as JBS Packerland Group, Central Valley Meat, Manning Beef, Nebraska Beef, and American Beef Packers. The company was founded in 1957.

	Annual Growth	10/15	10/16	10/17	10/18	10/19
Sales ($mil.)	(32.3%)	–	205.2	173.1	98.4	63.5
Net income ($ mil.)	301.6%	–	0.0	0.1	0.5	1.6
Market value ($ mil.)	–	–	–	–	–	–
Employees	–	–	–	–	–	30

HARLEY ELLIS DEVEREAUX CORP

123 W 5TH ST
ROYAL OAK, MI 480672527
Phone: 248 262-1500
Fax: –
Web: www.hed.design

CEO: J P Devereaux
CFO: –
HR: –
FYE: December 31
Type: Private

Harley Ellis Devereaux offers architecture, engineering, interior, landscaping, planning, preservation, and other services from about a half-dozen offices in the Chicago, Detroit, Los Angeles, and San Diego metro areas. The company serves corporations, health care firms, universities, and government agencies; it has done work for such clients as Comerica, General Motors, Stanford University, and Chicago's Lincoln Park Zoo. Companies affiliated with Harley Ellis Devereaux offer such specialized services as crime lab design, environmentally sustainable design consulting, and real estate services.

	Annual Growth	12/08	12/09	12/10	12/11	12/12
Sales ($mil.)	0.3%	–	–	36.9	34.6	37.1
Net income ($ mil.)	(40.3%)	–	–	0.3	(0.0)	0.1
Market value ($ mil.)	–	–	–	–	–	–
Employees	–	–	–	–	–	420

HARLEY-DAVIDSON INC

NYS: HOG

3700 West Juneau Avenue
Milwaukee, WI 53208
Phone: 414 342-4680
Fax: –
Web: www.harley-davidson.com

CEO: Jochen Zeitz
CFO: Jonathan Root
HR: –
FYE: December 31
Type: Public

Harley-Davidson is a major US motorcycle manufacturer that sells its bikes worldwide through a network of about 1,300 dealers. The company offers cruiser and touring models, standard, sport bikes, and dual models that can be used on- and off-road. The trademarks of motorcycles include Softail, H-D, and Sportster. Harley-Davidson also sells attitude with its brand-name products, which include a line of riding gear and apparel (MotorClothes). Harley-Davidson Financial Services (HDFS) offers financing to dealers and consumers in the US and Canada. The company conducts business on a global basis, with sales in the US, Canada, Europe/Middle East/Africa (EMEA), Asia Pacific, and Latin America.

	Annual Growth	12/19	12/20	12/21	12/22	12/23
Sales ($mil.)	2.1%	5,361.8	4,054.4	5,336.3	5,755.1	5,836.5
Net income ($ mil.)	13.6%	423.6	1.3	650.0	741.4	706.6
Market value ($ mil.)	(0.2%)	5,069.4	5,002.7	5,137.6	5,670.6	5,021.7
Employees	3.4%	5,600	5,200	5,800	6,300	6,400

HARLEYSVILLE FINANCIAL CORP

NBB: HARL

271 Main Street
Harleysville, PA 19438
Phone: 215 256-8828
Fax: –
Web: www.harleysvillesavings.com

CEO: –
CFO: –
HR: –
FYE: September 30
Type: Public

Get your moola runnin'! Harleysville Savings Financial is the holding company of Harleysville Savings Bank, which operates about a half-dozen branches in southeastern Pennsylvania's Montgomery County. The bank offers standard deposit products such as checking and savings accounts, CDs, and IRAs. Its lending activities consist primarily of single-family residential mortgages, which account for more than two-thirds of the company's loan portfolio; home equity loans account for nearly 15%. To a lesser extent, Harleysville Savings Bank also originates commercial mortgages, residential construction loans, and consumer lines of credit.

	Annual Growth	09/19	09/20	09/21	09/22	09/23
Assets ($mil.)	2.0%	779.3	854.9	892.6	912.1	842.3
Net income ($ mil.)	10.7%	8.1	7.1	7.3	8.8	12.2
Market value ($ mil.)	(0.2%)	83.7	80.4	94.3	93.6	83.0
Employees	–	–	–	–	–	–

HARMONIC, INC. — NMS: HLIT

2590 Orchard Parkway
San Jose, CA 95131
Phone: 408 542-2500
Fax: –
Web: www.harmonicinc.com

CEO: Patrick J Harshman
CFO: Walter Jankovic
HR: Joy Bautista
FYE: December 31
Type: Public

Harmonic Inc. is a leading global provider of versatile and high performance video delivery software, products, system solutions and services that enable its customers to efficiently create, prepare, store, playout and deliver a full range of high-quality broadcast and streaming video services to consumer devices, including televisions, personal computers, laptops, tablets and smart phones and cable access solutions that enable cable operators to more efficiently and effectively deploy high-speed internet, for data, voice and video services to consumers' homes. Harmonic company sells directly and through distributors and systems integrators. American customers account for about 75% of the Harmonic's revenue.

	Annual Growth	12/19	12/20	12/21	12/22	12/23
Sales ($mil.)	10.8%	402.9	378.8	507.1	625.0	607.9
Net income ($ mil.)	–	(5.9)	(29.3)	13.3	28.2	84.0
Market value ($ mil.)	13.7%	876.8	830.7	1,321.9	1,472.5	1,465.8
Employees	3.8%	1,172	1,169	1,267	1,340	1,359

HARNISH GROUP INC.

17035 W VALLEY HWY
TUKWILA, WA 981885519
Phone: 425 251-9800
Fax: –
Web: www.ncmachinery.com

CEO: John J Harnish
CFO: –
HR: –
FYE: December 31
Type: Private

Harnish Group Inc. (HGI) harnesses the power of the Caterpillar brand in some sparsely populated pieces of real estate. The equipment dealer services, rents, and sells new and used Caterpillar machines (including bulldozers, tractors, earthmovers, and graders) and parts in Washington and Alaska. It also distributes equipment made by other manufacturers and provides engines and power systems. HGI operates about 15 equipment branches under the name N C Machinery, as well as more than 15 rental locations as The Cat Rental Store. Descendants of founder J. J. Niehenke, including CEO John J. Harnish, own the company.

HARPER'S MAGAZINE FOUNDATION

666 BROADWAY FL 11
NEW YORK, NY 100122394
Phone: 212 420-5720
Fax: –
Web: www.harpers.org

CEO: –
CFO: –
HR: –
FYE: February 28
Type: Private

Percentage of people who crack a smile while reading Harper's Index: 99. Harper's Magazine Foundation publishes Harper's Magazine, renowned for its fiction, essays, and reporting, as well as its Harper's Index, a statistical snapshot of the world's economic, political, and cultural climate. The magazine was established in 1850 by Harper & Brothers (now HarperCollins) and has had several changes in ownership. When former parent Minneapolis Star and Tribune Company (now The Star Tribune Company) announced in 1980 that Harper's Magazine would cease publication, The John D. and Catherine T. MacArthur Foundation and the Atlantic Richfield Company formed the Harper's Magazine Foundation to run the magazine.

HARRINGTON MEMORIAL HOSPITAL, INC.

100 SOUTH ST
SOUTHBRIDGE, MA 015504047
Phone: 508 765-9771
Fax: –
Web: www.harringtonhospital.org

CEO: Edward Moore
CFO: –
HR: –
FYE: September 30
Type: Private

Harrington Memorial Hospital works to ensure that its patients feel less harried about health care. The health care facility, founded in 1931, serves south-central Massachusetts and northeastern Connecticut. Harrington Memorial boasts nearly 115 beds and some 180 physicians who provide general and emergency medical care. It offers such specialized services as obstetrics, physical therapy, pediatrics, diagnostic imaging, and substance abuse treatment. The hospital also provides patients with home health care services and operates health clinics. Harrington Memorial invests in nearby Hubbard Regional Hospital through a management agreement in an effort to shore up the finances of both facilities.

	Annual Growth	09/17	09/18	09/19	09/20	09/21
Sales ($mil.)	0.8%	–	135.6	146.6	120.5	138.8
Net income ($ mil.)	–	–	12.1	13.8	(0.4)	(0.1)
Market value ($ mil.)	–	–	–	–	–	–
Employees	–	–	–	–	–	1,100

HARTE HANKS INC — NMS: HHS

1 Executive Drive, Suite 103
Chelmsford, MA 01824
Phone: 512 434-1100
Fax: –
Web: www.hartehanks.com

CEO: Kirk Davis
CFO: Laurilee Kearnes
HR: Temicka Phillips
FYE: December 31
Type: Public

Harte-Hanks is one of the leading global customer experience company. The company operates through its business segments. Marketing Services, Customer Care, and Fulfillment & Logistics Services. The company provides integrated direct-marketing services in the US and internationally, including market research and analytics. It handles customer contracts through phone, e-mail, social media, text messaging, chat and digital self-service support. Customers include major retailers and companies from the financial services and health care. Its biggest market is the US, accounting for about 90% of total revenue.

	Annual Growth	12/18	12/19	12/20	12/21	12/22
Sales ($mil.)	(7.7%)	284.6	217.6	176.9	194.6	206.3
Net income ($ mil.)	20.3%	17.6	(26.3)	(1.7)	15.0	36.8
Market value ($ mil.)	48.3%	17.9	26.5	20.4	56.3	86.5
Employees	(2.4%)	2,983	2,430	2,434	3,092	2,704

HARTFORD FINANCIAL SERVICES GROUP INC. — NYS: HIG

One Hartford Plaza
Hartford, CT 06155
Phone: 860 547-5000
Fax: –
Web: www.thehartford.com

CEO: Christopher J Swift
CFO: Beth Costello
HR: Amy Coates
FYE: December 31
Type: Public

The Hartford Financial Services Group is a leader in property and casualty insurance, group benefits, and mutual funds. Its commercial operations include workers' compensation, auto, and liability coverage as well as specialty insurance policies. The Hartford also offers consumer homeowners and auto coverage. The company has been the direct auto and home insurance writer for AARP's members. In addition, the company provides group life, accident, and disability benefits. The Hartford also offers wholesale solutions through Navigators, a brand of The Hartford, and assumed reinsurance coverage through Navigators Re More than 95% of the company's revenue comes from US. The Hartford has been in business since 1810.

	Annual Growth	12/19	12/20	12/21	12/22	12/23
Assets ($mil.)	2.0%	70,817	74,111	76,578	73,022	76,780
Net income ($ mil.)	4.7%	2,085.0	1,737.0	2,365.0	1,815.0	2,504.0
Market value ($ mil.)	7.2%	18,138	14,619	20,607	22,633	23,991
Employees	(1.0%)	19,500	18,500	18,100	18,800	18,700

HARTFORD HEALTHCARE CORPORATION

100 PEARL ST
HARTFORD, CT 061034506
Phone: 860 263-4100
Fax: –
Web: www.hartfordhealthcare.org

CEO: Jeffrey A Flaks
CFO: Charles L Johnson III
HR: Nathania D Valle
FYE: September 30
Type: Private

Hartford Health Care provides a variety of health services to the descendants of our founding fathers. Founded in 1854, the health care system operates a network of hospitals, behavioral health centers, nursing and rehabilitation facilities, medical labs, and numerous community programs for residents in northern Connecticut. Medical specialties range from orthopedics and women's health to cancer and heart care. Hartford Health Care's flagship facility is the Hartford Hospital, an 870-bed teaching hospital affiliated with the University of Connecticut Medical School. Its network also includes MidState Medical Center (some 155 beds), Windham Hospital (145 beds), and The Hospital of Central Connecticut (415 beds).

	Annual Growth	09/17	09/18	09/19	09/20	09/22
Sales ($mil.)	15.2%	–	3,072.3	3,541.9	4,280.9	5,403.7
Net income ($ mil.)	(14.2%)	–	410.2	(101.3)	108.8	222.2
Market value ($ mil.)	–	–	–	–	–	–
Employees	–	–	–	–	–	12,500

HARVARD BIOSCIENCE INC.

NMS: HBIO

84 October Hill Road
Holliston, MA 01746
Phone: 508 893-8999
Fax: –
Web: www.harvardbioscience.com

CEO: –
CFO: –
HR: –
FYE: December 31
Type: Public

Toss an 850-page Harvard Bioscience catalog toward a bioscience researcher and it will keep him or her busy for hours. The company develops, manufactures, and markets the scientific gizmos and instruments used in pharmaceutical, biotechnology, academic, and government labs worldwide. Its 11,000-item product line focuses on molecular biology and ADMET (absorption, distribution, metabolism, elimination, and toxicology) testing. ADMET tests are used to screen drug candidates. Other products include spectrophotometers, multi-well plate readers, and protein calculators. Customers can shop directly online, from its printed Harvard Apparatus catalog, or through distributors.

	Annual Growth	12/19	12/20	12/21	12/22	12/23
Sales ($mil.)	(0.9%)	116.2	102.1	118.9	113.3	112.3
Net income ($ mil.)	–	(4.7)	(7.8)	(0.3)	(9.5)	(3.4)
Market value ($ mil.)	15.1%	132.4	186.2	305.9	120.2	232.2
Employees	(4.7%)	505	459	494	455	416

HARVARD STUDENT AGENCIES INC

67 MOUNT AUBURN ST
CAMBRIDGE, MA 021384961
Phone: 617 495-3030
Fax: –
Web: www.hsa.net

CEO: James McKellar
CFO: –
HR: –
FYE: January 31
Type: Private

Harvard Student Agencies (HSA) consists of nine businesses managed by Harvard students and claims to be the largest student-run corporation in the world. The businesses, which include several dry cleaners, a retail store, and book publishing companies, were created to provide an additional source of income for students and business management experience. The company was founded in 1957 and originally included only two businesses: HSA Cleaners and HSA Dorm Store, which provides students with rental equipment for their rooms including refrigerators, televisions, and water coolers. Its largest division, Let's Go Publications, publishes nearly 50 budget travel guides (written by students and updated yearly).

	Annual Growth	01/15	01/16	01/17	01/20	01/22
Sales ($mil.)	11.3%	–	1.9	2.1	3.3	3.6
Net income ($ mil.)	57.9%	–	0.1	0.5	0.5	1.8
Market value ($ mil.)	–	–	–	–	–	–
Employees	–	–	–	–	–	1,000

HARVEST NATURAL RESOURCES, INC.

5535 KEMPER CT
DALLAS, TX 752202245
Phone: 281 899-5700
Fax: –
Web: www.harvestnr.com

CEO: James A Edmiston
CFO: Stephen C Haynes
HR: –
FYE: December 31
Type: Private

Harvest Natural Resources is keen to harvest the natural resources of oil and gas. The independent's main exploration and production work takes place in Venezuela, where it operates in Venezuela through a 32% interest in exploration firm Petrodelta. It also has exploration and production assets in the western states and the Gulf Coast in the US, as well as in Indonesia (through a majority stake in Budong PSC), Oman, and China. In 2012 Harvest reported proved reserves of 39.4 million barrels of oil equivalent. However, the company is facing massive debts and is jettisoning assets to stay afloat.

HARVEST OIL & GAS CORP

NBB: HRST

1001 Fannin, Suite 750
Houston, TX 77002
Phone: 713 651-1144
Fax: –
Web: www.hvstog.com

CEO: Michael E Mercer
CFO: Ryan Stash
HR: –
FYE: December 31
Type: Public

Harvest Oil & Gas Corp (formerly EV Energy Partners) is a natural gas and oil exploration and production company which operates in the Appalachian Basin, primarily in West Virginia and Ohio, as well as in Kansas, Louisiana, Michigan, New Mexico, Oklahoma, and Texas. In 2018 Harvest Oil & Gas reported estimated proved reserves of 545 billion cu. ft. equivalent of oil and natural gas. EV Energy Partners filed Chapter 11 in April 2018 and emerged two months later under a new name -- Harvest Oil & Gas Corp. In 2018 Harvest Oil & Gas sold all its interests in the Barnett Shale, divested certain Mid-Continent assets, and announced it was exploring strategic alternatives for the company.

	Annual Growth	12/17*	05/18*	12/18	12/19	12/20
Sales ($mil.)	(51.2%)	225.7	111.0	138.6	113.8	26.3
Net income ($ mil.)	–	(134.2)	(610.5)	24.0	(138.3)	(8.9)
Market value ($ mil.)	–	–	–	18.5	6.6	21.2
Employees	–	1,185	–	5	5	–

*Fiscal year change

HARVEY INDUSTRIES, LLC

1400 MAIN ST FL 3
WALTHAM, MA 024511689
Phone: 800 598-5400
Fax: –
Web: www.harveybp.com

CEO: Thomas Bigony
CFO: Scott Lassonde
HR: Amy L Plante
FYE: February 28
Type: Private

Harvey Industries, also known as Harvey Building Products, designs and manufactures its line of vinyl and wood windows, as well as custom window shapes, doors, and patio enclosures. It provides services for architects, remodelers, restoration, multifamily builders, and light commercial, and single-family home builders. It is currently privately owned and has an expanded manufacturing footprint that provides windows and doors to customers in over half of the United States, from the East Coast to the Rockies, under the brands of Harvey Windows and Doors, SoftLite Windows & Doors, Thermo-Tech Windows & Doors, and Northeast Building Products. The company was incorporated in 1961.

HARVEY MUDD COLLEGE

301 PLATT BLVD
CLAREMONT, CA 917115901
Phone: 909 621-8000
Fax: –
Web: www.hmc.edu

CEO: –
CFO: Andrew Dorantes
HR: –
FYE: June 30
Type: Private

Mudders get down and dirty with math and science. About 800 undergraduate students (called "Mudders") attend Harvey Mudd College (HMC), a private non-profit liberal arts school that specializes in engineering, mathematics, and the sciences. HMC is a member of The Claremont Colleges, a confederation of five independent undergraduate colleges and two graduate schools that is managed by the Claremont University Consortium. The group shares resources and offers dual degree programs. HMC alums include Jonathan Gay, creator of Flash software, and Unison founder Rick Sontag.

	Annual Growth	06/18	06/19	06/20	06/21	06/22
Sales ($mil.)	11.8%	–	97.0	92.2	77.7	135.4
Net income ($ mil.)	110.0%	–	4.1	(1.5)	(0.4)	37.6
Market value ($ mil.)	–	–	–	–	–	250
Employees	–	–	–	–	–	–

HASBRO, INC.

1027 Newport Avenue
Pawtucket, RI 02861
Phone: 401 431-8697
Fax: –
Web: www.hasbro.com

NMS: HAS
CEO: Christian P Cocks
CFO: –
HR: –
FYE: December 31
Type: Public

Hasbro is one of the largest toy makers worldwide and the producer of such childhood favorites as Nerf, Magic: The Gathering, My Little Pony, Transformers, Play-Doh, Monopoly, Baby Alive, Dungeons & Dragons, Power Rangers, Peppa Pig and PJ Masks. Hasbro has a significant relationship with Disney, producing merchandise for the entertainment giant's megabrands including Star Wars, Marvel (including Spider-Man and The Avengers), Ghost Busters, and Frozen. Besides toys, Hasbro makes board games such as Scrabble, Monopoly, and Trivial Pursuit, as well as trading cards including Magic: The Gathering (through its Wizards of the Coast unit) and Dungeons & Dragons. About 60% of company's total revenue comes from the US operations.

	Annual Growth	12/19	12/20	12/21	12/22	12/23
Sales ($mil.)	1.5%	4,720.2	5,465.4	6,420.4	5,856.7	5,003.3
Net income ($ mil.)	–	520.5	222.5	428.7	203.5	(1,489.3)
Market value ($ mil.)	(16.6%)	14,678	12,928	13,590	8,078.9	7,086.5
Employees	(0.4%)	5,600	6,822	6,640	6,490	5,502

HASELDEN CONSTRUCTION, LLC

6950 S POTOMAC ST
CENTENNIAL, CO 801124039
Phone: 303 751-1478
Fax: –
Web: www.haselden.com

CEO: Ed J Haselden
CFO: Troy Schroeder
HR: Amanda Sparks
FYE: December 31
Type: Private

Haselden Construction eliminates some of the hassle for companies and institutions looking for full turnkey construction services. The company provides finance, design, engineering, construction, renovation, management, and maintenance services for the development of facilities, including schools, hospitals, resorts, hospitality facilities, and office buildings. The company primarily serves clients in Colorado, Wyoming, and other western states. Clients have included Isle of Capri Casinos and the University of Colorado. Family-owned Haselden Construction was founded in Denver in 1973.

HASTINGS ENTERTAINMENT, INC.

3601 PLAINS BLVD
AMARILLO, TX 791021098
Phone: 806 351-2300
Fax: –
Web: www.gohastings.com

CEO: –
CFO: –
HR: –
FYE: June 30
Type: Private

Hastings Entertainment has it all for a smaller-town Saturday night. The company operates about 125 superstores in nearly 20 Midwestern and western US states. Hastings' stores and website sell new and used CDs, movies, books, magazines, and video games, in addition to related electronics, such as video game consoles and DVD players. Hastings also rents DVDs and video games. Its store locations average 24,000 sq. ft. and offer such amenities as music listening stations, reading chairs, coffee bars, and children's play areas. Hastings' other store concepts include Sun Adventure Sports, which offers bicycles, skateboards, and other sporting goods, and Tradesmart, a seller of mostly used entertainment products.

HASTINGS MANUFACTURING CO

325 North Hanover Street
Hastings, MI 49058
Phone: 269 945-2491
Fax: 269 945-4667
Web: www.hastingsmanufacturing.com

CEO: –
CFO: –
HR: –
FYE: December 31
Type: Public

Hastings Manufacturing is one of the automotive industry's ring leaders. The company's core business is making piston rings for the automotive aftermarket. Customers include engine rebuilders, retailers, and warehouse distributors. Hastings also makes piston rings for OEM giants, such as Chrysler, as well as motorcycle, snowmobile, and all-terrain vehicle builders, Harley-Davidson and Polaris, and for smaller uses, such as lawn and garden, and marine gasoline engines. Hastings distributes its products, including top compression rings, oil control rings, and all steel nitride racing rings, throughout the US and Canada. The firm was founded in 1915; it is owned by Michigan-based investment firm Anderson Group.

	Annual Growth	12/98	12/99	12/00	12/01	12/02
Sales ($mil.)	(1.9%)	38.8	37.4	35.3	34.8	35.8
Net income ($ mil.)	(26.5%)	1.7	0.3	(0.5)	1.0	0.5
Market value ($ mil.)	(12.3%)	13.3	6.2	4.0	3.9	7.9
Employees	(2.9%)	465	442	417	379	413

HAUPPAUGE DIGITAL, INC.

91 Cabot Court
Hauppauge, NY 11788
Phone: 631 434-1600
Fax: –
Web: www.hauppauge.com

NBB: HAUP
CEO: –
CFO: –
HR: –
FYE: September 30
Type: Public

Wanna watch TV at work? Hauppauge Digital's WinTV analog and digital video boards let viewers videoconference, watch TV, and view input from VCRs and camcorders in a resizable window on a PC monitor. Hauppauge (pronounced "HAW-pog") also offers boards that accommodate radio and Internet broadcasts, and makes a line of PC video editing boards. The company outsources its manufacturing to companies in Europe and Asia. The company sells its products to contract electronics manufacturers, including ASUSTeK Computer and Hon Hai Precision Industry (Foxconn), and partners with companies such as Intel and Microsoft. Customers outside the US make up more than half of sales.

	Annual Growth	09/09	09/10	09/11	09/12	09/13
Sales ($mil.)	(13.0%)	59.3	56.9	42.3	44.6	34.0
Net income ($ mil.)	–	(7.1)	(1.8)	(5.8)	(2.5)	(4.0)
Market value ($ mil.)	(23.9%)	11.7	26.0	8.7	10.9	3.9
Employees	(12.5%)	169	167	146	132	99

HAVILAND ENTERPRISES, INC.

421 ANN ST NW
GRAND RAPIDS, MI 495042019
Phone: 616 361-6691
Fax: –
Web: www.havilandusa.com

CEO: Meg Post
CFO: –
HR: –
FYE: November 30
Type: Private

Haviland Enterprises distributes chemicals such as acids, alcohols, amines, chelating agents, lubricants, solvents, and surfactants. The company also provides contract blending and packaging, research and development, technical service, compliance training, and supply chain management services. It primarily serves customers in the Midwestern US but provides services to all 50 states and overseas as well. Associated companies include Haviland Contoured Plastics, which makes spiral-wound plastic hose, and Haviland Consumer Products, which blends and packages swimming pool chemicals for private-label customers.

	Annual Growth	12/01	12/02	12/03*	11/04	11/08
Sales ($mil.)	11.3%	–	–	49.1	–	83.7
Net income ($ mil.)	9.4%	–	–	1.3	–	2.0
Market value ($ mil.)	–	–	–	–	–	–
Employees	–	–	–	–	–	225

*Fiscal year change

HAWAI I PACIFIC HEALTH

55 MERCHANT ST STE 2500
HONOLULU, HI 968134306
Phone: 808 949-9355
Fax: –
Web: www.hawaiipacifichealth.org

CEO: Raymond Vara
CFO: David Okabe
HR: –
FYE: June 30
Type: Private

Hawaii may be paradise, but even in paradise's some residents get sick. That's when Hawai'i Pacific Health (HPH) surfs in to save the day. HPH is a not-for-profit health care system consisting of four hospitals (Kapi'olani Medical Center for Women & Children, Pali Momi Medical Center, Straub Clinic & Hospital, and Wilcox Memorial Hospital) across the islands with a combined capacity of 550 beds. The system offers a full array of tertiary, specialty, and acute care services through its hospitals, which also serve as teaching and research centers, as well as about 50 outpatient centers. Specialized services offered by HPH include cardiac care, maternity services, oncology, orthopedics, and pediatric care.

	Annual Growth	06/17	06/18	06/20	06/21	06/22
Sales ($mil.)	(36.2%)	–	1,351.8	1,369.4	198.1	224.2
Net income ($ mil.)	(44.0%)	–	130.8	(48.5)	4.5	12.8
Market value ($ mil.)	–	–	–	–	–	–
Employees	–	–	–	–	–	5,400

HAWAI I PACIFIC UNIVERSITY

1 ALOHA TOWER DR
HONOLULU, HI 968134815
Phone: 808 544-0200
Fax: –
Web: www.hpu.edu

CEO: –
CFO: Bruce Edwards
HR: Bernard Nunies
FYE: June 30
Type: Private

Hawai'i Pacific University infuses a little aloha spirit into the liberal arts. The state's largest private institution of higher education offers some 50 undergraduate degrees and about a dozen graduate programs to more than 7,000 students, with majors ranging from journalism to business administration. The university's main campus is located in downtown Honolulu, while two others also on the island of Oahu focus on environmental science, marine biology, oceanography, and nursing. Students come from more than 80 countries, making it one of the most diverse campuses in the world. Founded in 1965, the not-for-profit university's student/faculty ratio is 15:1.

	Annual Growth	06/18	06/19	06/20	06/21	06/22
Sales ($mil.)	7.7%	–	75.2	77.5	77.1	94.1
Net income ($ mil.)	–	–	(10.5)	(2.6)	13.3	(8.3)
Market value ($ mil.)	–	–	–	–	–	–
Employees	–	–	–	–	–	1,300

HAWAII DEPARTMENT OF TRANSPORTATION

869 PUNCHBOWL ST STE A
HONOLULU, HI 968135003
Phone: 808 587-1830
Fax: –
Web: hidot.hawaii.gov

CEO: –
CFO: –
HR: –
FYE: June 30
Type: Private

The State of Hawaii Department of Transportation (Hawaii DOT) makes sure the state's consumers get their consumables. Hawaii imports some 80% of what it utilizes. About 99% of this enters The 50th State through the commercial harbor system; a system that's planned, constructed, operated, and maintained by the Hawaii DOT. In addition to the state's 10 harbors, the agency operates a Highways Division, which manages about 2,400 lane miles of highway on six islands, and an Airports Division, responsible for 15 airports, serving commercial airlines and general aviation flights and handling more than 30 million passengers annually. The Hawaii DOT generates its own monies through independent special funds.

	Annual Growth	06/15	06/16	06/19	06/21	06/22
Sales ($mil.)	3.0%	–	475.0	440.8	494.2	568.2
Net income ($ mil.)	–	–	64.8	172.2	184.8	(8.3)
Market value ($ mil.)	–	–	–	–	–	–
Employees	–	–	–	–	–	2,215

HAWAIIAN ELECTRIC INDUSTRIES INC

NYS: HE

1001 Bishop Street, Suite 2900
Honolulu, HI 96813
Phone: 808 543-5662
Fax: 808 543-7966
Web: www.hei.com

CEO: Constance H Lau
CFO: Gregory C Hazelton
HR: –
FYE: December 31
Type: Public

Hawaiian Electric Industries (HEI) is principally engaged in banking, electric utility and non-regulated renewable/sustainable infrastructure businesses operating in the State of Hawaii. An unusual combination, HEI operates two regulated utility companies that provide electricity for approximately 95% of Hawaii residents mainly in Oahu, Hawaii, Maui, Lanai and Molokai. It also runs one of the state's largest financial institutions. The utilities serve about 469,670 customers across all islands except Kauai and generate the bulk of HEI's revenue and Banking serves both consumer and commercial customers and operates about 40 branches on the islands of Oahu, Maui, Hawaii, Kauai, and Molokai.

	Annual Growth	12/19	12/20	12/21	12/22	12/23
Sales ($mil.)	6.4%	2,874.6	2,579.8	2,850.4	3,742.0	3,682.2
Net income ($ mil.)	(2.2%)	219.9	199.7	248.1	243.0	201.1
Market value ($ mil.)	(25.8%)	5,161.7	3,898.3	4,571.3	4,609.9	1,563.1
Employees	(1.6%)	3,841	3,702	3,649	3,756	3,597

HAWAIIAN HOLDINGS INC

NMS: HA

3375 Koapaka Street, Suite G-350
Honolulu, HI 96819
Phone: 808 835-3700
Fax: –
Web: www.hawaiianairlines.com

CEO: Peter R Ingram
CFO: Shannon L Okinaka
HR: –
FYE: December 31
Type: Public

Hawaiian Holdings' main subsidiary is the Hawaiian Airlines. It is engaged in the scheduled air transportation of passengers and cargo amongst the Hawaiian Islands (the Neighbor Island routes), between the Hawaiian Islands and certain cities in the United States (the North America routes, and together with the Neighbor Island routes, the Domestic routes), and between the Hawaiian Islands and the South Pacific, Australia, New Zealand and Asia (the International routes). It operates a fleet of almost 20 Boeing 717-200 aircraft for the Neighbor Island routes and nearly 25 Airbus A330-200 aircraft and roughly 20 Airbus A32neofor the North America and International routes. In addition to its scheduled passenger and cargo operations, Hawaiian Airlines provides various charter flights. Domestic operations account for about 85% of total sales.

	Annual Growth	12/19	12/20	12/21	12/22	12/23
Sales ($mil.)	(1.0%)	2,832.2	844.8	1,596.6	2,641.3	2,716.3
Net income ($ mil.)	–	224.0	(510.9)	(144.8)	(240.1)	(260.5)
Market value ($ mil.)	(16.6%)	1,517.9	917.3	952.0	531.7	735.9
Employees	(0.3%)	7,437	5,278	6,674	7,108	7,362

HAWAIIAN MACADAMIA NUT ORCHARDS LP

688 Kinoole Street, Suite 121
Hilo, HI 96720
Phone: 808 747-8471
Fax: –
Web: www.rholp.com

CEO: Bradford C Nelson
CFO: Bradford C Nelson
HR: –
FYE: December 31
Type: Public

Business is nuts (and that's a good thing) at ML Macadamia Orchards. As the world's largest macadamia nut grower, the company owns or leases some 4,200 acres of macadamia orchards located on the southeastern portion of the island of Hawaii, where it produces a yearly average of 21 million pounds of nuts. ML Macadamia is strictly a nut grower; it sells its crop to Hawaiian nut processors, including the Mauna Loa Macadamia Nut Corporation, MacFarms of Hawaii, and others under various contract agreements. The company decided to become vertically integrated in 2008 and is looking to acquire processing operations in order to insulate itself from low commodity prices.

	Annual Growth	12/13	12/14	12/15	12/16	12/17
Sales ($mil.)	23.5%	13.9	16.0	18.5	26.7	32.2
Net income ($ mil.)	–	(3.7)	(6.2)	(2.2)	(2.0)	1.2
Market value ($ mil.)	(3.6%)	0.0	0.0	0.0	0.0	0.0
Employees	1.6%	279	269	265	244	297

HAWAIIAN TELCOM HOLDCO, INC.

1177 BISHOP ST
HONOLULU, HI 968132837
Phone: 877 643-3456
Fax: –
Web: ir.hawaiiantel.com

CEO: –
CFO: –
HR: Sunshine Topping
FYE: December 31
Type: Private

Hawaiian Telcom, through its operating subsidiaries, provides modern telecommunications services to residential and business customers in the island state. The company has almost 320,000 local access lines (aka landlines) in service. It also provides long-distance phone service to about 171,000 customers and broadband Internet access to about 100,000 customers. Hawaiian Telcom resells wireless communications services through an agreement with Sprint Nextel. Local voice services about for about 80% of revenue. The company has been in operation since 1883.

HAWKINS CONSTRUCTION COMPANY

2516 DEER PARK BLVD
OMAHA, NE 681053771
Phone: 402 342-1607
Fax: –
Web: www.hawkins1.com

CEO: Fred Hawkins Jr
CFO: –
HR: Kylie Tallant
FYE: December 31
Type: Private

Hawkins Construction provides both commercial building and heavy/highway contracting services. The diversified contractor has a project portfolio that includes regional banks, warehouses, schools, churches, and prisons. It also works on highways, bridges, site developments, and parking structures, and is one of the Midwest's largest road builders. Clients include the University of Nebraska, Mutual of Omaha, and Hewlett-Packard. The family-owned company began with a successful contract bid in 1922 by Kenneth Hawkins and his brother Earl for what is now Lincoln, Nebraska's Memorial Stadium; the firm was incorporated in 1960 by Kenneth and his son Fred.

HAWKINS INC

NMS: HWKN

2381 Rosegate
Roseville, MN 55113
Phone: 612 331-6910
Fax: –
Web: www.hawkinsinc.com

CEO: Patrick H Hawkins
CFO: Jeffrey P Oldenkamp
HR: Kelsey Joswiak
FYE: April 2
Type: Public

Hawkins distributes, blends and manufactures chemicals and specialty ingredients for its customers in a wide variety of industries. The company processes and distributes bulk specialty chemicals. Its Industrial segment makes bleach (sodium hypochlorite), repackages liquid chlorine, and custom blends other chemicals. Hawkins' Water Treatment segment distributes products and equipment used to treat drinking water, municipal and industrial wastewater, and swimming pools. In addition, the company operates a fleet of more than 200 commercial vehicles, primarily in its Water Treatment segment, which are highly regulated, including by the US Department of Transportation (DOT). Hawkins, Inc. was founded in 1938.

	Annual Growth	03/19	03/20	03/21*	04/22	04/23
Sales ($mil.)	13.9%	556.3	540.2	596.9	774.5	935.1
Net income ($ mil.)	25.2%	24.4	28.4	41.0	51.5	60.0
Market value ($ mil.)	4.4%	767.9	693.9	697.9	952.9	912.8
Employees	6.7%	657	656	742	813	851

*Fiscal year change

HAWTHORNE MACHINERY CO.

16945 CAMINO SAN BERNARDO
SAN DIEGO, CA 921272499
Phone: 858 674-7000
Fax: –
Web: www.hawthornecat.com

CEO: Tee K Ness
CFO: –
HR: Crystal Kantouth
FYE: December 31
Type: Private

Leader of the track, Hawthorne Machinery, a Caterpillar dealership, sells and rents more than 300 CAT equipment models, including tractors, trucks, loaders, compactors, harvesters, graders, excavators, and power systems. It also provides more than 73,000 parts and repair services for industrial and construction contractors, and other public and private customers around San Diego County. Hawthorne Machinery offers new and used equipment and rentals of brand-name equipment by such blue chip OEMs as Kubota, Spartan, and Sullair. The company was founded in 1956 by Tom Hawthorne.

	Annual Growth	12/01	12/02	12/03	12/06	12/07
Sales ($mil.)	13.9%	–	176.2	170.8	377.2	338.1
Net income ($ mil.)	–	–	–	44.8	7.6	0.4
Market value ($ mil.)	–	–	–	–	–	–
Employees	–	–	–	–	–	1,000

HAY HOUSE, LLC

2591 PIONEER AVE STE A
VISTA, CA 920818415
Phone: 760 431-7695
Fax: –
Web: www.hayhouse.com

CEO: Louise L Hay
CFO: –
HR: –
FYE: December 31
Type: Private

Self-help publisher Hay House publishes books and sells audio and video content covering topics such as self-help, sociology, philosophy, psychology, alternative health, and environmental issues. It has more than 300 print books and 350 audio programs from some 130 authors, including TV psychic John Edward, talk show host Montel Williams, and radio personality Tavis Smiley. In addition to its eponymous imprint, the company publishes under the New Beginnings Press, Princess Books, and Smiley Books labels; the firm has international divisions in Australia, the UK, India, and South Africa. Hay House was founded in 1984 by Louise Hay to self-publish her first two books, Heal Your Body and You Can Heal Your Life.

	Annual Growth	12/03	12/04	12/05	12/06	12/08
Sales ($mil.)	(56.3%)	–	–	723.9	57.0	60.5
Net income ($ mil.)	–	–	–	–	1.5	0.9
Market value ($ mil.)	–	–	–	–	–	–
Employees	–	–	–	–	–	92

HAYNES INTERNATIONAL, INC. NMS: HAYN

1020 West Park Avenue
Kokomo, IN 46904-9013
Phone: 765 456-6000
Fax: –
Web: www.haynesintl.com

CEO: Michael L Shor
CFO: Daniel W Maudlin
HR: –
FYE: September 30
Type: Public

Haynes International is one of the world's largest producer of alloys in flat product form such as sheet, coil, and plate. The company develops and manufactures nickel- and cobalt-based alloys?high-temperature alloys (HTAs) able to withstand extreme temperatures and corrosion-resistant alloys (CRAs) that stand up to corrosive substances and processes. HTAs are used in jet engines, gas turbines used for power generation, and waste incinerators, while CRAs have applications in chemical processing, power plant emissions control, and hazardous waste treatment. Haynes does the majority of its business in the US.

	Annual Growth	09/19	09/20	09/21	09/22	09/23
Sales ($mil.)	4.7%	490.2	380.5	337.7	490.5	590.0
Net income ($ mil.)	44.1%	9.7	(6.5)	(8.7)	45.1	42.0
Market value ($ mil.)	6.7%	456.3	217.6	474.3	447.1	592.3
Employees	2.2%	1,179	1,054	1,110	1,255	1,284

HAYS MEDICAL CENTER, INC.

2220 CANTERBURY DR
HAYS, KS 676012370
Phone: 785 623-5000
Fax: –
Web: www.haysmed.com

CEO: John H Jeter MD
CFO: William Overbey
HR: Jana Fross
FYE: June 30
Type: Private

Hays Medical Center brings big city health care to rural Kansas. The not-for-profit hospital, which has about 210 beds, provides both acute and tertiary medical care to the Midwestern plains, serving more than 13,000 emergency patients each year. In addition to medical, surgical, and pediatric care, Hays Medical Center offers home care, hospice, skilled nursing, rehabilitation, and behavioral health services. It operates centers for cardiac care (the DeBakey Heart Institute), fitness and rehabilitation (Center for Health Improvement), orthopedics (Hays Orthopedic Institute), and cancer treatment (the Dreiling/Schmidt Cancer Center). The organization also operates specialty and rural health clinics.

	Annual Growth	06/13	06/14	06/15	06/16	06/22
Sales ($mil.)	2.3%	–	198.7	201.6	199.5	238.7
Net income ($ mil.)	(20.4%)	–	21.0	8.6	2.6	3.4
Market value ($ mil.)	–	–	–	–	–	–
Employees	–	–	–	–	–	1,178

HAYWOOD HEALTH AUTHORITY

262 LEROY GEORGE DR
CLYDE, NC 287217430
Phone: 828 456-7311
Fax: –
Web: www.myhaywoodregional.com

CEO: Steve Heatherly
CFO: Gene Winters
HR: Jo Palmer
FYE: September 30
Type: Private

Got a bad case of hay fever? Head to Haywood! Haywood Regional Medical Center (HRMC) provides a wide range of health care services to the residents of western North Carolina. Specialty services include emergency medicine, home and hospice care, occupational health, immediate and prolonged physical rehabilitation, and surgery. Founded in 1927, the medical center offers imaging services, diabetes education, and health and fitness centers. HRMC also houses a state-funded adult psychiatric inpatient program managed by Smoky Mountain Center, a local provider of behavioral health care services. The HRMC Foundation provides charitable giving and administration services.

	Annual Growth	07/14	07/15	07/16*	09/21	09/22
Sales ($mil.)	(62.1%)	–	110.5	118.8	0.9	0.1
Net income ($ mil.)	–	–	(1.8)	(4.2)	0.5	(0.8)
Market value ($ mil.)	–	–	–	–	–	–
Employees	–	–	–	–	–	1,000

*Fiscal year change

HAZEN AND SAWYER, D.P.C.

498 FASHION AVE FL 11
NEW YORK, NY 100186710
Phone: 212 539-7000
Fax: –
Web: www.hazenandsawyer.com

CEO: –
CFO: –
HR: Rebecca Job
FYE: December 31
Type: Private

There is nothing hazy about Hazen and Sawyer's focus on water, wastewater, and solid waste infrastructure. The environmental engineering firm specializes in planning, designing, and constructing clean drinking water systems for public and private clients worldwide. Hazen and Sawyer's specific areas of expertise include architectural design, aquatic sciences, biosolids management, buried infrastructure, odor control, resource economics, risk management, utility management services, and wastewater and stormwater collection. The employee-owned firm operates from about 40 offices throughout the eastern US and several international branch offices in South America.

HBE CORPORATION

11330 OLIVE BLVD
SAINT LOUIS, MO 631417107
Phone: 314 567-9000
Fax: –
Web: www.hbecorp.com

CEO: Joseph Lehrer
CFO: –
HR: Judy Wilson
FYE: December 31
Type: Private

Could HBE stand for Hospital Builder Extraordinaire? This company would like to think so. With more than 1,100 commercial projects under its belt, HBE's experience lies in an integrated approach to designing and building hospitals and healthcare facilities in the US. It boasts particular expertise in hospital renovation and additions. Services include planning, estimating, interior design, construction, and project management. Certain architectural and engineering services are carried out by employees of affiliate Hospital Designers, Inc., so that HBE functions as a one-stop shop for hospital-building. Founded by CEO Fred Kummer in 1960, HBE is majority owned by Kramer and his wife June.

HCA FLORIDA ENGLEWOOD HOSPITAL

700 MEDICAL BLVD
ENGLEWOOD, FL 342233964
Phone: 941 475-6571
Fax: –
Web: www.hcafloridahealthcare.com

CEO: Michael Ehrat
CFO: James Ayerfman
HR: –
FYE: December 31
Type: Private

Englewood Community Hospital wants the community of Englewood to always feel better. The hospital, part of the HCA system of health care providers, is a 100-bed acute care hospital that serves Florida's Englewood area. Founded in 1985, Englewood Community Hospital offers emergency and general medical care, as well as specialty services including orthopedics and urology. The medical center includes a women's wellness center and a sleep disorder center; it also operates diagnostic imaging, rehabilitation therapy, wound healing, and cardiac care units.

	Annual Growth	12/07	12/08	12/14	12/16	12/17
Sales ($mil.)	4.5%	–	36.5	40.9	53.1	54.3
Net income ($ mil.)	–	–	(2.1)	(0.5)	3.6	1.3
Market value ($ mil.)	–	–	–	–	–	–
Employees	–	–	–	–	–	356

HCA HEALTHCARE INC   NYS: HCA

One Park Plaza
Nashville, TN 37203
Phone: 615 344-9551
Fax: –
Web: www.hcahealthcare.com

CEO: –
CFO: –
HR: –
FYE: December 31
Type: Public

HCA Healthcare is one of the leading healthcare services companies in the US. It operates about 175 hospitals, mostly acute care centers, five psychiatric facilities, and two rehabilitation hospitals in the US and UK. It also runs about 125 freestanding surgery centers and urgent care, rehab, and other outpatient centers that form healthcare networks in many communities it serves. In total, its hospitals are home to some 48,500 beds. HCA's facilities are located in about 20 states. About 45 of each of its hospitals are in Florida and Texas. The HCA International unit operates the company's hospitals and clinics in the UK.

	Annual Growth	12/19	12/20	12/21	12/22	12/23
Sales ($mil.)	6.1%	51,336	51,533	58,752	60,233	64,968
Net income ($ mil.)	10.6%	3,505.0	3,754.0	6,956.0	5,643.0	5,242.0
Market value ($ mil.)	16.3%	39,249	43,670	68,222	63,718	71,876
Employees	2.6%	280,000	355,000	284,000	294,000	310,000

HCI GROUP INC   NYS: HCI

3802 Coconut Palm Drive
Tampa , FL 33619
Phone: 813 849-9500
Fax: –
Web: www.hcigroup.com

CEO: Paresh Patel
CFO: Mark Harmsworth
HR: –
FYE: December 31
Type: Public

Floridian homeowners are picking HCI Group for their insurance needs -- by default. The company's Homeowners Choice Property and Casualty Insurance (HCPCI) subsidiary provides homeowners' insurance and other property/casualty coverage in the state. HCI sells policies through its two subsidiaries. Other HCI Group subsidiaries provide real estate, reinsurance, and information technology products and services. The firm changed its name from Homeowners Choice, Inc., to HCI Group in to reflect its diversified businesses.

	Annual Growth	12/19	12/20	12/21	12/22	12/23
Assets ($mil.)	22.6%	802.6	941.3	1,176.9	1,803.3	1,811.3
Net income ($ mil.)	31.3%	26.6	27.6	1.9	(58.5)	79.0
Market value ($ mil.)	17.6%	444.5	509.3	813.5	385.5	851.1
Employees	–	491	451	526	578	

HDR, INC.

1917 S 67TH ST
OMAHA, NE 681062973
Phone: 402 399-1000
Fax: –
Web: www.hdrinc.com

CEO: Eric Keen
CFO: Galen Meysenburg
HR: Amy Rodriguez
FYE: December 29
Type: Private

HDR is one of the largest 100% employee-owned firms in the US by employee count. It specializes in engineering, architecture, environmental and construction services. The company is most well-known for adding beauty and structure to communities through high-performance buildings and smart infrastructure. The company also provides mechanical and plumbing services, construction and project management, and utilities planning. It has operations in approximately 15 countries and has offices in more than 200 global locations. The employee-owned company was founded as Henningson Engineering in 1917 to build municipal plants in the rural Midwest.

	Annual Growth	12/14	12/15	12/16	12/17	12/18
Sales ($mil.)	(6.1%)	–	2,132.2	2,230.5	2,362.1	1,762.8
Net income ($ mil.)	15.9%	–	74.1	90.3	82.7	115.3
Market value ($ mil.)	–	–	–	–	–	–
Employees	–	–	–	–	–	10,000

HEA LEGACY, INC.

810 E 10TH ST
LAWRENCE, KS 660443018
Phone: 785 843-1234
Fax: –
Web: www.allenpress.com

CEO: Gerald Lillian
CFO: –
HR: –
FYE: December 31
Type: Private

Customers who are hard-pressed for printed pieces turn to Allen Press. The company is a commercial typesetting, printing, and publishing company. It also provides editing, marketing, advertising, online publishing, and distribution services. Clients include corporations, professional associations, scholarly societies, university presses, and commercial publishers of journals, magazines, and books. Harold Allen founded Allen Press in 1935 as a print shop in the basement of a downtown bank building. The company is still family-owned.

HEADWATERS INCORPORATED

10701 S RIVER FRONT PKWY STE 300
SOUTH JORDAN, UT 84095
Phone: 801 984-9400
Fax: –
Web: www.ecomaterial.com

CEO: Mike Kane
CFO: –
HR: –
FYE: September 30
Type: Private

Headwaters, Inc. is a broad-based natural resource management and consulting firm. The company has, for over 20 years, maintained a multi-faceted approach to natural resource management dealing with projects related to environmental management, regulatory compliance, permitting, wetlands mitigation banking, environmental assessments, forest resources management, wildlife and fisheries management, property management and conservation easements. Headwaters has and continues to serve as the principal environmental consulting firm for a broad spectrum of client sectors that includes several major corporations and State and Federal agencies across the southern US.

HEALTH DIAGNOSTICS, LLC

110 MARCUS DR
MELVILLE, NY 117473118
Phone: 631 420-3701
Fax: –
Web: www.hmca.com

CEO: –
CFO: –
HR: –
FYE: December 31
Type: Private

Health Diagnostics is willing to look right through you to get to the heart of the problem. The medical company provides diagnostic imaging services, such as CT (Computed Tomography) for cancer, cardiovascular disease, and infectious disease; mammography; ultrasound; X-ray; and various forms of MRI (Magnetic Resonance Imaging) for spinal, joint, and heart problems. It operates more than 20 outpatient facilities in California, Florida, and New York. Health Diagnostics' radiologists and sub-specialists also perform nuclear medicine imaging that helps to detect tumors and infection by evaluating organ function. The private company was formed in 2007.

HEALTH FIRST SHARED SERVICES, INC.

6450 US HIGHWAY 1
ROCKLEDGE, FL 329555747
Phone: 321 434-4300
Fax: –
Web: www.hf.org

CEO: James Shaw
CFO: Robert C Galloway
HR: Paula Just
FYE: September 30
Type: Private

Health First is Central Florida's only fully integrated delivery network (IDN). The health system includes four hospitals, over 500 providers, and the area's only Level II trauma center, plus First Flight, a state-of-the-art emergency helicopter transport service providing critical care when every second counts. Health First's biggest hospital is Holmes Regional Medical Center in Melbourne, with more than 500 beds. Its Cape Canaveral Hospital and Palm Bay Community Hospital have 150 and 120 beds, respectively. Its Viera Hospital is an 84-bed acute-care hospital. The system also runs outpatient clinics, a home health service, and a physicians group. In addition, it offers exceptional, convenient insurance options through Health First Health Plans, along with a suite of support services including its Family Pharmacy, Hospice, physical therapy, and much more.

	Annual Growth	09/10	09/11	09/13	09/14	09/15
Sales ($mil.)	76.5%	–	129.4	1,059.4	1,137.0	1,255.3
Net income ($ mil.)	–	–	(0.4)	51.1	90.2	19.9
Market value ($ mil.)	–	–	–	–	–	–
Employees	–	–	–	–	–	6,900

HEALTH INDUSTRY DISTRIBUTORS ASSOCIATION

510 KING ST
ALEXANDRIA, VA 223143132
Phone: 703 549-4432
Fax: –
Web: www.hida.org

CEO: Matthew Rowan
CFO: –
HR: –
FYE: December 31
Type: Private

Ever wonder where all that equipment at the doctor's office comes from? HIDA could tell you. The Health Industry Distributors Association (HIDA) is a trade association comprised of medical products distributors. The group provides legal information, networking, and educational programs for its more than 150 members. It also hosts expos and conferences for distributors and manufacturers, lobbies government on behalf of the industry, publishes newsletters and special issue reports, and conducts research on industry trends. The organization has separate groups for long term care, home health care, acute care, and physician or alternative care. HIDA was established in 1902.

	Annual Growth	12/16	12/17	12/18	12/21	12/22
Sales ($mil.)	2.1%	–	3.9	4.2	4.8	4.4
Net income ($ mil.)	–	–	0.0	0.2	1.0	(0.6)
Market value ($ mil.)	–	–	–	–	–	–
Employees	–	–	–	–	–	25

HEALTH PARTNERS PLANS, INC.

901 MARKET ST STE 500
PHILADELPHIA, PA 191074496
Phone: 215 849-9606
Fax: –
Web: www.healthpartnersplans.com

CEO: –
CFO: Kevin Clancy
HR: –
FYE: December 31
Type: Private

Health Partners is one of a few hospital-owned health maintenance organizations in the nation providing free and low-cost high-quality health insurance through its Medicaid, Medicare and CHIP plans. The company is a not-for-profit health plan that provides health benefits to over 291,000 members in the Philadelphia area. Its Health Partners Medicare plans offer three Medicare Advantage plans in the twelve-county area, all of which provide more benefits than Original Medicare with no or low monthly plan premiums. Its KidzPartners program is provided in partnership with the state of Pennsylvania's Children's Health Insurance Program (CHIP). Its provider network includes over 6,400 primary and specialty care doctors and more than 40 hospitals in the region. Health Partners was founded in 1984 by a group of hospitals in the Philadelphia area.

	Annual Growth	12/12	12/13	12/14	12/21	12/22
Sales ($mil.)	8.9%	–	1,000.3	910.2	1,902.2	2,146.7
Net income ($ mil.)	–	–	(0.2)	(8.5)	30.0	39.7
Market value ($ mil.)	–	–	–	–	–	–
Employees	–	–	–	–	–	620

HEALTH RESEARCH, INC.

150 BROADWAY STE 560
MENANDS, NY 122042732
Phone: 518 431-1200
Fax: –
Web: www.healthresearch.org

CEO: –
CFO: –
HR: –
FYE: March 31
Type: Private

Health Research, Inc. (HRI) knows where the money is. The group is a not-for-profit organization that helps the New York State Department of Health and its affiliated Roswell Park Cancer Institute solicit, evaluate, and administer financial support. Sources of that support come from federal and state government sources, other non-profits, and businesses. HRI's Technology Transfer office also assists the Department of Health in sharing its research findings with other public and private institutions and finding ways to create biomedical technologies through private sector development. HRI was founded in 1953 and has administered $7 billion over its lifetime.

	Annual Growth	03/13	03/14	03/15	03/20	03/22
Sales ($mil.)	8.3%	–	703.4	677.9	1,326.5	1,331.8
Net income ($ mil.)	15.1%	–	13.5	22.6	506.2	41.8
Market value ($ mil.)	–	–	–	–	–	–
Employees	–	–	–	–	–	1,400

HEALTHCARE DISTRIBUTION ALLIANCE

901 N GLEBE RD STE 1000
ARLINGTON, VA 222031854
Phone: 703 787-0000
Fax: –
Web: www.hda.org

CEO: John M Gray
CFO: –
HR: –
FYE: December 31
Type: Private

The Healthcare Distribution Management Association (HDMA) helps the medicine get where it's needed. HDMA is a trade association representing healthcare and pharmaceutical products distributors. Its members include hundreds of manufacturers and some 70 distributors, as well as numerous service providers that deliver to pharmacies, hospitals, nursing homes, and health clinics. The organization provides opportunities for members to share industry best practices, represents member concerns before Congress and regulatory agencies, and publishes newsletters and state by state information sheets for members.

HEALTHCARE SERVICES GROUP, INC.

3220 Tillman Drive, Suite 300
Bensalem, PA 19020
Phone: 215 639-4274
Fax: –
Web: www.hcsgcorp.com

NMS: HCSG
CEO: –
CFO: –
HR: –
FYE: December 31
Type: Public

Healthcare Services Group provides management, administrative and operating expertise and services to the housekeeping, laundry, linen, facility maintenance and dietary service departments of healthcare facilities, including nursing homes, retirement complexes, rehabilitation centers and hospitals located throughout the US. The company's dietary services purchase food and prepare meals for residents and monitor nutritional needs in more than 1,500 facilities. Healthcare Services Group also tidies up more than 3,000 facilities, mostly primarily providers of long-term care, many of which rely on Medicare, Medicaid, and third-party payors' reimbursement funds. Healthcare Services Group was established in 1976. All revenues are earned in the US.

	Annual Growth	12/19	12/20	12/21	12/22	12/23
Sales ($mil.)	(2.4%)	1,840.8	1,760.3	1,642.0	1,690.2	1,671.4
Net income ($ mil.)	(12.2%)	64.6	98.7	45.9	34.6	38.4
Market value ($ mil.)	(19.2%)	1,783.7	2,060.9	1,304.7	880.1	760.5
Employees	(10.0%)	51,000	44,200	39,200	35,700	33,400

HEALTHEAST DIVERSIFIED SERVICES, INC.

559 CAPITOL BLVD
SAINT PAUL, MN 551032101
Phone: 651 232-2300
Fax: –
Web: –

CEO: James Hereford
CFO: –
HR: Dianne Hahn
FYE: August 31
Type: Private

Having twins in the Twin Cities? Head to HealthEast. HealthEast Care System operates a number of hospitals and other health care facilities throughout the St. Paul, Minnesota metro area. Its hospitals include three general acute care facilities -- St. John's Hospital with about 185 beds; St. Joseph's Hospital with more than 400 beds; Woodwinds Health Campus, an 85-bed facility run in partnership with Children's Hospitals and Clinics of Minnesota. A fourth hospital, Bethesda Hospital, provides long term acute care. HealthEast Care System also features a number of primary care and specialty clinics located throughout its service area, as well as home health and community health care programs. In mid-2017 HealthEast merged with Fairview Health Services.

HEALTHEAST ST JOHN'S HOSPITAL

1575 BEAM AVE
SAINT PAUL, MN 551091126
Phone: 651 232-7000
Fax: –
Web: –

CEO: –
CFO: –
HR: –
FYE: December 31
Type: Private

St. John's Hospital provides health care to folks residing the suburbs of the Twin Cities. The hospital has about 185 beds and is an acute-care facility with emergency, inpatient, and outpatient medicine departments. Its facilities include specialty centers for breast care, cancer care, heart health, maternity services, and orthopedics, among other offerings. St. John's started in 1910 with a private home that was converted into a 25-bed hospital. St. John's Hospital is part of the HealthEast Care System, which includes other hospitals and health centers in the Minneapolis/St. Paul metropolitan area.

	Annual Growth	08/08	08/09*	12/18	12/19	12/20
Sales ($mil.)	(0.2%)	–	252.1	–	–	247.5
Net income ($ mil.)	–	–	18.6	–	–	(4.6)
Market value ($ mil.)	–	–	–	–	–	–
Employees	–	–	–	–	–	713

*Fiscal year change

HEALTHEQUITY INC

NMS: HQY

15 West Scenic Pointe Drive, Suite 100
Draper, UT 84020
Phone: 801 727-1000
Fax: –
Web: www.healthequity.com

CEO: Jon Kessler
CFO: Tyson Murdock
HR: –
FYE: January 31
Type: Public

HealthEquity is a leader and an innovator in providing technology-enabled services that empower consumers to make healthcare saving and spending decisions. The company's platform allows consumers to access their healthcare savings accounts, compare treatment options and pricing, evaluate and pay healthcare bills, receive personalized benefit and clinical information, earn wellness incentives, and make educated investment choices to grow their healthcare savings. HealthEquity can integrate with any healthcare plan or banking institution. The company's sole geographic market is the US.

	Annual Growth	01/20	01/21	01/22	01/23	01/24
Sales ($mil.)	17.1%	532.0	733.6	756.6	861.7	999.6
Net income ($ mil.)	8.9%	39.7	8.8	(44.3)	(26.1)	55.7
Market value ($ mil.)	3.4%	5,689.5	7,195.9	4,602.6	5,240.8	6,509.5
Employees	1.8%	2,931	3,039	3,715	3,208	3,150

HEALTHFIRST, INC.

100 CHURCH ST
NEW YORK, NY 100072601
Phone: 212 801-6000
Fax: –
Web: www.healthfirst.org

CEO: Pat Wang
CFO: John J Bermel
HR: –
FYE: December 31
Type: Private

If you want to be first in your field, it helps if your owners are first in theirs. Owned by some of the most prestigious hospitals in the region, Healthfirst might just have a leg-up on other health care management organizations. The not-for-profit has about 500,000 members throughout New York City, Long Island, and northern New Jersey. It offers government-sponsored health insurance programs, including Medicaid, Medicare, Family Health Plus, and Child Health Plus plans, to low-income and special needs clients. It also offers commercial HMO and point-of-service plans to individuals and small employer groups. Healthfirst was formed in 1993; its plans are administered by HF Management Services.

	Annual Growth	12/03	12/04	12/05	12/13	12/14
Assets ($mil.)	(4.3%)	–	–	269.8	181.1	181.1
Net income ($ mil.)	17.0%	–	–	8.7	32.8	35.8
Market value ($ mil.)	–	–	–	–	–	–
Employees	–	–	–	–	–	2

HEALTHPEAK PROPERTIES INC

NYS: DOC

4600 South Syracuse Street, Suite 500
Denver, CO 80237
Phone: 720 428-5050
Fax: 562 733-5200
Web: www.healthpeak.com

CEO: Scott M Brinker
CFO: Peter A Scott
HR: Jeanette Mungcal
FYE: December 31
Type: Public

Healthpeak Properties (formerly HCP, Inc.) is a self-administered real estate investment trust (REIT) that invests in, acquires, develops, owns, leases, and manages healthcare real estate across the US. Its real estate portfolio consists of lab and office space for biopharma and medical device companies, and medical office buildings. Healthpeak consolidated portfolio of investment consisted of interest in some 480 properties. The company was founded in 1985.

	Annual Growth	12/19	12/20	12/21	12/22	12/23
Sales ($mil.)	2.2%	1,997.4	1,644.9	1,896.2	2,061.2	2,181.0
Net income ($ mil.)	61.0%	45.5	413.6	505.5	500.4	306.0
Market value ($ mil.)	(12.9%)	18,860	16,541	19,747	13,717	10,834
Employees	(1.4%)	204	217	196	199	193

HEALTHPLAN HOLDINGS, INC.

4110 GEORGE RD STE 200
TAMPA, FL 336347411
Phone: 813 289-1000
Fax: –
Web: www.healthplan.com

CEO: –
CFO: –
HR: –
FYE: January 31
Type: Private

HealthPlan Holdings is the wind beneath the wings of health insurers across the US. The company, through its subsidiaries, is a third-party administrator of health plans; it processes claims, supports sales and distribution operations, and provides enrollment, customer service, and billing services for some 2 million consumers belonging to health plans offered by the likes of CIGNA and Humana. The firm's HealthPlan Services subsidiary primarily serves insurers in the small business, individual, and voluntary markets, and its American Benefit Plan Administrators unit caters to union trust benefit plans. Outsourcing firm Wipro is buying HealthPlan from private equity firm Water Street Healthcare Partners.

HEALTHSPAN INTEGRATED CARE

1701 MERCY HEALTH PL
CINCINNATI, OH 452376147
Phone: 216 621-5600
Fax: –
Web: www.payhealthspan.com

CEO: George Halverson
CFO: Thomas Revis
HR: –
FYE: December 31
Type: Private

Kaiser Foundation Health Plan of Ohio is a subsidiary of the Kaiser Foundation Health Plan and provides health care services to nearly 150,000 people at 10 medical facilities in the Akron and Cleveland metropolitan areas. It offers specialized services at The Cleveland Clinic, Lake Hospital System, and Summa Health System. More than 3,000 businesses offer their employees access to the company's health plans and care from more than 3,000 physicians in the network. Kaiser Foundation Health Plans have an integrated care model, offering both hospital and physician care through a network of hospitals and physician practices operating under the Kaiser name in 9 states and the District of Columbia.

	Annual Growth	12/10	12/11	12/12	12/13	12/14
Assets ($mil.)	(40.6%)	–	–	–	271.1	161.1
Net income ($ mil.)	–	–	–	–	(84.4)	(42.2)
Market value ($ mil.)	–	–	–	–	–	–
Employees	–	–	–	–	–	1,240

HEALTHSTREAM INC

NMS: HSTM

500 11th Avenue North, Suite 1000
Nashville, TN 37203
Phone: 615 301-3100
Fax: –
Web: www.healthstream.com

CEO: Robert A Frist Jr
CFO: Scott A Roberts
HR: –
FYE: December 31
Type: Public

HealthStream, Inc. is a leading healthcare technology platform for workforce solutions. The company provides primarily SaaS based applications for healthcare organizations?all designed to improve business and clinical outcomes by supporting the people who deliver patient care. It is focused on helping healthcare organizations meet their ongoing clinical development, talent management, training, education, assessment, competency management, safety and compliance, scheduling, and provider credentialing, privileging, and enrollment needs. The company was founded in 1999.

	Annual Growth	12/19	12/20	12/21	12/22	12/23
Sales ($mil.)	2.4%	254.1	244.8	256.7	266.8	279.1
Net income ($ mil.)	(0.9%)	15.8	14.1	5.8	12.1	15.2
Market value ($ mil.)	(0.2%)	824.1	661.7	798.7	752.6	819.0
Employees	5.7%	876	1,069	1,101	1,154	1,092

HEALTHWAREHOUSE.COM, INC.

NBB: HEWA

7107 Industrial Road
Florence, KY 41042
Phone: 800 748-7001
Fax: –
Web: www.healthwarehouse.com

CEO: Joseph Peters
CFO: –
HR: –
FYE: December 31
Type: Public

HealthWarehouse.com sells over-the-counter in more than one way. The online pharmacy sells prescription and over-the-counter drugs to more than 160,000 customers. It sources its products from suppliers including Masters Pharmaceutical and The Harvard Drug Group. HealthWarehouse went public through a reverse merger with OTC-traded Clacendix in 2009. Clacendix provided products that protected enterprise data and networks from security threats. Faced with declining sales and mounting losses, Clacendix sold its assets to API Cryptek for $3.2 million in 2008. Clacendix later merged with HealthWarehouse and changed its name in 2009. HealthWarehouse purchased the online assets of Hocks Pharmacy in 2011.

	Annual Growth	12/18	12/19	12/20	12/21	12/22
Sales ($mil.)	3.6%	15.7	15.8	17.2	16.1	18.1
Net income ($ mil.)	–	(0.8)	(0.1)	0.6	(0.6)	(1.0)
Market value ($ mil.)	(9.4%)	14.8	10.0	8.1	8.1	10.0
Employees	–	–	–	110	104	121

HEALTHY MOTHERS HEALTHY BABIES INC

4401 FORD AVE STE 300
ALEXANDRIA, VA 223021472
Phone: 703 837-4792
Fax: –
Web: www.cfah.org

CEO: Janice Frey-Angel
CFO: –
HR: –
FYE: December 31
Type: Private

The Healthy Mothers, Healthy Babies Coalition (HMHB) promotes maternal and infant health through a network of some 90 Healthy Mothers, Healthy Babies state and local coalitions and about 100 organizational members. HMHB's focuses include maternal and infant health, child and adolescent health, and family and community health. It encourages pregnant women to seek early care, eat well, avoid drugs and alcohol, and to breast feed their babies. The organization was founded in 1981 by the American Academy of Pediatrics, the American College of Obstetricians and Gynecologists, the American Nurses Association, the March of Dimes, the National Congress of Parents and Teachers, and the US Public Health Service.

	Annual Growth	12/07	12/08	12/12	12/13	12/14
Sales ($mil.)	58.9%	–	0.2	3.6	3.5	3.3
Net income ($ mil.)	–	–	(0.1)	0.0	(0.1)	0.1
Market value ($ mil.)	–	–	–	–	–	–
Employees	–	–	–	–	–	11

HEARST, WILLIAM RANDOLPH FOUNDATION

300 W 57TH ST FL 26
NEW YORK, NY 100193741
Phone: 212 586-5404
Fax: –
Web: www.hearstfdn.org

CEO: –
CFO: –
HR: –
FYE: December 31
Type: Private

The William Randolph Hearst Foundation is one of two foundations (the other being The Hearst Foundation) created by their namesake, publisher William Randolph Hearst. The William Randolph Hearst Foundation was established in 1948 as the California Charities Foundation and changed its name in 1951. Both foundations share a headquarters in New York, but the two entities divide the US in half to organize giving activities: The Hearst Foundation receives any grant requests or proposals made from organizations east of the Mississippi, and the former California Charities Foundation takes any applications from the western US. Philanthropic interests include culture, education, health, and social service.

	Annual Growth	12/95	12/96	12/97	12/98	12/14
Sales ($mil.)	6.2%	–	–	–	18.1	47.1
Net income ($ mil.)	–	–	–	–	(5.8)	13.3
Market value ($ mil.)	–	–	–	–	–	–
Employees	–	–	–	–	–	32

HEARTHSTONE UTILITIES, INC.

184 SHUMAN BLVD STE 300
NAPERVILLE, IL 605638420
Phone: 844 488-0530
Fax: –
Web: www.hearthstonecompany.com

CEO: Gregory J Osborne
CFO: James Sprague
HR: –
FYE: December 31
Type: Private

Gas Natural (formerly Energy Inc.) does what comes naturally -- it distributes, markets, transports, and produces natural gas. Its Energy West, Inc., unit has natural gas distribution operations in Maine, Montana, North Carolina, and Wyoming. Gas Natural also owns Orwell Natural Gas and Northeast Ohio Natural Gas which distribute gas in Ohio and Pennsylvania. All told, Gas Natural serves about 63,500 customers. The company's energy marketing subsidiary, Energy West Resources, primarily sells natural gas and power to customers in Maine, Montana, North Carolina, and Wyoming. It owns the Shoshone interstate and the Glacier gathering natural gas pipelines in Montana and Wyoming. It also has stakes in 160 gas wells.

HEARTLAND CO-OP

2829 WESTOWN PKWY STE 350
WEST DES MOINES, IA 502661340
Phone: 515 225-1334
Fax: –
Web: www.heartlandcoop.com

CEO: –
CFO: –
HR: Craig Mommer
FYE: June 30
Type: Private

Heartland Co-op has no need to go against the grain. The cooperative offers agricultural products and services for its central Iowa member/farmers. Heartland operates more than 50 grain elevators and service centers. It offers agronomy products and services, such as seed treatments and alfalfa fertilization; grain drying, storage, and merchandising; petroleum products for farm vehicles and home heating; livestock and pet feed; and personal and crop credit and financing. Headquartered in West Des Moines, Heartland was formed in 1987 when cooperatives in Dallas Center, Minburn, and Panora merged. Heartland, which has grown to more than 5,400-members, merged with Farm Service Company of Council Bluffs in 2013.

	Annual Growth	06/15	06/16	06/17	06/18	06/19
Sales ($mil.)	0.5%	–	854.4	932.4	901.7	867.6
Net income ($ mil.)	3.5%	–	16.0	17.9	20.1	17.7
Market value ($ mil.)	–	–	–	–	–	–
Employees	–	–	–	–	–	678

HEARTLAND EXPRESS, INC.

NMS: HTLD

901 Heartland Way
North Liberty, IA 52317
Phone: 319 645-7060
Fax: –
Web: www.heartlandexpress.com

CEO: Michael J Gerdin
CFO: Christopher A Strain
HR: Dave Dalmasso
FYE: December 31
Type: Public

Heartland Express primarily provides nationwide asset-based dry van truckload service for major shippers across the US, along with cross-border freight and other transportation services offered through third party partnerships in Mexico. The company operates about 35 terminal facilities throughout the contiguous US and one in Mexico, which are strategically located to concentrate on regional freight movements generally within a 500-mile radius of the terminals. Heartland customers represent primarily the consumer goods, appliances, food products, and automotive industries. Almost all of its operating revenue is derived from shipments within the US.

	Annual Growth	12/19	12/20	12/21	12/22	12/23
Sales ($mil.)	19.3%	596.8	645.3	607.3	968.0	1,207.5
Net income ($ mil.)	(32.9%)	73.0	70.8	79.3	133.6	14.8
Market value ($ mil.)	(9.3%)	1,663.8	1,430.6	1,329.4	1,212.5	1,127.1
Employees	–	–	4,050	3,780	3,180	4,710

HEARTLAND FINANCIAL USA, INC. (DUBUQUE, IA)

NMS: HTLF

1800 Larimer Street, Suite 1800
Denver, CO 80202
Phone: 303 285-9200
Fax: 563 589-2011
Web: www.htlf.com

CEO: Bruce K Lee
CFO: Bryan R McKeag
HR: Jennifer Smith
FYE: December 31
Type: Public

Founded in 1981, Heartland Financial USA (HTLF) is a $20.2 billion multi-bank holding company that owns flagship subsidiary Dubuque Bank and Trust (Iowa) and ten other banks that together operate over 130 branches in about a dozen states, primarily in the West and Midwest. In addition to the standard deposit, loan, and mortgage services, the banks also offer retirement, wealth management, insurance, and investment services. HTFL's principal services are FDIC-insured deposit accounts and related services, and loans to businesses and consumers. The loans consist primarily of commercial and industrial, owner-occupied commercial real estate, non-owner occupied commercial real estate, real estate construction, agricultural and agricultural real estate, residential real estate and consumer loans.

	Annual Growth	12/19	12/20	12/21	12/22	12/23
Assets ($mil.)	10.1%	13,210	17,908	19,275	20,244	19,412
Net income ($ mil.)	(14.4%)	149.1	137.9	219.9	212.2	79.9
Market value ($ mil.)	(6.7%)	2,123.3	1,723.3	2,160.4	1,990.1	1,605.5
Employees	0.8%	1,908	2,013	2,249	2,002	1,970

HEARTLAND PAYMENT SYSTEMS, LLC

10 GLENLAKE PKWY STE 324
ATLANTA, GA 303283495
Phone: 609 683-3831
Fax: –
Web: www.heartlandpaymentsystems.com

CEO: –
CFO: –
HR: –
FYE: December 31
Type: Private

Heartland Payment Systems (HPS), a wholly owned subsidiary of Global Payments Inc., is one of the largest payment processors in the US that delivers credit, debit, and prepaid card processing and security technology. Its client list includes restaurants, retailers, convenience stores, and professional service providers. The pioneer in modern payment processing is trusted by more than 750,000 customers to provide the financial technology to make money, move money, manage employees, and engage their customers. Other markets for the firm include K-12 school nutrition programs and payment processing for colleges and universities. Global Payments bought Heartland for $4.3 billion in 2016.

	Annual Growth	12/11	12/12	12/13	12/14	12/15
Sales ($mil.)	10.0%	–	2,013.4	2,135.4	2,311.4	2,682.4
Net income ($ mil.)	8.4%	–	66.5	78.1	31.9	84.7
Market value ($ mil.)	–	–	–	–	–	–
Employees	–	–	–	–	–	3,734

HEARTLAND REGIONAL MEDICAL CENTER

5325 FARAON ST
SAINT JOSEPH, MO 645063488
Phone: 816 271-6000
Fax: –
Web: www.mymlc.com

CEO: Mike Poore
CFO: –
HR: –
FYE: June 30
Type: Private

Heartland Regional Medical Center strives for healthy hearts, minds, and bodies in the US heartland. The acute care hospital, a subsidiary of Heartland Health, provides medical services to residents of St. Joseph, Missouri, and some 20 surrounding counties in northwest Missouri, southeast Nebraska, and northeast Kansas. Heartland Regional Medical Center encompasses specialty centers for trauma and long-term care, acute rehabilitation, cancer, heart disease, and birthing. As part of the services provided by the medical center, Heartland Regional Medical Center offers services such as arthritis, pain, and wound treatments, as well as home health and hospice care.

	Annual Growth	06/18	06/19	06/20	06/21	06/22
Sales ($mil.)	3.2%	–	645.9	714.3	672.9	710.4
Net income ($ mil.)	(25.2%)	–	38.3	84.3	47.6	16.0
Market value ($ mil.)	–	–	–	–	–	–
Employees	–	–	–	–	–	4,000

HEARTWARE INTERNATIONAL, INC.

500 OLD CONNECTICUT PATH
FRAMINGHAM, MA 017014574
Phone: 508 739-0950
Fax: –
Web: www.heartware.com

CEO: Douglas Godshall
CFO: Peter F McAree
HR: –
FYE: December 31
Type: Private

HeartWare International makes hardware for your heart. The firm's proprietary heart pump is an implantable device designed for patients suffering from advanced-stage heart failure. The pump, branded as HVAD (for HeartWare Ventricular Assist System), is used for people who can't undergo a heart transplant or who are on a waiting list for a heart to become available. The HVAD is small, fits above the diaphragm (not the abdomen, like other VADs, which makes it less invasive) and can generate up to 10 liters of blood flow per minute. HeartWare is a development-stage company; the HVAD is approved for sale in Europe and Australia. Medical device maker Medtronic acquired HeartWare for $1.1 billion in 2016.

HECLA MINING CO
NYS: HL

6500 Mineral Drive, Suite 200
Coeur d'Alene, ID 83815-9408
Phone: 208 769-4100
Fax: –
Web: www.hecla-mining.com

CEO: Phillips S Baker Jr
CFO: –
HR: –
FYE: December 31
Type: Public

Hecla Mining discovers, acquires and develops mines and other mineral interests and produce and market concentrates containing silver, gold (in the case of Greens Creek), lead and zinc; carbon material containing silver and gold; and unrefined dor containing silver and gold. In 2022, the mining and natural resource exploration company produced approximately 3.1 million ounces of silver, 7,580 ounces of gold, 18.6 million pounds of zinc, and 12 million pounds of lead. Hecla's Greens Creek is located in Alaska, the Lucky Friday is in Idaho, Keno Hill is in Canada's Yukon Teritorry, Casa Berardi is in Quebec, Canada, and the Nevada Operations is located in northern Nevada. Majority of the company's sales were generated outside the US.

	Annual Growth	12/19	12/20	12/21	12/22	12/23
Sales ($mil.)	1.7%	673.3	691.9	807.5	718.9	720.2
Net income ($ mil.)	–	(99.6)	(16.8)	35.1	(37.3)	(84.2)
Market value ($ mil.)	9.1%	2,088.6	3,992.4	3,216.1	3,425.6	2,963.5
Employees	2.3%	1,622	1,600	1,650	1,850	1,775

HEICO CORP
NYS: HEI

3000 Taft Street
Hollywood, FL 33021
Phone: 954 987-4000
Fax: –
Web: –

CEO: Laurans A Mendelson
CFO: Carlos L Macau
HR: –
FYE: October 31
Type: Public

HEICO Corporation is one of the world's largest providers of a jet engine and aircraft replacement parts. Its Flight Support Group makes FAA-approved replacement parts for jet engines that can be substituted for original parts, including fuel pumps, generators, fuel controls, pneumatic valves, starters and actuators, turbo compressors, and hydraulic pumps, among others. Flight Support also repairs, overhauls, and distributes jet engine parts as well as avionics and instruments for commercial air carriers. HEICO's second segment, Electronic Technologies Group, makes a variety of electronic equipment for the aerospace/defense, electronic, medical, and telecommunications industries. The company generates about 65% of revenue in the US.

	Annual Growth	10/19	10/20	10/21	10/22	10/23
Sales ($mil.)	9.6%	2,055.6	1,787.0	1,865.7	2,208.3	2,968.1
Net income ($ mil.)	5.3%	327.9	314.0	304.2	351.7	403.6
Market value ($ mil.)	6.5%	17,049	14,521	19,268	22,481	21,897
Employees	12.9%	5,900	5,200	5,600	6,500	9,600

HEIDRICK & STRUGGLES INTERNATIONAL, INC.
NMS: HSII

233 South Wacker Drive, Suite 4900
Chicago, IL 60606-6303
Phone: 312 496-1200
Fax: –
Web: www.heidrick.com

CEO: Krishnan Rajagopalan
CFO: Mark Harris
HR: Diana Su
FYE: December 31
Type: Public

Heidrick & Struggles International is a human capital leadership advisory firm providing executive search, consulting, and on-demand talent services to businesses and business leaders worldwide by helping them to improve the effectiveness of their leadership teams. The company has about 55 offices in about 30 countries that serves middle market and emerging growth companies, major US and non-US companies, governmental, higher education and not-for-profit organizations, Fortune 1000 companies, and other leading private and public entities. The company's fees are generally equal to approximately one-third of the estimated first-year compensation for the position to be filled. Americas generate some 55% of the company's total revenue.

	Annual Growth	12/19	12/20	12/21	12/22	12/23
Sales ($mil.)	9.4%	725.6	629.4	1,008.5	1,083.6	1,041.2
Net income ($ mil.)	3.8%	46.9	(37.7)	72.6	79.5	54.4
Market value ($ mil.)	(2.4%)	654.0	591.2	880.0	562.8	594.2
Employees	5.6%	1,780	1,563	1,846	2,141	2,212

HEIFER PROJECT INTERNATIONAL INC

1 WORLD AVE
LITTLE ROCK, AR 722023825
Phone: 501 907-2600
Fax: –
Web: www.heifer.org

CEO: Pierre Ferrari
CFO: Robert B Bloom
HR: Julie Wood
FYE: June 30
Type: Private

It's not just a handout; it's a new way of life. Heifer Project International (known as Heifer International) runs more than 925 projects that help millions of impoverished families become self-sufficient. Current recipients are located in more than 50 countries around the world, including about 28 US states. The non-profit organization provides more than 25 different kinds of breeding livestock and other animals (bees, rabbits, ducks) that can be used for food, income, or plowing power, in addition to training in sustainable agriculture techniques. In exchange, the family agrees to pass on not only the animals' first female offspring to another needy family, but their knowledge, too.

	Annual Growth	06/13	06/14	06/15	06/16	06/18
Sales ($mil.)	1.6%	–	–	125.3	114.3	131.3
Net income ($ mil.)	–	–	–	(0.3)	(9.0)	10.0
Market value ($ mil.)	–	–	–	–	–	–
Employees	–	–	–	–	–	304

HELEN KELLER INTERNATIONAL

1 DAG HAMMARSKJOLD PLZ FL 2
NEW YORK, NY 100172208
Phone: 212 532-0544
Fax: –
Web: www.helenkellerintl.org

CEO: Kathy Spahn
CFO: Elspeth Taylor
HR: Nancy Prail
FYE: June 30
Type: Private

Helen Keller International (HKI) has vision. The organization fights blindness by working with doctors, government agencies, partner groups, and individuals in 22 countries, citing that 80% of all blindness is avoidable. Its core areas of focus are eye health, overall health and nutrition, and poverty reduction. HKI distributes antibiotics, performs cataract surgery, and provides eye screenings, glasses, and education. The group works to combat malnutrition by promoting prenatal care, supplying Vitamin A, and helping others set up sustainable gardens and nutrition programs. It aims to reduce poverty through projects for literacy, pre-school, and clean water, and offers entrepreneurial support for women.

	Annual Growth	06/14	06/15	06/16	06/20	06/22
Sales ($mil.)	7.7%	–	72.1	69.2	81.8	121.1
Net income ($ mil.)	16.7%	–	9.8	(0.3)	9.2	29.0
Market value ($ mil.)	–	–	–	–	–	–
Employees	–	–	–	–	–	1,022

HELENA AGRI-ENTERPRISES, LLC

225 SCHILLING BLVD
COLLIERVILLE, TN 380177177
Phone: 901 761-0050
Fax: –
Web: www.helenaagri.com

CEO: Eric Cowling
CFO: –
HR: –
FYE: March 31
Type: Private

Call it cops for crops, if you will: Helena Chemical's mission is to protect and serve. The product line of the company, the agricultural products division of Japanese business group Marubeni's US subsidiary Marubeni America, is split into two units: Crop Protection and Crop Production. It produces agricultural chemicals, seeds, and fertilizers. Helena Chemical has four toll manufacturing sites -- in Arkansas, California, Georgia, and Iowa -- and sales, marketing, and distribution locations throughout the US. Ancillary product lines and services include forestry, aquatic, and vegetation management.

HELIOS & MATHESON ANALYTICS INC — NBB: HMNY

Empire State Building, 350 Fifth Avenue
New York, NY 10118
Phone: 212 979-8228
Fax: –
Web: www.hmny.com

CEO: –
CFO: –
HR: –
FYE: December 31
Type: Public

Helios & Matheson Analytics Inc. (formerly Helios & Matheson Information Technology Inc.) is a source (or outsource) of IT services. The company provides database management, project management, network design and implementation, application development, and Web enablement and related e-business services. The company also markets and distributes third-party software products. HMNA primarily serves global corporations and larger organizations in the financial services banking, insurance, and pharmaceutical industries. The company is controlled by India-based Helios & Matheson Information Technology Ltd.

	Annual Growth	12/13	12/14	12/15	12/16	12/17
Sales ($mil.)	(5.9%)	13.3	10.6	9.7	6.8	10.4
Net income ($ mil.)	–	0.4	(0.2)	(2.1)	(7.4)	(146.0)
Market value ($ mil.)	2.4%	137.9	48.0	33.3	79.1	151.3
Employees	12.7%	44	32	20	34	71

HELIOS TECHNOLOGIES INC — NYS: HLIO

7456 16th St. E.
Sarasota, FL 34243
Phone: 941 362-1200
Fax: –
Web: www.sunhydraulics.com

CEO: Josef Matosevic
CFO: –
HR: –
FYE: December 30
Type: Public

Helios Technologies is a global leader in highly engineered motion control and electronic controls technology for diverse end markets, including construction, material handling, agriculture, energy, recreational vehicles, marine, health, and wellness. The Hydraulics segment includes products sold under the Sun Hydraulics, Faster, Custom Fluidpower, Seungwon, NEM, Taimi, Daman, and Schultes brands. The Electronics segment includes products sold under the novation Controls, Murphy, Zero Off, HCT, Balboa Water Group, and Joyonway brands. Products are sold through value-add distributors, OEMs, and system integrators. The Americas represents almost 55% of its sales.

	Annual Growth	12/19*	01/21	01/22*	12/22	12/23
Sales ($mil.)	10.8%	554.7	523.0	869.2	885.4	835.6
Net income ($ mil.)	(11.2%)	60.3	14.2	104.6	98.4	37.5
Market value ($ mil.)	(0.1%)	1,506.1	1,763.9	3,481.1	1,802.0	1,501.1
Employees	8.3%	1,960	2,000	2,350	2,400	2,700

*Fiscal year change

HELIX BIOMEDIX INC — NBB: HXBM

22121 17th Avenue SE, Suite 112
Bothell, WA 98021
Phone: 425 402-8400
Fax: –
Web: www.helixbiomedix.com

CEO: R S Beatty
CFO: –
HR: –
FYE: December 31
Type: Public

Helix BioMedix wants to remove wrinkles and acne without leaving red, itchy skin. The company has a library of bioactive peptides with antimicrobial properties it hopes to exploit as it works to formulate wrinkle- and acne-fighting creams, along with topical treatments for skin and wound infections. The firm also hopes to use its peptides to develop a treatment that will speed the healing of wounds with minimal scarring, as well as to prevent drug resistant staph infections. Helix is looking to partner with large, better-funded drugmakers to develop some of its product candidates. The company also licenses its peptides to consumer products makers.

	Annual Growth	12/07	12/08	12/09	12/10	12/11
Sales ($mil.)	42.1%	0.5	0.6	0.4	0.9	1.9
Net income ($ mil.)	–	(3.4)	(4.5)	(3.8)	(7.7)	(2.5)
Market value ($ mil.)	(15.9%)	0.0	0.0	0.0	0.0	0.0
Employees	–	8	6	7	8	8

HELIX ENERGY SOLUTIONS GROUP INC — NYS: HLX

3505 West Sam Houston Parkway North, Suite 400
Houston, TX 77043
Phone: 281 618-0400
Fax: 281 618-0500
Web: www.helixesg.com

CEO: –
CFO: –
HR: –
FYE: December 31
Type: Public

Helix Energy Solutions Group, Inc. is an international offshore energy company that provides specialty services to the offshore energy industry, with a focus on its growing well intervention and robotics operations. Its services are centered on a three-legged business model well positioned to facilitate global energy transition by maximizing production of remaining oil and gas reserves, supporting renewable energy developments and decommissioning end-of-life oil and gas fields. Its well intervention unit primarily works in water depths ranging from 100 to 10,000 feet. The company makes use of remotely operated vehicles (ROV's) that support vessels under term charters as well as spot vessels as needed. About 50% of the company's total revenue comes from the US.

	Annual Growth	12/19	12/20	12/21	12/22	12/23
Sales ($mil.)	14.4%	751.9	733.6	674.7	873.1	1,289.7
Net income ($ mil.)	–	57.9	22.2	(61.5)	(87.8)	(10.8)
Market value ($ mil.)	1.6%	1,466.6	639.6	475.1	1,123.9	1,565.6
Employees	11.3%	1,650	1,536	1,327	2,280	2,531

HELMERICH & PAYNE, INC. — NYS: HP

1437 South Boulder Avenue, Suite 1400
Tulsa, OK 74119
Phone: 918 742-5531
Fax: 918 742-0237
Web: www.hpinc.com

CEO: John W Lindsay
CFO: Mark W Smith
HR: –
FYE: September 30
Type: Public

Contract driller Helmerich & Payne (H&P) deploys its fleet of over 410 rigs, mostly on the US mainland but also internationally and at sea. It is the largest provider of super-spec AC drive land rigs in the Western Hemisphere and had twelve land rigs contracted for work in locations outside of the US. One of H&P's key competitive strengths is its FlexRigs, its proprietary drilling platforms, which have evolved and taken on new technology over the years. Besides drilling, H&P has ancillary real estate operations, including a shopping center and office buildings in Tulsa.

	Annual Growth	09/19	09/20	09/21	09/22	09/23
Sales ($mil.)	0.7%	2,798.5	1,773.9	1,218.6	2,058.9	2,872.4
Net income ($ mil.)	–	(33.7)	(494.5)	(326.2)	7.0	434.1
Market value ($ mil.)	1.3%	3,984.0	1,456.6	2,725.3	3,675.8	4,191.8
Employees	(7.6%)	8,510	4,138	5,932	8,000	6,200

HELMSMAN MANAGEMENT SERVICES LLC

175 BERKELEY ST
BOSTON, MA 021165066
Phone: 857 224-1970
Fax: –
Web: www.helmsmantpa.com

CEO: –
CFO: –
HR: –
FYE: December 31
Type: Private

Helmsman Management Services helps businesses steer clear of risk. The third-party administrator provides risk management programs in the alternative risk marketplace for more than 300 clients across the US. The company's services, which are provided on a state, regional, or national basis, include claims management, litigation management, loss prevention, managed care and occupational health services, medical bill review, and utilization review. Helmsman Management Services is part of the Boston-based Liberty Mutual Insurance group. It utilizes Liberty Mutual's national network of claims and loss prevention specialists.

	Annual Growth	12/00	12/01	12/02	12/03	12/10
Assets ($mil.)	7.0%	–	–	–	74.6	119.9
Net income ($ mil.)	7.5%	–	–	–	3.8	6.3
Market value ($ mil.)	–	–	–	–	–	–
Employees	–	–	–	–	–	400

HEMAGEN DIAGNOSTICS INC

NBB: HMGN

9033 Red Branch Road
Columbia, MD 21045
Phone: 443 367-5500
Fax: –
Web: www.hemagen.com

CEO: William P Hales
CFO: M R Campbell
HR: –
FYE: September 30
Type: Public

Hemagen Diagnostics lets no disease go undetected. The company makes diagnostic kits and related components. Its Virgo product line is used to identify infectious and autoimmune diseases such as rheumatoid arthritis, lupus, measles, and syphilis. Physicians and veterinarians use its Analyst reagent system and related components to test blood for substances like cholesterol, glucose, and triglycerides. Hemagen sells products internationally primarily through distributors; its Brazilian subsidiary markets its products in South America.

	Annual Growth	09/08	09/09	09/10	09/11	09/12
Sales ($mil.)	(10.8%)	6.4	5.4	5.2	5.1	4.0
Net income ($ mil.)	–	0.4	(0.8)	(0.2)	(0.9)	(0.9)
Market value ($ mil.)	(26.5%)	1.9	1.2	0.9	0.5	0.5
Employees	(14.7%)	34	25	29	31	18

HENDRICK SOUTHWESTERN HEALTH DEVELOPMENT CORPORATION

1900 PINE ST
ABILENE, TX 796012432
Phone: 817 532-3032
Fax: –
Web: www.hendrickhealth.org

CEO: –
CFO: –
HR: –
FYE: August 31
Type: Private

Serving more than 20 counties in midwestern Texas, Hendrick Health System operates Hendrick Medical Center, which has some 500 beds. Specialty services include heart care, home health, respiratory care, and trauma services. The medical center also provides a women's center, a hospice program, and a center for rehabilitation. The company is expanding its children's hospital, birthing center, sterile processing area, and surgical services. The Hendrick Health System, which is affiliated with the Baptist General Convention of Texas, was founded in 1924.

HENRICKSEN & COMPANY, INC.

1101 W THORNDALE AVE
ITASCA, IL 601431334
Phone: 630 250-9090
Fax: –
Web: www.henricksen.com

CEO: –
CFO: Tim Osborn
HR: Kristen Vergiels
FYE: April 30
Type: Private

Henricksen is a full-service contract furniture dealership specializing in office, healthcare, education, government, senior living, and hospitality spaces. With more than 500 major and specialty manufacturing partners, Henricksen's offers an array of products from systems furniture, case goods, seating, lounge, and conference furnishings to architectural solutions including modular walls, flooring, lighting, sound masking, and technology equipment. Partners include among others AC Furniture, Clarus Glassboards, Allsteel, Gunlocke, HON, Rubbermaid, Stanley Furniture, Vitra, and Winco. Henricksen also offers its customers furniture warehousing, installation, maintenance, inventory, and project management. Customers have included Centro, Cision, Gogo, Enova, Hamilton House, Menasha Corporation, and Beckhoff Automation. The company was founded by the Henricksen family in 1962.

	Annual Growth	04/09	04/10	04/11	04/12	04/13
Sales ($mil.)	8.6%	–	–	129.6	147.4	153.0
Net income ($ mil.)	(37.4%)	–	–	0.3	0.1	0.1
Market value ($ mil.)	–	–	–	–	–	–
Employees	–	–	–	–	–	210

HENRY COUNTY BANCSHARES INC (STOCKBRIDGE, GA)

4806 N. Henry Boulevard
Stockbridge, GA 30281
Phone: 770 474-7293
Fax: –
Web: www.firststateonline.com

CEO: –
CFO: –
HR: –
FYE: December 31
Type: Public

Just like the home run king it shares a name with, Henry County Bancshares swings for the bleachers, especially when it comes to mortgages. The institution is the holding company for First State Bank, which serves the area south of Atlanta. With about half a dozen branches, the bank offers standard deposit products, including checking and savings accounts, money market accounts, IRAs, and CDs. Lending activities are heavily focused on real estate: construction loans account for about half of total loans, while mortgages account for another 40%. The company also provides mortgage banking products and services through subsidiary First Metro Mortgage; it originates loans for sale on the secondary market.

HENRY COUNTY MEMORIAL HOSPITAL

500 WILLIAMS ST
ANGOLA, IN 467031144
Phone: 260 665-2161
Fax: –
Web: www.hchcares.org

CEO: Paul F Janssen
CFO: –
HR: Callie Klein
FYE: December 31
Type: Private

Henry County east of Indianapolis is a perfect slice of the Midwest: farms, small towns, and its own county hospital system. Henry County Memorial Hospital actually serves parts of three counties with a 110-bed general hospital, medical offices, specialty centers, a long-term care unit, and an assisted living center. The hospital offers patients emergency care, general medical, obstetric, pediatric, hospice and surgical services. The Henry County Hospital Foundation funds a program to train nurses through the local schools and college. The hospital opened its doors in 1930.

	Annual Growth	12/15	12/16	12/17	12/18	12/21
Sales ($mil.)	11.9%	–	75.1	82.8	94.5	131.6
Net income ($ mil.)	–	–	(4.8)	(4.5)	2.0	6.9
Market value ($ mil.)	–	–	–	–	–	–
Employees	–	–	–	–	–	787

HENRY FORD HEALTH SYSTEM

1 FORD PL
DETROIT, MI 482023450
Phone: 313 916-2600
Fax: –
Web: www.henryford.com

CEO: Robert Riney
CFO: James M Connelly
HR: Kathleen M Oswald
FYE: December 31
Type: Private

Henry Ford Health provides a full continuum of services ? from primary and preventative care, to complex and specialty care, health insurance, a full suite of home health offerings, virtual care, pharmacy, eye care and other healthcare retail. It is one of the nation's leading academic medical centers, recognized for clinical excellence in cancer care, cardiology and cardiovascular surgery, neurology and neurosurgery, orthopedics and sports medicine, and multi-organ transplants. Henry Ford Health engages in more than 2,000 research projects annually. It trains more than 4,000 medical students, residents and fellows every year across about 50 accredited programs. Health Alliance Plan (HAP), a Henry Ford subsidiary, is a Michigan-based nonprofit health plan that provides health coverage to individuals and companies of all sizes.

	Annual Growth	12/13	12/14	12/17	12/18	12/21
Sales ($mil.)	4.5%	–	1,513.7	5,977.0	5,853.8	2,062.5
Net income ($ mil.)	–	–	(13.8)	203.0	89.3	(402.1)
Market value ($ mil.)	–	–	–	–	–	–
Employees	–	–	–	–	–	23,000

HENRY J KAISER FAMILY FOUNDATION

185 BERRY ST STE 2000
SAN FRANCISCO, CA 941071704
Phone: 650 854-9400
Fax: -
Web: www.kff.org

CEO: -
CFO: -
HR: -
FYE: December 31
Type: Private

The next time you watch a Very Special Episode of your favorite television sitcom, you might be seeing the work of a consultant at The Henry J. Kaiser Family Foundation. Kaiser specializes in researching and communicating health issues that affect the US and South Africa. Specific areas of concern include HIV/AIDS, Medicaid and Medicare, minority health issues, and women's health policy. The not-for-profit organization differs from other foundations by providing primarily information and analysis to policymakers, the media, and the general public on health care issues, rather than providing grant money to fund outside research or programs. The industrialist Henry J. Kaiser established the foundation in 1948.

	Annual Growth	12/11	12/12	12/13	12/19	12/22
Sales ($mil.)	8.5%	-	-	33.9	53.8	70.7
Net income ($ mil.)	-	-	-	(13.1)	(1.1)	(0.2)
Market value ($ mil.)	-	-	-	-	-	-
Employees	-	-	-	-	-	210

HENRY MAYO NEWHALL MEMORIAL HOSPITAL

23845 MCBEAN PKWY
VALENCIA, CA 913552001
Phone: 661 253-8000
Fax: -
Web: www.henrymayo.com

CEO: -
CFO: -
HR: -
FYE: September 30
Type: Private

Had a bit too much mayo? Arteries feeling a bit clogged? Henry Mayo Newhall Memorial Hospital exists for just this reason (among others). The hospital serves the healthcare needs of the Santa Clarita Valley in northern Los Angeles County. The not-for-profit community hospital houses more than 220 beds and provides general medical and surgical care, as well as trauma services (it is a Level II trauma center), outpatient services, psychiatric care, and emergency services, among other specialties. In operation since 1975, the hospital was built to serve the needs of the at-the-time unincorporated City of Santa Clara, on land donated by The Newhall Land and Farming Company.

	Annual Growth	09/18	09/19	09/20	09/21	09/22
Sales ($mil.)	3.7%	-	411.3	326.2	366.1	458.6
Net income ($ mil.)	(42.7%)	-	30.5	0.4	9.7	5.7
Market value ($ mil.)	-	-	-	-	-	-
Employees	-	-	-	-	-	1,600

HENRY MODELL & COMPANY, INC.

498 FASHION AVE FL 20
NEW YORK, NY 100186738
Phone: 212 822-1000
Fax: -
Web: www.modells.com

CEO: Mitchell B Modell
CFO: -
HR: -
FYE: February 02
Type: Private

Operating as Modell's Sporting Goods, retailer Henry Modell & Company sells sporting goods, fitness equipment, apparel, and brand-name athletic footwear. It is America's oldest family-owned and -operated sporting goods retailer. Its top brands are Asics, Champion, FILA and Smith's, to name a few. It also offers fan gear such as jerseys for football. It also boasts an online presence at Modells.com.

	Annual Growth	01/09	01/10	01/11	01/12*	02/13
Sales ($mil.)	4.3%	-	-	558.8	570.3	608.0
Net income ($ mil.)	-	-	-	(7.5)	(3.3)	0.6
Market value ($ mil.)	-	-	-	-	-	-
Employees	-	-	-	-	-	5,430

*Fiscal year change

HENRY WURST, INC.

1331 SALINE ST
NORTH KANSAS CITY, MO 641164410
Phone: 816 701-0825
Fax: -
Web: www.mittera.com

CEO: Michael S Wurst
CFO: Kate Stewart
HR: Melissa Conte
FYE: December 31
Type: Private

Henry Wurst provides printing and communications services. The company offers such services as Web and sheetfed printing, digital printing, mailing and fulfillment, and custom Web site development. The company serves the needs of small to large businesses, franchise operators, and advertising agencies. One of the nation's leading commercial printers, Henry Wurst boasts clients that include department store operator J. C. Penney and Quiznos subs franchises. The firm has a handful of printing facilities located in Colorado, Missouri, and North Carolina. Founded in 1937 by namesake Henry Wurst, today the family-owned and -operated company is run by Henry's grandson CEO Mike Wurst.

HENSEL PHELPS CONSTRUCTION CO.

420 6TH AVE
GREELEY, CO 806312332
Phone: 970 352-6565
Fax: -
Web: www.henselphelps.com

CEO: Mike Choutka
CFO: Stephen J Carrico
HR: -
FYE: December 31
Type: Private

Hensel Phelps Construction is a proven industry leader and trusted advisor. The employee-owned general contractor provides a full range of development, pre-construction, construction, and renovation services for commercial, institutional, and government projects throughout the US. Its project portfolio includes prisons, airports, arenas, laboratories, government complexes, offices, and more. Major public and private clients include the US Intercontinental San Diego, Masonic Temple Hotel, NASA, Samsung, US Air Force, and Cin polis Luxury Cinema. Hensel Phelps founded the eponymous company as a homebuilder in 1937.

	Annual Growth	12/18	12/19	12/20	12/21	12/22
Sales ($mil.)	3.6%	-	5,676.7	5,868.5	5,334.9	6,316.1
Net income ($ mil.)	10.5%	-	177.1	181.6	186.0	238.6
Market value ($ mil.)	-	-	-	-	-	-
Employees	-	-	-	-	-	2,065

HER INTERACTIVE, INC.

325 118TH AVE SE STE 209
BELLEVUE, WA 980053539
Phone: 425 460-8787
Fax: -
Web: www.herinteractive.com

CEO: Penny Milliken
CFO: Rob Klee
HR: -
FYE: December 31
Type: Private

The "her" at Her Interactive is that venerable teen detective Nancy Drew. The company started out in 1995, creating games specifically aimed at teenage girls. Two years later, Her Interactive published the first title in its Nancy Drew series, Secrets Can Kill , and other titles starring the young gumshoe followed, including Stay Tuned for Danger , Ghost Dogs of Moon Lake , and The Haunted Carousel . The Hardy Boys, Nancy Drew's occasional collaborators, are featured in some titles. The games that the company publishes are rated "E" (for everyone), are mainly for PC-based play, are designed for kids age 10 and up, and do not depict violence. Her Interactive is adding titles to play on Nintendo game consoles.

	Annual Growth	12/03	12/04	12/05	12/08	12/09
Sales ($mil.)	14.7%	-	-	5.5	8.9	9.5
Net income ($ mil.)	-	-	-	0.1	0.6	(0.8)
Market value ($ mil.)	-	-	-	-	-	-
Employees	-	-	-	-	-	25

HERBORIUM GROUP INC

NBB: HBRM

4306 Kenston Place
Houston, TX 77459
Phone: 201 647-3757
Fax: –
Web: www.acnease.com; www.herborium.com; www.acnease.fr

CEO: Agnes P Olszewski Dr
CFO: Agnes P Olszewski Dr
HR: –
FYE: November 30
Type: Public

No, it's not a bevy of vegetarians. Herborium Group is a developer and marketer of herbal nutritional supplements. Herborium's product line includes Traditional Chinese Medicine herbal blends designed to clear up acne (AcnEase), boost energy (Energy Restoration), and heighten sexual performance (Lasting Pleasure for women, MaleForce for men). Herborium sells it products in the US, the UK, and continental Europe through a network of distributors, specialty retailers, such as natural foods stores, and online marketplaces. The company's founder, president and CEO Agnes Olszewski and director James Gilligan hold about 70% of the company's shares.

	Annual Growth	11/16	11/17	11/18	11/19	11/20
Sales ($mil.)	4.2%	0.8	0.9	0.8	0.9	1.0
Net income ($ mil.)	–	(0.1)	(0.0)	(0.2)	(0.1)	0.0
Market value ($ mil.)	–	0.6	0.6	0.6	0.6	0.6
Employees	–	–	–	–	–	–

HERC HOLDINGS INC

NYS: HRI

27500 Riverview Center Blvd.
Bonita Springs, FL 34134
Phone: 239 301-1000
Fax: –
Web: www.hertz.com

CEO: Lawrence H Silber
CFO: Mark Humphrey
HR: Eric Resman
FYE: December 31
Type: Public

Herc Holdings is one of the leading equipment rental suppliers with about 355 locations primarily in North America. Its portfolio of equipment includes aerial, earthmoving, material handling, trucks and trailers, air compressors, compaction and lighting. Its equipment rental business is supported by ProSolutions, its industry-specific solutions-based services, which includes power generation, climate control, remediation and restoration, pump, trench shoring, studio, and production equipment, and its ProContractor professional grade tools. Its customers include construction, industrial, and infrastructure industry. The US accounts for about 90% of revenue.

	Annual Growth	12/19	12/20	12/21	12/22	12/23
Sales ($mil.)	13.2%	1,999.0	1,781.3	2,073.1	2,738.8	3,282.0
Net income ($ mil.)	64.4%	47.5	73.7	224.1	329.9	347.0
Market value ($ mil.)	32.1%	1,380.1	1,872.8	4,414.7	3,710.3	4,198.7
Employees	9.0%	5,100	4,800	5,600	6,600	7,200

HEREUARE, INC.

228 Hamilton Ave., 3rd floor
Palo Alto, CA 94301
Phone: 650 798-5288
Fax: –
Web: messaging.hereuare.com

CEO: –
CFO: –
HR: –
FYE: December 31
Type: Public

Need help finding out where you're at? Internet software and telecom solutions firm hereUare (formerly PeopleNet International Corporation) offers a suite of Web services that include searching, online classified ads, group and e-mail messaging software, voice over IP (VoIP) telephony, and social-networking portals. Throughout 2008, hereUare was primarily developing products and was not generating revenues. The company's search engine and classified advertising products remain in the Beta testing phase, while hereUare is marketing its e-messaging and groupware products to small and medium-sized businesses. It has an engineering and operations center in Vietnam.

	Annual Growth	12/05	12/06	12/07	12/08	12/09
Sales ($mil.)	(60.6%)	–	–	0.0	0.0	0.0
Net income ($ mil.)	–	–	–	(4.0)	(8.2)	(9.3)
Market value ($ mil.)	–	–	–	0.0	0.0	0.0
Employees	–	–	–	–	4	5

HERITAGE COMMERCE CORP

NMS: HTBK

224 Airport Parkway
San Jose, CA 95110
Phone: 408 947-6900
Fax: –
Web: www.heritagecommercecorp.com

CEO: Walter T Kaczmarek
CFO: Lawrence D McGovern
HR: –
FYE: December 31
Type: Public

Heritage Commerce is the holding company for Heritage Bank of Commerce, which operates about 15 branches in the southern and eastern regions of the San Francisco Bay area. Serving consumers and small to midsized businesses and their owners and managers, the bank offers savings and checking accounts, money market accounts, and CDs, as well as cash management services and loans. Commercial and commercial real estate loans make up most of the company's loan portfolio, which is rounded out by land, construction, and home equity loans.

	Annual Growth	12/19	12/20	12/21	12/22	12/23
Assets ($mil.)	6.0%	4,109.5	4,634.1	5,499.4	5,157.6	5,194.1
Net income ($ mil.)	12.3%	40.5	35.3	47.7	66.6	64.4
Market value ($ mil.)	(6.2%)	784.5	542.4	730.1	794.9	606.6
Employees	0.1%	357	335	329	340	359

HERITAGE FINANCIAL CORP (WA)

NMS: HFWA

201 Fifth Avenue SW
Olympia, WA 98501
Phone: 360 943-1500
Fax: –
Web: www.hf-wa.com

CEO: Jeffrey J Deuel
CFO: Donald J Hinson
HR: –
FYE: December 31
Type: Public

Heritage Financial is a bank holding company, primarily engaged in the business of planning, directing, and coordinating the business activities of its wholly owned subsidiary and single reportable segment, Heritage Bank. Heritage Bank operates about 50 branches throughout Washington and Oregon. Boasting nearly $7 billion in assets, the bank's business consists primarily of commercial lending and deposit relationships with small and medium-sized businesses and their owners in its market areas and attracting deposits from the general public.

	Annual Growth	12/19	12/20	12/21	12/22	12/23
Assets ($mil.)	6.6%	5,553.0	6,615.3	7,432.4	6,980.1	7,175.0
Net income ($ mil.)	(2.2%)	67.6	46.6	98.0	81.9	61.8
Market value ($ mil.)	(6.8%)	987.8	816.5	853.1	1,069.5	746.6
Employees	(2.5%)	884	856	767	829	799

HERITAGE INSURANCE HOLDINGS INC

NYS: HRTG

1401 N. Westshore Blvd
Tampa, FL 33607
Phone: 727 362-7200
Fax: –
Web: www.heritagepci.com

CEO: Ernie Garateix
CFO: Kirk H Lusk
HR: Simone McArty
FYE: December 31
Type: Public

Heritage Insurance Holdings is a super-regional property and casualty insurance holding company that primarily provides personal and commercial residential insurance through its insurance company subsidiaries. The company is vertically integrated and control or manage substantially all aspects of insurance underwriting, customer service, actuarial analysis, distribution, and claims processing and adjusting. Its subsidiary, Heritage Property & Casualty Insurance Company, offers personal and commercial residential property insurance and commercial general liability insurance. The company's other insurance subsidiaries are Narragansett Bay Insurance Company and Zephyr Insurance Company.

	Annual Growth	12/19	12/20	12/21	12/22	12/23
Assets ($mil.)	2.6%	1,939.7	2,089.4	1,980.8	2,392.6	2,153.2
Net income ($ mil.)	12.2%	28.6	9.3	(74.7)	(154.4)	45.3
Market value ($ mil.)	(16.2%)	400.4	306.1	177.7	54.4	197.0
Employees	1.7%	530	641	648	612	566

HERITAGE UNIVERSITY

3240 FORT RD
TOPPENISH, WA 989489562
Phone: 509 865-8500
Fax: –
Web: www.heritage.edu

CEO: –
CFO: –
HR: –
FYE: June 30
Type: Private

Those at Heritage University believe it's everyone's birthright to pursue a higher education. The four-year private liberal arts college serves students from diverse backgrounds. A majority of students are low-income and are the first in their families to attend college. About 40% of the college's 1,150 students are Hispanic, and a majority are women. In addition to its main campus on the Yakama Indian Reservation in Central Washington, the college has three other sites in the state. Heritage University offers associate, bachelor's, and master's degree programs in subjects including business, education, nursing, and social work.

	Annual Growth	06/17	06/18	06/20	06/21	06/22
Sales ($mil.)	(0.3%)	–	32.6	25.2	36.9	32.2
Net income ($ mil.)	(5.3%)	–	4.1	0.2	10.1	3.3
Market value ($ mil.)	–	–	–	–	–	–
Employees	–	–	–	–	–	255

HERITAGE VALLEY HEALTH SYSTEM, INC.

1000 DUTCH RIDGE RD
BEAVER, PA 150099727
Phone: 724 728-7000
Fax: –
Web: www.heritagevalley.org

CEO: Norman F Mitry
CFO: –
HR: Stan Elich
FYE: June 30
Type: Private

Heritage Valley Health System has a legacy of serving the health care needs of residents of southwestern Pennsylvania, eastern Ohio, and the West Virginia Panhandle. The two-hospital system includes the flagship Heritage Valley Beaver hospital in Beaver, Pennsylvania, with more than 330 beds and a smaller facility in nearby Sewickley with roughly 185 beds. In addition to its acute-care facilities, the system operates several satellite facilities and provides primary care through a network of three affiliated physician groups. Heritage Valley Health System was formed in 1996 when the two hospitals merged, but it has roots going back to 1894.

	Annual Growth	06/13	06/14	06/18	06/20	06/22
Sales ($mil.)	15.6%	–	5.2	450.7	14.3	16.4
Net income ($ mil.)	(1.0%)	–	4.5	30.8	6.6	4.2
Market value ($ mil.)	–	–	–	–	–	–
Employees	–	–	–	–	–	4,291

HEROIX LLC

163 BAY STATE DR
BRAINTREE, MA 021845203
Phone: 781 848-1701
Fax: –
Web: www.heroix.com

CEO: –
CFO: –
HR: –
FYE: December 31
Type: Private

Heroix believes you shouldn't be forced into heroic acts just to keep your technology infrastructure up and running. The company provides software used to manage application, system, and network availability and performance. Heroix's applications (sold under the Longitude, eQ, and RoboMon brand names) also include automated monitoring and reporting functionality, as well as centralized control of servers, switches, routers, bridges, and other information technology hardware. The company's customers come from a wide range of industries including financial services, manufacturing, education, and consumer goods. Clients have included University of Alaska and FIS. Heroix was founded by chairman Howard Reisman.

HERON THERAPEUTICS INC

NAS: HRTX

4242 Campus Point Court, Suite 200
San Diego, CA 92121
Phone: 858 251-4400
Fax: –
Web: www.herontx.com

CEO: Craig Collard
CFO: Ira Duarte
HR: –
FYE: December 31
Type: Public

Heron Therapeutics is a commercial-stage biotechnology company focused on improving the lives of patients by developing best-in-class treatments to address some of the most important unmet patient needs. The company's CINVANTI (aprepitant) injectable emulsion (CINVANTI) and SUSTOL (granisetron) extended-release injection (SUSTOL) are both approved in the US for the prevention of chemotherapy-induced nausea and vomiting. ZYNRELEF (bupivacaine and meloxicam) extended-release solution (ZYNRELEF) is approved in the US and about 30 European countries for the management of postoperative pain. Within its acute care franchise, it is also developing HTX-019, an investigational agent for the prevention of postoperative nausea and vomiting (PONV) and HTX-034, an investigational agent, its next-generation product candidate for the management of postoperative pain.

	Annual Growth	12/19	12/20	12/21	12/22	12/23
Sales ($mil.)	(3.4%)	146.0	88.6	86.3	107.7	127.0
Net income ($ mil.)	–	(204.7)	(227.3)	(220.7)	(182.0)	(110.6)
Market value ($ mil.)	(48.1%)	3,531.7	3,180.8	1,372.1	375.7	255.5
Employees	(14.1%)	231	223	302	203	126

HERR FOODS INCORPORATED

20 HERR DR
NOTTINGHAM, PA 193629788
Phone: 610 932-9330
Fax: –
Web: www.herrs.com

CEO: James M Herr
CFO: Gerry Kluis
HR: –
FYE: December 31
Type: Private

Herr Foods is a family-owned snack food manufacturer, made famous by its signature Herr's potato chip. The company, which celebrates over 70 years in business, makes more than 350 different kinds of snack foods. This line of quality snacks includes potato chips, pretzels, tortilla chips, cheese curls, corn chips, popcorn, baked crisps, snack friez, nuts, pork rinds, onion rings, and meat snacks. Herr Foods operates more than 500 sales routes, and two manufacturing facilities, and is distributed in some 20 regional branches. It produces up to one million pounds of potato chips every week and offers about 20 different flavors on both regular and ripple chips. The company was founded by James Stauffer Herr in 1946.

HERSCHEND ENTERTAINMENT COMPANY, LLC

157 TECHNOLOGY PKWY STE 100
PEACHTREE CORNERS, GA 300922944
Phone: 770 441-1940
Fax: –
Web: www.hfecorp.com

CEO: –
CFO: –
HR: –
FYE: January 03
Type: Private

Herschend Family Entertainment (HFE) makes more than a few silver dollars. The company owns and operates (or co-owns), more than 25 amusement parks in about 10 states. Properties include Silver Dollar City in Branson, Missouri and Tennessee's Dollywood, in partnership with country legend Dolly Parton. HFE also owns aquariums near Philadelphia and Cincinnati, and the Ride the Ducks amphibious tours in a handful of cities, including Atlanta and Philadelphia. The firm touts that it offers family entertainment "with Christian values and ethics". The family-owned company was founded in 1950 by Hugo and Mary Herschend to manage the Marvel Cave in the Ozarks, a tourist attraction that opened in 1894.

HERSHA HOSPITALITY TRUST

NYS: HT

44 Hersha Drive
Harrisburg, PA 17102
Phone: 717 236-4400
Fax: 717 774-7383
Web: www.hersha.com

CEO: –
CFO: –
HR: –
FYE: December 31
Type: Public

Hersha Hospitality Trust is a self-advised real estate investment trust (REIT) that invests in the high quality luxury, upscale, and upper midscale hotels in metropolitan markets with high barriers to entry and independent boutique hotels across the US. Its portfolio consists of about 20 hotels containing approximately 3,390 rooms, most of them are in New York, Washington, DC, Boston, Philadelphia, South Florida, and California. The properties are operated under such brand names as Marriott International, Hilton Worldwide, InterContinental, and Hyatt. The majority of its wholly-owned hotels are managed by Hersha Hospitality Management, a privately held, qualified management company owned primarily by other unaffiliated third party investors and in which certain of its trustees and executive officers have a minority investment.

	Annual Growth	12/18	12/19	12/20	12/21	12/22
Sales ($mil.)	(4.8%)	495.1	530.0	176.7	296.0	405.9
Net income ($ mil.)	95.8%	10.0	(3.7)	(166.3)	(40.2)	146.7
Market value ($ mil.)	(16.5%)	696.3	577.6	313.2	364.0	338.2
Employees	(15.9%)	54	49	32	28	27

HERSHEY COMPANY (THE)

NYS: HSY

19 East Chocolate Avenue
Hershey, PA 17033
Phone: 717 534-4200
Fax: 717 531-6161
Web: www.thehersheycompany.com

CEO: Michele G Buck
CFO: Steven E Voskuil
HR: –
FYE: December 31
Type: Public

With a portfolio of more than 100 global brands, the largest chocolate producer in North America has built a big business making such well-known chocolate and candy brands as Hershey's Kisses, Reese's peanut butter cups, Twizzlers, Cadbury and Almond Joy candy bars, York peppermint patties, and Kit Kat wafer bars. Hershey also makes grocery goods ? including baking products, toppings, sundae syrup, cocoa mix, snack bites, breath mints, and bubble gum ? and has expanded into popcorn and other savory snacks. Products are sold to wholesale distributors and retailers throughout North America and exported overseas; the US accounts for most of sales.

	Annual Growth	12/19	12/20	12/21	12/22	12/23
Sales ($mil.)	8.7%	7,986.3	8,149.7	8,971.3	10,419	11,165
Net income ($ mil.)	12.8%	1,149.7	1,278.7	1,477.5	1,644.8	1,861.8
Market value ($ mil.)	6.1%	30,042	31,135	39,544	47,331	38,107
Employees	6.2%	16,140	16,880	18,990	19,865	20,505

HERSHEY ENTERTAINMENT & RESORTS COMPANY

27 W CHOCOLATE AVE # 100
HERSHEY, PA 170331672
Phone: 717 534-3131
Fax: –
Web: www.thehotelhershey.com

CEO: –
CFO: –
HR: Elaine Gruin
FYE: December 31
Type: Private

Life is sweet for Hershey Entertainment & Resorts. The company owns the many chocolate-related entertainment destinations in Hershey, Pennsylvania. Its holdings include Hersheypark, one of the nation's top amusement parks with more than 65 rides and attractions; ZooAmerica wildlife park; the Hotel Hershey; and the Hershey Lodge. Hershey Entertainment also owns four golf courses and the Giant Center arena in Hershey. Hershey Entertainment & Resorts is fully owned by the Hershey Trust Company, which controls a majority stake in candymaker The Hershey Company. The Hershey Trust Co. also acts as trustee for the Milton Hershey School.

	Annual Growth	12/06	12/07	12/08	12/09	12/20
Sales ($mil.)	(57.2%)	–	1,333.8	274.0	271.0	0.0
Net income ($ mil.)	–	–	0.0	13.9	6.9	(0.0)
Market value ($ mil.)	–	–	–	–	–	–
Employees	–	–	–	–	–	7,300

HERTZ GLOBAL HOLDINGS INC (NEW)

NMS: HTZ

8501 Williams Road
Estero, FL 33928
Phone: 239 301-7000
Fax: –
Web: www.hertz.com

CEO: Mark Fields
CFO: Kenny K Cheung
HR: Chritina Federighi
FYE: December 31
Type: Public

Hertz Global Holdings is one of the largest worldwide vehicle rental companies. Hertz Global operates about 11,600 rental locations in about 160 countries under the Hertz, Dollar, and Thrifty brands. Its fleet includes a peak rental fleet in its Americas RAC and International RAC segments of approximately 428,700 vehicles and 118,700 vehicles, respectively. The company sells vehicles through Hertz Car Sales and operates the Firefly vehicle rental brand and Hertz 24/7 car sharing business in international markets. The majority of its revenue comes from the US.

	Annual Growth	12/19	12/20	12/21	12/22	12/23
Sales ($mil.)	(1.1%)	9,779.0	5,258.0	7,336.0	8,685.0	9,371.0
Net income ($ mil.)	–	(58.0)	(1,714.0)	366.0	2,059.0	616.0
Market value ($ mil.)	(9.9%)	4,806.6	390.6	7,626.4	4,696.7	3,170.8
Employees	(8.2%)	38,000	24,000	23,000	25,000	27,000

HESS CORP

NYS: HES

1185 Avenue of the Americas
New York, NY 10036
Phone: 212 997-8500
Fax: –
Web: www.hess.com

CEO: John B Hess
CFO: John P Rielly
HR: –
FYE: December 31
Type: Public

Hess Corporation is a global exploration and production company engaged in the exploration, development, production, transportation, purchase and sale of crude oil, natural gas liquids, and natural gas. It can profess to own about 720 billion barrels of oil equivalent worldwide. Its primary operations are in the US, but it also has producing interests in Malaysia and Thailand. It also offers midstream services, including gathering, compressing, and processing natural gas and fractionating and transporting crude oil and NGL as well as propane storage. Prospecting for oil since the 1920s, Hess generates about 65% of its revenue from the US.

	Annual Growth	12/19	12/20	12/21	12/22	12/23
Sales ($mil.)	13.1%	6,510.0	4,804.0	7,583.0	11,570	10,645
Net income ($ mil.)	–	(408.0)	(3,093.0)	559.0	2,096.0	1,382.0
Market value ($ mil.)	21.2%	20,521	16,215	22,739	43,561	44,280
Employees	(0.3%)	1,775	1,621	1,545	1,623	1,756

HESS MIDSTREAM LP

NYS: HESM

1501 McKinney Street
Houston, TX 77010
Phone: 713 496-4200
Fax: –
Web: www.hessmidstream.com

CEO: John B Hess
CFO: –
HR: –
FYE: December 31
Type: Public

Hess Midstream Partners is fueled up and ready to grow. A 2014 spin-off of Hess Corporation, it is a master limited partnership (MLP) that owns, operates, and acquires various midstream assets to service the needs of Hess Corporation and third-party customers. Through a shared ownership structure, Hess Midstream owns a 20% controlling interest in its asset portfolio, which is comprised of partially or wholly owned pipelines, gas compression facilities, storage facilities, and other related items. All assets were dropped into Hess Midstream by previous parent, Hess Corporation, and its partners. Hess Midstream conducts business primarily in the Williston Basin area of North Dakota. It sold a 30% ownership interest to the investing public in a 2017 initial public offering.

	Annual Growth	12/19	12/20	12/21	12/22	12/23
Sales ($mil.)	12.3%	848.3	1,091.9	1,203.8	1,275.2	1,348.6
Net income ($ mil.)	67.4%	15.1	24.0	46.4	83.9	118.6
Market value ($ mil.)	8.7%	5,132.7	4,428.9	6,252.9	6,771.2	7,158.2
Employees	4.6%	176	196	199	199	211

HEWLETT PACKARD ENTERPRISE CO   NYS: HPE

1701 East Mossy Oaks Road | CEO: Antonio F Neri
Spring, TX 77389 | CFO: Jeremy K Cox
Phone: 678 259-9860 | HR: –
Fax: – | FYE: October 31
Web: www.hpe.com | Type: Public

Hewlett Packard Enterprise (HPE), designs and sells servers, storage, and networking equipment, and provides technology services to help its large enterprise customers put together and deploy IT systems. HPE has software-defined IT offerings for private, public, and hybrid cloud environments, as well as technologies for industrial Internet of Things (IoT) applications. HPE is a global company and about 60% of its revenue comes from outside the US. It maintains a cache of around 13,000 worldwide patents. HPE traces its roots back to a partnership founded in 1939 by William R. Hewlett and David Packard.

	Annual Growth	10/19	10/20	10/21	10/22	10/23
Sales ($mil.)	–	29,135	26,982	27,784	28,496	29,135
Net income ($ mil.)	17.9%	1,049.0	(322.0)	3,427.0	868.0	2,025.0
Market value ($ mil.)	(1.6%)	21,054	11,085	18,796	18,308	19,733
Employees	0.2%	61,600	59,400	60,400	60,200	62,000

HEWLETT, WILLIAM AND FLORA FOUNDATION (INC)

2121 SAND HILL RD | CEO: –
MENLO PARK, CA 940256909 | CFO: –
Phone: 650 234-4500 | HR: Megan Rossi
Fax: – | FYE: December 31
Web: www.hewlett.org | Type: Private

The Hewlett Foundation is dedicated to helping solve the world's social and environmental problems. One of the nation's largest charitable institutions, it has some $8.6 billion in assets, and it disbursed approximately $240 million in grants and gifts in 2013. It provides grants in a diverse areas including education reform, environmental protection in the West, and population growth. The private foundation also promotes the performing arts in the San Francisco Bay Area and has funded conflict resolution and international relations programs in the past. The late Bill Hewlett, co-founder of Hewlett-Packard, founded the Hewlett Foundation with his wife and eldest son in 1967.

	Annual Growth	12/01	12/02	12/05	12/14	12/16
Sales ($mil.)	9.1%	–	94.2	–	624.6	317.5
Net income ($ mil.)	–	–	426.8	–	205.0	(164.8)
Market value ($ mil.)	–	–	–	–	–	–
Employees	–	–	–	–	–	60

HEXCEL CORP.   NYS: HXL

Two Stamford Plaza, 281 Tresser Boulevard | CEO: Nick L Stanage
Stamford, CT 06901-3238 | CFO: Patrick J Winterlich
Phone: 203 969-0666 | HR: –
Fax: – | FYE: December 31
Web: www.hexcel.com | Type: Public

Hexcel is a global leader in advanced lightweight composites technology. The company makes advanced structural materials used in everything from aircraft components to wind turbine blades. Its composite materials include structural adhesives, honeycomb, molding compounds, tooling materials, polyurethane systems and laminates that are incorporated into many applications, including military and commercial aircraft, wind turbine blades, recreational products, transportation. Aerospace is the largest market for honeycomb products. It designs and builds its products in over 20 manufacturing plants located in the US and Europe, as well as in China and Morocco. The US generates more than 50% of revenue.

	Annual Growth	12/19	12/20	12/21	12/22	12/23
Sales ($mil.)	(6.6%)	2,355.7	1,502.4	1,324.7	1,577.1	1,789.0
Net income ($ mil.)	(23.4%)	306.6	31.7	16.1	126.3	105.7
Market value ($ mil.)	0.1%	6,165.4	4,078.0	4,356.4	4,949.3	6,202.4
Employees	(5.4%)	6,977	4,647	4,863	5,328	5,590

HEXION INC

180 East Broad St. | CEO: Michael Lefenfeld
Columbus, OH 43215 | CFO: Mark Bidstrup
Phone: 614 225-4000 | HR: –
Fax: – | FYE: December 31
Web: www.hexion.com | Type: Public

Hexion is a leading, global producer of adhesives and performance materials that enable the production of engineered wood products and other specialty materials used in high-performance coatings for industrial applications. Hexion provides specialty products and technical support for customers in a diverse range of applications and industries, such as construction, agriculture, energy, automotive and infrastructure protection. Hexion offers a range of chemical platform options to meet a range of performance and process requirements including amino resins, resin coated proppants, Versatic Acids and Derivatives, wax emulsions, and formaldehyde and derivatives. Hexion serves more than 1,200 companies across approximately 60 countries. In 2022, the parent company of Hexion Inc. (Hexion Holdings Corp.) was acquired by affiliates of American Securities.

	Annual Growth	12/17	12/18*	07/19*	12/19	12/20
Sales ($mil.)	(11.3%)	3,591.0	3,797.0	1,778.0	1,596.0	2,510.0
Net income ($ mil.)	–	(234.0)	(162.0)	2,894.0	(89.0)	(230.0)
Market value ($ mil.)	–	–	–	–	–	–
Employees	(15.4%)	4,300	4,000	–	4,000	2,600

*Fiscal year change

HF SInclair CORP   NYS: DINO

2828 N. Harwood, Suite 1300 | CEO: Michael C Jennings
Dallas, TX 75201 | CFO: Richard L Voliva III
Phone: 214 871-3555 | HR: Daniel McGuire
Fax: – | FYE: December 31
Web: www.hollyfrontier.com | Type: Public

HF SInclair is an independent petroleum refiner and marketer that produces high-value light products such as gasoline, diesel fuel, jet fuel, specialty lubricant products and specialty and modified asphalt that sells its products to customers in the Southwest US, the Rocky Mountains (extending into the Pacific Northwest), and Plains states. The company operates refineries and other production facilities in Kansas, Oklahoma, New Mexico, Utah, and Wyoming as well as Texas, Arizona, and Ontario, Canada. HollyFrontier has over 45% stake in Holly Energy Partners (HEP), which operates crude oil and petroleum product pipelines. The company sells lubricants and other specialty products through its Petro-Canada Lubricants and Red Giant Oil subsidiaries.

	Annual Growth	12/19	12/20	12/21	12/22	12/23
Sales ($mil.)	16.3%	17,487	11,184	18,389	38,205	31,964
Net income ($ mil.)	19.8%	772.4	(601.4)	558.3	2,922.7	1,589.7
Market value ($ mil.)	2.3%	10,142	5,169.9	6,555.9	10,378	11,114
Employees	6.4%	4,074	3,891	4,208	5,223	5,218

HFB FINANCIAL CORP.   NBB: HFBA

1602 Cumberland Avenue | CEO: David B Cook
Middlesboro, KY 40965 | CFO: Stanley Alexander Jr
Phone: 606 242-1071 | HR: –
Fax: 606 242-3432 | FYE: December 31
Web: www.homefederalbank.com | Type: Public

HFB Financial Corporation is the holding company for Home Federal Bank, which provides community banking services to individuals and small to midsized businesses through three offices in southeastern Kentucky and two more in eastern Tennessee. Standard retail services include savings, checking, and money market accounts, as well as certificates of deposit, individual retirement accounts, and Keogh plans. Home Federal focuses on residential lending, but also originates commercial real estate, construction, business, and consumer loans. Home Federal Bank was founded as People's Building and Loan Association in 1920.

	Annual Growth	12/09	12/10	12/11	12/12	12/13
Assets ($mil.)	(0.6%)	342.4	348.0	347.1	344.3	334.8
Net income ($ mil.)	(10.9%)	3.1	1.9	1.4	2.0	2.0
Market value ($ mil.)	2.6%	20.3	23.3	21.1	21.5	22.4
Employees	–	90	–	–	–	–

HG HOLDINGS INC   NBB: STLY

2115 E. 7th Street, Suite 101
Charlotte, NC 28204
Phone: 850 772-0698
Fax: –
Web: www.hgholdingsinc.net

CEO: –
CFO: –
HR: –
FYE: December 31
Type: Public

Stanley Furniture needs lots of rooms to spread out. The company, established in 1924, primarily makes wood furniture that retails in the upper-medium price range. Its products include furniture for adult bedrooms, dining rooms, youth bedrooms, home offices, and living rooms, as well as for home entertainment centers. Youth furniture is made under the Young America brand. Stanley Furniture makes and markets furniture styles such as European and American traditional lines, as well as contemporary/transitional and country/casual. With a manufacturing facility in North Carolina, the company sells its products through furniture and department stores. International customers account for about 10% of sales.

	Annual Growth	12/18	12/19	12/20	12/21	12/22
Sales ($mil.)	–	–	–	–	2.4	14.5
Net income ($ mil.)	–	(1.4)	0.2	0.0	2.8	3.7
Market value ($ mil.)	100.3%	1.2	1.6	1.5	33.8	20.1
Employees	–	–	2	2	2	76

HHGREGG INC   NBB: HGGG Q

4151 East 96th Street
Indianapolis, IN 46240
Phone: 317 848-8710
Fax: –
Web: www.hhgregg.com

CEO: –
CFO: –
HR: –
FYE: March 31
Type: Public

Retailer hhgregg sells a range of electronics and appliances in nearly 220 stores in 20 US states and online. It offers TV and video products (LED TVs, Blu-ray disc players), home and car audio gear (CD players, home theater systems), appliances (refrigerators, washers and dryers), computers, gaming consoles, digital cameras, GPS navigators, and mattresses. The company also offers installation and tech services. Founded in 1955, Indianapolis-based hhgregg had expanded from southern states to the Midwest and mid-Atlantic regions. In early 2017 the company filed for Chapter 11 bankruptcy protection and was forced to liquidate its assets after failing to secure a buyer. It ceased operations in May 2017.

	Annual Growth	03/12	03/13	03/14	03/15	03/16
Sales ($mil.)	(5.8%)	2,493.4	2,474.8	2,338.6	2,129.4	1,960.0
Net income ($ mil.)	–	81.4	25.4	0.2	(132.7)	(54.9)
Market value ($ mil.)	(34.4%)	315.3	306.2	266.3	169.8	58.5
Employees	(6.6%)	6,700	6,300	6,100	5,400	5,100

HIBBETT INC   NMS: HIBB

2700 Milan Court
Birmingham, AL 35211
Phone: 205 942-4292
Fax: –
Web: www.hibbett.com

CEO: Michael E Longo
CFO: Robert J Volke
HR: –
FYE: February 3
Type: Public

Hibbett is a leading athletic-inspired fashion retailer primarily located in underserved communities. The company sells brand-name sports equipment, athletic apparel, and footwear in small to midsized markets in some 35 states, mainly in the South and Midwest. Its flagship Hibbett chain boasts more than 930 locations; stores are primarily found in malls and strip centers. Hibbett also operates approximately 185 of City Gear stores, which stock urban streewear, and about 15 mall-based Sports Additions shoe shops, most of which are situated near Hibbett stores. The company also trades online. The company was founded in 1945.

	Annual Growth	02/20*	01/21	01/22	01/23*	02/24
Sales ($mil.)	9.9%	1,184.2	1,419.7	1,691.2	1,708.3	1,728.9
Net income ($ mil.)	39.4%	27.3	74.3	174.3	128.1	103.2
Market value ($ mil.)	29.4%	292.3	665.8	702.1	779.9	818.5
Employees	5.2%	10,200	10,700	11,000	11,000	12,500

*Fiscal year change

HICKMAN, WILLIAMS & COMPANY

250 E 5TH ST STE 300
CINCINNATI, OH 452024198
Phone: 513 621-1946
Fax: –
Web: www.hicwilco.com

CEO: –
CFO: –
HR: –
FYE: March 31
Type: Private

Hickman, Williams makes carbon products (anthracite coal, metallurgical coke, and reactive char coke) and metals and alloys (chromium, manganese, and silicon) used by metals producers. The company also manufactures service injection systems and cored wire feeding units for metal production facilities. Hickman, Williams operates about 50 warehouse facilities throughout the nation. Founded by Richard Hickman and Harry Williams in 1891, the company is now owned by its employees.

	Annual Growth	03/12	03/13	03/14	03/15	03/16
Sales ($mil.)	(10.6%)	–	–	245.2	247.2	195.9
Net income ($ mil.)	–	–	–	–	4.6	2.8
Market value ($ mil.)	–	–	–	–	–	–
Employees	–	–	–	–	–	114

HIGH CONCRETE GROUP LLC

125 DENVER RD
DENVER, PA 175179315
Phone: 717 735-1060
Fax: –
Web: www.highconcrete.com

CEO: Michael F Shirk
CFO: Karen A Biondolillo
HR: –
FYE: December 31
Type: Private

High Concrete Group offers concrete solutions for your building needs. The company produces precast concrete structures, including walls, architectural facades, and floor slabs, to create everything from office buildings to sports arenas. It is one of the leading makers of precast parking structures in the US. Its StructureCare service provides preventive maintenance to extend the life of those structures. A subsidiary of High Industries, High Concrete Group counts architects, contractors, and building owners among its customers. It primarily serves the Mid-Atlantic, Midwest, and New England regions of the country, with projects that include the Baltimore Ravens' stadium and a Harrah's casino parking garage.

HIGH COUNTRY BANCORP, INC.   NBB: HCBC

7360 West US Highway 50
Salida, CO 81201
Phone: 719 539-2516
Fax: 719 539-6216
Web: –

CEO: Larry D Smith
CFO: –
HR: –
FYE: June 30
Type: Public

High Country Bancorp is in rarefied air. It is the holding company for High Country Bank, which was founded in 1886 as the first savings and loan association chartered in Colorado. Serving the state's tourist-oriented "Fourteener" region (for the number of mountain peaks exceeding 14,000 feet), the bank operates four branches in Salida, Buena Vista, and Canon City. It offers traditional services such as personal and business checking accounts, CDs, and IRAs, as well as financial planning and investment services. The bank's lending activities include residential and commercial mortgages, construction and land loans, and home equity and personal loans. High Country Bank focuses on real estate lending, with mortgages secured by one- to four-family residences comprising about 40% of the loan portfolio and commercial mortgages adding almost another quarter. The bank also makes business, consumer, construction, and land loans.

	Annual Growth	06/19	06/20	06/21	06/22	06/23
Assets ($mil.)	12.4%	275.4	331.8	404.3	455.4	439.9
Net income ($ mil.)	3.0%	4.0	4.3	4.9	4.2	4.6
Market value ($ mil.)	(4.0%)	45.7	35.7	45.9	44.4	38.7
Employees	–	–	–	–	–	–

HIGH COUNTRY FUSION COMPANY, INC.

20 N POLY FUSION PL
FAIRFIELD, ID 83327
Phone: 208 764-2000
Fax: –
Web: www.hcfusion.com

CEO: –
CFO: –
HR: –
FYE: December 31
Type: Private

High Country Fusion Company (HCFC) makes its path to success through its pipes. HCFC manufactures high-density polyethylene pipes (HDPE) and pipe fittings for use in industrial, marine, municipal, wastewater, and other types of projects. The company's HDPE pipes (in essence, dense plastic-based pipes) are capable of transporting water and wastewater, chemicals, compressed gases, and other substances. HCFC's customers include municipal and government agencies, as well as US and international construction companies. Based in a small town in Idaho, the company operates a 21,000-sq.-ft. facility, as well as a smaller facility in Utah. HCFC was founded in 1994 by president Steve Wilson and VP David Hanks.

	Annual Growth	12/10	12/11	12/12	12/13	12/14
Sales ($mil.)	17.9%	–	–	28.4	40.3	39.6
Net income ($ mil.)	(35.8%)	–	–	1.3	1.6	0.5
Market value ($ mil.)	–	–	–	–	–	–
Employees	–	–	–	–	–	54

HIGH HOTELS, LTD.

1853 WILLIAM PENN WAY
LANCASTER, PA 176016713
Phone: 717 747-0360
Fax: –
Web: www.highhotels.com

CEO: Michael F Shirk
CFO: Karen Biondolillo
HR: –
FYE: December 31
Type: Private

High Hotels wants to be at the top of the list for places to stay. The company develops, owns, and operates about 10 hotel and motel properties in Pennsylvania, Maryland, and New York. The company operates its hotels under the Hampton Inn, Homewood Suites, Courtyard by Marriott, and Hilton Garden Inn banners. The company's hotels are located in tourist areas and many offer special packages like Amish tours, Civil War packages, Hershey Entertainment's Hersheypark tickets, and shopping excursions. High Hotels was founded in 1988 by its parent company High Industries, as part of its real estate group.

	Annual Growth	12/04	12/05	12/06	12/07	12/08
Sales ($mil.)	2.4%	–	–	–	41.1	42.1
Net income ($ mil.)	6.1%	–	–	–	1.8	1.9
Market value ($ mil.)	–	–	–	–	–	–
Employees	–	–	–	–	–	526

HIGH INDUSTRIES INC.

1853 WILLIAM PENN WAY
LANCASTER, PA 176016713
Phone: 717 293-4444
Fax: –
Web: www.high.net

CEO: –
CFO: –
HR: –
FYE: December 31
Type: Private

High Industries has ascended to the top of the steel and construction business. Doing business as High Companies, its subsidiaries are active in heavy construction and materials, mostly along the East Coast. Its High Steel Structures is one of North America's largest steel bridge fabricators. Other group companies include High Steel Service Center (metal processing), High Concrete Group (precast concrete), High Transit (specialty hauler), and High Structural Erectors (field erection services). Affiliates of High Companies, such as High Hotels, are active in real estate. Tracing its roots to a welding shop founded by Sanford H. High in 1931, the family-owned company is controlled by the High Family Council.

	Annual Growth	12/05	12/06	12/07	12/08	12/09
Sales ($mil.)	(6.5%)	–	390.2	429.5	452.9	319.2
Net income ($ mil.)	–	–	25.9	23.1	31.9	–
Market value ($ mil.)	–	–	–	–	–	–
Employees	–	–	–	–	–	2,107

HIGH POINT REGIONAL HEALTH

601 N ELM ST
HIGH POINT, NC 272624331
Phone: 336 878-6011
Fax: –
Web: www.wakehealth.edu

CEO: Ernie Bovio
CFO: Kimberly Crews
HR: –
FYE: June 30
Type: Private

Hospital stays are usually not the high point of one's life, but High Point Regional Health System aims to make patients comfortable. Its main facility is High Point Regional Hospital, a medical/surgical facility with about 380 beds serving the Piedmont Triad region of North Carolina. The private, not-for-profit health care system also operates the Carolina Regional Heart Center, Neuroscience Center, Piedmont Joint Replacement Center, Emergency Center, Culp Women's Center, and Hayworth Cancer Center. Other operations include primary care physician practices, mental health, wound care, and home health care services. The hospital was founded in 1904. Parent company UNC Health Care System is selling High Point to Wake Forest Baptist Medical Center.

	Annual Growth	06/17	06/18	06/19	06/20	06/21
Sales ($mil.)	3654.9%	–	–	0.3	337.1	384.9
Net income ($ mil.)	1317.7%	–	–	0.3	27.2	56.5
Market value ($ mil.)	–	–	–	–	–	–
Employees	–	–	–	–	–	2,338

HIGH POINT SOLUTIONS INC.

5 GAIL CT
SPARTA, NJ 078713438
Phone: 973 940-0040
Fax: –
Web: www.highpoint.com

CEO: –
CFO: –
HR: –
FYE: December 31
Type: Private

High Point Solutions can solve your networking needs. The company supplies network hardware -- routers, switches, and access servers -- to telecommunications companies and other large enterprises. High Point's procurement specialists provide equipment from leading manufactures such as Cisco Systems and Nortel Networks. The company also provides services in repair, network design, and installation. Owners Mike and Tom Mendiburu maintain a lean-and-mean corporate philosophy: a small staff dedicated to procurement and focused on speed and service for a short list of large clients. The brothers founded High Point in 1996.

	Annual Growth	12/14	12/15	12/16	12/17	12/18
Sales ($mil.)	(5.6%)	–	145.9	111.5	104.5	122.7
Net income ($ mil.)	–	–	–	–	–	3.0
Market value ($ mil.)	–	–	–	–	–	–
Employees	–	–	–	–	–	50

HIGH STEEL STRUCTURES LLC

1915 OLD PHILADELPHIA PIKE
LANCASTER, PA 176023410
Phone: 717 299-5211
Fax: –
Web: www.highsteel.com

CEO: Michael F Shirk
CFO: Karen A Biondolillo
HR: –
FYE: December 31
Type: Private

Steel fabricator High Steel Structures helps to build bridges -- literally. The company manufactures structural steel beams and girders used to build bridges and elevated roads in the US. High Steel also makes steel structures for buildings such as manufacturing plants, power plants, and sports arenas, and offers erection services and emergency repair services. Working with contractors such as Balfour Beatty, Skanska, and Middlesex, High Steel has fabricated steel for thousands of bridges, mainly along the East Coast. The company has four fabrication plants in Pennsylvania and is a part of High Industries. High Steel traces its roots back to 1931, when it was founded as High Welding Company.

	Annual Growth	12/05	12/06	12/07	12/08	12/09
Sales ($mil.)	15.4%	–	–	136.0	131.5	181.0
Net income ($ mil.)	–	–	–	5.9	7.1	–
Market value ($ mil.)	–	–	–	–	–	–
Employees	–	–	–	–	–	600

HIGHER ONE HOLDINGS, INC.

18700 N HAYDEN RD
SCOTTSDALE, AZ 852556759
Phone: 203 776-7776
Fax: –
Web: –

CEO: –
CFO: –
HR: –
FYE: December 31
Type: Private

The higher ambition at Higher One is to facilitate higher education payments. Doing business as CASHNet, the firm provides payment processing and disbursement services to some 700 colleges and universities and more than 5 million enrolled students across the US. To make financial transactions more efficient, it offers Refund Management disbursement service, which schools use to electronically distribute financial aid and other funds to students; CASHNet Payment Solutions, which offer billing and tuition payment options to students and parents; and OneAccount banking and card services for students. Blackboard acquired Higher One in a $260 million deal in 2016.

HII MISSION TECHNOLOGIES CORP.

8350 BROAD ST STE 1400
MC LEAN, VA 221025154
Phone: 703 918-4480
Fax: –
Web: www.hii.com

CEO: Steve Schorer
CFO: Kevin Cook
HR: Donna Foster
FYE: September 30
Type: Private

Alion Science and Technology provides advanced engineering and R&D services in the areas of intelligence, surveillance, and reconnaissance, military training and simulation, cyber, data analytics and other next-generation technology based solutions to the DoD and intelligence community customers, with the U.S. Navy representing about one-third of current annual revenues. With global industry expertise in big data, analytics, and cyber security; artificial intelligence and machine learning; live, virtual, and constructive solutions; electronic warfare and C5ISR; and rapid prototyping and manufacturing, Alion delivers mission success where and when it matters most. In 2021, the company was acquired by Huntington Ingalls Industries, the America's largest military shipbuilding company and a provider of professional services to partners in government and industry, for approximately $1.65 billion in cash.

HIGHLANDS BANKSHARES INC.

NBB: HBSI

3 North Main Street, P.O. Box 929
Petersburg, WV 26847
Phone: 304 257-4111
Fax: –
Web: www.grantcountybank.com

CEO: John G Van Meter
CFO: Jeffrey B Reedy
HR: Marcie L Yokum
FYE: December 31
Type: Public

No matter if you take the high road or the low road, Highlands Bankshares will take of your money afore ye. The company (not to be confused with Highlands Bankshares, headquartered in Virginia) is the holding company for The Grant County Bank and Capon Valley Bank, which together operate about a dozen branches in Virginia and West Virginia. The banks offer standard retail products and services, including demand and time deposit accounts and business and consumer loans. Real estate loans account for about 80% of the company's loan book. Highlands Bankshares also offers credit life, accident, and health insurance through HBI Life.

	Annual Growth	12/19	12/20	12/21	12/22	12/23
Assets ($mil.)	7.0%	418.9	475.5	518.4	527.4	548.2
Net income ($ mil.)	0.2%	3.5	3.3	4.9	4.4	3.6
Market value ($ mil.)	(0.4%)	52.3	45.9	58.8	57.5	51.5
Employees	–	–	–	–	–	–

HIL TECHNOLOGY, INC.

94 HUTCHINS DR
PORTLAND, ME 041021930
Phone: 207 756-6200
Fax: –
Web: www.hydro-int.com

CEO: Stephen Hides
CFO: Anthony Hollox
HR: –
FYE: December 31
Type: Private

Understanding HIL Technology is similar to drinking out of a fire hydrant. A US subsidiary of UK-based Hydro International, HIL makes and distributes stormwater management, and water and wastewater treatment equipment. Its stormwater products control and treat runoff, managing quantity and rate of flow of excess rainwater, remove sand and grit, and collect and filter water, largely for existing urban sites, and new commercial and residential projects. Water and wastewater products treat water and wastewater at municipal sewage and drinking water plants, and industrial discharge. HIL also offers rainwater harvesting systems to capture runoff for re-use. The company operates under the Hydro International name.

	Annual Growth	12/03	12/04	12/05	12/06	12/07
Sales ($mil.)	38.4%	–	–	–	7.9	10.9
Net income ($ mil.)	(63.9%)	–	–	–	3.1	1.1
Market value ($ mil.)	–	–	–	–	–	–
Employees	–	–	–	–	–	30

HIGHWOODS PROPERTIES, INC.

NYS: HIW

150 Fayetteville Street, Suite 1400
Raleigh, NC 27601
Phone: 919 872-4924
Fax: 919 431-1439
Web: www.highwoods.com

CEO: –
CFO: –
HR: –
FYE: December 31
Type: Public

Highwoods Properties, Inc. is a fully integrated office real estate investment trust (REIT) that owns, develops, acquires, leases, and managed properties primarily in the best business districts (BBDs) of Atlanta, Charlotte, Nashville, Orlando, Pittsburgh, Raleigh, Richmond and Tampa. The company owns a total of about 27.4 million sq. ft. of leasable space and has about 90% occupancy rate. Its largest tenants include the federal government, Bank of America, and Bridgestone Americas.

	Annual Growth	12/19	12/20	12/21	12/22	12/23
Sales ($mil.)	3.2%	736.0	736.9	768.0	828.9	834.0
Net income ($ mil.)	2.1%	136.9	347.4	313.3	159.1	148.7
Market value ($ mil.)	(17.2%)	5,170.3	4,189.3	4,713.6	2,957.8	2,427.1
Employees	(5.1%)	431	359	348	345	349

HILAND DAIRY FOODS COMPANY., LLC

1133 E KEARNEY ST
SPRINGFIELD, MO 658033435
Phone: 417 862-9311
Fax: –
Web: www.hilanddairy.com

CEO: –
CFO: –
HR: –
FYE: September 30
Type: Private

Hiland Dairy Foods is a farmer-owned dairy foods company that offers dairy products, including ice cream, milk, butter, cheese, and yogurt. It has expanded beyond dairy and has a wide variety of other beverages, such as Red Diamond Tea, lemonade, and fresh juices. Hiland runs about 20 processing plants and has nearly 65 distribution centers across the region. It partners with a larger dairy co-operative, Prairie Farms Dairy, to market and sell products. Beyond dairy, Hiland supplies juices, bottled milk and coffee, as well as tea, water, and other to-go drinks. It features limited-run specialty items, such as peanut butter banana ice cream. Hiland was founded in 1938.

	Annual Growth	09/07	09/08	09/09	09/10	09/11
Sales ($mil.)	30.8%	–	–	559.9	588.6	958.2
Net income ($ mil.)	(53.0%)	–	–	39.3	24.6	8.7
Market value ($ mil.)	–	–	–	–	–	–
Employees	–	–	–	–	–	1,350

HILAND HOLDINGS GP, LP

205 W MAPLE AVE STE 1100
ENID, OK 737010032
Phone: 580 242-6040
Fax: -
Web: www.hilandpartners.com

CEO: -
CFO: -
HR: -
FYE: December 31
Type: Private

Hiland Holdings lets Hiland Partners do all the work. The company owns a 2% general partner interest in the natural gas gathering and processing company. Hiland Partners serves primarily the Mid-Continent and Rocky Mountain regions of the US. It maintains natural gas gathering systems, processing plants, treating facilities, and NGL fractionation facilities. Hiland Partners supplies natural gas and NGL products to transmission pipelines and various markets. Hiland Partners chairman Harold Hamm owns about 32% of Hiland Holdings and plans to take both companies private.

HILBERT COLLEGE

5200 S PARK AVE
HAMBURG, NY 140751597
Phone: 716 649-7900
Fax: -
Web: www.hilbert.edu

CEO: -
CFO: -
HR: -
FYE: May 31
Type: Private

Hilbert College is a four-year liberal arts institution in the Catholic, Franciscan tradition not far from New York's Niagara Falls. The school has some 1,100 students and offers four-year bachelor degree programs and two-year associate degree programs. For those seeking a college major with the promise of some job security, Hilbert has one of the few Economic Crime Investigation programs in the country. It also offers about a dozen other bachelor-level programs. The university was founded in 1957 by Sister Edwina Bogel and named for Mother Colette Hilbert, founder of the Franciscan Sisters of St. Joseph.

	Annual Growth	05/17	05/18	05/20	05/21	05/22
Sales ($mil.)	18.6%	-	12.7	18.7	25.4	25.0
Net income ($ mil.)	-	-	(1.3)	(1.9)	1.2	(2.1)
Market value ($ mil.)	-	-	-	-	-	-
Employees						120

HILITE INTERNATIONAL, INC.

2001 PEACH ST
WHITEHALL, MI 494611844
Phone: 972 242-2116
Fax: -
Web: www.hilite.com

CEO: Karl Hammer
CFO: Stefan Eck
HR: Teresa Nails
FYE: December 31
Type: Private

The highlight of Hilite International's day is to manufacture high-volume, high-tech auto components and systems. Its lineup is used in many powertrain (engine and transmission) applications. Hilite's hydraulic and electromagnetic products (on/off valves and variable pressure solenoids) enhance fuel efficiency, emissions control, and torque. Hilite sells to global auto OEMs such as GM, BMW, and Honda, and brake systems suppliers such as BorgWarner. The company, established in 1999, operates through eight locations spanning Asia, Europe, and North America.

HILL COUNTRY MEMORIAL HOSPITAL

1020 S STATE HIGHWAY 16
FREDERICKSBURG, TX 786244471
Phone: 830 997-4353
Fax: -
Web: www.sahealth.com

CEO: Steve Kading
CFO: Mark Jones
HR: Alysha Metzger
FYE: December 31
Type: Private

Hill Country Memorial takes care of the peaks and valleys in the wellness of area residents. The health system provides medical services to eight counties near Fredericksburg in Central Texas. Its hospital, Hill Country Memorial Hospital, has about 85 beds and a staff of close to 100 physicians. Specialties include cardiology, obstetrics, oncology, orthopedics, and emergency medicine. The health system also operates a wellness center that offers locals yoga, stress management, weight loss, and massage. Other community services include hospice and home care, and the administration of state-funded services for low income women, infants, children (WIC).

	Annual Growth	12/10	12/11	12/12	12/16	12/21
Sales ($mil.)	1.7%	-	63.7	70.6	76.5	75.6
Net income ($ mil.)	-	-	(9.7)	3.0	25.2	21.7
Market value ($ mil.)	-	-	-	-	-	-
Employees	-	-	-	-	-	626

HILL INTERNATIONAL, INC.

2005 MARKET ST FL 17
PHILADELPHIA, PA 191037042
Phone: 215 309-7700
Fax: -
Web: www.hillintl.com

CEO: Raouf S Ghali
CFO: Todd Weintraub
HR: -
FYE: December 31
Type: Private

Hill International is one of the largest construction management firms in the US. With more than 3,200 professionals in over 100 offices worldwide, provides program management, project management, construction management, project management oversight, construction claims, dispute resolution, advisory, facilities management, and other consulting services to clients in a variety of market sectors. In late 2022, Hill International was acquired by Global Infrastructure Solutions Inc., the largest privately owned construction manager in the commercial building, industrial and healthcare markets, and a leading project/construction manager in the environmental and public infrastructure sectors.

HILL PHYSICIANS MEDICAL GROUP, INC.

2409 CAMINO RAMON
SAN RAMON, CA 945834285
Phone: 800 445-5747
Fax: -
Web: www.hillphysicians.com

CEO: David Joyner
CFO: -
HR: -
FYE: December 31
Type: Private

Hill Physicians Medical Group is the doctors' answer to HMOs. The company is an independent practice association (IPA) serving some 300,000 health plan members in northern California. The company contracts with managed care organizations throughout the region -- including HMOs belonging to Aetna, CIGNA, and Health Net-- to provide care to health plan members through its provider affiliates. Its network includes about 3,800 primary care and specialty physicians, 38 hospitals, and 24 urgent care centers. The company also provides administrative services for doctors and patients. PriMed, a management services organization, created Hill Physicians Medical Group in 1984 and still runs the company.

	Annual Growth	12/04	12/05	12/06	12/10	12/15
Sales ($mil.)	2.0%	-	414.4	427.5	427.5	504.8
Net income ($ mil.)	(1.3%)	-	7.8	5.3	5.3	6.8
Market value ($ mil.)	-	-	-	-	-	-
Employees	-	-	-	-	-	600

HILLENBRAND INC   NYS: HI

One Batesville Boulevard
Batesville, IN 47006
Phone: 812 931-5000
Fax: –
Web: www.hillenbrand.com

CEO: Kimberly K Ryan
CFO: Robert M Vanhimbergen
HR: –
FYE: September 30
Type: Public

Hillenbrand is a global diversified industrial company with multiple leading brands that serve a wide variety of industries worldwide. It has three very distinct businesses: Advanced Process Solutions designs, develops, manufactures, and services highly engineered industrial equipment throughout the world; Molding Technology Solutions, a global leader in highly engineered and customized systems and service in plastic technology and processing; and Batesville, a recognized leader in the death care industry in North America. Founded by John A. Hillenbrand in 1906, Hillenbrand generates just about 45% of its sales in the US. In late 2022, Hillenbrand entered into a definitive agreement to sell its Batesville business segment to an affiliate of private equity firm, LongRange Capital, for approximately $761.5 million, which includes an $11.5 million sub-note.

	Annual Growth	09/19	09/20	09/21	09/22	09/23
Sales ($mil.)	11.8%	1,807.3	2,517.0	2,864.8	2,940.9	2,826.0
Net income ($ mil.)	47.2%	121.4	(60.1)	249.9	208.9	569.7
Market value ($ mil.)	8.2%	2,158.5	1,982.4	2,981.2	2,566.7	2,957.5
Employees	12.5%	6,500	11,000	10,500	11,000	10,400

HILLS BANCORPORATION   NBB: HBIA

131 Main Street
Hills, IA 52235
Phone: 319 679-2291
Fax: –
Web: www.hillsbank.com

CEO: Dwight O Seegmilleer
CFO: Joseph A Schueller
HR: –
FYE: December 31
Type: Public

There's gold in them thar hills! Hills Bancorporation is the holding company for Hills Bank and Trust, which has about a dozen branches located in the eastern Iowa counties of Johnson, Linn, and Washington. The bank provides standard commercial services to area individuals, businesses, government entities, and institutional customers. Offerings include deposit accounts, loans, and debit and credit cards. Hills Bank and Trust also administers estates, personal trusts, and pension plans, and provides farm management and investment advisory and custodial services. The bank traces its roots to 1904.

	Annual Growth	12/19	12/20	12/21	12/22	12/23
Assets ($mil.)	7.1%	3,300.9	3,780.6	4,044.6	3,980.5	4,341.7
Net income ($ mil.)	(4.2%)	45.3	38.6	48.1	47.8	38.2
Market value ($ mil.)	3.8%	598.4	564.5	618.9	650.0	694.3
Employees	1.7%	484	529	498	527	517

HILLSBOROUGH COUNTY AVIATION AUTHORITY

4160 GEORGE J BEAN PKWY STE 2400
TAMPA, FL 336071440
Phone: 813 870-8700
Fax: –
Web: www.tampaairport.com

CEO: Joe Lopano
CFO: –
HR: –
FYE: September 30
Type: Private

If you've ever flown to the Tampa area to catch the NFL's Buccaneers or Major League Baseball's Rays, then you've probably been through an airport managed by the Hillsborough County Aviation Authority. The agency operates Tampa International Airport, which handles more than 8.4 million passengers annually, plus three general aviation airports. Three of the agency's five board members are residents of Hillsborough County who are appointed by the governor of Florida; other board members include the mayor of the City of Tampa and a member of the Hillsborough County Board of Commissioners. The Hillsborough County Aviation Authority was established by the Florida Legislature in 1945.

	Annual Growth	09/17	09/18	09/19	09/20	09/22
Sales ($mil.)	7.4%	–	234.7	253.5	183.1	311.9
Net income ($ mil.)	2.5%	–	44.1	13.7	53.0	48.6
Market value ($ mil.)	–	–	–	–	–	–
Employees	–	–	–	–	–	600

HILLTOP HOLDINGS, INC.   NYS: HTH

6565 Hillcrest Avenue
Dallas, TX 75205
Phone: 214 855-2177
Fax: –
Web: www.hilltop-holdings.com

CEO: Jeremy B Ford
CFO: William B Furr
HR: Dudley Strawn
FYE: December 31
Type: Public

With about $16.3 billion in assets, diversified financial holding company Hilltop Holdings' provides banking, mortgage origination, insurance, and financial advisory services through its PlainsCapital Bank, PrimeLending, and Momentum Independent Network subsidiaries. Hilltop offers community, commercial, and private banking through about 65 branches throughout Texas and holds some $11.3 billion in deposits. PrimeLending generates mortgages in all 50 states and District of Columbia through approximately 1,100 loan officers. Momentum Independent Network is an investment bank and is among the US top financial advisors to municipalities based on transaction volume.

	Annual Growth	12/19	12/20	12/21	12/22	12/23
Assets ($mil.)	2.1%	15,172	16,944	18,689	16,259	16,467
Net income ($ mil.)	(16.5%)	225.3	447.8	374.5	113.1	109.6
Market value ($ mil.)	9.0%	1,624.3	1,792.4	2,289.5	1,955.2	2,294.0
Employees	(6.3%)	4,950	4,950	4,950	4,170	3,820

HILTON GRAND VACATIONS INC   NYS: HGV

6355 MetroWest Boulevard, Suite 180
Orlando, FL 32835
Phone: 407 613-3100
Fax: –
Web: www.hgv.com

CEO: Mark D Wang
CFO: Daniel J Mathewes
HR: –
FYE: December 31
Type: Public

Hilton Grand Vacations Inc. (HGV) is a global timeshare company engaged in developing, marketing, selling, managing, and operating timeshare resorts, timeshare plans, and ancillary reservation services, primarily under the Hilton Grand Vacations brand. Its vacation ownership interests (VOI) product allows customers to advance purchase a lifetime of vacations and its customers also benefit from the amenities and services at its Hilton-branded resorts and Diamond resorts. The company had over 150 properties located in the US, Europe, Mexico, the Caribbean, Canada, and Japan. A significant number of its properties and VOIs are concentrated in Florida, Nevada, Hawaii, Europe, California, Virginia, and Arizona.

	Annual Growth	12/19	12/20	12/21	12/22	12/23
Sales ($mil.)	21.3%	1,838.0	894.0	2,335.0	3,835.0	3,978.0
Net income ($ mil.)	9.7%	216.0	(201.0)	176.0	352.0	313.0
Market value ($ mil.)	4.0%	3,644.0	3,321.9	5,521.6	4,083.7	4,257.5
Employees	13.3%	9,110	6,700	13,000	14,500	15,000

HILTON WORLDWIDE HOLDINGS INC   NYS: HLT

7930 Jones Branch Drive, Suite 1100
McLean, VA 22102
Phone: 703 883-1000
Fax: –
Web: www.hiltonworldwide.com

CEO: Christopher J Nassetta
CFO: Kevin J Jacobs
HR: Dana S Grylli
FYE: December 31
Type: Public

Hilton is a hospitality company, with about 7,165 comprising about 1,127,430 rooms in about 125 countries and territories. Founded in 1919, Hilton's premier brand portfolio includes its luxury hotel brands, Waldorf Astoria Hotels & Resorts; its emerging lifestyle hotel brands, Canopy by Hilton; its full service hotel brands, Signia by Hilton; its focused service hotel brands, Hilton Garden Inn, Hampton by Hilton and Tru by Hilton; its all-suites hotel brands, Embassy Suites by Hilton, Homewood Suites by Hilton and Home2 Suites by Hilton; and its timeshare brand, Hilton Grand Vacations. The company has about 152 million Hilton Honors members. Almost 80% of the company's total revenue comes from US.

	Annual Growth	12/19	12/20	12/21	12/22	12/23
Sales ($mil.)	2.0%	9,452.0	4,307.0	5,788.0	8,773.0	10,235
Net income ($ mil.)	6.7%	881.0	(715.0)	410.0	1,255.0	1,141.0
Market value ($ mil.)	13.2%	28,114	28,203	39,542	32,031	46,158
Employees	0.7%	173,000	141,000	142,000	159,000	178,000

HINES INTERESTS LIMITED PARTNERSHIP

845 TEXAS ST STE 3300
HOUSTON, TX 77002
Phone: 713 621-8000
Fax: –
Web: www.hines.com

CEO: Jeffery Hines
CFO: Keith Montgomery
HR: Laura Delatorre
FYE: December 31
Type: Private

Hines is a real estate firm that invests in, develops, renovates, manages, and finances commercial real estate, including high-rise office buildings, industrial parks, medical facilities, mixed-use developments, and master-planned residential communities. Its portfolio boasts around 1,610 properties completed, under development, managed, or invested totaling over 537 million sq. ft. The firm's property and asset management portfolio include approximately 685 properties, representing roughly 216 million sq. ft. and it spans in about 395 cities in some 30 countries. Hines has around $95.79 billion of investment assets under management and more than 96 million square feet of assets for which Hines provides third-party property-level services. Gerald Hines founded the family-controlled firm in 1957.

HINGHAM INSTITUTION FOR SAVINGS

NMS: HIFS

55 Main Street
Hingham, MA 02043
Phone: 781 749-2200
Fax: 781 740-4889
Web: www.hinghamsavings.com

CEO: Robert H Gaughen Jr
CFO: Cristian A Melej
HR: –
FYE: December 31
Type: Public

The Hingham Institution for Savings serves businesses and retail customers in Boston's south shore communities, operating more than 10 branches in Massachusetts in Boston, Cohasset, Hingham, Hull, Norwell, Scituate, South Hingham, and South Weymouth. Founded in 1834, the bank offers traditional deposit products, such as checking and savings accounts, IRAs, and certificates of deposit. More than 90% of its loan portfolio is split between commercial mortgages and residential mortgages (including home equity loans), though the bank also originates construction, business, and consumer loans. More than 95% of the company's revenue comes from loan interest.

	Annual Growth	12/19	12/20	12/21	12/22	12/23
Assets ($mil.)	14.7%	2,590.3	2,857.1	3,431.2	4,193.8	4,483.9
Net income ($ mil.)	(9.3%)	38.9	50.8	67.5	37.5	26.4
Market value ($ mil.)	(1.9%)	454.5	467.1	907.9	596.7	420.4
Employees	0.3%	90	87	76	92	91

HINSHAW & CULBERTSON LLP

151 N FRANKLIN ST STE 2500
CHICAGO, IL 606061821
Phone: 312 704-3000
Fax: –
Web: www.hinshawlaw.com

CEO: –
CFO: –
HR: –
FYE: December 31
Type: Private

Hinshaw & Culbertson's more than 400 lawyers offer a wide range of legal services, though the firm specializes in commercial and defense litigation and corporate, environmental, employment and construction law. It represents professionals dealing with appellate, bankruptcy, restructuring, and workouts, corporate, health care, taxation, white collar crime, insurance coverage, immigration, intellectual property, securities, real estate liability, data management, privacy, and cybersecurity issues. The firm also offers legal advisement services to architects, engineers, and people residing in the financial services sector. Hinshaw has about 25 offices nationwide and membership in Global Access Lawyers. The firm was founded in 1934.

	Annual Growth	12/00	12/01	12/02	12/03	12/10
Sales ($mil.)	7.2%	–	108.5	116.2	124.6	202.8
Net income ($ mil.)	9.4%	–	44.0	50.2	53.7	98.4
Market value ($ mil.)	–	–	–	–	–	–
Employees	–	–	–	–	–	1,010

HIREQUEST INC

NAS: HQI

111 Springhall Drive
Goose Creek, SC 29445
Phone: 843 723-7400
Fax: –
Web: www.hirequest.com

CEO: Richard Hermanns
CFO: David S Burnett
HR: –
FYE: December 31
Type: Public

Command Center wouldn't mind being regarded as the George Patton of the temporary staffing market. The company operates about 50 temporary staffing stores across 20 US states. It specializes in the placement of workers in the event services, hospitality, construction, manufacturing, janitorial, telemarketing, administrative, clerical, and accounting fields. Command Center was formed in 2005 when Temporary Financial Services acquired Command Staffing and Harborview Software, then changed its name. Command Center's top executives own about 34% of the company.

	Annual Growth	12/18	12/19	12/20	12/21	12/22
Sales ($mil.)	(24.9%)	97.4	15.9	13.8	22.8	31.0
Net income ($ mil.)	89.1%	1.0	(0.3)	5.4	11.8	12.5
Market value ($ mil.)	43.1%	52.4	98.4	141.8	279.8	219.4
Employees	26.4%	32,230	67,050	57,040	73,070	82,223

HIROTEC AMERICA INC.

3000 HIGH MEADOW CIR
AUBURN HILLS, MI 483262837
Phone: 248 836-5100
Fax: –
Web: www.hirotecamerica.com

CEO: Katsutoshi Uno
CFO: Brian McGinnity
HR: –
FYE: December 31
Type: Private

HIROTEC AMERICA (formerly TESCO Engineering) designs and builds the robotic equipment used to make doors, hoods, and other body panels for automobile and motorcycle manufacturers around the world, including General Motors, Harley-Davidson, and Toyota, among others. HIROTEC AMERICA products are touted as modular; in other words, the same equipment can be used to make several different automobile makes and models, boosting efficiency and lowering costs. The company also offers various engineering, consulting, plant and integration, and try-out services. HIROTEC AMERICA is part of a larger group of companies that are collectively owned by Japan's HIROTEC Corporation.

HISTOGEN INC

NAS: HSTO

10655 Sorrento Valley Road, Suite 200
San Diego, CA 92121
Phone: 858 526-3100
Fax: –
Web: www.histogen.com

CEO: Richard W Pascoe
CFO: Susan A Knudson
HR: –
FYE: December 31
Type: Public

Conatus Pharmaceuticals is ready to deliver a sliver of hope to people suffering from liver disease. The biotechnology company is developing a drug named emricasan to treat patients with chronic liver failure or liver fibrosis (scarring) from Hepatitis C. Emricasan is designed to reduce the enzymes that cause inflammation and cell death in order to interrupt the progression of liver disease; currently, there's no other drug like it. Pfizer initially developed the drug; Conatus bought the rights to emricasan in 2010. It is beginning Phase III trials in Europe and Phase II trials in the US in 2014. Conatus went public in mid-2013, raising $66 million in its IPO. It will use the proceeds to further fund the drug's development.

	Annual Growth	12/18	12/19	12/20	12/21	12/22
Sales ($mil.)	(42.1%)	33.6	21.7	2.1	1.0	3.8
Net income ($ mil.)	–	(18.0)	(11.4)	(18.8)	(15.0)	(10.6)
Market value ($ mil.)	(16.8%)	7.4	1.7	3.2	1.4	3.5
Employees	(31.1%)	31	6	19	22	7

HITCHINER MANUFACTURING CO., INC.

594 ELM ST
MILFORD, NH 030554306
Phone: 603 673-1100
Fax: –
Web: www.hitchiner.com

CEO: John Morison IV
CFO: –
HR: Amy Demmons
FYE: December 31
Type: Private

There's no hitch in Hitchiner Manufacturing's business plan. The family-owned supplier of thin-wall investment castings, and subassemblies and components operates 4 businesses: Ferrous-USA produces countergravity castings for the auto, defense, and pump and valve industries; Gas Turbine specializes in hot-section parts utilizing vacuum-melted alloys for the jet engine component market; Hitchiner Manufacturing Company de Mexico makes component parts for auto OEMs; and Hitchiner S.A. de C.V., front-end casting services. Hitchiner is primarily a tier-two supplier (its parts go to another company that contracts directly with the OEM) for majors such as BorgWarner, Goodrich, General Motors, and General Electric.

	Annual Growth	12/18	12/19	12/20	12/21	12/22
Sales ($mil.)	5.2%	–	–	202.3	213.9	223.8
Net income ($ mil.)	25.4%	–	–	11.3	17.6	17.8
Market value ($ mil.)	–	–	–	–	–	–
Employees	–	–	–	–	–	1,843

HITT CONTRACTING, INC.

2900 FAIRVIEW PARK DR
FALLS CHURCH, VA 220424513
Phone: 703 846-9000
Fax: –
Web: www.hitt.com

CEO: Kimberly Roy
CFO: Paul J Ross
HR: –
FYE: December 31
Type: Private

HITT Contracting is one of the nation's largest general contractors, offering lifecycle construction services from small projects to high rises and headquarters campuses. The company provides turnkey construction services for corporate base building and interiors, healthcare, aviation, law, hospitality, technology, healthcare, multifamily, and institutional and governmental facilities. In addition to general contracting, HITT offers design, interior, paint, preconstruction, and construction management services. It handles eco-friendly projects, historic renovations, and infrastructure refits. The company was founded in 1937.

HKN, INC.

180 STATE ST STE 200
SOUTHLAKE, TX 760927619
Phone: 817 424-2424
Fax: –
Web: www.hkninc.com

CEO: Mikel D Faulkner
CFO: Kristina M Humphries
HR: –
FYE: December 31
Type: Private

HKN (formerly Harken Energy) harkens back to the days when a certain President George W. Bush was an oil man. HKN, which bought Bush's small oil company more than a decade ago, explores for and produces oil and gas primarily in the US, where it has interests in oil and gas wells in the Gulf Coast region of Texas and Louisiana, and holds coalbed methane assets in the Midwest. Internationally, it has stakes in exploration and production assets in South America (Global Energy Development, 34%) and in Canada (Spitfire Energy, 27%). In 2008 HKN reported proved reserves (all in the US) of 4.2 billion cu. ft. of gas and 1.5 million barrels of oil. Lyford Investments Enterprises owns 36% of the voting stock of HKN.

HKS, INC.

350 N SAINT PAUL ST STE 100
DALLAS, TX 752014200
Phone: 214 969-5599
Fax: –
Web: www.hksinc.com

CEO: Dan Noble
CFO: Samuel Mudro
HR: –
FYE: December 31
Type: Private

HKS is a global firm of architects, designers, advisors and makers driven by curiosity and devoted to creating places that combine beauty with performance. HKS has designed sports and entertainment, healthcare, hospitality, industrial, and corporate buildings in the US and overseas. The company offers structural engineering, architecture, project management, and interior and graphic design services. It provides planning and development, programming, branding, research, and advisory services. HKS was founded in 1939 by Harwood K. Smith.

	Annual Growth	09/13	09/14*	12/15	12/18	12/21
Sales ($mil.)	7.6%	–	237.1	368.2	387.6	396.3
Net income ($ mil.)	466.9%	–	0.0	19.1	2.2	14.3
Market value ($ mil.)	–	–	–	–	–	–
Employees	–	–	–	–	–	1,550

*Fiscal year change

HLSS MANAGEMENT LLC

2002 SUMMIT BLVD FL 6
BROOKHAVEN, GA 303191560
Phone: 561 682-7561
Fax: –
Web: www.ir.hlss.com

CEO: –
CFO: –
HR: –
FYE: December 31
Type: Private

Home Loan Servicing Solutions is looking to get a grip on subprime mortgage services. The company, founded in late 2010 by Ocwen Financial's chairman William Erbey, plans to purchase the rights to a large portion of Ocwen's HomEq Mortgage Servicing portfolio. The portfolio comprises mortgage servicing rights to subprime and Alt-A mortgages (Alt-A mortgages are less risky than subprime mortgages but riskier than prime loans). Mortgage servicing activity includes, among other things, tracking late payments and resolving delinquent loans. In an effort to raise funds for its acquisition efforts, Home Loan Servicing went public in 2012; however, it delisted from NASDAQ in 2015.

HMG/COURTLAND PROPERTIES, INC.

1870 S. Bayshore Drive
Coconut Grove, FL 33133
Phone: 305 854-6803
Fax: –
Web: www.hmgcourtland.com

ASE: HMG
CEO: Maurice Wiener
CFO: –
HR: –
FYE: December 31
Type: Public

Sun, sea, and sand are key parts of the business mix for HMG/Courtland Properties, a real estate investment trust (REIT) that owns and manages commercial properties in the Miami area. The company owns the posh Grove Isle -- a Coconut Grove-area luxury resort, which includes a hotel, restaurant, spa, and marina. The property, managed by Grand Heritage Hotel Group, accounts for about 70% of HMG/Courtland's rental income. The REIT also holds a 50% interest in a 16,000 sq. ft. seafood restaurant at the marina, in addition to a 5,000 sq. ft. corporate office building. HMG/Courtland has two properties held for development in Rhode Island and Vermont and has equity interests in other commercial real estate operations.

	Annual Growth	12/16	12/17	12/18	12/19	12/20
Sales ($mil.)	4.4%	0.0	0.0	0.0	0.0	0.0
Net income ($ mil.)	–	(0.4)	(0.3)	4.1	0.3	(1.1)
Market value ($ mil.)	0.1%	10.6	14.6	13.9	12.9	10.6
Employees	–	–	–	–	–	–

HMH HOSPITALS CORPORATION

343 THORNALL ST
EDISON, NJ 088372206
Phone: 201 996-2000
Fax: –
Web: www.hackensackmeridianhealth.org

CEO: Robert C Garrett
CFO: Robert Glenning
HR: –
FYE: December 31
Type: Private

Hackensack University Medical Center (HUMC) is an acute care teaching and research hospital that serves northern New Jersey and parts of New York. The hospital has about 775 beds and staffs more than 2,200 medical professionals. HUMC administers general medical, surgical, emergency, and diagnostic care. The center also includes specialized treatment centers including a children's hospital, a women's hospital, a cancer center, and a heart and vascular hospital. HUMC is part of the Hackensack University Health Network, which also includes a physician practice group and a joint venture that operates two community hospitals. In 2016 the network merged with Meridian Health to create Hackensack Meridian Health.

	Annual Growth	12/13	12/14	12/15	12/16	12/18
Sales ($mil.)	32.2%	–	1,309.1	1,357.1	1,707.9	3,999.7
Net income ($ mil.)	19.9%	–	106.6	83.1	41.2	220.3
Market value ($ mil.)	–	–	–	–	–	–
Employees	–	–	–	–	–	1,100

HMN FINANCIAL INC.

1016 Civic Center Drive NW
Rochester, MN 55901
Phone: 507 535-1200
Fax: –
Web: www.hmnf.com

NMS: HMNF
CEO: Bradley C Krehbiel
CFO: Jon J Eberle
HR: –
FYE: December 31
Type: Public

HMN Financial is the holding company for Home Federal Savings Bank, which operates about a dozen branches in southern Minnesota and central Iowa. Serving individuals and local businesses, the bank offers such deposit products as checking and savings accounts, CDs, and IRAs. Its lending activities include commercial mortgages (more than 30% of the company's loan portfolio), business loans (about 25%), residential mortgages, and construction, development, and consumer loans. The bank provides financial planning, investment management, and investment products through its Osterud Insurance Agency subsidiary and Home Federal Investment Management.

	Annual Growth	12/19	12/20	12/21	12/22	12/23
Assets ($mil.)	9.2%	777.6	909.6	1,069.5	1,096.2	1,107.1
Net income ($ mil.)	(6.3%)	7.8	10.3	13.6	8.0	6.0
Market value ($ mil.)	2.3%	93.7	76.7	110.0	95.1	102.5
Employees	(4.1%)	190	180	163	164	161

HMS HOLDINGS LLC

5615 HIGH POINT DR STE 100
IRVING, TX 750382453
Phone: 214 453-3000
Fax: –
Web: www.gainwelltechnologies.com

CEO: William C Lucia
CFO: Jeffrey S Sherman
HR: –
FYE: December 31
Type: Private

HMS Holdings is an industry-leading provider of cost containment and analytical solutions in the healthcare marketplace. The company provides solutions such as Coordination of Benefits (COB), Payment Integrity (PI), and Payment Health Management (PHM). Through subsidiary Health Management Systems, the company also assist in identifying third party insurance and recovering medical expenses where a number is involved in a casualty or tort incident. HMS Holdings serves state Medicaid agencies and Children's Health Insurance Programs, as well as federal agencies, health plans and PBMs, healthcare exchanges, employers, at-risk providers and ACOs, and other healthcare organizations.

	Annual Growth	12/16	12/17	12/18	12/19	12/20
Sales ($mil.)	8.9%	–	521.2	598.3	626.4	673.3
Net income ($ mil.)	20.5%	–	40.1	55.0	87.2	70.1
Market value ($ mil.)	–	–	–	–	–	–
Employees	–	–	–	–	–	3,100

HNI CORP

600 East Second Street, P.O. Box 1109
Muscatine, IA 52761-0071
Phone: 563 272-7400
Fax: 563 272-7114
Web: www.hnicorp.com

NYS: HNI
CEO: Jeffrey D Lorenger
CFO: Marshall H Bridges
HR: –
FYE: December 30
Type: Public

HNI Corporation is a manufacturer of workplace furnishings and residential building products. Workplace furnishing products include furniture systems, seating, storage, tables, and architectural products, and are marketed under brands such as HON, Allsteel, and Maxon. The company sells to furniture dealers, wholesalers, and wholesale distributors as well as retailers. HNI's Hearth & Home Technologies participates in the hearth products industry, manufactures and markets products under various brand names. The unit operates under the Fireside Hearth & Home banner. Residential Building products are sold through independent dealers and distributors as well as company-owned distribution centers, installing distributors, and retail outlets. Founded in 1944, HNI is North America's largest manufacturer and marketer of prefabricated fireplaces, hearth stoves, and related products.

	Annual Growth	12/19*	01/21	01/22*	12/22	12/23
Sales ($mil.)	2.0%	2,246.9	1,955.4	2,184.4	2,361.8	2,434.0
Net income ($ mil.)	(18.3%)	110.5	41.9	59.8	123.9	49.2
Market value ($ mil.)	2.9%	1,752.7	1,616.2	1,972.1	1,333.4	1,961.8
Employees	(0.6%)	8,500	7,700	8,100	7,300	8,300

*Fiscal year change

HO-CHUNK, INC.

1 MISSION DR
WINNEBAGO, NE 680715167
Phone: 402 878-4135
Fax: –
Web: www.hochunkinc.com

CEO: –
CFO: –
HR: –
FYE: December 31
Type: Private

Ho-Chunk, Inc. (HCI) the economic development corporation run by the Winnebago Tribe of Nebraska, manages about 18 subsidiaries in the fields of communications, construction, distribution, gasoline and convenience store retail (under the Heritage Express banner in Iowa and Nebraska), government contracting, lodging (The WinnaVegas Inn), marketing, used-vehicle sales, and more. The profits from these businesses are in turn managed by the Ho-Chunk Community Development Corporation, a not-for-profit organization that directs commercial growth and community infrastructure development for the tribe. "Ho-Chunk" is a modernized form of Hochungra, the Winnebago tribe's traditional name.

	Annual Growth	12/04	12/05	12/06	12/07	12/09
Sales ($mil.)	24.8%	–	63.6	113.0	121.4	154.3
Net income ($ mil.)	(27.7%)	–	16.4	0.7	1.1	4.5
Market value ($ mil.)	–	–	–	–	–	–
Employees	–	–	–	–	–	310

HOAG HOSPITAL FOUNDATION

330 PLACENTIA AVE STE 100
NEWPORT BEACH, CA 926633309
Phone: 949 764-7217
Fax: –
Web: www.hoaghospitalfoundation.org

CEO: Flynn A Andrizzi
CFO: –
HR: –
FYE: December 31
Type: Private

Hoag Hospital Foundation supports the Hoag Memorial Hospital Presbyterian by raising money for the hospital's operations, medical research, education, and community outreach activities. The foundation's volunteers are organized into groups such as the 552 Club and Circle 1000 who host events like the Christmas Carol Ball and the Toshiba Classic and encourage donors to make annual gifts. It raised about $40 million in 2012. Donations through the Hoag Hospital Foundation enabled completion of Phase I of the Hoag Heart & Vascular Institute renovation, as well as program development at the Mary & Dick Allen Diabetes Center and 80 new nursing scholarships.

HOAG MEMORIAL HOSPITAL PRESBYTERIAN

1 HOAG DR
NEWPORT BEACH, CA 926634162
Phone: 949 764-4624
Fax: –
Web: www.hoag.org

CEO: Robert Braithwaite
CFO: –
HR: –
FYE: December 31
Type: Private

Serving California's Orange County population, Hoag Memorial Hospital Presbyterian boasts several hospitals and even more clinics to cater to area residents. The not-for-profit health care system is home to two acute care hospitals, ten health centers, about 15 urgent care centers, and a network of more than 1,800 physicians. Its hospitals include Hoag Hospital Irvine, Hoag Orthopedic Institute and Hoag Hospital Newport Beach in Southern California. Combined, these hospitals provide a comprehensive range of medical and surgical services, with specialized expertise in a number of areas, such as cancer, heart and vascular, neurosciences, women's health, and orthopedics.

	Annual Growth	12/18	12/19	12/20	12/21	12/22
Sales ($mil.)	29.1%	–	–	–	1,275.1	1,646.5
Net income ($ mil.)	(88.6%)	–	–	–	403.0	45.8
Market value ($ mil.)	–	–	–	–	–	–
Employees		–	–	–	–	3,800

HOAK MEDIA, LLC

3963 MAPLE AVE STE 450
DALLAS, TX 752193236
Phone: 972 960-4840
Fax: –
Web: –

CEO: –
CFO: –
HR: –
FYE: December 31
Type: Private

From the icy conditions in Fargo to the heat waves in Texas, Hoak Media's TV stations are adept to all climates. As an owner and operator of about two dozen television stations, Hoak Media operates in small- to medium-sized markets, primarily in North and South Dakota, but also in Colorado, Nebraska, Louisiana, and other states. Its portfolio of stations contains affiliates of all four major networks, as well as The CW and MyNetworkTV affiliates. Hoak Media was founded in 2003 by Jim Hoak, CEO Eric Van den Branden, and other investors. The company has added stations to its portfolio in almost every year since its founding.

HOBART AND WILLIAM SMITH COLLEGES

300 PULTENEY ST
GENEVA, NY 144563304
Phone: 315 781-3337
Fax: –
Web: www.hws.edu

CEO: –
CFO: –
HR: –
FYE: June 30
Type: Private

Hobart and William Smith Colleges offer a liberal arts education on the shores of Seneca Lake. The schools operate in conjunction on adjacent campuses, making a nearly 200-acre complex in Geneva, New York. Male students attend Hobart College and female students go to William Smith College, for a total enrollment of about 2,400. The colleges have nearly 230 faculty members and offer degrees in arts, sciences, and teaching. Hobart and William Smith students hail from 41 US states and more than 30 other countries. About 86% of its students receive financial aid.

	Annual Growth	05/18	05/19	05/20	05/21*	06/22
Sales ($mil.)	18.5%	–	107.9	162.3	164.7	179.6
Net income ($ mil.)		–	–	(4.8)	(0.1)	12.5	17.5
Market value ($ mil.)		–	–	–	–	–
Employees		–	–	–	–	337

*Fiscal year change

HOBBY LOBBY STORES, INC.

7707 SW 44TH ST
OKLAHOMA CITY, OK 731794899
Phone: 405 745-1100
Fax: –
Web: www.hobbylobby.com

CEO: David Green
CFO: Jon Cargill
HR: Dana Cackey
FYE: December 31
Type: Private

Hobby Lobby is the largest privately-owned arts-and-crafts retailer in the world. The craft-and-fabric company operates more than 900 stores in more than 45 US states. It is primarily an arts-and-crafts store but also includes hobbies, picture framing, jewelry making, fabrics, floral and wedding supplies, cards and party ware, baskets, wearable art, home decor and holiday merchandise. Hobby Lobby also maintains offices in Hong Kong, Shenzhen, and Yiwu, China. In addition, the company operates Mardel Christian and Education Supply, which sells Christian, educational, and homeschooling products. CEO David Green, who owns the company, founded Hobby Lobby in 1972 and operates it according to biblical principles, including closing shop on Sunday.

	Annual Growth	12/02	12/03	12/04	12/06	12/17
Sales ($mil.)	27.5%	–	150.9	1,363.4	196.6	4,544.2
Net income ($ mil.)	13.7%	–	58.8	88.5	58.0	352.7
Market value ($ mil.)	–	–	–	–	–	–
Employees		–	–	–	–	23,000

HODGSON MILL, INC.

22 HAMILTON WAY
CASTLETON ON HUDSON, NY 120331015
Phone: 888 417-9343
Fax: –
Web: www.hodgsonmill.com

CEO: –
CFO: Jeff Masters
HR: –
FYE: December 31
Type: Private

When it comes to making whole grain products, Hodgson Mill is rock solid. The company touts its use of grinding stones (rather than the steel blades that the big companies use) to mill a variety of grains, including wheat, oats, rye, and corn. The Missouri mill was built in 1837; company founder Alva Hodgson purchased the mill after its second rebuilding in 1882. Hodgson Mill products include flours, flax seed, couscous, cereals, bread and baking mixes, batters, and non-gluten and soy products. It has added wholewheat and veggie dried pastas to its offerings, which are available at retail food outlets nationwide.

	Annual Growth	05/04	05/05	05/06*	12/07	12/08
Sales ($mil.)	9.3%	–	–	22.0	22.9	26.3
Net income ($ mil.)	(80.9%)	–	–	7.2	0.1	0.3
Market value ($ mil.)	–	–	–	–	–	–
Employees		–	–	–	–	6

*Fiscal year change

HOFFMAN CORPORATION

805 SW BROADWAY STE 2100
PORTLAND, OR 972053361
Phone: 503 221-8811
Fax: –
Web: www.hoffmancorp.com

CEO: –
CFO: Mario Nudo
HR: –
FYE: December 31
Type: Private

Hoffman is one of the largest general contractors in the US, with projects in over a dozen states and overseas. It serves such sectors as education, healthcare, hospitality, athletics, transportation, industrial, and government. It provides deep preconstruction and construction resources, renovations, tenant improvements, and other services. Its divisions include structural concrete, mechanical, electrical, instrumentation and controls and surveying. Some of its projects include Overlook Wall in Seattle; Idaho Central Credit Union Arena, Hayward Field, Oak Harbor Clean Water Facility and Alder Red Retail Store, among others. Lee Hawley Hoffman founded in the company in 1922.

HOFMANN INDUSTRIES, INC.

3145 SHILLINGTON RD
READING, PA 196081606
Phone: 610 678-8051
Fax: –
Web: www.hofmann.com

CEO: Stephen P Owens
CFO: –
HR: –
FYE: December 31
Type: Private

Offenbach does not work here. These tales of Hofmann come from the sales guys and are about tubing deals. Hofmann Industries is a beginning-to-end manufacturer of welded steel tubing, powder-coated tubing, zinc-plated tubing, and fabricated tubing. The company's main customers are in the agricultural equipment, automotive, fitness, furniture, lawn and garden, and recreational and sporting goods industries. Its tubes can be found in such products as bicycle racks, table legs, closet shelving, curtain rods, lawn mower handles, and flag poles. Hoffman has 13 tube mills and three powder coating lines; it provides large-run and contract manufacturing from its almost half-million square foot facility.

HOFSTRA UNIVERSITY

100 HOFSTRA UNIVERSITY
HEMPSTEAD, NY 115494001
Phone: 516 463-6600
Fax: –
Web: www.hofstra.edu

CEO: –
CFO: –
HR: –
FYE: August 31
Type: Private

Hofstra University is busy. Sponsoring some 500 cultural events each year, the private, nonsectarian four-year university has an annual enrollment of some 11,000 full- and part-time students. To encourage the success of its students, Hofstra maintains a low student-faculty ratio of 14 to 1. It offers more than 140 undergraduate program options and about 150 graduate program options in liberal arts and sciences; education, health, and human services; business; communications; and honors studies. It has a School of Law, School of Engineering and Applied Science, and Hofstra North Shore-LIJ School of Medicine. Hofstra University was founded in 1935 by trustees of the estate of William and Kate Hofstra.

	Annual Growth	08/08	08/09	08/10	08/11	08/12
Sales ($mil.)	1.5%	–	–	370.4	390.0	381.7
Net income ($ mil.)	(16.4%)	–	–	35.6	50.0	24.9
Market value ($ mil.)	–	–	–	–	–	–
Employees		–	–	–	–	2,000

HOHNER, INC.

12020 VOLUNTEER BLVD
MOUNT JULIET, TN 371221000
Phone: 800 446-6010
Fax: –
Web: www.hohnerusa.com

CEO: –
CFO: Eg Martin
HR: –
FYE: March 31
Type: Private

Hohner has made a big business of selling little harmonicas. Hohner (AKA Hohner HSS) is the US marketing and distribution arm of German instrument maker, Matth. Hohner. Established in the US in 1986, the company distributes Hohner harmonicas as well as accordions, recorders, melodicas, fretted instruments, HSS bags and cases, Sonor drums and percussion items, Lanikai ukuleles, and Rockwood drums and guitars. Hohner also makes music stands and accessories and has a separate line of musical instruments and toys for children (Hohner Kids) that includes shakers, whistles, finger castanets, and drums. Matthias Hohner founded the parent company in 1857 at age 24, to mass produce harmonicas.

HOLDER PROPERTIES, INC.

3300 CUMBERLAND BLVD SE STE 200
ATLANTA, GA 303398103
Phone: 770 988-3131
Fax: –
Web: www.holderproperties.com

CEO: John Holder
CFO: Lori Pisarcik
HR: –
FYE: March 31
Type: Private

Holder Properties can hold the fort and build it too. The company is a commercial real estate developer that builds and leases office and industrial space and offers property management services. Holder Properties has developed facilities for such companies as T-Mobile, Northrop Grumman, and Turner Broadcasting; it also builds speculative projects (properties built before tenants or buyers are lined up). The company's portfolio is located primarily in Georgia and other southeastern states, but it has expanded to midwestern, northwestern, and northeastern states in recent years. It manages more than 8 million sq. ft. of office and industrial space. Holder Properties was founded in 1980.

	Annual Growth	03/04	03/05	03/06	03/07	03/09
Assets ($mil.)	(7.4%)	–	9.3	7.2	6.9	6.8
Net income ($ mil.)	–	–	(0.0)	0.0	(0.0)	(0.0)
Market value ($ mil.)		–	–	–	–	–
Employees		–	–	–	–	32

HOLIDAY BUILDERS, INC.

2293 W EAU GALLIE BLVD
MELBOURNE, FL 329353184
Phone: 321 610-5156
Fax: –
Web: www.holidaybuilders.com

CEO: Bruce Assam
CFO: Mendy McCann
HR: –
FYE: December 31
Type: Private

Holiday Builders is out to make buying a new home a vacation-like experience. The company, a 100% employee-owned enterprise since 1999, builds single-family detached homes throughout Florida, and in Alabama, South Carolina, and Texas. Since its inception the company has built more than 30,000 homes, sold primarily to first-time and value-conscious buyers. The company offers full homebuying services to its clients through HBI Title Company, Holiday Builders Real Estate, HB Designs, and a partnership with Shelter Mortgage. Holiday Builders was founded in 1983.

	Annual Growth	12/03	12/04	12/05	12/06	12/07
Sales ($mil.)	(41.8%)	–	–	691.8	699.2	234.1
Net income ($ mil.)	–	–	–	42.4	40.5	(26.2)
Market value ($ mil.)		–	–	–	–	–
Employees		–	–	–	–	101

HOLIDAY INN CLUB VACATIONS INCORPORATED

9271 S JOHN YOUNG PKWY
ORLANDO, FL 328198607
Phone: 407 239-0000
Fax: –
Web: www.holidayinnclub.com

CEO: Charles K Swan III
CFO: –
HR: Tara Hunsinger
FYE: December 31
Type: Private

Holiday Inn Club Vacations (formerly Orange Lake Country Club) is a resort, real estate and travel company that offers many destinations and vacation experiences to discover exciting theme parks and dynamic cities to stunning mountainside vistas and relaxing beaches. The company is a timeshare company that offers points-based vacation ownership. Holiday Inn Club Vacations was founded by Kemmons Wilson and is majority owned by the Wilson family.

HOLIDAY ISLAND HOLDINGS INC   NBB: HIHI

193 Wild Turkey Drive
Holiday Island, AR 72631
Phone: 479 244-6047
Fax: –
Web: www.holidayislandholdings.com

CEO: –
CFO: –
HR: –
FYE: December 31
Type: Public

VillageEDOCS believes it takes their village of tools to help you solve your business problems. The company provides Software as a Service (SaaS) hosted services that offer outsourced Internet-based broadcast fax transmission services for invoices, billing statements, and purchase orders through its MessageVision subsidiary. It operates enhanced voice and data communications services through its GoSolutions unit, and provides document management and archiving services through subsidiary Questys. VillageEDOCS also provides consulting, installation, support, maintenance, and training. The company targets the financial services, health care, manufacturing, and local government markets as a whole.

HOLIDAY WHOLESALE, INC.

225 PIONEER DR
WISCONSIN DELLS, WI 539658397
Phone: 608 254-8321
Fax: –
Web: www.holidaywholesale.com

CEO: –
CFO: –
HR: –
FYE: February 28
Type: Private

Holiday Wholesale services most of south and central Wisconsin with confections, tobacco products, paper goods, and food products. The company's customers are primarily convenience stores and other small businesses. Holiday Wholesale also offers consultation services, including a demographic study of the customer's location, estimate of foot traffic, and evaluation of proposed floor plans. In addition to its wholesale business, the company also sells a number of its products (at wholesale prices) to the general public through its Showroom Store location. The company was founded in 1951 when it began operating out of a one-car garage.

	Annual Growth	02/05	02/06	02/07	02/08	02/09
Sales ($mil.)	4.3%	–	111.4	113.3	120.2	126.5
Net income ($ mil.)	(6.3%)	–	0.8	0.8	0.8	0.6
Market value ($ mil.)	–	–	–	–	–	–
Employees	–	–	–	–	–	250

HOLLAND COMMUNITY HOSPITAL AUXILIARY, INC.

602 MICHIGAN AVE
HOLLAND, MI 494234918
Phone: 616 748-9346
Fax: –
Web: www.hollandhospital.org

CEO: Dale Sowders
CFO: –
HR: Megan Scott
FYE: March 31
Type: Private

Holland Hospital (formerly Holland Community Hospital) provides a comprehensive range of health services to residents of western Michigan's Lakeshore region. The 190-bed, not-for-profit hospital provides a variety of medical care and health services, including primary, emergency, diagnostic, surgical, rehabilitative, and inpatient behavioral health care. Holland Hospital is home to centers of excellence in the treatment of sleep disorders, cancer, women's health issues, and cardiovascular ailments. The hospital provides community health and wellness education programs, and operates a regional community health clinic. Founded in 1917, Holland Hospital employs some 330 physicians across 14 medical specialties.

	Annual Growth	03/18	03/19	03/20	03/21	03/22
Sales ($mil.)	0.3%	–	258.6	258.3	267.6	260.9
Net income ($ mil.)	42.7%	–	6.4	(22.8)	61.0	18.6
Market value ($ mil.)	–	–	–	–	–	–
Employees	–	–	–	–	–	1,500

HOLLAND SOUTHWEST INTERNATIONAL, INCORPORATED

6831 SILSBEE ST
HOUSTON, TX 770331114
Phone: 713 644-1966
Fax: –
Web: www.hollandsw.com

CEO: –
CFO: –
HR: –
FYE: June 30
Type: Private

Distributor Holland Southwest International supplies forest products from vendors throughout the world. The company boasts inventory facilities in Baltimore, Houston and Memphis. It specializes in worldwide sourcing and inventory support to accommodate any requirement for industrial, commercial or OEM forest products. Holland's products may be ordered in truckload or LTL quantities. Among its dealer and industrial products include plywood paneling, Russian birch plywood, tileboard, NRP/FRP, and foils, among others. The company was founded by Gus Gillebaard, an immigrant from Holland, as a small import company in 1953.

	Annual Growth	12/02	12/03	12/04	12/05*	06/20
Sales ($mil.)	(34.2%)	–	–	28.5	29.4	0.0
Net income ($ mil.)	–	–	–	0.5	0.0	(0.0)
Market value ($ mil.)	–	–	–	–	–	–
Employees	–	–	–	–	–	30

*Fiscal year change

HOLLINGSWORTH OIL COMPANY, INC.

1503 MEMORIAL BLVD STE B
SPRINGFIELD, TN 371723269
Phone: 615 242-8466
Fax: –
Web: suddenservice.business.site

CEO: –
CFO: –
HR: –
FYE: December 31
Type: Private

The Hollingsworth Companies meets companies' industrial-strength needs. The company develops and builds industrial parks and facilities in the southeastern US. It provides build-to-suit and finish-to-suit structures, primarily on its SouthPoint Business Park pad-ready sites located in Alabama, North Carolina, Tennessee, and Virginia. Developments typically range from 50,000 sq. ft. to 500,000 sq. ft. Hollingsworth also provides facility expansion and funding services. All of the company's SouthPoint properties are located in areas convenient to interstate highways and airport services. CEO and owner Joe Hollingsworth, Jr., founded The Hollingsworth Companies in 1986.

	Annual Growth	12/13	12/14	12/16	12/17	12/18
Sales ($mil.)	(4.1%)	–	547.4	380.9	408.2	463.5
Net income ($ mil.)	9.4%	–	0.9	1.3	2.5	1.3
Market value ($ mil.)	–	–	–	–	–	–
Employees	–	–	–	–	–	300

HOLLINS UNIVERSITY CORPORATION

7916 WILLIAMSON RD
ROANOKE, VA 240194421
Phone: 540 362-6000
Fax: –
Web: www.hollins.edu

CEO: –
CFO: –
HR: –
FYE: June 30
Type: Private

Hollins University was founded in 1842 as the first chartered women's college in Virginia. It has about 600 female undergraduates, as well as some 200 students in its graduate school, which is coeducational. A private institution emphasizing the liberal arts, Hollins offers some 25 undergraduate majors and a dozen graduate degrees in subjects such as creative writing, liberal studies, children's literature, teaching, and film studies. Notable alumni include the first woman publisher at Time (Elizabeth Valk Long, '72) and the first woman to be named a White House correspondent (Ann Compton, '69).

	Annual Growth	06/17	06/18	06/19	06/20	06/21
Sales ($mil.)	25.4%	–	33.6	33.8	31.9	66.2
Net income ($ mil.)	153.7%	–	0.6	(6.4)	(12.8)	10.6
Market value ($ mil.)	–	–	–	–	–	–
Employees	–	–	–	–	–	380

HOLMES LUMBER & BUILDING CENTER, INC.

6139 S R 39
MILLERSBURG, OH 44654
Phone: 330 674-9060
Fax: –
Web: www.holmeslumber.com

CEO: –
CFO: –
HR: –
FYE: December 31
Type: Private

Try building a home -- or any other structure -- without the products that Holmes Lumber supplies. The building materials retailer sells lumber, blocks, bricks, cabinets, doors, paneling, ceiling tiles, hardware, and other building materials to professional contractors and consumers at three Holmes Lumber and Building Centers in Hartville, Millersburg, and Sugarcreek Ohio. Founded in 1952 as Holmes Door & Lumber Co., the business was acquired by family-owned Carter Lumber of Kent, Ohio in 2004, adding Holmes' operations to its 200-plus stores in 10 states.

	Annual Growth	12/04	12/05	12/06	12/07	12/08
Sales ($mil.)	5.1%	–	–	–	47.1	49.5
Net income ($ mil.)	–	–	–	–	0.4	(0.5)
Market value ($ mil.)	–	–	–	–	–	–
Employees	–	–	–	–	–	150

HOLMES REGIONAL MEDICAL CENTER, INC.

1350 HICKORY ST
MELBOURNE, FL 329013224
Phone: 321 434-7000
Fax: –
Web: www.hf.org

CEO: –
CFO: –
HR: –
FYE: September 30
Type: Private

If you're a Great Space Coaster, you might depend on Holmes Regional Medical Center in times of medical need. The general acute-care hospital, which houses about 515 beds and provides comprehensive medical and surgical care, serves residents of Brevard County on Florida's Space Coast. A member of not-for-profit health care system Health First, Holmes Regional Medical Center offers specialty care in a number of areas, including trauma, oncology, cardiology, orthopedics, pediatrics, and women's health. It also operates an air ambulance service, a stroke care center, a full-service endoscopy unit, and an outpatient diagnostic facility, as well as advanced robotic surgery and joint replacement centers.

	Annual Growth	09/12	09/13	09/14	09/19	09/22
Sales ($mil.)	8.5%	–	391.8	412.5	703.9	817.2
Net income ($ mil.)	62.2%	–	0.6	72.2	59.1	50.5
Market value ($ mil.)	–	–	–	–	–	–
Employees	–	–	–	–	–	2,778

HOLOBEAM, INC.

NBB: HOOB

217 First Street, P.O. Box 287
Ho-Ho-Kus, NJ 07423-0287
Phone: 201 445-2420
Fax: –
Web: –

CEO: –
CFO: –
HR: –
FYE: September 30
Type: Public

Holobeam develops and leases commercial real estate in New Jersey. The company owns two buildings in Paramus, New Jersey; with a total of approximately 95,000 sq. ft. of space. The properties house retail businesses. Befitting its scientific-sounding name, Holobeam developed and was granted several patents for surgical staple technology. However, it ditched that venture in the early 2000s after finding the demand wasn't strong enough to pursue. Chairman Melvin Cook and family (including his wife and company secretary, Beverly) own a majority of Holobeam.

	Annual Growth	09/02	09/03	09/04	09/05	09/06
Sales ($mil.)	0.9%	2.1	2.0	2.1	2.1	2.1
Net income ($ mil.)	21.9%	0.2	0.2	0.2	0.5	0.4
Market value ($ mil.)	11.0%	7.0	6.2	7.3	11.1	10.6
Employees	–	–	3	3	3	3

HOLOGIC INC

NMS: HOLX

250 Campus Drive
Marlborough, MA 01752
Phone: 508 263-2900
Fax: 781 280-0669
Web: www.hologic.com

CEO: Stephen P Macmillan
CFO: Karleen M Oberton
HR: –
FYE: September 30
Type: Public

Hologic develops, manufactures, and supplies a variety of women's health products focused on four areas: breast health, diagnostics, gynecological surgical health, and skeletal health. Its offerings include the Aptima line of diagnostic tests, the Dimensions 3D mammography platform, the ThinPrep Pap test for cervical cancer screening, the NovaSure System to treat excessive bleeding, and the Fluoroscan Mini C-arm Imaging system used to guide doctors during orthopedic surgery. Hologic sells its products to hospitals and clinical labs worldwide. Overall, the company generates the majority of its revenue in the US.

	Annual Growth	09/19	09/20	09/21	09/22	09/23
Sales ($mil.)	4.6%	3,367.3	3,776.4	5,632.3	4,862.8	4,030.4
Net income ($ mil.)	–	(203.6)	1,115.2	1,871.5	1,302.0	456.0
Market value ($ mil.)	8.8%	11,991	15,554	18,486	15,223	16,775
Employees	1.9%	6,478	5,814	6,705	6,944	6,990

HOLY CROSS HOSPITAL, INC.

4725 N FEDERAL HWY
FORT LAUDERDALE, FL 333084668
Phone: 954 771-8000
Fax: –
Web: www.holy-cross.com

CEO: Patrick Taylor
CFO: Linda Wilford
HR: Geoffrey Washburn
FYE: June 30
Type: Private

Holy Cross Hospital's patients have more than just doctors on their side. Holy Cross is a Catholic community hospital serving the Ft. Lauderdale, Florida, area. The hospital has about 560 beds and offers inpatient and outpatient medical services along with a cancer treatment center, heart and vascular center, women's health center, orthopedic unit, and home health division, as well as outpatient imaging centers. It also operates family health and specialist clinics in the region. Sponsored by the Sisters of Mercy, Holy Cross Hospital is a part of Trinity Health.

	Annual Growth	06/17	06/18	06/20	06/21	06/22
Sales ($mil.)	6.7%	–	470.4	526.0	599.4	609.4
Net income ($ mil.)	–	–	8.9	(19.7)	29.7	(3.4)
Market value ($ mil.)	–	–	–	–	–	–
Employees	–	–	–	–	–	2,300

HOMASOTE CO.

NBB: HMTC

932 Lower Ferry Road, P.O. Box 7240
West Trenton, NJ 08628-0240
Phone: 609 883-3300
Fax: 609 530-1584
Web: www.homasote.com

CEO: Warren L Flicker
CFO: Ronald Fasano
HR: Paul Volkoff
FYE: December 31
Type: Public

Homasote Company sees green when it comes to building materials. It manufactures environmentally friendly fiberboard for use in residential and commercial construction. The fiberboard is made from recycled paper and contains no asbestos or formaldehyde. Applications include roof decking, concrete forming, paneling, insulating, sound proofing, and industrial packaging purposes. Its Pak-Line division creates packaging materials for electronics. Homasote processes up to 250 tons of post-consumer paper daily, helping to conserve 1.4 million trees and eliminate 65 million pounds of waste per year. Formed in 1909, Homasote is the oldest manufacturer of post-consumer recycled paper building and packaging products.

	Annual Growth	12/17	12/18	12/19	12/20	12/21
Sales ($mil.)	(2.0%)	20.6	20.6	19.8	18.4	19.0
Net income ($ mil.)	–	1.4	1.0	0.4	1.2	(0.4)
Market value ($ mil.)	(10.7%)	2.9	3.7	3.3	3.3	1.8
Employees	–	–	–	–	–	–

HOME BANCORP INC
NMS: HBCP

503 Kaliste Saloom Road
Lafayette, LA 70508
Phone: 337 237-1960
Fax: 337 264-9280
Web: www.home24bank.com

CEO: John W Bordelon
CFO: David T Kirkley
HR: –
FYE: December 31
Type: Public

Making its home in Cajun Country, Home Bancorp is the holding company for Home Bank, a community bank which offers deposit and loan services to consumers and small to midsized businesses in southern Louisiana. Through about two dozen branches, the bank offers standard savings and checking accounts, as well as lending services such as mortgages, consumer loans, and credit cards. Its loan portfolio includes commercial real estate, commercial, and industrial loans, as well as construction and land loans. Home Bancorp also operates about half a dozen bank branches in west Mississippi, which were formerly part of Britton & Koontz Bank.

	Annual Growth	12/19	12/20	12/21	12/22	12/23
Assets ($mil.)	10.8%	2,200.5	2,591.9	2,938.2	3,228.3	3,320.1
Net income ($ mil.)	9.6%	27.9	24.8	48.6	34.1	40.2
Market value ($ mil.)	1.8%	319.7	228.4	338.7	326.6	342.7
Employees	–	–	–	–	445	484	477

HOME BANCSHARES INC
NYS: HOMB

719 Harkrider, Suite 100
Conway, AR 72032
Phone: 501 339-2929
Fax: –
Web: www.homebancshares.com

CEO: John W Allison
CFO: Brian S Davis
HR: –
FYE: December 31
Type: Public

Home BancShares is the holding company for Centennial Bank (the bank), which operates about 160 branches in Arkansas, Alabama, New York and Florida. The bank offers traditional services such as checking, savings, and money market accounts; IRAs; and CDs. It focuses on commercial real estate lending, including construction, land development, and agricultural loans, which make up about 60% of its lending portfolio. The bank also writes residential mortgage, business, and consumer loans. Nonbank subsidiaries offer trust and insurance services. The company has a total assets of $18.1 billion. Home BancShares was formed by an investor group led by John W. Allison, its Chairman, and Robert H. "Bunny" Adcock, Jr., its Vice Chairman in 1998.

	Annual Growth	12/19	12/20	12/21	12/22	12/23
Assets ($mil.)	10.8%	15,032	16,399	18,052	22,884	22,657
Net income ($ mil.)	7.9%	289.5	214.4	319.0	305.3	392.9
Market value ($ mil.)	6.5%	3,962.0	3,925.7	4,907.2	4,592.8	5,104.7
Employees	10.1%	1,920	2,018	1,992	2,774	2,819

HOME DEPOT INC
NYS: HD

2455 Paces Ferry Road
Atlanta, GA 30339
Phone: 770 433-8211
Fax: 770 431-2707
Web: www.homedepot.com

CEO: Edward P Decker
CFO: Richard V McPhail V
HR: –
FYE: January 28
Type: Public

Home Depot is the world's largest home improvement chain and one of the largest retailers in the US. The company operates more than 2,320 stores in North America. It targets the do-it-yourself (DIY), Do-It-For-Me (DIFM) and professional markets with its selection of up to 40,000 items, including lumber, flooring, plumbing supplies, garden products, tools, paint, and appliances. The Home Depot also offers installation services for cabinetry and other products for its do-it-for-me (DIFM) customers. It conducts e-commerce operations through its websites (including thecompanystore.com) and mobile apps. More than 90% of its total revenue is generated within the US.

	Annual Growth	02/20*	01/21	01/22	01/23	01/24
Sales ($mil.)	8.5%	110,225	132,110	151,157	157,403	152,669
Net income ($ mil.)	7.7%	11,242	12,866	16,433	17,105	15,143
Market value ($ mil.)	11.7%	226,275	268,653	363,608	314,156	352,458
Employees	2.7%	415,700	504,800	490,600	471,600	463,100

*Fiscal year change

HOME ENERGY SAVINGS CORP
NBB: HESV

710 Third Street
Roanoke, VA 24061
Phone: 540 345-3358
Fax: –
Web: –

CEO: Bruce Edwards
CFO: –
HR: –
FYE: June 30
Type: Public

Home is where the savings -- and the dreams -- are. Home Energy Savings (formerly Elite Flight Solutions) has grounded its aviation-related businesses and set a course for home improvements and financing. After selling its Optimum Aviation unit and air ambulance service provider American Air Network Alaska (AANA) in 2006, the company operates through subsidiaries DreamHome Solutions (sales and installation of energy-efficient products) and Aim American Mortgage (home improvement financing and mortgages). The company opened a DreamHome Solutions location in metropolitan Philadelphia in 2006.

	Annual Growth	06/00	06/01	06/02	06/03	06/04
Sales ($mil.)	2821.3%	–	–	–	0.2	4.9
Net income ($ mil.)	–	–	–	–	(0.9)	(6.0)
Market value ($ mil.)	(96.5%)	–	–	–	0.4	0.0
Employees	211.1%	–	–	–	9	28

HOME INSTEAD, INC.

13323 CALIFORNIA ST
OMAHA, NE 681545240
Phone: 402 498-4466
Fax: –
Web: www.homeinstead.com

CEO: Anthony Crosen
CFO: –
HR: Chris Purles
FYE: December 31
Type: Private

The company is the world's largest provider of home care franchise model. Home Instead professional CAREGivers are providing care services to ageing adults around the world. Home Instead has a network of almost 1,200 franchises operating throughout the US and in about 15 countries worldwide. Though global in scale, the Home Instead network remains grounded at a personal level - building personalized one-on-one relationships between care professionals and seniors in the comfort of home. Home Instead Senior Care was founded in 1994 by Paul and Lori Hogan.

	Annual Growth	12/04	12/05	12/06	12/07	12/08
Assets ($mil.)	(89.9%)	–	–	4.9	7.4	0.0
Net income ($ mil.)	–	–	–	7.7	8.5	(0.1)
Market value ($ mil.)	–	–	–	–	–	–
Employees	–	–	–	–	–	796

HOME LOAN FINANCIAL CORP
NBB: HLFN

413 Main Street
Coshocton, OH 43812
Phone: 740 622-0444
Fax: 740 622-5389
Web: www.homeloanfinancialcorp.com

CEO: Robert C Hamilton
CFO: Breann L Miller
HR: –
FYE: June 30
Type: Public

Home Loan Financial is the holding company for Home Loan Savings, which has about five branches in eastern Ohio's Coshocton and Knox counties. True to its name, the bank primarily originates one- to four-family residential mortgages, which account for more than two-thirds of its loan portfolio. It also issues commercial loans and mortgages, construction loans, and consumer loans. Founded in 1882 as The Home Building Savings and Loan, the bank offers standard deposit products including checking and savings accounts, CDs, and money market accounts. Home Loan Financial completed a reverse stock split transaction in August 2005, allowing it to deregister from the Nasdaq.

	Annual Growth	06/19	06/20	06/21	06/22	06/23
Assets ($mil.)	7.9%	214.7	244.7	252.6	254.6	291.2
Net income ($ mil.)	8.4%	3.7	3.6	3.8	4.2	5.2
Market value ($ mil.)	(4.9%)	49.0	41.6	45.5	46.9	40.1
Employees	–	–	–	–	–	–

HOME PRODUCTS INTERNATIONAL INC.

4501 West 47th Street
Chicago, IL 60632
Phone: 773 890 1010
Fax: –
Web: www.hpii.com

CEO: George Hamilton
CFO: Dennis Doheny
HR: –
FYE: January 1
Type: Public

Home Products International (HPI) helps folks get organized. The company makes an array of plastic storage containers, including carts, crates, bins, totes, and tubs (some with more than 60 gallons of stowing space). It also produces and markets closet organizers, clothing hampers, ironing boards, shower caddies, hangers, and hooks. HPI markets its products under the HOMZ brand and sells them in North and South America through retailers, such as Wal-Mart, Target, Staples, and Bed Bath & Beyond, as well as online via Amazon.com and other merchants. The company also markets its products to hotels and other clients in the hospitality industry.

	Annual Growth	12/00	12/01	12/02	12/03*	01/05
Sales ($mil.)	(3.2%)	297.0	249.7	249.2	233.6	260.3
Net income ($ mil.)	–	(71.5)	17.0	14.3	(11.3)	(4.6)
Market value ($ mil.)	6.5%	14.3	24.1	37.4	9.4	18.3
Employees	(10.4%)	1,345	1,215	1,255	883	865

*Fiscal year change

HOMESTREET INC

NMS: HMST

601 Union Street, Suite 2000
Seattle, WA 98101
Phone: 206 623-3050
Fax: –
Web: www.homestreet.com

CEO: –
CFO: –
HR: –
FYE: December 31
Type: Public

HomeStreet is a diversified financial services company with offices in Washington, Oregon, California, Hawaii, Arizona, Utah, and Idaho serving customers throughout the western US. HomeStreet is principally engaged in commercial banking, consumer banking, mortgage banking and consumer/retail banking activities. It provides commercial banking products and services to small and medium sized businesses, real estate investors and professional firms and consumer banking products and services to individuals. Founded in 1921, HomeStreet has some $9.4 billion assets.

	Annual Growth	12/19	12/20	12/21	12/22	12/23
Assets ($mil.)	8.4%	6,812.4	7,237.1	7,204.1	9,364.8	9,392.5
Net income ($ mil.)	–	17.5	80.0	115.4	66.5	(27.5)
Market value ($ mil.)	(25.8%)	639.5	634.8	978.1	518.8	193.7
Employees	(4.7%)	1,071	1,030	984	937	883

HOMETOWN AMERICA, L.L.C.

150 N WACKER DR STE 2800
CHICAGO, IL 606061610
Phone: 312 604-7500
Fax: –
Web: www.hometownamerica.com

CEO: Richard Cline
CFO: –
HR: –
FYE: December 31
Type: Private

There's no place like home for Hometown America. The company invests in and manages manufactured home parks throughout the US. Across 10 US states Hometown America owns more than 45 communities, many of which feature recreational facilities, such as swimming pools, clubhouses, and basketball courts. With California and Florida among its largest markets, Hometown America operates properties for all ages, as well as those that are targeted toward active seniors (under the Providence brand). It's expanding in California and Delaware. The company, founded in 1997, also offers home financing and insurance through agreements with third-party providers.

HOMEVESTORS OF AMERICA, INC.

6500 GREENVILLE AVE STE 400
DALLAS, TX 752061002
Phone: 972 761-0046
Fax: –
Web: www.homevestors.com

CEO: David Hicks
CFO: –
HR: –
FYE: December 31
Type: Private

HomeVestors has turned fixer-uppers into its bread and butter. Operating under the slogan "We Buy Ugly Houses," the company purchases single-family houses, condos, townhomes, row houses, duplexes, and fourplexes, usually from owners who are motivated to sell their properties quickly and at a discount. It also renovates, sells, and rents properties. HomeVestors has some 200 franchised offices in about 35 states. The company provides access to financing, training, research and analysis, and advertising -- billboards, radio and TV spots, and direct mail -- to its network of franchisees. The late Ken D'Angelo founded HomeVestors in 1989. Franchise Brands acquired majority ownership of the company in 2008.

	Annual Growth	12/10	12/11	12/12	12/13	12/14
Assets ($mil.)	47.9%	–	–	7.3	10.3	16.0
Net income ($ mil.)	132.7%	–	–	1.3	2.2	7.1
Market value ($ mil.)	–	–	–	–	–	–
Employees	–	–	–	–	–	20

HONEYWELL INTERNATIONAL INC

NMS: HON

855 South Mint Street
Charlotte, NC 28202
Phone: 704 627-6200
Fax: 973 455-4807
Web: www.honeywell.com

CEO: Lucian Boldea
CFO: Gregory P Lewis
HR: –
FYE: December 31
Type: Public

Incorporated in Delaware in 1985, Honeywell International Inc. invents and commercializes technologies that address some of the world's most critical challenges around energy, safety, security, air travel, productivity, and global urbanization. The company is a leading software-industrial company committed to introducing state of the art technology solutions to improve efficiency, productivity, sustainability, and safety in high growth businesses in broad-based, attractive industrial end markets. The major products and services, including Honeywell Forge solutions supported by Honeywell Connected Enterprise. The company does business worldwide, and generates around 60% its sales in the US.

	Annual Growth	12/19	12/20	12/21	12/22	12/23
Sales ($mil.)	–	36,709	32,637	34,392	35,466	36,662
Net income ($ mil.)	(2.0%)	6,143.0	4,779.0	5,542.0	4,966.0	5,658.0
Market value ($ mil.)	4.3%	115,369	138,638	135,907	139,681	136,689
Employees	(4.2%)	113,000	103,000	99,000	97,000	95,000

HONORHEALTH AMBULATORY

8125 N HAYDEN RD
SCOTTSDALE, AZ 852582463
Phone: 623 580-5800
Fax: –
Web: www.honorhealth.com

CEO: Thomas J Sadvary
CFO: Paul Briggs
HR: Judie Goe
FYE: December 31
Type: Private

HonorHealth is a non-profit, local community healthcare system serving an area of 1.6 million people in the greater Phoenix area. The network encompasses six acute-care hospitals, an extensive medical group, outpatient surgery centers, a cancer care network, clinical research, medical education, a foundation, and community services with approximately 13,700 employees, 3,700 affiliated providers, and nearly 800 volunteers. HonorHealth was formed by a merger between Scottsdale Healthcare and John C. Lincoln Health Network.

	Annual Growth	12/15	12/16	12/17	12/18	12/19
Sales ($mil.)	(87.5%)	–	1,716.5	1,763.2	1,967.2	3.4
Net income ($ mil.)	–	–	93.0	105.0	77.3	–
Market value ($ mil.)	–	–	–	–	–	–
Employees	–	–	–	–	–	17,000

HONSHY ELECTRIC CO., INC.

7345 SW 41ST ST
MIAMI, FL 331554503
Phone: 305 264-5500
Fax: –
Web: www.honshyelectric.com

CEO: –
CFO: –
HR: –
FYE: December 31
Type: Private

Honshy Electric Company is plugged into being a top Hispanic-owned business in Florida. The enterprise provides a full range of general electrical contracting services that includes organizing, installing, and repairing wiring and electricity systems, computer cabling and networking systems, and lighting. Honshy Electri specializes in high-rise buildings, but also works on education, government, hotel, commercial, institutional, and residential facilities. The firm also provides upgrades, troubleshooting, and inspection services. Company president Manuel Diaz owns the company, which was founded in 1973.

	Annual Growth	12/03	12/04	12/05	12/09	12/10
Sales ($mil.)	(8.2%)	–	10.1	1.3	8.2	6.0
Net income ($ mil.)	–	–	0.1	0.6	0.4	(0.0)
Market value ($ mil.)	–	–	–	–	–	–
Employees	–	–	–	–	–	192

HOOKER FURNISHINGS CORP

NMS: HOFT

440 East Commonwealth Boulevard
Martinsville, VA 24112
Phone: 276 632-2133
Fax: –
Web: www.hookerfurniture.com

CEO: Jeremy R Hoff
CFO: Paul A Huckfeldt
HR: –
FYE: January 29
Type: Public

Hooker Furniture is a designer, marketer, and importer of casegoods (wooden and metal furniture), leather furniture, fabric-upholstered furniture, and outdoor furniture for the residential, hospitality, and contract market. It also domestically manufactures premium residential custom leather and custom fabric-upholstered furniture. It sells furniture under the Samuel Lawrence Furniture by Home Meridian label. Hooker Furniture's popular Bradington-Young line includes residential upholstered upscale motion and stationary leather furniture. Hooker Furniture also offers home furnishings centered around an eclectic mix of unique pieces and materials that offer a fresh take on home fashion focused on e-commerce customers through Accentrics Home. International customers account for less than 5% of the company's revenue.

	Annual Growth	02/19	02/20*	01/21	01/22	01/23
Sales ($mil.)	(3.9%)	683.5	610.8	540.1	593.6	583.1
Net income ($ mil.)	–	39.9	17.1	(10.4)	11.7	(4.3)
Market value ($ mil.)	(8.4%)	327.0	275.9	337.4	235.6	229.8
Employees	(0.1%)	1,263	1,251	1,148	1,294	1,259

*Fiscal year change

HOOSIER ENERGY RURAL ELECTRIC COOPERATIVE INC

2501 S COOPERATIVE WAY
BLOOMINGTON, IN 474035175
Phone: 812 876-2021
Fax: –
Web: www.hoosierenergy.com

CEO: J S Smith
CFO: –
HR: Megan Miller
FYE: December 31
Type: Private

Who's yer daddy? In terms of providing electricity, for many Indianans (and some residents of Illinois) that would be Hoosier Energy Rural Electric Cooperative, which provides wholesale electric power to 18 member distribution cooperatives in 59 central and southern Indiana counties, and 11 counties in southeastern Illinois. These electric cooperatives serve 300,000 consumers (650,000 residents, businesses, industries and farms) in a 18,000 sq. ml. service area. Hoosier Energy operates six power plants and a 1,720-mile transmission system, and maintains the Tuttle Creek Reservoir in Southwest Indiana. Hoosier Energy is part of the Touchstone Energy network of electric cooperatives.

	Annual Growth	12/07	12/08	12/09	12/11	12/12
Sales ($mil.)	4.1%	–	–	575.0	649.6	647.9
Net income ($ mil.)	18.9%	–	–	16.6	30.3	27.9
Market value ($ mil.)	–	–	–	–	–	–
Employees	–	–	–	–	–	475

HOP ENERGY, LLC

4 INTERNATIONAL DR
PORT CHESTER, NY 105737015
Phone: 914 304-1300
Fax: –
Web: www.hopenergy.com

CEO: Michael Anton
CFO: Richard Nota
HR: –
FYE: September 30
Type: Private

HOP Energy (formerly Heating Oil Partners) hops to it when it comes to serving about 100,000 commercial and residential customers in an eight-state region from Boston to Philadelphia with heating oil, central air conditioning, commercial fuels, fleet fueling, and heating/air conditioning equipment (HVAC) services. The environmentally conscious company carefully maintains its own bulk storage fuel facilities ans supplies biofuels. HOP Energy also conducts inspections and performs preventative maintenance on its customers' heating equipment to help improve fuel efficiency and reduce particulate emissions. It also helps customer secure electricity services.

HOPTO INC

NBB: HPTO

189 North Main Street, Suite 102
Concord, NH 03301
Phone: 408 688-2674
Fax: –
Web: www.hopto.com

CEO: Jonathon R Skeels
CFO: Jonathon R Skeels
HR: –
FYE: December 31
Type: Public

GraphOn keeps its thin clients on a diet. The company provides business connectivity software that delivers applications to PCs and workstations from a host computer. The company's products enable clients to relocate desktop software to centralized servers and deploy and manage applications when needed, thus conserving computing resources. GraphOn's software can be used to provide access to applications through Linux, UNIX, and Windows platforms. The company serves clients in a variety of industries, including telecommunications, software development, manufacturing, financial services, and electronics.

	Annual Growth	12/18	12/19	12/20	12/21	12/22
Sales ($mil.)	5.5%	3.2	3.5	3.6	3.6	3.9
Net income ($ mil.)	–	(0.0)	0.6	0.7	1.1	0.1
Market value ($ mil.)	21.1%	4.3	7.5	8.8	8.5	9.2
Employees	1.7%	14	13	13	13	15

HORACE MANN EDUCATORS CORP.

NYS: HMN

1 Horace Mann Plaza
Springfield, IL 62715-0001
Phone: 217 789-2500
Fax: –
Web: www.horacemann.com

CEO: Marita Zuraitis
CFO: Bret A Conklin
HR: Michele Brown
FYE: December 31
Type: Public

Horace Mann Educators is an insurance holding company that primarily serves K-12 school teachers, administrators, and other employees of public schools and their families. Through its operating subsidiaries, the company offers personal lines of property and casualty insurance products, life insurance products, retirement products, worksite direct insurance products, and employer-sponsored group benefits products. Horace Mann employs agents, many of whom are former teachers themselves. Writing business in all 50 states and the US Virgin Islands and the District of Columbia, the top five states and their portion of total direct insurance premiums and contract deposits for the worksite direct business were California, Texas, Florida, North Carolina, and Louisiana. Horace Mann was founded in 1945 by two Springfield, Illinois, teachers who saw a need for quality, affordable auto insurance for teachers.

	Annual Growth	12/19	12/20	12/21	12/22	12/23
Assets ($mil.)	3.0%	12,479	13,472	14,384	13,447	14,050
Net income ($ mil.)	(29.7%)	184.4	133.3	142.8	(2.6)	45.0
Market value ($ mil.)	(7.0%)	1,782.9	1,716.8	1,580.4	1,526.1	1,335.4
Employees	2.5%	1,538	1,490	1,450	1,700	1,700

HORIZON BANCORP INC

NMS: HBNC

515 Franklin Street
Michigan City, IN 46360
Phone: 219 879-0211
Fax: -
Web: www.horizonbank.com

CEO: Craig M Dwight
CFO: Mark E Secor
HR: -
FYE: December 31
Type: Public

For those in Indiana and Michigan, Horizon Bancorp stretches as far as the eye can see. The company is the holding company for Horizon Bank (and its Heartland Community Bank division), which provides checking and savings accounts, IRAs, CDs, and credit cards to customers through more than 50 branches in north and central Indiana and southwest and central Michigan. Commercial, financial, and agricultural loans make up the largest segment of its loan portfolio, which also includes mortgage warehouse loans (loans earmarked for sale into the secondary market), consumer loans, and residential mortgages. Through subsidiaries, the bank offers trust and investment management services; life, health, and property/casualty insurance; and annuities.

	Annual Growth	12/19	12/20	12/21	12/22	12/23
Assets ($mil.)	10.9%	5,246.8	5,886.6	7,374.9	7,872.5	7,940.5
Net income ($ mil.)	(19.5%)	66.5	68.5	87.1	93.4	28.0
Market value ($ mil.)	(6.8%)	829.4	692.3	910.1	658.3	624.7
Employees	1.1%	839	815	912	923	876

HORIZON PHARMA, INC.

1 HORIZON WAY
DEERFIELD, IL 600153888
Phone: 224 383-3000
Fax: -
Web: www.horizontherapeutics.com

CEO: -
CFO: -
HR: -
FYE: December 31
Type: Private

Horizon Pharma sees commercial drug success in its future. The biopharmaceutical develops medicines for arthritis, pain, and inflammatory diseases through its three operating subsidiaries in the US, Switzerland, and Germany. Its DUEXIS and Vimovo pills combine two existing drugs to treat mild to moderate pain from rheumatoid arthritis while reducing the risk of stomach ulcers associated with some pain relievers. Its RAYOS (known as LODOTRA outside the US) is a form of prednisone, formulated to reduce morning stiffness from rheumatoid arthritis. Horizon Pharma sells its products in the US, Europe, the Middle East, and Africa. The company bought Raptor Pharmaceuticals in 2016 for some $800 million.

HORIZON PHARMACEUTICAL LLC

7 HAMILTON LANDING # 100
NOVATO, CA 949498209
Phone: 224 383-3699
Fax: -
Web: www.horizontherapeutics.com

CEO: -
CFO: -
HR: -
FYE: December 31
Type: Private

Raptor Pharmaceuticals is on the hunt for rare disease cures. The commercial-stage biopharmaceutical specializes in developing small molecule therapies to treat orphan diseases. It has two products on the market -- PROCYSBI (for the management of nephropathic cystinosis, approved in Europe) and QUINSAIR (for the management of chronic pulmonary infections in cystic fibrosis patients, also approved in Europe). The PROCYSBI molecule RP103 also holds US orphan drug designation for the treatment of Huntington's disease and other neurodegenerative diseases. Horizon Pharma acquired Raptor Pharmaceuticals for $800 million in October 2016 to expand its rare disease business.

HORIZON TELCOM, INC.

68 E MAIN ST
CHILLICOTHE, OH 456012503
Phone: 740 772-8200
Fax: -
Web: www.horizonconnects.com

CEO: -
CFO: -
HR: -
FYE: December 31
Type: Private

Horizon Telcom's reach spans telephone, pay television, Internet access, and information technology services. Serving home subscribers and businesses primarily in southern Ohio, the company offers local and long distance phone calling, digital cable (under the View Plus brand), as well high-speed DSL Internet services. In addition, Horizon Telcom offers its business customers such technology services as software development, business networking, and Web hosting. It also sells and installs business phone systems from vendors like NEC, as well as security systems for homes and businesses (Horizon Safe & Sound). Four of the company's directors own significant stakes in Horizon Telcom.

	Annual Growth	12/04	12/05	12/06	12/08	12/09
Sales ($mil.)	-	-	-	(74.4)	46.6	44.5
Net income ($ mil.)	1990.4%	-	-	0.0	4.0	5.7
Market value ($ mil.)	-	-	-	-	-	-
Employees	-	-	-	-	-	285

HORMEL FOODS CORP.

NYS: HRL

1 Hormel Place
Austin, MN 55912-3680
Phone: 507 437-5611
Fax: 507 437-5489
Web: www.hormelfoods.com

CEO: James P Snee
CFO: Jacinth C Smiley
HR: Katherine M Losness-Larson
FYE: October 29
Type: Public

Hormel Foods is a global branded food company bringing some of the most trusted and iconic brands to tables across the globe. It produces a slew of refrigerated processed meats and deli items, ethnic entrees, and frozen foods, sold under the flagship Hormel brand, as well as Don Miguel, MegaMex, and Lloyd's (barbeque). Food service offerings include Do a Maria, Cafe H, Austin Blues, Fast 'N Easy, and Bread Ready pre-sliced meats. Hormel is also a major US turkey and pork processor, churning out Jennie-O turkey, Cure 81 hams, and Always Tender pork. The vast majority of its total sales were from domestic operations.

	Annual Growth	10/19	10/20	10/21	10/22	10/23
Sales ($mil.)	6.3%	9,497.3	9,608.5	11,386	12,459	12,110
Net income ($ mil.)	(5.1%)	978.8	908.1	908.8	1,000.0	793.6
Market value ($ mil.)	(6.2%)	22,176	27,117	23,132	25,668	17,158
Employees	1.6%	18,800	19,100	20,000	20,000	20,000

HORNBLOWER YACHTS, LLC

PIER 3 THE EMBARCADERO
SAN FRANCISCO, CA 94111
Phone: 415 424-4309
Fax: -
Web: www.cityexperiences.com

CEO: Terry Macrae
CFO: -
HR: Gregory Shephard
FYE: December 31
Type: Private

Hornblower provides sightseeing, dining, and wedding cruises. The company has yachts sailing from about 20 California ports, including Berkeley, San Diego, Newport Beach, Marina del Rey, and San Francisco. Regularly scheduled tours include brunch, dinner, date night, and corporate events. City Cruises also provides cruises for private events, including corporate functions. Subsidiaries Alcatraz Cruises and Statue Cruises run a ferry service to Alcatraz in California and the Statue of Liberty National Monument and Ellis Island in New York through a deal with the National Park Service. CEO Terry MacRae founded Hornblower in 1980 with two yachts.

	Annual Growth	12/02	12/03	12/04	12/06	12/09
Sales ($mil.)	29.5%	-	-	32.2	35.2	117.6
Net income ($ mil.)	9.9%	-	-	7.5	2.0	11.9
Market value ($ mil.)	-	-	-	-	-	-
Employees	-	-	-	-	-	2,404

HORNE INTERNATIONAL INC

3975 University Drive, Suite 100
Fairfax, VA 22030
Phone: 703 641-1100
Fax: –
Web: www.horne.com

CEO: Dallas Evans
CFO: John E Donahue
HR: –
FYE: December 31
Type: Public

At the nexus where government agencies, national security, and environmental sustainability meet, you'll find Horne International. Through its primary operating subsidiary, Horne Engineering Services, the company offers military base and homeland security, missile defense, ecosystems management and restoration, and business process engineering services. It also offers public outreach services, including the organization of public meetings and drafting Congressional testimony. Not surprisingly, the US government's departments of Homeland Security, Defense, and Transportation are Horne's primary customers. Horne, which has struggled in the recession, owes nearly 85% of sales to its three largest customers.

	Annual Growth	12/08	12/09	12/10	12/11	12/12
Sales ($mil.)	(4.0%)	4.9	4.7	3.4	5.7	4.1
Net income ($ mil.)	–	(6.1)	(0.3)	(1.0)	(0.1)	(1.6)
Market value ($ mil.)	(8.5%)	1.4	4.3	7.1	6.2	1.0
Employees	–	–	–	–	–	–

HORRY TELEPHONE COOPERATIVE, INC.

3480 HIGHWAY 701 N
CONWAY, SC 295265702
Phone: 843 365-2151
Fax: –
Web: www.htcinc.net

CEO: Mike Hagg
CFO: Duane C Lewis Jr
HR: Gidget Johnson
FYE: December 31
Type: Private

Horry Telephone Cooperative (HTC) is the incumbent local exchange carrier (ILEC) serving rural Horry County in South Carolina (population: about 270,000). HTC offers local and long-distance voice service, Internet access, cable TV, home security service, and mobile phone service (through AT&T Mobility). It also offers business services such as remote recovery, LAN and WAN design, and firewall and network security and provides bundled telecommunications services to residential and business customers via its Bluewave fiber-to-the-home business. Membership in the cooperative is open to any customer who receives at least one of HTC's primary services.

	Annual Growth	12/05	12/06	12/07	12/08	12/09
Sales ($mil.)	–	–	–	(1,361.9)	162.9	172.8
Net income ($ mil.)	10020.7%	–	–	0.0	3.7	4.3
Market value ($ mil.)	–	–	–	–	–	–
Employees	–	–	–	–	–	690

HORTON (DR) INC

1341 Horton Circle
Arlington, TX 76011
Phone: 817 390-8200
Fax: –
Web: www.drhorton.com

NYS: DHI
CEO: –
CFO: –
HR: –
FYE: September 30
Type: Public

The largest US homebuilder by volume, D.R. Horton constructs single-family homes that range in size from 1,000 sq. ft. to more than 4,000 sq. ft. and sell for an average price range of about $200,000 to more than 1,000,000 under the D.R. Horton, America's Builder, Emerald Homes, Express Homes, and Freedom Homes. D.R. Horton is active in roughly 105 markets in about 35 states. Through its mortgage, title and insurance subsidiaries, D.R. Horton provides mortgage financing, title services and insurance services for its homebuyers. The company also constructs and sells both single-family and multi-family rental properties and is the majority owner of Forestar Group, a national residential lot development company.

	Annual Growth	09/19	09/20	09/21	09/22	09/23
Sales ($mil.)	19.2%	17,593	20,311	27,774	33,480	35,460
Net income ($ mil.)	30.9%	1,618.5	2,373.7	4,175.8	5,857.5	4,745.7
Market value ($ mil.)	19.5%	17,650	25,325	28,117	22,552	35,986
Employees	10.8%	8,916	9,716	11,788	13,237	13,450

HOSPICE OF MICHIGAN, INC.

400 GALLERIA OFFICENTRE STE 400
SOUTHFIELD, MI 480342162
Phone: 313 578-5000
Fax: –
Web: www.hom.org

CEO: Dottie Deremo
CFO: Robert Cahill
HR: –
FYE: December 31
Type: Private

When it comes to hospice care, experience counts. As the largest hospice provider in Michigan, Hospice of Michigan (HOM) has plenty of it. HOM provides specialized health care to patients with terminal illnesses. The organization's nurses, home health aids, and volunteers help patients manage pain and other symptoms, provide spiritual and emotional support, and offer grief counseling to family members. The organization works with about 1,000 patients on any given day at some 20 locations throughout Michigan's lower peninsula. Its services are offered in patient homes, as well as in hospitals and nursing homes. Hospice of Michigan was created in 1994 when several smaller hospice programs joined forces.

	Annual Growth	12/12	12/13	12/17	12/18	12/22
Sales ($mil.)	(13.6%)	–	66.0	18.0	15.4	17.8
Net income ($ mil.)	–	–	2.3	1.7	0.0	(2.0)
Market value ($ mil.)	–	–	–	–	–	–
Employees	–	–	–	–	–	500

HOSPIRA, INC.

275 N FIELD DR
LAKE FOREST, IL 600452510
Phone: 224 212-2000
Fax: –
Web: www.hospira.com

CEO: F M Ball
CFO: Thomas E Werner
HR: –
FYE: December 31
Type: Private

Pfizer Hospital US offers a comprehensive, diverse portfolio focused on therapeutic areas where quality and supply reliability are crucial, and where safety and ease of use are of utmost importance. It offers the broadest US portfolio of sterile injectable medications, including ready-to-use and surgical products. Some of its products are ABBOJECT (ready-to-use, prefilled emergency syringe), ADD-Vantage System (ready-to-mix IV dr), CARPUJECT Syringe System, NEXJECT (all-in-one, prefilled syringe) and ACT-O-VIAL System (dual-component vial system).

HOSPITAL AUTHORITY OF VALDOSTA AND LOWNDES COUNTY, GEORGIA

2501 N PATTERSON ST
VALDOSTA, GA 316021735
Phone: 229 333-1000
Fax: –
Web: www.sgmc.org

CEO: Ronald E Dean
CFO: John Moore
HR: Gracelynn Wiseman
FYE: September 30
Type: Private

Hospital Authority of Valdosta and Lowndes County, Georgia, oversees South Georgia Medical Center (SGMC), a 335-bed regional hospital serving southern Georgia and northern Florida. The hospital offers a range of services focusing on such specialties as diabetes management, pulmonary care, pediatrics, and women's health. SGMC's Pearlman Cancer Center is devoted to a holistic approach to cancer care. The medical center also operates a specialized wound healing center and orthopedic and spine centers. The public hospital was founded as Pineview General Hospital in 1955. Its governing board is appointed by the local city council and county commissioners.

	Annual Growth	09/15	09/16	09/17	09/18	09/21
Sales ($mil.)	13.3%	–	215.5	314.7	325.8	402.0
Net income ($ mil.)	1062.4%	–	0.0	11.8	(18.4)	78.7
Market value ($ mil.)	–	–	–	–	–	–
Employees	–	–	–	–	–	3,000

HOSPITAL OF CENTRAL CONNECTICUT

100 GRAND ST
NEW BRITAIN, CT 060522016
Phone: 860 224-5011
Fax: –
Web: www.thocc.org

CEO: Clarence J Silvia
CFO: Ralph Becker
HR: –
FYE: September 30
Type: Private

The Hospital of Central Connecticut, an acute care facility, serves the communities of central Connecticut from two campuses. With approximately 415 beds and more than 400 physicians, the hospital offers a full range of diagnostic and treatment services, as well as education and prevention programs. Its diabetes treatment program is an affiliate of the Boston-based Joslin Diabetes Center; the hospital is also affiliated with the University of Connecticut School of Medicine and other universities. Central Connecticut Health Alliance (CCHA) is the parent company of The Hospital of Central Connecticut and is part of the Hartford Health Care network.

	Annual Growth	09/16	09/17	09/20	09/21	09/22
Sales ($mil.)	10.8%	–	366.3	470.2	494.7	612.8
Net income ($ mil.)	(2.1%)	–	23.2	33.1	86.5	20.8
Market value ($ mil.)	–	–	–	–	–	–
Employees		–	–	–	–	2,500

HOSPITAL SERVICE DISTRICT 1 INC

1101 MEDICAL CENTER BLVD
MARRERO, LA 700723147
Phone: 504 347-5511
Fax: –
Web: www.lcmchealth.org

CEO: Nancy R Cassagne
CFO: –
HR: –
FYE: December 31
Type: Private

West Jefferson Medical Center keeps the suburbs of New Orleans in tune. A full-service community hospital located in Marrero, Louisiana, the not-for-profit hospital has about 430 beds and provides general medical-surgical care, as well as specialty care in a number of areas, including cardiovascular disease, neurosciences, orthopedics, women's health, and oncology. The medical center also operates several primary care clinics throughout its service area and provides behavioral health and occupational health services. The hospital is also part of The Louisiana Organ Procurement Agency.

	Annual Growth	12/05	12/06*	09/13*	12/14	12/16
Sales ($mil.)	(0.4%)	–	234.9	59.5	200.9	226.3
Net income ($ mil.)	–	–	(9.1)	2.3	(16.9)	(2.8)
Market value ($ mil.)	–	–	–	–	–	–
Employees		–	–	–	–	2,000

*Fiscal year change

HOSPITAL SERVICE DISTRICT 1 OF EAST BATON ROUGE PARISH

6300 MAIN ST
ZACHARY, LA 707914037
Phone: 225 658-4000
Fax: –
Web: www.lanermc.org

CEO: Randalt Olson
CFO: Claude Hacker
HR: –
FYE: June 30
Type: Private

Lane Regional Medical Center (formerly Lane Memorial Hospital) has 137 beds and provides a full range of medical services, including emergency care, surgery, occupational therapy, pediatrics, psychiatry, imaging, wound care, and sleep studies. The hospital also operates a 30-bed medical rehabilitation center, a 38-bed nursing home, a 12-bed skilled nursing unit, a family practice clinic, and a home health agency. Founded in 1960, the hospital has a staff of more than 100 physicians.

	Annual Growth	06/02	06/03	06/04	06/15	06/16
Sales ($mil.)	5.5%	–	38.1	40.4	72.6	76.8
Net income ($ mil.)	–	–	(1.3)	0.4	(0.2)	(0.4)
Market value ($ mil.)	–	–	–	–	–	–
Employees		–	–	–	–	605

HOSPITAL SERVICE DISTRICT NO. 1

8166 MAIN ST
HOUMA, LA 703603404
Phone: 985 873-4141
Fax: –
Web: www.tghealthsystem.com

CEO: Phyllis Peoples
CFO: –
HR: –
FYE: March 31
Type: Private

If you find yourself feeling puny in the parish, Terrebonne General Medical Center in southeastern Louisiana is there to help (TGMC). The not-for-profit health care system is anchored by a 320-bed hospital with a staff of more than 150 physicians. The hospital provides a range of health care services including cardiac care, women's health care, rehabilitation, and emergency medicine. TGMC also administers care through an outpatient surgery center, imaging and breast centers, and a psychiatric care program. The Mary Bird Perkins Cancer Center at TGMC offers a continuum of cancer care, from prevention and early detection to diagnosis and treatment. Programs include surgery, chemotherapy, and radiation therapy.

	Annual Growth	03/16	03/17	03/18	03/21	03/22
Sales ($mil.)	2.1%	–	185.4	271.1	345.6	205.8
Net income ($ mil.)	–	–	(3.1)	(6.2)	16.1	(12.7)
Market value ($ mil.)	–	–	–	–	–	–
Employees		–	–	–	–	1,400

HOSPITAL SISTERS HEALTH SYSTEM

4936 LAVERNA RD
SPRINGFIELD, IL 627079797
Phone: 217 523-4747
Fax: –
Web: www.hshsupdates.org

CEO: Andrew Bagnall
CFO: –
HR: Clay England
FYE: June 30
Type: Private

These sisters want their big family to benefit everyone in the community. Hospital Sisters Health System (HSHS), a Catholic ministry of the Hospital Sisters of the Third Order of St. Francis, operates more than a dozen hospitals located throughout Wisconsin and Illinois. Its facilities have a total of more than 2,500 beds and range from large-scale acute care facilities such as St. John's Hospital (Springfield, Illinois), St. Elizabeth's Hospital (Bellevue, Illinois), and St. Vincent Hospital (Green Bay, Wisconsin) to small community hospitals; it also operates regional outpatient clinics. While the organization was incorporated in 1978, the health care ministry of the HSHS goes back to 1875.

	Annual Growth	06/13	06/14	06/20	06/21	06/22
Sales ($mil.)	7.6%	–	166.7	285.8	323.1	299.0
Net income ($ mil.)	16.0%	–	4.1	36.3	50.7	13.4
Market value ($ mil.)	–	–	–	–	–	–
Employees		–	–	–	–	14,676

HOSPITAL SOLUTIONS, INC.

10700 NORTH FWY STE 475
HOUSTON, TX 770371156
Phone: 713 350-9900
Fax: –
Web: www.hospitalsolutionsinc.com

CEO: –
CFO: –
HR: –
FYE: September 30
Type: Private

Here to make sure those patients can pay is Hospital Solutions (HSI), a provider of health care debt collection and other revenue management services to hospitals and clinics nationwide. HSI also provides on-site screening services for self-pay patients to determine whether or not these patients can be reimbursed from various state or federal health care programs including Medicaid (not Medicare), Supplemental Security Income, County Indigent Health Care Program, and Victims of Crime. Founded in 1996, the company works with all types of commercial insurance carriers (HMO, PPO, etc.) on behalf of hospitals for claims resolution. HSI also provides medical lien filing services.

HOSS'S STEAK & SEA HOUSE, INC.

170 PATCHWAY RD
DUNCANSVILLE, PA 166358431
Phone: 814 695-7600
Fax: –
Web: www.hosss.com

CEO: –
CFO: –
HR: –
FYE: December 30
Type: Private

Don't expect to find any Cartwright memorabilia here, just plenty of hearty food. Hoss's Steak and Sea House operates about 40 of its signature family-style restaurants in Pennsylvania. The diners offer standard American fare and seafood for lunch and dinner, along with an all-you-can-eat soup and salad bar. Each restaurant sports local memorabilia as part of its d cor. The company also operates Hoss's Fresh Xpress, its own warehouse and distribution system used to supply the restaurants. CEO Bill Campbell, a former WesterN SizzliN franchisee, opened the first Hoss's in 1983.

	Annual Growth	12/03	12/04	12/05	12/06	12/07
Sales ($mil.)	(0.9%)	–	78.0	77.6	81.7	75.9
Net income ($ mil.)	–	–	1.3	0.7	0.7	(0.8)
Market value ($ mil.)	–	–	–	–	–	–
Employees	–	–	–	–	–	3,000

HOST HOTELS & RESORTS INC

4747 Bethesda Avenue, Suite 1300
Bethesda, MD 20814
Phone: 240 744-1000
Fax: –
Web: www.hosthotels.com

NMS: HST
CEO: James F Risoleo
CFO: Sourav Ghosh
HR: Pinit Nakor
FYE: December 31
Type: Public

Host Hotels & Resorts is the largest hospitality real estate investment trust (REIT) in the US and one of the top owners of luxury and upscale hotels. It owns around 80 luxury and upper upscale hotels mostly in the US (but also in Canada and Brazil) totaling some 42,200 rooms. Properties are managed by third parties; most operate under the Marriott brand and are managed by sister firm Marriott International. Other brands include Hyatt, Ritz-Carlton, Westin, and Hilton. In addition, Host owns non-controlling interests in seven domestic and one international joint venture that primarily own hotels. Host generates most of its revenue in the US.

	Annual Growth	12/19	12/20	12/21	12/22	12/23
Sales ($mil.)	(0.7%)	5,469.0	1,620.0	2,890.0	4,907.0	5,311.0
Net income ($ mil.)	(5.3%)	920.0	(732.0)	(11.0)	633.0	740.0
Market value ($ mil.)	1.2%	13,052	10,294	12,236	11,293	13,699
Employees	–	–	175	163	160	165	–

HOUCHENS INDUSTRIES, INC.

700 CHURCH ST
BOWLING GREEN, KY 421011816
Phone: 270 843-3252
Fax: –
Web: www.houchens.com

CEO: James P Gipson
CFO: James G Minter
HR: –
FYE: October 01
Type: Private

Houchens Industries is listed by Forbes as one of the largest 100% employee-owned companies in the world. The diversified company runs more than 300 retail grocery, convenience, and neighborhood markets across around 15 US states. Its construction and manufacturing companies include Air Hydro Power, LEE Building Products, Pan-Oston, Scotty's Contracting | TS Trucking, Stephens Pipe & Steel, Stewart Richey, and Tampico. In addition, Houchens' diversified portfolio includes retail, insurance, manufacturing, construction, restaurant, utilities, and fast food, among others. Houchens was originally founded in Glasgow, Kentucky by Ervin G. Houchens in 1917 as Houchens Foods.

	Annual Growth	10/12	10/13	10/14	10/15	10/16
Sales ($mil.)	(7.0%)	–	–	–	3,213.0	2,987.2
Net income ($ mil.)	4.1%	–	–	–	99.9	104.1
Market value ($ mil.)	–	–	–	–	–	–
Employees	–	–	–	–	–	16,290

HOUGHTON CHEMICAL CORPORATION

52 CAMBRIDGE ST
ALLSTON, MA 021341850
Phone: 617 254-1010
Fax: –
Web: www.houghton.com

CEO: –
CFO: –
HR: Patty Daly
FYE: December 31
Type: Private

From ethanol to antifreeze, Houghton Chemical has found a way into your life. The company makes and distributes its own lines of automotive fluids, heat transfer fluids, and water treatment and industrial chemicals. Its Automotive division makes and distributes antifreeze nationally under such brands as Security, MacGuard, and Pah|nol. The company's Heat Transfer Fluids unit makes the Wintrex and Safe-T-Therm brands for heating, cooling, and refrigeration systems. Houghton Chemical sold parts of its Industrial Chemical and Solvents division to Brenntag for $7 million in 2010. Founded in the mid-1920s, Houghton Chemical has remained a family-owned business; current CEO Bruce Houghton is the founder's grandson.

HOUGHTON MIFFLIN HARCOURT COMPANY

125 HIGH ST STE 900
BOSTON, MA 021102777
Phone: 617 351-5000
Fax: –
Web: ir.hmhco.com

CEO: John J Lynch Jr
CFO: Joseph P Abbott Jr
HR: –
FYE: December 31
Type: Private

Houghton Mifflin Harcourt Company (HMH) is a leading provider of Kindergarten through 12th grade (K-12) core curriculum, supplemental and intervention solutions, and professional learning services, HMH partners with educators and school districts to uncover solutions that unlock students' potential and extend teachers' capabilities. HMH estimates that it serves more than 50 million students and three million educators in about 150 countries. The company specializes in comprehensive core curriculum, supplemental and intervention solutions, and provides ongoing support in professional learning and coaching for educators and administrators.

	Annual Growth	12/17	12/18	12/19	12/20	12/21
Sales ($mil.)	(7.4%)	–	1,322.4	1,390.7	1,031.3	1,050.8
Net income ($ mil.)	–	–	(94.2)	(213.8)	(479.8)	213.6
Market value ($ mil.)	–	–	–	–	–	–
Employees	–	–	–	–	–	2,300

HOULIHAN LOKEY INC

10250 Constellation Blvd., 5th Floor
Los Angeles, CA 90067
Phone: 310 788-5200
Fax: –
Web: www.hl.com

NYS: HLI
CEO: Scott L Beiser
CFO: J L Alley
HR: –
FYE: March 31
Type: Public

Established in 1972, Houlihan Lokey, Inc. is a leading global independent investment bank with expertise in mergers and acquisitions (M&A), capital markets, financial restructurings, and financial and valuation advisory. The company serves a diverse set of clients worldwide, including corporations, financial sponsors and government agencies. The company serves clients in three primary business practices ? Corporate Finance, encompassing M&A and capital markets advisory; Financial Restructuring, both out-of-court and in formal bankruptcy or insolvency proceedings; and Financial and Valuation Advisory, including financial opinions and a variety of valuation and financial consulting services. About 70% of total revenue comes from US customers.

	Annual Growth	03/19	03/20	03/21	03/22	03/23
Sales ($mil.)	13.7%	1,084.4	1,159.4	1,525.5	2,270.0	1,809.4
Net income ($ mil.)	12.4%	159.1	183.8	312.8	437.8	254.2
Market value ($ mil.)	17.5%	3,149.3	3,580.0	4,568.4	6,030.7	6,009.4
Employees	17.8%	1,354	1,491	1,574	2,257	2,610

HOUSE OF REPRESENTATIVES, UNITED STATES

THE CAPITOL
WASHINGTON, DC 205150001
Phone: 202 224-3121
Fax: –
Web: www.house.gov

CEO: –
CFO: –
HR: –
FYE: September 30
Type: Private

The US House of Representatives is considered the lower chamber of the nation's Congress, sitting in deliberation on the opposite end of the Capitol from the Senate. Its members are elected to two-year terms. The number of representatives allotted to each state depends on its population as reckoned by the decennial census, but every state is guaranteed at least one congressman. The presiding officer is called the Speaker and is chosen by the members. By constitutional fiat, it is the House of Representatives that initiates all bills pertaining to revenue.

HOUSING FINANCE AGENCY, CALIFORNIA

500 CAPITOL MALL STE 1400
SACRAMENTO, CA 958144740
Phone: 916 326-8030
Fax: –
Web: calhfa.ca.gov

CEO: –
CFO: –
HR: –
FYE: June 30
Type: Private

The California Housing Finance Agency (CalHFA) strives to help renters and first-time home buyers by providing a variety of programs and financing for safe and affordable housing. CalHFA's portfolio includes some 32,000 home mortgage loans with a value of more than $6 billion. The agency offers services through its First-Time Homebuyer Lending, Homeownership, Mortgage Insurance, and Multifamily Lending divisions. In recent years, the agency has added Foreclosure Avoidance to its list of programs. CalHFA's programs are available throughout California. The agency was created by the state as its affordable housing bank in 1975.

HOUSTON AMERICAN ENERGY CORP.   ASE: HUSA

801 Travis Street, Suite 1425
Houston, TX 77002
Phone: 713 222-6966
Fax: –
Web: www.houstonamerican.com

CEO: John Terwilliger
CFO: –
HR: –
FYE: December 31
Type: Public

Houston-based, with North and South American properties, and energy focused, Houston American Energy explores for and produces oil and natural gas, primarily in Colombia, but also along the US Gulf Coast (Louisiana and Texas, although the oil and gas independent also holds some acreage in Oklahoma). In 2011 the company reported proved reserves of 115,627 barrels of oil equivalent. President and CEO John Terwilliger owns 27.5% of Houston American Energy; director Orrie Tawes, 10%. In 2012 the debt-plagued company was pursuing strategic alternatives.

	Annual Growth	12/18	12/19	12/20	12/21	12/22
Sales ($mil.)	(8.7%)	2.4	1.0	0.6	1.3	1.6
Net income ($ mil.)	–	(0.3)	(2.5)	(4.0)	(1.0)	(0.7)
Market value ($ mil.)	106.5%	2.0	1.5	18.1	14.8	35.5
Employees		2	2	2	2	2

HOUSTON COMMUNITY COLLEGE, INC.

3100 MAIN ST STE MC1148
HOUSTON, TX 770029331
Phone: 713 718-5001
Fax: –
Web: www.hccs.edu

CEO: –
CFO: –
HR: Willie Williams
FYE: September 30
Type: Private

The Houston Community College System (HCC) has an open admission policy and offers associate degrees, ongoing education, workforce training, and prerequisite coursework for students enrolled at universities. In addition to traditional classes, the system offers online classes and other distance education courses via video and broadcast TV. HCC is one of the largest community college in the US. It has six area colleges (Central, Coleman, Northeast, Northwest, Southeast, and Southwest) throughout Houston, and 57,200 students are enrolled each year. HCC was founded in 1971.

HOUSTON COUNTY HEALTHCARE AUTHORITY

1108 ROSS CLARK CIR
DOTHAN, AL 363013022
Phone: 334 793-8111
Fax: –
Web: www.southeasthealth.org

CEO: Rick Sutton
CFO: Derek Miller
HR: Bsp T Miller
FYE: September 30
Type: Private

The Houston County Health Authority is the governing body for Southeast Alabama Medical Center (SAMC), a not-for-profit acute-care hospital that serves Southeastern Alabama and adjacent parts of Georgia and Florida. In addition to providing comprehensive medical, surgical, and emergency care, the 420-bed SAMC provides specialty services including heart, cancer, and women's health care. The health system also operates primary care physician offices and clinics specializing in neurology, pain management, and cardiovascular care, as well as a home health agency. SAMC offers residency programs for medical students, most of whom attend the Alabama College of Osteopathic Medicine.

	Annual Growth	09/16	09/17	09/18	09/19	09/21
Sales ($mil.)	4.2%	–	381.6	386.0	427.4	450.6
Net income ($ mil.)	11.1%	–	16.2	11.6	21.9	24.8
Market value ($ mil.)	–	–	–	–	–	–
Employees	–	–	–	–	–	2,500

HOUSTON GRAND OPERA ASSOCIATION, INC.

510 PRESTON ST
HOUSTON, TX 770021504
Phone: 713 546-0200
Fax: –
Web: www.houstongrandopera.org

CEO: Beth Madison
CFO: –
HR: Melissa Kiesel
FYE: July 31
Type: Private

The Houston Grand Opera Association (HGO) is one of the top opera companies in the US. Mainly known for its innovative productions of new operas, it has produced some 30 world and six American premieres since 1974. The Houston Grand Opera had been under the artistic direction of David Gockley since 1972. Gockley moved to the San Francisco Opera at the beginning of 2006 and was replaced in Houston by Anthony Freud, from the Welsh National Opera. The company also has an apprenticeship program for young artists (Houston Grand Opera Studio) and conducts numerous outreach programs for students and the general public. HGO was founded in 1955.

	Annual Growth	07/18	07/19	07/20	07/21	07/22
Sales ($mil.)	(5.5%)	–	–	–	29.1	27.5
Net income ($ mil.)	–	–	–	–	7.4	(2.6)
Market value ($ mil.)	–	–	–	–	–	–
Employees	–	–	–	–	–	120

HOUSTON LIVESTOCK SHOW AND RODEO EDUCATIONAL FUND

3 NRG PARK
HOUSTON, TX 770541574
Phone: 832 667-1000
Fax: –
Web: www.rodeohouston.com

CEO: Joel Cowley
CFO: Jennifer Hazelton
HR: –
FYE: August 31
Type: Private

Everything is bigger in Texas, and this organization is no exception. The Houston Livestock Show and Rodeo puts on one of North America's largest festivals. Proceeds from the not-for-profit group's annual show support various scholarship programs. The show also is designed to promote better breeding and improved marketing of livestock. It draws thousands of entries, including both animals and works of art. Show winners are sold at auction for prices that run into the hundreds of thousands of dollars. Houston Livestock Show and Rodeo events are held at Reliant Stadium, home to the NFL's Houston Texans, and surrounding venues. The first show was held in 1932.

	Annual Growth	08/15	08/16	08/18	08/20	08/22
Sales ($mil.)	(1.9%)	–	22.6	18.0	14.0	20.1
Net income ($ mil.)	(6.7%)	–	3.5	(1.7)	(5.6)	2.3
Market value ($ mil.)	–	–	–	–	–	–
Employees	–	–	–	–	–	1,200

HOUSTON MUSEUM OF NATURAL SCIENCE

5555 HERMANN PARK DR
HOUSTON, TX 770301718
Phone: 713 639-4629
Fax: –
Web: www.hmns.org

CEO: –
CFO: Stephen Satchnik
HR: Dulce Hernandez
FYE: December 31
Type: Private

Mother Nature is under the microscope at the Houston Museum of Natural Science. The popular museum features displays on subjects such as space science, energy, paleontology, chemistry, gems and minerals, ancient Egyptians, Native Americans, and Texas wildlife. The museum also hosts traveling exhibitions detailing a variety of topics. Special features of the museum include an IMAX theater, the Burke Baker Planetarium, the Cockrell Butterfly Center, and the nearby George Observatory. The Houston Museum of Natural Science was founded in 1909 as the Houston Museum and Scientific Society; its permanent facility was established in 1964.

	Annual Growth	12/15	12/16	12/19	12/21	12/22
Sales ($mil.)	3.9%	–	36.6	51.6	71.6	46.2
Net income ($ mil.)	(10.4%)	–	9.0	15.3	21.3	4.6
Market value ($ mil.)	–	–	–	–	–	–
Employees	–	–	–	–	–	202

HOUSTON WIRE & CABLE COMPANY INC

10201 NORTH LOOP E
HOUSTON, TX 770291415
Phone: 713 609-2100
Fax: –
Web: www.houwire.com

CEO: –
CFO: –
HR: –
FYE: December 31
Type: Private

Houston Wire & Cable (HWC) may have a Texas name, but it can keep customers wired from Seattle to Tampa. The company is a conduit between cable manufacturers and electrical distributors and their customers. It distributes specialty (electrical and electronic) wire and cable products, such as cable terminators, fiber-optic cables, and bare copper and building wire, as well as voice, data, and premise wire. It also owns the brand LifeGuard, a low-smoke, zero-halogen cable. HWC operates a network of multiple distribution centers across the US and sells primarily to electrical distributors.

HOUSTON ZOO, INC.

6200 HERMANN PARK DR
HOUSTON, TX 770301710
Phone: 713 533-6500
Fax: –
Web: www.houstonzoo.org

CEO: Lee Ehmke
CFO: Leslie Forestier
HR: Charolette Carter
FYE: December 31
Type: Private

For getting down to earth in Space City, there's nothing like the Houston Zoo. The not-for-profit zoo occupies 55-acres in Hermann Park at the heart of Houston's cultural district. It is home to more than 4,500 animals from about 800 species and hosts about 1.5 million visitors per year. Facilities include the McGovern Children's Zoo, Kipp Aquarium, the tropical bird house, Texas Wetlands, and the Wildlife Carousel. The zoo participates in programs that oversee the breeding of more than 40 endangered animal species. Several of its facilities may be reserved for private functions and private tours are offered "behind the scenes." The Houston Zoo was founded in 1922 to house a bison donated by the US government.

	Annual Growth	06/08	06/09	06/10*	12/13	12/17
Sales ($mil.)	8.6%	–	37.0	30.6	50.1	71.3
Net income ($ mil.)	7.1%	–	13.1	6.2	15.4	22.7
Market value ($ mil.)	–	–	–	–	–	–
Employees	–	–	–	–	–	750

*Fiscal year change

HOVNANIAN ENTERPRISES, INC.

NYS: HOV

90 Matawan Road, 5th Floor
Matawan, NJ 07747
Phone: 732 747-7800
Fax: –
Web: www.khov.com

CEO: ARA K Hovnanian
CFO: Brad G O'Connor
HR: –
FYE: October 31
Type: Public

Hovnanian Enterprises designs, constructs, markets, and sells single-family detached homes, attached townhomes and condominiums, urban infill, and active lifestyle homes in planned residential developments and is one of the nation's largest builders of residential homes. It designs communities that offer homes with a diversity of architecture, textures, and colors, frequently with recreational amenities such as swimming pools, tennis courts, and clubhouses. Hovnanian offers a variety of home styles at base prices ranging from $156,000 to $1,485,000 with an average sales price, including options, of $513,000 in some 120 communities in about 30 markets in about 15 states throughout the US.

	Annual Growth	10/19	10/20	10/21	10/22	10/23
Sales ($mil.)	8.1%	2,016.9	2,343.9	2,782.9	2,922.2	2,756.0
Net income ($ mil.)	–	(42.1)	50.9	607.8	225.5	205.9
Market value ($ mil.)	29.0%	152.9	193.6	513.6	245.8	423.5
Employees	(2.1%)	1,868	1,697	1,784	1,866	1,715

HOWARD BUILDING CORPORATION

707 WILSHIRE BLVD STE 3750
LOS ANGELES, CA 900173535
Phone: 213 683-1850
Fax: –
Web: www.howardbuilding.com

CEO: Paul McGunnigle
CFO: –
HR: –
FYE: December 31
Type: Private

General contracting firm Howard Building provides preconstruction, design/build, engineering, construction, and management services primarily for commercial projects throughout California. The company's portfolio includes projects ranging from corporate, legal, and financial buildings to entertainment, showroom, and high-tech facilities. Clients include BAE Systems, Trammell Crow, Deutsche Bank, The Endeavor Agency, Fox Television, and Pacific Investment Management Company. Howard Building, founded in 1983, maintains offices in greater Los Angeles and Orange County, California.

HOWARD COMMUNITY COLLEGE

10901 LITTLE PATUXENT PKWY
COLUMBIA, MD 210443197
Phone: 410 518-1000
Fax: –
Web: www.howardcc.edu

CEO: –
CFO: –
HR: Lawrencia Darko
FYE: June 30
Type: Private

Howard Community College (HCC) provides academic programs to students in Maryland's Howard County. More than 14,500 of its students pursue studies leading to immediate employment upon graduation or transfer to four year colleges (many go to the University System of Maryland's University of Maryland, College Park; University of Maryland, Baltimore County; and Towson State University). Another 15,300 students take HCC courses for personal or professional development. In fiscal year 2013 some 75.6% of the college's credit student population were residents of Howard County.

	Annual Growth	06/14	06/15	06/16	06/18	06/19
Sales ($mil.)	–	–	34.4	34.2	33.8	34.4
Net income ($ mil.)	12.9%	–	9.4	25.4	15.6	15.2
Market value ($ mil.)	–	–	–	–	–	–
Employees	–	–	–	–	–	800

HOWARD HUGHES HOLDINGS INC NYS: HHH

9950 Woodloch Forest Drive, Suite 1100
The Woodlands, TX 77380
Phone: 281 719-6100
Fax: –
Web: www.howardhughes.com

CEO: –
CFO: –
HR: –
FYE: December 31
Type: Public

The Howard Hughes Corporation (THHC) is involved in neither planes, movies, or medical research, but one of the 20th century entrepreneur's later interests, real estate. The company arose from the bankruptcy restructuring of shopping mall developer General Growth Properties (GGP) to oversee much of GGP's non-retail assets. THHC owns GGP's former portfolio of four master planned communities outside Columbia, Maryland; Houston, Texas; and Summerlin, Nevada; as well as about two dozen other as-yet undeveloped sites and commercial properties in 16 states from New York to Hawaii, including GGP's own headquarters building in downtown Chicago. Unlike GGP, THHC does not operate as a REIT.

	Annual Growth	12/19	12/20	12/21	12/22	12/23
Sales ($mil.)	(5.8%)	1,300.5	699.5	1,427.9	1,608.5	1,024.1
Net income ($ mil.)	–	74.0	(26.2)	56.1	184.5	(551.8)
Market value ($ mil.)	(9.4%)	6,344.8	3,949.5	5,092.9	3,823.9	4,280.8
Employees	(20.2%)	1,500	600	530	565	608

HOWARD MILLER COMPANY

860 E MAIN AVE
ZEELAND, MI 494641365
Phone: 616 772-9131
Fax: –
Web: www.howardmiller.com

CEO: Philip Miller
CFO: –
HR: –
FYE: December 31
Type: Private

Few things run like clockwork like the nation's largest private clock manufacturer. Howard Miller Company, previously Howard Miller Clock Company, makes an array of grandfather, wall, and mantel clocks, curio cabinets, wine and spirits furnishings, rugs, and home furniture, as well as memorial urns. Products are sold primarily through dealers in the US, Canada, and Mexico. Since the 1920s, Howard Miller has specialized in clock-making as it grew through acquisitions, including furniture maker Hekman, German clock movement master Kieninger, and Pulaski Furniture's Ridgeway Clocks. Howard Miller also markets home storage and console units and other furnishings under celebrity Ty Pennington's brand name.

HOWARD YOUNG HEALTH CARE, INC

240 MAPLE ST
WOODRUFF, WI 545689190
Phone: 715 356-8000
Fax: –
Web: www.hyhc.com

CEO: Brian Kief
CFO: Cathy Bukowski
HR: –
FYE: June 30
Type: Private

A Ministry Health Care affiliate, Howard Young Health Care provides a comprehensive range of health services to residents of north central Wisconsin. At the center of the health system is Howard Young Medical Center, a 110-bed acute care rural community hospital. The medical center provides an array of inpatient, outpatient, emergency, diagnostic, and surgical services; as well as maternity care, behavioral health services, and care for the elderly. Howard Young Health Care also includes the Howard Young Health Care Foundation, which provides philanthropic support to the hospital and community. The system also offers local emergency transportation services.

	Annual Growth	06/17	06/18	06/19	06/21	06/22
Sales ($mil.)	(40.7%)	–	0.8	0.4	0.3	0.1
Net income ($ mil.)	–	–	0.0	(0.0)	(0.0)	(0.1)
Market value ($ mil.)	–	–	–	–	–	–
Employees	–	–	–	–	–	840

HOWMET AEROSPACE INC NYS: HWM

201 Isabella Street, Suite 200
Pittsburgh, PA 15212-5872
Phone: 412 553-1940
Fax: –
Web: www.howmet.com

CEO: John C Plant
CFO: Kenneth J Giacobbe
HR: –
FYE: December 31
Type: Public

Formerly known as Arconic Inc, the company is now renamed as Howmet Aerospace Inc., is a global leader in lightweight metals engineering and manufacturing. Most of its products are primarily made multi-material products, which include aluminum, titanium, and nickel. Created in 2016 when it was spun off from the aluminum giant Alcoa, Howmet has retained the parts businesses of its predecessor ? engineered products and forging businesses like engine products, fastening systems, engineered structures and forged wheels. With operations in some 20 countries, Howmet is a top provider of specialty materials to the aerospace, commercial transportation, automotive, defense, building and construction, and oil and gas industries. It generates more than 50% of its sales in the US.

	Annual Growth	12/19	12/20	12/21	12/22	12/23
Sales ($mil.)	(17.3%)	14,192	5,259.0	4,972.0	5,663.0	6,640.0
Net income ($ mil.)	13.0%	470.0	261.0	258.0	469.0	765.0
Market value ($ mil.)	15.2%	12,613	11,699	13,048	16,155	22,185
Employees	(13.6%)	41,700	19,700	19,900	21,400	23,200

HP INC NYS: HPQ

1501 Page Mill Road
Palo Alto, CA 94304
Phone: 650 857-1501
Fax: –
Web: www.hp.com

CEO: Enrique Lores
CFO: Timothy J Brown
HR: –
FYE: October 31
Type: Public

HP Inc., is one of two companies created from the breakup of Hewlett-Packard Co. in 2015. HP makes a full line of computing devices from desktops and laptops for commercial and consumer use to tablets and point-of-sale systems. Its printers include large format commercial printers and inkjet and laser printers as well as 3D printers. It sells to individual consumers, small- and medium-sized businesses (SMBs) and large enterprises, including customers in the government, health and education sectors. The company generates about 35% of its revenue in the US.

	Annual Growth	10/19	10/20	10/21	10/22	10/23
Sales ($mil.)	(2.2%)	58,756	56,639	63,487	62,983	53,718
Net income ($ mil.)	0.9%	3,152.0	2,844.0	6,503.0	3,203.0	3,263.0
Market value ($ mil.)	11.0%	17,179	17,762	29,996	27,316	26,040
Employees	0.9%	56,000	53,000	51,000	58,000	58,000

HR POLICY ASSOCIATION

4201 WILSON BLVD STE 110 PMB 368
ARLINGTON, VA 222031859
Phone: 202 789-8670
Fax: –
Web: www.hrpolicy.org

CEO: –
CFO: –
HR: –
FYE: December 31
Type: Private

HR policies don't just grow on trees, you know. They are molded, shaped, shepherded, and, eventually, shared at HR Policy Association. The group gives senior human resources executives of major corporations (those with annual revenues exceeding $750 million) an outlet through which they can share training strategies and propose changes to public policy relating to employment, labor, and workplace issues. The group offers networking opportunities, training, newsletters and other publications, and regular meetings and conferences. HR Policy Association was established in 1957 as the Labor Policy Association.

	Annual Growth	12/16	12/17	12/18	12/19	12/21
Sales ($mil.)	68.6%	–	1.3	1.1	10.5	10.2
Net income ($ mil.)	–	–	(0.0)	(0.0)	0.0	1.1
Market value ($ mil.)	–	–	–	–	–	–
Employees	–	–	–	–	–	15

HSBC USA, INC.

452 Fifth Avenue
New York, NY 10018
Phone: 212 525-5000
Fax: –
Web: www.us.hsbc.com

CEO: Michael Roberts
CFO: Kavita Mahtani
HR: –
FYE: December 31
Type: Public

HSBC USA, a subsidiary of British banking behemoth HSBC Holdings, operates HSBC Bank USA, one of the largest foreign-owned banks in the country. Through HSBC Bank USA, the company offers its customers a wide range of commercial and consumer banking products and related financial services. HSBC Bank USA is also an international dealer in derivative instruments denominated in US dollars and other currencies. More than 70% of HSBC USA's loan portfolio is made up of commercial loans, and around 65% of its total revenue comes from interest income.

	Annual Growth	12/19	12/20	12/21	12/22	12/23
Assets ($mil.)	(1.0%)	175,375	196,434	189,232	164,655	168,238
Net income ($ mil.)	36.6%	113.0	(940.0)	688.0	548.0	393.0
Market value ($ mil.)	–	–	–	–	–	–
Employees	(19.4%)	4,828	4,179	3,463	2,180	2,040

HSN, INC.

1 HSN DR
SAINT PETERSBURG, FL 337290001
Phone: 727 872-1000
Fax: –
Web: www.hsn.com

CEO: –
CFO: William Hunter
HR: –
FYE: December 31
Type: Private

HSN Inc. sells different types of apparel and accessories, crafts and sewing, jewelry, electronics, home, health, beauty, shoes, toys and games, and fitness products through its home shopping television network with and through fast-growing HSN.com. It also offers gift cards to its customers. The company also provides free shipping and handling only available within the continental US. Brands include Baby Delight, Connie Craig Carroll Jewelry, KidsMe, OXO, Azzaro, Gucci, Eagle Eyes, and many other leading brands.

HUB GROUP, INC.

2001 Hub Group Way
Oak Brook, IL 60523
Phone: 630 271-3600
Fax: –
Web: www.hubgroup.com

NMS: HUBG
CEO: David P Yeager
CFO: Geoffrey F Demartino
HR: –
FYE: December 31
Type: Public

Hub Group is a leading supply chain solutions provider that offers comprehensive transportation and logistics management services focused on reliability, visibility and value for its customers. It offers multi-modal supply chain management solutions that serve to strengthen and deepen its relationships with its customers and allow the company to provide a more cost effective and higher service solution. Operating throughout North America, the company provides services including comprehensive intermodal, truck brokerage, dedicated trucking, managed transportation, freight consolidation, warehousing, last mile delivery, international transportation and other logistics services. The company also offers complementary services such as temperature protected transportation.

	Annual Growth	12/19	12/20	12/21	12/22	12/23
Sales ($mil.)	3.5%	3,668.1	3,495.6	4,232.4	5,340.5	4,202.6
Net income ($ mil.)	11.8%	107.2	73.6	171.5	356.9	167.5
Market value ($ mil.)	15.7%	3,219.8	3,578.2	5,288.2	4,990.1	5,771.6
Employees	4.4%	5,000	5,000	4,700	5,900	5,950

HUBBELL INC.

40 Waterview Drive
Shelton, CT 06484
Phone: 475 882-4000
Fax: –
Web: www.hubbell.com

NYS: HUBB
CEO: Gerben W Bakker
CFO: William R Sperry
HR: Charlotte Malfant
FYE: December 31
Type: Public

Founded in 1888, Hubbell Incorporated manufactures utility and electrical solutions, with more than 75 brands used to operate infrastructure efficiently. Its utility segment includes electrical distribution, transmission, substation, and telecommunications products. This includes utility transmission & distribution (T&D) components such as arresters, insulators, connectors, anchors, bushings, enclosures, cutoffs and switches. The electrical segment includes wiring device products, rough-in electrical products, connector and grounding products, lighting fixtures, and other electrical equipment. The company's customers include distributors, wholesalers, electric utilities, OEMs, electrical contractors, telecommunications companies and retail and hardware outlets. Hubbell generates most of its sales in the US (more than 90%).

	Annual Growth	12/19	12/20	12/21	12/22	12/23
Sales ($mil.)	4.0%	4,591.0	4,186.0	4,194.1	4,947.9	5,372.9
Net income ($ mil.)	17.3%	400.9	351.2	399.5	545.9	759.8
Market value ($ mil.)	22.1%	7,942.5	8,424.4	11,190	12,609	17,674
Employees	(0.6%)	18,800	19,100	18,300	16,300	18,317

HUBSPOT INC

Two Canal Park
Cambridge, MA 02141
Phone: 888 482-7768
Fax: –
Web: www.hubspot.com

NYS: HUBS
CEO: Yamini Rangan
CFO: Kate Bueker
HR: –
FYE: December 31
Type: Public

HubSpot makes and sells cloud-based software designed to help its customers make sales and more. The company offers applications for sales, marketing, service and content management system, as well as other tools and integrations. Among functions handled by HubSpot's products are website pages, business blogging, smart content, landing pages and forms, search engine optimization tools, forms and lead flow, web analytics reporting, calls-to-action, and file manager. The company focuses on selling to mid-market business-to-business companies (up to 2,000 employees). The company boasts around 167,400 customers in over 120 countries but it generates most of its sales in the Americas.

	Annual Growth	12/19	12/20	12/21	12/22	12/23
Sales ($mil.)	33.9%	674.9	883.0	1,300.7	1,731.0	2,170.2
Net income ($ mil.)	–	(53.7)	(85.0)	(77.8)	(112.7)	(176.3)
Market value ($ mil.)	38.3%	7,996.0	20,000	33,253	14,586	29,287
Employees	22.6%	3,387	4,225	5,895	7,433	7,663

HUDSON GLOBAL INC
NMS: HSON

53 Forest Avenue, Suite 102
Old Greenwich, CT 06870
Phone: 475 988-2068
Fax: –
Web: www.hudsonrpo.com

CEO: Jacob Zabkowicz
CFO: Matthew K Diamond
HR: –
FYE: December 31
Type: Public

Hudson Global is a leading total talent solutions provider operating under the brand name Hudson RPO. The company delivers RPO recruitment and Contracting solutions tailored to the individual needs of primarily mid-to-large-cap multinational companies. The company's RPO delivery teams utilize state-of-the-art recruitment process methodologies and project management expertise in their flexible, turnkey solutions to meet clients' ongoing business needs. Its RPO services include complete recruitment outsourcing, project-based outsourcing, contingent workforce solutions, and recruitment consulting. Among the company's clients are mid-to-large-cap multinational businesses and government agencies. Almost 60% of the company's total sales come from Asia Pacific.

	Annual Growth	12/19	12/20	12/21	12/22	12/23
Sales ($mil.)	14.5%	93.8	101.4	169.2	200.9	161.3
Net income ($ mil.)	–	(1.0)	(1.2)	3.2	7.1	2.2
Market value ($ mil.)	6.7%	33.5	29.5	81.4	63.5	43.5
Employees	28.1%	390	380	1,300	1,440	1,050

HUDSON PACIFIC PROPERTIES INC
NYS: HPP

11601 Wilshire Blvd., Ninth Floor
Los Angeles, CA 90025
Phone: 310 445-5700
Fax: –
Web: –

CEO: –
CFO: –
HR: –
FYE: December 31
Type: Public

Hudson Pacific Properties is a fully integrated, self-administered and self-managed real estate investment trust (REIT). The company owns, manages, leases, acquires and develops real estate, consisting primarily of office properties, but also media and entertainment properties located throughout Northern and Southern California, the Pacific Northwest, Western Canada and Greater London, UK. It owns about 65 properties totaling some 20.1 million sq. ft., including three production studios on Hollywood's Sunset Boulevard. Its largest tenants range from tech giants such as Google, Netflix, Uber, Qualcomm, and Nutanix.

	Annual Growth	12/19	12/20	12/21	12/22	12/23
Sales ($mil.)	3.9%	818.2	805.0	896.8	1,026.2	952.3
Net income ($ mil.)	–	43.4	1.4	10.0	(34.3)	(170.5)
Market value ($ mil.)	(29.5%)	5,310.0	3,387.7	3,485.0	1,372.3	1,313.0
Employees	21.6%	347	375	560	885	758

HUDSON TECHNOLOGIES INC
NAS: HDSN

300 Tice Boulevard, Suite 290
Woodcliff Lake, NJ 07677
Phone: 845 735-6000
Fax: –
Web: www.hudsontech.com

CEO: Brian F Coleman
CFO: Nat Krishnamurti
HR: –
FYE: December 31
Type: Public

Hudson Technologies defends the ozone. Using proprietary reclamation technology to remove moisture and impurities from refrigeration systems, it recovers and reclaims chlorofluorocarbons (CFCs) used in commercial air-conditioning and refrigeration systems. The company sells both reclaimed and new refrigerants and also buys used refrigerants for reclamation and sale. In addition, Hudson Technologies offers on-site decontamination services, as well as services designed to improve the efficiency of customers' refrigeration systems. Customers include commercial and industrial enterprises and government entities, along with refrigerant contractors, distributors, and wholesalers and makers of refrigeration equipment.

	Annual Growth	12/19	12/20	12/21	12/22	12/23
Sales ($mil.)	15.6%	162.1	147.6	192.5	325.2	289.0
Net income ($ mil.)	–	(25.9)	(5.2)	32.3	103.8	52.2
Market value ($ mil.)	92.7%	44.5	49.6	202.0	460.5	613.8
Employees	–	–	234	221	217	232

HUGOTON ROYALTY TRUST (TX)
NBB: HGTX U

c/o The Corporate Trustee:, Argent Trust Company, 2911 Turtle Creek Blvd, Suite 850
Dallas, TX 75219
Phone: 855 588-7839
Fax: –
Web: www.hgt-hugoton.com

CEO: –
CFO: –
HR: –
FYE: December 31
Type: Public

Hugoton Royalty Trust was formed by Cross Timbers Oil Company (now XTO Energy) to pay royalties to shareholders based on the proceeds of sales from its oil and gas holdings. Payouts depend on oil and gas prices, the volume of gas and oil produced, and production and other costs. The trust receives 80% of the net proceeds from XTO Energy's properties, located in the Hugoton fields of Kansas, Oklahoma, and Texas; the Anadarko Basin of Oklahoma; and the Green River Basin of Wyoming. In 2008 the trust reported proved reserves of 3.3 million barrels of oil and 366.3 billion cu. ft. of natural gas. XTO Energy controls the trust, which is administered through Bank of America and has no officers.

	Annual Growth	12/18	12/19	12/20	12/21	12/22
Sales ($mil.)	86.6%	1.6	0.4	0.0	–	19.6
Net income ($ mil.)	158.7%	0.4	–	–	–	16.6
Market value ($ mil.)	37.3%	21.6	6.8	3.6	7.7	76.8
Employees	–	–	–	–	–	–

HUMAN PHEROMONE SCIENCES, INC.

84 West Santa Clara Street
San Jose, CA 95113
Phone: 408 938-3030
Fax: –
Web: www.erox.com

CEO: William P Horgan
CFO: Gregory S Fredrick
HR: –
FYE: December 31
Type: Public

Human Pheromone Sciences (HPS) hopes its animal magnetism makes consumers hot under the collar. It makes fragrances that contain a patented synthetic version of a pheromone produced by the human body to stimulate the senses. It also licenses its technology to partners in the personal care products industry. The company's products are sold through its website and through direct marketing under the Natural Attraction name. It has granted non-exclusive rights to the Natural Attraction brand in the US, Europe, and Japan. HPS also partners with makers of consumer products to license its patented technology; CrowdGather is launching a unisex scent EroxA in 2011 with HPS. Renovatio Global Funds owns 16% of the firm.

	Annual Growth	12/06	12/07	12/08	12/09	12/10
Sales ($mil.)	(10.0%)	1.2	1.3	1.0	0.9	0.8
Net income ($ mil.)	–	(0.1)	(0.0)	(0.2)	(0.3)	(0.1)
Market value ($ mil.)	(47.2%)	3.7	2.9	1.0	0.6	0.3
Employees	–	3	3	3	3	3

HUMAN RIGHTS WATCH, INC.

350 5TH AVE FL 34
NEW YORK, NY 101183499
Phone: 212 290-4700
Fax: –
Web: www.hrw.org

CEO: –
CFO: –
HR: –
FYE: June 30
Type: Private

Human Rights Watch (HRW) is watching out for everyone. The organization's mission is to prevent discrimination, uphold political freedom, protect people during wartime, and bring offenders to justice. HRW researches human rights violations around the world and publishes its findings to help generate publicity about the atrocities it uncovers. The nongovernmental organization (NGO) also meets with national and international governing officials to help steer policy change. Along with partner organizations, HRW won the 1997 Nobel Peace Prize for its International Campaign to Ban Landmines. HRW is an independent organization; all funds come from private contributors. The group was founded in 1978.

	Annual Growth	06/18	06/19	06/20	06/21	06/22
Sales ($mil.)	3.0%	–	85.6	70.5	96.7	93.5
Net income ($ mil.)	21.4%	–	0.7	(13.2)	13.1	1.3
Market value ($ mil.)	–	–	–	–	–	–
Employees	–	–	–	–	–	348

HUMANA INC.

NYS: HUM

500 West Main Street
Louisville, KY 40202
Phone: 502 580-1000
Fax: –
Web: www.humana.com

CEO: Bruce D Broussard
CFO: Susan Diamond
HR: –
FYE: December 31
Type: Public

Humana is a leading health and well-being company serving 17 million members in its medical benefit plans, as well as approximately five million members in its specialty products. Its range of clinical capabilities, resources and tools, such as in-home care, behavioral health, pharmacy services, data analytics and wellness solutions, combine to produce a simplified experience that makes health care easier to navigate and more effective. Additionally, Humana provides health insurance coverage under Centers for Medicare and Medicaid Services (CMS) contracts to approximately 4.6 million individual Medicare Advantage members, including approximately 771,900 members in Florida. It also provides its members with access through their networks of health care providers such outpatient surgery centers, primary care providers, specialist physicians, dentists, and providers of ancillary health care services.

	Annual Growth	12/19	12/20	12/21	12/22	12/23
Assets ($mil.)	12.8%	29,074	34,969	44,358	43,055	47,065
Net income ($ mil.)	(2.1%)	2,707.0	3,367.0	2,933.0	2,806.0	2,489.0
Market value ($ mil.)	5.7%	44,798	50,145	56,695	62,602	55,955
Employees	9.4%	47,200	49,600	96,900	67,100	67,600

HUMANGOOD NORCAL

1900 HUNTINGTON DR
DUARTE, CA 910102694
Phone: 925 924-7100
Fax: –
Web: www.humangood.org

CEO: David B Ferguson
CFO: –
HR: Barb Landis
FYE: December 31
Type: Private

American Baptist Homes of the West (ABHOW) preaches the gospel of the active senior lifestyle, operating more than 40 senior living facilities in four western states. Nearly three-fourths of ABHOW's communities are government-subsidized apartments for low-income seniors. About a dozen of its residences, however, are continuing care retirement communities, which offer a continuum of care -- residential living, assisted living, or skilled nursing -- depending on residents' needs. The communities also schedule social activities and offer wellness programs and transportation services. Parent company Cornerstone Affiliates acquires and develops communities with ABHOW.

	Annual Growth	12/16	12/17	12/18	12/21	12/22
Assets ($mil.)	(4.3%)	–	852.2	479.3	678.9	684.4
Net income ($ mil.)	158.3%	–	0.0	(1.8)	17.9	10.1
Market value ($ mil.)	–	–	–	–	–	–
Employees	–	–	–	–	–	2,500

HUMANIGEN INC

NBB: HGEN

830 Morris Turnpike, 4th Floor
Short Hills, NJ 07078
Phone: 973 200-3100
Fax: –
Web: www.humanigen.com

CEO: Cameron Durrant
CFO: Timothy E Morris
HR: –
FYE: December 31
Type: Public

KaloBios Pharmaceuticals seeks the "good life" (its meaning from the Greek) for patients afflicted with serious medical conditions, especially respiratory diseases and certain cancers. It is developing drugs containing antibodies produced via its own technology. The most advanced is in clinical trials and is engineered to fight common bacteria, found even in hospitals, that cause pneumonia in patients treated by mechanical ventilation. KaloBios has partnered with Sanofi Pasteur to further develop, manufacture, and market the drug. It also is working on antibodies to treat severe cases of asthma and blood disease. In July 2016 the company emerged from a six-month stint in Chapter 11 bankruptcy.

	Annual Growth	12/18	12/19	12/20	12/21	12/22
Sales ($mil.)	–	–	–	0.3	3.6	2.5
Net income ($ mil.)	–	(12.0)	(10.3)	(89.5)	(236.6)	(70.7)
Market value ($ mil.)	(35.7%)	83.4	58.1	2,083.9	443.0	14.3
Employees	18.9%	3	2	10	11	6

HUMANSCALE CORPORATION

1114 AVENUE OF THE AMERICAS FL 15A
NEW YORK, NY 100367703
Phone: 212 725-4749
Fax: –
Web: www.humanscale.com

CEO: Robert King
CFO: Michele Gerards
HR: Bruny Carlo
FYE: December 31
Type: Private

Humanscale is the pioneer and one of the leading manufacturers of ergonomic office products ? such as keyboard systems, monitor arms, foot rests, laptop holders, and chairs, and desk that are easy on the body. The company has locations in about 30 countries and has even gained attention from Hollywood, with products gracing the sets of hit television shows and films including The Newsroom, New Girl, 24, The Bourne Ultimatum, Mission: Impossible III, and Mr. & Mrs. Smith. It also sells its products online, international retail partners and provides products for use in healthcare environments. Humanscale was founded in 1983 by CEO Bob King.

HUMAX USA, INC.

1200 MAIN ST
IRVINE, CA 926146749
Phone: 714 389-1924
Fax: –
Web: americas.humaxdigital.com

CEO: –
CFO: –
HR: –
FYE: December 31
Type: Private

Humax USA prefers to connect with its customers through its products. The company develops and manufactures flat-panel TV sets and digital set-top boxes for satellite, cable, and terrestrial connections. Humax USA is the US-based subsidiary of Korean consumer electronics manufacturing firm Humax Co., which was founded in 1989. The brand has become one of the most popular worldwide among set-top boxes. Humax's products are available in more than 90 countries as well as in the US. The company primarily serves customers in Asia and Europe.

	Annual Growth	12/13	12/14	12/15	12/16	12/17
Sales ($mil.)	2.5%	–	448.9	373.2	360.5	482.8
Net income ($ mil.)	–	–	0.5	0.5	(0.1)	(4.6)
Market value ($ mil.)	–	–	–	–	–	–
Employees	–	–	–	–	–	29

HUNT (J.B.) TRANSPORT SERVICES, INC.

NMS: JBHT

615 J.B. Hunt Corporate Drive
Lowell, AR 72745
Phone: 479 820-0000
Fax: –
Web: www.jbhunt.com

CEO: John N Roberts III
CFO: John Kuhlow
HR: Jay Johnson
FYE: December 31
Type: Public

J.B. Hunt Transport Services is one of the largest transportation, delivery, and logistics companies in North America. Through its segments, the company transports freight, including general merchandise, specialty consumer items, appliances, forest and paper products, food and beverages, building materials, soaps and cosmetics, automotive parts, agricultural products, electronics, and chemicals. The company also offers dedicated contract services, truckload freight transportation, and transportation management and logistics services. The company was founded in 1961 and went public in 1983.

	Annual Growth	12/19	12/20	12/21	12/22	12/23
Sales ($mil.)	8.8%	9,165.3	9,636.6	12,168	14,814	12,830
Net income ($ mil.)	9.0%	516.3	506.0	760.8	969.4	728.3
Market value ($ mil.)	14.4%	12,054	14,105	21,098	17,997	20,617
Employees	4.6%	29,056	30,309	33,045	37,151	34,718

HUNT MEMORIAL HOSPITAL DISTRICT

4215 JOE RAMSEY BLVD E
GREENVILLE, TX 754017852
Phone: 903 408-5000
Fax: –
Web: www.huntregional.org

CEO: Richard Carter
CFO: Jerii Rich
HR: –
FYE: September 30
Type: Private

Hunt Memorial Hospital District doesn't want Hunt County residents to have to search high and low for a health care provider. The district, also known as Hunt Regional Healthcare, operates two Northeast Texas hospitals, the Hunt Regional Medical Center (HRMC) at Greenville and the Hunt Regional Community Hospital at Commerce. The hospitals offer specialized services including cardiac care, rehabilitation, cancer treatment, diabetes management, diagnostic imaging, surgery, and sleep disorder diagnosis. In addition, the district operates divisions that provide home health and EMS services, as well as family medicine, occupational health, and specialty outpatient medical clinics.

	Annual Growth	09/17	09/18	09/19	09/20	09/21
Sales ($mil.)	10.4%	–	137.0	149.5	158.6	184.3
Net income ($ mil.)	–	–	(1.6)	(0.3)	9.2	13.9
Market value ($ mil.)	–	–	–	–	–	–
Employees	–	–	–	–	–	900

HUNTERDON HEALTHCARE SYSTEM

2100 WESCOTT DR
FLEMINGTON, NJ 088224603
Phone: 908 788-6100
Fax: –
Web: –

CEO: –
CFO: –
HR: –
FYE: December 31
Type: Private

Hunting for health care in the Garden State? Hunterdon Healthcare System has you covered. The not-for-profit organization provides a full range of medical services through its 180-bed medical center. Among its specialty services are behavioral health care, maternity and newborn care, diagnostic imaging, and hospice. Its Hunterdon Regional Community Health segment provides home health care services that include skilled nursing, occupational and physical therapy, and home health aides. The organization also provides home-based psychiatric care. Outpatient services, including family medicine and primary care, are provided through a network of local clinics. The system, founded in 1953, is led by CEO Robert Wise.

	Annual Growth	12/05	12/06	12/09	12/13	12/14
Sales ($mil.)	(39.3%)	–	184.5	1.6	3.2	3.4
Net income ($ mil.)	(36.1%)	–	7.4	0.0	0.0	0.2
Market value ($ mil.)	–	–	–	–	–	–
Employees	–	–	–	–	–	1,720

HUNTINGTON BANCSHARES INC   NMS: HBAN

41 South High Street
Columbus, OH 43287
Phone: 614 480-2265
Fax: –
Web: www.huntington.com

CEO: Stephen D Steinour
CFO: Zachary J Wasserman
HR: –
FYE: December 31
Type: Public

Huntington Bancshares is a multi-state diversified regional bank holding company. The company operates more than 1,030 full-service branches, and private client group offices are primarily located in approximately 10 states. Through its subsidiaries, including its bank subsidiary, The Huntington National Bank (the bank), Huntington offers mortgage banking, capital market services, equipment financing, brokerage services, investment management, recreational vehicle and marine financing, and trust and estate services among others. The company's Vehicle finance business provides new and used automobile financing and dealer services throughout the Midwest. Founded in 1866, the company boasts total assets of approximately $189 billion.

	Annual Growth	12/19	12/20	12/21	12/22	12/23
Assets ($mil.)	14.8%	109,002	123,038	174,064	182,906	189,368
Net income ($ mil.)	8.4%	1,411.0	817.0	1,295.0	2,238.0	1,951.0
Market value ($ mil.)	(4.2%)	21,841	18,292	22,333	20,421	18,423
Employees	6.2%	15,664	15,578	18,442	19,920	19,955

HUNTINGTON HOSPITAL DOLAN FAMILY HEALTH CENTER, INC.

270 PARK AVE
HUNTINGTON, NY 117432787
Phone: 631 351-2000
Fax: –
Web: www.huntingtonhealth.org

CEO: Michael J Dowling
CFO: Kevin Lawlor
HR: Nicole Longaro
FYE: December 31
Type: Private

When residents of the Gold Coast feel poorly, Huntington Hospital is there to help. Part of the North Shore-Long Island Jewish Health System, Huntington Hospital is a 410-bed, not-for-profit tertiary care center providing a comprehensive range of medical services to residents of Huntington, New York, and surrounding communities. Along with general surgical services, the hospital provides specialty cardiac, cancer, maternity, pediatric, and psychiatric care. Huntington also operates a number of outpatient diagnostic and community clinics where patients can turn for primary care, physical rehabilitation, or specialized care for other ailments.

	Annual Growth	12/16	12/17	12/18	12/21	12/22
Sales ($mil.)	13.7%	–	336.9	351.9	457.6	641.2
Net income ($ mil.)	5.9%	–	19.3	(0.5)	58.0	25.8
Market value ($ mil.)	–	–	–	–	–	–
Employees	–	–	–	–	–	2,000

HUNTINGTON INGALLS INDUSTRIES, INC.   NYS: HII

4101 Washington Avenue
Newport News, VA 23607
Phone: 757 380-2000
Fax: –
Web: www.huntingtoningalls.com

CEO: –
CFO: –
HR: –
FYE: December 31
Type: Public

Huntington Ingalls Industries (HII) is the sole designer, builder, and refueler of the US Navy's nuclear aircraft carriers. The company is America's largest military shipbuilding company and a provider of professional services to partners in government and industry. In addition, HII builds expeditionary warfare ships, surface combatants, submarines, and Coast Guard surface ships and provides aftermarket fleet support. Almost all its offerings are sold to the US government. Although the company competes with General Dynamics, the company has a partnership with a division of General Dynamics, Electric Boat Corporation to build Virginia class (SSN 774) fast attack nuclear submarines.

	Annual Growth	12/19	12/20	12/21	12/22	12/23
Sales ($mil.)	6.5%	8,899.0	9,361.0	9,524.0	10,676	11,454
Net income ($ mil.)	5.5%	549.0	696.0	544.0	579.0	681.0
Market value ($ mil.)	0.9%	9,939.6	6,754.2	7,398.4	9,139.3	10,287
Employees	1.2%	42,000	42,000	44,000	43,000	44,000

HUNTSMAN CORP   NYS: HUN

10003 Woodloch Forest Drive
The Woodlands, TX 77380
Phone: 281 719-6000
Fax: –
Web: www.huntsman.com

CEO: Peter R Huntsman
CFO: Phil M Lister
HR: Heather Hubbert
FYE: December 31
Type: Public

Huntsman Corporation manufactures differentiated organic chemical products. It offers chemicals and formulations, which it markets globally to a diversified group of consumer and industrial customers. Products are used in various applications, including those in the adhesives, aerospace, automotive, construction products, durable and non-durable consumer products, electronics, insulation, packaging, coatings and construction, power generation. Key product lines also include MDI, amines, maleic anhydride, and epoxy-based polymer formulations. The US and Canada are Huntsman's biggest market, accounting for about 40% of sales. The company started in 1970 as a maker of small polystyrene plastics packaging.

	Annual Growth	12/19	12/20	12/21	12/22	12/23
Sales ($mil.)	(2.6%)	6,797.0	6,018.0	8,453.0	8,023.0	6,111.0
Net income ($ mil.)	(34.9%)	562.0	1,034.0	1,045.0	460.0	101.0
Market value ($ mil.)	1.0%	4,145.5	4,313.6	5,984.8	4,715.1	4,311.9
Employees	(12.0%)	10,000	9,000	9,000	7,000	6,000

HUNTSMAN INTERNATIONAL LLC

10003 WOODLOCH FOREST DR
THE WOODLANDS, TX 773801955
Phone: 281 719-6000
Fax: –
Web: www.huntsman.com

CEO: –
CFO: –
HR: –
FYE: December 31
Type: Private

Chemistry is key to any successful relationship, and good chemistry is what Huntsman is all about. Huntsman International operates in five business segments: polyurethanes, advanced materials, textile effects, performance products, and pigments. The company manufactures surfactants (used in cleaning and personal care products) and performance chemicals like polyurethanes, propylene oxides, and propylene glycol. Its polyurethanes segment is the company's largest, representing 39% of 2011 sales. Huntsman ranks among the largest makers of titanium dioxide, the most commonly used white pigment, with 15% of the world market. Huntsman International operates the business of parent Huntsman Corporation.

HUNZICKER BROTHERS, INC.

501 N VIRGINIA AVE
OKLAHOMA CITY, OK 731062638
Phone: 405 239-7771
Fax: –
Web: www.hunzicker.com

CEO: Myers Lockard
CFO: –
HR: Randy Witzel
FYE: December 31
Type: Private

Hunzicker Brothers distributes electrical equipment and supplies to customers from seven locations throughout Oklahoma. It also conducts educational classes in power quality, electric motors, and heat tracing, among others. The Hunzicker Lighting Gallery, complete with showroom, offers professional lighting design services. The Hunzicker family, now in its fourth generation of ownership, holds controlling interest. Hunzicker Sales was founded in 1920 by brothers Walter and Frederick Hunzicker; its name was changed to Hunzicker Brothers four years later. The brothers started the business by buying a rail car full of light bulbs and reselling them. It later expanded into electrical fixtures and related products.

HUNZINGER CONSTRUCTION COMPANY

21100 ENTERPRISE AVE
BROOKFIELD, WI 530455226
Phone: 262 797-0797
Fax: –
Web: www.hunzinger.com

CEO: –
CFO: –
HR: –
FYE: December 31
Type: Private

Hunzinger Construction Company (Hunzinger) provides general contracting, construction management, and design/build services to industrial, commercial, and aviation clients across Wisconsin. Projects have included health care facilities, hotels, churches, restaurants, shops, educational facilities, and the Milwaukee Bucks Entertainment Block and Miller Park. Hunzinger's Sustainable Building Solutions division specializes in eco-friendly projects. The company's roots reach back to 1907, when the Hunzinger brothers formed J.H. Hunzinger and Company. In 1928 brothers Frank and Fred moved to Milwaukee and founded Hunzinger Construction. The Hunzinger family continues to lead the company.

HURCO COMPANIES INC

One Technology Way
Indianapolis, IN 46268
Phone: 317 293-5309
Fax: 317 328-2811
Web: www.hurco.com

NMS: HURC
CEO: Gregory S Volovic
CFO: Sonja K McClelland
HR: –
FYE: October 31
Type: Public

Hurco is an international industrial technology company that designs and makes computerized metal cutting and forming machine tools, such as vertical machining (mills) and turning (lathes) centers, to companies in the metal cutting industry through a worldwide sales, service, and distribution network. Its machines are manufactured and assembled by Taiwan subsidiary Hurco Manufacturing, using components produced by neighboring contract suppliers. Hurco markets its five-axis machines through its TM/TMM, TMX and VMX series and other specialty product lines. It sells to customers in the aerospace, automotive, computers/electronics, energy, medical equipment, and transportation industries. About 60% of total revenue comes from outside the Americas.

	Annual Growth	10/19	10/20	10/21	10/22	10/23
Sales ($mil.)	(3.6%)	263.4	170.6	235.2	250.8	227.8
Net income ($ mil.)	(29.2%)	17.5	(6.2)	6.8	8.2	4.4
Market value ($ mil.)	(12.9%)	224.8	192.8	209.7	149.6	129.2
Employees	(2.3%)	785	710	706	735	716

HURLEN CORPORATION

9841 BELL RANCH DR
SANTA FE SPRINGS, CA 906702953
Phone: 562 941-5330
Fax: –
Web: www.hurlen-kenig.com

CEO: Jay Hurtado
CFO: –
HR: –
FYE: May 31
Type: Private

Hurlen distributes metals to aerospace companies through warehouses in California and Florida. The company, whose business in Florida operates through subsidiary Kenig Aerospace, specializes in aerospace and commercial-quality metals such as high-temperature refractory and nickel alloys, copper and copper alloys, hand forgings, aluminum alloys, and stainless steels. Hurlen also offers related treatment and processing services, including heat treating, cutting, sonic testing, grinding, and milling. Customers have included companies such as Boeing, Gulfstream, Lockheed Martin, and Northrop Grumman.

HURLEY MEDICAL CENTER

1 HURLEY PLZ
FLINT, MI 485035902
Phone: 810 262-9000
Fax: –
Web: www.hurleymc.com

CEO: Melanie Devalac
CFO: Kevin Murphy
HR: Tyree Walker
FYE: June 30
Type: Private

A community hospital owned by the City of Flint, Hurley Medical Center is a teaching hospital serving Genesee, Lapeer, and Shiawassee counties in eastern Michigan. The 440-bed acute care facility is affiliated with the medical schools of Michigan State University and The University of Michigan. It provides care in areas such as cancer, mental health, rehabilitation, surgery, and women's health, and it is a regional center for pediatrics. Hurley Medical Center also offers advanced specialty care, such as trauma care, neonatal intensive care, kidney transplantation, burn medicine, and bariatric (weight loss) surgery. The center was founded in 1908 and is owned by the state of Michigan.

	Annual Growth	03/07	03/08*	06/08	06/15	06/16
Sales ($mil.)	6.8%	–	250.1	350.2	378.5	422.1
Net income ($ mil.)	97.7%	–	0.2	3.8	24.3	44.8
Market value ($ mil.)	–	–	–	–	–	–
Employees	–	–	–	–	–	2,884

*Fiscal year change

HURON CONSULTING GROUP INC

NMS: HURN

550 West Van Buren Street
Chicago, IL 60607
Phone: 312 583-8700
Fax: –
Web: www.huronconsultinggroup.com

CEO: James H Roth
CFO: John D Kelly
HR: –
FYE: December 31
Type: Public

Huron Consulting Group provides a variety of consulting services designed to assist clients in achieving growth and profitability, improving quality of service, and managing corporate transitions, among other initiatives. Its Healthcare segment services clients such as hospitals, health systems, and medical groups, while Commercial segment includes all industries outside of healthcare and education, including, but not limited to, financial services and energy and utilities. Its Education segment provides research enterprise and student lifecycle; digital, technology and analytic solutions; and organizational transformation.

	Annual Growth	12/19	12/20	12/21	12/22	12/23
Sales ($mil.)	9.7%	965.5	871.0	927.0	1,159.0	1,398.8
Net income ($ mil.)	10.6%	41.7	(23.8)	63.0	75.6	62.5
Market value ($ mil.)	10.6%	1,268.9	1,088.5	921.4	1,340.5	1,898.1
Employees	14.7%	3,750	3,807	4,609	5,660	6,480

HURRICANES HOCKEY LIMITED PARTNERSHIP

1400 EDWARDS MILL RD
RALEIGH, NC 276073624
Phone: 919 467-7825
Fax: –
Web: www.nhl.com

CEO: –
CFO: –
HR: Allison Duino
FYE: July 31
Type: Private

Carolina Hurricanes Hockey Club is a professional hockey franchise that represents North Carolina in the National Hockey League. Originally founded in 1971 as the New England Whalers of the World Hockey Association (WHA), the team joined the NHL as the Hartford Whalers in 1979. Peter Karmanos, founder and chairman of Compuware, led a group that acquired the team in 1994, relocating it first to Greensboro, North Carolina, before settling in Raleigh in 1999. Playing host that the RBC Center, the team earned its first and only Stanley Cup championship in 2006.

HUSSEY SEATING COMPANY

38 DYER ST EXT
NORTH BERWICK, ME 039066763
Phone: 207 676-2271
Fax: –
Web: www.husseyseating.com

CEO: Timothy B Hussey
CFO: Charles W Nadeau
HR: –
FYE: April 02
Type: Private

Hussey Seating Company makes sure people in the back row are comfortable, even if the back row consists of hundreds of seats. The company makes bleachers for gymnasiums; plush seating for sports stadiums, auditoriums, and movie theaters; and upholstered chairs for convention centers and places of worship. Hussey Seating also serves corporate clients, such as casinos (entertainment seating) and justice buildings (court room environments). Its brand names include MAXAM, Fusion, Legend, and Quattro, among others. Still family-owned and -operated, the company started as a plow manufacturer when it was founded by namesake New Englander William Hussey in 1835.

HUSSON UNIVERSITY

1 COLLEGE CIR
BANGOR, ME 044012999
Phone: 207 941-7000
Fax: –
Web: www.husson.edu

CEO: Robert A Clark
CFO: –
HR: Carol Mandzik
FYE: June 30
Type: Private

If the hustle and bustle of college life attracts you, Husson University is probably not the place for you. The university, tucked away on 175 acres of fields and forests, primarily caters to rural and small town residents in its home state of Maine. Enrollment is about 2,500 students, about 20% of whom are seeking graduate degrees. The school has about 70 faculty members and a 19-to-1 student teacher ratio. Husson offers both undergraduate and graduate degreee programs in such academic disciplines as business, communications, education, health, language studies, and science and humanities. The school was founded in 1898.

	Annual Growth	06/13	06/14	06/20	06/21	06/22
Sales ($mil.)	5.4%	–	57.0	81.8	80.4	86.5
Net income ($ mil.)	3.0%	–	3.7	9.2	6.8	4.7
Market value ($ mil.)	–	–	–	–	–	–
Employees	–	–	–	–	–	520

HUTCHINSON & BLOODGOOD LLP

550 N BRAND BLVD FL 14
GLENDALE, CA 912031952
Phone: 818 637-5000
Fax: –
Web: www.hbllp.com

CEO: –
CFO: –
HR: Esmeralda Rendon
FYE: September 30
Type: Private

Hutchinson and Bloodgood LLP (HBLLP) makes good on its promise to serve clients in the Golden State. With five offices throughout California, the accounting and consulting firm offers a variety of services, including tax planning, auditing, human resources services, and business advisory. Its H&B Consulting Group provides technology consulting. Founded in 1922, Hutchinson and Bloodgood serves clients internationally through its affiliation with PKF International. Hutchinson and Bloodgood caters to clients in the financial services, construction, legal, health care, agribusiness, non-profit, and manufacturing sectors.

	Annual Growth	09/01	09/02	09/03	09/04	09/19
Sales ($mil.)	(28.5%)	–	13.0	13.7	14.9	0.0
Net income ($ mil.)	–	–	4.3	4.8	3.1	(0.0)
Market value ($ mil.)	–	–	–	–	–	–
Employees	–	–	–	–	–	125

HUTCHINSON TECHNOLOGY INCORPORATED

40 W HIGHLAND PARK DR NE
HUTCHINSON, MN 553509300
Phone: 320 587-3797
Fax: –
Web: hutchinson.tdk.com

CEO: Wayne M Fortun
CFO: David P Radloff
HR: Jerry Polzin
FYE: September 27
Type: Private

Hutchinson Technology (HTI) specializes in the design and manufacture of close-tolerance products that require chemical, mechanical, and electronic technologies. The company is a leading manufacturer of micro scale precision electromechanical products. Assembly operations rely heavily on its world class tool design and manufacturing capability to achieve leading edge tolerances. HTI has a number of core, highly capable manufacturing proficiencies for precision assembly, including precision locating, laser welding, shearing/cutting, die bonding, adhesive bonding, ultrasonic cleaning, and automated material handling and packaging. Hutchinson serves disk drive, smartphones, medical and microelectronics markets. Hutchinson has been part of TDK Corp. since 2016.

HUTTIG BUILDING PRODUCTS, INC.

555 MARYVILLE UNIVERSITY DR STE 400
SAINT LOUIS, MO 63141
Phone: 314 216-2600
Fax: –
Web: www.huttig.com

CEO: Jon P Vrabely
CFO: Philip W Keipp
HR: Theresa Kaelin
FYE: December 31
Type: Private

Huttig Building Products, now known as Woodgrain and is a part of Woodgrain's Distribution division, is one of the US's largest distributors of millwork, building materials, and wood products for new housing construction and in-home improvement, remodeling, and repair work. Huttig sells doors, windows, moldings, trusses, wall panels, lumber, and other supplies through approximately 25 distribution centers in about 40 states, covering a substantial portion of the US housing market. Its wholesale distribution centers sell principally to building materials dealers, national buying groups, home centers and industrial users, including makers of manufactured homes. In mid-2022, Woodgrain closed the Huttig Building Products acquisition for approximately $350 million.

HY-VEE, INC.

5820 WESTOWN PKWY
WEST DES MOINES, IA 502668223
Phone: 515 267-2800
Fax: –
Web: www.hy-vee.com

CEO: Randy Edeker
CFO: Mike Skokan
HR: Karee White
FYE: September 30
Type: Private

Hy-Vee is one of the largest privately-owned US supermarket chains, despite serving some modestly-sized towns in the Midwest. The company runs more than 285 stores in eight Midwestern states. It distributes products to its stores through several subsidiaries, including Amber Specialty Pharmacy, D & D Foods, Florist Distributing, Hy-Vee Pharmacy Solutions, Midwest Heritage, Perishable Distributors of Iowa, RedBox RX, Wall to Wall Wine and Spirits, and Vivid Clear RX. Hy-Vee is synonymous with quality, variety, convenience, healthy lifestyles, culinary expertise and superior customer service. Charles Hyde and David Vredenburg founded the employee-owned company in 1930. It takes its name from a combination of its founders' names.

	Annual Growth	09/18	09/19	09/20	09/21	09/22
Sales ($mil.)	6.5%	–	10,673	11,449	12,182	12,888
Net income ($ mil.)	–	–	–	–	–	–
Market value ($ mil.)	–	–	–	–	–	–
Employees	–	–	–	–	–	73,000

HYATT HOTELS CORP

NYS: H

150 North Riverside Plaza, 8th Floor
Chicago, IL 60606
Phone: 312 750-1234
Fax: –
Web: www.hyatt.com

CEO: Mark S Hoplamazian
CFO: Joan Bottarini
HR: –
FYE: December 31
Type: Public

Hyatt Hotels is one of the world's top operators of luxury hotels and resorts. The company has about 1,300 managed, franchised, and owned properties (more than 304,000 rooms) in about 70 countries. Its core Hyatt Regency brand offers hospitality services targeted primarily to business travelers and leisure guests. The company's hotel chains include the upscale, full service Hyatt, Grand Hyatt, and Andaz brands, as well as Park Hyatt (luxury) and Hyatt Place (select service). Hyatt also operates resorts under the names Hyatt Zilara and Hyatt Ziva. Domestic markets account for about 50% of total revenue.

	Annual Growth	12/19	12/20	12/21	12/22	12/23
Sales ($mil.)	7.4%	5,020.0	2,066.0	3,028.0	5,891.0	6,667.0
Net income ($ mil.)	(26.8%)	766.0	(703.0)	(222.0)	455.0	220.0
Market value ($ mil.)	9.8%	9,243.1	7,650.2	9,880.9	9,319.3	13,437
Employees	(1.9%)	55,000	37,000	44,000	189,000	51,000

HYCROFT MINING CORPORATION

8181 E TUFTS AVE STE 510
DENVER, CO 802372580
Phone: 775 358-4455
Fax: –
Web: www.hycroftmining.com

CEO: –
CFO: –
HR: –
FYE: December 31
Type: Private

All that glitters is not gold; some of it's silver. That's the story at Allied Nevada Gold, a mining company that produces gold, primarily, and silver as a by-product from its property in Nevada. Its wholly owned Hycroft Mine, sitting on 96 sq. mi., has proven and probable mineral reserves of about 3 million ounces of gold and nearly 50 million ounces of silver. The company is conducting feasibility studies for a mill on the property that would process sulfide and other high oxide ores. Allied Nevada Gold also explores for gold, silver, and other minerals on more than 100 properties in the state. The company was spun off from Vista Gold in 2007 when it acquired its former parent's Nevada mining operations.

HYDE GROUP, INC.

54 EASTFORD RD
SOUTHBRIDGE, MA 015503604
Phone: 800 872-4933
Fax: –
Web: www.hydegrp.com

CEO: –
CFO: –
HR: –
FYE: December 31
Type: Private

Hyde Group (dba as Hyde Tools) makes surface preparation hand tools for drywall, painting, and plumbing professionals. The niche manufacturing company makes about 2,000 products, including industrial knives and surface preparation tools (scrapers, trowels), are sold worldwide through retailers, such as McCoy Corp. and Sherwin-Williams and online. Hyde Manufacturing early investor Myron Clemence's son and grandson ran the company (which became Hyde Tools) during the 1970s. Some of his descendants are still involved in the business today, including CEO Rick Clemence.

HYDROMER, INC.

NBB: HYDI

4715 Corporate Dr. NW, Suite 200
Concord, NC 28027
Phone: 800 287-5208
Fax: –
Web: www.hydromer.com

CEO: Michael E Torti
CFO: Robert Y Lee
HR: –
FYE: June 30
Type: Public

Hydromer would say its products become lubricious when wet. Bon Jovi preferred the term "slippery," but it amounts to the same thing. The company makes lubricating and water-resistant coatings for use in medical, pharmaceutical, cosmetic, industrial, and veterinary markets. Its products include lubricated medical devices, hydro-gels for drugs, anti-fog coatings, marine hull protective coatings, barrier dips for dairy cows, and intermediaries for hair and skin care products. Services include research and development, medical device manufacturing (through subsidiary Biosearch Medical Products), and contract coating. Chairman and CEO Manfred Dyck owns a third of Hydromer.

	Annual Growth	06/18	06/19	06/20	06/21	06/22
Sales ($mil.)	(9.5%)	5.6	5.2	6.2	3.7	3.8
Net income ($ mil.)	–	0.0	4.5	(3.0)	(2.7)	(1.6)
Market value ($ mil.)	(6.6%)	2.0	5.7	7.3	3.8	1.5
Employees	–	–	34	–	–	–

HYDRON TECHNOLOGIES, INC.

9843 18th Street N, Suite 150
St. Petersburg, FL 33716
Phone: 727 342-5050
Fax: –
Web: www.hydron.com

CEO: –
CFO: –
HR: –
FYE: September 30
Type: Public

The magic is in the moisture at Hydron Technologies. The company focuses on developing skin care products that contain microbubbles of pure oxygen used in treating the epidermis and underlying tissues. Hydron Technologies also manufactures personal and oral care products that contain its moisture-attracting ingredient, the Hydron polymer. The company distributes about 40 skin, hair, and sun care products, as well as bath and body items, through its Web site. It also produces private-label skin care items and ships them to contract manufacturers.

	Annual Growth	12/05	12/06*	09/07	09/08	09/09
Sales ($mil.)	–	1.5	1.5	0.9	1.1	–
Net income ($ mil.)	–	(0.8)	(0.6)	(0.5)	(0.7)	(0.7)
Market value ($ mil.)	(41.9%)	6.9	3.3	2.9	0.4	0.8
Employees	–	15	19	17	22	

*Fiscal year change

HYNES INDUSTRIES, INC.

3805 HENDRICKS RD
YOUNGSTOWN, OH 445153046
Phone: 330 799-3221
Fax: –
Web: www.hynesindustries.com

CEO: Rick Organ
CFO: –
HR: –
FYE: December 31
Type: Private

Hynes Industries offers a variety of products to original equipment manufacturers in the appliance, automotive, agricultural, and hardware industries, as well as to other steel processors. The largest custom roll form fabricator in North America has produced precision-engineered custom roll form metal solutions with an unyielding commitment to quality, service, and performance. Its targeted experience in highly-engineered designs for truck/trailer manufacturing, solar, automated material handling, and industrial and commercial building products has made Hynes the preferred roll form fabricator for Fortune 500 and Global 2000 companies in North America. Hynes Industries was founded in 1925.

	Annual Growth	12/17	12/18	12/19	12/20	12/21
Sales ($mil.)	27.2%	–	–	–	13.5	17.1
Net income ($ mil.)	–	–	–	–	(0.3)	1.4
Market value ($ mil.)	–	–	–	–	–	–
Employees	–	–	–	–	–	171

HYPERDYNAMICS CORP

12012 Wickchester Lane, Suite 475
Houston, TX 77079
Phone: 713 353-9400
Fax: 713 353-9421
Web: www.hyperdynamics.com

NBB: HDYN Q
CEO: –
CFO: –
HR: –
FYE: June 30
Type: Public

Not as hyper as it was, but still dynamic, Hyperdynamics (which began life in 1996 as a value-added reseller of computer hardware and software) now focuses on oil and gas exploration in Africa. The company concentrates on developing an oil and gas concession located offshore in the Republic of Guinea in West Africa in partnership with Tullow Oil and Dana Petroleum. The oil and gas exploration and production company holds a 37% non-operator interest covering approximately 25,000 square kilometers in Guinea, one of the largest exploration and production licenses in West Africa.

	Annual Growth	06/13	06/14	06/15	06/16	06/17
Sales ($mil.)	–	–	–	–	–	–
Net income ($ mil.)	–	(18.5)	(17.1)	(13.4)	(22.8)	(21.5)
Market value ($ mil.)	33.5%	13.0	89.1	24.7	11.6	41.4
Employees	(5.4%)	20	17	11	10	16

HYSPAN PRECISION PRODUCTS, INC.

1685 BRANDYWINE AVE
CHULA VISTA, CA 919116020
Phone: 619 421-1355
Fax: –
Web: www.hyspan.com

CEO: Donald R Heye
CFO: Phillip Ensz
HR: –
FYE: June 30
Type: Private

Hyspan Precision Products comprehensive engineering, quality and production capability to design, develop and fabricate metal bellows and hose; and assemblies and products that incorporate these components. Products are sold directly from manufacturing facilities in the US, a plant in Mexico, and through distributors and Hyspan's sales force, for such end uses as auto, highway, industrial OEM, and HVAC. US defense agencies are among Hyspan's top accounts. Founded in 1968, Hyspan is a member of the Expansion Joint Manufacturers Assocation, Inc. (EJMA), an organization devoted to the development of design methods for metal bellows and related products.

	Annual Growth	06/06	06/07	06/08	06/09	06/10
Sales ($mil.)	(14.5%)	–	–	46.5	40.5	34.0
Net income ($ mil.)	(30.4%)	–	–	3.0	3.4	1.4
Market value ($ mil.)	–	–	–	–	–	–
Employees	–	–	–	–	–	480

HYSTER-YALE MATERIALS HANDLING INC

5875 Landerbrook Drive, Suite 300
Cleveland, OH 44124-4069
Phone: 440 449-9600
Fax: –
Web: www.hyster-yale.com

NYS: HY
CEO: Rajiv K Prasad
CFO: Kenneth C Schilling
HR: Darnell Hill
FYE: December 31
Type: Public

Hyster-Yale Materials Handling is a leading, globally integrated, full-line lift truck manufacturer that designs, manufactures, and sells a variety of forklifts and other lift truck products through its Hyster-Yale Group subsidiary. In addition, the company has a broad array of solutions aimed at meeting the specific materials handling needs of its customers, including attachments and hydrogen fuel cell power products, telematics, automation and fleet management services, as well as a variety of other power options for its lift trucks. Its trucks are primarily sold under the Hyster and Yale brands. The company, which operates facilities in the Americas, Europe, and Asia, gets about 55% of revenue from the US markets.

	Annual Growth	12/19	12/20	12/21	12/22	12/23
Sales ($mil.)	5.8%	3,291.8	2,812.1	3,075.7	3,548.3	4,118.3
Net income ($ mil.)	36.9%	35.8	37.1	(173.0)	(73.6)	125.9
Market value ($ mil.)	1.3%	1,013.3	1,023.4	706.3	435.0	1,068.8
Employees	–	7,900	7,600	8,100	8,200	–

I O INTERCONNECT, LTD.

7 OLD RANCH RD
LAGUNA NIGUEL, CA 926779210
Phone: 714 564-1111
Fax: –
Web: www.ioint.com

CEO: –
CFO: –
HR: –
FYE: December 31
Type: Private

I/O Interconnect is a contract manufacturer of interconnection devices, such as printed circuit boards and cables. Services include design, assembly, testing, packaging, and program management. I/O Interconnect is big on reading and writing, if not 'rithmetic -- it makes Universal Serial Bus (USB) drives for reading stored data, PC adapters that can turn any PC Card slot into a flash memory reader/writer, and external drives for burning CDs and DVDs. The company was established in 1986 and has facilities in China, Taiwan, the UK, and the US.

I-5 DESIGN BUILD INC.

9000 ORION DR NE
LACEY, WA 985166100
Phone: 360 459-3200
Fax: –
Web: www.i5design.com

CEO: –
CFO: Jack Frost
HR: –
FYE: December 31
Type: Private

I-5 is a highly skilled casino and retail design/build firm with a proven track record designing high impact gaming and food & beverage environments done in highly reduced timeframes to maximize revenue. Company offers nature motifs, imagery honoring tribal heritage, to vivacious nightclub settings, I-5 Design provides premier-quality casino design and renovation plans that deliver unforgettable guest experiences. I-5 design staff's broad expertise includes casino design, bar and lounge design, bank design, supermarket design, restaurant design and more.

I/OMAGIC CORPORATION

20512 CRESCENT BAY DR
LAKE FOREST, CA 926308847
Phone: 949 707-4800
Fax: –
Web: www.iomagic.com

CEO: Tony Shahbaz
CFO: –
HR: –
FYE: December 31
Type: Private

I/OMagic has some input regarding computer peripheral output. It designs and markets optical storage products, such as CD-ROM and DVD-ROM playback and read-write devices. Other products include audio cards, digital photo frames, external hard drives, headphones, and Web cameras. The company also markets LCD-based HDTVs and home theater speakers through its Digital Research Technologies (DRT) division. I/OMagic sells to retailers such as Staples (nearly half of sales), OfficeMax, and Costco in the US and Canada. Other significant customers include distributors Tech Data (29% of sales) and D&H Distributing. The company subcontracts the manufacturing of most of its products.

IAC INC

555 West 18th Street
New York, NY 10011
Phone: 212 314-7300
Fax: –
Web: www.iac.com

CEO: Faye Iosotaluno
CFO: Gary Swidler
HR: Bud Bartholomew
FYE: December 31
Type: Public

Match Group operates Match.com, one of the world's largest dating Web portals. Some of the company's well-known brands include Tinder, Match, Hinge, OkCupid, and OurTime, among others. Registered members post a personal profile and browse the site in search of a potential match. In addition to its flagship site, the company connects with web-bound singles in different countries via sites in over 40 languages.

	Annual Growth	12/19	12/20	12/21	12/22	12/23
Sales ($mil.)	12.7%	2,705.8	3,047.7	3,699.6	5,235.3	4,365.2
Net income ($ mil.)	84.6%	22.9	269.7	597.5	(1,170.2)	265.9
Market value ($ mil.)	–	–	–	–	–	–
Employees	10.4%	6,400	8,200	13,200	11,000	9,500

IAG CORP.

N114W18770 CLINTON DR
GERMANTOWN, WI 530223118
Phone: 262 251-3000
Fax: –
Web: www.pccweb.com

CEO: –
CFO: –
HR: –
FYE: December 31
Type: Private

Professional Control Corporation (PCC) is a consulting company with a focus on providing industrial automation and control distributor services to equipment manufacturers in Wisconsin and Minnesota. The company provides services ranging from Sensor Technologies, Power Distributions and Controls, Motion Control and Drives, Enclosures, and Safety Products. It distributes industrial computers, electronics, and controls from such suppliers as AMCI, iKey, Binder, FiBoX, and Larco. PCC is also an authorized trainer for Siemens products. PCC was founded in 1980.

	Annual Growth	12/18	12/19	12/20	12/21	12/22
Sales ($mil.)	(2.8%)	–	39.0	34.7	74.4	35.8
Net income ($ mil.)	–	–	4.1	5.1	16.8	(5.2)
Market value ($ mil.)	–	–	–	–	–	–
Employees	–	–	–	–	–	85

IAP WORLDWIDE SERVICES, INC.

7315 N ATLANTIC AVE
CAPE CANAVERAL, FL 329203721
Phone: 321 784-7100
Fax: –
Web: www.iapws.com

CEO: Terry Derosa
CFO: Charles Cosgrove
HR: –
FYE: December 31
Type: Private

Wherever US troops are marching, IAP Worldwide Services is there to support them. The company provides a variety of logistics and facility support services, chiefly for the US Department of Defense and other government customers, including US states and other countries; it also undertakes work for commercial enterprises. Services include base camp facilities support, logistics planning, and temporary staffing. The company operates through three distinct segments: global operations and logistics; facilities management and base operations support; and professional and technical services. Investment firm Cerberus Capital Management owns a controlling interest in IAP.

	Annual Growth	12/12	12/13	12/14	12/21	12/22
Assets ($mil.)	(55.6%)	–	–	247.9	0.4	0.4
Net income ($ mil.)	–	–	–	263.1	0.2	(0.1)
Market value ($ mil.)	–	–	–	–	–	–
Employees	–	–	–	–	–	110

IASIS HEALTHCARE LLC

117 SEABOARD LN BLDG E
FRANKLIN, TN 370672855
Phone: 615 844-2747
Fax: –
Web: www.iasishealthcare.com

CEO: –
CFO: –
HR: –
FYE: September 30
Type: Private

IASIS Healthcare owns and operates 17 acute care hospitals and a behavioral health facility (with some 3,600 beds total), as well as some 150 physician clinics in Arizona, Arkansas, Colorado, Louisiana, Texas, and Utah. IASIS also operates several outpatient facilities and other centers providing ancillary services, such as radiation therapy, diagnostic imaging, and ambulatory surgery. Its Health Choice subsidiary is a Medicaid and Medicare managed health plan that serves about 260,000 individuals in Arizona and Utah. An investor group led by TPG Capital owns the lion's share of the company, which plans to merge with Steward Health Care.

IBASIS, INC.

10 MAGUIRE RD STE 300
LEXINGTON, MA 024213120
Phone: 781 430-7500
Fax: –
Web: www.ibasis.com

CEO: Feddo Hazewindus
CFO: Ardjan Konijnenberg
HR: Lynne Tartaglia
FYE: December 31
Type: Private

iBasis has laid a foundation for digital phone service. The company, a subsidiary of Dutch telecommunications service provider KPN, primarily sells wholesale access to its international VoIP (voice-over-Internet protocol) network to more than 1,000 other voice and data service carriers and resellers in about 100 countries. Its long distance services are enabled through agreements with regional providers worldwide who handle termination of calls. While its core segment is wholesale VoIP access, the company also offers mobile data services such as hosted roaming and global mobile signaling and sells retail prepaid services through some 240 calling card brands and online.

	Annual Growth	12/03	12/04	12/07	12/16	12/17
Sales ($mil.)	3.5%	–	511.1	938.6	–	796.6
Net income ($ mil.)	–	–	(2.2)	16.1	–	2.9
Market value ($ mil.)	–	–	–	–	–	–
Employees	–	–	–	–	–	300

IBIQUITY DIGITAL CORPORATION

6711 COLUMBIA GATEWAY DR # 5
COLUMBIA, MD 210462294
Phone: 443 539-4290
Fax: –
Web: www.ibiquity.com

CEO: –
CFO: –
HR: –
FYE: September 30
Type: Private

iBiquity Digital wants to spread the news about digital radio. The company licenses in-band on-channel (IBOC) technology, branded as HD Radio, that allows AM or FM radio stations to transmit digital signals on the back of their normal analog signals. Customers include broadcast companies and more than 1,000 radio stations nationwide. The company also licenses HD Radio technology to home and car stereo receiver manufacuters including Boston Acoustics and Sanyo. iBiquity Digital has offices in Columbia, Maryland; Basking Ridge, New Jersey; and Pontiac, Michigan. In 2015 DTS agreed to acquire the company for about $172 million.

	Annual Growth	12/03	12/04	12/05*	09/07	09/08
Sales ($mil.)	34.4%	–	4.0	9.3	11.7	13.0
Net income ($ mil.)	–	–	(12.3)	(12.6)	(37.9)	(57.3)
Market value ($ mil.)	–	–	–	–	–	–
Employees	–	–	–	–	–	150

*Fiscal year change

IBW FINANCIAL CORP

NBB: IBWC

4812 Georgia Avenue, NW
Washington, DC 20021
Phone: 202 722-2000
Fax: –
Web: –

CEO: –
CFO: –
HR: –
FYE: December 31
Type: Public

IBW Financial is the holding company for Industrial Bank, one of the largest minority-owned banks in the US. Catering to the African-American community in and around Washington, DC, the bank offers standard personal and commercial services, such as checking and savings accounts, debit cards, and cash management. It primarily writes real estate loans, with residential mortgages and commercial mortgages each accounting for nearly 40% of its portfolio. Industrial Bank has about 10 branches and loan production offices in Washington, DC, and nearby parts of Maryland. The Mitchell family, including CEO B. Doyle Mitchell Jr., whose grandfather founded the bank in 1934, holds a controlling stake in IBW Financial.

	Annual Growth	12/99	12/00	12/01	12/02	12/03
Assets ($mil.)	2.5%	–	–	–	295.3	302.6
Net income ($ mil.)	(0.5%)	–	–	–	2.0	2.0
Market value ($ mil.)	21.2%	–	–	–	12.1	14.7
Employees	–	–	–	–	–	160

IC COMPLIANCE LLC

2520 RENAISSANCE BLVD STE 130
KING OF PRUSSIA, PA 194062676
Phone: 650 378-4150
Fax: –
Web: www.talentwave.com

CEO: Teresa Creech
CFO: Jim Hanrahan
HR: –
FYE: December 31
Type: Private

IC Compliance (doing business as ICon Professional Services) keeps the IRS off the backs of companies with contingent workforces. The consulting firm ensures that its clients are in compliance with tax rules for independent contractors, providing advice on employee classification guidelines, IRS audit support, tax reporting and invoice submission, and other services. Additionally, ICon offers outsourced payroll and benefits administration for certain classes of employees, including non-independent contractors, non-sourced workers, and former employees. The firm was established in 1997.

	Annual Growth	12/04	12/05	12/06	12/07	12/08
Sales ($mil.)	–	–	–	(104.3)	15.8	15.1
Net income ($ mil.)	339.3%	–	–	0.0	0.5	0.3
Market value ($ mil.)	–	–	–	–	–	–
Employees	–	–	–	–	–	5,500

ICAD INC

NAS: ICAD

98 Spit Brook Road, Suite 100
Nashua, NH 03062
Phone: 603 882-5200
Fax: –
Web: www.icadmed.com

CEO: Dana Brown
CFO: Eric Lonnqvist
HR: Michelle Keefe
FYE: December 31
Type: Public

Early detection is the best prevention in iCAD's eyes. The company targets the breast cancer detection market with its core SecondLook computer-aided detection (CAD) systems. The systems include workstations and analytical software that help radiologists better identify potential cancers in mammography images. iCAD sells models that can be used with film-based and digital mammography systems. In addition, the company also makes similar CAD systems that are used with magnetic resonance imaging (MRI) systems to detect breast and prostate cancers. iCAD markets its products directly and through sales partnerships with the likes of GE Healthcare, Siemens Medical Solutions, Fuji Medical, and Agfa.

	Annual Growth	12/18	12/19	12/20	12/21	12/22
Sales ($mil.)	2.2%	25.6	31.3	29.7	33.6	27.9
Net income ($ mil.)	–	(9.0)	(13.6)	(17.6)	(11.2)	(13.7)
Market value ($ mil.)	(16.1%)	93.5	196.3	333.4	181.9	46.2
Employees	3.0%	97	138	114	137	109

ICAHN ENTERPRISES LP

NMS: IEP

16690 Collins Avenue, PH-1
Sunny Isles Beach, FL 33160
Phone: 305 422-4100
Fax: –
Web: www.ielp.com

CEO: David Willetts
CFO: Ted Papapostolou
HR: –
FYE: December 31
Type: Public

Icahn Enterprises has investments in companies active across seven industry segments: investment, energy, automotive, food packaging, real estate, home fashion, and pharma. Subsidiaries include CVR Energy, Viskase, and WestPoint Home, among others. Icahn has investments in major brands such as Xerox, Herc Holdings, Inc. Newell Brands, Southwest Gas, and FirstEnergy.. Most of Icahn's revenue is in the US, which accounts for some 95% of revenue. Billionaire corporate raider Carl Icahn and his affiliates control his namesake firm.

	Annual Growth	12/19	12/20	12/21	12/22	12/23
Sales ($mil.)	4.8%	8,992.0	6,123.0	11,328	14,101	10,847
Net income ($ mil.)	–	(1,098.0)	(1,653.0)	(518.0)	(183.0)	(670.0)
Market value ($ mil.)	(27.3%)	26,386	21,739	21,276	21,731	7,375.1
Employees	(14.4%)	28,033	23,800	19,500	20,000	15,038

ICE DATA SERVICES, INC.

32 CROSBY DR STE 100
BEDFORD, MA 017301448
Phone: 781 687-8500
Fax: –
Web: –

CEO: –
CFO: –
HR: Lori Hannay
FYE: December 31
Type: Private

Interactive Data Corporation has something vital to the information superhighway -- the information. Its subscription services provide financial market data, analytics, and related services to financial institutions, active traders, and individual investors. Interactive Data conducts business through two segments: Institutional Services and Active Trader Services. Products include Interactive Data Fixed Income Analytics (fixed-income portfolio analytics for institutions), Interactive Data Pricing and Reference Data (securities information for institutions), and Interactive Data Desktop Solutions (real-time market data for individuals). Private-equity firms Silver Lake and Warburg Pincus agreed to sell IDC to Intercontinental Exchange in 2015.

	Annual Growth	12/09	12/10	12/11	12/12	12/13
Assets ($mil.)	(1.5%)	–	–	4,093.7	3,962.3	3,968.4
Net income ($ mil.)	–	–	–	(29.3)	1.0	33.5
Market value ($ mil.)	–	–	–	–	–	–
Employees	–	–	–	–	–	2,600

ICF INTERNATIONAL INC

NMS: ICFI

1902 Reston Metro Plaza
Reston, VA 20190
Phone: 703 934-3000
Fax: –
Web: www.icf.com

CEO: John M Wasson
CFO: Barry Broadus
HR: –
FYE: December 31
Type: Public

ICF International provides professional services and technology-based solutions to government and commercial clients, including management, marketing, technology, and policy consulting and implementation services, in the areas of energy, environment, and infrastructure; health, education, and social programs; safety and security; and consumer and financial. It offers services throughout the entire life cycle of a policy, program, project, or initiative, from research and analysis and assessment and advice to design and implementation of programs and technology-based solutions, and the provision of engagement services and programs. The company generates about 10% of its revenue from its international clients.

	Annual Growth	12/19	12/20	12/21	12/22	12/23
Sales ($mil.)	7.3%	1,478.5	1,506.9	1,553.0	1,780.0	1,963.2
Net income ($ mil.)	4.6%	68.9	55.0	71.1	64.2	82.6
Market value ($ mil.)	10.0%	1,726.6	1,400.8	1,932.6	1,866.6	2,527.0
Employees	6.5%	7,000	7,500	7,700	9,000	9,000

ICICLE SEAFOODS, INC.

4019 21ST AVE W
SEATTLE, WA 981991299
Phone: 206 282-0988
Fax: –
Web: www.icicleseafoods.com

CEO: –
CFO: –
HR: –
FYE: December 31
Type: Private

Icicle Seafoods is out fishing even when icicles hang low. The fishery and seafood-processing company catches, processes, and distributes fresh, canned, and frozen fish. Products include cod, herring, pollock, halibut, wild salmon, crab, and trout. Customers include food retailers, as well as industrial, wholesale, and food service operators worldwide. The company operates floating seafood processing plants, shoreline plants, and other facilities in Alaska and Washington. Its Alaskan cannery has been in operation since 1899. Icicle also participates in a Chilean trout- and salmon-farm JV. The seafood supplier is owned by private investment firm Paine & Partners, part of Fox Paine & Co.

ICIMS, INC.

101 CRAWFORDS CORNER RD STE 3100
HOLMDEL, NJ 07733
Phone: 800 889-4422
Fax: –
Web: www.icims.com

CEO: Steve Lucas
CFO: Valerie Rainey
HR: –
FYE: December 31
Type: Private

iCIMS provides Web-based applicant tracking and recruiting management software for corporate human resources professionals and third-party recruiters. The company's iCIMS Talent Platform, which is designed to help businesses make their hiring processes more efficient, includes software for screening and storing applicant information, enabling online job applications, tracking candidates, monitoring performance after recruitment, and managing post-employment processes. It sells its applications on a Software-as-a-Service basis. iCIMS targets recruiters, midsized companies, and large corporations. The company was founded in 1999 by Colin Day and George Lieu.

	Annual Growth	12/09	12/10	12/11	12/12	12/13
Sales ($mil.)	24.2%	–	–	30.7	37.3	47.4
Net income ($ mil.)	16.8%	–	–	3.7	(3.4)	5.0
Market value ($ mil.)	–	–	–	–	–	–
Employees	–	–	–	–	–	342

ICOA INC

NBB: ICOA

3651 Lindell Rd., Suite D
Las Vegas, NV 89103
Phone: 401 648-0690
Fax: –
Web: www.icoa.tech

CEO: –
CFO: Erwin Vahlsing Jr
HR: –
FYE: December 31
Type: Public

ICOA installs and operates Wi-Fi hotspots in public areas such as airports, apartment buildings, and retail businesses across the US. Retail users have included such restaurants as Panera Bread and Panda Express. Airport clients have included facilities in Fresno, California and Boise, Idaho. The company's iDockUSA subsidiary focuses on marinas while LinkSpot targets RV parks and outdoor recreation areas. All told, ICOA claims about 1,500 installations in 45 states. It also provides software called Tollbooth which is used to manage wireless network user authentication, billing, and customer service functions.

	Annual Growth	12/17	12/18	12/19	12/20	12/21
Sales ($mil.)	183.8%	0.0	0.0	0.0	0.0	2.3
Net income ($ mil.)	74.0%	0.4	0.6	(0.1)	(0.1)	3.9
Market value ($ mil.)	207.1%	0.6	0.6	0.6	1.2	53.3
Employees	–	–	–	–	–	–

ICON HEALTH & FITNESS, INC.

1500 South, 1000 West
Logan, UT 84321
Phone: 435 750-5000
Fax: –
Web: www.iconfitness.com

CEO: –
CFO: –
HR: –
FYE: May 31
Type: Public

iFIT Health & Fitness (iFIT), formerly known as ICON Health & Fitness, has brawn as one of the leading US makers of home fitness equipment. Targeted to consumers, iFIT manufactures and sells treadmills, elliptical trainers, and other fitness equipment under the NordicTrack, ProForm, Sweat, iFIT, and Weider brands. The company also offers commercial equipment through its FreeMotion Fitness business unit. Currently holds more than 400 active and pending technology patents, iFIT's workouts are streamed in English, Spanish, French and Mandarin Chinese. The company reaches the fitness industry's largest total addressable market in North America, Europe and around the world. The company was founded as a housewares importer in 1977.

	Annual Growth	05/02	05/03	05/04	05/05	05/06
Sales ($mil.)	(0.6%)	871.4	1,011.5	1,095.7	898.1	852.2
Net income ($ mil.)	–	19.4	26.7	23.4	(110.0)	(49.7)
Market value ($ mil.)	–	–	–	–	–	–
Employees	–	–	4,569	5,142	3,467	3,263

ICON IDENTITY SOLUTIONS, INC.

1701 GOLF RD STE 1-900
ROLLING MEADOWS, IL 600084246
Phone: 847 364-2250
Fax: –
Web: www.stratusunlimited.com

CEO: Tim Eippert
CFO: John Callan
HR: –
FYE: December 31
Type: Private

Icon Identity Solutions helps its customers avoid identity crises. The firm provides a variety of services related to the building of a company's brand through the use of signs and exterior graphics. Icon can help clients manage multiple sign projects on a global scale if needed. Its services include sign design, permitting, and manufacturing. Icon Identity Solutions is one arm of Icon Companies, which also operates subsidiaries East Coast Sign Advertising and ImageCare Maintenance Services (IMS). IMS provides sign repair and maintenance. Past clients have included BMW's Mini unit and Citigroup.

	Annual Growth	12/14	12/15	12/16	12/17	12/18
Sales ($mil.)	16.1%	–	107.7	119.1	110.2	168.7
Net income ($ mil.)	(42.1%)	–	4.1	5.0	2.9	0.8
Market value ($ mil.)	–	–	–	–	–	–
Employees	–	–	–	–	–	450

ICONIX BRAND GROUP, INC.

180 MAIN ST UNIT 4
WESTHAMPTON BEACH, NY 119782741
Phone: 212 730-0030
Fax: –
Web: www.iconixbrand.com

CEO: –
CFO: –
HR: –
FYE: December 31
Type: Private

Iconix International (formerly Iconix Brand Group) is a brand management company and owner of some 30 women's, men's, and home to retailers and manufacturers through more than 1,100 worldwide licenses. Brands include Candie's, Danskin, Ocean Pacific, Mossimo, London Fog, Mudd, and Rocawear. Among the company's home brands are Cannon, Fieldcrest, and Waverly. In addition, Iconix provides brand management, licensing, and other advisory services to owners of brand IP on a global basis. Through its in-house business development, strategy, merchandising, advertising, and public relations departments, Iconix manages these brands to drive greater consumer awareness, broader commercial reach, and greater brand valuations.

ICONMA, L.L.C.

850 STEPHENSON HWY STE 612
TROY, MI 480831127
Phone: 248 583-1930
Fax: –
Web: www.iconma.com

CEO: Claudine S George
CFO: –
HR: –
FYE: December 31
Type: Private

ICONMA offers companies a number of consulting and staffing services, with a focus on information technology. Its staffing services include contract, contract-to-hire, and direct hire IT placement, as well as staffing in the areas of engineering, accounting/finance, and professional. The firm also provides offshore software development services and other IT consulting and has a health care services division dedicated to the technology needs of insurance providers, hospitals and other medical companies. Clients include Deutsche Bank, Toyota, and Anthem. Established in 2000, ICONMA has offices across the US and one in India.

	Annual Growth	12/05	12/06	12/07	12/08	12/09
Sales ($mil.)	38.6%	–	–	27.7	40.5	53.2
Net income ($ mil.)	18.1%	–	–	1.2	1.2	1.7
Market value ($ mil.)	–	–	–	–	–	–
Employees	–	–	–	–	–	1,556

ICORE NETWORKS, INC.

7900 WESTPARK DR STE A315
MC LEAN, VA 221024235
Phone: 703 673-1350
Fax: –
Web: www.icore.com

CEO: –
CFO: –
HR: –
FYE: December 31
Type: Private

iCore Networks wants to get to the heart of your networking infrastructure problems. The company offers a variety of Voice over Internet Protocol (VoIP) telephony and telecommunications cabling services such as network installation, site survey studies, system testing, and service and support once the network systems have been placed. iCore Networks primarily caters to companies in Virginia and was established in 2001.

ICU MEDICAL INC

NMS: ICUI

951 Calle Amanecer
San Clemente, CA 92673
Phone: 949 366-2183
Fax: –
Web: www.icumed.com

CEO: Vivek Jain
CFO: Brian Bonnell
HR: Sara Grimaldo
FYE: December 31
Type: Public

ICU Medical (ICU) develops, manufactures, and sells infusion systems, infusion consumables and high-value critical care products used in hospital, alternate site and home care settings. Its product portfolio includes IV solutions, IV smart pumps with pain management and safety software technology, dedicated and non-dedicated IV sets and needle-free connectors designed to help meet clinical, safety and workflow goals. In addition, the company manufactures automated pharmacy IV compounding systems with workflow technology, closed system transfer devices for preparing and administering hazardous IV drugs and cardiac monitoring systems for critically ill patients. ICU, which sells its products to other equipment makers and distributors, gets most of its revenue from the US customers.

	Annual Growth	12/19	12/20	12/21	12/22	12/23
Sales ($mil.)	15.6%	1,266.2	1,271.0	1,316.3	2,280.0	2,259.1
Net income ($ mil.)	–	101.0	86.9	103.1	(74.3)	(29.7)
Market value ($ mil.)	(14.6%)	4,517.3	5,178.0	5,729.6	3,801.7	2,407.8
Employees	15.0%	8,000	7,900	8,500	14,500	14,000

IDACORP INC

NYS: IDA

1221 W. Idaho Street
Boise, ID 83702-5627
Phone: 208 388-2200
Fax: –
Web: www.idacorpinc.com

CEO: –
CFO: –
HR: –
FYE: December 31
Type: Public

IDACORP, operating through a subsidiary, Idaho Power Company, is an electric utility engaged in the generation, transmission, distribution, sale, and purchase of electric energy and capacity. Idaho Power provides electric utility service to approximately 604,000 retail customers in southern Idaho and eastern Oregon. Approximately 506,000 of these customers are residential. Other IDACORP subsidiaries include IDACORP Financial Services, Inc. (IFS), an investor in affordable housing and other real estate investments; and Ida-West Energy Company, an operator of small hydropower generation projects that satisfy the requirements of the Public Utility Regulatory Policies Act of 1978 (PURPA).

	Annual Growth	12/19	12/20	12/21	12/22	12/23
Sales ($mil.)	7.0%	1,346.4	1,350.7	1,458.1	1,644.0	1,766.4
Net income ($ mil.)	2.9%	232.9	237.4	245.6	259.0	261.2
Market value ($ mil.)	(2.0%)	5,405.7	4,860.6	5,735.2	5,458.8	4,976.5
Employees	1.5%	1,993	1,950	1,999	2,077	2,112

IDAHO POWER CO

1221 W. Idaho Street
Boise, ID 83702-5627
Phone: 208 388-2200
Fax: 208 388-6903
Web: www.idahopower.com

CEO: Lisa A Grow
CFO: Steven R Keen
HR: Scott Wright
FYE: December 31
Type: Public

Idaho Power provides electric utility service to retail customers in southern Idaho and eastern Oregon. The utility, a subsidiary of holding company IDACORP, provides electricity to approximately 618,000 residential, commercial, and industrial customers through a network of nearly 4,830 pole miles of high-voltage transmission and some 29,385 pole miles of distribution lines. Idaho Power holds franchises, typically in the form of right-of-way arrangements, in over 70 cities in Idaho and seven cities in Oregon. It reaches its highest all-time system peak demand of about 3,750 MW. In addition, through its Idaho Energy Resources unit, the company has a one-third interest in the Bridger Coal Company, which supplies fuel to the Jim Bridger generating plant in Wyoming.

	Annual Growth	12/18	12/19	12/20	12/21	12/22
Sales ($mil.)	4.7%	1,366.6	1,342.9	1,347.3	1,455.4	1,641.0
Net income ($ mil.)	3.5%	222.3	224.4	233.2	243.2	254.9
Market value ($ mil.)	–	–	–	–	–	–
Employees	1.1%	1,979	1,982	1,937	1,988	2,066

IDAHO STATE UNIVERSITY

921 S 8TH AVE
POCATELLO, ID 832090001
Phone: 208 282-0211
Fax: –
Web: www.isu.edu

CEO: –
CFO: –
HR: Angie Tamayo-Wojcik
FYE: June 30
Type: Private

Even couch potatoes know that Idaho State University (ISU) is the spud state's place to go for a good education. The state institution provides graduate and undergraduate instruction through departments in seven colleges. The school's 14,500 students can choose from about 280 certificate and degree programs in a range of subjects including arts and sciences, business, health professions, and technology. ISU is a Carnegie-classified doctoral research and teaching institution and it has student-teacher ratio of 17:1. In addition to its main campus in Pocatello, the school also has academic centers in Idaho Falls, Meridian, and Twin Falls as well as a research institute specialized in natural and physical sciences.

	Annual Growth	06/17	06/18	06/19	06/20	06/21
Sales ($mil.)	(51.4%)	–	123.4	123.1	15.0	14.2
Net income ($ mil.)	–	–	(0.6)	3.9	5.2	4.0
Market value ($ mil.)	–	–	–	–	–	–
Employees	–	–	–	–	–	1,900

IDAHO STRATEGIC RESOURCES INC

201 N. Third Street
Coeur d'Alene, ID 83814
Phone: 208 625-9001
Fax: –
Web: www.newjerseymining.com

ASE: IDR
CEO: –
CFO: –
HR: –
FYE: December 31
Type: Public

No product of the Garden State, New Jersey Mining seeks out gold, silver, and base metals in the Coeur d'Alene mining district of northern Idaho and western Montana. The development and exploration company maintains two Idaho-based joint ventures, one with Marathon Gold at the Golden Chest gold mine and another with United Mining Group involved in ore processing. The company also holds rights to several mineral properties, including the Niagara copper-silver deposit, Toboggan gold exploration project (formerly a JV with Newmont Mining), and Silver Strand mine. President Fred Brackebusch controls about a quarter of New Jersey Mining.

	Annual Growth	12/19	12/20	12/21	12/22	12/23
Sales ($mil.)	22.2%	6.1	5.7	7.6	9.6	13.7
Net income ($ mil.)	–	(0.6)	(0.6)	(3.2)	(2.5)	1.2
Market value ($ mil.)	–	–	–	–	70.7	78.5
Employees	15.0%	24	31	38	40	42

IDEAL SHIELD, L.L.C.

2525 CLARK ST
DETROIT, MI 482091337
Phone: 866 825-8659
Fax: –
Web: www.idealshield.com

CEO: –
CFO: –
HR: –
FYE: December 31
Type: Private

Diversity is the idea behind the Ideal Group. The group of companies provides construction, manufacturing, and materials management services for a variety of building and automotive markets. Among the group's divisions is Ideal Contracting (a joint venture with Barton Malow), which provides commercial and industrial construction management and general contracting services. It has built plants for auto companies, office buildings, hospitals, and schools. Ideal Shield makes steel guardrails, handrails, and bumper posts. Joint venture Ideal Setech provides third-party supply chain services. Ideal Surplus Sales provides customers with used industrial equipment made by Allen Bradley, Vickers, Honeywell, and others.

IDEMIA IDENTITY & SECURITY USA LLC

11951 FREEDOM DR STE 1800
RESTON, VA 201905642
Phone: 703 775-7800
Fax: –
Web: www.idemia.com

CEO: –
CFO: –
HR: –
FYE: December 31
Type: Private

Idemia Identity & Security USA (formerly MorphoTrust USA) has operated in the US for nearly half a century, developing technologies and products that enhance national security while simplifying lives of Americans. It is a global leader in Augmented Identity for an increasingly digital world. It is administered, managed and operated by US staff on US soil for all services provided to US government customers at the federal, state, local, and tribal levels.

	Annual Growth	12/12	12/13	12/14	12/15	12/16
Sales ($mil.)	17.1%	–	–	–	605.0	708.5
Net income ($ mil.)	–	–	–	–	–	(7.3)
Market value ($ mil.)	–	–	–	–	–	–
Employees	–	–	–	–	–	1,600

IDENTIV INC

2201 Walnut Avenue, Suite 100
Fremont, CA 94538
Phone: 949 250-8888
Fax: –
Web: www.identiv.com

NAS: INVE
CEO: Steven Humphreys
CFO: Justin Scarpulla
HR: –
FYE: December 31
Type: Public

Identive Group grants secure access to the digital world. The company makes hardware and software for securely accessing digital content and services. Its products include smart card readers for electronic IDs and driver's licenses, as well as health care, computer network, and facility access cards. Among other purposes, Identive's digital media readers are used in digital photo kiosks to transfer data to and from flash media. The company sells to computer makers, government contractors, systems integrators, financial institutions, and photo processing equipment makers. Identive has international facilities in Australia, Canada, Germany, Hong Kong, India, Japan, the Netherlands, Singapore, and Switzerland.

	Annual Growth	12/19	12/20	12/21	12/22	12/23
Sales ($mil.)	8.6%	83.8	86.9	103.8	112.9	116.4
Net income ($ mil.)	–	(1.2)	(5.1)	1.6	(0.4)	(5.5)
Market value ($ mil.)	9.9%	131.1	197.6	654.2	168.3	191.6
Employees	8.1%	289	326	329	343	394

IDEX CORPORATION
NYS: IEX

3100 Sanders Road, Suite 301
Northbrook, IL 60062
Phone: 847 498-7070
Fax: –
Web: www.idexcorp.com

CEO: Eric D Ashleman
CFO: William K Grogan
HR: Gary Rae
FYE: December 31
Type: Public

IDEX is an applied solutions provider serving niche markets worldwide. IDEX is a high-performing global enterprise committed to making trusted solutions that improve lives and are mission critical components in everyday life. Substantially all of the company's business activities are carried out through over 50 wholly-owned subsidiaries with shared values of trust, team and excellence. The company serves industries such as industrial, fire and safety, life sciences, energy, analytical instruments, water, as well as food & pharma, among other things. Founded in 1988, the company has manufacturing operations in more than 20 countries. The US accounts for around half of IDEX's sales.

	Annual Growth	12/19	12/20	12/21	12/22	12/23
Sales ($mil.)	7.0%	2,494.6	2,351.6	2,764.8	3,181.9	3,273.9
Net income ($ mil.)	8.8%	425.5	377.8	449.4	586.9	596.1
Market value ($ mil.)	6.0%	13,025	15,085	17,896	17,291	16,441
Employees	4.3%	7,439	7,075	7,536	8,868	8,800

IDEXX LABORATORIES, INC.
NMS: IDXX

One IDEXX Drive
Westbrook, ME 04092
Phone: 207 556-0300
Fax: 207 856-0346
Web: www.idexx.com

CEO: Jonathan J Mazelsky
CFO: Brian P McKeon
HR: Carla Savino
FYE: December 31
Type: Public

A leading animal health care company, IDEXX develops, manufactures, and distributes products for pets, livestock, dairy, and poultry markets. Veterinarians use the company's VetTest analyzers for blood and urine chemistry and its SNAP in-office test kits to detect heartworms, feline leukemia, and other diseases. The company also provides lab testing services and practice management software. In addition, IDEXX makes products to test for contaminants in water. The company offers solutions and products to customers in more than 175 countries, but the US account for around 65% of its total revenue.

	Annual Growth	12/19	12/20	12/21	12/22	12/23
Sales ($mil.)	11.1%	2,406.9	2,706.7	3,215.4	3,367.3	3,661.0
Net income ($ mil.)	18.6%	427.7	581.6	744.8	679.1	845.0
Market value ($ mil.)	20.7%	21,682	41,505	54,673	33,874	46,087
Employees	4.6%	9,200	9,300	10,350	10,780	11,000

IDI LOGISTICS, LLC

1197 PEACHTREE ST NE STE 600
ATLANTA, GA 303613502
Phone: 404 479-4000
Fax: –
Web: www.idilogistics.com

CEO: Mark Saturno
CFO: –
HR: –
FYE: December 31
Type: Private

Industrial Developments International (dba IDI Gazeley) gives industry space to grow. The company develops, owns, manages, and leases warehouse, distribution, and light manufacturing facilities throughout North America, Europe, and China. Boasting almost $4.5 billion in property holdings, it manages some 60 million square feet of industrial space, with land sites to develop another 55 million square feet of distribution facility space. Parent company Brookfield Property Partners merged IDI with sister logistics developer Gazeley to form IDI Gazeley in May 2014. The combined firm has developed more than 250 million square feet of industrial space since its founding more than 25 years ago.

IDS INTERNATIONAL, LLC

2500 WILSON BLVD STE 200
ARLINGTON, VA 222013834
Phone: 757 388-9807
Fax: –
Web: www.idsinternational.com

CEO: Chris Bauer
CFO: Constance O'Brien
HR: Holly Kerlin
FYE: December 31
Type: Private

This DECO has nothing to do with art and everything to do with security. The private, Native American-owned firm provides professional security services, including anti-terrorism training, armed and unarmed guards, escorts and patrols, security system monitoring, security consulting, and administrative staffing support, to federal, corporate, and tribal clients. Security services account for about 90% of the firm's revenue. The remainder comes from its contracting division, which offers construction services for large-scale remodeling projects and electrical and security system installations. DECO counts the US Department of Homeland Security, FAA, and US Environmental Protection Agency among its clients.

	Annual Growth	12/08	12/09	12/10	12/11	12/12
Sales ($mil.)	9.8%	–	–	82.9	94.9	100.0
Net income ($ mil.)	(59.5%)	–	–	0.6	1.2	0.1
Market value ($ mil.)	–	–	–	–	–	–
Employees	–	–	–	–	–	12

IDT CORP
NYS: IDT

520 Broad Street
Newark, NJ 07102
Phone: 973 438-1000
Fax: –
Web: www.idt.net

CEO: Shmuel Jonas
CFO: Marcelo Fischer
HR: –
FYE: July 31
Type: Public

IDT is a global provider of financial technology, or fintech, cloud communications, and traditional communications services. The communications holding company operates primarily through subsidiary IDT Telecom, which provides prepaid and rechargeable international calling cards and other payment services to customers across the world through the Boss Revolution brand. Its consumer businesses make it easier for families to connect, support, and share across international borders. It also enables businesses to transact and communicate with their customers with enhanced intelligence and insight. The company was founded by its Chairman, Howard Jonas, in 1990. Majority of its sales were generated in the US.

	Annual Growth	07/19	07/20	07/21	07/22	07/23
Sales ($mil.)	(3.2%)	1,409.2	1,345.8	1,447.0	1,364.1	1,238.9
Net income ($ mil.)	316.9%	0.1	21.4	96.5	27.0	40.5
Market value ($ mil.)	23.6%	256.8	164.5	1,258.6	657.9	599.5
Employees	–	1,285	1,256	1,650	1,690	–

IDW MEDIA HOLDINGS INC
ASE: IDW

520 Broad Street
Newark, NJ 07102
Phone: 323 433-6670
Fax: –
Web: www.idwmh.com

CEO: Howard Jonas
CFO: –
HR: –
FYE: October 31
Type: Public

CTM Media Holdings is not embarrassed by tourists. The company distributes travel-related print and online advertising and information. Offerings include visitor maps, brochures, and other destination guides. Its publications are found in strategically located display stands, primarily located in hotels, attractions, restaurants, and rest stops along high-traffic throughways and interstates. In addition, CTM Media publishes books and comics through its IDW Publishing subsidiary. The company was founded in 1983 as Creative Theatre Marketing. Previously known as IDT Capital, the company was spun off from telecommunications firm IDT Corporation in 2009.

	Annual Growth	10/18	10/19	10/20	10/21	10/22
Sales ($mil.)	(11.4%)	58.7	62.6	38.2	32.4	36.1
Net income ($ mil.)	–	(35.5)	(26.4)	(13.8)	(5.4)	(0.7)
Market value ($ mil.)	(37.6%)	365.9	167.1	45.8	55.6	55.6
Employees	–	–	–	–	81	85

iENTERTAINMENT NETWORK, INC.

NBB: IENT

124-126 Quade Drive
Cary, NC 27513
Phone: 919 678-8301
Fax: –
Web: www.imagicgames.com

CEO: –
CFO: –
HR: –
FYE: December 31
Type: Public

iEntertainment Network (iEN) has got more than just a little game. Once a CD-ROM game maker, the company has sold its CD-ROM business to focus solely on online games. iEN's subscription-based and pay-per-play games include battle simulators WarBirds and Dawn of Aces, as well as the fantasy role playing titles Helbreath and Savage Eden. From its I Am Game website, iEN also offers free, ad-based games such as video poker, blackjack, bingo, and trivia. In 2012 iEN announced an agreement to merge with Great Outdoors, LLC, a company owned by game executive Danny Hammett.

	Annual Growth	12/97	12/98	12/99	12/00	12/01
Sales ($mil.)	(44.0%)	16.5	12.6	4.3	6.9	1.6
Net income ($ mil.)	–	(4.3)	(11.7)	(11.7)	(5.3)	(1.6)
Market value ($ mil.)	–	–	127.7	58.7	7.5	2.2
Employees	(37.9%)	121	121	56	161	18

IES HOLDINGS INC

NMS: IESC

2 Riverway, Suite 1730
Houston, TX 77056
Phone: 713 860-1500
Fax: –
Web: www.ies-corporate.com

CEO: Jeffrey L Gendell
CFO: Tracy A McLauchlin
HR: –
FYE: September 30
Type: Public

IES specializes in designing and installing electrical and communications systems for residential, commercial, and industrial customers. Its services range from designing custom electrical and mechanical systems, including fire and intrusion alarms, audio and video, and data network systems, to construction and maintenance. The company also installs and constructs electrical and mechanical systems for industrial properties, including manufacturing plants, office buildings, chemical plants, data centers, and healthcare facilities. Banking investor Jeffrey Gendell, through Tontine Capital Partners, owns 57% of IES.

	Annual Growth	09/19	09/20	09/21	09/22	09/23
Sales ($mil.)	21.9%	1,077.0	1,190.9	1,536.5	2,166.8	2,377.2
Net income ($ mil.)	34.4%	33.2	41.6	66.7	34.8	108.3
Market value ($ mil.)	33.7%	415.8	641.6	922.7	557.8	1,330.2
Employees	11.8%	5,389	5,243	6,845	8,078	8,427

IFX CORP

15050 NW 79th Court, Suite 200
Miami Lakes, FL 33016
Phone: 305 512-1100
Fax: –
Web: –

CEO: Samuel Mezrahi
CFO: Michael Abramowitz
HR: –
FYE: June 30
Type: Public

Latin America is feeling the effect of IFX Corporation. The Florida-based company operates primarily as a telecom network service provider, offering network connectivity and related services in nine Latin American countries and the US. It offers wholesale bandwidth and DSL connections to corporations, Internet service providers, telecommunications carriers, and small to midsized businesses in Latin America. IFX also sells Internet telephony service to businesses and provides colocation and Web hosting from 8 data centers. Services are made possible using the company's fiber optic network and through agreements with local network operators in Argentina, Brazil, Chile, and Mexico among other countries.

	Annual Growth	06/98	06/99	06/00	06/01	06/02
Sales ($mil.)	16.2%	15.5	0.7	9.7	32.1	28.2
Net income ($ mil.)	–	3.4	1.4	(45.9)	(58.4)	(24.6)
Market value ($ mil.)	(18.3%)	0.0	0.7	0.5	0.0	0.0
Employees	77.3%	39	245	450	500	385

IGC PHARMA INC

ASE: IGC

10224 Falls Road
Potomac, MD 20854
Phone: 301 983-0998
Fax: –
Web: www.igcinc.us

CEO: Ram Mukunda
CFO: –
HR: –
FYE: March 31
Type: Public

India Globalization Capital (IGC) sounds like a finance firm but its business is much more concrete. It operates mines and quarries that produce cement, concrete, and other highway and heavy construction materials; builds roads, tunnels, and other infrastructure projects, exports iron ore, and provides related logistics. The US-based company serves the infrastructure industry in fast-growing India and China from four offices in India. It operates through three wholly owned subsidiaries, all bearing the IGC name, and one 77% owned subsidiary, Techni Bharathi Ltd, that has built highways and tunnels for the National Highway Authority of India and the Indian Railroad.

	Annual Growth	03/19	03/20	03/21	03/22	03/23
Sales ($mil.)	(35.0%)	5.1	4.1	0.9	0.4	0.9
Net income ($ mil.)	–	(4.1)	(7.3)	(8.8)	(15.0)	(11.5)
Market value ($ mil.)	(36.4%)	110.4	26.0	95.0	50.4	18.0
Employees	32.2%	20	50	50	52	61

IGENE BIOTECHNOLOGY, INC.

NBB: IGNE

9110 Red Branch Road
Columbia, MD 21045-2024
Phone: 410 997-2599
Fax: 410 730-0540
Web: www.igene.com

CEO: Stephen F Hiu
CFO: Edward J Weisberger
HR: –
FYE: December 31
Type: Public

IGENE Biotechnology makes vitamins for fish and humans alike. The company manufactures biochemical products for the human and animal nutrition industry. Its primary product is astaxanthin, a nutrient that is used as a coloring agent in farmed salmon feed under the AstaXin brand. Other uses for astaxanthin include feed for pigmentation of other types of fish and shrimp and for poultry (to enhance egg yolk coloring). The company primarily markets AstaXin through a joint venture, Naturxan, with agricultural giant Archer-Daniels-Midland. As astaxanthin is a potent antioxidant, IGENE is trying to further develop the commercial applications of the nutrient as an ingredient in consumer health products.

	Annual Growth	12/05	12/06	12/07	12/08	12/09
Sales ($mil.)	–	(0.4)	(0.1)	2.5	7.6	2.9
Net income ($ mil.)	–	(1.4)	(1.2)	(1.9)	(4.0)	(0.1)
Market value ($ mil.)	(31.3%)	70.2	46.8	20.3	9.4	15.6
Employees	8.5%	13	12	18	18	18

IHEARTMEDIA INC

NMS: IHRT

20880 Stone Oak Parkway
San Antonio, TX 78258
Phone: 210 822-2828
Fax: –
Web: www.iheartmedia.com

CEO: Robert W Pittman
CFO: Michael B McGuinness
HR: –
FYE: December 31
Type: Public

iHeartMedia is one of the world's leading radio companies. The firm owns and operates nearly 860 radio stations in about 160 markets. Its radio stations, podcasts and other content can be heard across a broad range of audio platforms, including our AM/FM broadcast radio stations; HD digital radio stations; satellite radio; on the Internet at iHeart.com, its radio stations' websites, and certain Metaverse platforms; and through its iHeartRadio mobile application on 250+ platforms and thousands of devices, including enhanced automotive dashes, on tablets, wearables and smartphones, on gaming consoles, via in-home entertainment (including smart televisions) and voice-controlled smart speaker devices. The company also operates an events business, which includes live and virtual events, and SmartAudio suite of data targeting and attribution products, among others.

	Annual Growth	12/19	12/20	12/21	12/22	12/23
Sales ($mil.)	9.5%	2,610.1	2,948.2	3,558.3	3,912.3	3,751.0
Net income ($ mil.)	–	112.5	(1,914.7)	(159.2)	(264.7)	(1,102.7)
Market value ($ mil.)	(37.0%)	2,461.4	1,890.5	3,064.4	892.8	388.9
Employees	(1.3%)	11,400	10,200	10,800	11,000	10,800

IHS INC.

15 INVERNESS WAY E
ENGLEWOOD, CO 801125710
Phone: 303 790-0600
Fax: —
Web: www.spglobal.com

CEO: Jerre L Stead
CFO: Todd Hyatt
HR: Kristen Esposito
FYE: November 30
Type: Private

IHS (Information Handling Services) does more than handle information. The company's core competency is sourcing data and transforming it into critical information and insight that businesses, governments, and others can use. Its experts process information from a variety of sources to provide analysis, business and market intelligence, and technical documents, which it distributes in electronic formats. Its products include collections of technical specifications and standards, regulations, parts data, and design guides. The company also offers economic-focused information and analysis through its IHS Global Insight subsidiary. IHS primarily earns revenue through subscription sales.

II-VI OPTOELECTRONIC DEVICES, INC.

141 MOUNT BETHEL RD
WARREN, NJ 070595128
Phone: 908 668-5000
Fax: —
Web: www.ii-vi.com

CEO: —
CFO: —
HR: Pinal Johnson
FYE: December 31
Type: Private

ANADIGICS makes chips that cook with GaAs. The company makes gallium arsenide (GaAs) radio-frequency integrated circuits for cellular wireless, WiFi, and infrastructure applications. GaAs ICs may be costlier than silicon, but their physical properties allow the compound materials to be used for chips that are smaller and faster or more energy-efficient than silicon chips. ANADIGICS' power amplifiers, switches, and other chips can be found in the cable modems, set-top boxes, wireless devices, and other gear of companies including Samsung, Huawei, and ZTE. The majority of customers come from Asia. In late 2015, ANADIGICS agreed to be acquired by GaAs Labs, a venture capital firm.

	Annual Growth	12/10	12/11	12/12	12/13	12/14
Sales ($mil.)	(12.5%)	—	—	112.6	134.2	86.3
Net income ($ mil.)	—	—	—	(69.9)	(54.0)	(38.9)
Market value ($ mil.)	—	—	—	—	—	—
Employees	—	—	—	—	—	477

IKANO COMMUNICATIONS, INC.

9221 CORBIN AVE STE 260
NORTHRIDGE, CA 913241625
Phone: 801 924-0900
Fax: —
Web: www.ikano.com

CEO: —
CFO: —
HR: —
FYE: June 30
Type: Private

IKANO Communications says "I can" to businesses looking for access to the Web. The company resells wholesale Internet service in North America through agreements with network operators such as Covad, enabling customers to resell Internet service under their own private brands. Clients include ISP's, as well as customers in such industries as health care, marketing, and higher education. IKANO serves broadband customers in California through subsidiary DSL Extreme. Other brands include Dialup USA and DNAMail. The company operates from satellite offices in Los Angeles, Seattle, Toronto, and Washington, DC. Founded in 1999, IKANO has received funding from investors including Insight Venture Partners.

	Annual Growth	06/01	06/02	06/04	06/05	06/08
Sales ($mil.)	10.4%	—	28.0	—	26.0	50.8
Net income ($ mil.)	—	—	(6.5)	—	(1.9)	13.5
Market value ($ mil.)	—	—	—	—	—	—
Employees	—	—	—	—	—	184

ILC INDUSTRIES, LLC

105 WILBUR PL
BOHEMIA, NY 117162426
Phone: 631 567-5600
Fax: —
Web: —

CEO: Clifford P Lane
CFO: Ken Sheedy
HR: —
FYE: December 31
Type: Private

You'd be forgiven if you thought that ILC Industries stood for I Love Companies. ILC is a holding company for a group of businesses. Its mainstay subsidiary, Data Device Corp. (DDC), makes and sells microelectronic components used in data conversion and networking products (cards, software, and fiber channel switches) by the defense, space, and aerospace industries. Its oldest subsidiary, ILC Dover, was spun-off in 2011, cutting ILC's ties to engineering and making softgoods for industrial, military, and space applications (blimps, spacesuits, and chemical-biological warfare protection gear). ILC customers have included Boeing, Lockheed Martin, and NASA. Buyout firm Behrman Capital owns a majority stake in ILC.

ILG, LLC

6262 SUNSET DR
SOUTH MIAMI, FL 331434843
Phone: 305 666-1861
Fax: —
Web: www.marriottvacationsworldwide.com

CEO: Craig M Nash
CFO: William L Harvey
HR: —
FYE: December 31
Type: Private

Your vacation time is worth something to Interval Leisure Group. The timeshare exchange broker offers services to some 2 million member-property owners. Its primary Interval Network is an exchange program that lets owners trade their timeshare intervals for accommodations at more than 2,900 resorts in approximately 80 countries. In addition, the company provides exchange services to owners at timeshare properties managed by vacation services subsidiary Trading Places International (TPI), while its Preferred Residences is a luxury branded membership program with Preferred Hotel Group. The company also provides resort management services.

ILITCH HOLDINGS, INC.

2211 WOODWARD AVE
DETROIT, MI 482013467
Phone: 313 983-6000
Fax: —
Web: www.ilitchnewshub.com

CEO: Christopher Ilitch
CFO: Scott Fisher
HR: Carmen Moritzswekel
FYE: December 31
Type: Private

This holding company rules over a Caesar, tames Tigers, and takes flight on the ice. Ilitch Holdings controls the business interests of the Ilitch family, which includes the Little Caesars pizza chain, the Detroit Tigers baseball team, and the Detroit Red Wings hockey team. Subsidiary Olympia Entertainment owns Detroit's Fox Theatre and operates Comerica Park, Joe Louis Arena, and Cobo Arena. Additional holdings include Blue Line Foodservice Distribution, a leading supplier of food and equipment to restaurant operators (including Little Caesars operators), and an interest in the MotorCity Casino Hotel. The Ilitches started Little Caesars in 1959 and formed Ilitch Holdings in 1999.

ILLINOIS DEPARTMENT OF EMPLOYMENT SECURITY

607 E ADAMS ST FL 10
SPRINGFIELD, IL 627012037
Phone: 217 785-5070
Fax: –
Web: www.illinoisskillsmatch.com

CEO: –
CFO: –
HR: –
FYE: June 30
Type: Private

The Illinois Department of Employment Security (IDES) plants employment seeds and tends to their growth throughout the Prairie State. The department is mostly known for administering Illinois' unemployment insurance program; however, it also provides numerous resources for job seekers and employers. Its Illinois Skills Match program offers the largest database of job openings in Illinois, helping job seekers find work and employers find workers. The IDES also analyzes and publishes information on careers and the Illinois economy, including unemployment statistics, employment projections, and occupational wage information. The department operates 70 offices and employment centers statewide.

ILLINOIS ENVIRONMENTAL PROTECTION AGENCY

1021 E NORTH GRAND AVE
SPRINGFIELD, IL 627024059
Phone: 217 782-3397
Fax: –
Web: epa.illinois.gov

CEO: –
CFO: –
HR: –
FYE: June 30
Type: Private

The Illinois Environmental Protection Agency (IEPA) wants Illinoisans to breathe easier. It works to enhance the quality of the state's air, land, and water through environmental monitoring, permits, performance standards, compliance inspections, and enforcement. Its Bureau of Air improves air quality, develops plans to attain new and existing national ambient air quality standards, runs an air permitting program, regularly inspects sources of pollution, and enforces applicable requirements. The Bureau of Land ensures hazardous and solid wastes are managed properly and oversees contaminated site cleanups. Keeping Illinois' rivers, streams, and lakes clean for aquatic life, recreation, and drinking water is the Bureau of Water.

	Annual Growth	06/16	06/17	06/18	06/19	06/22
Sales ($mil.)	40.0%	–	–	–	77.5	212.6
Net income ($ mil.)	0.4%	–	–	–	156.0	157.7
Market value ($ mil.)	–	–	–	–	–	–
Employees	–	–	–	–	–	1,487

ILLINOIS HISTORIC PRESERVATION AGENCY

1 OLD STATE CAPITOL PLZ
SPRINGFIELD, IL 627011512
Phone: 217 785-7930
Fax: –
Web: www.landmarks.org

CEO: –
CFO: –
HR: –
FYE: June 30
Type: Private

The Illinois Historic Preservation Agency (IHPA) is the keeper of Lincoln's Tomb, though the nose on the large bronze head at the tomb's base is kept polished not by the IHPA, but by visitors who rub it for good luck. The IHPA also operates more than 60 other state-owned historic sites and memorials. Additionally, it administers state and federal historic preservation programs; administers the Illinois History Exposition; develops publications for teachers, students, scholars, and history buffs; and oversees the Lincoln Legal Papers. In 2005 the IHPA opened the Abraham Lincoln Presidential Library and Museum, the nation's most extensive presidential library. The agency has an annual budget of roughly $31 million.

	Annual Growth	06/05	06/06	06/10	06/11	06/12
Sales ($mil.)	(65.5%)	–	31.0	0.0	0.4	0.0
Net income ($ mil.)	–	–	–	(0.1)	0.1	(0.2)
Market value ($ mil.)	–	–	–	–	–	–
Employees	–	–	–	–	–	200

ILLINOIS HOUSING DEVELOPMENT AUTHORITY (INC)

111 E WACKER DR STE 1000
CHICAGO, IL 606014306
Phone: 312 836-5200
Fax: –
Web: www.ihda.org

CEO: –
CFO: Robert Kugel
HR: Kate Hoctor
FYE: June 30
Type: Private

The Illinois Housing Development Authority (IHDA) wants every Illinoisan to have a safe, comfortable place to lay their head. The authority finances the construction and preservation of affordable housing for low- and moderate-income families throughout the state. Since its inception in 1967 the IHDA has allocated more than $6 billion and financed roughly 150,000 units of affordable housing. An independent and self-supporting authority, the IHDA raises private capital from bond markets and administers and manages a number of federal and state funding programs, including the Illinois Affordable Housing Trust Fund and the Illinois Affordable Housing Tax Credit Fund.

	Annual Growth	06/18	06/19	06/20	06/21	06/22
Sales ($mil.)	61.7%	–	191.1	38.4	578.0	808.1
Net income ($ mil.)	–	–	64.6	(61.7)	56.2	(51.3)
Market value ($ mil.)	–	–	–	–	–	–
Employees	–	–	–	–	–	200

ILLINOIS INSTITUTE OF TECHNOLOGY

10 W 35TH ST
CHICAGO, IL 606163717
Phone: 312 567-3000
Fax: –
Web: www.iit.edu

CEO: –
CFO: –
HR: Adam Stultz
FYE: May 31
Type: Private

Chicago has some cool architecture, due, in part, to the Illinois Institute of Technology (IIT). The school offers more than 100 undergraduate and graduate degree programs in engineering, science, psychology, architecture, business, law, humanities, and design. In addition to three campuses in Chicago, IIT also has locations in Summit-Argo (Moffet campus) and Wheaton (Daniel F. and Ada L. Rice campus). The institute has an enrollment of some 8,000 undergraduate, graduate, business school, and law school students, with a student-to-faculty ratio of 8:1.

	Annual Growth	05/17	05/18	05/19	05/21	05/22
Sales ($mil.)	(1.2%)	–	260.8	265.0	259.2	248.8
Net income ($ mil.)	(64.3%)	–	62.7	(10.1)	48.0	1.0
Market value ($ mil.)	–	–	–	–	–	–
Employees	–	–	–	–	–	1,662

ILLINOIS STATE BOARD OF EDUCATION

100 N 1ST ST STE 1
SPRINGFIELD, IL 627025011
Phone: 217 782-4321
Fax: –
Web: www.isbe.net

CEO: –
CFO: –
HR: –
FYE: June 30
Type: Private

The Illinois State Board of Education (ISBE) wants the state's public schools to get an A+ in all subjects. The board provides funding and support to the students, teachers, and administrators in Illinois' more than 850 public school districts and nearly 4,000 schools. Created in 1975, the nine-member board sets state educational policies and guidelines for elementary, middle, and high schools, and disburses and oversees more than $8 billion in state and federal funds annually.

ILLINOIS STATE OF TOLL HIGHWAY AUTHORITY

2700 OGDEN AVE
DOWNERS GROVE, IL 605151703
Phone: 630 241-6800
Fax: –
Web: www.illinois.gov

CEO: –
CFO: Mike Colsch
HR: –
FYE: December 31
Type: Private

The Illinois State Toll Highway Authority (ISTHA) is trying to give Illinois drivers a little relief from congestion, making their morning and afternoon commutes easier to swallow. The department maintains and operates about 275 miles of interstate tollways in 12 Northern Illinois counties. ISTHA is mid-way through its 10-year, $6.3 billion Congestion-Relief Program, which is conducting major improvements, including rebuilding, widening, and extending tollway segments; converting toll plazas to provide non-stop toll collection for I-PASS users; opening additional tollway oases; and adding electronic over-the-road signs to improve communication with tollway users.

	Annual Growth	12/18	12/19	12/20	12/21	12/22
Sales ($mil.)	1.5%	–	1,484.5	1,261.0	1,459.8	1,554.5
Net income ($ mil.)	33.2%	–	374.6	124.2	299.6	885.4
Market value ($ mil.)	–	–	–	–	–	–
Employees	–	–	–	–	–	1,750

ILLINOIS TOOL WORKS, INC.

155 Harlem Avenue
Glenview, IL 60025
Phone: 847 724-7500
Fax: –
Web: www.itw.com

NYS: ITW
CEO: E S Santi
CFO: Michael M Larsen
HR: –
FYE: December 31
Type: Public

Illinois Tool Works (ITW) manufactures and services equipment for the automotive, construction, electronics, food, beverage, decorative surfaces, and medical components industries. The company makes metal and plastic fasteners, components, and assemblies used in light vehicles, automobiles, and industrial applications. It also manufactures cooking equipment such as ovens, ranges, and broilers, equipment and software for testing and measuring materials, structures, gases, and fluids. The company's brands include Shakeproof, Instron, and Rain-X. ITW has operations in around 50 countries, but the customers in the US supply about 50% of the company's revenue. It was founded in 1912.

	Annual Growth	12/19	12/20	12/21	12/22	12/23
Sales ($mil.)	3.4%	14,109	12,574	14,455	15,932	16,107
Net income ($ mil.)	4.1%	2,521.0	2,109.0	2,694.0	3,034.0	2,957.0
Market value ($ mil.)	9.9%	53,763	61,021	73,867	65,936	78,399
Employees	–	–	45,000	43,000	45,000	46,000	45,000

ILLINOIS WESLEYAN UNIVERSITY

1312 PARK ST
BLOOMINGTON, IL 617011773
Phone: 309 556-1000
Fax: –
Web: www.iwu.edu

CEO: Craig Hart
CFO: –
HR: –
FYE: July 31
Type: Private

The Fightin' Titans of Illinois Wesleyan University cannot be accused of having a one-track mind. The small private university offers 50 majors and programs and is organized into three colleges: liberal arts, fine arts, and the school of nursing. As an undergraduate university with about 2,000 students, Illinois Wesleyan also offers pre-professional programs in fields including engineering, law, and medicine. Traditionally, about 80% of the student population is enrolled in the College of Liberal Arts. The school was founded in 1850 by civic and Methodist Church leaders.

	Annual Growth	07/19	07/20*	12/20*	07/21	07/22
Sales ($mil.)	(5.4%)	–	75.6	0.0	133.5	67.6
Net income ($ mil.)	(54.5%)	–	2.9	0.0	65.5	0.6
Market value ($ mil.)	–	–	–	–	–	–
Employees	–	–	–	–	–	500

*Fiscal year change

ILLINOIS WHOLESALE CASH REGISTER, INC.

2790 PINNACLE DR
ELGIN, IL 601247943
Phone: 847 310-4200
Fax: –
Web: www.weareiw.com

CEO: Al Moorhouse
CFO: –
HR: –
FYE: December 31
Type: Private

Ka-ching! The sound of cash registers is music to Illinois Wholesale Cash Register (IWCR). The company sells and services refurbished point-of-sale (POS) equipment from such manufacturers as IBM, MICROS Systems, NCR, and Panasonic, among others. Products include POS terminals, processors, scanners, printers, keyboards, and spare parts for that equipment. IWCR also offers printed circuit board repair and technical support services. Established in 1976, the company serves clients in such industries as hospitality, supermarkets, and general retail. Al Moorhouse, the president of IWCR, owns the company.

	Annual Growth	12/15	12/16	12/17	12/18	12/20
Sales ($mil.)	(0.5%)	–	34.0	32.1	31.9	33.3
Net income ($ mil.)	7.1%	–	1.6	1.1	1.7	2.1
Market value ($ mil.)	–	–	–	–	–	–
Employees	–	–	–	–	–	130

ILLUMINA INC

5200 Illumina Way
San Diego, CA 92122
Phone: 858 202-4500
Fax: –
Web: www.illumina.com

NMS: ILMN
CEO: –
CFO: –
HR: –
FYE: December 31
Type: Public

Illumina is a global leader in sequencing- and array-based solutions for genetic and genomic analysis. Its products and services serve customers in a wide range of markets, enabling the adoption of genomic solutions in research and clinical settings. Its proprietary BeadArray technology combines microscopic beads and a substrate in a proprietary manufacturing process to produce arrays that can perform many assays simultaneously. Customers include pharma and biotech companies, research centers, and academic institutions. More than half of Illumina's revenue comes from the US.

	Annual Growth	12/19*	01/21	01/22	01/23*	12/23
Sales ($mil.)	6.2%	3,543.0	3,239.0	4,526.0	4,584.0	4,504.0
Net income ($ mil.)	–	1,002.0	656.0	762.0	(4,404.0)	(1,161.0)
Market value ($ mil.)	(19.5%)	52,834	58,830	60,490	32,150	22,139
Employees	8.4%	7,700	9,350	10,750	12,960	10,640

*Fiscal year change

IMAGE API, LLC

2002 OLD SAINT AUGUSTINE RD STE D
TALLAHASSEE, FL 323014881
Phone: 850 222-1400
Fax: –
Web: www.imageapi.com

CEO: –
CFO: –
HR: –
FYE: December 31
Type: Private

Image API helps its clients to clean up their paper trails. The company provides content management software and offers services such as document conversion, online licensing and permitting, and business process outsourcing. Its offices are located in Connecticut, Florida, Pennsylvania, and Texas. Customers include government agencies and private businesses. Image API's products and services are used in a variety of document-intensive applications, such as corporate filings, professional licensing, medical records management, class action lawsuits, and claims administration. The company was founded in 1993.

	Annual Growth	12/12	12/13	12/14	12/15	12/16
Sales ($mil.)	(3.2%)	–	–	–	16.6	16.1
Net income ($ mil.)	–	–	–	–	(0.4)	(1.1)
Market value ($ mil.)	–	–	–	–	–	–
Employees	–	–	–	–	–	150

IMAGE MICROSYSTEMS INC.

4500 CAMBRIDGE RD STE 100
FORT WORTH, TX 761552236
Phone: 469 642-1400
Fax: –
Web: www.imagemicro.com

CEO: –
CFO: –
HR: –
FYE: December 31
Type: Private

You might not know what to do with an old computer, but Image Microsystems does. The company provides reverse logistics services for computer manufacturers. It repairs, recycles, and remarkets excess and returned inventory, handling everything from inspection and testing to repair and delivery. The firm handles the disposal and recycling of materials used in displays, circuit boards, enclosures and other components. It also tests and resells replacement parts for equipment from major computer makers. Image Microsystems has facilities in Austin, the Los Angeles area, and in Ohio and has partnerships with IT manufacturers including Dell, IBM, and Lexmark. The company was founded in 1992 by CEO Alex Abadi.

	Annual Growth	07/09	07/10	07/11*	12/12	12/15
Sales ($mil.)	13.4%	–	–	10.1	18.1	16.7
Net income ($ mil.)	30.0%	–	–	0.8	2.2	2.2
Market value ($ mil.)	–	–	–	–	–	–
Employees	–	–	–	–	–	145

*Fiscal year change

IMAGE SOFTWARE, INC.

6025 S. Quebec St., Suite 300
Englewood, CO 80111
Phone: 303 694-9180
Fax: –
Web: www.inimageinc.com

NBB: ISOL
CEO: David R Deyoung
CFO: –
HR: –
FYE: December 31
Type: Public

For 1mage Software, images are everything. 1mage helps organizations manage their paper and electronic files by providing software that captures, stores, and displays documents as electronic images. The company's software handles a wide range of documents, including e-mails, scanned forms, memos, letters, spreadsheets, databases, multimedia documents, faxes, and maps. Add-on modules include tools for faxing, printing, workflow, searching, reporting, and remote access. 1mage licenses its software to a wide range of clients including energy, manufacturing, transportation, and real estate firms, as well as government agencies and organizations.

	Annual Growth	12/00	12/01	12/02	12/03	12/04
Sales ($mil.)	(10.4%)	2.2	2.8	2.2	2.1	1.4
Net income ($ mil.)	–	0.0	0.2	(0.3)	0.0	(1.1)
Market value ($ mil.)	(27.6%)	2.2	2.0	1.2	1.0	0.6
Employees	(7.7%)	22	21	18	21	16

IMAGETREND, LLC

20855 KENSINGTON BLVD
LAKEVILLE, MN 550447486
Phone: 952 469-1589
Fax: –
Web: www.imagetrend.com

CEO: –
CFO: –
HR: –
FYE: December 31
Type: Private

ImageTrend hopes that the trend in your enterprise is towards increased efficiency. The company provides software development services and Web-based software used to address tasks such as content and document management, e-commerce development, database design, and back-office integration. ImageTrend, founded in 1998, also provides services including consulting, support, and training. The company's clients come from fields such as manufacturing, health care, financial services, and education and have included Russell Athletic, Goodyear Tire, HealthEast Care System, the University of Minnesota, Cargill, and FirstComp Insurance.

	Annual Growth	12/07	12/08	12/10	12/12	12/14
Sales ($mil.)	6.7%	–	11.0	11.0	12.7	16.2
Net income ($ mil.)	7.1%	–	2.4	0.5	(0.9)	3.7
Market value ($ mil.)	–	–	–	–	–	–
Employees	–	–	–	–	–	250

IMAGEWARE SYSTEMS INC

11440 West Bernardo Court, Suite 300
San Diego, CA 92127
Phone: 858 673-8600
Fax: –
Web: www.imageware.io

NBB: IWSY
CEO: Kristin Taylor
CFO: –
HR: –
FYE: December 31
Type: Public

Even if your face won't launch a thousand ships, ImageWare Systems will remember it. The company's identification products are used to manage and issue secure credentials, including national IDs, passports, driver's licenses, smart cards, and access-control credentials. Its software creates secure digital images and enables the enrollment and management of unlimited population sizes, while its digital booking products provide law enforcement agencies with integrated mug shot, fingerprint, and investigative capabilities. The company markets its products worldwide to governments, public safety agencies, and commercial enterprises, such as Unisys. The US government accounts for about 15% of revenue.

	Annual Growth	12/17	12/18	12/19	12/20	12/21
Sales ($mil.)	(5.2%)	4.3	4.4	3.5	4.8	3.5
Net income ($ mil.)	–	(10.1)	(12.6)	(11.6)	(7.3)	9.3
Market value ($ mil.)	(66.6%)	552.1	309.0	116.3	27.3	6.8
Employees	(20.2%)	64	73	75	44	26

IMAGINE SCHOOLS, INC.

1005 N GLEBE RD STE 610
ARLINGTON, VA 222015758
Phone: 703 527-2600
Fax: –
Web: www.imagineschools.org

CEO: –
CFO: –
HR: Heather Kelley
FYE: June 30
Type: Private

New solutions in education is not a stretch of the imagination for Imagine Schools. The company is one of the largest US operators of charter schools for students in kindergarten through 12th grade. Imagine Schools educates nearly 40,000 students at some 70 public charter schools in about a dozen states and Washington, DC. Imagine Schools was established in 2003 by CEO Dennis Bakke and his wife Eileen through a buyout of Chancellor Beacon Academies, the second-largest school management group in the US (behind Edison).

	Annual Growth	06/13	06/14	06/20	06/21	06/22
Sales ($mil.)	47.1%	–	1.5	32.9	30.9	31.9
Net income ($ mil.)	144.0%	–	0.0	17.4	11.9	15.2
Market value ($ mil.)	–	–	–	–	–	–
Employees	–	–	–	–	–	3,400

IMAGING BUSINESS MACHINES, L.L.C.

2750 CRESTWOOD BLVD
IRONDALE, AL 352101227
Phone: 205 956-4071
Fax: –
Web: www.ibml.com

CEO: –
CFO: –
HR: Barton Fisk
FYE: March 31
Type: Private

Imaging Business Machines (IBML) manufactures and markets high-speed document scanners and related software. Enterprises including airlines, banks, government agencies, and pharmaceutical companies use the company's products to scan and store documents. IBML's Conversion Assistance Services (CAS) division provides on-site and off-site document preparation and scanning services, as well as short-term rentals. Customers have included athenahealth, Bank of America, Mellon Bank, and the US federal government. The company has offices in Germany, the UK, and the US.

	Annual Growth	12/05	12/06	12/07	12/08*	03/10
Sales ($mil.)	2.0%	–	–	46.7	46.1	49.5
Net income ($ mil.)	28.8%	–	–	1.5	(1.3)	3.2
Market value ($ mil.)	–	–	–	–	–	–
Employees	–	–	–	–	–	17,395

*Fiscal year change

IMAGING DIAGNOSTIC SYSTEMS INC

618 E South St, Suite 500
Orlando, FL 32801
Phone: 954 581-9800
Fax: –
Web: www.imds.com

CEO: Linda B Grable
CFO: Allan L Schwartz
HR: –
FYE: June 30
Type: Public

Imaging Diagnostic Systems is a medical technology company involved in the research and development of breast-imaging devices used for detecting cancer. Using laser-based technology, the company has created a more comfortable, radiation-free breast examination that does not require breast compression. Its CTLM (Computed Tomography Laser Mammography) system, used in conjuction with X-ray mammography, may help improve early diagnosis of cancer. The company is also researching other breast screening systems using fluorescence imaging. It had been developing laser imaging products for research with lab animals, but it has licensed the technology to Bioscan in order to focus on the women's health market.

IMH FINANCIAL CORPORATION

7001 N SCOTTSDALE RD STE 2050
PARADISE VALLEY, AZ 852533698
Phone: 480 840-8400
Fax: –
Web: www.lat33cap.com

CEO: –
CFO: –
HR: –
FYE: December 31
Type: Private

IMH Financial deals in real estate lending and investment mainly in the southwestern US. Although its family of companies historically have focused on acquiring and originating short-term bridge loans to enable commercial real estate development and construction, market conditions -- mainly lack of mortgage capital availability -- are prompting the company to change course. Its focus now is to make investments across a more diverse set of target assets, including interim loans used to pay off construction or property loans and whole commercial real estate mortgage loans. Its primary markets include Arizona, California, and Texas. IMH filed to go public in 2010 but withdrew the next year.

IMMERSION CORP

2999 N.E. 191st Street, Suite 610
Aventura, FL 33180
Phone: 408 467-1900
Fax: –
Web: www.immersion.com

NMS: IMMR
CEO: Eric Singer
CFO: Aaron Akerman
HR: Lori Hioki
FYE: December 31
Type: Public

Immersion is a premier licensing company focused on the creation, design, development, and licensing of innovative haptic technologies that allow people to use their sense of touch to engage with products and experience the digital world around them. It is one of the leading experts in haptics, and its focus on innovation allows them to deliver world-class intellectual property (IP) and technology that enables the creation of products that delight end users. Immersion licenses its patents directly to Microsoft, Sony and Nintendo for use in their console gaming products. Additionally, the company has licensed its patents to third party gaming peripheral manufacturers and distributors for use in spinning mass and force feedback devices such as controllers, steering wheels and joysticks, to be used with PC platforms running on Microsoft Windows and other operating systems, as well as in connection with video game consoles made by Microsoft, Sony, Nintendo and others. The Asian markets hold the majority of the company's revenue.

	Annual Growth	12/19	12/20	12/21	12/22	12/23
Sales ($mil.)	(1.4%)	36.0	30.5	35.1	38.5	33.9
Net income ($ mil.)	–	(20.0)	5.4	12.5	30.7	34.0
Market value ($ mil.)	(1.3%)	234.3	356.0	180.0	221.6	222.6
Employees	(29.3%)	56	54	26	20	14

IMMIXGROUP, INC.

8444 WESTPARK DR STE 200
MC LEAN, VA 221025112
Phone: 703 752-0610
Fax: –
Web: www.immixgroup.com

CEO: Art Richer
CFO: Noel N Samuel
HR: –
FYE: May 31
Type: Private

immixGroup offers a blend of information technology (IT), business development, and consulting services to help tech firms do business with federal, state, and local government agencies. Through its technology sales division, the company is a hardware and software reseller for such manufacturers as IBM, Oracle, and Hewlett-Packard. It also offers customized public sector channel development programs, outsourced government contract management, and IT consulting and execution. Other services include market intelligence, sales training, and recruiting. immixGroup serves more than 250 tech manufacturers, and its government partner network includes more than 600 resellers, systems integrators, and other providers. Arrow Electronics acquired immixGroup in 2015.

	Annual Growth	05/09	05/10	05/11	05/12	05/13
Sales ($mil.)	(3.5%)	–	563.6	43.6	502.1	505.9
Net income ($ mil.)	0.8%	–	11.8	16.5	13.3	12.1
Market value ($ mil.)	–	–	–	–	–	–
Employees	–	–	–	–	–	201

IMMTECH PHARMACEUTICALS, INC.

93 PROSPECT AVE
MONTCLAIR, NJ 070421920
Phone: 212 791-2911
Fax: –
Web: –

CEO: Eric L Sorkin
CFO: –
HR: –
FYE: March 31
Type: Private

Immtech Pharmaceuticals has a vendetta against infectious diseases. The development-stage pharmaceutical company has focused its efforts on finding treatments for bacterial, viral, and fungal infections, including hepatitis C and hospital-acquired infections. Much of the company's work is in the early stages of research and development; it halted work on its clinical-stage candidate pafuramidine in 2008 because of safety issues. Immtech has licensed some of its other drug technology from academic researchers at the University of North Carolina at Chapel Hill and Georgia State University.

	Annual Growth	03/04	03/05	03/06	03/07	03/08
Sales ($mil.)	64.9%	–	–	3.6	4.3	9.7
Net income ($ mil.)	–	–	–	(15.5)	(11.1)	(10.5)
Market value ($ mil.)	–	–	–	–	–	–
Employees	–	–	–	–	–	7

IMMUCELL CORP.

56 Evergreen Drive
Portland, ME 04103
Phone: 207 878-2770
Fax: –
Web: www.immucell.com

NAS: ICCC
CEO: Michael F Brigham
CFO: –
HR: –
FYE: December 31
Type: Public

Many biotech companies focus on human health but ImmuCell has udder pursuits. The company develops products to help livestock farmers maintain the health of their herds. Its animal-health products include First Defense, which prevents diarrhea in calves; MASTiK, which diagnoses bovine mammary gland inflammation; and Wipe Out Dairy Wipes, moist towelettes used to disinfect the teat area of cows prior to milking. ImmuCell makes a product for preventing disease in humans -- Isolate (formerly called Crypto-Scan), a test for cryptosporidium in water. When present in municipal drinking water supplies, cryptosporidium can cause diarrheal disease in humans.

	Annual Growth	12/18	12/19	12/20	12/21	12/22
Sales ($mil.)	14.0%	11.0	13.7	15.3	19.2	18.6
Net income ($ mil.)	–	(2.3)	(1.3)	(1.0)	(0.1)	(2.5)
Market value ($ mil.)	(3.5%)	54.6	39.9	46.1	62.0	47.3
Employees	9.8%	51	54	61	67	74

IMMUCOR, INC.

3130 GATEWAY DR
PEACHTREE CORNERS, GA 300711189
Phone: 770 441-2051
Fax: –
Web: www.immucor.com

CEO: AVI Pelossof
CFO: –
HR: –
FYE: May 31
Type: Private

Immucor is a leading provider of transfusion and transplantation diagnostic products worldwide. The company strives to create a world where anyone, anywhere in need of blood or transplantation gets the right blood or transplant that is safe, accessible and affordable. Immucor is proud to partner with thousands of hospitals, clinical laboratories, reference laboratories and donor centers across the globe.

IMMUNE DESIGN CORP.

1616 EASTLAKE AVE E STE 310
SEATTLE, WA 98102
Phone: 206 682-0645
Fax: –
Web: www.immunedesign.com

CEO: Carlos Paya
CFO: –
HR: –
FYE: December 31
Type: Private

Immune Design wants to use nature's own design to build immunity. The clinical-stage pharmaceutical company is creating products to boost the human immune system's ability to fight cancer using naturally produced cytotoxic T cells (CTLs). Its combo approach includes a mechanism to induce the production of tumor-specific CTLs along with something to increase CTLs and activate other immunity functions. The company has two lead immuno-oncology candidates -- CMB305 and G100 -- that are being studied for the treatment of soft tissue sarcoma and follicular non-Hodgkin Lymphoma, respectively. Pharmaceutical giant Merck is buying Immune Design for some $300 million.

	Annual Growth	12/14	12/15	12/16	12/17	12/18
Sales ($mil.)	(38.6%)	–	9.5	13.3	7.2	2.2
Net income ($ mil.)	–	–	(39.4)	(53.5)	(51.9)	(54.8)
Market value ($ mil.)	–	–	–	–	–	–
Employees	–	–	–	–	–	56

IMMUNE PHARMACEUTICALS INC

1 Bridge Plaza North, Suite 270
Fort Lee, NJ 07024
Phone: 201 464-2677
Fax: –
Web: www.immunepharmaceuticals.com

CEO: –
CFO: –
HR: –
FYE: December 31
Type: Public

Immune Pharmaceuticals' drug development mission is to help patients avoid pain, leukemia remission, and other conditions. The company's research pipeline includes AmiKet, a topical analgesics for neuropathic pain conditions. Cancer drug candidate Ceplene is a remission maintenance therapy for acute myeloid leukemia (AML) patients; the drug is sold in the EU by Meda, and Immune Pharmaceuticals is developing Ceplene for additional markets. In February 2019, after some $5.5 million in expected development funding fell through, the company filed for Chapter 11 bankruptcy protection.

	Annual Growth	12/13	12/14	12/15	12/16	12/17
Sales ($mil.)	–	0.0	0.0	–	–	–
Net income ($ mil.)	–	(5.8)	(23.6)	(17.2)	(32.7)	(17.9)
Market value ($ mil.)	(29.5%)	48.3	39.7	15.4	3.8	12.0
Employees	(3.3%)	8	11	12	12	7

IMMUNIC INC

1200 Avenue of the Americas, Suite 200
New York, NY 10036
Phone: 332 255-9818
Fax: –
Web: www.imux.com

NMS: IMUX
CEO: Duane D Nash
CFO: Glenn Whaley
HR: –
FYE: December 31
Type: Public

Immunic (formerly Vital Therapies) develops therapies that treat chronic inflammatory and autoimmune diseases such as multiple sclerosis (MS), ulcerative colitis, Crohn's disease, and psoriasis. The company is developing three small molecule products: IMU-838, which inhibits intracellular metabolism in activated immune cells; IMU-935, an antibody therapy; and IMU-856, aimed at restoring the intestinal barrier function. IMU-838 for relapsing-remitting MS and ulcerative colitis in phase 2 clinical trials and Immunic has plans for phase 2 trials for Crohn's. Immunic is based in San Diego, but its primary research and development activities are conducted in Germany. In 2019, Vital Therapies acquired Immunic, Inc. and subsequently changed its name to Immunic.

	Annual Growth	12/19	12/20	12/21	12/22	12/23
Sales ($mil.)	–	–	–	–	–	–
Net income ($ mil.)	–	(34.9)	(44.0)	(92.9)	(120.4)	(93.6)
Market value ($ mil.)	(37.3%)	438.2	690.8	432.4	63.2	67.8
Employees	31.2%	26	28	55	66	77

IMPAC MORTGAGE HOLDINGS, INC.

4000 MacArthur Blvd., Suite 600
Newport Beach, CA 92660
Phone: 949 475-3600
Fax: –
Web: www.impaccompanies.com

ASE: IMH
CEO: –
CFO: –
HR: –
FYE: December 31
Type: Public

Impac Mortgage Holdings wants to make a positive impact on home ownership rates. The lender originates, sells, and services residential mortgage loans that are eligible to be sold to US government-sponsored enterprises such as Fannie Mae, Freddie Mac. It does the same for government-insured mortgage loans eligible for securitization that are issued through Ginnie Mae. Beyond lending, its Integrated Real Estate Services (IRES) subsidiary provides loan modifications, real estate brokerage, and monitoring and surveillance services. Other subsidiaries include Impac Mortgage Corp., IMH Assets Corp., and Impac Funding Corp. Founded in 1995, Impac originated and sold about $4.5 billion in loans.

	Annual Growth	12/18	12/19	12/20	12/21	12/22
Sales ($mil.)	(46.5%)	105.0	90.6	(8.1)	66.3	8.6
Net income ($ mil.)	–	(145.4)	(8.0)	(88.2)	(3.9)	(39.4)
Market value ($ mil.)	(53.9%)	138.2	192.4	111.2	40.6	6.2
Employees	(30.4%)	417	530	326	326	98

IMPERIAL DISTRIBUTORS, INC.

150 BLACKSTONE RIVER RD STE 1
WORCESTER, MA 016071455
Phone: 508 713-6500
Fax: –
Web: www.imperialdist.com

CEO: Michael Sleeper
CFO: Colleen Peloquin
HR: Dean Messier
FYE: April 02
Type: Private

Imperial Distributors is recognized as the leader in both distribution and merchandising of supermarket non-foods. Customers include independent retail stores and large supermarket chains such as Barnes & Noble, HyVee, Kmart, Palmer's, Whole Foods, Price Chopper, and Stop & Shop. Imperial Distributors offers more than 26,000 SKUs with store-specific planograms, merchandising strategy, ordering and stocking support, and distribution and EDI services. Its services include marketing and in-store merchandising, as well as logistics and distribution. The company was founded in 1939.

IMPERIAL IRRIGATION DISTRICT

333 E BARIONI BLVD
IMPERIAL, CA 922511773
Phone: 800 303-7756
Fax: –
Web: www.iid.com

CEO: Keven Kelly
CFO: –
HR: Nallie Merrill
FYE: December 31
Type: Private

Imperial Irrigation District (IID) keeps the lights on and the water flowing. A public agency, IID is the six largest public power utility in the state of California, providing generation, transmission, and distribution services to more than 145,000 residential, commercial, and industrial customers. It is also the largest irrigation district in the US, with more than 3,000 miles of canals and drains delivering water to active farmland and providing wholesale water to local municipalities primarily in the Southern California desert corridors of Imperial Valley and Coachella Valley. The district is governed by a five-member board of directors elected by district residents.

	Annual Growth	12/18	12/19	12/20	12/21	12/22
Sales ($mil.)	10.2%	–	642.2	705.5	795.7	859.5
Net income ($ mil.)	(23.2%)	–	51.5	115.4	107.7	23.3
Market value ($ mil.)	–	–	–	–	–	–
Employees	–	–	–	–	–	1,300

IMPERIAL PETROLEUM RECOVERY CORP.

4747 Research Forest Dr., Suite 180-257
The Woodlands, TX 77381
Phone: 713 542-7440
Fax: –
Web: www.irpc.com

CEO: Alan Springer
CFO: –
HR: –
FYE: October 31
Type: Public

Though it sticks to the sludge business, Imperial Petroleum Recovery isn't bogged down. The company makes and markets oil sludge remediation equipment for oil producers and refiners, pipelines, and tankers. Its Microwave Separation Technology system breaks down sludge with heat and recovers hydrocarbon compounds, salable oil, treatable water, and disposable solids. The trailer-mounted system consists of a microwave generator, a series of waveguides and tuners, and a sludge applicator. Imperial Petroleum Recovery has yet to post a profit, and the company's auditors have questioned whether it will be able to stay in business.

	Annual Growth	10/07	10/08	10/09	10/10	10/11
Sales ($mil.)	(52.8%)	5.7	1.3	0.2	0.3	0.3
Net income ($ mil.)	–	(0.3)	0.3	(0.7)	(0.8)	(0.9)
Market value ($ mil.)	(27.7%)	5.3	1.2	3.4	1.0	1.5
Employees	(6.9%)	8	2	2	2	6

IMPERVA, INC.

1 CURIOSITY WAY STE 203
SAN MATEO, CA 944032396
Phone: 650 345-9000
Fax: –
Web: www.imperva.com

CEO: Pam Murphy
CFO: Mike Burns
HR: Einat Lehamlivnat
FYE: December 31
Type: Private

Imperva is the cybersecurity leader that protects customers from cyber-attacks through all stages of digital transformation. With an integrated approach combining edge, application security, and data security, customers around the world trust Imperva to protect their applications, data, and websites from cyber-attacks. Imperva's security products are aimed at financial services, government, healthcare, telecoms, travel, and retail. Its customers include AARP, ALYN Hospital, Dubizzle, Belgian Telco, Tower, Sun Life, and Shutterfly, among others. In addition to the company's more than 15 office locations, the company has channel partners in approximately 70 countries worldwide. The company was founded in 2002 by Shlomo Kramer, Amichai Shulman, and Mickey Boodaei. In mid-2023, Imperva's parent company Thoma Bravo agreed to sell Imperva to Thales Group a global leader in advanced technologies for $3.6 billion.

IMPINJ INC

NMS: PI

400 Fairview Avenue North, Suite 1200
Seattle, WA 98109
Phone: 206 517-5300
Fax: –
Web: www.impinj.com

CEO: Chris Diorio
CFO: Cary Baker
HR: –
FYE: December 31
Type: Public

Impinj designs semiconductors to adapt to their surroundings. The company's "self-adaptive silicon" technology allows analog circuits -- which translate radio waves into data usable by electronic systems -- to be made smaller and more efficient, and allow for chip adjustment. The company focuses on designing communications chips, particularly UHF Gen 2 radio-frequency identification (RFID) devices. The RFID chips connect an item's identity to businesses' software for solutions that range from healthcare asset management and optimization to interactive product displays for retail stores. Impinj was founded in 2000 by chip design legend (and Caltech professor emeritus) Carver Mead and his former student, Chris Diorio.

	Annual Growth	12/19	12/20	12/21	12/22	12/23
Sales ($mil.)	19.1%	152.8	138.9	190.3	257.8	307.5
Net income ($ mil.)	–	(23.0)	(51.9)	(51.3)	(24.3)	(43.4)
Market value ($ mil.)	36.6%	702.5	1,137.4	2,409.6	2,966.0	2,445.8
Employees	4.1%	404	310	332	389	475

IMPRESO INC.

652 Southwestern Boulevard
Coppell, TX 75019
Phone: 972 462-0100
Fax: 972 462-7764
Web: www.impreso.com

CEO: Marshall D Sorokwasz
CFO: –
HR: –
FYE: August 31
Type: Public

Money is just paper to holding company Impreso. Impreso, a Spanish word meaning "printed matter," was founded in 1976. Through its primary subsidiary TST/Impreso, the company makes and distributes specialty paper and film imaging products. Its paper products include thermal fax, copier, wide-format, continuous-feed, and special surface papers, such as film transparencies. Impreso operates a number of manufacturing plants and distributes in North America through its warehouses to dealers and other resellers. Impreso owns two other subsidiaries: Hotsheet.com (provides links to popular websites), and Alexa Springs (a custom-label water bottling business). Impreso suspended its SEC reporting obligations in 2006.

	Annual Growth	08/13	08/14	08/15	08/16	08/17
Sales ($mil.)	4.2%	73.7	83.4	87.7	89.0	87.0
Net income ($ mil.)	(27.4%)	0.3	(0.1)	0.3	0.1	0.0
Market value ($ mil.)	(3.2%)	3.6	3.6	3.8	2.8	3.2
Employees	–	–	–	–	–	–

IMRIS INC

NBB: IMRS Q

5101 Shady Oak Rd.
Minnetonka, MN 55343
Phone: 763 203-6300
Fax: 866 992-3224
Web: www.imris.com

CEO: –
CFO: –
HR: –
FYE: December 31
Type: Public

IMRIS wants to give neurosurgeons the best and most convenient view of the brain. The company designs and manufactures image-guided therapy systems that use magnetic resonance (MR) and fluoroscopy to deliver high-resolution images of brain tissue during neurosurgical procedures. Flagship product IMRISneuro is a leading MR-guided imaging system in the US with customers that include some of the top hospitals and neurosurgery centers in the country. Additional products include IMRISNV neurovascular conditions such as stroke and IMRIScardio for heart disease. IMRIS' systems are marketed directly by sales personnel in Asia, Europe, and North America and through distributors in Southeast Asia and the Middle East.

	Annual Growth	12/10	12/11	12/12	12/13	12/14
Sales ($mil.)	(20.4%)	71.9	51.8	52.4	46.0	28.9
Net income ($ mil.)	–	(1.4)	(20.9)	(27.8)	(42.0)	(30.4)
Market value ($ mil.)	(38.1%)	359.9	169.0	231.0	99.5	52.7
Employees	(5.9%)	154	169	168	137	121

IMUNON INC

997 Lenox Drive, Suite 100
Lawrenceville, NJ 08648
Phone: 609 896-9100
Fax: –
Web: www.celsion.com

NAS: IMNN
CEO: Corinne L Goff
CFO: Jeffrey W Church
HR: –
FYE: December 31
Type: Public

Celsion is trying to turn up the heat on cancer. The company is developing a heat-activated cancer therapy in the form of its lead drug ThermoDox. ThermoDox combines a common oncology drug, doxorubicin, with a heat-activated liposome that may help deliver and release the drug more accurately. The drug is being studied as a treatment for liver cancer and breast cancer. Celsion was previously a device maker and developed the Prolieve Thermodilatation system, an FDA-approved device used to treat benign prostatic hyperplasia (prostate enlargement). Celsion sold the product line to Boston Scientific in 2007.

	Annual Growth	12/19	12/20	12/21	12/22	12/23
Sales ($mil.)	–	0.5	0.5	0.5	0.5	–
Net income ($ mil.)	–	(16.9)	(21.5)	(20.8)	(35.9)	(19.5)
Market value ($ mil.)	(20.6%)	16.1	6.7	5.1	12.7	6.4
Employees	–	–	29	27	29	31

IN-N-OUT BURGERS

4199 CAMPUS DR STE 900
IRVINE, CA 926128604
Phone: 949 509-6200
Fax: –
Web: www.in-n-out.com

CEO: –
CFO: –
HR: –
FYE: December 31
Type: Private

In-N-Out Burger owns and operates more than 385 popular burger joints located primarily in California and a handful of other western states as well as Texas. The chain's menu features just four basic items ? hamburgers, cheeseburgers, the Double-Double (two patties and two slices of cheese), and French fries ? but patrons are free to customize how their hamburger is prepared. In addition, In-N-Out customers can purchase shirts at all its locations, including company stores in Baldwin Park and Las Vegas, and through the company's website. Harry and Esther Snyder started the family-owned company in 1948.

	Annual Growth	12/14	12/15	12/16	12/17	12/19
Sales ($mil.)	26.8%	–	–	–	4.1	6.6
Net income ($ mil.)	62.0%	–	–	–	1.3	3.3
Market value ($ mil.)	–	–	–	–	–	–
Employees	–	–	–	–	–	10,000

IN-Q-TEL, INC

2107 WILSON BLVD STE 1100
ARLINGTON, VA 222013079
Phone: 703 248-3000
Fax: –
Web: www.iqt.org

CEO: Steve Bowsher
CFO: –
HR: –
FYE: March 31
Type: Private

Just where do spies go to get their toys? Well, James Bond had "Q," and the CIA has In-Q-Tel (IQT). While it doesn't deal in exploding pens or cars equipped with missiles, the not-for-profit venture capital firm does keep the CIA and the broader US intelligence community equipped with the latest in information technology by investing in innovative high-tech companies. IQT is known for investing in Keyhole, which created the 3-D mapping software now used by Google Earth. Formed in 1999 as "Peleus" and later renamed after the above-mentioned "007" series character, IQT was designed to help the CIA keep pace with the rapid technological advances of the private sector, an increasingly daunting task.

	Annual Growth	03/10	03/11	03/20	03/21	03/22
Sales ($mil.)	10.1%	–	57.8	133.4	324.4	166.2
Net income ($ mil.)	14.2%	–	11.6	22.1	217.4	49.8
Market value ($ mil.)	–	–	–	–	–	–
Employees	–	–	–	–	–	60

INC.JET HOLDING INC

One Winnenden Road
Norwich, CT 06360
Phone: 860 823-1427
Fax: 860 886-0135
Web: –

NBB: SORT
CEO: –
CFO: Christophe Turner
HR: –
FYE: December 31
Type: Public

When customers want help with their document processing, Gunther tells them to stuff it. Gunther International makes electronic publishing, mailing, and billing systems that automate the assembly of printed documents. Its equipment is used to staple, bind, match, and insert documents into envelopes for distribution. Gunther targets insurance companies such as Allstate and Metropolitan Life, as well as businesses in the government, retail, and service bureau sectors. Subsidiary inc.jet offers industrial inkjet printers that OEMs incorporate into other devices. Gunther International was established in 1977.

	Annual Growth	03/18*	12/18	12/19	12/20	12/21
Sales ($mil.)	9.3%	11.8	10.7	14.3	15.0	16.8
Net income ($ mil.)	–	(1.9)	0.5	1.3	1.8	1.8
Market value ($ mil.)	–	–	–	–	–	–
Employees	–	–	–	–	–	–

*Fiscal year change

INCOME OPPORTUNITY REALTY INVESTORS INC

1603 LBJ Freeway, Suite 800
Dallas, TX 75234
Phone: 469 522-4200
Fax: –
Web: www.incomeopp-realty.com

ASE: IOR
CEO: Bradley J Muth
CFO: Gene S Bertcher
HR: –
FYE: December 31
Type: Public

When opportunity knocks, Income Opportunity Realty Investors (IORI) is there to answer. The real estate investment firm owns commercial, retail, and industrial real estate and land parcels in Texas as well as an apartment complex in Indiana. Transcontinental Realty Investors (TRI) owns about 80% of IORI after buying out the majority stake of Syntek West, which had overseen IORI's daily activities. American Realty Investors shares executive officers and board members with both IORI and TRI; affiliates of Prime Income Asset Management manage IORI's properties, as well as those of TRI. In 2008 IORI sold six apartment properties in Texas (about half of its assets).

	Annual Growth	12/19	12/20	12/21	12/22	12/23
Sales ($mil.)	–	–	–	–	–	–
Net income ($ mil.)	14.0%	4.1	4.2	3.6	3.9	7.0
Market value ($ mil.)	0.4%	54.3	46.6	49.1	49.4	55.1
Employees	–	–	–	–	–	–

INCONTACT, INC.

75 W TOWNE RIDGE PKWY 1
SANDY, UT 840705528
Phone: 801 320-3200
Fax: –
Web: www.incontact.com

CEO: Paul Jarman
CFO: –
HR: Shanna Lelli
FYE: December 31
Type: Private

inContact specializes in serving organizations with inbound call (contact) centers with some 10- over 300 seats. It assists in researching, designing, testing and implementing procedures, technologies and strategies that reduce costs and improve profitability and customer management. It helps organizations attain world class performance in their contact centers by leveraging technology, operations, management and strategy. It also helps to navigate customers' way to implementing the latest technologies in contact centers through VOIP & Virtual Call Center, CTI (Computer Telephone Integration), Integrated Channels (Voice, Video, Data,), Remote (work at home) agents, Web Chat, and other.

INCREDIBLE PIZZA CO., INC.

2522 S CAMPBELL AVE
SPRINGFIELD, MO 658073502
Phone: 417 887-3030
Fax: –
Web: www.incrediblepizza.com

CEO: Rick Barsness
CFO: George Ward
HR: –
FYE: December 31
Type: Private

America's Incredible Pizza Company has room on its plate for your family to eat and be entertained. The company operates and franchises about 15 all-you-can-eat pizza buffet plus entertainment centers offering themed dining areas, private party rooms, and a fairgrounds-style fun center full of games, rides, and attractions, including go-karts and mini-golf. The chain's menu includes pasta, soups, and salads, as well as several styles of pizza, along with a full dessert bar. About half the buffet fun centers are found in Texas with other locations in Louisiana, Missouri, Oklahoma, and Tennessee. Rick Barsness and his wife Cheryl opened the first America's Incredible Pizza location in 1999.

INCYTE CORPORATION   NMS: INCY

1801 Augustine Cut-Off
Wilmington, DE 19803
Phone: 302 498-6700
Fax: –
Web: www.incyte.com

CEO: Herve Hoppenot
CFO: Christiana Stamoulis
HR: Paula J Swain
FYE: December 31
Type: Public

Incyte is a biopharmaceutical company focused on the discovery, development and commercialization of proprietary therapeutics. Its portfolio focuses on areas of high unmet medical need and includes compounds in various stages, ranging from preclinical to late stage development, and commercialized products JAKAFI (ruxolitinib), ICLUSIG (ponatinib), PEMAZYRE (pemigatinib) and OPZELURA (ruxolitinib) cream, as well as MINJUVI (tafasitamab) and MONJUVI (tafasitamab-cxix), which are co-commercialized. The company conducts clinical development and commercial operations from its European headquarters in Morges, Switzerland and its other offices across Europe, as well as its Japanese office in Tokyo and its Canadian headquarters in Montreal.

	Annual Growth	12/19	12/20	12/21	12/22	12/23
Sales ($mil.)	14.4%	2,158.8	2,666.7	2,986.3	3,394.6	3,695.6
Net income ($ mil.)	7.5%	446.9	(295.7)	948.6	340.7	597.6
Market value ($ mil.)	(7.9%)	19,585	19,508	16,463	18,015	14,083
Employees	14.7%	1,456	1,773	2,094	2,324	2,524

INDEPENDENT BANK (IONIA, MI)

230 W. Main St., P.O. Box 491
Ionia, MI 48846
Phone: 616 527-9450
Fax: –
Web: www.ibcp.com

CEO: William B Kessel
CFO: Robert N Shuster
HR: Angela Champagne
FYE: December 31
Type: Public

Independent Bank Corporation is the holding company for Independent Bank, which serves rural and suburban communities of Michigan's Lower Peninsula from more than 100 branches. The bank offers traditional deposit products, including checking and savings accounts and CDs. Loans to businesses account for about 40% of the bank's portfolio; real estate mortgages are more than a third. Independent Bank also offers additional products and services like title insurance through subsidiary Independent Title Services, and investments through agreement with third-party provider PrimeVest.

INDEPENDENT BANK CORP (MA)   NMS: INDB

2036 Washington Street
Hanover, MA 02339
Phone: 781 878-6100
Fax: –
Web: www.rocklandtrust.com

CEO: Christopher Oddleifson
CFO: Robert Cozzone
HR: –
FYE: December 31
Type: Public

Independent Bank is a state chartered, federally registered bank holding company. The company is the sole stockholder of Rockland Trust Company ("Rockland Trust"or the "Bank"). Its banking subsidiary, Rockland Trust, operates almost 95 retail branches as well two limited service branches located in Barnstable, Bristol, Dukes, and more in Eastern Massachusetts.Serving area consumers and small to midsized businesses, the bank offers standard services such as checking and savings accounts, CDs, and credit cards, in addition to insurance products, financial planning, trust services. Commercial loans, including industrial, construction, and small business loans. Incorporated in 1985, the bank boasts total assets of some $13.2 billion.

	Annual Growth	12/19	12/20	12/21	12/22	12/23
Assets ($mil.)	14.1%	11,395	13,204	20,423	19,294	19,347
Net income ($ mil.)	9.7%	165.2	121.2	121.0	263.8	239.5
Market value ($ mil.)	(5.7%)	3,569.2	3,131.5	3,495.5	3,619.8	2,821.5
Employees	7.3%	1,348	1,375	1,691	1,739	1,787

INDEPENDENT BANK CORPORATION (IONIA, MI)   NMS: IBCP

4200 East Beltline
Grand Rapids, MI 49525
Phone: 616 527-5820
Fax: –
Web: www.independentbank.com

CEO: William B Kessel
CFO: Robert N Shuster
HR: Angela Champagne
FYE: December 31
Type: Public

Independent Bank Corporation is the holding company for Independent Bank, which serves rural and suburban communities of Michigan's Lower Peninsula from more than 100 branches. The bank offers traditional deposit products, including checking and savings accounts and CDs. Loans to businesses account for about 40% of the bank's portfolio; real estate mortgages are more than a third. Independent Bank also offers additional products and services like title insurance through subsidiary Independent Title Services, and investments through agreement with third-party provider PrimeVest.

	Annual Growth	12/19	12/20	12/21	12/22	12/23
Assets ($mil.)	10.2%	3,564.7	4,204.0	4,704.7	4,999.8	5,263.7
Net income ($ mil.)	6.2%	46.4	56.2	62.9	63.4	59.1
Market value ($ mil.)	3.5%	471.9	384.8	497.3	498.4	542.1
Employees	(4.4%)	994	983	986	916	832

INDEPENDENT BANK GROUP INC.   NMS: IBTX

7777 Henneman Way
McKinney, TX 75070-1711
Phone: 972 562-9004
Fax: –
Web: www.ifinancial.com

CEO: David R Brooks
CFO: Paul Langdale
HR: –
FYE: December 31
Type: Public

The bank holding company, Independent Bank Group does business through subsidiary Independent Bank, which operates about 95 full-services branches, which more than 70 of these branches are company-owned. The company operates in the Dallas/North Texas area, Austin/Central Texas Area, and the Houston Texas metropolitan area. The banks offer standard personal and business accounts and services including some focused on small business owners. IBG has total assets of around $18.3 billion and loans of about $1.8 billion. The company traces its roots back 100 years but took its current shape in 2002.

	Annual Growth	12/19	12/20	12/21	12/22	12/23
Assets ($mil.)	6.2%	14,958	17,753	18,733	18,258	19,035
Net income ($ mil.)	(31.2%)	192.7	201.2	224.8	196.3	43.2
Market value ($ mil.)	(2.1%)	2,288.7	2,580.9	2,978.5	2,480.2	2,100.4
Employees	0.8%	1,469	1,513	1,543	1,547	1,517

INDEPENDENT CHEMICAL CORP

7119 80TH ST STE 8202　　　　　　　　　　　　　　　　　CEO: -
GLENDALE, NY 113857733　　　　　　　　　　　　　　　CFO: -
Phone: 718 894-0700　　　　　　　　　　　　　　　　　　HR: -
Fax: -　　　　　　　　　　　　　　　　　　　　FYE: December 31
Web: www.independentchemical.com　　　　　　　　　Type: Private

Independent Chemical Corporation distributes chemicals such as chelating agents, hydrogen peroxide, inorganics, and surfactants. It also offers custom blending and contract packaging for the textiles, pharmaceutical, cosmetics, and food industries. The organization partners with customers to create the services they need, including custom packaging, particle sizing, custom synthesis, and just-in-time stocking at US locations. It carries products from more than 70 major chemical manufacturers, including ASHTA, Dow Chemical, Innophos, and Shin-Etsu. Independent Chemical is a family-owned and -operated company and was founded in 1948 by Benjamin Spielman.

INDEPENDENT HEALTH ASSOCIATION, INC.

511 FARBER LAKES DR STE 2　　　　　　　　　　　　　CEO: -
WILLIAMSVILLE, NY 142218272　　　　　　　　　　　　CFO: -
Phone: 716 631-3001　　　　　　　　　　　　　　　　　　HR: -
Fax: -　　　　　　　　　　　　　　　　　　　　FYE: December 31
Web: www.independenthealth.com　　　　　　　　　　Type: Private

Independent Health (IH) is a not-for-profit organization that provides a range of health insurance and related products to more than 365,000 members primarily in western New York (it's licensed in 35 states). IH's plans include HAS, HMO, POS, PPO, indemnity, and Medicare Advantage plans. It also provides dental and vision coverage, as well as coverage for Medicaid recipients. The firm offers a variety of community-based health and fitness programs including it Encompass 65 and SilverSneakers wellness programs for seniors. The company's Healthy Options program helps local restaurants design healthy menus.

INDEX FRESH, INC.

1250 CORONA POINTE CT STE 401　　　　　　　　　　CEO: -
CORONA, CA 928791781　　　　　　　　　　　　　　　CFO: -
Phone: 909 877-0999　　　　　　　　　　　　　　　　　　HR: -
Fax: -　　　　　　　　　　　　　　　　　　　　FYE: October 31
Web: www.indexfresh.com　　　　　　　　　　　　　　Type: Private

Index Fresh is a worldwide marketer of avocados, sourcing from all major growing regions around the globe, including California, Mexico, Peru, Chile, and Colombia. Aside from Index's facilities in California, it also has distribution centers and preconditioning facilities in California, Texas, Pennsylvania, Iowa, Ohio, Illinois, and Colorado. Through its dedication to quality, consistency, and innovation, Index Fresh continues to be a leader in the industry. It serves the retail and food service industries. It works diligently to link avocado growers who produce the finest fruit to retailers who seek the finest fruit. The company used to organize, pack, and market lemons and oranges until the 1950s when it absorbed its sister cooperative, United Growers Association. It became a corporation in 1999.

	Annual Growth	10/03	10/04	10/06	10/07	10/17
Sales ($mil.)	24.6%	-	11.5	24.7	32.2	199.9
Net income ($ mil.)	(9.2%)	-	9.6	0.6	0.3	2.8
Market value ($ mil.)	-	-	-	-	-	-
Employees	-	-	-	-	-	57

INDIANA BOTANIC GARDENS INC

3401 W 37TH AVE　　　　　　　　　　　　　　CEO: Harvey Cleland
HOBART, IN 463421751　　　　　　　　　　　　　　　CFO: -
Phone: 219 947-4040　　　　　　　　　　　　　　　　　HR: -
Fax: -　　　　　　　　　　　　　　　　　　　　FYE: December 31
Web: www.botanicchoice.com　　　　　　　　　　　Type: Private

Indiana Botanic Gardens makes, markets, and sells herbal supplements, cosmetics, and other natural products. Its Botanic Choice and Botanic Spa lines feature such exotic ingredients as hoodia (an African desert plant), Indian Water Hyssop, and emu oil. In all, it sells about 1,700 items to customers throughout the US and abroad. The company does most of its business through its mail-order catalogue and online retail site; it also operates a retail store and offers wholesale sales for other retailers. Joseph E. Meyer, author of the classic reference book The Herbalist, founded Indiana Botanic Gardens in 1910. His great-grandson Tim Cleland is the company's president.

	Annual Growth	12/11	12/12	12/13	12/14	12/15
Sales ($mil.)	(3.9%)	-	21.3	20.8	19.1	18.8
Net income ($ mil.)	-	-	(0.1)	1.0	0.3	(0.3)
Market value ($ mil.)	-	-	-	-	-	-
Employees	-	-	-	-	-	157

INDIANA FARM BUREAU, INC.

225 S EAST ST　　　　　　　　　　　　　　　　　　　　CEO: -
INDIANAPOLIS, IN 462024002　　　　　　　　　　　　CFO: -
Phone: 317 692-7851　　　　　　　　　　　　　　　　　HR: -
Fax: -　　　　　　　　　　　　　　　　　　　　FYE: December 31
Web: www.infarmbureau.org　　　　　　　　　　　　Type: Private

The Indiana Farm Bureau serves those who like things down on the farm. The group is a membership organization that provides educational programs, public policy advocacy, and other benefits for farmers. It's Indiana's largest general farm organization. Some member benefits include farm supply discounts, Internet and long distance service, life insurance, online agriculture reports, travel discounts, and vet supply discounts. The group also provides training, scholarship programs, a publication (The Hoosier Farmer), and special programs for young farmers. Indiana Farm Bureau, which itself is a member of the American Farm Bureau Federation, is divided into 10 districts, or geographic regions.

	Annual Growth	10/06	10/07	10/08	10/09*	12/22
Sales ($mil.)	48.3%	-	-	-	0.0	11.7
Net income ($ mil.)	-	-	-	-	(0.0)	0.6
Market value ($ mil.)	-	-	-	-	-	-
Employees	-	-	-	-	-	1,501

*Fiscal year change

INDIANA HARBOR BELT RAILROAD CO

2721 161ST ST　　　　　　　　　　　　　　　　　CEO: Jim Roots
HAMMOND, IN 463231099　　　　　　　　　　CFO: Derek Smith
Phone: 219 989-4703　　　　　　　　　　　　　　HR: Dan Kelley
Fax: -　　　　　　　　　　　　　　　　　　　　FYE: December 31
Web: www.ihbrr.com　　　　　　　　　　　　　　　Type: Private

Indiana Harbor Belt Railroad provides switching services on its network of more than 50 miles of mainline track in Indiana and Illinois. The company serves the Chicago area, which is North America's primary railroad hub. Indiana Harbor Belt handles traffic from industrial customers, such as chemical and metal producers, and interchanges traffic with about 15 other rail lines. Steel companies account for the largest share of the company's freight traffic. Conrail, which is controlled by Norfolk Southern and CSX, owns 51% of Indiana Harbor Belt; Canadian Pacific Railway owns 49%. Indiana Harbor Belt Railroad was formed in 1907.

	Annual Growth	12/07	12/08	12/09	12/10	12/11
Sales ($mil.)	14.3%	-	-	85.1	107.3	111.1
Net income ($ mil.)	28.2%	-	-	3.8	9.7	6.3
Market value ($ mil.)	-	-	-	-	-	-
Employees	-	-	-	-	-	750

INDIANA MICHIGAN POWER COMPANY

1 RIVERSIDE PLZ
COLUMBUS, OH 432152355
Phone: 614 716-1000
Fax: –
Web: www.indianamichiganpower.com

CEO: Nicholas K Akins
CFO: Brian X Tierney
HR: –
FYE: December 31
Type: Private

Indiana Michigan Power flips the switch where the Hoosiers and the Wolverines live and work. The utility serves about 582,000 electricity customers over its 24,220-mile transmission and distribution system in eastern and northern Indiana and southwestern Michigan. The American Electric Power subsidiary also sells power wholesale to other energy market participants, and it has some 5,930 MW of capacity from its primarily fossil-fueled (61% of total capacity), and nuclear power plants. Indiana Michigan Power owns the Cook Plant in Michigan, which consists of two nuclear generating units with a capacity of 2,160 MW. Nuclear power accounts for about 36% of Indiana Michigan Power's generating capacity.

INDIANA MUNICIPAL POWER AGENCY

11610 N COLLEGE AVE
CARMEL, IN 460325602
Phone: 317 573-9955
Fax: –
Web: www.impa.com

CEO: Jack Alvey
CFO: Chris Rettig
HR: –
FYE: December 31
Type: Private

Indiana Municipal Power Agency (IMPA) supplies bulk electricity to 53 community-owned distribution utilities throughout Indiana. IMPA members deliver electric service to households, businesses, and industries across Indiana. The company has interests in fossil-fueled power plants that give it nearly 820 MW of generating capacity; it also buys electricity through supply contracts and through purchases on the wholesale market. IMPA also owns power tranmission assets, and it provides utility engineering and consulting services through its ISC subsidiary. The state's 72 public power systems provide about 6% of the state's power capacity.

	Annual Growth	12/15	12/16	12/17	12/18	12/19
Sales ($mil.)	4.2%	–	–	423.4	461.1	459.7
Net income ($ mil.)	21.0%	–	–	23.2	37.6	33.9
Market value ($ mil.)	–	–	–	–	–	–
Employees		–	–	–	–	60

INDIANA SYMPHONY SOCIETY, INC.

32 E WASHINGTON ST # 600
INDIANAPOLIS, IN 462043594
Phone: 317 262-1100
Fax: –
Web: www.indianapolissymphony.org

CEO: Simon P Crookall
CFO: –
HR: Deidra Biltz
FYE: August 31
Type: Private

It's not only about racecars in Indianapolis. The Indiana Symphony Society funds and operates the Indianapolis symphony, one of about 20 full-time symphonies in the US. The symphony plays about 200 concerts every year under the artistic leadership of music director Mario Venzago and pops conductor Jack Everly. In addition to performances at its home Hilbert Circle Theatre, the symphony plays each summer at the Marsh Symphony on the Prairie, on a twice weekly radio show, and to audiences across the US and in Europe. The Indiana Symphony Society was founded in 1930.

	Annual Growth	08/15	08/16	08/17	08/18	08/21
Sales ($mil.)	(70.2%)	–	35.4	26.1	0.2	0.0
Net income ($ mil.)		–	7.2	2.8	0.0	(0.0)
Market value ($ mil.)		–	–	–	–	–
Employees		–	–	–	–	170

INDIANA UNIVERSITY FOUNDATION, INC.

1500 N STATE ROAD 46 BYPASS
BLOOMINGTON, IN 47408
Phone: 812 855-8311
Fax: –
Web: iufoundation.iu.edu

CEO: J T Forbes
CFO: James Perin
HR: –
FYE: June 30
Type: Private

Hoosier favorite fund-raiser? If you're a fan of Indiana University, then it might well be the Indiana University Foundation (IUF). The not-for-profit foundation raises more than $100 million annually in donations from individuals, corporations, and institutional organizations; alumni gifts account for about half of IUF's funds. It manages an endowment of about $1 billion and provides administrative services for gift accounts and scholarship and fellowship accounts. The organization has offices in Bloomington and Indianapolis. IUF was established in 1936.

	Annual Growth	06/18	06/19	06/20	06/21	06/22
Sales ($mil.)	17.1%	–	309.5	228.5	362.9	496.9
Net income ($ mil.)	15.4%	–	69.8	(9.8)	131.7	107.1
Market value ($ mil.)	–	–	–	–	–	–
Employees		–	–	–	–	240

INDIANA UNIVERSITY HEALTH BALL MEMORIAL HOSPITAL, INC.

2401 W UNIVERSITY AVE
MUNCIE, IN 473033428
Phone: 765 751-1449
Fax: –
Web: www.accesschs.org

CEO: Michael Haley
CFO: –
HR: –
FYE: December 31
Type: Private

Humble glass canning jars built the fortune that founded Indiana University Health Ball Memorial Hospital. The 380-bed hospital serves east central Indiana and is part of the Indiana University Health (IU Health) system. The hospital provides general acute and specialist care. IU Health Ball Memorial also operates the smaller Blackford Community Hospital, as well as physician offices, pharmacies, and home health and hospice care programs. The main hospital serves as a teaching facility for Indiana University's School of Medicine, providing internships and residency programs in specialties including internal medicine and family practice. IU Health Ball Memorial was founded in 1929.

	Annual Growth	12/12	12/13	12/14	12/15	12/22
Sales ($mil.)	4.0%	–	–	–	421.7	556.1
Net income ($ mil.)	(18.2%)	–	–	–	100.4	24.6
Market value ($ mil.)	–	–	–	–	–	–
Employees		–	–	–	–	3,000

INDIANA UNIVERSITY HEALTH BLOOMINGTON, INC.

2651 E DISCOVERY PKWY
BLOOMINGTON, IN 474089059
Phone: 812 353-5252
Fax: –
Web: www.iuhealth.org

CEO: Matthew Bailey
CFO: Jim Myers
HR: –
FYE: December 31
Type: Private

Indiana University Health Bloomington wants to put a bloom back in patients' cheeks. The facility, operating as IU Health Bloomington, provides care in a ten-county region in south central Indiana. The not-for-profit hospital -- which includes a 350-bed main campus in Bloomington and a 25-bed rural hospital in Paoli -- provides care in a number of medical specialties, including cardiovascular disease, cancer, orthopedics, and neuroscience. It also runs home health and hospice, urgent care, lab, and specialty care facilities, as well as physician practices under the name Southern Indiana Physicians. IU Health Bloomington is part of the Indiana University Health (IU Health) system.

	Annual Growth	12/11	12/12	12/14	12/21	12/22
Sales ($mil.)	7.1%	–	355.7	382.3	515.6	705.1
Net income ($ mil.)		–	64.3	92.2	145.3	(45.0)
Market value ($ mil.)	–	–	–	–	–	–
Employees		–	–	–	–	3,200

INDIANA UNIVERSITY HEALTH, INC.

340 W 10TH ST
INDIANAPOLIS, IN 462023082
Phone: 317 962-2000
Fax: -
Web: www.iuhealth.org

CEO: -
CFO: -
HR: -
FYE: December 31
Type: Private

Indiana University Health (IU Health) is one of the largest health systems in Indiana. As an academic health center, IU Health works in partnership with IU School of Medicine to train physicians, blending breakthrough research and high-quality patient care. The largest, Riley Children's Health is Indiana's most skilled pediatric system, with more than 50 locations across the states. IU Health Physicians include more than 1,500 board-certified or board-eligible physicians, more than 200 locations statewide including more than 250 advanced practice providers. With more than 2,715 beds, IU Health offers a full range of specialty services for children and adults, including cancer, cardiovascular, neuroscience, orthopedics, pediatrics and transplant services.

	Annual Growth	12/04	12/05	12/06	12/08	12/19
Sales ($mil.)	(30.7%)	-	-	2,478.3	1,889.6	20.9
Net income ($ mil.)	-	-	-	159.1	(24.0)	(2.3)
Market value ($ mil.)	-	-	-	-	-	-
Employees	-	-	-	-	-	17,242

INDIANA UNIVERSITY OF PENNSYLVANIA

1090 SOUTH DR
INDIANA, PA 157051038
Phone: 724 357-2200
Fax: -
Web: www.iup.edu

CEO: -
CFO: -
HR: -
FYE: June 30
Type: Private

Indiana University of Pennsylvania (IUP) isn't geographically confused. It's named for the town of Indiana, which is located in Western Pennsylvania, east of Pittsburgh. The school serves more than 14,000 students on three campuses (Indiana, Northpointe, and Punxsutawney); it also has a center in Monroeville that offers classes on evenings and Saturdays for professionals pursuing master's or doctoral degrees. All told, the university offers some 140 undergraduate degree programs, about 40 master's programs, and nine doctoral programs. IUP was founded in 1875 as Indiana Normal School and was granted university status in 1965. It is part of the Pennsylvania State System of Higher Education.

	Annual Growth	06/11	06/12	06/13	06/16	06/18
Sales ($mil.)	(1.4%)	-	188.5	176.0	173.8	172.9
Net income ($ mil.)	14.5%	-	7.8	12.9	(8.5)	17.5
Market value ($ mil.)	-	-	-	-	-	-
Employees	-	-	-	-	-	1,846

INDIANA UNIVERSITY RESEARCH AND TECHNOLOGY CORPORATION

518 INDIANA AVE
INDIANAPOLIS, IN 462023106
Phone: 317 274-5905
Fax: -
Web: www.iu.edu

CEO: -
CFO: Mike Burton
HR: -
FYE: June 30
Type: Private

You might say this program is Indiana's best KEP secret. Kelley Executive Partners (KEP) is the executive education program at Indiana University's Kelley School of Business. KEP provides custom designed programs for clients, including Fortune 500 companies, multinational corporations, and midsize businesses. It also offers general management programs, public courses, and certificate programs, as well as consulting services in learning and organizational development. KEP offers its programs either at the location of a client's choice or via the William J. Godfrey Graduate & Executive Education Center in Bloomington, Indiana, or the University Place Conference Center & Hotel in Indianapolis.

INDIANAPOLIS COLTS, INC.

7001 W 56TH ST
INDIANAPOLIS, IN 462549698
Phone: 317 297-2658
Fax: -
Web: www.colts.com

CEO: Michael Chernoff
CFO: -
HR: Michelle Rodriguez
FYE: January 31
Type: Private

Fans of this team are can saddle up for football glory. The Indianapolis Colts trace a long and storied history as a franchise in the National Football League, boasting five championships since joining the league in 1953. Most of those glory days, though, took place when the team was the Baltimore Colts and boasted the likes of Johnny Unitas on its roster. The team relocated to Indianapolis in 1984, but fans there had to wait until the 2006 season for the team to make a successful Super Bowl run with the help of such talent as Peyton Manning and Marvin Harrison. Started by Carroll Rosenbloom, the team has been owned by CEO James Irsay and his family since 1972.

INDIANAPOLIS MOTOR SPEEDWAY FOUNDATION INC

4565 W 16TH ST
INDIANAPOLIS, IN 462222513
Phone: 317 492-6784
Fax: -
Web: www.imsmuseum.org

CEO: Anton H George
CFO: Jeffrey G Belskus
HR: Cortne Gander
FYE: December 31
Type: Private

The Brickyard might be stationary, but those who compete there are anything but. Indianapolis Motor Speedway Corporation (IMS) owns and operates the 2.5 mile race track also known as the Brickyard that is home to the famous Indianapolis 500. A spotlight event of the Indy Racing League (IRL) and American motorsports in general, the Indy 500 is held every Memorial Day weekend and draws more than 250,000 spectators. IMS also hosts the Brickyard 400, an event sanctioned by NASCAR, as well as the Red Bull Indianapolis GP. In addition to the track, IMS operates a hotel and an 18-hole golf course. The track was built in 1911 and acquired by Tony Hulman in 1945. His family continues to own IMS.

	Annual Growth	12/09	12/10	12/13	12/15	12/21
Sales ($mil.)	14.2%	-	1.3	2.1	2.5	5.7
Net income ($ mil.)	30.9%	-	0.0	0.4	0.7	1.6
Market value ($ mil.)	-	-	-	-	-	-
Employees	-	-	-	-	-	80

INDIEPUB ENTERTAINMENT INC.

11248 Cornell Park Drive, Suite 608
Blue Ash, OH 45242
Phone: 513 824-8297
Fax: -
Web: www.zoogamesinc.com

NBB: IPUB
CEO: -
CFO: -
HR: -
FYE: December 31
Type: Public

If your house feels like a zoo, Zoo Entertainment hopes you'll tame those animals with some family-friendly fun. The software company develops mass market video games that play on Nintendo, Sony, and Microsoft gaming equipment as well as on PCs, Apple's iPhone, and Facebook. It also runs the indiePub Games website, which offers game developers a place to compete for prizes and game players an opportunity to play and rate free games. Many of Zoo Entertainment's casual games feature licensing tie-ins with Jeep, Hello Kitty, and Remington; some branded titles are packaged with giveaways including steering wheels, bows, and guns. It aims for a steady stream of releases rather than sporadic blockbusters.

	Annual Growth	12/07	12/08	12/09	12/10	12/11
Sales ($mil.)	-	-	36.3	48.7	63.4	9.9
Net income ($ mil.)	-	(0.1)	(21.7)	(13.2)	(14.0)	(25.9)
Market value ($ mil.)	-	-	6.0	6.0	36.9	5.8
Employees	52.0%	3	24	30	32	16

INDOTRONIX INTERNATIONAL CORP

687 LEE RD STE 250
ROCHESTER, NY 146064257
Phone: 845 473-1137
Fax: –
Web: www.iic.com

CEO: –
CFO: –
HR: –
FYE: December 31
Type: Private

Indotronix provides information technology (IT) services from six US branch offices and two software development and call center facilities in India. It mainly develops customized business software using Microsoft, IBM, and open source applications to automate sales force, e-commerce, and office management functions, among others. Indotronix also provides consulting, staffing, IT hosting, and call center services. Clients come from such industries as financial services, health care, and technology, as well as from the public sector. The company has counted IBM, Merrill Lynch, and the US General Services Administration among its customers. Indotronix was founded in 1986.

	Annual Growth	12/04	12/05	12/06	12/07	12/08
Sales ($mil.)	(15.9%)	–	–	70.5	59.5	49.8
Net income ($ mil.)	–	–	–	0.1	(0.8)	(0.3)
Market value ($ mil.)	–	–	–	–	–	–
Employees	–	–	–	–	–	228

INDUS CORPORATION

1515 WILSON BLVD STE 1100
ARLINGTON, VA 222092440
Phone: 703 506-6700
Fax: –
Web: –

CEO: Shivram Krishnan
CFO: –
HR: –
FYE: December 31
Type: Private

INDUS hopes to capitalize on technology by providing a variety of information technology (IT) services to the federal government and commercial clients. The company's services include software design, consulting, application integration, systems engineering, and enterprise support services. Its areas of expertise include database management, data warehousing, and data mining; Web development; geographic information systems (GIS); telecommunications; and data security. The company has nine satellite offices in the US. Clients have included NASA, the Department of Defense, and Homeland Security agencies. INDUS CEO and majority owner Shiv Krishnan founded the company in 1993.

	Annual Growth	12/01	12/02	12/03	12/04	12/14
Sales ($mil.)	–	–	(153.6)	61.0	75.3	51.4
Net income ($ mil.)	229.6%	–	0.0	2.6	3.8	3.3
Market value ($ mil.)	–	–	–	–	–	–
Employees	–	–	–	–	–	450

INDUSTRIAL SCIENTIFIC CORPORATION

1 LIFE WAY
PITTSBURGH, PA 152057500
Phone: 412 788-4353
Fax: –
Web: www.indsci.com

CEO: –
CFO: Rowland Cromwell
HR: Mia Grazioso
FYE: June 30
Type: Private

Industrial Scientific is a leader in lifesaving products and technologies that improve in-the-moment safety outcomes for workers worldwide. The company makes, sells, rents, and services gas monitoring instruments, equipment, and related products to detect oxygen and combustible and toxic gases. Its Instrument Network (iNet) is a subscription service that covers gas detectors, shipping, calibration gas, docking stations, training, and more. The company pioneered numerous technologies, including the first 3-gas detector, 6-gas detector, and wireless gas detector. It began in 1976 as the Research Division of the National Mine Service Company (NMS) with a focus on developing instrumentation to detect methane gas.

	Annual Growth	01/04	01/05	01/06*	12/07*	06/15
Sales ($mil.)	(42.9%)	–	63.2	72.7	140.8	0.2
Net income ($ mil.)	(32.3%)	–	7.2	8.8	12.5	0.1
Market value ($ mil.)	–	–	–	–	–	–
Employees	–	–	–	–	–	549

*Fiscal year change

INDUSTRIAL SUPPLY ASSOCIATION

3435 CONCORD RD # 21889
YORK, PA 174021000
Phone: 866 460-2360
Fax: –
Web: www.isapartners.org

CEO: –
CFO: –
HR: –
FYE: December 31
Type: Private

The Industrial Supply Association (ISA) is a trade organization that comprises maintenance, repair, operating, and production suppliers. It represents about 500 companies. In addition to hosting conventions and other events, the group offers its members training and support on increasing productivity, improving sales and marketing, and reducing costs. It also conducts research, develops performance standards, and provides networking opportunities. The ISA was formed in 2004 by the merger of the ISMA and the Industrial Distributors Association. They were joined in 2005 by members of the defunct North American Industrial Representatives Association.

	Annual Growth	06/18	06/19*	12/19	12/21	12/22
Sales ($mil.)	292.2%	–	0.0	3.3	2.0	3.0
Net income ($ mil.)	119.2%	–	0.0	0.5	0.2	0.5
Market value ($ mil.)	–	–	–	–	–	–
Employees	–	–	–	–	–	6

*Fiscal year change

INDUSTRIAL TURNAROUND CORPORATION

13141 N ENON CHURCH RD
CHESTER, VA 238363120
Phone: 804 414-1100
Fax: –
Web: itac.us.com

CEO: –
CFO: –
HR: –
FYE: December 31
Type: Private

Facility builder Industrial TurnAround Corporation (ITAC) makes sure that wheels turn and conveyors churn at industrial plants around the world. ITAC provides architectural and design expertise, construction management, and electrical and mechanical engineering to clients whose facilities are based on heavy production, such as biofuels, chemical, metal, pharmaceutical, power, pulp and paper, and tobacco. It also offers on-site staffing (for clients who need temporary project managers, draftsmen, CAD operators, and other support staff), as well as hazard and fall prevention assessment, equipment, and training. Clients include Amtrak, Honeywell International, and NASA.

	Annual Growth	12/11	12/12	12/13	12/14	12/17
Sales ($mil.)	13.6%	–	42.5	50.7	64.5	80.4
Net income ($ mil.)	(26.7%)	–	3.0	4.0	6.1	0.6
Market value ($ mil.)	–	–	–	–	–	–
Employees	–	–	–	–	–	550

INDYNE, INC.

46561 EXPEDITION DR # 100
LEXINGTON PARK, MD 206532118
Phone: 703 903-6900
Fax: –
Web: www.indyneinc.com

CEO: –
CFO: –
HR: Margaret James
FYE: December 31
Type: Private

InDyne offers out-of-this-world technology expertise. The company provides information technology, science and engineering, and technical and administrative services, primarily to US government agencies, including NASA. It develops custom software, designs Web sites, and builds computer networks. InDyne's science and engineering division designs aerospace systems, provides space mission support and crew training, and offers structural and fluid analysis. Its technical and administrative services unit handles imagery operations, data management, media services, and operations support. InDyne's projects have included the development of custom database software for the CDC and the Department of Transportation.

	Annual Growth	12/06	12/07	12/08	12/09	12/10
Sales ($mil.)	(5.0%)	–	–	288.5	256.0	260.4
Net income ($ mil.)	(12.1%)	–	–	8.9	7.7	6.9
Market value ($ mil.)	–	–	–	–	–	–
Employees	–	–	–	–	–	1,700

INFINERA CORP

NMS: INFN

6373 San Ignacio Avenue
San Jose, CA 95119
Phone: 408 572-5200
Fax: –
Web: www.infinera.com

CEO: David W Heard
CFO: Nancy Erba
HR: –
FYE: December 31
Type: Public

Infinera is a semiconductor manufacturer and a global supplier of networking solutions comprised of networking equipment, optical semiconductors, software, and services. Its portfolio of solutions includes optical transport platforms, converged packet-optical transport platforms, compact modular platforms, optical line systems, coherent optical engines and subsystems, a suite of automation software offerings, and support and professional services. Infinera also optimizes the manufacturing process by using indium phosphide (INP) to build its PICs, which enables the integration of hundreds of optical functions onto a single, monolithic optical semiconductor chip. Customers include telecommunication service providers, internet content providers (ICPs), cable providers, wholesale carriers, research and education institutions, utilities, governments, and large enterprises. The company generates about 55% of revenue domestically.

	Annual Growth	12/18	12/19	12/20	12/21	12/22
Sales ($mil.)	13.6%	943.4	1,298.9	1,355.6	1,425.2	1,573.2
Net income ($ mil.)	–	(214.3)	(386.6)	(206.7)	(170.8)	(76.0)
Market value ($ mil.)	14.5%	864.0	1,714.8	2,417.9	2,104.9	1,485.5
Employees	(4.2%)	3,876	3,261	3,050	3,225	3,267

INFINITE ENERGY, LLC

5950 NW 1ST PL STE 100
GAINESVILLE, FL 326076063
Phone: 352 331-1654
Fax: –
Web: www.gassouth.com

CEO: –
CFO: –
HR: –
FYE: December 31
Type: Private

Infinite wisdom? No. Infinite energy? Yes. Infinite Energy does not provide its customers with the natural high of endorphins, or with the latest health diet, but with the more prosaic commodity of natural gas. The company supplies natural gas to clients in Florida, Georgia, and New York. Wholesale customers include municipalities, institutions, and utilities; Infinite Energy also sells to large and small commercial establishments (including restaurants) and to residential customers.

	Annual Growth	12/02	12/03	12/04	12/05	12/09
Sales ($mil.)	6.0%	–	335.8	474.0	583.9	477.6
Net income ($ mil.)	26.7%	–	3.1	8.7	4.5	13.0
Market value ($ mil.)	–	–	–	–	–	–
Employees	–	–	–	–	–	418

INFINITE GRAPHICS INCORPORATED

4611 E LAKE ST
MINNEAPOLIS, MN 554062397
Phone: 612 721-6283
Fax: –
Web: www.igi.com

CEO: Cliff Stritch
CFO: –
HR: –
FYE: April 30
Type: Private

Infinite Graphics Inc. (IGI) plots to provide chip makers with high-tech images. The company provides precision digital imaging services for the electronics industry. IGI transforms customers' circuit designs into precise graphic images, then transfers them onto film, quartz, or glass substrates. Customers reproduce and mass-produce the designs to make photochemically etched and plated parts, integrated circuits, and flat-panel displays. Infinite Graphics also designs printed circuit boards, provides a variety of computer-aided design (CAD) software and services, and resells imaging equipment. IGI was established in 1969.

	Annual Growth	01/02	01/03*	04/10	04/11	04/14
Sales ($mil.)	(26.1%)	–	259.9	6.6	7.1	9.3
Net income ($ mil.)	90.8%	–	0.0	(0.1)	0.3	0.3
Market value ($ mil.)	–	–	–	–	–	–
Employees	–	–	–	–	–	45

*Fiscal year change

INFINITE GROUP, INC.

NBB: IMCI

175 Sully's Trail, Suite 202
Pittsford, NY 14534
Phone: 585 385-0610
Fax: –
Web: www.igius.com

CEO: James Villa
CFO: –
HR: –
FYE: December 31
Type: Public

As far as Infinite Group Inc. (IGI) is concerned, it's capacity to handle its clients' IT outsourcing is unlimited -- particularly for government clients. The company provides infrastructure management, information security, systems engineering, server and desktop virtualization, enterprise architecture, and software development. US government contracts account for the majority of IGI's sales and some its government clients are the Department of Homeland Security and the US Navy. The company has offices in New York, Colorado, and Virginia (which serves its DC customers).

	Annual Growth	12/18	12/19	12/20	12/21	12/22
Sales ($mil.)	2.4%	6.4	7.1	7.2	7.2	7.0
Net income ($ mil.)	–	0.0	0.0	0.7	(1.6)	(3.6)
Market value ($ mil.)	278.4%	0.0	0.0	0.0	0.0	1.0
Employees	(0.9%)	57	59	60	65	55

INFINITY PHARMACEUTICALS INC

NBB: INFI

1100 Massachusetts Avenue, Floor 4
Cambridge, MA 02138
Phone: 617 453-1000
Fax: –
Web: www.infi.com

CEO: Seth Tasker
CFO: –
HR: –
FYE: December 31
Type: Public

Infinity Pharmaceuticals is a clinical-stage innovative biopharmaceutical company dedicated to developing novel medicines for people with cancer, including non-small cell lung cancer. The company combines proven scientific expertise with a passion for developing novel small molecule drugs that target disease pathways for potential applications in oncology. It focuses on advancing eganelisib, also known as IPI-549, an orally administered, clinical-stage, immuno-oncology product candidate that selectively inhibits the enzyme phosphoinositide-3-kinase-gamma, or PI3K-gamma. The company retains worldwide development and commercialization rights to eganelisib, subject to certain success-based milestone payment obligations to its licensor, Takeda Pharmaceutical Company Limited.

	Annual Growth	12/18	12/19	12/20	12/21	12/22
Sales ($mil.)	(41.5%)	22.1	3.0	1.7	1.9	2.6
Net income ($ mil.)	–	(11.3)	(47.1)	(40.5)	(45.3)	(44.4)
Market value ($ mil.)	(17.2%)	105.5	85.8	189.6	201.2	49.6
Employees	4.7%	25	25	23	33	30

INFINITY SOFTWARE DEVELOPMENT, INC.

1901 COMMONWEALTH LN
TALLAHASSEE, FL 323033196
Phone: 850 383-1011
Fax: –
Web: www.infinity-software.com

CEO: –
CFO: –
HR: –
FYE: December 31
Type: Private

Infinity Software Development hopes to take your technological efforts to new, immeasurable heights. The company provides information technology consulting and software development services to businesses and public organizations primarily in the Southeast. Infinity Software Development specializes in network services, and client server, main frame and Web development. Clients have included the Florida Department of Agriculture and Consumer Services, the Florida Department of Education, and the Florida Department of Law Enforcement. The company was founded in 1994.

	Annual Growth	12/06	12/07	12/08	12/09	12/10
Sales ($mil.)	(20.1%)	–	–	18.4	12.3	11.7
Net income ($ mil.)	–	–	–	0.4	(0.1)	(0.0)
Market value ($ mil.)	–	–	–	–	–	–
Employees	–	–	–	–	–	60

INFLUENCE HEALTH, INC.

3000 RIVERCHASE GALLERIA STE 800
HOOVER, AL 352442315
Phone: 205 982-5800
Fax: -
Web: -

CEO: Rupen Patel
CFO: Dave Morgan
HR: Linda Benedict
FYE: December 31
Type: Private

Hospitals searching for help with website development could find answers from MedSeek. The Web development company designs and manages websites and intranets for more than 1,100 hospitals. It offers a propriety content management software called eHealth ecoSystem and also provides custom application design. Its Web portals feature physician directories and job boards, and they provide secure access to clinical information and facilitate communication between doctors, patients, and hospitals. MedSeek was founded in 1996.

	Annual Growth	12/05	12/06	12/07	12/08	12/10
Sales ($mil.)	14.6%	-	-	23.0	25.1	34.6
Net income ($ mil.)	143.6%	-	-	0.2	1.6	2.4
Market value ($ mil.)	-	-	-	-	-	-
Employees	-	-	-	-	-	143

INFOBLOX INC.

2390 MISSION COLLEGE BLVD STE 501
SANTA CLARA, CA 950541554
Phone: 408 986-4000
Fax: -
Web: www.infoblox.com

CEO: Scott Harrell
CFO: Hoke Horne
HR: Veronica Gonzalez
FYE: July 31
Type: Private

Infoblox is the leader in next generation DNS management and security. It dramatically simplifies complex distributed networking and security by delivering modern, cloud-first networking and security services that automate and streamline NetOps, SecOps, DevOps and user experiences. Infoblox is uniquely able to support organizations in this challenging environment because its solutions support DNS, DHCP and IP address management. Its NetMRI product line automates network change and configuration management processes. Infoblox works more than 13,000 customers, including over 75% of the Fortune 500. The company revolutionized network services in 1999 when it delivers the first hardened DNS appliance.

	Annual Growth	07/11	07/12	07/13	07/14	07/15
Sales ($mil.)	16.6%	-	-	225.0	250.3	306.1
Net income ($ mil.)	-	-	-	(4.4)	(23.9)	(27.1)
Market value ($ mil.)	-	-	-	-	-	-
Employees	-	-	-	-	-	800

INFOCROSSING, LLC

20 MERCER ST
HACKENSACK, NJ 076015608
Phone: 201 840-4700
Fax: -
Web: www.infocrossing.com

CEO: Pinaki Kar
CFO: Yogesh Patel
HR: Albert Stichter
FYE: March 31
Type: Private

Infocrossing wants to make sure information keeps coursing through your IT assets. The company assists midsized and large enterprises with a variety of outsourced IT services, including computer facilities management, application development, remote monitoring, data center and data processing, and network management. The company also offers infrastructure management consulting, mainframe and open system outsourcing, managed hosting, and disaster recovery services. Its strategic partners include such vendors as CA , Cisco , and EMC . Infocrossing is a subsidiary of Wipro Technologies , one of India's largest providers of business process outsourcing (BPO) and IT services.

INFOGAIN CORPORATION

485 ALBERTO WAY STE 100
LOS GATOS, CA 950325476
Phone: 408 355-6000
Fax: -
Web: www.infogain.com

CEO: Sunil Bhatia
CFO: Kulesh Bansal
HR: -
FYE: March 31
Type: Private

Infogain is a digital platform and software engineering company. It is based in Silicon Valley with design and build centers around the globe. Infogain engineers business outcomes for Fortune 500 companies and digital natives in the technology, healthcare, insurance, travel, telecom, and retail/CPG industries. It accelerates experience-led transformation in the delivery of digital platforms using technologies such as cloud, microservices, automation, IoT, and artificial intelligence. Infogain is a multi-cloud expert across hyperscale cloud providers ? Microsoft Azure, Google Cloud Platform and Amazon Web Services.

	Annual Growth	03/17	03/18	03/19	03/20	03/21
Sales ($mil.)	28.4%	-	-	-	165.7	212.7
Net income ($ mil.)	29.2%	-	-	-	5.8	7.4
Market value ($ mil.)	-	-	-	-	-	-
Employees	-	-	-	-	-	597

INFONOW CORP.

NBB: INOW

1875 Lawrence Street, Suite 1100
Denver, CO 80202
Phone: 303 293-0212
Fax: 303 293-0213
Web: www.infonow.com

CEO: Mark Geene
CFO: -
HR: -
FYE: December 31
Type: Public

InfoNow doesn't mean to sound impatient -- it just wants sales channel partners to get the information they need. Its channel data management software tracks point-of-sale transactions and gives manufacturers detailed information on their partners and customers, enabling clients to track their products through third-party distribution and sales channels. The company also provides tools for partner analysis, sales credit assignment, and campaign generation, as well as applications to monitor and manage inventory data. InfoNow, which provides its software under the Software-as-a-Service model, markets its offerings primarily to companies in the financial services, industrial, and technology industries.

	Annual Growth	12/00	12/01	12/02	12/03	12/04
Sales ($mil.)	10.8%	7.2	14.0	12.8	12.4	10.9
Net income ($ mil.)	-	(6.8)	(1.8)	0.0	0.5	(0.7)
Market value ($ mil.)	(4.9%)	14.1	37.4	15.6	29.8	11.6
Employees	0.5%	106	114	115	91	108

INFOR, INC.

641 AVENUE OF THE AMERICAS FL 4
NEW YORK, NY 100112038
Phone: 646 336-1700
Fax: -
Web: www.infor.com

CEO: Kevin Samuelson
CFO: Jay Hopkins
HR: Imani Smith
FYE: April 30
Type: Private

Infor is a global leader in business cloud software products for companies in industry specific markets. Infor builds complete industry suites in the cloud and efficiently deploys technology that puts the user experience first, leverages data science, and integrates easily into existing systems. Over 65,000 organizations in more than 175 countries rely on Infor's 17,000 employees to help achieve their business goals. As a Koch company, company's financial strength, ownership structure, and long-term view empower us to foster enduring, mutually beneficial relationships with our customers.

INFORMATICA LLC

2100 SEAPORT BLVD
REDWOOD CITY, CA 940635596
Phone: 650 385-5000
Fax: –
Web: www.informatica.com

CEO: Amit Walia
CFO: Michael McLaughlin
HR: –
FYE: December 31
Type: Private

Informatica is an enterprise cloud data management leader that empowers businesses to realize the transformative power of data. It pioneers a new category of software, the Intelligent Data Management Cloud, or IDMC. Its AI-powered IDMC platform delivers best-of-breed solutions that enables enterprises to create a single source of truth for their data, allowing them to create compelling 360-degree customer experiences, automate data operations across enterprise-wide business processes like supply chain management, financial planning and operations, and provides governed and secure data access to their employees. The company has approximately 5,700 600 active customers in over 100 countries and territories worldwide, including 9 of the Fortune 10, about 85 of the Fortune 100 and nearly 925over 910 of the Global 2000. The company went public in late 2021. The North America accounts for more than 65about 70% of the company's revenue.

INFORMATION BUILDERS, INC.

11 PENN PLZ FL 8
NEW YORK, NY 100012049
Phone: 212 736-4433
Fax: –
Web: www.tibco.com

CEO: Frank J Vella
CFO: Frank Brunetti
HR: –
FYE: December 31
Type: Private

Information Builders Inc. (IBI) wants to help your business intelligently with its business intelligence tools. The company help organizations get their complex and disconnected data in order so they can build, embed, and automate intelligence in everything they do. IBI has known that the technological evolution requires an informed understanding of the role data in an enterprise. It continues to leverage both its forward-thinking and historical expertise to embed analytics into any product, application, portal, or process that requires enterprise-trusted data. In 2021, TIBCO Software Inc., a global leader in enterprise data, empowers its customers to connect, unify, and confidently predict business outcomes, solving the world's most complex data-driven challenges, announced it has successfully closed the acquisition of Information Builders, Inc.

INFORMATION SERVICES GROUP INC   NMS: III

2187 Atlantic Street
Stamford, CT 06902
Phone: 203 517-3100
Fax: –
Web: www.isg-one.com

CEO: Michael P Connors
CFO: Humberto P Alfonso
HR: –
FYE: December 31
Type: Public

True to its name, Information Services Group's (ISG) service is information. ISG provides technology insights, market intelligence, and advisory services to companies seeking to outsource their business operations. The company specializes in marketing, advertising, human resources, legal, supply chain management, and other business services. It targets North American, European, and Asia/Pacific markets, and has operations in some 20 countries. It serves such industries as telecom, financial services, health care, pharmaceutical, and utilities. ISG operates through subsidiaries TPI Advisory Services (data and advisory), Compass (benchmarking and analysis), and STA Consulting (public sector IT services).

	Annual Growth	12/19	12/20	12/21	12/22	12/23
Sales ($mil.)	2.3%	265.8	249.1	277.8	286.3	291.1
Net income ($ mil.)	16.5%	3.3	2.8	15.5	19.7	6.2
Market value ($ mil.)	16.8%	123.1	159.6	370.7	223.8	229.2
Employees	4.2%	1,287	1,258	1,335	1,599	1,518

INGERSOLL MACHINE TOOLS, INC.

707 FULTON AVE
ROCKFORD, IL 611034069
Phone: 815 987-6000
Fax: –
Web: en.machinetools.camozzi.com

CEO: Jeff Ahrstrom
CFO: Lawrence Mocadlo
HR: Kaylie Barber
FYE: December 31
Type: Private

At Ingersoll Machine Tools, folks want to talk shop. The company leads the conversation in global production, churning out advanced machine tools for other industries' goods. Products include general purpose equipment (vertical turning lathes, scalpers, and horizontal boring centers) to one-of-a-kind machines that produce aluminum and hard metal components, and structures from composite materials. Ingersoll's contract manufacturing services offer prototype machining and short production runs of windmill hubs to small engine parts. Customers include most of the world's aerospace, transportation, energy, and heavy industry OEMs, from Caterpillar to Lockheed Martin. Ingersoll is a company of Italy's Camozzi Group.

INGERSOLL RAND INC   NYS: IR

525 Harbour Place Drive, Suite 600
Davidson, NC 28036
Phone: 704 655-4000
Fax: –
Web: www.gardnerdenver.com

CEO: –
CFO: –
HR: –
FYE: December 31
Type: Public

Ingersoll Rand (formerly known as Gardner Denver Holdings, Inc.) is a global market leader with a broad range of innovative and mission-critical air, fluid, energy, and medical technologies, providing services and solutions to increase industrial productivity and efficiency. The company manufactures one of the broadest and most complete ranges of compressor, pump, vacuum and blower products in its markets, which, when combined with its global geographic footprint and application expertise, allows the company to provide differentiated product and service offerings to its customers. Its products are sold under more than 40 market-leading brands, including Ingersoll Rand and Gardner Denver. Around 40% of its sales comes from US.

	Annual Growth	12/19	12/20	12/21	12/22	12/23
Sales ($mil.)	29.4%	2,451.9	4,910.2	5,152.4	5,916.3	6,876.1
Net income ($ mil.)	48.7%	159.1	(33.3)	562.5	604.7	778.7
Market value ($ mil.)	20.5%	14,795	18,377	24,955	21,075	31,195
Employees	28.5%	6,600	15,900	16,000	17,000	18,000

INGEVITY CORP   NYS: NGVT

4920 O'Hear Avenue Suite 400
North Charleston, SC 29405
Phone: 843 740-2300
Fax: –
Web: www.ingevity.com

CEO: John C Fortson
CFO: Mary D Hall
HR: –
FYE: December 31
Type: Public

Ingevity produces chemicals and high-performance activated carbon materials. The company manufactures resins used to connect polymers that comprise rigid packaging, product assembly, hygiene, tapes, labels, construction and road markings. It makes other chemicals and products used within the asphalt paving, oil well service additives and production, downstream applications chemicals, agrochemicals, lubricants, adhesives and printing inks sectors. It also supplies automotive components that reduce gasoline vapor emissions. Ingevity sells its products to customers in about 80 countries and generates some 60% of total revenue from the US.

	Annual Growth	12/19	12/20	12/21	12/22	12/23
Sales ($mil.)	7.0%	1,292.9	1,216.1	1,391.5	1,668.3	1,692.1
Net income ($ mil.)	–	183.7	181.4	118.1	211.6	(5.4)
Market value ($ mil.)	(14.3%)	3,166.0	2,743.9	2,597.9	2,552.3	1,710.9
Employees	(2.1%)	1,850	1,750	1,850	2,050	1,700

INGLES MARKETS INC
NMS: IMKT A

2913 U.S. Hwy., 70 West, Black Mountain, NC
Asheville, NC 28711
Phone: 828 669-2941
Fax: –
Web: www.ingles-markets.com

CEO: –
CFO: –
HR: –
FYE: September 30
Type: Public

Ingles Markets is a leading supermarket chain in the southeast US that operates about 200 supermarkets, primarily in suburbs, small towns, and rural areas of six southeastern states. The stores largely operate under the Ingles name, although nine do business as Sav-Mor. In addition to brand-name goods, Ingles Markets stocks its shelves with its Laura Lynn and Harvest Farms private label products. The company also owns milk processing and packaging plant that sells approximately 75% of its products to Ingles stores and the rest to other retailers and distributors. Ingles Markets is also in the real estate business: it owns about 165 of its supermarkets, nearly all of which contain an Ingles store.

	Annual Growth	09/19	09/20	09/21	09/22	09/23
Sales ($mil.)	8.8%	4,202.0	4,610.6	4,987.9	5,678.8	5,892.8
Net income ($ mil.)	26.8%	81.6	178.6	249.7	272.8	210.8
Market value ($ mil.)	18.0%	737.6	693.1	1,243.9	1,553.4	1,430.8
Employees	(0.5%)	27,000	27,000	26,000	26,000	26,420

INGRAM MICRO INC.

3351 MICHELSON DR STE 100
IRVINE, CA 926120697
Phone: 714 566-1000
Fax: –
Web: corp.ingrammicro.com

CEO: Paul Bay
CFO: Mike Zilis
HR: Blake Wettstein
FYE: January 02
Type: Private

Ingram Micro is one of the largest global providers of technology, mobility, and cloud platform solutions. With about 135 logistics centers and service centers worldwide, the company offers a comprehensive portfolio of IT and mobility products, services, and capabilities globally. It provides thousands of products desktop and notebook PCs, storage devices, printers, software, and more to more than 160,000 customers in some 200 countries around the world. It sells products from more than 1,500 vendors, including many of the world's top manufacturers. Its vendor partners include Adobe, Cisco, Dell, Visiontek, and Schneider Electric, among others. Husband and wife Geza Czige and Lorraine Mecca founded the company in 1979. In mid-2021, Ingram Micro is now part of Platinum Equity.

INGREDION INC
NYS: INGR

5 Westbrook Corporate Center
Westchester, IL 60154
Phone: 708 551-2600
Fax: 708 551-2700
Web: www.ingredion.com

CEO: James P Zallie
CFO: James D Gray
HR: –
FYE: December 31
Type: Public

Ingredion is a leading global ingredients solutions provider that turns corn, tapioca, potatoes, plant-based stevia, grains, fruits, and vegetables into value-added ingredients and biomaterials for the food, beverage, brewing and other industries. The company's largest product line is starches, used in food for stabilization, feel, and texture and in paper, packaging, and other materials for quality, strength, and a host of other attributes. Its other product lines include sweeteners (high-fructose corn syrup, dextrose), specialty ingredients (products focused on health, affordability, and sustainability), and co-products (refined corn oil, corn gluten feed and meal). Ingredion operates worldwide, but generates most of its sales in North America.

	Annual Growth	12/19	12/20	12/21	12/22	12/23
Sales ($mil.)	7.1%	6,209.0	5,987.0	6,894.0	7,946.0	8,160.0
Net income ($ mil.)	11.7%	413.0	348.0	117.0	492.0	643.0
Market value ($ mil.)	4.0%	6,064.0	5,132.4	6,304.7	6,388.9	7,080.4
Employees	1.3%	11,000	12,000	12,000	11,700	11,600

INHIBITOR THERAPEUTICS INC
NBB: INTI

4905 South West Shore Blvd
Tampa, FL 33611
Phone: 813 864-2562
Fax: –
Web: www.inhibitortx.com

CEO: Francis E O'Donnell
CFO: James A McNulty
HR: –
FYE: December 31
Type: Public

Development-stage drug maker HedgePath Pharmaceuticals wants to move beyond fungal infections. The company is evaluating its primary product, the anti-fungal agent itraconazole, as a potential treatment for cancer. It is engaged in clinical trials, with initial emphasis on skin, prostate, and lung cancers in the US market. Founded in 1992 as Commonwealth Biotechnologies, the company filed for Chapter 11 bankruptcy in early 2011. It emerged in 2013 as publicly traded HedgePath Pharmaceuticals.

	Annual Growth	12/18	12/19	12/20	12/21	12/22
Sales ($mil.)	–	–	–	–	–	–
Net income ($ mil.)	–	(4.6)	(2.7)	(1.1)	(0.3)	12.1
Market value ($ mil.)	13.3%	10.3	9.6	6.0	25.7	17.0
Employees	(3.8%)	7	2	2	2	6

INNODATA INC
NMS: INOD

55 Challenger Road
Ridgefield Park, NJ 07660
Phone: 201 371-8000
Fax: –
Web: www.innodata.com

CEO: Jack S Abuhoff
CFO: Mark A Spelker
HR: Marcia Novero
FYE: December 31
Type: Public

Innodata handles information inundation. The company provides content management and process outsourcing services to businesses and government agencies mainly in the US and Europe. It oversees abstracting and indexing, data capture and entry, research and analysis, and technical writing, among other tasks. Innodata manages such tasks as digitizing paper documents into a more manageable electronic form. The company also provides IT services such as consulting, systems integration, and software and systems engineering. It primarily serves the media, publishing, and information services industries. Innodata's top clients are Apple, Wolters Kluwer, Bloomberg, and Reed Elsevier.

	Annual Growth	12/19	12/20	12/21	12/22	12/23
Sales ($mil.)	11.6%	55.9	58.2	69.8	79.0	86.8
Net income ($ mil.)	–	(1.6)	0.6	(1.7)	(11.9)	(0.9)
Market value ($ mil.)	63.5%	32.8	152.4	170.2	85.3	234.0
Employees	4.2%	3,640	3,769	4,931	4,209	4,296

INNOPHOS HOLDINGS, INC.

259 PROSPECT PLAINS RD BLDG A
CRANBURY, NJ 085123706
Phone: 609 495-2495
Fax: –
Web: www.innophos.com

CEO: Richard Hooper
CFO: Dennis Loughran
HR: Elaine Baez
FYE: December 31
Type: Private

Innophos Holdings adds a dash of its phosphate products to food, beverages, health and nutrition, and industrial specialties. Innophos manufactures specialty phosphates used in consumer products, and industrial applications. The applications for phosphates are wide-ranging and the company sets the industry standard with solutions and products designed to enhance quality of life. Its target markets include food and beverage, health and nutrition, and industrial specialties. It offers a broad portfolio of high-quality nutrition brands and specialty ingredients. Innophos' brands are Advantra Z, Bergavit, Maitake Gold, CranSmart, Chelamax, Physicor, and MycoFusions, among others.

INNOSIGHT CONSULTING, LLC

265 FRANKLIN ST STE 402
BOSTON, MA 021103159
Phone: 781 652-7200
Fax: –
Web: www.innosight.com

CEO: –
CFO: –
HR: –
FYE: December 31
Type: Private

Innosight hopes clients will think its ideas are outtasight. The consulting and training firm helps companies capitalize on disruptive change within their industries by creating a culture of innovation. Its consulting services are aimed at identifying and analyzing market opportunities through market research and advice on product development and deal-making. Innosight also offers tailored workshop series to managers and team members designed to foster innovation within the organization. Founded in 2000, the company has served such clients as Bell Canada, Dow Corning, SAP, and Lockheed Martin.

INNOSPEC INC

NMS: IOSP

8310 South Valley Highway, Suite 350
Englewood, CO 80112
Phone: 303 792-5554
Fax: –
Web: www.innospecinc.com

CEO: Patrick S Williams
CFO: Ian P Cleminson
HR: Debbie Hooker
FYE: December 31
Type: Public

Innospec develops, manufactures, blends, markets and supplies specialty chemicals for use as fuel additives, ingredients. Innospec's Fuel Specialties segment makes chemical additives that enhance fuel efficiency and engine performance, and its Performance Chemicals unit makes several products used in the personal care, home care, agrochemical and mining. Meanwhile, the Oilfield Services provide drilling and production chemical. The company generates about 45% of sales from the US and North America.

	Annual Growth	12/19	12/20	12/21	12/22	12/23
Sales ($mil.)	6.5%	1,513.3	1,193.1	1,483.4	1,963.7	1,948.8
Net income ($ mil.)	5.5%	112.2	28.7	93.1	133.0	139.1
Market value ($ mil.)	4.5%	2,572.3	2,256.5	2,246.6	2,557.9	3,064.7
Employees	4.7%	2,000	1,900	1,900	2,100	2,400

INNOVARO INC.

NBB: INNI

2109 Palm Avenue
Tampa, FL 33605
Phone: 813 754-4330
Fax: –
Web: www.innovaro.com

CEO: Asa Lanum
CFO: Carole R Wright
HR: –
FYE: December 31
Type: Public

Innovaro's mission in life is to turn innovations into profitable ventures. The company (formerly UTEK) provides consultation services to help clients to locate new markets, identify game-changing strategies, and develop new platforms; it also facilitates the sale of licensing deals for potential commercial use. Areas of expertise include biotechnology, energy, geology, manufacturing, and electronics. Founded in 1997, Innovaro has worked with hundreds of big-name clients such as Disney, Johnson & Johnson, and Nokia. The former UTEK changed its name to Innovaro in mid-2010, after a UK consulting firm it had acquired in 2008.

	Annual Growth	09/09*	12/09	12/10	12/11	12/12
Sales ($mil.)	(59.1%)	7.8	3.0	13.1	14.9	0.5
Net income ($ mil.)	–	(9.3)	(0.6)	(19.1)	(4.6)	(10.0)
Market value ($ mil.)	(62.6%)	75.6	68.6	23.1	15.5	4.0
Employees	–	–	61	39	31	7

*Fiscal year change

INNOVATE CORP

NYS: VATE

222 Lakeview Ave.., Suite 1660
West Palm Beach, FL 33401
Phone: 212 235-2691
Fax: –
Web: www.hc2.com

CEO: Paul K Voigt
CFO: Michael J Sena
HR: Will Trujillo
FYE: December 31
Type: Public

INNOVATE (formerly known as HC2 Holdings) is a diversified holding company, which seeks opportunities to grow businesses that can generate long-term sustainable free cash flow and attractive returns to maximize value for all stakeholders. INNOVATE has a diverse array of operating subsidiaries across multiple reportable segments, including Infrastructure, Spectrum, and Life Sciences, plus the company's Other segment. INNOVATE's largest operating subsidiary is DBM Global Inc., a family of companies providing fully integrated structural and steel construction services. Founded in 1994, the company announced in late 2021 its successful name change from HC2 Holdings, Inc. to INNOVATE Corp.

	Annual Growth	12/19	12/20	12/21	12/22	12/23
Sales ($mil.)	(8.0%)	1,984.1	1,005.8	1,205.2	1,637.3	1,423.0
Net income ($ mil.)	–	(31.5)	(92.0)	(227.5)	(35.9)	(35.2)
Market value ($ mil.)	(13.2%)	171.9	258.3	293.2	148.2	97.5
Employees	181.6%	64	2,803	3,902	3,761	4,024

INNOVATIVE CARD TECHNOLOGIES INC

633 West Fifth Street, Suite 2600
Los Angeles, CA 90071
Phone: 310 312-0700
Fax: –
Web: www.incardtech.com

CEO: Richard J Nathan
CFO: Richard J Nathan
HR: –
FYE: December 31
Type: Public

Innovative Card Technologies (ICT) is almost ready to make your plastic more powerful. The company has developed power inlay technology designed for information-bearing plastic cards. The company's primary product is the ICT DisplayCard, which incorporates a battery, circuit, and display on a card the size of a credit card. The DisplayCard offers increased security by ensuring the card is physically present; at the push of a button, the card displays a one-time password that must be used in conjunction with the card for the transaction to be authorized. The DisplayCard can be configured for use as a payment card (debit or credit) or as an RFID access card serving electronic banking or data access needs.

	Annual Growth	12/05	12/06	12/07	12/08	12/09
Sales ($mil.)	271.5%	0.0	0.0	0.4	2.8	4.1
Net income ($ mil.)	–	(2.6)	(6.9)	(14.3)	(8.9)	(5.9)
Market value ($ mil.)	(45.5%)	72.1	126.9	73.3	2.2	6.3
Employees	13.6%	6	12	15	7	10

INNOVATIVE SOFTWARE TECHNOLOGIES INC

2802 North Howard Avenue
Tampa, FL 33607
Phone: 813 920-9435
Fax: –
Web: –

CEO: William White
CFO: –
HR: –
FYE: March 31
Type: Public

Innovative Software Technologies (IST) is looking for a new field to focus on. The company provided business continuity services and products, primarily to small and midsized customers. ITS' offerings included its AcXess Application Continuity Xchange, which provided Web-based access to enterprise applications. IST entered the business continuity market through its 2006 purchase of AcXess; in late 2007 the company agreed to sell the AcXess operations to the AcXess management team. IST plans to acquire a software or services company at some point in the future.

	Annual Growth	03/06	03/07	03/08	03/09	03/10
Sales ($mil.)	–	–	0.1	0.2	0.4	–
Net income ($ mil.)	–	(0.5)	(2.9)	(1.5)	(1.0)	(0.4)
Market value ($ mil.)	(23.1%)	4.0	5.0	2.6	0.0	1.4
Employees	–	–	5	2	1	1

INNOVATIVE SOLUTIONS AND SUPPORT INC
NMS: ISSC

720 Pennsylvania Drive
Exton, PA 19341
Phone: 610 646-9800
Fax: –
Web: www.innovative-ss.com

CEO: Shahram Askarpour
CFO: –
HR: –
FYE: September 30
Type: Public

Pilots use products by Innovative Solutions and Support (IS&S) to gauge their success. The company makes flight information computers, electronic displays, and monitoring systems that measure flight information, such as airspeed, altitude, and engine and fuel data. IS&S's reduced vertical separation minimum (RVSM) system enables planes to fly closer together; engine and fuel displays help pilots track fuel and oil levels and other engine functions. IS&S offers flat-panel displays, which take up less cockpit space than conventional displays. Customers are the US DoD and other government agencies, defense contractors, and commercial/corporate air carriers.

	Annual Growth	09/19	09/20	09/21	09/22	09/23
Sales ($mil.)	18.6%	17.6	21.6	23.0	27.7	34.8
Net income ($ mil.)	34.3%	1.9	3.3	5.1	5.5	6.0
Market value ($ mil.)	12.8%	82.0	119.3	122.5	150.6	132.6
Employees	8.4%	71	86	85	81	98

INNOVIVA INC
NMS: INVA

1350 Old Bayshore Highway Suite 400
Burlingame, CA 94010
Phone: 650 238-9600
Fax: –
Web: www.inva.com

CEO: –
CFO: –
HR: –
FYE: December 31
Type: Public

Innoviva is a company with a portfolio of royalties that include respiratory assets partnered with Glaxo Group Limited (GSK). The company collaborates with GSK to develop and commercialize once-daily products for the treatment of chronic obstructive pulmonary disease (COPD) and asthma. The collaboration has developed three combination products, Relvar, once-daily combination medicine consisting of a LABA, vilanterol, and an inhaled corticosteroid, fluticasone furoate; Anoro Ellipta, once-daily medicine combining a long-acting muscarinic antagonist; and Trelegy Ellipta, once-daily combination medicine consisting of an inhaled corticosteroid, long-acting muscarinic antagonist, and LABA.

	Annual Growth	12/19	12/20	12/21	12/22	12/23
Sales ($mil.)	4.4%	261.0	336.8	391.9	331.3	310.5
Net income ($ mil.)	3.4%	157.3	224.4	265.9	213.9	179.7
Market value ($ mil.)	3.2%	896.4	784.4	1,092.0	838.8	1,015.4
Employees	107.9%	6	5	5	101	112

INNSUITES HOSPITALITY TRUST
ASE: IHT

InnSuites Hospitality Centre, 1730 E. Northern Avenue, Suite 122
Phoenix, AZ 85020
Phone: 602 944-1500
Fax: –
Web: www.innsuitestrust.com

CEO: James F Wirth
CFO: Sylvin Lange
HR: –
FYE: January 31
Type: Public

This company trusts you'll have a night full of sweet dreams while staying at one of its hotels. InnSuites Hospitality Trust wholly-owns and operates five studio and two-room suite hotels in Arizona, New Mexico, and southern California, four of which are co-branded as Best Westerns. The company also provides management services for nine hotels and trademark license services for 11 hotels. InnSuites Hospitality Trust primarily operates through the InnSuites Hotels & Suites and InnSuites Boutique Hotel Collection brands. InnSuites Hospitality Trust operates through its majority-owned affiliate RRF Limited Partnership, which in turn operates through subsidiary InnSuites Hotels.

	Annual Growth	01/19	01/20	01/21	01/22	01/23
Sales ($mil.)	3.7%	6.2	6.6	4.2	6.4	7.1
Net income ($ mil.)	(22.1%)	1.4	(1.7)	(1.6)	0.3	0.5
Market value ($ mil.)	(0.4%)	15.2	14.2	25.4	26.7	14.9
Employees	(9.9%)	120	140	140	76	79

INOGEN, INC
NMS: INGN

301 Coromar Drive
Goleta, CA 93117
Phone: 805 562-0500
Fax: –
Web: www.inogen.com

CEO: Kevin Smith
CFO: Mike Sergesketter
HR: Angela Zoes
FYE: December 31
Type: Public

Inogen is a medical technology company that primarily develops, manufactures and markets innovative portable oxygen concentrators used to provide supplemental oxygen by people with chronic respiratory conditions. The company's proprietary Inogen One systems concentrate the air around the patient to offer a single source of supplemental oxygen anytime, anywhere with a single battery and can be plugged into an outlet when at home, in a car, or in a public place with outlets available. Unlike most suppliers in the market, Inogen sells and rents directly to patients. The US accounts for about 75% of revenue. Inogen was formed in 2001 and went public in early 2014.

	Annual Growth	12/19	12/20	12/21	12/22	12/23
Sales ($mil.)	(3.4%)	361.9	308.5	358.0	377.2	315.7
Net income ($ mil.)	–	21.0	(5.8)	(6.3)	(83.8)	(102.4)
Market value ($ mil.)	(46.8%)	1,593.8	1,042.1	793.0	459.7	128.1
Employees	(4.9%)	1,020	938	1,021	1,026	834

INOTIV INC
NAS: NOTV

2701 Kent Avenue
West Lafayette, IN 47906
Phone: 765 463-4527
Fax: –
Web: www.inotivco.com

CEO: Robert W Leasure Jr
CFO: Beth A Taylor
HR: Jeff Krupp
FYE: September 30
Type: Public

Inotiv is a leading contract research organization (CRO) specializing in nonclinical and analytical drug discovery and development services to the pharmaceutical, chemical, and medical device industries, and sells analytical instruments to the pharmaceutical development and contract research industries. The company's products and services focus on bringing new drugs and medical devices through the discovery and preclinical phases of development, all while increasing efficiency, improving data, and reducing the cost of taking new drugs to market. The vast majority of its total revenue accounts in the US. The company has been providing services involving the research of products and treatment of diseases through products since 1974.

	Annual Growth	09/19	09/20	09/21	09/22	09/23
Sales ($mil.)	90.3%	43.6	60.5	89.6	547.7	572.4
Net income ($ mil.)	–	(0.8)	(4.7)	10.9	(337.0)	(105.1)
Market value ($ mil.)	(3.8%)	92.5	123.2	753.7	434.3	79.4
Employees	58.9%	322	421	567	2,204	2,055

INOVA HEALTH SYSTEM FOUNDATION

8095 INNOVATION PARK DR
FAIRFAX, VA 220314868
Phone: 703 289-2069
Fax: –
Web: www.inova.org

CEO: J S Jones
CFO: Alice H Pope
HR: –
FYE: December 31
Type: Private

Inova Health Foundation provides financial support and assistance to the Inova Health System, which operates a network of not-for-profit community hospitals in northern Virginia. It also supports home health services, heart care programs, clinical research and trials, emergency and urgent care centers, outpatient services and destination institutes. Inova Health serves more than 2 million individuals annually. Its five hospitals are consistently recognized by the Centers for Medicare and Medicaid Services (CMS), US News & World Report Best Hospitals and Leapfrog Hospital Safety Grades for excellence in healthcare. The organization is home to Northern Virginia's only Level 1 Trauma Center and Level 4 Neonatal Intensive Care Unit. Its hospitals have a total of more than 1,950 licensed beds.

	Annual Growth	12/14	12/15	12/17	12/19	12/21
Sales ($mil.)	(13.0%)	–	2,972.1	765.9	821.6	1,284.8
Net income ($ mil.)	31.9%	–	234.8	717.2	763.0	1,237.1
Market value ($ mil.)	–	–	–	–	–	–
Employees	–	–	–	–	–	16,000

INOVA TECHNOLOGY INC

2300 W. Sahara Ave., Suite 800
Las Vegas, NV 89102
Phone: 800 507-2810
Fax: –
Web: www.inovatechnology.com

CEO: –
CFO: –
HR: –
FYE: April 30
Type: Public

Inova Technology has innovative ways of keeping track of things. The company provides radio frequency identification (RFID) scanners and tags through its RighTag subsidiary. Its Trakkers subsidiary offers a tracking solution that allows trade show exhibitors to scan badges of attendees to capture contact information, then store the data in a specially designated Web site for access from any location. Inova Technology also offers IT consulting and computer network services through its Desert Communications subsidiary. Chairman and CEO Adam Radly controls more than half of the company.

	Annual Growth	04/09	04/10	04/11	04/12	04/13
Sales ($mil.)	(4.6%)	22.6	21.0	22.1	21.2	18.7
Net income ($ mil.)	–	–	(2.0)	(7.1)	(3.4)	(1.2)	(6.6)
Market value ($ mil.)	(74.9%)	2.4	1.9	0.1	0.0	0.0
Employees	–	–	–	–	–	75

INOVALON HOLDINGS, INC.

4321 COLLINGTON RD
BOWIE, MD 207162646
Phone: 301 809-4000
Fax: –
Web: www.inovalon.com

CEO: Keith R Dunleavy
CFO: Jonathan R Boldt
HR: –
FYE: December 31
Type: Private

Inovalon wants to innovate the cloud for health care companies. The company provides a cloud-based health care data analytics technology platform used by hospitals, physicians, clinical facilities and patients. Its products provide predictive analytics that can identify gaps in care, quality, data integrity, and financial performance. Inovalon's MORE 2 platform provides data and insight on more than 754,000 physicians; 248,000 clinical facilities; 120 million unique patients (spanning 98% of all U.S. counties); and 9.2 billion discrete entries relating to patient interactions, medical procedures, or changes in patients' medical conditions (which Inovalon refers to as medical events).

INOVIO PHARMACEUTICALS INC. NAS: ION

660 W. Germantown Pike, Suite 110
Plymouth Meeting, PA 19462
Phone: 267 440-4200
Fax: –
Web: www.inovio.com

CEO: –
CFO: –
HR: –
FYE: December 31
Type: Public

INOVIO is a biotechnology company focused on developing and commercializing DNA medicines to help treat and protect people from HPV-associated diseases, cancer, and infectious diseases. INOVIO's DNA medicines in development are delivered using its investigational proprietary smart device to produce immune responses against targeted pathogens and cancers. Its DNA medicines pipeline is comprised of three types of product candidates: prophylactic DNA vaccines, therapeutic DNA immunotherapies, and DNA encoded monoclonal and bispecific antibodies (dMAbs and dBTAs), all of which utilize the two components of its integrated platform, SynCon and CELLECTRA.

	Annual Growth	12/19	12/20	12/21	12/22	12/23
Sales ($mil.)	(32.9%)	4.1	7.4	1.8	10.3	0.8
Net income ($ mil.)	–	(119.4)	(166.4)	(303.7)	(279.8)	(135.1)
Market value ($ mil.)	(37.3%)	75.2	201.7	113.7	35.6	11.6
Employees	(10.9%)	194	262	317	184	122

INPHI CORPORATION

110 RIO ROBLES
SAN JOSE, CA 951341813
Phone: 408 217-7300
Fax: –
Web: www.marvell.com

CEO: –
CFO: Jean Hu
HR: Ryan Turner
FYE: December 31
Type: Private

Inphi is a fabless provider of high-speed analog and mixed signal semiconductor solutions for the communications and cloud markets. Its analog and mixed signal semiconductor solutions provide high signal integrity at leading-edge data speeds while reducing system power consumption. Its semiconductor solutions are designed to address bandwidth bottlenecks in networks, maximize throughput and minimize latency in communication and computing environments and enable the rollout of next generation communications and cloud infrastructures. About 55% of company's revenue comes from China. Inphi was acquired by Marvell Technology, in 2021, creating a US semiconductor powerhouse positioned for end-to-end technology leadership in data infrastructure.

	Annual Growth	12/15	12/16	12/17	12/18	12/19
Sales ($mil.)	2.5%	–	–	348.2	294.5	365.6
Net income ($ mil.)	–	–	–	(74.9)	(95.8)	(72.9)
Market value ($ mil.)	–	–	–	–	–	–
Employees	–	–	–	–	–	616

INRAD OPTICS INC NBB: INRD

181 Legrand Avenue
Northvale, NJ 07647
Phone: 201 767-1910
Fax: –
Web: www.inradoptics.com

CEO: Amy Eskilson
CFO: Theresa A Balog
HR: –
FYE: December 31
Type: Public

Inrad Optics (formerly Photonic Products Group) manufactures products for use in photonics, including custom optics, crystals, and components, and provides thin-film coating services on a contract basis. Its products find applications in laser systems, military gear, semiconductor production equipment, and telecommunications networks. The company's INRAD unit grows and finishes crystals used in commercial laser systems. Its custom optics segment includes waveplates, beam displacers, rotators, and phase-shift plates. Inrad Optics gets about 10% of its sales from overseas customers.

	Annual Growth	12/19	12/20	12/21	12/22	12/23
Sales ($mil.)	6.6%	10.0	9.0	11.4	10.6	12.9
Net income ($ mil.)	–	(0.8)	(0.9)	1.7	0.2	2.7
Market value ($ mil.)	(2.3%)	17.9	7.8	16.5	24.6	16.4
Employees	–	58	51	53	59	–

INROADS, INC.

10 S BROADWAY STE 300
SAINT LOUIS, MO 631021751
Phone: 314 241-7330
Fax: –
Web: www.inroads.org

CEO: Forest T Harper
CFO: Todd D Thomason
HR: –
FYE: August 31
Type: Private

INROADS is helping minority college students blaze trails into corporate America. The company provides a link between corporations and African-American, Hispanic, and Native American students through seminars, career counseling, and internship programs with companies like GE, PricewaterhouseCoopers, and Lockheed Martin. The organization's Retail Management Institute prepares its students for management careers specifically in the retail industry. INROADS, which today has offices all across the US, was founded in 1970 as part of an effort to get more people of color into corporate management positions.

	Annual Growth	05/11	05/12	05/13	05/14*	08/15
Sales ($mil.)	(15.2%)	–	5.2	5.3	4.5	3.2
Net income ($ mil.)	–	–	(0.0)	0.1	0.2	(1.5)
Market value ($ mil.)	–	–	–	–	–	–
Employees	–	–	–	–	–	200

*Fiscal year change

INSEEGO WIRELESS, INC.

9710 SCRANTON RD STE 200
SAN DIEGO, CA 921211744
Phone: 858 812-3400
Fax: –
Web: www.inseego.com

CEO: Ashish Sharma
CFO: Michael Newman
HR: Tina Brunhart
FYE: December 31
Type: Private

Novatel Wireless proves you can take it with you. The company designs wireless modems that let users access the Internet from anywhere. Its MiFi brand of mobile hotspot devices provides wireless connectivity for up to five users at the same time. Novatel also offers a series of wireless PC card modems (Merlin), embedded wireless modules for OEMs (Expedite), and desktop wireless gateway consoles (Ovation). Its MobiLink software, bundled with modems and embedded modules, connects mobile devices with wireless LANs. Novatel also offers activation, provisioning, and integration services. The company gets most sales from North America.

INSIGHT ENTERPRISES INC.   NMS: NSIT

2701 E. Insight Way
Chandler, AZ 85286
Phone: 480 333-3000
Fax: –
Web: www.insight.com

CEO: Kenneth T Lamneck
CFO: Glynis A Bryan
HR: –
FYE: December 31
Type: Public

Insight Enterprises distributes computer hardware and software and provides IT services for public and private sectors, schools, and government agencies. The company offers thousands of products from hundreds of manufacturers (including Microsoft, HP Inc., Dell, Lenovo, and Cisco), as well as cloud solutions. Geographically, Insight gets approximately 75% of sales from customers in the US, and, in terms of customers, its large business clients provide about 70% of sales. Insight began operations in Arizona in 1988, incorporated in Delaware in 1991 and completed its initial public offering in 1995.

	Annual Growth	12/19	12/20	12/21	12/22	12/23
Sales ($mil.)	4.4%	7,731.2	8,340.6	9,436.1	10,431	9,175.8
Net income ($ mil.)	15.3%	159.4	172.6	219.3	280.6	281.3
Market value ($ mil.)	26.0%	2,290.8	2,479.8	3,474.1	3,267.8	5,774.6
Employees	6.4%	11,261	11,006	11,624	13,448	14,437

INSMED INC   NMS: INSM

700 US Highway 202/206
Bridgewater, NJ 08807
Phone: 908 977-9900
Fax: –
Web: www.insmed.com

CEO: William H Lewis
CFO: Sara Bonstein
HR: –
FYE: December 31
Type: Public

Insmed Incorporated is a global biopharmaceutical company on a mission to transform the lives of patients with serious and rare diseases. Its first commercial products, inhaled Arikayce is for the treatment of lung disease in patients who haven't responded to conventional treatment. Insmed clinical-stage pipeline includes brensocatib and TPIP. Brensocatib is a small molecule, oral, reversible inhibitor of dipeptidyl peptidase 1 (DPP1), which the company is developing for the treatment of patients with bronchiectasis and other neutrophil-mediated diseases. TPIP is an inhaled formulation of the treprostinil prodrug treprostinil palmitil which may offer a differentiated product profile for pulmonary arterial hypertension (PAH) and pulmonary hypertension associated with interstitial lung disease (PH-ILD). Majority of its sales come from the US.

	Annual Growth	12/19	12/20	12/21	12/22	12/23
Sales ($mil.)	22.3%	136.5	164.4	188.5	245.4	305.2
Net income ($ mil.)	–	(254.3)	(294.1)	(434.7)	(481.5)	(749.6)
Market value ($ mil.)	6.7%	3,533.7	4,926.2	4,030.9	2,956.6	4,585.8
Employees	20.3%	435	521	613	736	912

INSPERITY INC   NYS: NSP

19001 Crescent Springs Drive
Kingwood, TX 77339
Phone: 281 358-8986
Fax: –
Web: www.insperity.com

CEO: Paul J Sarvadi
CFO: Douglas S Sharp
HR: –
FYE: December 31
Type: Public

Insperity handles and provides an array of human resources services to small and midsize companies in the US. As a professional employer organization (PEO), Insperity offers payroll and benefits administration, workers' compensation programs, and personnel records management through its flagship Workforce Optimization product. The company also offers recruiting, performance management, and training and development services. Through its cloud-based software solution, the company is able to offer other services such as organizational planning, employment screening, and insurance services, among others.

	Annual Growth	12/19	12/20	12/21	12/22	12/23
Sales ($mil.)	10.7%	4,314.8	4,287.0	4,973.1	5,938.8	6,485.9
Net income ($ mil.)	3.2%	151.1	138.2	124.1	179.4	171.4
Market value ($ mil.)	8.0%	3,207.7	3,035.4	4,403.3	4,235.1	4,370.1
Employees	5.9%	3,500	3,600	3,600	4,100	4,400

INSPIRA HEALTH NETWORK, INC.

2950 COLLEGE DR STE 2D
VINELAND, NJ 083606933
Phone: 856 641-8000
Fax: –
Web: www.inspirahealthnetwork.org

CEO: John A Diangelo
CFO: William Pelino
HR: Julie H Ellis
FYE: December 31
Type: Private

Inspira wants to inspire folks from South Jersey to stay healthy. The network operates health care facilities in a five-county area in southern New Jersey. Its three hospitals include Inspira Medical Centers located in Vineland (260-bed facility with specialty cancer and diagnostic centers), Elmer (100 beds), and Woodbury (300-beds). The system also includes the 65-bed Health Center Bridgeton, a mental health and hospice facility. Inspira also offers outpatient care, home care services, and about 60 community-based health clinics and wellness programs.

	Annual Growth	12/18	12/19	12/20	12/21	12/22
Sales ($mil.)	8.3%	–	–	–	29.6	32.0
Net income ($ mil.)	–	–	–	–	0.8	(0.5)
Market value ($ mil.)	–	–	–	–	–	–
Employees	–	–	–	–	–	3,063

INSTALLED BUILDING PRODUCTS INC   NYS: IBP

495 South High Street, Suite 50
Columbus, OH 43215
Phone: 614 221-3399
Fax: –
Web: www.installedbuildingproducts.com

CEO: Jeffrey W Edwards
CFO: Michael T Miller
HR: –
FYE: December 31
Type: Public

Installed Building Products, Inc. (IBP) is one of the nation's largest insulation installers for the residential new construction market and is also a diversified installer of complementary building products, including waterproofing, fire-stopping and fireproofing, garage doors, rain gutters, shower doors, closet shelving and mirrors, throughout the US. The company manages all aspects of the installation process for its customers, including direct purchases of materials from national manufacturers, supply of materials to job sites and quality installation. It offers its portfolio of services for new and existing single-family and multi-family residential and commercial building projects from its national network of branch locations.

	Annual Growth	12/19	12/20	12/21	12/22	12/23
Sales ($mil.)	16.4%	1,511.6	1,653.2	1,968.7	2,669.8	2,778.6
Net income ($ mil.)	37.5%	68.2	97.2	118.8	223.4	243.7
Market value ($ mil.)	27.6%	1,953.7	2,891.5	3,963.5	2,428.2	5,186.1
Employees	5.7%	8,500	8,950	9,500	10,300	10,600

INSTEEL INDUSTRIES, INC.   NYS: IIIN

1373 Boggs Drive
Mount Airy, NC 27030
Phone: 336 786-2141
Fax: –
Web: www.insteel.com

CEO: H O Woltz III
CFO: Scot R Jafroodi
HR: –
FYE: September 30
Type: Public

Insteel Industries manufactures steel welded wire reinforcement (WWR), which is used primarily in concrete construction materials; pre-stressed concrete strand (PC strand); engineered structural mesh (ESM); concrete pipe reinforcement (CPR); and standard welded wire reinforcement (SWWR). Its PC strand products are the spine for concrete structures, from bridges to parking garages. Insteel's customers include manufacturers of concrete products, distributors, and rebar fabricators and contractors. A majority of its sales come from manufacturers of non-residential concrete construction products. The US is responsible for a majority of the company's total sales. The company was founded in 1953 by Howard O. Woltz, Jr.

	Annual Growth	09/19*	10/20	10/21	10/22*	09/23
Sales ($mil.)	9.2%	455.7	472.6	590.6	826.8	649.2
Net income ($ mil.)	55.1%	5.6	19.0	66.6	125.0	32.4
Market value ($ mil.)	11.9%	402.9	368.7	758.7	516.1	631.5
Employees	1.5%	834	881	913	964	884

*Fiscal year change

INSTITUTE FOR DEFENSE ANALYSES INC

730 E GLEBE RD
ALEXANDRIA, VA 223053086
Phone: 703 845-2000
Fax: –
Web: www.ida.org

CEO: Norton Schwartz
CFO: –
HR: –
FYE: September 30
Type: Private

The Institute for Defense Analyses (IDA) provides technical analyses of weapons. The institute is a federally-funded organization that works for the US government's defense agencies, as well as for other government entities. The Institute for Defense Analyses' Science and Technology Policy Institute analyzes global science and tech trends to help the US government formulate policy.

	Annual Growth	09/18	09/19	09/20	09/21	09/22
Sales ($mil.)	6.1%	–	260.3	248.2	270.1	311.3
Net income ($ mil.)	58.4%	–	6.1	8.0	22.6	24.3
Market value ($ mil.)	–	–	–	–	–	–
Employees	–	–	–	–	–	1,500

INSTITUTE OF GAS TECHNOLOGY

1700 S MOUNT PROSPECT RD
DES PLAINES, IL 600181804
Phone: 847 768-0500
Fax: –
Web: www.gti.energy

CEO: David C Carroll
CFO: James Ingold
HR: Alyssa Ressinger
FYE: December 31
Type: Private

Natural gas burns more cleanly and efficiently thanks to the Institute of Gas Technology (dba Gas Technology Institute, or GTI), which provides engineering, research, development, and training services for energy and environmental companies, consumers, and government clients. GTI's research focuses on expanded energy supply, reduced energy delivery costs, efficient energy use, and clean energy systems, primarily in the natural gas sector. Natural gas companies, as well as large energy consumers and private industry firms comprise the majority of GTI's client base. The not-for-profit company's contract services range from market and technology analysis to product development, testing, and commercialization.

	Annual Growth	12/13	12/14	12/15	12/17	12/21
Sales ($mil.)	9.6%	–	56.8	71.8	79.9	107.5
Net income ($ mil.)	–	–	(1.4)	8.2	11.1	(0.2)
Market value ($ mil.)	–	–	–	–	–	–
Employees	–	–	–	–	–	281

INSTITUTE OF THE AMERICAS

10111 N TORREY PINES RD
LA JOLLA, CA 920371017
Phone: 858 453-5560
Fax: –
Web: www.iamericas.org

CEO: –
CFO: Nora Livesay
HR: –
FYE: December 31
Type: Private

Not to be confused with School of the Americas, the Institute of the Americas (IOA) works for peace and understanding among people of North and South America. The group is an independent, nonprofit and inter-American institution that promotes development, trade and investment, and good governance through cooperation between the public and private sectors throughout the Americas. IOA programs are focused on energy, healthcare, telecommunication and information technology, and water. The group holds an annual conference and about 15 smaller meetings through out Latin America that bring together public groups and private enterprises working in the region. The institute was formed in 1983.

	Annual Growth	12/17	12/18	12/19	12/21	12/22
Sales ($mil.)	7.3%	–	1.1	6.2	1.3	1.5
Net income ($ mil.)	–	–	(0.8)	4.5	(0.5)	(0.5)
Market value ($ mil.)	–	–	–	–	–	–
Employees	–	–	–	–	–	15

INSULET CORP   NMS: PODD

100 Nagog Park
Acton, MA 01720
Phone: 978 600-7000
Fax: –
Web: www.insulet.com

CEO: James R Hollingshead
CFO: Lauren Budden
HR: –
FYE: December 31
Type: Public

Insulet Corporation is primarily engaged in the development, manufacture and sale of its proprietary Omnipod System, a continuous insulin delivery system for people with insulin-dependent diabetes. The Omnipod System includes the Omnipod Insulin Management System (Omnipod), the Omnipod DASH Insulin Management System (Omnipod DASH), its digital mobile Omnipod platform and the Omnipod 5 Automated Insulin Delivery System (Omnipod 5). Most of its drug delivery revenue consists of sales of pods to Amgen for use in the Neulasta Onpro kit, a delivery system for Amgen's Neulasta to help reduce the risk of infection after intense chemotherapy. The US is the company's largest market which accounts for more than 70% of total revenue.

	Annual Growth	12/19	12/20	12/21	12/22	12/23
Sales ($mil.)	23.1%	738.2	904.4	1,098.8	1,305.3	1,697.1
Net income ($ mil.)	105.4%	11.6	6.8	16.8	4.6	206.3
Market value ($ mil.)	6.1%	11,968	17,870	18,600	20,580	15,168
Employees	22.1%	1,350	1,900	2,300	2,600	3,000

INTEGER HOLDINGS CORP   NYS: ITGR

5830 Granite Parkway, Suite 1150
Plano, TX 75024
Phone: 214 618-5243
Fax: –
Web: www.integer.net

CEO: Joseph W Dziedzic
CFO: Diron Smith
HR: Carlie Kohn
FYE: December 31
Type: Public

Integer Holdings is one of the world's largest medical devices outsource (MDO) manufacturing companies and serves the cardiac rhythm management, neuromodulation, orthopedics, vascular, advanced surgical, and portable medical markets. The company provides innovative, high quality medical technologies that enhance the lives of patients worldwide and develop batteries for high-end niche applications in energy, military, and environmental markets. Integer brands include Greatbatch Medical, Lake Region Medical, and Electrochem. The company's primary customers include large, multi-national original equipment manufacturers (OEMs) and their affiliated subsidiaries. The US is the company's largest single market, accounting for about 55% of total revenue.

	Annual Growth	12/19	12/20	12/21	12/22	12/23
Sales ($mil.)	6.1%	1,258.1	1,073.4	1,221.1	1,376.1	1,596.7
Net income ($ mil.)	(1.5%)	96.3	77.3	96.8	66.4	90.7
Market value ($ mil.)	5.4%	2,680.7	2,706.0	2,852.7	2,281.7	3,302.3
Employees	6.2%	8,250	7,500	9,000	10,000	10,500

INTEGRA LIFESCIENCES HOLDINGS CORP   NMS: IART

1100 Campus Road
Princeton, NJ 08540
Phone: 609 275-0500
Fax: -
Web: www.integralife.com

CEO: Peter J Arduini
CFO: Carrie Anderson
HR: Lisa Evoli
FYE: December 31
Type: Public

Integra LifeSciences is a global leader in regenerative tissue technologies and neurological solutions company. The company develops medical equipment used in cranial procedures, small bone and joint reconstruction, and the repair and reconstruction of soft tissue, nerves, and tendons. Integra's products include tissue ablation equipment, drainage catheters, bone fixation devices, regenerative technologies, and basic surgical instruments. Its products are marketed in more than 130 countries through direct sales and distributors. The US market accounts for more than 70% of revenue. Integra was founded in 1989 by Richard Caruso.

	Annual Growth	12/19	12/20	12/21	12/22	12/23
Sales ($mil.)	0.4%	1,517.6	1,371.9	1,542.4	1,557.7	1,541.6
Net income ($ mil.)	7.8%	50.2	133.9	169.1	180.6	67.7
Market value ($ mil.)	(7.0%)	4,555.7	5,074.7	5,236.5	4,382.9	3,404.3
Employees	(0.3%)	4,000	3,700	3,800	3,722	3,946

INTEGRAL TECHNOLOGIES INC.

412 Mulberry
Marietta, OH 45750
Phone: 812 550-1770
Fax: -
Web: www.itkg.net

CEO: Doug Bathauer
CFO: Eli Dusenbury
HR: -
FYE: June 30
Type: Public

Integral Technologies hopes to discover that technology truly is integral to everyday life. The company has developed what it calls its "ElectriPlast" product, an electrically conductive resin-based polymer that can be molded into any shape. The company's "PlasTenna" technology uses ElectriPlast for antenna design and other manufacturing processes. It can become part of the cell phone casing itself. Integral Technologies outsources its manufacturing and is marketing its products to cell phone and other wireless device manufacturers. The development stage company has yet to recognize any appreciable revenues from its products.

	Annual Growth	06/13	06/14	06/15	06/16	06/17
Sales ($mil.)	-	-	0.0	0.2	0.0	0.0
Net income ($ mil.)	-	(3.7)	(4.5)	(4.4)	(4.6)	(5.7)
Market value ($ mil.)	(51.2%)	113.4	60.7	128.4	32.4	6.5
Employees	-	-	-	-	-	-

INTEGRAL VISION INC.   NBB: INVI

49113 Wixom Tech Drive
Wixom, MI 48393
Phone: 248 668-9230
Fax: 248 668-9384
Web: www.iv-usa.com

CEO: -
CFO: -
HR: -
FYE: December 31
Type: Public

Integral Vision wants manufacturers to take a closer look. The company makes machine vision systems that monitor and control manufacturing processes in the small flat-panel display industry. Its systems inspect for both cosmetic and functional defects in display components used in camcorders, cell phones, digital still cameras, computer monitors, and handheld video games. Integral Vision also offers software for developing machine vision inspection applications. Customers have included Liquavista, QUALCOMM, Samsung Electronics, and Texas Instruments.

	Annual Growth	12/07	12/08	12/09	12/10	12/11
Sales ($mil.)	(17.8%)	1.2	1.0	1.8	1.6	0.5
Net income ($ mil.)	-	(3.0)	(10.7)	(2.8)	(2.4)	(3.1)
Market value ($ mil.)	(30.9%)	2.5	5.7	2.1	0.9	0.6
Employees	(10.5%)	14	14	10	9	9

INTEGRATED BIOPHARMA INC   NBB: INBP

225 Long Ave.
Hillside, NJ 07205
Phone: 888 319-6962
Fax: -
Web: www.integratedbiopharma.com

CEO: Christina Kay
CFO: Dina L Masi
HR: -
FYE: June 30
Type: Public

Integrated BioPharma has taken a bounty of businesses and coalesced them into the cohesive nutraceuticals manufacturer it is today. Through numerous subsidiaries Integrated BioPharma manufactures and distributes vitamins, nutritional supplements, herbal products, and natural chemicals. Subsidiaries include AgroLabs (nutritional drinks, vitamins, supplements), Chem International (vitamins), IHT Health Products (natural chemicals), Manhattan Drug Company (vitamins and nutritional supplements sold to distributors, multi-level marketers, and specialized health care providers), and Vitamin Factory (sells private-label Manhattan Drug products online and via mail order catalogue).

	Annual Growth	06/19	06/20	06/21	06/22	06/23
Sales ($mil.)	0.3%	50.0	52.8	63.6	56.2	50.7
Net income ($ mil.)	-	1.7	4.1	8.0	3.8	(0.0)
Market value ($ mil.)	9.5%	6.9	13.5	32.9	15.0	9.9
Employees	0.7%	137	143	147	147	141

INTEGRATED BUSINESS SYSTEMS & SERVICES, INC.   NBB: IBSS

115 Atrium Way, Suite 228
Columbia, SC 29223
Phone: 803 736-5595
Fax: 803 736-5639
Web: -

CEO: George Mendenhall
CFO: Michael P Bernard
HR: -
FYE: December 31
Type: Public

Integrated Business Systems and Services (IBSS) helps manufacturers make all sorts of ends meet. IBSS' software enables large and midsized manufacturers to enhance existing enterprise resource-planning software by automating manufacturing and printing processes and tying together supply chains. Its products include applications for automating shop floor operations, integrating disparate systems and programs, and collecting data through RFID. The company also resells third-party hardware and provides such services as consulting, implementation, and custom software design.

	Annual Growth	12/00	12/01	12/02	12/03	12/04
Sales ($mil.)	(3.9%)	2.4	3.7	3.4	3.3	2.0
Net income ($ mil.)	-	(4.2)	(11.3)	(3.2)	(0.8)	(1.9)
Market value ($ mil.)	(47.3%)	121.9	52.0	5.5	17.6	9.4
Employees	(15.1%)	54	40	27	27	28

INTEGRATED CONTROL SYSTEMS, INC.

4020 VASSAR DR NE STE H
ALBUQUERQUE, NM 871072058
Phone: 505 884-3503
Fax: -
Web: www.icsicontrols.com

CEO: -
CFO: -
HR: -
FYE: December 31
Type: Private

Integrated Control Systems, Inc. (ICSI) designs custom integration and automation systems to manage and control facility environments. Its systems monitor and control lighting, fire and security, heating, cooling, and ventilation equipment in commercial and institutional structures. Some of ICSI's product and service suppliers include Automated Logic, Veris, Siemens, and Dynacon. The company's clients have included The University of New Mexico Hospital, the Los Alamos National Laboratory, The University of Arizona, and the Center for Creative Leadership. ICSI operates through offices in the southwestern US. President Steven Chavez founded the company in 1996.

	Annual Growth	12/03	12/04	12/05	12/06	12/10
Sales ($mil.)	3.2%	-	-	13.3	12.1	15.5
Net income ($ mil.)	7.8%	-	-	1.2	0.2	1.7
Market value ($ mil.)	-	-	-	-	-	-
Employees	-	-	-	-	-	110

INTEGRATED DATA CORP

625 West Ridge Pike, Suite C-106
Conshohocken, PA 19428
Phone: 610 825-6224
Fax: –
Web: www.integrateddatacorp.com

CEO: David C Bryan
CFO: –
HR: –
FYE: June 30
Type: Public

Integrated Data Corp. (IDC) is a holding company with interests in technology, natural resources, and real estate. Its holdings include wholly owned wireless communications company C3 Technologies and stakes in IDC Palm Energy (oil and gas wells) and Montana Holdings (international property investor and developer of the Rum Bay Resort Marina in the Bahamas). Its majority-owned New England Land Resources also holds Bahamian resort interests. IDC is increasingly focused on its resort operations; it divested an Italian wireless subsidiary as well as its stake in DataWave Systems.

	Annual Growth	06/02	06/03	06/04	06/05	06/06
Sales ($mil.)	–	–	4.0	18.2	0.3	0.0
Net income ($ mil.)	–	(3.6)	2.9	(2.9)	(0.8)	0.4
Market value ($ mil.)	199.1%	0.0	30.7	8.0	7.9	3.2
Employees	–	–	2	2	2	–

INTEGRATED MANAGEMENT SERVICES, P.A.

126 E AMITE ST
JACKSON, MS 392012101
Phone: 601 968-9194
Fax: –
Web: www.imsengineers.com

CEO: John Calhoun
CFO: –
HR: –
FYE: December 31
Type: Private

Integrated Management Services, which operates as IMS Engineers, provides engineering, consulting, and construction management services. IMS offers its services to a variety of industries; projects include aviation, environmental, transportation, water, and wastewater facilities. It has offices in Jackson, Mississippi; Memphis; New Orleans (where it participates in Hurricane Katrina recovery work); and Detroit, Michigan. The city of Jackson, Mississippi and Nissan Motor are among the company's customers. The minority-owned IMS was formed in 1996 by CEO John Calhoun and President Rod Hill. It is a mainstay on Inc. magazine's list of the fastest-growing private companies in the US.

	Annual Growth	12/03	12/04	12/05	12/06	12/08
Sales ($mil.)	(30.1%)	–	–	13.6	17.3	4.6
Net income ($ mil.)	–	–	–	1.0	4.2	(0.4)
Market value ($ mil.)	–	–	–	–	–	–
Employees	–	–	–	–	–	45

INTEGRATED PROJECT MANAGEMENT COMPANY, INC.

60 N FRONTAGE RD STE 300
BURR RIDGE, IL 605277282
Phone: 630 789-8600
Fax: –
Web: www.ipmcinc.com

CEO: C R Panico
CFO: Joann Jackson
HR: Aby S Sph
FYE: January 31
Type: Private

Integrated Project Management (IPM) is a consulting company that specializes in providing onsite project management services and related consulting services to a wide range of corporate customers. Tackling complex projects, often for highly regulated industries, the company helps clients define project timelines and strategies and assists with establishing and maintaining budgets. The consulting firm also offers process improvement consulting once a project has been completed. It has offices in Chicago, Boston, San Francisco, Los Angeles, Minneapolis, and St. Louis.

	Annual Growth	01/02	01/03	01/04	01/06	01/07
Sales ($mil.)	7.4%	–	8.3	6.6	7.9	11.1
Net income ($ mil.)	34.6%	–	0.0	0.0	0.1	0.3
Market value ($ mil.)	–	–	–	–	–	–
Employees	–	–	–	–	–	80

INTEGRATED SILICON SOLUTION, INC.

1623 BUCKEYE DR
MILPITAS, CA 950357423
Phone: 408 969-6600
Fax: –
Web: www.issi.com

CEO: Jimmy Lee
CFO: –
HR: Amy Guiriba
FYE: September 30
Type: Private

Fabless semiconductor company Integrated Silicon Solution, Inc. (ISSI) has the right acronyms for the manufacturing process. ISSI primarily makes SRAM (static random-access memory) chips and DRAM (dynamic RAM) chips that are used in cars, computers, consumer electronics, cell phones, and networking devices. It sells its chips to dozens of electronics manufacturers, from the automotive, communications, consumer, industrial, medical, and military markets, either directly or through distributors and contract manufacturers. Customers include Bosch, Cisco, GE, and Samsung. Most of its sales come from Asia. In late 2015 ISSI was acquired by Uphill Investment.

INTEGRIS BAPTIST MEDICAL CENTER, INC.

3300 NW EXPRESSWAY
OKLAHOMA CITY, OK 731124418
Phone: 405 949-3011
Fax: –
Web: www.integrishealth.org

CEO: –
CFO: –
HR: –
FYE: June 30
Type: Private

INTEGRIS Baptist Medical Center seeks integrity by caring for citizens from across the state of Oklahoma. The Oklahoma City-based medical center is the flagship hospital of the not-for-profit INTEGRIS Health system. With about 510 beds, INTEGRIS Baptist is home to specialty care facilities for burns, women's and children's health, infertility, stroke treatment, cardiac care, organ transplantation, cancer treatment, and more. The company also has centers for wellness, hearing, sleep disorders, senior health, and weight loss, and it provides medical training and residency programs. INTEGRIS Baptist Medical Center opened its doors in 1959 with 200 beds.

	Annual Growth	06/17	06/18	06/20	06/21	06/22
Sales ($mil.)	6.6%	–	814.1	950.5	1,051.5	1,049.8
Net income ($ mil.)	–	–	67.7	(14.4)	192.0	(33.0)
Market value ($ mil.)	–	–	–	–	–	–
Employees	–	–	–	–	–	2,700

INTEGRIS HEALTH, INC.

3300 NW EXPRESSWAY
OKLAHOMA CITY, OK 731124418
Phone: 405 949-6066
Fax: –
Web: www.integrishealth.org

CEO: Bruce Lawrence
CFO: David Hadley
HR: –
FYE: June 30
Type: Private

INTEGRIS Health is Oklahoma's largest not-for-profit and owned health care systems, with hospitals, rehabilitation centers, physician clinics, mental health facilities and home health agencies throughout much of the state. Its flagship hospital, INTEGRIS Baptist Medical Center is a center of leading-edge medicine, housing nine Centers of Excellence, including a full-service heart hospital, a comprehensive transplant institute and one of the nation's foremost burn centers. Its Lakeside Women's Hospital is a fully Licensed Joint Commission accredited hospital designed exclusively for women. The hospitals provide services including primary care, breast health, cancer care, gynecology, surgery, lung care, transplant, and rehabilitation & physical care and more.

	Annual Growth	06/18	06/19	06/20	06/21	06/22
Sales ($mil.)	6.4%	–	1,950.1	2,078.0	2,250.5	2,346.1
Net income ($ mil.)	–	–	11.6	(172.0)	300.2	(40.6)
Market value ($ mil.)	–	–	–	–	–	–
Employees	–	–	–	–	–	9,500

INTEL CORP
NMS: INTC

2200 Mission College Boulevard
Santa Clara, CA 95054-1549
Phone: 408 765-8080
Fax: 408 765-2633
Web: www.intc.com

CEO: Patrick P Gelsinger
CFO: David A Zinsner
HR: –
FYE: December 30
Type: Public

Intel offers platform products that incorporate various components and technologies, including a microprocessor and chipset, a stand-alone SoC, or a multichip package. The company makes use of technology such as Artificial Intelligence, pervasive connectivity, cloud to edge, and ubiquitous computing to its operations and interact with its products. The company's latest data center solutions target a wide range of use cases within cloud computing, network infrastructure, and intelligent edge applications, and support high-growth workloads, including AI and 5G. About 74% of its revenue comes from international customers. Intel was founded in 1968.

	Annual Growth	12/19	12/20	12/21	12/22	12/23
Sales ($mil.)	(6.8%)	71,965	77,867	79,024	63,054	54,228
Net income ($ mil.)	(46.8%)	21,048	20,899	19,868	8,014.0	1,689.0
Market value ($ mil.)	(4.4%)	254,018	199,012	216,939	111,746	212,457
Employees	3.0%	110,800	110,600	121,100	131,900	124,800

INTELIQUENT, INC.

1 N WACKER DR STE 2500
CHICAGO, IL 606062825
Phone: 855 404-4768
Fax: –
Web: www.sinch.com

CEO: Ed O'Hara
CFO: Michael Donahue
HR: Angela Dyer
FYE: December 31
Type: Private

Inteliquent powers communications for the top communication service providers, unified communications as a service providers and partners. The foundation of Inteliquent's communications platform as a service (CPaaS) is its fully redundant, geo-diverse, carrier-grade tier 1 network. This network is trusted by the nation's largest service providers, as it provides the most expansive footprint of local phone numbers in the United States with over 12,200 on-net rate centers and 300 billion minutes of traffic on the network annually.

INTELLABRIDGE TECHNOLOGY CORP
NBB: KASH F

2060 Broadway Suite B1
Boulder, CO 80302
Phone: 303 578-3578
Fax: 604 682-4768
Web: www.intellabridge.com

CEO: –
CFO: –
HR: –
FYE: December 31
Type: Public

Afrasia Mineral Fields doesn't have mining operations in Africa or Asia, but it does do business in Canada. The company is looking to acquire or partner with other mineral exploration businesses in its sector. It found something it liked in 2010 when it agreed to buy a copper project in Arizona for about $12.5 million. Afrasia Mineral Fields is managed and administered by venture capital firm Varshney Capital. Praveen Varshney, CEO of Afrasia Mineral Fields, also heads up Varshney Capital.

INTELLECT DESIGN ARENA INC.

20 CORPORATE PL S
PISCATAWAY, NJ 088546144
Phone: 732 769-1037
Fax: –
Web: www.intellectai.com

CEO: Pranav Pasricha
CFO: –
HR: –
FYE: March 31
Type: Private

Seek and ye shall find a legacy of mainframe transformation. SEEC develops and supports software that readies legacy computer systems for the Internet. Its products automate the integration of older programs with newer applications by tying together business rule management, legacy software components, and Web services. The company also provides specialized software for the health care and insurance industry, as well as professional services, such as training and maintenance. Customers include Cognizant Technology Solutions, Computer Sciences, and SeeBeyond Technology. The company was acquired in 2008 by India-based Polaris Software Lab and does business as Intellect SEEC.

	Annual Growth	03/14	03/15	03/16	03/17	03/18
Sales ($mil.)	22.8%	–	7.8	10.8	12.6	14.4
Net income ($ mil.)	–	–	(4.2)	(5.6)	(1.0)	2.4
Market value ($ mil.)	–	–	–	–	–	–
Employees	–	–	–	–	–	100

INTELLICHECK INC
NMS: IDN

200 Broadhollow Road, Suite 207
Melville, NY 11747
Phone: 516 992-1900
Fax: –
Web: www.icmobil.com

CEO: –
CFO: –
HR: –
FYE: December 31
Type: Public

IntelliCheck Mobilisa will need to see some ID. The company provides handheld electronic card readers and related software for the commercial, government, and military markets. Used to secure military and federal government locations, its Defense ID System can read barcodes, magnetic stripes, optical character recognition (OCR), and radio frequency identification (RFID) codes. Its ID-Check systems are designed to verify the age and identity of customers who swipe a driver's license, military ID, or other magnetically encoded ID card. The company has installed systems in airports, bars, casinos, convenience stores, hotels, and stadiums.

	Annual Growth	12/18	12/19	12/20	12/21	12/22
Sales ($mil.)	37.8%	4.4	7.7	10.7	16.4	16.0
Net income ($ mil.)	–	(4.0)	(2.5)	0.6	(4.1)	(3.9)
Market value ($ mil.)	(1.7%)	40.6	142.0	216.2	87.6	37.9
Employees	11.7%	34	34	37	49	53

INTELLIDYNE, L.L.C.

1950 OLD GALLOWS RD STE 750
VIENNA, VA 221823990
Phone: 703 575-9715
Fax: –
Web: www.intellidyne-llc.com

CEO: –
CFO: Carlos Salazar
HR: Marisa Krafsig
FYE: December 31
Type: Private

IntelliDyne likes to think it takes a smarter approach to solving IT problems. The company consults with US government and commercial customers to help them plan, design, install, lease, and manage information technology systems and services. Its areas of expertise include network security, cloud computing, custom software development, business process management, and data center consolidation. IntelliDyne primarily serves defense, homeland security, law enforcement, and civilian agencies. The US Department of Defense, its largest client, uses its services primarily to support medical centers and hospitals. The company was established in 1999 by president Robert Grey.

INTELLISYS TECHNOLOGY, L.L.C.

700 COMMERCE DR STE 500
OAK BROOK, IL 605238736
Phone: 630 928-1111
Fax: –
Web: www.intellisystechnology.com

CEO: –
CFO: –
HR: –
FYE: December 31
Type: Private

Intellisys Technology tries to be smart about the information technology services it delivers. The company is an IT services provider with customers in such industries as financial services, banking, insurance, and retail. Intellisys' offerings include application development, consulting, outsourcing, systems design, support, training, legacy migration, maintenance, and network engineering. The company has overseas software development centers and sales offices in Australia, India, Singapore, and the UK. CEO Raju Iyer and company executive Vishi Viswanath founded Intellisys in 1997 and it became a subsidiary of India-based Ontrack Systems in 2006.

	Annual Growth	12/04	12/05	12/06	12/07	12/08
Sales ($mil.)	(5.3%)	–	4.2	4.0	3.8	3.5
Net income ($ mil.)	–	–	0.5	0.6	0.4	(0.2)
Market value ($ mil.)	–	–	–	–	–	–
Employees	–	–	–	–	–	24

INTER PARFUMS, INC.

NMS: IPAR

551 Fifth Avenue
New York, NY 10176
Phone: 212 983-2640
Fax: 212 983-4197
Web: www.interparfumsinc.com

CEO: Jean Madar
CFO: Russell Greenberg
HR: –
FYE: December 31
Type: Public

Inter Parfums manufactures, markets and distributes a wide array of prestige fragrance, and fragrance related products. Most of the fragrance developer and manufacturer's revenue is generated by sales of its prestige fragrance brands, including Karl Lagerfeld, Jimmy Choo, Lanvin, Montblanc, Repetto, S.T. Dupont, and Van Cleef & Arpels, among others. (The company owns the Lanvin and Jean Philippe brand names.) Customers include specialty shops and department stores, mass merchandisers, and perfumeries. Its fragrances are sold in more than 120 countries. Europe generates nearly 80% of Inter Parfums net sales. Inter Parfums was founded in 1982.

	Annual Growth	12/19	12/20	12/21	12/22	12/23
Sales ($mil.)	16.6%	713.5	539.0	879.5	1,086.7	1,317.7
Net income ($ mil.)	26.2%	60.2	38.2	87.4	120.9	152.7
Market value ($ mil.)	18.6%	2,327.1	1,936.0	3,421.3	3,089.1	4,609.0
Employees	10.9%	402	396	467	527	607

INTER-AMERICAN DEVELOPMENT BANK

1300 New York Avenue, N.W.
Washington, DC 20577
Phone: 202 623-1000
Fax: 202 623-3096
Web: www.iadb.org

CEO: –
CFO: Freddy Telleria
HR: Armando Justo
FYE: December 31
Type: Public

Inter-American Development Bank (IDB) is the world's oldest and largest regional, multilateral development bank. It provides grants and loans to help fund public and private projects, promote sustainable growth, modernize public institutions, foster free trade, and fight poverty and injustice. It also provides technical assistance and research services and gets involved in cross-border issues such as infrastructure and energy. Serves as the main source of multilateral financing for economic, social, and institutional development in Latin America and the Caribbean, governments, government organizations (such as state banks and universities), civil societies, and private-sector companies are all eligible to receive IDB loans. The institution was founded in 1959.

	Annual Growth	12/04	12/05	12/06	12/07	12/08
Sales ($mil.)	(16.0%)	2,797.0	2,830.0	3,097.0	2,942.0	1,393.0
Net income ($ mil.)	–	1,176.0	762.0	243.0	134.0	(22.0)
Market value ($ mil.)	–	–	–	–	–	–
Employees	–	1,884	1,852	1,824	1,745	–

INTERACT HOLDINGS GROUP INC

NBB: IHGP

8880 Rio San Diego Drive, 8th Floor
San Diego, CA 92108
Phone: 619 342-7443
Fax: –
Web: www.interactholdings.com

CEO: Jeffrey W Flannery
CFO: –
HR: –
FYE: December 31
Type: Public

Interact Holdings Group (formerly The Jackson Rivers Company) changed horses mid-stream and came out on the other bank as a technology company. Through its Diverse Networks subsidiary (acquired in 2005 via a reverse merger) the company provides wired and wireless communications network engineering services. After expanding its operations through various acquisitions, the company has pared back its holding in recent years, selling its JRC Global Products subsidiary and mutually agreeing to rescind the purchase of its UTSI International subsidiary.

	Annual Growth	12/03	12/04	12/05	12/06	12/07
Sales ($mil.)	39.8%	–	–	–	3.2	4.5
Net income ($ mil.)	–	–	–	–	(2.8)	(3.3)
Market value ($ mil.)	(90.0%)	–	–	–	0.0	0.0
Employees	–	–	–	–	–	–

INTERACTIVE BROKERS GROUP INC

NMS: IBKR

One Pickwick Plaza
Greenwich, CT 06830
Phone: 203 618-5800
Fax: –
Web: www.interactivebrokers.com

CEO: Milan Galik
CFO: Paul J Brody
HR: –
FYE: December 31
Type: Public

Interactive Brokers Group is an automated global electronic broker that custody and service accounts for hedge and mutual funds, exchange-traded funds (ETFs), registered investment advisors, proprietary trading groups, and introducing brokers and individual investors. Catering to institutional and individual investors, the company offers access to more than 150 electronic exchanges and trading centers worldwide, processing trades in stocks, options, futures, foreign exchange instruments, bonds, and mutual funds. The company also licenses its trading interface to large banks and brokerages through white branding agreements. Interactive Brokers operates worldwide but generates about 70% of its revenue in the US.

	Annual Growth	12/19	12/20	12/21	12/22	12/23
Sales ($mil.)	22.3%	1,937.0	2,218.0	2,714.0	3,067.0	4,340.0
Net income ($ mil.)	38.9%	161.0	195.0	308.0	380.0	600.0
Market value ($ mil.)	15.5%	4,990.5	6,521.2	8,501.6	7,744.8	8,874.1
Employees	15.6%	1,643	2,033	2,571	2,820	2,932

INTERACTIVE INTELLIGENCE GROUP, INC.

7601 INTERACTIVE WAY
INDIANAPOLIS, IN 462782727
Phone: 317 872-3000
Fax: –
Web: www.inin.com

CEO: –
CFO: –
HR: –
FYE: December 31
Type: Private

With PBX telephone systems going the way of the telegraph, Interactive Intelligence is taking its customers' communications to the cloud. The company provides software and cloud services for customer engagement, communications, and collaboration. It offers on-premises software, single-tenant cloud service, and multitenant cloud service. Interactive Intelligence's Customer Interaction Center software and its PureCloud Platform can process thousands of interactions per hour in telephone calls, emails, faxes, voice mail, internet chat sessions, IP telephony calls, text messages, and social media. More than 10,000 customers, including CarMax, IKEA, and Walgreens, run automated call centers on Interactive Intelligence's systems. It was acquired by Genesys in late 2016.

INTERBOND OF AMERICA, LLC

3200 SW 42ND ST
FORT LAUDERDALE, FL 333126813
Phone: 954 797-4000
Fax: –
Web: www.brandsmartusa.com

CEO: Michael O Perlman
CFO: Eric Beazley
HR: –
FYE: September 24
Type: Private

Interbond Corporation of America (doing business as BrandsMart USA) boasts more than 500 brand names across its nearly 50,000 electronics and entertainment products. It sells them in the US and internationally. It offers low-priced appliances, computers, TVs, car stereos, mobile phones, personal care gadgets, movie, music, games, and more. The retailer runs about 10 electronics stores under the BrandsMart USA banner in the South Florida and Atlanta metropolitan areas. Each stocks more than $8 million in merchandise. BrandsMart USA also sells products online, providing shipping for orders placed throughout the US, Latin America, and the Caribbean. Chairman Robert Perlman founded the company in 1977.

INTERCLOUD SYSTEMS INC

NBB: ICLD

1030 Broad Street, Suite 102
Shrewsbury, NJ 07702
Phone: 561 988-1988
Fax: –
Web: www.intercloudsys.com

CEO: Mark Munro
CFO: Timothy A Larkin
HR: –
FYE: December 31
Type: Public

It took a lot of storms to form InterCloud Systems. Formerly real estate firm Genesis Group Holdings, the company changed its name to InterCloud Systems in 2013 and now oversees a group of subsidiaries that serve the telecom industry. It owns ADEX Corporation, which provides engineering and installation services; structured cabling and DAS installers TNS and Tropical Communications; engineering firm Rives-Monteiro Engineering and equipment provider Rives-Monteiro Leasing; and AW Solutions, which provides network systems design and engineering services. Customers include wireless and wireline telcos (Sprint), cable broadband multiple system operators (Verizon), and original equipment manufacturers (Ericsson).

	Annual Growth	12/13	12/14	12/15	12/16	12/17
Sales ($mil.)	(9.5%)	51.4	76.2	74.9	78.0	34.5
Net income ($ mil.)	–	(24.4)	(18.8)	(65.8)	(26.5)	(44.3)
Market value ($ mil.)	(85.3%)	54.6	54.6	54.6	0.3	0.0
Employees	7.3%	354	483	529	422	469

INTERCONTINENTAL EXCHANGE INC

NYS: ICE

5660 New Northside Drive
Atlanta, GA 30328
Phone: 770 857-4700
Fax: 770 937-0020
Web: www.theice.com

CEO: Jeffrey C Sprecher
CFO: A W Gardiner
HR: –
FYE: December 31
Type: Public

Intercontinental Exchange (ICE) is a leading provider of regulated marketplaces and clearing services for global commodity trading, primarily of electricity, and agricultural commodities, metals, interest rates, equities, exchange traded funds, or ETFs, credit derivatives, digital assets, bonds and currencies, and also offer mortgage and technology services. It manages a handful of global over-the-counter (OTC) markets and regulated futures exchanges. The company also owns ICE Futures Europe, a leading European energy futures and options platform, as well as NYSE Holdings (including the New York Stock Exchange). The company serves clients in over 150 countries. ICE's largest geographical market is the US with more than 65% of the company's revenue.

	Annual Growth	12/19	12/20	12/21	12/22	12/23
Sales ($mil.)	10.9%	6,547.0	8,244.0	9,168.0	9,636.0	9,903.0
Net income ($ mil.)	5.2%	1,933.0	2,089.0	4,058.0	1,446.0	2,368.0
Market value ($ mil.)	8.5%	53,031	66,061	78,369	58,784	73,590
Employees	21.9%	5,989	8,890	8,858	8,911	13,222

INTERDENOMINATIONAL THEOLOGICAL CENTER, INC.

700 MARTIN LUTHER KING JR DR SW
ATLANTA, GA 303144143
Phone: 404 527-7700
Fax: –
Web: www.itc.edu

CEO: Michael A Battle
CFO: Elizabeth Littlejohn
HR: Idell Henderson
FYE: June 30
Type: Private

Interdenominational Theological Center (ITC) is a consortium of six denominational seminaries and a leading center of graduate theological education and religious training for African Americans. ITC offers six degree programs and is accredited by The Commission on Colleges of the Southern Association of Colleges and Schools and The Association of Theological Schools in the US and Canada. It is also a member institution of the Atlanta University Consortium, which includes Morehouse, Spelman, and Morris Brown colleges; Clark Atlanta University; and the Morehouse School of Medicine. ITC was chartered in 1958.

	Annual Growth	06/16	06/17	06/18	06/21	06/22
Sales ($mil.)	4.3%	–	8.7	7.3	10.7	10.8
Net income ($ mil.)	–	–	(0.0)	(1.3)	1.4	1.0
Market value ($ mil.)	–	–	–	–	–	–
Employees	–	–	–	–	–	98

INTERDENT, INC.

222 North Sepulveda Boulevard, Suite 740
El Segundo, CA 90245
Phone: 310 765-2400
Fax: –
Web: –

CEO: –
CFO: Robert W Hill
HR: Diane Stern
FYE: December 31
Type: Public

InterDent is looking to fill the gap in dental practice management. The company provides practice management services to more than 120 dental offices and multi-specialty dental practices in eight states west of the Mississippi River (nearly half are in California). Its clients include general dentists and specialists offering periodontics, oral surgery, and orthodontics. InterDent clients receive administrative, financial, and operations support and management as well as information systems and the benefits of economies of scale. InterDent was created by the 1998 merger of Gentle Dental Service and Dental Care Alliance, which became Wisdom Holdings before the company adopted its current name in 1999.

	Annual Growth	12/02*	09/03*	12/03	12/04	12/05
Sales ($mil.)	(5.3%)	250.1	171.6	52.8	214.3	212.1
Net income ($ mil.)	–	(97.1)	58.0	1.3	5.0	(3.1)
Market value ($ mil.)	–	–	–	–	–	–
Employees	(5.4%)	2,123	–	–	–	1,800

*Fiscal year change

INTERFACE INC.

NMS: TILE

1280 West Peachtree Street
Atlanta, GA 30309
Phone: 770 437-6800
Fax: –
Web: www.interface.com

CEO: Daniel T Hendrix
CFO: Bruce A Hausmann
HR: Pebbles Holcombe
FYE: December 31
Type: Public

Interface is a global flooring company specializing in carbon-neutral carpet tile and resilient flooring, including luxury vinyl tile (LVT), vinyl sheet, rigid core, and Nora rubber flooring. The Company manufactures modular carpets focusing on the high quality, designer-oriented sector of the market, sources resilient flooring including LVT from third parties and focuses on the same sector of the market, and provides specialized carpet replacement, installation, and maintenance services. Its Interface's other offerings include an antimicrobial chemical compound under the brand Intersept, which is incorporated in some of its modular carpet products, and the TacTiles carpet tile installation system. It also continues to provide "turnkey" project management services through its InterfaceSERVICES business.

	Annual Growth	12/19*	01/21	01/22	01/23*	12/23
Sales ($mil.)	(1.6%)	1,343.0	1,103.3	1,200.4	1,297.9	1,261.5
Net income ($ mil.)	(13.4%)	79.2	(71.9)	55.2	19.6	44.5
Market value ($ mil.)	(6.5%)	961.2	610.2	926.9	573.6	733.4
Employees	(4.4%)	4,335	3,858	3,897	3,847	3,619

*Fiscal year change

INTERGROUP CORP. (THE)   NAS: INTG

1516 S. Bundy Dr., Suite 200
Los Angeles, CA 90025
Phone: 310 889-2500
Fax: –
Web: www.intgla.com

CEO: John V Winfield V
CFO: –
HR: –
FYE: June 30
Type: Public

InterGroup buys, develops, and manages affordable housing and other projects with an eye toward social responsibility. The company owns around 20 apartment complexes, two commercial real estate properties, two single-family residences, and, through subsidiary Santa Fe Financial, majority interest in a San Francisco hotel. Its holdings are primarily concentrated in California and Texas. InterGroup also invests in securities and in real estate portfolios. It holds a stake in Comstock Mining, a precious metals producing company. Chairman and CEO John Winfield controls about 62% of the company. Winfield is also CEO of Santa Fe Financial and its subsidiary, Portsmouth Square.

	Annual Growth	06/19	06/20	06/21	06/22	06/23
Sales ($mil.)	(6.3%)	74.8	58.0	28.7	47.2	57.6
Net income ($ mil.)	–	1.5	(3.8)	10.4	(8.7)	(6.7)
Market value ($ mil.)	3.9%	67.6	58.5	94.9	93.4	78.7
Employees	3.4%	28	30	27	28	32

INTERIM HEALTHCARE INC.

1551 SAWGRASS CORPORATE PKWY STE 230
SUNRISE, FL 333232832
Phone: 800 338-7786
Fax: –
Web: www.interimhealthcare.com

CEO: Paul Mastrapa
CFO: David Waltzer
HR: Beverly Berkowitz
FYE: December 31
Type: Private

Interim HealthCare providers care for the whole person, regardless of diagnosis, providing the support needed to reach individual physical goals. With over 43,000 health care professionals across more than 40 states, Interim HealthCare provides nurses, therapists, aides and other health care personnel to approximately 173,000 people annually. Interim HealthCare Hospice offers the best in medical and nursing care, using state-of-the-art symptom management to control symptoms and promote comfort. Interim HealthCare was founded in 1966 as Medical Personnel Pool. The Caring Brands International is the leading franchisor of home healthcare services was acquired by Wellspring Capital Management in late 2021.

	Annual Growth	12/12	12/13	12/14	12/15	12/16
Sales ($mil.)	1.1%	–	–	–	68.5	69.3
Net income ($ mil.)	1.5%	–	–	–	8.8	9.0
Market value ($ mil.)	–	–	–	–	–	–
Employees	–	–	–	–	–	6,841

INTERIOR CONCEPTS CORPORATION

18525 TRIMBLE CT
SPRING LAKE, MI 494569794
Phone: 616 842-5550
Fax: –
Web: www.interiorconcepts.com

CEO: Donald Ott
CFO: Barb Szymanski
HR: Katie McCool
FYE: December 31
Type: Private

Interior Concepts Corporation is calling on those who call the man or woman of the house. The company's a custom manufacturer of furniture for use in call centers, computer labs, reception areas, technology stations, and school environments. Interior Concepts's primary product lines include thin-line paneling and wire-management systems. The company's products are sold under the Swurv, Pro-Fit Furniture, and Degrees brand names. The furniture, seating, and accessories at Interior Concepts are sold through the company's network of sales professionals.

	Annual Growth	12/06	12/07	12/08	12/09	12/10
Sales ($mil.)	(7.1%)	–	–	14.2	13.2	12.2
Net income ($ mil.)	(9.5%)	–	–	0.5	0.7	0.4
Market value ($ mil.)	–	–	–	–	–	–
Employees	–	–	–	–	–	43

INTERLINK ELECTRONICS INC   NAS: LINK

15707 Rockfield Boulevard, Suite 105
Irvine, CA 92618
Phone: 805 484-8855
Fax: 805 484-9457
Web: www.interlinkelectronics.com

CEO: Steven N Bronson
CFO: Ryan J Hoffman
HR: –
FYE: December 31
Type: Public

Interlink Electronics designs electronic signature capture devices and specialty interface products. The company's signature capture products include its ePad line of hardware devices and IntegriSign software. Its sensor interface components enable menu navigation, cursor control, and character input in devices such as computer mice and mobile phones. Interlink's patented force-sensing technology enables smaller, more touch-sensitive input devices. The company also provides design and integration services. Special Situations Technology Fund owns about 40% of the company.

	Annual Growth	12/19	12/20	12/21	12/22	12/23
Sales ($mil.)	17.5%	7.3	6.9	7.5	7.5	13.9
Net income ($ mil.)	–	(0.5)	0.1	(0.7)	1.7	(0.4)
Market value ($ mil.)	28.0%	46.8	88.7	95.5	80.5	125.9
Employees	–	–	86	89	98	107

INTERMARK INDUSTRIES, INC.

2980 NW 74TH AVE
MIAMI, FL 331221426
Phone: 305 591-8930
Fax: –
Web: www.intermarkindustries.com

CEO: –
CFO: –
HR: –
FYE: December 31
Type: Private

Intermark Industries is a wholesale and preferred distributor of electronic components, computer accessories, electronic test and measurement instruments, cable, car audio and professional audio products, tools and soldering products, and sound accessories; markets for the products include Latin America and the Caribbean region. The company also manufactures BK Electronics (microphones, headphones, mixers, etc.) and Blast King sound reinforcement speakers. President Bernard Kremen founded the company in 1978 and is the majority shareholder. In the early days of Intermark, he used his bedroom closet as the company's warehouse space. Robert Levine, the company's treasurer, owns 30% of Intermark.

INTERMATIC INCORPORATED

1950 INNOVATION WAY STE 300
LIBERTYVILLE, IL 600482079
Phone: 815 675-7000
Fax: –
Web: www.intermatic.com

CEO: G R Boutilier Jr
CFO: –
HR: Dana Berry
FYE: December 31
Type: Private

Intermatic offers an extensive catalog of lighting and energy controls, surge protection devices, weatherproof covers, and Wi-Fi enabled solutions as it continues to evolve and push the industry forward. Its product portfolio broadened to include industrial- and commercial-grade controls and would soon expand with a variety of progressive, energy-saving solutions. The company manufactures home timers that include pool and spa controls, timer controls, and in-wall controls. It also offers photocontrols that include fixed mount electronic, locking type electronic, fixed mount thermal, and locking type thermal photocontrols. Other products include occupancy/vacancy sensors, photo controls, LED and HID lighting, industrial surge protectors, weatherproof covers for electrical outlets, and enclosures.

	Annual Growth	12/99	12/00	12/03	12/04	12/17
Sales ($mil.)	(5.3%)	–	317.5	330.0	380.0	124.7
Net income ($ mil.)	(4.9%)	–	16.6	63.2	240.8	7.0
Market value ($ mil.)	–	–	–	–	–	–
Employees	–	–	–	–	–	746

INTERMETRO COMMUNICATIONS, INC. (NV)

NBB: IMTO

2685 Park Center Drive, Building A
Simi Valley, CA 93065
Phone: 805 433-8000
Fax: –
Web: www.intermetrocomm.net

CEO: Charles Rice
CFO: James Winter
HR: Lynne Gilbert
FYE: December 31
Type: Public

InterMetro Communications hopes to take over the VoIP market city by city. The company's national, private voice-over Internet Protocol (VoIP) network delivers long-distance phone service to telecoms providers and calling card users. InterMetro's more than 200 customers include traditional long-distance carriers, broadband companies, VoIP service providers, and wireless providers. Its VoIP network utilizes proprietary software, switching equipment, and fiber-optic lines to deliver carrier-quality VoIP services, which are typically more cost efficient than circuit-based technologies used in traditional long-distance networks. Chairman and CEO Charles Rice owns almost 40% of the company.

	Annual Growth	12/09	12/10	12/11	12/12	12/13
Sales ($mil.)	(15.1%)	22.3	28.0	21.3	20.1	11.6
Net income ($ mil.)	–	(4.9)	3.2	3.6	0.7	(2.5)
Market value ($ mil.)	49.5%	0.8	5.0	4.1	8.3	4.1
Employees	(2.9%)	27	29	23	30	24

INTERMOUNTAIN HEALTH CARE INC

36 S STATE ST STE 1600
SALT LAKE CITY, UT 841111633
Phone: 801 442-2000
Fax: –
Web: www.intermountainhealthcare.org

CEO: Rob Allen
CFO: Clay Ashdown
HR: Bruce Dent
FYE: December 31
Type: Private

Intermountain Healthcare is a non-profit system composed of 60,000 caregivers that serve the healthcare needs of people across the Intermountain West, primarily in Utah, Idaho, Nevada, Colorado, Montana, Wyoming, and Kansas. Intermountain Healthcare is an integrated, non-profit health system based, with clinics, a medical group, affiliate networks, hospitals, homecare, telehealth, health insurance plans, and other services, along with wholly-owned subsidiaries including SelectHealth, Saltzer Health, Castell, Tellica, and Classic Air Medical. Intermountain Healthcare was established in 1975 when The Church of Jesus Christ of Latter-day Saints donated its then 15-hospital system to the communities they served.

	Annual Growth	12/16	12/17	12/18	12/19	12/20
Sales ($mil.)	14.2%	–	–	7,724.2	8,812.0	10,082
Net income ($ mil.)	93.2%	–	–	420.9	1,212.0	1,571.0
Market value ($ mil.)	–	–	–	–	–	–
Employees	–	–	–	–	–	35,000

INTERNAP CORP

NBB: INAP Q

12120 Sunset Hills Road, Suite 330
Reston, VA 20190
Phone: 404 302-9700
Fax: –
Web: www.internap.com

CEO: –
CFO: –
HR: –
FYE: December 31
Type: Public

Internap (INAP) is a worldwide supplier of secure and efficient hybrid infrastructure solutions. Its offerings help technology leaders simplify their cloud migration and speed up innovation. INAP provides a wide array of services, including modern data centers, optimized networks, security solutions, and bare metal cloud, to help companies relocate their workloads to the most suitable destination at the right time. This ensures that their IT strategy is maximized, resulting in optimal outcomes.

	Annual Growth	12/15	12/16	12/17	12/18	12/19
Sales ($mil.)	(2.2%)	318.3	298.3	280.7	317.4	291.5
Net income ($ mil.)	–	(48.2)	(124.7)	(45.3)	(62.5)	(138.3)
Market value ($ mil.)	(35.6%)	170.0	40.9	417.2	110.2	29.2
Employees	(4.5%)	650	530	503	640	540

INTERNATIONAL ASSOCIATION OF AMUSEMENT PARKS AND ATTRACTIONS

4155 TAFT VINELAND RD
ORLANDO, FL 328374031
Phone: 321 319-7690
Fax: –
Web: www.iaapa.org

CEO: –
CFO: –
HR: –
FYE: December 31
Type: Private

Work is just a walk in the park for this group. The International Association of Amusement Parks and Attractions (IAAPA) is the world's largest trade organization for the amusement and theme park industry with 5,000 members in 80 countries. The not-for-profit group develops services, training products, and networking opportunities for its members which include zoo, museum, arcade, and family fun center operators. It holds annual trade shows, publishes FUNWORLD magazine, offers management and customer service advice, sets safety standards, and lobbies government on behalf of the industry. IAAPA was founded in 1918.

	Annual Growth	07/07	07/08*	12/13	12/21	12/22
Sales ($mil.)	3.7%	–	13.0	17.4	31.1	21.8
Net income ($ mil.)	–	–	0.7	1.4	14.5	(0.4)
Market value ($ mil.)	–	–	–	–	–	–
Employees	–	–	–	–	–	33

*Fiscal year change

INTERNATIONAL ASSOCIATION OF MACHINISTS AND AEROSPACE WORKERS

9000 MACHINISTS PL
UPPER MARLBORO, MD 207722675
Phone: 301 967-4500
Fax: –
Web: www.goiam.org

CEO: –
CFO: –
HR: –
FYE: December 31
Type: Private

Corporate executives who bargain with the International Association of Machinists and Aerospace Workers (IAM) don't like to hear the words, "IAM going on strike." The labor union represents almost 700,000 active and retired members through more than 5,000 contracts with employers in the US and Canada. The organization represents workers in about two dozen industries, although primarily in the air transportation, aerospace, metalworking and machinery, manufacturing, and automotive industries. In addition to negotiating wage, paid time-off, job security, and work environment issues, the union provides a pension plan and a healthcare plan. The union is affiliated with the AFL-CIO.

	Annual Growth	12/99	12/00	12/01	12/05	12/08
Sales ($mil.)	(44.9%)	–	–	122.0	0.1	1.9
Net income ($ mil.)	–	–	–	(2.4)	(0.0)	–
Market value ($ mil.)	–	–	–	–	–	–
Employees	–	–	–	–	–	400

INTERNATIONAL BALER CORP

NBB: IBAL

5400 Rio Grande Avenue
Jacksonville, FL 32254
Phone: 904 358-3812
Fax: –
Web: www.intl-baler.com

CEO: D R Griffin
CFO: William E Nielsen
HR: –
FYE: October 31
Type: Public

No need to bail on International Baler. This holding company, formerly known as Waste Technology, banks on its business being in the dumps. International Baler manufactures about 50 different types of waste baling equipment. It also sells replacement parts for waste haulers. In addition, International Baler produces accessories such as conveyor belts and "rufflers," which break down refuse for better compaction. Customers include rubber and polymer makers, solid-waste recycling facilities, power generating facilities, textile and paper mills, cotton gins, and supermarkets. International Baler makes about three-quarters of its sales in the US.

	Annual Growth	10/17	10/18	10/19	10/20	10/21
Sales ($mil.)	(1.2%)	10.5	11.1	9.5	9.0	10.0
Net income ($ mil.)	–	0.0	0.3	(0.3)	(0.4)	(0.1)
Market value ($ mil.)	(1.3%)	10.4	9.6	7.5	6.5	9.9
Employees	(6.5%)	59	57	50	49	45

INTERNATIONAL BANCSHARES CORP.   NMS: IBOC

1200 San Bernardo Avenue
Laredo, TX 78042-1359
Phone: 956 722-7611
Fax: –
Web: www.ibc.com

CEO: Dennis E Nixon
CFO: –
HR: –
FYE: December 31
Type: Public

International Bancshares is a registered multibank financial holding company providing a diversified range of commercial and retail banking services in its main banking and branch facilities located in north, south, central and southeast Texas and the State of Oklahoma. One of the largest independent commercial bank holding companies, it does business through some 170 facilities of International Bank of Commerce (IBC), IBC-Oklahoma, Commerce Bank, IBC Zapata, and IBC Brownsville. The company facilitates trade between the US and Mexico and serves Texas' growing Hispanic population. In addition to commercial and international banking services for small and midsized businesses, International Bancshares provides retail deposit services, insurance and investment products, mortgages, and consumer loans.

	Annual Growth	12/19	12/20	12/21	12/22	12/23
Assets ($mil.)	5.6%	12,113	14,029	16,046	15,501	15,066
Net income ($ mil.)	19.0%	205.1	167.3	253.9	300.2	411.8
Market value ($ mil.)	6.0%	2,673.6	2,324.1	2,631.4	2,840.6	3,372.0
Employees	(8.8%)	3,314	2,456	2,261	2,169	2,292

INTERNATIONAL BROTHERHOOD OF ELECTRICAL WORKERS

900 7TH ST NW BSMT 1
WASHINGTON, DC 200014089
Phone: 202 833-7000
Fax: –
Web: www.ibew.org

CEO: –
CFO: –
HR: John Dibiase
FYE: June 30
Type: Private

These brothers are held together with wire, steel girders, fiber optic cable, and conveyor belts. The International Brotherhood of Electrical Workers (IBEW) is about a 725,000-member labor union for workers in such industries as utilities, construction, telecommunications, and manufacturing in the US and Canada. The union lobbies government on behalf of its members, provides training and scholarships, maintains an electronic job board, and helps members secure higher wages, better health care, and safer working conditions. The union was formally organized in 1891 at a convention in St. Louis run by the original American Federation of Labor, a predecessor to the AFL-CIO, with which the union is affiliated.

	Annual Growth	06/15	06/16	06/19	06/20	06/22
Sales ($mil.)	6.9%	–	161.1	181.7	172.2	240.7
Net income ($ mil.)	21.0%	–	13.2	27.9	1.2	41.4
Market value ($ mil.)	–	–	–	–	–	–
Employees	–	–	–	–	–	970

INTERNATIONAL BROTHERHOOD OF TEAMSTERS

25 LOUISIANA AVE NW
WASHINGTON, DC 200012130
Phone: 202 624-6800
Fax: –
Web: www.teamster.org

CEO: –
CFO: –
HR: Kristin King
FYE: December 31
Type: Private

One of the largest and best-known labor unions in the US, the International Brotherhood of Teamsters has 1.4 million members. The Teamsters represents workers in nearly 25 industry sectors, including airlines, freight, parcel delivery, industrial trades, and public service. Most of the union's members are employees of package delivery giant United Parcel Service. Besides negotiating labor contracts with employers on behalf of its members, the union oversees pension funds and serves as an advocate in legislative and regulatory arenas. The union and its affiliates have about 1,900 local chapters in the US, Puerto Rico and Canada, including about 360 Teamsters locals. The Teamsters union was founded in 1903.

	Annual Growth	12/08	12/09	12/19	12/21	12/22
Sales ($mil.)	2.5%	–	172.8	–	211.8	238.1
Net income ($ mil.)	14.5%	–	12.5	–	51.2	72.8
Market value ($ mil.)	–	–	–	–	–	–
Employees	–	–	–	–	–	649

INTERNATIONAL BUILDING TECHNOLOGIES GROUP INC

17800 Castleton Street, Suite 638
City of Industry, CA 91748
Phone: 626 581-8500
Fax: –
Web: www.ibtgi.com

CEO: Kenneth Yeung
CFO: Kenneth Yeung
HR: –
FYE: December 31
Type: Public

International Building Technologies Group (INBG) has raced from business to business. Formerly a card game developer for casinos and a seller of racing and motorsports accessories and apparel, the company changed lanes in 2007. That's when it began a new life as a manufacturer of a specialty panel-based technology that helps buildings withstand earthquakes and hurricane-force winds. INBG also offers other services including site planning, engineering, contractor services, training, and supervision. In 2011 a a merger plan between INBG and Chinese petroleum storage company FHH Sino New Energies was terminated. The deal would have allowed INBG to move into yet another line of business -- the energy sector.

	Annual Growth	12/06	12/07	12/08	12/09	12/10
Sales ($mil.)	–	–	–	–	–	–
Net income ($ mil.)	–	(1.2)	(1.2)	(4.8)	(1.9)	0.7
Market value ($ mil.)	(71.4%)	256.2	34.2	1.3	0.9	1.7
Employees	–	–	1	–	1	1

INTERNATIONAL BUSINESS MACHINES CORP   NYS: IBM

One New Orchard Road
Armonk, NY 10504
Phone: 914 499-1900
Fax: 914 765-4190
Web: www.ibm.com

CEO: Arvind Krishna
CFO: James J Kavanaugh
HR: –
FYE: December 31
Type: Public

International Business Machines (IBM) is addressing the hybrid cloud and AI opportunity with a platform-centric approach, focused on providing two primary sources of client value ? technology and business expertise. It provide integrated solutions and products that leverage: data, information technology, deep expertise in industries and business processes, with trust and security and a broad ecosystem of partners and alliances. Its hybrid cloud platform and AI technology and services capabilities support clients' digital transformations and help them engage with their customers and employees in new ways. These solutions draw from an industry-leading portfolio of capabilities in software, consulting services, and a deep incumbency in mission-critical systems, all bolstered by one of the world's leading research organizations. The company generates about 40% of revenue from the US.

	Annual Growth	12/19	12/20	12/21	12/22	12/23
Sales ($mil.)	(5.4%)	77,147	73,620	57,350	60,530	61,860
Net income ($ mil.)	(5.6%)	9,431.0	5,590.0	5,743.0	1,639.0	7,502.0
Market value ($ mil.)	5.1%	122,648	115,182	122,301	128,916	149,650
Employees	(5.6%)	383,800	375,300	307,600	311,300	305,300

INTERNATIONAL CENTER FOR ENTREPRENEURIAL DEVELOPMENT INC

12715 TELGE RD
CYPRESS, TX 774292289
Phone: 281 256-4100
Fax: –
Web: www.parcelplus.com

CEO: Stephen B Hammerstein
CFO: Scott Kruger
HR: –
FYE: December 31
Type: Private

The International Center for Entrepreneurial Development (ICED) is a holding company that offers several franchise opportunities. The organization specializes in the computer education, health care, and mail center and printing industries. ICED offers a number of franchise brands including Kwik Kopy, Parcel Plus, and Women's Health Boutique. Its Computer Explorers (CE) unit is a franchise group that serves some 25,000 students through about 1,000 locations worldwide. CE boasts approximately 600 educators that ensure that children in some 2,000 schools are fully engaged in learning the latest technology. Bud Hadfield founded the company in 1967 when he began franchising his Kwik Kopy centers.

	Annual Growth	12/05	12/06	12/07	12/08	12/09
Sales ($mil.)	(18.3%)	–	–	14.0	13.0	9.3
Net income ($ mil.)	–	–	–	0.1	0.4	(0.6)
Market value ($ mil.)	–	–	–	–	–	–
Employees	–	–	–	–	–	150

INTERNATIONAL CENTER FOR RESEARCH ON WOMEN

1120 20TH ST NW STE 500N
WASHINGTON, DC 200363421
Phone: 202 797-0007
Fax: -
Web: www.icrw.org

CEO: -
CFO: -
HR: -
FYE: September 30
Type: Private

Don't let the name get you, no one is performing experiments on anyone here. The International Center for Research on Women (ICRW) strives to protect women's rights and improve women's quality of life around the world. It researches women's issues, advocates for policy development, and offers technical assistance to women in more than 40 countries. ICRW works to improve women's economic, health, and social status in developing nations around issues including HIV/AIDS, nutrition and food security, reproductive health, violence against women, and poverty reduction. The not-for-profit organization was formed in 1976 to help understand the role of women in developing nations.

	Annual Growth	09/18	09/19	09/20	09/21	09/22
Sales ($mil.)	0.5%	-	10.7	12.1	9.5	10.8
Net income ($ mil.)	-	-	(0.7)	1.5	(1.1)	(1.4)
Market value ($ mil.)	-	-	-	-	-	-
Employees	-	-	-	-	-	80

INTERNATIONAL DISPENSING CORP NBB: IDND

170 Pulaski Street
Southhampton, NY 11968
Phone: 212 464-7203
Fax: -
Web: www.idcinnovation.com

CEO: Gregory Abbott
CFO: -
HR: -
FYE: December 31
Type: Public

International Dispensing Corporation wants to be indispensable. The research and development company designs and manufactures cutting edge packaging and aseptic dispensing solutions for the foodservice industry. International Dispensing's core products include an aseptic flow valve (attached to a flexible bag, it allows liquids to be dispensed without bacteria or oxygen entering the package) and a disposable beverage carafe (consisting of a sterile, flexible, biax nylon pouch attached to a rigid plastic frame, with corrugated side panels that attach to the plastic frame). The firm primarily serves the foodservice, retail food, and specialty coffee sectors.

	Annual Growth	12/17	12/18	12/19	12/20	12/21
Sales ($mil.)	(43.7%)	0.4	0.3	0.3	0.0	0.0
Net income ($ mil.)	-	(1.5)	(1.2)	(0.3)	(1.6)	(1.1)
Market value ($ mil.)	(40.2%)	41.6	29.8	11.3	10.4	5.3
Employees	-	-	-	-	-	-

INTERNATIONAL FALLS MEMORIAL HOSPITAL ASSOCIATION

1400 HIGHWAY 71
INTERNATIONAL FALLS, MN 566492154
Phone: 218 283-4481
Fax: -
Web: www.rainylakemedical.com

CEO: Brian Long
CFO: Nancy Treacy
HR: -
FYE: December 31
Type: Private

Rainy Lake Medical Center (formerly Falls Memorial Hospital) works hard to give its patients a sunny future. The rural acute care facility is the result of the integration of Duluth Clinic International Falls and Falls Memorial Hospital. The not-for-profit hospital, which is designated a Critical Access Hospital, provides general medical and surgical care and emergency services to the International Falls community in northern Michigan. The 25-bed facility provides chemotherapy, maternity care, radiology, pharmacy, and laboratory services, among other things. It also offers specialty and primary care (in areas such as ophthalmology, pediatrics, physical therapy, and orthopedics) through the former Duluth clinic.

	Annual Growth	12/03	12/04	12/08	12/21	12/22
Sales ($mil.)	5.3%	-	13.9	16.7	31.9	35.0
Net income ($ mil.)	-	-	1.5	-	7.2	1.5
Market value ($ mil.)	-	-	-	-	-	-
Employees	-	-	-	-	-	165

INTERNATIONAL FINANCE CORP. (WORLD CORPORATIONS GOVT.) OPT WS

2121 Pennsylvania Avenue, N.W.
Washington, DC 20433
Phone: 202 473-3800
Fax: 202 974-4384
Web: www.ifc.org

CEO: -
CFO: -
HR: Dorothy H Berry
FYE: June 30
Type: Public

International Finance Corporation (IFC) is the largest global development institution focused exclusively on the private sector. IFC invested approximately $32.8 billion in total commitments, including $23.2 billion in long-term finance and $9.7 billion in short-term finance, to private companies and financial institutions in emerging and developing economies. It typically focuses on small and mid-sized businesses, financing projects in several industries, including manufacturing, agribusiness, health and education, infrastructure, tourism, retail, and property, among others. Established in 1956, IFC is a member of the World Bank Group, one of the world's largest sources of financing and knowledge for developing countries. It operates in more than 100 countries.

	Annual Growth	06/10	06/11	06/12	06/13	06/14
Sales ($mil.)	0.2%	3,383.0	3,178.0	3,120.0	2,514.0	3,415.0
Net income ($ mil.)	(4.0%)	1,746.0	1,579.0	1,328.0	1,018.0	1,483.0
Market value ($ mil.)	-	-	-	-	-	-
Employees	-	-	-	-	-	-

INTERNATIONAL FLAVORS & FRAGRANCES INC. NYS: IFF

521 West 57th Street
New York, NY 10019-2960
Phone: 212 765-5500
Fax: -
Web: www.iff.com

CEO: Frank K Clyburn Jr
CFO: -
HR: -
FYE: December 31
Type: Public

International Flavors & Fragrances (IFF) is one of the leading creators and manufacturers of food, beverage, health & biosciences, scent, and pharma solutions, and complementary adjacent products. The company serves food and beverage, pharmaceutical, health and wellness, home and personal care integrated solutions, and ingredients worldwide. As a leading creator of flavor offerings, the company helps its customers deliver on the promise of delicious and healthy foods and drinks. It also creates natural-focused compounds and ingredients for niche markets. About 70% of its revenue comes from outside North America.

	Annual Growth	12/19	12/20	12/21	12/22	12/23
Sales ($mil.)	22.2%	5,140.1	5,084.2	11,656	12,440	11,479
Net income ($ mil.)	-	455.9	363.2	270.0	(1,871.0)	(2,567.0)
Market value ($ mil.)	(11.0%)	32,937	27,786	38,459	26,764	20,671
Employees	12.1%	13,600	13,700	24,000	24,600	21,500

INTERNATIONAL FLEET SALES, INC.

476 MCCORMICK ST
SAN LEANDRO, CA 945771106
Phone: 510 569-9770
Fax: -
Web: www.internationalfleetsales.com

CEO: Michael Libasci
CFO: Peggy King
HR: -
FYE: December 31
Type: Private

By air, land, or sea, International Fleet Sales (IFS) can ship North American cars, trucks, and buses to international buyers. IFS is an authorized export distributor of Navistar and General Motors vehicles (including Chevrolet), as well as parts and service. It is also an export distributor of Blue Bird Bus and Volvo Trucks North America parts. Customers include auto retailers and distributors, governments, individual buyers, and humanitarian aid agencies. The company's US office handles sales in Central and South America, Asia (primarily in China), and Africa, while its Netherlands office supports sales in Europe. IFS was founded in 1999 by president and CEO Mike Libasci.

	Annual Growth	12/05	12/06	12/07	12/08	12/09
Sales ($mil.)	27.3%	-	-	39.1	37.5	63.4
Net income ($ mil.)	81.2%	-	-	1.5	2.0	5.0
Market value ($ mil.)	-	-	-	-	-	-
Employees	-	-	-	-	-	11

INTERNATIONAL INDUSTRIES, INC.

210 LARRY JOE HARLESS DR
GILBERT, WV 25621
Phone: 304 664-3227
Fax: –
Web: www.comfortinn.com

CEO: –
CFO: –
HR: –
FYE: December 31
Type: Private

International Industries markets the products of leading US and international hydrographic and oceanographic firms in the marine technology industry. The equipment, both owned and brokered, is leased worldwide to the professional trade. Its products include echosounders, side scan sonars, and other geophysical and oceanographic equipment. The company is led Morris Ransone, who has more than 40 years experience in marine operations, instrumentation, surveying and underwater exploration. James H. "Buck" Harless founded International Industries in 1947.

INTERNATIONAL ISOTOPES INC   NBB: INIS

4137 Commerce Circle
Idaho Falls, ID 83401
Phone: 208 524-5300
Fax: –
Web: www.intisoid.com

CEO: –
CFO: –
HR: –
FYE: December 31
Type: Public

Despite its name, International Isotopes is confined to a single US state. The firm operates primarily through subsidiary International Isotopes Idaho, where it makes calibration and measurement equipment used with nuclear imaging cameras. Most of its nuclear imaging products, including dose measurement devices and testing equipment, are made under contract with RadQual, a privately held firm that markets the devices; International Isotopes owns a minority stake in RadQual. The company partnered with RadQual in late 2010 to acquire Technology Imaging Services. The joint venture called TI Services LLC distributes products and services for nuclear medicine, nuclear cardiology, and PET imaging.

	Annual Growth	12/18	12/19	12/20	12/21	12/22
Sales ($mil.)	1.9%	10.4	9.0	9.4	9.7	11.2
Net income ($ mil.)	–	(0.8)	(1.5)	2.2	(0.9)	0.3
Market value ($ mil.)	(15.6%)	33.1	26.8	26.3	48.4	16.7
Employees	0.8%	32	37	32	32	33

INTERNATIONAL LEASE FINANCE CORP.

10250 Constellation Blvd., Suite 3400
Los Angeles, CA 90067
Phone: 310 788-1999
Fax: –
Web: www.ilfc.com

CEO: Henri Courpron
CFO: Elias Habayeb
HR: Mario Fernadez
FYE: December 31
Type: Public

John Travolta bought his own Boeing; if your company's cash flow is more limited, International Lease Finance Corporation (ILFC) will lease you one. The company, which leases the entire range of Boeing and Airbus commercial aircraft, is the world's second-largest lessor of new aircraft and widebody carriers. It boasts of owning the world's most valuable fleet of leasable aircraft -- about 930 planes. ILFC's airplane-parts management business maintains the aging aircraft in its fleet. Commercial airlines outside the US generate more than 95% of revenue; ILFC counts most of the world's airlines as customers. Former parent AIG (American International Group) sold the company to Netherlands-based AerCap Holdings in 2014.

	Annual Growth	12/09	12/10	12/11	12/12	12/13
Sales ($mil.)	(4.5%)	5,321.7	4,798.9	4,526.7	4,504.2	4,417.4
Net income ($ mil.)	–	895.6	(383.8)	(723.9)	410.3	(517.1)
Market value ($ mil.)	–	–	–	–	–	–
Employees	36.9%	180	194	497	564	632

INTERNATIONAL MANAGEMENT GROUP (OVERSEAS), LLC

1360 E 9TH ST STE 100
CLEVELAND, OH 441141730
Phone: 216 522-1200
Fax: –
Web: –

CEO: –
CFO: Arthur J La Fave Jr
HR: Christopher Magee
FYE: October 27
Type: Private

Show me the money! Founded by the late pioneer of sports marketing Mark McCormack, IMG Worldwide (previously International Management Group) is the world's largest sports talent and marketing agency, operating in some 30 countries. Its IMG Clients represents athletes (Venus Williams), models (Giselle Bundchen), and broadcasters (Bob Costas). IMG also represents corporate clients, and offers a variety of related services with divisions devoted to collegiate sports marketing (IMG College); sports programming production and distribution (IMG Media); consumer products licensing (IMG Licensing); and sponsorship and media consulting (IMG Consulting).

INTERNATIONAL MARKET BRANDS, INC.

13206 192ND AVE E
BONNEY LAKE, WA 983918357
Phone: 425 827-3849
Fax: –
Web: www.imbusa.com

CEO: –
CFO: –
HR: –
FYE: December 31
Type: Private

International Market Brands (IMB) provides export marketing, sales, and consulting services for companies that manufacture food, food service, and pet products. The company's consulting services help manufacturers develop new export markets by identifying foreign buyers, advising on costs and shipping, and navigating administrative hurdles for export. IMB also provides strategic sales and marketing planning and production services targeted to specific countries, cultures, and client needs.

INTERNATIONAL MONETARY SYSTEMS LTD   NBB: ITNM

16901 West Glendale Drive
New Berlin, WI 53151
Phone: 262 780-3640
Fax: –
Web: www.imsbarter.com

CEO: John E Strabley
CFO: David A Powell
HR: Jennifer Weber
FYE: December 31
Type: Public

Who says the barter system is dead? Not International Monetary Systems (IMS). IMS runs one of the world's largest trade exchanges, or barter networks, allowing businesses and professionals to convert excess inventory into goods and services. Its IMS Barter Network serves approximately 17,000 clients in major markets in the US and Canada. Users swap excess goods or services electronically with trade dollars, IMS' electronic currency. Founded in 1985, the company has expanded by acquiring other trade exchanges.

	Annual Growth	12/17	12/18	12/19	12/20	12/21
Sales ($mil.)	(3.8%)	11.4	11.4	11.7	9.7	9.7
Net income ($ mil.)	114.2%	0.0	0.4	0.4	0.9	2.1
Market value ($ mil.)	15.6%	2.6	2.5	2.1	2.3	4.6
Employees	–	–	–	–	–	–

INTERNATIONAL PAPER CO
NYS: IP

6400 Poplar Avenue
Memphis, TN 38197
Phone: 901 419-7000
Fax: –
Web: www.internationalpaper.com

CEO: Mark S Sutton
CFO: Timothy S Nicholls
HR: Cyndi Wood
FYE: December 31
Type: Public

International Paper (IP) is a global producer of renewable fiber-based packaging and pulp products with manufacturing operations in North America, Latin America, Europe and North Africa. Products include uncoated paper used in printers and market pulp for tissue and paper products. The company operated about 25 pulp and packaging mills, about 165 converting and packaging plants, around 15 recycling plants, and three bag facilities. It also runs a pulp and paper business in Russia via a 50/50 joint venture with Ilim S.A. More than 85% of IP's revenue comes from the US.

	Annual Growth	12/19	12/20	12/21	12/22	12/23
Sales ($mil.)	(4.1%)	22,376	20,580	19,363	21,161	18,916
Net income ($ mil.)	(30.4%)	1,225.0	482.0	1,752.0	1,504.0	288.0
Market value ($ mil.)	(5.9%)	15,933	17,203	16,255	11,982	12,508
Employees	(6.5%)	51,000	49,300	38,200	39,000	39,000

INTERNATIONAL SHIPHOLDING CORPORATION

11 N WATER ST
MOBILE, AL 366023809
Phone: 504 249-6088
Fax: –
Web: www.intship.com

CEO: –
CFO: –
HR: –
FYE: December 31
Type: Private

International Shipholding helps put the "car" in cargo. Most of the company's sales come from its time-charter vessels, including car and truck carriers, ships with strengthened hulls (used in polar regions), and coal and sulfur carriers. Its fleet consists of some nearly 40 US and international-flag vessels. International Shipholding's primary subsidiaries include Central Gulf Lines, Waterman Steamship Corp., LCI Shipholdings, CG Railway, and East Gulf Shipholding. The company has offices in Mobile, Alabama; New York City; Singapore; and Shanghai. Customers have included such big names as Toyota, Hyundai Motor, International Paper, and the US Navy's Military Sealift Command. A victim of a prolonged malaise in the shipping industry, the company filed for Chapter 11 bankruptcy protection in mid-2016 and emerged a year later, no longer as an independent company but as a subsidiary of SEACOR Holdings.

INTERNATIONAL SIGN ASSOCIATION INC

1001 N FAIRFAX ST STE 301
ALEXANDRIA, VA 223141587
Phone: 703 836-4012
Fax: –
Web: www.signs.org

CEO: Lori Anderson
CFO: –
HR: –
FYE: December 31
Type: Private

Signs, signs, everywhere there's signs, and you can thank ISA. The International Sign Association (ISA) is a business association that represents sign manufacturers, users, and suppliers. It promotes the on-site sign industry by improving codes and legislation, supporting research, and conducting trade shows. For members, ISA provides newsletters, discount programs, sales and marketing leads, and educational opportunities. The organization was founded in 1944.

	Annual Growth	12/16	12/17	12/18	12/21	12/22
Sales ($mil.)	(5.3%)	–	7.9	8.3	8.0	6.0
Net income ($ mil.)	–	–	0.2	0.5	3.1	(1.3)
Market value ($ mil.)	–	–	–	–	–	–
Employees	–	–	–	–	–	21

INTERNATIONAL SOFTWARE SYSTEMS, INC.

7337 HANOVER PKWY STE A
GREENBELT, MD 207703669
Phone: 301 982-9700
Fax: –
Web: www.issi-software.com

CEO: –
CFO: –
HR: Diane Jeffers
FYE: October 20
Type: Private

International Software Systems (ISSI) provides IT consulting services and develops custom software for various governmental departments and corporations. Customers have included the US Departments of Agriculture, Commerce, and Treasury; the US Navy and Marine Corps; the National Park Service; and such commercial clients as St. Clair Health Corporation, Software Corporation of America, and Sprint. Founded in 1995 by CEO and owner Bhaskar Ganti, the company has sales offices in the US and software development facilities in India.

	Annual Growth	12/03	12/04	12/05	12/14*	10/17
Sales ($mil.)	16.3%	–	2.7	5.0	11.5	19.1
Net income ($ mil.)	28.6%	–	0.1	0.0	0.1	2.6
Market value ($ mil.)	–	–	–	–	–	–
Employees	–	–	–	–	–	120

*Fiscal year change

INTERNATIONAL SPEEDWAY CORPORATION

1 DAYTONA BLVD
DAYTONA BEACH, FL 321141212
Phone: 386 254-2700
Fax: –
Web: www.internationalspeedwaycorporation.com

CEO: Lesa F Kennedy
CFO: Gregory S Motto
HR: Tammy Apple
FYE: November 30
Type: Private

International Speedway Corporation (ISC) doesn't believe in slow and steady. The company is the top motorsports operator in the US with more than a dozen racetracks hosting more than 100 events annually. Its race facilities include Daytona International Speedway (home of the Daytona 500), Talladega Superspeedway, and Michigan International Speedway. In addition, ISC operates the Daytona 500 EXperience theme park and museum and it owns 50% of motorsports merchandiser Motorsports Authentics with rival Speedway Motorsports. Former CEO James France and his family own about 70% control of the company. Events sanctioned by NASCAR, also controlled by the France family, account for about 90% of sales.

INTERNATIONAL UNION, UNTD AUTMBLE, ARSPCE AND AGRCLTRL IMPLMNT WRKRS OF AMRICA

8000 E JEFFERSON AVE
DETROIT, MI 482143963
Phone: 313 926-5000
Fax: –
Web: www.uaw.org

CEO: –
CFO: –
HR: –
FYE: December 31
Type: Private

At contract time, the International Union, UAW stands up (or sits down across the table) on behalf of some 390,000 active members and more than 600,000 retirees. The UAW (officially the United Automobile, Aerospace and Agricultural Implement Workers of America), represents workers at large and small companies, universities, and state agencies. The union has about 3,100 contracts with some 2,000 employers in the US, Canada, and Puerto Rico. Along with negotiating wages, benefits, and working conditions, the UAW provides education and training programs for its members, who belong to about 800 local unions. The organization was founded in Detroit in 1935.

	Annual Growth	12/05	12/06	12/07	12/08	12/22
Sales ($mil.)	45.3%	–	–	–	1.2	221.4
Net income ($ mil.)	–	–	–	–	–	(22.3)
Market value ($ mil.)	–	–	–	–	–	–
Employees	–	–	–	–	–	3,000

INTERNATIONAL WIRE GROUP, INC.

12 MASONIC AVE
CAMDEN, NY 133161202
Phone: 315 245-3800
Fax: –
Web: www.internationalwire.com

CEO: –
CFO: –
HR: –
FYE: December 31
Type: Private

International Wire Group (IWG) bares it all in the wire business. Through three divisions -- Bare Wire Products, Engineered Products - Europe, and High Performance Conductors -- IWG makes multi-gauge bare, silver-, nickel-, and tin-plated copper wire, as well as engineered wire products and performance conductors. The company's customers (General Cable is one of its largest) include suppliers and OEMs. IWG's wire products are used in industrial/energy, consumer electronics, aerospace and defense, medical electronics, automotive, and appliance applications.

	Annual Growth	12/04	12/05	12/06	12/07	12/08
Sales ($mil.)	–	–	–	(1,789.4)	730.8	736.4
Net income ($ mil.)	13597.3%	–	–	0.0	15.9	6.5
Market value ($ mil.)	–	–	–	–	–	–
Employees	–	–	–	–	–	1,600

INTERNET AMERICA INC

6210 ROTHWAY ST STE 100
HOUSTON, TX 770404600
Phone: 214 861-2500
Fax: –
Web: www.internetamerica.com

CEO: –
CFO: –
HR: –
FYE: June 30
Type: Private

Internet America is changing its "lines" of business. Traditionally a provider of dial-up Internet access and, to a lesser degree, of wire-line DSL broadband Internet access to rural and suburban markets in Texas, the company is battling dwindling subscriber numbers by expanding its wireless broadband Internet business. Total subscribers number more than 30,000 with about one quarter of those connecting wirelessly. Internet America also provides installation and maintenance services from its three Texas operational centers in Corsicana, San Antonio, and Stafford (near Houston). The ISP, founded in 1995, is known regionally for its 1-800-BE-A-GEEK sign-up number.

INTERNET CORPORATION FOR ASSIGNED NAMES AND NUMBERS

12025 WATERFRONT DR STE 300
LOS ANGELES, CA 900942536
Phone: 310 823-9358
Fax: –
Web: www.icann.org

CEO: –
CFO: –
HR: Liz Torres
FYE: June 30
Type: Private

Can anyone manage the Internet? This group says "ICANN." The Internet Corporation for Assigned Names and Numbers (ICANN) is a not-for-profit organization responsible for the management of the Internet's domain name system (DNS), allocation of Internet protocol (IP) addresses, and assignment of protocol parameters. The DNS allows people to type in an address like "www.hoovers.com" rather than the string of numbers that represents the underlying IP address. Internet users register some 20 domain names ending in .com, .org, .info, and .net, among others, through ICANN-accredited DNS registrars. The group is also managing the application process for a slew of new generic top-level domains (gTLDs).

	Annual Growth	06/13	06/14	06/15	06/19	06/20
Sales ($mil.)	2.7%	–	127.8	219.6	161.2	149.6
Net income ($ mil.)	23.2%	–	3.5	87.9	11.1	12.4
Market value ($ mil.)	–	–	–	–	–	–
Employees	–	–	–	–	–	160

INTERNETARRAY INC

7954 Transit Road, #232
Williamsville, NY 14221
Phone: 410 295-3388
Fax: –
Web: –

NBB: INAR
CEO: Michael Black
CFO: –
HR: –
FYE: June 30
Type: Public

InternetArray wants to align with an assortment of online companies. The firm, formerly U.S. MedSys, offers financing and advice to early-stage Internet companies. Calling its charges "partners," InternetArray provides marketing, sales, administrative, and other back-office assistance in exchange for a share of the partner company. The company owns social media developer Noobis, which is working with social networking sites in China, the US, the UK, and Canada. Noobis' Amplify product helps not-for-profits set up fundraising networks. InternetArray also owns BidSellBuy.com, an online auction and shopping network.

	Annual Growth	06/01	06/02	06/03	06/04	06/05
Sales ($mil.)	–	–	–	–	0.2	0.9
Net income ($ mil.)	–	–	–	(0.7)	(1.9)	(7.1)
Market value ($ mil.)	209.4%	–	–	0.0	0.0	0.0
Employees	–	–	–	–	–	31

INTERPACE BIOSCIENCES INC

Waterview Plaza, Suite 310, 2001 Route 46
Parsippany, NJ 07054
Phone: 855 776-6419
Fax: –
Web: www.interpace.com

NBB: IDXG
CEO: Thomas W Burnell
CFO: Thomas Freeburg
HR: –
FYE: December 31
Type: Public

PDI handles sales and marketing for pharmaceutical companies that would rather focus on product development. As a contract sales organization (CSO), the company provides sales teams dedicated to a single client and teams that represent multiple, non-competing brands. Sales teams typically are assigned to geographic territories on a client's behalf. Each year, contract sales services account for about 90% of PDI's revenue. The company's marketing and strategic consulting services operations are represented by its Pharmakon Interactive Healthcare Communications unit. PDI was established in 1987.

	Annual Growth	12/18	12/19	12/20	12/21	12/22
Sales ($mil.)	9.8%	21.9	24.1	32.4	41.3	31.8
Net income ($ mil.)	–	(12.2)	(26.7)	(26.5)	(14.9)	(22.0)
Market value ($ mil.)	6.8%	3.4	2.1	13.5	32.1	4.5
Employees	1.4%	89	178	152	147	94

INTERPUBLIC GROUP OF COMPANIES INC.

909 Third Avenue
New York, NY 10022
Phone: 212 704-1200
Fax: –
Web: www.interpublic.com

NYS: IPG
CEO: Arun Kumar
CFO: Ellen Johnson
HR: Linda Sorbera
FYE: December 31
Type: Public

The Interpublic Group of Companies (IPG) provides marketing, communications and business transformation services and has operations in over 100 countries. IPG specializes in data, creativity, media, consulting, commerce, behavioral science and communications. It provides innovative capabilities and scale in digital services, advertising and marketing services, e-commerce services, corporate and brand identity services, and strategic consulting, including IPG Mediabrands, UM, Initiative, Kinesso, FCB, IPG Health, and McCann Worldgroup. IPG also provides global public relations and communications services, live events, sports and entertainment marketing, and strategic consulting, including DXTRA Health, The Weber Shandwick Collective, and Golin. The US is IPG's largest market, accounting for almost 65% of the company's revenue.

	Annual Growth	12/19	12/20	12/21	12/22	12/23
Sales ($mil.)	1.6%	10,221	9,061.0	10,241	10,928	10,889
Net income ($ mil.)	13.8%	656.0	351.1	952.8	938.0	1,098.4
Market value ($ mil.)	9.0%	8,748.0	8,907.0	14,182	12,614	12,361
Employees	1.4%	54,300	50,200	55,600	58,400	57,400

INTERSECTIONS INC.

250 NORTHERN AVE STE 300
BOSTON, MA 022102035
Phone: 703 488-6100
Fax: –
Web: www.intersectionsweb.com

CEO: –
CFO: –
HR: –
FYE: December 31
Type: Private

Robert Johnson went to the crossroads to get the blues; consumers can go to Intersections to make sure they don't. Intersections provides credit management and identity theft protection to subscribers in North America. Its offerings include credit reports and ongoing record monitoring through major reporting agencies Equifax, Experian, and TransUnion. Its Intersections Insurance Services unit offers customers discounts on insurance products. Bank of America is the firm's #1 client, accounting for more than 40% of its revenue. Amid declining sales and profits, Intersections has exited the bail bonds and market intelligence businesses to focus on its core consumer protection services business.

INTERSTATE RESOURCES, INC.

600 PEACHTREE ST NE
ATLANTA, GA 303082269
Phone: 703 243-3355
Fax: –
Web: –

CEO: Neetmat Frem
CFO: Pierre Khatter
HR: –
FYE: December 31
Type: Private

Interstate Resources is not a fancy name for the latest US Highway Bill, but a paperboard and packaging products manufacturer. The company's offerings include linerboard, kraft paper (for bags), and corrugated medium board and packaging for consumer products and retail displays. It also produces timber and wood chips, and burns the waste to fuel its plants; it sells the excess to the local power grid. Interstate Resources operates about a dozen plants and produces 350,000 tons of linerboard and 180,000 tons of medium board per year. Its corrugated converting and packaging operations have a total annual capacity of 4 billion sq. ft. The company was acquired (80% of it) by UK-based DS Smith in 2017.

INTEST CORP.

804 East Gate Drive, Suite 200
Mt. Laurel, NJ 08054
Phone: 856 505-8800
Fax: 856 505-8801
Web: www.intest.com

ASE: INTT
CEO: Richard N Grant Jr
CFO: Duncan Gilmore
HR: Meghan Blount
FYE: December 31
Type: Public

When semiconductor makers are testing their chips, inTEST handles the trickiest chores. The semiconductor test equipment supplier offers test head manipulators, docking hardware, and systems for managing temperatures during integrated circuit (IC) production and testing. inTEST's products facilitate testing procedures by quickly moving and connecting IC components to handling and testing equipment. The company's clients include Analog Devices, Freescale Semiconductor, Intel, Sony, STMicroelectronics, and Texas Instruments (14% of sales). inTEST built up its product line through a series of acquisitions. The company gets most of its sales in the US.

	Annual Growth	12/19	12/20	12/21	12/22	12/23
Sales ($mil.)	19.3%	60.7	53.8	84.9	116.8	123.3
Net income ($ mil.)	41.6%	2.3	(0.9)	7.3	8.5	9.3
Market value ($ mil.)	23.0%	72.4	79.0	154.8	125.3	165.5
Employees	13.0%	198	204	316	346	323

INTEVAC, INC.

3560 Bassett Street
Santa Clara, CA 95054
Phone: 408 986-9888
Fax: –
Web: www.intevac.com

NMS: IVAC
CEO: Nigel Hunton
CFO: James Moniz
HR: –
FYE: December 30
Type: Public

Founded in 1991, Intevac is a leading provider of thin-film process technology and manufacturing platforms for high-volume manufacturing environments. The company leverages its core capabilities in high-volume manufacturing of small substrates to provide process manufacturing equipment solutions to the hard disk drive (HDD) and display cover panel (DCP) industries. Intevac's customers include manufacturers of hard disk media and DCPs. Intevac operates in a single segment: Thin-film Equipment (TFE). Product development and manufacturing activities occur in North America and Asia. Intevac also has field offices in Asia to support its customers. Intevac's products are highly technical and are sold primarily through Intevac's direct sales force. It generates most of its revenue internationally.

	Annual Growth	12/19*	01/21	01/22*	12/22	12/23
Sales ($mil.)	(16.6%)	108.9	97.8	38.5	35.8	52.7
Net income ($ mil.)	–	1.1	1.1	26.6	(17.1)	(12.2)
Market value ($ mil.)	(10.4%)	177.1	190.3	124.3	170.8	114.0
Employees	(17.2%)	272	269	151	166	128

*Fiscal year change

INTREPID CAPITAL CORPORATION

1400 MARSH LANDING PKWY STE 106
JACKSONVILLE BEACH, FL 322502493
Phone: 904 246-3383
Fax: –
Web: www.intrepidcapitalfunds.com

CEO: –
CFO: –
HR: –
FYE: December 31
Type: Private

Fear not! Intrepid Capital is here to help you face the sometimes frightening world of investing. Through subsidiary Intrepid Capital Management the company manages investments for institutional investors such as corporations, labor unions, foundations, and endowments, as well as wealthy individuals and families. Its products include small-cap and multi-cap equity, high-yield fixed-income, and balanced portfolios. The company invests in a variety of sectors including retail stores, consumer products, and sporting facilities. Chairman Forrest Travis founded Intrepid Capital in 1994 along with his son Mark, who is president and CEO of the firm.

INTREPID MUSEUM FOUNDATION, INC.

86 N RIVER PIERS FRNT 1
NEW YORK, NY 100061007
Phone: 212 245-0072
Fax: –
Web: www.intrepidmuseum.org

CEO: Arnold Fisher
CFO: Patricia Beene
HR: –
FYE: December 31
Type: Private

Intrepid Museum Foundation operates New York's Intrepid Sea, Air & Space Museum. Featuring the 900-foot-long aircraft carrier USS Intrepid and several military airplanes, the museum has drawn more than 10 million visitors since its opening in 1982 and attracts some 750,000 people each year. The USS Intrepid, which was built in 1943 and retired in 1974, is docked nearby on the Hudson River at Pier 86. Museum attendees also can tour the inside of the world's fastest commercial airplane, Concorde. The museum foundation also operates small rides, such as the Virtual Flight Zone, which puts civilians in the pilot's seat.

	Annual Growth	04/14	04/15	04/16*	12/21	12/22
Sales ($mil.)	(1.4%)	–	–	33.2	23.3	30.6
Net income ($ mil.)	–	–	–	(1.2)	(0.1)	(0.8)
Market value ($ mil.)	–	–	–	–	–	–
Employees	–	–	–	–	–	150

*Fiscal year change

INTREPID POTASH INC
NYS: IPI

707 17th Street, Suite 4200
Denver, CO 80202
Phone: 303 296-3006
Fax: –
Web: www.intrepidpotash.com

CEO: Robert P Jornayvaz III
CFO: Matthew D Preston
HR: Jamie Whyte
FYE: December 31
Type: Public

Intrepid Potash is a diversified mineral company that delivers potassium, magnesium, sulfur, salt, and water products essential for customer success in agriculture, animal feed and the oil and gas industry. The company is the only US producer of muriate of potash (sometimes referred to as potassium chloride or potash), which is applied as an essential nutrient for healthy crop development, utilized in several industrial applications, and used as an ingredient in animal feed. In addition, we produce a specialty fertilizer, Trio, which delivers three key nutrients, potassium, magnesium, and sulfate, in a single particle. It also provides water, magnesium chloride, brine and various oilfield products and services. Intrepid culls these minerals from a handful mines in New Mexico and Utah, where it also operates production facilities. The company has the capacity to annually produce about 390,000 tons of potash and 400,000 tons of Trio.

	Annual Growth	12/19	12/20	12/21	12/22	12/23
Sales ($mil.)	6.1%	220.1	197.0	270.3	337.6	279.1
Net income ($ mil.)	–	13.6	(27.2)	249.8	72.2	(35.7)
Market value ($ mil.)	72.3%	34.7	309.3	547.3	369.7	306.0
Employees	2.2%	445	440	440	473	485

INTRICON CORPORATION

1260 RED FOX RD
ARDEN HILLS, MN 551126944
Phone: 651 636-9770
Fax: –
Web: www.intricon.com

CEO: Scott Longval
CFO: Annalee Lutgen
HR: Sara Hill
FYE: December 31
Type: Private

IntriCon hears its future calling, and that future is in precision microminiature components and molded plastic parts, such as volume controls and switches, primarily used in hearing aids. IntriCon's components are also used in professional audio equipment, such as headsets and microphones, and in biotelemetry devices for such uses as diagnostic monitoring and drug delivery. The company has concentrated its product portfolio on what it terms "body-worn devices" through a series of acquisitions and divestitures, including the 2010 sale of its RTI Electronics business line to Shackleton Equity Partners.

INTRINSIX CORP.

100 CAMPUS DR FL 4
MARLBOROUGH, MA 017523041
Phone: 508 658-7600
Fax: –
Web: www.intrinsix.com

CEO: James Gobes Jr
CFO: Russell Cheung
HR: –
FYE: December 31
Type: Private

Intrinsix touts the intrinsic advantage of its design services. Founded in 1985, the company provides electronic design and verification services to manufacturers and semiconductor companies. Specializing in application-specific integrated circuits (ASICs), Intrinsix designs microchips, embedded systems (small, dedicated computer systems built into motherboards and other electronic circuits), and related software for such applications as digital media, networking, storage, and telecommunications. The company's owners include CTO Mark Beal and CEO James Gobes.

	Annual Growth	12/04	12/05	12/06	12/07	12/08
Sales ($mil.)	(26.0%)	–	–	12.3	10.7	6.7
Net income ($ mil.)	–	–	–	0.0	4.7	(0.9)
Market value ($ mil.)	–	–	–	–	–	–
Employees	–	–	–	–	–	50

INTRUSION INC
NAS: INTZ

101 East Park Blvd., Suite 1200
Plano, TX 75074
Phone: 972 234-6400
Fax: –
Web: www.intrusion.com

CEO: Anthony J Levecchio
CFO: –
HR: –
FYE: December 31
Type: Public

Think of Intrusion as a virtual police force protecting and serving your network. The security specialist sells network intrusion detection and security monitoring systems. Its products include software and stand-alone security appliances that guard against misuse of classified or private information and aid law enforcement agencies in battling cyber crimes. Intrusion also provides consulting, design, installation, and technical support services. The company sells its products directly and through distributors and resellers. Intrusion markets its products to government agencies, as well as businesses ranging from health care providers to telecommunications service operators.

	Annual Growth	12/18	12/19	12/20	12/21	12/22
Sales ($mil.)	(7.5%)	10.3	13.6	6.6	7.3	7.5
Net income ($ mil.)	–	2.3	4.5	(6.5)	(18.8)	(16.2)
Market value ($ mil.)	85.0%	5.7	5.7	373.3	72.9	67.0
Employees	21.2%	31	32	63	60	67

INTRUST FINANCIAL CORP.

105 North Main Street, Box One
Wichita, KS 67201
Phone: 316 383-1111
Fax: 316 383-1828
Web: –

CEO: C Q Chandler III
CFO: Jay L Smith
HR: –
FYE: December 31
Type: Public

INTRUST Financial wants to be entrusted with your cash. The holding company owns INTRUST Bank, which is the largest bank headquartered in Kansas. The bank operates about 40 branches in the Sunflower State, in addition to a handful of locations in Oklahoma and Arkansas. Serving consumers and small businesses, the bank offers a range of financial products, including savings, checking, and retirement accounts; CDs; credit cards; and loans and mortgages. INTRUST Bank was founded in 1876 as the Farmers and Merchants Bank. It has been run by the Chandler family for more than a century.

	Annual Growth	12/98	12/99	12/00	12/01	12/02
Assets ($mil.)	4.5%	2,115.5	2,338.5	2,418.5	2,555.5	2,524.5
Net income ($ mil.)	8.3%	19.5	22.5	25.1	26.5	26.9
Market value ($ mil.)	3.8%	302.2	311.5	278.9	303.0	351.0
Employees	4.1%	23	23	23	25	27

INTUIT INC
NMS: INTU

2700 Coast Avenue
Mountain View, CA 94043
Phone: 650 944-6000
Fax: –
Web: www.intuit.com

CEO: Sasan K Goodarzi
CFO: Michelle M Clatterbuck
HR: –
FYE: July 31
Type: Public

Intuit is a leading developer of software used for small business accounting (QuickBooks), and consumer tax preparation (TurboTax). The company helps consumers and small businesses prosper by delivering financial management, compliance, and marketing products and services. It also helps manage personal finances and budgeting with its online Mint service. Customers include individual consumers, accountants, and small businesses; Intuit claims about 100 million users for its products and services. Nearly all of the company's revenue is made in the US, although it has taken steps toward international expansion. More than 85% of revenue comes from services. The company was incorporated in 1984.

	Annual Growth	07/19	07/20	07/21	07/22	07/23
Sales ($mil.)	20.6%	6,784.0	7,679.0	9,633.0	12,726	14,368
Net income ($ mil.)	11.2%	1,557.0	1,826.0	2,062.0	2,066.0	2,384.0
Market value ($ mil.)	16.6%	77,764	85,913	148,615	127,920	143,491
Employees	18.0%	9,400	10,600	13,500	17,300	18,200

INTUITIVE SURGICAL INC

NMS: ISRG

1020 Kifer Road
Sunnyvale, CA 94086
Phone: 408 523-2100
Fax: –
Web: www.intuitive.com

CEO: –
CFO: –
HR: –
FYE: December 31
Type: Public

Intuitive Surgical is one of the pioneers of robotic-assisted surgery. The company develops the da Vinci Surgical System, a combination of software, hardware, and optics that allows doctors to perform robotically aided surgery from a remote console. The da Vinci system reproduces the doctor's hand movements during minimally invasive surgery in real time, performed by tiny electromechanical arms and instruments. The company's da Vinci products fall into five broad categories: da Vinci Surgical Systems, da Vinci instruments and accessories, da Vinci Stapling, da Vinci Energy, and da Vinci Vision, including Firefly Fluorescence imaging systems and da Vinci Endoscopes. It also provides a comprehensive suite of systems, learning, and services offerings. The US accounts for about 65% of the company's revenue.

	Annual Growth	12/19	12/20	12/21	12/22	12/23
Sales ($mil.)	12.3%	4,478.5	4,358.4	5,710.1	6,222.2	7,124.1
Net income ($ mil.)	6.9%	1,379.3	1,060.6	1,704.6	1,322.3	1,798.0
Market value ($ mil.)	(13.1%)	208,262	288,217	126,581	93,483	118,852
Employees	16.9%	7,326	8,031	9,793	12,120	13,676

INUVO INC

ASE: INUV

500 President Clinton Ave., Suite 300
Little Rock, AR 72201
Phone: 501 205-8508
Fax: –
Web: www.inuvo.com

CEO: Richard K Howe
CFO: Wallace D Ruiz
HR: Melanie Clayton
FYE: December 31
Type: Public

Inuvo provides online marketing and advertising services through its Exchange segment, which includes technology and analytics, and its Direct segment, which consists of websites designed to drive traffic to advertisers. Included in the Exchange segment is the Inuvo Platform, which offers affiliate marketing, search engine marketing, and lead generation services, helping customers drive Web traffic and convert that traffic into sales. Its Inuvo Search platform acts as a pay-per-click marketplace. Inuvo's Direct segment websites include BabytoBee (pregnancy advice) and Kowabunga (daily deals). In 2018 e-commerce tech company ConversionPoint Technologies agreed to acquire Inuvo.

	Annual Growth	12/19	12/20	12/21	12/22	12/23
Sales ($mil.)	4.7%	61.5	44.6	59.8	75.6	73.9
Net income ($ mil.)	–	(4.5)	(7.3)	(7.6)	(13.1)	(10.4)
Market value ($ mil.)	9.5%	40.8	62.5	73.1	30.6	58.6
Employees	–	–	64	71	81	87

INVACARE CORP

NBB: IVCR Q

One Invacare Way
Elyria, OH 44035
Phone: 440 329-6000
Fax: –
Web: www.invacare.com

CEO: Geoffrey P Purtill
CFO: Kathleen P Leneghan
HR: –
FYE: December 31
Type: Public

Invacare Corporation is a leading manufacturer and distributor in its markets for medical equipment used in non-acute care settings. Invacare is a leading company in custom power wheelchairs; custom manual wheelchairs; electromotive technology to augment wheelchairs and recreational products; recreational adaptive sports products; non-acute bed systems; and patient transfer and bathing equipment. The company sells its products to health care providers, consumers, and medical equipment dealers in North America, Europe, and the Asia Pacific region. Most of the company's revenue comes from international markets. Invacare emerged from Chapter 11 in mid-2023.

	Annual Growth	12/18	12/19	12/20	12/21	12/22
Sales ($mil.)	(6.5%)	972.3	928.0	850.7	872.5	741.7
Net income ($ mil.)	–	(43.9)	(53.3)	(28.3)	(45.6)	(101.1)
Market value ($ mil.)	(44.1%)	182.9	383.7	380.8	115.7	17.9
Employees	(9.6%)	4,200	3,900	3,400	3,000	2,800

INVENDA CORPORATION

7315 WISCONSIN AVE STE 400
BETHESDA, MD 208143202
Phone: 240 333-6100
Fax: –
Web: www.invenda.com

CEO: –
CFO: –
HR: –
FYE: December 31
Type: Private

Invenda Corporation wants to get inventive when it comes to consumer reviews. An interactive direct marketing firm, the company's primary operations, ConsumerReview.com, provides advertising and e-commerce services through its product interest Web communities, which foster communication and consumer reviews for various products. Websites within its network include PhotographyREVIEW.com, CarREVIEW.com, and AudioREVIEW.com, among others. In May 2010, Invenda sold two of its former divisions -- E-centives and Collabrys -- to shopper marketing giant Catalina Marketing. Both divisions developed software for database management, e-mail marketing, and promotions.

INVENSENSE, INC.

1745 TECHNOLOGY DR STE 200
SAN JOSE, CA 95110
Phone: 408 501-2200
Fax: –
Web: invensense.tdk.com

CEO: Behrooz Abdi
CFO: Mark Dentinger
HR: Aishwarya Rajasekaran
FYE: April 03
Type: Private

InvenSense, a TDK Group Company, is a world leading provider of MEMS sensor platforms found in Mobile, Wearables, Smart Home, Industrial, and Automotive products. The semiconductor manufacturer addresses the emerging need of many mass-market consumer applications via improved performance, accuracy, and intuitive motion-, gesture- sound-, and ultrasonic 3D- based interfaces. Its MotionTracking devices are rapidly becoming a key function in many consumer electronic devices such as smartphones, tablets, gaming consoles, and smart TVs to provide an intuitive way for consumers to interact with their electronic devices. The company was founded in 2003.

INVENTERGY GLOBAL INC

19925 Stevens Creek Blvd., #142
Cupertino, CA 95014
Phone: 408 389-3510
Fax: –
Web: www.inventergy.com

CEO: –
CFO: –
HR: –
FYE: December 31
Type: Public

eOn Communications knows it's been ages since you've had a good customer service experience. The company's products integrate voice and Internet communications for large call centers and e-commerce customer contact centers. eOn's communications servers feature automatic call distribution, e-mail queuing, and customer identification. It also sells the Millennium voice switching hardware platform, a private branch exchange (PBX) system with computer telephony integration. Customers include Lillian Vernon and Rockhurst University. eOn gets more than 90% of sales from the US. Chairman David Lee owns about 27% of the company.

	Annual Growth	07/12	07/13*	12/14	12/15	12/16
Sales ($mil.)	(47.0%)	22.5	20.6	0.7	4.9	1.8
Net income ($ mil.)	–	0.5	0.0	(20.1)	(11.7)	(7.7)
Market value ($ mil.)	(4.1%)	10.2	10.3	8.1	18.6	8.6
Employees	(56.3%)	82	75	15	8	3

*Fiscal year change

INVESCO LTD
NYS: IVZ

1331 Spring Street, Suite 2500
Atlanta, GA 30309
Phone: 404 892-0896
Fax: –
Web: www.invesco.com

CEO: –
CFO: –
HR: –
FYE: December 31
Type: Public

Invesco is a global independent investment management firm that offers a range of investment products and services, including mutual funds, exchange-traded funds, separately managed accounts, and savings plans. Invesco and its subsidiaries boast roughly $1.4 trillion in assets under management on behalf of retail and institutional clients in more than 110 countries in North America, Europe, the Middle East, Africa, and the Asia-Pacific region. Its subsidiary, Invesco Pensions Limited, is an insurance company that was established to facilitate retirement savings plans in the UK. Americas generates more than 75% of Invesco's total revenue.

	Annual Growth	12/19	12/20	12/21	12/22	12/23
Sales ($mil.)	(1.7%)	6,117.4	6,145.6	6,894.5	6,048.9	5,716.4
Net income ($ mil.)	–	688.3	761.6	1,629.8	920.7	(96.9)
Market value ($ mil.)	–	–	–	–	–	–
Employees	(1.0%)	8,821	8,512	8,513	8,611	8,489

INVESCO MORTGAGE CAPITAL INC
NYS: IVR

1555 Peachtree Street N.E., Suite 1800
Atlanta, GA 30309
Phone: 404 892-0896
Fax: –
Web: www.invescomortgagecapital.com

CEO: John M Anzalone
CFO: R L Phegley Jr
HR: –
FYE: December 31
Type: Public

Invesco Mortgage Capital is ready to roll now that the mortgage industry has finally reversed its course. Invesco Mortgage is a real estate investment trust (REIT) that finances and manages residential and commercial mortgage-backed securities and mortgage loans. It purchases agency-backed mortgages secured by the likes of Fannie Mae and Freddie Mac and is managed and advised by sibling Invesco Institutional, a subsidiary of Invesco Ltd. The firm's mortgage-backed securities portfolio is concentrated within the four populous states of California, Florida, Texas, and New York.

	Annual Growth	12/19	12/20	12/21	12/22	12/23
Assets ($mil.)	(30.3%)	22,347	8,632.9	8,443.8	5,097.4	5,284.2
Net income ($ mil.)	–	364.1	(1,674.4)	(90.0)	(402.9)	(15.9)
Market value ($ mil.)	–	806.9	163.8	134.7	–	–
Employees	–	–	–	–	–	–

INVESTAR HOLDING CORP
NMS: ISTR

10500 Coursey Boulevard
Baton Rouge, LA 70816
Phone: 225 227-2222
Fax: –
Web: www.investarbank.com

CEO: John J D'Angelo
CFO: Christopher L Hufft
HR: –
FYE: December 31
Type: Public

Investar is a community bank where the tellers are so personable they say, 'How's your mama and dem?' The holding company operates though subsidiary Investar Bank in south Louisiana. It offers checking and savings accounts as well as online banking services to individuals and small and midsized businesses. Investar Bank also provides loans: personal, business, mortgage, and construction. (The bank makes most of its money on interest income from loans and loan-related fees.) It has 10 branches in south Louisiana, stretching along the I-10 corridor in Lafayette, Baton Rouge, and New Orleans, and north of New Orleans in Hammond. Founded in 2006, Investar went public in 2014 and raised $40 million.

	Annual Growth	12/19	12/20	12/21	12/22	12/23
Assets ($mil.)	7.0%	2,148.9	2,321.2	2,513.2	2,753.8	2,815.2
Net income ($ mil.)	(0.2%)	16.8	13.9	8.0	35.7	16.7
Market value ($ mil.)	(11.2%)	234.0	161.2	179.5	209.9	145.3
Employees	0.5%	324	326	343	338	331

INVESTORS TITLE CO.
NMS: ITIC

121 North Columbia Street
Chapel Hill, NC 27514
Phone: 919 968-2200
Fax: –
Web: www.invtitle.com

CEO: J A Fine
CFO: James A Fine Jr
HR: Katy Cordell
FYE: December 31
Type: Public

Investors Title insures you in case your land is, well, not completely yours. It's the holding company for Investors Title Insurance and Northeast Investors Title Insurance, which underwrite land title insurance and sell reinsurance to other title companies. (Title insurance protects those who invest in real property against loss resulting from defective titles.) Investors Title Insurance serves customers from about 30 offices in North Carolina, South Carolina, Michigan, and Nebraska, and through branches or agents in 20 additional states. Northeast Investors Title operates through an agency office in New York. Founder and CEO J. Allen Fine and his family own more than 20% of Investors Title.

	Annual Growth	12/19	12/20	12/21	12/22	12/23
Assets ($mil.)	5.8%	263.9	282.9	331.5	339.8	330.6
Net income ($ mil.)	(8.9%)	31.5	39.4	67.0	23.9	21.7
Market value ($ mil.)	0.5%	301.0	289.3	372.8	279.0	306.6
Employees	9.2%	402	456	562	655	571

INVITATION HOMES INC
NYS: INVH

1717 Main Street, Suite 2000
Dallas, TX 75201
Phone: 972 421-3600
Fax: –
Web: www.invitationhomes.com

CEO: Dallas B Tanner
CFO: Ernest M Freedman
HR: –
FYE: December 31
Type: Public

Raised up from the foundations of Blackstone investment funds, Invitation Homes is a leading owner and operator of single-family rental homes in the US. The Real Estate Investment Trust (REIT) has a portfolio of over 80,000 homes in major metropolitan areas, with an emphasis in the Western US and Florida. A typical home is comprised of 3 bedrooms and 2 bathrooms, about 1,850 square feet, and rents for just under $2,000/month. Invitation Homes completed in late 2017 the acquisition of Starwood Waypoint Homes, and in the process gained a new CEO, Fred Tuomi, who previously led Starwood.

	Annual Growth	12/19	12/20	12/21	12/22	12/23
Sales ($mil.)	8.4%	1,764.7	1,822.8	1,996.6	2,238.1	2,432.3
Net income ($ mil.)	37.5%	145.5	196.2	261.4	383.3	519.5
Market value ($ mil.)	3.3%	18,340	18,175	27,746	18,138	20,874
Employees	8.1%	1,140	1,149	1,240	1,511	1,555

IO INTEGRATION INC.

1903 CENTRAL DR STE 201
BEDFORD, TX 760215876
Phone: 408 996-3420
Fax: –
Web: www.bluprintx.com

CEO: Mike Holt
CFO: Nigel Oswald
HR: –
FYE: December 31
Type: Private

IO Integration knows its way around digital imaging. The company, which does business as IOI, primarily sells and integrates software used in the graphic arts. The company primarily targets clients in the advertising, marketing, publishing, and printing industries. Applications for the products it sells include digital image capture, workflow automation, content management, and remote proofing. It has sales and service partnerships with such developers as Adobe, Apple and Quark. IOI's customers have included Advanstar, Quebecor World, and McCann Erickson.

IOCO

537 HAMILTON AVE
PALO ALTO, CA 943012012
Phone: 415 252-4388
Fax: –
Web: www.mckinsey.com

CEO: Jeff Smith
CFO: –
HR: –
FYE: December 31
Type: Private

When the moon hits your eye and you need some design, that's amore ... or maybe just Lunar Design. The firm offers industrial design, engineering, graphic design, brand development, and corporate identity services. The majority of Lunar's work is geared towards the high-tech industry; it designed Apple's first Powerbook, as well as the first Palm. Other product designs include the HP TouchSmart PC for Hewlett-Packard, sunglasses for DKNY, a toothbrush for Oral-B, and a catheter for Acuson Corporation. Lunar has offices in California, Hong Kong, and Germany. The design firm was founded in 1984 by CEO Jeff Smith and COO Gerard Furbershaw.

ION GEOPHYSICAL CORP

NBB: IOGP Q

2105 CityWest Blvd., Suite 100
Houston, TX 77042-2855
Phone: 281 933-3339
Fax: 281 879-3626
Web: www.iongeo.com

CEO: Christopher T Usher
CFO: Michael L Morrison
HR: –
FYE: December 31
Type: Public

There's a whole lotta shakin' goin' on at ION Geophysical. The seismic data-acquisition imaging and software systems company helps worldwide petroleum exploration contractors identify and measure subsurface geological structures that could contain oil and gas. Its data acquisition products are capable of processing 3-D, 4-D, and multi-component 3-C seismic data for land, marine, and transition areas (such as swamps, shoreline, marsh, and jungle). ION Geophysical also makes other products such as geophysical software, digital sensors, cables, and telemetry systems. Its marine positioning systems map the geography of the ocean's floor. Nearly 75% of total revenue accounts outside North America.

	Annual Growth	12/16	12/17	12/18	12/19	12/20
Sales ($mil.)	(8.2%)	172.8	197.6	180.0	174.7	122.7
Net income ($ mil.)	–	(65.1)	(30.2)	(71.2)	(48.2)	(37.2)
Market value ($ mil.)	(20.2%)	86.0	283.1	74.2	124.4	34.8
Employees	(2.8%)	480	478	496	519	428

IONIS PHARMACEUTICALS INC

NMS: IONS

2855 Gazelle Court
Carlsbad, CA 92010
Phone: 760 931-9200
Fax: –
Web: www.ionispharma.com

CEO: Brett P Monia
CFO: Elizabeth L Hougen
HR: Karen Horning
FYE: December 31
Type: Public

Ionis Pharmaceuticals develops biotech drugs to target neurological disorders and other conditions. Products are based on its antisense technology, in which drugs attach themselves to strands of RNA to prevent them from producing disease-causing proteins; the hoped-for result is a therapy that fights disease without harming healthy cells. Commercial medicines approved in major global markets include SPINRAZA for spinal muscular atrophy and TEGSEDI for polyneuropathy caused by hereditary TTR amyloidosis (marketed by Akcea). It also has a rich late-stage pipeline of medicines, primarily focused on its cardiovascular and neurology franchises. Its late-stage pipeline consists of seven medicines in Phase 3 development for nine indications.

	Annual Growth	12/19	12/20	12/21	12/22	12/23
Sales ($mil.)	(8.5%)	1,122.6	729.3	810.5	587.4	787.6
Net income ($ mil.)	–	294.1	(451.3)	(28.6)	(269.7)	(366.3)
Market value ($ mil.)	(4.3%)	8,719.6	8,161.0	4,392.3	5,451.7	7,302.2
Employees	–	–	817	757	600	796

IOWA FIRST BANCSHARES CORP.

NBB: IOFB

300 East Second Street
Muscatine, IA 52761
Phone: 563 263-4221
Fax: 563 262-4213
Web: www.fnbmusc.com

CEO: –
CFO: –
HR: –
FYE: December 31
Type: Public

Mark Twain remembered Muscatine for its sunsets, but Iowa First Bancshares is hoping you'll remember it for its banks. Iowa First Bancshares is the holding company for First National Bank of Muscatine (founded in 1870) and First National Bank in Fairfield (founded in 1865 and acquired by Iowa First Bancshares in 1985). The banks, which operate eight branches in the two southeastern Iowa towns for which they're named, offer individuals and businesses checking, savings, money market, and time deposit accounts, as well as other traditional products and services including loans, trust services, debit cards, credit-related insurance, Internet and telephone banking, and brokerage services.

	Annual Growth	12/01	12/02	12/03	12/04	12/05
Assets ($mil.)	0.1%	380.6	378.7	372.4	364.2	382.4
Net income ($ mil.)	(0.4%)	3.4	3.6	3.2	3.7	3.3
Market value ($ mil.)	13.0%	29.4	32.4	38.3	47.2	48.1
Employees	–	125	131	125	130	–

IOWA HEALTH SYSTEM

1776 WEST LAKES PKWY STE 400
WEST DES MOINES, IA 502668377
Phone: 515 241-6161
Fax: –
Web: www.unitypoint.org

CEO: David Williams
CFO: Doug Watson
HR: Daniel Tallon
FYE: December 31
Type: Private

Iowa Health System (IHS), which does business as UnityPoint Health, is the nations' fifth largest non-denominational health system. This overall system name also includes the UnityPoint Clinic (formerly known as Iowa Health Physicians & Clinic) and UnityPoint at Home and UnityPoint Hospice (formerly Iowa Health Home Care). As an industry leader in the Midwest, the system provides care throughout Iowa, Illinois, and Wisconsin through partnerships with more than 1,100 physicians and providers working in more than 280 UnityPoint Clinics, about 30 hospitals in metropolitan and rural communities, and home care services throughout its eight regions. UnityPoint Health was founded in 1993.

	Annual Growth	12/13	12/14	12/15	12/16	12/17
Sales ($mil.)	2.5%	–	–	–	4,054.8	4,157.2
Net income ($ mil.)	54.4%	–	–	–	148.7	229.5
Market value ($ mil.)	–	–	–	–	–	–
Employees	–	–	–	–	–	18,923

IOWA STATE UNIVERSITY OF SCIENCE AND TECHNOLOGY

515 MORRILL RD
AMES, IA 500112105
Phone: 515 294-6162
Fax: –
Web: www.iastate.edu

CEO: –
CFO: –
HR: Kristi Darr
FYE: June 30
Type: Private

Home to the Cyclones athletics teams, Iowa State University of Science and Technology (ISU) can be a whirlwind experience for some. ISU is a public land-grant institution offering higher education courses and programs with an emphasis on science, technology, and related areas. ISU's eight colleges offer more than 100 undergraduate degrees and nearly 200 fields of study leading to graduate and professional degrees. The university has an enrollment of more than 31,000 students and charges more than $7,720 in tuition and fees for resident students for two semesters.

	Annual Growth	06/18	06/19	06/20	06/21	06/22
Sales ($mil.)	2.7%	–	952.0	937.0	895.6	1,031.9
Net income ($ mil.)	(20.9%)	–	97.3	43.2	44.6	48.1
Market value ($ mil.)	–	–	–	–	–	–
Employees	–	–	–	–	–	5,800

IPALCO ENTERPRISES, INC.

1 MONUMENT CIR
INDIANAPOLIS, IN 462043025
Phone: 317 261-8261
Fax: –
Web: www.ipalco.com

CEO: Lisa Krueger
CFO: Gustavo Garavaglia
HR: –
FYE: December 31
Type: Private

IPALCO Enterprises ensures that the Indianapolis 500 track is lit up and the sound system is crackling. Through its regulated utility unit, Indianapolis Power & Light (IPL), IPALCO generates, transmits, and distributes electricity to about 470,000 customers in central Indiana. IPL has almost 3,500 MW of generating capacity; most of its power is generated from coal-burning plants. A member of The Midwest Independent Transmission System Operator the company provides wholesale power to the regional power grid operator at market rates. IPALCO's nonregulated subsidiary, Mid-America Capital Resources, has an interest in a small venture capital fund. IPALCO is a subsidiary of AES, a top independent power producer.

IPAYMENT, INC.

30721 RUSSELL RANCH RD STE 200
WESTLAKE VILLAGE, CA 913626317
Phone: 212 802-7200
Fax: –
Web: www.paysafe.com

CEO: –
CFO: Mark C Monaco
HR: –
FYE: December 31
Type: Private

iPayment doesn't want small businesses to pay an arm and a leg for credit and debit card processing. The company's approximately 153,000 clients are mostly small US merchants, firms taking money over the phone or Internet, and those that previously may have accepted only cash or checks as payment. iPayment markets through independent sales organizations and has grown by consolidating its niche, buying a dozen competitors and merchant portfolios since 2003. A typical iPayment merchant generates less than $185,000 of charge volume per year, with an average transaction value of about $70. In 2013, iPayment processed charge volume of nearly $22 billion. iPayments is owned by iPayment Holdings.

IPC HEALTHCARE, INC.

4605 LANKERSHIM BLVD STE 617
NORTH HOLLYWOOD, CA 916021856
Phone: 888 447-2362
Fax: –
Web: –

CEO: Adam D Singer
CFO: Richard H Kline III
HR: –
FYE: December 31
Type: Private

IPC Healthcare (formerly IPC The Hospitalist Company) is on the leading edge of a growing US trend toward hospitalist specialization. The staffing firm provides 1,900 hospitalists to more than 400 hospitals and 1,200 post-acute care facilities facilities in about 30 states. Hospitalists are health care providers (physicians, nurses, and physicians assistants) who oversee all of a patient's treatment from the beginning to the end of their stay. They answer questions and coordinate treatment programs to improve the quality of care and reduce the length of a patient's hospital stay. Team Health Holdings bought IPC for some $1.6 billion in late 2015.

IPCO US LLC

10 BLOOMFIELD AVE STE 8
PINE BROOK, NJ 070589743
Phone: 973 720-7000
Fax: –
Web: www.ipco.com

CEO: –
CFO: –
HR: –
FYE: December 31
Type: Private

IPCO's toughness is steel belted. The company manufactures machinery and steel belts for internal merchandise movement and management, which are used in the food, chemical, and material-handling industries. IPCO is made up of various product areas that include belts, process solutions like cooling systems and film and sheet casting, press plates for laminate production, and equipment and systems for heat recovery systems. IPCO (formerly Sandvik Process Systems) is owned by FAM AB, part of the Wallenberg group.

IPG PHOTONICS CORP

NMS: IPGP

377 Simarano Drive
Marlborough, MA 01752
Phone: 508 373-1100
Fax: –
Web: www.ipgphotonics.com

CEO: Eugene A Scherbakov
CFO: Timothy P Mammen V
HR: Bayli Lane
FYE: December 31
Type: Public

IPG Photonics develops, manufactures, and sells fiber lasers and amplifiers, and diode lasers, which are primarily used in materials processing applications such as welding and brazing, cutting, marking, and engraving, cleaning and stripping, and solar cell manufacturing. Its fiber lasers are also used in additive manufacturing such as laser sintering, 3D printing, and ablation. IPG design and manufacture a broad range of high-performance fiber lasers and amplifiers. It also makes packaged diodes, direct diode lasers, laser and non-laser systems, and communications components and systems. Many of its products are designed to be used as general-purpose energy or light sources, making them useful in diverse applications and markets. Deriving more than 75% of its sales outside North America, IPG Photonics has offices and applications laboratories worldwide.

	Annual Growth	12/19	12/20	12/21	12/22	12/23
Sales ($mil.)	(0.5%)	1,314.6	1,200.7	1,460.9	1,429.5	1,287.4
Net income ($ mil.)	5.0%	180.2	159.6	278.4	109.9	218.9
Market value ($ mil.)	(7.0%)	6,712.8	10,366	7,973.6	4,385.2	5,027.6
Employees	0.9%	5,960	6,060	6,580	6,230	6,180

IQVIA HOLDINGS INC

NYS: IQV

2400 Ellis Rd.
Durham, NC 27703
Phone: 919 998-2000
Fax: –
Web: www.quintiles.com

CEO: ARI Bousbib
CFO: Ronald E Bruehlman
HR: –
FYE: December 31
Type: Public

IQVIA Holdings provides advanced analytics, technology solution, and clinical research services to the life sciences industry. It also offers the IQVIA Connected Intelligence which delivers powerful insights that enable customers to accelerate clinical development and commercialization of medical treatments. It also boasts one of the largest and most comprehensive health information collections in the world, which includes patient records, prescription, and promotional data, medical, claims, genomic, social media, and many more. It has a diversified base of over 10,000 clients, including pharmaceutical companies, biotechnology companies, device and diagnostic companies and consumer health companies in over 100 countries. IQVIA gets about 50% of its revenue in the US.

	Annual Growth	12/19	12/20	12/21	12/22	12/23
Sales ($mil.)	7.8%	11,088	11,359	13,874	14,410	14,984
Net income ($ mil.)	63.3%	191.0	279.0	966.0	1,091.0	1,358.0
Market value ($ mil.)	10.6%	28,044	32,519	51,208	37,188	41,995
Employees	6.7%	67,000	70,000	79,000	86,000	87,000

IRBY CONSTRUCTION COMPANY

318 OLD HIGHWAY 49 S
RICHLAND, MS 392189449
Phone: 601 709-4729
Fax: –
Web: www.irbyconstruction.com

CEO: –
CFO: Robert A Croft Sr
HR: Amanda Lott
FYE: December 31
Type: Private

Irby Construction kicks high voltage into gear. The electrical contractor is a leader in power line construction. It also builds transmission and distribution systems and substations in rural US and international locations, including Central America. Services include stringing of conductors, erecting pole lines, and providing emergency manpower and equipment. Stuart Irby Sr. founded the company in 1919 as Stuart C. Irby Company, a wholesale electrical supplier and contractor that erected power lines throughout the Southeast under the aegis of the Rural Electrification Administration during the 1930s. Irby Construction is now a unit of specialized contracting services provider Quanta Services.

IREX CORPORATION

120 N LIME ST
LANCASTER, PA 176022923
Phone: 717 397-3633
Fax: –
Web: www.irex.com

CEO: Lori A Pickell
CFO: Devon E Liddell
HR: Allie Brouse
FYE: December 31
Type: Private

Irex is a network of specialty contracting companies delivering exceptional value in performance, quality, safety and service. The company specializes in S.I.P.A. Services (Scaffolding, Insulation, Painting, and Abatement), which includes mechanical insulation, scaffolding and access services, industrial coatings, and the abatement of asbestos, lead, and other hazardous materials. Acting as prime contractor or subcontractor, its companies provide new construction and maintenance services to industrial, commercial, and government customers. Irex traces its roots back to 1969.

IRC RETAIL CENTERS LLC

814 COMMERCE DR STE 300
OAK BROOK, IL 605238823
Phone: 877 206-5656
Fax: –
Web: www.pinetree.com

CEO: Mark E Zalatoris
CFO: Brett A Brown
HR: –
FYE: December 31
Type: Private

IRC Retail Centers (formerly Inland Real Estate Corporation) buys, leases, and operates retail properties, mainly in the Midwest, with a concentration in the Chicago and Minneapolis/St. Paul metropolitan markets. The self-managed real estate investment trust (REIT) owns about 150 properties, most of which are strip shopping centers anchored by a grocery or big-box store. It also invests in single-tenant retail properties and develops properties, usually through joint ventures. The REIT's portfolio totals about 14 million sq. ft. of leasable space in a dozen states. IRC Retail Centers was acquired by DRA Advisors in early 2015.

	Annual Growth	12/10	12/11	12/12	12/13	12/14
Assets ($mil.)	12.5%	–	–	1,243.4	1,529.9	1,573.0
Net income ($ mil.)	48.7%	–	–	17.7	111.7	39.1
Market value ($ mil.)	–	–	–	–	–	–
Employees	–	–	–	–	–	129

IRIDEX CORP.

NMS: IRIX

1212 Terra Bella Avenue
Mountain View, CA 94043-1824
Phone: 650 940-4700
Fax: –
Web: www.iridex.com

CEO: David I Bruce
CFO: Fuad Ahmad
HR: –
FYE: December 31
Type: Public

A meeting with IRIDEX can be an eye-opening experience. The company makes laser systems and peripheral devices used to treat serious eye conditions including the three major causes of blindness: macular degeneration, glaucoma, and diabetic retinopathy. The company markets its products under such brands as IQ and OcuLight through a direct sales staff in the US and through distributors in more than 100 countries worldwide. Its ophthalmic systems, including laser consoles, delivery devices, and disposable probes, are used by ophthalmologists in hospitals, surgery centers, and physician practice centers. IRIDEX exited its aesthetics business (lasers for dermatology and plastic surgery procedures) in 2012.

	Annual Growth	12/18	12/19*	01/21	01/22*	12/22
Sales ($mil.)	7.5%	42.6	43.4	36.3	53.9	57.0
Net income ($ mil.)	–	(12.8)	(8.8)	(6.3)	(5.2)	(7.5)
Market value ($ mil.)	(18.0%)	71.2	37.6	40.1	97.7	32.1
Employees	1.9%	152	132	128	170	164

*Fiscal year change

IRELL & MANELLA LLP

1800 AVENUE OF THE STARS STE 900
LOS ANGELES, CA 900674276
Phone: 310 277-1010
Fax: –
Web: www.irell.com

CEO: –
CFO: –
HR: –
FYE: December 31
Type: Private

Law firm Irell & Manella is known for its work related to the entertainment industry, and over the years its clients have included big movers and shakers like Pinnacle Entertainment and Wynn Resorts Limited. The firm employs attorneys that maintain a wide range of practices, including appellate, art, intellectual property transactions, mergers and acquisitions, securities litigation, taxation, and white collar defense. Irell & Manella operates from two Southern California locations. The firm was founded in 1941.

IRIDIUM COMMUNICATIONS INC

NMS: IRDM

1750 Tysons Boulevard, Suite 1400
McLean, VA 22102
Phone: 703 287-7400
Fax: –
Web: www.iridium.com

CEO: Matthew J Desch
CFO: Thomas J Fitzpatrick
HR: –
FYE: December 31
Type: Public

Iridium Communications (formerly Iridium Satellite) is the only commercial provider of communications services offering true global coverage, connecting people, organizations and assets to and from anywhere, in real time. The company offers mobile voice and data services, high speed data services and IoT services worldwide, targeting companies that operate in remote areas. While Iridium focuses on such commercial industries as energy, defense, maritime, and industrial, its main customer is the US government. Boeing primarily operates and maintains the Iridium satellite system, which consists of around 65 operational satellites with in-orbit and ground spares and related ground infrastructure. The mobile satellite communications company has operations center in Virginia and generates more than 50% of sales in the US.

	Annual Growth	12/19	12/20	12/21	12/22	12/23
Sales ($mil.)	9.0%	560.4	583.4	614.5	721.0	790.7
Net income ($ mil.)	–	(162.0)	(56.1)	(9.3)	8.7	15.4
Market value ($ mil.)	13.7%	3,025.2	4,828.2	5,069.4	6,310.7	5,053.5
Employees	10.6%	512	522	543	663	766

IROBOT CORP

NMS: IRBT

8 Crosby Drive
Bedford, MA 01730
Phone: 781 430-3000
Fax: –
Web: www.irobot.com

CEO: Colin M Angle
CFO: Julie Zeiler
HR: –
FYE: December 30
Type: Public

iRobot is a leading consumer robot company that designs and builds robots that empower people to do more around the globe. The company's portfolio of home robots and smart home devices features proprietary technologies for the connected home and advanced concepts in cleaning, mapping and navigation, human-robot interaction, and physical solutions. With approximately 17.6 million connected customers, iRobot sells its robotic floor care products through distributor and retail sales channels, as well as the online store on its website and through its Home App. It operates worldwide but generates more than 50% of its revenue in the US. Since its founding, iRobot has sold more than 50 million consumer robots around the world.

	Annual Growth	12/19*	01/21	01/22*	12/22	12/23
Sales ($mil.)	(7.5%)	1,214.0	1,430.4	1,565.0	1,183.4	890.6
Net income ($ mil.)	–	85.3	147.1	30.4	(286.3)	(304.7)
Market value ($ mil.)	(7.2%)	1,459.7	2,245.2	1,842.3	1,345.9	1,082.2
Employees	(0.3%)	1,128	1,209	1,372	1,254	1,113

*Fiscal year change

IRON EAGLE GROUP, INC.

61 West 62nd Street, Suite 23F
New York, NY 10023
Phone: 800 481-4445
Fax: –
Web: –

CEO: –
CFO: –
HR: –
FYE: December 31
Type: Public

Are diamonds or gold the ultimate token of return on investment? Pinnacle Resources says -- both! The firm invests in drilling and refinery projects in diamonds, gold, tantalum, and vanadium (used in the manufacture of high-strength steel). Its holdings include the South African Vanadium and Magnetite Exploration and Development, which has a mineral lease on land containing vanadium and titanium mines; and joint venture Diamonaire, engaged in the recovery of diamondiferous gravels from the ocean floor off the coast of South Africa. The firm owns a tantalum refinery and a gold drilling property in Ghana. Pinnacle Resources was founded in 1995.

	Annual Growth	12/07	12/08	12/09	12/10	12/11
Sales ($mil.)	–	–	–	–	–	–
Net income ($ mil.)	–	–	–	–	(0.9)	(3.3)
Market value ($ mil.)	(95.8%)	–	–	–	1.5	0.0
Employees	–	–	–	–	–	3

IRON MOUNTAIN INC (NEW)

NYS: IRM

85 New Hampshire Avenue, Suite 150
Portsmouth, NH 03801
Phone: 617 535-4766
Fax: –
Web: www.ironmountain.com

CEO: William L Meaney
CFO: Barry Hytinen
HR: –
FYE: December 31
Type: Public

Iron Mountain is a market leader in the physical ecosystem supporting information storage, operates about 1,400 facilities worldwide. The company stores physical records and data backup media, offers information management solutions and provides data center space for enterprise-class colocation and hyper-scale deployments. It offers comprehensive records and information management services, and data management services, along with the expertise and experience to address complex storage and information management challenges such as rising storage rental costs, legal and regulatory compliance, and disaster recovery requirements. It provides secure and reliable data center facilities to protect digital information and ensure the continued operation of its customers' IT infrastructure. Iron Mountain has about 225,000 customers in about 60 countries. It generates most of its sales in the US, almost 65% of sales.

	Annual Growth	12/19	12/20	12/21	12/22	12/23
Sales ($mil.)	6.5%	4,262.6	4,147.3	4,491.5	5,103.6	5,480.3
Net income ($ mil.)	(8.9%)	267.4	342.7	450.2	557.0	184.2
Market value ($ mil.)	21.7%	9,310.6	8,612.4	15,288	14,563	20,444
Employees	1.9%	25,000	24,000	25,000	26,000	27,000

IRONWOOD PHARMACEUTICALS INC

NMS: IRWD

100 Summer Street, Suite 2300
Boston, MA 02110
Phone: 617 621-7722
Fax: –
Web: www.ironwoodpharma.com

CEO: Thomas A McCourt
CFO: Gina Consylman
HR: –
FYE: December 31
Type: Public

Ironwood Pharmaceuticals develops internally discovered gastrointestinal drugs; its first commercial product, LINZESS (or linaclotide), a treatment for irritable bowel syndrome (IBS) and chronic constipation, is sold in the US and in Canada under the brand name Constella. To support the development and commercialization of linaclotide worldwide, it partnered with pharmaceutical companies including with AbbVie in the US and all countries worldwide other than China (including Hong Kong and Macau) with AstraZeneca and Japan with Astellas Pharma. Through collaboration with COUR Pharmaceutical, Ironwood has an option to acquire an exclusive license from COUR to research, develop, manufacture and commercialize, in the US, products containing CNP-104 for the potential treatment of PBC.

	Annual Growth	12/19	12/20	12/21	12/22	12/23
Sales ($mil.)	0.8%	428.4	389.5	413.8	410.6	442.7
Net income ($ mil.)	–	21.5	106.2	528.4	175.1	(1,002.2)
Market value ($ mil.)	(3.7%)	2,081.1	1,780.9	1,823.1	1,937.2	1,788.7
Employees	(4.2%)	317	232	219	219	267

IROQUOIS MEMORIAL HOSPITAL & RESIDENT HOME

200 E FAIRMAN AVE
WATSEKA, IL 609701644
Phone: 815 432-5841
Fax: –
Web: www.iroquoismemorial.com

CEO: Chuck Bohlmann
CFO: Richard Harning
HR: Tera Bivins
FYE: September 30
Type: Private

Iroquis Memorial Hospital and its clinics provide acute medical care and long-term nursing in eastern Illinois and western Indiana. The hospital has some 50 beds and about 80 physicians on its medical staff. Among its specialized services are emergency medicine, oncology, surgery, orthopedics, and cardiology. It receives more than 50,000 patient visits every year.

	Annual Growth	09/13	09/14	09/15	09/19	09/21
Sales ($mil.)	(2.6%)	–	37.2	33.7	0.0	31.0
Net income ($ mil.)	–	–	(0.5)	(0.8)	(1.3)	6.9
Market value ($ mil.)	–	–	–	–	–	–
Employees	–	–	–	–	–	385

ISCO INTERNATIONAL, INC.

444 E STATE PKWY STE A
SCHAUMBURG, IL 601736424
Phone: 630 283-3100
Fax: –
Web: www.iscointl.com

CEO: Gordon Reichard Jr
CFO: Gary Berger
HR: –
FYE: December 31
Type: Private

ISCO International, LLC doesn't want anything interfering with your cellular experience. The company makes filters, duplexers, and spectrum conditioners for cellular and PCS wireless telecommunications companies. Unlike conventional radio-frequency (RF) filters, the company's products use high-temperature superconductors to reject unwanted signals, improving call quality and decreasing the chance that calls will be blocked by interference. Its products support domestic and international frequencies. In 2009 ISCO's assets were sold by its lenders to a privately held company, also called ISCO International, and operations continued with the same product line.

ISG TECHNOLOGY, LLC

12980 METCALF AVE STE 550
OVERLAND PARK, KS 662132851
Phone: 785 823-1555
Fax: –
Web: www.isgtech.com

CEO: Ben Foster
CFO: –
HR: Ashley Olberding
FYE: March 31
Type: Private

ISG Technology hopes to help you capitalize on all of your technology operations. The company, which does business as Integrated Solutions Group, provides information technology (IT) and telecommunications services, primarily to small and midsized businesses in the midwestern US. ISG services include network design, hardware and software procurement, web development and hosting, and training. Clients come from fields such as financial services, manufacturing, telecommunications, and health care. The company has seven locations in the Midwest, including offices in Kansas, Missouri, and Oklahoma.

	Annual Growth	03/04	03/05	03/06	03/07	03/08
Sales ($mil.)	15.7%	–	–	41.3	44.4	55.3
Net income ($ mil.)	572.3%	–	–	0.3	0.2	12.5
Market value ($ mil.)	–	–	–	–	–	–
Employees	–	–	–	–	–	170

ISIGN SOLUTIONS INC

NBB: ISGN

2033 Gateway Place, Suite 662
San Jose, CA 95110
Phone: 650 802-7888
Fax: –
Web: www.isignnow.com

CEO: Philip S Sassower
CFO: Michael Engmann
HR: –
FYE: December 31
Type: Public

If your intelligent communication involves hunting and pecking, try Communication Intelligence Corp. (CIC). The company's handwriting recognition software, including its SignatureOne, Sign-it, and iSign products, recognizes character strokes of words from English, Chinese, and Western European languages and converts them to digital text. Industries served by CIC include banking, insurance, and financial services, which often require electronic signatures for legal documents. Customers have included Charles Schwab and Wells Fargo. CIC was founded in 1981 in conjunction with Stanford University's Research Institute. Phoenix Ventures is the company's largest shareholder, with a 37% stake.

	Annual Growth	12/18	12/19	12/20	12/21	12/22
Sales ($mil.)	1.9%	0.9	0.8	1.0	1.1	1.0
Net income ($ mil.)	–	(1.0)	(1.1)	(0.5)	(0.5)	(0.7)
Market value ($ mil.)	(15.9%)	4.4	2.8	2.0	12.1	2.2
Employees	14.4%	7	14	14	13	12

ISLE OF CAPRI CASINOS LLC

600 EMERSON RD STE 300
SAINT LOUIS, MO 631416762
Phone: 314 813-9200
Fax: –
Web: www.ladyluck.com

CEO: Eric L Hausler
CFO: Michael A Hart
HR: –
FYE: April 24
Type: Private

Rollin' on the river takes on new meaning when you're talking about Isle of Capri Casinos. The company owns and operates about 15 dockside, riverboat, and land-based casinos in Colorado, Iowa, Louisiana, Mississippi, Missouri, and Pennsylvania. In addition, the company has a pari-mutuel harness racetrack and casino in Pompano Beach, Florida. Most of the company's casinos have hotels and feature restaurants, live entertainment, and private lounges for high-rollers. Altogether, Isle of Capri's properties feature approximately 12,000 slot machines and 300 table games (including some 80 poker tables), as well as more than 2,200 hotel rooms and 40 restaurants.

ISO NEW ENGLAND INC.

1 SULLIVAN RD
HOLYOKE, MA 010402841
Phone: 413 535-4000
Fax: –
Web: www.iso-ne.com

CEO: Gordon V Welie
CFO: Robert Ludlow
HR: Janice S Dickstein
FYE: December 31
Type: Private

ISO New England is an independent, not-for-profit corporation responsible for keeping electricity flowing across Connecticut, Maine, Massachusetts, New Hampshire, Rhode Island, and Vermont and ensuring that the region has reliable, competitively priced wholesale electricity today and into the future. With approximately 7.2 million retail electricity customers, the company has about 31,500 MW of generating capability, and some 350 dispatchable generators. In addition to the company's 9,000 miles of high-voltage transmission lines (115 kV and above) and nearly 15 transmission interconnections to electricity systems in New York and Eastern Canada, ISO New England has about 500 buyers and sellers in the wholesale electricity marketplace.

	Annual Growth	12/18	12/19	12/20	12/21	12/22
Sales ($mil.)	2.8%	–	194.3	195.6	201.7	210.8
Net income ($ mil.)	–	–	–	–	–	–
Market value ($ mil.)	–	–	–	–	–	–
Employees	–	–	–	–	–	610

ISOMET CORP.

NBB: IOMT

5263 Port Royal Road
Springfield, VA 22151
Phone: 703 321-8301
Fax: 703 321-8546
Web: www.isomet.com

CEO: –
CFO: Jerry Rayburn
HR: –
FYE: December 31
Type: Public

Isomet never met a laser beam it couldn't control. The company makes acousto-optic systems that manipulate interactions between light and sound to control laser beams, especially in color image reproduction applications such as laser printing and phototypesetting. Isomet had long made graphic arts systems of its own -- including digital scanners and graphics plotters -- but has been winding down that business as it expands its production of birefringent materials (such as lead molybdate) used in fiber-optic applications. The company also offers components such as athermal filters, anti-reflection coatings, tunable filters, and optical switches.

	Annual Growth	12/15	12/16	12/17	12/18	12/19
Sales ($mil.)	(2.1%)	4.0	2.8	3.4	3.9	3.6
Net income ($ mil.)	–	0.0	(0.3)	(0.1)	0.0	(0.2)
Market value ($ mil.)	26.4%	0.0	0.0	0.0	0.0	0.1
Employees	–	–	–	–	–	–

ITA GROUP, INC

4600 WESTOWN PKWY STE 100
WEST DES MOINES, IA 502661042
Phone: 515 326-3400
Fax: –
Web: www.itagroup.com

CEO: Thomas J Mahoney
CFO: Brent V Waal V
HR: –
FYE: August 31
Type: Private

ITA Group (doing business as ITAGroup) bets it can make your company better. Specializing in performance marketing, ITAGroup (standing for "Ideas to Action") builds and manages programs that help clients increase sales and customer satisfaction through incentives and training. The company's services include research and program design, administration, fulfillment, and measurement for employee recognition and rewards programs, business-to-business loyalty programs, and sales incentive programs. ITAGroup also provides business meeting and event planning services.

ITC HOLDINGS CORP.

27175 ENERGY WAY
NOVI, MI 483773639
Phone: 248 946-3000
Fax: –
Web: www.itc-holdings.com

CEO: Linda H Apsey
CFO: Gretchen L Holloway
HR: –
FYE: December 31
Type: Private

ITC is the largest independent electricity transmission company in the US. The company provides transmission grid solutions to improve reliability, expand access to energy markets, allow new generating resources to interconnect to our systems and lower the overall cost of delivered energy. ITC connects a variety of customers at transmission-level voltages ? including generation and distribution utilities, municipal utility systems, rural electric utility cooperatives, and commercial and industrial customers which require high-voltage electricity. Through this work the company delivers power to customers through several Midwest states, spanning from metropolitan Detroit westward to the community of Dodge City, Kansas. ITC is a subsidiary of Fortis Inc., a leader in the North American regulated electric and gas utility industry.

ITG CIGARS INC.

5900 N ANDREWS AVE STE 1100
FORT LAUDERDALE, FL 333092367
Phone: 954 772-9000
Fax: –
Web: www.altadisusa.com

CEO: Gary R Ellis
CFO: –
HR: –
FYE: December 31
Type: Private

When the smoke clears, connoisseur puffers may find themselves holding a cigar crafted by Altadis USA. Created by the consolidation of HavaTampa Inc. and Consolidated Cigar Holdings, Altadis USA has grown to rival the world's largest cigar makers and generate a considerable share of US cigar sales. Altadis USA manufactures, markets, and sells both premium and mass-market cigars, under such well-known brand names as Montecristo, Romeo y Julieta, H. Upmann, and Trinidad. It also sells little cigars under the Dutch Treats and Supre Sweets brands, as well as humidors and cigar cases. Altadis USA is a wholly owned subsidiary of Britain's Imperial Brands.

ITERIS INC

1250 S. Capital of Texas Hwy., Building 1, Suite 330
Austin, TX 78746
Phone: 512 716-0808
Fax: –
Web: www.iteris.com

NAS: ITI
CEO: J J Bergera
CFO: Kerry A Shiba
HR: –
FYE: March 31
Type: Public

Iteris is a provider of smart mobility infrastructure management solutions. Its cloud-enabled solutions help public transportation agencies, municipalities, commercial entities and other transportation infrastructure providers monitor, visualize, and optimize mobility infrastructure to make mobility safe, efficient and sustainable for everyone. As a pioneer in intelligent transportation systems (ITS) technology, its intellectual property, advanced detection sensors, mobility and traffic data, software-as-a-service (SaaS) offerings, mobility consulting services and cloud-enabled managed services represent a comprehensive range of smart mobility infrastructure management solutions and its distributed to customers throughout the US and internationally. More than 10,000 public agencies and private-sector enterprises focused on mobility rely on Iteris. It was incorporated in 1987 and has operated in its current form since 2004.

	Annual Growth	03/19	03/20	03/21	03/22	03/23
Sales ($mil.)	12.0%	99.1	114.1	117.1	133.6	156.1
Net income ($ mil.)	–	(7.8)	(5.6)	10.1	(7.1)	(14.9)
Market value ($ mil.)	3.0%	178.5	137.0	264.1	127.6	200.8
Employees	4.4%	393	440	439	444	467

ITI TROPICALS INC.

30 GORDON AVE
LAWRENCEVILLE, NJ 086481033
Phone: 609 987-0550
Fax: –
Web: www.ititropicals.com

CEO: –
CFO: –
HR: –
FYE: December 31
Type: Private

ITI Tropicals packs a lot of fruity flavor into not very itty-bitty packages. The company imports tropical fruit purees, concentrates, waters, essences, and other products, focusing on banana, coconut, guava, mango, papaya, and passion fruit. It also carries more exotic fruits such as mangosteen, mora-berry, acerola, lulo, tamarind, and guanabana. ITI distributes its products, which come in frozen or aseptic packaging and range in size from 5-gallon pails to 220-gallon drums, to food manufacturers throughout the US. Founded in 1988, ITI Tropicals is owned by president Gert Van Manen.

	Annual Growth	12/06	12/07	12/09	12/11	12/12
Sales ($mil.)	9.5%	–	31.1	35.1	37.1	48.9
Net income ($ mil.)	–	–	–	0.7	–	–
Market value ($ mil.)	–	–	–	–	–	–
Employees	–	–	–	–	–	38

ITEX CORP

13555 SE 36th Street, Suite 210
Bellevue, WA 98006
Phone: 425 463-4000
Fax: 425 463-4040
Web: www.itex.com

NBB: ITEX
CEO: Steven White
CFO: Carolyn Young
HR: Mike Ryan
FYE: July 31
Type: Public

ITEX provides a business-to-business payment system for corporate members through a licensed broker network across the US and Canada. In lieu of cash, some 24,000 member businesses of the company's ITEX Marketplace barter time-sensitive, slow-moving, or surplus goods and services valued in ITEX dollars. Members represent a variety of industries including advertising, construction, dining, health care, hospitality, media, printing, and professional services. ITEX administers the trade exchange; it (or any of its 95 franchisees or licensed brokers) also acts as a record keeper for member transactions.

	Annual Growth	07/19	07/20	07/21	07/22	07/23
Sales ($mil.)	(7.1%)	8.9	7.9	6.9	6.7	6.6
Net income ($ mil.)	(0.4%)	0.8	0.8	0.8	0.6	0.8
Market value ($ mil.)	1.1%	6.7	5.9	7.0	6.0	7.0
Employees	–	–	–	–	–	–

ITIS HOLDINGS INC

10750 Hammerly Boulevard, Suite 300
Houston, TX 77043
Phone: 281 600-6000
Fax: 713 462-1950
Web: www.itisinc.com

CEO: –
CFO: –
HR: –
FYE: December 31
Type: Public

Is ITIS Holdings suffering from legalitis...or bronchitis? Until mid-2004 the company provided automated litigation support services, document and database management services, and operated pharmacies. ITIS had no revenue-producing operations and was exploring new business opportunities, until 2005 when the company began providing management and marketing services to third party companies. Chairman and CEO Hunter M. A. Carr owns 52% of ITIS Holdings.

	Annual Growth	12/01	12/02	12/03	12/04	12/05
Sales ($mil.)	(68.5%)	–	0.3	0.8	0.2	0.0
Net income ($ mil.)	–	–	(12.0)	(5.8)	(1.0)	(0.1)
Market value ($ mil.)	(39.6%)	–	0.5	0.3	0.2	0.1
Employees	–	–	–	–	3	3

ITRON INC
NMS: ITRI

2111 N Molter Road
Liberty Lake, WA 99019
Phone: 509 924-9900
Fax: –
Web: www.itron.com

CEO: –
CFO: –
HR: –
FYE: December 31
Type: Public

Itron is a leader in the Industrial Internet of Things (IoT), enabling utilities and cities to safely, securely, and reliably deliver critical infrastructure solutions for electric, natural gas, and water utilities. Its proven platform enables smart networks, software, services, devices, and sensors to help customers better manage their operations in the energy, water, and smart city spaces. It also offers end-to-end device solutions, networked solutions, and outcomes-based products and services to the utility and municipal sectors. The company also provides consulting, licensing hardware technology, and technical support services. Around 70% of Itron's total revenue comes from the US and Canada.

	Annual Growth	12/19	12/20	12/21	12/22	12/23
Sales ($mil.)	(3.5%)	2,502.5	2,173.4	1,981.6	1,795.6	2,173.6
Net income ($ mil.)	18.6%	49.0	(58.0)	(81.3)	(9.7)	96.9
Market value ($ mil.)	(2.6%)	3,820.7	4,364.6	3,118.5	2,305.2	3,436.6
Employees	(10.4%)	7,900	6,749	6,065	5,477	5,081

ITRON NETWORKED SOLUTIONS, INC.

230 W TASMAN DR
SAN JOSE, CA 951341714
Phone: 669 770-4000
Fax: –
Web: www.itron.com

CEO: –
CFO: –
HR: –
FYE: December 31
Type: Private

Silver Spring Networks helps utility companies plug into the 21st century. Its Smart Energy Platform modernizes a utility's existing power grid infrastructure into the "smart" grid, i.e. one that is connected to a digital network and more energy efficient. The Smart Energy Platform is a secure, Internet-based network made up of hardware, such as access points, communications modules, bridges, and relays; its UtilOS-brand network operating system; and software. It also offers managed services to maintain and regulate the network. Silver Spring sells its platform to electric, gas, and water utilities -- FPL, PG&E, and OG&E account for almost 80% of service revenue. The company went public in 2013.

ITRONICS INC.
NBB: ITRO

6490 South McCarran Boulevard, Building C, Suite 23
Reno, NV 89509
Phone: 775 689-7696
Fax: –
Web: www.itronics.com

CEO: –
CFO: –
HR: –
FYE: December 31
Type: Public

Mary, Mary, quite contrary, how does your garden grow? Silver (recycled) from X-rays and photowaste turns plants green all in a row. Itronics operates its two business segments through subsidiaries. Itronics Metallurgical recycles photochemicals and turns the results into its GOLD'n GRO animal repellent and liquid fertilizer. GOLD'n GRO products are sold primarily in the western US. Another subsidiary, Whitney & Whitney, provides mineral planning and technical services (mineral economics, geologic studies, and project management services) to the mining industry. In 2009 the company expanded its silver refining capacity from 24,000 to 2.4 million ounces per year, significantly cutting its operating expenses.

	Annual Growth	12/03	12/04	12/05	12/06	12/07
Sales ($mil.)	13.1%	–	1.6	1.4	1.9	2.3
Net income ($ mil.)	–	–	(2.8)	(4.9)	(3.8)	(10.5)
Market value ($ mil.)	(63.8%)	–	0.0	0.0	0.0	0.0
Employees						

ITT EDUCATIONAL SERVICES INC
NBB: ESIN Q

13000 North Meridian Street
Carmel, IN 46032-1404
Phone: 317 706-9200
Fax: –
Web: www.ittesi.com

CEO: –
CFO: –
HR: –
FYE: December 31
Type: Public

ITT Educational Services operates Daniel Webster College, a single-campus institution located in Nashua, New Hampshire. Daniel Webster offers undergraduate and graduate programs in arts and sciences, aviation sciences, business and management, and engineering and computer sciences. It has some 650 students and about 80 faculty members. In 2016, ITT Educational Services shut down its namesake ITT Technical Institutes, which provided technology-focused degrees in such areas as computer-aided design (CAD), engineering technology, and information technology, after the US government barred the schools from using federal financial aid to enroll new students. There were some 140 ITT Technical Institutes throughout the US.

	Annual Growth	12/11	12/12	12/13	12/14	12/15
Sales ($mil.)	(13.2%)	1,499.9	1,287.2	1,072.3	961.8	849.8
Net income ($ mil.)	(47.5%)	307.8	140.5	(27.0)	29.3	23.3
Market value ($ mil.)	(49.4%)	1,346.8	409.8	795.0	227.5	88.3
Employees	(4.3%)	10,000	9,800	9,500	8,900	8,400

ITT INC
NYS: ITT

100 Washington Boulevard, 6th Floor
Stamford, CT 06902
Phone: 914 641-2000
Fax: –
Web: www.itt.com

CEO: Denise L Ramos
CFO: Thomas M Scalera
HR: Jason Greenwood
FYE: December 31
Type: Public

ITT Corporation hopes its customers are pumped, moved, and energized about its products. A diversified manufacturer, ITT makes a range of industrial products through four operating segments: industrial process (pumping systems though Goulds Pumps, valves, and services for oil and gas and chemical companies); motion technologies (brake pads and friction materials for transportation markets); interconnect solutions (ICS, connectors for fiber optic, RF, power, and other electronic products); and control technologies (hydraulic valves, actuators, and switches for aerospace companies).

	Annual Growth	12/19	12/20	12/21	12/22	12/23
Sales ($mil.)	3.6%	2,846.4	2,477.8	2,765.0	2,987.7	3,283.0
Net income ($ mil.)	6.0%	325.1	72.5	316.3	367.0	410.5
Market value ($ mil.)	12.7%	6,068.0	6,323.3	8,389.8	6,658.3	9,796.2
Employees	0.2%	10,500	9,700	9,900	10,300	10,600

IVCI, LLC

601 OLD WILLETS PATH STE 100
HAUPPAUGE, NY 117884111
Phone: 800 224-7083
Fax: –
Web: www.ivci.com

CEO: –
CFO: –
HR: –
FYE: December 31
Type: Private

IVCi screens its calls. The company resells and installs cameras, video servers, speaker phones, and other equipment used for video, audio, and Web conferences. It supplies and supports equipment made by such industry leaders as Cisco and Polycom. In addition to installation, IVCi's Audio/Visual Division offers conference room design consulting, project management, on-site technical assistance, maintenance, and training services. Its private video communications network, enables 24-hour access to a secure managed conferencing environment. It serves customers in the education to health care industries, as well legal and federal and state government clients. IVCi was founded in 1995 by CEO Robert Swing.

	Annual Growth	06/13	06/14*	12/14	12/15	12/16
Sales ($mil.)	58.9%	–	32.3	65.6	69.4	81.5
Net income ($ mil.)	121.1%	–	0.5	1.0	0.7	2.5
Market value ($ mil.)						
Employees	–	–	–	–	–	180

*Fiscal year change

IVERIC BIO, INC.

1249 S RIVER RD STE 107
CRANBURY, NJ 085123633
Phone: 609 945-6050
Fax: –
Web: www.ivericbio.com

CEO: Samira Patel
CFO: –
HR: Beth Fucito
FYE: December 31
Type: Private

Iveric bio (formerly Ophthotech) isn't taking a wait-and-see attitude towards eye disease. The biopharmaceutical company is transitioning to become a gene therapy-focused firm developing treatments for orphan inherited retinal diseases. It had been developing Fovista, a drug for wet age-related macular degeneration (wet AMD) meant to be used in conjunction with Genentech's Lucentis, but that treatment failed in two clinical trials. The company's pipeline is now led by pre-clinical assets IC-100 and IC-200, which will be studied for their efficacy in treating rhodopsin-mediated autosomal dominant retinitis pigmentosa and Best disease. A legacy candidate, Zimura, is being developed for the treatment of geographic atrophy, a form of dry AMD.

IVEY MECHANICAL COMPANY, LLC

134 W WASHINGTON ST
KOSCIUSKO, MS 390903633
Phone: 662 289-3646
Fax: –
Web: www.iveymechanical.com

CEO: Larry Terrell
CFO: Randy Dew
HR: Courtney Burns
FYE: December 31
Type: Private

More blue-collar than Ivy League, Ivey Mechanical Company gets an "A" for its slate of mechanical services. The specialty contractor designs, fabricates, and manufactures sheet metal work, as well as air conditioning/heating, and medical gas and plumbing/piping systems. It also provides system repairs, maintenance, and emergency services. With projects covering 30 states, Ivey Mechanical drives preconstruction and construction, and prefabrication work for commercial and industrial facilities, correctional, health care, and government contracts. The company operates through service offices dotting the Southeast US. It is owned by CEO Larry Terrell along with members of Ivey Mechanical's management team.

IW GROUP

6300 WILSHIRE BLVD STE 2150
LOS ANGELES, CA 900485204
Phone: 213 262-6978
Fax: –
Web: www.iwgroup.agency

CEO: Bill Imada
CFO: –
HR: –
FYE: December 31
Type: Private

IW Group (formerly Imada Wong Communications Group) is a marketing communications firm which helps its clients reach Asian communities in the US. Services include advertising, public relations, media buying, direct marketing, research, and cross-cultural training. The company has experience working with the banking, retail, pharmaceutical, healthcare, automotive, insurance, and quick-service restaurants industries. Specific clients have included Wal-Mart, MetLife, and McDonald's. The agency was founded in 1990, and serves clients from offices in Los Angeles, New York City, and San Francisco.

	Annual Growth	12/03	12/04	12/05	12/06	12/08
Sales ($mil.)	–	–	–	(1,369.2)	29.0	23.9
Net income ($ mil.)	1606.3%	–	–	0.0	1.1	0.2
Market value ($ mil.)	–	–	–	–	–	–
Employees	–	–	–	–	–	68

IXIA

26601 AGOURA RD
CALABASAS, CA 913021959
Phone: 818 871-1800
Fax: –
Web: support.ixiacom.com

CEO: –
CFO: Jason Kary
HR: –
FYE: December 31
Type: Private

Ixia nixes network glitches. The company designs network validation testing hardware and software that provides visibility into traffic performance and also addresses the network applications. Hardware consists of optical and electrical interface cards and the chassis to hold them. Its software tests the functionality of video, voice, conformance, and security across ethernet, wi-fi, and 3G/LTE equipment and networks. Ixia primarily serves network equipment manufacturers (Cisco), service providers (AT&T), corporate customers (Bloomberg), the federal government (US Army), and its contractors (General Dynamics). In 2017 Ixia was acquired by Keysight Technologies, a provider of electronic measurement equipment, for $1.6 billion.

IXYS, LLC

1590 BUCKEYE DR
MILPITAS, CA 950357418
Phone: 408 457-9000
Fax: –
Web: www.ixys.com

CEO: –
CFO: –
HR: –
FYE: March 31
Type: Private

IXYS makes a variety of power semiconductors including power metal-oxide semiconductor field effect transistors (MOSFETs), insulated gate bipolar transistors (IGBTs) and BIMOSFETs, which convert and control electric power in electronic gear. Through its subsidiary, Clare Inc., IXYS designs optically isolated solid state relays, mixed-signal custom ASICs and ASSP integrated circuits (ICs). System-on-chip microcontrollers units, Radio Frequency power & systems are also sold through IXYS' subsidiaries. The company also offers products used for Solar and Wind energy. Its 2,500-plus customers ranges across industrial, transportation, telecommunications, computer, medical, consumer and clean tech markets. IXYS is a part of Littlefuse Inc.

J & D PRODUCE, INC.

7310 N EXPRESSWAY 281
EDINBURG, TX 785421232
Phone: 956 380-0353
Fax: –
Web: www.littlebearproduce.com

CEO: –
CFO: –
HR: –
FYE: December 31
Type: Private

J & D Produce is a leading vegetable and melon grower in the Rio Grande Valley of Texas. Marketing its produce under the Little Bear brand, the company harvests, packs, and ships such items as asparagus, carrots, and lettuce, along with cabbage, limes, and a variety of melons. It supplies fresh produce primarily to supermarkets, grocery stores, and other food retailers. J & D Produce was founded in the early 1980s by Jimmy Bassetti and his wife Diane.

	Annual Growth	12/07	12/08	12/12	12/13	12/14
Sales ($mil.)	(2.2%)	–	121.1	–	106.0	105.8
Net income ($ mil.)	(14.4%)	–	3.2	–	1.3	1.2
Market value ($ mil.)	–	–	–	–	–	–
Employees	–	–	–	–	–	420

J M SMITH CORPORATION

101 W SAINT JOHN ST STE 305
SPARTANBURG, SC 293065150
Phone: 864 542-9419
Fax: –
Web: www.jmsmith.com

CEO: Paula H Bethea
CFO: Philip Ryan
HR: Amy Thyen
FYE: February 28
Type: Private

J M Smith Corporation, the third-largest privately-held company in South Carolina, operates industry-leading healthcare and technology business units including Smith Drug Company, Integral Rx and Integral Rx Supplies. Founded in 1925 by James M. Smith Sr. as a single community pharmacy in Asheville, North Carolina, the company supplies services and technology to organizations across the US.

	Annual Growth	02/11	02/12	02/13	02/14	02/15
Sales ($mil.)	4.2%	–	–	2,362.8	2,370.0	2,566.2
Net income ($ mil.)	33.8%	–	–	26.3	38.4	47.1
Market value ($ mil.)	–	–	–	–	–	–
Employees	–	–	–	–	–	235

J&J SNACK FOODS CORP.

350 Fellowship Road
Mt. Laurel, NJ 08054
Phone: 856 665-9533
Fax: –
Web: www.jjsnack.com

NMS: JJSF
CEO: Daniel Fachner
CFO: Ken Plunk
HR: –
FYE: September 30
Type: Public

J & J Snack Foods manufactures snack foods and distributes frozen beverages which it markets nationally to the food service and retail supermarket industries. The company offers an assortment of brands, including SUPERPRETZEL, ICEE frozen drinks, Whole Fruit juice treats, Tio Pepe's churros, and Funnel Cake Factory funnel cakes. J & J also sells snacks such as Auntie Anne's pretzels, Sour Patch Kids sticks, and Minute Maid's frozen lemonade and juice bars. The company's customer base comprises small and large foodservice operators and supermarket chains. It also has approximately 128,000 company-owned and customer-owned frozen beverage dispensing machines. Products are manufactured in facilities in more than a dozen US states and reach customers via 180 warehouse and distribution facilities in the US as well as Canada and Mexico.

	Annual Growth	09/19	09/20	09/21	09/22	09/23
Sales ($mil.)	7.1%	1,186.5	1,022.0	1,144.6	1,380.7	1,558.8
Net income ($ mil.)	(4.5%)	94.8	18.3	55.6	47.2	78.9
Market value ($ mil.)	(3.8%)	3,700.1	2,491.7	2,970.4	2,640.8	3,163.7
Employees	2.1%	4,600	4,100	4,300	5,000	5,000

J. ALEXANDER'S HOLDINGS, INC.

3401 WEST END AVE STE 260
NASHVILLE, TN 372036862
Phone: 615 269-1900
Fax: –
Web: www.jalexandersholdings.com

CEO: Lonnie J Stout II
CFO: –
HR: –
FYE: January 03
Type: Private

J. Alexander's owns and operates three upscale dining restaurant concepts: J. Alexander's, Redlands Grill, and Stoney River Steakhouse and Grill. The company's J. Alexander's restaurants offer guests a contemporary American menu. The firm started it's Stoney River concept in February 2013. Stoney River locations provide 'white tablecloth' service and high quality food in a casual atmosphere. The company's newest concept, Redlands Grill, offers customers a slightly different contemporary American menu that J. Alexander's restaurants along with a unique architectural design and feel.

J. C. BLAIR MEMORIAL HOSPITAL

1225 WARM SPRINGS AVE
HUNTINGDON, PA 166522398
Phone: 814 643-8367
Fax: –
Web: www.phhealthcare.org

CEO: Adam Dimm
CFO: –
HR: Michael F Hubert
FYE: June 30
Type: Private

J. C. Blair Memorial Hospital serves Huntingdon County in central Pennsylvania. With more than 100 beds, the community hospital has about 40 physicians on staff representing a variety of specialties including cancer care, pediatrics, cardiology, and orthopedics. J. C. Blair also offers patients a range of hospital services including emergency, behavioral health, diagnostic, birthing, and surgical care, as well as ambulatory outpatient services. The hospital was established in 1911 by Kate Fisher Blair in memory of her husband, John Chalmers Blair.

	Annual Growth	06/15	06/16	06/20	06/21	06/22
Sales ($mil.)	2.4%	–	51.6	53.0	51.2	59.4
Net income ($ mil.)	(1.0%)	–	4.4	5.2	1.9	4.1
Market value ($ mil.)	–	–	–	–	–	–
Employees	–	–	–	–	–	479

J. CREW GROUP, LLC

225 LIBERTY ST
NEW YORK, NY 102811048
Phone: 434 385-5775
Fax: –
Web: www.jcrew.com

CEO: Libby Wadle
CFO: Vincent Zanna
HR: –
FYE: February 02
Type: Private

J. Crew Group is a retailer known for its preppy fashions, including t-shirts and tops, sweatshirts and sweatpants, matching sets, shirts, sweaters, and more sold to young professionals through its catalogs, and websites, and over 125 stores across the US. Clothing is sold under the J. Crew and Madewell banners. The company operates stores under its Madewell brand, a women's-only collection of hip, casual clothes. It is expert in signature categories: cashmere, coats, blazers, pants ? and also collaborate with the coolest brands out there. It also considers leopard a neutral, speak stripes fluently and live for a great gingham.

J. D. STREETT & COMPANY, INC.

144 WELDON PKWY
MARYLAND HEIGHTS, MO 630433102
Phone: 314 432-6600
Fax: –
Web: www.jdstreett.com

CEO: Newell A Baker Jr
CFO: James A Schuering
HR: Kristy Pedroli
FYE: December 31
Type: Private

Word on the street is that J. D. Streett tries to stay streets ahead of its rivals as it supplies its customers with a wide range of fuels, oxygenates, lubricants, transmission fluids, and antifreezes. The company operates more than 20 retail locations (convenience stores and gas stations) under its own ZX label and/or BP brand in Missouri and Illinois. J. D. Streett also serves more than 10 international markets. In addition, the company offers terminalling services for distillate, ethanol, and oil products, and owns and operates a chain of discount cigarette shops (most that also sell beer) across Missouri.

	Annual Growth	12/18	12/19	12/20	12/21	12/22
Sales ($mil.)	15.7%	–	189.0	156.8	226.0	292.9
Net income ($ mil.)	41.6%	–	2.5	6.2	7.2	7.2
Market value ($ mil.)	–	–	–	–	–	–
Employees	–	–	–	–	–	240

J. F. WHITE CONTRACTING COMPANY

10 BURR ST
FRAMINGHAM, MA 017014692
Phone: 508 879-4700
Fax: –
Web: www.jfwhite.com

CEO: –
CFO: –
HR: –
FYE: December 31
Type: Private

J.F. White Contracting has been at the bedrock of heavy civil construction in New England for more than 85 years. The group has civil, design/build, mechanical, electrical, and deep foundation divisions to provide a large range of engineering, construction, infrastructure, and equipment and wiring installation services. J.F. White also has a diving division that specializes in marine construction and underwater engineering. The company has worked on projects for Harvard University and was involved in building Boston's Central Artery/Tunnel project. J.F. also was tapped to rebuild the Chelsea Street Bridge -- a $125 million project funded by stimulus money. It was founded in 1924 by Joseph F. White, Sr.

J. H. FINDORFF & SON INC.

300 S BEDFORD ST
MADISON, WI 537033622
Phone: 608 257-5321
Fax: –
Web: www.findorff.com

CEO: –
CFO: Daniel L Petersen
HR: –
FYE: September 30
Type: Private

J.H. Findorff & Son has been building its resume since the 19th century. The company constructs commercial and institutional projects in the US Midwest. It provides general contracting, design/build, and construction management services. Projects include schools, government buildings, health care centers, hotels, condos, offices, and shopping complexes. Findorff also self-performs trade work including carpentry, concrete, masonry, drywall, and steel erection. Among its projects is Madison, Wisconsin's Children's Museum and the Overture Center for the Arts. It also built the Wisconsin Institutes for Discovery at The University of Wisconsin-Madison. John Findorff founded the company as J.H. Findorff in 1890.

	Annual Growth	09/05	09/06	09/08	09/11	09/12
Sales ($mil.)	7.4%	–	209.1	322.0	209.2	320.9
Net income ($ mil.)	(14.0%)	–	10.2	3.8	0.3	4.1
Market value ($ mil.)	–	–	–	–	–	–
Employees	–	–	–	–	–	500

J. LOHR WINERY CORPORATION

1000 LENZEN AVE
SAN JOSE, CA 951262739
Phone: 408 288-5057
Fax: –
Web: www.jlohr.com

CEO: Steven W Lohr
CFO: –
HR: –
FYE: December 31
Type: Private

J. Lohr Winery pours it on. It produces red, white, sparkling, and non-alcoholic wines. The family-owned winery's vintages are divided into tiers with the more expensive wines falling under the labels J. Lohr Cuv e Series, J. Lohr Vineyards Series, and J. Lohr Estates. The company's less expensive wines bear the Cypress Vineyards and Painter Bridge labels. The company also makes a line of non-alcoholic wines called ARIEL. J. Lohr Winery grows mainly red varietals of grapes on almost 3,700 acres that it owns and farms in three distinct wine growing regions in California. It sells its wines nationwide and in more than 25 other countries.

J. STOKES & ASSOC., INC.

1444 N MAIN ST STE 100
WALNUT CREEK, CA 945964677
Phone: 925 933-1624
Fax: –
Web: www.jstokes.com

CEO: –
CFO: –
HR: –
FYE: September 30
Type: Private

Subway, Mail Boxes Etc., and P.F. Chang's are all stoked, so to speak. They are all clients of advertising and public relations agency J. Stokes & Associates, which focuses on the restaurant and retail industry. In fact, J. Stokes & Associates represents more than 900 Subway restaurants in California. In addition to its advertising and PR capabilities, the agency also provides promotional and media buying services to retail and business-to-business oriented clients primarily in the San Francisco Bay area. Jim Stokes founded J. Stokes & Associates in 1974.

	Annual Growth	09/04	09/05	09/06	09/07	09/13
Sales ($mil.)	(57.1%)	–	2,011.2	12.5	13.0	2.3
Net income ($ mil.)	96.3%	–	0.0	(0.0)	2.6	0.0
Market value ($ mil.)	–	–	–	–	–	–
Employees	–	–	–	–	–	24

J.D. ABRAMS, L.P.

5811 TRADE CENTER DR BLDG 1
AUSTIN, TX 787441308
Phone: 512 322-4000
Fax: –
Web: www.jdabrams.com

CEO: Brad Everett
CFO: –
HR: –
FYE: December 31
Type: Private

J.D. Abrams, L.P. is a 100% employee-owned company with an Employee Stock Ownership Plan (ESOP) and 401(k) specializing in heavy civil construction. J.D. Abrams builds the infrastructure that helps travelers drive across Texas. While highway and bridge construction projects from the Texas Department of Transportation make up the bulk of its construction work, the civil engineering and construction company also works on flood control dams, reservoirs, waterways, railroad test tracks, airport taxiways, and other infrastructure projects in Texas and other construction market. J.D. Abrams also operates two subsidiaries, Transmountain Equipment and Austin PreStress, both located in Austin, Texas. Founded in 1966, the company operates from three Texas-based offices in Austin, Dallas, El Paso, and Houston.

	Annual Growth	12/06	12/07	12/08	12/09	12/12
Sales ($mil.)	42.4%	–	–	42.9	307.8	176.6
Net income ($ mil.)	–	–	–	1.2	15.0	(2.3)
Market value ($ mil.)	–	–	–	–	–	–
Employees	–	–	–	–	–	750

J.E. DUNN CONSTRUCTION COMPANY

1001 LOCUST ST
KANSAS CITY, MO 641061904
Phone: 816 474-8600
Fax: –
Web: www.jedunn.com

CEO: Gordon E Landsford III
CFO: Beth A Soukup
HR: Annzetta Davis
FYE: December 31
Type: Private

From first building designs to the last brick, J.E. Dunn Construction helps make building plans a done deal. The contractor offers general construction services, construction management, and design/build services nationwide. It's known for its work on campus, health care, and commercial projects, including the BayCare Health System, CHI Health - Creighton University Medical Center - Bergan Mercy, Seaton Hall/Regnier Hall, Decatur High School and Ron Clark Academy. Founded in 1924, the company is one of Kansas City's top commercial construction firms and has been listed as one of the nation's top 20 general building companies. It operates as a subsidiary of J.E. Dunn Construction Group.

	Annual Growth	12/13	12/14	12/15	12/16	12/17
Sales ($mil.)	9.5%	–	2,242.7	2,909.4	2,909.4	2,945.8
Net income ($ mil.)	–	–	–	–	–	–
Market value ($ mil.)	–	–	–	–	–	–
Employees	–	–	–	–	–	1,635

J.E. DUNN CONSTRUCTION GROUP, INC.

1001 LOCUST ST
KANSAS CITY, MO 641061904
Phone: 816 474-8600
Fax: –
Web: www.jedunn.com

CEO: Terrence P Dunn
CFO: Beth Soukup
HR: Jason Bowne
FYE: December 31
Type: Private

Owned by descendants of founder John Ernest Dunn, J.E. Dunn Construction Group operates as the holding company for a group of construction firms that includes flagship J.E. Dunn Construction and JE Dunn Capital Partners. With expertise across corporate environments, courthouse and justice, federal and military, education, life sciences, local and state government, and mixed use and retail industries, the company builds institutional, commercial, and industrial structures nationwide. It also provides construction and program management and design/build services. J.E. Dunn Construction, which is among the largest US general builders, is one of the first contractors to offer the construction management delivery method. Some of its major projects have included an IRS facility and the world headquarters for H&R Block, both located in Kansas City, Missouri. The company was founded in 1924.

	Annual Growth	12/12	12/13	12/14	12/15	12/19
Sales ($mil.)	11.6%	–	2,243.7	2,243.7	2,910.6	4,329.2
Net income ($ mil.)	–	–	–	–	–	–
Market value ($ mil.)	–	–	–	–	–	–
Employees	–	–	–	–	–	2,080

J.J. GUMBERG CO.

1051 BRINTON RD STE 201
PITTSBURGH, PA 152214571
Phone: 412 244-4000
Fax: –
Web: www.jjgumberg.com

CEO: Ira J Gumberg
CFO: –
HR: –
FYE: December 31
Type: Private

J.J. Gumberg does dyn-o-mite business in commercial real estate. The company invests in, develops, and manages commercial real estate, primarily large-scale retail space, in the eastern US. It owns some 30 shopping centers and malls around the country, along with commercial office properties, totaling approximately 15 million sq. ft. of leasable space. Its portfolio is Pennsylvania-heavy, with more than half of its properties located in that state; the company has seven additional properties in Ohio. It also maintains properties in Florida, Louisiana, Maryland, Michigan, and West Virginia. Joseph J. Gumberg founded J.J. Gumberg in 1927.

J.JILL INC   NYS: JILL

4 Batterymarch Park
Quincy, MA 02169
Phone: 617 376-4300
Fax: –
Web: www.jjill.com

CEO: Claire Spofford
CFO: Mark Webb
HR: Susan Noyes
FYE: January 28
Type: Public

J.Jill is a national lifestyle brand that provides apparel, footwear and accessories designed to help its customers move through a full life with ease. The brand represents an easy, thoughtful, and inspired style that celebrates the totality of all women and designs its products with its core brand ethos in mind: keep it simple and make it matter. J.Jill offers a high touch customer experience through over 200 stores nationwide and a robust ecommerce platform. J.Jill is headquartered outside Boston. J.Jill's products are marketed under the J.Jill brand name and sold primarily through two channels: its ecommerce platform and catalog and its retail stores.

	Annual Growth	02/19	02/20*	01/21	01/22	01/23
Sales ($mil.)	(3.4%)	706.3	691.3	426.7	585.2	615.3
Net income ($ mil.)	8.4%	30.5	(128.6)	(139.4)	(28.1)	42.2
Market value ($ mil.)	45.1%	59.4	12.1	41.0	152.0	263.3
Employees	(6.9%)	3,970	3,748	2,912	2,896	2,984

*Fiscal year change

J.M. HUBER CORPORATION

3100 CUMBERLAND BLVD SE STE 600
ATLANTA, GA 303395930
Phone: 678 247-7300
Fax: –
Web: www.huber.com

CEO: Mike Marberry
CFO: Michael L Marberry
HR: Bob Hossenlopp
FYE: December 31
Type: Private

J.M. Huber Corporation (Huber) is one of the largest privately-held companies in the US. It makes specialty additives and minerals used in a personal care, food and beverage, agricultural nutrients and adjuvants, building materials, flame retardants and smoke suppressants, as well as sustainable forestry services. The diverse company also makes and manages timberlands. Huber also makes pectin, gellan gum, xanthan gum, carrageenan and more unique biopolymers, among other products, through subsidiary CP Kelco, and innovative specialty products (AdvanTech flooring and ZIP System) roof and wall sheathing through Huber Engineered Woods. Huber has remained family-owned since its founding by Joseph Maria Huber in 1883.

JABIL INC   NYS: JBL

10800 Roosevelt Boulevard North
St. Petersburg, FL 33716
Phone: 727 577-9749
Fax: –
Web: www.jabil.com

CEO: Frederic McCoy
CFO: Michael Dastoor
HR: –
FYE: August 31
Type: Public

Jabil Inc. is one of the leading providers of worldwide manufacturing services and solutions. Some of its services include comprehensive electronics design, production and product management services to companies in various industries and end markets. The company distributes its products and has facilities globally, including China, Hungary, Malaysia, Mexico, Singapore, and the US. Its segments typically serve customers in the 5G, wireless and cloud, digital print and retail, industrial and semi-cap, and networking and storage industries. The company's customers include automotive and transportation, connected devices, healthcare and packaging, and mobility industries. The company generates some 15% of revenue from the US.

	Annual Growth	08/19	08/20	08/21	08/22	08/23
Sales ($mil.)	8.2%	25,282	27,266	29,285	33,478	34,702
Net income ($ mil.)	29.9%	287.1	53.9	696.0	996.0	818.0
Market value ($ mil.)	41.2%	3,782.6	4,483.7	8,111.4	7,917.1	15,023
Employees	4.2%	200,000	240,000	238,000	250,000	236,000

JACK HENRY & ASSOCIATES, INC.   NMS: JKHY

663 Highway 60, P.O. Box 807
Monett, MO 65708
Phone: 417 235-6652
Fax: –
Web: www.jackhenry.com

CEO: –
CFO: –
HR: –
FYE: June 30
Type: Public

Jack Henry & Associates (JKHY) provides an extensive array of products and services that includes processing transactions, automating business processes, and managing information for about 7,500 financial institutions and diverse corporate entities. Products include core processing systems, electronic funds transfer (EFT) systems, automated teller machines (ATMs), digital check and document imaging systems, Internet banking, and electronic payment solutions. Its products and services provide its customers with solutions that can be tailored to support their unique growth, service, operational, and performance goals. It primarily serves commercial banks and savings institutions with up to $50 billion in assets. The company sold select products and services primarily in Latin, America, the Caribbean, and Canada.

	Annual Growth	06/19	06/20	06/21	06/22	06/23
Sales ($mil.)	7.6%	1,552.7	1,697.1	1,758.2	1,942.9	2,077.7
Net income ($ mil.)	7.8%	271.9	296.7	311.5	362.9	366.6
Market value ($ mil.)	5.7%	9,762.0	13,415	11,919	13,122	12,197
Employees	2.7%	6,402	6,717	6,714	6,847	7,120

JACK IN THE BOX, INC.

NMS: JACK

9357 Spectrum Center Blvd.
San Diego, CA 92123
Phone: 858 571-2121
Fax: –
Web: www.jackintheboxinc.com

CEO: Darin S Harris
CFO: Brian Scott
HR: –
FYE: October 1
Type: Public

Jack in the Box is one of the nation's largest hamburger chains. The company operates and franchises approximately 2,200 Jack in the Box quick-service restaurants across nearly 20 states, and Del Taco, the second largest Mexican-American quick service restaurants chain by units in the US with approximately 600 restaurants across approximately 15 states. Jack in the Box offers such standard fast-food fare as burgers, burritos, fries, and ice cream as well as salads, tacos, curly fries, egg rolls, and breakfast items. Opened in 1951, the company allows its guests to customize their meals to their tastes and order any product when they want it, including breakfast items any time of day or night.

	Annual Growth	09/19	09/20*	10/21	10/22	10/23
Sales ($mil.)	15.5%	950.1	1,021.5	1,143.7	1,468.1	1,692.3
Net income ($ mil.)	8.5%	94.4	89.8	165.8	115.8	130.8
Market value ($ mil.)	(6.5%)	1,785.0	1,583.5	1,963.8	1,461.8	1,362.9
Employees	16.3%	5,200	5,200	5,300	12,083	9,523

*Fiscal year change

JACKSON COUNTY HOSPITAL DISTRICT

4250 HOSPITAL DR
MARIANNA, FL 324461917
Phone: 850 526-2200
Fax: –
Web: www.jackson-hospital.com

CEO: –
CFO: –
HR: –
FYE: September 30
Type: Private

Jackson County Hospital Corporation provides traditional medical and surgical care for the residents in Jackson County, Florida. The not-for-profit company manages the acute-care, 100-bed Jackson Hospital. Some of the services offered at the hospital include cardiac rehabilitation, intensive care, occupational therapy, radiology, a maternity center, and a sleep laboratory. The medical center also offers physical and speech therapy and laboratory services. Jackson County Hospital Corporation is managed by a board of trustees that is appointed by the governor of Florida.

JACKSON COUNTY MEMORIAL HOSPITAL AUTHORITY

1200 E PECAN ST
ALTUS, OK 735216141
Phone: 580 482-4781
Fax: –
Web: www.jcmh.com

CEO: Steve Hartgraves
CFO: Nancy Davidson
HR: –
FYE: June 30
Type: Private

If you happen to get hobbled in Hollis, get the gout in Gould, get tripped up in Tipton, or are ailing in Altus, chances are your best bet for care is at Jackson County Memorial Hospital Trust Authority (JCMHTA). JCMHTA provides medical care to residents of Southwest Oklahoma and North Texas through its 150-bed Jackson County Memorial Hospital and 55-bed Tamarack Assisted Living Center, an assisted-living facility. More than 20 specialized services include home health and hospice care, emergency medicine, pediatrics, and orthopedics. The hospital also offers an outpatient same-day surgery unit, a women's center, a cancer center, and an intensive care unit.

	Annual Growth	06/06	06/07	06/08	06/09	06/12
Sales ($mil.)	1.4%	–	–	73.0	70.5	77.2
Net income ($ mil.)	–	–	–	7.4	1.8	(1.5)
Market value ($ mil.)	–	–	–	–	–	–
Employees	–	–	–	–	–	800

JACKSON ELECTRIC MEMBERSHIP CORPORATION

850 COMMERCE RD
JEFFERSON, GA 305493329
Phone: 706 367-5281
Fax: –
Web: www.jacksonemc.com

CEO: Randall Pugh
CFO: Greg Keith
HR: Keith Johnson
FYE: December 31
Type: Private

Jackson EMC distributes electricity to more than 197,800 individual customers (more than 210,200 meters) in 10 counties around Atlanta and in northeastern Georgia. The majority of customers are residential, with commercial and industrial customers accounting for 42% of fiscal year 2013 revenues. One of the largest nonprofit power cooperatives in the US and the largest electric cooperative in Georgia, Jackson EMC is owned by its members. The cooperative's generation and transmission partners include Oglethorpe Power Corp., Georgia Systems Operation, and Georgia Transmission Corp.

	Annual Growth	05/19	05/20	05/21	05/22*	12/22
Sales ($mil.)	8.6%	–	585.6	593.1	598.7	690.4
Net income ($ mil.)	–	–	37.3	36.6	24.4	–
Market value ($ mil.)	–	–	–	–	–	–
Employees	–	–	–	–	–	445

*Fiscal year change

JACKSON ENERGY AUTHORITY

119 E COLLEGE ST
JACKSON, TN 383016201
Phone: 731 422-7500
Fax: –
Web: www.jaxenergy.com

CEO: Danny Wheeler
CFO: –
HR: Stacy Scoggins
FYE: June 30
Type: Private

Jackson Energy Authority has the power and the authority to provide for all of Jackson, Tennessee's energy needs. The municipal utility distributes electricity, natural gas, and water and provides wastewater services to about 40,000 residential, commercial, and industrial customers in Jackson and surrounding areas. Jackson Energy also sells propane and offers broadband telecommunications services (cable, Internet, and telephone). Other services provided by Jackson Energy Authority include the sale of outdoor security lights, surge protection systems, gas grills, and decorative lights.

	Annual Growth	06/18	06/19	06/20	06/21	06/22
Sales ($mil.)	2.0%	–	254.3	243.6	247.9	269.5
Net income ($ mil.)	(6.3%)	–	40.2	23.3	25.8	33.1
Market value ($ mil.)	–	–	–	–	–	–
Employees	–	–	–	–	–	425

JACKSON HEALTHCARE, LLC

2655 NORTHWINDS PKWY
ALPHARETTA, GA 300092280
Phone: 770 643-5500
Fax: –
Web: www.jacksonhealthcare.com

CEO: –
CFO: –
HR: –
FYE: December 31
Type: Private

Jackson Healthcare is a family of highly specialized healthcare staffing, search and technology companies. Its companies provide healthcare systems, hospitals and medical facilities of all sizes with the skilled and specialized labor and technologies they need to deliver high quality patient care and achieve the best possible outcomes ? while connecting healthcare professionals to the temporary engagements, contract assignments and permanent placement employment opportunities they desire. Jackson Healthcare allows to help health systems, hospitals and other healthcare facilities with temporary and permanent workforce needs. . Richard Jackson formed the company in 2000.

	Annual Growth	12/05	12/06	12/07	12/15	12/16
Sales ($mil.)	9.0%	–	–	385.0	696.9	838.1
Net income ($ mil.)	19.8%	–	–	18.3	70.8	93.0
Market value ($ mil.)	–	–	–	–	–	–
Employees	–	–	–	–	–	949

JACKSON HEWITT TAX SERVICE INC.

10 EXCHANGE PL FL 27
JERSEY CITY, NJ 073023922
Phone: 973 630-0708
Fax: –
Web: www.jacksonhewitt.com

CEO: –
CFO: –
HR: –
FYE: April 30
Type: Private

For Jackson Hewitt, there's no season like tax season. The tax preparer, ranked #2 in the US behind H&R Block, prepares tax returns for primarily low- and middle-income customers. Jackson Hewitt provides full-service individual federal and state income tax preparation through about 6,400 primarily franchised offices, including more than 3,200 locations within Wal-Mart and Sears stores in the US and Puerto Rico. The firm's tax preparers use its proprietary ProFiler decision-tree software to file millions of returns annually. It also offers online tax preparation at JacksonHewittOnline.com.

JACKSON HOSPITAL & CLINIC, INC.

1725 PINE ST
MONTGOMERY, AL 361061117
Phone: 334 293-8000
Fax: –
Web: www.jackson.org

CEO: –
CFO: –
HR: –
FYE: December 31
Type: Private

Jackson Hospital & Clinic looks after the health and well being of a large number of residents of Montgomery and central Alabama. The privately held not-for-profit medical institution has about 345 acute care beds. Specialized services include cardiac care, emergency medicine, neurology, orthopedics, oncology, and women's and infant's health care. The medical center also provides family medicine, primary care, and diagnostic services through its outpatient clinic facilities, and it offers medical laboratory services for other regional health care providers.

	Annual Growth	12/18	12/19	12/20	12/21	12/22
Sales ($mil.)	7.5%	–	268.1	270.5	270.8	332.9
Net income ($ mil.)	–	–	3.2	10.7	2.1	(8.4)
Market value ($ mil.)	–	–	–	–	–	–
Employees	–	–	–	–	–	1,400

JACKSON STATE UNIVERSITY

1400 J R LYNCH ST STE 206
JACKSON, MS 392170001
Phone: 601 979-2121
Fax: –
Web: www.jsums.edu

CEO: –
CFO: Arlitha Williams-Harmon
HR: –
FYE: June 30
Type: Private

Jackson State University (JSU) is a public, coeducational institution that offers more than 90 undergraduate and graduate degrees. It offers programs through five academic colleges covering business; education and human development; liberal arts; public service; and science, technology, and engineering. The historically black school now serves a diverse, 9,000-strong student body. JSU also operates the Mississippi Urban Research Center, which analyzes and distributes information relating to public policies and activities that affect urban life. The school was founded as Natchez Seminary in 1877; after multiple name changes, it became JSU in 1974 after achieving university status.

	Annual Growth	06/18	06/19	06/20	06/21	06/22
Sales ($mil.)	(9.5%)	–	153.5	105.5	98.4	113.8
Net income ($ mil.)	–	–	(10.9)	8.1	21.4	21.9
Market value ($ mil.)	–	–	–	–	–	–
Employees	–	–	–	–	–	2,000

JACKSONVILLE ELECTRIC AUTHORITY

21 W CHURCH ST FL 1
JACKSONVILLE, FL 322023139
Phone: 904 665-6000
Fax: –
Web: www.jea.com

CEO: Jay Stowe
CFO: Melissa Dykes
HR: Paul Parsons
FYE: September 30
Type: Private

As long as sparks are flying in Jacksonville, everything is A-OK with JEA. The community-owned, not-for-profit utility provides electricity to 438,000 customers in Jacksonville and surrounding areas in northeastern Florida. Managing an electric system that dates back to 1895, JEA has a net generating capacity of 3,747 MW. It owns an electric system with five primarily fossil-fueled generating plants. JEA also gets 12.8 MW of generating capacity from two methane-fueled landfill plants. The company resells electricity to other utilities, including NextEra Energy. JEA also provides water and wastewater services; it serves 321,600 water customers and 247,500 wastewater customers.

	Annual Growth	09/15	09/16	09/17	09/18	09/22
Sales ($mil.)	1.6%	–	–	1,875.2	1,790.0	2,029.9
Net income ($ mil.)	(14.3%)	–	–	254.6	126.5	117.4
Market value ($ mil.)	–	–	–	–	–	–
Employees	–	–	–	–	–	2,356

JACKSONVILLE JAGUARS, LLC

1 TIAA BANK FIELD DR
JACKSONVILLE, FL 322021917
Phone: 904 633-6000
Fax: –
Web: www.jaguars.com

CEO: –
CFO: –
HR: –
FYE: December 31
Type: Private

Gators might come to mind first when you think of Florida sports, but these big cats have a following, too. The Jacksonville Jaguars joined the National Football League as an expansion franchise in 1995, along with the Carolina Panthers. The team quickly gained respect by securing playoff berths the following four years, but the Jags have struggled to be a consistent contender in the years since. The team plays host at Jacksonville Municipal Stadium. Wayne Weaver, chairman and majority owner of retailer Shoe Carnival, owns 48% of the team, while a group of local businessmen owns the rest.

JACKSONVILLE UNIVERSITY

2800 UNIVERSITY BLVD N
JACKSONVILLE, FL 322113394
Phone: 904 256-8000
Fax: –
Web: www.ju.edu

CEO: –
CFO: –
HR: E'Lisa Green
FYE: June 30
Type: Private

To become a jack of all knowledgeable trades, you might head to Jacksonville University. The private liberal arts university has more than 4,000 students and offers more than 100 majors, minors, and programs, including degrees in Business, Marine Science, Engineering, Physics, and Nursing, as well as those in the more contemporary and specialized fields of Aviation, Communication Sciences and Disorders, Film, Animation, and Sport Business. Its Adult Degree Program (ADP) is designed for adults to complete a bachelor's degree without putting their career or family on hold.

	Annual Growth	06/17	06/18	06/20	06/21	06/22
Sales ($mil.)	17.3%	–	94.4	162.5	172.0	179.9
Net income ($ mil.)	–	–	(1.7)	(3.7)	12.5	3.1
Market value ($ mil.)	–	–	–	–	–	–
Employees	–	–	–	–	–	450

JACO ELECTRONICS, INC.

NBB: JACO

145 Oser Avenue
Hauppauge, NY 11788
Phone: 631 273-5500
Fax: 631 273-5528
Web: www.jacoelectronics.com

CEO: Joel H Girsky
CFO: Jeffrey D Gash
HR: –
FYE: June 30
Type: Public

Jaco Electronics, doing business as Jaco Display Solutions, offers information displays for a variety of industries. In 2009 Jaco sold the assets of its electronic components distribution business to WPG Americas, Inc., a subsidiary of Taiwan-based WPG Holdings. Jaco shifted its focus to distributing displays, embedded computing products, and inverters, while providing value-added services. The components distribution business is shifting to Asia, the company noted. Jaco also offers a number of services, including inventory management and flat-panel display system configuration, but discontinued contract manufacturing services. The company still provides engineering support services for its customers.

	Annual Growth	06/04	06/05	06/06	06/07	06/08
Sales ($mil.)	(6.1%)	249.1	231.8	228.5	240.2	193.7
Net income ($ mil.)	–	(0.6)	(4.9)	(7.0)	(3.1)	(9.1)
Market value ($ mil.)	(34.3%)	38.3	18.6	23.5	14.6	7.1
Employees	(17.2%)	412	202	205	205	194

JACO OIL COMPANY

3101 STATE RD
BAKERSFIELD, CA 933084931
Phone: 661 393-7000
Fax: –
Web: www.jaco.com

CEO: T J Jamieson
CFO: Brian Busacca
HR: –
FYE: December 31
Type: Private

Jaco Oil Company is jockeying for its piece of the convenience store pie. The company's Fastrip Food Stores subsidiary operates more than 50 convenience stores and gas stations primarily in and around Bakersfield, California, but also in Arizona. Besides offering customers traditional convenience-store fare, which includes coffee, milk, beer, snacks, tobacco, and the like, the Fastrip chain stocks a full range of grocery items and provides in-store financial service centers. Financial services include check cashing, payday loans, wire transfer services via The Western Union Company, refund anticipation loans, and other services, at many locations. Jaco Oil Company was founded in 1970.

	Annual Growth	12/17	12/18	12/19	12/20	12/21
Sales ($mil.)	16.0%	–	636.7	657.9	555.9	993.6
Net income ($ mil.)	(2.2%)	–	19.5	25.9	20.4	18.3
Market value ($ mil.)	–	–	–	–	–	–
Employees	–	–	–	–	–	350

JACOBS ENTERTAINMENT, INC.

12596 W BAYAUD AVE STE 100
LAKEWOOD, CO 802282035
Phone: 303 215-5196
Fax: –
Web: www.jacobsentertainmentinc.com

CEO: Jeffrey Jacobs
CFO: Brent Kramer
HR: Donna Berard
FYE: December 31
Type: Private

Jacobs Entertainment wants you to come out and play. The company operates gaming properties in Colorado, Louisiana, Nevada, and Virginia. Its portfolio includes five casinos: The Lodge Casino and The Gilpin Casino in Black Hawk, Colorado, and the Gold Dust West casinos in Reno, Carson City, and Elko, Nevada. The firm also has about 20 truck stop video gaming facilities throughout Louisiana. In Virginia it has The Colonial Downs horseracing track, which has ten satellite pari-mutuel wagering locations throughout the state. Chairman and CEO Jeffrey Jacobs is also responsible for the Nautica Entertainment Complex, a development on the Cleveland, Ohio waterfront. He owns Jacobs Entertainment through family trusts.

JACOBS FINANCIAL GROUP INC

179 Summers Street, Suite 307
Charleston, WV 25301
Phone: 304 343-8171
Fax: –
Web: www.thejacobsfinancialgroup.com

CEO: –
CFO: –
HR: –
FYE: May 31
Type: Public

If Jacob needed to bond his ladder, Jacobs Financial Group could provide the surety. Through subsidiaries, Jacobs Financial provides surety and insurance as well as investment advisory services. The company's FS Investments (FSI) is a holding company that develops surety business by creating companies engaged in the issuance of surety bonds (bonds collateralized by accounts managed by Jacobs & Co.). FSI's wholly owned subsidiary Triangle Surety Agency specializes in placing surety bonds with insurance companies, with an emphasis on clients in industries such as coal, oil, and gas. Jacobs Financial, whose background is in energy, has been expanding its insurance and surety operations through acquisitions.

	Annual Growth	05/13	05/14	05/15	05/16	05/17
Sales ($mil.)	20.9%	1.3	1.3	1.6	1.3	2.9
Net income ($ mil.)	–	(2.0)	(1.8)	(1.6)	(0.0)	(1.3)
Market value ($ mil.)	(25.9%)	3.2	2.3	1.1	1.0	1.0
Employees	10.7%	6	9	9	9	9

JACOBS SOLUTIONS INC

NYS: J

1999 Bryan Street, Suite 1200
Dallas, TX 75201
Phone: 214 583-8500
Fax: –
Web: www.jacobs.com

CEO: Steven J Demetriou
CFO: Kevin C Berryman
HR: –
FYE: September 29
Type: Public

Jacobs Engineering Group provides a full spectrum of professional services including consulting, technical, scientific, and project delivery for government, and private sector throughout the world. Jacobs handles project design, architectural, and engineering, construction and construction management services, operations and maintenance services, and process, scientific and systems consulting services. Around 70% of revenue comes from the US while the rest originates in other countries, primarily in Europe. PA consulting serves as the company's third segment at the moment.

	Annual Growth	09/19*	10/20	10/21*	09/22	09/23
Sales ($mil.)	6.4%	12,738	13,567	14,093	14,923	16,352
Net income ($ mil.)	(5.9%)	848.0	491.8	477.0	644.0	665.8
Market value ($ mil.)	10.8%	11,425	11,872	16,964	13,667	17,196
Employees	3.6%	52,000	55,000	55,000	63,300	60,000

*Fiscal year change

JACOBS, MALCOLM & BURTT

2258 CAMINO RAMON
SAN RAMON, CA 945831353
Phone: 415 285-0400
Fax: –
Web: www.jmb-produce.com

CEO: –
CFO: –
HR: –
FYE: December 31
Type: Private

Jacobs, Malcolm & Burtt may sound like a law office, but the only argument this company would make is to eat your vegetables. The firm is a California-based wholesaler and distributor of fruits and vegetables, such as asparagus, oranges, and berries. Jacobs and Malcolm founded the company in 1888 and Burtt joined the name in 1969. Leo Rolandelli owns 50% of the capital stock, the Wilson Family Trust owns 31%, and the rest is controlled by the other officers.

	Annual Growth	12/13	12/14	12/15	12/17	12/18
Sales ($mil.)	2.4%	–	54.9	59.0	75.5	60.3
Net income ($ mil.)	25.0%	–	0.4	0.5	0.8	0.9
Market value ($ mil.)	–	–	–	–	–	–
Employees	–	–	–	–	–	22

JACOBSON & COMPANY, INC

1079 E GRAND ST
ELIZABETH, NJ 072012655
Phone: 908 355-5200
Fax: -
Web: www.jacobsoncompany.com

CEO: Thomas D Jacobson
CFO: -
HR: -
FYE: December 31
Type: Private

If these walls could talk they might say something about Jacobson & Company. The long-standing company specializes in drywall and ceiling installations and has been working in around the metropolitan New York area for more than 120 years. When Jacobson & Company was established by Gustave Jacobson in 1889, it specialized in ornamental plaster contracting, working on iconic projects such as the Presidential Palace in Cuba, the Metropolitan Museum of Art, and the Hearst Castle. The company began offering acoustical ceiling products in the 1940s. More recent projects include Trump Tower and the renovation of Carnegie Hall. Fifth-generation family member Thomas Jacobson is the company's president and CEO.

JAFFE ASSOCIATES INCORPORATED

1300 PENN AVE NW STE 700
WASHINGTON, DC 200043024
Phone: 877 808-9600
Fax: -
Web: www.jaffepr.com

CEO: Jay M Jaffe
CFO: -
HR: -
FYE: December 31
Type: Private

Jaffe Associates makes sure its clients don't make any public gaffes. The company provides marketing consulting and public relations services to law firms and other clients in the legal profession. It also offers Web site design and interactive marketing services as well as business development consulting. The firm, started by CEO Jay Jaffe in 1979, is a "virtual" consultancy -- the firm's employees work from home instead of from a central location. Jaffe Associates serves clients, including Powell Goldstein, Potter Anderson & Corroon, and Wildman Harrold, throughout the US and Canada. It works through subsidiary Lehmann Communications in the UK and other parts of Europe.

	Annual Growth	12/95	12/96	12/97	12/08	12/10
Sales ($mil.)	(0.4%)	–	3.5	4.1	3.0	3.3
Net income ($ mil.)	–	–	(0.0)	(0.1)	0.0	0.1
Market value ($ mil.)	–	–	–	–	–	–
Employees	–	–	–	–	–	25

JAGGAER, LLC

3020 CARRINGTON MILL BLVD STE 100
MORRISVILLE, NC 275605433
Phone: 919 659-2100
Fax: -
Web: www.jaggaer.com

CEO: Jim Bureau
CFO: Jeff Laborde
HR: -
FYE: December 31
Type: Private

JAGGAER is an industry leader in sourcing and procurement software. The company develops and provides comprehensive source-to-settle SaaS-based solutions, including advanced Spend Analytics, Category Management, Supplier Management, Sourcing, Contracts, eProcurement, Invoicing, Supply Chain Management and Inventory Management. It offers end-to-end Software-as-a-Service (SaaS)-based procurement solutions that all reside on a single platform, JAGGAER ONE. It was founded in 1995.

JAGGED PEAK, INC.

7650 W COURTNEY CAMPBELL
TAMPA, FL 336077214
Phone: 813 637-6900
Fax: -
Web: www.id-logistics.com

CEO: -
CFO: -
HR: -
FYE: December 27
Type: Private

Jagged Peak rises up to help customers reach the peak of supply chain management. The company's E-Business Dynamic Global Engine (EDGE) software is a ready-to-use Web-based application that captures, processes, and distributes orders from multiple sources, sending them in real-time to warehouses. With automated purchases and orders, companies can streamline their supply chain processes to improve delivery, reduce costs, and integrate inventory information. Jagged Peak took its present form in 2005, when publicly traded Absolute Glass Protection acquired the private company and adopted its name, officers, and operations.

JAKKS PACIFIC INC

NMS: JAKK

2951 28th Street
Santa Monica, CA 90405
Phone: 424 268-9444
Fax: -
Web: www.jakks.com

CEO: -
CFO: -
HR: -
FYE: December 31
Type: Public

JAKKS Pacific is one of the US's top toy companies. It makes and sells action figures (including licenses for Harry Potter and Nintendo), die-cast and plastic cars, electronic products, dolls (such as Disney Princess and Fancy Nancy), Halloween costumes and dress-up products, and a host of other playthings. Its products are sold to US mass merchandisers such as Target and Wal-Mart, which together account for about 55% of sales. The company sells its products through e-commerce sites, including Walmart.com, Target.com, and Amazon.com. The US is the company's largest market by far.

	Annual Growth	12/19	12/20	12/21	12/22	12/23
Sales ($mil.)	4.4%	598.6	515.9	621.1	796.2	711.6
Net income ($ mil.)	–	(55.5)	(14.3)	(6.0)	91.4	38.4
Market value ($ mil.)	142.4%	10.4	50.3	102.6	176.6	358.9
Employees	8.4%	477	626	583	622	659

JAMBA, INC.

3001 DALLAS PKWY STE 140
FRISCO, TX 750348046
Phone: 469 294-9600
Fax: -
Web: locations.jamba.com

CEO: -
CFO: Michael J Dixon
HR: -
FYE: January 02
Type: Private

Jamba is the global lifestyle brand leader serving on-the-go freshly blended fruit and vegetable smoothies, made-to-order bowls, fresh-squeezed juices, shots, boosts, and bites. Jamba has nearly 800 locations operating in about 35 US states, as well as the Philippines, Taiwan, South Korea, Thailand, Singapore, and Guatemala. Its menu includes more than 30 varieties of custom smoothies (including Aloha Pineapple, Mango-a-go-go, and Strawberry Surf Rider) and Jamba Boosts (smoothies made with vitamin and protein supplements), along with other fruit juices and food items. Jamba Juice locations include freestanding units as well as on-site kiosks in high-traffic areas, including college campuses, gyms, and airports. Jamba is a part of the Focus Brands family of brands.

JAMES MADISON UNIVERSITY

800 S MAIN ST
HARRISONBURG, VA 228070002
Phone: 540 568-6211
Fax: –
Web: www.jmu.edu

CEO: –
CFO: –
HR: –
FYE: June 30
Type: Private

James Madison is known as the Father of the Constitution and America's fourth president, but he also has a public institution of higher education named after him. James Madison University (JMU) offers some 70 undergraduate and 40 graduate degrees through more than a half-dozen colleges, including arts and letters, business, education, visual and performing arts, and science and mathematics. The university enrolls about 20,000 students, mostly undergrads, with a faculty of 1,200 teachers and a student-to-faculty ratio of 16:1. JMU also has extensive men's and women's athletic programs. JMU was established in 1908 in Harrisonburg, Virginia.

	Annual Growth	06/06	06/07	06/08	06/11	06/13
Sales ($mil.)	6.2%	–	–	270.4	323.3	365.0
Net income ($ mil.)	0.7%	–	–	69.2	56.5	71.7
Market value ($ mil.)	–	–	–	–	–	–
Employees						1,700

JAMES RIVER COAL COMPANY

901 E BYRD ST FL 2
RICHMOND, VA 232194087
Phone: 804 780-3000
Fax: –
Web: www.registrar-transfers.com

CEO: Peter T Socha
CFO: –
HR: –
FYE: December 31
Type: Private

James River keeps the coal flowing. The company operates about 40 mines in Kentucky and West Virginia (in the Central Appalachian Basin) and Indiana (in the Illinois Basin) that produce more than 10 million tons of coal annually. Though a small percentage of the coal it sells comes from independent operators and third-party producers, the vast majority of James River's coal is produced from company-operated mines. It controls approximately 362.8 million tons of proved and probable reserves (92% in Appalachia). The company, which filed for chapter 11 bankruptcy in mid-2014, sells its coal to power stations in the southern US and to steel producers around the world.

JANEL CORP

80 Eighth Avenue
New York, NY 10011
Phone: 212 373-5895
Fax: 718 527-1689
Web: www.janelcorp.com

NBB: JANL
CEO: Darren C Seirer
CFO: Vincent A Verde
HR: –
FYE: September 30
Type: Public

Janel Corporation is a holding company with subsidiaries in three business segments: Logistics, Life Sciences Manufacturing. It provides cargo transportation logistics management services, including freight forwarding via air-, ocean- and land-based carriers, customs brokerage services, warehousing and distribution services, and other logistics services. Through a combined portfolio of approximately 3,000 products and a range of custom services, the Life Sciences segment provides the scientific community with high quality tools to support critical research efforts.

	Annual Growth	09/19	09/20	09/21	09/22	09/23
Sales ($mil.)	21.9%	84.4	82.4	146.4	316.9	186.4
Net income ($ mil.)	4.1%	0.6	(1.7)	5.2	(2.1)	0.7
Market value ($ mil.)	33.1%	10.7	10.7	27.3	62.9	33.5
Employees	16.1%	174	173	317	326	316

JANI-KING INTERNATIONAL, INC.

16885 DALLAS PKWY
ADDISON, TX 750015202
Phone: 972 991-0900
Fax: –
Web: www.janiking.com

CEO: –
CFO: Steve Hawkins
HR: –
FYE: December 31
Type: Private

Jani-King is the world's largest commercial cleaning franchise company. With more than 7,500 franchised businesses worldwide, the company provides cleaning services to office buildings, hospitals, hotels, manufacturing facilities, healthcare institutions, hotels, restaurants, universities, sports arenas, and more. Jani-King operates through 120 offices in around 10 countries. The company was founded in 1969 by Jim Cavanaugh.

JANONE INC

325 E. Warm Springs Road, Suite 102
Las Vegas, NV 89119
Phone: 702 997-5968
Fax: –
Web: www.janone.com

NAS: JAN
CEO: Tony Isaac
CFO: Virland A Johnson
HR: –
FYE: December 31
Type: Public

Appliance Recycling Centers of America (ARCA) retrieves, recycles, repairs, and resells household appliances. The company's retail business operates 20 ApplianceSmart Factory Outlet stores in Minnesota, Georgia, Ohio, and Texas that sell new, reconditioned, and "special-buy" appliances from manufacturers such as Electrolux, GE, and Whirlpool. ARCA provides recycling and replacement services for appliance makers, electric utilities, and energy-efficiency programs in North America. The firm also cashes in on byproducts, collecting fees for appliance disposal and selling scrap metal and reclaimed chlorofluorocarbon refrigerants from processed appliances. ARCA was founded in 1976 as a used appliance retailer.

	Annual Growth	12/18	12/19*	01/21	01/22*	12/22
Sales ($mil.)	1.9%	36.8	35.1	33.9	40.0	39.6
Net income ($ mil.)	–	(5.6)	(12.0)	(8.5)	(16.9)	11.0
Market value ($ mil.)	28.3%	1.6	9.2	15.4	12.9	4.3
Employees	6.8%	159	208	179	170	207

*Fiscal year change

JANUS CAPITAL GROUP INC.

151 DETROIT ST
DENVER, CO 802064928
Phone: 303 333-3863
Fax: –
Web: www.janushenderson.com

CEO: –
CFO: –
HR: –
FYE: December 31
Type: Private

Named after the Roman god with two faces, Janus Capital Group provides investment management and advisory services for institutional and individual customers. Known for its intensive equities research, the company manages dozens of mutual funds, including its flagship Janus Fund (formed in 1969), as well as separate accounts and sub-advised portfolios. Subsidiary INTECH manages institutional portfolios by utilizing investment strategies based on mathematical analysis of the stock market, while Perkins Investment Management focuses on long-term value investments. All told, Janus Capital and its subsidiaries have $183 billion of assets under management. Janus is merging with UK-based asset manager Henderson Group.

JAPAN SOCIETY, INC.

333 E 47TH ST
NEW YORK, NY 100172313
Phone: 212 832-1155
Fax: –
Web: www.japansociety.org

CEO: Joshua Walker
CFO: Lisa Bermudez
HR: Jane Fenton
FYE: June 30
Type: Private

Japan Society administrates many cultural and educational offerings including corporate outreach programs, policy discussions, journalistic fellowships, gallery exhibitions, public lectures, and film screenings. The Society also operates the C.V. Starr Library, which contains about 14,000 volumes on all aspects of Japan's culture, and the Toyota Language Center, which offers 12 levels of training in the Japanese language. The institution was founded in 1907 by business leaders in New York City to promote good relations between the US and Japan.

	Annual Growth	06/12	06/13	06/20	06/21	06/22
Sales ($mil.)	2.8%	–	13.5	9.8	10.5	17.4
Net income ($ mil.)	11.6%	–	2.1	(1.8)	0.3	5.7
Market value ($ mil.)	–	–	–	–	–	–
Employees	–	–	–	–	–	72

JARVIS CHRISTIAN UNIVERSITY

7631 E US HIGHWAY 80
HAWKINS, TX 757653466
Phone: 903 730-4890
Fax: –
Web: www.jarvis.edu

CEO: Ronald Hay
CFO: –
HR: –
FYE: June 30
Type: Private

At Jarvis Christian College, life is all about opining amongst the pines. The private, not-for-profit liberal arts college is located on 1,000 acres in the Piney Woods of East Texas. The four-year, historically black college enrolls about 550 students per semester. It operates divisions of arts and sciences, education, and business administration. Jarvis' Division of Arts and Sciences is especially well known for its programs in geosciences and astronomy. Other popular fields of study include religion, science and mathematics, and chemistry. Jarvis Christian College is named after Major J.J. Davis, who donated 456 acres of land in 1910 for the purpose of building the college.

	Annual Growth	06/13	06/14	06/15	06/16	06/22
Sales ($mil.)	5.4%	–	–	17.6	21.2	25.5
Net income ($ mil.)	–	–	–	(0.9)	0.3	2.0
Market value ($ mil.)	–	–	–	–	–	–
Employees	–	–	–	–	–	137

JAUREGUI, INC.

3660 STONERIDGE RD STE A102
AUSTIN, TX 78746
Phone: 512 328-7706
Fax: –
Web: www.jaureguiarchitect.com

CEO: –
CFO: –
HR: –
FYE: December 31
Type: Private

Jauregui, doing business as Jauregui Architect Builder, custom designs and builds luxury homes in Texas. The company offers architectural, interior design, brokerage, and construction services. Houses typically run in the multi-million dollar price range; architectural styles include contemporary, Tuscan, Mediterranean, and classical Italian. Jauregui Architect Builder operates primarily in the Austin and surrounding Hill Country area, but also has offices in Dallas and Houston.

JAVELIN MORTGAGE INVESTMENT CORP.

3001 OCEAN DR STE 201
VERO BEACH, FL 329631992
Phone: 772 617-4340
Fax: –
Web: www.armourreit.com

CEO: Jeffrey J Zimmer
CFO: James R Mountain
HR: –
FYE: December 31
Type: Private

JAVELIN Mortgage Investment is looking to spearhead a new effort in mortgage-related investments. The company formed in June 2012 as a real estate investment trust (REIT) with plans to invest in mortgage securities backed by government-supported enterprises such as Fannie Mae, Freddie Mac, and Ginnie Mae, as well as other mortgage securities. As a REIT, JAVELIN Mortgage Investment will be exempt from paying federal income tax as long as it makes a quarterly distribution to shareholders. It will be externally managed by ARMOUR Residential Management, LLC, the same external manager of sister company ARMOUR Residential REIT, Inc. The company went public in 2012.

	Annual Growth	12/11	12/12	12/13	12/14	12/15
Assets ($mil.)	(12.1%)	–	1,286.5	1,066.3	1,280.9	874.3
Net income ($ mil.)	–	–	6.1	(43.8)	(21.8)	(0.3)
Market value ($ mil.)	–	–	–	–	–	–
Employees	–	–	–	–	–	5

JAVO BEVERAGE COMPANY, INC.

1311 SPECIALTY DR
VISTA, CA 920818521
Phone: 760 560-5286
Fax: –
Web: www.javobeverage.com

CEO: –
CFO: –
HR: –
FYE: December 31
Type: Private

Javo puts the S-Q-U-E-E-Z-E on coffee. Javo Beverage Company makes and markets coffee and tea concentrates, drink mixes, iced and hot ready-to-drink beverages, and flavor and dispenser systems. Its national and international customers do business in the retail, health care, oil, food and beverage manufacturing, and food service industries. Of note is Javo's line of "bag-in-a-box" products that allows restaurants, hotels, and hospitals to offer fresh-tasting coffee without having to do any actual brewing. In May 2011 Javo emerged from Chapter 11 -- after four months in bankruptcy -- as a private company; it is majority owned by Coffee Holdings, an affiliate of Falconhead Capital.

JAYHAWK PIPELINE, L.L.C.

2000 S MAIN ST
MCPHERSON, KS 674609402
Phone: 620 241-9270
Fax: –
Web: –

CEO: –
CFO: –
HR: –
FYE: December 31
Type: Private

Jayhawk Pipeline is not the process for producing University of Kansas mascots. What it is is a subsidiary of National Cooperative Refinery Association that transports more than 110,000 barrels per day of crude oil via both intrastate and interstate pipelines in Kansas. It operates 1,200 miles of gathering and trunk lines throughout Kansas, Nebraska, Oklahoma, and Texas. It also manages the business of Kaw Pipe Line Company. National Cooperative Refinery Association provides three farm supply cooperatives (Cenex Harvest States, GROWMARK, and MFA Oil) with fuel through its oil refinery in Kansas.

JBG SMITH PROPERTIES　　　　　　　　　　　NYS: JBGS

4747 Bethesda Avenue Suite 200　　　　　　　　CEO: W M Kelly
Bethesda, MD 20814　　　　　　　　　　　　　CFO: M M Banerjee
Phone: 240 333-3600　　　　　　　　　　　　　HR: Carey Goldberg
Fax: –　　　　　　　　　　　　　　　　　　　FYE: December 31
Web: www.jbgsmith.com　　　　　　　　　　　　Type: Public

JBG SMITH Properties is a self-managed real estate investment trust (REIT) with holdings in high-growth office, multifamily, and retail properties located in the Washington, DC area. Approximately two-thirds of JBG SMITH's holdings are in the National Landing submarket in Northern Virginia, which is anchored by four key demand drivers: Amazon's new headquarters, which is being developed by JBG SMITH; Virginia Tech's under-construction $1 billion Innovation Campus; the submarket's proximity to the Pentagon; and JBG SMITH's deployment of next-generation public and private 5G digital infrastructure. Additionally, it has two under-construction multifamily assets with around 1,585 units and some 20 assets in the development pipeline totaling 12.5 million square feet (about 9.7 million square feet at its share) of estimated potential development density.

	Annual Growth	12/19	12/20	12/21	12/22	12/23
Sales ($mil.)	(1.7%)	647.8	602.7	634.4	605.8	604.2
Net income ($ mil.)	–	65.6	(62.3)	(79.3)	85.4	(80.0)
Market value ($ mil.)	(19.2%)	3,762.0	2,949.0	2,707.6	1,790.0	1,604.2
Employees	(4.6%)	1,017	1,050	997	912	844

JCK LEGACY COMPANY

1601 ALHAMBRA BLVD STE 100　　　　　　　　CEO: Tony Hunter
SACRAMENTO, CA 958167164　　　　　　　　　　CFO: –
Phone: 916 321-1844　　　　　　　　　　　　　HR: –
Fax: –　　　　　　　　　　　　　　　　　　　FYE: December 30
Web: www.mcclatchy.com　　　　　　　　　　　Type: Private

The McClatchy Company is one of the top newspaper businesses in the US. McClatchy has about 30 daily papers with a combined circulation of about 2.6 million. Its portfolio includes The Kansas City Star, The Miami Herald, The Charlotte Observer, The Sacramento Bee (California), and the Star-Telegram (Fort Worth, Texas). In addition, it has some 50% stake in The Seattle Times Company, weekly newspapers in the Puget Sound area and daily newspapers located in Walla Walla and Yakima, Washington, and their related websites and mobile applications. The company traces its roots back to the 1850s, when James McClatchy co-founded The Bee, his first newspaper.

JCM PARTNERS, LLC

3581 MT DIABLO BLVD STE 205　　　　　　　　CEO: –
LAFAYETTE, CA 945498306　　　　　　　　　　 CFO: –
Phone: 925 681-4393　　　　　　　　　　　　　HR: –
Fax: –　　　　　　　　　　　　　　　　　　　FYE: December 31
Web: www.jcmpartners.com　　　　　　　　　　Type: Private

At the northern end of the Golden State is where you'll find JCM Partners, which invests in, renovates, manages, markets, and sells multifamily residential and commercial real estate. The company also offers furnished corporate housing. JCM Partners owns about 45 properties, including apartment communities (containing a total of about 5,000 units), one multi-tenant office/retail property, office properties, and industrial properties. Nearly half of JCM Partners' residential properties are located in Sacramento County; the remainder are in San Joaquin, Solano, Stanislaus, and Contra Costa counties. JCM runs Rent-One.com -- an online apartment rental guide.

JDS UNIPHASE CANADA LTD

430 North McCarthy Boulevard　　　　　　　　CEO: Oleg Khaykin
Milpitas, CA 95035　　　　　　　　　　　　　 CFO: Ilan Daskal
Phone: 408 546-5000　　　　　　　　　　　　　HR: –
Fax: 408 546-4300　　　　　　　　　　　　　　FYE: June 29
Web: www.jdsu.com　　　　　　　　　　　　　　Type: Public

Viavi Solutions is a global provider of network test, monitoring, and assurance solutions that are used to build and improve communications equipment and broadband networks. Viavi's AvComm products are a global leader in test and measurement (T&M) instrumentation for communication and safety in the government, aerospace, and military markets. It also provides test products and services for private enterprise networks. Another Viavi offering is an optical technology, which includes tools for detecting counterfeit currency as well as optical filters for sensor applications. About a third of Viavi's revenue are to customers in the US. Viavi was created in 2015 when JDS Uniphase split into two companies.

	Annual Growth	06/04	06/05*	07/11*	06/12	06/13
Sales ($mil.)	14.4%	476.8	581.1	1,849.4	1,625.2	1,599.5
Net income ($ mil.)	–	(86.6)	(213.2)	74.3	(54.4)	54.4
Market value ($ mil.)	16.8%	783.4	406.0	4,865.1	2,374.0	3,166.9
Employees	–	–	5,022	–	–	–

*Fiscal year change

JEFFERIES FINANCIAL GROUP INC　　　　　　NYS: JEF

520 Madison Avenue　　　　　　　　　　　　　CEO: Lee Chun-Kee
New York, NY 10022　　　　　　　　　　　　　CFO: Matthew S Larson
Phone: 212 284-2300　　　　　　　　　　　　　HR: DOT Golden
Fax: 212 598-4869　　　　　　　　　　　　　　FYE: November 30
Web: www.jefferies.com　　　　　　　　　　　Type: Public

Jefferies Financial Group is a financial services company engaged in investment banking and securities firm. Its largest subsidiary, Jefferies LLC, a US broker-dealer and its first international operating subsidiary, Jefferies International Limited, a UK broker-dealer. The company's industry coverage groups include retail, energy, Institutions, healthcare, industrials, media, real estate, financial sponsors and public finance. Jefferies offers advisory, equity underwriting and debt underwriting, which include both mergers and acquisitions and restructuring and recapitalization expertise. Some of its holdings include Golden Queen, FXCM Group, JETX Energy, LLC and HomeFed. It also has interests in a gold and silver mining company, and a telecommunications business in Italy. About 80% of revenues come from US customers.

	Annual Growth	11/19	11/20	11/21	11/22	11/23
Sales ($mil.)	4.8%	3,893.0	6,010.9	8,185.3	5,978.8	4,700.4
Net income ($ mil.)	(26.8%)	964.7	775.2	1,674.4	785.4	277.7
Market value ($ mil.)	14.1%	4,402.1	4,787.5	7,915.3	8,001.7	7,464.6
Employees	12.0%	4,800	4,945	5,556	5,381	7,564

JEFFERIES GROUP LLC

520 MADISON AVE　　　　　　　　　　　　　　CEO: Richard B Handler
NEW YORK, NY 100224213　　　　　　　　　　　CFO: Matthew Larson
Phone: 212 284-2550　　　　　　　　　　　　　HR: –
Fax: –　　　　　　　　　　　　　　　　　　　FYE: November 30
Web: www.jefferies.com　　　　　　　　　　　Type: Private

Because smaller companies need hostile-takeover advice, too. A full-service investment bank founded in 1962, Jefferies Group (along with its main subsidiary Jefferies & Company) raises capital, performs securities trading and research, and provides advisory services for small and midsized companies in the US. Serving about 2,000 institutional clients worldwide, the company also trades derivatives and commodities and makes markets for some 5,000 US and international equities. With more than $45 billion in assets, Jefferies Group invests on behalf of investors, companies, and national and local governments. In a friendly deal, Jefferies became a subsidiary of its largest shareholder, Leucadia, in 2013.

JEFFERSON COUNTY HMA, LLC

110 HOSPITAL DR
JEFFERSON CITY, TN 377605281
Phone: 865 471-2500
Fax: –
Web: www.tennova.com

CEO: Colin McRae
CFO: –
HR: –
FYE: September 30
Type: Private

Jefferson Memorial Hospital provides acute-care services to residents of eastern Tennessee -- from Knoxville to Morristown. The hospital has approximately 60 beds and offers care in the areas of diagnostics, oncology, obstetrics, orthopedics, and outpatient surgery. The medical center boasts capability for eye surgery, gastroenterology, respiratory therapy, urology, and cardiology. It also operates rehabilitation centers. Jefferson Memorial Hospital is part of Tennova Healthcare (formerly Mercy Health Partners Tennessee), which was acquired by Health Management Associates from former parent Catholic Healthcare Partners in 2011.

	Annual Growth	09/11	09/12	09/13	09/14	09/15
Sales ($mil.)	(5.7%)	–	–	–	44.4	41.9
Net income ($ mil.)	(40.4%)	–	–	–	4.1	2.5
Market value ($ mil.)	–	–	–	–	–	–
Employees	–	–	–	–	–	330

JEFFERSON HEALTH - NORTHEAST

10800 KNIGHTS RD
PHILADELPHIA, PA 191144200
Phone: 215 612-4000
Fax: –
Web: www.jeffersonhealth.org

CEO: Kathleen Kinslow
CFO: –
HR: Elizabeth McGrath
FYE: June 30
Type: Private

Aria Health wants to get you back to singing arias in no time flat. Aria Health provides medical care from two acute care hospitals in Philadelphia (Frankford Campus and Torresdale Campus), as well as the Bucks County Campus in Langhorne, Pennsylvania. Combined the three facilities boast about 480 beds and offer a full range of specialty care, from anesthesiology and pain management to women's care and invasive oncology, as well as cardiac and surgical procedures. Aria Health also operates primary care and specialty outpatient facilities throughout its service area. In 2016, Aria announced plans to rejoin forces with Thomas Jefferson University Hospitals, eight years after the systems separated.

	Annual Growth	06/11	06/12	06/13	06/15	06/19
Sales ($mil.)	1.5%	–	–	460.0	432.0	501.7
Net income ($ mil.)	(29.4%)	–	–	52.0	31.7	6.4
Market value ($ mil.)	–	–	–	–	–	–
Employees	–	–	–	–	–	4,000

JEFFERSON HOMEBUILDERS, INC.

501 N MAIN ST
CULPEPER, VA 227012607
Phone: 540 825-5898
Fax: –
Web: www.culpeperwood.com

CEO: –
CFO: –
HR: –
FYE: September 30
Type: Private

Culpeper Wood Preservers may sound like the name of an environmental non-profit, but this Virginia-based building materials supplier has more commercial interests in mind. Jefferson Homebuilders, which does business as Culpeper Wood Preservers, manufactures and distributes pressure-treated lumber from plants located in the midwestern and northeastern US (pressure treating protects wood from damage by moisture and insects). Products include standard dimensional lumber, plywood, and timbers. The company also makes such specialty products as deck accessories, lattice, fencing, and landscaping items. It has ten plants in Virginia, Indiana, Maryland, North and South Carolina.

	Annual Growth	09/03	09/04	09/05	09/06	09/07
Sales ($mil.)	(10.3%)	–	–	195.5	166.0	157.2
Net income ($ mil.)	(32.1%)	–	–	6.9	5.1	3.2
Market value ($ mil.)	–	–	–	–	–	–
Employees	–	–	–	–	–	177

JEFFERSON HOSPITAL ASSOCIATION, INC.

1600 W 40TH AVE
PINE BLUFF, AR 716036301
Phone: 870 541-7100
Fax: –
Web: www.jrmc.org

CEO: –
CFO: –
HR: Paulette Skillman
FYE: June 30
Type: Private

Jefferson Regional Medical Center (JRMC) provides acute care and other health services to residents of Pine Bluff and an 11-county area of southern Arkansas. The not-for-profit, community-owned hospital has about 470 acute care beds and offers general medical and surgical care, as well as services in a range of specialties, including urology, orthopedics, cardiology, and oncology. It also has a 25-bed skilled nursing unit that cares for patients transitioning to long-term care or home care. A network of clinics offers outpatient surgery, diagnostic imaging, wound care, and other ambulatory health services. Additionally, the health system operates a nursing school and home health and hospice agencies.

	Annual Growth	06/18	06/19	06/20	06/21	06/22
Sales ($mil.)	8.1%	–	187.7	210.6	228.7	236.9
Net income ($ mil.)	–	–	(4.7)	(10.4)	12.0	2.4
Market value ($ mil.)	–	–	–	–	–	–
Employees	–	–	–	–	–	1,700

JEFFERSONVILLE BANCORP

NBB: JFBC

4864 State Route 52, P.O. Box 398
Jeffersonville, NY 12748
Phone: 845 482-4000
Fax: –
Web: www.jeffbank.com

CEO: George W Kinne Jr
CFO: John A Russell
HR: –
FYE: December 31
Type: Public

Jeffersonville Bancorp is the holding company for The First National Bank of Jeffersonville. The bank serves businesses and consumers through about 10 locations in southeastern New York's Sullivan County. First National Bank of Jeffersonville offers such standard retail services as demand deposit, savings, and money market accounts; NOW accounts; CDs; and IRAs to fund a variety of loans. Nearly 40% of the bank's loan portfolio consists of residential mortgages, while commercial mortgages account for another 35%. The bank also provides home equity, business, consumer, construction, and agricultural loans.

	Annual Growth	12/18	12/19	12/20	12/21	12/22
Assets ($mil.)	8.1%	506.7	511.6	616.6	704.9	693.0
Net income ($ mil.)	10.7%	6.2	6.5	4.8	5.9	9.3
Market value ($ mil.)	2.2%	76.9	76.3	72.2	93.2	83.8
Employees	–	–	–	–	–	–

JELD-WEN HOLDING INC

NYS: JELD

2645 Silver Crescent Drive
Charlotte, NC 28273
Phone: 704 378-5700
Fax: –
Web: www.jeld-wen.com

CEO: Kevin C Lilly
CFO: John R Linker
HR: Paula Ordway
FYE: December 31
Type: Public

JELD-WEN is a leading global manufacturer of high-performance interior and exterior building products, offering one of the broadest selections of windows, interior and exterior doors, and wall systems. It designs, produces, and distributes an extensive range of interior and exterior doors, windows, and other building products for use in the new construction and R&R of residential single and multi-family homes and, to a lesser extent, non-residential buildings. The company offers aluminum, vinyl, and wood windows; folding or sliding patio doors; and door frames and moldings. Products are marketed globally under the JELD-WEN brand as well as through regional brands, including DANA and Swedoor (Europe) and Corinthian, Stegbar, and Breezway (Australia). Tracing its roots to 1960, the company operates around 130 manufacturing sites in about 20 countries. The majority of its revenue comes from the US.

	Annual Growth	12/19	12/20	12/21	12/22	12/23
Sales ($mil.)	0.1%	4,289.8	4,235.7	4,771.7	5,129.2	4,304.3
Net income ($ mil.)	(0.2%)	63.0	91.6	168.8	45.7	62.4
Market value ($ mil.)	(5.2%)	1,997.1	2,163.4	2,248.8	823.2	1,610.6
Employees	(6.6%)	23,300	23,000	24,700	23,400	17,700

JELLY BELLY CANDY COMPANY

1 JELLY BELLY LN
FAIRFIELD, CA 945336741
Phone: 707 428-2800
Fax: –
Web: www.jellybelly.com

CEO: Robert M Simpson Jr
CFO: –
HR: –
FYE: June 30
Type: Private

This company has cheesecake, buttered popcorn, orange sherbet, and jalape o on the menu -- who could ask for anything more? You could and can. The Jelly Belly Candy Company makes Jelly Belly jelly beans in 50 "official" flavors, with new and sometimes startlingly flavored (and named) versions introduced periodically, such as Chili Mango. The company's other products include gumballs, gummies, and sour candies in Jelly Belly flavors. Its more than 100 confections also include candy corn, sour candies, jellies, novelty candy, chocolates, chocolate-covered nuts, cinnamon confections, and licorice, along with seasonal offerings. Jelly Belly's candy is sold in more than 70 countries worldwide.

JENNIFER CONVERTIBLES, INC.

1995 BROADHOLLOW RD
FARMINGDALE, NY 117351704
Phone: 516 496-1900
Fax: –
Web: www.jenniferfurniture.com

CEO: –
CFO: Rami Abada
HR: –
FYE: August 29
Type: Private

Houseguests are likely to get a good night's sleep thanks to Jennifer Convertibles. The company owns and operates about 80 namesake stores and some 10 Jennifer Leather stores that sell sofa beds, loveseats, recliners, and chairs. The furniture firm also is among one of the top dealers of Sealy sofa beds in the US. Besides its network of Jennifer-branded stores, the retailer also boasts half a dozen licensed Ashley Furniture HomeStores. Jennifer Convertibles sells name-brand products, as well as the company's private-label: the Bellissimo Collection. In early 2011 Jennifer Convertibles emerged from Chapter 11 bankruptcy protection, under new ownership and a new CEO.

JENZABAR, INC.

101 HUNTINGTON AVE # 2200
BOSTON, MA 021997603
Phone: 617 492-9099
Fax: –
Web: www.jenzabar.com

CEO: Robert Maginn Jr
CFO: Mimi Flanagan
HR: Pat Barnett
FYE: December 31
Type: Private

Raising the bar on higher learning, Jenzabar provides enterprise software for colleges and universities. The company's products and services help simplify the processes and tools that drive enrollment, retention, and advancement -- integrating them into a single Web-based portal. Jenzabar's Total Campus Management framework combines student information and business office systems with Internet portal, alumni, and student services modules to support the student lifecycle. Its e-Racer learning management system offers online learning tools and other software for students and faculty. Jenzabar, which counts more than 1,000 higher education institutions as clients, operates through five US offices and one in Ireland.

	Annual Growth	12/06	12/07	12/08	12/17	12/21
Sales ($mil.)	(7.3%)	–	–	1.0	1.5	0.4
Net income ($ mil.)	–	–	–	–	1.4	(0.6)
Market value ($ mil.)	–	–	–	–	–	–
Employees	–	–	–	–	–	275

JER INVESTORS TRUST INC

1650 Tysons Blvd., Suite 1600
McLean, VA 22102
Phone: 703 714-8000
Fax: 703 714-8100
Web: www.jerinvestorstrust.com

NBB: JERT
CEO: –
CFO: –
HR: –
FYE: December 31
Type: Public

A real estate investment trust (REIT), JER Investors Trust manages a portfolio of real estate structured finance products, primarily commercial mortgage-backed securities (CMBS), commercial mortgage loans, mezzanine loans, and other real estate investments. Founded in 2004, the company is managed by an affiliate of real estate investment management firm J.E. Robert Company (JER). It went public the following year. Due to the downturn in the mortgage industry and the credit industry overall, JER Investors Trust has turned its focus on managing its portfolio credit risk and maintaining liquidity. The REIT has sold some of its real property assets and CMBS investments.

	Annual Growth	12/05	12/06	12/07	12/08	12/09
Assets ($mil.)	(24.8%)	659.2	1,368.0	1,376.2	434.8	210.5
Net income ($ mil.)	–	19.6	31.7	23.1	(254.2)	(76.8)
Market value ($ mil.)	(70.7%)	98.8	120.5	62.8	5.4	0.7
Employees	–	–	–	–	–	–

JERRY BIGGERS CHEVROLET, INC.

1385 E CHICAGO ST
ELGIN, IL 601204715
Phone: 847 742-9000
Fax: –
Web: www.biggerschevy.com

CEO: –
CFO: –
HR: –
FYE: December 31
Type: Private

Jerry Biggers Chevrolet (dba Biggers Chevy Heaven) certainly enjoys its size. The company, which has been in business for more than 40 years, sells Chevy Camaros, Corvettes, Impalas, and Yukons along with Isuzu Rodeos, Ascenders, and Amigos at a dealership in Elgin, Illinois. It also offers a variety of used car models. In addition to cars, Biggers Chevrolet sells aftermarket accessories like DVD players and truck bed liners and offers parts, service, and fleet sales. Its Web site allows customers to apply for financing, search new and used inventory, and schedule service. Help is available in English, Spanish, and Polish. The big dog at Biggers is owner Jim Leichter.

	Annual Growth	12/03	12/04	12/05	12/06	12/08
Sales ($mil.)	(8.0%)	–	80.5	51.5	67.8	57.6
Net income ($ mil.)	–	–	–	(0.3)	0.0	(0.6)
Market value ($ mil.)	–	–	–	–	–	–
Employees	–	–	–	–	–	105

JERSEY CENTRAL POWER & LIGHT CO.

c/o FirstEnergy Corp., 76 South Main Street
Akron, OH 44308
Phone: 800 736-3402
Fax: –
Web: –

CEO: Donald M Lynch
CFO: Marlene A Barwood
HR: –
FYE: December 31
Type: Public

New Jersey native son Bruce Springsteen may be The Boss, but Jersey Central Power & Light (JCP&L) electrifies more fans than he does every day. The company, a subsidiary of multi-utility holding company FirstEnergy, transmits and distributes electricity to 1.1 million homes and businesses in 13 counties in central and northern New Jersey. JCP&L operates 22,670 miles of distribution lines; its 2,550-mile transmission system is overseen by regional transmission organization (RTO) PJM Interconnection. The utility also has some power plant interests.

	Annual Growth	12/08	12/09	12/10	12/11	12/12
Sales ($mil.)	(12.6%)	3,472.3	2,992.7	3,027.1	2,495.0	2,027.0
Net income ($ mil.)	(8.2%)	187.0	170.5	192.1	144.0	133.0
Market value ($ mil.)	–	–	–	–	–	–
Employees	(1.0%)	1,470	1,432	1,434	1,413	1,410

JERSEY CITY MEDICAL CENTER, INC.

355 GRAND ST
JERSEY CITY, NJ 073024321
Phone: 201 915-2000
Fax: –
Web: www.rwjbh.org

CEO: Joe Scott
CFO: –
HR: Christine Gregory
FYE: December 31
Type: Private

With roots extending back to 1882, Jersey City Medical Center (JCMC) may have history, but it's not stuck in the past. The 350-bed, acute-care hospital serves residents of New Jersey's Hudson County area. Operated by Liberty Healthcare, the hospital includes a trauma center, a perinatal center, and a heart institute. JCMC also offers pediatric, women's health, rehabilitation, and ambulatory care, and it is a teaching affiliate for the Mount Sinai School of Medicine. JCMC's modern incarnation came about in the Great Depression when it was constructed by a political ally of Franklin Roosevelt.

	Annual Growth	12/15	12/16	12/17	12/18	12/21
Sales ($mil.)	3.1%	–	354.6	385.1	402.5	413.4
Net income ($ mil.)	–	–	(2.7)	26.3	13.3	(15.6)
Market value ($ mil.)	–	–	–	–	–	–
Employees	–	–	–	–	–	1,942

JESCO, INC.

2020 MCCULLOUGH BLVD
TUPELO, MS 388017108
Phone: 662 842-3240
Fax: –
Web: www.jescoinc.net

CEO: William Yates Jr
CFO: –
HR: Jon Bramlett
FYE: November 27
Type: Private

When the South rises again, JESCO will be there to help with the rebuilding. The company does just about everything for commercial and industrial construction projects. Founded in 1941, JESCO offers turnkey services from design to equipment installation and maintenance. Services include engineering, construction, mechanical and electrical work, millwrighting, and steel fabrication. A unit of The Yates Companies, JESCO operates throughout the Southeast and east coast regions of the US. Customers include Caterpillar, Cooper Tire & Rubber, Kimberly-Clark Corp., Carquest, and UPS. The company has offices in Alabama, Mississippi, and Tennessee, and it is owned by the Yates family.

JETBLUE AIRWAYS CORP

NMS: JBLU

27-01 Queens Plaza North
Long Island City, NY 11101
Phone: 718 286-7900
Fax: –
Web: www.jetblue.com

CEO: –
CFO: –
HR: –
FYE: December 31
Type: Public

JetBlue is New York's hometown airlines and carries customers across the US, Caribbean and Latin America, and between New York and London. Domestic and Canada flights represent its largest market, accounting for about 65% of total company sales. Most of its flights arrive or depart from Boston, New York, Orlando, Fort Lauderdale, Los Angeles, and San Juan, Puerto Rico. The company's differentiated product and culture combined with its competitive cost structure enables the company to compete effectively in high-value geographies and serve customers to over 100 destinations. JetBlue is bringing that same human touch and innovative spirit across the travel industry through the airline and its two subsidiaries ? JetBlue Travel Products and JetBlue Technology Ventures.

	Annual Growth	12/19	12/20	12/21	12/22	12/23
Sales ($mil.)	4.4%	8,094.0	2,957.0	6,037.0	9,158.0	9,615.0
Net income ($ mil.)	–	569.0	(1,354.0)	(182.0)	(362.0)	(310.0)
Market value ($ mil.)	(26.2%)	6,364.8	4,943.6	4,841.6	2,203.2	1,887.0
Employees	2.0%	21,569	20,742	19,466	20,901	23,388

JEWETT-CAMERON TRADING CO. LTD.

NAS: JCTC F

32275 N.W. Hillcrest
North Plains, OR 97133
Phone: 503 647-0110
Fax: 503 647-2272
Web: www.jewettcameron.com

CEO: Chad Summers
CFO: Mitch V Domelen
HR: –
FYE: August 31
Type: Public

Jewett-Cameron Trading Company (JCTC) puts the lumber in lumberyards, the air in pneumatic tools, and greenhouses in the garden. Its JC USA subsidiary supplies wood and other building materials to home improvement chains in the western US from distribution centers in Oregon. The MSI-PRO subsidiary imports pneumatic air tools and industrial clamps from Asia. Jewett-Cameron Seed Company processes and distributes agricultural seed. Other brands are involved in supplying greenhouses, dog kennels, modular garages, and gate and fencing products. JCTC was incorporated in 1953.

	Annual Growth	08/19	08/20	08/21	08/22	08/23
Sales ($mil.)	4.5%	45.4	44.9	57.5	62.9	54.3
Net income ($ mil.)	–	2.1	2.8	3.5	1.2	(0.0)
Market value ($ mil.)	(13.4%)	28.1	26.4	37.1	22.3	15.8
Employees	23.7%	58	63	74	75	136

JFK HEALTH SYSTEM, INC.

80 JAMES ST
EDISON, NJ 088203938
Phone: 732 321-7000
Fax: –
Web: www.jfkhealthsystem.org

CEO: –
CFO: –
HR: –
FYE: December 31
Type: Private

JFK Health System provides medical services in a tri-county area in central New Jersey through flagship facility JFK Medical Center. The hospital has about 500 acute care beds and is one of the Garden State's major health care facilities. Included in the medical center complex are JFK Johnson Rehabilitation Institute, JFK New Jersey Neuroscience Institute, and a number of outpatient care and imaging centers. Other JFK Health System facilities provide primary and specialty services, as well as senior living, home health, and hospice care. In 2017 JFK Health agreed to merge with Hackensack Meridian; the combined system will operate 15 hospitals in New Jersey.

JG WENTWORTH CO (THE)

1200 Morris Drive, Suite 300
Chesterbrook, PA 19087
Phone: 484 434-2300
Fax: –
Web: www.jgw.com

CEO: Randi Sellari
CFO: Dwight Perry
HR: –
FYE: December 31
Type: Public

J.G. Wentworth Co. is for those who just can't wait for the big payoff. The company purchases the rights of claimants in lawsuits, insurance annuities, and lotteries so that instead of receiving a series of settlement payments, the claimants get a smaller lump sum payment up front. J.G. Wentworth Co. operates under the brands J.G. Wentworth and Peachtree Financial Solutions and advertises its structured settlement services heavily on TV, radio, and digital media. (Structured settlements became legal in 1982 with the Periodic Payment Settlement Act.) Founded in 1995, J.G. Wentworth went public in 2013. In late 2017 it filed for Chapter 11 bankruptcy protection.

	Annual Growth	12/13	12/14	12/15	12/16	12/17
Assets ($mil.)	3.1%	4,472.1	5,182.7	5,075.0	4,992.9	5,051.5
Net income ($ mil.)	–	(5.6)	31.2	(95.3)	(46.9)	(191.3)
Market value ($ mil.)	(85.6%)	425.0	260.5	44.0	9.2	0.2
Employees	18.0%	388	410	700	600	751

JIT MANUFACTURING, INC.

19240 144TH AVE NE BLDG 2
WOODINVILLE, WA 980724370
Phone: 425 487-0672
Fax: -
Web: www.jit-mfg.com

CEO: -
CFO: -
HR: -
FYE: March 31
Type: Private

When it is important to get your finished metals parts just in time, JIT Manufacturing can deliver. The company makes precision, high-tolerance sheet-metal parts for a wide range of industries. JIT Manufacturing operates its business in a 18,000 sq. ft. facility which houses precision measuring equipment that is calibrated yearly to the highest industry standards. The company produces everything from simple panels to complex assemblies. Through its relationship with specialty finishing houses in the region, JIT Manufacturing can customize finishes to suit its clients' specific requirements.

	Annual Growth	10/03	10/04	10/05*	03/13	03/21
Sales ($mil.)	6.7%	-	-	2.8	6.1	7.9
Net income ($ mil.)	-	-	-	0.1	0.5	(0.0)
Market value ($ mil.)	-	-	-	-	-	-
Employees	-	-	-	-	-	70

*Fiscal year change

JIVE SOFTWARE, INC.

2028 E BEN WHITE BLVD STE 240
AUSTIN, TX 787416966
Phone: 877 495-3700
Fax: -
Web: www.jivesoftware.com

CEO: Elisa A Steele
CFO: Bryan J Leblanc
HR: -
FYE: December 31
Type: Private

Jive Software is a top-tier Employee Experience Platform, seamlessly integrating people, knowledge, and content in a secure hub across mobile and desktop devices. It is an indispensable tool for millions of users and numerous successful organizations worldwide, who rely on Jive-powered collaboration hubs to achieve their work objectives. Its major customers include Dell, Citi, American Airlines, Verizon, Volkswagen, Pomerleau, and American Express. In 2023, Jive Software operates as a part of IgniteTech, one of the world's leading enterprise software companies and a member of the privately-held ESW Capital group of companies.

JLM COUTURE INC.

525 Seventh Avenue, Suite 1703
New York, NY 10018
Phone: 212 221-8203
Fax: -
Web: www.jlmcouture.com

NBB: JLMC Q
CEO: Daniel M Sullivan
CFO: -
HR: -
FYE: October 31
Type: Public

Here comes the bride, and she might be wearing a gown from JLM Couture. The company designs, manufactures, and markets bridal and bridesmaid gowns, veils, and related items in the US and the UK. Its bridal gowns, which boast price tags of several thousand dollars, are made under the Alvina Valenta, Jim Hjelm Couture, Jim Hjelm Visions, Tara Keely, and Lazaro names. JLM Couture markets its gowns through bridal magazines, trunk shows, and catalogs. The company's bridesmaid and flower girl collections are produced under the Jim Hjelm Occasions and Lazaro Bridesmaids labels; they're peddled through bridal boutiques and bridal departments in clothing stores. Its Party by JLM is a collection of evening wear.

	Annual Growth	10/17	10/18	10/19	10/20	10/21
Sales ($mil.)	(21.0%)	31.8	30.2	24.9	18.3	12.4
Net income ($ mil.)	-	1.2	0.9	(1.0)	(0.8)	(1.7)
Market value ($ mil.)	(9.0%)	5.1	15.1	9.7	3.3	3.5
Employees	-	-	-	-	-	-

JMP GROUP INC.

600 MONTGOMERY ST STE 1100
SAN FRANCISCO, CA 941112702
Phone: 415 835-8900
Fax: -
Web: www.jmpg.com

CEO: Joseph A Jolson
CFO: Raymond S Jackson
HR: -
FYE: December 31
Type: Private

JMP Group wants to get the jump on the competition. Positioning itself as an alternative to bulge-bracket firms, the company provides investment banking services such as strategic advice, corporate finance, and equity underwriting, sales, trading, and research to small and midsized growth companies. It focuses on the technology, health care, financial services, and real estate sectors. Its research department covers more than 300 small- and mid-cap public companies. JMP Group's Heartland Capital Strategies (HCS) subsidiary manages alternative investments such as equity hedge funds, middle-market corporate loans, and private equity for institutional and high-net-worth investors.

	Annual Growth	12/11	12/12	12/13	12/14	12/15
Assets ($mil.)	(28.2%)	-	709.9	1,121.9	-	262.8
Net income ($ mil.)	-	-	8.0	13.6	-	(9.3)
Market value ($ mil.)	-	-	-	-	-	-
Employees	-	-	-	-	-	228

JOANN INC

5555 Darrow Road
Hudson, OH 44236
Phone: 330 656-2600
Fax: -
Web: www.joann.com

NMS: JOAN
CEO: Darrell Webb
CFO: Scott Sekella
HR: -
FYE: January 28
Type: Public

JOANN is the nation's leading fabric and craft specialty retailer. Its store locations and website feature a variety of competitively priced merchandise used in sewing, crafting, and home decorating projects, including fabric, notions, crafts, frames, paper crafting supplies, artificial floral, finished seasonal, and home d cor items. JOANN offers an extensive assortment, which at its seasonal peak, averages more than 80,000 stock-keeping units (SKUs) in stores and over 200,000 SKUs online, across Creative Product categories. The company has approximately 81 million addressable customers in its vast database, approximately 20 million customers in its email database. JOANN Fabric and Craft Stores was founded in 1943 as a single retail store, and at the beginning of 2021 JOANN went public on the Nasdaq market under the trading symbol "JOAN."

	Annual Growth	02/19	02/20*	01/21	01/22	01/23
Sales ($mil.)	(1.2%)	2,324.8	2,241.2	2,762.3	2,417.6	2,216.9
Net income ($ mil.)	-	35.3	(546.6)	212.3	56.7	(200.6)
Market value ($ mil.)	-	-	-	-	412.6	154.1
Employees	-	-	27,700	27,500	22,000	20,000

*Fiscal year change

JOB OPTIONS, INCORPORATED

3465 CAMINO DEL RIO S STE 300
SAN DIEGO, CA 92108
Phone: 619 688-1784
Fax: -
Web: www.joboptionsinc.org

CEO: William Mead
CFO: Char Healy
HR: April Diaz
FYE: September 30
Type: Private

Job Options provides cleaning, stocking, laundry, maintenance, and grounds jobs for people with physical, mental, or psychological disabilities. The company also provides on-the-job training, support, and job search assistance for its employees. Employing more than 800 people, the not-for-profit corporation generates enough revenue from its operations to fund the business without charitable donations or grants. A number of the company's contracts are with Federal agencies that reserve certain contracts for companies that hire primarily disabled people. CEO Bill Mead and Chief Administrative Officer Bill Eastwood founded Job Options in 1987.

	Annual Growth	09/17	09/18	09/19	09/21	09/22
Sales ($mil.)	3.9%	-	53.7	54.1	65.4	62.5
Net income ($ mil.)	(12.5%)	-	0.1	0.6	5.4	0.0
Market value ($ mil.)	-	-	-	-	-	-
Employees	-	-	-	-	-	900

JOE GRANATO, INCORPORATED

46 S ORANGE ST STE D
SALT LAKE CITY, UT 841163185
Phone: 801 359-8651
Fax: –
Web: www.jgpro.com

CEO: –
CFO: –
HR: –
FYE: March 31
Type: Private

Joe Granato is a fresh fruit and vegetable wholesaler. The Salt Lake City company purchases produce from farmers in Arizona and California and distributes it to customers in Utah and neighboring states through a partnership with Pride Transport. It also imports produce from overseas. They partner with such companies as Taylor Farms, Sunkist Growers, Growers Express and Bolthouse Farms. The family-owned and -operated company was founded by its namesake, the late Joe Granato, in 1964.

	Annual Growth	03/13	03/14	03/15	03/16	03/17
Sales ($mil.)	1.8%	–	10.5	10.4	10.6	11.1
Net income ($ mil.)	–	–	0.0	(0.0)	(0.0)	(0.0)
Market value ($ mil.)	–	–	–	–	–	–
Employees	–	–	–	–	–	25

JOHN BEAN TECHNOLOGIES CORP

70 West Madison Street, Suite 4400
Chicago, IL 60602
Phone: 312 861-5900
Fax: –
Web: www.jbtcorporation.com

NYS: JBT
CEO: Brian A Deck
CFO: Matthew J Meister
HR: Susan Carter
FYE: December 31
Type: Public

John Bean Technologies Corporation (JBT) is a leading global technology solution and service provider to high-value segments of the food, beverage, and aviation support industry. JBT manufactures industrial equipment for the food processing and air transportation industries. Its JBT FoodTech segment provides comprehensive solutions throughout the food production value chain. JBT AeroTech markets its solutions and services to domestic and international airport authorities, passenger airlines, airfreight and ground handling companies, military forces and defense contractors. About 65% of JBT's revenue is generated in the US.

	Annual Growth	12/19	12/20	12/21	12/22	12/23
Sales ($mil.)	(3.8%)	1,945.7	1,727.8	1,868.3	2,166.0	1,664.4
Net income ($ mil.)	45.8%	129.0	108.8	118.4	130.7	582.6
Market value ($ mil.)	(3.1%)	3,581.4	3,619.9	4,881.6	2,903.4	3,161.5
Employees	(5.5%)	6,400	6,200	6,600	7,200	5,100

JOHN BROWN UNIVERSITY

2000 W UNIVERSITY ST
SILOAM SPRINGS, AR 727612121
Phone: 479 524-9500
Fax: –
Web: www.jbu.edu

CEO: –
CFO: –
HR: –
FYE: June 30
Type: Private

John Brown University is a non-denominational Christian university with a student body of some 2,300 and a student/faculty ratio of 13:1. Enrollment is comprised of about 1,300 undergrads, some 500 graduate students, and about 500 adult degree completion students. Popular undergraduate majors among the 40 offered include engineering, graphic and web design, family and human services, early childhood education, and business administration; the university also offers nine graduate degree programs such as international business and school counseling. John Brown University was founded in northwest Arkansas in 1919 by evangelist and broadcaster John E. Brown, Sr.

	Annual Growth	06/18	06/19	06/20	06/21	06/22
Sales ($mil.)	21.0%	–	45.3	44.8	45.2	80.4
Net income ($ mil.)	39.4%	–	3.1	1.0	49.8	8.4
Market value ($ mil.)	–	–	–	–	–	–
Employees	–	–	–	–	–	242

JOHN C. LINCOLN HEALTH NETWORK

2500 E DUNLAP AVE
PHOENIX, AZ 85020
Phone: 602 870-6060
Fax: –
Web: –

CEO: –
CFO: –
HR: –
FYE: December 31
Type: Private

John C. Lincoln Health Network takes care of the health of John Q. Public in Arizona. The not-for-profit health care network serves the northern Phoenix area and is home to two hospitals: John C. Lincoln Deer Valley Hospital, with more than 200 beds, and John C. Lincoln North Mountain Hospital, with roughly 260 beds (the Valley's first Magnet nursing hospital, an accredited Chest Pain Center, and the host of a Level 1 Trauma Center). The system also features a children's care facility, various physician and dental clinics, a food bank, and assisted living facilities for the elderly all operating under the Desert Mission moniker. John C. Lincoln Health Network is part of the Scottsdale Lincoln Health Network, along with Scottsdale Healthcare.

	Annual Growth	12/09	12/10	12/11	12/12	12/13
Sales ($mil.)	2.0%	–	551.2	486.8	509.2	584.5
Net income ($ mil.)	31.3%	–	19.5	17.5	32.7	44.1
Market value ($ mil.)	–	–	–	–	–	–
Employees	–	–	–	–	–	3,500

JOHN CARROLL UNIVERSITY

1 JOHN CARROLL BLVD
UNIVERSITY HEIGHTS, OH 441184581
Phone: 216 397-1886
Fax: –
Web: www.jcu.edu

CEO: –
CFO: –
HR: Leslie Beck
FYE: May 31
Type: Private

John Carroll University (JCU) is a Roman Catholic school that offers degree programs in more than 40 fields of the liberal arts, social sciences, natural sciences, business, and interdisciplinary studies at the undergraduate level, and in selected areas at the master's level. Operated by the Society of Jesus -- the Jesuits -- it provides instruction to about 3,600 students (including 2,950 undergraduates). The school is one of 28 Jesuit universities in the US and has been listed in U.S. News & World Report magazine's top 10 rankings of Midwest regional universities for more than 20 consecutive years.

	Annual Growth	05/14	05/15	05/16	05/20	05/22
Sales ($mil.)	9.2%	–	96.1	155.8	162.6	177.8
Net income ($ mil.)	3.6%	–	3.7	(2.8)	(7.6)	4.7
Market value ($ mil.)	–	–	–	–	–	–
Employees	–	–	–	–	–	2,343

JOHN D AND CATHERINE T MACARTHUR FOUNDATION

140 S DEARBORN ST
CHICAGO, IL 606035202
Phone: 312 332-0101
Fax: –
Web: www.macfound.org

CEO: –
CFO: –
HR: –
FYE: December 31
Type: Private

Granted, The John D. and Catherine T. MacArthur Foundation gives away a lot of money. With some $5.3 billion in assets, the private foundation issues more than $250 million in grants annually to groups and individuals working to improve the human condition. Its two primary programs are Human and Community Development (affordable housing, education reform, mental health) and Global Security and Sustainability (world peace, population reduction, conservation, human rights). The foundation also funds special initiatives and awards $500,000 MacArthur Fellowships to a variety of individuals. Since making its first grant in 1978, The John D. and Catherine T. MacArthur Foundation has distributed about $4 billion.

	Annual Growth	12/03	12/04	12/05	12/13	12/21
Sales ($mil.)	0.6%	–	–	705.8	430.1	781.3
Net income ($ mil.)	–	–	–	–	144.1	221.7
Market value ($ mil.)	–	–	–	–	–	–
Employees	–	–	–	–	–	150

JOHN F KENNEDY CENTER FOR THE PERFORMING ARTS

2700 F ST NW
WASHINGTON, DC 205660001
Phone: 202 416-8000
Fax: –
Web: www.kennedy-center.org

CEO: –
CFO: Lynne Pratt
HR: –
FYE: September 30
Type: Private

The John F. Kennedy Center for the Performing Arts, also known as The Kennedy Center, traces its roots to 1958 when president Dwight Eisenhower signed the National Cultural Center Act calling for a privately funded venture featuring a variety of classic and contemporary programming with an educational focus. The center was a pet project and fund raiser beneficiary of president Kennedy; it was named as a living memorial to him after his death. Located on 17 acres overlooking the Potomac River in Washington, D.C., the center opened in 1971 and presents some 2,000 events a year including musicals, dance performances, and jazz and orchestral concerts. It also produces TV programming, workshops, and lectures.

	Annual Growth	09/15	09/16	09/19	09/21	09/22
Sales ($mil.)	0.2%	–	236.2	326.5	131.9	239.7
Net income ($ mil.)	–	–	13.7	71.6	(6.6)	(13.0)
Market value ($ mil.)	–	–	–	–	–	–
Employees	–	–	–	–	–	1,144

JOHN F. KENNEDY UNIVERSITY

11355 N TORREY PINES RD
LA JOLLA, CA 920371013
Phone: 925 969-3300
Fax: –
Web: law.nu.edu

CEO: Charles Powell
CFO: Alexander Kramer
HR: –
FYE: June 30
Type: Private

You're never too old to learn something new -- that's the theory behind John F. Kennedy University. The private school caters to adult students in California. JFK University has an enrollment of approximately 2,000 students who attend classes at four campuses and facilities around the Bay Area. The university has about 800 faculty members (60 core and 740 adjunct) and offers undergraduate, graduate, and professional programs in the fields of education, liberal arts, management, psychology, holistic studies, and law. Classes are mostly offered in the late afternoon and evening. JFK University, named for the 35th president of the United States, was created in 1964 -- one year after his assassination.

	Annual Growth	06/14	06/15	06/17	06/18	06/20
Sales ($mil.)	(6.6%)	–	26.0	27.3	21.3	18.5
Net income ($ mil.)	4.1%	–	0.5	(0.3)	(5.5)	0.6
Market value ($ mil.)	–	–	–	–	–	–
Employees	–	–	–	–	–	487

JOHN HINE PONTIAC

12520 KIRKHAM CT STE 5
POWAY, CA 920646865
Phone: 619 297-4251
Fax: –
Web: www.hellomazdasandiego.com

CEO: –
CFO: –
HR: –
FYE: December 31
Type: Private

John Hine Mazda (formerly John Hine Pontiac) sells new and used Mazda brand vehicles to customers in the San Diego area. The dealership also offers parts, service, and collision repair through its John Hine Auto Body Center. Visitors to its Web site can check new and used inventory, get a quote on a vehicle, schedule service, order parts, and apply for financing. The company is a founding member of the California Sales Training Academy, a private training program that has become an associates degree program at a local community college. The company was established in 1957. Prior to the discontinuation of the Pontiac brand, the dealership sold Dodge and Pontiac vehicles in addition to Mazdas.

	Annual Growth	12/05	12/06	12/07	12/08	12/09
Sales ($mil.)	(11.6%)	–	69.0	–	58.7	47.7
Net income ($ mil.)	–	–	(0.2)	–	(0.4)	(0.1)
Market value ($ mil.)	–	–	–	–	–	–
Employees	–	–	–	–	–	201

JOHN MUIR HEALTH

1601 YGNACIO VALLEY RD
WALNUT CREEK, CA 945983122
Phone: 925 947-4449
Fax: –
Web: www.johnmuirhealth.com

CEO: Calvin Knight
CFO: –
HR: –
FYE: December 31
Type: Private

John Muir Health is a not-for-profit health care organization east of San Francisco serving patients in Contra Costa, eastern Alameda and southern Solano Counties. It includes a network of more than 1,000 primary care and specialty physicians, 6,500 employees, medical centers in Concord and Walnut Creek, including Contra Costa County's only trauma center, and a Behavioral Health Center. John Muir Health also has partnerships with UCSF Health, Tenet Healthcare/San Ramon Regional Medical Center, Stanford Children's Health, Optum and Carbon Health. The health system offers a full-range of medical services, including primary care, outpatient and imaging services, and is widely recognized as a leader in many specialties ? neurosciences, orthopedic, cancer, cardiovascular, trauma, emergency, pediatrics and high-risk obstetrics care.

	Annual Growth	12/16	12/17	12/20	12/21	12/22
Sales ($mil.)	1.1%	–	1,831.6	2,106.0	2,340.4	1,934.9
Net income ($ mil.)	–	–	92.3	178.2	239.4	(334.8)
Market value ($ mil.)	–	–	–	–	–	–
Employees	–	–	–	–	–	2,200

JOHN T. MATHER MEMORIAL HOSPITAL OF PORT JEFFERSON, NEW YORK, INC.

75 N COUNTRY RD
PORT JEFFERSON, NY 117772119
Phone: 631 476-2738
Fax: –
Web: www.matherhospital.org

CEO: –
CFO: –
HR: –
FYE: December 31
Type: Private

Shipbuilder John T. Mather envisioned a legacy that would keep his community of Port Jefferson in good health, and John T. Mather Memorial Hospital came to fruition in 1929, one year after it's namesake's death. The not-for-profit hospital has some 250 beds and provides a variety of health care services to the residents of Port Jefferson, New York, and surrounding areas of Suffolk County. Services include emergency care, occupational therapy, psychiatry, and radiology. Mather Hospital is a member of Long Island Health Network, an association of about a dozen affiliated hospitals all serving Long Island. It is also Magnet recognized hospital by the American Nurses Credentialing Center.

	Annual Growth	12/16	12/17	12/18	12/21	12/22
Sales ($mil.)	5.8%	–	320.1	315.7	379.5	424.6
Net income ($ mil.)	114.9%	–	0.4	5.5	18.0	18.5
Market value ($ mil.)	–	–	–	–	–	–
Employees	–	–	–	–	–	2,568

JOHNS HOPKINS ALL CHILDREN'S HOSPITAL, INC.

501 6TH AVE S
SAINT PETERSBURG, FL 337014634
Phone: 727 898-7451
Fax: –
Web: www.hopkinsmedicine.org

CEO: Jonathan Ellen
CFO: Sherron Rogers
HR: –
FYE: June 30
Type: Private

Johns Hopkins All Children's Hospital has about 260 beds, all dedicated to the health of west-central Florida's children. With about 645 pediatric physician specialists on board, the hospital offers its young patients (infants, children, and teens) a variety of services including a Neonatal Intensive Care Unit for premature and "at-risk" infants. Its heart, bone marrow, and kidney transplant programs are nationally renowned. The teaching hospital is also affiliated with the University of South Florida College of Medicine. All Children's Hospital is a member of the Johns Hopkins Medicine network.

	Annual Growth	06/13	06/14	06/15	06/16	06/21
Sales ($mil.)	4.8%	–	–	408.1	400.7	540.7
Net income ($ mil.)	–	–	–	(1.5)	21.7	144.9
Market value ($ mil.)	–	–	–	–	–	–
Employees	–	–	–	–	–	2,325

JOHNS HOPKINS BAYVIEW MEDICAL CENTER, INC.

4940 EASTERN AVE
BALTIMORE, MD 212242735
Phone: 410 550-0100
Fax: –
Web: www.hopkinsmedicine.org

CEO: –
CFO: –
HR: –
FYE: June 30
Type: Private

If you've just been pulled from the bay like an old empty crab trap, Johns Hopkins Bayview might be the first place you're taken. One of five member institutions in the Johns Hopkins Health System, Johns Hopkins Bayview Medical Center is a community teaching hospital. Its Baltimore-based operations include a neonatal intensive care unit, as well as centers devoted to trauma, geriatrics, sleep disorders, and weight management. It also features the state's only regional burn center. The facility includes a meditation labyrinth for patients, families, and staff to walk. Established in 1773, the medical center has more than 560 beds.

	Annual Growth	06/18	06/19	06/20	06/21	06/22
Sales ($mil.)	4.9%	–	648.1	669.1	716.9	749.1
Net income ($ mil.)	–	–	(39.1)	(41.0)	91.2	19.0
Market value ($ mil.)	–	–	–	–	–	–
Employees	–	–	–	–	–	3,300

JOHNSON & JENNINGS INC

3870 MURPHY CANYON RD STE 110
SAN DIEGO, CA 921234421
Phone: 858 623-1100
Fax: –
Web: www.johnsonandjennings.com

CEO: Donna J Vargo
CFO: Naomi Lohnes
HR: –
FYE: April 30
Type: Private

Johnson & Jennings General Contracting provides construction services in the San Diego area. Projects range from corporate office, health care, and retail construction to commercial and industrial facility tenant improvements. Services include project evaluation and consulting, estimating, and construction management. CEO Tom Johnson and president Jackie Jennings co-own the company they founded in 1981.

	Annual Growth	04/05	04/06	04/07	04/09	04/10
Sales ($mil.)	(10.2%)	–	–	46.2	27.6	33.4
Net income ($ mil.)	79.5%	–	–	0.0	0.0	0.2
Market value ($ mil.)	–	–	–	–	–	–
Employees	–	–	–	–	–	42

JOHNSON & JOHNSON

One Johnson & Johnson Plaza
New Brunswick, NJ 08933
Phone: 732 524-0400
Fax: 732 214-0332
Web: www.jnj.com

NYS: JNJ
CEO: Joaquin Duato
CFO: Joseph J Wolk
HR: –
FYE: December 31
Type: Public

Johnson & Johnson (J&J) is engaged in the research and development, manufacture and sale of a broad range of products in the healthcare field. The company is organized into three business segments: Pharmaceutical, Consumer Health, and MedTech. Its Pharmaceuticals segment is focused on manufacturing medicines for immunology, infectious diseases, neuroscience, cardiovascular, metabolism, pulmonary hypertension, and oncology ailments. Its MedTech segment includes a broad portfolio of products used in the Orthopaedic, Surgery, Interventional Solutions (cardiovascular and neurovascular), and Vision fields. Its Consumer segment makes over-the-counter (OTC) drugs and products for baby, skin, oral, women's, and first-aid care. The company operates worldwide but makes about half of its revenue in the US.

	Annual Growth	12/19*	01/21	01/22	01/23*	12/23
Sales ($mil.)	0.9%	82,059	82,584	93,775	94,943	85,159
Net income ($ mil.)	23.5%	15,119	14,714	20,878	17,941	35,153
Market value ($ mil.)	1.8%	350,832	378,826	411,779	425,210	377,285
Employees	(0.2%)	133,200	136,400	144,300	152,700	131,900

*Fiscal year change

JOHNSON & WALES UNIVERSITY INC

8 ABBOTT PARK PL
PROVIDENCE, RI 029033775
Phone: 401 598-1000
Fax: –
Web: www.jwu.edu

CEO: –
CFO: Joseph J Greene Jr
HR: –
FYE: June 30
Type: Private

Johnson & Wales University (JWU) is a private, not-for-profit, accredited institution that offers an upside-down curriculum, allowing students to take courses in their major during the first year, so they learn right away if their career choice is right for them. The university offers undergraduate and graduate degree programs in arts and sciences, business, engineering, food innovation, hospitality, nutrition, health, and wellness. It also offers undergraduate programs in culinary arts, dietetics, and design. Student-faculty ratio is 15:1. Founded in 1914, the school enrolls more than 8,180 graduate, undergraduate, and online students at its campuses in Providence, Rhode Island, and Charlotte, North Carolina.

	Annual Growth	06/18	06/19	06/20	06/21	06/22
Sales ($mil.)	6.7%	–	301.5	289.3	220.3	366.4
Net income ($ mil.)	–	–	(11.2)	(31.3)	16.0	20.3
Market value ($ mil.)	–	–	–	–	–	–
Employees	–	–	–	–	–	1,400

JOHNSON C. SMITH UNIVERSITY, INCORPORATED

100 BEATTIES FORD RD
CHARLOTTE, NC 282165302
Phone: 704 378-1000
Fax: –
Web: www.jcsu.edu

CEO: –
CFO: Teare Brewington
HR: –
FYE: June 30
Type: Private

Founded as Biddle Memorial Institute, Johnson C. Smith University is a private liberal arts school that enrolls about 1,400 students and boasts a student/faculty ratio of 11:1. The historically African-American university confers bachelor's degrees to hundreds of students each year in 22 different majors, including business administration, computer engineering, music, political science, and sport management. It was established in 1867 under the auspices of the Committee on Freedmen of the Presbyterian Church, U.S.A. The university took its original name from the late Major Henry Biddle, whose wife (Mary) was a generous fundraiser and donor; in 1923 Jane Smith endowed the school in memory of her late husband, Johnson C. Smith.

	Annual Growth	06/15	06/16	06/20	06/21	06/22
Sales ($mil.)	15.6%	–	46.5	52.0	73.3	110.8
Net income ($ mil.)	–	–	(9.7)	(1.0)	20.4	56.4
Market value ($ mil.)	–	–	–	–	–	–
Employees	–	–	–	–	–	280

JOHNSON CITY ENERGY AUTHORITY

2600 BOONES CREEK RD
JOHNSON CITY, TN 376154441
Phone: 423 952-5000
Fax: –
Web: www.brightridge.com

CEO: –
CFO: Brian Bolling
HR: Connie Crouch
FYE: June 30
Type: Private

Board members have real power (to dispense) on the Johnson City Power Board. Based in Johnson City, Tennessee, the Johnson City Power Board provides electricity and related programs, services, and products to approximately 68,000 residential and business customers in Washington County, as well as parts of Carter, Greene, and Sullivan Counties. The company is one of 158 power companies throughout, Alabama, Georgia, Kentucky, and Tennessee which purchase electricity from the Tennessee Valley Authority. Johnson City Power Board teams with cities, towns, governments, economic development, and Chambers of Commerce to promote business and industry in its service area.

	Annual Growth	06/17	06/18	06/19	06/21	06/22
Sales ($mil.)	2.0%	–	201.5	204.2	199.1	218.5
Net income ($ mil.)	5.6%	–	13.0	11.5	12.9	16.1
Market value ($ mil.)	–	–	–	–	–	–
Employees	–	–	–	–	–	174

JOHNSON CONTRACTORS, INC.

3635 2ND ST
MUSCLE SHOALS, AL 356611275
Phone: 256 383-0313
Fax: –
Web: www.johnsoncont.com

CEO: Clyde H Roberts
CFO: –
HR: –
FYE: December 31
Type: Private

Not only does Muscle Shoals, Alabama have the Swampers ("known to pick a song or two"), but it has the Johnson Contractors as well. Founded in 1918, Johnson Contractors is a general construction company that specializes in industrial plants, office buildings, apartments, commercial projects, schools, medical facilities, and water and sewage treatment plants. Its capabilities include heavy equipment installation, structural steel erection, concrete pouring, carpentry, excavation, and maintenance. The company is active throughout the Southeast. Johnson Contractors is a part of the Johnson family of companies, which also includes J. K. Johnson Mechanical Contractors and Johnson Electric Company.

	Annual Growth	04/06	04/07	04/08*	12/19	12/22
Sales ($mil.)	8.5%	–	–	31.6	66.6	99.6
Net income ($ mil.)	6.1%	–	–	0.7	1.3	1.7
Market value ($ mil.)	–	–	–	–	–	–
Employees	–	–	–	–	–	300

*Fiscal year change

JOHNSON CONTROLS FIRE PROTECTION LP

6600 CONGRESS AVE
BOCA RATON, FL 334871213
Phone: 561 988-7200
Fax: –
Web: –

CEO: –
CFO: –
HR: –
FYE: September 30
Type: Private

SimplexGrinnell handles emergencies well. The company provides integrated security alarm, fire suppression, healthcare communications, and emergency lighting systems. SimplexGrinnell reaches some 1 million customers in the US and Canada through more than 150 district offices located in the Americas, Europe, Asia, and other regions. In addition to providing security and fire related products, SimplexGrinnell operates a service division devoted to test and inspection, preventive maintenance, central station monitoring, and emergency services. The company's clients include members of local, state, and federal government agencies, corporations, oil and gas companies, hospitals, and educational facilities.

	Annual Growth	09/06	09/07	09/08	09/09	09/16
Sales ($mil.)	1.0%	–	–	–	1,750.5	1,871.4
Net income ($ mil.)	–	–	–	–	–	182.5
Market value ($ mil.)	–	–	–	–	–	–
Employees	–	–	–	–	–	9,500

JOHNSON CONTROLS, INC.

5757 N GREEN BAY AVE
MILWAUKEE, WI 532094408
Phone: 920 245-6409
Fax: –
Web: www.johnsoncontrols.com

CEO: George Oliver
CFO: Marc Vandiepenbeeck
HR: –
FYE: September 30
Type: Private

Climate control for offices, Johnson Controls manufactures, installs, and services energy-efficient heating, ventilation, and air conditioning (HVAC) systems. Its products cover everything needed to make a place of work comfortable and safe to be in, extending to fire detection and suppression and security measures such as electronic card site access. Originally an American company, Johnson Controls completed a reverse merger with Cork-based Tyco International and is now domiciled in Ireland (although the US remains its largest market by far). The company sold its car battery manufacturing operations in 2018 to Brookfield Business Partners.

	Annual Growth	09/11	09/12	09/13	09/14	09/15
Sales ($mil.)	(6.7%)	–	–	42,730	42,828	37,179
Net income ($ mil.)	13.8%	–	–	1,297.0	1,335.0	1,679.0
Market value ($ mil.)	–	–	–	–	–	–
Employees	–	–	–	–	–	126,377

JOHNSON OUTDOORS INC

555 Main Street
Racine, WI 53403
Phone: 262 631-6600
Fax: –
Web: www.johnsonoutdoors.com

NMS: JOUT
CEO: Helen P Johnson-Leipold
CFO: David W Johnson
HR: –
FYE: September 29
Type: Public

Founded in 1987, Johnson Outdoors keeps sports buffs from staying indoors. The company makes, markets, and sells camping and outdoor equipment (such as Jetboil cooking systems and Eureka! tents and backpacks). It also focuses on supplying equipment for water activities with its diving gear (Scubapro masks, fins, snorkels, and tanks), trolling motors (Minn Kota), fish finders (Humminbird), and watercraft (Old Town canoes). With GPS technologies and electric boat motors, The Johnson family, including CEO Helen Johnson-Leipold, controls the company. Most of the company's sales come from the US.

	Annual Growth	09/19*	10/20	10/21*	09/22	09/23
Sales ($mil.)	4.2%	562.4	594.2	751.7	743.4	663.8
Net income ($ mil.)	(21.5%)	51.4	55.2	83.4	44.5	19.5
Market value ($ mil.)	(1.7%)	601.0	883.4	1,124.2	526.0	560.6
Employees	3.9%	1,200	1,200	1,400	1,500	1,400

*Fiscal year change

JOHNSON SUPPLY AND EQUIPMENT CORPORATION

10151 STELLA LINK RD
HOUSTON, TX 770255398
Phone: 713 830-2300
Fax: –
Web: webstore.johnsonsupply.com

CEO: Carl I Johnson
CFO: Donald K Wile
HR: –
FYE: March 31
Type: Private

Global warming? Bring it on! Keeping Texas and Louisiana residents cool is no easy task, but Johnson Supply does what it can. Through about two dozen locations in hot spots like Houston and Lake Charles, Louisiana, Johnson Supply distributes air-conditioning and refrigeration equipment, controls, parts, and supplies from more than 200 manufacturers. Since those places also get cold, relatively speaking, the company sells heating and ventilation equipment as well. Its 200 suppliers include names like York, Friedrich, Warren, Mueller, and Johnson Controls. The company was founded in 1953 by Carl I. Johnson, Sr.

	Annual Growth	03/02	03/03	03/04	03/05	03/08
Sales ($mil.)	1.2%	–	97.9	105.8	110.3	103.9
Net income ($ mil.)	137.8%	–	0.3	22.4	80.0	24.9
Market value ($ mil.)	–	–	–	–	–	–
Employees	–	–	–	–	–	210

JOHNSONVILLE, LLC

N6928 JOHNSONVILLE WAY
SHEBOYGAN FALLS, WI 530851279
Phone: 920 453-6900
Fax: –
Web: www.johnsonville.com

CEO: Nick Meriggioli
CFO: –
HR: Leah Glaub
FYE: December 31
Type: Private

Johnsonville is the number one brand of sausage in America. It makes a variety of top-selling fresh, frozen, pre-cooked, and smoked sausage products. The company's portfolio includes summer sausage, naturals, chicken and turkey sausage, fresh breakfast sausage, and sausage strips. Other products are snack sausages and ground sausages. The company's link and bulk sausage meats are sold primarily through grocery stores and foodservice operators. Johnsonville sells and serves more than 70 different varieties of sausage across over 45 countries and in more than 75 US professional, semi-pro, and college sports stadiums. The privately-owned company was founded by Ralph F. and Alice Stayer in 1945.

JOHNSTON ENTERPRISES, INC.

411 W CHESTNUT AVE
ENID, OK 737012057
Phone: 580 249-4449
Fax: –
Web: –

CEO: Lew Meibergen
CFO: Gary Tucker
HR: –
FYE: April 30
Type: Private

Johnston Enterprises serves the harvesters of America's amber waves of grain. The company offers farmers in Oklahoma and other Midwestern states grain-processing and storage facilities and inland water transportation services through its Johnston Grain and Johnston Port Terminals divisions. Its Johnston Seed subsidiary sells wildflower and turf, wild, forage, and native grass seed, and wildlife feed. The company was founded in 1893 by W. B. Johnston and is owned and operated by the founder's descendants, president Lew Meibergen and COO Butch Meibergen.

	Annual Growth	04/08	04/09	04/10	04/11	04/12
Sales ($mil.)	45.7%	–	–	140.2	289.9	297.8
Net income ($ mil.)	147.4%	–	–	0.3	1.4	1.6
Market value ($ mil.)	–	–	–	–	–	–
Employees	–	–	–	–	–	335

JOINT COMMISSION ON ACCREDITATION OF HEALTHCARE ORGANIZATIONS

1 RENAISSANCE BLVD
OAKBROOK TERRACE, IL 601814294
Phone: 630 792-5000
Fax: –
Web: www.jointcommission.org

CEO: –
CFO: –
HR: Karen Fuchgruber
FYE: December 31
Type: Private

With an eye on improving performance and patient care, the Joint Commission on Accreditation of Health Care Organizations is a nonprofit that provides accreditation and certification services. The group evaluates and accredits more than 20,500 health care providers in the US. Its board of commissioners includes doctors, nurses, consumers, and administrators. They evaluate hospitals, health care networks, nursing homes and other long-term care facilities, laboratories, and health-related groups. The Joint Commission's Quality Check website includes each accredited organization's quality review. The group, also known simply as The Joint Commission, was founded in 1951.

	Annual Growth	12/01	12/02	12/19	12/21	12/22
Sales ($mil.)	3.0%	–	115.4	193.0	194.3	208.9
Net income ($ mil.)	1.7%	–	12.5	14.2	22.3	17.5
Market value ($ mil.)	–	–	–	–	–	–
Employees	–	–	–	–	–	936

JONATHAN SPROUTS, INC.

384 VAUGHAN HILL RD
ROCHESTER, MA 027702035
Phone: 508 763-2577
Fax: –
Web: singapore.tie.org

CEO: –
CFO: –
HR: –
FYE: March 31
Type: Private

Jonathan Sprouts is a fresh organic fruits and vegetables supplier that operates as Jonathan's Organic. It was founded in 1976 as an alfalfa-sprout grower. Today it sources organic produce from farmers in the US, as well as from Canada, Europe, Israel, Mexico, South Africa, and South America. Jonathan Sprouts was certified in 2002 as a "fair trade" company, paying higher prices to Third World suppliers of organic bananas and grapes. The company partners with Organic Farm Foods of the UK, which owns 51% of Jonathan Sprouts; the remainder is owned by company officers.

	Annual Growth	03/15	03/16	03/17	03/18	03/19
Sales ($mil.)	2.5%	–	4.0	4.5	4.4	4.3
Net income ($ mil.)	–	–	0.0	0.2	(0.0)	(0.1)
Market value ($ mil.)	–	–	–	–	–	–
Employees	–	–	–	–	–	25

JONES FINANCIAL COMPANIES LLLP

12555 Manchester Road
Des Peres, MO 63131
Phone: 314 515-2000
Fax: –
Web: www.edwardjones.com

CEO: –
CFO: –
HR: –
FYE: December 31
Type: Public

The Jones Financial Companies is the parent of Edward Jones, an investment brokerage network catering to individual investors. Serving some 7 million clients, the partnership has more than 15,000 offices in all 50 states and Canada. Financial advisors and BOAs provide tailored solutions and services to clients while leveraging the resources of the Partnership's home office. The Jones Financial Companies derives more than 95% of its revenue from its US operations. The business was founded as Edward D. Jones & Co. in 1922.

	Annual Growth	12/18	12/19	12/20	12/21	12/22
Sales ($mil.)	9.7%	8,469.0	9,369.0	10,063	12,279	12,269
Net income ($ mil.)	9.1%	990.0	1,092.0	1,285.0	1,605.0	1,404.0
Market value ($ mil.)	–	–	–	–	–	–
Employees	2.1%	47,000	49,000	50,000	50,000	51,000

JONES LANG LASALLE INC

NYS: JLL

200 East Randolph Drive
Chicago, IL 60601
Phone: 312 782-5800
Fax: 312 782-4339
Web: www.jll.com

CEO: –
CFO: –
HR: –
FYE: December 31
Type: Public

Jones Lang LaSalle (JLL) is a leading professional services firm specializing in real estate and investment management. It provides comprehensive, integrated real estate and investment management expertise on a local, regional and global level to owner, occupier and investor clients. The company's LaSalle Investment Management arm is a diversified real estate management firm with about $79.1 billion in assets under management. JLL has commercial real estate expertise across office, retail, healthcare, industrial, and multifamily residential properties. It manages approximately 4.6 billion sq. ft. worldwide. Operating in over 80 countries, the company generates some 60% of its total revenue from the US. JLL was formed through the 1999 merger of Jones Lang Wootton (founded in England in 1783) and LaSalle Partners (founded in the US in 1968).

	Annual Growth	12/19	12/20	12/21	12/22	12/23
Sales ($mil.)	3.7%	17,983	16,590	19,367	20,862	20,761
Net income ($ mil.)	(19.4%)	535.3	402.5	961.6	654.5	225.4
Market value ($ mil.)	2.1%	8,271.0	7,049.0	12,796	7,571.6	8,973.2
Employees	3.2%	93,400	90,800	98,200	103,300	106,000

JONES SODA CO.

NBB: JSDA

4786 1st Avenue South, Suite 103
Seattle, WA 98134
Phone: 206 624-3357
Fax: 206 624-6857
Web: www.jonessoda.com

CEO: Mark Murray
CFO: Joe Culp
HR: –
FYE: December 31
Type: Public

Keeping up with the Joneses at Jones Soda requires an adventurous palate. The beverage company makes, markets and sells brightly colored sodas with wacky names and flavors like Fufu Berry and Blue Bubblegum. Seasonal offerings include Turkey and Gravy for Thanksgiving and Chocolate Fudge for Valentine's Day. To keep things interesting, it regularly discontinues flavors and introduces new ones; labels also can be customized with photos submitted by customers. Jones Soda also sells Jones Zilch (zero calories) and the WhoopAss Energy Drink, an energy beverage that's available with or without sugar. Jones Soda's beverages are distributed throughout North America, as well as in Australia, the UK, and Ireland.

	Annual Growth	12/18	12/19	12/20	12/21	12/22
Sales ($mil.)	11.0%	12.6	11.5	11.9	14.8	19.1
Net income ($ mil.)	–	(2.1)	(2.8)	(3.0)	(1.8)	(6.4)
Market value ($ mil.)	3.0%	23.6	29.1	23.2	73.2	26.6
Employees	4.8%	24	29	21	23	29

JORDAN CF INVESTMENTS LLP

7700 CF JORDAN DR
EL PASO, TX 799128808
Phone: 915 877-3333
Fax: –
Web: www.jordanfosterconstruction.com

CEO: –
CFO: –
HR: –
FYE: December 31
Type: Private

A high-flier in construction services, C.F. Jordan is a top building contractor that offers preconstruction, design/build, development, and project management services. The company has traditionally built hotels and resorts, but has diversified into military, residential, highway, and school construction. Its contracts include projects for the Immigration and Naturalization Service for border patrol stations, health care centers, and detention centers. Other works have included Sea World in San Antonio, the Insights Science Museum in El Paso, and the Pearl Harbor Commissary and Exchange in Hawaii. Chairman Charles "Paco" Jordan started the Texas-based firm in 1988.

	Annual Growth	12/03	12/04	12/05	12/08	12/09
Sales ($mil.)	6.8%	–	–	260.0	337.9	337.9
Net income ($ mil.)	11.3%	–	–	2.5	3.9	3.9
Market value ($ mil.)	–	–	–	–	–	–
Employees	–	–	–	–	–	500

JOSEPH DROWN FOUNDATION

1999 AVE OF THE STS 233 STE 2330
LOS ANGELES, CA 90067
Phone: 310 277-4488
Fax: –
Web: www.jdrown.org

CEO: –
CFO: –
HR: –
FYE: March 31
Type: Private

The Joseph Drown Foundation helps Southern California non-profits and schools keep their heads above water. The foundation awards grants in community, health, and social services; education; medical and scientific research; and arts and the humanities with the aim of helping people become "successful, self-sustaining, contributing citizens". It has provided funding for such organizations as The Accelerated School (a charter school), Families in Schools, and HighTechHigh. Although most grants go to Southern California-based institutions, the foundation occasionally gives to non-SoCal causes, too. Joseph Warford Drown, the developer of the Hotel Bel-Air in Los Angeles, established the foundation in 1953.

	Annual Growth	03/08	03/09	03/10	03/11	03/17
Assets ($mil.)	4.8%	–	57.7	77.9	81.9	84.3
Net income ($ mil.)	–	–	–	(0.1)	(0.0)	(3.7)
Market value ($ mil.)	–	–	–	–	–	–
Employees	–	–	–	–	–	3

JOYCE LESLIE INC

20 COMMERCE DR STE 301
CRANFORD, NJ 070163618
Phone: 201 804-7800
Fax: –
Web: www.rainbowshops.com

CEO: Celia Clancy
CFO: Peter Left
HR: –
FYE: January 30
Type: Private

Club-hoppers (and high schoolers) hoping to look like Paris Hilton without spending like her do their shopping at Joyce Leslie. The northeastern retail chain specializes in trendy and inexpensive women's and junior's clothing aimed primarily at teens and tweens. It operates about 50 shops filled with high-fashion knockoffs in Connecticut, New Jersey, New York, and Pennsylvania. Joyce Leslie, named after the daughter of the company's founder Julius Gewirtz, was established in Brooklyn in 1945 and originally sold women's dresses. In February 2016, after struggling to find a business strategic partner to save the business, the company announced it would be closing its stores for good.

	Annual Growth	01/06	01/07	01/08	01/09	01/10
Sales ($mil.)	3.1%	–	–	95.0	100.9	101.0
Net income ($ mil.)	2.4%	–	–	1.2	1.2	1.3
Market value ($ mil.)	–	–	–	–	–	–
Employees	–	–	–	–	–	900

JPMORGAN CHASE & CO

383 Madison Avenue
New York, NY 10179
Phone: 212 270-6000
Fax: –
Web: www.jpmorganchase.com

NYS: JPM
CEO: James Dimon
CFO: Jeremy Barnum
HR: –
FYE: December 31
Type: Public

Boasting some $3.7 trillion in assets, JPMorgan Chase is the largest bank holding company in the US and a leader in investment banking, financial services for consumers and small businesses, commercial banking, financial transaction processing, and asset management. The company operates through approximately 4,790 branches in about 50 states and Washington DC. Its principal bank subsidiary is JPMorgan Chase Bank, National Association, a national banking association; while its principal non-bank subsidiary is J.P. Morgan Securities LLC, a US broker-dealer. Both of its subsidiaries operate nationally and overseas through branches, representative office, and subsidiary foreign banks. The North America accounts for about 75% of the company's total revenue.

	Annual Growth	12/19	12/20	12/21	12/22	12/23
Assets ($mil.)	9.6%	2,687,379	3,386,071	3,743,567	3,665,743	3,875,393
Net income ($ mil.)	8.0%	36,431	29,131	48,334	37,676	49,552
Market value ($ mil.)	5.1%	401,006	365,537	455,519	385,760	489,320
Employees	4.8%	256,981	255,351	271,025	293,723	309,926

JSD MANAGEMENT, INC.

1283 COLLEGE PARK DR
DOVER, DE 199048713
Phone: 302 735-4628
Fax: –
Web: www.jsdinc.net

CEO: –
CFO: –
HR: –
FYE: December 31
Type: Private

James, Stevens & Daniels is not just another Tom, Dick, or Harry. Also known as JSD for short, the privately owned collection agency performs commercial collections and accounts receivable portfolio management for businesses in the US and abroad. It customizes its efforts on a case-by-case basis and offers clients the ability to monitor collection activity via a secure online network. The company also provides related services such as skip tracing, legal referrals, and financial investigation reports. clients the ability to monitor collection activity via a secure online network. JSD was founded in 1997 by president Kelly Hedrick.

	Annual Growth	12/14	12/15	12/16	12/17	12/18
Sales ($mil.)	0.3%	–	2.3	2.2	2.8	2.4
Net income ($ mil.)	12.5%	–	0.0	0.0	0.4	0.1
Market value ($ mil.)	–	–	–	–	–	–
Employees	–	–	–	–	–	48

JSJ CORPORATION

700 ROBBINS RD
GRAND HAVEN, MI 494172603
Phone: 616 842-6350
Fax: –
Web: www.jsjcorp.com

CEO: Nelson Jacobson
CFO: Martin Jennings
HR: –
FYE: December 31
Type: Private

JSJ Corporation is the brain behind a number of brands. The company designs, develops, and markets durable goods through a variety of global businesses. Its izzy+ design operating company makes office furniture, seating, and countertops. The GHSP unit offers automotive gearshift and pedal assemblies. Other operating companies manufacture and distribute industrial equipment, conveyor belts, and fluid control products. Clients have included Herman Miller, Honda, and Proctor & Gamble. The company has nearly 30 locations in China, Japan, Mexico, and the US. JSJ was founded in 1919 by the Jacobson, Johnson, and Sherwood families; second and third generations of the founders continue to run the firm.

JUDLAU CONTRACTING, INC.

2615 ULMER ST
FLUSHING, NY 113541144
Phone: 718 554-2309
Fax: –
Web: www.ohla-usa.com

CEO: Ashok Patel
CFO: –
HR: Adam Ingber
FYE: December 31
Type: Private

Judlau Contracting takes on hefty jobs that help keep New York City hustling and bustling. One of eight firms under The Judlau Companies group banner, Judlau Contracting specializes in heavy construction and large public works projects primarily around the New York metropolitan area and northeastern US. It builds bridges, mass transit tunnels, roads, underground utility stations, and wastewater treatment plants. The general contractor also has expertise in electrical work and environmental remediation. Major clients have included Consolidated Edison, New York State Department of Transportation, and Verizon. Spanish construction group OHL acquired a majority of Judlau in late 2010.

	Annual Growth	12/09	12/10	12/11	12/12	12/14
Sales ($mil.)	52.6%	–	–	–	134.6	313.4
Net income ($ mil.)	77.1%	–	–	–	4.2	13.2
Market value ($ mil.)	–	–	–	–	–	–
Employees	–	–	–	–	–	140

JUNIATA COLLEGE

1700 MOORE ST
HUNTINGDON, PA 166522196
Phone: 814 641-3000
Fax: –
Web: www.juniata.edu

CEO: –
CFO: –
HR: –
FYE: May 31
Type: Private

Brothers and sisters are welcome at Juniata College, an independent, co-educational school affiliated with the Church of the Brethren. The college offers bachelor of arts (BA) and bachelor of science (BS) degrees in about 100 fields at its two dozen academic departments. Students are encouraged to design their own majors or "programs of emphasis" (POEs); nearly half do just that. Its most popular POEs include biology, pre-health, accounting, business, education, environmental science, psychology, chemistry, and sociology. Founded in 1876, Juniata College enrolls about 1,600 students.

	Annual Growth	05/15	05/16	05/17	05/20	05/22
Sales ($mil.)	2.5%	–	86.4	56.6	89.0	100.0
Net income ($ mil.)	21.8%	–	1.3	7.8	(1.6)	4.1
Market value ($ mil.)	–	–	–	–	–	–
Employees	–	–	–	–	–	500

JUNIATA VALLEY FINANCIAL CORP

NBB: JUVF

Bridge and Main Streets, P.O. Box 66
Mifflintown, PA 17059-0066
Phone: 855 582-5101
Fax: –
Web: www.jvbonline.com

CEO: Marcie A Barber
CFO: Joann N McMinn
HR: –
FYE: December 31
Type: Public

Juniata Valley Financial is the holding company for Juniata Valley Bank, which serves central Pennsylvania from some 15 locations. The bank offers standard products such as checking and savings accounts, money market accounts, certificates of deposit, individual retirement accounts, and credit cards. Residential estate mortgages account for about half the company's loan portfolio, which also includes commercial, construction, home equity, municipal, and personal loans. The bank offers trust and investment services, as well. Juniata Valley Bank was established in 1867.

	Annual Growth	12/19	12/20	12/21	12/22	12/23
Assets ($mil.)	6.8%	670.6	793.7	810.5	830.9	871.8
Net income ($ mil.)	3.1%	5.8	5.6	6.6	8.3	6.5
Market value ($ mil.)	(9.4%)	96.6	88.3	82.4	79.9	65.1
Employees	(2.5%)	177	167	157	158	160

JUNIOR ACHIEVEMENT USA

12320 ORACLE BLVD STE 325
COLORADO SPRINGS, CO 809212543
Phone: 719 540-8000
Fax: –
Web: www.juniorachievement.org

CEO: Jack Kosakowski
CFO: Edward Priem II
HR: –
FYE: June 30
Type: Private

Junior Achievement USA teaches smaller people about big business. Doing business as Junior Achievement (JA), the organization educates students in grades K-12 about business, economics, and free enterprise. The group conducts its activities in more than 110 countries. JA's programs reach about 10 million students each year and focus on such areas as citizenship, career development, financial literacy, entrepreneurship, and ethics, among others. Some 213,000 classroom volunteers assist with the organization's activities through about 140 chapters nationwide. The organization's funding comes from individual contributions and corporate donations. The group was established in 1919.

	Annual Growth	06/09	06/10	06/14	06/15	06/16
Sales ($mil.)	(6.2%)	–	33.8	24.5	28.4	23.0
Net income ($ mil.)	–	–	(3.9)	0.2	2.7	(1.8)
Market value ($ mil.)	–	–	–	–	–	–
Employees	–	–	–	–	–	65

JUNIPER GROUP INC.

20283 State Road 7, Suite 300
Boca Raton, FL 33498
Phone: 561 807-8990
Fax: –
Web: www.junipergroup.com

CEO: Vlado P Hreljanovic
CFO: –
HR: –
FYE: December 31
Type: Public

The Juniper Group is hoping to turn over a new leaf. The company primarily provides broadband installation and wireless infrastructure construction services through its Tower West Communications subsidiary, including tower erection and construction, site installation and surveying, and antenna installation. Its clients include national providers of wireless voice, messaging, and data services. Juniper also is involved in film distribution, acquiring motion picture rights from independent producers; that business line accounted for less than 2% of revenues in fiscal 2008.

	Annual Growth	12/06	12/07	12/08	12/09	12/10
Sales ($mil.)	(15.8%)	4.7	1.9	0.6	1.1	2.4
Net income ($ mil.)	–	(1.7)	(9.8)	(55.0)	45.7	(14.9)
Market value ($ mil.)	(71.4%)	68.0	4.5	3.4	34.2	0.5
Employees	–	–	–	9	17	9

JUNIPER NETWORKS INC

NYS: JNPR

1133 Innovation Way
Sunnyvale, CA 94089
Phone: 408 745-2000
Fax: 408 745-2100
Web: www.juniper.net

CEO: –
CFO: –
HR: –
FYE: December 31
Type: Public

Juniper Networks designs, develops, and sells products and services high-performance network offerings that are designed to meet the performance, reliability, and security requirements of the world's most demanding enterprises such as financial services; national, federal, state, and local government; as well as research and educational institutions. Its routers, switches and security technologies are high-performance networks that enable customers to build scalable, reliable, secure and cost-effective networks for their businesses, while achieving agility and improved operating efficiency through automation. Juniper sells directly and through resellers and distributors including Ingram Micro and Hitachi. More than half of the company's sales are made to customers based in the US. The company was founded in 1996.

	Annual Growth	12/19	12/20	12/21	12/22	12/23
Sales ($mil.)	5.8%	4,445.4	4,445.1	4,735.4	5,301.2	5,564.5
Net income ($ mil.)	(2.6%)	345.0	257.8	252.7	471.0	310.2
Market value ($ mil.)	4.6%	7,889.0	7,210.0	11,438	10,237	9,442.4
Employees	4.3%	9,419	2,880	10,191	10,901	11,144

JUNIPER PHARMACEUTICALS, INC.

33 ARCH ST STE 3110
BOSTON, MA 021101424
Phone: 617 639-1500
Fax: –
Web: www.catalent.com

CEO: –
CFO: –
HR: –
FYE: December 31
Type: Private

Columbia Laboratories knows the power hormones have over us. The company develops, manufactures, and markets hormone therapies. Its products in development include a progesterone product delivered through a propriety bioadhesive technology to reduce the risk of preterm births. Columbia Laboratories already developed two such products, PROCHIEVE and CRINONE, and is now working on a new generation in agreement with Watson Pharmaceuticals. The company relies upon third-party manufacturers to produce its products.

JUPITER MARINE INTERNATIONAL HOLDINGS, INC.
NBB: JMIH

1103 12th Avenue East
Palmetto, FL 34221
Phone: 941 729-5000
Fax: –
Web: www.jupitermarine.com

CEO: Carl M Herndon Sr
CFO: Lawrence S Tierney
HR: –
FYE: July 28
Type: Public

Women are from Venus, men are from Mars, and fishing boats are from Jupiter, as in Jupiter Marine International Holdings (JMIH). The company designs and manufactures offshore sport fishing boats under the Jupiter brand name; the nine model lineup ranges in size from a 29 foot forward seating outboard to a 39 foot cruiser. JMIH offers open center console and forward cabin models, as well as yacht-like amenities. A build-a-boat option allows color selection. The company builds all of its boats at its plant in Palmetto, Florida. Products are sold through US dealers, primarily on the East and Gulf Coast. President and CEO Carl Herndon, his family, and CFO Lawrence Tierney collectively own more than half of JMIH.

	Annual Growth	07/03	07/04	07/05	07/06	07/07
Sales ($mil.)	15.2%	–	–	11.5	15.2	15.2
Net income ($ mil.)	–	–	–	0.4	0.2	(1.4)
Market value ($ mil.)	(46.5%)	–	–	5.7	4.2	1.6
Employees	–	–	–	–	73	70

JUPITER MEDICAL CENTER, INC.

1210 S OLD DIXIE HWY
JUPITER, FL 334587205
Phone: 561 747-2234
Fax: –
Web: www.jupitermed.com

CEO: Donald McKenna
CFO: –
HR: –
FYE: September 30
Type: Private

Located in Palm Beach County and the Treasure Coast region, Jupiter Medical Center provides specialty services that include orthopedics and spine care; cancer care and oncology; cardiac and vascular care; neuroscience and stroke care; women's and children's services; urgent care; and other key areas. The not-for-profit medical center has about 250 beds and some 675 physicians. Jupiter Medical Center was built and opened its doors in 1979.

	Annual Growth	09/18	09/19	09/20	09/21	09/22
Sales ($mil.)	7.8%	–	319.6	255.5	305.7	400.5
Net income ($ mil.)	(36.2%)	–	31.4	21.2	7.6	8.1
Market value ($ mil.)	–	–	–	–	–	–
Employees	–	–	–	–	–	1,780

JUST BORN, INC.

1300 STEFKO BLVD
BETHLEHEM, PA 180176672
Phone: 610 867-7568
Fax: –
Web: www.justborn.com

CEO: David Shaffer
CFO: –
HR: Anne Cosenza
FYE: December 31
Type: Private

Just Born is the tenth largest candy company in the US that manufactures candies under well-known brands such as Peeps Brand, particularly the Peeps Chick and Peeps Bunny at Easter time. Other candy treats produced by the company include Just Born jelly beans, Hot Tamales jelly beans, Mike and Ike and Peanut Chews. Just Born operates the company's online store at www.peepsandcompany.com which carries all of its candy, branded gifts, apparel, and other fun merchandise. The third-generation family-owned and -operated company was founded by Sam Born in 1923.

K-MICRO, INC.

1618 STANFORD ST
SANTA MONICA, CA 904045368
Phone: 310 442-3200
Fax: –
Web: www.corpinfo.com

CEO: Michael Sabourian
CFO: –
HR: –
FYE: October 31
Type: Private

CorpInfo wants your technology to fit your enterprise to a T. The company offers information technology (IT) services including e-commerce consulting, network engineering, systems design, application development, systems architecture, support, training, application development, and program management. The company's clients come from a wide range of industries such as manufacturing, technology, health care, retail, manufacturing, and financial services. They include The Aerospace Corporation, Bank of the West, Countrywide Financial, and Honda.

	Annual Growth	10/09	10/10	10/11	10/12	10/13
Sales ($mil.)	5.7%	–	–	17.8	14.1	19.9
Net income ($ mil.)	35.1%	–	–	0.0	0.0	0.0
Market value ($ mil.)	–	–	–	–	–	–
Employees	–	–	–	–	–	96

K-TEL INTERNATIONAL INC

2491 Xenium Lane North
Plymouth, MN 55441
Phone: 763 559-5566
Fax: –
Web: www.ktel.com

CEO: Philip Kives
CFO: –
HR: –
FYE: June 30
Type: Public

K-tel International practically invented the commercial mix. The company produces and markets prerecorded albums (primarily compilations such as "Masters of Metal" and "Sound Explosion") that it creates with music from the approximately 6,000 titles in its catalog. K-tel sells its CDs and DVDs to wholesalers, retail stores, and and mass merchandisers; it also licenses music to other companies for a variety of uses, including soundtracks and TV commercials. In addition, K-tel distributes its music digitally through companies such as Napster, Amazon.com, and Apple's iTunes. The "K" in K-tel International stands for chairman and CEO Philip Kives, who founded the company in the late 1960s.

	Annual Growth	06/02	06/03	06/04	06/05	06/06
Sales ($mil.)	(8.6%)	6.9	7.2	6.7	6.0	4.8
Net income ($ mil.)	–	0.0	(1.0)	(0.1)	(0.5)	(1.2)
Market value ($ mil.)	(18.4%)	1.2	1.4	1.4	0.9	0.5
Employees	(16.7%)	27	21	17	17	13

K-VA-T FOOD STORES, INC.

1 FOOD CITY CIR E
ABINGDON, VA 242101100
Phone: 800 826-8451
Fax: –
Web: www.foodcity.com

CEO: Steven C Smith
CFO: Michael T Lockard
HR: Donnie Meadows
FYE: December 31
Type: Private

Food City actually dates back to 1918 when a store was opened in Greeneville, Tennessee, but K-VA-T Food Stores' official beginning took place in 1955 when founder Jack C. Smith--with his father, Curtis and uncle, Earl--opened the first store in Grundy, Virginia. The company have around 100 pharmacies and around 85 fuel stations. The company has also grown steadily by expansion into new market areas while remodeling and replacing existing locations as needed to best serve their customers.

K. V. MART CO.

990 CHERRY AVE STE 204
LONG BEACH, CA 908135939
Phone: 310 816-0200
Fax: –
Web: www.kvmart.com

CEO: –
CFO: –
HR: –
FYE: December 31
Type: Private

K.V. may as well be an acronym for knockout value. K.V. Mart Co. operates about 15 grocery stores primarily under the Top Valu Market and Buy Low Market banners. Other formats include ValuMart and Amar Ranch stores, primarily in Los Angeles County, California. The stores focus on serving low-income shoppers and catering to their surrounding ethic communities. K.V. Mart was founded in 1977 and is owned and operated by chairman and CEO Darioush Khaledi, who fled Iran in the late-1970s. K.V. Mart is one of the leading independent grocery chains in Southern California, as well as one of the largest minority-owned companies in the Los Angeles area.

KADANT INC

NYS: KAI

One Technology Park Drive
Westford, MA 01886
Phone: 978 776-2000
Fax: –
Web: www.kadant.com

CEO: Jeffrey L Powell
CFO: –
HR: Lauren Sharpe
FYE: December 30
Type: Public

Kadant is a global supplier of technologies and engineered systems that drive sustainable industrial processing. Its products and services play an integral role in enhancing efficiency, optimizing energy utilization, and maximizing productivity in process industries while helping its customers advance their sustainability initiatives with products that reduce waste or generate more yield with fewer inputs, particularly fiber, energy, and water. It develops and manufactures a range of products and equipment used in process industries such as paper, packaging, and tissue; wood products; mining; metals; food processing; and recycling and waste management, among others. Kadant's diverse customer base includes global and regional industrial manufacturers and distributors who participate in the broader resource transformation sector. Most of Kadant's revenues are generated outside the US.

	Annual Growth	12/19*	01/21	01/22*	12/22	12/23
Sales ($mil.)	8.0%	704.6	635.0	786.5	904.7	957.7
Net income ($ mil.)	22.2%	52.1	55.2	84.0	120.9	116.1
Market value ($ mil.)	27.6%	1,238.3	1,650.6	2,698.5	2,079.7	3,281.9
Employees	2.6%	2,800	2,600	2,900	3,100	3,100

*Fiscal year change

KADLEC REGIONAL MEDICAL CENTER

888 SWIFT BLVD
RICHLAND, WA 993523514
Phone: 509 946-4611
Fax: –
Web: www.kadlec.org

CEO: Lane Savitch
CFO: –
HR: –
FYE: December 31
Type: Private

Kadlec Regional Medical Center is an acute care hospital facility serving southeastern Washington and northeastern Oregon. In addition to providing comprehensive medical, surgical, and emergency services, the hospital provides neonatal intensive care, cardiopulmonary rehabilitation, interventional cardiology, neurology, cancer care, and other specialist services. Not-for-profit Kadlec Regional has some 270 inpatient beds, including pediatric, intensive, intermediate, and critical care capacity. It also operates outpatient physician offices and clinics in surrounding areas.

	Annual Growth	12/16	12/17	12/18	12/20	12/21
Sales ($mil.)	5.4%	–	595.8	640.4	675.4	736.2
Net income ($ mil.)	(12.8%)	–	87.3	51.1	72.8	50.4
Market value ($ mil.)	–	–	–	–	–	–
Employees	–	–	–	–	–	2,668

KAISER ALUMINUM CORP.

NMS: KALU

1550 West McEwen Drive, Suite 500
Franklin, TN 37067
Phone: 629 252-7040
Fax: –
Web: www.kaiseraluminum.com

CEO: Keith Harvey
CFO: Neal West
HR: Mark Krouse
FYE: December 31
Type: Public

Kaiser Aluminum manufactures and sells semi-fabricated aluminum mill products with nearly 15 production facilities in North America. The company's business focuses on producing rolled, extruded, and drawn aluminum products used principally for aerospace and defense, aluminum beverage and food packaging, automotive, and general engineering products that include consumer durables, electronics and products for electrical and machinery and equipment applications. The company purchases primary aluminum and recycled and scrap aluminum from third-party suppliers to make its fabricated products. Some of its facilities supply billet, log, and other intermediate materials to its other plants for use in production. Serving some 570 customers, Kaiser generates the majority of its revenue from the US.

	Annual Growth	12/19	12/20	12/21	12/22	12/23
Sales ($mil.)	19.5%	1,514.1	1,172.7	2,622.0	3,427.9	3,087.0
Net income ($ mil.)	(6.6%)	62.0	28.8	(18.5)	(29.6)	47.2
Market value ($ mil.)	(10.5%)	1,776.0	1,584.0	1,504.5	1,216.6	1,140.2
Employees	9.1%	2,820	2,575	3,957	4,000	4,000

KAISER FOUNDATION HEALTH PLAN, INC.

1 KAISER PLZ
OAKLAND, CA 946123610
Phone: 510 271-5800
Fax: –
Web: healthy.kaiserpermanente.org

CEO: Greg Adams
CFO: Kathy Lancaster
HR: Frank Hurtarte
FYE: December 31
Type: Private

Kaiser Foundation Health Plan, operates as Kaiser Permanente, serves around 12.7 million members in eight states and the District of Columbia. It is one of America's leading health care providers and nonprofit health plans. Kaiser has an integrated care model, offering both hospital and physician care through a network of hospitals and physician practices operating under the Kaiser Permanente name. Members of Kaiser health plans have access to hospitals and hundreds of other health care facilities operated by Kaiser Foundation Hospitals and Permanente Medical Groups.

	Annual Growth	12/18	12/19	12/20	12/21	12/22
Sales ($mil.)	4.0%	–	–	–	68,095	70,804
Net income ($ mil.)	–	–	–	–	924.6	(645.7)
Market value ($ mil.)	–	–	–	–	–	–
Employees	–	–	–	–	–	189,319

KAISER FOUNDATION HOSPITALS INC

1 KAISER PLZ
OAKLAND, CA 946123610
Phone: 510 271-6611
Fax: –
Web: www.kaisercenter.com

CEO: Gregory A Adams
CFO: Kathy Lancaster
HR: –
FYE: December 31
Type: Private

Kaiser Foundation Hospitals is on a roll. The hospital group operates nearly 40 acute care hospitals and 680 medical offices in eight states (California, Colorado, Georgia, Hawaii, Maryland, Oregon, Virginia, and Washington) and Washington D.C. The company's largest presence is in California, where the majority of its hospitals are located. Kaiser Foundation Hospitals employs more than 21,000 physicians, representing all medical specialties. Kaiser Foundation Hospital's doctors group is controlled by Permanente Medical Groups, and its HMO is offered through Kaiser Foundation Health Plan. Altogether, the group provides care for about 11.7 million members.

KAISER GROUP HOLDINGS, INC.   NBB: KGHI

9302 Lee Highway
Fairfax, VA 22031-1207
Phone: 703 934-3010
Fax: 703 934-3199
Web: www.icfkaiser.com/

CEO: Dorris Sewell
CFO: Zach Steinfeld
HR: –
FYE: December 31
Type: Public

This king has diminishing assets. The primary asset of Kaiser Group Holdings is its 50% stake in Kaiser-Hill Company, a joint venture with CH2M HILL that was formed to clean up the US Department of Energy's Rocky Flats site, a former nuclear weapons production facility in Colorado (completed ahead of schedule in 2005). Subsidiary Kaiser Analytical Management Services provides analytical management services in areas such as health and safety and environmental and waste management and accounted for all of the company's revenue in 2006, but the company expects no future revenues from this unit. Kaiser Group also has an insurance unit (MS Builders Insurance Company), but it has not written any policies.

	Annual Growth	12/02	12/03	12/04	12/05	12/06
Sales ($mil.)	–	–	–	1.0	1.8	0.2
Net income ($ mil.)	–	18.3	4.4	7.4	45.3	(2.4)
Market value ($ mil.)	47.7%	9.4	38.5	47.5	69.8	44.8
Employees	(25.5%)	13	11	14	12	4

KAISER-FRANCIS OIL COMPANY

6733 S YALE AVE
TULSA, OK 741363330
Phone: 918 494-0000
Fax: –
Web: www.kfoc.net

CEO: George B Kaiser
CFO: Don Millican
HR: Ronald Rackley
FYE: December 31
Type: Private

King of the Tulsa oil patch, oil and gas exploration and production independent Kaiser-Francis Oil Company buys, sells, and develops oil and gas properties, primarily in Arkansas, Colorado, Kansas, Nebraska, New Mexico, North Dakota, Oklahoma, Oregon, Texas, West Virginia, and Wyoming. The company teamed up with fellow Tulsa-based energy firm SemGas LP to help build the Wyckoff Gas Storage facility (5.1 billion cu. ft. of working gas storage) in Steuben County, New York. Tulsa billionaire George Kaiser owns and manages Kaiser-Francis Oil through GBK Corporation.

	Annual Growth	12/18	12/19	12/20	12/21	12/22
Sales ($mil.)	(18.7%)	–	–	–	8.1	6.6
Net income ($ mil.)	1.6%	–	–	–	0.4	0.4
Market value ($ mil.)	–	–	–	–	–	–
Employees	–	–	–	–	–	2,067

KALA BIO INC   NAS: KALA

1167 Massachusetts Avenue
Arlington, MA 02476
Phone: 781 996-5252
Fax: –
Web: www.kalarx.com

CEO: Mark Iwicki
CFO: Mary Reumuth
HR: –
FYE: December 31
Type: Public

KALA BIO, formerly known as Kala Pharmaceuticals, is a biopharmaceutical company that develops therapeutics with an initial focus on complex eye diseases. Its product candidate KPI-012 is a mesenchymal stem cell secretome, or MSC-S, and is currently in clinical development for the treatment of persistent corneal epithelial defects, or PCED, a rare disease of impaired corneal healing. In addition, the company has initiated preclinical studies under its KPI-014 program to evaluate the utility of its MSC-S platform for inherited retinal degenerative diseases, such as Retinitis Pigmentosa and Stargardt Disease.

	Annual Growth	12/18	12/19	12/20	12/21	12/22
Sales ($mil.)	–	–	6.1	6.4	11.2	3.9
Net income ($ mil.)	–	(66.7)	(94.3)	(104.3)	(142.6)	(44.8)
Market value ($ mil.)	67.1%	8.3	6.3	11.6	2.1	65.1
Employees	(28.5%)	130	136	188	192	34

KALEIDA HEALTH

726 EXCHANGE ST
BUFFALO, NY 142101484
Phone: 716 859-5600
Fax: –
Web: www.kaleidahealth.org

CEO: Don Boyd
CFO: Hugh P Chisholm
HR: Jerry Venable
FYE: December 31
Type: Private

Kaleida Health provides a kaleidoscope of services to residents of western New York. The health system operates five acute care hospitals including Buffalo General Hospital and Gates Vascular Institute (combined with about 550 beds), The Women & Children's Hospital of Buffalo (200), DeGraff Memorial Hospital (70), and Millard Fillmore Suburban Hospital (260). Community health needs are met through a network of some 80 medical clinics. Kaleida Health also operates skilled nursing care facilities and provides home health care through its Visiting Nursing Association. To help train future medical professionals, Buffalo General Hospital is a teaching affiliate of the State University of New York.

	Annual Growth	12/12	12/13	12/17	12/21	12/22
Sales ($mil.)	3.1%	–	1,139.2	1,331.2	1,422.5	1,502.4
Net income ($ mil.)	–	–	(14.3)	60.4	7.9	(9.0)
Market value ($ mil.)	–	–	–	–	–	–
Employees	–	–	–	–	–	9,000

KAMAN CORP.   NYS: KAMN

1332 Blue Hills Avenue
Bloomfield, CT 06002
Phone: 860 243-7100
Fax: –
Web: www.kaman.com

CEO: Ian K Walsh
CFO: –
HR: –
FYE: December 31
Type: Public

Kaman makes aircraft components for the aerospace, medical, and industrial distribution markets. The company manufactures Kaman-branded aircraft bearings and components in addition to metallic and composite aerostructures for commercial, military, and general aviation fixed and rotary wing aircraft. It also makes safety, and arming solutions for missile and bomb systems for the US and its allies; restores, modifies and supports its SH-2G Super Seasprite maritime helicopters; and manufactures and supports its K-MAX manned and unmanned medium-to-heavy lift helicopters. Customers have included such notable names as Airbus, Bell, Rolls-Royce, and Lockheed Martin. While it generates sales from most continents, the company's sales from North America make up most of its revenue.

	Annual Growth	12/19	12/20	12/21	12/22	12/23
Sales ($mil.)	0.5%	761.6	784.5	709.0	688.0	775.9
Net income ($ mil.)	(55.9%)	209.8	(69.7)	43.7	(46.2)	7.9
Market value ($ mil.)	(22.4%)	1,864.9	1,616.3	1,220.7	630.9	677.6
Employees	0.8%	2,935	3,193	2,846	3,063	3,031

KANE UPMC

4372 ROUTE 6
KANE, PA 167353060
Phone: 814 837-8585
Fax: –
Web: www.kanecommunityhospital.com

CEO: James Armstrong
CFO: –
HR: –
FYE: December 31
Type: Private

Injured Keystone Staters don't have to raise Cain to get medical care with Kane Community Hospital around. The 40-bed acute care hospital provides services that include cardiology, emergency care, general surgery, oncology, and women's care. Kane Community Hospital has an affiliation with the larger Hamot Medical Center (which has about 350 beds) through which the two organizations share resources and training, as well as physician recruitment opportunities. Additionally, their combined size allows them cut back on operating costs by purchasing supplies in volume. Kane Community Hospital, founded in 1929, also provides primary care to residents of northwestern Pennsylvania through its hospital-based clinics.

	Annual Growth	06/08	06/09	06/15	06/16*	12/22
Sales ($mil.)	(21.3%)	–	18.2	20.2	19.4	0.8
Net income ($ mil.)	–	–	(0.3)	(1.2)	(1.8)	(0.0)
Market value ($ mil.)	–	–	–	–	–	–
Employees	–	–	–	–	–	190

*Fiscal year change

KANSAS CITY BOARD OF PUBLIC UTILITIES

540 MINNESOTA AVE
KANSAS CITY, KS 661012930
Phone: 913 573-9000
Fax: –
Web: www.bpu.com

CEO: –
CFO: –
HR: Samuel D Leon
FYE: September 30
Type: Private

Goin' to ... Kansas City? The Board of Public Utilities of Kansas City, Kansas (known as the Kansas City Board of Public Utilities) will help light the way. The utility provides electric transmission and distribution services to 63,000 customers and water distribution services to 50,000 customers in the Kansas City metropolitan area (in Wyandotte and Johnson counties). Most electric customers are residential, but commercial and industrial customers account for the bulk of the utility's power revenues. The Kansas City Board of Public Utilities also has interests in coal, gas, and oil-fired power generation facilities. The utility is owned by the Unified Government of Wyandotte County and Kansas City.

	Annual Growth	09/18	09/19*	12/19	12/21*	09/22
Sales ($mil.)	3.7%	–	256.1	337.2	349.4	286.0
Net income ($ mil.)	(0.4%)	–	27.8	16.2	34.7	27.5
Market value ($ mil.)	–	–	–	–	–	–
Employees	–	–	–	–	–	545

*Fiscal year change

KANSAS CITY LIFE INSURANCE CO (KANSAS CITY, MO)

3520 Broadway
Kansas City, MO 64111-2565
Phone: 816 753-7000
Fax: 816 753-4902
Web: www.kclife.com

NBB: KCLI
CEO: Walter E Bixby
CFO: Tracy W Knapp
HR: –
FYE: December 31
Type: Public

Kansas City Life Insurance and its subsidiaries provide insurance products throughout the US to individuals (life and disability coverage and annuities) and to groups (life, dental, vision, and disability insurance). Subsidiary Grange Life sells traditional life insurance, universal life products and fixed annuities. The insurance companies sell through independent agents and agencies. Kansas City Life Insurance was established in 1895 and is based in Kansas City, Missouri. Chairman and CEO R. Philip Bixby and his family control the company.

	Annual Growth	12/18	12/19	12/20	12/21	12/22
Assets ($mil.)	–	4,971.5	5,219.9	5,463.0	5,433.4	4,965.1
Net income ($ mil.)	–	15.7	24.4	15.2	10.7	(16.2)
Market value ($ mil.)	(8.1%)	358.3	324.9	368.0	411.5	255.6
Employees	–	–	–	–	–	–

KANSAS DEPARTMENT OF TRANSPORTATION

700 SW HARRISON ST STE 500
TOPEKA, KS 666033964
Phone: 785 296-3501
Fax: –
Web: www.ksdot.org

CEO: –
CFO: –
HR: Melissa Tyrrell
FYE: June 30
Type: Private

The Kansas Department of Transportation (KDOT) helps connect the dots with residents who love to travel the 140,000-plus miles across the Sunflower State. The agency focuses on providing a transportation system for citizens in the state by offering a wide range of services such as maintaining roads and bridges, transportation planning, and designing construction projects. The department also provides federal fund program administration, as well as administrative support, travel information, and programs in traffic safety. KDOT traces its roots to the organization of interstate travel in 1917.

	Annual Growth	06/18	06/19	06/20	06/21	06/22
Sales ($mil.)	4.5%	–	1,583.0	1,540.2	1,624.9	1,804.2
Net income ($ mil.)	(22.4%)	–	312.1	104.5	21.2	145.6
Market value ($ mil.)	–	–	–	–	–	–
Employees	–	–	–	–	–	3,000

KANSAS ELECTRIC POWER COOPERATIVE, INC.

600 SW CORPORATE VW
TOPEKA, KS 666151233
Phone: 785 273-7010
Fax: –
Web: www.kepco.org

CEO: –
CFO: –
HR: –
FYE: December 31
Type: Private

If Dorothy lived in rural Kansas today, she'd probably hear that tornado warning and reach safety, thanks to the power supplied by Kansas Electric Power Cooperative (KEPCo). KEPCo operates power plants and purchases additional energy for its 19 member distribution cooperatives, which serve more than 110,000 rural customers. The generation and transmission utility's assets include a 6% stake in Wolf Creek Nuclear Operating Corporation, which operates Kansas' Wolf Creek Generating Station. Subsidiary KSI Engineering provides utility construction and infrastructure services. KEPCo, which was formed in 1975, is part of the alliance of Touchstone Energy Cooperatives.

	Annual Growth	12/16	12/17	12/18	12/21	12/22
Sales ($mil.)	1.3%	–	155.2	164.6	155.3	165.6
Net income ($ mil.)	(9.9%)	–	2.4	2.7	1.1	1.4
Market value ($ mil.)	–	–	–	–	–	–
Employees	–	–	–	–	–	24

KANSAS STATE UNIVERSITY

1301 MID CAMPUS DR N
MANHATTAN, KS 66506
Phone: 785 532-6011
Fax: –
Web: www.k-state.edu

CEO: Alysia Starkey
CFO: –
HR: –
FYE: December 31
Type: Private

K-State is a big deal in the Little Apple. Located in Manhattan, Kansas (aka the Little Apple), Kansas State University (K-State) is a land grant institution that has an enrollment of some 24,000 students. It offers more than 250 undergraduate majors, 65 master's degrees, 45 doctoral degrees, and more than 20 graduate certificate programs. Major fields of study include agriculture, technology, and veterinary medicine. Notable alumni include former White House press secretary Marlin Fitzwater and actor Gordon Jump. Along with the University of Kansas and other universities, technical schools, and community colleges in the state, K-State is governed by The Kansas Board of Regents.

	Annual Growth	06/08	06/09	06/10	06/17*	12/22
Sales ($mil.)	(35.9%)	–	420.6	459.8	620.2	1.3
Net income ($ mil.)	(26.5%)	–	10.7	50.5	50.8	0.2
Market value ($ mil.)	–	–	–	–	–	–
Employees	–	–	–	–	–	5,168

*Fiscal year change

KARYOPHARM THERAPEUTICS INC
NMS: KPTI

85 Wells Avenue, 2nd Floor
Newton, MA 02459
Phone: 617 658-0600
Fax: –
Web: www.karyopharm.com

CEO: Richard Paulson
CFO: Michael Mason
HR: Alexandria Jackson
FYE: December 31
Type: Public

Karyopharm Therapeutics is a commercial-stage pharmaceutical company that focuses on the treatment of cancer and other diseases. Its lead product, Xpovio (selinexor), is the first Selective Inhibitor of Nuclear Export (SINE) compound to receive FDA approval and is being marketed for use in adult patients with relapsed or refractory multiple myeloma. The company also has a number of other products lined up for approval, namely, Eltanexor, Verdinexor, and KPT-9274. The company caters to specialty distributors and specialty pharmacies that resell Karyopharm's products. The company was founded in 2008 by Dr. Sharon Shacham.

	Annual Growth	12/19	12/20	12/21	12/22	12/23
Sales ($mil.)	37.5%	40.9	108.1	209.8	157.1	146.0
Net income ($ mil.)	–	(199.6)	(196.3)	(124.1)	(165.3)	(143.1)
Market value ($ mil.)	(53.9%)	2,202.9	1,778.9	738.9	390.7	99.4
Employees	–	347	432	442	385	–

KASPIEN HOLDINGS INC
NBB: KSPN

2818 N. Sullivan Rd., Ste 130
Spokane, WA 99216
Phone: 509 900-6287
Fax: –
Web: www.kaspien.com

CEO: Brock Kowalchuk
CFO: Edwin Sapienza
HR: –
FYE: January 28
Type: Public

Just an F.Y.I., but Trans World Entertainment operates F.Y.E. and a handful of other retail ventures. F.Y.E. (aka For Your Entertainment) stores sell CDs, DVDs, video games, software, and related products at about 390 locations throughout the US, Puerto Rico, and the Virgin Islands. Trans World's other bricks-and-mortar operations include about 15 video stores under the Saturday Matinee and Suncoast Motion Pictures banners. Most of the firm's retail outlets are located in shopping malls. Trans World also sells entertainment products via its e-commerce sites (including fye.com, secondspin.com, and wherehouse.com). Chairman and CEO Bob Higgins founded the company in 1972.

	Annual Growth	02/19	02/20*	01/21	01/22	01/23
Sales ($mil.)	(25.6%)	418.2	325.9	158.3	143.7	128.2
Net income ($ mil.)	–	(97.4)	(58.7)	(3.9)	(8.0)	(19.0)
Market value ($ mil.)	10.2%	2.9	17.2	191.5	37.5	4.3
Employees	(56.3%)	2,200	155	136	141	80

*Fiscal year change

KATE SPADE HOLDINGS LLC

5822 HAVERFORD AVE STE 2
PHILADELPHIA, PA 191314848
Phone: 212 354-4900
Fax: –
Web: –

CEO: –
CFO: Thomas Linko
HR: –
FYE: December 31
Type: Private

Kate Spade is a global lifestyle brand synonymous with joy, delivering seasonal collections of handbags, ready-to-wear, jewelry, footwear, gifts, home d cor and more. The company operates freestanding flagship, specialty retail and outlet stores as well as concession shop-in-shops. These stores are located in regional shopping centers, metropolitan areas throughout the world and established outlet centers. Kate Spade has about 400 stores, including more than 205 stores in North America and around 190 stores in international operations. The majority of its sales were generated in North America.

KAYEM FOODS, INC.

75 ARLINGTON ST
CHELSEA, MA 021502365
Phone: 781 933-3115
Fax: –
Web: www.kayemfoods.com

CEO: –
CFO: –
HR: Yolanda Vegasantillan
FYE: October 31
Type: Private

Kayem Foods makes one of the top-selling hot dogs in New England and is a fixture at Fenway Park. Rolling out some 1 million dogs daily, the company also makes traditional Italian sausages, bratwurst, deli meats, spiral hams, and fresh gourmet chicken sausage. Products are sold under brand names Deutschmacher, Essem, Kayem, al fresco, Genoa Sausage, Meisterchef, Schonland's, and Triple M. Outside the New England states, Kayem sells its meats nationwide. US food customers include retailers Hannaford, Price Chopper, Kroger, and Town & Country. It also serves food service accounts the likes of U.S. Foodservice and SYSCO. Founded more than a century ago, Kayem is still owned and operated by the Monkiewicz family.

KB HOME
NYS: KBH

10990 Wilshire Boulevard
Los Angeles, CA 90024
Phone: 310 231-4000
Fax: 310 231-4222
Web: www.kbhome.com

CEO: Jeffrey T Mezger
CFO: Jeff J Kaminski
HR: Deanna Schmitt
FYE: November 30
Type: Public

KB Home is one of the largest and most recognized homebuilding companies in the US. The company constructs single-family (attached and detached) houses, townhouses, and condominiums suited mainly for first-time, move-up, and active adult buyers in nine states on the West Coast and in the Southwest, Central US, and Southeast. Its Built-to-Order brand allows buyers to customize their houses by choosing a floor plan as well as exterior and interior features. KB Home's average selling price for a house is in the range of $490,000 to $500,000. To help with the buying process, KB Home also offers mortgage banking, title services, and insurance. KB has built more than 670,000 homes since it was founded in 1957.

	Annual Growth	11/19	11/20	11/21	11/22	11/23
Sales ($mil.)	8.9%	4,552.7	4,183.2	5,724.9	6,903.8	6,410.6
Net income ($ mil.)	21.7%	268.0	296.2	564.7	816.7	590.2
Market value ($ mil.)	10.8%	2,855.3	2,906.5	3,302.1	2,591.9	4,302.0
Employees	0.8%	2,140	1,776	2,244	2,366	2,205

KBR INC
NYS: KBR

601 Jefferson Street, Suite 3400
Houston, TX 77002
Phone: 713 753-2000
Fax: –
Web: www.kbr.com

CEO: Stuart J Bradie
CFO: Mark W Sopp
HR: –
FYE: December 29
Type: Public

KBR delivers science, technology and engineering solutions to governments and companies around the world. The company's business capabilities and offerings include scientific research such as quantum science and computing; defense systems engineering such as rapid prototyping; operational support such as space domain awareness; Information operations such as cyber analytics and cybersecurity; and Sustainable decarbonization solutions that accelerate and enable energy transition and climate change solutions such as proprietary, sustainability-focused process licensing. Key customers include US DoD agencies such as the US Army, US Navy and US Air Force, Missile Defense Agency, National Geospatial-Intelligence Agency, National Reconnaissance Office, and other intelligence agencies. Operations in the US account for more than 55% of KBR's revenue.

	Annual Growth	12/19	12/20	12/21	12/22	12/23
Sales ($mil.)	5.4%	5,639.0	5,767.0	7,339.0	6,564.0	6,956.0
Net income ($ mil.)	–	202.0	(72.0)	18.0	190.0	(265.0)
Market value ($ mil.)	16.1%	4,119.6	4,177.6	6,431.9	7,131.6	7,484.1
Employees	5.0%	28,000	29,000	28,000	30,000	34,000

KBS, INC.

8050 KIMWAY DR
RICHMOND, VA 232282831
Phone: 804 262-0100
Fax: –
Web: www.kbsgc.com

CEO: –
CFO: James Lipscombe
HR: –
FYE: September 30
Type: Private

You would hit the nail right on the head if you were to call KBS a "regional contractor." The company provides design/build, planning, general contracting, and construction management services for commercial and multifamily residential projects in Virginia. Its projects include office buildings, apartment complexes, shopping centers, hotels, schools, jails, warehouses, and senior living facilities. Some 60% of the company's business comes in the form of repeat customers. Clients have included Cousins Properties, Forest City Enterprises, Ukrop's, Best Buy, Wal-Mart, and Virginia Commonwealth University. President Bill Paulette founded KBS in a sheet metal shop in 1975.

	Annual Growth	09/15	09/16	09/17	09/19	09/21
Sales ($mil.)	10.6%	–	200.4	244.8	276.7	331.7
Net income ($ mil.)	15.1%	–	4.9	8.5	10.9	9.8
Market value ($ mil.)	–	–	–	–	–	–
Employees	–	–	–	–	–	130

KEARNY FINANCIAL CORP (MD)

120 Passaic Avenue
Fairfield, NJ 07004
Phone: 973 244-4500
Fax: –
Web: www.kearnybank.com

NMS: KRNY
CEO: Craig L Montanaro
CFO: Keith Suchodolski
HR: –
FYE: June 30
Type: Public

Kearny Financial is the holding company for Kearny Bank (formerly Kearny Federal Savings Bank), which boasts over $7 billion in assets and more than 50 branches across northern New Jersey, Brooklyn, and New York. Kearny Bank offers such standard services as checking and savings accounts, CDs, ATM and debit cards, IRAs, and loans. Residential mortgages make up about 30% of its loan portfolio; multifamily and commercial mortgages and home equity loans round out most of the rest. Kearny also invests in mortgage-backed securities, government and municipal bonds, and other securities.

	Annual Growth	06/19	06/20	06/21	06/22	06/23
Assets ($mil.)	5.0%	6,634.8	6,758.2	7,283.7	7,719.9	8,064.8
Net income ($ mil.)	(0.8%)	42.1	45.0	63.2	67.5	40.8
Market value ($ mil.)	(14.7%)	875.3	538.8	787.1	731.7	464.3
Employees	(0.4%)	565	552	584	596	556

KECK GRADUATE INSTITUTE OF APPLIED LIFE SCIENCES

535 WATSON DR
CLAREMONT, CA 917114817
Phone: 909 621-8000
Fax: –
Web: www.kgi.edu

CEO: –
CFO: Robert W Caragher
HR: Michelle Vega
FYE: June 30
Type: Private

Those who attend Keck Graduate Institute (KGI) know good things come in small packages. The institute, which enrolls 82 students (and has 21 faculty members for a ratio of approximately 1-to-4), specializes in applied life sciences and is a member of The Claremont Colleges, maintained by the Claremont University Consortium. KGI offers a two-year graduate program that culminates in a Master of Bioscience (MBS) degree. Those who earn their MBS may put in an additional three years for a Ph.D. in Applied Life Sciences. Curriculum is designed to prepare students for careers in the biotech, medical device, and pharmaceutical industries. KGI was founded in 1997 with a $50 million grant from the W.M. Keck Foundation.

	Annual Growth	06/18	06/19	06/20	06/21	06/22
Sales ($mil.)	(0.2%)	–	42.1	36.0	38.2	41.9
Net income ($ mil.)	–	–	(0.5)	(0.3)	10.3	(0.3)
Market value ($ mil.)	–	–	–	–	–	–
Employees	–	–	–	–	–	265

KEENAN, HOPKINS, SCHMIDT AND STOWELL CONTRACTORS, INC.

5422 BAY CENTER DR STE 200
TAMPA, FL 336093437
Phone: 813 628-9330
Fax: –
Web: www.khss.com

CEO: Michael R Cannon
CFO: Lynda Licht
HR: –
FYE: December 31
Type: Private

Business is always looking up for KHS&S Contractors, which specializes in wall and ceiling construction, including interior, exterior, acoustical, and insulation work. KHS&S is one of the largest theme park contractors in the US, completing more than 5.5 million square feet of thematic finishes and providing water feature and rockwork technology and concrete/tilt-up construction. The specialty contractor has worked on projects for Busch Gardens Cheetah Hunt and Walt Disney Parks & Resorts. KHS&S also works on casinos, convention centers, health care facilities, office buildings, laboratories, and other commercial projects. Founded in 1984, the company is owned by its employees.

	Annual Growth	12/18	12/19	12/20	12/21	12/22
Sales ($mil.)	(6.3%)	–	146.7	101.4	112.9	120.8
Net income ($ mil.)	(18.1%)	–	15.6	13.2	7.0	8.6
Market value ($ mil.)	–	–	–	–	–	–
Employees	–	–	–	–	–	350

KELLANOVA

412 N. Wells Street
Chicago, IL 60654
Phone: 269 961-2000
Fax: –
Web: www.kelloggcompany.com

NYS: K
CEO: Steven A Cahillane
CFO: Amit Banati
HR: –
FYE: December 30
Type: Public

From the company's home base in Battle Creek, Michigan, Kellogg Company markets crackers, savory snacks, toaster pastries, cereal bars, granola bars and bites; and convenience foods, such as, ready-to-eat cereals, frozen waffles, veggie foods, and noodles. Kellogg, founded in 1906, boasts many familiar cereal brands, including Kellogg's Corn Flakes, Frosted Flakes, Froot Loops, Special K, and Rice Krispies. While the company works to fill the world's cereal bowls, it actually makes more money these days from its crackers, crisps, convenience brands such as Kellogg's, Cheez-It, Pringles, and Austin, Eggo and Morningstar Farms frozen foods, and Kashi and Bear Naked cereal bars. Though its products are sold worldwide, the company generates approximately 55% of its revenue domestically.

	Annual Growth	12/19*	01/21	01/22*	12/22	12/23
Sales ($mil.)	(0.9%)	13,578	13,770	14,181	15,315	13,122
Net income ($ mil.)	(0.2%)	960.0	1,251.0	1,488.0	960.0	951.0
Market value ($ mil.)	(5.2%)	23,555	21,195	21,941	24,264	19,042
Employees	(7.2%)	31,000	31,000	31,000	30,000	23,000

*Fiscal year change

KELLER NORTH AMERICA, INC.

7550 TEAGUE RD STE 300
HANOVER, MD 210761807
Phone: 410 551-8200
Fax: –
Web: www.keller-na.com

CEO: –
CFO: –
HR: –
FYE: December 31
Type: Private

Hayward Baker is well grounded. The company provides ground modification services used to prepare soil foundations prior to commercial and infrastructure construction. Its services include soil stabilization, underpinning, excavation support, foundation rehabilitation, and groundwater and settlement control. Hayward Baker has worked on projects including the Dalles Lock and Dam spanning the Columbia River in Oregon, levee work in New Orleans, and improvements to the Queretaro Bus Terminal in Queretaro, Mexico. Hayward Baker is a subsidiary of UK-based Keller Group and operates from offices in the US, Canada, and Latin America.

KELLSTROM AEROSPACE, LLC

3430 DAVIE RD STE 302
DAVIE, FL 333141637
Phone: 847 233-5800
Fax: –
Web: www.kellstromaerospace.com

CEO: –
CFO: –
HR: –
FYE: December 31
Type: Private

Does the spell-check at aircraft parts inventory service Kellstrom Aerospace correct "enginuity"? Using its ingenuity to specialize in engines made by CFM International, General Electric, Pratt & Whitney, and Rolls-Royce, the company supplies new and overhauled products for military and commercial aircraft. Kellstrom, doing business as Kellstrom Industries, also provides maintenance for military and commercial aircraft components. Customers include commercial airlines, US and foreign military forces, and maintenance, repair, and overhaul facilities. Kellstrom Aerospace was established in 1990 and has been privately owned since 2002.

	Annual Growth	12/07	12/08	12/09	12/10	12/11
Sales ($mil.)	(2.4%)	–	–	163.2	149.4	155.5
Net income ($ mil.)	(24.5%)	–	–	1.7	2.7	1.0
Market value ($ mil.)		–	–	–	–	–
Employees		–	–	–	–	83

KELLY SERVICES, INC.

999 West Big Beaver Road
Troy, MI 48084
Phone: 248 362-4444
Fax: –
Web: www.kellyservices.com

NMS: KELY A
CEO: Peter W Quigley
CFO: Olivier G Thirot
HR: –
FYE: December 31
Type: Public

Kelly Services is a talent solutions company that delivers staffing for office, professional, light industrial, contact center specialties, clinical research, engineering, technology, telecommunications, early childhood to higher education, outsourcing and consulting group. It is also one of the world's largest scientific and clinical research staffing providers. The company provides workforce solutions to a wide range of local, regional, and global clients in the Americas, Europe, and the Asia-Pacific region. Overall, Kelly Services assigned more than 300,000 temporary employees around the world. About 80% of revenue comes from US. Founded in 1946 by William Russell Kelly.

	Annual Growth	12/19*	01/21	01/22	01/23*	12/23
Sales ($mil.)	(2.5%)	5,355.6	4,516.0	4,909.7	4,965.4	4,835.7
Net income ($ mil.)	(24.6%)	112.4	(72.0)	156.1	(62.5)	36.4
Market value ($ mil.)	(0.7%)	784.0	726.1	592.0	596.6	763.2
Employees	(65.7%)	446,700	374,300	354,500	307,500	6,200

*Fiscal year change

KELSO & COMPANY, L.P.

299 PARK AVE
NEW YORK, NY 101716005
Phone: 212 350-7700
Fax: –
Web: www.kelso.com

CEO: –
CFO: –
HR: –
FYE: December 31
Type: Private

Kelso & Company is a North American middle market private equity firm that specializes in supporting management buyouts. The company's investments generally center on energy, financial services, healthcare, consumer, industrial, media, and services sectors. Kelso & Company was founded in 1971 by the late renowned economist Louis O. Kelso, and has more than 130 investments across a range of industries including American Beacon, Inmark, Del Laboratories, Sentinel Data Centers, Unilab, and Nortek. The company has invested approximately $15 billion of equity capital since 1980.

KELSO-BURNETT CO.

5200 NEWPORT DR
ROLLING MEADOWS, IL 600083806
Phone: 847 259-0720
Fax: –
Web: www.kelso-burnett.com

CEO: Stefan Lopata
CFO: Jim Smith
HR: –
FYE: December 31
Type: Private

Kelso-Burnett is keeping the city that works wired. One of the Chicago area's largest electrical contractors, Kelso-Burnett also ranks as one of the US's largest specialty contractors. Founded in 1908, the employee-owned firm provides electrical construction services to commercial, industrial, institutional, and utility customers. It also installs telecom, security, closed circuit TV, and sound systems and provides fire alarm and electrical systems testing. Customers include Abbott Laboratories, Kraft Foods, and Bass Pro Shops. Kelso-Burnett is part of the international Federated Electrical Contractors network.

KEMPER CORP (DE)

200 E. Randolph Street, Suite 3300
Chicago, IL 60601
Phone: 312 661-4600
Fax: –
Web: www.kemper.com

NYS: KMPR
CEO: Joseph P Lacher Jr
CFO: Bradley T Camden
HR: –
FYE: December 31
Type: Public

Kemper is a diversified insurance holding company, with subsidiaries that provide automobile, homeowners, life, health, and other insurance products to individuals and businesses. The Kemper family of companies is one of the nation's leading specialized insurers. With nearly $13.4 billion in assets, Kemper is improving the world of insurance by providing affordable and easy-to-use personalized solutions to individuals, families and businesses through its auto, personal insurance, life and health brands. Kemper serves more than 5.3 million ppolicyholders andis represented by more than 29,000 agents and brokers.

	Annual Growth	12/19	12/20	12/21	12/22	12/23
Assets ($mil.)	(0.5%)	12,989	14,342	14,917	13,364	12,743
Net income ($ mil.)	–	531.1	409.9	(120.5)	(301.2)	(272.1)
Market value ($ mil.)	(11.0%)	4,968.6	4,925.9	3,769.1	3,154.3	3,120.3
Employees	(2.3%)	8,900	2,100	2,250	9,500	8,100

KENERGY CORP.

6402 OLD CORYDON RD
HENDERSON, KY 424209392
Phone: 270 926-4141
Fax: –
Web: www.kenergycorp.com

CEO: –
CFO: –
HR: –
FYE: December 31
Type: Private

Kenergy kens energy, as the Scots might say. Electric distribution cooperative Kenergy serves about 55,000 customers in 14 counties (Breckinridge, Caldwell, Crittenden, Daviess, Hancock, Henderson, Hopkins, Livingston, Lyon, McLean, Muhlenberg, Ohio, Union and Webster) in Western Kentucky. Kenergy serves its customer base of households, commercial enterprises, and industries via more than 6,700 miles of power lines. The customer-owned company is part of Touchstone Energy Cooperatives, a national alliance of more than 600 local, consumer-owned electric utility cooperatives.

	Annual Growth	12/13	12/14	12/15	12/21	12/22
Sales ($mil.)	3.5%	–	474.8	375.7	473.6	624.0
Net income ($ mil.)	(17.3%)	–	0.1	0.1	0.2	0.0
Market value ($ mil.)		–	–	–	–	–
Employees		–	–	–	–	155

KENNAMETAL INC.
NYS: KMT

525 William Penn Place, Suite 3300
Pittsburgh, PA 15219
Phone: 412 248-8000
Fax: -
Web: www.kennametal.com

CEO: Christopher Rossi
CFO: Patrick S Watson
HR: -
FYE: June 30
Type: Public

Kennametal is a global industrial technology leader that helps customers across the aerospace and defense, earthworks, energy, general engineering, and transportation end markets build their products with precision and efficiency. The company's core expertise includes the development and application of tungsten carbides, ceramics, super-hard materials, and solutions used in metal cutting and extreme wear applications to keep customers up and running longer against conditions such as corrosion and high temperatures. Its standard and custom product offering spans metal cutting and wear applications including turning, milling, hole making, tooling systems and services, as well as specialized wear components and metallurgical powders. Kennametal generates 60% of its revenue in markets outside of the US, with principal international operations in Western Europe, China, and India.

	Annual Growth	06/19	06/20	06/21	06/22	06/23
Sales ($mil.)	(3.3%)	2,375.2	1,885.3	1,841.4	2,012.5	2,078.2
Net income ($ mil.)	(16.3%)	241.9	(5.7)	54.4	144.6	118.5
Market value ($ mil.)	(6.4%)	2,953.1	2,292.1	2,867.7	1,854.6	2,266.5
Employees	(4.3%)	10,400	9,000	8,635	8,732	8,739

KENNEDY HEALTH SYSTEM, INC.

1099 WHITE HORSE RD
VOORHEES, NJ 080434405
Phone: 856 566-5200
Fax: -
Web: -

CEO: -
CFO: -
HR: -
FYE: September 30
Type: Private

Like its namesake, The Kennedy Health System is all about service to the public. The system operates three acute care hospitals with more than 600 beds in southern interior New Jersey. Its operations include several outpatient centers and wellness programs, cancer care, dialysis centers, primary care facilities, and a nursing home. Its outpatient services are vast and varied, ranging from behavioral and occupational health centers to balance centers (to treat dizziness and balance problems) and sleep centers. Affiliated with the Rowan University School of Osteopathic Medicine, Kennedy Health System was founded in 1965 as John F. Kennedy Hospital. It plans to merge with Thomas Jefferson University Hospitals.

KENNEDY KRIEGER INSTITUTE, INC.

707 N BROADWAY
BALTIMORE, MD 212051888
Phone: 443 923-9200
Fax: -
Web: www.kennedykrieger.org

CEO: -
CFO: Michael Neuman
HR: Raymond Short
FYE: June 30
Type: Private

Kennedy Krieger Institute is internationally recognized for improving the lives of tens of thousands of children, adolescents and adults with neurological, rehabilitative or developmental needs through inpatient and day hospital programs, outpatient clinics, home and community services, education, and research. Altogether, the institute serves more than 25,000 individuals each year. Its inpatient pediatric hospital caters to children who suffer from feeding problems and severe behaviors, such as self-injury and aggression. Kennedy Krieger also runs schools for special-education students ages five to 21 that focuses on the development of academic, social, emotional and behavioral skills in an environment that recognizes and capitalizes on the individual strengths of each child.

	Annual Growth	06/08	06/09	06/13	06/19	06/22
Sales ($mil.)	0.1%	-	200.4	213.5	267.3	202.5
Net income ($ mil.)	-	-	(23.6)	13.9	(9.7)	1.0
Market value ($ mil.)	-	-	-	-	-	-
Employees	-	-	-	-	-	2,500

KENNEDY-WILSON HOLDINGS INC
NYS: KW

151 S. El Camino Drive
Beverly Hills, CA 90212
Phone: 310 887-6400
Fax: -
Web: www.kennedywilson.com

CEO: William J McMorrow
CFO: Justin Enbody
HR: -
FYE: December 31
Type: Public

Kennedy Wilson is a global real estate investment company. It owns, operates and develops real estate with the objective of maximizing earnings over the long run for itself and its equity partners. The company focuses primarily on multifamily and office properties located in the Western US, UK, and Ireland. Kennedy Wilson has about $21.6 billion in Real Estate Assets under Management (AUM). The real estate that it holds in its global portfolio consists primarily of multifamily apartments (about 55%) and commercial properties (about 45%) based on Consolidated NOI and JV NOI. Geographically, the company focuses on the Western US (about 60%), the UK (almost 20%) and Ireland (around 20%). Its investment activities in its Consolidated Portfolio involve ownership of multifamily units, office, retail and industrial space and one hotel. Its ownership interests in such consolidated properties make up its Consolidated Portfolio. About 60% of revenue comes from its domestic operations.

	Annual Growth	12/19	12/20	12/21	12/22	12/23
Sales ($mil.)	(0.3%)	569.7	450.9	453.6	540.0	562.6
Net income ($ mil.)	-	226.7	110.1	330.4	93.7	(303.8)
Market value ($ mil.)	(13.7%)	3,093.6	2,481.8	3,312.8	2,182.2	1,717.4
Employees	(5.0%)	318	202	220	230	259

KENNESAW STATE UNIVERSITY

1000 CHASTAIN RD NW
KENNESAW, GA 301445591
Phone: 770 423-6000
Fax: -
Web: www.kennesaw.edu

CEO: -
CFO: -
HR: -
FYE: June 30
Type: Private

Kennesaw State University (KSU) is a comprehensive university located on two suburban campuses in Kennesaw and Marietta, northwest of metro Atlanta. The college offers over 180 undergraduate and graduate degree programs, including bachelor's, master's, and doctorate programs in the core areas of nursing, business, and education, as well as such subjects as public administration, information technology, and social work. KSU enrolls nearly 43,000 students at its two campuses in the Atlanta metropolitan area. The university is the third largest member of the University System of Georgia, after University of Georgia and Georgia State.

	Annual Growth	06/06	06/07	06/08	06/09	06/19
Sales ($mil.)	10.2%	-	99.6	113.9	116.5	321.0
Net income ($ mil.)	(10.6%)	-	10.2	10.8	(0.7)	2.7
Market value ($ mil.)	-	-	-	-	-	-
Employees	-	-	-	-	-	3,000

KENNESTONE HOSPITAL AT WINDY HILL, INC.

677 CHURCH ST NE
MARIETTA, GA 300601101
Phone: 770 793-5000
Fax: -
Web: www.wellstar.org

CEO: Thomas E Hill
CFO: Dick Stovall
HR: -
FYE: June 30
Type: Private

Kennestone cures kidney stones and other ailments for residents of Cobb County, Georgia. WellStar Kennestone Hospital has more than 630 beds and a full range of specialty services. The hospital's physicians provide cardiac care, inpatient and outpatient surgery and rehabilitation, trauma, diabetes care, oncology, dialysis, and home health care. The hospital also operates centers specializing in women's health, senior living facilities, diagnostic clinics, and a wellness and fitness center. WellStar Kennestone Hospital is part of the not-for-profit WellStar Health System, which operates hospitals and other medical facilities throughout Georgia.

	Annual Growth	06/02	06/03	06/04	06/05	06/15
Sales ($mil.)	0.3%	-	792.4	878.0	481.8	821.3
Net income ($ mil.)	12.9%	-	24.8	50.2	54.2	106.2
Market value ($ mil.)	-	-	-	-	-	-
Employees	-	-	-	-	-	2,950

KENOSHA BEEF INTERNATIONAL, LTD.

3111 152ND AVE
KENOSHA, WI 531447630
Phone: 262 859-2272
Fax: –
Web: www.joinbt.com

CEO: Charles Vignieri
CFO: Jerome D King
HR: Phyllis Murray
FYE: June 30
Type: Private

Birchwood Meat & Provision, which does business as Birchwood Foods, is one of the largest US processors of raw, frozen, and pre-cooked beef and pork products for the quick-service restaurant and retail food industries. The company produces some 6 million pounds of beef patties, pizza toppings, and taco meat per week. Its four manufacturing facilities primarily serve the Midwestern US, although the company distributes to restaurant and foodservice customers throughout the US. In addition, family-owned and -operated Birchwood serves supermarkets, club stores, and convenience stores. It also offers custom product development and private-label services.

KENSINGTON PUBLISHING CORP.

119 W 40TH ST FL 21
NEW YORK, NY 100182522
Phone: 212 407-1500
Fax: –
Web: www.kensingtonbooks.com

CEO: Steven Zacharius
CFO: Michael Rosamilia
HR: –
FYE: September 30
Type: Private

Kensington Publishing holds court with readers. The independent publisher sells hardcover, trade, and mass market fiction and non-fiction books through its Kensington, Zebra, Pinnacle, and Citadel imprints. The company publishes about 600 titles a year and has a backlist of more than 3,000. Romance and women's fiction account for more than half of its titles published each year. Other niche topics covered include wicca, gambling, gay & lesbian, and military history. Readers can turn to the company's Rebel Base Books Web site to order titles such as I Hope They Serve Beer in Hell by Tucker Max, which sold more than 70,000 copies its first year and made the New York Times Bestseller list in 2006, 2007, and 2008.

	Annual Growth	09/03	09/04	09/05	09/06	09/11
Sales ($mil.)	5.3%	–	–	47.6	57.0	64.7
Net income ($ mil.)	19.2%	–	–	1.1	1.9	3.2
Market value ($ mil.)	–	–	–	–	–	–
Employees	–	–	–	–	–	81

KENT COUNTY MEMORIAL HOSPITAL

455 TOLL GATE RD
WARWICK, RI 028862770
Phone: 401 737-7000
Fax: –
Web: www.kentri.org

CEO: –
CFO: –
HR: Judy Karneeb
FYE: September 30
Type: Private

As one of Rhode Island's largest hospitals, Kent County Memorial Hospital offers Ocean Staters a sea of medical care options. The healthcare facility provides inpatient acute care, as well as outpatient services (such as diagnostic imaging) and primary care. It also offers a range of specialties, including cardiology, orthopedics, oncology, surgery, pediatrics, and women's health. A member of the Care New England Health System, Kent Hospital opened in 1951 with 90 beds; today the hospital has about 360 beds and a staff of some 600 doctors.

	Annual Growth	09/18	09/19	09/20	09/21	09/22
Sales ($mil.)	17.3%	–	372.8	357.3	454.4	601.1
Net income ($ mil.)	–	–	1.1	(16.7)	52.1	(33.2)
Market value ($ mil.)	–	–	–	–	–	–
Employees	–	–	–	–	–	1,850

KENT STATE UNIVERSITY

1500 HORNING RD
KENT, OH 442420001
Phone: 330 672-3000
Fax: –
Web: www.kent.edu

CEO: –
CFO: –
HR: –
FYE: June 30
Type: Private

Kent State University (KSU) knows all about learning from history. The school offers some 300 degrees in art, business management, technology, medicine, biology, psychology, and other fields. Through eight campuses located in northeastern Ohio, KSU educates some 43,000 students, making it Ohio's second-largest public university (behind Ohio State). Its campuses include more than 24 residence halls, and the university encourages on-campus living. The school has a student-teacher ratio of about 20:1, and it offers both graduate and undergraduate degrees. KSU was founded in 1910 for teacher training and is one of the state's oldest universities.

	Annual Growth	06/07	06/08	06/09	06/11	06/13
Sales ($mil.)	6.4%	–	–	358.8	420.3	460.1
Net income ($ mil.)	–	–	–	(63.5)	107.3	54.9
Market value ($ mil.)	–	–	–	–	–	–
Employees	–	–	–	–	–	5,466

KENTUCKY FIRST FEDERAL BANCORP

NMS: KFFB

655 Main Street
Hazard, KY 41702
Phone: 502 223-1638
Fax: –
Web: www.ffsbky.bank

CEO: Don D Jennings
CFO: R C Hulette
HR: –
FYE: June 30
Type: Public

Kentucky First Federal wants to be second to none for banking in the Bluegrass State. Formed in 2005 to be the holding company for First Federal Savings and Loan of Hazard and First Federal Savings Bank of Frankfort, which operate three branches in the state's capital and one in the town of Hazard. The banks offer traditional deposit products, such as checking and savings accounts, NOW and money market accounts, and CDs. Lending is focused on residential mortgages, but the banks also offer loans secured by churches and commercial real estate, as well as consumer and construction loans. Kentucky First Federal, which has received final regulatory approval, is merging with CKF Bancorp.

	Annual Growth	06/19	06/20	06/21	06/22	06/23
Assets ($mil.)	1.4%	330.8	321.1	338.1	328.1	349.0
Net income ($ mil.)	3.5%	0.8	(12.5)	1.8	1.6	0.9
Market value ($ mil.)	(5.7%)	63.5	54.6	59.5	64.5	50.2
Employees	(0.8%)	64	63	62	64	62

KENTUCKY MEDICAL SERVICES FOUNDATION, INC.

2333 ALUMNI PARK PLZ STE 200
LEXINGTON, KY 405174012
Phone: 859 257-7910
Fax: –
Web: www.kmsf.com

CEO: –
CFO: –
HR: –
FYE: June 30
Type: Private

Does the mailbox at your old Kentucky home contain doctors' bills? They might be from Kentucky Medical Services Foundation. The physician's practice group provides billing and other administrative services for the more than 600 physicians and other health care providers affiliated with the University of Kentucky's health system, UK HealthCare. The network provides more than 80 specialty services, offers educational programs, and operates acute medical centers including Chandler Hospital, Good Samaritan Hospital, and Kentucky Children's Hospital.

	Annual Growth	06/13	06/14	06/15	06/21	06/22
Sales ($mil.)	4.8%	–	236.2	306.7	425.4	344.3
Net income ($ mil.)	–	–	1.7	11.0	0.5	(0.8)
Market value ($ mil.)	–	–	–	–	–	–
Employees	–	–	–	–	–	150

KENTUCKY NEIGHBORHOOD BANK, INC.

1000 N DIXIE AVE
ELIZABETHTOWN, KY 427012526
Phone: 270 737-6000
Fax: –
Web: www.bankknb.com

CEO: –
CFO: –
HR: –
FYE: December 31
Type: Private

Kentucky National Bancorp is the holding company for Kentucky National Bank (KNB), which offers traditional banking services through two branches and a loan production office in Hardin County, Kentucky. Consumers get access to both fixed-rate and adjustable-rate mortgages, as well as construction loans for those in the market to build a new home. Business customers can choose a Business Analysis account, where the bank analyzes the activities of the business account and offsets the banking costs based on that activity. KNB was founded in 1997.

	Annual Growth	12/12	12/13	12/14	12/15	12/16
Assets ($mil.)	1.0%	–	128.7	132.0	134.6	132.5
Net income ($ mil.)	(22.2%)	–	1.3	0.9	1.0	0.6
Market value ($ mil.)	–	–	–	–	–	–
Employees	–	–	–	–	–	47

KENTUCKY POWER COMPANY

1 RIVERSIDE PLZ
COLUMBUS, OH 432152355
Phone: 614 716-2654
Fax: –
Web: www.aep.com

CEO: Michael G Morris
CFO: Holly K Koeppel
HR: –
FYE: December 31
Type: Private

The sun may shine bright on old Kentucky homes, but Kentucky Power provides light regardless of the sun's hue. Organized in 1919, the utility distributes electricity to about 175,000 homes and businesses across 20 counties in eastern Kentucky. An operating unit of holding company American Electric Power (AEP), Kentucky Power also sells electricity to wholesale customers and has coal-fired power plant interests that, combined, have a generating capacity of more than 1,060 MW. The company operates more than 11,040 miles of overhead transmission and distribution power lines.

	Annual Growth	12/04	12/05	12/06	12/15	12/16
Sales ($mil.)	2.0%	–	531.3	585.9	–	662.0
Net income ($ mil.)	8.3%	–	20.8	35.0	–	50.2
Market value ($ mil.)	–	–	–	–	–	–
Employees	–	–	–	–	–	466

KENTUCKY UTILITIES COMPANY INC

1 QUALITY ST
LEXINGTON, KY 405071462
Phone: 502 627-2000
Fax: –
Web: www.lge-ku.com

CEO: Paul W Thompson
CFO: Kent W Blake
HR: –
FYE: December 31
Type: Private

Kentucky Utilities may not be as bright as the blue moon of Kentucky, but it still shines bright on those in the Bluegrass State. The company, founded in 1912, was a subsidiary of E.ON U.S. It generates and distributes electricity to more than 485,250 industrial and residential customers in a 6,600 square mile area in Kentucky. The company's Old Dominion Power serves about 30,000 customers in five Virginia counties. Kentucky Utilities has a total generation capacity of approximately 4,570 MW. In 2010 E.ON U.S. was acquired by PPL as that company consolidated its holdings in the region.

KENYON COLLEGE

1 KENYON COLLEGE
GAMBIER, OH 430229623
Phone: 740 427-5000
Fax: –
Web: www.kenyon.edu

CEO: –
CFO: –
HR: –
FYE: June 30
Type: Private

Kenyon College is a small liberal arts school located approximately 45 miles northeast of Columbus, Ohio. With an enrollment of some 1,600 students, the school offers bachelor's degrees in more than 30 majors in fields such as fine arts, humanities, natural sciences, and social sciences. Notable alumni include actor Paul Newman and poet Robert Lowell. The college also produces renowned literary journal The Kenyon Review. The oldest private institution of higher education in Ohio, Kenyon College was founded in 1824 by Philander Chase, an Episcopal bishop.

	Annual Growth	06/05	06/06	06/08	06/16	06/17
Sales ($mil.)	(0.5%)	–	131.9	123.7	116.6	124.3
Net income ($ mil.)	(2.1%)	–	58.6	24.6	(9.2)	46.3
Market value ($ mil.)	–	–	–	–	–	–
Employees	–	–	–	–	–	450

KEPNER-TREGOE, INC.

103 CARNEGIE CTR STE 205
PRINCETON, NJ 085406235
Phone: 609 921-2806
Fax: –
Web: www.kepner-tregoe.com

CEO: William Baldwin
CFO: –
HR: –
FYE: December 31
Type: Private

Kepner-Tregoe provides management consulting and executive development services to clients in such industries as aerospace, consumer products manufacturing, financial services, and information technology. Through its years of research on effective management, the company trains organizations in their decision-making and management processes. Its training services include corporate on-site training and public workshops, as well as workforce development programs delivered through community and technical colleges in the US and Canada. Former RAND Corporation researchers Charles Kepner and Benjamin Tregoe started the firm in 1958.

	Annual Growth	12/02	12/03	12/04	12/05	12/07
Sales ($mil.)	0.5%	–	40.0	41.1	42.7	40.8
Net income ($ mil.)	(10.7%)	–	0.7	0.7	0.3	0.5
Market value ($ mil.)	–	–	–	–	–	–
Employees	–	–	–	–	–	175

KETTERING ADVENTIST HEALTHCARE

3535 SOUTHERN BLVD
DAYTON, OH 454291221
Phone: 937 298-4331
Fax: –
Web: www.ketteringhealth.org

CEO: Michael Gentry
CFO: –
HR: Amanda Koch
FYE: December 31
Type: Private

Kettering Adventist Healthcare, dba Kettering Health Network and named for famed inventor Charles F. Kettering, is an Ohio-based health care system. It comprises about 120 outpatient facilities, including seven acute care hospitals: Kettering Medical Center, Grandview Medical Center, Sycamore Medical Center, Southview Medical Center, Fort Hamilton Hospital, Greene Memorial Hospital, and Soin Medical Center. Other facilities include Kettering Behavioral Hospital and multiple outpatient, diagnostic, senior care, and urgent care clinics. Among its specialized services are heart care, rehabilitation, orthopedics, women's health, and emergency medicine.

	Annual Growth	12/16	12/17	12/19	12/21	12/22
Sales ($mil.)	7.0%	–	1,753.8	40.9	2,375.9	2,459.4
Net income ($ mil.)	–	–	171.3	3.0	192.9	(182.4)
Market value ($ mil.)	–	–	–	–	–	–
Employees	–	–	–	–	–	6,800

KETTERING UNIVERSITY

1700 UNIVERSITY AVE
FLINT, MI 485044898
Phone: 810 762-9500
Fax: –
Web: www.kettering.edu

CEO: –
CFO: –
HR: –
FYE: June 30
Type: Private

Sometimes referred to as the "West Point of Industry," Kettering University specializes in engineering, science, and mathematics programs. Other academic fields include business, pre-law, pre-med, and computer gaming. The private school offers about 15 undergraduate degrees and five graduate degrees to a small student body of more than 1,680. As part of its cooperative educational framework, the school provides academic credit for structured job experience. Kettering's students work with employers in aerospace, accounting, government, law, medical, and not-for-profits and research firms, in addition to companies in the manufacturing sector. Its student/faculty ratio is 13:1.

	Annual Growth	06/16	06/17	06/19	06/20	06/21
Sales ($mil.)	4.3%	–	65.0	82.1	64.1	76.8
Net income ($ mil.)	36.0%	–	11.1	19.2	(3.2)	37.8
Market value ($ mil.)	–	–	–	–	–	–
Employees						425

KEUKA COLLEGE

141 CENTRAL AVE
KEUKA PARK, NY 144789764
Phone: 315 279-5000
Fax: –
Web: www.keuka.edu

CEO: –
CFO: Jerry Hiller
HR: –
FYE: June 30
Type: Private

In 1890 Emily Dickinson's first volume of poetry was published, the Battle of Wounded Knee took place, Otto von Bismarck resigned as Germany's prime minister, and Keuka College was founded in New York's Finger Lakes region. Today the liberal arts school has about 1,600 students working toward around 35 undergraduate and graduate degrees; its focus is on experiential learning, which includes annual internship periods. An additional 3,000 Chinese students attend Keuka College in mainland China.

	Annual Growth	06/18	06/19	06/20	06/21	06/22
Sales ($mil.)	8.3%	–	41.1	42.6	55.5	52.3
Net income ($ mil.)	(20.8%)	–	1.5	4.4	4.0	0.7
Market value ($ mil.)	–	–	–	–	–	–
Employees						253

KEURIG DR PEPPER INC

NMS: KDP

53 South Avenue
Burlington, MA 01803
Phone: 781 418-7000
Fax: –
Web: www.keurig.com

CEO: Robert J Gamgort
CFO: Sudhanshu Priyadarshi
HR: Lindsay Devagno
FYE: December 31
Type: Public

Keurig Dr Pepper (KDP) is a leading beverage company in North America, with a diverse portfolio of flavored carbonated soft drinks, and non-carbonated beverages, including water (enhanced and flavored), ready-to-drink tea and coffee, juice, juice drinks, mixers and specialty coffee. It is a leading producer of innovative single-serve brewing systems. It owns the top single-serve coffee system in the US (Keurig) and one of the US's leading soft drinks (Dr Pepper), as well as Green Mountain coffee, Canada Dry, A&W root beer, Snapple tea and juice, and Mott's fruit juice, among many other products. Serving major retailers in the US, Canada, and Mexico, the company generates majority of its sales from the US.

	Annual Growth	12/19	12/20	12/21	12/22	12/23
Sales ($mil.)	7.4%	11,120	11,618	12,683	14,057	14,814
Net income ($ mil.)	14.8%	1,254.0	1,325.0	2,146.0	1,436.0	2,181.0
Market value ($ mil.)	3.6%	40,253	44,494	51,252	49,583	46,330
Employees	2.5%	25,500	27,000	27,500	28,000	28,100

KEURIG GREEN MOUNTAIN, INC.

1 ROTARIAN PL
WATERBURY, VT 056761582
Phone: 877 879-2326
Fax: –
Web: www.keurigdrpepper.com

CEO: Robert Gamgort
CFO: Peter Leemputt
HR: Johanna Starrett
FYE: September 27
Type: Private

Keurig Green Mountain's business amounts to far more than a hill of beans. The company (formerly Green Mountain Coffee Roasters) is a leader in the specialty coffee and coffeemaker business in North America. Its Keurig subsidiary makes single-cup coffee machines for home and office use, and roasts coffee for its K-Cups and Vue portion packs. Green Mountain also roasts and packages whole bean and ground coffee and supplies apple cider, teas, cocoa, and other beverages wholesale to food stores, resorts, and office-delivery services. The company markets coffee under the Newman's Own Organics , Tully's , and Green Mountain Coffee labels. In 2016 JAB Holding Co. completed a $13.9 billion acquisition of Keurig Green Mountain.

KEWAUNEE SCIENTIFIC CORPORATION

NMS: KEQU

2700 West Front Street
Statesville, NC 28677-2927
Phone: 704 873-7202
Fax: 704 873-5160
Web: www.kewaunee.com

CEO: Thomas D Hull III
CFO: Donald T Gardner III
HR: –
FYE: April 30
Type: Public

The nutty professor once wreaked havoc on furniture like that made by Kewaunee Scientific. The company makes furniture for laboratories, including wood and steel cabinets, fume hoods, and work surfaces. It also makes technical workstations, workbenches, and computer enclosures for local area networking applications. Kewaunee's primary customers are schools, health care institutions, and labs (pharmaceutical, biotech, industrial, chemical, and commercial research). The company's products are sold through VWR International, a school and lab products supplier, as well as through designated Kewaunee dealers. Kewaunee's subsidiaries in Singapore and India handle sales in the Asian and Middle Eastern markets.

	Annual Growth	04/19	04/20	04/21	04/22	04/23
Sales ($mil.)	10.6%	146.6	147.5	147.5	168.9	219.5
Net income ($ mil.)	(16.6%)	1.5	(4.7)	(3.7)	(6.1)	0.7
Market value ($ mil.)	(7.9%)	64.0	29.0	34.0	40.4	46.0
Employees	3.5%	856	912	838	893	982

KEY CITY FURNITURE COMPANY INC

1804 RIVER ST STE C
WILKESBORO, NC 286977657
Phone: 336 818-1161
Fax: –
Web: –

CEO: –
CFO: –
HR: –
FYE: January 01
Type: Private

Family-owned and -operated since 1927, Key City Furniture has a lock on handcrafting furniture. The company operates facilities in Wilkesboro and North Wilkesboro, North Carolina. More than 400 types of furniture are made to order, including sleeper sofas, sectionals, rockers, and ottomans. The company offers its customers some 1,200 different fabrics and leathers. Key City Furniture, founded by James E. Caudill, is run by his grandsons F.D. Forester III and James Caudill Forester.

	Annual Growth	12/05	12/06	12/07*	01/09	01/10
Sales ($mil.)	(19.0%)	–	–	18.0	13.1	9.5
Net income ($ mil.)		–	–	(0.5)	(2.2)	(0.8)
Market value ($ mil.)		–	–	–	–	–
Employees		–	–	–	–	105

*Fiscal year change

KEY ENERGY SERVICES INC (DE)   NBB: KEGX

1301 McKinney Street, Suite 1800
Houston, TX 77010
Phone: 713 651-4300
Fax: –
Web: www.keyenergy.com

CEO: J M Dodson
CFO: J M Dodson Sr
HR: Kendall Lasseigne
FYE: December 31
Type: Public

Key Energy Services provides a wide array of leading edge energy production solutions and services. The company provides services such as well servicing, rental services, and cementing and abandonment to major and independent oil companies. Through its highly trained and experienced crews, technical expertise, state-of-the-art data analytics, and fit for purpose equipment, it enables America's E&P companies, from small independents to majors, get the most out of the life of their wells.

	Annual Growth	12/16	12/16	12/17	12/18	12/19
Sales ($mil.)	1.2%	399.4	17.8	436.2	521.7	413.9
Net income ($ mil.)	–	(131.7)	(10.2)	(120.6)	(88.8)	(97.4)
Market value ($ mil.)	–	–	13.1	4.8	0.9	0.0
Employees	–	–	3,225	3,000	2,600	2,000

KEY FOOD STORES CO-OPERATIVE, INC.

100 MATAWAN RD STE 100
MATAWAN, NJ 077473913
Phone: 718 370-4200
Fax: –
Web: www.keyfood.com

CEO: Dean Janeway
CFO: –
HR: –
FYE: April 25
Type: Private

Key Food Stores Co-Operative is a friend to independent New York area grocers. The co-op provides retail support and other services to 150 independently owned food retailers in the New York City area. Key Food's member-owners run stores mainly in Brooklyn and Queens, but also in the other boroughs and surrounding counties. It operates stores primarily under the Key Food banner, but it also has Key Food Marketplace locations that feature expanded meat, deli, and produce departments. In addition, the co-op supplies Key Foods-branded products to member stores. Among its members are Pick Quick Foods, Dan's Supreme Super Markets, Gemstone Supermarkets, and Queens Supe rmarkets. Key Foods was founded in 1937.

KEY TECHNOLOGY, INC.

150 AVERY ST
WALLA WALLA, WA 993624703
Phone: 509 529-2161
Fax: –
Web: www.key.net

CEO: Michael J Kachmer
CFO: Craig Reuther
HR: –
FYE: September 30
Type: Private

Key Technology is a worldwide leader in food processing technology. The company makes conveyor and sorting systems for the pharmaceutical, nutraceutical, and leafy green industries, among others. It provides food processing technology, and ongoing innovations provide increased control, continuous processing, and longer machine life in processed food, fruits and vegetables, nuts, dried fruits, fresh cut produce and more. In addition, it is the premier choice for the most comprehensive source of digital sorting, conveying, and process automation technology. The company operates in around 80 countries and has grown to serve some 10 industries. Founded in 1948, Key Technology is a Duravant Company.

KEY TRONIC CORP   NMS: KTCC

4424 North Sullivan Road
Spokane Valley, WA 99216
Phone: 509 928-8000
Fax: –
Web: www.keytronic.com

CEO: Craig D Gates
CFO: Brett R Larsen
HR: –
FYE: July 1
Type: Public

Key Tronic is a leading independent manufacturer of keyboards for computers in the US. The company's unique strategic attributes are based on its core strengths of innovative design and engineering expertise in electronics, mechanical engineering, sheet metal fabrication and stamping, and precision plastics combined with high-quality, low cost production, and assembly on an international basis while providing exceptional customer service. Its fully integrated design, tooling, and automated manufacturing capabilities enabled it to rapidly respond to customers' needs for keyboards in production quantities worldwide. The company provides integrated electronic and mechanical engineering, precision plastic molding, sheet metal fabrication, printed circuit board (PCB) and complete product assembly, component selection, sourcing and procurement, and worldwide logistics. Customers in the US generate about 80% of revenue.

	Annual Growth	06/19	06/20*	07/21	07/22	07/23
Sales ($mil.)	6.1%	464.0	449.5	518.7	531.8	588.1
Net income ($ mil.)	–	(8.0)	4.8	4.3	3.4	5.2
Market value ($ mil.)	3.3%	53.6	56.6	70.5	46.0	61.0
Employees	7.6%	4,067	5,741	5,450	4,897	5,447

*Fiscal year change

KEYCORP   NYS: KEY

127 Public Square
Cleveland, OH 44114-1306
Phone: 216 689-3000
Fax: –
Web: www.key.com

CEO: Christopher M Gorman
CFO: –
HR: –
FYE: December 31
Type: Public

KeyCorp is one of the nation's largest bank-based financial services companies, with consolidated total assets of approximately $189.8 billion. KeyBank, a subsidiary of KeyCorp, operates more than 970 branches and a network of more than 1,265 ATMs in some 15 states across the US. Through KeyBank and certain other subsidiaries, the company provides a wide range of retail and commercial banking, commercial leasing, investment management, consumer finance, student loan refinancing, commercial mortgage servicing and special servicing, and investment banking products and services to individual, corporate, and institutional clients. The company also provides other financial services through various nonbank subsidiaries. These services include community development financing, securities underwriting, investment banking and capital markets products, brokerage, and merchant services to businesses. The company generates the majority of its revenue from the US customers.

	Annual Growth	12/19	12/20	12/21	12/22	12/23
Assets ($mil.)	6.8%	144,988	170,336	186,346	189,813	188,281
Net income ($ mil.)	(13.4%)	1,717.0	1,343.0	2,625.0	1,917.0	967.0
Market value ($ mil.)	(8.2%)	18,956	15,369	21,663	16,315	13,487
Employees	0.4%	17,045	16,826	17,654	18,891	17,333

KEYSIGHT TECHNOLOGIES INC   NYS: KEYS

1400 Fountaingrove Parkway
Santa Rosa, CA 95403
Phone: 800 829-4444
Fax: –
Web: www.investor.keysight.com

CEO: Satish C Dhanasekaran
CFO: Neil Dougherty
HR: –
FYE: October 31
Type: Public

Keysight Technologies provides electronic measurement instruments? oscilloscopes, meters, and network analyzers?and design, test, and measurement software used to make electronics equipment. It also offers instrument productivity and application services and instrument calibration and repair, as well as consulting services throughout the product life cycle. Keysight has more than 18,000 direct customers and approximately 30,000 customers and large, worldwide install base with accounts primarily in the communications, networking, and electronics industries. About 40% of total revenue comes from US customers.

	Annual Growth	10/19	10/20	10/21	10/22	10/23
Sales ($mil.)	6.2%	4,303.0	4,221.0	4,941.0	5,420.0	5,464.0
Net income ($ mil.)	14.2%	621.0	627.0	894.0	1,124.0	1,057.0
Market value ($ mil.)	4.9%	17,591	18,281	31,381	30,358	21,276
Employees	2.3%	13,600	13,900	14,300	15,000	14,900

KEYSTONE CONSOLIDATED INDUSTRIES, INC.

5430 LYNDON B JOHNSON FWY STE 1740
DALLAS, TX 752402601
Phone: 800 441-0308
Fax: –
Web: www.kci-corp.com

CEO: Chris Armstrong
CFO: Bert E Downing Jr
HR: –
FYE: December 31
Type: Private

Keystone Consolidated Industries can wire your world. The company, mainly through its Keystone Steel & Wire division (86% of the company's 2011 revenues), makes fabricated wire products, including fencing, barbed wire, welded wire, and woven wire mesh for the agricultural, construction, and do-it-yourself markets. Many of its products are sold under the Red Brand label. A vertically integrated company with its own steel mininmill, Keystone (which is a subsidiary of Contran), also makes industrial wire -- used to make such items as barbecue grills, coat hangers, and nails -- and carbon steel rod.

KEYSTONE DEDICATED LOGISTICS CO LLC

111 RYAN CT
PITTSBURGH, PA 152051310
Phone: 412 429-2141
Fax: –
Web: www.kdlog.com

CEO: –
CFO: –
HR: –
FYE: December 31
Type: Private

Keystone Dedicated Logistics (KDL) provides freight transportation management services. Working with a network of independent carriers, the company can arrange the transportation of shipments ranging in size from small packages to full truckloads. KDL also provides warehousing and distribution and supply chain management services, along with international air and ocean freight forwarding. Customers have included Calgon Carbon and RHI. KDL -- which does business as KDL Freight Management -- was founded in 1999 as a subsidiary of trucking company Pitt Ohio Express. Pitt Ohio Express spun off KDL in 2003.

	Annual Growth	12/06	12/07	12/08	12/09	12/10
Sales ($mil.)	(2.9%)	–	–	21.8	16.1	20.5
Net income ($ mil.)	26.7%	–	–	2.3	1.8	3.7
Market value ($ mil.)	–	–	–	–	–	–
Employees	–	–	–	–	–	50

KFORCE INC.

NMS: KFRC

1150 Assembly Drive, Suite 500
Tampa, FL 33607
Phone: 813 552-5000
Fax: –
Web: www.kforce.com

CEO: Joseph J Liberatore
CFO: David M Kelly
HR: Cynthia Jones
FYE: December 31
Type: Public

Kforce is a leading domestic provider of technology and finance and accounting talent solutions primarily to many innovative and industry-leading companies. Kforce provides career opportunities for approximately 25,000 highly skilled professionals on a temporary, consulting, or direct-hire basis. These professionals work with approximately 2,500 clients, including a significant majority of the Fortune 500, helping them conquer challenges and meet their digital transformation goals. Kforce serves clients across a diverse set of industries and organizations of all sizes, but the company places a particular focus on serving Fortune 500 and other large companies. While Kforce was incorporated in 1994 and completed its initial public offering in 1995, Kforce has been providing domestic staffing services through its predecessor companies since 1962.

	Annual Growth	12/19	12/20	12/21	12/22	12/23
Sales ($mil.)	3.3%	1,347.4	1,397.7	1,579.9	1,710.8	1,531.8
Net income ($ mil.)	(17.3%)	130.9	56.0	75.2	75.4	61.1
Market value ($ mil.)	14.2%	775.0	821.6	1,468.4	1,070.3	1,318.8
Employees	(38.9%)	12,900	13,900	13,000	12,000	1,800

KGBO HOLDINGS, INC.

4289 IVY POINTE BLVD
CINCINNATI, OH 452450002
Phone: 513 831-2600
Fax: –
Web: –

CEO: –
CFO: –
HR: Tracy Burnett
FYE: December 30
Type: Private

Total Quality Logistics sets a high standard for moving merchandise. The third-party logistics (non-asset based) provider specializes in arranging freight transportation using reefers (refrigerated trucks), vans, and flatbeds -- moving in excess of 500,000 loads each year. The trucking brokerage company serves more than 7,000 clients across the US, Canada, and Mexico, ranging from small businesses to Fortune 500 organizations. Founded in 1997 by company president Ken Oaks, Total Quality Logistics (TQL) has contracts with carriers that include single owner operators and large fleets. Customers have included Kroger, Dole Food, and Laura's Lean Beef.

	Annual Growth	12/08	12/09	12/10	12/11	12/12
Sales ($mil.)	34.9%	–	–	762.1	1,046.7	1,387.4
Net income ($ mil.)	–	–	–	–	–	–
Market value ($ mil.)	–	–	–	–	–	–
Employees	–	–	–	–	–	4,077

KID BRANDS, INC.

NBB: KIDB Q

301 Route 17 North, 6th Floor
Rutherford, NJ 07070
Phone: 201 405-2400
Fax: 204 405-7355
Web: www.kidbrands.com

CEO: –
CFO: –
HR: –
FYE: December 31
Type: Public

Kid Brands sells products for brand-new people: newborns to 3-year-olds. Through its subsidiaries, the company designs, imports, and markets infant and juvenile bedding and furniture, as well as related nursery accessories. It also peddles infant-development toys and teething, feeding, and bath and baby care products. Kid Brands' principal subsidiaries include Sassy, Kids Line, LaJobi, and CoCaLo. The company also makes juvenile products under license from Carters, Disney, Graco, and Serta. Founded in 1963 by the late Russell Berrie, the company (formerly Russ Berrie and Co.) changed its name to Kid Brands in 2009 to underscore its shift to infant and juvenile products.

	Annual Growth	12/09	12/10	12/11	12/12	12/13
Sales ($mil.)	(6.3%)	243.9	275.8	252.6	229.5	188.2
Net income ($ mil.)	–	11.7	34.7	(38.6)	(54.1)	(28.8)
Market value ($ mil.)	(30.5%)	96.7	188.8	69.8	34.2	22.5
Employees	(3.1%)	340	304	320	300	300

KID GALAXY, INC.

150 DOW ST STE 425B
MANCHESTER, NH 031011254
Phone: 603 645-6252
Fax: –
Web: www.kidgalaxy.com

CEO: –
CFO: –
HR: –
FYE: March 31
Type: Private

Kid Galaxy wants kids to think its toys are outta this world. The company makes land (DRV, Morphibians), air (Hyper Flyer planes), and water toys (submarines), as well as foam toys and mini remote control vehicles known as KG Racers, as well as pre-school lines called My First RC and Little Universe. Kid Galaxy sells its products in Australia, Canada, China, Japan, the UK, and the US, as well as through sales outlets in Hong Kong. The US is the biggest market for Kid Galaxy's toys. Founded in 1994, Kid Galaxy is a subsidiary of Lung Cheong International Holdings Limited, which acquired the toymaker in 2002.

	Annual Growth	03/15	03/16	03/17	03/18	03/19
Sales ($mil.)	32.8%	–	9.5	8.9	15.8	22.2
Net income ($ mil.)	–	–	0.5	(0.7)	(0.3)	(1.1)
Market value ($ mil.)	–	–	–	–	–	–
Employees	–	–	–	–	–	11

KILGORE JUNIOR COLLEGE DISTRICT

1100 BROADWAY BLVD
KILGORE, TX 756623299
Phone: 903 983-8105
Fax: -
Web: www.kilgore.edu

CEO: -
CFO: Duane J McNaney
HR: Jerri Saenz
FYE: August 31
Type: Private

Kilgore College is a community college that offers a variety of academic programs, as well as occupational and technical degrees and certificates, including Associate of Arts, Associate of Science, and Associate of Applied Science. The college offers training in cosmetology, nursing, law enforcement, manufacturing technology, and numerous other vocational fields. It is also the home of athletic program, an agriculture demonstration farm, the Rangerettes, the East Texas Oil Museum, and the Texas Shakespeare Festival. Kilgore College is accredited by the Commission on Colleges of the Southern Association of Colleges and Schools.

	Annual Growth	08/15	08/16	08/17	08/19	08/22
Sales ($mil.)	(26.0%)	-	14.9	16.4	4.6	2.5
Net income ($ mil.)	-	-	(1.7)	1.4	2.1	(0.8)
Market value ($ mil.)	-	-	-	-	-	-
Employees	-	-	-	-	-	310

KILLBUCK BANCSHARES, INC.

165 North Main Street, P.O. Box 407
Killbuck, OH 44637
Phone: 330 276-2771
Fax: 330 276-0216
Web: www.killbuckbank.com

NBB: KLIB
CEO: -
CFO: -
HR: -
FYE: December 31
Type: Public

Interestingly enough, if you want to save a buck, you can take your doe to Killbuck. Killbuck Bancshares is the holding company for The Killbuck Savings Bank, which operates about 10 branches in northeast Ohio. It offers traditional retail products to individuals and small to midsized businesses, including checking and savings accounts, credit cards, and IRAs. Residential and commercial mortgages make up about two-thirds of its loan portfolio, which also includes business loans and consumer loans. Killbuck Bancshares is the #1 financial institution in Holmes County, where most of its offices are located. It also has branches in Knox and Tuscarawas counties.

	Annual Growth	12/11	12/12	12/13	12/14	12/15
Assets ($mil.)	3.1%	436.5	460.4	461.8	479.8	492.3
Net income ($ mil.)	12.3%	2.9	3.3	3.6	4.1	4.6
Market value ($ mil.)	0.4%	65.4	65.2	61.9	67.0	66.4
Employees	-	-	121	-	-	-

KILROY REALTY CORP

12200 W. Olympic Boulevard, Suite 200
Los Angeles, CA 90064
Phone: 310 481-8400
Fax: -
Web: www.kilroyrealty.com

NYS: KRC
CEO: John Kilroy
CFO: Eliott Trencher
HR: Pauleen Hudson
FYE: December 31
Type: Public

Kilroy is a self-administered real estate investment trust (REIT), which operates in premier office and mixed-use submarkets in the US. Kilroy Realty owns, manages, and develops Class A office space, mostly in Greater Los Angeles, San Diego County, the San Francisco Bay Area, Greater Seattle and Austin, Texas. Its portfolio includes about 120 office properties encompassing about 15 million square feet of leasable space. In addition, the company also boasts six future development sites, which accounts for about 60 gross acres of undeveloped land. A majority of Kilroy Realty's more than 420 tenants are involved in technology, media, healthcare, and entertainment.

	Annual Growth	12/19	12/20	12/21	12/22	12/23
Sales ($mil.)	7.8%	837.5	898.4	955.0	1,097.0	1,129.7
Net income ($ mil.)	2.1%	195.4	187.1	628.1	232.6	212.2
Market value ($ mil.)	(17.0%)	9,836.4	6,729.6	7,791.7	4,533.7	4,670.8
Employees	(1.8%)	267	252	244	259	248

KIMBALL ELECTRONICS INC

1205 Kimball Boulevard
Jasper, IN 47546
Phone: 812 634-4000
Fax: -
Web: www.kimballelectronics.com

NMS: KE
CEO: Richard D Phillips
CFO: Michael K Sergesketter
HR: Bonnie Wininger
FYE: June 30
Type: Public

Kimball Electronics is a global, multifaceted manufacturing solutions provider of contract electronics manufacturing services (EMS) and diversified manufacturing services, including engineering and supply chain support, to customers in the automotive, medical, industrial, and public safety end markets. It offers a package of value that begins with its core competency of producing durable electronics and has expanded into diversified contract manufacturing services for non-electronic components, medical disposables, precision molded plastics, and production automation, test, and inspection equipment. It delivers award-winning service across its global footprint with an operations platform driven by highly integrated procedures, standardization, and teamwork. Kimball Electronics generates its largest revenue domestically. The company was founded in 1961 and incorporated in 1998.

	Annual Growth	06/19	06/20	06/21	06/22	06/23
Sales ($mil.)	11.5%	1,181.8	1,200.6	1,291.8	1,349.5	1,823.4
Net income ($ mil.)	15.3%	31.6	18.2	56.8	31.3	55.8
Market value ($ mil.)	14.2%	401.5	334.8	537.5	497.0	683.1
Employees	5.8%	6,300	6,400	6,400	7,200	7,900

KIMBALL MEDICAL CENTER INC.

600 RIVER AVE
LAKEWOOD, NJ 087015281
Phone: 732 363-1900
Fax: -
Web: www.saintbarnabas.com

CEO: -
CFO: -
HR: -
FYE: December 31
Type: Private

Kimball Medical Center knows that life on the Jersey Shore isn't always as beachy as it's cracked up to be. Kimball Medical Center is a 350-bed acute care hospital and part of the Saint Barnabas Health Care System. Located in Lakewood, the medical center serves the southern Monmouth and Ocean counties of New Jersey. Services include cancer treatment, rehabilitation, emergency care, maternity and pediatrics, and occupational medicine. The hospital also offers wellness and health education programs and support groups at its Center For Healthy Living.

	Annual Growth	12/07	12/08	12/12	12/15	12/16
Sales ($mil.)	(4.1%)	-	147.9	141.8	108.9	106.0
Net income ($ mil.)	-	-	(18.0)	(3.3)	9.7	5.2
Market value ($ mil.)	-	-	-	-	-	-
Employees	-	-	-	-	-	1,500

KIMBELL ART FOUNDATION

3333 CAMP BOWIE BLVD
FORT WORTH, TX 761072744
Phone: 817 336-6100
Fax: -
Web: www.kimbellart.org

CEO: -
CFO: -
HR: -
FYE: December 31
Type: Private

Kimbell Art Foundation, established in 1935 by Kay Kimbell, operates the Kimbell Art Museum in Fort Worth, Texas. The first-rate public art museum (opened in 1972 and built by American architect Louis Kahn) got started with a gift from Kimbell of of several hundred works of art. With a permanent collection comprised of fewer than 350 works of art, the collection is distinguished by its artistic quality and importance. Today, the museum houses pieces dating from antiquity into the 20th century. When Kimbell died in 1964, he left his fortune to the Kimbell Art Foundation to establish and support the Kimbell Art Museum.

	Annual Growth	12/15	12/16	12/17	12/18	12/21
Sales ($mil.)	18.0%	-	22.9	29.4	43.2	52.3
Net income ($ mil.)	-	-	(8.0)	2.6	16.1	14.2
Market value ($ mil.)	-	-	-	-	-	-
Employees	-	-	-	-	-	110

KIMBERLY-CLARK CORP.

NYS: KMB

P.O. Box 619100
Dallas, TX 75261-9100
Phone: 972 281-1200
Fax: –
Web: www.kimberly-clark.com

CEO: Michael D Hsu
CFO: Nelson Urdaneta
HR: Emily Swan
FYE: December 31
Type: Public

Kimberly-Clark is a global company that delivers products and solutions that provide better care. The company is principally engaged in the manufacturing and marketing of a wide range of products mostly made from natural or synthetic fibers using advanced technologies in fibers, nonwovens and absorbency. Kimberly-Clark's largest unit, Personal Care, makes products such as diapers (Huggies, Pull-Ups), feminine care items (Kotex), and incontinence care products (Poise, Depend). Through its Consumer Tissue segment, the manufacturer offers facial and bathroom tissues, paper towels, and other household items under the names Cottonelle, Kleenex, Viva, and Scott (plus the Scott Naturals line). Kimberly-Clark's K-C Professional unit makes WypAll commercial wipes, among other items. North America accounts for more than 50% of Kimberly-Clark's sales.

	Annual Growth	12/19	12/20	12/21	12/22	12/23
Sales ($mil.)	2.6%	18,450	19,140	19,440	20,175	20,431
Net income ($ mil.)	(4.9%)	2,157.0	2,352.0	1,814.0	1,934.0	1,764.0
Market value ($ mil.)	(3.1%)	46,354	45,438	48,164	45,748	40,949
Employees	0.6%	40,000	46,000	45,000	44,000	41,000

KIMCO REALTY CORP

NYS: KIM

500 North Broadway, Suite 201
Jericho, NY 11753
Phone: 516 869-9000
Fax: –
Web: www.kimcorealty.com

CEO: Conor C Flynn
CFO: Glenn G Cohen
HR: Paul Weinberg
FYE: December 31
Type: Public

Kimco Realty is a self-administered real estate investment trust (REIT) that owns or has interests in around 530 community shopping centers with some 90 million sq. ft. of leasable space in metropolitan areas in about 30 states. In addition, the company had about 25 other property interests, primarily through the company's preferred equity investments and other real estate investments, totaling 5.7 million square feet of GLA. Kimco properties are usually anchored by a grocery store, off-price retailer, discounter or service-oriented tenant. Home Depot, Ahold Delhaize, TJX, Albertsons, and Amazon are its largest tenants. Through subsidiaries, the company also develops shopping centers and provides real estate management and disposition services to retailers.

	Annual Growth	12/19	12/20	12/21	12/22	12/23
Sales ($mil.)	11.4%	1,158.9	1,057.9	1,364.6	1,727.7	1,783.4
Net income ($ mil.)	12.4%	410.6	1,000.8	844.1	126.0	654.3
Market value ($ mil.)	0.7%	12,838	9,304.3	15,280	13,129	13,209
Employees	7.1%	502	484	606	639	660

KINDER MORGAN INC.

NYS: KMI

1001 Louisiana Street, Suite 1000
Houston, TX 77002
Phone: 713 369-9000
Fax: –
Web: www.kindermorgan.com

CEO: Steven J Kean
CFO: David P Michels
HR: –
FYE: December 31
Type: Public

Kinder Morgan, Inc. (KMI) is one of the largest energy infrastructure companies in North America. It operates approximately 83,000 miles of pipelines and about 140 terminals that transport natural gas, renewable fuels, refined petroleum products, crude oil, condensate, CO2, and other products to its customers across America. Its terminals store and handle various commodities, including gasoline, diesel fuel, renewable fuel feedstocks, chemical, ethanol, metals, and petroleum coke. KMI owns and operates 37.5% of Natural Gas Pipeline Company of America (NGPL). It generates most of its revenue in the US.

	Annual Growth	12/19	12/20	12/21	12/22	12/23
Sales ($mil.)	3.8%	13,209	11,700	16,610	19,200	15,334
Net income ($ mil.)	2.2%	2,190.0	119.0	1,784.0	2,548.0	2,391.0
Market value ($ mil.)	(4.5%)	46,992	30,344	35,205	40,133	39,156
Employees	83.8%	954	10,524	10,529	10,525	10,891

KINETIC SYSTEMS, INC.

4309 HACIENDA DR STE 450
PLEASANTON, CA 945882737
Phone: 510 683-6000
Fax: –
Web: www.kinetics.net

CEO: –
CFO: –
HR: –
FYE: December 31
Type: Private

Kinetic Systems stays in motion. The company (known as Kinetics) provides process and mechanical systems primarily to the microelectronics, solar energy, and biopharmaceutical industries in the Americas, Asia, and Europe. It installs gas, chemical, water, and utility systems, as well as fabricated steel pipe, HVAC, and plumbing systems. While most of its work is done designing and constructing laboratories and manufacturing facilities, Kinetics also installs systems for data centers, condominiums, schools, and water treatment plants. Kinetics has served clients including AMD, Merck, and Pepsi. Founded in 1973, the firm is controlled by Ares Management.

	Annual Growth	12/14	12/15	12/16	12/17	12/18
Sales ($mil.)	53.0%	–	–	–	112.4	172.0
Net income ($ mil.)	129.5%	–	–	–	0.6	1.5
Market value ($ mil.)	–	–	–	–	–	–
Employees	–	–	–	–	–	500

KING FISH MEDIA, LLC

900 CUMMINGS CTR STE 307V
BEVERLY, MA 019156181
Phone: 978 745-4140
Fax: –
Web: www.kingfishmedia.com

CEO: –
CFO: Mary Miller
HR: –
FYE: December 31
Type: Private

Call it "Field of Dreams" marketing. King Fish Media will build the content in the hopes that sales will come. Providing an alternative to traditional advertising, the company offers custom publishing and content creation services serving business-to-business and business-to-consumer clients. The company creates custom content in the form of newsletters, magazines, Web sites, or Webcasts designed to enhance customer loyalty and retention by becoming a reliable source of information within their market. In addition to its publishing services, the company offers event planning options which help clients find new prospects and increase customer retention using seminars, roundtables, and conferences.

KING RANCH, INC.

3 RIVERWAY STE 1600
HOUSTON, TX 770561967
Phone: 832 681-5700
Fax: –
Web: www.king-ranch.com

CEO: –
CFO: Andy Reul
HR: –
FYE: December 31
Type: Private

Meanwhile, back at the ranch ... the quite-sprawling King Ranch, to be exact. Founded in 1853, King Ranch's operations extend beyond its original 825,000 Texan cattle-raising acres. The ranch is still home to cattle and horses, of course, but King Ranch oversees considerable farming interests in its home state and elsewhere, including cotton, sorghum, sod, citrus, pecans, vegetables, and cane sugar. It also has various retail operations, such as hardware, designer saddles, publishing, and printing. In addition, King Ranch also beefs up revenues with tourist dollars from birdwatchers, hunters, and sightseers who visit its Texas ranch lands. The descendants of founder Richard King own King Ranch.

KING'S COLLEGE

133 N RIVER ST
WILKES BARRE, PA 187110801
Phone: 570 208-5900
Fax: –
Web: www.kings.edu

CEO: –
CFO: –
HR: –
FYE: June 30
Type: Private

King's College emphasizes intelligence over royalty. The school is a Catholic university offering more than 35 majors in allied health, business, education, natural science, and humanities and social sciences. King's enrolls about 2,700 undergraduate and graduate students. The school also offers about a dozen pre-professional programs, as well as special concentration programs in ethics, forensic studies, and other fields. Founded in 1946 by the Holy Cross congregation from the University of Notre Dame, the school is part of a national network of Holy Cross colleges and universities.

	Annual Growth	06/18	06/19	06/20	06/21	06/22
Sales ($mil.)	(1.5%)	–	70.3	69.0	72.2	67.3
Net income ($ mil.)	–	–	8.3	2.0	44.1	(0.4)
Market value ($ mil.)	–	–	–	–	–	–
Employees	–	–	–	–	–	500

KINGSBROOK JEWISH MEDICAL CENTER INC

585 SCHENECTADY AVE
BROOKLYN, NY 112031809
Phone: 718 604-5000
Fax: –
Web: www.onebrooklynhealth.org

CEO: Linda Brady
CFO: John Schmitt
HR: –
FYE: December 31
Type: Private

Kingsbrook Jewish Medical Center (KJMC) cares for the health needs of all Brooklyn residents. Founded in 1925 to serve the area's Jewish community, the campus includes an acute care hospital with about 320 inpatient beds and an adult and pediatric long-term care facility with 540 beds. KJMC provides emergency, surgical, cardiology, gastroenterology, pulmonary, wound care, and diagnostic imaging services, as well as skilled nursing services. The hospital also serves as a training facility for medical, dental, and pharmacy residents. It also operates a primary and specialty care outpatient center and a rehabilitation institute.

	Annual Growth	12/13	12/14	12/15	12/16	12/17
Sales ($mil.)	4.5%	–	211.6	218.4	215.7	241.3
Net income ($ mil.)	28.7%	–	12.8	(1.1)	15.0	27.3
Market value ($ mil.)	–	–	–	–	–	–
Employees	–	–	–	–	–	2,100

KINGSTONE COMPANIES INC

15 Joys Lane
Kingston, NY 12401
Phone: 845 802-7900
Fax: –
Web: www.kingstonecompanies.com

NAS: KINS
CEO: Meryl S Golden
CFO: Jennifer L Gravelle
HR: –
FYE: December 31
Type: Public

Kingstone Companies (formerly DCAP Group) keeps things covered. While the company has transformed itself from a broker into an underwriter, its main business is still insurance. Its Kingstone Insurance Company (formerly Commercial Mutual Insurance Company) provides property/casualty insurance policies for individuals and businesses in New York State. Its products, including auto, business, and homeowners' policies, are sold through independent agents. The company has divested its former insurance brokerage business, which offered life and property/casualty policies through owned and franchised retail locations in New York and eastern Pennsylvania.

	Annual Growth	12/18	12/19	12/20	12/21	12/22
Sales ($mil.)	3.4%	113.8	145.6	131.4	161.2	130.2
Net income ($ mil.)	–	–	3.1	(6.0)	1.0	(7.4)	(22.5)
Market value ($ mil.)	(47.4%)	189.3	82.9	71.2	53.5	14.4
Employees	(1.5%)	101	97	87	91	95

KINGSWAY FINANCIAL SERVICES INC (DE)

10 S. Riverside Road, Suite 1520
Chicago, IL 60606
Phone: 312 766-2138
Fax: –
Web: www.kingsway-financial.com

NYS: KFS
CEO: –
CFO: –
HR: –
FYE: December 31
Type: Public

Kingsway Financial Services is an investment firm with an eye on the royal prize. Its portfolio has focused on insurance and warranty companies, which it typically holds for 15 - 30 years. Its current holdings include non-standard auto insurance (coverage for high-risk drivers) underwriter Mendota as well as three extended warranty firms -- Trinity, IWS Acquisition, and Professional Warranty Service. All are active in the US. Its Kingsway America holding provides non-standard (coverage of high-risk drivers) personal auto coverage in the US. However, Kingsway has decided to sell that business to focus on its other holdings.

	Annual Growth	12/19	12/20	12/21	12/22	12/23
Assets ($mil.)	(16.1%)	399.6	452.5	475.6	285.7	197.7
Net income ($ mil.)	–	(5.9)	(6.7)	(0.3)	24.7	23.6
Market value ($ mil.)	45.8%	50.4	127.4	148.5	214.9	227.7
Employees	23.3%	172	239	279	471	397

KINSALE CAPITAL GROUP INC

2035 Maywill Street, Suite 100
Richmond, VA 23230
Phone: 804 289-1300
Fax: 804 673-5697
Web: www.kinsalecapitalgroup.com

NYS: KNSL
CEO: Michael P Kehoe
CFO: Bryan P Petrucelli
HR: –
FYE: December 31
Type: Public

Kinsale Capital Group owns and operates Kinsale Insurance. Kinsale Insurance provides property and casualty insurance products. the company's commercial insurance offerings include construction, small business, general casualty, energy, excess casualty, professional liability, life sciences, product liability, allied health, health care, commercial property, environmental, management liability, and inland marine, as well as homeowners insurance. Kinsale Insurance markets and sells its insurance products online and through a network of independent insurance brokers. Kinsale Capital Group was founded in 2009 and went public in 2016.

	Annual Growth	12/19	12/20	12/21	12/22	12/23
Assets ($mil.)	36.4%	1,090.6	1,546.9	2,025.7	2,747.1	3,773.0
Net income ($ mil.)	48.5%	63.3	88.4	152.7	159.1	308.1
Market value ($ mil.)	34.7%	2,356.7	4,639.4	5,514.7	6,062.5	7,763.9
Employees	20.2%	275	335	375	466	574

KINSETH HOSPITALITY COMPANY, INC.

801 E 2ND AVE STE 200
CORALVILLE, IA 522412250
Phone: 319 626-5600
Fax: –
Web: www.kinseth.com

CEO: –
CFO: –
HR: –
FYE: December 31
Type: Private

Talk about Midwestern hospitality! Kinseth Hospitality Company owns or operates about 30 hotels (including Holiday Inn, Hampton Inn, and Best Western) and about a dozen restaurants (including Bennigan's and Green Mill) the Midwest. In addition to managing its own properties, the company also offers financial management, development, sales and marketing, and operational consulting services to third-party properties. The company opens or buys hotels and full-service restaurants next to each other to take advantage of the foot traffic. Kinseth Hospitality was founded by the Kinseth family, who own the company, in 1981.

	Annual Growth	12/95	12/96	12/97	12/98	12/09
Sales ($mil.)	(15.3%)	–	–	–	16.8	2.7
Net income ($ mil.)	–	–	–	–	(2.0)	0.2
Market value ($ mil.)	–	–	–	–	–	–
Employees	–	–	–	–	–	82

KIOR, INC.

13001 Bay Park Road
Pasadena, TX 77507
Phone: 281 694-8700
Fax: –
Web: www.kior.com

CEO: –
CFO: –
HR: –
FYE: December 31
Type: Public

Renewable crude oil. Wait - what? KiOR makes actual crude oil using renewable, non-food biomass like wood chips and switch grass. It also makes gasoline and diesel as well as blends for standard gasoline from its crude. Refined in standard petrochemical refinery equipment, the development stage company's products can be transported using existing oil and gas transportation infrastructure. Unlike ethanol and biodiesel KiOR's fuel is completely interchangeable with fossil fuels and can be "dropped in" to engines. The company claims it can produce a gallon of gas for $1.80 with an 80% reduction in greenhouse gas emissions compared to standard gasoline.

KIRBY CORP.

55 Waugh Drive, Suite 1000
Houston, TX 77007
Phone: 713 435-1000
Fax: 713 435-1010
Web: www.kirbycorp.com

NYS: KEX
CEO: David W Grzebinski
CFO: Raj Kumar
HR: –
FYE: December 31
Type: Public

Kirby Corporation is the nation's largest domestic tank barge operator, transporting bulk liquid products throughout the Mississippi River System, on the Gulf Intracoastal Waterway, and coastwise along all three US coasts. Its fleet, operated by subsidiary Kirby Inland Marine, consists of over 1,035 barges with a transportation capacity of approximately 23.1 million barrels and over 275 inland towboats. The vessels are used to transport petrochemicals, black oil, refined petroleum products, and agricultural chemicals. Its coastal operations are conducted through wholly owned subsidiaries, Kirby Offshore Marine and Kirby Ocean Transport. Kirby also offers diesel engine repair and overhaul services and parts for marine, oilfield, and power generation customers and manufactures oilfield service equipment.

	Annual Growth	12/19	12/20	12/21	12/22	12/23
Sales ($mil.)	2.2%	2,838.4	2,171.4	2,246.7	2,784.8	3,091.6
Net income ($ mil.)	11.9%	142.3	(272.5)	(247.0)	122.3	222.9
Market value ($ mil.)	(3.2%)	5,249.1	3,038.7	3,483.7	3,772.8	4,601.2
Employees	12.9%	3,350	5,400	5,125	5,200	5,450

KIRBY RISK CORPORATION

1815 SAGAMORE PKWY N
LAFAYETTE, IN 479041765
Phone: 765 448-4567
Fax: –
Web: www.kirbyrisk.com

CEO: James K Risk III
CFO: Jason J Bricker
HR: Angela Dimmich
FYE: December 31
Type: Private

Kirby Risk, named after one of its co-founders, is a full-service distributor of electrical, automation products, lighting, enterprise, and power distribution products and solutions. The company operates through four business units comprising Electrical Supply, Service Center, Mechanical Solutions and Service, and Precision Machining. The Electrical Supply distribution unit handles more than 90,000 products from over 2,000 manufacturers. Other operations include ARCO Electric Products (phase converters). CEO James Risk III owns the company that was founded in 1926.

	Annual Growth	12/10	12/11	12/12	12/13	12/14
Sales ($mil.)	3.4%	–	377.9	398.4	401.3	417.9
Net income ($ mil.)	–	–	–	–	–	–
Market value ($ mil.)	–	–	–	–	–	–
Employees	–	–	–	–	–	950

KIRKLAND'S INC

5310 Maryland Way
Brentwood, TN 37027
Phone: 615 872-4800
Fax: –
Web: www.kirklands.com

NMS: KIRK
CEO: –
CFO: –
HR: –
FYE: January 28
Type: Public

Kirkland's is a specialty retailer of home furnishings in the US. The company sells its products through nearly 345 stores in approximately 35 US states as well as an e-commerce website, www.kirklands.com, under the Kirkland's Home brand. It is known for stocking decorative home accessories and gifts, including holiday d cor, furniture, wall d cor, art, textiles, mirrors, fragrances, lamps, and other home decorating items. The majority of its stores are located in strip malls. It also adds seasonal holiday items to its merchandise mix. The company has a network of approximately 90 vendors that provide approximately 90% of its merchandise. Kirkland's was founded in 1966 by Carl Kirkland.

	Annual Growth	02/19	02/20*	01/21	01/22	01/23
Sales ($mil.)	(6.3%)	647.1	603.9	543.5	558.2	498.8
Net income ($ mil.)	–	3.8	(53.3)	16.6	22.0	(44.7)
Market value ($ mil.)	(22.5%)	130.2	14.7	324.7	198.2	47.1
Employees	(12.9%)	7,300	6,800	4,700	4,500	4,200

*Fiscal year change

KISH BANCORP INC.

4255 East Main Street
Belleville, PA 17004
Phone: 844 554-4748
Fax: –
Web: www.mykish.com

NBB: KISB
CEO: William P Hayes
CFO: Sangeeta Kishore
HR: –
FYE: December 31
Type: Public

Get your banking needs sealed with a Kish. Kish Bancorp is the holding company for Kishacoquillas Valley National Bank, commonly referred to as Kish Bank. The bank serves individual and business customers through about 10 offices in Centre, Huntingdon, and Mifflin counties in central Pennsylvania. It offers checking and savings accounts, IRAs, CDs, and other retail products, and uses funds from deposits to write primarily real estate loans (commercial and residential mortgages each account for about one-third of its loan portfolio). Other subsidiaries of Kish Bancorp provide insurance, investment management, financial planning, and travel services.

	Annual Growth	12/17	12/18	12/19	12/20	12/21
Assets ($mil.)	11.0%	811.2	850.5	918.3	1,106.6	1,232.8
Net income ($ mil.)	24.3%	4.1	6.0	7.0	8.0	9.9
Market value ($ mil.)	(10.8%)	152.6	84.2	80.9	75.0	96.4
Employees	–	–	–	–	–	–

KISHHEALTH SYSTEM

1 KISH HOSPITAL DR
DEKALB, IL 601159602
Phone: 815 756-1521
Fax: –
Web: www.nm.org

CEO: –
CFO: Loren Foelske
HR: Michele McClelland
FYE: April 30
Type: Private

KishHealth System takes care of the welfare of people all along the "Kish." Formerly Kishwaukee Health System, KishHealth System operates two community hospitals -- Kishwaukee and Valley West, which have a combined 125 staffed beds -- as well as several cancer centers, imaging facilities, and an eye institute that serve Dekalb County and surrounding areas in northern Illinois. Specialty services include cardiology, emergency care, neurosurgery, obstetrics, and orthopedics. The health system takes its name from Kishwaukee (a Potowatomi word for "river of the sycamore"). KishHealth became part of Northwestern Memorial HealthCare in late 2015.

	Annual Growth	04/05	04/06	04/09	04/10	04/15
Sales ($mil.)	(11.2%)	–	143.9	12.8	13.1	49.5
Net income ($ mil.)	(1.2%)	–	28.9	0.0	0.2	25.9
Market value ($ mil.)	–	–	–	–	–	–
Employees	–	–	–	–	–	150

KISSIMMEE UTILITY AUTHORITY (INC)

1701 W CARROLL ST
KISSIMMEE, FL 347416804
Phone: 407 933-7777
Fax: –
Web: www.kua.com

CEO: –
CFO: –
HR: –
FYE: September 30
Type: Private

Kissimmee Utility Authority (KUA) is committed to redoubling efforts to serve this Florida city with three double letters in its name. KUA operates the municipal power distribution system serving 58,000 commercial and industrial, and residential customers in Kissimmee and surrounding areas. It also offers its customers internet, telephone, and security services. In addition, the community-owned utility has stakes in and handful of power plants and has a total generating capacity of 410 MW. The venerable company is used to managing operations in a hurricane-prone area, and is equipped to mobilize maintenance crews to quickly restore power in the wake of infrastructure damage caused by severe storms.

	Annual Growth	09/09	09/10	09/11	09/21	09/22
Sales ($mil.)	2.3%	–	196.4	174.3	192.4	259.2
Net income ($ mil.)	(3.3%)	–	9.1	3.4	18.0	6.1
Market value ($ mil.)	–	–	–	–	–	–
Employees	–	–	–	–	–	300

KITCHELL CORPORATION

1707 E HIGHLAND AVE STE 100
PHOENIX, AZ 850164668
Phone: 602 264-4411
Fax: –
Web: www.kitchell.com

CEO: Wendy Cohen
CFO: –
HR: –
FYE: December 31
Type: Private

From the first structure design sketch to the last brick laid, Kitchell builds the whole kit and caboodle. The employee-owned company, which operates through half a dozen subsidiaries, offers general contracting, project and construction management, engineering and architectural services, and environmental services. Its projects run the gamut of public- and private-sector work and include bioscience labs, casinos, student housing, hotels, jails, custom homes, and performing arts centers. Kitchell is also active in facility and project management and real estate development, as well as fleet management and air conditioning equipment wholesale supply. While the western US is its primary area of focus, Kitchell boasts projects in about two dozen US states.

KITE PHARMA, INC.

2400 BROADWAY STE 100
SANTA MONICA, CA 904043058
Phone: 310 824-9999
Fax: –
Web: www.kitepharma.com

CEO: –
CFO: –
HR: –
FYE: December 31
Type: Private

Kite Pharma, a Gilead company, is a biopharmaceutical company that focused on cell therapy and potentially cure cancer. Its pipeline of cancer therapies in the areas of cell therapy, immuno-oncology, and targeted therapies includes investigational therapies and next-generation technologies that have the power to transform the way cancer is treated. The company's lead product candidate, YESCARTA (axicabtagene ciloleucal), is a treatment for non-Hodgkin lymphoma. Another candidate, TECARTUS (brexucabtagene autoleucel), is a treatment for mantle cell lymphoma. Kite is proud to have more than 350 authorized treatment centers (ATCs) where patients can receive CAR T-cell therapy across the globe, including more than 125 in the US.

KITE REALTY GROUP TRUST

30 S. Meridian Street, Suite 1100
Indianapolis, IN 46204
Phone: 317 577-5600
Fax: –
Web: www.kiterealty.com

NYS: KRG
CEO: John A Kite
CFO: Heath R Fear
HR: –
FYE: December 31
Type: Public

Kite Realty Group Trust is a publicly held real estate investment trust which, through its majority-owned subsidiary, Kite Realty Group, L.P., owns interests in various operating subsidiaries and joint ventures engaged in the ownership, operation, acquisition, development and redevelopment of high-quality, open-air shopping centers and mixed-use assets in select markets in the US. It owns interests in 180 operating retail properties totaling approximately 29.0 million square feet and one office property with 0.3 million square feet. Its largest tenants include Florida grocer Publix, and TJX Cos., though no single tenant accounts for more than 5% of the company's rental income.

	Annual Growth	12/19	12/20	12/21	12/22	12/23
Sales ($mil.)	27.1%	315.2	266.6	373.3	802.0	823.0
Net income ($ mil.)	–	(0.5)	(16.2)	(80.8)	(12.6)	47.5
Market value ($ mil.)	4.0%	4,285.8	3,282.9	4,779.6	4,619.4	5,016.6
Employees	14.6%	133	113	241	236	229

KITZ CORPORATION OF AMERICA

10750 CORPORATE DR
STAFFORD, TX 774774008
Phone: 281 491-7333
Fax: –
Web: www.kitzus-kca.com

CEO: –
CFO: –
HR: Suzanne Wood
FYE: December 31
Type: Private

Kitz Corp. of America (KCA) promotes the free flow of anything but fluids. The subsidiary of Kitz Corp. sells and markets, as well as distributes a slew of flow control valves. Through its divisions, KCA manufactures pressure seal, and high-pressure valves and valve actuators, in chrome, carbon steel, and exotic alloys. The lineup is used in gas and oil pipelines, oil refineries, petrochemical processing plants, and power plants. KCA's products are promoted directly to engineering companies and end users, notably petrochemical plants. KCA was created to represent its Japan-based parent KCA has evolved to also operate a network of valve modification shops in the US and Canada.

	Annual Growth	12/09	12/10	12/11	12/12	12/13
Sales ($mil.)	(36.3%)	–	–	67.9	91.8	27.5
Net income ($ mil.)	(41.3%)	–	–	2.9	1.4	1.0
Market value ($ mil.)	–	–	–	–	–	–
Employees	–	–	–	–	–	38

KIWANIS INTERNATIONAL, INC.

3636 WOODVIEW TRCE
INDIANAPOLIS, IN 462683196
Phone: 317 875-8755
Fax: –
Web: www.kiwanis.org

CEO: Stan Soderstrom
CFO: –
HR: Erin Sloan
FYE: September 30
Type: Private

Kiwanians focus on kids. Kiwanis International unites local clubs that serve children and young adults through various service projects. These projects are targeted to address one or more of the club's six permanent "Objects of Kiwanis," which include fostering spiritual values and higher social standards, developing a more aggressive citizenship, and increasing patriotism and goodwill. Kiwanis' Circle K is its collegiate club, Key Club is for high schoolers, Builders Club serves junior high and middle school students, K-Kids is for elementary kids, and Aktion Club helps adults with disabilities do service projects. Founded in 1915, Kiwanis International operates more than 8,000 clubs in about 95 countries.

	Annual Growth	09/16	09/17	09/20	09/21	09/22
Sales ($mil.)	(2.2%)	–	22.4	18.7	18.4	20.1
Net income ($ mil.)	–	–	(0.2)	(4.9)	6.4	(15.1)
Market value ($ mil.)	–	–	–	–	–	–
Employees	–	–	–	–	–	28,849

KIWIBOX.COM, INC.   NBB: KIWB

330 West 42nd Street, Suite 3210
New York, NY 10036
Phone: 347 836-4727
Fax: –
Web: www.kiwibox.com

CEO: Andre Scholz
CFO: Andre Scholz
HR: –
FYE: December 31
Type: Public

Kiwibox.com (formerly Magnitude Information Systems) offered a line of ergonomic software tools that helped employees avoid repetitive stress injuries in their use of computers. In 2007 Magnitude acquired Kiwibox Media, which operates a social networking site for teenagers. In late 2009 the company changed its name to Kiwibox.com as part of a shifting strategy to focus on its social networking operations. With social media only getting stronger, in 2012 it completed its purchase of European social network site KWICK!, based near Stuttgart, Germany, for about ?6.4 million ($8.3 million). KWICK! reports more than 10 million registered users and 1 million active users.

	Annual Growth	12/12	12/13	12/14	12/15	12/16
Sales ($mil.)	(70.1%)	1.5	0.9	0.0	0.0	0.0
Net income ($ mil.)	–	(14.0)	(7.0)	(4.7)	(4.4)	(4.9)
Market value ($ mil.)	(39.9%)	4.6	3.1	0.8	0.7	0.6
Employees	(30.7%)	13	3	4	3	3

KKR & CO INC   NYS: KKR

30 Hudson Yards
New York, NY 10001
Phone: 212 750-8300
Fax: –
Web: www.kkr.com

CEO: Joseph Y Bae
CFO: Robert H Lewin
HR: –
FYE: December 31
Type: Public

KKR is a leading global investment firm that offers alternative asset management as well as capital markets and insurance solutions. The global investment firm has about $504 billion in assets under management. Its insurance subsidiaries offer retirement, life and reinsurance products under the management of Global Atlantic. KKR completed more than 690 private equity investments in portfolio companies with a total transaction value in excess of $700 billion. Founded in 1976, KKR is led by co-founders Henry Kravis and George Roberts.

	Annual Growth	12/19	12/20	12/21	12/22	12/23
Sales ($mil.)	36.1%	4,220.9	4,230.9	16,236	5,721.2	14,499
Net income ($ mil.)	16.8%	2,005.0	2,002.5	4,666.5	(841.1)	3,732.3
Market value ($ mil.)	29.8%	25,816	35,834	65,933	41,082	73,323
Employees	34.2%	1,384	1,583	3,200	4,150	4,490

KKR FINANCIAL HOLDINGS LLC

555 CALIFORNIA ST FL 50
SAN FRANCISCO, CA 941041503
Phone: 415 315-3620
Fax: –
Web: www.kkrfinancial.com

CEO: William J Janetschek
CFO: Thomas N Murphy
HR: –
FYE: December 31
Type: Private

KKR Financial Holdings is a specialty finance company that invests in a variety of financial products, primarily below-investment-grade corporate debt, as well as public and private equity. Its portfolio, which weighs in at more than $8 billion, includes syndicated bank loans, mezzanine loans, high-yield corporate bonds, asset-backed securities, commercial real estate, and debt and equity securities. KKR Financial Holdings is externally managed by KKR Financial Advisors; both firms are affiliates of private equity and leveraged buyout giant KKR & Co.

KKR REAL ESTATE FINANCE TRUST INC   NYS: KREF

30 Hudson Yards, Suite 7500
New York, NY 10001
Phone: 212 750-8300
Fax: –
Web: www.kkrreit.com

CEO: Matthew A Salem
CFO: Mostafa Nagaty
HR: –
FYE: December 31
Type: Public

KKR Real Estate Finance Trust (KREF) will lend you a few bucks -- if you've got a big building as collateral. The company, a real estate finance company that focuses primarily on originating and acquiring senior loans secured by institutional-quality commercial real estate ("CRE") properties that are owned and operated by experienced and well-capitalized sponsors and located in liquid markets with strong underlying fundamentals.. Some 30% of its portfolio consists of properties in New York, California, and the Washington, D.C. area. Multifamily and office properties split about 85% of KREF's portfolio. KREF's assets total about $5.1 million.

	Annual Growth	12/19	12/20	12/21	12/22	12/23
Sales ($mil.)	23.9%	280.3	270.5	292.1	441.2	661.6
Net income ($ mil.)	–	90.0	54.4	137.2	38.1	(30.9)
Market value ($ mil.)	(10.3%)	1,415.4	1,242.1	1,443.8	967.6	917.0
Employees		–	–	–	–	–

KLA CORP   NMS: KLAC

One Technology Drive
Milpitas, CA 95035
Phone: 408 875-3000
Fax: –
Web: www.kla.com

CEO: Richard P Wallace
CFO: Bren D Higgins
HR: –
FYE: June 30
Type: Public

KLA is a supplier of process equipment, process control equipment, and data analytics products for a broad range of industries, including semiconductors, printed circuit boards (PCB), and displays. It provides advanced process control and process-enabling solutions for manufacturing and testing wafers and reticles, integrated circuits (IC), packaging, light-emitting diodes (LED), power devices, compound semiconductor devices, microelectromechanical systems (MEMS), data storage, PCBs, flat and flexible panel displays, and general materials research, as well as providing contracted and comprehensive support and services across its installed base. Customers in international markets account for nearly 90% of the company's revenue.

	Annual Growth	06/19	06/20	06/21	06/22	06/23
Sales ($mil.)	23.1%	4,568.9	5,806.4	6,918.7	9,211.9	10,496
Net income ($ mil.)	30.3%	1,175.6	1,216.8	2,078.3	3,321.8	3,387.3
Market value ($ mil.)	42.3%	16,164	26,595	44,336	43,634	66,326
Employees	11.0%	10,020	10,600	11,550	14,280	15,210

KLEINKNECHT ELECTRIC COMPANY, INC.

25 W 45TH ST
NEW YORK, NY 100364915
Phone: 212 728-1800
Fax: –
Web: www.kecny.com

CEO: –
CFO: –
HR: –
FYE: December 31
Type: Private

Kleinknecht Electric Company (KEC) offers electrical construction and electrical, data, and telecommunications installation and maintenance services in the metropolitan New York City area. The company has two divisions (maintenance and datacom) and specializes in high-rise data infrastructure and landmark building renovation projects. KEC has completed projects in office buildings, broadcast facilities, museums, concert halls, and manufacturing facilities. The family-owned company, which was founded by George Kleinknecht in 1916, is one of the largest electrical contractors in the US.

KNIGHT TRANSPORTATION, INC.

20002 N 19TH AVE
PHOENIX, AZ 850274271
Phone: 602 269-2000
Fax: –
Web: www.knighttrans.com

CEO: David A Jackson
CFO: Adam W Miller
HR: –
FYE: December 31
Type: Private

Knight Transportation is part of North America's largest truckload fleet, providing multiple truckload services with industry leading safety, service, and financial returns. The truckload has over 4,220 driving associates averaging about 1.2 million miles daily. From some 25 terminals, Knight provides the strength, capacity, and equipment needed to serve any of the customers' immediate and complex truckload needs. It has a fleet of more than 4,000 tractors and over 11,000 trailers. Knight Transportation was founded in 1990 by four cousins: brothers, Kevin and Keith Knight and brothers Randy and Gary Knight.

KNIGHT-SWIFT TRANSPORTATION HOLDINGS INC

NYS: KNX

2002 West Wahalla Lane
Phoenix, AZ 85027
Phone: 602 269-2000
Fax: –
Web: –

CEO: David Jackson
CFO: Adam Miller
HR: Lindsay Wilbert
FYE: December 31
Type: Public

Knight-Swift Transportation (formerly Swift Transportation) provides multiple truckload transportation, intermodal, and logistics services using a nationwide network of business units and terminals in the US and Mexico serving customers throughout North America. During 2022, the company's truckload segment operated an average of 18,110 tractors (comprised of 16,228 company tractors and 1,882 independent contractor tractors). Besides standard dry vans, Knight-Swift's services include refrigerated, flatbed, intermodal, and cross-border transportation of various products, goods, and materials.

	Annual Growth	12/19	12/20	12/21	12/22	12/23
Sales ($mil.)	10.2%	4,844.0	4,673.9	5,998.0	7,428.6	7,141.8
Net income ($ mil.)	(8.5%)	309.2	410.0	743.4	771.3	217.1
Market value ($ mil.)	12.6%	5,784.0	6,749.1	9,834.8	8,458.2	9,303.8
Employees	10.7%	22,800	22,900	27,900	28,500	34,300

KNIGHTS OF COLUMBUS

1 Columbus Plaza
New Haven, CT 06510-3326
Phone: 203 772-2130
Fax: –
Web: www.kofc.org

CEO: –
CFO: –
HR: –
FYE: December 31
Type: Public

The Knights of Columbus are men who lead, serve, protect, and defend, whether it is giving out Coats for Kids, lending a hand in disaster relief efforts, supporting local pregnancy centers by donating ultrasound machines, or providing top-quality financial products. The fraternal organization is also a force to be reckoned with in the insurance world, providing life insurance, annuities, and long-term care insurance to its members and their families. In addition, the group manages the Knights of Columbus Museum in New Haven, Connecticut. The group was founded in 1882 by Father Michael J. McGivney.

	Annual Growth	12/95	12/96	12/97	12/00	12/01
Assets ($mil.)	7.8%	–	6,338.8	6,920.8	8,553.2	9,212.2
Net income ($ mil.)	2.2%	–	83.3	88.4	114.0	93.0
Market value ($ mil.)	–	–	–	–	–	–
Employees	–	–	–	–	–	–

KNOUSE FOODS COOPERATIVE, INC.

800 PEACH GLEN IDAVILLE RD
PEACH GLEN, PA 173750001
Phone: 717 677-8181
Fax: –
Web: www.knouse.com

CEO: Lawrence Martin
CFO: Craig Hinkle
HR: –
FYE: June 30
Type: Private

Is there a Knouse in the house? Might be. With retail brand names such as Apple Time, Lucky Leaf, Musselman's, Lincoln, and Speas Farm, Knouse Foods Cooperative's apple products are in many a pantry. The company is a growers' co-op made up of some 150 Appalachian Mountain and Midwestern grower/members. It processes its members' apples for sale as canned and bottled applesauce, juice, cider vinegar, apple butter, pie fillings, and snack packs, all of which are available nationwide. In addition to stocking supermarket shelves, Knouse, founded in 1949, supplies foodservice operators and industrial-ingredient companies with bulk apple and other fruit products. It also offers private-label and co-packing services.

KNOWLES CORP

NYS: KN

1151 Maplewood Drive
Itasca, IL 60143
Phone: 630 250-5100
Fax: 630 250-0575
Web: www.knowles.com

CEO: Jeffrey S Niew
CFO: John S Anderson
HR: –
FYE: December 31
Type: Public

Knowles is a market leader and global provider of advanced micro-acoustic microphones and balanced armature speakers, audio solutions, high-performance capacitors, and radio frequency (RF) filtering products, serving the Medtech, defense, consumer electronics, electric vehicle, industrial, and communications markets. The company uses its leading position in SiSonic micro-electro-mechanical systems (MEMS) microphones and strong capabilities in audio processing technologies to optimize audio systems and improve the user experience across consumer applications. Knowles is also a leader in hearing health acoustics, high-performance capacitors, and RF solutions for a diverse set of markets. Knowles, founded in 1946, has facilities located in roughly 15 countries around the world. Although based in the US, Knowles generates about 60% of revenue in Asia region.

	Annual Growth	12/19	12/20	12/21	12/22	12/23
Sales ($mil.)	(4.6%)	854.8	764.3	868.1	764.7	707.6
Net income ($ mil.)	10.2%	49.1	6.6	150.4	(430.1)	72.4
Market value ($ mil.)	(4.1%)	1,884.3	1,642.0	2,080.3	1,462.9	1,595.7
Employees	(4.4%)	8,500	7,000	7,000	7,000	7,100

KNOX NURSERY, INC.

940 AVALON RD
WINTER GARDEN, FL 347879701
Phone: 407 654-1972
Fax: –
Web: www.knoxhort.com

CEO: –
CFO: –
HR: Bibi Sharzaman
FYE: December 31
Type: Private

Annuals are an everyday business for Knox Nursery. Founded in 1962, the company grows 13,000 varieties of flowering annuals for a variety of customers, including landscapers and home improvement chain stores, nationwide. For the production of seedling annuals, which account for most of the company's sales, Knox Nursery spent about $6 million to build a growing facility that uses automation to cut labor costs, about in half. It operates its business on more than 20 acres in Florida. The company's major customers have included Ball Seed, Walt Disney World, and DPT Brokerage. The Knox family took the company private in mid-2005, citing the high cost of Sarbanes-Oxley compliance.

	Annual Growth	12/04	12/05	12/06	12/07	12/08
Sales ($mil.)	1.3%	–	–	8.9	9.0	9.1
Net income ($ mil.)	–	–	–	0.0	(0.5)	(0.2)
Market value ($ mil.)	–	–	–	–	–	–
Employees	–	–	–	–	–	106

KNOXVILLE UTILITIES BOARD

445 S GAY ST
KNOXVILLE, TN 379021125
Phone: 865 594-7531
Fax: –
Web: www.kub.org

CEO: Mintha Roach
CFO: –
HR: Deanna Unger
FYE: June 30
Type: Private

Providing utility services to residential and business customers has proven to be an excellent idea for Knoxville Utilities Board (KUB), an independent agency that serves the city of Knoxville, and surrounding areas. The multi-utility provides services to 196,500 electric, 96,920 gas, 77,600 water, and 68,740 wastewater customers. The company accesses electric power from the Tennessee Valley Authority. KUB's natural gas supply comes from the East Tennessee Natural Gas pipeline. It also maintains five treatment plants, which provide water and wastewater services.

	Annual Growth	06/18	06/19	06/20	06/21	06/22
Sales ($mil.)	3.6%	–	815.4	803.8	822.3	905.8
Net income ($ mil.)	6.0%	–	65.3	78.0	75.5	77.8
Market value ($ mil.)	–	–	–	–	–	–
Employees	–	–	–	–	–	500

KOCH ENTERPRISES, INC.

14 S 11TH AVE
EVANSVILLE, IN 477125020
Phone: 812 465-9800
Fax: –
Web: www.kochenterprises.com

CEO: –
CFO: Susan E Parsons
HR: Glen Muehlbauer
FYE: December 31
Type: Private

Koch gets straight A's for diversification; it's a private holding company active in automobile parts manufacturing, metals recycling, wholesale distribution, and equipment design and construction. Subsidiaries include Audubon Metals (processes aluminum), George Koch Sons (engineers, installs, and services auto finishing systems), Koch Air (distributes Carrier HVAC equipment), Gibbs Die Casting (parts for making cars lighter), Brake Supply (repairs brakes and hydraulic systems for auto and mining equipment), and Uniseal (makes structural adhesives, thermoplastics, and sealant systems for industrial and auto markets). George Koch founded the company in 1873.

KOCH SUPPLY & TRADING, LP

4111 E 37TH ST N
WICHITA, KS 672203203
Phone: 713 544-4123
Fax: –
Web: www.ksandt.com

CEO: –
CFO: –
HR: –
FYE: December 31
Type: Private

Koch Supply & Trading (KS&T) knows the risks in being crude and refined at the same time. The company, a member of conglomerate Koch Industries' group of businesses, offers its clients global trading and risk management services. The company markets crude oil, refined petroleum products, chemicals, industrial and precious metals, steel, and other commodities. KS&T also offers logistics and technical management services. Risk management offerings include market research, derivative transactions, and price hedging. The company leverages the presence of Koch companies in about 60 countries in order to secure and execute contracts.

KOHL'S CORP.

NYS: KSS

N56 W17000 Ridgewood Drive
Menomonee Falls, WI 53051
Phone: 262 703-7000
Fax: 262 703-6373
Web: www.kohls.com

CEO: Thomas Kingsbury
CFO: Jill Timm
HR: –
FYE: February 3
Type: Public

Clothing retailer Kohl's operates some 1,170 namesake department stores across the US. Competing with discount and mid-level department stores, the company sells moderately priced name-brand and private-label apparel, shoes, accessories, and housewares. Its private-label brands include Apt. 9, Croft & Barrow, SO, Sonoma Goods for Life, and Jumping Beans. Kohl's also sells exclusive brands through agreements with Lauren Conrad, Vera Wang, and the Food Network, among others. Around 80% of the company's stores are in strip centers with the rest are freestanding and located community and regional in malls.

	Annual Growth	02/20*	01/21	01/22	01/23*	02/24
Sales ($mil.)	(3.3%)	19,974	15,955	19,433	18,098	17,476
Net income ($ mil.)	(17.7%)	691.0	(163.0)	938.0	(19.0)	317.0
Market value ($ mil.)	(11.4%)	4,745.3	4,890.7	6,677.8	3,495.4	2,930.4
Employees	(5.8%)	122,000	110,000	99,000	97,000	96,000

*Fiscal year change

KOHLER CO.

444 HIGHLAND DR
KOHLER, WI 530441500
Phone: 920 457-4441
Fax: –
Web: www.kohlercompany.com

CEO: K D Kohler
CFO: –
HR: Anne Blindauer
FYE: December 31
Type: Private

With more than 50 manufacturing locations worldwide, Kohler is a global leader in the design, innovation and manufacture of kitchen and bath products; luxury cabinetry, tile and lighting; engines, generators, and clean energy solutions; and owner/operator of two, five-star hospitality and golf resort destinations in Kohler, Wisconsin, and St. Andrews, Scotland. Kohler's Whistling Straits golf course recently hosted the 43rd Ryder Cup. The company also develops solutions to address pressing issues, such as clean water and sanitation, for underserved communities around the world to enhance the quality of life for current and future generations. The Kohler family controls the company since its founding year in 1873 by John Michael Kohler.

KOHN PEDERSEN FOX ASSOCIATES, PC

11 W 42ND ST FL 8
NEW YORK, NY 100368002
Phone: 212 977-6500
Fax: –
Web: www.kpf.com

CEO: –
CFO: –
HR: –
FYE: December 31
Type: Private

Kohn Pedersen Fox Associates (KPF) puts its stamp on buildings around the world. One of the top 10 architectural and planning firms in the US, the company offers services such as master planning, urban design, space planning, programming, building analysis, graphic and product, and interior design. It specializes in such projects as corporate headquarters, government offices, health care facilities, hotels, and educational facilities. KPF's structures range from small pavilions to entire cities. The firm operates from offices in New York, London, and Shanghai. Architects A. Eugene Kohn, William Pedersen, and Sheldon Fox founded the firm in 1976.

	Annual Growth	12/02	12/03	12/04	12/05	12/07
Sales ($mil.)	5.3%	–	–	62.4	64.1	72.8
Net income ($ mil.)	142.4%	–	–	0.4	22.2	6.3
Market value ($ mil.)	–	–	–	–	–	–
Employees	–	–	–	–	–	350

KOHR BROTHERS, INC.

2151 RICHMOND RD STE 200
CHARLOTTESVILLE, VA 229113636
Phone: 434 975-1500
Fax: –
Web: www.kohrbros.com

CEO: Randolph L Kohr
CFO: –
HR: –
FYE: October 31
Type: Private

Kohr Brothers operates and franchises more than 30 Kohr Bros. Frozen Custard outlets in about 10 states, a majority of which are in New Jersey. Most of its shops are in high traffic areas, such as shopping malls, airports, and sports arenas. School teacher Archie Kohr started the chain with his brothers in 1919 in order to sell more cream from the family's dairy business. The brothers began with a single ice cream shop on Coney Island's boardwalk.

	Annual Growth	10/14	10/15	10/16	10/17	10/18
Sales ($mil.)	1.3%	–	13.6	13.9	14.3	14.1
Net income ($ mil.)	(1.1%)	–	0.9	0.6	0.9	0.9
Market value ($ mil.)	–	–	–	–	–	–
Employees	–	–	–	–	–	250

KOIL ENERGY SOLUTIONS INC

NBB: KLNG

1310 Rankin Road
Houston, TX 77073
Phone: 281 517-5000
Fax: 281 517-5001
Web: www.deepdowninc.com

CEO: –
CFO: –
HR: –
FYE: December 31
Type: Public

Deep down, Deep Down understands itself to be in the subsea sector. The company (formerly medical equipment provider Mediquip Holdings) acquired Deep Down in a reverse merger, taking on that company's subsea service business as well as its name. An umbilical and flexible pipe installation engineering and installation management company, Deep Down also fabricates component parts for subsea distribution systems and assemblies that specialize in the development of offshore subsea fields. The company's product include umbilicals, flowlines, distribution systems, pipeline terminations, controls, winches, and launch and retrieval systems. It serves clients in the Gulf of Mexico and internationally.

	Annual Growth	12/18	12/19	12/20	12/21	12/22
Sales ($mil.)	(5.4%)	16.2	18.9	13.0	17.2	13.0
Net income ($ mil.)	–	(4.7)	(2.8)	(6.1)	2.3	(2.9)
Market value ($ mil.)	(13.6%)	10.0	8.0	5.1	7.4	5.6
Employees	(4.1%)	58	48	45	46	49

KOKOSING CONSTRUCTION COMPANY, INC.

6235 WESTERVILLE RD
WESTERVILLE, OH 430814041
Phone: 614 228-1029
Fax: –
Web: www.kokosing.biz

CEO: W B Burgett
CFO: James Geiser
HR: –
FYE: March 31
Type: Private

Regional general contractor Kokosing Construction is one of the largest non-residential builders in Ohio. The company operates with its primary business lines, including industrial, transportation, pipelines, water and wastewater, marine and renewable energy. Additionally, Kokosing owns construction material supply companies. The company's projects include commercial and institutional buildings, heavy industrial process plants, waste and water-treatment plants, underground sewer and utility lines, heavy/highway construction, and sports facilities. Kokosing's local office in the Midwest and Mid-Atlantic supports its operations across the US. The company, which was founded in 1951 by William Burgett and Les Rinehart, is owned and run by the Burgett family.

KOLORFUSION INTERNATIONAL INC

NBB: KOLR

16075 E. 32nd Ave, Suite A
Aurora, CO 80011
Phone: 303 340-9994
Fax: –
Web: www.kolorfusion.com

CEO: –
CFO: –
HR: –
FYE: June 30
Type: Public

Beauty might be more than skin-deep, but surface appearances are what matter most to Kolorfusion International. Via the Kolorfusion process, the company's customers can print colors and patterns onto coatings on metal, wood, and glass products, and directly onto plastic products. The company maintains production capabilities for clients in the US and Canada and licenses the process internationally to other clients. Customers have included Daisy Manufacturing, Moen, and Polaris. In mid-2010 the company voluntarily filed for Chapter 11 bankruptcy protection.

	Annual Growth	06/04	06/05	06/06	06/07	06/08
Sales ($mil.)	(13.5%)	–	2.3	2.1	1.6	1.5
Net income ($ mil.)	–	–	(0.6)	(0.3)	0.5	(0.5)
Market value ($ mil.)	(20.6%)	–	2.9	2.1	2.4	1.5
Employees	–	–	–	9	9	9

KOMATSU MINING CORP.

311 E GREENFIELD AVE
MILWAUKEE, WI 532042939
Phone: 414 670-8454
Fax: –
Web: www.mining.komatsu

CEO: Edward L Doheny II
CFO: James M Sullivan
HR: Dan Flournoy
FYE: October 28
Type: Private

Komatsu Mining Corporation (formerly Joy Global) makes heavy equipment for the mining industry through two subsidiaries. The company makes underground coal-mining equipment that includes armored face conveyors, roof supports, longwall shearers, and shuttle cars. Other operations make electric mining shovels, rotary blasthole drills, and other equipment used in surface open-pit mining; it also provides parts and service through its P&H MinePro Services network. The company was acquired in 2017 by construction equipment maker behemoth Komatsu.

KONGSBERG POWER PRODUCTS SYSTEMS I, LLC

300 S COCHRAN ST
WILLIS, TX 773789034
Phone: 936 856-2971
Fax: –
Web: –

CEO: –
CFO: –
HR: –
FYE: December 31
Type: Private

Kongsberg Power Products Systems (formerly Capro) makes motion control systems and cable assemblies. Its automotive products include cables that operate hood and fuel door releases, heating and air conditioning controls, trunk releases, seat recliners, and door and window systems. The company also makes mechanical control systems and cable assemblies for power and industrial equipment OEMs. Kongsberg Power Products offers services that include engineering, design, and prototyping. A former subsidiary of diversified manufacturer Teleflex, Capro was sold in 2008 to global auto supplier Kongsberg Automotive Holding ASA, which changed the company's name but kept the Capro brand.

KONTOOR BRANDS INC   NYS: KTB

400 N. Elm Street
Greensboro, NC 27401
Phone: 336 332-3400
Fax: –
Web: www.wrangler.com

CEO: Scott H Baxter
CFO: Joe Alkire
HR: –
FYE: December 30
Type: Public

Kontoor Brands is a global lifestyle apparel company, with a portfolio led by two of the world's most iconic consumer brands: Wrangler and Lee. The company designs, produces, procures, markets, distributes, and licenses apparel, footwear, and accessories, primarily under the brand names Wrangler and Lee. Its products are sold in the US through mass merchants, specialty stores, mid-tier and traditional department stores, company-operated stores, and online. The company's products are also sold internationally, primarily in the EMEA, and APAC regions, through department, specialty, company-operated, concession retail, and independently-operated partnership stores and online. With all brands accounting for approximately 157 million units of apparel sold in 2022, the company has a presence in more than 70 countries. The US accounts for the majority of the company's revenue.

	Annual Growth	12/19*	01/21	01/22*	12/22	12/23
Sales ($mil.)	0.6%	2,548.8	2,097.8	2,475.9	2,631.4	2,607.5
Net income ($ mil.)	24.3%	96.7	67.9	195.4	245.5	231.0
Market value ($ mil.)	10.1%	2,367.6	2,260.0	2,855.7	2,228.3	3,478.1
Employees	(2.4%)	15,100	14,000	14,000	14,400	13,700

*Fiscal year change

KOPIN CORP.   NAS: KOPN

125 North Drive
Westborough, MA 01581-3335
Phone: 508 870-5959
Fax: –
Web: www.kopin.com

CEO: Michael Murray
CFO: Richard A Sneider
HR: –
FYE: December 30
Type: Public

Kopin is a leading developer, manufacturer and seller of miniature displays and optical lenses for sale as individual displays, components, modules or higher-level subassemblies. The company also licenses its intellectual property through technology license agreements. Its component products are used in highly demanding high-resolution portable defense, enterprise and consumer electronic applications, training and simulation equipment, and 3D metrology equipment. Kopin's products enable its customers to develop and market an improved generation of products for these target applications. Kopin was founded in 1984 by engineers from the Massachusetts Institute of Technology's Electronic Materials Group, including co-founder and CEO John Fan. About 80% of the company's revenue comes from the US.

	Annual Growth	12/19	12/20	12/21	12/22	12/23
Sales ($mil.)	8.2%	29.5	40.1	45.7	47.4	40.4
Net income ($ mil.)	–	(29.5)	(4.4)	(13.4)	(19.3)	(19.7)
Market value ($ mil.)	48.3%	47.1	309.8	487.2	139.2	227.9
Employees	(1.5%)	153	160	181	177	144

KOPPERS HOLDINGS INC   NYS: KOP

436 Seventh Avenue
Pittsburgh, PA 15219
Phone: 412 227-2001
Fax: –
Web: www.koppers.com.

CEO: Leroy M Ball
CFO: Michael J Zugay
HR: –
FYE: December 31
Type: Public

Koppers Holdings is a leading integrated global provider of treated wood products, wood preservation chemicals, and carbon compounds for the railroad, specialty chemical, utility, residential lumber, agriculture, aluminum, steel, rubber, and construction industries around the world. Its carbon materials and chemicals unit make materials for the production of polyester resins, plasticizers, and alkyd paints. The railroad and utility products unit is the largest supplier of railroad crossties to the Class I railroads in North America. Additionally, the company is a leading supplier of fire-retardant chemicals (FlamePro) for the pressure treatment of wood, primarily in commercial construction. The US generates nearly 65% of the company's total sales.

	Annual Growth	12/19	12/20	12/21	12/22	12/23
Sales ($mil.)	5.0%	1,772.8	1,669.1	1,678.6	1,980.5	2,154.2
Net income ($ mil.)	7.6%	66.6	122.0	85.2	63.4	89.2
Market value ($ mil.)	7.6%	797.3	650.0	652.9	588.3	1,068.5
Employees	(0.1%)	2,120	2,061	2,088	2,119	2,108

KOPPERS UTILITY AND INDUSTRIAL PRODUCTS INC.

237 FORESTRY RD
EUTAWVILLE, SC 29048
Phone: 412 227-2001
Fax: –
Web: www.koppersuip.com

CEO: R M Johnson
CFO: –
HR: –
FYE: April 30
Type: Private

Koppers Utility & Industrial Products (KUIP) is the country's largest American-owned wood pole manufacturer, supplying quality poles and cross-arms to utilities nationwide. Its utility products and services division makes treated wood products used in utility poles, crossarms, and treatment types. Its marine products have included wood piling which is a mainstay of foundation systems. Engineers and contractors depend on wood piling to perform its intended function in all kinds of structures, including piers, docks, bulkheads, manufacturing plants and commercial buildings. It serves a broad customer base including investor-owned, cooperative and municipal utility companies.

KORN FERRY   NYS: KFY

1900 Avenue of the Stars, Suite 1500
Los Angeles, CA 90067
Phone: 310 552-1834
Fax: –
Web: www.kornferry.com

CEO: Gary D Burnison
CFO: Robert P Rozek
HR: –
FYE: April 30
Type: Public

Korn Ferry is a global organizational consulting firm helping private, public, middle market, and emerging growth companies, as well as government and not-for-profit clients organize their strategies and talent to drive superior business performance such as leadership and professional development, and rewards and benefits. The company invests and develops specialized technology and IP, including proprietary systems, processes and methodologies, such as Korn Ferry Advance and Talent Hub. The company also serves consumers through Korn Ferry Advance, which helps people looking to make their next career move, and provides career services to employees within organizations. Korn Ferry operates in about 100 offices in nearly 55 countries.

	Annual Growth	04/19	04/20	04/21	04/22	04/23
Sales ($mil.)	9.8%	1,973.9	1,977.3	1,819.9	2,643.5	2,863.8
Net income ($ mil.)	19.5%	102.7	104.9	114.5	326.4	209.5
Market value ($ mil.)	0.5%	2,457.7	1,506.9	3,548.5	3,211.4	2,510.0
Employees	5.4%	8,678	8,198	7,889	10,779	10,697

KORTE CONSTRUCTION COMPANY

5700 OAKLAND AVE STE 275
SAINT LOUIS, MO 631101375
Phone: 314 231-3700
Fax: –
Web: www.korteco.com

CEO: –
CFO: –
HR: –
FYE: December 31
Type: Private

The Korte Company provides design/build, design/build/furnish, construction management, and interior design services for a variety of commercial and industrial construction projects. The group works on projects that include warehouse/distribution centers, recreational centers, schools, office complexes, churches, and facilities for local, state, and federal government agencies, including Department of Defense. The Korte Company, which was founded in 1958, operates from offices in Las Vegas, St. Louis, and Highland, Illinois.

	Annual Growth	12/14	12/15	12/16	12/17	12/18
Sales ($mil.)	23.6%	–	119.9	268.5	341.2	226.3
Net income ($ mil.)	–	–	(2.5)	0.8	(3.9)	(0.3)
Market value ($ mil.)	–	–	–	–	–	–
Employees	–	–	–	–	–	170

KORU MEDICAL SYSTEMS INC

NAS: KRMD

100 Corporate Drive
Mahwah, NJ 07430
Phone: 845 469-2042
Fax: 845 469-5518
Web: www.korumedical.com

CEO: Linda Tharby
CFO: Andrew D Lafrence
HR: –
FYE: December 31
Type: Public

Repro-Med Systems (aka RMS Medical Products) doesn't want to repo your medical devices, it wants to supply you with them! The company manufactures portable medical devices for respiratory and infusion therapy. Most of RMS' products are designed for simplicity and do not require batteries or electricity. The company's biggest seller is a hand-powered airway suction device (RES-Q-VAC) used in emergency situations in hospitals and ambulances. Its other key product is a portable, self-powered infusion system (FREEDOM60) for ambulatory, home, and hospital use. The company also has a line of gynecological instruments. Founder CEO Andrew Sealfon owns 20% of the company he established in 1980.

	Annual Growth	12/18	12/19	12/20	12/21	12/22
Sales ($mil.)	12.6%	17.4	23.2	24.2	23.5	27.9
Net income ($ mil.)	–	0.9	0.6	(1.2)	(4.6)	(8.7)
Market value ($ mil.)	21.3%	75.0	296.7	273.6	136.3	162.2
Employees	3.1%	76	71	101	77	86

KOSCIUSKO 21ST CENTURY FOUNDATION, INC.

2170 N POINTE DR
WARSAW, IN 465829043
Phone: 574 267-3200
Fax: –
Web: www.k21healthfoundation.org

CEO: –
CFO: Doug Bement
HR: –
FYE: December 31
Type: Private

It's not an easy name to say, but don't let that keep you away! Kosciusko Community Hospital, which has just over 70 beds, provides 24-hour emergency care and general health care services to the residents of Kosciusko County in northern Indiana. The hospital has centers dedicated to health and wellness, women's imaging, wound care, and weight management. Kosciusko's Center of Hope offers a range of cancer treatment programs including chemotherapy and radiation therapy, home and hospice care, nutritional counseling, and pain and symptom management. The hospital, led by CEO Steve Miller, is part of the Lutheran Health Network.

	Annual Growth	02/07	02/08	02/09*	12/14	12/17
Sales ($mil.)	(33.9%)	–	–	98.8	4.1	3.6
Net income ($ mil.)	–	–	–	32.3	(0.1)	(0.9)
Market value ($ mil.)	–	–	–	–	–	–
Employees	–	–	–	–	–	839

*Fiscal year change

KOSMOS ENERGY LTD (DE)

NYS: KOS

8176 Park Lane
Dallas, TX 75231
Phone: 214 445-9600
Fax: –
Web: www.kosmosenergy.com

CEO: –
CFO: –
HR: –
FYE: December 31
Type: Public

Searching the cosmos for energy? No, searching Africa for oil and gas. Kosmos Energy is a US-based oil and gas exploration firm with about 30 producing wells off the coast of Ghana. The company also has leases on oil fields off the coasts of Cameroon and Morocco. It looks for underdeveloped or "misunderstood" energy assets off west Africa. Kosmos Energy owns about 31% and 18% of its two producing units off Ghana and 75% each in the other assets. The company was formed in 2003 by management before it was acquired by Hess Corporation. Kosmos went public in 2011. In 2016 BP agreed to acquire stakes in exploration blocks in Mauritania and Senegal from Kosmos for $916 million.

	Annual Growth	12/19	12/20	12/21	12/22	12/23
Sales ($mil.)	3.0%	1,509.9	896.2	1,333.8	2,299.8	1,701.5
Net income ($ mil.)	–	(55.8)	(411.6)	(77.8)	226.6	213.5
Market value ($ mil.)	4.2%	2,622.7	1,081.3	1,592.0	2,926.4	3,087.5
Employees	(9.4%)	360	252	229	236	243

KOSS CORP

NAS: KOSS

4129 North Port Washington Avenue
Milwaukee, WI 53212
Phone: 414 964-5000
Fax: –
Web: www.koss.com

CEO: Michael J Koss Jr
CFO: Kim M Schulte
HR: –
FYE: June 30
Type: Public

Koss makes sure you can turn up the volume without disturbing the neighbors. The company makes stereo headphones, or "stereophones," and related accessories for consumers and audio professionals. Its lineup includes full-size, noise-cancellation, portable, earbud, and wireless headphones. Products are sold through more than 17,000 US retail outlets, including specialty audio stores, discount stores, and mass merchandisers, as well as by catalogs and online merchants. The company also produces classical music recordings through its Koss Classics subsidiary. In addition to its US operations, Koss has an international sales office in Switzerland. Founded by John Koss, the firm has roots reaching back to the 1950s.

	Annual Growth	06/19	06/20	06/21	06/22	06/23
Sales ($mil.)	(12.0%)	21.8	18.3	19.5	17.6	13.1
Net income ($ mil.)	109.1%	0.4	(0.5)	0.5	1.3	8.3
Market value ($ mil.)	16.6%	18.5	12.6	214.4	64.2	34.2
Employees	(2.3%)	34	34	35	34	31

KPH HEALTHCARE SERVICES, INC.

29 E MAIN ST
GOUVERNEUR, NY 136421401
Phone: 315 287-3600
Fax: –
Web: www.kphhealthcareservices.com

CEO: Craig Painter
CFO: –
HR: Debbie Davis
FYE: December 31
Type: Private

Founded by Burt Orrin Kinney, who opened the company's first drugstore in 1903, Kinney Drugs has grown to number about 100 stores in central and northern New York and Vermont. Most of the company's stores are free-standing units, with pharmacies, one-hour photo developing services, and a growing selection of convenience foods. The 100%-employee-owned company maintains its own distribution warehouse and offers about 800 different products, including Kinney-branded over-the-counter medicines. Pharmacy accounts for 75% of sales. Besides retail stores, the firm operates ProAct prescription benefit management firm, HealthDirect institutional pharmacy services, and HealthDirect mail order pharmacy services.

	Annual Growth	12/18	12/19	12/20	12/21	12/22
Sales ($mil.)	7.9%	–	–	1,589.3	1,760.8	1,849.6
Net income ($ mil.)	(0.9%)	–	–	41.9	42.1	41.2
Market value ($ mil.)	–	–	–	–	–	–
Employees	–	–	–	–	–	4,300

KPMG LLP

345 PARK AVE
NEW YORK, NY 101540004
Phone: 212 758-9700
Fax: –
Web: www.home.kpmg

CEO: –
CFO: –
HR: Tina Caramagna
FYE: December 31
Type: Private

KPMG is the US firm of the KPMG global organization of independent professional services firms providing audit, tax, and advisory services. The KPMG global organization operates in about 145 countries and territories and has more than 265,000 people working in member firms worldwide. KPMG mostly serves a diverse client base across industries including investment and financial services, energy and natural resources, healthcare, life sciences, industrial manufacturing, consumer and retail, media, and the government and public sectors.

KPRS CONSTRUCTION SERVICES, INC.

2850 SATURN ST STE 110
BREA, CA 928216201
Phone: 714 672-0800
Fax: –
Web: www.kprsinc.com

CEO: –
CFO: –
HR: Carole Santamaria
FYE: September 30
Type: Private

KPRS Construction Services is a keeper of California construction. The company offers design/build, preconstruction, construction management, and general contracting mostly in and around Los Angeles. KPRS, which was founded in 1997, also has an office in Honolulu. The company targets the hospitality, education, entertainment, industrial, institutional, sports and recreational, medical, office, and retail markets. While the major construction market has cooled, KPRS has focused on tenant improvement and renovation services as a way to attract new clients. About a quarter of KPRS' business is tenant improvements, and the company has helped renovate spaces for clients such as Beckman Coulter and Whirlpool.

KRASDALE FOODS, INC.

65 W RED OAK LN
WHITE PLAINS, NY 106043614
Phone: 914 694-6400
Fax: –
Web: www.krasdalefoods.com

CEO: Charles Krasne
CFO: –
HR: Linda D Leon
FYE: January 02
Type: Private

Krasdale Foods keeps independent grocery stores' shelves stocked with a wholesale portfolio of more than 12,000 products. From its distribution center in the Bronx, the company provides food retailers with Krasdale-labeled, private-label, and regional brands, as well as ethnic and specialty food items. The wholesaler serves over 2,500 independent grocery stores in the New York metropolitan area, including C Town, Bravo, AIM, Market Fresh, Stop1, and Shop Smart. Krasdale Foods also provides merchandising and marketing services to its customers. The company adopted its current moniker in 1972.

KQED INC.

2601 MARIPOSA ST
SAN FRANCISCO, CA 941101426
Phone: 415 864-2000
Fax: –
Web: www.kqed.org

CEO: John Boland
CFO: Mitzie Kelley
HR: Debbie Jue
FYE: September 30
Type: Private

Public interest is a big concern for this West Coast broadcasting company. Publicly financed TV and radio broadcaster KQED serves the Northern California area through its flagship KQED Public Television 9 station. KQED produces and broadcasts educational programming focused on arts, science, and the humanities, as well as public interest shows highlighting local, national, and international issues. It creates most of its own programming but also specializes in broadcasting independent films and programs from PBS and other distributors. In addition, KQED Public Radio broadcasts to listeners across San Francisco and Sacramento, and its website provides event listings, resources, polls, podcasts, and blogs.

	Annual Growth	09/18	09/19	09/20	09/21	09/22
Sales ($mil.)	(3.4%)	–	121.5	103.4	115.9	109.7
Net income ($ mil.)	(35.4%)	–	32.0	11.4	24.8	8.7
Market value ($ mil.)	–	–	–	–	–	–
Employees	–	–	–	–	–	266

KRATON CORPORATION

15710 JOHN F KENNEDY BLVD STE 300
HOUSTON, TX 770322347
Phone: 281 504-4700
Fax: –
Web: www.kraton.com

CEO: Marcello Boldrini
CFO: Eun-Mi Kim
HR: Cindy Delancey
FYE: December 31
Type: Private

When the rubber meets the road, Kraton Polymers is responsible for both ends of the equation. It makes chemical ingredients used in both autos and in asphalt for road-building. As the operating subsidiary of holding company Kraton Performance Polymers, it is a leading global producer of styrenic block copolymers (SBCs). SBCs are a kind of polymer used in a variety of plastic, rubber, and chemical products, as well as for improving the stability of asphalt. Kraton Polymers splits its operations into four main end-use markets: Adhesives, Sealants, and Coatings; Advanced Materials; Paving and Roofing; and Cariflex, its brand for isopene rubber latex products. Kraton Polymers sells its products worldwide.

KRAFT HEINZ CO (THE)   NMS: KHC

One PPG Place
Pittsburgh, PA 15222
Phone: 412 456-5700
Fax: –
Web: www.kraftheinzcompany.com

CEO: Miguel Patricio
CFO: Andre Maciel
HR: –
FYE: December 30
Type: Public

The Kraft Heinz Company is one of the largest food and beverage companies in the world. In addition to its two namesakes, the company's portfolio of iconic brands include such names as Oscar Mayer, Capri Sun, Ore-Ida, Kool-Aid, Jell-O, Philadelphia, Lunchables, Maxwell House, and Velveeta. Kraft Heinz, which generates more than 45% of combined sales from condiments and sauces and cheese and dairy products, offers its goods through e-commerce platforms, retailers, and foodservice distributors. It manages its sales portfolio through six consumer-driven product platforms. The US accounts for about 70% of the company's total sales.

	Annual Growth	12/19	12/20	12/21	12/22	12/23
Sales ($mil.)	1.6%	24,977	26,185	26,042	26,485	26,640
Net income ($ mil.)	10.2%	1,935.0	356.0	1,012.0	2,363.0	2,855.0
Market value ($ mil.)	4.0%	38,513	42,606	42,935	49,585	45,042
Employees	(0.7%)	37,000	38,000	36,000	37,000	36,000

KRATOS DEFENSE & SECURITY SOLUTIONS, INC.   NMS: KTOS

1 Chisholm Trail, Suite 3200
Round Rock, TX 78681
Phone: 512 238-9840
Fax: –
Web: www.kratosdefense.com

CEO: –
CFO: –
HR: –
FYE: December 31
Type: Public

Kratos Defense & Security Solutions' primary focus areas are unmanned systems, space and satellite communications, microwave electronics, cybersecurity/warfare, rocket, hypersonic and missile defense systems, turbine technologies, Command, Control, Communication, Computing, Combat, Intelligence Surveillance and Reconnaissance (C5ISR) Systems, and training systems. Kratos was founded in 1995 and initially focused on commercial clients.

	Annual Growth	12/19	12/20	12/21	12/22	12/23
Sales ($mil.)	9.6%	717.5	747.7	811.5	898.3	1,037.1
Net income ($ mil.)	–	12.5	79.6	(2.0)	(36.9)	(8.9)
Market value ($ mil.)	3.4%	2,297.4	3,413.2	2,565.1	1,220.5	2,623.2
Employees	6.8%	3,000	3,200	3,300	3,600	3,900

KRAUS-ANDERSON, INCORPORATED

501 S 8TH ST
MINNEAPOLIS, MN 554041030
Phone: 612 332-7281
Fax: -
Web: www.krausanderson.com

CEO: Bruce Engelsma
CFO: -
HR: Diane Toll
FYE: December 31
Type: Private

Kraus-Anderson has built on experience since 1897. The group's Kraus-Anderson Construction firm works on projects of all types and sizes around the US. Serving as general contractor or construction manager, the firm builds hotels, churches, schools, wind farms, and sports arenas. Other subsidiaries include Kraus-Anderson Realty, which owns, leases and manages some 4 million sq. ft. of commercial property space in the Minneapolis area. Its Kraus-Anderson Insurance arm offers personal and business coverage, while Kraus-Anderson Development develops office, retail, medical office, hospitality, multi-family housing, and mixed-use projects. Chairman and CEO Bruce Engelsma and his family own the company.

	Annual Growth	12/01	12/02	12/03	12/05	12/19
Sales ($mil.)	(24.5%)	-	-	552.1	26.4	6.1
Net income ($ mil.)	-	-	-	3.7	2.1	(0.6)
Market value ($ mil.)	-	-	-	-	-	-
Employees	-	-	-	-	-	97

KRAUSE GENTLE, L.L.C.

1459 GRAND AVE
DES MOINES, IA 503093005
Phone: 515 226-0128
Fax: -
Web: www.krausechallenge.com

CEO: William A Krause
CFO: Brian Beckett
HR: Steve Kimmes
FYE: December 31
Type: Private

If you're in a hurry in Iowa, Krause Gentle provides an assist. The company runs more than 400 Kum & Go convenience stores, mostly in Iowa, but also in a dozen other Midwestern and western states. The stores provide basic gas station amenities, as well as the company's private-label line (Hiland) of coffee, potato chips, sandwiches, and other foods. The company has more than doubled its Kum & Go store count since 1997 mostly through acquisitions. Solar Transport, a petroleum products and fertilizer hauler, Liberty Bank, and the Des Moines Menace soccer team are affiliated with Krause Gentle, which was founded in 1959. The founding Krause and Gentle families still own and run Krause Gentle.

KREHER STEEL COMPANY, LLC

1550 N 25TH AVE
MELROSE PARK, IL 601601801
Phone: 708 345-8180
Fax: -
Web: www.kreher.com

CEO: -
CFO: -
HR: -
FYE: September 30
Type: Private

Kreher Steel is a nationwide distributor of alloy, carbon, stainless, and tool steel. It also offers sawing and turning services. A pioneer in just-in-time delivery, Kreher Steel operates warehouses throughout the US to serve automotive manufacturers, steel processors, aerospace companies, and other customers. It also owns Kreher Wire, which makes fasteners and industrial products from its facility in Michigan. A joint venture between specialty metals distributors A. M. Castle & Co. and European steel trader Duferco owns two-thirds of Kreher Steel; chairman Thomas Kreher owns the rest. Kreher Steel was founded in 1978.

	Annual Growth	12/02	12/03	12/05	12/06*	09/19
Sales ($mil.)	1.1%	-	95.8	130.9	131.0	114.1
Net income ($ mil.)	(8.1%)	-	6.4	8.6	8.6	1.7
Market value ($ mil.)	-	-	-	-	-	-
Employees	-	-	-	-	-	53

*Fiscal year change

KROENKE SPORTS HOLDINGS LLC

1000 CHOPPER CIR
DENVER, CO 802045805
Phone: 303 405-1100
Fax: -
Web: www.ballarena.com

CEO: -
CFO: -
HR: -
FYE: June 30
Type: Private

The Pepsi Center is Rocky Mountain High on entertaining the masses in Denver. The arena serves primarily as the home court for the Denver Nuggets basketball team and as home ice for the Colorado Avalanche professional hockey club. It also hosts more than 200 other sporting contests, concerts, and entertainment events. The Pepsi Center includes such amenities as casual and fine dining restaurants, as well as conference facilities. The arena opened in 1999 with a Celine Dion concert. The $180 million facility is owned by Kroenke Sports, and is located near Denver's LoDo entertainment district.

KROGER CO (THE)

1014 Vine Street
Cincinnati, OH 45202
Phone: 513 762-4000
Fax: 513 762-1400
Web: www.thekrogerco.com

NYS: KR
CEO: W R McMullen
CFO: Gary Millerchip
HR: -
FYE: January 28
Type: Public

The Kroger operates supermarkets under a variety of local banner names in approximately 35 states and the District of Columbia, the company operates either directly or through its subsidiaries, nearly 2,720 supermarkets, of which more than 2,250 have pharmacies and about 1,635 have fuel centers. The company offers Pickup and Harris Teeter ExpressLane ? personalized, order online, pick up at the store services ? at over 2,275 of its supermarkets and provides home delivery services to substantially all of Kroger households. It also has about 35 food production plants in the US, mostly bakeries and dairies.

	Annual Growth	02/19	02/20*	01/21	01/22	01/23
Sales ($mil.)	5.2%	121,162	122,286	132,498	137,888	148,258
Net income ($ mil.)	(7.8%)	3,110.0	1,659.0	2,585.0	1,655.0	2,244.0
Market value ($ mil.)	12.6%	20,098	19,232	24,702	31,125	32,256
Employees	(1.3%)	453,000	435,000	465,000	420,000	430,000

*Fiscal year change

KRONES, INC.

9600 S 58TH ST
FRANKLIN, WI 531329107
Phone: 414 409-4000
Fax: -
Web: www.kronesusa.com

CEO: Holger Beckmann
CFO: -
HR: -
FYE: December 31
Type: Private

Krones is in the business of keeping things all bottled up. The company develops, manufactures, and installs packaging machinery and systems that design, clean, rinse, and fill bottles, cans, and plastic containers. Its offerings include labeling and sealing machines, inspection and monitoring systems, and mixing and carbonating systems. Krones caters to companies in North and Central America and the Caribbean in the food and beverage, beer, wine and spirits, health and cosmetic, pharmaceutical, and household goods industries. Krones is a subsidiary of KRONES, which is owned largely by the founding Kronseder family.

	Annual Growth	12/04	12/05	12/06	12/07	12/08
Sales ($mil.)	(1.7%)	-	383.1	364.4	359.7	363.9
Net income ($ mil.)	58.2%	-	1.5	2.3	6.8	6.0
Market value ($ mil.)	-	-	-	-	-	-
Employees	-	-	-	-	-	570

KRONOS WORLDWIDE INC

NYS: KRO

5430 LBJ Freeway, Suite 1700
Dallas, TX 75240-2620
Phone: 972 233-1700
Fax: –
Web: www.kronostio2.com

CEO: James M Buch
CFO: Tim C Hafer
HR: –
FYE: December 31
Type: Public

Kronos Worldwide is a leading global producer and marketer of value-added titanium dioxide pigments, or TiO2, a base industrial product used in a wide range of applications. TiO2 is a white inorganic pigment used in a wide range of products for its exceptional durability and its ability to impart whiteness, brightness, and opacity. It is a critical component of everyday applications, such as coatings, plastics, and paper, as well as many specialty products such as inks, food, cosmetics, and pharmaceuticals. The company, along with its distributors and agents, sells and provides technical services for its products to approximately 4,000 customers in some 100 countries with the majority of its sales in Europe, North America, and the APAC region. The US generates about 40% of the company's revenue.

	Annual Growth	12/19	12/20	12/21	12/22	12/23
Sales ($mil.)	(0.9%)	1,731.1	1,638.8	1,939.4	1,930.2	1,666.5
Net income ($ mil.)	–	–	87.1	63.9	112.9	104.5	(49.1)
Market value ($ mil.)	(7.2%)	1,542.3	1,716.1	1,727.7	1,081.9	1,144.1
Employees	–	2,200	2,242	2,248	2,266	2,196

KRUEGER INTERNATIONAL, INC.

1330 BELLEVUE ST
GREEN BAY, WI 543022197
Phone: 920 468-8100
Fax: –
Web: www.ki.com

CEO: –
CFO: –
HR: –
FYE: December 31
Type: Private

Krueger International is one of the world's leading contract furniture manufacturers in the industry. The company, which does business as KI, makes ergonomic seating, cabinets, sleepers, occasional tables, and other furniture used by businesses, healthcare organizations, government agencies, and educational institutions. It offers everything from benches and beds to desks and tables, not to mention shelving, filing systems, and movable walls. KI markets its products through sales representatives, furniture dealers, architects, and interior designers worldwide. Founded in 1941, KI is 100% employee-owned.

	Annual Growth	12/08	12/09	12/10	12/11	12/15
Sales ($mil.)	–	–	–	(40.1)	649.7	617.3
Net income ($ mil.)	1047.2%	–	–	0.0	56.9	53.3
Market value ($ mil.)	–	–	–	–	–	–
Employees	–	–	–	–	–	2,300

KS BANCORP INC

NBB: KSBI

1031 North Brightleaf Blvd., P.O. Box 661
Smithfield, NC 27577
Phone: 919 938-3119
Fax: 919 938-2645
Web: www.ksbankinc.com

CEO: Earl W Worley
CFO: –
HR: –
FYE: December 31
Type: Public

KS Bancorp is the holding company for KS Bank, which serves the eastern North Carolina counties of Johnston, Wake, Wayne, and Wilson, including portions of the Raleigh metro area. Through nearly 10 branches, it offers standard deposit products such as checking, savings, and money market accounts, as well as individual retirement accounts and certificates of deposit. The bank specializes in real estate lending, including one- to four-family residential mortgages, commercial mortgages, and construction and land development loans, which together account for more than 90% of its loan portfolio. It also offers investment services. KS Bank was chartered in 1924.

	Annual Growth	12/99	12/00	12/01	12/02	12/03
Assets ($mil.)	9.7%	138.9	152.3	163.9	191.1	201.5
Net income ($ mil.)	4.8%	1.2	2.0	1.4	1.3	1.4
Market value ($ mil.)	2.6%	27.0	24.7	22.7	24.2	29.9
Employees	14.6%	44	44	54	62	76

KUAKINI HEALTH SYSTEM

347 N KUAKINI ST
HONOLULU, HI 968172382
Phone: 808 547-9148
Fax: –
Web: www.kuakini.org

CEO: –
CFO: Quin Ogawa
HR: –
FYE: June 30
Type: Private

Say aloha to better health! Kuakini Health System operates the non-profit Kuakini Medical Center, a 250-bed acute care hospital that provides specialty services including cancer treatment, cardiac care, and orthopedic surgery. The hospital serves as a teaching center for the University of Hawaii's John A. Burns School of Medicine. Kuakini Health System also operates the 234-bed Kuakini Geriatric Care facility, which offers nursing home and adult day care for Honolulu's senior citizens. The system also maintains two medical office buildings. The Kuakini Health System was founded by Japanese immigrants in 1900. It is a member of the Premier group purchasing alliance.

	Annual Growth	06/14	06/15	06/16	06/20	06/21
Sales ($mil.)	0.1%	–	–	148.3	144.9	148.8
Net income ($ mil.)	–	–	–	(23.8)	(14.4)	14.4
Market value ($ mil.)	–	–	–	–	–	–
Employees	–	–	–	–	–	1,400

KURT MANUFACTURING COMPANY, INC.

5280 MAIN ST NE
MINNEAPOLIS, MN 554211594
Phone: 763 572-1500
Fax: –
Web: www.kurt.com

CEO: Paul Lillyblad
CFO: Paul Lillyblad
HR: Deanna Jylha
FYE: October 31
Type: Private

Kurt Manufacturing helps its customers provide decisions on precision when it comes to the manufacturing process. It makes precision-machined parts and components on a contract basis for the aerospace, automotive, oil, and defense markets. Kurt operates through divisions including Hydraulics, Engineered Systems, Kinetic, and Workholding. These divisions make gauging systems, hydraulic coupling and hoses, vises and other workholding tools to a list of clients that have included such big names as ATK, Deere & Co., General Dynamics, General Electric, General Motors, Honeywell, IBM, and Lockheed Martin. Kurt is an employee owned company.

	Annual Growth	10/05	10/06	10/07*	11/08*	10/09
Sales ($mil.)	(22.2%)	–	–	112.1	108.9	67.8
Net income ($ mil.)	–	–	–	2.9	3.3	(1.3)
Market value ($ mil.)	–	–	–	–	–	–
Employees	–	–	–	–	–	510

*Fiscal year change

KUTAK ROCK LLP

1650 FARNAM ST FL 2
OMAHA, NE 681022103
Phone: 402 346-6000
Fax: –
Web: www.kutakrock.com

CEO: –
CFO: –
HR: Rita Garrett
FYE: December 31
Type: Private

Kutak Rock is a national law firm with more than 550 attorneys. Kutak Rock offers legal services that are aligned with the marketplace and showcase its attorneys' background, skill, and experience. The firm's practice areas include business, corporate, and securities, public finance, real estate, real estate capital markets, and litigation. Through a founding partnership featuring Robert Kutak and Harold Rock, Kutak Rock first opened its doors in Omaha in 1965 and has now grown to include almost 20 offices nationwide. Clients have included federal agencies, utilities, ESCOs, lenders, investors, state and local governments, and rating agencies.

KVH INDUSTRIES, INC.

50 Enterprise Center
Middletown, RI 02842
Phone: 401 847-3327
Fax: –
Web: www.kvh.com

NMS: KVHI
CEO: –
CFO: –
HR: –
FYE: December 31
Type: Public

KVH Industries is a leading provider of innovative, technology-driven connectivity and navigation solutions to maritime, defense and other commercial customers globally. Through its mobile connectivity business, it provides global high-speed Internet and voice services via satellite to mobile users at sea and on land. It is also a leading provider of commercially licensed entertainment, including news, sports, music, and movies, to commercial and leisure customers in the maritime, hotel, and retail markets. The company started in 1982 as Sailcomp Industries and was reincorporated as KVH Industries, Inc. in 1985.

	Annual Growth	12/19	12/20	12/21	12/22	12/23
Sales ($mil.)	(4.3%)	157.9	158.7	171.8	138.9	132.4
Net income ($ mil.)	–	33.3	(21.9)	(9.8)	24.1	(15.4)
Market value ($ mil.)	(17.1%)	218.3	222.6	180.2	200.4	103.2
Employees	(13.5%)	604	639	648	397	338

KWALU LLC

6160 PEACHTREE DUNWOODY RD BLDG C
ATLANTA, GA 303286068
Phone: 678 690-5600
Fax: –
Web: www.kwalu.com

CEO: –
CFO: –
HR: –
FYE: December 31
Type: Private

Kwalu knows that sturdy can be stylish, too. The company makes durable chairs, tables, case goods, and wall protection products (including handrails and kick plates) for contract interior design clients. The modular construction of its products enables customers to mix and match frame styles, finishes, and upholstery choices to create unique furnishings. Kwalu markets its goods to cruise ships, dining rooms, hospitals and other health care facilities, hotels, and primary schools and universities. It also serves the government, institutional, and special needs niches. The company was founded in 1984.

	Annual Growth	12/11	12/12	12/13	12/14	12/15
Sales ($mil.)	–	–	–	–	0.0	0.0
Net income ($ mil.)	–	–	–	–	(0.0)	–
Market value ($ mil.)	–	–	–	–	–	–
Employees	–	–	–	–	–	65

KWIK TRIP, INC.

1626 OAK ST
LA CROSSE, WI 546032308
Phone: 608 781-8988
Fax: –
Web: www.kwiktrip.com

CEO: –
CFO: Jeff Wrobel
HR: Tom Reinhart
FYE: September 27
Type: Private

Kwik Trip is a privately owned family company. Midwesterners who need to make a quick trip to get gas or groceries, cigarettes or donuts, race on over to Kwik Trip stores. Adding over 30 new stores each year, the company's more than 36,000 co-workers serve guests at more than 850 Kwik Trip, Kwik Star, Stop-N-Go, Tobacco Outlet Plus Grocery, and Tobacco Outlet Plus convenience stores throughout Iowa, Illinois, Minnesota, and Wisconsin. With its own bakery, kitchens, dairy, distribution, and transportation divisions, the company produces quality products for its customers. Kwik Trip opened its first store in 1965.

	Annual Growth	09/01	09/02	09/03	09/04	09/08
Sales ($mil.)	17.1%	–	–	1,651.1	1,887.1	3,640.4
Net income ($ mil.)	(0.2%)	–	–	24.1	24.7	23.9
Market value ($ mil.)	–	–	–	–	–	–
Employees	–	–	–	–	–	10,500

KYNECT, LTD.

2745 DALLAS PKWY STE 200
PLANO, TX 750938729
Phone: 214 800-4400
Fax: –
Web: www.mystream.com

CEO: Mark Schiro
CFO: David Faranetta
HR: Cydney White
FYE: December 31
Type: Private

If you'd like energy streamed right to your house or business for less cost, this company can help. Stream Gas & Electric, dba Stream Energy, competes with major utilities by supplying natural gas and electric services at lower prices to residential, business, and commercial customers in deregulated power and gas markets in Georgia, Maryland, New Jersey, Pennsylvania, and Texas. The company's marketing arm, Ignite, uses a multi-level marketing approach to sign up customers for energy services. Ignite oversees a network of independent agents who earn money for signing up customers and other sales agents as well as from utility sales. In 2019, Stream Energy agreed to be acquired by NRG Energy for $300 million.

L & L FRANCHISE, INC.

2138 ALGAROBA ST
HONOLULU, HI 968262714
Phone: 808 951-9888
Fax: –
Web: www.hawaiianbarbecue.com

CEO: Elisia Flores
CFO: –
HR: –
FYE: December 31
Type: Private

L&L Franchise brings Hawaiian-style quick-service dining to the US mainland. The company operates the L&L Hawaiian Barbecue chain with about 180 franchised locations in California, Hawaii, and about 10 other mostly Western states. The eateries feature Hawaiian plate lunches, which typically includes two scoops of rice and a scoop of macaroni salad flanking an entree of Hawaiian barbecued beef, chicken, or pork ribs. Other entrees include fried seafood and curry dishes. Founders Johnson Kam and Eddie Flores, Jr., bought their first restaurant in 1976 and began franchising in 1988.

	Annual Growth	12/05	12/06	12/07	12/08	12/20
Sales ($mil.)	67.9%	–	–	–	0.0	5.8
Net income ($ mil.)	–	–	–	–	(0.0)	2.5
Market value ($ mil.)	–	–	–	–	–	–
Employees	–	–	–	–	–	20

L & M COMPANIES INC.

2925 HUNTLEIGH DR STE 204
RALEIGH, NC 276043374
Phone: 919 981-8000
Fax: –
Web: www.lmcompanies.com

CEO: Jonathan C Oxford
CFO: –
HR: –
FYE: December 31
Type: Private

L & M Companies is a leading supplier of fresh fruits and vegetables under the Nature's Delight label. It grows much of its own produce through subsidiary L & M Farms, with locations throughout the US, as well as in Central and South America. The company's AG Warehouse & Packing and L & M Transportation divisions provide packaging and logistics services through more than a dozen distribution facilities. Its Carolina Refrigerated Trailer Sales (CRTS) sells freight vehicles and provides related parts and services. L & M was founded in 1964 by president Joe McGee.

L & S ELECTRIC, INC.

5101 MESKER ST
SCHOFIELD, WI 544763056
Phone: 715 359-3155
Fax: –
Web: www.lselectric.com
CEO: –
CFO: David Krause
HR: –
FYE: December 31
Type: Private

L&S Electric isn't a run of the mill distributor, even if its products run the mill. The company specializes in selling motors, controls, drives, and integrated systems used in power generation, railway, pulp and paper mill, mining, and other industrial applications. It also offers engineering and repair services worldwide through an engineering division and its L&S Electric of Canada subsidiary. L&S Electric has about eight locations in Wisconsin, Minnesota, and Michigan. The company was formed in the 1983 merger of Leverence Electric and Snapp Electric, two motor repair shops that dated back to the 1930s. L&S Electric is owned by the Lewitzke family.

	Annual Growth	12/12	12/13	12/14	12/15	12/16
Sales ($mil.)	(1.6%)	–	84.0	81.4	85.5	80.1
Net income ($ mil.)	–	–	5.8	2.6	1.6	(0.4)
Market value ($ mil.)	–	–	–	–	–	–
Employees	–	–	–	–	–	350

L&L ENERGY INC

130 Andover Park East, Suite 200
Seattle, WA 98188
Phone: 206 264-8065
Fax: 206 838-0488
Web: www.llenergyinc.com
CEO: –
CFO: –
HR: –
FYE: April 30
Type: Public

You'll excuse L & L Energy (formerly L & L International) if it's a bit jet lagged. Incorporated in Nevada with headquarters in Seattle, the company mines coal in China. Granted a license by the government to extract a set amount of coal in exchange for up-front fees, L & L owns mines in China's Yunnan and Guizhou provinces. The company currently extracts more than 630,000 tons of coal per year from the mines. It also processes coal to produce coke used in steel production, medium coal used for heating, and coal slurries used as a lower quality fuel. L & L is swapping a stake in a coking mine with Singapore-based Union Energy to acquire a 50% stake in the LuoZhou coal mine.

	Annual Growth	04/09	04/10	04/11	04/12	04/13
Sales ($mil.)	48.5%	40.9	109.2	223.9	143.6	199.0
Net income ($ mil.)	40.1%	10.0	32.9	36.8	14.2	38.4
Market value ($ mil.)	21.1%	68.6	411.5	264.8	85.7	147.4
Employees	3.3%	1,200	1,400	1,600	1,330	1,364

L&M TECHNOLOGIES, INC.

4700 LINCOLN RD NE STE 114
ALBUQUERQUE, NM 871092303
Phone: 505 343-0200
Fax: –
Web: www.lmtechnologies.com
CEO: –
CFO: Antonette Montoya
HR: –
FYE: December 31
Type: Private

L&M provides information technology and logistics services to government agencies and defense contractors. It builds large databases, manages IT and operational facilities, provides consulting services, and performs systems integration among other services. The company also specializes in purchasing, warehousing, and inventory control. L&M's clients have included NASA's White Sands Test Facility, the Department of Energy, and Sandia National Laboratories. It has operations in Florida, Maryland, New Mexico, and Texas. The company is owned by director Antonio Montoya.

	Annual Growth	11/04	11/05	11/06	11/07*	12/12
Sales ($mil.)	20.9%	–	–	–	13.8	35.7
Net income ($ mil.)	57.2%	–	–	–	0.0	0.9
Market value ($ mil.)	–	–	–	–	–	–
Employees	–	–	–	–	–	80

*Fiscal year change

L.D. MCFARLAND COMPANY, LIMITED

1640 E MARC ST
TACOMA, WA 98421
Phone: 253 572-5670
Fax: –
Web: www.ldm.com
CEO: –
CFO: –
HR: –
FYE: December 31
Type: Private

Some builders think it "wooden" be a project without McFarland Cascade. The company produces wood and composite products including pressure-treated utility poles, crossarms, lumber, and plywood. McFarland Cascade also packages and distributes consumer-oriented outdoor living products and develops computer software packages for assisting consumers in designing, estimating, and constructing such outdoor projects as decks. The company sells to customers in the US, Canada, the Middle East, and Asia, and operates four treating facilities in the Northwest and Mississippi. Founded in 1916, McFarland Cascade has agreed to be acquired by Stella-Jones Inc. for about $250 million.

L3HARRIS TECHNOLOGIES INC

1025 West NASA Boulevard
Melbourne, FL 32919
Phone: 321 727-9100
Fax: –
Web: www.l3harris.com
NYS: LHX
CEO: Christopher E Kubasik
CFO: Kenneth L Bedingfield
HR: –
FYE: December 29
Type: Public

L3Harris Technologies (formerly Harris Corp. and L3 Technologies) is a Trusted Disruptor for the aerospace and defense industry, delivering end-to-end technology solutions that meet customers' mission-critical needs that provide advanced defense and commercial technologies across air, land, sea, space, and cyber domains for government and commercial customers in approximately 100 countries. It makes tactical communications and other integrated vision solutions; air traffic management; and intelligence, surveillance, and reconnaissance systems. Although almost 75% of L3Harris' revenue comes from US government agencies, it also has customers in the international and commercial sectors. US operations account for approximately 90% of revenue.

	Annual Growth	01/20	01/21*	12/21	12/22	12/23
Sales ($mil.)	20.3%	9,263.0	18,194	17,814	17,062	19,419
Net income ($ mil.)	10.5%	822.0	1,119.0	1,846.0	1,062.0	1,227.0
Market value ($ mil.)	–	–	39,949	35,878	40,475	39,520	39,977
Employees	–	50,000	48,000	47,000	46,000	50,000

*Fiscal year change

LA FRANCE CORP.

ONE LAFRANCE WAY
CONCORDVILLE, PA 19331
Phone: 610 361-4300
Fax: –
Web: www.lafrancecorp.com
CEO: –
CFO: Thomas Sheehan
HR: –
FYE: December 31
Type: Private

LaFrance Corp., also known as LaFrance, makes nameplates, functional components, and other products through several divisions. It offers an array of alternatives for its customer's decorative or functional component. Its comprehensive product offering of metals and plastics can be combined to create unique emblems, logos, trim, and functional pieces. It uses electroform, metal letters, stainless steel, and more, to create its products. Starting out in the jewelry business in 1946, Joseph A. Teti, Jr., the founder, recognized a match between LaFrance's precision manufacturing capabilities and a market need for high-quality product branding.

	Annual Growth	12/09	12/10	12/11	12/12	12/13
Sales ($mil.)	14.1%	–	–	–	115.1	131.4
Net income ($ mil.)	(5.8%)	–	–	–	10.9	10.3
Market value ($ mil.)	–	–	–	–	–	–
Employees	–	–	–	–	–	2,400

LA INDIA PACKING CO.

1520 MARCELLA AVE
LAREDO, TX 780407900
Phone: 956 723-3772
Fax: –
Web: www.laindiaherbsandspices.com

CEO: –
CFO: –
HR: –
FYE: December 31
Type: Private

La India Packing Company is actually situated closer to el M xico than to the home of the Taj Mahal. Located in Laredo, Texas, the company sells authentic Hispanic herbs, spices, and teas. It offers tejano and fajita seasoning, pica rico (for seasoning fruits), Mexican chocolate and more. Its products are sold in bulk, boxed, and bagged. They are available online at La India's Web site and at the company's store in Laredo, where the owners also operate a small restaurant called the Tasting Room Cafe. La India's spices are also carried by such retail outlets in Texas as Albertsons, H.E.B, Kmart, and Wal-mart. Owned and operated by the Rodriguez family, La India Packing Company was founded in 1924.

LA JOLLA PHARMACEUTICAL COMPANY

35 GATEHOUSE DR STE E0
WALTHAM, MA 024511215
Phone: 617 715-3600
Fax: –
Web: www.lajollapharmaceutical.com

CEO: Pavel Raifeld
CFO: Michael Hearne
HR: –
FYE: December 31
Type: Private

La Jolla Pharmaceutical Company is dedicated to the commercialization of innovative therapies that improve outcomes in patients suffering from life-threatening diseases. GIAPREZA (angiotensin II) injection is approved by the US Food and Drug Administration (FDA) as a vasoconstrictor indicated to increase blood pressure in adults with septic or other distributive shock. XERAVA (eravacycline) is approved by the US FDA for the treatment of complicated intra-abdominal infections. In connection with the acquisition of Tetraphase, La Jolla acquired the following product candidates that are in early stage clinical or preclinical development: TP-6076, an IV formulation of a fully synthetic fluorocycline derivative for the treatment of certain multidrug-resistant gram-negative bacteria; TP-271, an IV and oral formulation of a fully synthetic fluorocycline for the treatment of respiratory disease caused by bacterial biothreat; and (iii) TP-2846, an IV formulation of a tetracycline for the treatment of acute myeloid leukemia. In mid-2022, Innoviva acquired the company for approximately $149 million.

LA QUINTA HOLDINGS INC.

909 HIDDEN RDG STE 600
IRVING, TX 750383822
Phone: 214 492-6600
Fax: –
Web: www.lq.com

CEO: Keith A Cline
CFO: James H Forson
HR: –
FYE: December 31
Type: Private

This hotel chain wants its hotels to be the affordable but nice place to stay in North America. La Quinta by Windham has hundreds of hotels throughout the North, Central, and South America, Canada, and Mexico under the La Quinta Inns and La Quinta Inn & Suites brands. La Quinta has some 940 hotels. It was a midscale hotel operated by Wyndham. Backed by investment firm, The Blackstone Group, the company went public, but it was acquired by Wyndham Worldwide.

LA-Z-BOY INC.

One La-Z-Boy Drive
Monroe, MI 48162-5138
Phone: 734 242-1444
Fax: –
Web: www.la-z-boy.com

NYS: LZB
CEO: Melinda D Whittington
CFO: Robert G Lucian
HR: –
FYE: April 29
Type: Public

La-Z-Boy is the leading global producer of reclining chairs and the second largest manufacturer/distributor of residential furniture in the US. The La-Z-Boy Furniture Galleries stores retail network is the third largest retailer of single-branded furniture in the US. It manufactures, markets, imports, exports, distributes, and retails upholstery furniture products under the La-Z-Boy, England, Kincaid, and Joybird tradenames, and the company imports, distributes, and retails accessories and casegoods (wood) furniture products under the Kincaid, American Drew, Hammary, and Joybird tradenames. La-Z-Boy sells its products through its company-owned stores and about 870 independent locations under the La-Z-Boy Furniture Galleries and La-Z-Boy Comfort Studio names. The company also sells furniture to retailers across the US, Canada, and approximately 55 other countries. The US is the company's largest market.

	Annual Growth	04/19	04/20	04/21	04/22	04/23
Sales ($mil.)	7.7%	1,745.4	1,704.0	1,734.2	2,356.8	2,349.4
Net income ($ mil.)	21.7%	68.6	77.5	106.5	150.0	150.7
Market value ($ mil.)	(3.0%)	1,405.7	912.7	1,872.2	1,138.4	1,244.5
Employees	2.0%	9,700	9,500	11,500	12,800	10,500

LABORATORY CORPORATION OF AMERICA HOLDINGS

358 South Main Street
Burlington, NC 27215
Phone: 336 229-1127
Fax: –
Web: www.labcorp.com

NYS: LH
CEO: Adam H Schechter
CFO: Glenn A Eisenberg
HR: –
FYE: December 31
Type: Public

Laboratory Corporation of America (LabCorp) is a leading global life sciences company that provides vital information to help doctors, hospitals, pharmaceutical companies, researchers, and patients make clear and confident decisions. Labcorp serves a broad range of customers, including MCOs, pharmaceutical, biotechnology, medical device and diagnostics companies, governmental agencies, physicians and other healthcare providers, hospitals and health systems, employers, patients and consumers, contract research organizations (CROs), and independent clinical laboratories. Services range from routine urinalyses, HIV tests, and Pap smears to specialty testing for diagnostic genetics, disease monitoring, forensics, identity, clinical drug trials, and allergies. Majority of the company's revenue comes from North America.

	Annual Growth	12/19	12/20	12/21	12/22	12/23
Sales ($mil.)	1.3%	11,555	13,979	16,121	14,877	12,162
Net income ($ mil.)	(15.6%)	823.8	1,556.1	2,377.3	1,279.1	418.0
Market value ($ mil.)	7.7%	14,193	17,078	26,362	19,757	19,070
Employees	0.8%	65,000	72,400	75,500	80,000	67,000

LADDER CAPITAL CORP

320 Park Avenue
New York, NY 10022
Phone: 212 715-3170
Fax: –
Web: www.laddercapital.com

NYS: LADR
CEO: Brian Harris
CFO: Marc Fox
HR: –
FYE: December 31
Type: Public

This specialty finance firm is looking to climb to the top of the commercial real-estate lending business. Ladder Capital Corp. is a non-bank operating company engaged in three major lines of business: commercial mortgage lending, mortgage backed securities, and real-estate assets. Its loans typically range from $5 million to $100 million. More than 50% of its loans originate in the Northeast. Hotel, retail, and office properties account for about three-quarters of Ladder's loan portfolio. Since its founding in 2008, the commercial real estate finance firm has originated $5.4 billion in conduit loans. Ladder Capital went public in 2014 with an offering valued at $225 million.

	Annual Growth	12/19	12/20	12/21	12/22	12/23
Assets ($mil.)	(4.6%)	6,669.2	5,881.2	5,851.3	5,951.2	5,512.7
Net income ($ mil.)	(4.7%)	122.6	(14.4)	56.5	142.2	101.1
Market value ($ mil.)	(10.6%)	2,289.5	1,241.2	1,521.7	1,274.2	1,460.8
Employees	(6.1%)	76	58	65	63	59

LADENBURG THALMANN FINANCIAL SERVICES INC   NBB: LTSA

4400 Biscayne Boulevard, 12th Floor
Miami, FL 33137
Phone: 305 572-4100
Fax: –
Web: www.ladenburg.com

CEO: Jamie Price
CFO: –
HR: Nancy Disilva
FYE: December 31
Type: Public

Ladenburg Thalmann Financial Services is a wholly-owned subsidiary of Advisor Group Holdings, Inc., which is owned by private investment funds sponsored by Reverence Capital Partners, LLC. Ladenburg's subsidiaries include industry-leading independent advisory and brokerage (IAB) firms Securities America, Triad Advisors, Securities Service Network, Investacorp and KMS Financial Services, as well as Premier Trust, Ladenburg Thalmann Asset Management, Highland Capital Brokerage, a leading independent life insurance brokerage company and full-service annuity processing and marketing company, and Ladenburg Thalmann & Co. Inc., an investment bank.

	Annual Growth	12/15	12/16	12/17	12/18	12/19
Sales ($mil.)	6.3%	1,152.1	1,107.0	1,268.2	1,391.1	1,469.3
Net income ($ mil.)	–	(11.2)	(22.3)	7.7	33.8	22.8
Market value ($ mil.)	0.3%	3,694.0	3,574.5	3,779.2	3,535.7	3,744.7
Employees	3.7%	1,307	1,299	1,379	1,512	1,510

LADIES PROFESSIONAL GOLF ASSOCIATION

100 INTERNATIONAL GOLF DR
DAYTONA BEACH, FL 321241082
Phone: 386 274-6200
Fax: –
Web: www.lpga.com

CEO: –
CFO: –
HR: Wendy Caves
FYE: December 31
Type: Private

This organization has chipped out a place for itself in the male-dominated sports world. The Ladies Professional Golf Association (LPGA) is the organizing body for women's golf, overseeing development and promotion of the game and its star players. It operates the LPGA Tour consisting of about 30 events a year. In addition to its high-profile golf tournaments, the organization runs the LPGA Teaching & Club Professional Division, which is the golf education and development subsidiary for its 1,200 members. The LPGA was founded in 1950, making it one of the oldest women's sports organizations in the world.

	Annual Growth	12/11	12/12	12/13	12/21	12/22
Sales ($mil.)	7.3%	–	89.1	102.9	165.8	180.1
Net income ($ mil.)	47.3%	–	0.2	1.2	9.1	7.6
Market value ($ mil.)	–	–	–	–	–	–
Employees	–	–	–	–	–	85

LADRX CORP   NBB: LADX

11726 San Vicente Blvd., Suite 650
Los Angeles, CA 90049
Phone: 310 826-5648
Fax: 310 826-6139
Web: www.cytrx.com

CEO: Stephen Snowdy
CFO: John Y Caloz
HR: –
FYE: December 31
Type: Public

CytRx is fighting cancer at the scene of the crime. The clinical-stage biopharmaceutical is researching and developing drug candidates to treat conditions such as like pancreatic cancer, head and neck cancer, triple negative breast cancer, colorectal cancer and soft-tissue sarcomas (malignant tumors). Its lead candidate is aldoxorubicin, a conjugate of the chemotherapic agent doxorubicin. CytRx subsidiary Centurion BioPharma is focused on specialized treatments that are delivered directly to solid tumors.

	Annual Growth	12/19	12/20	12/21	12/22	12/23
Sales ($mil.)	–	–	–	–	–	–
Net income ($ mil.)	–	(7.2)	(6.7)	(13.2)	(4.2)	0.4
Market value ($ mil.)	45.5%	0.1	0.9	0.3	0.0	0.6
Employees	(15.9%)	4	4	3	3	2

LAEMMLE THEATRES, LLC

11523 SANTA MONICA BLVD
LOS ANGELES, CA 900253007
Phone: 310 478-1041
Fax: –
Web: www.laemmle.com

CEO: –
CFO: –
HR: –
FYE: December 31
Type: Private

To get your art cinema fix, turn to Laemmle Theatres. The exhibitor (pronounced LEM-lee) specializes in art films, foreign films, and other independent fare. The company operates about 10 movie houses in Southern California, most of which are in the Los Angeles area. Locations include Beverly Hills, Hollywood, Pasadena, and Santa Monica. Laemmle Theatres has upgraded several of its properties in recent years, adding air conditioning and other amenities to aging art houses. The company was established in 1938 by Kurt and Max Laemmle, nephews of Carl Laemmle, the founder of Universal Pictures. Robert Laemmle, son of Max, owns the firm.

LAFAYETTE COLLEGE

730 SULLIVAN RD
EASTON, PA 180421760
Phone: 610 330-5000
Fax: –
Web: www.lafayette.edu

CEO: –
CFO: –
HR: –
FYE: June 30
Type: Private

Lafayette College has a revolutionary background. Named after the French hero of the American Revolution, the school offers bachelor's degrees in 37 areas of study in engineering, sciences, and the arts. Some 2,450 students -- all undergraduates -- are enrolled on the campus, located about 70 miles west of New York City and 60 miles north of Philadelphia. Students come from 46 US states and territories and from 48 other countries. Lafayette is a member of the Lehigh Valley Association of Independent Colleges, which also includes Cedar Crest College, DeSales University, Lehigh University, Moravian College, and Muhlenberg College.

	Annual Growth	06/14	06/15	06/20	06/21	06/22
Sales ($mil.)	–	–	265.7	228.5	234.2	266.4
Net income ($ mil.)	(14.1%)	–	73.3	(0.1)	28.6	25.2
Market value ($ mil.)	–	–	–	–	–	–
Employees	–	–	–	–	–	675

LAFAYETTE GENERAL MEDICAL CENTER, INC.

1214 COOLIDGE BLVD
LAFAYETTE, LA 705032621
Phone: 337 289-7991
Fax: –
Web: www.ochsner.org

CEO: –
CFO: –
HR: –
FYE: December 31
Type: Private

Serving the people of Acadiana (southern Louisiana), Lafayette General Medical Center (LGMC) provides general inpatient medical and surgical care, as well as specialized trauma care and neonatal intensive care. The nonprofit hospital, which has 365 beds, also offers a cancer center, home health services, outpatient care, occupational medicine, and mental health care. As part of umbrella group Lafayette Health, LGMC is affiliated with Lafayette General Surgical Hospital, Lafayette General Southwest, St. Martin Hospital, Acadia General Hospital, University Hospital and Clinics, and Abrom Kaplan Memorial Hospital. It's also a teaching hospital for LSU. Non-profit foundation Lafayette General Foundation supports and governs Lafayette Health.

	Annual Growth	09/19	09/20	09/21*	12/21	12/22
Sales ($mil.)	6.7%	–	492.5	474.8	589.2	560.2
Net income ($ mil.)	–	–	58.6	74.8	70.7	(11.3)
Market value ($ mil.)	–	–	–	–	–	–
Employees	–	–	–	–	–	1,626

*Fiscal year change

LAHEY HEALTH SYSTEM, INC.

41 MALL RD
BURLINGTON, MA 018050001
Phone: 781 744-5100
Fax: –
Web: www.lahey.org

CEO: Kevin Tabb
CFO: –
HR: Steven Walley
FYE: September 30
Type: Private

Physician-led Lahey Health System provides primary and tertiary care to residents of northeastern Massachusetts. Lahey Health System operates the Lahey Hospital & Medical Center in Burlington, which has about 320 beds and is a teaching hospital for Tufts University School of Medicine. It also operates four other area hospitals with a total of about 530 beds. The not-for-profit organization also operates several community-based primary care practices. It offers a range of health care services including cancer treatment, heart care, family medicine, and organ transplantation. Lahey Health System has agreed to merge with Beth Israel Deaconess Medical Center to create the state's second-largest health system.

	Annual Growth	09/11	09/12	09/13	09/14	09/15
Sales ($mil.)	(89.7%)	–	–	1,073.8	5.4	11.5
Net income ($ mil.)	–	–	–	1,073.8	–	–
Market value ($ mil.)	–	–	–	–	–	–
Employees	–	–	–	–	–	5,500

LAIRD & COMPANY

1 LAIRD RD
EATONTOWN, NJ 077249724
Phone: 732 542-0312
Fax: –
Web: www.lairdandcompany.com

CEO: –
CFO: –
HR: –
FYE: December 31
Type: Private

The North American settlers may have had a bit of applejack for breakfast, but don't think it was a sweet cereal. Applejack is a brandy distilled from -- you guessed it -- apples, and Robert Laird was among the first to make it in the New World. (Laird fought in the Revolutionary War under George Washington and supplied the Colonial troops with applejack.) He formally established the Laird distillery in 1780, and today the ninth generation of the Laird family continues to make applejack -- which is aged from four to eight years. The firm also imports (mostly Italian and French) wine and hard spirits (vodka, gin, grappa, tequila). Laird's beverages are distributed throughout the US.

	Annual Growth	12/14	12/15	12/16	12/17	12/18
Sales ($mil.)	(0.2%)	–	44.0	44.7	45.0	43.7
Net income ($ mil.)	17.5%	–	0.7	0.5	0.7	1.1
Market value ($ mil.)	–	–	–	–	–	–
Employees	–	–	–	–	–	56

LAKE AREA CORN PROCESSORS CO-OPERATIVE

46269 SD HIGHWAY 34
WENTWORTH, SD 570756934
Phone: 605 483-2676
Fax: –
Web: –

CEO: –
CFO: –
HR: –
FYE: December 31
Type: Private

Lake Area Corn Processors produces ethanol and its byproduct, distillers grains, which are used in livestock feed. Through its Dakota Ethanol unit, the company produces about 48 million gallons of ethanol per year. Dakota Ethanol had worked in tandem with Broin Companies, a manufacturer of ethanol processing plants, until Lake Area Corn Processors bought out Broin's minority stake in Dakota Ethanol in 2006. The following year, the company acquired a stake in its ethanol distributor, Renewable Products Marketing Group. Lake Area Corn Processors is owned by its 1,000 members.

	Annual Growth	12/04	12/05	12/06	12/07	12/10
Sales ($mil.)	3.8%	–	80.0	103.9	103.7	96.4
Net income ($ mil.)	(8.3%)	–	10.9	46.0	18.0	7.0
Market value ($ mil.)	–	–	–	–	–	–
Employees	–	–	–	–	–	25

LAKE FOREST COLLEGE

555 N SHERIDAN RD
LAKE FOREST, IL 600452338
Phone: 847 234-3100
Fax: –
Web: www.lakeforest.edu

CEO: –
CFO: –
HR: –
FYE: May 31
Type: Private

Living up to its name, Lake Forest College is a liberal arts school near the shores of Lake Michigan, just north of Chicago. The school sits on about a 100 acre campus 30 miles north of downtown Chicago and offers undergraduate and graduate programs to its approximately 1,500 students. With nearly 20 departmental and about 10 interdisciplinary majors, its subjects include economics, international studies, neuroscience, and pre-law. The College's Center for Chicago Programs facilitates research and internships at Chicago institutions as well as brings Chicago-based artists and artisans alike to the campus for lectures and performances.

	Annual Growth	05/18	05/19	05/20	05/21	05/22
Sales ($mil.)	8.5%	–	56.3	58.4	52.2	71.9
Net income ($ mil.)	–	–	4.2	(1.2)	24.9	(0.3)
Market value ($ mil.)	–	–	–	–	–	–
Employees	–	–	–	–	–	385

LAKE HOSPITAL SYSTEM, INC.

7590 AUBURN RD
CONCORD TOWNSHIP, OH 440779176
Phone: 440 375-8100
Fax: –
Web: www.uhhospitals.org

CEO: –
CFO: –
HR: Craig Ghidotti
FYE: December 31
Type: Private

Lake Health serves eight counties in Ohio. The not-for-profit health system comprises three main hospital campuses (Beachwood Medical Center, TriPoint Medical Center and West Medical Center), which provides patient- and family-centered care with a 24/7 Emergency Department, surgery center, labor and delivery suites, lab, imaging, physical therapy, retail pharmacy, and physician offices. The system's Lake Health Physician Group includes physicians ranging from family practitioners to vascular surgeons. Lake Health was founded in 1959.

	Annual Growth	12/15	12/16	12/17	12/18	12/21
Sales ($mil.)	1.0%	–	334.2	356.9	373.9	350.6
Net income ($ mil.)	–	–	(13.2)	33.3	(7.4)	20.6
Market value ($ mil.)	–	–	–	–	–	–
Employees	–	–	–	–	–	2,700

LAKE SHORE BANCORP INC

31 East Fourth Street
Dunkirk, NY 14048
Phone: 716 366-4070
Fax: –
Web: www.lakeshoresavings.com

NMS: LSBK
CEO: Kim C Liddell
CFO: Taylor Gilden
HR: –
FYE: December 31
Type: Public

Money washes up along this shore. Lake Shore Bancorp is the holding company for Lake Shore Savings Bank, which serves consumers and businesses through 11 branches in Chautauqua and Erie counties in western New York, near Lake Erie. Founded in 1891, the community oriented savings bank focuses on residential real estate lending, with one- to four-family mortgages accounting for a majority of its loan portfolio. Lake Shore Savings Bank also offers home equity loans and commercial and consumer loans, as well as checking and savings accounts, CDs, and IRAs. Mutual holding company Lake Shore, MHC owns about 60% of Lake Shore Bancorp.

	Annual Growth	12/19	12/20	12/21	12/22	12/23
Assets ($mil.)	4.4%	610.9	686.2	713.7	699.9	725.1
Net income ($ mil.)	4.2%	4.1	4.6	6.2	5.7	4.8
Market value ($ mil.)	(6.5%)	87.0	73.9	84.7	68.6	66.6
Employees	0.2%	116	118	107	120	117

LAKELAND BANCORP, INC.

NMS: LBAI

250 Oak Ridge Road
Oak Ridge, NJ 07438
Phone: 973 697-2000
Fax: –
Web: www.lakelandbank.com

CEO: Thomas J Shara
CFO: Thomas F Splaine Jr
HR: Sheri Picioccio
FYE: December 31
Type: Public

Lakeland Bancorp is the holding company for Lakeland Bank, which serves northern New Jersey from about 70 branch offices. Targeting individuals and small to midsized businesses, the bank offers standard retail products, such as checking and savings accounts, money market, certificates of deposit, online banking, secured and unsecured loans, consumer installment loans, mortgage loans, and safe deposit services. It also offers advisory services for consumers. The bank's lending activities primarily consist of commercial loans and mortgages (about 55% of the company's loan portfolio) and residential mortgages. Lakeland also offers commercial lease financing for office systems and heavy equipment.

	Annual Growth	12/19	12/20	12/21	12/22	12/23
Assets ($mil.)	13.5%	6,711.2	7,664.3	8,198.1	10,784	11,139
Net income ($ mil.)	4.6%	70.7	57.5	95.0	107.4	84.7
Market value ($ mil.)	(4.0%)	1,130.2	825.9	1,234.9	1,145.2	961.8
Employees	7.3%	692	711	717	911	916

LAKELAND COMMUNITY HOSPITAL, WATERVLIET

400 MEDICAL PARK DR
WATERVLIET, MI 490989225
Phone: 269 463-3111
Fax: –
Web: www.specthealthlakeland.org

CEO: Ray Cruse
CFO: Chris Kuhlmann
HR: –
FYE: December 31
Type: Private

If you're visiting the Arsenal City and you trip on an old cannon ball, Community Hospital Watervliet is there to fix your war wounds. The not-for-profit, acute care hospital provides medical care for the denizens of Watervliet, Michigan and surrounding townships. Among its specialized services are emergency medicine, obstetrics, cardiology, pediatrics, and pain management. Community Hospital is affiliated with Borgess Health. Community Hospital Watervliet also operates the Tri-City Medical Center, a medical group practice. The hospital -- originally a private residence and later a nursing home -- opened its doors in 1979.

	Annual Growth	09/17	09/18	09/19*	12/20	12/21
Sales ($mil.)	2.0%	–	44.1	44.0	38.6	46.8
Net income ($ mil.)	67.6%	–	1.5	2.6	0.3	7.2
Market value ($ mil.)	–	–	–	–	–	–
Employees	–	–	–	–	–	300

*Fiscal year change

LAKELAND FINANCIAL CORP

NMS: LKFN

202 East Center Street,
Warsaw, IN 46580
Phone: 574 267-6144
Fax: –
Web: www.lakecitybank.com

CEO: David M Findlay
CFO: Lisa M O'Neill
HR: –
FYE: December 31
Type: Public

Lakeland Financial is the holding company for Lake City Bank, which serves area business customers and individuals through around 50 branches scattered across about 15 northern and central Indiana counties. With $4.8 billion in assets, the community bank offers such standard retail services as checking and savings accounts, money market accounts, and CDs. Commercial loans, including agricultural loans and mortgages, make up about 90% of the bank's loan portfolio. Lake City Bank also offers investment products and services such as corporate and personal trust, brokerage, and estate planning.

	Annual Growth	12/19	12/20	12/21	12/22	12/23
Assets ($mil.)	7.2%	4,946.7	5,830.4	6,557.3	6,432.4	6,524.0
Net income ($ mil.)	1.9%	87.0	84.3	95.7	103.8	93.8
Market value ($ mil.)	7.4%	1,244.3	1,362.6	2,038.0	1,855.7	1,657.1
Employees	3.1%	568	585	616	652	643

LAKELAND INDUSTRIES, INC.

NMS: LAKE

1525 Perimeter Parkway, Suite 325
Huntsville, AL 35806
Phone: 256 350-3873
Fax: 256 350-0773
Web: www.lakeland.com

CEO: Charles D Roberson
CFO: –
HR: –
FYE: January 31
Type: Public

The wrong clothing can be hazardous to your health -- not based on style, but by OSHA and EPA standards. Lakeland makes protective clothing for on-the-job hazards. It uses DuPont specialty fabrics, such as Kevlar, TyChem, and Tyvek, as well as its own fabrics, to make industrial disposable garments, toxic-waste cleanup suits, fire- and heat-resistant apparel (including Fyrepel gear for firefighters), industrial work gloves, high-visibility garments, and industrial/medical garments. Lakeland manufactures its products in Brazil, China, India, Mexico, and the US. Customers -- nearly 65% are outside of the US -- include high tech electronics manufacturers, construction companies, hospitals, and laboratories.

	Annual Growth	01/19	01/20	01/21	01/22	01/23
Sales ($mil.)	3.3%	99.0	107.8	159.0	118.4	112.8
Net income ($ mil.)	6.4%	1.5	3.3	35.1	11.4	1.9
Market value ($ mil.)	6.8%	81.5	102.1	203.6	154.0	106.1
Employees	(0.5%)	1,632	1,829	2,000	1,800	1,600

LAKELAND REGIONAL MEDICAL CENTER, INC.

1324 LAKELAND HILLS BLVD
LAKELAND, FL 338054500
Phone: 863 687-1100
Fax: –
Web: www.mylrh.org

CEO: Elaine C Thompson
CFO: –
HR: Beverly Mack
FYE: September 30
Type: Private

Lakeland Regional Medical Center (LRMC) serves Florida's Polk County (roughly between Kissimmee and Tampa) through an acute care hospital with approximately 850 beds. Among its specialty services are cardiac care, cancer treatment, senior care, urology, emergency medicine, orthopedics, women's and children's health care, and surgery. LRMC also operates general care and specialty outpatient clinics. Additionally, the hospital provides medical training programs for radiology specialists. Its LRMC Foundation offers financial support for indigent patients facing ongoing treatment.

	Annual Growth	09/15	09/16	09/19	09/21	09/22
Sales ($mil.)	4.5%	–	790.3	905.4	875.4	1,028.3
Net income ($ mil.)	(3.4%)	–	84.5	65.7	96.7	68.5
Market value ($ mil.)	–	–	–	–	–	–
Employees	–	–	–	–	–	3,100

LAKESIDE INDUSTRIES, INC.

6505 226TH PL SE STE 200
ISSAQUAH, WA 980278905
Phone: 425 313-2600
Fax: –
Web: www.bongacams.com

CEO: Timothy Lee Jr
CFO: Dax Woolston
HR: Pollie Sengstake
FYE: November 30
Type: Private

Lakeside Industries is one of the largest highway contractors in the Pacific Northwest. A leading asphalt paving contractor and manufacturer, the company works on municipal, commercial, and industrial sites, as well as residential projects. It also sells hot-mix and cold asphalt to other paving contractors. It has about a dozen offices in western Washington, northwestern Oregon, and central Idaho. Owned by the founding Lee family, Lakeside Industries was established when the family combined their mining, sand and gravel, asphalt, and trucking businesses in 1972.

	Annual Growth	11/02	11/03	11/04	11/05	11/07
Sales ($mil.)	10.9%	–	136.1	–	147.5	206.0
Net income ($ mil.)	–	–	–	–	–	–
Market value ($ mil.)	–	–	–	–	6.0	–
Employees	–	–	–	–	–	750

LAM RESEARCH CORP
NMS: LRCX

4650 Cushing Parkway
Fremont, CA 94538
Phone: 510 572-0200
Fax: 510 572-6454
Web: www.lamresearch.com

CEO: Timothy M Archer
CFO: Douglas R Bettinger
HR: –
FYE: June 25
Type: Public

Lam Research is a leading manufacturer of equipment used to make semiconductors. It is a global supplier of innovative wafer fabrication equipment and services to the semiconductor industry. Its plasma etch process used to remove single crystal silicon and other materials deep into the wafer is collectively referred to as deep silicon etch. Its products and services are designed to help its customers build smaller and better-performing devices that are used in a variety of electronic products, including mobile phones, personal computers, servers, wearables, automotive vehicles, and data storage devices. Lam's customers include some of the world's largest chip makers, such as Micron Technology and Samsung Electronics. Customers in four Asian countries account for over 75% of Lam's revenue. The company traces its historical roots back to 1980.

	Annual Growth	06/19	06/20	06/21	06/22	06/23
Sales ($mil.)	15.9%	9,653.6	10,045	14,626	17,227	17,429
Net income ($ mil.)	19.8%	2,191.4	2,251.8	3,908.5	4,605.3	4,510.9
Market value ($ mil.)	34.2%	25,039	40,325	84,036	60,009	81,146
Employees	12.6%	10,700	11,300	14,100	17,700	17,200

LAMAR ADVERTISING CO (NEW)
NMS: LAMR

5321 Corporate Blvd.
Baton Rouge, LA 70808
Phone: 225 926-1000
Fax: –
Web: www.lamar.com

CEO: Sean E Reilly
CFO: Keith Istre
HR: Debra Watson
FYE: December 31
Type: Public

Lamar Advertising is one of the largest outdoor advertising companies in the US. The company maintains approximately 160,200 billboards in about 45 states and Canada. The company is also the largest provider of logo signs in the US, operating about two dozen privatized state logo sign contracts. It operates more than 139,000 logo sign advertising displays, over 47,500 transit advertising displays, and approximately 4,500 digital billboard advertising displays as well. In addition, Lamar Advertising offers generally large, illuminated, and generally smaller advertising structures that are located on major highways and streets and target vehicular and pedestrian traffic. Chairman Kevin Reilly Jr., together with members of his family, controls more than 60% voting stake in the company. The company was established in 1902.

	Annual Growth	12/19	12/20	12/21	12/22	12/23
Sales ($mil.)	4.7%	1,753.6	1,568.9	1,787.4	2,032.1	2,111.0
Net income ($ mil.)	7.4%	372.1	243.4	388.1	438.6	495.8
Market value ($ mil.)	4.5%	9,110.4	8,493.9	12,381	9,635.0	10,848
Employees	(0.3%)	3,600	3,300	3,350	3,500	3,550

LAMB WESTON HOLDINGS INC
NYS: LW

599 S. Rivershore Lane
Eagle, ID 83616
Phone: 208 938-1047
Fax: –
Web: www.lambweston.com

CEO: Thomas P Werner
CFO: Bernadette M Madarieta
HR: –
FYE: May 28
Type: Public

Lamb Weston Holdings Inc. (Lamb Weston) is the leading global producer, distributor, and marketer of value-added frozen potatoes products, producing a variety of French fries as well as appetizers such as baked potato skins, mozzarella sticks, and breaded onion rings. The company markets its products under Lamb Weston, Lamb Weston Private Reserve, Lamb Weston Stealth Fries, Lamb Weston Colossal Crisp, and Sweet Things brand names among others. It distributes its products to restaurants, grocery stores, specialty retailers, food service distributors, and educational institutions. The Idaho-based company has customers across the globe in over 100 countries but gets most of its sales from the US market. Lamb Weston was founded in 1950.

	Annual Growth	05/19	05/20	05/21	05/22	05/23
Sales ($mil.)	9.2%	3,756.5	3,792.4	3,670.9	4,098.9	5,350.6
Net income ($ mil.)	20.5%	478.6	365.9	317.8	200.9	1,008.9
Market value ($ mil.)	15.2%	9,050.2	8,748.7	12,016	9,903.8	15,943
Employees	7.9%	7,600	7,700	7,800	8,000	10,300

LANCASTER COLONY CORP
NMS: LANC

380 Polaris Parkway, Suite 400
Westerville, OH 43082
Phone: 614 224-7141
Fax: 614 469-8219
Web: www.lancastercolony.com

CEO: David A Ciesinski
CFO: Thomas K Pigott
HR: –
FYE: June 30
Type: Public

Lancaster Colony is a US-based manufacturer and marketer of specialty food products for the retail and foodservice channels. Specific products include garlic bread, salad dressings, yeast rolls and dinner rolls, salad toppings and croutons, and vegetable dips and fruit dips sold under brands such as New York Brand Bakery, Sister Schubert's, Marzetti, Simply Dressed, and Chatham Village. Lancaster Colony is dependent on a small number of large customers, with the top five Retail customers accounted for around 55% of this segment's total sales in 2022, while its top five Foodservice direct customers accounted for roughly 60% of this segment. It also partners with third-parties, including Olive Garden, Chick-fil-A, and Buffalo Wild Wings, to produce shelf-stable products. Lancaster has 10 main manufacturing facilities and seven warehouses.

	Annual Growth	06/19	06/20	06/21	06/22	06/23
Sales ($mil.)	8.7%	1,307.8	1,334.4	1,467.1	1,676.4	1,822.5
Net income ($ mil.)	(7.3%)	150.5	137.0	142.3	89.6	111.3
Market value ($ mil.)	7.9%	4,090.6	4,266.5	5,326.9	3,545.0	5,535.5
Employees	1.5%	3,200	3,200	3,200	3,200	3,400

LANCESOFT, INC.

2121 COOPERATIVE WAY STE 130
HERNDON, VA 20171
Phone: 703 889-6548
Fax: –
Web: www.lancesoft.com

CEO: Divya Gandhi
CFO: –
HR: Kumarjit Dey
FYE: December 31
Type: Private

At LanceSoft's Round Table, consultants battle problems of a technical nature. The company provides a variety of information technology and consulting services in areas such as applications and systems development, infrastructure management, and quality assurance. The company also offers business outsourcing, including helpdesk, medical transcription, and human resources support, as well as IT contract and contract-to-hire services. Among its clients are small, midsized, and large companies in the health care, manufacturing, retail, and telecommunications industries, among others. LanceSoft operates from locations in India, the UK, and the US.

LAND O' LAKES INC

4001 Lexington Avenue North
Arden Hills, MN 55126
Phone: 651 481-2222
Fax: –
Web: www.landolakesinc.com

CEO: –
CFO: –
HR: –
FYE: December 31
Type: Public

Land O'Lakes is one of America's premier agribusiness and food companies with over 3,100 members. It is a member-owned cooperative with industry-leading operations that span the spectrum from agricultural production to consumer foods. The company has four businesses: WinField United, Dairy Foods, Feed, and Truterra. Its businesses provide It also has approximately 1,600 dairy producers delivering products to consumers. In addition, it sells feed for farm and exotic animals through Purina Animal Nutrition, Mazuri, PMI, and Land O'Lakes Animal Milk Products. The co-op does business across the US and in more than 60 other countries. The farmer-owned company was formed in 1921.

	Annual Growth	12/11	12/12	12/13	12/14	12/15
Sales ($mil.)	0.3%	12,849	14,116	14,236	14,966	13,008
Net income ($ mil.)	14.0%	182.2	240.4	306.0	266.5	307.6
Market value ($ mil.)	–	–	–	–	–	–
Employees	–	–	–	9,600	10,000	–

LAND O'FROST, INC.

16850 CHICAGO AVE
LANSING, IL 604381121
Phone: 708 474-7100
Fax: –
Web: www.landofrost.com

CEO: David V Eekeren
CFO: –
HR: Antonio Dawkins
FYE: December 31
Type: Private

Land O'Frost makes meat that's sandwich-worthy. As the nation's largest family-owned brand of packaged deli meat, Land O'Frost produces lunch and deli meats, such as beef, chicken, turkey, Canadian bacon, and ham. It markets its meats under the DeliShaved, Land O'Frost, Bistro Favorites, Taste Escapes, and Premium names. Land O'Frost customers include food retailers, food processors, and foodservice companies across the US. It also provides meat-derived ingredients to other food makers and bulk products to foodservice providers. Operating plants in Illinois, Arkansas, Nebraska, and Kentucky, Land O'Frost is still owned and managed by descendants of founded Antoon Van Eekeren.

	Annual Growth	12/00	12/01	12/02	12/03	12/13
Sales ($mil.)	(27.7%)	–	–	–	195.0	7.6
Net income ($ mil.)	–	–	–	–	–	0.2
Market value ($ mil.)	–	–	–	–	–	–
Employees	–	–	–	–	–	900

LANDAUER, INC.

2 SCIENCE RD
GLENWOOD, IL 604251586
Phone: 708 755-7000
Fax: –
Web: www.landauer.com

CEO: Mike Kaminski
CFO: –
HR: –
FYE: September 30
Type: Private

Landauer is the leading global provider of technical and analytical services to determine occupational and environmental radiation exposure and the leading domestic provider of outsourced medical physics services. The company provides complete radiation dosimetry services to hospitals, medical and dental offices, universities, national laboratories, nuclear facilities, and other industries in which radiation poses a potential threat to employees. It provides dosimetry services to about 1.8 million individuals worldwide. In addition, the Medical Physics division provides therapeutic and imaging physics services throughout the country.

LANDCAR MANAGEMENT, LTD.

9350 S 150 E STE 1000
SANDY, UT 840702721
Phone: 801 563-4100
Fax: –
Web: www.lhmauto.com

CEO: David Hult
CFO: –
HR: –
FYE: December 31
Type: Private

You wouldn't hire the Larry H. Miller Group for your late-night bebop, but the firm does know a little something about all that jazz. The company operates 55 auto dealerships in seven western US states. It also owns the NBA's Utah Jazz, its home (EnergySolutions Arena), and Salt Lake City's KJZZ (the Jazz's TV home). The Larry H. Miller Group's other sports interests include the Salt Lake Bees (AAA affiliate of the Los Angeles Angels of Anaheim), Miller Motorsports Park, and Fanzz retail stores. Besides these athletic assets, the firm owns commercial real estate in 22 states and the 180-screen Megaplex Theatres business. The company was founded by Larry H. Miller in 1979.

LANDMARK BANCORP INC

701 Poyntz Avenue
Manhattan, KS 66502
Phone: 785 565-2000
Fax: –
Web: www.landmarkbancorpinc.com

NMS: LARK
CEO: Michael E Scheopner
CFO: Mark A Herpich
HR: –
FYE: December 31
Type: Public

Landmark Bancorp is a tourist attraction for Kansas money. It is the holding company for Landmark National Bank, which has about 15 branches in communities in central, eastern, and southwestern Kansas. The bank provides standard commercial banking products including checking, savings, and money market accounts, as well as CDs and credit and debit cards. It primarily uses funds from deposits to write residential and commercial mortgages and business loans. Landmark National Bank offers non-deposit investment services through its affiliation with Investment Planners.

	Annual Growth	12/19	12/20	12/21	12/22	12/23
Assets ($mil.)	11.8%	998.5	1,188.0	1,329.0	1,502.9	1,561.7
Net income ($ mil.)	3.5%	10.7	19.5	18.0	9.9	12.2
Market value ($ mil.)	(5.7%)	137.2	125.2	157.2	124.0	108.4
Employees	(1.7%)	289	292	270	286	270

LANDS' END INC

1 Lands' End Lane
Dodgeville, WI 53595
Phone: 608 935-9341
Fax: –
Web: www.landsend.com

NAS: LE
CEO: –
CFO: –
HR: –
FYE: January 27
Type: Public

Lands' End is a leading digital retailer of casual clothing, swimwear, outerwear, accessories, footwear, and home products. It markets traditionally-styled casual apparel for men, women, and children through its website, specialty catalogs, third-party online marketplaces, and approximately 30 free-standing retail stores, including shops in Germany and the UK. Lands' End also offers home goods, soft luggage, school uniforms, and logoed business apparel and products. Generates the vast majority of its sales online, it still produces its longstanding catalog. While the company fulfills orders to customers in approximately 140 countries outside the US, the US generates about 90% of the company's total revenue.

	Annual Growth	02/19*	01/20	01/21	01/22	01/23
Sales ($mil.)	1.7%	1,451.6	1,450.2	1,427.4	1,636.6	1,555.4
Net income ($ mil.)	–	11.6	19.3	10.8	33.4	(12.5)
Market value ($ mil.)	(15.6%)	579.4	380.1	900.8	591.5	294.0
Employees	(1.8%)	7,000	7,100	7,300	6,500	6,500

*Fiscal year change

LANDSCAPES UNLIMITED, L.L.C.

1201 ARIES DR
LINCOLN, NE 685129338
Phone: 402 423-6653
Fax: –
Web: www.landscapesunlimited.com

CEO: –
CFO: –
HR: Amanda Tucker
FYE: December 31
Type: Private

When this company thinks about landscapes, it envisions lush grass dotted with tees, holes, flagsticks, and sand traps. Landscapes Unlimited is best known for its design and construction of resort, private, and municipal golf courses. But it also goes beyond the fairways to work on other types of recreational landscape projects such as sports complexes, baseball fields, football fields, and city parks and playgrounds. Services include golf course renovation, irrigation, and project management services. Through its Landscapes Golf Group subsidiary, Landscapes Unlimited has ownership interests in more than 25 golf courses across the US. The company was founded in 1976 by CEO and landscape architect Bill Kubly.

	Annual Growth	12/03	12/04	12/05	12/08	12/09
Sales ($mil.)	(9.4%)	–	91.6	–	–	55.8
Net income ($ mil.)	–	–	1.3	–	–	–
Market value ($ mil.)	–	–	–	–	–	–
Employees	–	–	–	–	–	500

LANDSTAR SYSTEM, INC.

NMS: LSTR

13410 Sutton Park Drive South
Jacksonville, FL 32224
Phone: 904 398-9400
Fax: –
Web: www.landstar.com

CEO: James B Gattoni
CFO: Federico L Pensotti
HR: –
FYE: December 30
Type: Public

Landstar System is a US truckload freight carrier with a fleet more than 18,500 third-party trailers (including flatbed, step decks, drop decks, low boys, refrigerated, and standard dry vans). Its fleet is primarily operated by independent contractors under exclusive contracts and its services are marketed by sales agents. Landstar's freight carrier-units transport general commodities and goods such as automotive parts and assemblies, building materials, chemicals, electronics, metals, foodstuffs and heavy machinery retail, as well as military equipment. Customers include third-party logistics providers and government agencies such as the US Department of Defense. In addition to truckload transportation, Landstar offers logistics and customs brokerage services.

	Annual Growth	12/19	12/20	12/21	12/22	12/23
Sales ($mil.)	6.8%	4,089.6	4,136.4	6,540.4	7,439.7	5,313.5
Net income ($ mil.)	3.8%	227.7	192.1	381.5	430.9	264.4
Market value ($ mil.)	14.4%	4,042.4	4,834.6	6,151.8	5,818.2	6,916.5
Employees	2.4%	1,333	1,320	1,399	1,449	1,468

LANE COLLEGE

545 LANE AVE
JACKSON, TN 383014598
Phone: 731 426-7500
Fax: –
Web: www.lanecollege.edu

CEO: –
CFO: –
HR: Melvin Hamlett
FYE: June 30
Type: Private

For Lane College, the past is prologue. The small, private liberal arts school was established in 1882 by the Christian Methodist Episcopal (C.M.E.) Church to provide educational opportunities -- particularly in the areas of teaching and preaching -- for newly-freed slaves. Originally called C.M.E. High School, it was renamed Lane College (after its founder Bishop Isaac Lane) in 1896. Throughout its history, the preparation of professional educators has been a primary focus; however, the college also offers undergraduate degrees in such disciplines as computer science, business, and criminal justice. Lane College enrolls 800-1,000 students annually.

	Annual Growth	06/14	06/15	06/17	06/18	06/20
Sales ($mil.)	3.5%	–	24.2	27.4	27.7	28.8
Net income ($ mil.)	7.3%	–	0.7	(0.1)	(0.4)	1.1
Market value ($ mil.)	–	–	–	–	–	–
Employees	–	–	–	–	–	165

LANE POWELL PC

1420 5TH AVE STE 4200
SEATTLE, WA 981012314
Phone: 206 223-7000
Fax: –
Web: www.lanepowell.com

CEO: –
CFO: –
HR: Evan Hawthorne
FYE: December 31
Type: Private

Lane Powell PC brings the power of attorney to the Pacific Northwest. Operating out of offices in Washington, Oregon, Alaska, and internationally in London, the law firm specializes in a range of legal services including corporate finance, intellectual property, regulation and taxation, real estate, labor relations, and commercial litigation. Lane Powell employs more than 200 attorneys and around 300 support personnel handling local, national, and international clientele. The law firm traces its roots back to 1889 when it was named Strudwick, Peters & Collins. (John Powell arrived that same year while W. Byron Lane joined the firm in 1929.)

	Annual Growth	12/13	12/14	12/16	12/17	12/18
Sales ($mil.)	0.5%	–	91.5	99.5	94.4	93.4
Net income ($ mil.)	–	–	(0.2)	1.2	(0.6)	(0.2)
Market value ($ mil.)	–	–	–	–	–	–
Employees	–	–	–	–	–	420

LANIER PARKING HOLDINGS, INC.

233 PEACHTREE ST NE 2600 HARRIS TOWER
ATLANTA, GA 303031510
Phone: 404 881-6076
Fax: –
Web: www.lanierparking.com

CEO: Bijan Eghtedari
CFO: Brian Dubay
HR: Harry Jackson
FYE: December 31
Type: Private

Lanier Parking offers more than just a spot to park your car. It offers a full array of parking and transportation services, from shuttle and valet to design/build and financial consulting, at more than 300 locations throughout the Southeast. In addition to providing traditional parking management and facility operations, the company touts its planning capabilities at sites where there is likely to be insufficient space or heavy congestion, such as hospitals, hotels, municipalities, sports and entertainment venues, and universities. Its consulting services include feasibility, site selection, and master planning. The company was founded by J. Michael Robison in 1989.

	Annual Growth	12/06	12/07	12/08	12/09	12/10
Sales ($mil.)	1.9%	–	–	59.1	59.6	61.3
Net income ($ mil.)	32.7%	–	–	1.2	2.3	2.1
Market value ($ mil.)	–	–	–	–	–	–
Employees	–	–	–	–	–	2,000

LANNETT CO., INC.

NBB: LCIN

1150 Northbrook Drive, Suite 155
Trevose, PA 19053
Phone: 215 333-9000
Fax: –
Web: www.lannett.com

CEO: Timothy C Crew
CFO: John Kozlowski
HR: –
FYE: June 30
Type: Public

Lannett develops, manufactures, packages, markets, and distributes generic prescription drugs in the US, including Fluphenazine tablets for the management of psychotic disorders, Verapamil SR tablets for the treatment of high blood pressure, and Methylphenidate CD for the treatment of Attention Deficit Hyperactivity Disorder (ADHD). The company sells its pharmaceutical products to generic pharmaceutical distributors, drug wholesalers, chain drug retailers, private label distributors, mail-order pharmacies, other pharmaceutical companies and health maintenance organizations. It markets more than 100 products, mainly tablet, capsule or liquid oral generic medications, across multiple therapeutic categories.

	Annual Growth	06/18	06/19	06/20	06/21	06/22
Sales ($mil.)	(16.0%)	684.6	655.4	545.7	478.8	340.6
Net income ($ mil.)	–	28.7	(272.1)	(33.4)	(363.5)	(231.6)
Market value ($ mil.)	(54.6%)	138.4	61.7	73.9	47.5	5.9
Employees	(18.2%)	1,251	1,020	954	810	560

LANSING BOARD OF WATER AND LIGHT

1110 S PENNSYLVANIA AVE
LANSING, MI 489121635
Phone: 517 702-6714
Fax: –
Web: www.lbwl.com

CEO: –
CFO: Heather Shawa
HR: Michael Flowers
FYE: June 30
Type: Private

Letting off a little steam is a good thing for Lansing Board of Water and Light, which provides electricity to 95,000 residential, commercial, and industrial customers and water to about 55,000 customers in Lansing, Michigan. The city-owned utility also produces and distributes steam to 162 customers along 14 miles of steam line. Lansing Board of Water and Light can chill out too. Its chilled water system delivers up to 10,000 tons of chilled water capacity to 16 customers to cool the interior of buildings in the downtown area. Lansing Board of Water and Light is the largest municipally owned utility in the state. It is also a major employer in the Lansing area.

	Annual Growth	06/14	06/15	06/16	06/17	06/22
Sales ($mil.)	(40.3%)	–	–	–	371.4	28.2
Net income ($ mil.)	27.1%	–	–	–	4.3	14.3
Market value ($ mil.)	–	–	–	–	–	–
Employees	–	–	–	–	–	740

LANTRONIX INC.
NAS: LTRX

48 Discovery, Suite 250
Irvine, CA 92618
Phone: 949 453-3990
Fax: 949 453-3995
Web: www.lantronix.com

CEO: Saleel Awsare
CFO: Jeremy R Whitaker
HR: -
FYE: June 30
Type: Public

Lantronix is a provider of software as a service (SaaS), engineering services, and hardware for Edge Computing, the Internet of Things (IoT), and Remote Environment Management (REM). The company's products and services dramatically simplify operations through the creation, development, deployment, and management of IoT and IT projects across Robotics, Automotive, Wearables, Video Conferencing, Industrial, Medical, Logistics, Smart Cities, Security, Retail, Branch Office, Server Room, and Datacenter applications. Lantronix conducts its business globally and manages its sales teams by three geographic regions: the Americas; Europe, Middle East, and Africa (EMEA); and Asia Pacific Japan (APJ). The company's largest market is the Americas which accounts for around 60% of revenue.

	Annual Growth	06/19	06/20	06/21	06/22	06/23
Sales ($mil.)	29.3%	46.9	59.9	71.5	129.7	131.2
Net income ($ mil.)	-	(0.4)	(10.7)	(4.0)	(5.4)	(9.0)
Market value ($ mil.)	6.0%	122.8	136.8	190.3	198.4	155.2
Employees	15.2%	210	242	312	348	370

LAPHAM-HICKEY STEEL CORP.

5500 W 73RD ST
BEDFORD PARK, IL 606386506
Phone: 708 496-6111
Fax: -
Web: www.lapham-hickey.com

CEO: -
CFO: Michael Pilarczyk
HR: -
FYE: December 31
Type: Private

Lapham-Hickey Steel is a full line steel service center that provides processing services such as blanking, cut-to-length, edge conditioning, and shearing. The family-owned company's products include tin plate, bar steel, flat wire, and stainless steel. It also provides aluminum/stainless steel products, including rounds and squares, flats, angles, channels, pipes, square and rectangular tubing, and extrusions. The steel company's support services also include distribution, fabrication, logistics, and inventory management. Other service offerings include machining, pickling and oiling, painting, and ultrasonic testing. Lapham-Hickey Steel is a trusted leader in the metal industry since 1926.

LAPOLLA INDUSTRIES, LLC

3315 E DIVISION ST
ARLINGTON, TX 760116832
Phone: 281 219-4100
Fax: -
Web: www.lapollaindustries.com

CEO: -
CFO: -
HR: -
FYE: December 31
Type: Private

LaPolla Industries would hate for its customers to have leaky roofs over their heads or insufficiently protected exterior walls. The company makes foam products used to protect roofs and the "building envelope," which is the separation of the exterior and interior parts of a building. It also makes coatings for weatherproofing concrete and metal roofing and other materials. The company changed its name in 2005 when it absorbed subsidiary LaPolla Industries, a provider of roof coatings and polyurethane foam construction systems. The former IFT Corp., which had previously been called Urecoats, acquired LaPolla in 2005. Chairman Richard Kurtz owns 57% of LaPolla.

LARIMAR THERAPEUTICS INC
NMS: LRMR

Three Bala Plaza East, Suite 506
Bala Cynwyd, PA 19004
Phone: 844 511-9056
Fax: -
Web: www.larimartx.com

CEO: Carole S Ben-Maimon
CFO: Michael Celano
HR: -
FYE: December 31
Type: Public

Zafgen targets the severe obesity epidemic with an alternative to bariatric surgery. The biopharmaceutical company's lead product candidate ZGN-1061, a preclinical drug it hopes will successfully treat general obesity. In mid-2016, Zafgen shut down development of its previous lead candidate, beloranib, which was designed to treat obesity related to Willi-Prader syndrome (a complex genetic disorder including insatiable life-threatening hunger and hunger-related behaviors known an hyperphagia), after two patients died in trials. It now plans to focus on ZGN-1061. The company went public in 2014.

	Annual Growth	12/19	12/20	12/21	12/22	12/23
Sales ($mil.)	-	-	-	-	-	-
Net income ($ mil.)	-	(45.4)	(42.5)	(50.6)	(35.4)	(36.9)
Market value ($ mil.)	42.3%	48.7	940.1	473.8	181.3	199.8
Employees	56.5%	7	28	31	26	42

LARKIN COMMUNITY HOSPITAL, INC.

7031 SW 62ND AVE
SOUTH MIAMI, FL 331434701
Phone: 305 757-5707
Fax: -
Web: www.larkinhealth.com

CEO: -
CFO: -
HR: Maggie Campos
FYE: December 31
Type: Private

Larkin Community Hospital may be small, but it doesn't skimp on its array of health care services. The 110-bed hospital provides general medical and surgical services to the sun-drenched residents of the Miami-Dade County area of Florida. Larkin Community Hospital offers more than 40 specialties, including diagnostic radiology, intensive care, arthritis services, an inpatient psychiatric ward, surgery, cardiovascular care, and rehabilitation (including physical, occupational, and speech therapy). President and CEO Jack Michel owns the health care facility.

	Annual Growth	12/10	12/11	12/12	12/14	12/16
Sales ($mil.)	8.7%	-	-	74.4	101.5	103.7
Net income ($ mil.)	(23.6%)	-	-	2.3	4.7	0.8
Market value ($ mil.)	-	-	-	-	-	-
Employees	-	-	-	-	-	1,225

LARKIN ENTERPRISES, INC.

317 W BROADWAY
LINCOLN, ME 044574002
Phone: 207 794-8700
Fax: -
Web: www.larkinent.com

CEO: -
CFO: -
HR: -
FYE: December 31
Type: Private

Founded in 1994, Larkin Enterprises supplies technical and support personnel to the power generation and utility industries. The company provides expertise to clients in mechanical, electrical and instrumentation, as well as support and maintenance personnel on a national basis. Larkin Enterprises filed for Chapter 11 bankruptcy protection in 2005, citing a downturn in utilities construction.

	Annual Growth	12/13	12/14	12/15	12/16	12/17
Sales ($mil.)	18.8%	-	8.6	8.8	8.1	14.4
Net income ($ mil.)	24.9%	-	0.4	0.0	0.0	0.7
Market value ($ mil.)	-	-	-	-	-	-
Employees	-	-	-	-	-	60

LAS VEGAS EVENTS, INC.

770 E WARM SPRINGS RD STE 140
LAS VEGAS, NV 891194333
Phone: 702 260-8605
Fax: –
Web: www.lasvegasevents.com

CEO: –
CFO: –
HR: –
FYE: June 30
Type: Private

Las Vegas Events is an event management company designed to produce and promote events in Sin City. Also known as LVE, the company has staged events ranging from the Miss Universe pageant to the NHRA SummitRacing.com Nationals to the USA Table Tennis Championships. The events management firm is responsible for America's Party, the New Year's Eve event held in Las Vegas each year. The not-for-profit company was founded in 1983 and is funded directly from the city's hotel room tax. It has either presented or assisted with about 400 events since its founding.

	Annual Growth	06/11	06/12	06/14	06/19	06/21
Sales ($mil.)	(13.3%)	–	20.1	23.1	28.1	5.5
Net income ($ mil.)	–	–	(0.2)	0.0	(0.3)	(0.3)
Market value ($ mil.)	–	–	–	–	–	–
Employees	–	–	–	–	–	15

LAS VEGAS SANDS CORP

5420 S. Durango Dr.
Las Vegas, NV 89113
Phone: 702 923-9000
Fax: –
Web: www.sands.com

NYS: LVS
CEO: Robert G Goldstein
CFO: Randy Hyzak
HR: –
FYE: December 31
Type: Public

Las Vegas Sands Corp. is a Fortune 500 company and the leading global developer of destination projects that feature premium accommodations, world-class gaming, entertainment and retail malls, convention and exhibition facilities, celebrity chef restaurants and other amenities. Through its majority-owned Sands China subsidiary, the company operates The Venetian Macao on the Cotai Strip (the Chinese equivalent of the Las Vegas Strip), as well as four other properties in Macao, the only place in China where gambling is legal. LVSC's portfolio also includes the Marina Bay Sands in Singapore and The Venetian Resort and the Sands Expo and Convention Center in Las Vegas.

	Annual Growth	12/19	12/20	12/21	12/22	12/23
Sales ($mil.)	(6.8%)	13,739	3,612.0	4,234.0	4,110.0	10,372
Net income ($ mil.)	(18.0%)	2,698.0	(1,685.0)	(961.0)	1,832.0	1,221.0
Market value ($ mil.)	(8.1%)	51,987	44,879	28,343	36,197	37,055
Employees	(6.4%)	50,000	46,000	44,700	35,700	38,400

LAS VEGAS VALLEY WATER DISTRICT

1001 S VALLEY VIEW BLVD
LAS VEGAS, NV 891074447
Phone: 702 870-2011
Fax: –
Web: www.lvvwd.com

CEO: –
CFO: –
HR: Jerry Keating
FYE: June 30
Type: Private

If casinos can bloom in the desert, why can't water flow? It can, thanks to the Las Vegas Valley Water District (LVVWD), which provides water to some one million residents living in one of the driest places in the US. In addition to Las Vegas, the LVVWD serves residents of Blue Diamond, Coyote Springs, Jean, Kyle Canyon, Laughlin, Searchlight, and other parts of Clark County in Southern Nevada. The district delivers water to customers through some 4,500 miles of water transmission pipeline connected to 59 pumping stations, 104 wells, and 94 reservoirs and tanks. (Its tanks and reservoirs have the capacity to store more than 900 million gallons.) The LVVWD sources 90% of its water to the Colorado River.

	Annual Growth	06/05	06/06	06/07	06/18	06/20
Sales ($mil.)	(0.1%)	–	–	377.5	372.3	373.7
Net income ($ mil.)	4.7%	–	–	30.0	43.9	54.2
Market value ($ mil.)	–	–	–	–	–	–
Employees	–	–	–	–	–	1,200

LASALLE UNIVERSITY

1900 W OLNEY AVE
PHILADELPHIA, PA 191411199
Phone: 215 951-1000
Fax: –
Web: www.lasalle.edu

CEO: –
CFO: –
HR: Susan Rohanna
FYE: May 31
Type: Private

La Salle University is an independent Catholic institution of higher learning with an enrollment of more than 7,000 students. It offers about 40 undergraduate majors and 15 minors, as well as 15 graduate programs (including a doctoral program in Clinical Psychology), and about 40 certificate programs. The liberal arts university consists of three schools: arts and sciences, business, and nursing and health sciences, plus a College of Professional and Continuing Studies. Nursing, psychology, education, accounting, and communications are among the school's most popular undergraduate areas of study.

	Annual Growth	05/17	05/18	05/19	05/20	05/22
Sales ($mil.)	5.2%	–	114.7	162.2	156.1	140.6
Net income ($ mil.)	–	–	2.2	(0.8)	(1.9)	(2.1)
Market value ($ mil.)	–	–	–	–	–	–
Employees	–	–	–	–	–	900

LASER MASTER INTERNATIONAL, INC

1000 First Street
Harrison, NJ 07029
Phone: 973 482-7200
Fax: –
Web: –

NBB: LMTI
CEO: –
CFO: –
HR: –
FYE: November 30
Type: Public

Laser Master International sells gift wrap and packaging materials, which it buys from producers outside the US, to industrial and retail customers. The company formerly produced its own gift wrap and packaging materials at a printing plant in New Jersey, but it was unable to compete with lower-cost producers in China and other countries. Laser Master International sold its printing plant and equipment in 2006. CEO Mendel Klein owns 35% of the company.

	Annual Growth	11/03	11/04	11/06	11/07	11/08
Sales ($mil.)	3.0%	16.9	21.9	21.1	22.7	19.5
Net income ($ mil.)	–	1.2	0.2	5.1	0.3	(0.9)
Market value ($ mil.)	(31.5%)	5.7	2.8	3.8	3.3	0.9
Employees	(21.4%)	60	65	–	25	18

LASERSIGHT INC

6848 Stapoint Court
Winter Park, FL 32792
Phone: 407 678-9900
Fax: 407 678-9981
Web: www.lase.com

CEO: Danghui Liu
CFO: Dorothy M Cipolla
HR: –
FYE: December 31
Type: Public

LaserSight has an eye for vision care. The company's LaserSight Technologies subsidiary makes excimer lasers, which surgically correct nearsightedness, farsightedness, and astigmatism. LaserSight's LaserScan LSX system is approved by the FDA for photorefractive keratectomy (PRK) and laser-in-situ keratomileusis (LASIK) vision correction procedures. The company also sells ophthalmic equipment including forceps, scissors, and needle holders. Subsidiary TechnicaLaser sells laser products for industrial, laboratory, and other applications. LaserSight has facilities in China and the US and markets its products in more than 30 countries worldwide.

	Annual Growth	12/01	12/02	12/03	12/04	12/05
Sales ($mil.)	(17.2%)	13.5	10.5	6.4	7.9	6.3
Net income ($ mil.)	–	(26.2)	(13.6)	(23.5)	14.7	0.5
Market value ($ mil.)	(46.7%)	6.2	1.9	0.1	0.3	0.5
Employees	(35.6%)	116	56	23	25	20

LATINWORKS MARKETING LLC

828 W 6TH ST STE 150
AUSTIN, TX 787035468
Phone: 512 479-6200
Fax: –
Web: www.latinworks.com

CEO: –
CFO: –
HR: –
FYE: December 31
Type: Private

Sometimes just plain advertising works, and sometimes you need LatinWorks. LatinWorks Marketing provides advertising and marketing services to FORTUNE 1000 clients seeking to tap into the growing Hispanic market. Its portfolio includes TV, print, and digital work for such brands as Anheuser-Busch, Mars, ESPN, and Burger King. Renouncing stereotypes in its creative work, the agency has instead based its strategic development process on an understanding of how generational differences influence the Hispanic worldview -- from acculturation through assimilation. The Diversified Agency Services unit of Omnicom Group, the world's largest media services conglomerate, is an investor in LatinWorks.

LATTICE INC

7150 N. Park Drive, Suite 500
Pennsauken, NJ 08109
Phone: 856 910-1166
Fax: 856 910-1811
Web: www.latticeincorporated.com

NBB: LTTC
CEO: –
CFO: –
HR: –
FYE: December 31
Type: Public

Government IT contractor Lattice has constructed a diverse product framework. The company provides data management applications, Internet server technology, and information systems for federal agencies. Deriving the majority of its revenue from Dept. of Defense, it develops applications related to business management, geographic information systems (GIS), Web services, and geospatial systems. In addition, the company's Nexus Call Control System provides technology that allows correctional facilities to monitor and control inmate collect-only phone calls. Lattice, which began in the 1970s as a telephone services company, also offers direct telecom services to correctional facilities.

	Annual Growth	12/11	12/12	12/13	12/14	12/15
Sales ($mil.)	(9.8%)	11.4	10.8	8.3	8.9	7.6
Net income ($ mil.)	–	(6.1)	(0.6)	(1.0)	(1.8)	(5.5)
Market value ($ mil.)	(21.8%)	11.4	7.6	15.6	9.5	4.2
Employees	(11.5%)	44	37	26	23	27

LATTICE SEMICONDUCTOR CORP

5555 NE Moore Court
Hillsboro, OR 97124
Phone: 503 268-8000
Fax: –
Web: www.latticesemi.com

NMS: LSCC
CEO: James R Anderson
CFO: Sherri Luther
HR: –
FYE: December 30
Type: Public

Lattice Semiconductor is a developer of technologies that monetizes through different programmable logic semiconductor products, system solutions, design services, and licenses. Lattice is also the low power programmable leader that solves customer problems across the network, from Edge to the Cloud, in growing communications, computing, industrial, consumer, and automotive applications. Its field-programmable gate arrays (FPGAs) devices enable the company to provide its customers with a strong, growing base of control, connect, and compute technologies. The majority of sales come from Asia.

	Annual Growth	12/19*	01/21	01/22*	12/22	12/23
Sales ($mil.)	16.2%	404.1	408.1	515.3	660.4	737.2
Net income ($ mil.)	56.2%	43.5	47.4	95.9	178.9	259.1
Market value ($ mil.)	37.6%	2,641.0	6,292.9	10,583	8,910.6	9,475.1
Employees	11.5%	747	746	856	949	1,156

*Fiscal year change

LAUREATE EDUCATION INC

PMB 1158, 1000 Brickell Avenue, Suite 715
Miami, FL 33131
Phone: 786 209-3368
Fax: –
Web: www.laureate.net

NMS: LAUR
CEO: Eilif Serck-Hanssen
CFO: Richard M Buskirk
HR: Danielle Marsh
FYE: December 31
Type: Public

Laureate Education operates the Laureate International Universities network, which grants undergraduate and graduate degrees to students through campus-based, online, and hybrid programs. Approximately 423,000 students are enrolled at five institutions. The company operates primarily in Latin America, including Mexico, and Peru, where the market relies heavily on private colleges and universities. A vast majority of its students were enrolled at traditional, campus-based institutions offering multi-year degrees, similar to leading private and public higher education institutions in developed markets such as the US and Europe. Laureate emphasizes science, technology, engineering, and math (STEM) and business disciplines. Laureate Education generates most of its revenue internationally.

	Annual Growth	12/19	12/20	12/21	12/22	12/23
Sales ($mil.)	(17.8%)	3,250.3	1,024.9	1,086.7	1,242.3	1,484.3
Net income ($ mil.)	(41.8%)	938.5	(613.3)	192.4	69.6	107.6
Market value ($ mil.)	(6.1%)	2,775.1	2,294.5	1,928.9	1,516.0	2,160.5
Employees	(12.8%)	50,000	37,000	24,000	35,000	28,900

LAUREN ENGINEERS & CONSTRUCTORS, INC.

901 S 1ST ST
ABILENE, TX 796021502
Phone: 325 670-9660
Fax: –
Web: www.laurenec.com

CEO: –
CFO: –
HR: –
FYE: December 31
Type: Private

Lauren Engineers & Constructors is a contractor that targets the power, chemical and polymer, oil and gas, and refining industries. In addition to its core engineering, procurement, and construction capabilities, the company offers fabrication, project management, and mechanical and electrical maintenance services. With offices in the southern US, Lauren Engineers & Constructors serves about 25 states. It also operates in Canada, centered from its presence in Calgary. Some of its power and chemical customers include Flying J, Florida Power & Light, General Electric Company, and Procter & Gamble. The company was originally established in 1984 as a subsidiary of Comstock Mechanical.

	Annual Growth	12/12	12/13	12/14	12/15	12/16
Sales ($mil.)	14.7%	–	163.3	237.4	582.6	246.2
Net income ($ mil.)	–	–	(3.4)	3.9	14.2	7.3
Market value ($ mil.)	–	–	–	–	–	–
Employees	–	–	–	–	–	1,100

LAURENS COUNTY HEALTH CARE SYSTEM

22725 HIGHWAY 76 E
CLINTON, SC 293257527
Phone: 864 833-9100
Fax: –
Web: www.lchcs.org

CEO: –
CFO: –
HR: –
FYE: September 30
Type: Private

It may be on the small side, but that doesn't keep Laurens County Health Care System from keeping Lauren County, South Carolina's residents hearty and hale. Operating as Laurens County Hospital, the 90-bed facility provides general acute care medical services, as well as specialty care for diabetes, breast cancer, emergency medicine, pediatrics, and wound care. Laurens County Health Care System, founded in 1990, also provides a range of community wellness programs and classes on subjects such as smoking cessation and prenatal care. The hospital's 14-bed skilled nursing facility administers rehabilitation care to patients in recovery from accident or illness.

LAUTH PROPERTIES, LLC

111 CONGRESSIONAL BLVD STE 300
CARMEL, IN 46032
Phone: 317 848-6500
Fax: –
Web: www.lauth.net

CEO: –
CFO: –
HR: –
FYE: December 31
Type: Private

Lauth is no sloth when it comes to commercial development. Lauth Property Group has completed more than 275 projects in 35 states since it began in 1977. Focusing on office, industrial, retail, and health care facilities, the group has designed, developed, and built projects including corporate headquarters, warehouses, retail shopping centers, and medical clinics. Lauth also owns, manages, and provides financing for properties. Owned by its management, the company became Lauth Property Group when chairman Bob Lauth bought out partner Terry Eaton in 1995. It operates about a half-dozen offices in the US.

	Annual Growth	12/98	12/99	12/00	12/07	12/08
Assets ($mil.)	(25.1%)	–	8.6	13.6	–	0.6
Net income ($ mil.)	–	–	1.5	0.7	–	–
Market value ($ mil.)	–	–	–	–	–	–
Employees		–	–	–	–	425

LAWNWOOD MEDICAL CENTER, INC.

1700 S 23RD ST
FORT PIERCE, FL 349504899
Phone: 772 461-4000
Fax: –
Web: www.hcafloridahealthcare.com

CEO: Eric Goldman
CFO: Robert Dunwoody Jr
HR: –
FYE: September 30
Type: Private

Lawnwood Regional Medical Center & Heart Institute, part of the HCA system of health care providers, is a 340-bed acute-care hospital that serves Florida's Treasure Coast area. Its Heart Institute is a specialty cardiac facility. The hospital's 35-bed Lawnwood Pavilion facility provides inpatient mental health and physical rehabilitation services. The hospital also provides specialty services in the areas of women's and children's health, heart and prostate surgery, diagnostic imaging, and medical laboratory services. Lawnwood Regional is part of HCA's East Florida division.

	Annual Growth	03/07	03/08	03/09*	09/14	09/15
Sales ($mil.)	347.5%	–	–	0.0	283.9	300.1
Net income ($ mil.)	658.3%	–	–	0.0	59.3	54.2
Market value ($ mil.)	–	–	–	–	–	–
Employees						1,200

*Fiscal year change

LAWRENCE + MEMORIAL HOSPITAL, INC.

365 MONTAUK AVE
NEW LONDON, CT 063204769
Phone: 860 442-0711
Fax: –
Web: www.lmhospital.org

CEO: Bruce D Cummings
CFO: –
HR: Nicole Depolito
FYE: September 30
Type: Private

Lawrence & Memorial Hospital (L + M) connects residents of Connecticut with health care, whether they're near the Rhode Island border or enjoying the Connecticut River. The not-for-profit hospital, founded in 1912, provides services to a 10-town region on the Connecticut shoreline and neighboring areas in the Northeast. L + M has roughly 280 beds and provides general acute care including medical, surgical, rehabilitative, pediatric, psychiatric, and obstetrical services. The hospital also runs about a dozen community physician practices and specialty clinics.L + M is owned by Yale New Haven Health Services.

	Annual Growth	09/13	09/14	09/15	09/20	09/21
Sales ($mil.)	2.1%	–	337.1	339.3	329.7	390.8
Net income ($ mil.)	23.9%	–	6.0	14.6	(11.8)	26.7
Market value ($ mil.)	–	–	–	–	–	–
Employees						2,200

LAWRENCE R. MCCOY & CO., INC.

120 FRONT ST STE 800
WORCESTER, MA 016081415
Phone: 508 368-7700
Fax: –
Web: www.lrmccoy.com

CEO: Richard K Dale
CFO: –
HR: –
FYE: September 30
Type: Private

If only his name was Robert Lawrence, the company could have called itself the "RL McCoy". Lawrence R. McCoy & Co. (LR McCoy) is a wholesale distributor of lumber products, fencing materials, landscaping supplies, and wood flooring to contractors, home centers, retail outlets, and industrial clients in the Northeastern US and Canada. Customers can access accounts online through the My LR McCoy service. The Davenport Peters Company division of the company wholesales lumber. Lawrence Robert McCoy incorporated the company in 1922. Today, it is employee-owned.

LAYNE CHRISTENSEN COMPANY

9303 NEW TRAILS DR STE 200
SPRING, TX 77381
Phone: 281 475-2600
Fax: –
Web: www.graniteconstruction.com

CEO: Michael J Caliel
CFO: J M Anderson
HR: –
FYE: January 31
Type: Private

Layne, a Granite Company, provides sustainable solutions for water resources and mineral exploration. Originally established in 1882, Layne offers a rich history of delivering safe, professional, and reliable water and minerals solutions throughout North and South America. Its Water Resources Division provides comprehensive solutions for various markets. Areas of specialty include water well drilling and rehabilitation, maintenance, and repair of wells and pumps. Layne has drilled thousands of wells throughout the US and internationally, from 500 to 3,300 feet deep, small to large diameter, constructed from a variety of materials. Its Mineral Services Division is driven by the need to identify, define, and develop underground base and precious mineral deposits. Layne is one of the three largest providers of drilling services for the global mineral services industry.

LAYNE MARX & COMPANY

31300 ORCHARD LAKE RD
FARMINGTON HILLS, MI 483341319
Phone: 248 855-6777
Fax: –
Web: www.marxlayne.com

CEO: –
CFO: –
HR: –
FYE: December 31
Type: Private

Marx Layne & Company, a marketing and public relations agency, provides media relations, investor relations, public affairs, and crisis management services to its clients, in addition to marketing services such as graphic design, event marketing, and direct marketing. Throughout the US, the firm serves clients of all sizes and in a variety of sectors including the financial, retail, not-for-profit, health care, and hospitality industries. Marx Layne was founded in 1987.

LAZARE KAPLAN INTERNATIONAL INC.

19 West 44th Street
New York, NY 10036
Phone: 212 972-9700
Fax: –
Web: www.lazarediamonds.com

CEO: Maurice Tempelsman
CFO: William H Moryto
HR: Stacey Sacks
FYE: May 31
Type: Public

Sometimes plain old diamonds just aren't good enough. Lazare Kaplan International specializes in cutting, polishing, and marketing premium-priced diamonds, as well as diamond jewelry. The company buys rough diamonds (primarily from Diamond Trading Company, a sales arm of behemoth De Beers), cuts and polishes the gems for maximum sparkle, and laser-inscribes the branded Lazare Diamonds with the company's logo and an ID number. Lazare boasts manufacturing plants in Puerto Rico, Russia (in Moscow and Barnaul), and South Africa (specifically Namibia) to handle processing of the diamonds. As part of its business, Lazare sells to wholesalers, manufacturers, and authorized jewelry retailers worldwide.

	Annual Growth	05/04	05/05	05/06	05/07	05/08
Sales ($mil.)	11.9%	235.8	421.4	528.0	434.4	369.7
Net income ($ mil.)	31.6%	2.4	5.2	1.5	(3.0)	7.2
Market value ($ mil.)	0.8%	72.6	71.1	70.0	71.8	75.1
Employees	(7.1%)	199	214	223	178	148

LCC INTERNATIONAL INC.

7900 Westpark Drive
McLean, VA 22102
Phone: 703 873-2000
Fax: –
Web: www.lcc.com

CEO: –
CFO: Rebecca Stahl
HR: –
FYE: December 31
Type: Public

In the war of wireless standards, LCC International plays all sides -- from CDMA to GSM. The radio-frequency engineering and consulting firm serves wireless carriers in every stage of operations. It helps aspiring carriers apply for licenses, buy cell sites, and design and deploy networks; it aids established carriers in expanding and upgrading technology; and it helps mature wireless firms streamline their operations. It also provides outsourced daily operations and maintenance of networks. In addition to wireless service providers, the company serves telecommunications equipment vendors, systems integrators, and tower operators. Riley Investment Management owns more than 40% of LCC International.

	Annual Growth	12/03	12/04	12/05	12/06	12/07
Sales ($mil.)	7.7%	108.4	198.6	194.0	130.0	145.7
Net income ($ mil.)	–	(6.5)	(5.3)	(12.5)	(8.0)	(30.8)
Market value ($ mil.)	(23.9%)	0.0	0.0	0.0	0.0	0.0
Employees	14.8%	751	960	977	783	1,304

LCI INDUSTRIES

3501 County Road 6 East
Elkhart, IN 46514
Phone: 574 535-1125
Fax: –
Web: www.lcii.com

NYS: LCII

CEO: Jason D Lippert
CFO: Brian M Hall
HR: Erica Davis
FYE: December 31
Type: Public

LCI Industries makes components for recreational vehicle (RVs) and other original equipment manufacturers. Through its primary operating subsidiary, Lippert Components, the company makes windows and doors, chassis, furniture, and slide-out walls for travel trailers and fifth-wheel RVs. The company also serves adjacent markets including manufactured home, buses, trailers used to haul boats, livestock, equipment and other cargo, trucks, modular housing, and trains. LCI's aftermarket segment sells to RV and trailer dealers, distributors, and service centers. Over 90% of the company's sales came from its US customers.

	Annual Growth	12/19	12/20	12/21	12/22	12/23
Sales ($mil.)	12.4%	2,371.5	2,796.2	4,472.7	5,207.1	3,784.8
Net income ($ mil.)	(18.6%)	146.5	158.4	287.7	395.0	64.2
Market value ($ mil.)	4.1%	2,713.2	3,284.3	3,947.6	2,341.4	3,183.7
Employees	2.7%	10,500	12,400	13,900	12,900	11,700

LCNB CORP

2 North Broadway
Lebanon, OH 45036
Phone: 513 932-1414
Fax: –
Web: www.lcnb.com

NAS: LCNB

CEO: Eric J Meilstrup
CFO: Robert C Haines II
HR: –
FYE: December 31
Type: Public

It just makes cents that LCNB counts bucks in the Buckeye State. The firm is the holding company for LCNB National Bank, which operates some 36 offices across southwestern Ohio. The bank serves about 10 Ohio counties, offering personal and commercial banking services. such as checking and savings accounts, money markets, IRAs, and CDs. Residential mortgages account for nearly half of the company's loan book. Other offerings include commercial mortgages, consumer loans including credit cards, and business loans. It also provides trust services. LCNB's subsidiary Dakin Insurance Agency sells commercial and personal property/casualty insurance.

	Annual Growth	12/19	12/20	12/21	12/22	12/23
Assets ($mil.)	8.7%	1,639.3	1,745.9	1,903.6	1,919.1	2,291.6
Net income ($ mil.)	(9.6%)	18.9	20.1	21.0	22.1	12.6
Market value ($ mil.)	(4.9%)	254.2	193.5	257.3	237.1	207.7
Employees	1.0%	332	331	307	309	345

LDR HOLDING CORPORATION

13785 N HIGHWAY 183 STE 200
AUSTIN, TX 78750
Phone: 512 344-3333
Fax: –
Web: www.zimvie.com

CEO: Christophe Lavigne
CFO: Robert McNamara
HR: –
FYE: December 31
Type: Private

LDR Holdings is at the spinal frontier of medical devices. The company makes cervical disc replacements used in spinal implant surgeries. Its VerteBRIDGE fusion device is affixed to discs without using screws, and its Mobi-C non-fusion device is the only FDA approved implant for one- and two-level cervical disc surgeries. Mobi-C received FDA approval in 2013. LDR Holdings also makes and sells traditional fusion products under the brands C-Plate, Easyspine, MC+, ROI, and SpineTune. Its products are sold in more than 25 countries, but the US accounts for about 70% of sales. Founded in France in 2000, LDR Holdings went public in 2013. Zimmer Biomet is now buying LDR for $1 billion.

LE MOYNE COLLEGE

1419 SALT SPRINGS RD
SYRACUSE, NY 132141301
Phone: 315 445-4100
Fax: –
Web: www.lemoyne.edu

CEO: –
CFO: –
HR: Timothy Barrett
FYE: May 31
Type: Private

Le Moyne College offers more than 700 courses leading to Bachelor of Arts or Bachelor of Science degrees in 24 different majors. A Jesuit Catholic school, Le Moyne has approximately 2,200 undergraduate students and 700 students in the graduate program, which offers degrees in business administration and education. It has a 13-1 ratio of students to faculty. Le Moyne was founded in 1946.

	Annual Growth	05/17	05/18	05/20	05/21	05/22
Sales ($mil.)	3.2%	–	88.3	85.4	87.2	100.1
Net income ($ mil.)	–	–	17.8	(4.7)	62.6	(9.4)
Market value ($ mil.)	–	–	–	–	–	–
Employees	–	–	–	–	–	500

LEADVENTURE INC.

4949 MEADOWS RD STE 150
LAKE OSWEGO, OR 970353255
Phone: 971 252-6652
Fax: –
Web: www.arinet.com
CEO: Roy W Olivier
CFO: –
HR: Mary Pierson
FYE: July 31
Type: Private

ARI Network Services helps some very manly industries attract smart shoppers. The company makes and sells software for creating electronic catalogs and e-commerce websites (together more than 80% of sales) in industries such as outdoor power equipment, power sports, motorcycles, marine, and agricultural equipment. Dealers, manufacturers, and distributors use its applications, including its PartSmart software, which allows companies to access product information for their suppliers and dealers, who can use the database. In addition, the company's e-commerce and communication applications process orders, product registrations, and warranty claims and perform search engine optimization.

LEAF GROUP LTD.

1655 26TH ST
SANTA MONICA, CA 904044016
Phone: 310 656-6253
Fax: –
Web: www.leafgroup.com
CEO: –
CFO: –
HR: –
FYE: December 31
Type: Private

Leaf Group is a diversified consumer internet company that builds enduring, digital-first brands that reach passionate audiences in large and growing lifestyle categories, including fitness and wellness and art and design. Leaf Group's Marketplaces segment serve a global community of approximately 475,000 independent artists that empower artists to reach a global audience. It also include made-to-order marketplace business site Society6.com, and SaatchiArt.com, an online art gallery. Its media properties that educate and inform consumers on a broad range of topics reached more than 69 million unique visitors each month in the US. Around 85% of total revenue comes from domestic market.

LEAF SOFTWARE SOLUTIONS, INC.

14300 CLAY TERRACE BLVD STE 200
CARMEL, IN 460323636
Phone: 317 814-8000
Fax: –
Web: www.leafsoftwaresolutions.com
CEO: –
CFO: –
HR: –
FYE: December 31
Type: Private

Leaf Software Solutions can provide information technology services such as consulting, implementation, project management, technical support, and training. The company also resells enterprise software (including enterprise resource planning and document management applications) from providers such as Microsoft, FileNet, and SAP. The company's customers come from such industries as financial services, telecommunications, retail, manufacturing, retail, and technology. Clients have included Dealer Services Corporation and T2 Systems.

	Annual Growth	12/08	12/09	12/10	12/11	12/12
Sales ($mil.)	16.4%	–	4.5	4.2	5.0	7.1
Net income ($ mil.)	12.7%	–	0.8	0.5	0.5	1.2
Market value ($ mil.)	–	–	–	–	–	–
Employees						39

LEANLOGISTICS, INC.

1351 S WAVERLY RD
HOLLAND, MI 494238570
Phone: 616 738-6400
Fax: –
Web: www.blujaysolutions.com
CEO: –
CFO: –
HR: –
FYE: June 30
Type: Private

LeanLogistics provides logistics software and services that help corporations manage shipments. Its cloudbased-based transportation network, Lean Transportation Network, handles planning, execution, settlement, and procurement functions. Major shippers use LeanLogistics' tools to plan for carrier coverage, track inventory, and share information with their partners. The company also offers managed transportation services. Customers include Barilla, Chiquita, Ace Hardware, AEP Industries, Air Canada, and Ashley Furniture. LeanLogistics is a division of Brambles, the parent company of container and pallet lessor CHEP.

LEAPFROG ENTERPRISES, INC.

2200 POWELL ST STE 500
EMERYVILLE, CA 946081818
Phone: 510 420-5000
Fax: –
Web: www.leapfrog.com
CEO: –
CFO: –
HR: –
FYE: December 31
Type: Private

LeapFrog Enterprises is the leader in innovative solutions that encourage a child's curiosity and love of learning throughout their early developmental journey. The toy maker develops interactive reading systems, educational games, books, and learning toys in different languages, covering subjects from math to music. Its bestselling brands include LeapPad, LeapStart, and LeapBand. Products are sold to retailers, distributors, and schools worldwide, as well as to consumers via the company's website. LeapFrog's target markets are infants and children through age nine. Founded in 1995, LeapFrog is a member of VTech Group.

LEAR CORP.
NYS: LEA

21557 Telegraph Road
Southfield, MI 48033
Phone: 248 447-1500
Fax: 248 447-5250
Web: www.lear.com
CEO: Raymond E Scott
CFO: Jason M Cardew
HR: –
FYE: December 31
Type: Public

Lear Corporation is a global automotive technology leader in Seating and E-Systems, enabling superior in-vehicle experiences for consumers around the world. In addition to seating, the company's E-Systems business produces automotive electronics and manufactures wire harnesses, junction boxes, terminals and connectors, and body control modules. The company operates from about 255 facilities in over 35 countries. It generates over 75% of revenue outside the US. Its largest customers are General Motors, Ford, Daimler, Volkswagen and Stellantis. Lear traces its history back to 1917 when it was founded in Detroit as American Metal Products.

	Annual Growth	12/19	12/20	12/21	12/22	12/23
Sales ($mil.)	4.3%	19,810	17,046	19,263	20,892	23,467
Net income ($ mil.)	(6.6%)	753.6	158.5	373.9	327.7	572.5
Market value ($ mil.)	0.7%	7,817.5	9,061.4	10,424	7,066.5	8,046.0
Employees	3.3%	164,100	174,600	160,100	168,700	186,600

LEARNING ALLY, INC.

20 ROSZEL RD
PRINCETON, NJ 085406206
Phone: 609 452-0606
Fax: –
Web: www.learningally.org

CEO: Andrew Friedman
CFO: Tim Wilson
HR: Patricia Wilus
FYE: June 30
Type: Private

Transforming the printed word speaks volumes at Learning Ally. Formerly Recording for the Blind & Dyslexic, the nonprofit group serves more than 300,000 individuals with reading disabilities. It has digitally recorded some 75,000 downloadable titles, including textbooks, from kindergarten-to-graduate school level, as well as literature and non-fiction, and some reference and professional materials. In addition to individuals, 9,000-plus schools use Learning Ally to address learning differences. Its studios and offices operate in more than a dozen locations across the US. Funded by private donations and government support, Learning Ally was founded in 1948 to record textbooks for blind WWII veterans.

	Annual Growth	06/16	06/17	06/19	06/20	06/22
Sales ($mil.)	17.1%	–	14.2	18.4	17.2	31.4
Net income ($ mil.)	–	–	(2.1)	(1.1)	(3.4)	3.6
Market value ($ mil.)	–	–	–	–	–	–
Employees	–	–	–	–	–	425

LEARNING EXPRESS, INC.

29 BUENA VISTA ST
AYER, MA 014345025
Phone: 978 889-1000
Fax: –
Web: www.learningexpress.com

CEO: Sharon J Diminico
CFO: –
HR: Craig Styles
FYE: December 31
Type: Private

For kids (and parents) who want to get on board the educational entertainment train, Learning Express is the first stop. The specialty toy store franchiser has more than 100 locations in about 25 states. It sell toys for every age group with a focus on educational items. Major brands include Alex Toys (craft kits), Calico Critters (animal figures), Groovy Girls (dolls and accessories), Rokenbok (remote controlled vehicles and construction sets), and Thomas the Tank (wooden train sets and construction toys). It offerings are designed to spark creativity, teach diversity, and encourage development. CEO Sharon DiMinico founded the company in 1987.

	Annual Growth	12/08	12/09	12/10	12/11	12/12
Assets ($mil.)	(2.5%)	–	–	3.0	2.8	2.8
Net income ($ mil.)	–	–	–	0.3	0.1	(0.1)
Market value ($ mil.)	–	–	–	–	–	–
Employees	–	–	–	–	–	35

LEARNING TREE INTERNATIONAL INC

NBB: LTRE

13650 Dulles Technology Drive, Suite 400
Herndon, VA 20171
Phone: 703 709-9119
Fax: –
Web: www.learningtree.com

CEO: –
CFO: –
HR: –
FYE: September 28
Type: Public

This tree of knowledge won't trick you into eating evil apples. It will, however, further your knowledge of information. Information technology, that is. The Learning Tree International is the premier global provider of learning solutions serving over 65,000 national and multinational corporations, government agencies, education and non-profits. The company offers agile transformation, IT modernization, cybersecurity, project/program management, interpersonal skills, digital transformation, ITSM & digital transformation, and software development solutions. Its over 500 expert advisors serve the company's global customer footprint. Aside from its headquarters in Virginia, it has offices in Japan, the UK, Canada and Sweden.

	Annual Growth	10/14	10/15*	09/16	09/17	09/18
Sales ($mil.)	(14.1%)	118.2	94.9	81.6	70.7	64.3
Net income ($ mil.)	–	0.0	(12.6)	(12.7)	(2.1)	(2.1)
Market value ($ mil.)	(15.4%)	30.9	16.7	24.2	39.7	15.9
Employees	(5.4%)	1,006	948	288	257	806

*Fiscal year change

LEDTRONICS, INC.

23105 KASHIWA CT
TORRANCE, CA 905054026
Phone: 310 534-1505
Fax: –
Web: www.ledtronics.com

CEO: –
CFO: –
HR: –
FYE: December 31
Type: Private

LEDtronics knows how to get the LEDs out. The company makes light-emitting diode (LED) lamps, clusters, and arrays. LEDtronics' LEDs are made for a variety of applications, such as aerospace, architectural lighting, automotive, aviation, broadcasting, electronic instrumentation, elevators, entertainment and gaming, industrial automation and controls, the military, traffic and safety, transportation, and utilities. Customers include Boeing, General Dynamics, General Electric, General Motors, IBM, Lockheed Martin, Siemens, and Toyota. LEDtronics was founded in 1983 by president/CEO Pervaiz Lodhie and VP Almas Lodhie. Pervaiz Lodhie owns the company.

	Annual Growth	12/95	12/96	12/97	12/02	12/14
Sales ($mil.)	–	–	–	13.8	11.4	13.9
Net income ($ mil.)	(14.9%)	–	–	1.8	1.3	0.1
Market value ($ mil.)	–	–	–	–	–	–
Employees	–	–	–	–	–	130

LEE COUNTY ELECTRIC COOPERATIVE, INC.

4980 Bayline Drive
North Fort Myers, FL 33917-3998
Phone: 239 995-2121
Fax: –
Web: www.lcec.net

CEO: Dennie Hamilton
CFO: Donald Schleicher
HR: Bonnie Tate
FYE: December 31
Type: Public

If you are a Floridian who is a really early riser or a night owl, Lee County Electric Cooperative (LCEC) may help light your way. The electric cooperative provides power to more than 198,880 residential and commercial customers across five counties in southwestern Florida (Lee County and parts of Collier, Hendry, Charlotte, and Broward counties. The member-owned non-profit electric utility operates more than 8,000 miles of transmission and distribution lines and more than 20 substations. Tampa-based Seminole Electric Cooperative serves as LCEC's wholesale power supplier.

	Annual Growth	12/00	12/04	12/05	12/06	12/07
Sales ($mil.)	11.1%	176.9	253.5	301.7	357.7	369.4
Net income ($ mil.)	1.8%	15.8	14.6	10.9	18.3	17.8
Market value ($ mil.)	–	–	–	–	–	–
Employees	–	–	–	–	–	–

LEE ENTERPRISES, INC.

NMS: LEE

4600 E. 53rd Street
Davenport, IA 52807
Phone: 563 383-2100
Fax: –
Web: –

CEO: Kevin D Mowbray
CFO: Timothy R Millage
HR: –
FYE: September 24
Type: Public

Lee Enterprises is a digital-first subscription platform providing local markets with valuable, high-quality, trusted, intensely local news, information, advertising, and marketing services. The company has operations in more than 75 mid-sized markets across some 25 states. It operates in predominately mid-sized communities with products ranging from large daily newspapers and associated digital products, such as the St. Louis Post-Dispatch and The Buffalo News, to non-daily newspapers with news websites and digital platforms serving smaller communities. Lee also offers services including a full-service digital marketing agency in Amplified Digital Agency as well as one of the largest web-hosting and content management services providers in North America through their majority-owned subsidiary, BLOX Digital.

	Annual Growth	09/19	09/20	09/21	09/22	09/23
Sales ($mil.)	7.9%	509.9	618.0	794.6	781.0	691.1
Net income ($ mil.)	–	–	14.3	(3.1)	22.8	(2.0)	(5.3)
Market value ($ mil.)	52.9%	12.2	5.0	144.0	103.1	66.6
Employees	3.1%	2,954	5,613	5,130	4,365	3,342

LEE LEWIS CONSTRUCTION, INC.

7810 ORLANDO AVE
LUBBOCK, TX 794231942
Phone: 806 797-8400
Fax: –
Web: www.leelewis.com

CEO: –
CFO: –
HR: –
FYE: June 30
Type: Private

General builder Lee Lewis Construction has waltzed across Texas and beyond to keep in step with the top US contractors. The company provides construction-related services and construction management for commercial, institutional, and industrial projects. Among its projects is the Garland ISD Special Events Center in Garland, Texas; it also worked on the Grand Floridian Resort at Walt Disney World. The company earns much of its revenue from projects for Texas school systems. Projects for hometown neighbor Texas Tech University have generated a significant portion of the company's business. CEO Lee Lewis founded the company in 1976.

	Annual Growth	06/03	06/04	06/05	06/06	06/09
Sales ($mil.)	10.6%	–	138.8	176.5	245.1	229.5
Net income ($ mil.)	47.7%	–	0.9	2.3	4.3	6.3
Market value ($ mil.)	–	–	–	–	–	–
Employees	–	–	–	–	–	200

LEE MEMORIAL HEALTH SYSTEM FOUNDATION, INC.

2776 CLEVELAND AVE
FORT MYERS, FL 339015864
Phone: 239 343-2000
Fax: –
Web: www.leehealth.org

CEO: Lawrence Antonucci
CFO: –
HR: Debbie Marzella
FYE: September 30
Type: Private

Not feeling so bright in the Sunshine State? Lee Memorial Health System can help. Serving residents of Fort Myers and surrounding areas in Southwestern Florida's Lee County, the community-owned, not-for-profit health care system is home to four acute care hospitals (with a total of more than 1,400 beds), a home health agency, a 112-bed nursing home, and numerous outpatient treatment and diagnostic centers. The flagship Lee Memorial Hospital also houses a 60-bed inpatient rehabilitation hospital, and the HealthPark Medical Center location includes a dedicated 100-bed children's hospital. Lee Memorial Health Systems' corporate services include pre-employment screenings, drug screens, and wellness programs.

	Annual Growth	09/01	09/02	09/03	09/04	09/18
Sales ($mil.)	8.6%	–	477.3	522.6	585.3	1,790.0
Net income ($ mil.)	17.4%	–	7.7	51.0	46.8	101.0
Market value ($ mil.)	–	–	–	–	–	–
Employees	–	–	–	–	–	7,870

LEE UNIVERSITY

1120 N OCOEE ST STE 102
CLEVELAND, TN 373114475
Phone: 423 614-8000
Fax: –
Web: www.leeuniversity.edu

CEO: –
CFO: –
HR: –
FYE: June 30
Type: Private

Lee University is a Christian liberal arts college located in southeastern Tennessee. Boasting an enrollment of more than 4,250 students, the university offers academic programs at both baccalaureate and master's levels. Religion courses are a requirement of each student. Lee University is owned and operated by the Church of God. It was founded in 1918.

	Annual Growth	06/08	06/09	06/10	06/11	06/22
Sales ($mil.)	3.2%	–	–	74.8	75.2	108.8
Net income ($ mil.)	(9.7%)	–	–	9.7	4.6	2.8
Market value ($ mil.)	–	–	–	–	–	–
Employees	–	–	–	–	–	635

LEERINK PARTNERS LLC

53 STATE ST STE 40
BOSTON, MA 021093006
Phone: 617 918-4000
Fax: –
Web: www.svbsecurities.com

CEO: –
CFO: –
HR: –
FYE: December 31
Type: Private

If you're looking for an investment that will produce some healthy returns, Leerink Swann could have the right prescription. The investment bank provides brokerage, equity research, corporate finance, and strategic advisory services to companies and institutional investors in the health care and life sciences fields. Research areas include biotechnology, pharmaceuticals, medical devices, health care facilities, and health care technology. Leerink Swann also provides investment advisory services to life sciences companies, medical professionals, and high-net-worth investors. In January 2019, Leerink Holdings, parent company of Leerink Partners, was acquired by SVB Financial Group.

	Annual Growth	12/99	12/00	12/01	12/02	12/12
Sales ($mil.)	(65.1%)	–	–	30.5	–	0.0
Net income ($ mil.)	–	–	–	2.2	–	(0.0)
Market value ($ mil.)	–	–	–	–	–	–
Employees	–	–	–	–	–	200

LEGACY AWC, INC.

135 W CENTRAL BLVD STE 840
ORLANDO, FL 328012430
Phone: 407 633-7123
Fax: –
Web: www.allstates-worldcargo.com

CEO: Sam Digiralomo
CFO: Christopher Barna
HR: –
FYE: September 30
Type: Private

No relation to insurance giant Allstate, Allstates WorldCargo uses its "good hands" to provide freight forwarding and logistics services. The company arranges the transportation of its customers' cargo by plane, ship, and truck, for domestic or transborder shipping. Rather than maintaining its own transportation assets, it uses a network of air, ocean, and over-the-road carriers. The company operates from about 20 offices in the US, and it maintains agents and relationships with freight forwarders in Europe, South America, and the Asia/Pacific region. Freight forwarding within the US accounts for most of the company's sales. Company founder Joseph Guido is a majority shareholder of Allstates WorldCargo.

LEGACY EMANUEL HOSPITAL & HEALTH CENTER

2801 N GANTENBEIN AVE
PORTLAND, OR 972271623
Phone: 503 413-2200
Fax: –
Web: www.legacyhealth.org

CEO: George J Brown MD
CFO: –
HR: Sonja Steves
FYE: March 31
Type: Private

Legacy Emanuel Hospital and Health Center, part of the Legacy Health System, provides acute and specialized health care to residents of Portland, Oregon, and surrounding communities. The 420-bed teaching hospital's operations include centers devoted to trauma treatment, burn care, oncology, birthing, neurosurgery, orthopedics, and cardiology. It also houses a pediatric hospital and operates the region's Life Flight Network service, which is owned by a consortium of local hospitals. Legacy Emanuel's emergency department handles more than 15,600 visits every year.

	Annual Growth	03/13	03/14	03/15	03/17	03/20
Sales ($mil.)	7.0%	–	649.8	705.0	778.2	977.4
Net income ($ mil.)	–	–	31.0	29.5	(12.1)	(49.2)
Market value ($ mil.)	–	–	–	–	–	–
Employees	–	–	–	–	–	3,619

LEGACY FARMERS COOPERATIVE

6566 COUNTY ROAD 236
FINDLAY, OH 458409769
Phone: 419 423-2611
Fax: –
Web: www.legacyfarmers.com

CEO: –
CFO: –
HR: –
FYE: February 28
Type: Private

Supporting local farmers gives Blanchard Valley Farmers Cooperative (BVFC) roots and reach. Founded in 1989, BVFC has about 1,700 area members. The co-op owns more than a dozen locations, including four agronomy stations, two seasonal grain facilities, a farm and garden store, and two petroleum sites. Member-farmers benefit from the co-op's array of products and services, including seed, feed, fertilizer, grain, crop storage, crop applications, and farming equipment sales and rental. The feed store also sells mulch, birdseed, and pet supplies, as well as conducts soil testing and arranges seeding and fertilizer programs. BVFC's petroleum locations offer gasoline and home-heating oil, among several products.

	Annual Growth	02/18	02/19	02/20	02/21	02/22
Sales ($mil.)	12.5%	–	236.1	153.0	229.0	336.2
Net income ($ mil.)	31.4%	–	2.7	(3.7)	3.6	6.2
Market value ($ mil.)	–	–	–	–	–	–
Employees	–	–	–	–	–	122

LEGACY HEALTH

1919 NW LOVEJOY ST
PORTLAND, OR 972091503
Phone: 503 415-5600
Fax: –
Web: www.legacyhealth.org

CEO: –
CFO: –
HR: –
FYE: March 31
Type: Private

Legacy Health is a locally-owned, non-profit health system that offers a unique blend of health services across the Portland/Vancouver metro area and mid-Willamette Valley. Its services range from wellness and urgent care to dedicated children's services and advanced medical centers for patients of all ages. It operates half a dozen hospitals, including Legacy Emanuel Medical Center and Legacy Good Samaritan Medical Center, as well as the Randall Children's Hospital at Legacy Emanuel. Legacy Health has more than 70 primary care, specialty and urgent care clinics and its facilities provide such services as behavioral health, and outpatient and health education programs.

	Annual Growth	03/17	03/18	03/19	03/20	03/21
Sales ($mil.)	2.3%	–	2,117.9	2,219.4	2,336.5	2,266.0
Net income ($ mil.)	53.6%	–	100.2	84.1	(42.1)	363.3
Market value ($ mil.)	–	–	–	–	–	–
Employees	–	–	–	–	–	10,675

LEGACY IMBDS INC

6740 Shady Oak Road
Eden Prairie, MN 55344-3433
Phone: 952 943-6000
Fax: –
Web: www.imediabrands.com

NBB: IMBI Q
CEO: Landel C Hobbs
CFO: –
HR: –
FYE: January 29
Type: Public

iMedia Brands, Inc. (formerly known as EVINE Live Inc.) is a leading interactive media company managing a growing portfolio of niche television networks, niche national advertisers and media services. Its ShopHQ unit, nationally distributed shopping entertainment network, sells jewelry and watches, home goods and electronics, beauty and fitness products, and apparel and accessories. The shopping network reaches more than 80 million homes nationwide via cable and satellite TV. Programming is also streamed live across the Internet and on various mobile devices, as well as through social networking sites. Its entertainment business accounts for a growing portion of the company's sales. The US generates more than 90% of the company's revenue.

	Annual Growth	02/18	02/19	02/20*	01/21	01/22
Sales ($mil.)	(4.0%)	648.2	596.6	501.8	454.2	551.1
Net income ($ mil.)	–	0.1	(22.2)	(56.3)	(13.2)	(22.0)
Market value ($ mil.)	42.1%	25.9	12.1	78.7	124.3	105.5
Employees	(2.2%)	1,200	1,130	990	780	1,096

*Fiscal year change

LEGACY RESERVES LP

15 SMITH RD STE 3000
MIDLAND, TX 797055461
Phone: 432 689-5200
Fax: –
Web: www.revenirenergy.com

CEO: James D Westcott
CFO: Robert L Norris
HR: Wendy Engdahl
FYE: December 31
Type: Private

Legacy Reserves LP explores for oil and gas deposits in the Permian Basin of West Texas and southeast New Mexico and exploits those resources. The company owns interests in producing oil and natural gas properties in the Permian Basin, Texas Panhandle, Wyoming, North Dakota, Montana, Oklahoma and several other states. The company restructured and became a subsidiary of Legacy Reserves, Inc. in 2018; the parent entity filed for Chapter 11 bankruptcy protection in 2019.

LEGAL SERVICES CORPORATION

3333 K ST NW STE 1
WASHINGTON, DC 200073522
Phone: 202 295-1500
Fax: –
Web: www.lsc.gov

CEO: –
CFO: –
HR: –
FYE: September 30
Type: Private

Legal Services Corporation (LSC) works to deliver Francis Bellamy's pledge, "with liberty and justice for all." A private, not-for-profit entity established by Congress and President Richard Nixon in 1974, LSC helps poor Americans gain equal access to the judicial system. It doesn't provide legal services directly, but instead makes grants funds to independent local programs throughout the country. It makes grants to more than 130 programs and is the nation's single-largest funder of civil legal aid for the poor (with 811 offices across the US). LSC-funded programs handle about 1.8 million cases each year. About 64 million US citizens are eligible to receive assistance from the organization.

	Annual Growth	09/15	09/16	09/18	09/21	09/22
Sales ($mil.)	5.5%	–	387.9	428.3	471.4	535.7
Net income ($ mil.)	–	–	(0.3)	23.6	(0.4)	38.3
Market value ($ mil.)	–	–	–	–	–	–
Employees	–	–	–	–	–	130

LEGEND OIL & GAS LTD

555 North Point Center East, Suite 410
Alpharetta, GA 30022
Phone: 678 366-4587
Fax: –
Web: www.legendoilandgas.com

NBB: LOGL
CEO: –
CFO: –
HR: –
FYE: December 31
Type: Public

SIN Holdings owns and operates Senior-Inet.com (The Senior Information Network), a Web portal for senior citizens throughout the US seeking information about support services for senior citizens in ten cities in Colorado, as well as for the City of Houston. Information categories include health, housing, senior centers, travel services, rehabilitation, Alzheimer's, hospice and adult day care, and funeral services. James Vandeberg, an attorney from Seattle, acquired controlling interest in SIN Holdings from founder and former company president Steve Sinohui.

	Annual Growth	12/12	12/13	12/14	12/15	12/16
Sales ($mil.)	11.8%	2.5	2.0	0.7	4.7	3.9
Net income ($ mil.)	–	(9.3)	(12.3)	(2.4)	(15.0)	(6.2)
Market value ($ mil.)	(60.2%)	56.5	33.1	1.8	2.8	1.4
Employees	37.7%	5	4	–	17	18

LEGGETT & PLATT, INC.
NYS: LEG

No. 1 Leggett Road
Carthage, MO 64836
Phone: 417 358-8131
Fax: –
Web: www.leggett.com

CEO: J M Dolloff
CFO: –
HR: –
FYE: December 31
Type: Public

Leggett & Platt (L&P) is a diversified international manufacturer that conceives, designs, and produces a wide range of engineered components and products serving an array of industries, including bedding, automotive, aerospace, office furniture, and home furniture. Bedding-related products include steel coils used in mattress innersprings, specialty foam used in bedding and furniture, and mattresses. L&P also makes machinery for sewing mattress quilting, and other industrial sewing and finishing machines. Other products include automotive seating components (wire seat suspensions, and motors and actuators for vehicle power systems) and tubing used in aerospace fluid conveyance systems. The US accounts for approximately 65% of the company's total sales.

	Annual Growth	12/19	12/20	12/21	12/22	12/23
Sales ($mil.)	(0.1%)	4,752.5	4,280.2	5,072.6	5,146.7	4,725.3
Net income ($ mil.)	–	333.8	247.6	402.4	309.8	(136.8)
Market value ($ mil.)	(15.3%)	6,780.7	5,909.6	5,490.7	4,299.5	3,491.1
Employees	(3.2%)	22,000	20,400	20,300	19,900	19,700

LEHIGH UNIVERSITY

27 MEMORIAL DR W UNIT 8
BETHLEHEM, PA 180153005
Phone: 610 758-3000
Fax: –
Web: www.lehigh.edu

CEO: –
CFO: –
HR: Linda Parks
FYE: June 30
Type: Private

Lehigh University (LU), nestled in eastern Pennsylvania's Lehigh Valley, offers about 90 undergraduate programs and majors at colleges of arts and sciences, business and economics, engineering and applied sciences, and education. It also offers more than 40 masters and doctoral degree programs, as well as certificate programs. Tuition is more than $40,000 per year; more than half of students receive financial aid. LU has an enrollment of nearly 7,000 undergraduate and graduate students. The university was founded in 1865 by entrepreneur and philanthropist Asa Packer.

	Annual Growth	06/16	06/17	06/18	06/21	06/22
Sales ($mil.)	2.9%	–	396.6	416.3	390.7	458.4
Net income ($ mil.)	–	–	171.6	110.1	499.8	(82.4)
Market value ($ mil.)	–	–	–	–	–	–
Employees	–	–	–	–	–	1,693

LEHIGH VALLEY HEALTH NETWORK, INC.

2100 MACK BLVD
ALLENTOWN, PA 181035622
Phone: 610 402-8000
Fax: –
Web: www.lvhn.org

CEO: Elliot J Sussman
CFO: –
HR: –
FYE: June 30
Type: Private

Lehigh Valley Health Network (LVHN) is a not-for-profit health care provider operating through a dozen of full-service hospital campuses. LVHN serves as a regional referral center for trauma and burn care and organ transplantation, as well as specialty care such as cardiology, women's health, and pediatric surgery. LVHN also boasts a network of physician practices and community health centers, as well as home health and hospice units. Through Lehigh Valley Physician Group, LVHN has more than 2,000 primary care and specialty physicians, as well as more than 800 advanced practice clinicians. HNL Lab Medicine provides an extensive range of laboratory tests from the most critical medical applications to simple pre-employment drug screenings.

	Annual Growth	06/18	06/19	06/20	06/21	06/22
Sales ($mil.)	8.8%	–	2,978.2	3,129.7	3,437.0	3,833.7
Net income ($ mil.)	–	–	118.5	2.1	700.2	(102.6)
Market value ($ mil.)	–	–	–	–	–	–
Employees	–	–	–	–	–	12,000

LEHMAN BROTHERS HOLDINGS INC.

110 E 42ND ST RM 820
NEW YORK, NY 100178539
Phone: 646 285-9000
Fax: –
Web: –

CEO: –
CFO: William J Fox
HR: –
FYE: November 30
Type: Private

In what could be called the collapse heard 'round the world, venerable investment bank Lehman Brothers declared bankruptcy in September 2008, ending a reign of some 160 years in financial services. One of the top bulge-bracket firms and perennially among the industry leaders in M&A advice, debt and equity underwriting, and global finance suffered a knockout punch, reporting nearly $7 billion in losses in the heat of the global credit crisis. After acquisition talks with foreign investors fell through, Lehman tried to restructure, including selling off units for cash. The efforts were too little too late, though, and Lehman filed for Chapter 11 bankruptcy, shutting down operating subsidiary Lehman Brothers Inc.

LEHMAN TRIKES INC

#125 Industrial Drive
Spearfish, SD 57783
Phone: 780 423-3661
Fax: 780 426-1293
Web: www.lehmantrikes.com

CEO: –
CFO: –
HR: –
FYE: November 30
Type: Public

Lehman Trikes proudly proclaims that it is the "leader of the three-world." Through its US subsidiary, the company builds motorized tricycles by converting heavy-cruiser motorcycles manufactured by Honda, Victory, and Suzuki. In 2010 Lehman Trikes ended its supply agreement with Harley-Davidson, a customer that represented approximately 80% of the tricycle maker's sales. The company also produces and wholesales the kits for do-it-yourselfers to convert traditional two-wheelers into motor trikes. In addition, the company offers a line of accessories, including custom wheels, lights, racks, and running boards. The company's products are sold in the US and Canada through a dealer network located in the US.

	Annual Growth	11/06	11/07	11/08	11/09	11/10
Sales ($mil.)	14.9%	14.4	19.8	22.6	33.4	25.0
Net income ($ mil.)	–	0.0	(1.0)	(0.6)	0.6	(0.6)
Market value ($ mil.)	(50.1%)	19.3	11.2	4.6	2.8	1.2
Employees	–	–	–	–	–	–

LEIDOS HOLDINGS INC
NYS: LDOS

1750 Presidents Street
Reston, VA 20190
Phone: 571 526-6000
Fax: –
Web: www.leidos.com

CEO: Thomas A Bell
CFO: Christopher R Cage
HR: –
FYE: December 29
Type: Public

Leidos Holdings provides services and solutions in the defense, intelligence, civil and health markets, both domestically and internationally. Services include digital modernization, cyber operations, mission software systems, integrated systems and mission operations. The company's areas of expertise include operations and logistics; sensors; software development; and systems engineering. These services are then offered to customers including the US Department of Defense (DoD), the US Intelligence Community, the US Department of Homeland Security (DHs), the Federal Aviation Administration (FAA), the Department of Veterans Affairs ("VA") and many other U.S. civilian, state and local government agencies, foreign government agencies and commercial businesses. Most of the company's revenue (over 85%) comes from the US government.

	Annual Growth	01/20	01/21*	12/21	12/22	12/23
Sales ($mil.)	8.6%	11,094	12,297	13,737	14,396	15,438
Net income ($ mil.)	(26.1%)	667.0	628.0	753.0	685.0	199.0
Market value ($ mil.)	2.1%	13,506	14,272	12,070	14,281	14,695
Employees	8.4%	34,000	39,000	43,000	45,000	47,000

*Fiscal year change

LELAND STANFORD JUNIOR UNIVERSITY

450 JANE STANFORD WAY
STANFORD, CA 943052004
Phone: 650 723-2300
Fax: –
Web: www.stanford.edu

CEO: –
CFO: Randall S Livingston
HR: –
FYE: August 31
Type: Private

The Leland Stanford Junior University, better known as simply Stanford University, is one of the top universities in the US. It boasts respected programs across seven schools and about 20 interdisciplinary institutes, such as business, education, engineering, law, humanities and sciences, medicine, and Doerr School of Sustainability. Stanford serves about 17,325 students (taught by nearly 2,305 faculty members). Its student-teacher ratio sits at about 5:1. A private institution, Stanford is supported through an endowment of some $36.3 billion, one of the largest in the US. The university was established in 1885 by Leland Stanford Sr. It was named after his son, Leland Stanford Jr.

	Annual Growth	08/18	08/19	08/20	08/21	08/22
Sales ($mil.)	7.3%	–	12,262	12,455	13,939	15,132
Net income ($ mil.)	(62.8%)	–	1,961.4	1,983.9	845.4	101.0
Market value ($ mil.)	–	–	–	–	–	–
Employees	–	–	–	–	–	15,000

LEMAITRE VASCULAR INC

NMS: LMAT

63 Second Avenue
Burlington, MA 01803
Phone: 781 221-2266
Fax: –
Web: www.lemaitre.com

CEO: George W Lemaitre
CFO: Joseph P Pellegrino Jr
HR: Daniel J Mumford
FYE: December 31
Type: Public

LeMaitre Vascular is a global provider of medical devices and human tissue cryopreservation services largely used in the treatment of peripheral vascular disease, end-stage renal disease, and to a lesser extent cardiovascular disease. The company develops, manufactures, and markets vascular devices to address the needs of vascular surgeons and, to a lesser degree, other specialties such as cardiac surgeons, general surgeons, and neurosurgeons. Its diversified portfolio of devices consists of brand name products that are used in arteries and veins and are well known to vascular surgeons. Its principal product offerings are sold globally, primarily in the US, Europe, Canada, and Asia Pacific. Its US operation accounts for the highest geographic market.

	Annual Growth	12/19	12/20	12/21	12/22	12/23
Sales ($mil.)	13.3%	117.2	129.4	154.4	161.7	193.5
Net income ($ mil.)	13.8%	17.9	21.2	26.9	20.6	30.1
Market value ($ mil.)	12.1%	802.7	904.3	1,121.5	1,027.5	1,267.3
Employees	6.4%	479	403	488	617	614

LEMIEUX GROUP LP

1001 5TH AVE
PITTSBURGH, PA 152196201
Phone: 412 642-1300
Fax: –
Web: www.pittsburghpenguins.com

CEO: Mario Lemieux
CFO: –
HR: –
FYE: April 30
Type: Private

These Penguins do their thing on the ice in downtown Pittsburgh, not the Antarctic. The Lemieux Group owns and operates the Pittsburgh Penguins professional hockey franchise. The team has represented the Steel City in the National Hockey League since 1967 and boasts back-to-back Stanley Cup championships in 1991 and 1992. The team won a third title in 2009 and its fourth in 2016. Popular through good times and bad, fans root for the Pens at Pittsburgh's CONSOL Energy Center. Legendary forward Mario Lemieux, who played for Pittsburgh during the 1990s, has controlled the franchise since 1999.

	Annual Growth	06/12	06/13	06/14	06/15*	04/19
Sales ($mil.)	(4.7%)	–	3.4	2.7	2.6	2.5
Net income ($ mil.)	–	–	1.6	(0.8)	(1.1)	(0.0)
Market value ($ mil.)	–	–	–	–	–	–
Employees	–	–	–	–	–	175

*Fiscal year change

LEMOYNE-OWEN COLLEGE

807 WALKER AVE
MEMPHIS, TN 381266595
Phone: 901 435-1681
Fax: –
Web: www.loc.edu

CEO: –
CFO: –
HR: Brenda Massey
FYE: June 30
Type: Private

A private, historically black, liberal arts school, LeMoyne-Owen College offers about 20 majors and grants bachelor of arts, bachelor of business administration, and bachelor of science degrees. The college also offers a degree completion program intended for working adults. LeMoyne-Owen was formed in 1968 from the merger of LeMoyne College, which was founded in 1862, and Owen College, which was founded in 1947.

	Annual Growth	06/14	06/15	06/16	06/21	06/22
Sales ($mil.)	0.8%	–	19.6	19.0	23.4	20.7
Net income ($ mil.)	(18.7%)	–	1.0	0.5	4.7	0.2
Market value ($ mil.)	–	–	–	–	–	–
Employees	–	–	–	–	–	200

LENDINGTREE INC (NEW)

NMS: TREE

1415 Vantage Park Dr., Suite 700
Charlotte, NC 28203
Phone: 704 541-5351
Fax: –
Web: www.lendingtree.com

CEO: Douglas Lebda
CFO: Trent Ziegler
HR: –
FYE: December 31
Type: Public

LendingTree is the nation's leading online marketplace. Through multiple branded marketplaces, LendingTree empowers consumers to shop for financial services the same way they would shop for airline tickets or hotel stays, comparing multiple offers from a nationwide network of over 600 partners (refer to as Network Partners). Services include mortgage loans, mortgage refinances, auto loans, personal loans, business loans, student refinances, credit cards, insurance and more. In addition, it offer tools and resources, including free credit scores that facilitate comparison shopping for loans, deposit products, insurance and other offerings. Through the My LendingTree platform, consumers receive free credit scores, credit monitoring and recommendations to improve credit health.

	Annual Growth	12/19	12/20	12/21	12/22	12/23
Sales ($mil.)	(11.7%)	1,106.6	910.0	1,098.5	985.0	672.5
Net income ($ mil.)	–	17.8	(48.3)	69.1	(188.0)	(122.4)
Market value ($ mil.)	(43.8%)	3,957.3	3,570.6	1,598.9	278.2	395.4
Employees	(5.8%)	1,107	1,303	1,425	1,253	870

LENDWAY INC

NAS: LDWY

5000 West 36th Street, Suite 220
Minneapolis, MN 55416
Phone: 763 392-6200
Fax: –
Web: www.insigniasystems.com

CEO: Randy Uglem
CFO: –
HR: Kelly Hagglund
FYE: December 31
Type: Public

Insignia Systems believes all signs point to greater sales. The company's point of purchase (POP) software and services help retailers and consumer goods manufacturers create promotional signage and in-store advertising that's displayed close to products on store shelving. As part of its POPSign program, Insignia Systems creates customized signs based on information from retailers and manufacturers; it generates the majority of its revenue from its POPSign program. Its Stylus software suite is used to create signs, labels, and posters. Insignia Systems also sells specialized cardstock and other printing supplies for its systems. The company was founded in 1990.

	Annual Growth	12/18	12/19	12/20	12/21	12/22
Sales ($mil.)	(13.3%)	33.2	22.0	17.7	19.5	18.8
Net income ($ mil.)	63.7%	1.4	(5.0)	(4.3)	(3.5)	10.0
Market value ($ mil.)	51.3%	2.7	1.3	1.5	41.5	14.0
Employees	(14.1%)	57	54	40	32	31

LENNAR CORP   NYS: LEN

5505 Waterford District Drive
Miami, FL 33126
Phone: 305 559-4000
Fax: –
Web: www.lennar.com

CEO: Jonathan M Jaffe
CFO: Diane J Bessette
HR: –
FYE: November 30
Type: Public

Lennar is one of the largest homebuilding, land-owning, loan-making leviathans in the US. The company builds single-family attached and detached homes and multi-family rental properties primarily under the Lennar brand. Lennar targets first-time, move-up, active adult, and luxury homebuyers and markets its homes as "everything included". In addition, the company's homebuilding operations purchase, develop and sell land to third parties. The company delivered more about 66,400 homes in fiscal 2022 at an average price of around $480,000. Lennar traces its roots back to 1954 as a local Miami homebuilder and went public in 1971.

	Annual Growth	11/19	11/20	11/21	11/22	11/23
Sales ($mil.)	11.4%	22,260	22,489	27,131	33,671	34,233
Net income ($ mil.)	20.8%	1,849.1	2,465.0	4,430.1	4,614.1	3,938.5
Market value ($ mil.)	21.0%	16,759	21,313	29,514	24,676	35,939
Employees	5.0%	10,106	9,495	10,753	12,012	12,284

LENNOX INTERNATIONAL INC   NYS: LII

2140 Lake Park Blvd.
Richardson, TX 75080
Phone: 972 497-5000
Fax: –
Web: www.lennoxinternational.com

CEO: Alok Maskara
CFO: Michael Quenzer
HR: –
FYE: December 31
Type: Public

Lennox International makes climate control equipment such as heating, ventilation, air conditioning, and refrigeration (HVACR) units for residential, commercial and industrial uses. Its brands include Dave Lennox Signature Collection, Elite Series, Merit Series, iComfort, ComfortSense, Healthy Climate Solutions, Heatcraft Worldwide Refrigeration, Lennox VRF, Lennox National Account Services, Allied Commercial, and MagicPak, among others. The company's products and services are sold through a combination of direct sales, distributors and company-owned parts and supplies stores. Lennox's largest single market is the US, which accounts for about 90% of total revenue. Named after inventor Dave Lennox, the company was founded in 1895.

	Annual Growth	12/19	12/20	12/21	12/22	12/23
Sales ($mil.)	7.0%	3,807.2	3,634.1	4,194.1	4,718.4	4,981.9
Net income ($ mil.)	9.6%	408.7	356.3	464.0	497.1	590.1
Market value ($ mil.)	16.4%	8,681.0	9,748.4	11,541	8,512.3	15,924
Employees	3.0%	11,200	10,300	11,000	13,200	12,600

LENOX CORPORATION

1414 RADCLIFFE ST
BRISTOL, PA 190075413
Phone: 800 223-4311
Fax: –
Web: www.lenox.com

CEO: Bob Burbank
CFO: –
HR: Agatha Su
FYE: April 02
Type: Private

Lenox is a leading supplier of tabletop, giftware and home entertaining products. It offers dinnerware, flatware, kitchenware, drinkware, accessories, and home decors under the Lenox and Reed & Barton names. Lenox's legacy begins in a small art studio to appearances at the White House. Under licensing agreements, Lenox makes products under the additional name, such as Kate Spade New York. Lenox was founded in 1889 by Walter Scott Lenox as the Ceramic Art Company. It brings a rich history of craftsmanship to modern day life; where families and friends gather to celebrate using pieces that are versatile and timeless.

	Annual Growth	03/12	03/13	03/14	03/15*	04/16
Sales ($mil.)	8.1%	–	–	–	224.1	242.4
Net income ($ mil.)	(3.1%)	–	–	–	5.8	5.6
Market value ($ mil.)	–	–	–	–	–	–
Employees	–	–	–	–	–	1,030

*Fiscal year change

LEO A. DALY COMPANY

8600 INDIAN HILLS DR
OMAHA, NE 681144039
Phone: 402 391-8111
Fax: –
Web: www.leoadaly.com

CEO: Leo A Daly III
CFO: James B Brader II
HR: Marissa McQuitty
FYE: February 28
Type: Private

Firmly ensconced among the lions of design, Leo A Daly takes great pride in its work. The company provides architecture, engineering, design, and program management services for commercial, industrial, and public projects in more than 85 countries. Its project portfolio includes the award-winning First National Tower in its home state of Nebraska and the Lockheed Martin Center for Leadership Excellence in Maryland. Leo A Daly also owns engineering group Lockwood, Andrews & Newnam, which specializes in infrastructure management and consulting. Leo A Daly and its subsidiaries have more than 30 offices worldwide. Established in 1915 by Leo A. Daly Sr., the company is now led by his grandson, Leo A. Daly III.

	Annual Growth	02/14	02/15	02/16	02/17	02/18
Sales ($mil.)	(6.6%)	–	139.4	162.3	107.1	113.6
Net income ($ mil.)	–	–	(2.0)	3.2	(1.9)	0.8
Market value ($ mil.)	–	–	–	–	–	–
Employees	–	–	–	–	–	750

LEONARD GREEN & PARTNERS, L.P.

11111 SANTA MONICA BLVD STE 2000
LOS ANGELES, CA 900253353
Phone: 310 954-0444
Fax: –
Web: www.leonardgreen.com

CEO: –
CFO: –
HR: Buffy Upchurch
FYE: December 31
Type: Private

This private equity firm has a green thumb for growing businesses. Leonard Green & Partners (LGP) specializes in long-term investments in friendly buyouts, focusing on established retailers and consumer products companies, such as J. Crew, Varsity Brands, The Container Store, The Sports Authority, PETCO, and Tourneau. It also has holdings in the health care, media, and distribution sectors. All told, LGP has invested in 70 firms with an aggregate value of $74 billion, and manages more than $15 billion in committed equity capital. The firm typically targets companies worth up to $5 billion, does not invest in start-ups, and tends to avoid technology-centric ventures.

LEONARDO DRS INC   NMS: DRS

2345 Crystal Drive, Suite 1000
Arlington, VA 22202
Phone: 703 416-8000
Fax: –
Web: www.leonardodrs.com

CEO: William J Lynn III
CFO: Michael Dippold
HR: Stuart Gruskin
FYE: December 31
Type: Public

Leonardo DRS is an innovative and agile provider of advanced defense technology to US national security customers and allies around the world. Its offerings include avionics and aviation support; communications and networks; computing and information technology; defense systems; intelligence and security; power and propulsion; and sustainment, logistics and advanced services. It is a wholly owned subsidiary of Italy's Leonardo.

	Annual Growth	12/19	12/20	12/21	12/22	12/23
Sales ($mil.)	1.0%	2,714.0	2,778.0	2,879.0	2,693.0	2,826.0
Net income ($ mil.)	22.3%	75.0	85.0	154.0	405.0	168.0
Market value ($ mil.)	40.2%	1,362.5	2,559.6	2,473.0	3,355.1	5,261.0
Employees	–	–	6,500	6,575	6,400	6,600

LEOPARDO COMPANIES INC.

210 N CARPENTER ST STE 300
CHICAGO, IL 60607
Phone: 847 783-3000
Fax: –
Web: www.leopardo.com

CEO: –
CFO: –
HR: –
FYE: December 31
Type: Private

While Leonardo created masterpieces out of paint and canvas, Leopardo creates them from brick and mortar. One of the top contractors in Illinois, Leopardo Companies, which also has an office in South Carolina, provides an array of construction services from pre-construction and general contracting to construction management, design-build, green building, and real estate development. Projects include office buildings; health care facilities; senior housing; retail, office, and industrial space; airports; condos; and community projects, such as churches, libraries, and schools. It is also a top interiors contractor. CEO Jim Leopardo started the company in 1979.

LEPRINO FOODS COMPANY

1830 W 38TH AVE
DENVER, CO 802112225
Phone: 303 480-2600
Fax: –
Web: www.leprinofoods.com

CEO: James G Leprino
CFO: –
HR: –
FYE: October 31
Type: Private

Leprino Foods is the worldwide leader in mozzarella-making and is one of the largest privately-held companies in the US. It sells its soft, cream-colored cheese to food manufacturers, stores, restaurants, and pizza purveyors. The company's portfolio of products includes string cheeses, shredded and diced cheese, and blocks. Aside from its cheese business, Leprino Foods operates a dairy powders segment that provides whey protein concentrate, lactose, and functional proteins for use in sports nutrition, baby formula, confectionery, and baked goods. In addition to its manufacturing facilities in the US, Leprino Foods has two global joint ventures and sales offices in Asia. The company was founded in 1950 by Mike Leprino.

LESCARDEN INC

420 Lexington Avenue, Ste 212
New York, NY 10170
Phone: 212 687-1050
Fax: 212 687-1051
Web: www.lescarden.com

CEO: William E Luther
CFO: William E Luther
HR: –
FYE: May 31
Type: Public

Lescarden lessens scarring when it can. The company develops clinical dermatological, osteoarthritis, and wound care products. Lescarden focuses on developing natural therapies. Many of its products utilize bovine cartilage, which is said to possess beneficial healing qualities. Its lead product, the bovine-based and FDA-approved Catrix, is sold as a dressing for non-healing wounds such as diabetic ulcers. Lescarden also markets a line of Catrix-based skin care products targeting the plastic surgery, dermatology, and medical spa markets. Other products include Poly-Nag, an anti-arthritic compound made from chitin, a material found in the shells of invertebrates, and BIO-CARTILAGE, a nutritional supplement.

	Annual Growth	05/12	05/13	05/14	05/15	05/16
Sales ($mil.)	(26.9%)	0.4	0.4	0.4	0.3	0.1
Net income ($ mil.)	–	(0.2)	(0.3)	(0.2)	(0.2)	(0.1)
Market value ($ mil.)	(6.5%)	1.1	1.9	1.7	1.6	0.8
Employees	–	1	1	1	1	1

LESTER E. COX MEDICAL CENTERS

1423 N JEFFERSON AVE
SPRINGFIELD, MO 658021917
Phone: 417 269-3000
Fax: –
Web: www.coxhealth.com

CEO: Steven D Edwards
CFO: Jake McWay
HR: Denise Dunaway
FYE: September 30
Type: Private

Lester E. Cox Medical Centers (dba CoxHealth) is the area leader in health care and community involvement. CoxHealth's network includes six acute care hospitals (with about 1,195 licensed beds), five ERs, and more than 80 physician clinics. Centers for cardiac care, cancer treatment, orthopedics, and women's health are among CoxHealth's specialized care options. The organization was named after its primary fundraiser in 1949.

	Annual Growth	09/10	09/11	09/12	09/13	09/14
Sales ($mil.)	3.2%	–	–	843.2	858.3	898.4
Net income ($ mil.)	(13.0%)	–	–	66.9	106.0	50.6
Market value ($ mil.)	–	–	–	–	–	–
Employees	–	–	–	–	–	11,170

LEVCOR INTERNATIONAL INC.

462 Seventh Avenue
New York, NY 10018
Phone: 212 354-8500
Fax: –
Web: –

CEO: Robert A Levinson
CFO: Pramila D Shaheed
HR: –
FYE: December 31
Type: Public

Button. Button. Who's got the button? Levcor does. Buttons and other accoutrements are the core of Levcor International's business. The company makes and sells buttons, decorations, craft products, and complementary product lines, including iron-ons, kits, and fashion and jewelry accessories. Levcor's products are sold to the home sewing and craft markets through mass merchandisers and retailers, such as Wal-Mart and Jo-Ann Stores. The company is led by chairman, president, and CEO Robert Levinson. Levcor's roots reach back to 1964, when it was established as Pantepec International.

	Annual Growth	12/03	12/04	12/05	12/06	12/07
Sales ($mil.)	(10.9%)	30.8	33.7	29.4	21.9	19.4
Net income ($ mil.)	–	(6.0)	0.7	(8.3)	1.6	0.1
Market value ($ mil.)	(47.7%)	0.0	0.0	0.0	0.0	0.0
Employees	(9.9%)	150	140	130	118	99

LEVEL 3 PARENT, LLC

1025 ELDORADO BLVD STE 4000
BROOMFIELD, CO 800218255
Phone: 720 888-1000
Fax: –
Web: –

CEO: Jeff K Storey
CFO: Sunit S Patel
HR: –
FYE: December 31
Type: Private

Level 3 Communications, a wholly owned subsidiary of CenturyLink, provides infrastructure for the Information Superhighway as operator of one of the world's largest fiber-optic communications networks, connecting customers in more than 60 countries. Its services include broadband internet access, wholesale voice origination and termination, enterprise voice, content distribution, broadband transport, and colocation services. Wholesale customers include ISPs, telecom carriers, cable TV operators, wireless providers, and the US government. The company markets its products and services directly to businesses, government agencies, and schools. Its content delivery unit targets video distributors, web portals, online gaming and software companies, and social networking sites. CenturyLink bought Level 3 for $34 billion in 2017.

LEVENGER COMPANY

420 S CONGRESS AVE
DELRAY BEACH, FL 334454696
Phone: 561 276-2436
Fax: –
Web: www.levenger.com

CEO: –
CFO: –
HR: –
FYE: December 31
Type: Private

Levenger began when Lori Granger Leveen and her husband, Steve, said: "Let there be lighting!" The company, which got its start in 1987 by selling halogen lights for reading, has fashioned itself into the provider of "Tools for Serious Readers." It offers an assortment of home and office accessories and furniture, including briefcases, leather armchairs, lap desks, pens, stationery, and of course, lighting products. The company also operates a publishing division, Levenger Press. Levenger (which derives its name from combining Leveen and Granger) sells its merchandise through its catalog, website, and retail stores in Boston, Chicago, and the Washington, DC, area.

	Annual Growth	12/18	12/19	12/20	12/21	12/22
Sales ($mil.)	(9.8%)	–	–	–	0.2	0.1
Net income ($ mil.)	–	–	–	–	(0.0)	(0.0)
Market value ($ mil.)	–	–	–	–	–	–
Employees						150

LEVI STRAUSS & CO.

1155 BATTERY ST
SAN FRANCISCO, CA 941111264
Phone: 415.501-6000
Fax: –
Web: www.levistrauss.com

CEO: Charles V Bergh V
CFO: –
HR: –
FYE: November 25
Type: Private

Levi Strauss & Co. (LS&CO) is one of the world's largest brand-name apparel companies. LS&CO sells jeans and sportswear under the Levi's, Dockers, Signature by Levi Strauss, and Denizen labels in more than 110 countries. The company distributes its brand products through approximately 50,000 retail stores worldwide, which includes 3,200 brand-dedicated stores and shop-in-shops. It designs, markets, and sells ? directly or through third parties and licensees ? products that include jeans, pants, tops, shorts, skirts, dresses, jackets, footwear, and related accessories for men, women, and children. Over 50% of the company's total revenue comes from US operations. Founded In 1853, Levi Strauss opened a wholesale dry goods business in San Francisco that became known as Levi Strauss & Co.

	Annual Growth	11/14	11/15	11/16	11/17	11/18
Sales ($mil.)	7.4%	–	4,494.5	4,552.7	4,904.0	5,575.4
Net income ($ mil.)	10.8%	–	209.9	291.2	284.6	285.2
Market value ($ mil.)	–	–	–	–	–	–
Employees						18,000

LEVI STRAUSS & CO.

1155 Battery Street
San Francisco, CA 94111
Phone: 415 501-6000
Fax: –
Web: www.levistrauss.com

NYS: LEVI
CEO: Charles V Bergh V
CFO: –
HR: –
FYE: November 26
Type: Public

Levi Strauss & Co. (LS&CO) is one of the world's largest brand-name apparel companies. LS&CO sells jeans and sportswear under the Levi's, Dockers, Signature by Levi Strauss, and Denizen labels in more than 110 countries. The company distributes its brand products through approximately 50,000 retail stores worldwide, which includes 3,200 brand-dedicated stores and shop-in-shops. It designs, markets, and sells ? directly or through third parties and licensees ? products that include jeans, pants, tops, shorts, skirts, dresses, jackets, footwear, and related accessories for men, women, and children. Over 50% of the company's total revenue comes from US operations. Founded In 1853, Levi Strauss opened a wholesale dry goods business in San Francisco that became known as Levi Strauss & Co.

	Annual Growth	11/19	11/20	11/21	11/22	11/23
Sales ($mil.)	1.8%	5,763.1	4,452.6	5,763.9	6,168.6	6,179.0
Net income ($ mil.)	(10.8%)	394.6	(127.1)	553.5	569.1	249.6
Market value ($ mil.)	(2.4%)	6,750.9	7,613.2	10,808	6,401.3	6,115.2
Employees	4.9%	15,800	14,800	16,600	18,000	19,100

LEVINDALE HEBREW GERIATRIC CENTER AND HOSPITAL, INC.

2434 W BELVEDERE AVE STE 1
BALTIMORE, MD 212155267
Phone: 410 601-2400
Fax: –
Web: www.lifebridgehealth.org

CEO: Ronald Rothstein
CFO: –
HR: –
FYE: June 30
Type: Private

Levindale Hebrew Geriatric Center and Hospital is a Jewish-sponsored nursing home that also operates a specialty hospital. In addition to traditional skilled nursing services, the hospital provides subacute (short-term) medical care, inpatient and outpatient mental health care, and adult day-care services. Founded in 1890, the medical center has more than 290 beds. Among its specialized services are rehabilitation, pain management, and wound care, as well as hospice care. Levindale Hebrew is part of the LifeBridge Health network of facilities in the Baltimore area and is sponsored by the Jewish Community Federation of Baltimore.

	Annual Growth	06/18	06/19	06/20	06/21	06/22
Sales ($mil.)	5.9%	–	79.0	84.1	76.3	93.8
Net income ($ mil.)	45.7%	–	3.0	4.8	(7.1)	9.4
Market value ($ mil.)	–	–	–	–	–	–
Employees						461

LEWIS & CLARK COLLEGE

615 S PALATINE HILL RD
PORTLAND, OR 972198091
Phone: 503 768-7933
Fax: –
Web: www.lclark.edu

CEO: –
CFO: –
HR: Nicholas Smith
FYE: May 31
Type: Private

Lewis & Clark College sends students on an expedition to higher learning. The private university offers bachelor's degrees in more than two dozen majors through its College of Arts and Sciences. Fields of study include the humanities, art history, communications, psychology, natural sciences, and mathematics. The school also offers master's and doctoral degrees at its Graduate School of Education and Counseling and its School of Law. Lewis & Clark has an enrollment of more than 3,700 students. Founded as Albany Collegiate Institute in 1867, the college changed its name to Lewis & Clark when it moved to Portland, Oregon, in 1942.

	Annual Growth	05/18	05/19	05/20	05/21	05/22
Sales ($mil.)	3.1%	–	125.7	124.9	121.3	138.0
Net income ($ mil.)	56.2%	–	9.3	(2.2)	74.4	35.3
Market value ($ mil.)	–	–	–	–	–	–
Employees						800

LEWIS BROTHERS BAKERIES INC

500 N FULTON AVE
EVANSVILLE, IN 477151571
Phone: 812 425-4642
Fax: –
Web: www.lewisbakeries.net

CEO: R J Lewis Jr
CFO: –
HR: Ann Greenfield
FYE: March 31
Type: Private

Lewis Brothers Bakeries is a leading producer of baked goods in about a dozen states in the Midwest, anchored by its flagship brands Bunny Bread, Gateway, Hartford Farms, Healthy Life, and Indiana Spud potato bread. The company's products include whole grain and white breads, buns, muffins, and bagels. Boasting a handful of baking facilities in Indiana and Tennessee, it also provides frozen bakery products nationwide. In addition to its own brands, Lewis Bakeries makes and distributes bread products under such licensed names as Butternut, Cinnabon, Holsum, Sun-Maid, Roman Meal, and Sunbeam. The family-owned company was established in 1925 by the Lewis brothers: Amos, Armold, and Jack.

LEXICON PHARMACEUTICALS, INC.

NMS: LXRX

2445 Technology Forest Blvd., 11th Floor
The Woodlands, TX 77381
Phone: 281 863-3000
Fax: –
Web: www.lexpharma.com

CEO: Lonnel Coats
CFO: –
HR: Mary McKinney
FYE: December 31
Type: Public

Lexicon Pharmaceuticals is a biopharmaceutical company is focused on a handful of potential medicines in clinical and pre-clinical research stages. The company is developing sotagliflozin, an orally-delivered small molecule drug candidate, as a treatment for heart failure and type 1 diabetes, as well as LX9211, an orally-delivered small molecule drug candidate, as a treatment for neuropathic pain. Lexicon is conducting preclinical research and development and preparing to conduct clinical development of compounds from a number of additional drug programs originating from its internal drug discovery efforts. Through its Genome5000 program, Lexicon scientists studied the role and function of nearly 5,000 genes and identified more than 100 protein targets with significant therapeutic potential in a range of diseases.

	Annual Growth	12/19	12/20	12/21	12/22	12/23
Sales ($mil.)	(75.3%)	322.1	24.0	0.3	0.1	1.2
Net income ($ mil.)	–	130.1	(58.6)	(87.8)	(101.9)	(177.1)
Market value ($ mil.)	(22.1%)	1,016.4	837.6	965.0	467.8	374.7
Employees	–	–	184	78	87	135	–

LEXINGTON MEDICAL CENTER

2720 SUNSET BLVD
WEST COLUMBIA, SC 291694810
Phone: 803 791-2000
Fax: –
Web: www.lexmed.com

CEO: Tod Augsburger
CFO: Jeff Brillhart
HR: –
FYE: September 30
Type: Private

Lexington Medical Center is a not-for-profit health care organization serving the residents of South Carolina's Lexington County. Established in 1971, the medical center has some 415 beds and provides general, emergency, surgical, and diagnostic services. Specialty services include cancer treatment, cardiovascular care, women's health, and rehabilitation. Lexington Medical Center also operates a skilled nursing center, as well as a network of affiliated community health centers, urgent care clinics, and affiliated physician practices. The hospital is managed by the Lexington County Health Service District.

LEXMARK INTERNATIONAL, INC.

740 W NEW CIRCLE RD
LEXINGTON, KY 405111876
Phone: 859 232-2000
Fax: –
Web: www.lexmark.com

CEO: Allen Waugerman
CFO: Chuck Butler
HR: Jody Swanson
FYE: December 31
Type: Private

Lexmark creates innovative IoT- and cloud-enabled imaging technologies that help customers in more than 170 countries worldwide quickly realize business outcomes. It is a provider of printing and imaging products, software, solutions, and services that help customers save time and money. Lexmark small workgroup devices offer the performance, quality, and reliability of larger enterprise-class devices, skillfully scaled to fit in smaller spaces and designed for work teams of up to ten printing up to 3,000 pages per month. The company's customers are in retail, financial services, healthcare, manufacturing, education, and government among others.. The company was founded in 1991.

LGI HOMES, INC.

NMS: LGIH

1450 Lake Robbins Drive, Suite 430
The Woodlands, TX 77380
Phone: 281 362-8998
Fax: –
Web: www.lgihomes.com

CEO: Eric T Lipar
CFO: Charles Merdian
HR: –
FYE: December 31
Type: Public

LGI Homes is engaged in the design, construction, and sale of new homes in markets in West, Northwest, Central, Midwest, Florida, Southeast and Mid-Atlantic. Its product offerings include entry-level homes, including both detached and attached homes, and move-up homes, which are sold under its LGI Homes brand, and its luxury series homes, which are sold under its Terrata Homes brand. Its homes have an average price of about $292,105and ranged from 1,000 to 4,100 sq. ft. The builder's higher-quality Terrata Homes started at average sales price of $549,550 home. LGI Homes has constructed and closed over 50,000 homes since its founding in 2003.

	Annual Growth	12/19	12/20	12/21	12/22	12/23
Sales ($mil.)	6.4%	1,838.2	2,367.9	3,050.1	2,304.5	2,358.6
Net income ($ mil.)	2.8%	178.6	323.9	429.6	326.6	199.2
Market value ($ mil.)	17.2%	1,666.0	2,496.1	3,642.9	2,183.7	3,140.1
Employees	3.4%	953	938	952	952	1,089

LGL GROUP INC (THE)

ASE: LGL

2525 Shader Road
Orlando, FL 32804
Phone: 407 298-2000
Fax: –
Web: www.lglgroup.com

CEO: Michael J Ferrantino
CFO: James W Tivy
HR: –
FYE: December 31
Type: Public

The LGL Group is hoping that one isn't the loneliest number. Previously made up of two separate businesses, the company has a sole remaining line of business: its MtronPTI subsidiary. The subsidiary produces frequency control devices, such as crystals and oscillators, used primarily in communications equipment. MtronPTI was formed in the 2004 merger of M-tron Industries and Piezo Technology, Inc. In 2007 The LGL Group sold certain assets of its unprofitable Lynch Systems subsidiary for about $3 million. The company's sales are roughly split between the US and other countries.

	Annual Growth	12/18	12/19	12/20	12/21	12/22
Sales ($mil.)	(49.2%)	24.9	31.9	31.2	28.1	1.7
Net income ($ mil.)	–	1.4	7.0	1.0	14.6	(3.0)
Market value ($ mil.)	(9.7%)	32.7	80.3	67.1	61.0	21.7
Employees	(64.3%)	308	353	320	306	5

LHH CORPORATION

100 E 77TH ST
NEW YORK, NY 100751850
Phone: 212 434-2000
Fax: –
Web: lenoxhill.northwell.edu

CEO: –
CFO: –
HR: –
FYE: December 31
Type: Private

When Manhattanites are looking for health care, many of them head for the hill: Lenox Hill Hospital, to be exact. The 650-bed facility provides care to patients on Manhattan's Upper East Side -- about 45% of its patient base is from Manhattan, the rest from surrounding boroughs. Services include cardiac care, high-risk obstetrics, pediatrics, and orthopedics and sports medicine. Lenox Hill serves as a teaching affiliate for NYU Medical Center and also owns Manhattan Eye, Ear and Throat Hospital, a provider of specialty care for vision, hearing, and speech disorders. Today it's part of North Shore-Long Island Jewish Health System.

	Annual Growth	12/15	12/16	12/18	12/21	12/22
Sales ($mil.)	10.9%	–	960.6	1,064.5	1,305.1	1,790.2
Net income ($ mil.)	10.5%	–	21.8	73.9	31.2	39.7
Market value ($ mil.)	–	–	–	–	–	–
Employees	–	–	–	–	–	2,955

LIBERTY ENERGY INC

NYS: LBRT

950 17th Street, Suite 2400
Denver, CO 80202
Phone: 303 515-2800
Fax: –
Web: www.libertyfrac.com

CEO: Christopher A Wright
CFO: Michael Stock
HR: –
FYE: December 31
Type: Public

Liberty Energy, formerly known as Liberty Oilfield Services Inc., is a leading integrated oilfield services and technology company focused on providing innovative hydraulic services and related technologies to onshore oil and natural gas exploration and production (E&P) companies in North America. It offers customers hydraulic fracturing services, together with complementary services including wireline services, proppant delivery solutions, data analytics, related goods (including its sand mine operations), and technologies that will facilitate lower emission completions, thereby helping its customers reduce their emissions profile. It also has wireline operations after obtaining certain assets and liabilities of the OneStim business including OneStim's hydraulic fracturing pressure pumping services business in onshore US and Canada.

	Annual Growth	12/19	12/20	12/21	12/22	12/23
Sales ($mil.)	24.3%	1,990.3	965.8	2,470.8	4,149.2	4,747.9
Net income ($ mil.)	94.3%	39.0	(115.6)	(179.2)	399.6	556.3
Market value ($ mil.)	13.0%	1,852.7	1,717.8	1,616.1	2,667.4	3,022.3
Employees	20.9%	2,571	1,946	3,601	4,580	5,500

LIBERTY HOMES INC

1101 EISENHOWER DR N
GOSHEN, IN 465265309
Phone: 574 533-0438
Fax: –
Web: www.libertyhomesntx.com

CEO: –
CFO: Marc A Dosmann
HR: –
FYE: December 31
Type: Private

Liberty Homes gives home buyers the freedom to move about the land. The company builds modular homes for the US and Canada from seven manufacturing facilities. The company's floor plans range from two to five bedrooms and cost from $35,000 to about $125,000. Options include kitchen islands, utility rooms, and front porches. The company builds homes under the Liberty Homes, Waverlee Homes, and Badger Built Homes brand names. Independent dealers and company-owned retail centers sell the company's products. CEO Edward Hussey and his family control Liberty Homes.

	Annual Growth	12/04	12/05	12/06	12/07	12/08
Sales ($mil.)	(4.6%)	–	–	89.7	80.9	81.7
Net income ($ mil.)	–	–	–	(1.3)	(3.5)	(6.3)
Market value ($ mil.)	–	–	–	–	–	–
Employees	–	–	–	–	–	100

LIBERTY MEDIA CORP (DE)

NMS: FWON K

12300 Liberty Boulevard
Englewood, CO 80112
Phone: 720 875-5400
Fax: –
Web: www.libertymedia.com

CEO: Gregory B Maffei
CFO: Brian Wendling
HR: Ashley Guy
FYE: December 31
Type: Public

A media and entertainment holding company, Liberty Media Corporation operates three primary businesses. It generates the most revenue from its majority stake in satellite radio service SiriusXM Group, which serves some 35 million subscribers. The company also owns global motorsport business Formula 1, which includes motor racing events took place in more than 10 countries as part of the FIA Formula One World Championship, and the Atlanta Braves professional baseball team. In addition, it owns a minority stake in Live Nation Entertainment, a major promoter of music events and music festivals. Liberty Media generates about 80% of revenue in the US.

	Annual Growth	12/18	12/19	12/20	12/21	12/22
Sales ($mil.)	10.9%	8,040.0	10,292	9,363.0	11,400	12,164
Net income ($ mil.)	36.0%	531.0	106.0	(1,421.0)	398.0	1,815.0
Market value ($ mil.)	1.4%	22,684	29,530	26,690	31,193	24,003
Employees	11.6%	4,641	6,753	7,047	6,886	7,200

LIBERTY MEDIA CORP (DE) - COMMON SERIES B BRAVES GROUP

NGS: BATR B

12300 Liberty Boulevard
Englewood, CO 80112
Phone: 720 875-5400
Fax: –
Web: www.libertymedia.com

CEO: Gregory B Maffei
CFO: Brian Wendling
HR: Ashley Guy
FYE: December 31
Type: Public

A media and entertainment holding company, Liberty Media Corporation operates three primary businesses. It generates the most revenue from its majority stake in satellite radio service SiriusXM Group, which serves some 35 million subscribers. The company also owns global motorsport business Formula 1, which includes motor racing events took place in more than 10 countries as part of the FIA Formula One World Championship, and the Atlanta Braves professional baseball team. In addition, it owns a minority stake in Live Nation Entertainment, a major promoter of music events and music festivals. Liberty Media generates about 80% of revenue in the US.

	Annual Growth	12/12	12/13	12/14	12/15	12/16
Sales ($mil.)	2.4%	–	–	250.0	243.0	262.0
Net income ($ mil.)	–	–	–	(24.0)	(20.0)	(62.0)
Market value ($ mil.)	–	–	–	–	–	17.8
Employees	–	–	–	–	–	3,626

LIBERTY MEDIA CORP (DE) - FORMULA ONE GROUP

NMS: FWON A

12300 Liberty Boulevard
Engelwood, CO 80112
Phone: 720 875-5400
Fax: –
Web: www.libertymedia.com

CEO: Gregory B Maffei
CFO: Brian Wendling
HR: Ashley Guy
FYE: December 31
Type: Public

A media and entertainment holding company, Liberty Media Corporation operates three primary businesses. It generates the most revenue from its majority stake in satellite radio service SiriusXM Group, which serves some 35 million subscribers. The company also owns global motorsport business Formula 1, which includes motor racing events took place in more than 10 countries as part of the FIA Formula One World Championship, and the Atlanta Braves professional baseball team. In addition, it owns a minority stake in Live Nation Entertainment, a major promoter of music events and music festivals. Liberty Media generates about 80% of revenue in the US.

	Annual Growth	12/19	12/20	12/21	12/22	12/23
Sales ($mil.)	12.4%	2,022.0	1,145.0	2,136.0	2,573.0	3,222.0
Net income ($ mil.)	–	(311.0)	(596.0)	(190.0)	558.0	185.0
Market value ($ mil.)	–	10,271	8,913.0	13,922	12,536	–
Employees	(1.4%)	6,777	7,047	–	7,200	6,400

LIBERTY MUTUAL HOLDING CO., INC.

175 Berkeley Street
Boston, MA 02116
Phone: –
Fax: –
Web: www.libertymutualgroup.com

CEO: David H Long
CFO: Christopher L Peirce
HR: –
FYE: December 31
Type: Public

Liberty Mutual is one of the top property/casualty insurers in the US and among the top 10 providers of automobile insurance. The company also offers a wide range of insurance products and services, including homeowners' insurance, workers' compensation, general liability, surety, commercial multi-peril, and other lines for individuals, families, and small to large companies. Liberty Mutual operates through two business divisions: Global Retail Markets and Global Risk Solutions. It distributes its products through a blend of telesales counselors, independent agents, and brokers globally.

	Annual Growth	12/08	12/09	12/10	12/11	12/12
Sales ($mil.)	6.0%	–	31,035	33,193	34,671	36,944
Net income ($ mil.)	(6.8%)	–	1,023.0	1,678.0	365.0	829.0
Market value ($ mil.)	–	–	–	–	–	–
Employees	–	–	–	–	–	–

LIBERTY ORCHARDS COMPANY, INC.

117 MISSION AVE
CASHMERE, WA 988151007
Phone: 509 782-1000
Fax: –
Web: www.libertyorchards.com

CEO: –
CFO: –
HR: –
FYE: December 31
Type: Private

Liberty Orchards exercises its freedom to manufacture candies and baked goods. The company's signature products are aplets and cotlets -- jellied fruit candies made from apples and apricots. It also makes and sells chocolates and fruity breads and cookies. Liberty Orchards products are sold online and by major chain retail stores. The candy maker was founded in 1919 as a fruit dehydration and canning enterprise by Armenian immigrants, Mark Balaban and Armen Tertsagian.

	Annual Growth	12/02	12/03	12/05	12/06	12/07
Sales ($mil.)	1.2%	–	13.5	15.4	14.4	14.2
Net income ($ mil.)	–	–	(0.7)	0.1	0.2	0.2
Market value ($ mil.)	–	–	–	–	–	–
Employees	–	–	–	–	–	80

LIBERTY REGIONAL MEDICAL CENTER INC.

462 ELMA G MILES PKWY
HINESVILLE, GA 313134000
Phone: 912 369-9400
Fax: –
Web: www.libertyregional.org

CEO: Hugh S Kroell Jr
CFO: Martha Traylor
HR: –
FYE: November 30
Type: Private

Liberty Regional Medical Center takes patient liberties to heart. The medical center consists of a 50-bed acute care hospital and a long-term skilled nursing facility with about 110 beds. Hospital services include emergency medicine, physical therapy, radiology, pediatrics, cardiology, laboratory, surgery, rehabilitation, and women's health. Liberty Regional Medical Center's long-term care facility, Coastal Manor, offers rehabilitation therapies and Alzheimer's and dementia care. The medical center was established in 1961 as Liberty Memorial Hospital and is governed by the Hospital Authority of Liberty County.

	Annual Growth	11/15	11/16	11/19	11/20	11/21
Sales ($mil.)	91.4%	–	1.7	2.0	44.5	44.6
Net income ($ mil.)	–	–	(0.4)	(0.1)	4.8	8.8
Market value ($ mil.)	–	–	–	–	–	–
Employees	–	–	–	–	–	485

LIBRARY OF CONGRESS

101 INDEPENDENCE AVE SE
WASHINGTON, DC 205400002
Phone: 202 707-5000
Fax: –
Web: www.loc.gov

CEO: –
CFO: –
HR: –
FYE: December 31
Type: Private

"A room without books is like a body without a soul." If Cicero was correct, then this book repository's got it all. The Library of Congress is the oldest cultural institution in the US. The institution boasts more than 150 million items, 35 million books, and 650 miles of bookshelves, and it makes all the difference. Established in 1800, it's a multi-tasking marvel -- serving as a legislative library for Congress, the US Copyright Office, a center for scholarship that preserves materials in more than 460 languages, and a bookworm's paradise with more than 20 reading rooms. and the world's largest repository of print material, maps, recorded music, motion pictures, and TV programs.

	Annual Growth	12/03	12/04	12/05*	09/07*	12/09
Sales ($mil.)	10.8%	–	–	5.9	5.9	8.8
Net income ($ mil.)	(7.4%)	–	–	1.6	1.6	1.2
Market value ($ mil.)	–	–	–	–	–	–
Employees	–	–	–	–	–	4,213

*Fiscal year change

LICKING MEMORIAL HEALTH SYSTEMS

1320 W MAIN ST
NEWARK, OH 430551822
Phone: 220 564-4000
Fax: –
Web: www.lmhealth.org

CEO: Robert Montagnese
CFO: Rob Montagnese
HR: –
FYE: December 31
Type: Private

Here to help Buckeye Staters lick disease is Licking Memorial Health Systems. The the not-for-profit health care provider operates the 230-bed Licking Memorial Hospital. Specialty services at the hospital include cancer care, home health, occupational health, cardiology, rehabilitation, and obstetrics. Licking Memorial Hospital administers behavioral health care (including substance abuse treatments) through its Shepherd Hill department. The health system also includes area outpatient medical practices, largely through the multi-specialty physician group Licking Memorial Health Professionals which has 100-plus physicians in various practices.

	Annual Growth	12/08	12/09	12/10	12/11	12/13
Sales ($mil.)	1.8%	–	–	199.0	184.2	209.7
Net income ($ mil.)	108.7%	–	–	4.4	(7.7)	39.7
Market value ($ mil.)	–	–	–	–	–	–
Employees	–	–	–	–	–	1,900

LICT CORP

401 Theodore Fremd Avenue
Rye, NY 10580-1430
Phone: 914 921-8821
Fax: 914 921-6410
Web: www.lictcorp.com

NBB: LICT
CEO: Robert E Dolan
CFO: Daniel E Hopkins
HR: –
FYE: December 31
Type: Public

LICT (formerly Lynch Interactive) is a holding company that operates through 12 small (mostly rural) local-exchange phone companies located primarily in the Midwestern and Western US; it also has a limited presence in the Northeast. The company provides local telephone service over nearly 60,000 access lines while dial-up and broadband Internet service lines number about 50,000. Subsidiaries include JBN Telephone, Haviland Telephone, and Giant Communications in Kansas; CentraCom Interactive in Utah; and Bretton Woods Telephone in New Hampshire. Chairman Mario Gabelli owns 24% of LICT.

	Annual Growth	12/17	12/18	12/19	12/20	12/21
Sales ($mil.)	4.9%	106.7	115.8	118.0	124.2	129.2
Net income ($ mil.)	2.6%	22.4	25.8	26.2	37.3	24.8
Market value ($ mil.)	22.2%	208.2	258.2	321.7	318.1	464.6
Employees	14.1%	206	315	338	343	349

LIDESTRI FOODS, INC.

815 WHITNEY RD W
FAIRPORT, NY 144501030
Phone: 585 377-7700
Fax: –
Web: www.lidestrifoodanddrink.com

CEO: –
CFO: –
HR: –
FYE: June 30
Type: Private

LiDestri Food and Drink (formerly LiDestri Foods) is one of the premier sauce makers in the country, making more than 80 million cases of product annually at four locations coast to coast for some of the country's largest and most respected retail brand and national brand partners, including Wegmans Food Markets and Newman's Own. Its core competencies include a variety of hot and cold filled, aseptic and retorted products available in glass and plastic containers for retail and food service customers. In addition, the company also produces an extensive array of premium spirits, liqueurs and other products in the category that can be marketed under private labels. LiDestri's rich heritage dates back to its founding in 1975.

	Annual Growth	06/03	06/04	06/05	06/06	06/07
Sales ($mil.)	13.5%	–	209.5	–	–	306.2
Net income ($ mil.)	–	–	–	–	–	3.6
Market value ($ mil.)	–	–	–	–	–	–
Employees	–	–	–	–	–	1,387

LIFE CARE CENTERS OF AMERICA, INC.

3570 KEITH ST NW
CLEVELAND, TN 373124309
Phone: 423 472-9585
Fax: –
Web: www.lcca.com

CEO: –
CFO: –
HR: –
FYE: December 31
Type: Private

Life Care Centers of America is a privately-owned operator of more than 200 retirement and health care centers in over 25 states across the US. Life Care Centers of America offers inpatient and outpatient rehabilitation, post-acute short-term rehabilitation, and post-operative recovery. In addition, Life Care Centers of America offers short- and long-term, on-site rehabilitation in all of its nursing homes. Specialized programs and features vary in its facilities, but many offer fine dining, concierge and valet services, on-site physicians and state-of-the-art technologies such as the AlterG Anti-Gravity Treadmill. The Life Care Centers of America story began in 1970 when Garden Terrace Convalescent Center, now Life Care Center of Cleveland, was built in Cleveland, Tennessee.

	Annual Growth	09/05	09/06	09/08	09/15*	12/21
Sales ($mil.)	8.5%	–	40.8	82.9	10.4	139.2
Net income ($ mil.)	–	–	6.2	3.2	(0.1)	(10.7)
Market value ($ mil.)	–	–	–	–	–	–
Employees	–	–	–	–	–	40,000

*Fiscal year change

LIFEBRIDGE HEALTH, INC.

2401 W BELVEDERE AVE
BALTIMORE, MD 212155216
Phone: 410 601-5653
Fax: –
Web: www.lifebridgehealth.org

CEO: Neil M Meltzer
CFO: David Krajewski
HR: D ' Pratt
FYE: June 30
Type: Private

LifeBridge Health links patients to healthcare. Serving the Baltimore region, the not-for-profit company operates two general hospitals -- Sinai Hospital of Baltimore and Northwest Hospital -- with specialties including oncology, neurology, pediatrics, and sports medicine. The LifeBridge Health network also provides long-term care at the Levindale Hebrew Geriatric Center and Hospital (nursing, subacute, and adult day care services) and the Courtland Gardens Nursing & Rehabilitation Center. Altogether, the health system boasts some 1,190 beds. LifeBridge's Health Wellness division includes a health and fitness program and community fitness center.

	Annual Growth	06/18	06/19	06/20	06/21	06/22
Sales ($mil.)	(43.8%)	–	1,610.4	1,662.2	264.7	286.2
Net income ($ mil.)	–	–	65.5	54.5	9.7	(10.3)
Market value ($ mil.)	–	–	–	–	–	–
Employees	–	–	–	–	–	6,000

LIFECELL CORPORATION

1 MILLENNIUM WAY
BRANCHBURG, NJ 088763876
Phone: 908 947-1100
Fax: –
Web: www.abbvie.com

CEO: Lisa Colleran
CFO: –
HR: –
FYE: December 31
Type: Private

LifeCell puts new life into the tissue graft market. The company makes soft tissue material for surgeries ranging from complex hernia repair to breast reconstruction. Products include Strattice Reconstructive Tissue Matrix, AlloDerm Regenerative Tissue Matrix, and an injectable form of Alloderm called Cymetra MAT. Its SPY Elite intraoperative system assists surgeons in visualizing tissue perfusion (flow of blood into tissue) in plastic, reconstructive, micro, gastrointestinal, and cardiovascular surgery procedures. Holding company Acelity sold LifeCell to Allergan for $2.9 billion in early 2017.

LIFECORE BIOMEDICAL INC

NMS: LFCR

3515 Lyman Boulevard
Chaska, MN 55318
Phone: 952 368-4300
Fax: 650 368-9818
Web: www.landec.com

CEO: James G Hall
CFO: John D Morberg
HR: –
FYE: May 28
Type: Public

Landec designs, develops, manufactures, and sells differentiated products for food and biomaterials markets and license technology applications to partners. Its natural food company, Curation Foods, focuses on innovating and distributing plant-based foods with 100% clean ingredients to retail, club, and foodservice channels throughout North America. Its biomedical company, Lifecore Biomedical, offers highly differentiated capabilities in the development, fill and finish of sterile, injectable pharmaceutical products in syringes and vials including injectable grade Hyaluronic Acid. In mid-2022, Landec formally announced that it will become a CDMO-focused life sciences company with a planned corporate rebranding including renaming the company to Lifecore Biomedical and exploring potential sales opportunities of the company's remaining Curation Foods assets.

	Annual Growth	05/19	05/20	05/21	05/22	05/23
Sales ($mil.)	(34.4%)	557.6	590.4	544.2	185.8	103.3
Net income ($ mil.)	–	0.4	(38.2)	(32.7)	(97.4)	(99.6)
Market value ($ mil.)	(4.2%)	285.6	323.5	363.0	299.3	240.8
Employees	(11.1%)	736	796	905	689	459

LIFEQUEST WORLD CORP

NBB: LQWC

100 Challenger Road, 8th Floor
Ridgefield Park, NJ 07660
Phone: 646 201-5242
Fax: –
Web: www.lifequestcorp.com

CEO: Anthony C Jurak
CFO: –
HR: –
FYE: May 31
Type: Public

Tired? Run-down? Listless? Do you poop out at parties? Time to call Tonicman! LifeQuest World uses its Tonicman radio shows to help get the word out about its Jurak Classic Whole Body Tonic, but its main distribution is through multilevel marketing. The company's primary product is a liquid herbal formula created in 1943 by Carl Jurak, father of CEO Anthony Jurak (who owns 41% of the company). LifeQuest has acquired ImmunXT for about $2 million and since has invested heavily in marketing the immune stimulating dietary supplement (even hiring actor and body builder Peter Lupus as its spokesman). The company expects ImmunXT -- which is an algae-based botanical complex -- to become its flagship product.

	Annual Growth	05/19	05/20	05/21	05/22	05/23
Sales ($mil.)	159.5%	0.0	0.4	0.5	0.3	0.1
Net income ($ mil.)	–	(8.3)	(0.1)	(0.5)	(0.2)	(0.4)
Market value ($ mil.)	(54.8%)	69.7	38.3	20.2	3.9	2.9
Employees	–	–	–	–	–	–

LIFESPAN CORPORATION

10 DAVOL SQ STE 300
PROVIDENCE, RI 029034754
Phone: 401 421-4000
Fax: –
Web: www.lifespan.org

CEO: –
CFO: –
HR: –
FYE: September 30
Type: Private

Formed in 1994, Lifespan is a not-for-profit health system based in Providence, RI comprising three teaching hospitals of The Warren Alpert Medical School of Brown University: Rhode Island Hospital and its Hasbro Children's Hospital; The Miriam Hospital; and Bradley Hospital, the nation's first psychiatric hospital for children; Newport Hospital, a community hospital offering a broad range of health services; Gateway Healthcare, the state's largest provider of community behavioral health care; Lifespan Physician Group, the largest multi-specialty practice in Rhode Island; and Coastal Medical, a primary care driven medical practice.

	Annual Growth	09/14	09/15	09/19	09/21	09/22
Sales ($mil.)	6.2%	–	187.2	240.4	281.1	285.1
Net income ($ mil.)	–	–	1.4	1.9	7.9	(2.2)
Market value ($ mil.)	–	–	–	–	–	–
Employees	–	–	–	–	–	8,000

LIFESTORE FINANCIAL GROUP
NBB: LSFG

1441 Mt Jefferson Road
West Jefferson, NC 28694
Phone: 336 246-4344
Fax: –
Web: www.afgrp.com

CEO: Robert E Washburn
CFO: Melanie Miller
HR: –
FYE: June 30
Type: Public

LifeStore helps you prepeare for whatever life has in store. Formerly AF Financial Group, LifeStore Financial Group provides good ol' traditional banking and insurance services through subsidiaries LifeStore Bank and LifeStore Insurance Services. The bank operates seven offices in northwestern North Carolina's Alleghany, Ashe, and Watauga counties. It provides standard deposit products such as checking and savings accounts and CDs. Residential mortgages make up about half of its loan portfolio. The bank also offers investment products and services through a pact with a third-party provider. LifeStore Insurance Services sells bonds and auto, homeowners, health, and life insurance.

	Annual Growth	06/03	06/04	06/05	06/06	06/07
Assets ($mil.)	6.9%	–	–	–	229.4	245.3
Net income ($ mil.)	44.1%	–	–	–	1.0	1.5
Market value ($ mil.)	(10.3%)	–	–	–	20.0	17.9
Employees	–	–	–	–	–	111

LIFETIME BRANDS INC
NMS: LCUT

1000 Stewart Avenue
Garden City, NY 11530
Phone: 516 683-6000
Fax: –
Web: www.lifetimebrands.com

CEO: Robert B Kay
CFO: Laurence Winoker
HR: –
FYE: December 31
Type: Public

Lifetime Brands designs and distributes kitchenware, tableware, and functional home products, including cutlery, scales, thermometers, baking trays, food storage, and other products for the home. Its top brands (both owned and licensed), include Farberware, KitchenAid, Taylor, Mikasa, Pfaltzgraff, Rabbit, Kamenstein, and Built NY. The company sells its varied lines in the US, Canada, Mexico, Latin America, Europe, and Asia through high-end retailers, supermarkets, department stores, and discount chains (including Bed Bath & Beyond, Wal-Mart, and Target), as well as online. About 90% of the company's total sales are generated in the US.

	Annual Growth	12/19	12/20	12/21	12/22	12/23
Sales ($mil.)	(1.7%)	734.9	769.2	862.9	727.7	686.7
Net income ($ mil.)	–	(44.4)	(3.0)	20.8	(6.2)	(8.4)
Market value ($ mil.)	(0.9%)	151.6	331.6	348.4	165.6	146.4
Employees	(3.2%)	1,400	1,350	1,350	1,260	1,230

LIFEWAY CHRISTIAN RESOURCES OF THE SOUTHERN BAPTIST CONVENTION

200 POWELL PL STE 100
BRENTWOOD, TN 370277707
Phone: 615 251-2000
Fax: –
Web: www.lifeway.com

CEO: Ben Mandrell
CFO: Joe Walker
HR: –
FYE: September 30
Type: Private

LifeWay Christian Resources of the Southern Baptist Convention helps to spread the teachings of Jesus. The company is a not-for-profit Christian publisher. It also sells Bibles, audio, video, gifts, and other supplies. The retailer sells products online and through authorized dealers. LifeWay was founded in 1891 by Dr. J.M. Frost.

	Annual Growth	09/18	09/19	09/20	09/21	09/22
Sales ($mil.)	(2.7%)	–	266.5	206.6	214.8	245.7
Net income ($ mil.)	–	–	(82.7)	(109.0)	87.3	36.0
Market value ($ mil.)	–	–	–	–	–	–
Employees	–	–	–	–	–	5,000

LIFEWAY FOODS, INC.
NMS: LWAY

6431 West Oakton
Morton Grove, IL 60053
Phone: 847 967-1010
Fax: –
Web: www.lifewayfoods.com

CEO: Julie Smolyansky
CFO: Eric Hanson
HR: –
FYE: December 31
Type: Public

Lifeway Foods is a leading producer of kefir and a recognized leader in the market for probiotic products. Its primary product is drinkable kefir, a cultured dairy product. Lifeway Kefir is tart and tangy, high in protein, calcium and vitamin D. It manufactures (directly or through co-packers) and markets products under the Lifeway, Fresh Made, and Glen Oaks Farms brand names, as well as under private labels on behalf of certain customers. The company's other products are European-style soft cheeses, cream, ProBugs (kefir products designed for children), yogurt, and other dairy. Two customers collectively accounted for approximately 20% of its total sales.

	Annual Growth	12/19	12/20	12/21	12/22	12/23
Sales ($mil.)	14.3%	93.7	102.0	119.1	141.6	160.1
Net income ($ mil.)	123.8%	0.5	3.2	3.3	0.9	11.4
Market value ($ mil.)	61.1%	29.2	79.5	67.6	81.5	197.0
Employees	(1.5%)	307	316	282	291	289

LIGAND PHARMACEUTICALS INC
NMS: LGND

3911 Sorrento Valley Boulevard, Suite 110
San Diego, CA 92121
Phone: 858 550-7500
Fax: –
Web: www.ligand.com

CEO: John L Higgins
CFO: Matthew Korenberg
HR: –
FYE: December 31
Type: Public

Ligand Pharmaceuticals is a biopharmaceutical company focused on developing or acquiring technologies that help pharmaceutical companies discover and develop medicines. The company employs research technologies such as antibody discovery technologies, ion channel discovery technology, Pseudomonas fluorescens protein expression technology, formulation science and liver targeted pro-drug technologies to assist companies in their work toward securing prescription drug and biologic approvals. Its partners and licensees fund the development and commercialization of its portfolio and it is entitled to receive royalties and milestones on program success. Currently approved portfolio drugs include those that treat cancer, osteoporosis, fungal infections and low blood platelets, among others. Its partners and licensees have programs currently in clinical development targeting seizure, coma, cancer, diabetes, cardiovascular disease, muscle wasting, liver disease, and kidney disease, among others. The company has over 1,600 issued patents worldwide.

	Annual Growth	12/19	12/20	12/21	12/22	12/23
Sales ($mil.)	2.2%	120.3	186.4	277.1	196.2	131.3
Net income ($ mil.)	(46.3%)	629.3	(3.0)	57.1	(33.4)	52.2
Market value ($ mil.)	–	–	–	–	–	–
Employees	(15.7%)	115	155	154	76	58

LIGHT & WONDER INC
NMS: LNW

6601 Bermuda Road
Las Vegas, NV 89119
Phone: 702 897-7150
Fax: –
Web: www.scientificgames.com

CEO: Matt Wilson
CFO: Constance P James
HR: Chastity Cook
FYE: December 31
Type: Public

Light & Wonder, Inc. (L&W) is a leading cross-platform global games company with a focus on content and digital markets. Its portfolio of revenue-generating activities in its continuing operations primarily includes supplying game content and gaming machines, CMSs and table game products and services to licensed gaming entities; providing social casino and other mobile games, including casual gaming, to retail customers; and providing a comprehensive suite of digital gaming content, distribution platforms, player account management systems, as well as various other iGaming content and services. Social games are played on mobile apps and web platforms such as Amazon, Apple, Facebook, Google, and Microsoft. The company generates around 70% of its revenue in the US.

	Annual Growth	12/19	12/20	12/21	12/22	12/23
Sales ($mil.)	(3.9%)	3,400.0	2,724.0	2,153.0	2,512.0	2,902.0
Net income ($ mil.)	–	(130.0)	(569.0)	371.0	3,675.0	163.0
Market value ($ mil.)	32.3%	2,410.2	3,734.1	6,014.7	5,274.0	7,389.9
Employees	(9.8%)	9,800	9,000	5,600	6,100	6,500

LIGHTBRIDGE CORP
NAS: LTBR

11710 Plaza America Drive, Suite 2000
Reston, VA 20190
Phone: 571 730-1200
Fax: –
Web: www.ltbridge.com

CEO: Seth Grae
CFO: Larry Goldman
HR: –
FYE: December 31
Type: Public

Lightbridge is ready to illuminate the wonders of using thorium as a possible nuclear fuel. The development-stage company has been working on a new kind of nuclear fuel that uses thorium, a less radioactive element than uranium, to power nuclear reactors. Thorium's lessened radioactivity also means it doesn't produce enough plutonium to make nuclear weapons, unlike uranium. The company's ideas for thorium were developed by the late nuclear engineer Dr. Alvin Radkowsky, who co-founded Lightbridge's predecessor, Thorium Power, in 1992. While Lightbridge's plans for thorium power plants are not ready for commercialization, the company has earned some revenue as a nuclear energy consultant.

	Annual Growth	12/19	12/20	12/21	12/22	12/23
Sales ($mil.)	–	–	–	–	–	–
Net income ($ mil.)	–	(10.6)	(14.4)	(7.8)	(7.5)	(7.9)
Market value ($ mil.)	(8.1%)	61.6	57.9	90.8	53.3	44.0
Employees	(17.6%)	13	7	6	5	6

LIGHTHOUSE COMPUTER SERVICES, INC.

6 BLACKSTONE VALLEY PL STE 205
LINCOLN, RI 028651112
Phone: 401 334-0799
Fax: –
Web: www.convergetp.com

CEO: –
CFO: –
HR: –
FYE: December 31
Type: Private

Lighthouse Computer Services shines a light on companies' IT needs. The firm provides IT services to businesses, primarily FORTUNE 1000 and midsized companies in the New England region. Lighthouse's services include customization, implementation, data migration, network design, and systems administration. It also refurbishes and sells computer equipment from IBM and other vendors. The company's consultants employ products from a variety of software and hardware partners, including Cisco Systems, Microsoft, NetApp, STORServer, Symantec, and VMware. CEO Tom Mrva controls Lighthouse Computer Services, which he founded in 1995.

	Annual Growth	12/02	12/03	12/04	12/06	12/07
Sales ($mil.)	17.8%	–	62.1	51.8	97.5	119.7
Net income ($ mil.)	42.5%	–	0.7	0.0	2.6	2.7
Market value ($ mil.)	–	–	–	–	–	–
Employees	–	–	–	–	–	105

LIGHTING SCIENCE GROUP CORP
NBB: LSCG

1350 Division Road, Suite 204
West Warwick, RI 02893
Phone: 321 779-5520
Fax: –
Web: www.lsgc.com

CEO: Khim Lee
CFO: David Quigley
HR: –
FYE: December 31
Type: Public

Going green turns on Lighting Science (LSG). The company designs, manufactures, and markets eco-friendly, light-emitting diode (LED) technologies that conserve energy and eliminate the use of hazardous materials. LSG creates biological, horticultural and urban lighting solutions, with popular products such as the GoodNight, GoodDay, and Sleepy Baby LED bulbs for health and wellness, including sleep and productivity, and the groundbreaking horticulture light, the GroBar. The company, with over 400 patents, operates Healthe, VividGro, and Global Value Lighting and is a portfolio company of Pegasus Capital Advisors, a private equity firm. LSG's headquarters is located in West Warwick, Rhode Island, with R&D, Operations, Marketing and Finance located in Cocoa Beach, Florida

	Annual Growth	12/12	12/13	12/14	12/15	12/16
Sales ($mil.)	(19.8%)	127.1	83.2	91.3	79.6	52.7
Net income ($ mil.)	–	(111.3)	(89.8)	(65.6)	(27.1)	(20.2)
Market value ($ mil.)	(48.3%)	122.0	67.5	20.0	17.4	8.7
Employees	(34.8%)	377	177	94	78	68

LIGHTPATH TECHNOLOGIES, INC.
NAS: LPTH

2603 Challenger Tech Court, Suite 100
Orlando, FL 32826
Phone: 407 382-4003
Fax: 407 382-4007
Web: www.lightpath.com

CEO: Shmuel Rubin
CFO: Albert Miranda
HR: –
FYE: June 30
Type: Public

LightPath Technologies is lighting the optical networking way. The company, which has traditionally used its patented GRADIUM glass to make distortion-reducing lenses for inspection equipment, is developing new applications for its technologies in the optoelectronics and fiber-optic communications fields. Its optoelectronics products include collimators (optical network components) and optical isolators (filters that prevent light waves from reflecting backwards). LightPath serves such customers as CyOptics, Intel, Santur, ThorLabs, and T-Networks. The company targets aerospace, telecommunications, health care, instrumentation, and the military. LightPath gets about two-thirds of its sales in the US.

	Annual Growth	06/19	06/20	06/21	06/22	06/23
Sales ($mil.)	(0.6%)	33.7	35.0	38.5	35.6	32.9
Net income ($ mil.)	–	(2.7)	0.9	(3.2)	(3.5)	(4.0)
Market value ($ mil.)	10.4%	34.0	124.7	94.9	45.9	50.4
Employees	(1.7%)	350	372	361	334	327

LILLY (ELI) & CO
NYS: LLY

Lilly Corporate Center
Indianapolis, IN 46285
Phone: 317 276-2000
Fax: –
Web: www.lilly.com

CEO: David A Ricks
CFO: Anat Ashkenazi
HR: –
FYE: December 31
Type: Public

Eli Lilly is a leading pharmaceutical company that develops diabetes, oncology, immunology, and neuroscience medicines. Its top-selling drugs include Trulicity (treatment of type 2 diabetes in adults and pediatric patients 10 years of age and older, and reducing the risk of adverse cardiovascular events in adult patients with type 2 diabetes and cardiovascular risk factors); Verzenio (treatment of breast cancer and early breast cancer); and Taltz (for the treatment of adults and pediatric patients aged 6 years or older with moderate-to-severe plaque psoriasis, adults with active psoriatic arthritis, adults with ankylosing spondylitis, and adults with active non-radiographic axial spondyloarthritis). The company generates most of its revenue in the US.

	Annual Growth	12/19	12/20	12/21	12/22	12/23
Sales ($mil.)	11.2%	22,320	24,540	28,318	28,541	34,124
Net income ($ mil.)	(10.9%)	8,318.4	6,193.7	5,581.7	6,244.8	5,240.4
Market value ($ mil.)	45.1%	124,777	160,293	262,237	347,321	553,412
Employees	6.3%	33,625	35,000	35,000	39,000	43,000

LIMETREE BAY TERMINALS LLC

1 ESTATE HOPE
CHRISTIANSTED, VI 00820
Phone: 340 692-3000
Fax: –
Web: –

CEO: –
CFO: –
HR: –
FYE: December 31
Type: Private

HOVENSA brings together US and Latin American know-how and operations to handle oil products in the US Virgin Islands. HOVENSA is a joint venture of Hess and Venezuelan oil giant PDVSA (its major crude oil supplier). Once the largest private employer in the US Virgin Islands, the company operated a 500,000-barrels-per-day crude oil refinery on St. Croix, along with two specialized oil processing complexes, a 150,000-barrels-per-day fluid catalytic cracking unit, and a 58,000-barrels-per-day delayed coker unit. However, the St. Croix refinery had run up losses for years; it was shut down in 2012 and was put up for sale in 2013.

	Annual Growth	12/05	12/06	12/07	12/08	12/09
Sales ($mil.)	(42.5%)	–	–	–	17,480	10,048
Net income ($ mil.)	–	–	–	–	95.0	(451.2)
Market value ($ mil.)	–	–	–	–	–	–
Employees	–	–	–	–	–	1,300

LIMONEIRA CO
NMS: LMNR

1141 Cummings Road
Santa Paula, CA 93060
Phone: 805 525-5541
Fax: 805 525-8211
Web: www.limoneira.com

CEO: Harold S Edwards
CFO: Mark Palamountain
HR: –
FYE: October 31
Type: Public

Limoneira is an agribusiness company founded and based in Santa Paula, California, committed to responsibly using and managing its approximately 15,400 acres of land, water resources and other assets to maximize long-term stockholder value. Their current operations consist of fruit production, sales and marketing, rental operations, real estate and capital investment activities. In addition to growing lemons and avocados, Limoneira grows oranges and a variety of specialty citrus and other crops. Limoneira packs its own lemons and those of other growers.

	Annual Growth	10/19	10/20	10/21	10/22	10/23
Sales ($mil.)	1.2%	171.4	164.6	166.0	184.6	179.9
Net income ($ mil.)	–	(5.9)	(16.4)	(3.4)	(0.2)	9.4
Market value ($ mil.)	(6.8%)	339.4	248.1	289.4	214.0	256.4
Employees	(5.3%)	319	299	268	265	257

LIN HOLDINGS CORP.

Four Richmond Square, Suite 200
Providence, RI 02906
Phone: 401 454-2880
Fax: –
Web: –

CEO: –
CFO: –
HR: –
FYE: December 31
Type: Public

This company spells success with TV call letters. LIN Media owns and operates about 40 stations and seven digital channels serving about two dozen markets in some 15 states. Its portfolio of stations includes affiliates with all the major networks -- mostly CBS and FOX-- as well as stations affiliated with smaller networks The CW Network and MyNetworkTV. Many of the company's stations operate as duopolies with two stations serving a single market. In addition, LIN Media operates a host of affiliated web properties, apps, and mobile products as part of its digital media portfolio. Fellow TV station group Media General is acquiring the company.

	Annual Growth	12/97	12/98	12/99	12/00	12/01
Sales ($mil.)	12.7%	–	189.5	224.4	295.7	271.0
Net income ($ mil.)	–	–	(27.3)	(34.0)	(34.2)	(61.7)
Market value ($ mil.)	–	–	–	–	–	–
Employees	11.6%	–	1,104	1,454	1,645	1,535

LINCOLN BENEFIT LIFE CO

2940 South 84th Street
Lincoln, NE 68506
Phone: 402 479-4061
Fax: –
Web: –

CEO: Frederick F Cripe
CFO: –
HR: –
FYE: December 31
Type: Public

Lincoln Benefit Life produces a variety of life insurance, annuities, and other retirement and investment products (primarily deferred and immediate fixed annuities, interest-sensitive life, and traditional life insurance) that are sold by former parent Allstate's exclusive agents, as well as by independent agents and through securities dealers. Lincoln Benefit Life is authorized to offer its products in all US states except New York. Allstate sold the company to Resolution Life Holdings for $600 million in 2014.

	Annual Growth	12/04	12/05	12/06	12/07	12/08
Sales ($mil.)	15.3%	11.2	13.5	12.7	13.8	19.9
Net income ($ mil.)	15.4%	7.3	8.8	8.3	9.0	13.0
Market value ($ mil.)	–	–	–	–	–	–
Employees	–	–	–	–	–	–

LINCOLN CENTER FOR THE PERFORMING ARTS, INC.

70 LINCOLN CENTER PLZ
NEW YORK, NY 100236548
Phone: 212 875-5000
Fax: –
Web: www.lincolncenter.org

CEO: Debora L Spar
CFO: Daniel Rubin
HR: Liza Parker
FYE: June 30
Type: Private

One of the world's largest cultural hubs, Lincoln Center presents live music, theater, dance, and opera performances from its 16-acre complex in New York City. The Center also offers educational programming and provides a home base for such organizations as the School of American Ballet, the New York Philharmonic, the Metropolitan Opera, and The Film Society of Lincoln Center. More than 5,000 performances and educational programs are presented and more than 5 million people visit each year. The Lincoln Center was conceived by New York City movers and shakers including Robert Moses, Robert F. Wagner, Jr., and John D. Rockefeller III; construction of the complex took place between 1959 and 1972.

	Annual Growth	06/18	06/19	06/20	06/21	06/22
Sales ($mil.)	(7.1%)	–	131.8	207.7	278.3	105.7
Net income ($ mil.)	–	–	(23.0)	58.1	170.2	(23.9)
Market value ($ mil.)	–	–	–	–	–	–
Employees	–	–	–	–	–	525

LINCOLN EDUCATIONAL SERVICES CORP
NMS: LINC

14 Sylvan Way, Suite A
Parsippany, NJ 07054
Phone: 973 736-9340
Fax: –
Web: www.lincolnedu.com

CEO: Scott M Shaw
CFO: Brian K Meyers
HR: Donna Cabrera
FYE: December 31
Type: Public

Lincoln hopes its graduates are better " Abe -l" to get a career. Lincoln Educational Services provides vocational programs from schools including Lincoln Technical Institute and Nashville Auto-Diesel College. It offers programs in automotive technology and skilled trades (including HVAC and electronics). Some 14,000 students are enrolled at more than 30 campuses and five training sites more than 15 states throughout the US. Lincoln tends to grow by buying smaller schools and by opening campuses in new markets. It also expands its campus facilities to accommodate higher enrollment numbers. The company announced plans to divest its health care and other professions business in 2015.

	Annual Growth	12/19	12/20	12/21	12/22	12/23
Sales ($mil.)	8.4%	273.3	293.1	335.3	348.3	378.1
Net income ($ mil.)	89.5%	2.0	48.6	34.7	12.6	26.0
Market value ($ mil.)	38.9%	84.7	203.8	234.3	181.6	314.8
Employees	4.6%	1,922	1,933	2,056	2,121	2,300

LINCOLN ELECTRIC HOLDINGS, INC.
NMS: LECO

22801 St. Clair Avenue
Cleveland, OH 44117
Phone: 216 481-8100
Fax: 216 486-1751
Web: www.lincolnelectric.com

CEO: Christopher L Mapes
CFO: Gabriel Bruno
HR: –
FYE: December 31
Type: Public

Lincoln Electric is a worldwide broad-line manufacturer of welding, cutting, and brazing products, including arc welding equipment, plasma and oxyfuel cutting systems, wire feeding systems, fume control equipment, welding accessories, and specialty gas regulators, as well as a comprehensive portfolio of automated solutions for joining, cutting, material handling, module assembly, and end of line testing. The company also offers a line of brazing and soldering alloys. The company's products are sold in both domestic and international markets. The US accounts for around 55% of sales.

	Annual Growth	12/19	12/20	12/21	12/22	12/23
Sales ($mil.)	8.7%	3,003.3	2,655.4	3,234.2	3,761.2	4,191.6
Net income ($ mil.)	16.8%	293.1	206.1	276.5	472.2	545.2
Market value ($ mil.)	22.4%	5,511.3	6,623.4	7,946.4	8,232.4	12,390
Employees	2.2%	11,000	10,700	11,000	12,000	12,000

LINCOLN INDUSTRIES, INC.

600 W E ST
LINCOLN, NE 685221399
Phone: 402 475-3671
Fax: –
Web: www.lincolnindustries.com

CEO: Marc E Lebaron
CFO: Andrew Hunzeker
HR: –
FYE: December 31
Type: Private

Lincoln Industries is the largest privately-held metal finishing company in North America. Its capabilities include anodizing, coating, and nickel plating. The company has been leading the industry in metal finishing, supply chain management, customer service, innovation, and establishing a company culture that is nationally known. It also works hand in hand with customers to develop solutions that solve or prevent difficult product challenges. Solutions have included innovation, heat management, corrosion and wear, and cosmetics. Lincoln Industries, formerly known as Lincoln Plating, was founded in 1952 by Dale LeBaron.

	Annual Growth	09/03	09/04	09/05	09/06*	12/12
Sales ($mil.)	(49.2%)	–	56.6	62.6	85.3	0.3
Net income ($ mil.)	(36.7%)	–	8.9	9.6	11.4	0.2
Market value ($ mil.)	–	–	–	–	–	–
Employees	–	–	–	–	–	1,100

*Fiscal year change

LINCOLN INTERNATIONAL LLC

110 N WACKER DR # 51
CHICAGO, IL 606061513
Phone: 312 580-8339
Fax: –
Web: www.lincolninternational.com

CEO: James Fang
CFO: –
HR: –
FYE: December 31
Type: Private

Lincoln International offers capital raising, merger and acquisition (M&A) and debt advisory, and other corporate finance services. It has expertise in several industries, including aerospace and defense, consumer products, chemicals, and renewable energy. The Lincoln MMI is the only index that tracks changes in the enterprise value of US privately held middle market companies? primarily those owned by private equity firms. Lincoln International has more than 850 professionals across some 15 countries. The company made 400-plus transaction in 2021.

	Annual Growth	12/14	12/15	12/16	12/17	12/18
Assets ($mil.)	11.6%	–	69.3	47.9	61.9	96.3
Net income ($ mil.)	–	–	–	–	–	–
Market value ($ mil.)	–	–	–	–	–	–
Employees	–	–	–	–	–	190

LINCOLN NATIONAL CORP.

NYS: LNC
150 N. Radnor Chester Road, Suite A305
Radnor, PA 19087
Phone: 484 583-1400
Fax: –
Web: www.lfg.com

CEO: Ellen G Cooper
CFO: Randal J Freitag
HR: –
FYE: December 31
Type: Public

Lincoln National, which operates as Lincoln Financial Group, is a holding company, which operates multiple insurance and retirement businesses through subsidiary companies. It also offers group non-medical insurance products and services, including short- and long-term disability, statutory disability and paid family medical leave administration and absence management services, term life, dental, vision and accident and critical illness benefits and services to the employer marketplace through various forms of employee-paid and employer-paid plans. The company does business through such subsidiaries as Lincoln National Life Insurance, Lincoln Life & Annuity Company of New York, and First Penn-Pacific Life Insurance.

	Annual Growth	12/19	12/20	12/21	12/22	12/23
Assets ($mil.)	2.7%	334,761	365,948	387,301	335,437	372,413
Net income ($ mil.)	–	886.0	499.0	1,405.0	(2,227.0)	(752.0)
Market value ($ mil.)	(17.8%)	10,012	8,535.9	11,581	5,212.1	4,575.9
Employees	(0.7%)	11,357	10,966	10,848	11,316	11,024

LINDE PLC (NEW)

NMS: LIN
10 Riverview Drive
Danbury, CT 06810
Phone: 203 837-2000
Fax: –
Web: www.linde.com

CEO: Stephen F Angel
CFO: Matthew J White
HR: –
FYE: December 31
Type: Public

Linde Inc. (formerly Praxair, Inc.), a wholly-owned subsidiary of Linde plc since 2018, is a leading industrial gas company in North and South America and one of the largest worldwide. Linde produces, sells and distributes atmospheric, process and specialty gases. Its products, services, and technologies, which include a full range of atmospheric, process, industrial, and specialty gases, are offered to a wide variety of industries, including aerospace and aircraft, chemicals, food and beverage, electronics, energy, healthcare, manufacturing and materials processing, pharmaceuticals and biotechnology, and many others.

	Annual Growth	12/19	12/20	12/21	12/22	12/23
Sales ($mil.)	3.9%	28,228	27,243	30,793	33,364	32,854
Net income ($ mil.)	28.3%	2,285.0	2,501.0	3,826.0	4,147.0	6,199.0
Market value ($ mil.)	–	–	–	–	–	–
Employees	(4.5%)	79,886	74,207	72,327	65,010	66,323

LINDSAY CORP

NYS: LNN
18135 Burke Street, Suite 100
Omaha, NE 68022
Phone: 402 829-6800
Fax: 402 829-6834
Web: www.lindsay.com

CEO: Randy A Wood
CFO: Brian L Ketcham
HR: –
FYE: August 31
Type: Public

Lindsay Corporation is a global leader in providing a variety of proprietary water management and road infrastructure products and services. The company manufactures and markets center pivot, lateral move, and hose reel irrigation systems. The company also produces and markets irrigation controls, chemical injection systems, remote monitoring and irrigation scheduling systems. These products are used by farmers to increase or stabilize crop production while conserving water, energy, and labor. The company also manufactures and markets, through distributors and direct sales to customers, various infrastructure products, including moveable barriers for traffic lane management, crash cushions, preformed reflective pavement tapes, and other road safety devices, through its production facilities in the US and Italy, and has produced road safety products in irrigation manufacturing facilities in China and Brazil. In addition, the company's infrastructure segment produces railroad signals and structures. The US accounts for more than 50% of revenue.

	Annual Growth	08/19	08/20	08/21	08/22	08/23
Sales ($mil.)	11.0%	444.1	474.7	567.6	770.7	674.1
Net income ($ mil.)	140.3%	2.2	38.6	42.6	65.5	72.4
Market value ($ mil.)	8.9%	971.8	1,100.3	1,814.1	1,765.7	1,366.5
Employees	3.1%	1,069	1,125	1,235	1,262	1,209

LINEAGE CELL THERAPEUTICS INC

ASE: LCTX
2173 Salk Avenue, Suite 200
Carlsbad, CA 92008
Phone: 442 287-8990
Fax: –
Web: www.lineagecell.com

CEO: Brian M Culley
CFO: Jill A Howe
HR: –
FYE: December 31
Type: Public

Lineage Cell Therapeutics is a clinical-stage biotechnology company developing novel cell therapies to address unmet medical needs. Lineage Cell programs are based on its proprietary cell-based technology and associated development and manufacturing capabilities. From this platform, the company designs, develops, manufactures, and tests specialized human cells with anatomical and physiological functions which are similar or identical to cells found naturally in the human body. These cells which the company manufactures are created by developmental differentiation protocols applied to established and well-characterized, pluripotent, and self-renewing cell lines. These cells are transplanted into patients and are designed to replace or support cells that are absent or dysfunctional due to degenerative disease, aging, or traumatic injury, and restore or augment functional activity in the affected person.

	Annual Growth	12/19	12/20	12/21	12/22	12/23
Sales ($mil.)	26.3%	3.5	1.8	4.3	14.7	8.9
Net income ($ mil.)	–	(11.7)	(20.6)	(43.0)	(26.3)	(21.5)
Market value ($ mil.)	5.2%	155.7	308.0	428.7	204.7	190.7
Employees	10.5%	55	55	61	78	82

LINEAR TECHNOLOGY LLC

1630 MCCARTHY BLVD
MILPITAS, CA 950357417
Phone: 408 432-1900
Fax: –
Web: www.analog.com

CEO: –
CFO: –
HR: –
FYE: July 03
Type: Private

Linear Technology's high performance linear integrated circuits (ICs) create a connection from the analog world to the digital one. Its chips convert temperature, pressure, sound, speed, and other information into a digital form that can be read by digital devices. Linear Technology also makes linear devices that control power and regulate voltage in electronic systems. The company's products are used in a myriad of equipment from PCs to radar systems, satellites, and industrial instrumentation. It caters largely to communications and industrial markets, as well as to the computer, consumer goods, aerospace, and automotive markets. Linear was acquired by Analog Devices for about $15 billion in 2017.

LINKAGE, INC.

6 LIBERTY SQ
BOSTON, MA 021095800
Phone: 781 402-5555
Fax: –
Web: www.linkageinc.com

CEO: Matt Norquist
CFO: Richard Pumfrey
HR: –
FYE: December 31
Type: Private

Linkage hooks up corporate managers, executives, and human resource professionals with information on developing people, advancing organizations, and driving change. It focuses on leadership development and offers conferences, summits, workshops, on-site training, online training, and other distance learning programs. Linkage also performs management consulting and executive coaching. The company publishes books and other products related to its educational programs (through John Wiley & Sons, McGraw-Hill Education, or its own publishing arm, Linkage Press. CEO Phil Harkins founded Linkage in 1988. Since then more than 100,000 people have participated in its programs around the world.

	Annual Growth	12/03	12/04	12/05	12/06	12/07
Sales ($mil.)	1.4%	–	–	21.8	19.5	22.5
Net income ($ mil.)	17.3%	–	–	0.7	8.2	1.0
Market value ($ mil.)	–	–	–	–	–	–
Employees	–	–	–	–	–	60

LINKEDIN CORPORATION

1000 W MAUDE AVE
SUNNYVALE, CA 940852810
Phone: 650 687-3600
Fax: –
Web: www.linkedin.com

CEO: Ryan Roslansky
CFO: James Chuong
HR: Cemre Kaya
FYE: December 31
Type: Private

LinkedIn connects the world's professionals to make them more productive and successful and transforms the way companies hire, market, sell, and learn. The site has grown to reach more than 950 million users in more than 200 countries since its launch in 2003. LinkedIn is free to join; it offers a paid premium membership with additional tools and sells advertising. It additionally earns revenue through its job listing service, which allows companies to post job openings and search for candidates on LinkedIn. Linkedin is a subsidiary of Microsoft.

LINKMONT TECHNOLOGIES, INC.

4108 E AIR LN
PHOENIX, AZ 850343022
Phone: 303 433-2333
Fax: –
Web: –

CEO: –
CFO: –
HR: –
FYE: December 31
Type: Private

Plasticomm Industries (PCI) provides a wide range of engineering and installation services for the deployment of telecommunication networks. These services include network planning and engineering, cable manufacturing and laying, network auditing, warehousing and distribution, and program management. The company also offers consulting services related to communications networks, Internet commerce services, and wireless services. PCI distributes, installs, and maintains networking equipment from such information technology vendors as Cisco. Its clients have included ADTRAN, Verizon, and the State of Colorado.

	Annual Growth	12/01	12/02	12/03	12/06	12/08
Sales ($mil.)	1.1%	–	5.4	6.8	8.6	5.7
Net income ($ mil.)	–	–	(0.0)	0.0	(0.2)	(0.3)
Market value ($ mil.)	–	–	–	–	–	–
Employees	–	–	–	–	–	14

LION COPPER & GOLD CORP

143 S Nevada St.
Yerington, NV 89447
Phone: 917 371-2966
Fax: –
Web: www.lioncg.com

TVX: LEO
CEO: –
CFO: –
HR: –
FYE: December 31
Type: Public

Quaterra Resources may not have all four corners of the earth covered, but it does explore for gold, silver, copper, uranium, molybdenum, and other precious metals in the US and Mexico. Based in Canada, the exploration-stage company is trying to make mineral discoveries at two copper projects in Nevada; copper and molybdenum projects in Utah and Texas through joint ventures with subsidiaries of Freeport-McMoRan; a uranium project in Arizona; a molybdenum project in Montana; and a gold project in Alaska. In Mexico, Quaterra is developing the Nieves silver property, and it maintains a strategic alliance with Goldcorp to discover gold and silver in Zacatecas State.

	Annual Growth	12/18	12/19	12/20	12/21	12/22
Sales ($mil.)	–	–	–	–	–	–
Net income ($ mil.)	–	(1.4)	(1.7)	(1.0)	(3.0)	(1.8)
Market value ($ mil.)	3.0%	13.7	14.9	17.0	32.5	15.4
Employees	3.4%	7	7	–	8	8

LIONBRIDGE TECHNOLOGIES, LLC

890 WINTER ST
WALTHAM, MA 024511470
Phone: 781 434-6000
Fax: –
Web: www.lionbridge.com

CEO: John Fennelly
CFO: Marc Litz
HR: Robert Doyle
FYE: December 31
Type: Private

Lionbridge Technologies helps companies connect with their global customers and employees by delivering translation, testing, and localization solutions in more than 350 languages. Through its world-class platform, Lionbridge orchestrate a network of 500,000 passionate experts around the world, who partner with brands to create culturally rich experiences. The company offers a full range of multilingual content support services, including digital marketing for web and mobile, financial reports and regulatory materials, research services, thought leadership and specialist writing, and software and training material development. Lionbridge has more than 2,100 customers all over the world.

LIPSCOMB UNIVERSITY

1 UNIVERSITY PARK DR
NASHVILLE, TN 372043956
Phone: 615 966-1000
Fax: -
Web: www.lipscomb.edu

CEO: -
CFO: Danny Taylor
HR: Janice Cato
FYE: May 31
Type: Private

Lipscomb University was founded in 1891 as the Nashville Bible School by David Lipscomb and James A. Harding; it was renamed in Lipscomb's honor in 1918. The coeducational Christian school offers more than 150 programs of study in about 80 majors leading to bachelor's degrees, about eight of them, at colleges of arts and humanities, Bible and ministry, business, education, engineering, pharmacy and health sciences, and professional studies. It also offers graduate degrees in areas such as theology, accountancy, business administration, conflict management, counseling, and education, in addition to a doctorate degree in pharmacy. Lipscomb has an annual enrollment of approximately 4,500 students.

	Annual Growth	05/18	05/19	05/20	05/21	05/22
Sales ($mil.)	2.7%	-	152.2	151.8	153.2	164.7
Net income ($ mil.)	-	-	(5.3)	(7.6)	36.8	(6.9)
Market value ($ mil.)	-	-	-	-	-	-
Employees	-	-	-	-	-	550

LIQUID HOLDINGS GROUP INC
NBB: LIQD Q

800 Third Avenue, 38th Floor
New York, NY 10022
Phone: 212 293-1836
Fax: -
Web: www.liquidholdings.com

CEO: Peter R Kent
CFO: Peter R Kent
HR: -
FYE: December 31
Type: Public

Liquid Holdings Group's software keeps investment firms fluid. The newly formed company's software is used by investors for asset management operations, such as trading, real-time risk management, accounting, and reporting. Its software, called the Liquid Platform, consists of a risk metrics platform (LiquidMetrics), a trading platform (LiquidTrade), and an accounting platform (LiquidView) that allows users to manage portfolios and other functions in one agile system. Customers include small to midsized hedge fund managers, asset managers, wealth management offices, and financial institutions. Formed in 2012, Liquid Holdings went public in 2013; it filed for Chapter 11 bankruptcy protection in early 2016.

	Annual Growth	12/09	12/10	12/11	12/12	12/13
Sales ($mil.)	106.1%	-	-	-	2.3	4.8
Net income ($ mil.)	-	-	-	-	(38.2)	(46.6)
Market value ($ mil.)	-	-	-	-	-	169.9
Employees	(32.4%)	-	-	-	71	48

LIQUID INVESTMENTS, INC.

3840 VIA DE LA VALLE STE 300
DEL MAR, CA 920144268
Phone: 858 509-8510
Fax: -
Web: www.nextsolutions.us

CEO: Ron L Fowler
CFO: -
HR: -
FYE: December 31
Type: Private

Liquid Investments has nothing to do with your bank accounts, your retirement fund, or your broker. The company supplies beer, malt beverages, soda, energy drinks, and water to customers in parts of California and Colorado. It owns the Mesa Beverage Co. in Santa Rosa, California, which handles over 1,500 accounts in Sonoma and Marin counties. It also serves 475 accounts in the western slope area of Colorado through Colorado Beverage Distribution, which has locations in Grand Junction and Montrose, Colorado. Liquid distributes imported, domestic, and craft beers. It also offers regional and local beers, along with soda and bottled water. Its latest addition to its craft labels is Victoria lagers.

	Annual Growth	12/07	12/08	12/09	12/10	12/11
Sales ($mil.)	(0.5%)	-	95.3	93.2	91.8	93.7
Net income ($ mil.)	(79.0%)	-	128.0	0.4	(0.1)	1.2
Market value ($ mil.)	-	-	-	-	-	-
Employees	-	-	-	-	-	629

LIQUIDITY SERVICES INC
NMS: LQDT

6931 Arlington Road, Suite 200
Bethesda, MD 20814
Phone: 202 467-6868
Fax: -
Web: www.liquidityservices.com

CEO: -
CFO: -
HR: -
FYE: September 30
Type: Public

Liquidity Services (LSI) is a global commerce company. LSI provides connections for millions of buyers and thousands of buyers and thousands of sellers through the company's auction marketplaces, search engines, asset management software, and related services. The company was able to record more than 2.2 million transactions in the past fiscal year. LSI, founded in 1999, offers its assets to manufacturers, retailers, corporations, and government agencies. The US generates the majority of the company's total revenue.

	Annual Growth	09/19	09/20	09/21	09/22	09/23
Sales ($mil.)	8.5%	226.5	205.9	257.5	280.1	314.5
Net income ($ mil.)	-	(19.3)	(3.8)	50.9	40.3	21.0
Market value ($ mil.)	24.2%	227.2	229.1	663.6	499.3	541.1
Employees	1.0%	687	574	614	735	716

LIQUIDMETAL TECHNOLOGIES INC
NBB: LQMT

20321 Valencia Circle
Lake Forest, CA 92630
Phone: 949 635-2100
Fax: -
Web: www.liquidmetal.com

CEO: Tony Chung
CFO: -
HR: -
FYE: December 31
Type: Public

It's not liquid, it's not metal -- well, OK, it is metal. Still, Liquidmetal Technologies has built on research done at the California Institute of Technology by company officers William Johnson and Atakan Peker to sell amorphous metal alloys. Those products include an alloy that's lighter than titanium but twice as strong as conventional titanium alloys. The company's products are sold as bulk alloys, coatings, composites, and powders. Applications include casings for cell phones, defense products (armor-piercing ammunition), industrial coatings, and sporting goods (baseball bats, tennis rackets). Electronics giant Samsung is among the company's largest customers.

	Annual Growth	12/19	12/20	12/21	12/22	12/23
Sales ($mil.)	(21.9%)	1.4	1.0	0.8	0.4	0.5
Net income ($ mil.)	-	(7.4)	(2.6)	(3.4)	(2.4)	(2.0)
Market value ($ mil.)	(12.8%)	94.5	76.3	80.3	58.3	54.6
Employees	(2.9%)	9	8	8	8	8

LISATA THERAPEUTICS INC
NAS: LSTA

110 Allen Road, 2nd Floor
Basking Ridge, NJ 07920
Phone: 908 842-0100
Fax: -
Web: www.caladrius.com

CEO: David J Mazzo
CFO: -
HR: Gail Holler
FYE: December 31
Type: Public

Caladrius Biosciences has a vision, and it stems from life's building blocks. Operating in the US and China, the clinical-stage company is working on developing cell-based therapies. Its lead candidate, CLBS03, is in studies to treat recent-onset type 1 diabetes; it is targeted at adolescents. Another Caladius program aims to treat ischemia.

	Annual Growth	12/19	12/20	12/21	12/22	12/23
Sales ($mil.)	-	-	-	-	-	-
Net income ($ mil.)	-	(19.4)	(8.2)	(27.5)	(54.2)	(20.8)
Market value ($ mil.)	2.1%	20.5	11.7	6.9	20.6	22.2
Employees	(1.9%)	27	24	27	27	25

LITCO INTERNATIONAL, INC.

1 LITCO DR
VIENNA, OH 444739600
Phone: 330 539-5433
Fax: –
Web: www.litco.com

CEO: Lionel Trebilcock
CFO: –
HR: Chameika Patterson
FYE: December 31
Type: Private

Litco International is not about to let go of its leading role in the materials handling market. The company operates two strategic business units: The Molded Products Group and The Product Protection/Damage Prevention Team. The Molded Products Group focuses on the design, manufacture and sales of pallets and other products that are three-dimensional and primarily made of wood fiber. Litco International's Product Protection/Damage Prevention Team concentrates on the production of dunnage materials (air bags, corner protectors, corrugated pads, corrugated void fill products, and separator sheets).

LITEHOUSE, INC.

100 LITEHOUSE DR
SANDPOINT, ID 838640528
Phone: 208 920-2000
Fax: –
Web: www.litehousefoods.com

CEO: Kelly Prior
CFO: –
HR: Charmaine Cook
FYE: December 29
Type: Private

This company shines its light on salads. Litehouse is a leading maker of salad dressings, sauces, and vegetable dips under the Litehouse label. It produces a variety of dressings, including blue cheese, ranch, and vinaigrette, along with low fat and organic products. The company also makes fruit dips, glazes, and cheese crumbles, as well as apple cider, marinades, and freeze-dried herbs. With manufacturing facilities in Idaho, Utah, and Michigan, Litehouse products are sold through supermarkets and warehouse clubs in the US and Canada. Litehouse also supplies dressings and other products to food service distributors and restaurants. Founded by Edward Hawkins in 1963, Litehouse is run by the Hawkins family.

LITHIA MOTORS INC

NYS: LAD

150 N. Bartlett Street
Medford, OR 97501
Phone: 541 776-6401
Fax: –
Web: www.lithiainvestorrelations.com

CEO: Bryan B Deboer
CFO: Tina H Miller
HR: –
FYE: December 31
Type: Public

Lithia Motors is one of the largest automotive retailers in the US. It offers a wide selection of vehicles across global carmakers and providing a full suite of financing, leasing, repair, and maintenance options in about 295 locations representing almost 50 brands in two countries, across almost 30 US states and three Canadian provinces. Purchasing and owning a vehicle is easy and hassle-free with convenient solutions offered through its comprehensive network of locations, e-commerce platforms, and captive finance division. Founded in 1946 and incorporated in Oregon in 1968, the company completed its initial public offering in 1996.

	Annual Growth	12/19	12/20	12/21	12/22	12/23
Sales ($mil.)	25.1%	12,673	13,124	22,832	28,188	31,042
Net income ($ mil.)	38.6%	271.5	470.3	1,060.1	1,251.0	1,000.8
Market value ($ mil.)	22.3%	4,027.8	8,019.2	8,136.4	5,609.9	9,022.3
Employees	17.7%	14,320	14,538	21,150	21,875	27,446

LITTELFUSE INC

NMS: LFUS

8755 West Higgins Road, Suite 500
Chicago, IL 60631
Phone: 773 628-1000
Fax: –
Web: www.littelfuse.com

CEO: David W Heinzmann
CFO: Meenal A Sethna
HR: Maggie Chu
FYE: December 30
Type: Public

Littelfuse is a diversified, industrial technology manufacturing company empowering a sustainable, connected, and safer world. In addition to its fuses, Littelfuse's other circuit protection devices include positive temperature coefficient devices that limit current when too much is being supplied and electrostatic discharge suppressors that redirect transient high voltage. The company's thyristors protect telecommunications circuits from transient voltage caused by lightning strikes. Littelfuse's over 5,000 customers include industrial, transportations, and electronics markets.

	Annual Growth	12/19	12/20*	01/22*	12/22	12/23
Sales ($mil.)	12.0%	1,503.9	1,445.7	2,079.9	2,513.9	2,362.7
Net income ($ mil.)	16.9%	139.1	130.0	283.8	373.3	259.5
Market value ($ mil.)	8.6%	4,783.8	6,269.6	7,839.6	5,485.8	6,665.7
Employees	10.7%	11,300	12,200	17,000	18,000	17,000

*Fiscal year change

LITTLE LEAGUE BASEBALL INC

539 US ROUTE 15 HWY
WILLIAMSPORT, PA 177028541
Phone: 570 326-1921
Fax: –
Web: www.littleleague.org

CEO: Stephen Keener
CFO: David Houseknecht
HR: –
FYE: September 30
Type: Private

Little League Baseball's players might be small, but the organization's reach is anything but. Little League Baseball oversees more than 7,000 baseball and softball programs for about 3 million children in more than 100 countries worldwide, including the US, China, Israel, Russia, and Venezuela. On the local level, Little League Baseball programs are organized and operated by volunteers. The season ends with the annual Little League World Series played in Williamsport, Pennsylvania. The organization also runs the Peter J. McGovern Little League Museum in Pennsylvania, the Little League Foundation, and summer baseball camps. Little League Baseball was founded by Carl Stotz with only three teams in 1939.

	Annual Growth	09/13	09/14	09/19	09/20	09/22
Sales ($mil.)	2.6%	–	25.9	35.8	22.5	31.8
Net income ($ mil.)	–	–	(1.4)	3.1	(0.3)	(1.1)
Market value ($ mil.)	–	–	–	–	–	–
Employees	–	–	–	–	–	98

LITTLE SIOUX CORN PROCESSORS LLC

4808 F AVE
MARCUS, IA 510357070
Phone: 712 376-2800
Fax: –
Web: www.littlesiouxcornprocessors.com

CEO: Ron Wetherell
CFO: Gary Grotjohn
HR: –
FYE: September 30
Type: Private

Pursuing the corny American Heartland dream of profitable renewable energy, Little Sioux Corn Processors operates an ethanol plant in northwest Iowa. (It actually owns a 60% interest in the limited partnership that owns the ethanol facility.) The company converts bushels of corn into ethanol, distiller grains (used as feed for the dairy and beef industries), and corn oil. Ethanol is used as an additive to gasoline as well as a fuel enhancer for high-octane motors, and it burns more cleanly than normal gasoline thereby reducing carbon monoxide emissions. Little Sioux's production capacity is about 90 million gallons of ethanol annually, more than double its orginal capacity after successive expansions.

	Annual Growth	09/02	09/03	09/10	09/11	09/13
Sales ($mil.)	27.0%	–	31.8	–	329.7	346.7
Net income ($ mil.)	1.3%	–	4.1	–	9.5	4.6
Market value ($ mil.)	–	–	–	–	–	–
Employees	–	–	–	–	–	48

LITTLEFIELD CORP   NBB: LTFD

2501 N. Lamar Blvd.   CEO: –
Austin, TX 78705   CFO: –
Phone: 512 476-5141   HR: –
Fax: –   FYE: December 31
Web: www.ambingo.com   Type: Public

A fun game of bingo is serious business for this company. Littlefield Corporation owns and operates nearly 40 bingo halls in Texas, South Carolina, Alabama, and Florida. Its gaming locations generate revenue by renting out the space to charitable organizations that use the halls for fund raising activities, such as charity bingo and other events. More than 100 charities utilize Littlefield's properties. President and CEO Jeffrey Minch and his family own about 20% of the company.

	Annual Growth	12/11	12/12	12/13	12/14	12/15
Sales ($mil.)	(16.1%)	9.4	8.3	6.4	5.1	4.7
Net income ($ mil.)	–	(1.0)	(4.3)	0.9	0.0	0.0
Market value ($ mil.)	(23.2%)	9.0	4.3	4.3	7.8	3.1
Employees	–	32	–	–	–	–

LITTLER MENDELSON, P.C.

101 2ND ST   CEO: Michael Wilder
SAN FRANCISCO, CA 941053672   CFO: –
Phone: 415 433-1940   HR: –
Fax: –   FYE: December 31
Web: www.littler.com   Type: Private

Littler Mendelson is the largest law practice in the world exclusively devoted to representing management in employment, employee benefits and labor law matters. With more than 1,600 labor and employment attorneys, its specialty is representing management in all types of labor disputes and employee lawsuits. Practice areas include appellate work, business restructuring, employment taxes, unfair competition and trade secrets, and workplace violence prevention. Littler Mendelson has attorneys and offices throughout Asia Pacific, Europe, Latin America, Middle East and Africa, and North America. The firm was founded in San Francisco in 1942; it began expanding beyond California in the 1990s.

LIVANOVA USA, INC.

100 CYBERONICS BLVD STE 600   CEO: Daniel J Moore
HOUSTON, TX 770582069   CFO: Gregory H Browne
Phone: 281 228-7200   HR: Jonathan Brown
Fax: –   FYE: April 24
Web: www.livanova.com   Type: Private

It may sound futuristic, but Cyberonics is all about treating an age-old neurological disorder. The firm is the maker of the first medical device to gain clearance by the FDA for treating epilepsy. Its Vagus Nerve Stimulation Therapy system (VNS Therapy) is a pacemaker-like device that connects to the vagus nerve in the neck and delivers intermittent signals to the brain to control epileptic seizures. Physicians can program the signals by computer, and patients can start or stop signals with hand-held magnets. The firm also has CE marking for its VITARIA System for the treatment of chronic heart failure. Cyberonics merged with Italian medical device firm Sorin to create LivaNova in 2015.

LIVE CURRENT MEDIA INC   NBB: LIVC

10801 Thornmint Road, Suite 200   CEO: –
San Diego, CA 92127   CFO: –
Phone: 604 648-0500   HR: –
Fax: –   FYE: December 31
Web: www.cmnn.com   Type: Public

Live Current Media (formerly Communicate.com) hopes to translate straightforward Web domain names into money. The company owns, develops, markets, and sells hundreds of Web domain names through its subject-specific DestinationHubs products and services. It partners with retailers and gets a share of e-commerce proceeds from company-owned domains such as cologne.com, perfume.com, and wrestling.com. It also generates advertising revenue via referrals from its websites. Striving to brand itself as a new media company, Communicate.com changed its name to Live Current Media in mid-2008.

	Annual Growth	12/18	12/19	12/20	12/21	12/22
Sales ($mil.)	–	–	–	–	–	0.5
Net income ($ mil.)	–	(0.8)	0.0	0.2	(0.2)	(15.7)
Market value ($ mil.)	33.4%	9.6	5.8	6.6	78.5	30.5
Employees	96.8%	1	1	1	1	15

LIVE MICROSYSTEMS INC   NBB: LMSC

One Monarch Drive, Suite 203   CEO: –
Littleton, MA 01460   CFO: –
Phone: 978 742-3177   HR: –
Fax: 978 742-9794   FYE: December 31
Web: www.livemicrosystems.com/   Type: Public

LiveWire Mobile takes mobile communications personally. The company provides mobile content and subscriber management products to wireless service providers. Its caller personalization applications provide such functionality as musical ringback service. The company markets its services to mobile network operators worldwide. Previously a telecom equipment provider called NMS Communications, the company sold its platforms business (voice quality and echo cancellation systems) to Dialogic for $28 million in cash in 2008. NMS then changed its name to LiveWire Mobile. The company generates about two-thirds of its sales outside the Americas.

	Annual Growth	12/09	12/10	12/11	12/12	12/13
Sales ($mil.)	–	16.8	12.1	9.5	13.3	–
Net income ($ mil.)	–	(2.8)	(1.5)	(8.4)	(0.6)	7.0
Market value ($ mil.)	(35.6%)	2.9	2.9	0.9	0.6	0.5
Employees	–	–	–	–	–	–

LIVE NATION ENTERTAINMENT INC   NYS: LYV

9348 Civic Center Drive   CEO: Michael Rapino
Beverly Hills, CA 90210   CFO: Alex Klos
Phone: 310 867-7000   HR: Gena Gilbert
Fax: –   FYE: December 31
Web: www.livenationentertainment.com   Type: Public

Live Nation Entertainment is the world's largest ticket seller and promoter of live entertainment. It connects over 670 million fans across all of its concerts and ticketing platforms in about 50 countries. Ticketmaster provides ticket sales, marketing, and distribution globally through www.ticketmaster.com and www.livenation.com and other websites, mobile apps, retail outlets, and call centers, selling over 550 million tickets in 2022. It owns, operates, has exclusive booking rights for, or has an interest in about 340 venues, including House of Blues music venues and prestigious locations such as The Fillmore in San Francisco, Brooklyn Bowl, the Hollywood Palladium, the Ziggo Dome in Amsterdam, 3Arena in Ireland, Royal Arena in Copenhagen and Spark Arena in New Zealand. As a leading artist management firm, Live Nation has 90 managers providing services to more than 410 artists. It generates over 65% of revenue in the US.

	Annual Growth	12/19	12/20	12/21	12/22	12/23
Sales ($mil.)	18.5%	11,548	1,861.2	6,268.4	16,681	22,749
Net income ($ mil.)	68.5%	69.9	(1,724.5)	(650.9)	296.0	563.3
Market value ($ mil.)	7.0%	16,674	17,143	27,924	16,271	21,837
Employees	8.8%	10,500	8,200	10,200	12,800	14,700

LIVE VENTURES INC
NAS: LIVE

325 E. Warm Springs Road, Suite 102
Las Vegas, NV 89119
Phone: 702 997-5968
Fax: –
Web: www.liveventures.com

CEO: Jon Isaac
CFO: David Verret
HR: –
FYE: September 30
Type: Public

LiveDeal (formerly YP Corp.) is an Internet yellow pages and local online classifieds provider. The company offers goods and services listed for sale through its online classified marketplace at classifieds.livedeal.com; LiveDeal also publishes about 17 million business listings via its business directory at yellowpages.livedeal.com. Sources of revenue include advertising sales, a pay-per-lead program with major auto dealers, and optional listing upgrade and e-commerce/fraud prevention fees. The company changed its name from YP Corp. after its 2007 purchase of online local classifieds marketplace LiveDeal.

	Annual Growth	09/19	09/20	09/21	09/22	09/23
Sales ($mil.)	16.4%	193.3	191.7	273.0	286.9	355.2
Net income ($ mil.)	–	(4.0)	10.9	31.2	24.7	(0.1)
Market value ($ mil.)	34.8%	27.1	28.3	117.1	79.3	89.5
Employees	9.2%	1,000	1,150	1,253	1,249	1,424

LIVEPERSON INC
NMS: LPSN

530 7th Avenue, Floor M1
New York, NY 10018
Phone: 212 609-4200
Fax: –
Web: www.liveperson.com

CEO: –
CFO: –
HR: –
FYE: December 31
Type: Public

LivePerson makes life easier for people and brands everywhere through trusted Conversational AI. Conversational AI enables "the tango" of humans, AI and bots, whereby human agents act as bot managers, overseeing AI-powered conversations and seamlessly stepping into the flow when a personal touch is needed. The Conversational Cloud, its enterprise-class cloud-based platform, enables businesses to have conversations with millions of consumers as personally as they would with a single consumer. It powers conversations across each of a brand's primary digital channels, including mobile apps, mobile and desktop web browsers, SMS, social media, and third-party consumer messaging platforms. Customers in the US make up about 65% of sales. The company was founded by Robert LoCascio back in 1995.

	Annual Growth	12/19	12/20	12/21	12/22	12/23
Sales ($mil.)	8.4%	291.6	366.6	469.6	514.8	402.0
Net income ($ mil.)	–	(96.1)	(107.6)	(125.0)	(225.7)	(100.4)
Market value ($ mil.)	(43.4%)	3,250.0	5,466.1	3,137.6	890.7	332.9
Employees	(4.9%)	1,341	1,201	1,540	1,301	1,095

LIVERAMP HOLDINGS INC
NYS: RAMP

225 Bush Street, Seventeenth Floor
San Francisco, CA 94104
Phone: 888 987-6764
Fax: –
Web: www.liveramp.com

CEO: Chad Engelgau
CFO: Brett Madison
HR: Kathy Brand
FYE: March 31
Type: Public

Acxiom is a customer intelligence company that provides data-driven solutions to enable the world's best marketers to better understand their customers to create better experiences and business growth. Acxiom helps thousands of clients and partners around the globe work together to create millions of better customer experiences. It draws clients from various sectors including automotive, financial services, health care, and telecommunications. The company has operations in China, Europe, and the US. Acxiom is part of The Interpublic Group of Companies.

	Annual Growth	03/19	03/20	03/21	03/22	03/23
Sales ($mil.)	20.2%	285.6	380.6	443.0	528.7	596.6
Net income ($ mil.)	–	1,028.5	(124.5)	(90.3)	(33.8)	(118.7)
Market value ($ mil.)	(20.4%)	3,635.2	2,193.0	3,456.0	2,490.7	1,460.9
Employees	9.6%	950	1,150	1,200	1,400	1,370

LIVESTYLE, INC.

902 BROADWAY FL 8
NEW YORK, NY 100106037
Phone: 646 561-6400
Fax: –
Web: www.livestyle.com

CEO: Robert F Sillerman
CFO: Richard Rosenstein
HR: –
FYE: December 31
Type: Private

Livestyle (formerly SFX Entertainment) makes flashing strobe lights, popular musical acts, big crowds, and a driving dance beat its business. The company, founded in 2011, produces music festivals in North America and Europe that attract fans of 'electronic music culture' or EDM (electronic dance music). As much as a fifth of the company's sales come from digital music sales between and around its musical events, which earn revenue through sales of tickets, concessions, sponsorships, promotion fees, and advertising. In 2013 the company went public in a $260 million IPO. In 2016 the company filed for bankruptcy and later that year changed its name to Livestyle.

LIVEWORLD, INC.
NBB: LVWD

2105 S Bascom Ave., Suite 159
Campbell, CA 95008
Phone: 800 301-9507
Fax: –
Web: www.liveworld.com

CEO: Peter H Friedman
CFO: David Houston
HR: –
FYE: December 31
Type: Public

LiveWorld hopes that online collaboration is the key to its livelihood. Promoting itself as a "social brand flow" manager, the company designs websites and offers applications that can be added to a customers' existing site. It also offers customized pages on popular social media sites including Twitter and Facebook as well as moderators and community managers on these sites to keep the discussion headed in the right direction. LiveWorld has created online communities for prominent companies including HSBC, Johnson & Johnson, The Campbell Soup Company, and Warner Brothers. Chairman and CEO Peter Friedman and EVP Jenna Woodul founded LiveWorld in 1996 from remnants of Apple's now-defunct eWorld online service.

	Annual Growth	12/18	12/19	12/20	12/21	12/22
Sales ($mil.)	9.7%	7.7	7.4	8.6	10.1	11.1
Net income ($ mil.)	–	(0.6)	(0.4)	0.4	1.8	1.0
Market value ($ mil.)	114.0%	0.4	0.6	3.0	8.2	7.8
Employees		–	–	–	–	–

LIVINGSTONE COLLEGE, INC.

701 W MONROE ST
SALISBURY, NC 281445298
Phone: 704 216-6000
Fax: –
Web: www.livingstone.edu

CEO: –
CFO: –
HR: Alisha Byrd
FYE: June 30
Type: Private

Livingstone College is one of the more than 100 Historically Black Colleges and Universities (HBCUs) in the US. The school, which is affiliated with the African Methodist Episcopal Zion Church, offers undergraduate degrees in business, education and social work, liberal arts, and math and sciences. Academic programs include accounting, sports management, political science, and chemistry. Livingstone College also offers accelerated degree programs for non-traditional students with online coursework and evening and weekend classes. HBCUs collectively grant about one-fifth of the undergraduate degrees earned by African-Americans. Dr. Joseph Charles Price founded the school in 1879.

	Annual Growth	06/15	06/16	06/20	06/21	06/22
Sales ($mil.)	2.1%	–	37.0	38.0	42.5	41.8
Net income ($ mil.)	1.8%	–	2.3	2.5	3.8	2.6
Market value ($ mil.)	–	–	–	–	–	–
Employees	–	–	–	–	–	73

LKQ CORP
NMS: LKQ

500 West Madison Street, Suite 2800
Chicago, IL 60661
Phone: 312 621-1950
Fax: –
Web: www.lkqcorp.com

CEO: –
CFO: –
HR: –
FYE: December 31
Type: Public

LKQ is one of the leading providers of alternative vehicle collision replacement products and alternative vehicle mechanical replacement products, including replacement parts, components, and systems used in the repair and maintenance of vehicles, and specialty products and accessories to improve the performance, functionality and appearance of vehicles. LKQ also offers reconditioned, remanufactured, and refurbished parts, including wheels, bumpers, covers and light, and remanufactured engines and transmissions, as well as recycled parts that are reclaimed from salvage vehicles. Customers include collision repair and mechanical repair shops. LKQ, which generates more than half its sales in the US, was formed in 1998.

	Annual Growth	12/19	12/20	12/21	12/22	12/23
Sales ($mil.)	2.6%	12,506	11,629	13,089	12,794	13,866
Net income ($ mil.)	14.7%	541.3	638.4	1,090.9	1,149.0	936.0
Market value ($ mil.)	7.6%	9,539.0	9,416.1	16,040	14,271	12,769
Employees	(1.0%)	51,000	44,000	46,000	45,000	49,000

LL FLOORING HOLDINGS INC
NYS: LL

4901 Bakers Mill Lane
Richmond, VA 23230
Phone: 800 366-4204
Fax: –
Web: www.lumberliquidators.com

CEO: –
CFO: –
HR: –
FYE: December 31
Type: Public

LL Flooring Holdings (formerly known as Lumber Liquidators Holdings) is one of the nation's largest retailers of hardwood flooring. It sells an extensive assortment of domestic and exotic species of hardwoods from more than 440 stores in more than 45 states, online, by catalog, and from its Virginia call center. Seeks to offer the best customer experience online via LLFlooring.com and in stores, with more than 500 varieties of hard-surface floors featuring a range of quality styles and on-trend designs. The company also offers laminate flooring, moldings, underlayment, adhesives, tools, and installation products. Its brands include Avella, Bellawood, Builder's Pride, ReNature, and Virginia Mill Works. LL Flooring primarily sells to homeowners or contractors on behalf of homeowners, as well as to commercial (Pro) customers. The company was founded in 1994.

	Annual Growth	12/19	12/20	12/21	12/22	12/23
Sales ($mil.)	(4.6%)	1,092.6	1,097.7	1,152.3	1,110.7	904.7
Net income ($ mil.)	–	9.7	61.4	41.7	(12.1)	(103.5)
Market value ($ mil.)	(20.5%)	281.9	886.8	492.5	162.1	112.5
Employees	(1.2%)	2,200	2,230	2,400	2,300	2,100

LL&E ROYALTY TRUST CO.

The Bank of New York Mellon Trust Company, N.A., Global Corporate Trust, 919 Congress Avenue
Austin, TX 78701
Phone: 512 236-6599
Fax: 512 236-9275
Web: –

CEO: –
CFO: –
HR: –
FYE: December 31
Type: Public

In oil and gas, Enduro trusts. Enduro Royalty Trust is a Delaware trust formed in 2011 that owns royalty interests in oil and gas production properties in Texas, Louisiana, and New Mexico. The trust is entitled to receive 80% of net profits from the sale of oil and natural gas produced by privately held Enduro Sponsor at properties in the Permian Basin and in the East Texas/North Louisiana regions; it then makes monthly distributions to trust unitholders. Enduro Sponsor holds interests in more than 900 net producing wells that are operated by third-party oil and gas companies. Its properties have proved reserves of about 27 million barrels of oil equivalent. Enduro Royalty Trust filed to go public in 2011.

	Annual Growth	12/06	12/07	12/08	12/09	12/10
Sales ($mil.)	(47.5%)	3.1	2.0	0.7	1.3	0.2
Net income ($ mil.)	–	2.1	0.6	(0.3)	0.0	(0.6)
Market value ($ mil.)	(21.7%)	52.0	40.3	10.1	12.5	19.6
Employees	–	–	–	–	–	–

LLOYD STAFFING, INC.

445 BROADHOLLOW RD STE 119
MELVILLE, NY 117473631
Phone: 631 777-7600
Fax: –
Web: www.lloydstaffing.com

CEO: Merrill Banks
CFO: Vincent J Albanese
HR: –
FYE: December 31
Type: Private

Lloyd Staffing's army of temps can help strengthen your corporate reserves. Founded in 1971, Lloyd Staffing provides temporary and direct-hire staffing and other employment-related services such as vendor management, business consulting, and recruitment process outsourcing. It also provides retained executive recruiting services. The firm has specialty practices in industries ranging from accounting and finance to health care to sales and marketing. The company, which says it has nearly 10,000 "contingent workers" available, operates from about a dozen franchised locations across the US.

	Annual Growth	12/01	12/02	12/03	12/04	12/07
Sales ($mil.)	8.9%	–	–	–	28.9	37.3
Net income ($ mil.)	(27.1%)	–	–	–	6.3	2.4
Market value ($ mil.)	–	–	–	–	–	–
Employees	–	–	–	–	–	1,500

LMI AEROSPACE, INC.

3600 MUELLER RD
SAINT CHARLES, MO 633018004
Phone: 636 946-6525
Fax: –
Web: www.lmiaerospace.com

CEO: Cliff Stebe
CFO: Clifford C Stebe Jr
HR: Heidi Wilkinson
FYE: December 31
Type: Private

LMI Aerospace, also known as LMI, is a leading supplier of structural assemblies, kits, and components, and a provider of design engineering services to the commercial, business and regional, and defense aerospace markets. The company fabricates, machines, finishes, kits, and assembles machined and formed close tolerance aluminum, specialty alloy, and composite components. LMI's engineering services provide product lifecycle services to help its customers meet their most complex challenges. Customers include Gulfstream Aerospace, Boeing, Hamilton Sundstrand, Mitsubishi Heavy Industries, and Airbus. In addition to its operations in Mexico, the company has about 15 locations in the US. LMI is a subsidiary of Belgium-based Sonaca Group.

LOCAL CORP
NBB: LOCM Q

7555 Irvine Center Drive
Irvine, CA 92618
Phone: 949 784-0800
Fax: 949 784-0880
Web: www.localcorporation.com

CEO: Frederick G Thiel
CFO: Kenneth S Cragun
HR: –
FYE: December 31
Type: Public

Local.com traffics in keywords. Specializing in paid-search advertising, the company connects businesses to consumers online. It attracts more than 30 million visitors per month through its Local.com search site, its network of more than 1,000 regional media websites, and ones that distribute its advertising feeds to third-party sites. It makes money from direct advertisers who bid for placement (based on keywords) and pay per click, and from indirect advertising subscribers that gain inclusion on the network through paid-search firms including Yahoo! and SuperMedia. Local.com also offers search engine optimization and other advertising support services.

	Annual Growth	12/10	12/11	12/12	12/13	12/14
Sales ($mil.)	(0.3%)	84.1	78.8	97.8	94.4	83.1
Net income ($ mil.)	–	4.2	(14.6)	(24.2)	(10.4)	(5.5)
Market value ($ mil.)	(36.7%)	151.2	49.4	47.8	36.8	24.2
Employees	(11.9%)	116	227	146	88	70

LOEBER MOTORS, INC.

4255 W TOUHY AVE
LINCOLNWOOD, IL 607121933
Phone: 847 675-1000
Fax: –
Web: www.loebermotors.com

CEO: –
CFO: –
HR: –
FYE: December 31
Type: Private

Want to buy a car from a son of a son of a salesman? Go to Loeber Motors, family-owned and -operated for three generations. The company sells Mercedes-Benz, Porsche, and smart cars, vans, and trucks from its dealerships in Lincolnwood, Illinois. Loeber Motors also sells used cars and maintains parts and service departments. Loeber's Web site allows visitors to get quick quotes on new cars, schedule service appointments, order parts, apply for finance, and search for used vehicles. The site also provides a forum for owners to chat about their cars. Martin Loeber founded Loeber Motors in 1938.

	Annual Growth	12/14	12/15	12/16	12/17	12/18
Sales ($mil.)	0.2%	–	315.0	330.2	268.2	316.7
Net income ($ mil.)	0.4%	–	3.8	4.6	1.8	3.9
Market value ($ mil.)	–	–	–	–	–	–
Employees						110

LOEFFLER ASSOCIATES, INC.

6115 PARK SOUTH DR # 350
CHARLOTTE, NC 282103269
Phone: 704 364-8969
Fax: –
Web: www.lkmideas.com

CEO: –
CFO: –
HR: –
FYE: December 31
Type: Private

Loeffler Ketchum Mountjoy (LKM) provides a lot of services for such a little shop. The independent agency offers advertising, direct marketing, design, media planning, and public relations services. LKM serves clients primarily in the travel and leisure; B2B; sporting goods; and home building and decorating sectors; its largest clients have included Cargill and Koch Industries. The agency's portfolio includes creative work in print and broadcasting, as well as its share of interactive work. It has conducted tourism marketing for the state of North Carolina for the past decade, and it has also worked with U.S. National Whitewater Center (a recreational park) to manage its marketing and media relations.

	Annual Growth	12/02	12/03	12/04	12/05	12/07
Sales ($mil.)	(0.3%)	–	–	3.6	3.9	3.6
Net income ($ mil.)	(37.8%)	–	–	0.3	(0.0)	0.0
Market value ($ mil.)	–	–	–	–	–	–
Employees		–	–	–	–	30

LOEWS CORP.

NYS: L

9 West 57th Street
New York, NY 10019-2714
Phone: 212 521-2000
Fax: –
Web: www.loews.com

CEO: James S Tisch
CFO: Jane J Wang
HR: Amber Allen
FYE: December 31
Type: Public

Loews is a diversified company, with businesses in the insurance, energy, hospitality and packaging industries. The multi-industry holding company's main interest is insurance through publicly traded subsidiary CNA Financial, which offers commercial property casualty coverage. It also owns hotels in the US and Canada through its Loews Hotels subsidiary. The company's Boardwalk Pipelines is engaged in interstate natural gas transmission pipeline systems. Loews owns 52.7% of Altium Packaging, which is a packaging solutions provider and manufacturer in North America. Loews is controlled and run by the Tisch family, including co-chairmen and cousins Andrew and Jonathan.

	Annual Growth	12/19	12/20	12/21	12/22	12/23
Assets ($mil.)	(0.9%)	82,243	80,236	81,626	75,494	79,197
Net income ($ mil.)	11.4%	932.0	(931.0)	1,578.0	1,012.0	1,434.0
Market value ($ mil.)	7.3%	11,662	10,002	12,832	12,959	15,461
Employees	(9.9%)	18,605	12,200	10,340	12,050	12,280

LOGANSPORT FINANCIAL CORP.

NBB: LOGN

723 East Broadway
Logansport, IN 46947
Phone: 574 722-3855
Fax: 574 722-3857
Web: www.logansportsavings.com

CEO: –
CFO: –
HR: –
FYE: December 31
Type: Public

Community banking is the main sport at Logansport. Logansport Financial is the holding company for Logansport Savings Bank, which serves customers in Cass County, Indiana. From a single office in Logansport, the bank offers individuals and businesses a variety of financial services, including such deposit products as checking, savings, and NOW accounts, as well as IRAs and certificates of deposit. Logansport Savings Bank uses funds from deposits to originate residential mortgages, which account for almost half of its loan portfolio. The bank, originally chartered in 1925, also offers home equity, home improvement, commercial real estate, business, and consumer loans.

	Annual Growth	12/07	12/13	12/14	12/21	12/22
Assets ($mil.)	3.3%	156.8	166.0	159.7	247.7	255.0
Net income ($ mil.)	10.0%	0.8	1.7	1.8	3.2	3.2
Market value ($ mil.)	6.3%	9.5	15.3	17.4	28.4	23.8
Employees	–	–	–	–	–	–

LOGIC DEVICES INC

1375 Geneva Drive
Sunnyvale, CA 94089
Phone: 408 542-5400
Fax: –
Web: www.logicdevices.com

CEO: Bill Volz
CFO: Kimiko Milheim
HR: –
FYE: September 30
Type: Public

LOGIC Devices doesn't produce philosophical machines. Rather, LOGIC specializes in high-end digital signal processor (DSP) chips used in applications including medical imaging, instrumentation, telecommunications, and military weapons systems. The company outsources production of its chips to Asian foundries, primarily Taiwan Semiconductor Manufacturing. LOGIC works with sales representatives and international distributors, and also sells directly to OEMs, including Lockheed Martin, QUALCOMM, Raytheon, Sony, Teradyne, and Texas Instruments.

	Annual Growth	09/07	09/08	09/09	09/10	09/11
Sales ($mil.)	(26.0%)	4.7	3.4	3.0	2.2	1.4
Net income ($ mil.)	–	(1.5)	(4.0)	(0.8)	(1.1)	(1.1)
Market value ($ mil.)	(32.7%)	16.5	8.0	7.2	5.6	3.4
Employees	(19.1%)	21	15	14	13	9

LOGICAL VENTURES, INC.

338 CLUBHOUSE RD
HUNT VALLEY, MD 210311344
Phone: 410 771-9507
Fax: –
Web: www.syssrc.com

CEO: –
CFO: –
HR: –
FYE: November 30
Type: Private

Logical Ventures is in business for a very good reason. The company, doing business as System Source and PCs in a Pinch, sells and rents computer systems and audiovisual equipment. It offers technical training and provides IT services, including website development, hosting, and network design. Logical Ventures serves large and mid-sized companies in Maryland. The company was established in 1981 as a Computerland store franchise. It is owned by its officers.

LOGICALIS, INC.

2600 W BIG BEAVER RD STE 150
TROY, MI 480843323
Phone: 212 596-7160
Fax: –
Web: us.logicalis.com

CEO: Vince Deluca
CFO: Sally Brandtneris
HR: –
FYE: February 28
Type: Private

Logicalis believes enterprise technology should operate in a straightforward fashion. The company provides a variety of IT services such as consulting, implementation, systems integration, staffing, network design, and training. Logicalis also offers managed services for tasks such as network security, IT infrastructure management and monitoring, and application management. Customers come from a variety of fields including manufacturing, financial services, and health care. In the US, Logicalis operates from more than 30 offices. It is a subsidiary of UK-based Logicalis Group. Both are owned by South Africa-based Datatec Limited.

LOGICQUEST TECHNOLOGY INC

NBB: LOGQ

5 Independence Way, Suite 300
Princeton, NJ 08540
Phone: 609 514-5136
Fax: –
Web: –

CEO: –
CFO: Cheng Y Siong
HR: –
FYE: December 31
Type: Public

Bluegate holds the keys to the gates of medical information. The company provides information technology (IT) services to the health care industry. It specializes in medical-grade network and managed services that meet HIPAA compliance regulations. It serves hospitals, medical practices, and other centralized health care providers. The company operates a leading Medical Grade Network dedicated to health care-related security and privacy concerns; Bluegate markets it as the only such network in the US. Memorial Hermann Health Net Providers, a subsidiary of the Memorial Hermann Healthcare System, is a client; Bluegate also provides services to the Texas-based Renaissance Healthcare Systems.

	Annual Growth	12/18	12/19	12/20	12/21	12/22
Sales ($mil.)	–	–	–	–	–	–
Net income ($ mil.)	–	–	(0.6)	(0.4)	(0.4)	(0.4)	(0.2)
Market value ($ mil.)	1.5%	0.2	0.3	0.2	0.7	0.2
Employees	–	–	–	–	–	–

LOGILITY, INC.

470 E PACES FERRY RD NE
ATLANTA, GA 303053301
Phone: 800 762-5207
Fax: –
Web: www.logility.com

CEO: –
CFO: Vincent C Klinges
HR: –
FYE: April 30
Type: Private

Logility brings logic and agility to the task of managing global supply chains. The company's Voyager Solutions software, available in cloud and on-premise deployments, helps small businesses and large corporations manage relationships with raw materials suppliers, manufacturers, distributors, retailers, and customers. Compatible with a variety of enterprise resource planning software tools, its products address specific supply chain needs, such as reducing inventory, lowering the cost of logistics, and adjusting sales and operations planning response to market changes, new products, or production constraints. Logility's subsidiary Demand Management offers supply chain software for small and midsized businesses. Logility is a subsidiary of American Software.

LOGISTICS PLUS, INC.

1406 PEACH ST
ERIE, PA 165011879
Phone: 814 461-7600
Fax: –
Web: www.logisticsplus.com

CEO: James Berlin
CFO: Frank Humes
HR: Alyssa Davis
FYE: December 31
Type: Private

Logistics Plus works to find the shortest and most cost-effective way to move things from point A to point B. The company provides global logistics services for industrial, energy, and manufacturing companies. Typically, these companies need to move raw materials, inventory, or finished goods by air, rail, truck, or ship. Logistics Plus, which began as a logistics manager for GE Transportation (now part of GE Infrastructure), has provided services for other GE divisions, as well as customers like US Steel and auto parts manufacturer LORD Corporation. It acquired the staff of Horizon Logistics in mid-2011. Founded in 1996 by CEO Jim Berlin, Logistics Plus operates internationally.

LOJACK CORPORATION

2400 N GLNVLLE DR STE 225
RICHARDSON, TX 75082
Phone: 781 302-4200
Fax: –
Web: www.lojack.com

CEO: –
CFO: –
HR: –
FYE: December 31
Type: Private

LoJack's signature product helps police recover stolen vehicles -- a chilling thought for those driving hot cars. When a car equipped with a LoJack transmitter is stolen, its signal is activated and tracked by police. The company rents tracking computers to law enforcement agencies, then markets transponders to dealers and operators in 28 states and the District of Columbia, and roughly 30 countries internationally. It also sells products for tracking people, personal electronics, cargo, data, and commercial equipment. LoJack provides installation and maintenance of its units, which are manufactured by third parties.

	Annual Growth	12/11	12/12	12/13	12/14	12/15
Sales ($mil.)	(3.0%)	–	–	–	133.6	129.6
Net income ($ mil.)	–	–	–	–	(18.0)	3.3
Market value ($ mil.)	–	–	–	–	–	–
Employees	–	–	–	–	–	490

LOMA LINDA UNIVERSITY

11060 ANDERSON ST BLDG MAGAN
LOMA LINDA, CA 923501736
Phone: 909 558-4540
Fax: –
Web: home.llu.edu

CEO: –
CFO: –
HR: Evelyn Benitez
FYE: June 30
Type: Private

Loma Linda University (LLU) is a Seventh-day Adventist institution that focuses on health sciences. The university offers more than 50 degree (bachelor's, master's, and doctorate) and certificate programs in the fields of allied health, behavioral health, dentistry, medicine, nursing, pharmacy, public health, and religion. It has an enrollment of approximately 5,000 students. LLU is an affiliate of the Loma Linda University Adventist Health Sciences Center, where physicians and other health-care professionals provide medical care at the Loma Linda University Medical Center campuses. The school was founded in 1905 and is one of 15 Seventh-day Adventist universities.

	Annual Growth	06/18	06/19	06/20	06/21	06/22
Sales ($mil.)	13.1%	–	268.4	284.6	350.5	388.6
Net income ($ mil.)	–	–	(27.9)	(85.8)	22.1	43.5
Market value ($ mil.)	–	–	–	–	–	–
Employees	–	–	–	–	–	7,000

LOMA LINDA UNIVERSITY MEDICAL CENTER

11234 ANDERSON ST
LOMA LINDA, CA 923542871
Phone: 909 558-4000
Fax: –
Web: www.lluh.org

CEO: Richard H Hart
CFO: Steven Mohr
HR: –
FYE: June 30
Type: Private

Loma Linda University Medical Center is widely respected as a healthcare leader, known for advances in many disciplines. These include pioneering work in organ transplants, proton treatment for cancers, cardiac care, physical rehabilitation, neurology, neurosurgery, and acute care. LLUMC is the largest and only Level I Trauma Center in the San Bernardino, Riverside, Inyo, and Mono counties. With a total of approximately 320 beds, its hospital provides expert care in nearly every specialty to hundreds of thousands of patients a year.

	Annual Growth	12/15	12/16*	06/20	06/21	06/22
Sales ($mil.)	(1.9%)	–	1,776.7	1,439.2	1,511.1	1,588.0
Net income ($ mil.)	–	–	128.8	71.1	145.1	(26.9)
Market value ($ mil.)	–	–	–	–	–	–
Employees	–	–	–	–	–	5,766

*Fiscal year change

LONDON FRUIT, INC.

9010 S CAGE BLVD
PHARR, TX 785779769
Phone: 956 781-7799
Fax: –
Web: www.londonfruit.com

CEO: –
CFO: –
HR: –
FYE: August 31
Type: Private

Located in the Rio Grande Valley of Texas, London Fruit ships tropical fruits, vegetables, and fresh and dried peppers from Mexico to the US. The company provides produce including mangos, papayas, limes, tomatillos, and cactus pears to retail and wholesale customers. London Fruit was founded in 1981 by president Barry London, who owns the majority of the company.

	Annual Growth	08/16	08/17	08/18	08/19	08/20
Sales ($mil.)	(14.9%)	–	47.1	43.3	3.5	29.0
Net income ($ mil.)	–	–	0.1	0.3	0.0	(0.1)
Market value ($ mil.)	–	–	–	–	–	–
Employees	–	–	–	–	–	50

LONG BEACH MEDICAL CENTER

2801 ATLANTIC AVE FL 2
LONG BEACH, CA 908061701
Phone: 562 933-2000
Fax: –
Web: www.memorialcare.org

CEO: Barry Arbuckle PHD
CFO: Patti Pilgrim
HR: Darcel Noble
FYE: June 30
Type: Private

Long Beach Medical Center (LBMC) is an old-timer in the Long Beach health care market. A subsidiary of Memorial Care, LBMC provides a full range of health services to residents of the Long Beach, California, area. Services include primary, emergency, diagnostic, surgical, therapeutic, and rehabilitative care. The hospital is home to centers for treatment of cancer, heart, stroke, and women's and children's health concerns. It also provides home and hospice care programs, as well as occupational health services. Through Outpatient Wound Healing Center, LBMC provides full-services wound care for adults and children in Los Angeles County and Orange County.

	Annual Growth	06/10	06/11	06/15	06/16	06/18
Sales ($mil.)	(7.4%)	–	1,083.1	624.1	618.8	633.6
Net income ($ mil.)	0.1%	–	63.5	93.9	88.8	63.8
Market value ($ mil.)	–	–	–	–	–	–
Employees	–	–	–	–	–	6,000

LONG ISLAND COMMUNITY HOSPITAL AT NYU LANGONE HEALTH

101 HOSPITAL RD
EAST PATCHOGUE, NY 117724870
Phone: 631 654-7100
Fax: –
Web: www.licommunityhospital.org

CEO: Marc Adler
CFO: Brenda Farrell
HR: Patricia White
FYE: December 31
Type: Private

Brookhaven Memorial Hospital Medical Center is an acute-care facility with more than 300 beds that serves patients primarily in Suffolk County on Long Island, New York. The not-for-profit community hospital's Emergency, Trauma and Chest Pain Pavilion is one of the largest emergency rooms on Long Island. Founded in 1956, Brookhaven Memorial also offers behavioral health services, including inpatient and outpatient mental health and alcohol treatment services. In addition to hospital services, the medical center operates two community health clinics and a specialty center that provides hemodialysis, women's imaging, and home health and hospice services.

	Annual Growth	12/15	12/16	12/17	12/19	12/21
Sales ($mil.)	(0.6%)	–	261.3	271.4	272.2	254.0
Net income ($ mil.)	–	–	(1.2)	(6.9)	4.8	(2.1)
Market value ($ mil.)	–	–	–	–	–	–
Employees	–	–	–	–	–	2,100

LONG ISLAND JEWISH MEDICAL CENTER

27005 76TH AVE
NEW HYDE PARK, NY 110401496
Phone: 516 465-2600
Fax: –
Web: www.lijed.com

CEO: Michael J Dowling
CFO: –
HR: Joseph Moscola
FYE: December 31
Type: Private

Long Island Jewish Medical Center serves the western edge of Long Island and the eastern edge of the greater metropolitan New York area. The medical center campus includes Long Island Jewish Hospital, a general acute care hospital; Cohen Children's Medical Center of New York Hospital, which provides a full range of pediatric care services; and The Zucker Hillside Hospital, a psychiatric hospital for patients of all ages. The medical center's staff includes 1,200 physicians. Long Island Jewish Medical Center is the primary clinical and medical training facility of Northwell Health.

	Annual Growth	12/16	12/17	12/18	12/21	12/22
Sales ($mil.)	11.6%	–	2,222.7	2,448.9	2,779.1	3,849.0
Net income ($ mil.)	(11.1%)	–	154.3	56.1	175.2	85.7
Market value ($ mil.)	–	–	–	–	–	–
Employees	–	–	–	–	–	1,214

LONG ISLAND POWER AUTHORITY

333 EARLE OVINGTON BLVD STE 403
UNIONDALE, NY 115533606
Phone: 516 222-7700
Fax: –
Web: www.lipower.org

CEO: Matthew Cohen
CFO: Herbert L Hogue
HR: –
FYE: December 31
Type: Private

The long and short of it is that Long Island Power Authority (LIPA) owns the electric transmission and distribution system on Long Island that delivers power to more than 1.1 million retail customers. The company's network, which is managed and operated by the National Grid USA consists of nearly 14,000 miles of overhead and underground lines. LIPA offers energy conservation products and services, as well as incentive programs to encourage customers to purchase energy from "green" (environmentally friendly) power generation sources. LIPA is a municipally owned, not-for-profit utility company.

	Annual Growth	12/15	12/16	12/18	12/19	12/20
Sales ($mil.)	3.5%	–	3,399.1	3,576.3	3,516.4	3,900.7
Net income ($ mil.)	–	–	(26.4)	22.7	24.0	18.8
Market value ($ mil.)	–	–	–	–	–	–
Employees	–	–	–	–	–	100

LONG ISLAND UNIVERSITY WESTCHESTER & ROCKLAND ALUMNI ASSOCIATION LTD.

700 NORTHERN BLVD
GREENVALE, NY 115481319
Phone: 516 299-1926
Fax: -
Web: www.liu.edu

CEO: -
CFO: Robert Altholz
HR: -
FYE: December 31
Type: Private

Long Island University (LIU) helps students see a long future in professional fields including medicine and business. LIU has an enrollment of more than 24,000 students at multiple locations in New York State. The university employs more than 600 full-time faculty members and has a 12:1 student-to-teacher ratio. LIU offers 575 degree programs and certificates in fields including pharmacy, nursing, health sciences, education, liberal arts, sciences, business, and information studies. The school traces its roots to 1886 when the Brooklyn College of Pharmacy was founded.

	Annual Growth	08/10	08/11	08/14	08/15*	12/19
Sales ($mil.)	(69.0%)	-	468.6	501.7	396.8	0.0
Net income ($ mil.)	-	-	2.5	41.4	33.7	-
Market value ($ mil.)	-	-	-	-	-	5,581
Employees	-	-	-	-	-	-

*Fiscal year change

LONG WAVE INC.

1111 N LEE AVE STE 334
OKLAHOMA CITY, OK 731032620
Phone: 405 235-2217
Fax: -
Web: www.longwaveinc.com

CEO: -
CFO: -
HR: -
FYE: December 31
Type: Private

The long wave that Long Wave has been riding is wireless communications. The government contractor provides communications engineering, antenna and tower maintenance, IT and help desk support services, training and simulation, and program management services to a number of agencies. It specializes in military communications, particularly radio-frequency (RF) and high-frequency (HF) global communications systems. Long Wave's government customers include the US Navy and US Air Force. In addition, its commercial customers include Raytheon, Rockwell Collins, and EDS. Founded by president Phil Miller in 1995, Long Wave has program operations in 19 US states.

	Annual Growth	12/06	12/07	12/08	12/09	12/10
Sales ($mil.)	(5.5%)	-	-	26.2	17.9	23.4
Net income ($ mil.)	20.8%	-	-	0.6	0.7	0.9
Market value ($ mil.)	-	-	-	-	-	-
Employees	-	-	-	-	-	95

LOOP LLC

137 NORTHPARK BLVD
COVINGTON, LA 704335071
Phone: 985 276-6100
Fax: -
Web: www.loopllc.com

CEO: -
CFO: -
HR: -
FYE: December 31
Type: Private

LOOP (Louisiana Offshore Oil Port) offloads crude oil from tankers, stores it, and routes it to pipelines and refineries along the Gulf Coast and the Midwest. It is also the storage and terminalling facility for the MARS pipeline system and its supply of offshore Gulf of Mexico crude oil. Oil is stored in eight underground caverns leached out of a naturally occurring salt dome. These caverns are capable of storing about 50 million barrels of crude oil. The company is owned by Marathon Ashland Pipe Line, Murphy Oil, and Shell Oil. In addition to other services LOOP has an above-ground tank farm made up of six 600,000 barrel tanks.

	Annual Growth	12/05	12/06	12/08	12/09	12/16
Sales ($mil.)	1.7%	-	235.8	265.3	243.6	279.9
Net income ($ mil.)	1.9%	-	104.3	79.2	87.3	125.9
Market value ($ mil.)	-	-	-	-	-	-
Employees	-	-	-	-	-	128

LOOS & CO., INC.

16B MASHAMOQUET RD
POMFRET, CT 06258
Phone: 860 928-7981
Fax: -
Web: www.loosco.com

CEO: William Loos
CFO: -
HR: Lynn Bouthillier
FYE: October 31
Type: Private

Loose wires can be problems in industrial applications; Loos wires, however, offer solutions to those critical safety and quality issues. Loos & Co. manufactures stainless steel wire rope, stainless steel cable, cable assemblies, plastic coated steel cable and related products. Customers draw from aerospace, agricultural, consumer product, marine, natural resource, medical, fitness and public utility industries. Moreover, its products meet a roster of military, OEM, and international specifications from Bombardier Aerospace and General Dynamics to Boeing. A network of distributors pushes the lineup. The privately held company was founded in 1958.

LOPITO, ILEANA & HOWIE INC.

13 CALLE 1 EXT ALTS DE SAN PATRICIO
GUAYNABO, PR 009683128
Phone: 787 783-1160
Fax: -
Web: www.lih.com

CEO: -
CFO: -
HR: -
FYE: December 31
Type: Private

This ad agency is more than a little territorial. Lopito, Ileana & Howie (LIH) provides the full range of advertising services (including branding, sales promotion, event marketing, media buying, and public relations) in Puerto Rico. LIH mostly serves clients in the retail, fast-food, packaged goods, and alcoholic beverages sectors. The agency's creative portfolio has included campaigns for The Hershey Company, McDonald's, and UBS Financial Services, in the Caribbean, Latin America, and the US. Founded in 1972, LIH owns Plug, a public relations unit, and Kairos, which provides media buying.

	Annual Growth	12/14	12/15	12/16	12/17	12/21
Sales ($mil.)	11.0%	-	5.9	6.3	7.3	11.1
Net income ($ mil.)	48.0%	-	0.1	0.0	0.2	1.3
Market value ($ mil.)	-	-	-	-	-	-
Employees	-	-	-	-	-	80

LORAL SPACE & COMMUNICATIONS INC.

600 5TH AVE FL 16
NEW YORK, NY 100202324
Phone: 212 697-1105
Fax: -
Web: www.loral.com

CEO: -
CFO: -
HR: -
FYE: December 31
Type: Private

Loral Space & Communications is a holding company operates through majority stakes in two satellite companies: Canada's Telesat and XTAR, a joint venture with Spain's Hisdesat. Telesat leases satellite transponder capacity to cable and satellite broadcasters as well as voice and data networks, while XTAR provides satellite services to the US and Spanish governments. Telesat has more than 15satellites in-orbit, while XTAR has two satellites in-orbit. Loral owns more than 60% of Telesat and has over 55% stake in XTAR. Its customers from Canada accounts for nearly 45 of its sales. The company is headquartered in New York and has a presence in the US, Canada, Spain, and other allied countries.

LOS ANGELES DEPARTMENT OF WATER AND POWER

111 N HOPE ST
LOS ANGELES, CA 900122607
Phone: 213 367-1320
Fax: –
Web: www.ladwp.com

CEO: –
CFO: Ann M Santilli
HR: Reza Eskandari
FYE: June 30
Type: Private

The Los Angeles Department of Water and Power (LADWP) is the nation's largest municipal utility, with about 8,020 megawatt (MW) electric capacity and serving an average of 435 million gallons of water per day to the 4 million residents of the City of Los Angeles, its businesses and visitors. As a revenue-producing proprietary department, the LADWP transfers a portion of its annual estimated electric revenues to the City of Los Angeles general fund.

	Annual Growth	06/08	06/09	06/10	06/11	06/17
Sales ($mil.)	4.7%	–	–	812.4	3,126.0	1,118.5
Net income ($ mil.)	11.1%	–	–	67.3	57.6	140.5
Market value ($ mil.)	–	–	–	–	–	–
Employees	–	–	–	–	–	9,500

LOS ANGELES PHILHARMONIC ASSOCIATION

151 S GRAND AVE
LOS ANGELES, CA 900123034
Phone: 213 972-7300
Fax: –
Web: www.laphil.com

CEO: Chad Smith
CFO: Glenn Briffa
HR: –
FYE: September 30
Type: Private

The Los Angeles Philharmonic Association promotes its orchestra, which is one of Southern California's leading performing arts institutions. The orchestra, often known simply as the LA Phil, performs orchestral and chamber music, jazz, world music, and holiday concerts at the Walt Disney Concert Hall (in winter) and the Hollywood Bowl (in summer). The orchestra that would become the Los Angeles Philharmonic was originally founded and financed back in 1919 by copper baron and music enthusiast William Andrews Clark, Jr. The Association was officially formed in 1976 but traces its roots to the beginning of the orchestra.

	Annual Growth	09/13	09/14	09/19	09/21	09/22
Sales ($mil.)	1.0%	–	145.5	187.2	149.0	158.2
Net income ($ mil.)	–	–	27.7	20.9	43.7	(21.8)
Market value ($ mil.)	–	–	–	–	–	–
Employees	–	–	–	–	–	2,000

LOUD TECHNOLOGIES INC   NBB: LTEC

16220 Wood-Red Road, N.E.
Woodinville, WA 98072
Phone: 425 487-4333
Fax: 425 487--4337
Web: www.loudtechinc.com

CEO: Alex Nelson
CFO: –
HR: Lisa Wesolowski
FYE: December 31
Type: Public

LOUD Technologies helps musicians bring their music to the masses. Best known for its multi-channel mixing consoles, which allow sound engineers to combine some 100 sound channels, the firm also makes loudspeakers, commercial audio systems, amplifiers, audio and music software, guitars, and orchestral string instruments. Brands include Alvarez, Ampeg, Crate, Mackie, Martin Audio, and TAPCO, among others. It also owns loudspeaker maker Eastern Acoustic Works (EAW). LOUD Technologies' products are sold through retail outlets and a network of installed sound contractors in the US, as well as through distributors worldwide. LOUD Technologies is owned by an affiliate, Sun Mackie, of private equity firm Sun Capital.

	Annual Growth	12/03	12/04	12/05	12/06	12/07
Sales ($mil.)	12.3%	130.8	123.3	204.3	215.0	208.3
Net income ($ mil.)	–	(21.8)	(2.3)	3.8	0.6	(12.6)
Market value ($ mil.)	35.5%	9.3	9.2	73.9	69.5	31.4
Employees	3.3%	468	408	704	658	533

LOUISIANA TECH UNIVERSITY

1100 HULL ST
RUSTON, LA 712705551
Phone: 318 257-3267
Fax: –
Web: www.latech.edu

CEO: –
CFO: –
HR: Alicia K Foster
FYE: June 30
Type: Private

Louisiana Tech University, founded in 1894, has an annual enrollment of approximately 11,000 students. The public research university offers bachelor's, master's, and doctoral degrees through more than 80 undergraduate and more than 40 graduate academic programs at colleges of applied and natural sciences, business, education, engineering and science, and liberal arts. It also confers associate degrees and post-bachelor's certificates. The university's research centers focus on education and government, technology and commercialization, and economic development and community support. Louisiana Tech's student-athletes compete in more than 15 varsity sports.

	Annual Growth	06/18	06/19	06/20	06/21	06/22
Sales ($mil.)	0.8%	–	120.2	116.1	115.5	122.9
Net income ($ mil.)	(22.1%)	–	16.0	14.6	34.9	7.6
Market value ($ mil.)	–	–	–	–	–	–
Employees	–	–	–	–	–	1,230

LOUISIANA-PACIFIC CORP   NYS: LPX

1610 West End Avenue, Suite 200
Nashville, TN 37203
Phone: 615 986-5600
Fax: –
Web: www.lpcorp.com

CEO: W B Southern
CFO: Alan J Haughie
HR: Tim Hartnett
FYE: December 31
Type: Public

Louisiana-Pacific (LP) is a leading provider of high-performance building solutions that makes specialized wood products such as oriented strand board (a lower-cost version of plywood), siding, and laminated lumber and related products. Its offerings are used in new home construction, repair and remodeling, and outdoor structures markets. The company sells its products to a variety of specialized and broad-line wholesale distributors, and dealers, focused primarily on the supply of products for use by professional builders and contractors. It has production facilities throughout North and South America, but generates most of its revenue in the US.

	Annual Growth	12/19	12/20	12/21	12/22	12/23
Sales ($mil.)	2.8%	2,310.0	2,788.0	4,553.0	3,854.0	2,581.0
Net income ($ mil.)	–	(5.0)	499.0	1,377.0	1,086.0	178.0
Market value ($ mil.)	24.3%	2,140.9	2,682.0	5,653.4	4,271.6	5,110.8
Employees	(3.9%)	4,800	4,500	4,800	4,300	4,100

LOUISVILLE-JEFFERSON COUNTY METRO GOVERNMENT

527 W JEFFERSON ST STE 400
LOUISVILLE, KY 402022814
Phone: 502 574-2003
Fax: –
Web: www.louisville-police.org

CEO: –
CFO: Daniel Frockt
HR: Ernestine Boothhenry
FYE: June 30
Type: Private

Louisville is so much more than bourbon, baseball bats, and horse races. The largest city in Kentucky, Louisville counts about 600,000 people in the urban area, which has the same parameters as Jefferson County. Louisville is home to liquor company Brown-Forman; Hillerich & Bradsby, maker of Louisville Slugger baseball bats; and Churchill Downs, where the Kentucky Derby is held. In addition, Louisville has a few Fortune 500 companies in the city - fast food operator YUM! Brands and health care companies Humana and Kindred.

	Annual Growth	06/18	06/19	06/20	06/21	06/22
Sales ($mil.)	7.9%	–	873.6	860.2	1,037.2	1,098.8
Net income ($ mil.)	–	–	(38.4)	26.5	60.1	185.6
Market value ($ mil.)	–	–	–	–	–	–
Employees	–	–	–	–	–	6,500

LOW TEMP INDUSTRIES, INC.

1947 BILL CASEY PKWY
JONESBORO, GA 302366041
Phone: 888 584-2722
Fax: –
Web: www.lowtempind.com

CEO: William E Casey
CFO: Michael Moody
HR: –
FYE: October 31
Type: Private

Cooks kick it up a notch on Low Temp Industries' (LTI) commercial chef's counters and dish tables. Constructed of stainless steel, the tables and counters outfit the kitchens of restaurants, hospitals, schools, and cafeterias. The chef's counter can be custom built for the customer to include a variety of food warmers, shelves, self-contained sandwich units, cutting boards, and a sink. LTI also manufactures custom serving counters for dining areas and automatic dish conveyors with washing systems. LTI was established in 1947 as Low Temp Manufacturing by William B. Casey (Bill), his sister Bertha Casey Hammonds, and his brother-in-law Ed Rawls.

	Annual Growth	10/02	10/03	10/04	10/06	10/07
Sales ($mil.)	4.7%	–	19.6	20.3	24.4	23.5
Net income ($ mil.)	–	–	–	–	–	–
Market value ($ mil.)	–	–	–	–	–	–
Employees	–	–	–	–	–	150

LOWE'S COMPANIES INC

1000 Lowes Blvd.
Mooresville, NC 28117
Phone: 704 758-1000
Fax: –
Web: www.lowes.com

NYS: LOW
CEO: Marvin R Ellison
CFO: Brandon J Sink
HR: –
FYE: February 2
Type: Public

Lowe's Companies is a Fortune 50 company and the world's second largest home improvement retailer. With over two million additional items available through the company's online selling channels, its stores offer approximately 40,000 products for repair and improvement projects (such as lumber, paint, plumbing and electrical supplies, and tools), gardening and outdoor living, and home furnishing and decorating. It targets homeowners, renters, and professional customers with national brand-name merchandise. The company only operates in North America, with the vast majority of sales generated in the US.

	Annual Growth	01/20	01/21	01/22*	02/23	02/24
Sales ($mil.)	4.6%	72,148	89,597	96,250	97,059	86,377
Net income ($ mil.)	15.9%	4,281.0	5,835.0	8,442.0	6,437.0	7,726.0
Market value ($ mil.)	17.2%	66,722	95,772	134,884	123,967	125,987
Employees	(2.9%)	320,000	340,000	340,000	307,000	284,000

*Fiscal year change

LOWELL, CITY OF (INC)

375 MERRIMACK ST RM 27
LOWELL, MA 018525939
Phone: 978 970-4200
Fax: –
Web: www.lowellma.gov

CEO: –
CFO: Thomas Moses
HR: –
FYE: June 30
Type: Private

The City of Lowell is the fourth-largest city in Massachusetts, with a population of more than 100,000. The mayor and seven city council members (elected for two-year terms) govern the city by setting policies, as well as appointing heads of departments, boards, and commissions. The City of Lowell operates through nearly 30 departments and programs, including emergency management, recycling, and veterans' services. Located about 30 miles northwest of Boston, Lowell was established in 1826 as a planned industrial city. CVS and the Market Basket grocery store chain were both founded in Lowell.

LOWENSTEIN SANDLER LLP

1 LOWENSTEIN DR
ROSELAND, NJ 070681740
Phone: 973 597-2500
Fax: –
Web: www.lowenstein.com

CEO: Gary M Wingens
CFO: William B Farrell
HR: Deirdre Walsh
FYE: June 30
Type: Private

Lowenstein Sandler, a New Jersey law firm of around 350 attorneys, offers a full range of legal services. Its core practice areas include corporate, employment and employee benefits, life sciences, litigation, real estate, and trusts. Lowenstein Sandler is proud to have joined over 115 other law firms in a commitment to Mansfield 4.0/The Mansfield Rule, which aims to increase the representation of historically underrepresented lawyers among law firm leadership.

LOWER COLORADO RIVER AUTHORITY

3700 LAKE AUSTIN BLVD
AUSTIN, TX 787033504
Phone: 512 473-3200
Fax: –
Web: www.lcra.org

CEO: –
CFO: Richard Williams
HR: Michael Bailey
FYE: December 31
Type: Private

The Lower Colorado River Authority serves customers and communities throughout Texas by managing the lower Colorado River; generating and transmitting electric power; providing a clean, reliable water supply; and offering outdoor adventures at more than 40 parks along the Colorado River from the Texas Hill Country to the Gulf Coast. LCRA and its employees are committed to fulfilling its mission to enhance the quality of life of the Texans it serves through water stewardship, energy and community service. LCRA was created by the Texas Legislature in 1934 and receives no state appropriations.

	Annual Growth	06/09	06/10	06/11	06/12*	12/21
Sales ($mil.)	(52.4%)	–	–	1,185.8	1,261.7	0.7
Net income ($ mil.)	(44.5%)	–	–	48.9	101.4	0.1
Market value ($ mil.)	–	–	–	–	–	–
Employees	–	–	–	–	–	1,800

*Fiscal year change

LOWRY HOLDING COMPANY, INC.

9420 MALTBY RD
BRIGHTON, MI 481168801
Phone: 810 229-7200
Fax: –
Web: www.lowrysolutions.com

CEO: –
CFO: –
HR: –
FYE: December 31
Type: Private

Lowry Holding, doing business as Lowry Solutions, is one of the leading resellers of hardware, software, and supplies in the barcode industry. The company provides label and tag solutions, software solutions, and professional services. The company's premier partners are Honeywell, Getac, Paragon, Teklynx, Zebra, Impinj, and Teklynx. Its customers come from a range of industries, including manufacturing, transportation and logistics, warehouse and distribution, health care, government, automotive, small business, and retail. Lowry has a client base of more than 10,000 customers and was founded in 1974 as a data peripheral supplier.

LOYOLA MARYMOUNT UNIVERSITY

1 LMU DR STE 100
LOS ANGELES, CA 90045
Phone: 310 338-2700
Fax: –
Web: www.lmu.edu

CEO: Thomas O Fleming
CFO: Aimee Uen
HR: Gerlie Salazar
FYE: May 31
Type: Private

Loyola Marymount University (LMU) in Los Angeles is a Jesuit (Catholic) institution with an enrollment of more than 9,500 students. It offers more than 115 graduate and undergraduate programs through four colleges: Bellarmine College of Liberal Arts, College of Business Administration, College of Communication and Fine Arts, and Seaver College of Science and Engineering. There is also the School of Education and School of Film and Television. Other programs include the Graduate Division, Continuing Education Program, and Loyola Law School. LMU has an 11:1 student-to-faculty ratio. The university was formed in 1973 by the merger of Loyola College (founded in 1911) and Marymount Junior College.

	Annual Growth	05/18	05/19	05/20	05/21	05/22
Sales ($mil.)	4.6%	–	415.6	411.5	375.4	475.6
Net income ($ mil.)	54.4%	–	20.1	8.7	174.9	73.9
Market value ($ mil.)	–	–	–	–	–	–
Employees	–	–	–	–	–	1,449

LOYOLA UNIVERSITY MARYLAND, INC.

5000 YORK RD STE 200
BALTIMORE, MD 212124437
Phone: 410 617-2000
Fax: –
Web: www.loyola.edu

CEO: –
CFO: –
HR: –
FYE: May 31
Type: Private

Loyola University in Maryland is a Jesuit Catholic university that offers studies in liberal arts and sciences. In addition to its undergraduate programs, Loyola has graduate degree programs in education, speech pathology, finance, psychology, modern studies, pastoral counseling, and engineering science. The university annually enrolls about 3,500 undergraduate and some 2,600 graduate students. The school has more than 300 full-time faculty and a student-teacher ratio of about 12:1. Loyola was founded in 1852 by Father John Early and eight other Jesuits.

	Annual Growth	05/12	05/13	05/14	05/21	05/22
Sales ($mil.)	2.2%	–	263.0	285.6	289.3	319.2
Net income ($ mil.)	(4.3%)	–	19.5	27.7	19.1	13.2
Market value ($ mil.)	–	–	–	–	–	–
Employees	–	–	–	–	–	2,066

LOYOLA UNIVERSITY OF CHICAGO INC

1032 W SHERIDAN RD
CHICAGO, IL 606601537
Phone: 773 274-3000
Fax: –
Web: www.luc.edu

CEO: –
CFO: –
HR: Gary Soltys
FYE: June 30
Type: Private

Loyola University Chicago (LUC) is a private, coeducational, not-for-profit institution of higher education and research. In addition to its three Chicago-area campuses, the university also maintains campus in Italy. LUC provides educational services to about 17,000 students primarily in undergraduate degree programs as well as graduate and professional degree programs. The university performs research, training, and other services under grants and contracts with government agencies and other sponsoring organizations. LCU was founded in 1870 by Arnold Damen, S.J., as St. Ignatius College.

	Annual Growth	06/16	06/17	06/18	06/19	06/20
Sales ($mil.)	1.4%	–	–	594.8	614.2	611.4
Net income ($ mil.)	(53.8%)	–	–	109.5	78.7	23.4
Market value ($ mil.)	–	–	–	–	–	–
Employees	–	–	–	–	–	10,500

LOYOLA UNIVERSITY, NEW ORLEANS

6363 SAINT CHARLES AVE
NEW ORLEANS, LA 701186143
Phone: 504 865-2011
Fax: –
Web: www.loyno.edu

CEO: –
CFO: –
HR: –
FYE: July 31
Type: Private

Loyola University New Orleans provides law, nursing, and fine arts education programs in the Big Easy. The university is part of US network of Jesuit universities and enrolls nearly 4,550 students. The liberal arts university offers some 110 undergraduate and about 35 graduate and professional degree programs through five colleges: Business, Arts and Sciences, Nursing & Health, Law, Music and Media, as well as online studies. Loyola University New Orleans has a student-to-teacher ratio of 12:1. It is one of a network of 28 Jesuit colleges and universities across the US.

	Annual Growth	07/12	07/13	07/14	07/20	07/22
Sales ($mil.)	3.6%	–	154.3	135.0	180.7	211.9
Net income ($ mil.)	(14.7%)	–	26.3	3.2	(0.2)	6.3
Market value ($ mil.)	–	–	–	–	–	–
Employees	–	–	–	–	–	1,000

LOZIER CORPORATION

6336 JOHN J PERSHING DR
OMAHA, NE 681101122
Phone: 402 457-8000
Fax: –
Web: www.lozier.com

CEO: Andy Lozier
CFO: Matt Simon
HR: Gloria Jensen
FYE: December 31
Type: Private

Lozier is a leader in the manufacturing store fixtures industry. The company makes retail store fixtures, including gondolas, display shelving and freestanding displays, for pharmacies, groceries, food service, convenience stores, and hardware. It has manufacturing facilities and a distribution center in Alabama, Indiana, Missouri, Nebraska, and Pennsylvania. Lozier distributes fixtures across the US, as well as internationally. The company maintains a sales and service network for its international retailers. In addition to selling fixtures, Lozier also offers installation services. To expedite parcel pickup and simplify the order fulfillment process, the company offers Buy Online Pick Up In Store (BOPIS) products and solutions.

	Annual Growth	12/18	12/19	12/20	12/21	12/22
Sales ($mil.)	16.5%	–	–	451.4	573.6	613.0
Net income ($ mil.)	–	–	–	–	–	–
Market value ($ mil.)	–	–	–	–	–	–
Employees	–	–	–	–	–	2,210

LPL FINANCIAL HOLDINGS INC.

NMS: LPLA

4707 Executive Drive
San Diego, CA 92121
Phone: 800 877-7210
Fax: –
Web: www.lpl.com

CEO: Dan H Arnold
CFO: Matthew J Audette
HR: –
FYE: December 31
Type: Public

LPL Financial is a leader in the retail financial advice market and the nation's largest independent broker-dealer. It provides technology, research, clearing and compliance services and practice management to some 20,000 independent financial advisors, financial institutions (such as credit unions) across the country. LPL also supports some 2,800 financial advisors affiliated with insurance companies that use LPL's clearing and advisory platforms. LPL was formed in 1989 by the merger of Linsco and Private Ledger.

	Annual Growth	12/19	12/20	12/21	12/22	12/23
Sales ($mil.)	15.6%	5,624.9	5,871.6	7,720.8	8,600.8	10,053
Net income ($ mil.)	17.5%	559.9	472.6	459.9	845.7	1,066.3
Market value ($ mil.)	25.3%	6,887.0	7,780.7	11,952	16,138	16,993
Employees	17.9%	4,343	4,756	5,900	6,900	8,400

LRI HOLDINGS, INC.

3011 ARMORY DR STE 300
NASHVILLE, TN 372043721
Phone: 303 664-4000
Fax: –
Web: www.logansroadhouse.com

CEO: Hazem Ouf
CFO: Edmund J Schwartz
HR: –
FYE: August 02
Type: Private

LRI Holdings earns a lot of peanuts even though it gives them away for free. The company operates Logan's Roadhouse, a chain of casual restaurants that serve generous-sized plates of grilled steaks, chicken, barbecued ribs, and hamburgers. The chain prides itself on its affordable prices (the average bill is less than $15) while also offering free, all-you-can-eat buckets of shelled peanuts and rolls. LRI Holdings has 185 company-owned locations of Logan's Roadhouse across 20 states and 26 franchises in four states. LRI Holdings was formed in 2006 by a private investor group. The company agreed to be acquired by private equity firm Kelso & Co. in 2010.

LSB INDUSTRIES, INC.

NYS: LXU

3503 N.W. 63rd Street, Suite 500
Oklahoma City, OK 73116
Phone: 405 235-4546
Fax: –
Web: www.lsbindustries.com

CEO: Mark T Behrman
CFO: Cheryl A Maguire
HR: Crystal Schroeder
FYE: December 31
Type: Public

LSB Industries makes and markets a wide variety of chemicals (including nitric acid). Its chemical business makes grade ammonium nitrate fertilizers, urea ammonia nitrate, and nitric acids for agricultural, mining, and industrial markets. LSB Industries products are sold through distributors and directly to end customers throughout the US and parts of Mexico and Canada. It produces ammonia at its El Dorado, Cherokee and Pryor Facilities. The products it manufactures at its facilities are primarily derived from natural gas (a raw material feedstock). The company was formed in 1968.

	Annual Growth	12/19	12/20	12/21	12/22	12/23
Sales ($mil.)	12.9%	365.1	351.3	556.2	901.7	593.7
Net income ($ mil.)	–	(63.4)	(61.9)	43.5	230.3	27.9
Market value ($ mil.)	22.0%	307.1	247.9	807.9	972.5	680.7
Employees	(0.3%)	593	573	545	571	586

LRR ENERGY, L.P.

1111 BAGBY ST STE 4600
HOUSTON, TX 770022559
Phone: 713 292-9510
Fax: –
Web: www.lrrenergy.com

CEO: –
CFO: –
HR: –
FYE: December 31
Type: Private

What do Texas, Oklahoma, and New Mexico have in common? Oil, gas, and LRR Energy. An oil and natural gas producer, LRR Energy owns assets in the Permian Basin in West Texas and southern New Mexico, the Mid-Continent region in Oklahoma and East Texas, and along the Gulf Coast in Texas. The company's properties have proved reserves of more than 30 million barrels of oil equivalent. It operates more than 850 oil or gas-producing wells. Formed in April 2011 from assets held by investment fund Lime Rock Resources, LRR Energy and went public in November 2011.

LSI INDUSTRIES INC.

NMS: LYTS

10000 Alliance Road
Cincinnati, OH 45242
Phone: 513 793-3200
Fax: –
Web: www.lsicorp.com

CEO: James A Clark
CFO: James E Galeese
HR: Cecelia Winters
FYE: June 30
Type: Public

LSI Industries is a leading producer of non-residential lighting and retail display solutions. The company's strength in indoor and outdoor lighting applications creates opportunities for LSI to introduce additional solutions to its valued customers. Retail display solutions consist of graphics solutions, digital signage, and technically advanced food display equipment for strategic vertical markets. LSI's team of internal specialists also provide comprehensive project management services in support of large-scale product rollouts. It products are sold primarily throughout US, but also in Canada, Mexico, Australia, and Latin America (outside of US generates some 5% of total revenue). LSI was founded in 1976.

	Annual Growth	06/19	06/20	06/21	06/22	06/23
Sales ($mil.)	10.9%	328.9	305.6	315.6	455.1	497.0
Net income ($ mil.)	–	(16.3)	9.6	5.9	15.0	25.8
Market value ($ mil.)	36.2%	103.8	184.1	227.9	175.5	357.3
Employees	6.9%	1,246	1,101	1,335	1,529	1,627

LS GALLEGOS & ASSOCIATES INC

116 INVERNESS DR E STE 207
ENGLEWOOD, CO 801125112
Phone: 303 790-8474
Fax: –
Web: www.lsgallegos.com

CEO: –
CFO: –
HR: Michele Barnett
FYE: December 31
Type: Private

Founded in 1988, LS Gallegos (LSG) provides program and project management consulting and support to federal, state, and local government entities; it has special expertise in the public transportation industry. The company's LSG Technologies division designs and installs information technology systems for public and private clients. Customers include the Port Authority of New York and New Jersey, the US Department of Energy, CH2M HILL, and various state and local transportation agencies.

LSREF4 LIGHTHOUSE CORPORATE ACQUISITIONS, LLC

11459 CRONHILL DR
OWINGS MILLS, MD 211176280
Phone: 585 546-4900
Fax: –
Web: –

CEO: Edward Pettinella
CFO: David Gardner
HR: –
FYE: December 31
Type: Private

Home Properties invests in, develops, renovates, and operates multifamily residential properties, primarily in growth markets in the Northeast and Mid-Atlantic. The self-administered real estate investment trust (REIT) owns and manages a portfolio of more than 120 apartment communities with around 42,000 individual units. It invests in communities for which it can provide a little TLC (such as improved landscaping, interior upgrades, and amenities such as swimming pools) to boost property values post-rehabilitation. The REIT also develops new properties, usually on raw land adjacent to existing properties in its portfolio. Lone Star Funds acquired the REIT in late 2015, taking it private.

	Annual Growth	12/09	12/10	12/11	12/12	12/13
Sales ($mil.)	(7.8%)	–	6.1	5.9	6.1	4.7
Net income ($ mil.)	(35.5%)	–	0.2	0.0	0.0	0.0
Market value ($ mil.)	–	–	–	–	–	–
Employees						50

LTC PROPERTIES, INC.
NYS: LTC

2829 Townsgate Road, Suite 350
Westlake Village, CA 91361
Phone: 805 981-8655
Fax: –
Web: www.ltcreit.com

CEO: Wendy L Simpson
CFO: Pamela J Shelley-Kessler
HR: –
FYE: December 31
Type: Public

Specializing in TLC, LTC Properties sees long-term care real estate as a healthy investment. The self-administered real estate investment trust (REIT) mostly invests in health care and long-term care facilities. Its portfolio includes about 200 assisted living, skilled-nursing and other healthcare properties with more than 15,000 living units across about 30 states, with its largest markets being in Texas, Florida, Colorado, and Arizona. Its top tenant operators include Brookdale Senior Living, Carespring, Senior Care Centers, and Senior Lifestyle Corporation, which in aggregate contribute around 45% to its total rental income. The REIT also invests in mortgage loans tied to long-term care properties.

	Annual Growth	12/19	12/20	12/21	12/22	12/23
Sales ($mil.)	1.6%	185.3	159.3	155.3	175.2	197.2
Net income ($ mil.)	2.7%	80.5	95.3	55.9	100.0	89.7
Market value ($ mil.)	(8.0%)	1,926.1	1,674.0	1,468.8	1,528.6	1,381.9
Employees	1.1%	22	24	25	24	23

LUB LIQUIDATING TRUST.

Two Liberty Square,, 9th Floor
Boston, MA 02109
Phone: 617 570-4600
Fax: –
Web: www.lubysinc.com

CEO: –
CFO: –
HR: –
FYE: December 31
Type: Public

Luby's, Inc. operates as a multi-branded company in the restaurant industry and the contract food services industry. The company's core brands include Luby's Cafeteria, Fuddruckers - World's Greatest Hamburgers and Luby's Culinary Contract Services. In addition, the company owns several smaller chains and provides contract foodservices for organizations that offer on-site food service, such as healthcare facilities, colleges and universities, sports stadiums, businesses and institutions, as well as sales through retail grocery outlets.

LUCK STONE CORPORATION

515 STONE MILL DR
MANAKIN SABOT, VA 231033261
Phone: 804 784-6300
Fax: –
Web: www.luckstone.com

CEO: Charles S Luck IV
CFO: Roy B Goodman
HR: Britten Parker
FYE: October 31
Type: Private

Rock on! Construction aggregates supplier Luck Stone Corporation produces a wide range of crushed stone, concrete, asphalt, architectural stone, pavers, and sand and gravel products for customers throughout the mid-Atlantic US. The family-owned company has more than 15 crushed stone plants in Virginia and North Carolina, in addition to more than half a dozen retail architectural stone centers in those states and Maryland. It provides about 75 different product lines to the construction, homebuilding, remodeling, and agricultural markets. The company also produces mulch, topsoil, and other specialty products for turf, landscaping, and sports-surfacing applications.

LUCKEY FARMERS, INC.

1200 W MAIN ST
WOODVILLE, OH 434699701
Phone: 419 849-2711
Fax: –
Web: www.luckeyfarmers.com

CEO: Daniel Walski
CFO: –
HR: –
FYE: January 31
Type: Private

You don't have to be lucky to be a grain farmer in northwestern Ohio, but the members of Luckey Farmers agricultural cooperative might feel fortunate just the same. The co-op offers services such as grain storage and marketing for the corn, soybean, and wheat crops of its member-farmers. It supplies its members with grain marketing and agronomy services and information, feed and seed processing facilities, gas stations, and fuel-delivery services. Luckey Farmers, which has approximately 2,000 member/farmers, was established in 1919.

	Annual Growth	01/03	01/04	01/05	01/06	01/07
Sales ($mil.)	6.6%	–	–	71.6	72.3	81.4
Net income ($ mil.)	(9.0%)	–	–	0.8	0.9	0.7
Market value ($ mil.)	–	–	–	–	–	–
Employees	–	–	–	–	–	115

LUCY WEBB HAYES NATIONAL TRAINING SCHOOL FOR DEACONESSES AND MISSIONARIES

5255 LOUGHBORO RD NW
WASHINGTON, DC 200162633
Phone: 202 537-4257
Fax: –
Web: www.hopkinsmedicine.org

CEO: –
CFO: –
HR: Tim Souza
FYE: June 30
Type: Private

The Lucy Webb Hayes National Training School for Deaconesses and Missionaries, commonly known as Sibley Memorial Hospital, provides medical, surgical, therapeutic, assisted living, and home care services in Washington, DC. Sibley Memorial is a not-for-profit, acute-care community facility with some 320 beds. Sibley Memorial specializes in obstetrics, neurology, and thoracic care, among other medical areas. Lucy Webb Hayes was the wife of Rutherford B. Hayes, the 19th president of the United States. Troops commanded by her husband during the Civil War referred to Lucy Webb Hayes as as "Mother Lucy" for her tending of the wounded and dying. Sibley Memorial was acquired by Johns Hopkins Medicine in 2010.

	Annual Growth	06/15	06/16	06/19	06/20	06/22
Sales ($mil.)	12.8%	–	267.9	418.3	–	551.9
Net income ($ mil.)	45.4%	–	6.1	131.1	–	57.9
Market value ($ mil.)	–	–	–	–	–	–
Employees	–	–	–	–	–	2,000

LUMEN TECHNOLOGIES INC
NYS: LUMN

100 CenturyLink Drive
Monroe, LA 71203
Phone: 318 388-9000
Fax: 318 789-8656
Web: www.lumen.com

CEO: Kate Johnson
CFO: Christopher D Stansbury
HR: –
FYE: December 31
Type: Public

Lumen (formerly CenturyLink) is an international facilities-based technology and communications company focused on providing its business and mass markets customers with a broad array of integrated products and services necessary to fully participate in its ever-evolving digital world. Historically a regional wireline local and long-distance telephone provider, it is connecting with the times by transforming into a broadband and network services provider for business, residential, wholesale, and government clients. The company is the one of the largest US wireline telecom companies, with some 400,000 route miles of fiber optic cable globally. Serving more than 60 countries, most of its revenue comes from the US.

	Annual Growth	12/19	12/20	12/21	12/22	12/23
Sales ($mil.)	(10.2%)	22,401	20,712	19,687	17,478	14,557
Net income ($ mil.)	–	(5,269.0)	(1,232.0)	2,033.0	(1,548.0)	(10,298.0)
Market value ($ mil.)	(39.0%)	13,322	9,832.7	12,656	5,264.3	1,845.5
Employees	(9.9%)	42,500	39,000	36,000	29,000	28,000

LUMENTUM HOLDINGS INC
NMS: LITE

1001 Ridder Park Drive
San Jose, CA 95131
Phone: 408 546-5483
Fax: –
Web: www.lumentum.com

CEO: Alan S Lowe
CFO: Wajid Ali
HR: –
FYE: July 1
Type: Public

Lumentum is a market-leading designer and manufacturer of innovative optical and photonic products enabling optical networking and laser applications worldwide. It is a provider of optical and photonic products including Optical Communications (OpComms) and Commercial Lasers (Lasers) for manufacturing, inspection and life-science applications. Its 3-D sensing applications enables real time depth information to any photo or video image. The company also makes for manufacturing, inspection, and life-sciences applications. Lumentum is one of two companies created from the split of JDS Uniphase. The other company is called Viavi Solutions and comprises the former company's networking and security business. The company was incorporated in 2015. Lumentum generates the majority of its revenue in the Asia Pacific.

	Annual Growth	06/19	06/20*	07/21	07/22	07/23
Sales ($mil.)	3.1%	1,565.3	1,678.6	1,742.8	1,712.6	1,767.0
Net income ($ mil.)	–	(36.4)	135.5	397.3	198.9	(131.6)
Market value ($ mil.)	1.5%	3,546.4	5,055.0	5,542.4	5,167.2	3,766.9
Employees	9.8%	5,161	5,473	5,618	6,815	7,500

*Fiscal year change

LUMINEX CORPORATION

12212 TECHNOLOGY BLVD
AUSTIN, TX 787276100
Phone: 512 219-8020
Fax: –
Web: www.luminexcorp.com

CEO: –
CFO: –
HR: –
FYE: December 31
Type: Private

Luminex develops, manufactures, and sells a wide range of solutions applicable in diverse markets including clinical diagnostics, pharmaceutical drug discovery, biomedical research, genomic and proteomic research, and food safety. Its xMAP can simultaneously perform up to approximately 500 tests in a single run. Luminex also uses MultiCode real-time polymerase chain reaction and xTAG technology. The VERIGENE System utilizes advanced automation and proprietary chemistry to enable rapid, sample to result detection of nucleic acid and protein targets. Distributes its products worldwide, Luminex's systems are used by clinical and research laboratories and are distributed through strategic partnerships with other life sciences firms.

LUMINIS HEALTH ANNE ARUNDEL MEDICAL CENTER, INC

2001 MEDICAL PKWY
ANNAPOLIS, MD 214013773
Phone: 443 481-1000
Fax: –
Web: www.luminishealth.org

CEO: Florence B Kurdle
CFO: –
HR: –
FYE: June 30
Type: Private

The ill and infirm get the royal treatment at Anne Arundel Medical Center. The full-service, acute-care hospital serves the residents of Anne Arundel, Calvert, Prince George's, and Queen Anne counties in Maryland. With about 425 beds, the hospital administers care for women's health, oncology, pediatrics (it has a level III neonatal intensive care unit), neurology, orthopedics, and cardiovascular care. The medical center also has weight loss, sleep disorder, and rehabilitation centers. Anne Arundel, which opened its doors in 1902 and is part of the Anne Arundel Health System, has expanded its service offerings through various affiliations with regional specialty and primary care clinics. It also has a partnership with Johns Hopkins Medicine.

	Annual Growth	06/14	06/15	06/19	06/21	06/22
Sales ($mil.)	3.8%	–	526.0	579.4	650.3	685.2
Net income ($ mil.)	(16.7%)	–	40.0	17.1	59.9	11.2
Market value ($ mil.)	–	–	–	–	–	–
Employees	–	–	–	–	–	1,890

LUMINIS HEALTH DOCTORS COMMUNITY MEDICAL CENTER FOUNDATION, INC.

8118 GOOD LUCK RD
LANHAM, MD 207063574
Phone: 301 552-8118
Fax: –
Web: www.luminishealth.org

CEO: Philip B Down
CFO: –
HR: –
FYE: June 30
Type: Private

Doctors Community Hospital is an acute care and surgical hospital serving the Washington, DC area. The not-for-profit medical center admits 12,000 patients each year and has some 220 beds and offers standard and specialty services such as diagnostics, emergency and cardiac care, diagnostics, rehabilitation, wound care, and neurology. The hospital, which has some 600 doctors on staff, also includes a women's health center, a sleep therapy division, and the Joslin Diabetes Center. Established in 1975, Doctors Community Hospital provides community health services such as educational programs and support groups for specific medical conditions.

	Annual Growth	06/13	06/14	06/15	06/21	06/22
Sales ($mil.)	2.5%	–	188.2	197.2	230.3	229.6
Net income ($ mil.)	–	–	2.2	7.7	(0.7)	(14.2)
Market value ($ mil.)	–	–	–	–	–	–
Employees	–	–	–	–	–	1,509

LUMOS NETWORKS CORP.

1 LUMOS PLZ
WAYNESBORO, VA 229804549
Phone: 540 946-2000
Fax: –
Web: www.lumosfiber.com

CEO: Timothy G Biltz
CFO: Johan G Broekhuysen
HR: Joseph Brent
FYE: December 31
Type: Private

Lumos provides high speed Fiber Internet, wall to wall Wi-Fi, voice, and streaming TV services to more than 225,000 residential and business customers throughout North Carolina and Virginia. Its customers enjoy the fastest fiber speeds available built on a network they can truly count on ? all backed by local, expert customer care teams. It provides solutions for homes, which include fiber internet, wifi, TV, and phone services; and business-class fiber internet and data and cloud services. In mid-2022, North Carolina's NorthState and Virginia's Lumos Networks announced the launch of a new, unified brand, Lumos.

LUMOS PHARMA INC
NMS: LUMO

4200 Marathon Blvd #200
Austin, TX 78756
Phone: 512 215-2630
Fax: –
Web: www.lumos-pharma.com

CEO: –
CFO: Carl W Langren
HR: –
FYE: December 31
Type: Public

Lumos Pharma is hoping to give a boost to the immune systems of cancer patients. A biopharmaceutical company focused on discovering cancer treatments, Lumos Pharma develops and commercializes small-molecule immunotherapy therapies that stimulate patients' immune systems. The company's leading small-molecule product candidates currently in clinical development target the indoleamine-2, 3-dioxygenase (IDO) pathway, which is one of the key pathways for cancer immune escape. In 2020, Newlink Genetics merged with Lumos Pharma and took its name.

	Annual Growth	12/19	12/20	12/21	12/22	12/23
Sales ($mil.)	21.7%	0.9	0.2	0.2	1.5	2.1
Net income ($ mil.)	–	(43.0)	(5.7)	(30.4)	(31.1)	(34.0)
Market value ($ mil.)	5.9%	20.5	289.3	56.2	29.3	25.8
Employees	12.0%	21	32	32	32	33

LUNA INNOVATIONS INC

NAS: LUNA

301 First Street SW, Suite 200
Roanoke, VA 24011
Phone: 540 769-8400
Fax: -
Web: www.lunainc.com

CEO: Scott A Graeff
CFO: George Gomez-Quintero
HR: -
FYE: December 31
Type: Public

Luna Innovations is a research and development firm. The company makes practical use of cutting-edge technologies in the areas of molecular technology and sensing. Its molecular technology efforts focus on materials (including polymers, reagents, and nanomaterials) with enhanced performance characteristics; Luna has developed contrast agents for MRI testing, nanomaterials used in solar cells, and protective coatings. It has also created sensing technologies used in medical monitoring equipment, as well as wireless and fiber-optic monitoring systems for defense and industrial instrumentation. In mid-2015 Luna Innovations merged with Advanced Photonix.

	Annual Growth	12/18	12/19	12/20	12/21	12/22
Sales ($mil.)	26.4%	42.9	70.5	82.7	87.5	109.5
Net income ($ mil.)	(4.2%)	11.0	5.3	3.3	1.4	9.3
Market value ($ mil.)	27.3%	110.9	241.3	327.1	279.4	291.0
Employees	15.1%	196	267	426	392	344

LUNDBECK SEATTLE BIOPHARMACEUTICALS, INC.

11804 N CREEK PKWY S
BOTHELL, WA 980118801
Phone: 425 205-2900
Fax: -
Web: -

CEO: Robert Azelby
CFO: Carlos E Campoy
HR: Tamara Scott
FYE: December 31
Type: Private

Lundbeck Seattle BioPharmaceuticals (Lundbeck US) is engaged in the research and development, manufacturing, and commercialization of pharmaceuticals worldwide. Lundbeck US marketed pharmaceuticals in depression, bipolar disorder, schizophrenia, symptomatic neurogenic orthostatic hypotension (nOH) and migraine prevention. It works with industry partners, academic institutions and government agencies. Lundbeck US is the largest affiliate of H. Lundbeck A/S.

LUNDY SERVICES, L.L.C.

13525 DENTON DR
DALLAS, TX 752344716
Phone: 214 951-8181
Fax: -
Web: www.lundy-services.com

CEO: -
CFO: -
HR: Kelly Beers
FYE: December 31
Type: Private

Lundy Services is pretty handy when it comes to providing custom drywall and millwork services to the commercial construction industry in the Dallas/Fort Worth metropolitan area. The company's millwork shop makes base and trim moldings, laminate cabinetry, doors and frames, and custom architectural pieces. The company also works on exterior and interior wall construction, installs doors and frames, and constructs acoustical ceilings and wall panels. Customers include Burlington Northern and CompUSA. President James Lundy founded the company in 1988.

	Annual Growth	12/03	12/04	12/05	12/06	12/07
Sales ($mil.)	13.2%	-	23.0	28.4	32.8	33.3
Net income ($ mil.)		-	0.5	1.2	0.1	(0.1)
Market value ($ mil.)		-	-	-	-	-
Employees		-	-	-	-	377

LUPUS RESEARCH ALLIANCE, INC.

118 ESSEX ST
BROOKLYN, NY 112081129
Phone: 646 723-0911
Fax: -
Web: www.lupusresearch.org

CEO: -
CFO: -
HR: -
FYE: December 31
Type: Private

The Alliance for Lupus Research (ALR) is looking for answers to help cure a major disease. The not-for-profit organization was formed to fund research into the prevention, treatment, and cure of systemic lupus erythematosus (lupus or SLE). Lupus is a sometimes fatal autoimmune disease that causes pain and stiffness in joints, ligaments, tendons, and bones as well as kidney, heart, lung, and liver problems. The ALR is the largest source of private funds for lupus research (including a project to map the genetic makeup of at-risk people and targeted treatments for lupus).

	Annual Growth	12/14	12/15	12/16	12/18	12/22
Sales ($mil.)	2.7%	-	18.8	18.3	19.0	22.7
Net income ($ mil.)		-	3.6	(8.8)	(3.8)	(9.7)
Market value ($ mil.)		-	-	-	-	-
Employees		-	-	-	-	20

LUSTER PRODUCTS, INC.

1104 W 43RD ST
CHICAGO, IL 606093342
Phone: 773 579-1800
Fax: -
Web: www.lusterproducts.com

CEO: Jory Luster
CFO: -
HR: Jacqueline Fair
FYE: December 31
Type: Private

Luster Products wants its customers to win the best tressed award. The African-American-owned company makes professional and consumer hair care products for the ethnic market. Products are sold to men and women under several brand names, such as Renutrients, Pink, and S-Curl. Luster Products sells children's items under the name PCJ Pretty-n-Silky & Smooth Roots and products for stylists under the Designer Touch line, among others. The company sells worldwide through its own sales force and through specialty retailers. Luster Products operates manufacturing facilities in Illinois and international offices in South Africa and the UK. The company was founded in 1957 by hairstylist Fred Luster, Sr.

	Annual Growth	12/05	12/06	12/07	12/08	12/19
Sales ($mil.)	(2.1%)	-	-	-	0.0	0.0
Net income ($ mil.)		-	-	-	-	(0.0)
Market value ($ mil.)		-	-	-	-	-
Employees		-	-	-	-	401

LUTHER BURBANK CORP

NMS: LBC

520 Third Street, Fourth Floor
Santa Rosa, CA 95401
Phone: 844 446-8201
Fax: -
Web: www.lutherburbanksavings.com

CEO: Simone Lagomarsino
CFO: Laura Tarantino
HR: -
FYE: December 31
Type: Public

Luther Burbank is a lively lender on the US West Coast. Growing from a single bank branch in 1983 to more than a dozen bank and lending branches, it recently went public to raise capital for further expansion. It specializes in multi-family residential lending and in jumbo, non-conforming single family residential loans. It has some $5.3 billion in assets and has more than $4.5 billion loaned out to its customer base.

	Annual Growth	12/18	12/19	12/20	12/21	12/22
Assets ($mil.)	3.5%	6,937.2	7,045.8	6,906.1	7,180.0	7,974.6
Net income ($ mil.)	15.5%	45.1	48.9	39.9	87.8	80.2
Market value ($ mil.)	5.3%	460.7	588.9	500.5	717.1	567.4
Employees	(2.0%)	278	277	277	281	256

LUTHER COLLEGE

700 COLLEGE DR
DECORAH, IA 521011041
Phone: 563 387-1372
Fax: -
Web: www.luther.edu

CEO: -
CFO: -
HR: Marsha Wenthold
FYE: May 31
Type: Private

Luther College is an independent liberal arts school offering undergraduate and graduate programs to about 2,500 students from about 35 states and 40 countries. The college provides more than 60 majors and professional certificate programs. The Luther student body has more than 110 student-run clubs and organizations, 19 athletic teams, and 15 student music ensembles. Courses are conducted by 181 full-time teaching faculty members, 89% with Ph.D. or equivalent. The ratio of students to faculty is 12:1. Luther College is affiliated with the Evangelical Lutheran Church in America.

	Annual Growth	05/18	05/19	05/20	05/21	05/22
Sales ($mil.)	18.8%	-	71.5	68.6	126.0	120.0
Net income ($ mil.)	-	-	-	(2.2)	(1.6)	9.1	0.4
Market value ($ mil.)	-	-	-	-	-	-
Employees	-	-	-	-	-	550

LUTHERAN SERVICES IN AMERICA INC

100 MARYLAND AVE NE STE 500
WASHINGTON, DC 200025625
Phone: 410 230-2703
Fax: -
Web: www.lutheranservices.org

CEO: Jill A Schumann
CFO: -
HR: -
FYE: June 30
Type: Private

Lutheran Services in America doesn't refer to the services that happen in Lutheran churches across the country every Sunday. The not-for-profit group is the social services organization that carries out the mission of the Evangelical Lutheran Church and The Lutheran Church - Missouri Synod through nearly 300 health and human service organizations, including hospitals and homes for the elderly. It provides health care, disaster recovery, services for children and the elderly, and advocacy. Member organizations work directly in communities to provide services for disadvantaged populations. LSA provides those organizations with networking, training, publications, a vendor database, and an annual conference.

	Annual Growth	06/14	06/15	06/16	06/17	06/19
Sales ($mil.)	13.5%	-	2.4	3.2	3.5	4.1
Net income ($ mil.)	-	-	-	(0.0)	0.0	0.2	0.0
Market value ($ mil.)	-	-	-	-	-	-
Employees	-	-	-	-	-	12

LUXFER HOLDINGS PLC

8989 North Port Washington Road, Suite 211
Milwaukee, WI 53217
Phone: 414 269-2419
Fax: -
Web: www.luxfer.com

NYS: LXFR
CEO: -
CFO: -
HR: -
FYE: December 31
Type: Public

Luxfer Holdings is a global industrial company innovating niche applications in materials engineering. Luxfer focuses on value creation by using its broad array of technical know-how and proprietary technologies. Luxfer's high-performance materials, components and high-pressure gas containment devices are used in defense, first response and healthcare, transportation and general industrial applications. It focuses primarily on product lines related to magnesium alloys, zirconium chemicals and carbon composites. Luxfer has some 15 manufacturing plants in about five countries. The US is the largest single market accounting for over 55% of total sales.

	Annual Growth	12/19	12/20	12/21	12/22	12/23
Sales ($mil.)	(2.2%)	443.5	324.8	374.1	423.4	405.0
Net income ($ mil.)	-	3.1	20.0	29.9	26.9	(1.9)
Market value ($ mil.)	-	-	-	-	-	-
Employees	(3.3%)	1,600	1,400	1,400	1,400	1,400

LXP INDUSTRIAL TRUST

One Penn Plaza, Suite 4015
New York, NY 10119-4015
Phone: 212 692-7200
Fax: -
Web: www.lxp.com

NYS: LXP
CEO: T W Eglin
CFO: Beth Boulerice
HR: Sara Klein
FYE: December 31
Type: Public

LXP Industrial Trust is a real estate investment trust (REIT) that owns and manages approximately 115 consolidated real estate properties across some 20 states. Its diverse portfolio of properties includes single-tenant warehouse/distribution real estate investments totaling approximately 54 million square feet of rentable space. A majority of its properties are subject to net or similar leases, where the tenant bears all or substantially all of the costs, including cost increases, for real estate taxes, utilities, insurance and ordinary repairs. However, certain leases provide that the landlord is responsible for certain operating expenses. Prominent tenants include Amazon, Nissan, and Kellog.

	Annual Growth	12/19	12/20	12/21	12/22	12/23
Sales ($mil.)	1.1%	326.0	330.4	344.0	321.2	340.5
Net income ($ mil.)	(42.6%)	279.9	183.3	382.6	113.8	30.4
Market value ($ mil.)	(1.7%)	3,116.4	3,116.4	4,583.7	2,940.4	2,911.0
Employees	2.9%	57	56	63	67	64

LYDALL, INC.

1 COLONIAL RD
MANCHESTER, CT 060422307
Phone: 860 646-1233
Fax: -
Web: www.lydall.com

CEO: John Dandolph
CFO: -
HR: David Martin
FYE: December 31
Type: Private

Lydall, Inc. designs and manufactures specialty engineered non-woven filtration media, advanced technical materials, industrial thermal insulating solutions, and thermal and acoustical barriers for heat abatement and sound dampening applications. Lydall serves a number of markets with the majority of products sold to original equipment manufacturers and tier-one suppliers. The company serves customers via manufacturing operations and sales offices in North America, Europe and Asia.

LYFT INC

185 Berry Street, Suite 400
San Francisco, CA 94107
Phone: 844 250-2773
Fax: -
Web: www.lyft.com

NMS: LYFT
CEO: David Risher
CFO: Lisa Blackwood-Kapra
HR: -
FYE: December 31
Type: Public

Lyft Inc (Lyft) is a provider of Transportation-as-a-Service (TaaS) and one of the largest multimodal transportation networks in the US and Canada. The company offers ride sharing, bikes and scooters rental, access to autonomous vehicles and provision of transportation options through the platform and mobile-based applications. Lyft operates as a peer-to-peer marketplace between drivers and riders. It also offers various tools and solutions to businesses for managing the transportation needs of their customers in the corporate, healthcare, auto, education, and government sector. The company through its Lyft app connects rideshare, bikes, scooters, car rentals and transit in one place.

	Annual Growth	12/19	12/20	12/21	12/22	12/23
Sales ($mil.)	5.0%	3,616.0	2,364.7	3,208.3	4,095.1	4,403.6
Net income ($ mil.)	-	(2,602.2)	(1,752.9)	(1,009.4)	(1,584.5)	(340.3)
Market value ($ mil.)	(23.2%)	17,200	19,642	17,084	4,405.9	5,993.1
Employees	(15.2%)	5,683	4,675	4,453	4,419	2,945

LYNE LABORATORIES, INC.

10 BURKE DR
BROCKTON, MA 023015505
Phone: 508 583-8700
Fax: –
Web: www.lyne.com

CEO: –
CFO: –
HR: Danielle Kradin
FYE: December 31
Type: Private

Drug developers and marketers often leave the actual production of their products to companies like Lyne Laboratories. The contract pharmaceutical manufacturer specializes in oral liquid formulations (with a bitter-taste blocker available), as well as powder-form, semi-solid, and tablet medicines. The company also offers analytical services, such as quality control and testing, and regulatory support services. Lyne Laboratories can whip up both small test-size batches for clinical research and full production for commercial launches, and it can provide regulatory support along the way. An explosion-proof production and storage facility has expanded its ability to produce flammable drugs.

LYNTEGAR ELECTRIC COOPERATIVE, INC.

1701 US HWY 87 WEST ACCESS ROAD
TAHOKA, TX 79373
Phone: 806 561-4588
Fax: –
Web: www.lyntegar.coop

CEO: Greg Henley
CFO: –
HR: –
FYE: December 31
Type: Private

Lyntegar Electric Cooperative is based in the agricultural heart of the Texas Panhandle, where the summer heat sizzles and the winter ice storms freeze. The rural power cooperative provides electric utility services to customers in Borden, Dawson, Gaines, Garza, Hockley, Lynn, Martin, Terry, and Yoakum counties. The cooperative also sells electric grills and provides internet and television services. In addition, Lyntegar Electric Cooperative produces Typically Texas Cookbooks, which share collections of recipes used by cooperative member-consumers.

	Annual Growth	12/16	12/17	12/18	12/21	12/22
Sales ($mil.)	7.0%	–	70.9	71.6	86.6	99.6
Net income ($ mil.)	(32.0%)	–	7.2	10.5	5.5	1.1
Market value ($ mil.)	–	–	–	–	–	–
Employees	–	–	–	–	–	117

LYON COLLEGE

2300 HIGHLAND RD
BATESVILLE, AR 725013629
Phone: 870 793-9813
Fax: –
Web: www.lyon.edu

CEO: –
CFO: –
HR: Donald Taylor
FYE: June 30
Type: Private

You don't have to be Scottish (or Presbyterian) to attend Lyon College, but it can't hurt! The four-year liberal arts college is affiliated with the Presbyterian Church and touts its Scottish heritage. Located in the foothills of the Ozark Mountains (about 90 minutes northeast of Little Rock), the school offers undergraduate degrees in about 20 academic areas as well as pre-professional programs in medical sciences, law, education, and ministry. Lyon College is a small institution, with a total enrollment of approximately 500 and an average class size of about 15 students. The school was founded as Arkansas College in 1872.

	Annual Growth	06/14	06/15	06/16	06/21	06/22
Sales ($mil.)	1.1%	–	31.5	–	34.3	34.0
Net income ($ mil.)	–	–	1.5	–	(3.9)	(3.6)
Market value ($ mil.)	–	–	–	–	–	–
Employees	–	–	–	–	–	160

LYONDELLBASELL ADVANCED POLYMERS INC.

1221 MCKINNEY ST STE 300
HOUSTON, TX 770102036
Phone: 713 309-7200
Fax: –
Web: www.lyondellbasell.com

CEO: Bernard Rzepka
CFO: Thomas Aebischer
HR: Cathy Brown
FYE: August 31
Type: Private

A. Schulman is really into plastics. It is an international leader of designed and engineered plastic compounds, composites, color concentrates, size reduction services, and specialty molded parts. It provides products to end markets such as agriculture, building & construction, electronics, mobility, and packaging. End products that are built from its compounds include kitchen appliances, gas tanks, and kayaks. It operates more than 50 manufacturing locations worldwide and generates approximately 50% of its revenue in Europe, Middle East, & Africa (EMEA). It also serves as a distributor for polymer producers worldwide.

LYRIC OPERA OF CHICAGO

20 N WACKER DR STE 860
CHICAGO, IL 606062801
Phone: 312 332-2244
Fax: –
Web: www.lyricopera.org

CEO: Sylvia Neil
CFO: –
HR: –
FYE: June 30
Type: Private

The Lyric Opera of Chicago, housed in the majestic limestone Civic Opera House on North Wacker Drive, is one of the leading opera companies in the US. The company usually mounts several productions per season, running them in repertory. The Lyric Opera also supports a development program for young artists (Lyric Opera Center for American Artists) and numerous community outreach and education programs for teachers and students. The organization was founded in 1954.

	Annual Growth	06/16	06/17	06/20	06/21	06/22
Sales ($mil.)	5.2%	–	60.9	60.3	46.9	78.4
Net income ($ mil.)	–	–	(25.6)	(16.7)	1.0	8.1
Market value ($ mil.)	–	–	–	–	–	–
Employees	–	–	–	–	–	100

LYRIS, INC.

401 CONGRESS AVE STE 2650
AUSTIN, TX 787013708
Phone: 512 201-8287
Fax: –
Web: www.aurea.com

CEO: Scott Brighton
CFO: –
HR: –
FYE: June 30
Type: Private

Lyris sings a song of SaaS-pence. The company provides a variety of Software-as-a-Service (Saas) online marketing applications and services. Its more than 8,000 clients use the company's products to manage email lists and to create and monitor email marketing campaigns. More than three quarters of its revenues come from subscriptions to its cloud-based Lyris HQ hosted software application. Customers come from a wide range of industries including financial services, consumer goods, health care, retail, media, and transportation. The company also provides professional services such as consulting, support, and training. Formerly called J. L. Halsey, the company took its present name in 2007.